D1079789

ROTHMANS

FOOTBALL

YEARBOOK

2000-2001

ROTHMANS

EDITORS: GLENDA ROLLIN AND JACK ROLLIN

HEADLINE

Copyright © 2000 Rothmans Publications Ltd

First published in 2000
by HEADLINE BOOK PUBLISHING

10 9 8 7 6 5 4 3 2 1

All rights reserved. No part of this publication may be reproduced, stored in a retrieval system, or transmitted, in any form or by any means without the prior written permission of the publisher, nor be otherwise circulated in any form of binding or cover other than that in which it is published and without a similar condition including this condition being imposed on the subsequent purchaser.

Front cover photographs: (left) Paul Scholes (Manchester U and England) – *ASP*; (centre and background) Harry Kewell (Leeds U) – *ASP*; (right) Sami Hyypia (Liverpool) – *Colorsport*.

Back cover photographs: (top) Nwankwo Kanu (Arsenal) – *ASP*; (bottom) Oliver Tebily (Celtic) and Jonatan Johansson (Rangers) – *Actionimages*; (background) Paul Scholes (Manchester U and England) – *ASP*.

British Library Cataloguing in Publication Data
Rothmans Football Yearbook.—2000–2001
1. Association Football—Serials
796.334'05

ISBN 0 7472 7231 X (hardback)
ISBN 0 7472 7232 8 (trade paperback)

Typeset by Wearset, Boldon, Tyne and Wear

Printed and bound in Great Britain by
Mackays of Chatham PLC,
Chatham, Kent

HEADLINE BOOK PUBLISHING
A division of Hodder Headline
338 Euston Road
London NW1 3BH

www.headline.co.uk
www.hodderheadline.com

CONTENTS

IMPORTANT NOTICE

In spite of clubs adhering to a Football League directive and not supplying information for inclusion in this year's edition, we were pleased with a positive response from more than two-thirds of the members. However, for the remainder, some of the details relating to their pages may not be as up-to-date as we would have wished.

INTRODUCTION

The 31st edition of Rothmans Football Yearbook again features historical and record information for the 92 English clubs. This includes each club's full record in the previous ten seasons and the latest sequences recorded for wins, draws and defeats, etc. There is also an article by our guest writer Alan Curbishley, the manager of Charlton Athletic, who successfully guided the South London club back to the FA Carling Premiership.

Full coverage is given for the Euro 2000 competition both for the qualifying stages and the final tournament itself, with results, scorers, teams and attendances.

Detailed and varied coverage involves the FA Premier League, Football League, Scottish, Welsh and Irish football, amateur, schools, university, reserve team, extensive non-league information, awards, records and an international directory, the Football Trust, Football and the Law, coaching, women's football, referees and the work of chaplains.

Transfer fees are given where known. When two clubs have differed as to the amount of a record move, the lower figure has been quoted in both instances. For certain entries, the figure quoted in the list of transfers may be the original one without extra finance built in for appearances and other reasons, which would appear subsequently as a record fee on the relevant club page. Also the date when a player is signed often varies from the one given as his registration and the diary occasionally refers to the transfer fee originally discussed.

A frequent question asked is why Football League records have not been changed since the advent of the Premier League. The answer is simple: the Football League still considers its First Division to be a championship which has existed for over 100 years.

The Editors would like to thank Alan Elliott for the Scottish section, Bob Hennessy for the Milestones Diary and Ian Vosper for the obituaries. Thanks are also due to John English who provided invaluable and conscientious reading of the proofs. The Editors would like to pay tribute to the various organisations who have helped to make this edition complete, especially Mike Foster, Adrian Cook and Jonathan Hargreaves of the FA Premier League, and David C. Thomson of the Scottish League.

ACKNOWLEDGEMENTS

The Editors would like to express appreciation of the following individuals and organisations for their cooperation: Heather Elliott, Malcolm Brodie, Wally Goss (AFA), Paul Reaney for Nationwide Conference information, Rev. Nigel Sands, Edward Grayson, Ken Goldman, Grahame Lloyd, Marshall Gillespie, Ben Jerram, Valery Karpoushkin, Sara Thompson and Juliana Lessa (Headline Book Publishing).

Special thanks are due to Lorraine Jerram, Headline's Senior Editor for her generosity, expertise, constant support, unflagging patience, sincerity, understanding, perspicacity and appreciation, not to mention her unfailing humour, quick-wittedness and understated authority.

Finally, sincere thanks to John Anderson, Simon Dunnington, Geoff Turner, Brian Tait and the staff at Wearset for their efforts in the production of this book, which was much appreciated throughout the year.

VIEWPOINT

by Alan Curbishley

I wonder how many times this summer Joe Royle and George Burley, the respective managers of newly promoted Manchester City and Ipswich Town, have been asked how they intend to bridge the gap that undoubtedly exists between the Premiership and the Nationwide League? Of course, it is an obvious question – and it is one to which Joe, George and I must find the answer very quickly if we are to survive next season.

How has this gap appeared? The principal reason lies in the significant difference in the financial rewards available to the two leagues: since its formation the Premiership has benefited from huge television and commercial revenues, amounts which dwarf those available to the Nationwide League clubs. Since BSkyB secured the television rights to the Premiership, the gap has continued to widen season by season. If you compare what a Nationwide League Division One side has received for the last four seasons with that of a Premiership side over the same period, the difference would be in the order of £20–25 million.

The current television deal expires at the end of the 2000–2001 season and the massive income generated by the new deal will serve to deepen the divide to such an extent that it is quite feasible that no promoted Nationwide League clubs will be able to retain their new-found status. On average a Premiership club can expect to receive around £5–6 million per season from the existing TV deal. This contrasts sharply with the £1 million paid to Nationwide League clubs. The new deal could see the average Premiership side receiving £15 million compared with £2–3 million in the Nationwide League.

The majority of Premiership teams are now well established and have used the vast resources available to them to strengthen their clubs, both on and off the field. Many have invested not only in players but also in increasing the capacity of their stadia and in developing youth academies to produce their own home-grown talent. The level of investment that these Premiership sides have been able to make, and the strength this has given them as clubs, makes them infinitely more powerful than any promoted club.

Many clubs relegated from the Premiership have endured real financial hardship. Relegated sides do receive a 'parachute payment', currently some £2 million per year, the intention being to ensure that the higher wage costs incurred in the Premiership are, to some extent, covered. This payment lasts for two seasons and it does give the relegated sides some chance of 'bouncing back' at the first attempt, which is why, in recent years, clubs such as Crystal Palace, Bolton Wanderers and Middlesbrough have managed to do what we achieved last season. Having said this, there is a stark lesson for all of us in what happened to Crystal Palace last season and the severe financial problems they faced.

We must all take heart from the achievements of Bradford City in 1999–2000. The role models for us, however, are Leicester City and Derby County who have survived in the Premiership for a number of seasons. If we can use the resources placed at our disposal in the same way, it will help us realise our ambition of establishing Charlton Athletic as a Premiership club. It will not be easy and the fantastic team spirit and organisation, which have been the cornerstone of our achievements in recent years, will be key factors in our bid to retain our newly won status. We will strengthen our squad principally with British players but at the same time we will radically overhaul our existing scouting structures to improve our knowledge of the overseas market, something it is difficult for a Nationwide League club to do because of financial constraints.

With the continuing inflation in the cost of domestic players, more and more clubs will look to the overseas market where there is better value for money. This will serve to fuel further the current debate on the effect the continuing influx of foreign players is having on the Premiership and the national team. With regard to the latter, it is fairly self-evident

that if the number of foreign players continues to rise at the present rate, the number of players available to the national team manager will be seriously reduced. The trend could also have the effect of stifling the development of our very best young players. We must not allow this to happen and Kevin Keegan's fear that the national team manager will be looking to select players from the Nationwide League must not be permitted to become a reality.

Unlike when I played, many of today's youngsters will perhaps not get the opportunity to play in their first team at an early stage, unless of course they are exceptionally talented. If that talent is not given a platform on which to perform early on, there is a risk that some very gifted players may well drift out of the game. The advent of youth academies, and the effort that everyone in the game is making to produce quality young players, gives us all hope that the best players will come through. The difference nowadays is that they may need to demonstrate their talent instantly as there is little patience in the game at the top level.

However, I look at our current crop of England Under-21 players and am encouraged by the emergence of players like Richard Wright, Rio Ferdinand, Gareth Barry, Frank Lampard, Lee Hendrie, Emile Heskey and Michael Owen. If these players can continue to progress at their current rate, then perhaps the future for our national side may not be so bleak after all.

The more successful foreign players have, in fairness, brought a style of professionalism that has undoubtedly rubbed off on our own players. Foreign managers and coaches, too, have brought different attitudes and methods which have positively influenced our domestic coaches. I believe, though, that the time has come for the number of non-British players to be limited to a maximum of six per club although it is likely that the Bosman ruling in the European courts is only the start of increasing legislative control of the professional game and my proposal may fall down on legal grounds.

As the game progresses and attracts ever-increasing revenues, there is inevitably more pressure on clubs to succeed. It is vital, therefore, that we do everything we possibly can to assist referees in the very difficult job they have to do each week. I rarely criticise a referee's performance even when I feel that decisions may have gone against my team, because I realise what a difficult task it is. Nobody sets out to make a wrong decision, but such judgements are made and perhaps, to some extent, add something to the after-match debates. They certainly keep the soccer pundits fully employed! Football is an instant game requiring instant decisions but I do believe that we should look at the introduction of new technology to aid referees.

Decisions as to whether the ball has crossed the line or not, or whether a tackle was made inside or outside the penalty box, can end up costing clubs millions of pounds and it would not be difficult to introduce new methods of corroboration in such cases – for example, the results of instant video replays could be communicated straight to the referee on the pitch by the fourth official. I am not calling for the game to be stopped continuously as it would lose its flow and momentum, but it is vital that the right decisions are made. I also think referees should be allowed to study videos of matches after the game and re-examine key incidents. If a player has been incorrectly booked, is it so bad that the decision is subsequently overturned? Natural justice must come before everything else.

The drive for success is relentless. As the stakes are raised, it is inevitable that more managers will lose their jobs. There are significant rewards for success, but it is interesting that Sir Alex Ferguson, currently the most successful manager in the country, has been at Old Trafford for some thirteen years and I have been at Charlton for nine years. Both of us have had our problems but the lesson to be learned is that, in both cases, our clubs have achieved success because the chairmen have been patient. It is a lesson that chairmen up and down the country would do well to reflect upon.

EDITORIAL

History can spin on the most trivial turn of events. The first competitive victory over Germany for 34 years produces a euphoric atmosphere bordering on hysteria. Confidence is sky-high until one ill-timed tackle sends the team careering out of the competition and produces the most damming judgment on the state of our game.

Alas results still cloud our senses. We see everything in black and white, winning and losing. It is the grey areas which should be analysed whatever the score. And naive tactics, woeful lack of creation and inability to pass the ball at any distance makes sad reading for our finest. When will we learn to be more objective in our criticism? But the problem lies much deeper.

There is precious little point in claiming that there are too many foreigners in the English game. There always have been. With Scots, Welsh and Irish gracing our teams as long as the organised game has existed, today there are simply more players unqualified for England, only now they come from France, Holland, Norway and other places.

The root cause of the lack of success at international level is that we do not have the same level of world class skill possessed by the best continental and South American players. It may be argued that we have more players of a certain standard of ability sound enough for domestic needs, but elsewhere they have the edge with technique and flair, which alas is not our style.

Our stalwart characteristics of grit, determination and stamina have time and again proved inadequate against opponents who can withstand these onslaughts and override our deficiencies in the area of simply manipulating the ball.

It might seem like heresy to say so, but unless there is the greatest revolution in the way our game is taught, we may never again achieve international success.

However, there is a movement at grass roots level to change the way our youth is encouraged to play. It comes from Brazil. The aspiring lads of Rio, Sao Paulo and other states train with a smaller and heavier ball, which has to be firmly controlled and is ideal for short passing. More importantly, it is impossible for it to be used in the long ball game.

The thinking behind this innovation is that if it improves the ball control of our boys, the traditional assets of countless England teams down the years, will at last give us the opportunity of competing with the best without the embarrassment which accompanies inevitable defeat. Clearly the need is urgent; England Under-16s 1, Brazil 2 at the Stadium of Light, Sunderland in July beams the message distinctly enough.

This is the theory. Changing attitudes may not be as easy in practice. Youngsters are accustomed to play in formation at an early age, regardless of whether they have the basic ability to control the ball. Pure basic mastery, before thoughts of artistry with the ball, should be a priority instilled into them before they even play in a match.

At least in terms of the World Cup being staged in this country, the short-term is taken care of after the fiasco of the voting for the 2006 finals. We have time to make amends on the field before we ever have the chance of holding the finals here. A costly £10m presidential-style campaign was poorly presented and the government's last minute attempt at legislation to prevent the hooligan touring company from entertaining abroad in the wake of the Charleroi rioting at Euro 2000 merely put a pathetic last chapter on the entire sorry tale. The beautiful game continues to attract the ugly people. But while our society allows the civil rights of the perpetrators to take precedence over those of the victims, that will remain a serious concern.

On moral grounds the finals should have gone to South Africa, but the security aspect would have presented endless problems. But there has to be a system of rotation to enable every confederation to have the finals. If we are to ignore Africa for example, one has to revert to the previous system when the so-called minnows had minimum recognition. And presidents of FIFA arc not elected on that platform. Germany won the right to stage World Cup 2006, largely because everyone underestimated them as they frequently have done on the field and off it.

ROTHMANS FOOTBALL YEARBOOK HONOURS

For the fifth consecutive year, members of the Football Writers' Association selected their team of the season for Rothmans Football Yearbook. As in previous years, players eligible had to have appeared in FA Carling Premiership matches during the season.

This year, to mark the New Millennium, members were asked to cast their votes for the English League Manager of the Century, Player of the Century and Team of the Century. The manager was chosen for his overall achievements between 1900 and 2000 as was the player over the same period, but the team award was for a specific season.

For the 1999–2000 Premiership, most members again preferred selecting players in a 4-4-2 formation. Despite achieving their sixth such title in eight years, Manchester United's representation on the final selection was cut in half from last year with only Jaap Stam, David Beckham and Roy Keane retaining their places.

This trend enabled more clubs to be represented. Leeds United had a trio of their own in Nigel Martyn, Ian Harte and Harry Kewell, who had almost made the final team in 1998–99. Harte faced strong opposition from Manchester United's Denis Irwin and Silvinho the Brazilian at Arsenal, while Paul Scholes (Manchester United) and Patrick Vieira (Arsenal) received a substantial share of the votes in midfield.

Chelsea had two, right-back Albert Ferrer and midfield player Dennis Wise, while the Liverpool central defender Sami Hyypia was well supported among the back four. Newcastle United's Alan Shearer, who missed out in the previous season, returned up front to partner Kevin Phillips, whose first season in the Premiership netted him 30 goals at Sunderland.

Once again, Sir Alex Ferguson of Manchester United took the managerial award, while Marcel Desailly (Chelsea), Ryan Giggs (Manchester United) and Thierry Henry (Arsenal) were nominated as substitutes.

The Manager of the Century was Bob Paisley of Liverpool, the most successful English club manager, with twenty various trophies at home and abroad between 1974 and 1983. He had strong challenges from Sir Alex Ferguson and Bill Nicholson, who guided Tottenham Hotspur in the 1960's.

Player of the Century was George Best of Manchester United and United's treble winning team of 1998–99 took the team prize, from Liverpool in 1976–77 and Tottenham's double-winning team.

Rothmans Football Yearbook Team of the Season

Nigel Martyn
(*Leeds U*)

Albert Ferrer	Sami Hyypia	Jaap Stam	Ian Harte
(*Chelsea*)	(*Liverpool*)	(*Manchester U*)	(*Leeds U*)
David Beckham	Roy Keane	Dennis Wise	Harry Kewell
(*Manchester U*)	(*Manchester U*)	(*Chelsea*)	(*Leeds U*)

Alan Shearer
(*Newcastle U*)

Kevin Phillips
(*Sunderland*)

Manager:
Sir Alex Ferguson (*Manchester U*)

Substitutes:
Marcel Desailly (*Chelsea*)
Ryan Giggs (*Manchester U*)
Thierry Henry (*Arsenal*)

Rothmans Football Yearbook Millennium Awards

Manager of the Century	Player of the Century	Team of the Century
Bob Paisley	George Best	Manchester U
(*Liverpool*)	(*Manchester U*)	(*1998-99*)

MILESTONES DIARY 1999–2000

June 1999
Refs get increase ... Liverpool pay record fee ... Sporting secure Schmeichel ... Gunners accuse Real ... Chelsea entice Deschamps ... Huge increase in foreigners ... FA appoint chairman Thompson ... Hooijdonk crosses to Arnhem ... No FA Cup defence says Edwards

14 Chelsea off-load Brian Laudrup, selling the Dane to Ajax for around £2m. Premiership ref match fees will rise next season from £400 to £600. Adrian Heath, 38, is Blades new boss.
15 Paris St Germain defender Alain Goma joins Newcastle for £4.75m. Liverpool's £4m signing of Sander Westerveld from Vitesse Arnhem sets a British record for a goalie. Leeds clinch £4m signing of Danny Mills from Charlton.
16 Steve Parkin who took Mansfield to the verge of the play-offs is to become Rochdale's boss.
17 Villa sign Liverpool's David James for £1.7m to replace Mark Bosnich. Palmeiras will be Man U's opponents in November's Intercontinental Cup Final in Toyko.
18 Sporting Lisbon confident of securing Peter Schmeichel's signature on a 2-year contract.
19 FL will supply officials to help oversee substitutions, dug-out decorum and time-keeping in non-televised Premiership matches. Arsenal make official complaint to FIFA and the FA accusing Real Madrid of an illegal approach for unsettled Nicolas Anelka.
20 Largest crowd to attend a women's sporting event, 78,972, watch US beat Denmark 3-0 in the opening Group A match of the 1999 Women's World Cup at the Giants Stadium.
21 Chelsea capture Didier Deschamps, France's WC-winning captain from Juventus for £3m. Deschamps, capped 85 times, signs 3-year contract. All of Newcastle's 33,000 season-tickets snapped up. Participating in FIFA's Club World Championship in Brazil (Jan 5-14) may force holders Man U to field a weakened side or even to withdraw from this season's FA Cup.
22 Everton off-load Ibrahima Bakayoko to Marseille for a reported £4m. Chelsea's Dmitri Kharine joins Celtic on a free. Survey shows 172 foreigners at Premiership clubs compared to 63 in 1995.
23 Cheltenham Town's reward for reaching the Nationwide League is a Worthington Cup 1st rd trip to Norwich. Irving Scholar, former chairman at Spurs, resigns from Nottm Forest board.
24 Leicester's Neil Lennon signs 4-year contract.
25 Arsenal place U-21 midfielder Stephen Hughes on the list. Stockport sack manager Gary Megson. Wales dismiss assistant-coach Graham Williams 3 weeks after Bobby Gould's resignation.
26 FA appoint Geoffrey Thompson as new chairman after winning 53-31 majority over David Sheepshanks (Ipswich). In surprise twist the council appoint Oldham's Ian Stott as vice-chairman in preference to Premier League's David Richards. David Davies says he is trying to engineer a window in Man U's season to allow them take 10 days out to compete in the new FIFA Club World Championship in Brazil.
27 Atletico Madrid sack coach Raddy Antic, the former Luton player, an hour after losing the Spanish Cup Final 3-0 to Valencia.
28 Peter Shreeves is caretaker-boss at Nottm Forest on 3-month contract. Stockport give Andy Kilner, a former club winger, the manager's post. Former Boro favourite Juninho is up for sale at Atletico Madrid. Celtic's Alan Stubbs is to undergo immediate surgery after drugs test detects illness, believed to be testicular cancer. FA insist no government pressure put on Man U to opt out of the FA Cup. Torquay postpone their Aug 10 Worthington Cup tie with Portsmouth for a week because it is scheduled for the night before the solar eclipse and the town is expected to be packed with visitors.
29 Arsenal land Brazilian left back Silvinho from Corinthians after agreeing £4m fee. Pierre van Hooijdonk completes £3.5m Nottm Forest move to Vitesse Arnhem. Everton sell Olivier Dacourt to Lens for £6.5m which represents a healthy profit having bought the midfielder from Strasbourg for £3.8m last year. Premiership new boys Bradford pay £1.4m to Leeds for David Wetherall. French WC striker Christophe Dugarry fails a drugs test and faces a 6-month ban.
30 Confirming Man U will not be entering next season's FA Cup, Martin Edwards, says: 'the club had to consider that the England WC 2006 bid may have been at stake if we had not gone to Brazil – we are in a no-win situation.' Gillingham sack manager Tony Pulis for alleged 'gross misconduct.' Cwmbran draw Celtic in UEFA money-spinning qualifier which will keep the little Welsh club going for 2 seasons. In Champions League Rangers meet either Haka or HB Torshavn (Faeroe Islands).

July 1999
Stadium of Light beams for Bould ... Chelsea's £10m for Sutton ... Manager Pulis is out and in ... Two caught in drugs tests ... Owls splash on strikers ... Brown refutes bigot slur ... Wolves Bull has to quit ... Palace honours Gunner Adams ... Collymore heads to Cottagers ... Ferguson collects knighthood ... Anfield for £7.5m Hamann ... More Man U strips ... New Wembley – no Twin Towers ... Ince joins Boro ... 29 watch Clydebank

1 Welsh rugby union and the FA of Wales strike a deal for football internationals to be played at Cardiff's new £120m Millennium Stadium. Everton anticipate a hefty FA fine for having the worst Premiership disciplinary record last season, 112 yellow and 8 red cards. David Platt signs 3-year lucrative contract as manager to Nottm Forest.
2 Steve Bould ends his 11-year career at Arsenal joining Sunderland on a 2-year contract. Andriy Shevchenko becomes the 6th most expensive player in the all-time list of transfers joining AC Milan for £16m from Dynamo Kiev. Peter Beardsley links with England's U-16 backroom staff.
3 Wimbledon's Chris Perry is unveiled as Tottenham's new £4m arrival with the transaction to be completed in the next 48 hours.

4 John Barnes confirms the appointment of coach Terry McDermott as Celtic's 'social' manager. Alec Stock, 81, who led Yeovil Town to their greatest triumph against Sunderland in the 1949 FA Cup is to have a testimonial 50 years late. Yeovil play Fulham whom Stock managed to the 1975 FA Cup Final.

5 Chelsea pay Blackburn £10m for Chris Sutton; the fee is the third largest between British clubs and brings coach Vialli's spending to £22.6m on 9 new signings. Peter Storrie, former W Ham managing director, is the new chief executive at Southend. Tony Pulis becomes Bristol City's new boss one week after being sacked by Gillingham. Argentine Martin Palermo, known as 'El Loco,' creates a piece of history when he squanders a hat-trick of penalties during his country's 3-0 Copa America defeat against Colombia.

6 Gerard Houllier tells skipper Paul Ince he is not in future Liverpool plans.

7 Peter Taylor, former England U-21 boss, is the new manager at Gillingham. UEFA fine FA £3,000 for England's improper conduct (7 yellow and 1 red card) during EC 2000 qualifiers against Sweden and Bulgaria. Blueprint of Wembley's new building plan shows that the famous Twin Towers are not included.

8 FA reveal that 2 players were caught in 544 drugs tests; a trainee, 17, unnamed, at a Premiership club admitted to being addicted to heroin while Byron Glasgow, 20, tests positive for cocaine and cannabis misuse, and has been sacked at Reading. Everton sell Marco Materazzi to former club Perugia for £3m. Man City complete the £1m signing of Wimbledon's Mark Kennedy.

9 Bobby Robson is to return to England's set-up as 'mentor' for younger FA coaches. At FIFA's Los Angeles congress 43 Asian delegates walk out in protest at the number of places allocated to the continent in the WC 2002 Finals.

10 Sheff Wed complete £5m double signing of PSV Eindhoven striker Gilles de Bilde and Ajax forward Gerald Sibon on 4-year contracts. Record crowd for a women's football match of 90,185 see the US defeat China 5-4 on penalties in a goalless WC Final at the Rose Bowl in Pasadena.

11 Shockwaves in Scottish football as Craig Brown is portrayed as a religious bigot by the *News of the World* which claims to have a tape recording of the national coach, made as he returned from an Old Firm clash, singing anti-Catholic songs. Brown denies the accusations and is taking legal action.

12 Bells to be sponsors of the Scottish Football League and Challenge Cup, the deal worth £2m over 3 years. Chelsea's Michael Duberry signs on at Leeds for £4.75m.

13 Sunderland sign Thomas Helmer from Bayern Munich. Sheff Wed put Benito Carbone on the list. Wolves legend Steve Bull, 34, announces his retirement because of a persistent knee injury after netting 306 goals in 561 appearances. Dave Ewing, 70, a hero in Man City's 1956 FA Cup-winning side, dies after a long illness. In £22m deal TV giants Granada takes a 10 per cent stake in Liverpool to become Anfield's second-largest shareholders.

14 Gary Megson is the new manager at Stoke, on a 3-year contract. Tony Adams, Arsenal and England defender, collects his MBE from the Queen at Buckingham Palace. Newcastle agree £6m deal for Kieron Dyer, Ipswich's U-21 attacking midfielder.

15 Derby agree £3.5m sale of Paulo Wanchope to W Ham.

16 John Rudge, long-serving former Vale boss, joins rivals Stoke as football executive adviser. Poland switch England's EC tie on Sept 8 from 32,000-seater stadium in Chorzow to a Warsaw ground holding just 12,000. Real Mallorca's Marcelino Elena joins Newcastle for £5.8m.

17 Paul Kitson's goal gets W Ham's European venture off to a winning but unconvincing start in the Inter-Toto Cup against Jokerit.

18 Brazil beat Uruguay 3-0 to retain their Copa America crown with Rivaldo scoring twice. A weakened Australian side is sunk by Dwight Yorke's strike before 78,032 at Sydney's Olympic Stadium, as Man U follow up the early 2-0 defeat of the Socceroos.

19 Fulham take Villa's Stan Collymore on 3-month loan. Morocco WC midfielder Mustapha Hadji completes £4m move to Coventry from Deportivo La Coruna.

20 Sir Alex Ferguson collects his knighthood from the Queen. Villa complete the £4.5m signing of George Boateng from Coventry.

21 Swansea will quit the Vetch Field in 2001 to groundshare with the city's rugby union club at the new 25,000 capacity Morfa stadium. Barry Town crash out to Valletta (3-2 on agg) in Champions League 2nd leg qualifier. Celtic complete £5.5m signing of W Ham's Eyal Berkovic.

22 Laurie Scott, former Arsenal and England player, dies after long illness. He was 84. Ricardo Scimeca leaves Villa to link with Nottm Forest in £3m deal. Newcastle's Dietmar Hamann completes £7.5m transfer to Liverpool.

23 Leeds snap up Sunderland striker Michael Bridges for £5m. Man U launch their navy blue and black away strip, the club's 16th change in 8 seasons.

24 Brighton return to their home town after 2-year exile at Gillingham, when Nottm Forest visit for a friendly at the Seagulls' new Withdean base. In Hong Kong before 40,000 Man U win 2-0 against South China. Celtic lose 2-1 to Leeds at Parkhead before 51,500.

25 Bayern Munich's veteran Lothar Matthaus is the Footballer of the Year in Germany. Brazil crush Germany 4-0 in opening Confederations Cup match in Mexico.

26 Frank Lampard agrees a W Ham contract to run until 2005 and reported to be worth around £1m a year.

27 Dunfermline appoint Jimmy Nicholl, the former Raith boss, as asst manager. WBA sack manager Denis Smith and put John Gorman in joint-charge with coach Cyrille Regis. Scottish Premier League will be expanded to 12 teams in a year's time, with the League splitting after 33 games for title, European and relegation placings. Leicester's US international Kasey Keller agrees Bosman free move to Rayo Vallecano.

28 W Ham take a 1-0 Inter-Toto Cup lead to the away tie in Heerenveen. In the European Cup, Michael Mols, the new £4m Rangers recruit, scores twice in 4-1 win over Haka. Steve McManaman makes a successful debut for Real Madrid in the 1-0 win against Lausanne in Switzerland.

29 Twin Towers will not be part of the new £475m Wembley when it opens in the summer of 2003. At the unveiling of plans architects say England will have the finest three-tiered stadium in the world, seating 90,000. But controversy surrounds the halving of on-site car parking capacity to just 1,500. Stefan Schwarz becomes Sunderland's £4m record signing. The Swedish midfielder, who figured at Arsenal, has played recently with Fiorentina and

Valencia. New Minister of Sport Kate Hoey says Man U owe the country a duty to find a way of defending the FA Cup. Blackburn take Alan Kelly from Sheff Utd to cover for the £1m departure of Tim Flowers to Leicester.

30   Leeds turn down transfer request of Jimmy Floyd Hasselbaink who threatens to do an 'Anelka' and go on strike if the club block a £10m move to Atletico Madrid. Liverpool's Paul Ince joins Bryan Robson's Boro for £1m. Backlash in Germany as their team loses 2-0 to US.

31   Just 29 paying fans for Clydebank's League Cup 1st rd tie with East Stirlingshire, a record low in Scottish football. A boycott due to ground-sharing and the start of the tall ships race in Greenock were reasons given. A Chelsea club testimonal record 27,259 turn up for Dennis Wise's 0-0 benefit against Bologna.

August 1999

Arsenal win Charity Shield ... Sir Alex's £40,000 Russian 'present' ... Highbury welcomes Suker and Henry ... Little in at Albion ... Leeds get £12m for Hasselbaink ... Anelka heads to Spain ... Ferguson book blast at Kidd ... Shearer off in opener ... 60,253 start at Celtic ... Long BBC contracts for Lineker and Hansen ... Kid Keane is £6m Sky Blue ... Gullit quits Magpies ... BskyB buy stake in Leeds

1   Celtic hit 5 without reply at Aberdeen, the first match for new coach John Barnes. Arsenal come from behind in the Charity Shield to beat Man U 2-1. A freak electrical storm abandons Bolton's friendly with Preston after 55 min.

2   Sir Alex Ferguson's autobiography reveals he was handed £40,000 in a parcel by a Russian representing Andrei Kanchelskis. The money was kept in an Old Trafford safe and returned to agent Grigory Essaoulenko. Arsenal pay £1m to Real Madrid for Croatian Davor Suker, 31, Golden Boot winner at France 98. Roy Hodgson is new coach at Grasshoppers Zurich. Everton's Craig Short moves to Blackburn for £2.1m, depending on appearances.

3   Wales ask Mark Hughes to supervise the national side against Belarus and Switzerland. Arsenal splash £10m to take French WC winner Thierry Henry, 21, from Juventus, on a 5-year contract. Brian Little, previously at Wolves, Leicester, Villa and Stoke is the new boss at WBA with a 2-year deal.

4   Leeds off-load Jimmy Floyd Hasselbaink to Atletico Madrid in £12m transfer. Rangers set up clash with Parma after defeating Haka 3-0 (7-1 on agg).

5   Nicolas Anelka, Real Madrid's new £22.3m signing from Arsenal, is paraded at the Bernabeu Stadium. Tottenham agree £2.75m fee to take Oyvind Leonhardsen from Liverpool. At *Rothmans Football Yearbook* launch FIFA ref David Elleray calls for the introduction of a sin-bin in place of a yellow card believing this radical step could help reduce the number of fouls. Newcastle off-load Andreas Andersson to AIK Stockholm for £2m.

6   Brian Kidd declines to respond in detail to Sir Alex Ferguson's autobiography jibes that his former asst was insecure – the Man U boss also questioned Kidd's judgement of players. Sheff Wed chairman Dave Richards dismisses talk of a merger with Sheff Utd. After 10 red cards last term Arsène Wenger warns Arsenal staff to improve their discipline. Boro snap up Christian Ziege for £4m from AC Milan.

7   On Aug 15 1992, the opening of the Premiership, 9 foreigners figured. As the new season gets under way today the tally is 65. Chelsea hit 4 against promoted Sunderland, Arsenal beat Leicester 2-1 thanks to 90th min og, Bradford, out of the top division for 77 years pull off shock 1-0 win at Boro. On his 100th start for Newcastle, Shearer is controversially sent off for 1st time in his career as Magpies lose 1-0 to Villa. The Dons, under Norwegian coach Egil Olsen and reduced to 10-men for most of the match, win 3-2 at Watford. On their return home, after 2 seasons ground-sharing at Gillingham, Brighton get off to a magnificent 6-0 start against Mansfield. Cheltenham Town, newest Nationwide League club, attract 5,189 to their refurbished Whaddon Road ground – but lose 2-0 to Rochdale. Genk make extraordinary start to their title defence battling out a 6-6 draw at Westerlo in a game featuring 5 pens, 4 red cards and both sides ending with 9 men! 60,253 at Parkhead, Britain's highest attendance for a League match this decade, watch Celtic beat St Johnstone 2-0.

8   W Ham have 1-0 win over Spurs. Promoted Man City attract 31,755 but lose opener 1-0 to Wolves. Jaap Stam's late og gives Everton a 1-1 draw with Man U at Goodison.

9   SPL fine Celtic £45,000 for their part in Old Firm disturbances on May 2 when ref Hugh Dallas was struck by a coin. French defender Stephane Mahe singled out for blame. England present FIFA their WC 2006 bid involving Michael Owen at the ceremony in Zurich. The Dons sign defender Trond Andersen for £2.5m from Molde.

10   Bergkamp magic maintains Arsenal's 100 per cent start which clinches 2-1 win at Derby. Sunderland, watched by 40,000, beat Watford, while Boro record a success at the Dons.

11   In Champions League qualifier Chelsea beat Sknoto Riga 3-0. Rangers take 2-0 lead to Parma. Man U chalk up 4-0 win over Sheff Wed. Villa hit 3 without reply at Everton, Leeds win by same margin at Saints, Leicester defeat Coventry 1-0.

12   Under-fire Ruud Gullit gets board vote of confidence to continue his Newcastle revolution. Cwmbran's UEFA Cup adventure turns sour with a 6-0 Ninian Park thrashing by Celtic. David O'Leary smashes the Leeds transfer record by landing Darren Huckerby in a £5.5m deal from Coventry.

13   Gullit's misery continues with an FA misconduct charge levelled at him. Chelsea's £3.5m capture of Gabriele Ambrosetti from Vicenza brings to 9 the Italian connection at Stamford Bridge. Pundits Lineker and Hansen sign 5-year contracts with the BBC.

14   Man U defeat Leeds 2-0 with a Yorke double and are level at the top with Arsenal held scoreless at Sunderland. Spurs beat Everton 3-2, but the big early season shock is Watford winning 1-0 at Liverpool.

15   Newcastle's fragile defence crumbles losing 4-2 at The Dell, increasing speculation on Gullit's future. Mols scores all 4 as Rangers outclass Motherwell 4-1, while Celtic go under 2-1 at Dundee Utd.

16   W Ham's late sucker punch (2-2) denies Villa taking Premiership table lead. FA to crack down on abuse to refs from players and club officials.

17   FA will consider Cardiff's new 72,500-seater Millennium Stadium for 2001 FA Cup Final. Blackburn's Kevin Davies rejoins Saints in part-exchange with Egil Ostenstad after scoring just twice in 29 appearances at Ewood Park following his £7.5m move 14 months ago. Rovers to receive a cash adjustment of up to £1.2m.

18   NI lose 1-0 to France in Belfast friendly. FL may propose the introduction of an orange card as a final warning to players who have already been cautioned. England remain 14th in FIFA rankings, Scotland drop to 32nd, the ROI

are in 38th spot, NI in 71st while Wales slip to 86th. LMA ask Brian Kidd to drop legal action against Sir Alex Ferguson.

19   Robbie Keane, 19, Wolves' exciting striker, becomes the most expensive teenager in British football after joining Coventry for a £6m fee and a 5-year contract. Silvio Maric asks for a transfer 5 months after arriving at Newcastle for £3.5m fee. The 1961 FA Cup-Winners medal of Spurs centre-forward Bobby Smith, now 66, sells at auction for £11,200.

20   Kevin Ratcliffe resigns as manager of struggling Chester. In charge since April 1995, he once helped keep the club afloat by paying the water bill.

21   Agony continues for Gullit as Newcastle surrender a 2-goal lead in 3-3 home draw with the Dons. In clash of Premiership newcomers Watford beat Bradford 1-0, while Spurs win at Hillsborough to dump Sheff Wed bottom. Kid Keane marks his debut scoring twice against Derby. Everton enjoy 4-1 win over Saints, Boro beat Liverpool 1-0 in bad-tempered affair. Man City put 6 without reply past Sheff Utd, and Rangers beat Dundee Utd 4-1 to top the SPL.

22   Two Roy Keane scores give Man U 2-1 win at Highbury inflicting Arsenal's 1st home League defeat since Dec 1997. Football coverage for the 21st Century arrives in the nation's living rooms with Sky Sports Interactive Digital service giving access to different angles, highlights, replays and match stats.

23   An og from both Leeds and Liverpool but the Anfield side win 2-1 at Elland Road.

24   Howard Wilkinson launches his reign as England's U-21 boss, the vast majority of his squad for EC qualifiers v Luxembourg and Poland having enjoyed considerable success under sacked Peter Taylor. W Ham secure UEFA spot beating Inter-Toto Cup opponents Metz 3-1 (agg 3-2).

25   Shearer remains dumped on subs bench, but Gullit's gamble backfires as Newcastle lose 2-1 at home to Sunderland in near swamp-like conditions. Everton hand out 20,000 chocolate bars, then treat fans to sweet attacking football with 4-0 win over the Dons. Chelsea get scoreless draw in Skonto Riga to qualify for Champions League. Rangers fight rearguard battle losing 1-0 (agg 2-1) in Parma, but make the group stage of Champions League. Colchester boss Mick Wadsworth resigns.

26   Cwmbran lose 4-0 at Celtic (agg 10-0). Fellow non-leaguers Inter Cardiff beat Gorica 1-0 but go out on 2-1 on aggregate. St Johnstone go through against Vasas (agg 3-1) and Kilmarnock advance 2-0 v KR Reykjavik (agg 2-1). In Champions League draw, Arsenal is grouped with Barcelona, Fiorentina and AIK Stockholm. Man U have Marseille, Croatia Zagreb and Sturm Graz. Chelsea entertain AC Milan, Galatasaray and Hertha Berlin. Rangers have formidable opposition in Bayern Munich, PSV Eindhoven and Valencia. Watford Academy director Gary Johnson, 43, is named Latvia manager.

27   In UEFA Cup draw Leeds may need government guidance before heading to Belgrade to meet Partizan. Other ties: CSKA Sofia v Newcastle, Tottenham v Zimbru Chisinau, W Ham v Osijek, Celtic v Hapoel Tel Aviv, Monaco v St Johnstone, Kaiserslautern v Kilmarnock. Ian Wright teams up with Forest on loan. Jimmy Carter, 33, ex-Arsenal and Liverpool winger, is forced to retire.

28   Ruud Gullit quits as Newcastle boss and blames his departure on bad results and the constant scrutiny of his private life. The ex-Chelsea coach has spent £32m and his overall record reads: Pl 52, W 18, D 13, L 21, F 70, A 73. Steve Clarke is put in temporary charge. Leeds, reduced to 10 men, still win 2-1 at Spurs, Saints get 2-0 success over Sheff Wed side minus Carbone who storms from The Dell 15 min before start. Huddersfield destroy Palace 7-1, Barnet beat York 6-3.

29   Sunderland and Coventry draw 1-1. McManaman scores first League goal as Real Madrid beat promoted Numancia 4-1.

30   Ex-Magpie Andy Cole bags 4 in Man U's 5-1 demolition of Newcastle who have Dabizas sent off in 46 min. Leicester beat Watford 1-0, Brum net 5 against Crewe, and Ipswich hit Barnsley 6-1.

31   Man U pay £4.5m to Venezia for goalie Massimo Taibi, 27, who signs a 4-year contract. Confirmation that BskyB takes 9.1 per cent stake in Leeds giving the club a £13.8m cash injection.

September 1999

Wales burdened by baggage ... Robson takes helm at Newcastle ... Shearer's England hat-trick ... England rely on Sweden after Poland draw ... Scare closes QPR ... Refs wire up ... 14 nationalities in one match ... Female officials make history ... Forest honour returning Clough ... Magpies score 8 ... Yet another red for Hughes ... Todd quits Bolton ... Rix leaves prison ... 3 off in Merseyside clash

1   Tony Cottee and Andy Impey charged with misconduct over alleged distributing of tickets allocated for Leicester's Worthington Cup Final. Ipswich boss George Burley, John Benson (Wigan) and Peter Fox (Exeter) lift the Nationwide Manager of the Month awards. ROI top their EC group with a 2-1 win over favourites Yugoslavia. Juninho re-joins Boro from Atletico Madrid on a short-term contract until the end of season.

2   Embarrassed FAW exceed baggage weight by one and a half tons at Stansted airport before departure to Belarus, and 13 fans have to be persuaded to catch another flight!

3   In Euro U-21 ties England win 5-1 against Luxembourg, but Wales, NI and ROI all lose. Former Leeds great John Charles, 67, known as the Gentle Giant, reveals he is undergoing treatment for bowel cancer. Newcastle, joint bottom of the Premiership, unveil Bobby Robson, 66, as new manager with a contract until the end of the season. Durham-born, the ex-Ipswich and England boss with experience at PSV Eindhoven, Sporting Lisbon, Porto and Barcelona, says he is 'privileged' to be in charge but admits 'we have a fight on our hands.'

4   Shearer smashes his first hat-trick for England in 6-0 EC rout of part-timers Luxembourg at Wembley. Kieron Dyer's introduction proves big success. Scotland reinforce their 2nd place winning 2-1 in Bosnia, but still lie 13 points behind Czech Republic. Wales keep slim hopes alive with a late 2-1 winner from Giggs in Belarus, but NI in front of just 7,270 lose 3-0 to Turkey. ROI on the defensive, hold out until injury time in Zagreb, then concede last gasp 1-0 winner to Croatia's Suker.

5   Bolton and Brum share 6 goals in Div 1, Vale win 3-1 at home to Grimsby. UEFA fine W Ham £12,000 for 2 offences during their Inter-Toto campaign.

6   Scottish Media Group announce £8m investment in Hearts. Man U pip Liverpool and agree £3.2m fee for Inter defender Michael Silvestre.

7   Wolves pay £3.5m club record to land striker Ade Akinbiyi, 24, from Bristol City. UEFA reveal Man U's Taibi was registered too late for Champions League opening 6 matches. England U-21's, already qualified with 100 per cent record and without conceding a goal, lose 3-1 in Poland. Because of the Balkan conflict Leeds will play their UEFA tie v Partizan Belgrade in Holland.

8   England get dismal 0-0 draw against Poland in Warsaw, have Batty dismissed on 83 min and leave their Euro 2000 fate in the hands of Sweden. An anxious wait until Oct 9 to see if the Swedes, already assured of their place, beat Poland in Stockholm. Scotland remain on course with 0-0 result in Estonia, while Wales' slim hopes end after needing Italy to win, but Denmark pull off a 3-2 shock result in Naples. NI go under 4-0 in Germany while ROI blushes were spared in Malta by Staunton's 74th min free kick 3-2 winner. The Irish had led 2-0.

9   QPR is closed down after George Kulcsar is diagnosed suffering from potentially fatal meningitis. Saturday's home fixture against Sheff Utd is off. Bobby Robson offers coaching post to Mick Wadsworth who quit Colchester 2 weeks ago. Premier League and FL will resist UEFA attempts to introduce uniform transfer windows.

10   Two Belgian league games involving Bruges, Anderlecht, Beveren and Westerlo postponed this weekend after authorities fear planned violence between rival sets of supporters. Barnsley make it 4 wins in 5 games with 2-1 victory over Stockport.

11   Premiership action enters the electronic age today when refs and assistants communicate via two-way radios. Stuart Pearce breaks his left leg in W Ham's win over Watford. In morning start Man U get the better of Liverpool winning 3-2 at Anfield. Arsenal's Suker scores his 1st in 3-1 victory over Villa. Leboeuf's penalty provides Chelsea's 1-0 success over Newcastle to spoil Bobby Robson's 1st match in charge. The 2-2 Dons v Derby clash has 14 nationalities on show. Charlton, who have Stuart red-carded, win 2-1 against Bolton, down to 9 with the dismissals of Todd and Whitlow.

12   Rob Jones, the former Liverpool and England defender, 27, takes doctors' advice and retires after 4 knee ops. McManaman scores and assists in another as Real Madrid draw 2-2 with Bilbao. Bradford's McCall snatches injury-time 1-1 equaliser against Spurs.

13   History is made when an all-female trio, Wendy Toms, Janie Frampton and Amy Rayner, officiate at the Conference clash between Kidderminster and Nuneaton. QPR reopen their Acton training ground after meningitis scare.

14   Derby finally complete £2.3m signing of Argentine striker Esteban Fuertes. Liverpool appoint Craig Brown's asst Alex Miller as head of scouting. Man U's Champions League campaign stalls as Ossie Ardiles' Croatia Zagreb hold them scoreless at Old Trafford. Kanu misses 80th min pen as Arsenal give magnificent display in 0-0 draw at Fiorentina. Bowyer nets twice as Leeds secure 3-1 win against Partizan Belgrade in Heerenveen.

15   Brazil top the list but England climb 2 places to 12th in FIFA rankings. Scotland lie 28th, and the ROI up to 34th. NI named 71st and Wales 78th. Bury will appeal for a work permit to allow Baichung Bhutia, 22, to become the 1st Indian in English football. He has scored 25 in 40 internationals. Juninho receives his work permit clearance to play for Boro following an intervention from Tony Blair.

16   Newcastle fielding £52m of talent in their starting line-up, have comprehensive 2-0 win at CSKA Sofia. Celtic win by the same score over Hapoel Tel Aviv. W Ham dispose of Osijek 3-0 and by the same margin Spurs beat Zimbru. Reading sack Tommy Burns and asst Pat Bonner and put Alan Pardew and John Gorman in charge. Saints agree to sell The Dell to Barratt Homes for £5m and pay £4.3m for a disused gasworks, the proposed site for a 32,000-seat stadium costing £30m. Portsmouth boss Alan Ball signs 4-year contract. Charlton tie-up with Italian's Inter.

17   A civil court in Belgium overturns a life ban on Man U's Ronnie Wallwork imposed for an assault on a ref. Watford's Graham Taylor signs new 3-year deal.

18   Sub Jordi Cruyff saves Man U blushes with 1-1 equaliser at home to the Dons. Sunderland score 5 without reply at Derby, Watford shock Chelsea with 1-0 win, and Thierry Henry nets his 1st in Gunners 1-0 win at Saints. Peter Beardsley wins vote as North East football writers' Player of the Decade.

19   Brian Clough receives rapturous reception at Forest where he once delivered a League Championship, 2 European Cups and 4 League Cups during his 18-year tenure. Clough, 64, was back at the City Ground after an absence of 6 years to unveil a bronze bust in his image. But Ian Wright, on loan, spoils the occasion with his sending-off in home draw with Wolves. Newcastle fans can't believe it as they witness an 8-0 rout of Sheff Wed with Shearer bagging 5, the biggest Magpie win since Len Shackleton, on his debut, notched 6 in a 13-0 mauling of Newport in 1946. In serialised publication of his autobiography Paul Merson reveals he blew £35,000 at the bookies in one crazy month.

20   Southend Utd chairman Vic Jobson dies, aged 62. UEFA impose 2-match international ban on England's Batty for his dismissal against Poland.

21   Hertha Berlin capitalise on Chelsea blunders and win 2-1 at the Olympic Stadium. Rangers concede late Bayern Munich equaliser in Germany to finish 1-1. Juninho brings Riverside to a standstill and the kick-off delayed as over 26,000 flock to welcome him back to Boro, against Chesterfield in the League Cup. Bobby Moore's spare WC 66 shirt sells for world record £44,000 in Wolverhampton auction. Just 2,772 witness Premiership side Dons win 3-1 against Cardiff who bring a large following. FL announce a Wimbledon-style Worthington Cup 3rd draw; all 32 teams have a number and can chart their progress on a fixed grid plan. Fiery new Welsh boss Mark Hughes gets an 8th career red card as Saints beat Man City.

22   Injury-time strikes by Henry and Suker keeps Arsenal's Euro bid on course, as they beat AIK 3-1 before 71,227 at Wembley. Man U net 3 in 18 min 1st half spell to sink Sturm Graz, in Austria. In League Cup action Alan Knight, 38, appears as late sub to chalk up 800th appearance for Portsmouth at Blackburn, while Everton go out at home to Oxford. Colin Todd, nearly 4 years at Wanderers, walks away from Bolton after club sell Per Frandsen to Blackburn for £1.75m.

23   Derby transfer-list Lars Bohinen after he uses his own website to slate Jim Smith's selections and training methods. UEFA unveil plans for a mini European Championship to replace friendlies in the odd years between WC and EC.

24 Graham Rix, 41, is released from Prison halfway through his 12-month sentence. Chelsea promise to re-employ him.

25 Defensive howlers, notably by Italian goalie Taibi, means Man U draw 3-3 at home to Saints who avoid defeat for the 1st time in 11 visits. Gascoigne receives red card for mouthing obscenities at ref's asst as Boro lose to Chelsea. Villa concede 3 goals and skipper Southgate is dismissed at Leicester.

26 Scorer Hartson sees red in the Dons' 1-1 draw with Spurs. The Selhurst side still awaiting a home Premiership win since Jan 9.

27 Three off as Everton take the points (1-0) in explosive 161st Merseyside derby at Anfield. Jeffers, and Liverpool pair Gerrard and Westerveld dismissed with Staunton pressed into service as emergency goalie. Wales call up David Johnson for EC 2000 tie with Switzerland even though the Ipswich striker has played for England B and Jamaica.

28 Petrescu's 58th min score gives Chelsea vital 1st win in Champions League group against Galatasaray whose Brazilian goalie Taffarel is sent off after half an hour for deliberate handling outside his area. Albertz scores late winner to give Rangers a win at PSV. Andy Hunt nets a hat-trick in Charlton's 4-0 defeat of Stockport. Liverpool's Karlheinz Riedle, 34, joins Fulham.

29 Cole's overhead strike helps in Man U's 2-1 Champions League win over Marseille, and takes his European tally to 14, one behind Denis Law's club record. Grimandi's elbow challenge earns dismissal but Kanu's late equaliser caps a spirited 2nd half Arsenal performance at Barcelona.

30 Leeds negotiate their way into UEFA 2nd rd beating Partizan, Newcastle, W Ham and Spurs also advance. But exit for Kilmarnock and St Johnstone leaving Celtic as Scotland's only survivor. Graham Rix returns to Chelsea's training ground after his early release from Wandsworth Prison. Fulham's Paul Bracewell is Nationwide Manager of the Month with recognition for Gary Megson (Stoke) and Barnet's John Still.

October 1999

Gregory hits out at Owen ... Ref Harris gives cards galore ... Indian striker creates history ... Dalglish gets Geordie settlement ... Vieira apology for spitting ... 'Thank you' Sweden, says Keegan ... Cantona returns for Ferguson testimonial ... Portugal win Euro 2004 vote ... Red card mania ... McCoist breaks a leg ... Rice's medals stolen ... Allardyce in at Bolton ... Chelsea destroy Turks ... Larsson double leg break ... FIFA inspect grounds ... Molineux landmark ... Wright links with Celtic ... 'Budgie' Byrne dies

1 In UEFA Cup draw Spurs host stiff opposition in Kaiserslautern. Leeds and Newcastle have home ties with Lokomotiv Moscow and FC Zurich. W Ham travel to Steaua Bucharest and Celtic journey to Lyon. Villa boss John Gregory labels Michael Owen a 'baby-faced assassin,' a reference to the dreadful lunge at Everton's David Weir in recent Merseyside clash.

2 Kevin Phillips bags 2 and heads the Premiership chart with 10 following Sunderland's 4-0 win at Bradford. Rob Harris cautions 11 and sends off Staunton in Villa-Liverpool scoreless draw. Sheff Wed sweep aside the Dons 5-1 for their 1st win. Charlton leap-frog Brum to top Div 1. Riedle, on his Fulham debut, scores in 2-1 win at Norwich, a run of 13 unbeaten matches. The clash of York and Chester, bottom two in Div 3, ends 2-2. Bury's Bhutia is the 1st Indian to play in the FL when he comes on as half-time sub against Cardiff – and is booked after 2 min!

3 Poyet nets after 27 sec as Chelsea destroy Man U 5-0 with Butt dismissed after 20 min. Sent-off Vieira is accused of spitting at W Ham who have Marc-Vivien Foe red-carded in added time. Shearer's brace for Newcastle sinks Boro in Tyne-Tees derby. Irish soccer loses one of its most able administrators with the death of Dr Tony O'Neill, 54, a former FAI Gen Sec.

4 Newcastle and former manager Kenny Dalglish finally agree undisclosed compensation settlement figure. Dalglish, now Celtic's Director of Football, initially sought over £1m. Wimbledon complete £2m signing of Norwegian midfielder Martin Andresen from Stabaek. Mikkel Beck gets injury-time 3-3 equaliser at The Dell for Derby who were 3-1 down. Arsenal's Vieira issues an apology saying he is ashamed of his spitting behaviour.

5 A Collins pen confirms Scotland's place in next month's EC 2000 play-offs after crucial if unconvincing win over Bosnia. W Ham sign Gary Charles from Benfica.

6 FAI extend manager Mick McCarthy's contract by 2 years to Feb 2002. Chelsea's Leboeuf, in France on international duty, says he is frightened by violence in English football and claims he is scared before some matches. Martin Edwards sells half of his stake in Man U for almost £41m.

7 Ian Atkins steps down as Northampton manager with asst Kevin Wilson standing in. W Ham can continue in UEFA Cup despite fielding Igor Stimac who was ineligble against Osijek. He should have served a 2-match ban imposed in 1995. Bulgaria's inspirational forward Hristo Stoichkov, 33, retires.

8 Following a 3-match trial period Bolton put caretaker-manager Phil Brown in charge for the 'forseeable future'. With 5 Leeds players in the starting line-up England U-21's beat Denmark 4-1 at Bradford.

9 Kevin Keegan offers Sweden a 'thousand thanks' for earning England a place in the EC 2000 play-offs. Sweden's 2-0 victory over Poland in Stockholm gives England the lifeline for the two-legged ties on Nov 13 and 17. Scotland end their group with an impressive 3-0 display over Lithuania. Lack-lustre Wales slump to 2-0 home defeat by Switzerland. NI fail 4-1 in Finland. Heartache for ROI; leading 1-0 in Macedonia, and just 12 sec from automatic EC 2000 qualification, they concede added-time equaliser and must now try to make it through the play-offs.

10 In friendly at Stadium of Light, England get a half-time 'shake-up' from boss Keegan and win 2-1 against Belgium thanks to scores from Shearer, his 28th in 54 internationals, and Redknapp. Villa's Gareth Barry hits a hat-trick in 9-0 victory over San Marino, but England eliminated from U-18 Championships, having lost 2-0 to group winners, Spain.

11 Sir Alex Ferguson's testimonial draws 55,824 to watch Man U against a World X1 which includes Schmeichel and Cantona. Boss Ferguson has brought 15 trophies in 13 years to Old Trafford. Wimbledon complete £2.5m signing of Brentford's Hermann Hriedarsson. Ex-Spurs midfielder Vinny Samways gets his 16th suspension of his two and a half year career in Spanish football following his 10th red card for Las Palmas.

12 UEFA announce Portugal win by a narrow majority the right to host Euro 2004 beating confident favourites Spain and a joint Austria-Hungary bid. England receive £4,050 UEFA fine for supporters' misbehaviour at EC

Poland qualifier. Italian Cup tie between Sampdoria and Bologna – the country's first with two refs – ends in chaos, is halted because of crowd trouble, and is then abandoned shortly after half time. In Worthington Cup tie Newcastle slump out at Brum, the Dons defeat Sunderland, Arsenal struggle to get past Preston and Bradford lose to Barnsley.

13 UEFA EC 2000 play-off draw pairs Scotland and England, the oldest fixture in the international calendar. Israel will meet Denmark, Slovenia v Ukraine and the ROI face Turkey. In League Cup Villa humble Man U's under-strength team 3-0. Chelsea's second-string go out at home to Huddersfield, Saints grab dramatic injury-time winner over Liverpool and Derby lose to Bolton. Reading appoint Alan Pardew as successor to Tommy Burns.

14 Sam Allardyce stuns 2nd place Notts County with resignation. Over 1,000 in Dudley watch the unveiling of a statue to former Man U and England hero Duncan Edwards who died in the Munich plane disaster 41 years ago.

15 Lawrie McMenemy rejects a new NI contract offer. Failure to qualify for EC finals brings dismissal for Poland coach Janusz Wojcik.

16 On a record day of shame 26 players sent-off in England and Scotland (14 in England and 12 north of the border). Owen misses a pen as Liverpool win 1-0 against Chelsea who have Desailly and Wise (9th time in Stamford Bridge career) sent off. Coventry, with 4-1 success, heap problems on Newcastle. Lee Dixon scores his 1st for 3 years in Arsenal's 4-1 win over Everton. The Dons get their 1st win since the opening day, beating Bradford. P/Manager David Platt starts his 1st Forest match, but is dismissed in the final moments at Sheff Utd. Celtic hit 7 without reply against bottom club Aberdeen who endure worst defeat in 30 years. Kilmarnock's Ally McCoist suffers left leg fracture against Rangers. Bruce Grobbelaar, 42, makes FA Cup appearance for Northwich Victoria.

17 Boro end spell of 5 defeats in 6 games with 2-1 win over W Ham. Bristol's scoreless derby at Ashton Gate is watched by 16,011 and sees Rovers introduce Simon Bryant, 15 years and 11 months, as the youngest in this local clash.

18 Gills new boss Peter Taylor is punished with £500 fine and warned about his future conduct. Kasey Keller is celebrating Rayo Vallecano's top of the table spot in Spain, and has conceded just 5, the best record in the League. Pat Rice's 4 FA Cup Final medals stolen from his Herts home.

19 Sam Allardyce is named new boss of Bolton. In gripping Champions League tie Arsenal lose 4-2 at Wembley to cynical and clinical Barcelona. Bergkamp shines and scores, Overmars also nets. Title holders Man U surrender to 69th min Marseille score in the Velodrome, their 1st defeat in 21 Champions League ties since losing to Juventus 2 seasons back.

20 Chelsea, given a 'Welcome to Hell' arrival in Turkey answer back on the pitch with 5-0 trouncing of Galatasaray. Rangers storm to top of the group beating PSV 4-1. FA appoint Adam Crozier, 35, as new chief executive, and he takes up his post in January on a salary believed to be in the region of £300,000 a year. Bill Dodgin senior, former Saints, Fulham, Brentford and Sampdoria manager dies, age 90.

21 Free-flowing Leeds stop Lokomotiv Moscow in their tracks and set up healthy 4-1 lead for the away leg. Guest of honour Larry Hagman – JR Ewing in *Dallas* – meets Steaua Bucharest and W Ham players beforehand; and in bizarre evening when the Danish ref requests booked Di Canio be taken off by his own coaching staff, Hammers lose 2-0. Shearer's 12th this season seals a Newcastle 2-1 win at Zurich. Celtic striker Henrik Larsson suffers double left leg fracture as his side go down in a 1-0 defeat in Lyon.

22 Everton's Phelan joins Palace on loan. Pompey unveil plans for £30m all-seater stadium holding 35,000 behind Fratton Park. Home Sec Jack Straw meets 5-man FIFA inspection team on a whistle-stop tour of Wembley and other grounds, and tells them England is better prepared than any of its rivals to host WC 2006.

23 In front of watching FIFA delegation at Stamford Bridge, Kanu hits a stunning hat-trick as Arsenal come from 2-down with 15 min remaining to snatch 3-2 win. At sodden White Hart Lane Spurs win a stirring 3-1 tussle against Man U.

24 Goal glut at Goodison as Everton and Leeds draw 4-4 ending the Elland Road club's record 10-match winning run. After Boro's win at Watford boss Robson hints that injury-plagued Gascoigne is not now an automatic choice. Seven yellow cards as Sinclair's 89th min 1-1 equaliser deprives 10-man Sunderland of going top at W Ham.

25 In silent demonstration against new seating arrangements for season-ticket holders, Magpie fans without replica black & white shirts stand throughout, as their team climbs out of the relegation zone for the 1st time with 2-0 success over Derby. Mal Shotton, 42, resigns as manager of struggling Oxford Utd. Rikki Hunt quits as chairman of Swindon 4 days after the £1m sale of striker George Ndah to Wolves.

26 Chelsea disciplined performance before 74,855 in the San Siro and get a 1-1 reward and valuable point against AC Milan thanks to Wises's equaliser. Rangers fail to secure home victory needed to advance to last 16 and hopes remain on a knife edge after Valencia prove too smart winning 2-1. The 2,000th League game at Molineux sees Wolves beat Sheff Utd 1-0. Notts County confirm Gary Brazil in charge.

27 Ian Wright heads to Celtic after 3 months at Forest. Liverpool's Titi Camara hears about the death of his father hours beforehand, but despite offers of compassionate leave, opts to play and scores the winner against W Ham. A ferocious 75th min Batistuta strike ends Arsenal's interest in the elite Champions League as they squander chances against Fiorentina and will now compete in the UEFA Cup. Man U defeat average-looking Croatia Zagreb and top their group. In SPL Celtic, before 58,731, blow opportunity to go top losing 1-0 to 10-man Motherwell.

28 Spurs, twice winners of the UEFA Cup and in their 50th home European tie, gain slim 1-0 pen advantage over Kaiserslautern. Arsenal's Vieira gets a 6-match ban and record £45,000 fine following misconduct charge at W Ham. Ossie Ardiles loses his job as coach to Croatia Zagreb 4 months and 20 days after taking charge. John 'Budgie' Byrne, 60, former Palace, W Ham and England forward dies in S Africa from a heart attack.

29 Rushden & Diamonds provide FA Cup upset beating Scunthorpe 2-0. Scotland's ticket hotline for EC 2000 play-off against England crashes after 17,000 calls in the opening minutes of trading.

30 Leeds confirm their status as potential Premiership champs with a 1-0 emphatic win over W Ham with manager David O'Leary pointing out crowds under him have leaped from 29,000 to 40,190. Newcastle collect their 1st away point in scoreless affair at Arsenal. Boro blunt Everton's new found belief winning 2-1, while Man U's 3-0 score-

line against Villa was better, says manager Ferguson, than the performance. In FA Cup action Nigel Clough's Burton Albion draw with Rochdale. Enfield pull off 2-1 shock at Chesterfield, who reached the semi-finals 3 years ago, and Ilkeston Town put out Carlisle, while Conference side Hereford, no strangers to cup romance, defeat York.

31 Robbie Keane scores one and plays a key role in 3 as Coventry defeat Watford 4-0, Sunderland beat Spurs, and in Div 1 Black Country clash West Brom and Wolves draw 1-1. John Toshack's future looks uncertain in the wake of Real Madrid's humiliating 3-1 home defeat by neighbours Atletico Madrid.

November 1999
Blackburn sack Kidd ... Sir Alf Ramsey street ... 'Lucky' Losers FA Cup draw ... Dixon's testimonial windfall ... England beat Scotland in play-off ... Icelandic consortium buy Stoke ... Kaiser tops German poll ... Bruce on Huddersfield board ... £6,400 for Gazza's shirt ... Scotland win but England through ... Real dismiss Toshack ... Collins retires from Internationals ... Heath quits Blades ... Welsh appoint Hughes ... Man U are World Champs

1   Kevin Wilson lands the Northampton job for the remainder of this season. Derby say they are close to agreeing a deal for the return of Georgi Kinkladze from Ajax. Retired Mark Wright applies for managerial post at his former club Oxford Utd.

2   Arsenal's last Champions League involvement ends with anything but a flourish, eventually seeing off part-timers AIK 3-2 in Stockholm with 2 from Overmars and one from Suker. A stunning Solskjaer volley sets up Man U's 2-1 win over Sturm Graz and a top group spot. England's U-21 EC play-off with Yugoslavia is now a one-off match switched to Luxembourg on Nov 14 because of security fears. Coach Vialli accepts criticism of his rota-selection from chairman Ken Bates. Dunfermline boss Dick Campbell resigns.

3   Blackburn sack Brian Kidd after 11 months in charge and with two and half years to run on his contract. For the 3rd time, Tony Parkes deputises. The club lies 19th in Div 1 winning just 3 of 14 games. Kidd, who succeeded Roy Hodgson, spent £30m but did recoup some £27m. Chelsea conjure up perfect retort to their chairman, overwhelming Hertha Berlin to go top of their group, but have Sutton sent off. Rangers will compete in UEFA Cup after their failure to secure a point against Bayern in Munich. Sir Alf Ramsey has a street named after him in Ipswich. Ref Gary Willard, 40, becomes 1st to be dropped from Premiership for failing fitness test.

4   Spurs, with Ginola architect of their home 1-0 lead only a sub until the last 10 min, concede two 90th min scores and cruelly go out of UEFA Cup in Kaiserslautern. Newcastle advance against Zurich 3-1 (agg 5-2) as do Leeds 3-0 (agg 7-1) in Moscow against Lokomotiv. W Ham's home tie ends scoreless (agg 2-0) with Steaua going through, and Celtic depart losing at Parkhead 1-0 (agg 2-0) to Lyon.

5   Rangers' striker Mols is injured and out for the season. In UEFA Cup draw Leeds travel to Moscow, again, this time to meet Spartak, and Newcastle head to Roma. Arsenal start home to Nantes and Rangers have Ibrox date with Borussia Dortmund.

6   Derby cannot reverse the trend of not keeping a clean sheet at Anfield since 1970 – and concede twice to Liverpool. Boro's 34,793 record crowd sees bad-tempered N East derby with Sunderland end 1-1 with 11 bookings and Chris Makin sent off. Fans register their annoyance as Villa lose at home to Saints. Man U's 2-0 win over Leicester puts them top. In Div 1 Man City stay top despite draw at QPR, Notts County held 1-1 by Gillingham, but remain leaders of Div 2, while Posh are tops in Div 3.

7   Having gone 29 games without keeping a clean sheet the Dons shore up and beat Leeds 2-0. Persistent fouling makes a mockery of the game as Arsenal have 6 booked plus Ljungberg and Keown dismissed in 2-1 defeat at Spurs. In-form Shearer stretches his tally to 13 goals in 11 matches, 18 in total for the season, with a pen in 1-1 against Everton. Chelsea in goalless affair with W Ham who have Margas sent off. Rangers win Ibrox Old Firm clash 4-2 to ease 4 pts clear with a game in hand.

8   FA's Challenge Cup committee announce 63 rather than 64 teams in the first 3rd round draw; Man U's place being taken by one of the 20 clubs beaten in the 2nd round. A second draw will be held to find the 'lucky' losers. This is the FA's unprecedented decision to solve the embarrassment caused by the holders' withdrawal to play in the FIFA Club World Championship. Lee Dixon's testimonial draws 22,486 to Highbury as Arsenal beat Real Madrid 3-1, and earns the 35-year old defender, 12 years at the club, a £300,000 windfall.

9   Spurs fail to have UEFA Cup opponents Kaiserslautern thrown out on the technicality of breaking regulations regarding the timing of team selection. But the Germans pick up a £500 fine for their indiscretion. FA charge Boro striker Brian Deane with misconduct over an elbow incident against Sunderland's Paul Butler.

10 Chairman Peter Hill-Wood voices concern over Arsenal's disciplinary record, 26 red cards since Arsène Wenger took charge in Sept 1996. Pressure eases on Wrexham boss Brian Flynn after overcoming a potential banana-skin of a 1st rd Cup replay against Kettering.

11 Spanish ref Diaz Vega is to take charge of the Scotland-England play-off clash. England's U-21 play-off decider in Luxembourg this Sunday is postponed because Yugoslavia is unhappy with security.

12 England are 1/3 favourites to qualify for EC 2000 finals with Scotland earning a 9/4 quote. Tomorrow's Hampden Park clash is being relayed worldwide; taking both games live include Indonesia, Malaysia, Thailand, Uganda, Ethiopia, Mauritius, 11 European countries, 27 countries in the Middle East and North Africa, and 50 million homes in China. Ryman Premier side Aldershot Town pay club record £20,000 for Woking's Grant Payne.

13 In largely one-sided play-off England, showing more guile, give Scotland a lesson in finishing. Scholes takes his tally to 9 in 19 internationals netting twice in the opening half. He is one of 10 cautioned, 5 to each side, for over-celebrating his first goal. Yet again ROI are undone in closing moments allowing Turkey to grab an all-important 83rd min (pen) equaliser from Carsley's handball, and just 4 min after Robbie Keane sweeps the home side ahead. Keane needlessly picks up late caution and is out of away leg.

14 Keegan pleads for the Scotland team's anthem to be respected at Wembley. David Batty reveals he has played for almost a year with a heart problem and is on steroid medication.

15 Following £3.5m takeover by an Icelandic consortium the Stoke manager Gary Megson is replaced after just 4 months and 22 matches by former Icelandic national coach Gudjon Thordarsson. Shrewsbury appoint Kevin Ratcliffe, previously with Chester, as manager until the end of the season. Croatian striker Davor Suker, a keen

stock market investor, astounds Arsenal supporters by investing £20,000 in Man U. Franz Beckenbauer, a WC-winner playing and coaching, is Germany's Footballer of the Century.

16 Arsenal plan to move into a new stadium half a mile from Highbury, at Ashburton Grove, which houses Islington council's depots. Steve Bruce joins the Huddersfield board, following Steve Coppell (Palace) and Dario Gradi (Crewe) as the only managers to be directors at their clubs. Liverpool stars earned an incredible £36m last year while the club plunged £5.1m into the red. Gascoigne's Euro 96 No 8 shirt raises £6,400 at charity auction.

17 England survive a tartan onslaught in play-off decider 2nd leg. Honours go to Scotland, positive and attack-minded throughout and roused by a 38th min Hutchison headed goal. But England, opting for strike power and no wingers, take their EC 2000 finals place. Ireland's campaign comes to bitter end after scoreless draw in Turkey. They fail on the away goal after the earlier 1-1 result in Dublin. Tony Cascarino, involved in some unsavoury scenes at the finish, afterwards announces his retirement from the international scene. John Toshack, mid-way through a 16-month contract, is sacked at Real Madrid for the 2nd time.

18 FAI extend Mick McCarthy's contract by a further 2 years. Sheff Wed chairman Dave Richards says the club is almost £18m in debt. NI make official approach to Macclesfield about the availabilty of manager Sammy McIlroy.

19 Everton's John Collins, 31, announces his international retirement after helping Scotland defeat England.

20 Ian Rush, being paid a reported £50,000 for 2 guest appearances in Australia, plays his 600th career match for Sydney Olympic. Arsenal subject Boro to a humiliating 5-1 defeat with Overmars helping himself to a hat-trick. Leboeuf is sent off but Chelsea's Flo nets a 1-1 stoppage-time equaliser at Everton. Liverpool's 7-match unbeaten Premiership sequence continues at Sunderland. Evergreen Tony Cottee, 34, grabs 2 in Leicester win over the Dons. In FA Cup one of the finest performances comes from Enfield holding Preston, third in Div 2, to a scoreless draw at Deepdale. Boncho Guentchev, Bulgaria's former WC player, stars for Hendon who lose to Blackpool.

21 Hammers squeeze home 4-3 against Sheff Wed who were twice ahead, but have Danny Sonner dismissed. Ipswich dominate scoreless 67th East Anglian derby with Norwich.

22 Coventry's Keane nets the 2-1 winner in lively Midlands clash with Villa. Steve Walsh asks to come off the Leicester transfer list. Rangers solve a goalie crisis by snapping up Everton's Thomas Myhre on loan to play in UEFA tie with Borussia Dortmund.

23 In Champions League Bosnich has a blinder, but Keane is lucky to stay on, as Man U pay dearly for 2 defensive errors presenting goal opportunities to Fiorentina's Batistuta and Balbo. Barnsley improve manager Dave Bassett's contract to stave off any likely Blackburn interest. Sheff U chairman Mike McDonald resigns before 3-1 home defeat by Vale and Adrian Heath quits after it!

24 Chelsea make hard work of easy pickings (3-1) against inept Feyenoord who were virtually on the back foot throughout. Man City move 4 points clear beating Barnsley 3-1. Saints player Mark Hughes accepts a 4 and half year contract to manage Wales.

25 In UEFA action late goals from Winterburn (81) and Bergkamp (90) seals unconvincing 3-0 win over Nantes. Newcastle come away from Roma tie having conceded a 51st min pen. Leeds must play Spartak (no under-soil heating) in Bulgaria next Thursday after UEFA Cup tie is called off because the alternative Dinamo Moscow pitch is unplayable. FA fine Villa's Southgate £5,000 for remarks to the ref following his 1st career sending-off. Arsenal's Pat Rice declines opportunity to take charge of NI.

26 Villa boss John Gregory gets 28-day touchline ban. Roma coach Fabio Capello launches scathing attack on Newcastle's Shearer labelling the striker a cheat for diving.

27 Ex-Watford striker Kevin Phillips scores twice on his return to Vicarage Road, lifting Sunderland into 3rd spot. Owen is cautioned for diving as Liverpool go under at W Ham. Huddersfield, unbeaten in 10 matches, claim Man City's scalp at Maine Road. Graham Kelly, former FA chief executive, completes 184-mile charity walk from Peterborough to Teesside.

28 Classic strikes from Henry give Arsenal victory over Derby. Chelsea's 1-0 over Bradford is their 1st League victory in 6 games. Bridges nets against Saints and sees Leeds on top. Patched-up Newcastle conjure a 2-1 win over Spurs. Rangers to Dundee and Celtic to Motherwell lose on the same day. Sevilla, bottom of Spanish League, end their match with Malaga with 8 players – but still hang on for scoreless draw. Paraguayan goalie Jose Luis Chilavert hits a hat-trick for Velez Sarsfield in their 6-1 win against Ferro Carril Oeste and is believed to be the 1st such feat by a goalkeeper. Extrovert Chilavert takes his goals career tally to 46!

29 Pressure mounting on Celtic's John Barnes following 5 defeats in last 8 matches. FA agree to stage England's delayed EC U-21 play-off versus Yugoslavia, in Barcelona on March 29.

30 In Worthington Cup 4th rd Boro level (2-2) late in normal time and win the shoot-out to defeat Arsenal. Two late goals, including Joe Cole's 1st for the club, seal Hammers win at Brum. In FA Cup, Hull see off Hayes to earn pay-day with Chelsea. Rushden & Diamonds overcome Ilkeston for a date with Sheff Utd. Man U become the 1st British side to be crowned FIFA Club World Champions in Toyko through Keane's 35th min Toyota Cup goal against Palmeiras. Man of the match Giggs wins a car from the sponsors. However, to retain the No 1 status they will need to triumph in FIFA's new official 8-team Club World Championship starting in Brazil on Jan 6. Chelsea's Pierluigi Casiraghi has 8th knee operation.

December 1999

Kanu tops in Africa ... Warnock is Blades boss ... England and Germany in WC 2002! ... Keane ends speculation ... Pompey sack Ball ... Prison for Ipswich player ... England and Germany – again! ... Gradi game milestone ... Edwards ridicules Ferguson ... Dublin's neck injury ... Geordies swamp Spurs ... Worthington quits Blackpool ... Kenwright wins Everton control ... Chelsea's all foreign line-up ... Wigan yet to lose ... 8-man Cardiff get draw ... Grobbelaar becomes manager ... WC 66 heroes honoured

1   Spurs second best all night to Fulham who win Worthington Cup tie 3-1, while Villa before their lowest crowd for 5 years, 17,608, breeze past Saints 4-0. CIS Scottish Cup, Aberdeen knock out Rangers 1-0 and Celtic's 90th min score provides win over Dundee. Arsenal's Kanu is African Footballer of the Year. Celtic's Craig Burley joins Derby for £3m. Divisional awards go to Leicester's Martin O'Neill, Steve Bruce (Huddersfield), Peter Taylor

(Gillingham) and Kevin Wilson (Northampton). In 'Wild Card' draw for FA Cup 2nd rd losers, Darlington, beaten 3-1 by Gillingham, are back in again, and face a 3rd rd trip to Villa.

2 Sheff Utd appoint locally-born Neil Warnock as boss, their 5th manager in less than 3 years. In UEFA 3rd rd, 1st leg, Leeds go under 2-1 against Spartak Moscow in Russia, their 1st reverse in Europe this season and only their 2nd in 17 games. Raith Rovers manager, John McVeigh, leaves the club by mutual consent. Derby manager Jim Smith is charged with misconduct by FA.

3 A cartilage injury rules Liverpool's Redknapp out for 3 months. Wolves celebrate Colin Lee's 50th Div 1 match in charge, beating Man City 4-1.

4 Sunderland gain revenge for their opening day 4-0 defeat by destroying Chelsea 4-1. No jet-lag fatigue for Man U who return to the top of the table beating Everton 5-1 with Solskjaer bagging 4. Swaggering Arsenal outclass Leicester 3-0 at Filbert Street. The Dons hit 5 past a Watford side offering little. Huddersfield head Div 1 after beating QPR. Wigan and Preston joint top of Div 2 with 42 pts. Just 2,252 witness table-topping Barnet beat Chester in Div 3. Despite a £100,000 security operation organised violence marks Cardiff's visit to Millwall.

5 Sheff Wed go ahead at Anfield but Liverpool run out 4-1 winners. Ian Harte's stoppage-time penalty sends Leeds back top – and keeps Derby rooted in the bottom 3. Winter ravages SPL programme but 60,092 attend Parkhead to see Celtic triumph 4-0 over Hibs.

6 In lifeless (0-0) 100th meeting of Spurs and W Ham, Steve Lomas gets his marching orders. FA fine Forest £25,000 for admitting unauthorised payments to management and playing staff between 1984-1993. Newcastle to investigate how 72 complimentary FA Cup Final tickets from their game with Man U went on the black market.

7 At WC 2002 draw (European Qualifying Group) in Tokyo, England will meet Germany whom they have not beaten since 1985. 'It gives us a chance to settle the score from Euro 96' quips Keegan. Greece, Finland and Albania make up group 9. Scotland have a fair draw in with Belgium, Croatia, Latvia and San Marino. Wales face a mammoth task up against Norway, Ukraine, Poland, Armenia and Belarus. NI's incoming manager will not like the look of Czech Republic, Denmark, Bulgaria, Iceland and Malta. ROI's main hurdle is Holland and Portugal, with Cyprus, Andorra and Estonia completing their section. Coach Vialli is 'sent off' and watches on a monitor his Chelsea side survive to get a point in tense scoreless draw at Lazio. Rangers' 2-goal 1st leg lead is overturned with an injury-time Borussia Dortmund equaliser from Bobic (2-2), and after extra time the Germans win shoot-out.

8 Double boost at Old Trafford as skipper Keane signs a 4-year new contract worth around £52,000 a week, then he scores the opener in 3-0 win over Valencia in Champions League phase 2, group A.

9 UEFA Cup goal feast (3-3) in Nantes as Arsenal pass their French test winning 6-3 on agg. Lucas Radebe's 84th min winner beats Spartak Moscow as Leeds go through on away goal. Newcastle fail to break down Roma (0-0) and the Italians advance. Tranmere boss John Aldridge signs 2 and a half year contract. Alan Ball, 54, is sacked at Portsmouth and afterwards hints at permanent retirement. Bob McNab steps in.

10 Cambridge Utd's 2-0 win removes Palace from FA Cup. Leicester agree £3m fee to sign Darren Eadie from Norwich. Ipswich's Gary Croft, an £800,000 signing from Blackburn 3 months ago, is jailed for 4 months for a series of driving offences. Bristol-born Bob Houghton is sacked as coach of China.

11 In FA Cup 3rd rd Tranmere's spirit sinks W Ham while Watford's miserable season continues, losing to Brum. Hull cannot contain Chelsea and go out 6-1. Sir Alex Ferguson watches his son Darren score the winner as Wrexham take yet another scalp, this time Boro. Derby's confidence rock-bottom losing at home to Burnley. Heroic Hereford hold Leicester scoreless, and Exeter do likewise against Everton. The Dons attract just 4,505 to witness the 1-0 win over heavily-supported Barnsley.

12 Kevin Keegan is staggered as Euro 2000 draw in Belgium throws up yet another England-Germany show-down! They will meet in Charleroi on June 17. Group A fixtures also include Romania and Portugal. In FA Cup, Man City advance winning 4-1 at Chester. Huddersfield can concentrate on promotion after losing to Liverpool, while the Spurs-Newcastle full-blooded clash ends 1-1. Sheff Utd held at home 1-1 by Rushden & Diamonds. UEFA announce all 31 games in EC 2004 finals in Portugal will be available free on terrestrial television. Valencia, down to 8 players, survive to beat Atletico Madrid 2-1. Shimizu S-Pulse, coached by Steve Perryman, lose the J-League on shoot-out.

13 Arsenal steer safe passage in FA Cup beating Blackpool 3-1, and Dean Richards' header at Ipswich ensures Saints advance. PFA urge managers to stop their players diving.

14 In Worthington Cup, Bolton defeat the Dons, and Tranmere, having knocked out W Ham in the FA Cup, now eliminate Boro. The FA will no longer be run by the 92 councillors; instead, a 12-man board consisting of representatives from Premier, FL and the Amateur game, will be in charge of all major issues. Adrian Heath joins Sunderland as senior coach. Dario Gradi celebrates his 900th game at the helm with Crewe, against Wolves.

15 Sunderland complete £2.5m signing of West Brom winger Kevin Kilbane. In Worthington Cup quarter-final (2-2) Villa's Southgate misses in shoot-out, and W Ham go through. Leicester win 4th rd tie against Leeds in shoot-out. Long-serving Steve Chettle leaves Forest for Barnsley on a free.

16 Mark Wright, the former England and Liverpool defender, gets managerial start with Southport. FAW confirm Mark Hughes as manager and the ex-Man Utd coach Eric Harrison will be his asst. In new publication *Manchester Unlimited* chairman Martin Edwards says Sir Alex Ferguson is a trouble-maker and useless with money.

17 Leeds snap up Blackburn winger Jason Wilcox for £3m. Derby complete £3m signing of Belgian striker Branko Strupar from Genk. Chairman Tony Hale quits at West Brom in the wake of heavy criticism over his handling of Kilbane's move to Sunderland.

18 Arsenal, wasteful in front of goal, are held 1-1 by the Dons. Liverpool stars of yesterday honour Bill Shankly while on the pitch the Anfield reds chalk up their 6th straight win at home, over Coventry. W Ham cannot contain Man U who grab 3 goals in an opening 20-min spell for 4-2 win. Derby's Darryl Powell nets his 1st in 3 seasons at Leicester. Juninho's twinkling feet inspires Boro 2-1 victory over Spurs to end a miserable 7-match spell without a win.

19 Chelsea lose the plot in grudge match against Leeds, Leboeuf is sent off and others might have joined him as Stephen McPhail nets twice for O'Leary's side who stay top. Blackburn lose at Sheff Utd, their 1st defeat in 8

League games under Tony Parkes. Hospital reports say Villa's Dion Dublin broke his neck following a collision in yesterday's win over Sheff Wed.

20 Two office staff resign in the wake of W Ham's Worthington Cup fiasco over ineligible Manny Omoyinmi, who, whilst on loan to Gillingham, figured in the competition – and never spoke up.

21 Rushden & Diamonds' FA Cup dream ends after losing a shoot-out to Sheff Utd but Everton make heavy weather of defeating Exeter.

22 In FA Cup replay Newcastle inflict a 6-1 drubbing on Spurs, the Londoners' worst defeat in an event they have won 8 times. Blackburn end West Brom's interest, in extra-time. Hereford get a standing ovation at Filbert Street after going out 2-1 in injury time to Leicester. Controversial Jesus Gil is removed from his president's post at Atletico Madrid. Chelsea sign Emerson Thome, Sheff Wed's Brazilian defender for £2.5m.

23 Nigel Worthington resigns as boss of struggling Blackpool. FL name John McKeown, 49, as chief executive, to replace Richard Scudamore.

24 Everton vice-chairman Bill Kenwright completes a late Christmas Eve coup to win control of the club, signing a cut-price £20m deal with the major shareholder Peter Johnson.

25 Disturbed by the interpretation of earlier comments Kevin Keegan pledges to stand by his job even if England flop at Euro 2000.

26 Chelsea enter the history books by starting the game at Saints without a single British player in their line-up. Leeds maintain top spot beating Leicester. Everton hit 5 past Sunderland, and manager Walter Smith extends his contract by 2 years. Bradford hold out for 75 min at Old Trafford then cave in 4-0. Coventry's enterprise seals 3-2 win over Arsenal. Spurs crush Watford 4-0 but boos for boss Graham as he subs Ginola, for the 11th time this season. Wigan create new club record of 22 games without defeat and are the only unbeaten side in the country.

27 Fortune favours Rangers in 1-1 Old Firm clash at Parkhead. The non-league scene still thrives as Rushden & Diamonds regain leadership of the Conference beating Stevenage before 5,721, an attendance only marginally better than the 5,518 who watch Aldershot's Ryman League 1-0 win over neighbours Farnborough.

28 Prime Minister Blair, in the record 42,026 crowd at the Stadium of Light, sees Sunderland surrender a 2-goal lead and finish level with Man U. Ljungberg and Henry score as wise old Arsenal give a lesson to an arrogant Leeds side including 9 under the age of 22. Fowler notches his 150th Liverpool goal in win over the Dons. Leyton Orient who have not scored for 9 hours and 22 min accomplish the feat 5 times at Chester to swap places with their hosts at the foot of the table. Cardiff have 3 sent off but force a goalless draw at Cambridge.

29 Wise replaces Deschamps and inspires Chelsea, who again start without a British player, to 3-0 win over Sheff Wed. Boro's giant 'bubble' cover is inadequate as frozen pitch cancels match with Coventry. Bruce Grobbelaar is appointed manager to S African side Supersport Utd. Harry Kewell is Oceania Footballer of the Year.

30 A table constructed by accumulating points for all games in the First Division and the Premiership from Jan 1 1900 to Dec 28 1999 has Liverpool the champions of the 20th century, by a narrow margin over Arsenal. Five 'forgotten' WC 66 members – Ball, Stiles, Cohen, Wilson and Hunt – are recognised with MBEs in the New Year's Honours, a list which controversially also includes Ian Wright, the former Arsenal and W Ham striker.

31 Paul Scholes is withdrawn from next week's FIFA Club World Championship in Brazil in order to undergo surgery on a hernia problem. Stoke pay a club record £600,000 for Icelandic international Brynjar Gunnarsson.

January 2000
Pele says Rio heat will hamper Man U ... McIlroy gets NI post ... Maradona in drugs clinic ... Spending spirals to £348m ... Pele is 20th Century tops ... McMahon boss at Bloomfield ... Ref rumpus at Tranmere ... Player's electric tag ... Weah joins Chelsea ... Pulis for Pompey ... MP's want Wilson out ... Leeds duo questioned ... England–Germany WC clash looms ... Irwin bows out ... Rivaldo is top of the world ... Tranmere reach Wembley ... Hoddle in charge of Saints ... At last – an away penalty at Man U ... Its Turkey for Izzet

1 Dennis Wise becomes one of the first new fathers of the Millennium when girlfriend Claire presents him with a son, Henry, at 1.27 am.

2 Chelsea's Didier Deschamps insists Serie A football is better. Dons boss Egil Olsen targets £2m Norwegian striker Andreas Lund. Round-the-clock protection including ten armed police marksmen, greet Man U's arrival in Rio de Janeiro.

3 Leeds top despite 2-1 home defeat by Villa. Branko Strupar , Derby's £3m signing 8 days before Christmas, scores twice in the win over Watford. Newcastle let slip a 2-goal home lead late on to finish 2-2 with a W Ham side short of ten senior players. Bogey opponents Sheff Wed get a point with visitors Arsenal. Everton preserve unbeaten home Premiership record in 2-2 draw with Leicester. Leaders Man City are held at Crewe. Wigan take unbeaten sequence to 24 at Oxford. In their 1st meeting in 35 years Luton beat Scunthorpe 4-1.

4 Twice vulnerable Coventry take lead (54 & 81 min) and twice within a minute Chelsea equalise. Pele forecasts the heat in Rio will wreck Man U chances in FIFA's Club World Championship. Sammy McIlroy, 45, resigns as Macclesfield boss to take the national manager's post with N I on a 2-year contract. Brighton's Darren Freeman receives a magnum of champagne from Nationwide after scoring the 1st goal of the 21st Century in the 4-2 win over Exeter.

5 Diego Maradona, 39, tests positive for cocaine at an Uruguayan clinic. Clubs splash £348m on players during 1999 taking total spending in the 1990's beyond £1.8b. Pele voted Player of the 20th Century ahead of Johan Cruyff and Franz Beckenbauer in a poll by the International Federation of Football History and Statistics; Bobby Charlton is 10th.

6 Peter Davenport replaces Sammy McIlroy at Macclesfield. In baking heat Man U draw 1-1 with Necaxa but Beckham is red-carded for a thigh-high challenge, and boss Ferguson is sent from the bench following a verbal assault at the Argentine ref. Bar penalty-saver Mark Bosnich, the entire United party avoid the media, increasing criticism of their already poor PR image. Swindon, losing £25,000 each week, sack assistant manager Mike Walsh and 14 backroom staff. Chester put former Northampton boss Ian Atkins in charge.

7 Steve McMahon's 16-month exile from the game ends with his appointment at struggling Blackpool. Last unbeaten League record of the season ends when Oldham snatch a 1-0 win at Wigan who still remain top in Div 2 with 15 wins in 25 games. Vasco da Gama beat Man U 3-1 handing out a lesson in the art of finishing

8 In FA Cup 4th rd, Newcastle hit 4 against Sheff Utd. Villa and Charlton have 1-0 wins over Saints and QPR, while Coventry and Everton see off Burnley and Brum. Fulham put out The Dons. But Sunderland could appeal for their tie with Tranmere to be replayed after the home side, in touchline confusion over sent off player, illegally bring on a sub during the closing seconds which is not noticed by the fourth official.

9 Premiership pacesetters Leeds advance with 5-2 FA Cup win at Man City. Ten yellows and a red (to Darren Eadie) at Arsenal as Leicester hold out in scoreless tie. Exeter release Peter Fox from his managerial post.

10 Ipswich's Gary Croft is released from a Suffolk prison after serving 4 weeks for a motoring offence, and as a condition of being freed early must wear an electric tag for a month.

11 Watford complete £1.5m record signing of Heidar Helguson, 22, from Lillestrom. AC Milan's George Weah, 33, joins Chelsea on 6-month loan. Man U's 'reserve' side beat Sth Melbourne 2-0 in final Group B FIFA Club World Championship at the Maracana Stadium. In Worthington Cup 'rematch' W Ham lose 3-1(aet) to Villa.

12 Weah, cleared only at 5 pm, makes dream start, as sub, scoring Chelsea's winner against Spurs. Tony Banks, former Sports Minister spends £102,780 in 2 years promoting England's bid for WC 2006. Fulham collapse late at Leicester and after extra time (3-3) lose Worthington Cup quarter-final 3-0 on penalties.

13 FA suspend ref Rob Harris and assistant Tony Green who blundered in the Tranmere-Sunderland FA Cup substitution farce. Steve Lomas extends his W Ham contract to 2006.

14 Lowly Pompey put ex-Bristol City boss Tony Pulis in charge. Man U's Roy Keane is Carling Player of the Month. The vacant Exeter post attracts 42 applications. Four Sheffield MP's call for Wednesday manager Danny Wilson to be sacked. Corinthians beat Vasco da Gama on penalties to win FIFA's Club World Championship.

15 Arsenal level on points with second-placed Man U after 4-1 win over Sunderland. Vladimir Smicer, with his 1st goal for the club, is Liverpool's 3-2 match-winner at Watford. Ipswich's Mike Stockwell chalks up his 601st appearance, and scores, in win over Swindon. Forest pair Dave Beasant and Jon Olav Hjelde are sent off and assistant manager Denis Booth ejected from the ground at Grimsby. Ipswich sub Croft becomes the 1st electronically tagged offender to play in the FL, against Swindon.

16 Newcastle knock 5 past stunned Saints to gain revenge for an early August defeat under Gullit. Before 30,057 Man City score 4 without reply against Fulham who have Coleman sent off. Harry Cavan, former President of the Irish FA and Britain's rep on FIFA's Executive Committee for almost 3 decades, dies aged 83.

17 Following a communication to officials giving guidance and advising discretion the average number of Premiership bookings per month drops by almost a half. LMA calls on Government to publicly censure MP's David Blunkett, Joe Ashton, Clive Betts and Bill Michie who are campaigning for the sacking of Hillsborough boss Danny Wilson. Eric Cantona pips George Best on Man U's official web-site to find their player of the 20th Century.

18 Leeds players Lee Bowyer, 22, and Jonathan Woodgate, 19, are questioned for 5 hours and released on bail without being charged pending further inquiries in connection with an assault which leaves a young Asian man in hospital with serious injuries.

19 FA to stage both semi-finals of the FA Cup at Wembley. Sub goalie Peggy Arphexad is Leicester's shoot-out hero (6-5 on penalties) after FA Cup 4th rd tie with Arsenal ends scoreless. Chelsea, stung by chairman Ken Bates' programme comments, still struggle to beat Forest resistance. Noel Blake succeeds manager Fox at Exeter.

20 After 7 hours of discussion over WC group fixtures in Frankfurt, England start off the campaign against fierce rivals Germany on Oct 7 and end with a home tie against Greece in Oct 2001. Wigan's Pompey signing Alan McLoughlin retires from the ROI international scene.

21 Coventry pay £1.5m for Peruvian hit man Israel Zuniga. The 23 year old has won the S America Golden Boot award for scoring 32 goals in 26 games for his Melgar club. Ray Harford parts company with Oxford Utd after 6 weeks as technical director. Barnet receive warning they face expulsion unless they upgrade Underhill to a 6,000 capacity.

22 Sheff Wed lift off the foot of the table for the 1st time this season winning at Spurs. Hammers secure a 1st League win in 2 months at Leicester. Bradford push fellow-strugglers Watford a step closer to relegation winning 3-2. With Keegan watching, Owen limps out of Liverpool's stalemate with Boro. Charlton remain top winning 3-0 at Norwich, Barnsley put 5 past Blackburn. Wigan and Bristol Rovers joint top in Div 2. In Div 3 leaders Rotherham hit 5 past Exeter, and are level on 53 pts with close pursuers Barnet and Swansea. Rangers thrash bottom club Aberdeen 5-0 to go 7 pts ahead of Celtic. Denis Irwin, capped at 6 levels for Ireland, quits international action after 56 appearances.

23 Celtic's ex-Arsenal and Hammers striker Ian Wright is involved in tunnel bust-up following the 1-1 draw at Kilmarnock.

24 Patched-up Arsenal, playing their 7th match in 22 days, take 11th min lead through Ljungberg at Man U, but sub Sheringham taps in 73rd min equaliser. Rivaldo is FIFA's World Player of the Year coming out top in poll of 140 national team coaches. Beckham and Batistuta get the 2nd and 3rd spots. Darlington's pitch is the worst in the FL despite thousands of special worms being dumped on Feethams to help improve the surface.

25 Former Sheff Wed and Saints striker David Hirst, 32, retires after failing to overcome a knee injury.

26 Tranmere brush aside Bolton 3-0 (agg 4-0) to claim a Worthington Cup Final place, the club's 1st major competition final in it's 116-year history. Everton's Walter Smith signs a 2-year contract extension. Peter Beardsley signs for 3 games with Melbourne Knights.

27 The FA Cup 3rd rd will revert to the traditional January date. Next season's Premiership will commence on Aug 19, two weeks later than had originally been anticipated.

28 Glenn Hoddle is back in Premiership management, albeit as caretaker, at struggling Saints. The ex-England boss takes up a 12-month contract which allows Dave Jones leave of absence on full pay to concentrate on his Nov trial in relation to child abuse charges while he worked at a Liverpool childrens' home ten years ago. Oxford ref Rob Harris is suspended for a month.

29   Man U beat Boro 1-0 before 61,267, the biggest Premiership crowd so far, but the home team players are roundly condemned for acting like 'a pack of wolves' towards the ref, Andy D'Urso, who awards the visitors a penalty, the 1st team in more than 6 years to win a Premiership spot-kick at Old Trafford. In FA Cup action, Coventry lose to Charlton. Everton defeat Preston; Fulham, at home, go out to Tranmere, and The Gills shock Sheff Wed. Albion sell teenage midfielder Enzo Maresca to Juventus for a club record £4.3m. Blackpool player Martin Aldridge, 25, dies in a car crash just hours after appearing for Rushden & Diamonds.

30   In ill-tempered FA Cup clash Chelsea advance beating Leicester 2-1 but Walsh and Wise are red-carded, each for a career 11th time. Paul Merson is a bloodied hero as Villa colleague Benito Carbone cuts down Leeds with a hat-trick in 3-2 success. The FA Cup 6th rd draw pairs Chelsea v Gillingham, Everton v Villa, Bolton v Charlton and Tranmere against Blackburn/Newcastle.

31   Shearer's double, and his 250th club score, destroys Blackburn taking Newcastle, FA Cup runners-up for the last 2 years, to within 2 matches of another Wembley appearance. Ukraine accept England's friendly invitation on May 3. Leicester's London-born Muzzy Izzet opts to play for Turkey, birthplace of his father.

February 2000
Burrows out at Cardiff ... Leicester again at Wembley ... Swindon financial worries ... Smith back at Manor ... Nev heads to Bradford ... Wilkie in charge ... Rangers surge ahead ... Wendy for Wembley ... Inverness-Caley shock Celts ... Thompson out at York ... Barnes chop – Kenny recalled ... Foxes take Collymore ... Vodafone call Old Trafford with £30m ... Dolan at York ... FA warn all clubs ... Gazza's costly arm-smash ... Wright links with Burnley ... Fawthrop for Bristol ... Robson rolls on ... Fergie & Becks fall-out ... No action for Welsh boss Hughes ... Nation mourns Sir Stanley's loss ... Hammam sells up ... Shearer to end after Euro ... Elliott's winning double ... City freedom for Sir Alex

1   Chelsea's Vialli comes out of retirement to register for European and domestic action. Danny Wilson (Sheff Wed) is Carling Premiership Manager of the Month, with Charlton's Alan Curbishley, Ian Holloway (Bristol Rovers) and Billy Dearden (Mansfield) taking the Nationwide nominations. Cardiff and manager Frank Burrows part company. Marcus Stewart completes £2.5m Huddersfield to Ipswich move.

2   Elliott's header against Villa earns Leicester a Worthington Cup visit to Wembley, their 3rd League Cup Final in 4 years. Man U's 1st League win at Hillsborough since Oct 1993 takes them 3 pts clear of Leeds. Swindon, 8 pts adrift at the bottom of Div 1, a tax bill of £500,000 to pay and losing £25,000 weekly, go into Administration. The Games's ruling bodies FA and FL call for reform of the work permit system, and for the Premiership clubs to be limited to 2 players from outside Europe in an attempt to control the flood of foreign imports.

3   FA charge a further 8 Leicester players and backroom staff with misconduct relating to 'irresponsible distribution of tickets' for last year's Worthington Cup Final with Spurs. Denis Smith returns to Oxford Utd as manager 2 years after leaving for Albion. Refs Graham Barber, Paul Durkin and Graham Poll are among a provisional list of 30 to officiate at Euro 2000. Torquay cancel week to week contract of former Everton and Wales goalie Neville Southall, 41, who chalks up his 700th league appearance at Chester, but now links with Bradford.

4   In a further break with FA Cup tradition this season's semi-finals – both at Wembley – will be played a week apart, April 2 and 9. Villa's Gareth Southgate is Carling Player of the Month. Alan Wilkie, 48, who retires this season, will be in charge of the Worthington Cup Final.

5   Man U set up 6 pts lead beating Coventry 3-2. Bradford, with a 2-1 win, damage the Championship-chasing ambitions of Arsenal, visiting Valley Parade for the 1st time in 78 years. Liverpool, with 3 stunning strikes, rock Leeds. Leicester use 4 makeshift strikers and get victory over Boro. New boss Hoddle gets warm welcome and supervises Saints 2-1 win over W Ham. Villa trounce Watford 4-0. Sunderland and Newcastle share 4 goals, but Magpies defender Pistone breaks a leg. Chelsea extend their unbeaten run against Spurs to 22 matches dating back 13 years. Charlton stay top of Div 1, PNE and Bristol Rovers lead Div 2 with Rotherham out in front in Div 3.

6   The Dons, outplayed in every department, suffer a 1st home defeat since Aug, losing 3-0 to Everton. Rangers move 10 pts ahead of Celtic after drawing 2-2 at Hibs.

7   Ref Mike Reed is asked to explain why he appeared to 'celebrate' Patrik Berger's scorching goal for Liverpool during the win over Leeds. Wendy Toms will become the 1st woman to officiate in a major Wembley Cup Final when she runs the line in the Worthington Cup.

8   The future of Celtic coach John Barnes is in the balance after tiny Inverness Caledonian Thistle inflict one of the most stunning Scottish Cup shocks in the history of the competition, The Div 1 Highlanders humble the Glasgow giants easily winning 3-1 at Parkhead. The Dons agree switching their Premiership fixture against Liverpool on April 15 to the following day to avoid a clash with the 11th anniversary of the Hillsborough disaster.

9   York, 21st in Div 3, part company with manager Neil Thompson. Mark Hughes names his 1st Wales squad, against Qatar, and promises to break with tradition by fielding Ryan Giggs in a friendly – in 9 years the Man U winger has yet to figure.

10   After just 8 months of a 3-year Celtic contract John Barnes and assts Terry McDermott and Eric Black are dismissed with Kenny Dalglish stepping into the managerial hot seat warning under-achieving players to improve their attitude. Leicester clinch incentive-related deal with Stan Collymore which ties the striker to Filbert St for 18 months. Villa who paid £7m for him in 1997 will receive £250,000 after the 1st 18 appearances and the same payment on completion of 50 matches. FL Chairman Peter Middleton, 60, announces he is retiring because of family commitments after taking up the post in Nov 1998. The Dons pay £2.5m for Andreas Lund, Molde's Norwegian striker.

11   Man U agree 4-year shirt sponsorship deal with Vodafone worth upwards of £30m. York appoint Terry Dolan as new boss. Ref Reed is reprimanded and taken off a high-profile televised game after freely admitting his pleasure that a Berger goal for Liverpool came from an advantage he had played against Leeds.

12   Enforcing the work ethic Newcastle gain 3-0 win over Man U who have Keane dismissed, but boss Ferguson pins blame on the ref. In a snarling scrap with 8 cautions, Leeds beat Spurs. W Ham come from 4-2 behind to snatch a 5-4 win over Bradford. Sub Zola sparkles to help lethargic Chelsea overcome The Dons 3-1, but police are summoned after tunnel fighting.

13 Impressive and on a roll Liverpool take all 3 pts at Arsenal. Aberdeen reach Scottish League Cup Final with 1-0 success over Dundee Utd.

14 FA react to the latest show of Premiership indiscipline by charging Leeds, Spurs, Chelsea and Wimbledon; also 3 players and a coach with misconduct. Notifications have gone to all 92 League clubs warning they will be held responsible for collective dissent towards match officials. Boro's Gascoigne breaks his left arm in a cynical elbow challenge on Villa's George Boateng, the Midlanders winning 4-0. Ian Wright leaves Celtic for promotion-seeking Burnley.

15 Charlton go 7 pts ahead of Man City after win over Fulham. Bobby Robson begins Newcastle clear-out placing 13 players on the list. A swift response from the FA levels a misconduct charge on Boro's Gascoigne for his rash forearm smash on a Villa midfielder. W Ham's Stuart Pearce returns in a reserve game after breaking a leg in Sept.

16 Only 381 turn up to watch Lazio draw 2-2 at Venezia to reach the Italian Cup Final, thought to be the lowest attendance for a cup match between Serie A sides. Leicester players sent home in disgrace by managing director of their La Manga training complex after boisterous behaviour and Stan Collymore spraying a fire extinguisher in the hotel bar. Bristol City confirm appointment of Tony Fawthrop as caretaker manager.

17 Kevin Keegan includes 2 teenagers, Liverpool's Steven Gerrard and Villa's Gareth Barry in his squad to face Argentina. Man U shares burst through the £800m barrier, £170m more than BskyB were ready to pay a year ago.

18 Newcastle's Bobby Robson celebrates his 67th birthday signing a 12-month rolling contract. England's WC 2002 qualifier with Germany will be played on 1st Sept 2001 in Munich's Olympic Stadium. Shaun Goater nets his 22nd goal for Man City in the draw at Huddersfield.

19 In FA Cup quarter-final Bolton, down to 10-men for most of the 2nd half, defeat Charlton 1-0 to make the last 4 for the 1st time since Nat Lofthouse led them in 1958. Sheff Utd put 6 without reply past Albion. Boss Ferguson has training ground bust-up with Beckham and drops the midfielder for tomorrow's top of the table clash at Leeds. The arrival of Ian Wright at Burnley attracts 20,435 against Wigan, Turf Moor's biggest crowd for 5 years and drawing more, by 304, for a Div 2 match than Bolton could for their FA Cup clash.

20 The Gills, playing in the FA Cup 6th rd for the 1st time in their 87-year history, lose 5-0 at Chelsea. Carbone nets 2-1 winner but is sent off as Villa triumph at Everton, while in-form Tranmere, at home, fail to deny Newcastle their place in last 4. Semi-final draw pits Bolton against Villa and Newcastle meeting Chelsea. Man U, without the punished Beckham, win a difficult match at ambitous rivals Leeds thanks to Cole's 100th score for the club. Inverness Caledonian Thistle who sensationally knocked out Celtic in Scottish Cup, draw 1-1 with Aberdeen.

21 Dave Richards resigns after 9 years as Sheff Wed chairman to take up the Independent chairman's post at the Premier League. Coventry list striker Noel Whelan. Tommy Burns returns to Celtic in a coaching capacity until the end of the season. New Wales boss Mark Hughes confirms his retirement from the international scene after 72 caps and 16 goals

22 Sir Alex Ferguson confirms that the club tried to bring back sacked Blackburn boss Brian Kidd to help with youth development. Lee Hendrie's goal gives England U-21's a win over Argentina before 15,748. The winners of next year's Worthington Cup will continue to have a UEFA Cup place.

23 Sir Stanley Matthews dies in a Staffordshire hospital, a few miles from his Stoke birthplace. He was 85 and became ill after injuries to his neck in a fall last week while on a holiday in Tenerife. The Queen, politicians and sporting stars pay tribute to the 1st footballing Knight whose career, without a booking, with Stoke, Blackpool and England spanned 3 decades, until his final game 5 days after his 50th birthday. Before 74,008 at Wembley for the 0-0 friendly with Argentina all players wear armbands and observe a silent tribute. Sammy McIlroy's reign as NI manager gets off to a good start winning 3-1 in Luxembourg. Wales get a 1-0 result in Qatar, and ROI pull off a 2-1 win over the visiting Czech Republic. Germany's Lothar Matthaus becomes World's most capped player appearing in his 144th international against the Netherlands – 20 years after starting against the same opponents.

24 Chelsea's Dan Petrescu signs a new 2-year contract. Cayman Islands face a barrage of protests after recruiting 8 players from Britain to join their WC squad. Coventry agree £1m package linked to appearances with Rangers for experienced defender Colin Hendry.

25 Crazy days over? Wimbledon's Sam Hammam sells his final 20 per cent stake to now chairman Bjorn Rune Gjelsten – and is promptly dunked in a giant puddle at the training ground! The Lebanese businessman who sold his other 80 per cent for £28m 2 years ago remains, for the time being, as a director. Leeds long-server Gary Kelly agrees 5-year contract

26 Sheff Wed relegation fears deepen losing 2-0 at home to improving Newcastle. Afterwards, Shearer announces he will end his England career after Euro 2000, and that Kevin Keegan was aware of his intentions. Outclassed in skill The Dons hang on to limit Man U (2-2) to a single point. Arsenal beat Saints 3-1. A Hammer Horror show at Upton Park conceding 4 for the 2nd successive game, to Everton. Chelsea's 2-1 win over Watford takes the team's unbeaten run to 13. On the day football pays respect to Sir Stanley Matthews some supporters at his old club Stoke get involved in disgraceful fighting scenes at Wigan which play held up for 8 min. Charlton, Bristol Rovers and Rotherham all top their respective divisions.

27 Matt Elliott's headed brace from set-pieces wins Leicester the Worthington Cup over a spirited Tranmere hampered by Clint Hill's dismissal. The Birkenhead club come close to forcing extra-time after Kelly's 77th min score. Alan Wilkie is 1st ref to be stretchered off at Wembley with a pulled calf muscle. Rangers notch up 7-1 win at Dundee to extend their lead to 11 pts.

28 At a lavish ceremony Manchester hands the Freedom of the City to Sir Alex Ferguson, an honour bestowed on Sir Matt Busby in 1967. Reading's former Scottish U-21 winger Andy McLaren is charged with misconduct after testing positive for cocaine and cannabis abuse.

29 Amidst serious crowd disturbances, stuttering Chelsea offer a poor display at Stade Velodrome losing 1-0 to Marseille but still remain 2nd in group D. Spanish labour tribunal awards dismissed R Madrid coach John Toshack £650,000 in compensation.

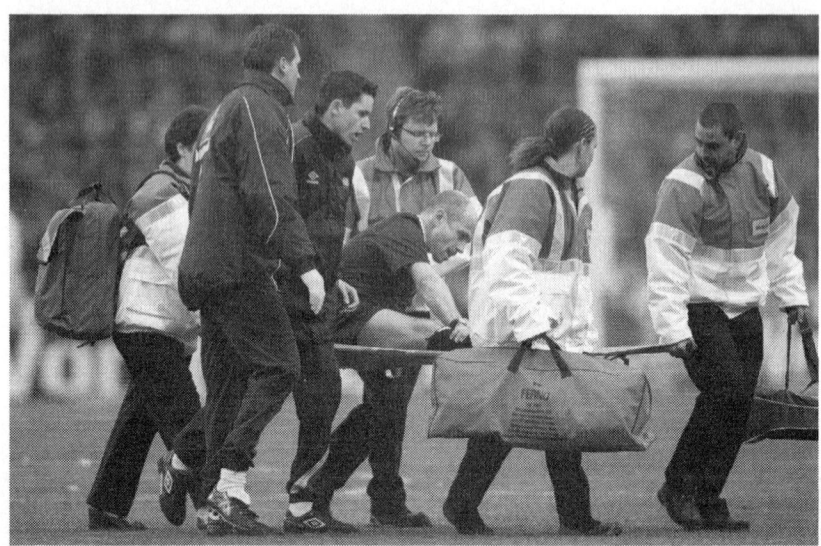

Alan Wilkie, suffering from a pulled calf muscle, becomes the first referee to be stretchered off at Wembley. (ASP)

March 2000
Sky take Chelsea stake ... Record Old Trafford attendance ... Albion sack Little ... £6m Spurs splash flounders ... Gunner Hughes leaves ... Pearce breaks a leg again ... Heskey heads to Anfield ... Rioch resigns ... Souness in at Blackburn ... Sparky joins Goodison ... England ban Leeds pair ... Cole equals Law record ... Phillips lands big contract ... Wenger reds now total 27 ... League Cup for Celtic ... Hay in at Livvy ... Owls sack Danny ... Chelsea's record ends ... Welsh ticket frenzy ... Parlour's Euro treble ... Spanish trips for Reds & Blues ... Hoey backs Conference request ... Whopping fine for Foxes ... Points deduction on the cards ... Bracewell leaves the Cottage.

1   Scores from the brilliant Giggs, and Sheringham, reward Man U with victory over Bordeaux. FA charge Portsmouth's Steve Claridge for betting on his side to beat Barnsley. Trevor Francis (Brum) Rotherham's Ronnie Moore, and Tony Fawthrop (Bristol City) win Nationwide League Manager of the Month divisional awards.

2   In UEFA clash at Highbury Deportivo La Coruna disintegrate following Djalminha's dismissal and Arsenal take advantage ramming in 5. Riding their luck at times Leeds do an excellent away job holding frustrated AS Roma scoreless. Liverpool will meet Celtic on May 16 in testimonial for Ronnie Moran who spent 50 years at Anfield. Boro's Gascoigne picks up a 3-match ban for his arm smash on Villa's Boateng. From this season, the Football Writers Association will re-name the Footballer of the Year prize as the Sir Stanley Matthews Trophy.

3   An estimated 100,000 throng the streets of Stoke to pay their respects as the funeral cortege of Sir Stanley Matthews passes through. At the Victoria Ground, now a piece of wasteland awaiting a housing estate, 4,000 are waiting. Sky announce they are to pay £40m for a 9.9 per cent stake in Chelsea. Two Wycombe Sunday League players gets unexpected call ups from St Vincent and Grenadines for a 2002 WC qualifier against US Virgin Islands.

4   In a rehearsal of their FA Cup semi-final clash Poyet's header seals it for Chelsea at Newcastle with PM Blair a spectator. Ed de Goey's 22nd clean sheet is a club record. Derby deepen Wimbledon gloom winning 4-0. Liverpool's Owen makes a re-appearance as late sub, after 6 weeks, nearly breaking the 1-1 deadlock at Man U. Old Trafford houses a Premiership record crowd of 61,592. After Tottenham's 1-1 with Bradford manager Graham announces a £6m deal has been agreed with The Dons for striker John Hartson. Peter Thorne becomes the 1st to score 4 times in a Britannia Stadium fixture as Stoke beat bottom club Chesterfield 5-1.

5   Collymore's hat-trick makes him the Leicester hero in 5-2 thrashing of Sunderland. Lee Dixon's 2nd score in 4 days rescues a point for Arsenal at Villa. Leeds trail Man U by just 4 pts after easily outclassing Coventry 3-0. Hibs defeat Celtic 2-1 to deflate Kenny Dalglish's side 4 days ahead of their Old Firm clash. Former Chelsea boss Ian Porterfield steers Trinidad & Tobago to a 5-0 winning start over Netherlands Antilles – 2 days after being appointed.

6   Brian Little is sacked at Albion 7 months into a 2-year contract. Dismissed John Barnes claims he got no credit for what he achieved at Celtic with people questioning decisions despite winning 12 out of his opening 13 matches. John Hartson's proposed £6m move to Tottenham dramatically collapses over doubts on a knee injury. Chris Balderstone who figured with Huddersfield and Carlisle, and also played cricket with Yorkshire and Leicestershire dies, aged 59.

7   Sub Solskjaer's late 2-1 winner over a 10-man Bordeaux sends Man U top of Champions League Group B. Arsenal's Stephen Hughes completes £3m move to Everton. Spurs place 6 on the list which includes Ruel Fox, Ramon Vega and Jose Dominguez. Charlton chalk up their 12th successive victory at Walsall.

8 Chelsea, with a 26th min Wise goal but lucky to still have 11 on the pitch, mount desperate defence to deny Marseille re-igniting hopes of a quarter-final place. Norwich set up a youth link with Serie A club Parma. Rod Wallace hits a stunning late winner to give Rangers a win at Celtic. Veteran Stuart Pearce breaks his left leg for the 2nd time in 6 months, as W Ham beat the Saints. Man U's value soars above £1b as shares rise to 402p.

9 Petit anchors the Gunners central defence as they survive a pounding at Deportivo La Coruna, losing 2-1 but advancing on agg 6-3. At Elland Road Kewell's winner, the 1st Roma has conceded in 528 min of Euro action, sweeps Leeds into the UEFA quarter-finals, as the Italians finish in disgrace having 2 sent off in a stoppage-time fracas. Gary Megson gets a 3-year deal at Albion, their 17th manager in 28 years. Scotland's Craig Brown appoints Everton's Archie Knox as No 2.

10 Leicester's Emil Heskey, 22, becomes the 3rd most expensive player to be transferred between Premiership clubs completing his £11m move to Liverpool. Manager Houllier denies it will mean the departure of either Owen or Fowler. Stoke boss Gudjon Thordarson pays £250,000 to Genk to sign up his son Bjarni.

11 Dwight Yorke nets a hat-trick in 3-1 win over Derby. Kevin Phillips hits his 25th of the season in 1-1 draw which dents Liverpool's hopes of a European Champions League place. Humiliating return to White Hart Lane for Hoddle as Saints get a 7-2 thrashing with Iversen collecting a hat-trick. St Mirren knock in 8 without reply against rock-bottom Clydebank.

12 Bradford, with Neville Southall, 41, pressed into service when Matt Clarke falls down the stairs at home, fight bravely but lose 2-1 to Leeds. Arsenal's patchwork side lose ground at Boro with Wenger blaming their Euro campaign for the inconsistent Premiership displays. Rangers progress to semi-finals of the Tennents Scottish Cup beating Hearts 4-1.

13 After less than 2 years in charge Bruce Rioch resigns from Norwich because of the lack of finances with Bryan Hamilton, the director of coaching, taking charge until the end of the season. Real Madrid suspend ex Arsenal striker Nicolas Anelka for 45 days, without pay.

14 Despite Leboeuf missing a penalty Chelsea give controlled performance to win 3-1 at Feyenoord, where scores from Zola, Wise and Flo puts Vialli's team into the Champions League quarter-final 2pts ahead of Lazio in the Group. Graeme Souness, 46, former Liverpool, Rangers and Saints boss, signs 3 and half year contract as Blackburn's new boss and vows to bring back good times to Ewood Park. Saints striker Mark Hughes signs a 14-month contract at Everton which will take him past his 37th birthday. Leeds pair Bowyer and Woodgate charged with GBH relating to a street attack on an Asian student, and are suspended by the FA from representing England pending the outcome of the case.

15 Champions League quarter-final beckons for Man U after dismissing formidable Fiorentina who have Rossitto sent off on the hour for hacking down Yorke who scores the 3rd. Cole's 20th min effort, his 14th in Europe's premier competition, equals the 31-year long record held by Denis Law. Liverpool are frustrated at home failing to break down a resolute Villa side with Owen missing a penalty and being subbed. Everton lose to a McAllister strike which ends Coventry's 8 and a half hour barren spell.

16 In UEFA quarter-final 1st leg, Arsenal establish a 2-goal lead over an unadventurous Werder Bremen. Scorers Kewell and Bowyer are guilty of alarming misses but Leeds take a 3-goal lead to Slavia Prague. Goal-grabber Phillips signs a 5-year contract which makes him the highest paid in Sunderland's history, likely to be around £25,000 a week. Since joining from Watford for £650,000 in the summer of 1997 the Saints reject has netted 85 times. Liverpool executive vice-chairman Peter Robinson, at the club 35 years, is to step down. PFA scrap the men-only policy for its annual awards dinner.

17 Former Newcastle striker Faustino Asprilla quits the international scene after being overlooked by Colombia for a WC qualifier. Misconduct from Chelsea fans at Marseille brings the club a £7,500 UEFA fine.

18 Branko Strupar misses opportunity to impress a 350-strong fan club from Belgium as Derby lose 2-0 to Liverpool. Brian Clough who played for both clubs is introduced at the interval in the Sunderland 1-1 clash with Boro. Bradford's position looking bleak after losing 4-0 at Coventry, while an 89th min winner gives Watford success over Sheff Wed. W Ham's niggly affair with Chelsea ends scoreless. Rangers beat Motherwell 6-2 and Falkirk hit 8 past Airdrie.

19 Arsenal gain their 50th league (2-1) victory in their 126th clash with rivals Spurs, and in spite of volatile Frenchman Grimandi getting another red card near the finish. Under Wenger the sending-off tally is 27. Revitalised Newcastle notch a late 2-0 win to ruin Everton's unbeaten home Premiership record, and shoot themselves into 11th position. Leeds refuse to allow a punishing schedule sidetrack them seeing off The Dons 4-1. Celtic capture the CIS Insurance League Cup beating Aberdeen at Hampden.

20 Scottish FA dish out a 2-match ban to Ian Wright for pushing the 4th official in a Celtic match at Kilmarnock. Coventry's Gordon Strachan gets a new 5-year contract. David Hay is the new coach at Livingston replacing sacked Ray Stewart. Tranmere boss John Aldridge is charged with misconduct for the 3rd time this season.

21 Second from bottom Sheff Wed sack Danny Wilson, and with 9 matches remaining put Peter Shreeves in charge. Wilson, Hillsborough's 4th boss in 5 years, the price for winning just 23 out of 78 League and Cup games. Mark Bosnich's towering display during the 0-0 in Valencia ensures Man U pole position in their Champions League Group, so avoiding Bayern Munich and Barcelona.

22 Without an English man in their line-up and after leading at the interval Chelsea are outplayed and go under 2-1 to Lazio. It surrenders a proud 42-year long record of European invincibility at Stamford Bridge, and only the 2nd time a visiting foreign side has scored more than a single goal. No stopping Charlton who put 4 without reply past Grimsby. Wales' experiment with slashing prices (entrance £5 and youngsters £3) results in 40,000 tickets being snapped up for Millennium Stadium friendly with Finland. Stoke receive a financial boost from local business man Phil Rawlin which could realise £1.5m.

23 Arsenal's 4-2 victory over Werder Bremen which includes a Parlour hat-trick eases them into the UEFA Cup semi-final, but the downside is Henry's 64th min dismissal – a decision the Gunners will contest. Below-par Leeds lose 2-1 to Slavia Prague but go through (agg 4-2) with Kewell's score effectively leaving the home side a mountain to climb. On transfer deadline day Sunderland complete the biggest deal signing Honduran, Milton Nunez for

£1.6m from PAOK Salonika. Bob Taylor who scored close on 100 goals at Albion rejoins from Bolton. Ipswich give manager George Burley a new 4 and half year deal.

24   Football chiefs will campaign against plans to end the traditional British season after FIFA announce a formula to harmonise an international calendar with a worldwide season running from Feb to Nov, and to be implemented by 2004. The Champions League quarter-final draw pairs Real Madrid v Man U, Chelsea v Barcelona, Porto against Bayern Munich and Lazio v Valencia. UEFA Cup semi-final pairing is: Galatasaray v Leeds, Arsenal v Lens. Former fearless striker George Kirby dies, aged 66. Mark Harrison, 39, former Oxford Utd assistant manager is to take charge of Bangladesh.

25   Man U open up 7-point lead with 4-0 win at Bradford. Lacklustre Chelsea rely on an og in 1-1 home draw with Saints. Liverpool sub Redknapp hits 88th min winner over Newcastle. Caretaker Shreeves is unable to conjure a Sheff Wed win at Boro. Merson sets up Villa goals in success over Derby. Phillips ends Sunderland's miserable run of 12 games without a win with his 26th Premiership strike. Spirited Watford earn 1-1 draw with Spurs. Chester, propping up Div 3, score 5 against mid-table Mansfield.

26   After his side's 2-1 defeat of Leicester, Leeds boss O'Leary concedes the title is destined for Old Trafford. Paolo Di Canio launches a spectacular angled volley to the Wimbledon net in Hammers' 2-1 Upton Park victory. Steve Ogrizovic, 42, answering a Coventry emergency call-up at Arsenal has little protection and picks the ball from the net 3 times. Rangers rout Celtic 4-0, their biggest Old Firm win in 12 years extending their Premier League lead to 15 pts and to a near certain 11th title in 12 years.

27   The appearance of new signing Milton Nunez helps attract 25,787 to the Stadium of Light for his debut in the 2-1 reserve win over Man U. Kate Hoey, the Sports Minister, gives her backing to additional promotion between the Nationwide Conference and FL which currently stands at 1 place. Howard Wilkinson, FA's technical director, wants players going into management to start preparing more thoroughly, 'like they do in Germany, France, Italy and Holland.' The ashes of Sir Stanley Matthews are buried beneath the centre circle at Stoke's Britannia Stadium.

28   FA fine 7 Leicester players and officials £75,000 plus £17,500 costs for 'breathtaking carelessness' in distributing Worthington Cup Final tickets. The heaviest punishment goes to Andy Impey with a £20,000 fine and £2,500 costs, in addition to the estimated £15,000 he had been docked by his club. NI land a resounding 3-0 victory over Malta in Valletta, and their U-21's notch a 2-1 win. But Scotland's U-21's go under 2-0 at home to France. *Four Four Two* magazine poll puts Sir Alex Ferguson the greatest British boss of all time, while Liverpool's Bob Paisley, the most successful, could only manage 6th.

29   FA dish out record £150,000 fines to Leeds and Tottenham for misconduct in their Feb Premiership clash. Concerned over mass-brawling outbreaks Lancaster Gate insist that a points deduction system will be an option in future for serious breaches. France have 6 of their WC-winning side in action as they overcome Scotland 2-0 with Arsenal's Henry netting in the closing moments. A sell-out 66,500 crowd pack Cardiff's Millennium Stadium but Wales lose 2-1 to Finland. England U-21's defeat Yugoslavia 3-0 to make the Euro Finals in Slovakia. Paul Bracewell gets the sack after 10 months in charge at Fulham with Karlheinz Reidle as caretaker boss.

30   The Div 3 chairmen agree in principle to increase promotion from Nationwide Conference. S African businessman and lifelong fan Dave King ploughs £20m into Rangers.

31   Roy Evans, out of work since leaving Liverpool, takes a consultancy role at Fulham. Table-topping Charlton grab late 2-1 winner over QPR, their 27th League victory and 30th in all of an incredible season so far.

April 2000

Accies on strike ... Leg break for unlucky Stan ... Leeds take Boundary stake ... Bosnich's Bernabeu brilliance ... Chelsea blitz Barca ... Death of fans shock Leeds ... Norwich name Hamilton ... 7 say yes to InterToto ... Chelsea off to Wembley ... Fulham choose Tigana ... Ref Poll tops poll ... Rugby rule beckons ... Duncan loses job ... Record low watch Dons ... New goalie rule ... Chelsea's tunnel fine ... Boss Graham in hospital ... Goodbye to Golden Boy ... Hillsborough remembered ... Stoke win Wembley shield ... Nightmare at Nou Camp ... Man U's real dream ends ... Kinkladze joins Rams ... Leeds pain; Arsenal joy ... Fulham ladies go pro ... Man U & Rangers take titles ... Hull welcome Little ... Ogrozovic calls it a day ... Man U's £18.5m Van Nistelrooy deal is off ... Kidderminster join FL ... Keane wins two awards

1   West Ham score 1st at Old Trafford but Man U turn on the style with a stunning 7-1 win. Everton condemn Watford to a 14th away defeat. Bradford depression continues losing 2-0 at Newcastle. Arsenal's Luzhny is sent off after 43 min at Wimbledon but Gunners still win 3-1. Chelsea leave out 6 of their most famous foreign signings and win 1-0 at Leeds. Blackburn hit 5 past Sheff Utd. Man City take 6,000 fans to Swindon, and win 2-0. Hamilton Academical players strike over non-payment of monies and fail to turn up for the Div 2 fixture with Stenhousemuir which is postponed.

2   Stan Collymore's chequered career takes an horrific turn for the worse when he breaks his left leg in an innocuous accident during Leicester's 3-0 defeat at Derby. Villa, hampered by Delaney's dismissal, win penalty shoot-out (4-1) after their scoreless FA Cup semi-final clash with Bolton. Late in extra time striker Holdsworth squanders a simple chance to send Wanderers to the Final. Two Bristol Rovers' fans launch an injury-time attack on Stoke goalie Gavin Ward. Holders Arsenal win their AXA Women's Premier League Cup crown beating Croydon 4-1.

3   In monsoon-like rain Boro's Ricard nets twice for a hat at Spurs. Kevin Keegan brushes aside fears over safety standards at 30,000-seater Charleroi's ground where England clash with Germany. Leeds buy 9.9 per cent stake in Oldham. Premier League chairmen challenge Television companies to come up with a £2b package that would revolutionise the way English football is screened. Divisional awards go to Dave Bassett (Barnsley) Preston's David Moyes, and Micky Adams of Brighton.

4   In quarter-final 1st leg scoreless draw at the Bernabeu Stadium and with Cantona in attendance, goalie Bosnich's brilliance keeps Man U hopes alive against R Madrid. Leaders Preston take another big stride towards promotion winning 1-0 at 2nd placed Wigan, before 15,993. Chief Executive of the FL John McKeown, 49, who only joined at Christmas, leaves his £175,000 a year post by mutual consent.

5 Chelsea overpower Spanish giants Barcelona on one of the great nights at Stamford Bridge with 3 goals in a remarkable 8 min 1st half spell. Zola's swerving free-kick and a double from Flo has Barca on the ropes, but the importance of Figo's 64th min score sets up a fascinating return. The death of two British supporters during rioting in Istanbul city centre throws into doubt the Galatasaray-Leeds UEFA Cup semi-final. Norwich name Bryan Hamilton as their new boss. Over 32,000 pack Maine Road for Man City's defeat of Bolton.

6 Subdued Leeds left with an uphill task in Istanbul conceding 2 first half goals to Galatasaray as tragedy overshadows their efforts to reach UEFA Final. The home side fail to wear arm bands and there is no minute silence, although Leeds fans turned away from the pitch to pause in memory of their dead friends. Arsenal fail to capitalise on Bergkamp's early goal and will face a tense return against Lens in the atmospheric Felix-Boilaert Stadium.

7 Brentford intend quitting Griffin Park for a new 15,000-seater stadium, the Feltham Arena. UEFA give Leeds the right to prevent Turkish fans from attending their return leg. Shearer admits he came close to quitting Newcastle during Gullit's reign. FA confirm 7 clubs have applied to compete in next season's InterToto Cup.

8 Saints ease fears of the drop winning at Bradford now 8 games without a win. A 4th consecutive defeat for The Dons at Sunderland. Charlton bus up 5,000 fans free of charge to Forest expecting to celebrate the inevitable return to the Premiership, but after the 1-1 result the party remains on hold. Rangers romp into the Scottish Cup Final beating Ayr 7-0 at Hampden.

9 In semi-final clash at Wembley two goals from Poyet ruins Newcastle hopes of a 3rd consecutive FA Cup Final, and seals Chelsea's place against Villa on May 20, the Londoners' 3rd in 7 seasons. Jean Tigana's 5-year managerial contract with Fulham, signed at Mohammed Fayed's Oxted, Surrey, home, amounts to a deal worth up to £7.5m. Aberdeen beat Hibs 2-1 to clinch a Scottish Cup Final spot with Rangers, and a place in next season's UEFA Cup.

10 Champions-elect Man U go 11 pts clear of the chasing pack led by Liverpool who win a thriller 4-3 at Boro. FL tribunal fine Bolton £45,000 for inducing manager Sam Allardyce to join from Notts Co. Graham Poll, England's sole rep at Euro 2000, gets the nod for this season's FA Cup Final.

11 Leeds warn UEFA they will consider withdrawing from clash with Galatasaray if the 2nd leg is moved to a neutral venue. The Premiership is to introduce rugby's 10-yard rule next season in an attempt to eliminate dissent and reduce suspensions. John Duncan is sacked at Chesterfield ending a 7-year spell.

12 Before just 8,248, the Premiership's lowest attendance, Wimbledon lose 2-0 to Sheff Wed. Wanchope's back header wins it late for the Hammers against Newcastle. Exeter give caretaker manager Noel Blake the job on a permanent basis. Calais make French Cup history becoming the 1st amateur team to reach the Final following their 3-1 win over League Champs Bordeaux before 41,000 in Lens. Vialli gives captain's armband to U-21 midfielder Jody Morris as Chelsea beat Coventry.

13 UEFA will implement the new FIFA 'six seconds' rule for goalies, due to replace the 'four-step rule' on July 1, for the whole of Euro 2000. FA fine Chelsea £50,000 for their part in the tunnel brawl at Stamford Bridge involving Wimbledon on Feb 12, and delay the cases against the visitors. Tottenham's George Graham is in hospital with chronic joint inflammation and extreme fever. Davor Suker who arrived from Real Madrid will be leaving Arsenal on a free.

14 Huddersfield's 1-0 win at The Valley keeps Charlton celebrations on hold. Wilf Mannion, former Boro and England forward who graced the game in the 1940's and was known as the Golden Boy, dies, aged 81. Last year Mannion was voted one of the FL's 100 greatest players.

15 Angry fans protest outside White Hart Lane after 4-2 home defeat by Villa. Boro's Ince apologises for a 'shambles' of a team performance losing at Coventry. Despite 'resting' many regulars Man U easily see off Sunderland 4-0 and head towards title number 6 with 14-point cushion. Leicester pull off their 1st League win on Tyneside in 15 years. Wanchope's match-winning double for W Ham plunges his former club Derby back into the relegation dog-fight. Saints all but rubber-stamp a 23rd consecutive season in top-flight action beating Watford 2-0. On an emotional day at Hillsborough Sheff Wed deserve their 2nd win in 4 days beating Chelsea 1-0. Bury's Baichung Bhutia, 23, becomes the 1st Indian-born player to score in the FL in the 1-1 with Chesterfield, but could not tell his parents as they don't have access to a telephone where they live in the Himalayas. All professional English clubs observe a minute silence before kick-off, put back to 3.06 as a mark of respect on the 11th anniversary of the Hillsborough tragedy. Clyde put 7 without reply past Stenhousemuir.

16 Liverpool's £11m signing Heskey guns down struggling Wimbledon with a brace, a win dedicated says coach Houllier to the memories of the 96 Anfield fans killed in the Hillsborough tragedy. Arsenal win 4-0 and leapfrog O'Leary's 10-men into a Champions League place, but tempers fray in ugly match with Harte off just before the break. Stoke win the Auto Windscreens Shield Final 2-1 at Wembley beating Bristol City before 75,057.

17 Paul Durkin is reprimanded by the Premier League for failing to send off Chelsea's Ed de Goey over a penalty incident at Sheff Wed. Galatasaray announce they will travel to Leeds- with 11 members of an anti-terrorist squad.

18 A nightmare for Chelsea at the Nou Camp. They were nearly there but crash out 5-1 (agg 6-4) torn apart by lethal Rivaldo. Vialli's men, pummelled and overun, fail to provide an attacking game which proves their undoing, yet from 2-down, Flo's 60th min score has the Londoner's right-back in it and with 7 min remaining are heading to the Champions League semis. Dani levels and shatters the dream, and in injury-time Rivaldo misses, then scores a penalty, and with Babayaro red-carded, Kluivert wraps it up. Denis Irwin, 34, signs a new contract to stay at Man U for an 11th season.

19 Man U's reign as European Champions ends in ruthless humiliating style . They are knocked off their pinnacle by Real Madrid who sweep into a shock 3-nil Old Trafford lead through Keane's og and two from Raul. Without the all-important away score, Utd were often denied by 18 year old goalie Casillas but rued numerous lost opportunities other than the goal from Beckham and the 88th min penalty from Scholes. West Ham reveal that Joe Cole broke his right leg in the weekend's match at Derby. Derby sign up Georgi Kinkladze from Ajax for a fee believed to be around £3m. Ginola gets 90th min Tottenham winner at Leicester. Hull sack manager Warren Joyce and assistant John McGovern.

20   Leeds, needing to claw back a 2-goal defeat, lose their way against Galatasaray on an emotional and volatile night at Elland Road. Bakke scores twice and Kewell is sent off in 2-2 draw, but the Turks who have Emre red-carded are never in danger and advance (agg 4-2). Tactically controlling the tie Arsenal reach the UEFA Cup Final deservedly winning in Lens 2-1 (agg 3-1). Ljungberg and Parlour shine, and Henry and Kanu finish, to give the Gunners their 1st Euro Final since losing to Zaragoza in 1995. Man U smash the British transfer record agreeing an £18.5m fee in Holland for PSV Eindhoven hit man, Ruud Van Nistelrooy, 23, although he cannot play for the club until next season. Hamilton Academical deducted 15 pts for failing to fulfill their April 1 fixture. Tranmere's John Aldridge fined £750 and warned about his behaviour. 5 women at Fulham Ladies FC make history by becoming Britain's 1st female professionals with insiders hinting their basic pay at £15,000 to £20,000 a year.

21   A bruising and bloodied 162nd Merseyside clash at Goodison ends scoreless. Locals lap up the 8-goal thriller equally shared by Bradford and Derby, a result which suits neither strugglers. More anti-climax as Charlton's promotion party is held up by the 1-1 result with Pompey. Mark Clattenburg will become the youngest league ref since WC official Jack Taylor when, at the age of 25, he joins the list for next season.

22   Sir Alex Ferguson hails his Man U heroes after claiming their 6th title in 8 seasons winning 3-1 at Saints. The English game has not known such dominance since Liverpool dictated terms throughout the 1980's, this being Ferguson's 15th trophy in the past ten years. Inspired by Di Canio West Ham slam 5 past Coventry. Chelsea drop Leboeuf and howls greet Vialli's decision to replace lively Zola followed by boos at the whistle after 1-1 with Boro. QPR's win over Ipswich guarantees Charlton a Premiership return. Preston's win over Scunthorpe means I point needed to claim promotion and title. In Div 3 six teams contest the title chase. Rangers are Premier League champions without kicking a ball as Celtic are held by Hibs.

23   Newcastle retrieve a 2-goal deficit to peg back Leeds thanks to Shearer's double. Despite almost blowing a 3-goal lead Arsenal, with 2 more from Henry, get full pts at Watford. Dick Advocaat resists the temptation to field a Rangers reserve selection for the 2-0 stroll at St Johnstone stretching their lead to 20 pts.

24   New signing Van Nistelrooy sees his Man U colleagues win 3-2 and switch to cruise control to deal with would-be rivals Chelsea. Derby's safety is virtually secure beating Saints. Bradford's dream of survival lives on thanks to an unexpected 1-0 away win at Sunderland. Preston go up despite losing at Cambridge Utd. Stockport score their 1st win of the Century and condemn Swindon to relegation. Charlton finally return to Premiership with 1-1 at Blackburn and Man City's draw at Pompey.

25   Ruud Van Nistelrooy's £18.5m British record transfer to Man U is in doubt after he fails a stringent medical test on a knee injury suffered 7 weeks ago. At the proposed press conference at Old Trafford his chair at the top table remains empty with the club's financial director David Gill reading out a statement. Hull confirm Brian Little as the new boss. Already guaranteed a play-off spot for the 4th time in as many years, Ipswich beat Palace to maintain a possible 2nd place. In U-21 friendlies Scotland lose 2-0 in Holland and ROI lose 2-1 to Greece. Leeds midfielder Lee Bowyer becomes the 1st Premiership player to clock up 14 bookings.

26   On an evening of European friendlies, Scotland produce an impressive away performance in a scoreless encounter in Arnhem against Holland. NI, after 2 rare victories over Luxembourg and Malta, lose 1-0 at home to Hungary. In dour Dublin event Greece score early then sit back against an ROI line-up missing 9 and introducing 5 new caps. Coventry's Steve Ogrozovic, the oldest in the Premiership at 42, announces his retirement.

27   Van Nistelrooy's transfer to Man U is off over a medical dispute with the club requesting to see the PSV Eindhoven striker in action before completing a deal. FA withdraw the England U-18's from an 8-team tournament in Turkey May 20-28.

28   The 10-yard law will be introduced into the Premiership and FA Cup next season, with the FL expected to follow suit having used it in the Auto Windscreens Shield. A new injury now threatens Man U transfer-target, Van Nistelrooy, as he dramatically collapses in agony, screaming aloud, while attempting to prove his fitness at PSV Eindhoven's ground. The 23 year old striker undergoes an immediate operation on a ruptured anterior cruciate ligament ruling him out for a year.

29   Butt and Hyde see red as Man U's 'reserve' side is dug out of trouble by Yorke in 3-2 win at Watford. An Overmars score sees the Gunners through at Everton. Stefan Schnoor is sent off and 10 cautions as Derby are denied a win by Tottenham's stoppage-time equaliser. Vialli's shaken-up selection triggers 2-0 win over Liverpool. Ipswich spring a late surprise winning 3-1 at already-promoted Charlton. Although losing at Woking, Jan Molby's Kidderminster capture the Nationwide Conference title to secure the FL place denied them 6 years ago. Rangers celebrate their 49th championship in style winning 3-0 over Dundee. Leaders Swansea clinch Div 2 promotion before 10,743, and Rotherham also book their place winning at Hartlepool.

30   Peter Beagrie's brace in 3-0 win provides a glimmer of hope but Wimbledon's cause not helped by the 50th min dismissal of John Hartson. Sheff Wed on the very brink of relegation after Leeds recover their poise and win 3-0. Roy Keane completes an awards double adding the PFA Player of the Year prize to the Football Writers' gong he already collected. He heads off Kevin Phillips and Harry Kewell who were also 2nd and 3rd in the journalist's poll. Kewell is Young Player of the Year. Mark Viduka, Celtic's leading scorer with 27 is the Scottish PFA's Player of the Year.

May 2000

Dons part with Olsen ... Robins replace Quinn with Todd ... Earle ill ... Chester drop out ... City in blue heaven ... Chairman quits dug out ... Owls off Premiership perch ... £50,000 Dons fine ... Carlisle sack boss ... Bradford stay, goodbye to Dons ... Premiership crowds up ... Law to run Chesterfield ... Spurs splash on Rebrov ... Gunners lose Euro final ... Bates buys turf ... Chelsea lift cup ... Wales and Brazil under roof ... Madrid glory for Macca ... Refs larger panel ... FA Soho move ... England hold Brazil ... Leighton's hurtful exit ... Gills up, Ipswich in top flight ... Spurs get Sullivan ... Barthez between Man U sticks ... Kidd accepts Leeds offer ... Cole misses out, England beat Ukraine ... Atkins out at Chester.

1   The Norwegian owners of Wimbledon, prompted by player power, part company with manager Egil Olsen after 11 months and 8 defeats on the trot, replacing him with assistant Terry Burton. Vialli hints at switching transfer activity to the British scene; since Ruud Gullit took charge 22 overseas players have arrived at Stamford Bridge.

2 Petit scores stoppage-time Arsenal 2-1 winner over W Ham who have Sinclair sent off. A thrilling 96th Tyne-Tees derby ends 2-2. Asaba's hat-trick for The Gills helps relegate Cardiff. Joe Royle (Man City) is Div 1 Manager of the month, Burnley's Stan Ternent wins the Div 2 award with Kevin Wilson (Northampton) taking the Div 3 honours. Relegated Swindon sack Jimmy Quinn after only 8 wins in 45 games. Liverpool land £21m shirt deal with Reebok. Auxerre coach Guy Roux is to step down after a record 39 years in charge.

3 Liverpool sweating on a European place after struggling to find form at Anfield and losing 2-0 to Leicester. Leeds shoot back into top 3 with comfortable win over doomed Watford. Just weeks after walking out of Stevenage former Colchester boss Steve Wignall is the new manager at Doncaster Rovers. Peter Thorne nets his 3rd hat-trick against Bury to clinch Stoke's 7th successive win.

4 Swindon appoint Colin Todd as new manager. Villa boss John Gregory agrees a new 3-year contract.

5 Darren Anderton rules himself out of Euro 2000 after being advised to rest an achilles tendon injury. Crewe's John Malpass tests positive for the drug Ecstasy. Wimbledon skipper Robbie Earle, seriously ill in hospital for 3 weeks, is improving after a further emergency operation on a blood clot.

6 Cantona receives a standing ovation as Man U parade and receive the Premiership League trophy after beating Spurs 3-1. Controversial sub striker Hartson heads an injury-time equaliser (2-2) to earn The Dons a priceless point against Villa. Results elsewhere go Bradford's way despite losing 3-0 at Leicester. Derby make certain of safety. Henry's brace seals Arsenal's 2-1 win over weary-looking Chelsea. Chester's 69-year long stay in the FL ends after losing to Posh, and Shrewsbury's surprise win at Exeter. Carlisle who survived the drop on the last day last season do it again -despite losing 1-0 at Brighton. In top of Div 3 decider which ends with crowd violence and the death of a Welsh supporter, Swansea capture the title at Rotherham.

7 With Fowler back in attack for his 1st start since Sept, Liverpool ambitions are stifled by the Saints in scoreless draw. Man City survive a battering then net 4 second-half goals at Blackburn to claim the Div 1 second automatic promotion spot. Swindon, Port Vale and Walsall, drop. In Div 2 Preston and Burnley go up; Cardiff, Blackpool, Scunthorpe and Chesterfield, drop down. In Div 3 Swansea, Rotherham and Northampton gain promotion; Chester relegated. In Scotland, Rangers are champs. In Div 1 St Mirren and Dunfermline will play higher. In Div 2 Clyde, Ross County and Alloa are promoted. In Div 3 Queens Park, Berwick and Forfar move up. A last min Nantes pen-winner ends the French Cup dream of amateur side Calais before 78,000 at the Stade de France.

8 Everton could not get a 1st league victory at Elland Road since 1951 but do Liverpool a favour restricting Leeds to a 1-1 draw. Hutchison and Dunne, and the home side's Duberry sent off. Macclesfield manager Peter Davenport apologises for walk out at the weekend and will continue. Lincoln chairman John Reames steps down from management duties. A financial report discloses top-flight Premiership players' wages last season rocketed by 31 per cent to £397m. Chester ordered to pay former manager Kevin Ratcliffe £200,000.

9 Sheff Wed say farewell at Highbury after a 2nd half providing 5 goals in 21 min as Arsenal fight back from 3-1 down to take a point. A header from Anelka effectively sends Real Madrid through against Bayern Munich to meet Barcelona or Valencia in their 11th European Cup Final. Derby's Jim Smith is charged with misconduct for the 2nd time this season.

10 FA punish Wimbledon with £50,000 fine and skipper Cunningham £5,000 for their part in the tunnel incident at Chelsea. Carlisle sack general manager Martin Wilkinson. FL to scrap away goals rule in favour of penalties for next season's play-off semi-finals.

11 Bradford cut short the loan of Jorge Cadete who started just 2 games and is returning to Benfica. Boro boss Bryan Robson denies Gascoigne is joining Australian club Joondalup City on loan this summer.

12 Chelsea's Jody Morris forfeits a Euro U-21 Championships spot because of a pending court case for an assault charge. Michael Knighton resigns as Carlisle chairman, but remains owner. The Football Trust who help finance the reconstruction of football stadiums with football pools money is to be replaced by the Football Foundation. Albion's Gary Megson is banned from the touchline for 28 days starting next season.

13 In Nationwide League play-off semi-finals 1st leg, Barnsley steal a commanding 4-0 lead at Brum. Hessenthaler's 30-yard strike 5 min into injury-time keeps Gillingham's Wembley hopes alive despite going under 3-2 at Stoke before a 22,214 crowd and a huge television audience in Ireland. Millwall are held scoreless by stubborn Wigan. Crowd violence and an ill-tempered affair on the pitch mars the NE clash at Hartlepool as Darlington take a 2-goal advantage. Posh win 2-1 at Barnet. The FA Umbro Trophy Final sees Kingstonian beat Kettering before 20,034.

14 The final day of the Premiership leaves an emotional North-South divide in football. Wimbledon end 14 years in the top flight losing 2-0 to Saints at The Dell. On this very day in 1977 The Dons joined the FL and this day 12 years ago they had their finest hour beating firm favourites Liverpool at Wembley in the FA Cup Final. Bradford, earmarked all season for the drop, take a 12th min lead over Liverpool with a Wetherall header, and contesting every ball, amazingly hang on and stay up with a meagre 36 pts, witnessed by joyful Valley Parade scenes at the close. Leeds book a deserved place in the Champions League against W Ham. Juninho nets a superb solo effort at Everton but his Boro long-term future remains in doubt. Sheringham's effort seals win at Villa for Man U who win the title by 18 pts, equalling the club record of only 3 defeats and beating Busby Babes' best of 27 league wins in a season. Sheff Wed bow out with 4-0 trouncing of Leicester. Shearer celebrates his 300th career score, his 200th league goal, and his 30th club goal of the season in 4-2 win over Arsenal. Chelsea warm-up for Wembley seeing off Derby 4-0. In Play-off 1st leg Bolton and Ipswich draw 2-2.

15 The FA Carling Premiership merit payments will give Wimbledon £696,606, Sheff Wed £464,404 and £232,202 to Watford. Arsène Wenger reports a clean bill of health before heading out to Wednesday's UEFA Cup Final in Copenhagen with Galatasaray.

16 Provisional figures released by the FA Premier League show a total of 11.66m fans passed through the turnstiles this season, an increase of 0.4 per cent. Chesterfield offer the managerial post to ex-League player, Nicky Law, the club's commercial officer. Ipswich and Leeds face charges following an investigation into the selling of tickets on the black market for England internationals at Wembley. After a medical David Pleat confirms Tottenham's £11m record signing of Ukrainian striker Sergei Rebrov, 25, from Dynamo Kiev on a 5-year contract worth

around £25,000 a week. Former Leeds striker Jimmy Floyd Hasselbaink and 17 of his colleagues at Atl Madrid are put on the transfer list following relegation.

17   In UEFA Cup Final Arsenal are foiled by inspired goalie Taffarel and fail to capitalise on Hagi's dismissal. Suker and Vieira strike penalty shoot-out efforts against the woodwork as Galatasaray become the first Turkish side to win a European trophy, with ex-Spurs defender Popescu snatching the spot-kick winner. In Nationwide League play-offs Ipswich's Magilton notches a hat-trick in thrilling 5-3 (agg 7-5) win over Bolton. The Gills complete 3-0 (agg 5-3) victory over a Stoke side up against it after the red-carding of Clarke and Kavanagh. Wigan are now 1 match away from Div 1 after a muscular 1-0 contest win over Millwall. Darlington are heading to Wembley beating rivals Hartlepool 1-0 (agg 3-0). Farrell nets a hat-trick for Posh as they see off Barnet (agg 5-1). Chelsea chairman Ken Bates pays £20,000 for a famous piece of Wembley turf, the exact spot where Geoff Hurst's disputed 3rd England goal is said to have crossed the line in the 1966 WC Final.

18   Sheff Wed's John Newsome, 29, is forced to retire. Barnsley, holding a 4-0 advantage, lose to Brum 2-1 (agg 5-2) and qualify for the club's 1st appearance at Wembley in their 113-year history where they will meet Ipswich for a Premiership spot.

19   Kevin Keegan calls up Malcolm Crosby, now at Swindon, for scouting duties during Euro 2000, and joins Nigel Spackman, Kenny Swain and Mike Pejic. Newcastle's Nikos Dabizas gets new 4-year contract.

20   Chelsea eventually take charge to win a generally poor and lack-lustre FA Cup Final against Villa, the last under the famous Twin Towers. Di Matteo, already with a place in FA Cup history having scored the quickest Wembley goal (42 sec) in 1997, nets the 73rd all-important close range strike after James fails to grasp Zola's teasing cross. Villa lack the creativity to disturb a defence well marshalled by Desailly who now has Cup Winners' medals from 3 countries.

21   Hearts beat rivals Hibs to retain 3rd spot and earn a place in UEFA Cup. Rangers lose their last game at Motherwell. Celtic's Larsson appears for 25 min showing no visible after-effects following his recovery from a broken leg. FAI joint-testimonial for Tony Cascarino and Steve Staunton attracts 36,000 against Liverpool Select. ITV's FA Cup Final broadcast, without opposition from BBC Grandstand, is viewed by only 7.2m, the lowest on terrestrial television.

22   Doug Ellis overules John Gregory and insists Villa enter the InterToto Cup. Jason Wilcox requires knee surgery ruling him out of Euro 2000 plans. Statisticians begin detailed check to see if Owen Price is indeed one of the world's fastest goalscorers, timed on video evidence at 4.07 sec. The 14 year old's effort for Tooting's Ernest Bevan College against Barking Abbey in the Heinz Ketchup Cup Final on May 18, at Highbury, is watched by a 1,000 crowd. Leicester's Muzzy Izzet makes Turkey's 27-man Euro 2000 panel.

23   Joe Kinnear is considering Sheff Wed's managerial job offer. Celtic remain confident of enticing Leicester's Martin O'Neill. The 1st major international in Britain in an enclosed dome attracts 72,000 at the £125m Millennium Stadium, Cardiff, to see Brazil beat Wales 3-0. Uriah Rennie and Paul Alcock are dropped from the Premiership ref's list.

24   Steve McManaman scores the goal of his life, and a place in history, helping Real Madrid capture the European Cup for the 8th time beating Valencia 3-0 in Paris. The ex- Liverpool winger notches a 67th min volley, Real's 2nd, becoming the 1st Englishman to score for a foreign side in a Euro Final. Bailiffs acting for former owner David Lloyd, reportedly owed £150,000 rent, lock Hull City out of Boothferry Park. FA serve Bolton with 8 misconduct charges relating to their controversial 5-3 play-off defeat at Ipswich.

25   Gary McAllister will join Liverpool on a free when his Coventry contract expires in July. Brent Council recommends approval for re-development of Wembley stadium, the £475m project commencing in October immediately following England's WC qualifier with Germany. Premier League to banish the elite group of refs, instead, a national list of 72 will also serve the Nationwide League. Man U named World Team of the Year at Laureas Sports awards in Monaco, beating the challenge of Australia's rugby WC winners and the US Women's soccer team.

26   Eleven Premier clubs decline the opportunity to qualify for Europe via the InterToto Cup leaving Villa and Bradford as representatives. Tony Fawthrop, a company director, resigns as Bristol City manager just 20 days after getting the job. Barry Fry does his customary touchline jig as his Posh team win promotion to Div 2 beating Darlington 1-0 in the play-off final. The FA is to sell off its famous Lancaster Gate HQ and lease a new home in Soho from Sept.

27   England, boasting no fewer than 7 goalscoring opportunities in the opening half against Brazil, step up their Euro 2000 preparations, by drawing 1-1 at Wembley with lively Owen stylishly firing ahead after 39 min. In Euro U-21 Championships in Bratislava, England lose their opener to Italy. In his farewell game after clocking up 839 senior appearances and winning 91 caps, Aberdeen's Jim Leighton, 41, breaks his jaw in a collision with Rod Wallace after only 2 min of the Scottish Cup Final which Rangers win comfortably 4-0, the 100th trophy in their 128-year history.

28   The Gills, with flashing headers from subs Butler and Thomson win an exciting play-off extra-time clash against a Wigan side who concede an og are reduced to 10-men, yet take a 2-1 lead only to get caught out twice from crosses. Tottenham sign Neil Sullivan, Wimbledon's 30 year old Scotland goalie on a Bosman free transfer.

29   Ipswich, 7 pts ahead of Barnsley in the division and who had gone out at the play-off semi-final stage in the last 3 seasons, come from behind in the Div 1 Wembley thriller, to deservedly win 4-2 and earn a return to the Premiership after a 5-year absence. W Ham's Lampard inspires England U-21's to an emphatic 6-0 beating of Turkey.

30   Barry Fry claims he has been sacked by Posh chairman Peter Boizot following a meeting to discuss the club's future. French goalie Fabien Barthez, at Old Trafford for talks, is believed to have agreed a 6-year contract worth around £45,000 a week, but the transfer from Monaco to Manchester hits a temporary stalemate. Arsenal complete the signing of Cameroon midfielder Lauren Bisan-Etame Mayer from Real Mallorca costing a fee of around £7m. Brian Kidd agrees a position of director of youth development at Leeds.

31   Nick Barmby, Gareth Barry and Steve Gerrard get the nod but Andy Cole, troubled with a minor foot problem, is left out of Kevin Keegan's Euro 2000 final squad. He is not present at Wembley to see England's 2-0 win over Ukraine thanks to goals from Fowler and Adams. Fabien Barthez finally joins Man U for a British record 'keeper

fee of £7.8m – but Sir Alex Ferguson is not at the ground to greet his new arrival as he is away on holiday. Barry Fry is staying at Posh despite having his youth policy questioned by directors. Chelsea agree £14m fee with Atl Madrid for Jimmy Floyd Hasselbaink. Newcastle sign midfielder Christian Bassedas, 26, from Velez Sarsfield for £3.5m. Chester City, relegated to the Nationwide Conference, part company with manager Ian Atkins.

June 2000
Burton in charge ... O'Neill takes Celtic post ... £15m gets Hasselbaink ... England win in Malta ... Higher fees for refs ... Wright retires ... Villa's Southgate wants to leave ... Busby babe Brennan dies ... Shearer jab ... Euro 2000 start ... Foxes appoint Taylor

1   The Dons appoint Terry Burton as manager on a permanent basis. Leicester's Martin O'Neill leaves Leicester and signs a lucrative 3-year contract becoming Celtic's 8th boss in 9 years as he took him only 2 and half seconds to agree to join the Glasgow giants. England slump out of the EC U-21 Championship losing 2-1 to host nation Slovakia. Blackburn pay £1.5m to Man U for U-21, reserve defender John Curtis.

2   Chelsea splash £15m for Jimmy Floyd Hasselbaink a year after the Dutch striker left Leeds for Atl Madrid in a £12m deal. Darlington will be docked a point next season if there is a repeat of the April 5 ugly scenes when a Quaker fan punched a Shrewsbury player.

3   With all-action Barmby the only plus point, Keegan admits if England repeat the stuttering form of the 2-1 victory in Malta, they face instant exit from Euro 2000. Goalie Richard Wright concedes 2 penalties, saves one, then crucially denies the Maltese in injury-time. In a clash resembling a practice match Keown and Shearer's replacement Heskey both score as the home nation utilise their reserves – all 11 of them!

4   Darren Debono complains that Shearer should have been sent off after the England skipper used an elbow and broke the Maltese defender's nose. Peter Schmeichel scores from a penalty in his 121st international as Denmark draw 2-2 with Belgium.

5   Premiership refs will double their match fees to £1,200 next season widening the gap with Nationwide League officials on £195. Dave Jones, relieved of managerial duties at Saints because of an impending court case, is taking the club to an independent tribunal maintaining he is sacked and is owed £300,000 contract monies. FIFA's Sepp Blatter suggests moving England's Euro clash with Germany from Charleroi to allay safety fears would make sense.

6   FIFA back down from enforcing a Premiership winter break and, instead, agree 12 dates between Feb and Dec for internationals and 16 for events such as the Champions League. But clubs must release players for internationals, African Nations Cup and the Gold Cup. An awards panel including Kevin Keegan selects Sunderland's Kevin Phillips as Carling's Player of the Year after netting 30 goals. FAW permit Mark Hughes to continue playing for a further 2 years remaining part-time national manager for half of the 4 years on his contract.

7   Strong speculation that S American voting countries will back S Africa's bid for WC 2006 in return for support to enable Brazil stage the bid for 2010. Ian Wright, 36, former Arsenal and England striker, shocks promoted Burnley by confirming he is retiring to concentrate on his television commitments. Liverpool pay £3m for French WC winger Bernard Diomede. The Duke of York, better known in sporting circles for his love of golf, is to succeed the Duke of Kent as the FA president. As England head to Euro 2000 Gareth Southgate requests a move from Villa. Ian Atkins is to take over at Carlisle.

8   Sheff Wed and Kilmarnock miss out on UEFA place through the Fair Play draw which goes to Lierse SK of Belgium and Spain's Rayo Vallecano. Liverpool's Jamie Redknapp is attending the famous Steadman-Hawkins clinic in Colorado awaiting a verdict on further knee surgery.

9   Arsenal will ban at least 40 fans involved in pre-match violence that marred the UEFA Cup Final against Galatasaray. Shay Brennan, a 1968 Man U European Cup hero, dies following a heart attack while playing golf in Waterford. Promoted Ipswich give £5m-rated goalie Richard Wright a 'sign or be sold' ultimatum.

10   England camp forced to issue a statement revealing skipper Shearer has received a controversial anti-inflammatory injection to help recover from a knee injury. As Euro 2000 gets under way before 50,000 at Stade Roi Baudouin in Brussels joint-hosts Belgium grab goals either side of the interval to gain a 2-1 victory over Sweden who had not conceded a score for 761 min in competitive football. Rushden & Diamonds break the non-League transfer record paying £180,000 for Morecambe striker Justin Jackson.

11   A dubious penalty 1 min from time gives the Dutch a lucky winning start over the Czech Rep who twice rattle the woodwork with headers. Never at their best but with the pace of Anelka and Henry a real threat, WC holders France open with a 3-0 win over Denmark. Italy's 2-1 start over Turkey in Arnhem is marred by crowd trouble and missile-throwing including a chair on the pitch after Inzaghi's 70th min controversial pen winner, awarded by Scotland's Hugh Dallas. In Nike Cup, won by the US, ROI beat S Africa with Niall Quinn's 2-1 winner equalling Frank Stapleton's record of 20 international scores.

12   England's assault on Euro 2000 suffers a severe setback when in an end to end encounter in Eindhoven they surrender a 2-goal lead and lose their opener 3-2 to a technically-superior Portugal team playing football of touch and skill. Scholes and McManaman, latching on to crosses, have England ahead in 18 min but the threat of a comeback is all too evident with Rui Costa and Luis Figo repeatedly sweeping through an overworked midfield and a back-pedalling defence. Far from impressive, champions Germany come from behind to share a 1-1 draw with Romania. Turkish FA receive £4,000 fine for bad fan behaviour against Italy. Peter Taylor, who has taken Gillingham into Div 1, becomes the new boss at Leicester agreeing a 3-year contract as successor to Martin O'Neill. Man City sign Alf Inge Haaland from Leeds for £2.5m.

13   Slovenia, 33-1 outsiders to win Group C, go 3 up against 10-man Yugoslavia who then score 3 in 8 min to grab the unlikeliest of draws with former Villa man Milosevic on as sub, netting twice. Norway, with 7 in their line-up at English clubs, snatch victory over Spain from Iversen's looping back-header. Rangers announce a £31m deal with main sponsors NTL. Ian Harte signs 5-year Leeds contract. England boss Keegan claims the abuse hurled at Beckham after the Portuguese defeat was the worst he had heard in football. Liverpool's Dumfries-born Dominic Matteo who has played at numerous levels for England is now pledging his future with Scotland.

ENGLISH LEAGUE TABLES 1999–2000

FA CARLING PREMIERSHIP

			Home			Goals	Away			Goals			
		P	W	D	L	F	A	W	D	L	F	A	GD	Pts
1	Manchester U	38	15	4	0	59	16	13	3	3	38	29	52	91
2	Arsenal	38	14	3	2	42	17	8	4	7	31	26	30	73
3	Leeds U	38	12	2	5	29	18	9	4	6	29	25	15	69
4	Liverpool	38	11	4	4	28	13	8	6	5	23	17	21	67
5	Chelsea	38	12	5	2	35	12	6	6	7	18	22	19	65
6	Aston Villa	38	8	8	3	23	12	7	5	7	23	23	11	58
7	Sunderland	38	10	6	3	28	17	6	4	9	29	39	1	58
8	Leicester C	38	10	3	6	31	24	6	4	9	24	31	0	55
9	West Ham U	38	11	5	3	32	23	4	5	10	20	30	−1	55
10	Tottenham H	38	10	3	6	40	26	5	5	9	17	23	8	53
11	Newcastle U	38	10	5	4	42	20	4	5	10	21	34	9	52
12	Middlesbrough	38	8	5	6	23	26	6	5	8	23	26	−6	52
13	Everton	38	7	9	3	36	21	5	5	9	23	28	10	50
14	Coventry C	38	12	1	6	38	22	0	7	12	9	32	−7	44
15	Southampton	38	8	4	7	26	22	4	4	11	19	40	−17	44
16	Derby Co	38	6	3	10	22	25	3	8	8	22	32	−13	38
17	Bradford C	38	6	8	5	26	29	3	1	15	12	39	−30	36
18	Wimbledon	38	6	7	6	30	28	1	5	13	16	46	−28	33
19	Sheffield W	38	6	3	10	21	23	2	4	13	17	47	−32	31
20	Watford	38	5	4	10	24	31	1	2	16	11	46	−42	24

NATIONWIDE FOOTBALL LEAGUE DIVISION 1

			Home			Goals	Away			Goals			
		P	W	D	L	F	A	W	D	L	F	A	GD	Pts
1	Charlton Ath	46	15	3	5	37	18	12	7	4	42	27	34	91
2	Manchester C	46	17	2	4	48	17	9	9	5	30	23	38	89
3	Ipswich T	46	16	3	4	39	17	9	9	5	32	25	29	87
4	Barnsley	46	15	4	4	48	24	9	6	8	40	43	21	82
5	Birmingham C	46	15	5	3	37	16	7	6	10	28	28	21	77
6	Bolton W	46	14	5	4	43	26	7	8	8	26	24	19	76
7	Wolverhampton W	46	15	5	3	45	20	6	6	11	19	28	16	74
8	Huddersfield T	46	14	5	4	43	21	7	6	10	19	28	13	74
9	Fulham	46	13	7	3	33	13	4	9	10	16	28	8	67
10	QPR	46	9	12	2	30	20	7	6	10	32	33	9	66
11	Blackburn R	46	10	9	4	33	20	5	8	10	22	31	4	62
12	Norwich C	46	11	6	6	26	22	3	9	11	19	28	−5	57
13	Tranmere R	46	10	8	5	35	27	5	4	14	22	41	−11	57
14	Nottingham F	46	9	10	4	29	18	5	4	14	24	37	−2	56
15	Crystal Palace	46	7	11	5	33	26	6	4	13	24	41	−10	54
16	Sheffield U	46	10	8	5	38	24	3	7	13	21	47	−12	54
17	Stockport Co	46	8	8	7	33	31	5	7	11	22	36	−12	54
18	Portsmouth	46	9	6	8	36	27	4	6	13	19	39	−11	51
19	Crewe Alex	46	9	5	9	27	31	5	4	14	19	36	−21	51
20	Grimsby T	46	10	8	5	27	25	3	4	16	14	42	−26	51
21	WBA	46	6	11	6	25	26	4	8	11	18	34	−17	49
22	Walsall	46	7	6	10	26	34	4	7	12	26	43	−25	46
23	Port Vale	46	6	6	11	27	30	1	9	13	21	39	−21	36
24	Swindon T	46	5	6	12	23	37	3	6	14	15	40	−39	36

NATIONWIDE FOOTBALL LEAGUE DIVISION 2

		P	W	D	L	F	A	W	D	L	F	A	GD	Pts
			Home			*Goals*		*Away*			*Goals*			
1	Preston NE	46	15	4	4	37	23	13	7	3	37	14	37	95
2	Burnley	46	16	3	4	42	23	9	10	4	27	24	22	88
3	Gillingham	46	16	3	4	46	21	9	7	7	33	27	31	85
4	Wigan Ath	46	15	3	5	37	14	7	14	2	35	24	34	83
5	Millwall	46	14	7	2	41	18	9	6	8	35	32	26	82
6	Stoke C	46	13	7	3	37	18	10	6	7	31	24	26	82
7	Bristol R	46	13	7	3	34	19	10	4	9	35	26	24	80
8	Notts Co	46	9	6	8	32	27	9	5	9	29	28	6	65
9	Bristol C	46	7	14	2	31	18	8	5	10	28	39	2	64
10	Reading	46	10	9	4	28	18	6	5	12	29	45	-6	62
11	Wrexham	46	9	6	8	23	24	8	5	10	29	37	-9	62
12	Wycombe W	46	11	4	8	32	24	5	9	9	24	29	3	61
13	Luton T	46	10	7	6	41	35	7	3	13	20	30	-4	61
14	Oldham Ath	46	8	5	10	27	28	8	7	8	23	27	-5	60
15	Bury	46	8	10	5	38	33	5	8	10	23	31	-3	57
16	AFC Bournemouth	46	11	6	6	37	19	5	3	15	22	43	-3	57
17	Brentford	46	8	6	9	27	31	5	7	11	20	30	-14	52
18	Colchester U	46	9	4	10	36	40	5	6	12	23	42	-23	52
19	Cambridge U	46	8	6	9	38	33	4	6	13	26	32	-1	48
20	Oxford U	46	6	5	12	24	38	6	4	13	19	35	-30	45
21	Cardiff C	46	5	10	8	23	34	4	7	12	22	33	-22	44
22	Blackpool	46	4	10	9	26	37	4	7	12	23	40	-28	41
23	Scunthorpe U	46	4	6	13	16	34	5	6	12	24	40	-34	39
24	Chesterfield	46	5	7	11	17	25	2	8	13	17	38	-29	36

NATIONWIDE FOOTBALL LEAGUE DIVISION 3

		P	W	D	L	F	A	W	D	L	F	A	GD	Pts
			Home			*Goals*		*Away*			*Goals*			
1	Swansea C	46	15	6	2	32	11	9	7	7	19	19	21	85
2	Rotherham U	46	13	5	5	43	17	11	7	5	29	19	36	84
3	Northampton T	46	16	2	5	36	18	9	5	9	27	27	18	82
4	Darlington	46	13	9	1	43	15	8	7	8	23	21	30	79
5	Peterborough U	46	14	4	5	39	30	8	8	7	24	24	9	78
6	Barnet	46	12	6	5	36	24	9	6	8	23	29	6	75
7	Hartlepool U	46	16	1	6	32	17	5	8	10	28	32	11	72
8	Cheltenham T	46	13	4	6	28	17	7	6	10	22	25	8	70
9	Torquay U	46	12	6	5	35	20	7	6	10	27	32	10	69
10	Rochdale	46	8	7	8	21	25	10	7	6	36	29	3	68
11	Brighton & HA	46	10	7	6	38	25	7	9	7	26	21	18	67
12	Plymouth Arg	46	12	10	1	38	18	4	8	11	17	33	4	66
13	Macclesfield T	46	9	7	7	36	30	9	4	10	30	31	5	65
14	Hull C	46	7	8	8	26	23	8	6	9	17	20	0	59
15	Lincoln C	46	11	6	6	38	23	4	8	11	29	46	-2	59
16	Southend U	46	11	5	7	37	31	4	6	13	16	30	-8	56
17	Mansfield T	46	9	6	8	33	26	7	2	14	17	39	-15	56
18	Halifax T	46	7	5	11	22	24	8	4	11	22	34	-14	54
19	Leyton Orient	46	7	7	9	22	22	6	6	11	25	30	-5	52
20	York C	46	7	10	6	21	21	5	6	12	18	32	-14	52
21	Exeter C	46	8	6	9	27	30	3	5	15	19	42	-26	44
22	Shrewsbury T	46	5	6	12	20	27	4	7	12	20	40	-27	40
23	Carlisle U	46	6	8	9	23	27	3	4	16	19	48	-33	39
24	Chester C	46	5	5	13	20	36	5	4	14	24	43	-35	39

FOOTBALL LEAGUE PLAY-OFFS 1999–2000

DIV 1 SEMI-FINALS FIRST LEG

13 MAY

Birmingham C (0) 0

Barnsley (1) 4 *(Shipperley 12, Dyer 48, 60, Hignett 84)*
26,492

Birmingham C: Myhre; Rowett, Johnson M, Hughes, Purse, (Ndlovu), Holdsworth, Grainger, O'Connor, Furlong (Adebola), Johnson A (Marcelo), Lazaridis.
Barnsley: Miller; Eaden, Barnard (Barker), Morgan, Chettle, Brown, Appleby, Hignett, Shipperley, Tinkler, Van der Laan (Thomas) (Dyer).

14 MAY

Bolton W (2) 2 *(Holdsworth 5, Gudjohnsen 26)*

Ipswich T (1) 2 *(Stewart 36, 65)*
18,814

Bolton W: Jaaskelainen; Bergsson, Whitlow, Warhurst, Fish, Ritchie (Phillips), Johansen (Elliott), Jensen, Gudjohnsen (Hansen), Holdsworth, Johnston.
Ipswich T: Wright R; Wilnis (Croft), Clapham, Thetis, Mowbray (Brown), Venus, Holland, Magilton, Johnson (Reuser), Scowcroft, Stewart.

DIV 2 SEMI-FINALS FIRST LEG

13 MAY

Millwall (0) 0

Wigan Ath (0) 0
14,091

Millwall: Warner; Lawrence, Ryan, Cahill, Nethercott, Tuttle, Neill, Livermore, Moody (Kinet), Harris, Ifill.
Wigan Ath: Stillie; Green, Sharp, McGibbon (Griffiths), Balmer, De Zeeuw, Kilford (Martinez), Sheridan, Haworth, Liddell, Redfearn.

Stoke C (2) 3 *(Gunnlaugsson 1, Lightbourne 8, Thorne 67)*

Gillingham (1) 2 *(Gooden 18, Hessenthaler 90)*
22,124

Stoke C: Ward; Hansson, Clarke, Mohan, Dryden (Jacobsen), Gunnlaugsson (Gudjonsson), Gunnarsson, Kavanagh G, Lightbourne (Connor), Thorne, O'Connor.
Gillingham: Bartram; Pennock, Edge, Smith (Browning), Ashby, Butters, Southall, Hessenthaler, Lewis, Onuora, Gooden.

DIV 3 SEMI-FINALS FIRST LEG

13 MAY

Barnet (1) 1 *(Arber 22)*

Peterborough U (1) 2 *(Lee 5, Clarke 68)*
4535

Barnet: Harrison; Stockley, Sawyers (Toms), Basham, Heald, Arber, Currie, Doolan, Charlery, McGleish, Wilson (Strevens).
Peterborough U: Tyler; Scott, Drury, Castle, Wicks, Edwards, Farrell, Oldfield, Clarke, Lee (Rea), Jelleyman (Gill).

Hartlepool U (0) 0

Darlington (1) 2 *(Liddle 35, Gabbiadini 76 (pen))*
6995

Hartlepool U: Hollund; Arnison (Dibble), Clark, Barron, Lee, Westwood, Coppinger (McAvoy), Miller, Beavers (Jones), Midgley, Stephenson.
Darlington: Collett; Liddle, Heckingbottom, Brumwell, Tutill, Gray, Heaney (Naylor), Oliver, Duffield (Nogan), Gabbiadini, Hyorth (Reed).

DIV 1 SEMI-FINALS SECOND LEG

17 MAY

Ipswich T (1) 5 *(Magilton 18 (pen), 49, 90, Clapham 94 (pen), Reuser 109)*

Bolton W (2) 3 *(Holdsworth 6, 39, Johnston 50)*
21,543

Ipswich T: Wright R; Croft, Clapham, Brown (Reuser), Mowbray, Venus, Holland, Magilton, Johnson, Scowcroft (Naylor), Stewart.
Bolton W: Jaaskelainen; Bergsson, Whitlow, Warhurst (Passi), Fish, Ritchie, Johansen (Phillips), Jensen, Holdsworth (Hansen), Elliott, Johnston.
(aet.)

18 MAY

Barnsley (0) 1 *(Dyer 54)*

Birmingham C (1) 2 *(Rowett 33, Marcelo 75)*
19,050

Barnsley: Miller; Eaden, Barnard (Curtis), Morgan, Chettle, Brown, Appleby, Hignett, Shipperley, Dyer, Tinkler.
Birmingham C: Myhre; Rowett, Johnson M (Lazaridis), Hughes, Purse, Holdsworth, Gill, O'Connor, Furlong (Johnson A), Marcelo, Ndlovu.

Andy Thomson swoops with a diving header to score the winning goal for Gillingham against Wigan Athletic.
(Actionimages)

Andy Clarke's goal-bound drive for Peterborough United was enough to overcome Darlington at Wembley.
(Colorsport)

DIV 2 SEMI-FINALS SECOND LEG

17 MAY

Gillingham (0) 3 *(Ashby 55, Onuora 102, Smith 118)*
Stoke C (0) 0   10,386
Gillingham: Bartram; Southall, Edge (Butler), Pennock, Ashby, Butters, Lewis, Hessenthaler, Asaba (Smith), Onuora (Nosworthy), Gooden.
Stoke C: Ward; Hansson, Clarke, Mohan, Jacobsen, Gunnarsson, Gudjonsson (Keen), Kavanagh G, Lightbourne (Connor), Gunnlaugsson (Melton), O'Connor.
(aet.)

Wigan Ath (0) 1 *(Sheridan 61)*
Millwall (0) 0   10,642
Wigan Ath: Stillie; Green, Sharp, McGibbon, Balmer, De Zeeuw, Kilford, Sheridan, Haworth, Liddell, Redfearn.
Millwall: Warner; Lawrence, Ryan (Shaw), Cahill, Nethercott, Tuttle, Neill (Kinet), Livermore, Moody, Harris, Ifill.

DIV 3 SEMI-FINALS SECOND LEG

17 MAY

Darlington (1) 1 *(Strodder 9 (og))*
Hartlepool U (0) 0   8238
Darlington: Collett; Liddle, Heckingbottom, Brumwell, Tutill (Reed), Gray, Heaney (Atkinson), Oliver, Duffield, Gabbiadini, Hyorth (Naylor).
Hartlepool U: Dibble; Arnison, Clark, Barron, Strodder, Westwood, Lee, Miller, Freestone, Jones (McAvoy), Stephenson (Fitzpatrick).

Peterborough U (1) 3 *(Farrell 28, 70, 89)*
Barnet (0) 0   10,515
Peterborough U: Tyler; Scott (Hooper), Drury, Castle, Rea, Edwards, Farrell, Oldfield, Clarke, Green (Hanlon), Jelleyman.
Barnet: Harrison (Bossu); Stockley, Toms, Basham, Heald, Arber, Currie, Doolan, Charlery, McGleish, Brown (King).

DIV 3 FINAL (at Wembley)

26 MAY

Peterborough U (0) 1 *(Clarke 25)*
Darlington (0) 0   33,383
Peterborough U: Tyler; Scott, Drury (Hanlon), Castle, Rea, Edwards, Farrell, Cullen, Clarke (Green), Oldfield, Jelleyman.
Darlington: Collett; Liddle, Heckingbottom (Naylor), Gray, Tutill, Aspin, Heaney, Oliver, Duffield (Nogan), Gabbiadini, Atkinson (Holsgrove).

DIV 2 FINAL (at Wembley)

28 MAY

Gillingham (1) 3 *(McGibbon 35 (og), Butler 114, Thomson 118)*
Wigan Ath (0) 2 *(Haworth 52, Barlow 99 (pen))* 53,764
Gillingham: Bartram; Southall, Edge (Smith), Pennock, Butters, Ashby (Butler), Lewis, Hessenthaler, Asaba, Onuora (Thomson), Gooden.
Wigan Ath: Stillie; Green, Sharp, McGibbon, Balmer, De Zeeuw, Kilford, Sheridan, Haworth (Peron), Liddell (Bradshaw), Redfearn (Barlow).
aet.

DIV 1 FINAL (at Wembley)

29 MAY

Ipswich T (1) 4 *(Mowbray 28, Naylor 52, Stewart 58, Reuser 90)*
Barnsley (1) 2 *(Wright R 6 (og), Hignett 78 (pen))* 73,427
Ipswich T: Wright R; Croft, Clapham, Venus, Mowbray, McGreal, Holland, Wright J (Wilnis), Johnson (Naylor), Magilton, Stewart (Reuser).
Barnsley: Miller; Curtis (Eaden), Barnard, Morgan, Chettle, Brown, Appleby, Hignett, Shipperley, Dyer (Hristov), Tinkler (Thomas).

LEADING GOALSCORERS 1999–2000

FA CARLING PREMIERSHIP	League	FA Cup	Worthington Cup	Other	Total
Kevin Phillips *(Sunderland)*	30	0	0	0	30
Alan Shearer *(Newcastle U)*	23	5	0	2	30
Dwight Yorke *(Manchester U)*	20	0	0	4	24
Andy Cole *(Manchester U)*	19	0	0	3	22
Michael Bridges *(Leeds U)*	19	0	0	2	21
Thierry Henry *(Arsenal)*	17	0	1	8	26
Paolo Di Canio *(West Ham U)*	16	0	0	1	17
Steffan Iversen *(Tottenham H)*	14	1	1	1	17
Chris Armstrong *(Tottenham H)*	14	0	0	0	14
Niall Quinn *(Sunderland)*	14	0	0	0	14
Tony Cottee *(Leicester C)*	13	0	0	0	13
Marian Pahars *(Southampton)*	13	0	0	0	13
Dion Dublin *(Aston Villa)*	12	1	2	0	15
Nwankwo Kanu *(Arsenal)*	12	0	1	4	17
Ole Gunnar Solskjaer *(Manchester U)*	12	0	0	3	15
Hamilton Ricard *(Middlesbrough)*	12	0	2	0	14
Paolo Wanchope *(West Ham U)*	12	0	0	3	15
Kevin Campbell *(Everton)*	12	0	0	0	12
Robbie Keane *(Coventry C)*	12	0	0	0	12

NATIONWIDE DIVISION 1

	League	FA Cup	Worthington Cup	Other	Total
Andy Hunt *(Charlton Ath)*	24	1	0	0	25
Shaun Goater *(Manchester C)*	23	3	3	0	29
David Johnson *(Ipswich T)*	22	0	1	0	23
Craig Hignett *(Barnsley)*	19	0	0	2	21
Iwan Roberts *(Norwich C)*	17	0	2	0	19
Wayne Allison *(Tranmere R)*	16	3	0	0	19
Marcus Stewart *(Ipswich T)*	16	0	1	3	20
(Including 14 League and 1 Worthington Cup goal for Huddersfield T)					
Ade Akinbiyi *(Wolverhampton W)*	16	0	0	0	16
Marcus Bent *(Sheffield U)*	15	1	0	0	16
Clyde Wijnhard *(Huddersfield T)*	15	0	1	0	16
Steve Claridge *(Portsmouth)*	14	0	0	0	14
Eidur Gudjohnsen *(Bolton W)*	13	4	3	1	21
Chris Kiwomya *(QPR)*	13	1	0	0	14
Darren Barnard *(Barnsley)*	13	0	2	0	15
Clinton Morrison *(Crystal Palace)*	13	0	2	0	15
James Scowcroft *(Ipswich T)*	13	0	2	0	15
Neil Shipperley *(Barnsley)*	13	0	1	1	15

NATIONWIDE DIVISION 2

	League	FA Cup	Worthington Cup	Other	Total
Andy Payton *(Burnley)*	27	0	0	0	27
Neil Harris *(Millwall)*	25	0	0	0	25
Peter Thorne *(Stoke C)*	24	0	1	5	30
Sean Devine *(Wycombe W)*	23	1	1	0	25
Jonathan Macken *(Preston NE)*	22	1	2	0	25
Jason Roberts *(Bristol R)*	22	0	3	0	25
Jamie Cureton *(Bristol R)*	22	0	1	1	24
Trevor Benjamin *(Cambridge U)*	20	3	0	0	23
Martin Butler *(Reading)*	18	2	3	0	23
(Including 14 League, 2 FA Cup and 3 Worthington Cup goals for Cambridge U)					
Stuart Barlow *(Wigan Ath)*	18	2	2	1	23
Darren Caskey *(Reading)*	17	3	2	1	23
Steve McGavin *(Colchester U)*	16	0	0	0	16
Robert Taylor *(Gillingham)*	15	2	1	0	18
David Reeves *(Chesterfield)*	14	0	2	2	18
Mark Stallard *(Notts Co)*	14	0	0	0	14

NATIONWIDE DIVISION 3

	League	FA Cup	Worthington Cup	Other	Total
Marco Gabbiadini *(Darlington)*	24	1	1	2	28
Martin Carruthers *(Southend U)*	19	0	0	0	19
Leo Fortune-West *(Rotherham U)*	17	0	0	0	17
Gary Alexander *(Exeter C)*	16	1	0	2	19
Anthony Bedeau *(Torquay U)*	16	1	0	0	17
Lee Thorpe *(Lincoln C)*	16	0	1	0	17
Richard Barker *(Macclesfield T)*	16	0	0	1	17
Andy Clarke *(Peterborough U)*	15	1	0	2	18
John Askey *(Macclesfield T)*	15	0	0	0	15
Luke Beckett *(Chester C)*	14	2	3	0	19
Tommy Miller *(Hartlepool U)*	14	0	1	1	16
Carlo Corazzin *(Northampton T)*	14	0	1	0	15
Paul McGregor *(Plymouth Arg)*	13	3	0	0	16
Ken Charlery *(Barnet)*	13	0	0	1	14

REVIEW OF THE SEASON

Manchester United's sixth FA Carling Premiership success in eight years brought with it problems for the competition as a whole and for those aspiring to emulate such triumphs.

The negative view is that United have such a wealth of playing resources that it is difficult for others to compete with them to the nth degree. A more positive point, however, is the need for aspiring challengers to improve levels of consistency, something in abundance at Old Trafford.

While United's performance did not quite match that of 1998-99 when they completed an unbeaten run of 33 matches grabbing the European Cup and the FA Cup as a treble-shooting honour in the process, it was a just reward.

With a forced winter break while the team was playing in the inaugural FIFA Club World Championship in Brazil, United were able to resume without too much of a problem. No League matches were played from 28 December when United were a point behind Leeds with a game in hand, until the 24 January when they were held to a 1-1 draw at Old Trafford by Arsenal. This left United three points behind Leeds, but with two games in hand, Arsenal on the same number of points yet having played three more matches than United.

A lesser team than United might well have been badly affected by this result against one of its main rivals, but though the early part of the game had seen Arsenal well on top, United levelled the scores late on.

Freed from the task of defending their FA Cup success and out of the Worthington Cup which had never really interested them, United had just twin sights: the League and the Champions Cup. While others were concerned with the fifth round of the FA Cup, United continued League fare and edged out Middlesbrough with a late David Beckham goal to go top on goal difference from Leeds – moreover with a precious game to the good over the Yorkshiremen.

The gap between the two teams gradually widened despite a slip when United crashed 3-0 at Newcastle early in February. As in many other instances, United's opponents failed to capitalize on such a gift. And more importantly, Manchester United won 1-0 at Leeds on 20 February, courtesy of an Andy Cole goal.

On 22 April United clinched the title with a 3-1 win at Southampton, typically bouncing back after losing to Real Madrid in the European Cup. By then their nearest challengers were Liverpool, but 13 points adrift with four matches still to be played.

United called upon the services of 29 different players. The strength of the squad system at Old Trafford being such that not one player was ever-present. Dwight Yorke with 20 goals was their leading marksman, while Cole had 19 and Ole Gunnar Solksjaer weighed in with a creditable 12 goals himself. Roy Keane took both PFA and Football Writers' accolades.

Liverpool just as Leeds had done before them had fallen away and it was Arsenal who finished runners-up some 18 points away. The Gunners' purple patch came with a run of eight successive wins. Alas this run straddled United taking the prize. Arsenal's European venture was interesting enough as it began in the European Cup and finished in the final of the UEFA Cup; such are the vageries of the modern game. Once again an English team fell foul of the penalty shoot-out.

There was much to commend in the largely youthful Leeds team, but they failed to take a point from either Manchester United or Arsenal, thus for no other reason, third place was appropriate. Liverpool's quiet start was stepped up from the middle of January, but again it came at the wrong time with the title about to fall into United's lap. But 13 unbeaten games was a creditable sequence, though it was followed by no goals from five matches.

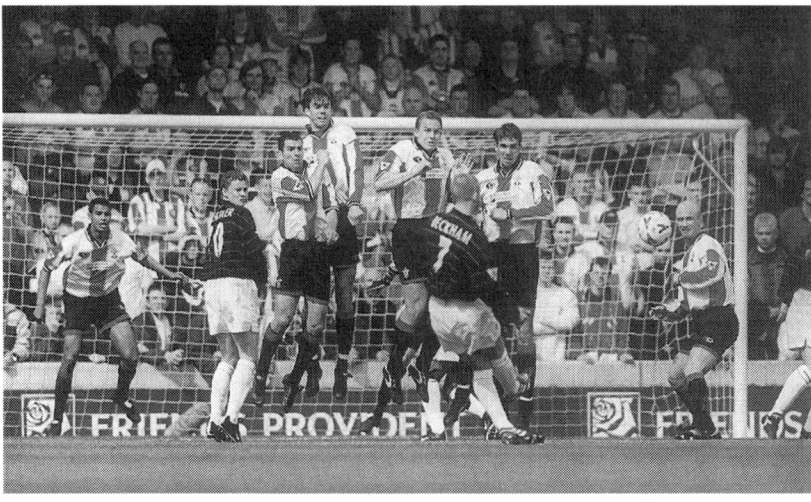

Manchester United clinched their sixth Premiership title by beating Southampton at The Dell on 22 April. Here David Beckham (7) scores for the champions. (Colorsport)

When Chelsea convincingly beat Manchester United 5-0 on 3 October prospects in the League could not have looked brighter, but defeats against Liverpool and Arsenal in the next two games put the situation into an entirely different light. But Chelsea's cavalier approach netted them the FA Cup.

Incredibly they, too, enjoyed their best run of the season at a time when United were well on their way. Again 16 matches without defeat was a worthy effort. Aston Villa also had a better second half of the season than the first in which they had to endure nine games without a win into December.

Sunderland after three years out of the Premier League climbed to an impressive third place until a 5-0 defeat at Everton on Boxing Day noticeably knocked them out of their stride. They did have the League's top marksman in Kevin Phillips with 30 League goals.

Fifth place was the highest Leicester managed throughout, though the Worthington Cup was a merited prize and West Ham having manfully struggled in late summer to wrest the Intertoto Cup, made a useful beginning to their League programme which was not maintained. As usual they were involved in several high-scoring and entertaining matches, though a 7-1 defeat against Manchester United hit their goals against column badly.

Only once in August did Tottenham manage as many as three wins in a row, but Newcastle ended a run of seven games with just one point by thrashing Sheffield Wednesday 8-0 with Alan Shearer scoring five goals to equal the Premiership record. Bobby Robson's appointment as manager came at the right time on Tyneside.

A mid-season blip in which only one win was registered in 11 games affected Middlesbrough and 14 drawn games, nine at Goodison Park kept Everton in check.

Coventry were stuck on 14th place for the last three months of the season, though above the relegation zone so familiar to them in recent years. But six games without a win and only three goals had the alarm bells ringing at The Dell by the end of December and manager Dave Jones was relieved of his duties and Glenn Hoddle came in to steer Southampton to safety.

Victories had to be hard won by Derby and goals were often scarce to worry them in the battle to avoid going down. While the favourite trio to be relegated was Bradford, Sheffield Wednesday and Watford, the collapse of Wimbledon who managed only one point out of a possible last 30 gave an unexpected reprieve for Bradford whose revival came late after six successive defeats and shipping 18 goals in the process.

Down with the Dons went Wednesday, who had only two wins in the first 20 matches and a manager with local MPs baying for his head, until Danny Wilson was eventually relieved of his position. Watford completed the threesome, with problems in attack and defence and rock bottom from 22 January.

Football League champions from Division One were Charlton though the champagne had to be put on ice a couple of times before they wrapped it up, no victories in the last seven outings taking a little of the shine off a splendid season.

Leeds United and Arsenal strove for the Premier crown themselves. Here the Gunners Dennis Bergkamp (left) disputes possession with Jonathan Woodgate (right) (Actionimages)

Chelsea and Liverpool had their Premier League moments, too. The Merseysiders Patrik Berger challenges Chelsea goalkeeper Ed de Goey with Frank Leboeuf on hand to defend. (Colorsport)

Manchester City ended the campaign confidently, unbeaten in the last 11 matches to achieve automatic promotion with them and were joined by Ipswich via the play-offs. Their best period had come from 18 games without defeat to the end of February, taking them to second place; a sequence spoiled by five games without a win.

It was Barnsley who lost out to Ipswich at Wembley, though they had made a useful job of trying to get back to the Premier League at the first attempt and they were never out of the frame after the start of the new year. Birmingham had been Barnsley's initial play-off victims. Their League season had been marred by some inconsistency having by 7 March promised a better run-in. Bolton timed their effort to perfection, snatching the last play-off berth after five wins in the last six outings, but they were beaten by Ipswich, having taken only one point from them in the League.

Once again Wolves just failed to make the cut. The seeds were sown early on when their second win was not forthcoming until 9 October. Huddersfield, too, slumped in the second half after heading the table on 18 December.

Eight games, no wins and the only goal from an opposing defender, virtually ended Fulham's hopes and fellow West Londoners Queens Park Rangers contrived six consecutive draws when two or three wins might have changed their fortunes.

A 2-0 win over Huddersfield on 15 January put Blackburn seventh, their highest all season and 15 draws inevitably kept Norwich City in mid-table. Tranmere had a marathon 60 League and Cup games during the season, the knock-out version clearly upsetting their League form.

Scoring goals became a problem for Nottingham Forest mid-way through the season, only six in 12 matches until a late recovery and similar problems hit Crystal Palace in February and March.

Two spells of ten and nine games chasing an elusive win said it all for Sheffield United and a healthy sixth place for Stockport was then totally ruined by 19 matches without one of their own.

Seventeen games without scoring was the cause of Portsmouth's ailment, but from mid-March improvement was noticeable in this direction. Crewe averaged just one goal a game themselves and ten games without a win plunged them into the relegation zone in February.

Grimsby slid dangerously near demotion with no wins in their last 11 outings and West Bromwich failed to average a goal a game until rescued by two wins and a draw from their last three.

The unlucky trio was composed of Walsall, Port Vale and Swindon. Walsall's best effort had been three wins in January, but from 23 November, Port Vale scrambled just two more wins and Swindon were rooted to the foot of the table from three days earlier.

Preston held on to top spot in the Second Division from mid-March their best run coming from 18 undefeated encounters to the turn of the year.

Fellow Lancastrians Burnley joined them in automatic uplift thanks to four wins in a row at the death. Gillingham who had finished third made it through the play-offs after looking a good bet from February.

Wigan lost out to Gillingham at Wembley after the best start any club could have wished – 24 unbeaten matches. But eight games passed before their next victory. Both Millwall and Stoke tripped up at this final stage.

Ipswich Town were understandably elated after their play-off success which enabled them to return to the Premiership elite. (Colorsport)

Winning only one of their last four did nothing for Millwall's automatic chances and Stoke's 13 without defeat only pushed them into play-off contention, leaving them with the Auto Windscreens Shield for the mantlepiece. Alas Bristol Rovers, top as late as mid-March, recorded merely one win in the last ten.

Notts County had been top on 6 November, Bristol City as low as 19th after sharing eight goals with Notts themselves on 27 November. Reading's improvement came in March after 13 minus a win bonus from November.

Lack of scoring power was evident from Wrexham with 11 games and only four goals at one time, while Wycombe only twice managed three wins in a row. Luton's bright opening was not maintained, but Oldham pulled themselves together after just three wins in the first 14.

Bury will never more than two consecutive wins and Bournemouth with merely isolated victories, were destined to a midway existence. Yet Brentford fell like a stone from fourth place in November recording only four more wins.

Colchester had to graft diligently following just two wins in the first 15 games, East Anglian neighbours Cambridge fell to the bottom by 15 January after only two goals in six matches and academically speaking, a poor scoring record was Oxford's major weakness.

Thirteen proved an unlucky number for Cardiff. This number of games without victory led to eventual relegation along with Blackpool, Scunthorpe and Chesterfield. Seventeen drawn affairs caused Blackpool dearly while Scunthorpe were unable to score more than two goals in any game after 12 November. For Chesterfield they were never out of the bottom two from 6 November.

The strength of Swansea's Third Division title came from nine wins in a row through the turn of the year and they also recovered from a late wobble. Rotherham and Northampton accompanied them, United having held top spot for four months and Northampton with six impressive wins at the end.

Darlington, who had been fourth, missed out in the final play-off against fifth placed Peterborough. They could not complain; they had won only two of their last 12. Peterborough had even been top in November.

Barnet's fortunes were dented in January after they had been leading the pack for months, but they held on for the play-offs with Hartlepool, there or thereabouts in the New Year.

Cheltenham made a useful bid in their first season, needing to win at Southend in the last game to push into the frame. Torquay's second half of the season never matched their first and six successive games without a goal underlined Rochdale's need.

Brighton, back home again, ran in for 14 without defeat at the end, but Plymouth disappointingly drew 18 times. Macclesfield's highest was sixth in January and the absence of scoring consistency hit Hull.

Eight games without loss was Lincoln's best and though fourth in September, Southend found their level just below half-way. Mansfield went eight games without a goal to the last but one outing and Halifax registered 19 games without a goal as did Leyton Orient, next to the foot after the half-way stage.

York needed those five wins from the last ten and Exeter went 15 games with just one win. It was left to Shrewsbury, Carlisle and Chester to finally dispute the relegation spot.

Shrewsbury were sucked into it by a lack of goals, but managed a crucial 2-1 win at Exeter on the last day. Carlisle had been in the bottom three since mid-December but despite losing 1-0 at Brighton in the final game, survived on a goal difference of two, because Chester similarly lost at home to Peterborough. Chester had briefly given the glimpse of staving off relegation with four wins in six games having appeared dead and buried much earlier. Their place will be taken by Kidderminster Harriers.

INTRODUCTION TO THE CLUB SECTION

For this year's Rothmans Football Yearbook, the players again appear under the club with whom they finished the season and in an A–Z form for easy reference (see pages 414–540). The names of Trainees, Scholars and Associated Schoolboys are also included under each club's name.

The club section again comprises four pages as last year, the first two feature increased historical and record details for each club, including new entries in the 'Did you know?' series. Record transfer fees are usually left to the discretion of the club concerned.

The third and fourth pages of this section present a complete record of the League season, including date, venue, opponents, results, half-time score, League position, goalscorers, attendances and complete line-ups including substitutes where used, for every League game in the 1999–2000 season. Again goal times have been added, though not official they give an indication of when goals were scored. These appear as superior figures [10, 20, 30].

Squad numbers have not been included; those used are the familiar ones, 1–11 while the introduction of a third outfield substitute has been recognised as follows:- the first substitute No. 12, the second No. 13 and the third No. 14. However, if there is a substitute goalkeeper he is represented by No. 15 but *only* if he replaces the first choice goalkeeper. Otherwise he adopts one of the other three substitute numbers, as there have been several instances where a goalkeeper has been used as an outfield player because of injuries during the game. Players replaced are respectively noted with superior figures [1], [2], [3] and [g] for goalkeeper. These third and fourth pages also include consolidated lists of goalscorers for the club in League, Worthington Cup and FA Cup matches plus a summary of results in these two main domestic competitions.

The continued increase in the number of matches played on Sundays has resulted in the League positions shown after every League result being taken on that day. Full holiday programmes are also recorded, but the position after mid-week fixtures will not normally have been updated. Attendance figures quoted for the Nationwide Football League are those which appeared in the Press at the time. But those in the FA Carling Premiership are official. The attendance statistics published on pages 567–569 are those officially issued by the FA Premier League but not the Football League at the end of the season.

In the totals at the top of each column on page 4, substitute appearances are listed separately by the '+', but have been amalgamated in the totals which feature in the players historical section in the directory mentioned above. Thus these appearances include those as substitute. In fact the directory again features those names appearing on the FA Premier League and Football League's Retained list, which is published at the end of May. Each player's height and weight where known, plus birth place, birth date and source together with total League goals and appearances for each club he has represented, can be found as in previous editions. The player's details remain under the club which retained him at the end of the season. An asterisk '*' by a player's name indicates that he was given a free transfer at the end of the 1999–2000 season, a dagger '†' against a name means that he is a non-contract player, a double dagger '‡' indicates that the player's registration was cancelled during the season and a section mark '§' shows the player to be a trainee or associated schoolboy who has made League appearances. The symbol # indicates players aged 24 and over who are out of contract but who were offered re-engagement by their clubs. Appearances by players in the play-offs are not included in their career totals.

FA Premiership **ARSENAL**

FOUNDATION

Formed by workers at the Royal Arsenal, Woolwich in 1886, they began as Dial Square (name of one of the workshops), and included two former Nottingham Forest players, Fred Beardsley and Morris Bates. Beardsley wrote to his old club seeking help and they provided the new club with a full set of red jerseys and a ball. The club became known as the 'Woolwich Reds' although their official title soon after formation was Woolwich Arsenal.

Arsenal Stadium, Highbury, London N5 1BU.
Telephone: (020) 7704 4000.
Fax: (020) 7704 4001.
Box Office: (020) 7413 3366.
Commercial & Marketing: (020) 7704 4100.
Recorded Information: (020) 7704 4242.
Clubline: 09068 202 021.
Ground Capacity: 38,500 all seated.
Record Attendance: 73,295 v Sunderland, Div 1, 9 March 1935.
At Wembley: 73,455 v Panathinaikos, European Cup Group E, 30 September 1998.
Record Receipts: £392,726.50 v Sampdoria, European Cup-Winners' Cup, semi-final first leg, 6 April 1995.
Pitch Measurements: 110yd x 73yd.
Life President: Sir Robert Bellinger GBE, D.SC.
Chairman: P. D. Hill-Wood.
Vice-Chairman: D. Dein.
Directors: R. G. Gibbs, C. E. B. L. Carr, R. C. L. Carr, D. D. Fiszman, K. J. Friar.
Managing Director: K. Edelman.
Manager: Arsène Wenger.
Assistant Manager: Pat Rice.
First Team Coach: Boro Primorac.
Head Youth Coach: Don Howe.
Head of Youth Development: Liam Brady.
Physio: Gary Lewin.
Reserve Coach: George Armstrong.
Company Secretary: David Miles.
Commercial Manager: John Hazell.
Stadium Manager: John Beattie.

HONOURS

FA Premier League: Champions 1997–98. Runners-up 1998–99, 1999–2000.

Football League: Division 1 – Champions 1930–31, 1932–33, 1933–34, 1934–35, 1937–38, 1947–48, 1952–53, 1970–71, 1988–89, 1990–91; Runners-up 1925–26, 1931–32, 1972–73; Division 2 – Runners-up 1903–04.

FA Cup: Winners 1930, 1936, 1950, 1971, 1979, 1993, 1998; Runners-up 1927, 1932, 1952, 1972, 1978, 1980.

Double performed: 1970–71, 1997–98.

Football League Cup: Winners 1987, 1993; Runners-up 1968, 1969, 1988.

European Competitions: Fairs Cup: 1963–64, 1969–70 (winners), 1970–71. *European Cup:* 1971–72, 1991–92, 1998–99, 1999–2000. *UEFA Cup:* 1978–79, 1981–82, 1982–83, 1996–97, 1997–98, 1999–2000 (runners-up). *European Cup-Winners' Cup:* 1979–80 (runners-up), 1993–94 (winners), 1994–95 (runners-up).

LATEST SEQUENCES
Longest Sequence of League Wins: 10, 11.3.98 – 3.5.98.
Longest Sequence of League Defeats: 7, 12.2.77 – 12.3.77.
Longest Sequence of League Draws: 6, 4.3.61 – 1.4.61.
Longest Sequence of Unbeaten League Matches: 26, 28.4.90 – 19.1.91.

Colours
Red shirts with white sleeves, white shorts, red and white hooped stockings.

Change Colours
Yellow and navy blue shirts, navy blue shorts, navy blue stockings.

Longest Sequence Without a League Win: 23, 28.9.12 – 1.3.13.

Year Formed: 1886.

Turned Professional: 1891.

Ltd Co: 1893.

Previous Names: 1886, Dial Square; 1886, Royal Arsenal; 1891, Woolwich Arsenal; 1914 Arsenal.

Club Nickname: 'Gunners'.

Previous Grounds: 1886, Plumstead Common; 1887, Sportsman Ground; 1888, Manor Ground; 1890, Invicta Ground; 1893, Manor Ground; 1913, Highbury.

First Football League Game: 2 September 1893, Division 2, v Newcastle U (h) D 2–2 – Williams; Powell, Jeffrey; Devine, Buist, Howat; Gemmell, Henderson, Shaw (1), Elliott (1), Booth.

Record League Victory: 12–0 v Loughborough T, Division 2, 12 March 1900 – Orr; McNichol, Jackson; Moir, Dick (2), Anderson (1); Hunt, Cottrell (2), Main (2), Gaudie (3), Tennant (2).

MANAGERS

Sam Hollis 1894–97
Tom Mitchell 1897–98
George Elcoat 1898–99
Harry Bradshaw 1899–1904
Phil Kelso 1904–08
George Morrell 1908–15
Leslie Knighton 1919–25
Herbert Chapman 1925–34
George Allison 1934–47
Tom Whittaker 1947–56
Jack Crayston 1956–58
George Swindin 1958–62
Billy Wright 1962–66
Bertie Mee 1966–76
Terry Neill 1976–83
Don Howe 1984–86
George Graham 1986–95
Bruce Rioch 1995–96
Arsène Wenger September 1996–

Record Cup Victory: 11–1 v Darwen, FA Cup 3rd rd, 9 January 1932 – Moss; Parker, Hapgood; Jones, Roberts, John; Hulme (2), Jack (3), Lambert (2), James, Bastin (4).

Record Defeat: 0–8 v Loughborough T, Division 2, 12 December 1896.

Most League Points (2 for a win): 66, Division 1, 1930–31.

Most League Points (3 for a win): 83, Division 1, 1990–91.

Most League Goals: 127, Division 1, 1930–31.

Highest League Scorer in Season: Ted Drake, 42, 1934–35.

Most League Goals in Total Aggregate: Cliff Bastin, 150, 1930–47.

Most League Goals in One Match: 7, Ted Drake v Aston Villa, Division 1, 14 December 1935.

Most Capped Player: Kenny Sansom, 77 (86), England, 1981–1988.

Most League Appearances: David O'Leary, 558, 1975–93.

Youngest League Player: Gerry Ward, 16 years 321 days v Huddersfield T, 22 August 1953 (Jermaine Pennant, 16 years 319 days v Middlesbrough, League Cup, 30 November 1999).

Record Transfer Fee Received: £22,900,000 from Real Madrid for Nicolas Anelka, August 1999.

Record Transfer Fee Paid: £10,000,000 to Juventus for Thierry Henry, August 1999.

Football League Record: 1893 Elected to Division 2; 1904–13 Division 1; 1913–19 Division 2; 1919–92 Division 1; 1992– FA Premier League.

TEN YEAR LEAGUE RECORD

		P	W	D	L	F	A	Pts	Pos
1989-90	Div 1	38	18	8	12	54	38	62	4
1990-91	Div 1	38	24	13	1	74	18	83	1
1991-92	Div 1	42	19	15	8	81	46	72	4
1992-93	PR Lge	42	15	11	16	40	38	56	10
1993-94	PR Lge	42	18	17	7	53	28	71	4
1994-95	PR Lge	42	13	12	17	52	49	51	12
1995-96	PR Lge	38	17	12	9	49	32	63	5
1996-97	PR Lge	38	19	11	8	62	32	68	3
1997-98	PR Lge	38	23	9	6	68	33	78	1
1998-99	PR Lge	38	22	12	4	59	17	78	2

DID YOU KNOW ?

On 2 March 2000, Arsenal beat Spanish League leaders Deportivo La Coruna 5-1 in the fourth round first leg of the UEFA Cup at Highbury, their first European success over a club from Spain.

ARSENAL 1999–2000 LEAGUE RECORD

Match No.	Date	Venue	Opponents	Result	H/T Score	Lg. Pos.	Goalscorers	Attendance
1	Aug 7	H	Leicester C	W 2-1	0-0	3	Bergkamp [65], Sinclair (og) [90]	38,026
2	10	A	Derby Co	W 2-1	1-1	—	Petit [40], Bergkamp [47]	25,901
3	14	A	Sunderland	D 0-0	0-0	2		40,037
4	22	H	Manchester U	L 1-2	1-0	8	Ljungberg [41]	38,147
5	25	H	Bradford C	W 2-0	2-0	—	Vieira [8], Kanu (pen) [17]	38,073
6	28	A	Liverpool	L 0-2	0-1	6		44,886
7	Sept 11	H	Aston Villa	W 3-1	1-1	5	Suker 2 [45, 49], Kanu [82]	38,093
8	18	A	Southampton	W 1-0	0-0	3	Henry [79]	15,242
9	25	H	Watford	W 1-0	0-0	3	Kanu [86]	38,127
10	Oct 3	A	West Ham U	L 1-2	0-1	5	Suker [77]	26,009
11	16	H	Everton	W 4-1	1-1	3	Dixon [40], Suker 2 [54, 61], Kanu [90]	38,042
12	23	A	Chelsea	W 3-2	0-1	2	Kanu 3 [75, 83, 90]	34,958
13	30	H	Newcastle U	D 0-0	0-0	4		38,106
14	Nov 7	A	Tottenham H	L 1-2	1-2	4	Vieira [39]	36,085
15	20	H	Middlesbrough	W 5-1	2-0	3	Overmars 3 [26, 61, 78], Bergkamp 2 [40, 49]	38,082
16	28	H	Derby Co	W 2-1	1-1	3	Henry 2 [11, 51]	37,964
17	Dec 4	A	Leicester C	W 3-0	1-0	3	Grimandi [23], Dixon [53], Overmars [75]	20,495
18	18	H	Wimbledon	D 1-1	0-1	4	Henry [61]	38,052
19	26	A	Coventry C	L 2-3	0-2	4	Ljungberg [67], Suker [86]	22,750
20	28	H	Leeds U	W 2-0	1-0	3	Ljungberg [32], Henry [58]	38,096
21	Jan 3	A	Sheffield W	D 1-1	1-0	3	Petit [40]	26,155
22	15	H	Sunderland	W 4-1	3-0	3	Henry 2 [3, 81], Suker 2 [27, 32]	38,039
23	24	A	Manchester U	D 1-1	1-0	—	Ljungberg [11]	58,293
24	Feb 5	A	Bradford C	L 1-2	1-1	3	Henry [13]	18,276
25	13	H	Liverpool	L 0-1	0-1	4		38,098
26	26	H	Southampton	W 3-1	2-0	3	Ljungberg 2 [22, 68], Bergkamp [36]	38,044
27	Mar 5	A	Aston Villa	D 1-1	0-0	4	Dixon [84]	36,930
28	12	A	Middlesbrough	L 1-2	0-0	5	Bergkamp [70]	32,244
29	19	H	Tottenham H	W 2-1	2-1	4	Armstrong (og) [20], Henry (pen) [45]	38,131
30	26	H	Coventry C	W 3-0	0-0	4	Henry [50], Grimandi [79], Kanu [80]	38,027
31	Apr 1	A	Wimbledon	W 3-1	2-1	4	Kanu 2 [33, 41], Henry (pen) [89]	25,858
32	16	A	Leeds U	W 4-0	1-0	3	Henry [21], Keown [70], Kanu [82], Overmars [90]	39,307
33	23	A	Watford	W 3-2	3-0	3	Henry 2 [18, 45], Parlour [43]	19,670
34	29	A	Everton	W 1-0	1-0	2	Overmars [34]	35,919
35	May 2	H	West Ham U	W 2-1	0-1	2	Overmars [69], Petit [90]	38,093
36	6	H	Chelsea	W 2-1	1-0	2	Henry 2 [21, 48]	38,119
37	9	H	Sheffield W	D 3-3	1-0	—	Dixon [34], Silvinho [78], Henry [79]	37,271
38	14	A	Newcastle U	L 2-4	1-2	2	Kanu [7], Malz [53]	36,450

Final League Position: 2

GOALSCORERS

League (73): Henry 17 (2 pens), Kanu 12 (1 pen), Suker 8, Overmars 7, Bergkamp 6, Ljungberg 6, Dixon 4, Petit 3, Grimandi 2, Vieira 2, Keown 1, Malz 1, Parlour 1, Silvinho 1, own goals 2.
Worthington Cup (4): Henry 1, Kanu 1, Malz 1, Suker 1.
FA Cup (3): Adams 1, Grimandi 1, Overmars 1.

Manninger A 14+1	Dixon L 28	Winterburn N 19+9	Vieira P 29+1	Keown M 27	Grimandi G 27+1	Parlour R 29+1	Kanu N 24+7	Petit E 24+2	Bergkamp D 23+5	Ljungberg F 22+4	Overmars M 22+9	Silvinho 23+8	Henry T 26+5	Upson M 5+3	Luzhny O 16+5	Boa Morte L —+2	Suker D 8+14	Vivas N 1+4	Adams T 21	Seaman D 24	Malz S 2+3	Hughes S 1+1	Barrett G —+2	Vernazza P 1+1	Black T —+1	Weston R 1	Cole A 1	McGovern B —+1	Gray J —+1	Match No.
1	2	3	4	5	6	7^1	8	9	10^3	11^2	12	13	14																	1
1	2	3	4	5		7^1	8^3	9	10		12		11^2		6		14		13											2
1	2		4	5		7	8	9^1	10^2		12	3	11		6		13													3
1	2		4	5		7	8^1	10	9		12	3	11^2		6		13													4
1			4	5	6	7	8^2	10^3	9		12	3	11^1		13		14		2											5
1	2	3	4	5		7^1	10	8	11^2		12	9	13		6															6
1	2	3	4	5	8	7	12		10^1	11^3		13	14		9^2		6													7
1	2	3	4	5	8	12	9^3	10	7		11^2		14		13		6													8
	2	3	4	5	8	7^2	12		10^1	11^3	14		9		6		1													9
	2		5			7	10	4^1	8^2	11^3	3	13			9		12		6	1				14						10
	3	4	5^3	8		12	7	13	11^2	10^1	14	2			9		6	1												11
	2	3	4	5	12		9^2	8^1	10	7	11				13		6	1												12
	2^1	3			5^2	7	9	4	10^3	8	11		13		14	12	6	1												13
1	3		4	7	12	9		10^1	11^3	8^2		5	2		13		6		14											14
1	2	3		4		8^3	9	7	11^2	10		5^5		2	12		6		13	14										15
1	2	3^1	6	8	9	7	11	4	10	5			12																	16
2	3		5	4^1	8	9	7	11	10			12			6		1													17
12	4		5	8	9^1	7	11	3^1	10^2			2			13		6		1											18
12	4		5	8^2	9	7	11^1	3	10			2			13		6		1											19
2		4	5	7		8	11^1	3	10^2	6	9				1		12		13											20
2	12	4	5	6	7		9	11	3^1	10			1		13		8^2													21
2	3		5	6	7		4	12	11			10			9		1		8^1											22
2		4	5	6	7		8^1	10^3	11^2	12	3	9			13		14		1											23
2		4	5	7	8	9	10^1	11	12	3					6		1													24
2	12	4	5	6^3	7	8	9^1	10^2		13	3	11	14		1															25
15	3	4		5	7^2	8	9	12	11^1		6	10	2		13		1^6													26
1	2	12			8	7	9		13	11^2	3	10^1	5		6															27
2	3	4		6	7	12	9	10^1	13^1	11^3		8^2			5		14													28
2	12	4	5	8	7	9^3		13	10^1	11^2	3		14		6		1													29
2	12	4	5	7	13	9^1	10^2	11	14	3			8^3		6		1													30
3	4	5	6	7		9	10		11^1	12^2	8		2				1								14					31
2^1	4			8	7	9		12	10	11	3		5		6		1													32
	2	12	5	4	7	8	9^1	10^2	11^3	3			6		1				14											33
2^1		4	8	7	9	12	10	11	3	5					6		1													34
2	12	4	5	7	13	9^3	10^2	11^1	3	8			14		6		1													35
2	3^2	4	5	8	7^1	9	12		11		13	10			6		1													36
1	11		5	7^1	8^3		12				2		9				10			4			6^2	3	13	14				37
1	11		5	7^1	8^3		12				2		9		10						4		6^2	3	13	14				38

Worthington Cup

Third Round	Preston NE	(h)	2-1
Fourth Round	Middlesbrough	(a)	2-2

FA Cup

Third Round	Blackpool	(h)	3-1
Fourth Round	Leicester C	(h)	0-0
		(a)	0-0

FA Premiership

ASTON VILLA

FOUNDATION

Cricketing enthusiasts of Villa Cross Wesleyan Chapel, Aston, Birmingham decided to form a football club during the winter of 1874–75. Football clubs were few and far between in the Birmingham area and in their first game against Aston Brook St Mary's Rugby team they played one half rugby and the other soccer. In 1876 they were joined by a Scottish soccer enthusiast George Ramsay who was immediately appointed captain and went on to lead Aston Villa from obscurity to one of the country's top clubs in a period of less than 10 years.

Villa Park, Trinity Rd, Birmingham B6 6HE.
Telephone: (0121) 327 2299. *Fax:* (0121) 322 2107. *Commercial Dept:* (0121) 327 5399.
Commercial Fax: (0121) 328 2099. *ClubCall:* 09068 121 148. *Ticketline:* 09068 121 848.
Ticket Information: (0121) 327 5353. *Club Shop:* (0121) 327 2800.
Ground Capacity: 39,217.
Record Attendance: 76,588 v Derby Co, FA Cup 6th rd, 2 March 1946.
Record Receipts: £1,196,712 Portugal v Czech Republic, Euro '96, 23 June 1996.
Pitch Measurements: 115yd × 72yd.
President: J. A. Alderson.
Chairman: H. D. Ellis.
Directors: S. M. Stride, M. J. Ansell.
PLC Non Executive Directors: D. M. Owen, A. Hales.
Manager: John Gregory.
First Team Coach: Steve Harrison.
Coaches: Kevin MacDonald, Gordon Cowans.
Physio: Jim Walker.
Reserve Team Manager: Kevin MacDonald.
Chief Scout: Ross MacLaren.
Fitness Consultant: Paul Barron.
Youth Team Manager: Tony McAndrew.
Youth Team Coach: Gordon Cowans.
Youth Development Officer: Alan Miller.
Secretary: Steven Stride.
Commercial Manager: Abdul Rashid.
Stadium Manager: Tony Diffley.
Football Academy Director: Bryan Jones.
Assistant Academy Director: Steve Burns.

LATEST SEQUENCES

Longest Sequence of League Wins: 9, 15.10.10 – 10.12.10.
Longest Sequence of League Defeats: 11, 23.3.63 – 4.5.63.
Longest Sequence of League Draws: 6, 12.9.81 – 10.10.81.
Longest Sequence of Unbeaten League Matches: 15, 12.3.49 – 27.8.49.
Longest Sequence Without a League Win: 12, 27.12.86 – 25.3.87.

HONOURS

FA Premier League: Runners-up 1992–93.

Football League: Division 1 – Champions 1893–94, 1895–96, 1896–97, 1898–99, 1899–1900, 1909–10, 1980–81; Runners-up 1888–89, 1902–03, 1907–08, 1910–11, 1912–13, 1913–14, 1930–31, 1932–33, 1989–90; Division 2 – Champions 1937–38, 1959–60; Runners-up 1974–75, 1987–88; Division 3 – Champions 1971–72.

FA Cup: Winners 1887, 1895, 1897, 1905, 1913, 1920, 1957; Runners-up 1892, 1924, 2000.

Double Performed: 1896–97.

Football League Cup: Winners 1961, 1975, 1977, 1994, 1996; Runners-up 1963, 1971.

European Competitions: European Cup: 1981–82 (winners), 1982–83.

UEFA Cup: 1975–76, 1977–78, 1983–84, 1990–91, 1993–94, 1994–95, 1996–97, 1997–98, 1998–99.

World Club Championship: 1982.

European Super Cup: 1982–83 (winners).

Colours

Claret shirts with sky blue sleeves, sky blue shorts, claret stockings with blue trim.

Change Colours

Black shirts with claret and blue trim, black shorts, black stockings with claret and blue trim.

Year Formed: 1874.

Turned Professional: 1885.

Ltd Co.: 1896.

Club Nickname: 'The Villans'.

Previous Grounds: 1874 Wilson Road and Aston Park (also used Aston Lower Grounds for some matches); 1876 Wellington Road, Perry Barr; 1897 Villa Park.

First Football League Game: 8 September 1888, Football League, v Wolverhampton W (a) D 1–1 – Warner; Cox, Coulton; Yates, H. Devey, Dawson; A. Brown, Green (1), Allen, Garvey, Hodgetts.

Record League Victory: 12–2 v Accrington S, Division 1, 12 March 1892 – Warner; Evans, Cox; Harry Devey, Jimmy Cowan, Baird; Athersmith (1), Dickson (2), John Devey (4), L. Campbell (4), Hodgetts (1).

Record Cup Victory: 13–0 v Wednesbury Old Ath, FA Cup 1st rd, 30 October 1886 – Warner; Coulton, Simmonds; Yates, Robertson, Burton (2); R. Davis (1), A. Brown (3), Hunter (3), Loach (2), Hodgetts (2).

Record Defeat: 1–8 v Blackburn R, FA Cup 3rd rd, 16 February 1889.

Most League Points (2 for a win): 70, Division 3, 1971–72.

Most League Points (3 for a win): 78, Division 2, 1987–88.

Most League Goals: 128, Division 1, 1930–31.

Highest League Scorer in Season: 'Pongo' Waring, 49, Division 1, 1930–31.

Most League Goals in Total Aggregate: Harry Hampton, 215, 1904–15.

Most League Goals in One Match: 5, Harry Hampton v Sheffield W, Division 1, 5 October 1912; 5, Harold Halse v Derby Co, Division 1, 19 October 1912; 5, Len Capewell v Burnley, Division 1, 29 August 1925; 5, George Brown v Leicester C, Division 1, 2 January 1932; 5, Gerry Hitchens v Charlton Ath, Division 1, 18 November 1959.

Most Capped Player: Paul McGrath, 51 (83), Republic of Ireland.

Most League Appearances: Charlie Aitken, 561, 1961–76.

Youngest League Player: Jimmy Brown, 15 years 349 days v Bolton W, 17 September 1969.

Record Transfer Fee Received: £12,600,000 from Manchester U for Dwight Yorke, August 1998.

Record Transfer Fee Paid: £7,000,000 to Liverpool for Stan Collymore, May 1997.

Football League Record: 1888 Founder Member of the League; 1936–38 Division 2; 1938–59 Division 1; 1959–60 Division 2; 1960–67 Division 1; 1967–70 Division 2; 1970–72 Division 3; 1972–75 Division 2; 1975–87 Division 1; 1987–88 Division 2; 1988–92 Division 1; 1992– FA Premier League.

MANAGERS

George Ramsay 1884–1926
(Secretary-Manager)
W. J. Smith 1926–34
(Secretary-Manager)
Jimmy McMullan 1934–35
Jimmy Hogan 1936–44
Alex Massie 1945–50
George Martin 1950–53
Eric Houghton 1953–58
Joe Mercer 1958–64
Dick Taylor 1964–67
Tommy Cummings 1967–68
Tommy Docherty 1968–70
Vic Crowe 1970–74
Ron Saunders 1974–82
Tony Barton 1982–84
Graham Turner 1984–86
Billy McNeill 1986–87
Graham Taylor 1987–90
Dr Jozef Venglos 1990–91
Ron Atkinson 1991–94
Brian Little 1994–1998
John Gregory February 1998–

TEN YEAR LEAGUE RECORD

		P	W	D	L	F	A	Pts	Pos
1989-90	Div 1	38	21	7	10	57	38	70	2
1990-91	Div 1	38	9	14	15	46	58	41	17
1991-92	Div 1	42	17	9	16	48	44	60	7
1992-93	PR Lge	42	21	11	10	57	40	74	2
1993-94	PR Lge	42	15	12	15	46	50	57	10
1994-95	PR Lge	42	11	15	16	51	56	48	18
1995-96	PR Lge	38	18	9	11	52	35	63	4
1996-97	PR Lge	38	17	10	11	47	34	61	5
1997-98	PR Lge	38	17	6	15	49	48	57	7
1998-99	PR Lge	38	15	10	13	51	46	55	6

DID YOU KNOW ?

Billy Walker, Tom Waring and George Brown (for England), plus Dai Astley (Wales) all appeared for Aston Villa in the 1931-32 season and all played at centre-forward in international football.

ASTON VILLA 1999–2000 LEAGUE RECORD

Match No.	Date		Venue	Opponents	Result		H/T Score	Lg. Pos.	Goalscorers	Atten- dance
1	Aug	7	A	Newcastle U	W	1-0	0-0	5	Joachim [75]	36,376
2		11	H	Everton	W	3-0	1-0	—	Joachim [9], Dublin [57], Taylor [85]	30,337
3		16	H	West Ham U	D	2-2	1-1	—	Dublin 2 [5, 52]	26,250
4		21	A	Chelsea	L	0-1	0-0	5		35,071
5		24	A	Watford	W	1-0	0-0	—	Delaney [68]	19,161
6		28	H	Middlesbrough	W	1-0	1-0	2	Dublin [5]	28,728
7	Sept	11	A	Arsenal	L	1-3	1-1	6	Joachim [44]	38,093
8		18	H	Bradford C	W	1-0	0-0	4	Dublin [71]	28,083
9		25	A	Leicester C	L	1-3	0-1	6	Dublin [73]	19,917
10	Oct	2	H	Liverpool	D	0-0	0-0	8		39,217
11		18	A	Sunderland	L	1-2	0-0	—	Dublin [46]	39,866
12		23	H	Wimbledon	D	1-1	1-1	9	Dublin [35]	27,160
13		30	A	Manchester U	L	0-3	0-2	11		55,211
14	Nov	6	H	Southampton	L	0-1	0-0	12		26,474
15		22	A	Coventry C	L	1-2	1-1	—	Dublin [41]	20,174
16		27	A	Everton	D	0-0	0-0	13		34,750
17	Dec	4	H	Newcastle U	L	0-1	0-0	15		34,531
18		18	H	Sheffield W	W	2-1	0-1	12	Merson [69], Taylor [82]	23,885
19		26	A	Derby Co	W	2-0	0-0	12	Boateng [68], Taylor [78]	33,222
20		29	H	Tottenham H	D	1-1	0-1	—	Taylor [75]	39,217
21	Jan	3	A	Leeds U	W	2-1	1-0	10	Southgate 2 [19, 62]	40,027
22		15	A	West Ham U	D	1-1	1-0	10	Taylor [24]	24,237
23		22	H	Chelsea	D	0-0	0-0	9		33,704
24	Feb	5	H	Watford	W	4-0	0-0	8	Stone [47], Merson 2 [57, 59], Walker [81]	27,647
25		14	A	Middlesbrough	W	4-0	1-0	—	Carbone [11], Summerbell (og) [65], Joachim 2 [70, 75]	31,591
26		26	A	Bradford C	D	1-1	1-0	8	Merson [38]	18,276
27	Mar	5	H	Arsenal	D	1-1	0-0	8	Walker [62]	36,930
28		11	H	Coventry C	W	1-0	1-0	7	Ehiogu [45]	33,177
29		15	A	Liverpool	D	0-0	0-0	—		43,615
30		18	A	Southampton	L	0-2	0-1	6		15,218
31		25	H	Derby Co	W	2-0	1-0	6	Carbone [40], Boateng [57]	28,613
32	Apr	5	A	Sheffield W	W	1-0	0-0	—	Thompson [90]	18,136
33		9	H	Leeds U	W	1-0	1-0	6	Joachim [39]	33,889
34		15	H	Tottenham H	W	4-2	0-1	6	Dublin 2 (1 pen) [62 (p), 69], Carbone [70], Wright [74]	35,304
35		22	A	Leicester C	D	2-2	1-1	6	Thompson [31], Merson [48]	31,229
36		29	H	Sunderland	D	1-1	0-0	6	Barry [60]	33,949
37	May	6	A	Wimbledon	D	2-2	0-1	6	Hendrie [54], Dublin [74]	19,188
38		14	H	Manchester U	L	0-1	0-0	6		39,217

Final League Position: 6

GOALSCORERS

League (46): Dublin 12 (1 pen), Joachim 6, Merson 5, Taylor 5, Carbone 3, Boateng 2, Southgate 2, Thompson 2, Walker 2, Barry 1, Delaney 1, Ehiogu 1, Hendrie 1, Stone 1, Wright 1, own goal 1.
Worthington Cup (16): Taylor 4, Hendrie 3, Joachim 3, Dublin 2, Boateng 1, Stone 1, Thompson 1, Watson 1.
FA Cup (8): Carbone 5, Dublin 1, Southgate 1, Stone 1.

James D 29	Delaney M 25 + 3	Wright A 31 + 1	Southgate G 31	Ehiogu U 31	Calderwood C 15 + 3	Taylor I 25 + 4	Boateng G 30 + 3	Dublin D 23 + 3	Joachim J 27 + 6	Thompson A 16 + 5	Stone S 10 + 14	Hendrie L 18 + 11	Merson P 24 + 8	Draper M — + 1	Vassell D 1 + 10	Enckelman P 9 + 1	Watson S 13 + 1	Barry G 30	Carbone B 22 + 2	Ghrayib N 1 + 4	Samuel J 5 + 4	Walker R 2 + 3	Cutler N — + 1	Bowers J — + 1	Match No.
1	2	3	4	5	6¹	7	8²	9	10	11	12	13													1
1	2	3	4	5	6	7	8¹	9³	10	11²	13	12	14												2
1	2	3	4	5	6	7	8¹	9	10	11²	13	12													3
1	2	3	4	5	6²	7		9	10	11¹	13³	8	12	14											4
1	2	3	4	5	6	7	12	9	11	8			10¹												5
1	2	3	4	5¹	6	7	12	9	11²	8			10				13								6
1⁶	2	3	4	5	6	7		9²	11	12		8	10		15		13								7
			4	5	6¹	7		9	10³	11²	12	13	8		14	1	2	3							8
	12		4	5	13	7	6	9	10	11²			8			1	2¹	3							9
	2		4		6²	7		9	10	11	12		8¹			1		3							10
1	2		4	5	6¹	7		9	11	12	8		13					3	10²						11
1	2		4	5	6¹	7		9	11²	8	12							3	10	13					12
1	2	12	4	5	6²	7		9	11¹	13	8	14						3	10³						13
1	2	3	4	5	12	9		11¹	7	10²								6	8	13					14
1	2¹	3	4	5	7	8		9	10	11²	6		13	12											15
1		3	4	5	7	8		9	10¹	11			2					6	12						16
1	2	3	4	5	7	8		9³	10	12²	11¹	13						6	14						17
1		3¹	4	5	13	7	8	9²	12	11	14	2						6	10³						18
1		3	4	5	7	8		9	12	11¹	13	2						6	10²						19
1		3²	4	5	7	8		9	13	11	12	2						6	10¹						20
1		3	4	5		8	9	7		11	12	2						6	10¹						21
1		3	4	5	12	7	8¹	9	2	11	13							6	10²						22
1	12	3	4	5	7	8	9²	14	11	13³	2¹							6	10						23
1	2	3		5	4	8²	9³	7	12	11¹								6	10	13	14				24
1⁶	2	3	4	5	12	8¹	9	7	13	11²								6	10			15			25
	2	3	4	5	12	8	9	7¹	13	11²						1		6	10						26
	2	3	4	5	8	9	7	12	11							1		6	10¹						27
	2	3	4	5	7	8	9²	12	11¹							1		6	10	13					28
	2	3	4¹	5	12	8	9³	7	13	11²								6	10	14					29
		3¹		5	4	8	13	12	7	11³	9					1	2	6	10	14					30
1	2	3		5	7²	8	12	9³	14	13	11							6	10¹		4				31
1	2²	3³		5		9	12	11	13	8	7						7	6	14	4	4	10¹			32
1		3³		5	8	12	9	13	7²	11						2		6	10¹	14	4				33
1	12²	3		5	8	9		11	7							2¹		6	10	4		13			34
1		3		5	8	9¹	12	11²	13	7						2		6	10	4					35
1	2		4	5	8	12	9¹	11²	13	7								6	10	3³	14				36
1	2	3¹	4	5	9¹	12	11	8	7									6	10	13					37
	2	3	4	5	12	8³	9	13	14	7¹	11					1		6	10²						38

Worthington Cup

Second Round	Chester C	(a)	1-0
		(h)	5-0
Third Round	Manchester U	(h)	3-0
Fourth Round	Southampton	(h)	4-0
Fifth Round	West Ham U	(a)	3-1
Semi-Final	Leicester C	(h)	0-0
		(a)	0-1

FA Cup

Third Round	Darlington	(h)	2-1
Fourth Round	Southampton	(h)	1-0
Fifth Round	Leeds U	(h)	3-2
Sixth Round	Everton	(a)	2-1
Semi-Final	Bolton W		0-0
(at Wembley)			
Final	Chelsea		0-1
(at Wembley)			

Division 3 **BARNET**

FOUNDATION

Barnet Football Club was formed in 1888 as an amateur organisation and they played at a ground in Queen's Road until they disbanded in 1901. A club known as Alston Works FC was then formed and they played at Totteridge Lane until changing to Barnet Alston FC in 1906. They moved to their present ground a year later, combining with The Avenue to form Barnet and Alston in 1912. The club progressed to senior amateur football by way of the Athenian and Isthmian Leagues, turning professional in 1965. It was as a Southern League and Conference club that they made their name.

Underhill Stadium, Barnet Lane, Barnet, Herts EN5 2BE.

Telephone: (020) 8441 6932.

Fax: (020) 8447 0655.

Ticket Office: (020) 8449 6325.

ClubCall: 09068 121 544.

Ground Capacity: 5560.

Record Attendance: 11,026 v Wycombe Wanderers. FA Amateur Cup 4th Round 1951–52.

Record Receipts: £31,202 v Portsmouth, FA Cup 3rd Round, 5 January 1991.

Pitch Measurements: 113yd × 72yd.

Chairman: A. Kleanthous.

Vice-Chairman: D. J. Buchler FCA.

Manager: John Still.

LATEST SEQUENCES

Longest Sequence of League Wins: 6, 28.8.93 – 25.9.99.

Longest Sequence of League Defeats: 11, 8.5.93 – 2.10.93.

Longest Sequence of League Draws: 4, 22.1.94 – 12.2.94.

Longest Sequence of Unbeaten League Matches: 12, 8.5.99 – 9.10.99.

Longest Sequence Without a League Win: 14, 11.12.93 – 8.3.94.

HONOURS

Football League: Division 2 best season: 24th, 1993–94.

FA Amateur Cup: Winners 1946.

FA Trophy: Finalists 1972.

GM Vauxhall Conference: Winners 1990–91.

FA Cup: never past 3rd rd.

League Cup: never past 2nd rd.

Colours

Amber shirts with black trim, amber shorts, amber stockings.

Change Colours

Green and blue.

Year Formed: 1888.

Turned Professional: 1965.

Previous Names: 1906, Barnet Alston FC; 1919 Barnet.

Club Nickname: The Bees.

Previous Grounds: 1888, Queens Road; 1901, Totteridge Lane, 1907 Barnet Lane.

First Football League Game: 17 August 1991, Division 4, v Crewe Alex (h) L 4–7 – Phillips; Blackford, Cooper (Murphy), Horton, Bodley (Stein), Johnson, Showler, Carter (2), Bull (2), Lowe, Evans.

Record League Victory: 6–0 v Lincoln C (a), Division 4, 4 September 1991 – Pape; Poole, Naylor, Bodley, Howell, Evans (1), Willis (1), Murphy (1), Bull (2), Lowe, Showler, (1 og).

Record Cup Victory: 6–1 v Newport Co, FA Cup 1st rd, 21 November 1970 – McClelland; Lye, Jenkins, Ward, Embery, King, Powell (1), Ferry, Adams (1), Gray, George (3), (1 og).

Record Defeat: 1–9 v Peterborough U, Division 3, 5 September 1998.

MANAGERS
Lester Finch
George Wheeler
Dexter Adams
Tommy Coleman
Gerry Ward
Gordon Ferry
Brian Kelly
Bill Meadows
Barry Fry
Roger Thompson
Don McAllister
Barry Fry
Edwin Stein
Gary Phillips *(Player-Manager)* 1993–94
Ray Clemence 1994–96
Alan Mullery *(Director of Football)* 1996–97
Terry Bullivant 1997
John Still June 1997–

Most League Points (3 for a win): 79, Division 3, 1992–93.

Most League Goals: 81, Division 4, 1991–92.

Highest League Scorer in Season: Dougie Freedman, 24, Division 3, 1994–95.

Most League Goals in Total Aggregate: Sean Devine, 47, 1995–99.

Most League Goals in One Match: 4, Dougie Freedman v Rochdale, Division 3, 13 September 1994; 4, Lee Hodges v Rochdale, Division 3, 8 April 1996.

Most Capped Player: Ken Charlery, St. Lucia.

Most League Appearances: Paul Wilson, 263, 1991–2000.

Youngest League Player: Kieran Adams, 17 years 71 days v Mansfield T, 31 December 1994.

Record Transfer Fee Received: £800,000 from Crystal Palace for Dougie Freedman, September 1995.

Record Transfer Fee Paid: £130,000 to Peterborough U for Greg Heald, August 1997.

Football League Record: Promoted to Division 4 from GMVC 1991; 1991–92 Division 4; 1992–93 Division 3; 1993–94 Division 2; 1994– Division 3.

TEN YEAR LEAGUE RECORD

		P	W	D	L	F	A	Pts	Pos
1989-90	Conf	42	26	7	9	81	41	85	2
1990-91	Conf	42	26	9	7	103	52	87	1
1991-92	Div 4	42	21	6	15	81	61	69	7
1992-93	Div 3	42	23	10	9	66	48	79	3
1993-94	Div 2	46	5	13	28	41	86	28	24
1994-95	Div 3	42	15	11	16	56	63	56	11
1995-96	Div 3	46	18	16	12	65	45	70	9
1996-97	Div 3	46	14	16	16	46	51	58	15
1997-98	Div 3	46	19	13	14	61	51	70	7
1998-99	Div 3	46	14	13	19	54	71	55	16

DID YOU KNOW ?

The first Barnet player to be capped was centre-forward George Sparrow for England in the Amateur International against Wales at Plymouth on 21 March 1925. Sparrow played all his senior football with the club.

BARNET 1999–2000 LEAGUE RECORD

Match No.	Date		Venue	Opponents	Result	H/T Score	Lg. Pos.	Goalscorers	Attendance
1	Aug	7	A	Chester C	W 2-0	2-0	2	Charlery [19], Arber [44]	2234
2		14	H	Exeter C	D 2-2	1-0	5	McGleish [40], Heald [88]	1973
3		21	A	Lincoln C	D 0-0	0-0	10		3113
4		28	H	York C	W 6-3	2-3	7	Toms [11], McGleish [16], Heald [49], Currie [64], Sawyers [66], Charlery [68]	1896
5		30	A	Cheltenham T	W 2-1	1-0	5	McGleish [12], Heald [77]	3518
6	Sept	5	H	Macclesfield T	W 2-1	1-0	1	McGleish 2 [39, 59]	2426
7		11	A	Swansea C	W 2-1	0-0	1	Currie [79], Charlery [90]	5167
8		18	H	Northampton T	W 2-1	2-1	1	Charlery 2 [22, 36]	3638
9		25	A	Torquay U	W 1-0	0-0	1	Heald [61]	2520
10	Oct	2	H	Hull C	D 0-0	0-0	1		3449
11		9	H	Rochdale	W 1-0	1-0	1	Charlery [22]	2765
12		16	A	Rotherham U	L 0-2	0-1	1		3596
13		19	A	Leyton Orient	D 0-0	0-0	—		3532
14		23	H	Torquay U	L 1-2	1-1	1	Charlery [21]	2334
15	Nov	2	A	Hartlepool U	L 0-3	0-1	—		2290
16		6	H	Darlington	W 1-0	0-0	2	McGleish [54]	2161
17		14	A	Plymouth Arg	L 1-4	0-2	2	Charlery [73]	6343
18		23	H	Carlisle U	W 3-0	1-0	—	Currie (pen) [32], King 2 [52, 58]	1769
19		27	A	Peterborough U	W 2-1	0-1	1	King 2 [60, 62]	8631
20	Dec	4	H	Chester C	W 2-0	1-0	1	Currie [8], McGleish [88]	2252
21		10	A	Southend U	W 3-1	1-1	—	Brown 2 [34, 88], King [90]	3521
22		18	H	Mansfield T	D 0-0	0-0	1		1997
23		26	A	Brighton & HA	D 1-1	0-0	1	Doolan [79]	5739
24		28	H	Halifax T	L 0-1	0-1	1		2450
25	Jan	3	A	Shrewsbury T	D 1-1	1-1	3	Arber [8]	3091
26		8	H	Southend U	W 2-1	2-1	2	Arber [12], Brown [36]	3057
27		15	A	Exeter C	D 0-0	0-0	3		2457
28		22	H	Lincoln C	W 5-3	3-1	2	Sawyers [23], Charlery [44], Smith (og) [45], Hackett [67], Doolan [83]	2504
29		29	A	York C	L 0-1	0-1	2		2497
30	Feb	5	H	Cheltenham T	W 3-2	2-1	2	Charlery 2 [14, 27], McGleish [90]	2727
31		12	A	Macclesfield T	L 0-2	0-1	3		2114
32		19	H	Peterborough U	L 0-2	0-2	4		3753
33		26	A	Northampton T	L 0-1	0-0	4		5862
34	Mar	4	H	Swansea C	L 0-1	0-1	5		2911
35		7	A	Darlington	L 0-4	0-2	—		5937
36		11	H	Hartlepool U	D 1-1	0-0	6	Charlery [90]	2925
37		18	A	Carlisle U	L 1-3	0-2	7	Currie [74]	2606
38		21	H	Plymouth Arg	W 1-0	0-0	—	McGleish [65]	2328
39		25	H	Brighton & HA	L 0-1	0-0	6		3721
40	Apr	1	A	Mansfield T	W 1-0	0-0	6	King [51]	1960
41		8	H	Shrewsbury T	D 1-1	0-0	7	McGleish [85]	2792
42		15	A	Halifax T	W 2-1	1-1	6	King 2 [15, 81]	1734
43		22	H	Rotherham U	W 1-0	0-0	6	Arber [59]	3239
44		24	A	Hull C	W 3-1	1-0	6	Heald [25], Charlery [66], Stockley [73]	4883
45		29	H	Leyton Orient	D 2-2	1-1	6	Arber [34], Wilson (pen) [87]	4030
46	May	6	A	Rochdale	D 1-1	0-0	6	Arber [67]	2347

Final League Position: 6

GOALSCORERS
League (59): Charlery 13, McGleish 10, King 8, Arber 6, Currie 5 (1 pen), Heald 5, Brown 3, Doolan 2, Sawyers 2, Hackett 1, Stockley 1, Toms 1, Wilson 1 (pen), own goal 1.
Worthington Cup (3): McGleish 2 (1 pen), Hackett 1.
FA Cup (0).

Harrison L 43	Stockley S 31 + 3	Hackett W 34	Currie D 44	Heald G 40	Arber M 43 + 2	Searle S 8 + 11	Doolan J 44	Charlery K 42 + 1	McGleish S 30 + 12	Toms F 27 + 12	Sawyers R 31 + 1	Wilson P 8 + 11	Naisbitt D 3 + 1	Gledhill L 8 + 2	King M 19 + 12	Brown D 20 + 4	Basham M 15	Barnes S 1 + 2	Strevens B — + 6	Davidson R 8 + 1	Darcy R 1 + 2	Ansell G — + 3	Goodhind W 5 + 4	Omoyinmi E 1 + 5	Bell L — + 1	Match No.
1	2	3	4^1	5	6	7^2	8	9	10	11	12	13														1
1	2	3	7	5	6		8	9	10	11				4												2
1	2	4	7	5	6		8	9	10	11		3														3
	2^2	4	7^1	5	6		8	9^3	10	11	12	3	1	13	14											4
	2	4	7	5	6		8	9	10	11		3	1													5
1	2^2	4	7	5	6		8	9^1	10	11		3		13	12											6
1		4	7	5	6		8	9	10	11		3^1		2	12											7
1		3	4	5	6		8	9	10^2	11	12			2	13	7^1										8
1		4	7	5	6	12	8	9	10^2	11		3^1		2	13											9
1^6	2^1	4	7	5	6	12	8	9	10^2	11		3			15	13										10
1		4	7	5	6		8	9	10	11		3		2												11
1		4^2	7	5	6	12	8	9^3	10	11		3		13	2^1	14										12
1		3	4		6	7	8	9	10^2	11^1				2	12	5	13									13
1		3	4		6		8	9	10	11^2				2	12	13	5			7^1						14
1		3	4		6		8	9	10^3	11^1				2^4	12	7	5			13		14				15
1	12	4	7	5	6		8	9	10	11				2^1	13	11							3^2			16
1	2^1		7	5	6	12	8	9^2	10^2						13	11	4						3			17
1		4	7	5	6	12	8	9^2						2^1		10	11			13			3			18
1		4	7	5	6		8	9						2		10	11						3			19
1		4	7	5	6	12	8	9^1				13		2^2		10	11						3			20
1	12	4	7	5	6		8	9^2				13		2	14	10	11^3						3^1			21
1		4	7	5	6	12	8	9^1				13		2^2		10	11						3			22
1	2	4	7	5	6	12	8^1	9		11		3				10										23
1	12	4^2	7	5	6	14	8	9		11^1		13		2		10							3^1			24
1	2	4	7	5	6	12	8	9^2	13	11^1		3				10										25
1	2	4	7^1	5	6	12	8	9^2	13	14		3				10	11^3									26
1	2	4	7	5	6	12	8	9				3				10^1	11									27
1	2	4	7		6		8	9	10			3				11	5									28
1	2^1	4^3	7		6		8	9	10			3^2				11	5		12	13		14				29
1	2	4	7		6	12	8	9	10			3^1				11^2	5			13						30
1	2	4	7	5	6			9	10		12	3^1			13		11						8^2			31
1	2	4		5	6	7^3	8	9^2	10		12	3			13		11^1							14		32
1	2	4	7^2	5	6	11	8	9^3	10		12	3^1			13									14		33
1	2^3	4	7	5	6	12	8	9	10	11^1		3^2			13	14										34
1	2	4^2		5	6	14	8	9	10^1	11^3	12	3			13					7						35
1	2^1	4		5	6	12	8	9	10^2	11		3			13					7^3				14		36
1	2^1	4	7	5	6	12	8	9	10	11		3^2			13											37
	2	4	7	5	6	12	8	9	10	11		3^1	1													38
1	2	4	7^2	5	6	12	8	9^1	10	11		3			13^3									14		39
1	2	4^1	7^2	5	6	12	8	9	10^3	11		3			13							14				40
1	2	4	7^2	5	6	12	8	9^1	10	11		3^2			13									14		41
1	2	4	7	5	6	12	8	9^2	10^1	11^3		3			13									14		42
1	2	4^1	7	5	6	12	8	9^2	10	11^3		3			13									14		43
1	2	4	7	5	6	12	8	9^3	10^1	11		3^2			13									14		44
1	2	4^2	7	5	6	12	8	9	10^1	11		3			13											45
1	2	4^2	7	5	6	12	8	9^1	10	11^3		3			13									14		46

Worthington Cup
First Round   Bournemouth   (a) 0-2
                                (h) 3-2

FA Cup
First Round   Burnley   (h) 0-1

Division 1 **BARNSLEY**

FOUNDATION

Many clubs owe their inception to the church and Barnsley are among them, for they were formed in 1887 by the Rev. T. T. Preedy, curate of Barnsley St Peter's and went under that name until it was dropped in 1897 a year before being admitted to the Second Division of the Football League.

Oakwell Stadium, Barnsley, South Yorkshire S71 1ET

Telephone: (01226) 211 211.

Fax: (01226) 211 444.

Website: barnsleyfc.co.uk

Email: thereds@barnsleyfc.co.uk

ClubCall: 09068 121 152.

Ground Capacity: 23,186.

Record Attendance: 40,255 v Stoke C, FA Cup 5th rd, 15 February 1936.

Record Receipts: undisclosed.

Pitch Measurements: 110yd × 75yd.

Chairman: J. A. Dennis.

Directors: C. B. Taylor (Vice-Chairman), M. Hanson, C. H. Harrison, M. R. Hayselden, J. N. Kelly, I. D. Potter.

Manager: Dave Bassett.

Assistant Manager: Peter Shirtliff.

Chief Coach: Eric Winstanley.

Physios: Michael Tarmey, Derek French.

General Manager/Secretary: Michael Spinks.

Lotteries Manager: Gerry Whewall.

Sales and Marketing Manager: Graham Barlow.

LATEST SEQUENCES

Longest Sequence of League Wins: 10, 5.3.55 – 23.4.55.

Longest Sequence of League Defeats: 9, 14.3.53 – 25.4.53.

Longest Sequence of League Draws: 7, 28.3.11 – 22.4.11.

Longest Sequence of Unbeaten League Matches: 21, 1.1.34 – 5.5.34.

Longest Sequence Without a League Win: 26, 13.12.52 – 26.8.53.

HONOURS

Football League: Division 1 – Runners-up 1996–97; Division 3 (N) – Champions 1933–34, 1938–39, 1954–55; Runners-up 1953–54; Division 3 – Runners-up 1980–81; Division 4 – Runners-up 1967–68; Promoted 1978–79.

FA Cup: Winners 1912; Runners-up 1910.

Football League Cup: best season: 5th rd, 1982.

Colours
Red shirts, white shorts, red stockings.

Change Colours
Royal blue and black striped shirts, black shorts, black stockings.

Year Formed: 1887.
Turned Professional: 1888.
Ltd Co.: 1899.
Previous Name: 1887, Barnsley St Peter's; 1897, Barnsley.
Club Nickname: 'The Tykes', 'Reds' or 'Colliers'.
First Football League Game: 1 September 1898, Division 2, v Lincoln C (a) L 0–1 – Fawcett; McArtney, Nixon; King, Burleigh, Porteous; Davis, Lees, Murray, McCullough, McGee.
Record League Victory: 9–0 v Loughborough T, Division 2, 28 January 1899 – Greaves; McArtney, Nixon; Porteous, Burleigh, Howard; Davis (4), Hepworth (1), Lees (1), McCullough (1), Jones (2). 9–0 v Accrington S, Division 3 (N), 3 February 1934 – Ellis; Cookson, Shotton; Harper, Henderson, Whitworth; Spence (2), Smith (1), Blight (4), Andrews (1), Ashton (1).
Record Cup Victory: 6–0 v Blackpool, FA Cup 1st rd replay, 20 January 1910 – Mearns; Downs, Ness; Glendinning, Boyle (1), Utley; Bartrop, Gadsby (1), Lillycrop (2), Tufnell (2), Forman. 6–0 v Peterborough U, League Cup 1st rd 2nd leg, 15 September 1981 – Horn; Joyce, Chambers, Glavin (2), Banks, McCarthy, Evans, Parker (2), Aylott (1), McHale, Barrowclough (1).
Record Defeat: 0–9 v Notts Co, Division 2, 19 November 1927.
Most League Points (2 for a win): 67, Division 3 (N), 1938–39.
Most League Points (3 for a win): 82, Division 1, 1999–2000.
Most League Goals: 118, Division 3 (N), 1933–34.
Highest League Scorer in Season: Cecil McCormack, 33, Division 2, 1950–51.
Most League Goals in Total Aggregate: Ernest Hine, 123, 1921–26 and 1934–38.
Most League Goals in One Match: 5, Frank Eaton v South Shields, Division 3N, 9 April 1927; 5, Peter Cunningham v Darlington, Division 3N, 4 February 1933; 5, Beau Asquith v Darlington, Division 3N, 12 November 1938; 5, Cecil McCormack v Luton T, Division 2, 9 September 1950.
Most Capped Player: Gerry Taggart, 35 (46), Northern Ireland.
Most League Appearances: Barry Murphy, 514, 1962–78.
Youngest League Player: Glyn Riley, 16 years 171 days v Torquay U, 11 January 1975.
Record Transfer Fee Received: £4,250,000 from Blackburn R for Ashley Ward, December 1998.
Record Transfer Fee Paid: £1,500,000 to Partizan Belgrade for Georgi Hristov, June 1997.
Football League Record: 1898 Elected to Division 2; 1932–34 Division 3 (N); 1934–38 Division 2; 1938–39 Division 3 (N); 1946–53 Division 2; 1953–55 Division 3 (N); 1955–59 Division 2; 1959–65 Division 3; 1965–68 Division 4; 1968–72 Division 3; 1972–79 Division 4; 1979–81 Division 3; 1981–92 Division 2; 1992–97 Division 1; 1997–98 FA Premier League; 1998– Division 1.

MANAGERS

Arthur Fairclough 1898–1901
(Secretary-Manager)
John McCartney 1901–04
(Secretary-Manager)
Arthur Fairclough 1904–12
John Hastie 1912–14
Percy Lewis 1914–19
Peter Sant 1919–26
John Commins 1926–29
Arthur Fairclough 1929–30
Brough Fletcher 1930–37
Angus Seed 1937–53
Tim Ward 1953–60
Johnny Steele 1960–71
(continued as General Manager)
John McSeveney 1971–72
Johnny Steele *(General Manager)* 1972–73
Jim Iley 1973–78
Allan Clarke 1978–80
Norman Hunter 1980–84
Bobby Collins 1984–85
Allan Clarke 1985–89
Mel Machin 1989–93
Viv Anderson 1993–94
Danny Wilson 1994–98
John Hendrie 1998–99
Dave Bassett June 1999–

TEN YEAR LEAGUE RECORD

		P	W	D	L	F	A	Pts	Pos
1989-90	Div 2	46	13	15	18	49	71	54	19
1990-91	Div 2	46	19	12	15	63	48	69	8
1991-92	Div 2	46	16	11	19	46	57	59	16
1992-93	Div 1	46	17	9	20	56	60	60	13
1993-94	Div 1	46	16	7	23	55	67	55	18
1994-95	Div 1	46	20	12	14	63	52	72	6
1995-96	Div 1	46	14	18	14	60	66	60	10
1996-97	Div 1	46	22	14	10	76	55	80	2
1997-98	PR Lge	38	10	5	23	37	82	35	19
1998-99	Div 1	46	14	17	15	59	56	59	13

DID YOU KNOW?

Although in Barnsley's 1954-55 Division Three North championship winning season, they did not score more than four goals in any game, six hat-tricks were recorded:- Lol Chappell (3), Frank Bartlett (2) and Bobby Brown (1).

BARNSLEY 1999–2000 LEAGUE RECORD

Match No.	Date	Venue	Opponents		Result	H/T Score	Lg. Pos.	Goalscorers	Attendance
1	Aug 7	A	Charlton Ath	L	1-3	1-2	21	Barnard [31]	19,268
2	14	H	Crystal Palace	L	2-3	1-1	24	Barnard (pen) [44], Sheron [63]	14,461
3	21	A	Blackburn R	W	2-1	0-0	17	Hristov [65], Shipperley [85]	19,537
4	28	H	Portsmouth	W	6-0	1-0	7	Van der Laan 2 [45,61], Barnard [54], Appleby 2 [59,75], Hignett [79]	13,792
5	30	A	Ipswich T	L	1-6	0-3	10	McClare [86]	18,037
6	Sept 3	H	Tranmere R	W	3-0	1-0	—	Sheron [35], Dyer [77], McClare [86]	12,865
7	10	H	Stockport Co	W	2-1	2-0	—	Sheron 2 [16,44]	13,173
8	18	A	Bolton W	D	2-2	1-1	6	Hignett [16], Barnard [54]	14,621
9	25	H	Huddersfield T	W	4-2	1-1	5	Barnard 2 (2 pens) [36,86], Sheron [65], Hignett [76]	17,765
10	Oct 1	A	Nottingham F	L	0-3	0-0	—		15,255
11	16	H	Wolverhampton W	L	1-2	0-2	8	Hignett [81]	14,923
12	19	H	Swindon T	W	1-0	0-0	—	Thomas [66]	12,026
13	23	A	Crewe Alex	W	1-0	1-0	6	Hignett [45]	5421
14	26	A	Huddersfield T	L	1-2	1-1	—	Sheron [19]	15,764
15	30	H	Nottingham F	W	1-0	0-0	7	Hignett (pen) [56]	14,727
16	Nov 6	H	Sheffield U	W	2-0	1-0	4	Shipperley 2 [18,79]	16,301
17	13	A	Fulham	W	3-1	1-1	—	Symons (og) [35], Dyer [61], Van der Laan [67]	10,634
18	20	H	Birmingham C	W	2-1	0-0	4	Tinkler [51], Hignett (pen) [57]	14,520
19	24	A	Manchester C	L	1-3	0-2	—	Thomas [64]	32,692
20	27	A	QPR	D	2-2	1-2	5	Thomas [11], Eaden [57]	11,054
21	Dec 4	H	Charlton Ath	D	1-1	1-1	5	Chettle [2]	14,553
22	18	H	Walsall	W	3-2	1-0	5	Hignett 3 [29,65,90]	13,300
23	26	A	Grimsby T	W	3-0	2-0	5	Hignett 2 [14,20], Appleby [58]	8742
24	28	H	Port Vale	W	3-1	0-0	5	Tinkler [63], Barnard [67], Shipperley [87]	16,855
25	Jan 3	A	WBA	W	2-0	1-0	4	Barnard 2 [4,66]	13,411
26	8	A	Norwich C	D	2-2	0-1	4	Dyer [58], Hignett [88]	14,039
27	15	A	Crystal Palace	W	2-0	2-0	4	Dyer [12], Barnard (pen) [15]	14,225
28	22	H	Blackburn R	W	5-1	4-1	3	Dyer 2 [5,72], Hignett [15], Shipperley [22], Barnard [32]	18,088
29	29	A	Portsmouth	L	0-3	0-2	3		12,201
30	Feb 5	H	Ipswich T	L	0-2	0-0	4		17,601
31	11	A	Tranmere R	D	2-2	1-1	—	Shipperley [44], Thomas [65]	7127
32	19	H	QPR	D	1-1	0-1	4	Hignett (pen) [90]	14,212
33	26	H	Bolton W	D	1-1	0-1	4	Tinkler [46]	14,604
34	Mar 3	A	Stockport Co	W	3-1	2-1	—	Hristov 2 [8,30], Shipperley [79]	6386
35	7	A	Sheffield U	D	3-3	2-1	—	Hristov [19], Barnard (pen) [38], Shipperley [68]	22,376
36	11	H	Manchester C	W	2-1	2-0	3	Curtis [4], Hignett [45]	22,650
37	18	A	Birmingham C	L	1-3	1-2	4	Hignett [13]	25,108
38	21	H	Fulham	W	1-0	1-0	—	Shipperley [41]	14,262
39	27	A	Grimsby T	W	3-0	1-0	4	Tinkler [25], Shipperley [63], Hignett [77]	14,613
40	Apr 1	A	Walsall	W	4-1	0-0	2	Sheron 2 [54,76], Shipperley [59], Appleby [80]	7218
41	8	H	WBA	D	2-2	0-0	4	Barnard [53], Shipperley [90]	16,329
42	15	A	Port Vale	D	2-2	1-1	4	Hignett [43], Curtis [66]	5918
43	22	A	Wolverhampton W	L	0-2	0-1	4		21,251
44	24	H	Norwich C	W	2-1	2-0	3	Chettle [41], Shipperley [45]	15,253
45	29	A	Swindon T	W	2-1	0-0	4	Appleby [53], Sheron [67]	6151
46	May 7	H	Crewe Alex	L	0-2	0-0	4		17,611

Final League Position: 4

GOALSCORERS

League (88): Hignett 19 (3 pens), Barnard 13 (5 pens), Shipperley 13, Sheron 9, Dyer 6, Appleby 5, Hristov 4, Thomas 4, Tinkler 4, Van der Laan 3, Chettle 2, Curtis 2, McClare 2, Eaden 1, own goal 1.
Worthington Cup (13): Barnard 2 (1 pen), Eaden 2, Hristov 2, Sheron 2, Van der Laan 2, Jones 1, Morgan 1, Shipperley 1.
FA Cup (0).

Bullock T 5+1	Austin K 3	Appleby M 33+3	Richardson K 4	Moses A 12	Jones S 20	Van der Laan R 23+9	Hignett C 38+4	Shipperley N 32+7	Dyer B 13+19	Barnard D 32+9	Tinkler E 28+5	Hristov G 5+13	Eaden N 38+4	Sheron M 28+8	Bullock M 1+3	Tuttle D 11+1	Miller K 41	McClare S 1+9	Barker C 28+1	Brown K 7+3	Morgan C 36+1	Thomas G 13+14	Curtis J 28	Chettle S 25	Jackson M 1	Match No.
1	2	3	4	5	6	7^1	8	9	10^2	11^3	12	13	14													1
1	2	3	4^1	5	6	7	8	9^2		11	13	12	10^3	14												2
1	2	3		5	6	8^1	13	9		11^2	12	10^3	7	14		4										3
		3	10^3	5	6	7^2	8		12	11		13	2	9^1	14	4	1									4
		3	7^3	5	6	10^1	8		12	11		13	2	9^2		4	1	14								5
		3^3			5	6	7^1	8	9^2	12		13	2	10		4	1	14	11							6
		3			5	6	11	8^1		13	12	10	7	9^2		4	1		2							7
		3			5	6	10	8^2	12	13	11		7	9^1		4	1		2							8
		3			5	6	10^2	8^1	12		11	7	2	9		4	1		13							9
		3^2			5	6	7	8	12	11		13	2	9^1		4	1		10							10
					6		8	12	10^2	11	4	13	2	9^1			1	7^3	3			5		14		11
		3			5	6	12	9	13	11^1	8^3	7	10^2			2	1				4	14				12
15		3	5^1	6			8^2	9	10^9	12	11	7				2	1				4	13				13
		3			6		8	9		11	7	2^1	10			5	1				4	12				14
		3			6		8	9	12		13	2	10^1	7^2		1			5		4	11				15
1		3			6	7^2	8^3	9	10^1	12	11	14	2				13	5			4					16
		3^1			6	7	8	9	10^2	12	11		2			1		5			4	13				17
						7^1	8	9	10^2	14	6	3		12		1	13	5^3			4	11	2			18
		3^2				8	9^1	12	13	6	7	10				1	14	5			4	11^3	2			19
		3				8	9	12	11		7	10^1				1					4	6	2	5		20
		3^1				8	9		11	7	10					1		6			4	12	2	5		21
						8			11^1	6	12	7	9			1		3			4	10	2	5		22
		10^3				8^2	12	13	11	6	7	9^1				1	14	3			4		2	5		23
		7^2				8	12	13	11	10	6	9^1				1		3^3	14		4		2	5		24
		7				8^1	12	13	11	10	6	9^2				1		3			4		2	5		25
		7^2				8	12	13	11^2	10	6	9^1				1	14	3			4		2	5		26
						8		9^1	10^2	11^3	7	12	5			1	13	3			4	14	2		6	27
		6				7	8	9	10^1	11^2		2	12	4^3		1		3	14			13		5		28
		6				10^1	8^2	9	12	11	7		13			1		3^1			4	14	2	5		29
		12				6^3	8	9	10^1	11	7		13			1		3^2			4	14	2	5		30
		3				12	8^1	9	13	7		10^2				1		6			4	11	2	5		31
						6^2	8	10^1	7	12		9				1	13	3			4	11	2	5		32
						6^1	8	9	12	11	13	7	10^2			1	14	3^3			4		2	5		33
						12		9	11^2	6	8^1	7	13			1		3			4	10	2	5		34
						12	13	9	11^1	10	8^2	7				1		3			4	6	2	5		35
						12	8	9	11^1	10		7				1		3			4	6	2	5		36
		12				6^3	8	9	13	10^1	14	7^2				1		3			4	11	2	5		37
		7^2				12	8	9	11	6^1	10^2	13				1		3			4	14	2	5		38
		7				12	8	9	10^2	11	6^1	13				1		3	14		4		2	5^1		39
		12				13	14	9	11^1	6^2	7^3	8				1		3			4	10	2	5		40
		7^2					8	9	11	6	13	12	10^2			1		3^1			4	14	2	5		41
		7^1				3	12	8	9	13	11	6		10^2		1					4		2	5		42
		3^3				12	8	9	13	11	6	10^2	14			1					4	7	2	5		43
		11^2				6	8	9	10^1	12	13	7				1		3			4		2	5		44
		8				6		9^1	12	11^2	7	10				1		3			4	13	2	5		45
1		8			5	6^1		10^1	11^2	12	7	9	13					3			4	14	2			46

Worthington Cup

First Round	Lincoln C	(a)	4-2	
		(h)	2-2	
Second Round	Stockport Co	(h)	1-1	
		(a)	3-3	
Third Round	Bradford C	(a)	3-2	
Fourth Round	Tranmere R	(a)	0-4	

FA Cup

Third Round	Wimbledon	(a)	0-1

Division 1 — BIRMINGHAM CITY

FOUNDATION

In 1875 cricketing enthusiasts who were largely members of Trinity Church, Bordesley, determined to continue their sporting relationships throughout the year by forming a football club which they called Small Heath Alliance. For their earliest games played on waste land in Arthur Street, the team included three Edden brothers and two James brothers.

St Andrews, Birmingham B9 4NH.

Telephone: 0709 111 25837.

Fax: (0121) 766 7866.

Website: www.bcfc.com

ClubCall: 09068 121 188.

Club Soccer Shop: 0709 111 25837 (ext. 8).

Ground Capacity: 30,009.

Record Attendance: 66,844 v Everton, FA Cup 5th rd, 11 February 1939.

Record Receipts: £262,000 v Watford, Play-off semi-final, 2nd leg, 20 May 1999.

Pitch Measurements: 110yd × 74yd.

Chairman: D. Gold.

Vice-Chairman: J. F. Wiseman.

Directors: D. Sullivan, R. Gold, B. Gold, H. Brandman, A. G. Jones, M. Wiseman.

Managing Director: K. R. Brady.

Manager: Trevor Francis.

Coach: Mick Mills.

Physio: N. McDiarmid.

Commercial Manager: Simon Bradley.

Stadium Manager: Brian Tew.

Secretary: A. G. Jones BA, MBA.

LATEST SEQUENCES

Longest Sequence of League Wins: 13, 17.12.1892 – 16.9.1893.

Longest Sequence of League Defeats: 8, 28.9.85 – 23.11.85.

Longest Sequence of League Draws: 8, 18.9.90 – 23.10.90.

Longest Sequence of Unbeaten League Matches: 20, 3.9.94 – 2.1.95.

Longest Sequence Without a League Win: 17, 28.9.85 – 18.1.86.

HONOURS

Football League: Division 1 best season: 4th, 1998–99; Division 2 – Champions 1892–93, 1920–21, 1947–48, 1954–55, 1994–95; Runners-up 1893–94, 1900–01, 1902–03, 1971–72, 1984–85; Division 3 Runners-up 1991–92.

FA Cup: Runners-up 1931, 1956.

Football League Cup: Winners 1963.

Leyland Daf Cup: Winners 1991.

Auto Windscreens Shield: Winners 1995.

European Competitions: European Fairs Cup: 1955–58, 1958–60 (runners-up), 1960–61 (runners-up), 1961–62.

Colours
Blue shirts, white shorts, blue and white stockings.

Change Colours
Yellow shirts, navy blue shorts and stockings.

Year Formed: 1875.

Turned Professional: 1885.

Ltd Co.: 1888.

Previous Names: 1875, Small Heath Alliance; 1888, dropped 'Alliance'; 1905, Birmingham; 1945, Birmingham City.

Club Nickname: 'Blues'.

Previous Grounds: 1875, waste ground near Arthur St; 1877, Muntz St, Small Heath; 1906, St Andrews.

First Football League game: 3 September 1892, Division 2, v Burslem Port Vale (h) W 5–1 – Charsley; Bayley, Speller; Ollis, Jenkyns, Devey; Hallam (1), Edwards (1), Short (1), Wheldon (2), Hands.

Record League Victory: 12–0 v Walsall T Swifts, Division 2, 17 December 1892 – Charsley; Bayley, Jones; Ollis, Jenkyns, Devey; Hallam (2), Walton (3), Mobley (3), Wheldon (2), Hands (2). 12–0 v Doncaster R, Division 2, 11 April 1903 – Dorrington; Goldie, Wassell; Beer, Dougherty (1), Howard; Athersmith (1), Leonard (3), McRoberts (1), Wilcox (4), Field (1). Aston, (1 og).

Record Cup Victory: 9–2 v Burton W, FA Cup 1st rd, 31 October 1885 – Hedges; Jones, Evetts (1); F. James, Felton, A. James (1); Davenport (2), Stanley (4), Simms, Figures, Morris (1).

Record Defeat: 1–9 v Sheffield W, Division 1, 13 December 1930. 1–9 v Blackburn R, Division 1, 5 January 1895.

Most League Points (2 for a win): 59, Division 2, 1947–48.

Most League Points (3 for a win): 89, Division 2, 1994–95.

Most League Goals: 103, Division 2, 1893–94 (only 28 games).

Highest League Scorer in Season: Joe Bradford, 29, Division 1, 1927–28.

Most League Goals in Total Aggregate: Joe Bradford, 249, 1920–35.

Most League Goals in One Match: 5, Walter Abbott v Darwen, Division 2, 26 November, 1898; 5, John McMillan v Blackpool, Division 2, 2 March 1901; 5, James Windridge v Glossop, Division 2, 23 January 1915.

Most Capped Player: Malcolm Page, 28, Wales.

Most League Appearances: Frank Womack, 491, 1908–28.

Youngest League Player: Trevor Francis, 16 years 7 months v Cardiff C, 5 September 1970.

Record Transfer Fee Received: £2,500,000 from Coventry C for Gary Breen, January 1997.

Record Transfer Fee Paid: £1,850,000 to Port Vale for Jon McCarthy, September 1997.

Football League Record: 1892 elected to Division 2; 1894–96 Division 1; 1896–1901 Division 2; 1901–02 Division 1; 1902–03 Division 2; 1903–08 Division 1; 1908–21 Division 2; 1921–39 Division 1; 1946–48 Division 2; 1948–50 Division 1; 1950–1955 Division 2; 1955–65 Division 1; 1965–72 Division 2; 1972–79 Division 1; 1979–80 Division 2; 1980–84 Division 1; 1984–85 Division 2; 1985–86 Division 1; 1986–89 Division 2; 1989–92 Division 3; 1992–94 Division 1; 1994–95 Division 2; 1995– Division 1.

MANAGERS

Alfred Jones 1892–1908
(Secretary-Manager)
Alec Watson 1908–10
Bob McRoberts 1910–15
Frank Richards 1915–23
Billy Beer 1923–27
Leslie Knighton 1928–33
George Liddell 1933–39
Harry Storer 1945–48
Bob Brocklebank 1949–54
Arthur Turner 1954–58
Pat Beasley 1959–60
Gil Merrick 1960–64
Joe Mallett 1965
Stan Cullis 1965–70
Fred Goodwin 1970–75
Willie Bell 1975–77
Jim Smith 1978–82
Ron Saunders 1982–86
John Bond 1986–87
Garry Pendrey 1987–89
Dave Mackay 1989–1991
Lou Macari 1991
Terry Cooper 1991–93
Barry Fry 1993–96
Trevor Francis May 1996–

TEN YEAR LEAGUE RECORD

		P	W	D	L	F	A	Pts	Pos
1989-90	Div 3	46	18	12	16	60	59	66	7
1990-91	Div 3	46	16	17	13	45	49	65	12
1991-92	Div 3	46	23	12	11	69	52	81	2
1992-93	Div 1	46	13	12	21	50	72	51	19
1993-94	Div 1	46	13	12	21	52	69	51	22
1994-95	Div 2	46	25	14	7	84	37	89	1
1995-96	Div 1	46	15	13	18	61	64	58	15
1996-97	Div 1	46	17	15	14	52	48	66	10
1997-98	Div 1	46	19	17	10	60	35	74	7
1998-99	Div 1	46	23	12	11	66	37	81	4

DID YOU KNOW ?

During October and November 1898, Birmingham scored 35 goals without reply in four League and FA Cup games:- v Chirk 8-0 (FAC); Luton Town 9-0 (Lge); Druids 10-0 (FAC); Darwen 8-0 (Lge).

BIRMINGHAM CITY 1999–2000 LEAGUE RECORD

Match No.	Date	Venue	Opponents	Result	H/T Score	Lg. Pos.	Goalscorers	Attendance
1	Aug 7	H	Fulham	D	2-2	0-1	7	Hughes [62], Lazaridis [85]	24,042
2	14	A	Norwich C	W	1-0	1-0	5	McCarthy [11]	15,261
3	21	H	Port Vale	W	4-2	3-2	3	Hughes 2 [8, 51], Furlong 2 [18, 34]	18,089
4	27	A	Stockport Co	L	0-2	0-0	—		6115
5	30	H	Crewe Alex	W	5-1	3-1	3	Johnson M [12], McCarthy [20], Furlong [30], Holdsworth [52], Ndlovu [77]	24,085
6	Sept 5	A	Bolton W	D	3-3	3-1	2	Holdsworth [26], Furlong 2 [37, 45]	11,668
7	11	H	WBA	D	1-1	1-0	3	Johnson A [43]	25,495
8	18	A	Ipswich T	W	1-0	1-0	2	Furlong (pen) [10]	19,758
9	25	H	QPR	W	2-0	1-0	1	Furlong 2 (2 pens) [44, 64]	18,748
10	Oct 2	A	Charlton Ath	L	0-1	0-1	4		19,753
11	8	A	Walsall	L	0-1	0-0	—		7164
12	16	H	Crystal Palace	W	2-0	1-0	3	Purse [10], McCarthy [48]	21,582
13	19	H	Manchester C	L	0-1	0-0	—		22,126
14	23	A	Grimsby T	D	1-1	1-1	5	Wreh [37]	6266
15	27	A	QPR	D	2-2	0-1	—	Marcelo 2 [74, 76]	11,196
16	30	H	Charlton Ath	W	1-0	1-0	4	Hughes [25]	19,172
17	Nov 6	A	Portsmouth	D	2-2	0-1	6	Lazaridis [59], Johnson M [62]	12,756
18	20	A	Barnsley	L	1-2	0-0	10	McCarthy [70]	14,520
19	23	H	Tranmere R	W	3-1	3-0	—	Grainger (pen) [2], Marcelo [27], Hyde [45]	21,132
20	27	H	Swindon T	D	1-1	1-0	7	Grainger [26]	22,620
21	Dec 4	A	Fulham	D	0-0	0-0	7		12,290
22	17	A	Wolverhampton W	L	1-2	1-1	—	Hughes [15]	19,724
23	26	H	Sheffield U	L	0-2	0-1	11		22,874
24	28	A	Nottingham F	L	0-1	0-0	13		20,821
25	Jan 3	H	Huddersfield T	W	1-0	1-0	12	Hughes [1]	19,558
26	15	H	Norwich C	W	2-0	2-0	11	Grainger 2 [16, 30]	21,007
27	22	A	Port Vale	L	1-3	0-1	11	Hughes [48]	7702
28	29	H	Stockport Co	W	2-1	0-0	8	Holdsworth [62], Hughes [72]	17,150
29	Feb 5	A	Crewe Alex	W	3-2	1-1	7	O'Connor (pen) [45], Hughes [54], Adebola [70]	6289
30	12	H	Bolton W	W	2-1	0-1	6	Rankin [50], Adebola [66]	18,426
31	15	H	Blackburn R	W	1-0	1-0	—	O'Connor [33]	20,719
32	19	A	Swindon T	W	4-1	3-1	5	Purse [11], Rankin [21], Adebola [26], Grainger [74]	7591
33	27	H	Ipswich T	D	1-1	1-1	5	Mowbray (og) [17]	20,493
34	Mar 4	A	WBA	W	3-0	2-0	5	Adebola 2 [6, 8], Marcelo [86]	17,029
35	7	H	Portsmouth	W	1-0	0-0	—	Marcelo [49]	19,573
36	11	A	Tranmere R	L	1-2	1-1	5	Rowett [45]	9232
37	18	H	Barnsley	W	3-1	2-1	5	Rankin 2 [25, 63], Holdsworth [45]	25,108
38	22	A	Blackburn R	L	0-1	0-0	—		18,096
39	25	A	Sheffield U	W	2-1	0-1	6	Kozluk (og) [52], Hughes [54]	15,486
40	Apr 1	H	Wolverhampton W	W	1-0	0-0	5	Holdsworth [54]	29,050
41	8	A	Huddersfield T	D	0-0	0-0	5		16,961
42	15	H	Nottingham F	L	0-1	0-1	6		23,006
43	22	A	Crystal Palace	W	2-0	1-0	5	Austin (og) [45], Furlong [61]	17,144
44	24	H	Walsall	W	2-0	0-0	5	Furlong 2 (1 pen) [70, 90 (p)]	24,268
45	28	A	Manchester C	L	0-1	0-1	—		32,062
46	May 7	H	Grimsby T	D	0-0	0-0	5		25,263

Final League Position: 5

GOALSCORERS

League (65): Furlong 11 (4 pens), Hughes 10, Adebola 5, Grainger 5 (1 pen), Holdsworth 5, Marcelo 5, McCarthy 4, Rankin 4, Johnson M 2, Lazaridis 2, O'Connor 2 (1 pen), Purse 2, Hyde 1, Johnson A 1, Ndlovu 1, Rowett 1, Wreh 1, own goals 3.

Worthington Cup (12): O'Connor 3 (2 pens), Adebola 1, Grainger 1, Holdsworth 1, Hyde 1, Johnson A 1, Purse 1, Rowett 1, own goals 2.

FA Cup (1): Rowett 1.

Poole K 18	Rowett G 45	Grainger M 34	Hughes B 41 + 4	Purse D 33 + 5	Johnson M 29 + 5	McCarthy J 21	O'Connor M 38 + 1	Furlong P 17 + 2	Adebola D 21 + 21	Lazaridis S 26 + 5	Forinton H — + 1	Holland C 2 + 12	Johnson A 15 + 7	Holdsworth D 43 + 1	Hyde G 20 + 11	Ndlovu P 2 + 11	Newton E 2 + 2	Beresford J 1	Bennett J 21	Johnston A 7 + 2	Haarhoff J — + 1	Bass J 5 + 3	Gill J 2 + 9	Wren C 6 + 1	Marcelo 14 + 11	Charlton S 19 + 1	Dyson J — + 2	Robinson S 5 + 1	Rankin I 11 + 2	Carrick M 1 + 1	Myhre T 7	Campbell S — + 2	Match No.
1	2	3¹	4	5²	6	7	8	9	10³	11	12	13	14																				1
1	2	3	4		6	7	8	9¹	12	11²			10	5	13																		2
1	2	3	4		6	7		9²	12	11²	13		10¹	5	8	14																	3
1	2	3	4		6	7¹	8	9	12	11²			10	5	13																		4
1	2	3	4		6	7	8³	9¹	12	11			10²	5	14	13																	5
1	2	3	4³	12	6		8	9	11¹	14			10²	5	7	13																	6
1	2	3¹	12		6	7	8	9²	13	11			10³	5	4	14																	7
1	2		12	5	6	7	8	9¹	13	3			4	10	11²																		8
1	2	4	13		6	7	8	9	14	3¹			10³	5	11	12²																	9
1	2	4²	5	3		7	8	9	12				10¹	6	11³	13	14																10
1	2	7	12		6		8	9²	13				14	10²	5	4¹	11	3															11
	2	4	5	3	7	8		9³					10¹	6	12		11²		1	13	14												12
	2	4	5	3²	7	8		9					10¹	6	12				1	11		13											13
	2	4¹	5		7	8		9					12	6			13		1	11³		14	3²	10									14
	2	12	5		7	8¹		13					14	6			4³		1	11²		3	10	9									15
	2	4	5		7²			12					8	6					1	11		3	13	10¹	9								16
	2	12	5	3	7	8		13	14				4	6					1	11³			10²	9¹									17
1	2	3	4		6	7	8		10	11			5							12		9¹											18
1	2	3	4¹	5		7³	12		13	11			6	8					14			10²	9										19
1	2	7	12²	5	13		8	9¹		14			6	4					11			10³	3										20
1	2	11¹	4²	9	6	8							5	7					10	12	13		3										21
1	5	11	4	9²	6	8			12					10¹					2			7²			3	14	13						22
1		11	4	12	6		8		10¹				13	5					2			9			3³	14	7²						23
1	5	11	4		6		8		10				12	13	7¹										2²	14	9	3³					24
	2	3	10	5²	6		8		13				14	4	7³				1			12			9			11¹					25
	2	11	4	5			8¹		12	13				6	7				1						9	3		10²					26
	2	11	4	5¹	12		8			13				6	7³				1						9	3²		10	14				27
	2	3	4		6		8		12	11¹		13		5	7				1						14			10³	9²				28
	2	11	4		6		8		9³	12				5	7¹				1						13	14	3	10²					29
	2	7³	4	5			8		9	11²			12	6	13				1						14	3		10¹					30
	2	7	4	5			8¹		9	11²				6	12				1						13	14	3	10³					31
	2	7	4¹	5			8		9³	11²			13	6	12				1						14	3		10					32
	2	11	4	5	6				9	12			7		13				1						14	3²		10¹	8³				33
	2	7	4	5					9²	11			12	6	8³				1						13	3		10¹	14				34
	2	7	4	5			8		9	11²			10¹	6	12				1						13	3		10³					35
	2	11	4	5	12		8		9				13	6					1						7	3¹		10²					36
	2	7	4	5			8		9	11				6					1						12	3		10¹					37
	2	7	4	5	12		8		9³	11				6	13				1						14	3¹		10²					38
	2	3	4	5	6		8		9¹	12		11²		7	13				1						10³			14					39
	2	7	4	5	3		8		9¹	12		11³		6					1						13			10²		1		14	40
	2	7	4	5	12		8³		13	9		11		6	14				1						10²	3¹				1			41
	2	8	4	5			7³		11²	11²		10		6	13				1						14	3				1			42
	2	11	4	5	3		7³		9²	12		10¹		6	8				1						13					1		14	43
	2	8³	4	5	3	7			12	9²		11		13	6	14			1						10¹					1			44
	2		4	5	3	7¹	8		9²	10		11		12	6		13		1						14					1			45
	2		4	5	3		8		9¹	12		11³		10	6	7²			1						13			14		1			46

Worthington Cup

First Round	Exeter C	(h)	3-0
		(a)	2-1
Second Round	Bristol R	(h)	2-0
		(a)	1-0
Third Round	Newcastle U	(h)	2-0
Fourth Round	West Ham U	(h)	2-3

FA Cup

Third Round	Watford	(a)	1-0
Fourth Round	Everton	(a)	0-2

Division 1   **BLACKBURN ROVERS**

FOUNDATION

It was in 1875 that some Public School old boys called a meeting at which the Blackburn Rovers club was formed and the colours blue and white adopted. The leading light was John Lewis, later to become a founder of the Lancashire FA, a famous referee who was in charge of two FA Cup Finals, and a vice-president of both the FA and the Football League.

Ewood Park, Blackburn BB2 4JF.
Telephone: (01254) 698 888.
Fax: (01254) 671 042.
Website: www.rovers.co.uk
Email: enquiries@rovers.co.uk
Ticket Hotline: (01254) 671 666.
ClubCall: 09068 121 179.
Mail Order: 08080 20 20 20.
Club Shop: (01254) 665 606.
Ground Capacity: 31,367.
Record Attendance: 62,522 v Bolton W, FA Cup 6th rd, 2 March 1929.
Record Receipts: £438,868 (gross) v Newcastle U, FA Cup 5th rd, 31 January 2000.
Pitch Measurements: 115yd × 72yd.
Chairman: R. D. Coar BSC.
Vice-Chairman: R. L. Matthewman.
Directors: R. D. Coar BSC, R. L. Matthewman, J. O. Williams BSC (Chief Executive), Tom Finn, K. C. Lee, G. R. Root, I. R. Stanners.
Manager: Graeme Souness.
Physio: Dave Fevre.
Assistant Manager: Tony Parkes.
Coach: Phil Boersma.
Commercial Manager: Ken Beamish.
Secretary: Tom Finn.
Stadium Manager: M. Highmore.

LATEST SEQUENCES
Longest Sequence of League Wins: 8, 1.3.80 – 7.4.80.
Longest Sequence of League Defeats: 7, 12.3.66 – 16.4.66.
Longest Sequence of League Draws: 5, 11.10.75 – 1.11.75.
Longest Sequence of Unbeaten League Matches: 23, 30.9.87 – 27.3.88.
Longest Sequence Without a League Win: 16, 11.11.78 – 24.3.79.

HONOURS

FA Premier League: Champions 1994–95; Runners-up 1993–94.

Football League: Division 1 – Champions 1911–12, 1913–14; Division 2 – Champions 1938–39; Runners-up 1957–58; Division 3 – Champions 1974–75; Runners-up 1979–80.

FA Cup: Winners 1884, 1885, 1886, 1890, 1891, 1928; Runners-up 1882, 1960.

Football League Cup: Semi-final 1962, 1993.

Full Members' Cup: Winners 1987.

European Competitions: European Cup: 1995–96. UEFA Cup: 1994–95, 1998–99.

Colours
Blue and white halved shirts, white shorts with navy blue strip, white stockings with navy blue trim.

Change Colours
Red and black striped shirts, red shorts with black panel, red and black stockings.

Year Formed: 1875.

Turned Professional: 1880.

Ltd Co.: 1897.

Club Nickname: Rovers.

Previous Grounds: 1875, all matches played away; 1876, Oozehead Ground; 1877, Pleasington Cricket Ground; 1878, Alexandra Meadows; 1881, Leamington Road; 1890, Ewood Park.

First Football League Game: 15 September 1888, Football League, v Accrington (h) D 5–5 – Arthur; Beverley, James Southworth; Douglas, Almond, Forrest; Beresford (1), Walton, John Southworth (1), Fecitt (1), Townley (2).

Record League Victory: 9–0 v Middlesbrough, Division 2, 6 November 1954 – Elvy; Suart, Eckersley; Clayton, Kelly, Bell; Mooney (3), Crossan (2), Briggs, Quigley (3), Langton (1).

Record Cup Victory: 11–0 v Rossendale, FA Cup 1st rd, 13 October 1884 – Arthur; Hopwood, McIntyre; Forrest, Blenkhorn, Lofthouse; Sowerbutts (2), J. Brown (1), Fecitt (4), Barton (3), Birtwistle (1).

Record Defeat: 0–8 v Arsenal, Division 1, 25 February 1933.

Most League Points (2 for a win): 60, Division 3, 1974–75.

Most League Points (3 for a win): 89, FA Premier League, 1994–95.

Most League Goals: 114, Division 2, 1954–55.

Highest League Scorer in Season: Ted Harper, 43, Division 1, 1925–26.

Most League Goals in Total Aggregate: Simon Garner, 168, 1978–92.

Most League Goals in One Match: 7, Tommy Briggs v Bristol R, Division 2, 5 February 1953.

Most Capped Player: Bob Crompton, 41, England.

Most League Appearances: Derek Fazackerley, 596, 1970–86.

Youngest League Player: Harry Dennison, 16 years 155 days v Bristol C, 8 April 1911.

Record Transfer Fee Received: £15,000,000 from Newcastle U for Alan Shearer, July 1996.

Record Transfer Fee Paid: £7,250,000 to Southampton for Kevin Davies, June 1998.

Football League Record: 1888 Founder Member of the League; 1936–39 Division 2; 1946–48 Division 1; 1948–58 Division 2; 1958–66 Division 1; 1966–71 Division 2; 1971–75 Division 3; 1975–79 Division 2; 1979–80 Division 3; 1980–92 Division 2; 1992–99 FA Premier League; 1999– Division 1.

MANAGERS

Thomas Mitchell 1884–96
(Secretary-Manager)
J. Walmsley 1896–1903
(Secretary-Manager)
R. B. Middleton 1903–25
Jack Carr 1922–26
*(Team Manager under
Middleton to 1925)*
Bob Crompton 1926–30
(Hon. Team Manager)
Arthur Barritt 1931–36
(had been Secretary from 1927)
Reg Taylor 1936–38
Bob Crompton 1938–41
Eddie Hapgood 1944–47
Will Scott 1947
Jack Bruton 1947–49
Jackie Bestall 1949–53
Johnny Carey 1953–58
Dally Duncan 1958–60
Jack Marshall 1960–67
Eddie Quigley 1967–70
Johnny Carey 1970–71
Ken Furphy 1971–73
Gordon Lee 1974–75
Jim Smith 1975–78
Jim Iley 1978
John Pickering 1978–79
Howard Kendall 1979–81
Bobby Saxton 1981–86
Don Mackay 1987–91
Kenny Dalglish 1991–95
Ray Harford 1995–97
Roy Hodgson 1997–98
Brian Kidd 1998–99
Tony Parkes 1999–2000
Graeme Souness March 2000–

TEN YEAR LEAGUE RECORD

		P	W	D	L	F	A	Pts	Pos
1989-90	Div 2	46	19	17	10	74	59	74	5
1990-91	Div 2	46	14	10	22	51	66	52	19
1991-92	Div 2	46	21	11	14	70	53	74	6
1992-93	PR Lge	42	20	11	11	68	46	71	4
1993-94	PR Lge	42	25	9	8	63	36	84	2
1994-95	PR Lge	42	27	8	7	80	39	89	1
1995-96	PR Lge	38	18	7	13	61	47	61	7
1996-97	PR Lge	38	9	15	14	42	43	42	13
1997-98	PR Lge	38	16	10	12	57	52	58	6
1998-99	PR Lge	38	7	14	17	38	52	35	19

DID YOU KNOW

Bob Crompton, arguably Blackburn's finest Rover of all, made his debut as a 17 year old centre-half in 1896, but delayed turning professional for two years as he was a keen amateur swimmer and apprentice plumber.

BLACKBURN ROVERS 1999–2000 LEAGUE RECORD

Match No.	Date	Venue	Opponents	Result	H/T Score	Lg. Pos.	Goalscorers	Attendance
1	Aug 7	H	Port Vale	D	0-0	0-0	13		20,530
2	13	A	Huddersfield T	L	2-3	0-1	—	Carsley [65], Broomes [89]	13,670
3	21	H	Barnsley	L	1-2	0-0	20	Carsley (pen) [81]	19,537
4	28	A	Norwich C	W	2-0	1-0	16	Ostenstad 2 [6, 51]	15,407
5	Sept 11	H	Tranmere R	W	2-0	0-0	15	Ward [82], Blake [87]	17,899
6	18	A	WBA	D	2-2	0-1	12	Dailly [57], Jansen [67]	16,902
7	25	H	Walsall	W	2-0	2-0	11	Ward [34], Carsley [44]	18,232
8	28	A	Swindon T	L	1-2	0-2	—	Ostenstad [85]	7354
9	Oct 2	A	QPR	D	0-0	0-0	13		14,002
10	16	H	Grimsby T	D	1-1	1-1	14	Carsley (pen) [45]	17,575
11	20	H	Crystal Palace	D	1-1	0-0	—	Frandsen [86]	15,819
12	23	A	Manchester C	L	0-2	0-1	17		33,027
13	26	A	Walsall	D	1-1	1-0	—	Carsley (pen) [28]	6484
14	30	H	QPR	L	0-2	0-1	19		17,491
15	Nov 6	H	Ipswich T	D	2-2	1-0	18	Carsley 2 (1 pen) [1, 67 (p)]	18,512
16	20	H	Fulham	W	2-0	1-0	16	Ostenstad [11], Duff [90]	18,543
17	23	A	Crewe Alex	D	0-0	0-0	—		6495
18	27	H	Stockport Co	W	2-0	1-0	17	Frandsen [44], Ostenstad [68]	17,592
19	30	A	Charlton Ath	W	2-1	1-1	—	Ward 2 [11, 48]	18,939
20	Dec 4	A	Port Vale	D	0-0	0-0	14		6084
21	7	H	Bolton W	W	3-1	0-0	—	Ward [56], McAteer [59], Blake [80]	21,046
22	19	A	Sheffield U	L	1-2	1-1	13	Ward [10]	10,437
23	26	H	Nottingham F	W	2-1	1-1	9	Frandsen [18], Carsley (pen) [68]	23,406
24	28	A	Portsmouth	W	2-1	2-1	7	Dailly [33], Ostenstad [44]	15,208
25	Jan 3	H	Wolverhampton W	D	1-1	1-1	9	Ostenstad [39]	24,743
26	15	H	Huddersfield T	W	2-0	2-0	7	Duff [29], Johnson [44]	21,420
27	22	A	Barnsley	L	1-5	1-4	8	Frandsen [7]	18,088
28	Feb 5	A	Bolton W	L	1-3	1-2	11	Blake [16]	17,687
29	12	H	Swindon T	D	0-0	0-0	12		16,938
30	15	A	Birmingham C	L	0-1	0-1	—		20,719
31	19	A	Stockport Co	W	1-0	0-0	9	McAteer [79]	7902
32	26	H	WBA	W	2-1	0-1	9	Gillespie [70], Dailly [76]	18,184
33	29	H	Norwich C	D	1-1	0-1	—	Frandsen [90]	15,671
34	Mar 4	A	Tranmere R	L	1-2	0-0	9	Dailly [90]	9502
35	7	A	Ipswich T	D	0-0	0-0	—		18,871
36	12	H	Crewe Alex	L	0-1	0-0	11		16,057
37	18	A	Fulham	D	2-2	1-1	11	Dunn [38], Gillespie [85]	15,108
38	22	H	Birmingham C	W	1-0	0-0	—	Dunn [90]	18,096
39	25	A	Nottingham F	W	1-0	1-0	9	Ward [7]	16,823
40	Apr 1	H	Sheffield U	W	5-0	2-0	9	Duff 2 [4, 82], Ward [42], Ostenstad [67], Jansen [89]	17,769
41	8	A	Wolverhampton W	L	1-2	0-1	10	Duff [54]	22,286
42	15	A	Portsmouth	D	1-1	1-1	10	Carsley (pen) [22]	19,263
43	22	A	Grimsby T	D	0-0	0-0	10		6558
44	24	H	Charlton Ath	D	1-1	0-1	10	Carsley (pen) [63]	18,587
45	29	A	Crystal Palace	L	1-2	1-0	11	Jansen [27]	18,272
46	May 7	H	Manchester C	L	1-4	1-0	11	Jansen [42]	29,913

Final League Position: 11

GOALSCORERS

League (55): Carsley 10 (7 pens), Ostenstad 8, Ward 8, Duff 5, Frandsen 5, Dailly 4, Jansen 4, Blake 3, Dunn 2, Gillespie 2, McAteer 2, Broomes 1, Johnson 1.
Worthington Cup (6): Jansen 2, Duff 1, Dunn 1, Gallacher 1, own goal 1.
FA Cup (6): Blake 2, Carsley 1 (pen), Duff 1, Frandsen 1, Jansen 1.

Filan J 16	Grayson S 31 + 3	Davidson C 28 + 2	Short C 17	Broomes M 13	Carsley L 30	Dunn D 17 + 5	Jansen M 16 + 14	Duff D 33 + 6	Davies K 2	Wilcox J 16 + 4	Johnson D 11 + 5	Gallacher K 3 + 2	Dailly C 43	Gillespie K 11 + 11	Flitcroft G 18 + 1	Blake N 17 + 11	Ward A 35 + 2	Ostenstad E 21 + 7	Kenna J 11	Peacock D 15 + 2	Frandsen P 26 + 5	Taylor M 4 + 2	McAteer J 24 + 4	Kelly A 29 + 1	Harkness S 17	Fettis A —+ 1	Miller A 1	Burgess B 1 + 1	Match No.
1	2	3	4	5	6	7^1	8^2	9	10	11	12	13																	1
1	2	3		5	6						12	10^1	11		9^2	4	7	8	13^1										2
1	2	3	4	5	6	12	13			11^2	14					7^3	8^1		9	10									3
1		3	4		6	7^1	8^2			11	14	13	5	12		9	10^3	2											4
1		3	4		6	7^1	8^2	13		11			5	12	14	9	10^3	2											5
1	2	3	4^3		6	7^1	8			11			5	12	13		9	10^2	14										6
1		3			6			12		11	10^1	8	5			9			2	4	7								7
1	2	3			6			12		11		7^1	5			10	9^2	13		4	8								8
1		3			6			12		11			5			7	9	10^1	2	4^2	8	13							9
1		3	4		6			12	13	11	7^3		5			9		10^1	2		8^2	14							10
1	2	3	4		6		8	7		11			5			9^1	12				10								11
1	12	3	4		6^2		8	7		11			5			9		2^1		10	13								12
1		3	4		6		8	7		11			5			9		2		10^1	12								13
1	12	3			6		8^2	7		11			5			9	13	2^1	4	10^3	14								14
	2				6	8^1		11^2	12				5			10	9	13			4	7	1	3					15
	2				6	8		11	12				5			9	10^1	4			13	7	1	3					16
	2		4		6	8^2		11^3	14				5			12	9	10^1			13	7	1	3					17
	2				6			11					5			12	9	10^1	4		8	7	1	3					18
	2				6			11^1	12				5			13	9	10^2	4		8	7	1	3					19
	2				6			11					5			12	9	10^1	4		8	7	1	3					20
	2				6			11					5			10	9		4		8	7	1	3					21
	2	12			6		13	11					5			10^2	9				8	4	7	1	3^1				22
	3				6	12		11	7				5			10^2	9^1	13	2		8	4	1						23
12	3				6	10		11	8				5			9	2^1				4	7	1^6	15					24
1		3			6	12	10^1	11	7				5			9		2			4	8							25
1^6	2	3			6			12	11				5			10	9^1	4			8^2	13	15						26
	2	3				12		11					5	13		10	9^1	4			8	7	1						27
	2	3				12		11^3	6				5	14		10	9^2	13			4	8	7^1	1					28
	2	3				12		11	6^3				5	14	13	10	9^1	4			8^2	7	1						29
	2	3	4			6^2	13	11					5	8	10	12	9^1					7	1						30
	2	3	4			10							5	8	11	9						7	1	6					31
	2	3	4			10^1	11^2						5	13	6	12	9					8	7	1					32
	2	3	4			12	11						5	8	6^2	9		10^1			13		7	1					33
	2	3	4				11						5	8	6	10	9				12	7^1	1						34
	2	3	4			12	11						5	7	6	10^1	9				8		1						35
	2	3^2	4			12	10	11					5	7	6^1	9	13				8		1						36
	2^1		4			6	12	11					8	7		9	5	10					1		3				37
	12	2				4	10	11					5	7	6^2	14	9^1				8^1		1		3				38
	2		4			6		11	8^1				5	12	7	10^2	9	13					1		3				39
			4			6	12	11					5	8^2	7	14	9^3	10^1					2	3	1				40
			4			6	12	11	8^3				5	14	7	13	9^1	10^2					2	1	3				41
	3	4			6	8		11					5	7^2		9	12	13					2	1			10^1		42
	3	2			6	4	12	11					5	8	10^1	9	13					7^2	1						43
	2^1	4			6	12	8						5	13	9^2	10^3	11					7	1	3	14				44
		4			6	10	11						5	12	7	9	8					2^1	1	3					45
	2		6			4	10	11					5	8	9		7	1	3										46

Worthington Cup

Second Round	Portsmouth	(a)	3-0
		(h)	3-1
Third Round	Leeds U	(a)	0-1

FA Cup

Third Round	WBA	(a)	2-2
		(h)	2-0
Fourth Round	Liverpool	(a)	1-0
Fifth Round	Newcastle U	(h)	1-2

Division 3   **BLACKPOOL**

FOUNDATION

Old boys of St John's School who had formed themselves into a football club decided to establish a club bearing the name of their town and Blackpool FC came into being at a meeting at the Stanley Arms Hotel in the summer of 1887. In their first season playing at Raikes Hall Gardens, the club won both the Lancashire Junior Cup and the Fylde Cup.

Bloomfield Rd Ground, Blackpool FY1 6JJ.

Telephone: (01253) 404 331 (Ticket/Credit Bookings), (01253) 405 331 (Shop/General Enquiries).

Fax: (01253) 405 011.

Website: www.blackpoolfc.co.uk

Email: info@blackpoolfc.co.uk

ClubCall: 09068 121 648

Ground Capacity: 11,295.

Record Attendance: 38,098 v Wolverhampton W, Division 1, 17 September 1955.

Record Receipts: £79,420 v Preston NE, Division 2, 21 November 1998.

Pitch Measurements: 112yd × 74yd.

Chairman: Mr K. Oyston.

Deputy Chairman: K. Chadwick.

Directors: C. Muir OBE, O. J. Oyston, G. Warburton, P. Smith, P. Whitehead.

Manager: Steve McMahon.

Secretary: Carol Banks.

Commercial Director: Geoff Warburton.

Physio: Paul Kelly.

Stadium Manager: John Turner.

LATEST SEQUENCES

Longest Sequence of League Wins: 9, 21.11.36 – 1.1.37.

Longest Sequence of League Defeats: 8, 26.11.1898 – 7.1.1899.

Longest Sequence of League Draws: 5, 4.12.76 – 1.1.77.

Longest Sequence of Unbeaten League Matches: 17, 6.4.68 – 21.9.68.

Longest Sequence Without a League Win: 19, 19.12.70 – 24.4.71.

HONOURS

Football League: Division 1 – Runners-up 1955–56; Division 2 – Champions 1929–30; Runners-up 1936–37, 1969–70; Division 4 – Runners-up 1984–85.

FA Cup: Winners 1953; Runners-up 1948, 1951.

Football League Cup: Semi-final 1962.

Anglo-Italian Cup: Winners 1971; Runners-up 1972.

Colours
All tangerine.

Change Colours
Tangerine and white.

Year Formed: 1887.

Turned Professional: 1887.

Ltd Co.: 1896.

Previous Name: 'South Shore' combined with Blackpool in 1899, twelve years after the latter had been formed on the breaking up of the old 'Blackpool St John's' club.

Club Nickname: 'The Seasiders'.

Previous Grounds: 1887, Raikes Hall Gardens; 1897, Athletic Grounds; 1899, Raikes Hall Gardens; 1899, Bloomfield Road.

First Football League game: 5 September 1896, Division 2, v Lincoln C (a) L 1–3 – Douglas; Parr, Bowman; Stuart, Strzaker, Norris; Clarkin, Donnelly, R. Parkinson, Mount (1), J. Parkinson.

Record League Victory: 7–0 v Reading, Division 2, 10 November 1928 – Mercer; Gibson, Hamilton, Watson, Wilson, Grant, Ritchie, Oxberry (2), Hampson (5), Tufnell, Neal. 7–0 v Preston NE (away), Division 1, 1 May 1948 – Robinson; Shimwell, Crosland; Buchan, Hayward, Kelly; Hobson, Munro (1), McIntosh (5), McCall, Rickett (1). 7–0 v Sunderland, Division 1, 5 October 1957 – Farm; Armfield, Garrett, Kelly (J), Gratrix, Kelly (H), Matthews, Taylor (2), Charnley (2), Durie (2), Perry (1).

Record Cup Victory: 7–1 v Charlton Ath, League Cup 2nd rd, 25 September 1963 – Harvey; Armfield, Martin; Crawford, Gratrix, Cranston; Lea, Ball (1), Charnley (4), Durie (1), Oates (1).

Record Defeat: 1–10 v Small Heath, Division 2, 2 March 1901 and v Huddersfield T, Division 1, 13 December 1930.

Most League Points (2 for a win): 58, Division 2, 1929–30 and Division 2, 1967–68.

Most League Points (3 for a win): 86, Division 4, 1984–85.

Most League Goals: 98, Division 2, 1929–30.

Highest League Scorer in Season: Jimmy Hampson, 45, Division 2, 1929–30.

Most League Goals in Total Aggregate: Jimmy Hampson, 246, 1927–38.

Most League Goals in One Match: 5, Jimmy Hampson v Reading, Division 2, 10 November 1928; 5, Jimmy McIntosh v Preston NE, Division 1, 1 May 1948.

Most Capped Player: Jimmy Armfield, 43, England.

Most League Appearances: Jimmy Armfield, 568, 1952–71.

Youngest League Player: Trevor Sinclair, 16 years 170 days v Wigan Ath, 19 August 1989.

Record Transfer Fee Received: £750,000 from QPR for Trevor Sinclair, August 1993.

Record Transfer Fee Paid: £275,000 to Millwall for Chris Malkin, October 1996.

Football League Record: 1896 Elected to Division 2; 1899 Failed re-election; 1900 Re-elected; 1900–30 Division 2; 1930–33 Division 1; 1933–37 Division 2; 1937–67 Division 1; 1967–70 Division 2; 1970–71 Division 1; 1971–78 Division 2; 1978–81 Division 3; 1981–85 Division 4; 1985–90 Division 3; 1990–92 Division 4; 1992–2000 Division 2; 2000– Division 3.

MANAGERS

Tom Barcroft 1903–33
  (Secretary-Manager)
John Cox 1909–11
Bill Norman 1919–23
Maj. Frank Buckley 1923–27
Sid Beaumont 1927–28
Harry Evans 1928–33
  (Hon. Team Manager)
Alex 'Sandy' Macfarlane 1933–35
Joe Smith 1935–58
Ronnie Suart 1958–67
Stan Mortensen 1967–69
Les Shannon 1969–70
Bob Stokoe 1970–72
Harry Potts 1972–76
Allan Brown 1976–78
Bob Stokoe 1978–79
Stan Ternent 1979–80
Alan Ball 1980–81
Allan Brown 1981–82
Sam Ellis 1982–89
Jimmy Mullen 1989–90
Graham Carr 1990
Bill Ayre 1990–94
Sam Allardyce 1994–96
Gary Megson 1996–97
Nigel Worthington 1997–99
Steve McMahon January 2000–

TEN YEAR LEAGUE RECORD

		P	W	D	L	F	A	Pts	Pos
1989-90	Div 3	46	10	16	20	49	73	46	23
1990-91	Div 4	46	23	10	13	78	47	79	5
1991-92	Div 4	42	22	10	10	71	45	76	4
1992-93	Div 2	46	12	15	19	63	75	51	18
1993-94	Div 2	46	16	5	25	63	75	53	20
1994-95	Div 2	46	18	10	18	64	70	64	12
1995-96	Div 2	46	23	13	10	67	40	82	3
1996-97	Div 2	46	18	15	13	60	47	69	7
1997-98	Div 2	46	17	11	18	59	67	62	12
1998-99	Div 2	46	14	14	18	44	54	56	14

DID YOU KNOW ?

Despite recording only one home win in the entire 1966-67 season, Blackpool produced a spectacular effort to beat Newcastle United 6-0 on 22 October. It was a week after their first win, 3-1 at Tottenham.

BLACKPOOL 1999–2000 LEAGUE RECORD

Match No.	Date	Venue	Opponents	Result		H/T Score	Lg. Pos.	Goalscorers	Attendance
1	Aug 7	H	Wrexham	W	2-1	2-0	2	Ormerod 2 [8, 37]	5008
2	14	A	Luton T	L	2-3	0-1	12	Ormerod [80], Nowland [86]	5176
3	21	H	Gillingham	D	1-1	0-1	11	Murphy [75]	4203
4	28	A	Brentford	L	0-2	0-2	18		5353
5	30	H	Oxford U	D	1-1	1-0	16	Carlisle [34]	3670
6	Sept 4	A	Bristol C	L	2-5	1-0	20	Ormerod [15], Murphy [85]	8439
7	11	A	Notts Co	L	1-2	0-0	21	Carlisle [75]	5512
8	18	H	Bournemouth	D	0-0	0-0	22		4471
9	25	H	Wycombe W	L	1-2	1-2	22	Ormerod [13]	3452
10	Oct 2	A	Bristol R	L	1-3	0-1	23	Murphy [89]	7715
11	9	A	Chesterfield	D	0-0	0-0	23		2804
12	16	H	Bury	L	0-5	0-1	23		5270
13	19	H	Oldham Ath	L	1-2	0-0	—	Murphy [90]	3845
14	23	A	Wycombe W	W	2-0	2-0	23	Nowland [43], Lee [45]	5021
15	Nov 2	A	Cardiff C	D	1-1	0-0	—	Murphy [57]	4523
16	6	H	Wigan Ath	D	2-2	2-0	21	Murphy [9], Durnin [22]	4535
17	14	A	Burnley	L	0-1	0-0	23		12,898
18	23	H	Millwall	L	1-2	1-2	—	Murphy [35]	2819
19	27	H	Cambridge U	W	2-1	2-0	22	Murphy [9], Clarkson [13]	4040
20	Dec 4	A	Wrexham	D	1-1	1-0	22	Hills (pen) [33]	2668
21	18	A	Preston NE	L	0-3	0-0	22		16,821
22	26	H	Stoke C	L	1-2	0-2	22	Nowland [67]	5274
23	28	A	Scunthorpe U	L	0-1	0-1	23		4476
24	Jan 3	H	Colchester U	D	1-1	1-0	22	Bent [21]	3462
25	8	A	Reading	D	1-1	0-0	22	Matthews [49]	7297
26	15	H	Luton T	D	3-3	1-1	22	Ablett [8], Clarkson [47], Bushell [56]	5262
27	22	A	Gillingham	W	3-1	2-0	21	Richardson [43], Bushell [45], Matthews [48]	6805
28	29	H	Brentford	L	0-1	0-1	22		5270
29	Feb 5	A	Oxford U	W	1-0	1-0	21	Murphy [18]	5179
30	8	H	Reading	L	0-2	0-0	—		4291
31	12	H	Bristol C	L	1-2	1-1	22	Murphy [42]	5066
32	19	A	Cambridge U	W	2-0	1-0	21	Carlisle [36], Newell [51]	4636
33	26	A	Bournemouth	L	0-2	0-1	22		4464
34	Mar 4	H	Notts Co	W	2-1	1-0	20	Lumsdon [45], Clarkson [75]	4277
35	7	A	Wigan Ath	L	1-5	1-1	—	Gill [2]	6451
36	11	H	Cardiff C	D	2-2	2-2	22	Gill [1], Hills (pen) [12]	5015
37	18	A	Millwall	D	1-1	1-1	23	Gill [37]	10,506
38	21	H	Burnley	D	1-1	0-0	—	Gill [48]	8029
39	25	A	Stoke C	L	0-3	0-0	23		10,002
40	Apr 1	H	Preston NE	D	0-0	0-0	23		9042
41	8	A	Colchester U	D	1-1	0-1	22	Thomas [66]	3351
42	15	H	Scunthorpe U	L	0-2	0-2	23		5542
43	22	A	Bury	L	2-3	0-1	23	Gill [68], Newell [71]	3857
44	24	H	Bristol R	W	2-1	0-1	22	Gill [65], Thomas [77]	5635
45	29	A	Oldham Ath	D	1-1	0-0	22	Carlisle [63]	6290
46	May 6	H	Chesterfield	D	2-2	1-0	22	Coid [35], Gill [57]	3860

Final League Position: 22

GOALSCORERS

League (49): Murphy 10, Gill 7, Ormerod 5, Carlisle 4, Clarkson 3, Nowland 3, Bushell 2, Hills 2 (2 pens), Matthews 2, Newell 2, Thomas 2, Ablett 1, Bent 1, Coid 1, Durnin 1, Lee 1, Lumsdon 1, Richardson 1.
Worthington Cup (3): Clarkson 2, Hughes 1.
FA Cup (5): Clarkson 2, Carlisle 1, Durnin 1, Nowland 1.

Barnes P 12	Bryan M 14 + 4	Hills J 32 + 1	Bardsley D 35	Carlisle C 43	Hughes I 31 + 3	Couzens A 12 + 3	Clarkson P 34 + 1	Murphy J 34 + 5	Bent J 18 + 10	Ormerod B 13	Wellens R 5 + 3	Jones E 1	Lambert R — + 3	Nowland A 5 + 16	Thompson P 2 + 1	Caig T 33	Whitley J 7 + 1	Aldridge M — + 5 (deceased)	Shuttleworth B 4 + 1	Robinson P 4 + 2	Forsyth R 10 + 3	Bushell S 17 + 7	Connell D 1 + 2	Rachel A 1	Garvey S 1 + 8	Coid D 13 + 8	Lee D 9	Durnin J 4 + 1	Beesley P 15 + 3	Qualley B 1	Matthews R 5 + 1	Ablett G 9 + 1	Richardson K 20	Jaszczun T 19	Lumsden C 6	Newell M 12 + 1	Byfield D 3	Gill W 12	Thomas J 9	Match No.
1	2	3	4	5	6	7¹	8	9	10²	11	12	13																												1
1	2¹	3	4	5	6	7	8	9	10	11	12																													2
	2	3¹	4	5	6	2	8	9	10	11²	12					1	7	13																						3
12			4	5	6	2	8	9	10²	11				13		1	7¹		3³	14																				4
	2	3		5	6		8	9	10¹	11²	12					1	7	13			4																			5
	2	3		5	6²	7	8	9	10¹	11	12					1		13			4																			6
	2	3	4	5		7³	8	9¹	10	11						1	12	14		13	6²																			7
	2	3	4	5	6			9	10²	11¹	12					1	7	13	8																					8
	2	3	4	5	6²			9	10³	11	12					1	7	14		13		8¹																		9
	2	3	4	5	6			9	10¹	11	12					1	7					8																		10
	2	3	4	5	6		8	9		11¹	12					1	7²				10								13											11
	2	3	4	5	6		8	9		11²	12					1	7¹				10								→13											12
12		3		5	6		8	9		11						1					10	4				2¹	7													13
12		3		5	6		8	9		11²		13				1					10³	4				2¹	14	7												14
12		3		5	6		8	9								1					10³	4				2¹	13	7	11²							14				15
	2	3		5	6		8	9²		12		13				1					7¹	4					14		11³								10			16
	2	3		5	6		8	9		12						1					7	4							11¹								10			17
	2	3		5³	6		8	9		12		13				1					7	4					14		11²								10¹			18
	3	2		5	6		8	9		12		13				1					7	4							11¹								10²			19
	2	3		5	6	12	8	9				13				1					7¹	4							11								10²			20
	3	4		5	6¹	2	8		10	9²						1					13					12	7		11											21
	3	2		5			8		10	9						1				6¹	4					13	12	7²	11											22
		2		5			8		10	9¹						1				3		4			12	6			11		7									23
		2		5			8		9	10¹						1				3	6	4			12				11		7									24
	3	2		5	6³	12	8		9							1				14	10¹	4				13			11		7²									25
		2		5			8		9¹	10						1					4				12				11		7	3	6							26
		2		5			8		9	10						1					4								11		9	6	7	3						27
	3	2		5			8		9	10						1					4¹								12		6	7	11							28
	3	2		5		12	8		9	10						1					4¹								11		6	7								29
	8	2		5		12			9	10²						1					4¹					13			6		7	3	11							30
11		2		5			8		9	12						1					6					4			3		7¹	10								31
11¹		2		5		12	8		9							1					6					4			3		7	10								32
		2		5	6		8		9							1					4					11			3		7	10								33
	7	2		5	12		8		9	13						1					6					4			3		11¹	10²								34
	7	2		5	12		8		9²	13			14			1					6					4¹			3		10³	11								35
	7²	2		5	6¹		8		12							1					11					13			4		3	9	10							36
		2		5	6	7	8		12							1										4			3		10	9¹	11							37
		2		5	6	7²	8		12			13														4			3		10	11	9¹							38
12		2		5	6	7³	8		13			14														4¹			3		10²	11	9							39
		2		5	6	7¹		9	13			12										8				4²			3		11	10								40
		2		5	6		9	8	7¹	12		13														4			3		12	11	10							41
		2		5	6²	9		7	12			13														4			3		10	11	8							42
	2³	5²		6			12		14			13										7				9¹			4		3	10	11	8						43
	2¹	5					12		8			13										7				6			4²		3	10	11	9						44
	2	5					12		8			13										7				6			4²		3	10¹	11	9						45
		6					12		8			13	2		14	1						4²				7			5³		3	10	11	9¹						46

Worthington Cup
First Round   Tranmere R   (h) 2-1
                                     (a) 1-3

FA Cup
First Round   Stoke C   (h) 2-0
Second Round   Hendon   (h) 2-0
Third Round   Arsenal   (a) 1-3

Division 1   **BOLTON WANDERERS**

FOUNDATION

In 1874 boys of Christ Church Sunday School, Blackburn Street, led by their master Thomas Ogden, established a football club which went under the name of the school and whose president was Vicar of Christ Church. Membership was 6d (two and a half pence). When their president began to lay down too many rules about the use of church premises, the club broke away and formed Bolton Wanderers in 1877, holding their earliest meetings at the Gladstone Hotel.

Reebok Stadium, Burnden Way, Lostock, Bolton BL6 6JW.

Telephone: (01204) 673 673.

Fax: (01204) 673 773.

Ticket Office: (01204) 673 601.

ClubCall: 09068 121 164.

Ground Capacity: 27,879.

Record Attendance: 69,912 v Manchester C, FA Cup 5th rd, 18 February 1933.

Record Receipts: £289,784 v West Ham U, FA Premier League, 21 February 1998.

Pitch Measurements: 114yd × 74yd.

President: Nat Lofthouse OBE.

Chairman: P. A. Gartside.

Directors: P. A. Gartside, G. Ball, G. Seymour, G. Warburton, W. B. Warburton, B. Scowcroft, G. Hargreaves, E. Davies OBE, D. Speakman.

Team Manager: Sam Allardyce.

Physio: Mark Leather.

Chief Executive & Secretary: Des McBain.

Commercial Director: G. Moores.

LATEST SEQUENCES

Longest Sequence of League Wins: 11, 5.11.04 – 2.1.05.

Longest Sequence of League Defeats: 11, 7.4.02 – 18.10.02.

Longest Sequence of League Draws: 6, 25.1.13 – 8.3.13.

Longest Sequence of Unbeaten League Matches: 23, 13.10.90 – 9.3.91.

Longest Sequence Without a League Win: 26, 7.4.02 – 10.1.03.

HONOURS

Football League: Division 1 – Champions 1996–97; Division 2 – Champions 1908–09, 1977–78; Runners-up 1899–1900, 1904–05, 1910–11, 1934–35, 1992–93; Division 3 – Champions 1972–73.
FA Cup: Winners 1923, 1926, 1929, 1958; Runners-up 1894, 1904, 1953.
Football League Cup: Runners-up 1995.
Freight Rover Trophy: Runners-up 1986.
Sherpa Van Trophy: Winners 1989.

Colours
White shirts, navy blue shorts, blue stockings.

Change Colours
Blue shirts with white sash, white shorts, blue stockings.

Year Formed: 1874.

Turned Professional: 1880.

Ltd Co.: 1895.

Previous Name: 1874, Christ Church FC; 1877, Bolton Wanderers.

Club Nickname: 'The Trotters'.

Previous Grounds: Park Recreation Ground and Cockle's Field before moving to Pike's Lane ground 1881; 1895, Burnden Park; 1997, Reebok Stadium.

First Football League Game: 8 September 1888, Football League, v Derby Co (h) L 3–6 – Harrison; Robinson, Mitchell; Roberts, Weir, Bullough, Davenport (2), Milne, Coupar, Barbour, Brogan (1).

Record League Victory: 8–0 v Barnsley, Division 2, 6 October 1934 – Jones; Smith, Finney; Goslin, Atkinson, George Taylor; George T. Taylor (2), Eastham, Milsom (1), Westwood (4), Cook, (1 og).

Record Cup Victory: 13–0 v Sheffield U, FA Cup 2nd rd, 1 February 1890 – Parkinson; Robinson (1), Jones; Bullough, Davenport, Roberts; Rushton, Brogan (3), Cassidy (5), McNee, Weir (4).

Record Defeat: 1–9 v Preston NE, FA Cup 2nd rd, 10 December 1887.

Most League Points (2 for a win): 61, Division 3, 1972–73.

Most League Points (3 for a win): 98, Division 1, 1996–97.

Most League Goals: 100, Division 1, 1996–97.

Highest League Scorer in Season: Joe Smith, 38, Division 1, 1920–21.

Most League Goals in Total Aggregate: Nat Lofthouse, 255, 1946–61.

Most League Goals in One Match: 5, Tony Caldwell v Walsall, Division 3, 10 September 1983.

Most Capped Player: Nat Lofthouse, 33, England.

Most League Appearances: Eddie Hopkinson, 519, 1956–70.

Youngest League Player: Ray Parry, 15 years 267 days v Wolverhampton W, 13 October 1951.

Record Transfer Fee Received: £4,500,000 from Liverpool for Jason McAteer, September 1995.

Record Transfer Fee Paid: £3,500,000 for Dean Holdsworth from Wimbledon, October 1997.

Football League Record: 1888 Founder Member of the League; 1899–1900 Division 2; 1900–03 Division 1; 1903–05 Division 2; 1905–08 Division 1; 1908–09 Division 2; 1909–10 Division 1; 1910–11 Division 2; 1911–33 Division 1; 1933–35 Division 2; 1935–64 Division 1; 1964–71 Division 2; 1971–73 Division 3; 1973–78 Division 2; 1978–80 Division 1; 1980–83 Division 2; 1983–87 Division 3; 1987–88 Division 4; 1988–92 Division 3; 1992–93 Division 2; 1993–95 Division 1; 1995–96 FA Premier League; 1996–97 Division 1; 1997–98 FA Premier League; 1998– Division 1.

MANAGERS

Tom Rawthorne 1874–85
(Secretary)
J. J. Bentley 1885–86
(Secretary)
W. G. Struthers 1886–87
(Secretary)
Fitzroy Norris 1887
(Secretary)
J. J. Bentley 1887–95
(Secretary)
Harry Downs 1895–96
(Secretary)
Frank Brettell 1896–98
(Secretary)
John Somerville 1898–1910
Will Settle 1910–15
Tom Mather 1915–19
Charles Foweraker 1919–44
Walter Rowley 1944–50
Bill Ridding 1951–68
Nat Lofthouse 1968–70
Jimmy McIlroy 1970
Jimmy Meadows 1971
Nat Lofthouse 1971
(then Admin. Manager to 1972)
Jimmy Armfield 1971–74
Ian Greaves 1974–80
Stan Anderson 1980–81
George Mulhall 1981–82
John McGovern 1982–85
Charlie Wright 1985
Phil Neal 1985–92
Bruce Rioch 1992–95
Roy McFarland 1995–96
Colin Todd 1996–99
Sam Allardyce October 1999–

TEN YEAR LEAGUE RECORD

		P	W	D	L	F	A	Pts	Pos
1989-90	Div 3	46	18	15	13	59	48	69	6
1990-91	Div 3	46	24	11	11	64	50	83	4
1991-92	Div 3	46	14	17	15	57	56	59	13
1992-93	Div 2	46	27	9	10	80	41	90	2
1993-94	Div 1	46	15	14	17	63	64	59	14
1994-95	Div 1	46	21	14	11	67	45	77	3
1995-96	PR Lge	38	8	5	25	39	71	29	20
1996-97	Div 1	46	28	14	4	100	53	98	1
1997-98	PR Lge	38	9	13	16	41	61	40	18
1998-99	Div 1	46	20	16	10	78	59	76	6

DID YOU KNOW?

Bolton Wanderers defeated QPR 6-4 on a frost-bound Burnden Park on 29 November 1969, despite finding themselves a goal down after 45 seconds. They were never behind again in this sequence:- 0-1; 1-1; 2-1; 3-1; 3-2; 4-2; 4-3; 5-3; 6-3; 6-4.

BOLTON WANDERERS 1999–2000 LEAGUE RECORD

Match No.	Date	Venue	Opponents	Result	H/T Score	Lg. Pos.	Goalscorers	Attendance
1	Aug 7	A	Tranmere R	D 0-0	0-0	14		7674
2	14	H	QPR	W 2-1	1-1	7	Holdsworth (pen) [11], Gudjohnsen [64]	13,019
3	21	A	Ipswich T	L 0-1	0-0	12		17,696
4	28	H	Manchester C	L 0-1	0-1	17		21,671
5	Sept 5	H	Birmingham C	D 3-3	1-3	18	Frandsen 2 [14, 53], Holdsworth (pen) [90]	11,668
6	11	A	Charlton Ath	L 1-2	1-1	20	Johansen [12]	19,028
7	18	H	Barnsley	D 2-2	1-1	20	Tuttle (og) [4], Gardner [85]	14,621
8	25	H	Nottingham F	W 3-2	1-0	16	Gardner [32], Holdsworth (pen) [65], Cox [90]	14,978
9	Oct 2	A	Swindon T	W 4-0	4-0	12	Cox [9], Holdsworth [22], Gardner [26], Elliott [43]	6711
10	9	A	Wolverhampton W	L 0-1	0-1	13		18,665
11	16	H	Huddersfield T	W 1-0	1-0	9	Gardner [45]	16,603
12	19	H	Crewe Alex	D 2-2	0-1	—	Gudjohnsen [44], Holdsworth [58]	12,676
13	24	A	Norwich C	L 1-2	0-0	12	Gardner [74]	12,468
14	27	A	Nottingham F	D 1-1	1-1	—	Gudjohnsen [20]	15,572
15	30	H	Swindon T	W 2-0	0-0	11	Taylor [87], Hansen [88]	12,486
16	Nov 6	H	Crystal Palace	W 2-0	0-0	11	Gudjohnsen [64], Jensen [82]	12,744
17	14	A	Sheffield U	W 2-1	2-1	12	Farrelly [2], Hansen [35]	10,013
18	20	H	Grimsby T	W 2-0	0-0	6	Hansen 2 [50, 69]	12,415
19	23	A	Fulham	D 1-1	1-1	—	Gudjohnsen [15]	9642
20	27	A	Portsmouth	D 0-0	0-0	8		10,431
21	Dec 4	H	Tranmere R	L 2-3	0-1	9	Gudjohnsen [64], Taylor [77]	13,534
22	7	A	Blackburn R	L 1-3	0-0	—	Elliott [57]	21,046
23	18	H	Stockport Co	L 0-1	0-0	11		13,285
24	28	H	WBA	D 1-1	0-0	14	Jensen [82]	16,269
25	Jan 3	A	Walsall	L 0-2	0-0	14		6873
26	15	A	QPR	W 1-0	0-0	14	Jensen [64]	11,396
27	22	H	Ipswich T	D 1-1	0-0	13	Holdsworth [66]	11,924
28	Feb 5	H	Blackburn R	W 3-1	2-1	12	Bergsson [17], Johansen [39], Gudjohnsen [69]	17,687
29	8	A	Port Vale	W 1-0	0-0	—	Gudjohnsen [77]	5092
30	12	A	Birmingham C	L 1-2	1-0	10	Johnston [20]	18,426
31	22	H	Portsmouth	W 3-0	1-0	—	Taylor [12], Jensen [68], Elliott [77]	12,672
32	26	A	Barnsley	D 1-1	1-0	10	Holdsworth (pen) [43]	14,604
33	Mar 4	H	Charlton Ath	L 0-2	0-0	10		13,788
34	7	A	Crystal Palace	D 0-0	0-0	—		15,236
35	11	H	Fulham	W 3-1	1-0	10	Holdsworth 2 (1 pen) [45 (p), 50], Gudjohnsen [90]	12,761
36	14	A	Stockport Co	D 0-0	0-0	—		6412
37	18	A	Grimsby T	W 1-0	1-0	9	Bergsson [39]	5289
38	21	H	Sheffield U	W 2-0	2-0	—	Johnston [32], O'Kane [45]	11,891
39	25	H	Port Vale	W 2-1	2-0	8	Gudjohnsen [16], Johnston [42]	12,292
40	Apr 5	A	Manchester C	L 0-2	0-2	—		32,927
41	8	H	Walsall	W 4-3	3-1	8	Johansen (pen) [2], Hansen 2 [13, 74], Phillips [25]	11,777
42	15	A	WBA	W 4-4	1-2	8	Hansen [36], Bergsson 2 [55, 90], Gudjohnsen [66]	12,802
43	22	A	Huddersfield T	W 3-0	2-0	8	Hansen 2 [9, 26], Whitlow [58]	16,404
44	29	A	Crewe Alex	W 3-1	1-1	8	Gudjohnsen [15], Holdsworth (pen) [71], Jensen [89]	8015
45	May 3	H	Wolverhampton W	W 2-1	0-1	—	Jensen [60], Gudjohnsen [70]	18,871
46	7	H	Norwich C	W 1-0	0-0	6	Holdsworth [72]	17,987

Final League Position: 6

GOALSCORERS

League (69): Gudjohnsen 13, Holdsworth 11 (6 pens), Hansen 9, Jensen 6, Gardner 5, Bergsson 4, Elliott 3, Johansen 3 (1 pen), Johnston 3, Taylor 3, Cox 2, Frandsen 2, Farrelly 1, O'Kane 1, Phillips 1, Whitlow 1, own goal 1.
Worthington Cup (17): Gudjohnsen 3, Johansen 3 (2 pens), Frandsen 2, Bergsson 1, Cox 1, Elliott 1, Fish 1, Gardner 1, Hansen 1, Holdsworth 1, Taylor 1, own goal 1.
FA Cup (7): Gudjohnsen 4, Taylor 2, Hansen 1.

Branagan K 11	Cox N 15	Whitlow M 35 + 2	Frandsen P 7	Strong G 6	Todd A 10 + 2	Johansen M 44 + 1	Jensen C 41 + 1	Gudjohnsen E 40 + 1	Hansen B 15 + 15	Gardner R 26 + 3	Holdsworth D 22 + 13	Phillips J 15 + 8	Aljofree H 3 + 5	Taylor B 15 + 12	Bergsson G 37 + 1	Elliott R 22 + 5	Warhurst P 15 + 4	Fish M 31	Jaaskelainen J 33 + 1	Farrelly G 8 + 3	Holden D 6 + 6	O'Kane J 7 + 4	Passi F 7 + 8	Holloway D 3 + 1	Ritchie P 13 + 1	Banks S 2	Johnston A 17 + 2	Kaprielian M — + 1	Nolan K — + 4	Match No.
1	2	3	4	5	6	7	8	9	10¹	11	12																			1
1	2	3	4	5	6¹	7	8	9	11²	10	12	13																		2
1	2	3	4	5	6	7	8	9	11					10																3
1	2	3	4	5	6	7	8²	9¹	12	11				13	10															4
1	2	3	4	5³	6²	7		12	11	9	13			10¹	14	8														5
1	2	3	4		6	7		12	10¹	11	9²			13	5³	8	14													6
1	2	3	4		6	7		9		11	12			10¹	5	8														7
1	2		7			9	12	11	10¹	3				5	8	4	6													8
1	2		7	12	9²		11	10¹	3				13	5	8	4	6													9
1	2	12		7	8³		13	11	9	3	14	10²	5	4¹		6														10
1⁹	2		12	7	8	9		11	10²	3		13	5	4¹		6	15													11
	2		4	7	8	9¹		11	10	3			5		12	6	1													12
	2	12		4	7²	8	9	13	11	10	3¹		5		14	6³	1													13
	2	3		4	7	8	9¹		11	10		12	5		6		1													14
	2	3		7	8	9¹	13	11	10²	4		12	5		6		1													15
		3		12	7¹	8	9	13	11	10²	2	14	5		4¹	6	1													16
		3		7²	8	9	10¹	11		2	13	12	5		6	1	4													17
		3		7	8	9	10	11		2	4		5		6	1														18
		3		7³	8	9	10¹	11		2²	4	12	5		6	1		13	14											19
		3		7	8	9²	10¹	11		12	5		6	1	4	13	2													20
		3		7²	8	9	10	11		2	6	12	13		5	1	4													21
			5	7¹	8	9	12	11		3	10³		2²	6	1	4	13		14											22
		3		7²	8	9	12	11		10¹	5		6	1	4	13		2												23
		3			8	9	12	11		10¹	5		4²	6	1	7		13	2											24
		3		12	8³	9		14	13		10²	5		6	1	7¹		11	2	4										25
		3		7	8	9²		10¹	6	12	5		11	2	4	13		1												26
		3		7	8¹	9		12	10	4	5	13		2	6²11		1													27
		3		7	8	9		11²	12	10¹	5	6	4		1	2		13												28
		3		7	8	9		12	10¹	5	6	4²		1	13	2	14	11³												29
			7	8	9	12	10³	13	5	6		1	4²	2	14	3	11¹													30
		3		7	8	9		12	13	10²	5	4	6³	1	2		14	11¹												31
		3		7²	8		12	11³	9	10¹	5	4	6	1	2	13		14												32
			7	8		12		9	10¹	2	3	5	1		4²		6	11³13	13	14										33
		3		7¹	8		9	10³	2	4	5	1	13	2	14	6	11²		14											34
		3		7	8	9		10¹		2	4	5	1	6	11		12													35
		3		7	8	9		10¹		12	2	4	5	1	6	11														36
		3		7	8	9	10¹		12	5²13		1	14	2	4²	6	11													37
		3		7	8	10		13		3	4³	5	1	12²	2	14	6	11¹												38
		3		7	8	9	12		10¹	2	3	5	1	13	4	6	11²													39
		3		7³	8	9	12		10¹13	4	6	5	1	2²		11	14													40
		3		7	8	9	10¹		12 13	2	6²14	5³	1	4		11														41
		3		7	8	9	10		12 13	2	6²	4	5	1		11¹														42
		3		7	8	9	10²		12	2	4³	5¹	1	13		14	6	11												43
		3		7	8	9¹	10¹		12 13	2	4	5	1	14		6²	11													44
		3		7	8	9	10¹		12 13	2	14	4³	5	1		6	11²													45
		3		7²	8	9¹	10¹		12	2	13	4	5	1		14	6	11												46

Worthington Cup

Round	Opponent	Venue	Score
First Round	Darlington	(a)	1-1
		(h)	5-3
Second Round	Gillingham	(a)	4-1
		(h)	2-0
Third Round	Derby Co	(a)	2-1
Fourth Round	Sheffield W	(h)	1-0
Fifth Round	Wimbledon	(h)	2-1
Semi-Final	Tranmere R	(h)	0-1
		(a)	0-3

FA Cup

Round	Opponent	Venue	Score
Third Round	Cardiff C	(h)	1-0
Fourth Round	Grimsby T	(a)	2-0
Fifth Round	Cambridge U	(a)	3-1
Sixth Round	Charlton Ath	(h)	1-0
Semi-Final	Aston Villa		0-0
(at Wembley)			

Division 2   AFC BOURNEMOUTH

FOUNDATION

There was a Bournemouth FC as early as 1875, but the present club arose out of the remnants of the Boscombe St John's club (formed 1890). The meeting at which Boscombe FC came into being was held at a house in Gladstone Road in 1899. They began by playing in the Boscombe and District Junior League.

Dean Court Ground, Bournemouth, Dorset BH7 7AF.

Telephone: (01202) 395 381.

Fax: (01202) 309 797.

Website: http://www.afcb.co.uk

ClubCall: 09068 121 163.

Ticket Office: (01202) 397 939.

Ground Capacity: 10,770.

Record Attendance: 28,799 v Manchester U, FA Cup 6th rd, 2 March 1957.

Record Receipts: £80,267 v Walsall, Auto Windscreens Shield Southern Area Final, 17 March 1998.

Pitch Measurements: 112yd × 74yd.

Chairman: T. S. Watkins.

Directors: A. H. Kaye (Vice-Chairman), K. R. Dando, P. W. Aldersey (Managing Director), A. Dawson (Deputy Managing Director), A. Swaisland.

Secretary: K. R. J. MacAlister.

Manager: Mel Machin.

Assistant Manager: John Williams.

First Team Coach: Sean O'Driscoll.

Physio: Steve Hardwick.

Corporate Manager: Miss D. Edwards.

Groundsman: D. Edwards.

LATEST SEQUENCES

Longest Sequence of League Wins: 7, 22.8.70 – 23.9.70.

Longest Sequence of League Defeats: 7, 13.8.94 – 13.9.94.

Longest Sequence of League Draws: 5, 10.11.79 – 21.12.79.

Longest Sequence of Unbeaten League Matches: 18, 6.3.82 – 28.8.82.

Longest Sequence Without a League Win: 14, 6.3.74 – 27.4.74.

HONOURS

Football League: Division 3 – Champions 1986–87; Division 3 (S) – Runners-up 1947–48; Division 4 – Runners-up 1970–71; Promotion from Division 4 1981–82 (4th).

FA Cup: best season: 6th rd, 1957.

Football League Cup: best season: 4th rd, 1962, 1964.

Associate Members' Cup: Winners 1984.

Auto Windscreens Shield: Runners-up 1998.

Colours

Red shirts with 3¾-inch black stripe and black collar with red and white trim, black shorts, black stockings.

Change Colours

Green shirts with 3¾-inch black stripe and black collar with green and white trim, green shorts, green stockings.

Year Formed: 1899.

Turned Professional: 1912.

Ltd Co.: 1914.

Previous Names: 1890, Boscombe St Johns; 1899, Boscombe FC; 1923, Bournemouth & Boscombe Ath FC; 1971, AFC Bournemouth.

Club Nickname: 'Cherries'.

Previous Grounds: 1899, Castlemain Road, Pokesdown; 1910, Dean Court.

First Football League Game: 25 August 1923, Division 3 (S), v Swindon T (a), L 1–3 – Heron; Wingham, Lamb; Butt, C. Smith, Voisey; Miller, Lister (1), Davey, Simpson, Robinson.

Record League Victory: 7–0 v Swindon T, Division 3 (S), 22 September 1956 – Godwin; Cunningham, Keetley; Clayton, Crosland, Rushworth; Siddall (1), Norris (2), Arnott (1), Newsham (2), Cutler (1). 10–0 win v Northampton T at start of 1939–40 expunged from the records on outbreak of war.

Record Cup Victory: 11–0 v Margate, FA Cup 1st rd, 20 November 1971 – Davies; Machin (1), Kitchener, Benson, Jones, Powell, Cave (1), Boyer, MacDougall (9 incl. 1p), Miller, Scott (De Garis).

Record Defeat: 0–9 v Lincoln C, Division 3, 18 December 1982.

Most League Points (2 for a win): 62, Division 3, 1971–72.

Most League Points (3 for a win): 97, Division 3, 1986–87.

Most League Goals: 88, Division 3 (S), 1956–57.

Highest League Scorer in Season: Ted MacDougall, 42, 1970–71.

Most League Goals in Total Aggregate: Ron Eyre, 202, 1924–33.

Most League Goals in One Match: 4, Jack Russell v Clapton Orient, Division 3S, 7 January 1933; 4, Jack Russell v Bristol C, Division 3S, 28 January 1933; 4, Harry Mardon v Southend U, Division 3S, 1 January 1938; 4, Jack McDonald v Torquay U, Division 3S, 8 November 1947.

Most Capped Player: Gerry Peyton, 7 (33), Republic of Ireland.

Most League Appearances: Sean O'Driscoll, 423, 1984–95.

Youngest League Player: Jimmy White, 15 years 321 days v Brentford, 30 April 1958.

Record Transfer Fee Received: £800,000 from Everton for Joe Parkinson, March 1994.

Record Transfer Fee Paid: £250,000 to Portsmouth for Steve Lovell, August 1999.

Football League Record: 1923 Elected to Division 3 (S) and remained a Third Division club for record number of years until 1970; 1970–71 Division 4; 1971–75 Division 3; 1975–82 Division 4; 1982–87 Division 3; 1987–90 Division 2; 1990–92 Division 3; 1992– Division 2.

MANAGERS

Vincent Kitcher 1914–23
(Secretary-Manager)
Harry Kinghorn 1923–25
Leslie Knighton 1925–28
Frank Richards 1928–30
Billy Birrell 1930–35
Bob Crompton 1935–36
Charlie Bell 1936–39
Harry Kinghorn 1939–47
Harry Lowe 1947–50
Jack Bruton 1950–56
Fred Cox 1956–58
Don Welsh 1958–61
Bill McGarry 1961–63
Reg Flewin 1963–65
Fred Cox 1965–70
John Bond 1970–73
Trevor Hartley 1974–75
John Benson 1975–78
Alec Stock 1979–80
David Webb 1980–82
Don Megson 1983
Harry Redknapp 1983–92
Tony Pulis 1992–94
Mel Machin August 1994–

TEN YEAR LEAGUE RECORD

		P	W	D	L	F	A	Pts	Pos
1989-90	Div 2	46	12	12	22	57	76	48	22
1990-91	Div 3	46	19	13	14	58	58	70	9
1991-92	Div 3	46	20	11	15	52	48	71	8
1992-93	Div 2	46	12	17	17	45	52	53	17
1993-94	Div 2	46	14	15	17	51	59	57	17
1994-95	Div 2	46	13	11	22	49	69	50	19
1995-96	Div 2	46	16	10	20	51	70	58	14
1996-97	Div 2	46	15	15	16	43	45	60	16
1997-98	Div 2	46	18	12	16	57	52	66	9
1998-99	Div 2	46	21	13	12	63	41	76	7

DID YOU KNOW ?

Right-back Jack Hayward made 309 League and Cup appearances in eight seasons up to 1933 for Bournemouth. He was the club's penalty taker and scored 33 goals.

AFC BOURNEMOUTH 1999–2000 LEAGUE RECORD

Match No.	Date		Venue	Opponents	Result		H/T Score	Lg. Pos.	Goalscorers	Attendance
1	Aug	7	H	Cambridge U	W	2-1	0-1	3	Mean [51], Howe [55]	5552
2		14	A	Bristol C	L	1-3	0-2	16	O'Neill [77]	11,315
3		21	H	Colchester U	W	4-0	1-0	7	Stein [15], Jorgensen [58], Fletcher S 2 [80, 89]	4508
4		28	A	Scunthorpe U	L	1-3	1-1	9	Stein [18]	3376
5		31	H	Luton T	W	1-0	0-0	—	Fletcher S [73]	4797
6	Sept	3	A	Burnley	L	1-2	1-1	—	Stein [39]	10,223
7		11	H	Reading	W	3-1	3-1	6	Grant (og) [22], Hughes [31], Casper (og) [43]	6007
8		18	A	Blackpool	D	0-0	0-0	6		4471
9		25	H	Bury	D	1-1	0-1	7	Stein [82]	4208
10	Oct	2	A	Chesterfield	W	1-0	1-0	7	Jorgensen [25]	2775
11		16	H	Stoke C	D	1-1	1-0	11	Robinson [24]	5990
12		19	H	Bristol R	L	0-1	0-1	—		5613
13		23	A	Bury	D	2-2	1-1	12	Warren [38], Robinson [52]	3701
14	Nov	3	A	Preston NE	L	0-3	0-2	—		9630
15		6	H	Cardiff C	W	1-0	0-0	13	Stein [64]	4471
16		12	A	Gillingham	L	1-4	1-2	13	Robinson [4]	6336
17		16	A	Wigan Ath	L	1-3	0-1	—	Fletcher S [59]	4338
18		23	H	Brentford	W	4-1	2-1	—	Warren [34], Jorgensen [42], Stein 2 [54, 74]	4202
19		27	H	Millwall	L	1-2	0-1	11	Fletcher C [56]	5121
20	Dec	4	A	Cambridge U	W	2-0	1-0	10	Robinson (pen) [36], Day [75]	3579
21		11	A	Notts Co	L	1-5	0-4	11	O'Neill [86]	4199
22		18	A	Oxford U	W	4-0	2-0	10	Fletcher S [18], Robinson (pen) [38], Jorgensen [48], Hayter [89]	4443
23		26	A	Wycombe W	L	1-2	1-1	10	Hayter [42]	5656
24		28	H	Wrexham	W	1-0	1-0	10	Stein [44]	5394
25	Jan	3	A	Oldham Ath	L	0-1	0-1	10		5160
26		8	H	Notts Co	D	1-1	0-0	10	Stein [47]	4344
27		15	H	Bristol C	L	2-3	0-1	11	Robinson [48], O'Neill [84]	5425
28		22	A	Colchester U	L	1-3	1-1	12	Robinson [35]	3767
29		29	H	Scunthorpe U	D	1-1	0-0	13	Stein [64]	4802
30	Feb	5	A	Luton T	W	2-1	1-0	12	Mean [34], Watts (og) [46]	5961
31		12	H	Burnley	L	0-1	0-1	13		5804
32		19	A	Millwall	L	1-3	1-1	16	O'Shea [3]	8463
33		26	H	Blackpool	W	2-0	1-0	13	Mean [3], Robinson (pen) [80]	4464
34	Mar	4	A	Reading	L	0-2	0-2	13		10,551
35		7	A	Cardiff C	W	2-1	0-0	—	Stein [65], Hughes [89]	4389
36		11	H	Preston NE	L	0-1	0-0	13		5317
37		18	A	Brentford	W	2-0	1-0	10	Jorgensen [26], Robinson (pen) [88]	4578
38		21	H	Gillingham	L	0-1	0-1	—		4443
39		25	H	Wycombe W	W	2-0	0-0	9	Elliott [50], Mean [81]	4393
40	Apr	1	A	Oxford U	L	0-1	0-1	12		5214
41		8	H	Oldham Ath	W	3-0	0-0	11	Sheerin [47], Fletcher S [71], Elliott [89]	3808
42		15	A	Wrexham	L	0-1	0-0	14		2597
43		22	A	Stoke C	L	0-1	0-0	14		15,022
44		25	H	Chesterfield	D	1-1	0-1	—	Fletcher C [78]	3481
45		29	A	Bristol R	D	2-2	1-1	16	Fletcher C [45], Fletcher S [52]	8847
46	May	6	H	Wigan Ath	D	2-2	2-0	16	Elliott [26], Jorgensen [44]	6512

Final League Position: 16

GOALSCORERS

League (59): Stein 11, Robinson 9 (4 pens), Fletcher S 7, Jorgensen 6, Mean 4, Elliott 3, Fletcher C 3, O'Neill 3, Hayter 2, Hughes 2, Warren 2, Day 1, Howe 1, O'Shea 1, Sheerin 1, own goals 3.
Worthington Cup (4): Stein 2, Hayter 1, Huck 1.
FA Cup (5): Fletcher S 2, Robinson 1 (pen), Stein 1, Warren 1.

Ovendale M 43	Young N 37	Warren C 39 + 2	Howe E 28	Cox I 28	Mean S 26 + 6	Jorgensen C 34 + 10	Hayter J 21 + 10	Stein M 36	Fletcher S 35 + 1	Rawlinson M 2 + 1	O'Neill J 18 + 12	Lovell S — + 1	Huck W 4 + 13	Hughes R 20 + 1	Robinson S 40	Watson G 2 + 4	Day J 9 + 2	Betsy K 1 + 4	Tindall J 4 + 4	Bailey J — + 1	Broadhurst K 16	Forbes T 3	Fletcher C 20 + 5	Stewart G 3	Elliott S 6 + 2	Stock B 4 + 1	O'Shea J 10	Elliott W 6 + 6	Fenton N 8	Keeler J — + 3	Sheerin J 3 + 3	Smith D — + 1	Ford J — + 2	Match No.
1	2	3	4	5	6	7	8¹	9²	10	11	12	13																						1
1	2	3	4	5	6²	7	8¹	9	10	11³	12		13	14																				2
1	2	3	4	5	6¹	7²	12	9	10		13			11	8																			3
1	2²	3³	4	5	6	7¹		9	10		12			11	8	13	14																	4
1	2	3	4	5	6			9³	10				7	11	8	12																		5
1	2	3	4	5	6	12		9	10			13		11¹							7²	14		8³										6
1	2	3	4	5	6²	12		9	10				7¹	11	8						13³	14												7
1	2		4	5	6	7		9¹	10					11	8		12				3													8
1	2	12	4	5	6²	7		9					13	11	8		10				3¹													9
1	2		4	5	6	7		9¹	10					11	8		12				3													10
1	2	3²	4¹	5	6	7		9	10				13	12	8						11													11
1	2	3		5	6	7		9	10					11¹	8	12							4											12
1	2	3		5		7		9	10						8						6		4		11									13
1	2	3¹		5		7²		9	10				14	12	8	13					6		4		11³									14
1	2	3		5		7	4	9	10					12	8						11¹		6											15
1	2	3		5		7	4¹	9	10					12	8						11		6											16
	2¹	3		5		7²	12	9	10				13		8						6		4	1	11									17
1	2	3		5		7		9	10					12	8						6¹		4		11									18
1	2	3¹		5		7	12	9	10			13	14		8						6³		4²		11									19
1	2	3		5	12	7²	13	9	10						8						11¹		4		6									20
1		3		5	12	7²	13	9	10				14		8						6¹		4		11³	2								21
1		3		5		7	4	9²	10¹						8	6	12				13		11		2³		14							22
1		3		5		7	4	9	10						8	6							11¹		12		2							23
1		3			13	7	4	9³	10¹						8	6	12²				14		11	5			2							24
1		3		5	6	7	4	9						11	8		10								2									25
1		3		5	12	7	4	9						11	8		2				10		6¹											26
		3		5	6	12		9	10					11	8	4²					2		13	1	7¹									27
1	2¹			5	6³	12	4	9					13	11	8		3				10²		14	7										28
1	2	3		5	6	12	10	9						7¹	8						11		4											29
1	2	3	5		6	12	10	9						7¹	8						11		4											30
1		3²	5³		6	12	10	9					7		8	14	2¹				11		13	4										31
1		3	5		6²	12	2	9					7¹	14	8	13	10³				11		4											32
1	2		5		6	7	10	9						11	8	3							4											33
1	2²		5		6³	7	10	9	12				13	11	8	3¹							4	14										34
1	2	12	5		6¹	7	3²	9	10				14	11	8						4		13³											35
1	2	3	5		6¹	7	12	9	10			13		11³	8	14							4²											36
1	2	3	5			7	10²	9	6¹					11	8	12							4	13										37
1	2	3	5		12	7	10	9	6					11¹	8	4²							13											38
1	2	3	5		12	7²	13	9	6³					11¹	8						10		4	14										39
1	2	3	5		6²	7		9	11¹						8	12							10	4	13									40
1	2	3	5		6¹	12	13	10						11³	8	14							7	9	4	8²								41
1	2	3	5		6¹	12	13	9	14					11	8							7	10³	4	8²									42
1	2³	3²	5			7		10	6					11	8	9¹							12	4	13	14								43
	2	3	5			7	12	9	6³					11	1	10²							13	4	8¹	14								44
1	2	3	5			7²		9	6¹					11	8	10							4	12	13									45
1	2	3	5			7		9	6²					11	8	10¹							4	12	13									46

Worthington Cup

First Round	Barnet	(h)	2-0
		(a)	2-3
Second Round	Charlton Ath	(a)	0-0
		(h)	0-0
Third Round	West Ham U	(a)	0-2

FA Cup

First Round	Notts Co	(a)	1-1
		(h)	4-2
Second Round	Bristol C	(h)	0-2

FA Premiership

BRADFORD CITY

FOUNDATION

Bradford was a rugby stronghold around the turn of the century but after Manningham RFC held an archery contest to help them out of financial difficulties in 1903, they were persuaded to give up the handling code and turn to soccer. So they formed Bradford City and continued at Valley Parade. Recognising this as an opportunity of spreading the dribbling code in this part of Yorkshire, the Football League immediately accepted the new club's first application for membership of the Second Division.

Bradford & Bingley Stadium, Valley Parade, Bradford BD8 7DY.

Telephone: (01274) 773 355 (Office).

Fax: (01274) 773 356.

Ticket Office: (01274) 770 022.

Website: www.bradfordcity.co.uk

Email: bradfordcityfc@compuserve.com

ClubCall: 09068 888 640.

Ground Capacity: 25,000 (during season 2000/2001).

Record Attendance: 39,146 v Burnley, FA Cup 4th rd, 11 March 1911.

Record Receipts: £164,567 v Sheffield Wednesday, FA Cup 5th rd, 16 February 1997.

Pitch Measurements: 110yd × 73yd.

Chairman: Geoffrey Richmond. *Vice-Chairman:* David Thompson FCA.

Directors: David Richmond, Elizabeth Richmond, Terry Goddard, Michael Richmond, Julian Rhodes, Prof. David Rhodes.

Managing Director: Shaun Harvey.

Manager: Chris Hutchings.

Assistant Manager: Stuart McCall.

Youth Coach: Steve Smith.

Physio: Steve Redmond.

Secretary: Jon Pollard.

Stadium Manager: Allan Gilliver.

LATEST SEQUENCES

Longest Sequence of League Wins: 10, 26.11.83 – 3.2.84.

Longest Sequence of League Defeats: 8, 21.1.33 – 11.3.33.

Longest Sequence of League Draws: 6, 30.1.76 – 13.3.76.

Longest Sequence of Unbeaten League Matches: 21, 11.1.69 – 2.5.69.

Longest Sequence Without a League Win: 16, 28.8.48 – 20.11.48.

HONOURS

Football League: Division 1 – Runners-up 1998–99; Division 2 – Champions 1907–08; Promoted from Division 2 1995–96 (play-offs); Division 3 – Champions 1984–85; Division 3 (N) – Champions 1928–29; Division 4 – Runners-up 1981–82.

FA Cup: Winners 1911.

Football League Cup: best season: 5th rd, 1965, 1989.

Colours
Claret and amber shirts, claret shorts, amber stockings.

Change Colours
White shirts, shorts and stockings with claret and amber trim.

Year Formed: 1903.

Turned Professional: 1903.

Ltd Co.: 1908.

Club Nickname: 'The Bantams'.

First Football League Game: 1 September 1903, Division 2, v Grimsby T (a) L 0–2 – Seymour; Wilson, Halliday; Robinson, Millar, Farnall; Guy, Beckram, Forrest, McMillan, Graham.

Record League Victory: 11–1 v Rotherham U, Division 3 (N), 25 August 1928 – Sherlaw; Russell, Watson; Burkinshaw (1), Summers, Bauld; Harvey (2), Edmunds (3), White (3), Cairns, Scriven (2).

Record Cup Victory: 11–3 v Walker Celtic, FA Cup 1st rd (replay), 1 December 1937 – Parker; Rookes, McDermott; Murphy, Mackie, Moore; Bagley (1), Whittingham (1), Deakin (4 incl. 1p), Cooke (1), Bartholomew (4).

Record Defeat: 1–9 v Colchester U, Division 4, 30 December 1961.

Most League Points (2 for a win): 63, Division 3 (N), 1928–29.

Most League Points (3 for a win): 94, Division 3, 1984–85.

Most League Goals: 128, Division 3 (N), 1928–29.

Highest League Scorer in Season: David Layne, 34, Division 4, 1961–62.

Most League Goals in Total Aggregate: Bobby Campbell, 121, 1981–84, 1984–86.

Most League Goals in One Match: 7, Albert Whitehurst v Tranmere R, Division 3N, 6 March 1929.

Most Capped Player: Harry Hampton, 9, Northern Ireland.

Most League Appearances: Cec Podd, 502, 1970–84.

Youngest League Player: Robert Cullingford, 16 years 141 days v Mansfield T, 22 April 1970.

MANAGERS

Robert Campbell 1903–05
Peter O'Rourke 1905–21
David Menzies 1921–26
Colin Veitch 1926–28
Peter O'Rourke 1928–30
Jack Peart 1930–35
Dick Ray 1935–37
Fred Westgarth 1938–43
Bob Sharp 1943–46
Jack Barker 1946–47
John Milburn 1947–48
David Steele 1948–52
Albert Harris 1952
Ivor Powell 1952–55
Peter Jackson 1955–61
Bob Brocklebank 1961–64
Bill Harris 1965–66
Willie Watson 1966–69
Grenville Hair 1967–68
Jimmy Wheeler 1968–71
Bryan Edwards 1971–75
Bobby Kennedy 1975–78
John Napier 1978
George Mulhall 1978–81
Roy McFarland 1981–82
Trevor Cherry 1982–87
Terry Dolan 1987–89
Terry Yorath 1989–90
John Docherty 1990–91
Frank Stapleton 1991–94
Lennie Lawrence 1994–95
Chris Kamara 1995–98
Paul Jewell 1998–2000
Chris Hutchings June 2000–

Record Transfer Fee Received: £2,000,000 from Newcastle U for Des Hamilton, March 1997.

Record Transfer Fee Paid: £1,400,000 to Leeds U for David Wetherall, July 1999.

Football League Record: 1903 Elected to Division 2; 1908–22 Division 1; 1922–27 Division 2; 1927–29 Division 3 (N); 1929–37 Division 2; 1937–61 Division 3; 1961–69 Division 4; 1969–72 Division 3; 1972–77 Division 4; 1977–78 Division 3; 1978–82 Division 4; 1982–85 Division 3; 1985–90 Division 2; 1990–92 Division 3; 1992–96 Division 2; 1996–99 Division 1; 1999– FA Premier League.

TEN YEAR LEAGUE RECORD

		P	W	D	L	F	A	Pts	Pos
1989-90	Div 2	46	9	14	23	44	68	41	23
1990-91	Div 3	46	20	10	16	62	54	70	8
1991-92	Div 3	46	13	19	14	62	61	58	16
1992-93	Div 2	46	18	14	14	69	67	68	10
1993-94	Div 2	46	19	13	14	61	53	70	7
1994-95	Div 2	46	16	12	18	57	64	60	14
1995-96	Div 2	46	22	7	17	71	69	73	6
1996-97	Div 1	46	12	12	22	47	72	48	21
1997-98	Div 1	46	14	15	17	46	59	57	13
1998-99	Div 1	46	26	9	11	82	47	87	2

DID YOU KNOW

In their first League Cup tie, Third Division Bradford City beat First Division Manchester United 2-1 in a second round match on 2 November 1960. United declined to enter the competition again until the 1966-67 season.

BRADFORD CITY 1999–2000 LEAGUE RECORD

Match No.	Date		Venue	Opponents	Result		H/T Score	Lg. Pos.	Goalscorers	Attendance
1	Aug	7	A	Middlesbrough	W	1-0	0-0	6	Saunders [89]	33,762
2		14	H	Sheffield W	D	1-1	0-1	9	Beagrie (pen) [89]	18,276
3		21	A	Watford	L	0-1	0-0	13		15,564
4		25	A	Arsenal	L	0-2	0-2	—		38,073
5		28	H	West Ham U	L	0-3	0-2	18		17,936
6	Sept	12	H	Tottenham H	D	1-1	0-0	18	McCall [90]	18,143
7		18	A	Aston Villa	L	0-1	0-0	18		28,083
8		25	A	Derby Co	W	1-0	0-0	17	Carbonari (og) [66]	31,035
9	Oct	2	H	Sunderland	L	0-4	0-1	18		18,204
10		16	A	Wimbledon	L	2-3	1-2	18	Mills [45], Windass [90]	10,029
11		23	H	Leicester C	W	3-1	2-1	16	Blake [12], Mills [40], Redfearn [66]	17,655
12	Nov	1	A	Liverpool	L	1-3	1-2	—	Windass [12]	40,483
13		6	H	Coventry C	D	1-1	1-1	17	Mills [43]	17,587
14		20	A	Leeds U	L	1-2	0-0	17	Windass [90]	39,937
15		28	A	Chelsea	L	0-1	0-1	17		31,591
16	Dec	4	H	Middlesbrough	D	1-1	0-1	17	Mills [60]	17,708
17		18	H	Newcastle U	W	2-0	0-0	17	Saunders [56], Wetherall [71]	18,276
18		26	A	Manchester U	L	0-4	0-0	17		55,188
19		28	H	Everton	D	0-0	0-0	17		18,276
20	Jan	3	A	Southampton	L	0-1	0-0	18		15,027
21		8	H	Chelsea	D	1-1	1-0	18	Mills [1]	18,276
22		15	A	Sheffield W	L	0-2	0-0	18		24,682
23		22	H	Watford	W	3-2	2-1	18	Beagrie (pen) [25], Whalley [37], O'Brien [49]	16,864
24	Feb	5	H	Arsenal	W	2-1	1-1	18	Windass [10], Saunders [57]	18,276
25		12	A	West Ham U	L	4-5	2-2	18	Windass [30], Beagrie (pen) [45], Lawrence 2 [47, 51]	25,417
26		26	H	Aston Villa	D	1-1	0-1	18	Windass [76]	18,276
27	Mar	4	A	Tottenham H	D	1-1	1-1	18	Lawrence [42]	35,472
28		12	H	Leeds U	L	1-2	0-1	18	Beagrie [75]	18,276
29		18	H	Coventry C	L	0-4	0-2	18		19,194
30		25	H	Manchester U	L	0-4	0-2	18		18,276
31	Apr	1	A	Newcastle U	L	0-2	0-1	18		36,572
32		8	H	Southampton	L	1-2	0-0	18	Blake [77]	17,439
33		15	A	Everton	L	0-4	0-2	19		31,646
34		21	H	Derby Co	D	4-4	4-3	—	Windass 3 [11, 18, 44], Beagrie (pen) [27]	18,276
35		24	A	Sunderland	W	1-0	0-0	18	Dreyer [60]	39,663
36		30	H	Wimbledon	W	3-0	1-0	17	Beagrie 2 (1 pen) [43 (p), 50], Windass [83]	18,276
37	May	6	A	Leicester C	L	0-3	0-0	18		21,103
38		14	H	Liverpool	W	1-0	1-0	17	Wetherall [13]	18,276

Final League Position: 17

GOALSCORERS

League (38): Windass 10, Beagrie 7 (5 pens), Mills 5, Lawrence 3, Saunders 3, Blake 2, Wetherall 2, Dreyer 1, McCall 1, O'Brien 1, Redfearn 1, Whalley 1, own goal 1.
Worthington Cup (5): Wetherall 2, Blake 1 (pen), Mills 1, Saunders 1.
FA Cup (3): Saunders 2, Blake 1.

Walsh G 11	Halle G 37+1	Jacobs W 22+2	O'Brien A 36	Wetherall D 38	Dreyer J 11+3	Redfearn N 14+3	Windass D 36+2	Mills L 19+2	Whalley G 16	Beagrie P 30+5	Saunders D 28+6	Lawrence J 19+4	Grant G —+1	Blake R 15+13	McCall S 33+1	Myers A 10+3	Rodriguez B —+2	Westwood A 1+4	Sharpe L 13+5	Clarke M 21	Rankin I —+9	Davison A 5+1	Cadete J 2+5	Southall N 1	Match No.
1	2	3	4	5	6	7	8^1	9	10	11	12														1
1	2	3		5	6	7	8	9	10	11	12				4^1										2
1	2	3		5	6	7^2	8	9	10	11	12			13	4^1										3
1	2^2	3	4	5	6	8	10	11	9	7^1	12			13											4
1	2	3	4^2	5	6	12	8^1	13	10	11	9^3	7		14											5
1	2	3^2		5	6		8^1	9	10	11	12	7^3	14	13	4										6
1	2		6	5		8	9^1	10	11	7	12	3			4										7
1	2	12	6	5		13	9	10	11^3	7^1	8^2	3	14		4										8
1	2		6	5		8	9	11	7	10		3			4										9
1	2	3	6	5		7	8	9	12	10					4						11^1				10
1	2		6	5		7	8	9	11^1	12	10	3			4										11
	2^1		6	5		7^2	8	9	11	12	10	3		13	4					1					12
	2^1		6	5		7	8	9	13	11^2	12	3	14		4	10^3				1					13
	2		6	5		7^1	8	9	10^2	3	12	13		11	4					1					14
	2		6	5		7	8	9^2	10^1	11	4	3		13	12					1					15
	12		6	5		7	8^1	9	11^2	2	10	3		13	4					1					16
	2		6	5		8	9	12	10	7	3	11^1			4					1					17
	2		6	5		10^1	8	9	13	12	7^2	3	14	11	4	3^1				1					18
	2		6	5		7	8^2	9	12	10	13	3^1		11	4					1					19
	2^3		6	5		12	8	9^1	11	10	7	13	14	3^2	4					1					20
	2		6	5		7	8^1	9	12	11	10	3			4					1					21
	2		6	5		8	12	13	11^2	9	7	3		10	4^1					1					22
	2	3	6	5		12	8	10^1	11	9^2	7	13		15	4					1^6					23
	2	3	6	5	12	8^1	10	11	9	7	4									1					24
	2	3	6	5		8	10	11	9	7	4									1					25
	2	3	6	5		8	10^2	11	9	7^1	12	13			4					1					26
	2	3	6	5	12	8	10^1	11	9^2	7	13				4					1					27
	2^2	3	6	5		8	10^1	11	9	7	12	13			4					1					28
	2^1	3	6	5		8	10^3	11	9	7	12	14			4			13		1					29
	2^2	3	6	5		8	10^1	11	9	7	12	13			4			10^1		1					30
	2	3	6	5	8^2	7	11	9	12		13	10^1			4					1					31
	2	3	6	5		8	11	9	12	10^1		7			4					1					32
	2	3^1	6	5	12	8	11	9^2	10	7	13				4					1					33
	2	3^2	6	9	7	8	11	12	10	5^1	13				4					1					34
	2	3	6	5	7	8	11^2	9^3	10^1	12	13	14			4					1					35
	2	3	6	5		8	7	11	9	10^1	12				4					1					36
	2	3^2	6	5		8^1	7	11^3	9	12	10	13	14		4					1					37
	2	12	6	5	10	8	11^1	9^2	7		13	3			4									1	38

Worthington Cup

Second Round	Reading	(h)	1-1
		(a)	2-2
Third Round	Barnsley	(h)	2-3

FA Cup

Third Round	Crewe Alex	(a)	2-1
Fourth Round	Gillingham	(a)	1-3

Division 2 **BRENTFORD**

FOUNDATION

Formed as a small amateur concern in 1889 they were very successful in local circles. They won the championship of the West London Alliance in 1893 and a year later the West Middlesex Junior Cup before carrying off the Senior Cup in 1895. After winning both the London Senior Amateur Cup and the Middlesex Senior Cup in 1898 they were admitted to the Second Division of the Southern League.

Griffin Park, Braemar Rd, Brentford, Middlesex TW8 0NT.
Telephone: (020) 8847 2511.
Fax: (020) 8568 9940.
Commercial Dept: (020) 8847 2511
Press Office: (020) 8847 2511.
ClubCall: 09068 121 108.
Ground Capacity: 12,763.
Record Attendance: 38,678 v Leicester C, FA Cup 6th rd, 26 February 1949.
Record Receipts: £162,314 v Tottenham H, Worthington Cup 2nd rd, 15 September 1998.
Pitch Measurements: 111yd × 74yd.
Chairman: Ron Noades.
President: E. J. Radley-Smith.
Managing Director: G. Hargraves.
Directors: S. R. Ebbs MS FRCS, J. Herting, D. Miller, E. Rogers, D. Tana.
Manager: Ron Noades.
First Team Coach: Ray Lewington.
Director of Youth Football: Geoff Taylor.
Coaches: Terry Bullivant, Ray Lewington, Wally Downes.
Youth Coach: Bob Booker.
Community Officer: Lee Doyle.
Secretary: Polly Kates.
Physio: Gerry Delahunt.
Safety Officer: Jill Dawson.
Communications Manager: Peter Gilham.
Corporate Sales Manager: Samantha Marmara.

LATEST SEQUENCES
Longest Sequence of League Wins: 9, 30.4.32 – 24.9.32.
Longest Sequence of League Defeats: 9, 20.10.28 – 25.12.28.
Longest Sequence of League Draws: 5, 16.3.57 – 6.4.57.
Longest Sequence of Unbeaten League Matches: 26, 20.2.99 – 16.10.99.
Longest Sequence Without a League Win: 16, 19.2.94 – 7.5.94.

HONOURS

Football League: Division 1 best season: 5th, 1935–36; Division 2 – Champions 1934–35; Division 3 – Champions 1991–92, 1998–99; Division 3 (S) – Champions 1932–33, Runners-up 1929–30, 1957–58; Division 4 – Champions 1962–63.

FA Cup: best season: 6th rd, 1938, 1946, 1949, 1989.

Football League Cup: best season: 4th rd, 1983.

Freight Rover Trophy: Runners-up 1985.

Colours
Red and white vertical striped shirts, black shorts, black stockings.

Change Colours
Blue and yellow shirts, blue shorts, yellow stockings.

Year Formed: 1889.

Turned Professional: 1899.

Ltd Co.: 1901.

Club Nickname: 'The Bees'.

Previous Grounds: 1889, Clifden Road; 1891, Benns Fields, Little Ealing; 1895, Shotters Field; 1898, Cross Road, S. Ealing; 1900, Boston Park; 1904, Griffin Park.

First Football League Game: 28 August 1920, Division 3, v Exeter C (a) L 0–3 – Young; Hodson, Rosier, Elliott J, Levitt, Amos, Smith, Thompson, Spreadbury, Morley, Henery.

Record League Victory: 9–0 v Wrexham, Division 3, 15 October 1963 – Cakebread; Coote, Jones; Slater, Scott, Higginson; Summers (1), Brooks (2), McAdams (2), Ward (2), Hales (1), (1 og).

Record Cup Victory: 7–0 v Windsor & Eton (away), FA Cup 1st rd, 20 November 1982 – Roche; Rowe, Harris (Booker), McNichol (1), Whitehead, Hurlock (2), Kamara, Joseph (1), Mahoney (3), Bowles, Roberts.

Record Defeat: 0–7 v Swansea T, Division 3 (S), 8 November 1924 and v Walsall, Division 3 (S), 19 January 1957.

Most League Points (2 for a win): 62, Division 3 (S), 1932–33 and Division 4, 1962–63.

Most League Points (3 for a win): 85, Division 2, 1994–95 and Division 3, 1998–99.

Most League Goals: 98, Division 4, 1962–63.

Highest League Scorer in Season: Jack Holliday, 38, Division 3 (S), 1932–33.

MANAGERS

Will Lewis 1900–03
(Secretary-Manager)
Dick Molyneux 1903–06
W. G. Brown 1906–08
Fred Halliday 1908–26
(only Secretary to 1922)
Ephraim Rhodes 1912–15
Archie Mitchell 1921–22
Harry Curtis 1926–49
Jackie Gibbons 1949–52
Jimmy Blain 1952–53
Tommy Lawton 1953
Bill Dodgin Snr 1953–57
Malcolm Macdonald 1957–65
Tommy Cavanagh 1965–66
Billy Gray 1966–67
Jimmy Sirrel 1967–69
Frank Blunstone 1969–73
Mike Everitt 1973–75
John Docherty 1975–76
Bill Dodgin Jnr 1976–80
Fred Callaghan 1980–84
Frank McLintock 1984–87
Steve Perryman 1987–90
Phil Holder 1990–93
David Webb 1993–97
Micky Adams 1997–98
Ron Noades July 1998–

Most League Goals in Total Aggregate: Jim Towers, 153, 1954–61.

Most League Goals in One Match: 5, Jack Holliday v Luton T, Division 3S, 28 January 1933; Billy Scott v Barnsley, Division 2, 15 December 1934; Peter McKennan v Bury, Division 2, 18 February 1949.

Most Capped Player: John Buttigieg, 22 (85), Malta.

Most League Appearances: Ken Coote, 514, 1949–64.

Youngest League Player: Danis Salman, 15 years 243 days v Watford, 15 November 1975.

Record Transfer Fee Received: £720,000 from Wimbledon for Dean Holdsworth, August 1992.

Record Transfer Fee Paid: £850,000 to Crystal Palace for Hermann Hreidarsson, September 1998.

Football League Record: 1920 Original Member of Division 3; 1921–33 Division 3 (S); 1933–35 Division 2; 1935–47 Division 1; 1947–54 Division 2; 1954–62 Division 3 (S); 1962–63 Division 4; 1963–66 Division 3; 1966–72 Division 4; 1972–73 Division 3; 1973–78 Division 4; 1978–92 Division 3; 1992–93 Division 1; 1993–98 Division 2; 1998 –99 Division 3; 1999– Division 2.

TEN YEAR LEAGUE RECORD

		P	W	D	L	F	A	Pts	Pos
1989-90	Div 3	46	18	7	21	66	66	61	13
1990-91	Div 3	46	21	13	12	59	47	76	6
1991-92	Div 3	46	25	7	14	81	55	82	1
1992-93	Div 1	46	13	10	23	52	71	49	22
1993-94	Div 2	46	13	19	14	57	55	58	16
1994-95	Div 2	46	25	10	11	81	39	85	2
1995-96	Div 2	46	15	13	18	43	49	58	15
1996-97	Div 2	46	20	14	12	56	43	74	4
1997-98	Div 2	46	11	17	18	50	71	50	21
1998-99	Div 3	46	26	7	13	79	56	85	1

DID YOU KNOW ?

Brentford fielded their youngest team when they defeated Aldershot 1-0 on 11 October 1966. They included three teenagers, two 20 year olds and one aged 21. But the 78th minute goal was scored by Ian Lawther, aged 27.

BRENTFORD 1999–2000 LEAGUE RECORD

Match No.	Date		Venue	Opponents	Result		H/T Score	Lg. Pos.	Goalscorers	Attendance
1	Aug	7	A	Bristol R	D	0-0	0-0	13		8514
2		14	H	Oldham Ath	W	2-0	0-0	4	Bryan [63], Hreidarsson [87]	5074
3		21	A	Bury	D	2-2	1-1	8	Partridge [44], Rowlands [83]	3491
4		28	H	Blackpool	W	2-0	2-0	5	Hreidarsson [11], Evans [33]	5353
5	Sept	11	A	Cambridge U	D	2-2	2-0	10	Scott [6], Evans [17]	4234
6		18	H	Luton T	W	2-0	0-0	8	Powell [55], Partridge [72]	7039
7		25	H	Preston NE	D	2-2	1-0	8	Partridge [43], Evans [73]	7100
8		28	H	Cardiff C	W	2-1	1-0	—	Scott [28], Owusu [66]	5247
9	Oct	2	A	Burnley	D	2-2	0-2	4	Partridge [54], Evans [80]	10,907
10		16	H	Oxford U	W	2-0	0-0	5	Owusu [66], Powell [88]	6237
11		19	H	Gillingham	L	1-2	0-2	—	Owusu [58]	6264
12		23	A	Preston NE	L	1-2	1-0	9	Mahon [4]	10,382
13		26	A	Notts Co	W	1-0	0-0	—	Evans [74]	5075
14	Nov	2	H	Reading	D	1-1	0-1	—	Folan [74]	6774
15		6	A	Wrexham	W	1-0	1-0	7	Marshall [22]	2473
16		12	H	Scunthorpe U	W	4-3	2-2	4	Partridge [30], Owusu 2 [33, 85], Mahon [57]	4657
17		19	A	Colchester U	W	3-0	0-0	—	Partridge [60], Owusu [65], Rowlands [90]	3464
18		23	A	Bournemouth	L	1-4	1-2	—	Owusu [27]	4202
19		27	A	Wycombe W	L	0-2	0-1	9		5879
20	Dec	4	H	Bristol R	L	0-3	0-1	9		6843
21		10	H	Chesterfield	D	1-1	1-0	—	Owusu [15]	4286
22		18	A	Wigan Ath	L	0-1	0-0	9		5498
23		26	H	Bristol C	W	2-1	0-0	9	Owusu [46], Rowlands [51]	6942
24		28	A	Millwall	L	2-3	0-0	9	Mahon [50], Rowlands [86]	12,077
25	Jan	3	H	Stoke C	L	0-1	0-0	9		6792
26		8	A	Chesterfield	L	0-1	0-0	9		2746
27		15	A	Oldham Ath	L	0-3	0-1	9		4967
28		22	H	Bury	W	2-1	0-0	9	Scott [50], Rowlands [66]	5605
29		29	A	Blackpool	W	1-0	1-0	8	Ingimarsson [10]	5270
30	Feb	5	H	Notts Co	L	0-2	0-1	9		5106
31		12	A	Cardiff C	D	1-1	1-0	9	Rowlands [26]	5478
32		19	H	Wycombe W	D	0-0	0-0	9		5981
33		26	A	Luton T	W	2-1	1-1	9	Owusu [45], Evans [62]	6029
34	Mar	4	H	Cambridge U	D	1-1	0-1	9	Evans (pen) [84]	4987
35		7	H	Wrexham	L	0-2	0-0	—		4055
36		11	A	Reading	L	0-1	0-0	9		11,427
37		18	H	Bournemouth	L	0-2	0-1	9		4578
38		21	A	Scunthorpe U	D	0-0	0-0	—		2686
39		25	A	Bristol C	L	0-1	0-0	12		8804
40	Apr	1	H	Wigan Ath	L	0-2	0-2	13		4479
41		8	A	Stoke C	L	0-1	0-1	15		9955
42		15	H	Millwall	L	1-3	1-2	15	Pinamonte [4]	6779
43		22	A	Oxford U	D	1-1	0-1	17	Owusu [46]	5342
44		24	A	Burnley	L	2-3	1-0	17	Owusu [43], Marshall [90]	6595
45		29	A	Gillingham	L	0-2	0-1	17		9001
46	May	6	H	Colchester U	D	0-0	0-0	17		5297

Final League Position: 17

GOALSCORERS

League (47): Owusu 12, Evans 7 (1 pen), Partridge 6, Rowlands 6, Mahon 3, Scott 3, Hreidarsson 2, Marshall 2, Powell 2, Bryan 1, Folan 1, Ingimarsson 1, Pinamonte 1.
Worthington Cup (0).
FA Cup (3): Marshall 1, Owusu 1, Quinn 1.

Woodman A 39	Boxall D 25	Anderson I 30 + 1	Quinn R 42 + 2	Powell D 36	Hreidarsson H 8	Evans P 33	Mahon G 37	Owusu L 39 + 2	Partridge S 38 + 3	Scott A 32 + 4	Rowlands M 38 + 2	Jenkins S 2 + 3	Bryan D 5 + 13	Folan T 1 + 8	Warner P 1 + 13	Theobald D 6 + 4	Kennedy R 4 + 5	Marshall S 22	Agyemang P 3 + 9	Ingimarsson I 21 + 4	Clement N 7 + 1	Graham G 5 + 8	Charles J — + 2	Einarsson G 1 + 2	Jones S 6 + 2	Pearcey J 6	Pinamonte L 5 + 10	Hutchings C 7 + 1	O'Connor K 6	Glass J 1 + 1	James C — + 1	Saroya N — + 1	Match No
1	2	3	4	5¹	6	7	8	9	10²	11³	12	13	14																				1
1	2	3	4¹	5	6	7	8	9²	10	11	12	13																					2
1	2	3	4	5		7	8	10¹	11	6	12	9																					3
1	2	3		5	6	7	8	10	11²	4									9¹	12	13												4
1		3	4	5	6	7	8	10	11	2									9¹	12													5
1		3	4	5	6	7	8¹	9²	10	11	2	13	12																				6
1		2	4	5	6	7	8	9	10	11¹	3		12																				7
1		2	4	5	6	7	8	9¹	10	11²	3³		12						14	13													8
1		2¹	4	5	6	7	8	9²	10	11	3³		12						14	13													9
1	2		14	6		7	8	9	10	11	3¹		13³	4²	12					5													10
1	2		4²	5		7	8	9	10	11	3¹				12					6	13												11
1	2		4	5		7	8	9²	10	11¹	3				12					6	13												12
1	2		4	5¹		7	8	9	10	11				3					12	6													13
1	2		4¹	5		7	8	9	10	11	3²				12					6	13												14
1	2		4	5		7²	8	9	10	11	3¹		12						13	6													15
1	2	3	4			8	9	10	11	6								12		5	7¹												16
1	2	3¹	4			8	9	10	11²	6	12		14					5	13³	7													17
1	2	3				8	9	10	6²					7¹		13	5	12	11	4													18
1	2		4			7	9	10	6							12	8	5	11¹	3													19
1	2		4			7	8	9	10		3		6¹	12				5	11														20
1	2		4			7	8²	9	10			6	11¹	12				5	13	3													21
1	2		4				8	9	10	6²		7¹						5	12	11	3	13											22
1		4				7	8	9¹	10²	6					2			5	12	11	3	13	13										23
1	2¹	4				7²	8	9	10	6						12		5	13³	11	3	14											24
1	12	4	5				8	9	10²						2	14	6³	7	11	3¹													25
1	3²	4	5				8	9	10³	6¹	12				2	7	14	11	13														26
1	2		4	5			8	9	12	6	13				3¹	7³	10	11²			14												27
1	2	3	4	5		7¹	8		10³	6	13	12						11			14	9²											28
	2	3	4	5		7		12²	9¹	10	6				13			11				8	1										29
1	2	3	4	5		7			10²	6					12			11		13	8	9¹											30
1	2	3		5		7	8	11	10	6								11¹			9²	13	4										31
1	2	3	4	5			8	9		6							13	11²		12	10¹	7											32
1	2¹	3	4	5		7	8	9	13	12	6							11			10²												33
1		3	4	5		7	6	9	10	12								11²			2³	8¹	13	14									34
1		3	4	5		7¹	8	9	10³	12	3						13	11²			13	1	14	6									35
	2		4			7²	8	9	12	10³	3							11			13	1	14	6	5¹								36
	2	12	5			7²	9	10	8³	6							13	11			1	14	4	3³									37
	2	4	5			8	9	10²	11	3								12	7¹		1	13	6										38
	2	4	5			8¹	9	10³	11	3						13		12²	7		1	14	6										39
	2	4	5			7		9	12	11	3					8²					1⁶	13	6	10¹	15								40
1		3	4	5		7		9²	10	11	8²					2¹	6		12			13				14							41
1		2	4	5			9	10	11	3							6				7		8										42
1			4	5		7		9¹	10	11						12	2²	6	13	3¹			8								14		43
1			4	5		7		9¹	11	10						12		6	3²	13			8										44
1		2	4	5		7		9	10	11						12	13	6					3²					8¹					45
		2	4	5		7		9	10	11³	3²					12		6			13			14			8¹	1					46

Worthington Cup
First Round   Ipswich T   (h) 0-2
                                (a) 0-2

FA Cup
First Round   Plymouth Arg   (h) 2-2
                                      (a) 1-2

Division 3   **BRIGHTON & HOVE ALBION**

FOUNDATION

A professional club Brighton United was formed in November 1897 at the Imperial Hotel, Queen's Road, but folded in March 1900 after less than two seasons in the Southern League at the County Ground. An amateur team, Brighton & Hove Rangers was then formed by some prominent United supporters and after one season at Withdean, decided to turn semi-professional and play at the County Ground. Rangers were accepted into the Southern League but then also folded June 1901. John Jackson the former United manager organised a meeting at the Seven Stars public house, Ship Street on 24 June 1901 at which a new third club Brighton & Hove United was formed. They took over Rangers' place in the Southern League and pitch at County Ground. The name was changed to Brighton & Hove Albion before a match was played because of objections by Hove FC.

Offices: Fifth floor, Hanover House, 118 Queens Road, Brighton BN1 3XG.
Telephone: (01273) 778 855.
Fax: (01273) 321 095.
Ground Address: Withdean Stadium, Tongdean Lane, Brighton BN1 5JD.
ClubCall: 09068 800 609.
Ground Capacity: 6960.
Record Attendance: 36,747 v Fulham, Division 2, 27 December 1958.
Record Receipts: £109,615.65 v Crawley T, FA Cup 3rd rd, 4 January 1992.
Pitch Measurements: 110yd × 70yd.
Directors: H. R. Knight (Chairman), Ray Bloom, Derek Chapman, M. J. Perry, R. L. Pinnock FCA.
Non-Executive Directors: R. O. Faulkner, Sir John Smith QPM.
Manager: Micky Adams.
Assistant Manager: Alan Cork.
Chief Executive: Martin Perry.
Secretary: Derek Allan.
Physio: Malcolm Stuart.
Youth Development Officer: Martin Hinshelwood.
Youth Team Coach: Dean Wilkins.

LATEST SEQUENCES
Longest Sequence of League Wins: 9, 2.10.26 – 20.11.26.
Longest Sequence of League Defeats: 12, 11.11.72 – 27.1.73.
Longest Sequence of League Draws: 6, 16.2.80 – 15.3.80.
Longest Sequence of Unbeaten League Matches: 16, 8.10.30 – 28.1.31.
Longest Sequence Without a League Win: 15, 21.10.72 – 27.1.73

HONOURS

Football League: Division 1 best season: 13th, 1981–82; Division 2 – Runners-up 1978–79; Division 3 (S) – Champions 1957–58; Runners-up 1953–54, 1955–56; Division 3 – Runners-up 1971–72, 1976–77, 1987–88; Division 4 – Champions 1964–65.

FA Cup: Runners-up 1983.

Football League Cup: best season: 5th rd, 1979.

Colours
Blue and white striped shirts, white shorts, blue stockings.

Change Colours
Red and black striped shirts, black shorts, black stockings.

Year Formed: 1901.

Turned Professional: 1901.

Ltd Co.: 1904.

Previous Grounds: 1901, County Ground; 1902, Goldstone Ground.

Club Nickname: 'The Seagulls'.

First Football League Game: 28 August 1920, Division 3, v Southend U (a) L 0–2 – Hayes; Woodhouse, Little; Hall, Comber, Bentley; Longstaff, Ritchie, Doran, Rodgerson, March.

Record League Victory: 9–1 v Newport Co, Division 3 (S), 18 April 1951 – Ball; Tennant (1p), Mansell (1p); Willard, McCoy, Wilson; Reed, McNichol (4), Garbutt, Bennett (2), Keene (1). 9–1 v Southend U, Division 3, 27 November 1965 – Powney; Magill, Baxter; Leck, Gall, Turner; Gould (1), Collins (1), Livesey (2), Smith (3), Goodchild (3).

Record Cup Victory: 10–1 v Wisbech, FA Cup 1st rd, 13 November 1965 – Powney; Magill, Baxter; Collins (1), Gall, Turner; Gould, Smith (2), Livesey (3), Cassidy (2), Goodchild (1), (1 og).

Record Defeat: 0–9 v Middlesbrough, Division 2, 23 August 1958.

Most League Points (2 for a win): 65, Division 3 (S), 1955–56 and Division 3, 1971–72.

Most League Points (3 for a win): 84, Division 3, 1987–88.

Most League Goals: 112, Division 3 (S), 1955–56.

Highest League Scorer in Season: Peter Ward, 32, Division 3, 1976–77.

Most League Goals in Total Aggregate: Tommy Cook, 114, 1922–29.

Most League Goals in One Match: 5, Jack Doran v Northampton T, Division 3S, 5 November 1921; 5, Adrian Thorne v Watford, Division 3S, 30 April 1958.

Most Capped Player: Steve Penney, 17, Northern Ireland.

Most League Appearances: 'Tug' Wilson, 509, 1922–36.

Youngest League Player: Ian Chapman, 16 years 259 days v Birmingham C, 14 February 1987.

Record Transfer Fee Received: £900,000 from Liverpool for Mark Lawrenson, August 1981.

Record Transfer Fee Paid: £500,000 to Manchester U for Andy Ritchie, October 1980.

Football League Record: 1920 Original Member of Division 3; 1921–58 Division 3 (S); 1958–62 Division 2; 1962–63 Division 3; 1963–65 Division 4; 1965–72 Division 3; 1972–73 Division 2; 1973–77 Division 3; 1977–79 Division 2; 1979–83 Division 1; 1983–87 Division 2; 1987–88 Division 3; 1988–96 Division 2; 1996– Division 3.

MANAGERS

John Jackson 1901–05
Frank Scott-Walford 1905–08
John Robson 1908–14
Charles Webb 1919–47
Tommy Cook 1947
Don Welsh 1947–51
Billy Lane 1951–61
George Curtis 1961–63
Archie Macaulay 1963–68
Fred Goodwin 1968–70
Pat Saward 1970–73
Brian Clough 1973–74
Peter Taylor 1974–76
Alan Mullery 1976–81
Mike Bailey 1981–82
Jimmy Melia 1982–83
Chris Cattlin 1983–86
Alan Mullery 1986–87
Barry Lloyd 1987–93
Liam Brady 1993–95
Jimmy Case 1995–96
Steve Gritt 1996–98
Brian Horton 1998–99
Jeff Wood 1999
Micky Adams February 1999–

TEN YEAR LEAGUE RECORD

		P	W	D	L	F	A	Pts	Pos
1989-90	Div 2	46	15	9	22	56	72	54	18
1990-91	Div 2	46	21	7	18	63	69	70	6
1991-92	Div 2	46	12	11	23	56	77	47	23
1992-93	Div 2	46	20	9	17	63	59	69	9
1993-94	Div 2	46	15	14	17	60	67	59	14
1994-95	Div 2	46	14	17	15	54	53	59	16
1995-96	Div 2	46	10	10	26	46	69	40	23
1996-97	Div 3	46	13	10	23	53	70	47	23
1997-98	Div 3	46	6	17	23	38	66	35	23
1998-99	Div 3	46	16	7	23	49	66	55	17

DID YOU KNOW

The first Football League goal of the New Millennium was scored by Darren Freeman, after 100 seconds of the match with Exeter City on 3 January. Brighton won 4-2.

BRIGHTON & HOVE ALBION 1999–2000 LEAGUE RECORD

Match No.	Date	Venue	Opponents	Result	H/T Score	Lg. Pos.	Goalscorers	Attendance
1	Aug 7	H	Mansfield T	W 6-0	2-0	1	Freeman 3 [14, 20, 70], Thomas [56], Newhouse 2 [79, 86]	5882
2	14	A	Leyton Orient	W 2-1	1-0	1	Crosby [20], Rogers [55]	7200
3	21	H	Torquay U	L 0-1	0-0	6		5717
4	28	A	Darlington	D 1-1	1-1	9	Hart [29]	6174
5	31	H	Hull C	W 3-0	1-0	—	Watson [11], Freeman (pen) [54], Crosby [75]	5856
6	Sept 5	A	Plymouth Arg	D 3-3	2-2	7	Freeman [17], Oatway 2 [44, 66]	5444
7	11	A	Halifax T	L 1-2	0-0	10	Freeman (pen) [49]	2532
8	18	H	Chester C	L 2-3	0-0	11	Hart [55], Cullip [83]	5810
9	25	H	Cheltenham T	W 1-0	0-0	8	Rogers [90]	5705
10	Oct 2	H	Peterborough U	D 0-0	0-0	10		7823
11	9	A	Carlisle U	W 1-0	0-0	6	Aspinall [73]	3059
12	16	H	York C	L 0-1	0-0	11		5862
13	19	H	Shrewsbury T	W 1-0	1-0	—	Hart [3]	5767
14	23	A	Cheltenham T	D 0-0	0-0	7		4050
15	Nov 2	A	Southend U	L 1-2	1-0	—	Watson [23]	4927
16	6	H	Hartlepool U	W 1-0	1-0	9	Campbell [6]	5746
17	14	A	Macclesfield T	D 1-1	0-0	11	Mayo [87]	2920
18	23	H	Lincoln C	D 2-2	1-1	—	Oatway [41], Rogers [62]	5714
19	27	H	Northampton T	L 1-3	1-1	12	Aspinall [31]	5935
20	Dec 10	H	Rochdale	L 3-4	2-2	—	Aspinall [39], Cullip [44], Hart [57]	5049
21	18	A	Swansea C	L 0-2	0-1	15		4555
22	26	H	Barnet	D 1-1	0-0	15	Watson [81]	5739
23	28	A	Rotherham U	W 3-1	0-0	15	Freeman [26], Oatway [53], Rogers [84]	5924
24	Jan 3	H	Exeter C	W 4-2	2-0	13	Freeman [2], Pinamonte 2 [45, 61], Rogers [76]	5746
25	8	A	Rochdale	L 0-1	0-1	14		2596
26	15	H	Leyton Orient	L 0-1	0-0	14		5863
27	22	A	Torquay U	D 0-0	0-0	14		2760
28	29	H	Darlington	D 1-1	0-0	16	Hart [69]	5715
29	Feb 1	A	Mansfield T	L 0-1	0-0	—		2541
30	5	A	Hull C	L 0-2	0-0	17		5167
31	12	H	Plymouth Arg	D 1-1	0-1	18	Zamora [49]	5654
32	19	A	Northampton T	L 0-1	0-1	18		5974
33	26	A	Chester C	W 7-1	2-0	18	Zamora 3 (1 pen) [18, 21, 54 (p)], McPherson [49], Brooker [52], Freeman [68], Rogers [88]	2743
34	Mar 4	H	Halifax T	W 2-1	0-1	17	Zamora 2 [65, 77]	5311
35	7	A	Hartlepool U	D 0-0	0-0	—		2734
36	11	H	Southend U	W 1-0	0-0	15	Hart [90]	5844
37	18	A	Lincoln C	W 3-1	1-0	15	Freeman [44], Rogers 2 [66, 79]	4288
38	21	H	Macclesfield T	W 5-2	2-2	—	Hart [21], Freeman 2 (1 pen) [45 (p), 48], Ramsay 2 [63, 88]	5596
39	25	A	Barnet	W 1-0	0-0	10	Hart [67]	3721
40	Apr 1	H	Swansea C	D 1-1	0-1	10	Hart [68]	5718
41	8	A	Exeter C	D 0-0	0-0	12		3426
42	15	H	Rotherham U	D 1-1	1-1	13	Watson [24]	5805
43	22	A	York C	D 0-0	0-0	12		3619
44	26	H	Peterborough U	D 0-0	0-0	—		5831
45	29	A	Shrewsbury T	W 2-1	0-0	12	Brooker [48], Ling [75]	7654
46	May 6	H	Carlisle U	W 1-0	1-0	11	Crosby [35]	5998

Final League Position: 11

GOALSCORERS

League (64): Freeman 12 (3 pens), Hart 9, Rogers 8, Zamora 6 (1 pen), Oatway 4, Watson 4, Aspinall 3, Crosby 3, Brooker 2, Cullip 2, Newhouse 2, Pinamonte 2, Ramsay 2, Campbell 1, Ling 1, Mayo 1, McPherson 1, Thomas 1.
Worthington Cup (0).
FA Cup (5): Cullip 1, Freeman 1, Mayo 1, Rogers 1, Watson 1.

Ormerod M 7	Wilder C 11	Campbell J 22+1	McPherson K 23+2	Crosby A 36	Hobson G 6	Freeman D 36+2	Rogers P 44+1	Hart G 42+1	Oatway C 42	Thomas R 14+20	Newhouse A 1+11	Armstrong P —+5	Cameron D 6+11	Johnson R 4+5	Watson P 40+2	Walton M 39	Arnott A —+1	Cullip D 32+1	Aspinall W 19+12	Mayo K 25+6	Ramsay S 8+16	Carr D 16+3	Palmer R 1	Wilkinson S —+2	Pinamonte L 8+1	McPhee C —+4	Culverhouse 11	Zamora B 6	Brooker P 15	Ling M 2+6	Match No.
1	2	3	4	5	6	7¹	8	9	10²	11³	12	13	14																		1
1		3	4	5	6	7	8¹	9²	10	12	13	14	11³	2																	2
1		3	4¹	5	6	7	8	9	10	12	13		11²	2³	14																3
	2	3	4	5		7¹	8	9²	10	11³	12		13	14	6	1															4
	2	3	4	5		7¹	8	9	10	11²	12				6	1	13														5
	2³	3	4	5		7²	8	9	10	11¹	13		12	14	6	1															6
	2	3	4	5		7¹	8	9		11²	12		13	6	10	1															7
	2	3	12	5¹		7	8	9		11³	13	14		6²	10	1		4													8
1	2	3	4			7	8	9		12	11¹			10				5	6												9
	2	3	4			7¹	8	9²	10	14	12		13		11	1		5	6³												10
	2	3	4		6		8	9¹	10	13	12		7²			1		5	11³	14											11
	2¹	3	4		6	7³	8	9	10	13					12	1		5	11²		14										12
	2	3		5		7¹	8	9²	10	11	12					1		6	4³	14	13										13
		3		5²		7	8	9	10	12		13	14	2	1			6	11¹			4³									14
		3	4¹			7²	8	9	10	12				2	1			5	11³	14	13	6									15
		3	4				8	9	10	7²		12		2	1			5	11¹	14	13	6³									16
		3	4				8	9¹	10	7		12	13	2	1			5	11³	14		6²									17
		3	4			12	8		10	7¹		9	13	2	1			5	11			6²									18
		3	4			12	8	13	10	7²		9¹		2	1			5	6	11³	14										19
		3		5	6³		8	9	10¹	12		13		2	1			14	11		7²	4									20
1		3	4	5			8		10					2				6	11²					7¹	12	9	13				21
			4	5			8	9²	10			12		2	1			6	11¹	3	13				7						22
				5		7	8	9¹	10			13		2	1			6	12	3		4			11²						23
				5		7¹	8	9²	10	13				2	1			6	12	3	14	4			11³						24
				5		7	8	9	10	12				2	1			6		3	13	4²			11¹						25
		3³		5		7	8	9²	10	12		13		2	1			6¹	14			4			11						26
				5		7¹	8	9	10	12				2	1			6		3	13	4			11²						27
				5		7	8	9¹	10	12				2	1			6		3	13	4			11²						28
				5³		7²	8¹	9	10	11				2	1			6	12	3	13	4			14						29
14						7	8	9		12		13³	10²	2	1			6	11	3		4					5¹				30
				5		7¹	8	9	10	12				2	1			6	4³	3	13				14			11²			31
				5		7		9	10					2	1			6		3	12							8³	11		32
			4	5		7	12	9	10					2	1			6¹		3	13							8²	11		33
			4	5		7	8	9	10					2	1				3									11	6		34
			4	5		7	8	9	10¹					2	1			12	3									11	6		35
			4	5		7²	8	9	10					2	1			12	3	13								11	6¹		36
				5		7	8		10²	12				2	1			6	13	3	9³	4¹				14		11			37
				5		7	8	9¹	10					2	1			6		3	11					12		4			38
				5		7	8	9³	10¹					2	1			6	12	3	11	13						4²	14		39
				5		7	8	9	10					2	1			6	12	3	11²							4¹	13		40
				5		7²	8¹	9	10					2	1			6	12	3	11³					13		4	14		41
				5		7¹	8	9	10	12				2	1			6	13	3	14							4³	11²		42
				5		7	8	9²	10	12				2	1			6		3		13						4	11¹		43
1				5			8	9¹	10	7				2				6	12	3	11²							4	13		44
1		12	5				8	9	10	11³				2				6		3	13	7²						4¹	14		45
			5			7²	8	9³	10	12				2	1			6	13	3	11							4¹	14		46

Worthington Cup

First Round	Gillingham	(h)	0-2		
		(a)	0-2		

FA Cup

First Round	Peterborough U	(a)	1-1
		(h)	3-0
Second Round	Plymouth Arg	(a)	0-0
		(h)	1-2

Division 2   **BRISTOL CITY**

FOUNDATION

The name Bristol City came into being in 1897 when the Bristol South End club, formed three years earlier, decided to adopt professionalism and apply for admission to the Southern League after competing in the Western League. The historic meeting was held at The Albert Hall, Bedminster. Bristol City employed Sam Hollis from Woolwich Arsenal as manager and gave him £40 to buy players. In 1901 they merged with Bedminster, another leading Bristol club.

Ashton Gate, Bristol BS3 2EJ.
Telephone: (0117) 963 0630 (5 lines).
Fax: (0117) 963 0700.
Website: www.bcfc.co.uk
Commercial: (0117) 963 0600.
Shop: (0117) 963 0637.
ClubCall: 09068 121 176.
Supporters Club: (0117) 966 5554.
Community Dept: (0117) 963 0636.
Ground Capacity: 21,479.
Record Attendance: 43,335 v Preston NE, FA Cup 5th rd, 16 February 1935.
Record Receipts: £251,612 v Everton, FA Cup 4th rd, 23 January 1999.
Pitch Measurements: 115yd × 75yd.
Executive Chairman: S. Davidson.
Directors: J. Laycock, J. Clapp, R. Neale, S. Lansdown, K. Dawe, A. Gooch.
Sales Manager: Elaine White.
General Manager: Ian Wilson.
Football Secretary: Michelle McDonald.
Manager: Danny Wilson.
Physio: Gill O'Shea.
Stadium Manager: Dave Lewis.
Safety Officer: Keith Draisey.

LATEST SEQUENCES

Longest Sequence of League Wins: 14, 9.9.05 – 2.12.05.
Longest Sequence of League Defeats: 7, 3.10.70 – 7.11.70.
Longest Sequence of League Draws: 4, 6.11.99 – 27.11.99.
Longest Sequence of Unbeaten League Matches: 24, 9.9.05 – 10.2.06.
Longest Sequence Without a League Win: 15, 29.4.33 – 4.11.33.

HONOURS

Football League: Division 1 – Runners-up 1906–07; Division 2 – Champions 1905–06; Runners-up 1975–76, 1997–98; Division 3 (S) – Champions 1922–23, 1926–27, 1954–55; Runners-up 1937–38; Division 3 – Runners-up 1964–65, 1989–90.

FA Cup: Runners-up 1909.

Football League Cup: Semi-final 1971, 1989.

Welsh Cup: Winners 1934.

Anglo-Scottish Cup: Winners 1978.

Freight Rover Trophy: Winners 1986; Runners-up 1987.

Auto Windscreens Shield: Runners-up 2000.

Colours
Red shirts, red shorts, white stockings.

Change Colours
White shirts, white shorts, white stockings.

Year Formed: 1894.

Turned Professional: 1897.

Ltd Co.: 1897. Bristol City Football Club Ltd.

Previous Name: 1894, Bristol South End; 1897, Bristol City.

Club Nickname: 'Robins'.

Previous Grounds: 1894, St John's Lane; 1904, Ashton Gate.

First Football League Game: 7 September 1901, Division 2, v Blackpool (a) W 2–0 – Moles; Tuft, Davies; Jones, McLean, Chambers; Bradbury, Connor, Boucher, O'Brien (2), Flynn.

Record League Victory: 9–0 v Aldershot, Division 3 (S), 28 December 1946 – Eddols; Morgan, Fox; Peacock, Roberts, Jones (1); Chilcott, Thomas, Clark (4 incl. 1p), Cyril Williams (1), Hargreaves (3).

Record Cup Victory: 11–0 v Chichester C, FA Cup 1st rd, 5 November 1960 – Cook; Collinson, Thresher; Connor, Alan Williams, Etheridge; Tait (1), Bobby Williams (1), Atyeo (5), Adrian Williams (3), Derrick, (1 og).

Record Defeat: 0–9 v Coventry C, Division 3 (S), 28 April 1934.

Most League Points (2 for a win): 70, Division 3 (S), 1954–55.

Most League Points (3 for a win): 91, Division 3, 1989–90.

Most League Goals: 104, Division 3 (S), 1926–27.

Highest League Scorer in Season: Don Clark, 36, Division 3 (S), 1946–47.

Most League Goals in Total Aggregate: John Atyeo, 314, 1951–66.

Most League Goals in One Match: 6, Tommy 'Tot' Walsh v Gillingham, Division 3S, 15 January 1927.

Most Capped Player: Billy Wedlock, 26, England.

Most League Appearances: John Atyeo, 597, 1951–66.

Youngest League Player: Nyrere Kelly, 16 years 213 days v Hartlepool U, 16 October 1982.

Record Transfer Fee Received: £3,000,000 from Wolverhampton W for Ade Akinbiyi, September 1999.

Record Transfer Fee Paid: £1,200,000 to Gillingham for Ade Akinbiyi, May 1998.

Football League Record: 1901 Elected to Division 2; 1906–11 Division 1; 1911–22 Division 2; 1922–23 Division 3 (S); 1923–24 Division 2; 1924–27 Division 3 (S); 1927–32 Division 2; 1932–55 Division 3 (S); 1955–60 Division 2; 1960–65 Division 3; 1965–76 Division 2; 1976–80 Division 1; 1980–81 Division 2; 1981–82 Division 3; 1982–84 Division 4; 1984–90 Division 3; 1990–92 Division 2; 1992–95 Division 1; 1995–98 Division 2; 1998–99 Division 1; 1999– Division 2.

MANAGERS

Sam Hollis 1897–99
Bob Campbell 1899–1901
Sam Hollis 1901–05
Harry Thickett 1905–10
Sam Hollis 1911–13
George Hedley 1913–15
Jack Hamilton 1915–19
Joe Palmer 1919–21
Alex Raisbeck 1921–29
Joe Bradshaw 1929–32
Bob Hewison 1932–49
    (under suspension 1938–39)
Bob Wright 1949–50
Pat Beasley 1950–58
Peter Doherty 1958–60
Fred Ford 1960–67
Alan Dicks 1967–80
Bobby Houghton 1980–82
Roy Hodgson 1982
Terry Cooper 1982–88
    (Director from 1983)
Joe Jordan 1988–90
Jimmy Lumsden 1990–92
Denis Smith 1992–93
Russell Osman 1993–94
Joe Jordan 1994–97
John Ward 1997–98
Benny Lennartsson 1998–99
Tony Pulis 1999
Tony Fawthrop 2000
Danny Wilson June 2000–

TEN YEAR LEAGUE RECORD

		P	W	D	L	F	A	Pts	Pos
1989-90	Div 3	46	27	10	9	76	40	91	2
1990-91	Div 2	46	20	7	19	68	71	67	9
1991-92	Div 2	46	13	15	18	55	71	54	17
1992-93	Div 1	46	14	14	18	49	67	56	15
1993-94	Div 1	46	16	16	14	47	50	64	13
1994-95	Div 1	46	11	12	23	42	63	45	23
1995-96	Div 2	46	15	15	16	55	60	60	13
1996-97	Div 2	46	21	10	15	69	51	73	5
1997-98	Div 2	46	25	10	11	69	39	85	2
1998-99	Div 1	46	9	15	22	57	80	42	24

DID YOU KNOW ?

On 30 April 1910, the final day of the season, Bristol City needed a win over Nottingham Forest to be sure of avoiding relegation. They won 4-0 with John Cowell scoring all their goals.

BRISTOL CITY 1999–2000 LEAGUE RECORD

Match No.	Date	Venue	Opponents	Result	H/T Score	Lg. Pos.	Goalscorers	Atten- dance
1	Aug 7	A	Reading	L 1-2	0-1	17	Tinnion [77]	13,348
2	14	H	Bournemouth	W 3-1	2-0	10	Akinbiyi 2 [24, 44], Brennan [47]	11,315
3	21	A	Wigan Ath	L 1-2	0-1	14	Thorpe (pen) [72]	7103
4	28	H	Bury	D 1-1	0-0	15	Taylor [90]	9537
5	Sept 4	H	Blackpool	W 5-2	0-1	12	Bell [49], Thorpe 2 [70, 79], Hutchings [83], Brennan [89]	8439
6	11	H	Millwall	D 0-0	0-0	14		9893
7	18	A	Scunthorpe U	W 2-1	0-0	11	Jones [79], Taylor [84]	4542
8	25	H	Burnley	D 0-0	0-0	13		11,510
9	Oct 2	A	Oxford U	L 0-3	0-2	14		6638
10	9	A	Preston NE	L 0-1	0-1	15		10,042
11	17	H	Bristol R	D 0-0	0-0	15		16,011
12	19	H	Colchester U	D 1-1	1-0	—	Tinnion [34]	7777
13	23	A	Burnley	L 0-2	0-1	16		10,175
14	Nov 2	A	Gillingham	L 0-3	0-0	—		6892
15	6	H	Cambridge U	D 1-1	1-1	17	Jones [35]	8646
16	14	A	Stoke C	D 1-1	0-0	17	Tinnion [85]	10,775
17	23	H	Oldham Ath	D 1-1	1-0	—	Beadle [39]	8214
18	27	A	Notts Co	D 4-4	1-2	19	Bell 2 [20, 75], Testimitanu [61], Beadle [64]	5374
19	Dec 4	H	Reading	W 3-1	1-0	14	Torpey [45], Taylor [50], Beadle [76]	8936
20	7	A	Chesterfield	W 2-0	1-0	—	Galloway (og) [45], Testimitanu [61]	2254
21	17	H	Wycombe W	D 0-0	0-0	—		8195
22	26	A	Brentford	L 1-2	0-0	14	Beadle [90]	6942
23	28	H	Luton T	D 0-0	0-0	14		11,832
24	Jan 3	A	Wrexham	W 1-0	0-0	14	Taylor [70]	4021
25	9	H	Cardiff C	D 0-0	0-0	15		10,568
26	15	A	Bournemouth	W 3-2	1-0	14	Millen [31], Thorpe 2 (1 pen) [61, 67 (p)]	5425
27	22	H	Wigan Ath	D 0-0	0-0	13		10,758
28	29	A	Bury	D 0-0	0-0	14		3435
29	Feb 5	H	Chesterfield	W 3-0	2-0	13	Thorpe [44], Murray [45], Beadle [75]	8837
30	12	A	Blackpool	W 2-1	1-1	11	Murray [21], Millen [48]	5066
31	19	H	Notts Co	D 2-2	2-0	11	Holmes (og) [35], Thorpe [43]	10,029
32	22	A	Cardiff C	D 0-0	0-0	—		6586
33	26	H	Scunthorpe U	W 2-1	2-1	10	Thorpe [18], Murray [40]	9897
34	Mar 4	A	Millwall	L 1-4	1-3	10	Meechan [45]	10,141
35	7	A	Cambridge U	L 0-3	0-1	—		3505
36	11	H	Gillingham	L 0-1	0-0	10		9332
37	18	A	Oldham Ath	D 1-1	0-0	11	Brown A [76]	4808
38	25	H	Brentford	W 1-0	0-0	10	Murray [77]	8804
39	28	H	Stoke C	D 2-2	1-2	—	Thorpe 2 [10, 78]	8103
40	Apr 1	A	Wycombe W	W 2-1	1-0	9	Thorpe [17], Spencer [65]	4754
41	8	A	Wrexham	W 4-0	0-0	9	Thorpe 2 [53, 78], Beadle [62], Meechan [90]	8639
42	18	A	Luton T	W 2-1	1-0	—	Murray [29], Bell [77]	4771
43	22	H	Bristol R	L 0-2	0-0	9		10,805
44	24	A	Oxford U	D 2-2	2-1	9	Meechan [22], Brown A [39]	9046
45	29	A	Colchester U	W 4-3	1-2	9	Murray [39], Meechan [63], Ferguson (og) [71], Bell [84]	4013
46	May 6	H	Preston NE	L 0-2	0-1	9		11,160

Final League Position: 9

GOALSCORERS

League (59): Thorpe 13 (2 pens), Beadle 6, Murray 6, Bell 5, Meechan 4, Taylor 4, Tinnion 3, Akinbiyi 2, Brennan 2, Brown A 2, Jones 2, Millen 2, Testimitanu 2, Hutchings 1, Spencer 1, Torpey 1, own goals 3.
Worthington Cup (5): Hutchings 1, Jordan 1, Mortimer 1, Thorpe 1, Torpey 1.
FA Cup (5): Murray 3, Tinnion 2.

Player appearances / goals grid (shirt number worn shown in each cell; superscript = goals). Boxed columns: **Hulbert R 1 + 1** and **Coles D — + 1**.

Phillips S 21	Lavin G 18+1	Brennan J 11+1	Mortimer P 22+1	Taylor S 25	Carey L 20+2	Goodridge G 13+8	Hutchings C 17+4	Hulbert R 1+1	Akinbiyi A 3	Coles D —+1	Brown A 10+3	Tinnion B 42+1	Pinamonte L 2+4	Murray S 31+10	Shail M —+1	Sebok V 8+3	Torpey S 15+5	Thorpe T 24+7	Bell M 34+2	Doherty T —+1	Meechan A 5+7	Jones S 12+2	Holland P 22+5	Testimtanui I 11+5	Brown M —+2	Beadle P 22+3	Mercer B 25	Burns J 6+5	Millen K 28	Black T 4	Burnell J 15+2	Hill M 8+6	Wright B —+2	Clist S 8+1	Hewlett M 5+2	Spencer D 6+3	Odejayi K —+3	Jordan A 8	Amankwaah K 4+1	Match No.
1	2	3	4	5	6	7¹	8²		9		10³	11	12	13	14																									1
1		3	4	5	6	7¹	8		9			11		13	12		2	10²																						2
1		3		5	6	7	8		9			11			4		2	10¹	12																					3
1	2			5		7	8²				11	12		4¹	6	10	9³	3		13	14																			4
1	2	12	4²	5	6	7	8				11			14	13	10³	9		3¹																					5
1	2¹	3	4	5	6²	7					11			8		13	10	9³	12		14																			6
1	2	3	4	5		7¹					11			8		6	10²	12	13		9																			7
1	2	3	4	5		7	12				11			10²		6		13	9	8¹																				8
1	2	3		5		7²	8³				11			13		6	12	10	4¹		9	14																		9
1	2		4	5	6²	7¹	8³				11			10	12	13		3		14	9																			10
1	2	3	4	5	6²	7¹	8				11			12		13	10³				9		14																	11
1	2	3	4	5		7²	8				11			12		6¹	13				9		14	10³																12
1	2	3	4	5			12				8	11		7		6¹	13	14			9²			10³																13
	2		4	5			8					11		7			12	3		6¹	9	10			1															14
	2¹		4	5			12²					11³		7				3	14		9	6	10		1		13													15
			4				12					8		11		6¹		3			9	7	5		10	1		2											16
12			4¹	5			13					11		7		14		3			9³	6	8²		10	1		2											17
2²			4	5								11		13		12		3			9¹	6	7		10	1		8											18
2			4²	5		7³	12					11		14		10		3			13	8¹	9		1			6											19
2				5			8					11				9		3			4	7			1			6											20
2				6			8¹					11				10		3			13	12	7		9	1		5	4²										21
2	12		6²				13		8			11¹				14		3			10	7³	9		1			5	4										22
2¹			4	6			8²					11		12		10³		14			3	13	9		1			5	7										23
			4²	6	2		12					11		8		9		3			14	10¹	13		1			5	7³										24
10¹			6	4	12							11		2		9		3³		7²	14	8		13	1			5											25
7					12							11		2		9		10²			6	8¹		1			5	4		3	13									26
4²					12							11		2¹		9		10			3	13	14	1		7³	6	8											27
4³					12							11		9		10²		2			7	13		1		5	6	3¹	14	8									28
					6							11		2		10³		3¹			8	9²	1		5		4	12		7	13	14							29
					6							11		2		10		3			8	9	1		5		4			7¹	12								30
					12	13		14				11		2		10		3				9	1		8²	5	4¹	6		7³									31
					6							11		2		10		3			8²	9	1		13	5	4		7¹										32
					6				8			11		2		10		3				9	1		5		4		7										33
					6				8²			11		2				3	10³		13	9	1		5		4¹	12	14	7									34
					6				12			11³		2		10		3			7²	9	1		13	5	4			8									35
1					6							11		10		12		8	9		4	5	2¹	3		7		9												36
1					6				8			11		2		10		9				12	3¹		7	4²			5			13								37
1							8					7		10		3		6				4			11	9			5		2									38
1					5²		8		12			7		10		3		6				4	13		11¹	9			2										39
1							8²					11		7		10		3			6	12		4	13	9¹			5		2									40
					2							11		7		10¹		3	12		6	9²	1		8	5			13		4									41
					2							11		7²		10³		3			6	9	1		14	5			13	12	8¹		4							42
					2		8					11		7		10¹		3			6	9²	1		5				12	13	4								43
1						13		14	8			11		7		10		3	12			4²	5		6³				9¹										44
1						10²			8¹			11		7		3		9			6	12	5		2				13	4							13	4	45
1												11		10		3		9			7	13	8		5¹	4²			12		14	6						2³		46

Worthington Cup

First Round	Cambridge U	(a)	2-2
		(h)	2-1
Second Round	Nottingham F	(a)	1-2
		(h)	0-0

FA Cup

First Round	Mansfield T	(h)	3-2
Second Round	Bournemouth	(a)	2-0
Third Round	Sheffield W	(a)	0-1

Division 2   **BRISTOL ROVERS**

FOUNDATION

Bristol Rovers were formed at a meeting in Stapleton Road, Eastville, in 1883. However, they first went under the name of the Black Arabs (wearing black shirts). Changing their name to Eastville Rovers in their second season, they won the Gloucestershire Senior Cup in 1888–89. Original members of the Bristol & District League in 1892, this eventually became the Western League and Eastville Rovers adopted professionalism in 1897.

Registered Offices: The Memorial Stadium, Filton Avenue, Horfield, Bristol BS7 0AQ. (0117) 909 6648.
Ground: The Memorial Stadium.
Training Ground: (0117) 977 2000.
Matchday Ticket Office: (0117) 909 8848.
ClubCall: 09068 121 131.
Fax: (0117) 924 4454.
Community Office: (0117) 977 3111.
Ticket Office: (0117) 924 3200.
Ground Capacity: 10,861.
Record Attendance: 9274 v Leyton Orient, FA Cup 4th rd, 23 January 1999 (Memorial Ground).
9464 v Liverpool, FA Cup 4th rd, 8 February 1992 (Twerton Park).
38,472 v Preston NE, FA Cup 4th rd, 30 January 1960 (Eastville).
Record Receipts: £75,935 v Leyton Orient, FA Cup 4th rd, 23 January 1999.
Pitch Measurements: 101m × 68m.
Vice-Presidents: Dr W. T. Cussen, A. I. Seager, R. Redmond.
Chairman: D. H. A. Dunford.
Vice-Chairman: G. M. H. Dunford.
Directors: R. Craig, B. Andrews, V. Stokes, B. Bradshaw.
Player/Manager: Ian Holloway.
Player-Coach: Gary Penrice.
Physio: Phil Kite.
Director of Youth: Phil Bater.
Community Scheme Organiser: Alan Walsh.
Chief Administrator/Club Secretary: Roger Brinsford.
Office Manager: Mrs Angela Mann.

LATEST SEQUENCES

Longest Sequence of League Wins: 12, 18.10.52 – 17.1.53.
Longest Sequence of League Defeats: 8, 29.4.61 – 9.9.61.
Longest Sequence of League Draws: 5, 1.11.75 – 22.11.75.
Longest Sequence of Unbeaten League Matches: 32, 7.4.73 – 27.1.74.
Longest Sequence Without a League Win: 20, 5.4.80 – 1.11.80.

HONOURS

Football League: Division 2 best season: 4th, 1994–95; Division 3 (S) – Champions 1952–53; Division 3 – Champions 1989–90; Runners-up 1973–74.

FA Cup: best season: 6th rd, 1951, 1958.

Football League Cup: best season: 5th rd, 1971, 1972.

Colours
Blue and white quartered shirts, white shorts, white stockings.

Change Colours
White shirts, black shorts, white stockings.

Year Formed: 1883.

Turned Professional: 1897.

Ltd Co.: 1896.

Previous Names: 1883, Black Arabs; 1884, Eastville Rovers; 1897, Bristol Eastville Rovers; 1898, Bristol Rovers.

Club Nickname: 'Pirates'.

Previous Grounds: 1883, Purdown; Three Acres, Ashley Hill; Rudgeway, Fishponds; 1897, Eastville; 1986, Twerton Park; 1996, The Memorial Stadium.

First Football League Game: 28 August 1920, Division 3, v Millwall (a) L 0–2 – Stansfield; Bethune, Panes; Boxley, Kenny, Steele; Chance, Bird, Sims, Bell, Palmer.

Record League Victory: 7–0 v Brighton & HA, Division 3 (S), 29 November 1952 – Hoyle; Bamford, Fox; Pitt, Warren, Sampson; McIlvenny, Roost (2), Lambden (1), Bradford (1), Petherbridge (2), (1 og). 7–0 v Swansea T, Division 2, 2 October 1954 – Radford; Bamford, Watkins; Pitt, Muir, Anderson; Petherbridge, Bradford (2), Meyer, Roost (1), Hooper (2), (2 og). 7–0 v Shrewsbury T, Division 3, 21 March 1964 – Hall; Hillard, Gwyn Jones; Oldfield, Stone (1), Mabbutt; Jarman (2), Brown (1), Biggs (1p), Hamilton, Bobby Jones (2).

Record Cup Victory: 6–0 v Merthyr Tydfil, FA Cup 1st rd, 14 November 1987 – Martyn; Alexander (Dryden), Tanner, Hibbitt, Twentyman, Jones, Holloway, Meacham (1), White (2), Penrice (3) (Reece), Purnell.

Record Defeat: 0–12 v Luton T, Division 3 (S), 13 April 1936.

Most League Points (2 for a win): 64, Division 3 (S), 1952–53.

Most League Points (3 for a win): 93, Division 3, 1989–90.

Most League Goals: 92, Division 3 (S), 1952–53.

Highest League Scorer in Season: Geoff Bradford, 33, Division 3 (S), 1952–53.

MANAGERS

Alfred Homer 1899–1920
(continued as Secretary to 1928)
Ben Hall 1920–21
Andy Wilson 1921–26
Joe Palmer 1926–29
Dave McLean 1929–30
Albert Prince-Cox 1930–36
Percy Smith 1936–37
Brough Fletcher 1938–49
Bert Tann 1950–68
(continued as General Manager to 1972)
Fred Ford 1968–69
Bill Dodgin Snr 1969–72
Don Megson 1972–77
Bobby Campbell 1978–79
Harold Jarman 1979–80
Terry Cooper 1980–81
Bobby Gould 1981–83
David Williams 1983–85
Bobby Gould 1985–87
Gerry Francis 1987–91
Martin Dobson 1991
Dennis Rofe 1992
Malcolm Allison 1992–93
John Ward 1993–96
Ian Holloway May 1996–

Most League Goals in Total Aggregate: Geoff Bradford, 242, 1949–64.

Most League Goals in One Match: 4, Sidney Leigh v Exeter C, Division 3S, 2 May 1921; 4, Jonah Wilcox v Bournemouth, Division 3S, 12 December 1925; 4, Bill Culley v QPR, Division 3S, 5 March 1927; Frank Curran v Swindon T, Division 3S, 25 March 1939; Vic Lambden v Aldershot, Division 3S, 29 March 1947; George Petherbridge v Torquay U, Division 3S, 1 December 1951; Vic Lambden v Colchester U, Division 3S, 14 May 1952; Geoff Bradford v Rotherham U, Division 2, 14 March 1959; Robin Stubbs v Gillingham, Division 2, 10 October 1970; Alan Warboys v Brighton & HA, Division 3, 1 December 1973; Jamie Cureton v Reading, Division 2, 16 January 1999.

Most Capped Player: Neil Slatter, 10 (22), Wales.

Most League Appearances: Stuart Taylor, 546, 1966–80.

Youngest League Player: Ronnie Dix, 15 years 180 days v Norwich C, 3 March 1928.

Record Transfer Fee Received: £2,000,000 from Fulham for Barry Hayles, November 1998.

Record Transfer Fee Paid: £370,000 to QPR for Andy Tillson, November 1992.

Football League Record: 1920 Original Member of Division 3; 1921–53 Division 3 (S); 1953–62 Division 2; 1962–74 Division 3; 1974–81 Division 2; 1981–90 Division 3; 1990–92 Division 2. 1992–93 Division 1; 1993– Division 2.

TEN YEAR LEAGUE RECORD

		P	W	D	L	F	A	Pts	Pos
1989-90	Div 3	46	26	15	5	71	35	93	1
1990-91	Div 2	46	15	13	18	56	59	58	13
1991-92	Div 2	46	16	14	16	60	63	62	13
1992-93	Div 1	46	10	11	25	55	87	41	24
1993-94	Div 2	46	20	10	16	60	59	70	8
1994-95	Div 2	46	22	16	8	70	40	82	4
1995-96	Div 2	46	20	10	16	57	60	70	10
1996-97	Div 2	46	15	11	20	47	50	56	17
1997-98	Div 2	46	20	10	16	70	64	70	5
1998-99	Div 2	46	13	17	16	65	56	56	13

DID YOU KNOW ?

On 4 December 1983 Bristol Rovers played a centenary match against Wotton Rovers, winning 4-0 as a celebration of the occasion when their forerunners, The Black Arabs AFC (Bristol), played Wotton-under-Edge on 1 December 1883.

BRISTOL ROVERS 1999–2000 LEAGUE RECORD

Match No.	Date		Venue	Opponents	Result	H/T Score	Lg. Pos.	Goalscorers	Attendance
1	Aug	7	H	Brentford	D 0-0	0-0	14		8514
2		14	A	Gillingham	W 1-0	0-0	9	Roberts [73]	6234
3		21	H	Oxford U	W 1-0	0-0	6	Roberts [60]	7617
4		28	A	Wrexham	L 1-2	0-0	7	Cureton [55]	3365
5		30	H	Burnley	W 1-0	1-0	4	Cureton (pen) [37]	7624
6	Sept	4	A	Scunthorpe U	W 2-0	1-0	1	Roberts 2 [24, 50]	4496
7		11	A	Wigan Ath	L 1-3	1-2	5	Roberts [28]	6927
8		18	H	Oldham Ath	W 3-2	2-1	2	Cureton 2 [26, 60], Foster [30]	6574
9		25	A	Notts Co	W 2-0	0-0	1	Cureton (pen) [54], Tillson [76]	6197
10	Oct	2	H	Blackpool	W 3-1	1-0	1	Cureton 2 (1 pen) [21 (p), 70], Roberts [76]	7715
11		9	H	Cardiff C	D 1-1	1-0	1	Thomson [31]	7363
12		17	A	Bristol C	D 0-0	0-0	1		16,011
13		19	A	Bournemouth	W 1-0	1-0	—	Cureton [24]	5613
14		23	H	Notts Co	L 0-1	0-0	3		8188
15	Nov	2	H	Bury	D 0-0	0-0	—		5397
16		6	A	Wycombe W	D 1-1	0-0	5	Ellington [57]	5167
17		20	A	Chesterfield	W 1-0	1-0	6	Pritchard [45]	2875
18		27	H	Luton T	W 3-0	2-0	4	Thomson [12], Walters [19], Cureton [48]	7805
19	Dec	4	A	Brentford	W 3-0	1-0	4	Roberts 2 [4, 90], Walters [77]	6843
20		11	H	Colchester U	W 2-1	0-0	3	Roberts 2 [31, 54]	7023
21		18	A	Stoke C	W 2-1	0-0	3	Roberts [72], Walters [84]	10,379
22		26	H	Millwall	W 1-0	0-0	2	Roberts [85]	10,077
23		28	A	Preston NE	L 1-2	1-0	3	Walters [43]	16,680
24	Jan	3	H	Cambridge U	W 1-0	0-0	3	Roberts [71]	9822
25		8	A	Colchester U	L 4-5	1-1	3	Roberts 2 [12, 46], Cureton (pen) [59], Ellington [86]	4482
26		15	H	Gillingham	W 2-1	0-0	2	Cureton [58], Roberts [66]	8331
27		22	A	Oxford U	W 5-0	1-0	2	Cureton 3 [30, 56, 80], Pethick [74], Ellington [75]	7355
28		29	H	Wrexham	W 3-1	1-0	1	Cureton [23], Trees [57], Roberts [76]	8196
29	Feb	5	A	Burnley	L 0-1	0-0	2		13,526
30		12	H	Scunthorpe U	D 1-1	1-0	2	Walters [11]	8236
31		19	A	Luton T	W 4-1	2-1	2	Roberts 2 [27, 90], Cureton 2 [38, 58]	6520
32		26	A	Oldham Ath	W 4-1	3-0	1	Cureton 2 (1 pen) [4, 6 (p)], Astafjevs [11], Thomson [48]	5839
33	Mar	4	H	Wigan Ath	D 1-1	1-1	1	Challis [19]	11,109
34		7	H	Wycombe W	W 1-0	1-0	—	Ellington [10]	8053
35		11	H	Bury	D 0-0	0-0	1		4049
36		18	H	Chesterfield	W 3-1	1-1	2	Walters [21], Cureton [71], Astafjevs [73]	8765
37		22	A	Reading	L 0-2	0-1	—		11,707
38		25	A	Millwall	L 0-3	0-1	2		12,858
39	Apr	1	H	Stoke C	D 3-3	2-1	3	Pethick [20], Cureton (pen) [32], Walters [69]	9312
40		4	H	Reading	L 0-1	0-0	—		7771
41		8	A	Cambridge U	D 1-1	0-1	3	Roberts [50]	4536
42		15	H	Preston NE	L 0-2	0-1	4		10,111
43		22	H	Bristol C	W 2-0	0-0	3	Roberts [53], Walters [69]	10,805
44		24	A	Blackpool	L 1-2	1-0	6	Roberts [36]	5635
45		29	H	Bournemouth	D 2-2	1-1	5	Walters [44], Cureton [76]	8847
46	May	6	A	Cardiff C	L 0-1	0-1	7		6655

Final League Position: 7

GOALSCORERS

League (69): Cureton 22 (6 pens), Roberts 22, Walters 9, Ellington 4, Thomson 3, Astafjevs 2, Pethick 2, Challis 1, Foster 1, Pritchard 1, Tillson 1, Trees 1.
Worthington Cup (4): Roberts 3, Cureton 1.
FA Cup (0).

Jones L 36	Pethick R 40+1	Challis T 36+4	Foster S 43	Thomson A 43	Tillson A 43	Mauge R 22	Hillier D 39	Pritchard D 21	Cureton J 46	Roberts J 41	Bennett F —+10	Andreasson M 6	Ellington N 12+25	Bryant S 9+6	Penrice G —+3	Taylor S 4	Leoni S 2+6	Zabek L 3+1	Zamora B —+4	Walters M 28+2	Trought M 2+2	White T 3	Parkin B 2+1	Meaker M —+2	Trees R 5+5	Byrne S 1+1	Astafjevs V 13+3	Evans R 4	Pierre N 1+2	Wolleaston R —+4	Stewart J 1+3	Match No.
1	2^1	3	4	5	6	7	8	9	10	11	12																					1
1	2	3	4		6	7	8	9	10^1	11^1	12	5	13																			2
1^2	2	3	4	5	6	7	8	9^1	10	11			12																			3
1	2	3	4	5	6		8	9	10	11	12		7^1																			4
1	2	3	4	5	6		8	9	10	11			7^1	12																		5
1	2	3	4	5	6		8	9	10	11			7^1	12																		6
1	2	3	4	5	6	7	8	9^1	10^2	11^1	12		13																			7
1	2	3	4	5	6	7	8	9	10	11^1	12																					8
	2	3	4	5	6	7	8^1		10	11	12									9			1									9
	2	3^3	4	5	6	7	8^2	9	10	11^1	12	13								14			1									10
	2	3	4	5	6	7	8	9	10	11										1												11
	2	3^4	4	5	6	7	8	9^2	10^1	11	12	13								14			1									12
1	2	3	4	5	6	7	8	9^1	10	11	12																					13
1	2	3	4	5	6	7^2	8	9^1	10	11	12	13																				14
1	2	3	4	5	6		8		10	11						7	9															15
1		3	4	5	6	7	8	2	10^2		12				9	11^1				13												16
1	2^2	3	4	5	6		8	9	10^1	11	13							12		7^3	14											17
1	2^1	12	4	5	6	7	8	3	10	11	13									9^1												18
1	2	12	4	5	6	7	8^1	3	10	11	13									9^2												19
1	2	12	4	5	6	7	8^1	3	10	11	13									9^2												20
1	2^1	12	4	5	6	7^2	8	3	10	11	14	13								9^1												21
1	2	3	4	5	6^2		8		10	11	12	7^1							13	9^2	14											22
1	2	3	4	5		7	8		10	11	12	2						13		9^1	6^2											23
1^6		3	4	5^1	6	7	8	2	10^2	11	12									9					15	13						24
1	12	7	4				8	2	10	11	13									9	5	6^1					3^2					25
	2	3	4	5	6	7			10^1	11	12									9	6	1			8							26
1	2	3		5	6	7^1			10		9^2					12				11	4				8	13						27
1	2^2	3	4	5	6	7			10	11	12									9^1					8	13						28
1		3^1	4	5	6	7			10	11	12								13	2					9^2	8						29
1	2		4	5	6		8		10	11	12									3					7	9^1						30
1	2	3	4	5	6		8		10	11										7						9						31
	2	3	4	5	6		8		10	11^3	12									7^1					13	9^2	1	14				32
	2	3	4	5	6		8		10	11								9^1		7					12		1					33
	2		4	5	6		8		10	11								9		7^1						1	12					34
	2		4	5	6		8		10	11	12							13		3^2					7	1	9^1					35
1	2	7	4^3	5	6		8^2		10	11									12	3^1					14	13	9					36
1	2	3	4	5	6^1		8		10	11									12	3^3						9	7					37
1	2	3	4^2	5	6				10	11							9^1			12						7			13	8		38
1	2	3		5	6		8		10	11^1	4	12								9						7^2		13				39
1	2	3^3		5	6		8^2		10^1	11	4	12								9						7		13	14			40
1	2	3^2	4	5	6		8		10	11									14	9						7^1			13^3			41
1	2^2		4	5	6		8		10	11									3^1	9						7		13	12			42
1	2		4	5	6		8		10	11	3	7								9												43
1	2		4	5	6		8		10	11	3^3	7^1	12^2							9							13	14				44
1	2	6		4	5		8^3		10	11	3^1	12	13							9^2	14							7				45
	2^3	3	4	5	6		8^1		10	11		7^2	12							9						1	13	14				46

Worthington Cup

First Round	Luton T	(a)	2-0
		(h)	2-2
Second Round	Birmingham C	(a)	0-2
		(h)	0-1

FA Cup

| First Round | Preston NE | (h) | 0-1 |

Division 1   **BURNLEY**

FOUNDATION

The majority of those responsible for the formation of the Burnley club in 1881 were from the defunct rugby club Burnley Rovers. Indeed, they continued to play rugby for a year before changing to soccer and dropping 'Rovers' from their name. The changes were decided at a meeting held in May 1882 at the Bull Hotel.

Turf Moor, Burnley BB10 4BX.

Telephone: (01282) 700 000.

Fax: (01282) 700 014.

ClubCall: 09068 121 153.

Ticket Office: (01282) 700 010.

Community Programme: (01282) 700 011.

Commercial Department: (01282) 700 007.

Ground Capacity: 22,546.

Record Attendance: 54,775 v Huddersfield T, FA Cup 3rd rd, 23 February 1924.

Record Receipts: £183,000 v Preston NE, Division 2, 4 March 2000.

Pitch Measurements: 114yd × 72yd.

Chairman: B. Kilby.

Vice-Chairman: R. Ingleby.

President: Dr R. D. Iven MRCS (Eng), LRCP (Lond), MRCGP.

Directors: F. J. Teasdale, C. Holt, R. Blakeborough, J. Turkington.

Manager: Stan Ternent.

General Manager: A. Watson.

Company Secretary: Cathy Pickup.

Coaches: Terry Pashley, Michael Docherty, James Robson.

Sales Manager: Anthony Fairclough.

LATEST SEQUENCES

Longest Sequence of League Wins: 10, 16.11.12 – 18.1.13.

Longest Sequence of League Defeats: 8, 2.1.95 – 25.2.95.

Longest Sequence of League Draws: 6, 21.2.31 – 28.3.31.

Longest Sequence of Unbeaten League Matches: 30, 6.9.20 – 25.3.21.

Longest Sequence Without a League Win: 24, 16.4.79 – 17.11.79.

HONOURS

Football League: Division 1 – Champions 1920–21, 1959–60; Runners-up 1919–20, 1961–62; Division 2 – Champions 1897–98, 1972–73; Runners-up 1912–13, 1946–47, 1999–2000; Promoted from Division 2, 1993–94 (play-offs); Division 3 – Champions 1981–82; Division 4 – Champions 1991–92. Record 30 consecutive Division 1 games without defeat 1920–21.

FA Cup: Winners 1914; Runners-up 1947, 1962.

Football League Cup: Semi-final 1961, 1969, 1983.

Anglo–Scottish Cup: Winners 1979.

Sherpa Van Trophy: Runners-up 1988.

European Competitions: European Cup: 1960–61. *European Fairs Cup:* 1966–67.

Colours

Claret body with blue sleeves, white shorts, white stockings.

Change Colours

Blue shirts, claret shorts, blue stockings.

Year Formed: 1882.

Turned Professional: 1883.

Ltd Co.: 1897.

Previous Name: 1881, Burnley Rovers; 1882, Burnley.

Club Nickname: 'The Clarets'.

Previous Grounds: 1881, Calder Vale; 1882, Turf Moor.

First Football League Game: 8 September 1888, Football League, v Preston NE (a) L 2–5 – Smith; Lang, Bury, Abrams, Friel, Keenan, Brady, Tait, Poland (1), Gallocher (1), Yates.

Record League Victory: 9–0 v Darwen, Division 1, 9 January 1892 – Hillman; Walker, McFettridge, Lang, Matthews, Keenan, Nicol (3), Bowes, Espie (1), McLardie (3), Hill (2).

Record Cup Victory: 9–0 v Crystal Palace, FA Cup 2nd rd (replay), 10 February 1909 – Dawson; Barron, McLean; Cretney (2), Leake, Moffat; Morley, Ogden, Smith (3), Abbott (2), Smethams (1). 9–0 v New Brighton, FA Cup 4th rd, 26 January 1957 – Blacklaw; Angus, Winton; Seith, Adamson, Miller; Newlands (1), McIlroy (3), Lawson (3), Cheesebrough (1), Pilkington (1). 9–0 v Penrith, FA Cup 1st rd, 17 November 1984 – Hansbury; Miller, Hampton, Phelan, Overson (Kennedy), Hird (3 incl. 1p), Grewcock (1), Powell (2), Taylor (3), Biggins, Hutchison.

Record Defeat: 0–10 v Aston Villa, Division 1, 29 August 1925 and v Sheffield U, Division 1, 19 January 1929.

Most League Points (2 for a win): 62, Division 2, 1972–73.

Most League Points (3 for a win): 88, Division 2, 1999–2000.

Most League Goals: 102, Division 1, 1960–61.

Highest League Scorer in Season: George Beel, 35, Division 1, 1927–28.

Most League Goals in Total Aggregate: George Beel, 178, 1923–32.

Most League Goals in One Match: 6, Louis Page v Birmingham C, Division 1, 10 April 1926.

Most Capped Player: Jimmy McIlroy, 51 (55), Northern Ireland.

Most League Appearances: Jerry Dawson, 522, 1907–28.

Youngest League Player: Tommy Lawton, 16 years 174 days v Doncaster R, 28 March 1936.

Record Transfer Fee Received: £750,000 from Luton T for Steve Davis, August 1995.

Record Transfer Fee Paid: £800,000 to Luton T for Steve Davis, December 1998.

Football League Record: 1888 Original Member of the Football League; 1897–98 Division 2; 1898–1900 Division 1; 1900–13 Division 2; 1913–30 Division 1; 1930–47 Division 2; 1947–71 Division 1; 1971–73 Division 2; 1973–76 Division 1; 1976–80 Division 2; 1980–82 Division 3; 1982–83 Division 2; 1983–85 Division 3; 1985–92 Division 4; 1992–94 Division 2; 1994–95 Division 1; 1995–2000 Division 2; 2000– Division 1.

MANAGERS

Arthur F. Sutcliffe 1893–96
(Secretary-Manager)
Harry Bradshaw 1896–99
(Secretary-Manager)
Ernest Magnall 1899–1903
(Secretary-Manager)
Spen Whittaker 1903–10
R. H. Wadge 1910–11
(Secretary-Manager)
John Haworth 1911–25
Albert Pickles 1925–32
Tom Bromilow 1932–35
Alf Boland 1935–39
(Secretary-Manager)
Cliff Britton 1945–48
Frank Hill 1948–54
Alan Brown 1954–57
Billy Dougall 1957–58
Harry Potts 1958–70
(General Manager to 1972)
Jimmy Adamson 1970–76
Joe Brown 1976–77
Harry Potts 1977–79
Brian Miller 1979–83
John Bond 1983–84
John Benson 1984–85
Martin Buchan 1985
Tommy Cavanagh 1985–86
Brian Miller 1986–89
Frank Casper 1989–91
Jimmy Mullen 1991–96
Adrian Heath 1996–97
Chris Waddle 1997–98
Stan Ternent June 1998–

TEN YEAR LEAGUE RECORD

		P	W	D	L	F	A	Pts	Pos
1989-90	Div 4	46	14	14	18	45	55	56	16
1990-91	Div 4	46	23	10	13	70	51	79	6
1991-92	Div 4	42	25	8	9	79	43	83	1
1992-93	Div 2	46	15	16	15	57	59	61	13
1993-94	Div 2	46	21	10	15	79	58	73	6
1994-95	Div 1	46	11	13	22	49	74	46	22
1995-96	Div 2	46	14	13	19	56	68	55	17
1996-97	Div 2	46	19	11	16	71	55	68	9
1997-98	Div 2	46	13	13	20	55	65	52	20
1998-99	Div 2	46	13	16	17	54	73	55	15

DID YOU KNOW ?

In successive seasons 1931-32 and 1932-33, Burnley finished in 19th place in Division 2 and managed to avoid relegation by two points on each occasion.

BURNLEY 1999–2000 LEAGUE RECORD

Match No.	Date	Venue	Opponents	Result	H/T Score	Lg. Pos.	Goalscorers	Attendance
1	Aug 7	A	Wycombe W	D 1-1	0-1	9	Cooke [68]	6119
2	14	H	Chesterfield	W 2-1	2-0	6	Payton (pen) [31], Johnrose [33]	10,615
3	21	A	Oldham Ath	W 1-0	1-0	4	Payton [31]	8543
4	28	H	Stoke C	W 1-0	0-0	3	Payton [75]	11,328
5	30	A	Bristol R	L 0-1	0-1	3		7624
6	Sept 3	H	Bournemouth	W 2-1	1-1	—	Branch [38], Davis [62]	10,223
7	11	A	Preston NE	D 0-0	0-0	4		13,708
8	18	H	Colchester U	W 3-0	2-0	1	Payton 3 (1 pen) [9, 38 (p), 51]	10,090
9	25	A	Bristol C	D 0-0	0-0	2		11,510
10	Oct 2	H	Brentford	D 2-2	2-0	3	Payton [23], Cook [31]	10,907
11	10	H	Scunthorpe U	L 1-2	0-1	5	Payton [59]	10,752
12	16	A	Millwall	D 1-1	1-0	6	Cooke [12]	8601
13	19	A	Cambridge U	W 1-0	1-0	—	Cooke [6]	4320
14	23	H	Bristol C	W 2-0	1-0	5	Cook [6], Cooke [61]	10,175
15	Nov 2	H	Wrexham	W 5-0	1-0	—	Mullin 2 [43, 70], Mellon [46], Little [49], Branch [82]	8944
16	6	A	Luton T	L 1-2	0-0	4	Cooke [50]	7205
17	14	H	Blackpool	W 1-0	0-0	4	Mellon [77]	12,898
18	24	A	Reading	D 0-0	0-0	—		6149
19	27	A	Wigan Ath	D 1-1	1-1	5	Payton [17]	11,986
20	Dec 4	H	Wycombe W	W 1-0	0-0	5	Payton [78]	9149
21	18	H	Cardiff C	W 2-1	1-1	5	Armstrong [34], Johnrose [68]	9753
22	26	A	Bury	L 2-4	0-4	6	Jepson [89], Mullin [90]	9115
23	28	H	Oxford U	W 3-2	1-1	5	Payton 3 (1 pen) [22 (p), 80, 89]	14,218
24	Jan 3	A	Notts Co	L 0-2	0-1	5		8229
25	15	A	Chesterfield	D 1-1	1-0	6	Payton [4]	4214
26	22	H	Oldham Ath	W 3-0	1-0	5	Cooke [24], Payton 2 [62, 80]	12,391
27	29	A	Stoke C	D 2-2	0-0	5	Payton 2 (1 pen) [76 (p), 83]	15,354
28	Feb 5	H	Bristol R	W 1-0	0-0	5	Little [69]	13,526
29	12	A	Bournemouth	W 1-0	1-0	4	Payton [32]	5804
30	19	A	Wigan Ath	D 0-0	0-0	5		20,435
31	26	A	Colchester U	W 2-1	2-1	5	Davis 2 [17, 38]	6194
32	Mar 4	H	Preston NE	L 0-3	0-1	5		22,310
33	7	H	Luton T	L 0-2	0-1	—		12,080
34	11	A	Wrexham	W 1-0	1-0	5	Payton [6]	6582
35	14	A	Gillingham	D 2-2	1-1	—	Payton [31], Wright [86]	7347
36	18	H	Reading	W 3-0	1-0	5	Davis [37], Payton [52], Wright [84]	14,436
37	21	A	Blackpool	D 1-1	0-0	—	Branch [72]	8029
38	25	H	Bury	D 2-2	0-0	5	Payton [50], Jepson [90]	13,297
39	Apr 1	A	Cardiff C	W 2-1	1-0	5	Davis [21], Payton [61]	6487
40	8	H	Notts Co	W 2-1	1-0	5	Payton [5], Wright [90]	13,022
41	15	A	Oxford U	W 2-1	0-1	5	Davis [85], Weller [90]	7549
42	18	H	Gillingham	L 0-3	0-1	—		17,026
43	22	H	Millwall	W 4-3	3-0	4	Cox [6], Cooke [28], Davis [43], Cook [52]	14,890
44	24	A	Brentford	W 3-2	0-1	3	Mullin 2 [61, 76], Wright [64]	6595
45	29	H	Cambridge U	W 2-0	2-0	2	Payton 2 [13, 31]	15,084
46	May 6	A	Scunthorpe U	W 2-1	1-1	2	Mellon [41], Little [73]	5862

Final League Position: 2

GOALSCORERS

League (69): Payton 27 (4 pens), Cooke 7, Davis 7, Mullin 5, Wright 4, Branch 3, Cook 3, Little 3, Mellon 3, Jepson 2, Johnrose 1, Armstrong 1, Cox 1, Weller 1.
Worthington Cup (0).
FA Cup (4): Cook 2, Cooke 1, Mullin 1.

Crichton P 46	West D 30+4	Thomas M 44	Mellon M 33+9	Davis S 42	Smith P 17+7	Little G 36+5	Cook P 44	Cooke A 33+3	Branch G 31+13	Mullin J 27+10	Jepson R 1+30	Payton A 39+2	Lee A 2+13	Cowan T 5+3	Armstrong G 22	Johnrose L 28+7	Robertson M —+1	Brass C 4+3	Weller P 1+6	Swan P —+2	Cox I 17	Wright I 4+11	Match No.
1	2	5	4	6	3	7	8¹	9	10²	11³	12	13	14										1
1	2	6	4	5²	12	8	14		13	9¹	10³	3	11	7									2
1	2	5	4		7		8²	9¹	12		13	10³	14	3	6	11							3
1	2	5	4¹		7	12	8²		14		13	9	10³	3	6	11							4
1	2	5	4			7	8¹	9	14	12	10			3²	11		13³	6					5
1	2	6	4	5	3³	7	8¹	9²		12	10		14	11	13								6
1	2	6	4¹	5	3³	7²	8		9	13		10	14	11	12								7
1	2	6	4¹	5	3	7²	8		9³	13		10	14	11	12								8
1	2	6	4	5	3	7²	8¹		9³	13	12	10		11	14								9
1	2	6	4²	5	3³	7	8	12	9¹	13		10		11	14								10
1	2	6	4²	5	3	7	8	12	9³	13		10		11¹					14				11
1	2	6	12	5	3	7¹	8	9²	13	11		10			4								12
1	2	6	12	5	3³	7¹	8	9	10²	11			13		4	14							13
1	2	6	12	5	3	7	8²	9³	14	11¹	13	10			4								14
1		6	4	5		7	8³	9¹	12	11	13	10²	14	3		2							15
1		6	4	5		7	8	9	12	11	14	10¹	13	3²		2³							16
1	2	6	4	5		7	8	9²	12	11¹	13	10		3									17
1	2	6	4	5		7	8	9¹	12	11		10²	13	3									18
1	2	6	4	5		7	8	9²	12	11		10	13	3¹									19
1	2²	6	4	5		7	8	9³	12	11¹	13	10		3	14								20
1	2¹	6	4³	5		7	8	9²	12	11	13	10		3	14								21
1	2¹		4²	5		7³		9	10	11	12		13	3	8		6	14					22
1	2¹	3	4	5	13	7	6³	9	8²	11	12	10							14				23
1	2³	3	4	5	13	7	6	9¹	8²	11	12	10						14					24
1	2	6			7	8	9¹	12		13	10	5	3³	11		14	4²						25
1	2	6	4¹	5	13		11³	9	8²	12	14	10		3	7								26
1	2²	6			5	13	12	7	9	8¹	11		10	3	4³			14					27
1		6	12	5		7¹	8²	9	14	11	13	10		3³	2						4		28
1	13	3	12	5		7	6³	9	8	11¹	14	10²		2							4		29
1	12	3		5	13	7¹	6	9³	8²	11	14			2						4	10		30
1		3		5		7	6	9	8	11	12			2						4	10		31
1	2		12	5	13	7	6¹	9³	8	11¹				3	14					4	10		32
1		3	12	5	13	7	6³	9	8²	11¹		14		2						4	10		33
1	12	6	11	5	3	7¹	8²	9³				13	10	2						4	14		34
1		3	11¹	5		7	6³	9²	8	12	13	10		2						4	14		35
1		3	11¹	5		7	6	9²	8	12		10³	13	2						4	14		36
1		3	11¹	5		7	6	9²	8	12		10		2						4	13		37
1		3	12	5		7	6²	9¹	8	11	13	10		2						4			38
1	12	6	13	5	3	7	8	9¹	11²			10³	14	2						4			39
1		6	11	5	3	7	8¹		10²		12	9¹	13	2						4	14		40
1	2³	6	11	5	3²		8¹		10			9	13	7			12			4	14		41
1	2¹	6	11	5	3²		8³		10		13	9		7			12			4	14		42
1		3	7	5		6¹	9³	8	11	2	10²	13					12			4	14		43
1		3	6	5		7¹		9	8	11	12	10²		2						4	13		44
1	2	3	4	5		12	6²	9³	8	11	13	10¹		7							14		45
1	2	3	4	5		12	6	9³	8¹	11	13	10²		7							14		46

Worthington Cup
First Round　　Manchester C　　(a)　0-5
　　　　　　　　　　　　　　　　(h)　0-1

FA Cup
First Round　　Barnet　　(a)　1-0
Second Round　Rotherham U　　(h)　2-0
Third Round　　Derby Co　　(a)　1-0
Fourth Round　Coventry C　　(a)　0-3

Division 2 **BURY**

FOUNDATION

A meeting at the Waggon & Horses Hotel, attended largely by members of Bury Wesleyans and Bury Unitarians football clubs, decided to form a new Bury club. This was officially formed at a subsequent gathering at the Old White Horse Hotel, Fleet Street, Bury on 24 April 1885.

Gigg Lane, Bury BL9 9HR.
Telephone: (0161) 764 4881.
Fax: (0161) 764 5521.
Commercial Dept: (0161) 705 2144.
Fax: (0161) 762 9620.
ClubCall: 09068 121 197.
Community Programme: (0161) 797 5423.
Social Club: (0161) 764 6771.
Ground Capacity: 11,841.
Record Attendance: 35,000 v Bolton W, FA Cup 3rd rd, 9 January 1960.
Record Receipts: £86,000 v Manchester C, Division 1, 12 September 1997.
Pitch Measurements: 112yd × 72yd.
Chairman: T. Robinson.
Directors: J. Smith, F. Mason, N. Neville.
Manager: Andy Preece.
Assistant Manager: Kevin Blackwell.
Coach: Alex Jones.
Physios: Alan Raw, Matthew Radcliffe.
Youth Development: Wayne Joyce.
Safety Officer: Wilf Linton.
Secretary: Jill Neville.
Commercial Manager: Neville Neville.

LATEST SEQUENCES

Longest Sequence of League Wins: 9, 26.9.60 – 19.11.60.
Longest Sequence of League Defeats: 6, 14.1.67 – 4.3.67.
Longest Sequence of League Draws: 6, 6.3.99 – 3.4.99.
Longest Sequence of Unbeaten League Matches: 18, 4.2.61 – 29.4.61.
Longest Sequence Without a League Win: 19, 1.4.11 – 2.12.11.

HONOURS

Football League: Division 1 best season: 4th, 1925–26; Division 2 – Champions 1894–95, 1996–97; Runners-up 1923–24; Division 3 – Champions 1960–61; Runners-up 1967–68; Promoted from Division 3 (3rd) 1995–96.
FA Cup: Winners 1900, 1903.
Football League Cup: Semi-final 1963.

Colours
White shirts, royal blue shorts, royal blue stockings.

Change Colours
Peach and blue.

Year Formed: 1885.

Turned professional: 1885.

Ltd Co.: 1897.

Club Nickname: 'Shakers'.

Club Sponsors: Birthdays.

First Football League Game: 1 September 1894, Division 2, v Manchester C (h) W 4–2 – Lowe; Gillespie, Davies; White, Clegg, Ross; Wylie, Barbour (2), Millar (1), Ostler (1), Plant.

Record League Victory: 8–0 v Tranmere R, Division 3, 10 January 1970 – Forrest; Tinney, Saile; Anderson, Turner, McDermott; Hince (1), Arrowsmith (1), Jones (4), Kerr (1), Grundy, (1 og).

Record Cup Victory: 12–1 v Stockton, FA Cup 1st rd (replay), 2 February 1897 – Montgomery; Darroch, Barbour; Hendry (1), Clegg, Ross (1); Wylie (3), Pangbourn, Millar (4), Henderson (2), Plant, (1 og).

Record Defeat: 0–10 v West Ham U, Milk Cup 2nd rd 2nd leg, 25 October 1983.

Most League Points (2 for a win): 68, Division 3, 1960–61.

Most League Points (3 for a win): 84, Division 4, 1984–85 and Division 2, 1996–97.

Most League Goals: 108, Division 3, 1960–61.

Highest League Scorer in Season: Craig Madden, 35, Division 4, 1981–82.

Most League Goals in Total Aggregate: Craig Madden, 129, 1978–86.

Most League Goals in One Match: 5, Eddie Quigley v Millwall, Division 2, 15 February 1947; 5, Ray Pointer v Rotherham U, Division 2, 2 October 1965.

Most Capped Player: Bill Gorman, 11 (13), Republic of Ireland and (4), Northern Ireland.

Most League Appearances: Norman Bullock, 506, 1920–35.

Youngest League Player: Brian Williams, 16 years 133 days v Stockport Co, 18 March 1972.

Record Transfer Fee Received: £1,100,000 from Ipswich T for David Johnson, November 1997.

Record Transfer Fee Paid: £200,000 to Ipswich T for Chris Swailes, November 1997 and to Swindon T for Darren Bullock, February 1999.

Football League Record: 1894 Elected to Division 2; 1895–1912 Division 1; 1912–24 Division 2; 1924–29 Division 1; 1929–57 Division 2; 1957–61 Division 3; 1961–67 Division 2; 1967–68 Division 3; 1968–69 Division 2; 1969–71 Division 3; 1971–74 Division 4; 1974–80 Division 3; 1980–85 Division 4; 1985–96 Division 3; 1996–97 Division 2; 1997–99 Division 1; 1999– Division 2.

MANAGERS

T. Hargreaves 1887
(Secretary-Manager)
H. S. Hamer 1887–1907
(Secretary-Manager)
Archie Montgomery 1907–15
William Cameron 1919–23
James Hunter Thompson 1923–27
Percy Smith 1927–30
Arthur Paine 1930–34
Norman Bullock 1934–38
Jim Porter 1944–45
Norman Bullock 1945–49
John McNeil 1950–53
Dave Russell 1953–61
Bob Stokoe 1961–65
Bert Head 1965–66
Les Shannon 1966–69
Jack Marshall 1969
Les Hart 1970
Tommy McAnearney 1970–72
Alan Brown 1972–73
Bobby Smith 1973–77
Bob Stokoe 1977–78
David Hatton 1978–79
Dave Connor 1979–80
Jim Iley 1980–84
Martin Dobson 1984–89
Sam Ellis 1989–90
Mike Walsh 1990–95
Stan Ternent 1995–98
Neil Warnock 1998–99
Andy Preece May 2000–

TEN YEAR LEAGUE RECORD

		P	W	D	L	F	A	Pts	Pos
1989-90	Div 3	46	21	11	14	70	49	74	5
1990-91	Div 3	46	20	13	13	67	56	73	7
1991-92	Div 3	46	13	12	21	55	74	51	21
1992-93	Div 3	42	18	9	15	63	55	63	7
1993-94	Div 3	42	14	11	17	55	56	53	13
1994-95	Div 3	42	23	11	8	73	36	80	4
1995-96	Div 3	46	22	13	11	66	48	79	3
1996-97	Div 2	46	24	12	10	62	38	84	1
1997-98	Div 1	46	11	19	16	42	58	52	17
1998-99	Div 1	46	10	17	19	35	60	47	22

DID YOU KNOW ?

Right-back Bill Gorman received his first full international cap for the Republic of Ireland against Switzerland on St Patrick's Day 17 March 1936, before making his first team debut which came on 17 April 1937 against Nottingham Forest.

BURY 1999–2000 LEAGUE RECORD

Match No.	Date		Venue	Opponents	Result		H/T Score	Lg. Pos.	Goalscorers	Attendance
1	Aug	7	H	Gillingham	W	2-1	0-0	4	Lawson [47], Littlejohn [53]	4014
2		14	A	Wrexham	L	0-1	0-1	14		4185
3		21	H	Brentford	D	2-2	1-1	12	Lawson [1], Swailes C [90]	3491
4		28	A	Bristol C	D	1-1	0-0	13	Littlejohn [67]	9537
5		30	H	Colchester U	W	5-2	2-1	7	Lawson 3 [12, 57, 68], Littlejohn [15], Preece [74]	3360
6	Sept	4	A	Luton T	D	1-1	0-0	7	Richardson [69]	4633
7		11	A	Oldham Ath	L	0-2	0-0	11		6541
8		18	H	Wycombe W	W	2-0	0-0	9	Preece [53], Bullock [87]	3293
9		25	A	Bournemouth	D	1-1	1-0	9	Lawson [24]	4208
10	Oct	2	H	Cardiff C	W	3-2	1-0	9	Lawson [2], Bullock [58], Preece [77]	3603
11		9	H	Notts Co	L	1-3	0-1	12	Billy [48]	3620
12		16	A	Blackpool	W	5-0	1-0	9	Swailes C [30], Hills (og) [50], Billy [57], Lawson [61], Barnes [82]	5270
13		20	A	Reading	L	0-2	0-1	—		5393
14		23	H	Bournemouth	D	2-2	1-1	10	Preece (pen) [41], Littlejohn [76]	3701
15	Nov	2	A	Bristol R	D	0-0	0-0	—		5397
16		6	H	Stoke C	D	0-0	0-0	11		4280
17		13	A	Oxford U	D	1-1	0-1	—	Lawson [80]	4318
18		23	H	Wigan Ath	D	2-2	1-1	—	Billy [19], Preece (pen) [61]	4086
19		27	H	Preston NE	L	1-3	0-1	13	Lawson [64]	6469
20	Dec	4	A	Gillingham	L	0-1	0-0	13		7036
21		18	A	Scunthorpe U	W	2-0	0-0	12	Logan (og) [48], Barnes [70]	3137
22		26	H	Burnley	W	4-2	4-0	11	Preece 2 (1 pen) [7, 11 (p)], Barrass [32], Littlejohn [41]	9115
23	Jan	4	H	Millwall	D	2-2	1-0	—	Reid [45], Redmond [90]	3375
24		15	H	Wrexham	L	0-2	0-1	15		3622
25		22	A	Brentford	L	1-2	0-0	16	Lawson [82]	5605
26		29	A	Bristol C	D	0-0	0-0	16		3435
27	Feb	5	A	Colchester U	W	3-1	1-1	15	Swailes D [23], James [53], Barnes [58]	3915
28		12	H	Luton T	W	1-0	0-0	14	Littlejohn [61]	3760
29		19	A	Preston NE	D	1-1	1-1	15	James [41]	13,901
30		22	H	Cambridge U	L	0-2	0-0	—		3088
31		26	A	Wycombe W	L	0-3	0-1	16		4909
32	Mar	4	H	Oldham Ath	D	2-2	0-1	16	Reid (pen) [47], Preece [90]	5306
33		11	H	Bristol R	D	0-0	0-0	17		4049
34		18	A	Wigan Ath	L	0-1	0-0	18		6567
35		21	H	Oxford U	L	1-2	0-1	—	Daws [89]	2606
36		25	H	Burnley	D	2-2	0-0	18	Swailes D [77], Daws [88]	13,297
37		28	A	Chesterfield	W	1-0	1-0	—	Swailes D [23]	1903
38	Apr	1	H	Scunthorpe U	W	3-0	1-0	15	Crowe [22], Preece (pen) [64], Barnes [90]	3546
39		4	A	Cambridge U	L	0-3	0-3	—		3016
40		8	A	Millwall	L	0-3	0-3	16		10,742
41		15	H	Chesterfield	D	1-1	1-0	17	Bhutia [39]	3021
42		22	H	Blackpool	W	3-2	1-0	16	Preece 2 (1 pen) [36, 48 (p)], Littlejohn [90]	3857
43		24	A	Cardiff C	W	2-0	0-0	15	Littlejohn 2 [59, 90]	6781
44		29	H	Reading	D	1-1	0-1	15	Preece [89]	3869
45	May	3	A	Stoke C	L	0-3	0-1	—		14,792
46		6	A	Notts Co	D	2-2	0-1	15	Bhutia [72], Billy [73]	4017

Final League Position: 15

GOALSCORERS

League (61): Preece 12 (5 pens), Lawson 11, Littlejohn 9, Barnes 4, Billy 4, Swailes D 3, Bhutia 2, Bullock 2, Daws 2, James 2, Reid (1 pen), Swailes C 2, Barrass 1, Crowe 1, Redmond 1, Richardson 1, own goals 2.
Worthington Cup (1): Lawson 1.
FA Cup (4): Billy 1, Bullock 1, James 1, Littlejohn 1.

Kenny P 46	Woodward A 14	Collins S 19	Daws N 43	Swailes C 27	Bullock D 22+5	Littlejohn A 34+8	Barnes P 13+17	Lawson I 20+5	Reid P 37+2	James L 17+6	Barrick D 12+5	Redmond S 28+5	Preece A 30+13	Williams P 22+4	Swailes D 18+6	Avdiu K 8+13	Billy C 32+4	Richardson L 5	Rocha C —+3	Bhutia B 6+8	Barrass M 24+1	Souter R 2+2	Forrest M 9+6	Crowe D 4	Bryan M 6+3	Linighan B 2+1	Hill N 4+1	Connell L 1+1	Halford S 1+1	Challinor P —+1	Buggie L —+1	Match No.
1	2	3	4	5	6¹	7²	8³	9	10	11	12	13	14																			1
1	2	5	4	6	7²	8		9	10	12				11³	3¹	13	14															2
1		3	4	5	6	7³		9	10²	11¹	12		8	13		14	2															3
1		6	4	5	12	7²		9	10	11		13	3			2	8¹															4
1		3	4	5		7¹		9²	10	11	12	8²		13		2	6	14														5
1		3	4	5	12	7		9	10	11²		6	13			2	8¹															6
1		3	4	5		7		9²	10	11²		6¹	12			13	2	8	14													7
1	3		4	5	14	7²	13	9	10		6³	12	11			2	8¹															8
1	3		4	5	7	8¹	13	9²	10		6	11²	12			2		14														9
1	3		4	5	7	8¹	14	9²	10		12	6	11			2		13³														10
1	3		4	5	8¹	7	13	9²	10		12	6³	11			14	2															11
1	3		4	5	7	12	13	9²	10¹	11		6	8³			2		14														12
1	3¹		4	5	8	13	14	9	10		7²	6	11³	12		2																13
1			4	5	8¹	12	13	9³	10		7	6	11	3²		2		14														14
1			4	5	8	9¹	13	12	10		6	11²	3	7³		2		14														15
1			4	5	7	8	9¹	12	10		6	11	3			2																16
1	2		4	5	6	12		9	10²	11³	13	8	3¹			7		14														17
1	3		4	5	7¹	8	13	9		12		6	10²	11		2¹																18
1	3		4	5	7	8	10³	9		13	11	6²		12	14	2¹																19
1	2³		4	5	7		8			6	12	3		13					9²	10	14	11¹										20
1	11		4	5		8²	9¹		10			6	12	3	13					2	7											21
1	11		4	5		8		12	10			6²	9¹	3	13	14				2	7³											22
1			4	5	12	8		13	10	14		6	9²	3			7³			2	11¹											23
1	5	4¹		13	8	12		10				6	9²	3		11				2	7											24
1		4			7	8²	12	14	10	13		6	9¹	3	5	11³				2												25
1		4			7		8	9¹	10			6	12	3	5	11				2												26
1		4			6	12	8²	9³	10	11¹		5	13	3	7		14			2												27
1		4			7	8		9¹	11²			6	10	3	5	13	12			2		14										28
1		4			7²	8¹	9		12	11³		6	10	3	5		13			2		14										29
1		4			7	8¹	9²		12	11		6	10	3	5	13				2												30
1		4			8	9¹		10	11²	3		6	12	5	13	7				2												31
1	4				8			10	12	3		6¹	13	5	11²	7				14	2		9³									32
1	5	4				8²	11	6		9	3¹	10	7							2	12	13										33
1	5	4		13		10	11	8	6³	12	3		9¹	7²						14	2											34
1	5	4		7	12			10	11¹	3	6	8		9²						13	2											35
1	6	4			12	13³		10	11¹	3	14	9		5		7				2			8²									36
1	6	4			8²	12		10		3³		9¹		5		7				2				13	11	14						37
1	6	4			8²	12		10	13			9¹	3²	5		7				2					11	14						38
1	6	4			8²	12		10	11			5		7						2²	3	13	9¹	14								39
1	6²	4			8	12		10				9		5						2¹	3	13		11	14							40
1		4			8	9¹		10				12	3	5	13	7				11²					2	6						41
1		4	5		8			9	3³	12			7							10²	2	13		11	6¹	14						42
1		4	5		8			9¹	12	11³		7								13²	2	10²		3	6	14						43
1		4	5		7	9¹		12				6¹³	13	8						2	10		3²		11	14						44
1		4	5		7²	12		8				9	6³	13	2					11¹		3	10			14						45
1		4			9²	8		6				12	2							11³		10			3	7	5				13	46

Worthington Cup

First Round	Notts Co	(h)	1-0
		(a)	0-2

FA Cup

First Round	Tamworth	(a)	2-2
		(h)	2-1
Second Round	Cardiff C	(h)	0-0
		(a)	0-1

Division 2   **CAMBRIDGE UNITED**

FOUNDATION

The football revival in Cambridge began soon after World War II when the Abbey United club (formed 1912) decided to turn professional in 1949. In 1951 they changed their name to Cambridge United. They were competing in the United Counties League before graduating to the Eastern Counties League in 1951 and the Southern League in 1958.

Abbey Stadium, Newmarket Rd, Cambridge, CB5 8LN.

Telephone: (01223) 566 500.

Fax: (01223) 566 502.

ClubCall: 09068 555 885.

Website: www.cambridgeunited.com

Ground Capacity: 9247.

Record Attendance: 14,000 v Chelsea, Friendly, 1 May 1970.

Record Receipts: £86,308 v Manchester U, Rumbelows Cup 2nd rd 2nd leg, 9 October 1991.

Pitch Measurements: 110yd × 74yd.

Chairman: R. H. Smart.

Vice-Chairman: R. F. Hunt.

Directors: G. Harwood, J. Howard, R. Hunt, G. Lowe, R. Summerfield, P. S. Barry, R. L. Sargent.

Manager: Roy McFarland.

Player/coach: David Preece.

Youth Manager: Dale Brooks.

Physio: Ken Steggles.

Secretary: Andrew Pincher.

General Manager: Colin Davies.

Stadium Manager: Ian Darler.

LATEST SEQUENCES

Longest Sequence of League Wins: 7, 19.2.77 – 1.4.77.

Longest Sequence of League Defeats: 7, 8.4.85 – 30.4.85.

Longest Sequence of League Draws: 6, 6.9.86 – 30.9.86.

Longest Sequence of Unbeaten League Matches: 14, 9.9.72 – 10.11.72.

Longest Sequence Without a League Win: 31, 8.10.83 – 23.4.84.

HONOURS

Football League: Division 2 best season: 5th, 1991–92; Division 3 – Champions 1990–91; Runners-up 1977–78, 1998–99; Division 4 – Champions 1976–77; Promoted from Division 4 1989–90 (play-offs).

FA Cup: best season: 6th rd, 1990 (shared record for Fourth Division club), 1991.

Football League Cup: best season: 5th rd, 1993.

Colours
Amber shirts with black trim, black shorts, amber stockings.

Change Colours
All white with navy blue trim.

Year Formed: 1912.

Turned Professional: 1949.

Ltd Co.: 1948.

Previous Name: 1919, Abbey United; 1951, Cambridge United.

Club Nickname: The 'U's'.

First Football League Game: 15 August 1970, Division 4, v Lincoln C (h) D 1–1 – Roberts; Thompson, Meldrum (1), Slack, Eades, Hardy, Leggett, Cassidy, Lindsey, McKinven, Harris.

Record League Victory: 6–0 v Darlington, Division 4, 18 September 1971 – Roberts; Thompson, Akers, Guild, Eades, Foote, Collins (1p), Horrey, Hollett, Greenhalgh (4), Phillips, (1 og). 6–0 v Hartlepool U, Division 4, 11 February 1989 – Vaughan; Beck, Kimble, Turner, Chapple (1), Daish, Clayton, Holmes, Taylor (3 incl. 1p), Bull (1), Leadbitter (1).

Record Cup Victory: 5–1 v Bristol C, FA Cup 5th rd second replay, 27 February 1990 – Vaughan; Fensome, Kimble, Bailie (O'Shea), Chapple, Daish, Cheetham (Robinson), Leadbitter (1), Dublin (2), Taylor (1), Philpott (1).

Record Defeat: 0–6 v Aldershot, Division 3, 13 April 1974; v Darlington, Division 4, 28 September 1974. 0–6 v Chelsea, Division 2, 15 January 1983 and v Brentford, Division 2, 28 January 1995.

Most League Points (2 for a win): 65, Division 4, 1976–77.

Most League Points (3 for a win): 86, Division 3, 1990–91.

Most League Goals: 87, Division 4, 1976–77.

Highest League Scorer in Season: David Crown, 24, Division 4, 1985–86.

Most League Goals in Total Aggregate: John Taylor, 83, 1988–92; 1996–2000.

Most League Goals in One Match: 5, Steve Butler v Exeter C, Division 2, 4 April 1994.

Most Capped Player: Tom Finney, 7 (15), Northern Ireland.

Most League Appearances: Steve Spriggs, 416, 1975–87.

Youngest League Player: Andy Sinton, 16 years 228 days v Wolverhampton W, 2 November 1982.

Record Transfer Fee Received: £1,000,000 from Manchester U for Dion Dublin, August 1992.

Record Transfer Fee Paid: £190,000 to Luton T for Steve Claridge, November 1992.

Football League Record: 1970 Elected to Division 4; 1973–74 Division 3; 1974–77 Division 4; 1977–78 Division 3; 1978–84 Division 2; 1984–85 Division 3; 1985–90 Division 4; 1990–91 Division 3; 1991–92 Division 2; 1992–93 Division 1; 1993–95 Division 2; 1995–99 Division 3; 1999– Division 2.

MANAGERS

Bill Whittaker 1949–55
Gerald Williams 1955
Bert Johnson 1955–59
Bill Craig 1959–60
Alan Moore 1960–63
Roy Kirk 1964–66
Bill Leivers 1967–74
Ron Atkinson 1974–78
John Docherty 1978–83
John Ryan 1984–85
Ken Shellito 1985
Chris Turner 1985–90
John Beck 1990–1992
Ian Atkins 1992–93
Gary Johnson 1993–95
Tommy Taylor 1995–96
Roy McFarland November 1996–

TEN YEAR LEAGUE RECORD

		P	W	D	L	F	A	Pts	Pos
1989-90	Div 4	46	21	10	15	76	66	73	6
1990-91	Div 3	46	25	11	10	75	45	86	1
1991-92	Div 2	46	19	17	10	65	47	74	5
1992-93	Div 1	46	11	16	19	48	69	49	23
1993-94	Div 2	46	19	9	18	79	73	66	10
1994-95	Div 2	46	11	15	20	52	69	48	20
1995-96	Div 3	46	14	12	20	61	71	54	16
1996-97	Div 3	46	18	11	17	53	59	65	10
1997-98	Div 3	46	14	18	14	63	57	60	16
1998-99	Div 3	46	23	12	11	78	48	81	2

DID YOU KNOW ?

At the start of the 1956-57 season, Cambridge United pulled off a major coup by signing England international inside-forward Wilf Mannion, then under a life ban imposed by the Football League.

CAMBRIDGE UNITED 1999–2000 LEAGUE RECORD

Match No.	Date	Venue	Opponents	Result	H/T Score	Lg. Pos.	Goalscorers	Attendance
1	Aug 7	A	Bournemouth	L	1-2	1-0	18	Butler [21]	5552
2	14	H	Reading	W	3-1	1-0	11	Kyd [35], Benjamin [59], Duncan [68]	4630
3	21	A	Chesterfield	L	2-4	1-1	17	Benjamin [8], Wanless [61]	2816
4	28	H	Notts Co	D	1-1	0-0	17	Butler [58]	4329
5	30	A	Wigan Ath	D	1-1	0-0	15	Taylor [77]	5976
6	Sept 4	H	Stoke C	L	1-3	0-1	19	Lightbourne (og) [47]	4007
7	11	H	Brentford	D	2-2	0-2	19	Butler (pen) [48], Benjamin [81]	4234
8	18	A	Millwall	L	1-2	0-0	21	Butler (pen) [53]	7278
9	25	A	Gillingham	D	2-2	0-1	21	Butler (pen) [60], Wanless [64]	4708
10	Oct 2	A	Preston NE	L	1-2	1-0	21	Butler [36]	9522
11	9	A	Wycombe W	L	0-1	0-1	22		5345
12	15	H	Colchester U	W	5-2	2-1	—	Butler 3 [29, 85, 89], Greene (og) [37], Benjamin [74]	5039
13	19	H	Burnley	L	0-1	0-1	—		4320
14	23	A	Gillingham	L	1-2	1-0	22	Youngs [17]	6417
15	Nov 2	H	Scunthorpe U	L	1-3	0-2	—	Kyd [64]	3285
16	6	A	Bristol C	D	1-1	1-1	22	Butler [2]	8646
17	12	H	Luton T	W	3-1	2-0	21	Butler [39], Benjamin [44], Kyd [59]	6211
18	23	A	Wrexham	D	1-1	1-0	—	Benjamin [20]	3467
19	27	A	Blackpool	L	1-2	0-2	21	Butler [82]	4040
20	Dec 4	H	Bournemouth	L	0-2	0-1	23		3579
21	18	H	Oldham Ath	L	2-3	1-2	23	Butler 2 [43, 72]	3162
22	26	A	Oxford U	L	0-1	0-0	23		6772
23	28	H	Cardiff C	D	0-0	0-0	22		4250
24	Jan 3	A	Bristol R	L	0-1	0-0	23		9822
25	15	A	Reading	D	0-0	0-0	24		6953
26	22	H	Chesterfield	W	2-0	1-0	23	Benjamin 2 [44, 66]	3819
27	Feb 5	H	Wigan Ath	D	1-1	0-1	24	Youngs [90]	3755
28	12	A	Stoke C	L	0-1	0-1	24		9662
29	15	A	Notts Co	W	3-2	1-2	—	Richardson (og) [15], Youngs [69], Benjamin [90]	4053
30	19	H	Blackpool	L	0-2	0-1	23		4636
31	22	A	Bury	W	2-0	0-0	—	Taylor [68], Eustace [75]	3088
32	26	H	Millwall	L	0-2	0-2	23		5116
33	Mar 4	A	Brentford	D	1-1	1-0	23	Benjamin [2]	4987
34	7	H	Bristol C	W	3-0	1-0	—	Youngs 2 [5, 76], Benjamin [87]	3505
35	11	A	Scunthorpe U	W	3-0	1-0	20	Taylor [15], Youngs [63], Benjamin [83]	3964
36	18	H	Wrexham	L	3-4	1-1	20	Youngs 2 [29, 53], Benjamin [90]	4591
37	21	A	Luton T	D	2-2	1-1	—	Benjamin [26], Ashbee [56]	5379
38	25	H	Oxford U	W	2-0	2-0	19	Benjamin [8], Hansen [44]	5127
39	Apr 1	A	Oldham Ath	L	0-1	0-0	20		4988
40	4	H	Bury	W	3-0	3-0	—	Wanless [7], Benjamin [25], Hansen [33]	3016
41	8	H	Bristol R	D	1-1	1-0	19	Benjamin [11]	4536
42	15	A	Cardiff C	W	4-0	1-0	19	Taylor 3 (1 pen) [20, 57 (pl), 61], Hunt [86]	6592
43	22	A	Colchester U	L	1-3	0-2	19	Benjamin [53]	4902
44	24	H	Preston NE	W	2-0	2-0	19	Hansen [8], Benjamin [44]	6068
45	29	A	Burnley	L	0-2	0-2	19		15,084
46	May 6	H	Wycombe W	L	1-2	1-1	19	Benjamin [36]	5335

Final League Position: 19

GOALSCORERS

League (64): Benjamin 20, Butler 14 (3 pens), Youngs 8, Taylor 6 (1 pen), Hansen 3, Kyd 3, Wanless 3, Ashbee 1, Duncan 1, Eustace 1, Hunt 1, own goals 3.
Worthington Cup (3): Butler 3.
FA Cup (7): Benjamin 3, Butler 2 (1 pen), Taylor 1, Wanless 1.

Van Heusden A 14 + 1	Chenery B 17 + 1	Ashbee I 43 + 2	Duncan A 13	Eustace S 34 + 2	Wilson C 27	Wanless P 39 + 3	Kyd M 12 + 6	Butler M 26	Benjamin T 42 + 2	Russell A 14 + 1	Mustoe N 28 + 5	Graham M — + 1	Taylor J 18 + 22	Cassidy J 4 + 4	Youngs T 12 + 9	Joseph M 27 + 6	Marshall S 23 + 1	Miller R — + 1	Byfield D 3 + 1	Paterson S 6	Preece D 1 + 11	MacKenzie N 19 + 3	McNeil M 29	Kavanagh J 19	Guinan S 4 + 2	Hansen J 12 + 4	Cowan T 4	Abbey Z 2 + 6	Perez L 9	Lamey N 2 + 1	Chillingworth D — + 3	Hunt J 3 + 4	Match No
1	2	3^1	4	5	6	7	8^3	9	10	11^2	12	13	14																				1
1	2	3	4	5	6	7	8^1	9	10	11			12																				2
1	2^2	3	4	5	6	7	8^1	9	10	11^3	12			13	14																		3
1	2	3	4	5	6	7	12	9	10	11				8^1																			4
1	2	3	4		6	7		9	10	11			12	8^1		5																	5
1^6	2	3	4^2	5	6	7	8^1	9	10	11			12			13		15															6
1	2	3	4			6^2	7^3	12	9	10			11			8^1	13	14	5														7
1^6	2	4^2	5	6	7	8^1	9	10	11			12				13	15																8
1	3	4				6^2	7^3	12	9	10			11			8^1	13	14	5														9
1	2	3	4	5		7^2		9	10				12			6					8^1	11	13										10
1	2^2	3	4	5	6	7			9	12	10^1					8^3	13					14	11										11
1		3	4	5^2	6		8^1	9	10		2		12			13						11^3	14	7									12
1		3	4^1		6^3	12	8^2	9	10		2		13			5						11	14	7									13
1	2	3		5	6^3	12		9^1			7		13	14	8^2	4						11	10										14
		3		5	6^1	7	8	9	10				4	12		2	1					11											15
		3			6	7	8^1	9	10^1				2	12		5	1					11	4										16
		3			6	7	8^1	9	10				2	12		5	1					11	4										17
		3			6	7	8	9^1	10				2	12		5	1					11	4										18
		3			6	7	8	9	10				2^2			12	5	1				13	11^1	4									19
		3			6	7	8	9	10				2	12		5	1					11^1	4										20
		3^1	13	6	7		9	10					12	8		5^2	1					14	11^3	4	2								21
		3		5	6		9	12	8^2	13					7^1	14	1					10^3	11	4	2								22
		3		5	6		9	10	8^1	7	12					1						11^1	4	2	13								23
		3		5	6		9	10	8	7^1	12					1						11^2	4	2	13								24
		3		5	6^2	7	9	10	8^1		12					13	1					11	4	2									25
	2	3		5		7	9	10	8	6							1					11	4										26
		3		5	6^1	7		10	8^3	2	12		14				1					13	11^2	4		9							27
	2	3		5	6	7	12	10					13	8^2			1					14	11^3	4		9^1							28
		3		5	6	7	12	10					8			11							4	2	9^1								29
		3		5	6^2	7		10		8			12			11	13						4^1	2	9^3	14							30
	12			5		7		10		3^2			8			11	6	1						2			9^1	4	13				31
	12			5		7	13	10		3			8			11^3	6	1						2^1			9^2	4	14				32
	2	3		5		7		10		11			8			12		1					4				9^1	6					33
	2	3		5		7		10		9^1			8^2			11	6	1			13	12	4				9^1						34
	2	3		5		7^2		10					8			11	6	1			13	12	4				9^1						35
	2	3		5		7		10					8^3			11	12^1	1				13	4				9^2	6^1	14				36
15	12	3		5		7		10					8			9^1	6	1^6				11^2	4	2	13								37
		3		5		7		10					12			6						11	4	2	9^2		13	1	8^1				38
		3		5		7				10			8^2			6							4	2^1	12		11	1		9^3	13	14	39
		3	5^1		7^3		10	11	8				6									12	4	2	9^2			1		13	14	40
		3		5		7		10			11		8^2			12	6						4	2	9^1		13	1			14		41
		3		5		7^1		10			11		8^3			13	6						4	2	9^2			1			14		42
		3^1			6	7		10			11^3		8			9^2	5						4	2	12		13	1			14		43
		3		5		7		10			12		8				6						4	2	9^1			1			11		44
		3		5		7		10^3	12							13	6						4	2	9^1		8^2	1			14	11	45
				5		12		10	7	6^1			8^3			13	3						4	2	9^2			1			14	11	46

Worthington Cup

First Round	Bristol C	(h)	2-2
		(a)	1-2

FA Cup

First Round	Gateshead	(h)	1-0
Second Round	Bamber Bridge	(h)	1-0
Third Round	Crystal Palace	(h)	2-0
Fourth Round	Wrexham	(a)	2-1
Fifth Round	Bolton W	(h)	1-3

Division 3   **CARDIFF CITY**

FOUNDATION

Credit for the establishment of a first class professional football club in such a rugby stronghold as Cardiff, is due to members of the Riverside club formed in 1899 out of a cricket club of that name. Cardiff became a city in 1905 and in 1908 the South Wales and Monmouthshire FA granted Riverside permission to call themselves Cardiff City.

Ninian Park, Cardiff CF1 8SX.

Telephone: (029) 2022 1001.

Fax: (029) 2034 1148.

Ticket Office: (029) 2022 2857/2022 2858.

ClubCall: 09068 121 171.

Website: www.cardiffcityfc.co.uk

Email: ccafc@baynet.co.uk

Ground Capacity: 15,585.

Record Attendance: 62,634, Wales v England, 17 October 1959.

Club Record Attendance: 57,893 v Arsenal, Division 1, 22 April 1953.

Record Receipts: £141,756 v Manchester C, FA Cup 4th rd, 29 January 1994.

Pitch Measurements: 120yd × 72yd.

Directors: Steve Borley (Chairman), Michael Isaac (Vice-Chairman), Bob Phillips, Paul Guy, David Temme, Kim Walker, Samesh Kumar.

Chief Executive: David Temme.

Acting Secretary: Jim Finney.

Manager: Billy Ayre.

Physios: Mike Davenport, Jimmy Goodfellow.

LATEST SEQUENCES

Longest Sequence of League Wins: 9, 26.10.46 – 28.12.46.

Longest Sequence of League Defeats: 7, 4.11.33 – 25.12.33.

Longest Sequence of League Draws: 6, 29.11.80 – 17.1.81.

Longest Sequence of Unbeaten League Matches: 21, 21.9.46 – 1.3.47.

Longest Sequence Without a League Win: 15, 21.11.36 – 6.3.37.

HONOURS

Football League: Division 1 – Runners-up 1923–24; Division 2 – Runners-up 1920–21, 1951–52, 1959–60; Division 3 (S) – Champions 1946–47; Division 3 – Champions 1992–93. Runners-up 1975–76, 1982–83; Division 4 – Runners-up 1987–88.

FA Cup: Winners 1927 (only occasion the Cup has been won by a club outside England); Runners-up 1925.

Football League Cup: Semi-final 1966.

Welsh Cup: Winners 21 times.

Charity Shield: Winners 1927.

European Competitions: *European Cup-Winners' Cup:* 1964–65, 1965–66, 1967–68 (semi-finalists), 1968–69, 1969–70, 1970–71, 1971–72, 1973–74, 1974–75, 1976–77, 1977–78, 1988–89, 1991–92, 1992–93, 1993–94.

Colours
Blue shirts, white shorts, blue stockings.

Change Colours
Yellow shirts, blue shorts, yellow stockings.

Year Formed: 1899.

Turned Professional: 1910.

Ltd Co.: 1910.

Previous Names: 1899, Riverside; 1902, Riverside Albion; 1908, Cardiff City.

Club Nickname: 'Bluebirds'.

Previous Grounds: Riverside, Sophia Gardens, Old Park and Fir Gardens. Moved to Ninian Park, 1910.

First Football League Game: 28 August 1920, Division 2, v Stockport Co (a) W 5–2 – Kneeshaw; Brittan, Leyton; Keenor (1), Smith, Hardy; Grimshaw (1), Gill (2), Cashmore, West, Evans (1).

Record League Victory: 9–2 v Thames, Division 3 (S), 6 February 1932 – Farquharson; E. L. Morris, Roberts; Galbraith, Harris, Ronan; Emmerson (1), Keating (1), Jones (1), McCambridge (1), Robbins (5).

Record Cup Victory: 8–0 v Enfield, FA Cup 1st rd, 28 November 1931 – Farquharson; Smith, Roberts; Harris (1), Galbraith, Ronan; Emmerson (2), Keating (3); O'Neill (2), Robbins, McCambridge.

Record Defeat: 2–11 v Sheffield U, Division 1, 1 January 1926.

Most League Points (2 for a win): 66, Division 3 (S), 1946–47.

Most League Points (3 for a win): 86, Division 3, 1982–83.

Most League Goals: 93, Division 3 (S), 1946–47.

Highest League Scorer in Season: Stan Richards, 30, Division 3 (S), 1946–47.

Most League Goals in Total Aggregate: Len Davies, 128, 1920–31.

Most League Goals in One Match: 5, Hugh Ferguson v Burnley, Division 1, 1 September 1928; 5, Walter Robbins v Thames, Division 3S, 6 February 1932; 5, William Henderson v Northampton T, Division 3S, 22 April 1933.

Most Capped Player: Alf Sherwood, 39 (41), Wales.

Most League Appearances: Phil Dwyer, 471, 1972–85.

Youngest League Player: John Toshack, 16 years 236 days v Leyton Orient, 13 November 1965.

Record Transfer Fee Received: £500,000 from Coventry C for Simon Haworth, June 1997.

Record Transfer Fee Paid: £180,000 to San Jose Earthquakes for Godfrey Ingram, September 1982.

Football League Record: 1920 Elected to Division 2; 1921–29 Division 1; 1929–31 Division 2; 1931–47 Division 3 (S); 1947–52 Division 2; 1952–57 Division 1; 1957–60 Division 2; 1960–62 Division 1; 1962–75 Division 2; 1975–76 Division 3; 1976–82 Division 2; 1982–83 Division 3; 1983–85 Division 2; 1985–86 Division 3; 1986–88 Division 4; 1988–90 Division 3; 1990–92 Division 4; 1992–93 Division 3; 1993–95 Division 2; 1995–99 Division 3; 1999–2000 Division 2; 2000– Division 3.

MANAGERS

Davy McDougall 1910–11
Fred Stewart 1911–33
Bartley Wilson 1933–34
B. Watts-Jones 1934–37
Bill Jennings 1937–39
Cyril Spiers 1939–46
Billy McCandless 1946–48
Cyril Spiers 1948–54
Trevor Morris 1954–58
Bill Jones 1958–62
George Swindin 1962–64
Jimmy Scoular 1964–73
Frank O'Farrell 1973–74
Jimmy Andrews 1974–78
Richie Morgan 1978–82
Len Ashurst 1982–84
Jimmy Goodfellow 1984
Alan Durban 1984–86
Frank Burrows 1986–89
Len Ashurst 1989–91
Eddie May 1991–94
Terry Yorath 1994–95
Eddie May 1995
Kenny Hibbitt *(Chief Coach)* 1995
Phil Neal 1996
Russell Osman 1996–97
Kenny Hibbitt 1996–98
Frank Burrows 1998–99
Billy Ayre December 1999–

TEN YEAR LEAGUE RECORD

		P	W	D	L	F	A	Pts	Pos
1989-90	Div 3	46	12	14	20	51	70	50	21
1990-91	Div 4	46	15	15	16	43	54	60	13
1991-92	Div 4	42	17	15	10	66	53	66	9
1992-93	Div 3	42	25	8	9	77	47	83	1
1993-94	Div 2	46	13	15	18	66	79	54	19
1994-95	Div 2	46	9	11	26	46	74	38	22
1995-96	Div 3	46	11	12	23	41	64	45	22
1996-97	Div 3	46	20	9	17	56	54	69	7
1997-98	Div 3	46	9	23	14	48	52	50	21
1998-99	Div 3	46	22	14	10	60	39	80	3

DID YOU KNOW ?

The club's nickname "The Bluebirds" was adopted in 1911/12 following the performance of a play in Cardiff – *The Blue Bird* – and as a result of the publicity, supporters called Cardiff City "The Bluebirds".

CARDIFF CITY 1999–2000 LEAGUE RECORD

Match No.	Date	Venue	Opponents	Result	H/T Score	Lg. Pos.	Goalscorers	Attendance
1	Aug 7	H	Millwall	D	1-1	1-1	10	Boland (pen) [45]	10,193
2	14	A	Oxford U	W	3-2	2-0	5	Faerber [17], Nugent 2 [41, 85]	6423
3	20	H	Wrexham	D	1-1	1-0	—	Bowen [37]	11,168
4	28	A	Luton T	L	0-1	0-0	14		5374
5	30	H	Scunthorpe U	D	1-1	0-1	13	Hughes [88]	8006
6	Sept 11	A	Wycombe W	L	1-3	1-1	18	Bowen [12]	4982
7	18	H	Notts Co	W	2-1	0-0	14	Bowen [62], Eckhardt [81]	6568
8	25	H	Wigan Ath	D	0-0	0-0	15		7679
9	28	A	Brentford	L	1-2	0-1	—	Cornforth [57]	5247
10	Oct 2	A	Bury	L	2-3	0-1	17	Nugent 2 [50, 65]	3603
11	9	A	Bristol R	D	1-1	0-1	16	Hill [73]	7363
12	16	H	Oldham Ath	D	1-1	0-1	16	Thomas [62]	5650
13	19	H	Stoke C	L	1-2	1-1	—	Legg [40]	6146
14	23	A	Wigan Ath	L	0-2	0-0	18		5728
15	Nov 2	H	Blackpool	D	1-1	0-0	—	Nugent [89]	4523
16	6	A	Bournemouth	L	0-1	0-0	20		4471
17	12	H	Chesterfield	W	2-1	0-0	17	Bowen 2 [10, 65]	4863
18	23	A	Colchester U	W	3-0	1-0	—	Humphreys 2 [37, 75], Brazier [51]	2557
19	27	H	Gillingham	L	1-2	1-2	17	Legg [18]	7608
20	Dec 4	A	Millwall	L	0-2	0-2	19		9044
21	18	A	Burnley	L	1-2	1-1	20	Thomas (og) [15]	9753
22	26	H	Reading	W	1-0	0-0	17	Nugent [75]	9791
23	28	A	Cambridge U	D	0-0	0-0	18		4250
24	Jan 3	H	Preston NE	L	0-4	0-0	18		10,142
25	9	A	Bristol C	D	0-0	0-0	17		10,568
26	15	H	Oxford U	D	1-1	0-1	17	Nugent [47]	6914
27	22	A	Wrexham	L	1-2	0-0	19	Low [48]	4350
28	30	H	Luton T	L	1-3	0-2	19	Bowen [89]	6185
29	Feb 5	A	Scunthorpe U	D	0-0	0-0	19		3614
30	12	H	Brentford	D	1-1	0-1	21	Fowler [59]	5478
31	22	H	Bristol C	D	0-0	0-0	—		6586
32	26	A	Notts Co	L	1-2	1-0	21	Carpenter [44]	5334
33	Mar 3	H	Wycombe W	D	2-2	1-1	—	Nugent [5], Low [89]	5011
34	7	A	Bournemouth	L	1-2	0-0	—	Earnshaw [69]	4389
35	11	A	Blackpool	D	2-2	2-2	23	Nugent (pen) [18], Bowen [44]	5015
36	17	H	Colchester U	W	3-2	1-1	—	Bowen 2 [34, 70], Nugent [83]	5174
37	21	A	Chesterfield	D	1-1	1-1	—	Perrett [31]	2348
38	25	A	Reading	W	1-0	0-0	20	Bowen [58]	10,044
39	Apr 1	H	Burnley	L	1-2	0-1	21	Cox (og) [66]	6487
40	8	A	Preston NE	D	0-0	0-0	21		13,794
41	15	H	Cambridge U	L	0-4	0-1	22		6592
42	22	A	Oldham Ath	W	2-1	1-1	20	Bowen [44], Brayson [51]	4549
43	24	H	Bury	L	0-2	0-0	21		6781
44	30	A	Stoke C	L	1-2	0-1	21	Young [71]	14,192
45	May 2	A	Gillingham	L	1-4	1-3	—	Bowen [2]	9178
46	6	H	Bristol R	W	1-0	1-0	21	Young [27]	6655

Final League Position: 21

GOALSCORERS
League (45): Bowen 12, Nugent 10 (1 pen), Humphreys 2, Legg 2, Low 2, Young 2, Boland 1 (pen), Brayson 1, Brazier 1, Carpenter 1, Cornforth 1, Earnshaw 1, Eckhardt 1, Faerber 1, Fowler 1, Hill 1, Hughes 1, Perrett 1, Thomas 1, own goals 2.
Worthington Cup (5): Bowen 2, Brazier 1, Hughes 1, Nugent 1 (pen).
FA Cup (5): Nugent 2 (1 pen), Brazier 1, Ford 1, Perrett 1.

Hallworth J 39	Faerber W 31 + 2	Legg A 42	Perrett R 26 + 1	Fowler J 28	Eckhardt J 39 + 2	Boland W 20 + 8	Bonner M 29 + 2	Bowen J 32 + 2	Thomas D 5 + 2	Hill D 12 + 11	Nugent K 37 + 2	Brazier M 20 + 10	Ford M 23 + 3	Jarman L — + 1	Cornforth J 6 + 4	Young S 20 + 2	Phillips L — + 3	Middleton C 7 + 3	Carpenter R 28 + 5	Hughes J — + 2	Roberts C 1 + 7	Vaughan T 14	Kelly S 7 + 1	Low J 12 + 5	Humphreys R 8 + 1	Schwinkendorf J 5	Earnshaw R 4 + 2	Brayson P 7 + 2	Nogan K 4 + 2	Match No.
1	2	3	4	5	6	7	8	9	10¹	11²	12	13																		1
1	2	3		5¹	6	7	8³	9			11²	10	13	4	12	14														2
1	2	3		5	6	7¹	8	9			11	10		4	12															3
1	2¹	3		5²	6			9			10	11	7		8³	4	12	13	14											4
1	2¹	3²		5	6	12		9			10	11	4		8³		7	13	14											5
1	2¹	3		5	7			9			10	11	8		4		6		12											6
1	2	3		5	6	7	9²				10		12	14	8¹		4³	13		11										7
1	2¹	3		5²	6	7		9	12	13	10			8	4				11											8
1	2	3		5²	6	7		9	13	10		12		8	4				11¹											9
	2	3		5	6	7²		9	13	12	10			8¹	4				11	1										10
1	2	3		5	7²			9	8¹	10	12	4		11³		13	14		6											11
1	2	3	4	8	5	7²		9	11¹	10	12					13			6											12
1	2	3¹	4	8	5	7		9	11	10	12								6											13
1	2	3	4	8¹	5³	7		9¹	11	10	12		13	14					6											14
1	2	3²		8	5			9¹	7³	10	11	4				13		12	6		14									15
1	2³	3	12	5	13			9	7²	10	11	4¹				8			6		14									16
1	2	3	4	5	12			9	7¹	11						8			10		6									17
1	2	3	4	5	12	7¹	9²			11						8			13		6			10						18
1	2	3	4	5		7²	9	13		11¹	12					8			14		6			10³						19
1	2	3¹	4	5	12	7²	9³	13		11						8			14		6			10						20
1	3²	4		5	12	7¹	9			14	13	2				11			8					10³	6					21
1	2	3	4	5			9									7			11			8		10¹	6	12				22
1	2	3	4¹	5	8		9									12	7	6				11	10							23
1	12	3		8	5		13	14		9	11					7³	4					2¹	10	6²						24
	3	4	7	5				12	9	11¹	10					8²	6	13				2								25
1	3			5	7	8	9		10			4				11						2	6							26
1	3¹			5	7	8³	9	13	10	12	4					11²						2	14	6						27
1	12	3	4		5¹	7²	8	13		9						11						2	10							28
1		3	4	7			8			9	11	6				5			10			2								29
1		3	4	7			8	12		9	11	6				5			10			2¹								30
1		3	4	5¹			8	9		10	11	2				6			7					12						31
1		3	4	5¹	12	13	8	14		10	11	2				6			7²					9³						32
1		3	4	8			12			10	11¹	2				5	7²	6				13		9						33
1		3	4	5³	6	12	8	13		14	10	11				3	7¹		2²					9						34
1		3	4	7	6		8	12		10	11					5			2					9¹						35
1		3	4	7²			8	9	13	10	11¹	6				5	12		14					2³						36
1		3	4	7	12		8	9	13		11²	6				5¹	10	14						2³						37
1	2	3	4	7	5		8	9				6				11			10											38
1	2	3	4	7²	5¹		8	9				6				11			12					13	10					39
1⁶	2	3	4		5		8	9		10		6				11			15						7					40
	2²	3	4¹		5		8	9		10		6		12		11			1					13	7					41
	2	3			5	7	8	9		10		4				6			1					11						42
	2	3			5	7	8¹	9		14	10	12		4		6³			1					11²	13					43
	2	3			5	7	8	9			10	6		4					1					11						44
	2	3			5	7	8¹	9³		12	10	13		4		6			1					11²	14					45
	2	3			5¹	7	8	9		6	10			4	12				1					11						46

Worthington Cup

First Round	QPR	(h)	1-2	
		(a)	2-1	
Second Round	Wimbledon	(h)	1-1	
		(a)	1-3	

FA Cup

First Round	Leyton Orient	(a)	1-1	
		(h)	3-1	
Second Round	Bury	(a)	0-0	
		(h)	1-0	
Third Round	Bolton W	(a)	0-1	

Division 3 **CARLISLE UNITED**

FOUNDATION

Carlisle United came into being in 1903 through the amalgamation of Shaddongate United and Carlisle Red Rose. The new club was admitted to the Second Division of the Lancashire Combination in 1905–06, winning promotion the following season. Devonshire Park was officially opened on 2 September 1905, when St Helens Town were the visitors. Despite defeat in a disappointing 3-2 start, a respectable mid-table position was achieved.

Brunton Park, Carlisle CA1 1LL.

Telephone: (01228) 526 237.

Fax: (01228) 530 138.

Commercial Dept: (01228) 524 014.

Information Line: 09068 230 011.

Ground Capacity: 16,651.

Record Attendance: 27,500 v Birmingham C, FA Cup 3rd rd, 5 January 1957 and v Middlesbrough, FA Cup 5th rd, 7 February 1970.

Record Receipts: £146,000 v Tottenham H, Coca-Cola Cup 2nd rd, 30 September 1997.

Pitch Measurements: 117yd × 72yd.

Directors: A. Doweck (Chairman), R. McKnight, H. A. Jenkins, P. Fletcher, S. Pattison, G. Crooks.

Manager: Ian Atkins.

Physio: Neil Dalton.

Secretary: Sarah McKnight.

LATEST SEQUENCES

Longest Sequence of League Wins: 6, 27.8.94 – 17.9.94.

Longest Sequence of League Defeats: 8, 8.11.86 – 3.1.87.

Longest Sequence of League Draws: 6, 11.2.78 – 11.3.78.

Longest Sequence of Unbeaten League Matches: 19, 1.10.94 – 11.2.95.

Longest Sequence Without a League Win: 14, 19.1.35 – 19.4.35.

HONOURS

Football League: Division 1 best season: 22nd, 1974–75; Promoted from Division 2 (3rd) 1973–74; Division 3 – Champions 1964–65, 1994–95; Runners-up 1981–82; Promoted from Division 3 1996–97; Division 4 – Runners-up 1963–64.

FA Cup: best season: 6th rd 1975.

Football League Cup: Semi-final 1970.

Auto Windscreens Shield: Winners 1997; Runners-up 1995.

Colours
Blue shirts, blue shorts, blue stockings.

Change Colours
All white with green and red trim.

Year Formed: 1903.

Ltd Co.: 1921.

Previous Name: 1903, Shaddongate United; 1904, Carlisle United.

Club Nickname: 'Cumbrians' or 'The Blues'.

Previous Grounds: 1903, Milholme Bank; 1905, Devonshire Park; 1909, Brunton Park.

First Football League Game: 25 August 1928, Division 3 (N), v Accrington S (a) W 3–2 – Prout; Coulthard, Cook; Harrison, Ross, Pigg; Agar (1), Hutchison, McConnell (1), Ward (1), Watson.

Record League Victory: 8–0 v Hartlepool U, Division 3 (N), 1 September 1928 – Prout; Smiles, Cook; Robinson (1) Ross, Pigg; Agar (1), Hutchison (1), McConnell (4), Ward (1), Watson. 8–0 v Scunthorpe U, Division 3 (N), 25 December 1952 – MacLaren; Hill, Scott; Stokoe, Twentyman, Waters; Harrison (1), Whitehouse (5), Ashman (2), Duffett, Bond.

Record Cup Victory: 6–0 v Shepshed Dynamo, FA Cup 1st rd, 16 November 1996 – Caig; Hopper, Archdeacon (pen), Walling, Robinson, Pounewatchy, Peacock (1), Conway (1) (Jansen), Smart (McAlindon (1)), Hayward, Aspinall (Thorpe), (2 og).

Record Defeat: 1–11 v Hull C, Division 3 (N), 14 January 1939.

Most League Points (2 for a win): 62, Division 3 (N), 1950–51.

Most League Points (3 for a win): 91, Division 3, 1994–95.

Most League Goals: 113, Division 4, 1963–64.

Highest League Scorer in Season: Jimmy McConnell, 42, Division 3 (N), 1928–29.

Most League Goals in Total Aggregate: Jimmy McConnell, 126, 1928–32.

Most League Goals in One Match: 5, Hugh Mills v Halifax T, Division 3N, 11 September 1937; 5, Jim Whitehouse v Scunthorpe U, Division 3N, 25 December 1952.

Most Capped Player: Eric Welsh, 4, Northern Ireland.

Most League Appearances: Allan Ross, 466, 1963–79.

Youngest League Player: Rory Delap, 16 years 306 days v Scarborough, 8 May 1993.

Record Transfer Fee Received: £1,500,000 from Crystal Palace for Matt Jansen, February 1998.

Record Transfer Fee Paid: £121,000 to Notts Co for David Reeves, December 1993.

Football League Record: 1928 Elected to Division 3 (N); 1958–62 Division 4; 1962–63 Division 3; 1963–64 Division 4; 1964–65 Division 3; 1965–74 Division 2; 1974–75 Division 1; 1975–77 Division 2; 1977–82 Division 3; 1982–86 Division 2; 1986–87 Division 3; 1987–92 Division 4; 1992–95 Division 3; 1995–96 Division 2; 1996–97 Division 3; 1997–98 Division 2; 1998– Division 3.

MANAGERS

Harry Kirkbride 1904–05
(Secretary-Manager)
McCumiskey 1905–06
(Secretary-Manager)
Jack Houston 1906–08
(Secretary-Manager)
Bert Stansfield 1908–10
Jack Houston 1910–12
Davie Graham 1912–13
George Bristow 1913–30
Billy Hampson 1930–33
Bill Clarke 1933–35
Robert Kelly 1935–36
Fred Westgarth 1936–38
David Taylor 1938–40
Howard Harkness 1940–45
Bill Clark 1945–46 *(Secretary-Manager)*
Ivor Broadis 1946–49
Bill Shankly 1949–51
Fred Emery 1951–58
Andy Beattie 1958–60
Ivor Powell 1960–63
Alan Ashman 1963–67
Tim Ward 1967–68
Bob Stokoe 1968–70
Ian MacFarlane 1970–72
Alan Ashman 1972–75
Dick Young 1975–76
Bobby Moncur 1976–80
Martin Harvey 1980
Bob Stokoe 1980–85
Bryan 'Pop' Robson 1985
Bob Stokoe 1985–86
Harry Gregg 1986–87
Cliff Middlemass 1987–91
Aidan McCaffery 1991–92
David McCreery 1992–93
Mick Wadsworth *(Director of Coaching)* 1993–96
Mervyn Day 1996–97
David Wilkes and John Halpin *(Directors of Coaching)*
Michael Knighton 1997–99
Martin Wilkinson 1999–2000
Ian Atkins June 2000–

TEN YEAR LEAGUE RECORD

		P	W	D	L	F	A	Pts	Pos
1989-90	Div 4	46	21	8	17	61	60	71	8
1990-91	Div 4	46	13	9	24	47	89	48	20
1991-92	Div 4	42	7	13	22	41	67	34	22
1992-93	Div 3	42	11	11	20	51	65	44	18
1993-94	Div 3	42	18	10	14	57	42	64	7
1994-95	Div 3	42	27	10	5	67	31	91	1
1995-96	Div 2	46	12	13	21	57	72	49	21
1996-97	Div 3	46	24	12	10	67	44	84	3
1997-98	Div 2	46	12	8	26	57	73	44	23
1998-99	Div 3	46	11	16	19	43	53	49	23

DID YOU KNOW ❓

On 1 June 1972, Carlisle United beat the Italian club Roma, coached by Helenio Herrera, 3-2 in the Anglo-Italian Cup in the Olympic Stadium.

CARLISLE UNITED 1999–2000 LEAGUE RECORD

Match No.	Date		Venue	Opponents	Result		H/T Score	Lg. Pos.	Goalscorers	Attendance
1	Aug	7	H	Leyton Orient	W	2-1	1-1	4	Tracey [21], Soley [69]	3895
2		14	A	Swansea C	L	0-1	0-0	12		5452
3		21	H	Hartlepool U	L	0-3	0-1	18		4033
4		28	A	Mansfield T	D	1-1	1-1	16	Baker [37]	2138
5		30	H	Plymouth Arg	W	4-2	2-0	12	Tracey 2 [41, 75], Black [44], Baker [47]	2863
6	Sept	4	A	Northampton T	D	0-0	0-0	15		4864
7		11	H	Lincoln C	W	1-0	0-0	13	Tracey [59]	3254
8		18	A	Shrewsbury T	L	1-4	1-0	14	Soley [45]	2393
9		25	A	Halifax T	L	2-5	1-3	16	Tracey [10], Gregory [76]	2545
10	Oct	2	H	Southend U	D	1-1	1-0	18	Clark [20]	2800
11		9	H	Brighton & HA	L	0-1	0-0	19		3059
12		16	A	Exeter C	D	1-1	0-0	18	Dobie [85]	3012
13		19	A	Darlington	L	1-3	0-1	—	Harries [77]	5016
14		23	H	Halifax T	D	1-1	0-1	19	Dobie [55]	2593
15	Nov	2	H	York C	L	0-1	0-1	—		2512
16		6	A	Cheltenham T	L	1-3	1-1	21	Dobie [18]	3118
17		12	H	Peterborough U	D	1-1	1-1	21	Dobie [8]	2515
18		23	A	Barnet	L	0-3	0-1	—		1769
19		27	H	Rotherham U	L	0-1	0-0	22		2649
20	Dec	4	A	Leyton Orient	W	1-0	0-0	21	Pitts [83]	3871
21		14	H	Torquay U	D	0-0	0-0	—		2028
22		18	A	Hull C	L	1-2	0-0	22	Tracey [90]	4727
23		26	H	Rochdale	L	1-2	1-0	22	Dalton [16]	3812
24		28	A	Macclesfield T	L	1-2	0-0	22	Tracey [62]	2836
25	Jan	3	H	Chester C	W	4-1	1-0	22	Dobie 2 [2, 51], Harries [71], Prokas [90]	4565
26		8	A	Torquay U	L	1-4	0-1	22	Soley [49]	2112
27		22	A	Hartlepool U	L	0-1	0-0	23		3530
28		29	H	Mansfield T	L	0-2	0-1	23		2501
29	Feb	5	A	Plymouth Arg	L	0-2	0-1	23		4009
30		19	A	Rotherham U	L	2-4	1-2	23	Halliday [43], Soley [69]	4271
31		26	H	Shrewsbury T	D	1-1	0-1	23	Halliday [46]	3105
32	Mar	4	A	Lincoln C	L	0-5	0-2	23		2945
33		11	A	York C	D	1-1	0-0	24	Halliday [60]	2976
34		18	H	Barnet	W	3-1	2-0	23	Soley [29], Halliday 2 [42, 51]	2606
35		21	A	Peterborough U	W	2-0	1-0	—	Durnin 2 [38, 62]	5178
36		25	H	Rochdale	L	2-3	1-2	23	Soley 2 (2 pens) [14, 71]	2417
37		28	H	Swansea C	W	2-0	1-0	—	Searle [37], Halliday [59]	2748
38	Apr	1	H	Hull C	L	0-4	0-2	22		3495
39		4	H	Cheltenham T	D	1-1	0-0	—	Soley [89]	2388
40		8	A	Chester C	W	1-0	0-0	22	Dobie [90]	5507
41		11	H	Northampton T	L	0-1	0-1	—		2855
42		15	H	Macclesfield T	L	0-1	0-0	22		3047
43		22	H	Exeter C	D	0-0	0-0	22		3567
44		24	A	Southend U	L	0-2	0-0	23		3053
45		29	H	Darlington	D	1-1	1-0	22	Halliday [38]	6525
46	May	6	A	Brighton & HA	L	0-1	0-1	23		5998

Final League Position: 23

GOALSCORERS

League (42): Soley 8 (2 pens), Dobie 7, Halliday 7, Tracey 7, Baker 2, Durnin 2, Harries 2, Black 1, Clark 1, Dalton 1, Gregory 1, Pitts 1, Prokas 1, Searle 1.
Worthington Cup (0).
FA Cup (1): Harries 1.

Weaver L 29	Pitts M 20+9	Clark P 42+1	Whitehead S 29	Brightwell D 37	Prokas R 28+7	Soley S 35+2	Hopper T 25+2	Walker A 3	Tracey R 25+11	Searle D 14+7	Barr B 28+1	Skelton G 1+6	Thorpe J 4+9	Roddie A 1+1	Harries P 6+14	Black T 5	Baker P 12+5	Clarke A 7	Gregory A 6+1	Keen P 6	Ingham M 7	Dobie S 25+9	Dibble A 2	Bowman R 12+3	Anthony G 12+6	Skinner S —+2	Durnin J 20+2	Dalton P 3	Reid P 17+2	Teale S 18	McKinnon R 8	Halliday S 16	Van der Kwaak P 2	Hore J 1	Match No.
1	2^1	3	4	5	6	7^2	8	9	10	11	12	13																							1
1	12	3	4	5	6		8	9	10^2	11^1	2	7^3	13	14																					2
1		3	4	5	6		8	9	10	11^1	2	12			7^2	13																			3
1	2	3		5	12	7	8		10	11^1	4		13		6		9^2																		4
1	2	3		5	6^1	7	8		10		4		12				11	9																	5
1		3	4	5		7	8		10		2	12	11^1		6		9																		6
1		3	4	5	12	7	8^1		10		2	13	6^3		14		9	11^2																	7
1		3	4	5		7			10^1		2	13			12	8	9^3	11^2	6																8
12		3	4	5^1	13	7			10		2		14		8		9^3	11^2	6	1															9
12		3	4	5	6	7^2	8		10		2	13			9^3			11^1			1	14													10
		3		5	6		8^1		10		2		12		13	11	7					9^2	1	4											11
		3		5		12			10		2	13	8^3	14	11	6^1						9^2	1	4	7										12
		3		5	12	7^1			10^2		2	14	13	8^3	11							9		4	6										13
		3		5	6	7			10^1		2	12	8									9		4	11										14
			4	5	12	7^3	14		13		2		8^1		10^2	11						9		3	6										15
		3	4	5	6	12	8^1		10^2		2		11		13							9		7											16
		3	4	5	6	7			10		2^1		8			11						9		12											17
	2			5		6^1	7	8^2	10	11	13	4					9^3						1	3			12	14							18
1	2	3	4	5		7			10		8						9^1								11		6		12						19
1	2	3	4	5	6	7			8													9			11		10								20
1	2	3	4	5	6	7					11		12									9			10^1		8								21
1	2^3	3	4	5	6				12	7			13									9^3		14	11		10		8^2						22
1	2^1	3	4	5	6				10	7		13	14									12			11		9^2		8^3						23
1	2	3	4	5	6				10			7^1	8									9		12	11										24
1	2^3	3		5		6			14			10^1	7	13	12							9		4	11		8^2								25
1	2	3	4	5	6		8^2		10^1	7		14			12							9			13		11^3								26
1	2	3^1		5		8	6		10^2	12	7				13							9		4^3	11				14						27
1	2	12			6	8			10^2	3	7				13							9		4	11^1				5						28
1	2	3^2			6^1	8			12	13	7				10^3	14						9		11					4	5					29
	2	3				8			7						12					1		9			10		4	5	6^1	11					30
12		6			10^3		8^2		7	2^1											9		13	14		4	5	3	11	1					31
	2	6			10^1		8		12												9		13	7^2		4	5	3	11	1					32
1		3	4	5	6	7	8														9					10	2	11						33
1	12	3	4	5	6	7^2	8^1		13													14		9^3			10	2	11						34
1		3	4	9	6^1	7	8		12													2		10			5	11							35
1		3	4	9	6^1	7	8	12			13	2^3										10^2		14	5		11								36
1	12	3	4	6^3	7	8^1	13	2							14							9^2		10	5		11								37
12	3^1	4	6^3	7	8	13	2						1			14						9^2		10	5		11								38
1	12	3	4	7	8^1	13	6^3				2^2			14								9		10	5		11								39
1	2	3	4	5	7				12													13		9^2			10	6	8^1	11					40
1	2	3	4	5	7				12	13												14		9^3			8^1	6	10^2	11					41
1	2	3^2	4	5	12	7			13													9					8^3	6	10^1	11					42
1		4	6	7	3				10	2												11		9			8	5							43
		4	6^2	7^1	8	12	2							14	1		13					9^3		3	5		10	11						44
		3	4	12	7	8	2								1		9					10	5	6^1	11									45
12		3	6	7	8^1	13	2								1		4^3					14		10	5		11				9^2		46

Worthington Cup

First Round	Grimsby T	(h)	0-0
		(a)	0-6

FA Cup

First Round	Ilkeston T	(a)	1-2

FA Premiership **CHARLTON ATHLETIC**

FOUNDATION

The club was formed on 9 June 1905, by a group of 14 and 15-year-old youths living in streets by the Thames in the area which now borders the Thames Barrier. The club's progress through local leagues was so rapid that after the First World War they joined the Kent League where they spent a season before turning professional and joining the Southern League in 1920. A year later they were elected to the Football League's Division 3 (South).

The Valley, Floyd Road, Charlton, London SE7 8BL.
Telephone: (020) 8333 4000.
Fax: (020) 8333 4001.
Website: www.cafc.co.uk
Email: info@cafc.co.uk
Box Office: (020) 8333 4010.
ClubCall: 09068 121 146.
Ground Capacity: 20,043.
Record Attendance: 75,031 v Aston Villa, FA Cup 5th rd, 12 February 1938 (at The Valley).
Record Receipts: £201,711 v QPR, FA Cup 5th rd, 8 January 2000.
Pitch Measurements: 111yd × 73yd.
Chairman: M. A. Simons.
Deputy Chairman: R. A. Murray.
Chief Executive: P. D. Varney.
Directors: R. N. Alwen, G. P. Bone, N. E. Capelin, R. D. Collins, D. J. Hughes, M. C. Stevens, D. C. Sumners, D. G. Ufton, R. C. Whitehand, G. B. C. Franklin, W. Perfect.
Manager: Alan Curbishley.
Assistant Manager: Keith Peacock.
First Team Coach: Mervyn Day.
Academy Director: Mick Browne.
Physio: Andy Jones.
Football Secretary: Chris Parkes.
Safety Officer: John Little.
Media and PR: Rick Everitt.

LATEST SEQUENCES

Longest Sequence of League Wins: 12, 26.12.99 – 7.3.00.
Longest Sequence of League Defeats: 10, 11.4.90 – 15.9.90.
Longest Sequence of League Draws: 6, 13.12.92 – 16.1.93.
Longest Sequence of Unbeaten League Matches: 15, 4.10.80 – 20.12.80.
Longest Sequence Without a League Win: 16, 26.2.55 – 22.8.55.

HONOURS

Football League: Division 1 – Champions 1999–2000; Runners-up 1936–37; Promoted from Division 1, 1997–98 (play-offs); Division 2 – Runners-up 1935–36, 1985–86; Division 3 (S) – Champions 1928–29, 1934–35; Promoted from Division 3 (3rd) 1974–75, 1980–81.

FA Cup: Winners 1947; Runners-up 1946.

Football League Cup: best season: 4th rd, 1963, 1966, 1979.

Full Members' Cup: Runners-up 1987.

Colours
Red shirts, white shorts, red stockings.

Change Colours
White shirts, red shorts, white stockings.

Year Formed: 1905.
Turned Professional: 1920.
Ltd Co.: 1919.
Club Nickname: 'Addicks'.

Previous Grounds: 1906, Siemen's Meadow; 1907, Woolwich Common; 1909, Pound Park; 1913, Horn Lane; 1920, The Valley; 1923, Catford (The Mount); 1924, The Valley; 1985, Selhurst Park; 1991, Upton Park; 1992, The Valley.

First Football League Game: 27 August 1921, Division 3 (S), v Exeter C (h) W 1–0 – Hughes; Mitchell, Goodman; Dowling (1), Hampson, Dunn; Castle, Bailey, Halse, Green, Wilson.

Record League Victory: 8–1 v Middlesbrough, Division 1, 12 September 1953 – Bartram; Campbell, Ellis; Fenton, Ufton, Hammond; Hurst (2), O'Linn (2), Leary (1), Firmani (3), Kiernan.

Record Cup Victory: 7–0 v Burton A, FA Cup 3rd rd, 7 January 1956 – Bartram; Campbell, Townsend; Hewie, Ufton, Hammond; Hurst (1), Gauld (1), Leary (3), White, Kiernan (2).

MANAGERS

Bill Rayner 1920–25
Alex McFarlane 1925–27
Albert Lindon 1928
Alex McFarlane 1928–32
Jimmy Seed 1933–56
Jimmy Trotter 1956–61
Frank Hill 1961–65
Bob Stokoe 1965–67
Eddie Firmani 1967–70
Theo Foley 1970–74
Andy Nelson 1974–79
Mike Bailey 1979–81
Alan Mullery 1981–82
Ken Craggs 1982
Lennie Lawrence 1982–91
Steve Gritt/Alan Curbishley 1991–95
Alan Curbishley June 1995–

Record Defeat: 1–11 v Aston Villa, Division 2, 14 November 1959.

Most League Points (2 for a win): 61, Division 3 (S), 1934–35.

Most League Points (3 for a win): 91, Division 1, 1999–2000.

Most League Goals: 107, Division 2, 1957–58.

Highest League Scorer in Season: Ralph Allen, 32, Division 3 (S), 1934–35.

Most League Goals in Total Aggregate: Stuart Leary, 153, 1953–62.

Most League Goals in One Match: 5, Wilson Lennox v Exeter C, Division 3S, 2 February 1929; 5, Eddie Firmani v Aston Villa, Division 1, 5 February 1955; 5, John Summers v Huddersfield T, Division 2, 21 December 1957; 5, John Summers v Portsmouth, Division 2, 1 October 1960.

Most Capped Player: John Robinson, 22, Wales.

Most League Appearances: Sam Bartram, 583, 1934–56.

Youngest League Player: Paul Konchesky, 16 years 93 days v Oxford U, 16 August 1997.

Record Transfer Fee Received: £4,370,000 from Leeds U for Danny Mills, June 1999.

Record Transfer Fee Paid: £1,017,000 to Barnsley for Neil Redfearn, July 1998.

Football League Record: 1921 Elected to Division 3 (S); 1929–33 Division 2; 1933–35 Division 3 (S); 1935–36 Division 2; 1936–57 Division 1; 1957–72 Division 2; 1972–75 Division 3; 1975–80 Division 2; 1980–81 Division 3; 1981–86 Division 2; 1986–90 Division 1; 1990–92 Division 2; 1992–98 Division 1; 1998–99 FA Premier League; 1999–2000 Division 1; 2000– FA Premier League.

TEN YEAR LEAGUE RECORD

		P	W	D	L	F	A	Pts	Pos
1989-90	Div 1	38	7	9	22	31	57	30	19
1990-91	Div 2	46	13	17	16	57	61	56	16
1991-92	Div 2	46	20	11	15	54	48	71	7
1992-93	Div 1	46	16	13	17	49	46	61	12
1993-94	Div 1	46	19	8	19	61	58	65	11
1994-95	Div 1	46	16	11	19	58	66	59	15
1995-96	Div 1	46	17	20	9	57	45	71	6
1996-97	Div 1	46	16	11	19	52	66	59	15
1997-98	Div 1	46	26	10	10	80	49	88	4
1998-99	PR Lge	38	8	12	18	41	56	36	18

DID YOU KNOW ?

On 1 October 1938 on the occasion of the 4-4 draw between Charlton Athletic and Birmingham at The Valley, the crowd included Prime Minister Neville Chamberlain and the Rector of Charlton, who offered prayers over the Munich crisis.

CHARLTON ATHLETIC 1999–2000 LEAGUE RECORD

Match No.	Date	Venue	Opponents	Result	H/T Score	Lg. Pos.	Goalscorers	Attendance
1	Aug 7	H	Barnsley	W 3-1	2-1	1	Mendonca 3 (2 pens) [8, 25 (p), 80 (p)]	19,268
2	21	H	Norwich C	W 1-0	0-0	4	Rufus [73]	19,623
3	28	A	Fulham	L 1-2	0-2	9	Melville (og) [52]	15,154
4	Sept 11	H	Bolton W	W 2-1	1-1	8	Stuart [21], Mendonca [50]	19,028
5	18	A	Sheffield U	W 2-1	1-1	7	Hunt 2 [31, 71]	13,216
6	25	A	Tranmere R	D 2-2	1-1	7	Mendonca (pen) [25], Kinsella [70]	5846
7	28	H	Stockport Co	W 4-0	0-0	—	Hunt 3 [48, 89, 90], Mendonca (pen) [63]	19,842
8	Oct 2	H	Birmingham C	W 1-0	1-0	1	Shields [27]	19,753
9	16	A	Portsmouth	W 2-0	1-0	1	Robinson [43], Salako [90]	14,812
10	19	A	Ipswich T	L 2-4	2-2	—	Hunt 2 [7, 11]	17,940
11	23	H	WBA	D 0-0	0-0	3		19,346
12	26	H	Tranmere R	W 3-2	0-2	—	Brown [47], Robinson [67], Rufus [80]	19,491
13	30	A	Birmingham C	L 0-1	0-1	3		19,172
14	Nov 2	A	Crewe Alex	W 2-0	2-0	—	Stuart [13], Pringle [30]	4741
15	6	H	Walsall	W 2-1	1-1	2	Hunt [45], Stuart [77]	18,663
16	12	A	Grimsby T	W 5-2	2-1	2	Rufus 2 [13, 35], Mendonca [62], Hunt [67], Groves (og) [75]	6849
17	20	H	Manchester C	L 0-1	0-0	3		20,043
18	23	A	Swindon T	W 2-1	2-1	—	Robinson [24], Newton [39]	6515
19	27	H	Port Vale	D 2-2	2-0	3	Mendonca 2 [16, 40]	19,266
20	30	H	Blackburn R	L 1-2	1-1	—	Newton [45]	18,939
21	Dec 4	A	Barnsley	D 1-1	1-1	3	Jones K [42]	14,553
22	18	A	QPR	D 0-0	0-0	4		14,709
23	26	H	Crystal Palace	W 2-1	2-1	3	Salako [13], Pringle [14]	20,043
24	28	A	Huddersfield T	W 2-1	2-0	3	Hunt [29], Robinson [35]	17,415
25	Jan 3	H	Nottingham F	W 3-0	1-0	2	Shields [6], Stuart [70], Hunt [77]	19,787
26	11	A	Wolverhampton W	W 3-2	2-1	—	Rufus [41], Pringle [45], Robinson [71]	18,464
27	15	H	Crewe Alex	W 1-0	1-0	1	Stuart [13]	19,125
28	22	A	Norwich C	W 3-0	1-0	1	Hunt 3 [42, 73, 78]	15,642
29	Feb 5	A	Stockport Co	W 3-1	2-1	1	Hunt 3 [41, 45, 88]	8185
30	12	H	Wolverhampton W	W 2-0	0-0	1	Stuart [48], Brown [69]	20,043
31	15	H	Fulham	W 1-0	0-0	—	Robinson [63]	19,940
32	26	H	Sheffield U	W 1-0	0-0	1	Robinson [47]	19,249
33	Mar 4	A	Bolton W	W 2-0	0-0	1	Pringle [80], Hunt [81]	13,788
34	7	A	Walsall	W 4-2	3-1	—	Hunt 2 [25, 33], Kinsella 2 [45, 66]	6227
35	11	H	Swindon T	L 0-1	0-1	1		19,569
36	19	A	Manchester C	D 1-1	1-1	1	Newton [43]	32,139
37	22	H	Grimsby T	W 4-0	1-0	—	Newton [7], Svensson [54], Hunt [60], Tiler [85]	19,364
38	25	A	Crystal Palace	W 1-0	0-0	1	Kitson [82]	22,577
39	31	H	QPR	W 2-1	1-0	—	Newton [2], Parker [87]	19,617
40	Apr 4	A	Port Vale	D 2-2	0-1	—	Rufus [63], Hunt [74]	4513
41	8	A	Nottingham F	D 1-1	1-0	1	Hunt [40]	20,922
42	14	A	Huddersfield T	L 0-1	0-1	—		19,739
43	21	H	Portsmouth	D 1-1	0-1	—	Stuart [64]	20,043
44	24	A	Blackburn R	D 1-1	1-0	1	Svensson [23]	18,587
45	29	H	Ipswich T	L 1-3	0-1	1	Hunt [81]	20,043
46	May 7	A	WBA	L 0-2	0-0	1		22,101

Final League Position: 1

GOALSCORERS

League (79): Hunt 24, Mendonca 9 (4 pens), Robinson 7, Stuart 7, Rufus 6, Newton 5, Pringle 4, Kinsella 3, Brown 2, Salako 2, Shields 2, Svensson 2, Jones K 1, Kitson 1, Parker 1, Tiler 1, own goals 2.
Worthington Cup (0).
FA Cup (6): Kinsella 2, Hunt 1, MacDonald 1, Newton 1, Robinson 1.

Kiely D 45	Brown S 29+11	Powell C 40	Stuart G 33+4	Rufus R 44	Youds E 23	Newton S 41+1	Kinsella M 38	Hunt A 43+1	Mendonca C 19	Robinson J 43+2	Jones K 16+1	Pringle M 12+20	Jones S 1+1	Parker S 5+10	Shields G 21	McCammon M 1+3	Salako J 4+23	Konchesky P 6+2	Barness A 17+2	Ilic S 1	Todd A 5+7	MacDonald C —+3	Svensson M 13+5	Tiler C 4+7	Kitson P 2+4	Match No.
1	2	3	4	5	6	7^1	8	9^2	10	11	12	13														1
1	2	3	4	5	6	7	8	9^2	10^1	11			12	13												2
1	2^2	3	4	5	6	7^3	8	12	10	11		13		9^1	14											3
1	12	3	4	5	6	7	8		10^1	11^3				9^2			2				13		14			4
1	12		4^1	5	6	7	8	9	10	11^2				2			13	3								5
1			5	6	7	8	10	11^2	12	4^3	2	9^1		13	3	14										6
1	13	3	5	6	7	8	9	10^1	11^3	12	4^2	2		14												7
1	12	3	5	6	7	8	9	10^2	11^3	13	4^1	2		14												8
1		3	5	6	7^2	8	9^1	10	11	4	12	2		13												9
1	12	3^3	4^2	5	6	7	8	9	11	10^1	2			13	14											10
1	12		5	6	7^2	8	9	10^1	11	4^3	2	14	13	3												11
1	12		4	5	6	7^1	9	10	11	8	2	13	3^2													12
1	12	3^2	4	5	6	9	10	11	8^2	13	14	2	7^1													13
1		5	3	4	6	12	8	9	11^1	7	10^2	2	13													14
1	12	3	4	5	6	8	9^1	11	7^3	10^2	2	14	13													15
	12	3	4	5	6^1	8^2	9	10	11	7	2	13								1						16
1	6	3	4^1	5	8	9	10	11	7	13	2^2	12														17
1	12	3	5	6	7^3	8	9	10^2	11	4	13	2^1									14					18
1	2	3	12	5	6	7^3	8	9^2	10	11	4^1			13					14							19
1	2	3^2	12	5	6	7	8	9	10	11^3	4^1			13					14							20
1	2	3		5	6	7	8	9	10^1	4	12	11^2									13					21
1		3		5	6	7^2	9	10	12	4	13	8	2	11^1												22
1	2	3		5	6	7	8	9	12	4^2	10	11^1									13					23
1	12	3		5	6^3	7^2	8^1	9	11	4	10	2									13		14			24
1	8	3	4^2	5		7	9^1	11	10^3	13	2	12										6	14			25
1	6	3	4^2	5		7	8	9	11^1	10^3	2	12										13	14			26
1	6		4	5		7^1	8	9	11^2	10	2	12					3					13				27
1	8	3	4	5		7	9	11	10	2												6				28
1	4	3	8	5		7	9	11^1	10^2	12	2											6	13			29
1	6	3	8	5		7	9	11	10^1	2	4												12			30
1	4	3	8	5		7	9	11	10^1	2^2	6											12	13			31
1	6	3	4	5		7	8	9^3	11^2	12	2^3	13										10	14			32
1	6	3^1	4	5		7	8	9	11^2	12	13	2										10^1	14			33
1	6	3	4^2	5		7	8	9	11	12	2											10^1	13			34
1	6	3^2	4	5		7	8	9^1	11	12	13	2										10				35
1	6	3	4			7	8	9	11	12	2											10^1	5			36
1	6^2	3	4	5		7	8	9^3	11^1	12	2											10	13	14		37
1		3	4	5		7^1	8	9^3	11^2	12	13	2										10	6	14		38
1	6	3	4	5		7^2	8	9	11	12	2^1											10^3	13	14		39
1	6	3	4	5		7	8	9	11^1	12	2^3											13	14	10^2		40
1	6	3	4	5		7^2	8	9	11	12	13	2										10^1				41
1	6	3^2	4	5		7	8	9	11	12	2											13	10			42
1	6	3	4	5		7	8	9	11	12	2											10				43
1	6	3	4	5		7	8	9^2	11^1	12	2											10	13			44
1	2	3	4^1	5		7	8	9	11	12	13	6										10^2				45
1	12			5		7^1	8	9	11	4	13	3	2									10^2		6		46

Worthington Cup
Second Round   Bournemouth   (h)   0-0
                               (a)   0-0

FA Cup
Third Round   Swindon T   (h)   2-1
Fourth Round   QPR   (h)   1-0
Fifth Round   Coventry C   (a)   3-2
Sixth Round   Bolton W   (a)   0-1

FA Premiership

CHELSEA

FOUNDATION

Chelsea may never have existed but for the fact that Fulham rejected an offer to rent the Stamford Bridge ground from Mr H. A. Mears who had owned it since 1904. Fortunately he was determined to develop it as a football stadium rather than sell it to the Great Western Railway and got together with Frederick Parker, who persuaded Mears of the financial advantages of developing a major sporting venue. Chelsea FC was formed in 1905, and when admission to the Southern League was denied, they immediately gained admission to the Second Division of the Football League.

Stamford Bridge, London SW6 1HS.
Telephone: (020) 7385 5545.
Fax: (020) 7381 4831.
ClubCall: 09068 121 159.
Ticket News and Promotions: 09068 121 011.
Ticket Credit Card Service: (020) 7386 7799.
Ground Capacity: 35,421 (during ground development); 41,000 (eventually).
Record Attendance: 82,905 v Arsenal, Division 1, 12 October 1935.
Record Receipts: £488,960 v Liverpool, FA Premier League, 30 December 1995.
Pitch Measurements: 113yd × 74yd.
Chairman: K. W. Bates.
Directors: C. Hutchinson (Managing), Ms Y. S. Todd.
Financial Director: M. Russell ACMA.
Player/Manager: Gianluca Vialli.
Assistant Manager: Gwyn Williams.
Coach: Graham Rix.
Physio: Michael Banks.
Reserve Team Manager: Mick McGiven.
Company Secretary: Alan Shaw.
Assistant Secretary: Claire Lait.
Commercial Manager: Carole Phair.
Safety Officer: Edward Ashwell MBE.

LATEST SEQUENCES
Longest Sequence of League Wins: 8, 15.3.89 – 8.4.89.
Longest Sequence of League Defeats: 7, 1.11.52 – 20.12.52.
Longest Sequence of League Draws: 6, 20.8.69 – 13.9.69.
Longest Sequence of Unbeaten League Matches: 27, 29.10.88 – 8.4.89.
Longest Sequence Without a League Win: 21, 3.11.87 – 2.4.88.

HONOURS

Football League: Division 1 – Champions 1954–55; Division 2 – Champions 1983–84, 1988–89; Runners-up 1906–07, 1911–12, 1929–30, 1962–63, 1976–77.

FA Cup: Winners 1970, 1997, 2000; Runners-up 1915, 1967, 1994.

Football League Cup: Winners 1965, 1998; Runners-up 1972.

Full Members' Cup: Winners 1986.

Zenith Data Systems Cup: Winners 1990.

European Competitions: *European Cup:* 1999–2000. *European Fairs Cup:* 1958–60, 1965–66, 1968–69. *European Cup-Winners' Cup:* 1970–71 (winners), 1971–72, 1994–95, 1997–98 (winners), 1998–99 (semi-finals). *Super Cup:* 1998–99 (winners).

Colours
Royal blue shirts and shorts with white and amber trim, white stockings with royal blue and amber trim.

Change Colours
Gold shirts with blue trim, blue shorts, gold stockings with blue turnover.

Year Formed: 1905.

Turned Professional: 1905.

Ltd Co.: 1905.

Club Nickname: 'The Blues'.

First Football League Game: 2 September 1905, Division 2, v Stockport Co (a) L 0–1 – Foulke; Mackie, McEwan; Key, Harris, Miller; Moran, J. T. Robertson, Copeland, Windridge, Kirwan.

Record League Victory: 9–2 v Glossop N E, Division 2, 1 September 1906 – Byrne; Walton, Miller; Key (1), McRoberts, Henderson; Moran, McDermott (1), Hilsdon (5), Copeland (1), Kirwan (1).

Record Cup Victory: 13–0 v Jeunesse Hautcharage, ECWC, 1st rd 2nd leg, 29 September 1971 – Bonetti; Boyle, Harris (1), Hollins (1p), Webb (1), Hinton, Cooke, Baldwin (3), Osgood (5), Hudson (1), Houseman (1).

Record Defeat: 1–8 v Wolverhampton W, Division 1, 26 September 1953.

Most League Points (2 for a win): 57, Division 2, 1906–07.

Most League Points (3 for a win): 99, Division 2, 1988–89.

Most League Goals: 98, Division 1, 1960–61.

Highest League Scorer in Season: Jimmy Greaves, 41, 1960–61.

MANAGERS

John Tait Robertson 1905–07
David Calderhead 1907–33
Leslie Knighton 1933–39
Billy Birrell 1939–52
Ted Drake 1952–61
Tommy Docherty 1962–67
Dave Sexton 1967–74
Ron Suart 1974–75
Eddie McCreadie 1975–77
Ken Shellito 1977–78
Danny Blanchflower 1978–79
Geoff Hurst 1979–81
John Neal 1981–85 *(Director to 1986)*
John Hollins 1985–88
Bobby Campbell 1988–91
Ian Porterfield 1991–93
David Webb 1993
Glenn Hoddle 1993–96
Ruud Gullit 1996–98
Gianluca Vialli February 1998–

Most League Goals in Total Aggregate: Bobby Tambling, 164, 1958–70.

Most League Goals in One Match: 5, George Hilsdon v Glossop, Division 2, 1 September 1906; 5, Jimmy Greaves v Wolverhampton W, Division 1, 30 August 1958; 5, Jimmy Greaves v Preston NE, Division 1, 19 December 1959; 5, Jimmy Greaves v WBA, Division 1, 3 December 1960; 5, Bobby Tambling v Aston Villa, Division 1, 17 September 1966; 5, Gordon Durie v Walsall, Division 2, 4 February 1989.

Most Capped Player: Dan Petrescu, 43 (92), Romania.

Most League Appearances: Ron Harris, 655, 1962–80.

Youngest League Player: Ian Hamilton, 16 years 138 days v Tottenham H, 18 March 1967.

Record Transfer Fee Received: £4,500,000 from Leeds U for Michael Duberry, July 1999.

Record Transfer Fee Paid: £15,000,000 to Atletico Madrid for Jimmy Floyd Hasselbaink, June 2000.

Football League Record: 1905 Elected to Division 2; 1907–10 Division 1; 1910–12 Division 2; 1912–24 Division 1; 1924–30 Division 2; 1930–62 Division 1; 1962–63 Division 2; 1963–75 Division 1; 1975–77 Division 2; 1977–79 Division 1; 1979–84 Division 2; 1984–88 Division 1; 1988–89 Division 2; 1989–92 Division 1; 1992– FA Premier League.

TEN YEAR LEAGUE RECORD

		P	W	D	L	F	A	Pts	Pos
1989-90	Div 1	38	16	12	10	58	50	60	5
1990-91	Div 1	38	13	10	15	58	69	49	11
1991-92	Div 1	42	13	14	15	50	60	53	14
1992-93	PR Lge	42	14	14	14	51	54	56	11
1993-94	PR Lge	42	13	12	17	49	53	51	14
1994-95	PR Lge	42	13	15	14	50	55	54	11
1995-96	PR Lge	38	12	14	12	46	44	50	11
1996-97	PR Lge	38	16	11	11	58	55	59	6
1997-98	PR Lge	38	20	3	15	71	43	63	4
1998-99	PR Lge	38	20	15	3	57	30	75	3

DID YOU KNOW ?

Chelsea fielded the first ever all-foreign starting XI when they won 2-1 at Southampton on 26 December 1999. But their last goal of the 20th Century was scored by an Englishman, Jody Morris, against Sheffield Wednesday three days later.

CHELSEA 1999–2000 LEAGUE RECORD

Match No.	Date		Venue	Opponents	Result	H/T Score	Lg. Pos.	Goalscorers	Attendance
1	Aug	7	H	Sunderland	W 4-0	2-0	1	Poyet 2 [20, 78], Zola [32], Flo [77]	34,831
2		14	A	Leicester C	D 2-2	0-1	7	Wise [48], Sinclair (og) [90]	21,068
3		21	H	Aston Villa	W 1-0	0-0	4	Ehiogu (og) [52]	35,071
4		28	A	Wimbledon	W 1-0	0-0	3	Petrescu [78]	22,167
5	Sept	11	H	Newcastle U	W 1-0	1-0	2	Leboeuf (pen) [37]	35,081
6		18	A	Watford	L 0-1	0-0	6		21,244
7		25	A	Middlesbrough	W 1-0	0-0	5	Lambourde [54]	34,183
8	Oct	3	H	Manchester U	W 5-0	2-0	4	Poyet 2 [1, 54], Sutton [16], Berg (og) [59], Morris [81]	34,909
9		16	A	Liverpool	L 0-1	0-0	6		44,826
10		23	H	Arsenal	L 2-3	1-0	7	Flo [38], Petrescu [52]	34,958
11		30	A	Derby Co	L 1-3	1-1	8	Leboeuf [10]	28,614
12	Nov	7	H	West Ham U	D 0-0	0-0	9		34,935
13		20	A	Everton	D 1-1	0-1	9	Flo [90]	38,225
14		28	H	Bradford C	W 1-0	1-0	8	Flo [16]	31,591
15	Dec	4	A	Sunderland	L 1-4	0-4	8	Poyet [81]	40,777
16		19	H	Leeds U	L 0-2	0-0	10		35,106
17		26	A	Southampton	W 2-1	2-0	9	Flo 2 [18, 43]	15,232
18		29	H	Sheffield W	W 3-0	2-0	—	Wise [31], Flo [34], Morris [83]	32,932
19	Jan	4	A	Coventry C	D 2-2	0-0	—	Flo 2 [55, 82]	20,152
20		8	A	Bradford C	D 1-1	0-1	7	Petrescu [58]	18,276
21		12	H	Tottenham H	W 1-0	0-0	—	Weah [87]	34,969
22		15	H	Leicester C	D 1-1	0-1	6	Wise [85]	35,063
23		22	A	Aston Villa	D 0-0	0-0	6		33,704
24	Feb	5	A	Tottenham H	W 1-0	0-0	5	Lambourde [52]	36,041
25		12	H	Wimbledon	W 3-1	0-0	5	Poyet [78], Weah [79], Morris [90]	34,814
26		26	H	Watford	W 2-1	1-1	5	Desailly [2], Harley [65]	34,944
27	Mar	4	A	Newcastle U	W 1-0	1-0	3	Poyet [22]	36,448
28		11	H	Everton	D 1-1	1-0	3	Wise [29]	35,113
29		18	A	West Ham U	D 0-0	0-0	5		26,041
30		25	H	Southampton	D 1-1	0-0	5	Richards (og) [75]	34,956
31	Apr	1	A	Leeds U	W 1-0	0-0	5	Harley [62]	40,162
32		12	H	Coventry C	W 2-1	0-1	—	Hendry (og) [53], Zola [58]	32,316
33		15	A	Sheffield W	L 0-1	0-0	5		21,743
34		22	H	Middlesbrough	D 1-1	1-1	5	Poyet [10]	34,467
35		24	A	Manchester U	L 2-3	2-2	5	Petrescu [22], Zola [36]	61,593
36		29	H	Liverpool	W 2-0	2-0	5	Weah [2], Di Matteo [14]	34,957
37	May	6	A	Arsenal	L 1-2	0-1	5	Poyet [79]	38,119
38		14	H	Derby Co	W 4-0	0-0	5	Zola [46], Poyet [56], Di Matteo [69], Flo [89]	35,084

Final League Position: 5

GOALSCORERS

League (53): Flo 10, Poyet 10, Petrescu 4, Wise 4, Zola 4, Morris 3, Weah 3, Di Matteo 2, Harley 2, Lambourde 2, Leboeuf 2 (1 pen), Desailly 1, Sutton 1, own goals 5.
Worthington Cup (0).
FA Cup (18): Poyet 6, Di Matteo 2, Weah 2, Flo 1, Leboeuf 1, Morris 1, Sutton 1, Terry 1, Wise 1, Zola 1 (pen), own goal 1.

De Goey E 37	Ferrer A 24 + 1	Le Saux G 6 + 2	Deschamps D 24 + 3	Leboeuf F 28	Desailly M 23	Petrescu D 24 + 5	Poyet G 25 + 8	Sutton C 21 + 7	Zola G 25 + 8	Wise D 29 + 1	Di Matteo R 14 + 4	Babayaro C 23 + 2	Flo T 20 + 14	Hogh J 6 + 3	Goldbaek B 2 + 4	Morris J 19 + 11	Ambrosetti G 9 + 7	Lambourde B 12 + 3	Harley J 13 + 4	Wolleaston R — + 1	Terry J 2 + 2	Emerson 18 + 2	Weah G 9 + 2	Dalla Bona S — + 2	Melchiot M 4 + 1	Cudicini C 1	Match No.
1	2	3	4	5	6	7[1]	8[2]	9[3]	10	11	12	13	14														1
1	2	3[2]		5		7	8	12	10[1]	11			4	9	6	13											2
1	2			5	6	7[2]	8	9	10[3]	11	3		12			13	4	14									3
1	2		4[2]	5	6	7[3]	8	12	10	11	3		9[1]			13		14									4
1	2	3[2]		5	6	12	13	9[3]	10	11	4		14					8[1]	7								5
1	2	3	4		6	12	9	13	10[2]	5	7[1]	8	11														6
1		3	4[3]	5	6	7	9	10[1]	8		13		12			14		11[2]				2					7
1	2	12	4	5		7[1]	8	9	10[2]	11[3]	3		13		6	14											8
1	2	12	4	5[1]	6	7[3]	8	9	10[2]	11	3		13					14									9
1	2	3[1]	4	5	6	7	12	9	13	11	8		10[2]														10
1	2	12	5[1]			7	9	10		8	3		6[2]			4		11[3]		13	14						11
1	2		4	5	6	7	8	10[1]		3	9					11	12										12
1	2[3]		4	5	6	7[1]	9	12	13	3	10		14			8	11[2]										13
1	2		4		6	7[1]	8	10		3	9		5			12	11										14
1					6[3]	8	10	11[2]	3	9	5	12	4					2				7[1]	13	14			15
1	2		4	5	6[2]	14	7	9	12	11	8		10[1]			13[3]		3									16
1	2		4	5		7[1]	10		8	3	9					12	11[2]	13				6					17
1		4[2]	5			7	10		12	13	8	3	9[1]			14	11[3]	2				6					18
1	2	4[3]		6		12	7[1]	13	10	11	8[2]	3	9			14						5					19
1	2		4			7	8[3]	9[1]	12	11[2]	13	3	10			14					6	5					20
1		5				7	10[1]	12	11	8	9[2]					2	3	6			4	13					21
1	2[2]	4[1]	5			7[3]	12	10	11	8	13					14	3				6	9					22
1		4	5[9]			7[2]	8[1]	13	11	12	14	10				2	3				6	9					23
1		4		6		7[2]	8	10[1]	11	12	13					2	3				5	9					24
1		4[2]	5			7[1]	8	10[3]	12	11	13	14				2	3				6	9					25
1	12		4		6	7	8	10		9	11					2[1]	3				5						26
1	2		5		12	7	9[2]	10	11	8[1]	3		13			4					6						27
1	2		5			12	9	10[2]	11	8	3		13			4		7[1]			6						28
1	2		4	5	6	7[1]	12	13	10	11	14	3				9[2]	8[3]										29
1	2			6		7	12	9[1]	10[2]	11	4		13			3					5	8					30
1	2		5				9		11	8	3					4	12	7[1]			6	10					31
1		5	2			7[1]	10		11	8[3]	9[2]	4				12	3					6	13	14			32
1	12				6	7[3]	8	9		3	13					4[1]	11[2]	2				5	10	14			33
1		4[2]			6		8	9	10[1]	11	12	13				3			7			14		2[2]	5		34
1		4[2]	5			7[1]	12	10		8	9	13	11[3]			3		14				6		2			35
1				5	6	12	13	10	11	8	3[1]					4[3]		7				14	9[2]	2			36
1	12	5[9]		6		13	7[2]	11	8	9	4[1]	3				14		10						2			37
	2[3]		4	5	6[2]	7[1]	10	11	8	3	9		12			13		14								1	38

Worthington Cup

Third Round	Huddersfield T	(h)	0-1

FA Cup

Third Round	Hull C	(a)	6-1
Fourth Round	Nottingham F	(h)	2-0
Fifth Round	Leicester C	(h)	2-1
Sixth Round	Gillingham	(h)	5-0
Semi-Final (at Wembley)	Newcastle U		2-1
Final (at Wembley)	Aston Villa		1-0

Division 3   **CHELTENHAM TOWN**

FOUNDATION

Although a scratch team representing Cheltenham played a match against Gloucester in 1884, the earliest recorded match for Cheltenham Town FC was a friendly against Dean Close School on 12 March 1892. The School won 4–3 and the match was played at Prestbury (half a mile from Whaddon Road). Cheltenham Town played Wednesday afternoon friendlies at a local cricket ground until entering the Mid Gloucester League. In those days the club played in deep red coloured shirts and were nicknamed 'the Rubies'. The club moved to Whaddon Lane for season 1901–02 and changed to red and white colours two years later.

Whaddon Road, Cheltenham, Gloucester GL52 5NA.

Telephone: (01242) 573 558.

Fax: (01242) 224 675.

ClubCall: 09066 555 833.

Ground Capacity: 6114.

Record Attendance: at Whaddon Road: 8326 v Reading, FA Cup 1st rd, 17 November 1956; at Cheltenham Athletic Ground: 10,389 v Blackpool, FA Cup 3rd rd, 13 January 1934.

Record Receipts: £40,000 v Yeovil T, Nationwide Conference, 22 April 1999.

Pitch Measurements: 111yd × 72yd.

Chairman: Paul Baker.

Directors: Rod Burge, Colin Farmer, Arthur Hayward, Brian Sandland, John Wood.

Chief Executive: Arthur Hayward.

Manager: Steve Cotterill.

Assistant Manager: Mike Davis.

First Team Coach: Graham Allner.

Youth Team Managers: Keith Hardcastle, Alan Gough.

Secretary: Reg Woodward.

Physio: Andy Mitchell.

HONOURS

Football Conference: Champions 1998–99, runners-up 1997–98.

FA Trophy: Winners 1997–98.

Southern League: Champions 1984–85; *Southern League Cup:* Winners 1957–58, runners-up 1968–69, 1984–85; *Southern League Merit Cup:* Winners 1984–85; *Southern League Championship Shield:* Winners 1985.

Gloucestershire Senior Cup: Winners 1998–99; *Gloucestershire Northern Senior Professional Cup:* Winners 30 times; *Midland Floodlit Cup:* Winners 1985–86, 1986–87, 1987–88; *Mid Gloucester League:* Champions 1896–97; *Gloucester and District League:* Champions 1902–03, 1905–06; *Cheltenham League:* Champions 1910–11, 1913–14; *North Gloucestershire League:* Champions 1913–14; *Gloucestershire Northern Senior League:* Champions 1928–29, 1932–33; *Gloucestershire Northern Senior Amateur Cup:* Winners 1929–30, 1930–31, 1932–33, 1933–34, 1934–35; *Leamington Hospital Cup:* Winners 1934–35.

Colours
Red and white striped shirts, white shorts, red stockings.

Change Colours
All white with blue and yellow trim.

Year Formed: 1892.

Turned Professional: 1932.

Ltd Co.: 1937.

Club Nickname: 'The Robins'.

Previous Grounds: Grafton Cricket Ground, Whaddon Lane, Carter's Field (pre 1932).

Record League Victory: 11–0 v Bourneville Ath, Birmingham Combination, 29 April 1933 – Davis; Jones, Williams; Lang (1), Blackburn, Draper; Evans, Hazard (4), Haycox (4), Goodger (1), Hill (1).

Record Cup Victory: 12–0 v Chippenham R, FA Cup 3rd qual. rd, 2 November 1935 – Bowles; Whitehouse, Williams; Lang, Devonport (1), Partridge (2); Perkins, Hackett, Jones (4), Black (4), Griffiths (1).

Record Defeat: 1–10 v Merthyr T, Southern League, 8 March 1952.

Most League Points (2 for a win): 60, Southern League Division 1, 1963–64.

Most League Points (3 for a win): 86, Southern League Premier Division, 1994–95.

Most League Goals: 115, Southern League, 1957–58.

Highest League Scorer in Season: Dave Lewis, 33 (53 in all competitions), Southern League Division 1, 1974–75.

Most League Goals in Total Aggregate: Dave Lewis, 205 (290 in all competitions), 1970–83.

Most League Appearances: Roger Thorndale, 523 (702 in all competitions), 1958–76.

Record Transfer Fee Received: £60,000 from Southampton for Christer Warren, 1995.

Record Transfer Fee Paid: £25,000 to Kidderminster H for Kim Casey, 1991.

MANAGERS

George Blackburn 1932–34
George Carr 1934–37
Jimmy Brain 1937–48
Cyril Dean 1948–50
George Summerbee 1950–52
William Raeside 1952–53
Arch Anderson 1953–58
Ron Lewin 1958–60
Peter Donnelly 1960–61
Tommy Cavanagh 1961
Arch Anderson 1961–65
Harold Fletcher 1965–66
Bob Etheridge 1966–73
Willie Penman 1973–74
Dennis Allen 1974–79
Terry Paine 1979
Alan Grundy 1979–82
Alan Wood 1982–83
John Murphy 1983–88
Jim Barron 1988–90
John Murphy 1990
Dave Lewis 1990–91
Ally Robertson 1991–92
Lindsay Parsons 1992–95
Chris Robinson 1995–97
Steve Cotterill 1997–

TEN YEAR LEAGUE RECORD

		P	W	D	L	F	A	Pts	Pos
1989–90	Conf	42	16	11	15	58	60	59	11
1990–91	Conf	42	12	12	18	54	72	48	16
1991–92	Conf	42	10	13	19	56	82	43	21
1992–93	Sth L	40	21	10	9	76	40	73	2
1993–94	Sth L	42	21	12	9	67	38	75	2
1994–95	Sth L	42	25	11	6	87	39	86	2
1995–96	Sth L	42	21	11	10	76	57	74	3
1996–97	Sth L	42	21	11	10	76	44	74	2
1997–98	Conf	42	23	9	10	63	43	78	2
1998–99	Conf	42	22	14	6	71	36	80	1

DID YOU KNOW ?

Locally-born Tim Ward, then a part-timer with Cheltenham Town, scored with his first kick on trial with Derby County A team and was signed for £100 in April 1937. He went on to win England honours.

CHELTENHAM TOWN 1999–2000 LEAGUE RECORD

Match No.	Date	Venue	Opponents	Result	H/T Score	Lg. Pos.	Goalscorers	Atten- dance
1	Aug 7	H	Rochdale	L	0-2	0-2	22		5189
2	14	A	Mansfield T	W	1-0	0-0	15	Grayson [64]	2348
3	21	H	Hull C	W	1-0	1-0	9	McAuley (pen) [26]	4427
4	28	A	Hartlepool U	W	1-0	1-0	6	Howarth [35]	2390
5	30	H	Barnet	L	1-2	0-1	8	Brough [81]	3518
6	Sept 12	H	Shrewsbury T	L	0-1	0-1	15		3704
7	18	A	Peterborough U	L	0-1	0-0	16		5943
8	25	A	Brighton & HA	L	0-1	0-0	19		5705
9	Oct 2	H	Rotherham U	L	0-2	0-1	21		3331
10	9	H	Southend U	W	2-1	1-0	18	Grayson [6], Milton [66]	3118
11	16	A	Darlington	L	0-1	0-1	21		4802
12	19	A	Chester C	L	1-2	0-0	—	Milton [75]	1705
13	23	H	Brighton & HA	D	0-0	0-0	21		4050
14	Nov 2	A	Halifax T	D	1-1	0-1	—	Milton (pen) [76]	1956
15	6	H	Carlisle U	W	3-1	1-1	20	Freeman [14], Victory [50], McAuley [57]	3118
16	12	A	Northampton T	L	2-3	1-2	20	McAuley [11], Grayson [83]	5837
17	16	A	Swansea C	D	0-0	0-0	—		4299
18	23	H	Plymouth Arg	W	2-0	1-0	—	Grayson 2 [5, 70]	5140
19	27	H	Leyton Orient	W	2-0	2-0	17	Howarth [17], Howells [33]	3604
20	Dec 4	A	Rochdale	W	2-0	0-0	16		2245
21	11	A	Macclesfield T	D	1-1	0-0	16	Collins (og) [83]	3107
22	26	H	Exeter C	W	3-1	3-0	14	Milton [6], Duff [24], Freeman [45]	5012
23	28	A	York C	W	2-1	2-0	14	Yates [13], Grayson [45]	2936
24	Jan 3	H	Lincoln C	L	0-2	0-1	15		4012
25	8	A	Macclesfield T	W	2-1	1-0	13	Grayson [14], Milton (pen) [75]	3221
26	15	H	Mansfield T	W	1-0	1-0	13	Grayson [12]	3150
27	22	A	Hull C	D	1-1	0-1	13	Devaney [65]	4691
28	29	H	Hartlepool U	W	2-1	2-0	10	McAuley [33], Grayson [45]	3630
29	Feb 5	A	Barnet	L	2-3	1-2	12	Devaney [2], Milton (pen) [90]	2727
30	13	H	Swansea C	D	0-0	0-0	13		4220
31	19	A	Leyton Orient	L	0-1	0-1	14		4884
32	26	H	Peterborough U	W	2-1	1-0	13	Freestone [17], Lee (og) [58]	4250
33	Mar 4	A	Shrewsbury T	W	2-0	1-0	12	Howells [6], Milton (pen) [90]	2876
34	11	H	Halifax T	W	3-0	1-0	9	Grayson [45], Milton [59], Freestone [79]	3478
35	14	A	Torquay U	D	1-1	1-0	—	Devaney [7]	2378
36	18	A	Plymouth Arg	L	0-1	0-1	11		4392
37	21	A	Northampton T	W	2-1	1-0	—	Duff [43], Victory [87]	4515
38	25	A	Exeter C	W	2-1	0-0	7	Victory [46], Devaney [63]	3007
39	Apr 1	H	Torquay U	W	2-0	1-0	7	Milton [34], Devaney [82]	5128
40	4	A	Carlisle U	D	1-1	0-0	—	Yates [62]	2388
41	8	A	Lincoln C	W	2-1	2-0	4	Victory [34], Devaney [37]	3133
42	15	H	York C	L	0-1	0-0	7		4722
43	22	H	Darlington	D	0-0	0-0	8		5059
44	24	A	Rotherham U	L	0-2	0-1	8		5447
45	29	H	Chester C	W	1-0	0-0	7	Brough [77]	5391
46	May 6	A	Southend U	L	1-2	1-1	8	Howells [7]	4977

Final League Position: 8

GOALSCORERS

League (50): Grayson 10, Milton 9 (4 pens), Devaney 6, McAuley 4 (1 pen), Victory 4, Howells 3, Brough 2, Duff 2, Freeman 2, Freestone 2, Howarth 2, Yates 2, own goals 2.
Worthington Cup (2): Grayson 1 (pen), Victory 1.
FA Cup (3): Brough 1, Howarth 1, Milton 1.

Book S 46	Griffin A 14 + 10	Victory J 46	Banks C 41 + 1	Freeman M 36 + 2	Brough J 15 + 22	Howells L 45	Bloomer B 1 + 10	Grayson N 39 + 4	Watkins D 4 + 5	Yates M 46	Howarth N 43 + 1	Devaney M 19 + 7	McAuley H 22 + 17	Walker R 6 + 1	Milton R 38	Jackson M — + 2	Duff M 31	Jones M 3	Hopkins G — + 1	Brissett J 5 + 3	Freestone C 5	Stevens I 1	Match No.
1	2	3	4	5	6¹	7	8²	9	10³	11	12	13	14										1
1	2	3	4	5		7	12	9	13	11	6	10¹	8²										2
1	2	3	4	5	12	7	13	9¹	14	11	6	10²	8³										3
1	2	3	4	5		7	12	9	13	11	6	10¹	8²										4
1	2	3	4	5	12	7		9	13	11	6	10²	8¹										5
1	2	3	4	5	12	7		9	13	11	6		8²		10¹								6
1	2³	3	4	5	12	7	13	9	10	11	6¹	14	8²										7
1	2¹	3	4	5		7	13	9	10³	11	6	12	14										8
1		3		5	12²	7		9	10¹	11	6	4³	13		8	14	2						9
1	4	3		5		7		9		11	6	12			8		2			10¹			10
1	4¹	3		5		7		9		11	6	12	13		8²		2			10			11
1		3	4	5		7		9		11	6	12			8		2			10¹			12
1		3	4	5	6¹	7		9		11	10	12			8		2						13
1		3	4	5	6	7		9		11	10				8		2						14
1		3	4	5	6¹	7	12			11	10		8²		9		2			13			15
1		3	4	5¹	12	7		9		11	6	10²			8		2			13			16
1		3	4	5	12	7		9		11	6	10²			8¹		2			13			17
1		3	4	5	12	7	13	9		11	6¹				8		2			10²			18
1	12	3		5	13	7		9		11	6²	4			8		2			10¹			19
1		3	12	5		7		9		11	6	4			8		2			10¹			20
1	12	3		5	13	7		9²		11	6	4¹			8		2			10			21
1	12	3	4	5	13		14	9¹		11	6		8²		10		2			7³			22
1	12	3	4	5	13	7		9²		11	6		8¹		10		2						23
1	5	3	4	12		7²		9		11	6¹		10		8		2			13			24
1	12	3	4	5	13	7		9¹		11	6		8²		10		2						25
1		3	4	5	12	7		9		11	6		8¹		10		2						26
1	2²	3	4	5	12	7		9		11	6	13	8¹		10								27
1		3	4	5	12	7		9		11	6		8¹		10		2						28
1	12	3	4	5	13	7		9²		11	6		8¹		10		2						29
1		3	4	5		7		9		11	6	12	13		8		2¹			10²			30
1		3	4	5	12	7		9		11¹	6	13			8		2			10²			31
1		3	4	5		7		9		11	6				8		2			10			32
1		3	4	5		7		9		11	6				8		2			10			33
1		3	4	5		7	12	9		11¹	6	13	14		8³		2			10²			34
1		3	4	5	12	7		9¹		11	6		10		8		2						35
1	12	3	4	5	6	7		9		11¹	10²	13			8		2						36
1		3	4	5		7	12	9		11	6	10			8¹		2						37
1	12	3	4	5	13	7		9		11	6¹	10²	14		8³		2						38
1		3	4	5		7	12	9		11	6	10²	13		8¹		2						39
1		3	4	5²		7		9		11	6	10¹	12	13	8		2						40
1		3	4	5		7		9		11	6	10			8		2						41
1	12	3	4	5	13	7		9²		11	6¹	10	14		8³		2						42
1		3	4	5	12	7	13	9¹		11	6	10			8²		2						43
1	12	3	4	5¹	13	7	14	9		11	6²	10			8³		2						44
1	2	3	4	5	6	7		9		11	12	10			8¹								45
1	2	3	4	5¹	6	7	12	9³		11²		13	10		8	14							46

Worthington Cup
First Round   Norwich C   (a) 0-2
                                        (h) 2-1

FA Cup
First Round   Gillingham   (h) 1-1
                                       (a) 2-3

Conference

CHESTER CITY

FOUNDATION

All students of soccer history have read about the medieval games of football in Chester, but the present club was not formed until 1884 through the amalgamation of King's School Old Boys with Chester Rovers. For many years Chester were overshadowed in Cheshire by Northwich Victoria and Crewe Alexandra who had both won the Senior Cup several times before Chester's first success in 1894–95. The final against Macclesfield saw Chester face the team that had not only beaten them in the previous year's final, but also knocked them out of the FA Cup two seasons in succession. The final was held at the Drill Field, Northwich and Chester had the support of more than 1000 fans. Chester won 2-1.

The Deva Stadium, Bumpers Lane, Chester CH1 4LT.

Telephone: (01244) 371 376, 371 809.

Fax: (01244) 390 265.

Commercial: (01244) 390 243.

ClubCall: 09068 121 633.

Ground Capacity: 6000.

Record Attendance: 20,500 v Chelsea, FA Cup 3rd rd (replay), 16 January 1952 (at Sealand Road).

Record Receipts: £30,609 v Sheffield W, FA Cup 4th rd, 31 January 1987.

Pitch Measurements: 115yd × 75yd.

Honorary President: C. Thompson.

Chairman: Terry Smith.

Manager: Graham Barrow.

Honorary Vice-Presidents: J. F. Kane, L. Lloyd, Dr. M. D. Swallow.

Secretary: Michael Fair.

Physio: Joe Hinnigan.

HONOURS

Football League: Division 3 – Runners-up 1993–94; Division 3 (N) – Runners-up 1935–36; Division 4 – Runners-up 1985–86.

FA Cup: best season: 5th rd, 1977, 1980.

Football League Cup: Semi-final 1975.

Welsh Cup: Winners 1908, 1933, 1947.

Debenhams Cup: Winners 1977.

LATEST SEQUENCES

Longest Sequence of League Wins: 8, 12.4.78 – 26.8.78.

Longest Sequence of League Defeats: 9, 30.4.94 – 13.9.94.

Longest Sequence of League Draws: 6, 11.10.86 – 1.11.86.

Longest Sequence of Unbeaten League Matches: 18, 27.10.34 – 16.2.35.

Longest Sequence Without a League Win: 25, 19.9.61 – 3.3.62.

Colours
Blue and white striped shirts, white shorts, blue and white stockings.

Change Colours
Claret and white.

Year Formed: 1885.

Turned Professional: 1902.

Ltd Co.: 1909.

Previous Name: Chester until 1983.

Club Nickname: 'Blues' and 'City'.

Previous Grounds: 1885, Faulkner Street; 1898, The Old Showground; 1901, Whipcord Lane; 1906, Sealand Road; 1990, Moss Rose Ground, Macclesfield; 1992, Deva Stadium, Bumpers Lane.

First Football League Game: 2 September 1931, Division 3 (N), v Wrexham (a) D 1–1 – Johnson; Herod, Jones; Keeley, Skitt, Reilly; Thompson, Ranson, Jennings (1), Cresswell, Hedley.

Record League Victory: 12–0 v York C, Division 3 (N), 1 February 1936 – Middleton; Common, Hall; Wharton, Wilson, Howarth; Horsman (2), Hughes, Wrightson (4), Cresswell (2), Sargeant (4).

Record Cup Victory: 6–1 v Darlington, FA Cup 1st rd, 25 November 1933 – Burke; Bennett, Little; Pitcairn, Skitt, Duckworth; Armes (3), Whittam, Mantle (2), Cresswell (1), McLachlan.

Record Defeat: 2–11 v Oldham Ath, Division 3 (N), 19 January 1952.

MANAGERS

Charlie Hewitt 1930–36
Alex Raisbeck 1936–38
Frank Brown 1938–53
Louis Page 1953–56
John Harris 1956–59
Stan Pearson 1959–61
Bill Lambton 1962–63
Peter Hauser 1963–68
Ken Roberts 1968–76
Alan Oakes 1976–82
Cliff Sear 1982
John Sainty 1982–83
John McGrath 1984
Harry McNally 1985–92
Graham Barrow 1992–94
Mike Pejic 1994–95
Derek Mann 1995
Kevin Ratcliffe 1995–99
Terry Smith 1999
Ian Atkins 2000
Graham Barrow July 2000–

Most League Points (2 for a win): 56, Division 3 (N), 1946–47 and Division 4, 1964–65.

Most League Points (3 for a win): 84, Division 4, 1985–86.

Most League Goals: 119, Division 4, 1964–65.

Highest League Scorer in Season: Dick Yates, 36, Division 3 (N), 1946–47.

Most League Goals in Total Aggregate: Stuart Rimmer, 135, 1985–88, 1991–98.

Most League Goals in One Match: 5, Tom Jennings v Walsall, Division 3N, 30 January 1932; 5, Barry Jepson v York C, Division 4, 8 February 1958.

Most Capped Player: Bill Lewis, 13 (27), Wales.

Most League Appearances: Ray Gill, 406, 1951–62.

Youngest League Player: Aidan Newhouse, 15 years 350 days v Bury, 7 May 1988.

Record Transfer Fee Received: £300,000 from Liverpool for Ian Rush, May 1980.

Record Transfer Fee Paid: £94,000 to Barnsley for Stuart Rimmer, August 1991.

Football League Record: 1931 Elected Division 3 (N); 1958–75 Division 4; 1975–82 Division 3; 1982–86 Division 4; 1986–92 Division 3; 1992–93 Division 2; 1993–94 Division 3; 1994–95 Division 2; 1995–2000 Division 3; 2000– Conference.

TEN YEAR LEAGUE RECORD

		P	W	D	L	F	A	Pts	Pos
1989-90	Div 3	46	13	15	18	43	55	54	16
1990-91	Div 3	46	14	9	23	46	58	51	19
1991-92	Div 3	46	14	14	18	56	59	56	18
1992-93	Div 2	46	8	5	33	49	102	29	24
1993-94	Div 3	42	21	11	10	69	46	74	2
1994-95	Div 2	46	6	11	29	37	84	29	23
1995-96	Div 3	46	18	16	12	72	53	70	8
1996-97	Div 3	46	18	16	12	55	43	70	6
1997-98	Div 3	46	17	10	19	60	61	61	14
1998-99	Div 3	46	13	18	15	57	66	57	14

DID YOU KNOW ?

The first time Chester scored as many as 100 League goals was in 1935-36 when they finished runners-up to Chesterfield in Division 3 (North).

CHESTER CITY 1999–2000 LEAGUE RECORD

Match No.	Date		Venue	Opponents		Result	H/T Score	Lg. Pos.	Goalscorers	Attendance
1	Aug	7	H	Barnet	L	0-2	0-2	23		2234
2		14	A	Rotherham U	L	0-4	0-0	23		2966
3		18	H	Northampton T	L	0-2	0-0	—		1904
4		28	A	Torquay U	D	2-2	1-0	23	Beckett [12], Berry [81]	2345
5		30	H	Rochdale	L	0-2	0-1	24		2644
6	Sept	3	A	Hull C	L	1-2	1-1	—	Richardson [23]	6137
7		11	H	Exeter C	D	1-1	0-0	24	Beckett [48]	1855
8		18	A	Brighton & HA	W	3-2	0-0	24	Beckett [69], Watson (og) [73], Agogo [90]	5810
9		25	H	Lincoln C	L	1-3	1-1	24	Blackwood [13]	2161
10	Oct	2	A	York C	D	2-2	0-0	24	Blackwood [54], Agogo [80]	2452
11		9	A	Peterborough U	L	1-2	1-2	24	Beckett [14]	4965
12		16	H	Macclesfield T	L	1-2	1-2	24	Agogo [16]	2506
13		19	H	Cheltenham T	W	2-1	0-0	—	Agogo 2 [61, 66]	1705
14		23	A	Lincoln C	L	1-4	1-1	24	Agogo [41]	3790
15	Nov	2	A	Shrewsbury T	W	1-0	0-0	—	Richardson [72]	2523
16		6	H	Plymouth Arg	L	0-1	0-1	23		2027
17		13	A	Hartlepool U	L	0-1	0-1	—		2266
18		23	H	Southend U	D	0-0	0-0	—		1906
19		27	H	Swansea C	L	0-1	0-0	24		2713
20	Dec	4	A	Barnet	L	0-2	0-1	24		2252
21		15	A	Darlington	L	1-3	0-2	—	Samways (og) [74]	3553
22		18	H	Halifax T	W	2-1	2-0	23	Laird [26], Eve [29]	2037
23		26	A	Mansfield T	L	1-2	0-1	23	Doughty [68]	3234
24		28	H	Leyton Orient	L	1-5	0-2	24	Wright [66]	3160
25	Jan	3	A	Carlisle U	L	1-4	0-1	24	Eve [89]	4565
26		8	H	Darlington	L	1-2	1-1	24	Beckett [37]	2067
27		15	H	Rotherham U	L	0-2	0-1	24		3398
28		22	A	Northampton T	L	1-3	1-1	24	Pickering [2]	5332
29		29	H	Torquay U	W	2-1	0-0	24	Eyjolfsson [47], Beckett [69]	2229
30	Feb	5	A	Rochdale	L	1-2	0-1	24	Beckett [82]	3093
31		12	H	Hull C	D	0-0	0-0	24		2802
32		18	A	Swansea C	L	1-2	1-0	—	Eyjolfsson [22]	6336
33		26	A	Brighton & HA	L	1-7	0-2	24	Beckett [78]	2743
34	Mar	4	H	Exeter C	W	2-0	2-0	24	Eyjolfsson [7], Beckett [22]	2391
35		7	A	Plymouth Arg	D	0-0	0-0	—		4140
36		11	H	Shrewsbury T	D	0-0	0-0	23		4002
37		18	A	Southend U	L	1-3	1-2	24	Beckett [45]	3483
38		21	A	Hartlepool U	D	1-1	1-0	—	Hemmings [24]	1816
39		25	H	Mansfield T	W	5-0	3-0	24	Heggs [17], Beckett [21], Hemmings [29], Eve 2 [59, 68]	1953
40	Apr	1	A	Halifax T	W	1-0	1-0	24	Beckett (pen) [14]	2431
41		8	H	Carlisle U	L	0-1	0-0	24		5507
42		15	A	Leyton Orient	W	2-1	1-1	23	Heggs [15], Fisher [56]	4123
43		22	A	Macclesfield T	L	1-1	0-1	24	Beckett [49]	3456
44		24	H	York C	W	2-0	0-0	22	Bower (og) [61], Beckett [63]	3503
45		29	A	Cheltenham T	L	0-1	0-0	23		5391
46	May	6	H	Peterborough U	L	0-1	0-0	24		4905

Final League Position: 24

GOALSCORERS

League (44): Beckett 14 (1 pen), Agogo 6, Eve 4, Eyjolfsson 3, Blackwood 2, Heggs 2, Hemmings 2, Richardson 2, Berry 1, Doughty 1, Fisher 1, Laird 1, Pickering 1, Wright 1, own goals 3.
Worthington Cup (6): Beckett 3 (2 pens), Jones 1, Richardson 1, Shelton 1.
FA Cup (6): Cross 3, Beckett 2, Richardson 1.

Brown W 46	Davidson R 9	Cross J 13+4	Reid S 10+3	Lancaster M 14+3	Woods M 40+2	Shelton A 9+2	Richardson N 31+5	Wright D 15+10	Beckett L 46	Fisher N 34+7	Moss D 28+7	Doughty M 19+14	Jones J 4+2	Blackburn C —+1	Berry P —+9	Blackwood M 9	Agogo M 10	Milosavljevic G 11+1	Nash M 12+4	Carver J 1+1	Finney S 4+9	Spooner N 9	Eve A 9+5	Laird K 2+1	Hobson G 20	Keister J 8+2	Eyjolfsson S 9	Pickering A 7	Hemmings T 19	Robinson J 9	Porter A 16	Hicks S 13	Heggs C 11	Carden P 9+2	Match No.
1	2	3	4	5	6	7^1	8	9	10	11^2	12	13																							1
1		3	4^2	5	6	7^1	8		10	11	2	12	9^3	13	14																				2
1	2	3	4	5	6	7	8	12	10	11					9^1																				3
1	2	3			6	7	4	9	10	11^1	5	8^1	12																						4
1	2	3			6	7	4	9	10	11^1	5	12	8^2	13																					5
1	2^1	3		5	6	7	4	12	10	11^2	13					9	8																		6
1	2	12		5	6	13	8	9^2	10	14	4	3^1				7	11^3																		7
1	2			5	6	12	8	9	10	13		3				7^2	11	4^1																	8
1	2			5	6^3			9	10	11^2		3	12			13	7^1	8	14	4															9
1				5	6		4	9	10	2	3					11	8	7																	10
1	2	12		5	6^1		8	9	10		4	3^2				7^3	11	13	14																11
1	3^1			5	6			9	10	11	12					13	7	8	4	2^2															12
1				5	6		8	9	10	2	3					7	11	4																	13
1				5	6		8		10	12	2	3				9	11	4^2	7^1	13															14
1					6^2	7^3	8	9	10	11	2	3^1				13	4	5	12	14															15
1	12				6		8	9^2	10	11	2	3					4	13	7^1	5															16
1	2					7	8^1	9	10	11	3					12	4^2	6	13	5															17
1		9	4^1	5			8		10	11	2	3					7^2	13	6																18
1		9	4^1	5			8		10	11	2	3					7	12	6																19
1			4	5			8	2	10	11	3						7	9	6																20
1		9	4	12	5		8^2	13	10	11	2	3	14						6^1		7^3														21
1		12					8	13	10	11	2	3							6^1		7	5	4	9^2											22
1	3^2				6		8	12	10	11	2	13							9		7^1	5^3	4	14											23
1	12				6		8^1	13	10	11	2	3									7	5	4	9^2											24
1	12	13					8	9^2	10	11	2	3							6		7^1	14	5^2	4											25
1	12	4^2			6		8^1	13	10	11	2	3													5	7	9								26
1	3			5	6		8^1	13	10	14									12						4	7	9^2	2^3							27
1	4^2	12			6		8	13	10	11	14														5	9^3	2^1	7	3						28
1	4^1				6		12		10	11									13						5	7	9^2	2	8	3					29
1					6				10	11^2	12	13							14						5	7	9	2	8^3	3	4				30
1		12			6				10		4	13													5	7	9	2	8^2	3	11				31
1		12			6				10		13	4													5	7	9	2	8^2	3	11				32
1					6				10		12	3						13	14						5	7^3	9	2	8^2	11	4				33
1					6				10	11	4^1	2													12	9			8	3	7	5			34
1		13			6				10	11	2^1	12		14											9^1	4			8^3	3	7	5			35
1			4^1		6				10	11	2														12	5		7	8	3			9^2	13	36
1					6				10	11^3	2	12							13						4					8^2	3^1	7	5	9	37
1					6				10	11^1	2	12							13						4					8	7	5	9^2	3	38
1	12				6				10^3	13	2	14						11							4					8	7	5	9^2	3^1	39
1					6				10	11	2	12													4					8	7	5	9^1	3	40
1					6				10		2	12						11							4					8	7	5	9^1	3	41
1					6				10	11^1	2	12							13						4					8^2	7	5	9	3	42
1					6				10	11	2														4					8^2	7	5	9	3	43
1					6				10	11^2	2	12							13						4					8^1	7	5	9	3	44
1					6				10	11^1	2^3	12	14						13						4					8^2	7	5	9	3	45
1		13			6				10	11^3	2^1	12	14												4					8^2	7	5	9	3	46

Worthington Cup					FA Cup				
First Round	Port Vale	(h)	2-1		First Round	Whyteleafe	(a)	0-0	
		(a)	4-4				(h)	3-1	
Second Round	Aston Villa	(h)	0-1		Second Round	Stalybridge C	(a)	2-1	
		(a)	0-5		Third Round	Manchester C	(h)	1-4	

Division 3   **CHESTERFIELD**

FOUNDATION

Chesterfield are fourth only to Stoke, Notts County and
Nottingham Forest in age for they can trace their existence as far
back as 1866, although it is fair to say that they were somewhat
casual in the first few years of their history playing only a few
friendlies a year. However, their rules of 1871 are still in existence
showing an annual membership of 2s (10p), but it was not until
1891 that they won a trophy (the Barnes Cup) and followed this a
year later by winning the Sheffield Cup, Barnes Cup and the
Derbyshire Junior Cup.

Recreation Ground, Chesterfield S40 4SX.
Telephone: (01246) 209 765.
Fax: (01246) 550 930.
Commercial Dept: (01246) 231 535.
ClubCall: 09068 555 818.
Ground Capacity: 8880.
Record Attendance: 30,968 v Newcastle U, Division 2, 7 April 1939.
Record Receipts: £45,000 v Mansfield T, Division 3 play-off semi-final, 17 May 1995.
Pitch Measurements: 113yd × 71yd.
President: His Grace the Duke of Devonshire MC, DL, JP.
Chairman: J. Norton Lea.
Vice-Chairman: B. W. Hubbard.
Directors: R. F. Pepper, M. L. Warner.
Manager: Nicky Law.
Assistant Manager: Kevin Randall.
Physio: Dave Rushbury.
Secretary: Stephanie Otter.
Commercial Manager: Jim Brown.
Stadium Manager: W. W. Kenworthy.

LATEST SEQUENCES
Longest Sequence of League Wins: 10, 6.9.33 – 4.11.33.
Longest Sequence of League Defeats: 9, 22.10.60 – 27.12.60.
Longest Sequence of League Draws: 5, 19.9.90 – 6.10.90.
Longest Sequence of Unbeaten League Matches: 21, 26.12.94 – 29.4.95.
Longest Sequence Without a League Win: 18, 11.9.99 – 3.1.00.

HONOURS
Football League: Division 2 best
season: 4th, 1946–47; Division 3 (N) –
Champions 1930–31, 1935–36;
Runners-up 1933–34; Division 4 –
Champions 1969–70, 1984–85.
FA Cup: Semi-final 1997.
Football League Cup: best season:
4th rd, 1965.
Anglo-Scottish Cup: Winners 1981.

Colours
All blue.

Change Colours
White shirts, blue shorts, white stockings.

Year Formed: 1866.

Turned Professional: 1891.

Ltd Co: 1871.

Previous Name: Chesterfield Town.

Club Nickname: 'Blues' or 'Spireites'.

First Football League Game: 2 September 1899, Division 2, v Sheffield W (a) L 1–5 – Hancock; Pilgrim, Fletcher; Ballantyne, Bell, Downie; Morley, Thacker, Gooing, Munday (1), Geary.

Record League Victory: 10–0 v Glossop NE, Division 2, 17 January 1903 – Clutterbuck; Thorpe, Lerper; Haig, Banner, Thacker; Tomlinson (2), Newton (1), Milward (3), Munday (2), Steel (2).

Record Cup Victory: 5–0 v Wath Ath (a), FA Cup 1st rd, 28 November 1925 – Birch; Saxby, Dennis; Wass, Abbott, Thompson; Fisher (1), Roseboom (1), Cookson (2), Whitfield (1), Hopkinson.

Record Defeat: 0–10 v Gillingham, Division 3, 5 September 1987.

Most League Points (2 for a win): 64, Division 4, 1969–70.

Most League Points (3 for a win): 91, Division 4, 1984–85.

Most League Goals: 102, Division 3 (N), 1930–31.

Highest League Scorer in Season: Jimmy Cookson, 44, Division 3 (N), 1925–26.

Most League Goals in Total Aggregate: Ernie Moss, 161, 1969–76, 1979–81 and 1984–86.

Most League Goals in One Match: 4, Jimmy Cookson v Accrington S, Division 3N, 16 January 1926; 4, Jimmy Cookson v Ashington, Division 3N, 1 May 1926; 4, Jimmy Cookson v Wigan Borough, Division 3N, 4 September 1926; 4, Tommy Lyon v Southampton, Division 2, 3 December 1938.

Most Capped Player: Walter McMillen, 4 (7), Northern Ireland; Mark Williams, 4 (11), Northern Ireland.

Most League Appearances: Dave Blakey, 613, 1948–67.

Youngest League Player: Dennis Thompson, 16 years 160 days v Notts Co, 26 December 1950.

Record Transfer Fee Received: £750,000 from Southampton for Kevin Davies, May 1997.

Record Transfer Fee Paid: £250,000 to Watford for Jason Lee, August 1998.

Football League Record: 1899 Elected to Division 2; 1909 failed re-election; 1921–31 Division 3 (N); 1931–33 Division 2; 1933–36 Division 3 (N); 1936–51 Division 2; 1951–58 Division 3 (N); 1958–61 Division 3; 1961–70 Division 4; 1970–83 Division 3; 1983–85 Division 4; 1985–89 Division 3; 1989–92 Division 4; 1992–95 Division 3; 1995–2000 Division 2; 2000– Division 3.

MANAGERS

E. Russell Timmeus 1891–95
(Secretary-Manager)
Gilbert Gillies 1895–1901
E. F. Hind 1901–02
Jack Hoskin 1902–06
W. Furness 1906–07
George Swift 1907–10
G. H. Jones 1911–13
R. L. Weston 1913–17
T. Callaghan 1919
J. J. Caffrey 1920–22
Harry Hadley 1922
Harry Parkes 1922–27
Alec Campbell 1927
Ted Davison 1927–32
Bill Harvey 1932–38
Norman Bullock 1938–45
Bob Brocklebank 1945–48
Bobby Marshall 1948–52
Ted Davison 1952–58
Duggie Livingstone 1958–62
Tony McShane 1962–67
Jimmy McGuigan 1967–73
Joe Shaw 1973–76
Arthur Cox 1976–80
Frank Barlow 1980–83
John Duncan 1983–87
Kevin Randall 1987–88
Paul Hart 1988–91
Chris McMenemy 1991–93
John Duncan 1993– 2000
Nicky Law May 2000–

TEN YEAR LEAGUE RECORD

		P	W	D	L	F	A	Pts	Pos
1989-90	Div 4	46	19	14	13	63	50	71	7
1990-91	Div 4	46	13	14	19	47	62	53	18
1991-92	Div 4	42	14	11	17	49	61	53	13
1992-93	Div 3	42	15	11	16	59	63	56	12
1993-94	Div 3	42	16	14	12	55	48	62	8
1994-95	Div 3	42	23	12	7	62	37	81	3
1995-96	Div 2	46	20	12	14	56	51	72	7
1996-97	Div 2	46	18	14	14	42	39	68	10
1997-98	Div 2	46	16	17	13	46	44	65	10
1998-99	Div 2	46	17	13	16	46	44	64	9

DID YOU KNOW ?

In 1935 Chesterfield manager Bill Harvey signed his unrelated namesake, a centre-forward called Bill Harvey from Eden Colliery, whose goals that season included a hat-trick against Wrexham.

CHESTERFIELD 1999–2000 LEAGUE RECORD

Match No.	Date	Venue	Opponents	Result		H/T Score	Lg. Pos.	Goalscorers	Attendance
1	Aug 7	H	Colchester U	L	0-1	0-0	22		2930
2	14	A	Burnley	L	1-2	0-2	21	Reeves (pen) [65]	10,615
3	21	H	Cambridge U	W	4-2	1-1	15	Reeves 4 (2 pens) [16 ipl, 56 ipl, 59, 79]	2816
4	28	A	Millwall	D	1-1	0-0	16	Reeves [74]	6256
5	Sept 4	A	Preston NE	W	2-0	0-0	13	Willis [51], Reeves [62]	8506
6	11	H	Stoke C	L	0-2	0-0	16		4285
7	18	A	Reading	L	0-1	0-0	17		6932
8	25	A	Scunthorpe U	D	0-0	0-0	17		4321
9	Oct 2	H	Bournemouth	L	0-1	0-1	18		2775
10	9	H	Blackpool	D	0-0	0-0	19		2804
11	16	A	Wrexham	D	1-1	1-0	19	Beaumont [35]	2603
12	19	A	Notts Co	L	0-1	0-0	—		4749
13	23	H	Scunthorpe U	D	1-1	1-0	19	Howard [7]	3464
14	Nov 2	A	Wigan Ath	L	0-3	0-1	—		4376
15	6	H	Oldham Ath	L	0-1	0-1	23		2737
16	12	A	Cardiff C	L	1-2	0-1	23	Willis [89]	4863
17	20	H	Bristol R	L	0-1	0-1	24		2875
18	27	H	Oxford U	D	0-0	0-0	24		2768
19	Dec 3	A	Colchester U	L	0-1	0-0	—		3027
20	7	H	Bristol C	L	0-2	0-1	—		2254
21	10	A	Brentford	D	1-1	0-1	—	Galloway [76]	4286
22	26	A	Luton T	D	1-1	0-1	24	Reeves [74]	5870
23	Jan 3	A	Wycombe W	L	0-3	0-1	24		5001
24	8	H	Brentford	W	1-0	0-0	23	Reeves [90]	2746
25	15	H	Burnley	D	1-1	0-1	23	Williams R [73]	4214
26	22	A	Cambridge U	L	0-2	0-1	24		3819
27	29	H	Millwall	W	2-0	1-0	23	Wilkinson [40], Beaumont [83]	3198
28	Feb 1	H	Gillingham	D	0-0	0-0	—		2898
29	5	A	Bristol C	L	0-3	0-2	23		8837
30	12	H	Preston NE	L	0-1	0-0	23		4726
31	19	A	Oxford U	L	1-2	0-1	24	Williams R [59]	5146
32	26	H	Reading	W	2-0	1-0	24	Payne [41], Breckin [71]	2986
33	Mar 4	A	Stoke C	L	1-5	0-3	24	Reeves [70]	11,968
34	11	H	Wigan Ath	D	1-1	1-0	24	Payne [21]	3106
35	18	A	Bristol R	L	1-3	1-1	24	Williams R [41]	8765
36	21	H	Cardiff C	D	1-1	1-1	—	Payne [32]	2348
37	25	H	Luton T	L	1-3	0-3	24	Howard [76]	2597
38	28	H	Bury	L	0-1	0-1	—		1903
39	Apr 1	A	Gillingham	L	0-1	0-0	24		6772
40	8	H	Wycombe W	L	1-2	1-0	24	Reeves (pen) [27]	2081
41	15	A	Bury	D	1-1	0-1	24	Carss [75]	3021
42	18	A	Oldham Ath	W	2-1	2-1	—	Williams R [29], Willis [43]	4012
43	22	H	Wrexham	L	0-3	0-1	24		2550
44	25	A	Bournemouth	L	1-1	1-0	—	Willis [17]	3481
45	29	H	Notts Co	W	2-1	0-1	24	Reeves 2 [66, 80]	2455
46	May 6	A	Blackpool	D	2-2	0-1	24	Williams R [81], Reeves [90]	3860

Final League Position: 24

GOALSCORERS

League (34): Reeves 14 (4 pens), Williams R 5, Willis 4, Payne 3, Beaumont 2, Howard 2, Breckin 1, Carss 1, Galloway 1, Wilkinson 1.
Worthington Cup (5): Reeves 2, Ebdon 1, own goals 2.
FA Cup (1): Lomas 1.

Leaning A 6	Hewitt J 38+2	Woods S 22+3	Curtis T 17+1	Payne S 15+3	Breckin I 37+1	Beaumont C 32+1	Holland P 4	Reeves D 43	Ebdon M 10+1	Bettney C 7+6	Lomas J 10+7	Willis R 20+8	Simpkins M 8+1	Williams D 3+2	Carss T 24+7	Gayle M 29+1	Blatherwick S 36	Dudley C —+2	Howard J 19+8	Wilkinson S 15+7	Perkins C 29+2	Lee J 3+3	Pearce G 8+2	Galloway M 14+1	Williams R 30	Agogo M 3+1	D'Auria D 4+1	Muggleton C 5	Pointon N 9+1	Vaughan J 3	Armstrong J 3	Barratt D —+2	Match No.
1	2	3	4	5	6	7	8	9	10¹	11²	12	13																					1
1	2	3¹	4		6		8	9	10	11					7	5	12																2
1⁸	2	3	4		6	12	8	9	10	11²					7	5¹			13	15													3
1	2	3¹	4		6	5	8	9	10	11					7		12																4
1	3		4		6		8	9	10	11¹	12				7		2²		13		5												5
1	2¹	3	4		6		8	9	10		12				7	11²	5		13														6
	2	3			6		8	9			12	10²	7³	4¹	11	1	5		13	14													7
	2	3			6		8	9				10¹	4	7	11	1	5		12														8
	2	3			6		8	9				10²	4	7¹	11	1	5		12	13													9
	2	3	12		6	7		9¹	10			13		4²	11	1	5				8												10
	2	3			6		8	9			12			4	11²	1	5	7¹	13	10													11
	2	3¹			6		8	9			12			4	11	1	5	7²	10	13													12
	2				6		4¹	9	10		12²				11	1	5		7	8	13					3							13
	2	3			6		4²	9	10		12				11	1	5¹		7	8	13												14
	2	3³			6¹			9	10				7	4	11	1	5		13		8			12²								14	15
	2			12				9²				13			11	1	5¹				7		3	4	10	6	8						16
	2²							9			12	13		4		1	5				7	14	3	11	10¹	6³	8						17
	2							9						4		1	5				7		3	11	10¹	6	8		12				18
	2¹		4		6			9								1	5				7		3	11	10		8		12				19
12			4		6	13		9							2	1	5				7		3¹	11²	10			8					20
	2	3¹	4		6			9			12					1	5		8		7			11	10								21
	2		3	4	6			9			12					1	5		7¹	13				11	10	8²							22
	2	3	4	12	6			9								1	5		7²	13	8			11¹	10								23
	2		4		6	7		9								1	5		12	8¹	13			11	10		3²						24
	2		4¹		6	7		9								1	5		12		8			11	10		3						25
	2		4		6			9			12					1	5		13	8²	7¹			11	10		3						26
	2		4		6			9								1	5			8	7			11	10		3						27
	2		4		6²			9			12	13				1	5			8¹	7			11	10		3						28
	2		4		12			9								1	5		6	8	7			11	10		3¹						29
	2		4					9								1	5		12	7²	13		8	6	10		3		11¹				30
	2				6	7		9						4		1	5		12	8¹				11	10		3						31
	2				6	8		9								1	5				7		4	11	10		3						32
	2		4	12	6	7		9								1	5		13		8			11	10²		3¹						33
	2		4	8	6	7		9								1	5							11	10		3						34
	2		4	8	6	7¹		9								1	5		12					11	10		3						35
	2		4		6	8		9								1	5¹		12		7			11	10		3						36
	2		4		6			9							7	1	5				8			11	10		3						37
	2				6	8		9		11¹					4	1	5		7	12					10		3						38
	2		4		6	8		9							7	1	5							11	10		3						39
	2		4		6			9								1	5		12	8¹	7			11	10		3						40
	2			12	6			9						4	7	1	5		13		8²			11	10¹		3						41
	2				6	8		9						4	7	1	5							11	10		3						42
	2			12	6	8		9				13		4	7	1	5³				3²			11¹	10							14	43
12²			4	5	6			9							2¹				13		7			11²	10³	8	3	1				14	44
	2		4	5	6			9											12		7			11²	10	8³	3¹	1			13	14	45
	2		4²	5	6			9											12	13	7			11	10	8¹	3	1					46

Worthington Cup

First Round	Rochdale	(a)	2-1	
		(h)	2-1	
Second Round	Middlesbrough	(h)	0-0	
		(a)	1-2	

FA Cup

First Round	Enfield	(h)	1-2

Division 2   **COLCHESTER UNITED**

FOUNDATION

Colchester United was formed in 1937 when a number of enthusiasts of the much older Colchester Town club decided to establish a professional concern as a limited liability company. The new club continued at Layer Road which had been the amateur club's home since 1909.

Layer Rd Ground, Colchester, Essex CO2 7JJ.
Telephone: (01206) 508 800.
Fax: (01206) 508 803.
Club Shop: (01206) 508 809.
Soccer Centre: (01206) 572 378.
Lottery: (01206) 508 820.
Ground Capacity: 7556.
Record Attendance: 19,072 v Reading, FA Cup 1st rd, 27 November 1948.
Record Receipts: £26,330 v Barrow, GM Vauxhall Conference, 2 May 1992.
Pitch Measurements: 110yd × 71yd.
Patron: The Mayor of Colchester.
Chairman: Peter Heard.
Directors: John Worsp, Peter Powell.
Manager: Steve Whitton.
Assistant Manager/Coach: Geraint Williams.
Youth Coach: Micky Cook.
Physio: Brian Owen.
Consultant Physio: Ray Cole.
Secretary: Mrs Marie Partner.
Marketing Manager: John Schultz.
Commercial Manager: Brian Wheeler.
Lottery Manager: John Cross.
Stadium Manager: David Blacknall.

LATEST SEQUENCES
Longest Sequence of League Wins: 7, 29.11.68 – 1.2.69.
Longest Sequence of League Defeats: 8, 9.10.54 – 4.12.54.
Longest Sequence of League Draws: 6, 21.3.77 – 11.4.77.
Longest Sequence of Unbeaten League Matches: 20, 22.12.56 – 19.4.57.
Longest Sequence Without a League Win: 20, 2.3.68 – 31.8.68.

HONOURS

Football League: Promoted from Division 3 – 1997–98 (play-offs); Division 4 – Runners-up 1961–62.

FA Cup: best season: 6th rd, 1971.

Football League Cup: best season: 5th rd, 1975.

Auto Windscreens Shield: Runners-up 1997.

GM Vauxhall Conference: Winners 1991–92.

FA Trophy: Winners 1992.

Colours
Blue and white striped shirts, navy shorts, white stockings.

Change Colours
Yellow shirts, blue shorts.

Year Formed: 1937.

Turned Professional: 1937.

Ltd Co.: 1937.

Club Nickname: 'The U's'.

First Football League Game: 19 August 1950, Division 3 (S), v Gillingham (a) D 0–0 – Wright; Kettle, Allen; Bearryman, Stewart, Elder; Jones, Curry, Turner, McKim, Church.

Record League Victory: 9–1 v Bradford C, Division 4, 30 December 1961 – Ames; Millar, Fowler; Harris, Abrey, Ron Hunt; Foster, Bobby Hunt (4), King (4), Hill (1), Wright.

Record Cup Victory: 7–1 v Yeovil T (away), FA Cup 2nd rd (replay), 11 December 1958 – Ames; Fisher, Fowler; Parker, Milligan, Hammond; Williams (1), McLeod (2), Langman (4), Evans, Wright. 7–1 v Yeading, FA Cup 1st rd (replay), 22 November 1994 – Cheesewright; Betts, English, Cawley, Caesar, Locke (Dennis), Fry, Brown (2), Whitton (2) (Thompson), Kinsella (1), Abrahams (2).

Record Defeat: 0–8 v Leyton Orient, Division 4, 15 October 1989.

Most League Points (2 for a win): 60, Division 4, 1973–74.

Most League Points (3 for a win): 81, Division 4, 1982–83.

Most League Goals: 104, Division 4, 1961–62.

Highest League Scorer in Season: Bobby Hunt, 38, Division 4, 1961–62.

Most League Goals in Total Aggregate: Martyn King, 130, 1956–64.

Most League Goals in One Match: 4, Bobby Hunt v Bradford C, Division 4, 30 December 1961; 4, Martyn King v Bradford C, Division 4, 30 December 1961; 4, Bobby Hunt v Doncaster R, Division 4, 30 April 1962.

Most Capped Player: None.

Most League Appearances: Micky Cook, 613, 1969–84.

Youngest League Player: Lindsay Smith, 16 years 218 days v Grimsby T, 24 April 1971.

Record Transfer Fee Received: £150,000 from Charlton Ath for Mark Kinsella, September 1996.

Record Transfer Fee Paid: £50,000 to Ipswich T for Neil Gregory, March 1998.

Football League Record: 1950 Elected to Division 3 (S); 1958–61 Division 3; 1961–62 Division 4; 1962–65 Division 3; 1965–66 Division 4; 1966–68 Division 3; 1968–74 Division 4; 1974–76 Division 3, 1976–77 Division 4; 1977–81 Division 3; 1981–90 Division 4; 1990–92 GM Vauxhall Conference; 1992–98 Division 3; 1998– Division 2.

MANAGERS

Ted Fenton 1946–48
Jimmy Allen 1948–53
Jack Butler 1953–55
Benny Fenton 1955–63
Neil Franklin 1963–68
Dick Graham 1968–72
Jim Smith 1972–75
Bobby Roberts 1975–82
Allan Hunter 1982–83
Cyril Lea 1983–86
Mike Walker 1986–87
Roger Brown 1987–88
Jock Wallace 1989
Mick Mills 1990.
Ian Atkins 1990–91
Roy McDonough 1991–94
George Burley 1994
Steve Wignall 1995–99
Mick Wadsworth 1999
Steve Whitton August 1999–

TEN YEAR LEAGUE RECORD

		P	W	D	L	F	A	Pts	Pos
1989-90	Div 4	46	11	10	25	48	75	43	24
1990-91	Conf	42	25	10	7	68	35	85	2
1991-92	Conf	42	28	10	4	98	40	94	1
1992-93	Div 3	42	18	5	19	67	76	59	10
1993-94	Div 3	42	13	10	19	56	71	49	17
1994-95	Div 3	42	16	10	16	56	64	58	10
1995-96	Div 3	46	18	18	10	61	51	72	7
1996-97	Div 3	46	17	17	12	62	51	68	8
1997-98	Div 3	46	21	11	14	72	60	74	4
1998-99	Div 2	46	12	16	18	52	70	52	18

DID YOU KNOW ?

Billy Bower serving at Colchester Garrison, was Colchester United's first post-war signing, having been their only ever present in the 1945-46 transitional season, in which he made 30 Southern League and Cup appearances at right-back.

COLCHESTER UNITED 1999–2000 LEAGUE RECORD

Match No.	Date	Venue	Opponents	Result	H/T Score	Lg. Pos.	Goalscorers	Attendance
1	Aug 7	A	Chesterfield	W 1-0	0-0	7	Dozzell [74]	2930
2	14	H	Notts Co	L 0-3	0-2	18		3986
3	21	A	Bournemouth	L 0-4	0-1	20		4508
4	28	H	Reading	W 3-2	1-1	12	Aspinall 2 (1 pen) [45, 88 (p)], Duguid [78]	3443
5	30	A	Bury	L 2-5	1-2	14	Wilkins [40], Lua-Lua [82]	3360
6	Sept 11	H	Scunthorpe U	L 0-1	0-0	20		3280
7	18	A	Burnley	L 0-3	0-2	23		10,090
8	25	A	Millwall	L 0-1	0-0	23		7161
9	Oct 1	H	Wrexham	D 2-2	0-0	—	Duguid [79], Wilkins [90]	3315
10	15	A	Cambridge U	L 2-5	1-2	—	Dozzell 2 [17, 54]	5039
11	19	A	Bristol C	D 1-1	0-1	—	Duguid [58]	7777
12	23	H	Millwall	L 1-2	1-1	24	McGavin [17]	3392
13	26	H	Wigan Ath	D 2-2	2-1	—	McGavin [7], Duguid [38]	2915
14	Nov 2	A	Oxford U	D 1-1	1-1	—	McGavin [33]	4444
15	6	H	Preston NE	D 2-2	1-0	24	Skelton [16], Lua-Lua [68]	3818
16	14	A	Oldham Ath	W 2-1	1-0	22	Lua-Lua [45], Greene (pen) [63]	5147
17	19	H	Brentford	L 0-3	0-0	—		3464
18	23	H	Cardiff C	L 0-3	0-1	—		2557
19	27	A	Stoke C	D 1-1	0-0	23	Skelton [71]	14,183
20	Dec 3	H	Chesterfield	W 1-0	0-0	—	Lua-Lua [52]	3027
21	11	A	Bristol R	L 1-2	0-1	20	Lua-Lua [66]	7023
22	17	H	Luton T	W 3-0	0-0	—	McGavin 2 [48, 54], Dozzell [74]	3049
23	26	A	Gillingham	L 1-2	0-2	20	McGavin [89]	7338
24	Jan 3	A	Blackpool	D 1-1	0-1	20	Duguid [52]	3462
25	8	H	Bristol R	W 5-4	1-1	16	McGavin 2 [36, 62], Duguid 2 [80, 82], Lua-Lua [89]	4482
26	15	A	Notts Co	W 2-1	2-0	16	McGavin 2 [30, 45]	4931
27	18	H	Wycombe W	W 1-0	0-0	—	Lua-Lua [81]	4075
28	22	H	Bournemouth	W 3-1	1-1	15	Moralee [33], Lua-Lua 2 [63, 83]	3767
29	29	A	Reading	L 0-2	0-1	15		7304
30	Feb 5	H	Bury	L 1-3	1-1	16	Duguid [16]	3915
31	12	A	Wigan Ath	W 1-0	1-0	16	McGavin [38]	6022
32	19	H	Stoke C	W 1-0	0-0	14	McGavin [87]	4364
33	26	H	Burnley	L 1-2	1-2	15	McGavin [19]	6194
34	Mar 4	A	Scunthorpe U	D 0-0	0-0	15		4253
35	7	A	Preston NE	W 3-2	1-0	—	Keith [14], Lua-Lua [57], Duguid [87]	11,323
36	11	H	Oxford U	L 1-2	0-1	14	Skelton [63]	4058
37	17	A	Cardiff C	L 2-3	1-1	—	Dozzell [43], Lua-Lua [51]	5174
38	21	A	Oldham Ath	L 0-1	0-1	—		3282
39	25	H	Gillingham	W 2-1	0-0	14	McGavin [60], Lock [66]	4337
40	Apr 1	A	Luton T	L 2-3	0-1	18	McGavin [52], Lock [59]	5125
41	8	H	Blackpool	D 1-1	1-0	17	Duguid [1]	3351
42	15	A	Wycombe W	L 0-3	0-0	18		4558
43	22	H	Cambridge U	W 3-1	2-0	18	Duguid [17], McGavin [22], Keeble [57]	4902
44	24	A	Wrexham	L 0-1	0-1	18		2460
45	29	H	Bristol C	L 3-4	2-1	18	Lua-Lua [12], Skelton (pen) [29], Duguid [46]	4013
46	May 6	A	Brentford	D 0-0	0-0	18		5297

Final League Position: 18

GOALSCORERS

League (59): McGavin 16, Duguid 12, Lua-Lua 12, Dozzell 5, Skelton 4 (1 pen), Aspinall 2 (1 pen), Lock 2, Wilkins 2, Greene 1 (pen), Keeble 1, Keith 1, Moralee 1.
Worthington Cup (3): Dozzell 1, Keith 1, Lua-Lua 1.
FA Cup (1): Lua-Lua 1.

Brown S 38	Duguid K 40 + 1	Keith J 45	Burton S 9	Greene D 29	Aspinall W 7	Wilkins R 23 + 1	Gregory D 45	Lua-Lua L 24 + 17	Launders B 6	Dozzell J 38 + 1	Germain S 1 + 2	Opara C 2 + 14	Pinault T 1 + 3	Richard F 13 + 1	Moralee J 20 + 7	Forbes S — + 2	Farley C 8 + 6	Lock T 12 + 12	Arnott A 4 + 8	McGavin S 30 + 4	Skelton A 27 + 6	Vaughan J 6	Johnson G 24 + 3	White A 4	Wignall J — + 1	Dunne J 19 + 1	Bramble T 2	Johnson R 17 + 1	Walker A 2	Sodje E 3	Ferguson B 5 + 1	Keeble C 2 + 3	Match No.
1	2	3	4	5	6	7	8	9	10^1	11^2	12	13																					1
1	2	3	4	5	6	7^1	8^2	9	10	11				12	13																		2
1	2	3	4	5	6	7	8	9	10^1	11^2				12	13																		3
1	2	3	4	5	6	7	8	9	10							11^1	12																4
1	2^1	3	4	5	6	7	8	9	10							11	12																5
1	2	3		5	6^1	7	8	9	10^2		13	12		4	11^3					14													6
1	2		4	5	6	7	8					12	13	11^3	14		10^1			9^2	3												7
1	2	3	4	5		7	8^2				12	13		11^1	9^2					6	14		10										8
1	10	3	4	5		7	8^2				12			11	9^1					2	13		6										9
1	10	3	4^2	5		7	8	9						11						2	6		12	13									10
1	10	3		5		7	8	9						11	12					2	6^2		13	4^1									11
1	6	3		5		7	8	9						11	12		13			2			10^1	4^2									12
1	6	3		5		7	8	9						11						2			10	4									13
1	8	3		5		7		9						11	4					2			10	6									14
1	2	3		5		7	8	9^2						11	4		12	13		10^1			6										15
	4^1	3		5		7	8	9^3						11	2^2		12	13		10	6	1	14										16
		3^3		5		7	8	9						11	4^2	2	12	13		10^1	6	1	14										17
	7	3		5			8^1	9^2						11	2^3		13	14	12	10	4	1	6										18
	7^1	3		5			8	9							2		13		12	10	4^2	1	11			6							19
	11^1	3		5			8	9		12					2					10	4	1	7			6							20
		3		5^2			8	9^1		12				11	2		13			10	4	1	7			6							21
1		3		5			8	9		11				4						10			7			6		2					22
1	7^1	3					8	9^2		11				4	12		13			10			5			6		2					23
1	7	3		5			8	9^1							12		13			10	11		6			4		2^2					24
1	7	3		5			8	9^1							12		13	14		10^2	11		6			4^3		2					25
1	7^1	3		5			8	9		11	12									10			6			4		2					26
1	7	3		5			8^1	9		11	12									10			6			4		2					27
	7	3		5			8	9^2		11					12		13^3	14		10^1			6			4		2	1				28
1	7	3		5			8	9^2		11					12		13	14		10^3	6^3					4		2					29
	7	3		5^1			8	9		11					12		13	14		10^3	6					4		2^2	1				30
1	7	3					8	9^1		11					12		13			10	6		5^2			4		2					31
1	7^2	3					8	9^1		11					12		13			10	6		5			4		2					32
1	7	3					8^1	9^2		11					12		13	14		10	6		5			4		2^3					33
1	7	3					8	9^1		11					12		13			10	6^2		5			4		2					34
1	7	3					8	9		11					12		13			10^2	6		5			4		2^1					35
1	2	3					8	9^1	7	11					12		13			10^2	6		5			4							36
1	2	3					8	9^2	7	11					12		13			10^1	6		5			4							37
1	2^2	3					8	9	7	11				4	12		13			10	6		5^1										38
1	2	3					8^3	9^2		11^1					12		13	14		10	6		5			4						7	39
1	2	3					8^3	9		11					12		13	14		10	6		5^1			4						7^2	40
1	7	3					8	9		11										10	6		5			4		2			11		41
1	7	3					8^2	9^3							12		13			10^1	6		5			4		2			11	14	42
1	4^2	3					8	9^1	7						12		13			10	6		5					2			11		43
1	12	3					8	9						4^1			13			10^2	6		5					2			11	7	44
1	4^1	3^2					8	9^3		11					12		13	14		10	6		5					2				7	45
1		3					8^2	9		11				4^1	12		13	14		10	6^3		5					2				7	46

FA Premiership **COVENTRY CITY**

FOUNDATION

Workers at Singers' cycle factory formed a club in 1883. The first success of Singers' FC was to win the Birmingham Junior Cup in 1891 and this led in 1894 to their election to the Birmingham and District League. Four years later they changed their name to Coventry City and joined the Southern League in 1908 at which time they were playing in blue and white quarters.

Highfield Road Stadium, King Richard Street, Coventry CV2 4FW.
Telephone: (024) 7623 4000.
Fax: (024) 7623 4099.
Ticket Office: (024) 7623 4020.
Ticket Office Fax: (024) 7623 4023.
Sales & Marketing: (024) 7623 4010.
ClubCall: 09068 121 166.
Website: http://www.ccfc.co.uk
Email: info@ccfc.co.uk
Ground Capacity: 23,611.
Record Attendance: 51,455 v Wolverhampton W, Division 2, 29 April 1967.
Record Receipts: £375,510 v Sheffield U, FA Cup 6th Rd, 7 March 1998.
Pitch Measurements: 110yd × 75yd.
President: G. Robinson MP.
Chairman: B. A. Richardson.
Deputy Chairman: M. C. McGinnity.
Directors: A. M. Jepson, J. F. W Reason, D. A. Higgs, Miss B. Price, G. P. Hover.
Company Secretary: Graham Hover.
Manager: Gordon Strachan.
Coaches: Garry Pendrey and Trevor Peake.
Physio: Stuart Collie.
Marketing: Ric Allison.
Stadium Manager: Don Blair.
Club Statistician: Jim Brown.

LATEST SEQUENCES
Longest Sequence of League Wins: 6, 25.4.64 – 5.9.64.
Longest Sequence of League Defeats: 9, 30.8.19 – 11.10.19.
Longest Sequence of League Draws: 6, 28.9.96 – 16.11.96.
Longest Sequence of Unbeaten League Matches: 25, 26.11.66 – 13.5.67.
Longest Sequence Without a League Win: 19, 30.8.19 – 20.12.19.

HONOURS

Football League: Division 1 best season: 6th, 1969–70; Division 2 – Champions 1966–67; Division 3 – Champions 1963–64; Division 3 (S) – Champions 1935–36; Runners-up 1933–34; Division 4 – Runners-up 1958–59.

FA Cup: Winners 1987.

Football League Cup: Semi-final 1981, 1990.

European Competitions: *European Fairs Cup:* 1970–71.

Colours
Sky blue and white striped shirts with a sky blue shoulder panel and black trim, white shorts with sky blue side panel, white stockings with sky blue cuff.

Change Colours
White shirts with black panels and red trim, black shorts, white stockings with black trim.

Year Formed: 1883.

Turned Professional: 1893.

Ltd Co.: 1907.

Previous Names: 1883, Singers FC; 1898, Coventry City FC.

Club Nickname: 'Sky Blues'.

Previous Grounds: 1883, Binley Road; 1887, Stoke Road; 1899, Highfield Road.

First Football League Game: 30 August 1919, Division 2, v Tottenham H (h) L 0–5 – Lindon; Roberts, Chaplin, Allan, Hawley, Clarke, Sheldon, Mercer, Sambrooke, Lowes, Gibson.

Record League Victory: 9–0 v Bristol C, Division 3 (S), 28 April 1934 – Pearson; Brown, Bisby; Perry, Davidson, Frith; White (2), Lauderdale, Bourton (5), Jones (2), Lake.

Record Cup Victory: 7–0 v Scunthorpe U, FA Cup 1st rd, 24 November 1934 – Pearson; Brown, Bisby; Mason, Davidson, Boileau; Birtley (2), Lauderdale (2), Bourton (1), Jones (1), Liddle (1).

Record Defeat: 2–10 v Norwich C, Division 3 (S), 15 March 1930.

Most League Points (2 for a win): 60, Division 4, 1958–59 and Division 3, 1963–64.

Most League Points (3 for a win): 63, Division 1, 1986–87.

Most League Goals: 108, Division 3 (S), 1931–32.

Highest League Scorer in Season: Clarrie Bourton, 49, Division 3 (S), 1931–32.

Most League Goals in Total Aggregate: Clarrie Bourton, 171, 1931–37.

Most League Goals in One Match: 5, Clarrie Bourton v Bournemouth, Division 3S, 17 October 1931; 5, Arthur Bacon v Gillingham, Division 3S, 30 December 1933.

Most Capped Player: Peter Ndlovu 26 (37), Zimbabwe.

Most League Appearances: Steve Ogrizovic, 507, 1984–2000.

Youngest League Player: Gary McSheffrey, 16 years 198 days v Aston Villa, 27 February 1999.

Record Transfer Fee Received: £5,750,000 from Aston Villa for Dion Dublin, November 1998.

Record Transfer Fee Paid: £6,000,000 to Wolverhampton W for Robbie Keane, August 1999.

Football League Record: 1919 Elected to Division 2; 1925–26 Division 3 (N); 1926–36 Division 3 (S); 1936–52 Division 2; 1952–58 Division 3 (S); 1958–59 Division 4; 1959–64 Division 3; 1964–67 Division 2; 1967–92 Division 1; 1992– FA Premier League.

MANAGERS

H. R. Buckle 1909–10
Robert Wallace 1910–13
(Secretary-Manager)
Frank Scott-Walford 1913–15
William Clayton 1917–19
H. Pollitt 1919–20
Albert Evans 1920–24
Jimmy Kerr 1924–28
James McIntyre 1928–31
Harry Storer 1931–45
Dick Bayliss 1945–47
Billy Frith 1947–48
Harry Storer 1948–53
Jack Fairbrother 1953–54
Charlie Elliott 1954–55
Jesse Carver 1955–56
Harry Warren 1956–57
Billy Frith 1957–61
Jimmy Hill 1961–67
Noel Cantwell 1967–72
Bob Dennison 1972
Joe Mercer 1972–75
Gordon Milne 1972–81
Dave Sexton 1981–83
Bobby Gould 1983–84
Don Mackay 1985–86
George Curtis 1986–87
(became Managing Director)
John Sillett 1987–90
Terry Butcher 1990–92
Don Howe 1992
Bobby Gould 1992–93
Phil Neal 1993–95
Ron Atkinson 1995–96
(became Director of Football)
Gordon Strachan November 1996–

TEN YEAR LEAGUE RECORD

		P	W	D	L	F	A	Pts	Pos
1989-90	Div 1	38	14	7	17	39	59	49	12
1990-91	Div 1	38	11	11	16	42	49	44	16
1991-92	Div 1	42	11	11	20	35	44	44	19
1992-93	PR Lge	42	13	13	16	52	57	52	15
1993-94	PR Lge	42	14	14	14	43	45	56	11
1994-95	PR Lge	42	12	14	16	44	62	50	16
1995-96	PR Lge	38	8	14	16	42	60	38	16
1996-97	PR Lge	38	9	14	15	38	54	41	17
1997-98	PR Lge	38	12	16	10	46	44	52	11
1998-99	PR Lge	38	11	9	18	39	51	42	15

DID YOU KNOW ?

Evergreen Coventry City goalkeeper Steve Ogrizovic holds the club record for the highest number of consecutive League appearances: 209 from August 1984 to September 1989.

COVENTRY CITY 1999–2000 LEAGUE RECORD

Match No.	Date	Venue	Opponents	Result	H/T Score	Lg. Pos.	Goalscorers	Atten- dance
1	Aug 7	H	Southampton	L 0-1	0-0	16		19,602
2	11	A	Leicester C	L 0-1	0-1	—		19,196
3	14	A	Wimbledon	D 1-1	0-0	16	McAllister (pen) [90]	10,635
4	21	H	Derby Co	W 2-0	1-0	12	Keane 2 [43, 67]	17,658
5	25	H	Manchester U	L 1-2	0-0	—	Aloisi [80]	22,022
6	29	A	Sunderland	D 1-1	1-0	16	Keane [33]	38,436
7	Sept 11	H	Leeds U	L 3-4	2-3	17	McAllister (pen) [2], Aloisi [17], Chippo [54]	21,528
8	19	A	Tottenham H	L 2-3	0-1	17	Keane [54], Chippo [75]	35,224
9	25	H	West Ham U	W 1-0	1-0	15	Hadji [36]	19,985
10	Oct 2	A	Everton	D 1-1	1-1	14	McAllister [11]	34,839
11	16	H	Newcastle U	W 4-1	3-0	13	Palmer [13], Williams [21], Keane [39], Hadji [90]	23,022
12	23	A	Sheffield W	D 0-0	0-0	13		23,296
13	31	H	Watford	W 4-0	2-0	13	Keane [17], Froggatt [33], Hadji [49], McAllister (pen) [62]	21,697
14	Nov 6	A	Bradford C	D 1-1	1-1	13	McAllister [1]	17,587
15	22	H	Aston Villa	W 2-1	1-1	—	Roussel [8], Keane [65]	20,174
16	27	H	Leicester C	L 0-1	0-0	12		22,016
17	Dec 4	A	Southampton	D 0-0	0-0	11		15,168
18	18	A	Liverpool	L 0-2	0-1	13		44,024
19	26	H	Arsenal	W 3-2	2-0	13	McAllister [6], Hadji [40], Keane [71]	22,750
20	Jan 4	H	Chelsea	D 2-2	0-0	—	Roussel [54], Keane [81]	20,152
21	15	H	Wimbledon	W 2-0	0-0	12	McAllister (pen) [56], Keane [74]	19,005
22	22	A	Derby Co	D 0-0	0-0	12		28,381
23	Feb 5	A	Manchester U	L 2-3	0-1	12	Roussel 2 [65, 90]	61,380
24	12	H	Sunderland	W 3-2	3-0	12	Keane [2], Hadji [13], Roussel [18]	22,099
25	19	A	Middlesbrough	L 0-2	0-2	12		32,793
26	26	H	Tottenham H	L 0-1	0-0	13		23,073
27	Mar 5	A	Leeds U	L 0-3	0-2	14		38,710
28	11	A	Aston Villa	L 0-1	0-1	14		33,177
29	15	H	Everton	W 1-0	0-0	—	McAllister [86]	18,513
30	18	H	Bradford C	W 4-0	2-0	12	Roussel [7], Whelan [21], Eustace [85], Zuniga [86]	19,194
31	26	A	Arsenal	L 0-3	0-0	14		38,027
32	Apr 1	H	Liverpool	L 0-3	0-2	14		23,084
33	12	A	Chelsea	L 1-2	1-0	—	McAllister [18]	32,316
34	15	H	Middlesbrough	W 2-1	1-0	14	Ince (og) [32], Keane [61]	19,430
35	22	A	West Ham U	L 0-5	0-2	14		24,719
36	29	A	Newcastle U	L 0-2	0-0	14		36,408
37	May 6	H	Sheffield W	W 4-1	1-0	14	McAllister 2 [38, 70], Zuniga [67], Hadji [80]	19,921
38	14	A	Watford	L 0-1	0-1	14		18,977

Final League Position: 14

GOALSCORERS
League (47): Keane 12, McAllister 11 (4 pens), Hadji 6, Roussel 6, Aloisi 2, Chippo 2, Zuniga 2, Eustace 1, Froggatt 1, Palmer 1, Whelan 1, Williams 1, own goal 1.
Worthington Cup (4): Chippo 2, McAllister 2.
FA Cup (8): Roussel 3, Chippo 2, Whelan 2, Eustace 1.

Hedman M 35	Edworthy M 10	Burrows D 11 + 4	Williams P 26 + 2	Shaw R 27 + 2	Chippo Y 33	Telfer P 26 + 4	Whelan N 20 + 6	Huckerby D 1	McAllister G 38	Hadji M 33	Froggatt S 21 + 5	Aloisi J 3 + 4	Breen G 20 + 1	Keane R 30 + 1	Strachan G 1 + 2	Konjic M 3 + 1	McSheffrey G — + 3	Quinn B 5 + 6	Hall M 7 + 2	Hall P — + 1	Palmer C 15	Roussel C 18 + 4	Normann R 1 + 7	Gustafsson T 7 + 3	Eustace J 12 + 4	Zuniga Y 3 + 3	Hendry C 9	Ogrizovic S 3	Betts R — + 2	Match No.
1	2	3	4	5	6¹	7	8	9²	10	11	12	13																		1
1	2	3	4	5	6	7	8		10	9	11¹	12																		2
1		3	4	5	6	7	8		10	11¹	12	9	2																	3
1	2	3	4	5	6	7¹	8		10	11²	12	13		9³	14															4
1	3		4	5	6²	12	8¹		10	7	11	13	2³	9	14															5
1	3		4	5	6	12			10	7¹	11	8²	2	9			13													6
1	3		4	5	6				10	7	11²	8³	9	12		13	2¹	14												7
1	2	3²	8	5	6				10	7	11¹		9	4			12	13												8
1	2		12	5	6¹	7			10²	11			9	4	13		3		8											9
1	2		12	5	6	7			10	11			9	4¹			3		8											10
1	2¹		4	5	6	7			10²	11	12		9				3		8	13										11
1			4	5	6¹	7			10	11	2		9				3		8	12										12
1			4	5		2			10	7	11		9				3	6	8											13
1			4	5	6	2			10	7	11		9				3		8											14
1	12	4		6¹	2	13			10	7			5	9			3		8	11²										15
1	3²	4		6	2	12			10	7	13		5	9					8	11¹										16
1		4		6	2	12			10	7	3		5	9					8	11¹										17
1		4		6	2	11¹			10	7²	3		5	9					8	12	13									18
1		4		6²	2	12			10	7	3		5	9¹					8	11		13								19
1		4		6	2	12			10	7	3		5	9					8	11¹										20
1		4			2	7			10		3		5	9					8	11¹	12				6					21
1		4			2	7			10		3		5	9	8¹			12		11		13			6²					22
1		4	3			7¹			10		11		5	9				6	8		2	12								23
1			5	8²					10	7	3¹		6	9			12			11	13	2	4							24
1	3³	4	5	6					10	7		12	9			13			8	11²		2¹	14							25
1		3	4¹	2	6		8²		10	7			5	9			12				13		11							26
1		2	12	6		8			10				5			3¹		11	13		7	9²	4							27
1	12		5	6		13			10	7	3		9²					11		2	8¹		4							28
1		3		5	6		9		10	7								11		2	8¹	12	4							29
1				5	6	12		9	10¹	7							3			11²		2	8	13	4					30
			5	6	12	9		10	7²	3									11	13		2¹	8			4		1		31
			5	6	2	9¹		10	7	3			12					13			11			8²		4		1		32
1	12			5	6	2	8²		10	7¹	3		9					11							13	4				33
1	12			6¹	2	8			10	7	3		5	9					11						4					34
1	5		12		2	8			10				6	9				11³		13	3²	7		4¹	14					35
1		4	3	6	2	8²			10	7			5	9					11¹			12			13					36
	4	3	6¹	2	8			10	7				5	9								12	11		1					37
1		4³	3	6	2	8			10	7			5	9					13					12²	14		11¹			38

Worthington Cup
Second Round Tranmere R (a) 1-5
                              (h) 3-1

FA Cup
Third Round Norwich C (a) 3-1
Fourth Round Burnley (h) 3-0
Fifth Round Charlton Ath (h) 2-3

Division 1 — CREWE ALEXANDRA

FOUNDATION

The first match played at Crewe was on 1 December 1877 against Basford, the leading North Staffordshire team of that time. During the club's history they have also played in a number of other leagues including the Football Alliance, Football Combination, Lancashire League, Manchester League, Central League and Lancashire Combination. Two former players, Aaron Scragg in 1899 and Jackie Pearson in 1911, had the distinction of refereeing FA Cup finals. Pearson was also capped for England against Ireland in 1892.

Football Ground, Gresty Road, Crewe CW2 6EB.

Telephone: (01270) 213 014.

Ground Capacity: 10,046.

ClubCall: 09068 121 647.

Record Attendance: 20,000 v Tottenham H, FA Cup 4th rd, 30 January 1960.

Record Receipts: £41,093 v Liverpool, FA Cup 3rd rd, 6 January 1992.

Pitch Measurements: 112yd × 74yd.

President: N. Rowlinson.

Chairman: J. Bowler.

Vice-Chairman: N. Hassall.

Directors: D. Rowlinson, R. Clayton, J. McMillan, D. Gradi.

Manager: Dario Gradi MBE.

Secretary: Mrs Gill Palin.

Marketing Manager: Alison Bowler.

LATEST SEQUENCES

Longest Sequence of League Wins: 7, 30.4.94 – 3.9.94.

Longest Sequence of League Defeats: 10, 16.4.79 – 22.8.79.

Longest Sequence of League Draws: 5, 31.8.87 – 18.9.87.

Longest Sequence of Unbeaten League Matches: 17, 25.3.95 – 16.9.95.

Longest Sequence Without a League Win: 30, 22.9.56 – 6.4.57.

HONOURS

Football League: Promoted from Division 2 1996–97 (play-offs).

FA Cup: Semi-final 1888.

Football League Cup: best season: 3rd rd, 1975, 1976, 1979, 1993, 1999, 2000.

Welsh Cup: Winners 1936, 1937.

Colours
Red shirts, white shorts, red stockings.

Change Colours
Blue shirts, white shorts, blue stockings.

Year Formed: 1877.

Turned Professional: 1893.

Ltd Co.: 1892.

Club Nickname: 'Railwaymen'.

First Football League Game: 3 September 1892, Division 2, v Burton Swifts (a) L 1–7 – Hickton; Moore, Cope; Linnell, Johnson, Osborne; Bennett, Pearson (1), Bailey, Barnett, Roberts.

Record League Victory: 8–0 v Rotherham U, Division 3 (N), 1 October 1932 – Foster; Pringle, Dawson; Ward, Keenor (1), Turner (1); Gillespie, Swindells (1), McConnell (2), Deacon (2), Weale (1).

Record Cup Victory: 8–0 v Hartlepool U, Auto Windscreens Shield 1st rd, 17 October 1995 – Gayle; Collins (1), Booty, Westwood (Unsworth), Macauley (1), Whalley (1), Garvey (1), Murphy (1), Savage (1) (Rivers (1p)), Lennon, Edwards, (1 og).

Record Defeat: 2–13 v Tottenham H, FA Cup 4th rd replay, 3 February 1960.

Most League Points (2 for a win): 59, Division 4, 1962–63.

Most League Points (3 for a win): 83, Division 2, 1994–95.

Most League Goals: 95, Division 3 (N), 1931–32.

Highest League Scorer in Season: Terry Harkin, 35, Division 4, 1964–65.

Most League Goals in Total Aggregate: Bert Swindells, 126, 1928–37.

Most League Goals in One Match: 5, Tony Naylor v Colchester U, Division 3, 24 April 1993.

Most Capped Player: Bill Lewis, 9 (27), Wales.

Most League Appearances: Tommy Lowry, 436, 1966–78.

Youngest League Player: Steve Walters, 16 years 119 days v Peterborough U, 6 May 1988.

Record Transfer Fee Received: £3,000,000 Derby Co for Seth Johnson, May 1999.

Record Transfer Fee Paid: £650,000 to Torquay U for Rodney Jack, June 1998.

Football League Record: 1892 Original Member of Division 2; 1896 Failed re-election; 1921 Re-entered Division 3 (N); 1958–63 Division 4; 1963–64 Division 3; 1964–68 Division 4; 1968–69 Division 3; 1969–89 Division 4; 1989–91 Division 3; 1991–92 Division 4; 1992–94 Division 3; 1994–97 Division 2; 1997– Division 1.

MANAGERS

W. C. McNeill 1892–94
(Secretary-Manager)
J. G. Hall 1895–96
(Secretary-Manager)
R. Roberts *(1st team Secretary-Manager)* 1897
J. B. Blomerley 1898–1911
(Secretary-Manager, continued as Hon. Secretary to 1925)
Tom Bailey *(Secretary only)* 1925–38
George Lillycrop *(Trainer)* 1938–44
Frank Hill 1944–48
Arthur Turner 1948–51
Harry Catterick 1951–53
Ralph Ward 1953–55
Maurice Lindley 1956–57
Willie Cook 1957–58
Harry Ware 1958–60
Jimmy McGuigan 1960–64
Ernie Tagg 1964–71
(continued as Secretary to 1972)
Dennis Viollet 1971
Jimmy Melia 1972–74
Ernie Tagg 1974
Harry Gregg 1975–78
Warwick Rimmer 1978–79
Tony Waddington 1979–81
Arfon Griffiths 1981–82
Peter Morris 1982–83
Dario Gradi June 1983–

TEN YEAR LEAGUE RECORD

		P	W	D	L	F	A	Pts	Pos
1989-90	Div 3	46	15	17	14	56	53	62	12
1990-91	Div 3	46	11	11	24	62	80	44	22
1991-92	Div 4	42	20	10	12	66	51	70	6
1992-93	Div 3	42	21	7	14	75	56	70	6
1993-94	Div 3	42	21	10	11	80	61	73	3
1994-95	Div 2	46	25	8	13	80	68	83	3
1995-96	Div 2	46	22	7	17	77	60	73	5
1996-97	Div 2	46	22	7	17	56	47	73	6
1997-98	Div 1	46	18	5	23	58	65	59	11
1998-99	Div 1	46	12	12	22	54	78	48	18

DID YOU KNOW ?

On 14 December 1999, Crewe Alexandra manager Dario Gradi celebrated his 900th game in charge of the club, as his team beat Wolverhampton Wanderers 1-0.

CREWE ALEXANDRA 1999–2000 LEAGUE RECORD

Match No.	Date		Venue	Opponents	Result	H/T Score	Lg. Pos.	Goalscorers	Attendance
1	Aug	7	A	Crystal Palace	D 1-1	0-0	9	Rivers [84]	13,664
2		21	A	Walsall	W 4-1	1-1	9	Charnock [14], Rivers [55], Lunt [56], Little [71]	6238
3		27	H	Grimsby T	D 1-1	0-0	—	Sorvel [84]	5440
4		30	A	Birmingham C	L 1-5	1-3	14	Cramb [3]	24,085
5	Sept	11	A	Norwich C	L 1-2	1-1	19	Cramb [31]	13,172
6		18	H	Swindon T	W 2-1	1-0	14	Street [13], Smith S (pen) [81]	5280
7		25	A	Fulham	L 0-3	0-3	18		12,156
8	Oct	3	H	Tranmere R	L 0-2	0-0	21		6169
9		9	H	Sheffield U	W 1-0	1-0	19	Sorvel [15]	5304
10		16	A	Stockport Co	L 1-2	1-1	22	Sorvel [16]	7571
11		19	A	Bolton W	D 2-2	1-1	—	Jack 2 [39, 87]	12,676
12		23	H	Barnsley	L 0-1	0-1	22		5421
13		26	H	Fulham	D 1-1	1-1	—	Little [45]	5493
14		30	A	Tranmere R	L 0-2	0-0	22		5987
15	Nov	2	H	Charlton Ath	L 0-2	0-2	—		4741
16		5	A	Port Vale	L 0-1	0-0	—		5584
17		20	A	Portsmouth	W 2-0	1-0	22	Jack [34], Tait [63]	11,550
18		23	H	Blackburn R	D 0-0	0-0	—		6495
19		27	A	Ipswich T	L 1-2	0-1	23	Rivers [75]	15,211
20	Dec	4	H	Crystal Palace	W 2-0	2-0	22	Tait [12], Macauley [34]	4923
21		7	H	WBA	W 2-0	0-0	—	Tait [48], Sorvel [84]	5419
22		14	H	Wolverhampton W	W 1-0	0-0	—	Tait [83]	6018
23		18	A	Nottingham F	L 0-1	0-0	17		15,289
24		26	H	Huddersfield T	D 1-1	0-0	15	Little [63]	8106
25		28	A	QPR	L 0-1	0-0	19		12,011
26	Jan	3	H	Manchester C	D 1-1	0-1	18	Jack [73]	10,066
27		15	A	Charlton Ath	L 0-1	0-1	20		19,125
28		22	H	Walsall	L 2-3	1-3	20	Macauley (pen) [34], Tait [67]	6275
29		29	A	Grimsby T	D 1-1	0-0	20	Lunt [51]	6147
30	Feb	5	H	Birmingham C	L 2-3	1-1	22	Macauley 2 [19, 90]	6289
31		12	A	WBA	L 0-1	0-1	22		12,406
32		19	H	Ipswich T	L 1-2	0-0	22	Tait [64]	6393
33		26	H	Swindon T	W 1-0	0-0	20	Cramb [54]	5003
34	Mar	4	H	Norwich C	W 1-0	1-0	19	Sorvel [5]	5450
35		7	H	Port Vale	W 2-1	1-0	—	Cramb [14], Lunt [88]	8044
36		12	A	Blackburn R	W 1-0	0-0	18	Cramb [80]	16,057
37		18	H	Portsmouth	L 1-3	0-1	19	Cramb [57]	6188
38		21	A	Wolverhampton W	L 0-2	0-1	—		20,444
39		25	A	Huddersfield T	L 0-3	0-1	20		14,014
40	Apr	1	H	Nottingham F	L 0-3	0-1	20		7014
41		8	A	Manchester C	L 0-4	0-1	21		32,433
42		15	H	QPR	W 2-1	1-1	20	Smith S (pen) [18], Rivers [55]	4741
43		22	H	Stockport Co	W 3-2	2-1	20	Rivers 2 [6, 56], Lightfoot [9]	5813
44		24	A	Sheffield U	D 1-1	0-0	20	Little [87]	9923
45		29	H	Bolton W	L 1-3	0-1	20	Rivers [30]	8015
46	May	7	A	Barnsley	W 2-0	0-0	19	Sorvel [55], Hulse [79]	17,611

Final League Position: 19

GOALSCORERS

League (46): Rivers 7, Cramb 6, Sorvel 6, Tait 6, Jack 4, Little 4, Macauley 4 (1 pen), Lunt 3, Smith S 2 (2 pens), Charnock 1, Hulse 1, Lightfoot 1, Street 1.
Worthington Cup (8): Little 4, Rivers 2, Cramb 1, Smith S 1 (pen).
FA Cup (1): Little 1.

Kearton J 46	Wright D 44 + 1	Smith S 30 + 1	Macauley S 35 + 2	Unsworth L 3 + 5	Charnock P 14 + 2	Little C 34 + 3	Lunt K 39 + 4	Jack R 21 + 2	Sorvel N 46	Grant J 1 + 3	Wright S 17 + 6	Rivers M 29 + 3	Tait P 19 + 14	Cramb C 33 + 4	Lightfoot C 16 + 5	Foran M 11 + 2	Smith P — + 6	Bignot M 25 + 2	Street K 20 + 8	Critchley N — + 1	Collins J 8 + 5	Boertien P 2	Walton D 8 + 3	Newby J 5 + 1	Hulse R — + 4	Ince C — + 1	Match No.
1	2	3	4	5^1	6^2	7	8	9	10	11^2	12	13	14														1
1	2	3	4	5	6	7^3	8		10		12	11^1	13	9^2	14												2
1	2	3			6	7	8		10				4	11	12	9^1		5									3
1	2	3	12		6	7^3	8^2		10				4	11	9	5^1		14	13								4
1	2	3	5	12^2	6	7^3	8	14	10				4^1	11	9	13											5
1	2	3	5	12	6	7^2	8		10	11		13^3		9				14	4^1								6
1	2	3			6^1	7	8^2		10	11	12	13	4	9^3	5				14								7
1	2	3	4		6	7^1	8		10		12	11		9				5									8
1	2	3	4	12	6	7^2	8^3		10			11		9		5^1		14	13								9
1	2	3^1	4		6^2	7	8		10		12	11	14	9^3				5		13							10
1	2	3	12	4^2	6	7	8		10	11		13		9		5^1											11
1	2	3			6	7	8		10		12	13		9^2				5	4^1		11						12
1	2	3				7	8		10		12	11		9^1				5	4		6						13
1	2	3				7	8^1		10		12	11	13	9^2				5	4		6						14
1	2	3	4		6	7	8		10		12			9				5			11^1						15
1		3	4	12		7	8		10			11	13	9^2				5	14	2^1	6^3						16
1	2	3			6	7	8^2		10		12	13		9^1				5	4		11						17
1	2	3	12		6	7	8		10			13		9^2		5^1			4		11						18
1	2	3	5			7	8		10			11		9					4		6						19
1	2	3	5			7^1	8		10			11		9					4	12	6						20
1	2	3	5			7	8		10			11		9					4	12	6^1						21
1	2	3	5			7	8		10			11	3	9^1					4	12	6						22
1	2		5	12		7	8		10^1			11	13	9^2	3				4		6						23
1	2	3	5			7	8		10			11		9					4		6						24
1	2	3	5			7	8		10			11		9^1					4	12	6						25
1	2		5			7	8		10		12	11		9			3		4		6^1						26
1	2		5			7	8		10^1		12	11	13	9			3^2		4		6						27
1	2		5			7	8		10			11		9			3		4		6						28
1	2		5			7	8		10^1			11		9			3		4	12	6						29
1	2			12	6	7^1	8		10			11	13	9			3^2	5	4								30
1	2	3	4	5^2	6^1	7	8		10		12	11	13	9													31
1	2			12	6	7	8		10			11	13	9^1			3^2	5	4								32
1	2	3	4		6	7^2	8		10^3		12	11	13	9		5^1	3						14				33
1	2	4			6^2	7	8		10^1			11		9			3			12			14	13^3			34
1	2^2	4	5		6	7	8		10		12	11	13	9^3			3^1						14				35
1	2	4	5		6	7^2	8		10^1		12	11		9			3		4			13					36
1	2	4	5		6	7	8		10^1		12	11		9			3		4								37
1	2		5	12		7^2	8		10			11	13	9^3		4^1	3				6		14				38
1^8	2	3	4	5		7	8		10		12	11		9							6^1				15		39
1	2	3	4	5	6^2	7	8^1		10		12	11^3	13	9									14				40
1	2	3	4	5		7	8		10			11		9							6						41
1	2	3	5			7	8		10			11	14	9^2					4	12	6^1		13^3				42
1	2	3				7^1	8		10			11	12	9	5^2				4		6		13				43
1	2	3				7	8		10		12	11	13	9^2				5	4		6^1						44
1	2	3	5			7	8		10		12	11^1	13	9^2					4		6						45
1	2	3	5			7^2	8		10^1		12	11		9					4		6		13				46

Worthington Cup

First Round	Hartlepool U	(a)	3-3
		(h)	1-0
Second Round	Ipswich T	(h)	2-1
		(a)	1-1
Third Round	Tottenham H	(a)	1-3

FA Cup

Third Round	Bradford C	(h)	1-2

Division 1   **CRYSTAL PALACE**

FOUNDATION

There was a Crystal Palace club as early as 1861 but the present organisation was born in 1905 after the formation of a club by the company that controlled the Crystal Palace (building), had been rejected by the FA who did not like the idea of the Cup Final hosts running their own club. A separate company had to be formed and they had their home on the old Cup Final ground until 1915.

Selhurst Park, London SE25 6PU.
Telephone: (020) 8768 6000. *Fax:* (020) 8771 5311.
Lottery Office: (020) 8768 6094.
Club Shop: (020) 8768 6100.
Dial-A-Seat Ticketline: (020) 8771 8841.
Palace Publications: (020) 8768 6021. *Fax:* (020) 8653 6312.
ClubCall: 09068 400 333.
Press Office: (020) 8768 6020. *Fax:* (020) 8768 6114.
Ground Capacity: 26,400.
Record Attendance: 51,482 v Burnley, Division 2, 11 May 1979.
Record Receipts: £327,124 v Manchester U, FA Premier League, 21 April 1993 (League); £336,583 v Chelsea, Coca-Cola Cup 5th rd, 6 January 1993.
Pitch Measurements: 110yd × 74yd.
Chairman: Simon Jordan.
Vice Chairman: Peter Brummet.
Director: S. Coppell.
Manager: Steve Coppell.
Physio: Gary Sadler.
Stadium Manager: Vic Worrall.
Club Secretary: Mike Hurst.
PR and Communications Manager: Terry Byfield.

LATEST SEQUENCES

Longest Sequence of League Wins: 8, 9.2.21 – 26.3.21.
Longest Sequence of League Defeats: 8, 10.1.98 – 14.3.98.
Longest Sequence of League Draws: 5, 30.12.78 – 24.2.79.
Longest Sequence of Unbeaten League Matches: 18, 22.2.69 – 13.8.69.
Longest Sequence Without a League Win: 20, 3.3.62 – 8.9.62.

HONOURS

Football League: Division 1 – Champions 1993–94; Promoted from Division 1, 1996–97 (play-offs); Division 2 – Champions 1978–79; Runners-up 1968–69; Division 3 – Runners-up 1963–64; Division 3 (S) – Champions 1920–21; Runners-up 1928–29, 1930–31, 1938–39; Division 4 – Runners-up 1960–61.

FA Cup: Runners-up 1990.

Football League Cup: Semi-final 1993, 1995.

Zenith Data Systems Cup: Winners 1991.

Colours
Red and blue vertical striped shirts, red shorts, red stockings with blue tops.

Change Colours
White shirts, royal blue shorts, royal blue stockings with red tops.

Year Formed: 1905.

Turned Professional: 1905.

Ltd Co.: 1905.

Club Nickname: 'The Eagles'.

Previous Grounds: 1905, Crystal Palace; 1915, Herne Hill; 1918, The Nest; 1924, Selhurst Park.

First Football League Game: 28 August 1920, Division 3, v Merthyr T (a) L 1–2 – Alderson; Little, Rhodes; McCracken, Jones, Feebury; Bateman, Conner, Smith, Milligan (1), Whibley.

Record League Victory: 9–0 v Barrow, Division 4, 10 October 1959 – Rouse; Long, Noakes; Truett, Evans, McNichol; Gavin (1), Summersby (4 incl. 1p), Sexton, Byrne (2), Colfar (2).

Record Cup Victory: 8–0 v Southend U, Rumbelows League Cup 2nd rd (1st leg), 25 September 1989 – Martyn; Humphrey (Thompson (1)), Shaw, Pardew, Young, Thorn, McGoldrick, Thomas, Bright (3), Wright (3), Barber (Hodges (1)).

Record Defeat: 0–9 v Burnley, FA Cup 2nd rd replay, 10 February 1909. 0–9 v Liverpool, Division 1, 12 September 1990.

Most League Points (2 for a win): 64, Division 4, 1960–61.

Most League Points (3 for a win): 90, Division 1, 1993–94.

Most League Goals: 110, Division 4, 1960–61.

Highest League Scorer in Season: Peter Simpson, 46, Division 3 (S), 1930–31.

Most League Goals in Total Aggregate: Peter Simpson, 153, 1930–36.

Most League Goals in One Match: 6, Peter Simpson v Exeter C, Division 3S, 4 October 1930.

Most Capped Player: Eric Young, 19 (21), Wales.

Most League Appearances: Jim Cannon, 571, 1973–88.

Youngest League Player: Phil Hoadley, 16 years 112 days v Bolton W, 27 April 1968.

Record Transfer Fee Received: £4,500,000 from Tottenham H for Chris Armstrong, June 1995.

Record Transfer Fee Paid: £2,750,000 to RC Strasbourg for Valerien Ismael, January 1998.

Football League Record: 1920 Original Members of Division 3; 1921–25 Division 2; 1925–58 Division 3 (S); 1958–61 Division 4; 1961–64 Division 3; 1964–69 Division 2; 1969–73 Division 1; 1973–74 Division 2; 1974–77 Division 3; 1977–79 Division 2; 1979–81 Division 1; 1981–89 Division 2; 1989–92 Division 1; 1992–93 FA Premier League; 1993–94 Division 1; 1994–95 FA Premier League; 1995–97 Division 1; 1997–98 FA Premier League; 1998– Division 1.

MANAGERS

John T. Robson 1905–07
Edmund Goodman 1907–25
(had been Secretary since 1905 and afterwards continued in this position to 1933)
Alec Maley 1925–27
Fred Mavin 1927–30
Jack Tresadern 1930–35
Tom Bromilow 1935–36
R. S. Moyes 1936
Tom Bromilow 1936–39
George Irwin 1939–47
Jack Butler 1947–49
Ronnie Rooke 1949–50
Charlie Slade and Fred Dawes *(Joint Managers)* 1950–51
Laurie Scott 1951–54
Cyril Spiers 1954–58
George Smith 1958–60
Arthur Rowe 1960–62
Dick Graham 1962–66
Bert Head 1966–72
(continued as General Manager to 1973)
Malcolm Allison 1973–76
Terry Venables 1976–80
Ernie Walley 1980
Malcolm Allison 1980–81
Dario Gradi 1981
Steve Kember 1981–82
Alan Mullery 1982–84
Steve Coppell 1984–93
Alan Smith 1993–95
Steve Coppell *(Technical Director)* 1995–96
Dave Bassett 1996–97
Steve Coppell 1997–98
Attilio Lombardo 1998
Terry Venables *(Head Coach)* 1998–99
Steve Coppell January 1999–

TEN YEAR LEAGUE RECORD

		P	W	D	L	F	A	Pts	Pos
1989-90	Div 1	38	13	9	16	42	66	48	15
1990-91	Div 1	38	20	9	9	50	41	69	3
1991-92	Div 1	42	14	15	13	53	61	57	10
1992-93	PR Lge	42	11	16	15	48	61	49	20
1993-94	Div 1	46	27	9	10	73	46	90	1
1994-95	PR Lge	42	11	12	19	34	49	45	19
1995-96	Div 1	46	20	15	11	67	48	75	3
1996-97	Div 1	46	19	14	13	78	48	71	6
1997-98	PR Lge	38	8	9	21	37	71	33	20
1998-99	Div 1	46	14	16	16	58	71	58	14

DID YOU KNOW ?

Crystal Palace celebrated the 75th anniversary of their move to Selhurst Park on 2 October 1999, by beating Portsmouth 4-0.

CRYSTAL PALACE 1999–2000 LEAGUE RECORD

Match No.	Date	Venue	Opponents	Result	H/T Score	Lg. Pos.	Goalscorers	Attendance
1	Aug 7	H	Crewe Alex	D	1-1	0-0	10	Rodger 67	13,664
2	14	A	Barnsley	W	3-2	1-1	4	Rodger 24, Austin 59, Bradbury 74	14,461
3	21	H	Swindon T	L	1-2	1-1	11	Morrison 11	12,726
4	28	A	Huddersfield T	L	1-7	0-3	21	Morrison 69	10,656
5	Sept 4	A	Sheffield U	L	1-3	0-2	23	Morrison 90	11,886
6	11	A	Manchester C	L	1-2	1-1	24	Morrison 39	31,541
7	18	H	Grimsby T	W	3-0	2-0	18	Morrison 5, Mullins 24, Svensson 49	13,294
8	25	A	WBA	D	0-0	0-0	19		13,219
9	28	H	Wolverhampton W	D	1-1	0-1	—	Bradbury 55	12,720
10	Oct 2	H	Portsmouth	W	4-0	1-0	14	Svensson 20, Carlisle 59, Zhiyi 63, Mullins 90	15,221
11	16	A	Birmingham C	L	0-2	0-1	18		21,582
12	20	A	Blackburn R	D	1-1	0-0	—	Mullins 55	15,819
13	23	H	Tranmere R	D	2-2	2-0	19	Svensson 34, Austin 45	18,645
14	26	H	WBA	L	0-2	0-2	—		12,203
15	30	A	Portsmouth	L	1-3	1-1	20	Linighan 22	13,018
16	Nov 6	A	Bolton W	L	0-2	0-0	21		12,744
17	14	H	QPR	W	3-0	1-0	22	McKenzie 1, Svensson 75, Mullins (pen) 90	15,861
18	20	A	Port Vale	D	2-2	0-1	19	McKenzie 54, Svensson 88	5170
19	23	H	Norwich C	W	1-0	0-0	—	Svensson 90	12,110
20	27	H	Nottingham F	W	2-0	1-0	16	McKenzie 33, Svensson 67	15,920
21	Dec 4	A	Crewe Alex	L	0-2	0-2	17		4923
22	7	H	Ipswich T	D	2-2	1-2	—	Svensson 5, Mowbray (og) 61	13,176
23	18	H	Fulham	D	0-0	0-0	16		17,480
24	26	A	Charlton Ath	L	1-2	1-2	18	Martin 2	20,043
25	28	H	Walsall	W	3-2	1-1	16	Svensson (pen) 42, Carlisle 64, Mullins 86	13,943
26	Jan 3	A	Stockport Co	W	2-1	0-0	15	Mullins 69, Carlisle 78	8570
27	15	H	Barnsley	L	0-2	0-2	15		14,225
28	21	A	Swindon T	W	4-2	1-1	—	Morrison 2 29, 88, Foster 55, Mullins (pen) 57	5214
29	29	H	Huddersfield T	D	2-2	0-2	15	Mullins 47, Linighan 77	14,290
30	Feb 5	A	Wolverhampton W	L	1-2	0-1	17	Martin 64	20,756
31	12	H	Sheffield U	D	1-1	0-0	17	Morrison 89	14,877
32	19	A	Nottingham F	L	0-2	0-1	17		16,421
33	26	A	Grimsby T	L	0-1	0-1	17		5421
34	Mar 4	H	Manchester C	D	1-1	1-1	18	Morrison 27	21,052
35	7	H	Bolton W	D	0-0	0-0	—		15,236
36	11	A	Norwich C	W	1-0	0-0	17	Morrison 79	15,064
37	18	H	Port Vale	D	1-1	0-0	17	Rougier (og) 64	18,954
38	22	A	QPR	W	1-0	0-0	—	Morrison 68	12,842
39	25	H	Charlton Ath	L	0-1	0-0	16		22,577
40	Apr 1	A	Fulham	L	0-1	0-1	17		16,356
41	8	H	Stockport Co	D	3-3	3-1	18	McKenzie 18, Forssell 2 29, 31	16,646
42	15	A	Walsall	D	2-2	0-0	18	Forssell 50, Mullins 67	6323
43	22	H	Birmingham C	L	0-2	0-1	18		17,144
44	25	A	Ipswich T	L	0-1	0-1	—		18,798
45	29	H	Blackburn R	W	2-1	0-1	18	Cole 60, Morrison 72	18,272
46	May 7	A	Tranmere R	W	2-1	2-0	15	Mullins 34, Morrison 39	8891

Final League Position: 15

GOALSCORERS
League (57): Morrison 13, Mullins 10 (2 pens), Svensson 9 (1 pen), McKenzie 4, Carlisle 3, Forssell 3, Austin 2, Bradbury 2, Linighan 2, Martin 2, Rodger 2, Cole 1, Foster 1, Zhiyi 1, own goals 2.
Worthington Cup (10): Morrison 2, Smith 2, Bradbury 1, Mullins 1, Rizzo 1, Rodger 1, Thomson 1, Zhiyi 1.
FA Cup (0).

Digby F 38	Smith J 27	Frampton A 6 + 3	Austin D 45	Carlisle W 23 + 3	Linighan A 44 + 1	Mullins H 45	Rodger S 34	Bradbury L 9 + 1	Morrison C 28 + 1	Rizzo N 2 + 15	Tuttle D — + 1	Evans S — + 1	Woozley D 14 + 9	Thomson S 17 + 4	Harris R 1 + 5	Hibburt J 1 + 3	Svensson M 20 + 4	Zhiyi F 29	Sharpling C 1 + 5	Fumaca J 2 + 1	De Ornelas F 5 + 4	Fullarton J 13	Phelan T 14	Martin A 10 + 9	Launders B 1 + 1	McKenzie L 24 + 1	Foster C 17 + 3	Kabba S 1	Mautone S 2	Forssell M 13	Cole A 14	Hankin S — + 1	Gregg M 6	Hunt S — + 3	Match No.
1	2	3	4	5	6^1	7	8	9	10	11^2	12	13																							1
1	2	3	4^1		6	7	8	9^3	10				5^2	11	12	13	14																		2
1	2	3^1	4		6	7	8	9	10	12			5^2	11^3	13		14																		3
1	2	3	4		12	7^2	8	9	10				13	11	5^1		14	6^3																	4
1	2		3		6	7	8	9^3	10	12			5	11^2	13			4^1	14																5
1	2		3		6	7	8	9^2	10	12			5^1	11^3			13	4		14															6
1	2	12	3		6^1	7	8	13	10					14			9	4	11^2	5^3															7
1	2		3		6	7	8^1	9^2	10					12			11	4	13	5															8
1	2		3		6	7	8^1	9	10^2	12			13	5			11	4																	9
1	2^2	12	3	5	6	7		9					13	11			10^3	4			14	8^1													10
1	2		3	5	6	7	8						12				10	4^1			9	11													11
1	2		3		6	7	8						5	10			9		12		4^1	11													12
1			2		6	7	8						5	10			9		12		4^1	11	3												13
1			2		6	7	8						5	10			9				4^1	11	3	12											14
1			2		6	7	8						5				9				4	11	3	12	10^1										15
1			2		6	7	8						5			4^1	9					11	3	10	12										16
1			2		6	7	8			14							9	4			12	11^2	3	5		10^1	13^3								17
1			2		6	7	8			12							9	4			13		3	10^2		11	5^1								18
1			2	12	6^2	7	8						13				9	4			14		3	10^1		11^3	5								19
1			2	12	6	7	8			13							9	4					3	10		11^1	5^2								20
1		3	2		6	7	8			12					13		9	4						10^1			5	11^2							21
1		3^1	2		6	7	8			12			13				9	4						10^2		11	5								22
1	2^1		5	12	6	7	8										9	4					3			11	10								23
1	2		4	5	6		8			13			12			14		7^3				11^2	3	9			10^1								24
	2		4	5	6	7	8										9					11	3	12		10^1			1						25
1	2		4	5	6	7	8										9					11	3			10									26
1	2			5^3	6	7	8		12				4				9^2					11^1	3	13		10	14								27
1	2		4	5	6	7	8		9^1														3	12		11	10								28
1	2		4	5	6	7	8		9				3											12		11^1	10								29
1	2		3^1	5	6	7	8		9	12								4						11			10								30
1	2		3	5^1	6	7	8		9	12			4					11	13					10^2											31
	2^2		3	5	6	7	8		9	12			4					10				11^1		13					1						32
1			2	5	6	7	8		9	11^1								4								12				10	3				33
1			2	5	6	7	8		9									4								11				10	3				34
1			2	5	6	7	8^2		9	12								4								11^1				10	3	13			35
1			2	5	6	7			9					8				4								11				10	3				36
1			2	5	6	7			9	12				8				4								11				10^1	3				37
1			2	5	6	7			9					8				4						12		11				10^1	3				38
1			2	5^2	6	7			9					8^1				4						13		11	12			10	3				39
			2	5^1	6	7			9									4								11	8			10	3		1	12	40
1			2	5	6	7			9									4								11	8			10	3				41
	2		5		6	7			9				12	13				4^1								11	8^2			10^3	3		1	14	42
	2		4	5	6	7			9					12												11	8^1			10^2	3		1	13	43
	2		4	5	6	7			9					10												11	8				3		1		44
	2		5		6^1	7			9				12	8												11	4			10	3		1		45
	2	12	5			7			9				6	8	13	14										11^3	4^1			10^2	3		1		46

Worthington Cup

First Round	Colchester U	(a)	2-2
		(h)	3-1
Second Round	Leicester C	(h)	3-3
		(a)	2-4

FA Cup

Third Round	Cambridge U	(a)	0-2

Division 3   **DARLINGTON**

FOUNDATION

A football club was formed in Darlington as early as 1861 but the present club began in 1883 and reached the final of the Durham Senior Cup in their first season, losing to Sunderland in a replay after complaining that they had suffered from intimidation in the first. On 5 April 1884, Sunderland had defeated Darlington 4-3. Darlington's objection was upheld by the referee and the replay took place on 3 May. The new referee for the match was Major Marindin, appointed by the Football Association to ensure fair play. Sunderland won 2-0. The following season Darlington won this trophy and for many years were one of the leading amateur clubs in their area.

Feethams Ground, Darlington DL1 5JB.

Telephone: (01325) 240 240.

Fax: (01325) 240 500.

Ground Capacity: 8500.

Record Attendance: 21,023 v Bolton W, League Cup 3rd rd, 14 November 1960.

Record Receipts: £32,300 v Rochdale, Division 4, 11 May 1991.

Pitch Measurements: 110yd × 74yd.

President: A. Noble.

Chairman: George Reynolds.

Vice-Chairman: G. Hodgson.

Manager: David Hodgson.

Assistant Manager: Ian Butterworth.

Coach: Gary Bennett.

Manager's Secretary: Lisa Charlton.

LATEST SEQUENCES

Longest Sequence of League Wins: 6, 6.2.00 – 7.3.00.

Longest Sequence of League Defeats: 8, 31.8.85 – 19.10.85.

Longest Sequence of League Draws: 5, 31.12.88 – 28.1.89.

Longest Sequence of Unbeaten League Matches: 17, 27.4.68 – 19.10.68.

Longest Sequence Without a League Win: 19, 27.4.88 – 8.11.88.

HONOURS

Football League: Division 2 best season: 15th, 1925–26; Division 3 (N) – Champions 1924–25; Runners-up 1921–22; Division 4 – Champions 1990–91; Runners-up 1965–66.

FA Cup: best season: 5th rd, 1958.

Football League Cup: best season: 5th rd, 1968.

GM Vauxhall Conference: Champions 1989–90.

Colours
Black and white with red piping.

Change Colours
Red and black.

Year Formed: 1883.

Turned Professional: 1908.

Ltd Co.: 1891.

Club Nickname: 'The Quakers'.

First Football League Game: 27 August 1921, Division 3 (N), v Halifax T (h) W 2–0 – Ward; Greaves, Barbour; Dickson (1), Sutcliffe, Malcolm; Dolphin, Hooper (1), Edmunds, Wolstenholme, Winship.

Record League Victory: 9–2 v Lincoln C, Division 3 (N), 7 January 1928 – Archibald; Brooks, Mellen; Kelly, Waugh, McKinnell; Cochrane (1), Gregg (1), Ruddy (3), Lees (3), McGiffen (1).

Record Cup Victory: 7–2 v Evenwood T, FA Cup 1st rd, 17 November 1956 – Ward; Devlin, Henderson; Bell (1p), Greener, Furphy; Forster (1), Morton (3), Tulip (2), Davis, Moran.

Record Defeat: 0–10 v Doncaster R, Division 4, 25 January 1964.

Most League Points (2 for a win): 59, Division 4, 1965–66.

Most League Points (3 for a win): 85, Division 4, 1984–85.

Most League Goals: 108, Division 3 (N), 1929–30.

Highest League Scorer in Season: David Brown, 39, Division 3 (N), 1924–25.

Most League Goals in Total Aggregate: Alan Walsh, 90, 1978–84.

Most League Goals in One Match: 5, Tom Ruddy v South Shields, Division 2, 23 April 1927; 5, Maurice Wellock v Rotherham U, Division 3N, 15 February 1930.

Most Capped Player: Jason Devos, 3, Canada.

Most League Appearances: Ron Greener, 442, 1955–68.

Youngest League Player: Dale Anderson, 16 years 254 days v Chesterfield, 4 May 1987.

Record Transfer Fee Received: £400,000 from Dundee U for Jason Devos, October 1998.

Record Transfer Fee Paid: £95,000 to Motherwell for Nick Cusack, January 1992.

Football League Record: 1921 Original Member Division 3 (N); 1925–27 Division 2; 1927–58 Division 3 (N); 1958–66 Division 4; 1966–67 Division 3; 1967–85 Division 4; 1985–87 Division 3; 1987–89 Division 4; 1989–90 GM Vauxhall Conference; 1990–91 Division 4; 1991– Division 3.

MANAGERS

Tom McIntosh 1902–11
W. L. Lane 1911–12
(Secretary-Manager)
Dick Jackson 1912–19
Jack English 1919–28
Jack Fairless 1928–33
George Collins 1933–36
George Brown 1936–38
Jackie Carr 1938–42
Jack Surtees 1942
Jack English 1945–46
Bill Forrest 1946–50
George Irwin 1950–52
Bob Gurney 1952–57
Dick Duckworth 1957–60
Eddie Carr 1960–64
Lol Morgan 1964–66
Jimmy Greenhalgh 1966–68
Ray Yeoman 1968–70
Len Richley 1970–71
Frank Brennan 1971
Ken Hale 1971–72
Allan Jones 1972
Ralph Brand 1972–73
Dick Conner 1973–74
Billy Horner 1974–76
Peter Madden 1976–78
Len Walker 1978–79
Billy Elliott 1979–83
Cyril Knowles 1983–87
Dave Booth 1987–89
Brian Little 1989–91
Frank Gray 1991–92
Ray Hankin 1992
Billy McEwan 1992–93
Alan Murray 1993–95
Paul Futcher 1995
David Hodgson/Jim Platt
(Director of Coaching) 1995
Jim Platt 1995–96
David Hodgson November 1996–

TEN YEAR LEAGUE RECORD

		P	W	D	L	F	A	Pts	Pos
1989-90	Conf	42	26	9	7	76	25	87	1
1990-91	Div 4	46	22	17	7	68	38	83	1
1991-92	Div 3	46	10	7	29	56	90	37	24
1992-93	Div 3	42	12	14	16	48	53	50	15
1993-94	Div 3	42	10	11	21	42	64	41	21
1994-95	Div 3	42	11	8	23	43	57	41	20
1995-96	Div 3	46	20	18	8	60	42	78	5
1996-97	Div 3	46	14	10	22	64	78	52	18
1997-98	Div 3	46	14	12	20	56	72	54	19
1998-99	Div 3	46	18	11	17	69	58	65	11

DID YOU KNOW ?

Darlington transferred centre-half Bob Thyne to Kilmarnock in October 1946 for £3250. He had played twice for Scotland shortly after being injured in the D-Day landings. After ten years with Kilmarnock, he became their chairman.

DARLINGTON 1999–2000 LEAGUE RECORD

Match No.	Date	Venue	Opponents	Result	H/T Score	Lg. Pos.	Goalscorers	Attendance
1	Aug 7	A	Halifax T	W 1-0	0-0	9	Gabbiadini [62]	3721
2	14	H	Macclesfield T	W 3-0	0-0	2	Gabbiadini 2 [82, 83], Duffield [90]	5117
3	21	A	Shrewsbury T	W 1-0	1-0	2	Heaney [25]	2181
4	28	H	Brighton & HA	D 1-1	1-1	2	Campbell (og) [19]	6174
5	30	A	Peterborough U	L 2-4	0-3	6	Gabbiadini 2 (1 pen) [48 (pl), 52]	6044
6	Sept 4	H	Exeter C	W 1-0	0-0	3	Russell [90]	5860
7	11	A	Rochdale	D 0-0	0-0	3		3253
8	18	H	Mansfield T	D 0-0	0-0	6		5027
9	25	H	Plymouth Arg	W 2-0	1-0	3	Nogan [23], Campbell [78]	5045
10	Oct 2	A	Hartlepool U	L 0-2	0-0	4		3957
11	9	A	Lincoln C	L 0-1	0-1	7		3747
12	16	H	Cheltenham T	W 1-0	1-0	6	Campbell [12]	4802
13	19	H	Carlisle U	W 3-1	1-0	—	Russell [45], Gabbiadini 2 [46, 50]	5016
14	23	A	Plymouth Arg	D 0-0	0-0	5		4362
15	Nov 2	H	Leyton Orient	W 3-1	2-0	—	Gabbiadini 2 [14, 69], Heaney [25]	4532
16	6	A	Barnet	L 0-1	0-0	5		2161
17	12	H	Torquay U	D 1-1	1-0	5	Gabbiadini [6]	5434
18	23	A	Swansea C	D 0-0	0-0	—		3748
19	27	A	Southend U	W 2-1	2-0	4	Gabbiadini [10], Heaney [35]	4134
20	Dec 4	H	Halifax T	W 4-0	3-0	3	Gabbiadini 2 (2 pens) [26, 37], Heaney [43], Duffield [46]	4581
21	15	H	Chester C	W 3-1	2-0	—	Duffield 2 [34, 36], Hyorth [88]	3553
22	18	A	Rotherham U	L 1-2	0-0	3	Berry (og) [58]	4234
23	26	H	Hull C	D 0-0	0-0	4		7058
24	28	A	Northampton T	W 3-0	2-0	4	Gabbiadini 2 [18, 53], Hyorth [38]	6823
25	Jan 8	A	Chester C	W 2-1	1-1	4	Liddle [8], Gabbiadini [63]	2067
26	15	A	Macclesfield T	L 1-2	1-2	4	Hyorth [12]	2399
27	18	H	York C	D 2-2	2-1	—	Gabbiadini 2 [26, 36]	5704
28	29	A	Brighton & HA	D 1-1	0-0	4	Duffield [66]	5715
29	Feb 6	H	Peterborough U	W 2-0	1-0	4	Gabbiadini [16], Wainwright [81]	4688
30	12	A	Exeter C	W 4-1	2-0	4	Heaney [14], Gabbiadini [29], Duffield [77], Wainwright [89]	3302
31	19	H	Southend U	W 1-0	0-0	3	Oliver [90]	4391
32	26	A	Mansfield T	W 2-1	1-0	3	Gabbiadini [11], Hyorth [78]	3114
33	Mar 4	H	Rochdale	W 4-1	3-1	3	Duffield 2 [2, 72], Wainwright [20], Gabbiadini [45]	5333
34	7	H	Barnet	W 4-0	2-0	—	Oliver [38], Duffield 2 [40, 59], Wainwright [68]	5937
35	11	A	Leyton Orient	L 1-2	0-0	3	Gabbiadini [46]	4053
36	18	H	Swansea C	D 1-1	1-0	3	Duffield [28]	6632
37	21	A	Torquay U	L 0-1	0-1	—		1938
38	25	A	Hull C	W 1-0	1-0	3	Nogan [45]	5617
39	Apr 1	H	Rotherham U	D 2-2	2-0	3	Gabbiadini [5], Naylor [43]	7401
40	5	H	Shrewsbury T	D 2-2	0-1	—	Hyorth [86], Naylor [90]	5031
41	8	A	York C	D 0-0	0-0	3		5308
42	15	H	Northampton T	L 0-1	0-1	3		5833
43	22	H	Cheltenham T	D 0-0	0-0	3		5059
44	24	A	Hartlepool U	D 1-1	0-1	4	Heckingbottom [59]	6746
45	29	A	Carlisle U	D 1-1	0-1	4	Naylor [80]	6525
46	May 6	H	Lincoln C	W 2-0	1-0	4	Hyorth [38], Duffield [77]	7145

Final League Position: 4

GOALSCORERS

League (66): Gabbiadini 24 (3 pens), Duffield 12, Hyorth 6, Heaney 5, Wainwright 4, Naylor 3, Campbell 2, Nogan 2, Oliver 2, Russell 2, Heckingbottom 1, Liddle 1, own goals 2.
Worthington Cup (4): Nogan 2, Gabbiadini 1, Oliver 1.
FA Cup (4): Duffield 1, Gabbiadini 1 (pen), Heckingbottom 1, Tutill 1.

Collett A 13	Liddle C 45	Heckingbottom P 44+1	Reed A 20+3	Bennett G 4+1	Aspin N 29	Gray M 40+1	Oliver M 35+2	Nogan L 19+12	Gabbiadini M 41+1	Atkinson B 26+4	Carruthers M —+6	Himsworth G 13+6	Heaney N 33+3	Duffield P 21+12	Campbell P 3+6	Russell C 11+1	Samways M 33+1	Brumwell P 9+9	Tutill S 25+2	Naylor G 8+17	Hyorth J 8+14	Taylor M 4	Kilty M 1+1	Wainwright N 16+1	Baker S 4+1	Holsgrove P 1+2	Match No
1	2	3	4	5	6	7	8	9¹	10	11²	12	13															1
1	2	3	4¹	5	6	7	8²	9³	10	11	12		13	14													2
1	2	3	4	5		7	12	9²	10	11	13	6	8¹														3
1	2	3	4²	5		7	9	10	11¹	12	6	8³	13	14													4
1	2	3	4³	5	6	7¹	9²	10	11	12	8		13	14													5
1	2	3	4	5²		7	8	9¹	10	11	12	6		13													6
1³	2	3	5	4²	8	9¹	10	11	6	12	7					15	13										7
	2	3	5	4	8	9¹	10	11	6²	12	7					1	13										8
	2	3	5	7	4¹	9	10²	11	12	13	8					1	6										9
	2	3	5	4	8²	9	10	11³	13	12	7					1	6¹	14									10
	2	3	5	4²	8	9³	11	6¹	7	12	10					1	13	14									11
	2	3	4³		8	9¹	12	11	13	10	6²				7	1	14	5									12
1	2	3			8	12	10	11	13	9	6²				7¹		4	5									13
1	2	3			8	9²	11	12	10	4¹	7				6		5	13									14
	2	3			8		10	11	6	7	9				1		4	5									15
	2	3	12	8	13	10	11²	6	7³	9					1	4¹	5	14									16
	2	3	4	8³	12	10¹	11	6	7	13	9²				1		5	14									17
2²	3	12	4	7	8	10	13	6	11¹	9³					1		5	14									18
	2	3	4	7	12	13	10	11	6¹	8²	9³				1		5	14									19
	2	3	12	6	4	8	10	11	7	9²					1		5¹	13									20
	2	3	5	4	8	10	11	7	9						1	6¹		12									21
	2	3	6	4	8	10	11	7	9¹						1	5		12									22
	2	3	6	4	8	10	11	7	9¹						1	5		12									23
	2	3	6	4	8	12	10²	11	7³	13					1	5		14	9¹								24
	2	3	12	6¹	4	8	10	11	7	13					1	5³		14	9²								25
	2	3	4	12		8³	10	11	6¹	7	13				1	5		14	9²								26
	2	3	4		6	8	10	11	7						1		12	9¹	5								27
	2	3	4		8		10	12	7	13					1	6¹		9²	5	11							28
	2	3	4		6	8	10		7	9¹					1		12	5	11								29
	2	3	4		6	8¹	10	7²	9						1		12	13	5	11							30
	2	3	4	5	6	8	10²	7	9						1		12	13		11¹							31
	2	3	4	5	6	8	12	10¹	7	9²					1			13		11							32
	2	3	4	5	6	8	10²	7	9						1		12	13		11¹							33
	2	3	4	5²	6	8	12	10	7	9					1		13			11¹							34
	2	3¹	4		6	8	10	12	7	9³					1	13	5		14	11²							35
	2	3	4¹		6	8²	12	10	7³	9					1	13	5		14	11							36
	2		4		6	8³	12	10	7²	9					1	13	5		11¹	14	3						37
	2	3			6	8	10		7¹	9²					1		5	12	13	11	4						38
	2	3			6	8²	12	10	9³						1	13	5	7	14	11¹	4						39
		3	2¹	4	6²	8	14	10	9						1	5	7	12	11		13³						40
	2	3	4	6¹	8²	10	12	13	9						1	5	7³	14	11								41
	2	3	4²	6		10	12	7³	9						1	5	13	14	11	8¹							42
1	2	3	4		7	9	10								5	8	11¹		12	6							43
1	2	3	6	7	9¹	10		12							5	8	13	11	4²								44
1	2	12	5	6²		13	10²	7	9						3	4	8¹	11		14							45
1	2	3	4³	6		9²	10	12	7	13					5	11	8¹		14								46

Worthington Cup

First Round	Bolton W	(h)	1-1
		(a)	3-5

FA Cup

First Round	Southport	(h)	2-1
Second Round	Gillingham	(a)	1-3
Third Round	Aston Villa	(a)	1-2

FA Premiership

DERBY COUNTY

FOUNDATION

Derby County was formed by members of the Derbyshire County Cricket Club in 1884, when football was booming in the area and the cricketers thought that a football club would help boost finances for the summer game. To begin with, they sported the cricket club's colours of amber, chocolate and pale blue, and went into the game at the top immediately entering the FA Cup.

Pride Park Stadium, Derby DE24 8XL.

Telephone: (01332) 202 202.

Fax: (01332) 667 519.

ClubCall: 09068 121 187.

Ground Capacity: 33,597.

Record Attendance: 41,826 v Tottenham H, Division 1, 20 September 1969.

Record Receipts: £425,804 v Huddersfield T, FA Cup 5th rd replay, 24 February 1999.

Pitch Measurements: 115yd × 75yd.

Chairman: L. V. Pickering.

Vice-Chairman: P. J. Gadsby.

Directors: J. N. Kirkland OBE, A. S. Webb, R. Clarke.

Manager: Jim Smith.

Assistant Manager: Billy McEwan.

Chief Scout: Bobby Roberts.

First Team Coach: Steve Round.

Physio: Peter Melville.

Stadium Manager: David Goodwin.

Chief Executive: Keith Loring.

Secretary: Keith Pearson ACIS.

Sales and Marketing Manager: Gary Hodder.

HONOURS

Football League: Division 1 – Champions 1971–72, 1974–75; Runners-up 1895–96, 1929–30, 1935–36, 1995–96; Division 2 – Champions 1911–12, 1914–15, 1968–69, 1986–87; Runners-up 1925–26; Division 3 (N) Champions 1956–57; Runners-up 1955–56.

FA Cup: Winners 1946; Runners-up 1898, 1899, 1903.

Football League Cup: Semi-final 1968.

Texaco Cup: Winners 1972.

European Competitions: European Cup: 1972–73, 1975–76. UEFA Cup: 1974–75, 1976–77. Anglo-Italian Cup: Runners-up 1993.

LATEST SEQUENCES

Longest Sequence of League Wins: 9, 15.3.69 – 19.4.69.

Longest Sequence of League Defeats: 8, 12.12.87 – 10.2.88.

Longest Sequence of League Draws: 6, 26.3.27 – 18.4.27.

Longest Sequence of Unbeaten League Matches: 22, 8.3.69 – 20.9.69.

Longest Sequence Without a League Win: 20, 15.12.90 – 23.4.91.

Colours

White shirts with black trim, black shorts with white stripes, white stockings.

Change Colours

Navy blue shirts, navy blue shorts with white trim, navy blue stockings.

Year Formed: 1884.

Turned Professional: 1884.

Ltd Co.: 1896.

Club Nickname: 'The Rams'.

Previous Grounds: 1884, Racecourse Ground; 1895, Baseball Ground; 1997, Pride Park.

First Football League Game: 8 September 1888, Football League, v Bolton W (a) W 6–3 – Marshall; Latham, Ferguson, Williamson; Monks, W. Roulstone; Bakewell (2), Cooper (2), Higgins, H. Plackett, L. Plackett (2).

Record League Victory: 9–0 v Wolverhampton W, Division 1, 10 January 1891 – Bunyan; Archie Goodall, Roberts; Walker, Chalmers, Roulston (1); Bakewell, McLachlan, Johnny Goodall (1), Holmes (2), McMillan (5). 9–0 v Sheffield W, Division 1, 21 January 1899 – Fryer; Methven, Staley; Cox, Archie Goodall, May; Oakden (1), Bloomer (6), Boag, McDonald (1), Allen, (1 og).

Record Cup Victory: 12–0 v Finn Harps, UEFA Cup 1st rd 1st leg, 15 September 1976 – Moseley; Thomas, Nish, Rioch (1), McFarland, Todd (King), Macken, Gemmill, Hector (5), George (3), James (3).

Record Defeat: 2–11 v Everton, FA Cup 1st rd, 1889–90.

MANAGERS
Harry Newbould 1896–1906
Jimmy Methven 1906–22
Cecil Potter 1922–25
George Jobey 1925–41
Ted Magner 1944–46
Stuart McMillan 1946–53
Jack Barker 1953–55
Harry Storer 1955–62
Tim Ward 1962–67
Brian Clough 1967–73
Dave Mackay 1973–76
Colin Murphy 1977
Tommy Docherty 1977–79
Colin Addison 1979–82
Johnny Newman 1982
Peter Taylor 1982–84
Roy McFarland 1984
Arthur Cox 1984–93
Roy McFarland 1993–95
Jim Smith June 1995–

Most League Points (2 for a win): 63, Division 2, 1968–69 and Division 3 (N), 1955–56 and 1956–57.

Most League Points (3 for a win): 84, Division 3, 1985–86 and Division 3, 1986–87.

Most League Goals: 111, Division 3 (N), 1956–57.

Highest League Scorer in Season: Jack Bowers, 37, Division 1, 1930–31; Ray Straw, 37 Division 3 (N), 1956–57.

Most League Goals in Total Aggregate: Steve Bloomer, 292, 1892–1906 and 1910–14.

Most League Goals in One Match: 6, Steve Bloomer v Sheffield W, Division 1, 2 January 1899.

Most Capped Player: Peter Shilton, 34 (125), England.

Most League Appearances: Kevin Hector, 486, 1966–78 and 1980–82.

Youngest League Player: Steve Powell, 16 years 33 days v Arsenal, 23 October 1971.

Record Transfer Fee Received: £5,300,000 from Blackburn R for Christian Dailly, August 1998.

Record Transfer Fee Paid: £3,000,000 rising to £4,000,000 for Lee Morris from Sheffield U, October 1999.

Football League Record: 1888 Founder Member of the Football League; 1907–12 Division 2; 1912–14 Division 1; 1914–15 Division 2; 1915–21 Division 2; 1921–26 Division 2; 1926–53 Division 1; 1953–55 Division 2; 1955–57 Division 3 (N); 1957–69 Division 2; 1969–80 Division 1; 1980–84 Division 2; 1984–86 Division 3; 1986–87 Division 2; 1987–91 Division 1; 1991–92 Division 2; 1992–96 Division 1; 1996– FA Premier League.

TEN YEAR LEAGUE RECORD

		P	W	D	L	F	A	Pts	Pos
1989-90	Div 1	38	13	7	28	43	40	46	16
1990-91	Div 1	38	5	9	24	37	75	24	20
1991-92	Div 2	46	23	9	14	69	51	78	3
1992-93	Div 1	46	19	9	18	68	57	66	8
1993-94	Div 1	46	20	11	15	73	68	71	6
1994-95	Div 1	46	18	12	16	66	51	66	9
1995-96	Div 1	46	21	16	9	71	51	79	2
1996-97	PR Lge	38	11	13	14	45	58	46	12
1997-98	PR Lge	38	16	7	15	52	49	55	9
1998-99	PR Lge	38	13	13	12	40	45	52	8

DID YOU KNOW ?

When Derby County supporters travelled for a sixth round FA Cup replay in 1933, four train loads were turned back eight miles before they reached Sunderland; the ground was already full with 75,120 inside. Derby won 1-0.

DERBY COUNTY 1999–2000 LEAGUE RECORD

Match No.	Date	Venue	Opponents	Result	H/T Score	Lg. Pos.	Goalscorers	Attendance
1	Aug 7	A	Leeds U	D	0-0	0-0	11		40,118
2	10	H	Arsenal	L	1-2	1-1	—	Delap [45]	25,901
3	14	H	Middlesbrough	L	1-3	1-2	17	Burton [41]	24,045
4	21	A	Coventry C	L	0-2	0-1	19		17,658
5	25	A	Sheffield W	W	2-0	0-0	—	Delap [54], Sturridge [79]	20,943
6	28	H	Everton	W	1-0	0-0	14	Fuertes [47]	26,550
7	Sept 11	A	Wimbledon	D	2-2	1-0	14	Carbonari [14], Johnson [81]	12,282
8	18	H	Sunderland	L	0-5	0-2	15		28,264
9	25	H	Bradford C	L	0-1	0-0	18		31,035
10	Oct 4	A	Southampton	D	3-3	1-2	—	Delap [21], Laursen [75], Beck [90]	14,208
11	16	H	Tottenham H	L	0-1	0-1	17		29,815
12	25	A	Newcastle U	L	0-2	0-1	—		35,614
13	30	H	Chelsea	W	3-1	1-1	16	Burton [7], Delap 2 [80, 88]	28,614
14	Nov 6	A	Liverpool	L	0-2	0-0	18		44,467
15	20	H	Manchester U	L	1-2	0-0	18	Delap [90]	33,370
16	28	A	Arsenal	L	1-2	1-1	18	Sturridge [2]	37,964
17	Dec 5	H	Leeds U	L	0-1	0-0	18		29,455
18	18	A	Leicester C	W	1-0	0-0	18	Powell [89]	18,581
19	26	H	Aston Villa	L	0-2	0-0	18		33,222
20	28	A	West Ham U	D	1-1	1-1	18	Sturridge [4]	24,998
21	Jan 3	H	Watford	W	2-0	1-0	17	Strupar 2 [2, 72]	28,072
22	15	A	Middlesbrough	W	4-1	1-0	16	Christie 2 [8, 59], Burton [47], Burley [90]	32,269
23	22	H	Coventry C	D	0-0	0-0	16		28,381
24	Feb 5	H	Sheffield W	D	3-3	0-1	17	Strupar [71], Burley [89], Srnicek (og) [90]	30,100
25	12	A	Everton	L	1-2	0-2	17	Nimni [59]	33,260
26	26	A	Sunderland	D	1-1	0-0	17	Christie [60]	41,619
27	Mar 4	H	Wimbledon	W	4-0	0-0	17	Kinkladze [65], Christie [71], Burton [89], Sturridge [90]	28,384
28	11	A	Manchester U	L	1-3	0-1	17	Strupar [66]	61,619
29	18	H	Liverpool	L	0-2	0-1	17		33,378
30	25	A	Aston Villa	L	0-2	0-1	17		28,613
31	Apr 2	H	Leicester C	W	3-0	3-0	17	Burley [15], Delap [44], Sturridge [45]	25,763
32	8	A	Watford	D	0-0	0-0	16		16,579
33	15	H	West Ham U	L	1-2	0-2	16	Sturridge [84]	31,202
34	21	A	Bradford C	D	4-4	3-4	—	Delap [1], Strupar [6], Burley 2 (2 pens) [36, 52]	18,276
35	24	H	Southampton	W	2-0	2-0	16	Powell [5], Christie [42]	29,403
36	29	A	Tottenham H	D	1-1	0-0	16	Carbonari [63]	33,061
37	May 6	H	Newcastle U	D	0-0	0-0	16		32,724
38	14	A	Chelsea	L	0-4	0-0	16		35,084

Final League Position: 16

GOALSCORERS

League (44): Delap 8, Sturridge 6, Burley 5 (2 pens), Christie 5, Strupar 5, Burton 4, Carbonari 2, Powell 2, Beck 1, Fuertes 1, Johnson 1, Kinkladze 1, Laursen 1, Nimni 1, own goal 1.
Worthington Cup (4): Beck 1, Borbokis 1, Fuertes 1, Sturridge 1.
FA Cup (0).

Poom M 28	Delap R 34	Dorigo T 20+3	Laursen J 36	Carbonari H 29	Prior S 15+5	Eranio G 17+2	Sturridge D 14+11	Baiano F 5+4	Johnson S 36	Powell D 31	Borbokis V 6+6	Burton D 15+4	Beck M 5+6	Schnoor S 22+7	Harper K —+5	Bohinen L 8+5	Hoult R 10	Fuertes E 8	Elliott S 18+2	Christie M 10+11	Murray A 1+7	Morris L 2+1	Robinson M 3+5	Nimni A 2+2	Kinkladze G 12+5	Burley C 18	Strupar B 13+2	Boertien P —+2	Jackson R —+2	Riggott C —+1	Match No
1	2	3	4	5	6	7^1	8^2	9^3	10	11	12	13	14																		1
1	2		4	5^1	6	7		9	10	11	13	12	8^3	3^2	14																2
1	2		4	5	6	7^3		9^1	3	11	12	10	8^2	13		14															3
1	3		4	5	6	7^3	8^2		10	11	2	9^1	12			13	14														4
	9		4	5	6	12	13		10	11	2^2	14	3			7^1	1	8^2													5
	9		4	5	6	12	13	14	10^3	11	2					3			7^1	1	8^2										6
2^1			4	5	6	7		13	10	11		8^2	14	3^3		12	1	9													7
2			4	5	6	7^3		12	10	11		9^1	3^2	13	14	1	8														8
7	3		5	6		8^2	9^3	10		2^1		12				1	11	4	13	14											9
7	3	4^3	5^2	6		8		10	11	14		12	2	13		1		9^1													10
7	3	4			2	12	13	10		6^1	8^2	9	5		1						14	11^3									11
7	3^1	4		12	2		9^2	10	11		13	8	5		1						14		6^2								12
2	3	4^1	5	12	7^2			10	11	13	8		6		1	9^3					14										13
2	3	4	5	12	7^3	13		10^1	11	14	8		6		1	9^2															14
1	7	3	4	5		8^1		10	11	2^2			6						13	12		9									15
1	2	3	4	5^1	6		8	10	11	9^2									12			13	7^1	14							16
1	2	13	4^1	5	12		8	3	11	9^3									6	14			10^2	7							17
1	7	3	4		6^1		10	11	8	12			5							9^2			2	13							18
1		3^1	4		6		10	11	8^3	12	7^2		5	13					14			2	9								19
1		4	5	6		8	3	11	12		7	10							9^1			2									20
1	7	3^2	4	5	12		8^3	11		13			6				14	10^1			2	9									21
1	2		5			3	11	8	6	10^2			4	9^1				13	12	7											22
1	2		4	5		3		8^2	10	11	6^1	13						12	7	9											23
1	2	3^1	4		7^2	12	10		5	6	11							13	8	9											24
1		3^3	4		6	2	8^2	11		5	12		13	14	10	7	9^1														25
1	2		4	5		7	12	3	11	13	6	14			10^1	8^2	9^3														26
1	2		4	5		7	12	3	11	13	14	8^3	6	9^1				10^2													27
1	2	3^1	4	5		7	12	11		8^2	6	9			10	13															28
1	2		4	5^1		7	13	3	11^2	12	6	8			10	9															29
1	2		4	5		7^1	12	8	11	3	6^2	13			10	9															30
1	2	12	4	5		8	3	11	6^2	13	14			10^1	7^3	9															31
1	2	12	4	5		8^2	3	11	6	13			10^1	7	9																32
1	2	3^1	4		8	10	11	5^2	6	13	12	7	9																		33
1	2	3	4	5		10	11	6	8	12	7	9^1																			34
1	2	6^2	4		3	11	5	8	12	10^1	7	9	13																		35
1	2		4	5		3	11	8^1	6	9	13	10^1	7	12^2																	36
1		3	2^1	5	12		11	8	6	13	9	4^2	10^1	7		14															37
1	2^1	6	4		10	3		8		11^2	5^3	9	12	7			13	14													38

Worthington Cup

Second Round	Swansea C	(a)	0-0
		(h)	3-1
Third Round	Bolton W	(h)	1-2

FA Cup

Third Round	Burnley	(h)	0-1

FA Premiership

EVERTON

FOUNDATION

St Domingo Church Sunday School formed a football club in 1878 which played at Stanley Park. Enthusiasm was so great that in November 1879 they decided to expand membership and changed the name to Everton playing in black shirts with a scarlet sash and nicknamed the 'Black Watch'. After wearing several other colours, royal blue was adopted in 1901.

Goodison Park, Liverpool L4 4EL.
Telephone: (0151) 330 2200.
Fax: (0151) 286 9112.
Ticket Infoline: 09068 121 599.
ClubCall: 09068 121 199.
Dial-A-Seat Service: (0151) 471 8000.
Ground Capacity: 40,260.
Record Attendance: 78,299 v Liverpool, Division 1, 18 September 1948.
Record Receipts: £693,000 v Preston NE, FA Cup 5th rd, 29 January 2000.
Pitch Measurements: 110yd × 71yd.
Chairman: Sir Philip Carter.
Vice-Chairman: Bill Kenwright.
Directors: Keith Tamlin, Arthur Abercromby, Lord Grantchester, Paul Gregg, Jon Woods.
Manager: Walter Smith OBE.
Assistant Manager: Archie Knox.
First Team Coach: Dave Watson.
Physio: Steve Hardwick.
Chief Executive: Michael J. Dunford.
Business Development Manager: Mal Brannigan.
Stadium Manager: A. Bowen.
Communications Manager: Alan Myers.

LATEST SEQUENCES

Longest Sequence of League Wins: 12, 24.3.1894 – 13.10.1894.
Longest Sequence of League Defeats: 6, 26.12.96 – 29.1.97.
Longest Sequence of League Draws: 5, 4.5.77 – 16.5.77.
Longest Sequence of Unbeaten League Matches: 20, 29.4.78 – 16.12.78.
Longest Sequence Without a League Win: 14, 6.3.37 – 4.9.37.

HONOURS

Football League: Division 1 – Champions 1890–91, 1914–15, 1927–28, 1931–32, 1938–39, 1962–63, 1969–70, 1984–85, 1986–87; Runners-up 1889–90, 1894–95, 1901–02, 1904–05, 1908–09, 1911–12, 1985–86; Division 2 – Champions 1930–31; Runners-up 1953–54.
FA Cup: Winners 1906, 1933, 1966, 1984, 1995; Runners-up 1893, 1897, 1907, 1968, 1985, 1986, 1989.
Football League Cup: Runners-up 1977, 1984.
League Super Cup: Runners-up 1986.
Simod Cup: Runners-up 1989.
Zenith Data Systems Cup: Runners-up 1991.
European Competitions: *European Cup:* 1963–64, 1970–71. *European Cup-Winners' Cup:* 1966–67, 1984–85 (winners), 1995–96. *European Fairs Cup:* 1962–63, 1964–65, 1965–66. *UEFA Cup:* 1975–76, 1978–79, 1979–80.

Colours
Royal blue shirts with white panels, white shorts with blue trim, blue stockings with white trim.

Change Colours
Amber shirts, dark royal blue shorts, amber stockings with royal trim.

Year Formed: 1878.

Turned Professional: 1885.

Ltd Co.: 1892.

Previous Name: 1878, St Domingo FC; 1879, Everton.

Club Nickname: 'The Toffees'.

Previous Grounds: 1878, Stanley Park; 1882, Priory Road; 1884, Anfield Road; 1892, Goodison Park.

First Football League Game: 8 September 1888, Football League, v Accrington (h) W 2–1 – Smalley; Dick, Ross; Holt, Jones, Dobson; Fleming (2), Waugh, Lewis, E. Chadwick, Farmer.

Record League Victory: 9–1 v Manchester C, Division 1, 3 September 1906 – Scott; Balmer, Crelley; Booth, Taylor (1), Abbott (1); Sharp, Bolton (1), Young (4), Settle (2), George Wilson. 9–1 v Plymouth Arg, Division 2, 27 December 1930 – Coggins; Williams, Cresswell; McPherson, Griffiths, Thomson; Critchley, Dunn, Dean (4), Johnson (1), Stein (4).

Record Cup Victory: 11–2 v Derby Co, FA Cup 1st rd, 18 January 1890 – Smalley; Hannah, Doyle (1); Kirkwood, Holt (1), Parry; Latta, Brady (3), Geary (3), Chadwick, Millward (3).

Record Defeat: 4–10 v Tottenham H, Division 1, 11 October 1958.

Most League Points (2 for a win): 66, Division 1, 1969–70.

Most League Points (3 for a win): 90, Division 1, 1984–85.

Most League Goals: 121, Division 2, 1930–31.

Highest League Scorer in Season: William Ralph 'Dixie' Dean, 60, Division 1, 1927–28 (All-time League record).

Most League Goals in Total Aggregate: William Ralph 'Dixie' Dean, 349, 1925–37.

Most League Goals in One Match: 6, Jack Southworth v WBA, Division 1, 30 December 1893.

Most Capped Player: Neville Southall, 92, Wales.

Most League Appearances: Neville Southall, 578, 1981–98.

Youngest League Player: Joe Royle, 16 years 282 days v Blackpool, 15 January 1966.

Record Transfer Fee Received: £8,000,000 from Fiorentina for Andrei Kanchelskis, February 1997.

Record Transfer Fee Paid: £5,750,000 to Middlesbrough for Nick Barmby, October 1996.

Football League Record: 1888 Founder Member of the Football League; 1930–31 Division 2; 1931–51 Division 1; 1951–54 Division 2; 1954–92 Division 1; 1992– FA Premier League.

MANAGERS

W. E. Barclay 1888–89
(Secretary-Manager)
Dick Molyneux 1889–1901
(Secretary-Manager)
William C. Cuff 1901–18
(Secretary-Manager)
W. J. Sawyer 1918–19
(Secretary-Manager)
Thomas H. McIntosh 1919–35
(Secretary-Manager)
Theo Kelly 1936–48
Cliff Britton 1948–56
Ian Buchan 1956–58
Johnny Carey 1958–61
Harry Catterick 1961–73
Billy Bingham 1973–77
Gordon Lee 1977–81
Howard Kendall 1981–87
Colin Harvey 1987–90
Howard Kendall 1990–93
Mike Walker 1994
Joe Royle 1994–97
Howard Kendall 1997–98
Walter Smith July 1998–

TEN YEAR LEAGUE RECORD

		P	W	D	L	F	A	Pts	Pos
1989-90	Div 1	38	17	8	13	57	46	59	6
1990-91	Div 1	38	13	12	13	50	46	51	9
1991-92	Div 1	42	13	14	15	52	51	53	12
1992-93	PR Lge	42	15	8	19	53	55	53	13
1993-94	PR Lge	42	12	8	22	42	63	44	17
1994-95	PR Lge	42	11	17	14	44	51	50	15
1995-96	PR Lge	38	17	10	11	64	44	61	6
1996-97	PR Lge	38	10	12	16	44	57	42	15
1997-98	PR Lge	38	9	13	16	41	56	40	17
1998-99	PR Lge	38	11	10	17	42	47	43	14

DID YOU KNOW ?

When Everton won the Charity Shield on 12 October 1932 at St James' Park by beating Newcastle United 5-3, Dixie Dean scored four, Tommy Johnson their other goal.

EVERTON 1999–2000 LEAGUE RECORD

Match No.	Date	Venue	Opponents	Result	H/T Score	Lg. Pos.	Goalscorers	Atten- dance
1	Aug 8	H	Manchester U	D	1-1	0-1	9	Stam (og) [86]	39,141
2	11	A	Aston Villa	L	0-3	0-1	—		30,337
3	14	A	Tottenham H	L	2-3	1-1	18	Unsworth 2 (2 pens) [24, 77]	34,308
4	21	H	Southampton	W	4-1	1-0	14	Gough [36], Lundekvam (og) [47], Jeffers [48], Campbell [54]	31,755
5	25	H	Wimbledon	W	4-0	1-0	—	Unsworth [16], Barmby [46], Jeffers [50], Campbell [68]	32,818
6	28	A	Derby Co	L	0-1	0-0	12		26,550
7	Sept 11	A	Sheffield W	W	2-0	2-0	9	Barmby [14], Gemmill [18]	23,539
8	19	H	West Ham U	W	1-0	0-0	7	Jeffers [64]	35,154
9	27	A	Liverpool	W	1-0	1-0	—	Campbell [4]	44,802
10	Oct 2	H	Coventry C	D	1-1	1-1	6	Jeffers [2]	34,839
11	16	A	Arsenal	L	1-4	1-1	7	Collins [16]	38,042
12	24	H	Leeds U	D	4-4	3-2	8	Campbell 2 [4, 28], Hutchison [37], Weir [90]	37,355
13	30	A	Middlesbrough	L	1-2	1-1	9	Campbell [3]	33,916
14	Nov 7	A	Newcastle U	D	1-1	0-0	10	Campbell [62]	36,164
15	20	H	Chelsea	D	1-1	1-0	11	Campbell [15]	38,225
16	27	H	Aston Villa	D	0-0	0-0	11		34,750
17	Dec 4	A	Manchester U	L	1-5	1-3	12	Jeffers [7]	55,193
18	18	A	Watford	W	3-1	2-0	11	Barmby [4], Hutchison [37], Unsworth (pen) [86]	17,346
19	26	H	Sunderland	W	5-0	3-0	8	Hutchison 2 [16, 26], Jeffers [41], Pembridge [61], Campbell [72]	40,017
20	28	A	Bradford C	D	0-0	0-0	8		18,276
21	Jan 3	H	Leicester C	D	2-2	1-2	9	Hutchison [16], Unsworth (pen) [56]	30,490
22	15	H	Tottenham H	D	2-2	1-2	9	Campbell [22], Moore [90]	36,144
23	22	A	Southampton	L	0-2	0-0	11		15,232
24	Feb 6	A	Wimbledon	W	3-0	0-0	10	Campbell 2 [53, 61], Moore [63]	13,172
25	12	H	Derby Co	W	2-1	2-0	7	Moore [24], Ball (pen) [45]	33,260
26	26	A	West Ham U	W	4-0	1-0	7	Barmby 3 [8, 64, 67], Moore [71]	26,025
27	Mar 4	H	Sheffield W	D	1-1	1-0	6	Weir [33]	32,020
28	11	A	Chelsea	D	1-1	0-1	8	Cadamarteri [69]	35,113
29	15	A	Coventry C	L	0-1	0-0	—		18,513
30	19	H	Newcastle U	L	0-2	0-0	10		32,512
31	25	A	Sunderland	L	1-2	1-1	10	Barmby [38]	41,155
32	Apr 1	H	Watford	W	4-2	3-1	9	Hughes M [18], Moore 2 [30, 36], Hughes S [86]	31,960
33	8	A	Leicester C	D	1-1	1-1	8	Hutchison [27]	18,705
34	15	H	Bradford C	W	4-0	2-0	9	Pembridge [2], Unsworth (pen) [15], Barmby [54], Collins [82]	31,646
35	21	H	Liverpool	D	0-0	0-0	—		40,052
36	29	H	Arsenal	L	0-1	0-1	10		35,919
37	May 8	A	Leeds U	D	1-1	0-1	—	Barmby [60]	37,713
38	14	H	Middlesbrough	L	0-2	0-1	13		34,663

Final League Position: 13

GOALSCORERS

League (59): Campbell 12, Barmby 9, Hutchison 6, Jeffers 6, Moore 6, Unsworth 6 (5 pens), Collins 2, Pembridge 2, Weir 2, Ball 1 (pen), Cadamarteri 1, Gemmill 1, Gough 1, Hughes M 1, Hughes S 1, own goals 2.
Worthington Cup (1): Cadamarteri 1.
FA Cup (6): Unsworth 3 (2 pens), Moore 2, Barmby 1.

Gerrard P 34	Weir D 35	Unsworth D 32+1	Ward M 6+4	Watson D 5+1	Gough R 29	Collins J 33+2	Barmby N 37	Campbell K 26	Hutchison D 28+3	Gemmill S 6+8	Cadamarteri D 3+14	Phelan T —+1	Ball M 14+11	Jeffers F 16+5	Pembridge M 29+2	Dunne R 27+4	Cleland A 3+6	Xavier A 18+2	Johnson T —+3	Grant T —+2	Moore J 11+4	Simonsen S —+1	Myhre T 4	Hughes S 11	Hughes M 9	Jevons P 2+1	Milligan J —+1	Match No.
1	2	3	4^1	5	6	7	8	9	10^2	11	12	13																1
1	2	5	4^1		6	7	8	9	10	11^2			3		12	13												2
1	2	3	4^3		6	7	8	9	12	11^1	13			10^2		5	14											3
1	2	3	12		6	7	8	9	10^2		13	14		11^3	4^1	5												4
1	2	3	7		6		8^3	9	10	12	13	14		11^2	4^1	5												5
1	2	3			6	7	8^1	9	10	12	13	14		11^2	4^3	5												6
1	2	3	7^2	5	6	12	8	9	13	11				10^1	4^3						14							7
1	2	3^1			6	7	8	9	10^2	12				13	11^3	5	14	4										8
1	2				6	7	8	9	10				3	11	4	5												9
1	2				6	7	8^1	9	10	13	12		3	11	4	5^2												10
1	2	5^2			6	7	8	9	10	11^1	12		3	13	4													11
1	2		4	5	6	7	8	9	10	11^1			3^2		12	13												12
1	2		4		6	7	8^2	9	10	12			3^1	11		5				13								13
1		3	4			7	8	9	10					11	12	5	2	6^1										14
1		3			6		8	9	10					11	4	5	2				7							15
1	2	3			6	7	8^1	9	10					11	4	5	12											16
1	2	3			6	7	8^2	9	12					10	11^3	5^1	13	4	14									17
1		3	4	12		7	8	9	10					11		5	2^1	6										18
1	2	3			6	7	8^1	9	10					11^2	4	5	12			13								19
1	2	3			6	7^1	8		10	13		14		11	4	5	12^2								9^3			20
1	2	3		5	6	7	8^1	9	10	12				11^2	4					13								21
1	2	3^1		5		7	8	9	10	12				11^2	4			6		13								22
1^9	2	3^1			6	7	8	9	10	12				11	4	5^2				13	15							23
	2	3			6		8	9	10^1					11	4	5	12				7		1					24
	2	12			6		8	9	10			7^1	3	11	4	5							1					25
	2	12	4	5		7	8^1	9					3	11				6			10		1					26
		5	4	2^1		7	8	9					3	11			12	6			10		1					27
1	2	5	3				8	9							4			6			7			10	11			28
1	2		12	5			8^2		10	13		14	3		4			6			7			11^1	9^3			29
1	2	3		5		7	8^1			13		14			4		12	6			10			11^3	9^2			30
1		3		5		7	8		12		13				4		2	6			10^2			11	9^1			31
1		5				7	8						3		4		2	6			10			11	9			32
1	2	3		5^1		7	8		10	13		14			4		12	6						11^3	9^2			33
1	2	5^1					8		10	13		14	3		4		12	6^2						11	9^3	7		34
1		5	4		12	7	8^1		10	13		14	3^2				2	6						11	9^3			35
1		5	3			7	8		10	12	13				4^3		2^1	6						11^2	9	14		36
1		5	4		12	7	8		10	13			3				2	6^1						11	9^2			37
1		5^2	4			7	8		10	12			3				2							11	9	6^1	13	38

Worthington Cup
Second Round Oxford U (a) 1-1
                        (h) 0-1

FA Cup
Third Round Exeter C (a) 0-0
                       (h) 1-0
Fourth Round Birmingham C (h) 2-0
Fifth Round   Preston NE   (h) 2-0
Sixth Round   Aston Villa   (h) 1-2

Division 3   **EXETER CITY**

FOUNDATION

Exeter City was formed in 1904 by the amalgamation of St. Sidwell's United and Exeter United. The club first played in the East Devon League and then the Plymouth & District League. After an exhibition match between West Bromwich Albion and Woolwich Arsenal was held to test interest as Exeter was then a rugby stronghold, Exeter City decided at a meeting at the Red Lion Hotel to turn professional in 1908.

St James Park, Exeter EX4 6PX.

Telephone: (01392) 254 073.

Fax: (01392) 425 885.

ClubCall: 09068 121 634.

Website: www.ecfc.demon.co.uk

Training Ground: (01395) 232784.

Ground Capacity: 10,570.

Record Attendance: 20,984 v Sunderland, FA Cup 6th rd (replay), 4 March 1931.

Record Receipts: £59,862.98 v Aston Villa, FA Cup 3rd rd, 8 January 1994.

Pitch Measurements: 114yd × 73yd.

Chairman: A. I. Doble.

Directors: P. Carter, I. M. Couch, S. W. Dawe, P. Dobson.

Associate Director: M. Shelbourne.

Manager: Noel Blake.

Physio: Simon Shakeshaft.

Chief Executive: Bernard Frowd OBE.

Secretary: Stuart Brailey.

Company Secretary: P. Carter.

Marketing Manager: Julie Richards.

LATEST SEQUENCES

Longest Sequence of League Wins: 7, 23.4.77 – 20.8.77.

Longest Sequence of League Defeats: 7, 14.1.84 – 25.2.84.

Longest Sequence of League Draws: 6, 13.9.86 – 4.10.86.

Longest Sequence of Unbeaten League Matches: 13, 23.8.86 – 25.10.86.

Longest Sequence Without a League Win: 18, 21.2.95 – 19.8.95.

HONOURS

Football League: Division 3 best season: 8th, 1979–80; Division 3 (S) – Runners-up 1932–33; Division 4 – Champions 1989–90; Runners-up 1976–77.

FA Cup: best season: 6th rd replay, 1931, 6th rd 1981.

Football League Cup: never beyond 4th rd.

Division 3 (S) Cup: Winners 1934.

Colours
Red and white striped shirts, red shorts, red stockings.

Change Colours
All purple.

Year Formed: 1904.

Turned Professional: 1908.

Ltd Co.: 1908.

Club Nickname: 'The Grecians'.

First Football League Game: 28 August 1920, Division 3, v Brentford (h) W 3–0 – Pym; Coleburne, Feebury (1p); Crawshaw, Carrick, Mitton; Appleton, Makin, Wright (1), Vowles (1), Dockray.

Record League Victory: 8–1 v Coventry C, Division 3 (S), 4 December 1926 – Bailey; Pollard, Charlton; Pullen, Pool, Garrett; Purcell (2), McDevitt, Blackmore (2), Dent (2), Compton (2). 8–1 v Aldershot, Division 3 (S), 4 May 1935 – Chesters; Gray, Miller; Risdon, Webb, Angus; Jack Scott (1), Wrightson (1), Poulter (3), McArthur (1), Dryden (1), (1 og).

Record Cup Victory: 14–0 v Weymouth, FA Cup 1st qual rd, 3 October 1908 – Fletcher; Craig, Bulcock; Ambler, Chadwick, Wake; Parnell (1), Watson (1), McGuigan (4), Bell (6), Copestake (2).

Record Defeat: 0–9 v Notts Co, Division 3 (S), 16 October 1948. 0–9 v Northampton T, Division 3 (S), 12 April 1958.

Most League Points (2 for a win): 62, Division 4, 1976–77.

Most League Points (3 for a win): 89, Division 4, 1989–90.

Most League Goals: 88, Division 3 (S), 1932–33.

Highest League Scorer in Season: Fred Whitlow, 33, Division 3 (S), 1932–33.

Most League Goals in Total Aggregate: Tony Kellow, 129, 1976–78, 1980–83, 1985–88.

Most League Goals in One Match: 4, Harold 'Jazzo' Kirk v Portsmouth, Division 3S, 3 March 1923; 4, Fred Dent v Bristol R, Division 3S, 5 November 1927; 4, Fred Whitlow v Watford, Division 3S, 29 October 1932.

Most Capped Player: Dermot Curtis, 1 (17), Eire.

Most League Appearances: Arnold Mitchell, 495, 1952–66.

Youngest League Player: Cliff Bastin, 16 years 31 days v Coventry C, 14 April 1928.

Record Transfer Fee Received: £500,000 from Manchester C for Martin Phillips, November 1995.

Record Transfer Fee Paid: £65,000 to Blackpool for Tony Kellow, March 1980.

Football League Record: 1920 Elected Division 3; 1921–58 Division 3 (S); 1958–64 Division 4; 1964–66 Division 3; 1966–77 Division 4; 1977–84 Division 3; 1984–90 Division 4; 1990–92 Division 3; 1992–94 Division 2; 1994– Division 3.

MANAGERS

Arthur Chadwick 1910–22
Fred Mavin 1923–27
Dave Wilson 1928–29
Billy McDevitt 1929–35
Jack English 1935–39
George Roughton 1945–52
Norman Kirkman 1952–53
Norman Dodgin 1953–57
Bill Thompson 1957–58
Frank Broome 1958–60
Glen Wilson 1960–62
Cyril Spiers 1962–63
Jack Edwards 1963–65
Ellis Stuttard 1965–66
Jock Basford 1966–67
Frank Broome 1967–69
Johnny Newman 1969–76
Bobby Saxton 1977–79
Brian Godfrey 1979–83
Gerry Francis 1983–84
Jim Iley 1984–85
Colin Appleton 1985–87
Terry Cooper 1988–91
Alan Ball 1991–94
Terry Cooper 1994–95
Peter Fox 1995–2000
Noel Blake May 2000–

TEN YEAR LEAGUE RECORD

		P	W	D	L	F	A	Pts	Pos
1989-90	Div 4	46	28	5	13	83	48	89	1
1990-91	Div 3	46	16	9	21	58	52	57	16
1991-92	Div 3	46	14	11	21	57	80	53	20
1992-93	Div 2	46	11	17	18	54	69	50	19
1993-94	Div 2	46	11	12	23	52	83	45	22
1994-95	Div 3	42	8	10	24	36	70	34	22
1995-96	Div 3	46	13	18	15	46	53	57	14
1996-97	Div 3	46	12	12	22	48	73	48	22
1997-98	Div 3	46	15	15	16	68	63	60	15
1998-99	Div 3	46	17	12	17	47	50	63	12

DID YOU KNOW

On 7 August 1999, Exeter City recorded their first home winning start to a season for a decade, thanks to half-time substitute Rob Speakman's late goal against Hull City.

EXETER CITY 1999–2000 LEAGUE RECORD

Match No.	Date	Venue	Opponents	Result	H/T Score	Lg. Pos.	Goalscorers	Attendance
1	Aug 7	H	Hull C	W 1-0	0-0	10	Speakman [84]	3834
2	14	A	Barnet	D 2-2	0-1	6	Nyamah [59], Rees [83]	1973
3	21	H	Rotherham U	W 3-1	2-1	4	Dewhurst [5], Holloway [41], McConnell (pen) [90]	2646
4	28	A	Rochdale	W 2-0	0-0	1	Gale [75], Speakman [77]	3113
5	30	H	Mansfield T	W 1-0	1-0	1	Alexander [34]	3109
6	Sept 4	A	Darlington	L 0-1	0-0	2		5860
7	11	A	Chester C	D 1-1	0-0	2	Dewhurst [90]	1855
8	18	H	York C	W 2-1	1-1	2	Alexander 2 (1 pen) [9 pl, 70]	2904
9	25	H	Macclesfield T	L 0-3	0-3	5		3202
10	Oct 2	A	Lincoln C	L 0-1	0-0	8		3557
11	9	A	Shrewsbury T	W 4-1	1-1	4	Bradley [3], Richardson [68], Alexander 2 [77, 80]	2052
12	16	A	Carlisle U	D 1-1	0-0	5	Rees [54]	3012
13	19	H	Swansea C	D 1-1	0-0	—	Rees [77]	2692
14	23	A	Macclesfield T	L 0-1	0-1	8		1893
15	Nov 2	A	Plymouth Arg	L 0-1	0-1	—		9412
16	6	H	Southend U	L 0-1	0-1	14		2353
17	12	A	Halifax T	L 0-1	0-0	15		2440
18	23	H	Northampton T	L 1-2	1-1	—	Rees (pen) [7]	2096
19	27	H	Torquay U	W 3-2	0-1	16	Boylan [50], Gittens [59], Alexander [75]	5263
20	Dec 4	A	Hull C	L 0-4	0-2	17		5683
21	18	H	Hartlepool U	L 1-2	0-1	18	Curran [74]	2261
22	26	A	Cheltenham T	L 1-3	0-3	19	Gittens [67]	5012
23	28	H	Peterborough U	D 2-2	0-1	19	Alexander [72], Speakman [88]	2695
24	Jan 3	A	Brighton & HA	L 2-4	0-2	19	Alexander [69], Flack [83]	5746
25	8	A	Leyton Orient	L 1-3	1-1	19	Alexander [38]	2434
26	15	H	Barnet	D 0-0	0-0	19		2457
27	22	A	Rotherham U	L 0-5	0-3	20		3402
28	29	H	Rochdale	W 2-0	2-0	20	Brown [27], Rowbotham [41]	2525
29	Feb 4	A	Mansfield T	D 1-1	0-0	—	Alexander [72]	3092
30	8	A	Leyton Orient	L 1-4	1-2	—	Buckle [43]	3855
31	12	H	Darlington	L 1-4	0-2	20	Alexander [61]	3302
32	19	A	Torquay U	L 0-1	0-1	20		3296
33	26	A	York C	D 0-0	0-0	20		3066
34	Mar 4	H	Chester C	L 0-2	0-2	20		2391
35	7	A	Southend U	W 2-1	0-0	—	Alexander [51], Cornforth (pen) [68]	3122
36	11	H	Plymouth Arg	D 1-1	1-0	20	Bennett [34]	4287
37	18	A	Northampton T	L 1-2	0-2	21	Rowbotham [57]	4989
38	21	H	Halifax T	W 1-0	1-0	—	Lovell [37]	1652
39	25	H	Cheltenham T	L 1-2	0-0	21	Alexander [90]	3007
40	Apr 1	A	Hartlepool U	L 1-2	0-0	21	Blake [52]	2668
41	8	H	Brighton & HA	D 0-0	0-0	21		3426
42	15	A	Peterborough U	L 1-3	0-3	21	Flack [47]	5276
43	22	A	Carlisle U	D 0-0	0-0	21		3567
44	24	H	Lincoln C	W 3-0	1-0	21	Cornforth (pen) [45], Alexander 2 [59, 65]	2568
45	29	A	Swansea C	L 0-3	0-3	21		10,743
46	May 6	H	Shrewsbury T	L 1-2	0-0	21	Alexander [84]	5213

Final League Position: 21

GOALSCORERS

League (46): Alexander 16 (1 pen), Rees 4 (1 pen), Speakman 3, Cornforth 2 (2 pens), Dewhurst 2, Flack 2, Gittens 2, Rowbotham 2, Bennett 1, Blake 1, Boylan 1, Bradley 1, Brown 1, Buckle 1, Curran 1, Gale 1, Holloway 1, Lovell 1, McConnell 1 (pen), Nyamah 1, Richardson 1.
Worthington Cup (1): McConnell 1 (pen).
FA Cup (4): Flack 2, Alexander 1, Gale 1.

Naylor S 31	Richardson J 35	Power G 28+1	Buckle P 27	Dewhurst R 21+2	Gittens J 38	Rowbotham D 13+5	Rees J 42+1	Flack S 19+21	Holloway C 20+4	Nyamah K 23+12	Breslan G 16+13	Speakman R 4+13	McConnell B 16+9	Gale S 18+5	Alexander G 37	Worrall B 1+3	Blake N 2+5	Matthews J 11+1	Curran C 36+2	Bradley S 6+2	Robinson J 11+1	Smith P 3+4	Waugh W —+3	Boylan L 3+3	Vanninen J 3+2	Potter D 4	Brown A 4+1	Bennett F 8+1	Cornforth J 12	Lee D 3+1	Inglethorpe A —+1	Ellington L —+1	Lovell S 4+1	Jarman L 7	Match No
1	2	3	4^1	5	6	7^2	8	9^3	10	11	12	13	14																						1
1	2	3		5	6		8	9	10	4	11^1				7	12																			2
1	2	3		5			8	12	10	4^2	11^1		7	6	9^3	13	14																		3
1^d	2	3		5	6		8	12	10	11	13	7^2	4		9^1	15																			4
1	2	3		5	6		8	12	10^2	11	4^1	7	14		9^3	13																			5
1	2	3		5	6		8	12	10^2	11^1		7	4		9	13																			6
1	2	3		5	6		8	12	10	4^2	11^3	13	7^1		9	14																			7
1	2	3		5	6		8		10	4^2	11^1	7^3	12		9	13	14																		8
1	2			5^1	6		8		10	11^2	12	13	14	3^3	9	4	7																		9
1	2			5^2	6				10	11	12	13	14	3^1	9	4	7^3	8																	10
1	2				6				10	4	12	13	7		9^2	8^3		11^1	5	3	14														11
1	2				6		8		10	4	12		7^2		9			11^1	5	3	13														12
1	2				6		8	11^3	10	4	12^2	7^1	13		9				5	14	3														13
1	2				6		8	11^2	10^3	4^1	12	13			9				5	7	3	14													14
1	2	12	4		6			9				13		3^2	11^3			7^1	5		8	14													15
1	2	3	4^2		6		8	9	10^1	11	12				7^1				5	13	14														16
1	2	3	4		6		8	9	10^1	11^2	12								5	7	13														17
1		3	4		6		8	11²	10^3	2¹	12	13			9			2^1	5	7	14	11^2													18
1		3	4^1		6		8	11	10^2	11	12	13	7		9				5		2														19
1	2		4^2		6		8	11	10^3	11	12	13	14	3^1	9				5	7															20
1	2	3		5^2	6	7^2	8		10	11^1	12		4		9	13	14																		21
1	2	3	10	5^2	6		8	11^2	12	7^1	12	7¹	4		9	13	14																		22
1	2	3	4^1		6		8	11^2	10	11	12	13			9				5	7															23
1	2	3^2		5	6	7^1	8	11	10	11	12		4		9	13																			24
1	2				6		8		10	12		13	14		9				5		3	7^2					4^1		11^3						25
	2		4^1		6		8		10	11	12		7^2	3	9			1	5		13														26
	2			5^1	6	7^2	8		10^3		12	13	14	3	9			1	4		11														27
1	2		4		6		8		10^1		12		7	3	9				5		11														28
1	2		4		6^2		8			12		13	7	3	9				5			10	11^1												29
1	2		4		6^2		8		10^1		12	13	7	3	9				5		11														30
1	2		4	5			8		10^2		12	13	7	3^1	9						6	11													31
			4		6		8		10^3		12	13	7^2	3	9^1	2		1	5			14	11												32
1			4				8	9^3		11	12					2	13	1	5								6^2	7^1	10	3	14				33
	2	3	4		6^2		8^1	9^1		11	12	13						1	5									7	10	14					34
1	2^1	3	4	5							12	13	14	7	9				6									11^2	10^3	8					35
		3	4	5^2			8		10		12			2^1	9	7		13			1	6							11						36
		3	4		6		8	9			12			2^2				1	5									7	10	11^1		13			37
		3	4		6		8	9			12	13	7	2				1	5										10^1				11^2		38
	2	3	4^1		6	7^2	8		10^3	11	12	13			9		14	1	5																39
		3	4^1		6	7	8		10		12	13			9^2				5		1	2												11	40
		3	4^2		6	7	8				12	13			9^1			14	5		1									10^3			11	2	41
		3			6	7^2	8				12	13			9^1		14		5		1	4							10				11	2^3	42
	2	3			6	7^2	8			11	12				9^1				5		1								10				13	4	43
	2	3			6	13	8			11	12				9^1				5		1								10				7^2	4	44
	2^2	3^1			6	7	8			11	12		14		9		13		5		1								10					4^3	45
			4	5	6		8			11	12	13	7^1	3	9		14				1								10^2					2^3	46

Worthington Cup
First Round   Birmingham C   (a)   0-3
                                      (h)   1-2

FA Cup
First Round   Eastwood T   (h)   2-1
Second Round   Aldershot T   (h)   2-0
Third Round   Everton   (h)   0-0
                                        (a)   0-1

Division 1 **FULHAM**

FOUNDATION

Churchgoers were responsible for the foundation of Fulham, which first saw the light of day as Fulham St Andrew's Church Sunday School FC in 1879. They won the West London Amateur Cup in 1887 and the championship of the West London League in its initial season of 1892–93. The name Fulham had been adopted in 1888.

Craven Cottage, Stevenage Rd, Fulham, London SW6 6HH.
Telephone: (020) 7893 8383.
Fax: (020) 7384 4715.
Website: http://www.fulhamfc.co.uk
ClubCall: 09068 440 044.
Ground Capacity: 19,250.
Record Attendance: 49,335 v Millwall, Division 2, 8 October 1938.
Record Receipts: £139,235 v Watford, Division 2, 2 May 1998.
Pitch Measurements: 110yd × 75yd.
Chairman: M. Al Fayed.
Directors: W. F. Muddyman (Vice-Chairman), Stuart Benson, Mark Griffiths, Andy Muddyman, Tim Delaney.
Managing Director: Michael Fiddy.
Manager: Jean Tigana.
Chief Scout: John Marshall.
Director of Youth: Alan Smith.
Youth Team Coach: Glenn Cockerill.
Community Officer: Gary Mulcahey (020) 7384 4759.
Stadium Manager: Francis Broughton.
Club Secretary: Etain Wist.
Sales and Marketing Director: Juliet Slot.
Communications Manager: Mark Maunders.

LATEST SEQUENCES

Longest Sequence of League Wins: 8, 6.3.99 – 13.4.99.
Longest Sequence of League Defeats: 11, 2.12.61 – 24.2.62.
Longest Sequence of League Draws: 6, 14.10.95 – 18.11.95.
Longest Sequence of Unbeaten League Matches: 15, 26.1.99 – 13.4.99.
Longest Sequence Without a League Win: 15, 25.2.50 – 23.8.50.

HONOURS

Football League: Division 1 best season: 10th, 1959–60; Division 2 – Champions 1948–49, 1998–99; Runners-up 1958–59; Division 3 (S) – Champions 1931–32; Division 3 – Runners-up 1970–71, 1996–97.
FA Cup: Runners-up 1975.
Football League Cup: best season: 5th rd, 1968, 1971, 2000.

Colours

White shirts, red and black trim, black shorts, white stockings red and black trim.

Change Colours

Red shirts with white and black trim, white shorts, black stockings.

Year Formed: 1879.
Turned Professional: 1898.
Ltd Co.: 1903.
Reformed: 1987.
Previous Name: 1879, Fulham St Andrew's; 1888, Fulham.
Club Nickname: 'Cottagers'.
Previous Grounds: 1879 Star Road, Fulham; c.1883 Eel Brook Common, 1884 Lillie Road; 1885 Putney Lower Common; 1886 Ranelagh House, Fulham; 1888 Barn Elms, Castelnau; 1889 Purser's Cross (Roskell's Field), Parsons Green Lane; 1891 Eel Brook Common; 1891 Half Moon, Putney; 1895 Captain James Field, West Brompton; 1896 Craven Cottage.

First Football League Game: 3 September 1907, Division 2, v Hull C (h) L 0–1 – Skene; Ross, Lindsay; Collins, Morrison, Goldie; Dalrymple, Freeman, Bevan, Hubbard, Threlfall.

Record League Victory: 10–1 v Ipswich T, Division 1, 26 December 1963 – Macedo; Cohen, Langley; Mullery (1), Keetch, Robson (1); Key, Cook (1), Leggat (4), Haynes, Howfield (3).

Record Cup Victory: 7–0 v Swansea C, FA Cup 1st rd, 11 November 1995 – Lange; Jupp (1), Herrera, Barkus (Brooker (1)), Moore, Angus, Thomas (1), Morgan, Brazil (Hamill), Conroy (3) (Bolt), Cusack (1).

Record Defeat: 0–10 v Liverpool, League Cup 2nd rd 1st leg, 23 September 1986.

Most League Points (2 for a win): 60, Division 2, 1958–59 and Division 3, 1970–71.

Most League Points (3 for a win): 101, Division 2, 1998–99.

Most League Goals: 111, Division 3 (S), 1931–32.

Highest League Scorer in Season: Frank Newton, 43, Division 3 (S), 1931–32.

Most League Goals in Total Aggregate: Gordon Davies, 159, 1978–84, 1986–91.

Most League Goals in One Match: 5, Fred Harrison v Stockport Co, Division 2, 5 September 1908; 5, Bedford Jezzard v Hull C, Division 2, 8 October 1955; 5, Jimmy Hill v Doncaster R, Division 2, 15 March 1958; 5, Steve Earle v Halifax T, Division 3, 16 September 1969.

Most Capped Player: Johnny Haynes, 56, England.

Most League Appearances: Johnny Haynes, 594, 1952–70.

Youngest League Player: Tony Mahoney, 17 years 38 days v Cardiff C, 6 November 1976.

Record Transfer Fee Received: £800,000 from Bristol C for Tony Thorpe, February 1998.

Record Transfer Fee Paid: £3,000,000 to Sunderland for Lee Clark, July 1999.

Football League Record: 1907 Elected to Division 2; 1928–32 Division 3 (S); 1932–49 Division 2; 1949–52 Division 1; 1952–59 Division 2; 1959–68 Division 1; 1968–69 Division 2; 1969–71 Division 3; 1971–80 Division 2; 1980–82 Division 3; 1982–86 Division 2; 1986–92 Division 3; 1992–94 Division 2; 1994–97 Division 3; 1997–99 Division 2; 1999– Division 1.

MANAGERS

Harry Bradshaw 1904–09
Phil Kelso 1909–24
Andy Ducat 1924–26
Joe Bradshaw 1926–29
Ned Liddell 1929–31
Jim MacIntyre 1931–34
Jimmy Hogan 1934–35
Jack Peart 1935–48
Frank Osborne 1948–64
(was Secretary-Manager or General Manager for most of this period)
Bill Dodgin Snr 1949–53
Duggie Livingstone 1956–58
Bedford Jezzard 1958–64
(General Manager for last two months)
Vic Buckingham 1965–68
Bobby Robson 1968
Bill Dodgin Jnr 1969–72
Alec Stock 1972–76
Bobby Campbell 1976–80
Malcolm Macdonald 1980–84
Ray Harford 1984–96
Ray Lewington 1986–90
Alan Dicks 1990–91
Don Mackay 1991–94
Ian Branfoot 1994–96
(continued as General Manager)
Micky Adams 1996–97
Ray Wilkins 1997–98
Kevin Keegan 1998–99
(Chief Operating Officer)
Paul Bracewell 1999–2000
Jean Tigana July 2000

TEN YEAR LEAGUE RECORD

		P	W	D	L	F	A	Pts	Pos
1989-90	Div 3	46	12	15	19	55	66	51	20
1990-91	Div 3	46	10	16	20	41	56	46	21
1991-92	Div 3	46	19	13	14	57	53	70	9
1992-93	Div 2	46	16	17	13	57	55	65	12
1993-94	Div 2	46	14	10	22	50	63	52	21
1994-95	Div 3	42	16	14	12	60	54	62	8
1995-96	Div 3	46	12	17	17	57	63	53	17
1996-97	Div 3	46	25	12	9	72	38	87	2
1997-98	Div 2	46	20	10	16	60	43	70	6
1998-99	Div 2	46	31	8	7	79	32	101	1

DID YOU KNOW ?

Rodney Marsh scored on his League debut for Fulham against Aston Villa on 23 March 1963, having registered 40 goals for the club's junior team.

FULHAM 1999–2000 LEAGUE RECORD

Match No.	Date	Venue	Opponents	Result	H/T Score	Lg. Pos.	Goalscorers	Attendance
1	Aug 7	A	Birmingham C	D 2-2	1-0	8	Horsfield 2 [36, 59]	24,042
2	14	H	Manchester C	D 0-0	0-0	13		16,754
3	21	A	Grimsby T	D 1-1	1-1	16	Finnan [4]	6196
4	28	H	Charlton Ath	W 2-1	2-0	10	Neilson [22], Peschisolido [42]	15,154
5	30	A	WBA	D 0-0	0-0	8		17,120
6	Sept 11	A	Port Vale	W 2-0	1-0	6	Peschisolido [36], Coleman [56]	6130
7	18	H	QPR	W 1-0	1-0	5	Peschisolido [17]	19,623
8	25	H	Crewe Alex	W 3-0	3-0	4	Horsfield [9], Hayles [16], Symons [36]	12,156
9	Oct 2	A	Norwich C	W 2-1	0-1	3	Riedle [73], Hayles [88]	16,332
10	16	H	Swindon T	W 1-0	0-0	2	Horsfield [84]	13,715
11	19	H	Wolverhampton W	L 0-1	0-0	—		13,160
12	23	A	Huddersfield T	D 1-1	1-0	4	Vincent (og) [7]	13,350
13	26	A	Crewe Alex	D 1-1	1-1	—	Coleman [10]	5493
14	30	H	Norwich C	D 1-1	1-0	6	Symons [9]	13,552
15	Nov 6	A	Stockport Co	L 1-2	0-2	8	Cadamarteri [66]	7200
16	9	H	Portsmouth	W 1-0	0-0	—	Collins [89]	13,229
17	13	H	Barnsley	L 1-3	1-1	—	Riedle [25]	10,634
18	20	A	Blackburn R	L 0-2	0-1	8		18,543
19	23	H	Bolton W	D 1-1	1-1	—	Peschisolido (pen) [18]	9642
20	26	A	Walsall	W 3-1	1-1	—	Riedle [35], Horsfield 2 [66, 84]	5449
21	Dec 4	A	Birmingham C	D 0-0	0-0	6		12,290
22	15	A	Nottingham F	D 0-0	0-0	—		14,250
23	18	A	Crystal Palace	D 0-0	0-0	7		17,480
24	26	H	Ipswich T	D 0-0	0-0	7		17,255
25	28	A	Sheffield U	L 0-2	0-0	9		17,375
26	Jan 3	H	Tranmere R	W 1-0	1-0	8	Roberts (og) [38]	11,377
27	16	A	Manchester C	L 0-4	0-1	10		30,057
28	22	H	Grimsby T	L 0-1	0-0	10		10,802
29	Feb 5	H	WBA	W 1-0	0-0	8	Riedle (pen) [48]	12,044
30	12	A	Portsmouth	W 1-0	0-0	8	Goldbaek [72]	17,337
31	15	A	Charlton Ath	L 0-1	0-0	—		19,940
32	19	H	Walsall	W 2-0	0-0	8	Phelan [53], Clark [84]	10,540
33	28	A	QPR	D 0-0	0-0	—		16,308
34	Mar 4	H	Port Vale	W 3-1	2-0	8	Clark 2 [18, 52], Melville [29]	10,418
35	7	H	Stockport Co	W 4-1	1-0	—	Hayles 2 [11, 65], Goldbaek [52], Finnan [70]	8688
36	11	A	Bolton W	L 1-3	0-1	8	Clark [71]	12,761
37	18	H	Blackburn R	D 2-2	1-1	8	Hayles [18], Riedle [75]	15,108
38	21	A	Barnsley	L 0-1	0-1	—		14,262
39	25	A	Ipswich T	L 0-1	0-0	10		20,168
40	Apr 1	H	Crystal Palace	W 1-0	1-0	10	Horsfield [16]	16,356
41	9	A	Tranmere R	D 1-1	0-0	10	Melville [88]	7132
42	15	H	Sheffield U	W 4-0	1-0	9	Phelan [12], Clark 2 [61, 63], Melville [72]	12,197
43	22	A	Swindon T	L 0-1	0-0	9		7556
44	24	H	Nottingham F	D 1-1	1-1	9	Coleman [30]	12,696
45	30	A	Wolverhampton W	L 0-3	0-0	9		19,912
46	May 7	H	Huddersfield T	W 3-0	1-0	9	Clark 2 (1 pen) [33, 68 (p)], Goldbaek [76]	13,728

Final League Position: 9

GOALSCORERS

League (49): Clark 8 (1 pen), Horsfield 7, Hayles 5, Riedle 5 (1 pen), Peschisolido 4 (1 pen), Coleman 3, Goldbaek 3, Melville 3, Finnan 2, Phelan 2, Symons 2, Cadamarteri 1, Collins 1, Neilson 1, own goals 2.
Worthington Cup (19): Horsfield 6, Peschisolido 3, Collins 2, Davis 2, Hayles 2, Clark 1, Coleman 1, Collymore 1, own goal 1.
FA Cup (9): Collins 2, Hayles 2, Coleman 1, Davis 1, Finnan 1, Hayward 1, Horsfield 1.

Taylor M 46	Finnan S 35	Brevett R 22+1	Melville A 40	Coleman C 40	Morgan S 26+2	Hughes S 3	Clark L 42	Horsfield G 28+3	Collymore S 3+3	Davis S 15+11	Trollope P 13+9	Hayward S 34+3	Peschisolido P 18+12	Betsy K —+2	Symons K 27+2	Neilson A 4+1	Hayles B 21+14	Collins W 6+13	Uhlenbeek G 11+5	Riedle K 15+6	Cadamarteri D 3+2	Ball K 15+3	Goldbaek B 16+2	Phelan T 17	Lewis E 6+2	Match No
1	2	3	4	5	6	7^1	8	9	10	11^2	12	13														1
1	2	3	4	5	6	7^1	8	9	10	11			12													2
1	2	3	4	5	6	7^1	8		10^2	11	12	14	9	13^2												3
1	2	12	4	5	6		8	9^1		11^3	13	7	10	12^2	14	3										4
1	2	12	4	5			8	9^3		11	13	7	10^2		6	3^1	14									5
1	2	3	4	5^1	12			9^2	13	11	8	7	10^3		6		14									6
1	2	3	4	5			8^2	9				7	11	10^1	6		12	13								7
1	2^3	3	4	5			8	9	12	13	11	7^2			6		10^1	14								8
1	2	3^1	4	5			8	9^3	12	13	7	11			6		14		10^2							9
1	2	3^3		5	4		8	12		13	7	11	10^2		6		14		9^1							10
1				5	4^3		8	9				7	11	12	6				3^2	13	14	2	10^1			11
1		3		5	4		8	9^2		12	7	11	10		6					13		2^1				12
1		3		5	4		8	9^1				7	11	10^2	6							12	2	13		13
1		3		5	4		8				10	7^1	11		6							12	2	9		14
1		3		5	4^1		8			2^2		7	11		6							12	13	9	10	15
1		3^1	4	5			8					7	11		6							12	2	9	10	16
1			4	5			8	7		3		11	12		6					13		2^2	9^1	10		17
1		3	4^2	5			8	9		11^1		7^3	10		6	2	12					13	14			18
1		3	4	5			8	9^1		11		7	10^2		6		12					2^3	13	14		19
1		3	4	5			8	9^1		11^2		7			6		12			13		2	10^1			20
1	2	3	4	5			8	9^1		11	14	7	12		6		10^2						13^2			21
1	2^2	3	4	5^1	12		8	9		11		7	10		6		13									22
1	2	3	4		6		8			11^1		7	9		5		10	12								23
1	2	3^2	4		6		8	9^1				11^3	12		5		10	7	13			14				24
1	2	3	4		6		8					11	9		5		10	7								25
1	2		4		6		8			12		7	13		5		9^1	11	3^2			10				26
1	2	3^1	4		6		8	9		12		10			5^2		7		13			11				27
1	2		4		6		8			10					5		7	9				11	3			28
1	2		4		6		8			12					5		10	13	9^1			11	7	3^2		29
1	2		4	5	6^1		8	9					12				10					11	7	3		30
1	2		4	5	6		8^1	9		12		13			10		14					11^2	7^3	3		31
1	2		4	5	6		8	9							10							11	7	3		32
1	2		4	5	6		8								10				9			11	7	3		33
1	2		4	5	6		8						10						9			11	7	3		34
1	2		4	5	6		8^1			12			9		10^2	13						11	7	3		35
1	2		4	5	6^1		8			12			9		10							11	7	3		36
1	2		4	5	6		8^1			12			7		10				9			11		3		37
1	2		4	5	6^3					11^2		9	12		10	13						8	7	3	14	38
1	2		4	5	6^2					12		7	8		10				9^3			11^1	13	3	14	39
1	2		4	5	6^3				9^1	12		11	10^2						13	14			7	3	8	40
1	2^3		4	5			8	9^1				11^2	12		10				7			13	14	3	6	41
1	2^3		4	5			8	9		12		11	13		10	14							7	3^1	6^2	42
1	2^3		4	5			8	9		11^2			12		10	13			14				7	3	6^1	43
1	6		4	5			8			12			13		10^2	2			9^1				7	3	11	44
1			4	5^1			8	9^3		12	7	10		6	13	14			2^2			11		3		45
1	2		4				8^1	9		12		13	11		5		10					14	7^3	3	6^2	46

Worthington Cup

First Round	Northampton T	(a)	2-1
		(h)	3-1
Second Round	Norwich C	(a)	4-0
		(h)	2-0
Third Round	WBA	(a)	2-1
Fourth Round	Tottenham H	(h)	3-1
Fifth Round	Leicester C	(a)	3-3

FA Cup

Third Round	Luton T	(h)	2-2
		(a)	3-0
Fourth Round	Wimbledon	(h)	3-0
Fifth Round	Tranmere R	(h)	1-2

Division 1   **GILLINGHAM**

FOUNDATION

The success of the pioneering Royal Engineers of Chatham excited the interest of the residents of the Medway Towns and led to the formation of many clubs including Excelsior. After winning the Kent Junior Cup and the Chatham District League in 1893, Excelsior decided to go for bigger things and it was at a meeting in the Napier Arms, Brompton, in 1893 that New Brompton FC came into being, buying and developing the ground which is now Priestfield Stadium.

Priestfield Stadium, Gillingham, ME7 4DD.

Telephone: (01634) 851 854/576 828.

Fax: (01634) 850 986.

ClubCall: 09068 332 211.

Ground Capacity: 10,600.

Record Attendance: 23,002 v QPR, FA Cup 3rd rd, 10 January 1948.

Record Receipts: £80,184 v Sheffield W, FA Cup 3rd rd, 7 January 1995.

Pitch Measurements: 114yd × 75yd.

Chairman/Chief Executive: P. D. P. Scally.

Director: P. A. Spokes.

Associate Director: Yvonne Paulley.

Player Manager: Andy Hessenthaler.

Assistant Manager: Steve Butler.

Coach: Steve Butler.

Physio: Wayne Jones.

Secretary: Mrs G. E. Poynter.

Sales and Marketing Manager: J. Swaby.

LATEST SEQUENCES

Longest Sequence of League Wins: 7, 18.12.54 – 29.1.55.

Longest Sequence of League Defeats: 10, 20.9.88 – 5.11.88.

Longest Sequence of League Draws: 5, 28.8.93 – 18.9.93.

Longest Sequence of Unbeaten League Matches: 20, 13.10.73 – 10.2.74.

Longest Sequence Without a League Win: 15, 1.4.72 – 2.9.72.

HONOURS

Football League: Promoted from Division 2 1999–2000 (play-offs); Division 3 – Runners-up 1995-96; Division 4 – Champions 1963–64; Runners-up 1973–74.

FA Cup: best season: 6th rd, 2000.

Football League Cup: best season: 4th rd, 1964, 1997.

Colours
Blue and black.

Change Colours
Red and black.

Year Formed: 1893.

Turned Professional: 1894.

Ltd Co.: 1893.

Previous Name: 1893, New Brompton; 1913, Gillingham.

Club Nickname: 'The Gills'.

First Football League Game: 28 August 1920, Division 3, v Southampton (h) D 1–1 – Branfield; Robertson, Sissons; Battiste, Baxter, Wigmore; Holt, Hall, Gilbey (1), Roe, Gore.

Record League Victory: 10–0 v Chesterfield, Division 3, 5 September 1987 – Kite; Haylock, Pearce, Shipley (2) (Lillis), West, Greenall (1), Pritchard (2), Shearer (2), Lovell, Elsey (2), David Smith (1).

Record Cup Victory: 10–1 v Gorleston, FA Cup 1st rd, 16 November 1957 – Brodie; Parry, Hannaway; Riggs, Boswell, Laing; Payne, Fletcher (2), Saunders (5), Morgan (1), Clark (2).

Record Defeat: 2–9 v Nottingham F, Division 3 (S), 18 November 1950.

Most League Points (2 for a win): 62, Division 4, 1973–74.

Most League Points (3 for a win): 85, Division 2, 1999–2000.

Most League Goals: 90, Division 4, 1973–74.

Highest League Scorer in Season: Ernie Morgan, 31, Division 3 (S), 1954–55; Brian Yeo, 31, Division 4, 1973–74.

Most League Goals in Total Aggregate: Brian Yeo, 135, 1963–75.

Most League Goals in One Match: 6, Fred Cheesmur v Merthyr T, Division 3S, 26 April 1930.

Most Capped Player: Tony Cascarino, 3 (88), Republic of Ireland.

Most League Appearances: John Simpson, 571, 1957–72.

Youngest League Player: Billy Hughes, 15 years 275 days v Southend U, 13 April 1976.

Record Transfer Fee Received: £1,500,000 from Manchester C for Robert Taylor, November 1999.

Record Transfer Fee Paid: £600,000 to Reading for Carl Asaba, August 1998.

Football League Record: 1920 Original Member of Division 3; 1921 Division 3 (S); 1938 Failed re-election; Southern League 1938–44; Kent League 1944–46; Southern League 1946–50; 1950 Re-elected to Division 3 (S); 1958–64 Division 4; 1964–71 Division 3; 1971–74 Division 4; 1974–89 Division 3; 1989–92 Division 4; 1992–96; Division 3; 1996–2000 Division 2; 2000– Division 1.

MANAGERS

W. Ironside Groombridge
1896–1906 *(Secretary-Manager)*
(previously Financial Secretary)
Steve Smith 1906–08
W. I. Groombridge 1908–19
(Secretary-Manager)
George Collins 1919–20
John McMillan 1920–23
Harry Curtis 1923–26
Albert Hoskins 1926–29
Dick Hendrie 1929–31
Fred Mavin 1932–37
Alan Ure 1937–38
Bill Harvey 1938–39
Archie Clark 1939–58
Harry Barratt 1958–62
Freddie Cox 1962–65
Basil Hayward 1966–71
Andy Nelson 1971–74
Len Ashurst 1974–75
Gerry Summers 1975–81
Keith Peacock 1981–87
Paul Taylor 1988
Keith Burkinshaw 1988–89
Damien Richardson 1989–93
Mike Flanagan 1993–95
Neil Smillie 1995
Tony Pulis 1995–99
Peter Taylor 1999–2000
Andy Hessenthaler June 2000–

TEN YEAR LEAGUE RECORD

		P	W	D	L	F	A	Pts	Pos
1989-90	Div 4	46	17	11	18	46	48	62	14
1990-91	Div 4	46	12	18	16	57	60	54	15
1991-92	Div 4	42	15	12	15	63	53	57	11
1992-93	Div 3	42	9	13	20	48	64	40	21
1993-94	Div 3	42	12	15	15	44	51	51	16
1994-95	Div 3	42	10	11	21	46	64	41	19
1995-96	Div 3	46	22	17	7	49	20	83	2
1996-97	Div 2	46	19	10	17	60	59	67	11
1997-98	Div 2	46	19	13	14	52	47	70	8
1998-99	Div 2	46	22	14	10	75	44	80	4

DID YOU KNOW ?

In the years before their return to the Football League in 1950, Gillingham's left-back George Dorling was a part-time player with the club and also employed on Tottenham Hotspur's maintenance staff.

GILLINGHAM 1999–2000 LEAGUE RECORD

Match No.	Date		Venue	Opponents	Result		H/T Score	Lg. Pos.	Goalscorers	Atten-dance
1	Aug	7	A	Bury	L	1-2	0-0	19	Thomson [76]	4014
2		14	H	Bristol R	L	0-1	0-0	22		6234
3		21	A	Blackpool	D	1-1	1-0	22	Ashby [40]	4203
4		28	H	Wycombe W	D	2-2	1-1	23	Taylor (pen) [37], McGlinchey [86]	6180
5		30	A	Stoke C	D	1-1	0-0	22	Taylor [90]	8369
6	Sept	4	H	Oldham Ath	W	2-1	2-0	17	Taylor [4], Omoyimni [6]	5884
7		11	A	Oxford U	W	2-1	0-0	12	Southall (pen) [53], Omoyimni [90]	5418
8		18	H	Preston NE	L	0-2	0-0	15		6610
9		25	A	Cambridge U	D	2-2	1-0	16	Taylor [26], Butters [69]	4708
10	Oct	2	H	Millwall	W	2-0	1-0	13	Lewis [22], Taylor [63]	6616
11		9	H	Wrexham	W	5-1	2-1	11	Thomson [26], Southall [45], Taylor 3 [65, 67, 70]	5997
12		16	A	Luton T	L	1-3	1-0	12	Lewis [16]	6394
13		19	A	Brentford	W	2-1	2-0	—	Omoyinmi [27], Saunders [29]	6264
14		23	H	Cambridge U	W	2-1	0-1	8	Thomson 2 [47, 84]	6417
15	Nov	2	H	Bristol C	W	3-0	0-0	—	Taylor 3 [60, 63, 89]	6892
16		6	A	Notts Co	D	1-1	1-1	9	Taylor [20]	6023
17		12	H	Bournemouth	W	4-1	2-1	6	Hessenthaler [12], Thomson [19], Taylor 2 [50, 59]	6336
18		23	A	Scunthorpe U	W	4-1	2-1	—	Taylor [24], Thomson [33], Lewis [52], Nosworthy [76]	3444
19		27	A	Cardiff C	W	2-1	2-1	3	Hessenthaler [1], Thomson [21]	7608
20	Dec	4	H	Bury	W	1-0	0-0	3	Edge [62]	7036
21		26	H	Colchester U	W	2-1	2-0	5	Rowe [13], Southall [42]	7338
22		28	A	Wigan Ath	L	0-2	0-1	6		8054
23	Jan	3	H	Reading	D	2-2	1-0	6	Southall [20], Thomson [90]	7453
24		15	A	Bristol R	L	1-2	0-0	8	Onuora [88]	8331
25		22	H	Blackpool	L	1-3	0-2	8	Southall [52]	6805
26	Feb	1	A	Chesterfield	D	0-0	0-0	—		2898
27		5	H	Stoke C	W	3-0	2-0	7	Onuora [13], Gooden [32], Rowe [73]	7801
28		12	A	Oldham Ath	W	3-1	2-1	7	Gooden [4], Ashby [41], Rowe [67]	5144
29		26	A	Preston NE	W	2-0	0-0	8	Asaba 2 [58, 69]	13,246
30	Mar	4	H	Oxford U	W	1-0	0-0	7	Lewis [89]	6966
31		7	H	Notts Co	L	0-1	0-0	—		6915
32		11	A	Bristol C	W	1-0	0-0	6	Hessenthaler [78]	9332
33		14	H	Burnley	D	2-2	1-1	—	Butters [4], Asaba [68]	7347
34		18	H	Scunthorpe U	W	3-1	1-1	6	Lewis [34], Thomson [55], Southall (pen) [73]	6822
35		21	A	Bournemouth	W	1-0	1-0	—	Onuora [44]	4443
36		25	A	Colchester U	L	1-2	0-0	6	Rowe [79]	4337
37		28	A	Wycombe W	L	0-1	0-0	—		4183
38	Apr	1	H	Chesterfield	W	1-0	0-0	6	Butler [75]	6772
39		7	A	Reading	D	2-2	0-1	—	Southall [49], Onuora [65]	11,064
40		15	H	Wigan Ath	W	2-1	1-1	6	Onuora [18], Lewis [82]	7746
41		18	A	Burnley	W	3-0	1-0	—	Gooden [21], Ashby [50], Smith [70]	17,026
42		22	H	Luton T	W	2-0	1-0	5	Hessenthaler [9], Southall [60]	8667
43		24	A	Millwall	D	2-2	2-2	4	Gooden [11], Hessenthaler [40]	17,929
44		29	H	Brentford	W	2-0	1-0	4	Onuora [37], Butler [87]	9001
45	May	2	H	Cardiff C	W	4-1	3-1	—	Asaba 3 [11, 36, 59], Southall [27]	9178
46		6	A	Wrexham	L	0-1	0-1	3		8811

Final League Position: 3

GOALSCORERS

League (79): Taylor 15 (1 pen), Southall 9 (2 pens), Thomson 9, Asaba 6, Lewis 6, Onuora 6, Hessenthaler 5, Gooden 4, Rowe 4, Ashby 3, Omoyimni 3, Butler 2, Butters 2, Edge 1, McGlinchey 1, Nosworthy 1, Saunders 1, Smith 1.
Worthington Cup (5): Hessenthaler 2, Southall 1, Taylor 1, own goal 1.
FA Cup (16): Thomson 4, Southall 3, Taylor 2, Ashby 1, Butters 1, Hodge 1, McGlinchey 1, Pennock 1, Saunders 1, own goal 1.

Bartram V 43	Patterson M 9	Ashby B 41	Smith P 43+1	Bryant M 3+3	Butters G 38+2	Southall N 45	Hessenthaler A 41+1	Thomson A 20+8	Pennock A 34	Nosworthy N 15+14	Taylor R 13+2	Lee C 1+2	Galloway M 1+1	McGlinchey B 6+7	Hodge J 1+14	Saunders M 20+6	Lewis J 37+5	Miller B 1+3	Williams A 2	Omoyimni E 7+2	Edge R 25+1	Pinnock J —+2	Butler S 2-8	Rowe R 8+14	Onuora I 21+1	Gooden T 15+1	Browning M —+1	Asaba C 7+4	Bass J 4+3	Matthews L 2+3	Mautone S 1	Match No.
1	2	3^1	4	5^2	6	7^3	8	9	10	11	12	13	14																			1
1		3	4	12	6^1	2	8	9^2	10	14	11			7		5^3	13															2
1		3	5	4^1		2	8	9	10	12	11					6	7															3
1	2	3	4		7^2	8	9^1			14	11					13	12	6	10	5^1	1											4
		3	5^2	4^1		2	8	13	10		11				9^2	12	6	7	14	1												5
1	3^1	5	4			2	8		10	12	11^1					13	6	7	14	9^2												6
1	3	5	4			2	8	12	10	9^1						6	11			7												7
	3^1	5	4			2	8		10	12	11					6^2	7	13	1	9												8
1	3	5	4	12		2	8	9^2	10		11^1	13				6	7															9
1	3^1	5	4	12		2	8	9	10		11^2					6	7			13												10
1		3	4	5		2	8	9	6	10^1	11^3					12	7^2				13	14										11
1	2		4^1	5^2			8	9	10	13					6	12	3	7		11												12
1		3	4	6	2		9^1			11^2					5	12	8	7		13	10											13
1		3	4	5		2	8	12	10	13					6	14	11^2	7^3		9^1												14
1		6	4	5	7	8	9^1	2		12						13	10^2	14		11^1	3											15
1		6	4	5	7	8		2		11						12	10^2	13		9^1	3											16
1		6	4	5	7	8^3	9^1	2		12	11					14	10				3^2											17
1		6	4	5	7	8^1	9^2	2		13	11^3						12	10			3		14									18
1		6	4	5	7	8	9^1	2		11							10				3		12									19
1		6	4	5	7	8	9^2	2		11						13	12^2	10^1			3		14									20
1		6	4	5	7	8	12	2		11^1						13	10				3		9^2									21
1		6	4	5	7	8	12	2^2		11^1						13	14	10			3		9^3									22
1		6	4	5	2	8	12									10	7				3		9^1	11								23
1	4	10	5	6^1	2	8^2										12	7				3		9	11	13							24
1	6	4	12	5	2	8^2										7					3^1		9	10	11	13						25
1	6		4	5	2	12	9^2									8^1	7				3		13	10	11							26
1	6	4		5	2	8^1	9^2									12	7				3		13	10	11							27
1	6	4		5	2	8^1				13						12	7				3		9	10^2	11							28
1		4		5	2	8	9^2	6	12							3^1	7						10	11	13							29
1	3	4		5	2	8	8^1	9	6							12	7				13	10^3	11	14								30
1		4^1		5	2	8	9^2	3	12					6		11	7				13	10^3		14								31
1		4		5	2	8		3	11							6	7				12	13	10^2		9^1							32
1		4	12	5	2	8		6	3					13		11^2	7				14	10^1		9^3								33
1		4		5	2	8	12	11	6							7				3	13	10^2		9^1								34
1	6	4		5	2			9^2	11^1	8					12		7				3	13	10									35
1	6	4		5	7			8						12		11^2				3^1	13	14	9	10^3			2					36
1	6			5	2			11						8^1		7				3	12	9	10^2			4	13					37
1	3	12		5	2	8		10^2								7					9	13	11			4^1	6					38
1	6	10		5	2	8										7				3	12	13	11			4^1	9^2					39
	6	4		5	7^2	8	2									10				3	13	12	9^1	11		1						40
1	3	4		5	7^2	8	2	6						12		10						9^2	11^1			14	13					41
1	3	4		5	7	6^1		2	12							10				8		11	9^2				13					42
1	6	4		5	7^3	8^1		2	12							10				3		13	9^2	11	14							43
1	6^3	4		5	7	8		2								12				3		13	10^2	11	9^1	14						44
1		5	4		6^3	7	8		2							12				3		13	10^2	11	9^1	14						45
1		5	4^1		6	7	8	12	2							13				3^2		14	10^3	11	9							46

Worthington Cup

First Round	Brighton & HA	(a)	2-0
		(h)	2-0
Second Round	Bolton W	(h)	1-4
		(a)	0-2

FA Cup

First Round	Cheltenham T	(a)	1-1
		(h)	3-2
Second Round	Darlington	(h)	3-1
Third Round	Walsall	(a)	1-1
		(h)	2-1
Fourth Round	Bradford C	(h)	3-1
Fifth Round	Sheffield W	(h)	3-1
Sixth Round	Chelsea	(a)	0-5

Division 1   **GRIMSBY TOWN**

FOUNDATION

Grimsby Pelham FC as they were first known, came into being at a meeting held at the Wellington Arms in September 1878. Pelham is the family name of big landowners in the area, the Earls of Yarborough. The receipts for their first game amounted to 6s. 9d. (approx. 39p). After a year, the club name was changed to Grimsby Town.

Blundell Park, Cleethorpes, North East Lincolnshire DN35 7PY.

Telephone: (01472) 605 050.

Fax: (01472) 693 665.

ClubCall: 09068 555 855.

Ground Capacity: 10,033.

Record Attendance: 31,657 v Wolverhampton W, FA Cup 5th rd, 20 February 1937.

Record Receipts: £119,799 v Aston Villa, FA Cup 4th rd, 29 January 1994.

Pitch Measurements: 111yd × 75yd.

Life Presidents: T. Aspinall, T. J. Lindley.

Chairman: D. P. Everitt FCA.

Vice-Chairman: B. Huxford.

Directors: J. Arnell, P. Furneaux, E. Graves, R. Jackson, A. King, R. Lake.

Manager: Alan Buckley.

Assistant Manager: John Cockerill.

Chief Executive/Company Secretary: Ian Fleming.

Commercial Manager: Tony Richardson.

Assistant Commercial Manager: Tim Harvey.

Physio: Paul Mitchell.

LATEST SEQUENCES

Longest Sequence of League Wins: 11, 19.1.52 – 29.3.52.

Longest Sequence of League Defeats: 9, 30.11.07 – 18.1.08.

Longest Sequence of League Draws: 5, 6.2.65 – 6.3.65.

Longest Sequence of Unbeaten League Matches: 19, 16.2.80 – 30.8.80.

Longest Sequence Without a League Win: 18, 10.10.81 – 16.3.82.

HONOURS

Football League: Division 1 best season: 5th, 1934–35; Division 2 – Champions 1900–01, 1933–34; Runners-up 1928–29; Promoted from Division 2 1997–98 (play-offs); Division 3 (N) – Champions 1925–26, 1955–56; Runners-up 1951–52; Division 3 – Champions 1979–80; Runners-up 1961–62; Division 4 – Champions 1971–72; Runners-up 1978–79; 1989–90.

FA Cup: Semi-finals, 1936, 1939.

Football League Cup: best season: 5th rd, 1980, 1985.

League Group Cup: Winners 1982.

Auto Windscreen Shield: Winners 1998.

Colours
Black and white striped shirts, black shorts, black stockings with red turnover.

Change Colours
Red shirts with blue collar and arm stripe, red shorts with blue stripe, blue stockings with red band.

Year Formed. 1878.

Turned Professional: 1890.

Ltd Co.: 1890.

Previous Name: 1878, Grimsby Pelham; 1879, Grimsby Town.

Club Nickname: 'The Mariners'.

Previous Grounds: 1880, Clee Park; 1889, Abbey Park; 1899, Blundell Park.

First Football League Game: 3 September 1892, Division 2, v Northwich Victoria (h) W 2–1 – Whitehouse; Lundie, T. Frith; C. Frith, Walker, Murrell; Higgins, Henderson, Brayshaw, Riddoch (2), Ackroyd.

Record League Victory: 9–2 v Darwen, Division 2, 15 April 1899 – Bagshaw; Lockie, Nidd; Griffiths, Bell (1), Nelmes; Jenkinson (3), Richards (1), Cockshutt (3), Robinson, Chadburn (1).

Record Cup Victory: 8–0 v Darlington, FA Cup 2nd rd, 21 November 1885 – G. Atkinson; J. H. Taylor, H. Taylor; Hall, Kimpson, Hopewell; H. Atkinson (1), Garnham, Seal (3), Sharman, Monument (4).

Record Defeat: 1–9 v Arsenal, Division 1, 28 January 1931.

Most League Points (2 for a win): 68, Division 3 (N), 1955–56.

Most League Points (3 for a win): 83, Division 3, 1990–91.

Most League Goals: 103, Division 2, 1933–34.

Highest League Scorer in Season: Pat Glover, 42, Division 2, 1933–34.

Most League Goals in Total Aggregate: Pat Glover, 180, 1930–39.

Most League Goals in One Match: 6, Tommy McCairns v Leicester Fosse, Division 2, 11 April 1896.

Most Capped Player: Pat Glover, 7, Wales.

Most League Appearances: Keith Jobling, 448, 1953–69.

Youngest League Player: Tony Ford, 16 years 143 days v Walsall, 4 October 1975.

Record Transfer Fee Received: £1,500,000 from Everton for John Oster, July 1997.

Record Transfer Fee Paid: £400,000 to Preston NE for Lee Ashcroft, August 1998.

Football League Record: 1892 Original Member Division 2; 1901–03 Division 1; 1903 Division 2; 1910 Failed re-election; 1911 re-elected Division 2; 1920–21 Division 3; 1921–26 Division 3 (N); 1926–29 Division 2; 1929–32 Division 1; 1932–34 Division 2; 1934–48 Division 1; 1948–51 Division 2; 1951–56 Division 3 (N); 1956–59 Division 2; 1959–62 Division 3; 1962–64 Division 2; 1964–68 Division 3; 1968–72 Division 4; 1972–77 Division 3; 1977–79 Division 4; 1979–80 Division 3; 1980–87 Division 2; 1987–88 Division 3; 1988–90 Division 4; 1990–91 Division 3; 1991–92 Division 2; 1992–97 Division 1; 1997–98 Division 2; 1998– Division 1.

MANAGERS

H. N. Hickson 1902–20
(Secretary-Manager)
Haydn Price 1920
George Fraser 1921–24
Wilf Gillow 1924–32
Frank Womack 1932–36
Charles Spencer 1937–51
Bill Shankly 1951–53
Billy Walsh 1954–55
Allenby Chilton 1955–59
Tim Ward 1960–62
Tom Johnston 1962–64
Jimmy McGuigan 1964–67
Don McEvoy 1967–68
Bill Harvey 1968–69
Bobby Kennedy 1969–71
Lawrie McMenemy 1971–73
Ron Ashman 1973–75
Tom Casey 1975–76
Johnny Newman 1976–79
George Kerr 1979–82
David Booth 1982–85
Mike Lyons 1985–87
Bobby Roberts 1987–88
Alan Buckley 1988–94
Brian Laws 1994–96
Kenny Swain 1997
Alan Buckley May 1997–

TEN YEAR LEAGUE RECORD

		P	W	D	L	F	A	Pts	Pos
1989-90	Div 4	46	22	13	11	70	47	79	2
1990-91	Div 3	46	24	11	11	66	34	83	3
1991-92	Div 2	46	14	11	21	47	62	53	19
1992-93	Div 1	46	19	7	20	58	57	64	9
1993-94	Div 1	46	13	20	13	52	47	59	16
1994-95	Div 1	46	17	14	15	62	56	65	10
1995-96	Div 1	46	14	14	18	55	69	56	17
1996-97	Div 1	46	11	13	22	60	81	46	22
1997-98	Div 2	46	19	15	12	55	37	72	3
1998-99	Div 1	46	17	10	19	40	52	61	11

DID YOU KNOW ?

In November 1954, Grimsby Town wanted to appoint as coach Emilio Berkessy, born in Transylvania, but a refugee from Hungary and coaching Real Zaragoza in Spain. He was refused a work permit.

GRIMSBY TOWN 1999–2000 LEAGUE RECORD

Match No.	Date	Venue	Opponents	Result	H/T Score	Lg. Pos.	Goalscorers	Attendance
1	Aug 7	H	Stockport Co	L 0-1	0-0	19		5528
2	14	A	Nottingham F	L 1-2	0-1	23	Groves (pen) [50]	17,121
3	21	H	Fulham	D 1-1	1-1	21	Black [43]	6196
4	27	A	Crewe Alex	D 1-1	0-0	—	Lester [56]	5440
5	30	H	Swindon T	W 1-0	1-0	15	Groves (pen) [30]	5705
6	Sept 5	A	Port Vale	L 1-3	0-2	19	Allen [60]	3737
7	11	H	Walsall	W 1-0	0-0	13	Allen [73]	6014
8	18	A	Crystal Palace	L 0-3	0-2	16		13,294
9	25	A	Portsmouth	W 2-1	1-1	13	Ashcroft [9], Coldicott [63]	12,073
10	Oct 2	H	Ipswich T	W 2-1	1-0	9	Donovan [39], Ashcroft [56]	6531
11	16	A	Blackburn R	D 1-1	1-1	11	Ashcroft (pen) [43]	17,575
12	19	A	Tranmere R	L 2-3	1-2	—	Allen 2 [30, 80]	5004
13	23	H	Birmingham C	D 1-1	1-1	15	Allen [34]	6266
14	26	H	Portsmouth	W 1-0	1-0	—	Awford (og) [24]	5912
15	30	A	Ipswich T	L 0-2	0-1	14		16,617
16	Nov 6	A	Wolverhampton W	W 0-3	0-1	15		19,036
17	12	H	Charlton Ath	L 2-5	1-2	15	Ashcroft (pen) [25], Donovan [46]	6849
18	20	A	Bolton W	L 0-2	0-0	17		12,415
19	23	H	QPR	W 2-1	0-1	—	Ashcroft 2 (2 pens) [57, 85]	4297
20	28	H	Norwich C	W 2-1	1-1	15	Ashcroft 2 (1 pen) [25 (p), 60]	5333
21	Dec 4	A	Stockport Co	L 1-2	0-1	16	Hamilton [88]	5581
22	14	H	WBA	D 1-1	1-1	—	Allen [31]	4036
23	18	A	Huddersfield T	L 1-3	1-2	18	Groves [44]	14,065
24	26	H	Barnsley	L 0-3	0-2	19		8742
25	28	A	Manchester C	L 1-2	1-1	20	Coldicott [27]	32,607
26	Jan 3	H	Sheffield U	D 2-2	1-1	20	Lester [16], Ashcroft [81]	7618
27	15	H	Nottingham F	W 4-3	2-1	17	Lester [29], Ashcroft 2 (1 pen) [32, 67 (p)], Donovan [83]	6738
28	22	A	Fulham	W 1-0	0-0	17	Lester [56]	10,802
29	29	H	Crewe Alex	D 1-1	0-0	17	Allen [89]	6147
30	Feb 5	A	Swindon T	W 1-0	0-0	15	Ashcroft [80]	5784
31	12	H	Port Vale	W 2-0	2-0	13	Clare [19], Allen [27]	6265
32	19	A	Norwich C	L 0-3	0-1	15		13,533
33	26	H	Crystal Palace	W 1-0	1-0	14	Smith D (pen) [45]	5421
34	Mar 4	A	Walsall	L 0-1	0-1	16		5384
35	7	A	Wolverhampton W	W 1-0	1-0	—	Clare [18]	5575
36	11	A	QPR	L 0-1	0-0	14		10,450
37	18	H	Bolton W	L 0-1	0-1	15		5289
38	22	A	Charlton Ath	L 0-4	0-1	—		19,364
39	27	A	Barnsley	L 0-3	0-1	—		14,613
40	Apr 1	H	Huddersfield T	D 0-0	0-0	16		6993
41	8	A	Sheffield U	D 0-0	0-0	17		11,612
42	15	H	Manchester C	D 1-1	1-1	16	Pouton [16]	8166
43	22	H	Blackburn R	D 0-0	0-0	16		6558
44	24	A	WBA	L 1-2	0-1	18	Black [52]	15,291
45	29	A	Tranmere R	L 1-2	1-1	19	Clare [37]	5427
46	May 7	A	Birmingham C	D 0-0	0-0	20		25,263

Final League Position: 20

GOALSCORERS

League (41): Ashcroft 12 (6 pens), Allen 8, Lester 4, Clare 3, Donovan 3, Groves 3 (2 pens), Black 2, Coldicott 2, Hamilton 1, Pouton 1, Smith D 1 (pen), own goal 1.
Worthington Cup (10): Lester 3, Groves 2, Ashcroft 1 (pen), Coldicott 1, Donovan 1, Gallimore 1, Smith D 1.
FA Cup (3): Livingstone 2, Allen 1.

Coyne D 44	Butterfield D 21 + 8	Smith D 34 + 2	Livingstone S 23 + 6	Smith R 19	Coldicott S 42 + 2	Donovan K 41	Black K 15 + 16	Ashcroft L 31 + 3	Allen B 12 + 19	Groves P 43	Pouton A 19 + 16	McDermott J 23 + 3	Lester J 23 + 3	Gallimore T 38 + 1	Lever M 35	Burnett W 7 + 3	Croudson S 2 + 1	Buckley A 8 + 5	Hamilton I 6	Clare D 13 + 4	Nicholls M 6	Bloomer M — + 2	Chapman B 1	Match No.
1	2[1]	3	4	5	6	7	8[2]	9	10[3]	11	12	13	14											1
1	2[3]	8[1]	4	5	6	7		9	10[2]	11	12	14	13	3										2
1		3		5	6	7	8	9[1]		11	12	2	10		4									3
1		3	12	5	6	7	8[2]	9		11	13	2	10		4[1]									4
1		3	4	5	6	7	8[1]	9		11		2	10		12									5
1	2[2]	10	4	5	6	7	8	9	13	11	12			3[1]										6
1		3[2]	4	5	6	7	12	9[1]	13	11	8		10	2										7
1	12	3[3]	4[1]	5	6	7		9[2]	13	11	8		10	2		14								8
1	2	8[3]		5	6	7	12	9[1]		11	13		10	3	4[2]			15						9
1	2			5	6	7		9		11	8		10	3	4									10
1	2	8[1]		5	6	7		9	13	11	12		10	3	4[2]									11
1	2			5	6	7	12	9[2]	13	11			10	3	4[1]			8						12
1	2	8		5				9		11	7		10	3	6	4								13
1	2	8	9[3]	5	12		13		14	11	7		10	3[2]	6	4[1]								14
1	2	8[3]			6		12	9[2]	13	11	7		10	3	5	4[1]	14							15
1	2	8		5	6			9[1]		11	12		10	3	4				7					16
1	2	8		5[2]		7		9		11	12		10	3	6	13	4[1]							17
1	2	11	12		6	7[1]		9[3]	14			13	10	3	5			8[2]		4				18
1	2	11			6	7	12	9					10	3	5	13		8[1]		4[2]				19
1	2	11			6	7	12	9					10	3	5			8[1]		4				20
1	2	4	12		6[3]	7		9[1]	13	11			10	3	5	14		8[2]						21
	12		9	4	6[2]	7			14	11	10[3]	2	13	3	5		1	8[1]						22
	12	8	9	4	6[2]	7				11	10[3]	2[1]	13	3	5	14	1							23
1			9	4	6[3]	7[1]	12		13	11	8	2	10[2]	3	5	14								24
1				4	6	7	12[2]	9	13	11		2	10	3	5			8[1]						25
1	8[2]			4	6	7		9		11	12	2	10	3	5[1]					13				26
1				4	6	7	8[1]	9	13	11	12	2	10	3	5[2]									27
1				4	6	7	8	9[2]	13	11	12	2	10[1]	3	5									28
1	12			4	6	7	8[2]	9		11		2	10[1]	3	5					13				29
1	12	3		4	6	7	8[2]	9		11		2	10[1]		5					13				30
1	12			4	6	7	8[3]	9	13	11		2	10	3[1]	5			14						31
1	12	3[1]		4	6	7		9[2]		11	8	2	10		5					13				32
1		3		4	6	7	8			11	12	2			5					10[1]	9			33
1	12			4	6	7	8[3]		13	11		2[1]		3	5			14		10[2]	9			34
1				4	6	7	12			11		2		3	5					10[1]	9			35
1	2		12	4	6	7			13	11	8			3[2]	5					10[1]	9			36
1				4	6	7	12			11		2		3	5					10[1]	9			37
1				4[1]	6	7	8		12	11		2	10	3	5						9			38
1	2			4[2]	6	7	8		12	11				3	5					10[1]	9	13		39
1	12	11		4	6	7		9[4]	13		8	2[1]		3	5					10				40
1	2	11	12	4	6	7		9	13		8			3[1]	5					10[2]				41
1	2	11	12	4	6	7		9			8			3	5					10[1]				42
1	2[3]	11[1]	10	4	6	7	12	9	13		8[2]			3	5	14								43
1	12	11[2]		4	6	7		9	13		8	2	10[3]	3[1]	5							14		44
1				4	6	7[2]	12	9[3]		11		2			5	13		8		10[1]		14	3	45
1	8			4	6	7	12	9		11		2		3	5					10[1]				46

Worthington Cup

First Round	Carlisle U	(a)	0-0
		(h)	6-0
Second Round	Leyton Orient	(h)	4-1
		(a)	0-1
Third Round	Leicester C	(a)	0-2

FA Cup

Third Round	Stockport Co	(h)	3-2
Fourth Round	Bolton W	(h)	0-2

Division 3 — **HALIFAX TOWN**

FOUNDATION

The real pioneer behind the setting up of the club was Mr A. E. Jones, who, using the *nom de plume* 'Old Sport', wrote to the *Halifax Evening Courier*. His letter suggesting a club be set up and inviting public opinion was published on 20 April 1911. A public meeting was held at the Saddle Hotel on 23 May 1911, whereafter Dr A. H. Muir became the club's first president and Joe McClelland its first secretary. Mr Jones proposed the following: "That this meeting of townsmen of Halifax heartily approves of the establishment of a town's Association football club on the basis of scheme 1 (the formation of a limited company) and pledges itself to adopt every legitimate means to that end". Mr Charles Deantry seconded the motion and the resolution was carried unanimously. The chairman asked for a show of hands of those willing to become guarantors of £1. There was an immediate response from 46 of the assembly.

The Shay Stadium, Shaw Hill, Halifax HX1 2YS.
Telephone: (01422) 345 543.
Fax: (01422) 349 487.
Souvenir Shop: (01422) 353 423.
ClubCall: 09068 121 649.
Ground Capacity: 9900.
Record Attendance: 36,885 v Tottenham H, FA Cup 5th rd, 15 February 1953.
Record Receipts: £36,267 v Bradford C, Worthington Cup, 2nd rd, 1st leg, 15 September 1998.
Pitch Measurements: 110yd × 70yd.
President: Robert Holmes.
Vice-Presidents: Jack Haymer and Bill King.
Chairman: S. J. Brown.
Directors: R. Crabtree, D. Tait, R. F. Walker.
General Manager: Tony Kniveton.
Manager: Mark Lillis.
Assistant Manager: Peter Butler.
Physio: Sarah Scott.
Youth Team Coach: Steve Thornber.
Acting Secretary: Mike Riley.

LATEST SEQUENCES

Longest Sequence of League Wins: 7, 22.2.64 – 21.3.64.
Longest Sequence of League Defeats: 8, 7.12.46 – 13.1.47.
Longest Sequence of League Draws: 7, 22.1.82 – 20.2.82.
Longest Sequence of Unbeaten League Matches: 17, 14.1.69 – 21.4.69.
Longest Sequence Without a League Win: 22, 26.8.78 – 10.2.79.

HONOURS

Football League: Division 3 best season: 3rd, 1970–71; Division 3 (N) – Runners-up 1934–35; Division 4: Runners-up 1968–69.

FA Cup: best season: 5th rd, 1933, 1953.

Football League Cup: best season: 4th rd, 1964.

Vauxhall Conference: Champions 1997–98.

Colours
Blue shirts with red trim, blue shorts, white stockings with blue band.

Change Colours
Green shirts with navy trim, green shorts, green stockings.

Year Formed: 1911.

Turned Professional: 1911.

Ltd Co.: 1911.

Club Nickname: 'The Shaymen'.

Previous Grounds: 1911, Sandhall; 1919, Exley; 1921, The Shay.

Club Sponsors: Nationwide.

First Football League Game: 27 August 1921, Division 3 (N), v Darlington (a) L 0-2 – Haldane; Hawley, Mackrill; Hall, Wellock, Challinor; Pinkey, Hetherington, Woods, Dent, Phipps.

Record League Victory: 6–0 v Bradford PA, Division 3 (N), 3 December 1955 – Johnson; Griffiths, Ferguson; Watson, Harris, Bell; Hampson (2), Baker (3), Watkinson (1), Capel, Lonsdale. 6–0 v Doncaster R, Division 4, 2 November 1976 – Gennoe; Trainer, Loska (Bradley), McGill, Dunleavy (1), Phelan, Hoy (2), Carroll (1), Bullock (1), Lawson (1), Johnston.

Record Cup Victory: 7–0 v Bishop Auckland, FA Cup 2nd rd (replay), 10 January 1967 – White; Russell, Bodell; Smith, Holt, Jeff Lee; Taylor (2), Hutchison (2), Parks (2), Atkins (1), McCarthy.

Record Defeat: 0–13 v Stockport Co, Division 3 (N), 6 January 1934.

Most League Points (2 for a win): 57, Division 4, 1968–69.

Most League Points (3 for a win): 66, Division 3, 1998–99.

Most League Goals: 83, Division 3 (N), 1957–58.

Highest League Scorer in Season: Albert Valentine, 34, Division 3 (N), 1934–35.

Most League Goals in Total Aggregate: Ernest Dixon, 129, 1922–30.

Most League Goals in One Match: 6, William Chambers v Hartlepools U, Division 3N, 7 April 1934.

Most Capped Player: None.

Most League Appearances: John Pickering, 367, 1965–74.

Youngest League Player: Robert Herbert, 16 years 13 days v Brighton & HA, 11 September 1999.

Record Transfer Fee Received: £350,000 from Fulham for Geoff Horsfield, October 1998.

Record Transfer Fee Paid: £150,000 to Scarborough for Chris Tate, July 1999.

Football League Record: 1921 Original Member of Division 3 (N); 1958–63 Division 3; 1963–69 Division 4; 1969–76 Division 3; 1976–92 Division 4; 1992–93 Division 3; 1993–98 Vauxhall Conference; 1998– Division 3.

MANAGERS

A. M. Ricketts 1911–12
(Secretary-Manager)
Joe McClelland 1912–30
Alec Raisbeck 1930–36
Jimmy Thomson 1936–47
Jack Breedon 1947–50
William Wootton 1951–52
Gerald Henry 1952–54
Willie Watson 1954–56
Billy Burnikell 1956
Harry Hooper 1957–62
Willie Watson 1964–66
Vic Metcalfe 1966–67
Alan Ball Snr 1967–70
George Kirby 1970–71
Ray Henderson 1971–72
George Mulhall 1972–74
Johnny Quinn 1974–76
Alan Ball Snr 1976–77
Jimmy Lawson 1977–78
George Kirby 1978–81
Mick Bullock 1981–84
Mick Jones 1984–86
Bill Ayre 1986–90
Jim McCalliog 1990–91
John McGrath 1991–92
Peter Wragg 1992–93
John Bird 1993–95
John Carroll 1996
George Mulhall 1996–98
Kieran O'Regan 1998–99
Mark Lillis June 1999–

TEN YEAR LEAGUE RECORD

		P	W	D	L	F	A	Pts	Pos
1989-90	Div 4	46	12	13	21	57	65	49	23
1990-91	Div 4	46	12	10	24	59	79	46	22
1991-92	Div 4	42	10	8	24	34	75	38	20
1992-93	Div 3	42	9	9	24	45	68	36	22
1993-94	Conf	42	13	16	13	55	49	55	13
1994-95	Conf	42	17	12	13	68	54	63	8
1995-96	Conf	42	13	13	16	49	63	52	15
1996-97	Conf	42	12	12	18	55	74	48	19
1997-98	Conf	42	25	12	5	74	43	87	1
1998-99	Div 3	46	17	15	14	58	56	66	10

DID YOU KNOW ?

At the start of the 1912-13 season, Halifax Town signed England international centre-foward Fred Pentland from Middlesbrough. They reached the first round proper of the FA Cup and Pentland ended the season with 22 goals.

HALIFAX TOWN 1999–2000 LEAGUE RECORD

Match No.	Date	Venue	Opponents	Result	H/T Score	Lg. Pos.	Goalscorers	Attendance
1	Aug 7	H	Darlington	L	0-1	0-0	18		3721
2	14	A	Hartlepool U	W	2-0	0-0	11	Stoneman [55], Murphy S [75]	2719
3	21	H	Plymouth Arg	L	0-1	0-0	16		2431
4	28	A	Leyton Orient	L	0-1	0-1	19		3703
5	31	H	Torquay U	W	2-0	2-0	—	Tate [18], Power [45]	1981
6	Sept 3	A	Rochdale	W	1-0	1-0	—	Mitchell [29]	4198
7	11	H	Brighton & HA	W	2-1	0-0	9	Paterson [71], Tate [90]	2532
8	18	A	Southend U	L	1-4	0-3	10	Stoneman [48]	4533
9	25	H	Carlisle U	W	5-2	3-1	7	Paterson 3 (2 pens) [32 (p), 40, 68 (p)], Painter [42], Stoneman [65]	2545
10	Oct 2	A	Shrewsbury T	D	0-0	0-0	9		2307
11	9	A	Macclesfield T	W	2-0	1-0	5	Rowe [12], Paterson [69]	2185
12	16	H	Peterborough U	W	2-1	1-0	3	Tate [23], Paterson (pen) [61]	3292
13	19	H	York C	L	0-2	0-2	—		2963
14	23	A	Carlisle U	D	1-1	1-0	6	Rowe [32]	2593
15	Nov 2	H	Cheltenham T	D	1-1	1-0	—	Painter [25]	1956
16	5	A	Swansea C	L	1-3	1-2	—	Tate [42]	3357
17	12	H	Exeter C	W	1-0	0-0	6	Bradshaw [76]	2440
18	23	A	Hull C	W	1-0	1-0	—	Painter [7]	6067
19	27	H	Mansfield T	L	0-1	0-0	8		2322
20	Dec 4	A	Darlington	L	0-4	0-3	10		4581
21	11	H	Rotherham U	D	0-0	0-0	9		2538
22	18	A	Chester C	L	1-2	0-2	11	Potter [78]	2037
23	26	H	Lincoln C	W	3-0	1-0	11	Cullen [12], Mitchell [15], Painter [87]	2371
24	28	A	Barnet	W	1-0	1-0	8	Cullen [3]	2450
25	Jan 3	H	Northampton T	D	2-2	1-1	9	Paterson (pen) [7], Cullen [90]	3001
26	8	A	Rotherham U	W	1-0	0-0	7	Potter [73]	4450
27	15	H	Hartlepool U	D	1-1	0-1	8	Cullen (pen) [86]	3546
28	22	A	Plymouth Arg	D	1-1	1-0	8	Painter [54]	4841
29	29	H	Leyton Orient	L	0-2	0-1	9		2655
30	Feb 5	A	Torquay U	L	0-4	0-2	11		1856
31	12	H	Rochdale	L	0-2	0-1	14		3504
32	19	A	Mansfield T	W	2-0	1-0	12	Painter [44], Cullen [50]	2476
33	26	H	Southend U	D	0-0	0-0	12		2068
34	Mar 4	A	Brighton & HA	L	1-2	1-0	14	Wilder [20]	5311
35	7	H	Swansea C	L	0-1	0-1	—		1657
36	11	A	Cheltenham T	L	0-3	0-1	16		3478
37	18	H	Hull C	L	0-1	0-0	17		2519
38	21	A	Exeter C	L	0-1	0-1	—		1652
39	25	A	Lincoln C	D	1-1	1-1	17	Jones [21]	3028
40	Apr 1	H	Chester C	L	0-1	0-0	18		2431
41	8	A	Northampton T	W	4-3	2-3	17	Painter [2], Stoneman [31], Middleton [51], Kerrigan [90]	5207
42	15	H	Barnet	L	1-2	1-1	17	Painter [35]	1734
43	22	A	Peterborough U	L	1-2	0-0	17	Kerrigan [47]	7194
44	24	H	Shrewsbury T	W	2-1	1-0	17	Tretton (og) [45], Kerrigan [90]	2123
45	29	A	York C	L	0-2	0-0	17		3079
46	May 6	H	Macclesfield T	L	0-1	0-0	18		2007

Final League Position: 18

GOALSCORERS

League (44): Painter 8, Paterson 7 (4 pens), Cullen 5 (1 pen), Stoneman 4, Tate 4, Kerrigan 3, Mitchell 2, Potter 2, Rowe 2, Bradshaw 1, Jones 1, Middleton 1, Murphy S 1, Power 1, Wilder 1, own goal 1.
Worthington Cup (1): Gaughan 1.
FA Cup (3): Mitchell 1, Paterson 1, Tate 1.

Adamson C 7	Russell M 3 + 4	Jules M 38 + 4	Mitchell G 45	Stoneman P 36 + 1	Sertori M 5	Paterson J 37 + 3	Gaughan S 29 + 9	Tate C 18	Painter R 38 + 4	Butler P 30	Hulme K 2 + 1	Jackson J — + 1	Murphy S 10 + 5	Power L 3 + 4	Newton C 4 + 4	Parks T 1	Bradshaw M 17 + 8	Stansfield J 10 + 2	Herbert R 1 + 3	Butler L 38	Rowe R 7 + 2	Clarke M 8 + 11	Wilder C 31	Lucas R 10 + 2	Holt G — + 4	Williams M 2 + 1	Reilly A 15 + 5	Potter L 13 + 6	Cullen J 11	Stamp D 5	Fitzpatrick 12 + 6	Middleton C 10	Richards I 5 + 1	Kerrigan S 7	Jones G 8	Clarke C — + 1	Match No.
1	2	3	4	5	6	7[1]	8	9	10[2]	11	12	13																									1
1		3	4	5	6	7	8	9	10	11							2																				2
1	12	3	4[2]	5	6	7	8	9	10	11[3]							2[1]	13	14																		3
	12	3	4	5[1]	6	7	8[2]	9	14	11					10		2[3]	13	1																		4
1	2	3	4		6	7		9		11					10		8	5																			5
1	2[2]	3	4	5		7	8	9	12	11							10[1]	6[3]		13	14																6
1		3	4[2]	5		7	8	9	10[1]								6	12	11	2	13																7
1		3	4	5		7	8	9	10								6	12	11[1]	2																	8
	12	3[1]	4	5		7	8	9	10								6	13		2			1				11[2]										9
		3	4	5		7	8	9	10[1]	11							12			2			1	6[2]			13										10
		3	4	5		7	8	9	10	11[1]							12			2			1	6[2]			13										11
		3	4	5		7	8	9	10	11										2			1	6													12
	12	3	4	5		7	8	9	10[2]	11							13			2[1]			1	6[3]			14										13
			4	5		7	8	9[1]	10	11							3						1	6	12	2											14
		3	4	5		7	8	9	10	11													1	12	6[1]	2											15
		3	4	5			8[3]	9[2]	10	11							7[1]						1	12	6	2	14	13									16
		3[1]	4	5		7			10[2]	11			13				12						1	8[3]	9	2	6	14									17
			4			7	8		10	11							3	5					1	9[1]		2	6	12									18
		3[1]	4			7	8		10	11			12				5						1	9[2]		2	6[3]	13	14								19
		3	4	5		7[1]	8	9	10	11							6						1		12		13	2[2]									20
		3	4	5			12	9	10	11[1]										1	8		2			6	7										21
		3	4	5[2]		8[1]		12	11				14	13						1	9[2]		2			10	6	7									22
		3	4			7	12	8	11[1]								5			1			2			9	6	10									23
		3	4			7	12	8	11				13	5						1			14	2		9[2]	6[2]	10[1]									24
		3[2]	4	12		7		8	11				13	5[1]						1			14	2		9	6[2]	10									25
			4	5		7	12	8[2]	11					3						1			13	2		9	6	10[1]									26
		3	4	5		7[2]	12	8	11[3]				13							1			2			9	6	10[1]									27
		3	4	5		7	12	8	11[5]				13							1			2			9[2]	6	10									28
		3	4	5		7		8[2]	11[5]				12							1			13	2		9	6	10									29
		3	4	5		7	6	8					12							1			13	2		9[2]	11[1]	10									30
		3		5		12		8	11[2]				13							1	7		2	4		9[1]	6	10									31
		3	4	5				8	11	6										1			2			7			10	9							32
		3	4	5		7	8		10[2]				6[1]							1			2	11		13	12	9									33
		3	4	5			8		10[3]	11			6[2]							1			2	7[1]		13	12	9	14								34
		3	4	5		12	8		10[2]	11[1]			6[3]							1			2	14		13	9	7									35
		3	4	5[1]		7	8	12		6										1	13		2	11		14	9[2]	10[3]									36
		3	4			7[1]	8	9		5										1	2		6			10	12	11									37
		3	4			7	8	9[2]		5	13									1	2		6[1]	12		10		11									38
		3	4			7				5										1	2		9	12		11	6	8[1]	10								39
		3	4			7				5										1	2		9[1]	12		11	6	8	10								40
	12		4	5		7	13	9[1]		3										1	2			11			6[2]	8	10								41
	12		4	5		7	13	9		3										1	2[1]		14	11[2]			6	8[3]	10								42
			4	5		7	12	9		3										1	2		13	11			6[1]	8[2]	10								43
	12		4	5[1]		7[2]	6	9[1]		3										1	2		13	11			8	10	14								44
	12		4	5		6	9[1]			3[3]			14							1	2		7	13			11	8[2]	10								45
	2		4	5		12	6[3]			3			7[1]	1									9	8[2]			13	11	14					10			46

Worthington Cup
First Round   WBA   (h) 0-0
                    (a) 1-5

FA Cup
First Round   Doncaster R   (a) 2-0
Second Round Reading   (a) 1-1
                        (h) 0-1

Division 3   HARTLEPOOL UNITED

FOUNDATION

The inspiration for the launching of Hartlepool United was the West Hartlepool club which won the FA Amateur Cup in 1904–05. They had been in existence since 1881 and their Cup success led in 1908 to the formation of the new professional concern which first joined the North-Eastern League. In those days they were Hartlepools United and won the Durham Senior Cup in their first two seasons.

Victoria Park, Clarence Road, Hartlepool TS24 8BZ.

Telephone: (01429) 272 584.

Commercial Dept: (01429) 272 584.

Fax: (01429) 863 007.

Website: www.hartlepoolunited.co.uk

Email: info@hartlepoolunited.co.uk

Football in the Community: (01429) 862 595.

Ground Capacity: 7229.

Record Attendance: 17,426 v Manchester U, FA Cup 3rd rd, 5 January 1957.

Record Receipts: £42,300 v Tottenham H, Rumbelows Cup 2nd rd, 2nd leg, 9 October 1990.

Pitch Measurements: 110yd × 75yd.

Chairman: K. Hodcroft.

Directors: H. Hornsey, I. Prescott, M. Downey.

Manager: Chris Turner.

Coach: Colin West.

Youth Coach: Mick Smith.

Physio: Gary Hinchley.

Commercial Manager: John Breward.

Secretary: Maureen Smith.

Football in the Community Officer: Keith Nobbs.

Safety Officer: Maurice Russell.

LATEST SEQUENCES

Longest Sequence of League Wins: 7, 1.4.68 – 26.4.68.

Longest Sequence of League Defeats: 8, 27.1.93 – 27.2.93.

Longest Sequence of League Draws: 4, 27.2.99 – 20.3.99.

Longest Sequence of Unbeaten League Matches: 17, 24.2.68 – 10.8.68.

Longest Sequence Without a League Win: 18, 9.1.93 – 3.4.93.

HONOURS

Football League: Division 3 (N) – Runners-up 1956–57.

FA Cup: best season: 4th rd, 1955, 1978, 1989, 1993.

Football League Cup, best season: 4th rd, 1975.

Colours
Royal blue and white striped shirts.

Change Colours
Yellow with blue trim.

Year Formed: 1908.

Turned Professional: 1908.

Ltd Co.: 1908.

Previous Names: 1908, Hartlepools United; 1968, Hartlepool; 1977, Hartlepool United.

Club Nickname: 'The Pool'.

First Football League Game: 27 August 1921, Division 3 (N), v Wrexham (a) W 2–0 – Gill; Thomas, Crilly; Dougherty, Hopkins, Short; Kessler, Mulholland (1), Lister (1), Robertson, Donald.

Record League Victory: 10–1 v Barrow, Division 4, 4 April 1959 – Oakley; Cameron, Waugh; Johnson, Moore, Anderson; Scott (1), Langland (1), Smith (3), Clark (2), Luke (2), (1 og).

Record Cup Victory: 6–0 v North Shields, FA Cup 1st rd, 30 November 1946 – Heywood; Brown, Gregory; Spelman, Lambert, Jones; Price, Scott (2), Sloan (4), Moses, McMahon.

Record Defeat: 1–10 v Wrexham, Division 4, 3 March 1962.

Most League Points (2 for a win): 60, Division 4, 1967–68.

Most League Points (3 for a win): 82, Division 4, 1990–91.

Most League Goals: 90, Division 3 (N), 1956–57.

Highest League Scorer in Season: William Robinson, 28, Division 3 (N), 1927–28; Joe Allon, 28, Division 4, 1990–91.

Most League Goals in Total Aggregate: Ken Johnson, 98, 1949–64.

Most League Goals in One Match: 5, Harry Simmons v Wigan Borough, Division 3N, 1 January 1931; 5, Bobby Folland v Oldham Ath, Division 3N, 15 April 1961.

Most Capped Player: Ambrose Fogarty, 1 (11), Republic of Ireland.

Most League Appearances: Wattie Moore, 447, 1948–64.

Youngest League Player: John McGovern, 16 years 205 days v Bradford C, 21 May 1966.

Record Transfer Fee Received: £300,000 from Chelsea for Joe Allon, August 1991.

Record Transfer Fee Paid: £60,000 to Barnsley for Andy Saville, March 1992.

Football League Record: 1921 Original Member of Division 3 (N); 1958–68 Division 4; 1968–69 Division 3; 1969–91 Division 4; 1991–92 Division 3; 1992–94 Division 2; 1994– Division 3.

MANAGERS

Alfred Priest 1908–12
Percy Humphreys 1912–13
Jack Manners 1913–20
Cecil Potter 1920–22
David Gordon 1922–24
Jack Manners 1924–27
Bill Norman 1927–31
Jack Carr 1932–35
    (had been Player-Coach since 1931)
Jimmy Hamilton 1935–43
Fred Westgarth 1943–57
Ray Middleton 1957–59
Bill Robinson 1959–62
Allenby Chilton 1962–63
Bob Gurney 1963–64
Alvan Williams 1964–65
Geoff Twentyman 1965
Brian Clough 1965–67
Angus McLean 1967–70
John Simpson 1970–71
Len Ashurst 1971–74
Ken Hale 1974–76
Billy Horner 1976–83
Johnny Duncan 1983
Mike Docherty 1983
Billy Horner 1984–86
John Bird 1986–88
Bobby Moncur 1988–89
Cyril Knowles 1989–91
Alan Murray 1991–93
Viv Busby 1993
John MacPhail 1993–94
David McCreery 1994–95
Keith Houchen 1995–96
Mick Tait 1996–99
Chris Turner March 1999–

TEN YEAR LEAGUE RECORD

		P	W	D	L	F	A	Pts	Pos
1989-90	Div 4	46	15	10	21	66	88	55	19
1990-91	Div 4	46	24	10	12	67	48	82	3
1991-92	Div 3	46	18	11	17	57	57	65	11
1992-93	Div 2	46	14	12	20	42	60	54	16
1993-94	Div 2	46	9	9	28	41	87	36	23
1994-95	Div 3	42	11	10	21	43	69	43	18
1995-96	Div 3	46	12	13	21	47	67	49	20
1996-97	Div 3	46	14	9	23	53	66	51	20
1997-98	Div 3	46	12	23	11	61	53	59	17
1998-99	Div 3	46	13	12	21	52	65	51	22

DID YOU KNOW ?

On 18 November 1967, injury-hit Hartlepool United were forced to field goalkeeper Ken Simpkins as a forward. He scored the winning goal in a 3-2 victory at Port Vale.

HARTLEPOOL UNITED 1999–2000 LEAGUE RECORD

Match No.	Date	Venue	Opponents	Result	H/T Score	Lg. Pos.	Goalscorers	Attendance
1	Aug 7	A	Peterborough U	L	1-2	1-1	13	Jones [39]	5886
2	14	H	Halifax T	L	0-2	0-0	22		2719
3	21	A	Carlisle U	W	3-0	1-0	15	Freestone 2 [3, 52], Miller [58]	4033
4	28	H	Cheltenham T	L	0-1	0-1	18		2390
5	31	A	Shrewsbury T	D	0-0	0-0	—		1803
6	Sept 4	H	Southend U	L	1-2	0-0	19	Stephenson [46]	1980
7	11	A	Northampton T	L	1-2	1-0	23	Miller [24]	4724
8	18	H	Plymouth Arg	W	3-0	2-0	19	Freestone [4], Lee [13], Henderson [88]	2242
9	25	A	Leyton Orient	L	1-2	1-2	22	Stephenson [14]	3889
10	Oct 2	H	Darlington	W	2-0	0-0	20	Shilton [46], Fitzpatrick [68]	3957
11	9	H	Hull C	W	2-0	0-0	14	Miller [50], Freestone [90]	3114
12	16	A	Mansfield T	W	3-2	1-1	13	Shilton [14], Stephenson [51], Miller (pen) [59]	2612
13	19	A	Rotherham U	L	0-3	0-3	—		3340
14	23	H	Leyton Orient	W	1-0	0-0	16	Henderson [49]	2397
15	Nov 2	H	Barnet	W	3-0	1-0	—	Miller 3 [27, 47, 85]	2290
16	6	A	Brighton & HA	L	0-1	0-1	13		5746
17	13	H	Chester C	W	1-0	1-0	—	Miller [35]	2266
18	23	H	Torquay U	D	0-0	0-0	—		2080
19	27	A	Macclesfield T	D	3-3	0-2	13	Clark 2 (1 pen) [47 (p), 90], Lee [84]	2351
20	Dec 4	H	Peterborough U	W	1-0	1-0	9	Jones [20]	2404
21	11	H	Swansea C	L	0-1	0-1	10		2397
22	18	A	Exeter C	W	2-1	1-0	9	Jones 2 [31, 78]	2261
23	26	H	York C	W	2-1	1-0	6	Henderson 2 [31, 73]	4668
24	28	A	Lincoln C	W	2-1	1-0	5	Clark [9], Miller [53]	3480
25	Jan 3	H	Rochdale	W	3-2	1-1	5	Miller (pen) [5], Jones [48], Clark [56]	4498
26	8	A	Swansea C	L	1-2	1-0	5	Henderson [40]	7163
27	15	A	Halifax T	D	1-1	1-0	5	Jones [24]	3546
28	22	H	Carlisle U	W	1-0	0-0	5	Miller [53]	3530
29	29	A	Cheltenham T	L	1-2	0-2	5	Lee [86]	3630
30	Feb 5	H	Shrewsbury T	W	1-0	0-0	6	Boyd [90]	2933
31	12	A	Southend U	L	1-2	1-1	6	Lee [45]	3337
32	19	H	Macclesfield T	L	1-4	1-3	8	Miller [39]	2823
33	26	A	Plymouth Arg	D	1-1	0-1	8	Shilton [59]	3917
34	Mar 4	H	Northampton T	W	2-1	2-1	7	Stephenson [6], Lee [29]	2878
35	7	H	Brighton & HA	D	0-0	0-0	—		2734
36	11	A	Barnet	D	1-1	0-0	7	Coppinger [73]	2925
37	18	H	Torquay U	W	2-0	1-0	6	Stephenson [10], Lee [77]	2766
38	21	A	Chester C	D	1-1	0-1	—	Fitzpatrick [78]	1816
39	25	A	York C	L	1-2	0-1	8	Coppinger [53]	4079
40	Apr 1	H	Exeter C	W	2-1	0-0	8	Arnison [62], Clark [63]	2668
41	8	A	Rochdale	L	0-2	0-1	8		2332
42	15	H	Lincoln C	W	2-0	2-0	8	Henderson [6], Miller [39]	2777
43	22	H	Mansfield T	W	1-0	0-0	7	Henderson [55]	3473
44	24	A	Darlington	D	1-1	1-0	7	Miller [45]	6746
45	29	H	Rotherham U	L	1-2	1-1	8	Clark [21]	4673
46	May 6	A	Hull C	W	3-0	3-0	7	Lee [2], Coppinger [8], Henderson [37]	7620

Final League Position: 7

GOALSCORERS

League (60): Miller 14 (2 pens), Henderson 8, Lee 7, Clark 6 (1 pen), Jones 6, Stephenson 5, Freestone 4, Coppinger 3, Shilton 3, Fitzpatrick 2, Arnison 1, Boyd 1.
Worthington Cup (3): Di Lella 1, Miller 1, Stephenson 1.
FA Cup (1): Jones 1.

Dibble A 6	Knowles D 43 + 1	Perkins C 7 + 1	Barron M 40	Lee G 38	Ingram D 6 + 1	Di Lella G 3	Miller T 44	Jones G 30 + 3	Freestone C 15 + 12	Stephenson P 46	Clark I 34 + 10	Strodder G 28 + 1	Midgley C 2 + 15	Henderson K 23 + 12	Tennebo T 6 + 5	Westwood C 33 + 4	Hollund M 40	Vindheim R 7	Fitzpatrick L 16 + 8	Shilton S 16 + 5	Boyd A — + 4	Mason G 5 + 1	McAvoy A 5 + 11	Coppinger J 6 + 4	West C — + 1	Arnison P 5 + 3	Beavers P 2 + 5	Match No
1	2	3	4	5	6		7^1	8	9	10	11	12																1
1	2	3	4^2	6			7^1	8	9	10^3	11	12	5	13	14													2
1	2	4^1	6	12			8	9^2	10^3	11	3	5	13	14	7													3
1	2^1	12	4	6	8^2		9	10	11	3	5	13	14	7^3														4
	3	6	8	9	11	2	5	10		7	4	1																5
	3	4	6	8^1	9^2	10	11	2	5	12	13	7		1														6
12	3	4	6	8	13	10^2	11	2^3	5^1	14	7	9	1															7
	2	3	4^2	5	8	9	10^1	11^3	7	12	13	1	6	14														8
	2	3^4	4	5	8	9^1	10	7^2	11	12	1	6	13	14														9
	2	4	5	8	9	11	12	10^1	13	1	6	3^2	7															10
	2	4	5	8	9^1	12	11	10	13	1	6	7^2	3															11
	2	4	5	8	9	12	11	13	10^1	1	6	7^2	3															12
1	2	4	5	8	9^1	12	11	13	10		6	7^2	3															13
	2	4	5	8	12	9^1	11^3	13	10	14	1	6	7^2	3														14
	2	4	5	8^2	9	10^1	11	7^2	12	13	3	14	1															15
	2	4	5	8	10	11^3	7	12^2	9^1	6	1	14	3	13														16
	2	4	5	8	9	10^2	11	12	13	6	1	7^1	3															17
	2	4	5	8	9	12	11	3	10^1	6	1		7															18
	2	4	5	9^1	12	11	3	13	10	14	6	1	7^2	8^3														19
	2	4	5	8	9	11	3	10^1	6	1	7	12																20
	2	4	5	8	9	11	3^2	12	6	1	13	7^1	10															21
	2	4	5	8	9^1	12	11	3	13	7^2	6	1	10															22
	2	4	8^3	9^1	12	11	3	5	7	6	1	13	10^2	14														23
	2	4	8	9	11	3	5	7^1	6	1	10	12																24
	2	4	9^2	12	11	7	5	13	10^1	6	1	3^3	14															25
	2	4	9	12	11	7	5	10^1	6	1	3																	26
	2	7	4	9^i	11	3	5	10	6	1	12																	27
	2^2	4	7	9	11	3^1	5	13	10^3	6	1	12	14															28
	2	4	6	9^1	12	11^2	5	14	7	1	13	3	10^3															29
	2	4	6	9^3	11	12	5	7^2	1	10^1	3	14	13															30
	2	4	9^1	11	12	5	13	14	6	1	7^3	3	10^2															31
1	2	4	6	8	12	11	10	5	9^1	7^2	3	13																32
	2	4	6	9^2	11	12	5	7	1	10^1	3	13																33
	2	4	6	9^1	11	3	5	7	1	10	12																	34
	2	4	5	8	9^3	11	3	10^2	6	1	7^1	12	13	14														35
	2	4	6	8	11^3	3	5	9^2	12	7	1	10^1	13	14														36
	2	4	10	8	12	11	3	5	13	6	1	7^2	9^1															37
	2	4	10^2	8	12	11	3	5	13	6	1	7	9^1															38
	2	4	8	9^1	11	3	5	12	13	6	1	7^2	10^3	14														39
	2	4	8	9^2	11	3	5	12	6	1	7^3	10^1	14	13														40
	2	4	8	11	3^2	5	12	14	6	1	13	10^1	7	9^3														41
	2	4	10^3	8	11^1	3	5	9^2	6	1	12	13	7	14														42
	2	4	5	8	11	3	12^2	10^1	6	1	13	14	7	9^3														43
	2	4	10	8	11	3	5	9	6^1	1	7	12																44
	2^2	4	10^3	8	11	3	5	9	6	1	12	14	7^1	13														45
	2^3	4	10	8	11	3	5	12	9^2	6	1	13	7^1	14														46

Worthington Cup
First Round   Crewe Alex   (h) 3-3
                           (a) 0-1

FA Cup
First Round   Millwall   (h) 1-0
Second Round Hereford U   (a) 0-1

Division 1   **HUDDERSFIELD TOWN**

FOUNDATION

A meeting, attended largely by members of the Huddersfield & District FA, was held at the Imperial Hotel in 1906 to discuss the feasibility of establishing a football club in this rugby stronghold. However, it was not until a man with both the enthusiasm and the money to back the scheme came on the scene, that real progress was made. This benefactor was Mr Hilton Crowther and it was at a meeting at the Albert Hotel in 1908, that the club formally came into existence with a capital of £2,000 and joined the North-Eastern League.

The Alfred McAlpine Stadium, Leeds Rd, Huddersfield HD1 6PX.
Telephone: (01484) 484 100.
Fax: (01484) 484 101.
Ticket Office: (01484) 484 123.
Club Shop: (01484) 484 144.
ClubCall: 09068 121 635.
Ground Capacity: 24,500.
Record Attendance: 67,037 v Arsenal, FA Cup 6th rd, 27 February 1932 (at Leeds Road); 23,678 v Liverpool, FA Cup 3rd rd, 12 December 1999 (at Alfred McAlpine Stadium).
Record Receipts: £243,081 v Liverpool, FA Cup 3rd rd, 12 December 1999.
Pitch Measurements: 115yd × 76yd.
President: Lawrence Batley OBE.
Chairman: Ian Ayre.
Directors: B. Rubery, G. Rubery, T. Cherry, A. Tarrant.
Manager: Steve Bruce.
First Team Coach: John Deehan
Secretary: Ann Hough.
Commercial Director: Brian Hewitt.
Physio: John Dickens.
Stadium Manager: Phil Armitage.

LATEST SEQUENCES

Longest Sequence of League Wins: 11, 5.4.20 – 4.9.20.
Longest Sequence of League Defeats: 7, 8.10.55 – 19.11.55.
Longest Sequence of League Draws: 6, 3.3.87 – 3.4.87.
Longest Sequence of Unbeaten League Matches: 27, 24.1.25 – 17.10.25.
Longest Sequence Without a League Win: 22, 4.12.71 – 29.4.72.

HONOURS

Football League: Division 1 – Champions 1923–24, 1924–25, 1925–26; Runners-up 1926–27, 1927–28, 1933–34; Division 2 – Champions 1969–70; Runners-up 1919–20, 1952–53; Promoted from Division 2 1994–95 (play-offs); Division 4 – Champions 1979–80.

FA Cup: Winners 1922; Runners-up 1920, 1928, 1930, 1938.

Football League Cup: Semi-final 1968.

Autoglass Trophy: Runners-up 1994.

Colours

Blue and white striped shirts, white shorts, white stockings with single navy hoop.

Change Colours

Red shirts, blue shorts, red stockings.

Year Formed: 1908.

Turned Professional: 1908.

Ltd Co.: 1908.

Club Nickname: 'The Terriers'.

Previous Ground: 1908, Leeds Road; 1994, The Alfred McAlpine Stadium.

First Football League Game: 3 September 1910, Division 2, v Bradford PA (a) W 1–0 – Mutch; Taylor, Morris; Beaton, Hall, Bartlett; Blackburn, Wood, Hamilton (1), McCubbin, Jee.

Record League Victory: 10–1 v Blackpool, Division 1, 13 December 1930 – Turner; Goodall, Spencer; Redfern, Wilson, Campbell; Bob Kelly (1), McLean (4), Robson (3), Davies (1), Smailes (1).

Record Cup Victory: 7–0 v Lincoln U, FA Cup 1st rd, 16 November 1991 – Clarke; Trevitt, Charlton, Donovan (2), Mitchell, Doherty, O'Regan (1), Stapleton (1) (Wright), Roberts (2), Onuora (1), Barnett (Ireland).

Record Defeat: 1–10 v Manchester C, Division 2, 7 November 1987.

Most League Points (2 for a win): 66, Division 4, 1979–80.

Most League Points (3 for a win): 82, Division 3, 1982–83.

Most League Goals: 101, Division 4, 1979–80.

Highest League Scorer in Season: Sam Taylor, 35, Division 2, 1919–20; George Brown, 35, Division 1, 1925–26.

Most League Goals in Total Aggregate: George Brown, 142, 1921–29; Jimmy Glazzard, 142, 1946–56.

Most League Goals in One Match: 5, Dave Mangnall v Derby Co, Division 1, 21 November 1931; 5, Alf Lythgoe v Blackburn R, Division 1, 13 April 1935.

Most Capped Player: Jimmy Nicholson, 31 (41), Northern Ireland.

Most League Appearances: Billy Smith, 520, 1914–34.

Youngest League Player: Denis Law, 16 years 303 days v Notts Co, 24 December 1956.

Record Transfer Fee Received: £2,700,000 from Sheffield W for Andy Booth, July 1996.

Record Transfer Fee Paid: £1,200,000 to Bristol R for Marcus Stewart, July 1996.

Football League Record: 1910 Elected to Division 2; 1920–52 Division 1; 1952–53 Division 2; 1953–56 Division 1; 1956–70 Division 2; 1970–72 Division 1; 1972–73 Division 2; 1973–75 Division 3; 1975–80 Division 4; 1980–83 Division 3; 1983–88 Division 2; 1988–92 Division 3; 1992–95 Division 2; 1995– Division 1.

MANAGERS

Fred Walker 1908–10
Richard Pudan 1910–12
Arthur Fairclough 1912–19
Ambrose Langley 1919–21
Herbert Chapman 1921–25
Cecil Potter 1925–26
Jack Chaplin 1926–29
Clem Stephenson 1929–42
David Steele 1943–47
George Stephenson 1947–52
Andy Beattie 1952–56
Bill Shankly 1956–59
Eddie Boot 1960–64
Tom Johnston 1964–68
Ian Greaves 1968–74
Bobby Collins 1974
Tom Johnston 1975–78
    (had been General Manager
    since 1975)
Mike Buxton 1978–86
Steve Smith 1986–87
Malcolm Macdonald 1987–88
Eoin Hand 1988–92
Ian Ross 1992–93
Neil Warnock 1993–95
Brian Horton 1995–97
Peter Jackson 1997–99
Steve Bruce June 1999–

TEN YEAR LEAGUE RECORD

		P	W	D	L	F	A	Pts	Pos
1989-90	Div 3	46	17	14	15	61	62	65	8
1990-91	Div 3	46	18	13	15	57	51	67	11
1991-92	Div 3	46	22	12	12	59	38	78	3
1992-93	Div 2	46	17	9	20	54	61	60	15
1993-94	Div 2	46	17	14	15	58	61	65	11
1994-95	Div 2	46	22	15	9	79	49	81	5
1995-96	Div 1	46	17	12	17	61	58	63	8
1996-97	Div 1	46	13	15	18	48	61	54	20
1997-98	Div 1	46	14	11	21	50	72	53	16
1998-99	Div 1	46	15	16	15	62	71	61	10

DID YOU KNOW?

Though not a regular goalscorer, England international wing-half Ken Willingham scored the club's fastest goal ten seconds after the start against Sunderland on 14 December 1935, the club he was to join ten years later.

HUDDERSFIELD TOWN 1999–2000 LEAGUE RECORD

Match No.	Date	Venue	Opponents	Result	H/T Score	Lg. Pos.	Goalscorers	Attendance
1	Aug 7	A	QPR	L 1-3	0-2	22	Wijnhard [65]	13,642
2	13	H	Blackburn R	W 3-2	1-0	—	Grayson (og) [26], Stewart [51], Edwards [90]	13,670
3	21	A	Tranmere R	L 0-1	0-1	18		6728
4	28	H	Crystal Palace	W 7-1	3-0	8	Beech [18], Wijnhard 3 [25,60,64], Irons [36], Stewart 2 [47,74]	10,656
5	30	A	Portsmouth	D 0-0	0-0	7		13,105
6	Sept 11	A	Wolverhampton W	W 1-0	0-0	5	Stewart (pen) [60]	20,385
7	18	H	Norwich C	W 1-0	0-0	4	Wijnhard [51]	12,823
8	25	A	Barnsley	L 2-4	1-1	6	Monkou [19], Stewart [71]	17,765
9	Oct 2	H	Sheffield U	W 4-1	2-0	6	Beech [14], Wijnhard [28], Stewart 2 [57,90]	14,238
10	9	H	Port Vale	D 2-2	2-0	6	Stewart (pen) [2], Irons [30]	11,885
11	16	A	Bolton W	L 0-1	0-1	7		16,603
12	19	A	Stockport Co	D 1-1	0-1	—	Sellars [89]	7305
13	23	H	Fulham	D 1-1	0-1	8	Wijnhard [75]	13,350
14	26	H	Barnsley	W 2-1	1-1	—	Wijnhard [13], Baldry [89]	15,764
15	30	A	Sheffield U	W 1-0	0-0	5	Dyson [51]	14,928
16	Nov 2	H	Ipswich T	W 3-1	1-1	—	Dyson [37], Beech [48], Stewart [57]	12,093
17	6	H	Swindon T	W 4-0	2-0	3	Beech [9], Thornley [35], Gorre 2 [57,63]	11,891
18	14	A	Nottingham F	W 3-1	2-1	3	Wijnhard 2 [22,63], Gray [34]	15,258
19	20	H	WBA	W 1-0	0-0	2	Gorre [55]	14,244
20	23	A	Walsall	L 0-2	0-2	—		5860
21	27	A	Manchester C	W 1-0	0-0	2	Beech [51]	32,936
22	Dec 4	H	QPR	W 1-0	1-0	1	Wijnhard [31]	13,027
23	18	H	Grimsby T	W 3-1	2-1	1	Wijnhard 2 [6,25], Stewart [63]	14,065
24	26	A	Crewe Alex	D 1-1	0-0	2	Beech [47]	8106
25	28	H	Charlton Ath	L 1-2	0-2	2	Stewart [80]	17,415
26	Jan 3	A	Birmingham C	L 0-1	0-1	5		19,558
27	15	A	Blackburn R	L 0-2	0-2	5		21,420
28	22	H	Tranmere R	W 1-0	1-0	5	Stewart [12]	12,653
29	29	A	Crystal Palace	D 2-2	2-0	5	Stewart 2 [34,41]	14,290
30	Feb 5	H	Portsmouth	L 0-1	0-0	5		12,753
31	12	A	Ipswich T	L 1-2	0-1	5	Gorre [56]	21,233
32	18	H	Manchester C	D 1-1	1-1	—	Wijnhard [32]	18,173
33	26	A	Norwich C	D 1-1	0-0	6	Vincent [65]	16,464
34	Mar 4	H	Wolverhampton W	W 2-0	2-0	6	Smith 2 [20,34]	17,214
35	7	A	Swindon T	L 0-2	0-1	—		4701
36	11	A	Walsall	D 1-1	0-0	6	Smith [78]	12,424
37	18	A	WBA	W 1-0	1-0	6	Smith [22]	15,484
38	21	H	Nottingham F	W 2-1	1-1	—	Beech [27], Holland [56]	12,893
39	25	H	Crewe Alex	W 3-0	1-0	5	Gray [14], Beech 2 [53,79]	14,014
40	Apr 1	A	Grimsby T	D 0-0	0-0	6		6993
41	8	H	Birmingham C	D 0-0	0-0	6		16,961
42	14	A	Charlton Ath	W 1-0	1-0	—	Wijnhard [25]	19,739
43	22	H	Bolton W	L 0-3	0-2	6		16,404
44	24	A	Port Vale	W 2-1	1-1	6	Vincent [6], Irons (pen) [54]	5828
45	29	H	Stockport Co	L 0-2	0-2	6		14,046
46	May 7	A	Fulham	L 0-3	0-1	8		13,728

Final League Position: 8

GOALSCORERS

League (62): Wijnhard 15, Stewart 14 (2 pens), Beech 9, Gorre 4, Smith 4, Irons 3 (1 pen), Dyson 2, Gray 2, Vincent 2, Baldry 1, Edwards 1, Holland 1, Monkou 1, Sellars 1, Thornley 1, own goal 1.
Worthington Cup (8): Irons 2, Beech 1, Gorre 1, Lucketti 1, Sellars 1, Stewart 1, Wijnhard 1.
FA Cup (0).

Vaesen N 46	Baker S 3	Vincent J 33 + 3	Armstrong C 37 + 2	Lucketti C 26	Irons K 39 + 1	Donis K 39 + 10	Beech C 34 + 1	Stewart M 29	Sellars S 23 + 11	Wijnhard C 45	Dyson J 22 + 6	Allison W — + 3	Thornley B 16 + 12	Edwards R 1 + 8	Baldry S 5 + 14	Monkou K 19	Horne B 6 + 8	Schofield D — + 2	Gorre D 26 + 2	Hodouto K 1 + 1	Jenkins S 33	Gray K 16 + 2	Edmondson D 2 + 3	May D 1	Smith M 10 + 2	Holland C 16 + 1	Facey D — + 2	Ngonge M — + 4	Armstrong A 4 + 2	Hay C 2 + 5	Heary T 1	Match No
1	3^4	4	5	6	7	8	9	10^3	11	12	13	14																				1
1	2	12	4^3	5	6	7^2	8^1	9	10	11	3		13	14																		2
1	2^2		4^1	5	6		8^3	9	10	11	3	12	7	13	14																	3
1		3	5	4^3		8	9	10^1	11	2	12	13	7			6^2	14															4
1		2	5	4		7^2	9^3	10	11	3	14	12	13			6	8^1															5
1		2	5	4	7^1		9	10	11^2	3						12	6	8	13													6
1		2	5	4	7	8	9^1	10	11	3^2						6			12	13												7
1		2	5	4^1	7		9	10	11	3^2	13					6	12		8													8
1	12	3	5	4		7	9	10	11	13						6			8^1	2^2												9
1		3	5	4	12	7	9	10^1	11							6			8	2												10
1		3	5^3	4	7^1	12	9	10^2	11	13						6			8	2	14											11
1	12	6		4	7	9	13	11	2^2	10			14				8^3		3^1	5												12
1		3	6	4	12	7	9	10	11	13						8^2			2^1	5												13
1		3		4	7^1	8	9	11	2	10	12								5	6												14
1		3	12	4	8	9^2		11	2	10	7					13			5^1	6												15
1		3		4	8	9		11	6	10	7								2^1	5	12											16
1		3		4	6	9^3	12	11	2	10^1	7^2	13				8				5	14											17
1		3		4	7	9	12	11	6	10						8^1			2	5												18
1		3	12	4	7	9		11	5	10						6			8^1	2												19
1		3		4	7	9	12	11	5^2	10^1						6			8	2	13											20
1		3		4	7	9	12	11		10						6			8^1	2	5											21
1		3	6	4		9	10	11	7^2	12	13								8^1	2	5											22
1		3		4		9	10^2	11	6	7^1	12					13			8	2	5											23
1		3	6		4	12	7	9^2	10^1	11	14					13			8	2		5^3										24
1		3	6^2		4	12	7	9		11	14	10^1				13			8	2		5^3										25
1		3	6		4	12	7	9	10^2	11	14					13			8^1	2		5^3										26
1		3	5		4	12	6	9	10^2	11						13	7^1		8^3	2	14											27
1		3	6		4		7	9		11	5					10			8	2												28
1		3	6		4	12	7^2	9	13	11^1	5					10			8	2												29
1		3	6		4^2	7				12	5		11			8^3	9		2^1						10	13	14					30
1			6		4^1				10	11	5	12	3			13	9^2		2						7	8						31
1		3	4	5	8				11	12						6			9	2^1					10	7						32
1		3	4	5	7^1				12	11			13			6			9	2					10^2	8						33
1		3	4	5	8^1				12	11			13	6^2	14				9	2					10^3	7						34
1		3	4	5	6				12	10^1	11		13						9	2					7	8^2						35
1		3	4	5	6				12	11^2	7^1		13						9	2					10	8						36
1		3	4	5		12	8^2			11^3			13						9^1	2	6				10	7		14				37
1	2		4	5		7^1	8			11	3		12	14						6					9^2	10		13^3				38
1	2		4	5	7	12	8			11^3	13					3			6^2					10			14	9^1				39
1		3	4	5	7^1	8				11	12					2			6						10			9^2	13			40
1		3	4	5			8		10^1	11^2	12						6			2					7		13	9^3	14			41
1		3	4	5	12		8		10^1	11	13						6			2					7			9^2				42
1		4^1		5			8		10^3	11	12						6			2					13	7		14	9^2			43
1		3	4	5			10^1	8		12	11^3						6			2					9^2	7		13	14			44
1		3	4^2	5		10^3	8			11	12					6			6^1		2					7	13		9	14		45
1		3		5			8^1		10^2	11			7^3	12					9	2					13	6				14	4	46

Worthington Cup

First Round	Scunthorpe U	(a)	2-0
		(h)	0-0
Second Round	Notts Co	(h)	2-1
		(a)	2-2
Third Round	Chelsea	(a)	1-0
Fourth Round	Wimbledon	(h)	1-2

FA Cup

| Third Round | Liverpool | (h) | 0-2 |

Division 3   HULL CITY

FOUNDATION

The enthusiasts who formed Hull City in 1904 were brave men indeed. More than that they were audacious for they immediately put the club on the map in this Rugby League fortress by obtaining a three-year agreement with the Hull Rugby League club to rent their ground! They had obtained quite a number of conversions to the dribbling code, before the Rugby League forbade the use of any of their club grounds by Association Football clubs. By that time, Hull City were well away having entered the FA Cup in their initial season and the Football League, Second Division after only a year.

Boothferry Park, Hull HU4 6EU.
Telephone: (01482) 575 263.
Fax: (01482) 565 752.
Club Shop: Ground: (01482) 575 263. Princes Quay: (01482) 227 654.
ClubCall: 09068 888 688.
Ground Capacity: 15,159.
Record Attendance: 55,019 v Manchester U, FA Cup 6th rd, 26 February 1949.
Record Receipts: £79,604 v Liverpool, FA Cup 5th rd, 18 February 1989.
Pitch Measurements: 115yd × 75yd.
Vice-President: S. Hinchliffe.
Chairman: Nick Buchanan.
Directors: Phillip Webster, Richard Ibbotson, David Capper, Andy Daykin.
Manager: Brian Little.
Physios: Keith Warner, Mick Mathews.
Director of Football Administration: David Capper.
Commercial Director: Andy Daykin (01482) 575 263.
Football in the Community Office: John Davies (01482) 568 088.
Marketing Manager: Rob Smith.
Ticket Office Manager: Carol Taylor.
Club Secretary: Jackie Bell.
Hon. Medical Officers: Mr F. R. Howell MA, FRCS, Dr T. Jackson.

LATEST SEQUENCES

Longest Sequence of League Wins: 10, 23.2.66 – 20.4.66.
Longest Sequence of League Defeats: 8, 7.4.34 – 8.9.34.
Longest Sequence of League Draws: 5, 30.3.29 – 15.4.29.
Longest Sequence of Unbeaten League Matches: 15, 23.4.83 – 18.10.83.
Longest Sequence Without a League Win: 27, 27.3.89 – 4.11.89.

HONOURS

Football League: Division 2 best season: 3rd, 1909–10; Division 3 (N) – Champions 1932–33, 1948–49; Division 3 – Champions 1965–66; Runners-up 1958–59; Division 4 – Runners-up 1982–83.

FA Cup: Semi-final 1930.

Football League Cup: best season: 4th, 1974, 1976, 1978.

Associate Members' Cup: Runners-up 1984.

Colours

Amber shirts with black side panels and black and white sleeves, black shorts, black stockings with amber turnovers.

Change Colours

All white.

Year Formed: 1904.

Turned Professional: 1905.

Ltd Co.: 1905.

Club Nickname: 'The Tigers'.

Previous Grounds: 1904, Boulevard Ground (Hull RFC); 1905, Anlaby Road (Hull CC); 1944, Boulevard Ground; 1946, Boothferry Park.

First Football League Game: 2 September 1905, Division 2, v Barnsley (h) W 4–1 – Spendiff; Langley, Jones; Martin, Robinson, Gordon (2); Rushton, Spence (1), Wilson (1), Howe, Raisbeck.

Record League Victory: 11–1 v Carlisle U, Division 3 (N), 14 January 1939 – Ellis; Woodhead, Dowen; Robinson (1), Blyth, Hardy; Hubbard (2), Richardson (2), Dickinson (2), Davies (2), Cunliffe (2).

Record Cup Victory: 8–2 v Stalybridge Celtic (a), FA Cup 1st rd, 26 November 1932 – Maddison; Goldsmith, Woodhead; Gardner, Hill (1), Denby; Forward (1), Duncan, McNaughton (1), Wainscoat (4), Sargeant (1).

Record Defeat: 0–8 v Wolverhampton W, Division 2, 4 November 1911.

Most League Points (2 for a win): 69, Division 3, 1965–66.

Most League Points (3 for a win): 90, Division 4, 1982–83.

Most League Goals: 109, Division 3, 1965–66.

Highest League Scorer in Season: Bill McNaughton, 39, Division 3 (N), 1932–33.

Most League Goals in Total Aggregate: Chris Chilton, 195, 1960–71.

Most League Goals in One Match: 5, Ken McDonald v Bristol C, Division 2, 17 November 1928; 5, Simon 'Slim' Raleigh v Halifax T, Division 3N, 26 December 1930.

Most Capped Player: Terry Neill, 15 (59), Northern Ireland.

Most League Appearances: Andy Davidson, 520, 1952–67.

Youngest League Player: Matthew Edeson, 16 years 63 days v Fulham, 10 October 1992.

Record Transfer Fee Received: £750,000 from Middlesbrough for Andy Payton, November 1991.

Record Transfer Fee Paid: £200,000 to Leeds U for Peter Swan, March 1989.

Football League Record: 1905 Elected to Division 2; 1930–33 Division 3 (N); 1933–36 Division 2; 1936–49 Division 3 (N); 1949–56 Division 2; 1956–58 Division 3 (N); 1958–59 Division 3; 1959–60 Division 2; 1960–66 Division 3; 1966–78 Division 2; 1978–81 Division 3; 1981–83 Division 4; 1983–85 Division 3; 1985–91 Division 2; 1991–92 Division 3; 1992–96 Division 2; 1996– Division 3.

MANAGERS

James Ramster 1904–05
(Secretary-Manager)
Ambrose Langley 1905–13
Harry Chapman 1913–14
Fred Stringer 1914–16
David Menzies 1916–21
Percy Lewis 1921–23
Bill McCracken 1923–31
Haydn Green 1931–34
John Hill 1934–36
David Menzies 1936
Ernest Blackburn 1936–46
Major Frank Buckley 1946–48
Raich Carter 1948–51
Bob Jackson 1952–55
Bob Brocklebank 1955–61
Cliff Britton 1961–70
(continued as General Manager to 1971)
Terry Neill 1970–74
John Kaye 1974–77
Bobby Collins 1977–78
Ken Houghton 1978–79
Mike Smith 1979–82
Bobby Brown 1982
Colin Appleton 1982–84
Brian Horton 1984–88
Eddie Gray 1988–89
Colin Appleton 1989
Stan Ternent 1989–91
Terry Dolan 1991–97
Mark Hateley 1997–98
Warren Joyce 1998–2000
Brian Little April 2000–

TEN YEAR LEAGUE RECORD

		P	W	D	L	F	A	Pts	Pos
1989-90	Div 2	46	14	16	16	58	65	58	14
1990-91	Div 2	46	10	15	21	57	85	45	24
1991-92	Div 3	46	16	11	19	54	54	59	14
1992-93	Div 2	46	13	11	22	46	69	50	20
1993-94	Div 2	46	18	14	14	62	54	68	9
1994-95	Div 2	46	21	11	14	70	57	74	8
1995-96	Div 2	46	5	16	25	36	78	31	24
1996-97	Div 3	46	13	18	15	44	50	57	17
1997-98	Div 3	46	11	8	27	56	83	41	22
1998-99	Div 3	46	14	11	21	44	62	53	21

DID YOU KNOW ?

On-loan goalkeeper Nick Culkin from Manchester United, kept his fifth consecutive clean sheet for Hull City against Leyton Orient on 3 January 2000, including a penalty save.

HULL CITY 1999–2000 LEAGUE RECORD

Match No.	Date	Venue	Opponents	Result	H/T Score	Lg. Pos.	Goalscorers	Attendance
1	Aug 7	A	Exeter C	L 0-1	0-0	19		3834
2	14	H	Lincoln C	D 1-1	1-0	17	Greaves [28]	7046
3	21	A	Cheltenham T	L 0-1	0-1	20		4427
4	28	H	Macclesfield T	L 2-3	1-1	21	Alcide [13], Brown [64]	6222
5	31	A	Brighton & HA	L 0-3	0-1	—		5856
6	Sept 3	H	Chester C	W 2-1	1-1	—	Eyre 2 [35, 77]	6137
7	11	A	Torquay U	W 1-0	1-0	18	Eyre (pen) [33]	2466
8	18	H	Swansea C	W 2-0	1-0	15	Brown [39], Wood [56]	5871
9	25	H	York C	D 1-1	1-1	14	Eyre [22]	8293
10	Oct 2	A	Barnet	D 0-0	0-0	16		3449
11	9	A	Hartlepool U	L 0-2	0-0	17		3114
12	16	H	Northampton T	L 0-1	0-0	20		6467
13	19	H	Plymouth Arg	L 0-1	0-0	—		4727
14	23	A	York C	D 1-1	0-1	20	Williams [67]	5109
15	Nov 2	A	Rochdale	W 2-0	1-0	—	Harper [8], Whitmore [90]	2265
16	6	H	Rotherham U	D 0-0	0-0	19		7045
17	12	A	Southend U	W 2-1	0-0	17	Greaves [74], Brabin [82]	4940
18	23	H	Halifax T	L 0-1	0-1	—		6067
19	27	A	Shrewsbury T	L 0-3	0-1	20		2577
20	Dec 4	H	Exeter C	W 4-0	2-0	19	Edwards [22], Harper 3 [45, 75, 89]	5683
21	18	H	Carlisle U	W 2-1	0-0	17	Wood [75], Eyre [87]	4727
22	26	A	Darlington	D 0-0	0-0	17		7058
23	28	H	Mansfield T	W 2-0	2-0	16	Greaves [31], Joyce [37]	7215
24	Jan 3	A	Leyton Orient	D 0-0	0-0	16		5169
25	8	H	Peterborough U	L 2-3	1-0	17	Brown [43], Eyre (pen) [55]	5898
26	15	A	Lincoln C	L 1-2	0-2	18	Brown [83]	4687
27	22	H	Cheltenham T	D 1-1	1-0	18	Whitmore [1]	4691
28	29	A	Macclesfield T	W 2-0	0-0	17	Eyre 2 [47, 54]	1900
29	Feb 5	H	Brighton & HA	W 2-0	0-0	15	Harris 2 [66, 82]	5167
30	12	A	Chester C	D 0-0	0-0	16		2802
31	19	H	Shrewsbury T	D 0-0	0-0	15		5100
32	22	A	Peterborough U	L 1-2	0-0	—	Brabin [48]	6668
33	26	A	Swansea C	D 0-0	0-0	16		6137
34	Mar 4	H	Torquay U	D 0-0	0-0	18		4668
35	7	A	Rotherham U	L 0-3	0-0	—		4881
36	11	H	Rochdale	D 2-2	1-0	18	Wood 2 [25, 81]	4219
37	18	A	Halifax T	W 1-0	0-0	18	Wood [77]	2519
38	21	H	Southend U	D 0-0	0-0	—		4150
39	25	H	Darlington	L 0-1	0-1	18		5617
40	Apr 1	A	Carlisle U	W 4-0	2-0	16	Prokas (og) [32], Harris 2 [45, 77], Morgan [80]	3495
41	8	H	Leyton Orient	W 2-0	1-0	16	Whitney [13], Brown [90]	4422
42	15	A	Mansfield T	W 1-0	0-0	14	Brown [83]	2213
43	21	A	Northampton T	L 0-1	0-1	—		6758
44	24	H	Barnet	L 1-3	0-0	14	Brabin [49]	4883
45	29	A	Plymouth Arg	W 1-0	1-0	14	Wood [21]	4233
46	May 6	H	Hartlepool U	L 0-3	0-3	14		7620

Final League Position: 14

GOALSCORERS

League (43): Eyre 8 (2 pens), Brown 6, Wood 6, Harper 4, Harris 4, Brabin 3, Greaves 3, Whitmore 2, Alcide 1, Edwards 1, Joyce 1, Morgan 1, Whitney 1, Williams 1, own goal 1.
Worthington Cup (6): Alcide 2, Brown 2, Eyre 2 (1 pen).
FA Cup (10): Brown 3, Edwards 2, Eyre 2, Greaves 1, Wood 1, own goal 1.

Bracey L 10	Swales S 17 + 3	Harper S 36 + 2	Perry J 1	Whittle J 38	Greaves M 38	Joyce W 19	Brabin G 37	Harris J 18 + 11	Alcide C 10 + 2	D'Auria D 10 + 2	Edwards M 36 + 4	Wood J 13 + 19	Brown D 39 + 6	Schofield J 13 + 12	Eyre J 24	Williams G 12 + 1	Baker M — + 2	Mann N 2	Wilson S 27	Morgan S 17 + 2	Whitney J 19 + 2	Harrison G 3	Knight R 1	Whitmore T 17	Goodison I 17 + 1	Bywater S 4	Bolder A 18 + 1	Betsy K 1 + 1	Culkin N 4	Morley B — + 1	Quigley M — + 3	Bradshaw G 5 + 7	Whitworth N — + 1	Match No.
1	2	3	4¹	5	6	7	8	9²	10³	11	12	13	14																					1
1	2	3		5	6		8	9	10¹		12	4	7	11																				2
1	2¹	12		5		7	8	9²	10		6	13	4	11	3																			3
1	2	3		5		7	8	12	10¹		6		9	4	11²	13	14																	4
1	2	3		5	6		8	12			7²	10	13	9	4	11¹																		5
1		3		5	6		8	12			7	4	13	9²		10	11¹	2																6
		3		5	6		8				12	7	10	13	9¹	4	11²		15	2	16													7
1	2		5	6			8				10¹	12	4	13	9²	7	11	3																8
1	2		5				8	12	10¹				4	13	9²	7	11	3			6													9
1	2		5				8		10¹			6		12	7	9	11					3	4											10
	2		5				8		10	7		4	12	13		9	3¹							6	11²	1								11
	12		5²			7	8		10	6		4	14	9	13	11³					1			3	2¹									12
	2		5	6			8				7	4	10	9		11	3			1														13
	2		5²	6			8		10	7		4		9	12	11¹	3			1	13													14
	2		5					12	11	4			9¹	7	10²	3			1	6				8	13									15
1	2²		5				13	12	4			9	7	10	3				6				8	11¹										16
	3		5				8		11	4	12	9	13	10¹					1	6				7²	2									17
	2		5	6			8	12		4	11	9	7						10	3¹	1													18
	2³		5	6²			12		4	11¹	9	7						13	10	3	1	14	8											19
	3		5		8		12		4	11¹	9²	7				6			10	2	1	13												20
	2	3		5	4	7				6	11¹	12		9				13				10²	1	8										21
	2	3		5	4	7	8			11	9							6				10	1											22
	2	3¹		5	4	7	8	13		11	9²							6	12			10	1											23
	2	3		5	6	7¹	8	13			9²	12	11			4						10	1											24
	2	3		5	6		8				12	9¹		11		1	4					10		7										25
	3		5		7	8				2	12	9		11		1	4	6						10¹										26
	2²	3			6	7	8			13	12	9		11			4					10¹	5		1									27
	2		5	6	7		14			4	12	9²	13	11¹		1						10³	3	8										28
	3		5	6	7		10			4		9		11		1		2					8¹			12								29
	2		5	6	7		10			4	12	9¹		11		1		3					8											30
	2		5	6	7		10			4	12	9		11¹		1		3					8											31
	2		5	6	7	8	11¹			4	14	9²	12			1		3					10					13³						32
	2		5	6	7	8	11			4		9				1		3					10											33
	3		5	2	7	8¹	11			4	12	9				1		6					10											34
	2	3		6	7	8	9²			4	12					1							10¹	5	11			13						35
	2	3		6		8	10			4	11	9¹				1							5	7				12						36
		3		5	4		8	10		12	11¹	9	13			1							2	7				6²						37
		3¹		5	4		8	10		12	11	9				1							6	7				2						38
12			5	4		8	3				11¹	9				1	7	6						10				2						39
12			5	4¹		8	11			2		9	13			1	7	3²				6						14	10³					40
12			5	2		8	11²			4		9				1	7	6		10	3¹							13						41
3			5	4		8	11²			2		9	12			1	7³							10¹	6			14	13					42
			5	2		8	11			4¹		9				1	7	6		10	3							12						43
2²			3			8				4	12	9	13			1	7	5		10	6							11¹						44
2			3			8¹				4	11²	9	12			1	7	5		10	6³								13	14				45
2		5	3			8¹				4²	11	9	12			1	7	6		10								13						46

Worthington Cup

First Round	Rotherham U	(a)	1-0	
		(h)	2-0	
Second Round	Liverpool	(h)	1-5	
		(a)	2-4	

FA Cup

First Round	Macclesfield T	(a)	0-0	
		(h)	4-0	
Second Round	Hayes	(a)	2-2	
		(h)	3-2	
Third Round	Chelsea	(h)	1-6	

FA Premiership

IPSWICH TOWN

FOUNDATION

Considering that Ipswich Town only reached the Football League in 1938, many people outside of East Anglia may be surprised to learn that this club was formed at a meeting held in the Town Hall as far back as 1878 when Mr T. C. Cobbold, MP, was voted president. Originally it was the Ipswich Association FC to distinguish it from the older Ipswich Football Club which played rugby. These two amalgamated in 1888 and the handling game was dropped in 1893.

Portman Road, Ipswich, Suffolk IP1 2DA.
Telephone: (01473) 400 500 (4 lines).
Fax: (01473) 400 040.
Ticket Office: (01473) 400 555.
Sales & Marketing Dept: (01473) 400 523.
ClubCall: 09068 121 068.
Ground Capacity: 22,700.
Record Attendance: 38,010 v Leeds U, FA Cup 6th rd, 8 March 1975.
Record Receipts: £105,950 v AZ 67 Alkmaar, UEFA Cup Final 1st leg, 6 May 1981.
Pitch Measurements: 112yd × 72yd.
Chairman and Chief Executive: David Sheepshanks (currently Chairman only).
Vice-Presidents: Kenneth H. Brightwell, Harold R. Smith.
Directors: P. Hope-Cobbold, R. Moore, John Kerr MBE, R. J. Finbow, Lord Ryder OBE.
Manager: George Burley.
Assistant Manager: Dale Roberts.
First Team Coach: Tony Mowbray.
Youth Team Coach: Paul Goddard.
Chief Scout: Colin Suggett.
Academy Director: Bryan Klug.
Physio: Dave Williams.
Secretary: David C. Rose.
Corporate Business Manager: Mike Noye.
Commercial Director: Paul Clouting.

LATEST SEQUENCES

Longest Sequence of League Wins: 8, 23.9.53 – 31.10.53.
Longest Sequence of League Defeats: 10, 4.9.54 – 16.10.54.
Longest Sequence of League Draws: 7, 10.11.90 – 21.12.90.
Longest Sequence of Unbeaten League Matches: 23, 8.12.79 – 26.4.80.
Longest Sequence Without a League Win: 21, 28.8.63 – 14.12.63.

HONOURS

Football League: Division 1 – Champions 1961–62; Runners-up 1980–81, 1981–82; Promoted from Division 1 1999–2000 (play-offs); Division 2 – Champions 1960–61, 1967–68, 1991–92; Division 3 (S) – Champions 1953–54, 1956–57.

FA Cup: Winners 1978.

Football League Cup: Semi-final 1982, 1985.

Texaco Cup: Winners 1973.

European Competitions: European Cup: 1962–63. *European Cup-Winners' Cup:* 1978–79. *UEFA Cup:* 1973–74, 1974–75, 1975–76, 1977–78, 1979–80, 1980–81 (winners), 1981–82, 1982–83.

Colours
Blue shirts, white shorts, blue stockings.

Change Colours
White shirts, black shorts, white stockings.

Year Formed: 1878.

Turned Professional: 1936.

Ltd Co.: 1936.

Club Nickname: 'Blues' or 'Town'.

First Football League Game: 27 August 1938, Division 3 (S), v Southend U (h) W 4–2 – Burns; Dale, Parry; Perrett, Fillingham, McLuckie; Williams, Davies (1), Jones (2), Alsop (1), Little.

Record League Victory: 7–0 v Portsmouth, Division 2, 7 November 1964 – Thorburn; Smith, McNeil; Baxter, Bolton, Thompson; Broadfoot (1), Hegan (2), Baker (1), Leadbetter, Brogan (3). 7–0 v Southampton, Division 1, 2 February 1974 – Sivell; Burley, Mills (1), Morris, Hunter, Beattie (1), Hamilton (2), Viljoen, Johnson, Whymark (2), Lambert (1) (Woods). 7–0 v WBA, Division 1, 6 November 1976 – Sivell; Burley, Mills, Talbot, Hunter, Beattie (1), Osborne, Wark (1), Mariner (1) (Bertschin), Whymark (4), Woods.

Record Cup Victory: 10–0 v Floriana, European Cup prel. rd, 25 September 1962 – Bailey; Malcolm, Compton; Baxter, Laurel, Elsworthy (1); Stephenson, Moran (2), Crawford (5), Phillips (2), Blackwood.

Record Defeat: 1–10 v Fulham, Division 1, 26 December 1963.

Most League Points (2 for a win): 64, Division 3 (S), 1953–54 and 1955–56.

Most League Points (3 for a win): 87, Division 1, 1999–2000.

Most League Goals: 106, Division 3 (S), 1955–56.

Highest League Scorer in Season: Ted Phillips, 41, Division 3 (S), 1956–57.

Most League Goals in Total Aggregate: Ray Crawford, 203, 1958–63 and 1966–69.

Most League Goals in One Match: 5, Alan Brazil v Southampton, Division 1, 16 February 1981.

Most Capped Player: Allan Hunter, 47 (53), Northern Ireland.

Most League Appearances: Mick Mills, 591, 1966–82.

Youngest League Player: Jason Dozzell, 16 years 56 days v Coventry C, 4 February 1984.

Record Transfer Fee Received: £6,000,000 from Newcastle U for Kieron Dyer, July 1999.

Record Transfer Fee Paid: £2,500,000 to Huddersfield T for Marcus Stewart, February 2000.

Football League Record: 1938 Elected to Division 3 (S); 1954–55 Division 2; 1955–57 Division 3 (S); 1957–61 Division 2; 1961–64 Division 1; 1964–68 Division 2; 1968–86 Division 1; 1986–92 Division 2; 1992–95 FA Premier League; 1995–2000 Division 1; 2000– FA Premier League.

MANAGERS

Mick O'Brien 1936–37
Scott Duncan 1937–55
(continued as Secretary)
Alf Ramsey 1955–63
Jackie Milburn 1963–64
Bill McGarry 1964–68
Bobby Robson 1969–82
Bobby Ferguson 1982–87
Johnny Duncan 1987–90
John Lyall 1990–94
George Burley December 1994–

TEN YEAR LEAGUE RECORD

		P	W	D	L	F	A	Pts	Pos
1989-90	Div 2	46	19	12	15	67	66	69	9
1990-91	Div 2	46	13	18	15	60	68	57	14
1991-92	Div 2	46	24	12	10	70	50	84	1
1992-93	PR Lge	42	12	16	14	50	55	52	16
1993-94	PR Lge	42	9	16	17	35	58	43	19
1994-95	PR Lge	42	7	6	29	36	93	27	22
1995-96	Div 1	46	19	12	15	79	69	69	7
1996-97	Div 1	46	20	14	12	68	50	74	4
1997-98	Div 1	46	23	14	9	77	43	83	5
1998-99	Div 1	46	26	8	12	69	32	86	3

DID YOU KNOW

Ipswich Town's first professional match was against Tunbridge Wells Rangers on 29 August 1936. It drew an attendance of 14,211 to Portman Road including Stanley Rous, the FA Secretary and the Scots Guards Band. Ipswich won 4-1.

IPSWICH TOWN 1999–2000 LEAGUE RECORD

Match No.	Date		Venue	Opponents	Result	H/T Score	Lg. Pos.	Goalscorers	Attendance
1	Aug	7	H	Nottingham F	W 3-1	2-0	2	Naylor [18], Johnson [20], Scowcroft [71]	20,830
2		15	A	Swindon T	W 4-1	1-1	1	Johnson 2 [44, 74], Naylor 2 [55, 68]	6195
3		21	H	Bolton W	W 1-0	0-0	1	Johnson [69]	17,696
4		28	A	Sheffield U	D 2-2	2-0	1	Scowcroft [3], Johnson [11]	12,455
5		30	H	Barnsley	W 6-1	3-0	1	Johnson 2 [14, 75], Venus [24], Naylor [45], Scowcroft [73], Magilton [90]	18,037
6	Sept	11	A	Portsmouth	D 1-1	0-0	1	Scowcroft [88]	16,034
7		18	H	Birmingham C	L 0-1	0-1	3		19,758
8		26	H	Manchester C	W 2-1	1-0	2	Johnson [43], Croft [67]	19,406
9	Oct	2	A	Grimsby T	L 1-2	0-1	5	Magilton [54]	6531
10		16	H	QPR	L 1-4	1-1	6	Holland [3]	17,544
11		19	H	Charlton Ath	W 4-2	2-2		Scowcroft [4], Venus [29], Johnson [66], Stockwell [76]	17,940
12		23	A	Walsall	W 1-0	0-0	2	Naylor [90]	6526
13		27	A	Manchester C	L 0-1	0-0	—		32,799
14		30	H	Grimsby T	W 2-0	1-0	2	Clapham [36], Naylor [60]	16,617
15	Nov	2	A	Huddersfield T	L 1-3	1-1	—	Holland [15]	12,093
16		6	A	Blackburn R	D 2-2	0-1	5	Holland [75], Mowbray [90]	18,512
17		12	H	Tranmere R	D 0-0	0-0	4		14,514
18		21	A	Norwich C	D 0-0	0-0	5		19,948
19		24	H	Wolverhampton W	W 1-0	0-0	—	Scowcroft [56]	15,731
20		27	H	Crewe Alex	W 2-1	1-0	4	Johnson 2 [4, 76]	15,211
21	Dec	5	A	Nottingham F	W 1-0	0-0	4	Holland [78]	15,724
22		7	A	Crystal Palace	D 2-2	2-1	—	Holland [11], Johnson [34]	13,176
23		18	H	WBA	W 3-1	2-0	3	Johnson [6], Scowcroft [27], Midgley [66]	14,712
24		26	A	Fulham	D 0-0	0-0	4		17,255
25		28	H	Stockport Co	W 1-0	1-0	4	Scowcroft [34]	20,671
26	Jan	3	A	Port Vale	W 2-1	1-0	3	Holland [43], Scowcroft [52]	6908
27		15	H	Swindon T	W 3-0	2-0	3	Stockwell [27], Naylor 2 [37, 82]	17,326
28		22	A	Bolton W	D 1-1	0-0	4	Holland [85]	11,924
29		29	H	Sheffield U	D 1-1	1-0	4	Johnson (pen) [45]	17,350
30	Feb	5	A	Barnsley	W 2-0	0-0	3	Scowcroft [59], Stewart [60]	17,601
31		12	H	Huddersfield T	W 2-1	1-0	3	Scowcroft [28], Stewart [73]	21,233
32		19	A	Crewe Alex	W 2-1	0-0	2	Clapham [60], Wright J [89]	6393
33		27	A	Birmingham C	D 1-1	1-1	2	Johnson [45]	20,493
34	Mar	4	H	Portsmouth	L 0-1	0-1	3		20,305
35		7	H	Blackburn R	D 0-0	0-0	—		18,871
36		11	A	Wolverhampton W	L 1-2	0-1	2	Scowcroft [75]	22,652
37		19	H	Norwich C	L 0-2	0-2	3		21,760
38		22	A	Tranmere R	W 2-0	1-0	—	Holland [18], Johnson [57]	6933
39		25	H	Fulham	W 1-0	0-0	2	Reuser [90]	20,168
40	Apr	4	A	WBA	D 1-1	0-1	—	Holland [68]	12,536
41		8	H	Port Vale	W 3-0	2-0	3	Scowcroft [12], Johnson [39], Holland [83]	19,663
42		15	A	Stockport Co	W 1-0	1-0	3	Johnson [44]	8501
43		22	A	QPR	L 1-3	0-0	3	Magilton (pen) [79]	14,920
44		25	H	Crystal Palace	W 1-0	1-0	3	Johnson [26]	18,798
45		29	A	Charlton Ath	W 3-1	1-0	3	Magilton [24], Johnson [58], Reuser [71]	20,043
46	May	7	H	Walsall	W 2-0	0-0	3	Johnson 2 [49, 60]	21,908

Final League Position: 3

GOALSCORERS
League (71): Johnson 22 (1 pen), Scowcroft 13, Holland 10, Naylor 8, Magilton 4 (1 pen), Clapham 2, Reuser 2, Stewart 2, Stockwell 2, Venus 2, Croft 1, Midgley 1, Mowbray 1, Wright J 1.
Worthington Cup (6): Clapham 2, Scowcroft 2, Johnson 1, Venus 1.
FA Cup (0).

Wright R 46	Stockwell M 21 + 14	Clapham J 44 + 2	Thetis M 15 + 1	Venus M 28	McGreal J 34	Holland M 46	Wright J 21 + 13	Johnson D 44	Scowcroft J 40 + 1	Naylor R 19 + 17	Wilnis F 30 + 5	Axeldal J 1 + 15	Brown W 20 + 5	Magilton J 33 + 5	Mowbray T 35 + 1	Croft G 14 + 7	Logan R — + 1	Friars S — + 1	Midgley N 1 + 3	Stewart M 9 + 1	Clegg M 3	Reuser M 2 + 6	Match No
1	2¹	3	4	5	6	7	8	9²	10	11	12	13											1
1	7	3	4	5²	6	8	11	9¹	10	2	12	13											2
1	2¹	3	4	5	6	7	8	9³	10	11³	12	13	14										3
1	12	3	4¹	5	6	7		9	10	11	2²			8	13								4
1	12	3	4	5³	6	7	8²	9	10	11	2¹		14	13									5
1	12	3		5	6	7	8	9²	10	11¹	2³	13	4	14									6
1	12	3	4²	5	6	7	8³	9	10	11	2¹			13	14								7
1	6²	12	4	5		7	8¹	9	10	13	2³		14	11		3							8
1	2	3	4¹	5	6	7		9	10	11	12			8									9
1	12	3	4	5	6	7	8	9²	10	13				11		2¹							10
1	8	3		4	6	7		9	10		2			11	5								11
1	8¹	3		4	6	7	13	9³	10	12	2		14	11²	5								12
1	8²	3		4	6	7		9¹	10	12	2³	13		11	5		14						13
1	10	3		4	6	7	8	9¹		11	2²	12			5		13						14
1	10³	3	4	5	6	7	8	9¹		11	2²	12			13	14							15
1	10	3		4	6	7	8			11	2	9			5								16
1	10	3		4	6	7	8²	9	12	11³	2¹	14		13	5								17
1	8¹	3	4		7		9	10	12	2			6	11	5								18
1	8¹	3		6		7	12	9²	10	13	2		4	11	5								19
1	8¹	3		6		7	12	9	10		4²	11	5	2	13								20
1	8¹	3		6		7	12	9	10		4	11	5	2									21
1	8¹	3		6		7	12	9²	10		13	4	11	5	2								22
1	2¹	3		6		7	12	9³	10	11²		13	4	8	5					14			23
1		3		6		7		9¹	10	11	2		4	8	5					12			24
1	12	3		4	6		7	13	9¹	10	11³	2		8²	5					14			25
1	12	3		4	6	7	8		10	11¹	2	13			5					9²			26
1	2³	3		4	6		7¹	12	9²	10	11		13		8	5	14						27
1	11¹	3		4	6	7	8	9	10		2²	12			5	13							28
1	12	3		4¹	6	7	8	9	10	11²		13			5	2							29
1		3²			6	7		9¹	10	12	13		4	11	5	2				8			30
1	14	3²			6	7		9¹	10	12	2		4	8	5	13³			11				31
1		4			6	7	12	9	10	11¹	3			8	5				2				32
1		3			6	7		9	10		4	8	5				11	2					33
1		3				7	12	9	10¹		6	4	8	5			11	2					34
1	12	3	4			7	8¹		13	2	6	10	5				11²						35
1		3			6	7	8¹	9	10	12	2		4	11	5								36
1	12	3	4¹	6		7		9	10	13	2		8	5				11²					37
1	12	4		6³		7	8	9²	10	13	2¹	14	11	5	3								38
1	12	3		4¹	6	7	8³	9	10²	13		11	5	2			14						39
1	2²	6		4		7	8	9¹	10	11		5	3			12	13						40
1		3		4³		7	12	9²	10	13	6	8	5	2			11¹	14					41
1	13	3		6¹	7	14	9	10	12²		4	11	5	2			8³						42
1	6			7	8¹	9	10	12	2		4	11	5	3²		13							43
1	3	4¹		7	12	9	10²	13	2		6	11	5			8							44
1	12	13	4²		7		9	10	2¹		6	8	5	3			11¹	14					45
1	3	4		7		9	10¹	12	2²		6	8	5	13			11³	14					46

Worthington Cup

First Round	Brentford	(a)	2-0
		(h)	2-0
Second Round	Crewe Alex	(a)	1-2
		(h)	1-1

FA Cup

Third Round	Southampton	(h)	0-1

Division 3   KIDDERMINSTER HARRIERS

FOUNDATION

Kidderminster Harriers were originally formed as a rugby team and played their first game as a soccer club on 18 September 1886 away to Wilden. Harriers won 2-1 with goals from Arthur Millward and William Colsey. Millward was vice-captain and later Kidderminster's first representative on the executive of the Birmingham County FA in 1897. Colsey was to die in tragic circumstances following an accidental injury sustained in a match only two months later.

Aggborough Stadium, Hoo Road, Kidderminster DY10 1NB.
Telephone: (01562) 823 931.
Fax: (01562) 827 329.
Website: www.harriers.co.uk
E-mail: info@harriers.co.uk
Ground Capacity: 6,293 (1,100 seated).
Record Attendance: 9,155 v Hereford U, 27 November 1948.
Chairman: L. Newton.
Vice Chairman: C. C. Youngjohns.
Directors: P. Byrne, G. R. Lane, T. Murrant.
Chief Executive: N. Morris.
Manager: Jan Molby.
Assistant Manager: Gary Barnett.
Reserve and Youth Team Manager: Ian Britton.
Medical Officers: Dr. K. O'Connor, Dr. V. P. Schreiber.
Physio: Jim Conway.
Commercial Manager: Mark Searl.
Financial Controller: Alan Biggs.
Football and Community Development Officer: Nick Griffiths.
Football Secretary: Roger Barlow.
Matchday Secretary: Dave Colwell.
Safety Officer: Peter Picken.
Stadium Manager: Roger Barlow.
Year Formed: 1886.
Club Nickname: 'Harriers'.
Record Transfer Fee Received: £380,000 from WBA for Lee Hughes, 1997.
Record Transfer Fee Paid: £100,000 to Nuneaton Borough for Andy Ducros, July 2000.

HONOURS

Conference: – Champions 1993–94, 1999–2000; Runners-up 1996–97.
FA Trophy: 1986–87 (winners); 1990–91, 1994–95 (runners-up).
League Cup: 1996–97 (winners).
Welsh FA Cup: 1985–86 (runners-up), 1988–89 (runners-up).
Southern League Cup: 1979–80 (winners).
Worcester Senior Cup: (21)
Birmingham Senior Cup: (7)
Staffordshire Senior Cup: (4)
West Midland League Champions: (6) Runners-up (3)
Southern Premier: Runners-up (1)
West Midland League Cup: Winners (7)
Keys Cup: Winners (7)
Border Counties Floodlit League Champions: (3)
Camkin Floodlit Cup: Winners (3)
Bass County Vase: Winners (1)
Conference Fair Play Trophy: (5)

Colours
Red shirts with white flash, red shorts and stockings with white trim.

Change Colours
Blue shirts with yellow flash, blue shorts and stockings with yellow trim.

KIDDERMINSTER HARRIERS ROLL CALL 1999–2000

Player	Date of Birth	Signed From	Debut
Gary Barnett	11-03-63	Barry T	v Yeovil T (17-08-99)
Dean Bennett	13-12-77	Bromsgrove	v Hayes (30-01-99
Stuart Brock	29-09-76	Aston Villa	v Kettering T (22-11-97)
Andrew Brownrigg	02-08-76	Rotherham U	v Yeovil T (17-08-99)
Adam Bugler			v Solihull B (16-04-00)
Richard Burgess	18-08-78	Stoke C (loan)	v Welling U (26-02-00)
Tim Clarke	16-05-65	Scunthorpe U	v Stevenage B (04-09-99)
Ian Clarkson	04-12-70	Northampton T	v Telford (06-11-99
James Collins	28-05-78	Crewe Alex (loan)	v Dover Ath (14-08-99)
Andy Corbett	20-02-82	Youth	v Solihull B (16-04-00)
Mark Creighton	08-10-81	Youth	v Solihull B (16-04-00)
Shaun Cunnington	04-01-66	Notts Co	v Kettering T (05-09-98)
Ben Davies	27-05-81	Walsall	v Solihull B (16-04-00)
Mark Druce	03-03-74	Hereford U	v Hayes (30-01-99
Ian Foster	11-11-76	Barrow	v Dover Ath (14-08-99)
Stewart Hadley	30-12-73	Mansfield T	v Morecambe (15-08-98)
Andy Hall	10-02-82	Youth	
Jez Harman	26-02-81	Shrewsbury T	v Welling U (16-10-99)
Leslie Hines	07-01-77	Aston V	v Forest Green R (21-09-98)
Craig Hinton	26-11-77	Birmingham C	v Forest Green R (21-09-98)
Kristian Kelsall		Boldmere St Michaels	v Solihull B (16-04-00)
Phil King	28-12-67	Brighton & H.A	v Dover Ath (14-08-99)
Mike Marsh	21-07-69	Southport	v Northwich Vic (20-11-99)
Neil Midgley	21-10-78	Ipswich T (loan)§	v Rushden & Diamonds (08-04-00)
Reny Petersen	22-08-73	St Truiden (Belgium)	v Dover Ath (14-08-99)
Steve Pope	08-09-76	Crewe Alex	v Telford U (07-02-98)
Thomas Skovbjerg	25-10-74	Esbjerg (Denmark)	v Dover Ath (14-08-99)
Adie Smith	11-08-73	Bromsgrove R	v Gateshead (23-08-97)
Scott Stamps	20-03-75	Colchester U	v Stevenage B (04-09-99)
Steve Taylor	07-01-70	Bromsgrove R	v Forest Green R (21-09-98)
Matt Tucker	07-09-81	Youth	v Solihull B (16-04-00)
Paul Webb	30-11-67	Bromsgrove R	v Farnborough T (20-08-94)
Martin Weir	04-07-68	Birmingham C	v Barnet (16-08-86)
Lee Williams	09-04-68	Rhyl	v Woking (28-08-99)

TEN YEAR LEAGUE RECORD

		P	W	D	L	F	A	Pts	Pos
1989-90	Conf.	42	15	9	18	64	67	54	13
1990-91	Conf.	42	14	10	18	56	67	52	13
1991-92	Conf.	42	12	9	21	56	77	45	19
1992-93	Conf.	42	14	16	12	60	60	58	9
1993-94	Conf.	42	22	9	11	63	35	75	1
1994-95	Conf.	42	16	9	17	63	61	57	11
1995-96	Conf.	42	18	10	14	78	66	64	7
1996-97	Conf.	42	26	7	9	84	42	85	2
1997-98	Conf.	42	11	14	17	56	63	47	17
1998-99	Conf.	42	14	9	19	56	52	51	15

DID YOU KNOW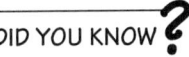

On 14 September 1955 floodlights were used for the first time in FA Cup history at Aggborough for the preliminary round replay against Brierley Hill Alliance. Kidderminster won 4-2 in front of a crowd of 2230.

KIDDERMINSTER HARRIERS 1999–2000 CONFERENCE RECORD

Match No.	Date		Venue	Opponents	Result	H/T Score	Goalscorers	Attendance
1	Aug	14	H	Dover Ath	L 1-2	0-2	Skovbjerg [53]	2175
2		17	A	Yeovil T	L 0-1	0-1		2473
3		21	A	Rushden & D	L 3-5	1-4	King [7], Foster [46], Petersen [53]	2728
4		28	H	Woking	W 3-2	1-1	Taylor [21], Foster (pen) [62], Bennett [90]	1729
5		30	A	Forest Green R	L 2-3	0-2	Foster (pen) [75], Bennett [80]	919
6	Sept	4	A	Stevenage B	W 2-0	0-0	Bennett [60], Brownrigg [78]	2894
7		11	H	Scarborough	W 2-0	1-0	Druce [37], Skovbjerg [52]	1784
8		13	H	Nuneaton B	L 1-2	1-0	Brownrigg [8]	3152
9		18	A	Morecambe	W 1-0	0-0	Bennett [84]	1411
10		25	H	Doncaster R	W 1-0	1-0	Foster [30]	2382
11	Oct	2	A	Hayes	L 0-2	0-0		635
12		9	H	Yeovil T	W 4-0	1-0	Druce [26], Hinton [64], Foster (pen) [71], Webb [78]	1769
13		23	H	Kettering T	W 1-0	0-0	Druce [53]	1708
14	Nov	1	A	Hednesford T	W 2-0	1-0	Stamps [19], Skovberg [84]	1522
15		6	A	Telford U	L 2-3	1-2	Bennett [34], Hadley [76]	1409
16		13	H	Southport	W 5-0	2-0	Druce 3 [22, 72, 84], Petersen 2 (1 pen) [34 (p), 63]	1404
17		20	A	Northwich Vic	D 1-1	0-0	Hadley [66]	1310
18	Dec	4	H	Kingstonian	W 2-0	0-0	Druce [61], Bennett [80]	1933
19		11	A	Scarborough	D 0-0	0-0		1125
20		18	H	Morecambe	W 2-1	0-1	Stamps [70], Hadley [72]	2189
21		27	A	Hereford U	D 1-1	0-1	Hadley [69]	4437
22	Jan	3	H	Hereford U	D 1-1	0-1	Foster [65]	4606
23		8	A	Nuneaton B	W 3-2	2-1	Foster 3 [6, 41, 51]	2596
24		15	H	Hayes	W 2-1	1-1	Foster 2 [13, 46]	2636
25		22	H	Sutton U	W 1-0	0-0	Hinton [48]	2818
26		29	A	Kingstonian	W 1-0	0-0	Foster [50]	1523
27	Feb	12	H	Hednesford T	W 3-0	1-0	Hadley 2 [33, 76], Smith [49]	2964
28		19	A	Kettering T	L 1-3	0-2	Bennett [49]	1815
29		26	H	Welling U	W 4-1	1-1	Marsh [45], Foster [60], Bennett [70], Skovberg [90]	2673
30	Mar	4	H	Stevenage B	W 3-1	0-1	Foster [77], Smith (og) [85], Hadley [90]	2832
31		7	A	Doncaster R	W 2-1	0-1	Bennett [86], Hadley [89]	2723
32		11	A	Altrincham	D 1-1	0-0	Marsh [55]	3054
33		18	A	Welling U	W 2-1	1-0	Foster [27], King [56]	867
34		25	H	Telford U	W 2-0	1-0	Hadley [28], Bennett [64]	3138
35	Apr	8	H	Rushden & D	W 2-0	0-0	Foster (pen) [61], Brownrigg [85]	6250
36		15	A	Southport	W 1-0	1-0	Midgley [9]	2033
37		22	H	Nortwich Vic	W 3-1	3-0	Midgley [19], Hadley [25], Marsh [40]	3443
38		24	A	Dover Ath	W 1-0	0-0	Foster (pen) [90]	1314
39		29	A	Woking	L 0-1	0-1		3210
40	May	1	H	Forest Green R	D 3-3	1-0	Hadley [14], Hinton [57], Barnett [69]	5301
41		3	A	Sutton U	W 3-0	2-0	Barnett [10], Marsh [31], Hadley [82]	579
42		6	A	Altrincham	D 0-0	0-0		176

GOALSCORERS

League (75): Foster 17 (5 pens), Hadley 12, Bennett 10, Druce 7, Marsh 4, Skovbjerg 4, Brownrigg 3, Hinton 3, Petersen 3 (1 pen), Barnett 2, King 2, Midgley 2, Stamps 2, Smith 1, Taylor 1, Webb 1, own goal 1.

FA Cup (0). *Trophy* (2): Clarkson 1, Pope 1.

Brock S 11+1	Hinton C 38+3	Hines L 6+5	Webb P 33+2	Weir M 1	Smith A 42	Collins J 5	Petersen R 16+2	Bennett D 35+4	Hadley S 26+12	Skovbjerg T 30+1	King P 7+7	Barnett G 4+5	Cunnington S 5+3	Foster I 34+3	Browning A 16+5	Taylor S 4+7	Davies B —+1	Williams L 2	Pope S 15+6	Clarke T 29+1	Stamps S 34+1	Druce M 15+7	Clarkson I 27+1	Marsh M 23+1	Burgess R —+3	Midgley N 4+1	Match No.
1	2	3	4	5^1	6	7	8	9^2	10	11	12			13													1
1	2	12	4		6	7	8		10^3	11^2	3^1	14		13	5	9											2
1	2	13	4		6	7^3	8		12	11^1	3^2	14		10	5	9											3
	2	13	4		6	7^3	8		12		3^2	14	11	10^1	5	9				1							4
	2^3	3	4		6	7^2	13		12		8^1	11		10	5	9				1	14						5
	13	12	4		6		7	14	8^2					11	10	2			5	1	3^1	9^3					6
	12		4		6		7^1	13	8^2			14	11^3	10		2			5	1	3	9					7
	2		4		6		7^1	12	8^2			13		10	11				5	1	3	9					8
1	2		4		6		7	12	8					10	11				5		3	9^1					9
	2		4		6		7	12	8^2			13		10	11				5	1	3	9^1					10
	2		4		6		7^1	13	8^2		12			10	11				5	1	3	9					11
	2	3	4		6		7	12	8					10	11				5	1		9^1					12
	2	3	4		6		7	8						11	10^1				5	1	12	9					13
	2	3	4		6		7	8		11	12			10					5	1		9^1					14
	2	3	4		6		7	8		11	13			10^2					5^1	1		9	12				15
		12	4		6		7^2	8	10	11	13								5	1	3	9^1	2				16
			4		6		7	8^1	10	11^2	12								5	1	3	9	2	13			17
	5	12	4		6		7	8	10^1					13						1	3	9^2	2	11			18
	5		4		6		7	12	8					10						1	3	9^1	2	11			19
	5		4		6		7	9	8					10						1	3		2	11			20
	5		4		6		7	9	8	11				10^1					12	1	3		2				21
	5	12	4^1		6		7	9	8		13			10^2						1	3		2	11			22
	5	12	4		6		7	9	8					10^1						1	3		2	11			23
	5		4		6		7^2	9^1	8		13			10					12	1	3		2	11			24
	5		4		6		7	9	8	11				10						1	3		2				25
	5		4^2		6		7	9^1	8		13			10					12	1	3		2	11			26
	5		4		6		7^1	9	8^3		12		14	10^2					13	1	3		2	11			27
	5		4		6		7	9	8					10^1					12	1	3		2	11			28
	5		4		6		7	9	8		13		14	10^1						1	3^2		2	11^3		12	29
	5		4		6		7	9	8		13									1	3	10	2	11		12	30
	5		4		6		7	9	8^1					10					12	1	3		2	11			31
	5		4^2		6		7	9^1	8^3		13		14	10						1	3		2	11		12	32
	5		4		6		7^1	9	8^2		12	13		10						1	3		2	11			33
1	5		4		6^1		7	9	8		12			10							3		2	11			34
	5		4		6		7	9^1	8^2		13			10					12	1	3		2	11			35
	5		4		6		7	13	8^2		12			10^1						1	3		2	11		9	36
1	5		4		6		7	13	8^1		12		14	10^2							3^3		2	11		9	37
1	5		4		6		7		8					10							3		2	11		9	38
1	5		4^1		6		7		8		12		14	10							3	13^3	2	11		9^2	39
1^1	5		4		6		7	9	8		13		14	10					12		3		2^2	11^3			40
1	5	12	4		6^2		7	9	8		13		14	10^3							3^1		2	11			41
1	5		4		6		7	9^1	8		12	13	14	10^2							3		2	11^3			42

FA Cup
Fourth Qual   Welling U   (a)   0-2

Trophy
Second Round   Telford U   (h)   2-4

FA Premiership   **LEEDS UNITED**

FOUNDATION

Immediately the Leeds City club (founded in 1904) was wound up by the FA in October 1919, following allegations of illegal payments to players, a meeting was called by a Leeds solicitor, Mr Alf Masser, at which Leeds United was formed. They joined the Midland League playing their first game in that competition in November 1919. It was in this same month that the new club had discussions with the directors of a virtually bankrupt Huddersfield Town who wanted to move to Leeds in an amalgamation. But Huddersfield survived even that crisis.

Elland Road, Leeds LS11 0ES.

Telephone: (0113) 226 6000.

Fax: (0113) 226 6050.

Website: www.lufc.co.uk

Ticket Information: 09068 121 680.

ClubCall: 09068 121 180.

Ground Capacity: 40,204.

Record Attendance: 57,892 v Sunderland, FA Cup 5th rd (replay), 15 March 1967.

Record Receipts: £780,697 v Tottenham Hotspur, FA Cup 5th rd, 13 February 1999.

Pitch Measurements: 105m × 68m.

President: The Right Hon. The Earl of Harewood KBE, LLD.

Chairman: Peter Ridsdale.

Directors: A. Hudson, A. Pearson, D. Spencer, I. Silvester.

Manager: David O'Leary.

Assistant Manager: Eddie Gray MBE.

Club Secretary: Ian Silvester.

Physio: David Swift.

Commercial Manager: Phil Brining.

Stadium Manager: Harry Stokey.

LATEST SEQUENCES

Longest Sequence of League Wins: 9, 26.9.31 – 21.11.31.

Longest Sequence of League Defeats: 6, 6.4.96 – 2.5.96.

Longest Sequence of League Draws: 5, 19.4.97 – 9.8.97.

Longest Sequence of Unbeaten League Matches: 34, 26.10.68 – 26.8.69.

Longest Sequence Without a League Win: 17, 1.2.47 – 26.5.47.

HONOURS

Football League: Division 1 – Champions 1968–69, 1973–74, 1991–92; Runners-up 1964–65, 1965–66, 1969–70, 1970–71, 1971–72; Division 2 – Champions 1923–24, 1963–64, 1989–90; Runners-up 1927–28, 1931–32, 1955–56.

FA Cup: Winners 1972; Runners-up 1965, 1970, 1973.

Football League Cup: Winners 1968; Runners-up 1996.

European Competitions: European Cup: 1969–70, 1974–75 (runners-up), 1992–93. *European Cup-Winners' Cup:* 1972–73 (runners-up). *European Fairs Cup:* 1965–66, 1966–67 (runners-up), 1967–68 (winners), 1968–69, 1970–71 (winners). *UEFA Cup:* 1971–72, 1973–74, 1979–80, 1995–96, 1998–99, 1999–2000 (semi-finalists).

Colours

All white with yellow and royal blue trim.

Change Colours

All yellow with royal blue trim.

Year Formed: 1919, as Leeds United after disbandment (by FA order) of Leeds City (formed in 1904).

Turned Professional: 1920.

Ltd Co.: 1920.

Club Nickname: 'United'.

First Football League Game: 28 August 1920, Division 2, v Port Vale (a) L 0–2 – Down; Duffield, Tillotson; Musgrove, Baker, Walton; Mason, Goldthorpe, Thompson, Lyon, Best.

Record League Victory: 8–0 v Leicester C, Division 1, 7 April 1934 – Moore; George Milburn, Jack Milburn; Edwards, Hart, Copping; Mahon (2), Firth (2), Duggan (2), Furness (2), Cochrane.

Record Cup Victory: 10–0 v Lyn (Oslo), European Cup 1st rd 1st leg, 17 September 1969 – Sprake; Reaney, Cooper, Bremner (2), Charlton, Hunter, Madeley, Clarke (2), Jones (3), Giles (2) (Bates), O'Grady (1).

Record Defeat: 1–8 v Stoke C, Division 1, 27 August 1934.

Most League Points (2 for a win): 67, Division 1, 1968–69.

Most League Points (3 for a win): 85, Division 2, 1989–90.

Most League Goals: 98, Division 2, 1927–28.

Highest League Scorer in Season: John Charles, 42, Division 2, 1953–54.

Most League Goals in Total Aggregate: Peter Lorimer, 168, 1965–79 and 1983–86.

Most League Goals in One Match: 5, Gordon Hodgson v Leicester C, Division 1, 1 October 1938.

Most Capped Player: Billy Bremner, 54, Scotland.

Most League Appearances: Jack Charlton, 629, 1953–73.

Youngest League Player: Peter Lorimer, 15 years 289 days v Southampton, 29 September 1962.

Record Transfer Fee Received: £12,000,000 from Atletico Madrid for Jimmy Floyd Hasselbaink, July 1999.

Record Transfer Fee Paid: £5,600,000 to Sunderland for Michael Bridges, July 1999.

Football League Record: 1920 Elected to Division 2; 1924–27 Division 1; 1927–28 Division 2; 1928–31 Division 1; 1931–32 Division 2; 1932–47 Division 1; 1947–56 Division 2; 1956–60 Division 1; 1960–64 Division 2; 1964–82 Division 1; 1982–90 Division 2; 1990–92 Division 1; 1992– FA Premier League.

MANAGERS

Dick Ray 1919–20
Arthur Fairclough 1920–27
Dick Ray 1927–35
Bill Hampson 1935–47
Willis Edwards 1947–48
Major Frank Buckley 1948–53
Raich Carter 1953–58
Bill Lambton 1958–59
Jack Taylor 1959–61
Don Revie OBE 1961–74
Brian Clough 1974
Jimmy Armfield 1974–78
Jock Stein CBE 1978
Jimmy Adamson 1978–80
Allan Clarke 1980–82
Eddie Gray MBE 1982–85
Billy Bremner 1985–88
Howard Wilkinson 1988–96
George Graham 1996–98
David O'Leary October 1998–

TEN YEAR LEAGUE RECORD

		P	W	D	L	F	A	Pts	Pos
1989-90	Div 2	46	24	13	9	79	52	85	1
1990-91	Div 1	38	19	7	12	65	47	64	4
1991-92	Div 1	42	22	16	4	74	37	82	1
1992-93	PR Lge	42	12	15	15	57	62	51	17
1993-94	PR Lge	42	18	16	8	65	39	70	5
1994-95	PR Lge	42	20	13	9	59	38	73	5
1995-96	PR Lge	38	12	7	19	40	57	43	13
1996-97	PR Lge	38	11	13	14	28	38	46	11
1997-98	PR Lge	38	17	8	13	57	46	59	5
1998-99	PR Lge	38	18	13	7	62	34	67	4

DID YOU KNOW ?

On 21 October 1999, when Leeds United beat Lokomotiv Moscow 4-1 in the UEFA Cup second round first leg, they created a club record with their 10th successive League and Cup win.

LEEDS UNITED 1999–2000 LEAGUE RECORD

Match No.	Date	Venue	Opponents	Result	H/T Score	Lg. Pos.	Goalscorers	Attendance
1	Aug 7	H	Derby Co	D 0-0	0-0	12		40,118
2	11	A	Southampton	W 3-0	1-0	—	Bridges 3 [11, 51, 72]	15,206
3	14	A	Manchester U	L 0-2	0-0	8		55,187
4	21	H	Sunderland	W 2-1	0-1	6	Bowyer [52], Mills [71]	39,064
5	23	H	Liverpool	L 1-2	1-1	—	Song (og) [20]	39,703
6	28	A	Tottenham H	W 2-1	0-1	5	Smith [53], Harte [83]	36,012
7	Sept 11	A	Coventry C	W 4-3	3-2	4	Bowyer [7], Huckerby [25], Harte (pen) [33], Bridges [60]	21,528
8	19	H	Middlesbrough	W 2-0	1-0	2	Bridges [14], Kewell [64]	34,122
9	25	H	Newcastle U	W 3-2	2-1	2	Bowyer [11], Kewell [39], Bridges [77]	40,192
10	Oct 3	A	Watford	W 2-1	1-1	1	Bridges [45], Kewell [70]	19,677
11	16	H	Sheffield W	W 2-0	0-0	1	Smith 2 [72, 78]	39,437
12	24	A	Everton	D 4-4	2-3	1	Bridges 2 [15, 67], Kewell [35], Woodgate [72]	37,355
13	30	H	West Ham U	W 1-0	0-0	1	Harte [57]	40,190
14	Nov 7	A	Wimbledon	L 0-2	0-1	2		18,747
15	20	H	Bradford C	W 2-1	0-0	2	Smith [54], Harte (pen) [80]	39,937
16	28	H	Southampton	W 1-0	0-0	1	Bridges [90]	39,288
17	Dec 5	A	Derby Co	W 1-0	0-0	1	Harte (pen) [90]	29,455
18	19	A	Chelsea	W 2-0	0-0	1	McPhail 2 [66, 87]	35,106
19	26	H	Leicester C	W 2-1	2-1	1	Bridges [29], Bowyer [45]	40,105
20	28	A	Arsenal	L 0-2	0-1	1		38,096
21	Jan 3	A	Aston Villa	L 1-2	0-1	1	Kewell [46]	40,027
22	23	A	Sunderland	W 2-1	1-0	1	Wilcox [24], Bridges [50]	41,633
23	Feb 5	A	Liverpool	L 1-3	0-1	2	Bowyer [62]	44,793
24	12	H	Tottenham H	W 1-0	1-0	2	Kewell [23]	40,127
25	20	H	Manchester U	L 0-1	0-0	2		40,160
26	26	A	Middlesbrough	D 0-0	0-0	2		34,800
27	Mar 5	H	Coventry C	W 3-0	2-0	2	Kewell [5], Bridges [42], Wilcox [85]	38,710
28	12	A	Bradford C	W 2-1	1-0	2	Bridges 2 [12, 63]	18,276
29	19	H	Wimbledon	W 4-1	3-1	2	Bakke 2 [23, 39], Harte (pen) [28], Kewell [83]	39,256
30	26	A	Leicester C	L 1-2	1-1	2	Kewell [38]	21,059
31	Apr 1	H	Chelsea	L 0-1	0-0	2		40,162
32	9	A	Aston Villa	L 0-1	0-1	3		33,889
33	16	H	Arsenal	L 0-4	0-1	4		39,307
34	23	A	Newcastle U	D 2-2	2-1	4	Bridges [12], Wilcox [17]	36,448
35	30	A	Sheffield W	W 3-0	1-0	4	Hopkin [1], Bridges [53], Kewell [68]	23,416
36	May 3	H	Watford	W 3-1	2-1	—	Bridges [20], Duberry [45], Huckerby [52]	36,324
37	8	H	Everton	D 1-1	1-0	—	Bridges [30]	37,713
38	14	A	West Ham U	D 0-0	0-0	3		26,044

Final League Position: 3

GOALSCORERS

League (58): Bridges 19, Kewell 10, Harte 6 (4 pens), Bowyer 5, Smith 4, Wilcox 3, Bakke 2, Huckerby 2, McPhail 2, Duberry 1, Hopkin 1, Mills 1, Woodgate 1, own goal 1.
Worthington Cup (1): Mills 1.
FA Cup (9): Bakke 4, Kewell 2, Bowyer 1, Harte 1, Smith 1.

Martyn N 38	Mills D 16 + 1	Harte I 33	Woodgate J 32 + 2	Radebe L 31	Batty D 16	Hopkin D 10 + 4	Smith A 20 + 6	Bridges M 32 + 2	Kewell H 36	Bowyer L 31 + 2	McPhail S 23 + 1	Duberry M 12 + 1	Jones M 5 + 6	Bakke E 24 + 5	Huckerby D 9 + 24	Hiden M — + 1	Kelly G 28 + 3	Haaland A 7 + 6	Wilcox J 15 + 5	Match No.
1	2	3	4	5	6	7	8^1	9	10	11^1	12									1
1	2	3	4	5	8	7^1		9	10^2	11		6		12	13					2
1	2	3^2	4	5	8	12		9	10^2	11		6		13			7	14		3
1	2	3	4	5	6	7	12	9	10	11				8						4
1	2	3	4	5	6	7^2	12	9	10	11		13		8						5
1	2^2	3	4^1	5	8	12	7	9^2	10	11		6		13			14			6
1	2	3^2	12	5	6	7		9	10	11		4^1		8			13			7
1	2	3	4	5	6	7^2	8	9	10	11				12			13			8
1		3	4	5	6		8^1	9	10	11	7^2			12			2	13		9
1	12	3	4	5^1	6	7^3	8	9^2	10	11				13		2		14		10
1	2		4	5	6	8	9^1	10	11	7		3		12						11
1		3	4	5	6	8^1	9	10	11	7				12			2			12
1		3	4	5	6	8^1	9	10	11	7				12			2			13
1		3	4^2	5	6	12	8^1	10	11^3	7		13	14		9			2		14
1		3	4	5	6	8^1	9	11	7	10				12			2			15
1	5	3	4	6^2	8^1	9	10	11	7			13		12			2			16
1		3	4	5	12	9	10	11	7^2			13		6	8^1		2			17
1		3	4	5				9^2	10	11^1	7	12		6	8		2	13		18
1		3	4	5				9	10	11	7			6	8^1		2	12		19
1		3	4	5			8^2	9	10	11^1	7			12	6		2	13		20
1		3	4	5	8^1			9	10	11^2	7	12			2	6		13		21
1		3	4	5	6			9^1	10	8	7			12			2		11	22
1		3	4	5	6		12	9^1	10	8	7^2			13			2		11	23
1		3	4	5	6^2		8	9	10^1	7				12			2	13	11	24
1		3	4	5			8	9	10	7				6			2		11	25
1	2	3	4	5		7^1	12	9^2	10	8				13			6		11	26
1		3	4^3	5				9^1	10	8^2	7	13		6	12		2	14	11	27
1		3	4	5		12		9^2	10	8	7^1			6	13		2		11	28
1		3	4	5		12		9	10^2	8	7		14	6^3	13		2		11	29
1		3	4	5				9^1	10	8	6			12			2	7	11	30
1		3	4	5				9	10	8	7			6			12	2	11^1	31
1		3	4	5				9^1	10	8	7			6			12	2	11	32
1		3	4		8			9^1	10	11	7	5		6			2	12		33
1	2	3^1	4	5			12	9^2	10	8	7			6	13				11	34
1		3	4	5				9^1	10	8	7			6^2	12		2	13	11	35
1	12	3	4	5^1				9	10	11	7	13		6	8^2		2			36
1		3	4	5				9^1	10	8	7			6	12		2	13	11^2	37
1		3	4	5		12		9^1	10	8	7	13		6^2	14		2		11^3	38

Worthington Cup

Third Round	Blackburn R	(h)	1-0
Fourth Round	Leicester C	(a)	0-0

FA Cup

Third Round	Port Vale	(h)	2-0
Fourth Round	Manchester C	(a)	5-2
Fifth Round	Aston Villa	(a)	2-3

FA Premiership

LEICESTER CITY

FOUNDATION

In 1884 a number of young footballers who were mostly old boys of Wyggeston School, held a meeting at a house on the Roman Fosse Way and formed Leicester Fosse FC. They collected 9d (less than 4p) towards the cost of a ball, plus the same amount for membership. Their first professional, Harry Webb from Stafford Rangers, was signed in 1888 for 2s 6d (12p) per week, plus travelling expenses.

City Stadium, Filbert St, Leicester LE2 7FL.
Telephone: (0116) 291 5000.
Fax: (0116) 247 0585.
Ticket Office: (0116) 291 5232.
ClubCall: 09068 121 185.
24hr Ticket Information: 09068 121 028.
Website: www.lcfc.co.uk
Ground Capacity: 22,215.
Record Attendance: 47,298 v Tottenham H, FA Cup 5th rd, 18 February 1928.
Record Receipts: £377,467 v Aston Villa, League Cup semi-final, 2nd leg, 2 February 2000.
Pitch Measurements: 110yd × 76yd.
President: T. W. Shipman.
Chairman: J. M. Elsom FCA.
Finance Director and Acting Chief Operating Officer: Steve Kind FCCA.
Directors: J. M. Elsom FCA, S. A. Kind FCCA, M. F. George.
Manager: Peter Taylor.
Assistant Manager: John Robertson.
First Team Coach: David Nish.
Physios: Alan Smith and Mick Yeoman.
Director of Media and Communications: Paul Mace.
Leicester City PLC Communications: Paul Barker.
Football Secretary: Andrew Neville.
Stadium Manager: John Petherick.

LATEST SEQUENCES

Longest Sequence of League Wins: 7, 28.2.93 – 27.3.93.
Longest Sequence of League Defeats: 7, 28.8.90 – 29.9.90.
Longest Sequence of League Draws: 6, 21.8.76 – 18.9.76.
Longest Sequence of Unbeaten League Matches: 19, 6.2.71 – 18.8.71.
Longest Sequence Without a League Win: 18, 12.4.75 – 1.11.75.

HONOURS

Football League: Division 1 – Runners-up 1928–29; Promoted from Division 1 1993–94 (play-offs) and 1995–96 (play-offs); Division 2 – Champions 1924–25, 1936–37, 1953–54, 1956–57, 1970–71, 1979–80; Runners-up 1907–08.

FA Cup: Runners-up 1949, 1961, 1963, 1969.

Football League Cup: Winners 1964, 1997, 2000; Runners-up 1965, 1999.

European Competitions: *European Cup-Winners' Cup:* 1961–62. *UEFA Cup:* 1997–98.

Colours
Royal blue shirts, white shorts, blue stockings.

Change Colours
White shirts, royal blue shorts, white stockings.

Year Formed: 1884.

Turned Professional: 1888.

Ltd Co: 1897.

Previous Name: 1884, Leicester Fosse; 1919, Leicester City.

Club Nickname: 'Foxes'.

Previous Grounds: 1884, Victoria Park; 1887, Belgrave Road; 1888, Victoria Park; 1891, Filbert Street.

First Football League Game: 1 September 1894, Division 2, v Grimsby T (a) L 3–4 – Thraves; Smith, Bailey; Seymour, Brown, Henrys; Hill, Hughes, McArthur (1), Skea (2), Priestman.

Record League Victory: 10–0 v Portsmouth, Division 1, 20 October 1928 – McLaren; Black, Brown; Findlay, Carr, Watson; Adcock, Hine (3), Chandler (6), Lochhead, Barry (1).

Record Cup Victory: 8–1 v Coventry C (a), League Cup 5th rd, 1 December 1964 – Banks; Sjoberg, Norman (2); Roberts, King, McDerment; Hodgson (2), Cross, Goodfellow, Gibson (1), Stringfellow (2), (1 og).

Record Defeat: 0–12 (as Leicester Fosse) v Nottingham F, Division 1, 21 April 1909.

Most League Points (2 for a win): 61, Division 2, 1956–57.

Most League Points (3 for a win): 77, Division 2, 1991–92.

Most League Goals: 109, Division 2, 1956–57.

Highest League Scorer in Season: Arthur Rowley, 44, Division 2, 1956–57.

Most League Goals in Total Aggregate: Arthur Chandler, 259, 1923–35.

Most League Goals in One Match: 6, John Duncan v Port Vale, Division 2, 25 December 1924; 6, Arthur Chandler v Portsmouth, Division 1, 20 October 1928.

Most Capped Player: John O'Neill, 39, Northern Ireland.

Most League Appearances: Adam Black, 528, 1920–35.

Youngest League Player: Dave Buchanan, 16 years 192 days v Oldham Ath, 1 January 1979.

Record Transfer Fee Received: £11,000,000 from Liverpool for Emile Heskey, March 2000.

Record Transfer Fee Paid: £3,000,000 to Norwich C for Darren Eadie, December 1999.

Football League Record: 1894 Elected to Division 2; 1908–09 Division 1; 1909–25 Division 2; 1925–35 Division 1; 1935–37 Division 2; 1937–39 Division 1; 1946–54 Division 2; 1954–55 Division 1; 1955–57 Division 2; 1957–69 Division 1; 1969–71 Division 2; 1971–78 Division 1; 1978–80 Division 2; 1980–81 Division 1; 1981–83 Division 2; 1983–87 Division 1; 1987–92 Division 2; 1992–94 Division 1; 1994–95 FA Premier League; 1995–96 Division 1; 1996– FA Premier League.

MANAGERS

Frank Gardner 1884–92
Ernest Marson 1892–94
J. Lee 1894–95
Henry Jackson 1895–97
William Clark 1897–98
George Johnson 1898–1912
Jack Bartlett 1912–14
Louis Ford 1914–15
Harry Linney 1915–19
Peter Hodge 1919–26
Willie Orr 1926–32
Peter Hodge 1932–34
Arthur Lochhead 1934–36
Frank Womack 1936–39
Tom Bromilow 1939–45
Tom Mather 1945–46
John Duncan 1946–49
Norman Bullock 1949–55
David Halliday 1955–58
Matt Gillies 1958–68
Frank O'Farrell 1968–71
Jimmy Bloomfield 1971–77
Frank McLintock 1977–78
Jock Wallace 1978–82
Gordon Milne 1982–86
Bryan Hamilton 1986–87
David Pleat 1987–91
Gordon Lee 1991
Brian Little 1991–94
Mark McGhee 1994–95
Martin O'Neill 1995–2000
Peter Taylor June 2000–

TEN YEAR LEAGUE RECORD

		P	W	D	L	F	A	Pts	Pos
1989-90	Div 2	46	15	14	17	67	79	59	13
1990-91	Div 2	46	14	8	24	60	83	50	22
1991-92	Div 2	46	23	8	15	62	55	77	4
1992-93	Div 1	46	22	10	14	71	64	76	6
1993-94	Div 1	46	19	16	11	72	59	73	4
1994-95	PR Lge	42	6	11	25	45	80	29	21
1995-96	Div 1	46	19	14	13	66	60	71	5
1996-97	PR Lge	38	12	11	15	46	54	47	9
1997-98	PR Lge	38	13	14	11	51	41	53	10
1998-99	PR Lge	38	12	13	13	40	46	49	10

DID YOU KNOW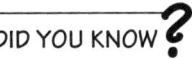

Wing-half Sep Smith was a senior Leicester City player from his League debut on 31 August 1929 until his final match on 7 May 1949. He appeared in 373 League and Cup games, plus 213 wartime matches for the club.

LEICESTER CITY 1999–2000 LEAGUE RECORD

Match No.	Date	Venue	Opponents	Result	H/T Score	Lg. Pos.	Goalscorers	Attendance
1	Aug 7	A	Arsenal	L 1-2	0-0	14	Cottee [57]	38,026
2	11	H	Coventry C	W 1-0	1-0	—	Izzet (pen) [24]	19,196
3	14	H	Chelsea	D 2-2	1-0	11	Heskey [10], Izzet (pen) [90]	21,068
4	21	A	West Ham U	L 1-2	1-1	15	Heskey [2]	23,631
5	24	A	Middlesbrough	W 3-0	2-0	—	Heskey 2 [35, 83], Cottee [38]	33,126
6	30	H	Watford	W 1-0	1-0	5	Izzet [44]	17,920
7	Sept 11	A	Sunderland	L 0-2	0-1	11		38,621
8	18	H	Liverpool	D 2-2	1-2	11	Cottee [2], Izzet [86]	21,623
9	25	H	Aston Villa	W 3-1	1-0	7	Izzet [40], Southgate (og) [48], Cottee [55]	19,917
10	Oct 3	A	Tottenham H	W 3-2	1-2	7	Izzet 2 (1 pen) [25 (p), 69], Taggart [76]	35,591
11	16	A	Southampton	W 2-1	2-0	5	Guppy [8], Cottee [39]	19,556
12	23	A	Bradford C	L 1-3	1-2	6	Impey [21]	17,655
13	30	H	Sheffield W	W 3-0	2-0	5	Taggart 2 [24, 36], Cottee [57]	19,046
14	Nov 6	A	Manchester U	L 0-2	0-1	7		55,191
15	20	H	Wimbledon	W 2-1	1-1	7	Cottee 2 [22, 58]	18,255
16	27	A	Coventry C	W 1-0	0-0	5	Heskey [60]	22,016
17	Dec 4	H	Arsenal	L 0-3	0-1	6		20,495
18	18	H	Derby Co	L 0-1	0-0	6		18,581
19	26	A	Leeds U	L 1-2	1-2	7	Cottee [10]	40,105
20	28	H	Newcastle U	L 1-2	0-1	7	Zagorakis [83]	21,225
21	Jan 3	A	Everton	D 2-2	2-1	8	Elliott 2 [26, 31]	30,490
22	15	A	Chelsea	D 1-1	1-0	8	Taggart [41]	35,063
23	22	H	West Ham U	L 1-3	1-2	10	Heskey [24]	19,019
24	Feb 5	H	Middlesbrough	W 2-1	2-0	9	O'Neill (og) [1], Schwarzer (og) [41]	17,550
25	12	A	Watford	D 1-1	1-0	10	Elliott [39]	16,814
26	Mar 5	H	Sunderland	W 5-2	2-0	10	Collymore 3 [17, 60, 87], Heskey [34], Oakes [90]	20,432
27	11	A	Wimbledon	L 1-2	0-1	11	Taggart [55]	14,316
28	18	H	Manchester U	L 0-2	0-1	13		22,170
29	26	H	Leeds U	W 2-1	1-1	11	Collymore [14], Guppy [48]	21,059
30	Apr 2	A	Derby Co	L 0-3	0-3	12		25,763
31	8	H	Everton	D 1-1	1-1	13	Taggart [8]	18,705
32	15	A	Newcastle U	W 2-0	1-0	10	Cottee [7], Savage [52]	36,426
33	19	H	Tottenham H	L 0-1	0-0	—		19,764
34	22	A	Aston Villa	D 2-2	1-1	11	Elliott [36], Lennon [67]	31,229
35	29	A	Southampton	W 2-1	1-1	11	Cottee [22], Izzet [60]	15,178
36	May 3	H	Liverpool	W 2-0	1-0	—	Cottee [2], Gilchrist [48]	43,456
37	6	H	Bradford C	W 3-0	0-0	8	Elliott 2 [59, 63], Cottee [68]	21,103
38	14	A	Sheffield W	L 0-4	0-2	8		21,656

Final League Position: 8

GOALSCORERS

League (55): Cottee 13, Izzet 8 (3 pens), Heskey 7, Elliott 6, Taggart 6, Collymore 4, Guppy 2, Gilchrist 1, Impey 1, Lennon 1, Oakes 1, Savage 1, Zagorakis 1, own goals 3.
Worthington Cup (15): Elliott 3, Marshall 3, Oakes 2 (1 pen), Fenton 1, Heskey 1, Izzet 1, Lennon 1, Taggart 1, Walsh 1, own goal 1.
FA Cup (3): Elliott 2, Izzet 1.

Flowers T 29	Impey A 28+1	Guppy S 29+1	Elliott M 37	Walsh S 5+6	Sinclair F 34	Lennon N 31	Izzet M 32	Cottee T 30+3	Savage R 35	Heskey E 23	Taggart G 30+1	Marshall I 2+19	Gilchrist P 17+10	Campbell S 1+3	Arphexad P 9+2	Oakes S 15+7	Zagorakis T 6+11	Eadie D 15+1	Thomas D —+3	Gunnlaugsson A 2	Fenton G 1+1	Goodwin T 1	Stewart J —+1	Collymore S 6	Dudfield L —+2	Match No.
1	2	3	4	5[1]	6	7	8	9	10	11[2]	12	13														1
1	2	3	4		6	7	8	9	10		5[1]	11[2]	12	13												2
1	2	3	4		6	7	8	9	10[1]	11	5[2]	12	13													3
1	2	3	4		6	7	8	9	10[1]	11	5[2]	12	13													4
1[6]	2	3	4		6	7	8	9[1]	10	11	5	12			15											5
		3	4		6	7	8	9[1]	2	11	5	12			1	10[2]	13									6
1	2	3	4		6	7	8	9[1]	10[2]	11	5	12	13													7
	2[2]	3	4		6	7	8	9[1]	10	11	5	12			1		13									8
1	2	3	4		6	7	8	9[1]	10[2]	11	12	5	13													9
1	2	3	4			7	8	9	10	11	5	12	6[1]													10
1	2	3	4		6	7	8	9[1]	10[3]	11	5[2]	12	13			14										11
1	2	3	4	12	6	7	8	9[1]	10[2]	11	5	13														12
1	2	3	4		6	7	8	9[2]	10[3]	11	5[1]	12	13			14										13
1	2	3	4	12	6	7	8	9[1]	10	11	5															14
1	2	3		5	6	7		9	10	11	4			8												15
1	2	3	4		6	7	8	9	10	11	5															16
1	2[1]	3	4		6	7	8	9	10[2]	11	5	12	13			14										17
1	2[1]		4	5		3	12	7		9	6				8	10	11									18
	4			2		8	9	3		11	5		6[1]		1	7	12	10								19
1			4		6	8[1]	9[2]	3		11	5	2			12	10	7	13								20
1[6]		10	5	6	7[2]	9	2	4			12			15	11	8[1]	3	13								21
	12		4	2		9	5	10[2]	6						1	11	8	3	7[1]	13						22
	4		7			11	6	2							1	8[2]	3	12	9[1]	10	5	13				23
1	2[1]	9	12		4	7	8	11		5	6				10		3							8		24
1	2		4	5		9	11			6					10	7	3							8		25
1		3	4		6	7[1]	8		2	9	5				12	11								10		26
1	2	3	4		6	7	8	9		11[2]	5	12	13											10		27
1		3	4		6	7	8	12	2		5	13			10[1]	11[2]								9		28
1		3	4		6[2]	7	8	12	2		5	13			10	11[1]								9		29
12		3	4		6[2]	7	8		2		5	14	13		1	10	11[1]							9[2]		30
1	2	3	4			7	8[1]	9[1]		11	5			13		6	10[2]	12							14	31
1	2	3	10		6	7	9	8[1]			5			13	4	11[2]	12									32
1	2	3[1]	10		6	8	9[2]	7			5			13	4	11	12									33
1		3	4		2	7	8[1]	9	10		5		6			11[2]	12							13		34
1	2	3	10	12	6	7	8	9[2]		11	5[1]				4		13									35
	2	3		5	6	7	8	9[2]	10			13		4	1	12	11[1]									36
	2[3]	3	5	12	6[2]	7	8	9	10					4[1]	1		13	11							14	37
	2[3]	3	5	12	6	7	8	9[2]	10					4[1]	1		14	11								38

Worthington Cup

Second Round	Crystal Palace	(a)	3-3
		(h)	4-2
Third Round	Grimsby T	(h)	2-0
Fourth Round	Leeds U	(h)	0-0
Fifth Round	Fulham	(h)	3-3
Semi-Final	Aston Villa	(a)	0-0
		(h)	1-0
Final	Tranmere R		2-1
(at Wembley)			

FA Cup

Third Round	Hereford U	(a)	0-0
		(h)	2-1
Fourth Round	Arsenal	(a)	0-0
		(h)	0-0
Fifth Round	Chelsea	(a)	1-2

Division 3

LEYTON ORIENT

FOUNDATION

There is some doubt about the foundation of Leyton Orient, and, indeed, some confusion with clubs like Leyton and Clapton over their early history. As regards the foundation, the most favoured version is that Leyton Orient was formed originally by members of Homerton Theological College who established Glyn Cricket Club in 1881 and then carried on through the following winter playing football. Eventually many employees of the Orient Shipping Line became involved and so the name Orient was chosen in 1888.

Leyton Stadium, Brisbane Road, Leyton, London E10 5NE.

Telephone: (020) 8926 1111.

Fax: (020) 8926 1110.

ClubCall: 09068 121 150.

Ground Capacity: 13,842.

Record Attendance: 34,345 v West Ham U, FA Cup 4th rd, 25 January 1964.

Record Receipts: £87,867.92 v West Ham U, FA Cup 3rd rd, 10 January 1987.

Pitch Measurements: 110yd × 80yd.

Chairman: Barry Hearn.

Chief Executive: Steve Dawson.

Directors: Tony Wood OBE, John Goldsmith FRIBA, David Dodd, Steve Davis, Nick Levene.

Team Manager: Tommy Taylor.

First Team Coach: Paul Clark.

Physio: Tony Flynn.

Secretary: Frank Woolf.

Commercial Manager: Lyn Newman.

Stadium Manager: Janet Hasler.

LATEST SEQUENCES

Longest Sequence of League Wins: 10, 21.1.56 – 30.3.56.

Longest Sequence of League Defeats: 9, 1.4.95 – 6.5.95.

Longest Sequence of League Draws: 6, 30.11.74 – 28.12.74.

Longest Sequence of Unbeaten League Matches: 13, 30.10.54 – 19.2.55.

Longest Sequence Without a League Win: 23, 6.10.62 – 13.4.63.

HONOURS

Football League: Division 1 best season: 22nd, 1962–63; Division 2 – Runners-up 1961–62; Division 3 – Champions 1969–70; Division 3 (S) – Champions 1955–56; Runners-up 1954–55; Promoted from Division 4 1988–89 (play-offs).

FA Cup: Semi-final 1978.

Football League Cup: best season: 5th rd, 1963.

Colours
White shirts with red V, black shorts, red stockings.

Change Colours
Blue and yellow.

Year Formed: 1881.

Turned Professional: 1903.

Ltd Co.: 1906.

Previous Names: 1881, Glyn Cricket and Football Club; 1886, Eagle Football Club; 1888, Orient Football Club; 1898, Clapton Orient; 1946, Leyton Orient; 1966, Orient; 1987, Leyton Orient.

Club Nickname: 'The O's'.

Previous Grounds: 1884, Glyn Road; 1896, Whittles Athletic Ground; 1900, Millfields Road; 1930, Lea Bridge Road; 1937, Brisbane Road.

First Football League Game: 2 September 1905, Division 2, v Leicester Fosse (a) L 1–2 – Butler; Holmes, Codling; Lamberton, Boden, Boyle; Kingaby (1), Wootten, Leigh, Evenson, Bourne.

Record League Victory: 8–0 v Crystal Palace, Division 3 (S), 12 November 1955 – Welton; Lee, Earl; Blizzard, Aldous, McKnight; White (1), Facey (3), Burgess (2), Heckman, Hartburn (2). 8–0 v Rochdale, Division 4, 20 October 1987 – Wells; Howard, Dickenson (1), Smalley (1), Day, Hull, Hales (2), Castle (Sussex), Shinners (2), Godfrey (Harvey), Comfort (2). 8–0 v Colchester U, Division 4, 15 October 1988 – Wells; Howard, Dickenson, Hales (1p), Day (1), Sitton (1), Baker (1), Ward, Hull (3), Juryeff, Comfort (1). 8–0 v Doncaster R, Division 3, 28 December 1997 – Hyde; Channing, Naylor, Smith (1p), Hicks, Clark, Ling, Joseph R, Griffiths (3) (Harris), Richards (2) (Baker (1)), Inglethorpe (1) (Simpson).

Record Cup Victory: 9–2 v Chester, League Cup 3rd rd, 15 October 1962 – Robertson; Charlton, Taylor; Gibbs, Bishop, Lea; Deeley (1), Waites (3), Dunmore (2), Graham (3), Wedge.

Record Defeat: 0–8 v Aston Villa, FA Cup 4th rd, 30 January 1929.

Most League Points (2 for a win): 66, Division 3 (S), 1955–56.

Most League Points (3 for a win): 75, Division 4, 1988–89.

Most League Goals: 106, Division 3 (S), 1955–56.

Highest League Scorer in Season: Tom Johnston, 35, Division 2, 1957–58.

Most League Goals in Total Aggregate: Tom Johnston, 121, 1956–58, 1959–61.

Most League Goals in One Match: 4, Wally Leigh v Bradford C, Division 2, 13 April 1906; 4, Albert Pape v Oldham Ath, Division 2, 1 September 1924; 4, Peter Kitchen v Millwall, Division 3, 21 April 1984.

Most Capped Players: Tunji Banjo, 7 (7), Nigeria; John Chiedozie, 7 (9), Nigeria; Tony Grealish, 7 (45), Eire.

Most League Appearances: Peter Allen, 432, 1965–78.

Youngest League Player: Paul Went, 15 years 327 days v Preston NE, 4 September 1965.

Record Transfer Fee Received: £600,000 from Notts Co, for John Chiedozie, August 1981.

Record Transfer Fee Paid: £175,000 to Wigan Ath for Paul Beesley, October 1989.

Football League Record: 1905 Elected to Division 2; 1929–56 Division 3 (S); 1956–62 Division 2; 1962–63 Division 1; 1963–66 Division 2; 1966–70 Division 3; 1970–82 Division 2; 1982–85 Division 3; 1985–89 Division 4; 1989–92 Division 3; 1992–95 Division 2; 1995– Division 3.

MANAGERS

Sam Omerod 1905–06
Ike Ivenson 1906
Billy Holmes 1907–22
Peter Proudfoot 1922–29
Arthur Grimsdell 1929–30
Peter Proudfoot 1930–31
Jimmy Seed 1931–33
David Pratt 1933–34
Peter Proudfoot 1935–39
Tom Halsey 1939
Bill Wright 1939–45
Willie Hall 1945
Bill Wright 1945–46
Charlie Hewitt 1946–48
Neil McBain 1948–49
Alec Stock 1949–59
Les Gore 1959–61
Johnny Carey 1961–63
Benny Fenton 1963–64
Dave Sexton 1965
Dick Graham 1966–68
Jimmy Bloomfield 1968–71
George Petchey 1971–77
Jimmy Bloomfield 1977–81
Paul Went 1981
Ken Knighton 1981
Frank Clark 1982–91 *(Managing Director)*
Peter Eustace 1991–94
Chris Turner/John Sitton 1994–95
Pat Holland 1995–96
Tommy Taylor November 1996–

TEN YEAR LEAGUE RECORD

		P	W	D	L	F	A	Pts	Pos
1989-90	Div 3	46	16	10	20	52	56	58	14
1990-91	Div 3	46	18	10	18	55	58	64	13
1991-92	Div 3	46	18	11	17	62	52	65	10
1992-93	Div 2	46	21	9	16	69	53	72	7
1993-94	Div 2	46	14	14	18	57	71	56	18
1994-95	Div 2	46	6	8	32	30	75	26	24
1995-96	Div 3	46	12	11	23	44	63	47	21
1996-97	Div 3	46	15	12	19	50	58	57	16
1997-98	Div 3	46	19	12	15	62	47	66	11
1998-99	Div 3	46	19	15	12	68	59	72	6

DID YOU KNOW ?

Leyton Orient's first 4-4 draw in the League came on 17 September 1949 at Ipswich. They were losing 4-2 with two minutes remaining, with ten men after 70 minutes through injury and three suffering from mild food poisoning.

LEYTON ORIENT 1999–2000 LEAGUE RECORD

Match No.	Date	Venue	Opponents	Result	H/T Score	Lg. Pos.	Goalscorers	Attendance
1	Aug 7	A	Carlisle U	L	1-2	1-1	14	Inglethorpe [13]	3895
2	14	H	Brighton & HA	L	1-2	0-1	20	Richards [70]	7200
3	21	A	Peterborough U	L	1-2	0-2	22	Lockwood [52]	6448
4	28	H	Halifax T	W	1-0	1-0	20	Simba [42]	3703
5	30	A	Southend U	D	1-1	1-0	17	Walschaerts [23]	5980
6	Sept 3	H	Shrewsbury T	L	1-2	0-0	—	Inglethorpe [72]	3742
7	11	A	Mansfield T	D	1-1	1-0	19	Simba [6]	2491
8	18	H	Torquay U	L	0-2	0-1	22		4452
9	25	H	Hartlepool U	W	2-1	2-1	21	Low [13], Smith [27]	3889
10	Oct 2	A	Plymouth Arg	L	0-5	0-2	22		3782
11	9	A	York C	L	1-2	1-0	23	Clark [13]	2320
12	16	H	Lincoln C	L	2-3	0-1	23	Lockwood (pen) [58], Simba [89]	4349
13	19	H	Barnet	D	0-0	0-0	—		3532
14	23	A	Hartlepool U	L	0-1	0-0	23		2397
15	Nov 2	A	Darlington	L	1-3	0-2	—	Brkovic [86]	4532
16	6	H	Northampton T	D	0-0	0-0	24		3928
17	12	A	Rotherham U	W	1-0	0-0	22	Ling [76]	4280
18	23	H	Rochdale	D	0-0	0-0	—		2990
19	27	A	Cheltenham T	L	0-2	0-2	23		3604
20	Dec 4	H	Carlisle U	L	0-1	0-0	23		3871
21	18	A	Macclesfield T	L	0-1	0-0	24		2303
22	26	H	Swansea C	L	0-1	0-1	24		4447
23	28	A	Chester C	W	5-1	2-0	23	Watts [8], Griffiths 3 (2 pens) [38 (p), 50 (p), 61], Christie [69]	3160
24	Jan 3	H	Hull C	D	0-0	0-0	23		5169
25	8	A	Exeter C	W	3-1	1-1	23	Watts [37], Smith [55], Christie [90]	2434
26	15	A	Brighton & HA	W	1-0	0-0	21	Brkovic [50]	5863
27	22	H	Peterborough U	D	1-1	1-1	21	Brkovic [4]	4795
28	29	A	Halifax T	W	2-0	1-0	21	Watts [15], Christie [90]	2655
29	Feb 5	H	Southend U	W	2-1	1-0	19	Watts [15], Brkovic [69]	5972
30	8	H	Exeter C	W	4-1	2-1	—	Walschaerts [11], Watts [33], Lockwood [70], Richards [83]	3855
31	12	A	Shrewsbury T	L	0-1	0-0	19		2740
32	19	H	Cheltenham T	W	1-0	1-0	19	Walschaerts [20]	4884
33	26	A	Torquay U	D	0-0	0-0	19		2470
34	Mar 4	H	Mansfield T	L	1-3	0-1	19	Smith [73]	4281
35	7	A	Northampton T	L	1-2	0-0	—	Christie [70]	5121
36	11	H	Darlington	W	2-1	0-0	19	Lockwood [64], Watts [90]	4053
37	18	A	Rochdale	W	4-1	2-0	19	Christie 2 [5, 59], Smith [28], Lockwood [74]	2472
38	21	A	Rotherham U	L	0-1	0-0	—		3959
39	25	A	Swansea C	D	0-0	0-0	19		6330
40	Apr 1	H	Macclesfield T	D	0-0	0-0	19		4302
41	8	A	Hull C	L	0-2	0-1	19		4422
42	15	H	Chester C	L	1-2	1-1	20	Griffiths [9]	4123
43	22	A	Lincoln C	D	0-0	0-0	20		2718
44	24	H	Plymouth Arg	W	3-0	1-0	19	McGhee [26], Brkovic [78], Christie [81]	4113
45	29	A	Barnet	D	2-2	1-1	19	Lockwood (pen) [45], Beall [85]	4030
46	May 6	H	York C	D	0-0	0-0	19		4594

Final League Position: 19

GOALSCORERS

League (47): Christie 7, Lockwood 6 (2 pens), Watts 6, Brkovic 5, Griffiths 4 (2 pens), Smith 4, Simba 3, Walschaerts 3, Inglethorpe 2, Richards 2, Beall 1, Clark 1, Ling 1, Low 1, McGhee 1.
Worthington Cup (4): Lockwood 2 (1 pen), Inglethorpe 1, Watts 1.
FA Cup (2): Ampadu 1, Smith 1.

Bayes A 17	Smith D 44	Lockwood M 41	Parsons D 1	Ling M 14	Morrison D 5+8	Harris A 11+4	Downer S 24	Ampadu K 43	Christie I 22+14	Inglethorpe A 12+4	Beall B 22+11	Richards T 9+8	Low J 2+3	Hicks S 13+1	Walscheerts W 32+4	Watts S 21+11	Barrett S 29	Joseph M 38+3	Clark S 19	Simba A 8+5	Holligan G 1	Gough N 1+3	Carter R —+2	Canham S 1	Hockton D 1+4	Webb S 3+1	Brkovic A 25+4	McGhee D 17+6	Rowbotham D 4+2	Griffiths C 11	McElholm B 3	Martin J 8	Shorey N 4+3	Ibehre J —+3	Murray J —+2	Joseph R —+1	Gould R —+2	McLean A —+3	Match No.
1	2	3		4^1	5^2	6	7	8	9	10	11	12	13																										1
	4	3		7^3	12	6		8	9	10	11^2	13			5	2^1	14	1																					2
2		3		7^3	12	6		8^1	9		11	10			5	13	14	1	4^2																				3
	4	3		7^3	12	6		8			13	11				2	9^2	1	14	5		10^1																	4
	4	3		7^1	14	6		8			10	11		13^3		2	9^2	1	12	5																			5
1	4	3		7	12	6		8		9		11^1				2	13	14	5^2	10^2																			6
1	4	3			5	6		8			10					2	12		7	11	9^1																		7
1	4	3		7^1		6		8^3					12	5^2				2	10			9	13	14	11														8
1	5	3			11	6	7	8	9^1	13	14	4^3					12		2			10^2																	9
1	5			4^3			7	8			9^2	11	12	6^1		2	13		3			10					14												10
1	4	3					6				9	11	10^2				12		2	5		13	14			7^3	8^1												11
	4	3					6^2		9		10	11		5				1	2			7^1	12			13	8	14											12
	4					6		8	9		11			5				1	2	3		10				7													13
	4	3		7^3	12			8	9^2		10	11		5				1	2			6				13	14												14
1	4	3			12			8	9		10^1	11		5^2		13			2			6				7													15
	4	3		7	12			8	9			13		5^1		11^2		1	2			6	14			10^5													16
	5	4					7	8	9^3		12	13				3^2		1	2			6	14				11	10^1											17
	4	3				6		8^2	9^3		12	11		5		13		1	2				14			7		10^1											18
	4					6^1		8			12	10	11	5^2		2		1	3				14			7	13	9^3											19
	4^3					6	5	7	8		12					2	14	1	3			10^2				11	9^1												20
		3						8	9		12			5				1	2	4						7	6^1					10	11						21
	4	3						11						5		7^2	9^1	1	2	6						13						12	10						22
	5	3					7	8			12					4	9^2	1	2	6						11						13	10^1						23
	6	3					7	8			12					5	9^1	1	2							11							10						24
	5	3					7	8			12	13				4	9^3	1	2							11	14						10^1	6^2					25
	5	3					7	8			10	12				4	9	1	2							11^1	13							6^2					26
	5	3					7	8			10^1	12				4	9	1	2							11							6						27
		3		14			7	8			12	13	10^1			4	9	1	2							11^3	6							5^2					28
	5	3					7	8			12	10^2				4	9	1	2							11	13							6^1					29
	5	3					7^2	8			12	10				4	9	1	2							11	13							6^1					30
	5	3		13				8			12	10				4	9^3	1	2							11	6^2							7^1	14				31
	5	3					7	8^2			12	10				4	9	1	2							11^2	13							6^1					32
	5	3					7	8			12	13	10			4	9	1	2							11^2	6^1												33
	5	3					7	8			12	14	10			4	9	1	2							11^3								6^1	13				34
	5	3					7	8^2	9		10					4^3	12	1	2							11	13							6^1	14				35
1	5	3					7	8			12	10^1	13			4	9		2							11^2	6												36
	5	3		12			7	8			10	13				9^2	2^1									11^2	4							6					37
	5	3					7	8^1	10		12					4^3	9		2							11^2	6							13	14				38
1	5	3^3					7		10^2		12					4	9		2							11	6							8^1	13	14			39
1	5	3					7	8			12	13				4			2			14				11^3	6						9^2	10^1					40
1	5	3					7	8^3	10		11					4	9^2		2			12				6^1								13		14			41
	5	3					7	8^1	12							4	9^2	1	2			11				6							10	13					42
	5	3						8	9			7				4		1	2							11	6						10^1				12		43
	5	3						8	9			7				4^1	12	1	2							11	6						10^2				13		44
	5	3		12				8^2	9			7				4^1	13		2	6							11						10^3				14		45
1	5	3	11^1					8	9			7^3				12			2								13	4					10	6^2			14		46

Worthington Cup
First Round	Swindon T	(a)	1-0
		(h)	1-1
Second Round	Grimsby T	(a)	1-4
		(h)	1-0

FA Cup
First Round	Cardiff C	(h)	1-1
		(a)	1-3

Division 3   LINCOLN CITY

FOUNDATION

Although there was a Lincoln club as far back as 1861, the present organisation was formed in 1884 winning the Lincolnshire Senior Cup in only their fourth season. They were founder members of the Midland League in 1889 and that competition's first champions.

Sincil Bank, Lincoln LN5 8LD.
Telephone: (01522) 880 011.
Fax: (01522) 880 020.
Website: www.redimps.com
ClubCall: 09068 555 900.
Ground Capacity: 11,729.
Record Attendance: 23,196 v Derby Co, League Cup 4th rd, 15 November 1967.
Record Receipts: £44,184.46 v Everton, Coca-Cola Cup 2nd rd 1st leg, 21 September 1993.
Pitch Measurements: 110yd × 71yd.
President: J. Jennison.
Chairman: K. J. Reames.
Vice-Chairman: J. Hicks.
Directors: N. Woolsey, P. Jackson, S. Tindall.
Chief Executive: J. Lonsdale.
Hon. Consultant Surgeon: Mr Brian Smith.
Hon. Club Doctor: Chris Batty.
Company Secretary: J. Hicks.
Manager: Phil Stant.
Assistant Manager: George Foster.
Physio: Keith Oakes.
Commercial Executive: K. France.
Secretary: F. J. Martin.
Stadium Manager: Nigel Dennis.

LATEST SEQUENCES

Longest Sequence of League Wins: 10, 1.9.30 – 18.10.30.
Longest Sequence of League Defeats: 12, 21.9.1896 – 9.1.1897.
Longest Sequence of League Draws: 5, 21.2.81 – 7.3.81.
Longest Sequence of Unbeaten League Matches: 18, 11.3.80 – 13.9.80.
Longest Sequence Without a League Win: 19, 22.8.78 – 23.12.78.

HONOURS

Football League: Division 2 best season: 5th, 1901–02; Promotion from Division 3, 1997–98; Division 3 (N) – Champions 1931–32, 1947–48, 1951–52; Runners-up 1927–28, 1930–31, 1936–37; Division 4 – Champions 1975–76; Runners-up 1980–81.

FA Cup: best season: 1st rd of Second Series (5th rd equivalent), 1887, 2nd rd (5th rd equivalent), 1890, 1902.

Football League Cup: best season: 4th rd, 1968.

GM Vauxhall Conference: Champions 1987–88.

Colours
Red and white striped shirts, black shorts, black stockings.

Change Colours
All purple.

Year Formed: 1884.

Turned Professional: 1892.

Ltd Co.: 1895.

Club Nickname: 'The Red Imps'.

Previous Grounds: 1883, John O'Gaunt's; 1894, Sincil Bank.

First Football League Game: 3 September 1892, Division 2, v Sheffield U (a) L 2–4 – W. Gresham; Coulton, Neill; Shaw, Mettam, Moore; Smallman, Irving (1), Cameron (1), Kelly, J. Gresham.

Record League Victory: 11–1 v Crewe Alex, Division 3 (N), 29 September 1951 – Jones; Green (1p), Varney; Wright, Emery, Grummett (1); Troops (1), Garvey, Graver (6), Whittle (1), Johnson (1).

Record Cup Victory: 8–1 v Bromley, FA Cup 2nd rd, 10 December 1938 – McPhail; Hartshorne, Corbett; Bean, Leach, Whyte (1); Hancock, Wilson (1), Ponting (3), Deacon (1), Clare (2).

Record Defeat: 3–11 v Manchester C, Division 2, 23 March 1895.

Most League Points (2 for a win): 74, Division 4, 1975–76.

Most League Points (3 for a win): 77, Division 3, 1981–82.

Most League Goals: 121, Division 3 (N), 1951–52.

Highest League Scorer in Season: Allan Hall, 42, Division 3 (N), 1931–32.

Most League Goals in Total Aggregate: Andy Graver, 144, 1950–55 and 1958–61.

Most League Goals in One Match: 6, Frank Keetley v Halifax T, Division 3N, 16 January 1932; 6, Andy Graver v Crewe Alex, Division 3N, 29 September 1951.

Most Capped Player: David Pugh, 3 (7), Wales; George Moulson, 3, Republic of Ireland.

Most League Appearances: Tony Emery, 402, 1946–59.

Youngest League Player: Shane Nicholson, 16 years 172 days v Burnley, 22 November 1986.

Record Transfer Fee Received: £500,000 from Port Vale for Gareth Ainsworth, September 1997.

Record Transfer Fee Paid: £75,000 to Carlisle U for Dean Walling, September 1997; £75,000 to Bury for Tony Battersby, August 1998.

Football League Record: 1892 Founder member of Division 2. Remained in Division 2 until 1920 when they failed re-election but also missed seasons 1908–09 and 1911–12 when not re-elected. 1921–32 Division 3 (N); 1932–34 Division 2; 1934–48 Division 3 (N); 1948–49 Division 2; 1949–52 Division 3 (N); 1952–61 Division 2; 1961–62 Division 3; 1962–76 Division 4; 1976–79 Division 3; 1979–81 Division 4; 1981–86 Division 3; 1986–87 Division 4; 1987–88 GM Vauxhall Conference; 1988–92 Division 4; 1992–98 Division 3; 1998–99 Division 2; 1999– Division 3.

MANAGERS

David Calderhead 1900–07
John Henry Strawson 1907–14
(had been Secretary)
George Fraser 1919–21
David Calderhead Jnr. 1921–24
Horace Henshall 1924–27
Harry Parkes 1927–36
Joe McClelland 1936–46
Bill Anderson 1946–65
(General Manager to 1966)
Roy Chapman 1965–66
Ron Gray 1966–70
Bert Loxley 1970–71
David Herd 1971–72
Graham Taylor 1972–77
George Kerr 1977–78
Willie Bell 1977–78
Colin Murphy 1978–85
John Pickering 1985
George Kerr 1985–87
Peter Daniel 1987
Colin Murphy 1987–90
Allan Clarke 1990
Steve Thompson 1990–93
Keith Alexander 1993–94
Sam Ellis 1994–95
Steve Wicks *(Head Coach)* 1995
John Beck 1995–98
Shane Westley 1998
John Reames 1998–99
Phil Stant May 2000–

TEN YEAR LEAGUE RECORD

		P	W	D	L	F	A	Pts	Pos
1989-90	Div 4	46	18	14	14	48	48	68	10
1990-91	Div 4	46	14	17	15	50	61	59	14
1991-92	Div 4	42	17	11	14	50	44	62	10
1992-93	Div 3	42	18	9	15	57	53	63	8
1993-94	Div 3	42	12	11	19	52	63	47	18
1994-95	Div 3	42	15	11	16	54	55	56	12
1995-96	Div 3	46	13	14	19	57	73	53	18
1996-97	Div 3	46	18	12	16	70	69	66	9
1997-98	Div 3	46	20	15	11	60	51	72	3
1998-99	Div 2	46	13	7	26	42	74	46	23

DID YOU KNOW ?

Billy Dinsdale scored a club record 14 FA Cup goals for Lincoln City in two spells between 1926 and 1929 and again 1930-31. Unusually they were composed of a hat-trick, five 2's and one single goal.

LINCOLN CITY 1999–2000 LEAGUE RECORD

Match No.	Date		Venue	Opponents	Result		H/T Score	Lg. Pos.	Goalscorers	Attendance
1	Aug	7	H	Rotherham U	W	2-1	0-0	5	Fleming (pen) [61], Philpott [63]	4494
2		14	A	Hull C	D	1-1	0-1	7	Gordon [67]	7046
3		21	H	Barnet	D	0-0	0-0	11		3113
4		27	A	Northampton T	L	0-1	0-1	—		5104
5		30	H	Swansea C	L	0-1	0-1	16		2893
6	Sept	4	A	Torquay U	L	2-5	1-4	17	Thorpe [11], Fleming (pen) [68]	1833
7		11	A	Carlisle U	L	0-1	0-0	20		3254
8		18	H	Macclesfield T	D	1-1	0-0	20	Barnett D [82]	2918
9		25	A	Chester C	W	3-1	1-1	17	Gordon [12], Thorpe [69], Stant [86]	2161
10	Oct	2	H	Exeter C	W	1-0	0-0	14	Peacock [58]	3557
11		9	H	Darlington	W	1-0	1-0	13	Gordon [4]	3747
12		16	A	Leyton Orient	W	3-2	1-0	12	Smith [5], Miller [60], Thorpe [86]	4349
13		19	A	Southend U	D	2-2	1-2	—	Barnett D [24], Thorpe [72]	3556
14		23	H	Chester C	W	4-1	1-1	9	Barnett D [10], Thorpe [59], Finnigan [75], Stant [90]	3790
15	Nov	2	H	Peterborough U	L	1-2	1-2	—	Philpott [6]	5032
16		6	A	Mansfield T	L	2-5	1-2	15	Philpott [37], Gordon [88]	2952
17		12	H	York C	W	4-2	1-1	12	Smith 2 [38, 63], Thorpe [56], Fleming (pen) [77]	2956
18		23	A	Brighton & HA	D	2-2	1-1	—	Miller [18], Stant [78]	5714
19		27	H	Rochdale	D	1-1	0-0	14	Gain [48]	3424
20	Dec	4	A	Rotherham U	D	1-1	0-1	12	Smith [52]	3674
21		18	H	Shrewsbury T	L	1-2	0-1	14	Agogo [54]	2907
22		26	A	Halifax T	L	0-3	0-2	16		2371
23		28	H	Hartlepool U	L	1-2	0-1	17	Miller [61]	3480
24	Jan	3	A	Cheltenham T	W	2-0	1-0	17	Miller [31], Finnigan [73]	4012
25		15	H	Hull C	W	2-1	2-0	15	Fleming (pen) [12], Battersby [45]	4687
26		22	A	Barnet	L	3-5	1-3	16	Gordon [20], Miller [48], Battersby (pen) [90]	2504
27		29	H	Northampton T	D	2-2	2-1	18	Henry [25], Battersby [45]	3717
28	Feb	4	A	Swansea C	L	1-2	0-2	—	Thorpe [88]	6847
29		12	H	Torquay U	W	2-1	0-0	17	Thorpe [48], Smith [77]	2919
30		19	A	Rochdale	D	1-1	0-1	17	Gordon [79]	3166
31		22	H	Plymouth Arg	W	3-0	1-0	—	Thorpe 2 [28, 46], Gordon [61]	2561
32		26	A	Macclesfield T	D	1-1	0-1	15	Miller [87]	2445
33	Mar	4	H	Carlisle U	W	5-0	2-0	15	Thorpe [1], Peacock 2 [6, 55], Gordon 2 [49, 81]	2945
34		7	H	Mansfield T	W	3-0	2-0	—	Fleming [36], Thorpe [37], Gain [51]	3445
35		11	A	Peterborough U	D	2-2	1-2	13	Miller [26], Thorpe [90]	7882
36		14	A	Plymouth Arg	D	1-1	1-1	—	Gordon [19]	4111
37		18	H	Brighton & HA	L	1-3	0-1	12	Thorpe [49]	4288
38		21	A	York C	L	0-2	0-0	—		2449
39		25	H	Halifax T	D	1-1	1-1	15	Thorpe [12]	3028
40	Apr	1	A	Shrewsbury T	W	2-1	1-0	13	Thorpe [13], Gordon [68]	2220
41		8	H	Cheltenham T	L	1-2	0-2	14	Holmes [76]	3133
42		15	A	Hartlepool U	L	0-2	0-2	15		2777
43		22	H	Leyton Orient	D	0-0	0-0	15		2718
44		24	A	Exeter C	L	0-3	0-1	15		2568
45		29	H	Southend U	W	1-0	1-0	15	Holmes [10]	2556
46	May	6	A	Darlington	L	0-2	0-1	15		7145

Final League Position: 15

GOALSCORERS

League (67): Thorpe 16, Gordon 11, Miller 7, Fleming 5 (4 pens), Smith 5, Barnett D 3, Battersby 3 (1 pen), Peacock 3, Philpott 3, Stant 3, Finnigan 2, Gain 2, Holmes 2, Agogo 1, Henry 1.
Worthington Cup (4): Fleming 1, Gordon 1, Peacock 1, Thorpe 1.
FA Cup (3): Barnett D 1, Gordon 1, Smith 1.

Vaughan J 6	Barnett J 17 + 1	Welsh S 32	Fleming T 41	Brown G 25 + 1	Barnett D 20 + 2	Peacock R 16 + 8	Finnigan J 36 + 1	Gordon G 39 + 2	Thorpe L 38 + 4	Philpott 18 + 5	Gain P 20 + 12	Miller P 37 + 3	Branston G 4	Poppleton D 4 + 1	Battersby T 7 + 9	Smith P 23 + 4	Bimson S 15 + 5	Lewis G 3 + 2	Richardson B 22	Stant P 3 + 15	Galloway M 5	Phillips D 6 + 2	Wilkins I 3 + 1	Henry A 14 + 3	Stones C — + 3	Agogo M 3	Mayo P 19	Marriott A 18	Holmes S 9	Lescott A 3 + 2	Match No.
1	2	3	4	5^1	6	7	8	9	10	11^2	12	13																			1
1	6	2				7	8	9	10	11^1	3	4	5	12																	2
1	5	2			6	7	8	9	10^2	11^1	3	4				13	12														3
1	6	4			2	7^1	8	9	10^2	3						5	11	13	12												4
1			4		6		8	9^2	12	11	3	13				5	7	10^2	2^1	14											5
1	6	2	12				8	9	10	11	3^2	4	5^1			7^3	13	14													6
		2	4	5	6	7^2	8	9^1	10	11	12						3		1		13										7
		2	4	5	6	7^1	8	9	10	11	12						3		1												8
		2	4	5	6	7	8	9	10^2	11^1	12						3		1		13										9
		2	4	5	6	7	8	9	10	11	12						3^1		1												10
		2	4	5	6	7^1	8	9	10	11	12						3		1												11
		2	4	5	6	7^1	8	9	10^2	11	12						3		1		13										12
		2	4	5	6	7	8	9	10	11^1	12						3		1												13
		2	4	5	6	7	8	9^1	10	11	12						3		1												14
		2^1	4	5		7	8	9	10	11^3	12^2						3	13	1	14		6									15
			4	5^3	6	7	8	9	10^1	11	12						3		1	14	2^2	13									16
		2	4		6	7	8	9	10	11							3		1		5										17
			4	5		7^2	8	9^1	10	11							3		1	12	2	6	13								18
			4	5		7	8^1	9	10	11							3		1	12	2	6	12								19
		2			6	7	8	9^1	10	11							3		1	12		4		5							20
		2		5		7	8	9^1	10								3		1	12	13	4		6^2		11					21
		2^3	4	5	6	7		9^2		11	12						3		1	14		13		8^1		10					22
		2		5	6	7	8	9^1		11	12						3^2		1				13	4		10					23
		2		5		7	8	9^1	10	11							3		1	12				4							24
		2^1		5	6	7	8	9^2	10	11	12						3		1				13	4							25
		11^1		5	6	7	8	9	10		12					2	3		1					4							26
		3^2		5	6	7	8	9	10^3	11	12					2^1			1	14			13	4							27
		11		5	6	7^1	8	9	10		12					2			1					4			3				28
				5	6	7	8	9	10	11						2								4			3	1			29
			4	5	6	7	8	9^2		11	12					2							13	10^1			3	1			30
			4	5	6	7	8	9^1	10	11	12					2											3	1			31
			4	5	6	7	8	9	10	11^2	12					2^1							13				3	1			32
			4	5		7^2	8	9	10	11						2							13	12			3	1	6^1		33
			4	5	6	7	8^3	9	10^2	11						2^1							13	12	14		3	1			34
			4	5	6	7	8^1	9	10	11^2	12					2							13				3	1			35
		11	4	5	6		8	9	10		12					2^1							13				3	1	7^2		36
			4	5	6	7	8^3	9	10		12					2							13		14		3^2	1		11^1	37
		2	4	5		7	8^2	9	10	11^1	12																3	1	6	13	38
		2	4	5		7	8^1	9	10	11	12																3	1	6		39
	2^3	2	4^2	5		7^1	8	9	10		12												13		14		3	1	6		40
	12	2		5		7	8	9	10	11													13				3^2	1	6	4^1	41
		2	4	5		7	8^1	9	10	11^2	12												13		14		3^3	1	6		42
		2	4	5		7^2	8	9^1	10	11	12												13				3	1	6		43
		2	4	5	6		8	9	10	11^1	12												13				3^2	1	7		44
		2	4	5^1		7	8	9^2	10	11	12												13				3	1	6		45
2^1				5	6	7	8	9^2	10^3	11	12												13	4	14		3	1			46

Worthington Cup
First Round   Barnsley   (h) 2-4
                                   (a) 2-2

FA Cup
First Round   Welling U   (h) 1-0
Second Round   Luton T   (a) 2-2
                                   (h) 0-1

FA Premiership

LIVERPOOL

FOUNDATION

But for a dispute between Everton FC and their landlord at Anfield in 1892, there may never have been a Liverpool club. This dispute persuaded the majority of Evertonians to quit Anfield for Goodison Park, leaving the landlord, Mr. John Houlding, to form a new club. He originally tried to retain the name 'Everton' but when this failed, he founded Liverpool Association FC on 15 March 1892.

Anfield Road, Liverpool L4 0TH.
Telephone: (0151) 263 2361. *Fax:* (0151) 260 8813.
Website: www.liverpoolfc.net
ClubCall: 09068 121 184.
Ticket and Match Information: (0151) 260 9999 (24-hour service) or (0151) 260 8680 (office hours).
Credit Card Bookings: (0151) 263 5727.
International Supporters Club: (0151) 261 1444.
Museum and Stadium Tours: (0151) 260 6677.
LFC Direct Mail Order: (0990) 532 532.
Ground Capacity: 45,362.
Record Attendance: 61,905 v Wolverhampton W, FA Cup 4th rd, 2 February 1952.
Record Receipts: £604,048 v Celtic, UEFA Cup, 30 September 1997.
Pitch Measurements: 111yd × 74yd.
Chairman: D. R. Moores.
Chief Executive: Rick Parry BSC, FCA.
Director of Finance: Les Wheatley.
Directors: N. White FSCA, T. D. Smith, J. Burns, K. E. B. Clayton FCA.
Vice-Presidents: H. E. Roberts, J. T. Cross, T. W. Saunders, P. B. Robinson.
Manager: Gerard Houllier.
Assistant Manager: Phil Thompson.
Physio: Dave Galley.
Secretary: Bryce Morrison.
Press Officer: Ian Cotton.
Stadium Manager: Ged Poynton.
Academy Director: Steve Heighway.

LATEST SEQUENCES
Longest Sequence of League Wins: 12, 21.4.90 – 6.10.90.
Longest Sequence of League Defeats: 9, 29.4.1899 – 14.10.1899.
Longest Sequence of League Draws: 6, 19.2.75 – 19.3.75.
Longest Sequence of Unbeaten League Matches: 31, 4.5.87 – 16.3.88.
Longest Sequence Without a League Win: 14, 12.12.53 – 20.3.54.

HONOURS

Football League: Division 1 – Champions 1900–01, 1905–06, 1921–22, 1922–23, 1946–47, 1963–64, 1965–66, 1972–73, 1975–76, 1976–77, 1978–79, 1979–80, 1981–82, 1982–83, 1983–84, 1985–86, 1987–88, 1989–90 (Liverpool have a record number of 18 League Championship wins); Runners-up 1898–99, 1909–10, 1968–69, 1973–74, 1974–75, 1977–78, 1984–85, 1986–87, 1988–89, 1990–91; Division 2 – Champions 1893–94, 1895–96, 1904–05, 1961–62.

FA Cup: Winners 1965, 1974, 1986, 1989, 1992; Runners-up 1914, 1950, 1971, 1977, 1988, 1996;

Football League Cup: Winners 1981, 1982, 1983, 1984, 1995; Runners-up 1978, 1987.

League Super Cup: Winners 1986.

European Competitions: European Cup: 1964–65, 1966–67, 1973–74, 1976–77 (winners), 1977–78 (winners), 1978–79, 1979–80, 1980–81 (winners), 1981–82, 1982–83, 1983–84 (winners), 1984–85 (runners-up). European Cup-Winners' Cup: 1965–66 (runners-up), 1971–72, 1974–75, 1992–93, 1996–97 (s-f.). European Fairs Cup: 1967–68, 1968–69, 1969–70, 1970–71. UEFA Cup: 1972–73 (winners), 1975–76 (winners), 1991–92, 1995–96, 1997–98, 1998–99. Super Cup: 1977 (winners), 1978, 1984. World Club Championship: 1981 (runners-up).

Colours
All red.

Change Colours
Gold shirts with navy blue side panels, navy blue shorts, navy blue stockings.

Year Formed: 1892.

Turned Professional: 1892.

Ltd Co.: 1892.

Club Nickname: 'Reds' or 'Pool'.

First Football League Game: 2 September 1893, Division 2, v Middlesbrough Ironopolis (a) W 2–0 – McOwen; Hannah, McLean; Henderson, McQue (1), McBride; Gordon, McVean (1), M. McQueen, Stott, H. McQueen.

Record League Victory: 10–1 v Rotherham T, Division 2, 18 February 1896 – Storer; Goldie, Wilkie; McCarthy, McQueen, Holmes; McVean (3), Ross (2), Allan (4), Becton (1), Bradshaw.

Record Cup Victory: 11–0 v Stromsgodset Drammen, ECWC 1st rd 1st leg, 17 September 1974 – Clemence; Smith (1), Lindsay (1p), Thompson (2), Cormack (1), Hughes (1), Boersma (2), Hall, Heighway (1), Kennedy (1), Callaghan (1).

MANAGERS

W. E. Barclay 1892–96
Tom Watson 1896–1915
David Ashworth 1920–23
Matt McQueen 1923–28
George Patterson 1928–36
(continued as Secretary)
George Kay 1936–51
Don Welsh 1951–56
Phil Taylor 1956–59
Bill Shankly 1959–74
Bob Paisley 1974–83
Joe Fagan 1983–85
Kenny Dalglish 1985–91
Graeme Souness 1991–94
Roy Evans January 1994–98
(then Joint Manager)
Gerard Houllier July 1998–

Record Defeat: 1–9 v Birmingham C, Division 2, 11 December 1954.

Most League Points (2 for a win): 68, Division 1, 1978–79.

Most League Points (3 for a win): 90, Division 1, 1987–88.

Most League Goals: 106, Division 2, 1895–96.

Highest League Scorer in Season: Roger Hunt, 41, Division 2, 1961–62.

Most League Goals in Total Aggregate: Roger Hunt, 245, 1959–69.

Most League Goals in One Match: 5, Andy McGuigan v Stoke C, Division 1, 4 January 1902; 5, John Evans v Bristol R, Division 2, 15 September 1954; 5, Ian Rush v Luton T, Division 1, 29 October 1983.

Most Capped Player: Ian Rush, 67 (73), Wales.

Most League Appearances: Ian Callaghan, 640, 1960–78.

Youngest League Player: Michael Owen, 17 years 144 days v Wimbledon, 6 May 1997.

Record Transfer Fee Received: £7,000,000 from Aston Villa for Stan Collymore, May 1997.

Record Transfer Fee Paid: £11,000,000 to Leicester C for Emile Heskey, March 2000.

Football League Record: 1893 Elected to Division 2; 1894–95 Division 1; 1895–96 Division 2; 1896–1904 Division 1; 1904–05 Division 2; 1905–54 Division 1; 1954–62 Division 2; 1962–92 Division 1; 1992– FA Premier League.

TEN YEAR LEAGUE RECORD

		P	W	D	L	F	A	Pts	Pos
1989-90	Div 1	38	23	10	5	78	37	79	1
1990-91	Div 1	38	23	7	8	77	40	76	2
1991-92	Div 1	42	16	16	10	47	40	64	6
1992-93	PR Lge	42	16	11	15	62	55	59	6
1993-94	PR Lge	42	17	9	16	59	55	60	8
1994-95	PR Lge	42	21	11	10	65	37	74	4
1995-96	PR Lge	38	20	11	7	70	34	71	3
1996-97	PR Lge	38	19	11	8	62	37	68	4
1997-98	PR Lge	38	18	11	9	68	42	65	3
1998-99	PR Lge	38	15	9	14	68	49	54	7

DID YOU KNOW ?

Matt McQueen played for Liverpool in their first season of 1892-93, made 87 League and Cup appearances, became a qualified Football League referee, appointed Director of Liverpool FC and finally manager of the club.

LIVERPOOL 1999–2000 LEAGUE RECORD

Match No.	Date		Venue	Opponents	Result		H/T Score	Lg. Pos.	Goalscorers	Attendance
1	Aug	7	A	Sheffield W	W	2-1	0-0	4	Fowler [75], Camara [84]	34,853
2		14	H	Watford	L	0-1	0-1	14		44,174
3		21	A	Middlesbrough	L	0-1	0-0	17		34,783
4		23	A	Leeds U	W	2-1	1-1	—	Camara [45], Radebe (og) [55]	39,703
5		28	H	Arsenal	W	2-0	1-0	8	Fowler [8], Berger [76]	44,886
6	Sept	11	H	Manchester U	L	2-3	1-3	12	Hyypia [23], Berger [68]	44,929
7		18	A	Leicester C	D	2-2	2-1	12	Owen 2 (1 pen) [23 (pl), 39]	21,623
8		27	H	Everton	L	0-1	0-1	—		44,802
9	Oct	2	A	Aston Villa	D	0-0	0-0	12		39,217
10		16	H	Chelsea	W	1-0	0-0	12	Thompson [47]	44,826
11		23	A	Southampton	D	1-1	0-1	12	Camara [81]	15,241
12		27	H	West Ham U	W	1-0	1-0	—	Camara [43]	44,012
13	Nov	1	H	Bradford C	W	3-1	2-1	—	Camara [21], Redknapp (pen) [42], Heggem [80]	40,483
14		6	H	Derby Co	W	2-0	0-0	5	Murphy [65], Redknapp [69]	44,467
15		20	A	Sunderland	W	2-0	0-0	5	Owen [63], Berger [85]	41,511
16		27	A	West Ham U	L	0-1	0-1	6		26,043
17	Dec	5	H	Sheffield W	W	4-1	2-1	5	Hyypia [21], Murphy [41], Gerrard [69], Thompson [79]	42,517
18		18	A	Coventry C	W	2-0	1-0	5	Owen [45], Camara [74]	44,024
19		26	A	Newcastle U	D	2-2	1-1	5	Owen 2 [31, 52]	36,445
20		28	H	Wimbledon	W	3-1	0-0	5	Owen [58], Berger [68], Fowler [80]	44,107
21	Jan	3	A	Tottenham H	L	0-1	0-1	5		36,044
22		15	A	Watford	W	3-2	2-1	4	Berger [10], Thompson [41], Smicer [71]	21,367
23		22	H	Middlesbrough	D	0-0	0-0	4		44,324
24	Feb	5	H	Leeds U	W	3-1	1-0	4	Hamann [19], Berger [69], Murphy [90]	44,793
25		13	A	Arsenal	W	1-0	1-0	3	Camara [18]	38,098
26	Mar	4	A	Manchester U	D	1-1	1-1	5	Berger [27]	61,592
27		11	H	Sunderland	D	1-1	1-0	4	Berger (pen) [2]	44,693
28		15	H	Aston Villa	D	0-0	0-0	—		43,615
29		18	A	Derby Co	W	2-0	1-0	3	Owen [17], Camara [86]	33,378
30		25	H	Newcastle U	W	2-1	0-0	3	Camara [51], Redknapp [88]	44,743
31	Apr	1	A	Coventry C	W	3-0	2-0	3	Owen 2 [23, 37], Heskey [80]	23,084
32		9	H	Tottenham H	W	2-0	1-0	2	Berger [34], Owen [61]	44,536
33		16	A	Wimbledon	W	2-1	1-0	2	Heskey 2 [36, 64]	26,102
34		21	A	Everton	D	0-0	0-0	—		40,052
35		29	H	Chelsea	L	0-2	0-2	3		34,957
36	May	3	H	Leicester C	L	0-2	0-1	—		43,456
37		7	H	Southampton	D	0-0	0-0	3		44,015
38		14	A	Bradford C	L	0-1	0-1	4		18,276

Final League Position: 4

GOALSCORERS

League (51): Owen 11 (1 pen), Berger 9 (1 pen), Camara 9, Fowler 3, Heskey 3, Murphy 3, Redknapp 3 (1 pen), Thompson 3, Hyypia 2, Gerrard 1, Hamann 1, Heggem 1, Smicer 1, own goal 1.
Worthington Cup (10): Murphy 3, Meijer 2, Riedle 2, Maxwell 1, Owen 1, Staunton 1.
FA Cup (2): Camara 1, Matteo 1.

Westerveld S 36	Heggem V 10+12	Matteo D 32	Hamann D 27+1	Carragher J 33+3	Hyypia S 38	Redknapp J 18+4	Smicer V 13+8	Fowler R 8+6	Camara T 22+11	Berger P 34	Thompson D 19+8	Staunton S 7+5	Meijer E 7+14	Gerrard S 26+3	Song R 14+4	Riedle K —+1	Owen M 22+5	Murphy D 9+14	Henchoz S 29	Friedel B 2	Newby J —+1	Heskey E 12	Match No.
1	2	3	4^1	5	6		7	8	9	10^3	11	12^2	13	14									1
1	2^3	3		5	6	4	8^1	9	10	11	13			7^2	14		12						2
1		3		5	4	8		9	10	11^1	12	6^2	13	7									3
1		3		5	6	4		9	10	11	8			7	2								4
1	12	3		5	6	4		9	10^2	11	8^1			7	2		13						5
1	12	3		5	6	4	13	9	10^3	11	8^2			7^1	2		14						6
1	2	3		5	6	4^2		9^1	11	8		12		7			10	13					7
1	2		4^2	5	6	7	8^1	9^3	12	11		3	13	14			10						8
1		4^1	12		6	7	8^3		13	11		3	9	14	2		10^2		5				9
	12			5	6	11	8			7	3	13			2		10^2	9^1	4	1			10
	12			5	6	11	8^1		10		13	3	7^3		2		14	9^2	4	1			11
1	12	3		5	6	7	13		10^2	11	8^1			9	2				4				12
1	12		4	13	6	7^2	8^3		9	11	10^1	3	14		2				5				13
1	2		7	5	6	11	8^2		9^3			3	14	12			10^1	13	4				14
1	12	3	4		6	7			11	13			14	8^2	2		10^1	9^3	5				15
1	4	3	7		6		11^1		12	13	14	8	2^3				10^2	9	5				16
1		3	4	12	6		13	9		11	14		7	2^1			10^2	8^3	5				17
1	12	3	4	2	6		13^3		9^1	11	8^2		7				10	14	5				18
1	12	3	4	5	6		13		9^1	11			7	2			10	8^2					19
1	2	3		5	6		12	13	9^3	11			7	14			10^1	8^2	4				20
1	2	3	8	5^2	6		10^1		9	11^3	13	12		7				14	4				21
1		3	4^1	2	6		12		9^2	11	8	13		7			10^3	14	5				22
1		3	4	2	6		9^3			11	8^2		12	7			10^1	13	5		14		23
1		3	4	2	6		8		9^1	11			10	7			12	5					24
1	12	3	4	2	6		8		9	11			10^2	7^1			13	5					25
1	2^1	3	4	7	6^3		8		9^2	11			10	12			13	14	5				26
1		3	4	7	6		12		11				10^2	8^3	2^1		13	14	5			9	27
1		3	4	2	6	12			13	11	8^3		14	7^1			10^2		5			9	28
1		3	4	2	6	12			13	11	8			7			10^2		5			9^1	29
1		3	4	2	6	12			10	11^3	8^2	13		7^1			14		5			9	30
1		3	4	2	6				12	11	8			7^3	13		10^1	14	5^2			9	31
1	12	3	4	2	6	13			14	11	8^2			10^3	7^1				5			9	32
1		3	4	2	6		12		13	11	8^1			7			10^3	14	5			9^2	33
1	12	3	4	2	6		13			11	8^1			7			10		5			9^4	34
1		3	4^1	2	6	13			14	12	11		7^2				10	8^3	5			9	35
1		3	4^2	2	6	7			13	12	11	8^3					10^1	14	5			9	36
1		3	12	4	6	7			10^4	8^3	11	13	14		2^1				5			9	37
1		3^2	4	2	6	8	12			13	11^2		14	7^1			10		5			9	38

Worthington Cup

Second Round	Hull C	(a)	5-1
		(h)	4-2
Third Round	Southampton	(a)	1-2

FA Cup

Third Round	Huddersfield T	(a)	2-0
Fourth Round	Blackburn R	(h)	0-1

Division 2   **LUTON TOWN**

FOUNDATION

Formed by an amalgamation of two leading local clubs, Wanderers and Excelsior a works team, at a meeting in Luton Town Hall in April 1885. The Wanderers had three months earlier changed their name to Luton Town Wanderers and did not take too kindly to the formation of another Town club but were talked around at this meeting. Wanderers had already appeared in the FA Cup and the new club entered in its inaugural season.

Kenilworth Road Stadium, 1 Maple Rd, Luton, Beds LU4 8AW.

Telephone: (01582) 411 622.

Ticket Office: (01582) 416 976.

Credit Hotline: (01582) 307 48 (24 hrs).

ClubCall: 09068 121 123.

Ground Capacity: 9975.

Record Attendance: 30,069 v Blackpool, FA Cup 6th rd replay, 4 March 1959.

Record Receipts: £115,541.20 v West Ham U, FA Cup 6th rd, 23 March 1994.

Pitch Measurements: 110yd × 72yd.

Chairman: M. Watson-Challis.

Directors: C. S. Bassett, C. T. F. Green, N. S. Terry.

Secretary: Cherry Newbery.

Sales and Marketing Manager: John Bailey Jnr.

Stadium Manager: Geoff Lovell.

Manager: Ricky Hill.

Coach: John Moore.

Physio: Clive Goodyear.

LATEST SEQUENCES

Longest Sequence of League Wins: 9, 22.1.77 – 8.3.77.

Longest Sequence of League Defeats: 8, 11.11.1899 – 6.1.1900.

Longest Sequence of League Draws: 5, 28.8.71 – 18.9.71.

Longest Sequence of Unbeaten League Matches: 19, 8.4.69 – 7.10.69.

Longest Sequence Without a League Win: 16, 9.9.64 – 6.11.64.

HONOURS

Football League: Division 1 best season: 7th, 1986–87; Division 2 – Champions 1981–82; Runners-up 1954–55, 1973–74; Division 3 – Runners-up 1969–70; Division 4 – Champions 1967–68; Division 3 (S) – Champions 1936–37; Runners-up 1935–36.
FA Cup: Runners-up 1959.
Football League Cup: Winners 1988; Runners-up 1989.
Simod Cup: Runners-up 1988.

Colours
Orange shirts with blue side panels and blue and white knitted collar, blue shorts with orange and white stripe, blue stockings with orange stripes.

Change Colours
White shirts with black side panels and black and orange knitted collar, black shorts with orange and white stripe, black stockings with white stripes.

Year Formed: 1885.

Turned Professional: 1890.

Ltd Co.: 1897.

Club Nickname: 'The Hatters'.

Previous Grounds: 1885, Excelsior, Dallow Lane; 1897, Dunstable Road; 1905, Kenilworth Road.

First Football League Game: 4 September 1897, Division 2, v Leicester Fosse (a) D 1–1 – Williams; McCartney, McEwen; Davies, Stewart, Docherty; Gallacher, Coupar, Birch, McInnes, Ekins (1).

Record League Victory: 12–0 v Bristol R, Division 3 (S), 13 April 1936 – Dolman; Mackey, Smith; Finlayson, Nelson, Godfrey; Rich, Martin (1), Payne (10), Roberts (1), Stephenson.

Record Cup Victory: 9–0 v Clapton, FA Cup 1st rd (replay after abandoned game), 30 November 1927 – Abbott; Kingham, Graham; Black, Rennie, Fraser; Pointon, Yardley (4), Reid (2), Woods (1), Dennis (2).

Record Defeat: 0–9 v Small Heath, Division 2, 12 November 1898.

Most League Points (2 for a win): 66, Division 4, 1967–68.

Most League Points (3 for a win): 88, Division 2, 1981–82.

Most League Goals: 103, Division 3 (S), 1936–37.

Highest League Scorer in Season: Joe Payne, 55, Division 3 (S), 1936–37.

Most League Goals in Total Aggregate: Gordon Turner, 243, 1949–64.

Most League Goals in One Match: 10, Joe Payne v Bristol R, Division 3S, 13 April 1936.

Most Capped Player: Mal Donaghy, 58 (91), Northern Ireland.

Most League Appearances: Bob Morton, 494, 1948–64.

Youngest League Player: Mike O'Hara, 16 years 32 days v Stoke C, 1 October 1960.

Record Transfer Fee Received: £2,500,000 from Arsenal for John Hartson, January 1995.

Record Transfer Fee Paid: £850,000 to Odense for Lars Elstrup, August 1989.

Football League Record: 1897 Elected to Division 2; 1900 Failed re-election; 1920 Division 3; 1921–37 Division 3 (S); 1937–55 Division 2; 1955–60 Division 1; 1960–63 Division 2; 1963–65 Division 3; 1965–68 Division 4; 1968–70 Division 3; 1970–74 Division 2; 1974–75 Division 1; 1975–82 Division 2; 1982–96 Division 1; 1996– Division 2.

MANAGERS

Charlie Green 1901–28
(Secretary-Manager)
George Thomson 1925
John McCartney 1927–29
George Kay 1929–31
Harold Wightman 1931–35
Ted Liddell 1936–38
Neil McBain 1938–39
George Martin 1939–47
Dally Duncan 1947–58
Syd Owen 1959–60
Sam Bartram 1960–62
Bill Harvey 1962–64
George Martin 1965–66
Allan Brown 1966–68
Alec Stock 1968–72
Harry Haslam 1972–78
David Pleat 1978–86
John Moore 1986–87
Ray Harford 1987–89
Jim Ryan 1900–91
David Pleat 1991–95
Terry Westley 1995
Lennie Lawrence 1995–2000
Ricky Hill July 2000–

TEN YEAR LEAGUE RECORD

		P	W	D	L	F	A	Pts	Pos
1989-90	Div 1	38	10	13	15	43	57	43	17
1990-91	Div 1	38	10	7	21	42	61	37	18
1991-92	Div 1	42	10	12	20	38	71	42	20
1992-93	Div 1	46	10	21	15	48	62	51	20
1993-94	Div 1	46	14	11	21	56	60	53	20
1994-95	Div 1	46	15	13	18	61	64	58	16
1995-96	Div 1	46	11	12	23	40	64	45	24
1996-97	Div 2	46	21	15	10	71	45	78	3
1997-98	Div 2	46	14	15	17	60	64	57	17
1998-99	Div 2	46	16	10	20	51	60	58	12

DID YOU KNOW ?

On 30 November 1946, Luton Town were 3-0 down to Newcastle United at half-time. They recovered to win 4-3. Their scorers were Billy Waugh, Allenby Driver, Hugh Billington and Mel Daniel.

LUTON TOWN 1999–2000 LEAGUE RECORD

Match No.	Date		Venue	Opponents	Result		H/T Score	Lg. Pos.	Goalscorers	Attendance
1	Aug	7	A	Notts Co	D	0-0	0-0	15		6141
2		14	H	Blackpool	W	3-2	1-0	7	Barnes (og) [21], George [73], Spring [81]	5176
3		21	A	Reading	W	2-1	0-0	3	Fotiadis [54], George [85]	8741
4		28	H	Cardiff C	W	1-0	0-0	2	Gray [81]	5374
5		31	A	Bournemouth	L	0-1	0-0	—		4797
6	Sept	4	H	Bury	D	1-1	0-0	5	Fotiadis [53]	4633
7		11	H	Wrexham	W	3-1	3-1	3	Taylor [5], Spring [14], George [36]	5121
8		18	A	Brentford	L	0-2	0-0	5		7039
9		25	H	Oxford U	W	4-2	3-0	3	George 2 [13, 45], Fraser [21], Locke [88]	6102
10	Oct	2	A	Wigan Ath	L	0-1	0-0	8		6866
11		9	A	Oldham Ath	L	1-2	0-0	10	Midgley [85]	4532
12		16	H	Gillingham	W	3-1	0-1	7	George 2 (1 pen) [51 (p), 73], Douglas [64]	6394
13		19	H	Wycombe W	D	1-1	0-1	—	Douglas [47]	5820
14		23	A	Oxford U	W	1-0	1-0	7	George [3]	5866
15	Nov	2	A	Millwall	L	0-1	0-0	—		6181
16		6	H	Burnley	W	2-1	0-0	8	Midgley 2 [49, 69]	7205
17		12	A	Cambridge U	L	1-3	0-2	9	George [90]	6211
18		23	H	Preston NE	L	0-2	0-2	—		5124
19		27	A	Bristol R	L	0-3	0-2	10		7805
20	Dec	4	H	Notts Co	D	2-2	2-0	11	Doherty [38], Thorpe [40]	5195
21		17	A	Colchester U	L	0-3	0-0	—		3049
22		26	H	Chesterfield	D	1-1	1-0	13	Locke [38]	5870
23		28	A	Bristol C	D	0-0	0-0	12		11,832
24	Jan	3	H	Scunthorpe U	W	4-1	3-0	11	Douglas [35], Gray [36], Spring 2 [38, 79]	5574
25		8	A	Stoke C	L	1-2	0-1	12	Spring (pen) [59]	10,016
26		15	A	Blackpool	D	3-3	1-1	13	Locke [27], Gray [82], Taylor [90]	5262
27		22	H	Reading	W	3-1	1-0	10	Watts [18], George 2 [69, 90]	6044
28		30	A	Cardiff C	W	3-1	2-0	10	Watts [22], Spring [45], George [57]	6185
29	Feb	5	H	Bournemouth	L	1-2	0-1	10	Boyce [58]	5961
30		8	H	Stoke C	W	2-1	0-1	—	Gray 2 [62, 78]	5396
31		12	A	Bury	L	0-1	0-0	10		3760
32		19	H	Bristol R	L	1-4	1-2	10	Gray [13]	6520
33		26	H	Brentford	L	1-2	1-1	12	Gray [9]	6029
34	Mar	4	A	Wrexham	L	0-1	0-0	12		2703
35		7	A	Burnley	W	2-0	1-0	—	White [26], Gray [55]	12,080
36		11	H	Millwall	L	0-2	0-2	11		6341
37		18	A	Preston NE	L	0-1	0-1	13		13,731
38		21	H	Cambridge U	D	2-2	1-1	—	Doherty [19], McLaren [90]	5379
39		25	A	Chesterfield	W	3-1	3-0	11	Doherty [1], Watts [17], George [42]	2597
40	Apr	1	H	Colchester U	W	3-2	1-0	10	Watts [9], Doherty [75], Taylor [82]	5125
41		8	A	Scunthorpe U	W	2-1	2-0	10	Gray [15], Doherty [45]	3811
42		18	H	Bristol C	L	1-2	0-1	—	Doherty [78]	4771
43		22	A	Gillingham	L	0-2	0-1	11		8667
44		24	H	Wigan Ath	D	1-1	0-1	13	Gray [56]	5010
45		29	A	Wycombe W	W	1-0	0-0	10	Taylor [87]	5379
46	May	6	H	Oldham Ath	D	1-1	1-0	13	Gray [9]	5963

Final League Position: 13

GOALSCORERS

League (61): George 13 (1 pen), Gray 11, Doherty 6, Spring 6 (1 pen), Taylor 4, Watts 4, Douglas 3, Locke 3, Midgley 3, Fotiadis 2, Boyce 1, Fraser 1, McLaren 1, Thorpe 1, White 1, own goal 1.
Worthington Cup (2): Doherty 1, Kandol 1.
FA Cup (9): Doherty 2, George 2, Spring 2, Douglas 1, Gray 1, Taylor 1.

Abbey N 32+1	Fraser S 20	Taylor M 39+2	Watts J 45	White A 16+3	Johnson M 44	Gray P 28+1	McLaren P 25+4	Douglas S 35+5	McIndoe M 2+15	Spring M 44+1	Boyce E 23+7	Doherty G 40	George L 35+7	Fotiadis A 8+15	Zahana-Oni L —+1	McKinnon R —+3	Sodje E 5+4	Kandol T 1+3	Locke A 27+7	Midgley N 8+2	Thorpe T 3+1	McGowan G 10+3	Scarlett A 2+1	Roberts B 14	Match No.
1	2	3¹	4	5	6	7	8	9	10	11	12														1
1	2	3	4		6		8¹	9²	12	11		5	7	10³	13	14									2
1	2	3	4		6	7	8		12	11		5	9	10¹											3
1	2	3	4		6	7	8²	12	13	11		5	9³	10¹	14										4
1	2	3	4		6	7	8²	12	13	11		5	9	10¹											5
1	2	3	4		6	7	8	12	13	11		5	9¹	10²											6
1	2	3	4		6³		8¹	9		11		5	7	10²			12	14	13						7
1	2	3	4		6			9		11		5	7				12	10¹	8						8
1	2	3	4		6			9	12	11		5	7					8	10¹						9
1	2	3	4		6		8¹	9	12	11		5	7						10²	13					10
1	2	3	4		6	7²	8¹	9³	12	11								5	13	10	14				11
1	2	3	4		6		8¹	9	12	11		5	7						13	10²					12
1	2	3	4		6		8	9	12	11		5	7							10¹					13
1	2	3	4		6		8	9²	12	11		5	7						13	10¹					14
1		3	4		6		8	9	12	11	2	5	7							10¹					15
1		3	4		6		8²	9¹	12	11	2	5	7					14	13	10³					16
1		3	4		6		8¹	9	12	11	2²	5	7				13	14	10³						17
	2³	3	4	13			8²	9	12	11	14	5	7			6			10¹						18
1	2		4¹	5			8		10	11	12		9²	7			6	3		13					19
1	2¹	3	4		6			9²		11	12		8	7			13	5	10						20
1	2	3	4		6				12	11		5	7¹				8	10	9						21
1		3	4		6	12	13	9		11²	2	5	7				8		10¹						22
1		3	4	5	6	7		9¹		11	2	10		12					8						23
1		3	4		6	10¹		9		11	2	5	7	12					8						24
1		3	4	5¹	6	10		9⁴		11	2		7	12	13				8						25
1		3	4		6	10		9		11	2	5	7¹	12					8						26
1			4		6	10		9¹			2	5	7	12					8			3	11		27
1	2		4			10		9¹		11	6	5	7	12								3	8		28
1			4		6	10		9¹		11	2	5	7	12					8			3²	13		29
1		3	4		6	10		9		11	2²	5	7¹	12								8	13		30
1		3	4	5²	6	10		9		11	14	8	13	12				7				2³			31
1		3	4	12	6	10		9		11¹	2	5	7²	13					8						32
		3	4	12	6	10		9¹		11	2²	5	7²	14					8			13		1	33
	2²	12	4		6	7		9		11	13	5	14	10¹					8			3¹		1	34
			4	5	6	7		9¹		11	2	8		12			10					3		1	35
	12			5	6	7		9²		11	2	8	14	13	4³		10					3¹		1	36
		3	4	5¹	6	7	12	9³		11	2	8	13	14			10²							1	37
		3	4	5	6		12	13		11¹	2	9	7	10²					8					1	38
		3	4	5	6		8	9²	12	11	2		7	13					10¹					1	39
		3	4	5	6	10	8			11	2	9	7											1	40
		3	4	5	6	10	8			11	2	9	7¹							12				1	41
		3	4	5	6	10¹	8²	12		11	2³	9	7						13		14			1	42
		3	4	5	6	10	8¹	9		11	2		7						12					1	43
		3	4	5	6	7	8	9¹		11			12							10		2		1	44
		3	4	5	6	7	8	9¹		11			12							10		2		1	45
15		3	4	5	6		8	9		11			12	7						10		2¹		1⁶	46

Worthington Cup

First Round	Bristol R	(h)	0-2
		(a)	2-2

FA Cup

First Round	Kingstonian	(h)	4-2
Second Round	Lincoln C	(h)	2-2
		(a)	1-0
Third Round	Fulham	(a)	2-2
		(h)	0-3

Division 3   **MACCLESFIELD TOWN**

FOUNDATION

From the mid-19th Century until 1874, Macclesfield Town FC played under rugby rules. In 1891 they moved to the Moss Rose and finished champions of the Manchester & District League in 1906 and 1908. By 1911, they had carried off the Cheshire Senior Cup five times. Macclesfield were founder members of the Cheshire County League in 1919.

The Moss Rose Ground, London Road, Macclesfield, Cheshire SK11 7SP.

Telephone: (01625) 264 686.

Fax: (01625) 264 692.

Website: www.mtfc.co.uk

Email: office@mtfc.co.uk

Commercial Office: (01625) 264 693.

Social Club: (01625) 424 324.

Press Box: (01625) 264 690/1.

ClubCall: 09066 555 835.

Ground Capacity: 6028 (seated 1053, standing 4975).

Record Attendance: 9008 v Winsford U, Cheshire Senior Cup 2nd rd, 4 February 1948.

Pitch Measurements: 100m × 66m.

Chairman: Alan Cash.

Directors: Harry Armstrong, John Brooks, Alan Cash, Reg Flowers, Colin Garlick, Roy Higginbotham, John Chesworth, Jeremy Turner, Andy White, Eddie Furlong, Mike Rance.

Assistant Manager: Peter Davenport.

Secretary: Colin Garlick.

Administration Manager: Dianne Hehir.

Commercial Manager: Jackie Birks.

Club Doctors: Dr Mike Whiteside and John Mackay.

Physio: Stephen Wade.

LATEST SEQUENCES

Longest Sequence of League Wins: 5, 16.10.99 – 6.11.99.

Longest Sequence of League Defeats: 6, 26.12.98 –6.2.99.

Longest Sequence of League Draws: 3, 27.9.97 – 11.10.97.

Longest Sequence of Unbeaten League Matches: 8, 16.10.99 – 27.11.99.

Longest Sequence Without a League Win: 10, 21.11.98 – 6.2.99.

HONOURS

Football League: Division 3 – Runners-up 1997–98.

Vauxhall Conference: Champions 1994–95, 1996–97.

FA Trophy: Winners 1969–70, 1995–96; Runners-up 1988–89.

Bob Lord Trophy: Winners 1993–94; Runners-up 1995–96, 1996–97.

Vauxhall Conference Championship Shield: Winners 1996, 1997, 1998.

Northern Premier League: Winners 1968–69, 1969–70, 1986–87; Runners-up 1984–85.

Northern Premier League Challenge Cup: Winners 1986–87; Runners-up 1969–70, 1970–71, 1982–83.

Northern Premier League Presidents Cup: Winners 1986–87; Runners-up 1984–85.

Cheshire Senior Cup: Winners 19 times; Runners-up 11.

Colours
Royal blue shirts, white shorts, blue stockings.

Change Colours
Old gold shirts, navy shorts, navy stockings.

Year formed: 1874.

Club Nickname: 'The Silkmen'.

Previous Ground: 1874, Rostron Field; 1891, Moss Rose.

First Football League Game: 9 August 1997, Division 3, v Torquay U (h) W 2–1 – Price; Tinson, Rose, Payne (Edey), Howarth, Sodje (1), Askey, Wood, Landon (1) (Power), Mason, Sorvel.

Record League Victory: 3–0 v Doncaster R, Division 3, 23 August 1997 – Price; Tinson, Rose, Payne, Howarth, Sodje, Askey (1) (Mitchell), Wood, Landon (1), Mason (Power), Sorvel, (1 og). 3–0 v Swansea C, Division 3, 13 September 1997 – Price; Tinson, Rose, Payne (Hitchen), Howarth, Sodje, Mitchell (Askey (1)), Gardiner (1), Peel (1), Power (Landon), Sorvel. 3–0 v Doncaster R (away), Division 3, 24 January 1998 – Price; Tinson, Howarth (Edey), Payne, McDonald, Sodje, Askey (Power), Wood (2), Chambers, Sorvel (1), Whittaker.

Record Win: 15–0 v Chester St Marys, Cheshire Senior Cup, 2nd rd, 16 February 1886.

Record Defeat: 1–13 v Tranmere R reserves, 3 May 1929.

Most League Points (3 for a win): 82, Division 3, 1997–98.

Most League Goals: 66, Division 3, 1999–2000.

Highest League Scorer in Season: Richard Barker, 16, Division 3, 1999–2000.

Most League Goals in Total Aggregate: John Askey, 25, 1997–2000.

Most League Appearances: Darren Tinson, 127, 1997–2000.

Youngest League Player: Peter Griffiths, 18 years 44 days v Reading, 26 September 1998.

Record Transfer Fee Received: £40,000 from Sheffield U for Mike Lake, 1988.

Record Transfer Fee Paid: £30,000 to Stevenage Borough for Efetobore Sodje, August 1997.

Football League Record: Promoted to Division 3 1997; 1998–99 Division 2; 1999– Division 3.

MANAGERS

Since 1967
Keith Goalen 1967–68
Frank Beaumont 1968–72
Billy Haydock 1972–74
Eddie Brown 1974
John Collins 1974
Willie Stevenson 1974
John Collins 1975–76
Tony Coleman 1976
John Barnes 1976
Brian Taylor 1976
Dave Connor 1976–78
Derek Partridge 1978
Phil Staley 1978–80
Jimmy Williams 1980–81
Brian Booth 1981–85
Neil Griffiths 1985–86
Roy Campbell 1986
Peter Wragg 1986–93
Sammy McIlroy 1993–2000
Peter Davenport January 2000–

TEN YEAR LEAGUE RECORD

		P	W	D	L	F	A	Pts	Pos
1989-90	Conf	42	17	15	10	66	41	66	4
1990-91	Conf	42	17	12	13	63	52	63	7
1991-92	Conf	42	13	13	16	50	50	52	13
1992-93	Conf	42	12	13	17	40	50	49	18
1993-94	Conf	42	16	11	15	48	49	59	7
1994-95	Conf	42	24	8	10	70	40	80	1
1995-96	Conf	42	22	9	11	66	49	75	4
1996-97	Conf	42	27	9	6	80	30	90	1
1997-98	Div 3	46	23	13	10	63	44	82	2
1998-99	Div 2	46	11	10	25	43	63	43	24

DID YOU KNOW ❓

On 8 April 2000, 20 year old Damien Whitehead made Macclesfield Town's first two goals and scored two more himself in the 4-2 win over Plymouth Argyle.

MACCLESFIELD TOWN 1999–2000 LEAGUE RECORD

Match No.	Date	Venue	Opponents	Result	H/T Score	Lg. Pos.	Goalscorers	Attendance
1	Aug 7	H	Northampton T	W	1-0	0-0	11	Barker [57]	2694
2	14	A	Darlington	L	0-3	0-0	16		5117
3	21	H	Swansea C	L	1-2	0-0	19	Askey [90]	2121
4	28	A	Hull C	W	3-2	1-1	13	Rioch 2 (1 pen) [39 (p), 55], Ware [88]	6222
5	30	H	Rotherham U	D	1-1	1-0	14	Barker [4]	2307
6	Sept 5	A	Barnet	L	1-2	0-1	16	Barker [70]	2426
7	11	H	Southend U	L	1-2	1-2	17	Barker [45]	2059
8	18	A	Lincoln C	D	1-1	0-0	18	Barker [58]	2918
9	25	A	Exeter C	W	3-0	3-0	13	Barker [9], Rioch [15], Durkan [45]	3202
10	Oct 2	H	Torquay U	L	1-2	1-1	19	Collins [22]	2002
11	9	H	Halifax T	L	0-2	0-1	21		2185
12	16	A	Chester C	W	2-1	2-1	16	Collins [8], Barker [30]	2506
13	19	A	Rochdale	W	1-0	1-0	—	Askey [5]	2397
14	23	H	Exeter C	W	1-0	1-0	15	Barker [25]	1893
15	Nov 2	H	Mansfield T	W	5-2	3-0	—	Priest [8], Barker 2 [10, 17], Sedgemore [82], Askey [86]	1541
16	6	A	York C	W	2-0	1-0	7	Sertori (og) [33], Barker [82]	2469
17	14	H	Brighton & HA	D	1-1	0-0	7	Askey [64]	2920
18	20	A	Peterborough U	D	2-2	2-1	7	Askey [33], Barker [44]	5083
19	27	H	Hartlepool U	D	3-3	2-0	9	Priest [5], Barker [28], Askey [67]	2351
20	Dec 4	A	Northampton T	L	0-2	0-1	11		5355
21	11	A	Cheltenham T	D	1-1	0-0	12	Durkan [52]	3107
22	18	H	Leyton Orient	W	1-0	0-0	10	Davies [58]	2303
23	26	A	Shrewsbury T	W	1-0	1-0	8	Durkan [44]	4302
24	28	H	Carlisle U	W	2-1	0-0	6	Priest 2 [82, 90]	2836
25	Jan 3	A	Plymouth Arg	L	2-3	1-2	6	Askey [13], Wood [53]	6128
26	8	H	Cheltenham T	L	1-2	0-1	10	Rioch (pen) [68]	3221
27	15	H	Darlington	W	2-1	2-1	7	Moore [14], Askey [34]	2399
28	22	A	Swansea C	L	0-1	0-0	9		6913
29	29	H	Hull C	L	0-2	0-0	11		1900
30	Feb 5	A	Rotherham U	L	1-2	1-2	14	Rioch (pen) [5]	4175
31	12	H	Barnet	W	2-0	1-0	9	Barker [18], Askey [64]	2114
32	19	A	Hartlepool U	W	4-1	3-1	9	Durkan [8], Barker 2 [22, 47], Askey [37]	2823
33	26	H	Lincoln C	D	1-1	1-0	9	Askey [26]	2445
34	Mar 3	A	Southend U	L	0-1	0-1	—		3725
35	7	H	York C	D	1-1	1-1	—	Durkan [22]	1581
36	11	A	Mansfield T	L	0-1	0-0	14		2327
37	18	H	Peterborough U	D	1-1	0-1	13	Moore [90]	2309
38	21	A	Brighton & HA	L	2-5	2-2	—	Askey [8], Whitehead [33]	5596
39	25	H	Shrewsbury T	W	4-2	2-1	12	Collins [8], Whitehead 2 [21, 60], Tomlinson [84]	1931
40	Apr 1	A	Leyton Orient	D	0-0	0-0	14		4302
41	8	H	Plymouth Arg	W	4-1	3-0	13	Askey [2], Durkan [15], Whitehead 2 [30, 89]	2231
42	15	A	Carlisle U	W	1-0	0-0	11	Whitehead [59]	3047
43	22	H	Chester C	D	1-1	1-0	11	Askey [30]	3456
44	24	A	Torquay U	L	2-3	2-1	12	Askey [8], Ware [18]	2139
45	29	H	Rochdale	L	1-2	1-2	13	Tomlinson [23]	2202
46	May 6	A	Halifax T	W	1-0	0-0	13	Tinson [53]	2007

Final League Position: 13

GOALSCORERS

League (66): Barker 16, Askey 15, Durkan 6, Whitehead 6, Rioch 5 (3 pens), Priest 4, Collins 3, Moore 2, Tomlinson 2, Ware 2, Davies 1, Sedgemore 1, Tinson 1, Wood 1, own goal 1.
Worthington Cup (1): Priest 1.
FA Cup (0).

Price R 11 + 1	Hitchen S 2 + 3	Rioch G 42	Collins S 37 + 2	Tinson D 46	Wood S 30 + 6	Askey J 37 + 3	Priest C 34 + 2	Barker R 35	Davies S 30 + 6	Durkan K 41 + 1	Ingram R 35 + 1	Sedgemore B 31 + 4	Tomlinson G 7 + 11	Abbey G 12 + 6	Whitehead D 10 + 13	Whittaker S 2 + 7	Brown G 2 + 3	Byrne C 5	Ware P 9 + 9	Martin L 21	Knight R 3	Moore N 12 + 3	Williams A 11	Munroe K 1 + 4	O'Neill P — + 1	Bamber M — + 1	Match No.
1	2¹	3	4	5	6	7²	8	9	10	11	12	13															1
1		3	4	5	6	7²	8	9	10²	11¹	2	12	13	14													2
1		3	4³	5	6	7	8	9		11²	12	2	13	10¹	14												3
1		3¹	4	5	6	7	8²	9	12		2			11								10	13				4
1		3²	4	5	6	7¹	14	9	13		2	12		11								10	8³				5
1		3		5	6	7²12		9	13	2¹	4			8	14							10	11³				6
1		3¹	4	5		7²	8	9	11	2	6	13	12									10					7
1		3	5		8	9	10	11¹	2		12	13							6			4²	7				8
1		3	4	5	6	7	8	9	10	11	2																9
1		3	4	5	6	8¹	9	10	11	2	12			7²13													10
1		3	4	5	6	7	8¹	9	10²	11	2	12		13													11
		3	4	5	6³	7	8	9	10²	11¹	2	13	12							1		14					12
		3	4	5		7	8	9	10	11	2	6								1							13
		3	4	5		7	8	9¹	10	11	2	6	12							1							14
		3	4	5	12	7	8	9	10¹	11	2	6								1							15
		3	4	5		7	8	9	10	11	2	6								1							16
		3	4	5		7	8	9	10	11	2	6								1							17
		3	4	5		7	8	9	10¹	11	2	6							12	1							18
15			4	5	12	7	8	9²	10¹	11	2	6	13						3	1⁶							19
		3	4	5		7	8		10	11	2²	6	9¹	13	12					1							20
		3	4	2	10	7	8	9		11		6							1	5							21
		3	4	5³	6	7¹	8	9²	12	11	10	13	2		14					1							22
		3		5	6	12	8	9	10¹	11	7	2								1		4					23
		3		5	6	12	8	9³	10²	11	7¹	2	13	14						1		4					24
		3		5	6	7		9	10	11¹	8	2	12							1		4					25
		3	5	2	6	12	8	9	10¹	11	7²		13							1		4					26
		3		5	6	7¹	8	9		11	2	10	12							1		4					27
		3		5	6	7²	8	9		11¹	2³	10	14	13	12					1		4					28
		3	12	5	6²		8	9		2	7¹		11	10								4		1		13	29
		3	11	5	6	7²	8¹	9	12	2		10	13									4		1			30
		3	4	5	12	7	8²	9	10	11	2	6¹							13			14		1			31
		3	4	5		7¹	8	9	10	11²	2	6	12						13					1			32
		3	4	5		7	8	9	10	11¹	2	6							12					1			33
		3²	4³	5	12	7	8	9	10	11	2	6¹							13			14		1			34
		3		5	6	7¹	8	9	10	11²	2	12							13			4		1			35
		3	12	5	6	7²	8	9¹	10	11³	2	14							13			4		1			36
		3	4¹	5	6	7	8²		10	11	2³	9	12						13			14		1			37
		3		5	6	7			11		8¹	9	10						2			4		1	12		38
		3	4	5	12	7²			11	2	6³	9	13	10					8					1		14	39
12			4	5	6		11	2	8	9¹	3	10							7²					1		13	40
12		3	4	5	6	7		10	11¹	2	8	9												1			41
		3	4	5	6	7		10	11³	2	8	9	12											1			42
12		3	4	5	6	7		10²	11	2¹	8	13	9											1			43
2		3	4	5	12	7²		10¹	11	13	9	6								1			8				44
		3	4	5	6²		12	11	8	10¹	2	9							7³	1			13	14			45
		3	4	5	6		12	11	2²	8	10¹	13	9						7	1							46

Worthington Cup
First Round   Stoke C   (h) 1-1   (a) 0-3

FA Cup
First Round   Hull C   (h) 0-0   (a) 0-4

FA Premiership　　　**MANCHESTER CITY**

FOUNDATION

Manchester City was formed as a Limited Company in 1894 after their predecessors Ardwick had been forced into bankruptcy. However, many historians like to trace the club's lineage as far back as 1880 when St Mark's Church, West Gorton added a football section to their cricket club. They amalgamated with Gorton Athletic in 1884 as Gorton FC. Because of a change of ground they became Ardwick in 1887.

Maine Road, Moss Side, Manchester M14 7WN.
Telephone: (0161) 232 3000.
Fax: (0161) 232 8999.
Ticket Office: (0161) 226 2224.
Dial-A-Seat: (0161) 227 9229.
Development Office: (0161) 226 3143.
ClubCall: 09068 121 191.
Ground Capacity: 34,026.
Record Attendance: 84,569 v Stoke C, FA Cup 6th rd, 3 March 1934 (British record for any game outside London or Glasgow).
Record Receipts: £512,235 Manchester U v Oldham Ath, FA Cup semi-final replay, 13 April 1994.
Pitch Measurements: 117yd × 78yd.
Chairman: D. A. Bernstein.
Directors: J. Wardle, D. Tueart, A. Lewis, A. Thomas, B. Bodek, C. Bird, A. Mackintosh.
General Secretary: J. B. Halford.
Manager: Joe Royle.
Head Coach: Willie Donachie.
Reserve Team Coach: Asa Hartford.
Physio: Roy Bailey.
Youth Team Coach: Alex Gibson.
Youth Academy Director: Jim Cassell.

LATEST SEQUENCES

Longest Sequence of League Wins: 9, 8.4.12 – 28.9.12.
Longest Sequence of League Defeats: 8, 23.8.95 – 14.10.95.
Longest Sequence of League Draws: 6, 5.4.13 – 6.9.13.
Longest Sequence of Unbeaten League Matches: 22, 16.11.46 – 19.4.47.
Longest Sequence Without a League Win: 17, 26.12.79 – 7.4.80.

HONOURS

Football League: Division 1 – Champions 1936–37, 1967–68; Runners-up 1903–04, 1920–21, 1976–77, 1999–2000; Division 2 – Champions 1898–99, 1902–03, 1909–10, 1927–28, 1946–47, 1965–66; Runners-up 1895–96, 1950–51, 1987–88; Promoted from Division 2 (play-offs) 1998–99.
FA Cup: Winners 1904, 1934, 1956, 1969; Runners-up 1926, 1933, 1955, 1981.
Football League Cup: Winners 1970, 1976; Runners-up 1974.
European Competitions: *European Cup:* 1968–69. *European Cup-Winners' Cup:* 1969–70 (winners), 1970–71. *UEFA Cup:* 1972–73, 1976–77, 1977–78, 1978–79.

Colours
Lazer blue shirts, white shorts, navy stockings.

Change Colours
Silver with yellow and navy striped shirts, navy shorts with yellow trim, yellow stockings.

Year Formed: 1887 as Ardwick FC; 1894 as Manchester City.
Turned Professional: 1887 as Ardwick FC.
Ltd Co.: 1894.
Previous Names: 1887, Ardwick FC (formed through the amalgamation of West Gorton and Gorton Athletic, the latter having been formed in 1880); 1894, Manchester City.
Club Nickname: 'Blues' or 'The Citizens'.
Previous Grounds: 1880, Clowes Street; 1881, Kirkmanshulme Cricket Ground; 1882, Queens Road; 1884, Pink Bank Lane; 1887, Hyde Road (1894–1923 as City); 1923, Maine Road.
First Football League Game: 3 September 1892, Division 2, v Bootle (h) W 7–0 – Douglas; McVickers, Robson; Middleton, Russell, Hopkins; Davies (3), Morris (2), Angus (1), Weir (1), Milarvie.
Record League Victory: 10–1 v Huddersfield T, Division 2, 7 November 1987 – Nixon; Gidman, Hinchcliffe, Clements, Lake, Redmond, White (3), Stewart (3), Adcock (3), McNab (1), Simpson.
Record Cup Victory: 10–1 v Swindon T, FA Cup 4th rd, 29 January 1930 – Barber; Felton, McCloy; Barrass, Cowan, Heinemann; Toseland, Marshall (5), Tait (3), Johnson (1), Brook (1).
Record Defeat: 1–9 v Everton, Division 1, 3 September 1906.
Most League Points (2 for a win): 62, Division 2, 1946–47.
Most League Points (3 for a win): 89, Division 1, 1999–2000.
Most League Goals: 108, Division 2, 1926–27.
Highest League Scorer in Season: Tommy Johnson, 38, Division 1, 1928–29.
Most League Goals in Total Aggregate: Tommy Johnson, 158, 1919–30.
Most League Goals in One Match: 5, Fred Williams v Darwen, Division 2, 18 February 1899; 5, Tom Browell v Burnley, Division 2, 24 October 1925; 5, Tom Johnson v Everton, Division 1, 15 September 1928; 5, George Smith v Newport Co, Division 2, 14 June 1947.
Most Capped Player: Colin Bell, 48, England.
Most League Appearances: Alan Oakes, 565, 1959–76.
Youngest League Player: Glyn Pardoe, 15 years 314 days v Birmingham C, 11 April 1961.
Record Transfer Fee Received: £4,925,000 from Ajax for Georgi Kinkladze, May 1998.
Record Transfer Fee Paid: £3,000,000 to Portsmouth for Lee Bradbury, July 1997.
Football League Record: 1892 Ardwick elected founder member of Division 2; 1894 Newly-formed Manchester C elected to Division 2; Division 1 1899–1902, 1903–09, 1910–26, 1928–38, 1947–50, 1951–63, 1966–83, 1985–87, 1989–92; Division 2 1902–03, 1909–10, 1926–28, 1938–47, 1950–51, 1963–66, 1983–85, 1987–89; 1992–96 FA Premier League; 1996–98 Division 1; 1998–99 Division 2; 1999–2000 Division 1; 2000– FA Premier League.

MANAGERS

Joshua Parlby 1893–95
(Secretary-Manager)
Sam Omerod 1895–1902
Tom Maley 1902–06
Harry Newbould 1906–12
Ernest Magnall 1912–24
David Ashworth 1924–25
Peter Hodge 1926–32
Wilf Wild 1932–46
(continued as Secretary to 1950)
Sam Cowan 1946–47
John 'Jock' Thomson 1947–50
Leslie McDowall 1950–63
George Poyser 1963–65
Joe Mercer 1965–71
(continued as General Manager to 1972)
Malcolm Allison 1972–73
Johnny Hart 1973
Ron Saunders 1973–74
Tony Book 1974–79
Malcolm Allison 1979–80
John Bond 1980–83
John Benson 1983
Billy McNeill 1983–86
Jimmy Frizzell 1986–87
(continued as General Manager)
Mel Machin 1987–89
Howard Kendall 1990
Peter Reid 1990–93
Brian Horton 1993–95
Alan Ball 1995–96
Steve Coppell 1996
Frank Clark 1996–98
Joe Royle February 1998–

TEN YEAR LEAGUE RECORD

		P	W	D	L	F	A	Pts	Pos
1989-90	Div 1	38	12	12	14	43	52	48	14
1990-91	Div 1	38	17	11	10	64	53	62	5
1991-92	Div 1	42	20	10	12	61	48	70	5
1992-93	PR Lge	42	15	12	15	56	51	57	9
1993-94	PR Lge	42	9	18	15	38	49	45	16
1994-95	PR Lge	42	12	13	17	53	64	49	17
1995-96	PR Lge	38	9	11	18	33	58	38	18
1996-97	Div 1	46	17	10	19	59	60	61	14
1997-98	Div 1	46	12	12	22	56	57	48	22
1998-99	Div 2	46	22	16	8	69	33	82	3

DID YOU KNOW ?

Manchester City clinched their initial First Division title in fine style, beating Sheffield Wednesday 4-1 on 24 April 1937, their first goal from Eric Brook after 19 minutes described as *"not so much a goal as a piece of forked lightning"*.

MANCHESTER CITY 1999–2000 LEAGUE RECORD

Match No.	Date		Venue	Opponents	Result		H/T Score	Lg. Pos.	Goalscorers	Attendance
1	Aug	8	H	Wolverhampton W	L	0-1	0-1	20		31,755
2		14	A	Fulham	D	0-0	0-0	20		16,754
3		21	H	Sheffield U	W	6-0	2-0	8	Horlock 2 (2 pens) [37, 43], Kennedy [62], Goater [66], Dickov [72], Taylor G [86]	30,110
4		28	A	Bolton W	W	1-0	1-0	4	Kennedy [32]	21,671
5		30	H	Nottingham F	W	1-0	1-0	2	Goater [13]	31,857
6	Sept	11	H	Crystal Palace	W	2-1	1-1	2	Jobson [42], Taylor G [50]	31,541
7		18	A	Walsall	W	1-0	1-0	1	Goater [34]	7260
8		26	A	Ipswich T	L	1-2	0-1	3	Goater [50]	19,406
9		28	A	Norwich C	L	0-1	0-1	—		15,130
10	Oct	2	H	Port Vale	W	2-1	2-0	2	Bishop 2 [30, 36]	31,608
11		16	A	Tranmere R	D	1-1	0-0	4	Horlock (pen) [50]	13,208
12		19	A	Birmingham C	W	1-0	0-0	—	Jobson [47]	22,126
13		23	H	Blackburn R	W	2-0	1-0	1	Edghill [39], Whitley Jeff [82]	33,027
14		27	H	Ipswich T	W	1-0	0-0	—	Horlock [58]	32,799
15		30	A	Port Vale	W	2-1	0-1	1	Snijders (og) [72], Granville [77]	10,250
16	Nov	3	H	Portsmouth	W	4-2	0-1	—	Whitley Jeff [46], Taylor G 2 [66, 69], Pollock [90]	31,660
17		6	A	QPR	D	1-1	0-1	1	Horlock [61]	19,002
18		20	A	Charlton Ath	W	1-0	0-0	1	Goater [48]	20,043
19		24	H	Barnsley	W	3-1	2-0	—	Taylor G [6], Goater [10], Horlock [73]	32,692
20		27	H	Huddersfield T	L	0-1	0-0	1		32,936
21	Dec	3	A	Wolverhampton W	L	1-4	1-3	—	Goater [30]	21,635
22		7	A	Stockport Co	L	1-2	0-0	—	Wiekens [49]	32,686
23		18	H	Swindon T	W	3-0	1-0	2	Pollock [29], Taylor R [47], Goater [59]	31,751
24		26	A	WBA	W	2-0	0-0	1	Granville [50], Goater [72]	19,589
25		28	H	Grimsby T	W	2-1	1-1	1	Horlock 2 [5, 90]	32,607
26	Jan	3	A	Crewe Alex	D	1-1	1-0	1	Crooks [6]	10,066
27		16	H	Fulham	W	4-0	1-0	1	Goater 3 [29, 77, 85], Horlock (pen) [87]	30,057
28		22	A	Sheffield U	L	0-1	0-1	2		23,862
29	Feb	5	A	Nottingham F	W	3-1	2-1	2	Taylor R [31], Goater 2 [35, 83]	25,846
30		12	H	Norwich C	W	3-1	1-1	2	Goater [3], Kennedy 2 [82, 83]	32,681
31		18	A	Huddersfield T	D	1-1	1-1	—	Goater [45]	18,173
32		26	H	Walsall	D	1-1	0-1	3	Goater [71]	32,438
33	Mar	4	A	Crystal Palace	D	1-1	1-1	2	Taylor R [8]	21,052
34		8	H	QPR	L	1-3	0-2	—	Whitley Jeff [84]	31,353
35		11	A	Barnsley	L	1-2	0-2	4	Goater [86]	22,650
36		19	H	Charlton Ath	D	1-1	1-1	2	Goater [32]	32,139
37		21	A	Stockport Co	D	2-2	1-2	—	Pollock [7], Jobson [79]	11,212
38		25	H	WBA	W	2-1	0-0	3	Kennedy [77], Goater [90]	32,072
39	Apr	1	A	Swindon T	W	2-0	1-0	3	Goater [43], Kennedy [57]	12,397
40		5	H	Bolton W	W	2-0	2-0	—	Horlock [18], Dickov [23]	32,927
41		8	H	Crewe Alex	W	4-0	1-0	2	Prior [42], Dickov 2 [68, 90], Kennedy [86]	32,433
42		15	A	Grimsby T	D	1-1	1-1	2	Prior [6]	8166
43		22	H	Tranmere R	W	2-0	1-0	2	Goater [10], Whitley Jeff [72]	32,842
44		24	A	Portsmouth	D	2-2	2-1	2	Prior [26], Taylor R [40]	19,015
45		28	H	Birmingham C	W	1-0	1-0	—	Taylor R [40]	32,062
46	May	7	A	Blackburn R	W	4-1	0-1	2	Goater [60], Dailly (og) [67], Kennedy [75], Dickov [81]	29,913

Final League Position: 2

GOALSCORERS

League (78): Goater 23, Horlock 10 (4 pens), Kennedy 8, Dickov 5, Taylor G 5, Taylor R 5, Whitley Jeff 4, Jobson 3, Pollock 3, Prior 3, Bishop 2, Granville 2, Crooks 1, Edghill 1, Wiekens 1, own goals 2.
Worthington Cup (9): Goater 3, Kennedy 2, Cooke 1, Dickov 1, Horlock 1 (pen), Taylor G 1.
FA Cup (6): Goater 3, Bishop 2, own goal 1.

Weaver N 45	Edghill R 40 + 1	Granville D 28 + 7	Wiekens G 32 + 2	Morrison A 12	Horlock K 36 + 2	Kennedy M 41	Whitley Jeff 41 + 1	Dickov P 22 + 12	Goater S 40	Cooke T 6 + 7	Crooks L 9 + 11	Taylor G 8 + 9	Tiatto D 26 + 9	Bishop I 25 + 12	Vaughan T — + 1	Jobson R 43 + 1	Allsopp D — + 4	Pollock J 17 + 7	Wright-Phillips S 2 + 2	Peacock L 4 + 4	Taylor R 14 + 2	Grant T 4 + 4	Wright T 1	Whitley Jim — + 1	Mills L 1 + 2	Prior S 9	Match No
1	2	3¹	4	5	6	7	8	9	10	11	12²	13															1
1			4	5	6	7¹	8	9	10		2		3	11	12												2
1	2		4	5²	6	7	8	9	10¹	11		12	3²	13		14											3
1	2		4		6	7	8	9	10¹	11³	13	12	3²	14		5											4
1	2		4		6	7	8	9	10¹	11²	14	12	3²	13		5											5
1	2		4		6	7	8	9¹	10	11²	13	12	3²	14		5											6
1	2		4¹		6	7	8	9	10		12		3	11		5											7
1	12		4		6	7	8	9	10	13	2		3¹	11²		5											8
1	3		4		6	7	8	9¹	10	14	2	12²		11		5³	13										9
1	3		4		6	7	8	9¹	10²	12	2			11		5	13										10
1	12	3	4		6	7¹	8	9		2	10			11		5											11
1	2	3	4		6	7	8	9²		12	10¹			11		5	13										12
1	2	3	4		6	7	8	9	10²	13	12			11¹		5											13
1	2	3	4		6	7³	8	9	10	13	12	14	11²			5											14
1	2	3	12	4¹		7	8	11³	6²	9		13				5	10	14									15
1	2	3	4¹		6	7	8	12		9	13	11³				5	14	10²									16
1	2	3			6	7²	8	12	4¹	9	13	11				5	10³	14									17
1	2	3	4		6		8		10	12		9	11¹			5		7									18
1	2	3	4		6		8		10¹	12	9	11²				5		7	13								19
1	2	3	4		6		8		10	12	9²	11¹				5		7	13								20
1	2	3¹	4		6	7	8²		10		12	11				5	13		9								21
1	2	3	4		6	7	8²		10	12		11				5	13		9¹								22
	2	3	4		6	7¹		10²		12	11	5	8				13	9					1				23
1	2	3	4			7²	8	12	10	13	11	5	6³	9¹			14										24
1	2	3	4		6		12	10	13	7¹	11²	5	8				9³	14									25
1		3¹	4		6	12	13	10	2	14	11	5	8				9²	7¹									26
1	2	3	4		6	7¹		10		12	11	5					9	8									27
1	3		6		7		12	10	2	4	11	5					9¹	8									28
1	2	12	4		6	7	8	13	10	3¹	11³	5	14	9²													29
1	2¹	3	4		6	7	8	9²	10	11	5	13	12														30
1	2	3	4		6¹	7	8	9	10	12	11²	5	13														31
1	2	3¹	4		6³	7	8	9¹	10	12	11	5	13	14													32
1	2	3¹	4		7	8	6		5	11	12	10	9														33
1	2	3¹	4	12	7	8	13	10	6¹	14	5	11²	9														34
1	2	3²	4	7	8	12	10	6		13	5	11¹	9														35
1	2	12	4	7	8	10	3	11¹	5	6	9																36
1	2	3	4	7	8	12	10	11¹	5	6	9																37
1	2	3²		7	8	12	10	6	5	11	9¹	13														4	38
1	2	12		7	8	9	10¹	3	13	5	6	11²														4	39
1	2	12	11	6	7	8	9	10²	3¹	5	13															4	40
1	2	11¹	6	7	8	9	10	3	12	5																4	41
1	2	11	6¹	7	8	9²	10	3	12	5	13															4	42
1	2	11	6	7¹	8²	9¹	10	3	12	5	13	14														4	43
1	2	12	11²	13	7¹	8	14	10	3	5	6	9³														4	44
1	2	12	11	6³	7¹	8	13	10	3	5	14	9²														4	45
1	2	12	6	7¹	8	13	10	3	14	5	11³	9²														4	46

Worthington Cup

First Round	Burnley		(h)	5-0
			(a)	1-0
Second Round	Southampton		(h)	0-0
			(a)	3-4

FA Cup

Third Round	Chester C	(a)	4-1
Fourth Round	Leeds U	(h)	2-5

FA Premiership **MANCHESTER UNITED**

FOUNDATION

Manchester United was formed as comparatively recently as 1902 after their predecessors, Newton Heath, went bankrupt. However, it is usual to give the date of the club's foundation as 1878 when the dining room committee of the carriage and waggon works of the Lancashire and Yorkshire Railway Company formed Newton Heath L and YR Cricket and Football Club. They won the Manchester Cup in 1886 and as Newton Heath FC were admitted to the Second Division in 1892.

Sir Matt Busby Way, Old Trafford, Manchester M16 0RA.
Telephone: (0161) 868 8000.
Textphone for Deaf/Impaired Hearing: (0161) 868 8668.
Fax: (0161) 868 8804.
Ticket and Match Information: (0161) 868 8020.
Membership and Supporters Club Enquiries:
(0161) 868 8450.
ClubCall: 09068 121 161.
Ground Capacity: 68,936.
Record Attendance: 76,962 Wolverhampton W v Grimsby T, FA Cup semi-final, 25 March 1939.
Club record: 70,504 v Aston Villa, Division 1, 27 December 1920.
Record Receipts: £723,650.22 (net of VAT), £850,289 (including VAT) v Liverpool, FA Cup 4th rd, 24 January 1999.
Pitch Measurements: 116yd × 76yd.
Chairman/Chief Executive: C. M. Edwards.
Directors: J. M. Edelson, Sir Bobby Charlton CBE, E. M. Watkins LL.M., R. L. Olive, P. F. Kenyon, D. A. Gill.
Manager: Sir Alex Ferguson CBE.
Assistant Manager: Steve McClaren
Secretary: Kenneth Merrett.
Stadium Manager: Alan Bird.

LATEST SEQUENCES
Longest Sequence of League Wins: 14, 15.10.04 – 3.1.05.
Longest Sequence of League Defeats: 14, 26.4.30 – 25.10.30.
Longest Sequence of League Draws: 6, 30.10.88 – 27.11.88.
Longest Sequence of Unbeaten League Matches: 29, 26.12.98 – 25.9.99.
Longest Sequence Without a League Win: 16, 19.4.30 – 25.10.30.

HONOURS

FA Premier League – Champions 1992–93, 1993–94, 1995–96, 1996–97, 1998–99, 1999–2000; Runners-up 1994–95, 1997–98.

Football League: Division 1 – Champions 1907–08, 1910–11, 1951–52, 1955–56, 1956–57, 1964–65, 1966–67; Runners-up 1946–47, 1947–48, 1948–49, 1950–51, 1958–59, 1963–64, 1967–68, 1979–80, 1987–88, 1991–92. Division 2 – Champions 1935–36, 1974–75; Runners-up 1896–97, 1905–06, 1924–25, 1937–38.

FA Cup: Winners 1909, 1948, 1963, 1977, 1983, 1985, 1990, 1994, 1996, 1999; Runners-up 1957, 1958, 1976, 1979, 1995.

Football League Cup: Winners 1992; Runners-up 1983, 1991, 1994.

European Competitions: European Cup: 1956–57 (s-f), 1957–58 (s-f), 1965–66 (s-f), 1967–68 (winners), 1968–69 (s-f), 1993–94, 1994–95, 1996–97 (s-f), 1997–98, 1998–99 (winners), 1999–2000. *European Cup-Winners' Cup:* 1963–64, 1977–78, 1983–84, 1990–91 (winners). 1991–92. *European Fairs Cup:* 1964–65. *UEFA Cup:* 1976–77, 1980–81, 1982–83, 1984–85, 1992–93, 1995–96. *Super Cup:* 1991 (winners), 1999 (runners-up). *Inter-Continental Cup:* 1999 (winners), 1968 (runners-up)

Colours
Red shirts, white shorts, black stockings.
Change Colours
All white.

Year Formed: 1878 as Newton Heath LYR; 1902, Manchester United.

Turned Professional: 1885. *Ltd Co.:* 1907.

Previous Name: 1880, Newton Heath; 1902, Manchester United.

Club Nickname: 'Red Devils'.

Previous Grounds: 1880, North Road, Monsall Road; 1893, Bank Street; 1910, Old Trafford (played at Maine Road 1941–49).

First Football League Game: 3 September 1892, Division 1, v Blackburn R (a) L 3–4 – Warner; Clements, Brown; Perrins, Stewart, Erentz; Farman (1), Coupar (1), Donaldson (1), Carson, Mathieson.

Record League Victory (as Newton Heath): 10–1 v Wolverhampton W, Division 1, 15 October 1892 – Warner; Mitchell, Clements; Perrins, Stewart (3), Erentz; Farman (1), Hood (1), Donaldson (3), Carson (1), Hendry (1).

Record League Victory (as Manchester U): 9–0 v Ipswich T, FA Premier League, 4 March 1995 – Schmeichel; Keane (1) (Sharpe), Irwin, Bruce (Butt), Kanchelskis, Pallister, Cole (5), Ince (1), McClair, Hughes (2), Giggs.

Record Cup Victory: 10–0 v RSC Anderlecht, European Cup prel. rd 2nd leg, 26 September 1956 – Wood; Foulkes, Byrne; Colman, Jones, Edwards; Berry (1), Whelan (2), Taylor (3), Viollet (4), Pegg.

MANAGERS

J. Ernest Mangnall 1903–12
John Bentley 1912–14
John Robson 1914–21
(Secretary-Manager from 1916)
John Chapman 1921–26
Clarence Hilditch 1926–27
Herbert Bamlett 1927–31
Walter Crickmer 1931–32
Scott Duncan 1932–37
Walter Crickmer 1937–45
(Secretary-Manager)
Matt Busby 1945–69
(continued as General Manager then Director)
Wilf McGuinness 1969–70
Sir Matt Busby 1970–71
Frank O'Farrell 1971–72
Tommy Docherty 1972–77
Dave Sexton 1977–81
Ron Atkinson 1981–86
Alex Ferguson November 1986–

Record Defeat: 0–7 v Blackburn R, Division 1, 10 April 1926. 0–7 v Aston Villa, Division 1, 27 December 1930. 0–7 v Wolverhampton W, Division 2, 26 December 1931.

Most League Points (2 for a win): 64, Division 1, 1956–57.

Most League Points (3 for a win): 92, FA Premier League, 1993–94.

Most League Goals: 103, Division 1, 1956–57 and 1958–59.

Highest League Scorer in Season: Dennis Viollet, 32, 1959–60.

Most League Goals in Total Aggregate: Bobby Charlton, 199, 1956–73.

Most Capped Player: Bobby Charlton, 106, England.

Most League Appearances: Bobby Charlton, 606, 1956–73.

Youngest League Player: Jeff Whitefoot, 16 years 105 days v Portsmouth, 15 April 1950.

Record Transfer Fee Received: £7,000,000 from Internazionale for Paul Ince, June 1995.

Record Transfer Fee Paid: £12,600,000 to Aston Villa for Dwight Yorke, August 1998.

Football League Record: 1892 Newton Heath elected to Division 1; 1894–1906 Division 2; 1906–22 Division 1; 1922–25 Division 2; 1925–31 Division 1; 1931–36 Division 2; 1936–37 Division 1; 1937–38 Division 2; 1938–74 Division 1; 1974–75 Division 2; 1975–92 Division 1; 1992– FA Premier League.

TEN YEAR LEAGUE RECORD

		P	W	D	L	F	A	Pts	Pos
1989-90	Div 1	38	13	9	16	46	47	48	13
1990-91	Div 1	38	16	12	10	58	45	59	6
1991-92	Div 1	42	21	15	6	63	33	78	2
1992-93	PR Lge	42	24	12	6	67	31	84	1
1993-94	PR Lge	42	27	11	4	80	38	92	1
1994-95	PR Lge	42	26	10	6	77	28	88	2
1995-96	PR Lge	38	25	7	6	73	35	82	1
1996-97	PR Lge	38	21	12	5	76	44	75	1
1997-98	PR Lge	38	23	8	7	73	26	77	2
1998-99	PR Lge	38	22	13	3	80	37	79	1

DID YOU KNOW ?

Manchester United's two highest individual scoring performances have been six goals: Harold Halse in the 1911 Charity Shield 6-4 v Swindon Town and George Best in the FA Cup against Northampton Town 8-2 in 1970.

MANCHESTER UNITED 1999–2000 LEAGUE RECORD

Match No.	Date	Venue	Opponents	Result	H/T Score	Lg. Pos.	Goalscorers	Attendance
1	Aug 8	A	Everton	D 1-1	1-0	10	Yorke [7]	39,141
2	11	H	Sheffield W	W 4-0	2-0	—	Scholes [9], Yorke [35], Cole [54], Solskjaer [84]	54,941
3	14	H	Leeds U	W 2-0	0-0	1	Yorke 2 [76, 80]	55,187
4	22	A	Arsenal	W 2-1	0-1	1	Keane 2 [58, 88]	38,147
5	25	A	Coventry C	W 2-1	0-0	—	Scholes [62], Yorke [75]	22,022
6	30	H	Newcastle U	W 5-1	1-1	1	Cole 4 [14, 46, 65, 71], Giggs [80]	55,190
7	Sept 11	A	Liverpool	W 3-2	3-1	1	Carragher (og) [3], Cole [18], Carragher (og) [44]	44,929
8	18	H	Wimbledon	D 1-1	0-1	1	Cruyff [73]	55,189
9	25	H	Southampton	D 3-3	2-1	1	Sheringham [34], Yorke 2 [37, 64]	55,249
10	Oct 3	A	Chelsea	L 0-5	0-2	2		34,909
11	16	H	Watford	W 4-1	3-0	2	Yorke [39], Cole 2 [42, 50], Irwin (pen) [44]	55,188
12	23	A	Tottenham H	L 1-3	1-2	4	Giggs [23]	36,072
13	30	H	Aston Villa	W 3-0	2-0	2	Scholes [30], Cole [45], Keane [65]	55,211
14	Nov 6	H	Leicester C	W 2-0	1-0	1	Cole 2 [30, 83]	55,191
15	20	A	Derby Co	W 2-1	0-0	1	Butt [53], Cole [83]	33,370
16	Dec 4	H	Everton	W 5-1	3-1	2	Irwin (pen) [26], Solskjaer 4 [29, 43, 52, 58]	55,193
17	18	A	West Ham U	W 4-2	3-1	2	Yorke 2 [9, 62], Giggs 2 [13, 19]	26,037
18	26	H	Bradford C	W 4-0	0-0	2	Fortune [75], Yorke [79], Cole [87], Keane [88]	55,188
19	28	A	Sunderland	D 2-2	1-2	2	Keane [27], Butt [86]	41,269
20	Jan 24	H	Arsenal	D 1-1	0-1	—	Sheringham [73]	58,293
21	29	H	Middlesbrough	W 1-0	0-0	1	Beckham [87]	61,267
22	Feb 2	A	Sheffield W	W 1-0	0-0	—	Sheringham [73]	39,640
23	5	H	Coventry C	W 3-2	1-0	1	Cole 2 [39, 54], Scholes [77]	61,380
24	12	A	Newcastle U	L 0-3	0-1	1		36,470
25	20	A	Leeds U	W 1-0	0-0	1	Cole [52]	40,160
26	26	H	Wimbledon	D 2-2	1-1	1	Cruyff [30], Cole [80]	26,129
27	Mar 4	H	Liverpool	D 1-1	1-1	1	Solskjaer [45]	61,592
28	11	H	Derby Co	W 3-1	1-0	1	Yorke 3 [12, 70, 72]	61,619
29	18	A	Leicester C	W 2-0	1-0	1	Beckham [33], Yorke [83]	22,170
30	25	A	Bradford C	W 4-0	2-0	1	Yorke 2 [37, 40], Scholes [71], Beckham [79]	18,276
31	Apr 1	H	West Ham U	W 7-1	3-1	1	Scholes 3 (1 pen) [24, 51, 63 (p)], Irwin (pen) [26], Cole [45], Beckham [66], Solskjaer [73]	61,611
32	10	A	Middlesbrough	W 4-3	0-1	—	Giggs [46], Cole [59], Scholes [74], Fortune [88]	34,775
33	15	H	Sunderland	W 4-0	1-0	1	Solskjaer 2 [2, 51], Butt [66], Berg [70]	61,612
34	22	A	Southampton	W 3-1	3-0	1	Beckham [7], Benali (og) [15], Solskjaer [29]	15,245
35	24	H	Chelsea	W 3-2	2-2	1	Yorke 2 [10, 69], Solskjaer [39]	61,593
36	29	A	Watford	W 3-2	0-1	1	Yorke [68], Giggs [75], Cruyff [96]	20,250
37	May 6	H	Tottenham H	W 3-1	3-1	1	Solskjaer [5], Beckham [34], Sheringham [36]	61,629
38	14	A	Aston Villa	W 1-0	0-0	1	Sheringham [66]	39,217

Final League Position: 1

GOALSCORERS
League (97): Yorke 20, Cole 19, Solskjaer 12, Scholes 9 (1 pen), Beckham 6, Giggs 6, Keane 5, Sheringham 5, Butt 3, Cruyff 3, Irwin 3 (3 pens), Fortune 2, Berg 1, own goals 3.
Worthington Cup (0).

Bosnich M 23	Neville P 25+4	Irwin D 25	Berg H 16+6	Keane R 28+1	Stam J 33	Beckham D 30+1	Solskjaer O 15+13	Cole A 23+5	Yorke D 29+3	Scholes P 27+4	Butt N 21+11	Giggs R 30	Sheringham T 15+12	Van der Gouw R 11+3	Culkin N —+1	Curtis J —+1	Clegg M —+2	Fortune Q 4+2	Neville G 22	Taibi M 4	Silvestre M 30+1	Wallwork R —+5	Cruyff J 1+7	Wilson M 1+2	Greening J 1+3	Higginbotham D 2+1	May D —+1	Johnsen R 2+1	Match No.
1	2	3	4	5	6	7	8[1]	9	10	11	12																		1
1	2	3	4	5	6	7[1]	13	9	10[3]	8	12	11[2]	14																2
1[6]	2	3	4	5	6	7		9	10[2]	8[1]	12	11	13	15															3
	2	3	4	5	6	7		9[2]	10	8[1]	12	11	13	1[6]	15														4
	2[3]	3	4	5	6	7	12	9	13	8[2]	11	10[1]		1				14											5
		3	4		6	7[1]		9	10	5[2]	8	11	12	1			13	14	2[2]										6
	2[1]		4		6	7		9	10	5	8[2]	11						12		1	3	13							7
	5	2	4		6	8[1]	12	9	7		11[2]	10								1	3	13							8
		2	4		6	7	11	9		5	8	10								1	3								9
	5	2	4		6	7[3]	12	9[1]	10	11[2]	8	13								1	3	14							10
1	2	3	12	6[1]		7	13	9[2]	10	5	8	11[3]									4		14						11
1	3	2[2]		5	6	7[1]	12	9	10	8		11									4		13						12
1	2	3		5	6	7	12	9[3]	10[1]	8		11[2]									4	13	14						13
1	2[1]		12	5	6	8		9	10	7		11									4					3[2]	13		14
	3	12		5	6	7[2]	13	9	10	8	11			1					2		4[1]								15
1[6]	12	3		5	6		9	13	7	8	11[2]	10		15					2		4[1]								16
	12	3[1]		5	6	7[2]		9	8	13	11	10		1					2		4								17
1	3			5	6[3]		9	12	13	7[2]	8		10[1]					11	2		4		14						18
1	12	3[2]		5	6	7[3]	14	9[1]	10	8		11							2		4		13						19
1	12	3[1]		5	6	7		9[2]	10	8		11							2		4		13						20
1		3[2]		5	6	7	13	12	9	14	8	11	10[1]						2[3]		4								21
1		3		5	6	7		9	12	8[1]	11	10							2		4								22
1	3			5	6	7	8[1]	9		11	12		10[2]						2		4		13						23
1		3[2]		5	6	7	12	9	13	8	11	10[1]							2		4								24
1	3			5	6		9	10[1]	7	8	11	12							2		4								25
1	3[2]	13		6		7	12	9	5	11	10							8[1]	2		4								26
	3			5	6	7	9[1]	12	10[2]	8	11	13		1					2		4								27
1	3	6	5[2]		7	9		10	11	12								8[1]	2		4		13						28
1	3	4	5	6	7		9[2]	10	8	12	11[1]	13							2										29
1	3	6	5[2]		7	12	9	10	8	11[1]									2		4		13						30
1	3	5[2]	6		7	12	9[2]	10	8[1]	13	14	11							2		4								31
1	3[2]	4	5[1]	6	7		9	10	8	12	11[3]							14	2		13								32
1[6]	3	12	5	6[1]	13	9		7[2]	8	10	15							11	2		4								33
	3			5	6	7	10[2]	9[1]	12	8	11[3]	13	1						2		4		14						34
	3	12	5[2]		7	9[3]		10	13	8	11			1					2[1]		4		14				6		35
	2		4			9		12	8	11	10		1								3		13	5[1]	7[2]	14		6[3]	36
	2	3	12		6[1]	7	9[2]		5	8[3]	11	10	1								4		13		14				37
	5	2	4			8[1]		9	7		11	10	1								6	13	12			3[2]			38

Worthington Cup
Third Round   Aston Villa   (a)   0-3

Division 3   **MANSFIELD TOWN**

FOUNDATION

The club was formed as Mansfield Wesleyans in 1897, and changed their name to Mansfield Wesley in 1906 and Mansfield Town in 1910. This was after the Mansfield Wesleyan Chapel trustees had requested that the club change its name as 'it has no longer had any connection with either the chapel or school'. The new club participated in the Notts and Derby District League, but in the following season 1911–12 joined the Central Alliance.

Field Mill Ground, Quarry Lane, Mansfield NG18 5DA.

Telephone: (01623) 623 567/658 070.

Fax: (01623) 625 014.

Marketing: (01623) 658 070.

Football in the Community: (01623) 625 197.

ClubCall: 09068 121 311.

Ground Capacity: 5289 (Undergoing re-development).

Record Attendance: 24,467 v Nottingham F, FA Cup 3rd rd, 10 January 1953.

Record Receipts: £46,915 v Sheffield W, FA Cup 3rd rd, 5 January 1991.

Pitch Measurements: 115yd × 70yd.

Chairman/Chief Executive: Keith Haslam.

Associate Directors: K. Woodcock, S. Whetton, M. Murphy.

Manager: Bill Dearden.

Physio: Barry Statham.

Community Scheme Organiser: John Gannon.

Secretary: Christine Reynolds.

Marketing Manager: Alan Prince.

LATEST SEQUENCES

Longest Sequence of League Wins: 7, 13.9.91 – 26.10.91.

Longest Sequence of League Defeats: 7, 18.1.47 – 15.3.47.

Longest Sequence of League Draws: 5, 18.10.86 – 22.11.86.

Longest Sequence of Unbeaten League Matches: 20, 14.2.76 – 21.8.76.

Longest Sequence Without a League Win: 12, 10.11.79 – 16.2.80.

HONOURS

Football League: Division 2 best season: 21st, 1977–78; Division 3 – Champions 1976–77; Division 4 – Champions 1974–75; Division 3 (N) – Runners-up 1950–51.

FA Cup: best season: 6th rd, 1969.

Football League Cup: best season: 5th rd, 1976.

Freight Rover Trophy: Winners 1987.

Colours
Amber shirts with royal blue trim, amber shorts with royal blue trim, amber stockings with blue hoops.

Change Colours
White shirts with maroon collar and trim, white shorts with burgundy trim, white stockings with burgundy hoop.

Year Formed: 1897.

Turned Professional: 1906.

Ltd Co.: 1922.

Previous Name: 1897, Mansfield Wesleyans; 1906, Mansfield Wesley; 1910, Mansfield Town.

Club Nickname: 'The Stags'.

First Football League Game: 29 August 1931, Division 3 (S), v Swindon T (h) W 3–2 – Wilson; Clifford, England; Wake, Davis, Blackburn; Gilhespy, Readman (1), Johnson, Broom (2), Baxter.

Record League Victory: 9–2 v Rotherham U, Division 3 (N), 27 December 1932 – Wilson; Anthony, England; Davies, S. Robinson, Slack; Prior, Broom, Readman (3), Hoyland (3), Bowater (3).

Record Cup Victory: 8–0 v Scarborough (a), FA Cup 1st rd, 22 November 1952 – Bramley; Chessell, Bradley; Field, Plummer, Lewis; Scott, Fox (3), Marron (2), Sid Watson (1), Adam (2).

Record Defeat: 1–8 v Walsall, Division 3 (N), 19 January 1933.

Most League Points (2 for a win): 68, Division 4, 1974–75.

Most League Points (3 for a win): 81, Division 4, 1985–86.

Most League Goals: 108, Division 4, 1962–63.

Highest League Scorer in Season: Ted Harston, 55, Division 3 (N), 1936–37.

Most League Goals in Total Aggregate: Harry Johnson, 104, 1931–36.

Most League Goals in One Match: 7, Ted Harston v Hartlepools U, Division 3N, 23 January 1937.

Most Capped Player: John McClelland, 6 (53), Northern Ireland.

Most League Appearances: Rod Arnold, 440, 1970–83.

Youngest League Player: Cyril Poole, 15 years 351 days v New Brighton, 27 February 1937.

Record Transfer Fee Received: £655,000 from Tottenham H for Colin Calderwood, July 1993.

Record Transfer Fee Paid: £150,000 to Carlisle U for Lee Peacock, October 1997.

Football League Record: 1931 Elected to Division 3 (S); 1932–37 Division 3 (N); 1937–47 Division 3 (S); 1947–58 Division 3 (N); 1958–60 Division 3; 1960–63 Division 4; 1963–72 Division 3; 1972–75 Division 4; 1975–77 Division 3; 1977–78 Division 2; 1978–80 Division 3; 1980–86 Division 4; 1986–91 Division 3; 1991–92 Division 4; 1992–93 Division 2; 1993– Division 3.

MANAGERS

John Baynes 1922–25
Ted Davison 1926–28
Jack Hickling 1928–33
Henry Martin 1933–35
Charlie Bell 1935
Harold Wightman 1936
Harold Parkes 1936–38
Jack Poole 1938–44
Lloyd Barke 1944–45
Roy Goodall 1945–49
Freddie Steele 1949–51
George Jobey 1952–53
Stan Mercer 1953–55
Charlie Mitten 1956–58
Sam Weaver 1958–60
Raich Carter 1960–63
Tommy Cummings 1963–67
Tommy Eggleston 1967–70
Jock Basford 1970–71
Danny Williams 1971–74
Dave Smith 1974–76
Peter Morris 1976–78
Billy Bingham 1978–79
Mick Jones 1979–81
Stuart Boam 1981–83
Ian Greaves 1983–89
George Foster 1989–93
Andy King 1993–96
Steve Parkin 1996–99
Bill Dearden July 1999–

TEN YEAR LEAGUE RECORD

		P	W	D	L	F	A	Pts	Pos
1989-90	Div 3	46	16	7	23	50	65	55	15
1990-91	Div 3	46	8	14	24	42	63	38	24
1991-92	Div 4	42	23	8	11	75	53	77	3
1992-93	Div 2	46	11	11	24	52	80	44	22
1993-94	Div 3	42	15	10	17	53	62	55	12
1994-95	Div 3	42	18	11	13	84	59	65	6
1995-96	Div 3	46	11	20	15	54	64	53	19
1996-97	Div 3	46	16	16	14	47	45	64	11
1997-98	Div 3	46	16	17	13	64	55	65	12
1998-99	Div 3	46	19	10	17	60	58	67	8

DID YOU KNOW ?

Michael Boulding, a striker signed by Mansfield Town from Hallam in the summer of 1999, was a former professional tennis player and room-mate of Tim Henman.

MANSFIELD TOWN 1999–2000 LEAGUE RECORD

Match No.	Date	Venue	Opponents	Result	H/T Score	Lg. Pos.	Goalscorers	Attendance
1	Aug 7	A	Brighton & HA	L	0-6	0-2	24		5882
2	14	H	Cheltenham T	L	0-1	0-0	24		2348
3	21	A	Southend U	L	0-1	0-1	24		3533
4	28	H	Carlisle U	D	1-1	1-1	24	Roscoe [14]	2138
5	30	A	Exeter C	L	0-1	0-1	23		3109
6	Sept 3	H	Peterborough U	W	3-1	2-0	—	Peacock 3 [6, 41, 65]	3338
7	11	H	Leyton Orient	D	1-1	0-1	21	Peacock [62]	2491
8	18	A	Darlington	D	0-0	0-0	21		5027
9	24	H	Shrewsbury T	W	4-0	3-0	—	Peacock 2 [24, 85], Sisson [42], Lormor [45]	2808
10	Oct 2	A	Swansea C	W	1-0	0-0	15	Lormor [57]	4263
11	9	A	Plymouth Arg	L	1-2	0-2	16	Peacock [64]	3809
12	16	H	Hartlepool U	L	2-3	1-1	19	Lormor [20], Hassell [79]	2612
13	19	H	Northampton T	D	0-0	0-0	—		2940
14	23	A	Shrewsbury T	W	2-1	1-1	18	Boulding [41], Lormor [74]	1785
15	Nov 2	A	Macclesfield T	L	2-5	0-3	—	Clarke [53], Blake [79]	1541
16	6	H	Lincoln C	W	5-2	2-1	18	Bacon [30], Clarke 2 [45, 70], Greenacre 2 [46, 85]	2952
17	14	A	Rochdale	L	1-2	0-0	19	Greenacre [52]	2709
18	23	H	Rotherham U	L	1-2	1-1	—	Lormor [13]	2937
19	27	A	Halifax T	W	1-0	0-0	19	Greenacre [54]	2322
20	Dec 18	A	Barnet	D	0-0	0-0	20		1997
21	26	H	Chester C	W	2-1	1-0	18	Richardson (og) [11], Boulding [72]	3234
22	28	A	Hull C	L	0-2	0-2	18		7215
23	Jan 3	H	Torquay U	W	4-3	3-2	18	Boulding 2 [4, 80], Clarke [19], Greenacre [32]	2876
24	8	A	York C	W	1-0	1-0	16	Sisson [44]	2458
25	15	A	Cheltenham T	L	0-1	0-1	17		3150
26	22	H	Southend U	W	3-1	2-1	15	Bromby [11], Lormor (pen) [38], Greenacre [77]	2215
27	29	A	Carlisle U	W	2-0	1-0	14	Lormor [3], Clarke [84]	2501
28	Feb 1	H	Brighton & HA	W	1-0	0-0	—	Lormor (pen) [77]	2541
29	4	H	Exeter C	D	1-1	0-0	—	Lormor [49]	3092
30	8	H	York C	W	1-0	0-0	—	Roscoe [57]	2571
31	12	A	Peterborough U	L	0-1	0-1	10		5472
32	19	H	Halifax T	L	0-2	0-1	13		2476
33	26	H	Darlington	L	1-2	0-1	14	Boulding [87]	3114
34	Mar 4	A	Leyton Orient	W	3-1	1-0	13	Clarke [3], Walschaerts (og) [52], Greenacre [89]	4281
35	7	A	Lincoln C	L	0-3	0-2	—		3445
36	11	H	Macclesfield T	W	1-0	0-0	12	Greenacre [58]	2327
37	17	A	Rotherham U	W	3-2	2-1	—	Boulding [8], Greenacre [14], Clarke [65]	5186
38	25	A	Chester C	L	0-5	0-3	14		1953
39	28	H	Rochdale	D	0-0	0-0	—		2275
40	Apr 1	H	Barnet	L	0-1	0-0	15		1960
41	8	A	Torquay U	L	0-4	0-3	15		1756
42	15	H	Hull C	L	0-1	0-0	16		2213
43	22	A	Hartlepool U	L	0-1	0-0	16		3473
44	24	H	Swansea C	L	0-1	0-1	16		2162
45	29	A	Northampton T	L	0-1	0-1	16		6901
46	May 6	H	Plymouth Arg	D	2-2	2-1	17	Andrews [5], Bacon [24]	2031

Final League Position: 17

GOALSCORERS

League (50): Greenacre 9, Lormor 9 (2 pens), Clarke 7, Peacock 7, Boulding 6, Bacon 2, Roscoe 2, Sisson 2, Andrews 1, Blake 1, Bromby 1, Hassell 1, own goals 2.
Worthington Cup (1): Peacock 1.
FA Cup (2): Blake 1, Lormor 1 (pen).

Richardson B 6	Williams L 46	Cowling L 3 + 5	Kerr D 10 + 8	Richardson N 31	Linighan D 28	Roscoe A 29 + 10	Peacock L 12	Lormor T 33	Thomas W 4 + 1	Tallon G 11 + 2	Boulding M 16 + 17	Sisson M 24 + 1	Hassell B 8 + 3	Blake M 40 + 3	Allardyce C 1 + 3	Asher A 29 + 6	Muggleton C 9	Camilleri C — + 2	Clarke D 39	Disley C 2 + 3	Williamson L — + 4	Bacon D 6 + 2	Porter A 5	Bowling I 10	Greenacre C 31	Andrews J 29 + 1	Bromby L 10	Thompson G 16	Fortune J 4	Lawrence L — + 2	Bassinder G 1 + 3	Evans A 4 + 2	Garratt M 4 + 2	Mimms B 5	Match No
1	2	3	4	5	6	7	8	9^1	10^2	11	12	13																							1
1	3	4	5	6	7	8	9^1	10^2	11^3	12						2	13	14																	2
1	3		5	6	7	8	9^1	10	11	12						2	4																		3
1	3		5	6	7	8	9	12	11^1	13	4^2	2^3	10			14																			4
1	2	12	5	6	7	8	9^2	10	11^1	13						4	3																		5
1	3^1	12	5	6	7	8^2	9	11	13	4						10	2																		6
	3		5	6	7	8	9	11^1		4				10		2	1	12																	7
	3		5	6	7	8	9			4		11^1		10		2	1	12	10																8
	3		5	6	7	8	9	11^2		4^1				10		2	1	12	13																9
	3	4	5	6	7	8	9			11^1				10		2	1	12																	10
	3	4^1	5	6	7	8	9			12				11		2	1	10																	11
	3		5	6	7		9	11^3		12	8	13	2^2	10		1	4^1	14																	12
	3		5	6	7^1	8	9	12				2	11	1		10	4																		13
	3		5	6	7		9	11^1		2	10		1	8			12	4																	14
	3^1		5	6	7		9	12		11	2^2	13	1	8		10	4																		15
	3^2		5	6	7		9	12				13		8^1		10	4	1	11	2															16
	3^2	5^1		6	7		9			12				13		8		10	4	1	11	2													17
	3		5	6	7		9					12		8		10	4^1	1	11	2															18
	3		5	6	12		9	7^1				4	13	8		10^2		1	11	2															19
	3		6			9		7		4				10			8						1	11	2	5									20
	3		6	12		9		7^1	13	4				10		14	8						1	11^2	2^3	5									21
	3		6	12		9		7^1	13	4^2				10			8						1	11	2	5									22
	3	12	6			9		13	7^2	4^1				10			8						1	11	2	5									23
	3	12	6			9		7^1	4					10			8						1	11	2	5									24
	3		6	12		9		7^1	4					10			8						1	11	2	5									25
	3	12				7		9		4				10^1		6	8							11	2	5	1								26
	3^1	13	12			7		9		4				10		6	8							11	2	5^2	1								27
	3	6				7		9		4				10		5	8							11	2		1								28
	3					7		9	12	4^1				10		6	8							11	2	5	1								29
	3	12				7		9		4				10		6	8							11	2^1	5	1								30
	3	4^1	6			7		9	12					10		5	8							11	2		1								31
	3^2	4^1	6			7		9	12					10		5	8							11				1	2	13				32
	3	12	6^1		7^3			9^2	13	4				10		5	8							11	14		1	2						33
	7	12	6	13				9^2	4^1					10		2	8							11	3		1	5						34
	7	4^1	5	6^2	12			9^3						10	13	2	8							11	3		1			14				35
	4	12	5			7^1		9		13				10		2	8							11	3		1			6^2				36
	7^1	12	6			9			4^2					10		2	8							11	3^2		1	5		13				37
	7	4	5^3	6	12				13					10		2^1	8							11	3^2		1	14	9					38
	4		6	12		9								5		10	2	8							11	3		1		7^1				39
	4		6^1	7^3		9								5		10	2	8							11	3		1		12^2	13	14		40
	4		6^2	7		9^1								5		10	2	8							11	3		1			12	13		41
	6		5					12		4^1				10		2	8							11	3		9	7				1		42
	6		5					12		4				10		2	8							11	3		9^1	7				1		43
	6		5			9				4				10^1		2	8							11	3			7				1		44
	6	12	5	13		9^2				4				10^3		2	8^1	14							11	3			7				1		45
	6^3		5	12		9^1				4				10		2	8	13	14	7^2					11	3						1		46

Worthington Cup
First Round Nottingham F (a) 0-3
(h) 1-0

FA Cup
First Round Bristol C (a) 2-3

FA Premiership   **MIDDLESBROUGH**

FOUNDATION

A previous belief that Middlesbrough Football Club was founded at a tripe supper at the Corporation Hotel has proved to be erroneous. In fact, members of Middlesbrough Cricket Club were responsible for forming it at a meeting in the gymnasium of the Albert Park Hotel in 1875.

Cellnet Riverside Stadium, Middlesbrough, Cleveland TS3 6RS.
Telephone: (01642) 877 700.
Fax: (01642) 877 840.
Website: www.mfc.co.uk
ClubCall: 09068 121 181.
Ticket Office: (01642) 877 745.
Ticket Information Line: (01642) 877 809.
Club Tours: (01642) 877 730.
Stadium Store: (01642) 877 720.
Town Centre Store: (01642) 877 849.
Mail Order: (01642) 866 642.
Lottery Office: (01642) 877 790.
Ground Capacity: 35,049.
Record Attendance: Ayresome Park: 53,536 v Newcastle U, Division 1, 27 December 1949. Cellnet Riverside Stadium: 34,800 v Leeds U, FA Premier League, 26 February 2000.
Record Receipts: £486,229 v Newcastle U, FA Premier League, 6 December 1998.
Pitch measurements: 105m × 68m.
Chairman: Steve Gibson.
Director: George Cooke.
Chief Executive: Keith Lamb.
Secretary: Karen Nelson.
Manager: Bryan Robson.
Assistant Manager: Viv Anderson.
Physio: Bob Ward.
First Team Coach: Gordon McQueen.
Reserve Team Coach: David Geddis.
Youth Academy Director: David Parnaby
Chief Scout: Ray Train.
General Manager Business Operations: Reg Corbidge.
Commercial Manager: Graham Fordy.
Public Relations Manager: Dave Allan.
Stadium Manager: Terry Tasker.

LATEST SEQUENCES

Longest Sequence of League Wins: 9, 16.2.74 – 6.4.74.
Longest Sequence of League Defeats: 8, 26.12.95 – 17.2.96.
Longest Sequence of League Draws: 8, 3.4.71 – 1.5.71.
Longest Sequence of Unbeaten League Matches: 24, 8.9.73 – 19.1.74.
Longest Sequence Without a League Win: 19, 3.10.81 – 6.3.82.

HONOURS

Football League: Division 1 – Champions 1994–95; Runners-up 1997–98; Division 2 – Champions 1926–27, 1928–29, 1973–74; Runners-up 1901–02, 1991–92; Division 3 – Runners-up 1966–67, 1986–87.

FA Cup: Runners-up 1997.

Football League Cup: Runners-up 1997, 1998.

Amateur Cup: Winners 1895, 1898.

Anglo-Scottish Cup: Winners 1976.

Zenith Data Systems Cup: Runners-up 1990.

Colours
Red and white.

Change Colours
White and purple.

Year Formed: 1876; re-formed 1986.

Turned Professional: 1889; became amateur 1892, and professional again, 1899.

Ltd Co: 1892.

Club Nickname: 'Boro'.

Previous Grounds: 1877, Old Archery Ground, Albert Park; 1879, Breckon Hill; 1882, Linthorpe Road Ground; 1903, Ayresome Park; 1995, Cellnet Riverside Stadium.

First Football League Game: 2 September 1899, Division 2, v Lincoln C (a) L 0–3 – Smith; Shaw, Ramsey; Allport, McNally, McCracken; Wanless, Longstaffe, Gettins, Page, Pugh.

Record League Victory: 9–0 v Brighton & HA, Division 2, 23 August 1958 – Taylor; Bilcliff, Robinson; Harris (2p), Phillips, Walley; Day, McLean, Clough (5), Peacock (2), Holliday.

Record Cup Victory: 7–0 v Hereford U, Coca-Cola Cup 2nd rd, 1st leg, 18 September 1996 – Miller; Fleming (1), Branco (1), Whyte, Vickers, Whelan, Emerson (1), Mustoe, Stamp, Juninho, Ravanelli (4).

Record Defeat: 0–9 v Blackburn R, Division 2, 6 November 1954.

Most League Points (2 for a win): 65, Division 2, 1973–74.

Most League Points (3 for a win): 94, Division 3, 1986–87.

Most League Goals: 122, Division 2, 1926–27.

Highest League Scorer in Season: George Camsell, 59, Division 2, 1926–27 (Second Division record).

Most League Goals in Total Aggregate: George Camsell, 325, 1925–39.

Most League Goals in One Match: 5, Andy Wilson v Nottingham F, Division 1, 6 October 1923; 5, George Camsell v Manchester C, Division 2, 25 December 1926; 5, George Camsell v Aston Villa, Division 1, 9 September 1935; 5, Brian Clough v Brighton & HA, Division 2, 22 August 1958.

Most Capped Player: Wilf Mannion, 26, England.

Most League Appearances: Tim Williamson, 563, 1902–23.

Youngest League Player: Stephen Bell, 16 years 323 days v Southampton, 30 January 1982; Sam Lawrie, 16 years 323 days v Arsenal, 3 November 1951.

Record Transfer Fee Received: £12,000,000 from Atletico Madrid for Juninho, July 1997.

Record Transfer Fee Paid: £7,000,000 to Juventus for Fabrizio Ravanelli, August 1996.

Football League Record: 1899 Elected to Division 2; 1902–24 Division 1; 1924–27 Division 2; 1927–28 Division 1; 1928–29 Division 2; 1929–54 Division 1; 1954–66 Division 2; 1966–67 Division 3; 1967–74 Division 2; 1974–82 Division 1; 1982–86 Division 2; 1986–87 Division 3; 1987–88 Division 2; 1988–89 Division 1; 1989–92 Division 2; 1992–93 FA Premier League; 1993–95 Division 1; 1995–97 FA Premier League; 1997–98 Division 1; 1998– FA Premier League.

MANAGERS

John Robson 1899–1905
Alex Mackie 1905–06
Andy Aitken 1906–09
J. Gunter 1908–10
(Secretary-Manager)
Andy Walker 1910–11
Tom McIntosh 1911–19
Jimmy Howie 1920–23
Herbert Bamlett 1923–26
Peter McWilliam 1927–34
Wilf Gillow 1934–44
David Jack 1944–52
Walter Rowley 1952–54
Bob Dennison 1954–63
Raich Carter 1963–66
Stan Anderson 1966–73
Jack Charlton 1973–77
John Neal 1977–81
Bobby Murdoch 1981–82
Malcolm Allison 1982–84
Willie Maddren 1984–86
Bruce Rioch 1986–90
Colin Todd 1990–91
Lennie Lawrence 1991–94
Bryan Robson May 1994–

TEN YEAR LEAGUE RECORD

		P	W	D	L	F	A	Pts	Pos
1989-90	Div 2	46	13	11	22	52	63	50	21
1990-91	Div 2	46	20	9	17	66	47	69	7
1991-92	Div 2	46	23	11	12	58	41	80	2
1992-93	PR Lge	42	11	11	20	54	75	44	21
1993-94	Div 1	46	18	13	15	66	54	67	9
1994-95	Div 1	46	23	13	10	67	40	82	1
1995-96	PR Lge	38	11	10	17	35	50	43	12
1996-97	PR Lge	38	10	12	16	51	60	39	19
1997-98	Div 1	46	27	10	9	77	41	91	2
1998-99	PR Lge	38	12	15	11	48	54	51	9

DID YOU KNOW ?

George Washington Elliott was leading scorer for Middlesbrough in seven out of nine peacetime seasons in a career of 213 League and Cup goals from 1909-10 to 1923-24.

MIDDLESBROUGH 1999–2000 LEAGUE RECORD

Match No.	Date	Venue	Opponents	Result	H/T Score	Lg. Pos.	Goalscorers	Attendance
1	Aug 7	H	Bradford C	L 0-1	0-0	17		33,762
2	10	A	Wimbledon	W 3-2	2-1	—	Ziege [23], Ricard 2 (1 pen) [28(p),64]	11,036
3	14	A	Derby Co	W 3-1	2-1	4	Deane [9], Ziege [20], Ricard (pen) [66]	24,045
4	21	H	Liverpool	W 1-0	0-0	3	Deane [49]	34,783
5	24	H	Leicester C	L 0-3	0-2	—		33,126
6	28	A	Aston Villa	L 0-1	0-1	10		28,728
7	Sept 11	H	Southampton	W 3-2	1-1	7	Pallister [17], Gascoigne (pen) [67], Deane [78]	32,157
8	19	A	Leeds U	L 0-2	0-1	10		34,122
9	25	H	Chelsea	L 0-1	0-0	11		34,183
10	Oct 3	A	Newcastle U	L 1-2	0-2	11	Deane [89]	36,421
11	17	H	West Ham U	W 2-0	0-0	11	Deane [51], Armstrong [88]	31,822
12	24	A	Watford	W 3-1	2-0	10	Williams (og) [2], Juninho [18], Ince [83]	16,081
13	30	H	Everton	W 2-1	1-1	6	Ziege [15], Deane [61]	33,916
14	Nov 6	H	Sunderland	D 1-1	0-0	8	Ricard [76]	34,793
15	20	A	Arsenal	L 1-5	0-2	8	Ricard [68]	38,082
16	27	H	Wimbledon	D 0-0	0-0	10		31,400
17	Dec 4	A	Bradford C	D 1-1	1-0	10	Ricard [13]	17,708
18	18	H	Tottenham H	W 2-1	1-1	8	Ziege [34], Deane [67]	33,113
19	26	A	Sheffield W	L 0-1	0-1	10		28,531
20	Jan 15	H	Derby Co	L 1-4	0-1	14	Campbell [71]	32,269
21	22	A	Liverpool	D 0-0	0-0	14		44,324
22	29	A	Manchester U	L 0-1	0-0	14		61,267
23	Feb 5	A	Leicester C	L 1-2	0-2	15	Campbell [52]	17,550
24	14	H	Aston Villa	L 0-4	0-1	—		31,591
25	19	H	Coventry C	W 2-0	2-0	14	Festa [8], Ricard [20]	32,793
26	26	H	Leeds U	D 0-0	0-0	14		34,800
27	Mar 4	A	Southampton	D 1-1	1-1	13	Ricard (pen) [44]	15,223
28	12	H	Arsenal	W 2-1	0-0	13	Ince [48], Ricard [63]	32,244
29	18	A	Sunderland	D 1-1	0-0	14	Ziege [82]	41,830
30	25	H	Sheffield W	W 1-0	1-0	13	Campbell [11]	32,802
31	Apr 3	A	Tottenham H	W 3-2	1-1	—	Carr (og) [40], Ricard 2 [64,78]	31,804
32	10	H	Manchester U	L 3-4	1-0	—	Campbell [18], Ince [86], Juninho [90]	34,775
33	15	A	Coventry C	L 1-2	0-1	13	Ziege (pen) [64]	19,430
34	22	A	Chelsea	D 1-1	1-1	13	Ricard [37]	34,467
35	29	A	West Ham U	W 1-0	0-0	13	Deane (pen) [60]	25,472
36	May 2	H	Newcastle U	D 2-2	1-2	—	Juninho [5], Festa [78]	34,744
37	6	H	Watford	D 1-1	1-0	13	Stockdale [27]	32,930
38	14	A	Everton	W 2-0	1-0	12	Deane [9], Juninho [86]	34,663

Final League Position: 12

GOALSCORERS
League (46): Ricard 12 (3 pens), Deane 9 (1 pen), Ziege 6 (1 pen), Campbell 4, Juninho 4, Ince 3, Festa 2, Armstrong 1, Gascoigne 1 (pen), Pallister 1, Stockdale 1, own goals 2.
Worthington Cup (6): Ricard 2 (1 pen), Ince 1, Juninho 1, Vickers 1, Ziege 1.
FA Cup (1): Deane 1.

Schwarzer M 37	Stamp P 13 + 3	Ziege C 29	Vickers S 30 + 2	Festa G 27 + 2	Gordon D 3 + 1	Mustoe R 18 + 10	Gascoigne P 7 + 1	Campbell A 16 + 9	Deane B 29	O'Neill K 14 + 2	Townsend A 3 + 2	Ricard H 28 + 6	Ince P 32	Armstrong A 3 + 9	Pallister G 21	Stockdale R 6 + 5	Maddison N 6 + 7	Gavin J 2 + 4	Summerbell M 16 + 3	Cooper C 26	Fleming C 27	Juninho 24 + 4	Marinelli C — + 2	Ormerod A — + 1	Beresford M 1	Cummins M — + 1	Kilgannon S — + 1	Match No.
1	2	3	4[1]	5	6	7	8	9[2]	10	11	12	13																1
1	2	3[2]	4	5	6	12	8	14	10	13	7	9[3]	11[1]															2
1	2	3	4	5	6[1]	7			10	11	12	9[2]	8	13														3
1	2[1]	3	4	5		12	8[3]	13	10	14	7	9[2]	11		6													4
1		3	4	5		7		13	10	11[1]		9	8		6						2	12[2]						5
1	2		4			7	12		10	11[2]		9[1]	8		6					3	5	13						6
1	2[1]	3	4[3]			7	8		10			9[2]	11	13	6					12	14	5						7
1		3	4	5		7			10	11	12	9[1]	8		6						2							8
1		3		5			12	13	10[2]		7	9	11[1]	14	6					4	2	8[2]						9
1		3	12	5		7	13					9	11	8	6[1]					4	2	10[2]						10
1		3	4						10		7	9[1]	11	12	6					5	2	8						11
1	12	3	4						10		7	9[2]	11	13	6					5	2	8[1]						12
1	5	3	4						10		7	9	11		6						2	8						13
1	2	3	4						10		7	9	11		6					5		8						14
1	2		4				14	12	10		7	9	11	13[3]	6					5	3[2]	8[1]						15
1	2	3	4		6		12		10		7	9[2]	11	13						5		8[1]						16
1	6	3	4	5		7	8[1]		10			9		13						12	2[2]	11						17
1		3[1]	4	5		7			10	11		9[2]		13	6	2				12		8						18
1	11[1]		4	5[2]		7			10		12	9[3]			6	2				13	3	8	14					19
1			4	5		7	12	9	10[1]	11					6	2[2]				13	3	8						20
1	2		4[2]			7		9[1]	10	11	12	13			6		13			5	3	8						21
1		3	4			7		9[3]	10[1]	11	12	13			6[2]					5	2	8	14					22
1		3	4			7		9	10[1]	11	12				6					5	2	8						23
12		3	4[1]	5		7		9	10[2]	11		13		14	6					7	2[3]	8			1			24
1		3	4			7		9	10	11	12				6					5	2	8[1]						25
1		3	12	4		7		9[1]	10[2]	11[3]		13			6					5	2	8	14					26
1		3[1]	4	12		7			10	11		9		13	6					5	2	8[2]						27
1		3	4	12		7	8[2]		10	11		9			6[1]					5	2	13						28
1		3[1]	4	12		7	8[2]		10	11		9[2]		13	6					5	2	14						29
1		3	4	12		7		9	10	11					6					5	2	8[1]						30
1		3	4		6	7	8	9	10	11										5	2							31
1		3	4	12	6[2]	7	8	9	10	11										5[1]	2	13						32
1	12	3	4	5	6	7[1]	8[3]	9	10	11				14							2[2]	13						33
1		3	4	5		7	8	9[1]	10	11	12				6						2							34
1	2	3	4	5		7		13	10	11	12	9[2]			6							8[1]						35
1		3[2]	4	5		7[1]		9	10[3]	11	12				6		13				2	8				14		36
1		3	4	5		7		9	10[1]	11		2			6							8	12					37
1	2[1]	3	4	5		7		9[2]	10	11	12	13			6							8						38

Worthington Cup

Second Round	Chesterfield	(a)	0-0	
		(h)	2-1	
Third Round	Watford	(h)	1-0	
Fourth Round	Arsenal	(h)	2-2	
Fifth Round	Tranmere R	(a)	1-2	

FA Cup

Third Round	Wrexham	(a)	1-2

Division 2

MILLWALL

FOUNDATION

Formed in 1885 as Millwall Rovers by employees of Morton & Co, a jam and marmalade factory in West Ferry Road. The founders were predominantly Scotsmen. Their first headquarters was The Islanders pub in Tooke Street, Millwall. Their first trophy was the East End Cup in 1887.

Millwall Football & Athletic Company (1985) plc, The Den, Zampa Road, Bermondsey SE16 3LN.
Telephone: (020) 7232 1222.
Ticket Office: (020) 7231 9999.
Club Shop: (020) 7231 9845.
Fax: (020) 7231 3663.
ClubCall: 09068 400 300.
Ground Capacity: 20,146 (all-seater).
Record Attendance: 20,093 v Arsenal, FA Cup 3rd rd, 10 January 1994.
Record Receipts: undisclosed.
Pitch Measurements: 100m × 68m.
Life President: Reg Burr.
Chairman: Theo Paphitis.
Directors: Reg Burr, Peter Mead, Steven Ring, Doug Woodward, David Sullivan.
Secretary: Yvonne Haines.
Joint Managers: Keith Stevens, Alan McLeary.
Reserve Team Coach: Steve Gritt.
Chief Scout: Ronnie Boyce.
Youth Development Officer & Senior Scout: Bob Pearson.
Assistant Youth Development Officer: Mick Beard.
Physio: Gerry Docherty.
Hon. Medical Officer: Dr. Charlotte Cowie.
Stadium Manager: Colin Sayer.
Sales and Promotions Manager: Mark Cole.

LATEST SEQUENCES

Longest Sequence of League Wins: 10, 10.3.28 – 25.4.28.
Longest Sequence of League Defeats: 11, 10.4.29 – 16.9.29.
Longest Sequence of League Draws: 5, 22.12.73 – 12.1.74.
Longest Sequence of Unbeaten League Matches: 19, 22.8.59 – 31.10.59.
Longest Sequence Without a League Win: 20, 26.12.89 – 5.5.90.

HONOURS

Football League: Division 1 best season: 3rd, 1993–94; Division 2 – Champions 1987–88; Division 3 (S) – Champions 1927–28, 1937–38; Runners-up 1952–53; Division 3 – Runners–up 1965–66, 1984–85; Division 4 – Champions 1961–62; Runners-up 1964–65.
FA Cup: Semi-final 1900, 1903, 1937 (first Division 3 side to reach semi-final).
Football League Cup: best season: 5th rd, 1974, 1977, 1995.
Football League Trophy: Winners 1983.
Auto Windscreens Shield: Runners-up 1999.

Colours
White with black trim.

Change Colours
All blue.

Year Formed: 1885.

Turned Professional: 1893.

Ltd Co.: 1894.

Previous Names: 1885, Millwall Rovers; 1889, Millwall Athletic; 1985, Millwall Football & Athletic Company.

Club Nickname: 'The Lions'.

Previous Grounds: 1885, Glengall Road, Millwall; 1886, Back of 'Lord Nelson'; 1890, East Ferry Road; 1901, North Greenwich; 1910, The Den, Cold Blow Lane; 1993, The Den, Bermondsey.

First Football League Game: 28 August 1920, Division 3, v Bristol R (h) W 2–0 – Lansdale; Fort, Hodge; Voisey (1), Riddell, McAlpine; Waterall, Travers, Broad (1), Sutherland, Dempsey.

Record League Victory: 9–1 v Torquay U, Division 3 (S), 29 August 1927 – Lansdale; Tilling, Hill; Amos, Bryant (3), Graham; Chance, Hawkins (3), Landells (1), Phillips (2), Black. 9–1 v Coventry C, Division 3 (S), 19 November 1927 – Lansdale; Fort, Hill; Amos, Collins (1), Graham; Chance, Landells (4), Cock (2), Phillips (2), Black.

Record Cup Victory: 7–0 v Gateshead, FA Cup 2nd rd, 12 December 1936 – Yuill; Ted Smith, Inns; Brolly, Hancock, Forsyth; Thomas (1), Mangnall (1), Ken Burditt (2), McCartney (2), Thorogood (1).

Record Defeat: 1–9 v Aston Villa, FA Cup 4th rd, 28 January 1946.

Most League Points (2 for a win): 65, Division 3 (S), 1927–28 and Division 3, 1965–66.

Most League Points (3 for a win): 90, Division 3, 1984–85.

Most League Goals: 127, Division 3 (S), 1927–28.

Highest League Scorer in Season: Richard Parker, 37, Division 3 (S), 1926–27.

Most League Goals in Total Aggregate: Teddy Sheringham, 93, 1984–91.

Most League Goals in One Match: 5, Richard Parker v Norwich C, Division 3S, 28 August 1926.

Most Capped Player: Eamonn Dunphy, 22 (23), Republic of Ireland.

Most League Appearances: Barry Kitchener, 523, 1967–82.

Youngest League Player: David Mehmet, 16 years 163 days v Burnley, 14 May 1977.

Record Transfer Fee Received: £2,300,000 from Liverpool for Mark Kennedy, March 1995.

Record Transfer Fee Paid: £800,000 to Derby Co for Paul Goddard, December 1989.

Football League Record: 1920 Original Members of Division 3; 1921 Division 3 (S); 1928–34 Division 2; 1934–38 Division 3 (S); 1938–48 Division 2; 1948–58 Division 3 (S); 1958–62 Division 4; 1962–64 Division 3; 1964–65 Division 4; 1965–66 Division 3; 1966–75 Division 2; 1975–76 Division 3; 1976–79 Division 2; 1979–85 Division 3; 1985–88 Division 2; 1988–90 Division 1; 1990–92 Division 2; 1992–96 Division 1; 1996– Division 2.

MANAGERS

F. B. Kidd 1894–99 *(Hon. Treasurer/Manager)*
E. R. Stopher 1899–1900 *(Hon. Treasurer/Manager)*
George Saunders 1900–11 *(Hon. Treasurer/Manager)*
Herbert Lipsham 1911–19
Robert Hunter 1919–33
Bill McCracken 1933–36
Charlie Hewitt 1936–40
Bill Voisey 1940–44
Jack Cock 1944–48
Charlie Hewitt 1948–56
Ron Gray 1956–57
Jimmy Seed 1958–59
Reg Smith 1959–61
Ron Gray 1961–63
Billy Gray 1963–66
Benny Fenton 1966–74
Gordon Jago 1974–77
George Petchey 1978–80
Peter Anderson 1980–82
George Graham 1982–86
John Docherty 1986–90
Bob Pearson 1990
Bruce Rioch 1990–92
Mick McCarthy 1992–96
Jimmy Nicholl 1996–97
John Docherty 1997
Billy Bonds 1997–98
Keith Stevens May 1998–
(then Joint Manager)
(plus Alan McLeary May 1999–)

TEN YEAR LEAGUE RECORD

		P	W	D	L	F	A	Pts	Pos
1989-90	Div 1	38	5	11	22	39	65	26	20
1990-91	Div 2	46	20	13	13	70	51	73	5
1991-92	Div 2	46	17	10	19	64	71	61	15
1992-93	Div 1	46	18	16	12	65	53	70	7
1993-94	Div 1	46	19	17	10	58	49	74	3
1994-95	Div 1	46	16	14	16	60	60	62	12
1995-96	Div 1	46	13	13	20	43	63	52	22
1996-97	Div 2	46	16	13	17	50	55	61	14
1997-98	Div 2	46	14	13	19	43	54	55	18
1998-99	Div 2	46	17	11	18	52	59	62	10

DID YOU KNOW ?

On 19 November 1927, Millwall defeated Coventry City 9-1 after going a goal behind in the 22nd minute. They equalised two minutes from half-time and scored eight in the second-half.

MILLWALL 1999–2000 LEAGUE RECORD

Match No.	Date	Venue	Opponents	Result	H/T Score	Lg. Pos.	Goalscorers	Attendance
1	Aug 7	A	Cardiff C	D	1-1	1-1	11	Harris (pen) [36]	10,193
2	14	H	Wigan Ath	D	3-3	0-1	19	Shaw [78], Cahill [80], Harris (pen) [90]	8165
3	22	A	Stoke C	L	1-3	0-1	21	Bircham [75]	7054
4	28	H	Chesterfield	D	1-1	0-0	20	Cahill [48]	6256
5	Sept 11	A	Bristol C	D	0-0	0-0	22		9893
6	18	H	Cambridge U	W	2-1	0-0	18	Harris [57], Cahill [72]	7278
7	25	H	Colchester U	W	1-0	0-0	14	Ifill [83]	7161
8	Oct 2	A	Gillingham	L	0-2	0-1	16		6616
9	9	A	Oxford U	W	3-1	1-0	14	Shaw 2 [25, 64], Cahill [72]	5392
10	16	H	Burnley	D	1-1	0-1	14	Cahill [70]	8601
11	19	H	Preston NE	L	0-2	0-0	—		6355
12	23	A	Colchester U	W	2-1	1-1	13	Moody [33], Ifill [82]	3392
13	Nov 2	H	Luton T	W	1-0	0-0	—	Cahill [75]	6181
14	6	A	Scunthorpe U	W	4-1	2-0	10	Harris 2 [2, 55], Ifill 2 [26, 49]	4550
15	9	A	Oldham Ath	L	1-2	0-1	—	Harris [62]	4209
16	12	H	Wrexham	D	0-0	0-0	10		6711
17	16	H	Reading	W	5-0	3-0	—	Moody 3 [8, 20, 54], Harris 2 [23, 69]	5202
18	23	A	Blackpool	W	2-1	2-1	—	Moody 2 [33, 45]	2819
19	27	A	Bournemouth	W	2-1	1-0	8	Harris 2 [7, 78]	5121
20	Dec 4	H	Cardiff C	W	2-0	2-0	6	Harris 2 [14, 28]	9044
21	11	A	Wycombe W	W	2-1	0-0	4	Ifill [51], Moody [76]	4777
22	18	H	Notts Co	W	1-0	0-0	4	Sadlier [79]	7917
23	26	A	Bristol R	L	0-1	0-0	4		10,077
24	28	H	Brentford	W	3-2	0-0	4	Harris [59], Shaw [89], Livermore [90]	12,077
25	Jan 4	A	Bury	D	2-2	0-1	—	Harris [56], Ifill [80]	3375
26	8	H	Wycombe W	D	1-1	1-1	4	Harris [45]	8945
27	15	A	Wigan Ath	D	1-1	0-0	4	Livermore [49]	6304
28	22	H	Stoke C	W	1-0	1-0	4	Gilkes [33]	11,548
29	29	A	Chesterfield	L	0-2	0-1	4		3198
30	Feb 5	H	Oldham Ath	W	1-0	0-0	4	Shaw (pen) [90]	8303
31	12	A	Reading	L	0-2	0-0	5		11,994
32	19	H	Bournemouth	W	3-1	1-1	4	Sadlier 2 [13, 76], Ifill [90]	8463
33	26	A	Cambridge U	W	2-0	2-0	3	Moody 2 [16, 22]	5116
34	Mar 4	H	Bristol C	W	4-1	3-1	3	Cahill 2 [8, 34], Ifill [30], Sadlier [57]	10,141
35	7	A	Scunthorpe U	L	1-2	1-0	—	Cahill [22]	8772
36	11	A	Luton T	W	2-0	2-0	3	Cahill 2 [18, 38]	6341
37	18	H	Blackpool	D	1-1	1-1	3	Harris (pen) [45]	10,506
38	21	A	Wrexham	D	1-1	0-1	—	Gilkes [90]	3019
39	25	H	Bristol R	W	3-0	1-0	4	Harris [28], Sadlier [78], Ifill [84]	12,858
40	Apr 1	A	Notts Co	D	1-1	1-0	4	Harris [13]	7032
41	8	H	Bury	W	3-0	3-0	4	Moody [7], Harris [34], Dolan [40]	10,742
42	15	A	Brentford	W	3-1	2-1	3	Harris 3 [10, 38, 64]	6779
43	22	A	Burnley	L	3-4	0-3	6	Harris 2 [59, 77], Cahill [87]	14,890
44	24	H	Gillingham	D	2-2	2-2	5	Moody [7], Harris [8]	17,929
45	29	A	Preston NE	L	2-3	0-3	6	Ifill [46], Neill [53]	19,407
46	May 6	H	Oxford U	W	1-0	1-0	5	Harris [7]	13,827

Final League Position: 5

GOALSCORERS

League (76): Harris 25 (3 pens), Cahill 12, Ifill 11, Moody 11, Sadlier 5, Shaw 5 (1 pen). Gilkes 2, Livermore 2, Bircham 1, Dolan 1, Neill 1.
Worthington Cup (1): Sadlier 1.
FA Cup (0).

Warner T 45	Bircham M 22	Ryan R 33 + 1	Cahill T 45	Nethercott S 37	Dolan J 16 + 1	Moody P 24 + 8	Odunsi L 1 + 3	Harris N 34 + 4	Shaw P 17 + 18	Neill L 27 + 4	Livermore D 29 + 3	Reid S 11 + 10	Ifill P 38 + 6	Fitzgerald S 31	Sadlier R 21 + 6	Gilkes M 26 + 3	Stuart J 9	Newman R 14	Bowry B 3 + 2	Bull R 5 + 4	Spink N 1	Bubb B — + 2	Kinet C — + 3	Tuttle D 7 + 1	Dyche S 1	Lawrence M 9	Match No
1	2	3	4	5	6	7	8¹	9	10	11	12																1
1	2	3	4	5	6	7²		9	10	11	8¹	12	13														2
1	2	3	4	5	6	7²		9	10	11	8¹	12	13														3
1	2	3	4	5		9¹		10	11	7	12	6	8														4
1	2	12	4	5		9²		13	10	14	7³	6	8	11¹	3												5
1	2		4	5	9	12		11³	7²	13	14	6	10¹	3	8												6
1	2		4	5				9¹	10²	11	7	12	6	13	3	8											7
1	2		4	5	12	9²	13	11¹	7	10²	14	6	8	3													8
1			4	5	7			10	11	12	8¹	6		3	2	9											9
1			4	5	9			10	7¹	12	11	6		3	2	8											10
1			4	5	9¹	12	10		7³	11	6	13	14	3	2²	8											11
1	2	3	4	5	9²	12	10¹	11	8³	7	6	13					14										12
1	2	3	4	5	12	9¹	11	10	7	6	8																13
1	2	3	4	5	9	11	10	7	6	8																	14
1	2	3	4	5	9	12	11	10	7²	6	8¹	13															15
1	2	3	4	5	9	8	10¹	7	6	12	11																16
1	2¹	3	4	5	8²	12	9	13	7	6	11	10															17
1	2	3	4	5	8	9	12	7¹	6	11	10																18
1	2	3		5	8	9	11	4	10	6	7																19
1	2	3	4	5	8	9¹	12	11	10	6	7																20
1	2	3	4	5	8	9	11	10	6	7																	21
1	2	3	4	5	6	8¹	9	11	13	10²	12	7															22
1	2		4	5	6	9	11	12	10	8	7¹	3															23
1	2	3	4¹	5	6	9	13	12	10	11	8²	7															24
1	2¹	3	4	5	6	12	9²	13	7	11	10	8															25
1		3	4	5	12	9	13	7	8	11	6	10¹		2²													26
		3	4	5	9		10	8	11¹	6	7		2	1	12												27
1		4	5	9¹		10	8	13	11²	6	12	7	2	3													28
1		4	5	6	9¹	10	8	11	12	7²	2	3			13												29
1		3	4	5	12	9	13	2	8	11	6	10¹	7²														30
1	3²	4	5	12	9	13	2	8	11	6	10¹	7															31
1	3	4	5¹	12	9³	2	8	11	6	10	7²			13		14											32
1	3	4		6	9	10	2	8	11	5	7¹			12													33
1	3	4	5	12	10	2	8	13	11²	9¹	7	6															34
1	3	4	5²	12	9	2	8	13	11	10¹	7³			14	6												35
1	3	4		12	9¹	2	11	8	7	10				5	6												36
1	3	4	6	9¹	12	2	8	11	10	7²			13	5													37
1	3	4	6	9	12	8	11¹	5	10	7																2	38
1	3	4	6	9¹	12	8	11	5	10	7																2	39
1	3	4	6	12	9	8	11²	5	10¹	7			13													2	40
1	3²	4	6	9¹	10	12	13	8	11²	5	7			14												2	41
1		4	6	9	10	8	11	5	7	3					2												42
1		4	6³	9¹	10	12	13	8	11	5	7²			3		14										2	43
1		4¹	5	9²	12	10	13	7³	8	11	14			3		6										2	44
1	3²	4	5	9	10	13	12	8	11	7¹						6										2	45
1	3	4	5	9¹	10	12	7	8	11	6																2	46

Worthington Cup
First Round   Swansea C   (a) 0-2
    (h) 1-1

FA Cup
First Round   Hartlepool U   (a) 0-1

FA Premiership   NEWCASTLE UNITED

FOUNDATION

It stemmed from a newly formed club called Stanley in 1881. In October 1882 they changed their name to Newcastle East End to avoid confusion with two other local clubs, Stanley Nops and Stanley Albion. Shortly afterwards another club Rosewood merged with them. Newcastle West End had been formed in August 1882 and they played on a pitch which was part of the Town Moor. Moved to Brandling Park 1885 and St James' Park 1886 (home of Newcastle Rangers). West End went out of existence after a bad run and the remaining committee men invited East End to move to St James' Park. They accepted and, at a meeting in Bath Lane Hall in 1892, changed their name to Newcastle United.

St James' Park, Newcastle-upon-Tyne NE1 4ST.
Telephone: (0191) 201 8400. *Fax:* (0191) 201 8600.
ClubCall: 09068 121 190. *Commercial Department:* (0191) 201 8715.
Ticket Office Hotline: (0191) 261 1571. *Mail Order:* (0990) 501 892. *Club Shop:* (0191) 201 8429.
Football in the Community Scheme: (0191) 235 3917. *Lottery Office:* (0191) 235 3901.
Travel Club: (0191) 201 8550. *Junior Magpies:* (0191) 201 8471. *Corporate Hospitality:* (0191) 201 8424.
Photographic Dept: (0191) 235 3906.
Ground Capacity: 52,167.
Record Attendance: 68,386 v Chelsea, Division 1, 3 September 1930.
Record Receipts: £830,271 v Everton, FA Cup 6th rd, 7 March 1999.
Pitch Measurements: 105m × 68m.
President: Sir John Hall.
Chairman: W. F. Shepherd. *Deputy Chairman:* D. S. Hall.
Chief Executive: D. Stonehouse.
Directors: W. F. Shepherd, D. Stonehouse, R. Jones, D. S. Hall.
Manager: Bobby Robson CBE.
Head Coach: Mick Wadsworth.
Coaches: John Carver, Tommy Craig.
Senior Physio: Derek Wright. *Physio:* Paul Ferris.
Fitness Coach: Paul Winsper.
Director of Football Administration and Secretary: Russell Cushing.
Operations Manager: Paul Stevens.
Assistant Secretary: Lee Charnley.
Academy Director: Alan Irvine.

LATEST SEQUENCES
Longest Sequence of League Wins: 13, 25.4.92 – 18.10.92.
Longest Sequence of League Defeats: 10, 23.8.77 – 15.10.77.
Longest Sequence of League Draws: 4, 20.1.90 – 24.2.90.
Longest Sequence of Unbeaten League Matches: 14, 22.4.50 – 30.9.50.
Longest Sequence Without a League Win: 21, 14.1.78 – 23.8.78.

HONOURS

FA Premier League: Runners-up 1995–96, 1996–97; *Football League:* Division 1 – Champions 1904–05, 1906–07, 1908–09, 1926–27, 1992–93; Division 2 – Champions 1964–65; Runners-up 1897–98, 1947–48.

FA Cup: Winners 1910, 1924, 1932, 1951, 1952, 1955; Runners-up 1905, 1906, 1908, 1911, 1974, 1998, 1999.

Football League Cup: Runners-up 1976.

Texaco Cup: Winners 1974, 1975.

European Competitions: European Cup: 1997–98. *European Fairs Cup:* 1968–69 (winners), 1969–70, 1970–71. *UEFA Cup:* 1977–78, 1994–95, 1996–97. *European Cup Winners' Cup:* 1998–99. *Anglo-Italian Cup:* Winners 1972–73.

Colours
Black and white striped shirts, black, white and blue shorts and stockings.

Change Colours
Black, powder blue and white shirts and shorts, black and white stockings.

Year Formed: 1881.

Turned Professional: 1889.

Ltd Co.: 1890.

Previous Names: 1881, Stanley; 1882, Newcastle East End; 1892, Newcastle United.

Club Nickname: 'Magpies'.

Previous Grounds: 1881, South Byker; 1886, Chillingham Road, Heaton, 1892, St James' Park.

First Football League Game: 2 September 1893, Division 2, v Royal Arsenal (a) D 2–2 – Ramsay; Jeffery, Miller; Crielly, Graham, McKane; Bowman, Crate (1), Thompson, Sorley (1), Wallace. Graham and not Crate scored according to some reports.

Record League Victory: 13–0 v Newport Co, Division 2, 5 October 1946 – Garbutt; Cowell, Graham; Harvey, Brennan, Wright; Milburn (2), Bentley (1), Wayman (4), Shackleton (6), Pearson.

Record Cup Victory: 9–0 v Southport (at Hillsborough), FA Cup 4th rd, 1 February 1932 – McInroy; Nelson, Fairhurst; McKenzie, Davidson, Weaver (1); Boyd (1), Jimmy Richardson (3), Cape (2), McMenemy (1), Lang (1).

Record Defeat: 0–9 v Burton Wanderers, Division 2, 15 April 1895.

Most League Points (2 for a win): 57, Division 2, 1964–65.

Most League Points (3 for a win): 96, Division 1, 1992–93.

Most League Goals: 98, Division 1, 1951–52.

MANAGERS

Frank Watt 1895–32
(Secretary-Manager)
Andy Cunningham 1930–35
Tom Mather 1935–39
Stan Seymour 1939–47
(Hon. Manager)
George Martin 1947–50
Stan Seymour 1950–54
(Hon. Manager)
Duggie Livingstone 1954–56
Stan Seymour 1956–58
(Hon. Manager)
Charlie Mitten 1958–61
Norman Smith 1961–62
Joe Harvey 1962–75
Gordon Lee 1975–77
Richard Dinnis 1977
Bill McGarry 1977–80
Arthur Cox 1980–84
Jack Charlton 1984
Willie McFaul 1985–88
Jim Smith 1988–91
Ossie Ardiles 1991–92
Kevin Keegan 1992–97
Kenny Dalglish 1997–98
Ruud Gullit 1998–1999
Bobby Robson September 1999–

Highest League Scorer in Season: Hughie Gallacher, 36, Division 1, 1926–27.

Most League Goals in Total Aggregate: Jackie Milburn, 177, 1946–57.

Most League Goals in One Match: 6, Len Shackleton v Newport Co, Division 2, 5 October 1946.

Most Capped Player: Alf McMichael, 40, Northern Ireland.

Most League Appearances: Jim Lawrence, 432, 1904–22.

Youngest League Player: Steve Watson, 16 years 223 days v Wolverhampton W, 10 November 1990.

Record Transfer Fee Received: £8,000,000 from Liverpool for Dieter Hamann, July 1999.

Record Transfer Fee Paid: £15,000,000 to Blackburn R for Alan Shearer, July 1996.

Football League Record: 1893 Elected to Division 2; 1898–1934 Division 1; 1934–48 Division 2; 1948–61 Division 1; 1961–65 Division 2; 1965–78 Division 1; 1978–84 Division 2; 1984–89 Division 1; 1989–92 Division 2; 1992–93 Division 1; 1993– FA Premier League.

TEN YEAR LEAGUE RECORD

		P	W	D	L	F	A	Pts	Pos
1989-90	Div 2	46	22	14	10	80	55	80	3
1990-91	Div 2	46	14	17	15	49	56	59	11
1991-92	Div 2	46	13	13	20	66	84	52	20
1992-93	Div 1	46	29	9	8	92	38	96	1
1993-94	PR Lge	42	23	8	11	82	41	77	3
1994-95	PR Lge	42	20	12	10	67	47	72	6
1995-96	PR Lge	38	24	6	8	66	37	78	2
1996-97	PR Lge	38	19	11	8	73	40	68	2
1997-98	PR Lge	38	11	11	16	35	44	44	13
1998-99	PR Lge	38	11	13	14	48	54	46	13

DID YOU KNOW ?

In 1924 Newcastle United won 4-2 at Portsmouth on the way to the FA Cup Final. In 1952 they repeated the scoreline there and again reached Wembley, this time with a successful outcome.

NEWCASTLE UNITED 1999–2000 LEAGUE RECORD

Match No.	Date		Venue	Opponents	Result	H/T Score	Lg. Pos.	Goalscorers	Attendance
1	Aug	7	H	Aston Villa	L	0-1	0-0	18		36,376
2		9	A	Tottenham H	L	1-3	1-2	—	Solano [16]	28,701
3		15	A	Southampton	L	2-4	1-0	20	Shearer (pen) [22], Speed [84]	15,030
4		21	H	Wimbledon	D	3-3	2-1	18	Speed [7], Domi [28], Solano (pen) [46]	35,809
5		25	H	Sunderland	L	1-2	1-0	—	Dyer [28]	36,420
6		30	A	Manchester U	L	1-5	1-1	19	Berg (og) [31]	55,190
7	Sept	11	A	Chelsea	L	0-1	0-1	19		35,081
8		19	H	Sheffield W	W	8-0	4-0	19	Hughes [11], Shearer 5 (2 pens) [30, 33 (p), 42, 61, 84 (p)], Dyer [46], Speed [78]	36,619
9		25	A	Leeds U	L	2-3	1-2	19	Shearer 2 [42, 54]	40,192
10	Oct	3	H	Middlesbrough	W	2-1	2-0	19	Shearer 2 [17, 44]	36,421
11		16	A	Coventry C	L	1-4	0-3	19	Domi [81]	23,022
12		25	H	Derby Co	W	2-0	1-0	—	Eranio (og) [41], Shearer [52]	35,614
13		30	A	Arsenal	D	0-0	0-0	17		38,106
14	Nov	7	H	Everton	D	1-1	0-0	16	Shearer (pen) [46]	36,164
15		20	A	Watford	D	1-1	0-0	16	Dabizas [59]	19,539
16		28	H	Tottenham H	W	2-1	1-1	15	Glass [5], Dabizas [58]	36,454
17	Dec	4	A	Aston Villa	W	1-0	0-0	14	Ferguson [65]	34,531
18		18	A	Bradford C	L	0-2	0-0	15		18,276
19		26	H	Liverpool	D	2-2	1-1	15	Shearer [12], Ferguson [67]	36,445
20		28	A	Leicester C	W	2-1	1-0	14	Ferguson [21], Shearer [53]	21,225
21	Jan	3	H	West Ham U	D	2-2	1-0	15	Dabizas [18], Speed [65]	36,314
22		16	A	Southampton	W	5-0	4-0	13	Ferguson 2 [3, 4], Solano [17], Dryden (og) [31], Monk (og) [83]	35,623
23		22	A	Wimbledon	L	0-2	0-0	15		22,118
24	Feb	5	A	Sunderland	D	2-2	2-1	13	Domi [11], Helder [21]	42,079
25		12	H	Manchester U	W	3-0	1-0	13	Ferguson [26], Shearer 2 [76, 86]	36,470
26		26	A	Sheffield W	W	2-0	1-0	12	Gallacher [11], Shearer [86]	29,212
27	Mar	4	H	Chelsea	L	0-1	0-1	12		36,448
28		11	H	Watford	W	1-0	0-0	12	Gallacher [59]	36,433
29		19	A	Everton	W	2-0	0-0	11	Hughes [79], Dyer [87]	32,512
30		25	A	Liverpool	L	1-2	0-0	12	Shearer [67]	44,743
31	Apr	1	H	Bradford C	W	2-0	1-0	11	Speed [7], Shearer [89]	36,572
32		12	A	West Ham U	L	1-2	0-0	—	Speed [48]	25,817
33		15	H	Leicester C	L	0-2	0-1	11		36,426
34		23	H	Leeds U	D	2-2	1-2	12	Shearer 2 [24, 48]	36,448
35		29	H	Coventry C	W	2-0	0-0	12	Shearer (pen) [78], Gavilan [84]	36,408
36	May	2	A	Middlesbrough	D	2-2	2-1	—	Speed [10], Pistone [18]	34,744
37		6	A	Derby Co	D	0-0	0-0	12		32,724
38		14	A	Arsenal	W	4-2	2-1	11	Speed 2 [6, 59], Shearer [22], Griffin [63]	36,450

Final League Position: 11

GOALSCORERS

League (63): Shearer 23 (5 pens), Speed 9, Ferguson 6, Dabizas 3, Domi 3, Dyer 3, Solano 3 (1 pen), Gallacher 2, Hughes 2, Gavilan 1, Glass 1, Griffin 1, Helder 1, Pistone 1, own goals 4.
Worthington Cup (0).
FA Cup (17): Shearer 5 (1 pen), Ferguson 3, Speed 3, Dabizas 2, Domi 1, Dyer 1, Gallacher 1, Lee 1.

Harper S 18	Barton W 33+1	Domi D 19+8	Marcelino E 10+1	Goma A 14	Solano N 29+1	Serrant C 2	Dumas F 6	Shearer A 36+1	Ketsbaia T 11+10	Speed G 36	Dyer K 27+3	Robinson P 2+9	Maric S 3+10	Hughes A 22+5	Karelse J 3	McClen J 3+6	Beharall D —+2	Ferguson D 17+6	Wright T 3	Dabizas N 29	Lee R 30	Glass S 1+6	Charvet L 1+1	Gallacher K 15+5	Given S 14	Pistone A 15	Helder R 8	Fumaca J 1+4	Gavilan D 2+4	Howey S 7+2	Griffin A 1+2	Match No.
1	2	3	4¹	5	6²	7³	8	9	10	11	12	13	14																			1
1	2	3		5	6		8¹	9	10	11	7	12	13	4²																		2
	2	3		5	6	11¹		9	10	8	7	13	12²	4	1																	3
	2	3	4	5¹	6			10²	11	7	9			1	8	12	13															4
	2	3		5	6		12	11	7	9²	8¹					10		13	1	4												5
	2			5	6²		9	11	7	12	3	14	13			10¹	1	4		8³												6
	6	3		5	8¹		9	11	2	14	13	12				10³	1	4		7²												7
1	2	3²		5	6		9	10²	11	7¹	12						4	13		8	14											8
1	2	3	4	5	6		9	10¹	11	7	12					8²					13											9
1	2	3		5	6²			9	11	7	12						4	8		13	10¹											10
	2	3			6			9	11	7		5					4	8			10	1										11
	2¹			5	6			9	11	7³	14	12				13		4		8	10²	1	3									12
	3		5		6¹	8	9	11				1				12		4		7	10	2										13
1	3			6		5	9	11		12						10¹		4		7	8	2										14
1		5		6	9	12	11					8²	2				4	7	13		10¹	3										15
1		6¹		9	10³				12	3				13	14	4	7	11	2			5	8²									16
1	12				2¹	5	9	10²	11					8³	13	14	4	7				3	6									17
1	2		6¹		9			11	12					5	10	7³	13	8²		3	4	14										18
1	2		6³		9	12	11			7²				5	10¹		4	8	13		14	3										19
1	2		5	6		9	11							10		4	7			8	3											20
1	2		5	6		9	12	11						10¹		4	7³	13		8²	3	14										21
1	2³	12		5	6²		9	13	11	7		14		10		4		8¹		3												22
1	2	12		5	6		9	11	7					10		4		8¹		3												23
1	2	11²			9		8	7	12					10		4	6³	13		3¹	5	14										24
1	2	12			9	13	11	7³						3		10²	4	6		8¹	5	14										25
	2	12			9	13	11	7						3		10²	4	6		8¹		5³	14	1								26
	2	3¹		12	9	13	11	7						6		10	4	8²			5			1								27
	2	12		6	9	11								3¹		10	4	7		8	5			1								28
	2	12		6²	9	11	13							3		10	4	7		8¹	5			1								29
	2	12		6¹	9		11	7						3		10	4	8²	13		5			1								30
1	2	11	4		9	12	8	7¹						3		10	6				5											31
	2	11	5	6	9	12	8	10¹						3			4²	7			1			13								32
	2	11	5	6¹	9	8	10²	12						3³			7				1			13	14	4						33
	2	11	12		9	10²	13							3			4	7			1			6¹	14	8²	5					34
	2	11¹			9	12	8	10						5		13	4	7²			1		3	6³	14							35
	2		6³		9	10¹	11	7²		12				5		13	4	8			1	3			14							36
	2	12	6²		9	10³	11	7						5		13	4	8	13		1	3¹		14								37
	3		6¹		9	10³	11	7		12				13			4	8²	14		1			5	2							38

Worthington Cup
Third Round   Birmingham C   (a)   0-2

FA Cup

Third Round	Tottenham H	(a)	1-1
		(h)	6-1
Fourth Round	Sheffield U	(h)	4-1
Fifth Round	Blackburn R	(a)	2-1
Sixth Round	Tranmere R	(a)	3-2
Semi-Final	Chelsea		1-2
(at Wembley)			

Division 2   NORTHAMPTON TOWN

FOUNDATION

Formed in 1897 by school teachers connected with the
Northampton and District Elementary Schools' Association, they
survived a financial crisis at the end of their first year when they
were £675 in the red and became members of the Midland League
– a fast move indeed for a new club. They achieved Southern
League membership in 1901.

Sixfields Stadium, Upton Way, Northampton NN5 5QA.

Telephone: (01604) 757 773.

Fax: (01604) 751 613.

Website: http://www.ntfc.co.uk

Email: secretary@ntfc.co.uk

Ticket Office: (01604) 588 338.

ClubCall: 09066 555 970.

Ground Capacity: 7653 (all seated).

Record Attendance: (at County Ground): 24,523 v Fulham, Division 1, 23 April 1966.
(at Sixfields Stadium): 7557 v Manchester C, Division 2, 26 September 1998.

Record Receipts (at Sixfields): £102,979 v Tottenham H, Worthington Cup 3rd rd, 27 October 1998.

Pitch Measurements: 116yd × 72yd.

Chairman: B. J. Stonhill.

Directors: B. Hancock, D. Kerr, C. Smith, T. Clarke MP, P. Randall.

Secretary: Norman Howells.

Company Secretary: B. J. Stonhill.

Manager: Kevin Wilson.

Coach: Kevan Broadhurst.

Physio: Dennis Casey.

Commercial Manager: Eric Broad.

Stadium Manager: Tom Holland.

LATEST SEQUENCES

Longest Sequence of League Wins: 8, 27.8.60 – 19.9.60.

Longest Sequence of League Defeats: 8, 26.10.35 – 21.12.35.

Longest Sequence of League Draws: 6, 18.9.83 – 15.10.83.

Longest Sequence of Unbeaten League Matches: 21, 27.9.86 – 6.2.87.

Longest Sequence Without a League Win: 18, 26.3.69 – 20.9.69.

HONOURS

Football League: Division 1 best
season: 21st, 1965–66; Division 2 –
Runners-up 1964–65; Division 3 –
Champions 1962–63; Promoted from
Division 3 1996–97 (play-offs);
Division 3 (S) – Runners-up 1927–28,
1949–50; Division 4 – Champions
1986–87; Runners-up 1975–76.

FA Cup: best season: 5th rd, 1934,
1950, 1970.

Football League Cup: best season:
5th rd, 1965, 1967.

Colours
Claret with white shirts, white shorts, white stockings.

Change Colours
White shirts with claret, claret shorts, claret stockings.

Year Formed: 1897.

Turned Professional: 1901.

Ltd Co.: 1901.

Previous Ground: 1897, County Ground; 1994, Sixfields Stadium.

Club Nickname: 'The Cobblers'.

First Football League Game: 28 August 1920, Division 3, v Grimsby T (a) L 0–2 – Thorpe; Sproston, Hewison; Jobey, Tomkins, Pease; Whitworth, Lockett, Thomas, Freeman, MacKechnie.

Record League Victory: 10–0 v Walsall, Division 3 (S), 5 November 1927 – Hammond; Watson, Jeffs; Allen, Brett, Odell; Daley, Smith (3), Loasby (3), Hoten (1), Wells (3).

Record Cup Victory: 10–0 v Sutton T, FA Cup prel rd, 7 December 1907 – Cooch; Drennan, Lloyd Davies, Tirrell (1), McCartney, Hickleton, Badenock (3), Platt (3), Lowe (1), Chapman (2), McDiarmid.

Record Defeat: 0–11 v Southampton, Southern League, 28 December 1901.

Most League Points (2 for a win): 68, Division 4, 1975–76.

Most League Points (3 for a win): 99, Division 4, 1986–87.

Most League Goals: 109, Division 3, 1962–63 and Division 3 (S), 1952–53.

Highest League Scorer in Season: Cliff Holton, 36, Division 3, 1961–62.

Most League Goals in Total Aggregate: Jack English, 135, 1947–60.

Most League Goals in One Match: 5, Ralph Hoten v Crystal Palace, Division 3S, 27 October 1928.

Most Capped Player: E. Lloyd Davies, 12 (16), Wales.

Most League Appearances: Tommy Fowler, 521, 1946–61.

Youngest League Player: Adrian Mann, 16 years 297 days v Bury, 5 May 1984.

Record Transfer Fee Received: £265,000 from Watford for Richard Hill, July 1987.

Record Transfer Fee Paid: £120,000 to Hartlepool U for Steve Howard, February 1999.

Football League Record: 1920 Original Member of Division 3; 1921 Division 3 (S); 1958–61 Division 4; 1961–63 Division 3; 1963–65 Division 2; 1965–66 Division 1; 1966–67 Division 2; 1967–69 Division 3; 1969–76 Division 4; 1976–77 Division 3; 1977–87 Division 4; 1987–90 Division 3; 1990–92 Division 4; 1992–97 Division 3; 1997–99 Division 2; 1999–2000 Division 3; 2000– Division 2.

MANAGERS

Arthur Jones 1897–1907
(Secretary-Manager)
Herbert Chapman 1907–12
Walter Bull 1912–13
Fred Lessons 1913–19
Bob Hewison 1920–25
Jack Tresadern 1925–30
Jack English 1931–35
Syd Puddefoot 1935–37
Warney Cresswell 1937–39
Tom Smith 1939–49
Bob Dennison 1949–54
Dave Smith 1954–59
David Bowen 1959–67
Tony Marchi 1967–68
Ron Flowers 1968–69
Dave Bowen 1969–72
(continued as General Manager and Secretary to 1985 when joined the board)
Billy Baxter 1972–73
Bill Dodgin Jnr 1973–76
Pat Crerand 1976–77
Bill Dodgin Jnr 1977
John Petts 1977–78
Mike Keen 1978–79
Clive Walker 1979–80
Bill Dodgin Jnr 1980–82
Clive Walker 1982–84
Tony Barton 1984–85
Graham Carr 1985–90
Theo Foley 1990–92
Phil Chard 1992–93
John Barnwell 1993–95
Ian Atkins 1995–99
Kevin Wilson November 1999–

TEN YEAR LEAGUE RECORD

		P	W	D	L	F	A	Pts	Pos
1989-90	Div 3	46	11	14	21	51	68	47	22
1990-91	Div 4	46	18	13	15	57	58	67	10
1991-92	Div 4	42	11	13	18	46	57	46	16
1992-93	Div 3	42	11	8	23	48	74	41	20
1993-94	Div 3	42	9	11	22	44	66	38	22
1994-95	Div 3	42	10	14	18	45	67	44	17
1995-96	Div 3	46	18	13	15	51	44	67	11
1996-97	Div 3	46	20	12	14	67	44	72	4
1997-98	Div 2	46	18	17	11	52	37	71	4
1998-99	Div 2	46	10	18	18	43	57	48	22

DID YOU KNOW

Northampton Town's Carlo Corazzin scored a 67th minute penalty for Canada against Colombia on 27 February 2000 in Los Angeles in the final of the Gold Cup. Canada won 2-0.

NORTHAMPTON TOWN 1999–2000 LEAGUE RECORD

Match No.	Date	Venue	Opponents	Result	H/T Score	Lg. Pos.	Goalscorers	Attendance
1	Aug 7	A	Macclesfield T	L	0-1	0-0	20		2694
2	14	H	Peterborough U	L	0-1	0-0	21		6253
3	18	A	Chester C	W	2-0	0-0	—	Hendon (pen) [61], Byfield [66]	1904
4	27	H	Lincoln C	W	1-0	1-0	—	Howard [5]	5104
5	30	A	York C	W	1-0	0-0	7	Spedding [72]	2597
6	Sept 4	H	Carlisle U	D	0-0	0-0	10		4864
7	11	H	Hartlepool U	W	2-1	0-1	5	Howard 2 [61, 71]	4724
8	18	A	Barnet	L	1-2	1-2	8	Corazzin [38]	3638
9	25	A	Rotherham U	L	0-3	0-1	12		3625
10	Oct 2	H	Rochdale	L	0-1	0-1	12		4860
11	9	H	Torquay U	W	3-0	1-0	11	Frain [34], Battersby [82], Sampson [86]	5003
12	16	A	Hull C	W	1-0	0-0	10	Sturridge [57]	6467
13	19	A	Mansfield T	D	0-0	0-0	—		2940
14	23	H	Rotherham U	L	0-1	0-0	14		5753
15	Nov 2	H	Swansea C	W	2-1	1-0	—	Corazzin [36], Sampson [73]	4495
16	6	A	Leyton Orient	D	0-0	0-0	11		3928
17	12	H	Cheltenham T	W	3-2	2-1	7	Savage [26], Corazzin [45], Clare [87]	5837
18	23	A	Exeter C	W	2-1	1-1	—	Corazzin [40], Hendon [78]	2096
19	27	A	Brighton & HA	W	3-1	1-1	5	Corazzin (pen) [8], Clare [53], Parrish [55]	5935
20	Dec 4	H	Macclesfield T	W	2-0	1-0	4	Hunter [12], Corazzin [54]	5355
21	11	A	Shrewsbury T	L	0-1	0-1	4		2339
22	17	H	Plymouth Arg	D	1-1	0-1	—	Corazzin [64]	5039
23	26	A	Southend U	D	2-2	0-0	5	Frain [61], Sampson [78]	5449
24	28	H	Darlington	L	0-3	0-2	7		6823
25	Jan 3	A	Halifax T	D	2-2	1-1	7	Peer [10], Parrish [87]	3001
26	8	H	Shrewsbury T	W	3-0	2-0	6	Green [8], Wilson [23], Clare [58]	4927
27	15	A	Peterborough U	L	0-1	0-0	6		9104
28	22	H	Chester C	W	3-1	1-1	6	Howard [31], Sampson [53], Corazzin [57]	5332
29	29	H	Lincoln C	D	2-2	1-2	6	Hunter [44], Corazzin [64]	3717
30	Feb 5	H	York C	W	3-0	1-0	5	Sampson [43], Howard [56], Parrish [66]	4958
31	19	A	Brighton & HA	W	1-0	1-0	5	Sampson [6]	5974
32	26	H	Barnet	W	1-0	0-0	5	Howard [50]	5862
33	Mar 4	A	Hartlepool U	L	1-2	1-2	6	Corazzin [33]	2878
34	7	H	Leyton Orient	W	2-1	0-0	—	Howard [68], Hunter [73]	5121
35	10	A	Swansea C	L	1-4	0-1	—	Corazzin [76]	7430
36	18	H	Exeter C	W	2-1	2-0	5	Green [25], Corazzin [36]	4989
37	21	A	Cheltenham T	L	1-2	0-1	—	Savage [77]	4515
38	25	H	Southend U	W	2-0	1-0	4	Savage [27], Forrester [71]	5426
39	Apr 1	A	Plymouth Arg	L	1-2	1-1	4	Corazzin [11]	5448
40	8	H	Halifax T	L	3-4	3-2	6	Savage [14], Forrester 2 [23, 45]	5207
41	11	A	Carlisle U	W	1-0	1-0	—	Forrester [30]	2855
42	15	A	Darlington	W	1-0	1-0	4	Howard [5]	5833
43	21	H	Hull C	W	1-0	1-0	—	Forrester [5]	6758
44	24	A	Rochdale	W	3-0	2-0	3	Howard [2], Hunt [40], Corazzin [83]	2891
45	29	H	Mansfield T	W	1-0	1-0	3	Savage [42]	6901
46	May 6	A	Torquay U	W	2-1	2-1	3	Forrester [26], Howard [40]	5010

Final League Position: 3

GOALSCORERS

League (63): Corazzin 14 (1 pen), Howard 10, Forrester 6, Sampson 6, Savage 5, Clare 3, Hunter 3, Parrish 3, Frain 2, Green 2, Hendon 2 (1 pen), Battersby 1, Byfield 1, Hunt 1, Peer 1, Spedding 1, Sturridge 1, Wilson 1.
Worthington Cup (2): Byfield 1, Corazzin 1 (pen).
FA Cup (1): Hendon 1.

Welch K 39	Clarkson I 1+1	Frain J 40	Hope R 14+3	Howey L 20	Parrish S 21+4	Savage D 43	Hunt J 33+4	Howard S 32+9	Sturridge S 10+8	Hendon I 44	Wilson K 4+4	Corazzin C 27+12	Gibb A 6+8	O'Reilly A 7	Sampson I 45	Byfield D 6	Spedding D 44	Matthew D —+1	Peer D 6+3	Battersby T —+3	Morrow A —+4	Hunter R 15+2	Dobson T 1	Clare D 9+1	Hughes G 1+1	Green R 21	Crowe D 3+2	Hodge J 5+3	Forrester J 9+1	Match No.
2		3	4	5	6¹	7	8	9	10²	11³	12	13	14																	1
		3		5	6¹	7	8³	9		2	13	12		1	4	10²	11	14												2
1		3	12	5		7	8	9		2	13		6¹		4	10²	11													3
1		3		5		7	8	9		2	12		6		4	10¹	11													4
1	12	3		5		7	8	9	13	2			6¹		4	10¹	11													5
1		3		5		7	8	9	12	2			6		4	10¹	11													6
1		3		5		7	8	9	12²	2		11			4	10¹			6			13								7
1		3		5		7	8	9	12	2		10			4		11		6¹											8
1		3		5		7	8	9²	10	2	12	11¹			4				6			13								9
1		3		5		7	8	9³	12	2	13	10²	6¹		4		11					14								10
1		3		5		7	8	9	10¹	2		11²			4				6			12		13						11
1		3		5		7	8	9	10¹	2	12				4		11		6											12
1		3		5		7	8	9	10¹	2	12	11²			4				6			13								13
1		3		5		7	8	9³	10¹	2	13	12			4		11		6²			14								14
1		3		5		7	8¹	9	12	2	13	10¹			4		11		6											15
1		3		5		7	8	9²		2		10			4		11¹		6			13		12						16
		3		5		7	8	9²	12	2	13	10¹		1	4		11		6											17
		3	12	5¹	6	7	8	9²	13	2		10		1	4		11									9²				18
		3		5	6	7	8	9¹	12	2		10		1	4		11												19
		3		5	6	7	8¹	9²	12	2³	13	10	14	1	4		11												20
		3		5	6¹	7	12	9	13	2		10²		1	4		11					8								21
1		3		5	6	7	8	9		2		10			4		11												22
1		3		5	6	7	12	9	13	2		10²			4		11					8¹								23
1		3		5	6¹	7	8	9²	12	2		10			4		11									13				24
1		3		5	6	7¹	8			2		10			4		11					12				9				25
1		3			6		8		10²	2¹					4		11		7			13				9	12	5		26
1		3			6		8¹		12	2		10			4		11		7							9		5		27
1		3			6		8			2		10			4		11		7							9		5		28
1		3			6	7		9		2		10			4		11					8				5				29
1		3¹			6	7	13	9	12	2		10²			4		11					8				5				30
1		3			6	7		9		2					4		11					8				5			10	31
1	12	3			6²	7	13	9		2					4¹		11					8				5			10	32
1		3¹				7	8	9		2		10			4		11		6							5			12	33
1						7	8	9		2		10			4		11¹		6							5	3	12		34
1						7	8²	9	12	2		10			4		11¹		6							5	3	13		35
1					6	7	8	9		2		10			4		11									5	3			36
1					6¹	7	8	9		2		10			4		11²					12				5	3	13		37
1	12	3²	13			7	8			2		10³	14		4		11¹								6	5			9	38
1	12	3			6²	7³	8¹		13	2		10			4		11									5		14	9	39
1		3				7	8		12	2		10			4		11¹		6							5			9	40
1		3			6	7		9		2		10			4		11									5			8	41
1		3			6	7	8	9	12	2					4		11									5			10¹	42
1		3			6	7	8	9	12	2					4		11									5			10¹	43
1		3			6	7	8	9²	12	2					4		11									5		13	10¹	44
1		3			6	7	8	9	12	2					4		11									5			10¹	45
1		3			6¹	7	8	9	12	2		13			4		11									5			10²	46

Worthington Cup
First Round   Fulham   (h) 1-2
                         (a) 1-3

FA Cup
First Round   Shrewsbury T   (a) 1-2

Division 1   **NORWICH CITY**

FOUNDATION

Formed in 1902, largely through the initiative of two local schoolmasters who called a meeting at the Criterion Cafe, they were shocked by an FA Commission which in 1904 declared the club professional and ejected them from the FA Amateur Cup. However, this only served to strengthen their determination. New officials were appointed and a professional club established at a meeting in the Agricultural Hall in March 1905.

Carrow Road, Norwich NR1 1JE.

Telephone: (01603) 760 760.

Fax: (01603) 613 886.

Box Office: (01603) 761 661.

ClubCall: 09068 121 144.

Ground Capacity: 21,414.

Record Attendance: 43,984 v Leicester C, FA Cup 6th rd, 30 March 1963.

Record Receipts: £261,918 v Internazionale, UEFA Cup 3rd rd 1st leg, 24 November 1993.

Pitch Measurements: 114yd × 74yd.

President: G. C. Watling.

Chairman: Bob Cooper.

Joint Vice-Chairmen: R. J. Munby, B. W. Lockwood.

Company Secretary: N. A. Doncaster.

Directors: M. M. Foulger, B. J. Skipper, M. Wynn Jones, D. Smith.

First Team Manager: Bryan Hamilton.

First Team Coach: Doug Livermore.

Director of Academy: Sammy Morgan.

Coaches: Keith Webb, Steve Foley, Dave Stringer.

Physio: Tim Sheppard MCSP, SRP.

Club Secretary: Kevin Platt.

LATEST SEQUENCES

Longest Sequence of League Wins: 10, 23.11.85 – 25.1.86.

Longest Sequence of League Defeats: 7, 1.4.95 – 6.5.95.

Longest Sequence of League Draws: 7, 15.1.94 – 26.2.94.

Longest Sequence of Unbeaten League Matches: 20, 31.8.50 – 30.12.50.

Longest Sequence Without a League Win: 25, 22.9.56 – 23.2.57.

HONOURS

FA Premier League: best season: 3rd 1992–93.

Football League: Division 2 – Champions 1971–72, 1985–86; Division 3 (S) – Champions 1933–34; Division 3 – Runners-up 1959–60.

FA Cup: Semi-finals 1959, 1989, 1992.

Football League Cup: Winners 1962, 1985; Runners-up 1973, 1975.

European Competitions: UEFA Cup: 1993–94.

Colours

Yellow shirts, green shorts, yellow stockings.

Change Colours

All white.

Year Formed: 1902.

Turned Professional: 1905.

Ltd Co.: 1905.

Club Nickname: 'The Canaries'.

Previous Grounds: 1902, Newmarket Road; 1908, The Nest, Rosary Road; 1935, Carrow Road.

First Football League Game: 28 August 1920, Division 3, v Plymouth Arg (a) D 1–1 – Skermer; Gray, Gadsden; Wilkinson, Addy, Martin; Laxton, Kidger, Parker, Whitham (1), Dobson.

Record League Victory: 10–2 v Coventry C, Division 3 (S), 15 March 1930 – Jarvie; Hannah, Graham; Brown, O'Brien, Lochhead (1); Porter (1), Anderson, Hunt (5), Scott (2), Slicer (1).

Record Cup Victory: 8–0 v Sutton U, FA Cup 4th rd, 28 January 1989 – Gunn; Culverhouse, Bowen, Butterworth, Linighan, Townsend (Crook), Gordon, Fleck (3), Allen (4), Phelan, Putney (1).

Record Defeat: 2–10 v Swindon T, Southern League, 5 September 1908.

Most League Points (2 for a win): 64, Division 3 (S), 1950–51.

Most League Points (3 for a win): 84, Division 2, 1985–86.

Most League Goals: 99, Division 3 (S), 1952–53.

Highest League Scorer in Season: Ralph Hunt, 31, Division 3 (S), 1955–56.

Most League Goals in Total Aggregate: Johnny Gavin, 122, 1945–54, 1955–58.

Most League Goals in One Match: 5, Tommy Hunt v Coventry C, Division 3S, 15 March 1930; 5, Roy Hollis v Walsall, Division 3S, 29 December 1951.

Most Capped Player: Mark Bowen, 35 (41), Wales.

Most League Appearances: Ron Ashman, 592, 1947–64.

Youngest League Player: Ian Davies, 17 years 29 days v Birmingham C, 27 April 1974.

MANAGERS

John Bowman 1905–07
James McEwen 1907–08
Arthur Turner 1909–10
Bert Stansfield 1910–15
Major Frank Buckley 1919–20
Charles O'Hagan 1920–21
Albert Gosnell 1921–26
Bert Stansfield 1926
Cecil Potter 1926–29
James Kerr 1929–33
Tom Parker 1933–37
Bob Young 1937–39
Jimmy Jewell 1939
Bob Young 1939–45
Cyril Spiers 1946–47
Duggie Lochhead 1947–50
Norman Low 1950–55
Tom Parker 1955–57
Archie Macaulay 1957–61
Willie Reid 1961–62
George Swindin 1962
Ron Ashman 1962–66
Lol Morgan 1966–69
Ron Saunders 1969–73
John Bond 1973–80
Ken Brown 1980–87
Dave Stringer 1987–92
Mike Walker 1992–94
John Deehan 1994–95
Martin O'Neill 1995
Gary Megson 1995–96
Mike Walker 1996–98
Bruce Rioch 1998–2000
Bryan Hamilton April 2000–

Record Transfer Fee Received: £5,000,000 from Blackburn R for Chris Sutton, July 1994.

Record Transfer Fee Paid: £1,000,000 to Leeds U for Jon Newsome, June 1994.

Football League Record: 1920 Original Member of Division 3; 1921 Division 3 (S): 1934–39 Division 2; 1946–58 Division 3 (S); 1958–60 Division 3; 1960–72 Division 2; 1972–74 Division 1; 1974–75 Division 2; 1975–81 Division 1; 1981–82 Division 2; 1982–85 Division 1; 1985–86 Division 2; 1986–92 Division 1; 1992–95 FA Premier League; 1995– Division 1.

TEN YEAR LEAGUE RECORD

		P	W	D	L	F	A	Pts	Pos
1989-90	Div 1	38	13	14	11	44	40	53	10
1990-91	Div 1	38	13	6	19	41	64	45	15
1991-92	Div 1	42	11	12	19	47	63	45	18
1992-93	PR Lge	42	21	9	12	61	65	72	3
1993-94	PR Lge	42	12	17	13	65	61	53	12
1994-95	PR Lge	42	10	13	19	37	54	43	20
1995-96	Div 1	46	14	15	17	59	55	57	16
1996-97	Div 1	46	17	12	17	63	68	63	13
1997-98	Div 1	46	14	13	19	52	69	55	15
1998-99	Div 1	46	15	17	14	62	61	62	9

DID YOU KNOW ?

On 19 October 1946 Ralph 'Ginger' Johnson, with 123 wartime goals for the club, scored after just ten seconds against Leyton Orient in a 5-0 win. In April 1947 he was transferred to Orient.

NORWICH CITY 1999–2000 LEAGUE RECORD

Match No.	Date	Venue	Opponents	Result	H/T Score	Lg. Pos.	Goalscorers	Attendance
1	Aug 7	A	WBA	D	1-1	0-0	11	Dalglish 49	16,196
2	14	H	Birmingham C	L	0-1	0-1	17		15,261
3	21	A	Charlton Ath	L	0-1	0-0	22		19,623
4	28	H	Blackburn R	L	0-2	0-1	24		15,407
5	30	A	Walsall	D	2-2	1-1	24	Marshall L 35, Coote 90	6187
6	Sept 11	H	Crewe Alex	W	2-1	1-1	21	Roberts 19, Eadie 83	13,172
7	18	A	Huddersfield T	L	0-1	0-0	22		12,823
8	25	A	Stockport Co	D	2-2	1-1	20	Roberts 40, Dalglish 50	7603
9	28	H	Manchester C	W	1-0	1-0	—	Roberts 37	15,130
10	Oct 2	H	Fulham	L	1-2	1-0	19	Forbes 29	16,332
11	16	A	Port Vale	W	1-0	0-0	17	Fleming 82	5790
12	19	A	Sheffield U	D	0-0	0-0	—		11,907
13	24	H	Bolton W	W	2-1	0-0	13	Russell 2 50, 82	12,468
14	26	H	Stockport Co	W	2-0	1-0	—	Flynn (og) 42, Roberts 89	16,880
15	30	A	Fulham	D	1-1	0-1	12	Roberts 53	13,552
16	Nov 6	H	Nottingham F	W	1-0	1-0	12	Sutch 27	15,818
17	12	A	Swindon T	D	0-0	0-0	11		7405
18	21	H	Ipswich T	D	0-0	0-0	12		19,948
19	23	A	Crystal Palace	L	0-1	0-0	—		12,110
20	28	A	Grimsby T	L	1-2	1-1	14	Kenton 11	5333
21	Dec 4	H	WBA	W	2-1	1-1	13	Roberts 45, Russell 87	15,183
22	17	A	Tranmere R	W	2-1	0-1	—	Roberts 2 63, 89	5863
23	26	H	QPR	W	2-1	1-1	8	Breacker (og) 25, Llewellyn 87	17,823
24	28	A	Wolverhampton W	L	0-1	0-0	12		25,072
25	Jan 3	A	Portsmouth	W	2-1	2-0	10	Fleming 9, Roberts (pen) 25	16,637
26	8	H	Barnsley	D	2-2	1-0	9	Roberts 2 3, 50	14,039
27	15	A	Birmingham C	L	0-2	0-2	12		21,007
28	22	H	Charlton Ath	L	0-3	0-1	12		15,642
29	Feb 5	A	Walsall	D	1-1	1-1	13	Llewellyn 11	16,837
30	12	A	Manchester C	L	1-3	1-1	14	Roberts 15	32,681
31	19	H	Grimsby T	W	3-0	1-0	14	McDermott (og) 11, Russell 64, Llewellyn 74	13,533
32	26	H	Huddersfield T	D	1-1	0-0	13	Roberts 75	16,464
33	29	A	Blackburn R	D	1-1	1-0	—	Sutch 25	15,671
34	Mar 4	A	Crewe Alex	L	0-1	0-1	12		5450
35	8	A	Nottingham F	D	1-1	1-1	—	Roberts 28	15,640
36	11	H	Crystal Palace	L	0-1	0-0	15		15,064
37	19	A	Ipswich T	W	2-0	2-0	13	Roberts 2 19, 45	21,760
38	22	H	Swindon T	L	0-2	0-0	—		13,662
39	25	A	QPR	D	2-2	1-0	13	Marshall L 2 14, 58	11,918
40	Apr 1	H	Tranmere R	D	1-1	1-1	12	Marshall L 15	13,734
41	8	A	Portsmouth	L	1-2	1-0	13	Marshall L 44	14,003
42	15	H	Wolverhampton W	W	1-0	0-0	12	Roberts 50	15,910
43	22	H	Port Vale	D	0-0	0-0	12		15,526
44	24	A	Barnsley	L	1-2	0-2	12	Bellamy 67	15,253
45	29	H	Sheffield U	W	2-1	2-0	12	Fleming 4, Bellamy 11	16,921
46	May 7	A	Bolton W	L	0-1	0-0	12		17,987

Final League Position: 12

GOALSCORERS

League (45): Roberts 17 (1 pen), Marshall L 5, Russell 4, Fleming 3, Llewellyn 3, Bellamy 2, Dalglish 2, Sutch 2, Coote 1, Eadie 1, Forbes 1, Kenton 1, own goals 3.
Worthington Cup (3): Roberts 2, Marshall L 1.
FA Cup (1): Llewellyn 1.

Marshall A 44	Sutch D 44 + 1	Fuglestad E 26	de Blasiis Y 26 + 2	Fleming C 38 + 1	Jackson M 38	Anselin C 15 + 4	Dalglish P 22 + 9	Roberts I 44	Mulryne P 7 + 2	Llewellyn C 24 + 12	Marshall L 21 + 12	Diop P 2 + 5	MacKay M 16 + 5	Coote A 4 + 7	Carey S 18 + 3	Wilson C 2 + 3	Eadie D 12 + 1	Russell D 28 + 5	Kenton D 23 + 3	Forbes A 15 + 10	Milligan M 9 + 2	Green R 2 + 1	Hamilton D 7	Brady G 6	De Waard R 4	Derveld F 5	Giallanza G 2 + 1	Bellamy C 2 + 2	McVeigh P — + 1	Match No.
1	2	3	4	5	6	7	8	9	10	11¹	12																			1
1	2	3²	4	5	6⁵	7	8	9	10	11³	12	13	14																	2
1	2	3	4	5		7²	8	9	10¹	11³	12	13			6		14													3
1	2	3	4³	5		7	8	9	10¹	11²	12				6		13	14												4
1	2³	3²		5		7	12	9¹		13	8	14			6	11	10	4												5
1	2	3		5		7²	8³	9	4¹	13					6	12	10	11	14											6
1	2	3²		5			12	9		13	4				6	11¹	10		8	7										7
1	2			5	6		8	9		11	4						10	7	3											8
1	2			5	6		8¹	9		12	4					11	10	7	3											9
1	12			5	6		8	9		13	2¹					10	11	4	3	7²										10
1		3		5	6			9			4						8	11	7	2	10									11
1	2		4	5	6		12	9		13	8					11²		7	3	10¹										12
1	2		4	5	6		12	9			10					11		7	3	8¹										13
1	2		4	5	6			9			10					11		7	3	8										14
1	2		4	5¹	6	14		9		12	10²					11		7	3	8	13³									15
1	2		4		6		12	9		7	5					11		3	8¹	10										16
1	2		4		6			9		12	5	13				11¹		7	3	8²	10									17
1	2		4	5	6					12	11²	13				7¹		8	3	9	10									18
1	2		4	5	6		8²	9		12	10							7	3	13	11¹									19
1	2		4	5	6		12	9		13	11							7	3²	8¹	10									20
1	2	3	4	5	6	7	8¹	9		11								10		12										21
1	2	3	4	5	6	7		9		11	12							8	10¹											22
1	2	3	4	5	6	7		9		11								10	8											23
1	2	3	4²	5	6	7¹		9		11	12							10	13	8										24
1	2	10	4³	5	6	7²		9		11	12						14	8¹	3	13										25
1	2	10²	4	5	6	7¹		9		11	12						13	8	3											26
1	2		4⁶		6	7¹	12	9		8	5					11		10	3	15										27
1	2	10¹			6		12	9		11	13				5		4²	7	3	8										28
	2	3			6		8¹	9		11	4				5	12		10	13	7²										29
	2	3	12		6		8	9		11	13				5		4²	7¹	14	10³			1							30
1	7	3	4¹		6		8	9		11					5		10	13	12	2²										31
1	4	3	12	13	6²		8	9		11³					5		10¹	7	2	14										32
1	7	3	4		6		8¹	9		11					5		10	2	12											33
1	7¹	3	4		6		8	9		11					5		10	2	12											34
1	7	3	4	5	6		8¹	9		11					12		10	2²	13											35
1	2	3	4²	5	6		8¹	9		11					12			7	13	10										36
1	2	3		5	6	12	8¹	9²		11					4			13	7	10										37
1	2	3		5	6	12	8			11²					4		9	7	13	10¹										38
1	2	3		5	6		8²	9		12					4		13						7	10	11¹					39
1	2	3		5	6¹			9		7³					4		12		14	13				8	10²	11				40
1	2			5	6			9		10³	12				4		13		14	3				8	7²	11¹				41
1	2			5	6			9		12	11³				4		13			10				8¹	7	3²	14			42
1	2			5	6	7¹		9		13					4		12							8²	11	3	10³	14		43
1	2			5			8	9		12					4		6			13				7³	10²	11¹	3	14		44
1	2			5	6			9		10	12				4		13			14				8²	11¹	3³	7			45
1	2			5	6	7¹		9		10	13				4		12¹								3	8³	11	14		46

Worthington Cup

First Round	Cheltenham T	(h)	2-0
		(a)	1-2
Second Round	Fulham	(h)	0-4
		(a)	0-2

FA Cup

Third Round	Coventry C	(h)	1-3

Division 1   **NOTTINGHAM FOREST**

FOUNDATION

One of the oldest football clubs in the world, Nottingham Forest was formed at a meeting in the Clinton Arms in 1865. Known originally as the Forest Football Club, the game which first drew the founders together was 'shinney', a form of hockey. When they determined to change to football in 1865, one of their first moves was to buy a set of red caps to wear on the field.

City Ground, Nottingham NG2 5FJ.
Telephone: (0115) 982 4444.
Fax: (0115) 982 4455.
Information Desk: (0115) 982 4449.
Commercial Office: (0115) 982 4450. *Fax:* (0115) 982 4410.
Ticket Office: (0115) 982 4445. *Souvenir Shop:* (0115) 982 4447. *Junior Reds:* (0115) 982 4454.
ClubCall: 09068 121 174.
Ground Capacity: 30,602.
Record Attendance: 49,946 v Manchester U, Division 1, 28 October 1967.
Record Receipts: £499,099 v Bayern Munich, UEFA Cup quarter-final 2nd leg, 19 March 1996.
Pitch Measurements: 116yd × 76yd.
Chairman: E. M. Barnes.
Chief Executive: M. A. Arthur.
Finance Director: J. D. Pelling.
Board of Directors: E. M. Barnes, M. A. Arthur, J. D. Pelling, N. G. Candeland, T. H. Farr, Sir David White.
Manager: David Platt.
First Team Coach: Steve Wigley.
Reserve Team Coach: Jimmy Gilligan.
Youth Academy Director: Paul Hart.
Physio: John Haselden.
Secretary: Paul White.
Public Relations Manager: Nick Lucy.
Football Press Officer: Fraser Nicholson.

LATEST SEQUENCES

Longest Sequence of League Wins: 7, 9.5.79 – 1.9.79.
Longest Sequence of League Defeats: 14, 21.3.13 – 27.9.13.
Longest Sequence of League Draws: 7, 29.4.78 – 2.9.78.
Longest Sequence of Unbeaten League Matches: 42, 26.11.77 – 25.11.78.
Longest Sequence Without a League Win: 19, 8.9.98 – 16.1.99.

HONOURS

Football League: Division 1 – Champions 1977–78, 1997–98; Runners-up 1966–67, 1978–79; Division 2 – Champions 1906–07, 1921–22; Runners-up 1956–57; Division 3 (S) – Champions 1950–51.

FA Cup: Winners 1898, 1959; Runners-up 1991.

Football League Cup: Winners 1978, 1979, 1989, 1990; Runners-up 1980, 1992.

Anglo-Scottish Cup: Winners 1977; *Simod Cup:* Winners 1989.

Zenith Data Systems Cup: Winners: 1992.

European Competitions: *European Fairs Cup:* 1961–62, 1967–68. *European Cup:* 1978–79 (winners), 1979–80 (winners), 1980–81. *Super Cup:* 1979–80 (winners), 1980–81 (runners-up). *World Club Championship:* 1980. *UEFA Cup:* 1983–84, 1984–85, 1995–96.

Colours

Red shirts, white shorts, red stockings.

Change Colours

White shirts, red shorts, white stockings.

Year Formed: 1865.

Turned Professional: 1889.

Ltd Co.: 1982.

Club Nickname: 'Reds'.

Previous Grounds: 1865, Forest Racecourse; 1879, The Meadows; 1880, Trent Bridge Cricket Ground; 1882, Parkside, Lenton; 1885, Gregory, Lenton; 1890, Town Ground; 1898, City Ground.

First Football League Game: 3 September 1892, Division 1, v Everton (a) D 2–2 – Brown; Earp, Scott; Hamilton, A. Smith, McCracken; McCallum, W. Smith, Higgins (2), Pike, McInnes.

Record League Victory: 12–0 v Leicester Fosse, Division 1, 12 April 1909 – Iremonger; Dudley, Maltby; Hughes (1), Needham, Armstrong; Hooper (3), Marrison, West (3), Morris (2), Spouncer (3 incl. 1p).

Record Cup Victory: 14–0 v Clapton (away), FA Cup 1st rd, 17 January 1891 – Brown; Earp, Scott; A. Smith, Russell, Jeacock; McCallum (2), 'Tich' Smith (1), Higgins (5), Lindley (4), Shaw (2).

Record Defeat: 1–9 v Blackburn R, Division 2, 10 April 1937.

Most League Points (2 for a win): 70, Division 3 (S), 1950–51.

Most League Points (3 for a win): 94, Division 1, 1997–98.

Most League Goals: 110, Division 3 (S), 1950–51.

Highest League Scorer in Season: Wally Ardron, 36, Division 3 (S), 1950–51.

Most League Goals in Total Aggregate: Grenville Morris, 199, 1898–1913.

Most League Goals in One Match: 4, Enoch West v Sunderland, Division 1, 9 November 1907; 4, Tommy Gibson v Burnley, Division 2, 25 January 1913; 4, Tom Peacock v Port Vale, Division 2, 23 December 1933; 4, Tom Peacock v Barnsley, Division 2, 9 November 1935; 4, Tom Peacock v Port Vale, Division 2, 23 November 1935; 4, Tom Peacock v Doncaster R, Division 2, 26 December 1935; 4, Tommy Capel v Gillingham, Division 3S, 18 November 1950; 4, Wally Ardron v Hull C, Division 2, 26 December 1952; 4, Tommy Wilson v Barnsley, Division 2, 9 February 1957; 4, Peter Withe v Ipswich T, Division 1, 4 October 1977.

Most Capped Player: Stuart Pearce, 76 (78), England.

Most League Appearances: Bob McKinlay, 614, 1951–70.

Youngest League Player: Gary Mills, 16 years 302 days v Arsenal, 9 September 1978.

Record Transfer Fee Received: £8,500,000 from Liverpool for Stan Collymore, June 1995.

Record Transfer Fee Paid: £3,500,000 to Celtic for Pierre van Hooijdonk, March 1997.

Football League Record: 1892 Elected to Division 1; 1906–07 Division 2; 1907–11 Division 1; 1911–22 Division 2; 1922–25 Division 1; 1925–49 Division 2; 1949–51 Division 3 (S); 1951–57 Division 2; 1957–72 Division 1; 1972–77 Division 2; 1977–92 Division 1; 1992–93 FA Premier League; 1993–94 Division 1; 1994–97 FA Premier League; 1997–98 Division 1; 1998–99 FA Premier League; 1999– Division 1.

MANAGERS

Harry Radford 1889–97
(Secretary-Manager)
Harry Haslam 1897–1909
(Secretary-Manager)
Fred Earp 1909–12
Bob Masters 1912–25
John Baynes 1925–29
Stan Hardy 1930–31
Noel Watson 1931–36
Harold Wightman 1936–39
Billy Walker 1939–60
Andy Beattie 1960–63
Johnny Carey 1963–68
Matt Gillies 1969–72
Dave Mackay 1972
Allan Brown 1973–75
Brian Clough 1975–93
Frank Clark 1993–96
Stuart Pearce 1996–97
Dave Bassett 1997–98 *(previously General Manager from February)*
Ron Atkinson 1998–99
David Platt July 1999–

TEN YEAR LEAGUE RECORD

		P	W	D	L	F	A	Pts	Pos
1989-90	Div 1	38	15	9	14	55	47	54	9
1990-91	Div 1	38	14	12	12	65	50	54	8
1991-92	Div 1	42	16	11	15	60	58	59	8
1992-93	PR Lge	42	10	10	22	41	62	40	22
1993-94	Div 1	46	23	14	9	74	49	83	2
1994-95	PR Lge	42	22	11	9	72	43	77	3
1995-96	PR Lge	38	15	13	10	50	54	58	9
1996-97	PR Lge	38	6	16	16	31	59	34	20
1997-98	Div 1	46	28	10	8	82	42	94	1
1998-99	PR Lge	38	7	9	22	35	69	30	20

DID YOU KNOW

On 7 May 1938, Nottingham Forest, reduced to ten men through injury, drew 2-2 at Barnsley to escape relegation while their opponents went down by one-200th part of a goal behind Forest, with both clubs on 36 points.

NOTTINGHAM FOREST 1999–2000 LEAGUE RECORD

Match No.	Date	Venue	Opponents	Result	H/T Score	Lg. Pos.	Goalscorers	Attendance
1	Aug 7	A	Ipswich T	L	1-3	0-2	23	Bart-Williams (pen) [76]	20,830
2	14	H	Grimsby T	W	2-1	1-0	12	Freedman [27], Palmer [87]	17,121
3	20	A	WBA	D	1-1	0-0	—	Freedman [62]	13,202
4	28	H	QPR	D	1-1	1-0	14	Wright [29]	18,442
5	30	A	Manchester C	L	0-1	0-1	16		31,857
6	Sept 4	H	Walsall	W	4-1	1-1	8	Freedman 2 [43, 76], Chettle (pen) [71], Wright [86]	15,081
7	11	A	Swindon T	D	0-0	0-0	9		8203
8	19	H	Wolverhampton W	D	1-1	0-1	11	Allou [46]	20,694
9	25	A	Bolton W	L	2-3	0-1	14	Freedman [47], Wright (pen) [50]	14,978
10	Oct 1	H	Barnsley	W	3-0	0-0	—	Rogers [63], Bonalair [68], Freedman [90]	15,255
11	16	A	Sheffield U	L	1-2	1-0	15	Freedman [43]	15,687
12	19	A	Port Vale	W	2-0	2-0	—	Bonalair [6], Wright [44]	5714
13	23	H	Stockport Co	D	1-1	1-1	11	Wright [16]	15,770
14	27	H	Bolton W	D	1-1	1-1	—	Harewood [32]	15,572
15	30	A	Barnsley	L	0-1	0-0	15		14,727
16	Nov 6	A	Norwich C	L	0-1	0-1	16		15,818
17	14	H	Huddersfield T	L	1-3	1-2	16	Rogers [45]	15,258
18	20	A	Tranmere R	L	0-3	0-0	18		6693
19	24	H	Portsmouth	W	2-0	2-0	—	John [6], Beck [11]	13,841
20	27	A	Crystal Palace	L	0-2	0-1	18		15,920
21	Dec 5	H	Ipswich T	L	0-1	0-0	19		15,724
22	15	H	Fulham	D	0-0	0-0	—		14,250
23	18	H	Crewe Alex	W	1-0	0-0	19	John [75]	15,289
24	26	A	Blackburn R	L	1-2	1-1	20	Johnson [31]	23,406
25	28	H	Birmingham C	W	1-0	0-0	17	Harewood [81]	20,821
26	Jan 3	A	Charlton Ath	L	0-3	0-1	17		19,787
27	15	A	Grimsby T	L	3-4	1-2	18	Rogers 2 [33, 90], Lever (og) [47]	6738
28	22	H	WBA	D	0-0	0-0	18		19,863
29	29	A	QPR	D	1-1	0-0	18	Quashie [12]	12,297
30	Feb 5	H	Manchester C	L	1-3	1-2	18	Bart-Williams [9]	25,846
31	12	A	Walsall	W	2-0	1-0	18	Rogers [43], Freedman [90]	8027
32	19	H	Crystal Palace	W	2-0	1-0	18	Rogers [13], Quashie [51]	16,421
33	26	A	Wolverhampton W	L	0-3	0-3	18		24,444
34	Mar 4	H	Swindon T	W	3-1	3-0	17	Rogers [32], Bart-Williams (pen) [36], Freedman [42]	19,748
35	8	H	Norwich C	D	1-1	1-1	—	Lester [1]	15,640
36	11	A	Portsmouth	L	1-2	0-0	19	Johnson [80]	14,336
37	18	H	Tranmere R	D	1-1	0-1	18	Harewood [66]	14,428
38	21	A	Huddersfield T	L	1-2	1-1	—	Harewood [21]	12,893
39	25	H	Blackburn R	L	0-1	0-1	19		16,823
40	Apr 1	A	Crewe Alex	W	3-0	1-0	19	Prutton [25], Rogers 2 [53, 79]	7014
41	8	H	Charlton Ath	D	1-1	0-1	19	Bart-Williams (pen) [81]	20,922
42	15	A	Birmingham C	W	1-0	1-0	17	Purse (og) [40]	23,006
43	22	H	Sheffield U	D	0-0	0-0	17		17,172
44	24	A	Fulham	D	1-1	1-1	17	Lester [20]	12,696
45	29	H	Port Vale	W	2-0	2-0	15	John [11], Prutton [34]	15,534
46	May 7	A	Stockport Co	W	3-2	2-1	14	Bart-Williams [33], Taylor (og) [37], Flynn (og) [55]	7756

Final League Position: 14

GOALSCORERS

League (53): Freedman 9, Rogers 9, Bart-Williams 5 (3 pens), Wright 5 (1 pen), Harewood 4, John 3, Bonalair 2, Johnson 2, Lester 2, Prutton 2, Quashie 2, Allou 1, Beck 1, Chettle 1 (pen), Palmer 1, own goals 4.
Worthington Cup (6): Allou 1, Bart-Williams 1, Freedman 1, Harewood 1, Quashie 1, Rogers 1.
FA Cup (4): Bart-Williams 2 (1 pen), Freedman 1, Rogers 1.

Crossley M 19+1	Louis-Jean M 26+1	Edds G 2	Cooper R —+1	Bonalair T 10+2	Mannini M 7+1	Matrecano S 11	Scimeca R 38	Bart-Williams C 38	Quashie N 25+3	Freedman D 28+6	Petrachi G 10+3	Rogers A 36+1	Harewood M 18+16	Aliou B 1+3	Chettle S 10+1	Palmer C 1+2	Guinan S —+1	Melton S 1+1	Wright I 10	Burns J 3	Platt D 1+2	Hjelde J 26+7	Beasant D 27	Prutton D 33+1	Doig C 8+3	Merino C 3+6	Woan I 1+10	Freeman D —+3	Brennan J 22+3	Johnson A 24+1	Gray A 12+10	Beck M 5	John S 13+4	Dawson K 4+3	Williams G —+2	Lester J 12+3	Vaughan T 10	Calderwood C 6	Terry J 5+1	Match No.
1	2	3^1	4	5	6	7	8	9	10^2	11	12	13																												1
1				4	5	11	7	8^1	9	2	3	10^2			6	12	13																							2
1	2			4^2	5	10	11	8	9	7^1	3	12			6	13																								3
1	2^3				5	11		8	9^1	7^2	3	12	13	4	6				14	10																				4
1	2			4^2	6			9	7^1	3	12	5							8	10		13																		5
	2			4	6		8	9	7	3		5							10	11^1	12		1																	6
1	2			4	6		8	9^1	7^3	3	12	5^2							10	11	14	13																		7
1	2	12		4	6		8	9^2		3	13	7	5^1						10	11^3		14																		8
	2^1	7	13	4^2	6		8	9		3		12							10		5	1	11																	9
1		2	4		6		8	9	7^3	3	12								10^1		5^2	11	13	14																10
1	2	7		5	6		8	9		3	12								10^1	4		11^2	13																	11
1	2	7		5^1	6	11	8^3	9		3^2									10		12		4	13	14															12
1	2	7			6	11	8^1	9		3								10		5	12	4																	13
1	2	7			6	11^1	8	9	12	3^2	10		13						5			4^1	14																	14
1	2	7^2			6	11^1		9	12		10^3	5							4	8			13	14	3															15
1	2					10		9	7^1			5							6	8		11		3	4	12														16
1		2^1				11		9^2	7^3	12		5							4	8			13	3	6	14	10													17
1			2^3			5	10^1	12			11								4	8		6^2	13	3	7	14	9													18
1			2^3			5	8	13	12		11^2								4	7	14			3	6		9	10^1												19
1						5	8^2	13	12		2								4	7	14			3	6	11^3	9^1	10												20
						6	11	8	12										4	1	7	2	5^2			3		13	9^1	10									21
						5	11	8	9^1			12							4	1	7						3	2		10	6								22
						5	11	8^2	9^1			12							4	1	7	6					3	13	2		10								23
						5	11^2					10							4	1	7	6	12				3	8	2^1		9		13						24
						5	11		12			10							4	1	7	6					3	8	2		9	5							25
						5	11	12				10^1							4	1	7						3	8^2	2		9	6	13						26
15	13^G	12				5	8		9		11								4	1	7						3		2^1	10	6^2								27
	2	6^2				5	8		9	13		12							4	1	7						3		11	10^1									28
1	2					5	10	8	9		11								7	6							3		4										29
	2					5^1	6	8^1	9		11	12								4^2	13						3	7			14	10							30
	2						11	8^2	12		3	9^1							4	1	7							6	13			10	5						31
	2						11	8	12		3	9^1							4	1	7							6			10	5							32
	2^3			4	6		8^1			3	9^2								1	7		13						11	14		12	10	5						33
	2			4	6	8	9			3	12								1	7							13	11^2			10	5							34
	2			4	6^3	8	9			3	12								1	7^2							13	11	14		10^1	5							35
	2			4^2	6	8				11	12								1			14					3	7	9^1		13	10	5^3						36
	2				6	8^2	9			11	12								1	7		13					3	4				10^1		5					37
	2^3				6		9^1			11	10								4	1	7^2		13				3	8	14	12				5					38
	2^3				6		9^1			11	10								4	1	7		13				3^2	8		12		14		5					39
						2	6			11	10								4^3	1	7^2		13				12	8		9^3		14	3^1	5					40
						2	6			11	10								4^3	1	7^3						3	8	12		9^2		13		5	14			41
						2	6			11	9								4	1	7						3	8			10		5^1	4					42
						2	11			3	9^1								4	1	7						8^2	13	12		10	5	6						43
						2	6			3	9^2								12	1	7						8	11	13		10	5^1	4						44
		3^2				2	6			11	10								12	1	7		13				8		9			5^1	4						45
		3	13	2	6					11^1	9^2								4	1	7		12				8				10		5						46

Worthington Cup

First Round	Mansfield T	(h)	3-0
		(a)	0-1
Second Round	Bristol C	(h)	2-1
		(a)	0-0
Third Round	Sheffield W	(a)	1-4

FA Cup

Third Round	Oxford U	(h)	1-1
		(a)	3-1
Fourth Round	Chelsea	(a)	0-2

Division 2

NOTTS COUNTY

FOUNDATION

According to the official history of Notts County 'the true date of Notts' foundation has to be the meeting at the George Hotel on 7 December 1864'. However, in the same opening chapter is the following: The Nottingham Guardian on 28 November 1862 carried the following report:- 'The opening of the Nottingham Football Club commenced on Tuesday last at Cremorne Gardens. A side was chosen by W. Arkwright and Chas Deakin. A very spirited game resulted in the latter scoring two goals and two rouges against one and one'.

County Ground, Meadow Lane, Nottingham NG2 3HJ.
Telephone: (0115) 952 9000. *Fax:* (0115) 955 3994.
Ticket Office: (0115) 955 7210. *ClubCall:* 09068 888 684.
Football in the Community: (0115) 955 7215.
Supporters Club: (0115) 955 7255.
Ground Capacity: 20,300.
Record Attendance: 47,310 v York C, FA Cup 6th rd, 12 March 1955.
Record Receipts: £124,539.10 v Manchester C, FA Cup 6th rd, 16 February 1991.
Pitch Measurements: 114yd × 74yd.
Chairman: D. C. Pavis.
Vice-Chairman: J. Mounteney.
Directors: W. Barrowcliffe, Mrs V. Pavis, M. Youdell MBE, G. Davey (Managing).
Manager: Jocky Scott.
Assistant Manager: Gary Brazil.
Youth Coach: John Gaunt.
Secretary: Tony Cuthbert.
Commercial Manager: Linda Patterson.
Conference & Banqueting Manager: Matthew Foote.
Physio: Roger Cleary.
Stadium Manager: Bob Davy.
Year Formed: 1862* (*see Foundation*).
Turned Professional: 1885.
Ltd Co.: 1888.
Club Nickname: 'Magpies'.
Previous Grounds: 1862, The Park; 1864, The Meadows; 1877, Beeston Cricket Ground; 1880, Castle Ground; 1883, Trent Bridge; 1910, Meadow Lane.

LATEST SEQUENCES
Longest Sequence of League Wins: 10, 3.12.97 – 31.1.98.
Longest Sequence of League Defeats: 7, 3.9.83 – 16.10.83.
Longest Sequence of League Draws: 5, 2.12.78 – 26.12.78.
Longest Sequence of Unbeaten League Matches: 19, 26.4.30 – 6.12.30.
Longest Sequence Without a League Win: 20, 3.12.96 – 31.3.97.

HONOURS

Football League: Division 1 best season: 3rd, 1890–91, 1900–01; Division 2 – Champions 1896–97, 1913–14, 1922–23; Runners-up 1894–95, 1980–81; Promoted from Division 2 1990–91 (play-offs); Division 3 (S) – Champions 1930–31, 1949–50; Runners-up 1936–37; Division 3 – Champions 1997–98; Runners-up 1972–73; Promoted from Division 3 1989–90 (play-offs); Division 4 – Champions 1970–71; Runners-up 1959–60.

FA Cup: Winners 1894; Runners-up 1891.

Football League Cup: best season: 5th rd, 1964, 1973, 1976.

Anglo-Italian Cup: Winners 1995; Runners-up 1994.

Colours
Black and white striped shirts, black shorts, black stockings.

Change Colours
All royal blue.

First Football League Game: 15 September 1888, Football League, v Everton (a) L 1–2 – Holland; Guttridge, McLean; Brown, Warburton, Shelton; Hodder, Harker, Jardine, Moore (1), Wardle.

Record League Victory: 11–1 v Newport Co, Division 3 (S), 15 January 1949 – Smith; Southwell, Purvis; Gannon, Baxter, Adamson; Houghton (1), Sewell (4), Lawton (4), Pimbley, Johnston (2).

Record Cup Victory: 15–0 v Rotherham T (at Trent Bridge), FA Cup 1st rd, 24 October 1885 – Sherwin; Snook, H. T. Moore; Dobson (1), Emmett (1), Chapman; Gunn (1), Albert Moore (2), Jackson (3), Daft (2), Cursham (4), (1 og).

Record Defeat: 1–9 v Blackburn R, Division 1, 16 November 1889. 1–9 v Aston Villa, Division 1, 29 September 1888. 1–9 v Portsmouth, Division 2, 9 April 1927.

Most League Points (2 for a win): 69, Division 4, 1970–71.

Most League Points (3 for a win): 99, Division 3, 1997–98.

Most League Goals: 107, Division 4, 1959–60.

Highest League Scorer in Season: Tom Keetley, 39, Division 3 (S), 1930–31.

Most League Goals in Total Aggregate: Les Bradd, 124, 1967–78.

Most League Goals in One Match: 5, Robert Jardine v Burnley, Division 1, 27 October 1888; 5, Daniel Bruce v Port Vale, Division 2, 26 February 1895; 5, Bertie Mills v Barnsley, Division 2, 19 November 1927.

Most Capped Player: Kevin Wilson, 15 (42), Northern Ireland.

Most League Appearances: Albert Iremonger, 564, 1904–26.

Youngest League Player: Tony Bircumshaw, 16 years 54 days v Brentford, 3 April 1961.

Record Transfer Fee Received: £2,500,000 from Derby Co for Craig Short, September 1992.

Record Transfer Fee Paid: £685,000 to Sheffield U for Tony Agana, November 1991.

Football League Record: 1888 Founder Member of the Football League; 1893–97 Division 2; 1897–1913 Division 1; 1913–14 Division 2; 1914–20 Division 1; 1920–23 Division 2; 1923–26 Division 1; 1926–30 Division 2; 1930–31 Division 3 (S); 1931–35 Division 2; 1935–50 Division 3 (S); 1950–58 Division 2; 1958–59 Division 3; 1959–60 Division 4; 1960–64 Division 3; 1964–71 Division 4; 1971–73 Division 3; 1973–81 Division 2; 1981–84 Division 1; 1984–85 Division 2; 1985–90 Division 3; 1990–91 Division 2; 1991–95 Division 1; 1995–97 Division 2; 1997–98 Division 3; 1998– Division 2.

MANAGERS

Edwin Browne 1883–93
  (Secretary-Manager)
Tom Featherstone 1893
  (Secretary-Manager)
Tom Harris 1893–1913 *(Secretary-Manager)*
Albert Fisher 1913–27
Horace Henshall 1927–34
Charlie Jones 1934–35
David Pratt 1935
Percy Smith 1935–36
Jimmy McMullan 1936–37
Harry Parkes 1938–39
Tony Towers 1939–42
Frank Womack 1942–43
Major Frank Buckley 1944–46
Arthur Stollery 1946–49
Eric Houghton 1949–53
George Poyser 1953–57
Tommy Lawton 1957–58
Frank Hill 1958–61
Tim Coleman 1961–63
Eddie Lowe 1963–65
Tim Coleman 1965–66
Jack Burkitt 1966–67
Andy Beattie *(General Manager)* 1967
Billy Gray 1967–68
Jimmy Sirrel 1969–75
Ron Fenton 1975–77
Jimmy Sirrel 1978–82
  (continued as General Manager to 1984)
Howard Wilkinson 1982–83
Larry Lloyd 1983–84
Richie Barker 1984–85
Jimmy Sirrel 1985–87
John Barnwell 1987–88
Neil Warnock 1989–93
Mick Walker 1993–94
Russell Slade 1994–95
Howard Kendall 1995
Colin Murphy June 1995
  (continued as General Manager to 1996)
Steve Thompson 1996
Sam Allardyce 1997–1999
Gary Brazil 1999–2000
Jocky Scott June 2000–

TEN YEAR LEAGUE RECORD

		P	W	D	L	F	A	Pts	Pos
1989-90	Div 3	46	25	12	9	73	53	87	3
1990-91	Div 2	46	23	11	12	76	55	80	4
1991-92	Div 1	42	10	10	22	40	62	40	21
1992-93	Div 1	46	12	16	18	55	70	52	17
1993-94	Div 1	46	20	8	18	65	69	68	7
1994-95	Div 1	46	9	13	24	45	66	40	24
1995-96	Div 2	46	21	15	10	63	39	78	4
1996-97	Div 2	46	7	14	25	33	59	35	24
1997-98	Div 3	46	29	12	5	82	43	99	1
1998-99	Div 2	46	14	12	20	52	61	54	16

DID YOU KNOW ?

Notts County twice broke the British transfer record, signing Tommy Lawton from Chelsea in November 1947 for £20,000 and transferring Jackie Sewell to Sheffield Wednesday in March 1951 for £34,500.

NOTTS COUNTY 1999–2000 LEAGUE RECORD

Match No.	Date	Venue	Opponents	Result	H/T Score	Lg. Pos.	Goalscorers	Attendance
1	Aug 7	H	Luton T	D	0-0	0-0	16		6141
2	14	A	Colchester U	W	3-0	2-0	3	Hughes [5], Stallard [35], Blackmore [79]	3986
3	21	H	Scunthorpe U	W	3-0	2-0	1	Ramage [31], Stallard 2 [33, 50]	5506
4	28	A	Cambridge U	D	1-1	0-0	4	Stallard [86]	4329
5	Sept 3	A	Wrexham	W	3-2	3-0	—	Darby 2 [25, 42], Stallard [44]	5030
6	11	H	Blackpool	W	2-1	0-0	2	Ramage [60], Stallard [81]	5512
7	18	A	Cardiff C	L	1-2	0-0	4	Stallard [55]	6568
8	25	H	Bristol R	L	0-2	0-0	5		6197
9	Oct 2	A	Oldham Ath	W	2-1	1-1	5	Darby [38], Ramage [67]	5143
10	9	A	Bury	W	3-1	1-0	2	Stallard [4], Blackmore [64], Owers [86]	3620
11	16	H	Wycombe W	W	2-1	1-1	2	Fenton [45], Richardson [49]	5710
12	19	H	Chesterfield	W	1-0	0-0	—	Ramage [82]	4749
13	23	A	Bristol R	W	1-0	0-0	1	Rapley [82]	8188
14	26	H	Brentford	L	0-1	0-0	—		5075
15	Nov 3	A	Stoke C	W	1-0	1-0	—	Dyer [23]	11,619
16	6	H	Gillingham	D	1-1	1-1	1	Allsopp [2]	6023
17	12	A	Preston NE	L	0-2	0-2	3		14,226
18	23	H	Oxford U	L	0-1	0-0	—		4020
19	27	H	Bristol C	D	4-4	2-1	6	Holland (og) [29], Stallard [30], Dyer [71], Warren [85]	5374
20	Dec 4	A	Luton T	D	2-2	0-2	7	Richardson [54], Owers [73]	5195
21	11	H	Bournemouth	W	5-1	4-0	6	Angell 3 [1, 8, 59], Richardson [6], Stallard [42]	4199
22	18	A	Millwall	L	0-1	0-0	7		7917
23	26	H	Wigan Ath	L	0-2	0-1	7		8176
24	28	A	Reading	D	0-0	0-0	7		7703
25	Jan 3	H	Burnley	W	2-0	1-0	7	Angell 2 [14, 62]	8229
26	8	A	Bournemouth	D	1-1	0-0	7	Owers [70]	4344
27	15	H	Colchester U	L	1-2	0-2	7	Stallard [65]	4931
28	22	A	Scunthorpe U	L	0-1	0-1	7		4035
29	Feb 5	A	Brentford	W	2-0	1-0	8	Tierney [11], Rapley [70]	5106
30	12	H	Wrexham	W	2-1	1-0	8	Dyer [35], Hughes [48]	5474
31	15	H	Cambridge U	L	2-3	2-1	—	Owers [2], Hughes (pen) [28]	4053
32	19	A	Bristol C	D	2-2	0-2	7	Liburd [60], Hughes (pen) [77]	10,029
33	26	H	Cardiff C	W	2-1	0-1	7	Hughes (pen) [80], Dyer [89]	5334
34	Mar 4	A	Blackpool	L	1-2	0-1	8	Stallard [59]	4277
35	7	A	Gillingham	W	1-0	0-0	—	Richardson [60]	6915
36	11	H	Stoke C	D	0-0	0-0	8		9677
37	18	A	Oxford U	W	3-2	3-1	7	Dyer [14], Hughes 2 (1 pen) [19, 39 (p)]	4544
38	21	H	Preston NE	W	1-0	1-0	—	Redmile [4]	6401
39	25	A	Wigan Ath	L	0-2	0-1	7		6094
40	Apr 1	H	Millwall	D	1-1	0-1	8	Darby [61]	7032
41	8	A	Burnley	L	1-2	0-1	8	Stallard [86]	13,022
42	15	H	Reading	L	1-2	0-0	8	Darby [58]	4791
43	21	A	Wycombe W	L	0-2	0-1	—		4369
44	24	H	Oldham Ath	L	0-1	0-0	8		3728
45	29	A	Chesterfield	L	1-2	1-0	8	Bolland [33]	2455
46	May 6	H	Bury	D	2-2	1-0	8	Dyer [21], Stallard [83]	4017

Final League Position: 8

GOALSCORERS

League (61): Stallard 14, Hughes 7 (4 pens), Dyer 6, Angell 5, Darby 5, Owers 4, Ramage 4, Richardson 4, Blackmore 2, Rapley 2, Allsopp 1, Bolland 1, Fenton 1, Liburd 1, Redmile 1, Tierney 1, Warren 1, own goal 1.
Worthington Cup (5): Blackmore 2, Ramage 2 (1 pen), Darby 1.
FA Cup (3): Rapley 1, Redmile 1, Tierney 1.

Notts County — appearance and goalscoring grid. Column headings give each player with total appearances (+ substitute appearances); superscript figures against shirt numbers denote goals scored.

Ward D 45	Holmes R 38+3	Blackmore C 21	Warren M 31+2	Redmile M 39+2	Richardson I 33	Liburd R 24+7	Ramage C 36+4	Stallard M 31+5	Beadle P 1+7	Murray S 4+5	Bolland P 18+7	Robson M —+2	Darby D 22+6	Owers G 45	Hughes A 32+3	Dyer A 21+9	Rapley K 11+18	Pearce D 14+6	Lindley J —+1	Fenton N 13	Tierney F 6+7	Allsopp D 3	Angell B 6	Webster A —+1	Farrell S —+9	Howell D —+1	Brough M 11	Gibson P 1	Heffernan P —+2	Cross D —+1	Ford R —+1	Match No.
1	2	3	4	5¹	6	7²	8	9³	10	11	12	13	14																			1
1	2	3	4	5	6		8¹	9²					13	11³	7	10	12	14														2
1	2	3¹	4	5	6	12	8	9²					13	11³	7	10	14															3
1	2²	3¹	4	5	6		8	9					13	11³	7	10	14	12														4
1	2	3	4	5	6		8³	9²	12				14	11¹	7	10	13															5
1	2¹	3	4	5	6		8	9				13	14	11²	7³	10	12															6
1⁶	2	3¹	4	5	6		8	9					13	11²	7	10	12			15												7
1	2	3	4	5	6		8³	9²	12					11¹	7	10	13	14														8
1	2	3	4	13	6		8	9						11¹	7	10	12²			5												9
1	2	3²		5			8	9¹					13	11	7	10	12				6		4									10
1	2			5	6²		8	9¹	12					11	7	10	13					3	4									11
1	2		3²	5	6		8	9						11¹	7	10	12			13			4									12
1	2	4		5	6	3¹	8	9³	12					11²	7	10	13	14														13
1	2	4		5	6	3	8	9	12					11²	7	10¹	13															14
1	2			5	6	3¹	8	9	12			14		11	7	10²	13						4³									15
1	2¹	3		5	6	4	8	9				13		11²	7	12	10															16
1	2	3¹		5	6	4	8	9	12					11¹	7	10²	13	14														17
1	2	3	12	5¹	6	4	8	9²			11	13		7	10																	18
1	2³	4		5		3	8	9¹			12	14		11	7	10	13				6²											19
1	2²	4		5	6	3	8¹	9	12		11	13		7	10																	20
1	2	3¹	4	5	6		8	9²					12	11	7	10	13									9²						21
1	2	3	4	5	6		8	9					12	11¹	7	10²	13									9						22
1	2	3	4	5	6	12	8	9						11²	7	10¹	13									9						23
1	2¹	3²	4	5³	6	12	8	9	10			14		11	7	10	13						11			9						24
1	2			5	6	3	8¹	10			12			11	7							4				9						25
1	2	4		5¹	6	3	8	10						11²	7	12	13									9						26
1	2³	4		5²	6	3	8	9				13		11¹	7	12	10	14														27
1	2	4			6	3	8							7	10	9¹	5				11				12							28
1	2	4			6	3	12	13						7¹	8	10	9²	5			11											29
1	2¹	4			6	3	12	13						7	10	8²	9	5			11											30
1	2	4			6	3	12	13						7	8	10²	9¹	5			11											31
1	2¹	4	12		6	3	13	14						7	8	10³	9	5			11²											32
1	12	4	5		6	3	8	9						10³	7	11¹	13	2²									14					33
1	2		5	3²			8	9						6¹	7	10	4	11									12	13				34
1	2		5	6		3	8²	9						11¹	7	10	12										13	4				35
1	2²		5	6		3	8	9	12					7	11¹	10											13	4				36
1	2	4	5			3	8²	9³	12			13		7	11	10	14										6¹					37
1	2	4	5			3	8¹	9²						7	11	10	12	13									6					38
1	2		5	6		3	8²	9¹						7	11	10	12	13					4									39
1	2²		5	6		3	8	9			11¹			7		4	10	12					13									40
1			5	6		3	8	9				2		10¹	7	11		12					4²				13					41
1	4¹		5			3	8	9	12			2		10	7	11		13									6					42
12		4	5			3	8	13			11¹	2		10	7	9							6²					1				43
1	12		5			3	8	9	11			2		6¹	7	10²	4													13		44
1	2¹	3	4	5				9³	11			7		8	10	12				6³										13	14	45
1		3	4	5²			12	11³	9			7	2	8	10¹	13				6											14	46

Worthington Cup

First Round	Bury	(a)	0-1	
		(h)	2-0	
Second Round	Huddersfield T	(a)	1-2	
		(h)	2-2	

FA Cup

First Round	Bournemouth	(h)	1-1	
		(a)	2-4	

Division 2   **OLDHAM ATHLETIC**

FOUNDATION

It was in 1895 that John Garland, the landlord of the Featherstall and Junction Hotel, decided to form a football club. As Pine Villa they played in the Oldham Junior League. In 1899 the local professional club Oldham County, went out of existence and one of the liquidators persuaded Pine Villa to take over their ground at Sheepfoot Lane and change their name to Oldham Athletic.

Boundary Park, Oldham OL1 2PA.
Telephone: (0161) 624 4972.
Fax: (0161) 627 5915.
Website: www.oldhamathletic.co.uk
Commercial Office: (0161) 627 1802.
Fax: (0161) 652 6501.
ClubCall: 09068 121 142.
Ground Capacity: 13,559.
Record Attendance: 47,671 v Sheffield W, FA Cup 4th rd, 25 January 1930.
Record Receipts: £138,680 v Manchester U, FA Premier League, 29 December 1993.
Pitch Measurements: 110yd × 74yd.
Chairman: D. A. Brierley.
Vice-Chairman: I. H. Stott.
Directors: G. T. Butterworth, D. R. Taylor, P. Chadwick, J. Slevin, N. Holden.
Manager: Andy Ritchie.
Chief Executive/Secretary: Alan Hardy.
Commercial Manager: Bob Gorrill.
Public Relations Office: Gordon A. Lawton.
Stadium Manager: Stuart Oddie.
Safety Officer: Frank Carlisle.
Senior Coach: Bill Urmson.
Physio: Alex Moreno MCSP SRP.
Youth Coaches: David Cross, Tony Philliskirk.

LATEST SEQUENCES

Longest Sequence of League Wins: 10, 12.1.74 – 12.3.74.
Longest Sequence of League Defeats: 8, 15.12.34 – 2.2.35.
Longest Sequence of League Draws: 5, 26.12.82 – 15.1.83.
Longest Sequence of Unbeaten League Matches: 20, 1.5.90 – 10.11.90.
Longest Sequence Without a League Win: 17, 4.9.20 – 18.12.20.

HONOURS

Football League: Division 1 – Runners-up 1914–15; Division 2 – Champions 1990–91; Runners-up 1909–10; Division 3 (N) – Champions 1952–53; Division 3 – Champions 1973–74; Division 4 – Runners-up 1962–63.
FA Cup: Semi-final 1913, 1990, 1994.
Football League Cup: Runners-up 1990.

Colours
All blue.

Change Colours
White shirts, claret shorts, claret stockings.

Year Formed: 1895.

Turned Professional: 1899.

Ltd Co.: 1906.

Previous Name: 1895, Pine Villa; 1899, Oldham Athletic.

Club Nickname: 'The Latics'.

Previous Grounds: 1895, Sheepfoot Lane; 1900, Hudson Field; 1906, Sheepfoot Lane; 1907, Boundary Park.

First Football League Game: 9 September 1907, Division 2, v Stoke (a) W 3–1 – Hewitson; Hodson, Hamilton; Fay, Walders, Wilson; Ward, W. Dodds (1), Newton (1), Hancock, Swarbrick (1).

Record League Victory: 11–0 v Southport, Division 4, 26 December 1962 – Hollands; Branagan, Marshall; McCall, Williams, Scott; Ledger (1), Johnstone, Lister (6), Colquhoun (1), Whitaker (3).

Record Cup Victory: 10–1 v Lytham, FA Cup 1st rd, 28 November 1925 – Gray; Wynne, Grundy; Adlam, Heaton, Naylor (1), Douglas, Pynegar (2), Ormston (2), Barnes (3), Watson (2).

Record Defeat: 4–13 v Tranmere R, Division 3 (N), 26 December 1935.

Most League Points (2 for a win): 62, Division 3, 1973–74.

Most League Points (3 for a win): 88, Division 2, 1990–91.

Most League Goals: 95, Division 4, 1962–63.

Highest League Scorer in Season: Tom Davis, 33, Division 3 (N), 1936–37.

Most League Goals in Total Aggregate: Roger Palmer, 141, 1980–94.

Most League Goals in One Match: 7, Eric Gemmell v Chester, Division 3N, 19 January 1952.

Most Capped Player: Gunnar Halle, 24 (63), Norway.

Most League Appearances: Ian Wood, 525, 1966–80.

Youngest League Player: Wayne Harrison, 15 years 11 months v Notts Co, 27 October 1984.

Record Transfer Fee Received: £1,700,000 from Aston Villa for Earl Barrett, February 1992.

Record Transfer Fee Paid: £750,000 to Aston Villa for Ian Olney, June 1992.

Football League Record: 1907 Elected to Division 2; 1910–23 Division 1; 1923–35 Division 2; 1935–53 Division 3 (N); 1953–54 Division 2; 1954–58 Division 3 (N); 1958–63 Division 4; 1963–69 Division 3; 1969–71 Division 4; 1971–74 Division 3; 1974–91 Division 2; 1991–92 Division 1; 1992–94 FA Premier League; 1994–97 Division 1; 1997– Division 2.

MANAGERS

David Ashworth 1906–14
Herbert Bamlett 1914–21
Charlie Roberts 1921–22
David Ashworth 1923–24
Bob Mellor 1924–27
Andy Wilson 1927–32
Jimmy McMullan 1933–34
Bob Mellor 1934–45
(continued as Secretary to 1953)
Frank Womack 1945–47
Billy Wootton 1947–50
George Hardwick 1950–56
Ted Goodier 1956–58
Norman Dodgin 1958–60
Jack Rowley 1960–63
Les McDowall 1963–65
Gordon Hurst 1965–66
Jimmy McIlroy 1966–68
Jack Rowley 1968–69
Jimmy Frizzell 1970–82
Joe Royle 1982–94
Graeme Sharp 1994–97
Neil Warnock 1997–98
Andy Ritchie May 1998–

TEN YEAR LEAGUE RECORD

		P	W	D	L	F	A	Pts	Pos
1989-90	Div 2	46	19	14	13	70	57	71	8
1990-91	Div 2	46	25	13	8	83	53	88	1
1991-92	Div 1	42	14	9	19	63	67	51	17
1992-93	PR Lge	42	13	10	19	63	74	49	19
1993-94	PR Lge	42	9	13	20	42	68	40	21
1994-95	Div 1	46	16	13	17	60	60	61	14
1995-96	Div 1	46	14	14	18	54	50	56	18
1996-97	Div 1	46	10	13	23	51	66	43	23
1997-98	Div 2	46	15	16	15	62	54	61	13
1998-99	Div 2	46	14	9	23	48	66	51	20

DID YOU KNOW ?

Billy Hibbert, centre-forward for Newton-le-Willows when they were beaten 11-0 by Oldham Athletic on 7 January 1905, eventually joined Oldham on 26 May 1922, having won international honours for England.

OLDHAM ATHLETIC 1999–2000 LEAGUE RECORD

Match No.	Date	Venue	Opponents	Result	H/T Score	Lg. Pos.	Goalscorers	Atten-dance
1	Aug 7	H	Preston NE	L	0-1	0-0	23		9432
2	14	A	Brentford	L	0-2	0-0	23		5074
3	21	H	Burnley	L	0-1	0-1	23		8543
4	28	A	Oxford U	L	0-1	0-1	24		5098
5	Sept 4	A	Gillingham	L	1-2	0-2	24	McNiven S [88]	5884
6	11	H	Bury	W	2-0	0-0	24	Allott [62], Duxbury [81]	6541
7	18	A	Bristol R	L	2-3	1-2	24	Sheridan [3], Allott [70]	6574
8	25	A	Reading	D	1-1	0-0	24	Allott [69]	7274
9	Oct 2	H	Notts Co	L	1-2	1-1	24	Thom [45]	5143
10	9	H	Luton T	W	2-1	0-0	21	McNiven D [66], Allott [90]	4532
11	16	A	Cardiff C	D	1-1	1-0	21	Graham [17]	5650
12	19	A	Blackpool	W	2-1	0-0	—	Duxbury [64], Allott [90]	3845
13	23	H	Reading	L	1-2	1-2	20	Dudley [20]	4963
14	Nov 2	H	Wycombe W	D	2-2	1-1	—	Rickers [3], Whitehall [90]	3807
15	6	A	Chesterfield	W	1-0	1-0	16	Adams [38]	2737
16	9	H	Millwall	W	2-1	1-0	—	Dudley [13], Whitehall [88]	4209
17	14	A	Colchester U	L	1-2	0-1	15	Dudley [46]	5147
18	23	A	Bristol C	D	1-1	0-1	—	Allott [83]	8214
19	27	H	Wrexham	D	0-0	0-0	14		4963
20	Dec 4	A	Preston NE	L	0-2	0-0	16		10,970
21	18	H	Cambridge U	W	3-2	2-1	15	Allott [11], Adams [34], Duxbury [78]	3162
22	26	H	Scunthorpe U	D	1-1	1-0	15	Whitehall [31]	5998
23	28	A	Stoke C	D	0-0	0-0	15		13,709
24	Jan 3	H	Bournemouth	W	1-0	1-0	15	Allott [27]	5160
25	7	A	Wigan Ath	W	1-0	0-0	—	Duxbury [86]	6487
26	15	H	Brentford	W	3-0	1-0	12	Holt [33], Allott 2 (1 pen) [61, 76 (p)]	4967
27	22	A	Burnley	L	0-3	0-1	14		12,391
28	29	H	Oxford U	W	2-0	1-0	11	Whitehall 2 [32, 88]	4780
29	Feb 5	A	Millwall	L	0-1	0-0	14		8303
30	12	H	Gillingham	L	1-3	1-2	15	Garnett [7]	5144
31	19	A	Wrexham	W	3-0	1-0	13	Graham [11], Whitehall [51], Dudley [73]	3603
32	26	H	Bristol R	L	1-4	0-3	14	Dudley [67]	5839
33	Mar 4	A	Bury	D	2-2	1-0	14	Whitehall [16], Rickers [66]	5306
34	11	A	Wycombe W	D	0-0	0-0	15		4471
35	18	H	Bristol C	D	1-1	0-0	15	Whitehall [46]	4808
36	21	A	Colchester U	W	1-0	1-0	—	Holt [22]	3282
37	25	A	Scunthorpe U	W	2-1	2-1	13	Garnett [4], Rickers [38]	3807
38	Apr 1	H	Cambridge U	W	1-0	0-0	11	Holt [75]	4988
39	4	H	Stoke C	L	0-1	0-1	—		4474
40	8	A	Bournemouth	L	0-3	0-0	13		3808
41	11	H	Wigan Ath	W	2-1	1-1	—	Tipton [42], Jones [87]	5697
42	18	H	Chesterfield	L	1-2	1-2	—	Whitehall [15]	4012
43	22	H	Cardiff C	L	1-2	1-1	12	Thom [15]	4549
44	24	A	Notts Co	W	1-0	0-0	11	Tipton [76]	3728
45	29	H	Blackpool	D	1-1	0-0	11	Sugden [90]	6290
46	May 6	A	Luton T	D	1-1	0-1	14	Tipton (pen) [90]	5963

Final League Position: 14

GOALSCORERS

League (50): Allott 10 (1 pen), Whitehall 9, Dudley 5, Duxbury 4, Holt 3, Rickers 3, Tipton 3 (1 pen), Adams 2, Garnett 2, Graham 2, Thom 2, Jones 1, McNiven D 1, McNiven S 1, Sheridan 1, Sugden 1.
Worthington Cup (1): Allott 1.
FA Cup (6): Whitehall 2, Adams 1, Dudley 1, Duxbury 1, Sheridan 1.

Kelly G 44	McNiven S 45	Holt A 46	Garnett S 32	Rickers P 40 + 1	Duxbury L 43	Adams N 29	Sheridan J 34 + 2	Allott M 28 + 4	Agogo M 2	Innes M 15 + 6	Tipton M 9 + 20	Beavers P 3 + 1	Sugden R 3 + 14	McLean I 1	McNiven D 3 + 1	Salt P 4 + 1	Tait J — + 1	Whitehall S 27 + 11	Graham R 14 + 3	Thom S 9	Dudley C 18 + 7	Hotte M 34 + 1	Futcher B 1 + 4	Walsh D — + 1	Jones P 16	Boshell D 4 + 4	Miskelly D 2	Match No.
1	2	3	4	5	6	7	8	9	10	11^1	12																	1
1	2	3	4	5	6	7	8	12	10	11^2		9^1	13															2
1	2	3	4	5		7^2	8	12		11		13	9^1			6		10										3
1	2	3	4	5	6^3	7	8	9			12	13						10^2	11^1	14								4
1	2	3	4	5	6	7	8	9^2		11^1	12							10^3	13			14						5
1	2	3	4^3	5	6	7	8	9		11^1	12		13					10^2	14									6
1	2	3		5	6	7	8	9		11	12							10^1				4						7
1	2	3		5	6	7	8	9^1		11	12							10				4						8
1	2	3		5	6	7	8	9^1		11	12		13					10^2				4						9
1	2	3		5	6	7	8	9		11	12							10				4^1						10
1	2	3		5	6	7^2	8	9		11	12		13					10^1				4						11
1	2	3		5	6	7		9		11	12							10	8^1			4						12
1	2	3^1		5	6	7		9		11	12^2		13					10	8			4						13
1	2	3		5	6	7^1	8	9^2		11	12		13					10				4						14
1	2	3		5	6	7	8	9^2		11	12		13					10^1				4^3	14					15
1	2	3		5	6	7	8	9^1		11	12							10				4						16
1	2	3		5	6	7^1	8	9^2			12		13					10	11			4						17
1	2	3	4	5	6		8	9		11^2	12							10^1	13			7						18
1	2	3	4	5	6		8	9		11	12							10^1				7						19
1	2	3	4	5	6		8	9		11^1	12							10				7						20
1	2	3	4	5	6	7	8	9^1			12							10^2	13			11						21
1	2	3	4	5	6	7	8	9^2			12							10^1	13						11			22
1	2	3	4	5	6	7	8	9^2			12							10^1	13			11						23
1	2	3	4	5	6	7	8	9										10^1			12	11						24
1	2	3	4	5	6	7	8	9			12							10^1				11						25
1	2	3	4	5^1	6^2	7	8	9			12	13						10				11						26
1	2	3	4	5	6	7	8	9			12							10^1				11						27
1	2	3	4	5^2	6	7	8	9^1			12							10	13			11						28
1	2	3	4	5	6	7		9										10		8		11						29
1	2	3	4	5^1	6	7		9^3			12	13						10^2		8		11	14					30
1		3	4	5	6	7					12							10	9^1	8		11			2			31
1	2	3	4	5	6	7^1					12	13						10^2	9	8		11						32
1	2	3	4	5			8			11	12							10^1	9			7			6			33
1	2	3		5	6^1		8			11								10	9			7	12			4		34
1	2	3	4	5	6		8				12							10	9^1			7	11					35
1	2	3	4	5^2	6		8				12		13					10^1	9			7	11					36
1	2	3	4	5	6		8	9			12							10^1				7	11					37
1	2	3	4	5^1	6		8	9			12		13					10^2				7	11					38
1	2	3	4	5	6			9^2			12							10		8	13	7	11^1					39
1	2	3	4^3		6		8	9^2		11	12							10^1			13	7	14		5			40
1	2	3		5	6		8^1	9		11	12							10				7				4		41
	2	3			6		8	9^1		11^2	12							10			13	7			5	4	1	42
	2	3	4		6		8^3				12							10^1	9		13	7^2	11	14	5		1	43
1	2	3^1	4		6		8				12							10^2	9		13	7	11		5	6		44
1	2	3^2	4		6						12		13					10^1	9^3	8		7	11	14	5			45
1	2	3	4		6					11	12		13					10^2	9^3	8^1		7	14	5				46

Worthington Cup

First Round   Stockport Co   (a)   0-2
          (h)   1-1

FA Cup

First Round   Chelmsford C   (h)   4-0
Second Round   Swansea C   (h)   1-0
Third Round   Preston NE   (a)   1-2

Division 2

OXFORD UNITED

FOUNDATION

There had been an Oxford United club around the time of World
War I but only in the Oxfordshire Thursday League and there is
no connection with the modern club which began as Headington in
1893, adding 'United' a year later. Playing first on Quarry Fields
and subsequently Wootten's Fields, they owe much to a Dr.
Hitchings for their early development.

Manor Ground, Headington, Oxford OX3 7RS.
Telephone: (01865) 761 503.
Fax: (01865) 741 820.
Website: www.oufc.co.uk
Email: oxford-united@community.co.uk
Supporters Club: (01865) 763 063.
ClubCall: 09068 440 055.
Ground Capacity: 9650.
Record Attendance: 22,730 v Preston NE, FA Cup 6th rd, 29 February 1964.
Record Receipts: £136,423 v Chelsea, FA Cup 4th rd, 25 January 1999.
Pitch Measurements: 110yd × 75yd.
President: The Duke of Marlborough.
Chairman: Firoz Kassam.
Directors: F. Higgins, A. Tawakley.
Manager: Denis Smith.
First Team Coach: Mickey Lewis.
Reserve/Assistant Coach: Les Taylor.
Technical Director: Ray Harford.
Physio: John Clinkard.
Secretary: Mick Brown.
Marketing Manager: Trevor Baxter.
Stadium Manager: Mick Moore.

LATEST SEQUENCES

Longest Sequence of League Wins: 6, 6.4.85 – 24.4.85.
Longest Sequence of League Defeats: 7, 4.5.91 – 7.9.91.
Longest Sequence of League Draws: 5, 7.10.78 – 28.10.78.
Longest Sequence of Unbeaten League Matches: 20,
17.3.84 – 29.9.84.
Longest Sequence Without a League Win: 27, 14.11.87 –
27.8.88.

HONOURS

Football League: Division 1 best
season: 12th, 1997–98; Division 2 –
Champions 1984–85; Runners-up
1995–96; Division 3 – Champions
1967–68, 1983–84; Division 4 –
Promoted 1964–65 (4th).

FA Cup: best season: 6th rd, 1964
(shared record for 4th Division club).

Football League Cup: Winners 1986.

Colours
Yellow shirts with navy trim, navy shorts, navy stockings.

Change Colours
Navy shirts with white trim, white shorts, white stockings.

Year Formed: 1893.

Turned Professional: 1949.

Ltd Co.: 1949.

Club Nickname: 'The U's'.

Previous Names: 1893, Headington; 1894, Headington United; 1960, Oxford United.

Previous Grounds: 1893, Headington Quarry; 1894, Wootten's Field; 1898, Sandy Lane Ground; 1902, Britannia Field; 1909, Sandy Lane; 1910, Quarry Recreation Ground; 1914, Sandy Lane; 1922, The Paddock Manor Road; 1925, Manor Ground.

First Football League Game: 18 August 1962, Division 4, v Barrow (a) L 2–3 – Medlock; Beavon, Quartermain; R. Atkinson, Kyle, Jones; Knight, G. Atkinson (1), Houghton (1), Cornwell, Colfar.

Record League Victory: 7–0 v Barrow, Division 4, 19 December 1964 – Fearnley; Beavon, Quartermain; R. Atkinson (1), Kyle, Jones; Morris, Booth (3), Willey (1), G. Atkinson (1), Harrington (1).

MANAGERS
Harry Thompson 1949–58
(Player-Manager) 1949-51
Arthur Turner 1959–69
(continued as General Manager to 1972)
Ron Saunders 1969
George Summers 1969–75
Mike Brown 1975–79
Bill Asprey 1979–80
Ian Greaves 1980–82
Jim Smith 1982–85
Maurice Evans 1985–88
Mark Lawrenson 1988
Brian Horton 1988–93
Denis Smith 1993–97
Malcolm Crosby 1997
Malcolm Shotton 1998–99
Denis Smith February 2000–

Record Cup Victory: 9–1 v Dorchester T, FA Cup 1st rd, 11 November 1995 – Whitehead; Wood (2), Ford M (1), Smith, Elliott, Gilchrist, Rush (1), Massey (Murphy), Moody (3), Ford R (1), Angel (Beauchamp (1)).

Record Defeat: 0–7 v Sunderland, Division 1, 19 September 1998.

Most League Points (2 for a win): 61, Division 4, 1964–65.

Most League Points (3 for a win): 95, Division 3, 1983–84.

Most League Goals: 91, Division 3, 1983–84.

Highest League Scorer in Season: John Aldridge, 30, Division 2, 1984–85.

Most League Goals in Total Aggregate: Graham Atkinson, 77, 1962–73.

Most League Goals in One Match: 4, Tony Jones v Newport Co, Division 4, 22 September 1962; 4, Arthur Longbottom v Darlington, Division 4, 26 October 1963; 4, Richard Hill v Walsall, Division 2, 26 December 1988; 4, John Durnin v Luton T, 14 November 1992.

Most Capped Player: Jim Magilton, 18 (40), Northern Ireland.

Most League Appearances: John Shuker, 478, 1962–77.

Youngest League Player: Jason Seacole, 16 years 149 days v Mansfield T, 7 September 1976.

Record Transfer Fee Received: £1,600,000 from Leicester C for Matt Elliott, January 1997.

Record Transfer Fee Paid: £475,000 to Aberdeen for Dean Windass, August 1998.

Football League Record: 1962 Elected to Division 4; 1965–68 Division 3; 1968–76 Division 2; 1976–84 Division 3; 1984–85 Division 2; 1985–88 Division 1; 1988–92 Division 2; 1992–94 Division 1; 1994–96 Division 2; 1996–99 Division 1; 1999– Division 2.

TEN YEAR LEAGUE RECORD

		P	W	D	L	F	A	Pts	Pos
1989-90	Div 2	46	15	9	22	57	66	54	17
1990-91	Div 2	46	14	19	13	69	66	61	10
1991-92	Div 2	46	13	11	22	66	73	50	21
1992-93	Div 1	46	14	14	18	53	56	56	14
1993-94	Div 1	46	13	10	23	54	75	49	23
1994-95	Div 2	46	21	12	13	66	52	75	7
1995-96	Div 2	46	24	11	11	76	39	83	2
1996-97	Div 1	46	16	9	21	64	68	57	17
1997-98	Div 1	46	16	10	20	60	64	58	12
1998-99	Div 1	46	10	14	22	48	71	44	23

DID YOU KNOW ?

The club's first appearance in the third round of the FA Cup was on 9 January 1954 at Stockport County. Some 2500 of the-then Headington United supporters saw a 0-0 draw. They won the replay with a Bobby Peart goal.

OXFORD UNITED 1999–2000 LEAGUE RECORD

Match No.	Date	Venue	Opponents	Result	H/T Score	Lg. Pos.	Goalscorers	Attendance
1	Aug 7	A	Stoke C	W 2-1	1-0	5	Murphy [28], Anthrobus [78]	11,300
2	14	H	Cardiff C	L 2-3	0-2	13	Murphy 2 (1 pen) [67 (p), 73]	6423
3	21	A	Bristol R	L 0-1	0-0	18		7617
4	28	H	Oldham Ath	W 1-0	1-0	11	Murphy (pen) [16]	5098
5	30	A	Blackpool	D 1-1	0-1	9	Lilley [57]	3670
6	Sept 4	H	Wycombe W	D 0-0	0-0	10		6306
7	11	H	Gillingham	L 1-2	0-0	15	Cook [90]	5418
8	18	A	Wrexham	L 0-1	0-1	16		4229
9	25	A	Luton T	L 2-4	0-3	19	Powell [59], Lilley [65]	6102
10	Oct 2	H	Bristol C	W 3-0	2-0	15	Beauchamp 2 [7, 33], Lilley [66]	6638
11	9	H	Millwall	L 1-3	0-1	17	Murphy (pen) [66]	5392
12	16	A	Brentford	L 0-2	0-0	18		6237
13	19	A	Scunthorpe U	L 0-1	0-0	—		3829
14	23	A	Luton T	L 0-1	0-1	21		5866
15	Nov 2	H	Colchester U	D 1-1	1-1	—	Lambert [1]	4444
16	7	A	Reading	W 2-1	1-0	18	Folland [7], Murphy [84]	10,101
17	13	H	Bury	D 1-1	1-0	—	Lambert [9]	4318
18	23	A	Notts Co	W 1-0	0-0	—	Warren (og) [85]	4020
19	27	A	Chesterfield	D 0-0	0-0	15		2768
20	Dec 4	H	Stoke C	D 1-1	1-0	15	Beauchamp [27]	5700
21	18	A	Bournemouth	L 0-4	0-2	16		4443
22	26	H	Cambridge U	W 1-0	0-0	16	Murphy [83]	6772
23	28	A	Burnley	L 2-3	1-1	16	Anthrobus [3], Whelan [52]	14,218
24	Jan 3	H	Wigan Ath	L 1-2	0-0	16	Cook [60]	5915
25	15	A	Cardiff C	D 1-1	1-0	18	Murphy [44]	6914
26	22	H	Bristol R	L 0-5	0-1	20		7355
27	29	A	Oldham Ath	L 0-2	0-1	21		4780
28	Feb 1	H	Preston NE	L 0-4	0-1	—		5164
29	5	H	Blackpool	L 0-1	0-1	22		5179
30	12	A	Wycombe W	W 1-0	1-0	20	Beauchamp [26]	6200
31	19	H	Chesterfield	W 2-1	1-0	20	Fear [10], Lilley [89]	5146
32	26	H	Wrexham	L 1-4	0-1	20	Edwards [71]	4988
33	Mar 4	A	Gillingham	L 0-1	0-0	21		6966
34	7	H	Reading	L 1-3	1-2	—	Powell [8]	7638
35	11	A	Colchester U	W 2-1	1-0	21	Weatherstone S [22], Whelan [90]	4058
36	14	A	Preston NE	L 1-3	0-1	—	Murphy [64]	12,008
37	18	H	Notts Co	L 2-3	1-3	21	Powell 2 (1 pen) [7, 76 (p)]	4544
38	21	A	Bury	W 2-1	1-0	—	Lilley [9], Cook [90]	2606
39	25	A	Cambridge U	L 0-2	0-2	21		5127
40	Apr 1	H	Bournemouth	W 1-0	1-0	19	Lilley [32]	5214
41	8	A	Wigan Ath	L 0-2	0-1	20		4848
42	15	H	Burnley	L 1-2	1-0	20	Murphy [13]	7549
43	22	H	Brentford	D 1-1	1-0	21	Lilley [41]	5342
44	24	A	Bristol C	D 2-2	1-2	20	Powell [10], Davis [68]	9046
45	29	H	Scunthorpe U	W 2-0	1-0	20	Murphy [26], Powell [70]	6752
46	May 6	A	Millwall	L 0-1	0-1	20		13,827

Final League Position: 20

GOALSCORERS

League (43): Murphy 11 (3 pens), Lilley 7, Powell 6 (1 pen), Beauchamp 4, Cook 3, Anthrobus 2, Lambert 2, Whelan 2, Davis 1, Edwards 1, Fear 1, Folland 1, Weatherstone S 1, own goal 1.
Worthington Cup (5): Murphy 3, Beauchamp 2.
FA Cup (9): Murphy 3, Powell 3, Abbey 1, Folland 1, Lilley 1.

Arendse A 13	Robinson L 46	Powell P 39 + 1	Murphy M 46	Watson M 34 + 1	Gilchrist P 1	Lilley D 36 + 8	Tait P 34	Anthrobus S 25 + 11	Weatherstone S 13 + 8	Beauchamp J 33 + 1	Folland R 17 + 6	Davis S 20 + 4	Banger N 1 + 2	Cook J 11 + 18	Whelan P 31	McGowan N 15 + 5	Lundin P 21 + 1	Lewis M 3 + 2	Lambert J 8 + 5	Fear P 13 + 6	Abbey B — + 10	Weatherstone R 3	Francis K — + 3	Knight R 12 + 1	Shepheard J 1 + 1	Jemson N 13 + 5	Russell C 5 + 1	Edwards C 5	Newton E 7	Hackett C — + 2	Match No.
1	2	3	4	5	6	7^1	8	9	10	11	12																				1
1	2	3	4	5		7^1	8	9	13	11			6	10^2	12																2
1	2	3^3	4	5		7	8	9	10^1	11		13	12			6^2	14														3
	2	3^3	4	5		7^1	8	9	10^2	11	6			12	13		14	1													4
	2	3^2	4	5		7	8	9	10^3	11	12			6^1	13		1		14												5
	2	3	4	5		7	8		10^3	11	12			13	6^1		1	14	9^2												6
	2	3^3	9	5		7^2	8		13	11	6			12		14	1		10^1	4											7
	2	6	7^3				12	8	9	11^1	10^2					13	3	1	5	14	4										8
1	2	3	7	12		13	8^2	9		11	10^3	5		14			6^1		4												9
	2	3	7	5		10^2		9		11	6			12			1		8^1	4	13										10
	2	3	10			7		9		11	6	5					1		8^1	4	12										11
1	2	3	10	5		7	8	9^2		11	6								12	4^1	13										12
1	2	3	10	5		7^2	8	9		11	6	12							4^1	13											13
1	2	3^2	9^3	5		7^1	8	12		11	6				13		10	14	4												14
1	2	3	9	5		7^2				11	10			12	6				8^1	4	13										15
	2		9	5		7				11	4				6	3	1		8^1		12	10									16
	2		9	5		7^2	8			11	4			12	6	3	1		10^1	13											17
	2		9	5		7^1	8	12		11	10	6				4	3	1													18
	2		9	5		7^1	8	12		11	10	6				4	3	1		13											19
	2		10	5^2		7^1		9		11	6					4	3	1	12	13		8									20
	2	12	9^3	5		7				11^2	10	6		8		4^1	3	1		13			14								21
1	2	6	9			7^2		12		11	10	5		8^1		4	3						13								22
1	2		9			7^1		8		11	10	6		12		4	3					5									23
1	2	3	9	5		7		8		11	10			4	6																24
	2	3	9			12	10	8		11	7	5		4^1	6		1														25
	2	7^2	9			12	10	8^3		11^1		5		4	6	3			13	14			1								26
	2	6	9	5		7^1	8	10^2						12	4	3^3	1			13							14	11			27
	2	3	9	5			8			11				4	6		1			12							7^1	10			28
	2	3	9	5		7^3	8	12	14	11	13			6			1			4^2								10^1			29
	2	3	9				8	12		11		5		6		1^6			4						15	10^1	7				30
	2	3	9			12	8^2	13		11^3		5				6	1	14		4							10	7^1			31
	2	3	9			12	8^2	5	11			13				1			4								10	7^1	6		32
1	2	3	9	5		12	8		13	11^2				6					4^1								10	7			33
1^6	2	3	9	5		12	8			11				6		15						13				10	7^2	4^1		34
	2	3	9	5		7^2	8	12	11^2					13	6	1										10^1	14	4		35
	2	3	9	5		7^2	8	12	11^3					13	6				14			1				10^1		4		36
	2	3	9	5		7	8	12	11^1					13	6				14			1				10^3		4^2		37
	2	3	9	5		7	8	10	11^1			12		4	6							1								38
	2	3	9	5^2		7	8	10	11^1			12		4	6							1				13				39
	2	3	9	5		7	8	10^1	12			13		4^3	6^2							1				14		11		40
	2	3	9	5		7	8	12			6			4^2								1				10^1		11	13	41
	2	3	9	5		7	8	10						4^1	6							1				12		11		42
	2	11	9	5		7^2	8	12	13			6		14	3							1				10^5		4^3		43
	2^2	11	9	5		7	10	8	12			14	6	13	3^3							1						4^1		44
	2	11^1	9			7		8	10^2	12			5		4	3						1				13		6		45
	2	11	9			7		8^3	10^2			12	5		4	3^1						1				13		6	14	46

Worthington Cup

First Round	Southend U	(a)	2-0
		(h)	1-0
Second Round	Everton	(h)	1-1
		(a)	1-0
Third Round	Tranmere R	(a)	0-2

FA Cup

First Round	Morecambe	(h)	3-2
Second Round	Shrewsbury T	(a)	2-2
		(h)	2-1
Third Round	Nottingham F	(a)	1-1
		(h)	1-3

Division 2   **PETERBOROUGH UNITED**

FOUNDATION

The old Peterborough & Fletton club, founded in 1923, was
suspended by the FA during season 1932–33 and disbanded. Local
enthusiasts determined to carry on and in 1934 a new professional
club Peterborough United was formed and entered the Midland
League the following year. Peterborough's first success came in
1939–40, but from 1955–56 to 1959–60 they won five successive
titles. During the 1958–59 season they were undefeated in the
Midland League. They reached the third round of the FA Cup,
won the Northamptonshire Senior Cup, the Maunsell Cup and
were runners-up in the East Anglian Cup.

London Road Ground, Peterborough PE2 8AL.
Telephone: (01733) 563 947.
Fax: (01733) 344 140.
ClubCall: 09068 121 654.
Website: www.theposh.com
Email: management@theposh.net
Ground Capacity: 15,314.
Record Attendance: 30,096 v Swansea T, FA Cup 5th rd, 20 February 1965.
Record Receipts: £51,315 v Brighton & HA, FA Cup 5th rd, 15 February 1986.
Pitch Measurements: 112yd × 71yd.
Chairman: Peter Boizot MBE, DL.
Vice-Chairman: Roger Terrell.
Directors: A. Hand, P. Sagar.
Chief Executive: Nigel Hards.
Company Secretary: Timothy Warren.
Club Secretary: Julie Etherington.
General Manager: David Gledhill.
First Team Manager: Barry Fry.
Assistant Manager: Paul Ashworth.
Youth Academy Director: Kit Carson.
Physio: Paul Showlen.

LATEST SEQUENCES

Longest Sequence of League Wins: 9, 1.2.92 – 14.3.92.
Longest Sequence of League Defeats: 5, 8.10.96 – 26.10.96.
Longest Sequence of League Draws: 8, 18.12.71 – 12.2.72.
Longest Sequence of Unbeaten League Matches: 17,
17.12.60 – 8.4.61.
Longest Sequence Without a League Win: 17, 23.9.78 –
30.12.78.

HONOURS

Football League: Division 1 best
season: 10th, 1992–93. Promoted from
Division 3 1999–2000 (play-offs);
Division 4 – Champions 1960–61,
1973–74.
FA Cup: best season: 6th rd, 1965.
Football League Cup: Semi-final 1966.

Colours
Royal blue shirts, white shorts, blue stockings with white tops.

Change Colours
Green shirts with navy trim, navy shorts, navy stockings.

Year Formed: 1934.

Turned Professional: 1934.

Ltd Co.: 1934.

Club Nickname: 'The Posh'.

First Football League Game: 20 August 1960, Division 4, v Wrexham (h) W 3–0 – Walls; Stafford, Walker; Rayner, Rigby, Norris; Hails, Emery (1), Bly (1), Smith, McNamee (1).

Record League Victory: 9–1 v Barnet (a) Division 3, 5 September 1998 – Griemink; Hooper (1), Drury (Farell), Gill, Bodley, Edwards, Davies, Payne, Grazioli (5), Quinn (2) (Rowe), Houghton (Etherington) (1).

Record Cup Victory: 7–0 v Harlow T, FA Cup 1st rd, 16 November 1991 – Barber; Luke, Johnson, Halsall (1), Robinson D, Welsh, Sterling (1) (Butterworth), Cooper G (2 incl. 1p), Riley (1) (Culpin (1)), Charlery (1), Kimble.

Record Defeat: 1–8 v Northampton T, FA Cup 2nd rd (2nd replay), 18 December 1946.

Most League Points (2 for a win): 66, Division 4, 1960–61.

Most League Points (3 for a win): 82, Division 4, 1981–82.

Most League Goals: 134, Division 4, 1960–61.

Highest League Scorer in Season: Terry Bly, 52, Division 4, 1960–61.

Most League Goals in Total Aggregate: Jim Hall, 122, 1967–75.

Most League Goals in One Match: 5, Guiliano Grazioli v Barnet, Division 3, 5 September 1998.

Most Capped Player: Tony Millington, 8 (21), Wales.

Most League Appearances: Tommy Robson, 482, 1968–81.

Youngest League Player: Matthew Etherington, 15 years 262 days v Brentford, 3 May 1997.

Record Transfer Fee Received: £700,000 from Tottenham H for Simon Davies, December 1999.

Record Transfer Fee Paid: £350,000 to Walsall for Martin O'Connor, July 1996.

Football League Record: 1960 Elected to Division 4; 1961–68 Division 3, when they were demoted for financial irregularities; 1968–74 Division 4; 1974–79 Division 3; 1979–91 Division 4; 1991–92 Division 3; 1992–94 Division 1; 1994–97 Division 2; 1997–2000 Division 3; 2000– Division 2.

MANAGERS

Jock Porter 1934–36
Fred Taylor 1936–37
Vic Poulter 1937–38
Sam Madden 1938–48
Jack Blood 1948–50
Bob Gurney 1950–52
Jack Fairbrother 1952–54
George Swindin 1954–58
Jimmy Hagan 1958–62
Jack Fairbrother 1962–64
Gordon Clark 1964–67
Norman Rigby 1967–69
Jim Iley 1969–72
Noel Cantwell 1972–77
John Barnwell 1977–78
Billy Hails 1978–79
Peter Morris 1979–82
Martin Wilkinson 1982–83
John Wile 1983–86
Noel Cantwell 1986–88
(continued as General Manager)
Mick Jones 1988–89
Mark Lawrenson 1989–90
Chris Turner 1991–92
Lil Fuccillo 1992–93
John Still 1994–95
Mick Halsall 1995–96
Barry Fry May 1996–

TEN YEAR LEAGUE RECORD

		P	W	D	L	F	A	Pts	Pos
1989-90	Div 4	46	17	17	12	59	46	68	9
1990-91	Div 4	46	21	17	8	67	45	80	4
1991-92	Div 3	46	20	14	12	65	58	74	6
1992-93	Div 1	46	16	14	16	55	63	62	10
1993-94	Div 1	46	8	13	25	48	76	37	24
1994-95	Div 2	46	14	18	14	54	69	60	15
1995-96	Div 2	46	13	13	20	59	66	52	19
1996-97	Div 2	46	11	14	21	55	73	47	21
1997-98	Div 3	46	18	13	15	63	51	67	10
1998-99	Div 3	46	18	12	16	72	56	66	9

DID YOU KNOW ?

At the start of each of Peterborough United's first three seasons in the Midland League, they were drawn away to Scarborough: 1935-36 (won 2-1); 1936-37 (won 1-0) and 1937-38 (lost 5-2).

PETERBOROUGH UNITED 1999–2000 LEAGUE RECORD

Match No.	Date		Venue	Opponents	Result	H/T Score	Lg. Pos.	Goalscorers	Atten- dance
1	Aug	7	H	Hartlepool U	W 2-1	1-1	6	Castle [34], Green [84]	5886
2		14	A	Northampton T	W 1-0	0-0	4	Davies [66]	6253
3		21	H	Leyton Orient	W 2-1	2-0	3	Etherington [19], Castle [45]	6448
4		28	A	Plymouth Arg	L 1-2	0-2	5	Farrell [90]	4189
5		30	H	Darlington	W 4-2	3-0	3	Shields [5], Martin [9], Farrell [17], Etherington [55]	6044
6	Sept	3	A	Mansfield T	L 1-3	0-2	—	Castle (pen) [78]	3338
7		11	A	York C	D 0-0	0-0	6		2832
8		18	H	Cheltenham T	W 1-0	0-0	5	Castle [68]	5943
9		25	A	Southend U	W 1-0	1-0	2	Davies [37]	6187
10	Oct	2	H	Brighton & HA	D 0-0	0-0	3		7823
11		9	H	Chester C	W 2-1	2-1	2	Forinton 2 [9, 43]	4965
12		16	A	Halifax T	L 1-2	0-1	2	Broughton [90]	3292
13		19	A	Torquay U	L 1-2	1-1	—	Etherington [19]	2000
14		23	H	Southend U	W 1-0	0-0	4	Chapple [85]	5860
15	Nov	2	A	Lincoln C	W 2-1	2-1	—	Forinton 2 [38, 43]	5032
16		6	H	Shrewsbury T	W 4-1	4-1	1	Clarke 2 [7, 29], Castle (pen) [19], Forinton [24]	5264
17		12	A	Carlisle U	D 1-1	1-1	1	Forinton [34]	2515
18		20	H	Macclesfield T	D 2-2	1-2	—	Clarke [19], Edwards [48]	5083
19		27	H	Barnet	L 1-2	1-0	3	Forinton [9]	8631
20	Dec	4	A	Hartlepool U	L 0-1	0-1	5		2404
21		26	H	Rotherham U	L 0-5	0-2	10		10,793
22		28	A	Exeter C	D 2-2	1-0	12	Clarke 2 [9, 61]	2695
23	Jan	3	H	Swansea C	L 2-3	2-0	12	Gill [2], Castle (pen) [45]	6439
24		8	A	Hull C	W 3-2	0-1	12	Clarke 2 [68, 90], Scott [75]	5898
25		15	H	Northampton T	W 1-0	0-0	9	Lee [72]	9104
26		22	A	Leyton Orient	D 1-1	1-1	10	Lee [19]	4795
27		29	H	Plymouth Arg	W 2-0	0-0	7	Castle [82], Clarke [88]	5694
28	Feb	6	A	Darlington	L 0-2	0-1	8		4688
29		12	H	Mansfield T	W 1-0	1-0	8	Lee [42]	5472
30		19	A	Barnet	W 2-0	2-0	6	Castle [21], Lee [45]	3753
31		22	H	Hull C	W 2-1	0-0	—	Drury [54], Scott [88]	6668
32		26	A	Cheltenham T	L 1-2	0-1	6	Clarke [72]	4250
33	Mar	4	H	York C	W 2-0	1-0	4	Clarke [40], Lee [80]	5578
34		7	A	Shrewsbury T	W 1-0	1-0	—	Clarke [18]	2018
35		11	H	Lincoln C	D 2-2	2-1	4	Farrell [11], Clarke [14]	7882
36		18	A	Macclesfield T	D 1-1	1-0	4	Scott [8]	2309
37		21	H	Carlisle U	L 0-2	0-1	—		5178
38		25	A	Rotherham U	D 1-1	1-1	5	Cullen [42]	5319
39	Apr	1	H	Rochdale	D 3-3	1-0	5	Clarke [17], Rea [68], Lee [82]	5587
40		8	A	Swansea C	D 0-0	0-0	5		6572
41		15	H	Exeter C	W 3-1	3-0	5	Clarke [2], Cullen [26], Edwards [32]	5276
42		18	A	Rochdale	W 2-1	2-1	—	Castle 2 (1 pen) [8, 40 (p)]	2816
43		22	H	Halifax T	W 2-1	0-0	4	Cullen [67], Clarke [70]	7194
44		26	A	Brighton & HA	D 0-0	0-0	—		5831
45		29	H	Torquay U	L 0-2	0-2	5		8242
46	May	6	A	Chester C	W 1-0	0-0	5	Hanlon [64]	4905

Final League Position: 5

GOALSCORERS

League (63): Clarke 15, Castle 10 (4 pens), Forinton 7, Lee 6, Cullen 3, Etherington 3, Farrell 3, Scott 3, Davies 2, Edwards 2, Broughton 1, Chapple 1, Drury 1, Gill 1, Green 1, Hanlon 1, Martin 1, Rea 1, Shields 1.
Worthington Cup (1): Shields 1.
FA Cup (1): Clarke 1.

Tyler M 32	Hooper D 28 + 1	Drury A 41 + 1	Gill M 7 + 13	Chapple P 15 + 1	Edwards A 44	Farrell D 33 + 2	Davies S 16	Shields T 15 + 9	Martin J 7 + 8	Castle S 36 + 3	Broughton D 5 + 5	Green F 8 + 12	Etherington M 19	Scott R 28 + 6	Wicks M 17 + 3	Koogi A — + 1	Clarke A 33 + 4	Forinton H 19 + 6	Rea S 11 + 3	Inman N — + 1	French D — + 6	Haley G 1	Griemink B 14	Hanlon R 9 + 7	Lee J 23	Jelleyman G 14 + 6	Connor D — + 1	Knight Z 8	Cullen J 12 + 1	Murray D 2	Oldfield D 9	Match No.
1	2	3	4¹	5	6	7	8	9²	10	11	12	13																				1
1	2	3		5	6	7	8	9	12	4	10			11¹																		2
1	2	3		5	6	7	8	9	12	4	10²	13		11³	14																	3
1	2	3		5²	6	7	8³	9¹	12	4	10			11			13	14														4
1	2¹	3		5	6	7		9	10	4	8	11	12					14														5
1	2	3	12	5	6	7³		9¹	10	8	4²	11		13				14														6
1	2	3			6	7¹		9	8	10	12	11	4	5																		7
1	2	3			6	7		12	9²	8		11		4	5		13	10¹														8
1	2²	3	14		6	7	8		12	4		11		13	5³			9¹	10													9
1	2	3		5	6	7³	8		12	4²			14	11	13			9	10¹													10
1	2	3	12	5²	6			9¹	10	7³	4	8		11			13	14														11
1	2	3	12	5	6		8¹	9	13	4³	11			7²			10	14														12
1	2	3			6		8	9²		4	12			7³	11		13	10	5¹		14											13
1		3		5	6		8	9¹		4				7²	11		12	10	13		2											14
1	2	3		5¹	6		8	7		4		11	12				9	10														15
1	2	3	12		6		8	7¹		4	13	14		11³	5		9²	10														16
1	2	3			6		8	7	12	4		11¹		5			9	10														17
1		3			6	7	8			4		11¹	2	5			9	10	12													18
1		3			6	7²	8	12		4¹	13	11	2	5			9	10														19
1	2	3			6	12	8	7¹		4		11		5			9	10														20
	2	3	4	5	6	7	8²				12			11¹			9	10					1			13						21
1	2¹	3	4	5	6	7		14	13³	8	12			9	10²											11						22
1	12	3	4²	5	6		8¹	7		2				9	14		13	11	10³													23
1	2	3	12	5	6		13	8	14	7²		4		9			11¹	10³														24
1	2	3			6	7¹	12	8²		5		9		13			11	10	4													25
1	2	3			6	7	12			5		9		10¹			11	8	4													26
1	2	3			6	7²	12	14	13	4		5		9			10¹	11³	8													27
1	2	3			6	7¹	8	12		4		5		9			13	11²	10													28
1	2	3	12		6	7¹	8			4		5		9			11²	10	13													29
1	2	3	12		6	7¹	8	13		4		5		9²	14		10	11³														30
1	2	3	12		6	7²	8			4		5		9			13	10	11¹													31
1⁰	2	3			6	7¹	8			4		9		12	13		10	11²								15		5				32
		3	4²		6	12		8		2		9		5			1	13	10		11¹			7								33
		3³			6	7	12	8		4¹		9		5			1	13	10		14		2	11²								34
		12			6	7²	13	8		4¹		9³	14	5			1	10	3		2			11								35
		12				7	13	8		4		10¹		5			1	9	3		2			11²		6						36
		12			6	7	8²	13		4		10		5	14		1	9	3		2¹			11³								37
		12			6		8			4		9		5			1	10	3		2			11¹		7						38
		12	13		6	7²	8³			4		9	14	5			1	10	3		2¹			11								39
		2			6	7	8			4		9		5			1	10	3¹		12			11								40
		3			6	7		4		2		9					1	10¹	3		8			5	11							41
		3			6	7²	4³	13		2	12	9		5¹			1	10	14		8				11							42
		3	4¹		6	7²		2		5		9					1	12	10		13			8	11							43
		2			6		4			5		9		1			11	10	3		8			7								44
		3			6	7²	4	12		2		5		9			1	13	10		14			8³	11¹							45
1		3	4		7	12		10		5		6		13			11¹	2²			8			9								46

Worthington Cup
First Round   Reading   (a) 0-0 / (h) 1-2

FA Cup
First Round   Brighton & HA   (h) 1-1 / (a) 0-3

Division 3   **PLYMOUTH ARGYLE**

FOUNDATION

The club was formed in September 1886 as the Argyle Football Club by former public and private school pupils who wanted to continue playing the game. The meeting was held in a room above the Borough Arms (a Coffee House), Bedford Street, Plymouth. It was common then to choose a local street/terrace as a club name and Argyle or Argyll was a fashionable name throughout the land due to Queen Victoria's great interest in Scotland.

Home Park, Plymouth, Devon PL2 3DQ.

Telephone: (01752) 562 561.

Fax: (01752) 606 167.

Pilgrim Shop: (01752) 558 292.

Ground Capacity: 19,630.

Record Attendance: 43,596 v Aston Villa, Division 2, 10 October 1936.

Record Receipts: £128,000 v Burnley, Division 2 play-off, 18 May 1994.

Pitch Measurements: 110yd × 72yd.

President: S. J. Rendell.

Chairman: D. McCauley.

Vice-Chairman: P. Bloom.

Directors: Paul Stapleton, John McNulty, Ken Jones, Roy Griggs.

Manager: Kevin Hodges.

Assistant Manager: Steve McCall.

Physio: Norman Medhurst.

Secretary/Chief Executive: Roger Matthews.

LATEST SEQUENCES

Longest Sequence of League Wins: 9, 8.3.86 – 12.4.86.

Longest Sequence of League Defeats: 9, 12.10.63 – 7.12.63.

Longest Sequence of League Draws: 5, 26.2.00 – 14.3.00.

Longest Sequence of Unbeaten League Matches: 22, 20.4.29 – 21.12.29.

Longest Sequence Without a League Win: 13, 27.4.63 – 2.10.63.

HONOURS

Football League: Division 2 best season: 4th, 1931–32, 1952–53; Division 3 (S) – Champions 1929–30, 1951–52; Runners-up 1921–22, 1922–23, 1923–24, 1924–25, 1925–26, 1926–27 (record of six consecutive years); Division 3 – Champions 1958–59; Runners-up 1974–75, 1985–86, Promoted 1995–96 (play-offs).
FA Cup: Semi-final 1984.
Football League Cup: Semi-final 1965, 1974.

Colours
Green and white shirts, white shorts, green, black and white stockings.
Change Colours
All white.

Year Formed: 1886.

Turned Professional: 1903.

Ltd Co.: 1903.

Previous Name: 1886, Argyle Athletic Club; 1903, Plymouth Argyle.

Club Nickname: 'The Pilgrims'.

First Football League game: 28 August 1920, Division 3, v Norwich C (h) D 1–1 – Craig; Russell, Atterbury; Logan, Dickinson, Forbes; Kirkpatrick, Jack, Bowler, Heeps (1), Dixon.

Record League Victory: 8–1 v Millwall, Division 2, 16 January 1932 – Harper; Roberts, Titmuss; Mackay, Pullan, Reed; Grozier, Bowden (2), Vidler (3), Leslie (1), Black (1), (1 og). 8–1 v Hartlepool U (a), Division 2, 7 May 1994 – Nicholls; Patterson (Naylor), Hill, Burrows, Comyn, McCall (1), Barlow, Castle (1), Landon (3), Marshall (1), Dalton (2).

Record Cup Victory: 6–0 v Corby T, FA Cup 3rd rd, 22 January 1966 – Leiper; Book, Baird; Williams, Nelson, Newman; Jones (1), Jackson (1), Bickle (3), Piper (1), Jennings.

Record Defeat: 0–9 v Stoke C, Division 2, 17 December 1960.

Most League Points (2 for a win): 68, Division 3 (S), 1929–30.

Most League Points (3 for a win): 87, Division 3, 1985–86.

Most League Goals: 107, Division 3 (S), 1925–26 and 1951–52.

Highest League Scorer in Season: Jack Cock, 32, Division 3 (S), 1925–26.

Most League Goals in Total Aggregate: Sammy Black, 180, 1924–38.

Most League Goals in One Match: 5, Wilf Carter v Charlton Ath, Division 2, 27 December 1960.

Most Capped Player: Moses Russell, 20 (23), Wales.

Most League Appearances: Kevin Hodges, 530, 1978–92.

Youngest League Player: Lee Phillips, 16 years 43 days v Gillingham, 29 October 1996.

Record Transfer Fee Received: £750,000 from Southampton for Mickey Evans, March 1997.

Record Transfer Fee Paid: £250,000 to Hartlepool U for Paul Dalton, June 1992.

Football League Record: 1920 Original Member of Division 3; 1921–30 Division 3 (S); 1930–50 Division 2; 1950–52 Division 3 (S); 1952–56 Division 2; 1956–58 Division 3 (S); 1958–59 Division 3; 1959–68 Division 2; 1968–75 Division 3; 1975–77 Division 2; 1977–86 Division 3; 1986–95 Division 2; 1995–96 Division 3; 1996–98 Division 2; 1998– Division 3.

MANAGERS

Frank Brettell 1903–05
Bob Jack 1905–06
Bill Fullerton 1906–07
Bob Jack 1910–38
Jack Tresadern 1938–47
Jimmy Rae 1948–55
Jack Rowley 1955–60
Neil Dougall 1961
Ellis Stuttard 1961–63
Andy Beattie 1963–64
Malcolm Allison 1964–65
Derek Ufton 1965–68
Billy Bingham 1968–70
Ellis Stuttard 1970–72
Tony Waiters 1972–77
Mike Kelly 1977–78
Malcolm Allison 1978–79
Bobby Saxton 1979–81
Bobby Moncur 1981–83
Johnny Hore 1983–84
Dave Smith 1984–88
Ken Brown 1988–90
David Kemp 1990–92
Peter Shilton 1992–95
Steve McCall 1995
Neil Warnock 1995–97
Mick Jones 1997–98
Kevin Hodges June 1998–

TEN YEAR LEAGUE RECORD

		P	W	D	L	F	A	Pts	Pos
1989-90	Div 2	46	14	13	19	58	63	55	16
1990-91	Div 2	46	12	17	17	54	68	53	18
1991-92	Div 2	46	13	9	24	42	64	48	22
1992-93	Div 2	46	16	12	18	59	64	60	14
1993-94	Div 2	46	25	10	11	88	56	85	3
1994-95	Div 2	46	12	10	24	45	83	46	21
1995-96	Div 3	46	22	13	12	68	49	79	4
1996-97	Div 2	46	12	18	16	47	58	54	19
1997-98	Div 2	46	12	13	21	55	70	49	22
1998-99	Div 3	46	17	10	19	58	54	61	13

DID YOU KNOW ?

On 6 December 1930, Plymouth lost goalkeeper Harry Cann with a head injury after 30 minutes against Tottenham Hotspur. Left-back Fred Titmuss took over and when Cann returned in the 85th minute, Plymouth were winning 2-0.

PLYMOUTH ARGYLE 1999–2000 LEAGUE RECORD

Match No.	Date	Venue	Opponents	Result		H/T Score	Lg. Pos.	Goalscorers	Attendance
1	Aug 7	A	Southend U	L	1-2	1-0	15	Barrett [21]	4981
2	14	H	Shrewsbury T	D	0-0	0-0	18		4919
3	21	A	Halifax T	W	1-0	0-0	12	Stonebridge [60]	2431
4	28	H	Peterborough U	W	2-1	2-0	10	Stonebridge [22], O'Sullivan [35]	4189
5	30	A	Carlisle U	L	2-4	0-2	13	Stonebridge 2 [59, 74]	2863
6	Sept 5	H	Brighton & HA	D	3-3	2-2	14	Gritton 2 [5, 38], Stonebridge [71]	5444
7	11	H	Rotherham U	D	1-1	1-0	14	Heathcote [15]	4075
8	18	A	Hartlepool U	L	0-3	0-2	17		2242
9	25	A	Darlington	L	0-2	0-1	20		5045
10	Oct 2	H	Leyton Orient	W	5-0	2-0	13	Leadbitter 2 [3, 48], McCarthy 2 [17, 53], Hargreaves [66]	3782
11	9	H	Mansfield T	W	2-1	2-0	12	Gritton [7], O'Sullivan [34]	3809
12	16	A	Rochdale	D	0-0	0-0	15		3105
13	19	A	Hull C	W	1-0	0-0	—	McGregor [49]	4727
14	23	H	Darlington	D	0-0	0-0	13		4362
15	Nov 2	H	Exeter C	W	1-0	1-0	—	McCarthy [22]	9412
16	6	A	Chester C	W	1-0	1-0	8	McCall [14]	2027
17	14	H	Barnet	W	4-1	2-0	6	McGregor 3 [19, 69, 79], Stonebridge [35]	6343
18	23	A	Cheltenham T	L	0-2	0-1	—		5140
19	27	A	York C	D	0-0	0-0	7		2745
20	Dec 4	H	Southend U	W	3-1	2-0	7	Bastow [23], Stonebridge [33], Hargreaves [68]	4679
21	17	A	Northampton T	D	1-1	1-0	—	McGregor [37]	5039
22	26	H	Torquay U	D	2-2	1-0	9	McCarthy [18], McGregor [69]	14,893
23	28	A	Swansea C	L	0-1	0-0	11		9075
24	Jan 3	H	Macclesfield T	W	3-2	2-1	8	Stonebridge 2 [35, 48], Taylor [38]	6128
25	15	A	Shrewsbury T	D	0-0	0-0	12		2458
26	22	H	Halifax T	D	1-1	0-0	12	McGregor [64]	4841
27	29	A	Peterborough U	L	0-2	0-0	13		5694
28	Feb 5	H	Carlisle U	W	2-0	1-0	10	Middleton [6], Gritton [85]	4009
29	12	A	Brighton & HA	D	1-1	1-0	12	Gritton [1]	5654
30	19	H	York C	W	2-0	2-0	11	Middleton [16], McCarthy [39]	4343
31	22	A	Lincoln C	L	0-3	0-1	—		2561
32	26	H	Hartlepool U	D	1-1	1-0	11	McGregor [39]	3917
33	Mar 4	A	Rotherham U	D	1-1	1-0	10	Hargreaves [23]	4496
34	7	H	Chester C	D	0-0	0-0	—		4140
35	11	A	Exeter C	D	1-1	0-1	10	Taylor [60]	4287
36	14	H	Lincoln C	D	1-1	1-1	—	Barrett [29]	4111
37	18	H	Cheltenham T	W	1-0	1-0	8	Gritton [43]	4392
38	21	A	Barnet	L	0-1	0-0	—		2328
39	25	A	Torquay U	W	4-0	2-0	9	Taylor [24], McGregor 3 [31, 71, 78]	4113
40	Apr 1	H	Northampton T	W	2-1	1-1	9	McGregor [23], Rowbotham [71]	5448
41	8	A	Macclesfield T	L	1-4	0-3	9	McCarthy [66]	2231
42	15	H	Swansea C	W	1-0	1-0	9	Barrett [6]	5881
43	22	A	Rochdale	D	1-1	0-0	10	McGregor [64]	6205
44	24	A	Leyton Orient	L	0-3	0-1	9		4113
45	29	H	Hull C	L	0-1	0-1	11		4233
46	May 6	A	Mansfield T	D	2-2	1-2	12	Guinan 2 [9, 72]	2031

Final League Position: 12

GOALSCORERS

League (55): McGregor 13, Stonebridge 9, Gritton 6, McCarthy 6, Barrett 3, Hargreaves 3, Taylor 3, Guinan 2, Leadbitter 2, Middleton 2, O'Sullivan 2, Bastow 1, Heathcote 1, McCall 1, Rowbotham 1.
Worthington Cup (2): Gritton 1, Stonebridge 1.
FA Cup (8): McGregor 3, Hargreaves 2, Bastow 1, Heathcote 1, Stonebridge 1.

Player appearances and goals (shirt number worn per match; superscript = goals scored).

Veysey K 5+1	Rowbotham J 7+4	Beswetherick J 44+1	Leadbitter C 28+3	Heathcote M 27+2	Barrett A 38+4	Bastow D 7+6	O'Sullivan W 45	McGregor P 44	Hargreaves C 44	Stonebridge I 27+4	Belgrave B 2+13	Sheffield J 41	McCall S 14+2	Ashton J 5+3	Taylor C 41	Gritton M 14+16	McCarthy S 21+8	Phillips L 3+14	Wotton P 21+2	Middleton C 6	Morrison-Hill J —+1	Wills K —+2	Barlow M 1+1	Paterson S 5	Gibbs P 3+4	Etherington C 4+1	Guinan S 8	Adams S 1	Match No.
1	2	3	4	5	6	7	8	9	10	11^1	12																		1
	2	3^1	4	5	6	7^2	8	9	10	11	12	1	13																2
	7	3	4^1		6	12	8	9^2	10	11	13	1			2		5												3
	2^1	3	4^2		6	13	8	9	10	11	14	1	12				5		7^3										4
1		3	4^1	5		12	8	9	10	11	13		6		2				7^2										5
		3	4^2	5^1	12	13	8	9^3	10	11	14	1	6		2				7										6
		3	4^2	5	12	7		9	10	11	13	1	6		2^1		8^3				14								7
		3	4	5^1		7	2	9^2	10	11	12	1	6				8	13											8
		3	4		6	7		9^1	10	12	13	1			2		5		8^2	11									9
		3	4		6	12	8	9	10	11^2		1			2^1		5	13	7										10
		3	4	12	6	7		9	10			1	2				5^1	8	11										11
12		3	4		6		8	9	10	11		1			2^1		5		7										12
12		3	4		6		8	9	10	11		1			2^1		5		7										13
12		3	4		6		8	9	10	11^3		1			2^1		5	13	7^2	14									14
		3	4		6		8	9	10	11		1			2		5		7										15
		3	4	12	6		8	9	10	11^2	13	1			2		5		7^1										16
		3	4	5	7		8	9	10	11^1	12	1			2		6												17
		3	4	5	7	12	8		10	11^1	9^2	1			2^3		6	13	14										18
		3	4	5	7	8	2	9	10	11^1		1					6		12										19
15		3	4	5	7	8	2	9^2	10	11^1		1^6			6		12	13											20
1		3	4	5	6	7	2	9	10	11							8												21
1		3	4	5	6	7	2	9	10	11	12						8^1												22
1		3	4^3	5	6	7^2	2	9	10	11^1	13						12	8		14									23
		3	4	5		8		9^1	10	11		1			2^2	6		7	12	13									24
		3	4	5		8		9	10	11		1			2	6		7											25
		4	5	3		2		9	10	11^1		1			6	12		7	8										26
		3	4	5	7			9		11^1	9^2	1			6	10^2	8		2	13									27
		3		5	7	2		9^2	10^3		11^1	1			6	12		13	8	4		14							28
		3		5	7	2		9^1	10		12	1			6	8^2		13	11	4									29
		3^1		5	12	2		9	10		13	1			6	8^2	7^3	14	11	4									30
		3		5	12	2		9^2	10		13	1			6	8^9	7^1	14	11	4									31
		3		5		2		9	10			1			6	8^1	7	12	11	4									32
		3	4	5	8	2		9^2	10			1			6	12	7^1		11				13						33
		3		5	4	2		9	10	12		1			6	13	8^3	14	11^1			7^2							34
		3		5	4^1	2		9	10	11		1			6	12		7					8						35
		3^2		5	7	2		9	10	12		1			6	8^1		11					4	13					36
		3		5^1	7	2		9	10^2			1			6	8		12	11				4	13					37
12		3			6	2		9	10	13		1			5	8^3		7^2	11				4^1	14					38
2		3			6	8		9^2	10			1			5	12	13		11							4	7^1		39
7		3			6	2		9	10			1			5	12	13		11							4^2	8^1		40
7		3^3			6	2		9	10			1			5	13	12^2		11				14		4^1	8		41
		3	12		6	2		9	10^1			1			5	13	7^2	14	11				4^3			8		42
		3	12		6	2		9	10			1			5	13	7^1		11				4^1			8		43
		3^3	12		6	2		9	10			1			5	13	7^1		11				4	14		8^2		44
		3	4		6	2		9	10	12		1			5	13		14	11^3				7^2			8^1		45
		3			6	2		9^2				1	7^3	12	5	13	11				14	10^1				8		4	46

Worthington Cup

First Round	Walsall	(a)	1-4
		(h)	1-4

FA Cup

First Round	Brentford	(a)	2-2
		(h)	2-1
Second Round	Brighton & HA	(h)	0-0
		(a)	2-1
Third Round	Reading	(a)	1-1
		(h)	1-0
Fourth Round	Preston NE	(h)	0-3

Division 1

PORTSMOUTH

FOUNDATION

At a meeting held in his High Street, Portsmouth offices in 1898, solicitor Alderman J. E. Pink and five other business and professional men agreed to buy some ground close to Goldsmith Avenue for £4,950 which they developed into Fratton Park in record breaking time. A team of professionals was signed up by manager Frank Brettell and entry to the Southern League obtained for the new club's September 1899 kick-off.

Fratton Park, Frogmore Rd, Portsmouth PO4 8RA.
Telephone: (01705) 731 204.
Fax: (01705) 734 129.
Commercial Dept: (01705) 731 204.
Ticket Office: (01705) 618 777/861 963.
Fax: (01705) 750 825.
Membership Office: (01705) 825 016.
ClubCall: 09068 121 182.
Ground Capacity: 19,179.
Record Attendance: 51,385 v Derby Co, FA Cup 6th rd, 26 February 1949.
Record Receipts: £233,000 v Chelsea, FA Cup 6th rd, 9 March 1997.
Pitch Measurements: 110yd × 72yd.
Chairman: Milan Mandaric.
Director: F. Dinenage.
Managing Director: David Deacon.
Manager: Tony Pulis.
First Team Coach: David Kemp.
Coach: Alan Knight.
Secretary: Paul Weld.
Youth Team Manager: Neil McNab.
Physio: Jonathan Trigg.

LATEST SEQUENCES
Longest Sequence of League Wins: 7, 22.1.83 – 26.2.83.
Longest Sequence of League Defeats: 9, 21.10.75 – 6.12.75.
Longest Sequence of League Draws: 5, 28.9.77 – 15.10.77.
Longest Sequence of Unbeaten League Matches: 15, 18.4.24 – 18.10.24.
Longest Sequence Without a League Win: 25, 29.11.58 – 22.8.59.

HONOURS

Football League: Division 1 – Champions 1948–49, 1949–50; Division 2 – Runners-up 1926–27, 1986–87; Division 3 (S) – Champions 1923–24; Division 3 – Champions 1961–62, 1982–83.

FA Cup: Winners 1939; Runners-up 1929, 1934.

Football League Cup: best season: 5th rd, 1961, 1986.

Colours
Blue shirts, white shorts, red stockings.

Change Colours
Gold shirts, blue shorts, white stockings.

Year Formed: 1898.

Turned Professional: 1898.

Ltd Co.: 1898.

Club Nickname: 'Pompey'.

First Football League Game: 28 August 1920, Division 3, v Swansea T (h) W 3–0 – Robson; Probert, Potts; Abbott, Harwood, Turner; Thompson, Stringfellow (1), Reid (1), James (1), Beedie.

Record League Victory: 9–1 v Notts Co, Division 2, 9 April 1927 – McPhail; Clifford, Ted Smith; Reg Davies (1), Foxall, Moffat; Forward (1), Mackie (2), Haines (3), Watson, Cook (2).

Record Cup Victory: 7–0 v Stockport Co, FA Cup 3rd rd, 8 January 1949 – Butler; Rookes, Ferrier; Scoular, Flewin, Dickinson; Harris (3), Barlow, Clarke (2), Phillips (2), Froggatt.

Record Defeat: 0–10 v Leicester C, Division 1, 20 October 1928.

Most League Points (2 for a win): 65, Division 3, 1961–62.

Most League Points (3 for a win): 91, Division 3, 1982–83.

Most League Goals: 91, Division 4, 1979–80.

Highest League Scorer in Season: Guy Whittingham, 42, Division 1, 1992–93.

MANAGERS
Frank Brettell 1898–1901
Bob Blyth 1901–04
Richard Bonney 1905–08
Bob Brown 1911–20
John McCartney 1920–27
Jack Tinn 1927–47
Bob Jackson 1947–52
Eddie Lever 1952–58
Freddie Cox 1958–61
George Smith 1961–70
Ron Tindall 1970–73
(General Manager to 1974)
John Mortimore 1973–74
Ian St. John 1974–77
Jimmy Dickinson 1977–79
Frank Burrows 1979–82
Bobby Campbell 1982–84
Alan Ball 1984–89
John Gregory 1989–90
Frank Burrows 1990–1991
Jim Smith 1991–95
Terry Fenwick 1995–98
Alan Ball 1998–99
Tony Pulis January 2000–

Most League Goals in Total Aggregate: Peter Harris, 194, 1946–60.

Most League Goals in One Match: 5, Alf Strange v Gillingham, Division 3, 27 January 1923; 5, Peter Harris v Aston Villa, Division 1, 3 September 1958.

Most Capped Player: Jimmy Dickinson, 48, England.

Most League Appearances: Jimmy Dickinson, 764, 1946–65.

Youngest League Player: Clive Green, 16 years 259 days v Wrexham, 21 August 1976.

Record Transfer Fee Received: £3,500,000 from Manchester C for Lee Bradbury, August 1997.

Record Transfer Fee Paid: £1,000,000 to Tottenham H for Rory Allen, July 1999.

Football League Record: 1920 Original Member of Division 3; 1921 Division 3 (S); 1924–27 Division 2; 1927–59 Division 1; 1959–61 Division 2; 1961–62 Division 3; 1962–76 Division 2; 1976–78 Division 3; 1978–80 Division 4; 1980–83 Division 3; 1983–87 Division 2; 1987–88 Division 1; 1988–92 Division 2; 1992– Division 1.

TEN YEAR LEAGUE RECORD

		P	W	D	L	F	A	Pts	Pos
1989-90	Div 2	46	15	16	15	62	65	61	12
1990-91	Div 2	46	14	11	21	58	70	53	17
1991-92	Div 2	46	19	12	15	65	51	69	9
1992-93	Div 1	46	26	10	10	80	46	88	3
1993-94	Div 1	46	15	13	18	52	58	58	17
1994-95	Div 1	46	15	13	18	63	58	58	18
1995-96	Div 1	46	13	13	20	61	69	52	21
1996-97	Div 1	46	20	8	18	59	53	68	7
1997-98	Div 1	46	13	10	23	51	63	49	20
1998-99	Div 1	46	11	14	21	57	73	47	19

DID YOU KNOW ?

On 22 September 1999, Alan Knight made his 800th first team appearance for Portsmouth in the Worthington Cup second round second leg game at Blackburn as an 84th minute substitute.

PORTSMOUTH 1999–2000 LEAGUE RECORD

Match No.	Date	Venue	Opponents	Result	H/T Score	Lg. Pos.	Goalscorers	Attendance
1	Aug 7	H	Sheffield U	W 2-0	1-0	4	Miglioranzi [26], Whittingham [88]	17,667
2	14	A	Wolverhampton W	D 1-1	1-0	3	Allen [36]	21,024
3	21	H	Stockport Co	W 2-0	0-0	2	Miglioranzi [65], Allen [74]	15,002
4	28	A	Barnsley	L 0-6	0-1	6		13,792
5	30	H	Huddersfield T	D 0-0	0-0	6		13,105
6	Sept 11	H	Ipswich T	D 1-1	0-0	11	Whittingham [48]	16,034
7	18	A	Tranmere R	W 4-2	3-0	9	Peron 2 [2, 17], Whittingham [39], Panopoulos [48]	5870
8	25	H	Grimsby T	L 1-2	1-1	10	McLoughlin (pen) [32]	12,073
9	Oct 2	A	Crystal Palace	L 0-4	0-1	15		15,221
10	16	H	Charlton Ath	L 0-2	0-1	19		14,812
11	19	H	Walsall	W 5-1	1-1	—	Thogersen 2 [44, 84], Bradbury [69], McLoughlin 2 (2 pens) [75, 79]	9042
12	23	A	QPR	D 0-0	0-0	14		13,303
13	26	A	Grimsby T	L 0-1	0-1	—		5912
14	30	H	Crystal Palace	W 3-1	1-1	13	Claridge 2 [43, 73], Bradbury [61]	13,018
15	Nov 3	A	Manchester C	L 2-4	1-0	—	Bradbury [6], Thogersen [57]	31,660
16	6	H	Birmingham C	D 2-2	1-0	13	McLoughlin 2 (2 pens) [35, 87]	12,756
17	9	A	Fulham	L 0-1	0-0	—		13,229
18	14	A	WBA	L 2-3	2-1	14	Whittingham [20], Awford [29]	11,483
19	20	H	Crewe Alex	L 0-2	0-1	15		11,550
20	24	A	Nottingham F	L 0-2	0-2	—		13,841
21	27	H	Bolton W	D 0-0	0-0	20		10,431
22	Dec 4	A	Sheffield U	L 0-1	0-1	20		10,834
23	18	H	Port Vale	D 0-0	0-0	22		11,869
24	26	A	Swindon T	D 1-1	0-1	22	Claridge [80]	10,279
25	28	H	Blackburn R	L 1-2	1-2	22	Claridge [14]	15,208
26	Jan 3	A	Norwich C	L 1-2	0-2	22	Bradbury [58]	16,637
27	15	H	Wolverhampton W	L 2-3	2-0	23	Igoe [19], Claridge [23]	13,255
28	22	A	Stockport Co	D 1-1	1-1	23	Hughes [44]	8008
29	29	H	Barnsley	W 3-0	2-0	23	Claridge 3 [8, 19, 64]	12,201
30	Feb 5	A	Huddersfield T	W 1-0	0-0	20	Claridge [74]	12,753
31	12	H	Fulham	L 0-1	0-0	20		17,337
32	22	A	Bolton W	L 0-3	0-1	—		12,672
33	Mar 1	H	Tranmere R	L 1-2	0-1	—	Claridge (pen) [83]	10,759
34	4	A	Ipswich T	W 1-0	1-0	21	Claridge [26]	20,305
35	7	A	Birmingham C	L 0-0	0-0	—		19,573
36	11	H	Nottingham F	W 2-1	0-0	21	Thogersen [84], Claridge [89]	14,336
37	18	A	Crewe Alex	W 3-1	1-0	20	Claridge [3], Thogersen [62], Harper [86]	6188
38	21	H	WBA	W 2-0	1-0	—	Claridge (pen) [26], Derry [85]	14,760
39	25	H	Swindon T	W 4-1	3-0	18	Whitbread [30], Bradbury 3 [42, 44, 49]	15,305
40	Apr 1	A	Port Vale	L 0-2	0-2	18		5426
41	8	H	Norwich C	W 2-1	0-1	15	Harper [51], Moore [71]	14,003
42	15	A	Blackburn R	D 1-1	1-1	15	Hughes [41]	19,263
43	21	A	Charlton Ath	D 1-1	0-1	—	Bradbury [40]	20,043
44	24	H	Manchester C	D 2-2	1-2	15	Bradbury 2 (1 pen) [44 (p), 84]	19,015
45	29	A	Walsall	L 0-1	0-1	17		8151
46	May 7	H	QPR	L 1-3	0-1	18	Allen [53]	16,301

Final League Position: 18

GOALSCORERS

League (55): Claridge 14 (2 pens), Bradbury 10 (1 pen), McLoughlin 5 (5 pens), Thogersen 5, Whittingham 4, Allen 3, Harper 2, Hughes 2, Miglioranzi 2, Peron 2, Awford 1, Derry 1, Igoe 1, Moore 1, Panopoulos 1, Whitbread 1.
Worthington Cup (4): Nightingale 2, Lovell 1, McLoughlin 1.
FA Cup (0).

Flahavan A 10	Robinson M 23 + 2	Harper K 12	Simpson F 17	Derry S 9	McLoughlin A 18 + 1	Cundy J 9	Myers A 4 + 4	Awford A 28 + 6	Newton A 1 + 2	Miglioranzi S 12 + 1	Allen R 10 + 5	Whittingham G 15 + 10	Peron J 9 + 1	Igoe S 14 + 12	Thogersen T 32 + 3	Petterson A 17	Whitbread A 38 + 1	Vlachos M 11 + 1	Nightingale L 1 + 6	Crowe J 21 + 4	Panopoulos M 18 + 4	Durnin J 2	Lovell S — + 3	Claridge S 31 + 3	Philips M 2 + 5	Bradbury L 35	Berntsen T 1 + 1	Waterman D 19 + 1	Pamarot N 1 + 1	Moore D 25	Brown M 4	Hiley S 4 + 4	Knight A 1	Vernazza P 7	Hoult R 18	Hughes C 15	O'Neil G — + 1	Birmingham D 1 + 1	Fenton A — + 1	Edinburgh J 11	Match No.
1	2	3	4	5	6	7¹	8	9	10	11²	12	13																													1
	2	3	4	5	6		8	9	10	11¹		12		7		1																									2
	2	3	4	5			8	9	10	11				7		1	6																								3
	2	3	4		6	12	8	9	10¹	11²				7		1	5	13																							4
	2	3	4		6	12	8¹	9	10²	11				7		1	5			13																					5
	12		6				8	9³	10²	11		13		7		1	5	3	14	2¹	4																				6
	3		4		6		8		10	11					2	1	5			7	9																				7
	3		4		6		8¹		10	11	12				2	1	5			7	9²	13																			8
	2	3	4		6	12			10²	11¹				7		1	5			8	9		13																		9
	12	3	4		6		8		10³	11		13			1		5		7²	14	2¹	9																			10
	12	3¹	4		6				11					7²	1		5	8		2				10	13	9															11
	3		4		6				12					11	7	1	5	8		2				10¹		9															12
	7	3	4		6				12					11		1	5	8²		2				10¹	13	9															13
	3²	11	4		6				12					7³	8	1	5			2	13			10¹	14	9															14
	3	11	4		6³				12					13	8	1	5			2	7²			10¹		9	14														15
	3	11³	4						10²					12	8¹	1	5			2	7			13		9		6	14												16
	3	10			6											1	5	7		2	11			12	8¹	9		4													17
1	3	11			6				10¹	12					8					2	7			13		9		4²	5												18
1	3	11	4						10²	12					5					2	7¹			13		9		6	8												19
1	3	8			6					12					5					2	7¹			10		9		13	4²	11											20
1	2	3	8¹	4	6					11					5					12				10		9			7												21
1	2		5	3			8	10²		14					6¹			12		7				13³		9		4	11												22
1	2			4	6		8¹			11					5					7		12		10		9			3												23
1			4	6					10	11					5			7¹		2				8	12	9			3												24
1	3				6				10¹	11					5					2				8	7	9		4	12												25
	3				6		8		12	11					5					2				10	7¹	9		4			1										26
	3				6					11²	12				5					2	7¹			8		9		4	13	10											27
	2				6										7		5							8		9	3	4		10	1	11									28
					3						12	13		10		5					7²			8¹		9		2	4	6³	1	11	14								29
					3						12			10		5					7²			8		9¹		2	4	13	6	1	11								30
					3³						12	13			6	5					7¹			8		9		2	4	14		1	11²								31
							12			11		5		13			2				7²			8		9¹		6	4	3³		10	1	14							32
							12							13	3		5			14	2	7³		8		9¹		6	4			10	1	11²							33
														11	7		5			2				8		9		10	4		6		1			3¹	12			3	34
		10															11			6				5		2		8	9	7	4		1							3	35
		10											13		11²	6	5									2	12	8	9¹	7	4		1							3	36
		10				7	12						13		6	5								8		9²		2	4				1			11¹				3	37
1		10				7									6	5								8		9		2	4				1			11				3	38
		10¹				7	12	14					13		6³	5								8²		9		2	4				1			11				3	39
		10				7	12	14							6²	5		13						8		9		2	4				1			11¹				3³	40
		10¹				7	12	14					13		6	5								8²		9		2	4				1			11				3³	41
		10				7	5	3							6									8		9			4				1			11				42
		10				7	13	14					12²		8									6	5³	9			4				1			11				3	43
		7				10¹	12	5					8		8								13			9		2²	4				1			11				3	44
		11					6³	5					8¹		7			12		13	14					9		2²	4				1			10				3	45
		11				7		2					8							6	5					9		2²	4				1			10				3	46

Worthington Cup

First Round	Torquay U	(a)	0-0
		(h)	3-0
Second Round	Blackburn R	(h)	0-3
		(a)	1-3

FA Cup

Third Round	Sunderland	(a)	0-1

Division 2
PORT VALE

FOUNDATION

Formed in 1876 as Port Vale, adopting the prefix 'Burslem' in 1884 upon moving to that part of the city. It was dropped in 1909.

Vale Park, Hamil Road, Burslem, Stoke-on-Trent ST6 1AW.

Telephone: (01782) 814 134.

Fax: (01782) 834 981.

Marketing Dept: (01782) 835 524.

ClubCall: 09068 121 636.

Marketing Fax: (01782) 836 875.

Club Shop: (01782) 833 545.

Community: (01782) 575 594.

Ground Capacity: 22,356.

Record Attendance: 49,768 v Aston Villa, FA Cup 5th rd, 20 February 1960.

Record Receipts: £170,349 v Everton, FA Cup 4th rd, 14 February 1996.

Pitch Measurements: 114yd × 77yd.

President: J. Burgess.

Chairman: W. T. Bell LAE, TECH. ENG, MIMI.

Directors: A. Belfield, I. McPherson, P. Wright, N. Hughes (Marketing Director).

Manager: Brian Horton.

Secretary: F. W. Lodey.

Coach:

Physio: Alan Rankin.

Medical Officer: Dr D. Phillips.

Safety Officer: W. Stevenson.

Groundsman: S. Speed.

Community Scheme Officer: Jim Cooper (01782 575594).

LATEST SEQUENCES

Longest Sequence of League Wins: 8, 8.4.1893 – 30.9.1893.

Longest Sequence of League Defeats: 9, 9.3.57 – 20.4.57.

Longest Sequence of League Draws: 6, 26.4.81 – 12.9.81.

Longest Sequence of Unbeaten League Matches: 19, 5.5.69 – 8.11.69.

Longest Sequence Without a League Win: 17, 7.12.91 – 21.3.92.

HONOURS

Football League: Division 2 – Runners-up 1993–94; Division 3 (N) – Champions 1929–30, 1953–54; Runners-up 1952–53; Division 4 – Champions 1958–59; Promoted 1969–70 (4th).

FA Cup: Semi-final 1954, when in Division 3.

Football League Cup: best season: 3rd rd 1992, 1997.

Autoglass Trophy: Winners 1993.

Anglo-Italian Cup: Runners-up 1996.

Colours
White shirts, black shorts, black and white stockings.

Change Colours
All yellow.

Year Formed: 1876.
Turned Professional: 1885.
Ltd Co.: 1911.
Previous Name: 1876, Burslem Port Vale; 1909, Port Vale.
Club Nickname: 'Valiants'.
Previous Grounds: 1876, Limekin Lane, Longport; 1881, Westport; 1884, Moorland Road, Burslem; 1886, Athletic Ground, Cobridge; 1913, Recreation Ground, Hanley; 1950, Vale Park.
First Football League Game: 3 September 1892, Division 2, v Small Heath (a) L 1–5 – Frail; Clutton, Elson; Farrington, McCrindle, Delves; Walker, Scarratt, Bliss (1), Jones. (Only 10 men).
Record League Victory: 9–1 v Chesterfield, Division 2, 24 September 1932 – Leckie; Shenton, Poyser; Sherlock, Round, Jones; McGrath, Mills, Littlewood (6), Kirkham (2), Morton (1).
Record Cup Victory: 7–1 v Irthlingborough, FA Cup 1st rd, 12 January 1907 – Matthews; Dunn, Hamilton; Eardley, Baddeley, Holyhead; Carter, Dodds (2), Beats, Mountford (2), Coxon (3).
Record Defeat: 0–10 v Sheffield U, Division 2, 10 December 1892. 0–10 v Notts Co, Division 2, 26 February 1895.
Most League Points (2 for a win): 69, Division 3 (N), 1953–54.
Most League Points (3 for a win): 89, Division 2, 1992–93.
Most League Goals: 110, Division 4, 1958–59.
Highest League Scorer in Season: Wilf Kirkham 38, Division 2, 1926–27.
Most League Goals in Total Aggregate: Wilf Kirkham, 154, 1923–29, 1931–33.
Most League Goals in One Match: 6, Stewart Littlewood v Chesterfield, Division 2, 24 September 1922.
Most Capped Player: Sammy Morgan, 7 (18), Northern Ireland.
Most League Appearances: Roy Sproson, 761, 1950–72.
Youngest League Player: Malcolm McKenzie, 15 years 347 days v Newport Co, 12 April 1966.
Record Transfer Fee Received: £2,000,000 from Wimbledon for Gareth Ainsworth, October 1998.
Record Transfer Fee Paid: £500,000 to Lincoln C for Gareth Ainsworth, September 1997.
Football League Record: 1892 Original Member of Division 2. Failed re-election in 1896; Re-elected 1898; Resigned 1907; Returned in Oct, 1919, when they took over the fixtures of Leeds City; 1929–30 Division 3 (N); 1930–36 Division 2; 1936–38 Division 3 (N); 1938–52 Division 3 (S); 1952–54 Division 3 (N); 1954–57 Division 2; 1957–58 Division 3 (S); 1958–59 Division 4; 1959–65 Division 3; 1965–70 Division 4; 1970–78 Division 3; 1978–83 Division 4; 1983–84 Division 3; 1984–86 Division 4; 1986–89 Division 3; 1989–94 Division 2; 1994–2000 Division 1; 2000– Division 2.

MANAGERS

Sam Gleaves 1896–1905
(Secretary-Manager)
Tom Clare 1905–11
A. S. Walker 1911–12
H. Myatt 1912–14
Tom Holford 1919–24 *(continued as Trainer)*
Joe Schofield 1924–30
Tom Morgan 1930–32
Tom Holford 1932–35
Warney Cresswell 1936–37
Tom Morgan 1937–38
Billy Frith 1945–46
Gordon Hodgson 1946–51
Ivor Powell 1951
Freddie Steele 1951–57
Norman Low 1957–62
Freddie Steele 1962–65
Jackie Mudie 1965–67
Sir Stanley Matthews *(General Manager)* 1965–68
Gordon Lee 1968–74
Roy Sproson 1974–77
Colin Harper 1977
Bobby Smith 1977–78
Dennis Butler 1978–79
Alan Bloor 1979
John McGrath 1980–83
John Rudge 1984–99
Brian Horton February 1999–

TEN YEAR LEAGUE RECORD

		P	W	D	L	F	A	Pts	Pos
1989-90	Div 2	46	15	16	15	62	57	61	11
1990-91	Div 2	46	15	12	19	56	64	57	15
1991-92	Div 2	46	10	15	21	42	59	45	24
1992-93	Div 2	46	26	11	9	79	44	89	3
1993-94	Div 2	46	26	10	9	79	46	88	2
1994-95	Div 1	46	15	13	18	58	64	58	17
1995-96	Div 1	46	15	15	16	59	66	60	12
1996-97	Div 1	46	17	16	13	58	55	67	8
1997-98	Div 1	46	13	10	23	56	66	49	19
1998-99	Div 1	46	13	8	25	45	75	47	21

DID YOU KNOW ?

In the summer of 1935, Port Vale should have registered the club's new name of Hanley Port Vale agreed at a shareholders meeting in March. However the decision was never acted upon and the new prefix never implemented.

PORT VALE 1999–2000 LEAGUE RECORD

Match No.	Date	Venue	Opponents	Result	H/T Score	Lg. Pos.	Goalscorers	Attendance
1	Aug 7	A	Blackburn R	D 0-0	0-0	15		20,530
2	14	H	WBA	L 1-2	1-1	18	Minton (pen) [38]	7891
3	21	A	Birmingham C	L 2-4	2-3	23	Rougier [30], Naylor [41]	18,089
4	28	H	Tranmere R	W 1-0	0-0	19	Naylor [64]	4657
5	31	A	QPR	L 2-3	0-1	—	Minton (pen) [75], Gardner [79]	9502
6	Sept 5	H	Grimsby T	W 3-1	2-0	13	Bent [21], Naylor [31], Foyle [85]	3737
7	11	H	Fulham	L 0-2	0-1	16		6130
8	18	A	Stockport Co	L 0-1	0-1	17		7632
9	25	H	Swindon T	W 2-0	0-0	15	Carragher [53], Talia (og) [72]	4629
10	Oct 2	A	Manchester C	L 1-2	0-2	17	Foyle [63]	31,608
11	9	A	Huddersfield T	D 2-2	0-2	17	Gardner [48], Foyle [71]	11,885
12	16	H	Norwich C	L 0-1	0-0	21		5790
13	19	H	Nottingham F	L 0-2	0-2	—		5714
14	23	A	Wolverhampton W	D 2-2	0-0	21	Walsh [80], Rougier [84]	20,488
15	26	A	Swindon T	L 1-2	1-1	—	Rougier [22]	5703
16	30	H	Manchester C	L 1-2	1-0	24	Foyle [40]	10,250
17	Nov 5	H	Crewe Alex	W 1-0	0-0	—	Rougier [75]	5584
18	12	A	Walsall	D 0-0	0-0	19		6190
19	20	H	Crystal Palace	D 2-2	1-0	20	Rougier [20], Foyle [78]	5170
20	23	A	Sheffield U	W 3-1	1-1	—	Eyre [45], Tankard [71], Gardner [80]	8965
21	27	A	Charlton Ath	D 2-2	0-2	19	Rougier [46], Foyle [55]	19,266
22	Dec 4	A	Blackburn R	D 0-0	0-0	18		6084
23	18	A	Portsmouth	D 0-0	0-0	21		11,869
24	28	A	Barnsley	L 1-3	0-0	21	Minton [71]	16,855
25	Jan 3	H	Ipswich T	L 1-2	0-1	21	Naylor [50]	6908
26	15	A	WBA	D 0-0	0-0	22		10,831
27	22	H	Birmingham C	W 3-1	1-0	22	Naylor [14], Widdrington (pen) [86], Rougier [90]	7702
28	Feb 5	H	QPR	D 1-1	1-1	23	Bullock [28]	5493
29	8	H	Bolton W	L 0-1	0-0	—		5092
30	12	A	Grimsby T	L 0-2	0-2	23		6265
31	26	H	Stockport Co	D 1-1	1-1	23	Widdrington [45]	5663
32	Mar 4	A	Fulham	L 1-3	0-2	23	Healy [74]	10,418
33	7	A	Crewe Alex	L 1-2	0-1	—	Viljanen [82]	8044
34	11	H	Sheffield U	L 2-3	1-1	23	Healy [45], Rougier [90]	5484
35	18	A	Crystal Palace	D 1-1	0-0	23	Widdrington (pen) [73]	18,954
36	21	H	Walsall	L 1-2	0-2	—	Cummins [59]	5737
37	25	A	Bolton W	L 1-2	0-2	23	Viljanen [53]	12,292
38	Apr 1	H	Portsmouth	W 2-0	2-0	23	Viljanen [15], Widdrington (pen) [43]	5426
39	4	H	Charlton Ath	D 2-2	1-0	—	Viljanen [39], Burton [68]	4513
40	8	A	Ipswich T	L 0-3	0-2	23		19,663
41	15	H	Barnsley	D 2-2	1-1	23	Burton [9], Widdrington (pen) [90]	5918
42	18	A	Tranmere R	L 1-2	1-0	—	Healy [41]	5602
43	22	A	Norwich C	D 0-0	0-0	23		15,526
44	24	H	Huddersfield T	L 1-2	1-1	23	Naylor [38]	5828
45	29	A	Nottingham F	L 0-2	0-2	23		15,534
46	May 7	H	Wolverhampton W	L 0-1	0-0	23		8525

Final League Position: 23

GOALSCORERS

League (48): Rougier 8, Foyle 6, Naylor 6, Widdrington 5 (4 pens), Viljanen 4, Gardner 3, Healy 3, Minton 3 (2 pens), Burton 2, Bent 1, Bullock 1, Carragher 1, Cummins 1, Eyre 1, Tankard 1, Walsh 1, own goal 1.
Worthington Cup (5): Naylor 2, Griffiths 1, Minton 1 (pen), Rougier 1.
FA Cup (0).

	Pilkington K 15	Brisco N 11 + 1	Walsh M 10 + 2	Brammer D 29	Carragher M 36 + 1	Gardner A 26	Rougier T 33 + 5	Bent M 7 + 1	Naylor T 25 + 11	Minton J 23	Barker S 3 + 2	Griffiths C — + 5	Eyre R 17 + 13	Tankard A 31 + 4	Smith A 9 + 4	Musselwhite P 30	Widdrington T 37 + 1	Foyle M 13 + 9	Butler T 15	Snijders M 18 + 3	Bogie I 8 + 1	Aldridge- M — + 3 (deceased)	Burns L 24	Rimmer S — + 2	Corden W — + 2	Burton S 19 + 1	Bullock M 6	Taylor G 4	Talbot S 6	O'Callaghan G 8 + 3	Donnelly P 4	Healy D 15 + 1	Viljanen V 11 + 4	Cummins M 12	Goodlad M 1	Match No.
	1	2	3	4	5	6	7	8	9¹	10	11²	12	13																							1
	1	2		4	5	6			8	9	10	11²	13	12	3	7¹																				2
		2		4	5	6	7		8¹	9²	10		3	12		1	11	13																		3
				4	5	6	7		9	10			8	2	11¹	1	12	3																		4
			12	4	5	6	7		9	11			13	8¹	2²	1	14	10²	3																	5
				4	5	6	7	8	9¹	10	13		11²	2		1		12	3¹	14																6
				4	5	6	12	8	9	10	11²		7¹	2		1		13	3																	7
			12	4	5	6	7	8	9	10			2¹			1	13	3	11²																	8
		2		4¹	5	6	7		9	10³	12		14	3²		1	13	8	11																	9
		2		4	5	6	7	8¹	9	10²						1	12	3	11	13																10
		2		4	5	6	7			10¹			13	12		1	8	9	3	11²																11
		2		4	5¹	6		13	9³	10²	11		12	1		7	8	3				14													12
		2¹		4	5	6	7		9				10	3		1	11	8							12											13
		2		4¹	3	6	13		9³	10²			11	12		1	7	14	5	8																14
		2¹		4	5	6	7						13	10	12	1	11	9²	3	8																15
				4	5	6	7						12	10¹	2	1	11	9	3	8																16
				4	3	6	7		12	10			8¹	2		1	11	9	5																	17
				4	3	6	7			10			12	2¹		1	11	9	5				8													18
				4	3	6	7		12	10¹			2			1	11	9	5				8													19
				4	3	6	7						10	2		1	11	9	5				8													20
		2		4¹	3	6	7		12				10			1	11	9	5				8													21
				4	3	6	7						10	2		1	11	9	5				8													22
		2			5	6	7		8	10			9	3		1	11		4																	23
					3	6	7		8¹	10			4			1	11	9	5²				2	13	12	8										24
		3		4	5	6	7		9	10¹			13	2		1	11²	12					8													25
				4	3	6¹	7		9	10			2			1	11		5						12	8										26
				4	3		12		9	10¹			2²	14		1	11		13				5		6	7³	8									27
			12	4			13		9²	10³			3	14		1	11						5		6	7	8	2¹									28
				4			12						13	3		7⁴	1	11³	9¹				5		6	8	10	2	14							29
				4²			9						12	3	8	1	11					13	5	14	6¹	7	10	2³								30
	1	2					9						12			11				6	5¹	7	4		13		8²				3	10²	14			31
	1						9²	10					12			11				5¹		7	4						2		3	8	13			32
		2					12						10	1	11					5	7¹				6					4	3	8	9			33
		2			12		13						14	10¹	1	11				5	7				6					4³	3	8	9²			34
	1		3		11								2	7		4						5		6					8¹		9	12	10			35
	1		3		11	12							2	7		4						5		6							8	9¹	10			36
	1		3		11	12							2			4²						5		6					7¹	13	8	9	10			37
	1		3		11¹								12	2		4		5						6					7		8	9	10			38
	1		3		11									2		4		5						6					7		8	9	10			39
	1		3		11	12								2		4		5						6					7¹		8	9	10			40
	1	2	3		11	12										4						5		6					7¹		8	9	10			41
	1	7	2		11	12							3			4						5		6							8	9	10¹			42
	1	2			11	12							7	3		4						5		6							8	9	10			43
	1	2¹		12²	11	9							7³	3		4		13				5		6							8	14	10			44
	1				11	9								12		4		5				2		6					3	7¹	8		10			45
			4¹	3					8²					7		11		5				2		6					12		13	9	10	1	46

Worthington Cup
First Round   Chester C   (a) 1-2
                          (h) 4-4

FA Cup
Third Round   Leeds U   (a) 0-2

Division 1   **PRESTON NORTH END**

FOUNDATION

North End Cricket and Rugby Club which was formed in 1863, indulged in most sports before taking up soccer in about 1879. In 1881 they decided to stick to football to the exclusion of other sports and even a 16–0 drubbing by Blackburn Rovers in an invitation game at Deepdale, a few weeks after taking this decision, did not deter them for they immediately became affiliated to the Lancashire FA.

Deepdale, Preston PR1 6RU.
Telephone: (01772) 902 020.
Fax: (01772) 653 266.
Website: www.prestonnorthend.co.uk
Email: enquiries@prestonnorthend.co.uk
Ticket Enquiries: (01772) 902 000.
Ticket Office Credit Card Bookings: (01772) 902 222.
Corporate Hospitality: (01772) 902 048.
Publishing: (01772) 902 046.
Community: (01772) 902 030.
Kit 1 Shop at Deepdale: (01772) 902 040.
Kit 2 Shop, Preston Town Centre: (01772) 887 088.
Kit 3 Shop, Leyland: (01772) 624 600.
ClubCall: 09068 121 173.
Ground Capacity: 21,412.
Record Attendance: 42,684 v Arsenal, Division 1, 23 April 1938.
Record Receipts: £68,650 v Sheffield W, FA Cup 3rd rd, 4 January 1992.
Pitch Measurements: 110yd × 77yd.
President: Sir Tom Finney OBE, JP.
Chairman: Bryan M. Gray.
Directors: K. W. Leeming and M. J. Woodhouse (snr) (Vice-Chairmen), D. Shaw (Non-Executive), T. Scholes (Finance Director/Company Secretary).
Manager: David Moyes.
Coach/Goalkeeping Coach: Kelham O'Hanlon.
Secretary: M. Wearmouth.

LATEST SEQUENCES
Longest Sequence of League Wins: 14, 25.12.50 – 27.3.51.
Longest Sequence of League Defeats: 8, 22.9.84 – 27.10.84.
Longest Sequence of League Draws: 6, 24.2.79 – 20.3.79.
Longest Sequence of Unbeaten League Matches: 23, 8.9.1888 – 14.9.1889.
Longest Sequence Without a League Win: 15, 14.4.23 – 20.10.23.

HONOURS

Football League: Division 1 – Champions 1888–89 (first champions) 1889–90; Runners-up 1890–91, 1891–92, 1892–93, 1905–06, 1952–53, 1957–58; Division 2 – Champions 1903–04, 1912–13, 1950–51, 1999–2000; Runners-up 1914–15, 1933–34; Division 3 – Champions 1970–71, 1995–96; Division 4 – Runners-up 1986–87.

FA Cup: Winners 1889, 1938; Runners-up 1888, 1922, 1937, 1954, 1964.

Double Performed: 1888–89.

Football League Cup: best season: 4th rd, 1963, 1966, 1972, 1981.

Colours
White shirts, navy shorts, white stockings.

Change Colours
All Royal blue.

Year Formed: 1881.

Turned Professional: 1885.

Ltd Co.: 1893.

Club Nicknames: 'The Lilywhites' or 'North End'.

First Football League Game: 8 September 1888, Football League, v Burnley (h) W 5–2 – Trainer; Howarth, Holmes; Robertson, W. Graham, J. Graham; Gordon (1), Ross (2), Goodall, Dewhurst (2), Drummond.

Record League Victory: 10–0 v Stoke, Division 1, 14 September 1889 – Trainer; Howarth, Holmes; Kelso, Russell (1), Graham; Gordon, Jimmy Ross (2), Nick Ross (3), Thomson (2), Drummond (2).

Record Cup Victory: 26–0 v Hyde, FA Cup 1st rd, 15 October 1887 – Addison; Howarth, Nick Ross; Russell (1), Thomson (5), Graham (1); Gordon (5), Jimmy Ross (8), John Goodall (1), Dewhurst (3), Drummond (2).

Record Defeat: 0–7 v Blackpool, Division 1, 1 May 1948.

Most League Points (2 for a win): 61, Division 3, 1970–71.

Most League Points (3 for a win): 95, Division 2, 1999–2000.

Most League Goals: 100, Division 2, 1927–28 and Division 1, 1957–58.

Highest League Scorer in Season: Ted Harper, 37, Division 2, 1932–33.

Most League Goals in Total Aggregate: Tom Finney, 187, 1946–60.

Most League Goals in One Match: 7, Jimmy Ross v Stoke, Division 1, 6 October 1888.

Most Capped Player: Tom Finney, 76, England.

Most League Appearances: Alan Kelly, 447, 1961–75.

Youngest League Player: Steve Doyle, 16 years 166 days v Tranmere R, 15 November 1974.

Record Transfer Fee Received: £1,250,000 from WBA for Kevin Kilbane, June 1997.

Record Transfer Fee Paid: £500,000 to Manchester U for Michael Appleton, August 1997.

Football League Record: 1888 Founder Member of League; 1901–04 Division 2; 1904–12 Division 1; 1912–13 Division 2; 1913–14 Division 1; 1914–15 Division 2; 1919–25 Division 1; 1925–34 Division 2; 1934–49 Division 1; 1949–51 Division 2; 1951–61 Division 1; 1961–70 Division 2; 1970–71 Division 3; 1971–74 Division 2; 1974–78 Division 3; 1978–81 Division 2; 1981–85 Division 3; 1985–87 Division 4; 1987–92 Division 3; 1992–93 Division 2; 1993–96 Division 3; 1996–2000 Division 2; 2000– Division 1.

MANAGERS

Charlie Parker 1906–15
Vincent Hayes 1919–23
Jim Lawrence 1923–25
Frank Richards 1925–27
Alex Gibson 1927–31
Lincoln Hayes 1931–1932
Run by committee 1932–36
Tommy Muirhead 1936–37
Run by committee 1937–49
Will Scott 1949–53
Scot Symon 1953–54
Frank Hill 1954–56
Cliff Britton 1956–61
Jimmy Milne 1961–68
Bobby Seith 1968–70
Alan Ball Sr 1970–73
Bobby Charlton 1973–75
Harry Catterick 1975–77
Nobby Stiles 1977–81
Tommy Docherty 1981
Gordon Lee 1981–83
Alan Kelly 1983–85
Tommy Booth 1985–86
Brian Kidd 1986
John McGrath 1986–90
Les Chapman 1990–92
John Beck 1992–94
Gary Peters 1994–98
David Moyes January 1998–

TEN YEAR LEAGUE RECORD

		P	W	D	L	F	A	Pts	Pos
1989-90	Div 3	46	14	10	22	65	79	52	19
1990-91	Div 3	46	15	11	20	54	67	56	17
1991-92	Div 3	46	15	12	19	61	72	57	17
1992-93	Div 2	46	13	8	25	65	94	47	21
1993-94	Div 3	42	18	13	11	79	60	67	5
1994-95	Div 3	42	19	10	13	58	41	67	5
1995-96	Div 3	46	23	17	6	78	38	86	1
1996-97	Div 2	46	18	7	21	49	55	61	15
1997-98	Div 2	46	15	14	17	56	56	59	15
1998-99	Div 2	46	22	13	11	78	50	79	5

DID YOU KNOW ❓

Preston North End established several club records in 1950-51 including their longest unbeaten run, successive sequence of wins, away wins and highest number of points.

PRESTON NORTH END 1999–2000 LEAGUE RECORD

Match No.	Date		Venue	Opponents	Result		H/T Score	Lg. Pos.	Goalscorers	Attendance
1	Aug	7	A	Oldham Ath	W	1-0	0-0	8	Macken [65]	9432
2		14	H	Stoke C	W	2-1	0-1	1	Nogan [52], Murdock [80]	11,465
3		21	A	Wycombe W	D	1-1	1-1	5	Nogan [23]	5091
4		28	H	Wigan Ath	L	1-4	1-1	8	Basham [18]	13,885
5	Sept	1	A	Reading	D	2-2	2-0	—	Eyres [32], Basham [39]	7628
6		4	H	Chesterfield	L	0-2	0-0	11		8506
7		11	H	Burnley	D	0-0	0-0	13		13,708
8		18	A	Gillingham	W	2-0	0-0	10	Macken [64], Gregan [71]	6610
9		25	H	Brentford	D	2-2	0-1	12	Macken [73], McKenna [81]	7100
10	Oct	2	H	Cambridge U	W	2-1	0-1	11	Macken 2 [55, 90]	9522
11		9	H	Bristol C	W	1-0	1-0	7	Mathie [36]	10,042
12		16	A	Scunthorpe U	D	1-1	1-0	8	Macken [40]	5336
13		19	A	Millwall	W	2-0	0-0	—	Cartwright [51], Nethercott (og) [57]	6355
14		23	H	Brentford	W	2-1	0-1	6	Alexander (pen) [60], Marshall (og) [87]	10,382
15	Nov	3	H	Bournemouth	W	3-0	2-0	—	McKenna [9], Macken [45], Alexander (pen) [74]	9630
16		6	A	Colchester U	D	2-2	0-1	3	Mathie [61], Nogan [85]	3818
17		12	H	Notts Co	W	2-0	2-0	2	Macken 2 [17, 27]	14,226
18		23	A	Luton T	W	2-0	2-0	—	Eyres 2 [32, 45]	5124
19		27	A	Bury	W	3-1	1-0	2	Jackson [24], Gregan [55], Macken [71]	6469
20	Dec	4	H	Oldham Ath	W	2-0	0-0	2	Macken 2 [60, 88]	10,970
21		18	H	Blackpool	W	3-0	0-0	2	Eyres 2 [71, 86], Appleton [75]	16,821
22		26	A	Wrexham	D	0-0	0-0	3		7872
23		28	H	Bristol R	W	2-1	0-1	2	Alexander (pen) [63], Macken [72]	16,680
24	Jan	3	A	Cardiff C	W	4-0	0-0	2	Edwards [46], Alexander 2 (1 pen) [55, 83 (p)], Nogan [63]	10,142
25		14	A	Stoke C	L	1-2	0-1	—	Alexander (pen) [84]	10,285
26		22	H	Wycombe W	W	3-2	2-1	3	Murdock [34], Macken 2 [45, 86]	10,969
27	Feb	1	A	Oxford U	W	4-0	1-0	—	Macken 2 [17, 50], Eyres [73], Appleton [90]	5164
28		5	H	Reading	D	2-2	0-1	1	Macken [53], Jackson [56]	12,618
29		12	A	Chesterfield	W	1-0	0-0	1	Gregan [78]	4726
30		19	H	Bury	D	1-1	1-1	1	Macken [17]	13,901
31		26	H	Gillingham	L	0-2	0-0	2		13,246
32	Mar	4	A	Burnley	W	3-0	1-0	2	Jackson [2], Macken [72], Edwards [77]	22,310
33		7	H	Colchester U	L	2-3	0-1	—	Angell 2 [71, 82]	11,323
34		11	A	Bournemouth	W	1-0	0-0	2	Angell [48]	5317
35		14	H	Oxford U	W	3-1	1-0	—	Angell 2 [42, 75], Macken [78]	12,008
36		18	H	Luton T	W	1-0	1-0	1	Anderson [8]	13,731
37		21	A	Notts Co	L	0-1	0-1	—		6401
38		25	H	Wrexham	W	1-0	0-0	1	Anderson [47]	12,481
39	Apr	1	D	Blackpool	D	0-0	0-0	1		9042
40		4	A	Wigan Ath	W	1-0	1-0	—	Jackson [17]	15,593
41		8	H	Cardiff C	D	0-0	0-0	1		13,794
42		15	A	Bristol R	W	2-0	1-0	1	Macken [41], Gunnlaugsson [67]	10,111
43		22	H	Scunthorpe U	W	1-0	1-0	1	Angell [42]	15,518
44		24	A	Cambridge U	L	0-2	0-2	1		6068
45		29	H	Millwall	W	3-2	3-0	1	Eyres [1], Jackson [8], Angell [40]	19,407
46	May	6	A	Bristol C	W	2-0	1-0	1	Angell [14], Appleton [53]	11,160

Final League Position: 1

GOALSCORERS

League (74): Macken 22, Angell 8, Eyres 7, Alexander 6 (5 pens), Jackson 5, Nogan 4, Appleton 3, Gregan 3, Anderson 2, Basham 2, Edwards 2, Mathie 2, McKenna 2, Murdock 2, Cartwright 1, Gunnlaugsson 1, own goals 2.
Worthington Cup (7): Macken 2, Mathie 2, Alexander 1, Appleton 1, Basham 1.
FA Cup (9): Alexander 3 (3 pens), Eyres 1, Gunnlaugsson 1, McKenna 1, Macken 1, own goals 2.

Lucas D 6	Alexander G 46	Ludden D 3	Murdock C 29+4	Jackson M 46	Gregan S 33	Appleton M 21+5	Rankine M 44	Nogan K 16+6	Macken J 40+4	Eyres D 26+15	Edwards R 37+4	Basham S 11+13	Kidd R 28+1	McKenna P 17+7	Cartwright L 22+8	Moilanen T 40+1	Mathie A 5+7	Gunnlaugsson B 12+14	Diaf F 1+2	Wright M —+2	Morgan P —	Darby J 2+1	Beresford D 1+3	Angell B 9+6	Anderson I 11+1	Beesley M —+1	Parkinson G —+1	Barry-Murphy B —+1	Match No
1	2	3^1	4	5	6	7	8	9^1	10	11	12	13																	1
1	2		4	5	6	7	8	9	10^1	11^2	12	3	13																2
1	2		4	5	6	7	8	9^1	10	11^2	12	3	13																3
1	2		4	5	6^2	7	8	12	9^1	11^6	10	3	13	15															4
1	2		4	5	6	7	8	9	10	11^2	12	3^1	13																5
1	2	6	4	5		8	9	12	10	11^3	3	10	7																6
	2	3	4	5	12^6	8	9	14	11^3	13	10		6^1	7	1														7
	2			5	6		8	9	11	3	4	12	7^1	1	10														8
	2			5	6		8	12	9	3	4	11	7^1	1	10														9
	2	12		5	6		8	9	13	3	4^1	11^2	7	1	10^3	14													10
	2			5	6		8	12	9	13	3	4	11^2	7	1	10^1													11
	2		4	5	6		8	12	9	13	3		11^2	7	1	10^1													12
	2		4	5	6		8	9^1	10^2	12	3		11	7	1	13													13
	2		4	5	6		8	9^4	10	12	3		11^1	7^3	1	13	14												14
	2		4	5	6		8	9^2	10^3		3		11^1	7	1	12	13	14											15
	2		4	5	6		8	9	10		3		7^2	1	12	13	11^1												16
	2		4	5	6		8	9^2	10^3	11^1	3	12	7	1	13		14												17
	2			5	6		8	10	9	11	3	4	7	1															18
	2			5	6	12	8	9	10^2	11^3	3	4	7^1	1	13	14													19
	2			5		7	8	9^1	10	11	3	4	1	12		6													20
	2			5	6	12	8	13	10^2	11	3	4	1	14	9^3				7^1										21
	2			5	6	7		12	10^2	11	3	13	4	1	9^1	14			8^3										22
	2	12		5	6	7	8	9	10	11^2	3		4^1	1	13														23
	2		4	5	6	7	8	9	10^1	11^2	3		1	12					13										24
	2		4	5	6	7^1	8	9	10	11^2	3		1	12					13										25
	2		4	5	6	11	8		10		3	12	7^1	1	9														26
	2		4	5	6^1	7	8	9^3	11	3	10^2	12	1	13											14				27
	2		4	5	6	7	8	9	11	3	10^1		1	12															28
	2		4	5	6	7		10	11	3	12	8^1	1	9^2			13												29
	2		4	5	6	7	8	10	11^3	3	12		1	9															30
	2		4	5	6	7^1	8	10	12	3	13		1	9^3			14	11^2											31
	2		4	5	6^2		8	10^3	12	3	9	7	13	1	14	11^1													32
	2^2		4	5			8	10	12	3	9^3	6	7	1	13	14	11^1												33
	2		4	5	12		8	10	11^1	3^2	14	6	13	7	1	9^3													34
	2		4	5			8	10^1	11	13	3	6	7^3	1	12	9^2	14												35
	2		4	5	6		8	10^2	11^1	12	13	3	14	1	9	7^3													36
	2		4	5			8	12	13	3	10^3	6^1	7	1	14	9	11^2												37
	2		4	5	6	12	8		10^3	3	13	7^1	1	14	9	11^2													38
	2			5	6		8	10^2	12	3	4	7	13	1	9	11^1													39
	2			5	6^3		8	10	12	3	14	4	7	13	1	9^1	11^2												40
	2			5			8	10^2	12	3	6^1	4	7	14	1	9	13^3	11											41
	2			5		7	8	10^1	12	3	4	6	13	1	9^3	14	11^2												42
	2			5		7	8	10^3	12	3	4	6^2	13	1	9	14	11^1												43
	2^3	12		5			11^2	8	13	3	14	4	6	7^1	1	10	9												44
	2	12		5		7	8	13	11	3^1	4	6	1	10^2	9														45
	2^2		4	5		7	8	10	11^3	3	12	6	1	9^1	13	14													46

Worthington Cup

First Round	Wrexham	(h)	1-0
		(a)	2-0
Second Round	Sheffield U	(a)	0-2
		(h)	3-0
Third Round	Arsenal	(a)	1-2

FA Cup

First Round	Bristol R	(a)	1-0
Second Round	Enfield	(h)	0-0
		(a)	3-0
Third Round	Oldham Ath	(h)	2-1
Fourth Round	Plymouth Arg	(a)	3-0
Fifth Round	Everton	(a)	0-2

Division 1   **QUEENS PARK RANGERS**

FOUNDATION

There is an element of doubt about the date of the foundation of this club, but it is believed that in either 1885 or 1886 it was formed through the amalgamation of Christchurch Rangers and St Jude's Institute FC. The leading light was George Wodehouse, whose family maintained a connection with the club until comparatively recent times. Most of the players came from the Queen's Park district so this name was adopted after a year as St Jude's Institute.

South Africa Road, London W12 7PA.
Telephone: (020) 8743 0262.
Fax: (020) 8749 0994.
Box Office: (020) 8740 2575.
Supporters Club: (020) 8740 2534.
Club Shop: (020) 8749 2509.
Commercial: (020) 8740 2547/2588.
Ticket Master: (020) 7344 9494.
ClubCall: 09068 121 162.
Ground Capacity: 19,148.
Record Attendance: 35,353 v Leeds U, Division 1, 27 April 1974.
Record Receipts: £218,475 v Manchester U, FA Premier League, 5 February 1994.
Pitch Measurements: 112yd × 72yd.
Chairman: Chris Wright.
Executive Directors: Nick Blackburn, Paul Hart, Simon Crane.
Non-Executive Directors: Lord Terence Burns GCB, Peter Ellis, Charles Levison, Ross Jones.
Associate Directors: Andrew Ellis, Tony Ingham, Chris O'Donnell, Keith Westcott, Ross Jones.
Manager: Gerry Francis.
Secretary: Sheila Marson.
Commercial Manager: Mark Devlin.
Physio: Brian Morris.
Year Formed: 1885* (*see Foundation*).
Turned Professional: 1898.
Ltd Co.: 1899.
Previous Name: 1885, St Jude's; 1887, Queens Park Rangers.
Club Nicknames: 'Rangers' or 'Rs'.

LATEST SEQUENCES
Longest Sequence of League Wins: 8, 7.11.31 – 28.12.31.
Longest Sequence of League Defeats: 9, 25.2.69 – 5.4.69.
Longest Sequence of League Draws: 6, 29.1.00 – 5.3.00.
Longest Sequence of Unbeaten League Matches: 20, 11.3.72 – 23.9.72.
Longest Sequence Without a League Win: 20, 7.12.68 – 7.4.69.

HONOURS

Football League: Division 1 – Runners-up 1975–76; Division 2 – Champions 1982–83; Runners-up 1967–68, 1972–73; Division 3 (S) – Champions 1947–48; Runners-up 1946–47; Division 3 – Champions 1966–67.

FA Cup: Runners-up 1982.

Football League Cup: Winners 1967; Runners-up 1986. (In 1966–67 won Division 3 and Football League Cup.)

European Competitions: UEFA Cup: 1976–77, 1984–85.

Colours
Blue and white hooped shirts, blue shorts, blue stockings.

Change Colours
White shirts, black shorts, black stockings.

Previous Grounds: 1885* (*see Foundation*), Welford's Fields; 1888–99; London Scottish Ground, Brondesbury, Home Farm, Kensal Rise Green, Gun Club Wormwood Scrubs, Kilburn Cricket Ground; 1899, Kensal Rise Athletic Ground; 1901, Latimer Road, Notting Hill; 1904, Agricultural Society, Park Royal; 1907, Park Royal Ground; 1917, Loftus Road; 1931, White City; 1933, Loftus Road; 1962, White City; 1963, Loftus Road.

First Football League Game: 28 August 1920, Division 3, v Watford (h) L 1–2 – Price; Blackman, Wingrove, Grant, O'Brien; Faulkner, Birch (1), Smith, Gregory, Middlemiss.

Record League Victory: 9–2 v Tranmere R, Division 3, 3 December 1960 – Drinkwater; Woods, Ingham; Keen, Rutter, Angell; Lazarus (2), Bedford (2), Evans (2), Andrews (1), Clark (2).

Record Cup Victory: 8–1 v Bristol R (away), FA Cup 1st rd, 27 November 1937 – Gilfillan; Smith, Jefferson; Lowe, James, March; Cape, Mallett, Cheetham (3), Fitzgerald (3) Bott (2). 8–1 v Crewe Alex, Milk Cup 1st rd, 3 October 1983 – Hucker; Neill, Dawes, Waddock (1), McDonald (1), Fenwick, Micklewhite (1), Stewart (1), Allen (1), Stainrod (3), Gregory.

Record Defeat: 1–8 v Mansfield T, Division 3, 15 March 1965. 1–8 v Manchester U, Division 1, 19 March 1969.

Most League Points (2 for a win): 67, Division 3, 1966–67.

Most League Points (3 for a win): 85, Division 2, 1982–83.

Most League Goals: 111, Division 3, 1961–62.

Highest League Scorer in Season: George Goddard, 37, Division 3 (S), 1929–30.

Most League Goals in Total Aggregate: George Goddard, 172, 1926–34.

Most League Goals in One Match: 4, George Goddard v Merthyr T, Division 3S, 9 March 1929; 4, George Goddard v Swindon T, Division 3S, 12 April 1930; 4, George Goddard v Exeter C, Division 3S, 20 December 1930; 4, George Goddard v Watford, Division 3S, 19 September 1931; 4, Tom Cheetham v Aldershot, Division 3S, 14 September 1935; 4, Tom Cheetham v Aldershot, Division 3S, 12 November 1938.

Most Capped Player: Alan McDonald, 52, Northern Ireland.

Most League Appearances: Tony Ingham, 519, 1950–63.

Youngest League Player: Frank Sibley, 16 years 97 days v Bristol C, 10 March 1964.

Record Transfer Fee Received: £6,000,000 from Newcastle U for Les Ferdinand, June 1995.

Record Transfer Fee Paid: £2,750,000 to Stoke C for Mike Sheron, July 1997.

Football League Record: 1920 Original Members of Division 3; 1921–48 Division 3 (S); 1948–52 Division 2; 1952–58 Division 3 (S); 1958–67 Division 3; 1967–68 Division 2; 1968–69 Division 1; 1969–73 Division 2; 1973–79 Division 1; 1979–83 Division 2; 1983–92 Division 1; 1992–96 FA Premier League; 1996– Division 1.

MANAGERS

James Cowan 1906–13
Jimmy Howie 1913–20
Ted Liddell 1920–24
Will Wood 1924–25
(had been Secretary since 1903)
Bob Hewison 1925–30
John Bowman 1930–31
Archie Mitchell 1931–33
Mick O'Brien 1933–35
Billy Birrell 1935–39
Ted Vizard 1939–44
Dave Mangnall 1944–52
Jack Taylor 1952–59
Alec Stock 1959–65
(General Manager to 1968)
Bill Dodgin Jnr 1968
Tommy Docherty 1968
Les Allen 1968–71
Gordon Jago 1971–74
Dave Sexton 1974–77
Frank Sibley 1977–78
Steve Burtenshaw 1978–79
Tommy Docherty 1979–80
Terry Venables 1980–84
Gordon Jago 1984
Alan Mullery 1984
Frank Sibley 1984–85
Jim Smith 1985–88
Trevor Francis 1988–90
Don Howe 1990–91
Gerry Francis 1991–94
Ray Wilkins 1994–96
Stewart Houston 1996–97
Ray Harford 1997–98
Gerry Francis October 1998–

TEN YEAR LEAGUE RECORD

		P	W	D	L	F	A	Pts	Pos
1989-90	Div 1	38	13	11	14	45	44	50	11
1990-91	Div 1	38	12	10	16	44	53	46	12
1991-92	Div 1	42	12	18	12	48	47	54	11
1992-93	PR Lge	42	17	12	13	63	55	63	5
1993-94	PR Lge	42	16	12	14	62	61	60	9
1994-95	PR Lge	42	17	9	16	61	59	60	8
1995-96	PR Lge	38	9	6	23	38	57	33	19
1996-97	Div 1	46	18	12	16	64	60	66	9
1997-98	Div 1	46	10	19	17	51	63	49	21
1998-99	Div 1	46	12	11	23	52	61	47	20

DID YOU KNOW ?

Jack Blackman scored 13 goals in seven consecutive League and FA Cup games for Queens Park Rangers in 1933-34, starting with a cup tie against New Brighton and ending with a League game against Brighton & Hove Albion.

QUEENS PARK RANGERS 1999–2000 LEAGUE RECORD

Match No.	Date		Venue	Opponents	Result		H/T Score	Lg. Pos.	Goalscorers	Attendance
1	Aug	7	H	Huddersfield T	W	3-1	2-0	3	Darlington [16], Kiwomya [38], Peacock [79]	13,642
2		14	A	Bolton W	L	1-2	1-1	10	Peacock (pen) [38]	13,019
3		21	H	Wolverhampton W	D	1-1	0-1	10	Peacock [75]	13,239
4		28	A	Nottingham F	D	1-1	0-1	12	Ready [89]	18,442
5		31	H	Port Vale	W	3-2	1-0	—	Wardley 2 [16, 63], Kiwomya [77]	9502
6	Sept	18	A	Fulham	L	0-1	0-1	13		19,623
7		25	A	Birmingham C	L	0-2	0-1	17		18,748
8	Oct	2	H	Blackburn R	D	0-0	0-0	18		14,002
9		9	H	Tranmere R	W	2-1	1-0	14	Steiner [3], Peacock [62]	9357
10		16	A	Ipswich T	W	4-1	1-1	10	Peacock [33], Wardley [65], Steiner 2 [71, 82]	17,544
11		19	A	WBA	W	1-0	0-0	—	Wardley [52]	9874
12		23	H	Portsmouth	D	0-0	0-0	9		13,303
13		27	H	Birmingham C	D	2-2	1-0	—	Steiner [40], Kiwomya [54]	11,196
14		30	A	Blackburn R	W	2-0	1-0	8	Wardley [40], Gallen [89]	17,491
15	Nov	2	A	Stockport Co	D	3-3	0-2	—	Gallen 2 [65, 89], Maddix [66]	4868
16		6	H	Manchester C	D	1-1	1-0	9	Kiwomya [39]	19,002
17		14	A	Crystal Palace	L	0-3	0-1	9		15,861
18		20	H	Walsall	W	2-1	2-1	7	Wardley [30], Kiwomya [33]	10,058
19		23	A	Grimsby T	L	1-2	1-0	—	Kiwomya [25]	4297
20		27	H	Barnsley	D	2-2	2-1	9	Darlington [21], Steiner [37]	11,054
21		30	H	Sheffield U	W	3-1	2-0	—	Steiner [8], Wardley [10], Breacker [50]	9922
22	Dec	4	A	Huddersfield T	L	0-1	0-1	8		13,027
23		18	H	Charlton Ath	D	0-0	0-0	8		14,709
24		26	A	Norwich C	L	1-2	1-1	10	Wardley [40]	17,823
25		28	H	Crewe Alex	W	1-0	0-0	8	Wardley [75]	12,011
26	Jan	3	A	Swindon T	W	1-0	0-0	7	Langley [89]	9460
27		15	H	Bolton W	L	0-1	0-0	8		11,396
28		22	A	Wolverhampton W	L	2-3	0-3	9	Peacock [79], Slade [89]	20,069
29		29	H	Nottingham F	D	1-1	0-1	10	Kiwomya [76]	12,297
30	Feb	5	A	Port Vale	D	1-1	1-1	10	Wardley [37]	5493
31		12	H	Stockport Co	D	1-1	0-1	11	Kiwomya [78]	10,531
32		19	A	Barnsley	D	1-1	1-0	10	Rose [43]	14,212
33		28	H	Fulham	D	0-0	0-0	—		16,308
34	Mar	5	A	Sheffield U	D	1-1	1-0	11	Beck [25]	11,554
35		8	A	Manchester C	W	3-1	2-0	—	Kiwomya [37], Wiekens (og) [45], Beck (pen) [73]	31,353
36		11	H	Grimsby T	W	1-0	0-0	9	Beck (pen) [77]	10,450
37		18	A	Walsall	W	3-2	2-1	10	Larusson (og) [11], Wardley [15], Kiwomya [73]	6414
38		22	H	Crystal Palace	L	0-1	0-0	—		12,842
39		25	H	Norwich C	D	2-2	0-1	11	Kiwomya 2 [47, 85]	11,918
40		31	A	Charlton Ath	L	1-2	0-1	—	Taylor [81]	19,617
41	Apr	8	H	Swindon T	W	2-1	2-1	11	Ready [23], Beck (pen) [29]	12,633
42		15	A	Crewe Alex	L	1-2	1-1	11	Langley [45]	4741
43		22	A	Ipswich T	W	3-1	0-0	11	Peacock [46], Koejoe [58], Kiwomya [90]	14,920
44		24	A	Tranmere R	D	1-1	1-0	11	Peacock (pen) [26]	7744
45		29	H	WBA	D	0-0	0-0	10		15,244
46	May	7	A	Portsmouth	W	3-1	1-0	10	Langley [30], Gallen [88], Myers (og) [89]	16,301

Final League Position: 10

GOALSCORERS

League (62): Kiwomya 13, Wardley 11, Peacock 8 (2 pens), Steiner 6, Beck 4 (3 pens), Gallen 4, Langley 3, Darlington 2, Ready 2, Breacker 1, Koejoe 1, Maddix 1, Rose 1, Slade 1, Taylor 1, own goals 3.
Worthington Cup (3): Langley 1, Peacock 1 (pen), own goal 1.
FA Cup (4): Wardley 3, Kiwomya 1.

Miklosko L 9	Breacker T 15 + 1	Baraclough I 45	Morrow S 6 + 1	Rose M 27 + 2	Maddix D 17	Langley R 36 + 5	Peacock G 26 + 4	Steiner R 24	Darlington J 34	Kiwomya C 42 + 2	Rowland K 5 + 10	Wardley S 41 + 2	Gallen K 7 + 24	Scully T 2 + 6	Ready K 32 + 1	Slade S 3 + 6	Harper L 37 + 1	Jeanne L 1 + 1	Bankole A — + 1	Murray P 21 + 9	Weare R — + 4	Plummer C 17 + 1	Kulcsar G 5 + 8	Koejoe S 5 + 6	Bruce P 11 + 1	Ward D 14	McGovern B 3 + 2	Beck M 10 + 1	Perry M 9 + 1	Taylor G 2 + 4	Match No
1	2	3	4	5	6	7^1	8	9	10^2	11^3	12	13	14																		1
1	2^2	3	4	5	6	7^1	8	9	10	11				12	13																2
1	2^2	3	4^1	5	6	7	8			11				10	12	9	13														3
1		3		5	6	7^2	8		4	11^1			13	9	10	12	2														4
1		3	13	5	6	7^2	8	9	4	12		11		10^1	2																5
1	2			5	6	4	8	9		11^1		10		12	7	3															6
1^6		3		5	6	7^1	8	9	4^2	11		10		12	13	2				15											7
		3		5	6	7^2	8		4	11		10		9^1	2	12	1			13											8
		3		5	6	7^1	8	9	4	11^2	12	10		13	2		1^6			15											9
	2	3			6^2	7	8^1	9	4	11^2	12	10		13	5		1			14											10
	2	3			6	7	8^2	9^1	4	11		10		12	5		1			13											11
	2	3		5	6	7	8	9		11		10			4		1			12											12
	2	3		5	6	7^1	8	9		11		10			4		1			12											13
		3		5	6	12		9^2	4	11		10	7^1	13	2		1			8											14
		3		5^2	6	12		9	2	11		10	8^1	13	4		1			7											15
		3		5^2	6	12		9	2	11		10	8^1	13	4		1			7											16
14		3		5^2	6	12		9	2	11		10	8	13^2	4		1			7^1											17
	2	3		5	6	7^1	8	9	4	11^2	12	10					1			13											18
	2	3	4			7^1	8	9	6	11		10					1			12	5										19
	2	3	4^3	5		12	8	9		11			10^2				1			7^1	13	14	6								20
	2	3		5^2		12	8	9^3		11		10	13				1			7^1	14	4	6								21
	2	3		5		12		9^3		11		13	10	8^2			1			7		4	6^1	14							22
	2						7^1	9	4	11			10				1			8		5	12		3	6					23
1	2	3				7		9	4	11			10	12						8^1		5				6					24
	2^1	3				7		9	4^3	11^2			10	12			1			8		5	13			6		14			25
		3				7		9		11			10				1			8		5		4	6		2				26
		3						9	4	11			10				1			8		5	7^2	12	2^1	6		13			27
		3				7			4	11	13		10	12	14		1			8^1			9^2	5^3		6		2			28
		3		5		7^2	8			11		10		4^3	12	9	1			13	14		6					2^1			29
		3		5		7^1	8		4	11			10	12	2		1			9^2			13			6					30
		3		5		7^1	8		4	11		13	10	12	2		1			9^2			6^3					14			31
		3		5			8		4	11^1			10		2	13	1			12			7			6		9^2			32
		3		5^1		7^1	8		2	11^2			10		4	13	1			12			14			6		9			33
		3				7	8		2^1	11^3		13	10	12	4	14	1			10		5				6		9^2			34
		3	12			7^1	8^2		2	11		13			4		1			10		5				6		9			35
		3	12			7^2			2	11		13	10		4		1			8^1		5				6		9			36
		3		5		7			2^1	11			10		4		1			8			6^2	12				9^3	13	14	37
		3		5		7^3				11			10	12	4		1			8^1			6^2	13				9	2	14	38
		3	12	5^3		7				11		13	10		4		1		6^1	8								9^2	2	14	39
		3				7			2^2	11		13	10	12	4		1			8^1				6				9^2	5	14	40
		3				7	6			11			10^2		4		1			12			13	14	5^1			9	2	8^3	41
		3				7^2	6			11		13	10	12	4		1			8			14	5^1					2	9^1	42
		3				7	8			11			10	12	4		1						5	13				9^1	6^2	2	43
1				5		7	8			11			10	12						4		13	6	9^1					3^2	2	44
				5		7	8			11			10	12			1			4		13	6	9^1					3^2	2	45
				5		7	8			11^1			10	12			1			4		14	6	13				9	3^2	2^3	46

Worthington Cup

First Round	Cardiff C	(a)	2-1	
		(h)	1-2	

FA Cup

Third Round	Torquay U	(h)	1-1	
		(a)	3-2	
Fourth Round	Charlton Ath	(a)	0-1	

Division 2 **READING**

FOUNDATION

Reading was formed as far back as 1871 at a public meeting held at the Bridge Street Rooms. They first entered the FA Cup as early as 1877 when they amalgamated with the Reading Hornets. The club was further strengthened in 1889 when Earley FC joined them. They were the first winners of the Berks and Bucks Cup in 1878–79.

Madejski Stadium, Junction 11, M4, Reading, Berks RG2 0FL.

Telephone: (0118) 968 1100.

Fax: (0118) 968 1101.

Website: www.readingfc.co.uk

Email: comments@readingfc.co.uk

Ticket Office: (0118) 968 1000.

Ticket Office Fax: (0118) 968 1001.

ClubCall: 09068 121 000.

Ground Capacity: 24,200.

Record Attendance: 33,042 v Brentford, FA Cup 5th rd, 19 February 1927.

Record Receipts: £171,203 v Manchester C, Division 2, 27 March 1999.

Pitch Measurements: 112yd × 77yd.

President: F. Orton.

Chairman: John Madejski.

Director: I. Wood-Smith.

Manager: Alan Pardew.

Chief Executive: Nigel Howe.

Physio: Paul Turner.

Commercial Manager: Kevin Girdler.

Secretary: Ms Andrea Barker.

LATEST SEQUENCES

Longest Sequence of League Wins: 13, 17.8.85 – 19.10.85.

Longest Sequence of League Defeats: 7, 10.4.98 – 15.8.98.

Longest Sequence of League Draws: 5, 11.10.97 – 1.11.97.

Longest Sequence of Unbeaten League Matches: 19, 21.4.73 – 27.10.73.

Longest Sequence Without a League Win: 14, 30.4.27 – 29.10.27.

HONOURS

Football League: Division 1 – Runners-up 1994–95; Division 2 – Champions 1993–94; Division 3 – Champions 1985–86; Division 3 (S) – Champions 1925–26; Runners-up 1931–32, 1934–35, 1948–49, 1951–52; Division 4 – Champions 1978–79.

FA Cup: Semi-final 1927.

Football League Cup: best season: 5th rd, 1996.

Simod Cup: Winners 1988.

Colours
Blue and white hooped shirts, blue shorts, blue stockings with white bands.

Change Colours
Orange with navy hoop, blue shorts, orange and blue hooped stockings.

Year Formed: 1871.

Turned Professional: 1895.

Ltd Co.: 1895.

Club Nickname: 'The Royals'.

Previous Grounds: 1871, Reading Recreation; Reading Cricket Ground; 1882, Coley Park; 1889, Caversham Cricket Ground; 1896, Elm Park; 1998, Madejski Stadium.

First Football League Game: 28 August 1920, Division 3, v Newport Co (a) W 1–0 – Crawford; Smith, Horler; Christie, Mavin, Getgood; Spence, Weston, Yarnell, Bailey (1), Andrews.

Record League Victory: 10–2 v Crystal Palace, Division 3 (S), 4 September 1946 – Groves; Glidden, Gulliver; McKenna, Ratcliffe, Young; Chitty, Maurice Edelston (3), McPhee (4), Barney (1), Deverell (2).

Record Cup Victory: 6–0 v Leyton, FA Cup 2nd rd, 12 December 1925 – Duckworth; Eggo, McConnell; Wilson, Messer, Evans; Smith (2), Braithwaite (1), Davey (1), Tinsley, Robson (2).

Record Defeat: 0–18 v Preston NE, FA Cup 1st rd, 1893–94.

Most League Points (2 for a win): 65, Division 4, 1978–79.

Most League Points (3 for a win): 94, Division 3, 1985–86.

Most League Goals: 112, Division 3 (S), 1951–52.

Highest League Scorer in Season: Ronnie Blackman, 39, Division 3 (S), 1951–52.

Most League Goals in Total Aggregate: Ronnie Blackman, 158, 1947–54.

Most League Goals in One Match: 6, Arthur Bacon v Stoke C, Division 2, 3 April 1931.

Most Capped Player: Jimmy Quinn, 17 (46), Northern Ireland.

Most League Appearances: Martin Hicks, 500, 1978–91.

Youngest League Player: Steve Hetzke, 16 years 184 days v Darlington, 4 December 1971.

Record Transfer Fee Received: £1,575,000 from Newcastle U for Shaka Hislop, August 1995.

Record Transfer Fee Paid: £800,000 to Brentford for Carl Asaba, August 1997 and £800,000 to Cambridge U for Martin Butler, February 2000.

Football League Record: 1920 Original Member of Division 3; 1921–26 Division 3 (S); 1926–31 Division 2; 1931–58 Division 3 (S); 1958–71 Division 3; 1971–76 Division 4; 1976–77 Division 3; 1977–79 Division 4; 1979–83 Division 3; 1983–84 Division 4; 1984–86 Division 3; 1986–88 Division 2; 1988–92 Division 3; 1992–94 Division 2; 1994–98 Division 1; 1998– Division 2.

MANAGERS

Thomas Sefton 1897–1901
(Secretary-Manager)
James Sharp 1901–02
Harry Matthews 1902–20
Harry Marshall 1920–22
Arthur Chadwick 1923–25
H. S. Bray 1925–26
(Secretary only since 1922 and 1926–35)
Andrew Wylie 1926–31
Joe Smith 1931–35
Billy Butler 1935–39
John Cochrane 1939
Joe Edelston 1939–47
Ted Drake 1947–52
Jack Smith 1952–55
Harry Johnston 1955–63
Roy Bentley 1963–69
Jack Mansell 1969–71
Charlie Hurley 1972–77
Maurice Evans 1977–84
Ian Branfoot 1984–89
Ian Porterfield 1989–91
Mark McGhee 1991–94
Jimmy Quinn/Mick Gooding 1994–97
Terry Bullivant 1997–98
Tommy Burns 1998–99
Alan Pardew October 1999–

TEN YEAR LEAGUE RECORD

		P	W	D	L	F	A	Pts	Pos
1989-90	Div 3	46	15	19	12	57	53	64	10
1990-91	Div 3	46	17	8	21	53	66	59	15
1991-92	Div 3	46	16	13	17	59	62	61	12
1992-93	Div 2	46	18	15	13	66	51	69	8
1993-94	Div 2	46	26	11	9	81	44	89	1
1994-95	Div 1	46	23	10	13	58	44	79	2
1995-96	Div 1	46	13	17	16	54	63	56	19
1996-97	Div 1	46	15	12	19	58	67	57	18
1997-98	Div 1	46	11	9	26	39	78	42	24
1998-99	Div 2	46	16	13	17	54	63	61	11

DID YOU KNOW ?

Reading won the Third Division South Cup in 1937-38. The final was held over until the following season with Magnus McPhee, who had not been signed the previous season, scoring four goals in the 6-1 first leg win over Bristol City.

READING 1999–2000 LEAGUE RECORD

Match No.	Date		Venue	Opponents	Result	H/T Score	Lg. Pos.	Goalscorers	Attendance
1	Aug	7	H	Bristol C	W 2-1	1-0	6	Brebner [15], Crawford [85]	13,348
2		14	A	Cambridge U	L 1-3	0-1	17	McIntyre [82]	4630
3		21	H	Luton T	L 1-2	0-0	19	Williams M [56]	8741
4		28	A	Colchester U	L 2-3	1-1	21	Forster [22], Williams M [64]	3443
5	Sept	1	H	Preston NE	D 2-2	0-2	—	Smith [71], Scott [79]	7628
6		11	A	Bournemouth	L 1-3	1-3	23	Caskey (pen) [9]	6007
7		18	H	Chesterfield	W 1-0	0-0	19	Caskey [58]	6932
8		25	H	Oldham Ath	D 1-1	0-0	18	Polston [90]	7274
9	Oct	2	A	Wycombe W	L 3-5	0-2	19	Forster 2 [58, 71], Caskey (pen) [86]	7042
10		9	A	Stoke C	L 1-2	0-0	20	Forster [52]	9621
11		16	H	Wigan Ath	L 0-2	0-1	22		7708
12		20	H	Bury	W 2-0	1-0	—	Scott [41], Williams M [90]	5393
13		23	A	Oldham Ath	W 2-1	2-1	17	Gurney [9], Caskey (pen) [45]	4963
14	Nov	2	A	Brentford	D 1-1	1-0	—	Gurney [17]	6774
15		7	H	Oxford U	L 1-2	0-1	19	McIntyre [77]	10,101
16		16	A	Millwall	L 0-5	0-3	—		5202
17		24	H	Burnley	D 0-0	0-0	—		6149
18		27	A	Scunthorpe U	D 1-1	0-0	20	Hunter [88]	6142
19	Dec	4	A	Bristol C	L 1-3	0-1	21	Caskey [56]	8936
20		18	H	Wrexham	D 2-2	1-1	21	Grant [39], Scott [62]	6223
21		26	A	Cardiff C	L 0-1	0-0	21		9791
22		28	H	Notts Co	D 0-0	0-0	21		7703
23	Jan	3	A	Gillingham	D 2-2	0-1	21	Nicholls [87], Williams M (pen) [90]	7453
24		8	H	Blackpool	D 1-1	0-0	21	Caskey [66]	7297
25		15	H	Cambridge U	D 0-0	0-0	21		6953
26		22	A	Luton T	L 1-3	0-1	22	Caskey [60]	6044
27		29	H	Colchester U	W 2-0	1-0	20	Caskey 2 [22, 78]	7304
28	Feb	5	A	Preston NE	D 2-2	1-0	20	Forster [39], Butler [60]	12,618
29		8	A	Blackpool	W 2-0	0-0	—	McIntyre [68], Butler [80]	4291
30		12	H	Millwall	W 2-0	0-0	17	Parkinson [65], Forster [87]	11,994
31		19	A	Scunthorpe U	D 2-2	1-2	17	Caskey (pen) [43], McIntyre [56]	4082
32		26	A	Chesterfield	L 0-2	0-1	18		2986
33	Mar	4	H	Bournemouth	W 2-0	2-0	18	Caskey [3], Forster [30]	10,551
34		7	A	Oxford U	W 3-1	2-1	—	Hodges 2 [11, 32], Caskey [61]	7638
35		11	H	Brentford	W 1-0	0-0	16	Williams A [80]	11,427
36		18	A	Burnley	L 0-3	0-1	17		14,436
37		22	H	Bristol R	W 2-0	1-0	—	Forster [24], Caskey [70]	11,707
38		25	H	Cardiff C	L 0-1	0-0	16		10,044
39	Apr	1	A	Wrexham	W 1-0	1-0	16	Butler [7]	2613
40		4	A	Bristol R	W 1-0	0-0	—	Caskey [65]	7771
41		7	H	Gillingham	D 2-2	1-0	—	Butler [43], Caskey [75]	11,064
42		15	A	Notts Co	W 2-1	0-0	13	Forster [46], Newman [60]	4791
43		22	A	Wigan Ath	L 0-1	0-1	13		5855
44		24	H	Wycombe W	W 2-1	0-0	12	Forster [55], Williams M [71]	11,834
45		29	A	Bury	D 1-1	1-0	12	Caskey [43]	3869
46	May	6	H	Stoke C	W 1-0	0-0	10	Caskey (pen) [81]	13,146

Final League Position: 10

GOALSCORERS

League (57): Caskey 17 (5 pens), Forster 10, Williams M 5 (1 pen), Butler 4, McIntyre 4, Scott 3, Gurney 2, Hodges 2, Brebner 1, Crawford 1, Grant 1, Hunter 1, Newman 1, Nicholls 1, Parkinson 1, Polston 1, Smith 1, Williams A 1.
Worthington Cup (5): Caskey 2 (1 pen), Scott 2, Hunter 1.
FA Cup (7): Caskey 3 (3 pens), Bernal 1, Hunter 1, McIntyre 1, Williams M 1.

Howie S 35 + 1	Gurney A 35 + 3	Gray S 12 + 3	Polston J 12 + 2	Hunter B 27 + 4	McLaren A 2	Hodges L 15 + 10	Caskey D 43 + 1	Williams M 22 + 7	Scott K 14 + 11	Brebner G 2	Crawford J 3 + 1	McIntyre J 15 + 11	Bernal A 19 + 4	Casper C 14 + 1	Brayson P — + 7	Grant P 27 + 2	Smith N 26 + 10	Forster N 31 + 5	Haddow A 1 + 1	Evers S 8 + 9	Primus L 27 + 1	Van der Kwaak P — + 1	Parkinson P 22	Whitehead P 11	Murty G 14 + 3	Lisbie K 1 + 1	Potter G 4	Sarr M — + 3	Nicholls M 4 + 1	Robinson M 19	Butler M 17	Williams A 15	Newman R 4 + 3	Henderson D 2 + 4	Igoe S 3 + 3	Tyson N — + 1	Match No.
1	2	3	4	5	6	7^1	8	9	10^2	11	12	13																									1
1	2	3	4^2	5		12		9^3	10	11	7	8	6^1	13	14																						2
1	2	3		5		8	9	10		7^1		6		4	11	12																					3
1		3		5		8	9	12		14	2	6		4	7	10^1	11^2	13^3																			4
1	2	3		11^1		8	9	12			5	6		4	7	10^2	13																				5
1	2	3^1		12		8	9	11^2		13	5	6		4	7	10																				6
1	2^1	3	13			8	12	14		9^3	4	6		11	7	10					5^2															7
1	2	3	12			14	8	13		9^2	4	6		11^3	7	10					5^1															8
1^6	2		12			7	8	9		11	4	6^1				10				5	15	3														9
						7^1	8^2	9		3	12	4	6			13	11	10			5	2	1													10
	2					7	8	9			12	4	6	13		11^2	10^1				5	3	1													11
	2		6			7	8^2	9	11^1		12	4				10	13				5	3	1													12
	2		4			8	9	10^1			12	7	6			11^2						13	5	3	1											13
	2^1		4			8^2	9	11^3			12	7	6			14	13					10	5	3	1											14
	2		4			8^3	9	10^1			12	7	6^2			14	13				11	5	3	1												15
	2^2	3	4	5		12	9					10	13	6^1		14					11^3				8	1	7									16
	2^1	12	5	6		8						9	4			13	10^2				11^3				3	1	7									17
15	2^1		4	5		8						9	6			12		13	10^2				3	1^6	7	11										18
1	2		4			8	9					10	6			7^2	12				11^1	5										13	3			19
1	2		6			8	9	12				4				10^2	13				11^1	5										7	3			20
1	2		4			8	9	10				6^2	12			7^1					13	5	3									11				21
1	2		4			8	9^2	10				12				7					11^1	5	3									6	13			22
1	2	13	4	12		7^2	8^3	9	10^1							11	14				5	3									6					23
1	2^2	3	4			8	9	10				12				7^3	13				5	11									14	6^1				24
1	2	3^2	4			8	9	10^1				7				12					5	11									13	6				25
1	2	3^2	4			8	12	10				7^1				11^2	9	13	5		6										14					26
1	2		4			12	8		13			9^1				7		10			5	11										6^2	3			27
1	2		4			12	8					7^1				11		10			5	6									3	9				28
1	2^2		4			12	8					7^1	13			11		10			5	6									3	9				29
1	2^1	12	4	7^2		8						14				11	13	10			5^1	6									3	9				30
1	2		4	12		8						7^1				11	13	10^2				6									3	9	5			31
1	2^2		4	12		8	13					7^3				11		10	14			6^1									3	9	5			32
1	2		4	12		8^2						7^1				11^3	6	10	14			13									3	9	5			33
1	2		4	7		8^1						14				11	6	10^3	12			13									3^2	9	5			34
1	2		4	8								12				13	6	7	10^1	3^2		11										9	5			35
1		2		7^1		8	12					6^2	4^3	10		5					11								3	9			13	14		36
1	12			7^1		8	13					2^3	4	10^2		5					11								3	9	6	14				37
1		12				7^3						2	4	10		5					11^1								3	9^2	6	2		14		38
1		6				7	8^3	12	13			2	4	10^1		11													3	9^2	5	13				39
1		4				7^1	8	12				2	6	10^1		11													3	9	5					40
1	12		4			7^2	8^3	13				2	6	10		11^1													3	9	5		14			41
1	2		4	12		8^2						6	10																3	9	5	7	13	11^1		42
1	2^2					7^1	8	12				11^3	4	10		5					13								3	9	6		14			43
1	12					14	8	13				2	6	10^1		5					7								3	9^2	4		11^3			44
				5		5^1	8						4^2	10		13	12				1	7							3			6	2	9^2	11	14	45
						8^1	9						4	10		12	5				1	7							3			6	2	13	11^2		46

Worthington Cup

First Round	Peterborough U	(h)	0-0
		(a)	2-1
Second Round	Bradford C	(a)	1-1
		(h)	2-2

FA Cup

First Round	Yeovil T	(h)	4-2
Second Round	Halifax T	(h)	1-1
		(a)	1-0
Third Round	Plymouth Arg	(h)	1-1
		(a)	0-1

Division 3 **ROCHDALE**

FOUNDATION

Considering the love of rugby in their area, it is not surprising that Rochdale had difficulty in establishing an Association Football club. The earlier Rochdale Town club formed in 1900 went out of existence in 1907 when the present club was immediately established and joined the Manchester League, before graduating to the Lancashire Combination in 1908.

Spotland, Sandy Lane, Rochdale OL11 5DS.

Telephone: (01706) 644 648.

Fax: (01706) 648 466.

Commercial: (01706) 647 521.

Ground Capacity: 10,249 (from October 2000).

Record Attendance: 24,231 v Notts Co, FA Cup 2nd rd, 10 December 1949.

Record Receipts: £46,000 v Burnley, Division 4, 5 May 1992.

Pitch Measurements: 114yd × 76yd.

President: Mrs L. Stoney.

Chairman: D. F. Kilpatrick.

Chief Executive: Francis Collins.

Directors: G. R. Brierley, C. Dunphy, J. Marsh, G. Morris, R. Bott.

Manager: Steve Parkin.

Secretary: Hilary Molyneux Horrocks.

Youth Development Manager: David Hamilton.

Lottery and Merchandising Manager: R. Wild.

Advertising & Sponsorship Manager: L. Duckworth.

Stadium Manager: Ronnie Cowgill.

Physio: Andy Thorpe.

LATEST SEQUENCES

Longest Sequence of League Wins: 8, 29.9.69 – 3.11.69.

Longest Sequence of League Defeats: 17, 14.11.31 – 12.3.32.

Longest Sequence of League Draws: 6, 17.8.68 – 14.9.68.

Longest Sequence of Unbeaten League Matches: 20, 15.9.23 – 19.1.24.

Longest Sequence Without a League Win: 28, 14.11.31 – 29.8.32.

HONOURS

Football League: Division 3 best season: 9th, 1969–70; Division 3 (N) – Runners-up 1923–24, 1926–27.

FA Cup: best season: 5th rd, 1990.

Football League Cup: Runners-up 1962 (record for 4th Division club).

Colours
Blue shirts with white trim, blue shorts, blue stockings with white hoop on turnover.

Change Colours
Jade green and black shirts, white shorts, black socks.

Year Formed: 1907.

Turned Professional: 1907.

Ltd Co.: 1910.

Club Nickname: 'The Dale'.

First Football League Game: 27 August 1921, Division 3 (N), v Accrington Stanley (h) W 6–3 – Crabtree; Nuttall, Sheehan; Hill, Farrer, Yarwood; Hoad, Sandiford, Dennison (2), Owens (3), Carney (1).

Record League Victory: 8–1 v Chesterfield, Division 3 (N), 18 December 1926 – Hill; Brown, Ward; Hillhouse, Parkes, Braidwood; Hughes, Bertram, Whitehurst (5), Schofield (2), Martin (1).

Record Cup Victory: 8–2 v Crook T, FA Cup 1st rd, 26 November 1927 – Moody; Hopkins, Ward; Braidwood, Parkes, Barker; Tompkinson, Clennell (3) Whitehurst (4), Hall, Martin (1).

Record Defeat: 1–9 v Tranmere R, Division 3 (N), 25 December 1931.

Most League Points (2 for a win): 62, Division 3 (N), 1923–24.

Most League Points (3 for a win): 68, Division 3, 1999–2000.

Most League Goals: 105, Division 3 (N), 1926–27.

Highest League Scorer in Season: Albert Whitehurst, 44, Division 3 (N), 1926–27.

Most League Goals in Total Aggregate: Reg Jenkins, 119, 1964–73.

Most League Goals in One Match: 6, Tommy Tippett v Hartlepools U, Division 3N, 21 April 1930.

Most Capped Player: None.

Most League Appearances: Graham Smith, 317, 1966–74.

Youngest League Player: Zac Hughes, 16 years 105 days v Exeter C, 19 September 1987.

Record Transfer Fee Received: £400,000 from West Ham U for Stephen Bywater, August 1998.

Record Transfer Fee Paid: £100,000 to Walsall for Clive Platt, September 1999.

Football League Record: 1921 Elected to Division 3 (N); 1958–59 Division 3; 1959–69 Division 4; 1969–74 Division 3; 1974–92 Division 4; 1992– Division 3.

MANAGERS

Billy Bradshaw 1920
Run by committee 1920–22
Tom Wilson 1922–23
Jack Peart 1923–30
Will Cameron 1930–31
Herbert Hopkinson 1932–34
Billy Smith 1934–35
Ernest Nixon 1935–37
Sam Jennings 1937–38
Ted Goodier 1938–52
Jack Warner 1952–53
Harry Catterick 1953–58
Jack Marshall 1958–60
Tony Collins 1960–68
Bob Stokoe 1967–68
Len Richley 1968–70
Dick Conner 1970–73
Walter Joyce 1973–76
Brian Green 1976–77
Mike Ferguson 1977–78
Doug Collins 1979
Bob Stokoe 1979–80
Peter Madden 1980–83
Jimmy Greenhoff 1983–84
Vic Halom 1984–86
Eddie Gray 1986–88
Danny Bergara 1988–89
Terry Dolan 1989–91
Dave Sutton 1991–94
Mick Docherty 1995–96
Graham Barrow 1996–99
Steve Parkin June 1999–

TEN YEAR LEAGUE RECORD

		P	W	D	L	F	A	Pts	Pos
1989-90	Div 4	46	20	6	20	52	55	66	12
1990-91	Div 4	46	15	17	14	50	53	62	12
1991-92	Div 4	42	18	13	11	57	53	67	8
1992-93	Div 3	42	16	10	16	70	70	58	11
1993-94	Div 3	42	16	12	14	63	51	60	9
1994-95	Div 3	42	12	14	16	44	67	50	15
1995-96	Div 3	46	14	13	19	57	61	55	15
1996-97	Div 3	46	14	16	16	58	58	58	14
1997-98	Div 3	46	17	7	22	56	55	58	18
1998-99	Div 3	46	13	15	18	42	55	54	19

DID YOU KNOW

Rochdale defeated First Division Coventry City 2-1 on 11 January 1971 to reach the fourth round of the FA Cup for the first time in their history with goals from David Cross and Dennis Butler.

ROCHDALE 1999–2000 LEAGUE RECORD

Match No.	Date		Venue	Opponents	Result		H/T Score	Lg. Pos.	Goalscorers	Atten-dance
1	Aug	7	A	Cheltenham T	W	2-0	2-0	3	Atkinson 26, Ford 42	5189
2		14	H	Southend U	W	2-0	2-0	3	Platt 12, Peake 32	2253
3		21	A	York C	W	3-0	1-0	1	Lancashire 33, Platt 56, Atkinson 61	3034
4		28	H	Exeter C	L	0-2	0-0	3		3113
5		30	A	Chester C	W	2-0	1-0	2	Atkinson 28, Platt 71	2644
6	Sept	3	H	Halifax T	L	0-1	0-1	—		4198
7		11	H	Darlington	D	0-0	0-0	4		3253
8		18	A	Rotherham U	W	1-0	0-0	3	Atkinson 90	3568
9		25	H	Swansea C	D	0-0	0-0	4		2975
10	Oct	2	A	Northampton T	W	1-0	1-0	2	Platt 41	4860
11		9	A	Barnet	L	0-1	0-1	3		2765
12		16	H	Plymouth Arg	D	0-0	0-0	4		3105
13		19	H	Macclesfield T	L	0-1	0-1	—		2397
14		22	A	Swansea C	L	0-1	0-0	—		4843
15	Nov	2	H	Hull C	L	0-2	0-1	—		2265
16		6	A	Torquay U	L	0-1	0-0	16		2351
17		14	H	Mansfield T	W	2-1	0-0	15	Platt 62, Ellis 64	2709
18		23	A	Leyton Orient	D	0-0	0-0	—		2990
19		27	A	Lincoln C	D	1-1	0-0	15	Jones 66	3424
20	Dec	4	H	Cheltenham T	D	0-0	0-0	15		2245
21		10	A	Brighton & HA	W	4-3	2-2	—	Bayliss 2, Atkinson 31, Platt 2 82, 88	5049
22		26	A	Carlisle U	W	2-1	0-1	12	Ellis 58, Flitcroft 62	3812
23		28	H	Shrewsbury T	W	2-1	1-0	9	Lancashire 11, Peake 59	2924
24	Jan	3	A	Hartlepool U	L	2-3	1-1	10	Westwood (og) 17, Ellis 65	4498
25		8	H	Brighton & HA	W	1-0	1-0	9	Lancashire 17	2596
26		15	A	Southend U	D	3-3	3-0	11	Jones 32, Lancashire 2 37, 39	3190
27		22	H	York C	W	2-1	0-1	7	Lancashire 59, Ellis 66	2580
28		29	A	Exeter C	L	0-2	0-2	8		2525
29	Feb	5	H	Chester C	W	2-1	1-0	7	Lancashire 9, Bayliss 89	3093
30		12	A	Halifax T	W	2-0	1-0	7	Lancashire 30, Peake 72	3504
31		19	H	Lincoln C	D	1-1	1-0	7	Bayliss 32	3166
32		26	H	Rotherham U	L	0-1	0-0	7		4131
33	Mar	4	A	Darlington	L	1-4	1-3	8	Ellis 24	5333
34		11	H	Hull C	D	2-2	0-1	11	Jones 2 (1 pen) 59 (p), 90	4219
35		18	H	Leyton Orient	L	1-4	0-2	14	Ellis 68	2472
36		25	H	Carlisle U	W	3-2	2-1	13	Monington 2 8, 45, Ellis 60	2417
37		28	A	Mansfield T	D	0-0	0-0	—		2275
38	Apr	1	A	Peterborough U	D	3-3	0-1	12	Ford 47, Ellis 58, Peake 72	5587
39		5	H	Torquay U	D	1-1	0-0	—	Jones 55	1529
40		8	H	Hartlepool U	W	2-0	1-0	11	Peake 14, Platt 55	2332
41		15	A	Shrewsbury T	W	4-2	2-1	10	Platt 7, Peake 15, Jones (pen) 48, Ellis 81	4158
42		18	H	Peterborough U	L	1-2	1-2	—	Jones (pen) 13	2816
43		22	A	Plymouth Arg	D	1-1	0-0	10	Ellis 90	6205
44		24	H	Northampton T	L	0-3	0-2	10		2891
45		29	A	Macclesfield T	W	2-1	2-1	9	Flitcroft 27, Evans 39	2202
46	May	6	H	Barnet	D	1-1	0-0	10	Ellis 83	2347

Final League Position: 10

GOALSCORERS

League (57): Ellis 11, Platt 9, Lancashire 8, Jones 7 (3 pens), Peake 6, Atkinson 5, Bayliss 3, Flitcroft 2, Ford 2, Monington 2, Evans 1, own goal 1.
Worthington Cup (2): Evans 1, Lancashire 1.
FA Cup (4): Atkinson 1, Dowe 1, Peake 1, Platt 1.

Edwards N 40	Evans W 46	Stokes D 18+1	Peake J 38+5	Bayliss D 26+3	Hill K 37+1	Flitcroft D 40+3	Ford T 28+6	Morris A 1+6	Lancashire G 21+8	Atkinson G 32+8	Platt C 31+10	Holt M 8+6	Jones G 31+8	Carden P 3+10	Monington M 22+2	Dowe J 1+6	Searle D 13+1	Green R 6	Ellis T 30+1	Bettney C 12+12	Peyton W 1	Priestley P 1+1	Gibson P 5	McAuley S 10+3	McClare S 5+4	Taylor D —+1	Wilson S —+1	Match No.
1	2	3	4	5	6	7	8	9	10²	11	12	13																1
1	2	3	4	5	6	7	8		10¹	11	9	12																2
1	2	3	4	5	6	7²	8³	12	10¹	11	9	13	14															3
1	2	3	4	5	6		8¹	13	10	11	9²	7	12															4
1	2	3⁴	4	5	6	7	8¹		10	11	9	13	12															5
1	2	3	4	5⁶	6	7	8²	12	10¹	11	9	13	14															6
1	2	3	4		6	7	8				11	9¹	10²	13	12		5											7
1	2	3	4		6	7	8¹				11	9	10³	12²	5	14	13											8
1	2		4			7					11	9	10¹	8	5	12	3	6										9
1	2		4		6	7	8¹				11	9	10²	12	13	3	5											10
1	2		4		6	7	8¹				11	9	10²	12	13	3	5											11
1	2		4		6	7					11	9	10³	12	8¹	13	3	5										12
1	2		4		6	7					11²	9	10³	12	8¹	13	14	3	5									13
1	2		4		6	7					11	9	12	8²	13	10¹	3	5										14
1	2	3	4		6	7¹	8				13	9³	14	12		5			11²	10								15
1	2	12			6²	7	8				11¹	9		4	5		3		10	13								16
1	2		4	6		13	8				11¹	9		7	5		3		10	12²								17
1	2		4	6			12	8³		13	11¹	9		7	5		3		10²	14								18
1	2		4	6			8		12	13	9¹			7	5		3		10	11²								19
1	2		4	6	5	12	8²		13	9				7			3		10	11¹								20
1	2	4²	6	5	7	14		12	11³	9				8			3		10¹	13								21
1	2	3	4	5	6	7		12	11	9¹				8					10									22
1	2	3	4	5	6	7	12	9²	11					8¹					10	13								23
1	2¹	3	4	5	6	7	12	9	11²					8					10	13								24
1	2	3	4		6	7		9²	12	13				8		5			10	11¹								25
1	2	3	4¹		6	7		9²	12	13				8		5			10	11								26
1	2	3¹	12		6			9	11²	13				8	14	5			10	7		4³						27
1⁴	2²	4¹	3			7	6	9	11	12				8		5			10	13				15				28
	2	3	4	6		7²	12	9		13				8		5			10²	11			1					29
	2	12	4	6		7	13	9³		14				8	5²				10	11			1	3¹				30
	2		4	5	6	7¹	12	13		14	9²			8					10	11³			1	3				31
	2			5	6	7	4¹	13		12	9			8					10²	11			1	3				32
	2		4¹	6	5	7	8²	13		11	9			12					10				1	3				33
	2	3²	12	5	6	7	4²	11¹	9					8					10	13			1		14			34
1	2		4		6	7⁴		12	13				9¹	8		5			10	11				3				35
1	2	12	6¹	13	7	3		9	11		14			8	5				10³						4¹			36
1	2	12	13	6²	7	3		9	11					8	5				10						4¹			37
1	2		4	5		7	6	9¹	11	12				8					10					3				38
1	3		4	5	6	7	2³	9²	11	12				8					10¹	13					14			39
1	2		4	5	6³	7	3	9²	11	10¹	12			8					13					14				40
1	3	4²		6	7	2		9¹	11	10				8	5				12						13			41
1	3		4	6	7²	2¹		12	11³	9				8	5				10					14	13			42
1	4	8		6	7²	2³		12		9¹			11		5				10	13				3	14			43
1	2	4²	6		7			12		9			8		5				10	13				3	11¹			44
1	2	12²	13	6	7			9³		14			8		5				10	11¹				3	4			45
1	2	3²		5	6	7		9	12					10	11³				8¹	4					13	14		46

Worthington Cup
First Round   Chesterfield   (h) 1-2
                               (a) 1-2

FA Cup
First Round   Burton A   (a) 0-0
                           (h) 3-0
Second Round   Wrexham   (a) 1-2

Division 2   **ROTHERHAM UNITED**

FOUNDATION

Rotherham were formed in 1870 before becoming Town in the late 1880s. Thornhill United were founded in 1877 and changed their name to Rotherham County in 1905. The Town amalgamated with Rotherham County to form Rotherham United in 1925.

Millmoor Ground, Rotherham S60 1HR.
Telephone: (01709) 512 434.
Fax: (01709) 512 762.
Commercial Dept: (01709) 512 760.
Fax: (01709) 512 763.
Football in the Community: (01709) 512 761.
ClubCall: 09068 121 637.
Ground Capacity: 11,514.
Record Attendance: 25,170 v Sheffield U, Division 2, 13 December 1952 and v Sheffield W, Division 2, 26 January 1952.
Record Receipts: £79,155 v Newcastle U, FA Cup 4th rd, 23 January 1993.
Pitch Measurements. 115yd × 75yd.
Chairman: K. F. Booth.
Directors: R. Hull (Vice-Chairman), C. A. Luckock, J. A. Webb, N. Freeman.
Chief Executive: Phil Henson.
Manager: Ronnie Moore.
Assistant Manager: John Breckin.
Youth Development Officer: Fraser Foster.
Physios: Paul Smith, Ian Bailey.
Coach: Billy Russell.
Stadium Manager/Safety Officer: David Sumner.
Commercial Manager: D. Nicholls.
Year Formed: 1870.
Turned Professional: 1905.
Ltd Co.: 1920.
Club Nickname: 'The Merry Millers'.

LATEST SEQUENCES

Longest Sequence of League Wins: 9, 2.2.82 – 6.3.82.
Longest Sequence of League Defeats: 8, 7.4.56 – 18.8.56.
Longest Sequence of League Draws: 6, 13.10.69 – 22.11.69.
Longest Sequence of Unbeaten League Matches: 18, 13.10.69 – 7.2.70.
Longest Sequence Without a League Win: 14, 8.10.77 – 2.1.78.

HONOURS

Football League: Division 2 best season: 3rd, 1954–55 (equal points with champions and runners-up); Division 3 – Champions 1980–81; Runners-up 1999–2000; Division 3 (N) – Champions 1950–51; Runners-up 1946–47, 1947–48, 1948–49; Division 4 – Champions 1988–89; Runners-up 1991–92.

FA Cup: best season: 5th rd, 1953, 1968.

Football League Cup: Runners-up 1961.

Auto Windscreens Shield: Winners 1996.

Colours
Red and white.

Change Colours
White shirts, black shorts, black stockings.

Previous Names: 1877, Thornhill United; 1905, Rotherham County; 1925, amalgamated with Rotherham Town under Rotherham United.

Previous Ground: 1870, Red House Ground; 1907, Millmoor.

First Football League Game: 2 September 1893, Division 2, Rotherham T v Lincoln C (a) D 1–1 – McKay; Thickett, Watson; Barr, Brown, Broadhead; Longden, Cutts, Leatherbarrow, McCormick, Pickering, (1 og). 30 August 1919, Division 2, Rotherham Co v Nottingham F (h) W 2–0 – Branston; Alton, Baines; Bailey, Coe, Stanton; Lee (1), Cawley (1), Glennon, Lees, Lamb.

Record League Victory: 8–0 v Oldham Ath, Division 3 (N), 26 May 1947 – Warnes; Selkirk, Ibbotson; Edwards, Horace Williams, Danny Williams; Wilson (2), Shaw (1), Ardron (3), Guest (1), Hainsworth (1).

Record Cup Victory: 6–0 v Spennymoor U, FA Cup 2nd rd, 17 December 1977 – McAlister; Forrest, Breckin, Womble, Stancliffe, Green, Finney, Phillips (3), Gwyther (2) (Smith), Goodfellow, Crawford (1). 6–0 v Wolverhampton W, FA Cup 1st rd, 16 November 1985 – O'Hanlon; Forrest, Dungworth, Gooding (1), Smith (1), Pickering, Birch (2), Emerson, Tynan (1), Simmons (1), Pugh. 6–0 v Kings Lynn, FA Cup 2nd rd, 6 December 1997 – Mimms; Clark, Hurst (Goodwin), Garner (1) (Hudson) (1), Warner (Bass), Richardson (1), Berry (1), Thompson, Druce (1), Glover (1), Roscoe.

Record Defeat: 1–11 v Bradford C, Division 3 (N), 25 August 1928.

Most League Points (2 for a win): 71, Division 3 (N), 1950–51.

Most League Points (3 for a win): 84, Division 3, 1999–2000.

Most League Goals: 114, Division 3 (N), 1946–47.

Highest League Scorer in Season: Wally Ardron, 38, Division 3 (N), 1946–47.

Most League Goals in Total Aggregate: Gladstone Guest, 130, 1946–56.

Most League Goals in One Match: 4, Roland Bastow v York C, Division 3N, 9 November 1935; 4, Roland Bastow v Rochdale, Division 3N, 7 March 1936; 4, Wally Ardron v Crewe Alex, Division 3N, 5 October 1946; 4, Wally Ardron v Carlisle U, Division 3N, 13 September 1947; 4, Wally Ardron v Hartlepools U, Division 3N, 13 October 1948.

Most Capped Player: Shaun Goater, 18, Bermuda.

Most League Appearances: Danny Williams, 459, 1946–62.

Youngest League Player: Kevin Eley, 16 years 72 days v Scunthorpe U, 15 May 1984.

Record Transfer Fee Received: £325,000 from Sheffield W for Matt Clarke, July 1996.

Record Transfer Fee Paid: £150,000 to Millwall for Tony Towner, August 1980; £150,000 to Port Vale for Lee Glover, August 1996.

Football League Record: 1893 Rotherham Town elected to Division 2; 1896 Failed re-election; 1919 Rotherham County elected to Division 2; 1923–51 Division 3 (N); 1951–68 Division 2; 1968–73 Division 3; 1973–75 Division 4; 1975–81 Division 3; 1981–83 Division 2; 1983–88 Division 3; 1988–89 Division 4; 1989–91 Division 3; 1991–92 Division 4; 1992–97 Division 2; 1997–2000 Division 3; 2000– Division 2.

MANAGERS

Billy Heald 1925–29 *(Secretary only for long spell)*
Stanley Davies 1929–30
Billy Heald 1930–33
Reg Freeman 1934–52
Andy Smailes 1952–58
Tom Johnston 1958–62
Danny Williams 1962–65
Jack Mansell 1965–67
Tommy Docherty 1967–68
Jimmy McAnearney 1968–73
Jimmy McGuigan 1973–79
Ian Porterfield 1979–81
Emlyn Hughes 1981–83
George Kerr 1983–85
Norman Hunter 1985–87
Dave Cusack 1987–88
Billy McEwan 1988–91
Phil Henson 1991–94
Archie Gemmill/John McGovern 1994–96
Danny Bergara 1996–97
Ronnie Moore May 1997–

TEN YEAR LEAGUE RECORD

		P	W	D	L	F	A	Pts	Pos
1989-90	Div 3	46	17	13	16	71	62	64	9
1990-91	Div 3	46	10	12	24	50	87	42	23
1991-92	Div 4	42	22	11	9	70	37	77	2
1992-93	Div 2	46	17	14	15	60	60	65	11
1993-94	Div 2	46	15	13	18	63	60	58	15
1994-95	Div 2	46	14	14	18	57	61	56	17
1995-96	Div 2	46	14	14	18	54	62	56	16
1996-97	Div 2	46	7	14	25	39	70	35	23
1997-98	Div 3	46	16	19	11	67	61	67	9
1998-99	Div 3	46	20	13	13	79	61	73	5

DID YOU KNOW ?

Cash-strapped Rotherham United were forced to transfer inside-forward Jackie Bestall to Grimsby Town in November 1926 for £700. He went on to play for England and had a street in Grimsby named after him.

ROTHERHAM UNITED 1999–2000 LEAGUE RECORD

Match No.	Date		Venue	Opponents	Result		H/T Score	Lg. Pos.	Goalscorers	Attendance
1	Aug	7	A	Lincoln C	L	1-2	0-0	16	Warne [90]	4494
2		14	H	Chester C	W	4-0	0-0	10	Martindale 2 (2 pens) [54, 58], Fortune-West [81], Watson [88]	2966
3		21	A	Exeter C	L	1-3	1-2	14	Garner [23]	2646
4		28	H	Shrewsbury T	W	4-0	4-0	11	Turner [2], Scott [3], Garner 2 [21, 33]	2708
5		30	A	Macclesfield T	D	1-1	0-1	11	Fortune-West [86]	2307
6	Sept	4	H	York C	W	1-0	0-0	9	Garner [59]	3171
7		11	A	Plymouth Arg	D	1-1	0-1	11	Berry [49]	4075
8		18	H	Rochdale	L	0-1	0-0	12		3568
9		25	H	Northampton T	W	3-0	1-0	9	Thompson 2 (2 pens) [14, 80], Fortune-West [52]	3625
10	Oct	2	A	Cheltenham T	W	2-0	1-0	5	Thompson (pen) [37], Warne [47]	3331
11		12	A	Swansea C	L	0-2	0-1	—		5287
12		16	H	Barnet	W	2-0	1-0	7	Fortune-West [10], Sedgwick [67]	3596
13		19	H	Hartlepool U	W	3-0	3-0	—	Garner 2 [7, 14], Berry [30]	3340
14		23	A	Northampton T	W	1-0	0-0	2	Warne [80]	5753
15	Nov	2	H	Torquay U	W	1-0	1-0	—	Berry [27]	3892
16		6	A	Hull C	D	0-0	0-0	3		7045
17		12	H	Leyton Orient	L	0-1	0-0	3		4280
18		23	A	Mansfield T	W	2-1	1-1	—	Berry [27], Sedgwick [90]	2937
19		27	A	Carlisle U	W	1-0	0-0	2	Hurst [90]	2649
20	Dec	4	H	Lincoln C	D	1-1	1-0	2	Garner [45]	3674
21		11	A	Halifax T	D	0-0	0-0	2		2538
22		18	H	Darlington	W	2-1	0-0	2	White 2 [83, 88]	4234
23		26	A	Peterborough U	W	5-0	2-0	2	Hudson [2], Warne 2 [34, 49], Thompson [71], Fortune-West [74]	10,793
24		28	H	Brighton & HA	L	1-3	0-1	2	Branston [83]	5924
25	Jan	3	A	Southend U	W	2-1	2-1	1	Fortune-West 2 [26, 40]	4788
26		8	H	Halifax T	L	0-1	0-0	1		4450
27		15	A	Chester C	W	2-0	1-0	1	Warne [21], Fortune-West [54]	3398
28		22	H	Exeter C	W	5-0	3-0	1	Fortune-West 2 [5, 7], Warne 2 [12, 86], Wilsterman [82]	3402
29		29	A	Shrewsbury T	D	0-0	0-0	1		2587
30	Feb	5	H	Macclesfield T	W	2-1	2-1	1	Sedgwick (pen) [31], Fortune-West [44]	4175
31		12	A	York C	W	2-1	1-0	1	Fortune-West [7], Branston [90]	4531
32		19	H	Carlisle U	W	4-2	2-1	1	Fortune-West 3 [22, 32, 73], Wilsterman [50]	4271
33		26	A	Rochdale	W	1-0	0-0	1	White [58]	4131
34	Mar	4	H	Plymouth Arg	D	1-1	0-1	1	Warne [76]	4496
35		7	H	Hull C	W	3-0	0-0	—	Wilsterman [74], Fortune-West [76], Warne [84]	4881
36		11	A	Torquay U	L	1-2	1-1	1	Thompson [42]	2655
37		17	H	Mansfield T	L	2-3	1-2	—	Sedgwick 2 [35, 69]	5186
38		21	A	Leyton Orient	W	1-0	0-0	—	Garner [58]	3959
39		25	H	Peterborough U	D	1-1	1-1	1	Hurst [14]	5319
40	Apr	1	A	Darlington	D	2-2	0-2	1	Branston [56], Tutill (og) [58]	7401
41		8	H	Southend U	D	0-0	0-0	1		4327
42		15	A	Brighton & HA	D	1-1	1-1	1	Thompson [32]	5805
43		22	A	Barnet	L	0-1	0-0	2		3239
44		24	H	Cheltenham T	W	2-0	1-0	2	Garner [12], White [84]	5447
45		29	A	Hartlepool U	W	2-1	1-1	2	Fortune-West [6], Branston [49]	4673
46	May	6	H	Swansea C	D	1-1	0-0	2	Glover (pen) [90]	10,863

Final League Position: 2

GOALSCORERS

League (72): Fortune-West 17, Warne 10, Garner 9, Thompson 6 (3 pens), Sedgwick 5 (1 pen), Berry 4, Branston 4, White 4, Wilsterman 3, Hurst 2, Martindale 2 (2 pens), Glover 1 (pen), Hudson 1, Scott 1, Turner 1, Watson 1, own goal 1.
Worthington Cup (0).
FA Cup (3): Garner 1, Martindale 1 (pen), Thompson 1.

Pollitt M 46	Varty W 26 + 1	Beech C 5 + 1	Dillon P 15	Wilsterman B 38 + 4	Ingledow J 2 + 2	Sedgwick C 29 + 9	Watson K 44	Fortune-West L 39	Martindale G 4 + 5	Turner A 26 + 6	Warne P 39 + 4	Scott R 33 + 1	Garner D 33 + 2	Thompson S 27 + 4	Berry T 18 + 18	Hurst P 25 + 5	Warner V 16 + 2	Hudson D 3 + 4	Branston G 30	Artell D — + 1	White J 8 + 12	Glover L — + 7	Match No
1	2	3¹	4	5	6	7²	8	9	10	11	12	13											1
1	2	3	4	5			8	9	10¹	11³	12	7²	6	13	14								2
1	2	3²	4	5			8	9		11	10	7¹	6		12	13							3
1	2		4	12	13		8	9²		11		3¹	6	10³	7	5	14						4
1	2		4	12			8	9		11		3¹	6²	10³	7	13	5	14					5
1	2		4	12	13		8	9		11²		3	6	10	7	5¹							6
1	2	3	4	5	12		8	9		11²	13	10	6	7¹									7
1	2		4	5	3		9¹	12		11²	13	10	6	8	7								8
1	2		4	5			8	9			10	3	6	7	11								9
1	2		4	5			8	9		12	10	3	6	11	7¹								10
1	2		4²	5	12		8	9			10	3¹	6	11	7			13					11
1	2			5	12		8	9²	13		10	3	4³	14	7¹	11			6				12
1	2			5	12		8	9			10	3	4	11	7¹				6				13
1	2			5			8	9			10	3	4	11	7				6				14
1	2			5			8	9		12	10	3	4	11²	7¹	13			6				15
1	2			5	12		8¹	9			10		11	4	7	3			6				16
1	2		4	5	12	13	8	9			10	3²	6	11¹	7								17
1	2		4	5	11¹	12	8	9²	13		10	3	6	7									18
1	2²		4	5	11		8			9³	10	3	6	7¹	12	13		14					19
1			4²	5	7	2		9³	11¹	10	3		8	12	13		6	14					20
1				5	7¹		8	9²		10	2	4	11	12	3		6	13					21
1				5	7¹		8	9		12	10	2	4	3	11²		6	13					22
1				5	7²		8	9	12	11	10¹			3	13	2	4	6					23
1				5	7		8	9	12	11²	10			3	13	2	4¹	6					24
1				5	7		8	9			10	3	4		2	11		6					25
1				5	7¹	8²	9			10	3	4³		12	2	11	13	6			14		26
1				5	7²	8	9			11	10	3	4	12	2			6					27
1	12			5¹	7²	8	9			11	10	3	4	13	2			6					28
1				5	7¹	8	9			11²	10	3	4	12	2			6	13				29
1				5	7		9			11	10¹	3	4		2			6	12		8		30
1				5	7		9			11¹	10	3	4	12	2			6	8				31
1				5	7	8	9¹			11	10²	3	4		2			6	12	13			32
1				5	7	8	9			11	10	3		12	2			6	4¹				33
1				5	7	8	9			11	10	3	12	4¹	2			6					34
1				5	7²	8	9			11	10	3¹	4	13	2	12		6					35
1				5	7²	8	9			11	10		4¹	12	2	3		6	13				36
1				5	7	8	9			11²	10	12	4¹	13	2³	3		6	14				37
1	2				7	8	9¹			11	10	4		3	5			6	12				38
1	2				7²	8		12		10	4	11¹	13	3	5			6	9³		14		39
1	2		12		7	8		11		10	4		3	5¹				6	9³		13		40
1	2				7	8		11		10¹	4²	12	3	5				6	9		13		41
1	2		12		7²	8		13		10	4		3	5¹	11			6	9				42
1	2			5	7²	8		11³		10	12	4¹	13	3				6	9		14		43
1	2			5	11¹	8	9²			10	4	7³	12	3				6	13		14		44
1	12			5	11	8	9			10	2¹	4	7	3				6	13		14		45
1	2			5	11²	8	9			12	10	4	7³	3¹				6	13		14		46

Worthington Cup

First Round   Hull C   (h) 0-1
                                             (a) 0-2

FA Cup

First Round   Worthing   (h) 3-0
Second Round   Burnley   (a) 0-2

Division 3   **SCUNTHORPE UNITED**

FOUNDATION

The year of foundation for Scunthorpe United has often been quoted as 1910, but the club can trace its history back to 1899 when Brumby Hall FC, who played on the Old Showground, consolidated their position by amalgamating with some other clubs and changing their name to Scunthorpe United. The year 1910 was when that club amalgamated with North Lindsey United as Scunthorpe and Lindsey United. The link is Mr W. T. Lockwood whose chairmanship covers both years.

Glanford Park, Scunthorpe, North Lincolnshire DN15 8TD.

Telephone: (01724) 848 077.

Fax: (01724) 857 986.

ClubCall: 09068 121 652.

Ground Capacity: 9183.

Record Attendance: Old Showground: 23,935 v Portsmouth, FA Cup 4th rd, 30 January 1954. Glanford Park: 8775 v Rotherham U, Division 4, 1 May 1989.

Record Receipts: £47,252 v Burnley, Division 2, 6 May 2000.

Pitch Measurements: 110yd × 71yd.

Vice-Presidents: I. T. Botham, G. Johnson, A. Harvey, R. Ashman, K. Waters, J. Brownsword, B. Heywood, Dr J. Zacarias.

Chairman: K. Wagstaff.

Vice-Chairman: R. Garton.

Directors: J. B. Borrill, B. Collen, J. A. C. Godfrey CBE, J. S. Wharton.

Team Manager: Brian Laws.

Chief Executive/Secretary: A. D. Rowing.

Commercial Manager: A. D. Rowing.

LATEST SEQUENCES

Longest Sequence of League Wins: 6, 18.10.69 – 25.11.69.

Longest Sequence of League Defeats: 8, 29.11.97 – 20.1.98.

Longest Sequence of League Draws: 6, 2.1.84 – 25.2.84.

Longest Sequence of Unbeaten League Matches: 15, 13.11.71 – 26.2.72.

Longest Sequence Without a League Win: 14, 22.3.75 – 6.9.75.

HONOURS

Football League: Division 2 best season: 4th, 1961–62; Division 3 (N) – Champions 1957-58. Promoted from Division 3 1998–99 (play-offs).

FA Cup: best season: 5th rd, 1958, 1970.

Football League Cup: never past 3rd rd.

Colours

White shirt with claret and blue trim, white shorts with claret and blue trim, white stockings with claret and blue top.

Change Colours

Lime green shirt with navy trim, navy shorts with lime trim, navy stockings with lime top.

Year Formed: 1899.

Turned Professional: 1912.

Ltd Co.: 1912.

Club Nickname: 'The Iron'.

Previous Names: Amalgamated first with Brumby Hall then North Lindsey United to become Scunthorpe & Lindsey United, 1910; dropped '& Lindsey' in 1958.

Previous ground: 1899, Old Showground; 1988, Glanford Park.

First Football League Game: 19 August 1950, Division 3 (N), v Shrewsbury T (h) D 0–0 – Thompson; Barker, Brownsword; Allen, Taylor, McCormick; Mosby, Payne, Gorin, Rees, Boyes.

Record League Victory: 8–1 v Luton T, Division 3, 24 April 1965 – Sidebottom; Horstead, Hemstead; Smith, Neale, Lindsey; Bramley (1), Scott, Thomas (5), Mahy (1), Wilson (1). 8–1 v Torquay U (a), Division 3, 28 October 1995 – Samways; Housham, Wilson, Ford (1), Knill (1), Hope (Nicholson), Thornber, Bullimore (Walsh), McFarlane (4) (Young), Eyre (2), Paterson.

Record Cup Victory: 9–0 v Boston U, FA Cup 1st rd, 21 November 1953 – Malan; Hubbard, Brownsword; Sharpe, White, Bushby; Mosby (1), Haigh (3), Whitfield (2), Gregory (1), Mervyn Jones (2).

Record Defeat: 0–8 v Carlisle U, Division 3 (N), 25 December 1952.

Most League Points (2 for a win): 66, Division 3 (N), 1956–57, 1957–58.

Most League Points (3 for a win): 83, Division 4, 1982–83.

Most League Goals: 88, Division 3 (N), 1957–58.

Highest League Scorer in Season: Barrie Thomas, 31, Division 2, 1961–62.

Most League Goals in Total Aggregate: Steve Cammack, 110, 1979–81, 1981–86.

Most League Goals in One Match: 5, Barrie Thomas v Luton T, Division 3, 24 April 1965.

Most Capped Player: None.

Most League Appearances: Jack Brownsword, 595, 1950–65.

Youngest League Player: Mike Farrell, 16 years 240 days v Workington, 8 November 1975.

Record Transfer Fee Received: £350,000 from Aston Villa for Neil Cox, February 1991.

Record Transfer Fee Paid: £200,000 to Bristol C for Steve Torpey, February 2000.

Football League Record: 1950 Elected to Division 3 (N); 1958–64 Division 2; 1964–68 Division 3; 1968–72 Division 4; 1972–73 Division 3; 1973–83 Division 4; 1983–84 Division 3; 1984–92 Division 4; 1992–99 Division 3; 1999–2000 Division 2; 2000– Division 3.

MANAGERS

Harry Allcock 1915–53
(Secretary-Manager)
Tom Crilly 1936–37
Bernard Harper 1946–48
Leslie Jones 1950–51
Bill Corkhill 1952–56
Ron Suart 1956–58
Tony McShane 1959
Bill Lambton 1959
Frank Soo 1959–60
Dick Duckworth 1960–64
Fred Goodwin 1964–66
Ron Ashman 1967–73
Ron Bradley 1973–74
Dick Rooks 1974–76
Ron Ashman 1976–81
John Duncan 1981–83
Allan Clarke 1983–84
Frank Barlow 1984–87
Mick Buxton 1987–91
Bill Green 1991–93
Richard Money 1993–94
David Moore 1994–96
Mick Buxton 1996–97
Brian Laws February 1997–

TEN YEAR LEAGUE RECORD

		P	W	D	L	F	A	Pts	Pos
1989-90	Div 4	46	17	15	14	69	54	66	11
1990-91	Div 4	46	20	11	15	71	62	71	8
1991-92	Div 4	42	21	9	12	64	59	72	5
1992-93	Div 3	42	14	12	16	57	54	54	14
1993-94	Div 3	42	15	14	13	64	56	59	11
1994-95	Div 3	42	18	8	16	68	63	62	7
1995-96	Div 3	46	15	15	16	67	61	60	12
1996-97	Div 3	46	18	9	19	59	62	63	13
1997-98	Div 3	46	19	12	15	56	52	69	8
1998-99	Div 3	46	22	8	16	69	58	74	4

DID YOU KNOW

Ted Gorin joined Scunthorpe United from Cardiff City on their election to the Football League in 1950. He had scored 12 goals for them in 26 successive League games, before being transferred to the other newcomers, Shrewsbury Town.

SCUNTHORPE UNITED 1999–2000 LEAGUE RECORD

Match No.	Date	Venue	Opponents	Result	H/T Score	Lg. Pos.	Goalscorers	Attendance
1	Aug 7	A	Wigan Ath	L	0-3	0-1	24		7481
2	14	H	Wycombe W	L	0-1	0-1	24		4092
3	21	A	Notts Co	L	0-3	0-2	24		5506
4	28	H	Bournemouth	W	3-1	1-1	22	Humphreys 2 (1 pen) [45, 76 (p)], Ipoua [61]	3376
5	30	A	Cardiff C	D	1-1	1-0	20	Ipoua [25]	8006
6	Sept 4	H	Bristol R	L	0-2	0-1	22		4496
7	11	A	Colchester U	W	1-0	0-0	17	Hodges [49]	3280
8	18	H	Bristol C	L	1-2	0-0	20	Guinan [56]	4542
9	25	H	Chesterfield	D	0-0	0-0	20		4321
10	Oct 2	A	Stoke C	L	0-1	0-0	20		13,068
11	10	A	Burnley	W	2-1	1-0	18	Ipoua 2 [25, 85]	10,752
12	16	H	Preston NE	D	1-1	0-1	17	Ipoua (pen) [47]	5336
13	19	A	Oxford U	W	1-0	0-0	—	Ipoua [88]	3829
14	23	A	Chesterfield	D	1-1	0-1	14	Fickling [56]	3464
15	Nov 2	A	Cambridge U	W	3-1	2-0	—	Hope [22], Harsley [36], Hodges [90]	3285
16	6	H	Millwall	L	1-4	0-2	14	Cornforth [65]	4550
17	12	A	Brentford	L	3-4	2-2	14	Ipoua (pen) [34], Harsley [42], Calvo-Garcia [88]	4657
18	23	H	Gillingham	L	1-4	1-2	—	Ipoua [8]	3444
19	27	A	Reading	D	1-1	0-0	16	Hodges [72]	6142
20	Dec 4	H	Wigan Ath	L	1-2	1-1	17	Hodges [7]	3463
21	18	H	Bury	L	0-2	0-0	19		3137
22	26	A	Oldham Ath	D	1-1	0-1	19	Hope [52]	5998
23	28	H	Blackpool	W	1-0	1-0	17	Omoyimni [39]	4476
24	Jan 3	A	Luton T	L	1-4	0-3	17	Hodges [78]	5574
25	15	A	Wycombe W	L	1-2	1-1	20	Sheldon [19]	4850
26	22	H	Notts Co	W	1-0	1-0	18	Ipoua [19]	4035
27	29	A	Bournemouth	D	1-1	0-0	18	Dawson [76]	4802
28	Feb 1	H	Wrexham	L	0-2	0-2	—		2851
29	5	H	Cardiff C	D	0-0	0-0	18		3614
30	12	H	Bristol R	D	1-1	0-1	19	Hope [52]	8236
31	19	H	Reading	D	2-2	2-1	18	Torpey [28], Quailey [40]	4082
32	26	A	Bristol C	L	1-2	1-2	19	Quailey [43]	9897
33	Mar 4	H	Colchester U	D	0-0	0-0	19		4253
34	7	A	Millwall	W	2-1	0-1	—	Logan [56], Quailey [69]	8772
35	11	A	Cambridge U	L	0-3	0-1	19		3964
36	18	A	Gillingham	L	1-3	1-1	19	Harsley [29]	6822
37	21	H	Brentford	D	0-0	0-0	—		2686
38	25	H	Oldham Ath	L	1-2	1-2	22	Quailey [14]	3807
39	28	A	Wrexham	L	1-3	0-2	—	Quailey [47]	2139
40	Apr 1	A	Bury	L	0-3	0-1	22		3546
41	8	H	Luton T	L	1-2	0-2	23	Dawson [71]	3811
42	15	A	Blackpool	W	2-0	2-0	21	Bull [26], Sheldon [27]	5542
43	22	A	Preston NE	L	0-1	0-1	22		15,518
44	24	H	Stoke C	L	0-2	0-2	23		5435
45	29	A	Oxford U	L	0-2	0-1	23		6752
46	May 6	H	Burnley	L	1-2	1-1	23	Hodges [21]	5862

Final League Position: 23

GOALSCORERS

League (40): Ipoua 9 (2 pens), Hodges 6, Quailey 5, Harsley 3, Hope 3, Dawson 2, Humphreys 2 (1 pen), Sheldon 2, Bull 1, Calvo-Garcia 1, Cornforth 1, Fickling 1, Guinan 1, Logan 1, Omoyinmi 1, Torpey 1.
Worthington Cup (0).
FA Cup (0).

Evans T 27 + 1	Harsley P 45 + 1	Dawson A 40 + 3	Logan R 39	Wilcox R 13 + 1	Hope C 43 + 1	Walker J 40 + 2	Hodges L 39 + 1	Gayle J 2 + 10	Graves W 9 + 10	Calvo-Garcia A 18	Stamp D 5 + 5	Marshall L 1 + 4	Humphreys R 6	Stanton N 27 + 7	Fickling A 24 + 6	Sheldon G 8 + 14	Ipoua G 28 + 12	Housham S 6 + 3	Sparrow M 2 + 9	Guinan S 2 + 1	Perez L 13	Marcelle C 8 + 2	Bull G 3 + 3	Cornforth J 2 + 2	McAuley S 8	Omoyinmi E 6	Hyldgaard M 5	Torpey S 15	Quailey B 13 + 1	Jackson M 6	Hodgson R 1	Clarke R 1	Turner R 1	Barwick T — + 1	Match No.
1	2	3	4	5	6	7	8	9³	10¹	11²	12	13		14																					1
1	2	3	4	5	6	7	8	12	11¹	9			10																						2
1	2	3		5	6	7	8		9¹	11	12			10³	4²	13	14																		3
1	2	3	4		6	7	8¹		11			12	10		5	9²	13																		4
1	2³	3	4		6	7	8¹		11			12	10	14	5	13	9²																		5
1	2	3	4		6	7³	8¹		11			10	12	5	13	9²	14																		6
1	2	3		5	6		8		11			10		4	7¹	9²	12	13																	7
1	2	3		5	6		8¹	12	11²			4			9	7	10																		8
1	2	3	4	5	6	7	8	12	11²					9		13	10¹																		9
1	2¹	3	4	5	6	7	8²	12		10				13	9		11																		10
	2	3	4	5¹	6	7	8²	14	11				12		9³		13		1	10															11
	2	3	4	5¹	6	7	8		11				12		9				1	10															12
	2	3	4		6	7	8	12	11				5		9				1	10¹															13
	2²	3	4		6	7	8	12	11				5		9¹		13		1	10															14
	2	3		5	6	7	8	12	11				13	4²		9¹			1	10³	14														15
	2	3		5²	6	7	8	12	11³				13	4		9			1	10¹		14													16
15	2²	3		5	6	7	8¹	13	12	11				4		9			1	10	10														17
	2²		4		6	7³	8	12	11				13	5		9			1	10¹		14	3												18
	2		7		6	12	8³	13		11²				4	5		9		1	14		10¹	3												19
	2	10			6	7	8	11						4¹	5		9		1	12			3												20
	2	3	11		6	7	8				10	12		4	5²	13			1		9¹														21
	2	3	4		6	7	8	10						5		12	9¹		1				11												22
	2	3	4		6¹	7	8	10						5	12		9		1				11												23
1	2	3¹	4	12		7³	8	10						6²	5		9	13	14				11												24
	6	12		5		7	8		10					2	4	11	9¹						3		1										25
	2	12	4		6	7	8¹		10					5	13	9²							3	11	1										26
	2	8	4		6	7¹			10²					14	5	13³	9		12				3	11	1										27
	2	3	4		6		8	12						13	5	14	9²						10³	7	11¹	1									28
	2	4	10		6	7	8							5			12							3		1	9	11¹							29
1	11	3	4		6	7¹	8	12						2	5		13										9	10¹							30
1	11	3	4		6		8¹	12						2	5	13		7									9	10²							31
1	11	3	4		6	12	8							2	5¹	13	9	7²										10							32
1	11	3	4		6	7								2	5³	12	9¹	8²	13					14				10							33
1	11	3	4		6	7		9						2	5	12²		8¹	13									10							34
1	11²	3	4		6	7		12						2		13												9	10	5	8¹				35
1	12	3	4		6	7		9²						2	5³		13		14									8	10	11¹					36
1	2	3	4		6	7		9						5		12	13											8	10¹	11²					37
1	2	3	4		6	7	12	9						5			13											8	10²	11¹					38
1	2	12	4		6³	7	8							5	14		13	11										9²	10			3¹			39
1	2	3	4		12	7	8		13					5		6	9²	11¹											10						40
1	2	3	4		6	7	8	12						5		11¹	9												10						41
1	2	3	4		6	7	8²	12						5	13	11¹	9³							14					10						42
1	2	3	4		6	7	8²	12		13				5		11¹	14							9³					10						43
1	2	3	4		6	7	8							5		11²	12							9¹					10	13					44
1	2	3	4		6	7	8		12					5			13												9¹	10	11²				45
	2	3	4		6	7²	8¹							5			12												9	10	11		1	13	46

Worthington Cup

First Round	Huddersfield T	(h)	0-2
		(a)	0-0

FA Cup

First Round	Rushden & D	(a)	0-2

Division 1 **SHEFFIELD UNITED**

FOUNDATION

In March 1889, Yorkshire County Cricket Club formed Sheffield United six days after an FA Cup semi-final between Preston North End and West Bromwich Albion had finally convinced Charles Stokes, a member of the cricket club, that the formation of a professional football club would prove successful at Bramall Lane. The United's first secretary, Mr J. B. Wostinholm was also secretary of the cricket club.

Bramall Lane Ground, Sheffield S2 4SU.
Telephone: (0114) 221 5757.
Fax: (0114) 272 3030.
Website: http://www.sufc.co.uk
Email: info@sufc.co.uk
ISDN: (0114) 221 3148.
Ticket Office: (0114) 221 1889.
Pools Office: (0114) 221 3131.
Club Shop: (0114) 221 3132.
Executive Suite: (0114) 221 3195.
Football in the Community: (0114) 276 9314
Ticket Info Line: (0645) 202 020
ClubCall: 09068 888 650.
Ground Capacity: 30,370.
Record Attendance: 68,287 v Leeds U, FA Cup 5th rd, 15 February 1936.
Record Receipts: £298,364 v Coventry C, FA Cup 6th rd replay, 17 March 1998.
Pitch Measurements: 112yd × 72yd.
Chairman: D. Dooley.
Directors: K. McCabe, B. Proctor, A. Lave, M. Dudley, Ron Reid.
Manager: Neil Warnock.
Assistant Manager: Kevin Blackwell.
Coach: Dougie Hodgson.
Physios: Denis Pettitt, Nigel Cox.
Stadium Manager: Roy Mitchell.
General Manager, Commercial: Adrian Danes.
Community Programme Organiser: Tony Currie,
Tel: (0114) 2769314.

LATEST SEQUENCES

Longest Sequence of League Wins: 8, 14.9.60 – 22.10.60.
Longest Sequence of League Defeats: 7, 19.8.75 – 20.9.75.
Longest Sequence of League Draws: 5, 16.12.95 – 20.1.96.
Longest Sequence of Unbeaten League Matches: 22, 2.9.1899 – 13.1.1900.
Longest Sequence Without a League Win: 19, 27.9.75 – 7.2.76.

HONOURS

Football League: Division 1 – Champions 1897–98; Runners-up 1896–97, 1899–1900; Division 2 – Champions 1952–53; Runners-up 1892–93, 1938–39, 1960–61, 1970–71, 1989–90; Division 4 – Champions 1981–82.

FA Cup: Winners 1899, 1902, 1915, 1925; Runners-up 1901, 1936.

Football League Cup: best season: 5th rd, 1962, 1967, 1972.

Colours
Red and white striped shirts with black trim, black shorts and stockings with red trim.

Change Colours
All white with red trim.

Year Formed: 1889.

Turned Professional: 1889.

Ltd Co.: 1899.

Club Nickname: 'The Blades'.

First Football League Game: 3 September 1892, Division 2, v Lincoln C (h) W 4–2 – Lilley; Witham, Cain; Howell, Hendry, Needham (1); Wallace, Dobson, Hammond (3), Davies, Drummond.

Record League Victory: 10–0 v Burslem Port Vale (a), Division 2, 10 December 1892 – Howlett; Witham, Lilley; Howell, Hendry, Needham (1), Wallace (1), Hammond (4), Davies (2), Watson (2).

Record Cup Victory: 5–0 v Newcastle U (a), FA Cup 1st rd, 10 January 1914 – Gough; Cook, English; Brelsford, Howley, Sturgess; Simmons (2), Gillespie (1), Kitchen (1), Fazackerley, Revill (1). 5–0 v Corinthians, FA Cup 1st rd, 10 January 1925 – Sutcliffe; Cook, Milton; Longworth, King, Green; Partridge, Boyle (1), Johnson (4), Gillespie, Tunstall. 5–0 v Barrow, FA Cup 3rd rd, 7 January 1956 – Burgin; Coldwell, Mason; Fountain, Johnson, Iley; Hawksworth (1), Hoyland (2), Howitt, Wragg (1), Grainger (1).

Record Defeat: 0–13 v Bolton W, FA Cup 2nd rd, 1 February 1890.

Most League Points (2 for a win): 60, Division 2, 1952–53.

Most League Points (3 for a win): 96, Division 4, 1981–82.

Most League Goals: 102, Division 1, 1925–26.

Highest League Scorer in Season: Jimmy Dunne, 41, Division 1, 1930–31.

Most League Goals in Total Aggregate: Harry Johnson, 205, 1919–30.

Most League Goals in One Match: 5, Harry Hammond v Bootle, Division 2, 26 November 1892; 5, Harry Johnson v West Ham U, Division 1, 26 December 1927.

Most Capped Player: Billy Gillespie, 25, Northern Ireland.

Most League Appearances: Joe Shaw, 629, 1948–66.

Youngest League Player: Julian Broddle, 17 years 62 days v Halifax T, 2 January 1982.

Record Transfer Fee Received: £2,700,000 from Leeds U for Brian Deane, July 1993.

Record Transfer Fee Paid: £1,200,000 to West Ham U for Don Hutchison, January 1996.

Football League Record: 1892 Elected to Division 2; 1893–1934 Division 1; 1934–39 Division 2; 1946–49 Division 1; 1949–53 Division 2; 1953–56 Division 1; 1956–61 Division 2; 1961–68 Division 1; 1968–71 Division 2; 1971–76 Division 1; 1976–79 Division 2; 1979–81 Division 3; 1981–82 Division 4; 1982–84 Division 3; 1984–88 Division 2; 1988–89 Division 3; 1989–90 Division 2; 1990–92 Division 1; 1992–94 FA Premier League; 1994– Division 1.

MANAGERS

J. B. Wostinholm 1889–1899
(Secretary-Manager)
John Nicholson 1899–1932
Ted Davison 1932–52
Reg Freeman 1952–55
Joe Mercer 1955–58
Johnny Harris 1959–68
(continued as General Manager to 1970)
Arthur Rowley 1968–69
Johnny Harris *(General Manager resumed Team Manager duties)* 1969–73
Ken Furphy 1973–75
Jimmy Sirrel 1975–77
Harry Haslam 1978–81
Martin Peters 1981
Ian Porterfield 1981–86
Billy McEwan 1986–88
Dave Bassett 1988–95
Howard Kendall 1995–97
Nigel Spackman 1997–98
Steve Bruce 1998–99
Adrian Heath 1999
Neil Warnock December 1999–

TEN YEAR LEAGUE RECORD

		P	W	D	L	F	A	Pts	Pos
1989-90	Div 2	46	24	13	9	78	58	85	2
1990-91	Div 1	38	13	7	18	36	55	46	13
1991-92	Div 1	42	16	9	17	65	63	57	9
1992-93	PR Lge	42	14	10	18	54	53	52	14
1993-94	PR Lge	42	8	18	16	42	60	42	20
1994-95	Div 1	46	17	17	12	74	55	68	8
1995-96	Div 1	46	16	14	16	57	54	62	9
1996-97	Div 1	46	20	13	13	75	52	73	5
1997-98	Div 1	46	19	17	10	69	54	74	6
1998-99	Div 1	46	18	13	15	71	66	67	8

DID YOU KNOW ?

For the first 21 League games of the 1958-59 season, the Sheffield United defence of goalkeeper, two full-backs and three half-backs, plus centre-forward were unchanged.

SHEFFIELD UNITED 1999–2000 LEAGUE RECORD

Match No.	Date	Venue	Opponents	Result	H/T Score	Lg. Pos.	Goalscorers	Attendance
1	Aug 7	A	Portsmouth	L	0-2	0-1	24		17,667
2	14	H	Walsall	D	1-1	1-1	21	Murphy [1]	12,581
3	21	A	Manchester C	L	0-6	0-2	24		30,110
4	28	H	Ipswich T	D	2-2	0-2	23	Smith [54], Murphy [83]	12,455
5	30	A	Tranmere R	W	3-1	3-1	17	Devlin 2 [5, 45], Smith [21]	5436
6	Sept 4	H	Crystal Palace	W	3-1	2-0	10	Marcelo 2 [19, 45], Ford [73]	11,886
7	18	H	Charlton Ath	L	1-2	1-1	15	Katchuro [2]	13,216
8	25	H	Wolverhampton W	W	3-0	0-0	12	Smith 2 [56, 69], Devlin [58]	14,163
9	Oct 2	A	Huddersfield T	L	1-4	0-2	16	Murphy [49]	14,238
10	9	A	Crewe Alex	L	0-1	0-1	20		5304
11	16	H	Nottingham F	W	2-1	0-1	13	Smith 2 [55, 57]	15,687
12	19	H	Norwich C	D	0-0	0-0	—		11,907
13	23	A	Swindon T	D	2-2	0-2	16	Smith 2 [52, 82]	5504
14	26	A	Wolverhampton W	L	0-1	0-0	—		24,402
15	30	H	Huddersfield T	L	0-1	0-0	18		14,928
16	Nov 6	A	Barnsley	L	0-2	0-1	19		16,301
17	14	H	Bolton W	L	1-2	1-2	20	Bent [32]	10,013
18	20	A	Stockport Co	D	1-1	1-0	21	Bent [17]	6614
19	23	H	Port Vale	L	1-3	1-1	—	Sandford [22]	8965
20	27	A	WBA	D	2-2	1-1	21	Smith [21], Ribeiro [60]	12,278
21	30	A	QPR	L	1-3	0-2	—	Devlin [87]	9922
22	Dec 4	H	Portsmouth	W	1-0	1-0	21	Devlin [20]	10,834
23	19	H	Blackburn R	W	2-1	1-0	20	Bent 2 [29, 71]	10,437
24	26	A	Birmingham C	W	2-0	1-0	16	Devlin [4], Smith [64]	22,874
25	28	H	Fulham	W	2-0	0-0	15	Devlin [84], Bent [86]	17,375
26	Jan 3	A	Grimsby T	D	2-2	1-1	16	Bent [23], Hall [60]	7618
27	15	A	Walsall	L	1-2	1-0	16	Devlin [26]	6222
28	22	H	Manchester C	W	1-0	1-0	16	Brown [40]	23,862
29	29	A	Ipswich T	D	1-1	0-1	16	Bent [54]	17,350
30	Feb 5	H	Tranmere R	W	3-1	0-0	14	Devlin [48], Bent [61], Ford [87]	14,219
31	12	A	Crystal Palace	D	1-1	0-0	15	Bent [49]	14,877
32	19	H	WBA	W	6-0	2-0	13	Bent 3 [2, 45, 51], Devlin [55], Notman [65], Brown [82]	14,519
33	26	A	Charlton Ath	L	0-1	0-0	15		19,249
34	Mar 5	H	QPR	D	1-1	0-1	14	Notman [54]	11,554
35	7	A	Barnsley	D	3-3	1-2	—	Notman [22], Brown [48], Bent [90]	22,376
36	11	A	Port Vale	W	3-2	1-1	12	Bent [23], Woodhouse [47], D'Jaffo [49]	5484
37	18	H	Stockport Co	W	1-0	0-0	12	Woodhouse [86]	14,907
38	21	H	Bolton W	L	0-2	0-2	—		11,891
39	25	H	Birmingham C	L	1-2	1-0	12	Bent [10]	15,486
40	Apr 1	A	Blackburn R	L	0-5	0-2	13		17,769
41	8	H	Grimsby T	D	0-0	0-0	12		11,612
42	15	A	Fulham	L	0-4	0-1	13		12,197
43	22	A	Nottingham F	D	0-0	0-0	14		17,172
44	24	H	Crewe Alex	D	1-1	0-0	14	Woodhouse [88]	9923
45	29	A	Norwich C	L	1-2	0-2	16	Devlin (pen) [78]	16,921
46	May 7	H	Swindon T	D	2-2	1-0	16	Quinn [14], Burley [73]	12,603

Final League Position: 16

GOALSCORERS

League (59): Bent 15, Devlin 11 (1 pen), Smith 10, Brown 3, Murphy 3, Notman 3, Woodhouse 3, Ford 2, Marcelo 2, Burley 1, D'Jaffo 1, Hall 1, Katchuro 1, Quinn 1, Ribeiro 1, Sandford 1.
Worthington Cup (8): Smith 4, Katchuro 2, Marcelo 2.
FA Cup (3): Bent 1, Derry 1, Smith 1.

Tracey S 45	Ford B 38 + 3	Quinn W 41 + 2	Woodhouse C 34 + 3	Murphy S 42	Sandford L 43	Smeets A 2 + 3	Derry S 31 + 3	Devlin P 40 + 4	Katchuro P 8 + 15	Hamilton I 3 + 4	Hunt J 8 + 6	Smith M 24 + 2	Kozluk R 36 + 3	Marcelo 9 + 1	Davison A 1 + 1	Gijsbrechts D 9 + 8	Craddock J 10	Burley A — + 2	Morris L — + 1	Ribeiro B 9 + 11	Bent M 32	Launders B — + 1	Doane B — + 1	Brown M 21 + 3	Hall P 1 + 3	Notman A 7 + 3	D'Jaffo L 6 + 9	Woodward A 2 + 1	Wilson S 4 + 2	Jagielka P — + 1	Match No.
1	2	3	4[1]	5	6		7	8	9	10[2]	11	12	13																		1
1	12	3		5	6	7[1]	4	9	10[2]	11		8	2	13																	2
1	4	3		5	6		7	9	10	8[9]	13	11[1]	2			15	12[2]														3
1	7	3[1]	11	5	6		8	12				10	2	9		4															4
1	7		11	5	6		8[1]	10	12			3	2	9		4															5
	7	12	4	5	3[1]		8[2]	10				11	2	9	1	6	13														6
1	2		11	5	6	12	3	8	10[1]		7		9			4															7
1	7[3]		11	5	3	12	4	8[1]	13	14	10	2	9[2]			6															8
1		3	11	5		4	8	12	7[1]	10	2	9				6															9
1		3	11[2]	5		4	8	12	7	10[1]	2	9				6	13														10
1	7	12	11	5	3[1]	4	8	13	10	2	9[2]					6															11
1	7	3	11		6	4[1]	8	12	10	2	9	5																			12
1		3	4	5		8	9	10	11	2					6						7										13
1		3	11	5	6	4	9	12	10	2		8									7[1]										14
1	12	3	11[2]	5	6	4	9	13	7	10	2[1]						8														15
1	7[2]	3	11	5	6	12	2	9[1]	13	4	10						8														16
1	7[1]	3	11	5	6	4	9	12	10	2							8														17
1	8	3	11[2]	5	6	12	9[1]	7			2	4					10	13[3]	14												18
1	7	3		5	6	8	12	9[3]	11[1]	13	2	4[2]				14	10														19
1	7	3	11	5	6	2	12			10		4				8	9[1]														20
1	7	3	11	5	6	2	12[2]	14	10[1]	13	4[3]					8	9														21
1	7	3		5	6	2	11	12	13	10[3]	14	4				8[2]	9[1]														22
1	2[1]	3	11	5	6	4	8[3]			10[2]	12	13					9				7					14					23
1		3		5	6	4	8[3]	12	14	11	10[1]	2					9[2]				7										24
1	12	3		5	6	4	8[3]	13	11[1]	10[2]	2						9				7					14					25
1	11	3	12	5	6	4		13		10[2]	2						9				7					8[1]					26
1	11	3[2]		5	6	4	8	12		10[1]	2					13	9				7					14					27
1	11	3	12	5	6	4[1]	8[3]	13		2		14					9				7					10[2]					28
1	11	3	4	5	6		8	10[1]		2						12	9				7										29
1	11	3	4[1]	5	6	12	8			2						13	9				7					10[2]					30
1	11	3	4[2]		6	12	8			2		5				13	9[3]				7					10[1]	14				31
1	11	3		5[2]	6	4[1]	8			2		13				12	9[3]				7					10	14				32
1	11[1]	3		5	6	4	8			2		12					9				7					10[2]	13				33
1	11	3	12	5	6	4[1]	8			2							9				7					10					34
1	11	3	4[2]	5	6	12	8			2[1]		13					9				7					10[3]	14				35
1	11	3	4	5	6		2					14					13				9[1]				7[2]	14	10[3]				36
1	11	3	4	5	6[1]		8			2		12					9				7					13	10[2]				37
1	11	3	4	5	6		8[3]	14		2[1]		12					9				7					13	10[2]				38
1	11	3	4	5	6		8			2[1]		5[2]					9				7					10	12	13			39
1	11	3	4	5	6		8			2							9[1]				7					12	2	10			40
1	11	3	4[1]	5	6		8			2							12	9			7					13	2	10[2]			41
1	11	3	4	5	6		8			2							12	9[2]			7					13	10[1]				42
1	11	3	4	5	6		7			2							8[1]	9			12					10					43
1	11	3	4	5	6		7			2							8[1]	9			12					10[2]	13				44
1	11	3	4		6		7	12		2		5[3]					8[2]	9			13					14	10[1]				45
1	11[2]	3[3]	4	5	6		10			2		12					8[1]	9			7					13			14		46

Worthington Cup

First Round	Shrewsbury T	(h)	3-0
		(a)	3-0
Second Round	Preston NE	(h)	2-0
		(a)	0-3

FA Cup

Third Round	Rushden & D	(h)	1-1
		(a)	1-1
Fourth Round	Newcastle U	(a)	1-4

Division 1   **SHEFFIELD WEDNESDAY**

FOUNDATION

Sheffield, being one of the principal centres of early Association Football, this club was formed as long ago as 1867 by the Sheffield Wednesday Cricket Club (formed 1825) and their colours from the start were blue and white. The inaugural meeting was held at the Adelphi Hotel and the original committee included Charles Stokes who was subsequently a founder member of Sheffield United.

Hillsborough, Sheffield S6 1SW.
Telephone: (0114) 221 2121.
Fax: (0114) 221 2122.
Website: www.swfc.co.uk
Email: enquiries@swfc.co.uk
Ticket Office: (0114) 221 2400.
ClubCall: 09068 121 186.
Ground Capacity: 39,859.
Record Attendance: 72,841 v Manchester C, FA Cup 5th rd, 17 February 1934.
Record Receipts: £533,918 Sunderland v Norwich C, FA Cup semi-final, 5 April 1992.
Pitch Measurements: 115yd × 74yd.
President: K. T. Addy.
Chairman: H. E. Culley.
Vice-Chairman: K. T. Addy.
Directors: G. K. Hulley, R. M. Grierson FCA, K. T. Addy, G. A. Thorpe, H. E. Culley.
Manager: Paul Jewell.
Physio: Rob Johnson.
Secretary: Alan D. Sykes.
Commercial Manager: Karen Walker.
Stadium Manager: Trevor Grayson.

LATEST SEQUENCES

Longest Sequence of League Wins: 9, 23.4.04 – 15.10.04.
Longest Sequence of League Defeats: 7, 7.1.1893 – 18.3.1893.
Longest Sequence of League Draws: 5, 24.10.92 – 28.11.92.
Longest Sequence of Unbeaten League Matches: 19, 10.12.60 – 8.4.61.
Longest Sequence Without a League Win: 20, 11.1.75 – 30.8.75.

HONOURS

Football League: Division 1 – Champions 1902–03, 1903–04, 1928–29, 1929–30; Runners-up 1960–61; Division 2 – Champions 1899–1900, 1925–26, 1951–52, 1955–56, 1958–59; Runners-up 1949–50, 1983–84.

FA Cup: Winners 1896, 1907, 1935; Runners-up 1890, 1966, 1993.

Football League Cup: Winners 1991; Runners-up 1993.

European Competitions: European Fairs Cup: 1961–62, 1963–64. *UEFA Cup:* 1992–93.

Colours
Blue and white striped shirts, black shorts, black stockings.

Change Colours
Yellow shirts, navy shorts, yellow/navy stockings.

Year Formed: 1867 (fifth oldest League club).

Turned Professional: 1887.

Ltd Co.: 1899.

Former Names: The Wednesday until 1929.

Club Nickname: 'The Owls'.

Previous Grounds: 1867, Highfield; 1869, Myrtle Road; 1877, Sheaf House; 1887, Olive Grove; 1899, Owlerton (since 1912 known as Hillsborough). Some games were played at Endcliffe in the 1880s. Until 1895 Bramall Lane was used for some games.

First Football League Game: 3 September 1892, Division 1, v Notts Co (a) W 1–0 – Allan; Tom Brandon (1), Mumford; Hall, Betts, Harry Brandon; Spiksley, Brady, Davis, R. N. Brown, Dunlop.

Record League Victory: 9–1 v Birmingham, Division 1, 13 December 1930 – Brown; Walker, Blenkinsop; Strange, Leach, Wilson; Hooper (3), Seed (2), Ball (2), Burgess (1), Rimmer (1).

Record Cup Victory: 12–0 v Halliwell, FA Cup 1st rd, 17 January 1891 – Smith; Thompson, Brayshaw; Harry Brandon (1), Betts, Cawley (2); Winterbottom, Mumford (2), Bob Brandon (1), Woolhouse (5), Ingram (1).

Record Defeat: 0–10 v Aston Villa, Division 1, 5 October 1912.

Most League Points (2 for a win): 62, Division 2, 1958–59.

Most League Points (3 for a win): 88, Division 2, 1983–84.

Most League Goals: 106, Division 2, 1958–59.

Highest League Scorer in Season: Derek Dooley, 46, Division 2, 1951–52.

Most League Goals in Total Aggregate: Andy Wilson, 199, 1900–20.

Most League Goals in One Match: 6, Doug Hunt v Norwich C, Division 2, 19 November 1938.

Most Capped Player: Nigel Worthington, 50 (66), Northern Ireland.

Most League Appearances: Andy Wilson, 502, 1900–20.

Youngest League Player: Peter Fox, 15 years 269 days v Orient, 31 March 1973.

Record Transfer Fee Received: £2,650,000 from Blackburn R for Paul Warhurst, September 1993.

Record Transfer Fee Paid: £4,700,000 to Celtic for Paolo Di Canio, August 1997.

Football League Record: 1892 Elected to Division 1; 1899–1900 Division 2; 1900–20 Division 1; 1920–26 Division 2; 1926–37 Division 1; 1937–50 Division 2; 1950–51 Division 1; 1951–52 Division 2; 1952–55 Division 1; 1955–56 Division 2; 1956–58 Division 1; 1958–59 Division 2; 1959–70 Division 1; 1970–75 Division 2; 1975–80 Division 3; 1980–84 Division 2; 1984–90 Division 1; 1990–91 Division 2; 1991–92 Division 1; 1992–2000 FA Premier League; 2000– Division 1.

MANAGERS

Arthur Dickinson 1891–1920
(Secretary-Manager)
Robert Brown 1920–33
Billy Walker 1933–37
Jimmy McMullan 1937–42
Eric Taylor 1942–58
(continued as General Manager to 1974)
Harry Catterick 1958–61
Vic Buckingham 1961–64
Alan Brown 1964–68
Jack Marshall 1968–69
Danny Williams 1969–71
Derek Dooley 1971–73
Steve Burtenshaw 1974–75
Len Ashurst 1975–77
Jackie Charlton 1977–83
Howard Wilkinson 1983–88
Peter Eustace 1988–89
Ron Atkinson 1989–91
Trevor Francis 1991–95
David Pleat 1995–97
Ron Atkinson 1997–98
Danny Wilson 1998–2000
Peter Shreeves (Acting) 2000
Paul Jewell June 2000–

TEN YEAR LEAGUE RECORD

		P	W	D	L	F	A	Pts	Pos
1989-90	Div 1	38	11	10	17	35	51	43	18
1990-91	Div 2	46	22	16	7	80	51	82	3
1991-92	Div 1	42	21	12	9	62	49	75	3
1992-93	PR Lge	42	15	14	13	55	51	59	7
1993-94	PR Lge	42	16	16	10	76	54	64	7
1994-95	PR Lge	42	13	12	17	49	57	51	13
1995-96	PR Lge	38	10	10	18	48	61	40	15
1996-97	PR Lge	38	14	15	9	50	51	57	7
1997-98	PR Lge	38	12	8	18	52	67	44	16
1998-99	PR Lge	38	13	7	18	41	42	46	12

DID YOU KNOW ?

Harry Chapman, a regular forward choice in Sheffield Wednesday's 1902-03 and 1903-04 championship teams, was the brother of the famous Huddersfield Town and Arsenal manager Herbert Chapman.

SHEFFIELD WEDNESDAY 1999–2000 LEAGUE RECORD

Match No.	Date	Venue	Opponents	Result	H/T Score	Lg. Pos.	Goalscorers	Attendance
1	Aug 7	H	Liverpool	L 1-2	0-0	15	Carbone [88]	34,853
2	11	A	Manchester U	L 0-4	0-2	—		54,941
3	14	A	Bradford C	D 1-1	1-0	19	Dreyer (og) [39]	18,276
4	21	H	Tottenham H	L 1-2	1-2	20	Carbone (pen) [23]	24,027
5	25	H	Derby Co	L 0-2	0-0	—		20,943
6	28	A	Southampton	L 0-2	0-0	20		14,815
7	Sept 11	H	Everton	L 0-2	0-2	20		23,539
8	19	A	Newcastle U	L 0-8	0-4	20		36,619
9	25	A	Sunderland	L 0-1	0-0	20		40,510
10	Oct 2	H	Wimbledon	W 5-1	2-1	20	Jonk [9], De Bilde 2 [23, 82], Rudi [70], Sibon [90]	18,077
11	16	A	Leeds U	L 0-2	0-0	20		39,437
12	23	H	Coventry C	D 0-0	0-0	20		23,296
13	30	A	Leicester C	L 0-3	0-2	20		19,046
14	Nov 6	H	Watford	D 2-2	0-1	20	De Bilde 2 (1 pen) [56 (p), 78]	21,658
15	21	A	West Ham U	L 3-4	1-1	20	Rudi [38], Jonk [48], Booth [66]	23,015
16	Dec 5	H	Liverpool	L 1-4	1-2	20	Alexandersson [18]	42,517
17	18	A	Aston Villa	L 1-2	1-0	20	De Bilde (pen) [20]	23,885
18	26	H	Middlesbrough	W 1-0	1-0	20	Atherton [28]	28,531
19	29	A	Chelsea	L 0-3	0-2	—		32,932
20	Jan 3	H	Arsenal	D 1-1	0-1	20	Sibon [56]	26,155
21	15	H	Bradford C	W 2-0	0-0	20	Alexandersson [52], O'Brien (og) [67]	24,682
22	22	A	Tottenham H	W 1-0	1-0	19	Alexandersson [38]	35,897
23	Feb 2	A	Manchester U	L 0-1	0-0	—		39,640
24	5	A	Derby Co	D 3-3	1-0	19	De Bilde [22], Sibon [68], Donnelly [88]	30,100
25	12	H	Southampton	L 0-1	0-1	19		23,470
26	26	H	Newcastle U	L 0-2	0-1	19		29,212
27	Mar 4	A	Everton	D 1-1	0-1	19	Quinn [49]	32,020
28	11	H	West Ham U	W 3-1	0-1	19	Cresswell [55], Hinchcliffe [63], Alexandersson [66]	21,147
29	18	A	Watford	L 0-1	0-0	19		15,840
30	25	A	Middlesbrough	L 0-1	0-1	19		32,802
31	Apr 5	H	Aston Villa	L 0-1	0-0	—		18,136
32	12	A	Wimbledon	W 2-0	1-0	—	De Bilde [39], Sibon [88]	8248
33	15	H	Chelsea	W 1-0	0-0	18	Jonk (pen) [51]	21,743
34	22	H	Sunderland	L 0-2	0-0	18		28,072
35	30	H	Leeds U	L 0-3	0-1	19		23,416
36	May 6	A	Coventry C	L 1-4	0-1	19	De Bilde [81]	19,921
37	9	A	Arsenal	D 3-3	0-1	—	Sibon [58], De Bilde [60], Quinn [70]	37,271
38	14	H	Leicester C	W 4-0	2-0	19	Quinn [14], Booth [42], Alexandersson [50], De Bilde [62]	21,656

Final League Position: 19

GOALSCORERS

League (38): De Bilde 10 (2 pens), Alexandersson 5, Sibon 5, Jonk 3 (1 pen), Quinn 3, Booth 2, Carbone 2 (1 pen), Rudi 2, Atherton 1, Cresswell 1, Donnelly 1, Hinchcliffe 1, own goals 2.
Worthington Cup (7): Alexandersson 2, Booth 1, Cresswell 1, De Bilde 1, Rudi 1, Sonner 1.
FA Cup (3): Alexandersson 1, Booth 1, Sibon 1.

Srnicek P 20	Newsome J 5+1	Hinchcliffe A 29	Donnelly S 3+9	Emerson 16+1	Walker D 37	Alexandersson N 37	Sibon G 12+16	De Bilde G 37+1	Rudi P 18+2	Sonner D 18+9	Briscoe L 7+9	Cresswell R 2+18	Carbone B 3+4	Atherton P 35	Pressman K 18+1	Jonk W 29+1	Booth A 20+3	Nolan I 28+1	Haslam S 16+7	Scott P 2+3	O'Donnell P —+1	Quinn A 18+1	McKeever M 1+1	Horne B 7	Match No.
1	2	3	4¹	5	6	7	8²	9³	10	11	12	13	14												1
1	2	3		5	6	7	8¹	9²	10	11³	14	13	12	4											2
2	3³	12		5	6	11		9²	10		14			8	4	1	7¹	13							3
				5	6	7		9	10¹					8	2	1	4¹²	3	11	13					4
12			5	6¹	7	13	9³	10				14	8	2	1	4	3	11²							5
6		12	5		7	13	9¹	10		3	8		2	1		4²	11								6
	12	5	6	7¹		9²	10³	11	2		13	4	1		8	3		14							7
2	4¹	5	6	7	12	9	10³	11		13		1		8²	3	14									8
1	4¹	5	6	7	12	9³	10²	11	3	14			13	8	2										9
1	12	5	6	7	13	9	10	11¹		2	4	8²	3												10
1	3	5	6	7		9	10	11		2	4	8													11
1	3²	5	6	7	12	9	10	11	13		2	4	8¹												12
1	3	5	6	7	8	9	10¹	11		12	2	4													13
	3	5	6	7²		9	10	11		13	2¹	1	4	8	12										14
	3	12	6	7		9	10²	11		13	5	1	4	8	2¹										15
	5	6	11	12	9²	10³		3¹	13		4	1	7	8	2		14								16
1	5	6	7	12	9		11		4	10¹	8	2	13		3²										17
1	3	6	7		9	11²	12	5	4	8	2	13		10¹											18
1	3	6	7	12	9	11³	10¹	13	5	4	8²	2	14												19
1	3	6	7	8¹	9	11	10²	12	5	4	2		13												20
1	3	12	6	7¹	8	9	5	4	2	10	11														21
1	3	12	6	7	8	9¹	5	4	2	10	13	11²													22
1	3	12	6	7	8³	9¹	13	14	5	4	2	10	11²												23
1	3	12	6	7³	8	9¹	13	5	4²	2	10	14	11												24
1	3	12	6	7	8	9¹	4²	13	5	14	2	10³	11												25
1	3	6	7	8	9²	12	11¹	13	5	2	10	4													26
1	3	6	7	8	9	11	12	5	2¹	10	4														27
1	3	6	7	8²	9	12	13	5	4¹	2	10	11													28
1⁰	3	6	7	12	9	8	5	15	4	2	10	11¹													29
	3	6	7	9²	8	12	13	5	1	4	2	10¹	11												30
	3	6	7	12	10¹	13	5	1	4	8²	2	11													31
	3	6	7	12	9¹	14	5	1	4²	10	2	13	11³	8											32
	3	6	7	12	9¹	13	5	1	4	10	2	11	8²												33
	3	6	7²	12	9	13	14	5	1	4	10³	2	11	8¹											34
	3	6	7³	12	9	13	14	5	1	4	10	2	14	11	8²										35
	3	6³	7¹	12	9	13	5	1	4	10	2	14	11	8²											36
	3	6	12	13	7²	14	5	1	4	9	2	10¹	11	8³											37
	3	6³	7¹	9	12	13	5	1	4	10	2	14	11	8²											38

Worthington Cup					**FA Cup**			
Second Round	Stoke C	(a)	0-0		Third Round	Bristol C	(h)	1-0
		(h)	3-1		Fourth Round	Wolverhampton W	(h)	1-1
Third Round	Nottingham F	(h)	4-1				(a)	0-0
Fourth Round	Bolton W	(a)	0-1		Fifth Round	Gillingham	(a)	1-3

Division 3   **SHREWSBURY TOWN**

FOUNDATION

Shrewsbury School having provided a number of the early
England and Wales international players it is not surprising that
there was a Town club as early as 1876 which won the Birmingham
Senior Cup in 1879. However, the present Shrewsbury Town club
was formed in 1886 and won the Welsh FA Cup as early as 1891.

Gay Meadow, Shrewsbury SY2 6AB.
Telephone: (01743) 360 111.
Fax: (01743) 236 384.
Commercial Dept: (01743) 356 316.
ClubCall: 09068 121 194.
Community Officer: Brian Williams (01743) 356 623.
Ground Capacity: 8000.
Record Attendance: 18,917 v Walsall, Division 3, 26 April 1961.
Record Receipts: £80,610 v Arsenal, FA Cup 5th rd, 27 February 1991.
Pitch Measurements: 114yd × 74yd.
President: F. C. G. Fry.
Life Vice-Presidents: Dr J. Millard Bryson, G. W. Nelson, W.H. Richards.
Chairman: R. Wycherley.
Directors: A. Hopkins, M. J. Starkey, K. R. Woodhouse, T. J. Allen, K. J. Sayfritz.
Associate Directors: M. R. Ashton, H. J. Wilson, A. T. Jones.
Manager: Kevin Ratcliffe.
Commercial Manager: M. Thomas.
Physio: Stuart Walker.
Coach: Dave Fogg.
Secretary: M. J. Starkey.
Operations Manager: M. R. Ashton.
Chaplain: Rev. Tim Welch.

LATEST SEQUENCES

Longest Sequence of League Wins: 7, 28.10.95 – 16.12.95.
Longest Sequence of League Defeats: 7, 17.10.87 – 14.11.87.
Longest Sequence of League Draws: 6, 30.10.63 – 14.12.63.
Longest Sequence of Unbeaten League Matches: 16, 30.10.93 – 26.2.94.
Longest Sequence Without a League Win: 17, 25.1.92 – 11.4.92.

HONOURS

Football League: Division 2 best
season: 8th, 1983–84, 1984–85;
Division 3 – Champions 1978–79,
1993–94; Division 4 – Runners-up
1974–75.

FA Cup: best season: 6th rd, 1979,
1982.

Football League Cup: Semi-final 1961.

Welsh Cup: Winners 1891, 1938, 1977,
1979, 1984, 1985; Runners-up 1931,
1948, 1980.

Auto Windscreens Shield: Runners-up
1996

Colours
Amber and blue striped shirts, blue shorts, blue stockings with amber trim.

Change Colours
Red shirts with black trim, black shorts, red stockings with black trim.

Year Formed: 1886.

Turned Professional: 1896.

Ltd Co.: 1936.

Club Nickname: 'Town', 'Blues' or 'Salop'. The name 'Salop' is a colloquialism for the county of Shropshire. Since Shrewsbury is the only club in Shropshire, cries of 'Come on Salop' are frequently used!

Previous Ground: Old Shrewsbury Racecourse.

First Football League Game: 19 August 1950, Division 3 (N), v Scunthorpe U (a) D 0–0 – Egglestone; Fisher, Lewis; Wheatley, Depear, Robinson; Griffin, Hope, Jackson, Brown, Barker.

Record League Victory: 7–0 v Swindon T, Division 3 (S), 6 May 1955 – McBride; Bannister, Skeech; Wallace, Maloney, Candlin; Price, O'Donnell (1), Weigh (4), Russell, McCue (2).

Record Cup Victory: 11–2 v Marine, FA Cup 1st rd, 11 November 1995 – Edwards, Seabury (Dempsey (1)), Withe (1), Evans (1), Whiston (2), Scott (1), Woods, Stevens (1), Spink (3) (Anthrobus), Walton, Berkley, (1 og).

Record Defeat: 1–8 v Norwich C, Division 3 (S), 13 September 1952. 1–8 v Coventry C, Division 3, 22 October 1963.

Most League Points (2 for a win): 62, Division 4, 1974–75.

Most League Points (3 for a win): 79, Division 3, 1993–94.

Most League Goals: 101, Division 4, 1958–59.

Highest League Scorer in Season: Arthur Rowley, 38, Division 4, 1958–59.

Most League Goals in Total Aggregate: Arthur Rowley, 152, 1958–65 (thus completing his League record of 434 goals).

Most League Goals in One Match: 5, Alf Wood v Blackburn R, Division 3, 2 October 1971.

Most Capped Player: Jimmy McLaughlin, 5 (12), Northern Ireland; Bernard McNally, 5, Northern Ireland.

Most League Appearances: Colin Griffin, 406, 1975–89.

Youngest League Player: Gerry Nardiello, 17 years 9 days v Blackburn R, 14 May 1983

Record Transfer Fee Received: £500,000 from Crew Alex for Dave Walton, October 1997.

Record Transfer Fee Paid: £100,000 to Aldershot for John Dungworth, November 1979 and £100,000 to Southampton for Mark Blake, August 1990.

Football League Record: 1950 Elected to Division 3 (N); 1951–58 Division 3 (S); 1958–59 Division 4; 1959–74 Division 3; 1974–75 Division 4; 1975–79 Division 3; 1979–89 Division 2; 1989–94 Division 3; 1994– Division 2.

MANAGERS

W. Adams 1905–12
(Secretary-Manager)
A. Weston 1912–34
(Secretary-Manager)
Jack Roscamp 1934–35
Sam Ramsey 1935–36
Ted Bousted 1936–40
Leslie Knighton 1945–49
Harry Chapman 1949–50
Sammy Crooks 1950–54
Walter Rowley 1955–57
Harry Potts 1957–58
Johnny Spuhler 1958
Arthur Rowley 1958–68
Harry Gregg 1968–72
Maurice Evans 1972–73
Alan Durban 1974–78
Richie Barker 1978
Graham Turner 1978–84
Chic Bates 1984–87
Ian McNeill 1987–90
Asa Hartford 1990–91
John Bond 1991–93
Fred Davies 1994–97
(previously Caretaker-Manager 1993–94)
Jake King 1997–99
Kevin Ratcliffe November 1999–

TEN YEAR LEAGUE RECORD

		P	W	D	L	F	A	Pts	Pos
1989-90	Div 3	46	16	15	15	59	54	63	11
1990-91	Div 3	46	14	10	22	61	68	52	18
1991-92	Div 3	46	12	11	23	53	68	47	22
1992-93	Div 3	42	17	11	14	57	52	62	9
1993-94	Div 3	42	22	13	7	63	39	79	1
1994-95	Div 2	46	13	14	19	54	62	53	18
1995-96	Div 2	46	13	14	19	58	70	53	18
1996-97	Div 2	46	11	13	22	49	74	46	22
1997-98	Div 3	46	16	13	17	61	62	61	13
1998-99	Div 3	46	14	14	18	52	63	56	15

DID YOU KNOW ?

On 13 January 1965, Shrewsbury Town defeated Manchester City 3-1 in a third round FA Cup replay, despite missing the penalty when they were a goal down. Fortunately, the culprit Bobby Ross was able to score their third goal.

SHREWSBURY TOWN 1999–2000 LEAGUE RECORD

Match No.	Date	Venue	Opponents	Result	H/T Score	Lg. Pos.	Goalscorers	Atten- dance
1	Aug 7	H	Torquay U	L	1-2	1-1	17	Brown [39]	2858
2	14	A	Plymouth Arg	D	0-0	0-0	19		4919
3	21	H	Darlington	L	0-1	0-1	21		2181
4	28	A	Rotherham U	L	0-4	0-4	22		2708
5	31	H	Hartlepool U	D	0-0	0-0	—		1803
6	Sept 3	A	Leyton Orient	W	2-1	0-0	—	Wilding [83], Steele [86]	3742
7	12	A	Cheltenham T	W	1-0	1-0	16	Steele [4]	3704
8	18	H	Carlisle U	W	4-1	0-1	13	Steele (pen) [56], Kerrigan [58], Cullen [78], Winstanley [84]	2393
9	24	A	Mansfield T	L	0-4	0-3	—		2808
10	Oct 2	H	Halifax T	D	0-0	0-0	17		2307
11	9	H	Exeter C	L	1-4	1-1	20	Kerrigan [18]	2052
12	16	A	Southend U	L	2-3	1-3	22	Jobling [42], Kerrigan [48]	3963
13	19	A	Brighton & HA	L	0-1	0-1	—		5767
14	23	H	Mansfield T	L	1-2	1-1	22	Steele [44]	1785
15	Nov 2	H	Chester C	L	0-1	0-0	—		2523
16	6	A	Peterborough U	L	1-4	1-4	22	Rigby [15]	5264
17	12	H	Swansea C	D	1-1	0-1	23	Brown [59]	2531
18	23	A	York C	L	0-1	0-1	—		1857
19	27	H	Hull C	W	3-0	1-0	21	Tretton [26], Jobling [49], Brown [53]	2577
20	Dec 4	A	Torquay U	L	1-3	0-0	22	Steele [73]	2050
21	11	H	Northampton T	W	1-0	1-0	21	Steele [3]	2339
22	18	A	Lincoln C	W	2-1	1-0	21	Steele 2 [14, 73]	2907
23	26	H	Macclesfield T	L	0-1	0-1	21		4302
24	28	A	Rochdale	L	1-2	0-1	21	Murray [76]	2924
25	Jan 3	H	Barnet	D	1-1	1-1	21	Tretton [41]	3091
26	8	A	Northampton T	L	0-3	0-2	21		4927
27	15	H	Plymouth Arg	D	0-0	0-0	22		2458
28	29	H	Rotherham U	D	0-0	0-0	22		2587
29	Feb 5	A	Hartlepool U	L	0-1	0-0	22		2933
30	12	H	Leyton Orient	W	1-0	0-0	22	Brown [66]	2740
31	19	A	Hull C	D	0-0	0-0	22		5100
32	26	A	Carlisle U	D	1-1	1-0	22	Thomas (pen) [45]	3105
33	Mar 4	H	Cheltenham T	L	0-2	0-1	22		2876
34	7	H	Peterborough U	L	0-1	0-1	—		2018
35	11	A	Chester C	D	0-0	0-0	22		4002
36	18	H	York C	L	0-1	0-1	22		2149
37	21	A	Swansea C	D	1-1	1-0	—	Sturridge [4]	6112
38	25	A	Macclesfield T	L	2-4	1-2	22	Wilding [5], Gayle [73]	1931
39	Apr 1	H	Lincoln C	L	1-2	0-1	23	Tretton [54]	2220
40	5	A	Darlington	D	2-2	1-0	—	Hughes [14], Gayle [85]	5031
41	8	A	Barnet	D	1-1	0-0	23	Jagielka [57]	2792
42	15	H	Rochdale	L	2-4	1-2	24	Brown 2 [32, 79]	4158
43	22	H	Southend U	W	2-1	0-1	23	Steele 2 (2 pens) [75, 84]	3540
44	24	A	Halifax T	L	1-2	0-1	24	Steele [89]	2123
45	29	H	Brighton & HA	L	1-2	0-0	24	Rodgers [87]	7654
46	May 6	A	Exeter C	W	2-1	0-0	22	Potter (og) [59], Brown [61]	5213

Final League Position: 22

GOALSCORERS
League (40): Steele 11 (3 pens), Brown 7, Kerrigan 3, Tretton 3, Gayle 2, Jobling 2, Wilding 2, Cullen 1, Hughes 1, Jagielka 1, Murray 1, Rigby 1, Rodgers 1, Sturridge 1, Thomas 1 (pen), Winstanley 1, own goal 1.
Worthington Cup (0).
FA Cup (5): Kerrigan 3, Jagielka 1, Wilding 1.

Edwards P 40	Seabury K 31+1	Hanmer G 31+2	Whelan S 16	Winstanley M 32+1	Wilding P 41	Brown M 35+9	Kerrigan S 20+5	Steele L 34+3	Jobling K 25+3	Berkley A 27+6	Rodgers L —+6	Jagielka S 14+19	Cullen J 10	Preece R 5	Tretton A 33	Rigby T 4+4	Hughes D 18+4	Spink D 1+3	Murray K 6+6	Gayle J 17+1	Aiston S 10	Tolley J —+2	Peer D 19	Thomas W 11+2	Dunbavin I 6+1	Sturridge S 10+1	Davidson R 9+1	Herbert C 1+1	Match No.
1	2	3	4	5	6	7	8¹	9²	10	11	12	13																	1
1	2	3	4	5	6	7		9¹	10				12	11	8														2
1	2	3		5	6		8¹	9	10	11			12	7	4														3
1	2	3		5	6	7	12	9	10¹			13		11	8	4²													4
1	2	3		5	6	10	8	9	4	11					7														5
1	2	3		5	6	10	8	9	4	11¹			12		7														6
1	2	3		5	6	10	8	9	4	11¹					7		12												7
1	2	3		5	6	10	8	9	4	11					7														8
1	2	3		5	6	10	8	9	4	11¹	12				7														9
1	2	3		5	6	10¹	8	9	4	11					7		12												10
1	2	3		5	6	10¹	8	9	4³	11²		13			7		12	14											11
1	2	3		5	6¹	12	8	9²	4	7				13	11					10									12
1	2	3		5		10	8		4	7			9		11		6												13
1	2	3		5		10	8	9	4	7¹			12	11²	13		6												14
1	2	3		5	6	10	8²	9	11¹	12					4	7	13												15
1	2	3		5	6	10²	8¹	12	11						4	7	9	13											16
1	2	3		5	6	10	8	9	12						4	7	11¹												17
1	2	3		5	11	8²	9		12						4	7¹	6	13		10									18
1	2	3		5	11	9		10	13						4		6	12	7²	8¹									19
1	2	3		5	11¹	9		10	12						4		6		7	8									20
1	2	3		5	7¹	9		11	8						4		6		12	10									21
1	2²	3¹	6	12	5	7		9	11			8			4				13	10									22
1	2	3	6	5	7	9		11	8						4					10									23
1	2	3	6	5²	7	9		11	8¹						4				12	10	13								24
1	2	3	6	5	12	9²		11	13						4				7	8	10¹								25
1	2	3	6	5	7							11²	12	8¹	4				13	9	10								26
1	2	6	3	5	7	9²		11				12	13		4								8¹	10					27
1	2	6²		5	11			9¹				7	12		4		13		10				3	8					28
1		6	3	5³	11	12						7¹	13		4	14				9¹			10	2		8			29
1		6	3	5	11	12						7²	13		4					9¹			10	2		8			30
1		6	3	5	11	12						7²	13		4					9¹			10¹	2		8			31
1		6	3	5	11							12	7		4					9	10¹			2		8			32
1⁶		6	3	5	11¹	12						7			13		4			9²				2	8	15	10		33
		6	3	5	11	10						7					4							2	8	1	9		34
		6³	5		7	8²		11¹	12			13			4		14						2	10	1	9	3		35
1	3				11	10	12		7			13			4		6		14				5	8¹		9²	2¹		36
1	12		5	6	13	10³	14		8						4		7						2	11¹		9²	3		37
1			5	6²	12		9¹	13				11			4		7		14				2	8³		10	3		38
1			5	6	12		9¹		7						4		11				10		2			8	3		39
1			5	6	12		9¹		7			13			4		11				10		2			8²	3	4	40
1			5	6	12		9		7			8			4		11				10¹		2				3		41
1	12		5¹	6	13		9		7³			14			4		11				10²		2			8	3		42
	12	3		6	11		9		7²	13		8			4		10						5		1		2¹		43
	2³	3		5	11¹		9		7	12		8			4		10						13	6²	1		14		44
	2	3		5²			9		7¹	12		8			4		6		10³				11	13	1	14			45
	2	3		5³	12		9					8			4		6		10¹				11	13	1	7²		14	46

Worthington Cup
First Round   Sheffield U   (a) 0-3
                                              (h) 0-3

FA Cup
First Round   Northampton T   (h) 2-1
Second Round   Oxford U   (h) 2-2
                                              (a) 1-2

FA Premiership **SOUTHAMPTON**

FOUNDATION

Formed largely by players from the Deanery FC, which had been established by school teachers in 1880. Most of the founders were connected with the young men's association of St Mary's Church. At the inaugural meeting held in November 1885 the club was named Southampton St Mary's and the church's curate was elected president.

The Dell, Milton Road, Southampton SO15 2XH.

Telephone: (023) 8022 0505.

Fax: (023) 8033 0360.

Website: www.soton.ac.uk/saints

Email: sfc@tcp.co.uk

Recorded Ticket Information: (023) 8022 8575.

ClubCall: 09068 121 178.

Ground Capacity: 15,000.

Record Attendance: 31,044 v Manchester U, Division 1, 8 October 1969.

Record Receipts: £215,450 v Portsmouth, FA Cup 3rd rd, 7 January 1996.

Pitch Measurements: 110yd × 72yd.

Chairman: R. J. G. Lowe.

Vice-Chairman: B. H. D. Hunt.

Directors: I. L. Gordon, K. St. J. Wiseman, M. R. Richards FCA, A. Cowen, R. M. Withers.

President: E. T. Bates.

Manager: Glenn Hoddle.

Joint Assistant Managers: John Mortimore, John Gorman.

Academy Director: John Sainty.

Physios: Don Taylor, Jim Joyce.

Secretary: Brian Truscott.

LATEST SEQUENCES

Longest Sequence of League Wins: 6, 3.3.92 – 4.4.92.

Longest Sequence of League Defeats: 5, 16.8.98 – 12.9.98.

Longest Sequence of League Draws: 7, 28.12.94 – 11.2.95.

Longest Sequence of Unbeaten League Matches: 19, 5.9.21 – 31.12.21.

Longest Sequence Without a League Win: 20, 30.8.69 – 27.12.69.

HONOURS

Football League: Division 1 – Runners-up 1983–84; Division 2 – Runners-up 1965–66, 1977–78; Division 3 (S) – Champions 1921–22; Runners-up 1920–21; Division 3 – Champions 1959–60.

FA Cup: Winners 1976; Runners-up 1900, 1902.

Football League Cup: Runners-up 1979.

Zenith Data Systems Cup: Runners-up 1992.

European Competitions: European Fairs Cup: 1969–70. UEFA Cup: 1971–72, 1981–82, 1982–83, 1984–85. European Cup-Winners' Cup: 1976–77.

Colours
Red and white striped shirts, black shorts, black stockings with red trim.

Change Colours
Dark navy shirts, dark navy shorts, yellow stockings.

Year Formed: 1885.

Turned Professional: 1894.

Ltd Co.: 1897.

Previous Name: 1885, Southampton St Mary's; 1897, Southampton.

Club Nickname: 'The Saints'.

Previous Grounds: 1885, Antelope Ground; 1897, County Cricket Ground; 1898, The Dell.

First Football League Game: 28 August 1920, Division 3, v Gillingham (a) D 1–1 – Allen; Parker, Titmuss; Shelley, Campbell, Turner; Barratt, Dominy (1), Rawlings, Moore, Foxall.

Record League Victory: 9–3 v Wolverhampton W, Division 2, 18 September 1965 – Godfrey; Jones, Williams; Walker, Knapp, Huxford; Paine (2), O'Brien (1), Melia, Chivers (4), Sydenham (2).

Record Cup Victory: 7–1 v Ipswich T, FA Cup 3rd rd, 7 January 1961 – Reynolds; Davies, Traynor; Conner, Page, Huxford; Paine (1), O'Brien (3 incl. 1p), Reeves, Mulgrew (2), Penk (1).

Record Defeat: 0–8 v Tottenham H, Division 2, 28 March 1936. 0–8 v Everton, Division 1, 20 November 1971.

Most League Points (2 for a win): 61, Division 3 (S), 1921–22 and Division 3, 1959–60.

Most League Points (3 for a win): 77, Division 1, 1983–84.

Most League Goals: 112, Division 3 (S), 1957–58.

Highest League Scorer in Season: Derek Reeves, 39, Division 3, 1959–60.

Most League Goals in Total Aggregate: Mike Channon, 185, 1966–77, 1979–82.

Most League Goals in One Match: 5, Charlie Wayman v Leicester C, Division 2, 23 October 1948.

Most Capped Player: Peter Shilton, 49 (125), England.

Most League Appearances: Terry Paine, 713, 1956–74.

Youngest League Player: Danny Wallace, 16 years 313 days v Manchester U, 29 November 1980.

Record Transfer Fee Received: £7,250,000 from Blackburn R, for Kevin Davies, June 1998.

Record Transfer Fee Paid: £2,000,000 to Sheffield Wednesday for David Hirst, October 1997.

Football League Record: 1920 Original Member of Division 3; 1921–22 Division 3 (S); 1922–53 Division 2; 1953–58 Division 3 (S); 1958–60 Division 3; 1960–66 Division 2; 1966–74 Division 1; 1974–78 Division 2; 1978–92 Division 1; 1992– FA Premier League.

MANAGERS

Cecil Knight 1894–95
(Secretary-Manager)
Charles Robson 1895–97
E. Arnfield 1897–1911
(Secretary-Manager)
(continued as Secretary)
George Swift 1911–12
Ernest Arnfield 1912–19
Jimmy McIntyre 1919–24
Arthur Chadwick 1925–31
George Kay 1931–36
George Gross 1936–37
Tom Parker 1937–43
J. R. Sarjantson stepped down
from the board to act as
Secretary-Manager 1943–47
with the next two listed being
team Managers during this
period
Arthur Dominy 1943–46
Bill Dodgin Snr 1946–49
Sid Cann 1949–51
George Roughton 1952–55
Ted Bates 1955–73
Lawrie McMenemy 1973–85
Chris Nicholl 1985–91
Ian Branfoot 1991–94
Alan Ball 1994–95
Dave Merrington 1995–96
Graeme Souness 1996–97
Dave Jones 1997–2000
Glenn Hoddle January 2000–

TEN YEAR LEAGUE RECORD

		P	W	D	L	F	A	Pts	Pos
1989-90	Div 1	38	15	10	13	71	63	55	7
1990-91	Div 1	38	12	9	17	58	69	45	14
1991-92	Div 1	42	14	10	18	39	55	52	16
1992-93	PR Lge	42	13	11	18	54	61	50	18
1993-94	PR Lge	42	12	7	23	49	66	43	18
1994-95	PR Lge	42	12	18	12	61	63	54	10
1995-96	PR Lge	38	9	11	18	34	52	38	17
1996-97	PR Lge	38	10	11	17	50	56	41	16
1997-98	PR Lge	38	14	6	18	50	55	48	12
1998-99	PR Lge	38	11	8	19	37	64	41	17

DID YOU KNOW ?

On 8 April 2000, Matt Le Tissier scored his 100th Premier League goal – his 48th successful penalty in 49 attempts for them. His only career failure even to hit the target was as a 15 year old in Guernsey, watched by Spurs player Glenn Hoddle.

SOUTHAMPTON 1999–2000 LEAGUE RECORD

Match No.	Date	Venue	Opponents	Result	H/T Score	Lg. Pos.	Goalscorers	Attendance
1	Aug 7	A	Coventry C	W 1-0	0-0	7	Ostenstad [85]	19,602
2	11	H	Leeds U	L 0-3	0-1	—		15,206
3	15	H	Newcastle U	W 4-2	0-1	6	Kachloul 2 [58, 68], Pakhar (Pahars) [66], Hughes M [78]	15,030
4	21	A	Everton	L 1-4	0-1	10	Pakhar (Pahars) [70]	31,755
5	28	H	Sheffield W	W 2-0	0-0	9	Kachloul [53], Oakley [84]	14,815
6	Sept 11	A	Middlesbrough	L 2-3	1-1	13	Kachloul [15], Pakhar (Pahars) [55]	32,157
7	18	H	Arsenal	L 0-1	0-0	13		15,242
8	25	A	Manchester U	D 3-3	1-2	13	Pakhar (Pahars) [17], Le Tissier 2 [51, 73]	55,249
9	Oct 4	H	Derby Co	D 3-3	2-1	—	Pakhar (Pahars) [22], Oakley [35], Ripley [66]	14,208
10	16	A	Leicester C	L 1-2	0-2	14	Pakhar (Pahars) [84]	19,556
11	23	H	Liverpool	D 1-1	1-0	14	Soltvedt [39]	15,241
12	30	A	Wimbledon	D 1-1	0-0	14	Pakhar (Pahars) [67]	15,754
13	Nov 6	A	Aston Villa	W 1-0	0-0	14	Richards [84]	26,474
14	20	H	Tottenham H	L 0-1	0-0	14		15,248
15	28	A	Leeds U	L 0-1	0-0	16		39,288
16	Dec 4	H	Coventry C	D 0-0	0-0	16		15,168
17	18	A	Sunderland	L 0-2	0-1	16		40,066
18	26	H	Chelsea	L 1-2	0-2	16	Davies [80]	15,232
19	28	A	Watford	L 2-3	0-2	16	Boa Morte [61], Davies [63]	18,459
20	Jan 3	H	Bradford C	W 1-0	0-0	16	Davies [55]	15,027
21	16	A	Newcastle U	L 0-5	0-4	17		35,623
22	22	H	Everton	W 2-0	0-0	17	Tessem [47], Oakley [56]	15,232
23	Feb 5	H	West Ham U	W 2-1	0-0	16	Pakhar (Pahars) [54], Charles (og) [86]	15,257
24	12	A	Sheffield W	W 1-0	1-0	14	Tessem [26]	23,470
25	26	A	Arsenal	L 1-3	0-2	16	Richards [61]	38,044
26	Mar 4	H	Middlesbrough	D 1-1	1-1	15	Pakhar (Pahars) [44]	15,223
27	8	A	West Ham U	L 0-2	0-1	—		23,484
28	11	A	Tottenham H	L 2-7	2-4	16	Tessem [26], El Khalej [33]	36,024
29	18	H	Aston Villa	W 2-0	1-0	15	Davies 2 [39, 63]	15,218
30	25	A	Chelsea	D 1-1	0-0	15	Tessem [69]	34,956
31	Apr 1	H	Sunderland	L 1-2	0-1	15	Le Tissier (pen) [90]	15,245
32	8	A	Bradford C	W 2-1	0-0	15	Windass (og) [56], Pakhar (Pahars) [76]	17,439
33	15	H	Watford	W 2-0	1-0	15	Davies [4], Pakhar (Pahars) [75]	15,242
34	22	H	Manchester U	L 1-3	0-3	15	Pakhar (Pahars) [83]	15,245
35	24	A	Derby Co	L 0-2	0-2	15		29,403
36	29	H	Leicester C	L 1-2	1-1	15	Kachloul [4]	15,178
37	May 7	A	Liverpool	D 0-0	0-0	15		44,015
38	14	H	Wimbledon	W 2-0	0-0	15	Bridge [57], Pakhar (Pahars) [79]	15,249

Final League Position: 15

GOALSCORERS

League (45): Pakhar (Pahars) 13, Davies 6, Kachloul 5, Tessem 4, Le Tissier 3 (1 pen), Oakley 3, Richards 2, Boa Morte 1, Bridge 1, El Khalej 1, Hughes M 1, Ostenstad 1, Ripley 1, Soltvedt 1, own goals 2.
Worthington Cup (6): Oakley 2, Richards 2, Dodd 1 (pen), Soltvedt 1.
FA Cup (1): Richards 1.

Jones P 31	Dodd J 30 + 1	Benali F 25 + 1	Marsden C 19 + 2	Lundekvam C 25 + 2	Richards D 35	Kachloul H 29 + 3	Le Tissier M 9 + 9	Ostenstad E 3	Hughes M 18 + 2	Pakhar (Pahars) M 31 + 2	Beresford J — + 3	Ripley S 18 + 5	Oakley M 26 + 5	Hiley S 3	Bridge W 15 + 4	Soltvedt T 17 + 7	Davies K 19 + 4	Bradley S — + 1	Boa Morte L 6 + 8	Beattie J 8 + 10	Almeida M — + 1	Colleter P 8	Tessem J 23 + 2	Moss N 7 + 2	Dryden R 1	Monk G 1 + 1	El Khalej T 11	Rodrigues D — + 2	Match No.
1	2	3	4	5	6	7^1	8^2	9	10	11	12	13																	1
1	2	3	4^1	5	6	7^2	8	9	10	11	13	12																	2
1		3		5	6	7^1	8^2	9	10	11		13	4^3	2	12	14													3
1		3		5	6	11^1	10	9^2	7	2	12	4	8	13															4
1	2	3		5	6	11^1	10	9	7	8	4	12																	5
1	2	3		5	6	11^3	10	9^2	7^1	12	13	4	8	14															6
1	2	3		5^2	6	7	12	10	8	11^1	4	9	13																7
1	2	3	12	5^1	6	11	13	10	9^3	7	8	4^2	14																8
1	5	3			6	11^4	8^1	10	9	7	4	2	13	12															9
1	2	3^2	4	5	6	11	12	10^3	9	7^1	8	14	13																10
1	2	3		5	6	11	7^1	10	9	12	8	4^2	13																11
1	2	3		5	6	11	10	9^1	7	8	4	12																	12
1	2			5	6	11	10	9	7^2	8	4^1	13	12		3														13
1				5	6	11^3	12		10^1	9	7	4	13	14	8^2	3	2												14
1	12			5	6	11	10^2	9^1	7	8	4	13			3	2													15
1			4	5	6	11	9^1	7	8	12	10				3	2													16
1^8		3	4	5	6	11	12	9	7^1	10	8	13			2^2	15													17
1	2	3		5	6	11^1	7	9	8^3	4	13	12	10^2	14															18
1	2	3		5	6	13	7^1	10^3	12^2	8	9	11	14	4															19
1	2		4	5	6	9	7			3		10	11		8														20
1	12				6	10	13	7			4	8	11^3	9	3^1	2							5^2	14					21
1		3	4	5	6	9	12		8^3		14	10^2	11^1		3^1	2													22
1	2	5	4		6	12	9^2	8		14	13	10	11^1		3^3	7													23
1	4	5	7	12	6	11	9	8		10					3^1	2													24
1	4	6	7	12	5	11		13	8			10	14	9^2	3^3	2^1													25
1	2	6	4	5		11^1	9	8	3	12	10	7																	26
1	2	6	4	5		11^1	9	8	3	12	10	7																	27
1		6	4	5		11^1	12	10	9	8	3	7											2						28
1	2	4			6	11	9^1	8	3	12	10	7											5						29
1	2	4			6	11	9	8	3		10	7											5						30
1^8	2	11	5	6		12	13	9	8^2	3	10	7^1											15				4		31
	2	3	4	6		9^1	12		7^2		11	13	10	8									1				5		32
	4	2	6		11	12	7	13	3	10		9^1		8^2	1												5		33
4	6^1	8	2	5	12	13	9	14	3		10^2	7			9^1								1				11^3		34
2	4^2	6			11^3	12	7	8	3	10	13		9^1			14							1				5		35
2	4^1	6			11	9	7^2	12	3	10	8												1				5	13	36
2		6			11	9	8	3	4	10	7												1				5		37
2	12	5			11^2	9	8	3	4^1	10	7												1				6	13	38

Worthington Cup
Second Round   Manchester C   (a)   0-0
                                      (h)   4-3
Third Round   Liverpool   (h)   2-1
Fourth Round   Aston Villa   (a)   0-4

FA Cup
Third Round   Ipswich T   (a)   1-0
Fourth Round   Aston Villa   (a)   0-1

Division 3   **SOUTHEND UNITED**

FOUNDATION

The leading club in Southend around the turn of the century was Southend Athletic, but they were an amateur concern. Southend United was a more ambitious professional club when they were founded in 1906, employing Bob Jack as secretary-manager and immediately joining the Second Division of the Southern League.

Roots Hall Football Ground, Victoria Avenue, Southend-on-Sea SS2 6NQ.
Telephone: (01702) 304 050.
Fax: (01702) 330 164.
Commercial: (01702) 304 050.
ClubCall: 09068 121 105.
Ticket Office: (01702) 304 090.
Ground Capacity: 12,306.
Record Attendance: 31,090 v Liverpool, FA Cup 3rd rd, 10 January 1979.
Record Receipts: £83,999 v West Ham U, Division 1, 7 April 1993.
Pitch Measurements: 110yd × 74yd.
President: N. J. Woodcock.
Chairman: J. J. W. R. Main.
Deputy-Chairman: G. King.
Secretary: Miss H. Giles.
Directors: J. A. Bridge, W. R. Kelleway, D. M. Markscheffel, R. J. Osborne, P. Robinson, D. A. J. Wilshire.
Manager: Alan Little.
Assistant Manager: Mick Gooding.
Physio: John Gowens.
Commercial Manager: David Comley.
Safety Officer: George Wright.
Club Nickname: 'The Blues' or 'The Shrimpers'.

LATEST SEQUENCES

Longest Sequence of League Wins: 7, 27.4.90 – 18.9.90.
Longest Sequence of League Defeats: 6, 29.8.87 – 19.9.87.
Longest Sequence of League Draws: 6, 30.1.82 – 19.2.82.
Longest Sequence of Unbeaten League Matches: 16, 20.2.32 – 29.8.32.
Longest Sequence Without a League Win: 17, 31.12.83 – 14.4.84.

HONOURS

Football League: Division 1 best season: 13th, 1994–95. Division 3 – Runners-up 1990–91; Division 4 – Champions 1980–81; Runners-up 1971–72, 1977–78.
FA Cup: best season: old 3rd rd, 1921; 5th rd, 1926, 1952, 1976, 1993.
Football League Cup: never past 3rd rd.

Colours
Royal blue/white.

Change Colours
All yellow.

Year Formed: 1906.

Turned Professional: 1906.

Ltd Co.: 1919.

Previous Grounds: 1906, Roots Hall, Prittlewell; 1920, Kursaal; 1934, Southend Stadium; 1955, Roots Hall Football Ground.

First Football League Game: 28 August 1920, Division 3, v Brighton & HA (a) W 2–0 – Capper; Reid, Newton; Wileman, Henderson, Martin; Nicholls, Nuttall, Fairclough (2), Myers, Dorsett.

Record League Victory: 9–2 v Newport Co, Division 3 (S), 5 September 1936 – McKenzie; Nelson, Everest (1); Deacon, Turner, Carr; Bolan, Lane (1), Goddard (4), Dickinson (2), Oswald (1).

Record Cup Victory: 10–1 v Golders Green, FA Cup 1st rd, 24 November 1934 – Moore; Morfitt, Kelly; Mackay, Joe Wilson, Carr (1); Lane (1), Johnson (5), Cheesmuir (2), Deacon (1), Oswald. 10–1 v Brentwood, FA Cup 2nd rd, 7 December 1968 – Roberts; Bentley, Birks; McMillan (1) Beesley, Kurila; Clayton, Chisnall, Moore (4), Best (5), Hamilton. 10–1 v Aldershot, Leyland Daf Cup Prel rd, 6 November 1990 – Sansome; Austin, Powell, Cornwell, Prior (1), Tilson (3), Cawley, Butler, Ansah (1), Benjamin (1), Angell (4).

Record Defeat: 1–9 v Brighton & HA, Division 3, 27 November 1965.

Most League Points (2 for a win): 67, Division 4, 1980–81.

Most League Points (3 for a win): 85, Division 3, 1990–91.

Most League Goals: 92, Division 3 (S), 1950–51.

Highest League Scorer in Season: Jim Shankly, 31, 1928–29; Sammy McCrory, 1957–58, both in Division 3 (S).

Most League Goals in Total Aggregate: Roy Hollis, 122, 1953–60.

Most League Goals in One Match: 5, Jim Shankly v Merthyr T, Division 3S, 1 March 1930.

Most Capped Player: George Mackenzie, 9, Eire.

Most League Appearances: Sandy Anderson, 452, 1950–63.

Youngest League Player: Phil O'Connor, 16 years 76 days v Lincoln C, 26 December 1969.

Record Transfer Fee Received: £3,570,000 from Nottingham F, for Stan Collymore, June 1993.

Record Transfer Fee Paid: £750,000 to Crystal Palace for Stan Collymore, November 1992.

Football League Record: 1920 Original Member of Division 3; 1921–58 Division 3 (S); 1958–66 Division 3; 1966–72 Division 4; 1972–76 Division 3; 1976–78 Division 4; 1978–80 Division 3; 1980–81 Division 4; 1981–84 Division 3; 1984–87 Division 4; 1987–89 Division 3; 1989–90 Division 4; 1990–91 Division 3; 1991–92 Division 2; 1992–97 Division 1; 1997–98 Division 2; 1998– Division 3.

MANAGERS

Bob Jack 1906–10
George Molyneux 1910–11
O. M. Howard 1911–12
Joe Bradshaw 1912–19
Ned Liddell 1919–20
Tom Mather 1920–21
Ted Birnie 1921–34
David Jack 1934–40
Harry Warren 1946–56
Eddie Perry 1956–60
Frank Broome 1960
Ted Fenton 1961–65
Alvan Williams 1965–67
Ernie Shepherd 1967–69
Geoff Hudson 1969–70
Arthur Rowley 1970–76
Dave Smith 1976–83
Peter Morris 1983–84
Bobby Moore 1984–86
Dave Webb 1986–87
Dick Bate 1987
Paul Clark 1987–88
Dave Webb *(General Manager)* 1988–92
Colin Murphy 1992–93
Barry Fry 1993
Peter Taylor 1993–95
Steve Thompson 1995
Ronnie Whelan 1995–97
Alvin Martin 1997–99
Alan Little March 1999–

TEN YEAR LEAGUE RECORD

		P	W	D	L	F	A	Pts	Pos
1989-90	Div 4	46	22	9	15	61	48	75	3
1990-91	Div 3	46	26	7	13	67	51	85	2
1991-92	Div 2	46	17	11	18	63	63	62	12
1992-93	Div 1	46	13	13	20	54	64	52	18
1993-94	Div 1	46	17	8	21	63	67	59	15
1994-95	Div 1	46	18	8	20	54	73	62	13
1995-96	Div 1	46	15	14	17	52	61	59	14
1996-97	Div 1	46	8	15	23	42	86	39	24
1997-98	Div 2	46	11	10	25	47	79	43	24
1998-99	Div 3	46	14	12	20	52	58	54	18

DID YOU KNOW ?

Lionel Louch, ex-Portsmouth and Clapton Orient, became Southend United's first international, winning his eighth cap and scoring four goals for England v Wales in the amateur international on 7 February 1914.

SOUTHEND UNITED 1999–2000 LEAGUE RECORD

Match No.	Date	Venue	Opponents	Result	H/T Score	Lg. Pos.	Goalscorers	Attendance
1	Aug 7	H	Plymouth Arg	W 2-1	0-1	7	Houghton [79], Tolson [81]	4981
2	14	A	Rochdale	L 0-2	0-2	14		2253
3	21	H	Mansfield T	W 1-0	1-0	8	Tolson [17]	3533
4	28	A	Swansea C	L 1-3	0-1	14	Roach [77]	4757
5	30	H	Leyton Orient	D 1-1	0-1	15	Roget [85]	5980
6	Sept 4	A	Hartlepool U	W 2-1	0-0	11	Coleman [63], Tolson (pen) [87]	1980
7	11	A	Macclesfield T	W 2-1	2-1	7	Tolson (pen) [2], Ingram (og) [29]	2059
8	18	H	Halifax T	W 4-1	3-0	4	Coleman 2 [12, 40], Tolson [28], Campbell [85]	4533
9	25	H	Peterborough U	L 0-1	0-1	6		6187
10	Oct 2	A	Carlisle U	D 1-1	0-1	7	Carruthers [62]	2800
11	9	A	Cheltenham T	L 1-2	0-1	9	Carruthers [72]	3118
12	16	H	Shrewsbury T	W 3-2	3-1	8	Tolson 2 [18, 34], Carruthers [30]	3963
13	19	H	Lincoln C	D 2-2	2-1	—	Carruthers 2 [22, 27]	3556
14	23	A	Peterborough U	L 0-1	0-0	11		5860
15	Nov 2	H	Brighton & HA	W 2-1	0-1	—	Carruthers [55], Jones [87]	4927
16	6	A	Exeter C	W 1-0	1-0	6	Coleman [44]	2353
17	12	H	Hull C	L 1-2	0-0	8	Beard [60]	4940
18	23	A	Chester C	D 0-0	0-0	—		1906
19	27	H	Darlington	L 1-2	0-2	11	Tolson (pen) [55]	4134
20	Dec 4	A	Plymouth Arg	L 1-3	0-2	13	Connelly [58]	4679
21	10	H	Barnet	L 1-3	1-1	—	Houghton [43]	3521
22	17	A	York C	D 2-2	1-0	—	Connelly [40], Carruthers [80]	2233
23	26	H	Northampton T	D 2-2	0-0	13	Carruthers [51], Tolson [81]	5449
24	28	A	Torquay U	W 1-0	0-0	13	Carruthers [75]	3138
25	Jan 3	H	Rotherham U	L 1-2	1-2	14	Pepper [36]	4788
26	8	A	Barnet	L 1-2	1-2	15	Heald (og) [15]	3057
27	15	H	Rochdale	D 3-3	0-3	16	Houghton [56], Carruthers (pen) [62], Roget [85]	3190
28	22	A	Mansfield T	L 1-3	1-2	17	Houghton [18]	2215
29	29	H	Swansea C	W 2-1	1-1	15	Carruthers 2 [33, 51]	3860
30	Feb 5	A	Leyton Orient	L 1-2	1-1	16	Tolson [26]	5972
31	12	H	Hartlepool U	W 2-1	1-1	15	Carruthers 2 [44, 46]	3337
32	19	A	Darlington	L 0-1	0-0	16		4391
33	26	A	Halifax T	D 0-0	0-0	17		2068
34	Mar 3	H	Macclesfield T	W 1-0	1-0	—	Carruthers [6]	3725
35	7	H	Exeter C	L 1-2	0-0	—	Carruthers (pen) [61]	3122
36	11	A	Brighton & HA	L 0-1	0-0	17		5844
37	18	H	Chester C	W 3-1	2-1	16	Jones S [17], Coleman [22], Carruthers (pen) [76]	3483
38	21	A	Hull C	D 0-0	0-0	—		4150
39	25	A	Northampton T	L 0-2	0-1	16		5426
40	Apr 1	H	York C	D 0-0	0-0	17		3364
41	8	A	Rotherham U	D 0-0	0-0	18		4327
42	22	A	Shrewsbury T	L 1-2	1-0	18	Carruthers [16]	3540
43	24	H	Carlisle U	W 2-0	0-0	18	Carruthers [79], Pepper [84]	3053
44	29	A	Lincoln C	L 0-1	0-1	18		2556
45	May 2	H	Torquay U	L 0-2	0-0	—		2563
46	6	H	Cheltenham T	W 2-1	1-1	16	Jones S [43], Jones N [90]	4977

Final League Position: 16

GOALSCORERS

League (53): Carruthers 19 (3 pens), Tolson 10 (3 pens), Coleman 5, Houghton 4, Connelly 2, Jones N 2, Jones S 2, Pepper 2, Roget 2, Beard 1, Campbell 1, Roach 1, own goals 2.
Worthington Cup (0).
FA Cup (0).

Capleton M 40+2	Booty M 28	Jones N 43	Morley D 29+3	Roget L 28+8	Coleman S 43	Beard M 38+3	Connelly G 29+4	Abiodun Y 1+2	Tolson N 29+2	Houghton S 42+1	Maher K 18+6	Fitzpatrick T 1+15	Tinkler M 41	Clarke A —+4	Cross G 7+1	Roach N 6+2	Gooding M —+2	Carruthers M 38	Campbell N 6+6	Kerrigan D —+4	Prudhoe M 6	Pepper N 9+3	Newman R 14+5	Hails J —+1	McDonald T 1+2	Jones S 9	Match No
1	2	3	4	5	6	7	8		9^1	10^2	11	12	13														1
1	2	3^1	4	5	6		8		10	11		7^2	12					9	13								2
1	2		4	5	6		8^2	12	10	11		7	13	3				9^1									3
1	2	3^1		5	6	7			10	11	12		8	4				9									4
1	2	3^3		5	6	7		12	10^1	11		13	8	14	4			9^2									5
1	2	3		5	6	4	8		10	11		12	7					9^1									6
1	2	3		5	6	4	7		10^1	11^2	12		8					9	13								7
1	2	3		5	6	4	7		10^2	11	12		8					9^1	13								8
1	2	3	12	5	6	4^1	7		10^2	11			8					9	13								9
1	2	3^1		5	6	4	7		10	11			8					9	12								10
1	2	3^2	12	5	6	4^1	7		10^2	11			8					9	13	14							11
1	2	3		5	6	4	7		10	11			8					9									12
1	2	3		5	6	4	7		10	11			8					9									13
1	2	3		5	6	4	7		10	11			8					9									14
1	2	3	4		6	5	7		10	11^1			8				12	9									15
1	2	3		5	6	4	7		10	11			8					9									16
1	2	3		5	6	4	7		10	11^1	12		8					9									17
	2	3	12	5	6	4	7		10	11		13	8^1					9^2			1						18
15	2	3		5	6	4	7^2		10	11			8				12	9^1	13	1^G							19
1	2^2		4	5	6	3	7		10^1	11			8				12	9	13								20
1	2	3	4	5	6		7		10	11	12		8^1					9									21
1	2	3	4		5	6	7		10	11	8							9									22
	2	3	4^1		5	12	7^2		10	11			8					9	13		1	6^2	14				23
	2	3			5	4			10	11	12		8^1					9			1	7	6				24
	2	3		5^2	6	4			10	11			8^2	12				9	13		1	7^1	14				25
15	2	3^2	4	12		6	7		10	11			8					9	13		1^G		5^1				26
1	2	3^1	4	12		6	7		11	13	14		8^2					10^3	9				5				27
1	2^2	3^3	4	5	6	10	7^1		12	11	8							9					13	14			28
1		3	4	12	6	2			10^1	11	7		8					9					5				29
1		3	4		6	2	12		10	11	7		8					9					5^1				30
1		3	4		6	2	13		10^1	11	7	12^2	8					9					5				31
1		3	4		6	2	12			11^1	7		8					9	10				5				32
1		3	4^1		6	2				11	7		8					9	10				5	12			33
1		3	4	12	6	2				11	7	13	8					9	10^2				5^1				34
1		3	4	12	6	2	11^1				7^3	13	8					9	10^2				14 5				35
1		3	4		6	2				11	7		8					9	10^1				12 5				36
1		3	4	12	6^1	2	13			11	7^2		8^3					9					14 5			10	37
1		3	4		6	2	7			11			8					9					11 5			10	38
1			4	12	6^1	13	7		11	3^2	14		8		2			9					5^3			10	39
1		3	4	5		2	7		11^1	12			8					9					6			10	40
1		3	4	5	6	2	7			12			8^1					9					11			10	41
1		3	4	5	6	2				12	7	10	8^1					9					11				42
1		3	4	5	6					11	7				2^1			9					8		12	10	43
1		3	4	5	6^3	12				11^1	7	13			2			9					8 14			10^2	44
1		3	4	12	6^1					11	7		8		2			9					5			10	45
1		3	4	5	6^3	2				12	11^1	7		8	13			9					14			10^2	46

Worthington Cup
First Round   Oxford U   (h)   0-2
                                        (a)   0-1

FA Cup
First Round   Torquay U   (a)   0-1

Division 1   **STOCKPORT COUNTY**

FOUNDATION

Formed at a meeting held at Wellington Road South by members of Wycliffe Congregational Chapel in 1883, they called themselves Heaton Norris Rovers until changing to Stockport County in 1890, a year before joining the Football Combination.

Edgeley Park, Hardcastle Road, Stockport, Cheshire SK3 9DD.
Telephone: (0161) 286 8888.
Fax: (0161) 286 8900.
Club Shop: (0161) 286 8899.
ClubCall: 09068 121 638.
Website: www.stockportcounty.com
Ground Capacity: 11,541.
Record Attendance: 27,833 v Liverpool, FA Cup 5th rd, 11 February 1950.
Record Receipts: £181,449 v Middlesbrough, Coca-Cola Cup Semi-final 1st leg, 26 February 1997.
Pitch Measurements: 111yd × 72yd.
Hon. Vice-Presidents: Freddie Pye, Andrew Barlow.
Chairman: Brendan Elwood.
Vice-Chairman: Grahame White.
Directors: Mike Baker, Michael Rains, Brian Taylor, David Jolley.
Secretary: Gary Glendenning BA (HONS), FCCA.
Manager: Andy Kilner.
Assistant Manager: David Moss.
Physio: Rodger Wylde.
Assistant Secretary: Andrea Dawson.
Commercial Manager: John Rutter.
Marketing Manager/Programme Editor: Steve Bellis.
Year Formed: 1883.
Turned Professional: 1891.
Ltd Co.: 1908.
Previous Names: 1883, Heaton Norris Rovers; 1888, Heaton Norris; 1890, Stockport County.
Club Nicknames: 'County' or 'Hatters'.

LATEST SEQUENCES

Longest Sequence of League Wins: 8, 26.12.27 – 28.1.28.
Longest Sequence of League Defeats: 9, 19.12.08 – 13.2.09.
Longest Sequence of League Draws: 7, 17.3.89 – 14.4.89.
Longest Sequence of Unbeaten League Matches: 18, 28.1.33 – 28.8.33.
Longest Sequence Without a League Win: 19, 28.12.99 – 22.4.00.

HONOURS

Football League: Division 1 best season: 8th, 1997–98; Division 2 – Runners-up 1996–97; Division 3 (N) – Champions 1921–22, 1936–37; Runners-up 1928–29, 1929-30; Division 4 – Champions 1966–67; Runners-up 1990–91.

FA Cup: best season: 5th rd, 1935, 1950.

Football League Cup: Semi-final 1997.

Autoglass Trophy: Runners-up 1992, 1993.

Colours
Blue shirts with vertical white chest band, blue shorts, white stockings.

Change Colours
Yellow shirts, yellow shorts, yellow stockings.

Previous Grounds: 1883 Heaton Norris Recreation Ground; 1884 Heaton Norris Wanderers Cricket Ground; 1885 Chorlton's Farm, Chorlton's Lane; 1886 Heaton Norris Cricket Ground; 1887 Wilkes' Field, Belmont Street; 1889 Nursery Inn, Green Lane; 1902 Edgeley Park.

First Football League Game: 1 September 1900, Division 2, v Leicester Fosse (a) D 2–2 – Moores; Earp, Wainwright; Pickford, Limond, Harvey; Stansfield, Smith (1), Patterson, Foster, Betteley (1).

Record League Victory: 13–0 v Halifax T, Division 3 (N), 6 January 1934 – McGann; Vincent (1p), Jenkinson; Robinson, Stevens, Len Jones; Foulkes (1), Hill (3), Lythgoe (2), Stevenson (2), Downes (4).

Record Cup Victory: 5–0 v Lincoln C, FA Cup 1st rd, 11 November 1995 – Edwards; Connelly, Todd, Bennett, Flynn, Gannon (Dinning), Beaumont, Oliver, Ware, Eckhardt (3), Armstrong (1) (Mike), Chalk, (1 og).

Record Defeat: 1–8 v Chesterfield, Division 2, 19 April 1902.

Most League Points (2 for a win): 64, Division 4, 1966–67.

Most League Points (3 for a win): 85, Division 2, 1993–94.

Most League Goals: 115, Division 3 (N), 1933–34.

Highest League Scorer in Season: Alf Lythgoe, 46, Division 3 (N), 1933–34.

Most League Goals in Total Aggregate: Jack Connor, 132, 1951–56.

Most League Goals in One Match: 5, Joe Smith v Southport, Division 3N, 7 January 1928; 5, Joe Smith v Lincoln C, Division 3N, 15 September 1928; 5, Frank Newton v Nelson, Division 3N, 21 September 1929; 5, Alf Lythgoe v Southport, Division 3N, 25 August 1934; 5, Billy McNaughton v Mansfield T, Division 3N, 14 December 1935; 5, Jack Connor v Workington, Division 3N, 8 November 1952; 5, Jack Connor v Carlisle U, Division 3N, 7 April 1956.

Most Capped Player: Martin Nash, 8, Canada.

Most League Appearances: Andy Thorpe, 489, 1978–86, 1988–92.

Youngest League Player: Jimmy Collier, 16 years 227 days v Bristol R, 8 April 1969.

Record Transfer Fee Received: £1,600,000 from Middlesbrough for Alun Armstrong, February 1998.

Record Transfer Fee Paid: £800,000 to Nottingham F for Ian Moore, July 1998.

Football League Record: 1900 Elected to Division 2; 1904 Failed re-election; 1905–21 Division 2; 1921–22 Division 3 (N); 1922–26 Division 2; 1926–37 Division 3 (N); 1937–38 Division 2; 1938–58 Division 3 (N); 1958–59 Division 3; 1959–67 Division 4; 1967–70 Division 3; 1970–91 Division 4; 1991–92 Division 3; 1992–97 Division 2; 1997– Division 1.

MANAGERS

Fred Stewart 1894–1911
Harry Lewis 1911–14
David Ashworth 1914–19
Albert Williams 1919–24
Fred Scotchbrook 1924–26
Lincoln Hyde 1926–31
Andrew Wilson 1932–33
Fred Westgarth 1934–36
Bob Kelly 1936–38
George Hunt 1938–39
Bob Marshall 1939–49
Andy Beattie 1949–52
Dick Duckworth 1952–56
Billy Moir 1956–60
Reg Flewin 1960–63
Trevor Porteous 1963–65
Bert Trautmann
   (General Manager) 1965–66
Eddie Quigley *(Team Manager)* 1965–66
Jimmy Meadows 1966–69
Wally Galbraith 1969–70
Matt Woods 1970–71
Brian Doyle 1972–74
Jimmy Meadows 1974–75
Roy Chapman 1975–76
Eddie Quigley 1976–77
Alan Thompson 1977–78
Mike Summerbee 1978–79
Jimmy McGuigan 1979–82
Eric Webster 1982–85
Colin Murphy 1985
Les Chapman 1985–86
Jimmy Melia 1986
Colin Murphy 1986–87
Asa Hartford 1987–89
Danny Bergara 1989–95
Dave Jones 1995–97
Gary Megson 1997–99
Andy Kilner July 1999–

TEN YEAR LEAGUE RECORD

		P	W	D	L	F	A	Pts	Pos
1989-90	Div 4	46	21	11	14	68	62	74	4
1990-91	Div 4	46	23	13	10	84	47	82	2
1991-92	Div 3	46	22	10	14	75	51	76	5
1992-93	Div 2	46	19	15	12	81	57	72	6
1993-94	Div 2	46	24	13	9	74	44	85	4
1994-95	Div 2	46	19	8	19	63	60	65	11
1995-96	Div 2	46	19	13	14	61	47	70	9
1996-97	Div 2	46	23	13	10	59	41	82	2
1997-98	Div 1	46	19	8	19	71	69	65	8
1998-99	Div 1	46	12	17	17	49	60	53	16

DID YOU KNOW ?

On 7 December 1999, Stockport County won 2-1 at Manchester City. Alan Bailey signed on a free transfer from City in the summer, equalised and was then brought down for the resulting penalty winner.

STOCKPORT COUNTY 1999–2000 LEAGUE RECORD

Match No.	Date	Venue	Opponents	Result	H/T Score	Lg. Pos.	Goalscorers	Attendance
1	Aug 7	A	Grimsby T	W 1-0	0-0	5	Smith [51]	5528
2	14	H	Tranmere R	W 2-1	0-1	2	Connelly [79], Dinning (pen) [85]	6555
3	21	A	Portsmouth	L 0-2	0-0	5		15,002
4	27	H	Birmingham C	W 2-0	0-0	—	Wilbraham [76], D'Jaffo [84]	6115
5	Sept 10	A	Barnsley	L 1-2	0-2	—	D'Jaffo [67]	13,173
6	18	H	Port Vale	W 1-0	1-0	8	Nicholson [15]	7632
7	25	H	Norwich C	D 2-2	1-1	8	D'Jaffo [26], Dinning [87]	7603
8	28	A	Charlton Ath	L 0-4	0-0	—		19,842
9	Oct 2	A	Walsall	W 2-1	1-0	8	Dinning 2 (1 pen) [32 (p), 46]	5492
10	9	A	Swindon T	D 1-1	1-1	7	Dinning [7]	5318
11	16	H	Crewe Alex	W 2-1	1-1	5	Connelly [45], D'Jaffo [59]	7571
12	19	H	Huddersfield T	D 1-1	1-0	—	Byrne C [21]	7305
13	23	A	Nottingham F	D 1-1	1-1	7	D'Jaffo [15]	15,770
14	26	A	Norwich C	L 0-2	0-1	—		16,880
15	30	H	Walsall	D 1-1	0-0	9	Byrne C [88]	6592
16	Nov 2	H	QPR	D 3-3	2-0	—	D'Jaffo [5], Moore [45], Briggs [56]	4868
17	6	H	Fulham	W 2-1	2-0	7	Moore [4], Cooper [22]	7200
18	20	H	Sheffield U	D 1-1	0-1	9	D'Jaffo [61]	6614
19	23	A	WBA	L 0-2	0-0	—		9201
20	27	A	Blackburn R	L 0-2	0-1	10		17,592
21	Dec 4	H	Grimsby T	W 2-1	1-0	10	Dinning (pen) [34], Cooper [58]	5581
22	7	A	Manchester C	W 2-1	0-0	—	Bailey [66], Dinning (pen) [86]	32,686
23	18	A	Bolton W	W 1-0	0-0	6	Dinning [60]	13,285
24	26	H	Wolverhampton W	W 3-2	1-2	6	Dinning [31], Moore 2 [51, 90]	10,278
25	28	A	Ipswich T	L 0-1	0-1	6		20,671
26	Jan 3	H	Crystal Palace	L 1-2	0-0	6	Moore [53]	8570
27	15	A	Tranmere R	D 0-0	0-0	6		7565
28	22	H	Portsmouth	D 1-1	1-1	7	Dinning (pen) [14]	8008
29	29	A	Birmingham C	L 1-2	0-0	7	Johnson M (og) [84]	17,150
30	Feb 5	H	Charlton Ath	L 1-3	1-2	9	Fradin [25]	8185
31	12	A	QPR	D 1-1	1-0	9	Matthews [18]	10,531
32	19	H	Blackburn R	L 0-1	0-0	11		7902
33	26	A	Port Vale	D 1-1	1-1	11	Wilbraham [9]	5663
34	Mar 3	H	Barnsley	L 1-3	1-2	—	Lawson [17]	6386
35	7	A	Fulham	L 1-4	0-1	—	Dinning (pen) [63]	8688
36	11	H	WBA	L 0-1	0-1	16		8238
37	14	H	Bolton W	D 0-0	0-0	—		6412
38	18	A	Sheffield U	L 0-1	0-0	16		14,907
39	21	H	Manchester C	D 2-2	2-1	—	Moore [28], Flynn [43]	11,212
40	25	A	Wolverhampton W	D 2-2	1-1	15	Lawson [16], Dinning [62]	25,065
41	Apr 8	A	Crystal Palace	D 3-3	1-3	16	Moore 2 [43, 63], Cooper [55]	16,646
42	15	H	Ipswich T	L 0-1	0-1	19		8501
43	22	A	Crewe Alex	L 2-3	1-2	19	Lawson [39], Moore [70]	5813
44	24	H	Swindon T	W 3-0	1-0	16	Moore [18], Lawson [51], Connelly [58]	5362
45	29	A	Huddersfield T	W 2-0	2-0	14	Cooper [12], Armstrong C (og) [12]	14,046
46	May 7	H	Nottingham F	L 2-3	1-2	17	Wilbraham 2 [4, 70]	7756

Final League Position: 17

GOALSCORERS

League (55): Dinning 12 (6 pens), Moore 10, D'Jaffo 7, Cooper 4, Lawson 4, Wilbraham 4, Connelly 3, Byrne C 2, Bailey 1, Briggs 1, Flynn 1, Fradin 1, Matthews 1, Nicholson 1, Smith 1, own goals 2.
Worthington Cup (7): Angell 1, Briggs 1, Cooper 1, Dinning 1 (pen), D'Jaffo 1, Wilbraham 1, Woodthorpe 1.
FA Cup (2): Bailey 1, Moore 1.

Nash C 38	Connelly S 42+1	Nicholson S 42	Dinning T 43+1	Flynn M 46	McIntosh M 17+3	Cooper K 44+2	Moore I 34+4	Angell B 5	Smith D 7+2	Wilbraham A 13+13	Woodthorpe C 12+14	Gannon J 20+9	Ellis T 1+3	D'Jaffo L 20+1	Byrne C 11+7	Monk G 2	Gibbens K 1+1	Briggs K 4+3	Bergersen K 10+7	Daly J —+4	Bailey A 5+9	Gray J 8+2	Allen C 10+6	Fradin K 19+2	Bennett T 8+1	Matthews R 3+1	Lawson I 13+2	Gibb A 13+1	Elliott S 4+1	Francis K 4	Taylor M 7	Ross N —+2	Match No
1	2	3	4	5	6	7^1	8^2	9	10	11^3	12	13	14																				1
1	2	3	4	5	6	7	8^3	9	10^2	11^1	12			14	13																		2
1	2^1	3	4	5	6	7	8	9	10^2		12			11	13																		3
1	2	3	4^2	5	6	7^3	8	9^1	10	12	14	13		11																			4
1	2	3	4	5		7	8		10^2	11	12			9				6^1	13														5
1	5	3	12	4		7^3	8			13	11			9			6^2	10^1	2	14													6
1	2	3	4	5	6	12	8			11^2		10	13	9				7^1															7
1	2	3	4	5	6	12	8^1			13	11^3	7	10^2	9				14															8
1	2	3	4	5	6	7	8			12	9^3	13		10^1				11^2	14														9
1	2	3	4	5	6	7	8^2			12				9	10			11^1				13											10
1	2	3	4	5	6	7	8			12				9^2	10			11^1				13											11
1	2	3	4	5	6	7	8^2			12				9	10			11^1				13											12
1	2	3	4	5	6	7	8			12				9	10			11^1															13
1	2	3^1	4	5	6	7	8			13	11^2	12		9	10																		14
1^6	2	3^2	4	5	6^1	7	8			11	12			9	10				15	13													15
	2		4	5	6	7	8			11	12			9	10	3^1			1														16
1	2		4	5	6	7	8^1			12	3	13		9	10^2				11														17
1	2	3		5	6	7	8	4^2		12	13			9^2	10				11^1														18
1	2	3	4	5	6	7	8^2	9		12				10^1				11^3	13	14													19
1	2^2	3	4	5		7	8			12	13	6		14					10^1	11^3	9												20
1		3	4	5		7	8				6					2		12	10^1		11	9^2	13										21
1		2	4	5	12	7	8				3	10						13		9^1	11	6^2											22
1	2	3	4	5		7	8			10	6							12	13	9^2	11^1												23
	2	3	4	5		7	12			13	10	6		9^2				11		8^1	1												24
	2	3	4	5		7^1	8			12	11^3	6		9^2				13		1	14	10											25
1	2^1	3	4	5		7	8			10^2	6			9					11^1	10	12	13											26
1^6	2	3	4	5	12	7	8			6				9^1					15	11	10												27
	2	3	4	5		7	8^2			12	6			9^1		2				13	1	11	10										28
	2	3	4	5	12	7	8^1	9			6								13	1	11^2	10											29
	2	3	4^1	5		7		9		6	12								1	13	10	8	11^2										30
	2	3	4^2	5		7		13	9^3	12	6							8^1	1	14	10												31
	2	3	4	5		7		12		6	1							10^1	8	11^2	9	13											32
1	2	6	5			7	12	10	3											4	13		9^1	11^2	8								33
1	2	3	4	5		7^1	12	9^3		6				13						14	10		8	11^2									34
1	12		4	5		7	13	9^2	3					14							10	6	8	11^3	2^1								35
1	2	3	4	5		7	8				6							11^1		10	12							9					36
1	2	3	4	5		7				12	6									10					8	11^1		9					37
1	2	3	4	5		7				12	13	6								10					8^1	11^2		9					38
1	2	3	4	5		7	8^2				6^1			12				13		10					14	11		9^2					39
1	2^2	3	4	5		7				12										10					9^1	11	13		6				40
1	2	3		5		7	8			12	13									10					9^1	11	4^2		6				41
1	2	3^1	4	5		7	8													10					9	11			6	12			42
1	2	3^1	4	5		7	8							12						10					9	11			6				43
1	2	3	4	5		7^3	8							12				13	14	10^1					9	11^2			6				44
1	2	3	4	5		7^1								12				13		10					9^3	11^2	8		6	14			45
1	2	3^1	4	5		7				8										10					9	11			6				46

Worthington Cup

First Round	Oldham Ath	(h)	2-0	
		(a)	1-1	
Second Round	Barnsley	(a)	1-1	
		(h)	3-3	

FA Cup

Third Round	Grimsby T	(a)	2-3

Divison 2

STOKE CITY

FOUNDATION

The date of the formation of this club has long been in doubt. The year 1863 was claimed, but more recent research by Wade Martin has uncovered nothing earlier than 1868, when a couple of Old Carthusians, who were apprentices at the local works of the old North Staffordshire Railway Company, met with some others from that works, to form Stoke Ramblers. It should also be noted that the old Stoke club went bankrupt in 1908 when a new club was formed.

Britannia Stadium, Stoke-on-Trent ST4 4EG.
Telephone: (01782) 592 222.
Fax: (01782) 592 221.
Commercial Dept: (01782) 592 211.
Football in the Community: (01782) 592 255.
ClubCall: 09068 121 040.
Ground Capacity: 24,054.
Record Attendance: 51,380 v Arsenal, Division 1, 29 March 1937.
Record Receipts: £160,000 v Newcastle U, Coca-Cola Cup 3rd rd, 25 October 1995.
Pitch Measurements: 116yd × 72yd.
Vice-President: Elfar Adalsteinsson.
Chairman: Gunnar Thor Gislason.
Directors: Asgeir Sigurvinsson, Peter Coates, Keith Humphreys.
Manager: Gudjon Thordarson
Physio: Stefan Steffanson.
Stadium Manager/Safety Officer: J. Alcock.
Chief Executive: J. Moxey.

LATEST SEQUENCES

Longest Sequence of League Wins: 8, 30.3.1895 – 21.9.1895.
Longest Sequence of League Defeats: 11, 6.4.85 – 17.8.85.
Longest Sequence of League Draws: 5, 21.3.87 – 11.4.87.
Longest Sequence of Unbeaten League Matches: 25, 5.9.92 – 20.2.93.
Longest Sequence Without a League Win: 17, 22.4.89 – 14.10.89.

HONOURS

Football League: Division 1 best season: 4th, 1935–36, 1946–47; Division 2 – Champions 1932–33, 1962–63, 1992–93; Runners-up 1921–22; Promoted 1978–79 (3rd); Division 3 (N) – Champions 1926–27.
FA Cup: Semi-finals 1899, 1971, 1972.
Football League Cup: Winners 1972.
Autoglass Trophy: Winners: 1992.
Auto Windscreens Shield: Winners: 2000.
European Competitions: UEFA Cup: 1972–73, 1974–75.

Colours
Red and white striped shirts, white shorts, red and white hooped stockings.

Change Colours
Navy blue shirts and shorts with red and white stripe on left hand side, navy blue stockings with red and white hoop at top.

Year Formed: 1863 *(see Foundation)*.

Turned Professional: 1885.

Ltd Co.: 1908.

Previous Names: 1868, Stoke Ramblers; 1870, Stoke; 1925, Stoke City.

Club Nickname: 'The Potters'.

Previous Grounds: 1875, Sweeting's Field; 1878, Victoria Ground (previously known as the Athletic Club Ground); 1997, Britannia Stadium.

First Football League Game: 8 September 1888, Football League, v WBA (h) L 0–2 – Rowley; Clare, Underwood; Ramsey, Shutt, Smith; Sayer, McSkimming, Staton, Edge, Tunnicliffe.

Record League Victory: 10–3 v WBA, Division 1, 4 February 1937 – Doug Westland; Brigham, Harbot; Tutin, Turner (1p), Kirton; Matthews, Antonio (2), Freddie Steele (5), Jimmy Westland, Johnson (2).

Record Cup Victory: 7–1 v Burnley, FA Cup 2nd rd (replay), 20 February 1896 – Clawley; Clare, Eccles; Turner, Grewe, Robertson; Willie Maxwell, Dickson, A. Maxwell (3), Hyslop (4), Schofield.

Record Defeat: 0–10 v Preston NE, Division 1, 14 September 1889.

Most League Points (2 for a win): 63, Division 3 (N), 1926–27.

Most League Points (3 for a win): 93, Division 2, 1992–93.

Most League Goals: 92, Division 3 (N), 1926–27.

Highest League Scorer in Season: Freddie Steele, 33, Division 1, 1936–37.

Most League Goals in Total Aggregate: Freddie Steele, 142, 1934–49.

Most League Goals in One Match: 7, Neville Coleman v Lincoln C, Division 2, 23 February 1957.

Most Capped Player: Gordon Banks, 36 (73), England.

Most League Appearances: Eric Skeels, 506, 1958–76.

Youngest League Player: Peter Bullock, 16 years 163 days v Swansea C, 19 April 1958.

Record Transfer Fee Received: £2,750,000 from QPR for Mike Sheron, July 1997.

Record Transfer Fee Paid: £600,000 to Orgryte for Brnynjar Gunnarsson, December 1999.

Football League Record: 1888 Founder Member of Football League; 1890 Not re-elected; 1891 Re-elected; relegated in 1907, and after one year in Division 2, resigned for financial reasons; 1919 re-elected to Division 2; 1922–23 Division 1; 1923–26 Division 3 (N); 1926–27 Division 3 (N); 1927–33 Division 2; 1933–53 Division 1; 1953–63 Division 2; 1963–77 Division 1; 1977–79 Division 2; 1979–85 Division 1; 1985–90 Division 2; 1990–92 Division 3; 1992–93 Division 2; 1993–98 Division 1; 1998– Division 2.

MANAGERS

Tom Slaney 1874–83
(Secretary-Manager)
Walter Cox 1883–84
(Secretary-Manager)
Harry Lockett 1884–90
Joseph Bradshaw 1890–92
Arthur Reeves 1892–95
William Rowley 1895–97
H. D. Austerberry 1897–1908
A. J. Barker 1908–14
Peter Hodge 1914–15
Joe Schofield 1915–19
Arthur Shallcross 1919–23
John 'Jock' Rutherford 1923
Tom Mather 1923–35
Bob McGrory 1935–52
Frank Taylor 1952–60
Tony Waddington 1960–77
George Eastham 1977–78
Alan A'Court 1978
Alan Durban 1978–81
Richie Barker 1981–83
Bill Asprey 1984–85
Mick Mills 1985–89
Alan Ball 1989–91
Lou Macari 1991–93
Joe Jordan 1993–94
Lou Macari 1994–97
Chic Bates 1997–98
Chris Kamara 1998
Brian Little 1998–99
Gary Megson 1999
Gudjon Thordarson
November 1999–

TEN YEAR LEAGUE RECORD

		P	W	D	L	F	A	Pts	Pos
1989-90	Div 2	46	6	19	21	35	63	37	24
1990-91	Div 3	46	16	12	18	55	59	60	14
1991-92	Div 3	46	21	14	11	69	49	77	4
1992-93	Div 2	46	27	12	7	73	34	93	1
1993-94	Div 1	46	18	13	15	57	59	67	10
1994-95	Div 1	46	16	15	15	50	53	63	11
1995-96	Div 1	46	20	13	13	60	49	73	4
1996-97	Div 1	46	18	10	18	51	57	64	12
1997-98	Div 1	46	11	13	22	44	74	46	23
1998-99	Div 2	46	21	6	19	59	63	69	8

DID YOU KNOW ?

Centre-forward Harry Connor was the last amateur to play as a Stoke City senior. He scored ten minutes into his League debut against Sunderland on 28 March 1953. Stoke won 3-0.

STOKE CITY 1999–2000 LEAGUE RECORD

Match No.	Date	Venue	Opponents	Result	H/T Score	Lg. Pos.	Goalscorers	Attendance
1	Aug 7	H	Oxford U	L 1-2	0-1	20	Kavanagh G 59	11,300
2	14	A	Preston NE	L 1-2	1-0	20	Thorne 9	11,465
3	22	H	Millwall	W 3-1	1-0	16	Thorne 15, Connor 51, Kavanagh G (pen) 84	7054
4	28	A	Burnley	L 0-1	0-0	19		11,328
5	30	H	Gillingham	D 1-1	0-0	19	Sigurdsson 87	8369
6	Sept 4	A	Cambridge U	W 3-1	1-0	14	Connor 19, Oldfield 81, Thorne 86	4007
7	11	A	Chesterfield	W 2-0	0-0	7	Lightbourne 2 50, 90	4285
8	18	H	Wigan Ath	D 1-1	0-1	12	Lightbourne 48	11,195
9	25	A	Wrexham	W 3-2	1-1	6	Thorne 27, Lightbourne 50, Mohan 78	5924
10	Oct 2	H	Scunthorpe U	W 1-0	0-0	6	Connor 90	13,068
11	9	H	Reading	W 2-1	0-0	3	Mohan 68, Jacobsen 89	9621
12	16	A	Bournemouth	D 1-1	0-1	4	Clarke 62	5990
13	19	A	Cardiff C	W 2-1	1-1	—	Thorne 23, O'Connor 84	6146
14	23	H	Wrexham	W 2-0	0-0	2	O'Connor 48, Kavanagh G 58	10,545
15	Nov 3	H	Notts Co	L 0-1	0-1	—		11,619
16	6	A	Bury	D 0-0	0-0	6		4280
17	14	H	Bristol C	D 1-1	0-0	7	Mohan 66	10,775
18	23	A	Wycombe W	W 4-0	2-0	—	Kavanagh G 44, Danielsson 45, Thorne 62, Mohan 71	4345
19	27	A	Colchester U	D 1-1	0-0	7	Lightbourne 82	14,183
20	Dec 4	A	Oxford U	D 1-1	0-1	8	Thorne 79	5700
21	18	H	Bristol R	L 1-2	0-0	8	Keen 52	10,379
22	26	A	Blackpool	W 2-1	2-0	8	Robinson 22, Kavanagh G 27	5274
23	28	A	Oldham Ath	D 0-0	0-0	8		13,709
24	Jan 3	A	Brentford	W 1-0	0-0	8	Thorne 60	6792
25	8	H	Luton T	W 2-1	1-0	5	Connor 24, Lightbourne 87	10,016
26	14	H	Preston NE	W 2-1	1-0	—	Kippe 4, O'Connor 87	10,285
27	22	A	Millwall	L 0-1	0-1	6		11,548
28	29	H	Burnley	D 2-2	0-0	6	Thorne 68, Davis (og) 71	15,354
29	Feb 5	A	Gillingham	L 0-3	0-2	6		7801
30	8	A	Luton T	L 1-2	1-0	—	O'Connor 32	5396
31	12	H	Cambridge U	W 1-0	1-0	6	Connor 29	9662
32	19	A	Colchester U	L 0-1	0-0	6		4364
33	26	A	Wigan Ath	W 2-1	1-1	6	Kavanagh G 28, O'Connor 76	9429
34	Mar 4	H	Chesterfield	W 5-1	3-0	6	Thorne 4 8, 18, 31, 61, Jacobsen 90	11,968
35	11	A	Notts Co	D 0-0	0-0	7		9677
36	18	H	Wycombe W	D 1-1	0-1	8	Gunnlaugsson (pen) 54	9738
37	25	H	Blackpool	W 3-0	0-0	8	Gunnarsson 62, Mohan 69, Gudjonsson 71	10,002
38	28	A	Bristol C	D 2-2	2-1	—	Lightbourne 26, Kavanagh G 40	8103
39	Apr 1	A	Bristol R	D 3-3	1-2	7	Thorne 3 10, 62, 79	9312
40	4	A	Oldham Ath	W 1-0	1-0	—	Thorne 23	4474
41	8	H	Brentford	W 1-0	1-0	6	Thorne 8	9955
42	22	H	Bournemouth	W 1-0	0-0	7	Thorne 81	15,022
43	24	A	Scunthorpe U	W 2-0	2-0	7	Thorne 2 24, 39	5435
44	30	H	Cardiff C	W 2-1	1-0	7	Gunnlaugsson 4, O'Connor 69	14,192
45	May 3	H	Bury	W 3-0	1-0	—	Thorne 3 11, 55, 81	14,792
46	6	A	Reading	L 0-1	0-0	6		13,146

Final League Position: 6

GOALSCORERS

League (68): Thorne 24, Kavanagh G 7 (1 pen), Lightbourne 7, O'Connor 6, Connor 5, Mohan 5, Gunnlaugsson 2 (1 pen), Jacobsen 2, Clarke 1, Danielsson 1, Gudjonsson 1, Gunnarsson 1, Keen 1, Kippe 1, Oldfield 1, Robinson 1, Sigurdsson 1, own goal 1.

Worthington Cup (5): Connor 1, Kavanagh G 1, Keen 1, O'Connor 1, Thorne 1.

FA Cup (0).

Ward G 46	Robinson P 14 + 8	Small B 5 + 3	Mohan N 40	Sigurdsson L 5	Keen K 20 + 3	Oldfield D 7 + 12	Kavanagh G 44 + 1	Connor P 15 + 11	Lightbourne K 35 + 5	Taaffe S 2	Aiston S 2 + 4	MacKenzie N — + 2	Crowe D — + 6	Clarke C 39 + 3	Thorne P 41 + 4	Jacobsen A 29 + 4	O'Connor J 42	Petty B 7 + 6	Short C 14	Heath R — + 3	Bullock M 4 + 3	Dryden R 11 + 2	Gislason S 4 + 4	Danielsson E 3 + 5	Hansson M 24 + 3	Kippe F 15	Gunnarsson B 21 + 1	Gunnlaugsson A 10 + 3	Gudjonsson B 7 + 1	Iwelumo C — + 3	Melton S — + 5	Match No
1	2	3	4	5	6¹	7²	8	9	10³	11	12	13	14																			1
1	2		4	5	6³	7	8	9²			11¹	12	13	3	10	14																2
1	2	12	4³	5	13	7	8	9					6¹	3²	10		11	14														3
1			4	5		7²	12	8	9			13	14	3	10³	6	11	2¹														4
1	12			5	13	6³	8	9				7²	14	3²	10	4	11	2														5
1	12	3	4		6	7		9	10¹					8		5	11	2														6
1	2		4		7	12	13	9²	10					3	8	6	11	5¹														7
1	2¹		4		7²	12	8		10	13				3	9	6	11	5														8
1	12			5	6	13	8	9¹	7²					3	10³	4	11	2	14													9
1			5		6	7¹	8	12	9				13	3	10²	4	11	2														10
1	2²	3	5		7³	12	8	13	9					10¹	6	11	4	14														11
1	2¹	3²	5		7		8	12	9³					13	10	6	11	4	14													12
1	12			5	7³		8	13	9²					3	10	6	11	14	2			4¹										13
1	12			5	6		8	9						3	10	4	11	2	7¹													14
1	2				7¹		8	12	9			13	3	10²	6		4	14	11³	5												15
1	2	3			7¹		8	12	9²				13	10	6	11	4³		14	5												16
1	12		4		7²	13	8		9					3	10	14	11	2¹		6³	5											17
1	2	4			7	12	8		9¹					3	10	6	11	14							5²	13³						18
1	2	4			7		8		9				12	3¹	10	6²	11	13							5							19
1	2	4			7¹		8		9					3²	10	6	11								5	12	13					20
1		4			7	12	8		9						10	6	11								3	5¹	2					21
1	2	4				12	8		9					3	10¹		11								5²	13	7	6				22
1		4			7²	12	8	9	10					3³	13		11								14	5¹	2	6				23
1		4					8	9¹	12					3	10²	5	11	7							13	2	6					24
1		4					8	9	12					3²	10¹	5	11	7³							13	2	6	14				25
1		4					8	9						3	10¹	5	11								12	2	6	7				26
1		4				12	8	13	9					3	10²	5¹	11								14	2³	6	7				27
1		4					8		9					3	10	5	11									2	6	7				28
1	12	4¹					8	13	9					3	10³	5	11²		14							2	6	7				29
1		4³				10¹	8	9²	12					3	13	5	11	14								2	6	7				30
1							8	9¹	10					3	12	5	11	4								2	6	7				31
1							8	9¹	10					3²	12	5	11	4							13	2	6	7				32
1	12	5				13	8		9²					3	10¹		11	4								2	6	7				33
1	12	13	5³				8							3²	10	14	11	4								2	6	7¹	9			34
1		4					8		12					3	10¹	5	11									2	6	7	9			35
1		4					8		12					3	10³	5²	11									2	6	7	9¹	13	14	36
1		4					8²	9³						3	10		11	12							5¹	2	6	13	7	14		37
1		4					8	9						3	10		11								5¹	2	6	12	7			38
1		4					8	9						3	10		11								5	12	6	7	2¹			39
1		4					8	9²						3	10		11								5	12	6	7¹	2³	13	14	40
1		4					8	9						3¹	10		11								12	2²	6	5	7	13		41
1		4					8	12	9¹					3²	10		11								13	2	5	6	7			42
1		4					8	9²						12	10	13	11								5¹	2	7	6	3³	14		43
1		4					8	9						3	10		11								5	2	7	6¹		12		44
1		4					8	12	9					3	10		11								5²	2	7	6¹		13		45
1		4	12				8	13	9²					3	10	6¹	11³								5	2	7	14				46

Worthington Cup

First Round	Macclesfield T	(a)	1-1
		(h)	3-0
Second Round	Sheffield W	(h)	0-0
		(a)	1-3

FA Cup

First Round	Blackpool	(a)	0-2

FA Premiership
SUNDERLAND

FOUNDATION

A Scottish schoolmaster named James Allan, working at Hendon Board School, took the initiative in the foundation of Sunderland in 1879 when they were formed as The Sunderland and District Teachers' Association FC at a meeting in the Adults School, Norfolk Street. Due to financial difficulties, they quickly allowed members from outside the teaching profession and so became Sunderland AFC in October 1880.

Sunderland Stadium of Light, Sunderland, Tyne and Wear SR5 1SU.
Telephone: (0191) 551 5000.
Fax: (0191) 551 5123.
Website: www.sunderland-afc.com
Ticket Office: (0191) 551 5151.
Club Shop: (0191) 551 5050.
Tour Hotline: (0191) 551 5055.
ClubCall: 09068 121 140.
Ground Capacity: 48,300.
Record Attendance: 42,079 v Newcastle U, FA Premier League, 5 February 2000.
Record Receipts: £605,310 v Sheffield U, Division 1 play-off semi-final, 13 May 1998.
Pitch Measurements: 105m × 68m.
Chairman: R. S. Murray.
Chief Executive: John Fickling.
Director: G. McDonnell.
Associate Directors: J. R. Featherstone, G. S. Wood, J. G. Wood.
Manager: Peter Reid.
Assistant Manager: Bobby Saxton.
Reserve Team Manager: Ricky Sbragia.
Physio: Gordon Ellis.
Academy Director: Ian Branfoot.
Community Programme Officer: Bob Oates.
Secretary: Mark Blackbourne.
Commercial Director: Grahame McDonnell.
Safety Officer: John Davidson.

LATEST SEQUENCES

Longest Sequence of League Wins: 13, 14.11.1891 – 2.4.1892.
Longest Sequence of League Defeats: 9, 23.11.76 – 15.1.77.
Longest Sequence of League Draws: 6, 26.3.49 – 19.4.49.
Longest Sequence of Unbeaten League Matches: 19, 3.5.98 – 14.11.98.
Longest Sequence Without a League Win: 14, 16.4.85 – 14.9.85.

HONOURS

Football League: Division 1 – Champions 1891–92, 1892–93, 1894–95, 1901–02, 1912–13, 1935–36, 1995–96, 1998–99; Runners-up 1893–94, 1897–98, 1900–01, 1922–23, 1934–35; Division 2 – Champions 1975–76; Runners-up 1963–64, 1979–80; Division 3 – Champions 1987–88.

FA Cup: Winners 1937, 1973; Runners-up 1913, 1992.

Football League Cup: Runners-up 1985.

European Competitions: European Cup-Winners' Cup: 1973–74.

Colours
Red and white striped shirts, black shorts, black stockings.

Change Colours
All white.

Year Formed: 1879.

Turned Professional: 1886.

Ltd Co.: 1906.

Previous Name: 1879, Sunderland and District Teacher's AFC; 1880, Sunderland.

Previous Grounds: 1879, Blue House Field, Hendon; 1882, Groves Field, Ashbrooke; 1883, Horatio Street; 1884, Abbs Field, Fulwell; 1886, Newcastle Road; 1898, Roker Park; 1997, Stadium of Light.

First Football League Game: 13 September 1890, Football League, v Burnley (h) L 2–3 – Kirtley; Porteous, Oliver; Wilson, Auld, Gibson; Spence (1), Miller, Campbell (1), Scott, D. Hannah.

Record League Victory: 9–1 v Newcastle U (a), Division 1, 5 December 1908 – Roose; Forster, Melton; Daykin, Thomson, Low; Mordue, Hogg (4), Brown, Holley (3), Bridgett (2).

Record Cup Victory: 11–1 v Fairfield, FA Cup 1st rd, 2 February 1895 – Doig; McNeill, Johnston; Dunlop, McCreadie (1), Wilson; Gillespie (1), Millar (5), Campbell, Hannah (3), Scott (1).

Record Defeat: 0–8 v West Ham U, Division 1, 19 October 1968. 0–8 v Watford, Division 1, 25 September 1982.

Most League Points (2 for a win): 61, Division 2, 1963–64.

Most League Points (3 for a win): 105, Division 1, 1998–99 (Football League Record).

Most League Goals: 109, Division 1, 1935–36.

Highest League Scorer in Season: Dave Halliday, 43, Division 1, 1928–29.

Most League Goals in Total Aggregate: Charlie Buchan, 209, 1911–25.

Most League Goals in One Match: 5, Charlie Buchan v Liverpool, Division 1, 7 December 1919; 5, Bobby Gurney v Bolton W, Division 1, 7 December 1935; 5, Dominic Sharkey v Norwich C, Division 2, 20 February 1962.

Most Capped Player: Charlie Hurley, 38 (40), Republic of Ireland.

Most League Appearances: Jim Montgomery, 537, 1962–77.

Youngest League Player: Derek Forster, 15 years 184 days v Leicester C, 22 August 1964.

Record Transfer Fee Received: £5,600,000 from Leeds U for Michael Bridges, July 1999.

Record Transfer Fee Paid: £3,500,000 to Valencia for Stefan Schwarz, July 1999.

Football League Record: 1890 Elected to Division 1; 1958–64 Division 2; 1964–70 Division 1; 1970–76 Division 2; 1976–77 Division 1; 1977–80 Division 2; 1980–85 Division 1; 1985–87 Division 2; 1987–88 Division 3; 1988–90 Division 2; 1990–91 Division 1; 1991–92 Division 2; 1992–96 Division 1; 1996–97 FA Premier League; 1997– 99 Division 1; 1999– FA Premier League.

MANAGERS

Tom Watson 1888–96
Bob Campbell 1896–99
Alex Mackie 1899–1905
Bob Kyle 1905–28
Johnny Cochrane 1928–39
Bill Murray 1939–57
Alan Brown 1957–64
George Hardwick 1964–65
Ian McColl 1965–68
Alan Brown 1968–72
Bob Stokoe 1972–76
Jimmy Adamson 1976–78
Ken Knighton 1979–81
Alan Durban 1981–84
Len Ashurst 1984–85
Lawrie McMenemy 1985–87
Denis Smith 1987–91
Malcolm Crosby 1992–93
Terry Butcher 1993
Mick Buxton 1993–95
Peter Reid March 1995–

TEN YEAR LEAGUE RECORD

		P	W	D	L	F	A	Pts	Pos
1989-90	Div 2	46	20	14	12	70	64	74	6
1990-91	Div 1	38	8	10	20	38	60	34	19
1991-92	Div 2	46	14	11	21	61	65	53	18
1992-93	Div 1	46	13	11	22	50	64	50	21
1993-94	Div 1	46	19	8	19	54	57	65	12
1994-95	Div 1	46	12	18	16	41	45	54	20
1995-96	Div 1	46	22	17	7	59	33	83	1
1996-97	PR Lge	38	10	10	18	35	53	40	18
1997-98	Div 1	46	26	12	8	86	50	90	3
1998-99	Div 1	46	31	12	3	91	28	105	1

DID YOU KNOW ?

In 1930 when Sunderland signed Tommy Urwin from Newcastle United, the winger achieved the distinction of playing for the North East's big three clubs, having been with Middlesbrough previously, despite being born near Sunderland.

SUNDERLAND 1999–2000 LEAGUE RECORD

Match No.	Date		Venue	Opponents	Result	H/T Score	Lg. Pos.	Goalscorers	Attendance
1	Aug	7	A	Chelsea	L 0-4	0-2	20		34,831
2		10	H	Watford	W 2-0	0-0	—	Phillips 2 (1 pen) 62 (p), 86	37,879
3		14	H	Arsenal	D 0-0	0-0	12		40,037
4		21	A	Leeds U	L 1-2	1-0	16	Phillips (pen) 37	39,064
5		25	A	Newcastle U	W 2-1	0-1	—	Quinn 64, Phillips 75	36,420
6		29	H	Coventry C	D 1-1	0-1	11	Phillips 73	38,436
7	Sept	11	H	Leicester C	W 2-0	1-0	8	Butler P 28, McCann 82	38,621
8		18	A	Derby Co	W 5-0	2-0	5	McCann 24, Phillips 3 42, 52, 85, Quinn 55	28,264
9		25	H	Sheffield W	W 1-0	0-0	4	Schwarz 51	40,510
10	Oct	2	A	Bradford C	W 4-0	1-0	3	Rae 17, Quinn 68, Phillips 2 (1 pen) 88, 90 (p)	18,204
11		18	H	Aston Villa	W 2-1	0-0	—	Phillips 2 (1 pen) 60 (p), 82	39,866
12		24	A	West Ham U	D 1-1	1-0	3	Phillips 24	26,022
13		31	H	Tottenham H	W 2-1	2-0	3	Quinn 2 10, 21	41,042
14	Nov	6	A	Middlesbrough	D 1-1	0-0	3	Reddy 78	34,793
15		20	H	Liverpool	L 0-2	0-0	4		41,511
16		27	A	Watford	W 3-2	2-1	4	Phillips 2 24, 33, McCann 70	21,590
17	Dec	4	H	Chelsea	W 4-1	4-0	4	Quinn 2 1, 38, Phillips 2 23, 36	40,777
18		18	H	Southampton	W 2-0	1-0	3	Phillips 2 30, 90	40,066
19		26	A	Everton	L 0-5	0-3	3		40,017
20		28	H	Manchester U	D 2-2	2-1	4	McCann 2, Quinn 13	41,269
21	Jan	3	A	Wimbledon	L 0-1	0-1	4		17,621
22		15	A	Arsenal	L 1-4	0-3	5	Quinn 46	38,039
23		23	H	Leeds U	L 1-2	0-1	5	Phillips 52	41,633
24	Feb	5	H	Newcastle U	D 2-2	1-2	6	Phillips 2 22, 82	42,079
25		12	A	Coventry C	L 2-3	0-3	6	Phillips 57, Rae 88	22,099
26		26	H	Derby Co	D 1-1	0-0	6	Rae 62	41,619
27	Mar	5	A	Leicester C	L 2-5	0-2	7	Phillips 53, Quinn 75	20,432
28		11	A	Liverpool	D 1-1	0-1	9	Phillips (pen) 77	44,693
29		18	H	Middlesbrough	D 1-1	0-0	8	Quinn 66	41,830
30		25	H	Everton	W 2-1	1-1	7	Summerbee 7, Phillips 77	41,155
31	Apr	1	A	Southampton	W 2-1	1-0	6	Quinn 14, Phillips (pen) 86	15,245
32		8	H	Wimbledon	W 2-1	0-0	7	Quinn 54, Kilbane 82	40,510
33		15	A	Manchester U	L 0-4	0-1	7		61,612
34		22	A	Sheffield W	W 2-0	0-0	7	Phillips 2 86, 90	28,072
35		24	H	Bradford C	L 0-1	0-0	7		39,663
36		29	A	Aston Villa	D 1-1	0-0	7	Quinn 85	33,949
37	May	6	H	West Ham U	W 1-0	1-0	7	Phillips 14	40,896
38		14	A	Tottenham H	L 1-3	1-1	7	Makin 20	36,083

Final League Position: 7

GOALSCORERS

League (57): Phillips 30 (6 pens), Quinn 14, McCann 4, Rae 3, Butler P 1, Kilbane 1, Makin 1, Reddy 1, Schwarz 1, Summerbee 1.

Worthington Cup (10): Dichio 4, Fredgaard 2, Ball 1, Roy 1, Williams 1, own goal 1.

FA Cup (1): McCann 1.

Sorensen T 37	Makin C 34	Gray M 32 + 1	Ball K 6 + 5	Bould S 19 + 1	Butler P 31 + 1	Summerbee N 29 + 3	Rae A 22 + 4	Quinn N 35 + 2	Phillips K 36	Lumsdon C 1	Fredgaard C — + 1	McCann G 21 + 3	Schwarz S 27	Oster J 4 + 6	Dichio D — + 12	Helmer T 1 + 1	Holloway D 8 + 7	Williams D 13 + 12	Roy E 19 + 5	Reddy M — + 8	Craddock J 18 + 1	Thirlwell P 7 + 1	Kibane K 17 + 3	Marriot A 1	Nunez M — + 1	Butler T — + 1	Match No
1	2	3	4¹	5	6	7	8	9	10	11²	12	13															1
1	2	3		5	6	7	8	9²	10		12	4	11¹	13													2
1	2	3	4	5²	6	7	8	12	9¹		13	10	11²		14												3
1	2	3¹	4²		6¹	7	8	12	9		11	10		13	5	14											4
1	2	3	12	5	6	7	8	9	10	11	4¹																5
1	2	3		5	6	7	8	9	10	11¹	4	12															6
1	2	3	4	5	6	7		9¹	10	11³	8²	12	13	14													7
1	2	3	4³	5	6	7	12	9²	10	11¹	8	13	14														8
1	2	3	4¹	5	6	7	12	9²	10	11	8	13															9
1	2	3		5	6	7	8²	9¹	10	11³	4	12	13	14													10
1	2	3	12	5	6	7³	8²	9	10	11¹	4	13	14														11
1	2	3²		5	6	7	8³	9¹	10	11	4	12	13	14													12
1	2	3	12	5	6	7³		9	10²	11	4	13	8¹														13
1	2	3³	12	5	6	7		9	10	11¹	4	13	8²	14													14
1		3			6	7	8¹	9	10	11		2	4	12	5												15
1		3	12		6	7		9	10²	11	8	2	4¹	13	5												16
1	2	3			7¹		9	10	8		12	6	11	5	4												17
1	2	3		5	6	7		9	10	11	8²	12	4¹	13													18
1	2	3²		5	6	7		9		11	8	12	4¹	13	10												19
1	2	3		5	6	7	8¹	9		11	4	12	13	10²													20
	2²	3		5	6	7¹		9	10	11	4	13	12	8	1												21
1	2¹	3		5	6	7²		9	10	11	8	12	4	13													22
1		3³	5²	6		7		9		11	8	14	2	4¹	12	13	10										23
1	2	3			6	7¹		9	10	11	4	12	5	8													24
1	3				6	7¹	12	9	10	11²	4	14	2³	13	5	8											25
1	3				6			8	9	10	12	2	7¹	5	4	11											26
1	3				6	12	8	9	10		7	13	2¹	4²	5	11											27
1	3						8	9	10		7	2	6	5	4	11											28
1	3				12		8	9	10		7	2	6	5	4¹	11											29
1	3			12	7	8	9	10			4¹	2	6	5	11												30
1	3	12			7¹	8	9²	10			13	2	6	4	5	11											31
1	3	7²			8	9	10				2	6	4¹	5	12	11	13										32
1	3	7²		12	13	8	9	10			2	6¹	4	5	11												33
1	3	7		6	8	9	10			13	12	2³	14	4	5	11²											34
1	2	3		6		8	9	10			12	13	4¹	7	5²	11											35
1	2	3		6	7		9	10			12		4	5	8	11¹											36
1	2	3		6	7		9¹	10			11²	12	13	4³	5	8	14										37
1	2²	3		6	7	12	9	10			11³	13	8	5	4¹	14											38

Worthington Cup

Second Round	Walsall	(h)	3-2	
		(a)	5-0	
Third Round	Wimbledon	(a)	2-3	

FA Cup

Third Round	Portsmouth	(h)	1-0
Fourth Round	Tranmere R	(a)	0-1

Division 2

SWANSEA CITY

FOUNDATION

The earliest Association Football in Wales was played in the
Northern part of the country and no international took place in
the South until 1894, when a local paper still thought it necessary
to publish an outline of the rules and an illustration of the pitch
markings. There had been an earlier Swansea club, but this has no
connection with Swansea Town (now City) formed at a public
meeting in June 1912.

Vetch Field, Swansea SA1 3SU.
Telephone: (01792) 474 114. *Fax:* (01792) 646 120.
Website: www.swansfc.co.uk
Email: swans.prom@btinternet.com
Club Shop: (01792) 462 584.
ClubCall: 09068 543 123.
Commercial Department: (01792) 465 087.
Youth Development: (01792) 465 610.
Ground Capacity: 10,402.
Record Attendance: 32,796 v Arsenal, FA Cup 4th rd, 17 February 1968.
Record Receipts: £36,477.42 v Liverpool, Division 1, 18 September 1982.
Pitch Measurements: 112yd × 74yd.
President: I. C. Pursey MBE.
Chairman: Steve Hamer. *Vice-Chairman:* Neil McClure.
Directors: Professor D. H. Farmer, R. G. Hamill,
Mike Lewis.
Chief Executive: Peter Day.
Commercial Director: Mike Lewis.
Manager: John Hollins MBE.
Assistant Manager: Alan Curtis.
Director of Youth Development: Malcolm Elias.
Physio: Richard Evans.
Centre of Excellence Director: Jeremy Charles.
Football Development Officer: Lyndon Jones.
Club Secretary: Victoria Townsend.
Safety Officer: Don Goss.
Programme Editor: Major Reg Pike (01792) 474114.

LATEST SEQUENCES
Longest Sequence of League Wins: 9, 27.11.99 – 22.100.
Longest Sequence of League Defeats: 9, 26.1.91 – 19.3.91.
Longest Sequence of League Draws: 5, 5.1.93 – 5.2.93.
Longest Sequence of Unbeaten League Matches: 19,
19.10.70 – 9.3.71.
Longest Sequence Without a League Win: 15, 25.3.89 –
2.9.89.

HONOURS

Football League: Division 1 best
season: 6th, 1981–82; Division 2 –
Promoted 1980–81 (3rd); Division 3
(S) – Champions 1924–25, 1948–49;
Division 3 – Champions 1999–2000;
Promoted 1978–79 (3rd); Division 4 –
Promoted 1969–70 (3rd), 1977–78
(3rd), 1987–88 (play-offs).
FA Cup: Semi-finals 1926, 1964.
Football League Cup: best season:
4th rd, 1965, 1977.
Welsh Cup: Winners 9 times;
Runners-up 8 times.
Autoglass Trophy: Winners 1994.
European Competitions: European
Cup-Winners' Cup: 1961–62, 1966–67,
1981–82, 1982–83, 1983–84, 1989–90,
1991–92.

Colours
White shirts with maroon and black facing, white shorts with maroon and
black trim, white stockings with maroon ring top.

Change Colours
Maroon shirts with black and white facings, maroon shorts with black and
white trim, maroon stockings with white band.

Year Formed: 1912.

Turned Professional: 1912.

Ltd Co.: 1912.

Previous Name: Swansea Town until February 1970.

Club Nickname: 'The Swans'.

First Football League Game: 28 August 1920, Division 3, v Portsmouth (a) L 0–3 – Crumley; Robson, Evans; Smith, Holdsworth, Williams; Hole, I. Jones, Edmundson, Rigsby, Spottiswood.

Record League Victory: 8–0 v Hartlepool U, Division 4, 1 April 1978 – Barber; Evans, Bartley, Lally (1) (Morris), May, Bruton, Kevin Moore, Robbie James (3 incl. 1p), Curtis (3), Toshack (1), Chappell.

Record Cup Victory: 12–0 v Sliema W (Malta), ECWC 1st rd 1st leg, 15 September 1982 – Davies; Marustik, Hadziabdic (1), Irwin (1), Kennedy, Rajkovic (1), Loveridge (2) (Leighton James), Robbie James, Charles (2), Stevenson (1), Latchford (1) (Walsh (3)).

Record Defeat: 0–8 v Liverpool, FA Cup 3rd rd, 9 January 1990. 0–8 v Monaco, ECWC, 1st rd 2nd leg, 1 October 1991.

Most League Points (2 for a win): 62, Division 3 (S), 1948–49.

Most League Points (3 for a win): 85, Division 3, 1999–2000.

Most League Goals: 90, Division 2, 1956–57.

Highest League Scorer in Season: Cyril Pearce, 35, Division 2, 1931–32.

Most League Goals in Total Aggregate: Ivor Allchurch, 166, 1949–58, 1965–68.

Most League Goals in One Match: 5, Jack Fowler v Charlton Ath, Division 3S, 27 December 1924.

Most Capped Player: Ivor Allchurch, 42 (68), Wales.

Most League Appearances: Wilfred Milne, 585, 1919–37.

Youngest League Player: Nigel Dalling, 15 years 289 days v Southport, 6 December 1974.

Record Transfer Fee Received: £400,000 from Bristol C for Steve Torpey, August 1997.

Record Transfer Fee Paid: £340,000 to Liverpool for Colin Irwin, August 1981.

Football League Record: 1920 Original Member of Division 3; 1921–25 Division 3 (S); 1925–47 Division 2; 1947–49 Division 3 (S); 1949–65 Division 2; 1965–67 Division 3; 1967–70 Division 4; 1970–73 Division 3; 1973–78 Division 4; 1978–79 Division 3; 1979–81 Division 2; 1981–83 Division 1; 1983–84 Division 2; 1984–86 Division 3; 1986–88 Division 4; 1988–92 Division 3; 1992–96 Division 2; 1996–2000 Division 3; 2000– Division 2.

MANAGERS

Walter Whittaker 1912–14
William Bartlett 1914–15
Joe Bradshaw 1919–26
Jimmy Thomson 1927–31
Neil Harris 1934–39
Haydn Green 1939–47
Bill McCandless 1947–55
Ron Burgess 1955–58
Trevor Morris 1958–65
Glyn Davies 1965–66
Billy Lucas 1967–69
Roy Bentley 1969–72
Harry Gregg 1972–75
Harry Griffiths 1975–77
John Toshack 1978–83
(resigned October re-appointed in December) 1983–84
Colin Appleton 1984
John Bond 1984–85
Tommy Hutchison 1985–86
Terry Yorath 1986–89
Ian Evans 1989–90
Terry Yorath 1990–91
Frank Burrows 1991–95
Kevin Cullis 1996
Jan Molby 1996–97
Micky Adams 1997
Alan Cork 1997–98
John Hollins July 1998–

TEN YEAR LEAGUE RECORD

		P	W	D	L	F	A	Pts	Pos
1989-90	Div 3	46	14	12	20	45	63	54	17
1990-91	Div 3	46	13	9	24	49	72	48	20
1991-92	Div 3	46	14	14	18	55	65	56	19
1992-93	Div 2	46	20	13	13	65	47	73	5
1993-94	Div 2	46	16	12	18	56	58	60	13
1994-95	Div 2	46	19	14	13	57	45	71	10
1995-96	Div 2	46	11	14	21	43	79	47	22
1996-97	Div 3	46	21	8	17	62	58	71	5
1997-98	Div 3	46	13	11	22	49	62	50	20
1998-99	Div 3	46	19	14	13	56	48	71	7

DID YOU KNOW ?

On 14 October 1981, Swansea City provided six players for the Welsh national team against Ireland: Dai Davies, John Mahoney, Jeremy Charles, Alan Curtis, Leighton James and Robbie James.

SWANSEA CITY 1999–2000 LEAGUE RECORD

Match No.	Date		Venue	Opponents	Result	H/T Score	Lg. Pos.	Goalscorers	Attendance
1	Aug	7	A	York C	L 0-1	0-1	21		3036
2		14	H	Carlisle U	W 1-0	0-0	13	Price 64	5452
3		21	A	Macclesfield T	W 2-1	0-0	7	Appleby 2 60, 85	2121
4		28	H	Southend U	W 3-1	1-0	4	Roberts 17, Watkin (pen) 88, Price 89	4757
5		30	A	Lincoln C	W 1-0	1-0	4	Price 9	2893
6	Sept	11	H	Barnet	L 1-2	0-0	8	Thomas 85	5167
7		18	A	Hull C	L 0-2	0-1	9		5871
8		25	A	Rochdale	D 0-0	0-0	11		2975
9	Oct	2	H	Mansfield T	L 0-1	0-0	11		4263
10		12	H	Rotherham U	W 2-0	1-0	—	Boyd 2 7, 82	5287
11		16	A	Torquay U	L 0-1	0-0	14		2488
12		19	A	Exeter C	D 1-1	0-0	—	Boyd 54	2692
13		22	H	Rochdale	W 1-0	0-0	—	Cusack 86	4843
14	Nov	2	A	Northampton T	L 1-2	0-1	—	Appleby 75	4495
15		5	H	Halifax T	W 3-1	2-1	—	Appleby 36, Coates 2 43, 81	3357
16		12	A	Shrewsbury T	D 1-1	1-0	13	Bound (pen) 7	2531
17		16	H	Cheltenham T	D 0-0	0-0	—		4299
18		23	H	Darlington	D 0-0	0-0	—		3748
19		27	A	Chester C	W 1-0	0-0	10	Cusack 54	2713
20	Dec	4	H	York C	W 1-0	0-0	8	Price 51	3812
21		11	A	Hartlepool U	W 1-0	1-0	5	Price 36	2397
22		18	H	Brighton & HA	W 2-0	1-0	4	Cusack 22, Coates 78	4555
23		26	A	Leyton Orient	W 1-0	1-0	3	Boyd 6	4447
24		28	H	Plymouth Arg	W 1-0	0-0	3	Boyd 66	9075
25	Jan	3	A	Peterborough U	W 3-2	0-2	2	Thomas 63, Alsop 77, Cusack 80	6439
26		8	H	Hartlepool U	W 2-1	0-1	1	Watkin 71, Smith 76	7163
27		22	A	Macclesfield T	W 1-0	0-0	3	Boyd 71	6913
28		29	A	Southend U	L 1-2	1-1	3	Cusack (pen) 43	3860
29	Feb	4	H	Lincoln C	W 2-1	2-0	—	Alsop 18, Coates 38	6847
30		13	A	Cheltenham T	D 0-0	0-0	2		4220
31		18	A	Chester C	W 2-1	0-1	—	Hobson (og) 84, Watkin 90	6336
32		26	H	Hull C	D 0-0	0-0	2		6137
33	Mar	4	A	Barnet	W 1-0	1-0	2	Watkin 27	2911
34		7	A	Halifax T	W 1-0	1-0	—	Watkin 30	1657
35		10	H	Northampton T	W 4-1	1-0	—	Watkin 18, Coates 56, Thomas 85, Bird 90	7430
36		18	A	Darlington	D 1-1	0-1	1	Cusack 49	6632
37		21	H	Shrewsbury T	D 1-1	0-1	—	Boyd 77	6112
38		25	A	Leyton Orient	D 0-0	0-0	2		6330
39		28	A	Carlisle U	L 0-2	0-1	—		2748
40	Apr	1	A	Brighton & HA	D 1-1	1-0	2	Alsop 19	5718
41		8	H	Peterborough U	D 0-0	0-0	2		6572
42		15	A	Plymouth Arg	L 0-1	0-1	2		5881
43		22	H	Torquay U	W 2-1	1-0	1	Watkin 28, Price 50	6396
44		24	A	Mansfield T	W 1-0	1-0	1	Cusack 37	2162
45		29	H	Exeter C	W 3-0	3-0	1	Thomas 12, Coates 24, Curran (og) 35	10,743
46	May	6	A	Rotherham U	D 1-1	0-0	1	Bound (pen) 88	10,863

Final League Position: 1

GOALSCORERS

League (51): Boyd 7, Cusack 7 (1 pen), Watkin 7 (1 pen), Coates 6, Price 6, Appleby 4, Thomas 4, Alsop 3, Bound 2 (2 pens), Bird 1, Roberts 1, own goals 2.
Worthington Cup (4): Bird 1 (pen), Bound 1 (pen), Price 1, Watkin 1.
FA Cup (2): Cusack 1, Watkin 1.

Freestone R 46	Jones S 34+4	Howard M 39+1	Cusack N 43	Smith J 43	Bound M 43	Appleby R 10+10	Thomas M 32+8	Alsop J 29+8	Watkin S 36+3	Coates J 41+1	Price J 35+4	Bird T 8+8	O'Leary K 9+11	Roberts S 9+2	Lacey D 14+2	Mutton T 1+1	Jenkins L 7+9	Boyd W 21+6	Keegan M 3+1	Casey R —+11	De-Vulgt L —+2	Phillips G 2+1	Evans K 1+1	Match No.
1	2	3	4^1	5	6	7	8	9^2	10	11^3	12	13	14											1
1		3	4	5	6	12	8^2	13	10		7	9^1	2	11										2
1		3	4	5	6	12	11	13	10^2		7	9	2^3	8^1	14									3
1	12	3	4^2	5	6	7		9	10^3	13	2	14		8^1	11									4
1	2	3		5	6	7	12	9	10	11^1	8		4											5
1	12	3		5	6	7^1	8	9	10	2	13	4^2	11^3	14										6
1	12	3		5	6		8	9^3	10^2	11	2	13	4	7^1	14									7
1	2	3	4	5	6		8	9		11	7				10									8
1	2	3^3	4	5	6	12	8	13		11	7^1	9						10^2	14					9
1	12		4	5	6		8			11^1	2			3	10		7	9						10
1			4	5	6	12	8	13		11	2			3	10^1		7^2	9						11
1	12	3	4	5	6		8		10	11	2						7^1	9						12
1	2	3	4	5	6		8^2	12	10	11		13	7^3					9^1	14					13
1		3	4	5	6	7^1	8	9	10	11^2	2							12	13					14
1		3	4	5	6	7		9	10	11	2		8											15
1		3	4	5	6	7^1		9	10^2	11^3	2		8					12	13	14				16
1		3	4	5	6	7^1	12	13	10	11^3	2		8					9^2		14				17
1	2	3^2	4	5	6	7^1	12	9	10	11^3			8					14		13				18
1	2	3^2	4	5	6	12		9	10	11	7^1		8					13						19
1	2	3	4	5	6	12		9	10	11	7		8^1											20
1	2	3	4	5	6	12		9	10^2	11	7^1		8					13						21
1	2	3	4	5	6			9	10	11^1	7		8					12						22
1	2	3	4	5	6			9					8					7^1	10	11	12			23
1	2	3	4	5	6	12		9^2	13	11	14		8^1					10	7^3					24
1	2	3^1	4	5	6	13	12		10	11^3			8	14				9	7^2					25
1	2		4	5	6		8	9	10	11					3			12	7^1					26
1	2^1		4	5	6		8	9	10	11					3			7			12			27
1	2		4	5	6^1			9	10	11	12							7	8^2	13	14	3^3		28
1	2		4	5^1	6			9	10	11	7							3	8		12			29
1	2		4			12		9	10	11	7							3^2	8	13		6^1	5	30
1	2	3	4	5	6	12			10	11^3	7	13	8^1					9		14				31
1	2	3	4	5	6		8	9^1	10	11^3	12	13						7^2		14				32
1	2	3	4	5	6		8^2	9	10	11	7^1		12					13						33
1	2	3	4	5	6		8	9	10^1	11	7^2		12					13						34
1	2	3	4	5	6		8^2	12	10^1	11	7		9					13						35
1	2	3	4	5	6		8	9^1		11	7				10			12						36
1	2	3	4	5	6	12	8			11^1	7^2	13			10			9						37
1	2	3^2	4	5	6	12	8		10	11^3	7^1	13						9		14				38
1	2	3^1	4	5	6	12	8		10	11^1	7^2		9					13		14				39
1	2	3	4	5	6		8	9	10	11^2	7^1		12					13						40
1	2	3	4	5	6	12	8^1	9	10	11^2	7^3	13								14				41
1	2	3	4^2	5	6	7	8	9	10^3	11^1	12	13								14				42
1	2	3	4	5	6		12	9^1		11	7	13						10^2						43
1	2	3	4	5	6		8		10	11	7							9						44
1	2	3	4	5	6	12	8		10^2	11	7^1	13						9						45
1	2	3	4		6		8			11	7	10	5					12	9^1					46

Worthington Cup

First Round	Millwall	(h)	2-0
		(a)	1-1
Second Round	Derby Co	(h)	0-0
		(a)	1-3

FA Cup

| First Round | Colchester U | (h) | 2-1 |
| Second Round | Oldham Ath | (a) | 0-1 |

Division 2

SWINDON TOWN

FOUNDATION

It is generally accepted that Swindon Town came into being in 1881, although there is no firm evidence that the club's founder, Rev. William Pitt, captain of the Spartans (an offshoot of a cricket club) changed his club's name to Swindon Town before 1883, when the Spartans amalgamated with St Mark's Young Men's Friendly Society.

County Ground, Swindon, Wiltshire SN1 2ED.
Telephone: (01793) 333 700. *Fax:* (01793) 333 703.
Marketing: (01793) 333 718. *Fax:* (01793) 333 719.
Superstore: (01793) 333 778. *Fax:* (01793) 333 780.
Community Office: (01793) 421 303.
ClubCall: 09068 121 640.
Ground Capacity: 15,728.
Record Attendance: 32,000 v Arsenal, FA Cup 3rd rd, 15 January 1972.
Record Receipts: £149,371 v Bolton W, Coca-Cola Cup semi-final, 1st leg, 12 February 1995.
Pitch Measurements: 110yd × 70yd.
Chief Executive: Peter Rowe.
Chairman: Cliff Puffett.
Directors: Sir Seton Wills Bt, P. R. Godwin CBE, J. M. Spearman, P. T. Archer, J. Wills, W. Carson OBE (Associate).
Manager: Colin Todd.
Coach: Andy King.
Physio: Dick Mackey.
Director of Finance/Company Secretary: Steve Jones.
Football Secretary: Steve Jones.
Community Officers: Clive Maguire and Jon Holloway.

LATEST SEQUENCES

Longest Sequence of League Wins: 8, 12.1.86 – 15.3.86.
Longest Sequence of League Defeats: 6, 2.5.93 – 25.8.93.
Longest Sequence of League Draws: 6, 22.11.91 – 28.12.91.
Longest Sequence of Unbeaten League Matches: 22, 12.1.86 – 23.8.86.
Longest Sequence Without a League Win: 19, 30.10.99 – 4.3.00.

HONOURS

FA Premier League: best season: 22nd 1993–94.

Football League: Division 2 – Champions 1995–96; Division 3 – Runners-up 1962–63, 1968–69; Division 4 – Champions 1985–86 (with record 102 points).

FA Cup: Semi-finals 1910, 1912.

Football League Cup: Winners 1969.

Anglo-Italian Cup: Winners 1970.

Colours
Red shirts, white shorts, red stockings.

Change Colours
Light blue/dark blue panelled shirts and shorts, light blue stockings.

Year Formed: 1881* (*see Foundation*).

Turned Professional: 1894.

Ltd Co.: 1894.

Club Nickname: 'Robins'.

Previous Ground: 1881, The Croft; 1896, County Ground.

First Football League Game: 28 August 1920, Division 3, v Luton T (h) W 9–1 – Nash; Kay, Macconachie; Langford, Hawley, Wareing; Jefferson (1), Fleming (4), Rogers, Batty (2), Davies (1), (1 og).

Record League Victory: 9–1 v Luton T, Division 3 (S), 28 August 1920 – Nash; Kay, Macconachie; Langford, Hawley, Wareing; Jefferson (1), Fleming (4), Rogers, Batty (2), Davies (1), (1 og).

Record Cup Victory: 10–1 v Farnham U Breweries (away), FA Cup 1st rd (replay), 28 November 1925 – Nash; Dickenson, Weston, Archer, Bew, Adey; Denyer (2), Wall (1), Richardson (4), Johnson (3), Davies.

Record Defeat: 1–10 v Manchester C, FA Cup 4th rd (replay), 25 January 1930.

Most League Points (2 for a win): 64, Division 3, 1968–69.

MANAGERS
Sam Allen 1902–33
Ted Vizard 1933–39
Neil Harris 1939–41
Louis Page 1945–53
Maurice Lindley 1953–55
Bert Head 1956–65
Danny Williams 1965–69
Fred Ford 1969–71
Dave Mackay 1971–72
Les Allen 1972–74
Danny Williams 1974–78
Bobby Smith 1978–80
John Trollope 1980–83
Ken Beamish 1983–84
Lou Macari 1984–89
Ossie Ardiles 1989–91
Glenn Hoddle 1991–93
John Gorman 1993–94
Steve McMahon 1994–99
Jimmy Quinn 1999–2000
Colin Todd May 2000–

Most League Points (3 for a win): 102, Division 4, 1985–86.

Most League Goals: 100, Division 3 (S), 1926–27.

Highest League Scorer in Season: Harry Morris, 47, Division 3 (S), 1926–27.

Most League Goals in Total Aggregate: Harry Morris, 216, 1926–33.

Most League Goals in One Match: 5, Harry Morris v QPR, Division 3S, 18 December 1926; 5, Harry Morris v Norwich C, Division 3S, 26 April 1930; 5, Keith East v Mansfield T, Division 3, 20 November 1965.

Most Capped Player: Rod Thomas, 30 (50), Wales.

Most League Appearances: John Trollope, 770, 1960–80.

Youngest League Player: Paul Rideout, 16 years 107 days v Hull C, 29 November 1980.

Record Transfer Fee Received: £1,500,000 from Manchester C for Kevin Horlock, January 1997.

Record Transfer Fee Paid: £800,000 to West Ham U for Joey Beauchamp, August 1994.

Football League Record: 1920 Original Member of Division 3; 1921–58 Division 3 (S); 1958–63 Division 2; 1963–65 Division 3; 1965–69 Division 3; 1969–74 Division 2; 1974–82 Division 3; 1982–86 Division 4; 1986–87 Division 3; 1987–92 Division 2; 1992–93 Division 1; 1993–94 FA Premier League; 1994–95 Division 1; 1995–96 Division 2; 1996–2000 Division 1; 2000– Division 2.

TEN YEAR LEAGUE RECORD								
		P	W	D	L	F	A	Pts	Pos
1989-90	Div 2	46	20	14	12	79	59	74	4
1990-91	Div 2	46	12	14	20	65	73	50	21
1991-92	Div 2	46	18	15	13	69	55	69	8
1992-93	Div 1	46	21	13	12	74	59	76	5
1993-94	PR Lge	42	5	15	22	47	100	30	22
1994-95	Div 1	46	12	12	22	54	73	48	21
1995-96	Div 2	46	25	17	4	71	34	92	1
1996-97	Div 1	46	15	9	22	52	71	54	19
1997-98	Div 1	46	14	10	22	42	73	52	18
1998-99	Div 1	46	13	11	22	59	81	50	17

DID YOU KNOW ?

On 11 March 2000, bottom club Swindon Town defeated First Division leaders Charlton Athletic 1-0 at The Valley, at a time when 54 points separated the two clubs in the table.

SWINDON TOWN 1999–2000 LEAGUE RECORD

Match No.	Date		Venue	Opponents	Result	H/T Score	Lg. Pos.	Goalscorers	Attendance
1	Aug	7	A	Walsall	D	0-0	0-0	16		6437
2		15	H	Ipswich T	L	1-4	1-1	22	Grazioli [15]	6195
3		21	A	Crystal Palace	W	2-1	1-1	15	Grazioli [32], Onuora [50]	12,726
4		28	H	WBA	L	1-2	1-0	20	Walters [4]	6565
5		30	A	Grimsby T	L	0-1	0-1	22		5705
6	Sept	11	H	Nottingham F	D	0-0	0-0	22		8203
7		18	A	Crewe Alex	L	1-2	0-1	23	Ndah [66]	5280
8		25	A	Port Vale	L	0-2	0-0	23		4629
9		28	H	Blackburn R	W	2-1	2-0	—	Walters [30], Howe [32]	7354
10	Oct	2	H	Bolton W	L	0-4	0-4	23		6711
11		9	H	Stockport Co	D	1-1	1-1	23	Hay [44]	5318
12		16	A	Fulham	L	0-1	0-0	24		13,715
13		19	A	Barnsley	L	0-1	0-0	—		12,026
14		23	H	Sheffield U	D	2-2	2-0	24	Hay 2 [11, 21]	5504
15		26	H	Port Vale	W	2-1	1-1	—	Onuora [1], Grazioli [89]	5703
16		30	A	Bolton W	L	0-2	0-0	23		12,486
17	Nov	6	A	Huddersfield T	L	0-4	0-2	24		11,891
18		12	H	Norwich C	D	0-0	0-0	23		7405
19		20	A	Wolverhampton W	D	1-1	1-0	24	Onuora (pen) [27]	19,917
20		23	H	Charlton Ath	L	1-2	1-2	—	Carrick [42]	6515
21		27	A	Birmingham C	D	1-1	0-1	24	Onuora [90]	22,620
22	Dec	4	A	Walsall	D	1-1	1-1	24	Carrick [38]	7186
23		18	A	Manchester C	L	0-3	0-1	24		31,751
24		26	H	Portsmouth	D	1-1	1-0	24	Hay [16]	10,279
25		28	A	Tranmere R	L	1-3	1-3	24	Hay [12]	8068
26	Jan	3	H	QPR	L	0-1	0-0	24		9460
27		15	A	Ipswich T	L	0-3	0-2	24		17,326
28		21	H	Crystal Palace	L	2-4	1-1	—	Reeves [21], Hall [61]	5214
29		29	A	WBA	D	1-1	0-0	24	Hall [77]	11,856
30	Feb	5	H	Grimsby T	L	0-1	0-0	24		5784
31		12	A	Blackburn R	D	0-0	0-0	24		16,938
32		19	H	Birmingham C	L	1-4	1-3	24	Hay [13]	7591
33		26	H	Crewe Alex	L	0-1	0-0	24		5003
34	Mar	4	A	Nottingham F	L	1-3	0-3	24	Hay (pen) [52]	19,748
35		7	A	Huddersfield T	W	2-0	1-0	—	Collins [11], Hay (pen) [89]	4701
36		11	A	Charlton Ath	W	1-0	1-0	24	Cowe [5]	19,569
37		18	H	Wolverhampton W	L	1-2	0-0	24	Williams A [82]	8748
38		22	A	Norwich C	W	2-0	0-0	—	Hay 2 (1 pen) [56 (p), 64]	13,662
39		25	A	Portsmouth	L	1-4	0-3	24	Gray [69]	15,305
40	Apr	1	H	Manchester C	L	0-2	0-1	24		12,397
41		8	A	QPR	L	1-2	1-2	24	Grazioli [35]	12,633
42		15	H	Tranmere R	W	3-1	2-1	24	Griffin [15], Grazioli [30], Gray [62]	4925
43		22	H	Fulham	W	1-0	0-0	24	Grazioli [83]	7556
44		24	A	Stockport Co	L	0-3	0-1	24		5362
45		29	H	Barnsley	L	1-2	0-0	24	Williams J [69]	6151
46	May	7	A	Sheffield U	D	2-2	0-1	24	Grazioli 2 [53, 55]	12,603

Final League Position: 24

GOALSCORERS

League (38): Hay 10 (3 pens), Grazioli 8, Onuora 4 (1 pen), Carrick 2, Gray 2, Hall 2, Walters 2, Collins 1, Cowe 1, Griffin 1, Howe 1, Ndah 1, Reeves 1, Williams A 1, Williams J 1.
Worthington Cup (1): Walters 1 (pen).
FA Cup (1): Gooden 1.

Talia F 31	Robinson M 40+2	Hall G 38+1	Leitch S 28+1	Hulbert R 5+7	Williams J 14+12	Walters M 11+2	Ndah G 12	Onuora J 18+6	Grazioli G 11+8	Gooden T 8+2	Taylor C 1+1	Griffin C 6+15	Willis A 16+7	Howe B 24+7	Hay C 27+4	McHugh F 9+5	Davies G 17	Reeves A 43	Davis S 24+5	Williams A 35+1	Thirlwell P 12	Glass J 8	Cowe S 12+5	Collins L 23+1	Carrick M 6	Quinn J 1+6	Mildenhall S 3+2	Cuervo P —+6	Campagna S 1+2	McCammon M 4	Griemink B 4	Gray W 8+4	Meaker M 6	Smith B —+1	Flanagan A —+1	Match No.
1	2	3	4	5^1	6	7	8	9	10^2	11	12	13																								1
1	2^2	3		5^1	6	12	8	9^3	10	4		13	14	7	11																					2
1	2	3			11		8	9	10^1						7	12		6	5	4																3
1	2	3			11		8^1	9				13	14	7	10^2	12		6	5^2	4																4
1	2	3	12		11		8	9^2					14	7	10^2	13		6	5^1	4																5
1	2	3					8	9^1				12		7	10			6	5	11	4															6
1	2^1	3				12	8	9^2				13		7	10			6	5	11	4															7
1	2	3				12	8	10				13		7	9^2			6^1	5	11	4															8
1	2		12^2		6		8^1	9	14	13		3		7	10^1			5		11	4															9
1	2		12		6^2		8	9	13			3		7^1	14	10^3		5		11	4															10
1	2	3					10^2	8	13	14	11		7	9^3			6^1	5		2	4															11
1	2	3					10	8	12				11^1		9			6	5	7	4															12
1	2	3					10	8^1	13	12		11^2		9^3	14			6	5	7	4															13
1		3				7^3	10^1	9	12	11		13	14	8				6^2	5	2	4															14
1	12	3^3		6				9^2	13	11		14	7	10				5	4	2^1	8															15
1		3		6^3		12		10^1	11^2	2		13	9					5	4	8				14	7											16
1	4	3	12		13			9				14	2	7^2	10			5^1	6		8			11^3												17
1	2	3^1	4^2		13			9^3		12				7	10			5	6	11		8	14													18
1	2	3	4					9^1						7	10			5	6	11		8	12													19
1	2	3	4		12			9^2						7^1	10			5	6	11		8	13													20
1	2	3	4^1					9				13		7^3	10^2			5	6	11		12	8	14												21
1	2	3	4					9			12			7^1				5	6	11		8	10													22
1	2		4		12			11						9^2	13	10		6	5	14	3^1		7^3	8												23
1		3	8^1	12	2			9				13			10			4^2	5	6	11		7^3		14											24
1	2	3	12		4^1			9						7^3	10			5	6	11^2		8		13	14											25
1	2	3	4	8^2								12			10	13		5	6	11		7				9^1										26
1	2^2	3	4	6^3	12									13	7	10	9	5		11		8^1			14											27
1		3	4		12										10	11		5	6^1	7		8^2			13	2	9									28
1^6	2	3	4	12											10	8^1	6	5		11		13	7^2		15		9									29
	2	3	4	8	12										10	6^1		5		11		7^2	14			9^3	1									30
	2	3	4	12	8							13		9^1	10			5	6	11		7^2					1									31
	2	3	4	8^1								12^2	14		10	13		6	5^3	9	11	7					1									32
	2	3^1	4											9	10		6	5	12	11		8^2	7	13				1								33
1		3	4^1									12		10		6	5	2	11^2		8^2	7		13				9								34
1	2		4									12	3	13	10		5	6	11		8^2	7						9^1								35
1	2	14	4		6							12^2	3		10		5		11^3		8^2	7		13				9^1								36
1	2		4^3	11							12			3	14	10		5	6	13		8^2	7					9^1								37
1	2	3^1	4									13	14		6	10		5	12	11		8^2	7					9^3								38
1	2	3	4		12							13			6			5	11^3		8^2	7^1	14					9	10							39
1	2	3^2	4									10		12	6			5		11		13	7					9^1	8							40
1	2		4									10		9^1	3			5	6	11		7						12	8							41
1	2	3	4									10^1		9^2	6			5		11		12	7					13	8							42
1	2	3	4									10^2		9^4	6			5	12	11^1		13	7					14	8							43
1	2	3	4		12									11^2	6			5^1	13			7		15				9^6	8							44
	2	3^1	4		12							10		9^2	11			5^3	6			8	7	1				13	14							45
	2	3		6^2								10		12	11	9	13	5	4			8^1	7	1^6					15							46

Division 3   **TORQUAY UNITED**

FOUNDATION

The idea of establishing a Torquay club was agreed by old boys of Torquay College and Torbay College, while sitting in Princess Gardens listening to the band. A proper meeting was subsequently held at Tor Abbey Hotel at which officers were elected. This was on 1 May 1899 and the club's first competition was the Eastern League (later known as the East Devon League). As an amateur club it played at Teignmouth Road, Torquay Recreation Ground and Cricket Field Road before settling down for four years at Torquay Cricket Ground where the rugby club now plays. They became Torquay United in 1921 after merging with Babbacombe FC.

Plainmoor Ground, Torquay, Devon TQ1 3PS.

Telephone: (01803) 328 666.

Fax: (01803) 323 976.

Ground Capacity: 6003.

Record Attendance: 21,908 v Huddersfield T, FA Cup 4th rd, 29 January 1955.

Record Receipts: £30,824 v Plymouth Arg, Division 3, 25 March 2000.

Pitch Measurements: 112yd × 74yd.

Chairman: M. Benney.

Managing Director: Miss H. Kindeleit.

Directors: M. Bateson, Mrs S. Bateson, I. Hayman, B. Palk.

Manager: Wes Saunders.

Physio: Norman Medhurst.

Company Secretary: Miss H. Kindeleit.

LATEST SEQUENCES

Longest Sequence of League Wins: 8, 24.1.98 – 3.3.98.

Longest Sequence of League Defeats: 8, 30.9.95 – 18.11.95.

Longest Sequence of League Draws: 8, 25.10.69 – 13.12.69.

Longest Sequence of Unbeaten League Matches: 15, 5.5.90 – 3.11.90.

Longest Sequence Without a League Win: 17, 5.3.38 – 10.9.38.

HONOURS

Football League: Division 3 best season: 4th, 1967–68; Division 3 (S) – Runners-up 1956–57; Division 4 – Promoted 1959–60 (3rd), 1965–66 (3rd), 1990–91 (play-offs).

FA Cup: best season: 4th rd, 1949, 1955, 1971, 1983, 1990.

Football League Cup: never past 3rd rd.

Sherpa Van Trophy: Runners-up 1989.

Colours
Yellow and white striped shirts, navy shorts, navy stockings with yellow tops.

Change Colours
Blue shirts with yellow sleeves, yellow shorts, yellow stockings with blue tops.

Year Formed: 1899.

Turned Professional: 1921.

Ltd Co.: 1921.

Previous Name: 1910, Torquay Town; 1921, Torquay United.

Club Nickname: 'The Gulls'.

Previous Grounds: 1899, Teignmouth Road; 1900, Torquay Recreation Ground; 1904, Cricket Field Road; 1906, Torquay Cricket Ground; 1910, Plainmoor Ground.

First Football League Game: 27 August 1927, Division 3 (S), v Exeter C (h) D 1–1 – Millsom; Cook, Smith; Wellock, Wragg, Connor, Mackey, Turner (1), Jones, McGovern, Thomson.

Record League Victory: 9–0 v Swindon T, Division 3 (S), 8 March 1952 – George Webber; Topping, Ralph Calland; Brown, Eric Webber, Towers; Shaw (1), Marchant (1), Northcott (2), Collins (3), Edds (2).

Record Cup Victory: 7–1 v Northampton T, FA Cup 1st rd, 14 November 1959 – Gill; Penford, Downs; Bettany, George Northcott, Rawson; Baxter, Cox, Tommy Northcott (1), Bond (3), Pym (3).

Record Defeat: 2–10 v Fulham, Division 3 (S), 7 September 1931. 2–10 v Luton T, Division 3 (S), 2 September 1933.

Most League Points (2 for a win): 60, Division 4, 1959–60.

Most League Points (3 for a win): 77, Division 4, 1987–88.

Most League Goals: 89, Division 3 (S), 1956–57.

Highest League Scorer in Season: Sammy Collins, 40, Division 3 (S), 1955–56.

Most League Goals in Total Aggregate: Sammy Collins, 204, 1948–58.

Most League Goals in One Match: 5, Robin Stubbs v Newport Co, Division 4, 19 October 1963.

Most Capped Player: Rodney Jack, St Vincent.

Most League Appearances: Dennis Lewis, 443, 1947–59.

Youngest League Player: David Byng, 16 years 36 days v Walsall, 14 August 1993.

Record Transfer Fee Received: £500,000 from Crewe Alex for Rodney Jack, July 1998.

Record Transfer Fee Paid: £70,000 to Barry T for Eifion Williams, March 1999.

Football League Record: 1927 Elected to Division 3 (S); 1958–60 Division 4; 1960–62 Division 3; 1962–66 Division 4; 1966–72 Division 3; 1972–91 Division 4; 1991– Division 3.

MANAGERS

Percy Mackrill 1927–29
A. H. Hoskins 1929 *(Secretary-Manager)*
Frank Womack 1929–32
Frank Brown 1932–38
Alf Steward 1938–40
Billy Butler 1945–46
Jack Butler 1946–47
John McNeil 1947–50
Bob John 1950
Alex Massie 1950–51
Eric Webber 1951–65
Frank O'Farrell 1965–68
Alan Brown 1969–71
Jack Edwards 1971–73
Malcolm Musgrove 1973–76
Mike Green 1977–81
Frank O'Farrell 1981–82
  (continued as General Manager to 1983)
Bruce Rioch 1982–84
Dave Webb 1984–85
John Sims 1985
Stuart Morgan 1985–87
Cyril Knowles 1987–89
Dave Smith 1989–91
John Impey 1991–92
Ivan Golac 1992
Paul Compton 1992–93
Don O'Riordan 1993–95
Eddie May 1995–96
Kevin Hodges *(Head Coach)* 1996–98
Wes Saunders July 1998–

TEN YEAR LEAGUE RECORD

		P	W	D	L	F	A	Pts	Pos
1989-90	Div 4	46	15	12	19	53	66	57	15
1990-91	Div 4	46	18	18	10	64	47	72	7
1991-92	Div 3	46	13	8	25	42	68	47	23
1992-93	Div 3	42	12	7	23	45	67	43	19
1993-94	Div 3	42	17	16	9	64	56	67	6
1994-95	Div 3	42	14	13	15	54	57	55	13
1995-96	Div 3	46	5	14	27	30	84	29	24
1996-97	Div 3	46	13	11	22	46	62	50	21
1997-98	Div 3	46	21	11	14	68	59	74	5
1998-99	Div 3	46	12	17	17	47	58	53	20

DID YOU KNOW ?

Sid Cann was one of Torquay United's most famous discoveries. A schoolboy international, he made his debut at 17 in 1928, became Southampton's manager and later taught the game to Prince Charles at Cheam.

TORQUAY UNITED 1999–2000 LEAGUE RECORD

Match No.	Date		Venue	Opponents	Result	H/T Score	Lg. Pos.	Goalscorers	Attendance
1	Aug	7	A	Shrewsbury T	W 2-1	1-1	8	Bedeau [7], O'Brien [82]	2858
2		14	H	York C	D 0-0	0-0	8		3005
3		21	A	Brighton & HA	W 1-0	0-0	5	Williams [78]	5717
4		28	H	Chester C	D 2-2	0-1	8	Bedeau [47], Williams [69]	2345
5		31	A	Halifax T	L 0-2	0-2	—		1981
6	Sept	4	H	Lincoln C	W 5-2	4-1	8	Healy 2 (1 pen) [2, 90 (p)], Bedeau 2 [3, 25], Williams [14]	1833
7		11	H	Hull C	L 0-1	0-1	12		2466
8		18	A	Leyton Orient	W 2-0	1-0	7	O'Brien [3], Simba (og) [84]	4452
9		25	H	Barnet	L 0-1	0-0	10		2520
10	Oct	2	A	Macclesfield T	W 2-1	1-1	6	Bedeau 2 [40, 63]	2002
11		9	A	Northampton T	L 0-3	0-1	10		5003
12		16	H	Swansea C	W 1-0	0-0	9	Bedeau [68]	2488
13		19	H	Peterborough U	W 2-1	1-1	—	Williams [39], Brandon [53]	2000
14		23	A	Barnet	W 2-1	1-1	3	Ingimarsson [45], Brandon [76]	2334
15	Nov	2	A	Rotherham U	L 0-1	0-1	—		3892
16		6	H	Rochdale	W 1-0	0-0	4	Bedeau [69]	2351
17		12	A	Darlington	D 1-1	1-1	4	Thomas [55]	5434
18		23	H	Hartlepool U	D 0-0	0-0	—		2080
19		27	A	Exeter C	L 2-3	1-0	6	O'Brien [19], Griffiths [87]	5263
20	Dec	4	H	Shrewsbury T	W 3-1	0-0	6	Bedeau [63], Watson [68], Hanmer (og) [76]	2050
21		14	A	Carlisle U	D 0-0	0-0	—		2028
22		26	A	Plymouth Arg	D 2-2	0-1	7	Williams [52], Hill [75]	14,893
23		28	H	Southend U	L 0-1	0-0	10		3138
24	Jan	3	A	Mansfield T	L 3-4	2-3	11	Bromby (og) [13], Platts [28], O'Brien (pen) [86]	2876
25		8	H	Carlisle U	W 4-1	1-0	8	Healy [11], Griffiths [51], Brandon [82], Bedeau [84]	2112
26		15	A	York C	D 2-2	1-1	10	Healy [40], Bedeau [79]	2427
27		22	H	Brighton & HA	D 0-0	0-0	11		2760
28		29	A	Chester C	L 1-2	0-0	12	Watson [72]	2229
29	Feb	5	H	Halifax T	W 4-0	2-0	9	Bedeau [14], Brandon [38], Williams [56], Healy (pen) [61]	1856
30		12	A	Lincoln C	L 1-2	0-0	11	Williams [81]	2919
31		19	H	Exeter C	W 1-0	1-0	10	Watson [30]	3296
32		26	H	Leyton Orient	D 0-0	0-0	10		2470
33	Mar	4	A	Hull C	D 0-0	0-0	9		4668
34		11	H	Rotherham U	W 2-1	1-1	8	Healy (pen) [12], Stocco [49]	2655
35		14	H	Cheltenham T	D 1-1	0-1	—	Williams [80]	2378
36		18	A	Hartlepool U	L 0-2	0-1	10		2766
37		21	H	Darlington	W 1-0	1-0	—	Bedeau [8]	1938
38		25	H	Plymouth Arg	L 0-4	0-2	11		4113
39	Apr	1	A	Cheltenham T	L 0-2	0-1	11		5128
40		5	A	Rochdale	D 1-1	0-0	—	Hill [65]	1529
41		8	H	Mansfield T	W 4-0	3-0	10	Stocco [10], Thomas [20], Brandon [31], Griffiths [89]	1756
42		22	A	Swansea C	L 1-2	0-0	13	Watson [67]	6396
43		24	A	Macclesfield T	W 3-2	1-2	11	Bedeau [17], Healy (pen) [80], Williams [90]	2139
44		29	H	Peterborough U	W 2-0	2-0	10	Bedeau [40], Thomas [45]	8242
45	May	2	A	Southend U	W 2-0	0-0	—	Healy 2 (1 pen) [59, 81 (p)]	2563
46		6	H	Northampton T	L 1-2	1-2	9	Bedeau [17]	5010

Final League Position: 9

GOALSCORERS

League (62): Bedeau 16, Healy 9 (5 pens), Williams 9, Brandon 5, O'Brien 4 (1 pen), Watson 4, Griffiths 3, Thomas 3, Hill 2, Stocco 2, Ingimarsson 1, Platts 1, own goals 3.
Worthington Cup (0).
FA Cup (7): O'Brien 2, Bedeau 1, Brandon 1, Donaldson 1, Hill 1, Thomas 1.

Southall N 28	Tully S 10 + 3	Herrera R 34 + 1	Aggrey J 22 + 5	Russell L 35	Watson A 43	Brandon C 41 + 1	Healy B 37 + 1	Bedeau A 37 + 1	Williams E 38 + 4	O'Brien M 25 + 5	Platts M 7 + 15	Hill K 39 + 4	Simb J 1 + 10	Donaldson O 4 + 11	Thomas W 38 + 2	Forrester M — + 1	Nichols J 1	Griffiths M 8 + 14	Ingimarsson I 4	Holmes P 30	Neil G 4 + 3	Northmore R 2 + 1	Jones S 16	Stocco T 2 + 6	Gutteridge L — + 1	Match No.
1	2	3	4	5	6	7[1]	8	9	10	11	12															1
1	2	3	4	5	6	7	8[1]	9[2]	10	11		12	13													2
1	2	3	4	5	6	7[1]	8	9	10	11		12														3
1	2	3	4	5	6	7	8	9[1]	10	11				12												4
1	2[1]	3	4	5	6	7	8		10	11		12		9[2]	13											5
1	2		4	5	6	7	8	9[3]	10[2]	11[1]	12	3	13	14												6
1	2[1]		4	5[3]	6	7	8	9[2]	10	11		3	12	13	14											7
1		3		5	6	7[1]	8	9	10[2]	11	12	2	13		4											8
1	2			5	6	7[1]	8	9	10[2]	11	12	3	13		4											9
1	2			5	6	7[1]	8	9	10[2]	11	12	3	13		4											10
1	12	2		5	6	7[1]	8	9	10[2]	11		3	13		4											11
1	12	3		5	6	7	8	9	10[2]	11[1]		2	13		4											12
1	12	3	13	5	6	7	8	9[3]	10[2]	11[1]		2			4	14										13
1	2	4		6	7			10[1]		11	12	13	5	3	9[2]			8								14
1	2			5	6	7	9	10[1]	11[2]	12		3	4		13			8								15
1	2			5	6	7	8	9	10[1]		3	12	4		11											16
1		3		5	6	7	8	9[2]	10	12	13	4			11[1]					2						17
1		3		5	6	7	9	10[2]	11[1]	8	12	13	4							2						18
1		3	12	5	6	7[1]	9[3]	11[2]	8	13	10	4								2						19
1		3	12	5	6	7	9[2]	11	8	10	4[1]	13								2						20
1		3	4	5	7	9[2]	12	11	8	10[1]	6	13								2						21
1		3	4[1]	5	12	9	10	11	7	8	6									2						22
1		3[3]	12	5	6	9[2]	10	11	7[1]	8	4	13								2	14					23
1				5	6	8	9	10	11	7	3	4[1]			12					2						24
1				5	6	7	8[1]	9	10[2]	11	12	3	14	4	13					2						25
1				5	6	7	8	9	12	11	13	3[2]	4	10[1]						2						26
1				5	6	7[1]	9	11	8	3	13	10[2]	4	12						2						27
1[8]				5	6	7	8	9	10	11[2]	12	3[1]	4	2	13	15										28
				5	6	7	8[1]	9[2]	10[3]	12	11	3	14	4	13	2							1			29
	12	4[1]		5	6	7[2]	8	9	10	11		3	13	2									1			30
		3		5	6	7	8	9	10	11		4	2										1			31
		3[1]		5	6	7[2]	8	9	10	12	13	11[3]	4	14	2								1			32
		3		5[1]	6	7[2]	8	9	11	12		4	2	10	1	13										33
		3	4	5		8	10[1]	11		6		9	2	7	1	12										34
		3	4[1]	5	12	8	13	10	11	6		9[2]	2	7	1	13										35
		3	12	6	7	8	9	10	11[2]	4		2	5[1]	1	13											36
		3	4	5	7	8	9	10[1]	11	6	12	2	1													37
		3		5	6	7	8	9[1]	10	11	4	12	2	1												38
		3[2]	4	5	6	7	8	9	12	11[1]	10	13	2	1												39
		3	4	5	7	8	12	11	6	10		2	1	9[1]												40
		3	4	5[3]	7	8[2]	12	11	6	10		2	13	1	9[1]	14										41
		3	4[1]	5	7[3]	8	9[2]	12	13	11	6	10	2	1	14											42
		3	4	5	7	8	9[1]	12	11	6	10	2	1	13												43
		3	4	5	7	8	9	10[2]	12	11[1]	6	2	1	13												44
		3	4	5	7	8	9	10	12	11[1]	6	2	1													45
		3[1]	4	5	7[2]	8	9	10	12	11	6	2	1	13												46

Worthington Cup
First Round   Portsmouth   (h) 0-0
                           (a) 0-3

FA Cup
First Round   Southend U   (h) 1-0
Second Round   Forest Green R (a) 3-0
Third Round   QPR   (a) 1-1
                               (h) 2-3

FA Premiership **TOTTENHAM HOTSPUR**

FOUNDATION

The Hotspur Football Club was formed from an older cricket club in 1882. Most of the founders were old boys of St John's Presbyterian School and Tottenham Grammar School. The Casey brothers were well to the fore as the family provided the club's first goalposts (painted blue and white) and their first ball. They soon adopted the local YMCA as their meeting place, but after a couple of moves settled at the Red House, which is still their headquarters, although now known simply as 748 High Road.

Bill Nicholson Way, 748 High Rd, Tottenham, London N17 0AP.
Telephone: (020) 8365 5000. *Fax:* (020) 8365 5005.
Commercial Dept: (020) 8365 5010. *Ticketline:* 09068 100 505.
Ticket Office: (020) 8365 5050.
Spurs match information line: (08700) 112 222
Spurs Line: 09068 100 500. *Members Ticketline:* (020) 8365 5100.
Ground Capacity: 36,236.
Record Attendance: 75,038 v Sunderland, FA Cup 6th rd, 5 March 1938.
Record Receipts: £336,702 v Manchester U, Division 1, 28 September 1991.
Pitch Measurements: 110yd × 73yd.
Directors: Sir A. M. Sugar (Chairman), J. Sedgwick (Finance Director), David Pleat (Director of Football).
Non-Executive Directors: C. M. Littner. M. S. Peters MBE, I. Yawetz, C. T. Sandy.
President: W. E. Nicholson OBE.
Vice-Presidents: N. Solomon, D. A. Alexiou, A. G. Berry.
Manager: George Graham.
Assistant Manager: Stewart Houston.
Reserve Team Manager: Chris Hughton.
Chief Physio: Alasdair Beattie.
Physio: Gareth Robinson.
Club Secretary: John Alexander.
Commercial Manager: Mike Rollo.
PRO: John Fennelly.

HONOURS

Football League: Division 1 –
Champions 1950–51, 1960–61;
Runners-up 1921–22, 1951–52,
1956–57, 1962–63; Division 2 –
Champions 1919–20, 1949–50;
Runners-up 1908–09, 1932–33;
Promoted 1977–78 (3rd).

FA Cup: Winners 1901 (as non-League club), 1921, 1961, 1962, 1967, 1981, 1982, 1991; Runners-up 1987.

Football League Cup: Winners 1971, 1973, 1999; Runners-up 1982.

European Competitions: *European Cup:* 1961–62. *European Cup-Winners' Cup:* 1962–63 (winners), 1963–64, 1967–68, 1981–82, 1982–83, 1991–92. *UEFA Cup:* 1971–72 (winners), 1972–73, 1973–74 (runners-up), 1983–84 (winners), 1984–85, 1999–2000.

LATEST SEQUENCES

Longest Sequence of League Wins: 13, 23.4.60 – 1.10.60.
Longest Sequence of League Defeats: 7, 1.1.94 – 27.2.94.
Longest Sequence of League Draws: 6, 9.1.99 – 27.2.99.
Longest Sequence of Unbeaten League Matches: 22, 31.8.49 – 31.12.49.
Longest Sequence Without a League Win: 16, 29.12.34 – 13.4.35.

Colours
White shirts, navy blue shorts, navy blue stockings.

Change Colours
Navy and white, white shorts, white stockings.

Year Formed: 1882.

Turned Professional: 1895.

Ltd Co.: 1898.

Previous Name: 1882–84, Hotspur Football Club.

Club Nickname: 'Spurs'.

Previous Grounds: 1882, Tottenham Marshes; 1888, Northumberland Park; 1899, White Hart Lane.

First Football League Game: 1 September 1908, Division 2, v Wolverhampton W (h) W 3–0 – Hewitson; Coquet, Burton; Morris (1), D. Steel, Darnell; Walton, Woodward (2), Macfarlane, R. Steel, Middlemiss.

Record League Victory: 9–0 v Bristol R, Division 2, 22 October 1977 – Daines; Naylor, Holmes, Hoddle (1), McAllister, Perryman, Pratt, McNab, Moores (3), Lee (4), Taylor (1).

Record Cup Victory: 13–2 v Crewe Alex, FA Cup 4th rd (replay), 3 February 1960 – Brown; Hills, Henry; Blanchflower, Norman, Mackay; White, Harmer (1), Smith (4), Allen (5), Jones (3 incl. 1p).

Record Defeat: 0–8 v Cologne, UEFA Inter Toto Cup, 22 July 1995.

Most League Points (2 for a win): 70, Division 2, 1919–20.

Most League Points (3 for a win): 77, Division 1, 1984–85.

MANAGERS
Frank Brettell 1898–99
John Cameron 1899–1906
Fred Kirkham 1907–08
Peter McWilliam 1912–27
Billy Minter 1927–29
Percy Smith 1930–35
Jack Tresadern 1935–38
Peter McWilliam 1938–42
Arthur Turner 1942–46
Joe Hulme 1946–49
Arthur Rowe 1949–55
Jimmy Anderson 1955–58
Bill Nicholson 1958–74
Terry Neill 1974–76
Keith Burkinshaw 1976–84
Peter Shreeves 1984–86
David Pleat 1986–87
Terry Venables 1987–91
Peter Shreeves 1991–92
Ossie Ardiles 1993–94
Gerry Francis 1994–97
Christian Gross *(Head Coach)* 1997–98
George Graham October 1998–

Most League Goals: 115, Division 1, 1960–61.

Highest League Scorer in Season: Jimmy Greaves, 37, Division 1, 1962–63.

Most League Goals in Total Aggregate: Jimmy Greaves, 220, 1961–70.

Most League Goals in One Match: 5, Ted Harper v Reading, Division 2, 30 August 1930; 5, Alf Stokes v Birmingham C, Division 1, 18 September 1957; 5, Bobby Smith v Aston Villa, Division 1, 29 March 1958.

Most Capped Player: Pat Jennings, 74 (119), Northern Ireland.

Most League Appearances: Steve Perryman, 655, 1969–86.

Youngest League Player: Ally Dick, 16 years 301 days v Manchester C, 20 February 1982.

Record Transfer Fee Received: £5,500,000 from Lazio for Paul Gascoigne, May 1992.

Record Transfer Fee Paid: £11,000,000 to Dynamo Kiev for Sergei Rebrov, May 2000.

Football League Record: 1908 Elected to Division 2; 1909–15 Division 1; 1919–20 Division 2; 1920–28 Division 1; 1928–33 Division 2; 1933–35 Division 1; 1935–50 Division 2; 1950–77 Division 1; 1977–78 Division 2; 1978–92 Division 1; 1992– FA Premier League.

TEN YEAR LEAGUE RECORD

		P	W	D	L	F	A	Pts	Pos
1989-90	Div 1	38	19	6	13	59	47	63	3
1990-91	Div 1	38	11	16	11	51	50	49	10
1991-92	Div 1	42	15	7	20	58	63	52	15
1992-93	PR Lge	42	16	11	15	60	66	59	8
1993-94	PR Lge	42	11	12	19	54	59	45	15
1994-95	PR Lge	42	16	14	12	66	58	62	7
1995-96	PR Lge	38	16	13	9	50	38	61	8
1996-97	PR Lge	38	13	7	18	44	51	46	10
1997-98	PR Lge	38	11	11	16	44	56	44	14
1998-99	PR Lge	38	11	14	13	47	50	47	11

DID YOU KNOW ?

In 1884-85, the club's name was changed to Tottenham Hotspur to prevent confusion with another club called London Hotspur. Tottenham had been receiving mail addressed to the other club.

TOTTENHAM HOTSPUR 1999–2000 LEAGUE RECORD

Match No.	Date		Venue	Opponents	Result		H/T Score	Lg. Pos.	Goalscorers	Attendance
1	Aug	7	A	West Ham U	L	0-1	0-1	19		26,010
2		9	H	Newcastle U	W	3-1	2-1	—	Iversen [29], Ferdinand [45], Sherwood [61]	28,701
3		14	H	Everton	W	3-2	1-1	5	Sherwood [34], Leonhardsen [82], Iversen [86]	34,308
4		21	A	Sheffield W	W	2-1	2-1	2	Ferdinand [19], Leonhardsen [41]	24,027
5		28	H	Leeds U	L	1-2	1-0	7	Sherwood [36]	36,012
6	Sept	12	A	Bradford C	D	1-1	0-0	10	Perry [76]	18,143
7		19	H	Coventry C	W	3-2	1-0	9	Iversen [7], Armstrong [50], Leonhardsen [51]	35,224
8		26	A	Wimbledon	D	1-1	0-0	8	Carr [76]	17,368
9	Oct	3	H	Leicester C	L	2-3	2-1	10	Iversen 2 [26, 35]	35,591
10		16	A	Derby Co	W	1-0	1-0	8	Armstrong [37]	29,815
11		23	H	Manchester U	W	3-1	2-1	5	Iversen [37], Scholes (og) [40], Carr [71]	36,072
12		31	A	Sunderland	L	1-2	0-2	7	Iversen [63]	41,042
13	Nov	7	H	Arsenal	W	2-1	2-1	6	Iversen [7], Sherwood [20]	36,085
14		20	A	Southampton	W	1-0	0-0	6	Leonhardsen [81]	15,248
15		28	A	Newcastle U	L	1-2	1-1	7	Armstrong [44]	36,454
16	Dec	6	H	West Ham U	D	0-0	0-0	—		36,233
17		18	A	Middlesbrough	L	1-2	1-1	7	Vega [7]	33,113
18		26	H	Watford	W	4-0	2-0	6	Ginola [28], Iversen [33], Sherwood 2 [56, 83]	36,089
19		29	A	Aston Villa	D	1-1	1-0	—	Sherwood [44]	39,217
20	Jan	3	H	Liverpool	W	1-0	1-0	6	Armstrong [23]	36,044
21		12	A	Chelsea	L	0-1	0-0	—		34,969
22		15	A	Everton	D	2-2	2-1	7	Armstrong [24], Watson (og) [28]	36,144
23		22	H	Sheffield W	L	0-1	0-1	7		35,897
24	Feb	5	H	Chelsea	L	0-1	0-0	7		36,041
25		12	A	Leeds U	L	0-1	0-1	8		40,127
26		26	A	Coventry C	W	1-0	0-0	9	Armstrong [82]	23,073
27	Mar	4	H	Bradford C	D	1-1	1-1	9	Iversen [14]	35,472
28		11	H	Southampton	W	7-2	4-2	6	Richards (og) [28], Anderton [39], Armstrong 2 [41, 64], Iversen 3 [45, 78, 90]	36,024
29		19	A	Arsenal	L	1-2	1-2	7	Armstrong [31]	38,131
30		25	H	Watford	D	1-1	0-0	9	Armstrong [51]	20,050
31	Apr	3	H	Middlesbrough	L	2-3	1-1	—	Armstrong [31], Ginola [83]	31,804
32		9	A	Liverpool	L	0-2	0-1	11		44,536
33		15	H	Aston Villa	L	2-4	1-0	12	Iversen [16], Armstrong [47]	35,304
34		19	A	Leicester C	W	1-0	0-0	—	Ginola [90]	19,764
35		22	H	Wimbledon	W	2-0	2-0	10	Armstrong [8], Anderton [36]	33,089
36		29	H	Derby Co	D	1-1	0-0	9	Clemence [90]	33,061
37	May	6	A	Manchester U	L	1-3	1-3	10	Armstrong [20]	61,629
38		14	H	Sunderland	W	3-1	1-1	10	Anderton (pen) [10], Sherwood [74], Carr [82]	36,083

Final League Position: 10

GOALSCORERS

League (57): Armstrong 14, Iversen 14, Sherwood 8, Leonhardsen 4, Anderton 3 (1 pen), Carr 3, Ginola 3, Ferdinand 2, Clemence 1, Perry 1, Vega 1, own goals 3.
Worthington Cup (4): Ginola 1, Iversen 1, Leonhardsen 1, Sherwood 1.
FA Cup (2): Ginola 1, Iversen 1.

Walker I 38	Carr S 34	Edinburgh J 7+1	Freund S 24+3	Campbell S 29	Perry C 36+1	Anderton D 22	Sherwood T 23+4	Iversen S 36	Dominguez J 2+10	Ginola D 36	Scales J 3+1	Ferdinand L 5+4	Leonhardsen O 21+1	Taricco M 29	Young L 11+9	Nielsen A 5+9	Armstrong C 29+2	Vega R 2+3	King L 2+1	Piercy J 1+2	Fox R 1+2	Clemence S 16+4	Korsten W 4+5	Etherington M 1+4	Davies S 1+2	McEwen D —+1	Doherty G —+2	Match No.
1	2	3	4	5^1	6	7	8	9	10^2	11^3	12	13	14															1
1	2	13	5	7	8	9	12^2	11	4	10^1	6	3^3	14															2
1	2	12	5	7^1	8	9	11	4	10	6	3																	3
1	2	12	4	7	8	9	11^1	10	6	3	5																	4
1	2		4	6	8	9	12^2	11	10^1	7	3	5	13															5
1	2		4	6	8	9	11^1	10^2	7	3	5	12	13															6
1	2		4	6	8	10	12	11^1	7	3	5	13	9^2															7
1	2		4	6	8	10	12	11	3	5	7	9^1																8
1	2		4	6	8	10	11^1	7	3	5^2	12	9	13															9
1	2		5	6	12	10	11^1	7	3	8^2	9^3	13	4	14														10
1	2		4	6	8	9	11	7	3	5^1	12	13	10^2															11
1	2		4	6	12	14	9	13	11^2	7^3	3	5	10^1	8														12
1	2	3		5	6	4	10	12	11^1	7^2	9	13	8															13
1		3	4	5	6	8	10	12	11^1	7	2	9																14
1		3	4^2	5	6	8	10	12	11	7	2	9^1	13															15
1			4	5	6	8^2	9	10^1	11	7	3	2	13	12														16
1	12		8^2	5	6	13	10	11^1	3	2	7	9^3	4					14										17
1	2		5	6	4	10	12	11^1	3	8	9	7																18
1	2		5	6	8	10	11	3	12	4^1	9	7																19
1	2		5	6	8	10	11	3	4	9	7																	20
1	2	3	5	6	7	8	10	11	9	4																		21
1	2	3^1	5	6	7	8	10	11^2	12	13	9	4																22
1	2	3^1	5	6	7	8	10	11	12	13	9^3	4^2	14															23
1	2		5	6	7^1	8	10^2	11	3	12	9	4	13															24
1	2		5	6	7	8	12	11^1	3	13	9	4^2	10															25
1	2	4	5	6	7	8^2	11	10	3^1	12	9	13																26
1	2	4	5	6	7	10	11	12	8^1	3^2	13	9																27
1	2	4	5	6^1	7	10	11	8	3	12	9																	28
1	2	4	5^1	6	7	10^2	11^3	13	8	3	12	9	14															29
1	2	4	6	7	10^1	11	5	12	8^2	3	9	13																30
1	2	4	5	6	7	10	11	3	9	12	8^1																	31
1	2	4	5	6	7	10	11^2	3	9	8^1	12	13																32
1	2	4	5	6	7	10	11	3	9	8																		33
1	2	4	5	6	7	10^3	11	3^1	12	9^2	8	13	14															34
1	2	4	5	6	7	10	11^1	9	3	8	12																	35
1	2		5	6	7	10^3	11^2	3	9	4	8^1	13	12	14														36
1	2	4	5	6	7	10^2		9^3	12	3	13	11^1	8	14														37
1	2	4	5	6	7	12	10^2	11	8^1	9	3	13																38

Worthington Cup

Third Round	Crewe Alex	(h)	3-1
Fourth Round	Fulham	(a)	1-3

FA Cup

Third Round	Newcastle U	(h)	1-1
		(a)	1-6

Division 1

TRANMERE ROVERS

FOUNDATION

Formed in 1884 as Belmont they adopted their present title the following year and eventually joined their first league, the West Lancashire League in 1889–90, the same year as their first success in the Wirral Challenge Cup. The club almost folded in 1899–1900 when all the players left en bloc to join a rival club, but they survived the crisis and went from strength to strength winning the 'Combination' title in 1907–08 and the Lancashire Combination in 1913–14. They joined the Football League in 1921 from the Central League.

Prenton Park, Prenton Road West, Prenton, Wirral CH42 9PY.

Telephone: (0151) 609 3333.

Fax: (0151) 608 4385.

Shop: (0151) 608 0438.

Ticket Office: (0151) 609 0137.

ClubCall: 09068 121 646

Ground Capacity: 16,789 (all seated).

Record Attendance: 24,424 v Stoke C, FA Cup 4th rd, 5 February 1972.

Record Receipts: £130,541 v Sunderland, FA Cup 4th rd, 24 January 1998.

Pitch Measurements: 110yd × 70yd.

Chairperson and Chief Executive: Lorraine Rogers.

Directors: Lorraine Rogers, Mick Horton, Richard Hughes.

Secretary: Mick Horton.

Manager: John Aldridge.

Assistant Manager: Kevin Sheedy.

Youth Development Officer: Warwick Rimmer.

Coach and Chief Scout: Dave Philpotts.

Reserve Team Coach: Ray Mathias.

Physio: Les Parry.

LATEST SEQUENCES

Longest Sequence of League Wins: 9, 9.2.90 – 19.3.90.

Longest Sequence of League Defeats: 8, 29.10.38 – 17.12.38.

Longest Sequence of League Draws: 5, 26.12.97 – 31.1.98.

Longest Sequence of Unbeaten League Matches: 18, 16.3.70 – 4.9.70.

Longest Sequence Without a League Win: 16, 8.11.69 – 14.3.70.

HONOURS

Football League Division 1 best season: 4th, 1992–93; Promoted from Division 3 1990–91 (play-offs); Division 3 (N) – Champions 1937–38; Promotion to 3rd Division: 1966–67, 1975–76; Division 4 – Runners-up 1988–89.

FA Cup: best season: 6th rd, 2000.

Football League Cup: Runners-up, 2000.

Welsh Cup: Winners 1935; Runners-up 1934.

Leyland Daf Cup: Winners 1990; Runners-up 1991.

Colours
White shirts, blue shorts.

Change Colours
Navy and sky blue.

Year Formed: 1884.

Turned Professional: 1912.

Ltd Co.: 1920.

Previous Name: 1884, Belmont AFC; 1885, Tranmere Rovers.

Club Nickname: 'The Rovers'.

Previous Grounds: 1884, Steeles Field; 1887, Ravenshaws Field/Old Prenton Park; 1912, Prenton Park.

First Football League Game: 27 August 1921, Division 3 (N), v Crewe Alex (h) W 4–1 – Bradshaw; Grainger, Stuart (1); Campbell, Milnes (1), Heslop; Moreton, Groves (1), Hyam, Ford (1), Hughes.

Record League Victory: 13–4 v Oldham Ath, Division 3 (N), 26 December 1935 – Gray; Platt, Fairhurst; McLaren, Newton, Spencer; Eden, MacDonald (1), Bell (9), Woodward (2), Urmson (1).

Record Cup Victory: 13–0 v Oswestry U, FA Cup 2nd prel rd, 10 October 1914 – Ashcroft; Stevenson, Bullough, Hancock, Taylor, Holden (1), Moreton (1), Cunningham (2), Smith (5), Leck (3), Gould (1).

Record Defeat: 1–9 v Tottenham H, FA Cup 3rd rd (replay), 14 January 1953.

Most League Points (2 for a win): 60, Division 4, 1964–65.

Most League Points (3 for a win): 80, Division 4, 1988–89 and Division 3, 1989–90.

Most League Goals: 111, Division 3 (N), 1930–31.

Highest League Scorer in Season: Bunny Bell, 35, Division 3 (N), 1933–34.

Most League Goals in Total Aggregate: Ian Muir, 142, 1985–95.

Most League Goals in One Match: 9, Bunny Bell v Oldham Ath, Division 3N, 26 December 1935.

Most Capped Player: John Aldridge, 30 (69), Republic of Ireland.

Most League Appearances: Harold Bell, 595, 1946–64 (incl. League record 401 consecutive appearances).

Youngest League Player: Dixie Dean, 16 years 355 days v Rotherham Co, 12 January 1924.

Record Transfer Fee Received: £3,300,000 from Everton for Steve Simonsen, September 1998.

Record Transfer Fee Paid: £450,000 to Aston Villa for Shaun Teale, August 1995.

Football League Record: 1921 Original Member of Division 3 (N): 1938–39 Division 2; 1946–58 Division 3 (N); 1958–61 Division 3; 1961–67 Division 4; 1967–75 Division 3; 1975–76 Division 4; 1976–79 Division 3; 1979–89 Division 4; 1989–91 Division 3; 1991–92 Division 2; 1992– Division 1.

MANAGERS

Bert Cooke 1912–35
Jackie Carr 1935–36
Jim Knowles 1936–39
Bill Ridding 1939–45
Ernie Blackburn 1946–55
Noel Kelly 1955–57
Peter Farrell 1957–60
Walter Galbraith 1961
Dave Russell 1961–69
Jackie Wright 1969–72
Ron Yeats 1972–75
John King 1975–80
Bryan Hamilton 1980–85
Frank Worthington 1985–87
Ronnie Moore 1987
John King 1987–96
John Aldridge April 1996–

TEN YEAR LEAGUE RECORD

		P	W	D	L	F	A	Pts	Pos
1989-90	Div 3	46	23	11	12	86	49	80	4
1990-91	Div 3	46	23	9	14	64	46	78	5
1991-92	Div 2	46	14	19	13	56	56	61	14
1992-93	Div 1	46	23	10	13	72	56	79	4
1993-94	Div 1	46	21	9	16	69	53	72	5
1994-95	Div 1	46	22	10	14	67	58	76	5
1995-96	Div 1	46	14	17	15	64	60	59	13
1996-97	Div 1	46	17	14	15	63	56	65	11
1997-98	Div 1	46	14	14	18	54	57	56	14
1998-99	Div 1	46	12	20	14	63	61	56	15

DID YOU KNOW ❓

In 1913-14 Tranmere Rovers won the championship of the Lancashire Combination. Stan Rowlands was leading scorer with 32 goals and received international recognition from Wales to achieve the club's first such honour.

TRANMERE ROVERS 1999–2000 LEAGUE RECORD

Match No.	Date	Venue	Opponents	Result	H/T Score	Lg. Pos.	Goalscorers	Attendance
1	Aug 7	H	Bolton W	D 0-0	0-0	17		7674
2	14	A	Stockport Co	L 1-2	1-0	19	Henry [30]	6555
3	21	H	Huddersfield T	W 1-0	1-0	13	Koumas [8]	6728
4	28	A	Port Vale	L 0-1	0-0	18		4657
5	30	H	Sheffield U	L 1-3	1-3	21	Yates [35]	5436
6	Sept 3	A	Barnsley	L 0-3	0-1	—		12,865
7	11	A	Blackburn R	L 0-2	0-0	23		17,899
8	18	H	Portsmouth	L 2-4	0-3	24	Kelly [82], Challinor [90]	5870
9	25	H	Charlton Ath	D 2-2	1-1	24	Santos [30], Allison [86]	5846
10	Oct 3	A	Crewe Alex	W 2-0	0-0	22	Allison 2 [74, 85]	6169
11	9	A	QPR	L 1-2	0-1	24	Hill [54]	9357
12	16	H	Manchester C	D 1-1	0-0	23	Mahon (pen) [82]	13,208
13	19	H	Grimsby T	W 3-2	2-1	—	Allison 2 [12, 31], Jones G [59]	5004
14	23	A	Crystal Palace	D 2-2	0-2	20	Jones G [82], Parkinson [90]	18,645
15	26	A	Charlton Ath	L 2-3	2-0	—	Roberts [37], Parkinson [38]	19,491
16	30	H	Crewe Alex	W 2-0	0-0	17	Hill [63], Allison [80]	5987
17	Nov 6	H	WBA	W 3-0	2-0	14	Parkinson 2 [34, 38], Mahon (pen) [82]	6623
18	12	A	Ipswich T	D 0-0	0-0	13		14,514
19	20	H	Nottingham F	W 3-0	0-0	13	Hill [53], Allison [66], Kelly [90]	6693
20	23	A	Birmingham C	L 1-3	0-3	—	Grainger (og) [78]	21,132
21	27	H	Wolverhampton W	W 1-0	0-0	12	Allison [50]	8017
22	Dec 4	H	Bolton W	W 3-2	1-0	12	Parkinson [18], Challinor [63], Taylor S [79]	13,534
23	17	A	Norwich C	L 1-2	1-0	—	Allison [14]	5863
24	26	A	Walsall	W 2-1	0-0	13	Parkinson [67], Allison [74]	7214
25	28	H	Swindon T	W 3-1	3-1	11	Hill [11], Allison 2 [13, 26]	8068
26	Jan 3	A	Fulham	L 0-1	0-1	13		11,377
27	15	H	Stockport Co	D 0-0	0-0	13		7565
28	22	A	Huddersfield T	L 0-1	0-1	14		12,653
29	Feb 5	A	Sheffield U	L 1-3	0-0	16	Taylor S [57]	14,219
30	11	H	Barnsley	D 2-2	1-1	—	Parkinson [16], Kelly [56]	7127
31	16	A	Wolverhampton W	L 0-4	0-2	—		18,186
32	Mar 1	A	Portsmouth	W 2-1	1-0	—	Hazell [33], Yates [90]	10,759
33	4	H	Blackburn R	W 2-1	0-0	15	Mahon (pen) [47], Allison [89]	9502
34	7	A	WBA	L 0-2	0-1	—		11,958
35	11	A	Birmingham C	W 2-1	1-1	13	Koumas [4], Jones G [83]	9232
36	18	A	Nottingham F	D 1-1	1-0	14	Allison [34]	14,428
37	22	H	Ipswich T	L 0-2	0-1	—		6933
38	25	H	Walsall	D 1-1	1-0	14	Allison [4]	6537
39	Apr 1	A	Norwich C	D 1-1	1-1	14	Sutch (og) [38]	13,734
40	9	H	Fulham	D 1-1	0-0	14	Kelly [72]	7132
41	15	A	Swindon T	L 1-3	1-2	14	Hill [37]	4925
42	18	H	Port Vale	W 2-1	0-1	—	Kelly 2 [60, 89]	5602
43	22	A	Manchester C	L 0-2	0-1	13		32,842
44	24	H	QPR	D 1-1	0-1	13	Mahon [52]	7744
45	29	A	Grimsby T	W 2-1	1-1	13	Challinor [12], Allison [82]	5427
46	May 7	H	Crystal Palace	L 1-2	0-2	13	Taylor S [46]	8891

Final League Position: 13

GOALSCORERS

League (57): Allison 16, Parkinson 7, Kelly 6, Hill 5, Mahon 4 (3 pens), Challinor 3, Jones G 3, Taylor S 3, Koumas 2, Yates 2, Hazell 1, Henry 1, Roberts 1, Santos 1, own goals 2.
Worthington Cup (23): Kelly 8, Taylor S 3, Hill 2, Parkinson 2, Black 1, Grant 1, Henry 1, Mahon 1 (pen), Morgan 1, Taylor P 1, Yates 1, own goal 1.
FA Cup (6): Allison 3, Henry 1, Jones G 1, Kelly 1.

Achterberg J 24 + 2	Yates S 32 + 1	Thompson A 10 + 5	Henry N 28 + 2	Allen G 21 + 3	Hazell R 21 + 2	Mahon A 33 + 3	Santos G 9 + 1	Parkinson A 30 + 7	Taylor S 23 + 12	Koumas J 9 + 14	Black M 7 + 15	Kelly D 25 + 7	Hill C 28 + 1	Roberts G 36 + 1	Matias P 1 + 3	Jones G 27 + 4	Challinor D 39 + 2	Allison W 40	Grant T 8 + 1	Jones L 3 + 11	Morgan A 20 + 6	Murphy J 21	Frail S 1 + 2	Nixon E 1 + 1	Babb P 4	Hinds R 5 + 1	Aldridge P — + 4	Hume I — + 3	Match No.
1	2	3	4	5	6	7¹	8	9²	10	11	12	13																	1
1	6	7	5	2²		8	14	10²	13	11	12	4	3	9¹															2
1	2	3	4	5		12	8	10²	11¹	7³	9	6					13	14											3
1	2	3		5		7	8	12	11¹	10³	6²	9	4				13	14											4
1	2	3	4	5		8	12	10¹	11²	7³	9	14					13	6											5
1	2	3	4²	5		8	12	14				13	9¹	11¹			6	10	7										6
1	2			5		7	8	9¹	10²	12			3	13			4	11³	6	14									7
1	2	3¹		5¹		8		9²	11	12	10			4			6		13	14	7								8
1	2			5²		7	8	12				9¹	4	3			6	10	11	13									9
1	2	12	13	5		7²	8	9³				4	3¹				6	10	11	14									10
1	2		4	5¹		7		12	11²			8	3				6	10	9	13									11
	2		4²			7		12	11³	14	5	3	13	6	10	8	9¹					1							12
	2	12	4			7	8¹		13		5	3	9	6	10	11²						1							13
15	2		4			7		12	13		5	3	9	6	10	8¹	11²					1⁶							14
	2	12	4	3²		7	8		13		5	11¹	9	6	10							1							15
	2		4			7	8	11¹	12		5	3	9	6	10							1							16
	2	12	4			7²	8	13		14	5	3	9³	6	10	11¹						1							17
	6¹	12	11	2	4	7	8²	13			5	3	9		10							1							18
	2			7¹		8	11²	12	13	14	5	3	9	6	10³	4	1												19
1	2	12		7²		8	11¹	13	14	5	3	9	6	10³	4														20
15	2	12		7¹		8		11	5	3	9	6	10	4	1⁶														21
	13	2	7			8	14	12²	11¹	5	3	9	6	10³	4	1													22
1		4	12	2	7¹	8	13	14	11²		3	9	6	10	5³														23
1	2	4³	3¹	7²		8	13	12	11			9	6	10	5		14												24
1	12	4²	2¹	13		8	11	7		5	3²	9	6	10	14														25
1	2²		8	12	7	11¹	5	3	9	6	10	4	13																26
1	2¹	12	7²	8	11³	13	14	5	3	9	6	10	4																27
		3	2	5	7	12	11¹	13	9²			10	14	4	8¹	1	6												28
1		3	4	2	7	8²	11³	12	13	14	9¹	5	10	6															29
1		3	4	2	7¹	8	9	12			6	10	11	5															30
1		3¹	4	2	7³	9²	11	13	12	5	10	14	8	6															31
8		4	2	7	11¹	12	5	3	9	6	10	1																	32
6		4	2	7²	11¹	12	8³	3	9	5	10	13	14	1															33
6		4¹	2	8²	13	7³	11	3	9	5	10	14	12	1															34
6		4	2	7¹	8²	11	3	9	5	10	13	12	1																35
5		4	2	7³	12	8²	11¹	3	9	10	13	6	1	14															36
4	6	2	8¹	12	13	11	3	9	5	10	7²	1																	37
4²	6	2	8	12	7¹	14	11³	3	9	5	10	13	1																38
1⁶		5	2	8	7	11	3	9	6	10	4	15																	39
4	5	2	12	8	11¹	9	3	13	6	10	7²	1																	40
4	7²	2	8²	12	11	5	3¹	9	6	10	1	13	14																41
1	12	2¹	8	11	5	3	9	6	10	4	7																		42
2	8³	12	11	5	3	9¹	6	10	4	1	7²	13	14																43
1	2	7	8	9	5	3	6	10	4	11																			44
1	2	7	8¹	13	12	9²	5	3	6	10	4³	11	14																45
2	7	8	9²	4¹	5	3	6	10	12	1	11³	14	13																46

Worthington Cup

First Round	Blackpool	(a)	1-2
		(h)	3-1
Second Round	Coventry C	(h)	5-1
		(a)	1-3
Third Round	Oxford U	(h)	2-0
Fourth Round	Barnsley	(h)	4-0
Fifth Round	Middlesbrough	(h)	2-1
Semi-Final	Bolton W	(a)	1-0
		(h)	3-0
Final (at Wembley)	Leicester C		1-2

FA Cup

Third Round	West Ham U	(h)	1-0
Fourth Round	Sunderland	(h)	1-0
Fifth Round	Fulham	(a)	2-1
Sixth Round	Newcastle U	(h)	2-3

Division 2

WALSALL

FOUNDATION

Two of the leading clubs around Walsall in the 1880s were Walsall Swifts (formed 1877) and Walsall Town (formed 1879). The Swifts were winners of the Birmingham Senior Cup in 1881, while the Town reached the 4th round (5th round modern equivalent) of the FA Cup in 1883. These clubs amalgamated as Walsall Town Swifts in 1888, becoming simply Walsall in 1895.

Bescot Stadium, Bescot Crescent, Walsall WS1 4SA.
Telephone: (01922) 622 791.
Fax: (01922) 613 202.
Commercial Dept: (01922) 651 412.
Website: www.saddlers.co.uk
Email: wfc@saddlers.co.uk
ClubCall: 09068 555 800.
Ground Capacity: 9000.
Record Attendance: 10,628 B International, England v Switzerland, 20 May 1991.
Record Receipts: £98,828 v Leeds U, FA Cup 3rd rd, 7 January 1995.
Pitch Measurements: 110yd × 73yd.
Chairman and Managing Director: M. N. Lloyd.
Directors: J. W. Bonser, R. E. Tisdale, C. Welch, K. R. Whalley.
Chief Executive: K. R. Whalley.
Director of Finance: K. Avery. *Director of Football:* P. Taylor.
Director of Conference and Banqueting Services: C. Deakin.
Manager: Ray Graydon.
General Manager: Paul Taylor.
Physio: Tom Bradley.
Secretary/Commercial Manager: Roy Whalley.
Year Formed: 1888.
Turned Professional: 1888.
Ltd Co.: 1921.
Previous Names: Walsall Swifts (founded 1877) and Walsall Town (founded 1879) amalgamated in 1888 and were known as Walsall Town Swifts until 1895.
Club Nickname: 'The Saddlers'.

LATEST SEQUENCES

Longest Sequence of League Wins: 7, 10.10.59 – 21.11.59.
Longest Sequence of League Defeats: 15, 29.10.88 – 4.2.89.
Longest Sequence of League Draws: 5, 7.5.88 – 17.9.88.
Longest Sequence of Unbeaten League Matches: 21, 6.11.79 – 22.3.80.
Longest Sequence Without a League Win: 18, 15.10.88 – 4.2.89.

HONOURS

Football League: Division 2: Runners-up, 1998–99; Division 3 – Runners-up 1960–61, 1994–95; Division 4 – Champions 1959–60; Runners-up 1979–80.

FA Cup: best season: 5th rd, 1939, 1975, 1978, 1987 and last 16 1889.

Football League Cup: Semi-final 1984.

Colours

Red shirts with black shoulder panel, black shorts with white trim, red stockings with white band.

Change Colours

Royal blue shirts with yellow side panel, royal blue shorts with yellow side panel, royal blue stockings with white band.

Previous Grounds: 1888, Fellows Park; 1990, Bescot Stadium.

First Football League Game: 3 September 1892, Division 2, v Darwen (h) L 12 – Hawkins; Withington, Pinches; Robinson, Whitrick, Forsyth; Marshall, Holmes, Turner, Gray (1), Pangbourn.

Record League Victory: 10–0 v Darwen, Division 2, 4 March 1899 – Tennent; E. Peers (1), Davies; Hickinbotham, Jenkyns, Taggart; Dean (3), Vail (2), Aston (4), Martin, Griffin.

Record Cup Victory: 7–0 v Macclesfield T (a), FA Cup 2nd rd, 6 December 1997 – Walker; Evans, Marsh, Viveash (1), Ryder, Peron, Boli (2 incl. 1p) (Ricketts), Porter (2), Keates, Watson (Platt), Hodge (2 incl. 1p).

Record Defeat: 0–12 v Small Heath, 17 December 1892. 0–12 v Darwen, 26 December 1896, both Division 2.

Most League Points (2 for a win): 65, Division 4, 1959–60.

Most League Points (3 for a win): 87, Division 2, 1998–99.

Most League Goals: 102, Division 4, 1959–60.

Highest League Scorer in Season: Gilbert Alsop, 40, Division 3 (N), 1933–34 and 1934–35.

Most League Goals in Total Aggregate: Tony Richards, 184, 1954–63; Colin Taylor, 184, 1958–63, 1964–68, 1969–73.

Most League Goals in One Match: 5, Gilbert Alsop v Carlisle U, Division 3N, 2 February 1935; 5, Bill Evans v Mansfield T, Division 3N, 5 October 1935; 5, Johnny Devlin v Torquay U, Division 3S, 1 September 1949.

Most Capped Player: Mick Kearns, 15 (18), Republic of Ireland.

Most League Appearances: Colin Harrison, 467, 1964–82.

Youngest League Player: Geoff Morris, 16 years 218 days v Scunthorpe U, 14 September 1965.

Record Transfer Fee Received: £600,000 from West Ham U for David Kelly, July 1988.

Record Transfer Fee Paid: £175,000 to Birmingham C for Alan Buckley, June 1979.

Football League Record: 1892 Elected to Division 2; 1895 Failed re-election; 1896–1901 Division 2; 1901 Failed re-election; 1921 Original Member of Division 3 (N); 1927–31 Division 3 (S); 1931–36 Division 3 (N); 1936–58 Division 3 (S); 1958–60 Division 4; 1960–61 Division 3; 1961–63 Division 2; 1963–79 Division 3; 1979–80 Division 4; 1980–88 Division 3; 1988–89 Division 2; 1989–90 Division 3; 1990–92 Division 4; 1992–95 Division 3; 1995–99 Division 2; 1999–2000 Division 1; 2000– Division 2.

MANAGERS

H. Smallwood 1888–91
(Secretary-Manager)
A. G. Burton 1891–93
J. H. Robinson 1893–95
C. H. Ailso 1895–96
(Secretary-Manager)
A. E. Parsloe 1896–97
(Secretary-Manager)
L. Ford 1897–98
(Secretary-Manager)
G. Hughes 1898–99
(Secretary-Manager)
L. Ford 1899–1901
(Secretary-Manager)
J. E. Shutt 1908–13
(Secretary-Manager)
Haydn Price 1914–20
Joe Burchell 1920–26
David Ashworth 1926–27
Jack Torrance 1927–28
James Kerr 1928–29
Sid Scholey 1929–30
Peter O'Rourke 1930–32
Bill Slade 1932–34
Andy Wilson 1934–37
Tommy Lowes 1937–44
Harry Hibbs 1944–51
Tony McPhee 1951
Brough Fletcher 1952–53
Major Frank Buckley 1953–55
John Love 1955–57
Billy Moore 1957–64
Alf Wood 1964
Reg Shaw 1964–68
Dick Graham 1968
Ron Lewin 1968–69
Billy Moore 1969–72
John Smith 1972–73
Doug Fraser 1973–77
Dave Mackay 1977–78
Alan Ashman 1978
Frank Sibley 1979
Alan Buckley 1979–86
Neil Martin *(Joint Manager with Buckley)* 1981–82
Tommy Coakley 1986–88
John Barnwell 1989–90
Kenny Hibbitt 1990–94
Chris Nicholl 1994–97
Jan Sorensen 1997–98
Ray Graydon May 1998–

TEN YEAR LEAGUE RECORD

		P	W	D	L	F	A	Pts	Pos
1989-90	Div 3	46	9	14	23	40	72	41	24
1990-91	Div 4	46	12	17	17	48	51	53	16
1991-92	Div 4	42	12	13	17	48	58	49	15
1992-93	Div 3	42	22	7	13	76	61	73	5
1993-94	Div 3	42	17	9	16	48	53	60	10
1994-95	Div 3	42	24	11	7	75	40	83	2
1995-96	Div 2	46	19	12	15	60	45	69	11
1996-97	Div 2	46	19	10	17	54	53	67	12
1997-98	Div 2	46	14	12	20	43	52	54	19
1998-99	Div 2	46	26	9	11	63	47	87	2

DID YOU KNOW ?

On 16 December 1957 the official opening of Fellows Park floodlights attracted a crowd of 6196 for the friendly visit of Falkirk. Walsall won 5-1 with Tom Brownlee scoring a hat-trick.

WALSALL 1999–2000 LEAGUE RECORD

Match No.	Date		Venue	Opponents	Result	H/T Score	Lg. Pos.	Goalscorers	Attendance
1	Aug	7	H	Swindon T	D	0-0	0-0	18		6437
2		14	A	Sheffield U	D	1-1	1-1	14	Wrack [38]	12,581
3		21	H	Crewe Alex	L	1-4	1-1	19	Robins [9]	6238
4		28	A	Wolverhampton W	W	2-1	2-1	15	Barras [3], Rammell [45]	24,439
5		30	H	Norwich C	D	2-2	1-1	11	Barras [3], Wrack [50]	6187
6	Sept	4	H	Nottingham F	L	1-4	1-1	15	Robins [4]	15,081
7		11	A	Grimsby T	L	0-1	0-0	17		6014
8		18	H	Manchester C	L	0-1	0-1	21		7260
9		25	A	Blackburn R	L	0-2	0-2	22		18,232
10	Oct	2	H	Stockport Co	L	1-2	0-1	24	Ricketts [90]	5492
11		8	H	Birmingham C	W	1-0	0-0	—	Rammell [74]	7164
12		16	A	WBA	W	1-0	0-0	20	Rammell [57]	19,562
13		19	A	Portsmouth	L	1-5	1-1	—	Wrack [10]	9042
14		23	H	Ipswich T	L	0-1	0-0	23		6526
15		26	H	Blackburn R	L	1-1	0-1	—	Ricketts [85]	6484
16		30	A	Stockport Co	D	1-1	0-0	21	Ricketts [71]	6592
17	Nov	6	A	Charlton Ath	L	1-2	1-1	22	Bukran [36]	18,663
18		12	H	Port Vale	D	0-0	0-0	21		6190
19		20	A	QPR	L	1-2	1-2	23	Ricketts [41]	10,058
20		23	H	Huddersfield T	W	2-0	2-0	—	Robins [7], Rammell [45]	5860
21		26	H	Fulham	L	1-3	1-1	—	Matias [45]	5449
22	Dec	4	A	Swindon T	D	1-1	1-1	23	Wrack [34]	7186
23		18	A	Barnsley	L	2-3	0-1	23	Keates [56], Roper [73]	13,300
24		26	H	Tranmere R	L	1-2	0-0	23	Bukran [47]	7214
25		28	A	Crystal Palace	L	2-3	1-1	23	Ricketts 2 [32, 82]	13,943
26	Jan	3	H	Bolton W	W	2-0	0-0	23	Ricketts [63], Matias [90]	6873
27		15	H	Sheffield U	W	2-1	0-1	21	Viveash [58], Robins [82]	6222
28		22	A	Crewe Alex	W	3-2	3-1	21	Bennett [17], Ricketts [33], Harper [45]	6275
29		29	A	Wolverhampton W	D	1-1	0-0	21	Barras [80]	9422
30	Feb	5	A	Norwich C	D	1-1	1-1	21	Ricketts [36]	16,837
31		12	H	Nottingham F	L	0-2	0-1	21		8027
32		19	A	Fulham	L	0-2	0-0	21		10,540
33		26	A	Manchester C	D	1-1	1-0	21	Matias [43]	32,438
34	Mar	4	H	Grimsby T	W	1-0	1-0	20	Robins [39]	5384
35		7	H	Charlton Ath	L	2-4	1-3	—	Robins (pen) [24], Vlachos [65]	6227
36		11	A	Huddersfield T	D	1-1	0-0	22	Eyjolfsson [75]	12,424
37		18	H	QPR	L	2-3	1-2	22	Barras [36], Hall [63]	6414
38		21	A	Port Vale	W	2-1	2-0	—	Matias [12], Fenton [45]	5737
39		25	A	Tranmere R	D	1-1	0-1	21	Ricketts (pen) [67]	6537
40	Apr	1	H	Barnsley	L	1-4	0-0	22	Hall [46]	7218
41		8	A	Bolton W	L	3-4	1-3	22	Hall [1], Ricketts [56], Bennett [83]	11,777
42		15	H	Crystal Palace	D	2-2	0-0	22	Matias [83], Hall [90]	6323
43		22	H	WBA	W	2-1	0-1	21	Rammell [48], Bennett [83]	9161
44		24	A	Birmingham C	L	0-2	0-0	22		24,268
45		29	H	Portsmouth	W	1-0	1-0	22	Matias [13]	8151
46	May	7	A	Ipswich T	L	0-2	0-0	22		21,908

Final League Position: 22

GOALSCORERS

League (52): Ricketts 11 (1 pen), Matias 6, Robins 6 (1 pen), Rammell 5, Barras 4, Hall 4, Wrack 4, Bennett 3, Bukran 2, Eyjolfsson 1, Fenton 1, Harper 1, Keates 1, Roper 1, Viveash 1, Vlachos 1.
Worthington Cup (10): Bukran 3, Eyjolfsson 3, Barras 1, Brissett 1, Keates 1, Robins 1.
FA Cup (2): Larusson 1, Robins 1 (pen).

Walker J 43	Marsh C 40	Pointon N 18	Viveash A 41+2	Barras T 19+5	Bukran G 33+4	Wrack D 34+10	Robins M 30+10	Rammell A 21+9	Keates D 27+8	Daley T 3+4	Larusson B 12+11	Ricketts M 21+11	Mavrak D 1+3	Eyjolfsson S 1+12	Roper J 32+2	Brissett J 5+2	Emberson C 3+2	Todd L 1	Carter A 1	Abou S 7+1	Matias P 30+3	Keister J —+1	Bica —+1	Padula G 23+2	Thomas W —+1	Gadsby M 1+2	Harper K 8+1	Forrester J 2+3	Bennett T 11	Brightwell I 9+1	Vlachos M 11	Fenton G 8+1	Hall P 10	Match No
1	2	3	4	5	6	7¹	8	9	10²	11	12	13																						1
1	2	3	4	5	6	7	8	9			11¹	10		12																				2
1	2	3²	4	5	6¹	7	8	9	12		11³	10	13	14																				3
1	2	3	4	5	6	7	8	9²	10	12					13						11¹													4
1	2	3	4	5	6	7	8²	9	10	12					13						11¹													5
1	2	3	4	5	6	7	8⁶	9²	10	12					13						11¹		15											6
1	2	3	4		6²	7	8		10	12	13	9³	14		5						11¹													7
	2			5	6	7	8¹		10	9	11²	12	4	13	1	3																		8
1	2	3	12	5	6	7	8²	9	10³		13	14	4								11¹													9
1	2	3	4	12	6²	7	13	9¹	10	14					5						11³			8										10
1	2	3	4		7	12	9	10²	8	13					5						6¹			11³	14									11
1	2	3	4	12	7		9¹	10	8	13					5						6³			11²	14									12
1⁶	2	3	4	12	7	13	9	10¹	8						5	15					6			11²										13
1	2	3	4		6	7	12	9	10						5	13					8²			11¹										14
1	2	3	4	12	6	7	13	9²	10		14				5¹						8³			11										15
1	2	3	4		6	7	9		10		12				5						8¹			11										16
1	2	3	4		6	7	9		8	10					5						12			11¹										17
1	2	3¹	4		6	7	9	8¹	10	12	5				11									13										18
1	2	3	4		6²	7	9	12	8	10¹					5						11³			14	13									19
1	2		4		6	7	8¹	9	10	12					5						11			3										20
1	2		4		6	7	8³	9	10¹	12	13				5						11²			3	14									21
1	2	3	4		6²	7	8	9¹	10	13	12				5						11			3										22
1	2		4		6	7	9	10	12	8¹					5						11²			3							13			23
1	2		4		6	7	8²	9	10	12	13				5						11¹			3										24
1	2		4		6	7	12	9¹	10²	13	8				14						11³			3										25
1	2		4	5	6	7	12	13	9¹		14				3						11³			8²		10								26
1	2		4		6	7³	12	13	9²	5					14						3			11		8¹	10							27
1	2		4	6¹	12	8³	13	14	9²	5					11						3			7		10								28
1	2		4	6	12	8²		9		5					11¹						3			7	13	10								29
1	2¹	12	4	6	7	8²		10	13	9					5³						3			14	11									30
1			4	5	6²	7	8³	12	10	13	9¹				3						11			14	2									31
1			4	5	6²	7	8	12³	10	13	9¹				3						11			14	2									32
1			4	5	6	7	12		9¹						11						3			10			2	8						33
1			4	5	6¹	7	8	12	13	9²					11						3						2	10						34
1			4	5	6¹	7	8²	12	9	13					11						3						2	10						35
1			4	5¹		7	8²	13	10	9³	14	12			11						3						2	6						36
1	2		4	5	12	9		10	13						11						3			6					8²			7¹		37
1	2		4¹	12	6	9		13		5					11						3³			14			10		8²			7		38
1	2		4¹	12		13	9²	14		5					11						6			3			10		8²			7		39
1	3		4	12		13	14	9²		5					11						6			2			10³		8			7¹		40
1	2		4		12	13	14	3	9³	5					11						6			10¹					8²			7		41
	3		4	12		13	14	9²		5		1			11						6			2			10³		8¹			7		42
	2		4	12	8²		9	10		5		1			11						3			6					13			7¹		43
1	2		4	12		13	8³	9	6	14		5¹			11²						3			10					7					44
1	2		4	12			9	10		5					11						3			6					8¹			7		45
1	2		4	12		13	14	9²	10	5					11						3¹			6					8³			7		46

Worthington Cup

First Round	Plymouth Arg	(h)	4-1	
		(a)	4-1	
Second Round	Sunderland	(a)	2-3	
		(h)	0-5	

FA Cup

Third Round	Gillingham	(h)	1-1	
		(a)	1-2	

Division 1

WATFORD

FOUNDATION

The club was formed as Watford Rovers in 1881. The name was changed to West Herts in 1893 and then the name Watford was adopted after rival club Watford St Mary's was absorbed in 1898.

Vicarage Road Stadium, Watford WD1 8ER.
Telephone: (01923) 496 000. ***Fax:*** (01923) 496 001.
Ticket and Prizeline: 09068 400 401. ***Ticket Office:*** (01923) 496 010. ***Ticket Office Fax:*** (01923) 351 145.
ClubCall: 09068 104 104. ***Club Shop:*** (01923) 496 005. ***Club Shop Fax:*** (01923) 496 238.
Catering: (01923) 252 323. ***Football in the Community:*** (01923) 440 449.
Junior Hornets Club: (01923) 496 256.
Marketing: (01923) 496 006. ***Press Office:*** (01923) 496 234.
Ground Capacity: 20,800.
Record Attendance: 34,099 v Manchester U, FA Cup 4th rd (replay), 3 February 1969.
Record Receipts: £440,349 v Chelsea, FA Premier League, 18 September 1999.
Pitch Measurements: 113yd × 73yd.
Life Presidents: Sir Elton John CBE, Geoff Smith.
Chairman: Sir Elton John CBE.
Vice Chairman: Haig Oundjian.
Directors: B. Anderson, D. Meller, D. Lester, C. Lissack, C. Norton, G. Simpson, M. Sherwood, N. Wray
Executive Director: Tim Shaw.
Football Secretary: Catherine Alexander.
Football Manager: Graham Taylor.
First Team Coach: Kenny Jackett.
Coach: Luther Blissett.
Reserve Team Manager: Tom Walley.
Academy Director: John McDermott.
Academy Assistant Directors: Chris Cummins, David Hockaday.
Press and Publications Officer: Andrew French.
Director of Marketing and Communications: Ed Coan.
Safety Officer: Paul Dumpleton.
Stadium Manager: Paddy Flavin.

LATEST SEQUENCES

Longest Sequence of League Wins: 7, 26.12.77 – 28.1.78.
Longest Sequence of League Defeats: 9, 26.12.72 – 27.2.73.
Longest Sequence of League Draws: 7, 30.11.96 – 27.1.97.
Longest Sequence of Unbeaten League Matches: 22, 1.10.96 – 1.3.97.
Longest Sequence Without a League Win: 19, 27.11.71 – 8.4.72.

HONOURS

Football League: Division 1 – Runners-up 1982–83, promoted from Division 1 1998–99 (play-offs); Division 2 – Champions 1997–98; Runners-up 1981–82; Division 3 – Champions 1968–69; Runners-up 1978–79; Division 4 – Champions 1977–78; Promoted 1959–60 (4th).

FA Cup: Runners-up 1984.

Football League Cup: Semi- final 1979.

European Competitions: UEFA Cup: 1983–84.

Colours

Yellow shirts with red and black piping on sleeves, black collar with red and yellow bands. Red shorts with yellow and black trim. Red stockings with yellow top.

Change Colours

White shirts with two black and one yellow band down either side. Black shorts with yellow trim. Black stockings with red and yellow trim.

Year Formed: 1881.

Turned Professional: 1897.

Ltd Co.: 1909.

Club Nickname: 'The Hornets'.

Previous Names: 1881, Watford Rovers; 1893, West Herts; 1898, Watford.

Previous Grounds: 1883, Vicarage Meadow, Rose and Crown Meadow; 1889, Colney Butts; 1890, Cassio Road; 1922, Vicarage Road.

First Football League Game: 28 August 1920, Division 3, v QPR (a) W 2–1 – Williams; Horseman, F. Gregory; Bacon, Toone, Wilkinson; Bassett, Ronald (1), Hoddinott, White (1), Waterall.

Record League Victory: 8–0 v Sunderland, Division 1, 25 September 1982 – Sherwood; Rice, Rostron, Taylor, Terry, Bolton, Callaghan (2), Blissett (4), Jenkins (2), Jackett, Barnes.

Record Cup Victory: 10–1 v Lowestoft T, FA Cup 1st rd, 27 November 1926 – Yates; Prior, Fletcher (1); F. Smith, 'Bert' Smith, Strain; Stephenson, Warner (3), Edmonds (3), Swan (1), Daniels (1), (1 og).

Record Defeat: 0–10 v Wolverhampton W, FA Cup 1st rd (replay), 24 January 1912.

Most League Points (2 for a win): 71, Division 4, 1977–78.

Most League Points (3 for a win): 88, Division 2, 1997–98.

Most League Goals: 92, Division 4, 1959–60.

Highest League Scorer in Season: Cliff Holton, 42, Division 4, 1959–60.

Most League Goals in Total Aggregate: Luther Blissett, 148, 1976–83, 1984–88, 1991–92.

Most League Goals in One Match: 5, Eddie Mummery v Newport Co, Division 3S, 5 January 1924.

Most Capped Player: John Barnes, 31 (79), England and Kenny Jackett, 31, Wales.

Most League Appearances: Luther Blissett, 415, 1976–83, 1984–88, 1991–92.

Youngest League Player: Keith Mercer, 16 years 125 days v Tranmere R, 16 February 1973.

Record Transfer Fee Received: £2,300,000 from Chelsea for Paul Furlong, May 1994.

Record Transfer Fee Paid: £1,500,000 to Lillestrom for Heidar Helguson, January 2000.

Football League Record: 1920 Original Member of Division 3; 1921–58 Division 3 (S); 1958–60 Division 4; 1960–69 Division 3; 1969–72 Division 2; 1972–75 Division 3; 1975–78 Division 4; 1978–79 Division 3; 1979–82 Division 2; 1982–88 Division 1; 1988–92 Division 2; 1992–96 Division 1; 1996–98 Division 2; 1998–99 Division 1; 1999–2000 FA Premier League; 2000– Division 1.

MANAGERS

John Goodall 1903–10
Harry Kent 1910–26
Fred Pagnam 1926–29
Neil McBain 1929–37
Bill Findlay 1938–47
Jack Bray 1947–48
Eddie Hapgood 1948–50
Ron Gray 1950–51
Haydn Green 1951–52
Len Goulden 1952–55
  (General Manager to 1956)
Johnny Paton 1955–56
Neil McBain 1956–59
Ron Burgess 1959–63
Bill McGarry 1963–64
Ken Furphy 1964–71
George Kirby 1971–73
Mike Keen 1973–77
Graham Taylor 1977–87
Dave Bassett 1987–88
Steve Harrison 1988–90
Colin Lee 1990
Steve Perryman 1990–93
Glenn Roeder 1993–96
Kenny Jackett 1996–97
Graham Taylor May 1997–
  (General Manager since February 1996)

TEN YEAR LEAGUE RECORD

		P	W	D	L	F	A	Pts	Pos
1989-90	Div 2	46	14	15	17	58	60	57	15
1990-91	Div 2	46	12	15	19	45	59	51	20
1991-92	Div 2	46	18	11	17	51	48	65	10
1992-93	Div 1	46	14	13	19	57	71	55	16
1993-94	Div 1	46	15	9	22	66	80	54	19
1994-95	Div 1	46	19	13	14	52	46	70	7
1995-96	Div 1	46	10	18	18	62	70	48	23
1996-97	Div 2	46	16	19	11	45	38	67	13
1997-98	Div 2	46	24	16	6	67	41	88	1
1998-99	Div 1	46	21	14	11	65	56	77	5

DID YOU KNOW ?

In the 1934-35 season Vic O'Brien an inside-forward scored a club record six goals in a 9-1 Football Combination win over QPR. He was subsequently converted to full-back and became a regular first team choice.

WATFORD 1999–2000 LEAGUE RECORD

Match No.	Date	Venue	Opponents	Result	H/T Score	Lg. Pos.	Goalscorers	Attendance
1	Aug 7	H	Wimbledon	L 2-3	1-2	13	Kennedy (pen) [17], Ngonge [71]	15,511
2	10	A	Sunderland	L 0-2	0-0	—		37,879
3	14	A	Liverpool	W 1-0	1-0	15	Mooney [14]	44,174
4	21	H	Bradford C	W 1-0	0-0	9	Mooney [71]	15,564
5	24	H	Aston Villa	L 0-1	0-0	—		19,161
6	30	H	Leicester C	L 0-1	0-1	15		17,920
7	Sept 11	A	West Ham U	L 0-1	0-0	15		25,310
8	18	H	Chelsea	W 1-0	0-0	14	Smart [57]	21,244
9	25	A	Arsenal	L 0-1	0-0	14		38,127
10	Oct 3	H	Leeds U	L 1-2	1-1	15	Williams [42]	19,677
11	16	A	Manchester U	L 1-4	0-3	16	Johnson [68]	55,188
12	24	H	Middlesbrough	L 1-3	0-2	18	Smith [53]	16,081
13	31	A	Coventry C	L 0-4	0-2	19		21,697
14	Nov 6	A	Sheffield W	D 2-2	1-0	19	Ngonge [21], Page [59]	21,658
15	20	H	Newcastle U	D 1-1	0-0	19	Ngonge [53]	19,539
16	27	H	Sunderland	L 2-3	1-2	19	Ngonge [4], Johnson (pen) [49]	21,590
17	Dec 4	A	Wimbledon	L 0-5	0-2	19		14,021
18	18	H	Everton	L 1-3	0-2	19	Ngonge [60]	17,346
19	26	A	Tottenham H	L 0-4	0-2	19		36,089
20	28	H	Southampton	W 3-2	2-0	19	Perpetuini [17], Gravelaine 2 [31, 65]	18,459
21	Jan 3	A	Derby Co	L 0-2	0-1	19		28,072
22	15	H	Liverpool	L 2-3	1-2	19	Johnson [44], Helguson [46]	21,367
23	22	A	Bradford C	L 2-3	1-2	20	Hyde [33], Helguson [88]	16,864
24	Feb 5	A	Aston Villa	L 0-4	0-0	20		27,647
25	12	H	Leicester C	D 1-1	0-1	20	Wooter [47]	16,814
26	26	A	Chelsea	L 1-2	1-1	20	Smart [39]	34,944
27	Mar 4	H	West Ham U	L 1-2	0-2	20	Helguson [61]	18,619
28	11	A	Newcastle U	L 0-1	0-0	20		36,433
29	18	H	Sheffield W	W 1-0	0-0	20	Smart [88]	15,840
30	25	H	Tottenham H	D 1-1	0-0	20	Smart [78]	20,050
31	Apr 1	A	Everton	L 2-4	1-3	20	Smart [35], Hyde [80]	31,960
32	8	H	Derby Co	D 0-0	0-0	20		16,579
33	15	A	Southampton	L 0-2	0-1	20		15,242
34	23	H	Arsenal	L 2-3	0-3	20	Helguson [58], Hyde [60]	19,670
35	29	H	Manchester U	L 2-3	1-0	20	Helguson [33], Smith [78]	20,250
36	May 3	A	Leeds U	L 1-3	1-2	—	Foley [25]	36,324
37	6	A	Middlesbrough	D 1-1	0-1	20	Ward [68]	32,930
38	14	H	Coventry C	W 1-0	1-0	20	Helguson [44]	18,977

Final League Position: 20

GOALSCORERS

League (35): Helguson 6, Ngonge 5, Smart 5, Hyde 3, Johnson 3 (1 pen), Gravelaine 2, Mooney 2, Smith 2, Foley 1, Kennedy 1 (pen), Page 1, Perpetuini 1, Ward 1, Williams 1, Wooter 1.
Worthington Cup (3): Easton 1, Hyde 1, Kennedy 1.
FA Cup (0).

Day C 11	Lyttle D 11	Easton C 13 + 4	Page R 36	Williams M 20 + 2	Palmer S 38	Ngonge M 16 + 7	Bonnot A 7 + 5	Mooney T 8 + 4	Johnson R 20 + 3	Kennedy P 17 + 1	Smith T 13 + 9	Brooker S — + 1	Gudmundsson J 1 + 8	Robinson P 29 + 3	Hyde M 33 + 1	Foley D 5 + 7	Bakalli A — + 2	Chamberlain A 27	Smart A 13 + 1	Wright N 1 + 3	Gibbs N 11 + 6	Wooter N 16 + 4	Miller C 9 + 5	Panayi J 2	Ward D 7 + 2	Cox N 20 + 1	Noel-Williams G 1 + 2	Gravelaine X 7	Perpetuini D 12 + 1	Helguson H 14 + 2	Match No
1	2	3	4^1	5	6	7	8	9	10	11	12^2	13																			1
1	2	3	4	5	6	7	8^1	9	10	11			12																		2
1	2	12	4	5	6	7^2			9	10^1	11			3	8	13															3
1	2	10	4	5	6	7^1			9		11			3	8	12															4
1	2	10^3	4	5	6	7^2	12	9			11		14	3	8^1	13															5
1	2	10^2	4	5	6	7^1		9			11		12	3	8				13												6
	2		4	5	6			12	9		11	13		3	8			1	10^2						7^1						7
		10	4	5	6				13	12^2	11			3	8			1	9^1		14			2	7^3						8
		12	4	5	6	7			13		11^1			3	8			1	9^2		14				10^3	2					9
	2^2	12	4	5	6			9			11^1			3	8^1	7^3		1			13	10	14								10
			4	5	6^2	9^1			10	11	13			3	8^1			1	12		14				7	2					11
		12	4	5	6				10	9				3	8			1	2^1		11				7						12
	2	3			6		12		10		7^2	13			8			1	4			9	11^1		5^3					14	13
		3	4		6			9^1	10		12				8			1			13	7^3	11		5^2	2				14	14
		11^2	4		6				10^1					3	8		13	1	12		5		2		9		7				15
			4	5	6			9^3						3	8	12		1	13		10^1	11^2	14		7	2					16
			4	5	6			9			11			3	8			1	10						7	2					17
			4	5	6			9		10	11			3	8^1	12		1							7	2					18
			4	5^3	6			9^1		10	11	13		3	8	12		1			14					2		7^2			19
				5	6			9^1		10		13		3	8^3	12		1	4		14					2		7^2	11		20
				5	6			9^2		10		13		3	8	12		1			2		4^1					7	11		21
			4^1	5	6			13	14	10^3	12			3	8			1								2		7	11	9^2	22
			4	5	6			12				13		3	8			1	10^2							2		7	11^1	9	23
1		11^1		5	6			8		10^2	12			3		7		13			4		14			2^3				9	24
1	4			5	6			12			8			3^2				13			7	11	10			2				9^1	25
			4	5	6			12			8^2			3		7		1			11	10^1	13			2				9	26
			4	5^2	6			8^1			12			3	13	7		1			11	10	14			2^2				9	27
		12	4	5	6			13			8^2			3	7			1			11	10^1				2				9	28
				5	6			8			12			3	7			1	4		11	10				2				9^1	29
		12		5^1	6			8			13			3	7^3			1	4		11	10	14			2				9^2	30
		7		5^2	6			8	9					3				1	4		11	10^1	12		13	2					31
		11^2		5	6			13		10	8				7			1	9^1				4			2		3	12		32
		11		5	6			8		10	12				7	13		1	9^2				4			2^1		3^2		14	33
				5	6			12		10		13		3	8			1	11^2				4			2		7^1		9	34
				5	6			12		10		13		3	8	11^1		1			14		4			2^3		7		9^2	35
1				5	6			12		10				3	8	11^1					13		4			2		7		9^2	36
1				5	6			12		10				3	8	11^2					13		4			2		7^1		9	37
1				5	6			8		10	11			3		12							4			2^1		7		9	38

Worthington Cup

Second Round	Wigan Ath	(h)	2-0
		(a)	1-3
Third Round	Middlesbrough	(a)	0-1

FA Cup

Third Round	Birmingham C	(h)	0-1

Division 1   **WEST BROMWICH ALBION**

> ### FOUNDATION
> There is a well known story that when employees of Salter's Spring Works in West Bromwich decided to form a football club, they had to send someone to the nearby Association Football stronghold of Wednesbury to purchase a football. A weekly subscription of 2d (less than 1p) was imposed and the name of the new club was West Bromwich Strollers.

The Hawthorns, West Bromwich B71 4LF.

Telephone: (0121) 525 8888 (all Depts).

Fax: (0121) 553 6634.

Registered Office: 'The Tom Silk Building', Halfords Lane, West Bromwich, West Midlands B71 4BR.

Ground Capacity: 25,396 (all seated).

Record Attendance: 64,815 v Arsenal, FA Cup 6th rd, 6 March 1937.

Record Receipts: £270,000 v Nottingham F, Div 1, 3 May 1998.

Pitch Measurements: 115yd × 74yd.

President: Sir F. A. Millichip.

Vice-President: John G. Silk LL.B (Lond).

Chairman: P. Thompson.

Directors: J. W. Brandrick, B. Hurst, C. Stapleton, J. D. Wile (Chief Executive).

Manager: Gary Megson.

Coaches: Cyrille Regis, Richard O'Kelly.

Secretary: Dr John J. Evans BA, PHD. (Wales).

Club Statistician: Tony Matthews.

Marketing Manager: Mark Ashton.

LATEST SEQUENCES

Longest Sequence of League Wins: 11, 5.4.30 – 8.9.30.

Longest Sequence of League Defeats: 11, 28.10.95 – 26.12.95.

Longest Sequence of League Draws: 5, 30.8.99 – 3.10.99.

Longest Sequence of Unbeaten League Matches: 17, 7.9.57 – 7.12.57.

Longest Sequence Without a League Win: 14, 28.10.95 – 3.2.96.

HONOURS

Football League: Division 1 – Champions 1919–20; Runners-up 1924–25, 1953–54; Division 2 – Champions 1901–02, 1910–11; Runners-up 1930–31, 1948–49; Promoted to Division 1 1975–76 (3rd).

FA Cup: Winners 1888, 1892, 1931, 1954, 1968; Runners-up 1886, 1887, 1895, 1912, 1935.

Football League Cup: Winners 1966; Runners-up 1967, 1970.

European Competitions: *European Cup-Winners' Cup:* 1968–69. *European Fairs Cup:* 1966–67. *UEFA Cup:* 1978–79, 1979–80, 1981–82.

Colours
Navy blue and white striped shirts, white shorts, blue and white stockings.

Change Colours
Yellow shirts with navy blue band, blue shorts with yellow stripe, yellow stockings.

Year Formed: 1878.

Turned Professional: 1885.

Ltd Co.: 1892.

Plc: 1996.

Previous Name: 1878, West Bromwich Strollers; 1871, West Bromwich Albion.

Club Nicknames: 'Throstles', 'Baggies', 'Albion'.

Previous Grounds: 1878, Coopers Hill; 1879, Dartmouth Park; 1881, Bunns Field, Walsall Street; 1882, Four Acres (Dartmouth Cricket Club); 1885, Stoney Lane; 1900, The Hawthorns.

First Football League Game: 8 September 1888, Football League, v Stoke (a) W 2–0 – Roberts; J. Horton, Green; E. Horton, Perry, Bayliss; Bassett, Woodhall (1), Hendry, Pearson, Wilson (1).

Record League Victory: 12–0 v Darwen, Division 1, 4 April 1892 – Reader; J. Horton, McCulloch; Reynolds (2), Perry, Groves; Bassett (3), McLeod, Nicholls (1), Pearson (4), Geddes (1), (1 og).

Record Cup Victory: 10–1 v Chatham (away), FA Cup 3rd rd, 2 March 1889 – Roberts; J. Horton, Green; Timmins (1), Charles Perry, E. Horton; Bassett (2), Perry (1), Bayliss (2), Pearson, Wilson (3), (1 og).

Record Defeat: 3–10 v Stoke C, Division 1, 4 February 1937.

Most League Points (2 for a win): 60, Division 1, 1919–20.

Most League Points (3 for a win): 85, Division 2, 1992–93.

Most League Goals: 105, Division 2, 1929–30.

Highest League Scorer in Season: William 'Ginger' Richardson, 39, Division 1, 1935–36.

Most League Goals in Total Aggregate: Tony Brown, 218, 1963–79.

Most League Goals in One Match: 6, Jimmy Cookson v Blackpool, Division 2, 17 September 1927.

Most Capped Player: Stuart Williams, 33 (43), Wales.

Most League Appearances: Tony Brown, 574, 1963–80.

Youngest League Player: Charlie Wilson, 16 years 73 days v Oldham Ath, 1 October 1921.

Record Transfer Fee Received: £4,300,000 from Juventus for Enzo Maresca, January 2000.

Record Transfer Fee Paid: £1,250,000 to Preston NE for Kevin Kilbane, June 1997.

Football League Record: 1888 Founder Member of Football League; 1901–02 Division 2; 1902–04 Division 1; 1904–11 Division 2; 1911–27 Division 1; 1927–31 Division 2; 1931–38 Division 1; 1938–49 Division 2; 1949–73 Division 1; 1973–76 Division 2; 1976–86 Division 1; 1986–91 Division 2; 1991–92 Division 3; 1992–93 Division 2; 1993– Division 1.

MANAGERS

Louis Ford 1890–92
(Secretary-Manager)
Henry Jackson 1892–94
(Secretary-Manager)
Edward Stephenson 1894–95
(Secretary-Manager)
Clement Keys 1895–96
(Secretary-Manager)
Frank Heaven 1896–1902
(Secretary-Manager)
Fred Everiss 1902–48
Jack Smith 1948–52
Jesse Carver 1952
Vic Buckingham 1953–59
Gordon Clark 1959–61
Archie Macaulay 1961–63
Jimmy Hagan 1963–67
Alan Ashman 1967–71
Don Howe 1971–75
Johnny Giles 1975–77
Ronnie Allen 1977
Ron Atkinson 1978–81
Ronnie Allen 1981–82
Ron Wylie 1982–84
Johnny Giles 1984–85
Ron Saunders 1986–87
Ron Atkinson 1987–88
Brian Talbot 1988–91
Bobby Gould 1991–92
Ossie Ardiles 1992–93
Keith Burkinshaw 1993–94
Alan Buckley 1994–97
Ray Harford 1997
Denis Smith 1997–2000
Gary Megson March 2000–

TEN YEAR LEAGUE RECORD

		P	W	D	L	F	A	Pts	Pos
1989-90	Div 2	46	12	15	19	67	71	51	20
1990-91	Div 2	46	10	18	18	52	61	48	23
1991-92	Div 3	46	19	14	13	64	49	71	7
1992-93	Div 2	46	25	10	11	88	54	85	4
1993-94	Div 1	46	13	12	21	60	69	51	21
1994-95	Div 1	46	16	10	20	51	57	58	19
1995-96	Div 1	46	16	12	18	60	68	60	11
1996-97	Div 1	46	14	15	17	68	72	57	16
1997-98	Div 1	46	16	12	17	50	56	61	10
1998-99	Div 1	46	16	11	19	69	76	59	12

DID YOU KNOW ?

West Bromwich Albion equalled their best start to a season since 1953-54 when they remained unbeaten in the first nine matches of the 1999-2000 season.

WEST BROMWICH ALBION 1999–2000 LEAGUE RECORD

Match No.	Date	Venue	Opponents	Result	H/T Score	Lg. Pos.	Goalscorers	Attendance
1	Aug 7	H	Norwich C	D 1-1	0-0	12	Raven [73]	16,196
2	14	A	Port Vale	W 2-1	1-1	6	Hughes [14], Kilbane [55]	7891
3	20	H	Nottingham F	D 1-1	0-0	—	Hughes [75]	13,202
4	28	A	Swindon T	W 2-1	0-1	3	Kilbane [48], Evans [64]	6565
5	30	H	Fulham	D 0-0	0-0	4		17,120
6	Sept 11	A	Birmingham C	D 1-1	0-1	7	Hughes [53]	25,495
7	18	H	Blackburn R	D 2-2	1-0	10	Kilbane 2 [20, 87]	16,902
8	25	H	Crystal Palace	D 0-0	0-0	9		13,219
9	Oct 3	A	Wolverhampton W	D 1-1	0-1	11	Carbon [76]	25,500
10	16	H	Walsall	L 0-1	0-0	16		19,562
11	19	H	QPR	L 0-1	0-0	—		9874
12	23	A	Charlton Ath	D 0-0	0-0	18		19,346
13	26	A	Crystal Palace	W 2-0	2-0	—	Flynn [32], Maresca [35]	12,203
14	31	H	Wolverhampton W	L 1-1	1-0	16	McDermott [13]	21,097
15	Nov 6	A	Tranmere R	L 0-3	0-2	17		6623
16	14	H	Portsmouth	W 3-2	1-2	17	Maresca [14], Van Blerk [59], Evans [89]	11,483
17	20	A	Huddersfield T	L 0-1	0-0	14		14,244
18	23	H	Stockport Co	W 2-0	0-0	—	Hughes 2 [87, 88]	9201
19	27	H	Sheffield U	D 2-2	1-1	13	Maresca [35], Evans [80]	12,278
20	Dec 4	A	Norwich C	L 1-2	1-1	15	Kilbane [28]	15,183
21	7	A	Crewe Alex	L 0-2	0-0	—		5419
22	14	A	Grimsby T	D 1-1	1-1	—	Hughes [42]	4036
23	18	A	Ipswich T	L 1-3	0-2	15	De Freitas [77]	14,712
24	26	H	Manchester C	L 0-2	0-0	17		19,589
25	28	A	Bolton W	D 1-1	0-0	18	Burgess [60]	16,269
26	Jan 3	H	Barnsley	L 0-2	0-1	19		13,411
27	15	H	Port Vale	D 0-0	0-0	19		10,831
28	22	A	Nottingham F	D 0-0	0-0	19		19,863
29	29	H	Swindon T	D 1-1	0-0	19	Hughes (pen) [73]	11,856
30	Feb 5	A	Fulham	L 0-1	0-0	19		12,044
31	12	H	Crewe Alex	W 1-0	1-0	19	Hughes [37]	12,406
32	19	A	Sheffield U	L 0-6	0-2	19		14,519
33	26	A	Blackburn R	L 1-2	1-0	19	Carbon [14]	18,184
34	Mar 4	H	Birmingham C	L 0-3	0-2	22		17,029
35	7	A	Tranmere R	W 2-0	1-0	—	Flynn [40], Hughes [50]	11,958
36	11	A	Stockport Co	W 1-0	1-0	20	Hughes [1]	8238
37	18	H	Huddersfield T	L 0-1	0-1	21		15,484
38	21	A	Portsmouth	L 0-2	0-1	—		14,760
39	25	A	Manchester C	L 1-2	0-0	22	Hughes [60]	32,072
40	Apr 4	H	Ipswich T	D 1-1	1-0	—	Hughes [43]	12,536
41	8	A	Barnsley	D 2-2	0-0	20	Sneekes (pen) [47], Taylor [55]	16,329
42	15	H	Bolton W	D 4-4	2-1	21	Sneekes (pen) [22], Flynn [38], Taylor [79], Oliver [88]	12,802
43	22	A	Walsall	L 1-2	1-0	22	Flynn [10]	9161
44	24	H	Grimsby T	W 2-1	1-0	21	Taylor 2 [14, 48]	15,291
45	29	A	QPR	D 0-0	0-0	21		15,244
46	May 7	H	Charlton Ath	W 2-0	0-0	21	Sneekes [65], Taylor [70]	22,101

Final League Position: 21

GOALSCORERS

League (43): Hughes 12 (1 pen), Kilbane 5, Taylor 5, Flynn 4, Evans 3, Maresca 3, Sneekes 3 (2 pens), Carbon 2, Burgess 1, De Freitas 1, McDermott 1, Oliver 1, Raven 1, Van Blerk 1.
Worthington Cup (11): Hughes 3, De Freitas 2, Kilbane 2, Evans 1, Flynn 1, Quinn 1, Raven 1.
FA Cup (2): Evans 1, Hughes 1.

Miller A 25	Gabbidon D 18	Potter G 6 + 4	Flynn S 36	Burgess D 23 + 3	Carbon M 33 + 1	Maresca E 19 + 6	Sneekes R 42	Evans M 16 + 17	Hughes L 36	Kilbane K 19	Raven P 27 + 5	Quinn J 30 + 7	De Freitas F 12 + 12	Van Blerk J 33 + 2	Oliver A 1 + 14	Sigurdsson L 27	Townsend A 15 + 3	McDermott A 10 + 3	Angel M — + 3	Adamson C 9	Chambers J 10 + 2	Hall P 4	Fredgaard C 5	Jensen B 12	Lyttle D 8 + 1	Clement N 7 + 1	Santos G 8	Butler T 7	Taylor B 8	Match No.
1	2¹	3	4	5	6	7²	8	9²	10	11	12	13	14																	1
1	2		4	5		12	8		10	11	6	7¹	9	3																2
1	2		4	5	12	7¹	8		10	11	6		9	3																3
1	2		4	5	6	12	8	9	10	11	7			3¹																4
1	2		4	5	6	7²	8	12	10	11			9¹	3		13														5
1	2	13	4		6	7³	8	12	10	11	5²		9¹	3		14														6
1	2		4		6		8¹		10	11	12	9		3		5	7													7
1	2		4		6	12	8		10	11		13	9²	3		5	7¹													8
1	2		4		6	12	8		10	11	7	13	9²	3¹		5														9
1	2²		4³	13		14	8		10¹	11	3	9	12	6		5	7													10
1			4		6	7	8	12		11	3	9				5	10¹	2												11
1			4		6	7	8	12	10	11	3	9¹				5		2												12
1			4		6	7	8		10	11	3	9				5		2												13
1			4		6	7	8		10	11	3	9				5		2												14
1			4		6	7		12	10	11	8	9		3		5		2¹												15
1			4	5		7	8	12	10		3	9		11		6		2¹												16
1			4	2		7¹	8	12	10	11	6	9²	13	3		5														17
1			4	2		7	8		10	11	6	9		3		5														18
1			4²	2¹		7	8	12		11	6	9	10³	3	14	5		13												19
1				2	6	7²	8	9²	10	11	3		12	13		5	4¹	14												20
1	2¹			4	6	12	8	13	10	11	3	9		7²		5														21
1	2			4	6		8		9	10	11	7		3		5														22
1	2				6	11²	8		9	10¹		4	7³	12	3		13	14												23
1	2¹		4			11	8		9	10		6	7	12	3		5													24
1			4			11²	8		9¹	10		2	7	12	3		5	6		13										25
	2	3	4			11	8	9				7	10			6	5		1											26
	2¹	3		5	6	11²	8³	13	10			9		12	14	7				1	4									27
	4¹	7		2	6		8	12	10			9		5			11			1	3									28
			12	4	2	6		8	13	10		9²		3		5	11			1	7¹									29
			3³	4		6		8	12	10		13	9		11	7¹	5		14	1	2²									30
				4		6		8³	9¹	10		3	12		14	5		1	2	7	11²									31
				4		6		8	9	10¹		3				5	12		1	2	7	11								32
				4		6¹		8	9	10		12				3			1	2	7¹	11								33
				4		6		9				8	12	3		5	10		1	2	7¹	11								34
			12	4		6		9²	10			7	13	3	14	5	8³	2				11¹	1							35
			3			6		9¹	10		13	7	12	11	14	5²	8	2¹		4			1							36
				4	12	6		8	9²	10		3³		13	11	14	7	2¹		5			1							37
	2³			4²	5	6		8	9	10		12	7		3	13	11¹						1	14						38
				4		6		8²				7¹			12				13					1	2	3	11	5	9	39
				4		6		8		10¹		7	12	3										1	2	5	11	6	9	40
				4³	12		8					6¹	13	7²	11	14								1	2	3	10	5	9	41
		12	4	5²	6		8					13	7³		14									1	2	3¹	11	10	9	42
				5	3¹	6		8	12			7²	11³	13										1	2	14	10	4	9	43
				4	5		8	12				9¹		11										1	2	3	7	6	10	44
				4	5	6	8	12				9²		11¹	13				14					1	2³	3	7		10	45
				4		6	8	12				9¹		11	13									1	2	3	7²	5	10	46

Worthington Cup						**FA Cup**			
First Round	Halifax T	(a)	0-0			Third Round	Blackburn R	(h)	2-2
		(h)	5-1					(a)	0-2
Second Round	Wycombe W	(h)	1-1						
		(a)	4-3						
Third Round	Fulham	(h)	1-2						

FA Premiership WEST HAM UNITED

FOUNDATION

Thames Ironworks FC was formed by employees of this shipbuilding yard in 1895 and entered the FA Cup in their initial season at Chatham and the London League in their second. Short of funds, the club was wound up in June 1900 and relaunched a month later as West Ham United. Connection with the Ironworks was not finally broken until four years later.

Boleyn Ground, Green Street, Upton Park, London E13 9AZ.
Telephone General Office: (020) 8548 2748.
Ticket Office: (020) 8548 2700.
Merchandise Shop: (020) 8548 2722.
Fax: (020) 8548 2758.
Membership Office: (020) 8548 2727.
Commercial: (020) 8548 2777.
Dial-a-seat: (020) 8548 2700.
Football in the Community: (020) 8548 2707.
ClubCall: 09068 121 165.
Ground Capacity: 26,054.
Record Attendance: 42,322 v Tottenham H, Division 1, 17 October 1970.
Record Receipts: £339,420 gross v Liverpool, FA Premier League, 22 November 1995.
Pitch Measurements: 112yd × 72yd.
Chairman: T. W. Brown FCIS, AII, FCCA.
Vice-Chairman: M. W. Cearns ACIB.
Directors: C. J. Warner, N. Igoe, P. Aldridge.
Manager: Harry Redknapp.
Assistant Manager: Frank Lampard.
Coaches: Roger Cross, Tony Carr.
Physio: John Green BSC, MCSP, SRP.
Secretary: Peter Barnes.
Stadium Manager: John Ball.
Press Officer: Peter Stewart.

LATEST SEQUENCES

Longest Sequence of League Wins: 9, 19.10.85 – 14.12.85.
Longest Sequence of League Defeats: 9, 28.3.32 – 29.8.32.
Longest Sequence of League Draws: 5, 7.9.68 – 5.10.68.
Longest Sequence of Unbeaten League Matches: 27, 27.12.80 – 10.10.81.
Longest Sequence Without a League Win: 17, 31.1.76 – 21.8.76.

HONOURS

Football League: Division 1 best season: 3rd, 1985–86; Division 2 – Champions 1957–58, 1980–81; Runners-up 1922–23, 1990–91.

FA Cup: Winners 1964, 1975, 1980; Runners-up 1923.

Football League Cup: Runners-up 1966, 1981.

European Competitions: European Cup-Winners' Cup: 1964–65 (winners), 1965–66, 1975–76 (runners-up), 1980–81. *UEFA Cup:* 1999–2000. *Intertoto Cup* (winners) 1999.

Colours

Claret shirts with blue sleeves, white shorts, light blue with claret hooped stockings.

Change Colours

White shirts with blue trim and claret trim, blue shorts, white stockings with blue and claret piping.

Year Formed: 1895.

Turned Professional: 1900.

Ltd Co.: 1900.

Previous Name: Thames Iron Works FC, 1895–1900.

Club Nickname: 'The Hammers'.

Previous Grounds: 1895, Memorial Recreation Ground, Canning Town; 1904, Boleyn Ground.

First Football League Game: 30 August 1919, Division 2, v Lincoln C (h) D 1–1 – Hufton; Cope, Lee; Lane, Fenwick, McCrae; D. Smith, Moyes (1), Puddefoot, Morris, Bradshaw.

MANAGERS

Syd King 1902–32
Charlie Paynter 1932–50
Ted Fenton 1950–61
Ron Greenwood 1961–74
(continued as General Manager to 1977)
John Lyall 1974–89
Lou Macari 1989–90
Billy Bonds 1990–94
Harry Redknapp August 1994–

Record League Victory: 8–0 v Rotherham U, Division 2, 8 March 1958 – Gregory; Bond, Wright; Malcolm, Brown, Lansdowne; Grice, Smith (2), Keeble (2), Dick (4), Musgrove. 8–0 v Sunderland, Division 1, 19 October 1968 – Ferguson; Bonds, Charles; Peters, Stephenson, Moore (1); Redknapp, Boyce, Brooking (1), Hurst (6), Sissons.

Record Cup Victory: 10–0 v Bury, League Cup 2nd rd (2nd leg), 25 October 1983 – Parkes; Stewart (1), Walford, Bonds (Orr), Martin (1), Devonshire (2), Allen, Cottee (4), Swindlehurst, Brooking (2), Pike.

Record Defeat: 2–8 v Blackburn R, Division 1, 26 December 1963.

Most League Points (2 for a win): 66, Division 2, 1980–81.

Most League Points (3 for a win): 88, Division 1, 1992–93.

Most League Goals: 101, Division 2, 1957–58.

Highest League Scorer in Season: Vic Watson, 42, Division 1, 1929–30.

Most League Goals in Total Aggregate: Vic Watson, 298, 1920–35.

Most League Goals in One Match: 6, Vic Watson v Leeds U, Division 1, 9 February 1929; 6, Geoff Hurst v Sunderland, Division 1, 19 October 1968.

Most Capped Player: Bobby Moore, 108, England.

Most League Appearances: Billy Bonds, 663, 1967–88.

Youngest League Player: Neil Finn, 17 years 3 days v Manchester C, 1 January 1996.

Record Transfer Fee Received: £7,500,000 from Wimbledon for John Hartson, January 1999.

Record Transfer Fee Paid: £4,200,000 to Lens for Marc-Vivien Foe, January 1999.

Football League Record: 1919 Elected to Division 2; 1923–32 Division 1; 1932–58 Division 2; 1958–78 Division 1; 1978–81 Division 2; 1981–89 Division 1; 1989–91 Division 2; 1991–93 Division 1; 1993– FA Premier League.

TEN YEAR LEAGUE RECORD

		P	W	D	L	F	A	Pts	Pos
1989-90	Div 2	46	20	12	14	80	57	72	7
1990-91	Div 2	46	24	15	7	60	34	87	2
1991-92	Div 1	42	9	11	22	37	59	38	22
1992-93	Div 1	46	26	10	10	81	41	88	2
1993-94	PR Lge	42	13	13	16	47	58	52	13
1994-95	PR Lge	42	13	11	18	44	48	50	14
1995-96	PR Lge	38	14	9	15	43	52	51	10
1996-97	PR Lge	38	10	12	16	39	48	42	14
1997-98	PR Lge	38	16	8	14	56	57	56	8
1998-99	PR Lge	38	16	9	13	46	53	57	5

DID YOU KNOW ?

In their three post-war FA Cup Final appearances in 1964, 1975 and 1980, West Ham United used 30 different players, 29 of them English. The odd man out was Ray Stewart, their Scottish full-back.

WEST HAM UNITED 1999–2000 LEAGUE RECORD

Match No.	Date	Venue	Opponents	Result		H/T Score	Lg. Pos.	Goalscorers	Attendance
1	Aug 7	H	Tottenham H	W	1-0	1-0	8	Lampard [45]	26,010
2	16	A	Aston Villa	D	2-2	1-1	—	Southgate (og) [7], Sinclair [90]	26,250
3	21	H	Leicester C	W	2-1	1-1	7	Wanchope [29], Di Canio [53]	23,631
4	28	A	Bradford C	W	3-0	2-0	4	Di Canio [34], Sinclair [44], Wanchope [49]	17,936
5	Sept 11	H	Watford	W	1-0	0-0	3	Di Canio [48]	25,310
6	19	H	Everton	L	0-1	0-0	8		35,154
7	25	A	Coventry C	L	0-1	0-1	10		19,985
8	Oct 3	H	Arsenal	W	2-1	1-0	9	Di Canio 2 [29, 72]	26,009
9	17	A	Middlesbrough	L	0-2	0-0	10		31,822
10	24	A	Sunderland	D	1-1	0-1	11	Sinclair [89]	26,022
11	27	A	Liverpool	L	0-1	0-1	—		44,012
12	30	A	Leeds U	L	0-1	0-0	12		40,190
13	Nov 7	A	Chelsea	D	0-0	0-0	11		34,935
14	21	H	Sheffield W	W	4-3	1-1	10	Wanchope [28], Di Canio (pen) [62], Foe [70], Lampard [76]	23,015
15	27	H	Liverpool	W	1-0	1-0	9	Sinclair [44]	26,043
16	Dec 6	A	Tottenham H	D	0-0	0-0	—		36,233
17	18	H	Manchester U	L	2-4	1-3	9	Di Canio 2 [23, 52]	26,037
18	26	A	Wimbledon	D	2-2	1-1	10	Sinclair [45], Lampard [81]	21,180
19	28	H	Derby Co	D	1-1	1-1	10	Di Canio [21]	24,998
20	Jan 3	A	Newcastle U	D	2-2	0-1	11	Lampard [84], Stimac [88]	36,314
21	15	H	Aston Villa	D	1-1	0-1	11	Di Canio [78]	24,237
22	22	A	Leicester C	W	3-1	2-1	8	Wanchope 2 [13, 45], Di Canio [60]	19,019
23	Feb 5	A	Southampton	L	1-2	0-0	11	Lampard [65]	15,257
24	12	H	Bradford C	W	5-4	2-2	9	Sinclair [35], Moncur [43], Di Canio (pen) [65], Cole [70], Lampard [83]	25,417
25	26	H	Everton	L	0-4	0-1	11		26,025
26	Mar 4	A	Watford	W	2-1	2-0	11	Lomas [3], Wanchope [35]	18,619
27	8	H	Southampton	W	2-0	1-0	—	Wanchope [18], Sinclair [48]	23,484
28	11	A	Sheffield W	L	1-3	1-0	10	Lampard [10]	21,147
29	18	H	Chelsea	D	0-0	0-0	9		26,041
30	26	H	Wimbledon	W	2-1	1-0	11	Di Canio [8], Kanoute [59]	22,438
31	Apr 1	A	Manchester U	L	1-7	1-3	8	Wanchope [11]	61,611
32	12	H	Newcastle U	W	2-1	0-0	—	Wanchope 2 [60, 89]	25,817
33	15	A	Derby Co	W	2-1	2-0	8	Wanchope 2 [15, 32]	31,202
34	22	H	Coventry C	W	5-0	2-0	8	Carrick [7], Margas [14], Di Canio 2 [48, 67], Kanoute [83]	24,719
35	29	H	Middlesbrough	L	0-1	0-0	8		25,472
36	May 2	A	Arsenal	L	1-2	1-0	—	Di Canio [40]	38,093
37	6	A	Sunderland	L	0-1	0-1	9		40,896
38	14	H	Leeds U	D	0-0	0-0	9		26,044

Final League Position: 9

GOALSCORERS

League (52): Di Canio 16 (2 pens), Wanchope 12, Lampard 7, Sinclair 7, Kanoute 2, Carrick 1, Cole 1, Foe 1, Lomas 1, Margas 1, Moncur 1, Stimac 1, own goal 1.
Worthington Cup (6): Lampard 2, Cole 1, Keller 1, Kitson 1, Lomas 1.
FA Cup (0).

Hislop S 22	Potts S 16 + 1	Minto S 15 + 3	Pearce I 1	Ferdinand R 33	Pearce S 8	Lampard F 34	Sinclair T 36	Wanchope P 33 + 2	Di Canio P 29 + 1	Foe M 25	Keller M 19 + 4	Cole J 17 + 5	Moncur J 20 + 2	Kitson P 4 + 6	Lomas S 25	Carrick M 4 + 4	Stimac I 24	Margas J 15 + 3	Newton A — + 2	Ruddock N 12 + 3	Forrest C 9 + 2	Byrne S — + 1	Charles G 2 + 2	Bywater S 3 + 1	Ilic S 1	Kanoute F 8	Feuer I 3	Match No.
1	2	3	4^1	5	6	7	8	9	10^2	11	12	13																1
1	2	3^1		5	6	4	8	9	10	11	12		7^2	13														2
1	6			5	3	4	8	9	10	11			7		2													3
1		4		5^1	6	8	2	9	10			3	7		11	12												4
1		4			6^2	8	2	9	10			3	7^1		11	12	5	13										5
1		4				8	2	9	10			3	7		11		5	6										6
1		4				8	2	9	10	11		3^1	7		6		5	12										7
1		4				8	2	9^1	10	11			7^2	12	3		5	13		6								8
1				5		8	2	9	10			3^1	12	7^6	11		4			6	15							9
1				5		7	2	9^1	10			3	8	13	12	11^2		6^9		4	14							10
1		4		5		7	2	9				3	8	10	11					6								11
1				5		8		9			11^1	3	12	7	10	2		4		6								12
				5		7	10	9			11	3	8^1		2		6	4	12		1							13
1		4		5		7	2	9	10	11		3	8							6								14
1				5		7	2	9^1	10			3	8	12	11		4			6								15
1	12	13		5		7	2	14	10^3	11		8	9^2		3		4^1			6								16
1		3		5		7	2	9	10			8			11		4			6								17
1		3		5		7	2	9	10	11		8					4			6								18
1	4	3^1		5		7	2	9	10	11	12	8								6								19
1	2	3		5		7		9				4	11^1	8			10	6			12							20
1				5		7	2	9	10			3	8		11		6	4										21
1	12			5		7	2	9	10			3^1	8			11^2	13			4	6	15						22
	3			5		7	10	9					8	12	11		6	4^1			1		2					23
1	3			5		7		9	10			8	11	12	4		6						2^1	15				24
				5	6		2	9				3	8	7	10	11		4							1			25
	3			5	6	8	10	9		11			7		2			4					1					26
	12			5	6^1	11	10	9		13		3	8^2	7	2			4					1					27
				5	8		3	9	10	11			12		7^1		2	4		6			1					28
	3			5	4	8		9^1	10	11		14	7^3		12^2		2	6		13	1							29
	3			5	4	8			10	11		12	7^1		2		6				1					9		30
	4	3		5	6	8		9		11			7		2						1					10		31
	3			5		7	12	10	11	2^3		8					4^2	13		6^1			14			9		32
	3			5		7	2	9	10	11		8^2					13	6^1		4			12				1	33
	3^1			5		7	2	9	10				8				6	4		12						11	1	34
				5		7	2	9	10	11		3					6	4								8	1	35
	2					11		9	10	5		3	7					4		6				1		8		36
	3			5			2	9	10	11			7				4	6						1		8		37
	2			5		11		9	10			3	7				6	4						1		8		38

Worthington Cup

Third Round	Bournemouth	(h)	2-0
Fourth Round	Birmingham C	(a)	3-2
Fifth Round	Aston Villa	(h)	1-3

FA Cup

Third Round	Tranmere R	(a)	0-1

Division 2   **WIGAN ATHLETIC**

FOUNDATION

Following the demise of Wigan Borough and their resignation from the Football League in 1931, a public meeting was called in Wigan at the Queen's Hall in May 1932 at which a new club Wigan Athletic, was founded in the hope of carrying on in the Football League. With this in mind, they bought Springfield Park for £2,250, but failed to gain admission to the Football League until 46 years later.

JJB Stadium, Robin Park Complex, Newtown, Wigan WN5 0UZ.
Website: www.wiganlatics.co.uk
Ticket Office: (01942) 770 410.
Telephone: (01942) 774 000.
Fax: (01942) 770 477.
Commercial Dept: (01942) 774 000.
Latics ClubCall: 09068 121 655.
Football in the Community: (01942) 824 599.
Ground Capacity: 25,000.
Record Attendance: 27,526 v Hereford U, 12 December 1953.
Record Receipts: £140,000 v Preston NE, Division 2, 4 April 2000.
Pitch Measurements: 115yd × 75yd.
President: S. Jackson.
Chairman: David Whelan.
Directors: D. Whelan, J. Winstanley, D. Sharpe, P. Williams, B. Ashcroft.
Chief Executive/Secretary: Mrs Brenda Spencer.
Assistant Secretary: Stuart Hayton.
Manager: Bruce Rioch.
Physio: Alex Cribley.
Safety Officer: David Johnson.
Groundsman: David Pinch.

LATEST SEQUENCES
Longest Sequence of League Wins: 6, 26.12.87 – 23.1.88.
Longest Sequence of League Defeats: 7, 6.4.93 – 4.5.93.
Longest Sequence of League Draws: 4, 9.5.89 – 19.8.89.
Longest Sequence of Unbeaten League Matches: 25, 8.5.99 – 3.1.00.
Longest Sequence Without a League Win: 14, 9.5.89 – 17.10.89.

HONOURS

Football League: Division 3 Champions, 1996–97; Division 4 – Promoted (3rd) 1981–82.
FA Cup: best season: 6th rd, 1987.
Football League Cup: best season: 4th rd, 1982.
Freight Rover Trophy: Winners 1985.
Auto Windscreens Shield: Winners 1999.

Colours
Blue shirts with white side panel, blue shorts and stockings.

Change Colours
White shirts with blue side panel, white shorts and stockings.

Year Formed: 1932.

Club Nickname: 'The Latics'.

First Football League Game: 19 August 1978, Division 4, v Hereford U (a) D 0–0 – Brown; Hinnigan, Gore, Gillibrand, Ward, Davids, Corrigan, Purdie, Houghton, Wilkie, Wright.

Record League Victory: 7–1 v Scarborough, Division 3, 11 March 1997 – Butler L, Butler J, Sharp (Morgan), Greenall, McGibbon (Biggins (1)), Martinez (1), Diaz (2), Jones (Lancashire (1)), Lowe (2), Rogers, Kilford.

Record Cup Victory: 6–0 v Carlisle U (away), FA Cup 1st rd, 24 November 1934 – Caunce; Robinson, Talbot; Paterson, Watson, Tufnell; Armes (2), Robson (1), Roberts (2), Felton, Scott (1).

Record Defeat: 1–6 v Bristol R, Division 3, 3 March 1990.

Most League Points (2 for a win): 55, Division 4, 1978–79 and 1979–80.

Most League Points (3 for a win): 91, Division 4, 1981–82.

Most League Goals: 84, Division 3, 1996–97.

Highest League Scorer in Season: Graeme Jones, 31, Division 3, 1996–97.

Most League Goals in Total Aggregate: David Lowe, 66, 1982–87 and 1995–99.

Most League Goals in One Match: Not more than three goals by one player.

Most Capped Player: Roy Carroll, 4, Northern Ireland.

Most League Appearances: Kevin Langley, 317, 1981–86, 1990–94.

Youngest League Player: Steve Nugent, 16 years 132 days v Leyton Orient, 16 September 1989.

Record Transfer Fee Received: £329,000 from Coventry C for Peter Atherton, August 1991.

Record Transfer Fee Paid: £600,000 to Coventry C for Simon Haworth, October 1998.

Football League Record: 1978 Elected to Division 4; 1982–92 Division 3; 1992–93 Division 2; 1993–97 Division 3; 1997– Division 2.

MANAGERS

Charlie Spencer 1932–37
Jimmy Milne 1946–47
Bob Pryde 1949–52
Ted Goodier 1952–54
Walter Crook 1954–55
Ron Suart 1955–56
Billy Cooke 1956
Sam Barkas 1957
Trevor Hitchen 1957–58
Malcolm Barrass 1958–59
Jimmy Shirley 1959
Pat Murphy 1959–60
Allenby Chilton 1960
Johnny Ball 1961–63
Allan Brown 1963–66
Alf Craig 1966–67
Harry Leyland 1967–68
Alan Saunders 1968
Ian McNeill 1968–70
Gordon Milne 1970–72
Les Rigby 1972–74
Brian Tiler 1974–76
Ian McNeill 1976–81
Larry Lloyd 1981–83
Harry McNally 1983–85
Bryan Hamilton 1985–86
Ray Mathias 1986–89
Bryan Hamilton 1989–93
Dave Philpotts 1993
Kenny Swain 1993–94
Graham Barrow 1994–95
John Deehan 1995–98
Ray Mathias 1998–99
John Benson 1999–2000
Bruce Rioch June 2000–

TEN YEAR LEAGUE RECORD

		P	W	D	L	F	A	Pts	Pos
1989-90	Div 3	46	13	14	19	48	64	53	18
1990-91	Div 3	46	20	9	17	71	54	69	10
1991-92	Div 3	46	15	14	17	58	64	59	15
1992-93	Div 2	46	10	11	25	43	72	41	23
1993-94	Div 3	42	11	12	19	51	70	45	19
1994-95	Div 3	42	14	10	18	53	60	52	14
1995-96	Div 3	46	20	10	16	62	56	70	10
1996-97	Div 3	46	26	9	11	84	51	87	1
1997-98	Div 2	46	17	11	18	64	66	62	11
1998-99	Div 2	46	22	10	14	75	48	76	6

DID YOU KNOW ?

Wigan Athletic manager John Benson appointed in June 1999, became the most successful to start a season with a new club. Wigan completed 24 League matches before defeat.

WIGAN ATHLETIC 1999–2000 LEAGUE RECORD

Match No.	Date	Venue	Opponents	Result	H/T Score	Lg. Pos.	Goalscorers	Attendance
1	Aug 7	H	Scunthorpe U	W 3-0	1-0	1	Haworth 2 [14, 73], Barlow (pen) [56]	7481
2	14	A	Millwall	D 3-3	1-0	2	Liddell [44], Balmer [54], Barlow [64]	8165
3	21	H	Bristol C	W 2-1	1-0	2	Barlow [8], Haworth [90]	7103
4	28	A	Preston NE	W 4-1	1-1	1	Barlow 3 (1 pen) [45 (p), 47, 88], Haworth [83]	13,885
5	30	H	Cambridge U	D 1-1	0-0	1	McGibbon [48]	5976
6	Sept 11	H	Bristol R	W 3-1	2-1	1	Sheridan [7], Barlow [20], Haworth [71]	6927
7	18	A	Stoke C	D 1-1	1-0	3	Mohan (og) [18]	11,195
8	25	A	Cardiff C	D 0-0	0-0	4		7679
9	Oct 2	H	Luton T	W 1-0	0-0	2	Barlow [75]	6866
10	16	A	Reading	W 2-0	1-0	3	Barlow [41], Bradshaw (pen) [90]	7708
11	19	A	Wrexham	D 1-1	0-0	—	Martinez [50]	3392
12	23	H	Cardiff C	W 2-0	0-0	4	Martinez [48], Kilford [88]	5728
13	26	A	Colchester U	D 2-2	1-2	—	Barlow [12], Liddell [90]	2915
14	Nov 2	H	Chesterfield	W 3-0	1-0	—	Liddell [30], Barlow 2 (1 pen) [75, 87 (p)]	4376
15	6	A	Blackpool	D 2-2	0-2	2	Jones [49], Barlow [52]	4535
16	12	H	Wycombe W	W 2-1	1-1	1	Barlow [42], Balmer [61]	5523
17	16	H	Bournemouth	W 3-1	1-0	—	Green [23], De Zeeuw [63], Barlow [87]	4338
18	23	A	Bury	D 2-2	1-1	—	Barlow [37], Haworth [58]	4086
19	27	H	Burnley	D 1-1	1-1	1	Haworth [41]	11,986
20	Dec 4	A	Scunthorpe U	W 2-1	1-1	1	Liddell [38], Martinez [84]	3463
21	18	H	Brentford	W 1-0	0-0	1	De Zeeuw [76]	5498
22	26	A	Notts Co	W 2-0	1-0	1	O'Neill [35], Liddell [74]	8176
23	28	H	Gillingham	W 2-0	1-0	1	McLoughlin [1], Sheridan [66]	8054
24	Jan 3	A	Oxford U	W 2-1	0-0	1	Haworth 2 [70, 88]	5915
25	7	H	Oldham Ath	L 0-1	0-0	—		6487
26	15	H	Millwall	D 1-1	0-0	1	O'Neill [87]	6304
27	22	A	Bristol C	D 0-0	0-0	1		10,758
28	Feb 5	A	Cambridge U	D 1-1	1-0	3	Barlow [10]	3755
29	12	H	Colchester U	L 0-1	0-1	3		6022
30	19	A	Burnley	D 0-0	0-0	3		20,435
31	26	H	Stoke C	L 1-2	1-1	4	Green [19]	9429
32	Mar 4	A	Bristol R	D 1-1	1-1	4	Liddell [4]	11,109
33	7	H	Blackpool	W 5-1	1-1	—	Liddell [6], Griffiths [56], Haworth [81], Barlow [89], Sheridan [90]	6451
34	11	A	Chesterfield	D 1-1	0-1	4	Cooke [83]	3106
35	18	H	Bury	W 1-0	0-0	4	Liddell [75]	6567
36	21	A	Wycombe W	W 2-0	0-0	—	De Zeeuw [59], Haworth [90]	3821
37	25	H	Notts Co	W 2-0	1-0	3	Redfearn 2 (1 pen) [6, 81 (p)]	6094
38	Apr 1	A	Brentford	W 2-0	2-0	2	Redfearn (pen) [18], Powell (og) [45]	4479
39	4	H	Preston NE	L 0-1	0-1	—		15,593
40	8	H	Oxford U	W 2-0	1-0	2	Haworth 2 [22, 90]	4848
41	11	A	Oldham Ath	L 1-2	1-1	—	Redfearn (pen) [40]	5697
42	15	A	Gillingham	L 1-2	1-1	2	Pennock (og) [20]	7746
43	22	H	Reading	W 1-0	1-0	2	Redfearn (pen) [34]	5855
44	24	A	Luton T	D 1-1	1-0	2	Redfearn (pen) [35]	5010
45	29	H	Wrexham	L 0-1	0-1	3		7245
46	May 6	A	Bournemouth	D 2-2	0-2	4	McGibbon [85], Roberts [89]	6512

Final League Position: 4

GOALSCORERS

League (72): Barlow 18 (3 pens), Haworth 13, Liddell 8, Redfearn 6 (5 pens), De Zeeuw 3, Martinez 3, Sheridan 3, Balmer 2, Green 2, McGibbon 2, O'Neill 2, Bradshaw 1 (pen), Cooke 1, Griffiths 1, Jones 1, Kilford 1, McLoughlin 1, Roberts 1, own goals 3.
Worthington Cup (6): Haworth 3, Barlow 2 (1 pen), Bradshaw 1 (pen).
FA Cup (6): Haworth 3, Barlow 2, Liddell 1.

Carroll R 34	Green S 32 + 1	Bowen M 7	Balmer S 41	De Zeeuw A 39	Kilford I 18 + 3	O'Neill M 30	Sheridan D 25 + 6	Haworth S 36 + 4	Liddell A 41	Barlow S 24 + 9	Porter A 2 + 3	Stillie D 12 + 1	McGibbon P 30 + 4	Martinez R 14 + 11	Jones G 1 + 2	Lee D — + 4	Bradshaw C 21 + 5	Sharp K 17 + 4	Griffiths G 10 + 6	Nicholls K 6 + 2	Peron J 19 + 4	McLoughlin A 11 + 4	Roberts N 8 + 1	Cooke T 10	Redfearn N 12	Clegg M 6	Match No
1	2	3	4	5	6	7	8¹	9	10	11	12																1
	2	3		5			8	9	10	12	7	1	4	6	11¹												2
1	2	3		5	6¹	7²	8	9	10	11	12		4				13										3
1	2	3¹		5	6	7	8	9	10	11			4	12													4
1	2			5	6²	7¹	8	9	10	11	3		4	12			13										5
1	2	3		5	6	7	8	9	10	11			4														6
1		3	4	5	6²	7	8	9	10¹	11			12				13	2									7
1		3²	4	5		7	8	9	10	11¹			12				2	6	13								8
1			4	5	6	7	8	9	10	11			12				2	3¹									9
1				5	6		8	9¹	10	11		3	4	12			2										10
1⁶				5	6		8	9¹	10	11	13	15	4	12			2²										11
12				5	6		8		10	11		1	4	9			2¹										12
	2			5	6		8		10	11		1	4	9													13
	2			5	6	8	7		10¹	11		1	4²	9	12		3	13									14
	2³			5	6	8	7	13	10	11		1	4¹	9²	12		14	3									15
	2			5	6	8	7	12	10	11		1	4	9			3¹										16
	2			5	6	8	7¹	12	10	11		1	4	9			3										17
	2			5	6	8	7		9	10	11	1	4				3										18
1	2			5	6	8²	7	12	9	10	11		4	13			3¹										19
1	2			5	6		7		9	10	11		4¹	8			3			12							20
1	4²			5	6	12	7¹		9	10	13						2	3		11	8						21
1	4			5	6		7		9	10							2	3		11	8						22
1	4			5²	6	14		8	9	10	12		13				2³	3		11¹	7						23
1	4¹				6		7		9	10	12		5				2	3		11	8						24
1	4				6	12	7¹		9	10	13		5				2²	3		11	8						25
1	2			5	6		7	12	9		4		10²				3¹	13		11	8						26
1	2			5			7		9	10	11¹		4				3	6		12	8						27
1				5			7¹	12	9	10	11²		4	6			2	3	13		8						28
1				5	6		7	12	9	10	11		13	4			2	3¹			8²						29
1	2			5			7	8	12	10	13		4	6³			3			11²	14	9¹					30
1	2			5	6		7	3³	12	10	13		4	8			14			11¹	9²						31
1	2			5	6		7³		9	10			4²	12			3		13	14	8¹	11					32
1	2			5	6			8	9	10	12		3	13			4				11¹	7²					33
1	2				6			8	9	10	11¹		4				3	5		12		7					34
1	2			5	6			8	9	10	12			13			3				11²	7¹			4		35
1	2			5	6			8	9	10							3				11		7		4		36
1				5	6			8	9	10	12						3				11		7		4	2¹	37
1			4	6			3²	8	9	10¹			5	13			12				11		7		4	2	38
1				5	6			8	9		12						3¹				11		10	7	4	2	39
1	3			5	6			8	9		12						13	11²			10		7¹		4	2	40
1	2¹			5	6			8	9				3	4	12						10		11	7			41
1				5	6			9			2	10		3			12	8²	11	13			4	7¹			42
				5	6			9	10		1	2	3					8	11	12		7¹	4				43
				5	6			9	10		1	2	12				3				8¹	11	13	7²	4		44
	2			5	6			9	10		1	12	13				3¹				8³	11	14	7²	4		45
	2				6			12	10		1	3	13				14				5	8¹	11³	7²	9	4	46

Worthington Cup

First Round	York C	(a)	1-0
		(h)	2-1
Second Round	Watford	(a)	0-2
		(h)	3-1

FA Cup

First Round	Cambridge C	(a)	2-0
Second Round	Wycombe W	(a)	2-2
		(h)	2-1
Third Round	Wolverhampton W	(h)	0-1

Division 1   **WIMBLEDON**

FOUNDATION

Old boys from Central School formed this club as Wimbledon Old Centrals in 1889. Their earliest successes were in the Clapham League before switching to the Southern Suburban League in 1902.

Selhurst Park, South Norwood, London SE25 6PY.
Telephone: (020) 8771 2233.
Fax: (020) 8768 0641.
Website: www.wimbledon-fc.co.uk
Box Office: (020) 8771 8841.
ClubCall: 09068 121 175.
Ground Capacity: 26,297.
Record Attendance: 30,115 v Manchester U, FA Premier League, 9 May 1993.
Record Receipts: £531,976 v Tottenham H, Worthington Cup semi-final, 2nd leg, 16 February 1999.
Pitch Measurements: 110yd × 74yd.
Chairman: B. R. Gjelsten.
Deputy Chairman: C. Koppel.
Directors: K. I. Røkke, S. Reed, J. H. Lelliott, P. R. Lloyd Cooper, P. E. Cork, P. J. B. Miller, M. Hauger, C. Stromberg.
Company Secretary: P. R. Lloyd Cooper.
Chief Executive: David Barnard.
Manager: Terry Burton.
Coaches: Mick Harford, Stewart Robson.
Club Secretary: Steve Rooke.
Marketing Manager: Sharon Sillitoe.
Press and PR Manager: Reg Davis.
Chief Scout: Ron Suart.
Physio: Steve Allen.
Stadium Manager: Vic Worrall.
Safety Officer: Bob Morrison.

LATEST SEQUENCES

Longest Sequence of League Wins: 7, 4.9.96 – 19.10.96.
Longest Sequence of League Defeats: 8, 19.3.00 – 30.4.00.
Longest Sequence of League Draws: 4, 26.10.96 – 23.11.96.
Longest Sequence of Unbeaten League Matches: 22, 15.1.83 – 14.5.83.
Longest Sequence Without a League Win: 14, 16.9.95 – 23.12.95.

HONOURS

FA Premier League: best season: 6th, 1993–94.

Football League: Division 3 – Runners-up 1983–84; Division 4 – Champions 1982–83.

FA Cup: Winners 1988.

Football League Cup: Semi-final 1996–97, 1998–99.

League Group Cup: Runners-up 1982.

Amateur Cup: Winners 1963; Runners-up 1935, 1947.

Colours
All navy blue with yellow trim.

Change Colours
All teal green with whie trim.

Year Formed: 1889.

Turned Professional: 1964.

Ltd Co.: 1964.

Previous Name: Wimbledon Old Centrals, 1899–1905.

Previous Ground: 1899, Plough Lane; 1991, Selhurst Park.

Club Nickname: 'The Dons', 'The Crazy Gang'.

First Football League Game: 20 August 1977, Division 4, v Halifax T (h) D 3–3 – Guy; Bryant (1), Galvin, Donaldson, Aitken, Davies, Galliers, Smith, Connell (1), Holmes, Leslie (1).

Record League Victory: 6–0 v Newport Co, Division 3, 3 September 1983 – Beasant; Peters, Winterburn, Galliers, Morris, Hatter, Evans (2), Ketteridge (1), Cork (3 incl. 1p), Downes, Hodges (Driver).

Record Cup Victory: 7–2 v Windsor & Eton, FA Cup 1st rd, 22 November 1980 – Beasant; Jones, Armstrong, Galliers, Mick Smith (2), Cunningham (1), Ketteridge, Hodges, Leslie, Cork (1), Hubbick (3).

Record Defeat: 0–8 v Everton, League Cup 2nd rd, 29 August 1978.

Most League Points (2 for a win): 61, Division 4, 1978–79.

Most League Points (3 for a win): 98, Division 4, 1982–83.

Most League Goals: 97, Division 3, 1983–84.

Highest League Scorer in Season: Alan Cork, 29, 1983–84.

Most League Goals in Total Aggregate: Alan Cork, 145, 1977–92.

Most League Goals in One Match: 4, Alan Cork v Torquay U, Division 4, 28 February 1979.

Most Capped Player: Kenny Cunningham, 31, Republic of Ireland.

Most League Appearances: Alan Cork, 430, 1977–92.

Youngest League Player: Kevin Gage, 17 years 15 days v Bury, 2 May 1981.

Record Transfer Fee Received: £7,000,000 from Newcastle U for Carl Cort, July 2000.

Record Transfer Fee Paid: £7,500,000 to West Ham U for John Hartson, January 1999.

Football League Record: 1977 Elected to Division 4; 1979–80 Division 3; 1980–81 Division 4; 1981–82 Division 3; 1982–83 Division 4; 1983–84 Division 3; 1984–86 Division 2; 1986–92 Division 1; 1992–2000 FA Premier League; 2000– Division 1.

MANAGERS

Les Henley 1955–71
Mike Everitt 1971–73
Dick Graham 1973–74
Allen Batsford 1974–78
Dario Gradi 1978–81
Dave Bassett 1981–87
Bobby Gould 1987–90
Ray Harford 1990–91
Peter Withe 1991
Joe Kinnear 1992–99
Egil Olsen 1999–2000
Terry Burton May 2000–

TEN YEAR LEAGUE RECORD

		P	W	D	L	F	A	Pts	Pos
1989-90	Div 1	38	13	16	9	47	40	55	8
1990-91	Div 1	38	14	14	10	53	46	56	7
1991-92	Div 1	42	13	14	15	53	53	53	13
1992-93	PR Lge	42	14	12	16	56	55	54	12
1993-94	PR Lge	42	18	11	13	56	53	65	6
1994-95	PR Lge	42	15	11	16	48	65	56	9
1995-96	PR Lge	38	10	11	17	55	70	41	14
1996-97	PR Lge	38	15	11	12	49	46	56	8
1997-98	PR Lge	38	10	14	14	34	46	44	15
1998-99	PR Lge	38	10	12	16	40	63	42	16

DID YOU KNOW

In 1930–31, Wimbledon won the Isthmian League Championship for the first time, won five cup competitions and suffered only seven defeats throughout, two of these by third division clubs.

WIMBLEDON 1999–2000 LEAGUE RECORD

Match No.	Date		Venue	Opponents	Result	H/T Score	Lg. Pos.	Goalscorers	Attendance
1	Aug	7	A	Watford	W 3-2	2-1	2	Cort 10, Gayle 28, Johnson (og) 78	15,511
2		10	H	Middlesbrough	L 2-3	1-2	—	Cort 17, Hartson 86	11,036
3		14	H	Coventry C	D 1-1	0-0	10	Cort 67	10,635
4		21	A	Newcastle U	D 3-3	1-2	11	Hughes M 44, Ainsworth 2 68, 90	35,809
5		25	A	Everton	L 0-4	0-1	—		32,818
6		28	H	Chelsea	L 0-1	0-0	17		22,167
7	Sept	11	H	Derby Co	D 2-2	0-1	16	Hartson 62, Euell 63	12,282
8		18	A	Manchester U	D 1-1	1-0	16	Badir 16	55,189
9		26	H	Tottenham H	D 1-1	0-0	16	Hartson 57	17,368
10	Oct	2	A	Sheffield W	L 1-5	1-2	17	Hartson 14	18,077
11		16	H	Bradford C	W 3-2	2-1	15	Hartson 2 22, 36, Cort 75	10,029
12		23	A	Aston Villa	D 1-1	1-1	15	Earle 26	27,160
13		30	H	Southampton	D 1-1	0-0	15	Gayle 90	15,754
14	Nov	7	H	Leeds U	W 2-0	1-0	15	Hartson 31, Gayle 65	18,747
15		20	A	Leicester C	L 1-2	1-1	15	Gayle 21	18,255
16		27	A	Middlesbrough	D 0-0	0-0	14		31,400
17	Dec	4	H	Watford	W 5-0	2-0	13	Cort 15, Earle 32, Hartson 61, Euell 67, Gayle 78	14,021
18		18	A	Arsenal	D 1-1	1-0	14	Cort 7	38,052
19		26	H	West Ham U	D 2-2	1-1	14	Hreidarsson 33, Ardley 85	21,180
20		28	A	Liverpool	L 1-3	0-0	15	Gayle 64	44,107
21	Jan	3	H	Sunderland	W 1-0	1-0	13	Cort 30	17,621
22		15	A	Coventry C	L 0-2	0-0	15		19,005
23		22	H	Newcastle U	W 2-0	0-0	13	Earle 48, Gayle 69	22,118
24	Feb	6	H	Everton	L 0-3	0-0	14		13,172
25		12	A	Chelsea	L 1-3	0-0	15	Lund 73	34,814
26		26	H	Manchester U	D 2-2	1-1	15	Euell 1, Cort 62	26,129
27	Mar	4	A	Derby Co	L 0-4	0-0	16		28,384
28		11	H	Leicester C	W 2-1	1-0	15	Ardley (pen) 33, Cort 87	14,316
29		19	A	Leeds U	L 1-4	1-3	16	Euell 2	39,256
30		26	A	West Ham U	L 1-2	0-1	16	Hughes M 75	22,438
31	Apr	1	H	Arsenal	L 1-3	1-2	16	Lund 12	25,858
32		8	A	Sunderland	L 1-2	0-0	17	Holloway (og) 73	40,510
33		12	H	Sheffield W	L 0-2	0-1	—		8248
34		16	H	Liverpool	L 1-2	0-1	17	Andresen 70	26,102
35		22	A	Tottenham H	L 0-2	0-2	17		33,089
36		30	A	Bradford C	L 0-3	0-1	18		18,276
37	May	6	H	Aston Villa	D 2-2	1-0	17	Ehiogu (og) 15, Hartson 90	19,188
38		14	A	Southampton	L 0-2	0-0	18		15,249

Final League Position: 18

GOALSCORERS

League (46): Cort 9, Hartson 9, Gayle 7, Euell 4, Earle 3, Ainsworth 2, Ardley 2 (1 pen), Hughes M 2, Lund 2, Andresen 1, Badir 1, Hreidarsson 1, own goals 3.
Worthington Cup (10): Cort 5, Earle 2, Euell 1, Hughes M 1, Kimble 1.
FA Cup (1): Cort 1.

Sullivan N 37	Cunningham K 37	Kimble A 24+4	Roberts A 14+2	Blackwell D 16+1	Pedersen T 6	Hughes M 13+7	Earle R 23+2	Hartson J 15+1	Cort C 32+2	Gayle M 35+1	Jupp D 6+3	Ardley N 10+7	Euell J 32+5	Thatcher B 19+1	Leaburn C 5+13	Andersen T 35+1	Ainsworth G —+2	Badir W 12+9	Hreidarsson H 24	Andresen M 4+10	Francis D 1+8	Willmott C 7	Gray W —+1	Lund A 10+2	Heald P 1	Match No
1	2	3	4	5	6	7¹	8	9²	10	11³	12	13	14													1
1	2	3¹	4	5	6	7²	8³	9	10	11			13	12	14											2
1	2		4¹	5	6	12	8²	9	10	11³			14	13	3		7									3
1	5	3	4		6	11²	8¹		10	9			12	2	13	7³	14									4
1	6	3	4²	5		11¹	8³		10	9			7	2	12	13	14									5
1	2	12	4		6¹	11	8³		10	9			13	3	14	5	7²									6
1	2		4		6		12	9	10	11			8	3		5	7¹									7
1	2		4	5				9	10¹	11	12		8	3		6	7									8
1	2	12	4	5				9	10	11			8	3		6¹	7									9
1	2	12	4³	5		13		9	10	11			8	3	14	6¹	7²									10
1	2	12	13	5²		8		9	10	11³			7	3¹	14	6		4								11
1	2	3				8		9²	10	11¹			7	5	12	6		4	13							12
1	2	3				8²		9	10	11			7	5	12	6¹		13	4							13
1	2	3				8		9¹	10³	11²			7	5	12	6		13	4	14						14
1	2	3	5¹			8		9	10	11			7			6		12	4							15
1	2	3				12	8		10	11			7	5	9¹	6		4								16
1	2	3³	12			13	8	9	10²	11			7	5¹		6		4	14							17
1	2	3	4			12	8	9	10²	11¹			7			6		13		4						18
1	2	3				12	8			11	7	10	9¹	5		6	4									19
1	2	3¹				8		12		11	10	5	9²	6		7³	4	13	14							20
1	2						9	11			12	8	3	6		7¹	4	10²	13	5						21
1	2	3				8		9			7¹	10	5	12	4	11	6²		13							22
1	2	3				8		10	11		12	7	9¹	5		6	4									23
1	2	3				8¹		10	11		12	7	9²	5		6³	4	13	14							24
1	2	3				8²		10			12	7		6		4	11¹	13	5	9						25
1	2	3						10	11		7²	8		6	12	4	13		5	9¹						26
1	2	3						10	11		7¹	8		6	12	4		5	9							27
	2	3				12	8	10	11		4¹	7		6			13		5	9²	1					28
1	2	3				12	8	10²	11		4	7		6	13				5	9¹						29
1	2	3				12	7	8³	11		4⁴	10	13	6			14	5¹	9							30
1	3	4²	5				11	2	12	10		6	13	8¹					9							31
1	3		5	7			11	2	8		12	6	10¹	4					9							32
1	3		5	7		12	11	2	8	13	6	10¹	4						9²							33
1	3	8	5¹	7		10	11	2		12	6		4	13					9²							34
1	5	3	8¹			11	10	9¹	2		7	6		4	12²	13			14							35
1	2		5¹	11		9	10	12	7	8	3	6		4												36
1	2²		5	11³		12	10¹	9	13	7	8	3	6		4	14										37
1	11³		5²			10	9¹	2	7	8	3	6		12	4	13		14								38

Worthington Cup

Second Round	Cardiff C	(a)	1-1
		(h)	3-1
Third Round	Sunderland	(h)	3-2
Fourth Round	Huddersfield T	(a)	2-1
Fifth Round	Bolton W	(a)	1-2

FA Cup

Third Round	Barnsley	(h)	1-0
Fourth Round	Fulham	(a)	0-3

Division 1 **WOLVERHAMPTON WANDERERS**

FOUNDATION

Another club where precise details of information are confused, due in part to the existence of an earlier Wolverhampton club which played rugby. However, it is now considered likely that it came into being in 1879 when players from St Luke's (founded 1877) and Wanderers Cricket Club joined forces to form Wolverhampton Wanderers FC.

Molineux Grounds, Wolverhampton WV1 4QR.

Telephone: (01902) 655 000.

Fax: (01902) 687 006.

ClubCall: 09068 121 103.

Ground Capacity: 28,525.

Record Attendance: 63,315 v Liverpool, FA Cup 5th rd, 11 February 1939.

Record Receipts: £319,141 v Arsenal, FA Cup 4th rd, 24 January 1999.

Pitch Measurements: 110yd × 75yd.

President: Sir Jack Hayward.

Chairman: Sir Jack Hayward.

Managing Director: John Richards.

Directors: Jack Harris, John Harris, Rachael Heyhoe Flint, Rick Hayward.

Manager: Colin Lee.

Assistant Manager: John Ward.

Stadium Manager: Clive Mountford.

Coach: Terry Connor.

Physio: Barry Holmes.

Secretary: Richard Skirrow.

LATEST SEQUENCES

Longest Sequence of League Wins: 8, 15.10.88 – 26.11.88.

Longest Sequence of League Defeats: 8, 5.12.81 – 13.2.82.

Longest Sequence of League Draws: 6, 22.4.95 – 20.8.95.

Longest Sequence of Unbeaten League Matches: 20, 24.11.23 – 5.4.24.

Longest Sequence Without a League Win: 19, 1.12.84 – 6.4.85.

HONOURS

Football League: Division 1 – Champions 1953–54, 1957–58, 1958–59; Runners-up 1937–38, 1938–39, 1949–50, 1954–55, 1959–60; Division 2 – Champions 1931–32, 1976–77; Runners-up 1966–67, 1982–83; Division 3 (N) – Champions 1923–24; Division 3 – Champions 1988–89; Division 4 – Champions 1987–88.

FA Cup: Winners 1893, 1908, 1949, 1960; Runners-up 1889, 1896, 1921, 1939.

Football League Cup: Winners 1974, 1980.

Texaco Cup: Winners 1971.

Sherpa Van Trophy: Winners 1988.

European Competitions: *European Cup:* 1958–59, 1959–60. *European Cup-Winners' Cup:* 1960–61. *UEFA Cup:* 1971–72 (runners-up), 1973–74, 1974–75, 1980–81.

Colours
Gold shirts, black shorts, gold stockings.

Change Colours
White shirts, white shorts.

Year Formed: 1877* (*see Foundation*).

Turned Professional: 1888.

Ltd Co.: 1982.

Previous Names: 1879, St Luke's combined with Wanderers Cricket Club to become Wolverhampton Wanderers (1923) Ltd until 1982.

Club Nickname: 'Wolves'.

Previous Grounds: 1877, Goldthorn Hill; 1879, John Harper's Field; 1881, Dudley Road; 1889, Molineux.

First Football League Game: 8 September 1888, Football League, v Aston Villa (h) D 1–1 – Baynton; Baugh, Mason; Fletcher, Allen, Lowder; Hunter, Cooper, Anderson, White, Cannon, (1 og).

Record League Victory: 10–1 v Leicester C, Division 1, 15 April 1938 – Sidlow; Morris, Dowen; Galley, Cullis, Gardiner; Maguire (1), Horace Wright, Westcott (4), Jones (1), Dorsett (4).

Record Cup Victory: 14–0 v Cresswell's Brewery, FA Cup 2nd rd, 13 November 1886 – I. Griffiths; Baugh, Mason; Pearson, Allen (1), Lowder; Hunter (4), Knight (2), Brodie (4), B. Griffiths (2), Wood. Plus one goal 'scrambled through'.

Record Defeat: 1–10 v Newton Heath, Division 1, 15 October 1892.

Most League Points (2 for a win): 64, Division 1, 1957–58.

Most League Points (3 for a win): 92, Division 4, 1988–89.

Most League Goals: 115, Division 2, 1931–32.

Highest League Scorer in Season: Dennis Westcott, 38, Division 1, 1946–47.

Most League Goals in Total Aggregate: Steve Bull, 250, 1986–99.

Most League Goals in One Match: 5, Joe Butcher v Accrington, Division 1, 19 November 1892; 5, Tom Phillipson v Barnsley, Division 2, 26 April 1926; 5, Tom Phillipson v Bradford C, Division 2, 25 December 1926; 5, Billy Hartill v Notts Co, Division 2, 12 October 1929; 5, Billy Hartill v Aston Villa, Division 1, 3 September 1934.

Most Capped Player: Billy Wright, 105, England (70 consecutive).

Most League Appearances: Derek Parkin, 501, 1967–82.

Youngest League Player: Jimmy Mullen, 16 years 43 days v Leeds U, 18 February 1939.

Record Transfer Fee Received: £2,000,000 from Crystal Palace for Neil Emblen, August 1997.

Record Transfer Fee Paid: £3,000,000 to Bristol C for Ade Akinbiyi, September 1999.

Football League Record: 1888 Founder Member of Football League: 1906–23 Division 2; 1923–24 Division 3 (N); 1924–32 Division 2; 1932–65 Division 1; 1965–67 Division 2; 1967–76 Division 1; 1976–77 Division 2; 1977–82 Division 1; 1982–83 Division 2; 1983–84 Division 1; 1984–85 Division 2; 1985–86 Division 3; 1986–88 Division 4; 1988–89 Division 3; 1989–92 Division 2; 1992– Division 1.

MANAGERS

George Worrall 1877–85
(Secretary-Manager)
John Addenbrooke 1885–1922
George Jobey 1922–24
Albert Hoskins 1924–26
(had been Secretary since 1922)
Fred Scotchbrook 1926–27
Major Frank Buckley 1927–44
Ted Vizard 1944–48
Stan Cullis 1948–64
Andy Beattie 1964–65
Ronnie Allen 1966–68
Bill McGarry 1968–76
Sammy Chung 1976–78
John Barnwell 1978–81
Ian Greaves 1982
Graham Hawkins 1982–84
Tommy Docherty 1984–85
Bill McGarry 1985
Sammy Chapman 1985–86
Brian Little 1986
Graham Turner 1986–94
Graham Taylor 1994–95
Mark McGhee 1995–98
Colin Lee November 1998–

TEN YEAR LEAGUE RECORD

		P	W	D	L	F	A	Pts	Pos
1989-90	Div 2	46	18	13	15	67	60	67	10
1990-91	Div 2	46	13	19	14	63	63	58	12
1991-92	Div 2	46	18	10	18	61	54	64	11
1992-93	Div 1	46	16	13	17	57	56	61	11
1993-94	Div 1	46	17	17	12	60	47	68	8
1994-95	Div 1	46	21	13	12	77	61	76	4
1995-96	Div 1	46	13	16	17	56	62	55	20
1996-97	Div 1	46	22	10	14	68	51	76	3
1997-98	Div 1	46	18	11	17	57	53	65	9
1998-99	Div 1	46	19	16	11	64	43	73	7

DID YOU KNOW ?

On 25 September 1920 in the match between Wolverhampton Wanderers and Bristol City at Molineux, a shot from Wolves' George Edmonds went straight through City net, but the referee refused to allow the goal. The match ended goalless.

WOLVERHAMPTON WANDERERS 1999–2000 LEAGUE RECORD

Match No.	Date		Venue	Opponents	Result	H/T Score	Lg. Pos.	Goalscorers	Attendance
1	Aug	8	A	Manchester C	W 1-0	1-0	6	Keane [30]	31,755
2		14	H	Portsmouth	D 1-1	0-1	8	Keane [48]	21,024
3		21	A	QPR	D 1-1	1-0	7	Corica [35]	13,239
4		28	H	Walsall	L 1-2	1-2	13	Robinson [31]	24,439
5	Sept	11	H	Huddersfield T	L 0-1	0-0	18		20,385
6		19	A	Nottingham F	D 1-1	1-0	19	Bazeley [18]	20,694
7		25	A	Sheffield U	L 0-3	0-0	21		14,163
8		28	A	Crystal Palace	D 1-1	1-0	—	Akinbiyi [43]	12,720
9	Oct	3	H	WBA	D 1-1	1-0	20	Akinbiyi [41]	25,500
10		9	H	Bolton W	W 1-0	1-0	18	Akinbiyi [3]	18,665
11		16	A	Barnsley	W 2-1	2-0	12	Taylor [5], Akinbiyi [33]	14,923
12		19	A	Fulham	W 1-0	0-0	—	Emblen [56]	13,160
13		23	H	Port Vale	D 2-2	0-0	10	Sedgley [47], Curle (pen) [89]	20,488
14		26	H	Sheffield U	W 1-0	0-0	—	Emblen [89]	24,402
15		31	A	WBA	D 1-1	0-1	10	Akinbiyi [82]	21,097
16	Nov	6	H	Grimsby T	W 3-0	1-0	10	Akinbiyi [3, 6, 79, 89]	19,036
17		20	H	Swindon T	D 1-1	0-1	11	Flo [81]	19,917
18		24	A	Ipswich T	L 0-1	0-0	—		15,731
19		27	A	Tranmere R	L 0-1	0-0	11		8017
20	Dec	3	H	Manchester C	W 4-1	3-1	—	Akinbiyi [5], Branch 2 [18, 40], Muscat [68]	21,635
21		14	A	Crewe Alex	L 0-1	0-0	—		6018
22		17	H	Birmingham C	W 2-1	1-1	—	Akinbiyi [39], Pollet [63]	19,724
23		26	A	Stockport Co	L 2-3	2-1	12	Emblen [12], Pollet [37]	10,278
24		28	H	Norwich C	W 1-0	0-0	10	Branch [57]	25,072
25	Jan	3	A	Blackburn R	D 1-1	1-1	11	Naylor [36]	24,743
26		11	H	Charlton Ath	L 2-3	1-2	—	Flo [18], Pringle (og) [76]	18,464
27		15	A	Portsmouth	W 3-2	0-2	9	Sedgley [73], Branch [85], Akinbiyi [89]	13,255
28		22	H	QPR	W 3-2	3-0	6	Sedgley [22], Branch [23], Akinbiyi [29]	20,069
29		29	A	Walsall	D 1-1	0-0	6	Emblen [76]	9422
30	Feb	5	H	Crystal Palace	W 2-1	1-0	6	Sedgley [15], Pollet [47]	20,756
31		12	A	Charlton Ath	L 0-2	0-0	7		20,043
32		16	H	Tranmere R	W 4-0	2-0	—	Akinbiyi 2 [35, 88], Naylor [45], Bazeley [69]	18,186
33		26	H	Nottingham F	W 3-0	3-0	7	Pollet [8], Bazeley [20], Branch [25]	24,444
34	Mar	4	A	Huddersfield T	L 0-2	0-2	7		17,214
35		7	A	Grimsby T	L 0-1	0-1	—		5575
36		11	H	Ipswich T	W 2-1	1-0	7	Flo 2 [4, 46]	22,652
37		18	A	Swindon T	W 2-1	0-0	7	Muscat [58], Robinson [85]	8748
38		21	H	Crewe Alex	W 2-0	1-0	—	Sedgley [14], Taylor [68]	20,444
39		25	H	Stockport Co	D 2-2	1-1	7	Curle (pen) [43], Emblen [90]	25,065
40	Apr	1	A	Birmingham C	L 0-1	0-0	7		29,050
41		8	H	Blackburn R	W 2-1	1-0	7	Muscat (pen) [40], Nielsen [72]	22,286
42		15	A	Norwich C	L 0-1	0-0	7		15,910
43		22	H	Barnsley	W 2-0	1-0	7	Akinbiyi 2 [43, 52]	21,251
44		30	H	Fulham	W 3-0	0-0	7	Nielsen [50], Muscat (pen) [60], Taylor [90]	19,912
45	May	3	A	Bolton W	L 1-2	1-0	—	Pollet [45]	18,871
46		7	A	Port Vale	W 1-0	0-0	7	Robinson [85]	8525

Final League Position: 7

GOALSCORERS
League (64): Akinbiyi 16, Branch 6, Emblen 5, Pollet 5, Sedgley 5, Flo 4, Muscat 4 (2 pens), Bazeley 3, Robinson 3, Taylor 3, Curle 2 (2 pens), Keane 2, Naylor 2, Nielsen 2, Corica 1, own goal 1.
Worthington Cup (3): Curle 1 (pen), Emblen 1, Larkin 1.
FA Cup (2): Robinson 1, Sedgley 1.

Stowell M 18	Muscat K 45	Naylor L 24+6	Robinson C 21+12	Curle K 44+1	Emblen N 45+1	Bazeley D 46	Osborn S 22+3	Flo H 9+10	Keane R 2	Sinton A 31+4	Sedgley S 32+6	Corica S 10+5	Simpson P 1+12	Larkin C 1	Pollet L 38+1	Akinbyi A 36+1	Niestroj R —+1	Jones M —+1	Taylor S 18+10	Ndah G 3+1	Oakes M 28	Branch M 25+2	Andrews K —+2	Williams A —+1	Nielsen A 7	Match No
1	2	3	4	5	6	7	8[1]	9	10[2]	11[3]	12	13	14													1
1	2	3	4	5	6	7		9	10	11	8															2
1	2	3	4	5	6	7		9		11	8	10[1]	12													3
1	3	12	4	5	6	2	8	9		11	13	7[1]			10[2]											4
1	2	3[1]	4[2]	5	6	7	8	9		11	12	13			10											5
1	2	3	4	5	6	7	8	12		11[3]	10[1]	13			9											6
1	2[2]	3	4	5	6	7	8			11[1]	10[1]	12			9	13	14									7
1	2	3	4	5	6	7	8			11[1]	12	10			9											8
1	3	4	5	7	2	8				11					6	9			10							9
1	3	12	5	7	2	8	4			11[2]	13				6	9			10[1]							10
1	3	12	13	5[1]	7	2	8	4		10[3]	14				6	9			11[2]							11
1	3	12	5	7	2	8	4			10[1]					6	9			11							12
1	3[2]	12	5	7	2	8	13	4							6	9			11[1]			10				13
1	3	5	7	2	8	12	4								6	9			11[1]			10				14
1	3	12	5	7	2	8	13	4			14				6[1]	9			11[2]			10[3]				15
1	3	12	5	6	2	8[2]	11	4		7[1]					13	9						10				16
1	3	5	4	2	8[1]	13	11	12		7[2]					6	9						10				17
1	3	7[1]	5	11	2	8[2]	12	13		4					6	9						10				18
	3	12	5	4[3]	2	8	13	11		14					6	9			10[2]		1	7[1]				19
	2	3	5	4	7	8				11[2]	12				6	9			13		1	10[1]				20
	2	3	5	4	7	8				11					6	9					1	10				21
	2	3	5	4	7	8				11					6	9			12		1	10[1]				22
	2	3	4	5	11	7	8[2]				12	13			6	9					1	10[1]				23
	2	3	4	5	8	7				11	12				6	9					1	10[1]				24
	2	3	4	5[3]	8	7				11[1]	12		14		6	9[2]			13		1	10				25
	2	3	4[2]	5	8	7		9		11	12	13			6[1]						1	10				26
	2	3	4[1]	5	8	7				11	12				6	9					1	10				27
	2	3	12	5	13	7	8[2]	4		11					6	9					1	10[1]				28
	2	3	4	5	8	7				11					6	9					1	10				29
	2	3	4	5	8	7				11					6	9					1	10				30
		3	4[2]	5	7	2	8			11[3]	12		14		6	9			13		1	10[1]				31
	2	3	12	5	8[2]	7	13	4		11[3]	14				6	9			10[1]		1					32
	2[2]	3	12	5	8	7	4[1]			11	13				6	9			14		1	10[3]				33
	2	3[1]	4	5	8	7				11	12				6	9			13		1	10[1]				34
	2	3	4	5	8	7				11		10[1]			6	9					1	12				35
	3	4	5	8	2	7				11					6	9					1	10				36
	3	12[1]	4	5	2	7	8			11					6[3]	9[1]					1	10	14	13		37
	3	4	5	8	2	7				11					6	9			10[1]		1	12				38
	3		4	5	2		8			11	12				6	9					1	10			7[1]	39
	2	3	4[1]	5		7				11[2]		10			6	9			13		1	12			8	40
	2	3	4[2]	5		7				11	12				6	9[1]			13		1	10			8	41
	2	3	4	5		7				11[1]	12				6	9					1	10			8	42
	2	3	4	5		7				11[1]	12				6	9			13		1	10			8[2]	43
	3	13	12	5	7	2	4			11[2]					6[1]	9			14		1	10			8[3]	44
	2	3	12	5		7	4			11					6	9			13		1	10[2]			8[1]	45
	2	3	12	5		7	8	4		11[2]		13			6	9					1	10[1]				46

Worthington Cup
First Round   Wycombe W   (a) 1-0
                            (h) 2-4

FA Cup
Third Round   Wigan Ath   (a) 1-0
Fourth Round   Sheffield W (a) 1-1
                            (h) 0-0

Division 2   **WREXHAM**

FOUNDATION

The club was formed on 28 September 1872 by members of Wrexham Cricket Club, so they could continue playing a sport during the winter months. This meeting was held at the Turf Hotel, which although rebuilt since, still stands at one corner of the present ground. Their first game was a few weeks later and matches often included 17 players on either side! By 1875 team formations were reduced to 11 men and a year later the club was among the founder members of the Cambrian Football Association, which quickly changed its title to the Football Association of Wales.

Racecourse Ground, Mold Road, Wrexham LL11 2AH.
Telephone: (01978) 262 129.
Fax: (01978) 357 821.
Commercial Dept: (01978) 352 536.
Community Office: (01978) 358 545.
ClubCall: 09068 121 642.
Ground Capacity: 15,500.
Record Attendance: 34,445 v Manchester U, FA Cup 4th rd, 26 January 1957.
Record Receipts: £126,012 v West Ham U, FA Cup 4th rd, 4 February 1992.
Pitch Measurements: 111yd × 71yd.
Chairman: W. P. Griffiths.
Managing Director: D. L. Rhodes.
Directors: C. Griffiths (Vice-Chairman), B. Williams.
Manager: Brian Flynn.
Assistant Manager: Kevin Reeves.
Secretary: D. L. Rhodes.
Player-Coach: Joey Jones.
Commercial Manager: Allan Thomas.
Physio: Mel Pejic.

LATEST SEQUENCES

Longest Sequence of League Wins: 7, 4.3.78 – 27.3.78.
Longest Sequence of League Defeats: 9, 2.10.63 – 30.10.63.
Longest Sequence of League Draws: 6, 12.11.99 – 26.12.99.
Longest Sequence of Unbeaten League Matches: 16, 3.9.66 – 19.11.66.
Longest Sequence Without a League Win: 16, 25.9.99 – 3.1.00.

HONOURS

Football League: Division 2 best season: 7th, 1997–98; Division 3 – Champions 1977–78; Runners-up 1992–93; Division 3 (N) – Runners-up 1932–33; Division 4 – Runners-up 1969–70.

FA Cup: best season: 6th rd, 1974, 1978, 1997.

Football League Cup: best season: 5th rd, 1961, 1978.

Welsh Cup: Winners 23 times (record); Runners-up 22 times (record).

FAW Premier Cup: Winners 1998, 2000.

European Competition: *European Cup-Winners' Cup:* 1972–73, 1975–76, 1978–79, 1979–80, 1984–85, 1986–87, 1990–91, 1995–96.

Colours
Red shirts, white shorts, red stockings.

Change Colours
Gold shirts, navy blue shorts, navy blue stockings.

Year Formed: 1872 (oldest club in Wales).

Turned Professional: 1912.

Ltd Co.: 1912.

Club Nickname: 'Robins'.

Previous Grounds: 1872, Racecourse Ground; 1883, Rhosddu Recreation Ground; 1887, Racecourse Ground.

First Football League Game: 27 August 1921, Division 3 (N), v Hartlepools U (h) L 0–2 – Godding; Ellis, Simpson; Matthias, Foster, Griffiths; Burton, Goode, Cotton, Edwards, Lloyd.

Record League Victory: 10–1 v Hartlepool U, Division 4, 3 March 1962 – Keelan; Peter Jones, McGavan; Tecwyn Jones, Fox, Ken Barnes; Ron Barnes (3), Bennion (1), Davies (3), Ambler (3), Ron Roberts.

Record Cup Victory: 11–1 v New Brighton, Football League Northern Section Cup 1st rd, 3 January 1934 – Foster; Alfred Jones, Hamilton, Bulling, McMahon, Lawrence, Bryant (3), Findlay (1), Bamford (5), Snow, Waller (1), (o.g. 1).

Record Defeat: 0–9 v Brentford, Division 3, 15 October 1963.

Most League Points (2 for a win): 61, Division 4, 1969–70 and Division 3, 1977–78.

Most League Points (3 for a win): 80, Division 3, 1992–93.

Most League Goals: 106, Division 3 (N), 1932–33.

Highest League Scorer in Season: Tom Bamford, 44, Division 3 (N), 1933–34.

MANAGERS
Selection Committee 1872–1924
Charlie Hewitt 1924–25
Selection Committee 1925–1929
Jack Baynes 1929–31
Ernest Blackburn 1932–37
James Logan 1937–38
Arthur Cowell 1938
Tom Morgan 1938–42
Tom Williams 1942–49
Les McDowell 1949–50
Peter Jackson 1950–55
Cliff Lloyd 1955–57
John Love 1957–59
Cliff Lloyd 1959–60
Billy Morris 1960–61
Ken Barnes 1961–65
Billy Morris 1965
Jack Rowley 1966–67
Alvan Williams 1967–68
John Neal 1968–77
Arfon Griffiths 1977–81
Mel Sutton 1981–82
Bobby Roberts 1982–85
Dixie McNeil 1985–89
Brian Flynn November 1989–

Most League Goals in Total Aggregate: Tom Bamford, 175, 1928–34.

Most League Goals in One Match: 5, Tom Bamford v Carlisle U, Division 3N, 17 March 1934.

Most Capped Player: Joey Jones, 29 (72), Wales.

Most League Appearances: Arfon Griffiths, 592, 1959–61, 1962–79.

Youngest League Player: Ken Roberts, 15 years 158 days v Bradford PA, 1 September 1951.

Record Transfer Fee Received: £800,000 from Birmingham C for Bryan Hughes, March 1997.

Record Transfer Fee Paid: £210,000 to Liverpool for Joey Jones, October 1978.

Football League Record: 1921 Original Member of Division 3 (N); 1958–60 Division 3; 1960–62 Division 4; 1962–64 Division 3; 1964–70 Division 4; 1970–78 Division 3; 1978–82 Division 2; 1982–83 Division 3; 1983–92 Division 4; 1992–93 Division 3; 1993– Division 2.

TEN YEAR LEAGUE RECORD

		P	W	D	L	F	A	Pts	Pos
1989-90	Div 4	46	13	12	21	51	67	51	21
1990-91	Div 4	46	10	10	26	48	74	40	24
1991-92	Div 4	42	14	9	19	52	73	51	14
1992-93	Div 3	42	23	11	8	75	52	80	2
1993-94	Div 2	46	17	11	18	66	77	62	12
1994-95	Div 2	46	16	15	15	65	64	63	13
1995-96	Div 2	46	18	16	12	76	55	70	8
1996-97	Div 2	46	17	18	11	54	50	69	8
1997-98	Div 2	46	18	16	12	55	51	70	7
1998-99	Div 2	46	13	14	19	43	62	53	17

DID YOU KNOW ?

On 11 December 1999, Wrexham beat Middlesbrough 2-1 in the FA Cup third round with six players under the age of 21 and five of the team former club trainees.

WREXHAM 1999–2000 LEAGUE RECORD

Match No.	Date	Venue	Opponents	Result	H/T Score	Lg. Pos.	Goalscorers	Attendance
1	Aug 7	A	Blackpool	L	1-2	0-2	21	Faulconbridge [85]	5008
2	14	H	Bury	W	1-0	1-0	15	Stevens [35]	4185
3	20	A	Cardiff C	D	1-1	0-1	—	Stevens [55]	11,168
4	28	H	Bristol R	W	2-1	0-0	6	Faulconbridge 2 [47, 88]	3365
5	31	A	Wycombe W	W	1-0	0-0	—	Barrett [66]	5393
6	Sept 3	H	Notts Co	L	2-3	0-3	—	Faulconbridge [61], Edwards [83]	5030
7	11	A	Luton T	L	1-3	1-3	9	Stevens [19]	5121
8	18	H	Oxford U	W	1-0	1-0	7	Stevens [4]	4229
9	25	H	Stoke C	L	2-3	1-1	11	Carey [6], Lowe [83]	5924
10	Oct 1	A	Colchester U	D	2-2	0-0	—	Owen [56], Morrell [85]	3315
11	9	A	Gillingham	L	1-5	1-2	13	Faulconbridge [45]	5997
12	16	H	Chesterfield	D	1-1	0-1	13	Roberts N [56]	2603
13	19	H	Wigan Ath	D	1-1	0-0	—	Roberts N (pen) [60]	3392
14	23	A	Stoke C	L	2-2	0-0	15		10,545
15	Nov 2	A	Burnley	L	0-5	0-1	—		8944
16	6	H	Brentford	L	0-1	0-1	15		2473
17	12	A	Millwall	D	0-0	0-0	16		6711
18	23	H	Cambridge U	D	1-1	0-1	—	Faulconbridge [73]	3467
19	27	A	Oldham Ath	D	0-0	0-0	18		4963
20	Dec 4	H	Blackpool	D	1-1	0-1	18	Faulconbridge [54]	2668
21	18	A	Reading	D	2-2	1-1	17	Owen [45], Roberts N [54]	6223
22	26	H	Preston NE	D	0-0	0-0	18		7872
23	28	A	Bournemouth	L	0-1	0-1	19		5394
24	Jan 3	H	Bristol C	L	0-1	0-0	19		4021
25	15	A	Bury	W	2-0	1-0	19	Roberts N 2 [45, 74]	3622
26	22	H	Cardiff C	W	2-1	0-0	17	Connolly [55], Ferguson [74]	4350
27	29	A	Bristol R	L	1-3	0-1	17	Roberts N [75]	8196
28	Feb 1	A	Scunthorpe U	W	2-0	2-0	—	Barrett [26], Connolly [30]	2851
29	5	H	Wycombe W	L	1-3	1-0	17	Faulconbridge [23]	2781
30	12	A	Notts Co	L	1-2	0-1	18	Connolly [88]	5474
31	19	H	Oldham Ath	L	0-3	0-1	19		3603
32	26	A	Oxford U	W	4-1	1-0	17	Connolly [15], Allsopp 2 [47, 78], Ferguson [88]	4988
33	Mar 4	H	Luton T	W	1-0	0-0	17	Allsopp [55]	2703
34	7	A	Brentford	W	2-0	0-0	—	Allsopp [67], Connolly [72]	4055
35	11	A	Burnley	L	0-1	0-1	18		6582
36	18	A	Cambridge U	W	4-3	1-1	16	Williams [9], Russell 2 [56, 80], Ferguson [59]	4591
37	21	H	Millwall	D	1-1	1-0	—	Owen [20]	3019
38	25	A	Preston NE	L	0-1	0-0	17		12,481
39	28	H	Scunthorpe U	W	3-1	2-0	—	Gibson [1], Russell [45], Ferguson (pen) [65]	2139
40	Apr 1	A	Reading	L	0-1	0-1	17		2613
41	8	A	Bristol C	L	0-4	0-0	18		8639
42	15	H	Bournemouth	W	1-0	1-0	16	Russell [19]	2597
43	22	A	Chesterfield	W	3-0	1-0	15	Connolly 3 (1 pen) [33, 48, 90 (p)]	2550
44	24	H	Colchester U	W	1-0	1-0	14	Hardy (pen) [26]	2460
45	29	A	Wigan Ath	W	1-0	1-0	13	Connolly [10]	7245
46	May 6	H	Gillingham	W	1-0	1-0	11	McGregor [11]	8811

Final League Position: 11

GOALSCORERS

League (52): Connolly 9 (1 pen), Faulconbridge 8, Roberts N 6 (1 pen), Allsopp 4, Ferguson 4 (1 pen), Russell 4, Stevens 4, Owen 3, Barrett 2, Carey 1, Edwards 1, Gibson 1, Hardy 1 (pen), Lowe 1, McGregor 1, Morrell 1, Williams 1. *Worthington Cup (0).*
FA Cup (8): Roberts N 2 (1 pen), Connolly 1, Faulconbridge 1, Ferguson 1, Gibson 1, Roberts S 1, Williams 1.

Dearden K 45	McGregor M 45	Hardy P 38	Owen G 35+4	Carey B 43	Ridler D 22+3	Williams M 14+2	Stevens I 14+2	Connolly K 35+6	Phillips W 3	Lowe D 4+6	Ryan M 4+3	Faulconbridge C 23+12	Russell K 29+4	Spink D 13+2	Barrett P 17+1	Brace D 3+3	Edwards J —+2	Ferguson D 37	Roberts S 16+3	Hannon K —+1	Chalk M 10+10	Morrell A 4+9	Jarrett J 1	Roberts N 18+1	Gibson R 18+6	Allsopp D 3	Thomas S —+2	Rogers K 1	Warren D 1	Match No
1	2	3¹	4	5	6	7	8	9	10	11²	12	13																		1
1	2	3	4	5	6	7	8²	9	10	12	13	11¹																		2
1	2	3	4	5	6	7	8¹	9	10³	12	13	11²	14																	3
1	2	12		6	7		8²	9				3	11	10	5	4¹		13												4
1	2		5	12	7	8		9				3¹	11²	10		4	6	13												5
1	2			5		8	9				7	3¹	11	10²	4	6	12	13												6
1	2	3	4	5		7	8	12				9¹	11	13	6³	10²	14													7
1	2	3	4	5			8	9¹				11	12		10			7	6											8
1	2		4	5	6		8¹	9				12	3³	11		7²		10	14	13										9
1	2	3	4	5	6		8²	12				11¹	9					10	7	13										10
1	2	3	4¹	5	6			9²				11		12	8			7	13	10										11
1	2	3	4	5		8	12					11²		10				9	6		7¹	13								12
1	2	3	4	5		9		12					10					8	6		7	11¹								13
1	2	3	4	5		9		12				13	11	6²				8	7¹			10								14
1	2	3	4	5		12	9¹					7						8	6		11	10								15
1	2	3²	4	5		7	8¹	12				13	10					9²	6		11	14								16
1	2	3	4	5	10		9					7						8	6		11									17
1	2	3	4³	5	12	11		9				13	7²					8	6¹		10	14								18
1	2	3	12	5	4¹	6		13				11²	7					8			9	10								19
1	2	3¹		5	4	12		11				10						8	6			9	7							20
1	2	3	4	5		12		11¹				7						8	6			9	10							21
1	2	3	4		6	7		11				10						8	5			9								22
1	2	3	4		6	7		11²				10¹						8	5		12	13	9							23
1	2	3²	12	5	6	4¹		10				7	13	11³				8			14	9								24
1	2		4		6			10				11		5	8	3			7			9								25
1	2	3	4	5	6	7		11¹				10						8			12	9								26
1	2	3	4				10	11				5	6					8	7¹			9	12							27
1	2	3	4		6		7	11				5	10					8				9								28
1	2	3²	4		6	11		7³				5	10¹					8	12		13	9	14							29
1	2		4	6	3	12	7	11¹				5	10²					8				9	13							30
1	2		4	6	7³	10²	9	12				13	8	3	5	11¹			14											31
1		3	12	6	13		9	7				4¹	2²		8	5			11	10										32
1	2	3	4	5	6		9	7										8			12			11	10					33
1	2	3	4	5	6		9	7										8				13	10¹	11						34
1	2	3²	4	5	6		9	12				7	8					8			13	10¹		11						35
1	2	3	4	5	6¹	7	9					10	12					8						11						36
1	2	3	4¹	5	7		9	10				6	8					8			12			11						37
1	2	3²	4	5	7¹		9	12				10	6					8	13					11						38
1	2	3	4	5	7	9²		13				10	6¹					8	12					11						39
1	2	3¹	4	5	7		11	10				8	6					8	6		12			9						40
1	2	3	4¹		6	7³	12	10				8	5					8	5		11	13		9²	14					41
1	2	3²	4	5	6	7¹		9				10	8					8	13		12			11						42
1	2	3	4¹	5	6	7		9				13	10³					8	12²		14			11						43
	2	3		5	6	7³		9				12	8	13				8	13			10¹		11			14	1	4²	44
1	2		4	5	6	9¹		10				8	3					8	3		7	12		11						45
1	2	3	4	5	6		9	12				10¹						8				7		11						46

Worthington Cup
First Round   Preston NE   (a) 0-1
                                (h) 0-2

FA Cup
First Round   Kettering T   (h) 1-1
                                (a) 2-0
Second Round   Rochdale   (h) 2-1
Third Round   Middlesbrough   (h) 2-1
Fourth Round   Cambridge U   (h) 1-2

Division 2   **WYCOMBE WANDERERS**

FOUNDATION

In 1887 a group of young furniture trade workers called a meeting at the Steam Engine public house with the aim of forming a football club and entering junior football. It is thought that they were named after the famous FA Cup winners, The Wanderers who had visited the town in 1877 for a tie with the original High Wycombe club. It is also possible that they played informally before their formation, although there is no proof of this.

Adams Park, Hillbottom Road, Sands, High Wycombe HP12 4HJ.
Telephone: (01494) 472 100.
Fax: (01494) 527 633.
Credit Card Hotline: (01494) 441 118.
Information Line: 0891 446 855.
Ground Capacity: 10,000; new stand now seats 7250.
Record Attendance: 9007 v West Ham U, FA Cup 3rd rd, 7 January 1995.
Record Receipts: £61,221 (net of VAT) v West Ham U, FA Cup 3rd rd, 7 January 1995.
Pitch Measurements: 115yd × 77yd.
Patron: J. Adams.
President: M. E. Seymour.
Chairman: I. L. Beeks JP.
Directors: G. Peart (Financial), G. Richards, B. R. Lee, A. Parry, A. Thibault, G. Cox.
Associate Director: J. Goldsworthy.
Secretary: Keith J. Allen.
Manager: Lawrie Sanchez.
Assistant Manager: Terry Gibson.
Physio: David Jones.
Youth Team Manager: Gary Goodchild.
Youth Development Officer: Adrian Cole.
Youth Physio: Terry Evans.
Marketing Manager: Mark Austin.
Promotions Manager: Mike Phillips.
Press Officer: Alan Hutchinson.

LATEST SEQUENCES
Longest Sequence of League Wins: 4, 26.2.94 – 19.3.94.
Longest Sequence of League Defeats: 4, 2.1.99 – 30.1.99.
Longest Sequence of League Draws: 4, 16.9.95 – 7.10.95.
Longest Sequence of Unbeaten League Matches: 14, 29.8.95 – 18.11.95.
Longest Sequence Without a League Win: 12, 8.8.98 – 10.10.98.

HONOURS

Football League: Division 2 best season: 6th, 1994–95.
FA Amateur Cup: Winners 1931.
FA Trophy: Winners 1991, 1993.
GM Vauxhall Conference: Winners 1992–93.
FA Cup: best season: 3rd rd 1975, 1986, 1994, 1995.
Football League Cup: never beyond 2nd rd.

Colours
Light & dark blue quartered shirts, light blue shorts, light blue stockings.
Change Colours
All yellow, red and white quarters.

Year Formed: 1887.

Turned Professional: 1974.

Club Nicknames: 'Chairboys' (after High Wycombe's tradition of furniture making), 'The Blues'.

Previous Grounds: 1887, The Rye; 1893, Spring Meadow; 1895, Loakes Park; 1899, Daws Hill Park; 1901, Loakes Park; 1990, Adams Park.

First Football League Game: 14 August 1993, Division 3 v Carlisle U (a) D 2–2: Hyde; Cousins, Horton (Langford), Kerr, Crossley, Ryan, Carroll, Stapleton, Thompson, Scott, Guppy (1) (Hutchinson), (1 og).

Record League Victory: 5–0 v Burnley, Division 2, 15 April 1997 – Parkin; Cousins, Bell, Kavanagh, McCarthy, Forsyth, Carroll (2p) (Simpson), Scott (Farrell), Stallard (1), McGavin (1) (Read (1)), Brown.

Record Cup Victory: 5–0 v Hitchin T (a), FA Cup 2nd rd, 3 December 1994 – Hyde; Cousins, Brown, Crossley, Evans, Ryan (1), Carroll, Bell (1), Thompson, Garner (3) (Hemmings), Stapleton (Langford).

Record Defeat: 0–5 v Walsall, Auto Windscreens Shield 1st rd, 7 November 1995.

Most League Points: 78, Division 2, 1994–95.

Most League Goals: 67, Division 3, 1993–94.

Highest League Goalscorer in Season: Sean Devine 23, 1999–2000.

Most League Goals in Total Aggregate: Dave Carroll, 38, 1993–2000.

Most League Goals in One Match: 3, Miguel Desouza v Bradford C, Division 2, 26 March 1996; 3, Mark Stallard v Walsall, Division 2, 21 October 1997; 3, Sean Devine v Reading, Division 2, 2 October 1999; 3, Sean Devine v Bury, Division 2, 26 February 2000.

Most Capped Player: None.

Most League Appearances: Dave Carroll, 278, 1993–2000.

Youngest League Player: Roger Johnson, 17 years 8 days v Cambridge U, 6 May 2000.

Record Transfer Fee Received: £375,000 from Swindon T for Keith Scott, November 1993.

Record Transfer Fee Paid: £220,000 to Barnet for Sean Devine, 15 April 1999.

Football League Record: Promoted to Division 3 from GMVC in 1993; 1993–94 Division 3; 1994– Division 2.

MANAGERS

First coach appointed 1951.
Prior to Brian Lee's appointment in 1969 the team was selected by a Match Committee which met every Monday evening.
James McCormack 1951–52
Sid Cann 1952–61
Graham Adams 1961–62
Don Welsh 1962–64
Barry Darvill 1964–68
Brian Lee 1969–76
Ted Powell 1976–77
John Reardon 1977–78
Andy Williams 1978–80
Mike Keen 1980–84
Paul Bence 1984–86
Alan Gane 1986–87
Peter Suddaby 1987–88
Jim Kelman 1988–90
Martin O'Neill 1990–95
Alan Smith 1995–96
John Gregory 1996–98
Neil Smillie 1998–99
Lawrie Sanchez February 1999–

TEN YEAR LEAGUE RECORD

		P	W	D	L	F	A	Pts	Pos
1989-90	Conf	42	17	10	15	64	56	61	10
1990-91	Conf	42	21	11	10	75	46	74	5
1991-92	Conf	42	30	4	8	84	35	94	2
1992-93	Conf	42	24	11	7	84	37	83	1
1993-94	Div 3	42	19	13	10	67	53	70	4
1994-95	Div 2	46	21	15	10	60	46	78	6
1995-96	Div 2	46	15	15	16	63	59	60	12
1996-97	Div 2	46	15	10	21	51	56	55	18
1997-98	Div 2	46	14	18	14	51	53	60	14
1998-99	Div 2	46	13	12	21	52	58	51	19

DID YOU KNOW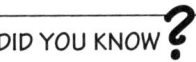

When Wycombe Wanderers won the Amateur Cup in 1931 beating Hayes 1-0 at Highbury with an Alf Britnell goal, there was only one non-local player in the team and he was Doug Vernon, serving in the RAF at nearby Halton.

WYCOMBE WANDERERS 1999–2000 LEAGUE RECORD

Match No.	Date	Venue	Opponents	Result	H/T Score	Lg. Pos.	Goalscorers	Attendance
1	Aug 7	H	Burnley	D 1-1	1-0	12	McSporran [27]	6119
2	14	A	Scunthorpe U	W 1-0	1-0	8	Devine [42]	4092
3	21	H	Preston NE	D 1-1	1-1	10	Devine [28]	5091
4	28	A	Gillingham	D 2-2	1-1	10	Brown (pen) [34], McCarthy [80]	6180
5	31	H	Wrexham	L 0-1	0-0	—		5393
6	Sept 4	A	Oxford U	D 0-0	0-0	15		6306
7	11	H	Cardiff C	W 3-1	1-1	8	Lawrence [18], McSporran [75], Baird [79]	4982
8	18	A	Bury	L 0-2	0-0	13		3293
9	25	A	Blackpool	W 2-1	2-1	10	McSporran [38], Devine [40]	3452
10	Oct 2	H	Reading	W 5-3	2-0	10	Ryan [8], Carroll [45], Devine 3 [52, 69, 83]	7042
11	9	H	Cambridge U	W 1-0	1-0	6	Devine [7]	5345
12	16	A	Notts Co	L 1-2	1-1	10	Devine (pen) [20]	5710
13	19	A	Luton T	D 1-1	1-0	—	Cousins [25]	5820
14	23	H	Blackpool	L 0-2	0-2	11		5021
15	Nov 2	A	Oldham Ath	D 2-2	1-1	—	Devine [2], Baird [88]	3807
16	6	H	Bristol R	D 1-1	0-0	12	Devine [67]	5167
17	12	A	Wigan Ath	L 1-2	1-1	12	McSporran [26]	5523
18	23	H	Stoke C	L 0-4	0-2	—		4345
19	27	H	Brentford	W 2-0	1-0	12	Devine 2 (1 pen) [44 (p), 59]	5879
20	Dec 4	A	Burnley	L 0-1	0-0	12		9149
21	11	H	Millwall	L 1-2	0-0	12	Ryan [61]	4777
22	17	A	Bristol C	D 0-0	0-0	—		8195
23	26	H	Bournemouth	W 2-1	1-1	12	Brown [26], Devine [55]	5656
24	Jan 3	H	Chesterfield	W 3-0	1-0	12	Devine 2 [40, 59], Bulman [90]	5001
25	8	A	Millwall	D 1-1	1-1	11	Devine [13]	8945
26	15	H	Scunthorpe U	W 2-1	1-1	10	Bates [30], Ryan [58]	4850
27	18	A	Colchester U	L 0-1	0-0	—		4075
28	22	A	Preston NE	L 2-3	1-2	11	Brady [5], Lawrence [57]	10,969
29	Feb 5	A	Wrexham	W 3-1	0-1	11	Brady [54], Carroll [77], Senda [90]	2781
30	12	H	Oxford U	L 0-1	0-1	12		6200
31	19	A	Brentford	D 0-0	0-0	12		5981
32	26	H	Bury	W 3-0	1-0	11	Devine 3 (1 pen) [40, 57 (p), 85]	4909
33	Mar 3	A	Cardiff C	D 2-2	1-1	—	McSporran [18], Devine (pen) [55]	5011
34	7	A	Bristol R	L 0-1	0-1	—		8053
35	11	H	Oldham Ath	D 0-0	0-0	12		4471
36	18	A	Stoke C	D 1-1	1-0	12	McSporran [23]	9738
37	21	H	Wigan Ath	L 0-2	0-0	—		3821
38	25	A	Bournemouth	L 0-2	0-0	15		4393
39	28	H	Gillingham	W 1-0	0-0	—	Baird [83]	4183
40	Apr 1	H	Bristol C	L 1-2	0-1	14	Devine [62]	4754
41	8	A	Chesterfield	W 2-1	0-1	12	Ryan [51], Devine [76]	2081
42	15	H	Colchester U	W 3-0	0-0	11	Ryan 2 [62, 67], Brown [90]	4558
43	21	H	Notts Co	W 2-0	1-0	—	Devine [40], McSporran [77]	4369
44	24	A	Reading	L 1-2	0-0	10	McSporran [64]	11,834
45	29	H	Luton T	L 0-1	0-0	14		5379
46	May 6	A	Cambridge U	W 2-1	1-1	12	Baird [35], McSporran [86]	5335

Final League Position: 12

GOALSCORERS

League (56): Devine 23 (4 pens), McSporran 9, Ryan 6, Baird 4, Brown 3 (1 pen), Brady 2, Carroll 2, Lawrence 2, Bates 1, Bulman 1, Cousins 1, McCarthy 1, Senda 1.
Worthington Cup (8): McSporran 2, Brown 1 (pen), Carroll 1, Devine 1, McCarthy 1, Ryan 1, own goal 1.
FA Cup (5): Baird 1, Brown 1, Devine 1, Ryan 1, Simpson 1.

Taylor M 42	Lawrence M 29	Vinnicombe C 33+2	Ryan K 38	McCarthy P 21+1	Bates J 30+2	Carroll D 36	Simpson M 42+1	McSporran J 32+6	Devine S 39	Brown S 34+5	Senda D 5+22	Holtsgrove L 5+4	Emblen P 12+4	Cousins J 30+7	Baird A 20+10	Beeton A 10+6	Harkin M 2+15	Bulman D 10+19	Westhead M 1+1	Bywater S 2	Osborn M 1	Rogers M 19+6	Ablett G 4	Brady M 4+3	Thompson R 1+5	Lee M 3+1	Townsend B 1	Johnson L —+1	Match No.
1	2	3	4	5	6	7^1	8^2	9	10	11	12	13																	1
1	2		4	5	6	7	8^3	9^1	10	11	12	13		3^2	14														2
1	2^2		4	5	6	7	8	9^1	10	11	12			3^3	13	14													3
1	2		4	5	6	7^3	8^1	9		10		12	13	11^2	3	14													4
1	2^1		4	5	6	7	8	9		11	12	13		10	3^2														5
1	2		4	5	6	7	8^2	9		11^1	12	13		10^3	3		14												6
1	2	12	4	5	6	7	13	9^1	10	11	8^3			14	3^1														7
1^6	2		4		6	7^2	8	9	10	12	11			5	13	3^1						15							8
	2	12	4	5	6	7	8	9^3	10	11^2		13	14	3^1						1									9
	2	3	4		6	7	8^3	9^1	10	12	11^2			5	13		14			1									10
	2	3	4		6	7^1	8	9^2	10	12	11			5	13						1								11
1	2	3^1	4		6		8^3	9	10	11	13			7^2	5	12						14							12
1	2	3	4		6		8	9^1	10	11	13			7^1	5	12													13
1	2	3^2	4		6		8	9	10	11^3	14			7^1	5	12	13												14
1	3	2	4				8^2		10^1	11^3	12	13		5	9	7	14					6							15
1	3^1		4				8	12	10	11	13		2	5	9^2	7	14					6							16
1	2^1		4				8	9	10	11	12			7^2	5	3	13					6							17
1	2	3^1	4		6	7	8	9	10	11^2				5	12			13											18
1	2	3	4		6	7	8	9^1	10	12^2				5	11^3		13	14											19
1	2	3^1	4			7	8	9^1	10^2				12	5	11		14	13				6							20
1	2^3	3^2	4		6	7^1	8		10				12	5	9		14	13						11					21
1	2		4		6	7^1	8		10^2	9				5	11	12		13				3							22
1	2	3	4		6		8^1	9	10	11^2	12			5	13	7													23
1	2	3	4^2		6	7	8	9^1	10	11^3				5	12	13	14												24
1	2	3	4		6	7	8	12	10^1	9^2				5	11^2	13	14												25
1	2	3	4		6	7^1	8		10	9^3	13			5	11^2	12	14		1										26
1	2	3	4	12	6^1	7^3	8		10^2	9	13			5	11		14												27
1	2	3	4	5^1		7	8^2		10	9	13			12			14					6		11^3					28
1	2	3	4	5		7	12	9^3	10^1						13	8	14					6		11^2					29
1	2	3^1	4		6	7^2	8		10	9^3				5	11	12	13	14											30
1	2^2	3	4		6	7	8	9^1	10	11				5	12							13							31
1	3	2	4			7^3	8	9^1	10^1	11^2				5	12		14	13				6							32
1	3		4^2			7	8	9	10^1	11^2	12		13	5	2		14					6							33
1	3					7	8	9	10	11				5	2^2	4^1	12	13				6							34
1	3					7	8	9		11	12		4	5	2			13				6				10^1			35
1	3^1	2	4			7	8	9	10^2	11				5		12		13				6							36
1	3		4^1			7	8	9	10^2	11				5	2	12		13				6							37
1	3	4				7	8	9^3	10^1	11			12	5			14	13				6		2^2					38
1	2	4				7	8	9^1	10^3	11			12	5^2	3		14	13				6							39
1	3^1		4^2	5	12	7	8		10	9^3	13			11	2		14					6							40
1	3	2	4	12		7	8^2		10^3	9	13			5^1	11		14					6							41
1	3	2	4	5		7^1	8	12	10	9				11								6							42
1	3		4	5		7	8	9	10	12					2^2							6		11^1	13				43
1	3		4	5^1			8^2	9	10	11	12				13	2						6				7			44
1	3		4^2	5			8	9	10	11^1	12		14		13	2						6				7^2			45
1	3						8^1	9	10		12			5	11		2	13				6				7^3	4^2	14	46

Worthington Cup

First Round	Wolverhampton W	(h)	0-1
		(a)	4-2
Second Round	WBA	(a)	1-1
		(h)	3-4

FA Cup

First Round	Oxford C	(h)	1-1
		(a)	1-0
Second Round	Wigan Ath	(h)	2-2
		(a)	1-2

Division 3

YORK CITY

FOUNDATION

Although there was a York City club formed in 1903 by a soccer enthusiast from Darlington, this has no connection with the modern club because it went out of existence during World War I. Unlike many others of that period who restarted in 1919, York City did not re-form until 1922 and the tendency now is to ignore the modern club's pre-1922 existence.

Bootham Crescent, York YO30 7AQ.

Telephone: (01904) 624 447.

Fax: (01904) 631 457.

ClubCall: 09068 121 643

Ground Capacity: 9534.

Record Attendance: 28,123 v Huddersfield T, FA Cup 6th rd, 5 March 1938.

Record Receipts: £63,680 v Manchester U, Coca-Cola Cup 2nd rd, 2nd leg, 3 October 1995.

Pitch Measurements: 115yd × 74yd.

Chairman: D. M. Craig OBE, JP, BSC, FICE, FI, MUN E, FCI ARB, M CONS E.

Directors: C. Webb, E. B. Swallow, J. E. H. Quickfall FCA.

Manager: Terry Dolan.

First Team Coach: Adie Shaw.

Secretary: Keith Usher.

Commercial Manager: James Richardson.

Physio: Jeff Miller.

Hon. Orthopaedic Surgeon: Mr Peter De Boer MA, FRCS.

Medical Officer: Dr R. Porter.

LATEST SEQUENCES

Longest Sequence of League Wins: 7, 31.10.64 – 26.12.64.

Longest Sequence of League Defeats: 8, 14.11.66 – 31.12.66.

Longest Sequence of League Draws: 6, 26.12.92 – 22.1.93.

Longest Sequence of Unbeaten League Matches: 21, 10.9.73 – 12.1.74.

Longest Sequence Without a League Win: 17, 4.5.87 – 24.10.87.

HONOURS

Football League: Division 3 – Promoted 1973–74 (3rd); Division 4 – Champions 1983–84.

FA Cup: Semi-finals 1955, when in Division 3.

Football League Cup: best season: 5th rd, 1962.

Colours
Red shirts, navy shorts, red stockings.

Change Colours
All green and white.

Year Formed: 1922.

Turned Professional: 1922.

Ltd Co.: 1922.

Club Nickname: 'Minstermen'.

Previous Grounds: 1922, Fulfordgate; 1932, Bootham Crescent.

First Football League Game: 31 August 1929, Division 3 (N), v Wigan Borough (a) W 2–0 – Farmery; Archibald, Johnson; Beck, Davis, Thompson; Evans, Gardner, Cowie (1), Smailes, Stockhill (1).

Record League Victory: 9–1 v Southport, Division 3 (N), 2 February 1957 – Forgan; Phillips, Howe; Brown (1), Cairney, Mollatt; Hill, Bottom (4 incl. 1p), Wilkinson (2), Wragg (1), Fenton (1).

Record Cup Victory: 6–0 v South Shields (away), FA Cup 1st rd, 16 November 1968 – Widdowson; Baker (1p), Richardson; Carr, Jackson, Burrows; Taylor, Ross (3), MacDougall (2), Hodgson, Boyer.

Record Defeat: 0–12 v Chester, Division 3 (N), 1 February 1936.

Most League Points (2 for a win): 62, Division 4, 1964–65.

Most League Points (3 for a win): 101, Division 4, 1983–84.

Most League Goals: 96, Division 4, 1983–84.

Highest League Scorer in Season: Bill Fenton, 31, Division 3 (N), 1951–52; Arthur Bottom, 31, Division 3 (N), 1954–55 and 1955–56.

Most League Goals in Total Aggregate: Norman Wilkinson, 125, 1954–66.

Most League Goals in One Match: 5, Alf Patrick v Rotherham U, Division 3N, 20 November 1948.

Most Capped Player: Peter Scott, 7 (10), Northern Ireland.

Most League Appearances: Barry Jackson, 481, 1958–70.

Youngest League Player: Reg Stockill, 15 years 281 days v Wigan Borough, 31 August 1929.

Record Transfer Fee Received: £1,000,000 from Manchester U for Jonathan Greening, March 1998.

Record Transfer Fee Paid: £140,000 to Burnley for Adrian Randall, December 1995.

Football League Record: 1929 Elected to Division 3 (N); 1958–59 Division 4; 1959–60 Division 3; 1960–65 Division 4; 1965–66 Division 3; 1966–71 Division 4; 1971–74 Division 3; 1974–76 Division 2; 1976–77 Division 3; 1977–84 Division 4; 1984–88 Division 3; 1988–92 Division 4; 1992–93 Division 3; 1993–99 Division 2; 1999– Division 3.

MANAGERS

Bill Sherrington 1924–60 *(was Secretary for most of this time but virtually Secretary-Manager for a long pre-war spell)*
John Collier 1929–36
Tom Mitchell 1936–50
Dick Duckworth 1950–52
Charlie Spencer 1952–53
Jimmy McCormick 1953–54
Sam Bartram 1956–60
Tom Lockie 1960–67
Joe Shaw 1967–68
Tom Johnston 1968–75
Wilf McGuinness 1975–77
Charlie Wright 1977–80
Barry Lyons 1980–81
Denis Smith 1982–87
Bobby Saxton 1987–88
John Bird 1988–91
John Ward 1991–93
Alan Little 1993–99
Neil Thompson 1999–2000
Terry Dolan February 2000–

TEN YEAR LEAGUE RECORD

		P	W	D	L	F	A	Pts	Pos
1989-90	Div 4	46	16	16	14	55	53	64	13
1990-91	Div 4	46	11	13	22	45	57	46	21
1991-92	Div 4	42	8	16	18	42	58	40	19
1992-93	Div 3	42	21	12	9	72	45	75	4
1993-94	Div 2	46	21	12	13	64	40	75	5
1994-95	Div 2	46	21	9	16	67	51	72	9
1995-96	Div 2	46	13	13	20	58	73	52	20
1996-97	Div 2	46	13	13	20	47	68	52	20
1997-98	Div 2	46	14	17	15	52	58	59	16
1998-99	Div 2	46	13	11	22	56	80	50	21

DID YOU KNOW?

Jimmy Cowie scored six of York City's FA Cup goals in the 7-1 win over Stockton on 29 September 1928. He also achieved the remarkable feat of 56 League and Cup goals in 56 Midland League matches that season.

YORK CITY 1999–2000 LEAGUE RECORD

Match No.	Date	Venue	Opponents	Result	H/T Score	Lg. Pos.	Goalscorers	Attendance
1	Aug 7	H	Swansea C	W 1-0	1-0	12	Atkins [18]	3036
2	14	A	Torquay U	D 0-0	0-0	9		3005
3	21	H	Rochdale	L 0-3	0-1	13		3034
4	28	A	Barnet	L 3-6	3-2	17	Atkins [14], Conlon 2 [34, 39]	1896
5	30	H	Northampton T	L 0-1	0-0	18		2597
6	Sept 4	A	Rotherham U	L 0-1	0-0	23		3171
7	11	H	Peterborough U	D 0-0	0-0	22		2832
8	18	A	Exeter C	L 1-2	1-1	23	Hulme [25]	2904
9	25	A	Hull C	D 1-1	1-1	23	Williams (og) [28]	8293
10	Oct 2	H	Chester C	D 2-2	0-0	23	Williams M [73], Lancaster (og) [78]	2452
11	9	H	Leyton Orient	W 2-1	0-1	22	Conlon 2 [52, 65]	2320
12	16	A	Brighton & HA	W 1-0	0-0	17	Hocking [90]	5862
13	19	A	Halifax T	W 2-0	2-0	—	Conlon [31], Williams M [41]	2963
14	23	H	Hull C	D 1-1	1-0	17	Hulme [43]	5109
15	Nov 2	A	Carlisle U	W 1-0	1-0	—	Williams J [9]	2512
16	6	H	Macclesfield T	L 0-2	0-1	17		2469
17	12	A	Lincoln C	L 2-4	1-1	18	Hulme [35], Williams M (pen) [88]	2956
18	23	H	Shrewsbury T	W 1-0	1-0	—	Alcide [9]	1857
19	27	H	Plymouth Arg	D 0-0	0-0	18		2745
20	Dec 4	A	Swansea C	L 0-1	0-0	18		3812
21	17	H	Southend U	D 2-2	0-1	—	Williams M [70], Jordan [76]	2233
22	26	A	Hartlepool U	L 1-2	1-0	20	Conlon [57]	4668
23	28	H	Cheltenham T	L 1-2	0-2	20	Williams M [67]	2936
24	Jan 8	H	Mansfield T	L 0-1	0-1	20		2458
25	15	H	Torquay U	D 2-2	1-1	20	Turley [16], Fox [69]	2427
26	18	A	Darlington	D 2-2	1-2	—	Conlon [20], Williams J [87]	5704
27	22	A	Rochdale	L 1-2	1-0	19	Jones [32]	2580
28	29	H	Barnet	W 1-0	1-0	19	Hocking [42]	2497
29	Feb 5	A	Northampton T	L 0-3	0-1	21		4958
30	8	A	Mansfield T	L 0-1	0-0	—		2571
31	12	H	Rotherham U	L 1-2	0-1	21	Conlon [74]	4531
32	19	A	Plymouth Arg	L 0-2	0-2	21		4343
33	26	H	Exeter C	D 0-0	0-0	21		3066
34	Mar 4	A	Peterborough U	L 0-2	0-1	21		5578
35	7	A	Macclesfield T	D 1-1	1-1	—	Hulme [29]	1581
36	11	H	Carlisle U	D 1-1	0-0	21	Conlon [86]	2976
37	18	A	Shrewsbury T	W 1-0	1-0	20	Conlon [14]	2149
38	21	H	Lincoln C	W 2-0	0-0	—	Bower [49], Conlon [62]	2449
39	25	H	Hartlepool U	W 2-1	1-0	20	Williams J [11], Alcide [90]	4079
40	Apr 1	A	Southend U	D 0-0	0-0	20		3364
41	8	H	Darlington	D 0-0	0-0	20		5308
42	15	A	Cheltenham T	W 1-0	0-0	19	Sertori [80]	4722
43	22	H	Brighton & HA	D 0-0	0-0	19		3619
44	24	A	Chester C	L 0-2	0-0	20		3503
45	29	H	Halifax T	W 2-0	0-0	20	Turley [63], Jordan [90]	3079
46	May 6	A	Leyton Orient	D 0-0	0-0	20		4594

Final League Position: 20

GOALSCORERS

League (39): Conlon 11, Williams M 5 (1 pen), Hulme 4, Williams J 3, Alcide 2, Atkins 2, Hocking 2, Jordan 2, Turley 2, Bower 1, Fox 1, Jones 1, Sertori 1, own goals 2.
Worthington Cup (1): Rowe 1.
FA Cup (0).

Howarth R 5+1	Hocking M 26+6	Hall W 23	Atkins M 10	Jones B 35+2	Fairclough C 25+1	Dawson A 11+6	Dixon K 3	Conlon B 31+9	Rowe R 3+4	Bullock L 16+8	Garratt M 2+5	Williams M 11+11	Williams J 28+8	Jordan S 26+2	Fox C 28+6	Thompson N 6	Sertori M 37+3	Mimms B 28	Hulme K 23	Turley J 9+2	Ormerod A 9+3	Agnew S 20+2	Alcide C 9+6	Keegan J 2+1	Skinner C 1+4	Reed M 7+1	Bower M 15	Hawkins P 14	Fettis A 13	Talbot P 5+1	Thompson M 9+1	Swan P 9	Edmondson D 7	Darlow K —+2	Match No.
1	2	3	4	5	6	7^1	8	9	10^2	11	12	13																							1
1	2	3	4	5	6	7	8	9	12	11				10^1																					2
1	2	3	4	5	6	7^1	8^3	9	12	11^2		13	10	14																					3
1	2	3	4	12	6	7^1		9	13	11			10^2	5	8																				4
	2	11	4	5	6			10	12				9	8	7^1	3		1																	5
	2	11	4		6	12		10	13				9^2	8	7	3^1	5	1																	6
	2^1	11	4		6	12		9	13	14			10^2		7	3^2	5	1	8																7
	2	3	4^1		6			9	12	11^3		13	14		7		5	1	8	10^2															8
	2	3	4		6			9	10						7		5	1	8	12	11^1														9
	2^1	3	4	12	6				10	13			14		7		5	1	8	9^2	11^3														10
		3		4	6			12				13	2	9^1	10^2	7^3	5	1	8			11	14												11
12		3		4	6	7		9					2^1	10			5	1	8			11													12
12		3		4	6	2		9		11^1				10			5	1	8			7													13
		3		4	6	7		9					2^1	10	13		5	1	8			12	11^2												14
12		3		4	6			9					13	10^1	2	7	5	1	8			11^2													15
10^1		3		4	6			9					12	2	7		5	1	8			11													16
		3		4	6			9^1					12	10	2	7	5	1	8			11													17
		3		4	6	12							13	10^2	8	2	7	5	1			11^1	9												18
12		3^1		4	6	2								8	10	7	5	1				11	9												19
		3		4^1	6	12				13				10	2	7	5	1	8^2			11	9												20
	2				6	11^1					12				3	12	8	7	5	1						10	9	4							21
	2			4							12				3	10^2	8	7	5	1						13	11	9^1	6						22
	2			4	6^3						12				3	10^2	8	7	5	1						13	11	9^1	14						23
	2			4							12		13	6	10	8^2	7	3	5	1						11	9^1								24
	2	11			6								9	4	12	10	7	3^2	5	1		8^1				13									25
	2				6			12					9	4	13	10	7	5	1			11^2	8^1			3									26
	2	3		4		8^1		9					6		13	10^1	12	7	5	1		11^2													27
	2	3			6			9					11	10	8	7	5	1											4						28
	2^2	3^1			6			9		11		12	10	8	7	5	1										13		4						29
	2			5		12		9					6^1	11	10	8	7	3^2	13	1									4						30
	2				6			9					11	10	8	7	5	1									3	4							31
15	2			6		7^2							11	10	8		5	1^6	9	12						13		4			3^1				32
1	2			6				9		12		13	14	8^2	7		5	10^1								4	3		11^3						33
	2^2			5				9		6		12		10	8		13									4	3	1	7^1	11					34
		5						12		6^2		13	9		8	7		10								4	3	1	2^1	11				35
		5						12		6^3		13	14	9	8	7^2	10								4	3	1	2^1	11				36
		2						9^2				10^1	12	8	7			11	13			4	3	1		6	5								37
		2						9		12		10		8^2	7			11	13			4	3	1		6^1	5								38
		2						9		13		10^3	12	8^2	7		11	14			4	3^1	1			5	6								39
12		2		5^1				9^3				10^2	13	8	7		11	14			4	3	1			5	6								40
		2						9^2		12			7^1	10	8		11	13			4	3	1			5	6								41
		2^1	12					9^2				13	7^3	10	8		11	14			4	3	1			5	6								42
				2^2				9^3		12		8		10			11	7^1		13	4	3	1	14		5	6								43
			2					9				10	8		12		11^1		14	4	3	1	7^3	13	5	6^2									44
								12				13	8			10^1	11	9^2		2	4	3	1	7^3	6	5		14							45
12								9					8		13		10	11		2^4	4	3^3	1		7	5^1	6	14							46

Worthington Cup
First Round   Wigan Ath   (h)   0-1
                                       (a)   1-2

FA Cup
First Round   Hereford U   (a)   0-1

ENGLISH LEAGUE PLAYERS DIRECTORY

*Free transfer, †Non-contract, ‡Registration cancelled, §Trainee/Scholar/Schoolboy
#Players over age 24, out of contract but who have been made an offer of re-engagement

Player	Ht	Wt	Pos	Birth Date	Birth Place	Source	Clubs	League App	League Gls
ARSENAL									
Adams Tony	6 3	13 02	D	10 10 66	Romford	Apprentice	Arsenal	468	31
Aliadiere Jeremie			F	30 3 83	France	Scholar	Arsenal	—	—
Anelka Nicolas	5 11	12 03	F	14 3 79	Versailles		Paris St Germain	10	1
(Transferred to Real Madrid, August 1999)							Arsenal	65	23
Barrett Graham	5 10	11 07	F	6 10 81	Dublin	Trainee	Arsenal	2	—
Bergkamp Dennis	6 0	12 05	F	18 5 69	Amsterdam		Ajax	185	103
							Internazionale	52	11
							Arsenal	147	57
Bernard Narada*			M	30 1 81	Bristol	Trainee	Arsenal	—	—
Black Tommy	5 7	11 04	M	26 11 79	Chigwell	Trainee	Arsenal	1	—
							Carlisle U (loan)	5	1
							Bristol C (loan)	4	—
Bothroyd Jay			F	5 5 82	London	Trainee	Arsenal	—	—
Canoville Lee			D	14 3 81	Ealing	Trainee	Arsenal	—	—
Cole Ashley	5 8	10 08	D	20 12 80	Stepney	Trainee	Arsenal	1	—
							Crystal Palace (loan)	14	1
Diawara Kaba	5 11	11 08	F	16 12 75	Toulon	Toulon	Bordeaux	43	9
(Transferred to Marseille, July 1999)							Rennes	12	3
							Bordeaux	17	5
							Arsenal	12	—
Dixon Lee	5 9	10 12	D	17 3 64	Manchester	Local	Burnley	4	—
							Chester C	16	1
							Chester	41	—
							Bury	45	5
							Stoke C	71	5
							Arsenal	416	24
Gray Julian	6 1	11 00	M	21 9 79	Lewisham	Trainee	Arsenal	1	—
Grimandi Gilles	5 10	11 08	M	11 11 70	Gap	FC Gap	Monaco	90	3
							Arsenal	58	3
Grondin David	5 9	11 11	D	8 5 80	Paris	St Etienne	Arsenal	1	—
(On loan to St Etienne)									
Harper James			M	9 11 80	Chelmsford	Trainee	Arsenal	—	—
Henry Thierry	6 2	13 01	F	17 8 77	Paris		Monaco	105	20
							Juventus	16	3
							Arsenal	31	17
Kanu Nwankwo	6 5	12 01	F	1 8 76	Owerri		Federation Works	30	9
							Iwanyanwu	30	6
							Ajax	54	25
							Internazionale	12	1
							Arsenal	43	18
Keown Martin	6 1	12 04	D	24 7 66	Oxford	Apprentice	Arsenal	22	—
							Brighton & HA (loan)	16	—
							Brighton & HA (loan)	7	1
							Aston Villa	112	3
							Everton	96	—
							Arsenal	226	4
Lincoln Greg			M	23 3 80	Cheshunt	Trainee	Arsenal	—	—
Ljungberg Frederik	5 9	10 13	M	16 4 77	Halmstad		Halmstad	79	10
							Arsenal	42	7
Lukic John	6 4	13 07	G	11 12 60	Chesterfield	Apprentice	Leeds U	146	—
							Arsenal	223	—
							Leeds U	209	—
							Arsenal	15	—
Luzhny Oleg	5 10	12 01	D	5 8 68	Ukraine		Dynamo Kiev	240	11
							Arsenal	21	—
MacDonald James	6 0	12 05	M	21 2 79	Inverness	Trainee	Arsenal	—	—
Malz Stefan	5 10	12 01	M	15 6 72	Ludwigshafen	Mannheim	Munich 1860	36	2
							Arsenal	5	1
Manninger Alex	6 2	13 03	G	4 6 77	Salzburg		Vorwaerts Steyr	5	—
							Salzburg	1	—
							Graz	23	—
							Arsenal	28	—
McGovern Brian	6 3	12 07	D	28 4 80	Dublin	Cherry Orchard	Arsenal	1	—
							QPR (loan)	5	—
McLeod Allan*			D	19 4 80	Islington	Trainee	Arsenal	—	—
Mendez Alberto	5 11	11 09	M	24 10 74	Nuremberg	FC Feucht	Arsenal	4	—
(On loan to Unterhaching)									
Norbert Guilliaume*			M	14 10 80	Chatenoy Malabry	Trainee	Arsenal	—	—

Overmars Marc	5 8	11 05	F	29 3 73	Emst		Go Ahead	11	1
							Willem II	31	1
							Ajax	135	36
							Arsenal	100	25
Parlour Ray	5 10	11 12	M	7 3 73	Romford	Trainee	Arsenal	235	18
Pennant Jermaine			M	15 1 83	Nottingham		Notts Co	—	—
							Arsenal	—	—
Petit Emmanuel	6 1	12 04	M	22 9 70	Dieppe	ES Arques	Monaco	222	4
							Arsenal	85	9
Seaman David	6 3	13 00	G	19 9 63	Rotherham	Apprentice	Leeds U	—	—
							Peterborough U	91	—
							Birmingham C	75	—
							QPR	141	—
							Arsenal	336	—
Silvinho	5 7	10 06	D	12 4 74	Sao Paulo	Corinthians	Arsenal	31	1
Suker Davor*	6 0	12 03	F	1 1 68	Osijek		Osijek	91	40
							Dynamo Zagreb	60	34
							Sevilla	153	75
							Real Madrid	86	38
							Arsenal	22	8
Taylor Stuart	6 4	13 07	G	28 11 80	Romford	Trainee	Arsenal	—	—
							Bristol R (loan)	4	—
Upson Matthew	6 1	11 04	D	18 4 79	Hartismere	Trainee	Luton T	1	—
							Arsenal	18	—
Vernazza Paulo	5 10	10 13	M	1 11 79	Islington	Trainee	Arsenal	3	—
							Ipswich T (loan)	2	—
							Portsmouth (loan)	7	—
Vieira Patrick	6 4	13 00	M	23 6 76	Dakar		Cannes	49	2
							AC Milan	2	—
							Arsenal	128	9
Vivas Nelson	5 5	10 06	D	18 10 69	San Nicolas	Lugano	Arsenal	28	—
(On loan to Celta Vigo)									
Volz Moritz			D	21 1 83	Germany		Arsenal	—	—
Weston Rhys	6 0	12 03	D	27 10 80	Kingston	Trainee	Arsenal	1	—
Winterburn Nigel	5 10	10 07	D	11 12 63	Nuneaton	Local	Birmingham C	—	—
							Oxford U	—	—
							Wimbledon	165	8
							Arsenal	440	8
Wreh Christopher	5 9	11 05	F	14 5 75	Monrovia		Monaco	13	3
(On loan to Den Bosch)							Guincamp	33	10
							Arsenal	28	3
							Birmingham C (loan)	7	1

Scholars
Brown, Jermaine A; Chilvers, Liam C; Chorley, Benjamin F; Halls, John; Itonga, Carlin D; Noble, David J; Oates, Greg W; Osei-Kuffour, Jonathan; Ricketts, Rohan A; Santry, Stephen M; Sidwell, Steven J; Stack, Graham; Thomas, Jerome W

ASTON VILLA

Barry Gareth	5 11	12 06	D	23 2 81	Hastings	Trainee	Aston Villa	64	3
Bartlet Gustavo‡			F	2 9 74	Buenos Aires		Aston Villa	—	—
(On loan from Roma, February 2000)									
Bewers Jonathan	5 8	9 13	D	10 9 82	Kettering	Trainee	Aston Villa	1	—
Blackwood Michael*	5 11	11 10	F	30 9 79	Birmingham	Trainee	Aston Villa	—	—
							Chester C (loan)	9	2
Boateng George	5 9	10 12	M	5 9 75	Nkawkaw		Excelsior	9	—
							Feyenoord	68	1
							Coventry C	47	5
							Aston Villa	33	2
Byfield Darren*	5 11	11 11	F	29 9 76	Sutton Coldfield	Trainee	Aston Villa	7	—
							Preston NE (loan)	5	1
							Northampton T (loan)	6	1
							Cambridge U (loan)	4	—
							Blackpool (loan)	3	—
Carbone Benito	5 6	10 06	F	14 8 71	Begnara		Torino	8	—
							Reggina	31	5
							Casert	31	4
							Ascoli	28	6
							Torino	28	3
							Napoli	29	5
							Internazionale	32	2
							Sheffield W	96	25
							Aston Villa	24	3
Cooke Stephen			M	15 2 83	Walsall		Aston Villa	—	—
Curtolo David	5 9	11 00	M	30 9 80	Stockholm		Aston Villa	—	—
Cutler Neil	6 1	12 00	G	3 9 76	Birmingham	Trainee	WBA	—	—
							Coventry C (loan)	—	—
							Chester C (loan)	1	—
							Crewe Alex	—	—
							Chester C (loan)	5	—
							Chester C	23	—
							Aston Villa	1	—

Player	Ht	Wt	Pos	Born	Birthplace	From	Club	Apps	Gls
De Bolla Mark			F	1 1 83	London	Trainee	Aston Villa	—	—
Delaney Mark	6 1	11 07	D	13 5 76	Haverfordwest	Carmarthen T	Cardiff C	28	—
							Aston Villa	30	1
Draper Mark	5 10	12 04	M	11 11 70	Long Eaton	Trainee	Notts Co	222	40
(On loan to Rayo Vallecano)							Leicester C	39	5
							Aston Villa	120	7
Dublin Dion	6 2	12 04	F	22 4 69	Leicester	Oakham U	Norwich C	—	—
							Cambridge U	156	52
							Manchester U	12	2
							Coventry C	145	61
							Aston Villa	50	23
Edwards Rob			D	25 12 82	Telford	Trainee	Aston Villa	—	—
Ehiogu Ugo	6 2	14 10	D	3 11 72	Hackney	Trainee	WBA	2	—
							Aston Villa	235	12
Enckelman Peter	6 2	12 05	G	10 3 77	Turku	TPS Turku	Aston Villa	10	—
Evans Graham‡	5 8	11 01	F	16 6 80	Wrexham	Caersws	Aston Villa	—	—
Evans Stephen	5 8	10 08	F	12 11 80	Coventry	Trainee	Aston Villa	—	—
Fahey Keith			M	15 1 83	Dublin		Aston Villa	—	—
Ferraresi Fabio‡	5 9	11 02	M	24 5 79	Fano	Cesena	Aston Villa	—	—
Ghent Matthew	6 3	14 01	G	5 10 80	Burton	Trainee	Aston Villa	—	—
Ghrayib Najwan	5 8	11 04	D	30 1 74	Nazareth		Maccabi Haifa	23	4
							Maccabi P-T	49	14
							Hapoel Haifa	55	9
							Aston Villa	5	—
Harding David*	5 8	9 04	D	30 3 81	Barnet	Trainee	Aston Villa	—	—
Hendrie Lee	5 10	10 02	F	18 5 77	Birmingham	Trainee	Aston Villa	85	7
Hylton Leon			D	27 1 83	Birmingham		Aston Villa	—	—
James David	6 5	14 02	G	1 8 70	Welwyn	Trainee	Watford	89	—
							Liverpool	214	—
							Aston Villa	29	—
Joachim Julian	5 6	12 00	F	20 9 74	Boston	Trainee	Leicester C	99	25
							Aston Villa	121	32
Kearns James*			M	16 9 80	Northampton	Trainee	Aston Villa	—	—
Lescott Aaron	5 8	10 10	M	2 12 78	Birmingham	Trainee	Aston Villa	—	—
							Lincoln C (loan)	5	—
McGrath John	5 10	10 04	M	27 3 80	Limerick	Belvedere	Aston Villa	—	—
McSeveney Gary‡	6 1	12 05	D	30 9 81	Lanark	Trainee	Aston Villa	—	—
Melaugh Gavin	5 7	9 07	M	9 7 81	Derry	Trainee	Aston Villa	—	—
Merson Paul	6 0	13 02	F	20 3 68	Northolt	Apprentice	Arsenal	327	78
							Brentford (loan)	7	—
							Middlesbrough	48	11
							Aston Villa	58	10
Mulholland Brian‡			D	22 8 81	Alexandria	Trainee	Aston Villa	—	—
Nkubi Isaac			F	5 3 81	Uganda	Vasteras	Aston Villa	—	—
Price Michael*			M	28 5 81	Wrexham	Trainee	Aston Villa	—	—
Prince Luke*			M	8 10 80	Oxford	Trainee	Aston Villa	—	—
Samuel J Lloyd	5 11	11 04	D	29 3 81	Trinidad	Charlton Ath	Aston Villa	9	—
Southgate Gareth	6 0	12 03	D	3 9 70	Watford	Trainee	Crystal Palace	152	15
							Aston Villa	160	5
Standing Michael	5 10	10 07	M	20 3 81	Brighton	Trainee	Aston Villa	—	—
Stone Steve	5 8	12 07	M	20 8 71	Gateshead	Trainee	Nottingham F	193	23
							Aston Villa	34	1
Tarrant Neil	6 1	11 05	F	24 6 79	Darlington	Trainee	Darlington	—	—
(On loan to Ayr U)							Shamrock R	2	—
							Ross Co	44	20
							Aston Villa	—	—
Taylor Ian	6 1	12 00	M	4 6 68	Birmingham	Moor Green	Port Vale	83	28
							Sheffield W	14	1
							Aston Villa	175	21
Thompson Alan	6 0	12 08	M	22 12 73	Newcastle		Newcastle U	16	—
							Bolton W	157	33
							Aston Villa	46	4
Thornley Stuart	5 8	11 04	D	28 10 80	Wrexham	Trainee	Aston Villa	—	—
Vassell Darius	5 7	12 00	F	13 6 80	Birmingham	Trainee	Aston Villa	17	—
Walker Richard	6 0	12 00	F	8 11 77	Sutton Coldfield	Trainee	Aston Villa	6	2
							Cambridge U (loan)	21	3
Watson Steve	6 1	12 07	D	1 4 74	North Shields	Trainee	Newcastle U	208	12
							Aston Villa	41	—
Willetts Benjamin			D	10 2 83	Sandwell		Aston Villa	—	—
Wright Alan	5 4	9 09	D	28 9 71	Ashton-under-Lyme	Trainee	Blackpool	98	—
							Blackburn R	74	1
							Aston Villa	191	4

Scholars
Berks, David; Dillon, Sean; Folds, Liam J; Haynes, Daniel; Jackman, Daniel J; Marfell, Andrew K; Myhill, Glyn O; Nicholas, Alexis P; Smith, Adam A; Smith, Jay A

BARNET

Name				Birth date	Birthplace	Source	Club	Apps	Gls
Ansell Gary*	5 10	12 00	M	8 11 78	Redbridge		Barnet	3	—
Arber Mark	6 1	12 11	D	8 10 77	Johannesburg	Trainee	Tottenham H	—	—
							Barnet	80	8
Barnes Steve*	5 4	10 09	M	5 1 76	Harrow	Welling U	Birmingham C	3	—
							Brighton & HA (loan)	12	—
							Barnet	15	—
Basham Mike	6 2	13 09	D	27 9 73	Barking	Trainee	West Ham U	—	—
							Colchester U (loan)	1	—
							Swansea C	29	1
							Peterborough U	19	1
							Barnet	67	2
Bell Leon	5 7	9 07	M	19 12 80	Hitchin	Trainee	Barnet	1	—
Bossu Bertrand	6 7	14 00	G	14 10 80	Calais		Barnet	—	—
Brown Daniel	6 0	12 06	M	12 9 80	Bethnal Green	Trainee	Leyton Orient	—	—
							Barnet	24	3
Butterfield John*	5 9	11 00	M	18 1 81	Peckham	Trainee	Barnet	—	—
Chapman Danny	6 2	12 07	D	19 4 81	London	Trainee	Barnet	—	—
Charlery Ken	6 1	13 12	F	28 11 64	Stepney	Beckton U	Maidstone U	59	11
							Peterborough U	51	19
							Watford	48	13
							Peterborough U	70	24
							Birmingham C	17	4
							Southend U (loan)	3	—
							Peterborough U	56	12
							Stockport Co	10	—
							Barnet	117	34
Currie Darren	5 10	12 07	M	29 11 74	Hampstead	Trainee	West Ham U	—	—
							Shrewsbury T (loan)	17	2
							Leyton Orient (loan)	10	—
							Shrewsbury T	66	8
							Plymouth Arg	7	—
							Barnet	82	9
Darcy Ross	6 0	12 02	D	21 3 78	Balbriggan	Trainee	Tottenham H	—	—
							Barnet	3	—
Doolan John	6 1	13 00	M	7 5 74	Liverpool	Trainee	Everton	—	—
							Mansfield T	131	10
							Barnet	103	4
Gledhill Lee	5 10	11 02	D	7 11 80	Bury	Trainee	Barnet	11	—
Goodhind Warren	5 11	11 02	D	16 8 77	Johannesburg	Trainee	Barnet	62	2
Hackett Warren	6 0	12 05	D	16 12 71	Plaistow	Tottenham H	Leyton Orient	72	3
							Doncaster R	46	2
							Mansfield T	117	5
							Barnet	41	1
Harrison Lee	6 2	12 07	G	12 9 71	Billericay	Trainee	Charlton Ath	—	—
							Fulham (loan)	—	—
							Gillingham (loan)	2	—
							Fulham (loan)	—	—
							Fulham	12	—
							Barnet	153	—
Heald Greg	6 1	13 01	D	26 9 71	Enfield	Enfield	Peterborough U	105	6
							Barnet	102	10
King Marlon	6 1	12 03	F	26 4 80	Dulwich	Trainee	Barnet	53	14
McCann Peter	5 6	10 09	D	27 6 82	Paisley	Trainee	Barnet	—	—
McGleish Scott	5 10	11 07	F	10 2 74	Camden Town	Edgware T	Charlton Ath	6	—
							Leyton Orient (loan)	6	1
							Peterborough U	13	—
							Colchester U (loan)	15	6
							Cambridge U (loan)	10	7
							Leyton Orient	36	7
							Barnet	115	31
Naisbitt Danny	6 1	11 12	G	25 11 78	Bishop Auckland	Trainee	Walsall	—	—
							Barnet	4	—
Sawyers Robert	5 10	11 03	D	20 11 78	Dudley	Wolverhampton W	Barnet	55	2
Searle Stevie	5 10	11 08	M	7 3 77	Lambeth	Sittingbourne	Barnet	84	5
Stockley Sam	6 0	12 00	D	5 9 77	Tiverton	Trainee	Southampton	—	—
							Barnet	137	1
Strevens Ben	6 1	11 00	F	24 5 80	Islington	Wingate & Finchley	Barnet	6	—
Toms Frazer	6 1	11 00	M	13 9 79	Ealing	Trainee	Charlton Ath	—	—
							Barnet	39	1
Wilson Paul#	5 9	12 00	M	26 9 64	Forest Gate	Barking	Barnet	263	24

Trainees
Lovett, Scott C; Obili, Shaun; Pluck, Lee K; Taylor, Mark J; White Ross A

Scholars
Cattle, Lee CD; Field, John D; Kent, Ryan D; Olayinka, Ade J; Oshitola, Oloruntobi O; Pope, Craig; Purches, John R

Non-Contract
Collis, Stephen P; Hall, Fitz

BARNSLEY

Appleby Matty	5 10	11 08	D	16 4 72	Middlesbrough	Trainee	Newcastle U	20	—
							Darlington (loan)	10	1
							Darlington	79	7
							Barnsley	120	5
Austin Kevin	6 1	15 00	D	12 2 73	Hackney	Saffron Walden	Leyton Orient	109	3
							Lincoln C	129	2
							Barnsley	3	—
Austin Neil	5 10	11 00	D	26 4 83	Barnsley	Trainee	Barnsley	—	—
Bagshaw Paul‡	5 10	12 02	M	29 5 79	Sheffield	Trainee	Barnsley	1	—
							Carlisle U (loan)	9	—
Barker Christopher	6 0	11 08	D	2 3 80	Sheffield	Alfreton	Barnsley	29	—
Barnard Darren	5 9	12 03	D	30 11 71	Rinteln	Wokingham T	Chelsea	29	2
							Reading (loan)	4	—
							Bristol C	78	15
							Barnsley	102	19
Bengtsson Robert‡	5 10	12 00	D	4 6 68	Gothenburg		Vastra Frolunda	229	18
							Barnsley	—	—
Bernard Curtis	5 10	12 05	F	3 7 80	Leeds	Trainee	Barnsley	—	—
Brown Keith	5 11	11 02	D	24 12 79	Edinburgh	Trainee	Blackburn R	—	—
							Barnsley	10	—
Bullock Martin	5 6	9 04	M	5 3 75	Derby	Eastwood T	Barnsley	167	3
							Port Vale (loan)	6	1
Bullock Tony*	6 1	14 01	G	18 2 72	Warrington	Leek T	Barnsley	38	—
Cataroche David‡	5 7	11 07	M	13 12 80	Leeds	Trainee	Barnsley	—	—
Chettle Steve	6 1	13 07	D	27 9 68	Nottingham	Apprentice	Nottingham F	415	11
							Barnsley	25	2
Crookes Dale*	5 9	12 03	M	10 3 80	Sheffield	Trainee	Barnsley	—	—
Dudgeon James	6 2	12 04	D	19 3 81	Newcastle	Trainee	Barnsley	—	—
Dyer Bruce	5 11	12 06	F	13 4 75	Ilford	Trainee	Watford	31	6
							Crystal Palace	135	37
							Barnsley	60	13
Eaden Nicky#	5 9	12 02	D	12 12 72	Sheffield	Trainee	Barnsley	293	10
Evans Andy	6 2	12 02	F	25 11 75	Aberystwyth	Trainee	Cardiff C	15	—
						Aberysthwyth T	Mansfield T (loan)	6	—
Fallon Rory	6 2	11 09	F	20 3 82	Gisbourne	North Shore U	Barnsley	—	—
Goodyear Craig	5 7	10 07	M	7 11 80	Barnsley	Trainee	Barnsley	—	—
Gregory Andrew*	5 10	11 04	M	8 10 76	Barnsley	Trainee	Barnsley	—	—
							Carlisle U (loan)	7	1
Hendrie John†	5 7	12 02	F	24 10 63	Lennoxtown	Apprentice	Coventry C	21	2
							Hereford U (loan)	6	—
							Bradford C	173	46
							Newcastle U	34	4
							Leeds U	27	5
							Middlesbrough	192	44
							Barnsley	65	17
Hignett Craig	5 9	11 03	M	12 1 70	Whiston	Liverpool	Crewe Alex	121	42
							Middlesbrough	156	33
							Aberdeen	13	2
							Barnsley	66	28
Hood Nathan	5 5	10 05	M	24 2 82	Rotherham		Barnsley	—	—
Hristov Georgi	6 0	12 09	F	30 1 76	Bitola		Partizan Belgrade	37	12
							Barnsley	44	8
Jackson Paul	5 8	11 04	F	14 5 81	Rochdale	Trainee	Barnsley	—	—
Jones Scott	5 10	12 01	D	1 5 75	Sheffield	Trainee	Barnsley	83	4
							Mansfield T (loan)	6	—
							Notts Co (loan)	—	—
Kay Antony	5 11	11 08	M	21 10 82	Barnsley	Trainee	Barnsley	—	—
Krizan Ales‡	5 11	12 09	D	25 7 71	Maribor		Branik Maribor	159	—
							Barnsley	13	—
Marcelle Clint‡	5 5	10 00	M	9 11 68	Port of Spain	Rio Ave	Falgueiras	51	3
							Barnsley	69	8
							Scunthorpe U (loan)	10	—
Markstedt Peter	6 2	13 05	D	11 1 72	Vasteras		Vasteras	23	4
(Transferred to Helsingborg, August 1999)							Barnsley	9	—
McClare Sean	5 11	11 08	M	12 1 78	Rotherham	Trainee	Barnsley	40	5
							Rochdale (loan)	9	—
Miller Kevin	6 1	16 00	G	15 3 69	Falmouth	Newquay	Exeter C	163	—
							Birmingham C	24	—
							Watford	128	—
							Crystal Palace	66	—
							Barnsley	41	—
Morgan Chris	6 1	12 09	D	9 11 77	Barnsley	Trainee	Barnsley	67	—
Moses Adrian	6 0	12 07	D	4 5 75	Doncaster	School	Barnsley	137	3
O'Callaghan Brian	6 1	12 01	D	24 2 81	Limerick	Pike Rovers	Barnsley	—	—
Parkin Jonathan	6 4	13 07	F	30 12 81	Barnsley	Scholar	Barnsley	2	—
Ravenhill Richard	5 10	11 01	M	16 1 81	Doncaster	Trainee	Barnsley	—	—

Name							Club	Apps	Gls
Richardson Kevin‡	5 9	11 08	M	4 12 62	Newcastle	Apprentice	Everton	109	16
							Watford	39	2
							Arsenal	96	5
							Real Sociedad	37	—
							Aston Villa	143	13
							Coventry C	78	—
							Southampton	28	—
							Barnsley	30	—
							Blackpool (loan)	20	1
Rose Karl	5 10	11 00	F	12 10 78	Barnsley		Barnsley	4	—
							Mansfield T (loan)	1	—
Sheron Mike	5 10	12 07	F	11 1 72	Liverpool	Trainee	Manchester C	100	24
							Bury (loan)	5	1
							Norwich C	28	2
							Stoke C	69	34
							QPR	63	19
							Barnsley	51	11
Shipperley Neil	6 0	14 01	F	30 10 74	Chatham	Trainee	Chelsea	37	7
							Watford (loan)	6	1
							Southampton	66	12
							Crystal Palace	61	20
							Nottingham F	20	1
							Barnsley	39	13
Siddall Richard	6 1	11 06	G	24 1 82	Sheffield	Scholar	Barnsley	—	—
Smith Andrew‡	5 9	11 04	M	13 1 80	Blackpool	Trainee	Barnsley	—	—
Thomas Geoff#	6 1	13 03	M	5 8 64	Manchester	Local	Rochdale	11	1
							Crewe Alex	125	20
							Crystal Palace	195	26
							Wolverhampton W	46	8
							Nottingham F	25	4
							Barnsley	27	4
Tinkler Eric#	6 2	13 08	M	30 7 70	Roodepoort		Vitoria Setubal	57	1
							Cagliari	20	—
							Barnsley	83	9
Turner Mike	6 2	13 03	F	2 4 76	Stoke	Bilston T	Barnsley	13	1
							Lincoln C (loan)	—	—
Van der Laan Robin#	5 11	13 08	M	5 9 68	Schiedam	Wageningen	Port Vale	176	24
							Derby Co	65	8
							Wolverhampton W (loan)	7	—
							Barnsley	49	4
Walker Leigh	5 10	12 06	G	12 2 81	Sheffield	Trainee	Sheffield U	—	—
							Barnsley	—	—
Watson David	6 0	12 09	G	10 11 73	Barnsley	Trainee	Barnsley	178	—
Young Darren	5 8	10 07	M	20 2 81	Whitehaven		Barnsley	—	—

Scholars
Rarrowclough, Carl; Christie, Jeremy J; Miller, Christopher T; Mulligan, David; Pearce, Allan D; Reece, Gary L; Richards, Duncan; Sedgwick, Craig D; Welch, Michael F

Non-Contract
Hendrie, John G; Shirtliff, Peter A

Player who does not hold a current contract but his registration has been retained by the club
Bernard, Curtis J

BIRMINGHAM CITY

Name							Club	Apps	Gls
Adebola Dele	6 3	12 08	F	23 6 75	Lagos	Trainee	Crewe Alex	124	39
							Birmingham C	98	25
Bass Jonathan	6 0	12 02	D	1 1 76	Weston-Super-Mare	Trainee	Birmingham C	67	—
							Carlisle U (loan)	3	—
							Gillingham (loan)	7	—
Bennett Ian	6 0	12 10	G	10 10 71	Worksop	Newcastle U	Peterborough U	72	—
							Birmingham C	208	—
Capaldi Tony	6 0	12 00	D	12 8 81	Porsgrunn	Trainee	Birmingham C	—	—
Charlton Simon*	5 8	11 00	D	25 10 71	Huddersfield	Trainee	Huddersfield T	124	1
							Southampton	114	2
							Birmingham C	72	—
Dyson James	6 2	12 00	D	20 4 79	Wordsley	Trainee	Birmingham C	2	—
Furlong Paul	6 0	11 00	F	1 10 68	London	Enfield	Coventry C	37	4
							Watford	79	37
							Chelsea	64	13
							Birmingham C	116	49
Gill Jeremy	5 11	11 00	D	8 9 70	Clevedon	Yeovil T	Birmingham C	17	—
Grainger Martin	5 10	11 07	D	23 8 72	Enfield	Trainee	Colchester U	46	7
							Brentford	101	12
							Birmingham C	138	14
Haarhoff Jimmy	5 5	10 02	M	27 5 81	Lusaka	Trainee	Birmingham C	1	—
Hey Tony‡	5 9	11 07	M	19 9 70	Berlin		Fortuna Cologne	32	9
							Birmingham C	9	—
Holdsworth David	6 1	12 10	D	8 11 68	Walthamstow	Trainee	Watford	258	10
							Sheffield U	93	4
							Birmingham C	52	6
Hughes Bryan	5 9	10 00	M	19 6 76	Liverpool	Trainee	Wrexham	94	12
							Birmingham C	124	18

Name	Ht	Wt	Pos	Birthdate	Birthplace	Previous	Club	Apps	Gls
Hyde Graham	5 7	12 04	M	10 11 70	Doncaster	Trainee	Sheffield W	172	11
							Birmingham C	44	1
Johnson Andrew	5 7	10 00	F	10 2 81	Bedford	Trainee	Birmingham C	26	1
Johnson Michael	5 11	11 00	D	4 7 73	Nottingham	Trainee	Notts Co	107	—
							Birmingham C	185	10
Lazaridis Stan	5 9	12 00	M	16 8 72	Perth	West Adelaide	West Ham U	69	3
							Birmingham C	31	2
Luntala Tresor	5 9	11 00	M	31 5 82	Dreux		Birmingham C	—	—
Marcelo	6 0	13 04	F	11 10 69	Niteroi	Alaves	Sheffield U	66	24
							Birmingham C	25	5
Marsh Simon	5 11	12 00	D	29 1 77	Ealing	Trainee	Oxford U	56	3
							Birmingham C	7	—
McCarthy Jon	5 9	11 05	M	18 8 70	Middlesbrough		Hartlepool U	1	—
						Shepshed	York C	199	31
							Port Vale	94	11
							Birmingham C	105	8
McKeown Francis‡	5 9	11 07	M	11 2 81	Belfast		Sunderland	—	—
							Birmingham C	—	—
Ndlovu Peter	5 8	10 02	F	25 2 73	Zimbabwe	Highlanders	Coventry C	177	37
							Birmingham C	95	20
O'Connor Martin	5 8	10 08	M	10 12 67	Walsall	Bromsgrove R	Crystal Palace	2	—
							Walsall (loan)	10	1
							Walsall	94	21
							Peterborough U	18	3
							Birmingham C	133	11
Parker Sonny			M	28 2 83	Middlesbrough	Trainee	Birmingham C	—	—
Pinkney Grant			M	31 1 83	Evesham		Birmingham C	—	—
Poole Kevin	5 10	11 11	G	21 7 63	Bromsgrove	Apprentice	Aston Villa	28	—
							Northampton T (loan)	3	—
							Middlesbrough	34	—
							Hartlepool U (loan)	12	—
							Leicester C	163	—
							Birmingham C	55	—
Purse Darren	6 2	13 08	D	14 2 76	Stepney	Trainee	Leyton Orient	55	3
							Oxford U	59	5
							Birmingham C	66	2
Robinson Steve	5 9	11 00	M	17 10 75	Nottingham	Trainee	Birmingham C	77	—
							Peterborough U (loan)	5	—
Rowett Gary	6 0	12 10	D	6 3 74	Bromsgrove	Trainee	Cambridge U	63	9
							Everton	4	—
							Blackpool (loan)	17	—
							Derby Co	105	2
							Birmingham C	87	6
Russo Marco‡			M	25 4 82	Gariati		Birmingham C	—	—
Scheppel Danny*	5 7	10 00	M	27 4 81	Worcester	Trainee	Birmingham C	—	—
Wassall Darren‡	6 0	12 07	D	27 6 68	Edgbaston		Nottingham F	27	—
							Hereford U (loan)	7	—
							Bury (loan)	7	1
							Derby Co	98	—
							Manchester C (loan)	15	—
							Birmingham C (loan)	8	—
							Birmingham C	17	—
Williams Jacques	5 9	11 00	M	25 4 81	Wallasey		Birmingham C	—	—

Scholars
Davies, Clint; Diamond, Ross; Evans, Richard G; Fagan, Craig A; Gilbert, Peter; Hart, Steven; Hider, Allan J; Horrigan, Darren; Hutchinson, Jonathan; Jameson, Michael; Robertson, Daniel; Tearney, Trevor L; Wood, Paul A

BLACKBURN ROVERS

Name	Ht	Wt	Pos	Birthdate	Birthplace	Previous	Club	Apps	Gls
Andersson Anders	5 9	11 09	M	15 3 74	Tomelilla		Malmo	126	19
(Transferred to Aalborg, July 1999)							Blackburn R	4	—
Baldacchino Ryan	5 9	12 03	F	13 1 81	Leicester	Trainee	Blackburn R	—	—
Bingham Michael	6 0	12 05	G	21 5 81	Preston	Trainee	Blackburn R	—	—
Blake Nathan	5 11	13 12	F	27 1 72	Cardiff	Chelsea	Cardiff C	131	35
							Sheffield U	69	34
							Bolton W	107	38
							Blackburn R	39	6
Blakeman Liam			M	6 9 82	Southport	Scholar	Blackburn R	—	—
Broomes Marlon	6 1	13 00	D	28 11 77	Meriden	Trainee	Blackburn R	30	1
							Swindon T (loan)	12	1
Burgess Ben	6 3	14 04	F	9 11 81	Buxton	Trainee	Blackburn R	2	—
Carsley Lee	5 10	12 06	M	28 2 74	Birmingham	Trainee	Derby Co	138	5
							Blackburn R	38	10
Chamberlain Robert			M	5 6 82	Chester	Trainee	Blackburn R	—	—
Corbett Jimmy	5 10	12 00	F	6 7 80	Hackney	Trainee	Gillingham	16	2
							Blackburn R	—	—
Dahlin Martin	6 1	13 03	F	16 4 68	Lund	Lund BK	Malmo	79	39
(Retired)							Moenchengladbach	106	50
							Roma	3	—
							Blackburn R	26	4

Name			Pos				Club		
Dailly Christian	6 0	12 10	D	23 10 73	Dundee		Dundee U	141	18
							Derby Co	67	4
							Blackburn R	60	4
Davidson Callum	5 10	12 07	D	25 6 76	Stirling		St Johnstone	44	4
							Blackburn R	65	1
Douglas Jonathan			M	22 11 81	Monaghan	Trainee	Blackburn R	—	—
Doyle Robert			M	15 4 82	Dublin	Trainee	Blackburn R	—	—
Duff Damien	5 9	11 07	F	2 3 79	Ballyboden	Lourdes Celtic	Blackburn R	94	10
Dunn David	5 10	12 06	M	27 12 79	Gt Harwood	Trainee	Blackburn R	37	3
Dunning Darren	5 6	11 12	M	8 1 81	Scarborough	Trainee	Blackburn R	—	—
Dunning Richard*	5 7	11 10	D	8 1 81	Scarborough	Trainee	Blackburn R	—	—
							Oldham Ath (loan)	—	—
Filan John	6 2	12 12	G	8 2 70	Sydney	Budapest St George	Cambridge U	68	—
							Nottingham F (loan)	—	—
							Coventry C	16	—
							Blackburn R	49	—
Flitcroft Garry	6 0	11 08	M	6 11 72	Bolton	Trainee	Manchester C	115	13
							Bury (loan)	12	—
							Blackburn R	91	5
Flitcroft Steven	5 10	11 01	M	17 10 81	Bolton	Trainee	Blackburn R	—	—
Forsyth Paul	5 8	10 05	F	11 4 81	Dublin	Trainee	Blackburn R	—	—
Foster Steve	5 9	13 01	F	30 12 81	Manchester	Trainee	Blackburn R	—	—
Frandsen Per	5 11	12 10	M	6 2 70	Copenhagen		B 1903	25	15
							Lille	109	19
							FC Copenhagen	55	19
							Bolton W	130	17
							Blackburn R	31	5
Gillespie Keith	5 10	11 03	F	18 2 75	Bangor	Trainee	Manchester U	9	1
							Wigan Ath (loan)	8	4
							Newcastle U	113	11
							Blackburn R	38	3
Grayson Simon	6 0	13 07	D	16 12 69	Ripon	Trainee	Leeds U	2	—
							Leicester C	188	4
							Aston Villa	48	—
							Blackburn R	34	—
Hamilton Gary			F	6 10 80	Bambridge	Trainee	Blackburn R	—	—
Harkness Steve	5 9	11 09	D	27 8 71	Carlisle	Trainee	Carlisle U	13	—
							Liverpool	102	2
							Huddersfield T (loan)	5	—
							Southend U (loan)	6	—
							Benfica	9	—
							Blackburn R	17	—
Hawe Steven			F	23 12 80	Machbrafelt	Trainee	Blackburn R	—	—
Howson Stuart			M	30 9 81	Chorley	Trainee	Blackburn R	—	—
Jansen Matt	5 11	12 06	F	20 10 77	Carlisle	Trainee	Carlisle U	42	10
							Crystal Palace	26	10
							Blackburn R	41	6
Johnson Damien	5 9	11 07	M	18 11 78	Lisburn	Trainee	Blackburn R	37	2
							Nottingham F (loan)	6	—
Kelly Alan	6 3	14 02	G	11 8 68	Preston	Trainee	Preston NE	142	—
							Sheffield U	216	—
							Blackburn R	30	—
Kenna Jeff	5 11	12 03	D	28 8 70	Dublin	Trainee	Southampton	114	4
							Blackburn R	149	1
Konde Oumar	6 2	13 00	M	19 8 79	Basle	Binningen	Basle	35	—
(Transferred to Freiburg, June 1999)							Blackburn R	—	—
Lawless Michael	5 6	10 13	M	15 8 81	Dublin	Trainee	Blackburn R	—	—
McAteer Jason	5 11	12 04	M	18 6 71	Birkenhead	Marine	Bolton W	114	8
							Liverpool	100	3
							Blackburn R	41	3
McCann Peter	5 6	10 13	D	18 8 81	Dublin	Trainee	Blackburn R	—	—
McKinlay Billy	5 8	11 06	M	22 4 69	Glasgow	Hamilton Th	Dundee U	222	23
							Blackburn R	90	3
McNamee David	5 11	11 02	D	10 10 80	Glasgow	St Mirren BC	St Mirren	31	—
							Blackburn R	—	—
Miller Alan	6 3	14 06	G	29 3 70	Epping	Trainee	Arsenal	8	—
							Plymouth Arg (loan)	13	—
							WBA (loan)	3	—
							Birmingham C (loan)	15	—
							Middlesbrough	57	—
							Huddersfield T (loan)	—	—
							Grimsby T (loan)	3	—
							WBA	98	—
							Blackburn R	1	—
Murphy Peter	5 11	12 10	D	27 10 80	Dublin	Trainee	Blackburn R	—	—
Murray Frederick			M	22 5 82	Clonmel	Trainee	Blackburn R	—	—
O'Brien Burton	5 10	10 12	M	10 6 81	South Africa	S Form	St Mirren	22	1
							Blackburn R	—	—
Ostenstad Egil	5 11	13 00	F	2 1 72	Haugesund		Viking	128	54
							Southampton	96	28
							Blackburn R	28	8

Peacock Darren	6 2	12 12	D	3 2 68	Bristol	Apprentice	Newport Co	28	—
							Hereford U	59	4
							QPR	126	6
							Newcastle U	133	2
							Blackburn R	47	—
Perez Sebastian	5 10	12 00	D	24 11 73	Saint-Chamond		St Etienne	55	2
(Transferred to Marseille, July 1999)							Bastia	63	10
							Blackburn R	5	1
Richards Marc			M	8 7 82	Wolverhampton	Trainee	Blackburn R	—	—
Richardson Leam	5 8	11 04	D	19 11 79	Leeds	Trainee	Blackburn R	—	—
Scates Garth*			M	27 8 79	Dundonald	Trainee	Blackburn R	—	—
Short Craig	6 1	11 10	D	25 6 68	Bridlington	Pickering T	Scarborough	63	7
							Notts Co	128	6
							Derby Co	118	9
							Everton	99	4
							Blackburn R	17	—
Taylor Martin	6 4	14 00	D	9 11 79	Ashington	Trainee	Blackburn R	9	—
							Darlington (loan)	4	—
							Stockport Co (loan)	7	—
Taylor Michael			M	21 11 82	Liverpool	Scholar	Blackburn R	—	—
Taylor Stuart			M	14 9 81	Rochdale	Trainee	Blackburn R	—	—
Thomas James	6 1	13 04	F	16 1 79	Swansea	Trainee	Blackburn R	—	—
							WBA (loan)	3	—
							Blackpool (loan)	9	2
Ward Ashley	6 1	12 04	F	24 11 70	Manchester	Trainee	Manchester C	1	—
							Wrexham (loan)	4	2
							Leicester C	10	—
							Blackpool (loan)	2	1
							Crewe Alex	61	25
							Norwich C	53	18
							Derby Co	40	9
							Barnsley	46	20
							Blackburn R	54	13
Williams Anthony*	6 1	12 13	G	20 9 77	Ogwr	Trainee	Blackburn R	—	—
							QPR (loan)	—	—
							Macclesfield T (loan)	4	—
							Huddersfield T (loan)	—	—
							Bristol R (loan)	9	—
							Gillingham (loan)	2	—
							Macclesfield T (loan)	11	—

Scholars
Byrne, Mark J; Creasy, Neil; Danns, Neil A; Derbyshire, Robert W; Gibson, Benjamin J; Hardy, Lee; Hevicon, Ryan; Hill, David JP; Hind, Matthew; Hockenhull, Darren; Martin, Anthony P; Murray, Philip D; Nutter, John RW; Renton, Keiron; Robinson, Ryan; Stone, Daniel JC; Woodhead; Robert A

Associated Schoolboys who have accepted the Club's offer of a Traineeship/Scholarship/Contract
Atkinson, Lee P; Donnelly Ciaran; McLean, Matthew; Willis, David J

BLACKPOOL

Ablett Gary*	6 2	11 04	D	19 11 65	Liverpool	Apprentice	Liverpool	109	1
							Derby Co (loan)	6	—
							Hull C (loan)	5	—
							Everton	128	5
							Sheffield U (loan)	12	—
							Birmingham C	104	1
							Wycombe W (loan)	4	—
							Blackpool	10	1
Aldridge Martin	5 11	12 02	F	4 12 74	Northampton	Trainee	Northampton T	70	17
(Deceased)							Oxford U	72	19
							Southend U (loan)	11	1
							Blackpool	27	7
							Port Vale (loan)	3	—
Bardsley David*	5 10	11 07	D	11 9 64	Manchester	Apprentice	Blackpool	45	—
							Watford	100	7
							Oxford U	74	7
							QPR	253	4
							Blackpool	64	—
Barnes Phil	6 1	11 01	G	2 3 79	Rotherham	Trainee	Rotherham U	2	—
							Blackpool	14	—
Beesley Paul	6 1	12 06	D	21 7 65	Liverpool	Marine	Wigan Ath	155	3
							Leyton Orient	32	1
							Sheffield U	168	7
							Leeds U	22	—
							Manchester C	13	—
							Port Vale (loan)	5	—
							WBA (loan)	8	—
							Port Vale	35	3
							Blackpool	18	—
Bent Junior	5 5	10 06	F	1 3 70	Huddersfield	Trainee	Huddersfield T	36	6
							Burnley (loan)	9	3
							Bristol C	183	20
							Stoke C (loan)	1	—
							Shrewsbury T (loan)	6	—
							Blackpool	103	5
Bushell Steve	5 9	11 06	M	28 12 72	Manchester	Trainee	York C	174	10
							Blackpool	55	5

Name	Ht	Wt	Pos	DOB	Birthplace	Source	Club	Apps	Gls
Caig Tony	6 1	12 00	G	11 4 74	Whitehaven	Trainee	Carlisle U	223	—
							Blackpool	43	—
Carlisle Clarke	6 1	12 07	D	14 10 79	Preston	Trainee	Blackpool	93	7
Clarkson Phil	5 10	12 05	M	13 11 68	Garstang	Fleetwood T	Crewe Alex	98	27
							Scunthorpe U	52	19
							Blackpool	141	30
Coid Daniel§	5 11	11 07	M	3 10 81	Liverpool	Trainee	Blackpool	22	1
Connell Darren§	5 8	10 08	M	3 2 82	Blackpool	Trainee	Blackpool	3	—
Conroy Mike‡	6 0	13 03	F	31 12 65	Glasgow	Apprentice	Coventry C	—	—
							Clydebank	114	38
							St Mirren	10	1
							Reading	80	7
							Burnley	77	30
							Preston NE	57	22
							Fulham	94	32
							Blackpool	14	—
							Chester C (loan)	15	3
Couzens Andy*	5 10	11 11	M	4 6 75	Shipley	Trainee	Leeds U	28	1
							Carlisle U	42	2
							Blackpool	21	—
Darlington Stephen‡			M	14 12 78	Manchester		Blackpool	—	—
Forsyth Richard	5 11	13 00	M	3 10 70	Dudley	Kidderminster H	Birmingham C	26	2
							Stoke C	95	17
							Blackpool	13	—
Garvey Steve	5 9	11 01	M	22 11 73	Stalybridge	Trainee	Crewe Alex	108	8
							Chesterfield (loan)	3	—
							Blackpool	17	1
Gill Wayne	5 9	11 00	M	28 11 75	Chorley	Trainee	Blackburn R	—	—
							Dundee U	2	—
							Blackburn R	—	—
							Blackpool	12	7
Hills John	5 8	10 08	D	21 4 78	St Annes-on-Sea	Trainee	Blackpool	—	—
							Everton	3	—
							Swansea C (loan)	11	—
							Swansea C (loan)	7	1
							Blackpool	80	4
Hughes Ian	5 10	12 08	M	2 8 74	Bangor	Trainee	Bury	175	1
							Blackpool	88	1
Jaszczun Tommy	5 11	11 02	D	16 9 77	Kettering	Trainee	Aston Villa	—	—
							Blackpool	19	—
Jones Eifion	6 3	13 00	D	28 9 80	Llanrug	Trainee	Liverpool	—	—
							Blackpool	1	—
Lambert Ricky§	6 2	12 01		16 2 82	Liverpool	Trainee	Blackpool	3	—
Murphy John	6 2	14 00	F	18 10 76	Whiston	Trainee	Chester C	103	20
							Blackpool	39	10
Newell Mike	6 0	13 00	F	27 1 65	Liverpool	Liverpool	Crewe Alex	3	—
							Wigan Ath	72	25
							Luton T	63	18
							Leicester C	81	21
							Everton	68	15
							Blackburn R	130	28
							Birmingham C	15	1
							West Ham U (loan)	7	—
							Bradford C (loan)	7	—
							Aberdeen	44	6
							Crewe Alex	4	—
							Blackpool	13	2
Nowland Adam	5 11	11 06	F	6 7 81	Preston	Trainee	Blackpool	59	5
Ormerod Brett	5 11	11 04	F	18 10 76	Blackburn	Accrington S	Blackpool	66	15
Rachel Adam	5 11	12 08	G	10 12 76	Birmingham	Trainee	Aston Villa	1	—
							Blackpool	1	—
Robinson Phil*	5 9	11 00	D	28 9 80	Manchester	Trainee	Blackpool	11	—
Shuttleworth Barry*	5 8	11 00	D	9 7 77	Accrington	Trainee	Bury	—	—
							Rotherham U	—	—
							Blackpool	19	1
Thompson Phil	5 11	12 00	D	1 4 81	Blackpool	Trainee	Blackpool	26	2
Wellens Richard	5 9	11 05	M	26 3 80	Manchester	Trainee	Manchester U	—	—
							Blackpool	8	—
Worthington Nigel‡	5 11	12 06	D	4 11 61	Ballymena	Ballymena U	Notts Co	67	4
							Sheffield W	338	12
							Leeds U	43	1
							Stoke C	12	—
							Blackpool	9	—

Trainees
Coid, Daniel J; Connell, Darren S; Ellison Gavin; Fahey, Mark A; Gilmore, Gavin; Lambert, Rickie L; Lynch, Patrick A; Manchester, Brian N; Sidebotham, Paul G

Scholars
Carroll, John D; Connors, John J; Maden, Wayne T; Robinson, Craig; Robinson, Daniel M; Smyth, Marc

BOLTON WANDERERS

Name	Ht	Wt	Pos	DOB	Birthplace	Source	Club	Apps	Gls
Aljofree Hasney*	6 0	12 06	D	11 7 78	Manchester	Trainee	Bolton W	14	—
Banks Steve	6 0	13 12	G	9 2 72	Hillingdon	Trainee	West Ham U	—	—
							Gillingham	67	—
							Blackpool	150	—
							Bolton W	11	—

Name					Born	Birthplace	From	Club	Apps	Gls
Bergsson Gudni*	6 1	12 11	D	21	7 65	Reykjavik	Valur	Tottenham H	71	2
								Bolton W	165	13
Boutsianis Con#	5 11	13 00	M	27	12 71	Melbourne	Perth Glory	Bolton W	—	—
Crumblehulme Danny	5 6	10 07	M	7	2 82	Blackpool	Trainee	Bolton W	—	—
Dawson Chris*	5 10	10 02	D	22	8 79	Coventry	Trainee	Bolton W	—	—
Elliott Robbie	5 10	12 03	M	25	12 73	Gosforth	Trainee	Newcastle U	79	9
								Bolton W	53	3
Evans James	6 0	12 00	G	27	1 82	Glasgow	Scholar	Bolton W	—	—
Farrelly Gareth	6 1	13 07	M	28	8 75	Dublin	Home Farm	Aston Villa	8	—
								Rotherham U (loan)	10	2
								Everton	27	1
								Bolton W	11	1
Fish Mark	6 4	13 06	D	14	3 74	Cape Town	Arcadia Shepherds	Jomo Cosmos	55	2
								Orlando Pirates	75	6
								Lazio	15	1
								Bolton W	89	3
Gardner Ricardo	5 9	11 01	M	25	9 78	St Andrews	Harbour View	Bolton W	59	7
Glennon Matthew	6 2	14 09	G	8	10 78	Stockport	Trainee	Bolton W	—	—
								Port Vale (loan)	—	—
								Stockport Co (loan)	—	—
Gregson Neil*	5 9	10 10	M	11	9 80	Fazackerley	Liverpool	Bolton W	—	—
Gudjohnsen Eidur	6 0	13 09	F	15	9 78	Reykjavik		Valur	17	7
								PSV Eindhoven	13	3
								KR	6	—
								Bolton W	55	18
Hansen Bo	6 1	12 02	F	16	6 72	Jutland		Brondby	102	43
								Bolton W	38	9
Haveron Gary	6 1	14 00	D	6	3 81	Belfast	Wolverhampton W	Bolton W	—	—
Holden Dean	6 0	12 03	D	15	9 79	Salford		Bolton W	12	—
Holdsworth Dean	5 11	13 06	F	8	11 68	Walthamstow	Trainee	Watford	16	3
								Carlisle U (loan)	4	1
								Port Vale (loan)	6	2
								Swansea C (loan)	5	1
								Brentford (loan)	7	1
								Brentford	110	53
								Wimbledon	169	58
								Bolton W	87	26
Jaaskelainen Jussi	6 3	13 05	G	19	4 75	Mikkeli		MP	64	—
								VPS	54	—
								Bolton W	68	—
Jensen Claus	5 11	12 13	M	29	4 77	Nykobing		Naestved	4	—
								Lyngby	62	14
								Bolton W	86	8
Johansen Michael*	5 6	10 08	M	22	7 72	Glostrup		KB Copenhagen	15	1
								B 1903	26	1
								FC Copenhagen	114	17
								Bolton W	137	16
Johnston Allan#	5 7	9 07	F	14	12 73	Glasgow		Hearts	84	12
								Rennes	23	2
								Sunderland	86	19
								Birmingham C (loan)	9	—
								Bolton W	19	3
Kaprielian Mickael	5 10	11 00	F	6	10 80	Marseille		Bolton W	1	—
Morrison Peter	5 11	10 00	M	29	6 80	Manchester	Trainee	Bolton W	—	—
Nolan Kevin	6 0	14 00	M	24	6 82	Liverpool	Scholar	Bolton W	4	—
Norris David	5 7	11 06	M	22	2 81	Peterborough	Boston U	Bolton W	—	—
O'Kane John	5 10	12 06	D	15	11 74	Nottingham	Trainee	Manchester U	2	—
								Wimbledon (loan)	—	—
								Bury (loan)	13	3
								Bradford C (loan)	7	—
								Everton	14	—
								Burnley (loan)	8	—
								Bolton W	11	1
O'Malley Carl*	5 10	13 00	D	10	1 81	Salford	Trainee	Bolton W	—	—
Passi Franck‡	5 10	12 08	M	28	3 66	Bergerac		Toulon	77	2
(On loan from Compostela, November 1999)								Monaco	15	—
								Compostela	142	4
								Bolton W	15	—
Phillips Jimmy*	6 0	13 06	D	8	2 66	Bolton	Apprentice	Bolton W	108	2
								Rangers	25	—
								Oxford U	79	8
								Middlesbrough	139	6
								Bolton W	221	3
Power Alan‡	5 8	10 06	M	18	9 80	Dublin	Trainee	Bolton W	—	—
Ritchie Paul*	6 1	13 06	D	21	8 75	Glasgow		Hearts	133	4
								Bolton W	14	—
Roberts John*	5 10	12 00	M	15	3 81	Bangor	Liverpool	Bolton W	—	—
Smith Gordon*	6 0	12 00	F	18	12 80	Glasgow	Trainee	Bolton W	—	—
Snorrason Olaf	5 10	11 00	F	22	4 82	Reykjavik		Bolton W	—	—
Staton Luke*	5 7	10 07	M	10	3 79	Doncaster	Trainee	Blackburn R	—	—
								Bolton W	—	—

Strong Greg	6 2	14 04	D	5 9 75	Bolton	Trainee	Wigan Ath	35	3
							Bolton W	12	1
							Blackpool (loan)	11	1
							Stoke C (loan)	5	1
							Motherwell (loan)	10	—
Warhurst Paul	6 0	13 07	D	26 9 69	Stockport	Trainee	Manchester C		
							Oldham Ath	67	2
							Sheffield W	66	6
							Blackburn R	57	4
							Crystal Palace	27	4
							Bolton W	39	—
Whitlow Mike	6 1	13 03	D	13 1 68	Northwich	Witton Alb	Leeds U	77	4
							Leicester C	147	8
							Bolton W	78	1

Scholars
Astle, Brook M; Buchanan, Wayne B; Downey, Christopher A; Flanagan, Daniel J; Laidlaw, Simon G; Letson, Craig W; McDonagh, Christopher; O'Connor, Kieran J; O'Hare, Alan PJ; Ross, Clive; Ryan, Ciaran P; Stephan, Matthew P; Tagoe, Darrel J; Williams, Christopher

AFC BOURNEMOUTH

Bailey John	5 8	10 02	M	6 5 69	London	Enfield	Bournemouth	149	6
Beardsmore Russell‡	5 8	10 04	M	28 10 69	Wigan	Apprentice	Manchester U	56	4
							Blackburn R (loan)	2	—
							Bournemouth	178	4
Boli Roger‡	5 8	10 12	F	26 9 65	Adjame	Lille	Lens	164	40
							Le Havre	26	4
							Walsall	41	12
							Dundee U	3	—
							Bournemouth	6	—
Broadhurst Karl	6 1	11 07	D	18 3 80	Portsmouth	Trainee	Bournemouth	16	—
Colgan Nick	6 1	13 06	G	19 9 73	Drogheda	Drogheda	Chelsea	1	—
(Transferred to Hibernian, July 1999)							Crewe Alex (loan)	—	—
							Grimsby T (loan)	—	—
							Millwall (loan)	—	—
							Brentford (loan)	5	—
							Reading (loan)	5	—
							Bournemouth	—	—
Day Jamie	5 10	11 04	M	13 9 79	Sidcup	Trainee	Arsenal	—	—
							Bournemouth	13	1
Dean Michael*	5 9	11 10	M	9 3 78	Weymouth	Trainee	Bournemouth	34	—
Elliott Wade	5 9	11 01	F	14 12 78	Southampton	Trainee	Bournemouth	12	3
Fletcher Carl	5 10	11 07	M	7 4 80	Camberley	Trainee	Bournemouth	27	3
Fletcher Steve	6 2	14 09	F	26 6 72	Hartlepool	Trainee	Hartlepool U	32	4
							Bournemouth	266	51
Ford James	5 8	11 00	M	23 10 81	Portsmouth	Trainee	Bournemouth	2	—
Hayter James	5 9	10 13	F	9 4 79	Newport (IW)	Trainee	Bournemouth	58	4
Howe Eddie	5 9	11 02	D	29 11 77	Amersham	Trainee	Bournemouth	131	4
Huck Willie	5 10	11 09	M	17 3 79	Paris	Monaco	Arsenal	—	—
							Bournemouth	25	—
Hughes Richard	6 2	12 00	M	25 6 79	Glasgow	Atalanta	Arsenal	—	—
							Bournemouth	65	4
Jorgensen Claus	5 10	10 06	M	27 4 76	Holstebro	AC Horsens	Bournemouth	44	6
Keeler Justin	5 11	11 06	F	17 4 78	Hillingdon	Christchurch	Bournemouth	3	—
Mean Scott*	5 11	13 08	M	13 12 73	Crawley	Trainee	Bournemouth	74	8
							West Ham U	3	—
							Port Vale (loan)	1	—
							Bournemouth	32	4
O'Neill Jon*	5 11	12 00	F	2 1 74	Glasgow	Queen's Park BC	Queen's Park	91	30
							Celtic	1	—
							Bournemouth	121	10
Ovendale Mark	6 2	13 10	G	22 11 73	Leicester	Wisbech T	Northampton T	6	—
						Barry T	Bournemouth	89	—
Rawlinson Mark*	5 10	11 04	M	9 6 75	Bolton	Trainee	Manchester U	—	—
							Bournemouth	79	2
Robinson Steve	5 9	11 02	F	10 12 74	Crumlin	Trainee	Tottenham H	2	—
							Leyton Orient (loan)	—	—
							Bournemouth	240	51
Sheerin Joe	6 1	12 13	F	1 2 79	Hammersmith	Trainee	Chelsea	1	—
							Bournemouth	6	1
Smith Daniel	5 11	11 04	D	17 8 82	Southampton	Trainee	Bournemouth	1	—
Stein Mark*	5 6	11 07	F	29 1 66	Capetown		Luton T	54	19
							Aldershot (loan)	2	1
							QPR	33	4
							Oxford U	82	18
							Stoke C	94	50
							Chelsea	50	21
							Stoke C (loan)	11	4
							Ipswich T (loan)	7	2
							Bournemouth (loan)	11	4
							Bournemouth	79	26
Stewart Gareth	6 0	12 08	G	3 2 80	Preston	Trainee	Blackburn R	—	—
							Bournemouth	3	—
Stock Brian	5 11	11 02	F	24 12 81	Winchester	Trainee	Bournemouth	5	—

Name	Ht	Wt	Pos	Born	Birthplace	Source	Clubs	Apps	Gls
Tindall Jason	6 1	12 01	M	15 11 77	Stepney	Trainee	Charlton Ath	—	—
							Bournemouth	25	1
Town David	5 7	11 13	F	9 12 76	Bournemouth	Trainee	Bournemouth	56	2
(Transferred to Rushden & Diamonds, June 1999)									
Warren Christer*	5 10	11 12	F	10 10 74	Poole	Cheltenham T	Southampton	8	—
							Brighton & HA (loan)	3	—
							Fulham (loan)	11	1
							Bournemouth	103	13
Watson Gordon‡	5 10	14 11	F	20 3 71	Sidcup	Trainee	Charlton Ath	31	7
							Sheffield W	66	15
							Southampton	52	8
							Bradford C	21	5
							Bournemouth	6	—
Young Neil	5 9	12 00	D	31 8 73	Harlow	Trainee	Tottenham H	—	—
							Bournemouth	242	3

Trainees
Lattimer, James D

BRADFORD CITY

Name	Ht	Wt	Pos	Born	Birthplace	Source	Clubs	Apps	Gls
Beagrie Peter	5 8	12 00	M	28 11 65	Middlesbrough	Local	Middlesbrough	33	2
							Sheffield U	84	11
							Stoke C	54	7
							Everton	114	11
							Sunderland (loan)	5	1
							Manchester C	52	3
							Bradford C	112	19
							Everton (loan)	6	—
Blake Robbie	5 8	11 00	F	4 3 76	Middlesbrough	Trainee	Darlington	68	21
							Bradford C	106	26
Bower Mark	5 10	10 11	D	23 1 80	Bradford	Trainee	Bradford C	3	—
							York C (loan)	15	1
Cadete Jorge‡	5 11	11 11	F	27 8 68	Mozambique	Benfica	Sporting	6	—
(On loan from Benfica, February 2000)							Vitoria Setubal	29	8
							Sporting	158	63
							Celtic	37	30
							Celta Vigo	36	8
							Benfica	16	3
							Celtic	—	—
							Bradford C	7	—
Clarke Matthew	6 3	12 02	G	3 11 73	Sheffield	Trainee	Rotherham U	124	—
							Sheffield W	4	—
							Bradford C	21	—
Davison Aidan	6 1	13 12	G	11 5 68	Sedgefield	Billingham Syn	Notts Co	1	—
							Leyton Orient (loan)	—	—
							Bury	—	—
							Chester C (loan)	—	—
							Blackpool (loan)	—	—
							Millwall	34	—
							Bolton W	37	—
							Ipswich T (loan)	—	—
							Hull C (loan)	9	—
							Bradford C	10	—
							Grimsby T	77	—
							Sheffield U	2	—
							Bradford C	6	—
Dreyer John	6 1	13 02	D	11 6 63	Alnwick	Wallingford T	Oxford U	60	2
							Torquay U (loan)	5	—
							Fulham (loan)	12	2
							Luton T	214	13
							Stoke C	49	3
							Bolton W (loan)	2	—
							Bradford C	80	2
Grant Gareth	5 10	10 04	F	6 9 80	Leeds	Trainee	Bradford C	9	—
							Halifax T (loan)	3	—
							Bolton W (loan)	—	—
Halle Gunnar	6 0	12 07	D	11 8 65	Lillestrom	Lillestrom	Oldham Ath	188	17
							Leeds U	70	4
							Bradford C	38	—
Jacobs Wayne	5 8	11 02	D	3 2 69	Sheffield	Apprentice	Sheffield W	6	—
							Hull C	129	4
							Rotherham U	42	2
							Bradford C	209	9
Jewell Paul‡	5 8	12 01	F	28 9 64	Liverpool	Apprentice	Liverpool	—	—
							Wigan Ath	137	35
							Bradford C	269	56
							Grimsby T (loan)	5	1
Lawrence Jamie	6 0	12 00	M	8 3 70	Balham	Cowes	Sunderland	4	—
							Doncaster R	25	3
							Leicester C	47	1
							Bradford C	101	8
McCall Stuart	5 9	11 04	M	10 6 64	Leeds	Apprentice	Bradford C	238	37
							Everton	103	6
							Rangers	194	14
							Bradford C	77	4
Mills Lee	6 2	12 09	F	10 7 70	Mexborough	Stocksbridge PS	Wolverhampton W	25	2
							Derby Co	16	7
							Port Vale	109	35
							Bradford C	65	28
							Manchester C (loan)	3	—

Myers Andy	5 10	13 11	D	3 11 73	Hounslow	Trainee	Chelsea	84	2
							Bradford C	13	—
							Portsmouth (loan)	8	—
O'Brien Andrew	5 10	10 06	D	29 6 79	Harrogate	Trainee	Bradford C	115	3
Patterson Andrew‡	5 10	10 04	F	26 11 80	Kirkaldy	Trainee	Bradford C	—	—
Rankin Isiah	5 10	11 00	F	22 5 78	London	Trainee	Arsenal	1	—
							Colchester U (loan)	11	5
							Bradford C	36	4
							Birmingham C (loan)	13	4
Rodriguez Bruno‡	6 1	12 01	F	25 11 72	Bastia		Monaco	3	—
							Bastia	61	23
							Strasbourg	14	2
							Metz	46	17
							Paris St Germain	18	6
							Bradford C	2	—
Saunders Dean	5 8	10 06	F	21 6 64	Swansea	Apprentice	Swansea C	49	12
							Cardiff C (loan)	4	—
							Brighton & HA	72	21
							Oxford U	59	22
							Derby Co	106	42
							Liverpool	42	11
							Aston Villa	112	37
							Galatasaray	27	15
							Nottingham F	43	5
							Sheffield U	43	17
							Benfica	17	5
							Bradford C	34	3
Sharpe Lee	6 0	12 10	M	27 5 71	Halesowen	Trainee	Torquay U	14	3
							Manchester U	193	21
							Leeds U	30	5
							Bradford C (loan)	9	2
							Sampdoria	3	—
							Bradford C	18	—
Southall Neville†	6 1	13 00	G	16 9 58	Llandudno	Winsford U	Bury	39	—
							Everton	578	—
							Port Vale (loan)	9	—
							Southend U (loan)	9	—
							Stoke C	12	—
							Torquay U	53	—
							Bradford C	1	—
Todd Lee	5 7	11 01	D	7 3 72	Hartlepool	Hartlepool U	Stockport Co	225	2
							Southampton	10	—
							Bradford C	15	—
							Walsall (loan)	1	—
Walsh Gary	6 3	14 11	G	21 3 68	Wigan	Apprentice	Manchester U	50	—
							Airdrieonians (loan)	3	—
							Oldham Ath (loan)	6	—
							Middlesbrough	44	—
							Bradford C	92	—
Westwood Ashley	5 11	11 02	D	31 8 76	Bridgnorth	Trainee	Manchester U	—	—
							Crewe Alex	98	9
							Bradford C	24	2
Wetherall David	6 4	13 05	D	14 3 71	Sheffield	School	Sheffield W	—	—
							Leeds U	202	12
							Bradford C	38	2
Whalley Gareth	5 10	11 06	M	19 12 73	Manchester	Trainee	Crewe Alex	180	9
							Bradford C	61	3
Windass Dean	5 10	12 06	F	1 4 69	Hull	N. Ferriby	Hull C	176	57
							Aberdeen	73	21
							Oxford U	33	15
							Bradford C	50	13
Wright Stephen‡	5 10	11 09	D	27 8 71	Bellshill		Aberdeen	147	2
							Rangers	7	—
							Wolverhampton W (loan)	3	—
							Bradford C	22	—

Scholars
Bolton, Scott; Dufton, Jack P; Fishlock, Craig C; Hardy, Adam N; Hatton, Philip D; Jones, Kingsley B; Kerr, Scott; Lee, Andrew J; Lo Piccolo, Giuseppe M; Rutherford, James; Tarsuslugil, Edward JM; Tyson, Garry W; Worsnop, Jon A

BRENTFORD

Anderson Ijah	5 8	10 06	D	30 12 75	Hackney	Tottenham H	Southend U	—	—
							Brentford	157	4
Boxall Danny	5 8	11 06	D	24 8 77	Croydon	Trainee	Crystal Palace	8	—
							Oldham Ath (loan)	18	—
							Brentford	63	1
Bryan Derek	5 10	11 05	F	11 11 74	London	Hampton	Brentford	49	7
Charles Julian	5 9	11 00	M	5 2 77	Plaistow	Hampton & Richmond B	Brentford	2	—
Clark Dean‡	5 10	12 06	M	31 3 80	Hillingdon	Trainee	Brentford	4	—
Dobson Michael	5 11	12 04	D	9 4 81	Isleworth	Trainee	Brentford	—	—
Einarsson Gunnar‡	5 11	11 04	D	7 7 76	Reykjavik	Roda	Maastricht	23	—
							Brentford	3	—
Evans Paul	5 8	11 06	M	1 9 74	Oswestry	Trainee	Shrewsbury T	198	26
							Brentford	47	10
Folan Tony	5 11	11 08	F	18 9 78	Lewisham	Trainee	Crystal Palace	1	—
							Brentford	38	5

	ht	wt	pos	DOB	birthplace	source	club	apps	goals
Glass Jimmy†	6 1	13 04	G	1 8 73	Epsom	Trainee	Crystal Palace	—	—
							Portsmouth (loan)	3	—
							Bournemouth	94	—
							Swindon T	11	—
							Carlisle U (loan)	3	1
							Cambridge U	—	—
							Brentford	2	—
Graham Gareth	5 7	10 02	M	6 12 78	Belfast	Trainee	Crystal Palace	1	—
							Brentford	13	—
Ingimarsson Ivar	6 0	12 07	M	20 8 77	Reykjavik		Valur	45	5
							IBV	36	5
							Torquay U	4	1
							Brentford	25	1
James Clement‡	5 10	11 00	F	10 3 81	Berkshire	Trainee	Brentford	1	—
Jenkins Steve*	6 1	13 00	D	2 1 80	Bristol	Trainee	Southampton	—	—
							Brentford (loan)	1	—
							Brentford	5	—
Kennedy Richard	5 8	10 05	M	28 8 78	Waterford	Trainee	Crystal Palace	—	—
							Wycombe W	—	—
							Brentford	9	—
Mahon Gavin	6 0	13 02	M	2 1 77	Birmingham	Trainee	Wolverhampton W	—	—
							Hereford U	11	1
							Brentford	66	7
Marshall Scott	6 2	12 12	D	1 5 73	Edinburgh	Trainee	Arsenal	24	1
							Rotherham U (loan)	10	1
							Oxford U (loan)	—	—
							Sheffield U (loan)	17	—
							Southampton	2	—
							Celtic	2	—
							Southampton	—	—
							Brentford	22	2
O'Connor Kevin	5 11	12 00	D	24 2 82	Blackburn	Trainee	Brentford	6	—
Owusu Lloyd	6 0	14 00	F	12 12 76	Slough	Slough T	Brentford	87	34
Partridge Scott	5 9	11 02	F	13 10 74	Leicester	Trainee	Bradford C	5	—
							Bristol C	57	7
							Torquay U (loan)	5	2
							Plymouth Arg (loan)	7	2
							Scarborough (loan)	7	—
							Cardiff C	37	2
							Torquay U	34	12
							Brentford	55	13
Pearcey Jason	6 1	13 12	G	23 7 71	Leamington Spa	Trainee	Mansfield T	77	—
							Grimsby T	49	—
							Brentford	23	—
Pinamonte Lorenzo	6 3	13 04	F	9 5 78	Foggia	Foggia	Bristol C	7	1
							Brighton & HA (loan)	9	2
							Brentford	15	1
Powell Darren	6 3	13 02	D	10 3 76	Hammersmith	Hampton	Brentford	69	4
Quinn Robert	5 11	11 02	D	8 11 76	Sidcup	Trainee	Crystal Palace	23	1
							Brentford	87	2
Rowlands Martin	5 9	10 10	M	8 2 79	Hammersmith	Farnborough T	Brentford	76	10
Saroya Nevin	6 3	14 00	M	15 9 80	Hillingdon	Trainee	Brentford	1	—
Scott Andy	6 1	11 05	F	2 8 72	Epsom	Sutton U	Sheffield U	75	6
							Chesterfield (loan)	5	3
							Bury (loan)	8	—
							Brentford	96	15
Theobald David	6 2	11 00	D	15 12 78	Cambridge	Trainee	Ipswich T	—	—
							Brentford	10	—
Townley Leon‡	6 2	13 06	D	16 2 76	Loughton	Trainee	Tottenham H	—	—
							Brentford	16	2
Woodman Andy	6 3	13 07	G	11 8 71	Camberwell	Apprentice	Crystal Palace	—	—
							Exeter C	6	—
							Northampton T	163	—
							Brentford	61	—
							Peterborough U (loan)	—	—

Trainees
Coleman, Danny; Fieldwick, Lee P; Johnson, Lee L; Julian, Alan J; King, Daryl; Oakley, Russell J; Rehman, Rizwan; Smith, Jay; Somner, Matthew J; Taggart, Anthony C; Williams, Mark R; Windell, Gavin J; Woodhouse, Paul

BRIGHTON & HOVE ALBION

	ht	wt	pos	DOB	birthplace	source	club	apps	goals
Andrews Ben	6 1	12 13	D	18 11 80	Burton-on-Trent	Trainee	Brighton & HA	4	—
Armstrong Paul*	5 10	10 09	M	5 10 78	Dublin	Trainee	Brighton & HA	53	2
Aspinall Warren*	5 9	11 12	M	13 9 67	Wigan	Apprentice	Wigan Ath	10	1
							Everton	7	—
							Wigan Ath (loan)	41	21
							Aston Villa	44	14
							Portsmouth	132	21
							Swansea C (loan)	5	—
							Bournemouth	33	9
							Carlisle U (loan)	7	1
							Carlisle U	100	11
							Brentford	43	5
							Colchester U	22	5
							Brighton & HA	31	3

Name							Club	Apps	Gls
Cameron David‡	6 1	12 05	F	24 8 75	Bangor		St Mirren	11	2
							Brighton & HA	17	—
Campbell Jamie	6 1	12 07	D	21 10 72	Birmingham	Trainee	Luton T	36	1
							Mansfield T (loan)	3	1
							Cambridge U (loan)	12	—
							Barnet	67	5
							Cambridge U	91	6
							Brighton & HA	23	1
Carr Darren	6 2	13 07	D	4 9 68	Bristol	Trainee	Bristol R	30	—
							Newport Co	9	—
							Sheffield U	13	1
							Crewe Alex	104	5
							Chesterfield	86	4
							Gillingham	30	2
							Brighton & HA	19	—
Crosby Andy	6 2	13 07	D	3 3 73	Rotherham	Leeds U	Doncaster R	51	—
							Darlington	181	3
							Chester C	41	4
							Brighton & HA	36	3
Cullip Danny	6 1	12 07	D	17 9 76	Bracknell	Trainee	Oxford U	—	—
							Fulham	50	2
							Brentford	15	—
							Brighton & HA	33	2
Culverhouse Ian*	5 10	11 02	D	22 9 64	Bishop's Stortford	Apprentice	Tottenham H	2	—
							Norwich C	296	—
							Swindon T	97	—
						Kingstonian	Brighton & HA	36	—
Davis Danny	5 10	11 04	M	3 10 80	Brighton	Trainee	Brighton & HA	1	—
Freeman Darren	5 11	13 00	F	22 8 73	Brighton	Horsham T	Gillingham	12	—
							Fulham	46	9
							Brentford	22	6
							Brighton & HA	38	12
Hart Gary	5 9	12 08	F	6 11 75	Harlow	Stansted	Brighton & HA	87	21
Ling Martin‡	5 7	10 08	M	15 7 66	West Ham	Apprentice	Exeter C	116	14
							Swindon T	2	—
							Southend U	138	31
							Mansfield T (loan)	3	—
							Swindon T (loan)	1	—
							Swindon T	149	10
							Leyton Orient	148	8
							Brighton & HA	8	1
Mayo Kerry	5 8	11 07	D	21 9 77	Cuckfield	Trainee	Brighton & HA	124	8
McArthur Duncan	5 9	12 06	M	6 5 81	Brighton	Trainee	Brighton & HA	3	—
McPhee Christopher§				20 3 83	Eastbourne	Scholar	Brighton & HA	4	—
McPherson Keith*	5 11	11 10	D	11 9 63	Greenwich	Apprentice	West Ham U	1	—
							Cambridge U (loan)	11	1
							Northampton T	182	8
							Reading	271	8
							Brighton & HA	35	1
Newhouse Aidan‡	6 2	13 10	F	23 5 72	Wallasey	Trainee	Chester C	44	6
							Wimbledon	23	2
							Tranmere R (loan)	—	—
							Port Vale (loan)	2	—
							Portsmouth (loan)	6	1
							Torquay U (loan)	4	2
							Fulham	8	1
							Swansea C	14	—
							Brighton & HA	12	2
Oatway Charlie	5 7	10 10	M	28 11 73	Hammersmith	Yeading	Cardiff C	32	—
							Torquay U	67	1
							Brentford	57	—
							Lincoln C (loan)	3	—
							Brighton & HA	42	4
Ormerod Mark*	6 0	11 06	G	5 2 76	Bournemouth	Trainee	Brighton & HA	85	—
Packham Will	6 2	13 00	G	13 1 81	Brighton	Trainee	Brighton & HA	—	—
Palmer Ryan*	6 1	11 02	D	2 2 80	Dulwich	Trainee	Fulham	—	—
							Brighton & HA	1	—
Ramsay Scott	6 0	13 00	F	16 10 80	Hastings	Trainee	Brighton & HA	24	2
Rogers Paul	6 0	13 02	M	21 3 65	Portsmouth	Sutton U	Sheffield U	125	10
							Notts Co	22	2
							Wigan Ath	100	5
							Brighton & HA	45	8
Thomas Rod	5 6	11 11	F	10 10 70	London	Trainee	Watford	84	9
							Gillingham (loan)	8	1
							Carlisle U	146	16
							Chester C	44	7
							Brighton & HA	46	4
Walton Mark#	6 4	15 08	G	1 6 69	Merthyr	Swansea C	Luton T	—	—
							Colchester U	40	—
							Norwich C	22	—
							Wrexham (loan)	6	—
							Dundee	—	—
							Bolton W	3	—
						Fakenham T	Fulham	40	—
							Gillingham (loan)	1	—
							Norwich C (loan)	—	—
							Brighton & HA	58	—

Watson Paul	5 8	10 10	D	4 1 75	Hastings	Trainee	Gillingham	62	2
							Fulham	50	4
							Brentford	37	—
							Brighton & HA	42	4
Westcott John*	5 9	10 03	F	31 5 79	Eastbourne	Trainee	Brighton & HA	38	
Wilkinson Shaun§				12 9 81	Portsmouth	Scholar	Brighton & HA	2	—
Winter Neil‡	5 10	11 12	D	25 9 80	Chichester	Trainee	Brighton & HA	—	—

Scholars
Beech, Andrew P; Dallaway, Steven J; Davis, Adam R; Hammond, Dean J; Hemsley, Kevin C; Jackson, Mark A; Marney, Daniel G; McCurdy, Conor M; McPhee, Christopher Sl; Sansom, Rupert; Wilkinson, Shaun F; Wojciechowski, Stefan

Non-Contract
Adams, Michael R; Wilkins, Dean M

Player who does not hold a current contract but his registration has been retained by the club
McArthur, Duncan E

BRISTOL CITY

Amankwaah Kevin§	6 1	12 00		19 5 82	London	Scholar	Bristol C	5	—
Andersen Bo‡	6 0	13 10	G	26 3 76	Slagelse		Lyngby	120	—
							Bristol C	10	—
Andersen Soren‡	5 11	12 06	F	31 1 70	Denmark		Vejle	59	22
(Transferred to Odense, August 1999)							Aarhus	12	11
							Rayo Vallecano	10	1
							Norrkoping	10	4
							Aalborg	67	30
							Bristol C	39	10
Ashley Neil	5 9	11 04	M	16 9 80	Chesterfield	Nottingham F	Leicester C	—	—
							Bristol C	—	—
Ashton Lee‡	6 0	11 03	D	8 11 79	Yeovil	Trainee	Bristol C	—	—
Ball Alex	5 9	10 06	D	4 8 81	Bristol	Trainee	Bristol C	—	—
Beadle Peter	6 2	14 07	F	13 5 72	Lambeth	Trainee	Gillingham	67	14
							Tottenham H	—	—
							Bournemouth (loan)	9	2
							Southend U (loan)	8	1
							Watford	23	1
							Bristol R	109	39
							Port Vale	23	6
							Notts Co	22	3
							Bristol C	25	6
Bell Mickey	5 8	11 13	D	15 11 71	Newcastle	Trainee	Northampton T	153	10
							Wycombe W	118	6
							Bristol C	113	20
Brown Aaron	5 10	11 12	M	14 3 80	Bristol	Trainee	Bristol C	27	2
							Exeter C (loan)	5	1
Brown Marvin§	5 9	11 01	F	6 7 83	Bristol		Bristol C	2	—
Burnell Joe	5 9	11 11	D	10 10 80	Bristol	Trainee	Bristol C	17	—
Burns John	5 8	11 04	M	4 12 77	Dublin	Belvedere	Nottingham F	3	—
							Bristol C	11	—
Carey Louis	5 10	12 05	D	22 1 77	Bristol	Trainee	Bristol C	166	—
Clist Simon	5 9	11 00	M	13 6 81	Bournemouth	Tottenham H	Bristol C	9	—
Coles Daniel§	6 1	11 05		30 10 81	Bristol	Scholar	Bristol C	1	—
Doherty Tom	5 8	11 07	M	17 3 79	Bristol	Trainee	Bristol C	54	3
Edwards Jamie			M	18 2 83	Hereford	Scholar	Bristol C	0	—
Goodridge Greg#	5 6	11 02	M	10 7 71	Barbados	Lambada	Torquay U	38	4
							QPR	7	1
							Bristol C	110	14
Hewlett Matt*	6 2	12 12	M	25 2 76	Bristol	Trainee	Bristol C	127	9
							Burnley (loan)	2	—
Hill Matt	5 8	11 09	D	26 3 81	Bristol	Trainee	Bristol C	17	—
Holland Chris*	6 0	10 06	M	29 8 80	Taunton	Bournemouth	Bristol C	—	—
Holland Paul	5 9	13 05	M	8 7 73	Lincoln	School	Mansfield T	149	25
							Sheffield U	18	1
							Chesterfield	114	11
							Bristol C	27	—
Hulbert Robin	5 9	10 05	M	14 3 80	Plymouth	Trainee	Swindon T	29	—
							Newcastle U (loan)	—	—
							Bristol C	2	—
Hussey Stuart*	5 10	11 11	M	4 12 80	Southampton	Portsmouth	Bristol C	—	—
Hutchings Carl	6 1	12 00	M	24 9 74	Hammersmith	Trainee	Brentford	162	7
							Bristol C	42	3
							Brentford (loan)	8	—
Jones Steve	6 1	12 07	F	17 3 70	Cambridge	Billericay T	West Ham U	16	4
							Bournemouth	74	26
							West Ham U	8	—
							Charlton Ath	52	8
							Bournemouth (loan)	5	4
							Bristol C	14	2
							Brentford (loan)	8	—
							Southend U (loan)	9	2

Jordan Andrew	6 2	13 04	D	14 12 79	Manchester	Trainee	Bristol C	9	—
Langan Kevin*	5 11	11 02	D	7 4 78	Jersey	Trainee	Bristol C	4	—
Lavin Gerard	5 10	11 10	D	5 2 74	Corby	Trainee	Watford	126	3
							Millwall	74	—
							Bristol C	19	—
Malessa Antony	5 11	11 12	G	13 11 80	Ascot		Bristol C	—	—
Meechan Alex	5 8	10 06	F	29 1 80	Plymouth	Trainee	Swindon T	1	—
							Bristol C	13	4
Mercer Billy	6 1	11 00	G	22 5 69	Liverpool	Trainee	Liverpool	—	—
							Rotherham U	104	—
							Sheffield U	4	—
							Nottingham F (loan)	—	—
							Chesterfield	149	—
							Bristol C	25	—
Millen Keith	6 1	13 02	D	26 9 66	Croydon	Juniors	Brentford	305	17
							Watford	165	5
							Bristol C	28	2
Mortimer Paul	5 9	12 13	M	8 5 68	Kensington	Fulham	Charlton Ath	113	17
							Aston Villa	12	1
							Crystal Palace	22	2
							Brentford (loan)	6	—
							Charlton Ath	86	15
							Bristol C	23	—
Morrison Scott*			M	31 8 81	Bristol	Trainee	Bristol C	—	—
Muntasser Jehad‡	5 10	9 11	M	26 7 78	Tripoli	Prosesto	Arsenal	—	—
							Bristol C	—	—
Murray Scott	5 8	11 00	M	26 5 74	Aberdeen	Fraserburgh	Aston Villa	4	—
							Bristol C	96	9
Odejayi Kayode§	6 2	12 02		21 2 82	Ibadon	Scholar	Bristol C	3	—
Phillips Steve	6 1	12 07	G	6 5 78	Bath	Paulton R	Bristol C	36	—
Pike James			M	15 11 82	Bristol	Scholar	Bristol C	—	—
Scope Tynan	6 3	13 08	G	30 7 79	Sydney		Coventry C	—	—
							Bristol C	—	—
Sebok Vilmos‡	6 3	12 10	D	13 6 73	Budapest	Ujpesti	Bristol C	23	—
Shail Mark*	6 1	12 06	D	15 10 66	Sweden	Yeovil T	Bristol C	128	4
Spencer Damien§	6 1	14 05	F	19 9 81	Ascot	Scholar	Bristol C	9	1
Stowell Matt‡	6 0	12 07	D	1 3 77	Reading	Trainee	Reading	—	—
						Slough T	Bristol C	—	—
Taylor Shaun#	6 1	12 10	D	26 2 63	Plymouth	Bideford	Exeter C	200	16
							Swindon T	212	30
							Bristol C	105	7
Testimitanu Ivan	5 10	11 02	M	27 4 74	Moldova		Zimbru Chisinau	79	24
							Bristol C	24	2
Thorpe Tony	5 8	12 06	F	10 4 74	Leicester	Leicester C	Luton T	120	50
							Fulham	13	3
							Bristol C	47	15
							Reading (loan)	6	1
							Luton T (loan)	8	4
							Luton T (loan)	4	1
Tinnion Brian	5 11	12 13	M	23 2 68	Stanley	Apprentice	Newcastle U	32	2
							Bradford C	145	22
							Bristol C	271	20
Turner Danny	6 3	13 02	M	8 1 81	Maidstone		Bristol C	—	—
Wilmot Ellis‡	5 9	12 00	D	2 11 79	Bournemouth	Trainee	Bristol C	—	—
Woodman Craig			M	22 12 82	Tiverton	Trainee	Bristol C	—	—
Wright Ben	6 1	13 07	F	1 7 80	Munster	Kettering T	Bristol C	2	—

Scholars
Amankwaah, Kevin; Blake, David J; Brown, Marvin R; Burnett, Michael A; Claridge, Jamie L; Cleverley, Benjamin R; Coles, Daniel R; Dew, Simon J; Harrison, Jamie; Horseman, David J; Jones, Darren L; Jordan, Thomas M; King, Rohan; McLay, Steven; Odejayi, Olukayode; Palmer, Marc K; Reynolds, Nicholas; Shorey, Adam C; Spencer, Damian M; Walters, James M; Williams, Paul J; Wilson, Martin J

Associated Schoolboys who have accepted the Club's offer of a Traineeship/Scholarship/Contract
Platt, Daniel; Rosenior, Liam; Simpson, Sekani; Trace, Ben

BRISTOL ROVERS

Andreasson Marcus	6 4	13 02	D	13 7 78	Liberia		Osters	12	—
							Bristol R	11	—
Astafjevs Vitalijs	5 11	12 05	M	3 4 71	Riga		Skonto Riga	154	60
							FK Austria (loan)	26	1
							Bristol R	16	2
Basford Luke‡	5 6	9 02	D	6 1 80	Lambeth	Trainee	Bristol R	16	—
Bater Geraint‡	5 8	10 08	D	26 7 80	Bristol		Bristol R	—	—
Bennett Frankie‡	5 7	12 10	F	13 1 69	Birmingham	Halesowen T	Southampton	19	1
							Shrewsbury T (loan)	4	3
							Bristol R	44	4
							Exeter C (loan)	9	1
Bryant Simon	5 11	12 11	M	22 11 82	Bristol	Scholar	Bristol R	15	—
Challis Trevor	5 8	11 06	D	23 10 75	Paddington	Trainee	QPR	13	—
							Bristol R	78	1

Name			Pos	DOB	Birthplace	Source	Club	Apps	Gls
Claridge Rob‡	6 0	11 10	F	13 3 80	Bristol	Trainee	Bristol R	—	—
Cureton Jamie	5 7	11 00	F	28 8 75	Bristol	Trainee	Norwich C	29	6
							Bournemouth (loan)	5	—
							Bristol R	173	71
Ellington Nathan	5 10	12 10	F	2 7 81	Bradford	Walton & Hersham	Bristol R	47	5
Ellis Clinton			M	7 7 77	Ealing		Bristol R	0	—
Foster Stephen	6 1	13 00	D	3 12 74	Mansfield	Trainee	Mansfield T	5	—
						Woking	Bristol R	120	2
French James‡	6 1	12 02	F	24 10 79	Germany	Trainee	Bristol R	—	—
Hillier David	5 10	12 07	M	19 12 69	Blackheath	Trainee	Arsenal	104	2
							Portsmouth	67	4
							Bristol R	52	—
Hogg Lewis	5 8	10 07	M	13 9 82	Bristol	Trainee	Bristol R	—	—
Holloway Ian*	5 7	10 10	M	12 3 63	Kingswood	Apprentice	Bristol R	111	14
							Wimbledon	19	2
							Brentford (loan)	13	2
							Brentford	17	—
							Torquay U (loan)	5	—
							Bristol R	179	26
							QPR	147	4
							Bristol R	107	1
Johnston Ray*	6 1	13 13	G	5 5 81	Bristol	Trainee	Bristol R	1	—
							Southampton (loan)	—	—
Jones Lee	6 3	14 10	G	9 8 70	Pontypridd	Porth	Swansea C	6	—
							Crewe Alex (loan)	—	—
							Bristol R	76	—
Kuipers Michels*	6 2	14 03	G	26 6 74	Amsterdam		Bristol R	1	—
Leoni Stephane*	5 9	13 00	D	1 9 76	Metz		Bristol R	38	—
Mauge Ronnie	5 10	10 06	M	10 3 69	Islington	Trainee	Charlton Ath	—	—
							Fulham	50	2
							Bury	108	10
							Manchester C (loan)	—	—
							Plymouth Arg	135	14
							Bristol R	22	—
Meaker Michael	5 11	12 12	M	18 8 71	Greenford	Trainee	QPR	34	1
							Plymouth Arg (loan)	4	—
							Reading	67	2
							Bristol R	22	2
							Swindon T (loan)	6	—
Parkin Brian†	6 4	14 05	G	12 10 65	Birkenhead	Local	Oldham Ath	6	—
							Crewe Alex (loan)	12	—
							Crewe Alex	86	—
							Crystal Palace (loan)	—	—
							Crystal Palace	20	—
							Bristol R	241	—
							Wycombe W	25	—
							Notts Co	1	—
							Bristol R	3	—
Penrice Gary†	5 8	12 10	F	23 3 64	Bristol	Bristol C	Bristol R	188	54
							Watford	43	18
							Aston Villa	20	1
							QPR	82	20
							Watford	39	2
							Bristol R	69	6
Pethick Robbie	5 10	12 07	D	8 9 70	Tavistock	Weymouth	Portsmouth	189	3
							Bristol R	50	2
Pierre Nigel	5 11	11 11	F	2 6 79	Port of Spain	Joe Public	Bristol R	3	—
Pritchard David	5 7	12 00	D	27 5 72	Wolverhampton	Telford U	WBA	5	—
						Telford U	Bristol R	158	1
Roberts Jason	6 1	13 06	F	25 1 78	Park Royal	Hayes	Wolverhampton W	—	—
							Torquay U (loan)	14	6
							Bristol C (loan)	3	1
							Bristol R	78	38
Shore Jamie	5 9	12 05	M	1 9 77	Bristol	Trainee	Norwich C	—	—
							Bristol R	24	2
Smith Mark	6 0	13 07	D	13 9 79	Bristol	Trainee	Bristol R	14	—
Thomson Andy	6 3	14 03	D	28 3 74	Swindon	Trainee	Swindon T	22	—
							Portsmouth	93	3
							Bristol R	64	4
Tillson Andy	6 2	13 05	D	30 6 66	Huntingdon	Kettering T	Grimsby T	105	5
							QPR	29	2
							Grimsby T (loan)	4	—
							Bristol R	253	11
Trees Robert	5 10	12 07	M	18 12 77	Manchester	Trainee	Manchester U	—	—
						Witton Alb	Bristol R	46	1
Trought Michael	6 2	14 03	D	19 10 80	Bristol	Trainee	Bristol R	13	—
Walters Mark	5 9	11 05	M	2 6 64	Birmingham	Apprentice	Aston Villa	181	39
							Rangers	106	32
							Liverpool	94	14
							Stoke C (loan)	9	2
							Wolverhampton W (loan)	11	3
							Southampton	5	—
							Swindon T	112	25
							Bristol R	30	9

White Tom*	5 11	14 03	D	26 1 76	Bristol	Trainee	Bristol R	54	1
Zabek Lee	6 0	13 08	M	13 10 78	Bristol	Trainee	Bristol R	29	1
Zamora Bobby	6 1	11 08	F	16 1 81	Barking	Trainee	Bristol R	4	—
							Brighton & HA (loan)	6	6

Scholars
Chambers, Andrew J; Clarke, Ryan J; Cordy, John Dwain; Cozens, Leon; Crowley, Jonathan; Gilroy, David M; Parker, Christian; Pope, Mark; Powell, Gary N; Scott, Robert T; Shore, Andrew J; Spencer, Lance JM; Zabek, James K

Non-Contract
Parkin, Brian; Penrice, Garry K; Thompson, Garry L

Associated Schoolboys who have accepted the Club's offer of a Traineeship/Scholarship/Contract
Arndale, Neil D; Davis, Anthony

BURNLEY

Armstrong Gordon	6 0	13 04	D	15 7 67	Newcastle	Apprentice	Sunderland	349	50
							Bristol C (loan)	6	—
							Northampton T (loan)	4	1
							Bury	71	4
							Burnley	62	3
Branch Graham#	6 2	12 02	F	12 2 72	Liverpool	Heswall	Tranmere R	102	10
							Bury (loan)	4	1
							Wigan Ath (loan)	3	—
							Stockport Co	14	3
							Burnley	64	4
Brass Chris	5 9	12 06	D	24 7 75	Easington	Trainee	Burnley	134	1
							Torquay U (loan)	7	—
Cook Paul#	5 11	11 00	M	22 6 67	Liverpool	Marine	Wigan Ath	83	14
							Norwich C	6	—
							Wolverhampton W	193	19
							Coventry C	37	3
							Tranmere R	60	4
							Stockport Co	49	3
							Burnley (loan)	12	1
							Burnley	44	3
Cooke Andy	5 11	12 08	F	20 1 74	Stoke	Newtown	Burnley	160	50
Cowan Tom‡	5 8	11 10	D	28 8 69	Bothwell	Netherdale BC	Clyde	16	2
							Rangers	12	—
							Sheffield U	45	—
							Stoke C (loan)	14	—
							Huddersfield T (loan)	10	—
							Huddersfield T	127	8
							Burnley	20	—
							Cambridge U (loan)	4	—
Cox Ian	6 0	12 00	D	25 3 71	Croydon	Carshalton Ath	Crystal Palace	15	—
							Bournemouth	172	16
							Burnley	17	1
Crichton Paul	6 1	13 08	G	3 10 68	Pontefract	Apprentice	Nottingham F	—	—
							Notts Co (loan)	5	—
							Darlington (loan)	5	—
							Peterborough U (loan)	4	—
							Darlington (loan)	3	—
							Swindon T (loan)	4	—
							Rotherham U (loan)	6	—
							Torquay U (loan)	13	—
							Peterborough U	47	—
							Doncaster R	77	—
							Grimsby T	133	—
							WBA	32	—
							Aston Villa (loan)	—	—
							Burnley	75	—
Davis Steve	6 2	14 07	D	30 10 68	Hexham	Trainee	Southampton	7	—
							Burnley (loan)	9	—
							Notts Co (loan)	2	—
							Burnley	162	22
							Luton T	138	21
							Burnley	61	11
Devenney Michael	5 8	10 05	D	8 2 80	Bolton	Trainee	Burnley	—	—
Grant Stephen‡	6 1	12 00	F	14 4 77	Birr	Athlone T / Shamrock R	Sunderland	—	—
							Stockport Co	29	4
							Burnley	—	—
Heywood Matthew	6 3	14 00	D	26 8 79	Chatham	Trainee	Burnley	13	—
Jepson Ronnie#	6 0	14 00	D	12 5 63	Stoke	Nantwich T	Port Vale	22	—
							Peterborough U (loan)	18	5
							Preston NE	38	8
							Exeter C	54	21
							Huddersfield T	107	36
							Bury	47	9
							Oldham Ath	9	4
							Burnley	46	3
Johnrose Lenny	5 11	12 06	M	27 11 69	Preston	Trainee	Blackburn R	42	11
							Preston NE (loan)	3	1
							Hartlepool U	66	11
							Bury	188	19
							Burnley	47	3
Kelly Eammon‡	5 10	11 05	M	24 12 80	Manchester	Trainee	Burnley	—	—
Kevan Alex	5 10	11 00	M	23 2 81	Liverpool	Trainee	Burnley	—	—

Name	Ht	Wt	Pos	DOB	Birthplace	Source	Club	Apps	Gls
Lee Alan	6 2	13 09	F	21 8 78	Galway	Trainee	Aston Villa	—	—
							Torquay U (loan)	7	2
							Port Vale (loan)	11	2
							Burnley	15	—
Little Glen	6 3	13 00	M	15 10 75	Wimbledon	Trainee	Crystal Palace	—	—
							Glentoran	6	2
							Burnley	108	12
Mawson Craig	6 2	13 04	G	16 5 79	Keighley	Trainee	Burnley	—	—
Maylett Bradley	5 8	10 07	M	24 12 80	Manchester	Trainee	Burnley	17	—
Mellon Micky	5 10	12 11	D	18 3 72	Paisley	Trainee	Bristol C	35	1
							WBA	45	6
							Blackpool	124	14
							Tranmere R	57	3
							Burnley	62	5
Mullin John	6 0	11 05	F	11 8 75	Bury	School	Burnley	18	2
							Sunderland	35	4
							Preston NE (loan)	7	—
							Burnley (loan)	6	—
							Burnley	37	5
Payton Andy	5 9	11 13	F	23 10 67	Burnley	Apprentice	Hull C	143	55
							Middlesbrough	19	3
							Celtic	36	15
							Barnsley	108	41
							Huddersfield T	43	17
							Burnley	100	55
Robertson Mark	5 9	11 09	M	6 4 77	Sydney	Marconi	Burnley	36	1
Scott Christopher	5 11	12 05	D	12 2 80	Burnley	Trainee	Burnley	14	—
Smith Paul	6 0	13 03	M	22 7 76	Leeds	Trainee	Burnley	98	4
Thomas Mitchell#	6 2	14 00	D	2 10 64	Luton	Apprentice	Luton T	107	1
							Tottenham H	157	6
							West Ham U	38	3
							Luton T	185	5
							Burnley	44	—
Vindheim Rune‡	5 11	12 04	D	15 5 72	Hoyanguer		Burnley	8	2
							Hartlepool U (loan)	7	—
Weller Paul	5 8	11 02	M	6 3 75	Brighton	Trainee	Burnley	103	6
West Dean	5 10	11 07	D	5 12 72	Leeds	Leeds U	Lincoln C	119	20
							Bury	110	8
							Burnley	34	—
Williamson John	6 1	11 06	D	3 3 81	Derby	Trainee	Burnley	1	—
Wright Ian#	5 10	11 08	F	3 11 63	Woolwich	Greenwich Bor	Crystal Palace	225	89
							Arsenal	221	128
							West Ham U	22	9
							Nottingham F (loan)	10	5
							Celtic	8	3
							Burnley	15	4

Scholars
Bowden, Anthony; Clark, Christopher; Davis, Earl A; Leeson, Andrew; Paxton, Andrew J; Robertshaw, Duncan; Shandran, Anthony M; Waine, Andrew P

Associated Schoolboys who have accepted the Club's offer of a Traineeship/Scholarship/Contract
Barrett, Paul J

BURY

Name	Ht	Wt	Pos	DOB	Birthplace	Source	Club	Apps	Gls
Avdiu Kemajl*	5 10	12 08	M	22 12 76	Yugoslavia	Esbjerg	Bury	27	1
							Partick T (loan)	6	1
Ball Nicholas*			M	14 8 81	Mexborough	Trainee	Bury	—	—
Barnes Paul	5 11	13 00	F	16 11 67	Leeds	Apprentice	Notts Co	53	14
							Stoke C	24	3
							Chesterfield (loan)	1	—
							York C	148	76
							Birmingham C	15	7
							Burnley	65	30
							Huddersfield T	30	2
							Bury	38	4
Barrass Matt	5 11	12 00	D	28 2 81	Bury	Trainee	Bury	25	1
Barrick Dean	5 8	12 00	D	30 9 69	Hemsworth	Trainee	Sheffield W	11	2
							Rotherham U	99	7
							Cambridge U	91	3
							Preston NE	109	1
							Bury	37	1
							Ayr U (loan)	11	—
Beal Philip*			M	18 2 81	Doncaster	Trainee	Bury	—	—
Bhutia Baichung	5 8	10 02	F	15 6 76	Sikkim	East Bengal	Bury	14	2
Billy Chris	5 11	12 06	D	2 1 71	Huddersfield	Trainee	Huddersfield T	94	4
							Plymouth Arg	118	9
							Notts Co	6	—
							Bury	73	4
Borg John‡	5 7	10 07	M	22 2 80	Salford	Trainee	Doncaster R	1	—
							Bury	—	—
Bryan Marvin†	6 0	12 02	D	2 8 75	Paddington	Trainee	QPR	—	—
							Doncaster R (loan)	5	1
							Blackpool	182	4
							Bury	9	—

Player	Ht	Wt	Pos	DOB	Birthplace	Source	Club	Apps	Goals
Buggie Lee	5 9	11 00	F	11 2 81	Bury	Trainee	Bolton W	—	—
							Bury	1	—
Bullock Darren	5 9	12 10	M	12 2 69	Worcester	Nuneaton Bor	Huddersfield T	128	16
							Swindon T	66	2
							Bury	39	3
Challinor Paul*	6 1	12 02	D	6 4 76	Newcastle under Lyme	Trainee	Birmingham C	—	—
							Lincoln C	—	—
						Telford U	Bury	1	—
Collins Sam	6 2	14 04	D	5 6 77	Pontefract	Trainee	Huddersfield T	37	—
							Bury	19	—
Connell Lee	6 0	12 00	D	24 6 81	Bury	Trainee	Bury	2	—
Daws Nick	5 11	12 13	M	15 3 70	Salford	Altrincham	Bury	325	13
Debenham Rob‡	5 8	10 07	D	28 11 79	Doncaster	Trainee	Doncaster R	6	—
							Bury	—	—
Donnelly Mark*	6 1	12 07	D	22 12 79	Leeds	Trainee	Doncaster R	11	1
							Bury	—	—
Forrest Martyn	5 10	12 02	M	2 1 79	Bury	Trainee	Bury	16	—
Halford Stephen	5 10	12 10	M	21 9 80	Bury	Trainee	Bury	2	—
Hill Nicky	6 0	12 03	D	26 2 81	Accrington	Trainee	Bury	5	—
Hoggeth Gary‡	6 0	11 07	G	7 10 79	South Shields	Trainee	Doncaster R	8	—
							Bury	—	—
Hutchinson Ian‡			M	23 12 80	Bury	Trainee	Bury	—	—
James Lutel	5 8	11 00	F	2 6 72	Manchester		Scarborough	6	—
						Hyde U	Bury	40	4
Kenny Paddy	6 1	14 06	G	17 5 78	Halifax	Bradford PA	Bury	46	—
Linighan Brian*	6 4	11 04	D	2 11 73	Hartlepool	Trainee	Sheffield W	1	—
							Bury	3	—
Littlejohn Adrian	5 10	11 00	M	26 9 71	Wolverhampton	WBA	Walsall	44	1
							Sheffield U	69	12
							Plymouth Arg	110	29
							Oldham Ath	21	5
							Bury	62	10
Messer Gary‡	6 1	13 00	F	22 9 79	Consett	Trainee	Doncaster R	14	1
							Bury	—	—
Preece Andy	6 1	12 00	F	27 3 67	Evesham	Evesham U	Northampton T	1	—
						Worcester C	Wrexham	51	7
							Stockport Co	97	42
							Crystal Palace	20	4
							Blackpool	126	35
							Bury	82	15
Redmond Steve#	5 11	13 00	D	2 11 67	Liverpool	Apprentice	Manchester C	235	7
							Oldham Ath	205	4
							Bury	59	1
Reid Paul	5 10	10 12	M	19 1 68	Oldbury	Apprentice	Leicester C	162	21
							Bradford C (loan)	7	—
							Bradford C	82	15
							Huddersfield T	77	6
							Oldham Ath	93	6
							Bury	39	2
Souter Ryan	5 10	12 00	M	5 2 78	Bedford	Weston-Super-Mare	Bury	5	—
Swailes Chris	6 2	13 07	D	19 10 70	Gateshead	Bridlington T	Doncaster R	49	—
							Ipswich T	33	1
							Bury	83	6
Swailes Danny	6 3	12 06	D	1 4 79	Bolton	Trainee	Bury	24	3
Tedaldi Domenico*	5 11	12 00	M	22 10 80	Aberystwyth	Trainee	Doncaster R	2	1
							Bury	—	—
Williams Paul*	5 7	11 07	M	11 9 69	Leicester	Trainee	Leicester C	—	—
							Stockport Co	70	4
							Coventry C	14	—
							WBA (loan)	5	—
							Huddersfield T (loan)	9	—
							Plymouth Arg	131	4
							Gillingham	10	1
							Bury	41	1

Scholars
Abbiss, Graham P; Armstrong, Christopher; Evans, Gary L; Gaynor, John; Gleaves, Carl M; Joseph, Daniel; Lobban, Alexander; Martin, Adam T; Morris, James P; O'Shaughnessy, Paul J; Thompson, Nicholas A

Non-Contract
Bryan, Marvin L

Associated Schoolboys
Kennedy, Matthew

Associated Schoolboys who have accepted the Club's offer of a Traineeship/Scholarship/Contract
Thompson, David J

Player who does not hold a current contract but his registration has been retained by the club
Borley, David

CAMBRIDGE UNITED

Name	Ht	Wt	Pos	Born	Birthplace	From	Club	Apps	Gls
Abbey Zema	6 1	12 11	F	17 4 77	Luton	Hitchin T	Cambridge U	8	—
Armstrong Dean‡	5 8	11 08	D	7 9 79	Chiswick	Trainee	Cambridge U	—	—
Ashbee Ian	6 1	14 04	M	6 9 76	Birmingham	Trainee	Derby Co	1	—
							Cambridge U	121	6
Benjamin Trevor	6 2	14 02	F	8 2 79	Kettering	Trainee	Cambridge U	123	35
Cassidy Jamie	5 9	11 05	M	21 11 77	Liverpool	Trainee	Liverpool	—	—
							Cambridge U	8	—
Chenery Ben*	6 1	12 03	D	28 1 77	Ipswich	Trainee	Luton T	2	—
							Cambridge U	98	2
Chillingworth Daniel	6 0	12 06	F	13 9 81	Cambridge	Scholar	Cambridge U	3	—
Cockrill Darren‡	6 1	14 02	F	28 2 80	Great Yarmouth	Trainee	Cambridge U	—	—
Duncan Andy	5 11	14 03	D	20 10 77	Hexham	Trainee	Manchester U	—	—
							Cambridge U	77	2
Eustace Scott#	6 1	15 03	D	13 6 75	Leicester	Trainee	Leicester C	1	—
							Mansfield T	98	6
							Cambridge U	52	1
Gibson Mark‡			M	24 8 81	Hitchin	Trainee	Cambridge U	—	—
Graham Mark‡	5 7	10 08	M	24 10 74	Newry	Trainee	QPR	18	—
							Cambridge U	1	—
Hansen John	5 11	13 01	M	17 9 73	Mannheim		Esbjerg	6	—
							Cambridge U	16	3
Ingham Andrew*	5 9	11 01	F	21 8 81	Leeds	Trainee	Cambridge U	—	—
Joseph Marc	6 1	13 00	D	10 11 76	Leicester	Trainee	Cambridge U	123	—
Kavanagh Jason	5 9	12 13	D	23 11 71	Meriden	Birmingham C	Derby Co	99	1
							Wycombe W	90	1
							Stoke C	8	—
							Cambridge U	19	—
Kyd Michael*	5 8	13 03	F	21 5 77	Hackney	Trainee	Cambridge U	124	23
Lamey Nathan	5 10	13 04	F	14 10 80	Sandwell	Trainee	Wolverhampton W	—	—
							Cambridge U	3	—
MacKenzie Neil	6 2	13 06	M	15 4 76	Birmingham	WBA	Stoke C	42	1
							Cambridge U (loan)	4	1
							Cambridge U	22	—
Marshall Shaun	6 1	13 03	G	3 10 78	Fakenham	Trainee	Cambridge U	46	—
McAvoy Larry‡	5 8	11 04	D	7 9 79	Lambeth	Trainee	Cambridge U	1	—
McNeil Martin	6 0	13 02	D	28 9 80	Rutherglen	Trainee	Cambridge U	35	—
Miller Rob‡	5 8	11 08	D	28 3 80	Bedford	West Ham U	Coventry C	—	—
							Cambridge U	1	—
Mustoe Neil	5 9	12 02	M	5 11 76	Gloucester	Trainee	Manchester U	—	—
							Cambridge U	67	3
Preece David	5 6	11 05	M	28 5 63	Bridgnorth	Apprentice	Walsall	111	5
							Luton T	336	21
							Derby Co	13	1
							Birmingham C (loan)	6	—
							Swindon T (loan)	7	1
							Cambridge U	73	2
Russell Alex	5 8	11 12	M	17 3 73	Crosby	Burscough	Rochdale	102	14
							Cambridge U	52	6
Tann Adam	6 0	11 05	D	12 5 82	Fakenham	Scholar	Cambridge U	—	—
Taylor John	6 2	15 00	F	24 10 64	Norwich	Local Sudbury T	Colchester U	—	—
							Cambridge U	160	46
							Bristol R	95	44
							Bradford C	36	11
							Luton T	37	3
							Lincoln C (loan)	5	2
							Colchester U (loan)	8	5
							Cambridge U	135	37
Van Heusden Arjan*	6 4	14 05	G	11 12 72	Alphen	Noordwijk	Port Vale	27	—
							Oxford U (loan)	11	—
							Cambridge U	42	—
Wanless Paul	6 1	14 08	M	14 12 73	Banbury	Trainee	Oxford U	32	—
							Lincoln C	8	—
							Cambridge U (loan)	14	1
							Cambridge U	159	22
Wilde Adam‡	5 9	11 11	M	22 5 79	Southampton	Trainee	Cambridge U	4	—
Wilson Clive*	5 7	11 08	D	13 11 61	Manchester	Local	Manchester C	98	9
							Chester (loan)	21	2
							Chelsea	81	5
							Manchester C (loan)	11	—
							QPR	172	12
							Tottenham H	70	1
							Cambridge U	27	—
Youngs Tom	5 9	11 01	F	31 8 79	Bury St Edmunds	Trainee	Cambridge U	35	8

Scholars
Bridges, David S; Cox, Darren M; Haniver, Matthew G; Kamara, Alim S; Lockhart, Duncan G; Mercer, James F; Nacca, Francesco; Paynter, Owen; Revell, Alexander D

Player who does not hold a current contract but his registration has been retained by the club
Millership, Jamie C

CARDIFF CITY

Name								Club	Apps	Gls
Boland Willie	5 9	11 02	M	6 8 75	Ennis	Trainee		Coventry C	63	—
								Cardiff C	28	1
Bonner Mark	5 8	11 00	M	7 6 74	Ormskirk	Trainee		Blackpool	178	14
								Cardiff C	56	1
								Hull C (loan)	1	1
Bowen Jason	5 8	11 02	F	24 8 72	Merthyr	Trainee		Swansea C	124	26
								Birmingham C	48	7
								Southampton (loan)	3	—
								Reading	15	1
								Cardiff C	56	14
Brazier Matt	5 8	11 08	M	2 7 76	Whipps Cross	Trainee		QPR	49	2
								Fulham	9	1
								Cardiff C (loan)	11	2
								Cardiff C	30	1
Cadette Nathan‡	5 8	11 11	M	6 1 80	Cardiff	Trainee		Cardiff C	4	—
Carpenter Richard#	6 0	13 01	M	30 9 72	Sheppey	Trainee		Gillingham	122	4
								Fulham	58	7
								Cardiff C	75	2
Earnshaw Robert	5 6	9 09	F	6 4 81	Zambia	Trainee		Cardiff C	16	2
								Middlesbrough (loan)	—	—
								Morton (loan)	3	2
Eckhardt Jeff*	6 0	12 00	D	7 10 65	Sheffield			Sheffield U	74	2
								Fulham	249	25
								Stockport Co	62	7
								Cardiff C	132	14
Faerber Winston	5 11	12 06	D	27 3 71	Surinam			Den Haag	28	—
								Cardiff C	33	1
Ford Mike*	6 0	12 12	D	9 2 66	Bristol	Apprentice Devizes T		Leicester C	—	—
								Cardiff C	145	13
								Oxford U	289	18
								Cardiff C	51	—
Fowler Jason#	6 3	12 04	M	20 8 74	Bristol	Trainee		Bristol C	25	—
								Cardiff C	140	14
Hallworth Jon#	6 3	14 08	G	26 10 65	Stockport	School		Ipswich T	45	—
								Swindon T (loan)	—	—
								Fulham (loan)	—	—
								Bristol R (loan)	2	—
								Oldham Ath	174	—
								Cardiff C	123	—
Hill Danny#	5 8	11 08	M	1 10 74	Edmonton	Trainee		Tottenham H	10	—
								Birmingham C (loan)	5	—
								Watford (loan)	1	—
								Cardiff C (loan)	7	—
								Oxford U	9	—
								Cardiff C	49	3
Hughes Jamie	6 0	13 05	F	5 4 77	Liverpool	Trainee Connahs Quay Nomads		Tranmere R	—	—
								Cardiff C	2	1
Kelly Seamus	6 1	13 13	G	6 5 74	Tullamore	UCD		Cardiff C	13	—
Legg Andy	5 8	11 01	D	28 7 66	Swansea	Briton Ferry		Swansea C	163	29
								Notts Co	89	9
								Birmingham C	45	5
								Ipswich T (loan)	6	1
								Reading	12	—
								Peterborough U (loan)	5	—
								Cardiff C	66	4
Low Josh	6 0	14 00	F	15 2 79	Bristol	Trainee		Bristol R	22	—
								Leyton Orient	5	1
								Cardiff C	17	2
Nogan Kurt	5 10	11 01	F	9 9 70	Cardiff	Trainee		Luton T	33	3
								Peterborough U	—	—
								Brighton & HA	97	49
								Burnley	92	33
								Preston NE	93	27
								Cardiff C	6	—
Nugent Kevin	6 2	13 00	F	10 4 69	Edmonton	Trainee		Leyton Orient	94	20
								Plymouth Arg	131	32
								Bristol C	70	14
								Cardiff C	84	25
Perrett Russell	6 2	13 00	D	18 6 73	Barton-on-Sea	AFC Lymington		Portsmouth	72	2
								Cardiff C	27	1
Phillips Lee*	6 0	12 10	D	18 3 79	Aberdare	Trainee		Cardiff C	16	—
Roberts Chris	5 10	12 03	F	22 10 79	Cardiff	Trainee		Cardiff C	23	3
Schwinkendorf Jorn	6 7	13 00	D	27 1 71	Hamburg	Norderstedt		St Pauli	41	2
								Wuppertal	31	3
								Saarbrucken	24	—
								Fortuna Dusseldorf	18	—
							Freiburg	Waldhof Mannheim	9	—
								Cardiff C	5	—
Thomas Dai	5 11	13 07	F	26 9 75	Caerphilly	Trainee		Swansea C	56	10
								Watford	16	3
								Cardiff C	31	5
Young Scott	6 2	13 04	D	14 1 76	Llwynypia	Trainee		Cardiff C	187	7

Trainees
Buttery, Paul A; Darbyshire, Jonathan R; Davis, Craig A; Givans, Warren AL; Higginson, Matthew; Phillips, Darryl J; Skelly, Lee

Scholars
Busby, Dean C; Collins, James M; Evans, Gari; Giles, Martyn; Hajgato, Gezza; Heal, Simon AF; Wallis, Tony

Non-Contract
Owen, Philip NR; Pascoe, Colin J

CARLISLE UNITED

Anthony Graham*	5 7	11 02	M	9 8 75	South Shields	Trainee	Sheffield U	3	—
							Scarborough (loan)	2	—
							Swindon T	3	—
							Plymouth Arg	5	—
							Carlisle U	69	3
Baker Paul‡	6 2	14 04	F	5 1 63	Newcastle	Bishop Auckland	Southampton	—	—
							Carlisle U	71	11
							Hartlepool U	197	67
							Motherwell	9	1
							Gillingham	62	16
							York C	48	18
							Torquay U	30	8
							Scunthorpe U	21	9
							Hartlepool U	35	9
							Carlisle U	17	2
Barr Billy*	5 11	11 02	D	21 1 69	Halifax	Trainee	Halifax T	196	13
						Halifax T	Crewe Alex	85	7
							Carlisle U	91	3
Blom Jonny‡			M	14 11 72	Halmeford		Carlisle U	—	—
Bowman Rob*	6 1	12 10	D	21 11 75	Durham	Trainee	Leeds U	7	—
							Rotherham U	13	—
							Carlisle U	46	2
Brightwell David*	6 2	12 09	D	7 1 71	Lutterworth	Trainee	Manchester C	43	1
							Chester C (loan)	6	—
							Lincoln C (loan)	5	—
							Stoke C (loan)	1	—
							Bradford C	24	—
							Blackpool (loan)	2	—
							Northampton T	35	1
							Carlisle U	78	4
Clark Peter	6 1	12 04	D	10 12 79	Romford	Arsenal	Carlisle U	79	1
Dobie Scott	6 2	12 09	F	10 10 78	Workington	Trainee	Carlisle U	92	14
							Clydebank (loan)	6	—
Douglas Andrew‡	5 9	10 05	F	27 5 80	Penrith	Trainee	Carlisle U	1	—
Durnin John‡	5 10	12 08	M	18 8 65	Liverpool	Waterloo Dock	Liverpool	—	—
							WBA (loan)	5	2
							Oxford U	161	44
							Portsmouth	181	31
							Blackpool	5	1
							Carlisle U	22	2
Halliday Stephen‡	5 10	12 07	F	3 5 76	Sunderland	Charlton Ath	Hartlepool U	140	25
							Motherwell	4	—
							Carlisle U	16	7
Harries Paul	6 1	13 00	F	19 11 77	Sydney	NSWSF	Portsmouth	1	—
							Crystal Palace	—	—
							Torquay U (loan)	5	—
							Carlisle U	20	2
Heritage Paul*	6 2	14 00	G	17 4 79	Sheffield	Trainee	Sheffield U	—	—
							Barnsley	—	—
							Carlisle U	—	—
Hopper Tony	5 11	12 08	M	31 5 76	Carlisle	Trainee	Carlisle U	100	1
Hore John§	5 11	11 12		18 8 82	Liverpool	Trainee	Carlisle U	1	—
Keen Peter	6 0	11 10	G	16 11 76	Middlesbrough	Trainee	Newcastle U	—	—
							Carlisle U	6	—
McKinnon Rob	5 11	11 01	D	31 7 66	Glasgow	Rutherglen	Newcastle U	1	—
						Glencairn	Hartlepool U	247	7
							Manchester U (loan)	—	—
							Motherwell	152	8
							Twente	50	1
							Hearts	19	—
							Hartlepool U (loan)	7	—
							Carlisle U (loan)	8	—
Pitts Matthew	5 11	12 06	D	25 12 79	Middlesbrough	Trainee	Sunderland	—	—
							Carlisle U	29	1
Prokas Richard	5 9	11 05	M	22 1 76	Penrith	Trainee	Carlisle U	175	3
Reid Paul	6 2	11 08	D	18 2 82	Carlisle	Trainee	Carlisle U	19	—
Roddie Andrew‡	5 9	11 00	M	4 11 71	Glasgow	S Form	Aberdeen	27	5
							Motherwell	55	—
							Notts Co	—	—
						Lungskile	St Mirren	19	1
						Happy Valley	Carlisle U	2	—
Searle Damon#	5 10	11 00	M	26 10 71	Cardiff	Trainee	Cardiff C	234	3
							Stockport Co	41	—
							Carlisle U	66	3
							Rochdale (loan)	14	—
Skelton Gavin	5 7	10 00	M	27 3 81	Carlisle	Trainee	Carlisle U	7	—

Name	Ht	Wt	Pos	Born	Birthplace	From	Club	Apps	Gls
Skinner Stephen§	6 0	12 03		25 11 81	Whitehaven	Trainee	Carlisle U	2	—
Soley Steve	5 11	12 08	M	22 4 71	Widnes	Leek T	Portsmouth	8	—
							Macclesfield T (loan)	10	—
							Carlisle U	37	8
Teale Shaun†	6 0	13 07	D	10 3 64	Southport	Weymouth	Bournemouth	100	4
							Aston Villa	147	2
							Tranmere R	54	—
							Preston NE (loan)	5	—
						Happy Valley	Motherwell	29	1
							Carlisle U	18	—
Thorpe Jeff*	5 11	12 08	M	17 11 72	Cockermouth	Trainee	Carlisle U	176	6
Thurston Mark	6 2	11 08	M	10 2 80	Carlisle	Trainee	Carlisle U	—	—
Tracey Richard*	5 11	12 04	F	9 7 79	Muirfield	Trainee	Sheffield U	—	—
							Rotherham U	3	—
							Carlisle U	47	10
Walker Andy‡	5 8	11 05	F	6 4 65	Glasgow	Baillieston Jun	Motherwell	76	17
							Celtic	108	30
							Newcastle U (loan)	2	—
							Bolton W	67	44
							Celtic	42	9
							Sheffield U	52	20
							Hibernian (loan)	8	3
							Raith R (loan)	7	2
							Ayr U	33	15
							Carlisle U	3	—
Weaver Luke	6 2	13 02	G	26 6 79	Woolwich	Trainee	Leyton Orient	9	—
							West Ham U (loan)	—	—
							Sunderland	—	—
							Scarborough (loan)	6	—
							Carlisle U	29	—
Whitehead Stuart	6 0	12 02	D	17 7 76	Bromsgrove	Bromsgrove R	Bolton W	—	—
							Carlisle U	66	—

Trainees
Allan, Jonathan M; Andrews, Lee D; Antony, Paul M; Ballantyne, Paul; Clark, Barry J; Graham, Ricky; Heggie, John A; Hetherington, Philip M; Hoolickin, Lee; Hore, John; Jack, Michael L; Johnston, Craig B; Lewis, Craig; May, Kyle; Rooke, Steven; Skinner, Stephen K; Thwaites, Adam

Non-Contract
Dalton, Neil J; Teale, Shaun

Associated Schoolboys
Hewson, David L

CHARLTON ATHLETIC

Name	Ht	Wt	Pos	Born	Birthplace	From	Club	Apps	Gls
Allman Anthony	5 9	10 07	D	14 12 80	Sidcup	Trainee	Charlton Ath	—	—
Barbe Steven‡	6 1	11 13	M	15 1 79	Asse		Charlton Ath	—	—
Barness Anthony*	5 11	11 10	D	25 3 73	Lewisham	Trainee	Charlton Ath	27	1
							Chelsea	14	—
							Middlesbrough (loan)	—	—
							Southend U (loan)	5	—
							Charlton Ath	96	3
Berti Nicola	6 1	12 02	M	14 4 67	Salsomaggiore Terme		Parma	28	—
							Fiorentina	80	8
							Internazionale	229	29
							Tottenham H	21	3
							Alaves	—	—
							Charlton Ath	—	—
Brown Steve	6 1	14 04	D	13 5 72	Brighton	Trainee	Charlton Ath	200	7
Cobian Juan‡	5 6	10 10	D	11 9 75	Buenos Aires	Boca Juniors	Sheffield W	9	—
							Charlton Ath	—	—
Collis David	5 11	12 00	M	8 11 81	London	Trainee	Charlton Ath	—	—
Curbishley Alan*	5 10	11 07	M	8 11 57	Forest Gate	Apprentice	West Ham U	85	5
							Birmingham C	130	11
							Aston Villa	36	1
							Charlton Ath	63	6
							Brighton & HA	116	13
							Charlton Ath	28	—
Fortune Jonathan	6 2	11 00	D	23 8 80	Islington	Trainee	Charlton Ath	—	—
							Mansfield T (loan)	4	—
Hales Lee	5 10	11 00	F	1 5 81	Gillingham	Trainee	Charlton Ath	—	—
Hockley David	5 11	11 05	M	23 2 81	Gillingham	Trainee	Charlton Ath	—	—
Holmes Matty*	5 7	11 01	M	1 8 69	Luton	Trainee	Bournemouth	114	8
							Cardiff C (loan)	1	—
							West Ham U	76	4
							Blackburn R	9	1
							Charlton Ath	16	1
Hunt Andy	6 0	12 02	F	9 6 70	Thurrock	Kettering T	Newcastle U	43	11
							WBA (loan)	10	9
							WBA	202	67
							Charlton Ath	78	31
Ifejiagwa Emeka*	6 3	14 00	D	30 10 77	Nigeria	Udoji U	Charlton Ath	—	—
							Brighton & HA (loan)	2	1
Ilic Sasa	6 4	14 00	G	18 7 72	Melbourne	St Leonards Stamcroft	Charlton Ath	38	—
							West Ham U (loan)	1	—

Izzet Kemal	5 8	10 05	M	29 9 80	Whitechapel	Trainee	Charlton Ath	—	—
James Kevin*	5 9	10 07	F	3 1 80	Southwark	Trainee	Charlton Ath	—	—
Jones Keith	5 9	11 07	M	14 10 65	Dulwich	Apprentice	Chelsea	52	7
							Brentford	169	13
							Southend U	90	11
							Charlton Ath	158	6
Kiely Dean	6 0	12 13	G	10 10 70	Salford	WBA	Coventry C	—	—
							Ipswich T (loan)	—	—
							York C (loan)	—	—
							York C	210	—
							Bury	137	—
							Charlton Ath	45	—
Kinsella Mark	5 9	11 07	M	12 8 72	Dublin	Home Farm	Colchester U	180	27
							Charlton Ath	159	17
Konchesky Paul	5 10	11 07	D	15 5 81	Barking	Trainee	Charlton Ath	13	—
Lisbie Kevin	5 9	11 00	F	17 10 78	Hackney	Trainee	Charlton Ath	43	2
							Gillingham (loan)	7	4
							Reading (loan)	2	—
MacDonald Charlie	5 9	11 00	F	13 2 81	Southwark	Trainee	Charlton Ath	3	—
McCammon Mark	6 2	14 06	F	7 8 78	Barnet	Cambridge C	Cambridge U	4	—
							Charlton Ath	4	—
							Swindon T (loan)	4	—
Mendonca Clive	5 10	12 07	F	9 9 68	Islington	Apprentice	Sheffield U	13	4
							Doncaster R (loan)	2	—
							Rotherham U	84	27
							Sheffield U	10	1
							Grimsby T (loan)	10	3
							Grimsby T	156	56
							Charlton Ath	84	40
Newton Shaun	5 8	11 04	F	20 8 75	Camberwell	Trainee	Charlton Ath	230	20
Parker Scott	5 9	10 12	M	13 10 80	Lambeth	Trainee	Charlton Ath	22	1
Powell Chris	5 10	11 10	D	8 9 69	Lambeth	Trainee	Crystal Palace	3	—
							Aldershot (loan)	11	—
							Southend U	248	3
							Derby Co	91	1
							Charlton Ath	78	—
Pringle Martin	6 2	12 02	F	18 11 70	Gothenburg	Stenungsund	Helsingborg	64	15
							Benfica	41	6
							Charlton Ath	50	7
Robinson John	5 10	11 08	F	29 8 71	Bulawayo	Apprentice	Brighton & HA	62	6
							Charlton Ath	262	32
Royal Mark	5 11	11 00	F	20 12 81	London	Chelsea	Charlton Ath	—	—
Royce Simon#	6 2	12 10	G	9 9 71	Forest Gate	Heybridge Swifts	Southend U	149	—
							Charlton Ath	8	—
Rufus Richard	6 1	12 10	D	12 1 75	Lewisham	Trainee	Charlton Ath	216	7
Salako John	5 9	12 03	F	11 2 69	Nigeria	Trainee	Crystal Palace	215	22
							Swansea C (loan)	13	3
							Coventry C	72	4
							Bolton W	7	—
							Fulham	10	1
							Charlton Ath	27	2
Shields Greg	5 10	11 06	D	21 8 76	Falkirk		Rangers	7	—
							Dunfermline Ath	72	—
							Charlton Ath	21	2
Shittu Daniel	6 3	16 00	D	2 9 80	Lagos		Charlton Ath	—	—
Stuart Graham	5 8	11 12	M	24 10 70	Tooting	Trainee	Chelsea	87	14
							Everton	136	22
							Sheffield U	53	11
							Charlton Ath	46	11
Svensson Mathias	6 0	12 06	F	24 9 74	Boras		Elfsborg	22	15
							Portsmouth	45	10
							Tirol	Crystal Palace	32	10
							Charlton Ath	18	2
Tiler Carl	6 2	13 10	D	11 2 70	Sheffield	Trainee	Barnsley	71	3
							Nottingham F	69	1
							Swindon T (loan)	2	—
							Aston Villa	12	1
							Sheffield U	23	2
							Everton	21	1
							Charlton Ath	38	2
Todd Andy	5 10	10 11	D	21 9 74	Derby	Trainee	Middlesbrough	8	—
							Swindon T (loan)	13	—
							Bolton W	84	2
							Charlton Ath	12	—
Turner John*	6 1	12 05	G	9 9 80	Pontypool	Trainee	Charlton Ath	—	—
Youds Eddie	6 1	14 09	D	3 5 70	Liverpool	Trainee	Everton	8	—
							Cardiff C (loan)	1	—
							Wrexham (loan)	20	2
							Ipswich T	50	1
							Bradford C	85	8
							Charlton Ath	53	2

Scholars

Bolangi, Pierre M; Brown, Jason R; Campbell-Ryce, Jamal J; Ford, Simon G; Gibbs, Dean P; Lewis, Yohance O; McCarthy, Paul D; Martin, Alexander; Smith, Richard R; Tambue, Joe; Taylor, Kris J

CHELSEA

Name	Ht	Wt	Pos	Born	Birthplace	From	Club	Apps	Gls
Aleksidze Rati	6 0	12 02	M	6 8 78	Georgia		Dynamo Tbilisi	63	21
							Chelsea	—	—
Ambrosetti Gabriele	5 11	11 05	M	7 8 73	Varese		Varese	50	11
							Brescia	34	10
							Venezia	18	3
							Brescia	9	2
							Vicenza	103	18
							Chelsea	16	—
Babayaro Celestine	5 9	11 09	D	29 8 78	Kaduna	Plateau U	Anderlecht	75	8
							Chelsea	61	3
Broad Stephen	6 0	11 05	D	10 6 80	Epsom	Trainee	Chelsea	—	—
Casiraghi Pierluigi	6 1	13 05	F	4 3 69	Monza		Monza	94	28
							Juventus	98	20
							Lazio	140	41
							Chelsea	10	1
Clement Neil	6 0	14 07	D	3 10 78	Reading	Trainee	Chelsea	1	—
							Reading (loan)	11	1
							Preston NE (loan)	4	—
							Brentford (loan)	8	—
							WBA (loan)	8	—
Crittenden Nick*	5 8	10 11	M	11 11 78	Bracknell	Trainee	Chelsea	2	—
							Plymouth Arg (loan)	2	—
Cudicini Carlo	6 1	12 02	G	6 9 73	Milan		AC Milan	—	—
							Como	6	—
							Prato	30	—
							Lazio	1	—
							Castel di Sangro	46	—
							Chelsea	1	—
Cummings Warren	5 9	11 05	D	15 10 80	Aberdeen	Trainee	Chelsea	—	—
Dalla Bona Samuele	6 0	13 04	F	6 2 81	San Dona di Piave		Atalanta	—	—
							Chelsea	2	—
De Goey Ed	6 6	14 05	G	20 12 66	Gouda		Sparta	145	—
							Feyenoord	201	—
							Chelsea	100	—
Demetrious Shayne	5 9	10 01	M	6 12 80	Perivale	Trainee	Chelsea	—	—
Desailly Marcel	6 0	13 05	D	7 9 68	Accra		Nantes	164	5
							Marseille	46	1
							AC Milan	137	5
							Chelsea	54	1
Deschamps Didier	5 8	12 11	M	15 10 68	Bayonne		Nantes	110	3
							Marseille	17	1
							Bordeaux	37	3
							Marseille	106	5
							Juventus	120	4
							Chelsea	27	—
Di Matteo Roberto	5 10	12 04	M	29 5 70	Schaffhausen		Schaffhausen	50	2
							Zurich	34	6
							Aarau	32	1
							Lazio	88	7
							Chelsea	112	15
Emerson	6 1	13 12	D	30 3 72	Porto Alegre	Benfica	Sheffield W	61	1
							Chelsea	20	—
Evans Rhys	6 1	12 02	G	27 1 82	Swindon	Trainee	Chelsea	—	—
							Bristol R (loan)	4	—
Ferrer Albert	5 9	12 02	D	6 6 70	Barcelona		Tenerife	17	—
							Barcelona	205	1
							Chelsea	55	—
Flo Tore Andre	6 4	13 08	F	15 6 73	Strin		Sogndal	22	5
							Tromso	26	18
							Brann	40	28
							Chelsea	98	31
Forssell Mikael	6 0	12 08	F	15 3 81	Steinfurt		HJK Helsinki	17	1
							Chelsea	10	1
							Crystal Palace (loan)	13	3
Hampshire Steve‡	5 10	10 12	M	17 10 79	Edinburgh	Trainee	Chelsea	—	—
(Transferred to Dunfermline Ath, January 2000)									
Harley Jon	5 9	11 05	D	26 9 79	Maidstone	Trainee	Chelsea	20	2
Hitchcock Kevin	6 1	13 00	G	5 10 62	Custom House	Barking	Nottingham F	—	—
							Mansfield T (loan)	14	—
							Mansfield T	168	—
							Chelsea	96	—
							Northampton T (loan)	17	—
							West Ham U (loan)	—	—
Hogh Jes	6 0	11 11	D	7 5 66	Aalborg		Aalborg	95	13
							Brondby	79	6
							Aalborg	14	4
							Fenerbahce	115	6
							Chelsea	9	—
Keenan Joseph	5 8	10 00	M	14 10 82	Southampton	Trainee	Chelsea	—	—
Knight Leon	5 4	9 06	F	16 9 82	Hackney	Trainee	Chelsea	—	—

Name							Club	Apps	Gls
Lambourde Bernard	6 0	13 05	D	11 5 71	Pointe-A-Pitre		Cannes	13	1
							Angers	36	1
							Cannes	28	1
							Bordeaux	28	1
							Chelsea	39	2
Le Saux Graeme	5 10	11 09	D	17 10 68	Jersey	St Pauls	Chelsea	90	8
							Blackburn R	129	7
							Chelsea	65	1
Leboeuf Franck	6 1	11 11	D	22 1 68	Marseille		Hyeres	14	1
							Meaux	39	3
							Laval	69	10
							Strasbourg	189	49
							Chelsea	119	17
Melchiot Mario	6 2	11 11	D	4 11 76	Amsterdam		Ajax	73	1
							Chelsea	5	—
Morris Jody	5 5	10 03	M	22 12 78	Hammersmith	Trainee	Chelsea	73	5
Nicholls Mark	5 10	10 12	M	30 5 77	Hillingdon	Trainee	Chelsea	36	3
							Reading (loan)	5	1
							Grimsby T (loan)	6	—
Nicholls Paul*	5 10	11 00	G	12 10 80	Newham	Trainee	Chelsea	—	—
Parkin Sam	6 2	13 00	F	14 3 81	Roehampton	School	Chelsea	—	—
Percassi Luca	5 9	11 09	M	25 8 80	Milan		Atalanta	—	—
							Chelsea	—	—
Petrescu Dan	5 10	11 02	M	22 12 67	Bucharest		Steaua	95	26
							FC Olt (loan)	24	—
							Foggia	55	7
							Genoa	24	1
							Sheffield W	37	3
							Chelsea	150	18
Poyet Gustavo	6 1	13 00	M	15 11 67	Montevideo	Bella Vista	Zaragoza	239	63
							Chelsea	75	25
Reddington Stuart			D	21 2 78	Lincoln	Lincoln U	Chelsea	—	—
(On loan to Kalmar)									
Richardson Jay	5 9	11 09	M	14 11 79	Keston	Trainee	Chelsea	—	—
Slatter Danny	5 8	10 02	D	15 11 80	Cardiff	Trainee	Chelsea	—	—
Sutton Chris	6 3	13 08	F	10 3 73	Nottingham	Trainee	Norwich C	102	35
							Blackburn R	130	47
							Chelsea	28	1
Terry John	6 1	12 13	D	7 12 80	Barking	Trainee	Chelsea	6	—
							Nottingham F (loan)	6	—
Thornton Paul	5 7	11 00	D	7 1 83	Surrey	Trainee	Chelsea	—	—
Vialli Gianluca	5 10	13 06	F	9 7 64	Cremona		Cremonese	105	23
							Sampdoria	223	85
							Juventus	102	38
							Chelsea	58	21
Weah George	6 1	12 10	F	1 10 66	Liberia	Tonnerre	Monaco	103	47
(On loan from AC Milan)							Paris St Germain	96	32
							AC Milan	114	46
							Chelsea	11	3
Wise Dennis	5 6	10 11	M	16 12 66	Kensington	Southampton	Wimbledon	135	27
							Chelsea	296	50
Wolleaston Robert	5 11	11 07	M	21 12 79	Perivale	Trainee	Chelsea	1	—
							Bristol R (loan)	4	—
Zola Gianfranco	5 6	10 08	F	5 7 66	Oliena		Nuorese	31	10
							Torres	88	21
							Napoli	105	32
							Parma	102	49
							Chelsea	120	33

Scholars
Baldwin, Patrick M; Byle, Leslie D; Cousins, Scott R; Pitt, Courtney; Ross, Andrew C; Sheppard, Kyle D

CHELTENHAM TOWN

Name								Club	Apps	Gls
Banks Chris	5 11	12 04	D	22 11 65	Stone	Local		Port Vale	65	1
								Exeter C	45	1
						Bath C		Cheltenham T	42	—
Benbow Steve	5 10	10 07	G	5 4 82	Cheltenham			Cheltenham T	—	—
Bloomer Bob	5 10	12 07	M	21 6 66	Sheffield			Chesterfield	141	15
								Bristol R	22	—
								Cheltenham T	11	—
Book Steve	5 11	11 02	G	7 7 69	Bournemouth			Brighton & HA	—	—
								Lincoln C	—	—
						Forest Green R		Cheltenham T	46	—
Brough John	6 0	12 11	D	8 1 73	Ilkeston	Trainee		Notts Co	—	—
								Shrewsbury T	16	1
						Telford U		Hereford U	79	3
								Cheltenham T	37	2
Devaney Martin	5 11	12 06	F	1 6 80	Cheltenham	Trainee		Coventry C	—	—
								Cheltenham T	26	6
Duff Michael	6 1	11 08	D	11 1 78	Belfast	Trainee		Cheltenham T	31	2
Freeman Mark	6 2	13 08	D	27 1 70	Walsall	Bilston T		Wolverhampton W	—	—
						Gloucester C		Cheltenham T	38	2

Name	Ht	Wt	Pos	DOB	Birthplace	Source	Club	Apps	Gls
Grayson Neil	5 10	12 09	F	1 11 64	York	Rowntree	Doncaster R	29	6
						Mackintosh	York C	1	—
							Chesterfield	15	—
						Boston U	Northampton T	120	31
						Hereford U	Cheltenham T	43	10
Griffin Anthony	5 11	11 03	M	22 3 79	Bournemouth	Trainee	Bournemouth	6	—
							Cheltenham T	24	—
Higgs Shane	6 3	14 02	G	13 5 77	Oxford	Trainee	Bristol R	10	—
						Worcester C	Cheltenham T	—	—
Hopkins Gareth	6 2	13 08	F	14 6 80	Cheltenham	Trainee	Cheltenham T	1	—
Howarth Neil	6 2	13 06	D	15 11 71	Bolton	Trainee	Burnley	1	—
						Macclesfield T	Macclesfield T	60	3
							Cheltenham T	44	2
Howells Lee	5 11	11 02	M	14 10 68	Fremantle	Apprentice	Bristol R	—	—
						Brisbane Lions	Cheltenham T	45	3
Jackson Michael D	5 7	10 10	M	26 6 80	Cheltenham	Trainee	Cheltenham T	2	—
Marker Nicky‡	6 0	13 09	D	3 5 65	Exeter	Apprentice	Exeter C	202	3
							Plymouth Arg	202	13
							Blackburn R	54	1
							Sheffield U	61	5
							Plymouth Arg (loan)	4	—
							Cheltenham T	—	—
McAuley Hugh	5 10	11 06	F	13 5 77	Plymouth	Leek T	Cheltenham T	39	4
Milton Russell	5 8	12 01	M	12 1 69	Folkestone	Apprentice	Arsenal	—	—
						Dover Ath	Cheltenham T	38	9
Mitchinson Stuart	5 6	10 08	F	15 10 80	Cheltenham	Trainee	Cheltenham T	—	—
Victory Jamie	5 11	12 02	D	14 11 75	London	Trainee	West Ham U	—	—
							Bournemouth	16	1
							Cheltenham T	46	4
Walker Richard	5 10	11 09	D	9 11 71	Derby	Trainee	Notts Co	67	4
							Mansfield T (loan)	4	—
						Hereford U	Cheltenham T	7	—
Watkins Dale‡	5 8	11 12	F	4 11 71	Peterborough	Trainee	Peterborough U	10	—
						Gloucester C	Cheltenham T	9	—
Yates Mark	5 11	13 02	M	24 1 70	Birmingham	Trainee	Birmingham C	54	6
							Burnley	18	1
							Lincoln C (loan)	14	—
							Doncaster R	34	4
						Kidderminster H	Cheltenham T	46	2

CHESTER CITY

Name	Ht	Wt	Pos	DOB	Birthplace	Source	Club	Apps	Gls
Ajetunmobi Adewale			M	27 10 77	Glasgow		Chester C	—	—
Beckett Luke	5 11	11 06	F	25 11 76	Sheffield	Trainee	Barnsley	—	—
							Chester C	74	25
Bennett Gary*	5 11	12 00	F	20 9 62	Kirby	Kirby T	Wigan Ath	20	3
							Chester C	126	36
							Southend U	42	6
							Chester C	80	15
							Wrexham	121	77
							Tranmere R	29	9
							Preston NE	24	4
							Wrexham	15	5
							Chester C	48	13
Berry Paul	5 9	10 08	M	6 12 78	Warrington	Warrington T	Chester C	9	1
Blackburn Chris§	5 7	10 06	M	2 8 82	Crewe	Scholar	Chester C	1	—
Brown Wayne	6 1	11 06	G	14 1 77	Southampton	Trainee	Bristol C	1	—
						Weston-Super-Mare	Chester C	84	—
Carden Paul	5 9	11 10	M	29 3 79	Liverpool	Trainee	Blackpool	1	—
							Rochdale	45	—
							Chester C	11	—
Carson Danny‡	5 6	10 07	M	2 2 81	Huyton	Trainee	Chester C	2	—
Carver Joe‡	5 10	11 00		11 6 71	Illinois	Hampton Rd Mariners	Chester C	2	—
Conkie Matthew‡			M	6 11 80	Chester	Trainee	Chester C	—	—
Cross Jonathan*	5 10	11 07	D	2 3 75	Wallasey	Trainee	Wrexham	119	12
							Hereford U (loan)	5	1
							Tranmere R (loan)	—	—
							Chester C	52	1
Doughty Matt§	5 8	10 00	D	2 11 81	Warrington	Scholar	Chester C	33	1
Eve Angus	5 7	11 02	M	23 2 72	Trinidad	Joe Public	Chester C	14	1
Finney Steve	5 11	12 08	F	31 10 73	Hexham	Trainee	Preston NE	6	1
							Manchester C	—	—
							Swindon T	73	18
							Cambridge U (loan)	7	2
							Carlisle U	33	6
							Leyton Orient	5	—
						Barrow	Chester C	13	—
Fisher Neil	5 10	10 09	M	7 11 70	St Helens	Trainee	Bolton W	24	1
							Chester C	157	5

Name							Club	Apps	Gls
Heggs Carl	6 1	12 10	F	11 10 70	Leicester	Paget R	WBA	40	3
(On loan from Rushden & Diamonds)							Bristol R (loan)	5	1
							Swansea C	46	7
							Northampton T	46	5
						Rushden & D	Chester C	11	2
Hemmings Tony	5 10	12 09	F	21 9 67	Burton	Northwich Vic	Wycombe W	49	12
						Ilkeston T	Chester C	19	2
Hicks Stuart	6 1	13 03	D	30 5 67	Peterborough	Wisbech T	Colchester U	64	—
							Scunthorpe U	67	1
							Doncaster R	36	—
							Huddersfield T	22	1
							Preston NE	12	—
							Scarborough	85	2
							Leyton Orient	78	1
							Chester C	13	—
Hobson Gary*	6 2	13 02	D	12 11 72	North Ferriby	Trainee	Hull C	142	—
							Brighton & HA	98	1
							Chester C	20	—
Jones Jon*	5 9	11 05	F	27 10 78	Wrexham	Trainee	Chester C	38	2
Keister John*	5 8	11 00	M	11 11 70	Manchester	Faweh FC	Walsall	106	2
							Chester C	10	—
Laird Kamu‡	5 8	11 04		23 12 75	Port of Spain	Dulwich H	Chester C	3	1
Lancaster Martin	6 0	12 07	D	10 11 80	Wigan	Trainee	Chester C	28	—
Malone Steve*	5 7	10 06	M	28 4 78	Glasgow	Knightswood	Chester C	—	—
Milosavljevic Goran*	6 4	12 00		11 4 67	Kraljevo	US Montelimar	Chester C	12	—
Moss Darren	5 10	11 00	M	24 5 81	Wrexham	Trainee	Chester C	42	—
Nash Martin‡	5 11	12 03	M	27 12 75	Regina	Regina	Stockport Co	11	—
						Vancouver 89ers	Chester C	16	—
Pickering Ally‡	5 9	11 07	D	22 6 67	Manchester	Buxton	Rotherham U	88	2
							Coventry C	65	—
							Stoke C	83	1
							Burnley	21	1
						Altrincham	Chester C	7	1
Reid Shaun*	5 8	12 02	M	13 10 65	Huyton	Local	Rochdale	133	4
							Preston NE (loan)	3	—
							York C	106	7
							Rochdale	107	10
							Bury	21	—
							Chester C	62	2
Rendell Carl‡			M	23 9 80	Liverpool	Trainee	Chester C	—	—
Richardson Nick	6 0	12 06	M	11 4 67	Halifax	Local	Halifax T	101	17
							Cardiff C	111	13
							Wrexham (loan)	4	2
							Chester C (loan)	6	1
							Bury	5	—
							Chester C	169	11
Robinson Jamie	6 1	12 08	D	26 2 72	Liverpool	Trainee	Liverpool	—	—
							Barnsley	9	—
							Carlisle U	57	4
							Torquay U	75	1
							Exeter C	12	—
							Chester C	9	—
Shelton Andy	5 10	12 00	M	19 6 80	Sutton Coldfield	Trainee	Chester C	35	1
Shelton Gary*	5 7	11 02	M	21 3 58	Nottingham	Apprentice	Walsall	24	—
							Aston Villa	24	7
							Notts Co (loan)	8	—
							Sheffield W	198	18
							Oxford U	65	1
							Bristol C	150	24
							Rochdale (loan)	3	—
							Chester C	69	6
Spooner Nicky‡	5 10	11 09	D	5 6 71	Manchester	Trainee	Bolton W	23	2
							Oldham Ath (loan)	2	—
							Chester C	9	—
Woods Matt	6 1	12 03	D	9 9 76	Gosport	Trainee	Everton	—	—
							Chester C	135	4
Wright Darren	5 6	10 00	F	7 9 79	Warrington	Trainee	Chester C	48	2

Scholars
Blackburn, Christopher R; Cooper, Joseph D; Donnelly, Christopher; Doughty, Matthew L; Hopwood, Christopher P; Howell, Marc T; Kilgannon Wesley M; Kincaid, James E; Lloyd-Hughes, Lee A; O'Brien, John P; Roberts, Paul; Sefton Lee; Williams, Michael A; Woodyatt, Lee M

Non-Contract
Croft, Brian GA; De Bartolo, Alejandro P

CHESTERFIELD

Name							Club	Apps	Gls
Armstrong Joel§	5 11	12 07	G	25 9 81	Chesterfield	Scholar	Chesterfield	3	—
Barratt Danny	6 0	11 12	D	25 9 80	Bradford	Trainee	Chesterfield	2	—
Beaumont Chris#	5 11	11 12	M	5 12 65	Sheffield	Denaby U	Rochdale	34	7
							Stockport Co	258	39
							Chesterfield	144	6
Blatherwick Steve	6 1	15 00	D	20 9 73	Nottingham	Notts Co	Nottingham F	10	—
							Wycombe W (loan)	2	—
							Hereford U (loan)	10	1
							Reading (loan)	7	—
							Burnley	24	—
							Chesterfield	50	1

Breckin Ian	5 11	11 07	D	24 2 75	Rotherham	Trainee	Rotherham U	132	6
							Chesterfield	125	4
Carss Tony*	5 10	11 08	M	31 3 76	Alnwick	Bradford C	Blackburn R	—	—
							Darlington	57	2
							Cardiff C	42	1
							Chesterfield	35	1
Curtis Tom	5 8	10 08	M	1 3 73	Exeter	School	Derby Co	—	—
							Chesterfield	240	12
D'Auria David	5 9	11 11	M	26 3 70	Swansea	Trainee	Swansea C	45	6
						Barry T	Scarborough	52	8
							Scunthorpe U	107	18
							Hull C	54	4
							Chesterfield	5	—
Danysz Lee‡	6 0	12 00	D	5 10 80	Doncaster		Chesterfield	—	—
Dooley James*			M	26 3 81	Chesterfield	Trainee	Chesterfield	—	—
Ebdon Marcus	5 10	11 02	M	17 10 70	Pontypool	Trainee	Everton	—	—
							Peterborough U	147	15
							Chesterfield	96	4
Galloway Mick	5 11	11 05	M	13 10 74	Nottingham	Trainee	Notts Co	21	—
							Gillingham (loan)	9	1
							Gillingham	66	4
							Lincoln C (loan)	5	—
							Chesterfield	15	1
Gayle Mark*	6 2	12 03	G	21 10 69	Bromsgrove	Trainee	Leicester C	—	—
							Blackpool	—	—
						Worcester C	Walsall	75	—
							Crewe Alex	83	—
							Liverpool (loan)	—	—
							Birmingham C (loan)	—	—
							Chesterfield	35	—
							Luton T (loan)	—	—
Hewitt Jamie#	5 10	10 08	M	17 5 68	Chesterfield	School	Chesterfield	249	14
							Doncaster R	33	—
							Chesterfield	256	12
Howard Jonathan	5 11	11 07	F	7 10 71	Sheffield	Trainee	Rotherham U	36	5
							Chesterfield	176	29
Leaning Andy*	6 0	13 00	G	18 5 63	Howden	Rowntree	York C	69	—
						Mackintosh	Sheffield U	21	—
							Bristol C	75	—
							Lincoln C	36	—
							Chesterfield	22	—
Lomas Jamie*	5 11	10 09	M	18 10 77	Chesterfield	Trainee	Chesterfield	30	—
Payne Steve	5 11	12 05	D	1 8 75	Castleford	Trainee	Huddersfield T	—	—
							Macclesfield T	77	2
							Chesterfield	18	3
Pearce Greg	6 0	11 00	M	26 5 80	Bolton	Trainee	Chesterfield	11	—
Perkins Chris	5 11	10 09	D	9 1 74	Nottingham	Trainee	Mansfield T	8	—
							Chesterfield	147	3
							Hartlepool U	8	—
							Chesterfield	31	—
Pointon Neil*	5 10	12 10	D	28 11 64	Warsop Vale	Apprentice	Scunthorpe U	159	2
							Everton	102	5
							Manchester C	74	2
							Oldham Ath	94	3
							Hearts	67	3
							Walsall	61	—
							Chesterfield	10	—
Reeves David#	6 0	12 06	F	19 11 67	Birkenhead	Heswall	Sheffield W	17	2
							Scunthorpe U (loan)	4	2
							Scunthorpe U (loan)	6	4
							Burnley (loan)	16	8
							Bolton W	134	29
							Notts Co	13	2
							Carlisle U	127	48
							Preston NE	47	12
							Chesterfield	109	29
Simpkins Mike	6 0	11 11	D	28 11 78	Sheffield	Trainee	Sheffield W	—	—
							Chesterfield	10	—
Wilkinson Steve*	5 11	11 11	F	1 9 68	Lincoln	Apprentice	Leicester C	9	1
							Rochdale (loan)	—	—
							Crewe Alex (loan)	5	2
							Mansfield T	232	83
							Preston NE	52	13
							Chesterfield	75	13
Williams Danny	5 9	9 13	M	2 3 81	Sheffield	Trainee	Chesterfield	5	—
Williams Ryan	5 4	11 02	F	31 8 78	Chesterfield	Trainee	Mansfield T	26	3
							Tranmere R	5	—
							Chesterfield	30	5
Willis Roger#	6 0	12 00	M	17 6 67	Islington	Dunkirk	Grimsby T	9	—
						Barnet	Barnet	44	13
							Watford	36	2
							Birmingham C	19	5
							Southend U	31	7
							Peterborough U	40	6
							Chesterfield	79	12
Woods Steve	5 11	11 13	D	15 12 76	Davenham	Trainee	Stoke C	34	—
							Plymouth Arg (loan)	5	—
							Chesterfield	25	—

Scholars
Armstrong, Joel; Atkinson, Joe; Hogg, Timothy G; James, Richard; Mitchell, Alistair; Renshaw, Lee; Richmond, Andrew J; Rushbury, Andrew J; Rushbury, Ian D; Stone, Joseph; Tuckwood, Stephen A; Wilding, Craig; Worthington, Matthew A; Young, Matthew P

COLCHESTER UNITED

Arnott Andy	6 0	13 07	M	18 10 73	Chatham	Trainee	Gillingham	73	12
							Manchester U (loan)	—	—
							Leyton Orient	50	6
							Fulham	1	—
							Brighton & HA	28	2
							Colchester U	12	—
Brown Simon	6 2	15 01	G	3 12 76	Chelmsford	Trainee	Tottenham H	—	—
							Lincoln C (loan)	1	—
							Fulham (loan)	—	—
							Colchester U	38	—
Dozzell Jason#	6 2	13 07	M	9 12 67	Ipswich	School	Ipswich T	332	52
							Tottenham H	84	13
							Ipswich T	8	1
							Northampton T	21	4
							Colchester U	68	9
Duguid Karl	5 11	11 00	F	21 3 78	Letchworth	Trainee	Colchester U	131	23
Dunne Joe	5 9	11 08	D	25 5 73	Dublin	Trainee	Gillingham	115	1
							Colchester U	121	3
Farley Craig	6 0	11 00	D	17 3 81	Oxford		Colchester U	14	—
Forbes Steve‡	6 1	13 03	M	24 12 75	Hackney	Sittingbourne	Millwall	5	—
							Colchester U	53	4
							Peterborough U (loan)	3	—
Germain Steve‡	5 10	11 00	F	22 6 81	Cannes		Colchester U	9	—
Greene David*	6 3	14 03	D	26 10 73	Luton	Trainee	Luton T	19	—
							Colchester U (loan)	14	1
							Brentford (loan)	11	—
							Colchester U	153	15
Gregory David#	5 10	12 03	M	23 1 70	Polstead	Trainee	Ipswich T	32	2
							Hereford U (loan)	2	—
							Peterborough U	3	—
							Colchester U	181	17
Gregory Neil‡	6 0	12 10	F	7 10 72	Ndola	Trainee	Ipswich T	45	9
							Chesterfield (loan)	3	1
							Scunthorpe U (loan)	10	7
							Torquay U (loan)	5	—
							Peterborough U (loan)	3	1
							Colchester U	53	11
Johnson Gavin	5 11	11 07	D	10 10 70	Eye	Trainee	Ipswich T	132	11
							Luton T	5	—
							Wigan Ath	84	8
							Dunfermline Ath	18	—
							Colchester U	27	—
Johnson Ross	6 0	13 00	D	2 1 76	Brighton	Trainee	Brighton & HA	132	2
							Colchester U	18	—
Keeble Chris	5 9	11 00	M	17 9 78	Colchester	Trainee	Ipswich T	1	—
							Colchester U	5	1
Keith Joey	5 7	10 06	D	1 1 78	London	Trainee	West Ham U	—	—
							Colchester U	45	1
Lock Tony†	6 0	12 04	F	3 9 76	Harlow	Trainee	Colchester U	88	11
Lua-Lua Lomano	5 8	10 00	F	28 12 80	Zaire		Colchester U	54	13
McGavin Steve	5 9	12 08	F	24 1 69	North Walsham	Sudbury T	Colchester U	58	17
							Birmingham C	23	2
							Wycombe W	120	15
							Southend U	11	—
							Northampton T	—	—
							Colchester U	34	16
Moralee Jamie*	5 11	11 00	F	2 12 71	Wandsworth	Trainee	Crystal Palace	6	—
							Millwall	67	19
							Watford	49	7
							Crewe Alex	16	—
							Brighton & HA	31	3
							Colchester U	27	1
Okafor Samuel§	5 9	12 00	M	17 3 82	Xtian		Colchester U	1	—
Opara Chris-Santos§	6 0	12 06	F	21 12 81	Oweri Imo State	Trainee	Colchester U	17	—
Pinault Thomas	5 10	11 01	M	4 12 81	Grasse	Cannes	Colchester U	4	—
Richard Fabrice‡	6 1	13 00	D	16 8 73	Saintes		Colchester U	24	—
Sale Mark‡	6 5	14 09	F	27 2 72	Burton-on-Trent	Trainee	Stoke C	2	—
							Cambridge U	—	—
							Birmingham C	21	—
							Torquay U	44	8
							Preston NE	13	7
							Mansfield T	45	12
							Colchester U	80	12
							Plymouth Arg (loan)	8	1
Skelton Aaron#	6 0	12 08	M	22 11 74	Welwyn	Trainee	Luton T	8	—
							Colchester U	81	11
Sodje Efetobar#	6 1	12 00	D	5 10 72	Greenwich	Stevenage Bor	Macclesfield T	83	6
							Luton T	9	—
							Colchester U	3	—
Walker Andy§			G	30 9 81	Bexley		Colchester U	3	—
Webster Adrian‡	5 8	10 09	M	11 10 80	New Zealand	Charlton Ath	Colchester U	—	—
Wignall Jack§	6 1	11 07	D	26 9 81	Liverpool	Trainee	Colchester U	1	—
Wiles Ian‡	6 0	11 13	D	28 4 80	Epping	Trainee	Colchester U	1	—

Wilkins Richard#	6 0	12 04	M	25 5 65	Streatham	Haverhill R	Colchester U	152	22
							Cambridge U	81	7
							Hereford U	77	5
							Colchester U	127	11
Williams Geraint#	5 8	13 00	M	5 1 62	Cwmpare	Apprentice	Bristol R	141	8
							Derby Co	277	9
							Ipswich T	217	3
							Colchester U	39	—

Scholars
Canham, Marc D; Chambers, Tristan; Gyoury, Nicky D; Hadrava, David L; Heighway, Gregg; Hillier, Sean E; Metcalfe, Ricki J; Okafor, Samuel A; Opara, Kelechi C; Taylor, Andrew C; Walker, Andrew W; Wignall, Jack D; Williamson, Glenn A

Non-Contract
Lock, Anthony C

Associated Schoolboys
Swindells, Adam C

Associated Schoolboys who have accepted the Club's offer of a Traineeship/Scholarship/Contract
Hearn, Matthew J; Morgan, Dean

COVENTRY CITY

Aloisi John	6 1	12 06	F	5 2 76	Adelaide		Cremonese	26	2
							Portsmouth	60	25
							Coventry C	23	7
Barnett Christopher‡	5 11	12 00	M	20 12 78	Derby	Trainee	Coventry C	—	—
Betts Robert	5 10	11 00	D	21 12 81	Doncaster	School	Doncaster R	3	—
							Coventry C	2	—
Breen Gary	6 1	11 12	D	12 12 73	London	Charlton Ath	Maidstone U	19	—
							Gillingham	51	—
							Peterborough U	69	1
							Birmingham C	40	2
							Coventry C	85	1
Burrows David*	5 8	11 08	D	25 10 68	Dudley	Apprentice	WBA	46	1
							Liverpool	146	3
							West Ham U	29	1
							Everton	19	—
							Coventry C	111	—
Burrows Mark*	6 3	12 08	D	14 8 80	Kettering	Trainee	Coventry C	—	—
Caruso Antonio‡			M	23 5 80	Catania		Coventry C	—	—
Chippo Youssef	5 11	12 00	M	10 6 73	Morocco	Al Arabi	Porto	30	2
							Coventry C	33	2
Clement Philippe	6 2	13 00	M	22 3 74	Antwerp		Genk	53	2
(Transferred to FC Brugge)							Coventry C	12	—
Colwell Richard‡	5 9	11 02	D	2 9 79	Wordsley	Trainee	Coventry C	—	—
Cudworth Thomas	5 10	11 00	D	3 8 82	Coventry	Trainee	Coventry C	—	—
Davenport Calum	6 4	14 00	D	1 1 83	Bedford	Trainee	Coventry C	—	—
Delorge Laurent	5 10	11 12	M	21 7 79	Leuven		Gent	10	5
							Coventry C	—	—
Doyle Daire	5 10	11 06	M	18 10 80	Dublin	Cherry Orchard	Coventry C	—	—
Edworthy Marc	5 11	10 03	D	24 12 72	Barnstaple	Trainee	Plymouth Arg	69	1
							Crystal Palace	126	—
							Coventry C	32	—
Eribenne Chukkie*	5 10	11 12	F	2 11 80	London	Trainee	Coventry C	—	—
Eustace John	5 11	11 12	M	3 11 79	Solihull	Trainee	Coventry C	—	—
							Dundee U	11	1
							Coventry C	16	1
Ferguson Barry	6 3	13 00	D	7 9 79	Dublin	Home Farm	Coventry C	—	—
							Colchester U (loan)	6	—
Ford Brian	5 11	12 00	D	23 9 82	Edinburgh	Trainee	Coventry C	—	—
Froggatt Steve	5 11	11 00	F	9 3 73	Lincoln	Trainee	Aston Villa	35	2
							Wolverhampton W	106	7
							Coventry C	49	2
Grant Martin	5 7	10 10	F	16 1 82	Kirkcaldy	Trainee	Coventry C	—	—
Gustafsson Tomas	5 10	11 00	D	7 5 73	Stockholm		Brommapojkarna	47	—
							AIK Stockholm	75	2
							Coventry C	10	—
Hadji Mustapha	6 0	12 00	M	16 11 71	Ifrane		Nancy	139	31
							Sporting	27	3
							La Coruna	31	2
							Coventry C	33	6
Hall Daniel	5 8	10 06	D	29 12 81	Rugby	Trainee	Coventry C	—	—
Hall Marcus	6 1	12 02	D	24 3 76	Coventry	Trainee	Coventry C	82	1
Hedman Magnus	6 3	14 00	G	19 3 73	Stockholm		AIK Stockholm	127	—
							Coventry C	85	—
Hendry Colin	6 1	12 07	D	7 12 65	Keith	Islavale	Dundee	41	2
							Blackburn R	102	22
							Manchester C	63	5
							Blackburn R	234	12
							Rangers	19	—
							Coventry C	9	—
Hyldgaard Morten	6 6	14 00	G	26 1 78	Herning	Ikast	Coventry C	—	—
							Scunthorpe U (loan)	5	—

Name	Ht	Wt	Pos	Date	Birthplace	Source	Club	Apps	Gls
Keane Robbie	5 9	11 07	F	8 7 80	Dublin	Trainee	Wolverhampton W	73	24
							Coventry C	31	12
Kirkland Christopher	6 3	11 07	G	2 5 81	Leicester	Trainee	Coventry C	—	—
Konjic Muhamed	6 3	13 00	D	14 5 70	Bosnia		Tuzla	8	—
							Belisce	18	—
							Zagreb	63	5
							Zurich	36	5
							Monaco	37	2
							Coventry C	8	—
Mathie Graeme	6 1	12 00	D	17 10 82	Lanark	Trainee	Coventry C	—	—
McAllister Gary	6 1	11 11	M	25 12 64	Motherwell	Fir Park BC	Motherwell	59	6
							Leicester C	201	47
							Leeds U	231	31
							Coventry C	119	20
McConnell Peter	5 10	11 12	M	16 9 82	Rutherglen	Trainee	Coventry C	—	—
McPhee Gary	6 0	12 00	F	18 4 80	Glasgow	Trainee	Coventry C	—	—
McPhee Stephen	5 7	10 08	M	5 6 81	Glasgow	Trainee	Coventry C	—	—
McSheffrey Gary	5 8	10 06	F	13 8 82	Coventry	Trainee	Coventry C	4	—
Mooney Gerard*	5 9	11 00	D	28 8 80	Glasgow	Trainee	Coventry C	—	—
Normann Runar	5 11	12 00	M	1 3 78	Harstad	Harstad	Lillestrom	41	6
							Coventry C	8	—
Nuzzo Raffaele‡	6 2	14 00	G	21 2 73	Monza		Coventry C	—	—
Ogrizovic Steve*	6 3	15 00	G	12 9 57	Mansfield	ONRYC	Chesterfield	16	—
							Liverpool	4	—
							Shrewsbury T	84	—
							Coventry C	507	1
Palmer Carlton	6 3	13 00	M	5 12 65	Oldbury	Trainee	WBA	121	4
							Sheffield W	205	14
							Leeds U	102	5
							Southampton	45	3
							Nottingham F	16	1
							Coventry C	15	1
Pead Craig	5 9	11 06	M	15 9 81	Bromsgrove	Trainee	Coventry C	—	—
Prenderville Barry‡	6 0	12 08	D	16 10 76	Dublin	Trainee	Coventry C	—	—
							Hibernian (loan)	13	2
Quinn Barry	6 0	12 02	M	9 5 79	Dublin	Trainee	Coventry C	18	—
Roussel Cedric	6 3	13 00	F	6 1 78	Mons	La Louviere	Gent	31	8
							Coventry C	22	6
Shaw Richard	5 9	12 08	D	11 9 68	Brentford	Apprentice	Crystal Palace	207	3
							Hull C (loan)	4	—
							Coventry C	155	—
Strachan Craig	5 8	10 06	M	19 5 82	Aberdeen	Trainee	Coventry C	—	—
Strachan Gavin	5 10	11 07	M	23 12 78	Aberdeen	Trainee	Coventry C	12	—
							Dundee (loan)	6	—
Telfer Paul	5 9	11 06	M	21 10 71	Edinburgh	Trainee	Luton T	144	19
							Coventry C	160	6
Whelan Noel	6 2	12 03	F	30 12 74	Leeds	Trainee	Leeds U	48	7
							Coventry C	134	31
Williams Paul	5 11	12 10	D	26 3 71	Burton	Trainee	Derby Co	160	26
							Lincoln C (loan)	3	—
							Coventry C	134	5
Zuniga Ysrael	5 9	11 00	F	27 8 76	Lima		Melgar	25	19
							Coventry C	6	2

Scholars
Ashby, Jascon C; Brush, David J; Cook, Matthew; Fowler, Lee A; Hope, Shaun; Jones, Daniel R; Magennis, Mark A; Montgomery, Gary S; Muir, Richard AD; Parkinson, Simon A; Shanahan, Aaron M

CREWE ALEXANDRA

Name	Ht	Wt	Pos	Date	Birthplace	Source	Club	Apps	Gls
Bignot Marcus#	5 9	11 00	D	28 8 74	Birmingham	Kidderminster H	Crewe Alex	95	—
Charles Anthony	6 0	12 00	D	11 3 81	Isleworth	Brook House	Crewe Alex	—	—
Charnock Phil	5 10	11 03	M	14 2 75	Southport	Trainee	Liverpool	—	—
							Blackpool (loan)	4	—
							Crewe Alex	125	7
Collins James	5 8	10 00	M	28 5 78	Liverpool	Trainee	Crewe Alex	20	1
Cramb Colin	6 0	12 09	F	23 6 74	Lanark	Hamilton A BC	Hamilton A	48	10
							Southampton	1	—
							Falkirk	8	1
							Hearts	6	1
							Doncaster R	62	25
							Bristol C	53	9
							Walsall (loan)	4	4
							Crewe Alex	37	6
Critchley Neil*	5 9	10 05	M	18 10 78	Crewe	Trainee	Crewe Alex	1	—
Foran Mark#	6 3	13 04	D	30 10 73	Aldershot	Trainee	Millwall	—	—
							Sheffield U	11	1
							Rotherham U (loan)	3	—
							Wycombe W (loan)	5	—
							Peterborough U	25	1
							Lincoln C (loan)	2	—
							Oldham Ath (loan)	1	—
							Crewe Alex	31	1

Foster Stephen	5 11	11 00	D	10 9 80	Warrington	Trainee	Crewe Alex	1	—
Grant John	5 11	10 08	F	9 8 81	Manchester	Trainee	Crewe Alex	4	—
Hoult Stephen*			M	17 1 80	Rhyl	Trainee	Crewe Alex	—	—
Hulse Robert	6 1	12 00	F	25 10 79	Crewe	Trainee	Crewe Alex	4	1
Ince Clayton	6 3	13 00	G	13 7 72	Trinidad	Defence Force	Crewe Alex	1	—
Jack Rodney	5 7	10 07	F	28 9 72	Kingston, Jamaica	Lambada	Torquay U	87	24
							Crewe Alex	62	13
Jones Robert‡			M	19 2 81	Chester	School	Crewe Alex	—	—
Kearton Jason	6 1	12 03	G	9 7 69	Ipswich (Aus)	Brisbane Lions	Everton	6	—
							Stoke C (loan)	16	—
							Blackpool (loan)	14	—
							Notts Co (loan)	10	—
							Preston NE (loan)	—	—
							Crewe Alex	165	—
Laurie Carl*			F	3 12 80	Crewe	Trainee	Crewe Alex	—	—
Lightfoot Chris	6 1	12 00	D	1 4 70	Penketh	Trainee	Chester C	277	32
							Wigan Ath	14	1
							Crewe Alex	87	4
Little Colin	5 10	11 00	F	4 11 72	Wythenshaw	Hyde U	Crewe Alex	143	28
Lunt Kenny	5 10	10 00	M	20 11 79	Runcorn	Trainee	Crewe Alex	102	6
Macauley Steve	6 1	12 03	D	4 3 69	Lytham	Fleetwood T	Crewe Alex	222	25
Rivers Mark	5 10	11 00	F	26 11 75	Crewe	Trainee	Crewe Alex	170	36
Smith Peter	5 10	10 00	F	15 9 78	Rhuddlan	Trainee	Crewe Alex	17	—
							Macclesfield T (loan)	12	3
Smith Shaun	5 10	11 00	D	9 4 71	Leeds	Trainee	Halifax T	7	—
							Crewe Alex	315	36
Sorvel Neil	6 0	12 09	M	2 3 73	Widnes	Trainee	Crewe Alex	9	—
							Macclesfield T	86	7
							Crewe Alex	46	6
Street Kevin	5 10	11 00	M	25 11 77	Crewe	Trainee	Crewe Alex	83	7
Tait Paul#	6 1	11 00	F	24 10 74	Newcastle	Trainee	Everton	—	—
							Wigan Ath	5	—
						Northwich Vic	Crewe Alex	33	6
Trainer Phil	6 0	12 00	M	3 7 81	Wolverhampton		Crewe Alex	—	—
Unsworth Lee*	5 11	11 02	D	25 2 73	Eccles	Ashton U	Crewe Alex	126	—
Walker Richard	6 2	13 00	D	17 9 80	Stafford	Trainee	Crewe Alex	—	—
Walton David	6 2	14 07	D	10 4 73	Bellingham	Trainee	Sheffield U	—	—
							Shrewsbury T	128	10
							Crewe Alex	76	1
Welsby Kevin	6 0	10 06	G	27 8 80	Crewe	Trainee	Crewe Alex	—	—
Wright David	5 11	10 09	D	1 5 80	Warrington	Trainee	Crewe Alex	68	1

Scholars
Baylis, Philip; Bell, Lee; Betts, Thomas G; Blake, Mathew L; Bostock, Andrew M; Coverley, Neil; Edwards, Paul; Frost, Carl R; Harris, Paul J; Jeffs, Ian D; Liddle, Gareth JC; Lunt, Gary T; Malpass, John; Marrow, James FJ; Marsh, Nicholas J; McCready, Christopher J; Morris, Alexander, S; Rix, Benjamin; Swiggs, Craig B; Vaughan, David O; Westwood, Lee K; Whiting, Louie A; Wilcock, James W; Yates, Adam P

Non-Contract
Wilson, Nicholas D

Associated Schoolboys
Ashton, Dean; Booth, Martin T; Higdon, Michael; Jenkins, Byron K; Malbon, Craig D; Platt, Matthew; Roberts, Mark A; Robinson, James G

CRYSTAL PALACE

Amsalem David	6 1	12 01	D	4 9 71	Israel		Hapoel Tel Aviv	27	4
(Transferred to Hapoel Haifa, June 1999)							Beitar Jerusalem	85	5
							Crystal Palace	10	—
Austin Dean*	5 11	11 11	D	26 4 70	Hemel Hempstead	St. Albans C	Southend U	96	2
							Tottenham H	124	—
							Crystal Palace	65	3
Boardman Jonathan			M	27 1 81	Reading	Trainee	Crystal Palace	—	—
Carlisle Wayne	6 0	11 06	M	9 9 79	Lisburn	Trainee	Crystal Palace	32	3
Curcic Sasa	5 9	11 00	M	14 2 72	Belgrade		OFK Belgrade	49	5
(Transferred to NY/NJ Metro Stars, June 1999)							Partizan Belgrade	74	16
							Bolton W	28	4
							Aston Villa	29	—
							Crystal Palace	23	5
De Ornelas Fernando	6 0	11 07	M	29 7 76	Caracas	Happy Valley	Crystal Palace	9	—
(Transferred to Zaragoza, December 1999)									
Del Rio Walter	6 0	12 06	D	16 6 76	Buenos Aires	Boca Juniors	Crystal Palace	2	—
Digby Fraser	6 1	12 12	G	23 4 67	Sheffield	Apprentice	Manchester U	—	—
							Oldham Ath (loan)	—	—
							Swindon T (loan)	—	—
							Swindon T	417	—
							Manchester U (loan)	—	—
							Crystal Palace	56	—
Dimond Kristian			M	1 2 83	Cardiff	Trainee	Crystal Palace	—	—
Dsane Roscoe			M	16 10 80	Epsom	Trainee	Crystal Palace	—	—
Evans Stephen	5 11	11 02	M	25 9 80	Caerphilly	Trainee	Crystal Palace	5	—

Player							Club	Apps	Gls
Foster Craig	5 11	12 00	M	15 4 69	Melbourne	Marconi	Portsmouth	16	2
							Crystal Palace	52	3
Fowler Michael			M	22 8 81	Cardiff	Trainee	Crystal Palace	—	
Frampton Andrew	5 11	10 10	D	3 9 79	Wimbledon	Trainee	Crystal Palace	15	—
Fullarton Jamie*	5 9	10 09	M	20 7 74	Bellshill		St Mirren	102	3
							Bastia	17	—
							Crystal Palace	45	1
							Bolton W (loan)	1	—
Gregg Matt	5 11	12 00	G	30 11 78	Cheltenham	Trainee	Torquay U	32	—
							Crystal Palace	6	—
							Swansea C (loan)	5	—
Hankin Sean	5 11	12 04	M	28 2 81	Camberley	Trainee	Crystal Palace	1	—
Harris Richard	5 11	10 09	D	23 10 80	Croydon	Trainee	Crystal Palace	7	—
Hibburt James	6 0	12 08	D	30 10 79	Ashford	Trainee	Crystal Palace	6	—
Howell Richard			M	29 8 82	Hitchin		Crystal Palace	—	—
Hunt Steve	5 9	12 06	M	1 8 81	Laois	Trainee	Crystal Palace	3	—
Jihai Sun	5 10	10 07	D	30 9 77	Dalian	Dalian Wanda	Crystal Palace	23	—
(Transferred to Dalian Wanda, July 1999)									
Kabba Steven	5 10	11 12	D	7 3 81	Lambeth	Trainee	Crystal Palace	1	—
Kendall Lee	5 10	10 05	G	8 1 81	Newport	Trainee	Crystal Palace	—	—
Linighan Andy*	6 4	13 10	D	18 6 62	Hartlepool	Smiths BC	Hartlepool U	110	4
							Leeds U	66	3
							Oldham Ath	87	6
							Norwich C	86	8
							Arsenal	118	5
							Crystal Palace	110	4
							QPR (loan)	7	—
Martin Andrew	6 0	10 12	F	28 2 80	Cardiff	Trainee	Crystal Palace	22	2
McKenzie Leon	5 10	10 03	F	17 5 78	Croydon	Trainee	Crystal Palace	77	7
							Fulham (loan)	3	—
							Peterborough U (loan)	14	8
Morrison Clinton	6 1	11 02	F	14 5 79	Tooting	Trainee	Crystal Palace	67	26
Mullins Hayden	6 0	11 12	M	27 3 79	Reading	Trainee	Crystal Palace	85	15
Ormshaw Gareth‡	6 0	12 10	G	8 7 79	Durban	Ramblers	Crystal Palace	—	—
Petric Gordan	6 1	12 03	D	30 7 69	Belgrade		Dundee U	60	3
							Rangers	65	3
							Crystal Palace	18	1
Rizzo Nicky	5 10	12 00	M	9 6 79	Sydney	Sydney Olympic	Liverpool	—	—
							Crystal Palace	36	1
Rodger Simon	5 9	11 09	M	3 10 71	Shoreham	Trainee	Crystal Palace	207	10
							Manchester C (loan)	8	1
							Stoke C (loan)	5	—
Sharpling Christopher	5 11	11 10	F	21 4 81	Bromley	Trainee	Crystal Palace	6	—
Smith Jamie	5 8	11 02	D	17 9 74	Birmingham	Trainee	Wolverhampton W	87	—
							Crystal Palace	71	—
							Fulham (loan)	9	1
Thomson Steve	5 8	10 04	M	23 1 78	Glasgow	Trainee	Crystal Palace	37	—
Walsh Ronald			M	15 9 82	Glasnevin	Scholar	Crystal Palace	—	—
Woozley David	6 0	12 10	D	6 12 79	Berkshire	Trainee	Crystal Palace	30	—
Zhiyi Fan	6 0	12 01	M	22 1 70	Shanghai	Shanghai Shenhua	Crystal Palace	58	3

Scholars
Amoako, Adolf; Antwee, William; Elsegood, Christopher J; Gooding, Scott O; Hateley, Gary J; Hunt, David; Leacock, Jamie H; Maxwell, Daniel R; Nicholas, Mark P; Smith, Robert; Surey, Ben D; Williams, Gareth A; Williams, Ryan

Non-Contract
Kember, Robert J

DARLINGTON

Player							Club	Apps	Gls
Aspin Neil	6 0	13 00	D	12 4 65	Gateshead	Apprentice	Leeds U	207	5
							Port Vale	348	3
							Darlington	29	—
Atkinson Brian	5 10	12 10	M	19 1 71	Darlington	Trainee	Sunderland	141	4
							Carlisle U (loan)	2	—
							Darlington	135	6
Bennett Gary*	6 2	12 01	D	4 12 61	Manchester	Amateur	Manchester C	—	—
							Cardiff C	87	11
							Sunderland	369	23
							Carlisle U	26	5
							Scarborough	88	18
							Darlington	34	4
Brumwell Phil*	5 8	11 00	M	8 8 75	Darlington	Trainee	Sunderland	—	—
							Darlington	156	1
Campbell Paul	6 1	11 00	M	29 1 80	Middlesbrough	Trainee	Darlington	24	4
Carter Michael*	6 0	11 08	F	13 11 80	Darlington	Trainee	Darlington	1	1
Collett Andy*	6 0	12 10	G	28 10 73	Stockton	Trainee	Middlesbrough	2	—
							Bristol R	107	—
							Darlington	13	—

Name							Club	Apps	Gls
Dorner Mario‡	5 10	13 02	F	21 3 70	Baden	Modling	Motherwell	2	—
							Darlington	49	13
Duffield Peter	5 6	10 04	F	4 2 69	Middlesbrough	Apprentice	Middlesbrough	—	—
							Sheffield U	58	14
							Halifax T (loan)	12	6
							Rotherham U (loan)	17	4
							Blackpool (loan)	5	1
							Bournemouth (loan)	—	—
							Stockport Co (loan)	7	4
							Crewe Alex (loan)	2	—
							Hamilton A	72	39
							Airdrieonians	24	6
							Raith R	42	10
							Darlington	47	14
Gabbiadini Marco	5 10	13 04	F	21 1 68	Nottingham	Apprentice	York C	60	14
							Sunderland	157	74
							Crystal Palace	15	5
							Derby Co	188	50
							Birmingham C (loan)	2	—
							Oxford U (loan)	5	1
							Stoke C	8	—
							York C	7	1
							Darlington	82	47
Gray Martin	5 9	11 05	M	17 8 71	Stockton	Trainee	Sunderland	64	1
							Aldershot (loan)	5	—
							Fulham (loan)	6	—
							Oxford U	121	4
							Darlington	41	—
Heaney Neil	5 11	12 00	M	3 11 71	Middlesbrough	Trainee	Arsenal	7	—
							Hartlepool U (loan)	3	—
							Cambridge U (loan)	13	4
							Southampton	61	5
							Manchester C	18	1
							Charlton Ath (loan)	6	—
							Bristol C (loan)	3	—
							Darlington	36	5
Heckingbottom Paul	6 0	12 03	D	17 7 77	Barnsley	Manchester U	Sunderland	—	—
							Scarborough (loan)	29	—
							Hartlepool U (loan)	5	1
							Darlington (loan)	10	—
							Darlington	45	1
Hickey Ben‡	6 0	12 00	M	11 11 74	Birmingham	New Jersey Imp.	Darlington	—	—
Himsworth Gary	5 8	11 00	M	19 12 69	York	Trainee	York C	88	8
							Scarborough	92	6
							Darlington	94	8
							York C	69	3
							Darlington	33	1
Hjorth Jesper	6 0	12 04	F	3 4 75	Denmark		Odense	61	9
						FC Midtjylland	Darlington	22	6
Holsgrove Paul‡	6 2	13 03	M	26 8 69	Wellington	Trainee	Aldershot	3	—
							Wimbledon (loan)	—	—
							WBA (loan)	—	—
						Wokingham T	Luton T	2	—
						Heracles	Millwall	11	—
							Reading	70	6
							Grimsby T (loan)	10	—
							Crewe Alex	8	1
							Stoke C	12	1
							Brighton & HA	—	—
							Hibernian	18	1
							Brighton & HA	—	—
							Darlington	3	—
Hunt David*	5 10	12 00	D	5 3 80	Durham	Trainee	Darlington	1	—
Keegan Justin*	6 2	12 06	D	9 7 81	Easington Lane	Trainee	Darlington	—	—
Kilty Mark	6 0	12 00	D	24 6 81	Sunderland	Trainee	Darlington	4	—
Leah John*	5 9	12 00	M	3 8 78	Shrewsbury	Newtown	Darlington	—	—
Liddle Craig	5 11	12 07	D	21 10 71	Chester-le-Street	Blyth Spartans	Middlesbrough	25	—
							Darlington (loan)	15	—
							Darlington	89	4
Naylor Glenn*	5 10	11 10	F	11 8 72	York	Trainee	York C	111	30
							Darlington (loan)	4	1
							Darlington	146	31
Nogan Lee	5 10	11 00	F	21 5 69	Cardiff	Apprentice	Oxford U	64	10
							Brentford (loan)	11	2
							Southend U (loan)	6	1
							Watford	105	26
							Southend U (loan)	5	—
							Reading	91	26
							Notts Co (loan)	6	—
							Grimsby T	74	10
							Darlington	31	2
Oliver Michael*	5 10	11 04	M	2 8 75	Middlesbrough	Trainee	Middlesbrough	—	—
							Stockport Co	22	1
							Darlington	151	14
Pepper Carl	5 11	11 00	D	26 7 80	Darlington	Trainee	Darlington	6	—
Preece David	6 2	11 11	G	26 8 76	Sunderland	Trainee	Sunderland	—	—
(Transferred to Aberdeen, July 1999)							Darlington	91	—

Name							Clubs	Apps	Goals
Radigan Neil*	5 10	11 00	M	4 7 80	Middlesbrough	Trainee	Scarborough	9	—
							Darlington	—	—
Reed Adam	6 1	11 00	D	18 2 75	Bishop Auckland	Trainee	Darlington	52	1
							Blackburn R	—	—
							Darlington (loan)	14	—
							Rochdale (loan)	10	—
							Darlington	52	2
Samways Mark*	6 2	14 01	G	11 11 68	Doncaster	Trainee	Doncaster R	121	—
							Scunthorpe U (loan)	8	—
							Scunthorpe U	172	—
							York C (loan)	—	—
							York C	29	—
							Darlington	34	—
Skelton Craig*	5 9	11 11	D	14 9 80	Middlesbrough	Trainee	Darlington	—	—
Tutill Steve	5 10	12 06	D	1 10 69	Derwent	Trainee	York C	301	6
							Darlington	70	—
Wells David	5 9	12 00	D	19 2 81	Stockton	Trainee	Darlington	—	—

Scholars
Birrell, Adam P; Bowes, Michael G; Bromley, Kevin; Ellenden, John; Finch, Keith J; Jackson, Neil P; Jarvis, Marc; Liddle, Graham B; McGuirk, David; Scroggins, Lee P; Sheeran, Mark J; Trainer, Lee GE; Williamson, Garry

Non-Contract
Porter, Christopher I; Walklate, Steven

DERBY COUNTY

Name							Clubs	Apps	Goals
Baiano Francesco	5 6	10 07	F	24 2 68	Naples		Napoli	4	—
(Transferred to Ternana, November 1999)							Empoli	26	2
							Napoli	1	—
							Parma	25	4
							Empoli	38	14
							Avellino	32	6
							Foggia	69	38
							Fiorentina	118	29
							Derby Co	64	16
Beck Mikkel	6 2	12 13	F	4 5 73	Aarhus	Kolding	B 1909	13	2
(On loan to Aalborg)							Fortuna Cologne	79	26
							Middlesbrough	91	24
							Derby Co	18	2
							Nottingham F (loan)	5	1
							QPR (loan)	11	4
Boertien Paul	5 10	11 07	D	21 1 79	Carlisle	Trainee	Carlisle U	17	1
							Derby Co	3	—
							Crewe Alex (loan)	2	—
Bohinen Lars	6 1	12 03	M	8 9 69	Vadso		Valerengen	33	5
							Viking	10	—
							Young Boys	58	6
							Nottingham F	64	7
							Blackburn R	58	7
							Derby Co	54	1
Bolder Adam	5 8	11 05	M	25 10 80	Hull	Trainee	Hull C	20	—
							Derby Co	—	—
Borbokis Vassilis	5 9	12 02	D	10 2 69	Serres		Apollon	29	2
(Transferred to PAOK Salonika, December 1999)							AEK Athens	86	9
							Sheffield U	55	4
							Derby Co	16	—
Bridge-Wilkinson Marc*	5 6	10 08	M	16 3 79	Nuneaton	Trainee	Derby Co	1	—
							Carlisle U (loan)	7	—
Burley Craig	6 2	13 03	M	24 9 71	Ayr	Trainee	Chelsea	113	7
							Celtic	56	19
							Derby Co	18	5
Burton Deon	5 9	12 02	F	25 10 76	Reading	Trainee	Portsmouth	62	10
							Cardiff C (loan)	5	2
							Derby Co	69	16
							Barnsley (loan)	3	—
Carbonari Horace Angel	6 3	14 03	D	2 5 73	Rosario	Rosario Central	Derby Co	58	7
Christie Malcolm	6 0	11 11	F	11 4 79	Peterborough	Nuneaton B	Derby Co	23	5
Delap Rory	6 2	13 00	D	6 7 76	Sutton Coldfield	Trainee	Carlisle U	65	7
							Derby Co	70	8
Doherty Gerard			M	24 8 81	Derry	Derry C	Derby Co	—	—
Dorigo Tony*	5 9	11 03	D	31 12 65	Adelaide	Apprentice	Aston Villa	111	1
							Chelsea	146	11
							Leeds U	171	5
							Torino	30	2
							Derby Co	41	1
Elliott Steve	6 2	14 03	D	29 10 78	Derby	Trainee	Derby Co	34	—
Eranio Stefano	5 10	12 04	M	29 12 68	Genoa		Genoa	213	13
							AC Milan	98	6
							Derby Co	67	5
Evatt Ian			D	19 11 81	Coventry	Trainee	Derby Co	—	—
Fuertes Esteban	6 1	13 12	F	26 12 72	Coronel Dorredo	Colon de Santa Fe	Derby Co	8	1
(On loan to Colon, February 2000)									
Gummer Sean*			M	14 4 81	Derby	Trainee	Derby Co	—	—
Jackson Richard	5 8	10 00	D	18 4 80	Whitby	Trainee	Scarborough	22	—
							Derby Co	2	—

Name	Ht	Wt	Pos	Date of Birth	Birthplace	Source	Clubs	Apps	Gls
Johnson Seth	5 10	11 11	M	12 3 79	Birmingham	Trainee	Crewe Alex	93	6
							Derby Co	36	1
Kinkladze Georgiou	5 8	11 05	M	6 7 73	Tbilisi		Mretebi	80	18
							Dynamo Tbilisi	44	27
							Saarbrucken	11	—
							Dynamo Tbilisi	21	14
							Manchester C	106	20
							Ajax	12	—
							Derby Co	17	1
Knight Richard*	6 1	14 00	G	3 8 79	Burton	Burton Alb	Derby Co	—	—
							Carlisle U (loan)	6	—
							Birmingham C (loan)	—	—
							Hull C (loan)	1	—
							Macclesfield T (loan)	3	—
							Oxford U (loan)	13	—
Laursen Jacob	6 0	12 13	D	6 10 71	Vejle		Vejle	55	1
							Silkeborg	125	8
							Derby Co	137	3
Le Geyt Sinclair*			M	10 7 80	Port Elizabeth		Derby Co	—	—
Lyons Michael*			M	24 7 81	Derby	Trainee	Derby Co	—	—
Morris Lee	5 9	10 12	F	30 4 80	Driffield	Trainee	Sheffield U	26	6
							Derby Co	3	—
Murray Adam	5 8	10 12	M	30 9 81	Birmingham	Trainee	Derby Co	12	—
Nimni Avi‡	6 0	12 07	M	26 4 72	Tel Aviv		Maccabi Tel Aviv	148	55
							Atletico Madrid	7	—
							Maccabi Tel Aviv	24	17
							Derby Co	4	1
Oakes Andy	6 3	10 12	G	11 1 77	Crewe		Bury	—	—
						Winsford U	Hull C	19	—
							Derby Co	—	—
							Port Vale (loan)	—	—
Poom Mart	6 4	13 04	G	3 2 72	Tallinn		Flora Tallinn	22	—
						FC Wil	Portsmouth	4	—
							Flora Tallinn	7	—
							Portsmouth	—	—
							Flora Tallinn	12	—
							Derby Co	85	—
Porter Danny*	5 10	12 00	D	23 1 79	Portsmouth	Portsmouth	Derby Co	—	—
Powell Darryl	6 0	13 01	M	15 11 71	Lambeth	Trainee	Portsmouth	132	16
							Derby Co	157	8
Riggott Chris	6 2	12 05	D	1 9 80	Derby	Trainee	Derby Co	1	—
Robinson Marvin	6 0	12 13	F	11 4 80	Crewe	Trainee	Derby Co	9	—
Schnoor Stefan	6 2	12 11	D	24 4 71	Neumunster		Hamburg	131	8
							Derby Co	52	2
Sidhu Amrit*			F	16 12 81	Coventry	Trainee	Derby Co	—	—
Strupar Branko	6 3	14 00	F	9 2 70	Zagreb	Spansko	Genk	110	61
							Derby Co	15	5
Sturridge Dean	5 8	12 02	F	27 7 73	Birmingham	Trainee	Derby Co	176	52
							Torquay U (loan)	10	5

Scholars
Adams, Wayne A; Brown, Karl E; Canning, Brendan; Cleary, Sean J; Grant, Lee A; Holmes, Gareth P; Hunt, Lewis J; Isik, Adam A; McArdle, Fiachra; McKeown, Gareth D; O'Halloran, Matthew V; Osborne, Jason G; Rickards, Scott; Stapleton-Smith, Matthew K; Tudgay, Marcus

EVERTON

Name	Ht	Wt	Pos	Date of Birth	Birthplace	Source	Clubs	Apps	Gls
Bakayoko Ibrahima	5 11	12 10	F	31 12 76	Seguela	Stade Abidjan	Montpellier	76	24
(Transferred to Marseille, July 1999)							Everton	23	4
Ball Michael	5 10	12 02	D	2 10 79	Liverpool	Trainee	Everton	92	5
Barmby Nick	5 8	11 04	F	11 2 74	Hull	Trainee	Tottenham H	87	20
							Middlesbrough	42	8
							Everton	116	18
Bilic Slaven‡	6 2	14 05	D	11 9 68	Split		Hajduk Split	109	13
							Karlsruhe	54	5
							West Ham U	48	2
							Everton	28	—
Cadamarteri Danny	5 9	12 10	F	12 10 79	Bradford	Trainee	Everton	74	9
							Fulham (loan)	5	1
Campbell Kevin	6 1	13 08	F	4 2 70	Lambeth	Trainee	Arsenal	166	46
							Leyton Orient (loan)	16	9
							Leicester C (loan)	11	5
							Nottingham F	80	32
							Trabzonspor	17	5
							Everton	34	21
Chadwick Nick	6 0	12 04	F	26 10 82	Stoke		Everton	—	—
Clarke Peter	6 0	12 00	D	3 1 82	Southport	Trainee	Everton	—	—
Cleland Alex	5 9	11 07	D	10 12 70	Glasgow		Dundee U	151	8
							Rangers	96	4
							Everton	27	—
Collins John	5 7	10 13	M	30 1 68	Galashiels		Hibernian	163	16
							Celtic	217	47
							Monaco	53	7
							Everton	55	3
Curran Damien	5 9	12 01	M	17 10 81	Antrim	Trainee	Everton	—	—

Player	Ht	Wt	Pos	Born	Birthplace	Source	Club	Apps	Gls
Dacourt Olivier	5 9	11 00	M	25 9 74	Montreuil		Strasbourg	127	4
(Transferred to Lens, June 1999)							Everton	30	2
Degn Peter	5 10	12 06	M	6 4 77	Denmark		Aarhus	76	5
							Everton	4	—
Delany Dean*			G	15 9 80	Dublin		Everton	—	—
Dempsey Gary*			F	15 1 81	Wexford	Trainee	Everton	—	—
Dunne Richard	6 2	14 06	D	21 9 79	Dublin	Trainee	Everton	57	—
Farley Adam*	6 2	10 08	D	12 1 80	Liverpool	Trainee	Everton	1	—
Gemmill Scot	5 9	11 11	M	2 1 71	Paisley	School	Nottingham F	245	21
							Everton	21	2
Gerrard Paul	6 2	14 00	G	22 1 73	Heywood	Trainee	Oldham Ath	119	1
							Everton	43	—
							Oxford U (loan)	16	—
Gough Richard	6 0	12 00	D	5 4 62	Stockholm		Dundee U	165	23
							Tottenham H	49	2
							Rangers	294	25
							Kansas City W	17	—
							Rangers	24	1
							San Jose Clash	19	2
							Nottingham F	7	—
							Everton	29	1
Hibbert Anthony	5 8	11 01	M	20 2 81	Liverpool	Trainee	Everton	—	—
Hogg Craig	6 1	11 12	D	8 10 81	Liverpool	Trainee	Everton	—	—
Howarth Carl*			M	27 9 80	Burnley	Trainee	Everton	—	—
Hughes Mark	5 11	13 00	F	1 11 63	Wrexham	Apprentice	Manchester U	89	37
							Barcelona	28	4
							Bayern Munich (loan)	18	6
							Manchester U	256	82
							Chelsea	95	25
							Southampton	52	2
							Everton	9	1
Hughes Stephen	6 0	12 12	M	18 9 76	Wokingham	Trainee	Arsenal	47	4
							Fulham	3	—
							Arsenal	2	—
							Everton	11	1
Hutchison Don	6 1	12 05	M	9 5 71	Gateshead	Trainee	Hartlepool U	24	2
							Liverpool	45	7
							West Ham U	35	11
							Sheffield U	78	5
							Everton	75	10
Jeffers Francis	5 10	10 05	F	25 1 81	Liverpool	Trainee	Everton	37	12
Jevons Phil	5 10	11 12	F	1 8 79	Liverpool	Trainee	Everton	4	—
Johnson Tommy	5 11	12 07	F	15 1 71	Newcastle	Trainee	Notts Co	118	47
							Derby Co	98	30
							Aston Villa	57	13
							Celtic	19	13
							Everton (loan)	3	—
Kearney Thomas	5 9	10 12	M	7 10 81	Liverpool	Trainee	Everton	—	—
Knowles David*			M	4 8 80	Wrexham	Trainee	Everton	—	—
Lester John	5 11	12 09	M	5 8 82	Dublin	Trainee	Everton	—	—
Materazzi Marco	6 4	14 00	D	19 8 73	Perugia	Tor di Quinto	Messina	—	—
(Transferred to Perugia, July 1999)							Marsala	25	4
							Trapani	13	2
							Perugia	1	—
							Carpi	18	7
							Perugia	46	7
							Everton	27	1
McAlpine Joseph‡			D	12 9 81	Glasgow		Everton	—	—
McKay Matt	6 0	11 05	M	21 1 81	Warrington	Trainee	Chester C	5	—
							Everton	—	—
McLeod Kevin	5 11	11 00	M	12 9 80	Liverpool	Trainee	Everton	—	—
Milligan Jamie	5 7	9 12	M	3 1 80	Blackpool	Trainee	Everton	4	—
Moore Joe-Max	5 8	11 06	F	23 2 71	USA		New England Rev	77	37
							Everton	15	6
Myhre Thomas	6 4	13 12	G	16 10 73	Sarpsborg		Viking	94	—
							Everton	64	—
							Birmingham C (loan)	7	—
O'Hanlon Sean	6 1	12 02	D	2 1 83	Liverpool		Everton	—	—
Osman Leon	5 8	9 11	M	17 5 81	Billinge	Trainee	Everton	—	—
Parkinson Joe‡	6 0	14 06	M	11 6 71	Eccles	Trainee	Wigan Ath	119	6
							Bournemouth	30	1
							Everton	90	3
Pembridge Mark	5 7	11 09	M	29 11 70	Merthyr	Trainee	Luton T	60	6
							Derby Co	110	28
							Sheffield W	93	11
							Benfica	19	1
							Everton	31	2
Penman Craig	5 11	11 06	D	9 9 82	Falkirk	Trainee	Everton	—	—
Pilkington George	5 11	11 00	D	7 11 81	Rugeley	Trainee	Everton	—	—
Price Michael	5 8	11 01	D	29 4 82	Wrexham	Trainee	Everton	—	—
Regan Carl	6 0	11 05	D	9 9 80	Liverpool	Trainee	Everton	—	—
Simonsen Steve	6 3	13 11	G	3 4 79	South Shields	Trainee	Tranmere R	35	—
							Everton	1	—

Southern Keith			M	24 4 81	Gateshead	Trainee	Everton	—	—
Unsworth Dave	6 1	14 09	D	16 10 73	Chorley	Trainee	Everton	116	11
							West Ham U	32	2
							Aston Villa	—	—
							Everton	67	7
Valentine Ryan	5 10	11 07	M	19 8 82	Wrexham	Trainee	Everton	—	—
Ward Mitch	5 8	11 13	D	19 6 71	Sheffield	Trainee	Sheffield U	154	11
							Crewe Alex (loan)	4	1
							Everton	24	—
Watson Dave	6 1	13 10	D	20 11 61	Liverpool	Amateur	Liverpool	—	—
							Norwich C	212	11
							Everton	423	23
Weir David	6 3	13 13	D	10 5 70	Falkirk		Falkirk	133	8
							Hearts	92	8
							Everton	49	2
Williamson Danny	6 0	13 13	M	5 12 73	West Ham	Trainee	West Ham U	51	5
							Doncaster R (loan)	13	1
							Everton	15	—
Wright John*			M	23 10 80	Liverpool	Trainee	Everton	—	—
Xavier Abel	6 2	13 06	M	30 11 72	Mozambique	Amadora	Benfica	46	4
							Bari	8	—
							Oviedo	58	—
							PSV Eindhoven	19	2
							Everton	20	—

Scholars
Eaton, David F; Woodcock, Colin

EXETER CITY

Blake Noel#	6 2	14 05	D	12 1 62	Kingston, Jamaica	Sutton Coldfield T	Aston Villa	4	—
							Shrewsbury T (loan)	6	—
							Birmingham C	76	5
							Portsmouth	144	10
							Leeds U	51	4
							Stoke C	75	3
							Bradford C (loan)	6	—
							Bradford C	39	3
							Dundee	54	2
							Exeter C	142	10
Boylan Lee‡	5 6	11 06	F	2 9 78	Witham	Trainee	West Ham U	1	—
							Trelleborg	5	—
							Exeter C	6	1
Breslan Geoff	5 9	10 05	M	4 6 80	Torbay	Trainee	Exeter C	64	4
Buckle Paul	5 8	11 08	M	16 12 70	Welwyn	Trainee	Brentford	57	1
							Torquay U	59	9
							Exeter C	22	2
							Northampton T	—	—
							Wycombe W	—	—
							Colchester U	105	7
							Exeter C	27	1
Cornforth John	5 11	14 06	M	7 10 67	Whitley Bay	Apprentice	Sunderland	32	2
							Doncaster R (loan)	7	3
							Shrewsbury T (loan)	3	—
							Lincoln C (loan)	9	1
							Swansea C	149	16
							Birmingham C	8	—
							Wycombe W	47	6
							Peterborough U (loan)	4	—
							Cardiff C	10	1
							Scunthorpe U	4	1
							Exeter C	12	2
Curran Chris	5 11	12 12	D	17 9 71	Birmingham	Trainee	Torquay U	152	4
							Plymouth Arg	30	—
							Exeter C	81	5
Dewhurst Rob*	6 3	14 07	D	10 9 71	Keighley	Trainee	Blackburn R	13	—
							Darlington (loan)	11	1
							Huddersfield T (loan)	7	—
							Hull C	138	13
							Exeter C	23	2
Ellington Lee‡	5 10	11 07	F	3 7 80	Bradford	Trainee	Hull C	15	2
							Exeter C	1	—
Flack Steve	6 1	14 07	F	29 5 71	Cambridge	Cambridge C	Cardiff C	11	1
							Exeter C	152	31
Fox Peter‡	5 11	13 10	G	5 7 57	Scunthorpe	Apprentice	Sheffield W	49	—
							West Ham U (loan)	—	—
							Barnsley (loan)	1	—
							Stoke C	409	—
							Wrexham (loan)	—	—
							Exeter C	108	—
Gale Shaun*	6 1	12 00	D	8 10 69	Reading	Trainee	Portsmouth	3	—
							Barnet	114	5
							Exeter C	93	5

Gittens Jon*	5 11	13 04	D	22 1 64	Moseley	Paget R	Southampton	18	—
							Swindon T	126	6
							Southampton	19	—
							Middlesbrough (loan)	12	1
							Middlesbrough	13	—
							Portsmouth	83	2
							Torquay U	78	9
							Exeter C	82	4
Holloway Chris	5 10	11 10	M	5 2 80	Swansea	Trainee	Exeter C	64	2
Jarman Lee‡	6 3	14 01	D	16 12 77	Cardiff	Trainee	Cardiff C	94	1
						Merthyr T	Exeter C	7	—
Matthews Jason*	6 0	12 02	G	13 3 75	Paulton	Nuneaton Borough	Exeter C	12	—
McConnell Barry*	5 11	10 10	F	1 1 77	Exeter	Trainee	Exeter C	105	12
Naylor Stuart*	6 4	13 12	G	6 12 62	Wetherby	Yorkshire Amat	Lincoln C	49	—
							Peterborough U (loan)	8	—
							Crewe Alex (loan)	38	—
							Crewe Alex (loan)	17	—
							WBA	355	—
							Bristol C	37	—
							Mansfield T (loan)	6	—
							Walsall	—	—
							Exeter C	31	—
Nyamah Kofi*	5 10	11 09	M	20 6 75	Islington	Trainee	Cambridge U	23	2
						Kettering T	Stoke C	17	—
							Luton T	—	—
							Cambridge U	—	—
							Exeter C	35	1
Potter Danny*	5 11	13 07	G	18 3 79	Ipswich	Chelsea	Colchester U	—	—
							Exeter C	9	—
Power Graeme	5 11	11 07	D	7 3 77	Northwick Park	Trainee	QPR	—	—
							Bristol R	26	—
							Exeter C	69	—
Rees Jason*	5 5	10 05	M	22 12 69	Aberdare	Trainee	Luton T	82	—
							Mansfield T (loan)	15	1
							Portsmouth	43	3
							Exeter C (loan)	7	—
							Cambridge U	20	—
							Exeter C	87	5
Richardson Jon	6 1	12 02	D	29 8 75	Nottingham	Trainee	Exeter C	247	8
Rowbotham Darren*	5 10	12 12	F	22 10 66	Cardiff	Trainee	Plymouth Arg	46	2
							Exeter C	118	47
							Torquay U	14	3
							Birmingham C	36	6
							Hereford U (loan)	8	2
							Mansfield T (loan)	4	—
							Crewe Alex	61	21
							Shrewsbury T	40	9
							Exeter C	118	37
							Leyton Orient (loan)	6	—
Smith Peter	5 10	11 00	M	31 10 80	Skelmersdale	Trainee	Exeter C	8	—
Speakman Robert	5 10	11 07	F	5 12 80	Swansea	Trainee	Exeter C	18	3
Vanninen Jukka	5 7	12 01	M	31 1 77	Riihimaki	Rops	Exeter C	5	—
Waugh Warren*	6 0	13 07	F	9 10 80	Harlesden	Trainee	Exeter C	10	—
Wilkinson John	5 9	10 06	M	24 8 79	Exeter	Trainee	Exeter C	19	2

Trainees
Casey, Emmett R; Cooper, Michael EC; Cronin, Glenn; Gross, Marcus J; Hallam, Robin S; Hensor, Stephen J; Jee, Russell; Kent, Stephen; Mudge, James RM; Pointing, Neil T; Price, Oliver

Associated Schoolboys
Hunt, Ben S

FULHAM

Ball Kevin	5 10	12 04	M	12 11 64	Hastings	Apprentice	Portsmouth	105	4
							Sunderland	339	21
							Fulham	18	—
Betsy Kevin	6 0	12 02	F	20 3 78	Seychelles	Woking	Fulham	9	1
							Bournemouth (loan)	5	—
							Hull C (loan)	2	—
Bracewell Paul	5 9	12 03	M	19 7 62	Heswall	Apprentice	Stoke C	129	5
							Sunderland	38	4
							Everton	95	7
							Sunderland	113	2
							Newcastle U	73	3
							Sunderland	77	—
							Fulham	62	1
Brevett Rufus	5 8	11 09	D	24 9 69	Derby	Trainee	Doncaster R	109	3
							QPR	152	1
							Fulham	79	1
Brooker Paul	5 8	10 01	F	25 11 76	Hammersmith	Trainee	Fulham	56	4
							Brighton & HA (loan)	15	2
Clark Lee	5 8	11 08	M	27 10 72	Wallsend	Trainee	Newcastle U	195	23
							Sunderland	73	16
							Fulham	42	8

Name					Birthplace	Source	Club	Apps	Gls
Coleman Chris	6 2	15 00	D	10 6 70	Swansea	Apprentice	Swansea C	160	2
							Crystal Palace	154	13
							Blackburn R	28	—
							Fulham	111	8
Collins Wayne	5 10	12 01	M	4 3 69	Manchester	Winsford U	Crewe Alex	117	14
							Sheffield W	31	6
							Fulham	53	4
Cornwall Luke	5 10	11 00	F	23 7 80	Lambeth	Trainee	Fulham	4	1
Davis Sean	5 11	12 07	M	20 9 79	Clapham	Trainee	Fulham	33	—
Finnan Steve	6 0	12 04	D	20 4 76	Limerick	Welling U	Birmingham C	15	1
							Notts Co (loan)	17	2
							Notts Co	80	5
							Fulham	57	4
Goldbaek Bjarne	5 9	12 08	M	6 10 68	Denmark		Kaiserslautern	55	7
							Tennis Borussia	24	5
							Cologne	30	2
							FC Copenhagen	74	16
							Chelsea	29	5
							Fulham	18	3
Hahnemann Marcus	6 3	16 02	G	15 6 72	Seattle		Colorado Rapids	66	—
							Fulham	—	—
Hammond Elvis	5 10	10 09	F	6 10 80	Accra	Trainee	Fulham	—	—
Hayles Barry	5 9	13 02	F	17 4 72	London	Stevenage Bor	Bristol R	62	32
							Fulham	65	13
Hayward Steve	5 11	13 00	M	8 9 71	Walsall	Trainee	Derby Co	26	1
							Carlisle U	90	13
							Fulham	114	7
Horsfield Geoff	6 1	13 07	F	1 11 73	Barnsley		Scarborough	12	1
						Witton Alb	Halifax T	10	7
							Fulham	59	22
Hudson Mark	6 1	12 01	D	30 3 82	Guildford	Trainee	Fulham	—	—
Hutchinson Tom	6 0	11 03	D	23 2 82	Hammersmith		Fulham	—	—
Keevill Sam	5 8	10 01	M	8 5 81	Lewisham	Trainee	Fulham	—	—
Knight Zatyiah	6 6	13 08	D	2 5 80	Solihull		Fulham	—	—
							Peterborough U (loan)	8	—
Lewis Eddie	5 9	11 12	M	17 5 74	California		San Jose Clash	115	9
							Fulham	8	—
Marshall John‡	5 10	12 04	D	18 8 64	Surrey	Apprentice	Fulham	411	28
McAnespie Steve*	5 9	10 09	D	1 2 72	Kilmarnock	Vasterhauringe	Raith R	40	—
							Bolton W	24	—
							Fulham	7	—
							Bradford C (loan)	7	—
McGuckin Ian*	6 2	14 01	D	24 4 73	Middlesbrough	Trainee	Hartlepool U	152	8
							Fulham	—	—
							Hartlepool U (loan)	8	—
Melville Andy	6 0	13 02	D	29 11 68	Swansea	School	Swansea C	175	22
							Oxford U	135	13
							Sunderland	204	14
							Bradford C (loan)	6	1
							Fulham	40	3
Morgan Simon	5 11	12 05	D	5 9 66	Birmingham	Trainee	Leicester C	160	3
							Fulham	352	48
Neilson Alan	5 11	12 06	D	26 9 72	Wegburg	Trainee	Newcastle U	42	1
							Southampton	55	—
							Fulham	26	2
Peschisolido Paul	5 7	10 09	F	25 5 71	Canada	Toronto Blizzard	Birmingham C	43	16
							Stoke C	66	19
							Birmingham C	9	1
							WBA	45	18
							Fulham	95	24
Phelan Terry	5 6	10 06	D	16 3 67	Manchester	Trainee	Leeds U	14	—
							Swansea C	45	—
							Wimbledon	159	1
							Manchester C	103	1
							Chelsea	15	—
							Everton	25	—
							Crystal Palace (loan)	14	—
							Fulham	17	2
Riedle Karlheinz	5 11	11 07	F	16 9 65	Weiler	Augsburg	Blau-Weiss 90	34	10
							Werder Bremen	86	38
							Lazio	84	30
							Borussia Dortmund	87	24
							Liverpool	60	11
							Fulham	21	5
Selley Ian*	5 10	10 09	M	14 6 74	Chertsey	Trainee	Arsenal	41	—
							Southend U (loan)	4	—
							Fulham	3	—
Symons Kit	6 3	13 00	D	8 3 71	Basingstoke	Trainee	Portsmouth	161	10
							Manchester C	124	4
							Fulham	74	13
Taylor Maik	6 3	14 02	G	4 9 71	Hildeshein	Farnborough T	Barnet	70	—
							Southampton	18	—
							Fulham	120	—

Thompson Glyn	6 3	11 03	G	24 2 81	Shrewsbury	Trainee	Shrewsbury T	1	—
							Fulham	—	—
							Mansfield T (loan)	16	—
Trollope Paul	5 11	11 04	M	3 6 72	Swindon	Trainee	Swindon T	—	—
							Torquay U (loan)	10	—
							Torquay U	96	16
							Derby Co	65	5
							Grimsby T (loan)	7	1
							Crystal Palace (loan)	9	—
							Fulham	66	5
Tucker Anthony	5 11	11 04	G	12 10 81	Barking	Trainee	Fulham	—	—
Uhlenbeek Gus*	5 9	12 05	D	20 8 70	Paramaribo		Ajax	2	—
							Cambuur	39	—
							TOPS SV	22	3
							Ipswich T	89	4
							Fulham	39	1

Scholars

Browning, Robert; Clark, Darren; Howard, Antony D; Hunter, Jermaine A; Johnson, Michael; Lampton, Neil J; McCracken, Gary W; Pomroy, John S; Read, Paul; Upsher, Tom P; Wilson, Justin F; Yhdego, Esayes Y

GILLINGHAM

Asaba Carl	6 2	13 00	F	28 1 73	London	Dulwich Hamlet	Brentford	54	25
							Colchester U (loan)	12	2
							Reading	33	8
							Gillingham	52	26
Ashby Barry	6 2	13 08	D	2 11 70	London	Trainee	Watford	114	3
							Brentford	121	4
							Gillingham	122	4
Bartram Vince	6 2	13 04	G	8 8 68	Birmingham	Local	Wolverhampton W	5	—
							Blackpool (loan)	9	—
							WBA (loan)	—	—
							Bournemouth	132	—
							Arsenal	11	—
							Wolverhampton W (loan)	—	—
							Huddersfield T (loan)	12	—
							Gillingham	96	—
Browning Marcus	6 0	12 10	M	22 4 71	Bristol	Trainee	Bristol R	174	13
							Hereford U (loan)	7	5
							Huddersfield T	33	—
							Gillingham	5	—
Bryant Matthew	6 1	13 01	D	21 9 70	Bristol	Trainee	Bristol C	203	7
							Walsall (loan)	13	—
							Gillingham	103	—
Butler Steve	6 1	12 02	F	21 1 62	Birmingham	Wokingham T	Brentford	21	3
						Maidstone U	Maidstone U	76	41
							Watford	62	9
							Bournemouth (loan)	1	—
							Cambridge U	109	51
							Gillingham	108	20
							Peterborough U	14	2
							Gillingham	10	2
Butters Guy	6 3	13 12	D	30 10 69	Hillingdon	Trainee	Tottenham H	35	1
							Southend U (loan)	16	3
							Portsmouth	154	6
							Oxford U (loan)	3	1
							Gillingham	124	12
Edge Roland	5 10	11 10	D	25 11 78	Gillingham	Trainee	Gillingham	34	1
Gooden Ty	5 8	12 06	M	23 10 72	Canvey Island	Wycombe W	Swindon T	146	9
							Gillingham	16	4
Hessenthaler Andy	5 7	11 05	M	17 6 65	Gravesend	Redbridge Forest	Watford	195	11
							Gillingham	161	14
Lee Christian	6 2	11 07	F	8 10 76	Aylesbury	Doncaster R	Northampton T	59	8
							Gillingham	3	—
Lee David*	6 3	14 10	D	26 11 69	Kingswood	Trainee	Chelsea	151	11
							Reading (loan)	5	5
							Plymouth Arg (loan)	9	1
							Portsmouth (loan)	5	—
							Sheffield U (loan)	5	—
							Bristol R	11	1
							Colchester U	—	—
							Exeter C	4	—
							Gillingham	—	—
Lewis Junior	6 2	11 08	F	9 10 73	Wembley	Trainee	Fulham	6	—
						Hendon	Gillingham	42	6
Mautone Steve‡	6 2	13 02	G	10 8 70	Myrtleford	Canberra Cosmos	West Ham U	1	—
							Crewe Alex (loan)	3	—
							Reading	29	—
							Wolverhampton W	—	—
							Crystal Palace	2	—
							Gillingham	1	—
McGlinchey Brian	5 8	10 05	D	26 10 77	Derry	Trainee	Manchester C	—	—
							Port Vale	15	1
							Gillingham	13	1

Miller Barry	6 0	11 07	D	29 3 76	Greenford Ealing		Gillingham	4	—
Mitten Charlie	6 2	12 07	G	9 10 74	Woolwich	Dover Ath	Gillingham	—	—
Nosworthy Nayron	6 1	12 07	M	11 10 80	London	Trainee	Gillingham	32	1
Onuora Iffy	6 1	13 10	F	28 7 67	Glasgow	British Univ	Huddersfield T	165	30
							Mansfield T	28	8
							Gillingham	62	23
							Swindon T	73	25
							Gillingham	22	6
Patterson Mark	5 9	12 04	D	13 9 68	Leeds	Trainee	Carlisle U	22	—
							Derby Co	51	3
							Plymouth Arg	134	3
							Gillingham	74	2
Pennock Adrian	6 1	13 05	M	27 3 71	Ipswich	Trainee	Norwich C	1	—
							Bournemouth	131	9
							Gillingham	120	2
Pinnock James	5 9	11 05	F	1 8 78	Dartford	Trainee	Gillingham	9	—
Rowe Rodney	5 8	12 08	F	30 7 75	Plymouth	Trainee	Huddersfield T	34	2
							Scarborough (loan)	14	1
							Bury (loan)	3	—
							York C	97	20
							Halifax T (loan)	9	2
							Gillingham	22	4
Saunders Mark	5 11	11 12	M	23 7 71	Reading	Tiverton	Plymouth Arg	72	11
							Gillingham	60	5
Smith Paul	5 11	12 08	M	18 9 71	East Ham	Trainee	Southend U	20	1
							Brentford	159	11
							Gillingham	135	10
Southall Nicky	5 10	12 12	M	28 1 72	Middlesbrough	Trainee	Hartlepool U	138	24
							Grimsby T	72	5
							Gillingham	110	15
Statham Brian‡	5 7	11 06	D	21 5 69	Zimbabwe	Apprentice	Tottenham H	24	—
							Reading (loan)	8	—
							Bournemouth (loan)	2	—
							Brentford (loan)	18	—
							Brentford	148	1
							Gillingham	20	—
Thomson Andy	5 10	11 05	F	1 4 71	Motherwell	Jerviston BC	Q of S	175	93
							Southend U	122	28
							Oxford U	38	7
							Gillingham	28	9

Trainees
Austin, Simon; Chamberlain, Dean; Collis, Adam M; Cornwall, Joseph M; Hafner, Stephen; Lovell, Mark; Morris, Dean; Neal, Jon; Phillips, Michael E; Rose, Richard A; Spiller, Daniel; Watts, Luke; White, Ben; White, Liam JC

GRIMSBY TOWN

Allen Bradley	5 8	11 00	F	13 9 71	Harold Wood	School	QPR	81	27
							Charlton Ath	40	9
							Colchester U (loan)	4	1
							Grimsby T	31	8
Ashcroft Lee	5 9	12 07	F	7 9 72	Preston	Trainee	Preston NE	91	13
							WBA	90	17
							Notts Co (loan)	6	—
							Preston NE	64	22
							Grimsby T	61	15
Black Kingsley*	5 10	12 00	M	22 6 68	Luton	School	Luton T	127	26
							Nottingham F	98	14
							Sheffield U (loan)	11	2
							Millwall (loan)	3	1
							Grimsby T	136	8
Bloomer Matthew	6 0	11 08	D	3 11 78	Cleethorpes	Trainee	Grimsby T	6	—
Buckley Adam	5 9	11 07	M	2 8 79	Nottingham	WBA	Grimsby T	15	—
Burnett Wayne#	5 11	12 07	M	4 9 71	Lambeth	Trainee	Leyton Orient	40	—
							Blackburn R	—	—
							Plymouth Arg	70	3
							Bolton W	2	—
							Huddersfield T	50	—
							Grimsby T	51	3
Butterfield Danny	5 10	11 06	D	21 11 79	Boston	Trainee	Grimsby T	48	—
Chapman Ben	5 6	11 05	D	2 3 79	Scunthorpe	Trainee	Grimsby T	2	—
Clare Daryl	5 9	12 05	F	1 8 78	Jersey	Trainee	Grimsby T	62	9
							Northampton T (loan)	10	3
Coldicott Stacy	5 8	12 08	M	29 4 74	Worcester	Trainee	WBA	104	3
							Cardiff C (loan)	6	—
							Grimsby T	81	2
Coyne Danny	6 0	13 04	G	27 8 73	Prestatyn	Trainee	Tranmere R	111	—
							Grimsby T	44	—
Crossley Gerard‡			M	5 2 80	Belfast		Grimsby T	—	—
Croudson Steve	6 0	11 12	G	14 9 79	Grimsby	Trainee	Grimsby T	5	—

Donovan Kevin	5 8	11 13	F	17 12 71	Halifax	Trainee	Huddersfield T	20	1
							Halifax T (loan)	6	—
							WBA	168	19
							Grimsby T	115	19
Gallimore Tony	5 11	13 04	D	21 2 72	Crewe	Trainee	Stoke C	11	—
							Carlisle U (loan)	16	—
							Carlisle U (loan)	8	1
							Carlisle U	116	8
							Grimsby T	169	4
Goodhand Paul‡	5 10	11 04	M	14 12 80	Cleethorpes		Grimsby T	—	—
Groves Paul	5 11	13 04	M	28 2 66	Derby	Burton Alb	Leicester C	16	1
							Lincoln C (loan)	8	1
							Blackpool	107	21
							Grimsby T	184	38
							WBA	29	4
							Grimsby T	135	24
Handyside Peter	6 1	13 07	D	31 7 74	Dumfries	Trainee	Grimsby T	171	3
Lever Mark#	6 3	14 03	D	29 3 70	Hull	Trainee	Grimsby T	361	8
Livingstone Steve	6 1	15 03	F	8 9 68	Middlesbrough	Trainee	Coventry C	31	5
							Blackburn R	30	10
							Chelsea	1	—
							Port Vale (loan)	5	—
							Grimsby T	224	33
Love Andrew‡	6 1	14 08	G	28 3 79	Grimsby	Trainee	Grimsby T	12	—
McDermott John	5 7	10 13	D	3 2 69	Middlesbrough	Trainee	Grimsby T	437	7
McKenzie Matt‡	6 1	12 12	D	3 4 79	Nottingham	Dunkerque	Grimsby T	—	—
Oswin Matthew*	5 9	11 11	M	2 10 79	Grimsby	Trainee	Grimsby T	—	—
Pouton Alan	6 0	12 10	M	1 2 77	Newcastle	Newcastle U	Oxford U	—	—
							York C	90	7
							Grimsby T	35	1
Rowan Jonathan	5 10	11 00	M	29 11 81	Grimsby	Trainee	Grimsby T	—	—
Smith David	5 7	11 11	M	29 5 68	Gloucester	Apprentice	Coventry C	154	19
							Bournemouth (loan)	1	—
							Birmingham C	38	3
							WBA	102	2
							Grimsby T	84	7
Smith Richard	6 0	13 11	D	3 10 70	Leicester	Trainee	Leicester C	98	1
							Cambridge U (loan)	4	—
							Grimsby T	81	—

Trainees
Chapman, Benjamin CR; Cocksworth, Matthew R; Darby, Stuart; McPherson, Lee; Partner, Dean R; Pritchard, Gareth J; Rowan, Jonathan R; Thompson, Mark S

Scholars
Butterwood, Michael S; Gibson, Thomas W; Moran, Gary; Pounder, Andrew; Shinn, Adam P; Smithson, Luke R; White, Russell

Non-Contract
Smith, Andrew A

HALIFAX TOWN

Ayscough Martin‡			M	26 2 81	Halifax	Trainee	Halifax T	—	—
Bradshaw Mark#	5 10	11 00	D	7 9 69	Ashton-under-Lyne		Blackpool	42	1
							York C (loan)	1	—
						Macclesfield T	Halifax T	66	5
Butler Lee	6 1	13 08	G	30 5 66	Sheffield	Haworth Colliery	Lincoln C	30	—
							Aston Villa	8	—
							Hull C (loan)	4	—
							Barnsley	120	—
							Scunthorpe U (loan)	2	—
							Wigan Ath	63	—
							Dunfermline Ath	35	—
							Halifax T	38	—
Butler Peter	5 9	11 01	M	27 8 66	Halifax	Apprentice	Huddersfield T	5	—
							Cambridge U (loan)	14	1
							Bury	11	—
							Cambridge U	55	9
							Southend U	142	9
							Huddersfield T (loan)	7	—
							West Ham U	70	3
							Notts Co	20	—
							Grimsby T (loan)	3	—
							WBA (loan)	9	—
							WBA	51	—
							Halifax T	63	1
Clarke Chris	6 3	12 02	D	18 12 80	Leeds	Wolverhampton W	Halifax T	1	—
Clarke Matthew	6 3	13 00	F	18 12 80	Leeds	Wolverhampton W	Halifax T	19	—
Fitzpatrick Ian	5 9	10 00	F	22 9 80	Manchester	Trainee	Manchester U	—	—
							Halifax T	8	—
Gaughan Steve	5 11	11 08	M	14 4 70	Doncaster	Hatfield Main	Doncaster R	67	3
							Sunderland		
							Darlington	171	15
							Chesterfield	20	—
							Darlington	47	3
							Halifax T	38	—
Herbert Robert§	5 10	11 00	M	29 8 83	Durham	Scholar	Halifax T	4	—

Player	Ht	Wt	Pos	DOB	Birthplace	From	Club	Apps	Gls
Holt Grant	6 0	12 06	M	12 4 81	Carlisle	Workington	Halifax T	4	—
Jackson Justin‡	5 11	11 06	F	10 12 74	Nottingham	Woking	Notts Co	25	1
							Rotherham U (loan)	2	1
							Halifax T	17	3
Jules Mark	5 7	10 09	D	5 9 71	Bradford	Trainee	Bradford C	—	—
							Scarborough	77	16
							Chesterfield	186	4
							Halifax T	42	—
Kerrigan Steve	6 1	12 04	F	9 10 72	Bailleston	Newmains J	Albion R	53	14
							Clydebank	30	—
							Stranraer	21	5
							Ayr U	33	17
							Shrewsbury T	76	15
							Halifax T	7	3
Lucas Richard*	5 10	12 06	M	22 9 70	Chapeltown	Trainee	Sheffield U	10	—
							Preston NE	50	—
							Lincoln C (loan)	4	—
							Scarborough	116	—
							Hartlepool U	49	2
							Halifax T	48	—
Middleton Craig	5 11	12 00	M	10 9 70	Nuneaton	Trainee	Coventry C	3	—
							Cambridge U	59	10
							Cardiff C	119	8
							Plymouth Arg (loan)	6	2
							Halifax T	10	1
Mitchell Graham	6 1	13 01	D	16 2 68	Shipley	Apprentice	Huddersfield T	244	2
							Bournemouth (loan)	4	—
							Bradford C	65	1
							Raith R	23	—
							Cardiff C	46	—
							Halifax T	45	2
Murphy Jamie‡	6 1	13 00	D	25 2 73	Manchester	Trainee	Blackpool	55	1
							Doncaster R	54	—
							Cambridge U	—	—
							Halifax T	23	1
Murphy Stephen*	5 11	11 06	M	5 4 78	Dublin	Belvedere	Huddersfield T	—	—
							Halifax T	27	1
Newton Chris*	6 0	11 02	M	5 11 79	Leeds	Huddersfield T	Halifax T	22	1
O'Regan Kieran‡	5 8	10 12	M	9 11 63	Cork		Brighton & HA	86	2
							Swindon T	26	1
							Huddersfield T	199	25
							WBA	25	2
							Halifax T	19	2
Ord Michael	6 1	11 06	M	22 5 81	Huddersfield	Ripon C	Halifax T	—	—
Painter Robbie	5 10	12 02	F	26 1 71	Ince	Trainee	Chester C	84	8
							Maidstone U	30	5
							Burnley	26	2
							Darlington	115	28
							Rochdale	112	30
							Halifax T	42	8
Parks Tony#	5 10	11 05	G	28 1 63	Hackney	Apprentice	Tottenham H	37	—
							Oxford U (loan)	5	—
							Gillingham (loan)	2	—
							Brentford	71	—
							QPR (loan)	—	—
							Fulham	2	—
							West Ham U	6	—
							Stoke C	2	—
							Falkirk	112	—
							Blackpool	—	—
							Burnley	—	—
							Doncaster R (loan)	6	—
						Barrow	Scarborough	15	—
							Halifax T	1	—
Paterson Jamie#	5 3	10 02	M	26 4 73	Dumfries	Trainee	Halifax T	86	18
							Falkirk	4	—
							Scunthorpe U	55	2
							Halifax T	64	17
Potter Lee	5 11	12 10	F	3 9 78	Salford	Trainee	Bolton W	—	—
							Halifax T	19	2
Power Lee‡	6 0	12 08	F	30 6 72	Lewisham	Trainee	Norwich C	44	10
							Charlton Ath (loan)	5	—
							Sunderland (loan)	3	—
							Portsmouth (loan)	2	—
							Bradford C	30	5
							Millwall (loan)	—	—
							Peterborough U	38	6
							Hibernian	11	2
							Plymouth Arg	16	—
							Halifax T	25	5
Reilly Alan	5 11	12 01	M	22 8 80	Dublin	Trainee	Manchester C	—	—
							Halifax T	20	—
Richards Ian	5 8	11 04	M	5 10 79	Barnsley	Trainee	Blackburn R	—	—
							Halifax T	6	—
Russell Matt‡	5 11	12 00	D	17 1 78	Dewsbury	Trainee	Scarborough	44	3
							Doncaster R (loan)	5	—
							Halifax T	7	—
Stansfield James	6 1	13 04	D	18 9 78	Dewsbury	Trainee	Huddersfield T	—	—
							Halifax T	24	1

Stoneman Paul	6 0	13 06	D	26 2 73	Whitley Bay		Blackpool	43	—
							Colchester U (loan)	3	1
							Halifax T	77	9
Tate Chris‡	6 0	12 03	F	27 12 77	York	York C	Sunderland	—	—
							Scarborough	49	13
							Halifax T	18	4
Wilder Chris#	5 11	12 07	D	23 9 67	Stocksbridge	Apprentice	Southampton	—	—
							Sheffield U	93	1
							Walsall (loan)	4	—
							Charlton Ath (loan)	1	—
							Charlton Ath (loan)	2	—
							Leyton Orient (loan)	16	1
							Rotherham U	132	11
							Notts Co	46	—
							Bradford C	42	—
							Sheffield U	12	—
							Northampton T (loan)	1	—
							Lincoln C (loan)	3	—
							Brighton & HA	11	—
							Halifax T	31	1
Williams Michael‡	5 10	12 00	M	21 11 69	Bradford	Maltby MW	Sheffield W	23	1
							Halifax T (loan)	9	1
							Huddersfield T (loan)	2	—
							Peterborough U (loan)	6	—
							Burnley	16	1
							Oxford U	2	—
							Halifax T	3	—
Wills David*	5 5	9 04	D	9 3 79	Ashton	Trainee	Manchester C	—	—
							Halifax T	—	—

Scholars
Boulton, Matthew J; Dunnan, Ryan P; Herbert, Robert; Lawler, Alex; Liversidge, Gareth J; Moores, Andrew M; Myers, Peter W; Sarbaz-Rezai, Carl; Speight, Simon; Tyrell-Nestor, James A; Underwood, Steven; Winder, Nathan J

HARTLEPOOL UNITED

Arnison Paul	5 10	11 08	D	18 9 77	Hartlepool	Trainee	Newcastle U	—	—
							Hartlepool U	8	1
Barron Micky	5 11	11 11	D	22 12 74	Lumley	Trainee	Middlesbrough	3	—
							Hartlepool U (loan)	16	—
							Hartlepool U	111	1
Boyd Adam	5 9	10 12	F	25 5 82	Hartlepool	Scholar	Hartlepool U	4	1
Briggs John‡	5 11	10 10	M	9 11 79	Stockton	Trainee	Hartlepool U	—	—
Clark Ian#	5 10	11 04	F	23 10 74	Stockton	Stockton	Doncaster R	45	3
							Hartlepool U	107	15
Cooper Paul‡	5 9	11 06	M	8 10 80	Easington	Trainee	Hartlepool U	—	—
Di Lella Gus‡	5 9	11 11	M	6 10 73	Buenos Aires		Darlington	5	—
						Blyth S	Hartlepool U	31	4
Dibble Andy*	6 2	16 07	G	8 5 65	Cwmbran	Apprentice	Cardiff C	62	—
							Luton T	30	—
							Sunderland (loan)	12	—
							Huddersfield T (loan)	5	—
							Manchester C	115	—
							Aberdeen (loan)	5	—
							Middlesbrough (loan)	19	—
							Bolton W (loan)	13	—
							WBA (loan)	9	—
							Oldham Ath (loan)	—	—
							Rangers	7	—
							Luton T	1	—
							Middlesbrough	2	—
						Altrincham	Hartlepool U	6	—
							Carlisle U (loan)	2	—
Downey Gareth*	6 1	13 11	G	8 2 81	Sunderland	Trainee	Hartlepool U	—	—
Downey Glen‡	6 1	13 00	D	20 9 78	Newcastle		Hartlepool U	—	—
Dunwell Micky*	5 11	12 11	F	6 1 80	Stockton	Trainee	Hartlepool U	1	—
Evans Nicky‡	5 8	12 05	M	12 5 80	Carmarthen	Trainee	Hartlepool U	1	—
Fitzpatrick Lee	5 10	11 02	M	31 10 78	Manchester	Trainee	Blackburn R	—	—
							Hartlepool U	24	2
Forster Richard*	5 11	12 09	D	16 8 81	Easington	Trainee	Hartlepool U	—	—
Freestone Chris	5 11	12 05	F	4 9 71	Nottingham	Arnold T	Middlesbrough	9	1
							Carlisle U (loan)	5	2
							Northampton T	57	13
							Hartlepool U	37	7
							Cheltenham T (loan)	5	2
Hay Andy*	5 11	12 04	F	20 10 80	Stockton	Trainee	Hartlepool U	—	—
Henderson Kevin	5 11	13 04	F	8 6 74	Ashington	Morpeth T	Burnley	14	1
							Hartlepool U	35	8
Hollund Martin	6 2	12 09	G	11 8 74	Stord		Brann	24	—
							Hartlepool U	109	—
Hughes Danny*	5 10	12 13	M	13 2 80	Bangor	Trainee	Wolverhampton W	—	—
							Hartlepool U	8	—
Ingram Denny*	5 11	11 13	D	27 6 76	Sunderland	Trainee	Hartlepool U	199	10

Player	Ht	Wt	Pos	Born	Birthplace	Source	Club	App	Gls
Jones Gary	6 1	12 08	F	6 4 69	Huddersfield	Rossington Main Boston U	Doncaster R	20	2
							Southend U	70	16
							Lincoln C (loan)	4	2
							Notts Co	117	38
							Scunthorpe U (loan)	11	5
							Hartlepool U	45	7
							Halifax T (loan)	8	1
Knowles Darren	5 6	11 02	D	8 10 70	Sheffield	Trainee	Sheffield U	—	—
							Stockport Co	63	—
							Scarborough	144	2
							Hartlepool U	143	1
Lake Craig*	5 11	10 01	D	10 2 80	Stockton	Trainee	Hartlepool U	—	—
Lee Graeme	6 2	13 07	D	31 5 78	Middlesbrough	Trainee	Hartlepool U	129	13
McAvoy Andy	6 0	13 06	M	28 8 79	Middlesbrough	Trainee	Blackburn R	—	—
							Hartlepool U	16	—
Midgley Craig	5 7	11 03	F	24 5 76	Bradford	Trainee	Bradford C	11	1
							Scarborough (loan)	16	1
							Scarborough (loan)	6	2
							Darlington (loan)	1	—
							Hartlepool U	55	10
Miller Tommy	6 1	12 01	M	8 1 79	Easington	Trainee	Hartlepool U	91	19
Provett Jim§	5 11	11 12	G	22 12 82	Stockton	Trainee	Hartlepool U	—	—
Robinson Mark	5 9	11 00	D	24 7 81	Guisborough	Trainee	Hartlepool U	—	—
Shilton Sam	5 11	11 06	M	21 7 78	Nottingham	Schoolboy	Plymouth Arg	3	—
							Coventry C	7	—
							Hartlepool U	21	3
Smith Jeff‡	5 10	11 01	M	28 6 80	Middlesbrough	Trainee	Hartlepool U	3	—
Stephenson Paul#	5 10	12 06	M	2 1 68	Wallsend	Apprentice	Newcastle U	61	1
							Millwall	98	6
							Gillingham (loan)	12	2
							Brentford	70	2
							York C	97	8
							Hartlepool U	76	7
Strodder Gary	6 1	13 07	D	1 4 65	Cleckheaton	Apprentice	Lincoln C	132	6
							West Ham U	65	2
							WBA	140	8
							Notts Co	121	10
							Rotherham U (loan)	3	—
							Hartlepool U	42	—
Tennebo Thomas	6 2	12 00	M	19 3 75	Bergen	Fana	Hartlepool U	11	—
West Colin#	6 1	13 11	F	13 11 62	Wallsend	Apprentice	Sunderland	102	21
							Watford	45	20
							Rangers	10	2
							Sheffield W	45	8
							WBA	73	22
							Port Vale (loan)	5	1
							Swansea C	33	12
							Leyton Orient	142	42
							Northampton T (loan)	2	—
						Northwich Vic	Hartlepool U	1	—
Westwood Chris	5 11	12 03	D	13 2 77	Dudley	Trainee	Wolverhampton W	4	1
							Hartlepool U	41	—

Scholars
Davison, Craig T; Dunkerley, Mark G; Flett, Martyn J; Hill, Terence; Lawlor, Terence S; Lines, Craig; McLean, Stephen; Nesbit, Mark A; Piggott, David J; Provett, Robert J; Ross, Brian S; Wear, Joseph M

HUDDERSFIELD TOWN

Player	Ht	Wt	Pos	Born	Birthplace	Source	Club	App	Gls
Armstrong Craig	5 11	12 10	D	23 5 75	South Shields	Trainee	Nottingham F	40	—
							Burnley (loan)	4	—
							Bristol R (loan)	14	—
							Gillingham (loan)	10	—
							Watford (loan)	15	—
							Huddersfield T	52	1
Atkinson Robert*			M	18 11 80	Bridlington	Trainee	Huddersfield T	—	—
Baldry Simon	5 10	11 06	M	12 2 76	Huddersfield	Trainee	Huddersfield T	85	4
							Bury (loan)	5	—
Beech Chris	5 10	11 12	M	16 9 74	Blackpool	Trainee	Blackpool	82	4
							Hartlepool U	94	22
							Huddersfield T	52	11
Beresford David	5 7	10 06	M	11 11 76	Middleton	Trainee	Oldham Ath	64	2
							Swansea C (loan)	6	—
							Huddersfield T	33	3
							Preston NE (loan)	4	—
Brennan Damien*	6 0	12 00	D	30 8 80	Dublin	Belvedere	Huddersfield T	—	—
Brown Nathaniel	6 2	12 05	F	15 6 81	Sheffield	Trainee	Huddersfield T	—	—
Crossley Ryan*	6 0	11 00	D	23 7 80	Halifax	Trainee	Huddersfield T	—	—
Cuss Paul‡	6 1	12 00	G	17 4 79	Minden	Trainee	Huddersfield T	—	—
Dalton Paul‡	5 11	12 06	M	25 4 67	Middlesbrough	Brandon U	Manchester U	—	—
							Hartlepool U	151	37
							Plymouth Arg	98	25
							Huddersfield T	98	25
							Carlisle U (loan)	3	1

Donis George	6 0	13 00	F	29 10 69	Greece		Yannina	22	3
							Panathinaikos	136	34
							Blackburn R	22	2
							AEK Athens	13	—
							Sheffield U	7	1
							Huddersfield T	20	—
Dyson Jon	6 1	12 09	D	18 12 71	Mirfield	School	Huddersfield T	183	6
Edwards Rob	5 9	12 04	M	23 2 70	Manchester	Trainee	Crewe Alex	155	44
							Huddersfield T	138	14
Facey Delroy	6 0	13 00	F	22 4 80	Huddersfield	Trainee	Huddersfield T	28	3
Gorre Dean	5 8	11 07	M	10 9 70	Surinam		SVV/Dordrecht	32	8
							Feyenoord	42	6
							Groningen	80	18
							Ajax	35	4
							Huddersfield T	28	4
Gray Kevin	6 0	14 00	D	7 1 72	Sheffield	Trainee	Mansfield T	141	3
							Huddersfield T	169	5
Hay Chris	5 11	11 07	F	28 8 74	Glasgow		Celtic	25	4
							Swindon T	94	30
							Huddersfield T	7	—
Heary Thomas*	5 10	11 03	D	14 2 79	Dublin	Trainee	Huddersfield T	12	—
Hodouto Kwami‡	5 11	11 12	D	31 10 74	Lome		Cannes	26	—
							Auxerre	—	—
							Huddersfield T	2	—
Holland Chris	5 9	11 05	M	11 9 75	Whalley	Trainee	Preston NE	1	—
							Newcastle U	3	—
							Birmingham C	70	—
							Huddersfield T	17	1
Horsley Jamie*	5 7	10 05	M	3 9 80	Halifax		Huddersfield T	—	—
Irons Kenny	5 10	11 02	M	4 11 70	Liverpool	Trainee	Tranmere R	351	54
							Huddersfield T	40	3
Jenkins Steve	5 11	12 03	D	16 7 72	Merthyr	Trainee	Swansea C	165	1
							Huddersfield T	162	3
Johnson Grant*	5 10	10 08	M	24 3 72	Dundee		Dundee U	85	7
							Huddersfield T	65	5
Lucketti Chris	6 1	13 04	D	21 9 71	Littleborough	Trainee	Rochdale	1	—
							Stockport Co	—	—
							Halifax T	78	2
							Bury	235	8
							Huddersfield T	26	—
Margetson Martyn	6 0	14 00	G	8 9 71	West Neath	Trainee	Manchester C	51	—
							Bristol R (loan)	3	—
							Bolton W (loan)	—	—
							Luton T (loan)	—	—
							Southend U	32	—
							Huddersfield T	—	—
Mattis Dwayne	5 10	11 00	M	31 7 81	Huddersfield	Trainee	Huddersfield T	2	—
Monkou Ken	6 3	14 06	D	29 11 64	Surinam	Feyenoord	Chelsea	94	2
							Southampton	198	10
							Huddersfield T	19	1
Muangsem Kiatisuk			M	11 8 76	Thailand		Huddersfield T	—	—
Richardson Lee J	5 11	10 06	M	12 3 69	Halifax	Trainee	Halifax T	56	2
(Transferred to Livingston, February 2000)							Watford	41	1
							Blackburn R	62	3
							Aberdeen	64	6
							Oldham Ath	88	21
							Stockport Co (loan)	6	—
							Huddersfield T	36	3
							Bury (loan)	5	1
Schofield Danny	5 10	11 06	F	10 4 80	Doncaster	Brodsworth	Huddersfield T	3	—
Scott Paul	5 11	12 00	M	5 11 79	Wakefield	Trainee	Huddersfield T	—	—
Sellars Scott	5 7	9 10	M	27 11 65	Sheffield	Apprentice	Leeds U	76	12
							Blackburn R	202	35
							Leeds U	7	—
							Newcastle U	81	5
							Bolton W	111	15
							Huddersfield T	34	1
Senior Michael	5 9	11 06	M	3 3 81	Huddersfield	Trainee	Huddersfield T	—	—
Senior Philip			M	30 10 82	Huddersfield	Trainee	Huddersfield T	—	—
Smith Martin	5 11	12 00	F	13 11 74	Sunderland	Trainee	Sunderland	119	25
							Sheffield U	26	10
							Huddersfield T	12	4
Thornley Ben	5 9	11 08	F	21 4 75	Bury	Trainee	Manchester U	9	—
							Stockport Co (loan)	10	1
							Huddersfield T (loan)	12	2
							Huddersfield T	63	5
Vaesen Nico	6 1	13 08	G	28 9 69	Hasselt		CS Brugge	16	—
							Aalst	34	—
							Huddersfield T	89	—
Vincent Jamie	5 10	11 09	D	18 6 75	London	Trainee	Crystal Palace	25	—
							Bournemouth (loan)	8	—
							Bournemouth	105	5
							Huddersfield T	43	2

Wijnhard Clyde	5 10	13 04	F	1 11 73	Paramaribo		Ajax	4	2
							Groningen	23	3
							Ajax	—	—
							RKC	50	18
							Willem II	29	14
							Leeds U	18	3
							Huddersfield T	45	15

Scholars
Austin, Ben; Brown, Christopher T; Clarke, Doni J; Clarke, Nathan; Fowler, Adam M; Greaves, Robert A; Hay, Nathan A; Senior, Christopher M; Simpson, Neil; Stead, Jonathan G; Trueman, Daniel P; Worthington, Jonathan A

Associated Schoolboys who have accepted the Club's offer of a Traineeship/Scholarship/Contract
Clapham, Daniel D; Kelly, Gregory; Lloyd, Anthony F

HULL CITY

Baker Matthew*	6 0	14 00	G	18 12 79	Harrogate	Trainee	Hull C	2	—
Blythe Michael*			M	21 9 80	Hull	Trainee	Hull C	—	—
Brabin Gary	5 11	14 08	M	9 12 70	Liverpool	Trainee	Stockport Co	2	—
						Runcorn	Doncaster R	59	11
							Bury	5	—
							Blackpool	63	5
							Lincoln C (loan)	4	—
							Hull C	58	7
Bracey Lee	6 2	13 02	G	11 9 68	Barking	Trainee	West Ham U	—	—
							Swansea C	99	—
							Halifax T	73	—
							Bury	67	—
							Ipswich T (loan)	—	—
							Ipswich T	—	—
							Hull C	10	—
Bradshaw Gary§	5 6	10 06		30 12 82	Beverley	Scholar	Hull C	12	—
Brown David	5 10	12 07	F	2 10 78	Bolton	Trainee	Manchester U	—	—
							Hull C (loan)	7	2
							Hull C	87	17
Edwards Michael	6 1	12 00	D	25 4 80	Hessle	Trainee	Hull C	91	1
Eyre John	6 0	12 06	F	9 10 74	Hull	Trainee	Oldham Ath	10	1
							Scunthorpe U (loan)	9	8
							Scunthorpe U	164	43
							Hull C	24	8
French Jon*	5 10	10 10	M	25 9 76	Bristol	Trainee	Bristol R	17	1
							Hull C	15	—
Goodison Ian	6 1	12 06	D	5 8 72	St James, Jamaica	Olympic Gardens	Hull C	18	—
Greaves Mark	6 1	13 00	D	22 1 75	Hull	Brigg Town	Hull C	118	7
Harper Steve	5 10	11 12	M	3 2 69	Newcastle-under-Lyme	Trainee	Port Vale	28	2
							Preston NE	77	10
							Burnley	69	8
							Doncaster R	65	11
							Mansfield T	160	18
							Hull C	38	4
Harris Jason	6 1	11 07	F	24 11 76	Sutton	Trainee	Crystal Palace	2	—
							Bristol R (loan)	6	2
							Lincoln C (loan)	1	—
							Leyton Orient	37	7
							Preston NE	34	6
							Hull C	29	4
Hateley Mark‡	6 2	13 00	F	7 11 61	Liverpool	Apprentice	Coventry C	93	25
							Portsmouth	38	22
							AC Milan	66	17
							Monaco	59	22
							Rangers	165	85
							QPR	27	3
							Leeds U (loan)	6	—
							Rangers	4	1
							Hull C	21	3
Hawes Steve‡	5 8	12 04	M	17 7 78	High Wycombe	Trainee	Sheffield U	4	—
							Doncaster R (loan)	11	—
							Hull C	19	—
Joyce Warren	5 9	12 00	M	20 1 65	Oldham	School	Bolton W	184	17
							Preston NE	177	34
							Plymouth Arg	30	3
							Burnley	70	9
							Hull C (loan)	9	3
							Hull C	138	12
Mann Neil	5 10	12 01	M	19 11 72	Nottingham	Grantham T	Hull C	162	9
Morgan Steve*	5 11	12 00	M	19 9 68	Oldham	Apprentice	Blackpool	144	10
							Plymouth Arg	121	6
							Coventry C	68	2
							Bristol R (loan)	5	—
							Wigan Ath	36	2
							Bury (loan)	5	—
							Burnley	17	—
							Hull C	19	1

Name			Pos	Born	Birthplace	From	Club	Apps	Gls
Morley Ben	5 9	10 01	M	22 12 80	Hull	Trainee	Hull C	21	—
Perry Jason	5 11	11 12	D	2 4 70	Newport	Trainee	Cardiff C	281	5
							Bristol R	25	—
							Lincoln C	12	—
							Hull C	9	—
Quigley Michael*	5 7	11 04	M	2 10 70	Manchester	Trainee	Manchester C	12	—
							Wrexham (loan)	4	—
							Hull C	54	3
Schofield Jon*	5 10	11 08	D	16 5 65	Barnsley	Gainsborough T	Lincoln C	231	11
							Doncaster R	110	12
							Mansfield T	86	—
							Hull C	25	—
Swales Steve	5 8	10 06	D	26 12 73	Whitby	Trainee	Scarborough	54	1
							Reading	43	1
							Hull C	42	—
Tucker Dexter‡	6 1	12 02	F	22 9 79	Pontefract	Trainee	Hull C	7	—
Whitmore Theodore	6 2	12 10	M	21 11 72	Jamaica	Seba U	Hull C	17	2
Whitney Jon	5 10	13 08	D	23 12 70	Nantwich	Winsford U	Huddersfield T	18	—
							Wigan Ath (loan)	12	—
							Lincoln C	101	8
							Hull C	42	2
Whittle Justin	6 1	12 12	D	18 3 71	Derby	Celtic	Stoke C	79	1
							Hull C	62	1
Whitworth Neil*	6 0	12 13	D	12 4 72	Ince		Wigan Ath	2	—
							Manchester U	1	—
							Preston NE (loan)	6	—
							Barnsley (loan)	11	—
							Rotherham U (loan)	8	1
							Blackpool (loan)	3	—
							Kilmarnock	76	3
							Wigan Ath	4	—
							Hull C	19	2
Williams Gareth‡	6 0	12 02	M	12 3 67	Newport (IW)	Gosport Bor	Aston Villa	12	—
							Barnsley	34	6
							Hull C (loan)	4	—
							Hull C (loan)	16	2
							Bournemouth	1	—
							Northampton T	50	1
							Scarborough	105	27
							Hull C	38	2
Wilson Paul*			M	22 9 80	Hull	Trainee	Hull C	—	—
Wilson Steve	5 10	10 12	G	24 4 74	Hull	Trainee	Hull C	181	—
Wood Jamie	5 10	13 04	F	21 9 78	Salford	Trainee	Manchester U	—	—
							Hull C	32	6

Scholars

Bolder, Christopher J; Bowsley, Anthony J; Bradshaw, Gary; Burton, Steven PG; Ebanks, Lemuel N; Flower, Clayton J; Kaveney, Glen; Lafferty, Mark A; McIntosh, Neil G; Peat, Nathan NM; Poole, Philip J; Waslin, Daniel; Woodward, Oliver

IPSWICH TOWN

Name			Pos	Born	Birthplace	From	Club	Apps	Gls
Artun Erdem			D	11 11 82	London	Trainee	Ipswich T	—	—
Axeldal Jonas*	5 11	12 00	F	2 9 70	Holm	Foggia	Ipswich T	16	—
Bramble Titus	6 1	13 10	D	21 7 81	Ipswich	Trainee	Ipswich T	4	—
							Colchester U (loan)	2	—
Branagan Keith#	6 1	14 03	G	10 7 66	Fulham		Cambridge U	110	—
							Millwall	46	—
							Brentford (loan)	2	—
							Gillingham (loan)	1	—
							Fulham (loan)	—	—
							Bolton W	214	—
							Ipswich T	—	—
Brown Wayne	6 0	12 00	D	20 8 77	Barking	Trainee	Ipswich T	27	—
							Colchester U (loan)	2	—
Clapham Jamie	5 9	11 08	D	7 12 75	Lincoln	Trainee	Tottenham H	1	—
							Leyton Orient (loan)	6	—
							Bristol R (loan)	5	—
							Ipswich T	114	5
Cowell Claydon‡			M	3 9 80	Colchester	Arsenal	Ipswich T	—	—
Croft Gary	5 8	10 08	D	17 2 74	Stafford	Trainee	Grimsby T	149	3
							Blackburn R	40	1
							Ipswich T	21	1
Daly Colm			M	4 1 82	Dublin		Ipswich T	—	—
Durrant George*	5 8	10 05	M	2 9 82	Plaistow	Academy	Ipswich T	—	—
Friars Sean	5 8	10 07	M	15 5 79	Derry	Trainee	Liverpool	—	—
							Ipswich T	1	—
Holland Matt	5 10	11 10	M	11 4 74	Bury	Trainee	West Ham U	—	—
							Bournemouth	104	18
							Ipswich T	138	25
Holster Marco‡	5 6	10 11	M	4 12 71	Weesp	Huizen	AZ	90	17
							Heracles	28	6
							Ipswich T	10	—

Inglis Kevin*	5 9	11 03	M	26 8 80	Rutherglen	Trainee	Ipswich T	—	—
Johnson David	5 6	12 00	F	15 8 76	Kingston, Jam	Trainee	Manchester U	—	—
							Bury	97	18
							Ipswich T	117	55
Kennedy John*	5 8	10 07	D	19 8 78	Cambridge	Trainee	Ipswich T	8	—
Logan Richard	6 0	12 00	F	4 1 82	Bury St Edmunds	Trainee	Ipswich T	3	—
Magilton Jim	6 0	14 13	M	6 5 69	Belfast	Apprentice	Liverpool	—	—
							Oxford U	150	34
							Southampton	130	13
							Sheffield W	27	1
							Ipswich T	57	7
Maurel Patrice*	5 5	11 00	M	16 10 78	Cayenne		Toulouse	5	1
							Ipswich T	—	—
McGreal John	5 11	11 00	D	2 6 72	Birkenhead	Trainee	Tranmere R	195	1
							Ipswich T	34	—
Midgley Neil	5 11	11 08	F	21 10 78	Cambridge	Trainee	Ipswich T	4	1
							Luton T (loan)	10	3
Miller Justin	6 0	11 07	D	16 12 80	Johannesburg	Academy	Ipswich T	—	—
Mowbray Tony#	6 1	13 07	D	22 11 63	Saltburn	Apprentice	Middlesbrough	348	25
							Celtic	78	6
							Ipswich T	128	5
Naylor Richard	6 0	13 07	F	28 2 77	Leeds	Trainee	Ipswich T	98	19
Niven Stuart	5 11	12 08	M	24 12 78	Glasgow	Trainee	Ipswich T	2	—
Petta Bobby	5 7	11 05	M	6 8 74	Rotterdam		Ipswich T	70	9
(Transferred to Celtic, July 1999)									
Pullen James	6 2	14 00	G	18 3 82	Chelmsford	Heybridge S	Ipswich T	—	—
Reuser Martijn*	5 7	11 07	M	1 2 75	Amsterdam		Ajax	42	6
							Vitesse	56	14
							Ipswich T	8	2
Salmon Mike	6 2	14 00	G	14 7 64	Leyland	Local	Blackburn R	1	—
							Chester C (loan)	16	—
							Stockport Co	118	—
							Bolton W	26	—
							Wrexham (loan)	17	—
							Wrexham	83	—
							Charlton Ath	148	—
							Oxford U (loan)	1	—
							Ipswich T	—	—
Scowcroft James	6 2	14 02	F	15 11 75	Bury St Edmunds	Trainee	Ipswich T	168	43
Stewart Marcus	5 10	10 06	F	7 11 72	Bristol	Trainee	Bristol R	171	57
							Huddersfield T	133	58
							Ipswich T	10	2
Stockwell Mick*	5 7	11 07	M	14 2 65	Chelmsford	Apprentice	Ipswich T	506	35
Thetis Manuel	6 3	14 13	D	5 11 71	France	Sevilla	Ipswich T	47	2
Venus Mark	6 1	12 12	D	6 4 67	Hartlepool		Hartlepool U	4	—
							Leicester C	61	1
							Wolverhampton W	287	7
							Ipswich T	86	12
Wilnis Fabian	5 8	12 06	D	23 8 70	Paramaribo	Sparta	NAC	134	3
							De Graafschap	107	1
							Ipswich T	53	1
Wright Carl‡			M	19 12 80	Nottingham	Trainee	Ipswich T	—	—
Wright Jermaine	5 10	11 09	M	21 10 75	Greenwich	Trainee	Millwall	—	—
							Wolverhampton W	20	—
							Doncaster R (loan)	13	—
							Crewe Alex	49	5
							Ipswich T	34	1
Wright Richard	6 2	13 02	G	5 11 77	Ipswich	Trainee	Ipswich T	204	—

Scholars
Asiamah, Justin; Chibogu, Edmund; Duncan, Fraser TD; Hulyer, Lee A; Logan, Stewart A; Mayes, Mark D; Miller, Adam E; Moffat, Steven J; Niemi, Tomi J; O'Neill, Lee G; Riley, Dominic M; Snowdon, William R

Associated Schoolboys who have accepted the Club's offer of a Traineeship/Scholarship/Contract
Beevers, Lee-Jon; Burton, Steven P; Wasylyczyn, Wayne M

LEEDS UNITED

Allaway Shaun			M	16 2 83	Reading	Trainee	Reading	—	—
							Leeds U	—	—
Bakke Eirik	6 1	13 11	M	13 9 77	Sogndal		Sogndal	76	17
							Leeds U	29	2
Batty David	5 8	11 10	M	2 12 68	Leeds	Trainee	Leeds U	211	4
							Blackburn R	54	1
							Newcastle U	83	3
							Leeds U	26	—
Bowyer Lee	5 9	10 09	M	3 1 77	London	Trainee	Charlton Ath	46	8
							Leeds U	125	21
Boyle Wes	5 10	11 01	F	30 3 79	Portadown	Trainee	Leeds U	1	—
Bridges Michael	6 1	11 00	F	5 8 78	North Shields	Trainee	Sunderland	79	16
							Leeds U	34	19

Name							Club		
Cansdell-Sheriff Shane	6 0	12 00	M	10 11 82	Sydney	NSW Academy	Leeds U	—	—
Cawley Alan	6 2	10 01	M	3 1 82	Sligo	Belvedere	Leeds U	—	—
Cramer Martin	5 4	10 01	M	15 11 82	Dublin	Maryland Boys	Leeds U	—	—
Crawford Dale‡	5 9	11 01	F	14 9 81	Sunderland	Trainee	Leeds U	—	—
Dixon Kevin	5 9	12 03	M	27 6 80	Easington	Trainee	Leeds U	—	—
							York C (loan)	3	—
Duberry Michael	6 1	14 00	D	14 10 75	Enfield	Trainee	Chelsea	86	1
							Bournemouth (loan)	7	—
							Leeds U	13	1
Evans Gareth	6 0	11 11	D	15 2 81	Leeds	Trainee	Leeds U	—	—
Evans Kevin	6 2	12 10	D	16 12 80	Carmarthen	Trainee	Leeds U	—	—
							Swansea C (loan)	2	—
Farrell Craig	5 11	12 00	F	5 12 82	Middlesbrough	Trainee	Leeds U	—	—
Feeney Warren	5 10	11 00	F	17 1 81	Belfast	Trainee	Leeds U	—	—
Ferguson Steven	5 6	9 03	M	25 2 83	Newry	St Andrew's	Leeds U	—	—
Folan Caleb	6 1	12 00	F	26 10 82	Leeds	Trainee	Leeds U	—	—
Haaland Alf-Inge	6 1	12 06	M	23 11 72	Stavanger	Bryne	Nottingham F	75	7
							Leeds U	74	8
Hackett Kristian‡			M	10 12 80	Rotherham	Trainee	Leeds U	—	—
Hackworth Tony	6 1	13 07	F	19 5 80	Durham	Trainee	Leeds U	—	—
(On loan to Sogndal)									
Harte Ian	6 0	12 04	D	31 8 77	Drogheda	Trainee	Leeds U	98	12
Hasselbaink Jimmy Floyd	6 0	13 08	F	27 3 72	Paramaribo		Campomairorense	31	12
(Transferred to Atletico Madrid, August 1999)							Boavista	29	20
							Leeds U	69	34
Hay Danny	6 4	14 11	D	15 5 75	Auckland	Perth Glory	Leeds U	—	—
Henderson Robbie‡			D	11 10 82	Bellshill	Trainee	Leeds U	—	—
Hiden Martin	6 1	12 00	D	11 3 73	Stainz		Sturm Graz	53	5
							Salzburg	58	2
							Sturm Graz	28	3
							Rapid Vienna	20	—
							Leeds U	26	—
Hopkin David	6 1	13 13	M	21 8 70	Greenock	Pt Glasgow R BC	Morton	18	—
							Chelsea	40	1
							Crystal Palace	83	21
							Leeds U	73	6
Huckerby Darren	5 11	11 04	F	23 4 76	Nottingham	Trainee	Lincoln C	28	5
							Newcastle U	1	—
							Millwall (loan)	6	3
							Coventry C	94	28
							Leeds U	33	2
Jones Matthew	5 11	11 09	M	1 9 80	Llanelli	Trainee	Leeds U	19	—
Kelly Gary	5 8	11 00	D	9 7 74	Drogheda	Home Farm	Leeds U	221	2
Kennedy Alan‡	5 8	11 00	F	17 10 81	Dublin	Trainee	Leeds U	—	—
Kewell Harry	6 0	12 10	F	22 9 78	Sydney	NSW Academy	Leeds U	106	21
Knarvik Tommy‡	5 8	11 00	M	1 11 79	Bergen	Skjerjard	Leeds U	—	—
Lagan Brian‡	5 5	10 00	M	3 10 80	Magherafelt	Trainee	Leeds U	—	—
Lanns Jason	5 8	10 07	D	2 11 81	Birmingham	Birmingham C	Leeds U	—	—
Lennon Anthony	5 9	10 08	F	16 5 82	Leeds	Trainee	Leeds U	—	—
Loughran Anthony‡	6 0	11 12	D	11 11 81	Liverpool	Trainee	Leeds U	—	—
Lynch Damien	5 10	11 00	D	31 7 79	Dublin		Leeds U	—	—
Martin Alan	5 10	11 05	D	21 11 81	Dublin	Trainee	Leeds U	—	—
Martyn Nigel	6 2	14 10	G	11 8 66	St Austell	St Blazey	Bristol R	101	—
							Crystal Palace	272	—
							Leeds U	146	—
Matthews Lee	6 2	13 05	F	6 1 79	Middlesbrough	Trainee	Leeds U	3	—
							Notts Co (loan)	5	—
							Gillingham (loan)	5	—
Maybury Alan	5 9	10 04	D	8 8 78	Dublin	Trainee	Leeds U	13	—
							Reading (loan)	8	—
McCargo Gerard	5 4	9 02	F	3 11 82	Belfast	Celtic (Belfast) Boy	Leeds U	—	—
McChrystal Brian‡	6 3	13 01	D	20 1 81	Dundalk	Bellurgan U	Leeds U	—	—
McMaster Jamie	5 10	11 12	M	29 11 82	Sydney	NSW Academy	Leeds U	—	—
McPhail Stephen	5 10	11 06	M	9 12 79	London	Trainee	Leeds U	45	2
Mills Danny	5 11	11 09	D	18 5 77	Norwich	Trainee	Norwich C	66	—
							Charlton Ath	45	3
							Leeds U	17	1
Milosevic Dejan	6 3	14 12	G	26 6 78	Carlton	Perth Glory	Leeds U	—	—
Molenaar Robert	6 2	14 09	D	27 2 69	Zaandam		Volendam	124	3
							Leeds U	51	5
O'Brien Carl‡	5 9	10 10	M	6 11 81	Dublin	Trainee	Leeds U	—	—
Porter Graeme‡	5 6	10 00	F	24 11 81	Liverpool	Trainee	Leeds U	—	—
Powell Graham‡			G	15 10 81	Liverpool	Trainee	Leeds U	—	—
Radebe Lucas	6 1	12 04	D	12 4 69	Johannesburg	Kaiser Chiefs	Leeds U	144	—
Richardson Frazer	5 11	11 08	D	29 10 82	Rotherham	Trainee	Leeds U	—	—
Robertson David‡	5 11	13 01	D	17 10 68	Aberdeen		Aberdeen	135	2
							Rangers	183	15
							Leeds U	26	—

Robinson Paul	6 4	14 04	G	15 10 79	Beverley	Trainee	Leeds U	5	—
Santos Nuno	6 1	13 00	G	20 4 73	Setubal		Setubal	42	—
(Transferred to Benfica, July 1999)							Leeds U	—	—
Shepherd Paul‡	5 11	12 00	D	17 11 77	Leeds	Trainee	Leeds U	1	—
							Ayr U (loan)	6	1
							Tranmere R (loan)	1	—
Singh Harpal	5 7	10 02	F	15 9 81	Bradford	Trainee	Leeds U	—	—
Smith Alan	5 9	10 13	F	28 10 80	Leeds	Trainee	Leeds U	48	11
Travers Mervyn‡			G	22 11 82	Dublin	Trainee	Leeds U	—	—
Watson Simon	5 9	10 00	M	22 9 80	Strabane	Trainee	Leeds U	—	—
Wilcox Jason	6 0	11 00	F	15 7 71	Bolton	Trainee	Blackburn R	269	31
							Leeds U	20	3
Woodgate Jonathan	6 2	12 09	D	22 1 80	Middlesbrough	Trainee	Leeds U	59	3
Wright Andy‡	5 8	9 06	M	21 10 78	Leeds	Trainee	Leeds U	—	—
							Reading (loan)	2	—

Scholars
Farren, Larry T; Groves, Bradley M; Harpur, Chad L; Johnson, Simon A; Matharu, Ravinder S; Newey, Thomas; Sherman, David TG

LEICESTER CITY

Allen Lee‡	5 10	10 08	F	12 3 79	Islington		Leicester C	—	—
Arphexad Pegguy	6 2	13 13	G	18 5 73	Abymes		Lens	3	—
							Leicester C	21	—
Bacon Carl*	5 10	11 06	D	15 12 80	Leicester	Trainee	Leicester C	—	—
Boateng Danny	5 10	12 07	F	14 11 80	London	Arsenal	Leicester C	—	—
Brennan Karl‡	5 6	11 00	M	19 3 81	Leicester	Trainee	Leicester C	—	—
Campbell Stuart	5 10	10 13	M	9 12 77	Corby	Trainee	Leicester C	37	—
							Birmingham C (loan)	2	—
Collymore Stan	6 3	13 10	F	22 1 71	Cannock	Stafford R	Crystal Palace	20	1
							Southend U	30	15
							Nottingham F	65	41
							Liverpool	61	26
							Aston Villa	45	7
							Fulham (loan)	6	—
							Leicester C	6	4
Cottee Tony	5 10	12 06	F	11 7 65	West Ham	Apprentice	West Ham U	212	92
							Everton	184	72
							West Ham U	67	23
						Selangor	Leicester C	83	27
							Birmingham C (loan)	5	1
Dudfield Lawrie	6 0	12 04	F	7 5 80	London	Kettering T	Leicester C	2	—
Eadie Darren	5 7	10 09	F	10 6 75	Chippenham	Trainee	Norwich C	168	35
							Leicester C	16	—
Elliott Matt	6 3	15 00	D	1 11 68	Roehampton	Epsom & Ewell	Charlton Ath	—	—
							Torquay U	124	15
							Scunthorpe U (loan)	8	1
							Scunthorpe U	53	7
							Oxford U	148	21
							Leicester C	127	19
Emerson Paul‡	6 1	11 06	D	29 8 78	Newtonards	Trainee	Leicester C	—	—
Flowers Tim	6 2	14 00	G	3 2 67	Kenilworth	Apprentice	Wolverhampton W	63	—
							Southampton (loan)	—	—
							Southampton	192	—
							Swindon T (loan)	2	—
							Swindon T (loan)	5	—
							Blackburn R	177	—
							Leicester C	29	—
Fox Martin‡	5 8	11 02	D	21 4 79	Sutton-in-Ashfield	Trainee	Leicester C	—	—
Gilchrist Phil	6 0	13 03	D	25 8 73	Stockton	Trainee	Nottingham F	—	—
							Middlesbrough	—	—
							Hartlepool U	82	—
							Oxford U	177	10
							Leicester C	27	1
Goodwin Tommy	6 0	12 07	D	8 11 79	Leicester	Trainee	Leicester C	1	—
Gough Steven*	6 0	11 11	M	16 9 80	Burton	Trainee	Nottingham F	—	—
							Leicester C	—	—
Gunnlaugsson Arnar	5 10	11 06	F	6 3 73	Akranes		IA Akranes	30	18
							Feyenoord	9	—
							Nuremberg	28	8
							IA Akranes	9	16
							Bolton W	42	13
							Leicester C	11	—
							Stoke C (loan)	13	2
Guppy Steve	5 11	11 11	M	29 3 69	Winchester	Southampton	Wycombe W	41	8
							Newcastle U	—	—
							Port Vale	105	12
							Leicester C	118	8
Hodges John*	6 0	11 13	G	22 1 80	Leicester	Trainee	Leicester C	—	—
Impey Andrew	5 8	11 06	M	13 9 71	Hammersmith	Yeading	QPR	187	13
							West Ham U	27	—
							Leicester C	47	1

Izzet Muzzy	5 10	11 02	M	31 10 74	Hackney	Trainee	Chelsea	—	—
							Leicester C (loan)	9	1
							Leicester C	134	20
Lennon Neil	5 9	13 02	M	25 6 71	Belfast	Trainee	Manchester C	1	—
							Crewe Alex	147	15
							Leicester C	155	6
Marshall Ian*	6 2	14 09	F	20 3 66	Liverpool	Apprentice	Everton	15	1
							Oldham Ath	170	36
							Ipswich T	84	32
							Leicester C	83	18
McCann Tim	5 9	12 00	M	22 3 80	Belfast	Trainee	Leicester C	—	—
Mortimer Alex	5 10	10 06	D	28 11 82	Manchester	Trainee	Leicester C	—	—
Oakes Stefan	5 11	12 08	M	6 9 78	Leicester	Trainee	Leicester C	25	1
Pasquinelli Fernando*			M	13 3 80	Canada de Gomez	Boca Juniors	Leicester C	—	—
Piper Matthew	6 1	13 02	M	29 9 81	Leicester	Trainee	Leicester C	—	—
Savage Robbie	5 11	11 01	M	18 10 74	Wrexham	Trainee	Manchester U	—	—
							Crewe Alex	77	10
							Leicester C	104	4
Sinclair Frank	5 10	12 03	D	3 12 71	Lambeth	Trainee	Chelsea	169	7
							WBA (loan)	6	1
							Leicester C	65	1
Stewart Jordan	6 0	12 04	M	3 3 82	Birmingham	Trainee	Leicester C	1	—
							Bristol R (loan)	4	—
Taggart Gerry	6 2	14 01	D	18 10 70	Belfast	Trainee	Manchester C	12	1
							Barnsley	212	16
							Bolton W	69	4
							Leicester C	46	6
Thomas Danny	5 7	10 10	D	1 5 81	Leamington Spa	Trainee	Nottingham F	—	—
							Leicester C	3	—
Ullathorne Robert‡	5 8	10 10	D	11 10 71	Wakefield	Trainee	Norwich C	94	7
							Osasuna	18	—
							Leicester C	31	1
Walsh Steve	6 3	15 02	D	3 11 64	Fulwood	Local	Wigan Ath	126	4
							Leicester C	368	53
Wilson Stuart	5 8	10 03	F	16 9 77	Leicester	Trainee	Leicester C	22	3
							Sheffield U (loan)	6	—
Zagorakis Theo*	5 9	12 00	M	27 10 71	Kavala	PAOK Salonika	Leicester C	50	3

Scholars
Ashton, Jonathan J; Hallows, Dominic K; Heath, Matthew P; Noble, Karl N; Nurse, Matthew J; Price, Michael; Purdie, Robert J; Reeves, Martin L; Savage, Michael J; Stevenson, Jonathan A; Webb, Mark A

LEYTON ORIENT

Ampadu Kwame*	5 10	11 10	M	20 12 70	Bradford	Belvedere	Arsenal	2	—
							Plymouth Arg (loan)	6	1
							WBA (loan)	7	1
							WBA	42	3
							Swansea C	147	12
							Leyton Orient	72	1
Andrews Barry‡	6 1	13 06	G	30 8 80	Dublin	QPR	Leyton Orient	—	—
Baker Joe‡	5 8	10 07	F	9 4 77	Islington	Charlton Ath	Leyton Orient	75	3
Barrett Scott	5 11	13 00	G	2 4 63	Ilkeston	Ilkeston T	Wolverhampton W	30	—
							Stoke C	51	—
							Colchester U (loan)	13	—
							Stockport Co (loan)	10	—
							Colchester U	—	—
							Gillingham	51	—
							Cambridge U	119	—
							Leyton Orient	49	—
Bayes Ashley	6 1	13 05	G	19 4 72	Lincoln	Trainee	Brentford	4	—
							Torquay U	97	—
							Exeter C	127	—
							Leyton Orient	17	—
Beall Billy	5 6	12 00	M	4 12 77	Enfield	Trainee	Cambridge U	81	7
							Leyton Orient	56	3
Brkovic Ahmet*	5 7	10 02	M	23 9 74	Dubrovnik	Dubrovnik	Leyton Orient	29	5
Canham Scott*	5 10	10 08	M	5 11 74	Stratford	Trainee	West Ham U	—	—
							Torquay U (loan)	3	—
							Brentford (loan)	14	—
							Brentford	35	1
							Leyton Orient	9	—
Carter Rob§	6 1	12 01	M	23 4 82	Stepney	Trainee	Leyton Orient	2	—
Christie Iyseden	5 10	12 02	F	14 11 76	Coventry	Trainee	Coventry C	1	—
							Bournemouth (loan)	4	—
							Mansfield T (loan)	8	—
							Mansfield T	81	18
							Leyton Orient	36	7
Clark Simon*	6 0	12 10	D	12 3 67	Boston	Stevenage Bor	Peterborough U	107	4
							Leyton Orient	98	9
Curran Danny‡	5 8	10 03	F	13 6 81	Basildon	Trainee	Leyton Orient	1	—
Downer Simon	5 11	12 08	D	19 10 81	Romford	Trainee	Leyton Orient	25	—
Gough Neil§	5 11	11 08	F	1 9 81	Harlow	Trainee	Leyton Orient	4	—

Gould Ronnie§	5 11	11 05	M	27 9 82	London	Trainee	Leyton Orient	2	—
Griffiths Carl	5 9	11 04	F	15 7 71	Welshpool	Trainee	Shrewsbury T	143	54
							Manchester C	18	4
							Portsmouth	14	2
							Peterborough U	16	2
							Leyton Orient	70	32
							Wrexham (loan)	4	3
							Port Vale	8	1
							Leyton Orient	11	4
Harris Andy	5 10	12 02	D	26 2 77	Springs	Trainee	Liverpool	—	—
							Southend U	72	—
							Leyton Orient	15	—
Ibehre Jabo§	6 2	12 10	M	28 1 83	London	Trainee	Leyton Orient	3	—
Inglethorpe Alex*	5 11	11 04	F	14 11 71	Epsom	School	Watford	12	2
							Barnet (loan)	6	3
							Leyton Orient	123	32
							Exeter C (loan)	1	—
Joseph Matt#	5 7	10 02	D	30 9 72	Bethnal Green	Trainee	Arsenal	—	—
							Gillingham	—	—
							Cambridge U	159	6
							Leyton Orient	89	1
Joseph Roger*	5 11	11 10	D	24 12 65	Paddington	Juniors	Brentford	104	2
							Wimbledon	162	—
							Millwall (loan)	5	—
							Leyton Orient	15	—
							WBA	2	—
							Leyton Orient	50	—
Lockwood Matt	5 9	10 12	D	17 10 76	Rochford	Trainee	QPR	—	—
							Bristol R	63	1
							Leyton Orient	78	9
Martin John	5 5	10 00	M	15 7 81	Bethnal Green	Trainee	Leyton Orient	10	—
McElholm Brendan§	5 11	12 02	M	7 7 82	Omagh	Trainee	Leyton Orient	3	—
McGhee Dave	6 0	12 01	D	19 6 76	Worthing	Trainee	Brentford	117	8
						Stevenage Borough	Leyton Orient	23	1
McLean Aaron§	5 6	10 02	F	25 5 83	Hammersmith	Trainee	Leyton Orient	3	—
Morrison Dave*	5 11	12 10	F	30 11 74	Waltham Forest	Chelmsford C	Peterborough U	77	12
							Leyton Orient	46	3
Murray Jade§	5 9	11 05	F	23 9 81	Islington	Trainee	Leyton Orient	2	—
Parsons David§	6 1	12 07	M	25 2 82	Greenwich	Trainee	Leyton Orient	1	—
Richards Tony	6 0	13 06	F	17 9 73	Newham	Sudbury T	Cambridge U	42	5
							Leyton Orient	63	11
Shorey Nicky	5 9	10 08	D	19 2 81	Romford	Trainee	Leyton Orient	7	—
Simba Amara*	6 1	13 00	F	23 12 61	Senegal		Paris St Germain	40	7
							Cannes	28	10
							Paris St Germain	38	10
							Monaco	32	4
							Caen	37	12
							Lille	39	4
						Lyon	Leyton Orient	37	13
Smith Dean	6 0	13 00	D	19 3 71	West Bromwich	Trainee	Walsall	142	2
							Hereford U	117	19
							Leyton Orient	124	22
Uka Niam	5 7	10 01	M	26 10 81	Kosovo	Partizani	Leyton Orient	—	—
Walschaerts Wim	5 11	12 00	M	5 11 72	Antwerp	FC Tielen	Leyton Orient	80	6
Watts Steve	6 1	13 00	F	11 7 76	Peckham	Fisher Ath	Leyton Orient	60	12
Webb Simon*	5 10	11 03	M	19 1 78	Ballyhaunis	Trainee	Tottenham H	—	—
							Leyton Orient	4	—

Trainees
Akontoh, Raymond; Carter, Robert HA; Crowe, Michael W; Dorrian, Chris S; Goodfellow, Mark; Gough, Neil; Gould, Ronnie D; Grimsdell, Daniel B; Ibehre, Jabo O; Jones, William K; McElholm, Brendan A; McLean, Aaron; Morgan, Thomas; Murray, Jade A; Parsons, David; White, Lee; Wolton, Lee

LINCOLN CITY

Allcock Adam‡			M	4 4 81	Farnworth		Lincoln C	—	—
Barnett Dave	6 0	12 08	D	16 4 67	Birmingham	Windsor & Eton	Colchester U	20	—
							WBA	—	—
							Walsall	5	—
						Kidderminster H	Barnet	59	3
							Birmingham C	46	—
							Dunfermline Ath	21	1
							Port Vale	36	1
							Lincoln C	22	3
Barnett Jason	5 9	10 10	D	21 4 76	Shrewsbury	Trainee	Wolverhampton W	—	—
							Lincoln C	148	3

Name	Ht	Wt	Pos	Date of birth	Birthplace	Source	Clubs	Apps	Gls
Battersby Tony	6 0	12 09	F	30 8 75	Doncaster	Trainee	Sheffield U	10	1
							Southend U (loan)	8	1
							Notts Co	39	8
							Bury (loan)	11	2
							Bury	37	6
							Lincoln C	55	10
							Northampton T (loan)	3	1
Bimson Stuart	5 11	11 08	D	29 9 69	Liverpool	Macclesfield T	Bury	36	—
							Lincoln C	78	3
Brown Grant	6 0	11 12	D	19 11 69	Sunderland	Trainee	Leicester C	14	—
							Lincoln C	351	13
Finnigan John	5 8	10 11	M	29 3 76	Wakefield	Trainee	Nottingham F	—	—
							Lincoln C (loan)	6	—
							Lincoln C	74	3
Fleming Terry#	5 8	10 01	M	5 1 73	Marston Green	Trainee	Coventry C	13	—
							Northampton T	31	1
							Preston NE	32	2
							Lincoln C	183	8
Gain Peter	5 9	11 00	M	2 11 76	Hammersmith	Trainee	Tottenham H	—	—
							Lincoln C	36	2
Gordon Gavin	6 2	12 00	F	24 6 79	Manchester	Trainee	Hull C	38	9
							Lincoln C	81	19
Henry Anthony	6 0	13 00	D	13 9 79	London	Trainee	West Ham U	—	—
							Lincoln C	17	1
Holmes Steve	6 2	13 00	D	13 1 71	Middlesbrough	Guisborough T	Preston NE	13	1
							Hartlepool U (loan)	5	2
							Lincoln C	143	18
Lewis Graham§	5 10	11 00	F	15 2 82	Reading	Trainee	Lincoln C	5	—
Marriott Alan	5 11	12 05	G	3 9 78	Bedford	Trainee	Tottenham H	—	—
							Lincoln C	18	—
Mayo Paul	5 11	11 09	D	13 10 81	Lincoln	Scholar	Lincoln C	19	—
Miller Paul	6 0	11 07	M	31 1 68	Bisley	Trainee	Wimbledon	80	10
							Newport Co (loan)	6	2
							Bristol C (loan)	3	—
							Bristol R	105	22
							Lincoln C	96	11
Peacock Richard	6 1	11 05	M	29 10 72	Sheffield	Sheffield FC	Hull C	174	21
							Lincoln C	34	3
Phillips David*	5 10	12 04	M	29 7 63	Wegberg	Apprentice	Plymouth Arg	73	15
							Manchester C	81	13
							Coventry C	100	8
							Norwich C	152	18
							Nottingham F	126	5
							Huddersfield T	52	3
							Lincoln C	17	—
Philpott Lee*	5 11	11 08	M	21 2 70	Barnet	Trainee	Peterborough U	4	—
							Cambridge U	134	17
							Leicester C	75	3
							Blackpool	71	5
							Lincoln C	47	3
Poppleton David‡	5 10	11 00	M	19 12 79	Doncaster	Trainee	Everton	—	—
							Lincoln C	5	—
Rice Dominic‡			M	30 4 81	Sunderland		Lincoln C	—	—
Richardson Barry*	6 1	12 01	G	5 8 69	Wallsend	Trainee	Sunderland	—	—
							Scunthorpe U	—	—
							Scarborough	30	—
							Northampton T	96	—
							Preston NE	20	—
							Lincoln C	131	—
							Mansfield T (loan)	6	—
							Sheffield W (loan)	—	—
Rocha Carlos‡	6 1	12 07	F	4 12 74	Lisbon	Boston Bulldogs	Bury	3	—
							Lincoln C	—	—
Smith Paul	5 11	11 07	M	25 1 76	Hastings	Hastings T	Nottingham F	—	—
							Lincoln C (loan)	17	3
							Lincoln C	55	7
Stant Phil†	5 11	12 07	F	13 10 62	Bolton	Camberley Army	Reading	4	2
							Hereford U	89	38
							Notts Co	22	6
							Blackpool (loan)	12	5
							Lincoln C (loan)	4	—
							Huddersfield T (loan)	5	1
							Fulham	19	5
							Mansfield T	57	32
							Cardiff C	79	34
							Mansfield T (loan)	4	1
							Bury	62	23
							Northampton T (loan)	5	2
							Lincoln C	64	20
Stones Craig*	5 10	11 11	M	31 5 80	Scunthorpe	Trainee	Lincoln C	21	—

Name	Ht	Wt	Pos	DOB	Birthplace	From	Club	Apps	Gls
Thorpe Lee	6 0	11 06	F	14 12 75	Wolverhampton	Trainee	Blackpool	12	—
							Lincoln C	124	38
Vaughan John*	5 11	13 01	G	26 6 64	Isleworth	Apprentice	West Ham U	—	—
							Charlton Ath (loan)	6	—
							Bristol R (loan)	6	—
							Wrexham (loan)	4	—
							Bristol C (loan)	2	—
							Fulham	44	—
							Bristol C (loan)	3	—
							Cambridge U	178	—
							Charlton Ath	6	—
							Preston NE	66	—
							Lincoln C	66	—
							Colchester U (loan)	5	—
							Colchester U (loan)	6	—
							Chesterfield (loan)	3	—
Walling Dean‡	6 0	10 08	D	17 4 69	Leeds	Apprentice	Leeds U	—	—
							Rochdale	65	8
					Guiseley		Carlisle U	236	22
							Lincoln C	38	5
Welsh Steve	6 0	12 03	D	19 4 68	Glasgow	Wimborne T	Cambridge U	1	—
							Peterborough U	146	2
							Preston NE (loan)	—	—
							Partick T	55	—
							Peterborough U (loan)	6	—
							Dunfermline Ath	26	—
							Ayr U	25	—
							Lincoln C	32	—
Wilkins Ian*	5 11	12 00	D	3 4 80	Lincoln	Trainee	Lincoln C	6	—

Trainees
Funnell, Gary; Gray, Darren K; Lewis, Graham; Pitter, Dominic J

Scholars
Bent, Daniel; Bone, Liam K; Byrne, Richard A; Greenwood, David; Kinsella, Sean I; McConville, Christopher

Non-Contract
Stant, Philip

LIVERPOOL

Name	Ht	Wt	Pos	DOB	Birthplace	From	Club	Apps	Gls
Armstrong Ian			F	16 11 81	Fazackerley	Trainee	Liverpool	—	—
Babb Phil*	6 0	12 03	D	30 11 70	Lambeth	Trainee	Millwall	—	—
							Bradford C	80	14
							Coventry C	77	3
							Liverpool	128	1
							Tranmere R (loan)	4	—
Berger Patrik	6 1	12 06	M	10 11 73	Prague		Slavia Prague	89	24
							Borussia Dortmund	25	4
							Liverpool	111	25
Bjornebye Stig Inge	5 10	11 09	D	11 12 69	Elverum		Strammen	19	—
(Transferred to Brondby, March 2000)							Kongsvinger	62	3
							Rosenborg	21	3
							Liverpool	139	2
Boardman John*			D	6 9 80	Liverpool	Trainee	Liverpool	—	—
Camara Titi	6 0	13 00	F	17 11 72	Donka		St Etienne	94	16
							Lens	63	14
							Marseille	61	8
							Liverpool	33	9
Carragher Jamie	6 1	13 00	M	28 1 78	Liverpool	Trainee	Liverpool	92	2
Doherty Kevin			M	18 4 80	Dublin		Liverpool	—	—
Dundee Sean	6 1	13 00	F	7 12 72	Durban	D'Alberton Carries	Stuttgart Kickers	7	—
(Transferred to Stuttgart, July 1999)						Ditzingen	Karlsruhe	85	36
							Liverpool	3	—
Ferri Jean-Michel	6 0	12 00	M	7 2 69	Lyon		Nantes	290	21
(Transferred to Sochaux, July 1999)						Istanbul	Liverpool	2	—
Foley-Sheridan Michael			M	9 3 83	Dublin		Liverpool	—	—
Fowler Robbie	5 11	11 10	F	9 4 75	Liverpool	Trainee	Liverpool	199	109
Friedel Brad	6 3	14 00	G	18 5 71	Lakewood		Columbus Crew	38	—
							Liverpool	25	—
Gerrard Steven	6 1	13 00	M	30 5 80	Whiston	Trainee	Liverpool	41	1
Gudnason Haukar	5 10	12 00	F	8 9 78	Keflavik		Keflavik	34	11
(On loan to KR)							Liverpool	—	—
Hamann Dietmar	6 2	12 06	M	27 8 73	Waldasson	Wacker Munich	Bayern Munich	105	6
							Newcastle U	23	4
							Liverpool	28	1
Heggem Vegard	5 11	12 00	D	13 7 75	Trondheim		Rosenborg	57	5
							Liverpool	51	3
Henchoz Stephane	6 1	12 08	D	7 9 74	Billens	Bulle	Neuchatel Xamax	91	1
							Hamburg	49	2
							Blackburn R	70	—
							Liverpool	29	—
Heskey Emile	6 2	14 03	F	11 1 78	Leicester	Trainee	Leicester C	154	40
							Liverpool	12	3

Name	Ht	Wt	Pos	Born	Birthplace	Source	Clubs	Apps	Gls
Hyypia Sami	6 4	14 00	D	7 10 73	Porvoo	KuMu	MyPa 47	63	3
							Willem II	100	3
							Liverpool	38	2
Kippe Frode	6 4	14 10	D	17 1 78	Oslo		Lillestrom	34	2
							Liverpool	—	—
							Stoke C (loan)	15	1
Kvarme Bjorn	5 11	12 04	D	17 6 72	Trondheim		Rosenborg	88	2
(Transferred to St Etienne, August 1999)							Liverpool	45	—
Matteo Dominic	6 1	11 10	D	24 4 74	Dumfries	Trainee	Liverpool	127	1
							Sunderland (loan)	1	—
Maxwell Leyton	5 8	11 00	M	3 10 79	St Asaph	Trainee	Liverpool	—	—
McManaman Steve	6 0	10 06	M	11 2 72	Liverpool	School	Liverpool	272	46
(Transferred to Real Madrid, June 1999)									
Meijer Erik	6 2	13 05	F	2 8 69	Meersen		Fortuna Sittard	10	1
							Antwerp	—	—
							Eindhoven	14	5
							Fortuna Sittard	26	5
							Maastricht	66	34
							PSV Eindhoven	39	13
							Uerdingen	32	11
							Leverkusen	84	16
							Liverpool	21	—
Miles John			F	28 9 81	Fazackerley	Trainee	Liverpool	—	—
Murphy Danny	5 9	10 08	M	18 3 77	Chester	Trainee	Crewe Alex	134	27
							Liverpool	40	3
							Crewe Alex (loan)	16	1
Murphy Neil*	5 9	11 00	D	19 5 80	Liverpool	Trainee	Liverpool	—	—
Navarro Alan			D	31 5 81	Liverpool	Trainee	Liverpool	—	—
Newby Jon	6 0	12 00	F	28 11 78	Warrington	Trainee	Liverpool	1	—
							Crewe Alex (loan)	6	—
Nielsen Jorgen*	6 0	13 00	G	6 5 71	Nykobing		Naestved	2	—
							Hvidovre*	—	—
							Liverpool	—	—
							Wolverhampton W (loan)	—	—
O'Brien Chris			M	13 1 82	Liverpool	Trainee	Liverpool	—	—
O'Mara Paul*	5 9	11 00	D	23 11 80	Dublin	Trainee	Liverpool	—	—
Otsemobor John			D	23 3 83	Liverpool	Trainee	Liverpool	—	—
Owen Michael	5 8	11 00	F	14 12 79	Chester	Trainee	Liverpool	95	48
Partridge Richie	5 8	10 10	M	12 9 80	Dublin	Trainee	Liverpool	0	—
Redknapp Jamie	6 0	12 10	M	25 6 73	Barton-on-Sea	Trainee	Bournemouth	13	—
							Liverpool	233	29
Smicer Vladimir	5 10	11 10	M	24 5 73	Degin		Slavia Prague	81	26
							Lens	91	16
							Liverpool	21	1
Song Rigobert	6 0	13 00	D	1 7 76	Nkenlicock	Tonnerre	Metz	123	3
							Salernitana	4	1
							Liverpool	31	—
Staunton Steve	6 1	12 11	D	19 1 69	Drogheda	Dundalk	Liverpool	65	—
							Bradford C (loan)	8	—
							Aston Villa	208	16
							Liverpool	43	—
Thompson David	5 7	10 00	M	12 9 77	Birkenhead	Trainee	Liverpool	48	5
							Swindon T (loan)	10	—
Torpey Steve			M	16 9 81	Fazackerley	Trainee	Liverpool	—	—
Traore Djimi	6 3	13 10	D	1 3 80	Saint Ouen	Laval	Liverpool	—	—
Warnock Stephen			M	12 12 81	Ormskirk	Trainee	Liverpool	—	—
Westerveld Sander	6 4	14 00	G	23 10 74	Enschede	Tubanters	Twente	14	—
							Vitesse	100	—
							Liverpool	36	—
Wright Stephen	6 0	12 00	D	8 2 80	Liverpool	Trainee	Liverpool	—	—
							Crewe Alex (loan)	23	—

Scholars

Bock, Lee T; Cavanagh, Peter J; Coupe, Alan E; Crookes, Peter; Culshaw, Paul R; Grace, Stephen; Hogg, Matthew W; McIlroy, Brian P; Mellor, Neil A; Morton, Anthony P; Olsen, James P; Parry, Mathew; Prince, Neil M; Thompson, Christopher M

LUTON TOWN

Name	Ht	Wt	Pos	Born	Birthplace	Source	Clubs	Apps	Gls
Abbey Nathan*	6 1	11 13	G	11 7 78	Islington	Trainee	Luton T	35	—
Ayres James	6 3	13 00	D	18 9 80	Luton	Trainee	Luton T	—	—
Boyce Emmerson	5 11	11 02	D	24 9 79	Aylesbury	Trainee	Luton T	31	1
Castro-Pearson David‡			M	30 10 80	Leamington Spa	Coventry C	Luton T	—	—
Davis Ryan‡	5 7	10 02	D	16 11 79	Stoke	Trainee	Sheffield W	—	—
							Luton T	—	—
Douglas Stuart	5 8	11 05	F	9 4 78	London	Trainee	Luton T	116	14
Fotiadis Andrew	5 11	11 07	F	6 9 77	Hitchin	School	Luton T	76	8
Fraser Stuart	5 9	10 06	D	9 1 80	Edinburgh	Trainee	Luton T	29	1
George Liam	5 9	11 04	F	2 2 79	Luton	Trainee	Luton T	55	13

Gray Phil*	5 9	12 07	F	2 10 68	Belfast	Apprentice	Tottenham H	9	—
							Barnsley (loan)	3	—
							Fulham (loan)	3	—
							Luton T	59	22
							Sunderland	115	34
							Nancy	16	4
							Fortuna Sittard	12	1
							Luton T	81	21
Johnson Marvin*	6 1	13 00	D	29 10 68	Wembley	Apprentice	Luton T	346	6
Kandol Tresor*	6 1	11 07	F	30 8 81	Banga	Trainee	Luton T	8	—
Locke Adam	5 11	12 07	M	20 8 70	Croydon	Trainee	Crystal Palace	—	—
							Southend U	73	4
							Colchester U (loan)	4	—
							Colchester U	79	8
							Bristol C	65	4
							Luton T	34	3
McGowan Gavin	5 10	12 06	D	16 1 76	Blackheath	Trainee	Arsenal	6	—
							Luton T (loan)	2	—
							Luton T (loan)	8	—
							Luton T	44	—
McIndoe Michael‡	5 8	10 06	M	2 12 79	Edinburgh	Trainee	Luton T	39	—
McKinnon Ray‡	5 10	11 08	M	5 8 70	Dundee		Dundee U	53	6
							Nottingham F	6	1
							Aberdeen	26	—
							Dundee U	44	6
							Luton T	33	2
McLaren Paul	6 1	13 00	M	17 11 76	High Wycombe	Trainee	Luton T	132	2
Moses Jerry*	5 9	11 05	M	22 2 81	Kampala		Luton T	—	—
O'Connor Richard‡	5 9	10 07	F	30 8 78	Wandsworth	Trainee	Wimbledon	—	—
							Luton T	—	—
Scarlett Andre	5 4	9 12	M	11 1 80	Brent	Trainee	Luton T	9	1
Spring Matthew	5 11	11 07	M	17 11 79	Harlow	Trainee	Luton T	102	9
Standen Dean			M	23 3 82	Lewisham	Welling U	Luton T	—	—
Stirling Jude	6 2	11 12	D	29 6 82	Enfield	Trainee	Luton T	—	—
Tate Daniel*	5 11	11 12	G	12 11 80	Bedford	Trainee	Luton T	—	—
Taylor Matthew	5 10	11 08	D	27 11 81	Oxford	Trainee	Luton T	41	4
Ward Scott	6 2	13 00	G	5 10 81	Brent	Trainee	Luton T	—	—
Watts Julian	6 2	13 06	D	17 3 71	Sheffield	Trainee	Rotherham U	20	1
							Sheffield W	16	1
							Shrewsbury T (loan)	9	—
							Leicester C	38	1
							Crewe Alex (loan)	5	—
							Huddersfield T (loan)	8	—
							Bristol C	17	1
							Lincoln C (loan)	2	—
							Blackpool (loan)	9	—
							Luton T	45	4
White Alan*	6 1	13 07	D	22 3 76	Darlington	Derby Co	Middlesbrough	—	—
							Luton T	80	3
							Colchester U (loan)	4	—
Zahana-Oni Landry*	5 9	10 09	M	8 8 76	Ivory Coast	Bromley	Luton T	9	—

Trainees
Minton, Alex

Scholars
Carroll, John M; Clarke, Duane L; Dogbe, Steven YS; James-Barriteau, Rene WJ; Mansell, Lee RS; Mortara, Dean P

MACCLESFIELD TOWN

Abbey George	5 8	10 08	D	20 10 78	Port Harcourt	Sharks	Macclesfield T	18	—
Askey John	6 0	12 02	F	4 11 64	Stoke	Port Vale	Macclesfield T	117	25
Bamber Michael	5 7	10 02	M	1 10 80	Preston	Blackpool	Macclesfield T	1	—
Barker Richard	8 1	13 12	F	30 5 75	Sheffield	Trainee	Sheffield W	—	—
							Doncaster R (loan)	6	—
						Linfield	Brighton & HA	60	12
							Macclesfield T	35	16
Brown Greg‡	5 10	12 02	D	31 7 78	Wythenshawe	Trainee	Chester C	4	—
							Macclesfield T	12	—
Brown Steve‡	6 0	13 10	F	6 12 73	Rochford	Trainee	Southend U	10	2
							Scunthorpe U	—	—
							Colchester U	62	17
							Gillingham	9	2
							Lincoln C	72	8
							Macclesfield T	2	—
Collins Simon	6 0	13 00	D	16 12 73	Pontefract	Trainee	Huddersfield T	52	3
							Plymouth Arg	84	5
							Macclesfield T	39	3
Davenport Peter†	6 0	12 08	M	24 3 61	Birkenhead	Everton	Nottingham F	118	54
							Manchester U	92	22
							Middlesbrough	59	7
							Sunderland	99	15
							Airdrie	38	9
							St Johnstone	22	4
							Stockport Co	6	1
						Southport	Macclesfield T	5	1

Davies Simon#	5 11	12 04	M	23 4 74	Davenham	Trainee	Manchester U	11	—
							Exeter C (loan)	6	1
							Huddersfield T (loan)	3	—
							Luton T	22	1
							Macclesfield T	48	3
Durkan Kieron	5 10	12 09	M	1 12 73	Chester	Trainee	Wrexham	50	3
							Stockport Co	64	4
							Macclesfield T	72	9
Griffiths Peter‡	5 9	11 06	M	13 3 80	St Helier	Trainee	Macclesfield T	4	1
Hitchen Steve	5 8	11 07	D	28 11 76	Salford	Trainee	Blackburn R	—	—
							Macclesfield T	42	—
Ingram Rae	5 11	12 09	D	6 12 74	Manchester	Trainee	Manchester C	23	—
							Macclesfield T (loan)	5	—
							Macclesfield T	65	—
Lomax Michael‡	5 10	10 12	D	7 12 79	Whithington		Macclesfield T	1	—
Martin Lee	6 0	13 07	G	9 9 68	Huddersfield	Trainee	Huddersfield T	54	—
							Blackpool	98	—
							Bradford C (loan)	—	—
							Rochdale	—	—
							Halifax T	37	—
							Macclesfield T	21	—
Mason Michael*	5 11	11 04	F	7 8 79	Walsall		Macclesfield T	—	—
Moore Neil‡	6 1	12 07	D	21 9 72	Liverpool	Trainee	Everton	5	—
							Blackpool (loan)	7	—
							Oldham Ath (loan)	5	—
							Carlisle U (loan)	13	—
							Rotherham U (loan)	11	—
							Norwich C	2	—
							Burnley	52	3
							Macclesfield T	15	2
Munroe Karl†	6 0	10 08	D	23 9 79	Manchester	Trainee	Swansea C	1	—
							Macclesfield T	5	—
O'Neill Paul§	5 11	11 02		17 6 82	Bolton	Trainee	Macclesfield T	1	—
Pates Bradley‡	5 9	11 02	M	21 12 79	Burnley		Macclesfield T	—	—
Price Ryan‡	6 6	14 00	G	13 3 70	Wolverhampton	Stafford R	Birmingham C	—	—
							Macclesfield T	100	—
Priest Chris	5 10	12 00	M	18 10 73	Leigh	Trainee	Everton	—	—
							Chester C	167	26
							Macclesfield T	36	4
Rioch Greg	5 10	12 08	D	24 6 75	Sutton Coldfield	Trainee	Luton T	—	—
							Barnet (loan)	3	—
							Peterborough U	18	—
							Hull C	91	6
							Macclesfield T	42	5
Sedgemore Ben	6 0	12 07	M	5 8 75	Wolverhampton	Trainee	Birmingham C	—	—
							Northampton T (loan)	1	—
							Mansfield T (loan)	9	—
							Peterborough U	17	—
							Mansfield T	67	6
							Macclesfield T	75	3
Tinson Darren	6 0	13 07	D	15 11 69	Birmingham	Northwich V	Macclesfield T	127	1
Tomlinson Graeme	5 10	12 00	F	10 12 75	Watford	Trainee	Bradford C	17	6
							Manchester U	—	—
							Luton T (loan)	7	—
							Bournemouth (loan)	7	1
							Millwall (loan)	3	1
							Macclesfield T	46	6
Ware Paul	5 9	11 05	M	7 11 70	Congleton	Trainee	Stoke C	115	10
							Stockport Co	54	4
							Cardiff C (loan)	5	—
						Hednesford T	Macclesfield T	18	2
Whitehead Damien	5 10	12 00	F	24 4 79	Whiston	Warrington T	Macclesfield T	23	6
Whittaker Stuart*	5 7	10 06	M	2 1 75	Liverpool	Liverpool	Bolton W	3	—
							Wigan Ath (loan)	3	—
							Macclesfield T	67	5
Wood Steve#	5 9	10 10	M	23 6 63	Oldham	Ashton U	Macclesfield T	121	18

Trainees
Booth, Daniel R; Buckley, Matthew TH; Cain, Philip; Came, Shaun R; Hulse, Paul G; Hutchinson, Neil W; Leonard, Christopher; Marsh, Adam R; Morris, Adam S; O'Neill, Paul D

Non-Contract
Davenport, Peter; Munroe, Karl A

MANCHESTER CITY

Allsopp Danny	6 0	12 08	F	10 8 78	Melbourne	Port Melbourne	Manchester C	28	4
							Notts Co (loan)	3	1
							Wrexham (loan)	3	4
Bishop Ian#	5 10	12 00	M	29 5 65	Liverpool	Apprentice	Everton	1	—
							Crewe Alex (loan)	4	—
							Carlisle U	132	14
							Bournemouth	44	2
							Manchester C	19	2
							West Ham U	254	12
							Manchester C	68	2

Cooke Terry	5 8	10 03	F	5 8 76	Marston Green	Trainee	Manchester U	4	—
							Sunderland (loan)	6	—
							Birmingham C (loan)	4	—
							Wrexham (loan)	10	—
							Manchester C	34	7
							Wigan Ath (loan)	10	1
Crooks Lee	6 1	12 09	D	14 1 78	Wakefield	Trainee	Manchester C	74	2
Day Rhys	6 1	12 08	M	31 8 82	Bridgend	Scholar	Manchester C	—	—
Dickov Paul	5 5	11 09	F	1 11 72	Glasgow	Trainee	Arsenal	21	3
							Luton T (loan)	15	1
							Brighton & HA (loan)	8	5
							Manchester C	128	29
Duff Greg*	5 11	10 08	D	16 10 80	Manchester	Trainee	Manchester C	—	—
Dunfield Terry	5 7	10 03	M	20 2 82	Canada	Trainee	Manchester C	—	—
Edghill Richard	5 9	11 00	D	23 9 74	Oldham	Trainee	Manchester C	164	1
Etuhu Dixon			M	8 6 82	Kano	Scholar	Manchester C	—	—
Fenton Nick	6 1	11 08	D	23 11 79	Preston	Trainee	Manchester C	15	—
							Notts Co (loan)	13	1
							Bournemouth (loan)	8	—
Garfield Darren*	5 9	10 06	F	27 1 81	Tameside	Trainee	Manchester C	—	—
Goater Shaun	6 0	12 10	F	25 2 70	Bermuda		Manchester U	—	—
							Rotherham U	209	70
							Notts Co (loan)	1	—
							Bristol C	75	40
							Manchester C	90	43
Grant Tony	5 10	10 08	M	14 11 74	Liverpool	Trainee	Everton	61	2
							Swindon T (loan)	3	1
							Tranmere R (loan)	9	—
							Manchester C	8	—
Granville Danny	6 1	12 11	D	19 1 75	Islington	Trainee	Cambridge U	99	7
							Chelsea	18	—
							Leeds U	9	—
							Manchester C	35	2
Hodgson Steven	5 11	11 00	G	23 12 81	Macclesfield	Scholar	Manchester C	—	—
Holmes Shaun	5 9	10 07	D	27 12 80	Derry	Trainee	Manchester C	—	—
Horlock Kevin	6 0	12 00	M	1 11 72	Erith	Trainee	West Ham U	—	—
							Swindon T	163	22
							Manchester C	118	28
Jobson Richard	6 2	12 12	D	9 5 63	Holderness	Burton Alb	Watford	28	4
							Hull C	221	17
							Oldham Ath	189	10
							Leeds U	22	1
							Southend U (loan)	8	1
							Manchester C	50	4
Jordan Stephen	6 0	11 00	M	6 3 82	Warrington	Scholar	Manchester C	—	—
Joyce Damien			M	8 3 83	Dublin	Scholar	Manchester C	—	—
Kennedy Mark	5 11	11 00	F	15 5 76	Dublin	Belvedere	Millwall	43	9
							Liverpool	16	—
							QPR (loan)	8	2
							Wimbledon	21	—
							Manchester C	41	8
Killen Chris	5 11	11 03	F	8 10 81	Wellington	Miramar R	Manchester C	—	—
Kneen Jason*	5 8	12 00	F	20 10 80	Stockport	Trainee	Manchester C	—	—
Laycock David	5 10	10 07	M	1 10 80	Hull	Trainee	Manchester C	—	—
Mason Gary	5 8	10 01	M	15 10 79	Edinburgh	Trainee	Manchester C	19	—
							Hartlepool U (loan)	6	—
McKinney Richard			G	18 5 79	Ballymoney	Ballymena U	Manchester C	—	—
Mike Leon	6 0	12 02	F	4 9 81	Manchester	Scholar	Manchester C	—	—
Morrison Andy	5 11	12 12	D	30 7 70	Inverness	Trainee	Plymouth Arg	113	6
							Blackburn R	5	—
							Blackpool	47	3
							Huddersfield T	45	2
							Manchester C	34	4
Murphy Brian			M	7 5 83	Waterford		Manchester C	—	—
Peacock Lee	6 1	13 12	F	9 10 76	Paisley	Trainee	Carlisle U	76	11
							Mansfield T	89	29
							Manchester C	8	—
Pollock Jamie	6 0	13 03	M	16 2 74	Stockton	Trainee	Middlesbrough	155	17
							Osasuna	—	—
							Bolton W	46	5
							Manchester C	58	5
Prior Spencer	6 1	13 00	D	22 4 71	Rochford	Trainee	Southend U	135	3
							Norwich C	74	1
							Leicester C	64	—
							Derby Co	54	1
							Manchester C	9	3
Russell Craig	5 10	12 07	F	4 2 74	Jarrow	Trainee	Sunderland	150	31
							Manchester C	31	2
							Tranmere R (loan)	4	—
							Port Vale (loan)	8	1
							Darlington (loan)	12	2
							Oxford U (loan)	6	—
							St Johnstone (loan)	1	1

Name	Ht	DOB	Pos	Debut	Birthplace	Source	Club	Apps	Gls
Shelia Murtaz‡	6 0	13 02	D	7 9 68	Georgia		Dynamo Tbilisi	10	2
							Alania	62	9
							Manchester C	15	2
Shuker Chris	5 5	9 03	M	9 5 82	Liverpool	Scholar	Manchester C	—	—
Taylor Gareth	6 1	12 02	F	25 2 73	Weston-Super-Mare	Southampton	Bristol R	47	16
							Crystal Palace	20	1
							Sheffield U	84	25
							Manchester C	43	9
							Port Vale (loan)	4	—
							QPR (loan)	6	1
Taylor Robert	6 1	13 08	F	30 4 71	Norwich	Trainee	Norwich C	—	—
							Leyton Orient (loan)	3	1
							Birmingham C	—	—
							Leyton Orient	73	20
							Brentford	173	56
							Gillingham	58	31
							Manchester C	16	5
Tiatto Danny	5 8	11 01	D	22 5 73	Melbourne	Baden	Stoke C	15	1
							Manchester C	52	—
Tskhadadze Kakhabor‡	6 1	12 04	D	7 9 68	Rustavi		Dynamo Tbilisi	41	1
							Sundsvall	4	—
							Spartak Moscow	7	—
							Eintracht Frankfurt	64	1
							Alania	17	1
							Manchester C	12	2
Weaver Nick	6 3	13 01	G	2 3 79	Sheffield	Trainee	Mansfield T	1	—
							Manchester C	90	—
Whitley Jeff	5 9	10 10	M	28 1 79	Zambia	Trainee	Manchester C	90	7
							Wrexham (loan)	9	2
Whitley Jim	5 9	10 12	M	14 4 75	Zambia	Trainee	Manchester C	38	—
							Blackpool (loan)	8	—
Wiekens Gerard	6 0	12 06	D	25 2 73	Tolhuiswyk		Veendam	33	1
							Manchester C	113	8
Wright-Phillips Shaun	5 6	10 01	F	25 10 81	London		Manchester C	4	—
Wright Tommy#	6 1	14 05	G	29 8 63	Belfast	Linfield	Newcastle U	73	—
							Hull C (loan)	6	—
							Nottingham F	11	—
							Reading (loan)	17	—
							Manchester C	33	—
							Wrexham (loan)	16	—
							Newcastle U (loan)	3	—

Scholars
Browne, Gary; Furnival, Gary R; Hogan Barry; Maguire, Gary J; McCarthy, Patrick; Paisley, Stephen; Parkhouse, Stephen; Pavey, Andrew; Tunnicliffe, Andrew J; Whelan, Glenn

Non-Contract
Barton, Joseph; Elliott, Stephen; Mears, Tyrone

Associated Schoolboys
Anderson-Hodgson, David

Associated Schoolboys who have accepted the Club's offer of a Traineeship/Scholarship/Contract
McDowall, Ryan; Orr, Adrian

MANCHESTER UNITED

Name	Ht	DOB	Pos	Debut	Birthplace	Source	Club	Apps	Gls
Beckham David	6 0	11 13	M	2 5 75	Leytonstone	Trainee	Manchester U	175	35
							Preston NE (loan)	5	2
Berg Henning	6 0	12 04	D	1 9 69	Eidsvoll	Lillestrom	Blackburn R	159	4
							Manchester U	65	2
Blomqvist Jesper	5 9	11 03	F	5 2 74	Tavelsjo		Umea	38	8
							IFK Gothenburg	71	19
							AC Milan	20	1
							Parma	28	1
							Manchester U	25	1
Bosnich Mark	6 2	15 07	G	13 1 72	Fairfield	Croatia Sydney	Manchester U	3	—
							Aston Villa	179	1
							Manchester U	23	
Brown Wes	6 1	13 11	D	13 10 79	Manchester	Trainee	Manchester U	16	—
Butt Nicky	5 10	11 11	M	21 1 75	Manchester	Trainee	Manchester U	178	16
Chadwick Luke	5 11	11 08	F	18 11 80	Cambridge	Trainee	Manchester U	—	—
Clegg George	5 10	11 11	F	16 11 80	Manchester	Trainee	Manchester U	—	—
Clegg Michael	5 8	11 10	D	3 7 77	Ashton-under-Lyne	Trainee	Manchester U	9	—
							Ipswich T (loan)	3	—
							Wigan Ath (loan)	6	—
Coates Craig	5 7	10 11	F	26 10 82	Dryburn	Trainee	Manchester U	—	—
Cole Andy	5 11	12 02	F	15 10 71	Nottingham	Trainee	Arsenal	1	—
							Fulham (loan)	13	3
							Bristol C (loan)	12	8
							Bristol C	29	12
							Newcastle U	70	55
							Manchester U	165	80
Cosgrove Stephen	5 9	10 06	M	29 12 80	Glasgow	Trainee	Manchester U	—	—
Cruyff Jordi*	6 1	11 00	F	9 2 74	Amsterdam	Ajax	Barcelona	41	11
							Manchester U	34	7

Name							Club	Apps	Gls
Culkin Nick	6 2	13 09	G	6 7 78	York	York C	Manchester U	1	—
							Hull C (loan)	4	—
Curtis John	5 10	11 13	D	3 9 78	Nuneaton	Trainee	Manchester U	13	—
							Barnsley (loan)	28	2
Davis James	5 8	11 05	F	6 2 82	Bromsgrove	Trainee	Manchester U	—	—
Djordjic Bojan	5 10	11 01	M	6 2 82	Belgrade		Manchester U	—	—
Dodd Ashley	5 10	10 02	M	7 1 82	Stafford	Trainee	Manchester U	—	—
Evans Wayne	5 9	9 08	M	23 10 80	Carmarthen	Trainee	Manchester U	—	—
Fortune Quinton	5 9	11 09	M	21 5 77	Cape Town	Tottenham H	Mallorca	8	—
							Atletico Madrid	3	—
							Atletico Madrid B	30	2
							Atletico Madrid	1	—
							Atletico Madrid B	31	1
							Atletico Madrid	2	—
							Manchester U	6	2
Giggs Ryan	5 11	11 00	F	29 11 73	Cardiff	School	Manchester U	290	59
Greening Jonathan	6 0	11 13	F	2 1 79	Scarborough	Trainee	York C	25	2
							Manchester U	7	—
Healy David	5 8	11 01	F	5 8 79	Downpatrick	Trainee	Manchester U	—	—
							Port Vale (loan)	16	3
Higginbotham Danny	6 1	12 07	D	29 12 78	Manchester	Trainee	Manchester U	4	—
Hilton Kirk	5 7	10 01	D	2 4 81	Flixton	Trainee	Manchester U	—	—
Howard Joshua*	5 8	10 06	M	15 11 80	Ashton-under-Lyne	Trainee	Manchester U	—	—
Irwin Denis	5 8	10 11	D	31 10 65	Cork	Apprentice	Leeds U	72	1
							Oldham Ath	167	4
							Manchester U	335	22
Johnsen Ronny	6 3	13 06	D	10 6 69	Sandefjord	Eik	Lyn	31	7
							Lillestrom	23	4
							Besiktas	22	1
							Manchester U	78	5
Jones Rhodri	6 0	12 04	D	19 1 82	Cardiff	Trainee	Manchester U	—	—
Keane Roy	5 11	11 10	M	10 8 71	Cork	Cobh Ramb	Nottingham F	114	22
							Manchester U	185	24
Lynch Mark	5 11	11 03	D	2 9 81	Manchester	Trainee	Manchester U	—	—
Marsh Allan*	6 0	11 01	G	10 9 80	Wigan	Trainee	Manchester U	—	—
May David	6 0	13 05	D	24 6 70	Oldham	Trainee	Blackburn R	123	3
							Manchester U	80	6
							Huddersfield T (loan)	1	—
McDermott Alan	6 1	11 07	D	22 1 82	Dublin	Trainee	Manchester U	—	—
Molloy Eric*	5 9	10 03	F	21 12 81	Galway	Trainee	Manchester U	—	—
Muirhead Ben	5 9	10 05	F	5 1 83	Doncaster	Trainee	Manchester U	—	—
Nardiello Daniel	5 11	11 04	F	22 10 82	Coventry	Trainee	Manchester U	—	—
Neville Gary	5 11	12 04	D	18 2 75	Bury	Trainee	Manchester U	171	2
Neville Phil	5 11	12 00	D	21 1 77	Bury	Trainee	Manchester U	131	1
Nevland Erik	5 10	11 12	F	10 11 77	Stavanger		Viking	14	5
(Transferred to Viking, December 1999)							Manchester U	1	—
Notman Alex	5 7	10 11	F	10 12 79	Edinburgh	Trainee	Manchester U	—	—
							Aberdeen (loan)	2	—
							Sheffield U (loan)	10	3
O'Shea John	6 3	12 10	D	30 4 81	Waterford	Waterford	Manchester U	—	—
							Bournemouth (loan)	10	1
Rachubka Paul	6 1	13 01	G	21 5 81	San Luis Obispo	Trainee	Manchester U	—	—
Roche Lee	5 10	10 10	D	28 10 80	Bolton	Trainee	Manchester U	—	—
Rose Michael	5 11	11 01	D	28 7 82	Salford	Trainee	Manchester U	—	—
Rose Stephen*	6 00	10 10	D	23 11 80	Salford	Trainee	Manchester U	—	—
Schmeichel Peter	6 4	16 00	G	18 11 63	Gladsaxe		Hvidovre	88	6
(Transferred to Sporting Lisbon, July 1999)							Brondby	119	2
							Manchester U	292	—
Scholes Paul	5 7	11 00	M	16 11 74	Salford	Trainee	Manchester U	160	41
Sheringham Teddy	6 0	12 09	F	2 4 66	Highams Park	Apprentice	Millwall	220	93
							Aldershot (loan)	5	—
							Nottingham F	42	14
							Tottenham H	166	75
							Manchester U	75	16
Silvestre Mikael	6 0	13 01	D	9 8 77	Chambray les Tours		Rennes	49	—
							Internazionale	18	1
							Manchester U	31	—
Solskjaer Ole Gunnar	5 10	11 11	F	26 2 73	Kristiansund		Molde	42	31
							Manchester U	102	47
Stam Jaap	6 3	15 00	D	17 7 72	Kampen		Zwolle	32	1
							Cambuur	66	3
							Willem II	19	1
							PSV Eindhoven	76	12
							Manchester U	63	1
Stewart Michael	5 11	11 11	M	26 2 81	Edinburgh	Trainee	Manchester U	—	—
Strange Gareth	5 9	10 05	M	3 10 81	Bolton	Trainee	Manchester U	—	—
Studley Dominic*	5 5	9 08	D	9 10 80	Manchester	Trainee	Manchester U	—	—
Studley Mark	5 6	10 00	D	21 12 81	Manchester	Trainee	Manchester U	—	—
Szmid Marek	5 8	11 06	D	2 3 82	Nuneaton	Trainee	Manchester U	—	—

Name	Ht	Wt	Pos	Born	Birthplace	Source	Club	Apps	Gls
Taibi Massimo *(On loan to Reggina)*	6 3	14 09	G	18 2 70	Palermo		Licata	1	—
							Trento	23	—
							AC Milan	—	—
							Como	34	—
							Piacenza	177	—
							AC Milan	17	—
							Venezia	34	—
							Manchester U	4	—
Teather Paul	6 0	11 13	D	28 12 77	Rotherham	Trainee	Manchester U	—	—
							Bournemouth (loan)	10	—
Twiss Michael*	5 11	13 03	M	28 12 77	Salford	Trainee	Manchester U	—	—
							Sheffield U (loan)	12	1
Van der Gouw Raimond	6 3	13 09	G	24 3 63	Oldenzaal		Go Ahead	97	—
							Vitesse	258	—
							Manchester U	26	—
Walker Joshua	6 1	11 01	M	20 12 81	Birmingham	Trainee	Manchester U	—	—
Wallwork Ronnie	5 10	13 01	D	10 9 77	Manchester	Trainee	Manchester U	6	—
							Carlisle U (loan)	10	1
							Stockport Co (loan)	7	—
Webber Danny	5 9	10 08	F	28 12 81	Manchester	Trainee	Manchester U	—	—
Wheatcroft Paul* *(On loan to FC Fortune)*	5 9	9 11	F	22 11 80	Manchester	Trainee	Manchester U	—	—
Williams Matthew	5 8	9 11	F	5 11 82	St Asaph		Manchester U	—	—
Wilson Mark	6 0	12 07	M	9 2 79	Scunthorpe	Trainee	Manchester U	3	—
							Wrexham (loan)	13	4
Wood Neil	5 10	13 02	F	4 1 83	Manchester	Trainee	Manchester U	—	—
Yorke Dwight	5 10	12 03	F	3 11 71	Canaan	St Clair's	Aston Villa	231	73
							Manchester U	64	38

Scholars

Baxter, Nicholas P; Clegg, Steven J; Grogan, Kevin M; Moran, David; Pugh, Daniel; Rankin, John; Sampson, Gary JF; Tate, Alan; Taylor, Andrew J; Tierney, Paul T; Whiteman, Marc C

MANSFIELD TOWN

Name	Ht	Wt	Pos	Born	Birthplace	Source	Club	Apps	Gls
Allardyce Craig‡	5 10	11 10	D	9 6 75	Bolton	Trainee	Preston NE	1	—
							Blackpool	1	—
						Chorley	Chesterfield	1	—
							Peterborough U	4	—
							Mansfield T	10	—
Andrews John	6 1	12 08	D	27 9 78	Cork	Trainee	Coventry C	—	—
						Grantham T	Mansfield T	30	1
Asher Alistair	5 11	11 07	D	14 10 80	Leicester	Trainee	Mansfield T	35	—
Bacon Danny	5 10	10 12	D	20 9 80	Mansfield	Trainee	Mansfield T	8	2
Bassinder Gavin*	5 8	11 01	D	24 9 79	Mexborough	Trainee	Barnsley	—	—
							Mansfield T	4	—
Blake Mark#	5 11	13 05	M	16 12 70	Nottingham		Aston Villa	31	2
							Wolverhampton W (loan)	2	—
							Portsmouth	15	—
							Leicester C	49	4
							Walsall	61	5
							Mansfield T	43	1
Boulding Mick	5 10	11 03	F	8 2 76	Sheffield	Hallam	Mansfield T	33	6
Bowling Ian*	6 3	14 06	G	27 7 65	Sheffield	Gainsborough T	Lincoln C	59	—
							Hartlepool U (loan)	1	—
							Bradford C (loan)	7	—
							Bradford C	29	—
							Mansfield T	170	—
Camilleri Carlo‡	5 11	12 02	M	14 5 75	Brussels		Charleroi	6	—
							Mansfield T	2	—
Clarke Darrell	5 10	11 06	M	16 12 77	Mansfield	Trainee	Mansfield T	129	18
Cowling Lee*	5 10	12 01	D	22 9 77	Doncaster	Trainee	Nottingham F	—	—
							Mansfield T	8	—
Disley Craig	5 10	10 12	M	24 8 81	Worksop	Trainee	Mansfield T	5	—
Garratt Martin‡	5 10	11 00	M	22 2 80	York		York C	45	1
							Mansfield T	6	—
Gibbons Scott*	5 9	11 00	M	1 5 81	Nottingham	Trainee	Mansfield T	—	—
Greenacre Chris	5 11	10 06	F	23 12 77	Halifax	Trainee	Manchester C	8	1
							Cardiff C (loan)	11	2
							Blackpool (loan)	4	—
							Scarborough (loan)	12	2
							Mansfield T	31	9
Hassell Bobby	5 9	12 04	D	4 6 80	Derby	Trainee	Mansfield T	23	1
Kerr David	6 0	12 11	M	6 9 74	Dumfries	Trainee	Manchester C	6	—
							Mansfield T (loan)	5	—
							Mansfield T	80	4
Lawrence Liam§	5 10	11 03		14 12 81	Retford	Trainee	Mansfield T	2	—
Linighan David‡	6 1	13 08	D	9 11 65	Hartlepool	Local	Hartlepool U	91	5
							Leeds U (loan)	—	—
							Derby Co	—	—
							Shrewsbury T	65	1
							Ipswich T	277	12
							Blackpool	100	5
							Dunfermline Ath	1	—
							Mansfield T	38	—

Lormor Tony	6 1	14 02	F	29 10 70	Ashington	Trainee	Newcastle U	8	3
							Norwich C (loan)	—	—
							Lincoln C	100	30
							Peterborough U	5	—
							Chesterfield	113	35
							Preston NE	12	3
							Notts Co (loan)	7	—
							Mansfield T	74	20
Milner Jonathan‡	5 8	11 07	F	30 3 81	Mansfield	Trainee	Mansfield T	7	—
Mimms Bobby#	6 3	14 01	G	12 10 63	York	Halifax T	Rotherham U	83	—
							Everton	29	—
							Notts Co (loan)	2	—
							Sunderland (loan)	4	—
							Blackburn R (loan)	6	—
							Manchester C (loan)	3	—
							Tottenham H	37	—
							Aberdeen (loan)	6	—
							Blackburn R	128	—
							Crystal Palace	1	—
							Preston NE	27	—
							Rotherham U	43	—
							York C	63	—
							Mansfield T	5	—
Parkin Steve‡	5 6	11 01	D	7 11 65	Mansfield	Apprentice	Stoke C	113	5
							WBA	48	2
							Mansfield T	87	3
Richardson Neil*	5 11	14 03	D	3 3 68	Sunderland	Brandon U	Rotherham U	184	9
							Exeter C (loan)	14	—
							Mansfield T	31	—
Roscoe Andy*	5 9	12 00	M	4 6 73	Liverpool	Trainee	Liverpool	—	—
							Bolton W	3	—
							Rotherham U	202	18
							Mansfield T	39	2
Sisson Michael	5 10	11 05	M	24 11 78	Sutton-in-Ashfield	Trainee	Mansfield T	27	2
Tallon Gary	5 10	11 10	M	5 9 73	Drogheda	Trainee	Blackburn R	—	—
							Kilmarnock	4	—
							Chester C (loan)	1	—
							Mansfield T	75	2
Williams Lee#	5 7	11 08	D	3 2 73	Edgbaston	Trainee	Aston Villa	—	—
							Shrewsbury T (loan)	3	—
							Peterborough U	91	1
							Tranmere R	—	—
							Mansfield T	134	5
Williamson Lee§	5 10	10 04		7 6 82	Derby	Trainee	Mansfield T	4	—
Willis Scott			M	20 2 82	Liverpool	Wigan Ath	Mansfield T	—	—

Trainees
Archbold, Shaun J; Jervis, David J; Jones, Adam L; Lawrence, Liam; Mitchell, Dean J; Overton, Paul D; Sweeney, Dean; Tye, Kevin; Williamson, Lee T

Scholars
Clarke, James W; Elliott, Dominic S; Gibson, Christopher J; Murcott, Scott A; Stringfellow, Daniel J; Swinscoe, Craig A

MIDDLESBROUGH

Armstrong Alun	6 0	13 08	F	22 2 75	Gateshead	School	Newcastle U	—	—
							Stockport Co	159	48
							Middlesbrough	29	9
							Huddersfield T (loan)	6	—
Baker Steve	6 0	12 06	D	8 9 78	Pontefract	Trainee	Middlesbrough	8	—
							Huddersfield T (loan)	3	—
							Darlington (loan)	5	—
Bennion Chris	6 2	12 00	G	30 8 80	Edinburgh	Trainee	Middlesbrough	—	—
Beresford Marlon	6 1	13 08	G	2 6 69	Lincoln	Trainee	Sheffield W	—	—
							Bury (loan)	1	—
							Ipswich T (loan)	—	—
							Northampton T (loan)	13	—
							Crewe Alex (loan)	3	—
							Northampton T (loan)	15	—
							Burnley	240	—
							Middlesbrough	8	—
Bernhardt Arturo	6 1	12 00	F	27 8 82	Santa Catarina	Nova Hamburgo	Middlesbrough	—	—
Campbell Andy	6 0	11 13	F	18 4 79	Middlesbrough	Trainee	Middlesbrough	45	4
							Sheffield U (loan)	11	3
Canavan Michael*	6 1	12 02	F	17 9 80	South Shields	Trainee	Middlesbrough	—	—
Close Brian			M	27 1 82	Belfast		Middlesbrough	—	—
Cooper Colin	5 11	11 11	D	28 2 67	Sedgefield		Middlesbrough	188	6
							Millwall	77	6
							Nottingham F	180	20
							Middlesbrough	58	1
Deane Brian	6 3	14 00	F	7 2 68	Leeds	Apprentice	Doncaster R	66	12
							Sheffield U	197	82
							Leeds U	138	32
							Sheffield U	24	11
						Benfica	Middlesbrough	55	15

Player							Clubs	App	Gls
Festa Gianluca	5 11	13 00	D	15 3 69	Cagliari		Cagliari	156	—
							Fersuicis (loan)	26	2
							Internazionale	66	3
							Roma (loan)	21	1
							Middlesbrough	105	7
Fleming Curtis	5 10	12 05	D	8 10 68	Manchester	St Patrick's Ath	Middlesbrough	228	3
Gascoigne Paul	5 10	12 09	M	27 5 67	Gateshead	Apprentice	Newcastle U	92	21
							Tottenham H	92	19
							Lazio	41	6
							Rangers	74	30
							Middlesbrough	41	4
Gavin Jason	6 0	11 12	D	14 3 80	Dublin	Trainee	Middlesbrough	8	—
Gordon Dean	6 0	13 08	D	10 2 73	Thornton Heath	Trainee	Crystal Palace	201	20
							Middlesbrough	42	3
Hanson Christian	6 1	11 05	D	3 8 81	Middlesbrough	Trainee	Middlesbrough	—	—
Harrison Craig	6 0	11 08	D	10 11 77	Gateshead	Trainee	Middlesbrough	24	—
							Preston NE (loan)	6	—
Hudson Mark	5 10	11 03	M	24 10 80	Bishop Auckland	Trainee	Middlesbrough	—	—
Ince Paul	5 10	12 04	M	21 10 67	Ilford	Trainee	West Ham U	72	7
							Manchester U	206	24
							Internazionale	54	9
							Liverpool	65	14
							Middlesbrough	32	3
Jones Bradley	6 3	12 01	G	19 3 82	Armadale	Trainee	Middlesbrough	—	—
Jones Thomas	5 10	11 02	F	26 3 80	Middlesbrough	Trainee	Middlesbrough	—	—
Juninho	5 5	10 00	F	22 2 73	Sao Paulo	Ituano	Sao Paulo	25	1
(On loan from Atletico Madrid)							Middlesbrough	56	14
							Atletico Madrid	55	14
							Middlesbrough	28	4
Kell Richard	6 1	10 13	M	15 9 79	Bishop Auckland	Trainee	Middlesbrough	—	—
Kelly Brian*	6 2	11 12	D	6 2 81	Dublin	Trainee	Middlesbrough	—	—
Kilgannon Sean	5 11	11 08	M	8 3 81	Stirling	Trainee	Middlesbrough	1	—
Kinder Vladimir‡	5 9	12 03	D	9 3 69	Bratislava	Karlovy Vary	Slovan Bratislava	161	22
							Middlesbrough	37	5
Maddison Neil	5 10	11 10	M	2 10 69	Darlington	Trainee	Southampton	169	19
							Middlesbrough	56	4
Marinelli Carlos	5 8	11 06	M	14 3 82	Buenos Aires	Boca Juniors	Middlesbrough	2	—
McStea Anthony	5 10	11 07	D	16 5 81	Gateshead	Trainee	Middlesbrough	—	—
Moat David	5 8	11 02	D	1 10 81	Gateshead	Trainee	Middlesbrough	—	—
Moore Alan	5 10	11 02	M	25 11 74	Dublin	Rivermount	Middlesbrough	118	14
							Barnsley (loan)	5	—
Mustoe Robbie	6 0	12 03	M	28 8 68	Oxford		Oxford U	91	10
							Middlesbrough	304	23
O'Loughlin John‡	5 8	10 12	M	31 1 79	Letterkenny	Bruncrana Hearts	Middlesbrough	—	—
O'Neill Keith	6 1	12 13	F	16 2 76	Dublin	Trainee	Norwich C	73	9
							Middlesbrough	22	—
Ormerod Anthony	5 11	12 00	M	31 3 79	Middlesbrough	Trainee	Middlesbrough	19	3
							Carlisle U (loan)	5	—
							York C (loan)	12	—
Pallister Gary	6 5	15 02	D	30 6 65	Ramsgate	Billingham T	Middlesbrough	156	5
							Darlington (loan)	7	—
							Manchester U	317	12
							Middlesbrough	47	1
Parnaby Stuart	5 11	11 00	M	19 7 82	Durham City	Trainee	Middlesbrough	—	—
Prunty Sean*	5 9	10 11	M	10 7 80	Dublin	Belvedere	Middlesbrough	—	—
Ricard Hamilton	6 1	13 12	F	12 1 74	Choco	Deportivo Cali	Middlesbrough	79	29
Roberts Ben	6 2	13 05	G	22 6 75	Bishop Auckland	Trainee	Middlesbrough	16	—
							Hartlepool U (loan)	4	—
							Wycombe W (loan)	15	—
							Bradford C (loan)	2	—
							Millwall (loan)	11	—
							Luton T (loan)	14	—
Robinson Gerard			M	9 6 82	Dublin	Trainee	Middlesbrough	—	—
Schwarzer Mark	6 5	15 01	G	6 10 72	Sydney	Dynamo Dresden	Kaiserslautern	4	—
							Bradford C	13	—
							Middlesbrough	113	—
Stamp Phil	5 11	14 09	M	12 12 75	Middlesbrough	Trainee	Middlesbrough	91	5
Stockdale Robbie	6 0	12 03	D	30 11 79	Redcar	Trainee	Middlesbrough	31	1
Summerbell Mark	5 9	11 01	M	30 10 76	Durham	Trainee	Middlesbrough	44	—
Taylor Andrew	5 11	11 01	D	6 9 81	Middlesbrough	Trainee	Middlesbrough	—	—
Vickers Steve	6 2	13 01	D	13 10 67	Bishop Auckland	Spennymoor U	Tranmere R	311	11
							Middlesbrough	227	8
Walklate Steve‡	5 11	12 00	M	27 9 79	Durham	Trainee	Middlesbrough	—	—
Wilford Aaron	6 3	14 01	D	14 1 82	Scarborough	Harrogate College	Middlesbrough	—	—
Wiltshire Luke			M	2 10 81	Australia		Middlesbrough	—	—
Ziege Christian	6 2	12 13	D	1 2 72	Berlin		Bayern Munich	172	41
							AC Milan	39	4
							Middlesbrough	29	6

Scholars
Brackstone, Stephen; Burton, Andrew; Crager, Paul M; Dove, Craig; Gulliver, Philip S; Russel, Samuel I; Ryan, Leon M; Skirving, Richard M; Smith, Liam; Stephenson, Paul

MILLWALL

Name	Ht	Wt	Pos	DOB	Birthplace	Source	Club	Apps	Gls
Barnard Richard*	6 1	12 13	G	27 12 80	Frimley	Trainee	Millwall	—	—
Bircham Marc	5 11	12 02	D	11 5 78	Brent	Trainee	Millwall	60	1
Bowry Bobby	5 9	10 08	M	19 5 71	Croydon		QPR	—	—
						Carshalton Ath	Crystal Palace	50	1
							Millwall	139	5
Braniff Kevin	5 11	12 00	F	4 3 83	Belfast	Scholar	Millwall	—	—
Bubb Byron	5 7	10 05	M	17 12 81	Harrow	Scholar	Millwall	5	—
Bull Ronnie	5 7	10 11	D	27 12 80	Hackney	Trainee	Millwall	10	—
Cahill Tim	5 10	10 10	M	6 12 79	Sydney	Sydney U	Millwall	82	18
Cook Andy‡	5 9	12 04	M	10 8 69	Romsey	Apprentice	Southampton	16	1
							Exeter C	70	1
							Swansea C	62	—
							Portsmouth	9	—
							Millwall	5	—
Cort Leon	6 2	12 13	D	11 9 79	Southwark	Dulwich H	Millwall	—	—
Dolan Joe	6 3	13 05	D	27 5 80	Harrow	Chelsea	Millwall	26	2
Dunne Alan	5 10	11 12	D	23 8 82	Dublin		Millwall	—	—
Dyche Sean	6 0	13 07	D	28 6 71	Kettering	Trainee	Nottingham F	—	—
							Chesterfield	231	8
							Bristol C	17	—
							Luton T (loan)	14	1
							Millwall	1	—
Fitzgerald Scott#	5 11	12 08	D	13 8 69	Westminster	Trainee	Wimbledon	106	1
							Sheffield U (loan)	6	—
							Millwall (loan)	7	—
							Millwall	81	1
Gilkes Michael#	5 8	10 10	M	20 7 65	Hackney	Leicester C	Reading	393	43
							Chelsea (loan)	1	—
							Southampton (loan)	6	—
							Wolverhampton W	38	1
							Millwall	29	2
Grant Kim	5 10	11 05	F	25 9 72	Ghana	Trainee	Charlton Ath	123	18
(Transferred to Lommel, August 1999)							Luton T	35	5
							Millwall	55	11
							Notts Co (loan)	6	1
Harris Neil	5 11	12 04	F	12 7 77	Orsett	Cambridge C	Millwall	80	40
Hicks Mark	5 8	10 04	F	24 7 81	Belfast	Trainee	Millwall	1	—
Hockton Danny‡	6 1	12 08	F	7 2 79	Barking	Trainee	Millwall	36	4
							Leyton Orient (loan)	5	—
Ifill Paul	6 0	12 09	M	20 10 79	Brighton	Trainee	Millwall	59	12
Kinet Christophe	5 8	10 12	M	31 12 74	Huy		Ekeren	38	4
							Strasbourg	27	2
							Millwall	3	—
Law Brian*	6 2	14 08	D	1 1 70	Merthyr	Apprentice	QPR	20	—
							Wolverhampton W	31	1
							Millwall	45	4
Lawrence Matthew	6 1	12 12	D	19 6 74	Northampton	Grays Ath	Wycombe W	16	1
							Fulham	59	—
							Wycombe W	63	4
							Millwall	9	—
Livermore David	5 11	12 04	M	20 5 80	Edmonton	Trainee	Arsenal	—	—
							Millwall	32	2
McLeary Alan*	5 11	11 09	D	6 10 64	Lambeth	Apprentice	Millwall	307	5
							Sheffield U (loan)	3	—
							Wimbledon (loan)	4	—
							Charlton Ath	66	3
							Bristol C	34	—
							Millwall	36	—
Mead Billy‡	5 10	10 02	D	7 1 81	London		Millwall	—	—
Meade Darren	5 9	11 00	F	3 2 82	Dublin	Belvedere	Millwall	—	—
Moody Paul	6 3	14 08	F	13 6 67	Portsmouth	Waterlooville	Southampton	12	—
							Reading (loan)	5	1
							Oxford U	136	49
							Fulham	40	19
							Millwall	32	11
Neill Lucas	6 0	12 03	M	9 3 78	Sydney	NSW Academy	Millwall	124	10
Nethercott Stuart	6 0	13 00	D	21 3 73	Chadwell Heath	Trainee	Tottenham H	54	—
							Maidstone U (loan)	13	1
							Barnet (loan)	3	—
							Millwall	84	2
Newman Ricky	5 10	12 06	M	5 8 70	Guildford	Trainee	Crystal Palace	48	3
							Maidstone U (loan)	10	1
							Millwall	150	5
							Reading (loan)	7	1
Odunsi Leke	5 9	11 07	M	5 12 80	Walworth	Trainee	Millwall	7	—
Phillips Mark	6 2	13 00	D	27 1 82	Lambeth	Scholar	Millwall	—	—
Rees Matthew	6 3	13 06	D	2 9 82	Swansea	Trainee	Millwall	—	—

Name	Ht	Wt	Pos	Born	Birthplace	Source	Club	Apps	Gls
Reid Steven	6 0	12 03	F	10 3 81	Kingston	Trainee	Millwall	47	—
Ryan Robbie	5 10	12 03	D	6 5 77	Dublin	Belvedere	Huddersfield T	15	—
							Millwall	76	—
Sadlier Richard	6 2	13 01	F	14 1 79	Dublin	Belvedere	Millwall	72	13
Shaw Paul	5 10	12 10	F	4 9 73	Burnham	Trainee	Arsenal	12	2
							Burnley (loan)	9	4
							Cardiff C (loan)	6	—
							Peterborough U (loan)	12	5
							Millwall	109	26
Smith Phil	6 1	13 11	G	14 12 79	Harrow	Trainee	Millwall	5	—
Spink Nigel*	6 2	15 07	G	8 8 58	Chelmsford	Chelmsford C	Aston Villa	361	—
							WBA	19	—
							Millwall	44	—
Stevens Keith*	6 0	12 12	D	21 6 64	Merton	Apprentice	Millwall	462	9
Stuart Jamie	5 9	11 10	D	15 10 76	Southwark	Trainee	Charlton Ath	50	3
							Millwall	44	—
Tuttle David	6 2	14 02	D	6 2 72	Reading	Trainee	Tottenham H	13	—
							Peterborough U (loan)	7	—
							Sheffield U	63	1
							Crystal Palace	81	5
							Charlton Ath (loan)	—	—
							Barnsley	12	—
							Millwall	8	—
Tyne Tommy	6 1	12 05	F	2 3 81	Lambeth		Millwall	—	—
Warner Tony	6 4	15 01	G	11 5 74	Liverpool	School	Liverpool	—	—
							Swindon T (loan)	2	—
							Celtic (loan)	3	—
							Aberdeen (loan)	6	—
							Millwall	45	—

Scholars
Alderton, Rio; Alimi, Bashiru; Deegan, Darren S; Karaiskos, Andreas; Kevin, Joseph S; Robinson, Paul MJ; Taylor, William B; Worsfold, Dean C

Non-Contract
Lombardo, Daniel CR; Steele, Daniel

Associated Schoolboys who have accepted the Club's offer of a Traineeship/Scholarship/Contract
Booth, Stuart; Hearn, Charley; Idaewor, Ambrose; Redmond, Gary

---

NEWCASTLE UNITED

Name	Ht	Wt	Pos	Born	Birthplace	Source	Club	Apps	Gls
Albert Philippe	6 3	12 04	D	10 8 67	Bouillon		Charleroi	65	7
(Transferred to Charleroi, July 1999)							Mechelen	87	5
							Anderlecht	50	9
							Newcastle U	96	8
							Fulham (loan)	13	2
Ameobi Foluwashola	6 2	12 00	F	12 10 81	Zaria	Trainee	Newcastle U	—	—
Andersson Andreas	6 1	12 01	F	10 4 74	Osterhoninge	Hova	Tidaholm	9	6
(Transferred to AIK Stockholm, August 1999)							Degerfors	40	16
							IFK Gothenburg	39	32
							AC Milan	13	1
							Newcastle U	27	4
Barton Warren	6 0	12 00	D	19 3 69	Islington	Leytonstone/Ilford	Maidstone U	42	—
							Wimbledon	180	10
							Newcastle U	130	4
Beharall David	6 2	11 07	D	8 3 79	Newcastle	Trainee	Newcastle U	6	—
Boyd Mark	5 9	11 02	M	22 10 81	Carlisle	Trainee	Newcastle U	—	—
Brady Garry	5 10	11 02	M	7 9 76	Glasgow	Trainee	Tottenham H	9	—
							Newcastle U	9	—
							Norwich C (loan)	6	—
Brennan Stephen	5 8	10 03	D	26 3 83	Dublin		Newcastle U	—	—
Caldwell Gary	5 11	11 10	D	12 4 82	Stirling	Trainee	Newcastle U	—	—
Caldwell Stephen	6 0	11 05	D	12 9 80	Stirling	Trainee	Newcastle U	—	—
Charvet Laurent	5 11	12 03	D	8 5 73	Beziers		Cannes	99	19
							Chelsea	11	2
							Newcastle U	33	1
Cominelli Lucas*	6 1	12 06	M	25 12 76	Buenos Aires	Granada	Newcastle U	—	—
(On loan from Granada)									
Coppinger James	5 7	10 03	F	18 1 81	Middlesbrough	Darlington	Newcastle U	—	—
							Hartlepool U (loan)	10	3
Cowan David	5 11	11 10	D	5 3 82	Carlisle	Trainee	Newcastle U	—	—
Cunningham David‡			M	8 9 81	Broxburn	Trainee	Newcastle U	—	—
Dabizas Nikos	6 1	12 07	D	3 8 73	Amindeo		Olympiakos	104	8
							Newcastle U	70	7
Domi Didier	5 10	11 03	D	2 5 78	Sarcelles		Paris St Germain	48	—
							Newcastle U	41	3
Dumas Franck	5 11	12 00	D	9 1 68	Bayeux		Caen	148	9
(Transferred to Marseille, January 2000)							Monaco	222	2
							Newcastle U	6	—
Dyer Kieron	5 7	9 07	M	29 12 78	Ipswich	Trainee	Ipswich T	91	9
							Newcastle U	30	3

Elliott Stuart	5 8	11 05	D	27 8 77	London	Trainee	Newcastle U	—	—
							Hull C (loan)	3	—
							Swindon T (loan)	2	—
							Gillingham (loan)	5	—
							Hartlepool U (loan)	5	—
							Wrexham (loan)	9	—
							Bournemouth (loan)	8	—
							Stockport Co (loan)	5	—
Ferguson Duncan	6 4	14 06	F	27 12 71	Stirling	Carse T	Dundee U	77	28
							Rangers	14	2
							Everton	116	37
							Newcastle U	30	8
Fumaca Jose Antunes	6 0	11 08	M	15 7 76	Belem	Catunese	Birmingham C	—	—
							Colchester U	1	—
							Barnsley	—	—
							Crystal Palace	3	—
							Newcastle U	5	—
Gall Kevin	5 9	11 01	F	4 2 82	Merthyr	Trainee	Newcastle U	—	—
Gallacher Kevin	5 8	11 03	F	23 11 66	Clydebank	Duntocher BC	Dundee U	131	27
							Coventry C	100	28
							Blackburn R	144	46
							Newcastle U	20	2
Gavilan Diego	5 8	10 07		1 3 80	Asuncion	Cerro Porteno	Newcastle U	6	1
Georgiadis George	5 8	10 11	M	8 3 72	Kavala		Doxa	55	10
(Transferred to PAOK Salonika, August 1999)							Panathinaikos	176	59
							Newcastle U	10	—
Given Shay	6 1	13 04	G	20 4 76	Lifford	Celtic	Blackburn R	2	—
							Swindon T (loan)	—	—
							Swindon T (loan)	5	—
							Sunderland (loan)	17	—
							Newcastle U	69	—
Glass Stephen	5 9	10 11	M	23 5 76	Dundee		Aberdeen	106	7
							Newcastle U	29	4
Goma Alain	6 0	13 00	D	5 10 72	Sault		Auxerre	166	4
							Paris St Germain	30	—
							Newcastle U	14	—
Green Stuart	5 10	11 00	M	15 6 81	Whitehaven	Trainee	Newcastle U	—	—
Griffin Andy	5 9	10 10	D	7 3 79	Billinge	Trainee	Stoke C	57	2
							Newcastle U	21	1
Hamilton Des	5 11	13 02	M	15 8 76	Bradford	Trainee	Bradford C	88	5
							Newcastle U	12	—
							Sheffield U (loan)	6	—
							Huddersfield T (loan)	10	1
							Norwich C (loan)	7	—
Harper Steve	6 2	13 00	G	14 3 75	Easington	Seaham Red Star	Newcastle U	26	—
							Bradford C (loan)	1	—
							Stockport Co (loan)	—	—
							Hartlepool U (loan)	15	—
							Huddersfield T (loan)	24	—
Harris Michael*	6 0	12 03	D	6 12 80	Liverpool	Trainee	Newcastle U	—	—
Helder Rodrigues	5 11	13 00	D	21 3 71	Luanda		Estoril	33	2
							Benfica	93	8
							La Coruna	37	1
							Newcastle U	8	1
Howey Steve	6 2	11 12	D	26 10 71	Sunderland	Trainee	Newcastle U	191	6
Hughes Aaron	6 1	11 02	D	8 11 79	Cookstown	Trainee	Newcastle U	45	2
Karelse John	6 3	13 07	G	17 5 70	Kapelle		NAC Breda	382	—
							Newcastle U	3	—
Kerr Brian	5 8	11 00	M	12 10 81	Motherwell	Trainee	Newcastle U	—	—
Ketsbaia Temuri	5 8	10 12	M	18 3 68	Gale	Dynamo Sukhumi	Dynamo Tbilisi	54	8
							Anorthosis	76	36
							AEK Athens	84	24
							Newcastle U	78	7
Knight Paul*	5 7	10 07	F	16 10 80	Dublin	Trainee	Newcastle U	—	—
Lee Robert	5 10	11 13	M	1 2 66	Plaistow	Hornchurch	Charlton Ath	298	59
							Newcastle U	265	43
Marcelino Elena	6 2	13 00	D	26 9 71	Gijon		Gijon	14	—
							Mallorca	103	9
							Newcastle U	11	—
Maric Silvio	5 9	11 02	M	20 3 75	Zagreb		Croatia Zagreb	4	—
							Segesta Sisak	9	1
							Croatia Zagreb	87	28
							Newcastle U	23	—
Martin Ian*	6 0	12 03	G	22 10 80	Ballymoney	Trainee	Newcastle U	—	—
McClen Jamie	5 8	10 07	M	13 5 79	Newcastle	Trainee	Newcastle U	10	—
McMahon David	6 1	11 05	F	17 1 81	Dublin	Trainee	Newcastle U	—	—
Perez Lionel	5 11	13 04	G	24 4 67	Bagnols Coze		Nimes	111	—
							Bordeaux	16	—
							Laval	42	—
							Sunderland	75	—
							Newcastle U	—	—
							Scunthorpe U (loan)	13	—
							Cambridge U (loan)	9	—

Pistone Alessandro	5 11	11 05	D	27 7 75	Milan		Vicenza	—	—
							Solbiatese	20	1
							Crevalcore	29	4
							Vicenza	6	—
							Internazionale	45	1
							Newcastle U	46	1
Robinson Paul	5 11	12 11	F	20 11 78	Sunderland	Trainee	Darlington	26	3
							Newcastle U	11	—
Serrant Carl	5 11	11 02	D	12 9 75	Bradford	Trainee	Oldham Ath	90	1
							Newcastle U	6	—
							Bury (loan)	15	—
Shearer Alan	6 0	12 06	F	13 8 70	Newcastle	Trainee	Southampton	118	23
							Blackburn R	138	112
							Newcastle U	115	64
Solano Nolberto	5 9	11 06	M	12 12 74	Callao		Sporting Cristal	75	32
							Boca Juniors	32	5
							Newcastle U	59	9
Speed Gary	5 10	10 12	M	8 9 69	Mancot	Trainee	Leeds U	248	39
							Everton	58	16
							Newcastle U	87	14
Walker Andrew*	5 10	12 00	M	2 1 81	Salford	Trainee	Newcastle U	—	—

Scholars
Barr, Keith; Brain, Jonathon R; Cowie, Oliver JC; Dixon, Kevin P; Dunn, Paul J; Grindlay, Stephen J; Heiniger, Carl S; Hogg, Ryan; Kendrick, Joseph; Mann, Jonathan J; Orr, Bradley J; Pringle, Phillip C; Wealleans, Kevin; Wright, Peter D

NORTHAMPTON TOWN

Clarkson Ian‡	5 10	12 00	D	4 12 70	Solihull	Trainee	Birmingham C	136	—
							Stoke C	75	—
							Northampton T	94	1
Corazzin Carlo*	5 10	12 07	F	25 12 71	Canada	Vancouver 86ers	Cambridge U	105	39
							Plymouth Arg	74	22
							Northampton T	78	30
Dobson Tony*	6 1	13 10	D	5 2 69	Coventry	Apprentice	Coventry C	54	1
							Blackburn R	41	—
							Portsmouth	53	2
							Oxford U (loan)	5	—
							Peterborough U (loan)	4	—
							WBA	11	—
							Gillingham (loan)	2	—
							Northampton T	12	—
Frain John	5 10	12 04	D	8 10 68	Birmingham	Apprentice	Birmingham C	274	23
							Northampton T	139	3
Green Richard#	6 1	13 07	D	22 11 67	Wolverhampton	Apprentice	Shrewsbury T	125	5
							Swindon T	—	—
							Gillingham	216	16
							Walsall	30	1
							Rochdale (loan)	6	—
							Northampton T	21	2
Hendon Ian	6 1	13 08	D	5 12 71	Ilford	Trainee	Tottenham H	4	—
							Portsmouth (loan)	4	—
							Leyton Orient (loan)	6	—
							Barnsley (loan)	6	—
							Leyton Orient	131	5
							Birmingham C (loan)	4	—
							Notts Co	82	6
							Northampton T	51	2
Hodge John	5 7	11 06	F	1 4 69	Skelmersdale	Exmouth	Exeter C	65	10
							Swansea C	112	10
							Walsall	76	12
							Gillingham	49	1
							Northampton T	8	—
Hodgson Dougie‡	6 2	13 10	D	27 2 69	Frankston	Heidelberg	Sheffield U	30	—
							Plymouth Arg (loan)	5	—
							Burnley (loan)	1	—
							Oldham Ath	41	4
							Northampton T	8	1
Hope Richard	6 3	13 05	D	22 6 78	Stockton	Trainee	Blackburn R	—	1
							Darlington	63	1
							Northampton T	36	—
Howard Steve	6 3	14 06	F	10 5 76	Durham	Tow Law T	Hartlepool U	142	27
							Northampton T	53	10
Howey Lee	6 3	14 06	D	1 4 69	Sunderland	AC Hemptinne	Sunderland	69	8
							Burnley	26	—
							Northampton T	45	6
Hughes Garry	6 0	12 00	D	19 11 79	Birmingham	Trainee	Northampton T	2	—
Hunt James	5 11	12 07	M	17 12 76	Derby	Trainee	Notts Co	19	1
							Northampton T	93	3
Hunter Roy	5 10	12 08	M	29 10 73	Saltburn	Trainee	WBA	9	1
							Northampton T	133	13
Matthew Damian‡	5 10	12 04	M	23 9 70	Islington	Trainee	Chelsea	21	—
							Luton T (loan)	5	—
							Crystal Palace	24	1
							Bristol R (loan)	8	—
							Burnley	59	7
							Northampton T	2	—

Name					Birthplace				
Morrow Andrew	5 8	9 07	F	5 10 80	Bangor	Trainee	Northampton T	4	—
Parrish Sean*	5 10	11 05	M	14 3 72	Wrexham	Trainee	Shrewsbury T	3	—
						Telford U	Doncaster R	66	8
							Northampton T	109	13
Sampson Ian	6 2	13 05	D	14 11 68	Wakefield	Goole T	Sunderland	17	1
							Northampton T (loan)	8	—
							Northampton T	244	21
Savage Dave	6 2	13 00	M	30 7 73	Dublin	Longford T	Millwall	132	6
							Northampton T	70	10
Spedding Duncan	6 2	12 01	M	7 9 77	Frimley	Trainee	Southampton	7	—
							Northampton T	68	2
Sturridge Simon*	5 6	11 08	F	9 12 69	Birmingham	Trainee	Birmingham C	150	30
							Stoke C	71	14
							Blackpool (loan)	5	1
							Northampton T	18	1
							Shrewsbury T (loan)	11	1
Turley Billy‡	6 4	14 10	G	15 7 73	Wolverhampton	Evesham U	Northampton T	28	—
							Leyton Orient (loan)	14	—
Welch Keith	6 2	13 07	G	3 10 68	Bolton	Trainee	Bolton W	—	—
							Rochdale	205	—
							Bristol C	271	—
							Northampton T	39	—
Wilkinson Paul*	6 1	12 04	F	30 10 64	Louth	Apprentice	Grimsby T	71	27
							Everton	31	7
							Nottingham F	34	5
							Watford	134	52
							Middlesbrough	166	49
							Oldham Ath (loan)	4	1
							Watford (loan)	4	—
							Luton T (loan)	3	—
							Barnsley	49	9
							Millwall	30	3
							Northampton T	15	1
Wilson Kevin#	5 8	11 04	F	18 4 61	Banbury	Banbury U	Derby Co	122	30
							Ipswich T	98	34
							Chelsea	152	42
							Notts Co	69	3
							Bradford C (loan)	5	—
							Walsall	125	38
							Northampton T	25	2

Trainees
Binder, Paul M; Dickson, Mark S; Gould, James R; Thompson, Ryan JD

Scholars
Champelovier, Neil M; Faulds, Peter J; Laws, Michael J; Meade, Nathan S; Nash, Ryan M; Spooner, Mark S; Taylor, Matthew A; Thompson, Christopher D

NORWICH CITY

Name					Birthplace				
Anselin Cedric	5 7	11 02	M	24 7 77	Lens		Bordeaux	8	—
							Lille	14	1
							Bordeaux	1	—
							Norwich C	26	1
Bellamy Craig	5 8	11 00	F	13 7 79	Cardiff	Trainee	Norwich C	83	32
Carey Shaun‡	5 10	10 12	M	13 5 76	Kettering	Trainee	Norwich C	68	—
Coote Adrian	6 1	11 11	F	30 9 78	Gt Yarmouth	Trainee	Norwich C	40	3
Dalglish Paul	5 10	11 00	F	18 2 77	Glasgow	X Form	Celtic	—	—
							Liverpool	—	—
							Newcastle U	11	1
							Bury (loan)	12	—
							Norwich C (loan)	5	—
							Norwich C	31	2
De Waard Raymond	6 1	12 03	F	27 3 73	Rotterdam		Excelsior	91	9
							Cambuur	23	—
							Norwich C	4	—
Derveld Fernando	6 2	13 00	D	22 10 76	Vlissingen		Willem II	40	1
							Haarlem	37	—
							Norwich C	5	—
Diop Pape‡	5 9	11 00	D	12 1 79	Dakar		Lens	1	—
							Norwich C	7	—
Fitzsimon Ross‡	5 9	10 12	M	26 9 80	Edgware	Tottenham H	Norwich C	—	—
Fleming Craig	5 11	12 10	D	6 10 71	Halifax	Trainee	Halifax T	57	—
							Oldham Ath	164	1
							Norwich C	98	7
Forbes Adrian	5 7	11 04	F	23 1 79	Greenford	Trainee	Norwich C	83	5
Fuglestad Erik‡	5 10	11 06	D	13 8 74	Randaberg		Viking	74	4
							Norwich C	74	2
Giallanza Gaetano#	5 11	11 09	F	6 6 74	Basle		Basle	32	19
							Nantes	12	2
							Bolton W	3	—
							Lugano	21	8
							Norwich C	3	—
Green Robert	6 3	13 00	G	18 1 80	Chertsey	Trainee	Norwich C	5	—

Jackson Matt	6 0	12 09	D	19 10 71	Leeds	School	Luton T	9	—
							Preston NE (loan)	4	—
							Everton	138	4
							Charlton Ath (loan)	8	—
							QPR (loan)	7	—
							Birmingham C (loan)	10	—
							Norwich C	135	6
Joynson Matthew‡	5 8	10 10	D	21 3 81	Liverpool	Trainee	Norwich C	—	—
Kenton Darren	5 11	11 10	D	13 9 78	Wandsworth	Trainee	Norwich C	59	2
Llewellyn Chris	6 0	11 11	F	29 8 79	Merthyr	Trainee	Norwich C	82	9
MacKay Malky	6 3	13 03	D	19 2 72	Bellshill		Queen's Park	70	6
							Celtic	37	4
							Norwich C	48	1
Marshall Andy	6 2	13 08	G	14 4 75	Bury	Trainee	Norwich C	154	—
							Bournemouth (loan)	11	—
							Gillingham (loan)	5	—
Marshall Lee	6 2	12 00	M	21 1 79	Islington	Enfield	Norwich C	81	8
McVeigh Paul	5 6	10 06	F	6 12 77	Belfast	Trainee	Tottenham H	3	1
							Norwich C	1	—
Milligan Mike‡	5 10	11 06	M	20 2 67	Manchester	Trainee	Oldham Ath	162	17
							Everton	17	1
							Oldham Ath	117	6
							Norwich C	124	5
Mulryne Phil	5 9	11 05	M	1 1 78	Belfast	Trainee	Manchester U	1	—
							Norwich C	16	2
Parker Kevin‡	5 10	11 06	F	20 9 79	Plymouth	Trainee	Norwich C	—	—
Roberts Iwan	6 3	13 01	F	26 6 68	Bangor	Trainee	Watford	63	9
							Huddersfield T	142	50
							Leicester C	100	41
							Wolverhampton W	33	12
							Norwich C	120	41
Russell Darel	6 0	12 02	M	22 10 80	Mile End	Trainee	Norwich C	47	5
Scott Kevin‡	6 3	14 03	D	17 12 66	Easington	Middlesbrough	Newcastle U	227	8
							Tottenham H	18	1
							Port Vale (loan)	17	1
							Charlton Ath (loan)	4	—
							Norwich C	33	—
							Darlington (loan)	4	—
Sutch Daryl	5 11	12 06	D	11 9 71	Lowestoft	Trainee	Norwich C	246	9
Way Darren‡	5 7	11 00	M	21 11 79	Plymouth	Trainee	Norwich C	—	—
Wilson Che‡	5 11	11 10	D	17 1 79	Ely	Trainee	Norwich C	22	—
de Blasiis Yves	5 9	11 05	M	25 9 73	Bordeaux	Red Star 93	Norwich C	28	—

Scholars
Bilham, Neil; Blois, Lewis P; Gay, Daniel K; Gilman, Lee D; Goodchild, Richard I; Merrick, Michael T; Ngopwani, Pitshou M; Oxby, Andrew D; Parry, Matthew G; Thompson, Ian R

Associated Schoolboys who have accepted the Club's offer of a Traineeship/Scholarship/Contract
Thompson, Ben

NOTTINGHAM FOREST

Allou Bernard	5 8	11 00	M	19 6 75	Cocody		Paris St Germain	41	3
						Grampas 8	Nottingham F	6	1
Bart-Williams Chris	5 11	12 07	M	16 6 74	Freetown	Trainee	Leyton Orient	36	2
							Sheffield W	124	16
							Nottingham F	144	13
Beasant Dave	6 4	14 02	G	20 3 59	Willesden	Edgware T	Wimbledon	340	—
							Newcastle U	20	—
							Chelsea	133	—
							Grimsby T (loan)	6	—
							Wolverhampton W (loan)	4	—
							Southampton	88	—
							Nottingham F	94	—
Bonalair Thierry†	5 9	10 08	D	14 6 66	Paris		Amiens	26	3
							Nantes	145	2
							Auxerre	25	1
							Lille	69	5
							Neuchatel Xamax	68	9
							Nottingham F	71	5
Brennan Jim	5 9	11 06	D	8 5 77	Toronto	Sora Lazio	Bristol C	55	3
							Nottingham F	25	—
Calderwood Colin	6 0	13 00	D	20 1 65	Stranraer	Amateur	Mansfield T	100	1
							Swindon T	330	20
							Tottenham H	163	6
							Aston Villa	26	—
							Nottingham F	6	—
Carter Nicky‡	5 11	11 07	F	29 11 81	Stoke	Trainee	Nottingham F	—	—
Cash Brian			M	24 11 82	Dublin	Trainee	Nottingham F	—	—
Cooper Richard	5 9	10 07	D	27 9 79	Nottingham	Trainee	Nottingham F	1	—
Crossley Mark*	6 0	15 09	G	16 6 69	Barnsley	Trainee	Nottingham F	303	—
							Manchester U (loan)	—	—
							Millwall (loan)	13	—

Name			Pos	DOB	Birthplace	From	Club	Apps	Gls
Dawson Kevin	6 0	10 07	D	18 6 81	Northallerton	Trainee	Nottingham F	7	—
Doig Chris	6 2	12 06	D	13 2 81	Dumfries	Trainee	Nottingham F	13	—
Doyle Kevin	5 11	12 02	D	13 10 80	Wexford	Trainee	Leeds U	—	—
							Nottingham F	—	—
Edds Gareth	5 11	10 12	M	3 2 81	Sydney	Trainee	Nottingham F	2	—
Edwards Christian	6 2	12 03	D	23 11 75	Caerphilly	Trainee	Swansea C	115	4
							Nottingham F	12	—
							Bristol C (loan)	3	—
							Oxford U (loan)	5	1
Fenton Paul			M	8 3 83	Cork	Scholar	Nottingham F	—	—
Foy Keith	5 11	12 03	M	30 12 81	Crumlin	Trainee	Nottingham F	—	—
Freedman Dougie	5 9	12 05	F	21 1 74	Glasgow	Trainee	QPR	—	—
							Barnet	47	27
							Crystal Palace	90	31
							Wolverhampton W	29	10
							Nottingham F	65	18
Freeman David	5 10	11 07	F	25 11 79	Dublin	Cherry Orchard	Nottingham F	3	—
Gray Andy	6 0	13 00	M	15 11 77	Harrogate	Trainee	Leeds U	22	—
							Bury (loan)	6	1
							Nottingham F	30	—
							Preston NE (loan)	5	—
							Oldham Ath (loan)	4	—
Harewood Marlon	6 1	13 03	F	25 8 79	Hampstead	Trainee	Nottingham F	58	5
							Ipswich T (loan)	6	1
Hjelde Jon Olav	6 2	13 05	D	30 7 72	Levanger		Rosenborg	27	1
							Nottingham F	78	2
Hudson Niall	5 10	10 02	M	7 1 82	Ilkeston	Trainee	Nottingham F	—	—
Jenas Jermaine			M	18 2 83	Nottingham	Scholar	Nottingham F	—	—
John Stern	6 1	13 07	F	30 10 76	Trinidad		Columbus Crew	55	44
							Nottingham F	17	3
Johnson Andy	6 1	13 03	M	2 5 74	Bristol	Trainee	Norwich C	66	13
							Nottingham F	87	6
Kearney Liam			M	10 1 83	Dublin	Scholar	Nottingham F	—	—
Lester Jack	5 10	11 10	F	8 10 75	Sheffield	Trainee	Grimsby T	133	17
							Doncaster R (loan)	11	1
							Nottingham F	15	2
Louis-Jean Mathieu	5 9	10 08	D	22 2 76	Mont-St-Aignan		Le Havre	78	—
							Nottingham F	43	—
Love Gordon			M	17 3 83	Bellshill	Scholar	Nottingham F	—	—
Mannini Moreno‡	6 1	13 00	D	15 8 62	Imola		Imola	25	2
							Forli	10	1
							Como	53	5
							Sampdoria	377	9
							Nottingham F	8	—
Matrecano Salvatore	6 2	14 00	D	5 10 70	Naples		Ercolanese	1	—
							V.Lamezia	4	—
							Audax Ravag	20	2
							Turris	33	—
							Foggia	28	—
							Parma	36	1
							Napoli	17	—
							Udinese	19	—
							Perugia	87	3
							Nottingham F	11	—
Mattsson Jesper	6 1	13 01	D	18 4 68	Visby		Hacken	24	3
							Halmstad	101	8
							Nottingham F	6	—
McNamara Niall	5 11	11 09	F	26 1 82	Eire	Trainee	Nottingham F	—	—
Merino Carlos	5 8	10 04	M	15 3 80	Bilbao	Urdaneta	Nottingham F	9	—
Pascolo Marco	6 2	14 04	G	2 5 66	Sion		Sion	17	1
(Transferred to Zurich, June 1999)							Neuchatel Xamax	52	—
							Servette	163	—
							Cagliari	14	—
							Nottingham F	5	—
Petrachi Gianluca	5 9	11 05	M	14 1 69	Lecce		Lecce	5	—
							Nola	29	—
							Taranto	—	—
							Arezzo	19	1
							Fedelis Andria	65	9
							Venezia	34	6
							Torino	1	—
							Palermo	27	2
							Cremonese	44	1
							Ancona	28	5
							Perugia	28	5
							Nottingham F	13	—
Platt David†	5 10	11 12	M	10 6 66	Chadderton	Chadderton	Manchester U	—	—
							Crewe Alex	134	55
							Aston Villa	121	50
							Bari	29	11
							Juventus	16	3
							Sampdoria	55	17
							Arsenal	88	13
							Nottingham F	3	—

Prutton David	6 1	11 06	D	12 9 81	Hull	Trainee	Nottingham F	34	2
Quashie Nigel	5 9	12 08	M	20 7 78	Nunhead	Trainee	QPR	57	3
							Nottingham F	44	2
Reid Andrew			M	29 7 82	Dublin	Trainee	Nottingham F	—	—
Roche Barry	6 4	12 06	G	6 4 82	Dublin	Trainee	Nottingham F	—	—
Rogers Alan	5 10	12 08	D	3 1 77	Liverpool	Trainee	Tranmere R	57	2
							Nottingham F	117	13
Scimeca Riccardo	6 0	13 11	D	13 6 75	Leamington Spa	Trainee	Aston Villa	73	2
							Nottingham F	38	—
Shevlin Anthony			M	9 12 82	Dublin	Trainee	Nottingham F	—	—
Thompson John			M	12 10 81	Dublin		Nottingham F	—	—
Turner Matthew*	5 9	10 00	F	29 12 81	Nottingham	Trainee	Nottingham F	—	—
Van Hooijdonk Pierre	6 4	13 07	F	29 11 69	Steenbergen		RBC	69	33
(Transferred to Vitesse, July 1999)							NAC	99	71
							Celtic	69	44
							Nottingham F	71	36
Vaughan Tony	6 1	12 10	D	11 10 75	Manchester	Trainee	Ipswich T	67	3
							Manchester C	58	2
							Cardiff C (loan)	14	—
							Nottingham F	10	—
Williams Gareth	5 11	11 08	M	16 12 81	Glasgow	Trainee	Nottingham F	2	—
Woan Ian*	5 10	12 07	F	14 12 67	Wirrall	Runcorn	Nottingham F	221	31

Scholars
Gray, Steven

Non-Contract
Platt, David A

Associated Schoolboys who have accepted the Club's offer of a Traineeship/Scholarship/Contract
Dawson, Michael R; Haskins, Andrew E

NOTTS COUNTY

Blackmore Clayton*	5 8	11 10	D	23 1 64	Neath	Apprentice	Manchester U	186	19
							Middlesbrough	53	4
							Bristol C (loan)	5	1
							Barnsley	7	—
							Notts Co	21	2
Bolland Paul	6 0	12 01	M	23 12 79	Bradford	Trainee	Bradford C	12	—
							Notts Co	38	1
Brough Michael	6 0	11 07	M	1 8 81	Nottingham	Trainee	Notts Co	11	—
Cross David§	5 10	10 07		7 9 82	Bromley	Scholar	Notts Co	1	—
Darby Duane	6 0	13 02	F	17 10 73	Birmingham	Trainee	Torquay U	108	26
							Doncaster R	17	4
							Hull C	78	27
							Notts Co	28	5
							Hull C (loan)	8	—
Dyer Alex	6 1	13 01	M	14 11 65	Forest Gate	Watford	Blackpool	108	19
							Hull C	60	14
							Crystal Palace	17	2
							Charlton Ath	78	13
							Oxford U	76	6
							Lincoln C	1	—
							Barnet	35	2
							Huddersfield T	12	1
							Notts Co	69	6
Farrell Sean	6 2	13 01	F	28 1 69	Watford	Apprentice	Luton T	25	1
							Colchester U (loan)	9	1
							Northampton T (loan)	4	1
							Fulham	94	31
							Peterborough U	66	20
							Notts Co	69	19
Ford Ryan	5 10	10 05	M	3 9 78	Worksop	Trainee	Manchester U	—	—
							Notts Co	1	—
Gibson Paul	6 3	13 00	G	1 11 76	Sheffield	Trainee	Manchester U	—	—
							Mansfield T (loan)	13	—
							Hull C (loan)	4	—
							Notts Co	2	—
							Rochdale (loan)	5	—
Heffernan Paul	5 10	11 00	F	29 12 81	Dublin	Newton	Notts Co	2	—
Holmes Richard	5 11	10 12	D	7 11 80	Grantham	Trainee	Notts Co	49	—
Howell Dean*	6 1	12 05	M	29 11 80	Burton-on-Trent	Trainee	Notts Co	1	—
Hughes Andy	6 0	12 07	M	2 1 78	Manchester	Trainee	Oldham Ath	33	1
							Notts Co	80	12
Liburd Richard	5 9	11 06	D	26 9 73	Nottingham	Forest Ath	Middlesbrough	41	1
							Bradford C	78	3
							Carlisle U	9	—
							Notts Co	66	2
Lindley James	6 1	13 00	G	23 7 81	Sutton-in-Ashfield	Trainee	Notts Co	1	—

Murray Shaun	5 8	10 12	M	7 10 70	Newcastle	Trainee	Tottenham H	—	—
							Portsmouth	34	1
							Millwall (loan)	—	—
							Scarborough	29	5
							Bradford C	130	8
							Notts Co	44	3
Owers Gary	6 0	12 09	M	3 10 68	Newcastle	Apprentice	Sunderland	268	25
							Bristol C	126	9
							Notts Co	84	7
Pearce Dennis	5 9	11 07	D	10 9 74	Wolverhampton	Trainee	Aston Villa	—	—
							Wolverhampton W	9	—
							Notts Co	91	3
Ramage Craig	5 11	12 10	M	30 3 70	Derby	Trainee	Derby Co	42	4
							Wigan Ath (loan)	10	2
							Watford	104	27
							Peterborough U (loan)	7	—
							Bradford C	35	1
							Notts Co	40	4
Rapley Kevin	5 10	11 07	F	21 9 77	Reading	Trainee	Brentford	51	12
							Southend U (loan)	9	4
							Notts Co	45	4
Redmile Matt	6 3	15 03	D	12 11 76	Nottingham	Trainee	Notts Co	139	7
Richardson Ian	5 10	12 00	D	22 1 70	Barking	Dagenham & Red.	Birmingham C	7	—
							Notts Co	120	14
Stallard Mark	6 0	12 13	F	24 10 74	Derby	Trainee	Derby Co	27	2
							Fulham (loan)	4	3
							Bradford C	43	10
							Preston NE (loan)	4	1
							Wycombe W	70	23
							Notts Co	50	18
Tierney Fran*	5 10	12 07	M	10 9 75	Liverpool	Trainee	Crewe Alex	87	10
							Notts Co	33	4
Ward Darren	5 11	12 09	G	11 5 74	Worksop	Trainee	Mansfield T	81	—
							Notts Co	216	—
Warren Mark	6 0	12 08	D	12 11 74	Clapton	Trainee	Leyton Orient	152	5
							West Ham U (loan)	—	—
							Oxford U (loan)	4	—
							Notts Co	51	1
Webster Adam‡	6 1	12 05	F	3 7 80	Leicester	Thurmaston	Notts Co	1	—

Scholars
Berry, Dean; Briggs, Andrew; Cross, David B; Davies, Andrew M; Deeney, Saul; Dunn, Mark A; Housley, Craig; McCaul, Matthew J; Osborne, Calum G; Poznanski, Lee J; Riley, Paul A; Skevington, Matthew

Associated Schoolboys
Hartshorn, Michael

Associated Schoolboys who have accepted the Club's offer of a Traineeship/Scholarship/Contract
Clarke, Ryan; Screaton, Iain

OLDHAM ATHLETIC

Adams Neil	5 9	11 04	M	23 11 65	Stoke	Local	Stoke C	32	4
							Everton	20	—
							Oldham Ath (loan)	9	—
							Oldham Ath	129	23
							Norwich C	182	25
							Oldham Ath	29	2
Allott Mark	5 11	10 12	F	16 3 78	Middleton	Trainee	Oldham Ath	100	20
Beavers Paul	6 3	14 07	F	2 10 78	Blackpool	Trainee	Sunderland	—	—
							Shrewsbury T (loan)	2	—
							Oldham Ath (loan)	7	2
							Oldham Ath	4	—
							Hartlepool U (loan)	7	—
Boshell Daniel	5 11	11 10	M	30 5 81	Bradford	Trainee	Oldham Ath	8	—
Campbell Jamie			G	2 12 80	Glasgow	Trainee	Oldham Ath	—	—
Clitheroe Lee‡	5 10	10 07	F	18 11 78	Chorley	Trainee	Oldham Ath	5	—
Dudley Craig	5 11	11 02	F	12 9 79	Ollerton	Trainee	Notts Co	31	3
							Shrewsbury T (loan)	4	—
							Hull C (loan)	7	2
							Oldham Ath	25	5
							Chesterfield (loan)	2	—
Duxbury Lee	5 10	10 07	M	7 10 69	Keighley	Trainee	Bradford C	209	25
							Rochdale (loan)	10	—
							Huddersfield T	29	2
							Bradford C	63	7
							Oldham Ath	134	16
Futcher Ben	6 6	12 02	D	4 6 81	Bradford	Trainee	Oldham Ath	5	—
Gardiner Gareth*			M	25 3 81	Bury	Trainee	Oldham Ath	—	—
Garnett Shaun	6 2	13 01	D	22 11 69	Wallasey	Trainee	Tranmere R	112	5
							Chester C (loan)	9	—
							Preston NE (loan)	10	2
							Wigan Ath (loan)	13	1
							Swansea C	15	—
							Oldham Ath	126	8

Graham Richard#	6 2	12 09	D	28 11 74	Dewsbury	Trainee	Oldham Ath	150	14
Holt Andy	6 1	11 02	D	21 5 78	Manchester	Trainee	Oldham Ath	104	9
Hotte Mark	5 11	11 00	M	27 9 78	Bradford	Trainee	Oldham Ath	37	—
Innes Mark	5 10	12 04	D	27 9 78	Bellshill	Trainee	Oldham Ath	38	1
Johnston Patrick‡			M	21 12 80	Liverpool	Trainee	Oldham Ath	—	—
Jones Paul	6 1	11 09	D	3 6 78	Liverpool	Trainee	Tranmere R	—	—
							Blackpool (loan)	—	—
						Leigh RMI	Oldham Ath	16	1
Kelly Gary	5 11	12 08	G	3 8 66	Fulwood	Apprentice	Newcastle U	53	—
							Blackpool (loan)	5	—
							Bury	236	—
							West Ham U (loan)	—	—
							Oldham Ath	157	—
McGinlay John‡	5 10	12 02	F	8 4 64	Inverness	Elgin C	Shrewsbury T	60	27
							Bury	25	9
							Millwall	34	10
							Bolton W	192	87
							Bradford C	17	3
							Oldham Ath	7	1
McLaughlin Gerard			M	26 9 81	Rutherglen	Trainee	Oldham Ath	—	—
McLean Ian*	5 10	11 04	D	13 9 78	Leeds	Trainee	Bradford C	—	—
							Oldham Ath	6	—
McNiven David*	5 10	12 00	F	27 5 78	Leeds	Trainee	Oldham Ath	26	2
McNiven Scott	5 10	10 08	D	27 5 78	Leeds	Trainee	Oldham Ath	142	3
Miskelly David	6 0	12 02	G	3 9 79	Ards	Trainee	Oldham Ath	3	—
Mohan John‡	6 1	11 04	M	4 7 80	York	York C	Oldham Ath	—	—
Pashley Adam‡			M	12 2 81	Blackpool	Trainee	Oldham Ath	—	—
Philliskirk Tony	6 2	12 12	F	10 2 65	Sunderland	Amateur	Sheffield U	80	20
							Rotherham U (loan)	6	1
							Oldham Ath	10	1
							Preston NE	14	6
							Bolton W	141	51
							Peterborough U	43	15
							Burnley	40	9
							Carlisle U (loan)	3	1
							Cardiff C	61	5
							Macclesfield T (loan)	10	1
							Oldham Ath	—	—
Rickers Paul	5 10	11 04	M	9 5 75	Dewsbury	Trainee	Oldham Ath	199	16
Ritchie Andy	5 11	12 04	F	28 11 60	Manchester	Apprentice	Manchester U	33	13
							Brighton & HA	89	23
							Leeds U	136	40
							Oldham Ath	217	82
							Scarborough	68	17
							Oldham Ath	26	2
Roberts Glen*			M	3 9 80	Gravesend	Trainee	Oldham Ath	—	—
Salt Philip	5 10	11 02	M	2 3 79	Huddersfield	Trainee	Oldham Ath	16	—
Sheridan John	5 10	11 12	M	1 10 64	Stretford	Local	Leeds U	230	47
							Nottingham F	—	—
							Sheffield W	197	25
							Birmingham C (loan)	2	—
							Bolton W	32	2
							Oldham Ath	66	3
Spurr Jonathan‡			M	21 8 81	Leeds	Trainee	Oldham Ath	—	—
Sugden Ryan	6 0	12 07	F	26 12 80	Bradford	Trainee	Oldham Ath	19	1
Swan Iain*	6 2	11 03	D	4 7 80	Glasgow	Trainee	Oldham Ath	1	—
							Partick T (loan)	2	—
Tait Jordan	5 10	11 05	D	27 9 79	Berwick	Trainee	Newcastle U	—	—
							Oldham Ath	1	—
Thom Stuart	6 3	13 01	D	27 12 76	Dewsbury	Trainee	Nottingham F	—	—
							Mansfield T (loan)	5	—
							Oldham Ath	34	3
Tipton Matthew	5 10	11 02	F	29 6 80	Bridgend	Trainee	Oldham Ath	60	5
Walsh Danny	5 11	12 03	M	16 9 78	Manchester	Trainee	Oldham Ath	2	—
Wardle Darren*	5 11	12 04	F	2 1 81	Bury		Oldham Ath	—	—
Wharton Nathan*			M	2 11 80	Oldham	Trainee	Oldham Ath	—	—
Whitehall Steve	5 11	11 09	F	8 12 66	Bromborough	Southport	Rochdale	238	75
							Mansfield T	43	24
							Oldham Ath	74	13 0

Scholars
Clark, Liam J; Donnelly, Anthony M; Doran, Joseph R; Duncan, Kevin; Froggatt, Jonathon P; Haining, William W; Hall, Colin AT; McLean, Michael J; Oliver, Alun M; Otto, Alastair J; Robertson, Benjamin A; Robinson, Thomas J; Rock, Alexander P; Saunders, John J; Smith, Benjamin; Sutcliffe, Arren; Thompson, Darren M; Whittle, Thomas J; Wright, Matthew

Associated Schoolboys who have accepted the Club's offer of a Traineeship/Scholarship/Contract
Chadderton, Daniel; Davenport, Michael J; Hall, Daniel; Lavery, Carl; Robinson, Christopher; Wademan, Gareth

OXFORD UNITED

Abbey Ben	5 7	11 00	F	13 5 78	London	Crawley T	Oxford U	10	—
Anthrobus Steve	6 2	14 07	F	10 11 68	Lewisham		Millwall	21	4
							Southend U (loan)	—	—
							Wimbledon	28	—
							Peterborough U (loan)	2	—
							Chester C (loan)	7	—
							Shrewsbury T	72	16
							Crewe Alex	61	9
							Oxford U	36	2
Arendse Andre	6 1	11 08	G	27 6 67	Cape Town	Cape Town S	Fulham	6	—
							Oxford U	13	—
Banger Nicky	5 8	11 10	F	25 2 71	Southampton	Trainee	Southampton	55	8
(Transferred to Dundee, October 1999)							Oldham Ath	64	10
							Oxford U	63	8
Beauchamp Joey#	5 10	12 07	M	13 3 71	Oxford	Trainee	Oxford U	124	20
							Swansea C (loan)	5	2
							West Ham U	—	—
							Swindon T	45	3
							Oxford U	192	35
Cook Jamie	5 10	10 10	F	2 8 79	Oxford	Trainee	Oxford U	68	6
Davis Steve#	6 1	13 05	D	26 7 65	Birmingham	Stoke C	Crewe Alex	145	1
							Burnley	147	11
							Barnsley	107	10
							York C (loan)	2	1
							Oxford U	42	3
Fear Peter	5 10	11 10	M	10 9 73	Sutton	Trainee	Wimbledon	73	4
							Oxford U	19	1
Folland Robbie	5 9	10 07	F	16 9 79	Swansea	Trainee	Oxford U	25	1
Hackett Christopher	6 0	11 06	D	1 3 83	Oxford	Scholar	Oxford U	2	—
Jemson Nigel#	5 11	13 00	F	10 8 69	Preston	Trainee	Preston NE	32	8
							Nottingham F	47	13
							Bolton W (loan)	5	—
							Preston NE (loan)	9	2
							Sheffield W	51	9
							Grimsby T (loan)	6	2
							Notts Co	14	1
							Watford (loan)	4	—
							Coventry C (loan)	—	—
							Rotherham U (loan)	16	5
							Oxford U	68	27
							Bury	29	1
							Oxford U	18	—
Lambert Jamie‡	5 8	12 06	M	14 9 73	Henley	School	Reading	125	16
							Walsall (loan)	6	—
							Oxford U	13	2
Lewis Mickey†	5 8	12 04	M	15 2 65	Birmingham	School	WBA	24	—
							Derby Co	43	1
							Oxford U	305	7
Lilley Derek	5 9	11 10	F	9 2 74	Paisley	Everton BC	Morton	180	57
							Leeds U	21	1
							Bury (loan)	5	1
							Hearts (loan)	4	1
							Oxford U	44	7
Lundin Paul‡	6 4	14 00	G	21 11 64	Osby	Malmo	Osters	144	—
							Umea	7	—
							Osters	38	—
							Oxford U	29	—
McGowan Neil	5 8	11 07	D	15 4 77	Glasgow	Bonnyton Th	Stranraer	4	—
							Albion R	62	—
							Oxford U	20	—
Murphy Matt	6 0	12 02	M	20 8 71	Northampton	Corby T	Oxford U	206	32
							Scunthorpe U (loan)	3	—
Newton Eddie#	5 11	12 11	M	13 12 71	Hammersmith	Trainee	Chelsea	165	8
							Cardiff C (loan)	18	4
							Birmingham C	4	—
							Oxford U	7	—
Powell Paul	5 8	11 01	M	30 6 78	Wallingford	Trainee	Oxford U	108	10
Richards Andrew‡			M	11 9 80	Haverfordwest	Trainee	Oxford U	—	—
Ricketts Sam			M	11 10 81	Aylesbury	Trainee	Oxford U	—	—
Robinson Les#	5 9	12 02	D	1 3 67	Shirebrook	Local	Mansfield T	15	—
							Stockport Co	67	3
							Doncaster R	82	12
							Oxford U	384	3
Shepheard Jon	6 2	12 04	D	31 3 81	Oxford	Trainee	Oxford U	2	—
Tait Paul	5 11	11 10	M	31 7 71	Sutton Coldfield	Trainee	Birmingham C	170	14
							Millwall (loan)	—	—
							Northampton T (loan)	3	—
							Oxford U	51	—
Watson Mark#	6 0	12 04	D	8 9 70	Vancouver		Watford	18	—
							Osters	24	—
							Oxford U	58	—
Weatherstone Ross	5 11	11 10	D	16 5 81	Reading	Trainee	Oxford U	3	—
Weatherstone Simon	5 10	12 04	F	26 1 80	Reading	Trainee	Oxford U	45	3

Whelan Phil#	6 4	14 04	D	7 3 72	Stockport		Ipswich T	82	2
							Middlesbrough	22	1
							Oxford U	54	2
							Rotherham U (loan)	13	4
Whitehead Dean	5 11	12 01	M	12 1 82	Oxford	Trainee	Oxford U	—	—

Trainees
Hamp, Adam RM

Scholars
Brooks, Jamie P; Holder, Jorden A; Jones, Brynmor R; King, Simon DR; McIntosh, Kelvin R; Newton, Andrew J; Spence, Brynley J; Wilson, Philip J

Non-Contract
Lewis, Michael

Associated Schoolboys
Kershaw, Richard J; Stalcup, Gregory M

Associated Schoolboys who have accepted the Club's offer of a Traineeship/Scholarship/Contract
Costelloe, Michael W; Lovegrove, Robert T; Mills, Jonathan P

Player who does not hold a current contract but his registration has been retained by the Club
Wickens, Gary J

PETERBOROUGH UNITED

Broughton Drewe	6 3	12 04	F	25 10 78	Hitchin	Trainee	Norwich C	9	1
							Wigan Ath (loan)	4	—
							Brentford	1	—
							Peterborough U	35	8
Cable Aaron*	5 8	11 06	F	12 10 80	Aberdare	Trainee	Peterborough U	—	—
Campbell James	6 2	11 12	D	16 11 79	Kent	Trainee	Peterborough U	—	—
Carr Shaun*			M	15 12 80	Iserlohn		Peterborough U	—	—
Castle Steve#	5 11	11 07	M	17 5 66	Ilford	Apprentice	Orient	243	55
							Plymouth Arg	101	35
							Birmingham C	23	1
							Gillingham (loan)	6	1
							Leyton Orient (loan)	4	1
							Peterborough U	102	17
Chapple Phil	6 2	13 01	D	21 11 66	Norwich	Apprentice	Norwich C	—	—
							Cambridge U	187	19
							Charlton Ath	142	15
							Peterborough U	17	1
Clarke Andy	5 10	11 07	F	22 7 67	Islington	Barnet	Wimbledon	170	17
							Port Vale (loan)	6	—
							Northampton T (loan)	4	—
							Peterborough U	37	15
Cleaver Chris‡	5 11	12 06	F	24 3 79	Hitchin	Trainee	Peterborough U	29	3
Connor Dan	6 2	13 04	G	31 1 81	Dublin	Trainee	Peterborough U	3	—
Cullen Jon	6 0	13 00	M	10 1 73	Durham	Trainee	Doncaster R	9	—
						Morpeth T	Hartlepool U	34	12
							Sheffield U	4	—
							Shrewsbury T (loan)	10	1
							Halifax T (loan)	11	5
							Peterborough U	13	3
Danielsson Helgi	6 0	12 00	M	13 7 81	Reykjavik	Fylkir	Peterborough U	—	—
Drury Adam	5 10	11 04	D	29 8 78	Cottenham	Trainee	Peterborough U	119	2
Edwards Andy	6 2	12 13	D	17 9 71	Epping	Trainee	Southend U	147	5
							Birmingham C	40	1
							Peterborough U	156	6
Farrell Dave	5 11	11 08	M	11 11 71	Birmingham	Redditch U	Aston Villa	6	—
							Scunthorpe U (loan)	5	1
							Wycombe W	60	8
							Peterborough U	114	13
Forinton Howard	5 11	12 04	F	18 9 75	Boston	Yeovil T	Birmingham C	5	1
							Plymouth Arg (loan)	9	3
							Peterborough U	25	7
French Daniel	5 11	11 00	M	25 11 79	Peterborough	Trainee	Peterborough U	6	—
Gill Matthew	5 11	11 07	M	8 11 80	Cambridge	Trainee	Peterborough U	48	1
Green Francis	5 9	11 04	F	23 4 80	Derby	Ilkeston T	Peterborough U	31	3
Griemink Bart*	6 3	15 02	G	29 3 72	Holland	WKE	Birmingham C	20	—
							Barnsley (loan)	—	—
							Peterborough U	58	—
							Swindon T (loan)	4	—
Haley Grant	5 8	10 02	D	20 9 79	Bristol	Trainee	Peterborough U	1	—
Hanlon Ritchie	6 1	12 13	M	25 5 78	Kenton	Chelsea	Southend U	2	—
						Rushden & D	Peterborough U	20	2
Hann Matthew	5 9	10 04	F	6 9 80	Saffron Walden	Trainee	Peterborough U	4	—
Hooper Dean	5 11	12 06	D	13 4 71	Harefield	Hayes	Swindon T	4	—
							Peterborough U (loan)	4	—
						Kingstonian	Peterborough U	67	2
Inman Niall	5 9	11 06	M	6 2 78	Wakefield	Trainee	Peterborough U	12	2
Jelleyman Gareth	5 10	10 03	D	14 11 80	Holywell	Trainee	Peterborough U	20	—
Kenna Warren‡	6 0	13 06	D	18 5 80	Southampton	Trainee	Peterborough U	—	—
Koogi Anders*	5 10	10 11	M	8 9 79	Roskilde	Trainee	Peterborough U	2	—

Lee Jason	6 3	13 03	F	9 5 71	Newham	Trainee	Charlton Ath	1	—
							Stockport Co (loan)	2	—
							Lincoln C	93	21
							Southend U	24	3
							Nottingham F	76	14
							Charlton Ath (loan)	8	3
							Grimsby T (loan)	7	1
							Watford	37	11
							Chesterfield	28	1
							Peterborough U	23	6
Lewis Neil	5 8	10 05	D	28 6 74	Wolverhampton	Trainee	Leicester C	67	1
							Peterborough U	34	—
Lyttle Gerard	5 9	11 04	D	27 11 77	Belfast	Star of the Sea	Celtic	—	—
							Peterborough U	—	—
Martin Jae*	5 10	13 02	M	5 2 76	London	Trainee	Southend U	8	—
							Leyton Orient (loan)	4	—
							Birmingham C	7	—
							Lincoln C	41	5
							Peterborough U	19	1
Murray Dan	6 2	12 12	D	16 5 82	Cambridge	Scholar	Peterborough U	2	—
Oldfield David	6 1	13 04	M	30 5 68	Perth (Aus)	Apprentice	Luton T	29	4
							Manchester C	26	6
							Leicester C	188	26
							Millwall (loan)	17	6
							Luton T	117	18
							Stoke C	65	7
							Peterborough U	9	—
Rea Simon	6 1	13 00	D	20 9 76	Coventry	Trainee	Birmingham C	1	—
							Peterborough U	14	1
Rowe Zeke‡	5 10	11 08	F	30 10 73	Stoke Newington	Trainee	Chelsea	—	—
							Barnet (loan)	10	2
							Brighton & HA (loan)	9	3
							Peterborough U	35	3
							Doncaster R (loan)	6	2
Sadler Chris‡	5 11	11 09	D	18 2 81	Ipswich	Trainee	Peterborough U	—	—
Scott Richard	5 11	12 08	M	29 9 74	Dudley	Trainee	Birmingham C	12	—
							Shrewsbury T	105	18
							Peterborough U	61	7
Shields Tony	5 8	10 01	M	4 6 80	Derry	Trainee	Peterborough U	34	1
Showler Paul	5 10	11 00	M	10 10 66	Doncaster	Altrincham	Barnet	71	12
							Bradford C	88	15
							Luton T	27	6
							Peterborough U	—	—
Tanner Adam#	6 0	13 00	M	25 10 73	Maldon	Trainee	Ipswich T	73	7
							Peterborough U	—	—
Tyler Mark	5 11	12 00	G	2 4 77	Norwich	Trainee	Peterborough U	113	—
Wicks Matthew	6 2	13 05	D	8 9 78	Reading	Manchester U	Arsenal	—	—
							Crewe Alex	6	—
							Peterborough U	31	—

Scholars
Bishop, James; Brewster, Jorden; Byrne, Matthew J; De'ath, Frederick AB; Duncliffe, John P; Evans, Louie; Hardy, Luke; Lang, Adam B; O'Flynn, John; Rusk, Simon; Vaughan, Jonathan R

Player who does not hold a current contract but his registration has been retained by the club
Lewis, Neil A; McCormick, Charles

PLYMOUTH ARGYLE

Adams Steve	6 0	12 00	D	25 9 80	Plymouth	Trainee	Plymouth Arg	1	—
Ashton Jon*	6 0	13 00	D	4 8 79	Plymouth	Trainee	Plymouth Arg	34	—
Barlow Martin#	5 7	10 03	M	25 6 71	Barnstable	Trainee	Plymouth Arg	309	24
Barrett Adam	5 10	12 00	M	29 11 79	Dagenham		Plymouth Arg	43	3
Bastow Darren	5 11	12 00	M	22 12 81	Torquay	Trainee	Plymouth Arg	42	3
Belgrave Barrington*	5 9	11 00		16 9 80	Bedford	Norwich C	Plymouth Arg	15	—
Beswetherick John	5 11	11 04	D	15 1 78	Liverpool	Trainee	Plymouth Arg	69	—
Dungey James‡	5 8	12 00	G	7 2 78	Plymouth	Trainee	Plymouth Arg	10	—
							Exeter C	1	—
						Bodmin T	Plymouth Arg	7	—
Ford Liam*	5 7	10 03	F	8 9 79	Bradford	Trainee	Plymouth Arg	1	—
Gibbs Paul#	5 10	11 09	D	26 10 72	Gorleston	Diss T	Colchester U	53	3
							Torquay U	41	7
							Plymouth Arg	34	3
Gritton Martin	6 1	12 02	F	1 6 78	Glasgow	Porthleven	Plymouth Arg	32	6
Guinan Stephen	6 1	13 06	F	24 12 75	Birmingham	Trainee	Nottingham F	7	—
							Darlington (loan)	3	1
							Burnley (loan)	6	—
							Crewe Alex (loan)	3	—
							Halifax T (loan)	12	2
							Plymouth Arg (loan)	11	7
							Scunthorpe U (loan)	3	1
							Cambridge U	6	—
							Plymouth Arg	8	2

Hapgood Leon‡	5 6	10 00	F	7 8 79	Torbay	Trainee	Torquay U	40	3
							Plymouth Arg	—	—
Hargreaves Chris#	5 11	12 02	M	12 5 72	Cleethorpes	Trainee	Grimsby T	51	5
							Scarborough (loan)	3	—
							Hull C	49	—
							WBA	1	—
							Hereford U (loan)	17	2
						Hereford U	Hereford U	44	4
							Plymouth Arg	76	5
Heathcote Mike#	6 2	12 08	D	10 9 65	Durham	Spennymoor U	Sunderland	9	—
							Halifax T (loan)	7	1
							York C (loan)	3	—
							Shrewsbury T	44	6
							Cambridge U	128	13
							Plymouth Arg	194	13
Leadbitter Chris	5 9	10 06	M	17 10 67	Middlesbrough	Apprentice	Grimsby T	—	—
							Hereford U	36	1
							Cambridge U	176	18
							Bournemouth	54	3
							Plymouth Arg	52	1
							Torquay U	63	2
							Plymouth Arg	31	2
McCall Steve#	5 11	12 10	M	15 10 60	Carlisle	Apprentice	Ipswich T	257	7
							Sheffield W	29	2
							Carlisle U (loan)	6	—
							Plymouth Arg	100	5
							Torquay U	51	2
							Plymouth Arg	33	1
McCarthy Sean	6 1	12 05	F	12 9 67	Bridgend	Bridgend	Swansea C	91	25
							Plymouth Arg	70	19
							Bradford C	131	60
							Oldham Ath	140	42
							Bristol C (loan)	7	1
							Plymouth Arg	45	9
McGovern Brendan‡	5 10	12 07	M	9 2 80	Camborne	Trainee	Plymouth Arg	2	—
McGregor Paul	5 10	11 06	F	17 12 74	Liverpool	Trainee	Nottingham F	30	3
							Carlisle U (loan)	10	3
							Preston NE	4	—
							Plymouth Arg	44	13
Morrison-Hill Jamie	5 8	10 04	M	8 6 81	Plymouth	Trainee	Plymouth Arg	1	—
O'Sullivan Wayne	5 7	10 11	M	25 2 74	Akrotiri	Trainee	Swindon T	89	3
							Cardiff C	85	4
							Plymouth Arg	45	2
Paterson Scott‡	5 11	11 09	D	13 5 72	Aberdeen	Cove Rangers	Liverpool	—	—
							Bristol C	50	1
							Cardiff C (loan)	5	—
							Carlisle U	19	1
							Cambridge U	6	—
							Plymouth Arg	5	—
Phillips Lee	5 10	12 00	F	16 9 80	Penzance	School	Plymouth Arg	44	1
Rowbotham Jason*	5 9	11 09	D	3 1 69	Cardiff	Trainee	Plymouth Arg	9	—
							Shrewsbury T	—	—
							Hereford U	5	1
							Raith R	56	1
							Wycombe W	27	—
							Plymouth Arg	51	1
Sheffield Jon#	5 11	11 06	G	1 2 69	Bedworth	Apprentice	Norwich C	1	—
							Aldershot (loan)	11	—
							Ipswich T (loan)	—	—
							Aldershot (loan)	15	—
							Cambridge U (loan)	2	—
							Cambridge U	54	—
							Colchester U (loan)	6	—
							Swindon T (loan)	2	—
							Hereford U (loan)	8	—
							Peterborough U	62	—
							Watford (loan)	—	—
							Oldham Ath (loan)	—	—
							Plymouth Arg	126	—
Stonebridge Ian	6 0	11 04	F	30 8 81	Lewisham	Tottenham H	Plymouth Arg	31	9
Taylor Craig	6 1	12 03	D	24 1 74	Plymouth	Dorchester T	Swindon T	55	2
							Plymouth Arg (loan)	6	1
							Plymouth Arg	41	3
Veysey Kenneth*	5 11	12 07	G	8 6 67	Hackney	Arsenal	Torquay U	72	—
							Oxford U	57	—
							Sheffield U (loan)	—	—
							Exeter C	12	—
						Dorchester T	Torquay U	37	—
							Plymouth Arg	6	—

Wills Kevin	5 7	10 04	F	15 10 80	Torbay	Trainee	Plymouth Arg	4	—
Wotton Paul	5 11	11 08	M	17 8 77	Plymouth	Trainee	Plymouth Arg	110	3

Trainees
Berry, Stuart; Broad, Joseph R; Cusack, Aaron; Mallett, Neil; Prosser, Owain M

Scholars
Baker, Paul M; Bance, Daniel R; Curtis, Karl G; Edwards, Darren P; McCormick, Luke M; McGowan, Jamie P; McGowan, Matthew J; Sundercombe, Thomas J

Non-Contract
Hodges, Kevin

PORTSMOUTH

Allen Rory	5 11	11 10	F	17 10 77	Beckenham	Trainee	Tottenham H	21	2
							Luton T (loan)	8	6
							Portsmouth	15	3
Andreasson Svein#			M	3 7 68	Hadsel		Lillestrom	15	4
							Portsmouth	2	—
Awford Andy	5 9	11 09	D	14 7 72	Worcester	Worcester C	Portsmouth	311	3
Berntsen Tommy‡	5 9	12 02	D	18 12 73	Oslo		Lillestrom	22	5
(On loan from Lillestrom, November 1999)							Portsmouth	2	—
Birmingham David	5 8	11 01	D	16 4 81	Portsmouth	Bournemouth	Portsmouth	2	—
Bradbury Lee	6 2	13 10	F	3 7 75	Isle of Wight	Cowes	Portsmouth	54	15
							Exeter C (loan)	14	5
							Manchester C	40	10
							Crystal Palace	32	6
							Birmingham C (loan)	7	—
							Portsmouth	35	10
Claridge Steve	5 9	12 09	F	10 4 66	Portsmouth	Fareham T	Bournemouth	7	1
						Weymouth	Crystal Palace	—	—
							Aldershot	62	19
							Cambridge U	79	28
							Luton T	16	2
							Cambridge U	53	18
							Birmingham C	88	35
							Leicester C	63	16
							Portsmouth (loan)	10	2
							Wolverhampton W	5	—
							Portsmouth	73	23
Connolly Gary*	5 9	11 05	D	11 9 80	Portsmouth	Trainee	Portsmouth	—	—
Crowe Jason	5 9	11 02	D	30 9 78	Sidcup	Trainee	Arsenal	—	—
							Crystal Palace (loan)	8	—
							Portsmouth	25	—
Cundy Jason	6 0	13 11	D	12 11 69	Wimbledon	Trainee	Chelsea	41	1
							Tottenham H (loan)	10	—
							Tottenham H	16	1
							Crystal Palace (loan)	4	—
							Bristol C (loan)	6	1
							Ipswich T	58	5
							Portsmouth	9	—
Derry Shaun	5 10	13 02	M	6 12 77	Nottingham	Trainee	Notts Co	79	4
							Sheffield U	72	—
							Portsmouth	9	1
Edinburgh Justin	5 10	12 01	D	18 12 69	Basildon	Trainee	Southend U	37	—
							Tottenham H (loan)	—	—
							Tottenham H	213	1
							Portsmouth	11	—
Fenton Anthony*	5 10	11 12	D	23 11 79	Preston	Trainee	Manchester C	—	—
							Portsmouth	1	—
Flahavan Aaron	6 1	11 12	G	15 12 75	Southampton	Trainee	Portsmouth	73	—
Griffiths Ben			M	27 11 81	Bournemouth	Trainee	Portsmouth	—	—
Harper Kevin	5 7	12 00	F	15 1 76	Oldham		Hibernian	96	15
							Derby Co	32	1
							Walsall (loan)	9	1
							Portsmouth	12	2
Hiley Scott	5 8	11 08	D	27 9 68	Plymouth	Trainee	Exeter C	210	12
							Birmingham C	49	—
							Manchester C	9	—
							Southampton	32	—
							Portsmouth	8	—
Holbrook Adam	5 9	11 06	D	17 10 80	Newport (IW)	Trainee	Portsmouth	—	—
Hoult Russell	6 4	14 07	G	22 11 72	Ashby	Trainee	Leicester C	10	—
							Lincoln C (loan)	2	—
							Blackpool (loan)	—	—
							Bolton W (loan)	4	—
							Lincoln C (loan)	15	—
							Derby Co (loan)	15	—
							Derby Co	108	—
							Portsmouth	18	—
Hughes Ceri	5 10	12 07	M	26 2 71	Pontypridd	Trainee	Luton T	175	17
							Wimbledon	31	1
							Portsmouth	15	2
Knight Alan†	6 1	13 11	G	3 7 61	Balham	Apprentice	Portsmouth	683	—

Name				DOB	Birthplace	Source	Club	Apps	Gls
Lovell Stephen	5 11	11 08	F	6 12 80	Amersham	Trainee	Bournemouth	8	—
							Portsmouth	3	—
							Exeter C (loan)	5	1
McNab Joe	5 4	9 00	M	29 10 80	Brighton	Manchester C	Portsmouth	—	—
McNab Neil	5 6	10 03	M	29 10 80	Brighton	Manchester C	Portsmouth	—	—
Miglioranzi Stefani	6 1	12 12	M	20 9 77	Pacos de Caldas	St Johns Univ	Portsmouth	20	2
Mitchell Robert*	5 11	11 07	G	7 3 81	Southampton	Bournemouth	Portsmouth	—	—
Moore Darren	6 3	15 08	D	22 4 74	Birmingham	Trainee	Torquay U	103	8
							Doncaster R	76	7
							Bradford C	62	3
							Portsmouth	25	1
Nightingale Luke	5 11	11 07	F	22 12 80	Portsmouth	Trainee	Portsmouth	26	3
O'Neil Gary§	5 10	11 00		18 5 83	Beckenham	Trainee	Portsmouth	1	—
Pamarot Noe*	5 10	13 08	D	14 4 79	Paris	Nice	Portsmouth	2	—
Panopoulos Mike	6 1	12 10	M	9 10 76	Melbourne	Heidelberg U	Aris Salonika	22	3
							Portsmouth	22	1
Pettefer Carl	5 7	10 02	M	22 3 81	Taplow	Trainee	Portsmouth	—	—
Petterson Andy	6 2	15 02	G	29 9 69	Fremantle		Luton T	19	—
							Swindon T (loan)	—	—
							Ipswich T (loan)	—	—
							Ipswich T (loan)	1	—
							Charlton Ath	72	—
							Bradford C (loan)	3	—
							Ipswich T (loan)	1	—
							Plymouth Arg (loan)	6	—
							Colchester U (loan)	5	—
							Portsmouth (loan)	13	—
							Portsmouth	17	—
							Wolverhampton W (loan)	—	—
Phillips Martin	5 8	10 03	M	13 3 76	Exeter	Trainee	Exeter C	52	5
							Manchester C	15	—
							Scunthorpe U (loan)	3	—
							Exeter C (loan)	8	—
							Portsmouth	24	1
							Bristol R (loan)	2	—
Simpson Fitzroy *(Transferred to Hearts, December 1999)*	5 10	11 12	D	26 2 70	Trowbridge	Trainee	Swindon T	105	9
							Manchester C	71	4
							Bristol C (loan)	4	—
							Portsmouth	148	10
Simpson Robbie‡	5 10	11 06	F	3 3 76	Luton	Trainee	Tottenham H	—	—
							Portsmouth	2	—
Stoner Craig			M	5 11 81	Chichester	Trainee	Portsmouth	—	—
Tardif Chris	5 11	12 07	G	19 9 79	Guernsey	Trainee	Portsmouth	—	—
Thogersen Thomas	6 2	13 01	M	2 4 68	Copenhagen		Frem	57	7
							Brondby	111	22
							Portsmouth	69	5
Waterman David	5 10	12 02	D	16 5 77	Guernsey	Trainee	Portsmouth	49	—
Whitbread Adrian	6 0	12 12	D	22 10 71	Epping	Trainee	Leyton Orient	125	2
							Swindon T	36	1
							West Ham U	10	—
							Portsmouth (loan)	13	—
							Portsmouth	134	2
Whittingham Guy	6 1	12 04	F	10 11 64	Evesham	Yeovil T, Army	Portsmouth	160	88
							Aston Villa	25	5
							Wolverhampton W (loan)	13	8
							Sheffield W	113	22
							Wolverhampton W (loan)	10	1
							Portsmouth (loan)	9	7
							Watford (loan)	5	—
							Portsmouth	25	4
Wilson Michael			M	5 10 81	Guernsey	Trainee	Portsmouth	—	—

Trainees
Barnett, Phillip; Dodd, Jonathon; Osborne, Benjamin H; Riddington, Charles AT; White, Thomas

Scholars
Chin, Gordon R; Molyneaux, Lee A; O'Neil, Gary P; Pook, Robbie J; Vine, Rowan L

Non-Contract
Knight, Alan E

Associated Schoolboys who have accepted the Club's offer of a Traineeship/Scholarship/Contract
Breslin, Neil J; Buxton, Lewis E; Cooper, Shaun A; Hunt, Warren D; Parker, Terry J

PORT VALE

Name				DOB	Birthplace	Source	Club	Apps	Gls
Barker Simon‡	5 8	11 07	M	4 11 64	Farnworth	Apprentice	Blackburn R	182	35
							QPR	315	33
							Port Vale	32	2
Bogie Ian*	5 7	11 10	M	6 12 67	Newcastle	Apprentice	Newcastle U	14	—
							Preston NE	79	12
							Millwall	51	1
							Leyton Orient	65	5
							Port Vale	154	9
Brammer Dave	5 11	12 00	M	28 2 75	Bromborough	Trainee	Wrexham	137	12
							Port Vale	38	—

Name	Ht	Wt	Pos	DOB	Birthplace	Signed	Club	Apps	Gls
Brisco Neil	5 11	13 01	M	26 1 78	Billinge	Trainee	Manchester C	—	—
							Port Vale	13	—
Burns Liam	6 0	13 03	D	30 10 78	Belfast	Trainee	Port Vale	29	—
Burton Sagi	6 2	13 06	D	25 11 77	Birmingham	Trainee	Crystal Palace	25	1
							Colchester U	9	—
							Sheffield U	—	—
							Port Vale	20	2
Carragher Matthew	5 9	11 06	D	14 1 76	Liverpool	Trainee	Wigan Ath	119	—
							Port Vale	73	1
Clitheroe Stuart*	5 4	10 00	M	28 11 80	Preston	Trainee	Port Vale	—	—
Corden Wayne*	5 10	11 05	M	1 11 75	Leek	Trainee	Port Vale	66	1
Cummins Michael	6 0	12 08	M	1 6 78	Dublin	Trainee	Middlesbrough	2	—
							Port Vale	12	1
Donnelly Paul	5 7	11 00	D	16 2 81	Newcastle under Lyme	Trainee	Port Vale	4	—
Eyre Richard	5 8	11 08	M	15 9 76	Poynton	Trainee	Port Vale	42	1
Foyle Martin#	5 10	12 00	F	2 5 63	Salisbury	Amateur	Southampton	12	1
							Blackburn R (loan)	—	—
							Aldershot	98	35
							Oxford U	126	36
							Port Vale	296	83
Goodlad Mark	6 0	13 02	G	9 9 80	Barnsley	Trainee	Nottingham F	—	—
							Scarborough (loan)	3	—
							Port Vale	1	—
Minton Jeffrey	5 10	12 04	F	28 12 73	Hackney	Trainee	Tottenham H	2	1
							Brighton & HA	174	31
							Port Vale	23	3
Musselwhite Paul*	6 2	14 04	G	22 12 68	Portsmouth	Apprentice	Portsmouth	—	—
							Scunthorpe U	132	—
							Port Vale	312	—
Naylor Tony	5 4	10 07	F	29 3 68	Manchester	Droylsden	Crewe Alex	122	45
							Port Vale	211	57
O'Callaghan George	6 1	10 05	M	5 9 79	Cork	Trainee	Port Vale	15	—
Pilkington Kevin*	6 1	13 00	G	8 3 74	Hitchin	Trainee	Manchester U	6	—
							Rochdale (loan)	6	—
							Rotherham U (loan)	17	—
							Port Vale	23	—
Rimmer Steve*	6 3	13 02	D	23 5 79	Liverpool	Trainee	Manchester C	—	—
							Port Vale	2	—
Rougier Tony	5 10	14 07	F	17 7 71	Trinidad		Raith R	56	2
							Hibernian	35	4
							Port Vale	51	8
Smith Alex	5 8	10 06	M	15 2 76	Liverpool	Trainee	Everton	—	—
							Swindon T	31	1
							Huddersfield T	6	—
							Chester C	32	2
							Port Vale	21	—
Snijders Mark*	6 2	14 04	D	12 3 72	Alkmaar		Port Vale	55	2
Talbot Stuart*	5 11	13 07	M	14 6 73	Birmingham	Moor Green	Port Vale	137	10
Tankard Allen	5 10	13 04	D	21 5 69	Fleet	Trainee	Southampton	5	—
							Wigan Ath	209	4
							Port Vale	242	7
Tarr Anthony*	6 0	12 00	F	9 10 80	Stoke	Trainee	Port Vale	—	—
Taylor Paul	5 11	12 06	M	16 9 80	Stoke	Trainee	Port Vale	—	—
Viljanen Ville#	6 2	13 05		2 2 71	Helsinki	Sandarna	Hacken	71	15
							Port Vale	15	4
Walsh Michael	6 0	12 08	D	5 8 77	Rotherham	Trainee	Scunthorpe U	103	1
							Port Vale	31	2
Widdrington Tommy	5 9	11 12	M	1 10 71	Newcastle	Trainee	Southampton	75	3
							Wigan Ath (loan)	6	—
							Grimsby T	89	8
							Port Vale (loan)	9	1
							Port Vale	38	5

Scholars
Barker, Philip; Byrne, Paul; Carrigan, Benjamin D; Fairbrother, Craig; Fairhurst, Neil A; Farr, David J; Gowan, Christopher J; Maye, Daniel P; Olaoye, Dolapo; Rowland, Stephen J; Simpson, Benjamin J; Taylor, Andrew

Associated Schoolboys who have accepted the Club's offer of a Traineeship/Scholarship/Contract
Birchall, Christopher; Eldershaw, Simon; Kirkham, Shane; Paynter, William; Reid, Levi SJ; Sneade, Adam; Stevenson, Matthew

PRESTON NORTH END

Name	Ht	Wt	Pos	DOB	Birthplace	Signed	Club	Apps	Gls
Alexander Graham	5 10	12 00	D	10 10 71	Coventry	Trainee	Scunthorpe U	159	18
							Luton T	150	15
							Preston NE	56	6
Anderson Iain	5 8	9 07	F	23 7 77	Glasgow		Dundee	126	15
							Toulouse	3	—
							Preston NE	12	2
Appleton Michael	5 8	11 00	M	4 12 75	Salford	Trainee	Manchester U	—	—
							Lincoln C (loan)	4	—
							Grimsby T (loan)	10	3
							Preston NE	89	7

Barry-Murphy Brian	6 0	12 04	M	27 7 78	Cork		Cork City	80	2
							Preston NE	1	—
Basham Steve	5 11	12 05	F	2 12 77	Southampton	Trainee	Southampton	19	1
							Wrexham (loan)	5	—
							Preston NE (loan)	17	10
							Preston NE	24	2
Beesley Mark*	5 11	11 10	F	10 11 81	Burscough	Trainee	Preston NE	1	—
Cartwright Lee	5 8	10 07	F	19 9 72	Rossendale	Trainee	Preston NE	289	21
Darby Julian*	6 0	11 04	M	3 10 67	Bolton	Trainee	Bolton W	270	36
							Coventry C	55	5
							WBA	39	1
							Preston NE	35	1
							Rotherham U (loan)	3	—
Diaf Farid*	5 8	10 12	M	19 4 71	Carcassonne	Rennes	Preston NE	3	—
Eaton Adam	5 10	11 08	D	2 5 80	Wigan	Trainee	Everton	—	—
							Preston NE	—	—
Edwards Robert	6 0	12 07	D	1 7 73	Kendal	Trainee	Carlisle U	48	5
							Bristol C	216	5
							Preston NE	41	2
Eyres David#	5 11	11 06	F	26 2 64	Liverpool	Rhyl	Blackpool	158	38
							Burnley	175	37
							Preston NE	103	19
Gregan Sean	6 2	12 03	M	29 3 74	Stockton	Trainee	Darlington	136	4
							Preston NE	130	9
Gunnlaugsson Bjarki	5 9	11 05	F	6 3 73	Iceland		IA Akranes	24	6
							Feyenoord	—	—
							Nuremberg	27	5
							IA Akranes	7	3
							Waldhof Mannheim	26	6
							Molde	18	6
							KR	16	11
							Preston NE	26	1
Jackson Michael	5 11	11 10	D	4 12 73	Chester	Trainee	Crewe Alex	5	—
							Bury	125	9
							Preston NE	137	15
Kidd Ryan	5 11	10 10	D	16 10 71	Radcliffe	Trainee	Port Vale	1	—
							Preston NE	238	9
King Stuart	5 11	10 00	M	20 3 81	Derry	Trainee	Preston NE	—	—
Lucas David	6 1	11 06	G	23 11 77	Preston	Trainee	Preston NE	46	—
							Darlington (loan)	6	—
							Darlington (loan)	7	—
							Scunthorpe U (loan)	6	—
Ludden Dominic#	5 7	10 09	D	30 3 74	Basildon	Trainee	Leyton Orient	58	1
							Watford	33	—
							Preston NE	35	—
Macken Jonathan	5 10	12 00	F	7 9 77	Manchester	Trainee	Manchester U	—	—
							Preston NE	115	36
Mathie Alex	5 10	11 13	F	20 12 68	Bathgate	Celtic BC	Celtic	11	—
							Morton	74	31
							Port Vale (loan)	3	—
							Newcastle U	25	4
							Ipswich T	109	38
							Dundee U	34	4
							Preston NE	12	2
McDonald Neil‡	6 0	13 10	D	2 11 65	Wallsend	Wallsend BC	Newcastle U	180	24
							Everton	90	4
							Oldham Ath	24	1
							Bolton W	4	—
							Preston NE	33	—
McKenna Paul	5 8	11 11	M	20 10 77	Chorley	Trainee	Preston NE	70	3
Moilanen Teuvo	6 5	12 09	G	12 12 73	Oulu		Ilves	63	—
							Jaro	26	—
							Preston NE	102	—
							Scarborough (loan)	4	—
							Darlington (loan)	16	—
Morgan Paul	6 0	11 05	D	23 10 78	Belfast	Trainee	Preston NE	—	—
Moyes David†	6 1	12 12	D	25 4 63	Glasgow	Drumchapel Amat	Celtic	24	—
							Cambridge U	79	1
							Bristol C	83	6
							Shrewsbury T	96	11
							Dunfermline Ath	105	13
							Hamilton A	5	—
							Preston NE	143	15
Murdock Colin	6 1	12 00	D	2 7 75	Ballymena	Trainee	Manchester U	—	—
							Preston NE	93	4

O'Hanlon Kelham†	6 1	13 12	G	16 5 62	Saltburn		Middlesbrough	87	—
							Rotherham U	248	—
							Carlisle U	83	—
							Preston NE	23	—
							Dundee U	30	—
							Preston NE	13	—
Parkinson Gary#	5 10	11 10	D	10 1 68	Middlesbrough	Everton	Middlesbrough	202	5
							Southend U (loan)	6	—
							Bolton W	3	—
							Burnley	135	4
							Preston NE	73	6
Rankine Mark	5 9	11 05	M	30 9 69	Doncaster	Trainee	Doncaster R	164	20
							Wolverhampton W	132	1
							Preston NE	144	4
Wright Mark	5 10	11 05	F	4 9 81	Chorley	Schoolboy	Preston NE	3	—

Scholars
Douglas, Adam M; Hallam Anthony T; Hollis, John; Keane, Michael T; Lin, Paul; Madin Lee P; McMillan, Anthony T; Nesa, Remo; O'Neill, Joseph; Underwood, Jeffrey H; Wilkinson, Craig; Wright, Ronnie M

Non-Contract
Moyes, David W; O'Hanlon, Kelham Gerard

Associated Schoolboys
Lonergan, Andrew; Mercer, Richard M

QUEENS PARK RANGERS

Bankole Ademola	6 3	14 11	G	9 9 69	Lagos	Leyton Orient	Crewe Alex	6	—
							QPR	1	—
							Grimsby T (loan)	—	—
							Bradford C (loan)	—	—
Baraclough Ian	6 1	12 10	D	4 12 70	Leicester	Trainee	Leicester C	—	—
							Wigan Ath (loan)	9	2
							Grimsby T (loan)	4	—
							Grimsby T	1	—
							Lincoln C	73	10
							Mansfield T	47	5
							Notts Co	111	10
							QPR	96	1
Brady Richard	5 8	10 04	F	17 9 82	Dartford	Trainee	QPR	—	—
Breacker Tim	6 0	13 00	D	2 7 65	Bicester	Apprentice	Luton T	210	3
							West Ham U	240	8
							QPR	34	2
Brown Carlos	6 0	11 07	D	22 4 81	Edmonton	Trainee	QPR	—	—
Browne Rickey	6 1	12 05	D	19 10 81	Edmonton	Scholar	QPR	—	—
Bruce Paul	5 10	12 06	F	18 2 78	London	Trainee	QPR	17	1
							Cambridge U (loan)	4	—
Bubb Alvin	5 4	10 03	F	11 10 80	Paddington	Trainee	QPR	—	—
Bull Nikki	6 1	11 13	G	2 10 81	Hastings	Scholar	QPR	—	—
Cass Matthew*	5 9	12 00	M	16 12 79	Liverpool	Trainee	QPR	—	—
Cochrane Justin	5 11	11 07	M	26 1 82	Hackney	Scholar	QPR	—	—
Currie Michael	5 10	11 00	F	19 10 79	Westminster	Trainee	QPR	—	—
D'Austin Ryan	5 9	10 13	M	29 11 82	Edgware	Trainee	QPR	—	—
Darlington Jermaine	5 9	13 00	D	11 4 74	Hackney	Aylesbury U	QPR	38	2
Dowie Iain#	6 1	14 06	F	9 1 65	Hatfield	Hendon	Luton T	66	16
							Fulham (loan)	5	1
							West Ham U	12	4
							Southampton	122	30
							Crystal Palace	19	6
							West Ham U	68	8
							QPR	30	2
Duncan Lyndon	5 8	11 02	D	12 1 83	Ealing	Trainee	QPR	—	—
Gallen Kevin	5 11	13 05	F	21 9 75	Hammersmith	Trainee	QPR	171	36
Graham Richard	5 8	10 06	M	5 8 79	Newry	Trainee	QPR	2	—
Harper Lee	6 1	14 07	G	30 10 71	Chelsea	Sittingbourne	Arsenal	1	—
							QPR	89	—
Heinola Antti	5 10	12 03	D	20 3 73	Helsinki		HJK Helsinki	80	5
							Emmen	19	—
							Heracles	31	3
							QPR	33	—
Jeanne Leon	5 8	10 10	F	17 11 80	Cardiff	Trainee	QPR	12	—
Jones Vinnie‡	6 0	11 12	M	5 1 65	Watford	Wealdstone	Wimbledon	77	9
							Leeds U	46	5
							Sheffield U	35	2
							Chelsea	42	4
							Wimbledon	177	12
							QPR	9	1

Name	Ht	Wt	Pos	DOB	Birthplace	Status	Club	Apps	Gls
Kiwomya Chris#	5 9	10 07	F	2 12 69	Huddersfield	Trainee	Ipswich T	225	51
							Arsenal	14	3
							Le Havre (loan)	7	—
							QPR	60	19
Koejoe Sammy	6 2	14 07	F	17 8 74	Surinam		Lustenau	29	7
							Salzburg	52	9
							QPR	11	1
Kulcsar George	6 1	12 08	M	12 8 67	Budapest		Antwerp	66	1
							Bradford C	26	1
							QPR	42	1
Langley Richard	5 10	11 04	M	27 12 79	London	Trainee	QPR	49	4
Lopez Rik*	5 9	11 13	M	25 10 79	Northwick Park	Arsenal	QPR	—	—
Lusardi Mario	5 9	12 00	F	27 9 79	Islington	Trainee	QPR	—	—
Maddix Danny	5 11	12 00	D	11 10 66	Ashford	Apprentice	Tottenham H	—	—
							Southend U (loan)	2	—
							QPR	292	13
Mahoney-Johnson Michael*	5 10	12 02	F	6 11 76	Paddington	Trainee	QPR	3	—
							Wycombe W (loan)	4	2
							Brighton & HA (loan)	4	—
McFlynn Terry	5 9	11 11	M	27 3 81	Magherafelt	Trainee	QPR	—	—
Miklosko Ludek#	6 5	14 00	G	9 12 61	Protesov	Banik Ostrava	West Ham U	315	—
							QPR	40	—
Mills Danny	6 0	12 07	G	8 9 82	Sidcup	Trainee	QPR	—	—
Morrow Steve	6 0	12 06	D	2 7 70	Bangor	Trainee	Arsenal	62	1
							Reading (loan)	10	—
							Watford (loan)	8	—
							Reading (loan)	3	—
							Barnet (loan)	1	—
							QPR	67	2
Murphy Danny	5 6	10 04	D	4 12 82	London	Trainee	QPR	—	—
Murray Paul	5 8	10 05	M	31 8 76	Carlisle	Trainee	Carlisle U	41	1
							QPR	134	7
Newall John*	5 11	12 01	D	22 9 80	West Bromwich	Trainee	QPR	—	—
Ord Richard‡	6 2	13 00	D	3 3 70	Easington	Trainee	Sunderland	243	7
							York C (loan)	3	—
							QPR	—	—
Owen Karl‡	5 11	12 03	D	12 10 79	Coventry	Trainee	QPR	—	—
Pacquette Richard	6 0	12 07	F	28 1 83	Paddington	Trainee	QPR	—	—
Peacock Gavin	5 9	11 08	M	18 11 67	Eltham	Apprentice	QPR	17	1
							Gillingham	70	11
							Bournemouth	56	8
							Newcastle U	105	35
							Chelsea	103	17
							QPR	138	30
Perry Mark	5 11	13 06	M	19 10 78	Perivale	Trainee	QPR	21	1
Piercewright Brad	6 0	12 00	D	21 9 80	Northampton	Northampton T	QPR	—	—
Plummer Chris	6 2	12 12	D	12 10 76	Isleworth	Trainee	QPR	34	—
Purser Wayne*	5 9	11 13	F	13 4 80	Basildon	Trainee	QPR	—	—
Ready Karl	6 3	13 08	D	14 8 72	Neath	Trainee	QPR	203	10
Rose Matthew	5 11	11 09	D	24 9 75	Dartford	Trainee	Arsenal	5	—
							QPR	74	1
Rowland Keith	5 10	10 07	M	1 9 71	Portadown	Trainee	Bournemouth	72	2
							Coventry C (loan)	2	—
							West Ham U	80	1
							QPR	52	3
Rustem Adam	6 0	11 07	F	18 9 81	Whipps Cross	Scholar	QPR	—	—
Scully Tony	5 7	11 06	M	12 6 76	Dublin	Trainee	Crystal Palace	3	—
							Bournemouth (loan)	10	—
							Cardiff C (loan)	14	—
							Manchester C	9	—
							Stoke C (loan)	7	—
							QPR	38	2
Slade Steve*	5 11	11 00	F	6 10 75	Hackney	Trainee	Tottenham H	5	—
							QPR	68	6
							Brentford (loan)	4	—
Steiner Rob	6 2	13 05	F	20 6 73	Finsprong		Norrkoping	41	14
							Bradford C	15	4
							Norrkoping	6	1
							Bradford C	37	10
							QPR (loan)	12	3
							Walsall (loan)	10	3
							QPR	24	6
Wardley Stuart	5 11	12 03	M	10 9 75	Cambridge	Saffron Walden T	QPR	43	11
Weare Ross	6 2	13 09	F	19 3 77	Perivale	East Ham U	QPR	4	—
Whittle David‡	5 10	12 07	D	2 12 78	Waterford	Trainee	QPR	—	—
Wright Danny	5 7	10 13	M	24 9 81	London	Trainee	QPR	—	—

Scholars
Burgess, Oliver D; Dick, Alexander R; Gradley, Patrick J; Nugent, Marcel E; Patrick-Heselton, Alistair; Robertson, Kristoffer R; Walshe, Benjamin M

Associated Schoolboys
Bean, Marcus; Daly, Wesley JP; Egan, Richard L; Fitzgerald, Brian M; Wattley, David A

READING

Name			Pos		Birthplace	Source	Club	Apps	Gls
Allaway Ricky	6 2	11 08	D	16 2 83	Reading	Trainee	Reading	—	—
Arkins Stephen*			M	9 8 81	Dublin	Trainee	Reading	—	—
Ashdown Jamie	6 3	14 07	G	30 11 80	Wokingham		Reading	—	—
Beasley Adam‡			M	22 4 81	Crewe	Trainee	Reading	—	—
Bernal Andy*	5 10	12 05	D	16 7 66	Canberra	Sporting Gijon	Ipswich T	9	—
						Sydney Olympic	Reading	187	2
Brayson Paul	5 4	10 10	F	16 9 77	Newcastle	Trainee	Newcastle U	—	—
							Swansea C (loan)	11	5
							Reading	41	1
							Cardiff C (loan)	9	1
Brebner Grant	5 10	11 11	M	6 12 77	Edinburgh	Trainee	Manchester U	—	—
(Transferred to Hibernian, August 1999)							Cambridge U (loan)	6	1
							Hibernian (loan)	9	1
							Reading	41	10
Butler Martin	6 0	11 07	F	15 9 74	Wordsley	Trainee	Walsall	74	8
							Cambridge U	103	41
							Reading	17	4
Caskey Darren	5 8	11 09	M	21 8 74	Basildon	Trainee	Tottenham H	32	4
							Watford (loan)	6	1
							Reading	159	26
Casper Chris	6 0	11 02	D	28 4 75	Burnley	Trainee	Manchester U	2	—
							Bournemouth (loan)	16	1
							Swindon T (loan)	9	1
							Reading	47	—
Crawford Jimmy	5 10	11 00	M	1 5 73	Chicago	Bohemians	Newcastle U	2	—
							Rotherham U (loan)	11	—
							Dundee U (loan)	2	—
							Reading	21	1
Evers Sean	5 9	9 07	M	10 10 77	Hitchin	Trainee	Luton T	52	6
							Reading	18	—
Forster Nicky	5 9	10 11	F	8 9 73	Caterham	Horley T	Gillingham	67	24
							Brentford	109	39
							Birmingham C	68	11
							Reading	36	10
Glasgow Byron‡	5 6	10 11	M	18 2 79	Tooting	Trainee	Reading	39	1
Grant Peter‡	5 8	11 07	M	30 8 65	Bellshill		Celtic	363	15
							Norwich C	68	3
							Reading	29	1
Gray Stuart	5 11	12 00	D	18 12 73	Harrogate		Celtic	28	1
							Reading	49	2
Gurney Andy	5 8	10 08	D	25 1 74	Bristol	Trainee	Bristol R	108	9
							Torquay U	64	10
							Reading	46	2
Haddow Alex	5 8	11 02	M	8 1 82	Fleet	Trainee	Reading	2	—
Hadland Philip*			M	20 10 80	Warrington	Trainee	Reading	—	—
Hammond Nicky‡	6 0	11 13	G	7 9 67	Hornchurch	Apprentice	Arsenal	—	—
							Bristol R (loan)	3	—
							Peterborough U (loan)	—	—
							Aberdeen (loan)	—	—
							Swindon T	67	—
							Plymouth Arg	4	—
							Reading	25	—
Henderson Darius	6 1	13 09	F	7 9 81	Doncaster	Trainee	Reading	6	—
Hodges Lee#	5 11	11 06	M	4 9 73	Epping	Trainee	Tottenham H	—	—
							Plymouth Arg (loan)	7	2
							Wycombe W (loan)	4	—
							Barnet	105	26
							Reading	50	8
Howie Scott	6 4	13 07	G	4 1 72	Motherwell		Clyde	55	—
							Norwich C	2	—
							Motherwell	69	—
							Reading	85	—
Hunter Barry#	6 4	12 00	D	18 11 68	Coleraine	Crusaders	Wrexham	91	4
							Reading	61	3
							Southend U (loan)	5	2
Igoe Sammy	5 6	10 08	M	30 9 75	Spelthorne	Trainee	Portsmouth	160	11
							Reading	6	—
Kromheer Elroy‡	6 4	12 07	D	15 1 70	Amsterdam		Volendam	72	6
							Motherwell	12	—
							Volendam	53	2
							Zwolle	53	5
							Reading	11	—
Lockwood Adam	6 0	12 00	D	26 10 81	Wakefield	Trainee	Reading	—	—
Mackie John	6 0	12 06	D	5 7 76	London	Sutton U	Reading	—	—
McIntyre Jim	5 11	11 05	F	24 5 72	Alexandria	Duntocher BC	Bristol C	1	—
							Exeter C (loan)	15	3
							Airdrieonians	54	10
							Kilmarnock	46	9
							Reading	64	10

Name	Ht	Wt	Pos	DOB	Birthplace	From	Club	Apps	Gls
McLaren Andy‡	5 10	10 06	M	5 6 73	Glasgow		Dundee U	165	12
							Reading	9	1
							Linvingston (loan)	9	—
Murty Graeme	5 10	11 10	M	13 11 74	Saltburn	Trainee	York C	117	7
							Reading	26	—
Osborne Steven*			M	26 10 80	Hillingdon	Trainee	Reading	—	—
Parkinson Phil	6 0	11 06	M	1 12 67	Chorley	Apprentice	Southampton	—	—
							Bury	145	5
							Reading	279	14
Polston John	5 11	11 12	D	10 6 68	Walthamstow	Apprentice	Tottenham H	24	1
							Norwich C	215	8
							Reading	18	1
Primus Linvoy*	6 0	12 04	D	14 9 73	Forest Gate	Trainee	Charlton Ath	4	—
							Barnet	127	7
							Reading	95	1
Robinson Matt	5 10	11 02	D	23 12 74	Exeter	Trainee	Southampton	14	—
							Portsmouth	69	1
							Reading	19	—
Sarr Mass‡	5 9	12 02	M	6 2 73	Monrovia		Ales	57	10
							Hajduk Split	59	17
							Reading	31	3
Scott Keith	6 3	14 03	F	9 6 67	Westminster	Leicester U	Lincoln C	16	2
						Wycombe W	Wycombe W	15	10
							Swindon T	51	12
							Stoke C	25	3
							Norwich C	25	5
							Bournemouth (loan)	8	1
							Watford (loan)	6	2
							Wycombe W (loan)	9	3
							Wycombe W	54	17
							Reading	34	5
Smith Christopher	5 11	11 01	D	30 6 81	Derby	Trainee	Reading	—	—
Smith Neil	5 9	12 00	M	30 9 71	Lambeth	Trainee	Tottenham H	—	—
							Gillingham	212	10
							Fulham	73	1
							Reading	36	1
Stamp Neville	5 11	12 07	D	7 7 81	Reading	Trainee	Reading	1	—
Tyson Nathan	6 0	10 01	F	4 5 82	Reading	Trainee	Reading	1	—
Van der Kwaak Peter‡	6 4	15 00	G	12 10 68	Haarlem	Ajax	Dordrecht	50	—
							Reading	4	—
							Carlisle U (loan)	2	—
Whitehead Phil	6 3	13 07	G	17 12 69	Halifax	Trainee	Halifax T	42	—
							Barnsley	16	—
							Halifax T (loan)	9	—
							Scunthorpe U (loan)	8	—
							Scunthorpe U (loan)	8	—
							Bradford C (loan)	6	—
							Oxford U	207	—
							WBA	26	—
							Reading	11	—
Williams Martin*	5 9	11 12	F	12 7 73	Luton	Leicester C	Luton T	40	2
							Colchester U (loan)	3	—
							Reading	128	26

Trainees
Hill, Emlyn R; Martin, Paul

Scholars
Alcott, Joseph D; Birnie, Matthew T; Brown, Craig; Campion, Adam J; Kurton, Stuart M; O'Hara, Declan M; Tonna, Michael J; Williams, Scott

Non-Contract
Gosby, Stuart G

ROCHDALE

Name	Ht	Wt	Pos	DOB	Birthplace	From	Club	Apps	Gls
Atkinson Graeme	5 7	11 04	D	11 11 71	Hull	Trainee	Hull C	149	23
							Preston NE	79	6
							Rochdale (loan)	6	—
							Brighton & HA	16	—
							Scunthorpe U	1	—
							Scarborough	15	1
							Rochdale	40	5
Bayliss Dave	5 11	12 00	D	8 6 76	Liverpool	Trainee	Rochdale	136	6
Bettney Chris*	5 9	11 02	F	27 10 77	Chesterfield	Trainee	Sheffield U	1	—
							Hull C (loan)	30	1
							Chesterfield	13	—
							Rochdale	24	—
Dowe Julian*	5 11	12 10	F	9 9 75	Manchester	Trainee	Wigan Ath	—	—
						Marbella	Ayr U	7	1
						Colne	Rochdale	7	—
Edwards Neil	5 9	11 11	G	5 12 70	Aberdare	Trainee	Leeds U	—	—
							Huddersfield T (loan)	—	—
							Stockport Co	164	—
							Rochdale	112	—

Ellis Tony#	5 11	11 00	F	20 10 64	Salford	Northwich Vic	Oldham Ath	8	—
							Preston NE	86	26
							Stoke C	77	19
							Preston NE	72	48
							Blackpool	146	54
							Bury	38	8
							Stockport Co	20	6
							Rochdale	31	11
Evans Wayne	5 10	12 03	D	25 8 71	Welshpool	Welshpool	Walsall	183	1
							Rochdale	46	1
Flitcroft David	5 11	13 05	M	14 1 74	Bolton	Trainee	Preston NE	8	2
							Lincoln C (loan)	2	—
							Chester C	167	18
							Rochdale	43	2
Ford Tony	5 9	13 00	M	14 5 59	Grimsby	Apprentice	Grimsby T	355	55
							Sunderland (loan)	9	1
							Stoke C	112	13
							WBA	114	14
							Grimsby T	68	3
							Bradford C (loan)	5	—
							Scunthorpe U	76	9
						Barrow	Mansfield T	103	7
							Rochdale	34	2
Hicks Graham	5 10	13 05	D	17 2 81	Oldham	Trainee	Rochdale	1	—
Hill Keith	6 1	12 07	D	17 5 69	Bolton	Apprentice	Blackburn R	96	3
							Plymouth Arg	123	2
							Rochdale	151	6
Holt Michael*	5 10	11 03	F	28 7 77	Barnoldswick	Trainee	Blackburn R	—	—
							Preston NE	36	5
							Macclesfield T (loan)	4	1
							Rochdale	38	7
Jones Gary	5 11	11 07	M	3 6 77	Birkenhead	Caernarfon Town	Swansea C	8	—
							Rochdale	76	9
Lancashire Graham#	5 9	12 04	F	19 10 72	Blackpool	Trainee	Burnley	31	8
							Halifax T (loan)	2	—
							Chester C (loan)	11	7
							Preston NE	23	2
							Wigan Ath	30	12
							Rochdale	67	20
Lenagh Steve*	6 2	12 12	D	21 3 79	Durham	Sheffield W	Chesterfield	13	1
							Rochdale	—	—
McAuley Sean	5 9	11 13	D	23 6 72	Sheffield	Trainee	Manchester U	—	—
							St Johnstone	62	—
							Chesterfield (loan)	1	1
							Hartlepool U	84	1
							Scunthorpe U	69	1
							Scarborough (loan)	7	—
							Rochdale	13	—
Monington Mark#	6 1	13 07	D	21 10 70	Mansfield	School	Burnley	84	5
							Rotherham U	79	3
							Rochdale	61	5
Morris Andy*	6 4	14 07	F	17 11 67	Sheffield	School	Rotherham U	7	—
							Chesterfield	266	56
							Exeter C (loan)	7	2
							Rochdale	32	7
Peake Jason#	5 11	12 13	M	29 9 71	Leicester	Trainee	Leicester C	8	1
							Hartlepool U (loan)	6	1
							Halifax T	33	1
							Rochdale	95	6
							Brighton & HA	30	1
							Bury	6	—
							Rochdale	81	11
Peyton Warren*	5 9	11 03	M	13 12 79	Manchester		Rochdale	1	—
Platt Clive	6 3	12 13	F	27 10 77	Wolverhampton	Trainee	Walsall	32	4
							Rochdale	41	9
Priestley Phil	6 0	12 09	G	30 3 76	Wigan	Atherton LR	Rochdale	3	—
Stoker Gareth‡	5 9	11 04	M	22 2 73	Bishop Auckland	Leeds U	Hull C	30	2
							Hereford U	70	6
							Cardiff C	37	4
							Rochdale	12	1
Stokes Dean*	5 8	11 02	D	23 5 70	Birmingham	Halesowen T	Port Vale	60	—
							Rochdale	30	—
Taylor Danny§	6 0	11 11	D	28 7 82	Oldham	Scholar	Rochdale	1	—
Wilson Scott*	5 7	9 08	M	25 10 80	Farnworth	Trainee	Rochdale	1	—

Scholars
Bell, Colin; Cantello, Stuart L; Crowe, Alex; Duffy, Lee; Duffy, Matthew J; Gilks, Matthew; Harvey, John D; Hill, Stephen B; Manousios, Nicholas G; Rudd, Paul G; Taylor, Daniel J; Taylor, Warren D; Walsh, David A

Non-Contract
Fielding, David P; Hampson, James JS; Taylor, Andrew; Weir, Scott; Westmorland, Darren P; Wilkinson, J

ROTHERHAM UNITED

Name	Ht	Wt	Pos	Born	Birthplace	From	Club	Apps	Gls
Artell David	6 2	13 00	D	22 11 80	Rotherham	Trainee	Rotherham U	1	—
Beech Chris	5 9	12 09	D	5 11 75	Congleton	Trainee	Manchester C	—	—
							Cardiff C	46	1
							Rotherham U	30	—
Berry Trevor#	5 6	11 00	M	1 8 74	Haslemere	Bournemouth	Aston Villa	—	—
							Rotherham U	162	20
Branston Guy	6 1	13 11	D	9 1 79	Leicester		Leicester C	—	—
						Trainee	Colchester U (loan)	12	1
							Colchester U (loan)	1	—
							Plymouth Arg (loan)	7	1
							Lincoln C (loan)	4	—
							Rotherham U	30	4
Dillon Paul	5 9	10 11	D	22 10 78	Limerick	Trainee	Rotherham U	70	2
Fortune-West Leo	6 4	13 01	F	9 4 71	Stratford	Stevenage Bor	Gillingham	67	18
							Leyton Orient (loan)	5	—
							Lincoln C	9	1
							Brentford	11	—
							Rotherham U	59	29
Garner Darren#	5 9	12 07	M	10 12 71	Plymouth	Trainee	Plymouth Arg	27	1
						Dorchester T	Rotherham U	176	19
Glover Lee*	5 11	11 09	F	24 4 70	Kettering	Trainee	Nottingham F	76	9
							Leicester C (loan)	5	1
							Barnsley (loan)	8	—
							Luton T (loan)	1	—
							Port Vale	52	7
							Rotherham U	85	29
							Huddersfield T (loan)	11	—
Hudson Danny	5 8	10 03	M	25 6 79	Mexborough	Trainee	Rotherham U	43	5
Hurst Paul#	5 4	9 00	D	25 9 74	Sheffield	Trainee	Rotherham U	179	8
Ingledow Jamie*	5 7	11 01	M	23 8 80	Barnsley	Trainee	Rotherham U	25	2
Knill Alan*	6 4	13 00	D	8 10 64	Slough	Apprentice	Southampton	—	—
							Halifax T	118	6
							Swansea C	89	3
							Bury	144	8
							Cardiff C (loan)	4	—
							Scunthorpe U	131	8
							Rotherham U	74	6
Martindale Gary*	6 1	11 13	F	24 6 71	Liverpool	Burscough	Bolton W	—	—
							Peterborough U	31	15
							Notts Co	66	13
							Mansfield T (loan)	5	2
							Rotherham U	27	6
Monkhouse Andy	6 0	13 09	F	23 10 80	Leeds	Trainee	Rotherham U	5	1
Pettinger Paul	6 0	13 00	G	1 10 75	Sheffield	Barnsley	Leeds U	—	—
							Torquay U (loan)	3	—
							Rotherham U (loan)	1	—
							Gillingham	—	—
							Carlisle U	—	—
							Rotherham U	3	—
Pollitt Mike#	6 3	14 12	G	29 2 72	Farnworth	Trainee	Manchester U	—	—
							Oldham Ath (loan)	—	—
							Bury	—	—
							Lincoln C	57	—
							Darlington	55	—
							Notts Co	10	—
							Oldham Ath (loan)	16	—
							Gillingham (loan)	6	—
							Brentford (loan)	5	—
							Sunderland	—	—
							Rotherham U	92	—
Roden Craig*	6 2	13 03	D	4 11 80	Rotherham	Trainee	Rotherham U	—	—
Scott Rob	6 1	12 04	F	15 8 73	Epsom	Sutton U	Sheffield U	6	1
							Scarborough (loan)	8	3
							Northampton T (loan)	5	—
							Fulham	84	17
							Carlisle U (loan)	7	3
							Rotherham U	40	2
Sedgwick Chris	5 11	10 10	F	28 4 80	Sheffield	Trainee	Rotherham U	75	9
Thompson Steve*	5 11	13 00	M	2 11 64	Oldham	Apprentice	Bolton W	335	49
							Luton T	5	—
							Leicester C	127	18
							Burnley	49	1
							Rotherham U	103	14
Turner Andy	5 10	11 10	M	23 3 75	Woolwich	Trainee	Tottenham H	20	3
							Wycombe W (loan)	4	—
							Doncaster R (loan)	4	1
							Huddersfield T (loan)	5	1
							Southend U (loan)	6	—
							Portsmouth	40	3
							Crystal Palace	2	—
							Wolverhampton W	—	—
							Rotherham U	32	1

Name	Ht	Wt	Pos	Born	Birthplace	Source	Club	Apps	Gls
Varty Will	6 0	12 00	D	1 10 76	Workington	Trainee	Carlisle U	82	1
							Rotherham U (loan)	14	—
							Rotherham U	27	—
Warne Paul	5 8	11 01	F	8 5 73	Norwich	Wroxham	Wigan Ath	36	3
							Rotherham U	62	18
Warner Vance*	6 0	13 04	D	3 9 74	Leeds	Trainee	Nottingham F	5	—
							Grimsby T (loan)	3	—
							Rotherham U	62	1
Watson Kevin	5 10	12 08	M	3 1 74	Hackney	Trainee	Tottenham H	5	—
							Brentford (loan)	3	—
							Bristol C (loan)	2	—
							Barnet (loan)	13	—
							Swindon T	63	1
							Rotherham U	44	1
White Jason*	6 1	12 12	F	19 10 71	Meriden	Derby Co	Scunthorpe U	68	16
							Darlington (loan)	4	1
							Scarborough	63	20
							Northampton T	77	18
							Rotherham U	73	22
Williams Mark*	6 0	11 02	D	10 11 78	Liverpool	Trainee	Rochdale	14	1
							Rotherham U	11	—
Wilsterman Brian	6 1	14 02	D	19 11 66	Surinam	Beerschot	Oxford U	42	2
							Rotherham U	42	3

Scholars
Alabi, Stephen; Barker, Shaun; Barraclough, Simon D; Beggs, John A; Boyd, Darren; Capill, Stephen L; Connor, Gareth A; Hoyler, Ian D; Lees, Scott; McCoy, James TG; Sandland, Guy; Shelton, Lee M

SCUNTHORPE UNITED

Name	Ht	Wt	Pos	Born	Birthplace	Source	Club	Apps	Gls
Barwick Terry§	5 11	10 12		11 1 83	Sheffield	Scholar	Scunthorpe U	1	—
Bull Gary*	5 10	12 02	F	12 6 66	Tipton	Swindon T	Southampton	—	—
							Cambridge U	19	4
					Barnet		Barnet	83	37
							Nottingham F	12	1
							Birmingham C (loan)	10	6
							Brighton & HA (loan)	10	2
							Birmingham C (loan)	6	—
							York C	83	11
							Scunthorpe U	30	1
Calvo-Garcia Alexander	5 11	11 10	M	1 1 72	Ordizia	Eibar	Scunthorpe U	118	17
Clarke Richard‡	5 11	10 10	D	15 2 80	Enfield	Trainee	Luton T	—	—
							Scunthorpe U	1	—
Clarke Tim‡	6 3	15 12	G	19 9 68	Stourbridge	Halesowen T	Coventry C	—	—
							Huddersfield T	70	—
							Rochdale (loan)	2	—
							Shrewsbury T	31	—
					Witton Alb		York C	17	—
							Scunthorpe U	78	—
Dawson Andrew	5 9	11 05	D	20 10 78	Northallerton	Trainee	Nottingham F	—	—
							Scunthorpe U	67	2
Evans Tom	6 1	13 02	G	31 12 76	Doncaster	Trainee	Sheffield U	—	—
							Crystal Palace	—	—
							Coventry C (loan)	—	—
							Scunthorpe U	57	—
Fickling Ashley#	5 10	11 08	D	15 11 72	Sheffield	Trainee	Sheffield U	—	—
							Darlington (loan)	14	—
							Darlington (loan)	1	—
							Grimsby T	39	2
							Darlington (loan)	8	—
							Scunthorpe U	59	1
Graves Wayne	5 8	10 09	M	18 9 80	Scunthorpe	Trainee	Scunthorpe U	22	—
Harsley Paul	5 10	11 03	M	29 5 78	Scunthorpe	Trainee	Grimsby T	—	—
							Scunthorpe U	95	4
Hodges Lee	5 5	11 00	M	2 3 78	Newham	Trainee	West Ham U	3	—
							Exeter C (loan)	17	—
							Leyton Orient (loan)	3	—
							Plymouth Arg (loan)	9	—
							Ipswich T (loan)	4	—
							Southend U (loan)	10	1
							Scunthorpe U	40	6
Hodgson Richard‡	5 10	11 06	F	1 10 79	Sunderland	Trainee	Nottingham F	—	—
							Scunthorpe U	1	—
Hope Chris	6 1	12 08	D	14 11 73	Sheffield	Darlington	Nottingham F	—	—
							Scunthorpe U	287	19
Housham Steven	5 10	12 03	M	24 2 76	Gainsborough	Trainee	Scunthorpe U	115	4
Ipoua Guy	6 1	13 02	F	14 1 76	Douala	Novelda	Bristol R	24	3
							Scunthorpe U	40	9
Jackson Mark	5 11	12 04	D	30 9 77	Barnsley	Trainee	Leeds U	19	—
							Huddersfield T (loan)	5	—
							Barnsley (loan)	1	—
							Scunthorpe U	6	—

Name	Ht	Wt	Pos	Date of birth	Birthplace	Signed from	Clubs	Apps	Gls
Laws Brian*	5 9	12 04	D	14 10 61	Wallsend	Apprentice	Burnley	125	12
							Huddersfield T	56	1
							Middlesbrough	107	12
							Nottingham F	147	4
							Grimsby T	46	2
							Darlington	10	—
							Scunthorpe U	18	—
Logan Richard*	6 0	13 03	M	24 5 69	Barnsley	Gainsborough T	Huddersfield T	45	1
							Plymouth Arg	86	12
							Scunthorpe U	80	7
Marshall Lee*	5 10	10 08	M	1 8 75	Nottingham	Trainee	Nottingham F	—	—
						Grantham T	Stockport Co	1	—
						Eastwood T	Scunthorpe U	45	2
Naisbett Philip‡			G	2 1 79	Easington	Trainee	Sunderland	—	—
							Scarborough	2	—
						Spennymoor U	Scunthorpe U	—	—
Pounewatchy Stephane‡	6 0	15 00	D	10 2 68	Paris		Martigues	44	2
							Gueugnon	30	—
							Carlisle U	81	3
							Dundee	3	—
							Port Vale	2	—
							Colchester U	15	1
							Scunthorpe U	—	—
Quailey Brian	6 0	13 04	F	21 3 78	Leicester	Nuneaton B	WBA	7	—
							Exeter C (loan)	12	2
							Blackpool (loan)	1	—
							Scunthorpe U	14	5
Sheldon Gareth	5 11	12 06	F	31 1 80	Birmingham	Trainee	Scunthorpe U	34	3
Sparrow Matthew§	5 11	10 06		3 10 83	Scunthorpe	Scholar	Scunthorpe U	11	—
Stamp Darryn	6 1	11 10	F	21 9 78	Beverley		Scunthorpe U	45	5
							Halifax T (loan)	5	—
Stanton Nathan	5 9	12 06	D	6 5 81	Nottingham	Trainee	Scunthorpe U	39	—
Torpey Steve	6 3	13 06	F	8 12 70	Islington	Trainee	Millwall	7	—
							Bradford C	96	22
							Swansea C	162	44
							Bristol C	70	13
							Notts Co (loan)	6	1
							Scunthorpe U	15	1
Turner Ross‡	5 11	12 00		17 6 79	Sheffield	Worsbrough Bridge	Scunthorpe U	1	—
Walker Justin*	6 0	13 03	M	6 9 75	Nottingham	Trainee	Nottingham F	—	—
							Scunthorpe U	132	2
Wilcox Russ#	6 0	12 13	D	25 3 64	Hemsworth	Apprentice	Doncaster R	1	—
						Frickley Ath	Northampton T	138	9
							Hull C	100	7
							Doncaster R	81	6
							Preston NE	62	1
							Scunthorpe U	73	3

Scholars
Anderson, Mark J; Barwick, Terence P; Burraway, David; Cotterill, James M; Herrick, Leigh; Marsh, Craig; Masson, Daniel P; McCombe, Jamie; Mulchinock, Daniel T; Ridley, Lee; Ridley, Steven; Sparrow, Matthew

SHEFFIELD UNITED

Name	Ht	Wt	Pos	Date of birth	Birthplace	Signed from	Clubs	Apps	Gls
Bent Marcus	6 2	12 04	F	19 5 78	Hammersmith	Trainee	Brentford	70	8
							Crystal Palace	28	5
							Port Vale	23	1
							Sheffield U	32	15
Brown Michael R	5 9	10 07	M	25 1 77	Hartlepool	Trainee	Manchester C	89	2
							Hartlepool U (loan)	6	1
							Portsmouth (loan)	4	—
							Sheffield U	24	3
Burke Paul*	5 10	11 08	F	17 7 81	Doncaster	Trainee	Sheffield U	—	—
Burley Adam	5 10	12 06	M	27 11 80	Sheffield	Trainee	Sheffield U	2	1
Camm Mark*	5 8	10 12	D	1 10 81	Mansfield	Trainee	Sheffield U	—	—
Cryan Colin			M	23 3 81	Dublin	Scholar	Sheffield U	—	—
D'Jaffo Laurent	6 0	13 05	F	5 11 70	Aquitane		Montpellier	36	3
						Niort	Ayr U	24	10
							Bury	37	8
							Stockport Co	21	7
							Sheffield U	15	1
Davies Kevin*	6 0	13 02	M	15 11 78	Sheffield	Trainee	Sheffield U	—	—
Dellas Traianos‡	6 4	15 00	D	31 1 76	Salonika	Aris Salonika	Sheffield U	26	3
Devlin Paul	5 8	11 08	F	14 4 72	Birmingham	Stafford R	Notts Co	141	25
							Birmingham C	76	28
							Sheffield U	87	17
							Notts Co (loan)	5	—
Doane Ben	5 10	10 05	D	22 12 79	Sheffield	Trainee	Sheffield U	1	—

Name							Club	Apps	Gls
Duke Matt*	6 5	13 04	G	16 7 77	Sheffield	Alfreton T	Sheffield U	—	—
El Banna Wassim	5 11	12 04	F	10 5 79	Zambia		Odense	12	4
							Northampton T	—	—
							Oldham Ath	—	—
							Sheffield U	—	—
Ford Bobby	5 8	10 07	M	22 9 74	Bristol	Trainee	Oxford U	116	7
							Sheffield U	94	3
Gijsbrechts Davy	6 1	13 08	D	20 9 72	Heusden		Mechelen	181	8
							Lokeren	47	—
							Sheffield U	17	—
Hamilton Ian	5 10	12 07	M	14 12 67	Stevenage	Apprentice	Southampton		
							Cambridge U	24	1
							Scunthorpe U	145	18
							WBA	240	23
							Sheffield U	45	3
							Grimsby T (loan)	6	1
Hunt Jonathan	5 10	11 13	M	2 11 71	London	Slough T	Barnet	33	—
							Southend U	49	6
							Birmingham C	77	18
							Derby Co	25	2
							Sheffield U	27	2
							Ipswich T (loan)	6	—
							Cambridge U (loan)	7	1
Jagielka Philip	5 11	12 08	M	17 8 82	Manchester	Scholar	Sheffield U	1	—
James Owen‡	5 11	12 00	D	1 9 78	Derby	Trainee	Sheffield U	—	—
Katchuro Petr‡	6 0	13 00	F	2 8 72	Minsk		Dynamo 93	15	7
							Dynamo Minsk	60	52
							Sheffield U	95	19
Kozluk Robert	5 8	10 07	D	5 8 77	Sutton-in-Ashfield	Trainee	Derby Co	16	—
							Sheffield U	49	—
Launders Brian‡	5 8	11 10	M	8 1 76	Dublin	Trainee	Crystal Palace	4	—
							Oldham Ath (loan)	—	—
							Crewe Alex	9	—
							Veendam	20	3
							Derby Co	1	—
							Colchester U (loan)	1	—
							Colchester U	6	—
							Crystal Palace	2	—
							Sheffield U	1	—
Macari Paul*	5 8	11 11	F	23 8 76	Manchester	Trainee	Stoke C	3	—
							Sheffield U	—	—
Mbome Kingsley			M	21 11 81	Yaounde		Sheffield U	—	—
McAughtrie Craig*	6 2	14 07	D	3 3 81	Burton-on-Trent	Trainee	Sheffield U	—	—
Mosley Matt*	5 10	11 07	D	12 9 80	Chesterfield	Trainee	Sheffield U	—	—
Murphy Shaun	6 1	13 10	D	5 11 70	Sydney	Perth Italia	Notts Co	109	5
							WBA	71	7
							Sheffield U	42	3
O'Connor Jon*	6 0	12 03	D	29 10 76	Darlington	Trainee	Everton	5	—
							Sheffield U	4	—
Quinn Wayne	5 10	12 10	D	19 11 76	Truro	Trainee	Sheffield U	115	4
Ribeiro Bruno	5 8	12 07	M	22 10 75	Setubal		Setubal	39	4
							Leeds U	42	4
							Sheffield U	20	1
Sandford Lee	6 0	13 06	D	22 4 68	Basingstoke	Apprentice	Portsmouth	72	1
							Stoke C	258	8
							Sheffield U	123	3
							Reading (loan)	5	—
Smeets Axel*	5 10	12 01	M	12 7 74	Karawa		Gent	20	1
							Salamanca	1	—
							Kortrijk	23	1
							Sheffield U	5	—
Smith Andy	5 11	11 10	F	25 9 80	Lisburn		Sheffield U	—	—
Tebily Oliver	6 0	13 00	D	19 12 75	Abidjan	Chateauroux	Sheffield U	8	—
(Transferred to Celtic, July 1999)									
Tracey Simon	6 0	14 00	G	9 12 67	Woolwich	Apprentice	Wimbledon	1	—
							Sheffield U	251	—
							Manchester C (loan)	3	—
							Norwich C (loan)	1	—
							Wimbledon (loan)	1	—
Whitehouse Dane‡	5 10	12 06	M	14 10 70	Sheffield	Trainee	Sheffield U	231	39
Woodhouse Curtis	5 8	11 06	M	17 4 80	Driffield	Trainee	Sheffield U	79	6
Woodward Andy	6 0	13 04	D	13 9 73	Stockport	Trainee	Crewe Alex	20	—
							Bury	115	1
							Sheffield U	3	—
Yohanna Buba			M	16 6 82	Yaounde		Sheffield U	—	—

Scholars

Adams, Carl; Anderson, Michael; Baum, Adam P; Brown, Thomas P; Clarke, Stuart; Crutchley, Wayne; Dempsey, Paul; Fayenuwo, Victor O; Hayden, John; Kendrick, Scott; Killeen, Lewis K; Lopez, Richard; Montgomery, Nicholas A; Spencer, Steven L; Thompson, Tyrone; Thornley, Carl; Tonge, Michael W

SHEFFIELD WEDNESDAY

Name			Pos	Born	Birthplace	From	Club	Apps	Gls
Agogo Manuel‡	5 11	11 09	M	1 8 79	Accra	Willesden	Sheffield W	2	—
							Oldham Ath (loan)	2	—
							Chester C (loan)	10	6
							Chesterfield (loan)	4	—
							Lincoln C (loan)	3	1
Alexandersson Niclas	6 2	11 08	M	29 12 71	Halmstad		Halmstad	145	25
							IFK Gothenburg	52	13
							Sheffield W	75	8
Atherton Peter	5 11	13 12	D	6 4 70	Orrell	Trainee	Wigan Ath	149	1
							Coventry C	114	—
							Sheffield W	214	9
Bennett Neil‡	6 0	12 02	G	29 10 80	Dewsbury	Trainee	Sheffield W	—	—
Bettney Scott	5 9	13 00	D	12 3 80	Hull	Trainee	Sheffield W	—	—
Billington David	5 9	10 06	D	15 10 80	Oxford	Trainee	Peterborough U	5	—
							Sheffield W	—	—
Booth Andy	6 0	13 00	F	6 12 73	Huddersfield	Trainee	Huddersfield T	123	54
							Sheffield W	115	25
Brennan Dean‡	5 9	11 08	M	17 6 80	Dublin		Sheffield W	—	—
Briscoe Lee	5 11	11 12	D	30 9 75	Pontefract	Trainee	Sheffield W	78	1
							Manchester C (loan)	5	1
Bromby Leigh	5 11	11 06	D	2 6 80	Dewsbury		Sheffield W	—	—
							Mansfield T (loan)	10	1
Coubrough James‡	5 7	10 01	F	4 10 80	Bradford	Trainee	Sheffield W	—	—
Crane Anthony	6 1	12 06	M	8 9 82	Liverpool	Trainee	Sheffield W	—	—
Cresswell Richard	6 0	11 08	F	20 9 77	Bridlington	Trainee	York C	95	21
							Mansfield T (loan)	5	1
							Sheffield W	27	2
De Bilde Gilles	5 11	11 04	F	9 6 71	Brussels		Alost	33	21
							Anderlecht	46	22
							PSV Eindhoven	49	24
							Sheffield W	38	10
Donnelly Simon	5 9	10 06	M	1 12 74	Glasgow		Celtic	146	30
							Sheffield W	12	1
Douglas Andrew*	5 7	10 06	F	7 2 80	Edmonton	Arsenal	Sheffield W	—	—
Geary Derek	5 6	10 08	D	19 6 80	Dublin		Sheffield W	—	—
Hamshaw Matthew	5 9	11 09	M	1 1 82	Rotherham	Trainee	Sheffield W	—	—
Haslam Nathan‡	5 8	11 12	M	13 1 81	Middlesbrough	Trainee	Sheffield W	—	—
Haslam Steven	5 11	10 10	D	6 9 79	Sheffield	Trainee	Sheffield W	25	—
Hibbins John*	6 2	12 02	M	17 11 79	Sheffield	Trainee	Sheffield W	—	—
Higgins Alex	5 9	11 04	M	22 7 81	Sheffield	Trainee	Sheffield W	—	—
Hinchcliffe Andy	5 10	13 07	D	5 2 69	Manchester	Apprentice	Manchester C	112	8
							Everton	182	7
							Sheffield W	76	5
Hiner Daniel‡			M	4 10 78	Sheffield	Trainee	Sheffield W	—	—
Holmes Peter	5 10	10 00	M	18 11 80	Bishop Auckland	Trainee	Sheffield W	—	—
Horne Barry*	5 10	12 03	M	18 5 62	St Asaph	Rhyl	Wrexham	136	17
							Portsmouth	70	7
							Southampton	112	6
							Everton	123	3
							Birmingham C	33	—
							Huddersfield T	64	1
							Sheffield W	7	—
Houlahan Martin	6 0	12 13	M	17 9 81	Bishop Auckland	Trainee	Sheffield W	—	—
Humphreys Richie	5 11	14 07	F	30 11 77	Sheffield	Trainee	Sheffield W	60	4
							Scunthorpe U (loan)	6	2
							Cardiff C (loan)	9	2
Hutton John	5 10	11 07	F	23 9 80	Easington	Trainee	Sheffield W	—	—
Jonk Wim	6 0	12 02	M	12 10 66	Volendam		Volendam	59	28
							Ajax	96	18
							Internazionale	54	8
							PSV Eindhoven	89	20
							Sheffield W	68	5
McKeever Mark	5 9	11 08	M	16 11 78	Derry	Trainee	Peterborough U	3	—
							Sheffield W	5	—
							Bristol R (loan)	7	—
							Reading (loan)	7	2
Morrison Owen	5 8	11 12	F	8 12 81	Derry	Trainee	Sheffield W	1	—
Muller Adam			M	17 4 82	Leeds		Sheffield W	—	—
Newsome Jon*	6 2	13 11	D	6 9 70	Sheffield	Trainee	Sheffield W	7	—
							Leeds U	76	3
							Norwich C	62	7
							Sheffield W	54	4
							Bolton W (loan)	6	—
Nicholson Kevin	5 9	11 07	D	2 10 80	Derby	Trainee	Sheffield W	—	—
Nolan Ian	6 0	12 01	D	9 7 70	Liverpool	Marine	Tranmere R	88	1
							Sheffield W	165	4
O'Donnell Phil	5 10	11 07	M	25 3 72	Bellshill		Motherwell	124	15
							Celtic	90	15
							Sheffield W	1	—

Oakes Scott‡	6 2	11 08	M	5 8 72	Leicester	Trainee	Leicester C	3	—
							Luton T	173	27
							Sheffield W	24	1
Pressman Kevin	6 1	15 05	G	6 11 67	Fareham	Apprentice	Sheffield W	266	—
							Stoke C (loan)	4	—
Quinn Alan	5 9	10 02	F	13 6 79	Dublin	Cherry Orchard	Sheffield W	21	3
Rand Craig	6 1	11 00	M	24 6 82	Bishop Auckland	Trainee	Sheffield W	—	—
Rudi Petter	6 2	12 00	M	17 9 73	Kristiansund		Molde	116	7
							Sheffield W	76	8
Sanetti Francesco‡	5 11	12 07	F	11 1 79	Rome	Genoa	Sheffield W	5	1
Scott Philip	5 9	11 01	M	14 11 74	Perth		St Johnstone	134	27
							Sheffield W	9	1
Sibon Gerald	6 3	13 04	F	19 4 74	Emmen		Twente	3	—
							VVV	53	34
							Roda	34	13
							Ajax	23	4
							Sheffield W	28	5
Sonner Danny	5 11	12 08	M	9 1 72	Wigan	Wigan Ath	Burnley	6	—
							Bury (loan)	5	3
						Erzgebirge Aue	Ipswich T	56	3
							Sheffield W	53	3
Srnicek Pavel	6 2	14 09	G	10 3 68	Bohumin	Banik Ostrava	Newcastle U	149	—
						Banik Ostrava	Sheffield W	44	—
Staniforth Thomas	5 10	13 00	D	15 12 80	Carlisle	Trainee	Sheffield W	—	—
Walker Des	5 11	11 13	D	26 11 65	Enfield	Apprentice	Nottingham F	264	1
							Sampdoria	30	—
							Sheffield W	264	—
Wilkinson Kraig‡			M	24 9 79	Durham	Billingham Syn	Sheffield W	—	—

Scholars
Barrett, Jamie J; Byne, Nicholas F; Callery, Alex J; Cropper, Dene J; Jubb, Ryan G; Nelson, Craig M; Quinn, Adam R; Stringer, Christopher; Strutt, Luke M; Tevendale, James R; Young, Gregory J

SHREWSBURY TOWN

Berkley Austin*	5 9	10 10	M	28 1 73	Gravesend	Trainee	Gillingham	3	—
							Swindon T	1	—
							Shrewsbury T	172	12
Brown Mickey#	5 9	10 12	F	8 2 68	Birmingham	Apprentice	Shrewsbury T	190	9
							Bolton W	33	3
							Shrewsbury T	67	11
							Preston NE	16	1
							Rochdale (loan)	5	—
							Shrewsbury T	127	12
Cooksey Scott‡	6 3	13 10	G	24 6 72	Birmingham	Bromsgrove R	Peterborough U	15	—
						Hednesford T	Shrewsbury T	2	—
Craven Dean‡	5 6	10 10	M	17 2 79	Shrewsbury	WBA	Shrewsbury T	11	—
Davidson Ross	5 9	12 04	D	13 11 73	Chertsey	Walton & Hersham	Sheffield U	2	—
							Chester C	132	5
							Barnet	9	—
							Shrewsbury T	10	—
Drysdale Leon	5 9	10 12	D	3 2 81	Walsall	Trainee	Shrewsbury T	2	—
Dunbavin Ian	6 1	10 10	G	27 5 80	Knowsley	Trainee	Liverpool	—	—
							Shrewsbury T	7	—
Edwards Paul	6 1	12 05	G	22 2 65	Liverpool	St. Helens T	Crewe Alex	29	—
							Shrewsbury T	286	—
Gayle John	6 3	15 04	F	30 7 64	Bromsgrove	Burton Alb	Wimbledon	20	2
							Birmingham C	44	10
							Walsall (loan)	4	1
							Coventry C	3	—
							Burnley	14	3
							Stoke C	26	4
							Gillingham (loan)	9	3
							Northampton T	48	7
							Scunthorpe U	49	4
							Shrewsbury T	18	2
Hanmer Gary	5 6	10 02	D	12 10 73	Shrewsbury	Newtown	WBA	—	—
							Shrewsbury T	118	1
Herbert Craig*	5 10	11 00	D	9 11 75	Coventry	Torquay U	WBA	8	—
							Shrewsbury T	34	—
Hughes David	6 4	13 06	D	1 2 78	Wrexham	Trainee	Aston Villa	7	—
							Carlisle U (loan)	1	—
							Shrewsbury T	22	1
Jagielka Steve	5 8	11 03	F	10 3 78	Manchester	Trainee	Stoke C	—	—
							Shrewsbury T	80	3
Jobling Kevin*	5 8	12 00	M	1 1 68	Sunderland	Apprentice	Leicester C	9	—
							Grimsby T	285	10
							Scunthorpe U (loan)	—	—
							Shrewsbury T	69	3
Jones Matthew	6 1	11 03	M	11 10 80	Shrewsbury	Trainee	Shrewsbury T	1	—
Murray Karl	5 10	12 00	M	24 6 82	Islington	Trainee	Shrewsbury T	12	1

Player							Club	Apps	Gls
Peer Dean	6 2	12 04	M	8 8 69	Stourbridge	Trainee	Birmingham C	120	8
							Mansfield T (loan)	10	—
							Walsall	45	8
							Northampton T	128	6
							Shrewsbury T	19	—
Preece Roger‡	5 8	10 13	M	9 6 69	Much Wenlock	Coventry C	Wrexham	110	12
							Chester C	170	4
							Shrewsbury T	52	3
Rigby Tony‡	5 10	13 12	M	10 8 72	Ormskirk	Barrow	Bury	166	19
							Scarborough (loan)	5	1
						Altrincham	Shrewsbury T	8	1
Rodgers Luke§	5 6	10 05	F	1 1 82	Birmingham	Trainee	Shrewsbury T	6	1
Seabury Kevin	5 10	11 06	D	24 11 73	Shrewsbury	Trainee	Shrewsbury T	218	7
Steele Lee#	5 8	12 05	F	2 12 73	Liverpool	Northwich V	Shrewsbury T	113	37
Thomas Wayne	5 11	11 10	M	28 8 78	Walsall	Trainee	Walsall	37	—
							Mansfield T	5	—
							Walsall	1	—
							Shrewsbury T	13	1
Tolley Jamie§	6 1	10 08	M	12 5 83	Shrewsbury	Scholar	Shrewsbury T	2	—
Tretton Andrew	6 0	12 08	D	9 10 76	Derby	Trainee	Derby Co	—	—
							Chesterfield	—	—
							Shrewsbury T	70	4
Whelan Spencer	6 2	13 00	D	17 9 71	Liverpool	Liverpool	Chester C	215	8
							Shrewsbury T	25	—
Wilding Peter	6 1	12 09	D	28 11 68	Shrewsbury	Telford U	Shrewsbury T	117	3
Winstanley Mark*	6 1	12 07	D	22 1 68	St Helens	Trainee	Bolton W	220	3
							Burnley	152	5
							Shrewsbury T (loan)	8	—
							Scunthorpe U (loan)	—	—
							Preston NE	—	—
							Shrewsbury T	33	1

Trainees
Impey, Daniel E; Rodgers, Luke J; Woodley, Frederick R

Scholars
Corbett, Mark; Hart, Timothy J; Johnson, Mathew T; Murphy, Christopher P; Silgram, James; Tolley, Jamie C

Non-Contract
Howarth, Paul A

SOUTHAMPTON

Player							Club	Apps	Gls
Almeida Marco‡	6 2	12 10	D	4 4 77	Lisbon	Sporting	Southampton	1	—
Beattie James	6 1	13 03	F	27 2 78	Lancaster	Trainee	Blackburn R	4	—
							Southampton	53	5
Benali Francis	5 9	11 01	M	30 12 68	Southampton	Apprentice	Southampton	302	1
Beresford John	5 7	12 00	M	4 9 66	Sheffield	Apprentice	Manchester C	—	—
							Barnsley	88	5
							Portsmouth	107	8
							Newcastle U	179	3
							Southampton	17	—
							Birmingham C (loan)	1	—
Bevan Scott	6 6	15 07	G	16 9 79	Southampton	Trainee	Southampton	—	—
Bleidelis Imants	5 9	12 00	M	16 8 75	Latvia		Interskonto Riga	11	1
							Skonto Riga	118	24
							Southampton	—	—
Boa Morte Luis	5 9	11 10	F	4 8 77	Lisbon	Sporting Lisbon	Arsenal	25	—
							Southampton	14	1
Bradley Shayne	6 0	13 12	F	8 12 79	Gloucester	Trainee	Southampton	4	—
							Swindon T (loan)	7	—
							Exeter C (loan)	8	1
Bridge Wayne	5 10	12 07	F	5 8 80	Southampton	Trainee	Southampton	42	1
Colleter Patrick	5 10	11 04	D	6 11 65	Brest		Brest	127	8
							Montpellier	31	—
							Paris St Germain	157	1
							Bordeaux	30	1
							Marseille	41	—
							Southampton	24	1
Collins Chris‡	6 0	13 04	D	26 9 79	Chatham	Trainee	Southampton	—	—
Davies Kevin	6 0	14 10	F	26 3 77	Sheffield	Trainee	Chesterfield	129	22
							Southampton	25	9
							Blackburn R	23	1
							Southampton	23	6
Dodd Jason	5 8	12 07	D	2 11 70	Bath	Bath C	Southampton	290	8
Dryden Richard	6 0	13 04	D	14 6 69	Stroud	Trainee	Bristol R	13	—
							Exeter C	51	7
							Manchester C (loan)	—	—
							Notts Co	31	1
							Plymouth Arg (loan)	5	—
							Birmingham C	48	—
							Bristol C	37	2
							Southampton	47	1
							Stoke C (loan)	13	—

Name			Pos	DOB	Birthplace	Source	Clubs	Apps	Gls
El Khalej Tahar	6 2	13 08	D	16 6 68	Morocco	KAC Marrakesh	Uniao Leiria	43	8
							Benfica	68	10
							Southampton	11	1
Gibbens Kevin	5 10	14 02	M	4 11 79	Southampton	Trainee	Southampton	6	—
							Stockport Co (loan)	2	—
Gray Steven			M	17 10 81	Dublin		Southampton	—	—
Hirst David‡	5 11	15 01	F	7 12 67	Cudworth	Apprentice	Barnsley	28	9
							Sheffield W	294	106
							Southampton	30	9
Howard Brian			M	23 1 83	Winchester	Trainee	Southampton	—	—
Howells David‡	6 0	12 02	M	15 12 67	Guildford	Trainee	Tottenham H	277	22
							Southampton	9	1
							Bristol C (loan)	8	1
Hughes David	5 11	11 01	M	30 12 72	St Albans	Trainee	Southampton	54	3
Hughes Paul	6 0	12 05	M	19 4 76	Hammersmith	Trainee	Chelsea	21	2
							Stockport Co (loan)	7	—
							Norwich C (loan)	4	1
							Crewe Alex (loan)	—	—
							Southampton	—	—
Jones Paul	6 3	15 00	G	18 4 67	Chirk	Kidderminster H	Wolverhampton W	33	—
							Stockport Co	46	—
							Southampton	100	—
Kachloul Hassan	6 2	13 02	M	19 2 73	Agadir		Nimes	86	26
							Dunkerque	28	6
							Metz	7	—
							St Etienne	16	—
							Southampton	54	10
Le Tissier Matthew	6 1	14 01	F	14 10 68	Guernsey	Trainee	Southampton	431	160
Leal Bruno*	5 11	11 05	D	1 12 80	Lisbon	Sporting	Southampton	—	—
Lundekvam Claus	6 4	12 12	D	22 2 73	Austevoll		Brann	53	1
							Southampton	120	—
Marsden Chris	6 0	12 08	M	3 1 69	Sheffield	Trainee	Sheffield U	16	1
							Huddersfield T	121	9
							Coventry C (loan)	7	—
							Wolverhampton W	8	—
							Notts Co	10	—
							Stockport Co	65	3
							Birmingham C	52	3
							Southampton	35	2
Monk Gary	6 0	13 12	D	6 3 79	Bedford	Trainee	Torquay U	5	—
							Southampton	6	—
							Torquay U (loan)	6	—
							Stockport Co (loan)	2	—
Moss Neil	6 3	14 00	G	10 5 75	New Milton	Trainee	Bournemouth	22	—
							Southampton	19	—
							Gillingham (loan)	10	—
Oakley Matthew	5 10	12 00	M	17 8 77	Peterborough	Trainee	Southampton	125	9
Pakhar (Pahars) Marian	5 8	10 08	F	5 8 76	Latvia		Pardaugava Riga	17	3
							Skonto/Metals Riga	16	4
							Skonto Riga	85	44
							Southampton	39	16
Paul Mark‡	5 6	10 10	F	3 1 79	Peterborough	Kings Lynn	Southampton	—	—
Richards Dean	6 2	14 01	D	9 6 74	Bradford	Trainee	Bradford C	86	4
							Wolverhampton W (loan)	10	2
							Wolverhampton W	112	5
							Southampton	35	2
Ripley Stuart	6 0	13 09	F	20 11 67	Middlesbrough	Apprentice	Middlesbrough	249	26
							Bolton W (loan)	5	1
							Blackburn R	187	13
							Southampton	45	1
Rodrigues Danny	5 11	11 05	F	3 3 80	Madeira	Farense	Bournemouth	5	—
							Southampton	2	—
Sims Adam‡	5 9	11 04	M	19 1 81	Bristol	Trainee	Southampton	—	—
Soltvedt Trond Egil	6 0	12 09	M	15 2 67	Vaksdal		Viking	65	10
							Brann	64	34
							Rosenborg	60	18
							Coventry C	57	3
							Southampton	24	1
Stensgaard Michael	6 2	13 11	G	1 9 74	Denmark	Hvidovre	Liverpool	—	—
(Transferred to FC Copenhagen, July 1999)							FC Copenhagen	17	—
							Southampton	—	—
Tealdi Daniele			M	15 11 82	Italy	Atletico 2000	Southampton	—	—
Tessem Jo	6 2	13 05	M	28 2 72	Norway		Lyn	22	15
							Molde	78	22
							Southampton	25	4
Warner Phil	5 10	11 09	D	2 2 79	Southampton	Trainee	Southampton	6	—
							Brentford (loan)	14	—

Scholars
Ashford, Ryan M; Baird, Christopher P; Blayney, Alan; Carter, Samuel J; Davies, Matthew D; Gordon, Scott B; Grimshaw, Steven; Halliwell, William A; Huxley, Matthew S; Lewis, Christopher W; Madgwick, Benjamin; McManus, Garry L; Stallard, Adam J; Wallace, Adam J; Webb, Daniel J

Non-Contract
Graham, Mark D

SOUTHEND UNITED

Abiodun Yemi	5 10	10 07	F	29 12 80	Clapton	Norwich C	Southend U	3	—
Beard Mark*	5 8	10 12	M	8 10 74	Roehampton	Trainee	Millwall	45	2
							Sheffield U	38	—
							Southend U (loan)	8	—
							Southend U	78	1
Booty Martyn	5 8	12 03	D	30 5 71	Kirby Muxloe	Trainee	Coventry C	5	—
							Crewe Alex	96	5
							Reading	64	1
							Southend U	48	—
Burns Alex	5 9	12 09	F	4 8 73	Bellshill		Motherwell	76	8
(Transferred to Raith R, July 1999)						Heracles	Southend U	31	5
Byrne Paul	5 11	13 00	M	30 6 72	Dublin	Trainee	Oxford U	6	—
						Bangor	Celtic	28	4
							Brighton & HA (loan)	8	1
							Southend U	83	6
Campbell Neil‡	6 1	13 10	F	26 1 77	Middlesbrough	Trainee	York C	12	1
							Scarborough	45	7
							Southend U	24	3
Capleton Mel	6 0	13 00	G	24 10 73	London	Trainee	Southend U	—	—
							Blackpool	11	—
							Leyton Orient	—	—
						Grays Ath	Southend U	56	—
Carruthers Martin	5 10	12 02	F	7 8 72	Nottingham	Trainee	Aston Villa	4	—
							Hull C (loan)	13	6
							Stoke C	91	13
							Peterborough U	67	21
							York C (loan)	6	—
							Darlington	17	2
							Southend U	38	19
Clarke Adrian*	5 9	11 04	M	28 9 74	Cambridge	Trainee	Arsenal	7	—
							Rotherham U (loan)	2	—
							Southend U (loan)	7	—
							Southend U	73	8
							Carlisle U (loan)	7	—
Coleman Simon*	6 1	12 10	D	13 6 68	Mansfield	Apprentice	Mansfield T	96	7
							Middlesbrough	55	2
							Derby Co	70	2
							Sheffield W	16	1
							Bolton W	34	5
							Wolverhampton W (loan)	4	—
							Southend U	99	9
Connelly Gordon	6 0	12 04	F	1 11 76	Glasgow		Airdrieonians	33	1
							York C	28	4
							Southend U	33	2
Cross Garry	5 9	12 00	D	7 10 80	Chelmsford	Trainee	Southend U	8	—
Fitzpatrick Trevor	6 1	13 00	F	19 2 80	Surrey	Trainee	Southend U	42	5
Gooding Mick†	5 8	10 10	M	12 4 59	Newcastle	Bishop Auckland	Rotherham U	102	10
							Chesterfield	12	—
							Rotherham U	156	33
							Peterborough U	47	21
							Wolverhampton W	44	4
							Reading	314	26
							Southend U	25	—
Hails Julian‡	5 10	10 07	M	20 11 67	Lincoln	Hemel Hempstead	Fulham	109	12
							Southend U	161	7
Houghton Scott	5 5	12 02	M	22 10 71	Hitchin	Trainee	Tottenham H	10	2
							Ipswich T (loan)	8	1
							Cambridge U (loan)	—	—
							Gillingham (loan)	3	—
							Charlton Ath (loan)	6	—
							Luton T	16	1
							Walsall	78	14
							Peterborough U	70	13
							Southend U	70	7
Johnson Leon	6 0	12 00	M	10 5 81	London	Scholar	Southend U	—	—
Jones Nathan#	5 7	10 05	D	28 5 73	Rhondda	Merthyr T	Luton T	—	—
						Numaicia	Southend U	99	2
							Scarborough (loan)	9	—
Kerrigan Danny§	5 7	10 04	M	4 7 82	Basildon	Trainee	Southend U	4	—
Livett Simon‡	5 10	13 07	M	8 1 69	Plaistow	Trainee	West Ham U	1	—
							Leyton Orient	24	—
							Cambridge U	12	—
						Billericay T	Southend U	23	1
Maher Kevin	5 11	13 04	M	17 10 76	Ilford	Trainee	Tottenham H	—	—
							Southend U	76	5
McDonald Thomas	6 2	12 00	D	15 9 80	London	Trainee	Southend U	3	—
Morley David	6 2	13 05	D	25 9 77	St Helens	Trainee	Manchester C	3	1
							Ayr U (loan)	4	—
							Southend U	59	—
Morrish Adam‡	6 1	13 05	D	28 6 80	Greenwich	Trainee	Southend U	—	—

Newman Rob*	6 1	14 03	D	13 12 63	Bradford-on-Avon	Apprentice	Bristol C	394	52
							Norwich C	205	14
							Motherwell (loan)	11	—
							Wigan Ath (loan)	8	—
							Southend U	55	7
Pepper Nigel	5 10	11 13	M	25 4 68	Rotherham	Apprentice	Rotherham U	45	1
(On loan from Aberdeen)							York C	235	39
							Bradford C	52	11
							Aberdeen	14	—
							Southend U	12	2
Perkins Chris	5 11	13 08	D	1 3 80	Stepney	Trainee	Southend U	5	—
Prudhoe Mark	6 0	14 00	G	8 11 63	Washington	Apprentice	Sunderland	7	—
							Hartlepool U (loan)	3	—
							Birmingham C	1	—
							Walsall	26	—
							Doncaster R (loan)	5	—
							Sheffield W (loan)	—	—
							Grimsby T (loan)	8	—
							Hartlepool U (loan)	13	—
							Bristol C (loan)	3	—
							Carlisle U	34	—
							Darlington	146	—
							Stoke C	82	—
							Peterborough U (loan)	6	—
							Liverpool (loan)	—	—
							York C (loan)	2	—
							Bradford C	8	—
							Darlington (loan)	—	—
						Guiseley	Southend U	6	—
Roach Neville*	5 11	11 09	F	29 9 78	Reading	Trainee	Reading	16	1
							Southend U	16	2
Roget Leo	6 1	12 02	D	1 8 77	Ilford	Trainee	Southend U	94	3
Spittle Stephen‡	6 5	13 05	G	9 4 81	Walsall	Trainee	Southend U	—	—
Tinkler Mark	6 2	13 00	M	24 10 74	Bishop Auckland	Trainee	Leeds U	25	· —
							York C	90	8
							Southend U	41	—
Tolson Neil	6 2	12 11	F	25 10 73	Wordsley	Trainee	Walsall	9	1
							Oldham Ath	3	—
							Bradford C	63	12
							Chester C (loan)	4	—
							York C	84	18
							Southend U	31	10
Whyte David‡	5 8	12 00	F	20 4 71	Greenwich	Greenwich Bor	Crystal Palace	27	4
							Charlton Ath (loan)	8	2
							Charlton Ath	85	28
							Ipswich T	2	—
							Bristol R	4	—
							Southend U	26	3

Scholars
Ayres, Kevin C; Boot, Anthony RD; Bourgeois, Daryl TA; Davey, Thomas; Edwards, Craig A; Fisher, James D; Harding, Dean J; Hunter, Leon D; Ing, Martin P; Kerrigan, Daniel A; Lunan, Jamie T; McSweeney, David; Pitts, Daniel J; Simmons, Michael K; Window, James S; Wray, Matthew K

Non-Contract
Gooding, Michael C

Player who does not hold a current contract but his registration has been retained by the club
Byrne, Paul P

STOCKPORT COUNTY

Allen Chris*	5 11	12 04	M	18 11 72	Oxford	Trainee	Oxford U	150	12
							Nottingham F (loan)	3	1
							Nottingham F	25	—
							Luton T (loan)	14	1
							Cardiff C (loan)	4	—
							Port Vale	5	1
							Stockport Co	16	—
Alsaker Paul#	5 9	10 10	M	6 11 73	Bergen	Flora Tallinn	Stockport Co	1	—
Angell Brett	6 2	13 10	F	20 8 68	Marlborough	Cheltenham T	Derby Co	—	—
							Stockport Co	70	28
							Southend U	115	47
							Everton (loan)	1	—
							Everton	19	1
							Sunderland	10	—
							Sheffield U (loan)	6	2
							WBA (loan)	3	—
							Stockport Co	126	50
							Notts Co (loan)	6	5
							Preston NE (loan)	15	8
Bailey Alan	5 11	12 03	F	1 11 78	Macclesfield	Trainee	Manchester C	—	—
							Macclesfield T (loan)	10	1
							Stockport Co	14	1

Name			Pos	DOB	Birthplace	From	Club	Apps	Gls
Bennett Tom	5 11	11 08	M	12 12 69	Falkirk	Trainee	Aston Villa	—	—
							Wolverhampton W	115	2
							Stockport Co	110	5
							Walsall (loan)	11	3
Bergersen Kent	5 10	11 07	M	8 2 67	Oslo	Drobbak/Frogn	Lyn	40	5
							Rosenborg	43	14
							Valerengen	44	10
							Panionios	42	2
							Stromsgodset	10	4
							Stockport Co	17	—
Briggs Keith	6 0	11 00	D	11 12 81	Glossop	Trainee	Stockport Co	7	1
Byrne Chris	5 9	10 02	M	9 2 75	Hulme	Macclesfield T	Sunderland	8	—
							Stockport Co	55	11
							Macclesfield T (loan)	5	—
Clare Robert			M	28 2 83	Belper	Trainee	Stockport Co	—	—
Connelly Sean	5 10	11 10	D	26 6 70	Sheffield	Hallam	Stockport Co	289	6
Cooper Kevin	5 8	10 07	F	8 2 75	Derby	Trainee	Derby Co	2	—
							Stockport Co (loan)	12	3
							Stockport Co	122	13
Daly Jon	6 3	12 00	F	8 1 83	Dublin	Trainee	Stockport Co	4	—
Dinning Tony	6 0	12 04	M	12 4 75	Wallsend	Trainee	Newcastle U	—	—
							Stockport Co	185	25
Evans Lee			M	30 11 81	Cardiff	Trainee	Stockport Co	—	—
Flynn Mike	6 0	11 02	D	23 2 69	Oldham	Trainee	Oldham Ath	40	1
							Norwich C	—	—
							Preston NE	136	7
							Stockport Co	317	14
Fradin Karim	5 11	12 00	M	2 2 72	Ste Martin d'Hyeres		Niort	174	4
							Nice	7	—
							Stockport Co	21	1
Francis Kevin*	6 7	16 12	F	6 12 67	Moseley	Mile Oak R	Derby Co	10	—
							Stockport Co	152	88
							Birmingham C	73	13
							Oxford U	36	8
							Stockport Co	4	—
Gannon Jim#	6 2	13 00	D	7 9 68	Southwark	Dundalk	Sheffield U	—	—
							Halifax T (loan)	2	—
							Stockport Co	383	52
							Notts Co (loan)	2	—
Gibb Ali	5 9	11 07	F	17 2 76	Salisbury	Trainee	Norwich C	—	—
							Northampton T	131	4
							Stockport Co	14	—
Gray Ian#	6 2	13 00	G	25 2 75	Manchester	Trainee	Oldham Ath	—	—
							Rochdale (loan)	12	—
							Rochdale	66	—
							Stockport Co	16	—
Hancock Glynn	6 0	12 02	D	24 5 82	Biddulph	Trainee	Stockport Co	—	—
Johnson Ben	6 0	12 00	D	27 8 80	Manchester	Trainee	Stockport Co	—	—
Larsson Jonas			M	1 4 82	Vanersborg	Trainee	Stockport Co	—	—
Lawson Ian	5 11	11 00	F	4 11 77	Huddersfield	Trainee	Huddersfield T	42	5
							Blackpool (loan)	9	3
							Bury	25	11
							Stockport Co	15	4
Lillis Adam*	6 3	13 04	F	15 12 80	Middleton	Trainee	Stockport Co	—	—
Mannion Sean*	5 8	11 05	M	3 3 80	Dublin	Stella Maris	Stockport Co	1	—
Matthews Rob	6 0	12 05	F	14 10 70	Slough	Loughborough Univ	Notts Co	43	11
							Luton T	11	—
							York C	17	1
							Bury	74	11
							Stockport Co	27	3
							Blackpool (loan)	6	2
McIntosh Martin	6 3	12 05	D	19 3 71	East Kilbride	Tottenham H	St Mirren	4	—
(Transferred to Hibernian, February 2000)							Clydebank	65	10
							Hamilton A	99	12
							Stockport Co	99	5
Moore Ian	5 11	12 02	F	26 8 76	Birkenhead	Trainee	Tranmere R	58	12
							Bradford C (loan)	6	—
							Nottingham F	15	1
							West Ham U (loan)	1	—
							Stockport Co	76	13
Nash Carlo	6 5	14 01	G	13 9 73	Bolton	Clitheroe	Crystal Palace	21	—
							Stockport Co	81	—
Nicholson Shane	5 10	11 10	D	3 6 70	Newark	Trainee	Lincoln C	133	6
							Derby Co	74	1
							WBA	52	—
							Chesterfield	24	—
							Stockport Co	42	1
Phelan Mike‡	5 11	11 01	D	24 9 62	Nelson	Apprentice	Burnley	168	9
							Norwich C	156	9
							Manchester U	102	2
							WBA	21	—
							Blackpool	—	—
							Stockport Co	—	—

Name	Ht	Wt	Pos	Birth date	Birthplace	Source	Clubs	Apps	Gls
Ross Neil	6 1	12 02	F	10 8 82	West Bromwich	Trainee	Leeds U	—	—
						Leeds U	Stockport Co	2	—
Smith David	5 10	12 11	M	26 12 70	Liverpool	Trainee	Norwich C	18	—
							Oxford U	198	2
							Stockport Co	26	2
Travis Simon‡	5 7	10 00	D	22 3 77	Preston	Trainee	Torquay U	8	—
						Holywell T	Stockport Co	22	2
Wilbraham Aaron	6 3	12 04	F	21 10 79	Knutsford	Trainee	Stockport Co	59	5
Woodthorpe Colin	6 0	11 08	D	13 1 69	Ellesmere Pt	Apprentice	Chester C	155	6
							Norwich C	43	1
							Aberdeen	48	1
							Stockport Co	95	3

Trainees
Andrews, Martyn; Carratt, Philip; Fenna, Stuart; Hennessy, Michael P; Johansson, Gustav; Kietly, Anthony; McLachlan, Fraser M; Mudd, Lee C; Rowley, Paul; Thomas, Andrew; Villers, Lee W; Welsh, Andrew; Wild, Peter

Player who does not hold a current contract but his registration has been retained by the club
Byrne, Desmond

STOKE CITY

Name	Ht	Wt	Pos	Birth date	Birthplace	Source	Clubs	Apps	Gls
Bullock Matthew	5 8	11 00	M	1 11 80	Stoke	Trainee	Stoke C	7	—
Burgess Richard‡	5 8	11 00	F	18 8 78	Bromsgrove	Trainee	Aston Villa	—	—
							Stoke C	—	—
Cartwright Jamie‡	5 7	9 06	M	11 10 79	Lichfield	Trainee	Stoke C	—	—
Clarke Clive	6 1	12 03	D	14 1 80	Dublin	Trainee	Stoke C	44	1
Collins Lee	6 1	12 06	D	10 9 77	Birmingham	Trainee	Aston Villa	—	—
							Stoke C	4	—
Connor Paul	6 2	11 08	F	12 1 79	Bishop Auckland	Trainee	Middlesbrough	—	—
							Hartlepool U (loan)	5	—
							Stoke C (loan)	3	2
							Stoke C	26	5
Crowe Dean	5 5	11 02	F	6 6 79	Stockport	Trainee	Stoke C	60	12
							Northampton T (loan)	5	—
							Bury (loan)	4	1
Danielsson Einar‡	5 8	11 03	M	19 1 70	Reykjavik		KR	125	32
							Stoke C	8	1
Dixon Calvin*			M	20 10 80	Walsall	Trainee	Stoke C	—	—
Evans Jamie*			M	3 12 80	Birmingham	Trainee	Stoke C	—	—
Fraser Stuart*	6 0	12 00	G	1 8 78	Cheltenham	Cheltenham T	Stoke C	1	—
Gislason Sigursteinn‡	5 9	11 03	D	25 6 68	Iceland		IA	41	6
							IA*	—	—
							IA	103	6
							KR	16	1
							Stoke C	8	—
Godbold Jamie*	5 4	9 0	M	10 1 80	Great Yarmouth	Trainee	Stoke C	—	—
Goodfellow Marc			M	20 9 81	Burton		Stoke C	—	—
Gudjonsson Bjarni	5 8	11 02	F	26 2 79	Reykjavik		IA Akranes	25	15
							Newcastle U	—	—
							Genk	14	—
							Stoke C	8	1
Gunnarsson Brynjar	6 1	11 00	M	16 10 75	Reykjavik		KR	50	1
							Moss	5	2
							Stoke C	22	1
Hansson Mikael	5 8	11 08	D	15 3 68	Norrkoping		Soderkopings	40	7
							Norrkoping	204	19
							Stoke C	27	—
Heath Robert	5 9	10 00	M	31 8 78	Newcastle-Under-Lyme		Stoke C	19	—
Henry Karl			M	26 11 82	Wolverhampton	Trainee	Stoke C	—	—
Iwelumo Chris	6 4	13 00	F	1 8 78	Coatbridge	Juniors	St Mirren	26	—
							Aarhus Fremad	27	4
							Stoke C	3	—
Jacobsen Anders*	6 2	12 09	D	18 4 69	Oslo	Start	Sheffield U	12	—
							Stoke C	33	2
Kavanagh Graham	5 10	12 06	M	2 12 73	Dublin	Home Farm	Middlesbrough	35	3
							Darlington (loan)	5	—
							Stoke C	163	27
Keen Kevin*	5 6	10 10	M	25 2 67	Amersham	Apprentice	West Ham U	219	21
							Wolverhampton W	42	7
							Stoke C	177	10
Lightbourne Kyle	6 2	12 00	F	29 9 68	Bermuda		Scarborough	19	3
							Walsall	165	65
							Coventry C	7	—
							Fulham (loan)	4	2
							Stoke C	89	16
McGeough David*			M	10 11 80	Drogheda		Stoke C	—	—

Name	Ht	Wt	Pos	Born	Birthplace	Source	Club	Apps	Gls
Melton Steve*	5 10	10 08	M	31 10 78	Lincoln	Trainee	Nottingham F	3	—
							Stoke C	5	—
Mohan Nicky	6 1	14 00	D	6 10 70	Middlesbrough	Trainee	Middlesbrough	99	4
							Hull C (loan)	5	1
							Leicester C	23	—
							Bradford C	83	4
							Wycombe W	58	2
							Stoke C	55	5
Muggleton Carl#	6 2	13 00	G	13 9 68	Leicester	Apprentice	Leicester C	46	—
							Chesterfield (loan)	17	—
							Blackpool (loan)	2	—
							Hartlepool U (loan)	8	—
							Stockport Co (loan)	4	—
							Liverpool (loan)	—	—
							Stoke C (loan)	6	—
							Sheffield U (loan)	—	—
							Celtic	12	—
							Stoke C	137	—
							Rotherham U (loan)	6	—
							Sheffield U (loan)	1	—
							Mansfield T (loan)	9	—
							Chesterfield (loan)	5	—
Neal Lewis			M	14 7 81	Leicester		Stoke C	—	—
O'Connor James	5 8	11 00	M	1 9 79	Dublin	Trainee	Stoke C	46	6
Petty Ben	6 0	12 05	D	22 3 77	Solihull	Trainee	Aston Villa	—	—
							Stoke C	24	—
Robinson Phil*	5 10	11 07	D	6 1 67	Stafford	Apprentice	Aston Villa	3	1
							Wolverhampton W	71	8
							Notts Co	66	5
							Birmingham C (loan)	9	—
							Huddersfield T	75	5
							Northampton T (loan)	14	—
							Chesterfield	61	17
							Notts Co	77	5
							Stoke C	62	2
Scheuber Stuart*			M	3 4 81	Rhuddlan	Trainee	Stoke C	—	—
Short Chris	5 10	12 04	D	9 5 70	Munster	Pickering T	Scarborough	43	1
							Manchester U (loan)	—	—
							Notts Co	94	2
							Huddersfield T (loan)	6	—
							Sheffield U	44	—
							Stoke C	35	—
Sigurdsson Kris	5 11	11 11	D	7 10 80	Akureyri		KA	15	—
							Stoke C	—	—
Small Bryan*	5 9	11 09	D	15 11 71	Birmingham	Trainee	Aston Villa	36	—
							Birmingham C (loan)	3	—
							Bolton W	12	—
							Luton T (loan)	15	—
							Bradford C (loan)	5	—
							Bury	18	1
							Stoke C	45	—
Taaffe Steven	5 7	9 00	F	10 9 79	Stoke	Trainee	Stoke C	8	—
Thorne Peter	6 0	13 07	F	21 6 73	Manchester	Trainee	Blackburn R		
							Wigan Ath (loan)	11	—
							Swindon T	77	27
							Stoke C	115	45
Ward Gavin	6 2	12 02	G	30 6 70	Sutton Coldfield	Aston Villa	Shrewsbury T	—	—
							WBA	—	—
							Cardiff C	59	—
							Leicester C	38	—
							Bradford C	36	—
							Bolton W	22	—
							Burnley (loan)	17	—
							Stoke C	52	—
Wooliscroft Ashley	5 10	11 02	D	28 12 79	Stoke	Trainee	Stoke C	1	—

Scholars
Commons, Kristian A; Cromie, Mark; Gibson, Alexander J; Hemmings, Andrew P; Machin, Jonathan P; Meadows, Colin D; Owen, Gareth D; Shaw, Martyn P; Wilson, Brian

SUNDERLAND

Name	Ht	Wt	Pos	Born	Birthplace	Source	Club	Apps	Gls
Aiston Sam	6 0	13 09	M	21 11 76	Newcastle	Newcastle U	Sunderland	20	—
							Chester C (loan)	14	—
							Chester C (loan)	11	—
							Stoke C (loan)	6	—
							Shrewsbury T (loan)	10	—
Bould Steve	6 4	14 02	D	16 11 62	Stoke	Apprentice	Stoke C	183	6
							Torquay U (loan)	9	—
							Arsenal	287	5
							Sunderland	20	—
Butler Paul	6 3	14 09	D	2 11 72	Manchester	Trainee	Rochdale	158	10
							Bury	84	4
							Sunderland	76	3
Butler Thomas	5 7	10 06	M	25 4 81	Ballymun	Trainee	Sunderland	1	—
Byrne Clifford			M	27 4 82	Dublin		Sunderland	—	—

Name			Pos	DOB	Birthplace		Club	Apps	Gls
Convery Mark	5 6	10 05	F	29 5 81	Newcastle	Trainee	Sunderland	—	—
Craddock Jody	6 2	12 05	D	25 7 75	Bromsgrove	Christchurch	Cambridge U	145	4
							Sunderland	57	—
							Sheffield U (loan)	10	—
Dichio Danny	6 4	13 09	F	19 10 74	Hammersmith	Trainee	QPR	75	20
							Barnet (loan)	9	2
							Sampdoria	—	—
							Lecce	4	1
							Sunderland	61	10
Dickman Jonjo	5 8	10 05	D	22 9 81	Hexham		Sunderland	—	—
Duke David	5 10	11 01	M	7 11 78	Inverness	Redby CA	Sunderland	—	—
Fredgaard Carsten	6 1	12 01	M	20 5 76	Hillesod		Sunderland	1	—
							WBA (loan)	5	—
Gray Michael	5 9	11 01	D	3 8 74	Sunderland	Trainee	Sunderland	259	14
Graydon Keith			M	10 2 83	Dublin		Sunderland	—	—
Harrison Gerry*	5 10	12 12	M	15 4 72	Lambeth	Trainee	Watford	9	—
							Bristol C	38	1
							Cardiff C (loan)	10	1
							Hereford U (loan)	6	—
							Huddersfield T	—	—
							Burnley	124	3
							Sunderland	—	—
							Luton T (loan)	14	—
							Hull C (loan)	8	—
							Hull C (loan)	3	—
							Burnley (loan)	—	—
Harrison Steve			D	3 2 82	Hexham	Scholar	Sunderland	—	—
Helmer Thomas	6 1	12 04	D	21 4 65	Herford	Bad Salzuflen	Arminia Bielefeld	39	5
							Borussia Dortmund	182	16
							Bayern Munich	191	24
							Sunderland	2	—
Holloway Darren	6 0	12 09	D	3 10 77	Crook	Trainee	Sunderland	53	—
							Carlisle U (loan)	5	—
							Bolton W (loan)	4	—
Ingham Michael	6 4	13 10	G	9 7 80	Preston	Malachians	Cliftonville	18	—
							Sunderland	—	—
							Carlisle U (loan)	7	—
Kennedy Jon			G	30 11 80	Rotherham	Worksop T	Sunderland	—	—
Kilbane Kevin	6 2	13 07	M	1 2 77	Preston	Trainee	Preston NE	47	3
							WBA	106	15
							Sunderland	20	1
Kyle Kevin	5 8	12 00	F	7 6 81	Stranraer		Sunderland	—	—
Lumsdon Chris	5 10	10 09	M	15 12 79	Newcastle	Trainee	Sunderland	2	—
							Blackpool (loan)	6	1
Lynch Finbar	5 8	10 01	F	24 1 82	Dublin		Sunderland	—	—
Makin Chris	5 11	12 11	D	8 5 73	Manchester	Trainee	Oldham Ath	94	4
							Wigan Ath (loan)	15	2
							Marseille	29	—
							Sunderland	97	1
Maley Mark	6 0	13 00	D	26 1 81	Newcastle	Trainee	Sunderland	—	—
Marriott Andy	6 2	13 04	G	11 10 70	Sutton-in-Ashfield	Trainee	Arsenal	—	—
							Nottingham F	11	—
							WBA (loan)	3	—
							Blackburn R (loan)	2	—
							Colchester U (loan)	10	—
							Burnley (loan)	15	—
							Wrexham	213	—
							Sunderland	2	—
McCann Gavin	6 1	12 08	M	10 1 78	Blackpool	Trainee	Everton	11	—
							Sunderland	35	4
McCartney George	6 0	12 06	D	29 4 81	Belfast	Trainee	Sunderland	—	—
McGill Brendan	5 8	9 02	M	22 3 81	Dublin		Sunderland	—	—
Nunez Milton	5 5	10 08	F	30 10 72	Honduras		PAOK Salonika	5	—
							Sunderland	1	—
Oster John	5 9	10 09	M	8 12 78	Boston	Trainee	Grimsby T	24	3
							Everton	40	1
							Sunderland	10	—
Phillips Kevin	5 8	11 05	F	25 7 73	Hitchin	Baldock T	Watford	59	24
							Sunderland	105	82
Porter Christopher‡			M	10 11 79	Sunderland	Trainee	Sunderland	—	—
Proctor Michael	6 0	11 08	F	3 10 80	Sunderland	Trainee	Sunderland	—	—
Quinn Niall	6 5	14 08	F	6 10 66	Dublin		Arsenal	67	14
							Manchester C	203	66
							Sunderland	123	48
Rae Alex	5 10	11 09	M	30 9 69	Glasgow	Bishopbriggs	Falkirk	83	20
							Millwall	218	63
							Sunderland	93	10
Reddy Michael	6 1	11 07	F	24 3 80	Graignamanagh	Kilkenny C	Sunderland	8	1
Roy Eric	6 2	13 00	M	26 9 67	Nice		Nice	86	4
							Toulon	34	2
							Lyon	111	9
							Marseille	87	9
							Sunderland	24	—

Name	Ht	Wt	Pos	Born	Birthplace	Source	Club	Apps	Gls
Schwarz Stefan	6 0	12 00	M	18 4 69	Malmo		Malmo	32	—
							Benfica	77	7
							Arsenal	34	2
							Fiorentina	78	2
							Valencia	30	4
							Sunderland	27	1
Shannon Greg*	6 0	11 00	G	15 2 81	Maghreafelt	Trainee	Sunderland	—	—
Sorensen Thomas	6 4	14 08	G	12 6 76	Odense	Odense	Sunderland	82	—
Summerbee Nicky	5 11	12 03	M	26 8 71	Altrincham	Trainee	Swindon T	112	6
							Manchester C	131	6
							Sunderland	93	7
Thirlwell Paul	5 11	12 00	M	13 2 79	Springwell Village	Trainee	Sunderland	10	—
							Swindon T (loan)	12	—
Wainwright Neil	6 1	11 07	M	4 11 77	Warrington	Trainee	Wrexham	11	3
							Sunderland	2	—
							Darlington (loan)	17	4
Williams Darren	5 11	12 00	D	28 4 77	Middlesbrough	Trainee	York C	20	—
							Sunderland	97	4

Scholars
Black, Christopher; Capper, Stephen; Clark, Benjamin; Dowell, Adam; James Craig P; Lacey, Glenn; Marchant, Ross; McGhie, Gareth; Mordey, Gareth; Morgan, David; Ramsden, Simon; Rossiter, Mark; Turns, Craig; Vickers, Thomas A

SWANSEA CITY

Name	Ht	Wt	Pos	Born	Birthplace	Source	Club	Apps	Gls
Alsop Julian#	6 5	14 08	F	28 5 73	Nuneaton	Halesowen T	Bristol R	33	4
							Swansea C	90	16
Appleby Ritchie	5 9	11 04	M	18 9 75	Stockton	Trainee	Newcastle U	—	—
							Darlington (loan)	—	—
							Ipswich T	3	—
							Swansea C	105	11
Barwood Danny	5 9	11 00	F	7 7 80	Caerphilly	Trainee	Swansea C	3	1
Bird Tony*	5 11	12 10	F	1 9 74	Cardiff	Trainee	Cardiff C	75	13
						Barry T	Swansea C	86	18
Bound Matthew#	6 2	14 00	D	9 11 72	Bradford-on-Avon	Trainee	Southampton	5	—
							Hull C (loan)	7	1
							Stockport Co	44	5
							Lincoln C (loan)	4	—
							Swansea C	116	4
Boyd Walter#	5 11	11 10	F	1 1 72	Kingston	Arnett Gardens	Swansea C	27	7
Casey Ryan	6 2	12 05	M	3 1 79	Coventry	Trainee	Swansea C	37	1
Coates Jonathan	5 8	11 04	M	27 6 75	Swansea	Trainee	Swansea C	186	17
Cusack Nick	6 0	12 05	M	24 12 65	Rotherham	Alvechurch	Leicester C	16	1
							Peterborough U	44	10
							Motherwell	77	17
							Darlington	21	6
							Oxford U	61	10
							Wycombe W (loan)	4	—
							Fulham	116	14
							Swansea C	118	8
Davies Jamie*	6 0	11 09	F	12 12 80	Swansea	Trainee	Swansea C	1	—
De-Vulgt Leigh	5 10	10 07	M	17 3 81	Swansea	Trainee	Swansea C	2	—
Freestone Roger	6 2	14 04	G	19 8 68	Newport	Trainee	Newport Co	13	—
							Chelsea	42	—
							Swansea C (loan)	14	—
							Hereford U (loan)	8	—
							Swansea C	396	3
Hartfield Charlie‡	6 0	13 08	M	4 9 71	London	Trainee	Arsenal	—	—
							Sheffield U	56	1
							Fulham (loan)	2	—
							Swansea C	22	2
							Lincoln C (loan)	3	1
Howard Mike	5 7	10 07	D	2 12 78	Birkenhead	Tranmere R	Swansea C	82	1
Jenkins Lee	5 8	11 02	M	28 6 79	Pontypool	Trainee	Swansea C	72	2
Jones Jason	6 2	12 10	G	10 5 79	Wrexham	Liverpool	Swansea C	4	—
Jones Steve	5 10	12 09	D	25 12 70	Bristol	Cheltenham T	Swansea C	133	3
Keegan Michael	5 10	11 00	M	12 5 81	Liskeard	Trainee	Swansea C	4	—
Lacey Damien	5 8	11 10	D	3 8 77	Bridgend	Trainee	Swansea C	60	1
Morgan Bari	5 6	10 08	M	13 8 80	Carmarthen	Trainee	Swansea C	—	—
Mutton Tommy	5 8	10 02	F	17 1 78	Huddersfield	Bangor C	Swansea C	2	—
O'Leary Kristian	6 0	13 07	D	30 8 77	Port Talbot	Trainee	Swansea C	81	3
Phillips Gareth	5 7	11 02	M	19 8 79	Pontypridd	Trainee	Swansea C	11	—
Price Jason	6 2	11 05	D	12 4 77	Aberdare	Aberaman Ath	Swansea C	103	13
Roberts Stuart	5 6	9 08	M	22 7 80	Carmarthen	Trainee	Swansea C	43	4
Smith Jason	6 3	14 00	D	6 9 74	Bromsgrove	Tiverton	Coventry C	—	—
						Tiverton T	Swansea C	85	5
Thomas Carl*	6 1	12 01	G	30 1 81	Swansea	Trainee	Swansea C	—	—
Thomas Martin	5 8	11 00	M	12 9 73	Lyndhurst	Trainee	Southampton	—	—
							Leyton Orient	5	2
							Fulham	90	8
							Swansea C	70	7

Walker Keith‡	6 0	12 08	D	7 4 66	Edinburgh	ICI Juveniles	Stirling Albion	91	17
							St Mirren	43	6
							Swansea C	270	9
Watkin Steve	5 10	11 12	F	16 6 71	Wrexham	School	Wrexham	200	55
							Swansea C	114	27

Trainees
Berry, James A; Davies, Alex J; Di Battista, Santino P; Draper, Craig JE; Gregson, Lyndon; Healey, Stephen J; James, Grant R; James, Robert K; Jenkins, Dean; Kern, Jamie T; Mazurczak, Ross P; Middleton, Luke; Morgan, Ian K; Mounty, Carl T; O'Sullivan, Christopher; Todd, Christopher

SWINDON TOWN

Burke Nicky‡	5 9	11 00	F	3 1 81	Waterford	Trainee	Swindon T	—	—
Campagna Sam	6 1	11 07	D	19 11 80	Worcester	Trainee	Swindon T	5	—
Collins Lee#	5 8	10 08	M	3 2 74	Bellshill	Possil U	Albion R	45	1
							Swindon T	63	2
Cowe Steve#	5 7	10 10	F	29 9 74	Gloucester	Trainee	Aston Villa	—	—
							Swindon T	88	10
Cuervo Philippe*	5 11	12 06	M	13 8 69	Ris-Orangis		St Etienne	21	—
							Swindon T	35	—
Culbertson Richard‡			M	10 8 80	Ballymena	Trainee	Swindon T	—	—
Davies Gareth	6 1	11 12	D	11 12 73	Hereford	Trainee	Hereford U	95	1
							Crystal Palace	27	2
							Cardiff C (loan)	6	2
							Reading	19	—
							Swindon T	23	—
Davis Sol	5 8	11 00	D	4 9 79	Cheltenham	Trainee	Swindon T	60	—
Flanagan Alan*	6 1	13 07	G	9 10 80	Drogheda	Trainee	Swindon T	1	—
Grazioli Guiliano	5 11	12 11	F	23 3 75	London	Wembley	Peterborough U	41	16
							Swindon T	19	8
Griffin Charlie	6 0	12 07	F	25 6 79	Bath	Bristol R	Swindon T	26	2
Hall Gareth	5 8	12 00	D	20 3 69	Croydon	Apprentice	Chelsea	138	4
							Sunderland	48	—
							Brentford (loan)	6	—
							Swindon T	80	3
Howe Bobby	5 7	10 04	M	6 11 73	Annisford	Trainee	Nottingham F	14	2
							Ipswich T (loan)	3	—
							Swindon T	64	4
Hughes Alun‡			M	9 11 80	Cardiff	School	Swindon T	—	—
Leitch Scott*	5 9	12 08	M	6 10 69	Motherwell	Shettleston Jun	Dunfermline Ath	89	16
							Hearts	55	2
							Swindon T	122	1
McAreavey Paul	5 10	11 00	M	3 12 80	Belfast	Trainee	Swindon T	2	—
McHugh Frazer	5 9	12 05	M	14 7 81	Nottingham	Trainee	Swindon T	15	—
Mildenhall Steve	6 5	13 05	G	13 5 78	Swindon	Trainee	Swindon T	10	—
Mills Jamie	5 10	11 00	M	31 8 81	Swindon	Trainee	Swindon T	—	—
Quinn Jimmy‡	6 0	13 10	F	18 12 59	Belfast	Oswestry T	Swindon T	49	10
							Blackburn R	71	17
							Swindon T	64	30
							Leicester C	31	6
							Bradford C	35	14
							West Ham U	47	18
							Bournemouth	43	19
							Reading	182	71
							Peterborough U	49	25
							Swindon T	7	—
Reeves Alan	6 0	12 00	D	19 11 67	Birkenhead	Heswall	Norwich C	—	—
							Gillingham (loan)	18	—
							Chester C	40	2
							Rochdale	121	9
							Wimbledon	57	4
							Swindon T	67	3
Robinson Mark#	5 9	12 04	D	21 11 68	Rochdale	Trainee	WBA	2	—
							Barnsley	137	6
							Newcastle U	25	—
							Swindon T	227	3
Smith Bryan§	6 1	12 00		26 8 83	Swindon	Trainee	Swindon T	1	—
Talia Frank*	6 1	13 06	G	20 7 72	Melbourne	Sunshine GC	Blackburn R	—	—
							Hartlepool U (loan)	14	—
							Swindon T	107	—
Williams Andy	5 10	10 10	M	8 10 77	Bristol	Trainee	Southampton	21	—
							Swindon T	36	1
Williams James	5 7	10 08	M	15 7 82	Liverpool	Trainee	Swindon T	29	1
Willis Adam	6 1	12 02	D	21 9 76	Nuneaton	Trainee	Coventry C	—	—
							Swindon T	34	—
							Mansfield T (loan)	10	—
Worrall Ben‡	5 5	10 04	M	7 12 75	Swindon	Trainee	Swindon T	3	—
							Scarborough	67	3
							Exeter C	4	—
							Swindon T	—	—

Trainees
Evans, Scott; Jeffrey, Danny; Martin, Lee; McRobie, Craig; McSherry, Ian GR; Ratcliffe, David P

Scholars
Andersen, Paul A; Bishop, Leslie M; Collier, Adam J; Collins, Christopher J; Edwards, Nathan M; Halliday, Kevin J; Reed, Paul S; Scarlett, Philip J; Smith, Bryan J; Thomas, Joshua C; Young, Alan J

Player who does not hold a current contract but his registration has been retained by the club
Kitchen, Luke F

TORQUAY UNITED

Name	Ht	Wt	Pos	Born	Birthplace	From	Club	Apps	Gls
Aggrey Jimmy	6 3	13 06	D	26 10 78	London	Chelsea	Fulham	—	—
							Torquay U	52	—
Bedeau Anthony	5 10	11 00	F	24 3 79	Hammersmith	Trainee	Torquay U	120	31
Brandon Chris	5 7	10 00	M	7 4 76	Bradford	Bradford PA	Torquay U	42	5
Donaldson O'Neill*	6 0	12 04	F	24 11 69	Birmingham	Hinckley	Shrewsbury T	28	4
							Doncaster R	9	2
							Mansfield T (loan)	4	6
							Sheffield W	14	3
							Oxford U (loan)	6	2
							Stoke C	2	—
							Torquay U	27	1
Forrester Mark‡	5 8	10 02	F	15 4 81	Stockton	Trainee	Torquay U	6	—
Griffiths Michael*	5 11	13 04		14 3 70	Birmingham	Boldmere St Michaels	Torquay U	22	3
Gutteridge Luke§	5 5	8 06	M	27 3 82	Barnstaple	Trainee	Torquay U	1	—
Healy Brian	6 1	13 02	M	27 12 68	Glasgow	Morecambe	Torquay U	57	11
Herrera Robbie	5 7	10 06	D	12 6 70	Torbay	Trainee	QPR	6	—
							Torquay U (loan)	11	—
							Torquay U (loan)	5	—
							Fulham	145	1
							Torquay U	75	—
Hill Kevin	5 8	10 03	M	6 3 76	Exeter	Torrington	Torquay U	115	14
Holmes Paul	5 10	11 00	D	18 2 68	Stocksbridge	Apprentice	Doncaster R	47	1
							Torquay U	138	4
							Birmingham C	12	—
							Everton	21	—
							WBA	103	1
							Torquay U	30	—
Jermyn Mark‡	5 11	12 00	D	16 4 81	West Germany	Trainee	Torquay U	1	—
Jones Stuart	6 0	13 07	G	24 10 77	Bristol	Weston-Super-Mare	Sheffield W	—	—
							Crewe Alex (loan)	—	—
							Torquay U	16	—
Neil Gary	6 0	12 10	F	16 8 78	Glasgow	Trainee	Leicester C	—	—
							Torquay U	14	—
Nichols Jon*	6 0	11 10	D	10 9 80	Plymouth	Trainee	Torquay U	7	—
Northmore Ryan	6 1	13 00	G	5 9 80	Plymouth	Trainee	Torquay U	3	—
O'Brien Mick	5 5	10 06	M	25 9 79	Liverpool	Trainee	Everton	—	—
							Torquay U	30	4
Patterson Jamie‡	5 8	10 02	M	11 2 81	Paignton	Trainee	Torquay U	—	—
Platts Mark	5 8	11 12	F	23 5 79	Sheffield	Trainee	Sheffield W	2	—
							Torquay U	30	1
Russell Lee	5 10	11 09	D	3 9 69	Southampton	Trainee	Portsmouth	123	3
							Bournemouth (loan)	3	—
							Torquay U (loan)	9	—
							Torquay U	35	—
Simb Jean-Pierre‡	6 1	11 05	F	4 9 74	Paris	FC Paris	Torquay U	20	1
Stocco Tom§	6 2	12 05	F	4 1 83	London	Trainee	Torquay U	8	2
Thomas Wayne	5 11	11 02	D	17 5 79	Gloucester	Trainee	Torquay U	123	5
Tully Stephen	5 7	10 04	M	10 2 80	Paignton	Trainee	Torquay U	59	2
Watson Alex	6 1	12 00	D	5 4 68	Liverpool	Apprentice	Liverpool	4	—
							Derby Co (loan)	5	—
							Bournemouth	151	5
							Gillingham (loan)	10	1
							Torquay U	172	8
Williams Eifion	5 11	11 00	F	15 11 75	Bangor	Barry T	Torquay U	49	14
Worthington Martin‡	5 10	11 11	F	25 1 81	Torquay	Trainee	Torquay U	1	—

Trainees
Ashington, Ryan D; Barwell, Thomas; Benefield, James P; Dawkins, Luke A; Douglin, Troy-Alexander; Ennis, Robert; Grinsill, Justin A; Guttridge, Luke; Higgins, Dean RJ; Hockley, Matthew; Jones, James P; Law, Gareth M; Legg, Scott G; Lyons, Simon R; Smith, Robert R; Stephens, Nicholas J; Stocco, Tom L; Tomkinson, David J; Worthington, David M

Non-Contract
Hancox, Richard C

TOTTENHAM HOTSPUR

Name	Ht	Wt	Pos	Born	Birthplace	From	Club	Apps	Gls
Anderton Darren	6 1	12 05	F	3 3 72	Southampton	Trainee	Portsmouth	62	7
							Tottenham H	201	28
Armstrong Chris	6 0	12 10	F	19 6 71	Newcastle	Llay Welfare	Wrexham	60	13
							Millwall	28	5
							Crystal Palace	118	45
							Tottenham H	132	46
Baardsen Espen	6 5	13 03	G	7 12 77	San Rafael	San Francisco AB	Tottenham H	23	—
Campbell Sol	6 21	14 04	D	18 9 74	Newham	Trainee	Tottenham H	234	8
Carr Stephen	5 9	12 04	D	29 8 76	Dublin	Trainee	Tottenham H	136	3
Clemence Stephen	5 11	11 07	M	31 3 78	Liverpool	Trainee	Tottenham H	55	1
Consorti Maurizio			M	6 3 82	Rome	Trainee	Tottenham H	—	—
Crouch Peter	6 2	11 12	F	30 1 81	Macclesfield	Trainee	Tottenham H	—	—
(On loan to Hassleholm)									

Player	Ht	Wt	Pos	Born	Birthplace	From	Club	Apps	Gls
Davies Simon	5 10	11 04	M	23 10 79	Haverfordwest	Trainee	Peterborough U	65	6
							Tottenham H	3	—
Doherty Gary	6 2	13 01	D	31 1 80	Carndonagh	Trainee	Luton T	70	12
							Tottenham H	2	—
Dominguez Jose	5 3	10 00	F	16 2 74	Lisbon	Benfica	Birmingham C	35	3
							Sporting Lisbon	62	4
							Tottenham H	43	4
Etherington Matthew	5 10	11 02	F	14 8 81	Truro	School	Peterborough U	51	6
							Tottenham H	5	—
Fenn Neale	5 10	12 08	F	18 1 77	Edmonton	Trainee	Tottenham H	8	—
							Leyton Orient (loan)	3	—
							Norwich C (loan)	7	1
							Swindon T (loan)	4	—
							Lincoln C (loan)	4	—
Ferdinand Les	5 11	13 05	F	8 12 66	Paddington	Hayes	QPR	163	80
							Brentford (loan)	3	—
							Besiktas (loan)	24	14
							Newcastle U	68	41
							Tottenham H	54	12
Fox Ruel	5 6	10 05	F	14 1 68	Ipswich	Apprentice	Norwich C	172	22
							Newcastle U	58	12
							Tottenham H	106	13
Freund Steffen	5 11	12 06	M	19 1 70	Brandenburg		Brandenburg	31	—
							Schalke	53	3
							Borussia Dortmund	117	6
							Tottenham H	44	—
Gardner Anthony	6 5	13 11	D	19 9 80	Stafford	Trainee	Port Vale	41	4
							Tottenham H	—	—
Ginola David	5 11	11 10	F	25 1 67	Gassin		Toulon	81	4
							Racing Paris	61	8
							Brest	50	10
							Paris St Germain	115	32
							Newcastle U	58	6
							Tottenham H	100	12
Gower Mark	5 11	11 12	M	5 10 78	Edmonton	Trainee	Tottenham H	—	—
							Motherwell (loan)	9	1
Hillier Ian	5 11	11 05	D	26 12 79	Neath	Trainee	Tottenham H	—	—
Iversen Steffen	6 1	11 08	F	10 11 76	Oslo		Rosenborg	25	10
							Tottenham H	92	28
Jackson Johnnie			M	15 8 82	Camden	Trainee	Tottenham H	—	—
Kamanan Yannick			F	5 10 82	St Pol-sur-Mer	Le Mans	Tottenham H	—	—
Kelly Gavin	6 0	13 05	G	3 6 81	Hammersmith	Trainee	Tottenham H	—	—
King Ledley	6 2	13 08	D	12 10 80	London	Trainee	Tottenham H	4	—
Korsten Willem	6 4	13 04	F	21 1 75	Boxtel		NEC	4	—
							Vitesse	71	12
							Leeds U	7	2
							Tottenham H	9	—
Lee David‡	5 11	11 08	M	28 3 80	Basildon	Trainee	Tottenham H	—	—
Leonhardsen Oyvind	5 10	11 02	M	17 8 70	Kristiansund	Clausenengen	Molde	64	9
							Rosenborg	63	20
							Wimbledon	76	13
							Liverpool	37	7
							Tottenham H	22	4
McEwen Dave	6 0	11 00	F	2 11 77	Westminster	Dulwich H	Tottenham H	1	—
Nielsen Allan	5 8	11 02	M	13 3 71	Esbjerg	Esbjerg	Bayern Munich	1	—
							Sion	—	—
							Odense	55	9
							FC Copenhagen	26	3
							Brondby	42	11
							Tottenham H	97	12
							Wolverhampton W (loan)	7	2
Partin Jonatan			M	24 2 83	Kungsbacka	Edsbyns	Tottenham H	—	—
Perry Chris	5 8	10 08	D	26 4 73	Carshalton	Trainee	Wimbledon	167	?
							Tottenham H	37	1
Piercy John	5 11	11 12	M	18 9 79	Forest Gate	Trainee	Tottenham H	3	—
Saib Moussa	5 9	11 08	M	5 3 69	Theniet-El-Had		Auxerre	134	23
							Valencia	14	—
							Tottenham H	13	1
(Transferred to Al Nasr, December 1999)									
Scales John*	6 2	13 05	D	4 7 66	Harrogate		Leeds U	—	—
							Bristol R	72	2
							Wimbledon	240	11
							Liverpool	65	2
							Tottenham H	33	—
Sherwood Tim	6 1	12 09	M	2 2 69	St Albans	Trainee	Watford	32	2
							Norwich C	71	10
							Blackburn R	246	25
							Tottenham H	41	10
Taricco Mauricio	5 8	11 05	D	10 3 73	Buenos Aires		Argentinos Juniors	21	—
							Ipswich T	137	4
							Tottenham H	42	—
Thelwell Alton	6 0	12 07	D	5 9 80	London	Trainee	Tottenham H	—	—
(On loan to Hassleholm)									
Toner Ciaran	6 1	12 02	M	30 6 81	Craigavon	Trainee	Tottenham H	—	—

Tramezzani Paolo	6 1	13 06	D	30 7 70	Reggio-Emilia		Internazionale	—	—
(Transferred to Pistoese, February 2000)							Prato	29	—
							Cosenza	15	—
							Lucchese	30	1
							Internazionale	26	—
							Venezia	25	—
							Cesena	19	2
							Piacenza	57	2
							Tottenham H	6	—
Van Hughf Wayne‡			M	19 8 82	Middlesbrough		Tottenham H	—	—
Vaughan Wayne*	5 11	11 11	F	18 2 80	Barking	Trainee	Tottenham H	—	—
Vega Ramon	6 3	13 00	D	14 6 71	Olten	Trimbach	Grasshoppers	156	13
							Cagliari	14	—
							Tottenham H	54	7
Walker Ian	6 2	13 01	G	31 10 71	Watford	Trainee	Tottenham H	255	—
							Oxford U (loan)	2	—
							Ipswich T (loan)	—	—
Young Luke	6 0	12 04	M	19 7 79	Harlow	Trainee	Tottenham H	35	—

Scholars
Adams, Terry P; Attwell, Jamie W; Brennan, Martin I; Burke, Andrew J; Darbo, Roy; Di Giulantonio, Luca; Fortune, Clayton A; Lacy, Neil D; Makumbu, Destin; Quilter, James E; Saker, Blake M; Snee, George

Non-Contract
Segers, Hans

TRANMERE ROVERS

Achterberg John	6 1	13 00	G	8 7 71	Utrecht	Utrecht	NAC	9	—
							Eindhoven	32	—
						Utrecht	Tranmere R	50	—
Aldridge Paul	5 11	11 07	F	2 12 81	Liverpool	Scholar	Tranmere R	4	—
Allen Graham	6 0	12 00	D	8 4 77	Bolton	Trainee	Everton	6	—
							Tranmere R	65	5
Allison Wayne	6 0	14 07	F	16 10 68	Huddersfield		Halifax T	84	23
							Watford	7	—
							Bristol C	195	48
							Swindon T	101	31
							Huddersfield T	74	15
							Tranmere R	40	16
Black Michael	5 8	11 08	M	6 10 76	Chigwell	Trainee	Arsenal	—	—
							Millwall (loan)	13	2
							Tranmere R	22	—
Challinor Dave	6 1	12 00	D	2 10 75	Chester	Brombrough Pool	Tranmere R	112	6
Frail Stephen	5 11	12 03	D	10 8 69	Glasgow		Dundee	101	1
(Transferred to St Johnstone, February 2000)							Hearts	54	4
							Tranmere R	14	—
Gibson Neil*	5 11	11 08	M	10 10 79	St Asaph	Trainee	Tranmere R	1	—
Hay Alexander	5 10	11 05	F	14 10 81	Wirral	Scholar	Tranmere R	—	—
Hazell Reuben	5 11	11 11	D	24 4 79	Birmingham	Trainee	Aston Villa	—	—
							Tranmere R	23	1
Henry Nick	5 6	10 12	M	21 2 69	Liverpool	Trainee	Oldham Ath	273	19
							Sheffield U	16	—
							Walsall	8	—
							Tranmere R	30	1
Hill Clint	6 0	11 06	D	19 10 78	Liverpool	Trainee	Tranmere R	76	9
Hinds Richard	6 2	12 00	D	22 8 80	Sheffield	Schoolboy	Tranmere R	8	—
Holmes Tommy*	6 0	12 06	D	1 9 79	Bevington	Trainee	Tranmere R	—	—
Hume Iain‡	5 7	11 02		31 10 83	Liverpool		Tranmere R	3	—
Jones Gary#	6 3	13 05	F	10 5 75	Chester	Trainee	Tranmere R	178	28
Jones Lee*	5 8	10 06	F	29 5 73	Wrexham	Trainee	Wrexham	39	10
							Liverpool	3	—
							Crewe Alex (loan)	8	1
							Wrexham (loan)	20	9
							Wrexham (loan)	6	—
							Tranmere R (loan)	8	5
							Tranmere R	78	11
Joy Ian‡	5 10	11 00	M	14 7 81	San Diego	Trainee	Tranmere R	—	—
Kelly David#	5 11	11 10	F	25 11 65	Birmingham	Alvechurch	Walsall	147	63
							West Ham U	41	7
							Leicester C	66	22
							Newcastle U	70	35
							Wolverhampton W	83	26
							Sunderland	34	2
							Tranmere R	88	21
Koumas Jason	5 10	11 06	M	25 9 79	Wrexham	Trainee	Tranmere R	46	5
Mahon Alan	5 9	11 05	M	4 4 78	Dublin	Crumplin U	Tranmere R	120	13
Moran Andy*	5 11	11 02	F	7 10 79	Wigan	Trainee	Tranmere R	—	—
Morgan Alan	5 9	11 00	D	2 11 73	Aberystwyth	Trainee	Tranmere R	56	1
Murphy Joe	6 2	13 06	G	21 8 81	Dublin	Trainee	Tranmere R	21	—

Nixon Erict	6 4	14 00	G	4 10 62	Manchester	Curzon Ashton	Manchester C	58	—
							Wolverhampton W (loan)	16	—
							Bradford C (loan)	3	—
							Southampton (loan)	4	—
							Carlisle U (loan)	16	—
							Tranmere R (loan)	8	—
							Tranmere R	333	—
							Blackpool (loan)	20	—
							Bradford C (loan)	12	—
							Stockport Co	43	—
							Wigan Ath	3	—
							Tranmere R	2	—
Parkinson Andy	5 8	10 12	F	27 5 79	Liverpool	Liverpool	Tranmere R	84	10
Roberts Gareth	5 8	11 00	D	6 2 78	Wrexham	Trainee	Liverpool	—	—
							Tranmere R	37	1
Rogers Peter‡			M	5 12 80	Dublin	Trainee	Tranmere R	—	—
Sharps Ian	6 3	13 05	M	23 10 80	Warrington	Trainee	Tranmere R	1	—
Taylor Perry	5 11	12 02	M	29 1 81	Birkenhead	Trainee	Tranmere R	—	—
Taylor Scott	5 10	11 06	F	5 5 76	Chertsey	Staines	Millwall	28	—
							Bolton W	12	1
							Rotherham U (loan)	10	3
							Blackpool (loan)	5	1
							Tranmere R	71	12
Thompson Andy‡	5 5	10 06	D	9 11 67	Cannock	Apprentice	WBA	24	1
							Wolverhampton W	376	43
							Tranmere R	96	4
Yates Steve	5 10	12 02	D	29 1 70	Bristol	Trainee	Bristol R	197	—
							QPR	134	2
							Tranmere R	33	2

Scholars
Baker, Phillip; Climo, Daniel P; Costello, Michael R; Dreves, Thomas; Evans, Dylan T; Farren, Mark J; Garry, Spencer D; Harrison, Daniel R; Ralph, Andrew O; Taylor, Craig; Thornton, Sean; Walsham, Paul J

Non-Contract
Nixon, Eric W

Associated Schoolboys
Roberts, Paul; Thurston, Dean

Associated Schoolboys who have accepted the Club's offer of a Traineeship/Scholarship/Contract
Linwood, Paul A

WALSALL

Barras Tony	6 0	13 00	D	29 3 71	Billingham	Trainee	Hartlepool U	12	—
							Stockport Co	99	5
							Rotherham U (loan)	5	1
							York C	171	11
							Reading	6	1
							Walsall	24	4
Bica‡	6 2	12 07	F	12 3 72	Sao Paulo	Sport Boys Callao	Sunderland	—	—
							Walsall	1	—
Birch Gary			M	8 10 81	Birmingham	Trainee	Walsall	—	—
Brightwell Ian#	5 9	12 05	M	9 4 68	Lutterworth	Congleton T	Manchester C	321	18
							Coventry C	—	—
							Walsall	10	—
Brissett Jason*	5 10	12 07	F	7 9 74	Redbridge	Arsenal	Peterborough U	35	—
							Bournemouth	124	8
							Walsall	42	2
							Cheltenham T (loan)	8	—
Bukran Gabby	5 11	12 01	M	16 11 75	Eger	Xerxes	Walsall	37	2
Carter Alfie	5 10	10 05	F	13 8 80	Birmingham	Trainee	Walsall	2	—
Daley Tony‡	5 9	11 00	M	18 11 67	Birmingham	Apprentice	Aston Villa	233	31
							Wolverhampton W	21	3
							Watford	12	1
							Walsall	7	—
Emberson Carl	6 2	14 07	G	13 7 73	Epsom	Trainee	Millwall	—	—
							Colchester U (loan)	13	—
							Colchester U	179	—
							Walsall	5	—
Eyjolfsson Siggi	6 2	12 07	F	1 12 73	Reykjavik		IA Akranes	13	7
						From IA Akranes	Walsall	23	2
							Chester C (loan)	9	3
Fenton Graham#	5 10	12 12	F	22 5 74	Wallsend	Trainee	Aston Villa	32	3
							WBA (loan)	7	3
							Blackburn R	27	7
							Leicester C	34	3
							Walsall	9	1

Forrester Jamie*	5 6	10 12	F	1 11 74	Bradford	Auxerre	Leeds U	9	—
							Southend U (loan)	5	—
							Grimsby T (loan)	9	1
							Grimsby T	41	6
							Scunthorpe U	101	37
							Utrecht	1	—
							Walsall	5	—
							Northampton T (loan)	10	6
Gadsby Matthew	6 1	11 12	D	6 9 79	Sutton Coldfield	Trainee	Walsall	10	—
Hall Paul#	5 8	10 02	F	3 7 72	Manchester	Trainee	Torquay U	93	1
							Portsmouth	188	37
							Coventry C	10	—
							Bury (loan)	7	—
							Sheffield U (loan)	4	1
							WBA (loan)	4	—
							Walsall	10	4
Keates Dean	5 5	10 06	M	30 6 78	Walsall	Trainee	Walsall	113	4
Larusson Bjarni*	5 10	12 10	M	11 3 76	Iceland		IBV	60	5
							Hibernian	7	1
							Walsall	59	3
Marsh Chris	5 11	13 02	D	14 1 70	Dudley	Trainee	Walsall	385	23
Matias Pedro	6 0	12 00	M	11 10 73	Madrid		Logrones	12	—
							Macclesfield T	22	2
							Tranmere R	4	—
							Walsall	33	6
Mavrak Darko‡	6 1	12 00	M	19 1 69	Mostar		Norrkoping	26	1
							Walsall	17	2
Padula Gino	5 9	12 01	D	11 7 76	Buenos Aires	Xerex	Bristol R	—	—
							Walsall	25	—
Rammell Andy	6 1	13 12	F	10 2 67	Nuneaton	Atherstone U	Manchester U	—	—
							Barnsley	185	44
							Southend U	69	13
							Walsall	69	23
Ricketts Michael	6 2	11 12	F	4 12 78	Birmingham	Trainee	Walsall	76	14
Robins Mark#	5 8	11 08	F	22 12 69	Ashton-under-Lyne	Apprentice	Manchester U	48	11
							Norwich C	67	20
							Leicester C	56	12
							Reading (loan)	5	—
						Panionios	Manchester C	2	—
							Walsall	40	6
Roper Ian	6 3	14 00	D	20 6 77	Nuneaton	Trainee	Walsall	103	2
Scott Dion	5 11	11 00	D	24 12 80	Bearwood	Trainee	Walsall	—	—
Viveash Adrian*	6 2	12 13	D	30 9 69	Swindon	Trainee	Swindon T	54	2
							Reading (loan)	5	—
							Reading (loan)	6	—
							Barnsley (loan)	2	1
							Walsall	202	13
Vlachos Michalis*	5 11	12 08	D	20 9 67	Athens		Apollon	80	10
							Olympiakos	47	2
							AEK Athens	105	3
							Portsmouth	57	—
							Walsall	11	1
Walker James	5 11	12 13	G	9 7 73	Sutton-in-Ashfield	Trainee	Notts Co	—	—
							Walsall	232	—
Wrack Darren	5 9	12 02	F	5 5 76	Cleethorpes	Trainee	Derby Co	26	1
							Grimsby T	13	1
							Shrewsbury T (loan)	4	—
							Walsall	90	17

Scholars
Bate, Ross; Bishop, Andrew J; Bissell, James; Fitzpatrick, Andrew J; Gaunt, Ian TF; Hawley, Carl L; Hunt, David T; Jones, Craig R; Smith, Nicholas A; Stanley, Craig; Teesdale, Richard C; Wright, Mark

Non-Contract
Ayres, Lee T

WATFORD

Bakalli Adrian	6 3	13 00	M	22 11 76	Brussels	Molenbeek	Watford	2	—
Bonnot Alex	5 8	11 05	M	31 7 73	Poissy	Angers	Watford	16	—
Brooker Stephen	5 10	12 04	F	21 5 81	Newport Pagnell	Trainee	Watford	1	—
Chamberlain Alec	6 2	13 10	G	20 6 64	March	Ramsey T	Ipswich T	—	—
							Colchester U	184	—
							Everton	—	—
							Tranmere R (loan)	15	—
							Luton T	138	—
							Chelsea (loan)	—	—
							Sunderland	90	—
							Liverpool (loan)	—	—
							Watford	123	—
Cook Lee			F	3 8 82	Hammersmith	Aylesbury U	Watford	—	—
Cox Neil	6 0	12 01	D	8 10 71	Scunthorpe	Trainee	Scunthorpe U	17	1
							Aston Villa	42	3
							Middlesbrough	106	3
							Bolton W	80	7
							Watford	21	—

Name			Pos	DOB	Birthplace	Source	Club	Apps	Gls
Day Chris‡	6 3	13 06	G	28 7 75	Walthamstow	Trainee	Tottenham H	—	—
							Crystal Palace	24	—
							Watford	11	—
Easton Clint	5 11	10 04	M	1 11 77	Barking	Trainee	Watford	53	1
Fisken Gary			M	27 10 81	Watford	Scholar	Watford	—	—
Foley Dominic	6 1	12 08	F	7 7 76	Cork	St James Gate	Wolverhampton W	20	3
							Watford (loan)	8	1
							Notts Co (loan)	2	—
							Watford	12	1
Gibbs Nigel	5 7	11 06	D	20 11 65	St Albans	Apprentice	Watford	401	5
Gravelaine Xavier	6 0	11 02	F	5 10 68	Tours	Pau	Saint-Seurin	30	10
(Transferred to Le Havre, January 2000)							Laval	32	12
							Caen	69	26
							Paris St Germain	21	2
							Strasbourg	33	9
							Paris St Germain	5	1
							Guingamp	17	7
							Marseille	62	25
							Montpellier	18	3
							Watford	7	2
Gudmundsson Johann	6 0	11 07	M	5 12 77	Reykjavik		Keflavik	49	13
							Watford	22	2
Hazan Alon‡	6 1	13 08	M	14 9 67	Ashdod	Ironi Ashdod	Watford	33	2
Helguson Heidar	5 10	11 00	F	22 8 77	Akureyri	Throttur	Lillestrom	44	18
							Watford	16	6
Hyde Micah	5 10	11 07	M	10 11 74	Newham	Trainee	Cambridge U	107	13
							Watford	118	9
Ifil Jerel			D	27 6 82	London	Academy	Watford	—	—
Iroha Ben‡	5 8	11 06	D	29 11 69	Calabar	Elche	Bristol R	—	—
							Watford	10	—
Johnson Lee	5 6	10 07	M	7 6 81	Newmarket	Trainee	Watford	—	—
Johnson Richard	5 10	11 13	M	27 4 74	Kurri Kurri	Trainee	Watford	227	20
Kennedy Peter	5 10	11 11	M	10 9 73	Lisburn	Portadown	Notts Co	22	—
							Watford	98	18
Kodra Elis			M	20 5 82	Pristina	Academy	Watford	—	—
Langston Matthew	6 2	12 04	D	2 4 81	Brighton	Trainee	Watford	—	—
Lyttle Des	5 9	12 00	D	24 9 71	Wolverhampton	Worcester C	Swansea C	46	1
							Nottingham F	185	3
							Port Vale (loan)	7	—
							Watford	11	—
							WBA (loan)	9	—
Miller Charlie	5 7	12 02	M	18 3 76	Glasgow		Rangers	83	10
							Leicester C (loan)	4	—
							Watford	14	—
Mooney Tommy	5 11	12 10	F	11 8 71	Teeside North	Trainee	Aston Villa	—	—
							Scarborough	107	30
							Southend U	14	5
							Watford (loan)	10	2
							Watford	201	39
Ngonge Michel	6 0	12 00	F	10 1 67	Huy	La Louviere	Harelbeke	31	14
							Samsunspor	52	1
							Watford	45	9
							Huddersfield T (loan)	4	—
Noel-Williams Gifton	6 1	12 04	F	21 1 80	Islington	Trainee	Watford	92	19
Page Robert	6 0	12 05	D	9 9 74	Llwynipia	Trainee	Watford	180	1
Palmer Steve	6 1	12 03	M	31 3 68	Brighton	Cambridge University	Ipswich T	111	2
							Watford	196	7
Panayi James	6 1	12 06	D	24 1 80	Hammersmith	Trainee	Watford	2	—
Perpetuini David	5 9	10 00	D	26 9 79	Hitchin	Trainee	Watford	14	1
Pluck Colin	6 0	12 10	D	6 9 78	London	Trainee	Watford	1	—
(Transferred to Morton, February 2000)									
Robinson Paul	5 9	11 11	D	14 12 78	Watford	Trainee	Watford	95	2
Rosenthal Ronny‡	5 11	13 04	F	4 10 63	Haifa	Standard Liege	Luton T (loan)	—	—
							Liverpool (loan)	8	7
							Liverpool	66	14
							Tottenham H	88	4
							Watford	30	8
Smart Allan	6 2	12 04	F	8 7 74	Perth		Caledonian Th	4	—
							Preston NE	21	6
							Carlisle U (loan)	4	—
							Northampton T (loan)	1	—
							Carlisle U	44	16
							Watford	49	12
Smith Tommy	5 9	10 00	F	22 5 80	Hemel Hempstead	Trainee	Watford	31	4
Walker Herwig‡	6 1	13 00	G	4 5 72	Linz	Linz ASK	Steyr	54	—
							Watford	—	—
Ward Darren	6 3	12 11	D	13 9 78	Kenton	Trainee	Watford	18	1
							QPR (loan)	14	—
Warner David			F	27 4 81	Hillingdon	Brook House	Watford	—	—
Williams Mark	6 0	12 04	D	28 9 70	Stalybridge	Newtown	Shrewsbury T	102	3
							Chesterfield	168	12
							Watford	22	1

Name	Ht	Wt	Pos	Born	Birthplace	Source	Club	Apps	Gls
Wooter Nordin	5 6	10 08	F	24 8 76	Breda		Ajax	58	6
							Zaragoza	33	1
							Watford	20	1
Wright Nick	5 10	11 08	F	15 10 75	Derby	Trainee	Derby Co	—	—
							Carlisle U	25	5
							Watford	37	6
Yates Dean	6 2	12 08	D	26 10 67	Leicester	Apprentice	Notts Co	314	33
							Derby Co	68	3
							Watford	9	1

Scholars
Brathwaite, Daniel SC; Deamer, William D; Doyley, Lloyd C; Edghill, Luke P; Forde, Fabian W; Godfrey, Elliott J; Lee, Richard A; Neill, Thomas E; Saunders, Neil C; Sinclair, Steve; Swonnell, Sam A

WEST BROMWICH ALBION

Name	Ht	Wt	Pos	Born	Birthplace	Source	Club	Apps	Gls
Adamson Chris	6 3	12 00	G	4 11 78	Ashington	Trainee	WBA	12	—
							Mansfield T (loan)	2	—
							Halifax T (loan)	7	—
Angel Mark*	5 8	11 02	M	23 8 75	Newcastle	Trainee	Sunderland	—	—
							Oxford U	73	4
							WBA	25	1
Burgess Daryl	5 11	11 04	D	24 1 71	Birmingham	Trainee	WBA	329	10
Butler Tony	6 2	12 00	D	28 9 72	Stockport	Trainee	Gillingham	148	5
							Blackpool	99	—
							Port Vale	19	—
							WBA	7	—
Carbon Matt	6 2	12 05	D	8 6 75	Nottingham	Trainee	Lincoln C	69	10
							Derby Co	20	—
							WBA	89	5
Chambers Adam	5 10	11 08	D	20 11 80	Sandwell	Trainee	WBA	—	
Chambers James	5 10	11 08	D	20 11 80	Sandwell	Trainee	WBA	12	—
De Freitas Fabian	6 0	12 00	F	28 7 72	Paramaribo	Volendam	Bolton W	40	7
							Osasuna	25	4
							WBA	61	8
Evans Micky	6 0	12 03	F	1 1 73	Plymouth	Trainee	Plymouth Arg	163	38
							Blackburn R (loan)	—	—
							Southampton	22	4
							WBA	63	6
Flynn Sean*	5 8	11 09	M	13 3 68	Birmingham	Halesowen T	Coventry C	97	9
							Derby Co	59	3
							Stoke C (loan)	5	—
							WBA	109	8
Gabbidon Daniel	5 10	11 02	D	8 8 79	Cwmbran	Trainee	WBA	20	—
Hughes Lee	5 10	11 06	F	22 5 76	Birmingham	Kidderminster H	WBA	115	57
Jensen Brian	6 1	12 04	G	8 6 75	Copenhagen		AZ	1	—
							WBA	12	—
Lezzi Massamiliano			M	1 2 81	Rome		WBA	—	—
Mardon Paul	6 0	11 10	D	14 9 69	Bristol	Trainee	Bristol C	42	—
							Doncaster R (loan)	3	—
							Birmingham C	64	—
							WBA	139	3
							Oldham Ath (loan)	12	3
Maresca Enzo	5 11	12 00	M	10 2 80	Salerno		WBA	47	5
(Transferred to Juventus, January 2000)									
McDermott Andy*	5 9	11 03	D	24 3 77	Sydney	Aust Inst of Sport	QPR	6	2
							WBA	52	1
Morris Elliott			M	4 5 81	Belfast	Trainee	WBA	—	—
Oliver Adam	5 9	11 02	M	25 10 80	Sandwell	Trainee	WBA	16	1
Potter Graham*	6 1	11 12	D	20 5 75	Solihull	Trainee	Birmingham C	25	2
							Wycombe W (loan)	3	—
							Stoke C	45	1
							Southampton	8	—
							WBA	43	—
							Northampton T (loan)	4	—
							Reading (loan)	4	—
Quinn James	6 1	12 10	F	15 12 74	Coventry	Trainee	Birmingham C	4	—
							Blackpool	151	37
							Stockport Co (loan)	1	—
							WBA	93	8
Raven Paul	6 1	12 11	D	28 7 70	Salisbury	School	Doncaster R	52	4
							WBA	259	15
							Doncaster R (loan)	7	—
							Rotherham U (loan)	11	2
Richards Justin	6 0	11 10	F	16 10 80	Sandwell	Trainee	WBA	1	—
Santos Georges#	6 3	14 08	D	15 8 70	Marseille	Toulon	Tranmere R	47	2
							WBA	8	—
Sigurdsson Larus	6 0	13 11	D	4 6 73	Akureyri	Thor	Stoke C	200	7
							WBA	27	—

Name				DOB	Birthplace	Prev club	Club	Apps	Gls
Sneekes Richard	5 11	12 03	M	30 10 68	Amsterdam		Ajax	3	—
							Volendam	31	7
							Fortuna Sittard	126	20
					Locarno		Bolton W	55	7
							WBA	182	28
Taylor Bob	5 11	13 05	F	3 2 67	Easington	Horden CW	Leeds U	42	9
							Bristol C	106	50
							WBA	238	96
							Bolton W (loan)	12	3
							Bolton W	65	18
							WBA	8	5
Townsend Andy	6 0	13 05	M	27 7 63	Maidstone	Weymouth	Southampton	83	5
							Norwich C	71	8
							Chelsea	110	12
							Aston Villa	134	8
							Middlesbrough	77	3
							WBA	18	—
Van Blerk Jason	6 1	13 00	D	16 3 68	Sydney	Go Ahead	Millwall	73	2
							Manchester C	19	—
							WBA	73	1

Scholars
Adams, Richard; Adams, Ross I; Ball, Jamie C; Briggs, Mark J; Bruce, Kevin; Collins, Matthew J; Fox, James E; McFarlane, Dwaine W; Mkandawire, Tamika P; Perry, Joshua; Scott, Mark; Watson, Anthony C

Player who does not hold a current contract but his registration has been retained by the club
Blake, Mosiah N

WEST HAM UNITED

Name				DOB	Birthplace	Prev club	Club	Apps	Gls
Abou Samassi*	6 1	12 08	F	4 4 73	Gagnoa		Martigues	23	7
							Lyon	58	4
							Cannes	37	5
							West Ham U	22	5
							Ipswich T (loan)	5	1
							Walsall (loan)	8	—
Alexander Gary	6 0	12 00	F	15 8 79	South London	Trainee	West Ham U	—	—
							Exeter C (loan)	37	16
Angus Stevland	6 0	12 00	D	16 9 80	Essex	Trainee	West Ham U	—	—
Berkovic Eyal	5 7	10 02	M	2 4 72	Haifa		Maccabi Haifa	128	25
(Transferred to Celtic, July 1999)							Southampton	28	4
							West Ham U	65	10
Briggs Ryan*			M	6 4 81	Maidenhead	Trainee	West Ham U	—	—
Britton Leon			M	16 9 82	London	Trainee	West Ham U	—	—
Bullard Jimmy	5 10	11 07	M	23 10 78	Newham	Gravesend & N	West Ham U	—	—
Byrne Shaun	5 9	11 08	D	21 1 81	Taplow	Trainee	West Ham U	1	—
							Bristol R (loan)	2	—
Bywater Steve	6 2	12 00	G	7 6 81	Manchester	Trainee	Rochdale	—	—
							West Ham U	4	—
							Wycombe W (loan)	2	—
							Hull C (loan)	4	—
Carrick Michael	6 0	11 10	M	28 7 81	Wallsend	Trainee	West Ham U	8	1
							Swindon T (loan)	6	2
							Birmingham C (loan)	2	—
Charles Gary	5 9	11 03	D	13 4 70	East London	Trainee	Nottingham F	56	1
							Leicester C (loan)	8	—
							Derby Co	61	3
							Aston Villa	79	3
							Benfica	4	1
							West Ham U	4	—
Cole Joe	5 7	9 08	M	8 11 81	Islington	Trainee	West Ham U	30	1
Coyne Chris‡	6 1	13 10	D	20 12 78	Brisbane	Porth SC	West Ham U	1	—
							Brentford (loan)	7	—
							Southend U (loan)	1	—
Defoe Jermaine	5 7	10 04	F	7 10 82	Beckton	Charlton Ath	West Ham U	—	—
Di Canio Paolo	5 9	11 09	F	9 7 68	Rome		Lazio	—	—
							Ternana	27	2
							Lazio	54	4
							Juventus	78	6
							Napoli	26	5
							Juventus	—	—
							AC Milan	37	6
							Celtic	26	12
							Sheffield W	41	15
							West Ham U	43	19
Dicks Julian‡	5 10	13 00	D	8 8 68	Bristol	Apprentice	Birmingham C	89	1
							West Ham U	159	29
							Liverpool	24	3
							West Ham U	103	21
Etherington Craig	6 0	11 10	M	16 9 79	Basildon	Trainee	West Ham U	—	—
						Trainee	Halifax T (loan)	4	—
							Plymouth Arg (loan)	5	—
Ferdinand Rio	6 2	12 00	D	8 11 78	Peckham	Trainee	West Ham U	115	2
							Bournemouth (loan)	10	—

Name							Club		
Ferrante Michael			M	28 4 81	Melbourne	Australia IOS	West Ham U	—	—
Feuer Ian	6 6	15 06	G	20 5 71	Las Vegas	Los Angeles Salsa	West Ham U	—	—
							Peterborough U (loan)	16	—
							Luton T	97	—
							New England Rev	26	—
							Colorado Rapids	19	—
							Cardiff C	—	—
							West Ham U	3	—
Foe Marc Vivien‡	6 4	12 07	M	1 5 75	Yaounde	Canon Yaounde	Lens	85	11
							West Ham U	38	1
Forbes Terrell	6 0	12 05	D	17 8 81	Southwark		West Ham U	—	—
						Trainee	Bournemouth (loan)	3	—
Forrest Craig	6 4	14 04	G	20 9 67	Vancouver	Apprentice	Ipswich T	263	—
							Colchester U (loan)	11	—
							Chelsea (loan)	3	—
							West Ham U	26	—
Garcia Richard			F	4 9 81	Perth	Trainee	West Ham U	—	
Hislop Shaka	6 4	14 04	G	22 2 69	Hackney	Howard Univ	Reading	104	—
							Newcastle U	53	—
							West Ham U	59	—
Holligan Gavin	5 10	13 00	F	13 6 80	Lambeth	Kingstonian	West Ham U	1	—
							Leyton Orient (loan)	1	—
Iriekpen Ezomo	6 1	12 02	D	14 5 82	East London	Trainee	West Ham U	—	—
Kanoute Frederic	6 3	12 04	F	2 9 77	Ste. Foy-Les-Lyon		Lyon	41	9
							West Ham U	8	2
Keller Marc	5 10	11 05	M	14 1 68	Colmar		Mulhouse	118	15
							Strasbourg	149	35
							Karlsruhe	61	13
							West Ham U	44	5
Kitson Paul	5 11	10 12	F	9 1 71	Murton	Trainee	Leicester C	50	6
							Derby Co	105	36
							Newcastle U	36	10
							West Ham U	54	15
							Charlton Ath (loan)	6	1
Lampard Frank	6 0	11 12	M	20 6 78	Romford	Trainee	West Ham U	118	16
							Swansea C (loan)	9	1
Laurie Steve			D	30 10 82	Melbourne		West Ham U	—	
Lomas Steve	6 0	12 08	M	14 3 72	Hanover	Trainee	Manchester C	111	8
							West Ham U	95	4
Margas Javier	6 1	13 00	D	10 5 69	Santiago	Colo Colo	America (Mexico)	9	1
							Univ Catolica	18	2
							West Ham U	21	1
McCann Grant			M	14 4 80	Belfast	Trainee	West Ham U	—	
Minto Scott	5 10	10 00	D	6 8 71	Wirral	Trainee	Charlton Ath	180	7
							Chelsea	54	4
							Benfica	31	—
							West Ham U	15	—
							Benfica	10	—
							West Ham U	18	—
Moncur John	5 8	9 10	M	22 9 66	Mile End	Apprentice	Tottenham H	21	1
							Cambridge U (loan)	4	—
							Doncaster R (loan)	4	—
							Portsmouth (loan)	7	—
							Brentford (loan)	5	1
							Ipswich T (loan)	6	—
							Nottingham F (loan)	—	—
							Swindon T	58	5
							West Ham U	133	6
Newton Adam	5 10	11 00	D	4 12 80	Ascot	Trainee	West Ham U	2	—
							Portsmouth (loan)	3	—
O'Reilly Alex			G	15 9 79	Epping	Trainee	West Ham U	—	—
							Northampton T (loan)	7	—
Omoyinmi Emmanuel*	5 7	10 01	M	28 12 77	Nigeria	Trainee	West Ham U	9	2
							Bournemouth (loan)	7	—
							Dundee U (loan)	4	—
							Leyton Orient (loan)	4	1
							Gillingham (loan)	9	3
							Scunthorpe U (loan)	6	1
							Barnet (loan)	6	—
Pearce Ian	6 3	14 04	D	7 5 74	Bury St Edmunds	Schoolboy	Chelsea	4	—
							Blackburn R	62	2
							West Ham U	64	3
Pearce Stuart	5 10	12 13	D	24 4 62	Shepherds Bush	Wealdstone	Coventry C	51	4
							Nottingham F	401	63
							Newcastle U	37	—
							West Ham U	8	—
Potts Steve	5 7	10 11	D	7 5 67	Hartford (USA)	Apprentice	West Ham U	391	1
Purches Stephen*			M	14 1 80	Essex	Trainee	West Ham U	—	—
Riza Omer			F	8 11 79	Edmonton	Trainee	Arsenal	—	—
							West Ham U	—	—

Ruddock Neil	6 2	12 12	D	9 5 68	Wandsworth	Apprentice	Millwall	—	—
							Tottenham H	9	
							Millwall	2	1
							Southampton	107	9
							Tottenham H	38	3
							Liverpool	115	11
							QPR (loan)	7	—
							West Ham U	42	2
Sinclair Trevor	5 10	12 05	F	2 3 73	Dulwich	Trainee	Blackpool	112	15
							QPR	167	16
							West Ham U	86	21
Sjolund Danny			M	22 4 83	Sweden		West Ham U	—	—
Stimac Igor	6 2	13 00	D	6 9 67	Metkovic	Cibalia Vinkovci	Hajduk Split	1	—
							Cadiz	62	4
							Hajduk Split	21	2
							Derby Co	84	3
							West Ham U	24	1
Wanchope Paulo	6 4	12 00	F	31 7 76	Heredia	Herediano	Derby Co	72	23
							West Ham U	35	12
Williams Thomas			M	8 7 80	Carshalton	Walton & Hersham	West Ham U	—	—

Scholars
Birch, Francis A; Brooker, Matthew A; Chandler, Martin A; Clark, Steven T; Cleaver, Dean; Foyewa, Amos; Jjunju, Moses; McMahon, William C; Riddle, Louis S; Sealey, Joe HJ; Smith, Dean G; Taylor, Sam AJ; Tobolewski, Ross J; Uddin, Anwar

Non-Contract
Sealey, Leslie J

WIGAN ATHLETIC

Balmer Stuart	6 0	13 02	D	20 9 69	Falkirk	Celtic BC	Celtic	—	—
							Charlton Ath	227	8
							Wigan Ath	77	3
Barlow Stuart#	5 10	11 03	F	16 7 68	Liverpool	School	Everton	71	10
							Rotherham U (loan)	—	—
							Oldham Ath	93	31
							Wigan Ath	83	40
Bowen Mark‡	5 8	11 11	D	7 12 63	Neath	Apprentice	Tottenham H	17	2
							Norwich C	320	24
							West Ham U	17	1
						Shimizu	Charlton Ath	42	—
							Wigan Ath	7	—
Bradshaw Carl#	5 10	12 00	D	2 10 68	Sheffield	Apprentice	Sheffield W	32	4
							Barnsley (loan)	6	1
							Manchester C	5	—
							Sheffield U	147	8
							Norwich C	65	2
							Wigan Ath	93	8
Carroll Roy	6 2	13 12	G	30 9 77	Enniskillen	Trainee	Hull C	46	—
							Wigan Ath	106	—
De Zeeuw Arjan	6 3	13 07	D	16 4 70	Castricum	Vitesse 22	Telstar	102	5
							Barnsley	138	7
							Wigan Ath	39	3
Fitzhenry Neil*	6 0	12 06	D	24 9 78	Billinge	Trainee	Wigan Ath	4	—
Green Scott#	5 10	12 09	D	15 1 70	Walsall	Trainee	Derby Co	—	—
							Bolton W	220	25
							Wigan Ath	108	3
Greenall Colin†	5 11	12 12	D	30 12 63	Billinge	Apprentice	Blackpool	183	9
							Gillingham	62	4
							Oxford U	67	2
							Bury (loan)	3	—
							Bury	68	5
							Preston NE	29	1
							Chester C	42	1
							Lincoln C	43	3
							Wigan Ath	162	14
Griffiths Gareth	6 4	14 01	D	10 4 70	Winsford	Rhyl	Port Vale	94	4
							Shrewsbury T (loan)	6	—
							Wigan Ath	36	1
Haworth Simon	6 1	14 02	F	30 3 77	Cardiff	Trainee	Cardiff C	37	9
							Coventry C	11	—
							Wigan Ath	60	23
Jones Graeme	6 0	13 11	F	13 3 70	Gateshead	Bridlington T	Doncaster R	92	26
(Transferred to St Johnstone, November 1999)							Wigan Ath	96	44
Kilford Ian#	5 10	11 04	M	6 10 73	Bristol	Trainee	Nottingham F	1	—
							Wigan Ath (loan)	8	3
							Wigan Ath	169	27
Lee David*	5 7	11 00	F	5 11 67	Whitefield	Blackburn Schools	Bury	208	35
							Southampton	20	—
							Bolton W	155	17
							Wigan Ath	83	11
							Blackpool (loan)	9	1
Liddell Andy	5 8	11 05	F	28 6 73	Leeds	Trainee	Barnsley	198	34
							Wigan Ath	69	18
Martinez Roberto	5 11	12 03	M	13 7 73	Balaguer	Balaguer	Wigan Ath	153	17

Name	Ht	Wt	Pos	DOB	Birthplace	Signed from	Club	Apps	Gls
McGibbon Pat#	6 2	13 09	D	6 9 73	Lurgan	Portadown	Manchester U	—	—
							Swansea C (loan)	1	—
							Wigan Ath (loan)	10	1
							Wigan Ath	105	7
McLaughlin Brian	5 5	9 02	M	14 5 74	Bellshill		Celtic	75	5
							Airdrieonians (loan)	—	—
							Dundee U	3	—
							Wigan Ath	—	—
McLoughlin Alan	5 8	10 10	M	20 4 67	Manchester	Local	Manchester U	—	—
							Swindon T	9	—
							Torquay U	24	4
							Swindon T	97	19
							Southampton	24	1
							Aston Villa (loan)	—	—
							Portsmouth	309	54
							Wigan Ath	15	1
Nicholls Kevin	5 11	12 04	M	2 1 79	Newham	Trainee	Charlton Ath	12	1
							Brighton & HA (loan)	4	1
							Wigan Ath	8	—
O'Neill Michael*	5 11	12 04	M	5 7 69	Portadown	Coleraine	Newcastle U	48	15
							Dundee U	64	11
							Hibernian	98	19
							Coventry C	5	—
							Reading (loan)	9	1
							Wigan Ath	66	2
Peron Jeff*	5 8	10 04	M	11 10 65	St Omer	Caen	Walsall	38	1
							Portsmouth	48	3
							Wigan Ath	23	—
Porter Andy	5 9	12 03	M	17 9 68	Holmes Chapel	Trainee	Port Vale	357	22
							Wigan Ath	21	1
							Mansfield T (loan)	5	—
							Chester C (loan)	16	—
Redfearn Neil	5 8	12 00	M	20 6 65	Dewsbury	Nottingham F	Bolton W	35	1
							Lincoln C (loan)	10	1
							Lincoln C	90	12
							Doncaster R	46	14
							Crystal Palace	57	10
							Watford	24	3
							Oldham Ath	62	16
							Barnsley	292	71
							Charlton Ath	30	3
							Bradford C	17	1
							Wigan Ath	12	6
Roberts Neil	5 10	11 02	F	7 4 78	Wrexham	Trainee	Wrexham	75	17
							Wigan Ath	9	1
Sharp Kevin	5 9	11 04	D	19 9 74	Ontario	Auxerre	Leeds U	17	—
							Wigan Ath	145	10
Sheridan Darren	5 6	11 04	M	8 12 67	Manchester	Winsford U	Barnsley	171	5
							Wigan Ath	31	3
Smeets Jorg‡	5 6	10 04	F	5 11 70	Bussum		Heracles	8	2
							Wigan Ath	24	3
							Chester C (loan)	3	—
Stillie Derek	6 0	12 05	G	3 12 73	Cumnock		Aberdeen	23	—
							Wigan Ath	13	—

Trainees
Addison, Carl W; Court, Mark; Cunningham, Craig J; Ellis, Lee P; Greenwood, Stephen; Haley, Danny; Johnson, Ian R; Johnson, Joel; Kay, Stephen B; McMahon, Francis; Mitchell, Paul A; Morris, Andrew; Pitts, Douglas J; Rae, Gary J; Speakman, Craig A; Spearritt, Thomas J

Non-Contract
Greenall, Colin A

Associated Schoolboys who have accepted the Club's offer of a Traineeship/Scholarship/Contract
Clegg, Michael J; Lee, Paul K; Robinson Nigel T

WIMBLEDON

Name	Ht	Wt	Pos	DOB	Birthplace	Signed from	Club	Apps	Gls
Agyemang Patrick	6 1	12 00	F	29 9 80	Walthamstow	Trainee	Wimbledon	—	—
							Brentford (loan)	12	—
Ainsworth Gareth	5 9	11 00	M	10 5 73	Blackburn	Blackburn R	Preston NE	5	—
							Cambridge U	4	1
							Preston NE	82	12
							Lincoln C	83	37
							Port Vale	55	10
							Wimbledon	10	2
Andersen Trond	6 0	11 06	M	6 1 75	Kristiansund	Clausenengen	Molde	105	4
							Wimbledon	36	—
Andresen Martin	5 11	11 04	M	2 2 77	Norway		Moss	24	7
							Viking	26	8
							Stabaek	47	16
							Wimbledon	14	1
Ardley Neal	5 11	11 09	M	1 9 72	Epsom	Trainee	Wimbledon	179	12
Badir Walid	5 10	12 07	M	12 3 74	Kafr Kasm		Hapoel P-T	153	19
							Wimbledon	21	1
Blackwell Dean	6 1	12 10	D	5 12 69	Camden	Trainee	Wimbledon	199	1
							Plymouth Arg (loan)	7	—

Name	Ht	Wt	Pos	DOB	Birthplace	Source	Club	Apps	Gls
Castledine Stewart*	6 1	12 00	M	22 1 73	Wandsworth	Trainee	Wimbledon	28	4
							Wycombe W (loan)	7	3
Cort Carl	6 4	12 07	F	1 11 77	Southwark	Trainee	Wimbledon	73	16
							Lincoln C (loan)	6	1
Cunningham Kenny	5 11	11 04	D	28 6 71	Dublin	Tolka R	Millwall	136	1
							Wimbledon	201	—
Davis Kelvin	6 1	11 02	G	29 9 76	Bedford	Trainee	Luton T	92	—
							Torquay U (loan)	2	—
							Hartlepool U (loan)	2	—
							Wimbledon	—	—
Earle Robbie*	5 9	10 10	M	27 1 65	Newcastle-Under-Lyme	Stoke C	Port Vale	294	77
							Wimbledon	284	59
Ekoku Efan	6 2	12 00	F	8 6 67	Manchester	Sutton U	Bournemouth	62	21
(Transferred to Grasshoppers, August 1999)							Norwich C	37	15
							Wimbledon	123	37
Euell Jason	5 11	11 02	F	6 2 77	Lambeth	Trainee	Wimbledon	105	22
Favata Seb*	5 10	11 07	D	18 10 80	Carshalton	Trainee	Wimbledon	—	—
Flinn Stephen‡			D	15 10 80	Raynes Park	Trainee	Wimbledon	—	—
Francis Damien	6 0	10 10	M	27 2 79	Wandsworth	Trainee	Wimbledon	11	—
Gayle Marcus	6 1	12 09	F	27 9 70	Hammersmith	Trainee	Brentford	156	22
							Wimbledon	204	34
Gier Robert	5 9	11 07	M	6 1 80	Ascot	Trainee	Wimbledon	—	—
Goodman Jon‡	6 0	12 03	F	2 6 71	Walthamstow	Bromley	Millwall	109	35
							Wimbledon	60	11
Gray Wayne	5 10	11 10	F	7 11 80	South London	Trainee	Wimbledon	1	—
							Swindon T (loan)	12	2
Halliwell Bryn‡	5 11	12 00	G	1 1 80	Leatherhead	Trainee	Wimbledon	—	—
Hartson John	6 0	13 07	F	5 4 75	Swansea	Trainee	Luton T	54	11
							Arsenal	53	14
							West Ham U	60	24
							Wimbledon	30	11
Hawkins Peter	6 0	11 04	D	19 9 78	Maidstone	Trainee	Wimbledon	—	—
							York C (loan)	14	—
Heald Paul	6 2	12 05	G	20 9 68	Wath-on-Dearne	Trainee	Sheffield U	—	—
							Leyton Orient	176	—
							Coventry C (loan)	2	—
							Crystal Palace (loan)	—	—
							Swindon T (loan)	2	—
							Wimbledon	21	—
Hinds Leigh	5 9	10 10	F	17 8 78	Beckenham	Trainee	Wimbledon	—	—
Hodges Danny*	6 0	12 07	D	14 9 76	Greenwich	Trainee	Wimbledon	—	—
Hreidarsson Hermann	6 3	11 12	D	11 7 74	Iceland		IBV	66	5
							Crystal Palace	37	2
							Brentford	41	6
							Wimbledon	24	1
Hughes Michael	5 6	10 08	M	2 8 71	Larne	Carrick R	Manchester C	26	1
							Strasbourg	83	9
							West Ham U (loan)	17	2
							West Ham U (loan)	28	—
							West Ham U	38	3
							Wimbledon	79	8
Jupp Duncan	6 0	12 11	D	25 1 75	Guildford	Trainee	Fulham	105	2
							Wimbledon	24	—
Kimble Alan	5 10	12 04	D	6 8 66	Poole		Charlton Ath	6	—
							Exeter C (loan)	1	—
							Cambridge U	299	24
							Wimbledon	181	—
Leaburn Carl	6 3	13 00	F	30 3 69	Lewisham	Apprentice	Charlton Ath	322	53
							Northampton T (loan)	9	—
							Wimbledon	56	4
Lund Andreas	6 1	11 04	F	7 5 75	Kristiancand		Start	37	13
							Molde	59	42
							Wimbledon	12	2
McAllister Brian*	5 11	12 05	D	30 11 70	Glasgow	Trainee	Wimbledon	85	—
							Plymouth Arg (loan)	8	—
							Crewe Alex (loan)	13	1
Mensing Simon	5 10	11 06	M	27 6 82	Wolfenbuttel		Wimbledon	—	—
Owusu Ansah	5 11	11 02	M	22 11 79	Hackney	Trainee	Wimbledon	—	—
(On loan to Raith R)									
Pedersen Tore	6 0	11 00	D	29 9 69	Fredrikstad	Fredrikstad	IFK Gothenburg	64	—
							Brann	22	—
							Oldham Ath	10	—
							Brann	1	—
						Sanfrecce	St Pauli	37	—
							Blackburn R	5	—
							Eintracht Frankfurt	20	1
							Wimbledon	6	—
Roberts Andy	5 10	13 00	M	20 3 74	Dartford	Trainee	Millwall	138	5
							Crystal Palace	108	2
							Wimbledon	56	3
Sullivan Neil*	6 0	12 01	G	24 2 70	Sutton	Trainee	Wimbledon	181	—
							Crystal Palace (loan)	1	—
Tapp Alex	5 8	11 10	M	7 6 82	Redhill	Trainee	Wimbledon	—	—

Name							Club	Apps	Gls
Thatcher Ben	5 11	12 00	D	30 11 75	Swindon	Trainee	Millwall	90	1
							Wimbledon	86	—
Thurgood Sean*	6 2	12 09	D	1 2 80	Hayling Island	Alton T	Wimbledon	—	—
Waehler Kjetil	5 10	11 00	M	16 3 76	Oslo		Lyn	88	6
							Wimbledon	—	—
Williamson Russ*	5 4	8 10	D	17 3 80	Epping	Trainee	Wimbledon	—	—
Willmott Chris	5 11	10 12	D	30 9 77	Bedford	Trainee	Luton T	14	—
							Wimbledon	7	—
Willy Mark*	5 11	12 00	D	5 8 80	Sidcup	Trainee	Wimbledon	—	—

Scholars
Cook, Paul T; Gore, Shane S; Innocent, Anton L; Jenkins, Neil; Leigertwood, Mikele B; Lewington, Craig J; McAnuff, Joel J; Morgan, Lionel A; Murphy, David C; O'Shea, Anthony S; Oflynn, Stephen J; Okikiolu, Samuel K; Shirley, Mark D; Sloma, Samuel M; Taylor, Glenn J; Unal, Mehmet

WOLVERHAMPTON WANDERERS

Name							Club	Apps	Gls
Akinbiyi Ade	6 1	13 09	F	10 10 74	Hackney	Trainee	Norwich C	49	3
							Hereford U (loan)	4	2
							Brighton & HA (loan)	7	4
							Gillingham	63	28
							Bristol C	47	21
							Wolverhampton W	37	16
Andrews Keith	5 10	12 04	M	13 9 80	Dublin	Trainee	Wolverhampton W	2	—
Barrett Shane	5 10	11 00	F	23 11 81	Luton	Trainee	Wolverhampton W	—	—
Bazeley Darren	5 11	10 09	D	5 10 72	Northampton	Trainee	Watford	240	21
							Wolverhampton W	46	3
Branch Michael	5 10	11 09	F	18 10 78	Liverpool	Trainee	Everton	41	3
							Manchester C (loan)	4	—
							Wolverhampton W	27	6
Bull Steve*	5 11	11 04	F	28 3 65	Tipton	Apprentice	WBA	4	2
							Wolverhampton W	474	250
Corica Steve‡	5 8	10 10	M	24 3 73	Cairns	Marconi	Leicester C	16	2
							Wolverhampton W	100	5
Crowe Seamie	5 7	11 07	M	18 11 80	Galway	Trainee	Wolverhampton W	—	—
Curle Keith	6 0	12 07	D	14 11 63	Bristol	Apprentice	Bristol R	32	4
							Torquay U	16	5
							Bristol C	121	1
							Reading	40	—
							Wimbledon	93	3
							Manchester C	171	11
							Wolverhampton W	150	9
Downes Lee	6 0	12 00	M	27 2 83	Wolverhampton	Trainee	Wolverhampton W	—	—
Emblen Neil	6 1	13 03	M	19 6 71	Bromley	Sittingbourne	Millwall	12	—
							Wolverhampton W	95	9
							Crystal Palace	13	—
							Wolverhampton W	79	7
Flo Havard	6 2	13 08	F	4 4 70	Volda	Sogndal	Aarhus	53	27
							Werder Bremen	55	5
							Wolverhampton W	38	9
Green Ryan	5 8	10 10	D	20 10 80	Cardiff	Danes Court	Wolverhampton W	1	—
Hackett Stephen‡			D	17 9 80	Dublin	Trainee	Wolverhampton W	—	—
Hagan Conor	5 10	11 07	D	31 3 82	Belfast	Trainee	Wolverhampton W	—	—
Jones Mark*	5 10	12 07	F	7 9 79	Walsall	Trainee	Wolverhampton W	3	—
							Cheltenham T (loan)	3	—
Larkin Colin	5 9	11 07	F	27 4 82	Dundalk	Trainee	Wolverhampton W	1	—
Leonard Gerard	5 9	11 04	F	7 7 82	Drogheda	Trainee	Wolverhampton W	—	—
Lescott Jolean	6 2	13 00	D	16 8 82	Birmingham	Trainee	Wolverhampton W	—	—
Loughlin Paul	5 10	11 00	D	5 10 81	Dublin	Stella Maris	Wolverhampton W	—	—
Middleton Darren‡	6 1	11 13	F	28 12 78	Lichfield	Trainee	Aston Villa	—	—
							Wolverhampton W	—	—
Murray Matt	6 3	13 07	G	2 5 81	Solihull	Trainee	Wolverhampton W	—	—
Muscat Kevin	5 11	11 07	D	7 8 73	Crawley	South Melbourne	Crystal Palace	53	2
							Wolverhampton W	106	11
Naylor Lee	5 8	12 00	D	19 3 80	Bloxwich	Trainee	Wolverhampton W	69	3
Ndah George	6 1	11 04	F	23 12 74	Dulwich	Trainee	Crystal Palace	78	8
							Bournemouth (loan)	12	2
							Gillingham (loan)	4	—
							Swindon T	67	14
							Wolverhampton W	4	—
Niestroj Robert	5 10	11 03	M	2 12 74	Oppeln	Fortuna Dusseldorf	Wolverhampton W	6	—
Oakes Michael	6 2	14 07	G	30 10 73	Northwich	Trainee	Aston Villa	51	—
							Scarborough (loan)	1	—
							Tranmere R (loan)	—	—
							Wolverhampton W	28	—
Osborn Simon	5 10	11 04	M	9 1 72	New Addington	Apprentice	Crystal Palace	55	5
							Reading	32	5
							QPR	9	1
							Wolverhampton W	142	11

Pollet Ludovic	6 0	12 06	D	18 6 70	Vieux-conde		Cannes	38	3
							Le Havre	102	—
							Wolverhampton W	39	5
Proudlock Adam	6 0	13 00	M	9 5 81	Wellington	Trainee	Wolverhampton W	—	—
Robinson Carl	5 10	12 10	M	13 10 76	Llandrindod Wells	Trainee	Wolverhampton W	101	14
							Shrewsbury T (loan)	4	—
Sedgley Steve*	6 1	13 13	D	26 5 68	Enfield	Apprentice	Coventry C	84	3
							Tottenham H	164	9
							Ipswich T	105	15
							Wolverhampton W	101	8
Simms Gordon	6 2	12 06	D	23 3 81	Larne	Trainee	Wolverhampton W	—	—
Simpson Paul	5 8	11 11	M	26 7 66	Carlisle	Apprentice	Manchester C	121	18
							Oxford U	144	43
							Derby Co	186	48
							Sheffield U (loan)	6	—
							Wolverhampton W	52	6
							Walsall (loan)	10	1
Sinton Andy	5 7	10 07	M	19 3 66	Newcastle	Apprentice	Cambridge U	93	13
							Brentford	149	28
							QPR	160	22
							Sheffield W	60	3
							Tottenham H	83	6
							Wolverhampton W	35	—
Stowell Mike	6 2	13 10	G	19 4 65	Portsmouth	Leyland Motors	Preston NE	—	—
							Everton	—	—
							Chester C (loan)	14	—
							York C (loan)	6	—
							Manchester C (loan)	14	—
							Port Vale (loan)	7	—
							Wolverhampton W (loan)	7	—
							Preston NE (loan)	2	—
							Wolverhampton W	377	—
Taylor Scott#	5 9	11 05	M	23 11 70	Portsmouth	Trainee	Reading	207	24
							Leicester C	64	6
							Wolverhampton W	28	3
Tudor Shane	5 8	11 00	M	10 2 82	Wolverhampton	Trainee	Wolverhampton W	—	—
Williams Adrian*	6 2	12 06	D	16 8 71	Reading	Trainee	Reading	196	14
							Wolverhampton W	27	—
							Reading (loan)	15	1

Trainees
Clegg, Dean R; Easter, Jermaine M; Eccleston, Neil G; Lee, Marc CW; McQuade, Scott; Melligan, John J

Scholars
Clyde, Mark G; Coleman, Kenneth J; Dickson, Andrew W; Gilmore, Craig C; Kerr, Aaron G; Morrow, Andrew J; Tower, Andrew R; Ward, Graham W; Willis, James R

Associated Schoolboys
Clark, David; Rollins, Mark

Associated Schoolboys who have accepted the Club's offer of a Traineeship/Scholarship/Contract
Bampfield, Steve D; Clark, Nicholas; Danks, Mark; Jones, Jimmi L; Slater, Christopher; Solly, Lewis

Player who does not hold a current contract but his registration has been retained by the club
Mitchell, Patrick J

WREXHAM

Barrett Paul	5 9	11 04	M	13 4 78	Newcastle	Trainee	Newcastle U	—	—
							Wrexham	28	2
Brace Deryn*	5 7	10 12	D	15 3 75	Haverfordwest	Trainee	Norwich C	—	—
							Wrexham	88	2
Carey Brian	6 3	13 02	D	31 5 68	Cork	Cork C	Manchester U	—	—
							Wrexham (loan)	3	—
							Wrexham (loan)	13	1
							Leicester C	58	1
							Wrexham	160	4
Cartwright Mark	6 2	13 06	G	13 1 73	Chester	York C	Wrexham	37	—
Chalk Martyn	5 6	11 03	F	30 8 69	Swindon	Louth U	Derby Co	7	1
							Stockport Co	43	6
							Wrexham	136	6
Connolly Karl#	5 10	11 01	F	9 2 70	Prescot	Napoli (Liverpool)	Wrexham	358	88
Cooper Steve*	5 9	11 03	D	10 12 79	Pontypridd		Wrexham	—	—
Dearden Kevin	5 11	12 06	G	8 3 70	Luton	Trainee	Tottenham H	1	—
							Cambridge U (loan)	15	—
							Hartlepool U (loan)	10	—
							Oxford U (loan)	—	—
							Swindon T (loan)	1	—
							Peterborough U (loan)	7	—
							Hull C (loan)	3	—
							Rochdale (loan)	2	—
							Birmingham C (loan)	12	—
							Portsmouth (loan)	—	—
							Brentford	205	—
							Barnet (loan)	1	—
							Huddersfield T (loan)	—	—
							Wrexham	45	—

Player							Club	Apps	Gls
Edwards Jake*	6 1	12 08	F	11 5 76	Manchester	USA College	Wrexham	11	2
Faulconbridge Craig	6 1	13 00	F	20 4 78	Nuneaton	Trainee	Coventry C	—	—
							Dunfermline Ath	13	1
							Coventry C	—	—
							Hull C (loan)	10	—
							Wrexham	35	8
Ferguson Darren	5 10	11 10	M	9 2 72	Glasgow	Trainee	Manchester U	27	—
							Wolverhampton W	117	4
							Wrexham	37	4
Gibson Robin	5 7	10 07	F	15 11 79	Crewe	Trainee	Wrexham	31	2
Hannon Kevin†	5 11	11 05	D	4 5 80	Whiston	Trainee	Wrexham	1	—
Hardy Phil	5 7	11 08	D	9 4 73	Chester	Trainee	Wrexham	336	1
Humes Tony*	6 0	12 00	D	19 3 66	Blyth	Apprentice	Ipswich T	120	10
							Wrexham	199	8
Jarrett Jason‡	6 0	12 04	M	14 9 79	Bury	Trainee	Blackpool	2	—
							Wrexham	1	—
Lowe David	5 10	11 04	F	30 8 65	Liverpool	Apprentice	Wigan Ath	188	40
							Ipswich T	134	37
							Port Vale (loan)	9	2
							Leicester C	94	22
							Port Vale (loan)	19	5
							Wigan Ath	108	26
							Wrexham	10	1
McGregor Mark	5 10	11 05	D	16 2 77	Chester	Trainee	Wrexham	201	6
Morrell Andy#	5 11	11 06	F	28 9 74	Doncaster	Newcastle Blue Star	Wrexham	20	1
Owen Gareth	5 8	12 00	M	21 10 71	Chester	Trainee	Wrexham	328	34
Phillips Wayne	5 11	11 00	M	15 12 70	Bangor	Trainee	Wrexham	207	16
							Stockport Co	22	—
							Wrexham	3	—
Ridler Dave	6 0	12 02	D	12 3 76	Liverpool	Prescot T	Wrexham	92	1
Rishworth Steve‡	5 11	11 09	M	8 6 80	Chester	Schoolboy	Wrexham	4	—
Roberts Steve	6 2	11 06	D	24 2 80	Wrexham	Trainee	Wrexham	19	—
Rogers Kristian	6 0	11 07	G	2 10 80	Chester		Wrexham	1	—
Russell Kevin	5 9	10 12	M	6 12 66	Portsmouth	Brighton & HA	Portsmouth	4	1
							Wrexham	84	43
							Leicester C	43	10
							Peterborough U (loan)	7	3
							Cardiff C (loan)	3	—
							Hereford U (loan)	3	1
							Stoke C (loan)	5	1
							Stoke C	40	5
							Burnley	28	6
							Bournemouth	30	1
							Notts Co	11	—
							Wrexham	161	13
Ryan Mike*	5 9	11 00	D	3 10 79	Stockport	Trainee	Manchester U	—	—
							Wrexham	7	—
Spink Dean*	6 1	12 12	D	22 1 67	Halesowen	Halesowen T	Aston Villa	—	—
							Scarborough (loan)	3	2
							Bury (loan)	6	1
							Shrewsbury T	273	52
							Wrexham	85	9
							Shrewsbury T (loan)	4	—
Stevens Ian*	5 10	12 07	F	21 10 69	Malta	Trainee	Preston NE	11	2
							Stockport Co	2	—
						Lancaster C	Bolton W	47	7
							Bury	110	38
							Shrewsbury T	111	37
							Carlisle U	78	26
							Wrexham	16	4
							Cheltenham T (loan)	1	—
Thomas Steve	5 10	11 07	M	23 6 79	Hartlepool	Trainee	Wrexham	6	—
Walsh Dave	6 1	12 05	G	29 4 79	Wrexham	Trainee	Wrexham	—	—
Warren David†	5 10	11 05	M	28 2 81	Cork	Mayfield U	Wrexham	1	—
Williams Danny	6 2	13 01	M	12 7 79	Wrexham	Trainee	Liverpool	—	—
							Wrexham	24	1
Wolfe Anthony‡	5 10	11 07	D	10 4 81	Cork	Mayfield U	Wrexham	—	—

Scholars
Arkell, Adam N; Campbell, Luke; Cocks, Ian T; Evans, Mark G; Harrison David; Horan, George J; Jackson, Mark G; Johnson, Darren M; Jones, Darren; Lee, Kenneth; Moody, Adrian JH; Moody, Craig; Pejic, Shaun M; Pybus, David Arthur; Sweet, David; Watkin, Daniel T; Whitfield, Paul M

Non-Contract
Hannon, Kevin M; Warren, David JP

Associated Schoolboys
Bates, Matthew J; Brand, Benjamin J; Cargill, Gary S; Entwistle, Mark R; Graham, Adam; Jones, Adam; O'Toole, Dominic; Taylor, Michael J

WYCOMBE WANDERERS

Name			Pos		DOB	Birthplace	Source	Club	Apps	Gls
Baird Andy	5 10	11 13	F	18	1 79	East Kilbride	Trainee	Wycombe W	60	10
Bates Jamie	6 2	14 06	D	24	2 68	Croydon	Trainee	Brentford	419	18
								Wycombe W	41	1
Beeton Alan	5 11	11 13	D	4	10 78	Watford	Trainee	Wycombe W	52	—
Brady Matt	5 10	10 04	M	27	10 77	Barnet	Trainee	Barnet	10	—
							Boreham Wood	Wycombe W	7	2
Brown Steve	5 10	11 12	M	6	7 66	Northampton		Northampton T	158	19
								Wycombe W	238	17
Bulman Dannie	5 9	11 12	M	24	1 79	Ashford	Ashford T	Wycombe W	40	2
Carroll Dave	5 10	11 12	M	20	9 66	Paisley	Ruislip Manor	Wycombe W	278	38
Cousins Jason	5 10	12 07	D	4	10 70	Hayes	Trainee	Brentford	21	—
							Wycombe W	Wycombe W	245	6
Devine Sean	5 11	13 00	F	6	9 72	Lewisham	Omonia	Barnet	126	47
								Wycombe W	51	31
Emblen Paul	5 9	12 12	M	3	4 76	Bromley	Tonbridge A	Charlton Ath	4	—
								Brighton & HA (loan)	15	4
								Wycombe W	51	2
Gray Edward*			M	4	9 80	Ascot	Trainee	Wycombe W	—	—
Harkin Maurice	5 8	11 05	M	16	8 79	Derry	Trainee	Wycombe W	58	2
Holsgrove Lee*	6 1	12 06	D	13	12 79	Wendover	Trainee	Millwall	—	—
								Wycombe W	10	—
Holsgrove Peter			M	16	4 82	Wendover	Scholar	Wycombe W	—	—
Johnson Roger	6 3	11 00	D	28	4 83	Ashford		Wycombe W	1	—
Leach Nicholas*			M	30	1 81	Hemel Hempstead	Trainee	Wycombe W	—	—
Lee Martyn	5 6	9 00	M	10	8 80	Guilford	Trainee	Wycombe W	7	—
McCarthy Paul	5 10	13 10	D	4	8 71	Cork	Trainee	Brighton & HA	181	6
								Wycombe W	122	3
McSporran Jermaine	5 10	10 12	F	1	1 77	Manchester	Oxford C	Wycombe W	64	13
Osborn Mark	6 0	14 01	G	19	6 81	Bletchley	Trainee	Wycombe W	1	—
Robson Mark	5 10	10 00	M	22	5 69	Newham	Trainee	Exeter C	26	7
								Tottenham H	8	—
								Reading (loan)	7	—
								Watford (loan)	1	—
								Plymouth Arg (loan)	7	—
								Exeter C (loan)	8	1
								West Ham U	47	8
								Charlton Ath	105	9
								Notts Co	32	4
								Wycombe W	4	—
Rogers Mark	5 11	12 12	D	3	11 75	Geulph		Wycombe W	25	—
Ryan Keith	5 10	12 06	M	25	6 70	Northampton	Berkhamsted T	Wycombe W	195	19
Senda Danny	5 10	10 02	F	17	4 81	Harrow	Southampton	Wycombe W	33	1
Simpson Michael	5 8	11 07	M	28	2 74	Nottingham	Trainee	Notts Co	49	3
								Plymouth Arg (loan)	12	—
								Wycombe W	117	5
Taylor Martin#	6 0	13 11	G	9	12 66	Tamworth	Mile Oak R	Derby Co	97	—
								Carlisle U (loan)	10	—
								Scunthorpe U (loan)	8	—
								Crewe Alex (loan)	6	—
								Wycombe W (loan)	4	—
								Wycombe W	131	—
Thompson Richard*	5 7	12 02	F	2	5 74	Lambeth	Crawley T	Wycombe W	6	—
Townsend Ben§	5 10	11 03		8	10 81	Reading	Scholar	Wycombe W	1	—
Vinnicombe Chris	5 9	10 12	D	20	10 70	Exeter	Trainee	Exeter C	39	1
								Rangers	23	1
								Burnley	95	3
								Wycombe W	76	—
Westhead Mark	6 1	14 05	G	19	7 75	Blackpool		Bolton W	—	—
							Telford U	Wycombe W	4	—
Wraight Gary‡	5 9	11 13	D	5	3 79	Epping	Trainee	Wycombe W	7	—

Scholars
Coltman, Mark J; Dash, Scott; Gostick, Ryan J; Johnson, Paul M; Johnson, Roger; Leach, Marc T; McCullagh, Ryan; Phelan, Leeyon; Powell, Kevin; Reeks, Stuart J; Simpemba, Ian F; Townsend, Ben; Williams, Steven

Associated Schoolboys who have accepted the Club's offer of a Traineeship/Scholarship/Contract
Cook, Lewis L; Dixon, Jonathan J

YORK CITY

Name			Pos		DOB	Birthplace	Source	Club	Apps	Gls
Agnew Steve	5 10	10 06	M	9	11 65	Shipley	Apprentice	Barnsley	194	29
								Blackburn R	2	—
								Portsmouth (loan)	5	—
								Leicester C	56	4
								Sunderland	63	9
								York C	42	2
Alcide Colin	6 2	13 11	F	14	4 72	Huddersfield	Emley	Lincoln C	121	26
								Hull C	29	4
								York C	15	2

Name					Birthplace	Source	Club	Apps	Gls
Atkins Mark‡	6 1	12 00	M	14 8 68	Doncaster		Scunthorpe U	48	2
							Blackburn R	257	35
							Wolverhampton W	126	9
							York C	10	2
Bullock Lee	6 1	12 07	M	22 5 81	Stockton	Trainee	York C	24	—
Conlon Barry	6 2	13 07	F	1 10 78	Drogheda	QPR	Manchester C	7	—
							Plymouth Arg (loan)	13	2
							Southend U	34	7
							York C	40	11
Darlow Kieran§	6 0	13 12		9 11 82	Bedford	Trainee	York C	2	—
Dawson Andrew	6 0	12 00	D	8 12 79	York	Trainee	York C	28	1
Dibie Michael‡			M	20 3 81	Ngbidi		York C	—	—
Edmondson Darren#	6 0	12 10	D	4 11 71	Ulverston	Trainee	Carlisle U	214	9
							Huddersfield T	37	—
							Plymouth Arg (loan)	4	—
							York C	7	—
Fairclough Chris	5 11	11 07	D	12 4 64	Nottingham	Apprentice	Nottingham F	107	1
							Tottenham H	60	5
							Leeds U	193	21
							Bolton W	90	8
							Notts Co	16	1
							York C (loan)	11	—
							York C	26	—
Fettis Alan#	6 2	13 00	G	1 2 71	Newtownards	Ards	Hull C	135	2
							WBA (loan)	3	—
							Nottingham F	4	—
							Blackburn R	11	—
							Leicester C (loan)		
							York C	13	—
Fox Christian	5 11	11 00	M	11 4 81	Auchenbrae	Trainee	York C	34	1
Hall Wayne#	5 9	10 06	D	25 10 68	Rotherham	Darlington	York C	354	9
Hocking Matt	5 11	12 00	D	30 1 78	Boston	Trainee	Sheffield U	—	—
							Hull C	57	2
							York C (loan)	6	—
							York C	32	2
Howarth Russell	6 1	12 00	G	27 3 82	York	Scholar	York C	6	—
Hulme Kevin	5 10	13 07	M	7 12 67	Farnworth	Radcliffe Borough	Bury	110	21
							Chester C (loan)	4	—
							Doncaster R	34	8
							Bury	29	—
							Lincoln C	5	—
						Macclesfield T	Halifax T	33	4
							York C	23	4
Jones Barry#	5 10	11 07	D	20 6 70	Prescot	Prescot T	Liverpool	—	—
							Wrexham	195	5
							York C	105	5
Jordan Scott	5 9	11 02	M	19 7 75	Newcastle	Trainee	York C	155	12
Keegan John§	5 11	11 09	G	5 8 81	Liverpool	Scholar	York C	3	—
McMillan Andy‡	5 11	11 09	D	22 6 68	Bloemfontein		York C	421	5
Reed Martin	5 11	11 07	D	10 1 78	Scarborough	Trainee	York C	44	—
Rennison Graham‡	6 1	12 00	D	2 10 78	Northallerton	Trainee	York C	1	—
Sertori Mark	6 2	14 02	D	1 9 67	Manchester		Stockport Co	4	—
							Lincoln C	50	9
							Wrexham	110	3
							Bury	13	1
							Scunthorpe U	83	2
							Halifax T	45	—
							York C	40	1
Skinner Craig	5 8	11 00	M	21 10 70	Bury	Trainee	Blackburn R	16	—
							Plymouth Arg	53	4
							Wrexham	87	10
							York C	10	—
Swan Peter	6 2	14 02	D	28 9 66	Leeds	Local	Leeds U	49	11
							Hull C	80	24
							Port Vale	111	5
							Plymouth Arg	27	2
							Burnley	49	7
							Bury	37	6
							Burnley	19	—
							York C	9	—
Talbot Paul*	5 10	10 09	D	11 8 79	Gateshead	Trainee	Newcastle U	—	—
							York C	6	—
Thompson Marc§	5 10	12 03		15 1 82	York		York C	10	—
Thompson Neil‡	6 0	13 08	D	2 10 63	Beverley	Nottingham F	Hull C	31	—
						Scarborough	Scarborough	87	15
							Ipswich T	206	19
							Barnsley	27	5
							Oldham Ath (loan)	8	—
							York C	42	8

Turley James	5 8	10 07	F	24 6 81	Manchester	Trainee	York C	11	2
Walters Steve‡	5 10	11 00	D	6 12 80	York	Trainee	York C	—	—
Williams John	6 2	13 08	F	11 5 68	Birmingham	Cradley T	Swansea C	39	11
							Coventry C	80	11
							Notts Co (loan)	5	2
							Stoke C (loan)	4	—
							Swansea C (loan)	7	2
							Wycombe W	48	9
							Hereford U	11	3
							Walsall	1	—
							Exeter C	36	4
							Cardiff C	43	12
							York C	36	3
Williams Marc	5 9	11 07	F	8 2 73	Bangor	Bangor C	Stockport Co	18	1
							Halifax T	24	6
							York C	33	9
Woods Neil‡	6 0	12 11	F	30 7 66	York	Apprentice	Doncaster R	65	16
							Rangers	3	—
							Ipswich T	27	5
							Bradford C	14	2
							Grimsby T	226	42
							Wigan Ath (loan)	1	—
							Scunthorpe U (loan)	2	—
							Mansfield T (loan)	6	—
							York C	8	—

Scholars
Collinson, Jonathan E; Darlow, Kieran B; Emmerson, Scott; Fielding, John R; Gowen, Christopher J; Hakami, Darren R; Keegan, John KP; Marshall, Christopher; Ormston, Gary; Rhodes, Benjamin; Russell, Adam J; Salvati, Marc R; Thompson, Marc; Vasey, Peter WJ; Whitfield, Richard; Wood, Leigh J

THE FOREIGN (INTERNATIONAL) LEGION

The following full international players born outside the UK played in the FA Premier League and Nationwide Football League in 1999-2000.

	Player	Club	From	Fee £s
ARGENTINA	Nelson Vivas	Arsenal	Lugano	1,600,000
AUSTRALIA	John Aloisi	Coventry C	Portsmouth	650,000
	Andy Bernal	Reading	Syndey Olympic	30,000
	Mark Bosnich	Manchester U	Aston Villa	Free
	Tim Cahill	Millwall	Sydney U	undisclosed
	Steve Corica	Wolverhampton W	Leicester C	1,100,000
	John Filan	Blackburn R	Coventry C	700,000
	Craig Foster	Crystal Palace	Portsmouth	Free
	Harry Kewell	Leeds U	NSW Soccer Academy	Free
	George Kulcsar	QPR	Bradford C	250,000
	Stan Lazaridis	Birmingham C	West Ham U	1,600,000
	Shaun Murphy	Sheffield U	WBA	undisclosed
	Kevin Muscat	Wolverhampton W	Crystal Palace	exch.
	Lucas Neill	Millwall	NSW Soccer Academy	Free
	Mark Schwarzer	Middlesbrough	Bradford C	1,500,000
	Danny Tiatto	Manchester C	Stoke C	300,000
	Jason Van Blerk	WBA	Manchester C	50,000
AUSTRIA	Martin Hiden	Leeds U	Rapid Vienna	1,300,000
	Alex Manninger	Arsenal	Graz	
BARBADOS	Greg Goodridge	Bristol C	QPR	50,000
BELARUS	Petr Katchuro	Sheffield U	Dynamo Minsk	650,000
BELGIUM	Gilles De Bilde	Sheffield W	PSV Eindhoven	3,000,000
	Branko Strupar	Derby Co	Genk	3,000,000
BERMUDA	Shaun Goater	Manchester C	Bristol C	500,000
	Kyle Lightbourne	Stoke C	Coventry C	500,000
BOSNIA	Muhamed Konjic	Coventry C	Monaco	2,000,000
BRAZIL	Juninho	Middlesbrough	Atletico Madrid	Loan
	Silvinho	Arsenal	Corinthians	4,000,000
CAMEROON	Marc-Vivien Foe	West Ham U	Lens	4,200,000
	Rigobert Song	Liverpool	Salernitana	2,720,000
CANADA	Marc Bircham	Millwall	Trainee	No fee
	Jim Brennan	Nottingham F	Bristol C	1,500,000
	Carlo Corazzin	Northampton T	Plymouth Arg	Free
	Craig Forrest	West Ham U	Ipswich T	500,000
	Martin Nash	Chester C	Vancouver 89ers	Free
	Paul Peschisolido	Fulham	WBA	1,100,000
	Mark Watson	Oxford U	Osters	Free
CHILE	Javier Margas	West Ham U	Univ Catolica	2,000,000
CHINA	Fan Zhiyi	Crystal Palace	Shanghai	500,000
COLOMBIA	Hamilton Ricard	Middlesbrough	Deportivo Cali	200,000
CONGO DR	Michel Ngonge	Watford	Samsun	Free
COSTA RICA	Paulo Wanchope	Derby Co	Heridiano	600,000
CROATIA	Silvio Maric	Newcastle U	Croatia Zagreg	3,650,000
	Igor Stimac	West Ham U	Derby Co	600,000
	Davor Suker	Arsenal	Real Madrid	Free
CZECH REPUBLIC	Patrik Berger	Liverpool	Borussia Dortmund	3,250,000
	Ludek Miklosko	QPR	West Ham U	50,000
	Vladimir Smicer	Liverpool	Lens	3,750,000
	Pavel Srnicek	Sheffield W	Banik Ostrava	undisclosed
DENMARK	Mikkel Beck	Derby Co	Middlesbrough	500,000
	Per Frandsen	Blackburn R	Bolton W	1,750,000
	Bjarni Goldbaek	Fulham	Chelsea	500,000
	Bo Hansen	Bolton W	Brondby	1,000,000
	Jes Hogh	Chelsea	Fenerbahce	300,000
	Jacob Laursen	Derby Co	Silkeborg	500,000
	Allan Nielsen	Tottenham H	Brondby	1,650,000
	Thomas Sorensen	Sunderland	Odense	500,000
ESTONIA	Mart Poom	Derby Co	Flora	500,000
FINLAND	Peter Enckleman	Aston Villa	TPS Turku	200,000
	Mikael Forssell	Chelsea	HJK Helsinki	Free
	Sami Hyypia	Liverpool	Willem II	2,600,000
	Jussi Jaaskelainen	Bolton W	VPS Vaasa	100,000
	Teuvo Moilanen	Preston NE	Jaro	undisclosed
	Ville Viljanen	Port Vale	Vastra Frolunda	Free

FRANCE	Marcel Desailly	Chelsea	AC Milan	4,600,000
	Didier Deschamps	Chelsea	Juventus	3,000,000
	David Ginola	Tottenham H	Newcastle U	2,000,000
	Alain Goma	Newcastle U	Paris St Germain	4,750,000
	Xavier Gravelaine	Watford	Paris St Germain	Free
	Thierry Henry	Arsenal	Juventus	10,000,000
	Marc Keller	West Ham U	Karlsruhe	Free
	Frank Leboeuf	Chelsea	Strasbourg	2,500,000
	Emmanuel Petit	Arsenal	Monaco	3,500,000
	Amara Simba	Leyton Orient	Leon	Free
	Patrick Vieira	Arsenal	AC Milan	3,500,000
GEORGIA	Temuri Ketsbaia	Newcastle U	AEK Athens	Free
	Georgi Kinkladze	Derby Co	Ajax	Loan
GERMANY	Steffen Freund	Tottenham H	Borussia Dortmund	750,000
	Dietmar Hamann	Liverpool	Newcastle U	8,000,000
	Thomas Helmer	Sunderland	Bayern Munich	Free
	Karlheinz Riedle	Fulham	Liverpool	250,000
	Christian Ziege	Middlesbrough	AC Milan	4,000,000
GREECE	Vassilis Borbokis	Derby Co	Sheffield U	600,000
	Nikos Dabizas	Newcastle U	Olympiakos	2,000,000
	George Donis	Huddersfield T	AEK Athens	Free
	Michalis Vlachos	Walsall	Portsmouth	Free
	Theo Zagorakis	Leicester C	PAOK Salonika	750,000
GRENADA	Jason Roberts	Bristol R	Wolverhampton W	250,000
GUINEA	Titi Camara	Liverpool	Marseille	2,600,000
HOLLAND	Dennis Bergkamp	Arsenal	Inter Milan	7,500,000
	Jordi Cruyff	Manchester U	Barcelona	1,400,000
	Ed De Goey	Chelsea	Feyenoord	2,250,000
	Wim Jonk	Sheffield W	PSV Eindhoven	2,500,000
	Erik Meijer	Liverpool	Leverkusen	Free
	Marc Overmars	Arsenal	Ajax	5,000,000
	Martijn Reuser	Ipswich T	Vitesse	undisclosed
	Jaap Stam	Manchester U	PSV Eindhoven	10,500,000
	Sander Westerveld	Liverpool	Vitesse	4,000,000
HONDURAS	Milton Nunez	Sunderland	PAOK Salonika	1,600,000
HUNGARY	Vilmos Sebok	Bristol C	Ujpest	200,000
ICELAND	Gudni Bergsson	Bolton W	Tottenham H	65,000
	Einar Danielsson	Stoke C	KR	Loan
	Gunnar Einarsson	Brentford	MVV	undisclosed
	Sigursteinn Gislason	Stoke C	IA	undisclosed
	Eidur Gudjohnsen	Bolton W	PSV Eindhoven	Free
	Bjarni Gudjonsson	Stoke C	Genk	250,000
	Johann Gudmunsson	Watford	Keflavik	undisclosed
	Brynjar Gunnarsson	Stoke C	Orgryte	600,000
	Arnar Gunnlaugsson	Leicester C	Bolton W	2,000,000
	Bjarke Gunnlaugsson	Preston NE	KR	Free
	Heidar Helguson	Watford	Lillestrom	1,500,000
	Hermann Hreidarsson	Wimbledon	Brentford	2,500,000
	Ivar Ingimarsson	Brentford	Torquay U	Free
	Larus Sigurdsson	WBA	Stoke C	325,000
ISRAEL	Walid Badir	Wimbledon	Hapoel Petah Tikva	900,000
	Najwan Ghrayib	Aston Villa	Hapoel Haifa	1,000,000
	Avi Nimni	Derby Co	Maccabi Tel Aviv	undisclosed
ITALY	Francesco Baiano	Derby Co	Fiorentina	650,000
	Roberto Di Matteo	Chelsea	Lazio	4,900,000
	Stefano Eranio	Derby Co	AC Milan	Free
	Moreno Mannini	Nottingham F	Sampdoria	Free
	Gianfranco Zola	Chelsea	Parma	4,500,000
JAMAICA	Walter Boyd	Swansea C	Arnett Gardens	Free
	Deon Burton	Derby Co	Portsmouth	1,500,000
	Robbie Earle	Wimbledon	Port Vale	775,000
	Ricardo Gardner	Bolton W	Harbour View	1,000,000
	Marcus Gayle	Wimbledon	Brentford	250,000
	Ian Goodison	Hull C	Olympic Gardens	Free
	Paul Hall	Walsall	Coventry C	Free
	David Johnson	Ipswich T	Bury	800,000
	Darryl Powell	Derby Co	Portsmouth	750,000
	Fitzroy Simpson	Portsmouth	Manchester C	200,000
	Frank Sinclair	Leicester C	Chelsea	2,000,000
	Theodore Whitmore	Hull C	Seba U	Free
LATVIA	Marian Pakhar (Pahars)	Southampton	Skonto Riga	800,000
	Vitalijs Astafjevs	Bristol R	Skonto Riga	150,000
LIBERIA	Mass Saar	Reading	Hajduk Split	158,000
	George Weah	Chelsea	AC Milan	Loan
	Christopher Wreh	Arsenal	Guingamp	300,000
MACEDONIA	Georgi Hristov	Barnsley	Partizan Belgrade	1,500,000
MOLDOVA	Ivan Testimetanu	Bristol C	Zimbru Chisinau	225,000

MOROCCO	Tahar El Khalej	Southampton	Benfica	300,000
	Hassan Kachloul	Southampton	St Etienne	Free
	Youssef Chippo	Coventry C	Porto	1,200,000
	Mustapha Hadji	Coventry C	La Coruna	4,000,000
NIGERIA	Celestine Babayaro	Chelsea	Anderlecht	2,250,000
	Nwankwo Kanu	Arsenal	Internazionale	4,500,000
NORWAY	Trond Andersen	Wimbledon	Molde	2,500,000
	Eirik Bakke	Leeds U	Sogndal	1,000,000
	Henning Berg	Manchester U	Blackburn R	5,000,000
	Lars Bohinen	Derby Co	Blackburn R	1,450,000
	Harvard Flo	Wolverhampton W	Werder Bremen	370,000
	Tore Andre Flo	Chelsea	Brann	300,000
	Alf Inge Haaland	Leeds U	Tottenham H	1,600,000
	Gunnar Halle	Bradford C	Leeds U	200,000
	Vegard Heggem	Liverpool	Rosenborg	3,500,000
	Steffen Iversen	Tottenham H	Rosenborg	2,600,000
	Anders Jacobsen	Stoke C	Sheffield U	Free
	Ronny Johnsen	Manchester U	Besiktas	1,200,000
	Oyvind Leonhardsen	Tottenham H	Liverpool	3,000,000
	Andreas Lund	Wimbledon	Molde	2,500,000
	Claus Lundekvam	Southampton	Brann	400,000
	Thomas Myhre	Everton	Viking Stavanger	800,000
	Egil Ostenstad	Blackburn R	Southampton	exch
	Tore Pedersen	Wimbledon	Eintracht Frankfurt	Free
	Petter Rudi	Sheffield W	Molde	800,000
	Ole Gunnar Solskjaer	Manchester U	Molde	1,500,000
	Trond Egil Soltvedt	Southampton	Coventry C	300,000
PARAGUAY	Diego Gavilan	Newcastle U	Cerro Porteno	2,000,000
PERU	Nolberto Solano	Newcastle U	Boca Juniors	2,500,000
	Ysrael Zuniga	Coventry C	Melgar	750,000
PORTUGAL	Jose Dominguez	Tottenham H	Sporting Lisbon	1,600,000
	Jorge Cadete	Bradford C	Benfica	Loan
	Rodriguez Helder	Newcastle U	La Coruna	Loan
	Abel Xavier	Everton	PSV Eindhoven	1,500,000
ROMANIA	Dan Petrescu	Chelsea	Sheffield W	2,300,000
SIERRA LEONE	John Keister	Chester C	Walsall	Free
SOUTH AFRICA	Andre Arendse	Oxford U	Fulham	30,000
	Mark Fish	Bolton W	Lazio	2,000,000
	Quinton Fortune	Manchester U	Atletico Madrid	1,500,000
	Lucas Radebe	Leeds U	Kaiser Chiefs	250,000
	Eric Tinkler	Barnsley	Cagliari	650,000
SPAIN	Albert Ferrer	Chelsea	Barcelona	2,200,000
	Marcelino	Newcastle U	Mallorca	5,800,000
ST KITTS & NEVIS	Lutel James	Bury	Hyde U	Free
ST LUCIA	Ken Charlery	Barnet	Stockport Co	80,000
	Warren Hackett	Barnet	Mansfield T	Free
ST VINCENT	Rodney Jack	Crewe Alex	Torquay U	500,000
SWEDEN	Niclas Alexandersson	Sheffield W	IFK Gothenburg	750,000
	Tomas Gustafsson	Coventry C	AIK Stockholm	250,000
	Mikael Hansson	Stoke C	Norrkoping	Free
	Magnus Hedman	Coventry C	AIK Stockholm	500,000
	Fredrik Ljungberg	Arsenal	Halmstad	3,000,000
	Martin Pringle	Charlton Ath	Benfica	Loan
	Stefan Schwarz	Sunderland	Valencia	3,500,000
	Robert Steiner	QPR	Bradford C	215,000
	Mathias Svensson	Charlton Ath	Crystal Palace	600,000
SWITZERLAND	Stephane Henchoz	Liverpool	Blackburn R	3,750,000
	Ramon Vega	Tottenham H	Cagliari	3,750,000
TRINIDAD & TOBAGO	Angus Eve	Chester C	Joe Public	undisclosed
	Shaka Hislop	West Ham U	Newcastle U	Free
	Stern John	Nottingham F	Columbus Crew	1,500,000
	Clint Marcelle	Barnsley	Felgueiras	Free
	Ronnie Mauge	Bristol R	Plymouth Arg	Free
	Nigel Pierre	Bristol R	Joe Public	50,000
	Tony Rougier	Port Vale	Hibernian	175,000
	Dwight Yorke	Manchester U	Aston Villa	12,600,000
TURKEY	Muzzy Izzet	Leicester C	Chelsea	650,000
UKRAINE	Oleg Luzhny	Arsenal	Dynamo Kiev	1,800,000
URUGUAY	Gustavo Poyet	Chelsea	Zaragoza	Free
USA	Brad Friedel	Liverpool	Columbus Crew	1,000,000
	Joe-Max Moore	Everton	New England Rev	Free
VENEZUELA	Fernando De Ornelas	Crystal Palace	Happy Valley	undisclosed
YUGOSLAVIA	Sasa Ilic	Charlton Ath	St Leonards Stamcroft	undisclosed
ZIMBABWE	Peter Ndlovu	Birmingham C	Coventry C	1,600,000

TRANSFERS 1999–2000

May 1999	From	To	Fee in £
25 Brown, Daniel	Leyton Orient	Barnet	Free
28 Burton, Sagi	Crystal Palace	Colchester United	undisclosed
13 Eaton, Jason	Cheltenham Town	Yeovil Town	undisclosed
26 Hocking, Matthew J.	Hull City	York City	30,000
21 Johnson, Seth A.M.	Crewe Alexandra	Derby County	3,000,000
27 Kiely, Dean L.	Bury	Charlton Athletic	1,000,000
27 Low, Joshua D.	Bristol Rovers	Leyton Orient	Free
27 Read, David	Telford United	Stafford Rangers	undisclosed
27 Spiller, Lee M.	Margate	Gravesend & Northfleet	undisclosed
29 Walling, Dean A.	Lincoln City	Doncaster Rovers	25,000
Temporary transfers			
8 Varty, John W.	Carlisle United	Rotherham United	
8 Whelan, Philip J.	Oxford United	Rotherham United	
June 1999			
11 Dalglish, Paul	Newcastle United	Norwich City	300,000
29 Eaton, Adam P.	Everton	Preston North End	undisclosed
25 Forster, Nicholas	Birmingham City	Reading	650,000
4 Gray, Martin	Oxford United	Darlington	Free
11 Halle, Gunnar	Leeds United	Bradford City	200,000
21 Higgs, Shane P.	Worcester City	Cheltenham Town	10,000
17 Irons, Kenneth	Tranmere Rovers	Huddersfield Town	450,000
23 James, David B.	Liverpool	Aston Villa	1,700,000
14 Lucketti, Christopher	Bury	Huddersfield Town	750,000
21 Nicholls, Kevin J.	Charlton Athletic	Wigan Athletic	250,000
7 Oakes, Andrew M.	Hull City	Derby County	460,000
5 Town, David	AFC Bournemouth	Rushden & Diamonds	20,000
15 Turley, William L.	Northampton Town	Rushden & Diamonds	130,000
19 Varty, John W.	Carlisle United	Rotherham United	Free
July 1999			
16 Allen, Rory W.	Tottenham Hotspur	Portsmouth	1,000,000
28 Barras, Anthony	Reading	Walsall	20,000
7 Basham, Steven	Southampton	Preston North End	200,000
22 Boateng, George	Coventry City	Aston Villa	4,500,000
9 Bould, Stephen A.	Arsenal	Sunderland	500,000
9 Brazier, Matthew R.	Fulham	Cardiff City	100,000
2 Burns, Alexander	Southend United	Raith Rovers	Free
14 Carr, Darren J.	Gillingham	Brighton & Hove Albion	25,000
13 Catlin, Neil	Hayes	Chesham United	undisclosed
2 Christie, Iyseden	Mansfield Town	Leyton Orient	40,000
13 Clark, Lee R.	Sunderland	Fulham	3,000,000
2 Collins, Sam J.	Huddersfield Town	Bury	75,000
20 Conlon, Barry J.	Southend United	York City	100,000
1 Connelly, Gordon J.	York City	Southend United	50,000
28 Crosby, Andrew K.	Chester City	Brighton & Hove Albion	10,000
7 Crowe, Jason W.R.	Arsenal	Portsmouth	750,000
15 Davis, Kelvin G.	Luton Town	Wimbledon	600,000
8 Dyche, Sean M.	Bristol City	Millwall	150,000
16 Dyer, Kieron C.	Ipswich Town	Newcastle United	6,000,000
23 Endersby, Lee A.	Slough Town	Farnborough Town	undisclosed
30 Flowers, Timothy D.	Blackburn Rovers	Leicester City	1,100,000
31 Francis, Delton M.	Kingstonian	Nuneaton Borough	undisclosed
14 Gaughan, Steven E.	Darlington	Halifax Town	Free
29 Grayson, Simon N.	Aston Villa	Blackburn Rovers	750,000
27 Griffin, Antony R.	AFC Bournemouth	Cheltenham Town	20,000
23 Hamann, Dietmar	Newcastle United	Liverpool	8,000,000
12 Harris, Jason A.S.	Preston North End	Hull City	30,000
20 Henchoz, Stephane	Blackburn Rovers	Liverpool	3,750,000
8 Hodges, Lee L.	West Ham United	Scunthorpe United	130,000
30 Kelly, Alan T.	Sheffield United	Blackburn Rovers	675,000
19 Kennedy, Mark J.	Wimbledon	Manchester City	1,000,000
16 Lawson, Ian J.	Huddersfield Town	Bury	75,000
29 Lazaridis, Stan	West Ham United	Birmingham City	1,600,000
8 Lee, Alan D.	Aston Villa	Burnley	150,000
1 Mills, Daniel J.	Charlton Athletic	Leeds United	4,370,000
20 Mitchell, Graham L.	Cardiff City	Halifax Town	45,000
21 Moody, Paul	Fulham	Millwall	150,000
16 Myers, Andrew	Chelsea	Bradford City	800,000
9 Oatway, Anthony P.	Brentford	Brighton & Hove Albion	10,000
8 Payne, Stephen J.	Macclesfield Town	Chesterfield	undisclosed
21 Perrett, Russell	Portsmouth	Cardiff City	10,000
7 Perry, Christopher J.	Wimbledon	Tottenham Hotspur	4,000,000
23 Phillips, Wayne	Stockport County	Wrexham	50,000
30 Preece, David	Darlington	Aberdeen	300,000
5 Russell, Matthew L.	Scarborough	Halifax Town	50,000
24 Sale, Mark D.	Colchester United	Rushden & Diamonds	30,000
23 Scimeca, Riccardo	Aston Villa	Nottingham Forest	3,000,000
7 Shipperley, Neil J.	Nottingham Forest	Barnsley	700,000
29 Steiner, Robert H.	Bradford City	Queens Park Rangers	215,000
16 Sutton, Christopher R.	Blackburn Rovers	Chelsea	10,000,000
5 Tate, Christopher D.	Scarborough	Halifax Town	150,000
8 Tebily, Olivier	Sheffield United	Celtic	1,250,000
28 Wanchope, Watson P.	Derby County	West Ham United	3,250,000
21 Wardley, Stuart	Saffron Walden Town	Queens Park Rangers	15,000
7 Watson, Paul D.	Brentford	Brighton & Hove Albion	20,000
7 Wetherall, David	Leeds United	Bradford City	1,400,000
22 Wijnhard, Clyde	Leeds United	Huddersfield Town	750,000
15 Willmott, Christopher A.	Luton Town	Wimbledon	350,000
12 Winston, Samuel A.	Chesham United	Sutton United	undisclosed
23 Wright, Jermaine M.	Crewe Alexandra	Ipswich Town	500,000
Temporary transfers			
1 Adamson, Christopher	West Bromwich Albion	Halifax Town	

18 Agogo, Manuel	Sheffield Wednesday	Oldham Athletic	
19 Collymore, Stanley V.	Aston Villa	Fulham	
26 Hughes, Stephen J.	Arsenal	Fulham	
30 Livermore, David	Arsenal	Millwall	
2 Newton, Adam L.	West Ham United	Portsmouth	
9 Warner, Philip	Southampton	Brentford	

August 1999

12 Ashe, Ryan	Ruislip Manor	Chertsey Town	undisclosed
4 Bailey, Alan	Manchester City	Stockport County	Free
9 Bailey, Dennis L.	Cheltenham Town	Forest Green Rovers	undisclosed
9 Beavers, Paul M.	Sunderland	Oldham Athletic	undisclosed
27 Boa Morte, Pereira L.	Arsenal	Southampton	500,000
19 Brebner, Grant I.	Reading	Hibernian	400,000
13 Carty, Paul	Hednesford Town	Worcester City	undisclosed
6 Cramb, Colin	Bristol City	Crewe Alexandra	200,000
18 Davies, Kevin C.	Blackburn Rovers	Southampton	1,250,000
13 D'Jaffo, Laurent	Bury	Stockport County	100,000
27 Edwards, Matthew	Hucknall Town	Yeading	undisclosed
10 Gilchrist, Philip A.	Oxford United	Leicester City	500,000
12 Hanlon, Ritchie K.	Peterborough United	Welling United	Free
23 Hannigan, Al J.	Yeovil Town	Slough Town	undisclosed
6 Heaney, Neil A.	Manchester City	Darlington	Free
12 Huckerby, Darren C.	Coventry City	Leeds United	4,000,000
6 Illingworth, Jeremy M.	Wisbech Town	Ashton United	undisclosed
3 Ince, Paul E.C.	Liverpool	Middlesbrough	1,000,000
20 Keane, Robert D.	Wolverhampton Wanderers	Coventry City	6,000,000
21 Kirkby, Martin J.	Workington	Bedlington Terriers	undisclosed
3 Lee, Christian	Northampton Town	Gillingham	Free
6 Leonhardsen, Oyvind	Liverpool	Tottenham Hotspur	3,000,000
6 Lilley, Derek	Leeds United	Oxford United	75,000
13 Lovell, Stephen W.H.	AFC Bournemouth	Portsmouth	250,000
12 Margetson, Martyn W.	Southend United	Huddersfield Town	undisclosed
19 McGowan, Neil	Albion Rovers	Oxford United	undisclosed
4 McGreal, John	Tranmere Rovers	Ipswich Town	650,000
24 McKimm, Steven	Farnborough Town	Hayes	undisclosed
26 McKinney, Richard	Ballymena United	Manchester City	15,000
27 Miller, Kevin	Crystal Palace	Barnsley	250,000
27 Morton, Neil	Morecambe	Lancaster City	undisclosed
6 Murphy, John J.	Chester City	Blackpool	undisclosed
18 Ostenstad, Egil	Southampton	Blackburn Rovers	exch.
6 Oster, John	Everton	Sunderland	1,000,000
24 Reddington, Stuart	Lincoln United	Chelsea	undisclosed
3 Redfearn, Neil D.	Charlton Athletic	Bradford City	250,000
11 Robinson, Ian B.	Ilkeston Town	Hednesford Town	undisclosed
31 Samuels, Anthony	Boreham Wood	Stevenage Borough	undisclosed
26 Shields, Greg	Dunfermline Athletic	Charlton Athletic	580,000
4 Short, Craig J.	Everton	Blackburn Rovers	1,700,000
20 Smith, Neil J.	Fulham	Reading	100,000
13 Soley, Steven	Portsmouth	Carlisle United	undisclosed
13 Soltvedt, Trond E.	Coventry City	Southampton	300,000
20 Taylor, Craig	Swindon Town	Plymouth Argyle	30,000
13 Tinkler, Mark R.	York City	Gillingham	40,000
18 Tuttle, David P.	Crystal Palace	Southend United	150,000
6 Whitehead, Damien S.	Warrington Town	Macclesfield Town	undisclosed
12 Williams, John	Cardiff City	York City	20,000
3 Witney, Scott	St Albans City	Bishop's Stortford	undisclosed

Temporary transfers

2 Adamson, Christopher	West Bromwich Albion	Halifax Town	
6 Aiston, Sam J.	Sunderland	Stoke City	
19 Alexander, Gary G.	West Ham United	Exeter City	
13 Baker, Joseph P.J.	Leyton Orient	Welling United	
6 Baker, Steven R.	Middlesbrough	Huddersfield Town	
25 Black, Thomas R.	Arsenal	Carlisle United	
10 Branston, Guy P.B.	Leicester City	Lincoln City	
24 Brunskill, Iain R.	Hednesford Town	Runcorn	
13 Byfield, Darren	Aston Villa	Northampton Town	
27 Byrne, Christopher T.	Stockport County	Macclesfield Town	
13 Chapman, Danny P.	Barnet	Crawley Town	
20 Clark, Dean W.	Brentford	Crawley Town	
14 Collins, James I.	Crewe Alexandra	Kidderminster Harriers	
17 Cook, Aaron	Havant & Waterlooville	Bognor Regis Town	
13 Cooksey, Scott A.	Shrewsbury Town	Weymouth	
13 Coward, Ronell	Woking	Whyteleafe	
27 Craddock, Jody D.	Sunderland	Sheffield United	
13 Cullen, David J.	Sheffield United	Shrewsbury Town	
5 Dixon, Kevin R.	Leeds United	York City	
20 Dudley, Craig B.	Oldham Athletic	Chesterfield	
28 Fenton, Darren T.	Hitchen Town	Baldock Town	
7 Granville, Daniel P.	Leeds United	Manchester City	
13 Hendry, Iain	Woking	St Leonards	
13 Humphreys, Richie J.	Sheffield Wednesday	Scunthorpe United	
4 Knight, Richard	Derby County	Birmingham City	
19 Love, Andrew M.	Grimsby Town	Ilkeston Town	
6 Margetson, Martyn W.	Southend United	Huddersfield Town	
26 Martin, John	Leyton Orient	Cambridge City	
27 McCann, Grant S.	West Ham United	Livingston	
21 Mildenhall, Stephen J.	Swindon Town	Salisbury City	
14 Newell, Paul C.	St Albans City	Dagenham & Redbridge	
1 Newton, Adam L.	West Ham United	Portsmouth	
20 Oakes, Andrew M.	Derby County	Port Vale	
6 O'Reilly, Alexander	West Ham United	Northampton Town	
13 Ovens, Steven	Witney Town	Tiverton Town	
16 Payne, Stuart	Kidderminster Harriers	Bromsgrove Rovers	
5 Platt, Clive L.	Walsall	Rochdale	
5 Pouton, Alan	York City	Grimsby Town	
24 Rea, Simon	Birmingham City	Peterborough United	

5 Richardson, Barry	Lincoln City	Mansfield Town
27 Richardson, Lee J.	Huddersfield Town	Bury
27 Ritchie, Stuart A.	Havant & Waterlooville	Wokingham Town
20 Salako, John A.	Fulham	Charlton Athletic
13 Samuels, Anthony	Boreham Wood	Stevenage Borough
13 Slinn, Kevin P.	Boston United	Stamford
6 Soley, Steven	Portsmouth	Carlisle United
13 Tardif, Christopher L.	Portsmouth	Havant & Waterlooville
6 Thomas, Wayne	Walsall	Mansfield Town
20 Townley, Leon	Brentford	Slough Town
12 Turkington, Edmund B.	Altrincham	Leigh RMI
6 Watts, Julian	Bristol City	Luton Town
6 Weaver, Luke D.S.	Sunderland	Carlisle United
20 Whitley, James	Manchester City	Blackpool
26 Whittle, David L.J.	Queens Park Rangers	Waterford United
5 Williams, Anthony S.	Blackburn Rovers	Gillingham
27 Wright, Ian E.	West Ham United	Nottingham Forest
6 Wright, Stephen J.	Liverpool	Crewe Alexandra
25 Wright, Thomas J.	Manchester City	Newcastle United

September 1999

29 Abbey, Benjamin	Crawley Town	Oxford United	30,000
7 Akinbiyi, Adeola P.	Bristol City	Wolverhampton Wanderers	3,500,000
24 Albrighton, Mark	Atherstone United	Telford United	undisclosed
6 Allison, Wayne A.	Huddersfield Town	Tranmere Rovers	300,000
24 Butler, Lee S.	Dunfermline Athletic	Halifax Town	undisclosed
22 Charles, Anthony D.	Brook House	Crewe Alexandra	5000
10 Coupe, Matthew W.E.	Gloucester City	Clevedon Town	undisclosed
21 Croft, Gary	Blackburn Rovers	Ipswich Town	800,000
23 Forinton, Howard L.	Birmingham City	Peterborough United	250,000
16 Francis, Ruben M.	Burton Albion	Rocester	undisclosed
22 Frandsen, Per	Bolton Wanderers	Blackburn Rovers	1,750,000
30 Graham, Gareth L.	Crystal Palace	Brentford	undisclosed
23 Holland, Paul	Chesterfield	Bristol City	200,000
15 Holt, Grant	Workington	Halifax Town	undisclosed
22 Hughes, Robert D.	Aston Villa	Shrewsbury Town	Free
14 Hulme, Kevin	Halifax Town	York City	undisclosed
10 Jones, Stephen G.	Charlton Athletic	Bristol City	425,000
6 Livermore, David	Arsenal	Millwall	30,000
28 McGrath, Stephen M.	Aldershot Town	Yeading	3000
10 Platt, Clive L.	Walsall	Rochdale	70,000
7 Pouton, Alan	York City	Grimsby Town	150,000
28 Rachel, Adam	Aston Villa	Blackpool	Free
28 Riedle, Karlheinz	Liverpool	Fulham	250,000
3 Sertori, Mark A.	Halifax Town	York City	25,000
17 Sigurdsson, Larus O.	Stoke City	West Bromwich Albion	325,000
3 Sparks, Christopher	Hayes	Yeovil Town	undisclosed
23 Telemaque, Errol	Stevenage Borough	Hayes	undisclosed
17 Townsend, Andrew D.	Middlesbrough	West Bromwich Albion	50,000
9 Watts, Julian	Bristol City	Luton Town	Free
9 Weaver, Luke D.S.	Sunderland	Carlisle United	Free
30 West, Mark	Farnborough Town	Thame United	undisclosed

Temporary transfers

13 Adams, Darren S.	Welling United	Hampton & Richmond Borough
3 Adamson, Christopher	West Bromwich Albion	Halifax Town
3 Agogo, Manuel	Sheffield Wednesday	Chester City
6 Aiston, Sam J.	Sunderland	Stoke City
29 Aldridge, Martin J.	Blackpool	Port Vale
19 Alexander, Gary G.	West Ham United	Exeter City
3 Allison, Wayne A.	Huddersfield Town	Tranmere Rovers
10 Ansell, Gary S.	Barnet	Hayes
24 Arnott, Andrew J.	Brighton & Hove Albion	Colchester United
24 Aspinall, Warren	Colchester United	Brighton & Hove Albion
21 Baillie, Lewis	Bishop's Stortford	Witham Town
24 Battersby, Anthony	Lincoln City	Northampton Town
3 Betsy, Kevin E.L.	Fulham	AFC Bournemouth
3 Blackwood, Michael	Aston Villa	Chester City
17 Bradley, Shayne	Southampton	Exeter City
10 Brown, John K.	Blackburn Rovers	Barnsley
21 Brunskill, Iain R.	Hednesford Town	Runcorn
17 Byfield, Darren	Aston Villa	Cambridge United
24 Bywater, Stephen M.	West Ham United	Wycombe Wanderers
9 Cadette, Nathan D.	Cardiff City	Aberystwyth Town
17 Carruthers, Martin G.	Darlington	Southend United
10 Claridge, Robert R.	Clevedon Town	Yate Town
21 Clark, Dean W.	Brentford	Crawley Town
10 Clarke, Adrian J.	Southend United	Carlisle United
3 Clarke, Tim	Scunthorpe United	Kidderminster Harriers
13 Connell, Lee A.	Bury	Workington
13 Cooksey, Scott A.	Shrewsbury Town	Weymouth
30 Craddock, Jody	Sunderland	Sheffield United
3 Culbertson, Richard D.J.	Swindon Town	Ballymena United
10 Cullen, David J.	Sheffield United	Shrewsbury Town
17 Cullip, Daniel	Brentford	Brighton & Hove Albion
17 Davies, Jamie	Swansea City	Bangor
28 Downey, Glen	Hartlepool United	Bishop Auckland
16 Dunwell, Michael	Hartlepool United	Whitby Town
17 Fettis, Alan	Blackburn Rovers	Leicester City
17 Fitzpatrick, Lee G.	Blackburn Rovers	Hartlepool United
29 Galloway, Michael A.	Gillingham	Lincoln City
6 Gant, Adam S.	Enfield	Bishop's Stortford
9 Gibbens, Kevin	Southampton	Stockport County
10 Glennon, Matthew W.	Bolton Wanderers	Port Vale
28 Graham, Gareth L.	Crystal Palace	Brentford
2 Grant, Anthony J.	Everton	Tranmere Rovers
24 Green, Richard E.	Walsall	Rochdale
17 Gregory, Andrew	Barnsley	Carlisle United
10 Guinan, Stephen	Nottingham Forest	Scunthorpe United

3 Hammatt, Bryan	Slough Town	Billericay Town
24 Hill, Graham E.	Chorley	Winsford United
13 Hockton, Danny J.	Millwall	Leyton Orient
17 Holligan, Gavin V.	West Ham United	Leyton Orient
17 Janney, Mark	Dagenham & Redbridge	Braintree Town
24 Johnson, Thomas	Celtic	Everton
16 Johnston, Ray	Bristol Rovers	Southampton
3 Knight, Richard	Derby County	Birmingham City
18 Love, Andrew	Grimsby Town	Ilkeston Town
24 McGrath, Stephen M.	Aldershot Town	Yeading
17 Mathie, Alexander	Dundee United	Preston North End
24 Midgley, Neil A.	Ipswich Town	Luton Town
9 Monk, Garry A.	Southampton	Stockport County
21 Morris, Andrew D.	Rochdale	Scarborough
9 Muggleton, Carl D.	Stoke City	Mansfield Town
8 Ndekine, Malcolm S.	Rushden & Diamonds	Spalding United
1 Newton, Adam L.	West Ham United	Portsmouth
3 Omoyimni, Emmanuel	West Ham United	Gillingham
24 Ormerod, Anthony	Middlesbrough	York City
17 Palmer, Carlton L.	Nottingham Forest	Coventry City
24 Payne, Stuart	Kidderminster Harriers	Halesowen Town
17 Prudhoe, Mark	Bradford City	Darlington
27 Ritchie, Stuart A.	Havant & Waterlooville	Wokingham Town
24 Rowe, Rodney C.	York City	Halifax Town
3 Russell, Craig S.	Manchester City	Darlington
20 Salako, John A.	Fulham	Charlton Athletic
17 Searle, Damon P.	Carlisle United	Rochdale
3 Simpson, Philip M.	Yeovil Town	Enfield
13 Slinn, Kevin P.	Boston United	Stamford AFC
11 Smith, Christopher G.	Blakenall	Solihull Borough
10 Smith, Philip A.	Millwall	Ashford Town
18 Stoker, Gareth	Rochdale	Scarborough
17 Stowell, Matthew D.	Bristol City	Yeovil Town
23 Sucharwycz, Gary	Hucknall Town	Spalding United
24 Taylor, Stuart J.	Arsenal	Bristol Rovers
8 Thirlwell, Paul	Sunderland	Swindon Town
17 Todd, Lee	Bradford City	Walsall
24 Trees, Robert V.	Bristol Rovers	Altrincham
22 Turner, Michael C.	Barnsley	Lincoln City
15 Vaughan, Anthony J.	Manchester City	Cardiff City
10 Walker, Keith C.	Swansea City	Merthyr Tydfil
24 Webster, Adam	Notts County	Grantham Town
10 Westcott, John P.J.	Brighton & Hove Albion	Newport (IW)
20 Whitley, James	Manchester City	Blackpool
8 Williams, Andrew P.	Southampton	Swindon Town
6 Williams, Anthony S.	Blackburn Rovers	Gillingham
27 Wright, Ian E.	West Ham United	Nottingham Forest
8 Wright, Stephen J.	Liverpool	Crewe Alexandra

October 1999

25 Arnott, Andrew J.	Brighton & Hove Albion	Colchester United	undisclosed
25 Aspinall, Warren	Colchester United	Brighton & Hove Albion	Free
21 Beadle, Peter C.	Notts County	Bristol City	200,000
28 Bent, Marcus N.	Port Vale	Sheffield United	300,000
14 Bradbury, Lee M.	Crystal Palace	Portsmouth	380,000
21 Carbone, Benito	Sheffield Wednesday	Aston Villa	undisclosed
18 Carruthers, Martin G.	Darlington	Southend United	50,000
18 Cullip, Daniel	Brentford	Brighton & Hove Albion	50,000
1 Gallacher, Kevin W.	Blackburn Rovers	Newcastle United	700,000
14 Hreidarsson, Hermann	Brentford	Wimbledon	2,500,000
14 MacKenzie, Neil D.	Stoke City	Cambridge United	45,000
25 Marcelo	Sheffield United	Birmingham City	500,000
29 Marshall, Scott R.	Southampton	Brentford	250,000
28 Mercer, William	Chesterfield	Bristol City	300,000
1 Miller, Charles D.	Rangers	Watford	350,000
8 Mitten, Charles H.	Dover Athletic	Gillingham	undisclosed
15 Morris, Lee	Sheffield United	Derby County	1,800,000
21 Ndah, George E.	Swindon Town	Wolverhampton Wanderers	1,000,000
22 Nwadike, Chukweumeka B.	Grantham Town	Kings Lynn	undisclosed
29 Oakes, Michael C.	Aston Villa	Wolverhampton Wanderers	400,000
1 Pullen, James	Heybridge Swifts	Ipswich Town	Free
25 Ribeiro, Bruno M.F.	Leeds United	Sheffield United	500,000
22 Russell, Matthew L.	Halifax Town	Scarborough	Free
20 Salako, John A.	Fulham	Charlton Athletic	150,000
21 Thompson, Glyn W.	Shrewsbury Town	Fulham	50,000
7 Whitehead, Philip M.	West Bromwich Albion	Reading	undisclosed
22 Wilder, Christopher J.	Brighton & Hove Albion	Halifax Town	Free
8 Williams, Andrew P.	Southampton	Swindon Town	undisclosed

Temporary transfers

1 Abou, Samassi	West Ham United	Walsall
4 Agogo, Manuel	Sheffield Wednesday	Chester City
18 Agyemang, Patrick	Wimbledon	Brentford
21 Alexander, Gary G.	West Ham United	Exeter City
29 Ansell, Gary S.	Barnet	Carshalton Athletic
29 Barry, Peter L.	Nuneaton Borough	Racing Club Warwick
1 Bartley, Daniel R.	Cambridge City	Bishop Stortford
19 Beadle, Peter C.	Notts County	Bristol City
7 Beresford, John	Southampton	Birmingham City
15 Bignall, Michael G.	Aylesbury United	Boreham Wood
4 Blackwood, Michael	Aston Villa	Chester City
21 Bradley, Shayne	Southampton	Exeter City
15 Branston, Guy P.B.	Leicester City	Rotherham United
29 Brennan, James G.	Bristol City	Nottingham Forest
30 Brockett, Luke	Chesham United	Chalfont St Peter
22 Brown, Greg J.	Macclesfield Town	Morecambe
21 Canham, Scott W.	Leyton Orient	Chesham United
22 Cartwright, Mark N.	Wrexham	Newry Town
10 Clarke, Adrian J.	Southend United	Carlisle United

	Player	From	To	Fee
29	Cleaver, Christopher W.	Peterborough United	Kings Lynn	
14	Conner, Stephen J.	Dagenham & Redbridge	Billericay Town	
29	Cooper, Mark N.	Rushden & Diamonds	Telford United	
30	Corns, Stuart R.	Telford United	Droylsden	
1	Dean, Michael J.	AFC Bournemouth	Basingstoke Town	
8	Dibble, Andrew G.	Hartlepool United	Carlisle United	
11	Di Lella, Gustavo M.	Hartlepool United	Blyth Spartans	
9	Douglas, Andrew S.	Carlisle United	Gretna	
1	Everitt, Leigh A.	Nuneaton Borough	Stafford Rangers	
7	Fenton, Nicholas L.	Manchester City	Notts County	
30	Fiore, Mark J.	Chesham United	Chalfont St Peter	
18	Fitzpatrick, Lee G.	Blackburn Rovers	Hartlepool United	
18	Forbes, Terrell	West Ham United	AFC Bournemouth	
11	Glennon, Matthew	Bolton Wanderers	Port Vale	
4	Grant, Anthony J.	Everton	Tranmere Rovers	
4	Green, Richard E.	Walsall	Rochdale	
8	Griffin, Charles J.	Swindon Town	Yeovil Town	
1	Harrison, Gerald R.	Sunderland	Hull City	
14	Hockton, Danny J.	Millwall	Leyton Orient	
15	Housham, Steven J.	Scunthorpe United	Gainsborough Trinity	
15	Hulse, Robert W.	Crewe Alexandra	Hyde United	
15	Hume, Mark A.	Doncaster Rovers	Gainsborough Trinity	
1	Ingham, Michael G.	Sunderland	Carlisle United	
16	Janney, Mark	Dagenham & Redbridge	Braintree Town	
15	Johnston, Allan	Sunderland	Birmingham City	
10	Johnston, Ray	Bristol Rovers	Southampton	
4	Jones, Mark A.	Wolverhampton Wanderers	Cheltenham Town	
15	Kelly, Paul L.M.	Chesham United	Boreham Wood	
30	Killick, Thomas M.	Basingstoke Town	Walton & Hersham	
7	Knight, Richard	Derby County	Hull City	
18	Lee, David M.	Wigan Athletic	Blackpool	
10	Marcelle, Clinton S.	Barnsley	Scunthorpe United	
15	Marshall, Scott R.	Southampton	Brentford	
13	McLaren, Andrew	Reading	Livingston	
25	Midgley, Neil	Ipswich Town	Luton Town	
11	Miller, Matthew	Hampton & Richmond Borough	Fleet Town	
14	Morris, Andrew D.	Rochdale	Scarborough	
18	Morrish, Adam	Southend United	Dartford	
11	Muggleton, Carl D.	Stoke City	Mansfield Town	
30	Naylor, Dominic J.	Stevenage Borough	Dagenham & Redbridge	
7	Omoyimni, Emmanuel	West Ham United	Gillingham	
4	Pates, Bradley J.	Macclesfield Town	Winsford Town	
8	Perez, Lionel	Newcastle United	Scunthorpe United	
7	Perkins, Christopher P.	Hartlepool United	Chesterfield	
23	Phelan, Terrence M.	Everton	Crystal Palace	
23	Pinnock, James E.	Gillingham	Margate	
22	Porter, Andrew M.	Wigan Athletic	Mansfield Town	
22	Reece, Dominic M.A.	Hednesford Town	Atherstone United	
22	Ribeiro, Bruno M.F.	Leeds United	Sheffield United	
24	Rowe, Rodney C.	York City	Halifax Town	
3	Russell, Craig S.	Manchester City	Darlington	
18	Searle, Damon	Carlisle United	Rochdale	
8	Simpson, Philip M.	Yeovil Town	Enfield	
11	Smith, Philip A.	Millwall	Ashford Town	
16	Smyth, Peter W.	Leigh RMI	Radcliffe Borough	
11	Stoker, Gareth	Rochdale	Scarborough	
20	Stowell, Matthew D.	Bristol City	Yeovil Town	
19	Strong, Grant	Chelmsford City	Whitham Town	
14	Thirlwell, Paul	Sunderland	Swindon Town	
12	Thompson, Richard O.	Wycombe Wanderers	Kingstonian	
14	Thurstan, Mark R.	Carlisle United	Gretna	
26	Turkington, Edmond B.	Altrincham	Leigh RMI	
30	Turpin, Simon J.	Leigh RMI	Winsford United	
22	Westcott, John P.J.	Brighton & Hove Albion	Bognor Regis Town	
29	Williams, Richard J.	Nuneaton Borough	Stafford Rangers	
22	Wilmot, Ellis J.	Bristol City	Weymouth	
30	Winter, Steven D.	Forest Green Rovers	Basingstoke Town	
22	Wreh, Christopher	Arsenal	Birmingham City	

November 1999

	Player	From	To	Fee
24	Alcide, Colin J.	Hull City	York City	80,000
19	Branston, Guy P.B.	Leicester City	Rotherham United	50,000
3	Brennan, James G.	Bristol City	Nottingham Forest	undisclosed
5	Burns, John C.	Nottingham Forest	Bristol City	100,000
19	Carr, Graeme	Scarborough	Workington	undisclosed
5	Cox, Neil J.	Bolton Wanderers	Watford	500,000
30	Cutler, Neil A.	Chester City	Aston Villa	Free
25	D'Auria, David A.	Hull City	Chesterfield	50,000
19	Ejiofor, Emeke	Moor Green	Rocester	undisclosed
5	Galloway, Michael A.	Gillingham	Chesterfield	15,000
25	Gayle, John	Scunthorpe United	Shrewsbury Town	Free
30	Gibbons, Daniel	Weston-Super-Mare	Newport (IW)	undisclosed
1	Granville, Daniel P.	Leeds United	Manchester City	undisclosed
11	Gutzmore, Leon	Aldershot Town	Bedford Town	6000
19	Jones, Graeme A.	Wigan Athletic	St Johnstone	100,000
24	McAvoy, Andrew D.	Blackburn Rovers	Hartlepool United	undisclosed
12	Millen, Keith D.	Watford	Bristol City	35,000
15	Moore, Darren M.	Bradford City	Portsmouth	500,000
12	Payne, Grant	Woking	Aldershot Town	20,000
5	Peacock, Lee A.	Mansfield Town	Manchester City	undisclosed
4	Perkins, Christopher P.	Hartlepool United	Chesterfield	undisclosed
30	Peron, Jean F.	Portsmouth	Wigan Athletic	Free
2	Rea, Simon	Birmingham City	Peterborough United	Free
25	Rowe, Rodney C.	York City	Gillingham	45,000
4	Rowland, Lynden J.	Halesowen Town	Kings Lynn	undisclosed
19	Smith, Danny	Kingstonian	Hampton & Richmond Borough	undisclosed
30	Taylor, Robert A.	Gillingham	Manchester City	1,500,000
18	Todd, Andrew J.J.	Bolton Wanderers	Charlton Athletic	750,000

17 Walters, Mark E.	Swindon Town	Bristol Rovers	Free

Temporary transfers

11 Agogo, Manuel	Sheffield Wednesday	Chesterfield	
18 Agyemang, Patrick	Wimbledon	Brentford	
23 Alcide, Colin J.	Hull City	York City	
5 Allsop, Daniel	Manchester City	Notts County	
30 Barry, Peter L.	Nuneaton Borough	Racing Club Warwick	
12 Beck, Mikkel	Derby County	Nottingham Forest	
19 Bernard, Curtis J.	Barnsley	Emley	
26 Betsy, Kevin E.L.	Fulham	Hull City	
9 Blaney, Steven D.	Billericay Town	Heybridge Swifts	
27 Bonfield, Darren	Hitchen Town	Hemel Hempstead Town	
11 Brady, Matthew J.	Boreham Wood	Wycombe Wanderers	
25 Branch, Paul M.	Everton	Wolverhampton Wanderers	
11 Brissett, Jason C.	Walsall	Cheltenham Town	
19 Brown, Michael R.	Manchester City	Portsmouth	
23 Bywater, Stephen M.	West Ham United	Hull City	
4 Cadamarteri, Daniel L.	Everton	Fulham	
22 Canham, Scott W.	Leyton Orient	Chesham United	
12 Carmody, Michael	Altrincham	Ashton United	
12 Carrick, Michael	West Ham United	Swindon Town	
26 Chettle, Stephen	Nottingham Forest	Barnsley	
12 Clare, Daryl A.	Grimsby Town	Northampton Town	
12 Clarke, Daniel N.	Enfield	Leyton Pennant	
13 Cleeve, Anthony G.	Basingstoke Town	Hampton & Richmond Borough	
23 Clement, Neil	Chelsea	Brentford	
27 Corns, Stuart R.	Telford United	Droylsden	
18 Critchley, Neil	Crewe Alexandra	Hyde United	
19 Curtis, John C.K.	Manchester United	Barnsley	
24 Davies, Jamie	Swansea City	Llanelli	
9 Di Lella, Gustavo M.	Hartlepool United	Blyth Spartans	
18 Donnelly, Mark P.	Bury	Whitby Town	
12 Douglas, Andrew S.	Carlisle United	Gretna	
3 Dryden, Richard A.	Southampton	Stoke City	
1 Durnin, John P.	Portsmouth	Blackpool	
12 Farrelly, Gareth	Everton	Bolton Wanderers	
7 Fenton, Nicholas L.	Manchester City	Notts County	
12 Gibbons, Daniel	Weston-Super-Mare	Newport (IW)	
18 Graham, Gareth L.	Brentford	Crawley Town	
5 Greenacre, Christopher M.	Manchester City	Mansfield Town	
9 Grime, Dominic	Boreham Wood	Chertsey Town	
4 Hamilton, Ian R.	Sheffield United	Grimsby Town	
15 Hulse, Robert W.	Crewe Alexandra	Hyde United	
19 Hume, Mark A.	Doncaster Rovers	Barrow	
22 Humphreys, Ritchie J.	Sheffield Wednesday	Cardiff City	
7 Johnston, Ray	Bristol Rovers	Southampton	
4 Keeble, Shaun R.	Kings Lynn	Raunds Town	
28 Lee, David M.	Wigan Athletic	Blackpool	
1 Linger, Paul H.	Billericay Town	Braintree Town	
26 Lisbie, Kevin A.	Charlton Athletic	Reading	
5 Lynch, Paul E.	Accrington Stanley	Netherfield Kendal	
20 Marcelle, Clinton S.	Barnsley	Scunthorpe United	
19 Marshall, Dwight W.	Kingstonian	Slough Town	
12 Mason, Gary	Manchester City	Hartlepool United	
18 Messer, Gary M.	Bury	Whitby Town	
12 Miller, Matthew	Hampton & Richmond Borough	Fleet Town	
15 Morris, Andrew D.	Rochdale	Scarborough	
19 Morrish, Adam	Southend United	Dartford	
9 Niemi, Antti	Rangers	Charlton Athletic	
19 O'Kane, John A.	Everton	Bolton Wanderers	
1 Ormerod, Anthony	Middlesbrough	York City	
1 Perez, Lionel	Newcastle United	Scunthorpe United	
1 Perkins, Christopher P.	Southend United	Kettering Town	
25 Phelan, Terrence M.	Everton	Crystal Palace	
30 Planck, Thomas	Margate	Sittingbourne	
5 Potter, Daniel R.J.	Exter City	Weymouth	
22 Price, Ryan	Macclesfield Town	Telford United	
4 Ritchie, Stuart A.	Havant & Waterlooville	Wokingham Town	
11 Rowbotham, Darren	Exeter City	Leyton Orient	
3 Russell, Craig S.	Manchester City	Darlington	
11 Sailesman, Neil A.	Burton Albion	Rocester	
17 Searle, Damon	Carlisle United	Rochdale	
15 Smith, Philip A.	Millwall	Ashford Town	
5 Soares, Clifton J.	Newport (IW)	Wokingham Town	
1 Spink, Dean P.	Wrexham	Shrewsbury Town	
11 Stoker, Gareth	Rochdale	Scarborough	
25 Stowell, Matthew D.	Bristol City	Rushden & Diamonds	
26 Thorpe, Anthony	Bristol City	Luton Town	
12 Thurstan, Mark R.	Carlisle United	Gretna	
23 Vaughan, John	Lincoln City	Colchester United	
19 Watkins, Dale A.	Cheltenham Town	Kettering Town	
19 Watts, Stephen	Leyton Orient	Welling United	
23 Westcott, John P.J.	Brighton & Hove Albion	Bognor Regis Town	
26 White, Alan	Luton Town	Colchester United	
5 Wilkinson, Lee A.	Spalding United	Hucknall Town	
30 Williams, Richard J.	Nuneaton Borough	Stafford Rangers	
10 Williams, Ryan N.	Tranmere Rovers	Chesterfield	
12 Wright, Stephen J.	Liverpool	Crewe Alexandra	

December 1999

23 Appleton, Arthur	Yeovil Town	Mangotsfield United	undisclosed
9 Ball, Kevin A.	Sunderland	Fulham	200,000
21 Brady, Matthew	Boreham Wood	Wycombe Wanderers	undisclosed
20 Brown, John K.	Blackburn Rovers	Barnsley	100,000
2 Burley, Craig W.	Celtic	Derby County	3,000,000
23 Campbell, Stephen J.	Chippenham Town	Devizes Town	undisclosed
15 Chettle, Stephen	Nottingham Forest	Barnsley	Free
15 Dunne, Joseph J.	Dover Athletic	Colchester United	undisclosed

10	Eadie, Darren M.	Norwich City	Leicester City	3,000,000
1	Ellender, Paul	Altrincham	Scarborough	undisclosed
23	Emerson, Augusto T.	Sheffield Wednesday	Chelsea	2,700,000
6	Everitt, Leigh A.	Nuneaton Borough	Stafford Rangers	undisclosed
17	Farrelly, Gareth	Everton	Bolton Wanderers	Free
10	Goodwin, Shaun	Doncaster Rovers	Altrincham	undisclosed
24	Grant, Anthony J.	Everton	Manchester City	450,000
16	Griffiths, Carl B.	Port Vale	Leyton Orient	80,000
17	Hanlon, Ritchie K.	Welling United	Peterborough United	Free
3	Hiley, Scott P.	Southampton	Portsmouth	200,000
16	Kilbane, Kevin D.	West Bromwich Albion	Sunderland	2,500,000
10	McLoughlin, Alan F.	Portsmouth	Wigan Athletic	250,000
24	Nartey, Joseph H.	Aldershot Town	Chesham United	3000
17	O'Connor, Joseph N.	Nuneaton Borough	Kingstonian	undisclosed
22	O'Kane, John A.	Everton	Bolton Wanderers	undisclosed
8	Ovens, Steven	Witney Town	Tiverton Town	undisclosed
17	Palmer, Carlton L.	Nottingham Forest	Coventry City	500,000
3	Reilly, Alan	Manchester City	Halifax Town	undisclosed
7	Riza, Omer K.	Arsenal	West Ham United	20,000
8	Simpson, Fitzroy	Portsmouth	Hearts	100,000
24	Stevens, David P.	Dulwich Hamlet	Hayes	undisclosed
21	Stowell, Matthew D.	Bristol City	Rushden & Diamonds	undisclosed
16	Tate, Christopher D.	Halifax Town	Scarborough	80,000
3	Tate, Steven K.	Havant & Waterlooville	Weymouth	undisclosed
17	Walker, Leigh D.	Sheffield United	Barnsley	Free
22	Watkins, Dale A.	Cheltenham Town	Kettering Town	undisclosed
17	Wilcox, Jason M.	Blackburn Rovers	Leeds United	3,000,000
10	Williams, Gareth J.	Hull City	Scarborough	10,000

Temporary transfers

3	Ablett, Gary I.	Birmingham City	Wycombe Wanderers
17	Agogo, Manuel	Sheffield Wednesday	Lincoln City
21	Agyemang, Patrick	Wimbledon	Brentford
24	Aiston, Sam J.	Sunderland	Shrewsbury Town
21	Aldridge, Martin J.	Blackpool	Rushden & Diamonds
30	Allsop, Michael P.	Burton Albion	Belper Town
9	Angell, Brett A.M.	Stockport County	Notts County
27	Barry, Peter L.	Nuneaton Borough	Redditch United
30	Bennett, Thomas M.	Stockport County	Walsall
17	Beresford, David	Huddersfield Town	Preston North End
3	Bird, Anthony	Swansea City	Merthyr Tydfil
17	Black, Thomas R.	Arsenal	Bristol City
3	Blake, Marvin	Nuneaton Borough	Atherstone United
10	Bolt, Daniel A.	Woking	Dover Athletic
29	Bramble, Titus M.	Ipswich Town	Colchester United
13	Brissett, Jason C.	Walsall	Cheltenham Town
23	Broad, Stephen	Chelsea	Hayes
2	Brockett, Luke	Chesham United	Chalfont St Peter
10	Bromby, Leigh	Sheffield Wednesday	Mansfield Town
7	Brough, Michael	Notts County	Spalding United
17	Brown, Michael R.	Manchester City	Sheffield United
3	Cadette, Nathan D.	Cardiff City	Inter-Cardiff
22	Canham, Scott W.	Leyton Orient	Chesham United
17	Carrick, Michael	West Ham United	Swindon Town
20	Cartwright, Mark N.	Wrexham	Bury
10	Carty, Paul	Worcester City	Nuneaton Borough
24	Chambers, Leroy D.	Altrincham	Kettering Town
3	Cheal, Mark	Lancaster City	Netherfield Kendal
12	Clare, Daryl A.	Grimsby Town	Northampton Town
10	Clark, Dean W.	Brentford	Uxbridge
21	Clement, Neil	Chelsea	Brentford
20	Critchley, Neil	Crewe Alexandra	Hyde United
17	Culbertson, Richard D.J.	Swindon Town	Larne
24	Culkin, Nicholas J.	Manchester United	Hull City
17	Cullen, David J.	Sheffield United	Halifax Town
20	Curtis, John C.K.	Manchester United	Barnsley
16	Dalton, Paul	Huddersfield Town	Carlisle United
2	Davidson, Daniel	Burton Albion	Belper Town
3	Davison, Aidan J.	Sheffield United	Bradford City
13	Donnelly, Mark P.	Bury	Whitby Town
2	Dowe, Julian L.	Rochdale	Burton Albion
6	Dryden, Richard A.	Southampton	Stoke City
3	Durnin, John P.	Portsmouth	Carlisle United
9	Ellington, Lee S.	Hull City	Altrincham
3	Elliott, Stuart T.	Newcastle United	AFC Bournemouth
7	Fenton, Nicholas L.	Manchester City	Notts County
4	Flitter, Matthew A.H.	Chesham United	Hampton & Richmond Borough
6	Greenacre, Christopher M.	Manchester City	Mansfield Town
7	Gregory, Neil R.	Colchester United	Canvey Island
22	Grime, Dominic	Boreham Wood	Gravesend & Northfleet
16	Hadland, Philip J.	Reading	Aldershot Town
17	Hall, Paul A.	Coventry City	Sheffield United
17	Harper, Kevin P.	Derby County	Walsall
10	Hendry, Iain	Woking	Molesey
14	Holloway, Darren	Sunderland	Bolton Wanderers
7	Howell, Dean G.	Notts County	Spalding United
24	Hughes, John P.	Chelsea	Crewe Alexandra
17	Hulse, Robert W.	Crewe Alexandra	Hyde United
19	Hume, Mark A.	Doncaster Rovers	Barrow
21	Hurdle, Augustus A.J.	Basingstoke Town	Ashford Town
3	Kelly, Gavin R.	Tottenham Hotspur	Chelmsford City
3	Kenna, Warren J.	Peterborough United	Cambridge City
26	Killick, Thomas M.	Basingstoke Town	Fleet Town
24	Kippe, Frode	Liverpool	Stoke City
3	Knight, Richard	Derby County	Macclesfield Town
10	Lindley, James E.	Notts County	Ilkeston Town
2	Lynch, Paul E.	Accrington Stanley	Netherfield Kendal
2	Lyttle, Gerard F.	Peterborough United	Kingstonian

24 McGovern, Brian	Arsenal	Queens Park Rangers
3 Makel, Lee R.	Heart of Midlothian	Portsmouth
19 Marshall, Dwight W.	Kingstonian	Slough Town
15 Mason, Gary	Manchester City	Hartlepool United
28 Matthews, Robert D.	Stockport County	Blackpool
24 May, David	Manchester United	Huddersfield Town
3 Meredith, Thomas J.A.	St Albans City	Boreham Wood
15 Messer, Gary	Bury	Whitby Town
10 Metcalfe, Christian W.	Hayes	Boreham Wood
25 Mings, Adrian	Forest Green Rovers	Yate Town
17 Morrison, David E.	Leyton Orient	Stevenage Borough
11 Mputu, Fiston	Hampton & Richmond Borough	Chertsey Town
9 Muggleton, Carl D.	Stoke City	Chesterfield
3 Newton, Christopher J.	Halifax Town	Barrow
30 Nicholls, Mark	Chelsea	Reading
21 Omoyimni, Emmanuel	West Ham United	Scunthorpe United
1 Ormerod, Anthony	Middlesbrough	York City
24 Pepper, Colin N.	Aberdeen	Southend United
2 Perez, Lionel	Newcastle United	Scunthorpe United
1 Perkins, Christopher P.	Southend United	Kettering Town
30 Phelan, Terrence M.	Everton	Crystal Palace
17 Pinamonte, Lorenzo	Bristol City	Brighton & Hove Albion
2 Potter, Graham S.	West Bromwich Albion	Reading
17 Potter, Lee	Bolton Wanderers	Halifax Town
3 Quailey, Brian S.	West Bromwich Albion	Blackpool
1 Quinton, Bradley L.J.	Bishop's Stortford	Leyton Pennant
17 Randall, Adrian J.	Forest Green Rovers	Weymouth
10 Rew, Ian K.	Newport (IW)	Wokingham Town
17 Rigby, Malcolm	Stafford Rangers	Northwich Victoria
22 Ritchie, Paul M.	Heart of Midlothian	Bolton Wanderers
24 Scope, Tynan G.A.	Bristol City	Chesham United
3 Shuttlewood, Justin	Forest Green Rovers	Salisbury City
16 Smith, Christopher A.	Reading	Hayes
3 Thompson, Christopher N.	Ilkeston Town	Stamford
1 Thorpe, Anthony L.	Bristol City	Luton Town
3 Walker, Richard S.	Crewe Alexandra	Northwich Victoria
17 Ward, Darren P.	Watford	Queens Park Rangers
16 Ware, Paul D.	Macclesfield Town	Nuneaton Borough
3 Webster, Adam	Notts County	Bedworth United
17 White, Daniel A.J.	Hampton & Richmond Borough	Leatherhead
28 Williams, Richard J.	Nuneaton Borough	Stafford Rangers
14 Williams, Ryan N.	Tranmere Rovers	Chesterfield
13 Woolsey, Jeffrey A.	Dagenham & Redbridge	Enfield
21 Xavier, Mark J.	Basingstoke Town	Ashford Town
30 Zamora, Robert L.	Bristol Rovers	Bath City

January 2000

26 Barry, Peter L.	Nuneaton Borough	Redditch United	undisclosed
20 Branch, Paul M.	Everton	Wolverhampton Wanderers	500,000
14 Brown, Michael R.	Manchester City	Sheffield United	375,000
10 Davies, Simon	Peterborough United	Tottenham Hotspur	700,000
17 Dunbavin, Ian S.	Liverpool	Shrewsbury Town	Free
10 Etherington, Matthew	Peterborough United	Tottenham Hotspur	700,000
27 Fitzpatrick, Lee G.	Blackburn Rovers	Hartlepool United	Free
28 Gardner, Anthony	Port Vale	Tottenham Hotspur	undisclosed
18 Goldbaek, Bjarne	Chelsea	Fulham	500,000
1 Gooden, Ty M.	Swindon Town	Gillingham	75,000
24 Greenacre, Christopher M.	Manchester City	Mansfield Town	Free
21 Hemmings, Anthony G.	Ilkeston Town	Chester City	30,000
21 Hughes, Ceri M.	Wimbledon	Portsmouth	150,000
20 Jaszczun, Anthony J.	Aston Villa	Blackpool	30,000
28 Lester, Jack W.	Grimsby Town	Nottingham Forest	300,000
5 Onuora, Ifem	Swindon Town	Gillingham	125,000
21 Potter, Lee	Bolton Wanderers	Halifax Town	30,000
12 Rigby, Malcolm R.	Stafford Rangers	Northwich Victoria	undisclosed
28 Svensson, Matthias	Crystal Palace	Charlton Athletic	600,000
21 Williams, Gary L.	Accrington Stanley	Doncaster Rovers	undisclosed
27 Williams, Richard J.	Nuneaton Borough	Stafford Rangers	undisclosed

Temporary transfers

24 Aiston, Sam J.	Sunderland	Shrewsbury Town
5 Aldridge, Martin J.	Blackpool	Rushden & Diamonds
14 Armstrong, Paul	Stevenage Borough	Aylesbury United
21 Babb, Philip A.	Liverpool	Tranmere Rovers
28 Baker, Matthew C.	Hull City	Bradford Park Avenue
29 Barker, Daniel T.	Basingstoke Town	Fleet Town
24 Behzadi, Bobby	Stevenage Borough	Wealdstone
17 Beresford, David	Huddersfield Town	Preston North End
21 Bettney, Scott	Sheffield Wednesday	Hednesford Town
3 Bonfield, Darren	Hitchin Town	Hemel Hempstead Town
4 Branch, Paul M.	Everton	Wolverhampton Wanderers
4 Brockett, Luke	Chesham United	Chalfont St Peter
12 Bromby, Leigh	Sheffield Wednesday	Mansfield Town
6 Brough, Michael	Notts County	Spalding United
6 Brown, Aaron W.	Bristol City	Exeter City
14 Bullock, Martin J.	Barnsley	Port Vale
7 Byrne, Shaun R.	West Ham United	Bristol Rovers
3 Cheal, Mark	Lancaster City	Netherfield Kendal
12 Clare, Daryl A.	Grimsby Town	Northampton Town
10 Clark, Dean W.	Brentford	Uxbridge
28 Cooksey, Scott A.	Shrewsbury Town	Hereford United
28 Critchley, Neil	Crewe Alexandra	Hyde United
21 Cullen, David J.	Sheffield United	Halifax Town
7 Curran, Danny	Leyton Orient	Purfleet
4 Davison, Aidan J.	Sheffield United	Bradford City
18 Doane, Ben N.D.C.	Sheffield United	Kettering Town
21 Drake, Kieron A.	Maidenhead United	Burnham
19 Dunwell, Richard K.	Enfield	Gravesend & Northfleet
20 Earnshaw, Robert	Cardiff City	Greenock Morton

21 Edwards, Ross P.	Gravesend & Northfleet	Croydon	
5 Elliott, Stuart T.	Newcastle United	AFC Bournemouth	
17 Evans, Kevin	Leeds United	Swansea City	
7 Eyjolfsson, Sigurdur	Walsall	Chester City	
14 Gledhill, Lee	Barnet	Slough Town	
18 Glennon, Matthew W.	Bolton Wanderers	Stockport County	
14 Gordon, Daniel	Aylesbury United	Tring Town	
7 Green, Richard E.	Walsall	Northampton Town	
7 Greenacre, Christopher M.	Manchester City	Mansfield Town	
4 Gregory, Neil R.	Colchester United	Canvey Island	
19 Harper, Kevin P.	Derby County	Walsall	
14 Hendry, Iain	Woking	Molesey	
21 Hibbins, John J.	Sheffield Wednesday	Hednesford Town	
7 Hobson, Gary	Brighton & Hove Albion	Chester City	
6 Hodson, Benjamin M.	Hayes	Wealdstone	
21 Holmshaw, James	Worksop Town	Matlock Town	
20 Holt, Michael A.	Rochdale	Northwich Victoria	
21 Hoult, Russell	Derby County	Portsmouth	
18 Housham, Steven J.	Scunthorpe United	Barrow	
6 Howell, Dean G.	Notts County	Spalding United	
21 Hughes, James J.	Cardiff City	Cwmbran Town	
22 Hurdle, Augustus A.J.	Basingstoke Town	Crawley Town	
7 Hylgaard, Morten L.	Coventry City	Scunthorpe United	
14 Jackson, Mark G.	Leeds United	Barnsley	
27 Johnston, Allan	Sunderland	Bolton Wanderers	
28 Jones, Jonathan B.	Chester City	Caernafon Town	
21 Jones, Stephen G.	Bristol City	Brentford	
14 Kadi, Junior	Kingstonian	Hampton & Richmond Borough	
6 Kelly, Gavin R.	Tottenham Hotspur	Chelmsford City	
28 Kelly, Seamus	Cardiff City	Merthyr Tydfil	
23 Kippe, Frode	Liverpool	Stoke City	
19 Knight, Richard	Derby County	Oxford United	
3 Lee, Jason	Chesterfield	Peterborough United	
7 Lindley, James E.	Notts County	Ilkeston Town	
3 McCammon, Mark J.	Charlton Athletic	Swindon Town	
28 McCormack, Francis	St Albans City	Sutton United	
20 McCoy, Barry J.	Aldershot Town	Fleet Town	
23 McGovern, Brian	Arsenal	Queens Park Rangers	
1 Meredith, Thomas J.A.	St Albans City	Boreham Wood	
13 Metcalfe, Christian W.	Hayes	Boreham Wood	
20 Morrison, David E.	Leyton Orient	Dover Athletic	
10 Muggleton, Carl D.	Stoke City	Chesterfield	
20 Notman, Alexander M.	Manchester United	Sheffield United	
23 Omoyimni, Emmanuel	West Ham United	Scunthorpe United	
3 Onuora, Ifem	Swindon Town	Gillingham	
18 O'Shea, John F.	Manchester United	AFC Bournemouth	
18 Pinamonte, Lorenzo	Bristol City	Brighton & Hove Albion	
28 Potter, Daniel R.J.	Exeter City	Salisbury City	
22 Randall, Adrian J.	Forest Green Rovers	Weymouth	
19 Rankin, Isiah	Bradford City	Birmingham City	
13 Rew, Ian K.	Newport (IW)	Wokingham Town	
10 Richardson, Kevin	Barnsley	Blackpool	
14 Roberts, Christian J.	Cardiff City	Drogheda	
20 Saunders, Lee	Ilkeston Town	Shepshed Dynamo	
29 Shaw, Darren R.	Stafford Rangers	Sutton Coldfield Town	
14 Shuttlewood, Justin	Forest Green Rovers	Salisbury City	
20 Strevens, Benjamin J.	Barnet	Slough Town	
21 Sucharwycz, Gary	Hucknall Town	Matlock Town	
21 Taylor, Gareth K.	Manchester City	Port Vale	
18 Taylor, Martin	Blackburn Rovers	Darlington	
28 Taylor, Stephen C.	Kidderminster Harriers	Halesowen Town	
27 Thomas, David J.	Cardiff City	Drogheda	
20 Thomas, Wayne	Walsall	Shrewsbury Town	
21 Thompson, Glyn W.	Fulham	Mansfield Town	
21 Turner, Michael C.	Barnsley	Finn Harps	
22 Vaughan, John	Lincoln City	Chesterfield	
14 Vernazza, Paulo A.P.	Arsenal	Portsmouth	
4 Walker, Richard S.	Crewe Alexandra	Northwich Victoria	
14 Ward, Darren P.	Watford	Queens Park Rangers	
13 Ware, Paul D.	Macclesfield Town	Nuneaton Borough	
1 Webster, Adam	Notts County	Bedworth United	
28 Westcott, John P.J.	Brighton & Hove Albion	Sutton United	
28 White, Thomas M.	Bristol Rovers	Hereford United	
28 Williams, Anthony S.	Blackburn Rovers	Macclesfield Town	
21 Wilson, Scott A.	Rochdale	Altrincham	
12 Yorke-Johnson, Ross	Brighton & Hove Albion	Colchester United	

February 2000

11 Abbey, Zema	Hitchin Town	Cambridge United	undisclosed
11 Baptiste, Rocky	Wealdstone	Staines Town	undisclosed
24 Bennett, Gary	Sudbury AFC	Chelmsford City	undisclosed
1 Butler, Martin N.	Cambridge United	Reading	750,000
11 Collymore, Stanley V.	Aston Villa	Leicester City	Free
4 Cox, Ian G.	AFC Bournemouth	Burnley	500,000
4 D'Jaffo, Laurent	Stockport County	Sheffield United	100,000
1 Ford, Ryan	Manchester United	Notts County	Free
4 Frail, Stephen	Tranmere Rovers	St Johnstone	undisclosed
18 Gibb, Alistair S.	Northampton Town	Stockport County	50,000
4 Gregory, Neil R.	Colchester United	Canvey Island	Free
11 Hayes, Adrian M.	Diss Town	Boston United	undisclosed
3 Holland, Christopher J.	Birmingham City	Huddersfield Town	150,000
17 Lawson, Ian J.	Bury	Stockport County	150,000
10 McIntosh, Martin	Stockport County	Hibernian	250,000
4 Marshall, Dwight W.	Kingstonian	Slough Town	undisclosed
28 Melton, Stephen	Nottingham Forest	Stoke City	Free
15 Miller, Alan J.	West Bromwich Albion	Blackburn Rovers	50,000
7 Moore, Christian	Ilkeston Town	Burton Albion	undisclosed
11 Newell, Michael C.	Doncaster Rovers	Blackpool	Free

2 Norris, David M.	Boston United	Bolton Wanderers	50,000
4 Pinamonte, Lorenzo	Bristol City	Brentford	undisclosed
3 Quailey, Brian S.	West Bromwich Albion	Scunthorpe United	Free
18 Roberts, Neil W.	Wrexham	Wigan Athletic	450,000
28 Sheerin, Joseph E.	Chelsea	AFC Bournemouth	Free
3 Smith, Martin	Sheffield United	Huddersfield Town	300,000
1 Stewart, Marcus P.	Huddersfield Town	Ipswich Town	2,500,000
22 Thomas, Wayne	Walsall	Shrewsbury Town	Free
4 Torpey, Stephen D.J.	Bristol City	Scunthorpe United	200,000
18 Watson, Liam	Runcorn	Accrington Stanley	undisclosed
14 Williams, Ryan N.	Tranmere Rovers	Chesterfield	80,000
14 Yorke-Johnson, Ross	Brighton & Hove Albion	Colchester United	Free

Temporary transfers

25 Allsop, Daniel	Manchester City	Wrexham
24 Angell, Brett A.M.	Stockport County	Preston North End
11 Armstrong, Paul	Stevenage Borough	Aylesbury United
26 Ayres, James M.	Luton Town	Stevenage Borough
18 Barnett, David K.	Lincoln City	Forest Green Rovers
11 Beck, Mikkel	Derby County	Queens Park Rangers
21 Behzadi, Bobby	Stevenage Borough	Wealdstone
3 Bennett, Frank	Bristol Rovers	Exeter City
11 Boertien, Paul	Derby County	Crewe Alexandra
17 Bower, Mark J.	Bradford City	York City
18 Brooker, Paul	Fulham	Brighton & Hove Albion
4 Broughton, Drewe O.	Peterborough United	Nuneaton Borough
29 Burgess, Richard D.	Stoke City	Kidderminster Harriers
25 Campbell, James R.	Peterborough United	Spalding United
15 Canoville, Trevor	Hampton & Richmond Borough	Chertsey Town
11 Carmody, Michael	Altrincham	Ashton United
23 Carrick, Michael	West Ham United	Birmingham City
1 Cheal, Mark	Lancaster City	Netherfield Kendal
9 Clarke, Daniel N.	Enfield	Hertford Town
11 Cleaver, Christopher W.	Peterborough United	Cambridge United
16 Clegg, Michael J.	Manchester United	Ipswich Town
25 Cole, Ashley	Arsenal	Crystal Palace
26 Conner, Stephen J.	Dagenham & Redbridge	Billericay Town
28 Cooksey, Scott A.	Shrewsbury Town	Hereford United
18 Cort, Wayne	Harlow Town	Thame United
22 Cowan, Thomas	Burnley	Cambridge United
11 Crowe, Dean A.	Stoke City	Northampton Town
6 Curran, Danny	Leyton Orient	Purfleet
4 Davison, Aidan J.	Sheffield United	Bradford City
4 Dean, Michael J.	AFC Bournemouth	Dorchester Town
15 Doane, Ben N.D.C.	Sheffield United	Kettering Town
18 Donnelly, Mark P.	Bury	Workington
11 Durnin, John P.	Portsmouth	Carlisle United
24 Edwards, Christian N.H.	Nottingham Forest	Oxford United
29 Edwards, Ross P.	Gravesend & Northfleet	Croydon
25 Elliott, Stuart T.	Newcastle United	Stockport County
25 Evans, Rhys K.	Chelsea	Bristol Rovers
10 Eyjolfsson, Sigurdur	Walsall	Chester City
23 Forssell, Mikael K.	Chelsea	Crystal Palace
18 Fortune, Jonathan J.	Charlton Athletic	Mansfield Town
9 Fredgaard, Karsten	Sunderland	West Bromwich Albion
11 Freestone, Christopher M.	Hartlepool United	Cheltenham Town
4 Gibson, Paul R.	Notts County	Rochdale
14 Gledhill, Lee	Barnet	Slough Town
5 Griemink, Bart	Peterborough United	Swindon Town
2 Grime, Dominic	Boreham Wood	Gravesend & Northfleet
10 Hall, Paul A.	Coventry City	West Bromwich Albion
4 Hanson, David	Nuneaton Borough	Ashton United
21 Harper, Kevin P.	Derby County	Walsall
22 Hawkins, Peter S.	Wimbledon	York City
10 Healy, Brett W.	Nuneaton Borough	Solihull Borough
25 Healy, David J.	Manchester United	Port Vale
15 Hoult, Russell	Derby County	Portsmouth
11 Hutchings, Carl E.	Bristol City	Brentford
11 Hyldgaard, Morten	Coventry City	Scunthorpe United
24 Ilic, Sasa	Charlton Athletic	West Ham United
24 Inglethorpe, Alex M.	Leyton Orient	Exeter City
27 Johnston, Allan	Sunderland	Bolton Wanderers
27 Jones, Stephen G.	Bristol City	Brentford
3 Jones, Stuart C.	Sheffield Wednesday	Torquay United
18 Key, Lance W.	Northwich Victoria	Altrincham
27 Kippe, Frode	Liverpool	Stoke City
25 Knight, Zatyiah	Fulham	Peterborough United
25 Koogi, Anders B.	Peterborough United	Cambridge City
7 Lee, Jason	Chesterfield	Peterborough United
25 Lockwood, Adam B.	Reading	Maidenhead United
18 Love, Andrew M.	Grimsby Town	Ilkeston Town
3 Lumsdon, Christopher	Sunderland	Blackpool
22 Martin, Jae A.	Peterborough United	Welling United
25 McAlindon, Gareth E.	Scarborough	Gateshead
22 McCoy, Barry J.	Aldershot Town	Fleet Town
14 McKinnon, Robert	Heart of Midlothian	Carlisle United
11 McNiven, David J.	Oldham Athletic	Scarborough
10 Metcalfe, Christian W.	Hayes	Boreham Wood
21 Morrison, David E.	Leyton Orient	Dover Athletic
25 Muir, Ian J.	Nuneaton Borough	Moor Green
24 Nicholls, Mark	Chelsea	Grimsby Town
22 Notman, Alexander M.	Manchester United	Sheffield United
25 Omoyimni, Emmanuel	West Ham United	Barnet
8 Osborn, Mark	Wycombe Wanderers	Marlow
18 O'Shea, John F.	Manchester United	AFC Bournemouth
15 Petterson, Andrew K.	Portsmouth	Wolverhampton Wanderers
5 Porter, Andrew M.	Wigan Athletic	Chester City
25 Randall, Adrian J.	Forest Green Rovers	Weymouth

#	Player	From	To	Fee
20	Rankin, Isaiah	Bradford City	Birmingham City	
11	Richardson, Kevin	Barnsley	Blackpool	
24	Roberts, Ben J.	Middlesbrough	Luton Town	
18	Rose, Stephen D.	Manchester United	AFC Bournemouth	
11	Russell, Craig S.	Manchester City	Oxford United	
5	Ryder, Stuart H.	Nuneaton Borough	Stafford Rangers	
2	Samuels, Anthony	Stevenage Borough	Boreham Wood	
16	Saunders, Lee	Ilkeston Town	Shepshed Dynamo	
24	Searle, Stuart A.	Aldershot Town	Molesey	
11	Skelton, Craig E.	Darlington	Altrincham	
12	Smyth, Peter W.	Leigh RMI	Chorley	
18	Stamp, Darryn M.	Scunthorpe United	Halifax Town	
16	Swan, Iain	Oldham Athletic	Leigh RMI	
18	Telemaque, Errol	Hayes	Molesey	
3	Thomas, Anton	Burton Albion	Hinckley United	
21	Thompson, Glyn	Fulham	Mansfield Town	
25	Tremble, David G.	Scarborough	Gateshead	
22	Van der Kwaak, Peter	Reading	Carlisle United	
8	Vaughan, Anthony J.	Manchester City	Nottingham Forest	
23	Vaughan, John	Lincoln City	Chesterfield	
4	Wainwright, Neil	Sunderland	Darlington	
5	Walker, Richard S.	Crewe Alexandra	Northwich Victoria	
25	Wall, James	Hereford United	Burton Albion	
14	Ward, Darren P.	Watford	Queens Park Rangers	
19	White, Devon W.	Ilkeston Town	Stafford Rangers	
27	White, Thomas M.	Bristol Rovers	Hereford United	
15	Williams, Adrian	Wolverhampton Wanderers	Reading	
29	Williams, Anthony S.	Blackburn Rovers	Macclesfield Town	
26	Woolsey, Jeffrey A.	Dagenham & Redbridge	Billericay Town	
1	Zamora, Robert L.	Bristol Rovers	Brighton & Hove Albion	

March 2000

#	Player	From	To	Fee
7	Allaway, Shaun	Reading	Leeds United	300,000
24	Arnison, Paul S.	Newcastle United	Hartlepool United	Free
23	Butler, Philip A.	Port Vale	West Bromwich Albion	140,000
15	Calderwood, Colin	Aston Villa	Nottingham Forest	70,000
20	Campbell, Neil A.	Southend United	Doncaster Rovers	10,000
17	Conner, Stephen J.	Dagenham & Redbridge	Billericay Town	undisclosed
17	Cort, Wayne	Harlow Town	Thame United	undisclosed
3	Cullen, David J.	Sheffield United	Peterborough United	35,000
17	Cummins, Michael T.	Middlesbrough	Port Vale	Free
16	Davison, Aidan J.	Sheffield United	Bradford City	undisclosed
16	Derry, Shaun P.	Sheffield United	Portsmouth	300,000
9	Edinburgh, Justin C.	Tottenham Hotspur	Portsmouth	175,000
1	Fettis, Alan	Blackburn Rovers	York City	Free
2	Fitzpatrick Ian M.	Manchester United	Halifax Town	Free
10	Francis, Kevin M.D.	Oxford United	Stockport County	Free
6	Gill, Wayne J.	Blackburn Rovers	Blackpool	undisclosed
23	Goodlad, Mark	Nottingham Forest	Port Vale	undisclosed
21	Hall, Paul A.	Coventry City	Walsall	Free
6	Harper, Kevin P.	Derby County	Portsmouth	300,000
23	Hay, Christopher D.	Swindon Town	Huddersfield Town	70,000
3	Hendry, Edward C.J.	Rangers	Coventry City	750,000
10	Heskey, Emile W.	Leicester City	Liverpool	11,000,000
8	Hodge, John	Gillingham	Northampton Town	25,000
23	Horne, Barry	Huddersfield Town	Sheffield Wednesday	Free
30	Hoult, Russell	Derby County	Portsmouth	300,000
10	Hughes, Stephen J.	Arsenal	Everton	500,000
23	Hulbert, Robin J.	Swindon Town	Bristol City	25,000
23	Igoe, Samuel G.	Portsmouth	Reading	100,000
23	Jones, Eifion P.	Liverpool	Blackpool	Free
10	Jones, Stuart C.	Sheffield Wednesday	Torquay United	30,000
23	Kerrigan, Steven J.	Shrewsbury Town	Halifax Town	undisclosed
31	Kiely, Paul	Leek Town	Stafford Rangers	undisclosed
22	Lawrence, Matthew J.	Wycombe Wanderers	Millwall	200,000
15	Lee, Jason B.	Chesterfield	Peterborough United	50,000
23	Lewis, Ben	Heybridge Swifts	Chelmsford City	undisclosed
23	McVeigh, Paul F.	Tottenham Hotspur	Norwich City	undisclosed
21	Messer, Gary	Bury	Workington	undisclosed
16	Middleton, Craig D.	Cardiff City	Halifax Town	25,000
22	Nogan, Kurt	Preston North End	Cardiff City	50,000
23	Prior, Spencer J.	Derby County	Manchester City	500,000
17	Redfearn, Neil D.	Bradford City	Wigan Athletic	112,500
22	Ritchie, Paul M.	Heart of Midlothian	Bolton Wanderers	Free
23	Santos, Georges	Tranmere Rovers	West Bromwich Albion	25,000
16	Standen, Dean	Welling United	Luton Town	undisclosed
23	Taylor, Robert	Bolton Wanderers	West Bromwich Albion	90,000
2	Tuttle, David P.	Barnsley	Millwall	200,000
23	Vaughan, Anthony J.	Manchester City	Nottingham Forest	350,000
23	Wellens, Richard P.	Manchester United	Blackpool	undisclosed
23	Woodward, Andrew S.	Bury	Sheffield United	35,000
17	Wormull, Simon J.	Dover Athletic	Rushden & Diamonds	undisclosed
10	Young, Ryan	Chasetown	Nuneaton Borough	undisclosed

Temporary transfers

#	Player	From	To
30	Arkins, Steven	Reading	Basingstoke Town
23	Armstrong, Alun	Middlesbrough	Huddersfield Town
10	Armstrong, Paul	Stevenage Borough	Aylesbury United
10	Arnison, Paul S.	Newcastle United	Hartlepool United
31	Bailey, Jermaine A.	Ilkeston Town	VS Rugby
23	Baker, Steven R.	Middlesbrough	Darlington
23	Bankole, Ademola	Queens Park Rangers	Bradford City
21	Banya, Sahr M.	Kettering Town	Bedford Town
1	Barker, Daniel T.	Basingstoke Town	Fleet Town
30	Barnes, Steven L.	Barnet	Welling United
23	Bass, Jonathan D.M.	Birmingham City	Gillingham
10	Batty, Laurence W.	Woking	Chesham United
23	Beavers, Paul M.	Oldham Athletic	Hartlepool United
13	Beck, Mikkel	Derby County	Queens Park Rangers
30	Belgrave, Barrington	Plymouth Argyle	Yeovil Town
23	Bennett, Thomas M.	Stockport County	Walsall
3	Blake, Marvin	Nuneaton Borough	Halesowen Town
10	Bonfield, Darren	Hitchin Town	Gravesend & Northfleet
10	Bradshaw, Mark	Halifax Town	Nuneaton Borough

22 Brady, Gary	Newcastle United	Norwich City
6 Branagan, Keith G.	Bolton Wanderers	Ipswich Town
16 Brayson, Paul	Reading	Cardiff City
19 Brooker, Paul	Fulham	Brighton & Hove Albion
5 Broughton, Drewe O.	Peterborough United	Nuneaton Borough
27 Bullock, Darren J.	Bury	Rushden & Diamonds
2 Burke, Paul	Sheffield United	Whitby Town
27 Butterfield, John P.	Barnet	Boreham Wood
6 Byfield, Darren	Aston Villa	Blackpool
17 Campagna, Samuel P.P.	Swindon Town	Bath City
27 Campbell, James R.	Peterborough United	Spalding United
23 Campbell, Stuart P.	Leicester City	Birmingham City
18 Canoville, Trevor	Hampton & Richmond Borough	Chertsey Town
3 Charles, Julian	Brentford	Woking
3 Clark, Dean W.	Brentford	Uxbridge
14 Cleaver, Christopher W.	Peterborough United	Cambridge City
23 Clegg, Michael J.	Manchester United	Wigan Athletic
23 Clement, Neil	Chelsea	West Bromwich Albion
31 Connolly, Gary M.	Portsmouth	Havant & Waterlooville
7 Cooke, Terence J.	Manchester City	Wigan Athletic
23 Cook, Robert P.	Forest Green Rovers	Gloucester City
16 Cooksey, Scott A.	Shrewsbury Town	Hereford United
10 Coppinger, James	Newcastle United	Hartlepool United
3 Crouch, Peter J.	Tottenham Hotspur	Dulwich Hamlet
23 Crowe, Dean A.	Stoke City	Bury
5 Dean, Michael J.	AFC Bournemouth	Dorchester Town
23 Dryden, Richard A.	Southampton	Stoke City
21 Dunning, Richard	Blackburn Rovers	Oldham Athletic
6 Edinburgh, Justin C.	Tottenham Hotspur	Portsmouth
29 Elliott, Stuart T.	Newcastle United	Stockport County
23 Etherington, Craig	West Ham United	Plymouth Argyle
22 Evans, David A.	Barnsley	Mansfield Town
23 Fenton, Nicholas L.	Manchester City	AFC Bournemouth
23 Ferguson, Barry	Coventry City	Colchester United
21 Forrester, Jamie M.	Walsall	Northampton Town
17 Friars, Sean M.	Ipswich Town	Portadown
30 Girdler, Stuart K.	Woking	Basingstoke Town
17 Gordon, Daniel	Aylesbury United	Tring Town
23 Grant, Gareth M.	Bradford City	Bolton Wanderers
3 Gray, Wayne W.	Wimbledon	Swindon Town
30 Gummer, Sean M.	Derby County	Southport
3 Gunnlaugsson, Arnar B.	Leicester City	Stoke City
17 Hall, Paul A.	Coventry City	Walsall
22 Hamilton, Derrick V.	Newcastle United	Norwich City
23 Harrison, Gerald R.	Sunderland	Burnley
10 Harrison, Ross	Stevenage Borough	Basingstoke Town
30 Harvey, Lee	St Albans City	Boreham Wood
27 Hawkins, Peter S.	Wimbledon	York City
26 Healy, David J.	Manchester United	Port Vale
10 Heggs, Carl S.	Rushden & Diamonds	Chester City
17 Hendry, Iain	Woking	Kingstonian
31 Hibbins, John J.	Sheffield Wednesday	Worksop Town
7 Hodge, John	Gillingham	Northampton Town
24 Holbrook, Adam P.	Portsmouth	Havant & Waterlooville
3 Holmshaw, James	Worksop Town	Matlock Town
3 Holt, Grant	Halifax Town	Barrow
31 Hooker, Jonathan W.	Harlow Town	Braintree Town
23 Hoult, Russell	Derby County	Portsmouth
31 Hughes, James J.	Cardiff City	Cwmbran Town
23 Hunt, Jonathan R.	Sheffield United	Cambridge United
19 Hurdle, Augustus A.J.	Basingstoke Town	Crawley Town
13 Hutchings, Carl E.	Bristol City	Brentford
21 Ingram, Stuart D.	Hartlepool United	Scarborough
31 James, Kevin E.	Charlton Athletic	Farnborough Town
27 Johnston, Allan	Sunderland	Bolton Wanderers
23 Jones, Gary	Hartlepool United	Halifax Town
17 Jones, Stephen G.	Bristol City	Southend United
24 Kielty, Gerrard T.	Altrincham	Leigh RMI
21 Kitson, Paul	West Ham United	Charlton Athletic
13 Knight, Richard	Derby County	Oxford United
27 Knight, Zatyiah	Fulham	Peterborough United
16 Kotylo, Krystof J.	Nuneaton Borough	Redditch United
21 Lawrence, Matthew J.	Wycombe Wanderers	Millwall
14 Lescott, Aaron A.	Aston Villa	Lincoln City
31 Lindley, James E.	Notts County	Moor Green
20 Lovell, Stephen W.H.	Portsmouth	Exeter City
21 Lyttle, Desmond	Watford	West Bromwich Albion
24 Martindale, Gary	Rotherham United	Telford United
18 Martin, Jae A.	Peterborough United	Welling United
17 Matassa, Vincent	Basingstoke Town	Salisbury City
23 Matthews, Lee J.	Leeds United	Gillingham
31 McAlindon, Gareth E.	Scarborough	Gateshead
22 McClare, Sean P.	Barnsley	Rochdale
18 McCormack, Francis	St Albans City	Harrow Borough
17 McDonnell, Nicholas	Croydon	Tonbridge Angels
24 McNiven, David J.	Oldham Athletic	Southport
23 Meaker, Michael J.	Bristol Rovers	Swindon Town
30 Midgley, Neil	Ipswich Town	Kidderminster Harriers
3 Miller, Barry S.	Gillingham	Woking
10 Mills, Rowan L.	Bradford City	Manchester City
26 Morrison, David E.	Leyton Orient	Dover Athletic
23 Myers, Andrew	Bradford City	Portsmouth
31 Myhre, Thomas	Everton	Birmingham City
24 Naylor, Stuart W.	Exeter City	Rushden & Diamonds
3 Newby, Jon P.R.	Liverpool	Crewe Alexandra
17 Newman, Richard A.	Millwall	Reading
17 Ngonge, Felix M.	Watford	Huddersfield Town
28 Nicholls, Mark	Chelsea	Grimsby Town
23 Nielsen, Allan	Tottenham Hotspur	Wolverhampton Wanderers
6 Pepper, Colin N.	Aberdeen	Southend United
23 Perez, Lionel	Newcastle United	Cambridge United
24 Perkins, Christopher P.	Southend United	Kettering Town
7 Porter, Andrew M.	Wigan Athletic	Chester City
4 Randall, Adrian J.	Forest Green Rovers	Newport (IW)

21 Rankin, Isaiah	Bradford City	Birmingham City	
17 Reece, Dominic M.A.	Hednesford Town	Redditch United	
30 Reed, Ian P.	Nuneaton Borough	Halesowen Town	
23 Richardson, Barry	Lincoln City	Sheffield Wednesday	
24 Roberts, Ben J.	Middlesbrough	Luton Town	
13 Roden, Craig L.	Rotherham United	Gainsborough Trinity	
29 Russell, Craig S.	Manchester City	St Johnstone	
5 Ryder, Stuart H.	Nuneaton Borough	Stafford Rangers	
16 Samuels, Anthony	Stevenage Borough	Dagenham & Redbridge	
17 Saunders, Edward	Woking	Kingstonian	
23 Searle, Stuart A.	Aldershot Town	Molesey	
10 Shaw, Darren R.	Stafford Rangers	Solihull Borough	
24 Simba, Amara S.	Leyton Orient	Kingstonian	
20 Stevens, Ian D.	Wrexham	Cheltenham Town	
23 Stewart, Jordan B.	Leicester City	Bristol Rovers	
31 Stones, Craig	Lincoln City	Grantham Town	
17 Strong, Greg	Bolton Wanderers	Motherwell	
2 Sturridge, Simon A.	Stoke City	Shrewsbury Town	
17 Swan, Iain	Oldham Athletic	Partick Thistle	
25 Tallentire, Dean	Corby Town	Aylesbury United	
1 Tardif, Christopher L.	Portsmouth	Newport (IW)	
15 Taylor, Gareth K.	Manchester City	Queens Park Rangers	
23 Taylor, Martin	Blackburn Rovers	Stockport County	
22 Terry, John G.	Chelsea	Nottingham Forest	
30 Thomas, Anthony	Burton Albion	Worcester City	
21 Thomas, James A.	Blackburn Rovers	Blackpool	
20 Thompson, Glyn	Fulham	Mansfield Town	
31 Tremble, David G.	Scarborough	Gateshead	
31 Trundle, Lee C.	Southport	Bamber Bridge	
4 Wainwright, Neil	Sunderland	Darlington	
24 Wardle, Darren C.	Oldham Athletic	Stalybridge Celtic	
24 Wall, James	Hereford United	Burton Albion	
24 Wardle, Darren	Oldham Athletic	Stalybridge Celtic	
24 Waugh, Warren A.	Exeter City	Dorchester Town	
31 Webb, Simon J.	Leyton Orient	Purfleet	
6 Whetton, Lee D.	Hucknall Town	Spennymoor United	
24 White, Devon W.	Ilkeston Town	Stafford Rangers	
27 White, Thomas M.	Bristol Rovers	Hereford United	
17 Wilkins, Ian J.	Lincoln City	Ballymena United	
22 Williams, Adrian	Wolverhampton Wanderers	Reading	
23 Wilson, Stuart K.	Leicester City	Sheffield United	
23 Wolleaston, Robert A.	Chelsea	Bristol Rovers	
23 Woodman, Andrew J.	Brentford	Peterborough United	
26 Woolsey, Jeffrey A.	Dagenham & Redbridge	Billericay Town	

April 2000

| 4 Bolder, Adam P. | Hull City | Derby County | undisclosed |
| 27 Doherty, Gary M.T. | Luton Town | Tottenham Hotspur | undisclosed |

Temporary transfers

24 Armstrong, Alun	Middlesbrough	Huddersfield Town	
30 Barnes, Steven L.	Barnet	Welling United	
25 Bass, Jonathan	Birmingham City	Gillingham	
17 Bower, Mark	Bradford City	York City	
2 Burke, Paul	Sheffield United	Whitby Town	
24 Campbell, Stuart P.	Leicester City	Birmingham City	
3 Charles, Julian	Brentford	Woking	
7 Cooke, Terence J.	Manchester City	Wigan Athletic	
10 Coppinger, James	Newcastle United	Hartlepool United	
25 Dryden, Richard A.	Southampton	Stoke City	
27 Elliott, Stuart T.	Newcastle United	Stockport County	
23 Fenton, Nicholas L.	Manchester City	AFC Bournemouth	
28 Forssell, Mikael K.	Chelsea	Crystal Palace	
3 Gray, Wayne W.	Wimbledon	Swindon Town	
3 Gunnlaugsson, Arnar B.	Leicester City	Stoke City	
26 Holbrook, Adam P.	Portsmouth	Havant & Waterlooville	
18 Ingram, Stuart D.	Hartlepool United	Scarborough	
7 James, Kevin E.	Charlton Athletic	Farnborough Town	
27 Jones, Gary	Hartlepool United	Halifax Town	
10 Knight, Richard	Derby County	Oxford United	
20 Matassa, Vincent	Basingstoke Town	Salisbury City	
23 McClare, Sean P.	Barnsley	Rochdale	
18 McCormack, Francis	St Albans City	Harrow Borough	
3 Miller, Barry S.	Gillingham	Woking	
29 Myhre, Thomas	Everton	Birmingham City	
4 Naylor, Stuart W.	Exeter City	Rushden & Diamonds	
25 Nielsen, Allan	Tottenham Hotspur	Wolverhampton Wanderers	
24 Perkins, Christopher P.	Southend United	Kettering Town	
10 Porter, Andrew M.	Wigan Athletic	Chester City	
22 Reece, Dominic M.A.	Hednesford Town	Redditch United	
23 Searle, Stuart A.	Aldershot Town	Molesey	
3 Sturridge, Simon A.	Northampton Town	Shrewsbury Town	
27 Taylor, Martin	Blackburn Rovers	Stockport County	
4 Wainwright, Neil	Sunderland	Darlington	
20 White, Devon W.	Ilkeston Town	Stafford Rangers	
25 Wilson, Stuart K.	Leicester City	Sheffield United	

May 2000

17 Alford, Carl P.	Stevenage Borough	Doncaster Rovers	
24 Carlisle, Clarke J.	Blackpool	Queens Park Rangers	500,000
24 Kelly, James	Hednesford Town	Doncaster Rovers	undisclosed
22 Marsh, Michael A.	Kidderminster Harriers	Southport	undisclosed
25 Matthews, Colin E.	Bognor Regis Town	Newport (IW)	undisclosed
9 Morrison, Peter A.	Bolton Wanderers	Scunthorpe United	undisclosed
25 Robinson, Stephen	AFC Bournemouth	Preston North End	undisclosed

Temporary transfers

8 Coppinger, James	Newcastle United	Hartlepool United	
5 Gunnlaugsson, Arnar B.	Leicester City	Stoke City	
8 Hendry, Iain	Woking	Kingstonian	
9 Myhre, Thomas	Everton	Birmingham City	
6 Saunders, Edward	Woking	Kingstonian	
7 Simba, Amara S.	Leyton Orient	Kingstonian	
6 Stewart, Jordan B.	Leicester City	Bristol Rovers	
1 Trundle, Lee C.	Southport	Bamber Bridge	
7 Webb, Simon J.	Leyton Orient	Purfleet	

THE THINGS THEY SAID . . .

George Best's tongue-in-cheek reference to David Beckham:
"He can't head the ball, tackle or kick with his left foot and doesn't score enough goals."

Mark Lawrenson on his days as a Liverpool defender:
"I'm going to sue Alan Hansen as he used to make me head all the balls. If I get Alzheimer's in 10 years, I'm going to take civil action against him!"

Arsene Wenger after the shoot-out failure which cost the UEFA Cup:
"We practise penalties and it was frustrating that the two we missed hit the post and bar."

John Gregory on the changing faces in his Villa squad:
"I looked at my subs bench sometimes and there were just babies sitting there. Most of the people outside of Birmingham wouldn't know their names – and some in Birmingham for that matter."

Leicester's Tony Cottee recalling his wish 17 years earlier when he began at West Ham:
"I can remember back in 1983 looking at 2000 and thinking it would be lovely to be playing then – but I never believed it would happen."

Wimbledon manager Egil Olsen explaining Ben Thatcher's elbow assault on Sunderland's Nicky Summerbee:
"He was running with his arms out and it's impossible to put them down and that was the contact."

Graham Taylor refusing to spend millions at Watford amd still be relegated:
"You can spend £2m and find the player cannot trap the ball."

Paul Bracewell after Fulham's wobbly festive period:
"All I've picked up over Christmas is a few more grey hairs."

Burnley's journeyman pro Ronnie Jepson on coaching opportunities:
"It's a question of getting on the roundabout of who you know and I won't kiss anyone's arse to get there."

Martin O'Neill on Leicester's demanding programme:
"Players keep looking at the wall diary in my office and at the black dot that's there for a week in February – international week and a rest for some of them."

Max Clifford, Fulham's new PR on his relationship with chairman Mohamed Al Fayed:
"My job will be to try to make sure he scores more goals than own goals."

US based Sasa Curcic who would make a comeback if a club waived payment and instead offered 15 women:
"I can't achieve an orgasm looking at a team mate, but it would be a totally different matter with Cindy Crawford."

Provost Bill Smith hoisting a flag at the Town House following the sensational cup defeat of Celtic:
"The team have not only put Inverness on the football map, but on the tourist, industrial and commercial maps as well."

Graham Rix praising the dressing-room calming effect of Chelsea's Vialli:
"If you get angry all the time people don't take notice. If you're cool, calm and collected and then suddenly throw one (a tea cup) it has greater effect."

Sheffield Wednesday striker Gilles de Bilde shooting from the hip:
"English players love to compensate their lack of ideas with three important qualities; they are powerful, run for everything and fight for every centimetre."

Derby's Jim Smith on the magic of Kinkladze:
"Georgi does things you will never see any other player do better. but if I'm honest he can be a bit of a luxury."

Harry Redknapp about Di Canio's display in a 5-4 win:
"What a footballer, the man is a genius."

David O'Leary on an ugly brawl:
"It's not my fault if Tottenham players can't stand on their feet. Bowyer's tackle was fair, unfortunately he didn't get the ball."

Bobby Robson before leading Newcastle out in FA Cup semi-final:
"Wembley is a cathedral and it is for unique matches."

Roy Keane on the hounding of the official when 'Boro got a penalty:
"What happened was unfortunate … although if he (ref Andy D'Urso) had stood still I don't think we would have been chasing him, but he kept running and we kept chasing."

Jimmy Armfield's tribute to Sir Stanley Matthews:
"He was the first great superstar. With only newspapers and radio and TV just starting, everybody knew Stanley Matthews."

Ex-Swansea player, now Qatar coach Dzemal Hadziabdic:
"If I was Mark Hughes and my best players didn't turn up, they wouldn't play again."

Graeme Souness on inevitable selection mistakes and purchasing errors:
"You're trapped inside a coconut shy. Every time you duck, someone else is ready to let fly at you."

Sami Hyypia, a school kid fan and now Anfield's Finnish skipper:
"When I bring friends over for a visit, I take them to the museum at the club. The winning tradition at Liverpool is clear."

Cowdenbeath's Craig Levein taking exception to East Fife's physical approach:
"I don't think six ice packs were enough for our dressing room."

Ray Parlour, feeling sorry for newcomer Oleg Luzhny:
"I would hate to be stuck in the middle of Ukraine without being able to speak the language."

Under-fire Peter Reid after Sunderland's failure to win in 13 matches:
"Three hundred fans would probably have 300 different opinions, so I'd have to sign 300 players to satisfy them."

Gareth Southgate ending his link with high profile management company:
"Although I've done that Pizza Hut advert I've turned down lots of others offering to go down the missed-penalty route."

Ian St John remembering Shankly's do's and don'ts:
"At first he told us to wear boxing gloves in bed on Friday nights, then later he would tell us to send the wife to her mother."

Bryan Robson's warning to players thinking of opting out at 'Boro's £10m training complex:
"We have a one-sided window looking over the players' gym from our physio room. It means we can keep an eye on them – and they don't know if we are there or not."

Tim Flowers cannot see another club following small-town Blackburn buying a team to beat Manchester United:
"They (star players) only want to go to two places, London or Manchester United."

Sheffield Wednesday's Pavel Srnicek on the tensions that a relegation battle brings:
"You have to be diplomatic, but sometimes in training we kick each other because we don't like our teammates."

Everton's Kevin Campbell explains about his boss Walter Smith:
"He can be as quiet as a mouse or he can go absolutely ballistic."

Former crowd-pleaser Frank Worthington on why he made so few England appearances:
"Down to one man, Don Revie. He preferred the workhorse type of player."

Kevin Keegan casting a glance at the 8 to 1 odds offered by bookies William Hill:
"I reckon we are worth a bet for Euro 2000 along with nations like France and Holland."

The great Eusebio, obviously not unduly worried when England went two up:
"Portugal controlled the game even when they were losing."

TV pundit Ron Atkinson seeing extrovert goalkeeper Barthez hoisting a trade-mark left-footed clearance high into the crowd:
"He might be the first player to kick the ball out of Old Trafford."

Leicester's two-goal Wembley hero Matt Elliott who kept in touch with heavily-pregnant wife Cathy by signalling to her throughout the game:
"I did have a real panic at one point because I lost track of her for 10 minutes."

Marcel Desailly on adjusting to Premiership life after five years in Serie A:
"When you go to Derby four days after playing in Milan, you still have a picture of the San Siro in your head and it can be a shock."

Bobby Robson, reflection on lifting morale at Newcastle:
"Under Gullit the best players were on the bench ... we have to face the fact he did nothing for this club."

David Beckham telling OK! magazine about the irritating distractions eating-out celebrities encounter:
"In the Ivy they don't let anyone ask for autographs. I know this because Michael Jordan was in there one night and I wasn't able to get his signature."

Glenn Hoddle on England's 1-0 success over Germany:
"It wasn't brilliant football, but it was effective."

Honest Keegan as England headed home after Romania's dramatic late win:
"They outplayed and outpassed us, and probably deserved the result."

Alan Shearer bowing out with a booking for a blatant dive:
"That was in desperation. I was wanting to do something for my country."

Ex-Chelsea and England striker Peter Osgood, not surprised by the Euro exit of Keegan's team:
"Outplayed by Portugal, outplayed by Romania, and we only beat the Germans because they are a worse team than we are."

Martin Keown's blunt summing-up of England's campaign:
"We were inept tactically and exposed against teams we could have beaten."

Headline on the front of sports daily 'Marca' after Spain's 4-3 victory over Yugoslavia:
"Long live the mother who gave birth to you."

Belgium's coach Robert Waseige showing he hadn't forgotten the finer points of coaching:
"We have to improve in two key areas: defence and attack."

Soccer fan Scott Vessey who believes Phil Neville's concession of a last minute penalty against Romania merited the same punishment handed down to hooligans:
"Phil Neville should have his passport confiscated and not be allowed to leave the country."

Portugal's Paulo Sousa delivers the damming verdict on England at Euro 2000:
"I was even laughing on the bench when I saw their defenders heading back to towards their own penalty area rather than trying to tackle Figo or Rui Costa."

TV pundit Dion Dublin after the Spain v Yugoslavia game from which Hierro was absent:
"Hierro has been magnificent for the Spaniards tonight."

Arsenal's Liam Brady believing there is no mystery to England's current lack of technique and talent:
"I would say that 85 percent of the teams we play at youth level kick the ball long and by-pass midfield. They play for territory."

Celtic's Kenny Dalglish overlooking the small matter of losing the League by 21 points:
"I've been sacked and I don't know why."

FA CHARITY SHIELD WINNERS 1908-99

1908	Manchester U v QPR	4-0 after 1-1 draw		1961	Tottenham H v FA XI	3-2
1909	Newcastle U v Northampton T		2-0	1962	Tottenham H v Ipswich T	5-1
1910	Brighton v Aston Villa		1-0	1963	Everton v Manchester U	4-0
1911	Manchester U v Swindon T		8-4	1964	Liverpool v West Ham U	2-2*
1912	Blackburn R v QPR		2-1	1965	Manchester U v Liverpool	2-2*
1913	Professionals v Amateurs		7-2	1966	Liverpool v Everton	1-0
1920	WBA v Tottenham H		2-0	1967	Manchester U v Tottenham H	3-3*
1921	Tottenham H v Burnley		2-0	1968	Manchester C v WBA	6-1
1922	Huddersfield T v Liverpool		1-0	1969	Leeds U v Manchester C	2-1
1923	Professionals v Amateurs		2-0	1970	Everton v Chelsea	2-1
1924	Professionals v Amateurs		3-1	1971	Leicester C v Liverpool	1-0
1925	Amateurs v Professionals		6-1	1972	Manchester C v Aston Villa	1-0
1926	Amateurs v Professionals		6-3	1973	Burnley v Manchester C	1-0
1927	Cardiff C v Corinthians		2-1	1974	Liverpool† v Leeds U	1-1
1928	Everton v Blackburn R		2-1	1975	Derby Co v West Ham U	2-0
1929	Professionals v Amateurs		3-0	1976	Liverpool v Southampton	1-0
1930	Arsenal v Sheffield W		2-1	1977	Liverpool v Manchester U	0-0*
1931	Arsenal v WBA		1-0	1978	Nottingham F v Ipswich T	5-0
1932	Everton v Newcastle U		5-3	1979	Liverpool v Arsenal	3-1
1933	Arsenal v Everton		3-0	1980	Liverpool v West Ham U	1-0
1934	Arsenal v Manchester C		4-0	1981	Aston Villa v Tottenham H	2-2*
1935	Sheffield W v Arsenal		1-0	1982	Liverpool v Tottenham H	1-0
1936	Sunderland v Arsenal		2-1	1983	Manchester U v Liverpool	2-0
1937	Manchester C v Sunderland		2-0	1984	Everton v Liverpool	1-0
1938	Arsenal v Preston NE		2-1	1985	Everton v Manchester U	2-0
1948	Arsenal v Manchester U		4-3	1986	Everton v Liverpool	1-1*
1949	Portsmouth v Wolverhampton W		1-1*	1987	Everton v Coventry C	1-0
1950	World Cup Team v Canadian Touring Team	4-2		1988	Liverpool v Wimbledon	2-1
1951	Tottenham H v Newcastle U		2-1	1989	Liverpool v Arsenal	1-0
1952	Manchester U v Newcastle U		4-2	1990	Liverpool v Manchester U	1-1*
1953	Arsenal v Blackpool		3-1	1991	Arsenal v Tottenham H	0-0*
1954	Wolverhampton W v WBA		4-4*	1992	Leeds U v Liverpool	4-3
1955	Chelsea v Newcastle U		3-0	1993	Manchester U† v Arsenal	1-1
1956	Manchester U v Manchester C		1-0	1994	Manchester U v Blackburn R	2-0
1957	Manchester U v Aston Villa		4-0	1995	Everton v Blackburn R	1-0
1958	Bolton W v Wolverhampton W		4-1	1996	Manchester U v Newcastle U	4-0
1959	Wolverhampton W v Nottingham F		3-1	1997	Manchester U† v Chelsea	1-1
1960	Burnley v Wolverhampton W		2-2*	1998	Arsenal v Manchester U	3-0

Each club retained shield for six months. † Won on penalties.

AXA FA CHARITY SHIELD 1999

Arsenal (0) 2, Manchester U (1) 1

At Wembley, 1 August 1999, attendance 70,185

Arsenal: Manninger; Dixon, Winterburn, Vieira, Keown, Grimandi, Parlour (Luzhny), Kanu, Petit, Ljungberg, Silvinho (Boa Morte).

Scorers: Kanu 67 (pen), Parlour 77.

Manchester U: Bosnich; Neville P, Irwin, Berg, Scholes, Stam (May), Beckham, Butt (Sheringham), Cole, Yorke, Cruyff (Solskjaer).

Scorer: Yorke 36.

Referee: G. Barber (Tring).

ENGLISH LEAGUE HONOURS 1888 to 2000

FA PREMIER LEAGUE
Maximum points: a 126; b 114.

	First	Pts	Second	Pts	Third	Pts
1992–93a	Manchester U	84	Aston Villa	74	Norwich C	72
1993–94a	Manchester U	92	Blackburn R	84	Newcastle U	77
1994–95a	Blackburn R	89	Manchester U	88	Nottingham F	77
1995–96a	Manchester U	82	Newcastle U	78	Liverpool	71
1996–97b	Manchester U	75	Newcastle U*	68	Arsenal*	68
1997–98b	Arsenal	78	Manchester U	77	Liverpool	65
1998–99b	Manchester U	79	Arsenal	78	Chelsea	75
1999–2000b	Manchester U	91	Arsenal	73	Leeds U	69

FIRST DIVISION
Maximum points: 138

	First		Second		Third	
1992–93	Newcastle U	96	West Ham U*	88	Portsmouth††	88
1993–94	Crystal Palace	90	Nottingham F	83	Millwall††	74
1994–95	Middlesbrough	82	Reading††	79	Bolton W	77
1995–96	Sunderland	83	Derby Co	79	Crystal Palace††	75
1996–97	Bolton W	98	Barnsley	80	Wolverhampton W††	76
1997–98	Nottingham F	94	Middlesbrough	91	Sunderland††	90
1998–99	Sunderland	105	Bradford C	87	Ipswich T††	86
1999–2000	Charlton Ath	91	Manchester C	89	Ipswich T	87

SECOND DIVISION
Maximum points: 138

	First		Second		Third	
1992–93	Stoke C	93	Bolton W	90	Port Vale††	89
1993–94	Reading	89	Port Vale	88	Plymouth Arg*††	85
1994–95	Birmingham C	89	Brentford††	85	Crewe Alex††	83
1995–96	Swindon T	92	Oxford U	83	Blackpool††	82
1996–97	Bury	84	Stockport Co	82	Luton T††	78
1997–98	Watford	88	Bristol C	85	Grimsby T	72
1998–99	Fulham	101	Walsall	87	Manchester C	82
1999–2000	Preston NE	95	Burnley	88	Gillingham	85

THIRD DIVISION
Maximum points: a 126; b 138.

	First		Second		Third	
1992–93a	Cardiff C	83	Wrexham	80	Barnet	79
1993–94a	Shrewsbury T	79	Chester C	74	Crewe Alex	73
1994–95a	Carlisle U	91	Walsall	83	Chesterfield	81
1995–96b	Preston NE	86	Gillingham	83	Bury	79
1996–97b	Wigan Ath*	87	Fulham	87	Carlisle U	84
1997–98b	Notts Co	99	Macclesfield T	82	Lincoln C	72
1998–99b	Brentford	85	Cambridge U	81	Cardiff C	80
1999–2000b	Swansea C	85	Rotherham U	84	Northampton T	82

††*Not promoted after play-offs.*

FOOTBALL LEAGUE
Maximum points: a 44; b 60

	First	Pts	Second	Pts	Third	Pts
1888–89a	Preston NE	40	Aston Villa	29	Wolverhampton W	28
1889–90a	Preston NE	33	Everton	31	Blackburn R	27
1890–91a	Everton	29	Preston NE	27	Notts Co	26
1891–92b	Sunderland	42	Preston NE	37	Bolton W	36

FIRST DIVISION to 1991–92
Maximum points: a 44; b 52; c 60; d 68; e 76; f 84; g 126; h 120; k 114.

	First		Second		Third	
1892–93c	Sunderland	48	Preston NE	37	Everton	36
1893–94c	Aston Villa	44	Sunderland	38	Derby Co	36
1894–95c	Sunderland	47	Everton	42	Aston Villa	39
1895–96c	Aston Villa	45	Derby Co	41	Everton	39
1896–97c	Aston Villa	47	Sheffield U*	36	Derby Co	36
1897–98c	Sheffield U	42	Sunderland	37	Wolverhampton W*	35
1898–99d	Aston Villa	45	Liverpool	43	Burnley	39
1899–1900d	Aston Villa	50	Sheffield U	48	Sunderland	41
1900–01d	Liverpool	45	Sunderland	43	Notts Co	40
1901–02d	Sunderland	44	Everton	41	Newcastle U	37
1902–03d	The Wednesday	42	Aston Villa*	41	Sunderland	41
1903–04d	The Wednesday	47	Manchester C	44	Everton	43
1904–05d	Newcastle U	48	Everton	47	Manchester C	46
1905–06e	Liverpool	51	Preston NE	47	The Wednesday	44
1906–07e	Newcastle U	51	Bristol C	48	Everton*	45
1907–08e	Manchester U	52	Aston Villa*	43	Manchester C	43
1908–09e	Newcastle U	53	Everton	46	Sunderland	44
1909–10e	Aston Villa	53	Liverpool	48	Blackburn R*	45
1910–11e	Manchester U	52	Aston Villa	51	Sunderland*	45
1911–12e	Blackburn R	49	Everton	46	Newcastle U	44
1912–13e	Sunderland	54	Aston Villa	50	Sheffield W	49
1913–14e	Blackburn R	51	Aston Villa	44	Middlesbrough*	43
1914–15e	Everton	46	Oldham Ath	45	Blackburn R*	43
1919–20f	WBA	60	Burnley	51	Chelsea	49
1920–21f	Burnley	59	Manchester C	54	Bolton W	52

Won or placed on goal average (ratio), goal difference or most goals scored.

	First	Pts	Second	Pts	Third	Pts
1921–22f	Liverpool	57	Tottenham H	51	Burnley	49
1922–23f	Liverpool	60	Sunderland	54	Huddersfield T	53
1923–24f	Huddersfield T*	57	Cardiff C	57	Sunderland	53
1924–25f	Huddersfield T	58	WBA	56	Bolton W	55
1925–26f	Huddersfield T	57	Arsenal	52	Sunderland	48
1926–27f	Newcastle U	56	Huddersfield T	51	Sunderland	49
1927–28f	Everton	53	Huddersfield T	51	Leicester C	48
1928–29f	Sheffield W	52	Leicester C	51	Aston Villa	50
1929–30f	Sheffield W	60	Derby Co	50	Manchester C*	47
1930–31f	Arsenal	66	Aston Villa	59	Sheffield W	52
1931–32f	Everton	56	Arsenal	54	Sheffield W	50
1932–33f	Arsenal	58	Aston Villa	54	Sheffield W	51
1933–34f	Arsenal	59	Huddersfield T	56	Tottenham H	49
1934–35f	Arsenal	58	Sunderland	54	Sheffield W	49
1935–36f	Sunderland	56	Derby Co*	48	Huddersfield T	48
1936–37f	Manchester C	57	Charlton Ath	54	Arsenal	52
1937–38f	Arsenal	52	Wolverhampton W	51	Preston NE	49
1938–39f	Everton	59	Wolverhampton W	55	Charlton Ath	50
1946–47f	Liverpool	57	Manchester U*	56	Wolverhampton W	56
1947–48f	Arsenal	59	Manchester U*	52	Burnley	52
1948–49f	Portsmouth	58	Manchester U*	53	Derby Co	53
1949–50f	Portsmouth*	53	Wolverhampton W	53	Sunderland	52
1950–51f	Tottenham H	60	Manchester U	56	Blackpool	50
1951–52f	Manchester U	57	Tottenham H*	53	Arsenal	53
1952–53f	Arsenal*	54	Preston NE	54	Wolverhampton W	51
1953–54f	Wolverhampton W	57	WBA	53	Huddersfield T	51
1954–55f	Chelsea	52	Wolverhampton W*	48	Portsmouth*	48
1955–56f	Manchester U	60	Blackpool*	49	Wolverhampton W	49
1956–57f	Manchester U	64	Tottenham H*	56	Preston NE	56
1957–58f	Wolverhampton W	64	Preston NE	59	Tottenham H	51
1958–59f	Wolverhampton W	61	Manchester U	55	Arsenal*	50
1959–60f	Burnley	55	Wolverhampton W	54	Tottenham H	53
1960–61f	Tottenham H	66	Sheffield W	58	Wolverhampton W	57
1961–62f	Ipswich T	56	Burnley	53	Tottenham H	52
1962–63f	Everton	61	Tottenham H	55	Burnley	54
1963–64f	Liverpool	57	Manchester U	53	Everton	52
1964–65f	Manchester U*	61	Leeds U	61	Chelsea	56
1965–66f	Liverpool	61	Leeds U*	55	Burnley	55
1966–67f	Manchester U	60	Nottingham F*	56	Tottenham H	56
1967–68f	Manchester C	58	Manchester U	56	Liverpool	55
1968–69f	Leeds U	67	Liverpool	61	Everton	57
1969–70f	Everton	66	Leeds U	57	Chelsea	55
1970–71f	Arsenal	65	Leeds U	64	Tottenham H*	52
1971–72f	Derby Co	58	Leeds U*	57	Liverpool*	57
1972–73f	Liverpool	60	Arsenal	57	Leeds U	53
1973–74f	Leeds U	62	Liverpool	57	Derby Co	48
1974–75f	Derby Co	53	Liverpool*	51	Ipswich T	51
1975–76f	Liverpool	60	QPR	59	Manchester U	56
1976–77f	Liverpool	57	Manchester C	56	Ipswich T	52
1977–78f	Nottingham F	64	Liverpool	57	Everton	55
1978–79f	Liverpool	68	Nottingham F	60	WBA	59
1979–80f	Liverpool	60	Manchester U	58	Ipswich T	52
1980–81f	Aston Villa	60	Ipswich T	56	Arsenal	53
1981–82g	Liverpool	87	Ipswich T	83	Manchester U	78
1982–83g	Liverpool	82	Watford	71	Manchester U	70
1983–84g	Liverpool	80	Southampton	77	Nottingham F*	74
1984–85g	Everton	90	Liverpool*	77	Tottenham H	77
1985–86g	Liverpool	88	Everton	86	West Ham U	84
1986–87g	Everton	86	Liverpool	77	Tottenham H	71
1987–88h	Liverpool	90	Manchester U	81	Nottingham F	73
1988–89k	Arsenal*	76	Liverpool	76	Nottingham F	64
1989–90k	Liverpool	79	Aston Villa	70	Tottenham H	63
1990–91k	Arsenal†	83	Liverpool	76	Crystal Palace	69
1991–92g	Leeds U	82	Manchester U	78	Sheffield W	75

No official competition during 1915–19 and 1939–46; Regional Leagues operated.
†2 pts deducted

SECOND DIVISION to 1991–92
Maximum points: a 44; *b* 56; *c* 60; *d* 68; *e* 76; *f* 84; *g* 126; *h* 132; *k* 138.

	First	Pts	Second	Pts	Third	Pts
1892–93a	Small Heath	36	Sheffield U	35	Darwen	30
1893–94b	Liverpool	50	Small Heath	42	Notts Co	39
1894–95c	Bury	48	Notts Co	39	Newton Heath*	38
1895–96c	Liverpool*	46	Manchester C	46	Grimsby T*	42
1896–97c	Notts Co	42	Newton Heath	39	Grimsby T	38
1897–98c	Burnley	48	Newcastle U	45	Manchester C	39
1898–99d	Manchester C	52	Glossop NE	46	Leicester Fosse	45
1899–1900d	The Wednesday	54	Bolton W	52	Small Heath	46
1900–01d	Grimsby T	49	Small Heath	48	Burnley	44
1901–02d	WBA	55	Middlesbrough	51	Preston NE*	42
1902–03d	Manchester C	54	Small Heath	51	Woolwich A	48

Won or placed on goal average (ratio)/goal difference.

	First	Pts	Second	Pts	Third	Pts
1903–04*d*	Preston NE	50	Woolwich A	49	Manchester U	48
1904–05*d*	Liverpool	58	Bolton W	56	Manchester U	53
1905–06*e*	Bristol C	66	Manchester U	62	Chelsea	53
1906–07*e*	Nottingham F	60	Chelsea	57	Leicester Fosse	48
1907–08*e*	Bradford C	54	Leicester Fosse	52	Oldham Ath	50
1908–09*e*	Bolton W	52	Tottenham H*	51	WBA	51
1909–10*e*	Manchester C	54	Oldham Ath*	53	Hull C*	53
1910–11*e*	WBA	53	Bolton W	51	Chelsea	49
1911–12*e*	Derby Co*	54	Chelsea	54	Burnley	52
1912–13*e*	Preston NE	53	Burnley	50	Birmingham	46
1913–14*e*	Notts Co	53	Bradford PA*	49	Woolwich A	49
1914–15*e*	Derby Co	53	Preston NE	50	Barnsley	47
1919–20*f*	Tottenham H	70	Huddersfield T	64	Birmingham	56
1920–21*f*	Birmingham*	58	Cardiff C	58	Bristol C	51
1921–22*f*	Nottingham F	56	Stoke C*	52	Barnsley	52
1922–23*f*	Notts Co	53	West Ham U*	51	Leicester C	51
1923–24*f*	Leeds U	54	Bury*	51	Derby Co	51
1924–25*f*	Leicester C	59	Manchester U	57	Derby Co	55
1925–26*f*	Sheffield W	60	Derby Co	57	Chelsea	52
1926–27*f*	Middlesbrough	62	Portsmouth*	54	Manchester C	54
1927–28*f*	Manchester C	59	Leeds U	57	Chelsea	54
1928–29*f*	Middlesbrough	55	Grimsby T	53	Bradford PA*	48
1929–30*f*	Blackpool	58	Chelsea	55	Oldham Ath	53
1930–31*f*	Everton	61	WBA	54	Tottenham H	51
1931–32*f*	Wolverhampton W	56	Leeds U	54	Stoke C	52
1932–33*f*	Stoke C	56	Tottenham H	55	Fulham	50
1933–34*f*	Grimsby T	59	Preston NE	52	Bolton W*	51
1934–35*f*	Brentford	61	Bolton W*	56	West Ham U	56
1935–36*f*	Manchester U	56	Charlton Ath	55	Sheffield U*	52
1936–37*f*	Leicester C	56	Blackpool	55	Bury	52
1937–38*f*	Aston Villa	57	Manchester U*	53	Sheffield U	53
1938–39*f*	Blackburn R	55	Sheffield U	54	Sheffield W	53
1946–47*f*	Manchester C	62	Burnley	58	Birmingham C	55
1947–48*f*	Birmingham C	59	Newcastle U	56	Southampton	52
1948–49*f*	Fulham	57	WBA	56	Southampton	55
1949–50*f*	Tottenham H	61	Sheffield W*	52	Sheffield U*	52
1950–51*f*	Preston NE	57	Manchester C	52	Cardiff C	50
1951–52*f*	Sheffield W	53	Cardiff C*	51	Birmingham C	51
1952–53*f*	Sheffield U	60	Huddersfield T	58	Luton T	52
1953–54*f*	Leicester C*	56	Everton	56	Blackburn R	55
1954–55*f*	Birmingham C*	54	Luton T*	54	Rotherham U	54
1955–56*f*	Sheffield W	55	Leeds U	52	Liverpool*	48
1956–57*f*	Leicester C	61	Nottingham F	54	Liverpool	53
1957–58*f*	West Ham U	57	Blackburn R	56	Charlton Ath	55
1958–59*f*	Sheffield W	62	Fulham	60	Sheffield U*	53
1959–60*f*	Aston Villa	59	Cardiff C	58	Liverpool*	50
1960–61*f*	Ipswich T	59	Sheffield U	58	Liverpool	52
1961–62*f*	Liverpool	62	Leyton Orient	54	Sunderland	53
1962–63*f*	Stoke C	53	Chelsea*	52	Sunderland	52
1963–64*f*	Leeds U	63	Sunderland	61	Preston NE	56
1964–65*f*	Newcastle U	57	Northampton T	56	Bolton W	50
1965–66*f*	Manchester C	59	Southampton	54	Coventry C	53
1966–67*f*	Coventry C	59	Wolverhampton W	58	Carlisle U	52
1967–68*f*	Ipswich T	59	QPR*	58	Blackpool	58
1968–69*f*	Derby Co	63	Crystal Palace	56	Charlton Ath	50
1969–70*f*	Huddersfield T	60	Blackpool	53	Leicester C	51
1970–71*f*	Leicester C	59	Sheffield U	56	Cardiff C*	53
1971–72*f*	Norwich C	57	Birmingham C	56	Millwall	55
1972–73*f*	Burnley	62	QPR	61	Aston Villa	50
1973–74*f*	Middlesbrough	65	Luton T	50	Carlisle U	49
1974–75*f*	Manchester U	61	Aston Villa	58	Norwich C	53
1975–76*f*	Sunderland	56	Bristol C*	53	WBA	53
1976–77*f*	Wolverhampton W	57	Chelsea	55	Nottingham F	52
1977–78*f*	Bolton W	58	Southampton	57	Tottenham H*	56
1978–79*f*	Crystal Palace	57	Brighton & HA*	56	Stoke C	56
1979–80*f*	Leicester C	55	Sunderland	54	Birmingham C*	53
1980–81*f*	West Ham U	66	Notts Co	53	Swansea C*	50
1981–82*g*	Luton T	88	Watford	80	Norwich C	71
1982–83*g*	QPR	85	Wolverhampton W	75	Leicester C	70
1983–84*g*	Chelsea*	88	Sheffield W	88	Newcastle U	80
1984–85*g*	Oxford U	84	Birmingham C	82	Manchester C	74
1985–86*g*	Norwich C	84	Charlton Ath	77	Wimbledon	76
1986–87*g*	Derby Co	84	Portsmouth	78	Oldham Ath††	75
1987–88*h*	Millwall	82	Aston Villa*	78	Middlesbrough	78
1988–89*k*	Chelsea	99	Manchester C	82	Crystal Palace	81
1989–90*k*	Leeds U*	85	Sheffield U	85	Newcastle U††	80
1990–91*k*	Oldham Ath	88	West Ham U	87	Sheffield W	82
1991–92*k*	Ipswich T	84	Middlesbrough	80	Derby Co	78

No official competition during 1915–19 and 1939–46; Regional Leagues operated.
Won or placed on goal average (ratio)/goal difference.
††*Not promoted after play-offs.*

THIRD DIVISION to 1991–92
Maximum points: 92; 138 from 1981–82.

	First	Pts	Second	Pts	Third	Pts
1958–59	Plymouth Arg	62	Hull C	61	Brentford*	57
1959–60	Southampton	61	Norwich C	59	Shrewsbury T*	52
1960–61	Bury	68	Walsall	62	QPR	60
1961–62	Portsmouth	65	Grimsby T	62	Bournemouth*	59
1962–63	Northampton T	62	Swindon T	58	Port Vale	54
1963–64	Coventry C*	60	Crystal Palace	60	Watford	58
1964–65	Carlisle U	60	Bristol C*	59	Mansfield T	59
1965–66	Hull C	69	Millwall	65	QPR	57
1966–67	QPR	67	Middlesbrough	55	Watford	54
1967–68	Oxford U	57	Bury	56	Shrewsbury T	55
1968–69	Watford*	64	Swindon T	64	Luton T	61
1969–70	Orient	62	Luton T	60	Bristol R	56
1970–71	Preston NE	61	Fulham	60	Halifax T	56
1971–72	Aston Villa	70	Brighton & HA	65	Bournemouth*	62
1972–73	Bolton W	61	Notts Co	57	Blackburn R	55
1973–74	Oldham Ath	62	Bristol R*	61	York C	61
1974–75	Blackburn R	60	Plymouth Arg	59	Charlton Ath	55
1975–76	Hereford U	63	Cardiff C	57	Millwall	56
1976–77	Mansfield T	64	Brighton & HA	61	Crystal Palace*	59
1977–78	Wrexham	61	Cambridge U	58	Preston NE*	56
1978–79	Shrewsbury T	61	Watford*	60	Swansea C	60
1979–80	Grimsby T	62	Blackburn R	59	Sheffield W	58
1980–81	Rotherham U	61	Barnsley*	59	Charlton Ath	59
1981–82	Burnley*	80	Carlisle U	80	Fulham	78
1982–83	Portsmouth	91	Cardiff C	86	Huddersfield T	82
1983–84	Oxford U	95	Wimbledon	87	Sheffield U*	83
1984–85	Bradford C	94	Millwall	90	Hull C	87
1985–86	Reading	94	Plymouth Arg	87	Derby Co	84
1986–87	Bournemouth	97	Middlesbrough	94	Swindon T	87
1987–88	Sunderland	93	Brighton & HA	84	Walsall	82
1988–89	Wolverhampton W	92	Sheffield U*	84	Port Vale	84
1989–90	Bristol R	93	Bristol C	91	Notts Co	87
1990–91	Cambridge U	86	Southend U	85	Grimsby T*	83
1991–92	Brentford	82	Birmingham C	81	Huddersfield T	78

FOURTH DIVISION (1958–1992)
Maximum points: 92; 138 from 1981–82.

	First	Pts	Second	Pts	Third	Pts	Fourth	Pts
1958–59	Port Vale	64	Coventry C*	60	York C	60	Shrewsbury T	58
1959–60	Walsall	65	Notts Co*	60	Torquay U	60	Watford	57
1960–61	Peterborough U	66	Crystal Palace	64	Northampton T*	60	Bradford PA	60
1961–62†	Millwall	56	Colchester U	55	Wrexham	53	Carlisle U	52
1962–63	Brentford	62	Oldham Ath*	59	Crewe Alex	59	Mansfield T*	57
1963–64	Gillingham*	60	Carlisle U	60	Workington	59	Exeter C	58
1964–65	Brighton & HA	63	Millwall*	62	York C	62	Oxford U	61
1965–66	Doncaster R*	59	Darlington	59	Torquay U	58	Colchester U*	56
1966–67	Stockport Co	64	Southport*	59	Barrow	59	Tranmere R	58
1967–68	Luton T	66	Barnsley	61	Hartlepools U	60	Crewe Alex	58
1968–69	Doncaster R	59	Halifax T	57	Rochdale*	56	Bradford C	56
1969–70	Chesterfield	64	Wrexham	61	Swansea C	60	Port Vale	59
1970–71	Notts Co	69	Bournemouth	60	Oldham Ath	59	York C	56
1971–72	Grimsby T	63	Southend U	60	Brentford	59	Scunthorpe U	57
1972–73	Southport	62	Hereford U	58	Cambridge U	57	Aldershot*	56
1973–74	Peterborough U	65	Gillingham	62	Colchester U	60	Bury	59
1974–75	Mansfield T	68	Shrewsbury T	62	Rotherham U	59	Chester*	57
1975–76	Lincoln C	74	Northampton T	68	Reading	60	Tranmere R	58
1976–77	Cambridge U	65	Exeter C	62	Colchester U*	59	Bradford C	59
1977–78	Watford	71	Southend U	60	Swansea C*	56	Brentford	56
1978–79	Reading	65	Grimsby T*	61	Wimbledon*	61	Barnsley	61
1979–80	Huddersfield T	66	Walsall	64	Newport Co	61	Portsmouth*	60
1980–81	Southend U	67	Lincoln C	65	Doncaster R	56	Wimbledon	55
1981–82	Sheffield U	96	Bradford C*	91	Wigan Ath	91	Bournemouth	88
1982–83	Wimbledon	98	Hull C	90	Port Vale	88	Scunthorpe U	83
1983–84	York C	101	Doncaster R	85	Reading*	82	Bristol C	82
1984–85	Chesterfield	91	Blackpool	86	Darlington	85	Bury	84
1985–86	Swindon T	102	Chester*	84	Mansfield T	81	Port Vale	79
1986–87	Northampton T	99	Preston NE	90	Southend U	80	Wolverhampton W††	79
1987–88	Wolverhampton W	90	Cardiff C	85	Bolton W	78	Scunthorpe U††	77
1988–89	Rotherham U	82	Tranmere R	80	Crewe Alex	78	Scunthorpe U††	77
1989–90	Exeter C	89	Grimsby T	79	Southend U	75	Stockport Co††	74
1990–91	Darlington	83	Stockport Co*	82	Hartlepool U	82	Peterborough U	80
1991–92†*	Burnley	83	Rotherham U*	77	Mansfield T	77	Blackpool	76

* *Won or placed on goal average (ratio)/goal difference.*
†*Maximum points: 88 owing to Accrington Stanley's resignation.* ††*Not promoted after play-offs.*
†**Maximum points: 126 owing to Aldershot being expelled (and only 23 teams started the competition).*

THIRD DIVISION—SOUTH (1920–1958)
1920–21 season as Third Division.
Maximum points: a 84; b 92.

	First	Pts	Second	Pts	Third	Pts
1920–21a	Crystal Palace	59	Southampton	54	QPR	53
1921–22a	Southampton*	61	Plymouth Arg	61	Portsmouth	53
1922–23a	Bristol C	59	Plymouth Arg*	53	Swansea T	53
1923–24a	Portsmouth	59	Plymouth Arg	55	Millwall	54
1924–25a	Swansea T	57	Plymouth Arg	56	Bristol C	53
1925–26a	Reading	57	Plymouth Arg	56	Millwall	53
1926–27a	Bristol C	62	Plymouth Arg	60	Millwall	56
1927–28a	Millwall	65	Northampton T	55	Plymouth Arg	53
1928–29a	Charlton Ath*	54	Crystal Palace	54	Northampton T*	52
1929–30a	Plymouth Arg	68	Brentford	61	QPR	51
1930–31a	Notts Co	59	Crystal Palace	51	Brentford	50
1931–32a	Fulham	57	Reading	55	Southend U	53
1932–33a	Brentford	62	Exeter C	58	Norwich C	57
1933–34a	Norwich C	61	Coventry C*	54	Reading*	54
1934–35a	Charlton Ath	61	Reading	53	Coventry C	51
1935–36a	Coventry C	57	Luton T	56	Reading	54
1936–37a	Luton T	58	Notts Co	56	Brighton & HA	53
1937–38a	Millwall	56	Bristol C	55	QPR*	53
1938–39a	Newport Co	55	Crystal Palace	52	Brighton & HA	49
1939–46	Competition cancelled owing to war. Regional Leagues operated.					
1946–47a	Cardiff C	66	QPR	57	Bristol C	51
1947–48a	QPR	61	Bournemouth	57	Walsall	51
1948–49a	Swansea T	62	Reading	55	Bournemouth	52
1949–50a	Notts Co	58	Northampton T*	51	Southend U	51
1950–51b	Nottingham F	70	Norwich C	64	Reading*	57
1951–52b	Plymouth Arg	66	Reading*	61	Norwich C	61
1952–53b	Bristol R	64	Millwall*	62	Northampton T	62
1953–54b	Ipswich T	64	Brighton & HA	61	Bristol C	56
1954–55b	Bristol C	70	Leyton Orient	61	Southampton	59
1955–56b	Leyton Orient	66	Brighton & HA	65	Ipswich T	64
1956–57b	Ipswich T*	59	Torquay U	59	Colchester U	58
1957–58b	Brighton & HA	60	Brentford*	58	Plymouth Arg	58

THIRD DIVISION—NORTH (1921–1958)
Maximum points: a 76; b 84; c 80; d 92.

	First	Pts	Second	Pts	Third	Pts
1921–22a	Stockport Co	56	Darlington*	50	Grimsby T	50
1922–23a	Nelson	51	Bradford PA	47	Walsall	46
1923–24b	Wolverhampton W	63	Rochdale	62	Chesterfield	54
1924–25b	Darlington	58	Nelson*	53	New Brighton	53
1925–26b	Grimsby T	61	Bradford PA	60	Rochdale	59
1926–27b	Stoke C	63	Rochdale	58	Bradford PA	55
1927–28b	Bradford PA	63	Lincoln C	55	Stockport Co	54
1928–29b	Bradford C	63	Stockport Co	62	Wrexham	52
1929–30b	Port Vale	67	Stockport Co	63	Darlington*	50
1930–31b	Chesterfield	58	Lincoln C	57	Wrexham*	54
1931–32c	Lincoln C*	57	Gateshead	57	Chester	50
1932–33b	Hull C	59	Wrexham	57	Stockport Co	54
1933–34b	Barnsley	62	Chesterfield	61	Stockport Co	59
1934–35b	Doncaster R	57	Halifax T	55	Chester	54
1935–36b	Chesterfield	60	Chester*	55	Tranmere R	55
1936–37b	Stockport Co	60	Lincoln C	57	Chester	53
1937–38b	Tranmere R	56	Doncaster R	54	Hull C	53
1938–39b	Barnsley	67	Doncaster R	56	Bradford C	52
1939–46	Competition cancelled owing to war. Regional Leagues operated.					
1946–47b	Doncaster R	72	Rotherham U	60	Chester	56
1947–48b	Lincoln C	60	Rotherham U	59	Wrexham	50
1948–49b	Hull C	65	Rotherham U	62	Doncaster R	50
1949–50b	Doncaster R	55	Gateshead	53	Rochdale*	51
1950–51d	Rotherham U	71	Mansfield T	64	Carlisle U	62
1951–52d	Lincoln C	69	Grimsby T	66	Stockport Co	59
1952–53d	Oldham Ath	59	Port Vale	58	Wrexham	56
1953–54d	Port Vale	69	Barnsley	58	Scunthorpe U	57
1954–55d	Barnsley	65	Accrington S	61	Scunthorpe U*	58
1955–56d	Grimsby T	68	Derby Co	63	Accrington S	59
1956–57d	Derby Co	63	Hartlepools U	59	Accrington S*	58
1957–58d	Scunthorpe U	66	Accrington S	59	Bradford C	57

* Won or placed on goal average (ratio).

PROMOTED AFTER PLAY-OFFS
(Not accounted for in previous section)

1986–87	Aldershot to Division 3.
1987–88	Swansea C to Division 3.
1988–89	Leyton Orient to Division 3.
1989–90	Cambridge U to Division 3; Notts Co to Division 2; Sunderland to Division 1.
1990–91	Notts Co to Division 1; Tranmere R to Division 2; Torquay U to Division 3.
1991–92	Blackburn R to Premier League; Peterborough U to Division 1.
1992–93	Swindon T to Premier League; WBA to Division 1; York C to Division 2.

1993–94 Leicester C to Premier League; Burnley to Division 1; Wycombe W to Division 2.
1994–95 Huddersfield T to Division 1.
1995–96 Leicester C to Premier League; Bradford C to Division 1; Plymouth Arg to Division 2.
1996–97 Crystal Palace to Premier League; Crewe Alex to Division 1; Northampton T to Division 2.
1997–98 Charlton Ath to Premier League; Colchester U to Division 2.
1998–99 Watford to Premier League; Scunthorpe U to Division 2.

LEAGUE TITLE WINS

FA PREMIER LEAGUE – Manchester U 6, Arsenal 1, Blackburn R 1.

LEAGUE DIVISION 1 – Liverpool 18, Arsenal 10, Everton 9, Sunderland 8, Manchester U 7, Aston Villa 7, Newcastle U 5, Sheffield W 4, Huddersfield T 3, Leeds U 3, Wolverhampton W 3, Blackburn R 2, Portsmouth 2, Preston NE 2, Burnley 2, Manchester C 2, Nottingham F 2, Tottenham H 2, Derby Co 2, Bolton W, Charlton Ath, Chelsea, Crystal Palace, Sheffield U, WBA, Ipswich T, Middlesbrough 1 each.

LEAGUE DIVISION 2 – Leicester C 6, Manchester C 6, Sheffield W 5, Birmingham C (one as Small Heath) 5, Derby Co 4, Liverpool 4, Preston NE 4, Ipswich T 3, Leeds U 3, Notts Co 3, Middlesbrough 3, Stoke C 3, Bury 2, Grimsby T 2, Norwich C 2, Nottingham F 2, Tottenham H 2, WBA 2, Aston Villa 2, Burnley 2, Chelsea 2, Manchester U 2, West Ham U 2, Wolverhampton W 2, Bolton W 2, Fulham 2, Swindon T, Huddersfield T, Bristol C, Brentford, Bradford C, Everton, Sheffield U, Newcastle U, Coventry C, Blackpool, Blackburn R, Sunderland, Crystal Palace, Luton T, QPR, Oxford U, Millwall, Oldham Ath, Reading 1, Watford 1 each.

LEAGUE DIVISION 3 – Portsmouth 2, Oxford U 2, Shrewsbury T 2, Carlisle U 2, Preston NE 2, Brentford 2, Plymouth Arg, Southampton, Bury, Northampton T, Coventry C, Hull C, QPR, Watford, Leyton Orient, Aston Villa, Bolton W, Oldham Ath, Blackburn R, Hereford U, Mansfield T, Wrexham, Grimsby T, Rotherham U, Burnley, Bradford C, Bournemouth, Reading, Sunderland, Wolverhampton W, Bristol R, Cambridge U, Cardiff C, Swansea C, Wigan Ath, Notts Co 1 each.

LEAGUE DIVISION 4 – Chesterfield 2, Doncaster R 2, Peterborough U 2, Port Vale, Walsall, Millwall, Brentford, Gillingham, Brighton & HA, Stockport Co, Luton T, Notts Co, Grimsby T, Southport, Mansfield T, Lincoln C, Cambridge U, Watford, Reading, Huddersfield T, Southend U, Sheffield U, Wimbledon, York C, Swindon T, Northampton T, Wolverhampton W, Rotherham U, Exeter C, Darlington, Burnley 1 each.

To 1957–58

DIVISION 3 (South) – Bristol C 3; Charlton Ath, Ipswich T, Millwall, Notts Co, Plymouth Arg, Swansea T 2 each; Brentford, Bristol R, Cardiff C, Crystal Palace, Coventry C, Fulham, Leyton Orient, Luton T, Newport Co, Nottingham F, Norwich C, Portsmouth, QPR, Reading, Southampton, Brighton & HA 1 each.

DIVISION 3 (North) – Barnsley, Doncaster R, Lincoln C 3 each; Chesterfield, Grimsby T, Hull C, Port Vale, Stockport Co 2 each; Bradford PA, Bradford C, Darlington, Derby Co, Nelson, Oldham Ath, Rotherham U, Stoke C, Tranmere R, Wolverhampton W, Scunthorpe U 1 each.

RELEGATED CLUBS

1891–92 League extended. Newton Heath, Sheffield W and Nottingham F admitted. *Second Division formed* including Darwen.
1892–93 In Test matches, Sheffield U and Darwen won promotion in place of Notts Co and Accrington S.
1893–94 In Tests, Liverpool and Small Heath won promotion. Newton Heath and Darwen relegated.
1894–95 After Tests, Bury promoted, Liverpool relegated.
1895–96 After Tests, Liverpool promoted, Small Heath relegated.
1896–97 After Tests, Notts Co promoted, Burnley relegated.
1897–98 Test system abolished after success of Stoke C and Burnley. League extended. Blackburn R and Newcastle U elected to First Division. *Automatic promotion and relegation introduced.*

FA PREMIER LEAGUE TO DIVISION 1

1992–93 Crystal Palace, Middlesbrough, Nottingham F
1993–94 Sheffield U, Oldham Ath, Swindon T
1994–95 Crystal Palace, Norwich C, Leicester C, Ipswich T
1995–96 Manchester C, QPR, Bolton W

1996–97 Sunderland, Middlesbrough, Nottingham F
1997–98 Bolton W, Barnsley, Crystal Palace
1998–99 Charlton Ath, Blackburn R, Nottingham F
1999–2000 Wimbledon, Sheffield W, Watford

DIVISION 1 TO DIVISION 2

1898–99 Bolton W and Sheffield W
1899–1900 Burnley and Glossop
1900–01 Preston NE and WBA
1901–02 Small Heath and Manchester C
1902–03 Grimsby T and Bolton W
1903–04 Liverpool and WBA
1904–05 League extended. Bury and Notts Co, two bottom clubs in First Division, re-elected.
1905–06 Nottingham F and Wolverhampton W
1906–07 Derby Co and Stoke C
1907–08 Bolton W and Birmingham C
1908–09 Manchester C and Leicester Fosse
1909–10 Bolton W and Chelsea
1910–11 Bristol C and Nottingham F
1911–12 Preston NE and Bury
1912–13 Notts Co and Woolwich Arsenal
1913–14 Preston NE and Derby Co
1914–15 Tottenham H and Chelsea*
1919–20 Notts Co and Sheffield W
1920–21 Derby Co and Bradford PA
1921–22 Bradford C and Manchester U
1922–23 Stoke C and Oldham Ath
1923–24 Chelsea and Middlesbrough
1924–25 Preston NE and Nottingham F
1925–26 Manchester C and Notts Co

1926–27 Leeds U and WBA
1927–28 Tottenham H and Middlesbrough
1928–29 Bury and Cardiff C
1929–30 Burnley and Everton
1930–31 Leeds U and Manchester U
1931–32 Grimsby T and West Ham U
1932–33 Bolton W and Blackpool
1933–34 Newcastle U and Sheffield U
1934–35 Leicester C and Tottenham H
1935–36 Aston Villa and Blackburn R
1936–37 Manchester U and Sheffield W
1937–38 Manchester C and WBA
1938–39 Birmingham C and Leicester C
1946–47 Brentford and Leeds U
1947–48 Blackburn R and Grimsby T
1948–49 Preston NE and Sheffield U
1949–50 Manchester C and Birmingham C
1950–51 Sheffield W and Everton
1951–52 Huddersfield T and Fulham
1952–53 Stoke C and Derby Co
1953–54 Middlesbrough and Liverpool
1954–55 Leicester C and Sheffield W
1955–56 Huddersfield T and Sheffield U
1956–57 Charlton Ath and Cardiff C
1957–58 Sheffield W and Sunderland

1958–59 Portsmouth and Aston Villa
1959–60 Luton T and Leeds U
1960–61 Preston NE and Newcastle U
1961–62 Chelsea and Cardiff C
1962–63 Manchester C and Leyton Orient
1963–64 Bolton W and Ipswich T
1964–65 Wolverhampton W and Birmingham C
1965–66 Northampton T and Blackburn R
1966–67 Aston Villa and Blackpool
1967–68 Fulham and Sheffield U
1968–69 Leicester C and QPR
1969–70 Sunderland and Sheffield W
1970–71 Burnley and Blackpool
1971–72 Huddersfield T and Nottingham F
1972–73 Crystal Palace and WBA
1973–74 Southampton, Manchester U, Norwich C
1974–75 Luton T, Chelsea, Carlisle U
1975–76 Wolverhampton W, Burnley, Sheffield U
1976–77 Sunderland, Stoke C, Tottenham H
1977–78 West Ham U, Newcastle U, Leicester C
1978–79 QPR, Birmingham C, Chelsea

1979–80 Bristol C, Derby Co, Bolton W
1980–81 Norwich C, Leicester C, Crystal Palace
1981–82 Leeds U, Wolverhampton W, Middlesbrough
1982–83 Manchester C, Swansea C, Brighton & HA
1983–84 Birmingham C, Notts Co, Wolverhampton W
1984–85 Norwich C, Sunderland, Stoke C
1985–86 Ipswich T, Birmingham C, WBA
1986–87 Leicester C, Manchester C, Aston Villa
1987–88 Chelsea**, Portsmouth, Watford, Oxford U
1988–89 Middlesbrough, West Ham U, Newcastle U
1989–90 Sheffield W, Charlton Ath, Millwall
1990–91 Sunderland and Derby Co
1991–92 Luton T, Notts Co, West Ham U
1992–93 Brentford, Cambridge U, Bristol R
1993–94 Birmingham C, Oxford U, Peterborough U
1994–95 Swindon T, Burnley, Bristol C, Notts Co
1995–96 Millwall, Watford, Luton T
1996–97 Grimsby T, Oldham Ath, Southend U
1997–98 Manchester C, Stoke C, Reading
1998–99 Bury, Oxford U, Bristol C
1999–2000 Walsall, Port Vale, Swindon T

**Relegated after play-offs.*
Subsequently re-elected to Division 1 when League was extended after the War.

DIVISION 2 TO DIVISION 3

1920–21 Stockport Co
1921–22 Bradford PA and Bristol C
1922–23 Rotherham Co and Wolverhampton W
1923–24 Nelson and Bristol C
1924–25 Crystal Palace and Coventry C
1925–26 Stoke C and Stockport Co
1926–27 Darlington and Bradford C
1927–28 Fulham and South Shields
1928–29 Port Vale and Clapton Orient
1929–30 Hull C and Notts Co
1930–31 Reading and Cardiff C
1931–32 Barnsley and Bristol C
1932–33 Chesterfield and Charlton Ath
1933–34 Millwall and Lincoln C
1934–35 Oldham Ath and Notts Co
1935–36 Port Vale and Hull C
1936–37 Doncaster R and Bradford C
1937–38 Barnsley and Stockport Co
1938–39 Norwich C and Tranmere R
1946–47 Swansea T and Newport Co
1947–48 Doncaster R and Millwall
1948–49 Nottingham F and Lincoln C
1949–50 Plymouth Arg and Bradford PA
1950–51 Grimsby T and Chesterfield
1951–52 Coventry C and QPR
1952–53 Southampton and Barnsley
1953–54 Brentford and Oldham Ath
1954–55 Ipswich T and Derby Co
1955–56 Plymouth Arg and Hull C
1956–57 Port Vale and Bury
1957–58 Doncaster R and Notts Co
1958–59 Barnsley and Grimsby T
1959–60 Bristol C and Hull C
1960–61 Lincoln C and Portsmouth
1961–62 Brighton & HA and Bristol R
1962–63 Walsall and Luton T
1963–64 Grimsby T and Scunthorpe U
1964–65 Swindon T and Swansea T
1965–66 Middlesbrough and Leyton Orient

1966–67 Northampton T and Bury
1967–68 Plymouth Arg and Rotherham U
1968–69 Fulham and Bury
1969–70 Preston NE and Aston Villa
1970–71 Blackburn R and Bolton W
1971–72 Charlton Ath and Watford
1972–73 Huddersfield T and Brighton & HA
1973–74 Crystal Palace, Preston NE, Swindon T
1974–75 Millwall, Cardiff C, Sheffield W
1975–76 Oxford U, York C, Portsmouth
1976–77 Carlisle U, Plymouth Arg, Hereford U
1977–78 Blackpool, Mansfield T, Hull C
1978–79 Sheffield U, Millwall, Blackburn R
1979–80 Fulham, Burnley, Charlton Ath
1980–81 Preston NE, Bristol C, Bristol R
1981–82 Cardiff C, Wrexham, Orient
1982–83 Rotherham U, Burnley, Bolton W
1983–84 Derby Co, Swansea C, Cambridge U
1984–85 Notts Co, Cardiff C, Wolverhampton W
1985–86 Carlisle U, Middlesbrough, Fulham
1986–87 Sunderland**, Grimsby T, Brighton & HA
1987–88 Huddersfield T, Reading, Sheffield U**
1988–89 Shrewsbury T, Birmingham C, Walsall
1989–90 Bournemouth, Bradford C, Stoke C
1990–91 WBA and Hull C
1991–92 Plymouth Arg, Brighton & HA, Port Vale
1992–93 Preston NE, Mansfield T, Wigan Ath, Chester C
1993–94 Fulham, Exeter C, Hartlepool U, Barnet
1994–95 Cambridge U, Plymouth Arg, Cardiff C,
         Chester C, Leyton Orient
1995–96 Carlisle U, Swansea C, Brighton & HA, Hull C
1996–97 Peterborough U, Shrewsbury T, Rotherham U,
         Notts Co
1997–98 Brentford, Plymouth Arg, Carlisle U, Southend U
1998–99 York C, Northampton T, Lincoln C,
         Macclesfield T
1999–2000 Cardiff C, Blackpool, Scunthorpe U,
         Chesterfield

DIVISION 3 TO DIVISION 4

1958–59 Rochdale, Notts Co, Doncaster R, Stockport Co
1959–60 Accrington S, Wrexham, Mansfield T, York C
1960–61 Chesterfield, Colchester U, Bradford C,
         Tranmere R
1961–62 Newport Co, Brentford, Lincoln C, Torquay U
1962–63 Bradford PA, Brighton & HA, Carlisle U,
         Halifax T
1963–64 Millwall, Crewe Alex, Wrexham, Notts Co
1964–65 Luton T, Port Vale, Colchester U, Barnsley
1965–66 Southend U, Exeter C, Brentford, York C
1966–67 Doncaster R, Workington, Darlington, Swansea T
1967–68 Scunthorpe U, Colchester U, Grimsby T,
         Peterborough U (demoted)
1968–69 Oldham Ath, Crewe Alex, Hartlepool,
         Northampton T
1969–70 Bournemouth, Southport, Barrow, Stockport Co

1970–71 Reading, Bury, Doncaster R, Gillingham
1971–72 Mansfield T, Barnsley, Torquay U, Bradford C
1972–73 Rotherham U, Brentford, Swansea C,
         Scunthorpe U
1973–74 Cambridge U, Shrewsbury T, Southport,
         Rochdale
1974–75 Bournemouth, Tranmere R, Watford,
         Huddersfield T
1975–76 Aldershot, Colchester U, Southend U, Halifax T
1976–77 Reading, Northampton T, Grimsby T, York C
1977–78 Port Vale, Bradford C, Hereford U, Portsmouth
1978–79 Peterborough U, Walsall, Tranmere R, Lincoln C
1979–80 Bury, Southend U, Mansfield T, Wimbledon
1980–81 Sheffield U, Colchester U, Blackpool, Hull C
1981–82 Wimbledon, Swindon T, Bristol C, Chester
1982–83 Reading, Wrexham, Doncaster R, Chesterfield

1983–84 Scunthorpe U, Southend U, Port Vale, Exeter C
1984–85 Burnley, Orient, Preston NE, Cambridge U
1985–86 Lincoln C, Cardiff C, Wolverhampton W,
        Swansea C
1986–87 Bolton W**, Carlisle U, Darlington, Newport Co

1987–88 Doncaster R, York C, Grimsby T, Rotherham U**
1988–89 Southend U, Chesterfield, Gillingham, Aldershot
1989–90 Cardiff C, Northampton T, Blackpool, Walsall
1990–91 Crewe Alex, Rotherham U, Mansfield T
1991–92 Bury, Shrewsbury T, Torquay U, Darlington

** *Relegated after play-offs. N.B. Relegated clubs not featured in exact order of finishing.*

APPLICATIONS FOR RE-ELECTION
FOURTH DIVISION

Eleven: Hartlepool U.
Seven: Crewe Alex.
Six: Barrow (lost League place to Hereford U 1972), Halifax T, Rochdale, Southport (lost League place to Wigan Ath 1978), York C.
Five: Chester C, Darlington, Lincoln C, Stockport Co, Workington (lost League place to Wimbledon 1977).
Four: Bradford PA (lost League place to Cambridge U 1970), Newport Co, Northampton T.
Three: Doncaster R, Hereford U.
Two: Bradford C, Exeter C, Oldham Ath, Scunthorpe U, Torquay U.
One: Aldershot, Colchester U, Gateshead (lost League place to Peterborough U 1960), Grimsby T, Swansea C, Tranmere R, Wrexham, Blackpool, Cambridge U, Preston NE.
Accrington S resigned and Oxford U were elected 1962.
Port Vale were forced to re-apply following expulsion in 1968.
Aldershot expelled March 1992. Maidstone U resigned August 1992.

THIRD DIVISIONS NORTH & SOUTH

Seven: Walsall.
Six: Exeter C, Halifax T, Newport Co.
Five: Accrington S, Barrow, Gillingham, New Brighton, Southport.
Four: Rochdale, Norwich C.
Three: Crystal Palace, Crewe Alex, Darlington, Hartlepool U, Merthyr T, Swindon T.
Two: Aberdare Ath, Aldershot, Ashington, Bournemouth, Brentford, Chester, Colchester U, Durham C, Millwall, Nelson, QPR, Rotherham U, Southend U, Tranmere R, Watford, Workington.
One: Bradford C, Bradford PA, Brighton & HA, Bristol R, Cardiff C, Carlisle U, Charlton Ath, Gateshead, Grimsby T, Mansfield T, Shrewsbury T, Torquay U, York C.

LEAGUE STATUS FROM 1986–87

RELEGATED FROM LEAGUE

1986–87	Lincoln C
1987–88	Newport Co
1988–89	Darlington
1989–90	Colchester U
1990–91	—
1991–92	—
1992–93	Halifax T
1993–94	—
1994–95	—
1995–96	—
1996–97	Hereford U
1997–98	Doncaster R
1998–99	Scarborough
1999–2000	Chester C

PROMOTED TO LEAGUE

Scarborough
Lincoln C
Maidstone U
Darlington
Barnet
Colchester U
Wycombe W
—
—

Macclesfield T
Halifax T
Cheltenham T
Kidderminster H

LEAGUE ATTENDANCES SINCE 1946–47

Season	Matches	Total	Div. 1	Div. 2	Div. 3 (S)	Div. 3 (N)
1946–47	1848	35,604,606	15,005,316	11,071,572	5,664,004	3,863,714
1947–48	1848	40,259,130	16,732,341	12,286,350	6,653,610	4,586,829
1948–49	1848	41,271,414	17,914,667	11,353,237	6,998,429	5,005,081
1949–50	1848	40,517,865	17,278,625	11,694,158	7,104,155	4,440,927
1950–51	2028	39,584,967	16,679,454	10,780,580	7,367,884	4,757,109
1951–52	2028	39,015,866	16,110,322	11,066,189	6,958,927	4,880,428
1952–53	2028	37,149,966	16,050,278	9,686,654	6,704,299	4,708,735
1953–54	2028	36,174,590	16,154,915	9,510,053	6,311,508	4,198,114
1954–55	2028	34,133,103	15,087,221	8,988,794	5,996,017	4,051,071
1955–56	2028	33,150,809	14,108,961	9,080,002	5,692,479	4,269,367
1956–57	2028	32,744,405	13,803,037	8,718,162	5,622,189	4,601,017
1957–58	2028	33,562,208	14,468,652	8,663,712	6,097,183	4,332,661

Season	Matches	Total	Div. 1	Div. 2	Div. 3	Div. 4
1958–59	2028	33,610,985	14,727,691	8,641,997	5,946,600	4,276,697
1959–60	2028	32,538,611	14,391,227	8,399,627	5,739,707	4,008,050
1960–61	2028	28,619,754	12,926,948	7,033,936	4,784,256	3,874,614
1961–62	2015	27,979,902	12,061,194	7,453,089	5,199,106	3,266,513
1962–63	2028	28,885,852	12,490,239	7,792,770	5,341,362	3,261,481
1963–64	2028	28,535,022	12,486,626	7,594,158	5,419,157	3,035,081
1964–65	2028	27,641,168	12,708,752	6,984,104	4,436,245	3,512,067
1965–66	2028	27,206,980	12,480,644	6,914,757	4,779,150	3,032,429
1966–67	2028	28,902,596	14,242,957	7,253,819	4,421,172	2,984,648
1967–68	2028	30,107,298	15,289,410	7,450,410	4,013,087	3,354,391
1968–69	2028	29,382,172	14,584,851	7,382,390	4,339,656	3,075,275
1969–70	2028	29,600,972	14,868,754	7,581,728	4,223,761	2,926,729
1970–71	2028	28,194,146	13,954,337	7,098,265	4,377,213	2,764,331
1971–72	2028	28,700,729	14,484,603	6,769,308	4,697,392	2,749,426
1972–73	2028	25,448,642	13,998,154	5,631,730	3,737,252	2,081,506
1973–74	2027	24,982,203	13,070,991	6,326,108	3,421,624	2,163,480
1974–75	2028	25,577,977	12,613,178	6,955,970	4,086,145	1,992,684
1975–76	2028	24,896,053	13,089,861	5,798,405	3,948,449	2,059,338
1976–77	2028	26,182,800	13,647,585	6,250,597	4,152,218	2,132,400
1977–78	2028	25,392,872	13,255,677	6,474,763	3,332,042	2,330,390
1978–79	2028	24,540,627	12,704,549	6,153,223	3,374,558	2,308,297
1979–80	2028	24,623,975	12,163,002	6,112,025	3,999,328	2,349,620
1980–81	2028	21,907,569	11,392,894	5,175,442	3,637,854	1,701,379
1981–82	2028	20,006,961	10,420,793	4,750,463	2,836,915	1,998,790
1982–83	2028	18,766,158	9,295,613	4,974,937	2,943,568	1,552,040
1983–84	2028	18,358,631	8,711,448	5,359,757	2,729,942	1,557,484
1984–85	2028	17,849,835	9,761,404	4,030,823	2,667,008	1,390,600
1985–86	2028	16,488,577	9,037,854	3,551,968	2,490,481	1,408,274
1986–87	2028	17,379,218	9,144,676	4,168,131	2,350,970	1,715,441
1987–88	2030	17,959,732	8,094,571	5,341,599	2,751,275	1,772,287
1988–89	2036	18,464,192	7,809,993	5,887,805	3,035,327	1,791,067
1989–90	2036	19,445,442	7,883,039	6,867,674	2,803,551	1,891,178
1990–91	2036	19,508,202	8,618,709	6,285,068	2,835,759	1,768,666
1991–92	2064*	20,487,273	9,989,160	5,809,787	2,993,352	1,694,974

Season	Matches	Total	FA Premier	Div. 1	Div. 2	Div. 3
1992–93	2028	20,657,327	9,759,809	5,874,017	3,483,073	1,540,428
1993–94	2028	21,683,381	10,644,551	6,487,104	2,972,702	1,579,024
1994–95	2028	21,856,020	11,213,168	6,044,293	3,037,752	1,560,807
1995–96	2036	21,844,416	10,469,107	6,566,349	2,843,652	1,965,308
1996–97	2036	22,783,163	10,804,762	6,931,539	3,195,223	1,851,639
1997–98	2036	24,692,608	11,092,106	8,330,018	3,503,264	1,767,220
1998–99	2036	25,435,542	11,620,326	7,543,369	4,169,697	2,102,150
1999-2000	2036	25,341,090	11,668,497	7,810,208	3,700,433	2,161,952

*Figures include matches played by Aldershot.

ENGLISH LEAGUE ATTENDANCES 1999–2000

FA CARLING PREMIERSHIP ATTENDANCES

	Average Gate			Season 1999/2000	
	1998/99	1999/2000	+/−%	Highest	Lowest
Arsenal	38,042	38,033	−0.02	38,147	37,271
Aston Villa	36,937	31,697	−14.19	39,217	23,885
Bradford City	14,289	18,030	+26.18	18,276	16,864
Chelsea	34,754	34,531	−0.64	35,113	31,591
Coventry City	20,773	20,786	+0.06	23,084	17,658
Derby County	29,193	29,351	+0.54	33,378	24,045
Everton	36,202	34,880	−3.65	40,052	30,490
Leeds United	35,773	39,155	+9.45	40,192	34,122
Leicester City	20,469	19,825	−3.15	22,170	17,550
Liverpool	43,231	44,074	+1.95	44,929	40,483
Manchester United	55,188	58,017	+5.13	61,629	54,941
Middlesbrough	34,386	33,263	−3.27	34,800	31,400
Newcastle United	36,690	36,311	−1.03	36,619	35,614
Sheffield Wednesday	26,745	24,855	−7.07	39,640	18,077
Southampton	15,140	15,132	−0.05	15,257	14,208
Sunderland	38,745	40,495	+4.52	42,079	37,879
Tottenham Hotspur	34,149	34,902	+2.21	36,233	28,701
Watford	11,822	18,544	+56.86	21,590	15,511
West Ham United	25,639	25,093	−2.13	26,044	22,438
Wimbledon	18,207	17,156	−5.77	26,129	8,248

TOTAL ATTENDANCES: 11,668,497 (380 games)
                                  Average 30,707 (+0.42%)
HIGHEST: 61,629 Manchester United v Tottenham Hotspur
LOWEST: 8,248 Wimbledon v Sheffield Wednesday
HIGHEST AVERAGE: 58,017 Manchester United
LOWEST AVERAGE: 15,132 Southampton

NATIONWIDE FOOTBALL LEAGUE: DIVISION ONE ATTENDANCES

	Average Gate			Season 1999/2000	
	1998/99	1999/2000	+/−%	Highest	Lowest
Barnsley	16,269	15,412	−5.3	22,650	12,026
Birmingham City	20,794	21,895	+5.3	29,050	17,150
Blackburn Rovers	25,773	19,253	−25.3	29,913	15,671
Bolton Wanderers	18,240	14,244	−21.9	21,671	11,668
Charlton Athletic	19,816	19,558	−1.3	20,043	18,663
Crewe Alexandra	5,269	6,222	+18.1	10,066	4,741
Crystal Palace	17,123	15,662	−8.5	22,577	12,110
Fulham	11,387	13,092	+15.0	19,623	8,688
Grimsby Town	6,681	6,157	−7.8	8,742	4,036
Huddersfield Town	12,976	14,029	+8.1	18,173	10,656
Ipswich Town	16,920	18,524	+9.5	21,908	14,514
Manchester City	28,261	32,088	+13.5	33,027	30,057
Norwich City	15,761	15,539	−1.4	19,948	12,468
Nottingham Forest	24,415	17,196	−29.6	25,846	13,841
Port Vale	6,991	5,997	−14.2	10,250	3,737
Portsmouth	11,973	13,906	+16.1	19,015	9,042
Queens Park Rangers	11,793	12,589	+6.7	19,002	9,357
Sheffield United	16,243	13,718	−15.5	23,862	8,965
Stockport County	7,900	7,411	−6.2	11,212	4,868
Swindon Town	8,651	6,977	−19.4	12,397	4,701
Tranmere Rovers	6,930	7,273	+4.9	13,208	5,004
Walsall	5,457	6,779	+24.2	9,422	5,384
West Bromwich Albion	14,585	14,584	0.0	22,101	9,201
Wolverhampton Wanderers	22,620	21,470	−5.1	25,500	18,186

TOTAL ATTENDANCES: 7,810,208 (552 games)
                                  Average 14,149 (+3.5%)
HIGHEST: 33,027 Manchester City v Blackburn Rovers
LOWEST: 3,737 Port Vale v Grimsby Town
HIGHEST AVERAGE: 32,088 Manchester City
LOWEST AVERAGE: 5,997 Port Vale

NATIONWIDE FOOTBALL LEAGUE: DIVISION TWO ATTENDANCES

	Average Gate			Season 1999/2000	
	1998/99	1999/2000	+/- %	Highest	Lowest
AFC Bournemouth	7,117	4,917	−30.9	6,512	3,481
Blackpool	5,116	4,841	−5.4	9,042	2,819
Brentford	5,444	5,742	+5.5	7,100	4,055
Bristol City	12,860	9,803	−23.8	16,011	7,777
Bristol Rovers	6,263	8,402	+34.2	11,109	5,397
Burnley	10,605	12,937	+22.0	22,310	8,944
Bury	5,476	4,025	−26.5	9,115	2,606
Cambridge United	4,583	4,403	−3.9	6,211	3,016
Cardiff City	7,131	6,895	−3.3	11,168	4,389
Chesterfield	4,564	2,935	−35.7	4,726	1,903
Colchester United	4,479	3,782	−15.6	6,194	2,557
Gillingham	6,339	7,088	+11.8	9,178	5,884
Luton Town	5,527	5,658	+2.4	7,205	4,633
Millwall	6,958	9,260	+33.1	17,929	5,202
Notts County	5,617	5,667	+0.9	9,677	3,728
Oldham Athletic	5,628	5,391	−4.2	9,432	3,807
Oxford United	7,040	5,790	−17.8	7,638	4,318
Preston North End	11,926	12,819	+7.5	19,407	8,506
Reading	11,265	8,985	−20.2	13,348	5,393
Scunthorpe United	3,741	4,064	+8.6	5,862	2,686
Stoke City	12,732	11,426	−10.3	15,354	7,054
Wigan Athletic	4,250	7,007	+64.9	15,993	4,338
Wrexham	3,948	3,952	+0.1	8,811	2,139
Wycombe Wanderers	5,121	5,101	−0.4	7,042	3,821

TOTAL ATTENDANCES:	3,700,433 (552 games)
	Average 6,704 (−11.3%)
HIGHEST:	22,310 Burnley v Preston North End
LOWEST:	1,903 Chesterfield v Bury
HIGHEST AVERAGE:	12,937 Burnley
LOWEST AVERAGE:	2,935 Chesterfield

NATIONWIDE FOOTBALL LEAGUE: DIVISION THREE ATTENDANCES

	Average Gate			Season 1999/2000	
	1998/99	1999/2000	+/- %	Highest	Lowest
Barnet	2,107	2,743	+30.2	4,030	1,769
Brighton & Hove Albion	3,253	5,733	+76.2	5,998	5,049
Carlisle United	3,319	3,192	−3.8	6,525	2,028
Cheltenham Town	3,112	4,125	+32.6	5,391	3,107
Chester City	2,526	2,686	+6.3	5,507	1,705
Darlington	3,181	5,523	+73.6	7,401	3,553
Exeter City	3,154	3,014	−4.4	5,263	1,652
Halifax Town	2,541	2,536	−0.2	3,721	1,657
Hartlepool United	2,690	2,982	+10.9	4,673	1,980
Hull City	6,051	5,736	−5.2	8,293	4,150
Leyton Orient	4,672	4,357	−6.7	7,200	2,990
Lincoln City	4,654	3,405	−26.8	5,032	2,556
Macclesfield Town	3,311	2,304	−30.4	3,456	1,541
Mansfield Town	2,963	2,594	−12.5	3,338	1,960
Northampton Town	6,073	5,459	−10.1	6,901	4,495
Peterborough United	5,306	6,568	+23.8	10,793	4,965
Plymouth Argyle	5,323	5,372	+0.9	14,893	3,782
Rochdale	2,125	2,774	+30.5	4,198	1,529
Rotherham United	3,988	4,426	+11.0	10,863	2,708
Shrewsbury Town	2,575	2,832	+10.0	7,654	1,785
Southend United	4,317	4,138	−4.1	6,187	2,563
Swansea City	5,225	5,895	+12.8	10,743	3,357
Torquay United	2,600	2,555	−1.7	5,010	1,756
York City	3,646	3,048	−16.4	5,308	1,857

TOTAL ATTENDANCES:	2,161,952 (552 games)
	Average 3,917 (+2.9%)
HIGHEST:	14,893 Plymouth Argyle v Torquay United
LOWEST:	1,529 Rochdale v Torquay United
HIGHEST AVERAGE:	6,568 Peterborough United
LOWEST AVERAGE:	2,304 Macclesfield Town

LEAGUE CUP FINALISTS 1961–2000

Played as a two-leg final until 1966. All subsequent finals at Wembley.

Year	Winners	Runners-up	Score
1961	Aston Villa	Rotherham U	0-2, 3-0 (aet)
1962	Norwich C	Rochdale	3-0, 1-0
1963	Birmingham C	Aston Villa	3-1, 0-0
1964	Leicester C	Stoke C	1-1, 3-2
1965	Chelsea	Leicester C	3-2, 0-0
1966	WBA	West Ham U	1-2, 4-1
1967	QPR	WBA	3-2
1968	Leeds U	Arsenal	1-0
1969	Swindon T	Arsenal	3-1 (aet)
1970	Manchester C	WBA	2-1 (aet)
1971	Tottenham H	Aston Villa	2-0
1972	Stoke C	Chelsea	2-1
1973	Tottenham H	Norwich C	1-0
1974	Wolverhampton W	Manchester C	2-1
1975	Aston Villa	Norwich C	1-0
1976	Manchester C	Newcastle U	2-1
1977	Aston Villa	Everton	0-0, 1-1 (aet), 3-2 (aet)
1978	Nottingham F	Liverpool	0-0 (aet), 1-0
1979	Nottingham F	Southampton	3-2
1980	Wolverhampton W	Nottingham F	1-0
1981	Liverpool	West Ham U	1-1 (aet), 2-1

MILK CUP
1982	Liverpool	Tottenham H	3-1 (aet)
1983	Liverpool	Manchester U	2-1 (aet)
1984	Liverpool	Everton	0-0 (aet), 1-0
1985	Norwich C	Sunderland	1-0
1986	Oxford U	QPR	3-0

LITTLEWOODS CUP
1987	Arsenal	Liverpool	2-1
1988	Luton T	Arsenal	3-2
1989	Nottingham F	Luton T	3-1
1990	Nottingham F	Oldham Ath	1-0

RUMBELOWS LEAGUE CUP
1991	Sheffield W	Manchester U	1-0
1992	Manchester U	Nottingham F	1-0

COCA-COLA CUP
1993	Arsenal	Sheffield W	2-1
1994	Aston Villa	Manchester U	3-1
1995	Liverpool	Bolton W	2-1
1996	Aston Villa	Leeds U	3-0
1997	Leicester C	Middlesbrough	1-1 (aet), 1-0 (aet)
1998	Chelsea	Middlesbrough	2-0 (aet)

WORTHINGTON CUP
1999	Tottenham H	Leicester C	1-0
2000	Leicester C	Tranmere R	2-1

LEAGUE CUP WINS
Aston Villa 5, Liverpool 5, Nottingham F 4, Leicester C 3, Tottenham H 3, Arsenal 2, Chelsea 2, Manchester C 2, Norwich C 2, Wolverhampton W 2, Birmingham C 1, Leeds U 1, Luton T 1, Manchester U 1, Oxford U 1, QPR 1, Sheffield W 1, Stoke C 1, Swindon T 1, WBA 1.

APPEARANCES IN FINALS
Aston Villa 7, Liverpool 7, Nottingham F 6, Arsenal 5, Leicester C 5, Manchester U 4, Norwich C 4, Tottenham H 4, Chelsea 3, Manchester C 3, WBA 3, Everton 2, Leeds U 2, Luton T 2, Middlesbrough 2, QPR 2, Sheffield W 2, Stoke C 2, West Ham U 2, Wolverhampton W 2, Birmingham C 1, Bolton W 1, Newcastle U 1, Oldham Ath 1, Oxford U 1, Rochdale 1, Rotherham U 1, Southampton 1, Sunderland 1, Swindon T 1, Tranmere R 1.

APPEARANCES IN SEMI-FINALS
Aston Villa 11, Liverpool 10, Arsenal 9, Tottenham H 9, Manchester U 7, West Ham U 7, Chelsea 6, Nottingham F 6, Leeds U 5, Leicester C 5, Manchester C 5, Norwich C 5, Middlesbrough 4, WBA 4, Birmingham C 3, Bolton W 3, Burnley 3, Everton 3, QPR 3, Sheffield W 3, Sunderland 3, Swindon T 3, Wimbledon 3, Blackburn R 2, Bristol C 2, Coventry C 2, Crystal Palace 2, Ipswich T 2, Luton T 2, Oxford U 2, Plymouth Arg 2, Southampton 2, Stoke C 2, Tranmere R 2, Wimbledon 2, Blackpool 1, Bury 1, Cardiff C 1, Carlisle U 1, Chester C 1, Derby Co 1, Huddersfield T 1, Newcastle U 1, Oldham Ath 1, Peterborough U 1, Rochdale 1, Rotherham U 1, Shrewsbury T 1, Stockport Co 1, Walsall 1, Watford 1.

WORTHINGTON CUP 1999-2000

FIRST ROUND, FIRST LEG

10 AUG

Birmingham C (2) 3 *(Johnson A 17, Richardson 42 (og), Adebola 75)*
Exeter C (0) 0 18,976
Birmingham C: Poole; Rowett, Grainger, Hughes, Purse, Holdsworth, O'Connor, Holland (McCarthy), Furlong (Adebola), Johnson A, Lazaridis (Forinton).
Exeter C: Naylor; Richardson, Power, Nyamah, Dewhurst, Gittens, McConnell (Wilkinson), Rees, Flack, Holloway, Breslan (Speakman).

Blackpool (1) 2 *(Hughes 26, Clarkson 65)*
Tranmere R (1) 1 *(Thompson 21 (og))* 3298
Blackpool: Barnes P; Couzens, Hills (Bryan), Bardsley, Carlisle, Hughes, Bent (Nowland), Clarkson, Murphy, Thompson, Ormerod.
Tranmere R: Achterberg; Hazell, Thompson, Henry, Allen, Yates, Mahon, Koumas (Frail), Parkinson (Kelly), Matias, Taylor S.

Bournemouth (1) 2 *(Hayter 6, Huck 72)*
Barnet (0) 0 3281
Bournemouth: Ovendale; Young, Warren, Howe, Cox, Mean (Hughes), Jorgensen, Hayter, Stein, Fletcher S (Huck), Rawlinson (O'Neill).
Barnet: Harrison; Stockley, Sawyers, Hackett, Heald, Arber, Wilson, Doolan, Charlery, McGleish (King), Toms (Brown).

Bury (0) 1 *(Lawson 73)*
Notts Co (0) 0 1893
Bury: Kenny; Woodward, James (Avdiu), Daws, Collins, Swailes C, Bullock, Littlejohn (Barrick), Lawson, Preece, Reid.
Notts Co: Ward; Holmes, Blackmore, Ward (Owers), Redmile, Richardson, Hughes, Ramage, Stallard, Beadle (Darby), Murray.

Cambridge U (0) 2 *(Butler 50, 86)*
Bristol C (0) 2 *(Hutchings 51, Mortimer 90)* 2813
Cambridge U: Van Heusden; Chenery, Ashbee, Duncan, Eustace, Wilson, Mustoe, Kyd (Taylor), Butler, Benjamin, Russell.
Bristol C: Phillips; Sebok, Brennan, Mortimer, Taylor, Carey, Murray (Goodridge), Hutchings (Doherty), Akinbiyi, Torpey (Pinamonte), Tinnion.

Cardiff C (0) 1 *(Bowen 67)*
QPR (1) 2 *(Langley 32, Fowler 65 (og))* 5702
Cardiff C: Hallworth; Faerber, Legg, Ford, Fowler (Jarman), Eckhardt, Boland, Bonner (Cornforth), Bowen, Nugent, Hill (Brazier).
QPR: Miklosko (Harper); Baraclough, Currie, Morrow, Ready, Maddix, Langley, Peacock, Kulcsar, Slade, Kiwomya (Gallen).

Carlisle U (0) 0
Grimsby T (0) 0 3000
Carlisle U: Weaver; Pitts (Barr), Clark, Brightwell, Whitehead, Prokas, Skelton (Anthony), Hopper, Walker, Tracey, Searle (Thorpe).
Grimsby T: Coyne; Butterfield (McDermott), Smith D, Livingstone, Smith R, Coldicott, Donovan, Black (Pouton), Ashcroft, Lester (Allen), Groves.

Chester C (1) 2 *(Richardson 7, Beckett 72 (pen))*
Port Vale (1) 1 *(Rougier 15)* 2102
Chester C: Brown; Davidson, Cross, Reid, Lancaster, Woods, Shelton, Richardson, Jones (Moss), Beckett, Fisher.
Port Vale: Pilkington; Walsh, Smith, Brammer, Carragher, Gardner, Rougier, Bent, Naylor (Griffiths), Minton, Barker (Eyre).

Colchester U (1) 2 *(Dozzell 36, Lua-Lua 63)*
Crystal Palace (0) 2 *(Smith 62, Rodger 90)* 4242
Colchester U: Brown; Duguid, Keith, Burton, Greene, Aspinall, Wilkins (Walker), Gregory D, Lua-Lua, Launders (Richard), Dozzell.
Crystal Palace: Digby; Smith, Frampton (Rizzo), Austin, Tuttle, Woozley, Mullins (Evans), Rodger, Bradbury, Morrison, Thomson (Harris).

Darlington (1) 1 *(Oliver 45)*
Bolton W (0) 1 *(Frandsen 71)* 5361
Darlington: Collett; Liddle, Heckingbottom, Reed, Aspin, Himsworth (Hickey), Gray, Oliver, Nogan (Duffield), Gabbiadini (Carruthers), Atkinson.
Bolton W: Branagan; Cox, Whitlow, Frandsen (Aljofree), Strong, Todd, Johansen, Jensen, Gudjohnsen, Hansen (Holdsworth), Gardner.

Halifax T (0) 0
WBA (0) 0 2451
Halifax T: Parks; Murphy S, Jules, Mitchell, Stoneman, Sertori, Paterson, Gaughan, Tate, Painter (Power), Butler.
WBA: Whitehead; Raven, Van Blerk, Flynn, Burgess, Carbon (Gabbidon), Quinn, Sneekes, De Freitas (Evans), Hughes, Kilbane.

Hartlepool U (1) 3 *(Miller 3, Di Lella 48, Stephenson 60)*
Crewe Alex (1) 3 *(Little 11, 54, Cramb 69)* 1836
Hartlepool U: Dibble; Knowles, Perkins, Barron, Lee, Ingram, Di Lella, Miller, Jones, Freestone (Midgley), Stephenson.
Crewe Alex: Kearton; Bignot, Smith S, Macauley, Unsworth, Charnock, Little, Lunt, Jack, Cramb, Sorvel.

Lincoln C (1) 2 *(Fleming 45, Thorpe 54)*
Barnsley (3) 4 *(Shipperley 16, Van der Laan 26, 31, Eaden 58)* 3426
Lincoln C: Vaughan; Barnett J (Poppleton), Welsh, Fleming, Branston, Smith (Peacock), Miller (Philpott), Finnigan, Gordon, Thorpe, Gain.
Barnsley: Bullock T; Eaden, Appleby, Austin, Moses, Jones, Van der Laan, Tinker (McClare), Shipperley (Dyer), Sheron (Hristov), Bullock M.

Luton T (0) 0
Bristol R (1) 2 *(Roberts 39, 60)* 2984
Luton T: Abbey; Fraser, Taylor, Watts, White (Doherty), Boyce, Gray, McLaren, Douglas (George), Spring, McIndoe (Fotiadis).
Bristol R: Jones; Pethick, Challis, Foster, Thomson, Tillson, Mauge (Trees), Hillier, Pritchard, Cureton, Roberts.

Macclesfield T (0) 1 *(Priest 76)*
Stoke C (1) 1 *(Keen 8)* 2551
Macclesfield T: Price; Ingram, Rioch, Collins, Tinson, Sedgemore (Wood), Davies, Priest, Barker, Tomlinson (Askey), Whittaker (Durkan).
Stoke C: Ward; Kavanagh J, Small (Clarke), Mohan, Sigurdsson, Keen, Oldfield, Kavanagh G, Connor, Lightbourne (Crowe), Taaffe.

Northampton T (0) 1 *(Corazzin 66 (pen))*
Fulham (0) 2 *(Davis 60, Horsfield 85)* 4415
Northampton T: O'Reilly; Hendon (Gibb), Frain, Sampson, Howey, Savage, Hunter (Corazzin), Hunt, Howard, Wilson (Clarkson), Spedding.
Fulham: Taylor; Symons, Brevett, Melville, Coleman, Morgan, Hughes, Clark, Horsfield, Collymore, Davis.

Norwich C (2) 2 *(Roberts 14, 37)*
Cheltenham T (0) 0 12,276
Norwich C: Marshall A; Sutch, Fuglestad, de Blasiis, Fleming, Jackson, Anselin (Diop), Dalglish (Coote), Roberts, Mulryne, Llewellyn (Marshall L).
Cheltenham T: Book; Griffin, Victory, Banks, Freeman, Howarth, Howells, McAuley (Watkins), Grayson (Brough), Daveney (Bloomer), Yates.

Preston NE (1) 1 *(Appleton 40)*
Wrexham (0) 0 4930
Preston NE: Lucas; Alexander, Edwards, Murdock, Jackson, Gregan, Appleton, Rankine, Nogan (Basham), Macken, McKenna.
Wrexham: Dearden; McGregor, Hardy, Owen, Carey, Ridler, Lowe (Faulconbridge), Stevens, Connolly, Phillips, Williams.

Rochdale (1) 1 *(Lancashire 18)*
Chesterfield (0) 2 *(Reeves 47, Hill 49 (og))* 1910
Rochdale: Edwards; Evans, Stokes, Peake, Bayliss, Hill, Flitcroft, Ford (Carden), Morris (Holt), Lancashire, Atkinson G.
Chesterfield: Leaning; Hewitt, Woods, Curtis, Payne (Simpkins), Breckin, Beaumont (Willis), Holland, Reeves, Ebdon, Bettney (Williams D).

Rotherham U (0) 0
Hull C (1) 1 *(Eyre 18)* 3294
Rotherham U: Pollitt; Varty, Beech, Watson, Wilsterman, Dillon, Sedgwick (Warne), Ingledow (Garner), Fortune-West, Martindale (Scott), Turner.
Hull C: Bracey; Swales, Harper, Schofield, Whittle, Greaves, Eyre, Brabin, Brown (Harris), Alcide, Williams.

Scunthorpe U (0) 0
Huddersfield T (1) 2 *(Lucketti 41, Beech 80)* 3398
Scunthorpe U: Evans; Harsley, Dawson, Logan, Wilcox, Hope, Walker, Hodges, Gayle (Stamp), Calvo-Garcia (Marshall), Graves.
Huddersfield T: Vaesen; Edwards, Dyson, Armstrong (Allison), Lucketti, Irons, Donis (Schofield), Beech, Stewart, Wijnhard, Thornley.

Sheffield U (0) 3 *(Katchuro 49, Smith 51, 90)*
Shrewsbury T (0) 0 6419
Sheffield U: Tracey; Ford, Quinn, Derry, Murphy, Sandford, Smeets, Hamilton, Devlin (Burley), Katchuro, Hunt (Smith).
Shrewsbury T: Edwards; Seabury, Hanmer, Whelan, Winstanley, Wilding, Brown, Kerrigan (Jagielka), Steele, Jobling, Murray.

Southend U (0) 0
Oxford U (0) 2 *(Murphy 53, Beauchamp 81)* 2618
Southend U: Capleton; Booty, Jones N (Clarke), Morley, Roget, Coleman, Maher, Connelly, Abiodun (Roach), Tolson, Houghton.
Oxford U: Arendse; Robinson, Powell, Cook (Banger), Watson, Davis, Lilley, Tait, Murphy, Anthrobus (Weatherstone S), Beauchamp.

Stockport Co (0) 2 *(Cooper 62, Angell 65)*
Oldham Ath (0) 0 3017
Stockport Co: Nash; Connelly, Nicholson, Dinning, Flynn, McIntosh, Cooper, Moore, Angell (Ellis), Smith (Gannon), Wilbraham.
Oldham Ath: Kelly; McNiven S, Holt, Garnett, Thom, Duxbury, Adams, Sheridan, Tipton (Beavers), Allott (Sugden), Innes.

Swindon T (0) 0
Leyton Orient (0) 1 *(Inglethorpe 77)* 3587
Swindon T: Talia; Robinson, Hall (Taylor), Leitch, Davis, Hulbert (Howe), Walters, Ndah, Onuora, Grazioli (Griffin), Williams J.
Leyton Orient: Barrett; Walschaerts (Morrison), Lockwood, Smith, Hicks, Harris, Ling, Ampadu, Christie (Simba), Inglethorpe (Richards), Beall.

Walsall (1) 4 *(Bukran 35, Robins 74, Eyjolfsson 84, 88)*
Plymouth Arg (1) 1 *(Stonebridge 43)* 3502
Walsall: Walker; Marsh, Pointon, Viveash, Barras, Bukran, Wrack, Robins, Rammell (Eyjolfsson), Keates (Larusson), Daley (Mavrak).
Plymouth Arg: Veysey; Rowbotham, McCall, Leadbitter, Heathcote, Barrett, Bastow, O'Sullivan, McGregor, Hargreaves, Stonebridge.

Wycombe W (0) 0
Wolverhampton W (0) 1 *(Curle 54 (pen))* 4564
Wycombe W: Taylor; Lawrence, Vinnicombe, Bates, McCarthy, Holsgrove (Simpson), Ryan, Brown, McSporran, Devine (Carroll), Emblen (Cousins).
Wolverhampton W: Stowell; Muscat, Naylor, Robinson, Curle, Emblen, Bazeley, Sedgley, Flo, Corica (Keane), Simpson.

York C (0) 0
Wigan Ath (0) 1 *(Haworth 73)* 1921
York C: Howarth; Hocking, Hall, Atkins, Jones, Fairclough, Dawson, Dixon, Conlon, Rowe, Bullock.
Wigan Ath: Carroll; Green, Bowen, Balmer, De Zeeuw (McGibbon), Kilford, O'Neill, Sheridan, Haworth, Liddell (Porter), Barlow.

11 AUG

Brentford (0) 0
Ipswich T (0) 2 *(Johnson 64, Clapham 70)* 4825
Brentford: Woodman; Boxall, Anderson, Quinn (Rowlands), Powell, Hreidarsson, Evans, Mahon, Owusu (Folan), Scott (Bryan), Partridge.
Ipswich T: Wright R; Stockwell, Clapham, Thetis, Venus, McGreal, Holland, Wright J, Johnson (Axeldal), Scowcroft, Naylor (Wilnis).

Brighton & HA (0) 0
Gillingham (1) 2 *(Ormerod 45 (og), Hessenthaler 67)* 5613
Brighton & HA: Ormerod; Wilder, Campbell, McPherson (Cameron), Crosby, Hobson, Freeman, Rogers, Hart, Oatway (Johnson), Thomas (Armstrong).
Gillingham: Bartram; Southall, McGlinchey, Smith, Ashby, Butters, Nosworthy, Hessenthaler, Lee (Taylor) (Hodge), Pennock, Saunders (Bryant).

Manchester C (1) 5 *(Goater 36, Kennedy 48, 82, Horlock 62 (pen), Taylor G 74)*
Burnley (0) 0 11,074
Manchester C: Weaver; Crooks, Tiatto, Wiekens, Morrison, Horlock, Kennedy, Jeff Whitley, Dickov (Allsopp), Goater (Taylor G), Cooke (Bishop).
Burnley: Crichton; West, Cowan, Mellon, Davis, Thomas, Little (Grant), Cook (Jepson), Branch (Lee), Payton, Johnrose.

Nottingham F (1) 3 *(Bart-Williams 44, Quashie 68, Allou 81)*
Mansfield T (0) 0 8300
Nottingham F: Crossley; Louis-Jean (Bonalair), Rogers (Allou), Metrecano, Chettle, Scimeca, Petrachi, Quashie, Freedman, Harewood, Bart-Williams.
Mansfield T: Richardson B; Hassell, Williams, Kerr, Richardson N, Linighan (Allardyce), Roscoe, Peacock, Lormor, Sisson, Tallon (Boulding).

Reading (0) 0
Peterborough U (0) 0 4651
Reading: Howey; Gurney, Gray, Polston, Hunter, McLaren (Bernal), Hodges (McIntyre), Caskey (Crawford), Williams M, Scott, Brebner.
Peterborough U: Tyler; Hooper, Drury, Castle, Wicks, Edwards, Farrell, Davies, Shields, Martin (Green), Broughton (Inman).

Swansea C (1) 2 *(Watkin 45, Price 47)*
Millwall (0) 0 3793
Swansea C: Freestone; O'Leary, Howard (Coates), Cusack, Smith, Bound, Price, Roberts (Appleby), Bird, Watkin (Alsop), Thomas.
Millwall: Warner; Bircham, Ryan, Cahill, Nethercott, Dolan, Moody, Livermore, Shaw (Harris), Reid, Neill.

17 AUG

Torquay U (0) 0
Portsmouth (0) 0 3209
Torquay U: Southall; Tully, Herrera (Simb), Aggrey, Russell, Watson, Brandon, Platts (Hill), Bedeau, Williams, O'Brien.
Portsmouth: Flahavan; Crowe, Robinson, Vlachos, Whitbread, Thogersen, Newton (Miglioranzi), Nightingale, Lovell (Allen), Phillips (Simpson), Igoe.

FIRST ROUND, SECOND LEG

24 AUG

Barnet (2) 3 *(McGleish 25, 43 (pen), Hackett 63)*
Bournemouth (2) 2 *(Stein 12, 21)* 1697
Barnet: Naisbitt; Stockley (King), Sawyers (Ansell), Hackett, Heald, Arber, Currie, Doolan, Charlery (Strevens), McGleish, Toms.
Bournemouth: Ovendale; Young, Warren, Howe, Cox, Mean (Hayter), Jorgensen (Day), Robinson, Stein (Watson), Fletcher S, Hughes.
Bournemouth won 4-3 on aggregate.

Barnsley (0) 2 *(Sheron 74, Eaden 79)*
Lincoln C (1) 2 *(Gordon 36, Peacock 52)* 7047
Barnsley: Bullock T; Austin (Barnard), Jones, Morgan, Moses, Bullock M (Eaden), Tinkler, Hignett, Shipperley (Hristov), Sheron, Van der Laan.
Lincoln C: Vaughan; Barnett D, Gain, Fleming, Branston, Poppleton, Peacock, Finnigan, Gordon, Thorpe (Stant), Philpott (Smith).
Barnsley won 6-4 on aggregate.

Bolton W (2) 5 *(Reed 5 (og), Gardner 6, Taylor 50, Frandsen 55, Johansen 71 (pen))*
Darlington (2) 3 *(Nogan 34, 41, Gabbiadini 75)* 4991
Bolton W: Branagan; Cox, Whitlow, Frandsen, Strong, Fish, Johansen, Aljofree, Gudjohnsen, Taylor, Gardner.
Darlington: Collett; Liddle, Heckingbottom, Reed, Bennett, Himsworth (Oliver), Gray, Heaney, Nogan, Gabbiadini (Duffield), Atkinson (Carruthers).
Bolton W won 6-4 on aggregate.

Bristol C (2) 2 *(Torpey 18, Thorpe 36)*
Cambridge U (0) 1 *(Butler 87)* 5352
Bristol C: Phillips; Carey, Brennan, Goodridge, Sebok, Taylor, Murray, Hutchings, Thorpe, Torpey (Pinamonte), Tinnion.
Cambridge U: Van Heusden; Chenery, Ashbee, Duncan, Eustace, Wilson, Mustoe (Taylor), Wanless (Cassidy), Butler, Benjamin, Kyd (Youngs).
Bristol C won 4-3 on aggregate.

Burnley (0) 0
Manchester C (0) 1 *(Cooke 65)* 3647
Burnley: Crichton; Robertson, Cowan, Mellon (West), Thomas, Armstrong, Little, Brass, Lee (Jepson), Branch (Grant), Johnrose.
Manchester C: Weaver; Crooks, Edghill, Wiekens (Vaughan), Jobson, Pollock, Kennedy, Bishop, Taylor (Allsopp), Brown, Cooke (Wright-Phillips).
Manchester C won 6-0 on aggregate.

Cheltenham T (0) 2 *(Grayson 47 (pen), Victory 69)*
Norwich C (0) 1 *(Marshall L 100)* 4203
Cheltenham T: Book; Griffin, Victory, Banks, Freeman, Howarth, Howells, McAuley (Watkins), Grayson, Daveney (Bloomer), Yates (Jackson).
Norwich C: Marshall A; Sutch, Wilson, Marshall L, Fleming, Mackay, Anselin (de Blasiis), Dalglish (Diop), Roberts, Mulryne, Llewellyn.
aet; Norwich C won 3-2 on aggregate.

Chesterfield (1) 2 *(Bayliss 4 (og), Ebdon 78)*
Rochdale (1) 1 *(Evans 39)* 2067
Chesterfield: Gayle; Hewitt, Woods, Curtis, Simpkins (Beaumont), Breckin, Willis, Holland, Reeves, Ebdon, Bettney.
Rochdale: Edwards; Evans, Stokes, Peake, Bayliss, Hill, Flitcroft, Ford (Carden), Lancashire, Holt (Morris), Atkinson.
Chesterfield won 4-2 on aggregate.

Crewe Alex (0) 1 *(Little 88)*
Hartlepool U (0) 0 5095
Crewe Alex: Kearton; Bignot, Smith S, Wright S, Foran, Charnock, Little, Lunt, Cramb, Sorvel, Rivers.
Hartlepool U: Dibble; Knowles, Clark, Barron, Lee (Ingram) (Henderson), Strodder, Tennebo, Miller (Di Lella), Jones, Freestone, Stephenson.
Crewe Alex won 4-3 on aggregate.

Crystal Palace (2) 3 *(Smith 18, Morrison 37, Rizzo 87)*
Colchester U (0) 1 *(Keith 75)* 5471
Crystal Palace: Digby; Smith, Frampton, Austin, Woozle, Harris, Morrison, Svensson (Carlisle), Bradbury, Rodger (Rizzo), Thomson.
Colchester U: Walker; Duguid, Keith, Burton, Greene, Aspinall, Wilkins, Gregory D, Lua-Lua (Pinault), Launders, Dozzell (Moralee).
Crystal Palace won 5-3 on aggregate.

Exeter C (0) 1 *(McConnell 75 (pen))*
Birmingham C (1) 2 *(Richardson 22 (og), O'Connor 50)* 2338
Exeter C: Naylor (Matthews); Richardson, Gale, Holloway, Dewhurst (Speakman), Rees, McConnell, Flack, Alexander, Worrall (Smith), Breslan.
Birmingham C: Poole (Knight); Gill, Bass, Newton, Purse, Wassall, Holland, O'Connor (Dyson), Adebola, Forinton, Ndlovu.
Birmingham C won 5-1 on aggregate.

Fulham (3) 3 *(Horsfield 6, 43, 44)*
Northampton T (1) 1 *(Byfield 30)* 5515
Fulham: Taylor; Finnan, Brevett (Hayward), Melville, Coleman, Morgan (Symons), Trollope, Clark, Horsfield, Peschisolido, Davis.
Northampton T: Welch; Hendon, Frain, Sampson, Howey, Hunt, Savage, Corazzin (Wilson), Howard, Byfield, Spedding.
Fulham won 5-2 on aggregate.

Gillingham (2) 2 *(Taylor 19, Southall 31)*
Brighton & HA (0) 0 4592
Gillingham: Bartram; Southall, Patterson, Saunders, Ashby, Pennock, Hodge, Hessenthaler (McGlinchey), Thomson (Miller), Lewis, Taylor (Lee).
Brighton & HA: Ormerod; Wilder, Campbell, Watson, Crosby, Hobson (Johnson), Newhouse (Freeman), Rogers (Hart), Arnott, Oatway, Thomas.
Gillingham won 4-0 on aggregate.

Grimsby T (3) 6 *(Lester 11, 35, 67, Groves 30, Coldicott 53, Donovan 86)*
Carlisle U (0) 0 2696
Grimsby T: Coyne; McDermott, Smith D, Livingstone, Smith R, Coldicott, Donovan, Black, Ashcroft (Clare), Lester (Allen), Groves (Pouton).
Carlisle U: Weaver; Pitts (Anthony), Clark, Whitehead (Thorpe), Brightwell, Prokas, Barr, Hopper, Walker, Tracey, Searle.
Grimsby T won 6-0 on aggregate.

Huddersfield T (0) 0
Scunthorpe U (0) 0 4345
Huddersfield T: Vaesen; Edwards, Armstrong, Irons, Lucketti, Monkou (Dyson), Thornley, Horne (Baldry), Stewart, Sellars, Wijnhard.
Scunthorpe U: Evans; Harsley, Dawson, Hope, Fickling, Stanton, Walker, Hodges, Sheldon, Anderson (Graves) (Sparrow), Calvo-Garcia (Housham).
Huddersfield won 2-0 on aggregate.

Hull C (1) 2 *(Alcide 10, Brown 73)*
Rotherham U (0) 0 4373
Hull C: Bracey; Swales, Harper, Schofield, Whittle, Edwards, Joyce (D'Auria), Brabin, Eyre (Wood), Alcide, Brown.
Rotherham U: Pollitt; Varty, Beech, Dillon (Warner), Wilsterman, Garner, Scott, Watson, Fortune-West (Berry), Warne, Turner.
Hull C won 3-0 on aggregate.

Ipswich T (2) 2 *(Scowcroft 41, Clapham 90)*
Brentford (0) 0 9748
Ipswich T: Wright R; Wilnis, Clapham, Thetis, Brown, McGreal, Holland, Wright J (Stockwell), Johnson (Axeldal), Scowcroft (Naylor), Magilton.
Brentford: Pearcey; Boxall, Anderson, Rowlands, Powell (Quinn), Hreidarsson, Evans, Mahon, Bryan (Warner), Partridge, Folan (Scott).
Ipswich T won 4-0 on aggregate.

Leyton Orient (0) 1 *(Lockwood 83)*
Swindon T (0) 1 *(Walters 57 (pen))* 2750
Leyton Orient: Barrett; Walschaerts (Joseph M), Lockwood, Smith, Hicks, Harris, Ling, Ampadu, Christie (Watts), Richards (Simba), Beall.
Swindon T: Talia; Robinson (Williams J), Hall, Davis, Reeves, Davies, Howe, Ndah (McHugh), Onuora, Grazioli (Hay), Walters.
Leyton Orient won 2-1 on aggregate.

Mansfield T (0) 1 *(Peacock 54)*
Nottingham F (0) 0 3072
Mansfield T: Richardson B; Hassell, Williams, Sisson, Richardson N, Linighan, Roscoe, Peacock, Lormor, Blake, Boulding (Allardyce).
Nottingham F: Beasant; Melton, Rogers (Gray), Hjelde, Chettle, Scimeca, Bart-Williams (Doig), Quashie, Guinan (Merino), Harewood, Allou.
Nottingham F won 3-1 on aggregate.

Millwall (1) 1 *(Sadlier 29)*
Swansea C (0) 1 *(Bird 90 (pen))* 4542
Millwall: Warner; Bircham, Ryan (Moody), Cahill, Nethercott, Fitzgerald, Livermore (Gilkes), Sadlier, Harris, Shaw, Neill.
Swansea C: Freestone; Price, Lacey, Smith, Cusack, Bound (Jones S), Appleby, Thomas, Alsop, Watkin (Bird), Coates.
Swansea C won 3-1 on aggregate.

Notts Co (0) 2 *(Blackmore 71, Ramage 83 (pen))*
Bury (0) 0 2494
Notts Co: Ward; Holmes, Blackmore (Pearce), Warren (Beadle), Redmile, Richardson, Owers, Ramage (Bolland), Stallard, Darby, Hughes.
Bury: Kenny; Billy, Collins, Daws, Swailes C, Bullock (Barnes), Littlejohn, Reid, Lawson, Preece (Barrick), James (Avdiu).
Notts Co won 2-1 on aggregate.

Oldham Ath (0) 1 *(Allott 85)*
Stockport Co (1) 1 *(Woodthorpe 41)* 2885
Oldham Ath: Miskelly; McNiven S, Holt, Garnett, Rickers, Swan (Sheridan), Adams, Sugden (Allott), Salt, McNiven D, Innes (Tait).
Stockport Co: Gray; Briggs, Nicholson (Cooper), Gannon, Flynn, McIntosh, Woodthorpe, Moore (Bailey), D'Jaffo (Wilbraham), Byrne C, Ellis.
Stockport Co won 3-1 on aggregate.

Oxford U (0) 1 *(Murphy 61)*
Southend U (0) 0 4162
Oxford U: Lundin; Robinson, Powell (McGowan), Weatherstone S (Cook), Watson, Folland, Lilley, Tait (Lewis), Murphy, Anthrobus, Beauchamp.
Southend U: Capleton; Booty, Cross, Morley, Roget, Coleman, Clarke (Jones N), Tinkler, Roach (Abiodun), Tolson, Houghton.
Oxford U won 3-0 on aggregate.

Peterborough U (1) 1 *(Shields 20)*
Reading (1) 2 *(Caskey 18, Scott 71)* 4109
Peterborough U: Tyler; Hooper, Drury, Castle, Wicks, Edwards, Farrell, Davies, Shields, Broughton (Martin), Etherington (Rea).
Reading: Howey; Bernal, Gray, Grant, Hunter, Casper, Smith, Caskey (Evers), Williams M (Brayson), Forster (Scott), Haddow.
Reading won 2-1 on aggregate.

Plymouth Arg (1) 1 *(Gritton 45)*
Walsall (3) 4 *(Keates 4, Barras 22, Bukran 44, Eyjolfsson 87)* 1834
Plymouth Arg: Sheffield; Ashton, Beswetherick, O'Sullivan, Barrett, McCall, Bastow, Gritton (McCarthy), McGregor, Hargreaves, Stonebridge (Belgrave).
Walsall: Emberson; Marsh, Pointon (Roper), Viveash, Barras, Bukran, Wrack (Mavrak), Robins (Ricketts), Eyjolfsson, Keates, Brissett.
Walsall won 8-2 on aggregate.

Port Vale (2) 4 *(Naylor 35, 64, Minton 45 (pen), Griffiths 84)*
Chester C (2) 4 *(Beckett 5 (pen), 13, Shelton 71, Jones 77)* 2625
Port Vale: Musselwhite; Walsh, Tankard, Brammer, Carragher, Gardner, Rougier (Eyre), Foyle, Naylor, Minton, Smith (Griffiths).
Chester C: Brown; Cross, Davidson, Shelton, Moss, Woods, Richardson, Reid (Jones), Wright, Beckett, Fisher.
Chester C won 6-5 on aggregate.

Portsmouth (2) 3 *(Nightingale 1, 55, Lovell 26)*
Torquay U (0) 0 8741
Portsmouth: Flahavan (Knight); Crowe, Simpson, Newton (Robinson), Awford, Thogersen, Nightingale, Phillips, Lovell (Durnin), Vlachos, Igoe.
Torquay U: Southall; Tully (Simb), Herrera, Aggrey, Russell, Watson, Brandon, Healy, Bedeau, Williams, O'Brien.
Portsmouth won 3-0 on aggregate.

Shrewsbury T (0) 0
Sheffield U (2) 3 *(Marcelo 37, 62, Smith 45)* 1723
Shrewsbury T: Thompson; Seabury, Hanmer, Tretton, Winstanley, Wilding (Kerrigan), Brown, Murray, Steele, Jobling, Berkley.
Sheffield U: Tracey; Kozluk (Doane), Quinn, Ford, Murphy, Sandford, Hunt, Derry, Marcelo (Katchuro), Hamilton (Burley), Smith.
Sheffield U won 6-0 on aggregate.

Tranmere R (2) 3 *(Taylor S 26, Kelly 45, 55)*
Blackpool (0) 1 *(Clarkson 64)* 4800
Tranmere R: Achterberg; Allen, Thompson, Hill, Yates, Black (Frail), Mahon, Santos, Kelly, Koumas (Parkinson), Taylor S.
Blackpool: Caig; Couzens, Shuttleworth, Bardsley, Carlisle, Hughes, Whitley, Clarkson, Nowland (Aldridge), Bent, Ormerod.
Tranmere R won 4-3 on aggregate.

WBA (4) 5 *(Kilbane 11, 40, Hughes 16, De Freitas 44, Evans 79)*
Halifax T (0) 1 *(Gaughan 76)* 8316
WBA: Miller; Gabbidon, Van Blerk, Flynn (Carbon), Burgess, Raven, Maresca, Sneekes (Potter), De Freitas (Evans), Hughes, Kilbane.
Halifax T: Parks; Murphy S, Jules (Russell), Mitchell, Stoneman, Sertori, Paterson, Gaughan, Tate, Painter, Butler.
WBA won 5-1 on aggregate.

Wigan Ath (1) 2 *(Barlow 21 (pen), 67)*
York C (0) 1 *(Rowe 89)* 3396
Wigan Ath: Stillie; Green, Bowen, McGibbon, Balmer, Kilford, O'Neill, Sheridan (Lee), Haworth (Jones), Liddell (McLoughlin), Barlow.
York C: Howarth; Fox, Hall, Atkins, Jones (Hocking), Fairclough, Dawson, Jordan, Conlon, Williams J (Rowe), Garratt.
Wigan Ath won 3-1 on aggregate.

Wolverhampton W (0) 2 *(Larkin 71, Emblen 89)*
Wycombe W (2) 4 *(Muscat 11 (og), McSporran 26, 59, Ryan 85)* 13,723
Wolverhampton W: Stowell; Muscat, Naylor, Robinson, Curle, Emblen, Bazeley, Sedgley, Flo (Simpson), Corica (Larkin), Sinton.
Wycombe W: Taylor; Lawrence, Ryan (Emblen), Holsgrove (Beeton), Bates, Cousins, Carroll, Brown, McSporran, Devine (Baird), Simpson.
Wycombe W won 4-3 on aggregate.

Wrexham (0) 0
Preston NE (1) 2 *(Basham 11, Macken 49)* 2911
Wrexham: Dearden; McGregor, Hardy, Owen (Thomas), Carey, Ridler, Williams, Stevens, Connolly, Russell, Faulconbridge.
Preston NE: Moilanen; Alexander, Edwards (Murphy), Kidd, Jackson, Gregan, Appleton (Eyres), Murdock, Macken (Nogan), Basham, McKenna.
Preston NE won 3-0 on aggregate.

25 AUG

Bristol R (0) 2 *(Roberts 60, Cureton 72)*
Luton T (0) 2 *(Kandol 46, Doherty 80)* 4414
Bristol R: Jones; Pethick, Challis, Foster, Thomson, Tillson, Mauge (Bryant), Hillier, Pritchard, Cureton, Roberts.
Luton T: Abbey; Locke, Boyce, Watts, White, Sodje, Gray, McIndoe, Douglas (Doherty), Kandol (Fotiadis), McKinnon.
Bristol R won 4-2 on aggregate.

QPR (0) 1 *(Peacock 103 (pen))*
Cardiff C (1) 2 *(Brazier 40, Hughes 115)* 6185
QPR: Miklosko; Breacker (Scully), Baraclough, Morrow (Rowland), Ready, Maddix, Langley (Slade), Peacock, Gallen, Rose, Kiwomya.
Cardiff C: Hallworth; Faerber (Phillips), Legg, Ford, Young, Eckhardt, Middleton, Bonner (Cornforth), Bowen (Hughes), Nugent, Brazier.
aet; Cardiff C won 3-2 on penalties.

Stoke C (0) 3 *(Connor 59, Thorne 69, O'Connor 75)*
Macclesfield T (0) 0 5003
Stoke C: Ward; Robinson (Short), Clarke, Jacobsen, Sigurdsson, Oldfield (Keen), Aiston, Kavanagh G, Connor (Crowe), Thorne, O'Connor.
Macclesfield T: Price; Abbey, Rioch (Brown), Sedgemore, Tinson, Wood (Tomlinson), Askey, Priest, Barker, Davies, Ware (Whittaker).
Stoke C won 4-1 on aggregate.

SECOND ROUND, FIRST LEG

14 SEPT

Barnsley (1) 1 *(Barnard 34)*
Stockport Co (1) 1 *(Briggs 32)* 6966
Barnsley: Miller; Bassinder, Barker, Bullock M, Moses, Jones, McClare, Van der Laan (Eaden), Dyer (Hristov), Thomas (Parkin), Barnard.
Stockport Co: Nash; Briggs, Nicholson, Flynn, Connelly, Monk, Gibbens, Moore (Cooper), Angell, Wilbraham, Woodthorpe.

Birmingham C (0) 2 *(O'Connor 51 (pen), Holdsworth 67)*
Bristol R (0) 0 17,457
Birmingham C: Poole; Rowett, Lazaridis (Newton), Hyde, Holdsworth, Johnson M, McCarthy, O'Connor, Adebola, Johnson A (Gill), Ndlovu (Forinton).
Bristol R: Jones; Pethick, Leoni, Foster, Thomson, Tillson, Mauge, Hillier (Bennett), Pritchard (Bryant), Cureton, Roberts.

Bradford C (1) 1 *(Blake 43 (pen))*
Reading (0) 1 *(Caskey 67 (pen))* 4961
Bradford C: Clarke; Wright, Myers, Redfearn, Westwood, Dreyer, Moore, Windass, Blake (Mills), Whalley (Grant), Rodriguez (Saunders).
Reading: Howey; Gurney, Gray, Grant, Bernal, Casper, Smith, Caskey (Hodges), McIntyre (McLaren), Forster, Crawford.

Cardiff C (1) 1 *(Nugent 23 (pen))*
Wimbledon (0) 1 *(Hughes M 73)* 7613
Cardiff C: Hallworth; Faerber, Legg, Young, Fowler (Brazier), Eckhardt, Boland, Ford, Bowen (Hughes), Nugent, Carpenter.
Wimbledon: Sullivan; Jupp, Kimble, Roberts (Francis), Blackwell, Anderson, Badir (Leaburn), Euell, Hartson (Earle), Cort, Hughes M.

Charlton Ath (0) 0
Bournemouth (0) 0 10,346
Charlton Ath: Kiely; Shields, Konchesky, Stuart, Rufus, Parker, Newton (Kinsella), Pringle (McCammon), Robinson, Mendonca, Brown.
Bournemouth: Ovendale; Young, Warren (Bailey), Howe, Cox, Mean, Broadhurst, Robinson, Stein, Fletcher S, Hughes.

Chester C (0) 0
Aston Villa (0) 1 *(Hendrie 77)* 4364
Chester C: Brown; Davidson, Doughty, Shelton, Lancaster, Woods, Richardson, Milosavaljevic (Berrry), Wright, Beckett, Fisher.
Aston Villa: Enckelman; Watson, Ghrayib, Barry, Ehiogu, Calderwood, Taylor, Hendrie, Joachim, Merson (Vassell), Thompson.

Chesterfield (0) 0
Middlesbrough (0) 0 4941
Chesterfield: Leaning (Gayle); Hewitt, Woods, Curtis (Lomas), Blatherwick, Breckin, Willis, Beaumont, Reeves, Ebdon, Carss.
Middlesbrough: Schwarzer; Stockdale, Fleming, Cooper, Gavin, Pallister, Mustoe, Gascoigne (Summerbell), Ricard, Armstrong, Maddison.

Crewe Alex (0) 2 *(Rivers 66, Little 86)*
Ipswich T (1) 1 *(Venus 30)* 4759
Crewe Alex: Kearton; Bignot (Little), Smith S, Wright D, Macauley, Charnock (Grant), Sorvel, Lunt, Jack (Street), Cramb, Rivers.
Ipswich T: Wright R; Stockwell, Clapham, Thetis, Venus, McGreal, Holland, Wright J, Johnson (Scowcroft), Magilton, Naylor (Axeldal).

Crystal Palace (1) 3 *(Morrison 23, Zhiyi 71, Mullins 74)*
Leicester C (2) 3 *(Digby 17 (og), Lennon 34, Taggart 58)* 5006
Crystal Palace: Digby; Smith, Austin, Zhiyi, Woozley (Rizzo), Linighan, Mullins, Rodger, Bradbury, Morrison, Fumaca.
Leicester C: Arphexad (Flowers); Savage, Guppy, Elliott (Taggart), Gilchrist, Sinclair, Lennon, Izzet, Marshall, Zagorakis, Heskey (Fenton).

Gillingham (0) 1 *(Hessenthaler 55)*
Bolton W (2) 4 *(Cox 17, Gudjohnsen 44, 58, Bergsson 64)* 4996
Gillingham: Williams; Southall, McGlinchey, Smith, Ashby, Saunders (Miller), Hodge (Pinnock), Hessenthaler, Thomson, Pennock, Omoyimni (Nosworthy).
Bolton W: Banks; Cox, Whitlow (Hansen), Frandsen, Bergsson (Warhurst), Todd, Johansen, Elliott, Gudjohnsen, Taylor, Gardner.

Grimsby T (2) 4 *(Smith D 8, Gallimore 45, Ashcroft 52 (pen), Groves 69)*
Leyton Orient (1) 1 *(Lockwood 33 (pen))* 2238
Grimsby T: Coyne; Butterfield, Gallimore, Smith D (Buckley), Livingstone, Coldicott, Donovan (Clare), Pouton, Ashcroft, Lester (Allen), Groves.
Leyton Orient: Bayes; Joseph M, Lockwood, Smith, Clark, Harris, Ling, Ampadu, Watts (Downer), Morrison (Walschaerts), Hockton (Curran).

Huddersfield T (1) 2 *(Wijnhard 17, Stewart 58)*
Notts Co (1) 1 *(Ramage 18)* 6900
Huddersfield T: Vaesen; Armstrong, Dyson, Irons, Lucketti, Monkou, Donis (Baldry), Horne (Senior), Stewart, Wijnhard, Thornley (Beresford).
Notts Co: Ward; Pearce, Blackmore (Holmes), Warren, Redmile, Richardson, Owers, Ramage (Bolland), Stallard, Darby (Beadle), Hughes.

Hull C (0) 1 *(Brown 58)*
Liverpool (2) 5 *(Murphy 10, 30, Meijer 48, 75, Staunton 89)* 10,034
Hull C: Bracey; Harper, Mann (Swales), Greaves, Whittle, Edwards, Schofield, Brabin, Brown, Eyre (Wood), D'Auria (Alcide).
Liverpool: Westerveld; Heggem, Staunton, Traore, Carragher, Hyypia, Murphy, Thompson, Smicer (Berger), Owen (Camara), Meijer.

Norwich C (0) 0
Fulham (1) 4 *(Peschisolido 24, Coote 64 (og), Clark 74,*
Collins 82) 11,760
Norwich C: Marshall A; Sutch, Wilson (Fuglestad), Diop,
Fleming, Mackay, Russell, Eadie, Roberts, Carey, Coote.
Fulham: Taylor; Finnan, Brevett, Melville, Coleman,
Symons, Trollope, Clark (Collins), Horsfield (Hayles),
Peschisolido (Collymore), Hayward.

Oxford U (1) 1 *(Murphy 21)*
Everton (1) 1 *(Cadamarteri 29)* 7345
Oxford U: Arendse; Robinson, Powell, Fear, Davis,
Lewis, Lilley (Cook), Tait, Murphy, Folland (McGowan),
Beauchamp.
Everton: Simonsen; Cleland, Ball, Weir, Unsworth,
Xavier, Collins (Campbell), Gemmill, Cadamarteri
(Jeffers), Hutchison, Phelan (Ward).

Portsmouth (0) 0
Blackburn R (0) 3 *(Cundy 58 (og), Jansen 72, 78)* 8542
Portsmouth: Flahavan (Petterson); Crowe, Robinson,
McLoughlin, Whitbread (Pamarot), Cundy, Panopoulos,
Miglioranzi, Whittingham, Thogersen, Peron
Blackburn R: Kelly; Kenna, Davidson, Gill, Dailly,
Peacock, Gillespie (Harkness), Dunn, Ward, Blake,
Johnson (Jansen).

Sheffield U (2) 2 *(Smith 12, Katchuro 40)*
Preston NE (0) 0 5350
Sheffield U: Tracey; Kozluk, Quinn, Derry, Murphy,
Ford, Smeets (Hunt), Katchuro, Devlin, Smith,
Woodhouse.
Preston NE: Moilanen; Alexander, Ludden (Kidd),
Murdock, Jackson, Edwards, Cartwright, Rankine,
Macken, McKenna, Eyres.

Stoke C (0) 0
Sheffield W (0) 0 9313
Stoke C: Ward; Short, Clarke, Robinson, Jacobsen,
Mohan, Keen (Connor), Kavanagh G, Lightbourne,
Thorne, O'Connor.
Sheffield W: Pressman; Briscoe, Nolan, Atherton
(Donnelly), Emerson, Walker, Alexandersson, Booth,
De Bilde (Carbone), Rudi, Sonner.

Sunderland (1) 3 *(Dichio 17, Barras 46 (og), Williams 77)*
Walsall (2) 2 *(Bukran 9, Brissett 41)* 14,388
Sunderland: Marriott; Maley (Gray), Holloway, Roy,
Williams, Wainwright, Fredgaard, Rae (Butler T),
Dichio, Oster, Lumsdon.
Walsall: Walker; Marsh, Pointon, Roper, Barras, Bukran,
Wrack, Robins (Keister), Ricketts, Keates, Brissett
(Eyjolfsson).

Swansea C (0) 0
Derby Co (0) 0 6260
Swansea C: Freestone; Price, Howard, O'Leary, Smith,
Bound, Roberts, Thomas, Bird (Alsop), Watkin, Coates.
Derby Co: Hoult; Borbokis (Boertien), Dorigo, Elliott,
Carbonari, Prior, Bohinen, Fuertes (Harper), Baiano
(Christie), Johnson, Beck.

Tranmere R (0) 5 *(Taylor S 50, 90, Kelly 58, 63, 80)*
Coventry C (1) 1 *(McAllister 7)* 6759
Tranmere R: Achterberg; Yates, Roberts, Henry
(Thompson), Allen, Challinor, Mahon, Morgan, Kelly,
Parkinson, Taylor S.
Coventry C: Nuzzo; Edworthy, Burrows, Williams, Shaw,
Breen (Konjic), Strachan, Eustace, McSheffrey (Hall M),
McAllister, Froggatt.

Watford (0) 2 *(Easton 57, Hyde 70)*
Wigan Ath (0) 0 6628
Watford: Chamberlain; Lyttle (Easton), Robinson, Page,
Williams, Palmer, Ngonge (Smart), Hyde, Mooney,
Wright (Gudmundsson), Kennedy.
Wigan Ath: Carroll; Bradshaw, Green, Balmer, De
Zeeuw, Kilford, O'Neill, Sheridan, Haworth, Liddell,
Barlow (Lee).

WBA (0) 1 *(Flynn 64)*
Wycombe W (0) 1 *(McCarthy 58)* 9383
WBA: Miller; McDermott, Van Blerk, Flynn, Gabbidon,
Carbon, De Freitas, Sneekes (Potter), Evans (Maresca),
Hughes, Kilbane.
Wycombe W: Taylor; Lawrence, Beeton, Ryan,
McCarthy, Bates, Carroll, Simpson, McSporran, Devine,
Baird (Emblen).

15 SEPT

Manchester C (0) 0
Southampton (0) 0 17,476
Manchester C: Weaver; Edghill, Tiatto, Morrison
(Crooks), Jobson, Horlock, Kennedy, Jeff Whitley,
Taylor (Allsopp), Goater, Cooke (Bishop).
Southampton: Jones; Dodd, Benali, Soltvedt (Marsden),
Lundekvam, Richards, Kachloul, Oakley, Pahars
(Beattie), Hughes M, Bridge.

Nottingham F (1) 2 *(Harewood 12, Rogers 56)*
Bristol C (1) 1 *(Jordan 13)* 5015
Nottingham F: Crossley; Louis-Jean, Rogers, Hjelde,
Chettle, Scimeca (Bonalair), Petrachi (Allou), Quashie,
Freedman (Merino), Harewood, Burns.
Bristol C: Phillips; Brennan, Bell (Brown A), Jordan,
Taylor, Sebok, Murray, Mortimer, Jones, Meechan
(Brown M), Tinnion.

SECOND ROUND, SECOND LEG

21 SEPT

Aston Villa (2) 5 *(Boateng 17, Taylor 31, Hendrie 46, 47,*
Thompson 50)
Chester C (0) 0 22,613
Aston Villa: Enckelman; Watson, Barry (Samuel),
Southgate, Ehiogu, Boateng, Taylor (Merson), Hendrie,
Dublin (Joachim), Vassell, Thompson.
Chester C: Brown; Davidson, Doughty, Richardson,
Lancaster, Woods, Shelton (Berry), Milosavaljevic
(Jones), Wright, Beckett, Fisher (Carson).
Aston Villa won 6-0 on aggregate.

Bolton W (2) 2 *(Hansen 4, Holdsworth 7)*
Gillingham (0) 0 3673
Bolton W: Banks; Aljofree (Potter), Phillips, Warhurst,
Strong, Todd, Johansen, Bergsson (Fish), Hansen,
Holdsworth, Gardner (Staton).
Gillingham: Williams; Pennock, McGlinchey, Smith,
Ashby, Miller, Butters, Hessenthaler (Galloway),
Thomson, Lewis, Omoyimni (Nosworthy).
Bolton W won 6-1 on aggregate.

Bournemouth (0) 0
Charlton Ath (0) 0 4369
Bournemouth: Ovendale; Young, Broadhurst, Howe,
Cox, Mean, Jorgensen, Robinson, Stein, Fletcher S, Day
(Huck).
Charlton Ath: Kiely; Shields, Konchesky, Stuart
(Kinsella), Rufus, Youds, Newton (Parker), Brown,
Hunt, Pringle (Mendonca), Robinson.
aet; Bournemouth won 3-1 on penalties.

Bristol R (0) 0
Birmingham C (0) 1 *(Rowett 48)* 5456
Bristol R: Jones; Pethick (Meaker), Challis, Foster,
Thomson, Tillson, Mauge, Hillier (Zamora), Pritchard
(Bryant), Cureton, Roberts.
Birmingham C: Poole; Rowett, Lazaridis (Newton),
Holdsworth, Purse, Johnson M, McCarthy, O'Connor,
Furlong (Adebola), Johnson A (Ndlovu), Hughes.
Birmingham C won 3-0 on aggregate.

Fulham (1) 2 *(Hayles 20, Davis 84)*
Norwich C (0) 0 5246
Fulham: Taylor; Finnan, Brevett, Melville, Coleman,
Morgan, Hayward (Davis), Clark, Horsfield
(Uhlenbeek), Trollope, Hayles.
Norwich C: Marshall A; Sutch, Wilson (Kenton),
Mackay, Fleming, Jackson, Marshall L, Russell, Roberts
(Dalglish), Carey, Eadie (Llewellyn).
Fulham won 6-0 on aggregate.

Ipswich T (1) 1 *(Scowcroft 38)*
Crewe Alex (0) 1 *(Rivers 86)* 9689
Ipswich T: Wright R; Stockwell, Clapham, Brown, Venus, McGreal, Holland, Magilton, Johnson, Scowcroft, Naylor.
Crewe Alex: Kearton; Wright D, Smith S, Macauley (Lightfoot), Unsworth, Charnock, Little, Lunt, Cramb, Sorvel, Rivers.
Crewe Alex won 3-2 on aggregate.

Leyton Orient (1) 1 *(Watts 44)*
Grimsby T (0) 0 1036
Leyton Orient: Bayes; Joseph M, Lockwood, Low, Smith, Harris, Downer, Ampadu (Canham), Watts (Gough), Holligan, Carter (Morrison).
Grimsby T: Coyne; Butterfield, Smith D, Pouton (Burnett), Smith R, Coldicott, Donovan, Black, Ashcroft (Allen), Lester, Groves.
Grimsby T won 4-2 on aggregate.

Liverpool (1) 4 *(Murphy 33, Maxwell 46, Riedle 65, 89)*
Hull C (0) 2 *(Eyre 51 (pen), Alcide 56)* 24,318
Liverpool: Friedel; Song, Staunton, Traore, Henchoz (Newby), Maxwell, Thompson, Murphy (Heggem), Riedle, Smicer (Kippe), Meijer.
Hull C: Bracey; Harper, Williams, Wood (Baker), Whittle, Edwards, Schofield (D'Auria), Brabin, Brown, Alcide (Harris), Eyre.
Liverpool won 9-3 on aggregate.

Middlesbrough (1) 2 *(Ince 24, Vickers 87)*
Chesterfield (0) 1 *(Reeves 85)* 25,602
Middlesbrough: Schwarzer; Fleming, Ziege, Cooper, Gavin (Stockdale), Pallister (Vickers), Mustoe, Juninho, Ricard (Campbell), Armstrong, Ince.
Chesterfield: Gayle; Hewitt, Woods, Simpkins (Holland), Blatherwick, Breckin, Carss (Willis), Beaumont, Reeves, Lomas, Bettney (Howard).
Middlesbrough won 2-1 on aggregate.

Notts Co (2) 2 *(Blackmore 19, Darby 35)*
Huddersfield T (2) 2 *(Irons 19, Gorre 30)* 4104
Notts Co: Gibson; Holmes, Blackmore, Warren, Redmile (Beadle), Richardson, Owers (Bolland), Ramage, Stallard, Darby, Hughes (Tierney).
Huddersfield T: Vaesen; Armstrong, Hodouto (Vincent), Irons, Lucketti, Gray, Beech, Horne, Stewart, Gorre (Donis), Wijnhard.
Huddersfield T won 4-3 on aggregate.

Preston NE (1) 3 *(Alexander 13, Mathie 57, 90)*
Sheffield U (0) 0 5658
Preston NE: Moilanen; Alexander, Edwards, Kidd, Jackson, Gregan, Cartwright, Rankine, Macken, Mathie, McKenna.
Sheffield U: Tracey; Derry, Gijsbrechts (Quinn), Woodhouse, Murphy, Sandford, Ford, Devlin, Marcello (Hunt), Katchuro, Smith.
Preston NE won 3-2 on aggregate.

Southampton (2) 4 *(Dodd 16 (pen), Oakley 28, 57, Richards 92)*
Manchester C (1) 3 *(Dickov 10, Goater 76, 82)* 10,960
Southampton: Jones; Dodd, Benali, Soltvedt, Lundekvam, Richards, Kachloul, Oakley, Beattie (Le Tissier), Hughes M, Ripley (Boa Morte).
Manchester C: Weaver; Crooks, Tiatto (Cooke), Edghill (Fenton), Jobson, Horlock, Kennedy, Jeff Whitley, Dickov (Allsopp), Goater, Bishop.
aet; Southampton won 4-3 on aggregate.

Stockport Co (2) 3 *(Wilbraham 15, D'Jaffo 45, Dinning 114 (pen))*
Barnsley (0) 3 *(Hristov 69, 99, Jones 80)* 3332
Stockport Co: Nash; Connelly, Woodthorpe (Cooper), Dinning, Flynn, Monk, Gannon, Moore, D'Jaffo, Wilbraham (McIntosh), Gibbens (Angell).
Barnsley: Miller; Barnard, Barker, Morgan, Moses, Jones, McClare (Appleby), Bullock M, Hristov, Sheron (Van der Laan), Thomas (Tinkler).
aet; Barnsley won on away goals.

Walsall (0) 0
Sunderland (2) 5 *(Dichio 10, 72, Roy 21, Fredgaard 60, 76)* 5109
Walsall: Walker; Marsh, Todd (Pointon), Roper, Barras, Bukran, Wrack, Robins (Eyjolfsson), Ricketts, Keates, Mavrak (Carter).
Sunderland: Marriott; Holloway, Gray, Roy, Williams, Butler P, Wainwright (Bica), Rae, Dichio, Oster, Fredgaard.
Sunderland won 8-2 on aggregate.

Wigan Ath (1) 3 *(Haworth 18, 78, Bradshaw 89 (pen))*
Watford (0) 1 *(Kennedy 62)* 5006
Wigan Ath: Carroll; Bradshaw (Lee), Bowen (Jones), Balmer, De Zeeuw, Martinez, O'Neill, Sheridan, Haworth, Sharp, Barlow.
Watford: Chamberlain; Gibbs, Robinson, Page, Williams, Palmer, Kennedy, Hyde, Smart (Foley), Wright (Ngonge), Easton.
aet; Watford won on away goals.

Wimbledon (0) 3 *(Cort 52, Earle 54, 73)*
Cardiff C (1) 1 *(Bowen 26)* 2772
Wimbledon: Sullivan; Jupp, Kimble, Roberts (Francis), Cunningham, Blackwell, Badir, Earle, Hartson (Goodman), Cort, Euell.
Cardiff C: Hallworth; Faerber, Legg, Young, Fowler (Brazier), Eckhardt, Boland, Ford, Bowen (Hughes), Nugent, Cornforth (Carpenter).
Wimbledon won 4-2 on aggregate.

Wycombe W (1) 3 *(Devine 4, Carroll 70, Brown 119 (pen))*
WBA (2) 4 *(Raven 15, De Freitas 33, Quinn 105, Hughes 115)* 5047
Wycombe W: Westhead (Osborn); Lawrence, Beeton, Ryan, Cousins, Bates, Carroll (Baird), Simpson, McSporran, Devine (Emblen), Brown.
WBA: Miller; Gabbidon (Quinn), Raven, Flynn, Burgess, Carbon, Townsend, Sneekes (Maresca), De Freitas (Evans), Hughes, Kilbane.
aet; WBA won 5-4 on aggregate.

22 SEPT

Blackburn R (0) 3 *(Duff 59, Dunn 64, Gallacher 90)*
Portsmouth (1) 1 *(McLoughlin 7)* 7512
Blackburn R: Kelly; Kenna, Harkness (Grayson), Gill, Peacock, Taylor, Dunn, Gillespie (Johnson), Blake, Ostenstad (Gallacher), Duff.
Portsmouth: Petterson (Knight); Robinson, Simpson, McLoughlin, Awford, Vlachos, Panopoulos, Miglioranzi, Durnin (Igoe), Whittingham (Lovell), Peron.
Blackburn R won 6-1 on aggregate.

Bristol C (0) 0
Nottingham F (0) 0 8259
Bristol C: Phillips; Lavin, Brennan, Goodridge (Brown A), Taylor, Sebok, Murray (Thorpe), Mortimer, Jones, Pinamonte (Torpey), Tinnion.
Nottingham F: Crossley (Beasant); Louis-Jean, Rogers, Doig, Hjelde, Bonalair, Allou (Gray), Quashie, Freedman, Harewood, Prutton.
Nottingham F won 2-1 on aggregate.

Coventry C (3) 3 *(McAllister 21, Chippo 44, 45)*
Tranmere R (1) 1 *(Taylor P 22)* 12,433
Coventry C: Kirkland; Edworthy, Hall M, Konjic, Shaw, Chippo, Telfer, Palmer, Hadji, McAllister, McSheffrey (Eustace).
Tranmere R: Achterberg; Yates, Roberts, Hill, Allen, Challinor, Mahon, Morgan, Kelly, Taylor P (Parkinson), Thompson.
Tranmere R won 6-4 on aggregate.

Derby Co (1) 3 *(Fuertes 26, Sturridge 66, Borbokis 76)*
Swansea C (0) 1 *(Bound 87 (pen))* 19,152
Derby Co: Hoult; Borbokis, Dorigo, Laursen (Sturridge), Elliott, Prior, Delap, Fuertes (Harper), Baiano, Bohinen, Powell (Johnson).
Swansea C: Freestone; Price, Howard, Smith, Bound, Roberts (Appleby), Thomas (Phillips), O'Leary, Alsop, Bird (Mutton), Coates.
Derby Co won 3-1 on aggregate.

Everton (0) 0
Oxford U (1) 1 *(Beauchamp 12)*   10,006
Everton: Simonsen; Cleland, Ball, Weir, Dunne, Jevons (Campbell), Ward, Farrelly (Barmby), Degn (Jeffers), Cadamarteri, Gemmill.
Oxford U: Arendse; Robinson, Powell, Fear, Lewis, Davis, Folland, Tait, Murphy, Anthrobus (Lilley), Beauchamp.
Oxford U won 2-1 on aggregate.

Leicester C (1) 4 *(Oakes 19 (pen), 88, Marshall 53, Fenton 79)*
Crystal Palace (0) 2 *(Thomson 61, Bradbury 86)*   12,762
Leicester C: Arphexad; Impey, Savage, Gilchrist, Taggart, Sinclair, Lennon (Fenton), Oakes, Marshall, Zagorakis, Heskey (Wilson).
Crystal Palace: Digby; Smith (Woozley), Frampton, Zhiyi, Austin, Linighan (Bradbury), Mullins (Thomson), Rodger, Morrison, Svensson, Fumaca.
Leicester C won 7-5 on aggregate.

Reading (1) 2 *(Scott 9, Hunter 98)*
Bradford C (0) 2 *(Saunders 73, Wetherall 108)*   6892
Reading: Howey; Gurney, Gray, Bernal, Hunter, Casper, Smith (Hodges), Caskey, Scott, Forster (Williams M), Grant (Crawford).
Bradford C: Walsh; Wright, Myers, McCall, Wetherall, O'Brien, Saunders, Windass (Blake), Grant (Rodriguez), Whalley, Beagrie (Jacobs).
aet; Bradford C won on away goals.

Sheffield W (2) 3 *(Alexandersson 5, 66, De Bilde 25)*
Stoke C (0) 1 *(Kavanagh G 73)*   10,993
Sheffield W: Srnicek; Nolan, Briscoe (Haslam), Donnelly, Emerson, Walker, Alexandersson, Booth, De Bilde (Sibon), Rudi (Cresswell), Sonner.
Stoke C: Ward; Short, Clarke, Jacobsen, Mohan, Keen, Petty (Oldfield), Kavanagh G, Lightbourne, Thorne (Connor), O'Connor (Heath).
Sheffield W won 3-1 on aggregate.

THIRD ROUND

12 OCT

Arsenal (1) 2 *(Kanu 31, Malz 61)*
Preston NE (1) 1 *(Macken 39)*   15,239
Arsenal: Seaman; Luzhny, Winterburn, Grimandi, Upson, Vernazza (Overmars), Parlour, Malz, Kanu (Wreh), Henry, Silvinho.
Preston NE: Moilanen; Alexander, Edwards, Kidd, Jackson, Gregan, Cartwright, Rankine, Macken (Nogan), Mathie (Gunnlaugsson), McKenna (Eyres).

Birmingham C (1) 2 *(O'Connor 45 (pen), Purse 60)*
Newcastle U (0) 0   19,795
Birmingham C: Bennett; Rowett, Johnson M, Hughes, Purse, Holdsworth, McCarthy, O'Connor (Hyde), Adebola, Newton (Holland), Ndlovu (Johnson A).
Newcastle U: Harper; Barton, Domi, Dabizas, Goma, Solano (Given), Lee (Pistone), Maric, Shearer (Robinson), Glass, Speed.

Bradford C (1) 2 *(Mills 18, Wetherall 87)*
Barnsley (2) 3 *(Sheron 22, Morgan 36, Barnard 55 (pen))*
                                                      8583
Bradford C: Walsh; Wright (Redfearn), Jacobs, McCall, Wetherall, O'Brien, Halle (Sharpe), Windass, Mills, Blake, Beagrie (Rodriguez).
Barnsley: Miller; Eaden, Barker, Tinkler, Jones, Morgan, Appleby (McClare), Hignett, Sheron, Dyer (Shipperley), Barnard.

Tranmere R (0) 2 *(Yates 57, Grant 63)*
Oxford U (0) 0   5328
Tranmere R: Murphy; Yates, Roberts, Henry, Hill, Challinor, Mahon, Grant, Kelly, Jones L (Black), Taylor P (Parkinson).
Oxford U: Arendse; Robinson, Powell, Fear, Davis, Whelan, Folland (Cook), Tait, Murphy, Anthrobus (Lilley), Beauchamp.

WBA (1) 1 *(Hughes 12)*
Fulham (1) 2 *(Peschisolido 3, Collymore 48)*   10,556
WBA: Miller; Gabbidon (Maresca), McDermott, Flynn, Raven, Carbon (Van Blerk), Townsend, Sneekes, De Freitas (Quinn), Hughes, Kilbane.
Fulham: Taylor; Finnan (Neilson), Brevett (Collymore), Morgan, Coleman, Symons, Trollope, Clark, Hayles, Peschisolido (Davis), Hayward.

Wimbledon (0) 3 *(Cort 69, 104, 111)*
Sunderland (0) 2 *(Dichio 67, Ball 120)*   *(aet)* 4790
Wimbledon: Sullivan; Cunningham, Kimble, Roberts (Jupp) (Willmott), Blackwell, Thatcher, Euell, Earle, Leaburn (Francis), Cort, Gayle.
Sunderland: Marriott; Makin, Gray, Roy (Ball), Williams, Butler P, Summerbee, Rae (McCann), Dichio, Oster (Reddy), Fredgaard.

13 OCT

Aston Villa (1) 3 *(Joachim 18, Taylor 49, Stone 90)*
Manchester U (0) 0   33,815
Aston Villa: Enckelman; Delaney, Barry, Calderwood, Ehiogu (Watson), Boateng, Taylor, Hendrie, Dublin, Joachim (Vassell), Thompson (Stone).
Manchester U: Bosnich; Clegg, Curtis, Higginbotham (Healy), Wallwork, O'Shea, Twiss (Wellens), Cruyff, Solskjaer, Greening, Chadwick.

Chelsea (0) 0
Huddersfield T (0) 1 *(Irons 77)*   21,008
Chelsea: Cudicini; Lambourde (Nicholls), Le Saux, Goldbaek, Terry, Hogh, Ambrosetti, Di Matteo (Wolleaston), Flo, Forssell, Morris.
Huddersfield T: Vaesen; Jenkins, Armstrong, Irons, Lucketti, Monkou, Donis, Gorre, Stewart, Beech, Wijnhard (Vincent).

Derby Co (1) 1 *(Beck 27)*
Bolton W (1) 2 *(Fish 45, Johansen 88)*   20,242
Derby Co: Hoult; Borbokis, Dorigo, Laursen, Elliott (Schnoor), Prior, Eranio, Sturridge (Burton), Beck, Harper, Delap.
Bolton W: Branagan; Cox, Phillips, Todd, Bergsson, Fish, Johansen, Jensen, Gudjohnsen, Holdsworth, Gardner.

Leeds U (0) 1 *(Mills 90)*
Blackburn R (0) 0   24,353
Leeds U: Martyn; Mills, Kelly, Woodgate, Radebe, Batty, Hopkin (McPhail), Smith, Bridges (Huckerby), Kewell, Bakke.
Blackburn R: Filan; Kenna, Richardson, Short, Taylor, Gill, Duff, Jansen, Ward, Dunn, Johnson.

Leicester C (1) 2 *(Izzet 28, Heskey 58)*
Grimsby T (0) 0   13,701
Leicester C: Flowers; Impey, Guppy (Wilson), Gilchrist, Taggart, Sinclair, Lennon, Izzet, Cottee (Fenton), Oakes, Heskey (Zagorakis).
Grimsby T: Croudson; Butterfield, Gallimore, Burnett (Smith D), Smith R, Coldicott, Donovan, Pouton, Ashcroft (Lever), Lester, Groves.

Middlesbrough (0) 1 *(Juninho 63)*
Watford (0) 0   8843
Middlesbrough: Schwarzer; Fleming, O'Neill (Ziege), Vickers, Cooper, Pallister, Maddison, Juninho, Armstrong (Ricard), Deane, Ince.
Watford: Chamberlain; Gibbs, Robinson, Miller (Smith), Page, Palmer, Kennedy, Hyde, Ngonge, Wooter, Johnson.

Sheffield W (1) 4 *(Cresswell 45, Booth 60, Sonner 71, Rudi 82)*
Nottingham F (0) 1 *(Freedman 85)*   15,524
Sheffield W: Srnicek; Atherton, Hinchcliffe (Nolan), Jonk (Briscoe), Emerson, Walker, Alexandersson (Donnelly), Booth, Cresswell, Rudi, Sonner.
Nottingham F: Crossley; Bonalair (Louis-Jean), Rogers, Mannini, Chettle, Metrecano, Merino, Quashie (Harewood), Freedman, Scimeca, Prutton.

Southampton (0) 2 *(Richards 67, Soltvedt 90)*
Liverpool (0) 1 *(Owen 53)* 13,822
Southampton: Jones; Dodd, Benali, Soltvedt, Lundekvam, Richards, Ripley (Beattie), Oakley (Marsden), Pahars (Davies), Le Tissier, Kachloul.
Liverpool: Friedel; Song (Heggem), Staunton, Henchoz, Carragher, Hyypia, Thompson (Camara), Redknapp, Meijer, Owen, Berger.

Tottenham H (0) 3 *(Leonhardsen 55, Ginola 63, Sherwood 88)*
Crewe Alex (0) 1 *(Smith S 70 (pen))* 25,486
Tottenham H: Walker; Carr, Taricco, Freund, Campbell, Perry, Leonhardsen, Sherwood, Armstrong, Piercy (Iversen), Ginola.
Crewe Alex: Kearton; Wright D, Smith S, Macauley, Foran, Charnock (Collins), Little, Lunt (Street), Cramb, Sorvel, Rivers (Grant).

West Ham U (0) 2 *(Keller 62, Lampard 77)*
Bournemouth (0) 0 22,067
West Ham U: Hislop; Sinclair, Keller, Stimac, Ferdinand, Ruddock, Lampard, Cole, Wanchope (Kitson), Di Canio, Foe.
Bournemouth: Ovendale; Young, Warren (Huck), Howe, Cox, Mean, Jorgensen (O'Neill), Robinson, Stein, Fletcher S, Broadhurst.

FOURTH ROUND

30 NOV

Birmingham C (0) 2 *(Hyde 8, Grainger 44)*
West Ham U (1) 3 *(Lomas 21, Kitson 87, Cole 89)* 17,728
Birmingham C: Poole; Rowett, Bass, Hyde (Hughes), Holdsworth, Johnson M, Holland, O'Connor, Purse, Johnston, Grainger.
West Ham U: Hislop; Charles (Cole), Keller, Margas (Sinclair), Ferdinand, Ruddock, Lampard, Foe, Wanchope (Kitson), Di Canio, Lomas.

Bolton W (0) 1 *(Elliott 53)*
Sheffield W (0) 0 12,543
Bolton W: Jaaskelainen; O'Kane (Holden), Whitlow, Aljofree, Bergsson (Elliott), Fish, Johansen, Jensen, Gudjohnsen, Hansen (Taylor), Gardner.
Sheffield W: Pressman; Nolan, Hinchcliffe (Emerson), Jonk, Atherton, Walker (Sonner), Alexandersson, Booth, De Bilde, Rudi, Sibon (McKeever).

Huddersfield T (1) 1 *(Sellars 40)*
Wimbledon (0) 2 *(Kimble 60, Euell 101)* *(aet)* 13,312
Huddersfield T: Vaesen; Jenkins, Vincent, Irons, Gray, Monkou (Dyson), Beech (Sellars), Gorre, Stewart, Thornley (Armstrong), Wijnhard.
Wimbledon: Sullivan; Cunningham, Kimble, Roberts, Blackwell, Thatcher, Badir (Andersen), Euell, Leaburn (Hughes M), Cort, Gayle.

Middlesbrough (1) 2 *(Ricard 8, 83 (pen))*
Arsenal (1) 2 *(Henry 38, Suker 80)* 23,157
Middlesbrough: Schwarzer; Fleming, Ziege, Vickers, Festa, Cooper, O'Neill (Stamp), Juninho, Ricard, Deane (Gascoigne), Ince (Mustoe).
Arsenal: Manninger; Luzhny (Weston), Silvinho, Vivas, Upson, Black (Pennant), Parlour (Cole), Vernazza, Suker, Henry, Malz.
aet; Middlesbrough won 3-1 on penalties.

Tranmere R (2) 4 *(Parkinson 3, Morgan 45, Hill 56, Black 86)*
Barnsley (0) 0 7039
Tranmere R: Murphy (Nixon); Hazell, Roberts, Morgan, Hill, Challinor, Mahon (Black), Parkinson, Jones G, Kelly, Taylor S (Koumas).
Barnsley: Miller; Bengtsson, Barker, Morgan, Krizan, McClare, Bullock M, Hristov, Dyer (Evans), Tinkler, Barnard.

1 DEC

Aston Villa (1) 4 *(Watson 22, Joachim 66, Dublin 72, 90)*
Southampton (0) 0 17,608
Aston Villa: James; Watson, Wright, Southgate, Calderwood, Barry, Taylor (Stone), Boateng, Dublin, Joachim (Merson), Hendrie (Thompson).
Southampton: Jones; Tessem, Colleter, Soltvedt (Le Tissier), Lundekvam, Richards, Ripley (Dodd), Oakley, Pahars, Hughes M, Kachloul (Boa Morte).

Fulham (2) 3 *(Hayles 10, Collins 44, Horsfield 77)*
Tottenham H (1) 1 *(Iversen 43)* 18,134
Fulham: Taylor; Uhlenbeek, Brevett, Melville, Coleman, Symons, Collins (Trollope), Clark, Horsfield, Hayles, Hayward.
Tottenham H: Walker; Taricco, Edinburgh (Young), Freund, Campbell, Perry (Vega), Leonhardsen, Sherwood, Armstrong (Dominguez), Iversen, Ginola.

15 DEC

Leicester C (0) 0
Leeds U (0) 0 16,125
Leicester C: Flowers; Impey, Savage, Elliott, Walsh, Taggart, Lennon (Zagorakis), Izzet, Cottee (Gunnlaugsson), Oakes, Heskey.
Leeds U: Martyn; Kelly, Harte, Woodgate, Radebe, Batty (Jones), McPhail, Bakke, Bridges (Duberry), Kewell, Bowyer.
aet; Leicester C won 4-2 on penalties.

FIFTH ROUND

14 DEC

Bolton W (2) 2 *(Gudjohnsen 34, Johansen 39 (pen))*
Wimbledon (1) 1 *(Cort 17)* 9463
Bolton W: Jaaskelainen; Holden, Whitlow, Elliott, Bergsson, Fish, Johansen, Jensen, Gudjohnsen (Hansen), Taylor (Passi), Gardner (Aljofree).
Wimbledon: Sullivan; Ardley (Leaburn), Kimble, Roberts, Cunningham, Andersen, Euell, Earle, Hartson, Cort, Gayle.

Tranmere R (1) 2 *(Kelly 39, Parkinson 71)*
Middlesbrough (0) 1 *(Ziege 79)* 10,581
Tranmere R: Murphy (Achterberg); Hazell, Roberts, Henry, Morgan, Challinor, Mahon (Allen), Parkinson, Jones G, Taylor S (Koumas), Kelly.
Middlesbrough: Schwarzer; Stamp, Ziege, Vickers, Festa, Stockdale (Campbell), Mustoe, Juninho, Ricard, Deane, O'Neill.

15 DEC

West Ham U (0) 2
Aston Villa (1) 2
aet; West Ham U won 5-4 on penalties; match ordered to be replayed, West Ham U fielded an ineligible player.

11 JAN

West Ham U (0) 1 *(Lampard 47)*
Aston Villa (0) 3 *(Taylor 80, 118, Joachim 93)(aet)* 25,592
West Ham U: Hislop; Lomas, Minto, Potts (Ruddock), Ferdinand, Stimac, Lampard, Cole, Sinclair (Keller), Di Canio, Foe.
Aston Villa: James; Watson (Thompson), Wright, Southgate, Ehiogu, Barry, Taylor, Boateng (Calderwood), Joachim, Merson (Vassell), Stone.

12 JAN

Leicester C (0) 3 *(Marshall 85, 111, Walsh 87)*
Fulham (0) 3 *(Peschisolido 58, Horsfield 75, Coleman 90)* 13,576
Leicester C: Arphexad; Impey (Gunnlaugsson), Sinclair, Elliott, Walsh, Taggart, Savage, Zagorakis (Gilchrist), Marshall, Oakes (Fenton), Heskey.
Fulham: Taylor; Finnan, Morgan, Melville, Symons, Coleman, Collins, Trollope, Horsfield, Peschisolido (Brevett), Hayward.
aet; Leicester C won 3-0 on penalties.

SEMI-FINALS, FIRST LEG

12 JAN

Bolton W (0) 0
Tranmere R (1) 1 *(Hill 22)*   13,303
Bolton W: Banks; O'Kane, Whitlow, Passi, Bergsson, Ritchie, Johansen (Warhurst), Jensen, Gudjohnsen, Hansen (Holdsworth), Gardner.
Tranmere R: Achterberg; Yates, Roberts, Morgan, Hill, Challinor, Mahon, Parkinson, Jones G, Kelly, Taylor S (Frail).

25 JAN

Aston Villa (0) 0
Leicester C (0) 0   28,037
Aston Villa: James; Watson (Walker), Wright, Southgate, Ehiogu, Barry, Taylor, Boateng, Joachim, Merson, Stone (Delaney).
Leicester C: Flowers; Impey (Campbell), Guppy (Zagorakis), Sinclair, Taggart, Gilchrist, Savage, Izzet (Walsh), Elliott, Oakes, Heskey.

SEMI-FINALS, SECOND LEG

26 JAN

Tranmere R (2) 3 *(Henry 5, Mahon 20 (pen), Kelly 70)*
Bolton W (0) 0   15,834
Tranmere R: Achterberg; Hazell, Thompson (Allen), Henry, Babb, Challinor, Mahon (Koumas), Parkinson, Jones G, Kelly (Black), Taylor S.
Bolton W: Banks; Holden, Phillips, Passi (Warhurst), Bergsson, Whitlow (Johansen), Elliott, Jensen, Gudjohnsen, Holdsworth (Taylor), Gardner.
Tranmere R won 4-0 on aggregate.

2 FEB

Leicester C (1) 1 *(Elliott 45)*
Aston Villa (0) 0   21,843
Leicester C: Flowers; Savage, Guppy (Impey), Sinclair, Taggart, Gilchrist, Lennon (Campbell), Izzet (Zagorakis), Elliott, Oakes, Heskey.
Aston Villa: James; Watson (Delaney) (Hendrie), Wright, Southgate, Ehiogu, Barry, Stone, Boateng, Joachim, Walker (Taylor), Merson.
Leicester C won 1-0 on aggregate.

FINAL (at Wembley)

27 FEB

Leicester C (1) 2 *(Elliott 29, 81)*
Tranmere R (0) 1 *(Kelly 77)*   74,313
Leicester C: Flowers; Savage, Guppy, Elliott, Taggart, Sinclair, Lennon, Izzet, Cottee (Marshall), Oakes (Impey), Heskey.
Tranmere R: Murphy; Hazell, Roberts, Henry, Hill, Challinor, Mahon, Parkinson (Yates), Jones G, Kelly, Taylor S.
Referee: A. Wilkie (Chester-le-Street).
(P. Richards (Preston) (substitute 57 minutes)).

Matt Elliott was Leicester City's Worthington Cup Final scoring hero against Tranmere Rovers. (ASP)

FOOTBALL LEAGUE COMPETITION ATTENDANCES

LEAGUE CUP ATTENDANCES

Season	Attendances	Games	Average
1960/61	1,204,580	112	10,755
1961/62	1,030,534	104	9,909
1962/63	1,029,893	102	10,097
1963/64	945,265	104	9,089
1964/65	962,802	98	9,825
1965/66	1,205,876	106	11,376
1966/67	1,394,553	118	11,818
1967/68	1,671,326	110	15,194
1968/69	2,064,647	118	17,497
1969/70	2,299,819	122	18,851
1970/71	2,035,315	116	17,546
1971/72	2,397,154	123	19,489
1972/73	1,935,474	120	16,129
1973/74	1,722,629	132	13,050
1974/75	1,901,094	127	14,969
1975/76	1,841,735	140	13,155
1976/77	2,236,636	147	15,215
1977/78	2,038,295	148	13,772
1978/79	1,825,643	139	13,134
1979/80	2,322,866	169	13,745
1980/81	2,051,576	161	12,743
1981/82	1,880,682	161	11,681
1982/83	1,679,756	160	10,498
1983/84	1,900,491	168	11,312
1984/85	1,876,429	167	11,236
1985/86	1,579,916	163	9,693
1986/87	1,531,498	157	9,755
1987/88	1,539,253	158	9,742
1988/89	1,552,780	162	9,585
1989/90	1,836,916	168	10,934
1990/91	1,675,496	159	10,538

Season	Attendances	Games	Average
1991/92	1,622,337	164	9,892
1992/93	1,558,031	161	9,677
1993/94	1,744,120	163	10,700
1994/95	1,530,478	157	9,748
1995/96	1,776,060	162	10,963
1996/97	1,529,321	163	9,382
1997/98	1,484,297	153	9,701
1998/99	1,555,856	153	10,169

WORTHINGTON CUP 1999-2000

Round	Aggregate	Games	Average
One	322,094	70	4,601
Two	430,799	50	8,616
Three	263,152	16	16,447
Four	125,646	8	15,706
Five	59,212	4	14,803
Semi-finals	79,017	4	19,754
Final	74,313	1	74,313
Total	1,354,233	153	8,851

AUTO WINDSCREENS SHIELD 1999-2000

Round	Aggregate	Games	Average
One	29,099	16	1,819
Two	43,888	17	2,582
Area Quarter-finals	26,399	8	3,300
Area Semi-finals	16,742	4	4,186
Area finals	36,788	4	9,197
Final	75,057	1	75,057
Total	227,973	50	4,559

FA CUP ATTENDANCES 1967–2000

	1st Round	2nd Round	3rd Round	4th Round	5th Round	6th Round	Semi-Finals & Final	Total	No. of matches	Average per match
1999-2000	181,485	127,728	514,030	374,795	182,511	105,443	214,921	1,700,913	158	10,765
1998-99	191,954	132,341	609,486	431,613	359,398	181,005	202,150	2,107,947	155	13,599
1997-98	204,803	130,261	629,127	455,557	341,290	192,651	172,007	2,125,696	165	12,883
1996-97	209,521	122,324	651,139	402,293	199,873	67,035	191,813	1,843,998	151	12,211
1995-96	185,538	115,669	748,997	391,218	274,055	174,142	156,500	2,046,199	167	12,252
1994-95	219,511	125,629	640,017	438,596	257,650	159,787	174,059	2,015,249	161	12,517
1993-94	190,683	118,031	691,064	430,234	172,196	134,705	228,233	1,965,146	159	12,359
1992-93	241,968	174,702	612,494	377,211	198,379	149,675	293,241	2,047,670	161	12,718
1991-92	231,940	117,078	586,014	372,576	270,537	155,603	201,592	1,935,340	160	12,095
1990-91	194,195	121,450	594,592	530,279	276,112	124,826	196,434	2,038,518	162	12,583
1989-90	209,542	133,483	683,047	412,483	351,423	123,065	277,420	2,190,463	170	12,885
1988-89	212,775	121,326	690,199	421,255	206,781	176,629	167,353	1,966,318	164	12,173
1987-88	204,411	104,561	720,121	443,133	281,461	119,313	177,585	2,050,585	155	13,229
1986-87	209,290	146,761	593,520	349,342	263,550	119,396	195,533	1,877,400	165	11,378
1985-86	171,142	130,034	486,838	495,526	311,833	184,262	192,316	1,971,951	168	11,738
1984-85	174,604	137,078	616,229	320,772	269,232	148,690	242,754	1,909,359	157	12,162
1983-84	192,276	151,647	625,965	417,298	181,832	185,382	187,000	1,941,400	166	11,695
1982-83	191,312	150,046	670,503	452,688	260,069	193,845	291,162	2,209,625	154	14,348
1981-82	236,220	127,300	513,185	356,987	203,334	124,308	279,621	1,840,955	160	11,506
1980-81	246,824	194,502	832,578	534,402	320,530	288,714	339,250	2,756,800	169	16,312
1979-80	267,121	204,759	804,701	507,725	364,039	157,530	355,541	2,661,416	163	16,328
1978-79	243,773	185,343	880,345	537,748	243,683	263,213	249,897	2,604,002	166	15,687
1977-78	258,248	178,930	881,406	540,164	400,751	137,059	198,020	2,594,578	160	16,216
1976-77	379,230	192,159	942,523	631,265	373,330	205,379	258,216	2,982,102	174	17,139
1975-76	255,533	178,099	867,880	573,843	471,925	206,851	205,810	2,759,941	161	17,142
1974-75	283,956	170,466	914,994	646,434	393,323	268,361	291,369	2,968,903	172	17,261
1973-74	214,236	169,114	840,142	747,909	346,012	233,307	273,051	2,779,952	167	16,646
1972-73	259,432	169,114	938,741	735,825	357,386	241,934	226,543	2,928,975	160	18,306
1971-72	277,726	236,127	986,094	711,399	486,378	230,292	248,546	3,158,562	160	19,741
1970-71	329,687	230,942	956,683	757,852	360,687	304,937	279,644	3,220,432	162	19,879
1969-70	345,229	195,102	925,930	651,374	319,893	198,537	390,700	3,026,765	170	17,805
1968-69	331,858	252,710	1,094,043	883,675	464,915	188,121	216,232	3,431,554	157	21,857
1967-68	322,121	236,195	1,229,519	771,284	563,779	240,095	223,831	3,586,824	160	22,418

AUTO WINDSCREENS SHIELD 1999–2000

FIRST ROUND

7 DEC

Brighton & HA (0) 1 *(Hart 90)*
Millwall (0) 0   2407
Brighton & HA: Walton; Watson, Campbell, Carr, Crosby, Hobson, Ramsay, Rogers, Hart, Oatway, Aspinall.
Millwall: Warner; Ryan, Neill, Cahill, Nethercott, Fitzgerald, Livermore, Moody (Sadlier), Harris (Shaw), Reid, Ifill.

Gillingham (0) 0
Torquay U (0) 3 *(Hill 52, Griffiths 75, 81)*   2718
Gillingham: Mitten; Pennock, McGlinchey, Smith (Hessenthaler), Ashby, Butters, Lewis, Nosworthy (Saunders), Rowe, Pinnock (Butler), Southall.
Torquay U: Northmore; Tully, Holmes, Aggrey, Neil, Thomas, Brandon (Worthington), Platts (Patterson), Williams (Simb), Griffiths, Hill.

Hartlepool U (1) 1 *(Henderson 14)*
Halifax T (0) 0   1482
Hartlepool U: Hollund; Knowles, Clark, Barron, Lee, Westwood, Mason, McAvoy (Midgley), Freestone (Boyd), Henderson, Stephenson.
Halifax T: Butler L; Wilder, Jules (Herbert), Stansfield, Stoneman, Gaughan, Holt (Lucas), Painter, Reilly, Clarke, Williams.

Mansfield T (1) 2 *(Lormor 42 (pen), Roscoe 105)*
Bury (1) 1 *(Bullock 45)*   1205
Mansfield T: Bowling; Andrews (Kerr), Williams, Sisson (Roscoe), Richardson, Linighan (Asher), Tallon, Clarke, Lormor, Blake, Greenacre.
Bury: Kenny; Barrass, Williams, Daws, Swailes C, Redmond, Billy, Barnes, Lawson (Avdiu), Littlejohn, Bullock.
aet; Mansfield T won on sudden death.

Northampton T (0) 1 *(Parrish 69)*
Cardiff C (0) 0   2431
Northampton T: O'Reilly; Morrow, Peer, Hope, Howey, Parrish, Savage, Hunt, Howard, Gibb, Spedding.
Cardiff C: Hallworth; Faerber (Low), Young, Perrett, Vaughan, Carpenter, Boland, Hill (Middleton), Bowen (Roberts), Humphreys, Brazier.

Notts Co (0) 0
Blackpool (1) 1 *(Clarkson 10)*   1167
Notts Co: Ward; Tierney (Dyer), Pearce, Warren, Redmile (Blackmore), Richardson, Owers, Rapley, Stallard, Fenton, Hughes (Bolland).
Blackpool: Barnes; Bardsley, Hills, Bushell, Carlisle, Hughes (Forsyth), Lee (Bent), Clarkson, Murphy, Quailey (Nowland), Beesley.

Oxford U (1) 2 *(Powell 40 (pen), 48 (pen))*
Luton T (0) 0   1220
Oxford U: Lundin; Robinson, McGowan, Fear, Weatherstone R, Whelan, Powell, Cook (Abbey), Weatherstone S, Anthrobus, Beauchamp (Whitehead).
Luton T: Abbey; Fraser, Boyce, Sodje, Doherty, Johnson, George, Ayres, Douglas (Read), Locke (Scarlett), Spring.

Preston NE (3) 4 *(Gunnlaugsson 2, 21, 74, Edwards 4)*
Wrexham (1) 1 *(Faulconbridge 29)*   3306
Preston NE: Moilanen; Alexander (Eaton), Edwards (King), Kidd, Diaf, Darby, Barry-Murphy, Appleton, Gunnlaugsson, Macken (Nogan), Mathie.
Wrexham: Walsh; Brace, Cooper, Owen, Spink, Ridler, Williams, Barrett, Connolly, Morrell, Faulconbridge.

Rotherham U (1) 2 *(Hanmer 18 (og), Sedgwick 72)*
Shrewsbury T (0) 1 *(Jagielka 71)*   1166
Rotherham U: Pollitt; Hurst, Scott, Garner, Wilsterman, Branston, Sedgwick (Berry), Watson (Ingledow), White, Warne (Martindale), Thompson.
Shrewsbury T: Edwards; Seabury, Hanmer, Tretton, Wilding, Hughes, Brown, Jagielka, Steele (Rodgers), Gayle, Jobling.

Southend U (0) 0
Cheltenham T (1) 1 *(Milton 15)*   1227
Southend U: Capleton; Cross, Johnson, Morley, Roget, Coleman (Jones), Connelly, Tinkler, Carruthers (Fitzpatrick), Kerrigan, Campbell (Roach).
Cheltenham T: Book; Yates, Victory, Banks, Freeman, Howarth, Howells, McAuley, Grayson, Milton, Brissett.

Stoke C (2) 3 *(Lightbourne 25, 93, Reed 40 (og))*
Darlington (1) 2 *(Nogan 4, Gabbiadini 81)*   3341
Stoke C: Ward; Robinson (Lightbourne), Crowe (Petty), Mohan, Gislason, Jacobsen, Hansson, Kavanagh G, Danielsson, Thorne (Oldfield), O'Connor.
Darlington: Samways; Liddle, Heckingbottom, Reed, Aspin, Brumwell (Campbell), Gray, Oliver, Nogan, Gabbiadini, Naylor (Hyorth).
aet; Stoke C won on sudden death.

Swansea C (2) 3 *(Mutton 16, Thomas 19, Watkin 75)*
Colchester U (0) 1 *(Moralee 56)*   1222
Swansea C: Freestone; Jones S, Appleby, Smith, Bound, Thomas, Jenkins (Coates), Mutton (Watkin), Alsop, Keegan (Roberts), Casey.
Colchester U: Brown; Farley, Keith, Skelton, White (Wignall), Lock (Opara), Moralee, Gregory D, Lua-Lua, McGavin, Dozzell.

Wigan Ath (1) 2 *(Bradshaw 39 (pen), Morris 105)*
Burnley (1) 1 *(Lee 26)*   2085
Wigan Ath: Carroll; Bradshaw (Martinez), Sharp, McGibbon (Mitchell), Griffiths, Kilford, McLoughlin (Morris), Sheridan, Haworth, Peron, Barlow.
Burnley: Crichton; West (Robertson), Thomas, Weller (Brass), Davis, Johnrose, Little, Lee (Cowan), Payton, Branch, Mullin.
aet; Wigan Ath won on sudden death.

York C (0) 0
Hull C (1) 1 *(Morgan 20)*   1005
York C: Mimms; Hocking, Dawson, Jordan, Sertori, Fairclough, Fox, Hulme, Alcide, Williams J, Ormerod (Conlon).
Hull C: Baker; Swales, Williams, Morgan, Perry, Greaves, Quigley, Bolder, Eyre (French), Betsy, Harris.

8 DEC

Reading (1) 1 *(Bernal 21)*
Leyton Orient (0) 0   1561
Reading: Howey; Gurney, Bowen, Polston, Primus, Bernal (Evers), Brayson, Caskey (Crawford), Williams, Potter (Sarr), Smith.
Leyton Orient: Bayes; Walschaerts, Clark, Martin (Joseph M), Hicks (Rowbotham), McGhee, Downer, Ampadu, Christie, Richards, Brkovic (McLean).

11 JAN

Cambridge U (1) 1 *(Youngs 27)*
Barnet (0) 2 *(Charlery 80, Toms 97)*   1556
Cambridge U: Van Heusden; Joseph, Chenery, Cassidy, Tann, Wilson, Wanless, Kyd, Preece (MacKenzie), Guinan (Chillingworth), Youngs.
Barnet: Harrison; Stockley, Sawyers (Toms), Currie, Heald, Arber, Searle, Doolan, King (Charlery), McGleish, Brown (Basham).
aet; Barnet won on sudden death.

SECOND ROUND

8 JAN

Lincoln C (0) 1 *(Henry 67)*
Scunthorpe U (1) 2 *(Hodges 17, Sheldon 89)*   3617
Lincoln C: Richardson; Smith, Bimson, Henry, Welsh (Philpott), Barnett D, Finnigan, Miller, Gordon, Battersby, Fleming.
Scunthorpe U: Hyldgaard; Harsley, McAuley, Fickling, Wilcox, Stanton, Walker, Hodges, Stamp, Sheldon, Omoyimni (Sparrow).

10 JAN

Preston NE (0) 1 *(Gunnlaugsson 65)*
Hartlepool U (0) 2 *(Midgley 83, Miller 86)* 3635
Preston NE: Lucas; Darby, Edwards (McKenna), Kidd, Ludden, Murdock, Appleton (Cartwright), Diaf, Gunnlaugsson, Macken (Beesley), Beresford.
Hartlepool U: Dibble; Knowles, Shilton (Clark), Barron, Strodder, Westwood, Tennebo, Miller, Freestone (Jones), Midgley, Stephenson (Boyd).

11 JAN

Bournemouth (0) 1 *(Hayter 102)*
Brighton & HA (0) 0 4325
Bournemouth: Ovendale; Broadhurst, Tindall, Hayter, Day, Mean, Rawlinson, Robinson, Stein, Fletcher C (Jorgensen), O'Neill.
Brighton & HA: Walton; Watson, Campbell, Carr, Crosby, Cullip, Freeman, Rogers, Hart (Cameron), Oatway, Aspinall.
aet; Bournemouth won on sudden death.

Exeter C (1) 2 *(Alexander 40, Buckle 51)*
Swansea C (0) 0 964
Exeter C: Matthews; Richardson, Gale, Buckle, Curran (Robinson), Gittens, Breslan (Nyamah), Rees, Alexander (Speakman), Flack, Holloway.
Swansea C: Freestone; Phillips, De Vulgt, Roberts, Smith, Bound, Keegan, Thomas (Appleby), Boyd (Bird), Mutton, Jenkins (Morgan).

Hull C (1) 2 *(Joyce 33, Morgan 76)*
Chester C (0) 0 1680
Hull C: Bracey; Harper, Edwards, Morgan (Perry), Whittle, Whitney, Joyce, Bolder, Brown (Harris), Schofield, Eyre (Wood).
Chester C: Brown; Moss, Cross, Reid (Shelton), Milosavijevic, Lancaster, Keister, Richardson (Wright), Eyjolfsson (Eve), Beckett, Fisher.

Mansfield T (0) 0
Blackpool (1) 1 *(Matthews 44)* 1844
Mansfield T: Bowling; Asher, Andrews, Sisson, Bromby, Williams, Boulding, Clarke, Lormor (Lawrence), Blake, Greenacre.
Blackpool: Caig; Bardsley, Ablett, Bushell, Carlisle, Couzens, Matthews, Richardson, Coid (Robinson), Bent (Nowland), Beesley.

Northampton T (0) 0
Bristol R (0) 0 2443
Northampton T: Welch; Hendon, Parrish, Gibb (Thompson), Green, Hope, Morrow (Dickson), Hunt, Hunter, Hughes (Gould), Spedding.
Bristol R: Parkin; Pethick, Byrne, Foster, Trought, Warne, Mauge (Bennett), Hillier (Trees), Ellington, Cureton (Walters), Roberts.
aet; Bristol R won 5-3 on penalties.

Oldham Ath (0) 0
Stoke C (0) 1 3673
abandoned after 56 mins; floodlight failure.

Oxford U (1) 1 *(Powell 21 (pen))*
Wycombe W (1) 1 *(McSporran 40)* 1798
Oxford U: Lundin; Robinson, Shepheard, Fear, Watson (Davis), Whelan, Cook, Anthrobus (Francis) (Beauchamp), Murphy, Tait, Powell.
Wycombe W: Taylor; Lawrence, Vinnicombe, Bulman, McCarthy, Harkin (Brady), Rogers, Simpson (Senda), McSporran (Thompson), Brown, Baird.
aet; Oxford U won 5-3 on penalties.

Peterborough U (0) 0
Brentford (1) 1 *(Owusu 45)* 2430
Peterborough U: Tyler; Hooper (Shields), Drury, Scott, Chapple (Jelleyman), Edwards, Gill, Martin (Green), Clarke, Lee, Hanlon.
Brentford: Woodman; Boxall, Theobald, Quinn, Powell, Rowlands, Mahon, Kennedy, Owusu, Partridge, Ingimarsson.

Plymouth Arg (0) 0
Torquay U (1) 1 *(Donaldson 35)* 3124
Plymouth Arg: Sheffield; Ashton, Beswetherick, Leadbitter, Barrett, Morrison-Hill (Stonebridge), O'Sullivan, Gritton, Phillips, Hargreaves, Wotton.

Torquay U: Northmore; Tully, Hill (Holmes), Aggrey, Neil, Thomas, Brandon, Healy, Donaldson (Bedeau), Griffiths, Platts.

Rochdale (0) 3 *(Monington 57, 82, Lancashire 106)*
Macclesfield T (2) 2 *(Davies 10, Barker 14)* 1123
Rochdale: Edwards; Evans, Stokes, Peake, Monington, Hill, Bettney, Flitcroft, Platt, Ellis (Lancashire), Atkinson (Jones).
Macclesfield T: Martin; Collins (Ingram), Rioch, Moore, Tinson, Wood, Askey (Whitehead), Sedgemore, Barker (Whittaker), Davies, Durkan.
aet; Rochdale won on sudden death.

Rotherham U (0) 1 *(White 61)*
Chesterfield (2) 4 *(Branston 4 (og), Wilsterman 29 (og), Wilkinson 58, Reeves 86)* 1997
Rotherham U: Pollitt; Scott (Varty), Ingledow, Hudson (Berry), Wilsterman, Branston, Sedgwick, Watson, White, Warne, Turner.
Chesterfield: Armstrong; Hewitt, Perkins, Beaumont (Williams D), Blatherwick, Breckin, Carss (Woods), Wilkinson, Reeves (Payne), Williams R, Galloway.

12 JAN

Bristol C (1) 3 *(Holland 28, Goodridge 54, Beadle 90)*
Cheltenham T (0) 1 *(McAuley 89)* 4123
Bristol C: Mercer; Lavin (Hill), Carey, Goodridge (Murray), Millen, Holland, Testimetanu, Hutchings, Meechan (Torpey), Beadle, Tinnion.
Cheltenham T: Book; Duff, Victory, Banks, Freeman, Howarth, Howells, McAuley, Grayson (Brough), Milton (Brissett), Yates (Bloomer).

18 JAN

Barnet (0) 1 *(Hackett 54)*
Reading (1) 2 *(Caskey 21, Scott 94)* 1109
Barnet: Harrison; Sawyers, Davidson (Darcy), Hackett, Basham, Arber, Currie, Doolan, Charlery (King), McGleish, Brown (Searle).
Reading: Howie; Gurney, Bernal, Hunter, Primus, Parkinson, Smith (Sarr), Caskey, Nicholls (Forster), Scott, Evers (Murty).
aet; Reading won on sudden death.

Oldham Ath (0) 0
Stoke C (0) 1 *(O'Connor 116)* 4682
Oldham Ath: Kelly; McNiven S, Holt, Garnett (Jones), Rickers (Tipton), Duxbury, Adams, Sheridan, Allott, Whitehall (Beavers), Hotte.
Stoke C: Ward; Hansson, Clarke, Mohan, Jacobsen, Kippe, Gunnarsson (Petty), Kavanagh G, Connor (Gislason), Lightbourne, O'Connor.
aet; Stoke C won on sudden death.

25 JAN

Carlisle U (2) 2 *(Pitts 32, Soley 39)*
Wigan Ath (0) 1 *(Martinez 72)* 1321
Carlisle U: Weaver; Pitts (Hopper), Barr, Reid, Brightwell, Prokas, Soley, Searle, Dobie, Tracey (Harries), Anthony (Gregory).
Wigan Ath: Carroll; Green (Barlow), Sharp, McGibbon, Balmer, Griffiths, O'Neill, Sheridan (Martinez), Haworth, Liddell, McLoughlin (Morris).

NORTHERN QUARTER-FINALS

25 JAN

Blackpool (1) 1 *(Jaszczun 39)*
Stoke C (1) 2 *(Gunnarsson 19, Kavanagh G 79)* 4943
Blackpool: Caig; Bardsley, Jaszczun, Ablett, Carlisle, Richardson, Matthews, Clarkson, Bent, Bushell, Beesley (Murphy).
Stoke C: Ward; Hansson (Connor), Clarke, Mohan, Jacobsen, Kippe, Gunnarsson, Kavanagh G, Lightbourne, Gislason, O'Connor.

Rochdale (0) 0
Hull C (0) 0 1745
Rochdale: Edwards; Evans, Bayliss, Flitcroft, Monington, Hill (Ford) (Carden), Bettney, Jones, Platt (Ellis), Lancashire, Atkinson.
Hull C: Wilson; Greaves (Edwards), Harper, Whitney, Whittle, Goodison, Joyce (Bolder) Brabin (Schofield), Brown, Whitmore, Wood.
aet; Rochdale won 5-4 on penalties.

Scunthorpe U (1) 1 *(Stamp 34)*
Chesterfield (1) 2 *(Blatherwick 45, Reeves 70)* 2532
Scunthorpe U: Hyldgaard; Harsley, Dawson, Pounewatchy (Sheldon), Wilcox, Hope, Stanton, Stamp, Ipoua, Cornforth, Graves.
Chesterfield: Vaughan; Hewitt, Pointon, Lomas (Perkins), Blatherwick, Breckin, Beaumont, Howard (Wilkinson), Reeves, Williams R, Galloway.

22 FEB

Carlisle U (1) 2 *(Halliday 13, McKinnon 51)*
Hartlepool U (0) 1 *(Lee 85)* 2399
Carlisle U: Van der Kwaak; Pitts, Clark, Reid, Teale, Searle, Soley (Hopper), Dobie, Durnin (Prokas), McKinnon, Halliday.
Hartlepool U: Hollund; Knowles, Shilton, Barron (Clark) (West), Strodder, Westwood, Fitzpatrick (McAvoy), Miller, Jones, Lee, Stephenson.

SOUTHERN QUARTER-FINALS

24 JAN

Bristol R (0) 1 *(Cureton 54 (pen))*
Reading (2) 2 *(Nicholls 11, 30)* 4948
Bristol R: Jones; Pethick, Byrne (Walters), Foster, Thomson, Tillson (Ellington), Mauge, Challis, Pritchard, Cureton, Roberts.
Reading: Howie; Gurney, Gray, Hunter, Primus, Grant, Nicholls (Scott), Caskey, Williams (Murty), Forster, Evers (McIntyre).

25 JAN

Brentford (0) 2 *(Bryan 62, Scott 90)*
Oxford U (0) 0 2942
Brentford: Woodman; Boxall, Anderson, Quinn, Powell, Rowlands, Evans, Mahon (Partridge), Jones (Bryan) (Einarsson), Scott, Ingimarsson.
Oxford U: Lundin; Robinson, McGowan, Cook, Weatherstone R (Beauchamp), Whelan, Lilley (Abbey), Tait, Murphy, Shepheard, Folland.

Bristol C (1) 1 *(Hewlett 16)*
Bournemouth (1) 1 *(Stein 35)* 4291
Bristol C: Mercer; Carey, Bell, Hill, Millen, Holland, Murray, Hewlett, Torpey (Beadle), Thorpe, Testimetanu (Clist).
Bournemouth: Ovendale; Young, Warren, O'Shea, Cox, Mean, Jorgensen (Watson) (Keeler), Robinson, Stein, Hayter, Hughes.
aet; Bristol C won 4-1 on penalties.

Exeter C (1) 1 *(Speakman 41)*
Torquay U (0) 0 2599
Exeter C: Naylor; Richardson, Gale, Buckle, Curran, Gittens, Breslan (Speakman) (Dewhurst), Rees, Alexander, Holloway, Nyamah.
Torquay U: Northmore; Tully, Nichols, Aggrey, Russell, Thomas, Neil, Hill, Donaldson (Simb), Griffiths, O'Brien (Bedeau).

NORTHERN SEMI-FINALS

15 FEB

Chesterfield (0) 0
Stoke C (0) 1 *(O'Connor 82)* 3825
Chesterfield: Gayle; Hewitt, Pointon (Carss), Beaumont, Blatherwick, Breckin, Perkins, Wilkinson, Reeves, Williams R, Galloway (Willis).
Stoke C: Ward; Hansson, Clarke (Gislason), Petty, Jacobsen, Kippe, Gunnarsson, Kavanagh G (Robinson), Connor (Thorne), Lightbourne, O'Connor.

7 MAR

Carlisle U (0) 0
Rochdale (0) 1 *(Hill 56)* 1792
Carlisle U: Van der Kwaak; Searle, McKinnon (Prokas), Reid, Teale, Brightwell, Soley (Tracey), Hopper, Dobie, Anthony, Halliday.
Rochdale: Priestley; Evans, Stokes, Ford, Hill, Bayliss, Flitcroft, Jones, Platt, Ellis (Bettney), Atkinson.

SOUTHERN SEMI-FINALS

15 FEB

Bristol C (2) 4 *(Beadle 35, Murray 70, Thorpe 39, 68)*
Reading (0) 0 8733
Bristol C: Mercer; Burnell, Bell, Hill, Millen, Holland (Hewlett), Murray, Clist, Beadle (Spencer), Thorpe, Tinnion (Brown A).
Reading: Howie; Bernal (Smith), Robinson, Hunter, Williams A, Parkinson, McIntyre (Hodges), Caskey, Butler, Forster, Grant (Scott).

Exeter C (2) 3 *(Breslan 27, Alexander 43, Powell 83 (og))*
Brentford (1) 2 *(Powell 45, Evans 59 (pen))* 2392
Exeter C: Matthews; McConnell, Richardson, Buckle, Vanninen (Gale), Gittens, Breslan, Rees, Alexander, Flack, Nyamah.
Brentford: Woodman; Boxall, Anderson, Quinn, Powell, Rowlands, Evans, Mahon, Jones (Owusu), Scott (Pinamonte), Ingimarsson (O'Connor).

SOUTHERN FINAL FIRST LEG

29 FEB

Bristol C (1) 4 *(Thorpe 4, Beadle 63, Murray 68, Burnell 75)*
Exeter C (0) 0 12,742
Bristol C: Mercer; Carey, Bell, Burnell, Millen, Hewlett (Burns), Murray, Brown A, Beadle (Brown M), Thorpe, Tinnion.
Exeter C: Matthews; Richardson, Powell (Nyamah), Buckle, Curran, Lee (Blake), McConnell, Rees, Alexander, Flack (Speakman), Inglethorpe.

NORTHERN FINAL FIRST LEG

14 MAR

Rochdale (0) 1 *(Holt 86)*
Stoke C (3) 3 *(Hansson 4, Thorne 21, 27)* 4241
Rochdale: Edwards; Ford (Atkinson), Evans, Peake, Monington, Hill, Flitcroft, Jones, Platt (Holt), Ellis, Bettney.
Stoke C: Ward; Hansson (Gudjonsson), Clarke, Mohan, Jacobsen, Kippe, Gunnarsson (Melton), Kavanagh G, Gunnlaugsson (Petty), Thorne, O'Connor.

SOUTHERN FINAL SECOND LEG

14 MAR

Exeter C (1) 1 *(Speakman 30)*
Bristol C (0) 1 *(Beadle 65)* 2929
Exeter C: Matthews; Lee, Power, Buckle, Curran, Gittens, Breslan (Jarman), Rees, Waugh (Ellington), Speakman (Blake), McConnell.
Bristol C: Phillips; Burnell, Carey, Burns, Millen, Hill, Murray, Brown A, Spencer (Beadle), Thorpe, Testimetanu (Clist).
Bristol C won 5–1 on agg.

NORTHERN FINAL SECOND LEG

22 MAR

Stoke C (0) 1 *(Thorne 86)*
Rochdale (0) 0 16,876
Stoke C: Ward; Hansson, Clarke, Petty, Mohan, Kippe, Gunnarsson, Kavanagh G, Gunnlaugsson (Gudjonsson), Thorne, O'Connor.
Rochdale: Edwards; Ford (Bettney), Evans, Peake, Monington, Bayliss, Flitcroft, Jones, Lancashire (Holt), Ellis, Atkinson.
Stoke C won 4–1 on agg.

FINAL (at Wembley)

16 APR

Bristol C (0) 1 *(Spencer 73)*
Stoke C (1) 2 *(Kavanagh G 31, Thorne 81)* 75,057
Bristol C: Mercer; Carey (Amankwaah), Bell, Jordan, Millen, Holland, Murray, Brown A (Spencer), Beadle, Thorpe, Tinnion.
Stoke C: Ward; Hansson, Clarke, Mohan, Gudjonsson, Gunnlaugsson (Dryden), Gunnarsson, Kavanagh G, Lightbourne (Iwelumo), Thorne, O'Connor.
Referee: K. Lynch (Kirk Hammerton).

FA CUP FINALS 1872–2000

1872 and 1874–92	Kennington Oval	1911	Replay at Old Trafford
1873	Lillie Bridge	1912	Replay at Bramall Lane
1886	Replay at Derby (Racecourse Ground)		
1893	Fallowfield, Manchester	1915	Old Trafford, Manchester
1894	Everton	1920–22	Stamford Bridge
1895–1914	Crystal Palace	1923 to date	Wembley
1901	Replay at Bolton	1970	Replay at Old Trafford
1910	Replay at Everton		

Year	Winners	Runners-up	Score
1872	Wanderers	Royal Engineers	1-0
1873	Wanderers	Oxford University	2-0
1874	Oxford University	Royal Engineers	2-0
1875	Royal Engineers	Old Etonians	2-0 (after 1-1 draw aet)
1876	Wanderers	Old Etonians	3-0 (after 1-1 draw aet)
1877	Wanderers	Oxford University	2-1 (aet)
1878	Wanderers*	Royal Engineers	3-1
1879	Old Etonians	Clapham R	1-0
1880	Clapham R	Oxford University	1-0
1881	Old Carthusians	Old Etonians	3-0
1882	Old Etonians	Blackburn R	1-0
1883	Blackburn Olympic	Old Etonians	2-1 (aet)
1884	Blackburn R	Queen's Park, Glasgow	2-1
1885	Blackburn R	Queen's Park, Glasgow	2-0
1886	Blackburn R†	WBA	2-0 (after 0-0 draw)
1887	Aston Villa	WBA	2-0
1888	WBA	Preston NE	2-1
1889	Preston NE	Wolverhampton W	3-0
1890	Blackburn R	Sheffield W	6-1
1891	Blackburn R	Notts Co	3-1
1892	WBA	Aston Villa	3-0
1893	Wolverhampton W	Everton	1-0
1894	Notts Co	Bolton W	4-1
1895	Aston Villa	WBA	1-0
1896	Sheffield W	Wolverhampton W	2-1
1897	Aston Villa	Everton	3-2
1898	Nottingham F	Derby Co	3-1
1899	Sheffield U	Derby Co	4-1
1900	Bury	Southampton	4-0
1901	Tottenham H	Sheffield U	3-1 (after 2-2 draw)
1902	Sheffield U	Southampton	2-1 (after 1-1 draw)
1903	Bury	Derby Co	6-0
1904	Manchester C	Bolton W	1-0
1905	Aston Villa	Newcastle U	2-0
1906	Everton	Newcastle U	1-0
1907	Sheffield W	Everton	2-1
1908	Wolverhampton W	Newcastle U	3-1
1909	Manchester U	Bristol C	1-0
1910	Newcastle U	Barnsley	2-0 (after 1-1 draw)
1911	Bradford C	Newcastle U	1-0 (after 0-0 draw)
1912	Barnsley	WBA	1-0 (aet, after 0-0 draw)
1913	Aston Villa	Sunderland	1-0
1914	Burnley	Liverpool	1-0
1915	Sheffield U	Chelsea	3-0
1920	Aston Villa	Huddersfield T	1-0 (aet)
1921	Tottenham H	Wolverhampton W	1-0
1922	Huddersfield T	Preston NE	1-0
1923	Bolton W	West Ham U	2-0
1924	Newcastle U	Aston Villa	2-0
1925	Sheffield U	Cardiff C	1-0
1926	Bolton W	Manchester C	1-0
1927	Cardiff C	Arsenal	1-0
1928	Blackburn R	Huddersfield T	3-1
1929	Bolton W	Portsmouth	2-0
1930	Arsenal	Huddersfield T	2-0
1931	WBA	Birmingham	2-1
1932	Newcastle U	Arsenal	2-1
1933	Everton	Manchester C	3-0
1934	Manchester C	Portsmouth	2-1
1935	Sheffield W	WBA	4-2
1936	Arsenal	Sheffield U	1-0
1937	Sunderland	Preston NE	3-1
1938	Preston NE	Huddersfield T	1-0 (aet)
1939	Portsmouth	Wolverhampton W	4-1
1946	Derby Co	Charlton Ath	4-1 (aet)
1947	Charlton Ath	Burnley	1-0 (aet)
1948	Manchester U	Blackpool	4-2
1949	Wolverhampton W	Leicester C	3-1
1950	Arsenal	Liverpool	2-0
1951	Newcastle U	Blackpool	2-0
1952	Newcastle U	Arsenal	1-0

Year	Winners	Runners-up	Score
1953	Blackpool	Bolton W	4-3
1954	WBA	Preston NE	3-2
1955	Newcastle U	Manchester C	3-1
1956	Manchester C	Birmingham C	3-1
1957	Aston Villa	Manchester U	2-1
1958	Bolton W	Manchester U	2-0
1959	Nottingham F	Luton T	2-1
1960	Wolverhampton W	Blackburn R	3-0
1961	Tottenham H	Leicester C	2-0
1962	Tottenham H	Burnley	3-1
1963	Manchester U	Leicester C	3-1
1964	West Ham U	Preston NE	3-2
1965	Liverpool	Leeds U	2-1 (aet)
1966	Everton	Sheffield W	3-2
1967	Tottenham H	Chelsea	2-1
1968	WBA	Everton	1-0 (aet)
1969	Manchester C	Leicester C	1-0
1970	Chelsea	Leeds U	2-1 (aet)
		(after 2-2 draw, after extra time)	
1971	Arsenal	Liverpool	2-1 (aet)
1972	Leeds U	Arsenal	1-0
1973	Sunderland	Leeds U	1-0
1974	Liverpool	Newcastle U	3-0
1975	West Ham U	Fulham	2-0
1976	Southampton	Manchester U	1-0
1977	Manchester U	Liverpool	2-1
1978	Ipswich T	Arsenal	1-0
1979	Arsenal	Manchester U	3-2
1980	West Ham U	Arsenal	1-0
1981	Tottenham H	Manchester C	3-2
		(after 1-1 draw, after extra time)	
1982	Tottenham H	QPR	1-0
		(after 1-1 draw, after extra time)	
1983	Manchester U	Brighton & HA	4-0
		(after 2-2 draw, after extra time)	
1984	Everton	Watford	2-0
1985	Manchester U	Everton	1-0 (aet)
1986	Liverpool	Everton	3-1
1987	Coventry C	Tottenham H	3-2 (aet)
1988	Wimbledon	Liverpool	1-0
1989	Liverpool	Everton	3-2 (aet)
1990	Manchester U	Crystal Palace	1-0
		(after 3-3 draw, after extra time)	
1991	Tottenham H	Nottingham F	2-1 (aet)
1992	Liverpool	Sunderland	2-0
1993	Arsenal	Sheffield W	2-1 (aet)
		(after 1-1 draw, after extra time)	
1994	Manchester U	Chelsea	4-0
1995	Everton	Manchester U	1-0
1996	Manchester U	Liverpool	1-0
1997	Chelsea	Middlesbrough	2-0
1998	Arsenal	Newcastle U	2-0
1999	Manchester U	Newcastle U	2-0
2000	Chelsea	Aston Villa	1-0

* *Won outright, but restored to the Football Association.*
† *A special trophy was awarded for third consecutive win.*

FA CUP WINS

Manchester U 10, Tottenham H 8, Arsenal 7, Aston Villa 7, Blackburn R 6, Newcastle U 6, Everton 5, Liverpool 5, The Wanderers 5, WBA 5, Bolton W 4, Manchester C 4, Sheffield U 4, Wolverhampton W 4, Chelsea 3, Sheffield W 3, West Ham U 3, Bury 2, Nottingham F 2, Old Etonians 2, Preston NE 2, Sunderland 2, Barnsley 1, Blackburn Olympic 1, Blackpool 1, Bradford C 1, Burnley 1, Cardiff C 1, Charlton Ath 1, Clapham R 1, Coventry C 1, Derby Co 1, Huddersfield T 1, Ipswich T 1, Leeds U 1, Notts Co 1, Old Carthusians 1, Oxford University 1, Portsmouth 1, Royal Engineers 1, Southampton 1, Wimbledon 1.

APPEARANCES IN FINALS

Manchester U 15, Arsenal 13, Newcastle U 13, Everton 12, Liverpool 11, Newcastle U 12, Aston Villa 10, WBA 10, Tottenham H 9, Blackburn R 8, Manchester C 8, Wolverhampton W 8, Bolton W 7, Preston NE 7, Chelsea 6, Old Etonians 6, Sheffield U 6, Sheffield W 6, Huddersfield T 5, *The Wanderers 5, Derby Co 4, Leeds U 4, Leicester C 4, Oxford University 4, Royal Engineers 4, Sunderland 4, West Ham U 4, Blackpool 3, Burnley 3, Nottingham F 3, Portsmouth 3, Southampton 3, Barnsley 2, Birmingham C 2, *Bury 2, Cardiff C 2, Charlton Ath 2, Clapham R 2, Notts Co 2, Queen's Park (Glasgow) 2, *Blackburn Olympic 1, *Bradford C 1, Brighton & HA 1, Bristol C 1, *Coventry C 1, Crystal Palace 1, Fulham 1, *Ipswich T 1, Luton T 4, Middlesbrough 1, *Old Carthusians 1, QPR 1, Watford 1, *Wimbledon 1.
* *Denotes undefeated.*

APPEARANCES IN SEMI-FINALS

Everton 23, Manchester U 22, Arsenal 20, Liverpool 20, Aston Villa 19, WBA 19, Blackburn R 16, Newcastle U 16, Sheffield W 16, Tottenham H 16, Chelsea 14, Wolverhampton W 14, Bolton W 13, Derby Co 13, Nottingham F 12, Sheffield U 12, Sunderland 11, Manchester C 10, Preston NE 10, Southampton 10, Birmingham C 9, Burnley 8, Leeds U 8, Leicester C 8, Huddersfield T 7, Old Etonians 6, Oxford University 6, West Ham U 6, Fulham 5, Notts Co 5, Portsmouth 5, The Wanderers 5, Luton T 4, Queen's Park (Glasgow) 4, Royal Engineers 4, Blackpool 3, Cardiff C 3, Clapham R 3, Crystal Palace (professional club) 3, Ipswich T 3, Millwall 3, Norwich C 3, Old Carthusians 3, Oldham Ath 3, Stoke C 3, The Swifts 3, Watford 3, Barnsley 2, Blackburn Olympic 2, Bristol C 2, Bury 2, Charlton Ath 2, Grimsby T 2, Swansea C 2, Swindon T 2, Wimbledon 2, Bradford C 1, Brighton & HA 1, Cambridge University 1, Chesterfield 1, Coventry C 1, Crewe Alex 1, Crystal Palace (amateur club) 1, Darwen 1, Derby Junction 1, Glasgow R 1, Hull C 1, Marlow 1, Old Harrovians 1, Middlesbrough 1, Orient 1, Plymouth Arg 1, Port Vale 1, QPR 1, Reading 1, Shropshire W 1, York C 1.

FA CUP 1999–2000

SPONSORED BY AXA

PRELIMINARY AND QUALIFYING ROUNDS

PRELIMINARY ROUND

Shildon v Thornaby-on-Tees	1-3
Glasshoughton Welfare v Hebburn	0-1
Brandon United v Ossett Town	0-3
Bradford Park Avenue v Prescot Cables	1-0
Workington v Burscough	1-2
Garforth Town v Armthorpe Welfare	0-4
Dunston FB v Maine Road	1-0
Atherton Collieries v Ramsbottom United	1-2
Marske United v Ashington	1-1, 2-1
Cheadle Town v Warrington Town	0-3
Morpeth Town v Harrogate Town	2-1
Tow Law Town v Tadcaster Albion	6-0
Chester-Le-Street Town v St Helens Town	1-3
Hallam v Liversedge	1-2
Billingham Town v Fleetwood Freeport	1-2
Farsley Celtic v Guisborough Town	1-1, 1-0
Accrington Stanley v Peterlee Newtown	3-0
Rossendale United v Chadderton	2-1
Netherfield Kendal v Oldham Town	3-0
Harrogate Railway Athletic v Willington	1-0
Bootle v Jarrow Roofing Boldon CA	0-0, 1-1
Jarrow Roofing Boldon CA won 5-4 on penalties.	
Crook Town v Yorkshire Amateur	2-0
Louth United v Kennek Ryhope CA	2-1
Flixton v Northallerton Town	2-1
Ashton United v Clitheroe	2-1
Goole v Trafford	1-1, 3-6
Woodleigh Sports v Ossett Albion	2-1
Pickering Town v Horden CW	4-1
Denaby United v Chorley	0-2
Darwen v Billingham Synthonia	0-1
Brodsworth v South Shields	1-0
Mossley v Atherton LR	2-1
Parkgate v Eccleshill United	1-5
Thackley v Consett	0-1
North Ferriby United v Witton Albion	1-0
Penrith v Shotton Comrades	4-0
Salford City v Evenwood Town	2-0
Radcliffe Borough v Durham City	2-1
Selby Town v Bedlington Terriers	0-3
Bacup Borough v Sheffield	2-2, 0-4
Curzon Ashton v Brigg Town	0-1
Skelmersdale United v Whitley Bay	5-2
Easington Colliery v Newcastle Blue Star	2-2, 0-4
Seaham Red Star v West Auckland Town	2-1
Gretna v Rossington Main	5-0
Brackley Town v Long Buckby	2-1
Stourbridge v Bromsgrove Rovers	3-1
Blackstone v Willenhall Town	0-0, 2-4
Rocester v Spalding United	2-3
Stamford v Corby Town	3-1
Belper Town v Stourport Swifts	2-2, 2-1
Boston Town v Boldmere St Michaels	1-0
Stratford Town v Leek CSOB	4-1
Borrowash Victoria v Sutton Coldfield Town	0-1
Matlock Town v Chasetown	1-0
Moor Green v Paget Rangers	3-0
Barwell v Staveley MW	1-1, 3-5
Redditch United v Kings Norton Town	1-0
Stafford Rangers v Glossop North End	2-0
Lincoln United v Mickleover Sports	1-2
Alfreton Town v Congleton Town	1-2
Ford Sports Daventry v Nantwich Town	1-2
Racing Club Warwick v Blakenall	1-2
Shepshed Dynamo v Raunds Town	0-3
Bilston Town v Oadby Town	2-4
Wednesfield v Oldbury United	1-6
Desborough Town v Northampton Spencer	2-3
Glapwell v Stapenhill	3-1
Bridgnorth Town v Hinckley United	1-3
Wellingborough Town v Kidsgrove Athletic	3-0
Gresley Rovers v Eastwood Town	0-1
Holbeach United v Pelsall Villa	2-0

VS Rugby v Solihull Borough	1-2
Bourne Town v Stewarts & Lloyds	0-2
Knypersley Victoria v Bedworth United	0-2
Shifnal Town v Rushall Olympic	3-3, 1-0
Arnold Town v Yaxley	2-2, 2-1
Halesowen Harriers v West Midlands Police	4-0
St Neots Town v Hornchurch	2-1
Potters Bar Town v Flackwell Heath	3-3, 0-1
Great Wakering Rovers v Staines Town	0-0, 0-5
Chalfont St Peter v Barking	0-6
Stotfold v Wembley	0-0, 1-2
Grays Athletic v Basildon United	7-1
Diss Town v Sudbury	1-6
Ely City v Witham Town	2-3
Berkhamsted Town v Bishop's Stortford	2-2, 3-3
Bishop's Stortford won 4-3 on penalties.	
Tiptree United v London Colney	2-0
Wealdstone v Clacton Town	1-0
Fakenham Town v Brook House	3-2
Southend Manor v Ilford	4-0
Southall v Witney Town	2-5
Felixstowe Port & Town v Wingate & Finchley	1-3
Wotton United v Arlesey Town	0-1
Saffron Walden Town v Kempston Rovers	5-0
Romford v Maldon Town	1-0
Burnham v Wisbech Town	0-1
Harwich & Parkeston v Harlow Town	2-3
Warboys Town v Bury Town	3-3, 2-2
Warboys Town won 4-3 on penalties.	
Concord Rangers v East Thurrock United	2-2, 2-4
Uxbridge v Wroxham	0-1
Ruislip Manor v Leighton Town	2-0
Gorleston v Lowestoft Town	1-1, 2-1
Wivenhoe Town v Bedford Town	0-1
Banbury United v Milton Keynes City	2-0
Burnham Ramblers v Hoddesdon Town	1-2
Great Yarmouth Town v Tilbury	5-3
Braintree Town v Leyton Pennant	1-1, 2-1
Hemel Hempstead Town v Harpenden Town	4-0
Soham Town Rangers v Buckingham Town	7-0
Aveley v Stansted	1-0
Histon v Hullbridge Sports	1-0
Wotton Blue Cross v Cheshunt	0-2
Waltham Abbey v Yeading	1-1, 3-1
Ware v Newmarket Town	3-0
Stowmarket Town v Welwyn Garden City	3-0
Baldock Town v Potton United	6-0
Bowers United v Hanwell Town	4-0
Ford United v Edgware Town	5-1
Woodbridge Town v Chelmsford City	1-5
Halstead Town v Royston Town	1-3
Beaconsfield SYCOB v Eynesbury Rovers	3-0
Hertford Town w.o. v Barkingside removed	
Northwood v Clapton	8-0
Marlow v Barton Rovers	2-2, 3-1
Kingsbury Town v Tring Town	2-1
East Cowes Victoria v Sittingbourne	0-1
Folkestone Invicta v Croydon Athletic	4-2
Bracknell Town v Camberley Town	2-2, 3-1
Cobham v Farnham Town	1-1, 2-3
Ashford Town (Middlesex) v Langney Sports	1-2
Saltdean United v Beckenham Town	1-0
Eastbourne Town v Three Bridges	0-0, 1-1
Eastbourne Town won 4-3 on penalties.	
Ash United v Chatham Town	1-2
Newport (IW) v North Leigh	2-0
Erith & Belvedere v Wick	0-2
Abingdon Town v Peacehaven & Telscombe	6-0
Thamesmead Town v Reading Town	2-2, 0-1
Chipstead v Tonbridge Angels	0-5
Hillingdon Borough v St Leonards	0-0, 1-4
Leatherhead v Cowes Sports	0-1
Merstham v Corinthian Casuals	1-5
Halesham Town v Littlehampton Town	5-4

Molesey v Ringmer	3-1
Bedfont v Tunbridge Wells	4-0
Raynes Park Vale v Fisher Athletic	1-2
Viking Greenford v Whitstable Town	3-2
Erith Town v Dorking	0-0, 2-1
Ashford Town v East Preston	2-1
Shoreham v Abingdon United	1-2
Windsor & Eton v Bromley	0-0, 0-3
Oxford City v Gosport Borough	5-1
Herne Bay v Canterbury City	1-0
Epsom & Ewell v Worthing	0-3
Redhill v Slade Green	2-0
Deal Town v Greenwich Borough	5-0
Fleet Town v Lewes	1-3
Hastings Town v Southwick	6-1
Bognor Regis Town v Didcot Town	2-1
Sandhurst Town v Newbury	0-0, 2-5
Thatcham Town v Lordswood	4-2
Chichester City v Selsey	2-2, 2-4
Wokingham Town v Sheppey United	1-4
Cray Wanderers v Portfield	2-2, 3-2
Whyteleafe v Lancing	4-3
Whitehawk v Maidenhead United	0-1
Egham Town v Croydon	2-0
Metropolitan Police v Chertsey Town	2-1
Horsham v Hassocks	0-1
Fareham Town v Carterton Town	0-1
Godalming & Guildford v Horsham YMCA	1-2
Hythe United v Burgess Hill Town	0-0, 0-3
Arundel v Portsmouth Royal Navy	1-2
Banstead Athletic v Thame United	0-2
Ramsgate v Dartford	2-1
Christchurch v Bridport	1-1, 4-2
Frome Town v Cinderford Town	0-4
Mangotsfield United v Hungerford Town	3-0
Falmouth Town v Bideford	1-2
Bridgwater Town v Lymington & New Milton	0-5
Minehead Town v Elmore	1-3
Totton v Weston-Super-Mare	1-2
Bashley v Calne Town	6-1
Chippenham Town v Bournemouth	1-0
Street v Eastleigh	0-1
Welton Rovers v Warminster Town	4-0
Yate Town v Taunton Town	0-3
Tiverton Town v Pershore Town	7-1
Bemerton Heath Harlequins v Brislington	0-1
Melksham Town v Evesham United	1-3
Downton v Barnstaple Town	3-6
St Blazey v Brockenhurst	3-1
Backwell United v Andover	5-1
Westbury United v Devizes Town	0-1
Paulton Rovers v Odd Down	1-2
Cirencester Town v BAT Sports	3-0

Byes: Newcastle Town, Stocksbridge Park Steels, Tooting & Mitcham United, Torrington, Tuffley Rovers and Wimborne Town.

FIRST QUALIFYING ROUND

Crook Town v Armthorpe Welfare	5-0
Rossendale United v Ossett Town	1-1, 0-2
Consett v Accrington Stanley	0-2
Liversedge v Woodleigh Sports	3-2
Bradford (Park Avenue) v Skelmersdale United	2-1
Thornaby-on-Tees v Tow Law Town	1-5
Brigg Town v Harrogate Railway Athletic	4-0
St Helens Town v Pickering Town	1-1, 2-3
Trafford v Jarrow Roofing Boldon CA	3-3, 3-1
Hebburn v Louth United	2-2, 2-4
Ramsbottom United v Fleetwood Freeport	1-2
Farsley Celtic v Burscough	1-1, 3-0
Mossley v Gretna	0-2
Eccleshill United v Marske United	4-0
Ashton United v Flixton	2-0
Radcliffe Borough v Warrington Town	8-1
Chorley v Seaham Red Star	3-0
Penrith v Morpeth Town	0-2
Sheffield v Brodsworth	1-0
North Ferriby United v Netherfield Kendal	3-2
Newcastle Blue Star v Billingham Synthonia	1-1, 3-0
Dunston FB v Salford City	1-0
Bedlington Terriers v Stocksbridge Park Steels	2-0
Stourbridge v Belper Town	0-2
Stafford Rangers v Matlock Town	2-2, 4-0
Northampton Spencer v Boston Town	1-1, 6-4

Hinckley United v Glapwell	1-0
Solihull Borough v Sutton Coldfield Town	1-0
Wellingborough Town v Newcastle Town	2-2, 2-1
Oldbury United v Stratford Town	2-0
Willenhall Town v Oadby Town	1-1, 1-3
Stamford v Brackley Town	3-1
Shifnal Town v Congleton Town	2-3
Bedworth United v Redditch United	1-3
Moor Green v Mickleover Sports	3-2
Staveley MW v Blakenall	1-3
Eastwood Town v Holbeach United	3-0
Halesowen Harriers v Arnold Town	1-4
Nantwich Town v Stewarts & Lloyds	3-0
Spalding United v Raunds Town	1-0
Bishop's Stortford v Hemel Hempstead Town	4-2
Banbury United v Gorleston	6-3
Cheshunt v Waltham Abbey	1-0
Wingate & Finchley v Braintree Town	3-2
Great Yarmouth Town v Warboys Town	2-3
East Thurrock United v Baldock Town	1-2
Romford v Southend Manor	4-1
Fakenham Town v Staines Town	1-3
Saffron Walden Town v Hoddesdon Town	3-1
Wisbech Town v Wroxham	3-1
Ruislip Manor v Beaconsfield SYCOB	0-1
Barking v Grays Athletic	0-1
Sudbury v Flackwell Heath	1-0
Hertford Town v Royston Town	0-2
Arlesey Town v Bowers United	4-1
Wealdstone v Ford United	1-1, 3-2
Marlow v Histon	7-2
Kingsbury Town v Chelmsford City	0-1
Tiptree United v Witney Town	1-2
Ware v Soham Town Rangers	1-1, 1-2
Wembley v Harlow Town	3-1
Bedford Town v Aveley	0-0, 2-1
Northwood v Stowmarket Town	2-0
St Neots Town v Witham Town	0-4
Ashford Town v Fisher Athletic	0-2
Farnham Town v Selsey	3-0
Hailsham Town v Sittingbourne	1-3
Bedfont v Reading Town	5-1
Worthing v Saltdean United	2-1
Maidenhead United v Viking Greenford	5-0
Horsham YMCA v Cray Wanderers	3-0
Folkestone Invicta v Ramsgate	1-3
St Leonards v Bognor Regis Town	0-1
Eastbourne Town v Langney Sports	0-4
Lewes v Erith Town	3-3, 4-3
Tonbridge Angels v Abingdon Town	3-0
Molesey v Hastings Town	0-3
Thame United v Wick	3-1
Abingdon United v Oxford City	0-6
Deal Town v Metropolitan Police	2-0
Thatcham Town v Cowes Sports	4-6
Carterton Town v Herne Bay	1-4
Corinthian Casuals v Sheppey United	4-0
Hassocks v Bromley	1-1, 1-2
Redhill v Burgess Hill Town	1-1, 0-3
Newbury v Portsmouth Royal Navy	3-1
Chatham Town v Newport (IW)	2-3
Egham Town v Whyteleafe	1-3
Bracknell Town v Tooting & Mitcham United	2-4
Elmore v Welton Rovers	0-3
Lymington & New Milton v Bideford	3-0
Devizes Town v Weston-Super-Mare	0-2
Mangotsfield United v Odd Down	1-1, 2-1
Backwell United v Bashley	5-0
Cinderford Town v Barnstaple Town	0-1
Tiverton Town v Evesham United	4-3
Christchurch v Brislington	1-0
Cirencester Town v Taunton Town	2-2, 0-4
Torrington v Wimborne Town	0-2
Chippenham Town v St Blazey	2-1
Tuffley Rovers v Eastleigh	2-1

SECOND QUALIFYING ROUND

Guiseley v Pickering Town	6-0
Gateshead v Winsford United	3-0
Ossett Town v Spennymoor United	2-1
Morpeth Town v Tow Law Town	2-1
Worksop Town v Bishop Auckland	2-3
Lancaster City w.o. v Fleetwood Freeport	

Fleetwood removed for playing an ineligible player in preliminary round.

Gainsborough Trinity v Eccleshill United	2-0
Leigh RMI v Blyth Spartans	5-3
Hyde United v Crook Town	1-1, 1-2
Barrow v Marine	2-2, 2-3
Ashton United v Brigg Town	0-2
Accrington Stanley v Whitby Town	0-2
Trafford v Bamber Bridge	2-2, 1-2
Billingham Synthonia v North Ferriby United	1-2
Liversedge v Dunston FB	1-2
Stalybridge Celtic v Colwyn Bay	1-0
Emley v Louth United	2-0
Sheffield v Farsley Celtic	0-0, 0-2
Runcorn v Gretna	2-0
Bradford (Park Avenue) v Droylsden	2-2, 1-2
Radcliffe Borough v Chorley	0-1
Frickley Athletic v Bedlington Terriers	0-1
Nantwich Town v Hucknall Town	1-0
Solihull Borough v Ilkeston Town	3-4
Moor Green v Atherstone United	2-1
Redditch United v Burton Albion	0-1
Tamworth v Spalding United	6-2
Boston United v Oldbury United	3-1
Oadby Town v Halesowen Town	2-1
Leek Town v Blakenall	0-2
Belper Town v Arnold Town	4-2
Grantham Town v Northampton Spencer	6-0
Hinckley United v Wellingborough Town	2-0
Stamford v Congleton Town	1-1, 0-2
Stafford Rangers v Eastwood Town	1-3
Wisbech Town v Billericay Town	1-3
Bishop's Stortford v Wingate & Finchley	1-1, 2-3
Warboys Town v Witney Town	0-2
Sudbury v Dagenham & Redbridge	1-2
Canvey Island v Boreham Wood	3-1
Heybridge Swifts v Romford	1-2
Purfleet v Banbury United	0-0, 1-0
Northwood v Rothwell Town	3-3, 0-2
Cambridge City v Arlesey Town	3-1
Beaconsfield SYCOB v Kings Lynn	0-3
Saffron Walden Town v Hitchin Town	1-4
Aylesbury United v Chelmsford City	1-3
Bedford Town v St Albans City	0-2
Chesham United v Baldock Town	1-3
Royston Town v Wembley	1-3
Soham Town Rangers v Enfield	1-3
Staines Town v Wealdstone	0-3
Marlow v Harrow Borough	1-4
Hendon v Grays Athletic	2-0
Cheshunt v Witham Town	0-0, 2-0
Aldershot Town v Lewes	6-1
Thame v Whyteleafe	0-1
Hampton & Richmond Borough v Bognor Regis Town	1-1, 0-0

Bognor Regis Town won 5-4 on penalties.

Ramsgate v Margate	0-3
Burgess Hill Town v Bedfont	2-2, 2-0
Walton & Hersham v Maidenhead United	0-2
Tooting & Mitcham United v Oxford City	0-2
Farnham Town v Herne Bay	2-2, 0-1
(abandoned: 66 mins, floodlight failure), 1-1	

Herne Bay won 3-2 on penalties; ordered to be replayed after Herne Bay used four substitutes. Herne Bay won 2-1.

Hastings Town v Newbury	3-1
Carshalton Athletic v Sittingbourne	2-2, 1-0
Tonbridge Angels v Farnborough Town	0-2
Horsham YMCA v Corinthian Casuals	4-0
Newport (IW) v Dulwich Hamlet	1-1, 1-4
Slough Town v Cowes Sports	3-1
Havant & Waterlooville v Langney Sports	2-2, 1-2
Bromley v Crawley Town	4-1
Gravesend & Northfleet v Fisher Athletic	1-1, 1-2
Deal Town v Worthing	2-2, 0-3
Christchurch v Worcester City	2-3
Clevedon Town v Tiverton Town	2-1
Taunton Town v Dorchester Town	3-0
Newport County v Wimborne Town	1-1, 3-0
Barnstaple Town v Backwell United	2-3
Weymouth v Gloucester City	0-0, 1-2
Bath City v Weston-Super-Mare	4-0
Lymington & New Milton v Tuffley Rovers	1-1, 5-0
Welton Rovers v Salisbury City	1-3
Chippenham Town v Mangotsfield United	2-0
Basingstoke Town v Merthyr Tydfil	0-0, 1-2

THIRD QUALIFYING ROUND

Dunston FB v Runcorn	0-2
Bamber Bridge v Morpeth Town	3-0
Stalybridge Celtic v Farsley Celtic	4-2
Bishop Auckland v Bedlington Terriers	1-1, 1-0
Lancaster City v Whitby Town	2-2, 2-2
Lancaster City won 4-2 on penalties.	
Marine v Chorley	2-0
North Ferriby United v Guiseley	1-3
Droylsden v Gainsborough Trinity	2-2, 2-1
Leigh RMI v Crook Town	1-1, 1-2
Gateshead v Brigg Town	4-0
Ossett Town v Emley	0-0, 1-4
Enfield v Billericay Town	2-0
Wembley v Canvey Island	0-3
Chelmsford City v Moor Green	1-0
Belper Town v Tamworth	1-2
Wingate & Finchley v Ilkeston Town	0-5
Hitchin Town v Grantham Town	2-1
Eastwood Town v Oadby Town	3-0
Romford v Congleton Town	6-0
Cambridge City v Kings Lynn	1-0
Baldock Town v Cheshunt	5-1
Wealdstone v Rothwell Town	1-1, 0-2
Dagenham & Redbridge v Burton Albion	0-2
St Albans City v Nantwich Town	4-2
Hendon v Blakenall	2-1
Boston United v Purfleet	4-0
Witney Town v Hinckley United	2-1
Chippenham Town v Worthing	1-1, 1-3
Dulwich Hamlet v Hastings Town	2-1
Bath City v Farnborough Town	3-1
Maidenhead United v Salisbury City	0-1
Gloucester City v Merthyr Tydfil	2-3
Whyteleafe v Langney Sports	1-0
Backwell United v Oxford City	2-4
Bognor Regis Town v Bromley	1-0
Fisher Athletic v Aldershot Town	1-2
Herne Bay v Horsham YMCA	0-3
Worcester City v Harrow Borough	3-2
Slough Town v Carshalton Athletic	1-0
Newport County v Burgess Hill Town	1-2
Lymington & New Milton v Clevedon Town	3-1
Taunton Town v Margate	0-3

FOURTH QUALIFYING ROUND

Nuneaton Borough v Guiseley	2-3
Droylsden v Eastwood Town	0-2
Telford United v Gateshead	0-0, 1-2
Scarborough v Tamworth	0-1
Doncaster Rovers v Crook Town	7-0
Southport v Emley	1-1, 2-0
Northwich Victoria v Hednesford Town	2-2, 0-1
Morecambe v Bishop Auckland	1-0
Marine v Runcorn	1-1, 2-3
Altrincham v Stalybridge Celtic	0-0, 1-2
Match ordered to be replayed; Stalybridge Celtic included an ineligible player.	
Lancaster City v Bamber Bridge	0-0, 3-4
Worthing v Dover Athletic	1-1, 1-0
Oxford City v Salisbury City	2-1
Hendon v Margate	1-0
Bognor Regis Town v Whyteleafe	0-1
Welling United v Kidderminster Harriers	2-0
Merthyr Tydfil v Hitchin Town	2-0
Dulwich Hamlet v Hayes	0-0, 0-3
Kingstonian v Boston United	0-0, 3-0
Rushden & Diamonds v Sutton United	4-1
Ilkeston Town v Romford	3-0
Worcester City v Forest Green Rovers	2-5
Yeovil Town v Witney Town	2-1
Woking v Burton Albion	1-1, 1-3
Enfield v Baldock Town	1-1, 2-2
Enfield won 4-3 on penalties.	
Lymington & New Milton v Aldershot Town	1-3
Rothwell Town v Kettering Town	1-1, 1-2
Canvey Island v St Albans City	3-3, 1-2
Stevenage Borough v Bath City	1-1, 0-1
Horsham YMCA v Chelmsford City	2-3
Hereford United v Burgess Hill Town	4-1
Slough Town v Cambridge City	1-1, 2-3

FA CUP 1999–2000
SPONSORED BY AXA

COMPETITION PROPER

FIRST ROUND

29 OCT

Rushden & D (0) 2 *(Warburton 48, Hamsher 76 (pen))*
Scunthorpe U (0) 0   4112
Rushden & D: Turley; Brady, Bradshaw (Wooding), McElhatton, Peters, Warburton, Butterworth, Hamsher, De Souza, Collins, Underwood.
Scunthorpe U: Evans; Harsley, Dawson, Logan (Stanton), Fickling, Hope, Walker, Hodges, Ipoua, Marcelle (Bull), Calvo-Garcia (Sheldon).

30 OCT

Aldershot T (0) 1 *(Abbott 56)*
Hednesford T (0) 1 *(Robinson 51)*   3269
Aldershot T: Pape; Coll, Chewins, Adedeji, Pearce, Fielder, Sugrue (Nartey), Bentley, Abbott, Gell, Hathaway (Bassey).
Hednesford T: Morgan; Evans, Colkin, Lake, Brindley, Robinson, Rhodes (Mike), Twynham, Davis, Goodwin, Kimmins.

Bath C (0) 0
Hendon (0) 2 *(Gentle 87, Guentchev 90)*   1690
Bath C: Jackson; Clode (Tisdale), Bodin, Harrington (Walker), Towler, Lloyd, Davis, James, Colbourne, Paul (Frazer), Holloway.
Hendon: McCann; White, Clarke, Daly, Towler, Fitzgerald, Binns, Hyatt, Whitmarsh (Guentchev), Watson (McKoy), Gentle.

Blackpool (1) 2 *(Carlisle 5, Nowland 90)*
Stoke C (0) 0   4721
Blackpool: Caig; Bryan (Bent), Hills, Bushell, Carlisle, Hughes, Robinson, Clarkson, Murphy, Nowland, Coid (Forsyth).
Stoke C: Ward; Robinson (Bullock), Clarke (Heath), Jacobsen, Short, Keen, Wooliscroft, Kavanagh G, Lightbourne, Thorne (Connor), O'Connor.

Brentford (0) 2 *(Owusu 56, Marshall 63)*
Plymouth Arg (1) 2 *(Stonebridge 43, McGregor 83)* 4287
Brentford: Woodman; Boxall, Jenkins (Rowlands), Quinn, Powell, Marshall, Evans, Mahon, Owusu, Partridge, Scott.
Plymouth Arg: Sheffield; Rowbotham, Beswetherick, Leadbitter, Heathcote, Taylor, Barrett, O'Sullivan (Belgrave), McGregor, Hargreaves, Stonebridge.

Bristol C (1) 3 *(Tinnion 44, 50, Murray 65)*
Mansfield T (1) 2 *(Lormor 10 (pen), Blake 89)* 5411
Bristol C: Phillips; Lavin, Bell, Mortimer (Testimitanu), Taylor, Holland, Murray, Hutchings, Jones (Meechan), Beadle (Goodridge), Tinnion.
Mansfield T: Bowling; Hassell (Asher), Williams (Boulding), Richardson, Linighan, Porter, Roscoe, Disley (Bacon), Lormor, Clarke, Blake.

Burton A (0) 0
Rochdale (0) 0   3103
Burton A: Goodwin; Davies, March, Lyons, Blount, Forsyth, Stride, Anderson, Thomas (Webster), Clough, Holmes.
Rochdale: Edwards; Evans, Stokes, Peake, Hicks, Monington, Flitcroft, Ford, Platt, Dowe (Holt), Atkinson (Jones).

Cambridge C (0) 0
Wigan Ath (2) 2 *(Barlow 30, 44)*   4024
Cambridge C: Davies; Coburn, Wenlock, Holden, Thompson (Gawthrop), Tovey, Pincher (Reeder), Stringfellow, Kirkup (Leete), Cambridge, Wilde.
Wigan Ath: Stillie; Green, Kilford, McGibbon, Balmer, De Zeeuw, O'Neill, Sheridan (Sharp), Martinez, Liddell, Barlow.

Cambridge U (0) 1 *(Taylor 79)*
Gateshead (0) 0   2970
Cambridge U: Marshall; Joseph, Ashbee, Paterson (Taylor), Eustace, Wilson, Wanless, Mustoe, Butler, Benjamin, MacKenzie.
Gateshead: Swan; Watson (Scott), Lynch, Kitchen, Hall, Bowey, Thompson, Fletcher, Alderson (Ross), Raitt (Proudlock), Hine.

Cheltenham T (0) 1 *(Brough 77)*
Gillingham (1) 1 *(Southall 37)*   3188
Cheltenham T: Book; Duff, Victory, Banks, Freeman, Brough, Howells, Milton, Grayson (Hopkins), Howarth, Yates.
Gillingham: Bartram; Southall, Ashby, Smith, McGlinchey (Edge), Butters, Lewis, Hessenthaler, Butler (Nosworthy), Pennock, Saunders.

Chesterfield (0) 1 *(Lomas 49)*
Enfield (1) 2 *(Bunn 23, Brown 67)*   2506
Chesterfield: Gayle; Hewitt, Beaumont, Lomas (Lee), Blatherwick, Breckin, Howard, Wilkinson, Reeves, Ebdon, Carss (Willis).
Enfield: John; Protheroe, Cooper, Brown, Southgate, Annon (Morgan), Tomlinson, Jones, Moran, Bunn, Dunwell.

Darlington (1) 2 *(Tutill 35, Gabbiadini 77 (pen))*
Southport (0) 1 *(Bolland 52)*   4313
Darlington: Collett (Finch); Liddle, Heckingbottom, Campbell (Himsworth), Tutill, Brumwell (Naylor), Heaney, Oliver, Nogan, Gabbiadini, Atkinson.
Southport: Dickinson; Clark, Grayston, Guyett (Elam), Bolland, Ryan, Woods, Gouck, Arnold (Furlong), Ellison, Stuart.

Doncaster R (0) 0
Halifax T (0) 2 *(Tate 51, Paterson 82)*   5588
Doncaster R: Warrington; Marples, Maxfield, McIntyre, Walling, Sutherland (Warren), Maamria (Penney), Goodwin, Kirkwood (Duerden), Newell, Cauldwell.
Halifax T: Butler L; Wilder, Jules, Mitchell, Stoneman, Clarke, Paterson, Gaughan, Tate, Painter, Butler P.

Exeter C (1) 2 *(Flack 40, Gale 47)*
Eastwood T (0) 1 *(Smith 56)*   2441
Exeter C: Naylor; Richardson, Robinson, Gale, Curran, Gittens, Smith (Buckle), Rees, Flack, Bradley, Nyamah (Breslan).
Eastwood T: Bryant; Gould (Kennerdale), Bonser, Flint, King (Breach), Castledine, Smith, Bonsall, Eaton, Worboys (Todd), Tomlinson.

Forest Green R (4) 6 *(Hunt 1, 31, 62, McGregor 25, Drysdale 38, Sykes 51)*
Guiseley (0) 0   1047
Forest Green R: Perrin; Hedges (Honor), Forbes, Randall, Clark, Burns (Hatswell), Daley, Sykes, McGregor, Hunt (Cook), Drysdale.
Guiseley: Shutt; Saunders (Hook), Hogarth, Nettleton, Gallacher, Parsley (Bulgin), Poole (Zoll), Williams, Parke, Agana, Shuttleworth.

Hayes (1) 2 *(Bunce 25, Charles 90 (pen))*
Runcorn (1) 1 *(McDonald 45)* 890
Hayes: Hodson; Boyce (Coppard), Flynn, Watts, Bunce, Goodliffe, McKimm (Trebble), Moore, Spencer (Roddis), Charles, Telemaque.
Runcorn: Acton; Salt, Ness, Nolan, Burke, Ruffer, Brunskill, Rose (Robinson), McNally, McDonald, Watson (Griffiths).

Hereford U (0) 1 *(May 77)*
York C (0) 0 2787
Hereford U: Jones; Clarke, Sturgess, Snape, Wright, James, Parry, Taylor, May, Williams, Rodgerson.
York C: Mimms; Williams M (Williams J), Hall, Jones, Sertori, Fairclough, Dawson (Hocking), Fox, Conlon, Hulme, Jordan.

Ilkeston T (1) 2 *(Moore 39, Raynor 62)*
Carlisle U (1) 1 *(Harries 18)* 1748
Ilkeston T: Beattie; Fairclough, Wright, Middleton, Fearon, Knapper, Eshelby, Hemmings (Hurst), Helliwell, Moore, Raynor (Ludlam).
Carlisle U: Thompson; Barr, Clark, Bowman, Brightwell, Prokas, Anthony, Harries, Dobie, Tracey, Soley.

Leyton Orient (0) 1 *(Ampadu 56)*
Cardiff C (1) 1 *(Nugent 39 (pen))* 3109
Leyton Orient: Bayes; Joseph M, Lockwood, Smith, Hicks, Clark, Brkovic (Inglethorpe), Ampadu, Christie, Simba (Watts), Beall.
Cardiff C: Hallworth; Faerber, Legg, Perrett, Young, Ford, Boland (Carpenter), Fowler, Bowen, Nugent, Hill.

Lincoln C (1) 1 *(Smith 30)*
Welling U (0) 0 2766
Lincoln C: Richardson; Fleming, Phillips, Finnigan, Wilkins, Barnett D, Smith, Miller, Gordon (Stant), Thorpe, Philpott.
Welling U: Wilkerson; Watts, Hone, Budden, Harle, Chapman (Riviere), Hanlon, Rutherford, Dennis, Rowe, Braithwaite.

Luton T (1) 4 *(Gray 11, George 66, Spring 76, Taylor 79)*
Kingstonian (1) 2 *(Crossley 35, Leworthy 47)* 4682
Luton T: Abbey; Fraser (Boyce), Taylor, Watts, Doherty, Johnson, George, McLaren, Douglas, Gray (McIndoe), Spring.
Kingstonian: Farrelly; Harris, Crossley, Allan, Mustafa, Smith (Kadi), Pitcher, Luckett, Wingfield, Leworthy, Marshall.

Macclesfield T (0) 0
Hull C (0) 0 2401
Macclesfield T: Martin; Ingram (Abbey), Rioch, Collins, Tinson, Sedgemore, Askey (Tomlinson), Priest, Barker, Davies (Wood), Durkan.
Hull C: Wilson; Harper, Williams, Edwards, Greaves, Morgan, D'Auria, Brabin, Brown (Alcide), Whitmore (Schofield), Eyre.

Notts Co (1) 1 *(Rapley 17)*
Bournemouth (0) 1 *(Warren 53)* 3674
Notts Co: Ward; Holmes, Warren, Richardson, Pearce, Dyer (Tierney), Rapley, Ramage, Stallard, Hughes, Bolland.
Bournemouth: Ovendale; Young, Warren, Forbes, Cox, Day, Jorgensen, Robinson, Stein, Fletcher S (Watson), Fletcher C.

Oldham Ath (2) 4 *(Dudley 28, Sheridan 29, Duxbury 70, Whitehall 83)*
Chelmsford C (0) 0 4392
Oldham Ath: Kelly; McNiven S, Hotte, Graham (Futcher), Rickers, Duxbury, Adams, Sheridan, Allott (Tipton), Dudley (Whitehall), Innes.
Chelmsford C: Catley; Girling B, Girling J, Dobinson, Wardley, Bishop, Vincent (Sonnex), Lakin, Reeve (Shirley), Berquez, Bell.

Oxford U (1) 3 *(Lilley 12, Powell 58, Abbey 87)*
Morecambe (1) 2 *(Wright 28, Jackson 47)* 3504
Oxford U: Arendse; Robinson, Powell, Fear, Watson, Whelan, Lilley, Lambert (Abbey), Murphy, Folland (McGowan), Beauchamp.
Morecambe: Banks; Fensome, Farrell, McKearney, Wright, Knowles (Smith), Drummond, Burns, Lyons (Keeling), Jackson, Hardy (Eastwood).

Peterborough U (1) 1 *(Clarke 24)*
Brighton & HA (1) 1 *(Freeman 35)* 7260
Peterborough U: Tyler; Hooper, Drury, Castle, Chapple, Edwards, Green (French), Davies, Clarke, Forinton, Etherington.
Brighton & HA: Walton; Watson, Campbell, McPherson, Cullip, Carr, Freeman (Newhouse), Rogers, Hart, Oatway (Mayo), Aspinall.

Reading (1) 4 *(Bernal 31, Caskey 63 (pen), Hunter 80, Williams M 87)*
Yeovil T (1) 2 *(Foster 36, Eaton 90)* 8032
Reading: Whitehead; Gurney, Parkinson (Grant), Hunter, Primus, Casper, Bernal (Murty), Caskey, Williams M, Evers, Scott (McIntyre).
Yeovil T: Pennock; Piper, Pitman, Sparks, Brown, Stowell, Hayfield, Stott (Cousins), Patmore, Foster (Eaton), Pounder (Smith).

Rotherham U (1) 3 *(Thompson 31, Garner 81, Martindale 90 (pen))*
Worthing (0) 0 3716
Rotherham U: Pollitt; Varty, Scott, Dillon (Sedgwick), Wilsterman, Garner, Berry, Watson, Fortune-West (Martindale), Warne, Thompson (Hurst).
Worthing: Bray; Rutherford M, James, Cox (Miles), Knee, Rutherford G, Thomas (Weston), Burt, Kennett, Funnell (Holden), Carrington.

Shrewsbury T (1) 2 *(Kerrigan 24, Wilding 70)*
Northampton T (1) 1 *(Hendon 43)* 2584
Shrewsbury T: Edwards; Seabury, Hanmer, Jobling, Winstanley, Wilding, Rigby, Kerrigan, Steele, Hughes, Brown.
Northampton T: Welch; Hendon, Gibb (Wilson), Sampson, Howey, Peer (Hope), Savage, Hunt, Sturridge (Howard), Corazzin, Spedding.

St Albans C (0) 0
Bamber Bridge (1) 2 *(Whittaker 45, Carroll 89)* 1127
St Albans C: Roberts; Pratt, James (Randall), Vickers, Harvey, Rooney, Pollard, Hunter (McCormack), Clark, Andrews (Duru), McMenamin.
Bamber Bridge: Dootson; Brown, Bryson, Jones, Baldwin, Maddock, Smith, Aspinall, Greenwood (Carroll), Whittaker (Spencer), Turner.

Swansea C (0) 2 *(Cusack 83, Watkin 89)*
Colchester U (0) 1 *(Lua-Lua 52)* 3622
Swansea C: Freestone; Price, Howard, Cusack, Smith, Bound, Keegan (Casey), Appleby, Boyd (Watkin), Alsop, O'Leary (Lacey).
Colchester U: Brown; Farley, Keith, Richard, Greene, Skelton, Duguid, Gregory D (Lock), Lua-Lua, McGavin, Dozzell.

Tamworth (1) 2 *(Haughton 8, Hallam 75)*
Bury (1) 2 *(Bullock 1, Littlejohn 68)* 2743
Tamworth: Acton; Warner, Mutchell, Grocutt, Hatton, Foy, Gray, Colley, Hallam, Haughton, Wolsey.
Bury: Kenny; Billy, Woodward (Barrick), Daws, Swailes C, Redmond (Williams), Bullock, Littlejohn, Bhutia (Lawson), Reid, Preece.

Torquay U (0) 1 *(O'Brien 75)*
Southend U (0) 0 2520
Torquay U: Southall; Tully, Nichols, Thomas, Russell, Watson, Brandon, Hill, Bedeau (Griffiths), Williams (Donaldson), O'Brien.
Southend U: Capleton; Booty (Kerrigan), Jones N (Morley), Beard, Roget, Coleman, Connelly, Tinkler, Carruthers, Tolson (Campbell), Houghton.

Whyteleafe (0) 0
Chester C (0) 0 2164
Whyteleafe: Rose; Alger, Golley, Arkwright, McKay, Ahmet, Fisher, Howland, Thornton, Lunn (George), Scott (Milton).
Chester C: Brown; Moss, Doughty, Richardson, Lancaster, Woods, Nash (Jones), Milosavljevic, Wright, Beckett, Fisher (Shelton).

Wrexham (0) 1 *(Roberts N 85 (pen))*
Kettering T (0) 1 *(Brown 48)* 2701
Wrexham: Dearden; McGregor, Hardy (Morrell), Owen, Carey, Barrett (Russell), Connolly, Ferguson, Spink, Roberts N, Faulconbridge (Stevens).
Kettering T: Sollitt; Diuk, Adams, Brown, Vowden, Norman, Fisher (Banya), Ridgway, McNamara, Hudson (Hopkins), Setchell.

Wycombe W (0) 1 *(Simpson 67)*
Oxford C (0) 1 *(Pierson 87)* 2963
Wycombe W: Taylor; Rogers, Beeton, Ryan, Cousins, Bates, Brown (Harkin), Simpson, McSporran (Emblen), Devine, Baird.
Oxford C: Foster; Thorp, Dark, Pierson, Hayward, Sweeney, Lee (Whitehead), Hulbert (Emsden), McCleary, Davy, Wimble (Strong).

31 OCT

Barnet (0) 0
Burnley (0) 1 *(Cook 74)* 2563
Barnet: Harrison; Gledhill (Strevens), Hackett, Brown (Barnes), Heald (Basham), Arber, Searle, Doolan, Charlery, McGleish, Toms.
Burnley: Crichton; West, Smith (Armstrong), Mellon, Davis (Jepson), Thomas, Little, Cook, Cooke, Payton (Lee), Mullin.

Bristol R (0) 0
Preston NE (0) 1 *(McKenna 52)* 6145
Bristol R: Jones; Pethick, Challis (Ellington), Foster, Thomson, Tillson, Mauge (Penrice), Hillier, Zabek, Cureton (Zamora), Roberts.
Preston NE: Moilanen; Alexander, Edwards, Murdock, Jackson, Gregan, Cartwright, Rankine, Nogan, Macken (Gunnlaugsson), McKenna.

Hartlepool U (0) 1 *(Jones 90)*
Millwall (0) 0 2847
Hartlepool U: Hollund; Westwood, Shilton, Barron, Lee, Clark, Knowles, Miller, Jones, Freestone, Stephenson.
Millwall: Warner; Bircham, Ryan, Cahill, Nethercott, Fitzgerald, Ifill, Reid, Shaw (Harris), Sadlier, Neill.

2 NOV

Merthyr T (0) 2 *(Mitchell 50, 84)*
Stalybridge C (2) 2 *(Parr 9, Sullivan 42)* 871
Merthyr T: Thomas; Regan, Power, Abraham, Lima, Walker (Carter), Price, Griffith, Sloane (Mitchell), Needs, Ramasut.
Stalybridge C: Ingham; Ward, Scott, Ogley, Johnston, Bauress, Williamson, Parr, Steele, Jones, Sullivan (Filson).

FIRST ROUND REPLAYS

8 NOV

Hednesford T (1) 1 *(Lake 44)*
Aldershot T (0) 2 *(Chewins 68, Abbott 87)* 1719
Hednesford T: Morgan; Evans, Colkin (Goodwin), Comyn, Brindley, Robinson, Kimmins, Norman, Davis, Lake, O'Connor.
Aldershot T: Pape; Coll, Chewins, Adedeji, Pearce, Fielder, Sugrue (Gell), Bentley, Abbott, Bassey (Nartey), Hathaway.

9 NOV

Bournemouth (1) 4 *(Fletcher S 44, 67, Stein 89, Robinson 90 (pen))*
Notts Co (0) 2 *(Redmile 78, Tierney 84)* 4026
Bournemouth: Ovendale; Young, Warren, Hayter, Cox, Fletcher C, Jorgensen, Robinson, Stein, Fletcher S, Watson (Mean).
Notts Co: Ward; Holmes (Rapley), Blackmore, Liburd, Redmile, Richardson, Owers, Ramage, Murray, Dyer, Hughes (Tierney).

Brighton & HA (1) 3 *(Rogers 9, Watson 63, Mayo 88)*
Peterborough U (0) 0 5612
Brighton & HA: Walton; Watson, Campbell, McPherson, Cullip, Carr, Thomas (Cameron), Rogers, Hart (Ramsay), Oatway, Aspinall (Mayo).
Peterborough U: Tyler; Hooper, Drury, Gill, Wicks, Edwards, Shields, Davies (Jelleyman), Clarke, Forinton, Etherington.

Bury (0) 2 *(Billy 86, James 95)*
Tamworth (1) 1 *(Haughton 15)* 2531
Bury: Kenny; Billy, Williams, Daws, Swailes C, Redmond (Woodward), Bullock, Littlejohn, Lawson, Barnes (Bhutia), Reid (James).
Tamworth: Acton; Warner, Mutchell, Grocutt, Hatton, Gray (Howard), Foy, Colley, Hallam, Haughton (Smith), Wolsey (Cotter).
(aet)

Cardiff C (1) 3 *(Brazier 22, Perrett 51, Nugent 54)*
Leyton Orient (1) 1 *(Smith 2)* 3095
Cardiff C: Hallworth; Faerber, Legg, Perrett, Eckhardt, Ford, Hill (Boland), Carpenter, Bowen, Nugent (Roberts), Brazier.
Leyton Orient: Barrett; Joseph M, Lockwood, Walschaerts (Ling), Smith, Clark, Downer, Ampadu, Watts, Simba (Inglethorpe), Brkovic (Christie).

Chester C (1) 3 *(Cross 35, 52, Beckett 48)*
Whyteleafe (1) 1 *(Lunn 8)* 2183
Chester C: Brown; Moss (Nash), Doughty, Milosavljevic, Malone (Lancaster), Shelton, Wright, Richardson, Cross, Beckett, Fisher.
Whyteleafe: Rose; Alger, Howland, Golley, Arkwright, McKay (Elliott), Ahmet (George), Fisher, Scott (Milton), Lunn, Thornton.

Gillingham (2) 3 *(Thomson 24, Pennock 41, McGlinchey 77)*
Cheltenham T (0) 2 *(Milton 56, Howarth 70)* 4352
Gillingham: Bartram; Pennock, McGlinchey, Smith, Ashby, Butters, Hodge, Saunders (Nosworthy), Thomson (Hessenthaler), Edge, Taylor (Lewis).
Cheltenham T: Book; Duff, Victory, Banks, Freeman, Brough (Grayson), Howells, McAuley, Milton, Howarth, Yates.

Hull C (3) 4 *(Eyre 3, 61, Greaves 7, Brown 29)*
Macclesfield T (0) 0 4844
Hull C: Bracey; Goodison, Harper, Edwards, Greaves, Morgan, D'Auria (Schofield), Brabin (Whittle), Brown (Wood), Whitmore, Eyre.
Macclesfield T: Martin; Ingram, Rioch, Collins, Tinson (Abbey), Sedgemore, Askey, Priest, Barker (Whittaker), Davies, Durkan (Tomlinson).

Oxford C (1) 1
Wycombe W (0) 1 2586
Abandoned after extra time; fire.

Plymouth Arg (0) 2 *(McGregor 67, 112)*
Brentford (0) 1 *(Quinn 82)* 5409
Plymouth Arg: Veysey; Ashton (Bastow), Beswetherick, Leadbitter (McCall), Heathcote, Taylor, Barrett, O'Sullivan, McGregor, Hargreaves, Stonebridge.
Brentford: Woodman; Boxall, Rowlands (Folan), Quinn, Powell, Marshall, Agyemang (Partridge), Mahon, Owusu, Warner (Bryan), Scott.
(aet)

Rochdale (1) 3 *(Platt 5, Peake 48, Dowe 82)*
Burton A (0) 0 2633
Rochdale: Edwards; Evans, Stokes, Peake (Flitcroft), Monington, Bayliss, Jones, Ford (Carden), Platt, Holt (Dowe), Atkinson.
Burton A: Goodwin; Davies, March, Glasser, Blount, Forsyth (George), Stride, Anderson, Thomas (Webster), Clough, Holmes (Lyons).

Stalybridge C (2) 3 *(Bauress 2 (pen), Pickford 24, Sullivan 86)*
Merthyr T (1) 1 *(Lima 3)* 1399
Stalybridge C: Ingham; Ward, Scott, Ogley, Johnston (Filson), Bauress, Pickford, Parr, Steele, Jones (Sullivan), Williamson.
Merthyr T: Thomas; Evans (Sloane), Power (Ryan), Needs, Lima, Walker, Price, Griffith, Mitchell, Carter (Shepherd), Ramasut.

10 NOV

Kettering T (0) 0
Wrexham (2) 2 *(Roberts S 11, Williams 22)* 2611
Kettering T: Sollitt; Diuk (Shutt), Adams, Cox, Vowden, Norman (Ridgway), Fisher, Brown, Hudson, McNamara, Setchell.
Wrexham: Dearden; McGregor, Hardy, Owen, Carey, Roberts S, Williams, Ferguson, Connolly, Roberts N, Russell.

16 NOV

Oxford C (0) 0
Wycombe W (0) 1 *(Brown 51)* 4004
Oxford C: Foster; Morisey (McCleary), Dark, Pierson, Hayward, Smart, Lee, Sweeney, Wimble, Strong (Hulbert), Davy.
Wycombe W: Taylor; Lawrence, Rogers, Ryan (Bulman), Bates, Beeton, Carroll, Simpson, McSporran (Emblen), Devine, Brown.

SECOND ROUND

19 NOV

Luton T (0) 2 *(Doherty 63, 84)*
Lincoln C (1) 2 *(Gordon 14, Barnett D 81)* 4291
Luton T: Abbey; Fraser, Taylor, Watts, Doherty, Johnson, George, McLaren, Douglas, Locke (Sodje), Spring.
Lincoln C: Richardson; Fleming, Bimson, Finnigan, Barnett D, Henry, Smith (Phillips), Miller, Gordon (Stant), Thorpe, Gain.

20 NOV

Blackpool (0) 2 *(Clarkson 69, Durnin 73)*
Hendon (0) 0 2975
Blackpool: Caig; Bryan, Hills, Bushell, Carlisle, Hughes, Coid (Forsyth), Clarkson, Murphy, Lee (Bent), Durnin (Nowland).
Hendon: McCann; White, Clarke, Daly, Towler, Fitzgerald, Guentchev, Hyatt, Whitmarsh (Sakala), McKoy (Maran), Gentle.

Bournemouth (0) 0
Bristol C (1) 2 *(Murray 21, 53)* 5223
Bournemouth: Ovendale; Young, Warren (Watson), Broadhurst, Cox, Day, Jorgensen, Robinson, Stein, Fletcher S, Fletcher C.
Bristol C: Mercer; Murray, Bell, Holland, Millen, Taylor, Testimitanu (Hutchings), Mortimer, Jones, Beadle, Tinnion.

Burnley (0) 2 *(Cook 67, Mullin 75)*
Rotherham U (0) 0 8110
Burnley: Crichton; West, Armstrong (Branch), Mellon, Davis, Thomas, Little, Cook (Jepson), Cooke (Lee), Payton, Mullin.
Rotherham U: Pollitt; Varty, Scott, Dillon, Wilsterman, Garner, Berry (Martindale), Watson, Fortune-West (Sedgwick), Warne, Thompson (Hurst).

Bury (0) 0
Cardiff C (0) 0 2603
Bury: Kenny; Billy, Woodward, Daws, Swailes C, Redmond, Bullock, Littlejohn, Lawson (Bhutia), Preece, James (Swailes D).
Cardiff C: Hallworth; Faerber, Legg, Perrett, Eckhardt, Ford, Carpenter, Bonner, Bowen, Roberts, Brazier.

Cambridge U (0) 1 *(Butler 71 (pen))*
Bamber Bridge (0) 0 3303
Cambridge U: Van Heusden; Mustoe, Ashbee, McNeil, Joseph, Wilson, Wanless, Kyd (Taylor), Butler, Benjamin, MacKenzie.
Bamber Bridge: Dootson; Brown, Bryson, Jones, Baldwin, Cliff, Smith (Turner), Aspinall, Greenwood, Whittaker, Carroll (Vickers).

Exeter C (2) 2 *(Alexander 32, Flack 35)*
Aldershot T (0) 0 4151
Exeter C: Naylor; Richardson, Power, Buckle (Dewhurst), Curran, Gittens, Robinson, Rees, Alexander (Speakman), Flack, Boylan (Holloway).
Aldershot T: Pape; Coll, Chewins, Adedeji, Pearce (Nartey), Fielder, Sugrue (Bell), Bentley, Abbott, Gell, Hathaway.

Gillingham (2) 3 *(Butters 17, Taylor 43, 47)*
Darlington (0) 1 *(Duffield 55)* 5168
Gillingham: Bartram; Pennock, McGlinchey, Saunders (Nosworthy), Ashby, Butters, Southall, Lewis, Butler, Edge, Taylor.
Darlington: Samways; Liddle, Heckingbottom, Aspin, Tutill, Himsworth, Gray, Oliver, Duffield, Nogan (Hyorth), Heaney (Naylor).
Darlington progressed to Third Round as 'Lucky Losers'.

Hayes (1) 2 *(Charles 21, 63 (pen))*
Hull C (1) 2 *(Roddis 4 (og), Edwards 56)* 2749
Hayes: Gothard; Boyce, Watts, Bunce, Goodliffe, Flynn, McKimm, Roddis, Moore (Telemaque), Trebble (Spencer), Charles.
Hull C: Wilson; Harper, Goodison, Morgan (Whittle), Greaves, Edwards, D'Auria, Brabin, Brown, Whitmore (Alcide), Wood.

Ilkeston T (1) 1 *(Eshelby 18)*
Rushden & D (0) 1 *(De Souza 51)* 2737
Ilkeston T: Beattie; Fairclough, Wright, Middleton, Fearon, Knapper, Eshelby (Hurst), Clifford, Raynor (Ludlum), Helliwell, Moore.
Rushden & D: Turley; Wooding, Rodwell, McElhatton, Peters, Warburton, Butterworth, Brady (Town), De Souza, Collins, Underwood.

Oldham Ath (1) 1 *(Whitehall 45)*
Swansea C (0) 0 4332
Oldham Ath: Kelly; McNiven S, Holt, Garnett, Rickers, Duxbury, Dudley, Sheridan, Allott, Whitehall, Graham.
Swansea C: Freestone; Jones S, Howard, Cusack, Smith, Bound, Appleby (Boyd), Lacey, Alsop, Watkin, Coates.

Plymouth Arg (0) 0
Brighton & HA (0) 0 7414
Plymouth Arg: Sheffield; McCall (Bastow), Beswetherick, Leadbitter, Heathcote, Taylor, Barrett (Belgrave), O'Sullivan, McGregor, Hargreaves.
Brighton & HA: Walton; Watson, Campbell, McPherson, Cullip, Carr (Hobson), Freeman, Rogers, Cameron (Thomas), Oatway, Aspinall (Mayo).

Preston NE (0) 0
Enfield (0) 0 11,566
Preston NE: Lucas; Alexander, Edwards, Kidd, Jackson, Gregan, Cartwright (Nogan), Rankine, Gunnlaugsson, Mathie (Macken), Eyres.
Enfield: John; Annon, Morgan, Cooper (Southgate), Witter (Protheroe), Brown, Deadman, Jones, Bunn, Moran, Dunwell.

Reading (0) 1 *(Caskey 75 (pen))*
Halifax T (0) 1 *(Mitchell 60)*   5918
Reading: Whitehead; Gurney, Polston, Bernal, Hunter (Grant), Parkinson, Murty (Gray), Caskey, Williams M (McIntyre), Forster, Evers.
Halifax T: Butler L; Wilder, Bradshaw, Mitchell, Stoneman, Lucas, Paterson, Clarke, Rowe (Newton), Painter, Butler P.

Shrewsbury T (1) 2 *(Kerrigan 8, 54)*
Oxford U (0) 2 *(Murphy 63, Folland 77)*   3357
Shrewsbury T: Edwards; Seabury, Hanmer, Tretton, Wilding, Hughes, Rigby, Kerrigan, Steele (Jagielka), Brown, Murray (Tolley).
Oxford U: Lundin; Robinson, McGowan, Whelan, Watson, Folland, Lilley (Anthrobus), Tait, Murphy, Lambert (Cook), Beauchamp.

Stalybridge C (1) 1 *(Scott 8)*
Chester C (1) 2 *(Cross 45, Beckett 69)*   3312
Stalybridge C: Ingham; Ward, Scott, Ogley, Johnston, Bauress, Pickford (Mason), Parr, Steele, Jones (Philson), Williamson (Sullivan).
Chester C: Brown; Moss, Doughty, Reid, Milosavljevic (Woods), Spooner, Richardson (Shelton), Nash, Cross, Beckett, Fisher.

Wrexham (1) 2 *(Roberts N 15, Faulconbridge 88)*
Rochdale (1) 1 *(Atkinson 33)*   3408
Wrexham: Dearden; McGregor, Hardy (Ridler), Owen, Carey, Roberts S, Williams, Ferguson (Faulconbridge), Connolly, Roberts N, Russell (Gibson).
Rochdale: Edwards; Evans, Stokes, Peake, Monington, Bayliss, Jones, Ford (Bettney), Platt, Ellis, Atkinson (Flitcroft).

Wycombe W (1) 2 *(Devine 20, Ryan 90)*
Wigan Ath (1) 2 *(Haworth 45, 61)*   2992
Wycombe W: Taylor; Lawrence (Emblen), Rogers (Cousins), Ryan, Bates, Beeton, Carroll, Simpson, McSporran, Devine, Brown.
Wigan Ath: Stillie; Bradshaw (Sharp), Green, McGibbon, Balmer, Griffiths, O'Neill, Kilford, Haworth, Martinez (Sheridan), Barlow.

21 NOV

Forest Green R (0) 0
Torquay U (0) 3 *(Brandon 77, Hill 81, Donaldson 87)*   2962
Forest Green R: Perrin; Hedges, Hatswell, Clark, Kilgour (Randall), Burns, Daley, Sykes, McGregor, Mehew (Hunt), Cook (Bailey).
Torquay U: Southall; Holmes, Herrera, Thomas, Russell, Watson, Brandon, Hill, Bedeau (Simb), Williams (Donaldson), O'Brien (Aggrey).

Hereford U (0) 1 *(Elms 54)*
Hartlepool U (0) 0   4914
Hereford U: Jones; Lane, Sturgess, Snape, Wright, James, Parry, Taylor, Elms (May), Williams (Rodgerson), Fewings.
Hartlepool U: Hollund; Knowles, Shilton, Barron, Lee, Vindheim (Stephenson), Mason (Henderson), Miller, Jones (Clark), Freestone, Westwood.

SECOND ROUND REPLAYS

30 NOV

Brighton & HA (0) 1 *(Cullip 63)*
Plymouth Arg (1) 2 *(Bastow 9, Hargreaves 65)*   5710
Brighton & HA: Walton; Watson, Johnson, Hobson, Crosby, Cullip, Freeman (Mayo), Rogers, Cameron (Ramsay), Oatway, Thomas.
Plymouth Arg: Sheffield; O'Sullivan, Beswetherick, Leadbitter, Heathcote, Taylor, Barrett, Bastow, McGregor (Phillips), Hargreaves, Stonebridge.

Cardiff C (0) 1 *(Ford 120)*
Bury (0) 0   4511
Cardiff C: Hallworth; Faerber, Legg, Perrett, Eckhardt, Ford, Carpenter, Bonner (Fowler), Bowen (Boland), Roberts (Thomas), Brazier.
Bury: Kenny; Woodward, Williams, Daws, Swailes C, Redmond, Swailes D, Bullock, Lawson (Bhutia), Barnes, Barrick (James) (Collins).
(aet)

Enfield (0) 0
Preston NE (0) 3 *(Eyres 52, Alexander 60 (pen), Gunnlaugsson 83)*   1808
Enfield: John; Annon, Protheroe, Morgan, Cooper (Tomlinson), Brown (Southgate), Deadman, Jones, Bunn (Alleyne), Rattray, Dunwell.
Preston NE: Moilanen; Alexander, Edwards, Kidd, Jackson (Murdock), Gregan, Appleton, Darby, Nogan, Macken (Mathie), Eyres (Gunnlaugsson).
(at St Albans)

Halifax T (0) 0
Reading (0) 1 *(Caskey 64 (pen))*   2156
Halifax T: Butler L; Wilder, Jules, Mitchell, Stansfield, Williams (Bradshaw), Paterson, Gaughan, Tate, Painter, Butler P (Lucas).
Reading: Howie; Gurney, Polston, Bernal, Primus, Parkinson, Murty, Caskey, McIntyre, Forster (Williams M), Evers (Grant).

Hull C (0) 3 *(Brown 49, Edwards 97, Wood 112)*
Hayes (0) 2 *(Gallen 78, Charles 114)*   5947
Hull C: Bracey; Harper, Greaves (Goodison), Edwards, Whittle, Whitney, Schofield, Joyce, Brown, Whitmore (Harris), Wood.
Hayes: Gothard; Boyce, Flynn (Gallen), Watts, Bunce, Goodliffe, McKimm (Onwere), Charles, Trebble, Moore, Spencer (Telmaque).
(aet)

Lincoln C (0) 0
Luton T (0) 1 *(Douglas 85)*   3822
Lincoln C: Richardson; Fleming, Bimson, Finnigan, Barnett D, Henry, Smith (Stant), Miller, Gordon, Thorpe, Gain (Philpott).
Luton T: Abbey; Fraser, Taylor, Watts, Doherty, Johnson, George, McLaren (Locke), Douglas, Sodje, Spring.

Oxford U (0) 2 *(Murphy 90, 117)*
Shrewsbury T (1) 1 *(Jagielka 27)*   4096
Oxford U: Lundin; Robinson, Powell (Cook), Whelan, Watson, Davis, Lilley (Lambert), Tait (Folland), Murphy, Anthrobus, Beauchamp.
Shrewsbury T: Edwards; Seabury, Hanmer, Tretton, Wilding, Hughes, Murray (Tolley), Jagielka, Steele (Rodgers), Jobling (Whelan), Brown.
(aet)

Rushden & D (2) 5 *(Wooding 2, Town 17, Collins 86)*
Ilkeston T (0) 0   4226
Rushden & D: Turley; Wooding, Burgess, McElhatton, Rodwell, Warburton, Butterworth, Brady, Town (Heggs), Collins, Underwood.
Ilkeston T: Beattie; Fairclough, Wright (Clifford), Middleton, Fearon, Knapper, Eshelby, Hemmings, Helliwell, Moore, Raynor.

Wigan Ath (1) 2 *(Liddell 28, Haworth 80)*
Wycombe W (1) 1 *(Baird 23)*   3967
Wigan Ath: Carroll; Green, Sharp, McGibbon, Balmer, De Zeeuw, O'Neill, Kilford (Martinez), Haworth, Liddell, Barlow.
Wycombe W: Taylor; Lawrence, Vinnicombe, Ryan, Cousins (Harkin), Bates, Carroll (Brown), Simpson, McSporran, Devine, Baird.

THIRD ROUND

10 DEC

Cambridge U (0) 2 *(Benjamin 75, Wanless 81)*
Crystal Palace (0) 0 5631
Cambridge U: Marshall; Kavanagh, Ashbee, McNeil, Joseph, Wilson, Wanless, Taylor, Butler, Benjamin, MacKenzie.
Crystal Palace: Digby; Austin, Frampton (Woozley), Zhiyi, Foster, Linighan, Mullins, Rodger, Svensson, Rizzo (Smith), McKenzie.

Nottingham F (1) 1 *(Freedman 39)*
Oxford U (0) 1 *(Powell 75)* 8079
Nottingham F: Beasant; Doig, Brennan, Hjelde, Scimeca, Bart-Williams, Prutton, Quashie, Freedman, John, Gray.
Oxford U: Lundin; Robinson, McGowan, Whelan, Watson, Folland (Powell), Lilley, Weatherstone R (Fear), Murphy, Anthrobus (Cook), Beauchamp.

11 DEC

Aston Villa (1) 2 *(Carbone 43, Dublin 63)*
Darlington (0) 1 *(Heckingbottom 71)* 22,101
Aston Villa: James; Delaney, Wright, Southgate, Ehiogu, Barry, Taylor, Carbone (Joachim), Dublin, Merson, Thompson (Stone).
Darlington: Samways; Liddle, Heckingbottom, Gray (Reed), Tutill, Aspin, Heaney, Oliver, Duffield, Nogan (Hyorth), Atkinson (Brumwell).

Charlton Ath (0) 2 *(Kinsella 48, 61)*
Swindon T (0) 1 *(Gooden 54)* 10,939
Charlton Ath: Kiely; Shields, Powell, Brown, Rufus, Todd (Jones), Newton, Kinsella, Hunt, Mendonca, Salako (Youds).
Swindon T: Mildenhall; Robinson, Hall (Davies), Leitch, Davis (Griffin), Willis, Williams A (Hay), Collins, Onuora, Quinn, Gooden.

Crewe Alex (0) 1 *(Little 75)*
Bradford C (0) 2 *(Blake 53, Saunders 83)* 6571
Crewe Alex: Kearton; Wright D, Smith S, Bignot, Macauley, Street, Little (Collins), Lunt, Cramb, Tait, Sorvel.
Bradford C: Clarke; Halle (Saunders), Myers, McCall, Wetherall, O'Brien, Lawrence, Redfearn, Mills, Blake, Beagrie (Sharpe).

Derby Co (0) 0
Burnley (0) 1 *(Cooke 62)* 23,400
Derby Co: Poom; Borbokis (Beck), Dorigo, Elliott, Carbonari, Nimni (Burton), Burley, Sturridge, Delap, Kinkladze (Johnson), Powell.
Burnley: Crichton; West, Armstrong (Jepson), Mellon, Davis, Thomas, Little, Cook (Johnrose), Cooke, Payton (Branch), Mullin.

Exeter C (0) 0
Everton (0) 0 6045
Exeter C: Naylor (Matthews); Richardson, Power, Buckle, Curran, Gittens, Dewhurst, Rees, Alexander, Breslan (Flack), Boylan (McConnell).
Everton: Gerrard; Weir, Unsworth, Pembridge (Moore), Dunne, Xavier, Collins, Barmby (Ball), Campbell, Hutchison, Jeffers.

Fulham (2) 2 *(Horsfield 11, Davis 14)*
Luton T (1) 2 *(George 6, Spring 82)* 8251
Fulham: Taylor; Finnan, Brevett, Melville, Coleman, Symons, Davis (Collins), Clark, Horsfield, Hayles, Hayward (Trollope).
Luton T: Abbey; Fraser, Taylor, Watts, Doherty, Johnson, George, Locke, Douglas, Sodje, Spring.

Grimsby T (1) 3 *(Livingstone 34, 89, Allen 90)*
Stockport Co (0) 2 *(Bailey 63, Moore 81)* 3400
Grimsby T: Croudson; Butterfield (McDermott), Gallimore, Smith R, Lever, Coldicott (Pouton), Donovan, Buckley, Livingstone, Lester (Allen), Groves.
Stockport Co: Nash; Connelly, Nicholson, Dinning, Flynn, Bennett (Woodthorpe), Cooper, Moore, Bailey, Gannon, Bergersen (Allen).

Hereford U (0) 0
Leicester C (0) 0 7795
Hereford U: Jones; Lane, Sturgess, Wright, James, Parry, Elmes, Taylor, Fowings (Rodgerson), Snape, Williams.
Leicester C: Flowers; Impey, Guppy, Elliott, Taggart, Sinclair (Walsh), Lennon, Izzet, Cottee, Savage, Heskey.

Hull C (1) 1 *(Brown 38)*
Chelsea (2) 6 *(Poyet 8, 49, 58, Sutton 30, Di Matteo 47, Edwards 90 (og))* 10,279
Hull C: Bracey; Harper, Goodison, Edwards, Whittle, Whitney, Schofield (Morgan), Joyce, Brown (Eyre), Whitmore, Wood.
Chelsea: De Goey; Ferrer, Harley, Deschamps (Morris), Leboeuf, Hogh (Terry), Poyet, Di Matteo, Sutton, Zola (Flo), Wise.

Norwich C (0) 1 *(Llewellyn 66)*
Coventry C (0) 3 *(Whelan 58, Roussel 76, Eustace 84)* 15,702
Norwich C: Marshall A; Sutch, Fuglestad, de Blasiis, Fleming, Jackson, Anselin (Kenton), Dalglish (Forbes), Roberts, Russell, Llewellyn.
Coventry C: Hedman; Telfer, Froggatt, Williams (Eustace), Breen, Chippo, Whelan (Roussel), Palmer, Keane, McAllister, Hadji.

Preston NE (1) 2 *(Macken 6, Alexander 69 (pen))*
Oldham Ath (0) 1 *(Adams 85)* 9940
Preston NE: Moilanen; Alexander, Edwards, Kidd, Jackson, Gregan, Darby (Diaf), Rankine, Gunnlaugsson (Nogan), Macken (Mathie), Eyres.
Oldham Ath: Kelly; McNiven S, Holt, Garnett, Rickers, Duxbury, Adams, Sheridan, Allott (Tipton), Whitehall (Dudley), Hotte.

QPR (1) 1 *(Wardley 9)*
Torquay U (0) 1 *(O'Brien 82)* 8843
QPR: Harper (Miklosko); Breacker, Baraclough, Darlington, Plummer, Bruce, Langley, Murray, Steiner, Wardley, Kiwomya (Koejoe).
Torquay U: Southall; Holmes, Herrera (Griffiths), Aggrey, Russell, Thomas, Brandon (Platts), Hill, Bedeau, Donaldson, O'Brien.

Reading (1) 1 *(McIntyre 37)*
Plymouth Arg (0) 1 *(Hargreaves 82)* 8536
Reading: Howie; Gurney (Sarr), Polston, Bernal, Primus, Parkinson, Murty, Caskey, Williams M (Scott), McIntyre, Evers (Grant).
Plymouth Arg: Sheffield; O'Sullivan, Beswetherick, Wotton, Heathcote, Barrett, McCarthy (Gritton), Bastow, McGregor, Hargreaves, Stonebridge.

Sheffield W (1) 1 *(Booth 24)*
Bristol C (0) 0 11,644
Sheffield W: Srnicek; Atherton, Hinchcliffe (McKeever), Jonk (Sibon), Emerson, Walker, Alexandersson, Booth, De Bilde (Quinn), Nolan, Sonner.
Bristol C: Mercer; Lavin (Jones), Bell, Holland, Millen, Taylor, Testimitanu (Murray), Hutchings, Torpey, Beadle, Tinnion.

Sunderland (1) 1 *(McCann 24)*
Portsmouth (0) 0 26,535
Sunderland: Sorensen; Makin, Gray, Roy (Thirlwell), Bould, Butler P, Summerbee, Schwarz, Quinn, Phillips, McCann.
Portsmouth: Flahavan; Hiley, Robinson, Moore (Crowe), Cundy, Awford, Panopoulos, Miglioranzi (Claridge), Bradbury, Whittingham, Vlachos.

Tranmere R (1) 1 *(Henry 21)*
West Ham U (0) 0 13,629
Tranmere R: Murphy; Hazell, Roberts, Henry, Morgan, Challinor, Mahon, Parkinson, Jones G, Allison, Kelly (Taylor S).
West Ham U: Hislop; Potts (Kitson), Minto, Lomas, Ferdinand, Ruddock, Lampard, Cole, Sinclair, Di Canio (Wanchope), Foe.

Walsall (0) 1 *(Robins 75 (pen))*
Gillingham (1) 1 *(Southall 27)* 4314
Walsall: Walker; Marsh, Padula, Viveash, Roper, Keates, Wrack, Robins, Rammell (Eyjolfsson), Larusson, Matias (Ricketts).
Gillingham: Bartram; Southall, McGlinchey (Lewis), Smith, Ashby, Butters, Saunders, Hessenthaler, Nosworthy, Pennock, Edge.

Watford (0) 0
Birmingham C (0) 1 *(Rowett 66)* 8144
Watford: Chamberlain; Cox, Robinson, Hyde (Brooker), Page, Palmer, Wright (Gibbs), Miller, Ngonge, Wooter (Gudmundsson), Johnson.
Birmingham C: Poole; Bass, Charlton, Gill (Robinson), Rowett, Johnson M, Hyde, Holland, Purse, Hughes, Grainger.

WBA (0) 2 *(Hughes 66, Evans 80)*
Blackburn R (0) 2 *(Frandsen 65, Blake 70)* 10,609
WBA: Adamson; Burgess, Gabbidon (Evans), Raven, Sigurdsson, Carbon, Maresca, Sneekes, Quinn, Hughes, Kilbane.
Blackburn R: Kelly; Davidson, Harkness, Peacock, Dailly, Carsley (Johnson), McAteer, Frandsen, Ward, Blake, Grayson.

Wigan Ath (0) 0
Wolverhampton W (0) 1 *(Robinson 90)* 10,531
Wigan Ath: Carroll; Bradshaw, Sharp, Green, Balmer, De Zeeuw, O'Neill, Martinez, Haworth, Liddell, Peron.
Wolverhampton W: Oakes; Muscat, Naylor, Robinson, Curle, Pollet, Bazeley, Corica (Flo), Akinbiyi, Emblen, Sinton (Simpson).

Wimbledon (1) 1 *(Cort 34)*
Barnsley (0) 0 4505
Wimbledon: Sullivan; Cunningham, Kimble, Hreidarsson, Andersen, Roberts, Euell, Earle (Badir), Hartson (Hughes M), Cort, Gayle.
Barnsley: Miller; Bengtsson, Barker (Dyer), Morgan, Tuttle, Tinkler, Eaden, Hignett, Shipperley (Sheron), Thomas, Barnard (Parkin).

Wrexham (0) 2 *(Gibson 50, Ferguson 68)*
Middlesbrough (1) 1 *(Deane 42)* 11,755
Wrexham: Dearden; McGregor, Hardy, Roberts S (Ridler), Carey, Williams, Russell, Ferguson, Roberts N, Gibson (Owen), Faulconbridge (Connolly).
Middlesbrough: Schwarzer; Stamp, Ziege, Vickers, Festa, Pallister (Gavin), Mustoe, Gascoigne, Ricard, Deane, Juninho.

12 DEC

Chester C (1) 1 *(Richardson 27)*
Manchester C (1) 4 *(Goater 19, 89, Bishop 78, Doughty 90 (og))* 5469
Chester C: Brown; Moss, Doughty, Reid, Woods, Spooner, Nash (Berry), Richardson, Wright (Cross), Beckett, Fisher.
Manchester C: Weaver; Edghill, Granville (Jeff Whitley), Wiekens, Jobson, Horlock, Kennedy, Pollock, Peacock, Goater, Bishop.

Huddersfield T (0) 0
Liverpool (1) 2 *(Camara 36, Matteo 59)* 23,678
Huddersfield T: Vaesen; Jenkins, Vincent, Irons, Gray (Dyson), Armstrong, Thornley (Donis), Gorre, Stewart (Schofield), Sellars, Wijnhard.
Liverpool: Westerveld; Carragher, Staunton (Matteo), Hamann, Henchoz, Hyypia, Gerrard, Smicer (Song), Camara, Owen, Murphy.

Leeds U (0) 2 *(Bakke 61, 68)*
Port Vale (0) 0 11,912
Leeds: Martyn; Kelly, Harte, Woodgate, Radebe, Bakke, McPhail, Smith (Jones), Huckerby, Kewell, Bowyer (Bridges).
Port Vale: Musselwhite; Brisco, Tankard (Naylor), Burns, Snijders, Gardner, Rougier, Eyre, Foyle, Minton, Widdrington.

Sheffield U (1) 1 *(Bent 14)*
Rushden & D (1) 1 *(Brady 45)* 10,104
Sheffield U: Tracey; Ford, Quinn, Derry, Murphy, Woodhouse, Hunt (Smeets), Devlin, Bent, Smith (Katchuro), Ribeiro (Hamilton).
Rushden & D: Turley; Wooding, Burgess (De Souza), Rodwell, Warburton, McElhatton, Butterworth, Brady, Town (Heggs), Collins, Underwood.

Tottenham H (0) 1 *(Iversen 57)*
Newcastle U (0) 1 *(Speed 77)* 33,116
Tottenham H: Walker; Young, Edinburgh (Vega), Freund, Campbell, Perry, Fox, Nielsen, Iversen, Dominguez (Armstrong), Ginola.
Newcastle U: Harper; Barton, Pistone, Dabizas, Charvet, Helder (Glass), Dyer (Ketsbaia), Lee, Shearer, Ferguson (Gallacher), Speed.

13 DEC

Arsenal (1) 3 *(Grimandi 23, Adams 65, Overmars 89)*
Blackpool (1) 1 *(Clarkson 38)* 34,143
Arsenal: Manninger; Dixon, Silvinho, Grimandi, Luzhny, Adams, Ljungberg (Hughes), Petit, Suker (Kanu), Henry, Overmars.
Blackpool: Caig; Bardsley, Hills, Bushell, Carlisle, Hughes, Lee, Clarkson, Murphy, Nowland, Beesley.

Ipswich T (0) 0
Southampton (1) 1 *(Richards 40)* 14,383
Ipswich T: Wright R; Wilnis (Wright J), Clapham, Brown, Mowbray, McGreal, Holland, Stockwell (Naylor), Johnson (Axeldahl), Scowcroft, Magilton.
Southampton: Jones; Tessem, Bridge, Dodd, Lundekvam, Richards, Ripley, Soltvedt, Pahars, Hughes M (Beattie), Oakley.

21 DEC

Bolton W (1) 1 *(Gudjohnsen 29)*
Cardiff C (0) 0 5734
Bolton W: Banks; Holden, Whitlow, Passi, Bergsson, Fish, Johansen, Jensen, Gudjohnsen, Taylor (Aljofree), Gardner.
Cardiff C: Hallworth; Low, Legg (Faerber), Perrett, Eckhardt, Schwinkendorf (Hill), Fowler, Carpenter, Bowen, Humphreys, Ford (Middleton).

THIRD ROUND REPLAYS

21 DEC

Everton (0) 1 *(Barmby 85)*
Exeter C (0) 0 16,869
Everton: Gerrard; Cleland, Unsworth, Weir, Dunne, Pembridge, Collins, Barmby, Campbell, Hutchison, Jeffers.
Exeter C: Naylor; Richardson, Power, Buckle, Curran, Gittens, Dewhurst, Rees, Alexander, Robinson (Flack), Breslan (McConnell).

Luton T (0) 0
Fulham (0) 3 *(Hayles 57, 60, Hayward 63)* 8170
Luton T: Abbey; Fraser (Boyce), Taylor, Watts, Doherty, Johnson, George, McLaren, Douglas, Locke, Spring.
Fulham: Taylor; Finnan, Brevett, Morgan, Melville (Trollope), Symons, Collins, Clark, Horsfield, Hayles, Hayward.

Plymouth Arg (0) 0 *(Heathcote 88)*
Reading (0) 0 8965
Plymouth Arg: Veysey; O'Sullivan, Beswetherick, Leadbitter, Heathcote, Barrett, McCarthy (Gritton), Bastow, McGregor, Hargreaves, Stonebridge.
Reading: Howey; Gurney, Polston, Parkinson, Primus, Casper, Murty, Caskey, Williams, Scott (Brayson), Smith.

Rushden & D (0) 1 *(Warburton 105)*
Sheffield U (0) 1 *(Derry 103)* 6010
Rushden & D: Turley; Wooding, Burgess (Hamsher), Rodwell, Warburton, McElhatton, Butterworth, Brady, Town (De Souza), Collins, Underwood.
Sheffield U: Tracey; Kozluk, Quinn, Derry, Murphy, Sandford, Hunt (Katchuro), Devlin, Bent, Smith (Hamilton), Woodhouse.
aet; Sheffield U won 6-5 on penalties.

Torquay U (0) 2 *(Bedeau 52, Thomas 80)*
QPR (0) 3 *(Wardley 56, 74, Kiwomya 71)* 5232
Torquay U: Southall; Tully (Griffiths), Holmes, Aggrey, Russell, Thomas, Brandon (Platts), Hill, Bedeau, Williams (Simb), O'Brien.
QPR: Harper (Miklosko); Breacker, Bruce, Darlington, Plummer, Kulcsar, Langley, Murray, Koejoe (Weare), Wardley, Kiwomya.

22 DEC

Blackburn R (0) 2 *(Duff 94, Carsley 114 (pen))*
WBA (0) 0 11,766
Blackburn R: Kelly; Kenna, Davidson, Taylor, Dailly, Carsley, McAteer (Johnson), Frandsen, Ward, Blake (Ostenstad), Duff.
WBA: Miller; Gabbidon, Van Blerk, Oliver, Raven, Carbon, De Freitas (McDermott), Sneekes, Evans (Richards), Hughes, Angel.
(aet)

Leicester C (0) 2 *(Elliott 78, Izzet 104)*
Hereford U (1) 1 *(Fewings 40)* 12,157
Leicester C: Arphexad; Savage, Oakes, Elliott, Taggart, Gilchrist, Gunnlaugsson (Fenton), Izzet, Cottee, Walsh (Impey), Zagorakis (Campbell).
Hereford U: Jones; Lane, Sturgess, Snape, Wright, James, Parry, Taylor, Elmes (May), Williams, Fewings (Rodgerson).
(aet)

Newcastle U (3) 6 *(Speed 5, Dabizas 27, Ferguson 45, Dyer 73, Shearer 83 (pen), 85)*
Tottenham H (1) 1 *(Ginola 34)* 35,415
Newcastle U: Harper; Barton, Hughes, Dabizas, Helder (Marcelino), Solano, Lee, Gallacher (Dyer), Shearer, Ferguson (Ketsbaia), Speed.
Tottenham H: Walker; Young (Fox) (Armstrong), Taricco, Vega, Campbell, Perry, Nielsen, Sherwood, Iversen, Clemence, Ginola (Dominguez).

8 JAN

Gillingham (1) 2 *(Barras 38 (og), Thomson 100)*
Walsall (1) 1 *(Larusson 44)* 6538
Gillingham: Bartram; Southall, Edge, Smith, Ashby, Butters, Lewis, Hessenthaler, Thomson, Saunders (Butler), Nosworthy (Hodge).
Walsall: Walker; Marsh (Gadsby), Padula, Viveash, Barras, Keates (Bukran), Wrack (Rammell), Larusson, Robins, Ricketts, Matias.
(aet)

Oxford U (0) 1 *(Powell 72)*
Nottingham F (0) 3 *(Bart-Williams 81, 83 (pen), Rogers 89)* 7191
Oxford U: Lundin; Robinson, Powell, Cook, Watson, Whelan, Lilley (Arendse), Anthrobus, Murphy, Folland (Francis), Beauchamp.
Nottingham F: Beasant; Gray, Brennan, Williams (Rogers), Scimeca, Dawson, Prutton, Johnson, John, Harewood (Freedman), Bart-Williams.

FOURTH ROUND

8 JAN

Aston Villa (1) 1 *(Southgate 20)*
Southampton (0) 0 25,025
Aston Villa: James; Watson (Stone), Wright, Southgate, Ehiogu, Barry, Taylor, Boateng, Joachim (Vassell), Carbone, Merson (Hendrie).
Southampton: Jones; Dodd (Kachloul), Bridge, Marsden (Soltvedt), Lundekvam, Benali, Ripley, Tessem, Pahars (Hughes M), Davies, Boa Morte.

Charlton Ath (0) 1 *(MacDonald 68)*
QPR (0) 0 16,798
Charlton Ath: Kiely; Shields, Powell, Stuart, Brown, Todd, MacDonald (Lisbie), Kinsella, Hunt, Salako (Parker), Robinson (Newton).
QPR: Harper; Baraclough, Bruce, Darlington (Rowland), Plummer, Ward, Langley, Gallen (Dowie), Steiner, Wardley, Murray (Scully).

Coventry C (1) 3 *(Chippo 11, 69, Whelan 75)*
Burnley (0) 0 22,774
Coventry C: Hedman; Telfer (Gustafsson), Froggatt, Williams, Breen, Chippo, Hadji, Palmer (Eustace), Keane, McAllister, Roussel (Whelan).
Burnley: Crichton; West (Branch), Armstrong, Mellon, Davis, Thomas, Little, Cook, Cooke, Payton, Mullin.

Everton (0) 2 *(Unsworth 75 (pen), 90 (pen))*
Birmingham C (0) 0 25,405
Everton: Gerrard; Weir, Unsworth, Pembridge, Dunne (Watson), Gough, Collins, Barmby, Campbell, Hutchison, Jeffers (Gemmill).
Birmingham C: Bennett; Rowett, Charlton, Hughes, Holdsworth, Johnson M, Hyde, O'Connor, Marcelo (Lazaridis), Robinson (Newton), Grainger (Adebola).

Fulham (2) 3 *(Collins 22, 77, Finnan 25)*
Wimbledon (0) 0 16,877
Fulham: Taylor; Finnan, Morgan, Melville, Symons, Coleman, Collins, Clark, Horsfield, Hayles (Peschisolido), Ball.
Wimbledon: Sullivan; Cunningham, Francis (Gray), Hreidarsson, Willmott, Andersen, Andresen, Euell, Leaburn (Ardley), Cort, Gayle.

Grimsby T (0) 0
Bolton W (1) 2 *(Gudjohnsen 33, Hansen 54)* 4270
Grimsby T: Coyne; McDermott, Chapman (Butterfield), Livingstone, Lever, Coldicott, Donovan, Pouton, Ashcroft, Lester (Allen), Buckley (Black).
Bolton W: Banks; O'Kane, Whitlow, Passi, Fish, Ritchie, Johansen, Jensen, Gudjohnsen (Taylor), Hansen (Holden), Gardner (Aljofree).

Newcastle U (1) 4 *(Shearer 5, Dabizas 47, Ferguson 59, Gallacher 69)*
Sheffield U (1) 1 *(Smith 17)* 36,220
Newcastle U: Harper; Barton, Pistone (Domi), Dabizas, Marcelino, Solano, Dyer (Fumaca), Gallacher (Ketsbaia), Shearer, Ferguson, Speed.
Sheffield U: Tracey; Kozluk, Quinn (Ribeiro), Derry (Hamilton), Gysbrechts, Sandford, Ford, Hunt, Bent (Katchuro), Smith, Woodhouse.

Plymouth Arg (0) 0
Preston NE (1) 3 *(O'Sullivan 39 (og), Alexander 60 (pen), Beswetherick 77 (og))* 10,824
Plymouth Arg: Sheffield; McCall (Barrett), Beswetherick, Leadbitter, Heathcote, Taylor, McCarthy (Gritton), O'Sullivan, McGregor, Hargreaves.
Preston NE: Moilanen; Alexander, Edwards, Murdoch, Jackson, Gregan, Appleton, Rankine, Nogan (Gunnlaugsson), Macken (Beresford), Eyres.

Sheffield W (1) 1 *(Alexanderson 9)*
Wolverhampton W (0) 1 *(Sedgley 68)* 18,506
Sheffield W: Srnicek; Nolan (Scott), Hinchcliffe, Jonk (Donnelly), Atherton, Walker, Alexanderson, Sibon, De Bilde (Cresswell), Haslam, Sonner.
Wolverhampton W: Oakes; Muscat, Naylor, Robinson, Sedgley, Pollet, Bazeley, Emblen, Akinbiyi (Flo), Branch, Sinton.

Tranmere R (1) 1 *(Allison 25)*
Sunderland (0) 0 15,469
Tranmere R: Achterberg; Yates, Roberts, Henry, Hill, Challinor, Koumas (Mahon), Parkinson (Frail), Jones G, Allison, Kelly (Taylor S).
Sunderland: Sorensen; Makin, Gray, Roy, Bould (Craddock), Butler P, Summerbee, Rae, Phillips, Schwarz (Ready), McCann.

Wrexham (1) 1 *(Connolly 44)*
Cambridge U (1) 2 *(Benjamin 15, Butler 52)* 7186
Wrexham: Dearden; McGregor, Hardy, Carey (Spink), Ridler, Williams (Barrett), Connolly, Ferguson, Roberts N, Stevens (Faulconbridge), Russell.
Cambridge U: Marshall; Kavanagh, Ashbee, McNeil, Eustace, Wilson, Mustoe, Russell (Wanless), Butler, Benjamin (Guinan), MacKenzie.

9 JAN

Arsenal (0) 0
Leicester C (0) 0 35,710
Arsenal: Seaman; Dixon, Silvinho, Vieira, Keown, Grimandi, Ljungberg, Malz (Kanu), Suker, Henry, Petit.
Leicester C: Arphexad; Savage, Eadie, Sinclair, Taggart, Walsh, Lennon (Marshall), Oakes, Elliott, Zagorakis (Campbell), Heskey.

Manchester C (2) 2 *(Goater 2, Bishop 11)*
Leeds U (3) 5 *(Bakke 8, Smith 20, Kewell 4l, 88, Bowyer 66)* 29,240
Manchester C: Weaver; Edghill, Granville (Peacock), Wiekens, Jobson, Horlock, Kennedy, Grant (Jeff Whitley), Dickov, Goater, Bishop.
Leeds U: Martyn; Kelly, Harte, Woodgate, Radebe, Bakke, McPhail, Bowyer, Smith (Huckerby), Kewell, Wilcox.

10 JAN

Liverpool (0) 0
Blackburn R (0) 1 *(Blake 84)* 32,839
Liverpool: Westerveld; Carragher (Newby), Matteo, Hamann, Henchoz, Hyypia, Gerrard, Smicer, Camara, Murphy (Thompson), Berger.
Blackburn R: Filan; Kenna (Grayson), Davidson, Peacock, Dailly, Carsley, Johnson, Frandsen, Ostenstad (Dunn), Blake (Gillespie), Duff.

11 JAN

Gillingham (1) 3 *(Thomson 39, Ashby 54, Hodge 78)*
Bradford C (0) 1 *(Saunders 77)* 7091
Gillingham: Bartram; Southall, Edge, Bryant, Ashby, Butters, Smith, Hessenthaler, Thomson (Nosworthy), Lewis, Hodge.
Bradford C: Clarke; Halle (Lawrence), Sharpe, O'Brien, Westwood, Redfearn, Saunders, Windass (Rankin), Mills (McCall), Blake, Beagrie.

19 JAN

Chelsea (0) 2 *(Leboeuf 57, Wise 86)*
Nottingham F (0) 0 30,125
Chelsea: De Goey; Lambourde, Harley, Deschamps (Morris), Leboeuf, Terry, Petrescu (Percassi), Poyet, Flo, Zola, Wise.
Nottingham F: Beasant; Louis-Jean, Brennan, Hjelde, Scimeca, Bart-Williams, Gray (Harewood), Prutton, Freedman, John, Rogers.

FOURTH ROUND REPLAYS

18 JAN

Wolverhampton W (0) 0
Sheffield W (0) 0 25,201
Wolverhampton W: Oakes; Bazeley, Naylor, Robinson (Osborn), Curle, Pollett, Sedgley, Emblen, Akinbiyi (Corica), Branch, Sinton (Simpson).
Sheffield W: Srnicek; Nolan, Hinchcliffe, Jonk, Atherton, Walker, Scott (Donnelly), Sibon, De Bilde (Cresswell), Haslam, Quinn (Sonner).
aet; Sheffield W won 4-3 on penalties.

19 JAN

Leicester C (0) 0
Arsenal (0) 0 15,235
Leicester C: Flowers (Arphexad); Savage, Guppy (Fenton), Elliott, Taggart, Gilchrist, Gunnlaugsson, Zagorakis, Heskey, Oakes, Eadie (Campbell).
Arsenal: Seaman; Dixon, Silvinho, Vieira, Grimandi, Keown, Parlour, Malz (Hughes), Suker, Henry, Petit.
aet; Leicester C won 6-5 on penalties.

FIFTH ROUND

29 JAN

Cambridge U (1) 1 *(Benjamin 29)*
Bolton W (0) 3 *(Taylor 53, 75, Gudjohnsen 86)* 7523
Cambridge U: Marshall; Kavanagh, Ashbee, McNeil, Eustace, Mustoe (Guinan), Wanless, Russell, Butler, Benjamin, MacKenzie (Taylor).
Bolton W: Jaaskelainen; Holden, Whitlow, Warhurst, Bergsson, Ritchie (Gardner), Johansen, Jensen, Holdsworth (Gudjohnsen), Taylor (Farrelly), Elliott.

Coventry C (2) 2 *(Roussel 15, 21)*
Charlton Ath (2) 3 *(Robinson 40, Newton 45, Hunt 88)* 23,400
Coventry C: Hedman; Telfer, Froggatt, Williams (Shaw), Breen, Eustace (Gustafsson), Normann (Delorge), Palmer, Keane, McAllister, Roussel.
Charlton Ath: Kiely; Shields, Powell, Stuart (Salako), Rufus, Brown, Newton, Kinsella (Todd), Hunt, Pringle, Robinson (Konchesky).

Everton (0) 2 *(Unsworth 64, Moore 90)*
Preston NE (0) 0 37,486
Everton: Myhre; Weir, Ball, Unsworth, Dunne, Gough, Pembridge (Cadamarteri), Barmby, Campbell, Hutchison, Jeffers (Moore).
Preston NE: Moilanen; Alexander, Edwards, Murdock, Jackson, Gregan, Appleton (Basham), Rankine, Gunnlaugsson, Macken, Eyres (Cartwright) (McKenna).

Fulham (1) 1 *(Coleman 18)*
Tranmere R (1) 2 *(Allison 9, Kelly 70)* 13,859
Fulham: Taylor; Finnan, Goldbaek, Melville, Symons, Coleman, Collins (Davis), Clark, Riedle, Peschisolido, Ball (Hayles).
Tranmere R: Achterberg; Hazell, Thompson, Henry, Babb, Challinor, Mahon, Parkinson, Jones G (Morgan), Allison, Taylor S (Kelly).

Gillingham (0) 3 *(Saunders 70, Thomson 72, Southall 82)*
Sheffield W (1) 1 *(Sibon 27)* 10,130
Gillingham: Bartram; Southall, Edge, Smith, Ashby, Butters, Hodge (Nosworthy), Hessenthaler, Thomson, Pennock, Browning (Saunders).
Sheffield W: Srnicek; Nolan, Hinchcliffe, Jonk, Atherton, Walker, Alexandersson, Sibon, De Bilde (Donnelly), Haslam (Cresswell), Quinn (Rudi).

30 JAN

Aston Villa (1) 3 *(Carbone 32, 58, 69)*
Leeds U (2) 2 *(Harte 13, Bakke 38)* 30,026
Aston Villa: James; Watson (Delaney), Wright, Southgate, Ehiogu, Barry, Stone, Boateng, Joachim, Carbone, Merson (Hendrie).
Leeds U: Martyn; Kelly, Harte, Woodgate, Duberry (Mills), Bakke (Huckerby), Bowyer, McPhail, Bridges (Smith), Kewell, Wilcox.

Chelsea (1) 2 *(Poyet 35, Weah 48)*
Leicester C (0) 1 *(Elliott 90)* 30,141
Chelsea: De Goey; Lambourde, Harley, Deschamps, Hogh (Terry), Desailly, Petrescu, Poyet, Sutton (Flo), Weah, Wise.
Leicester C: Arphexad; Impey (Stewart), Eadie, Elliott, Taggart, Gilchrist, Savage, Zagorakis (Fenton), Walsh, Sinclair, Heskey (Gunnlaugsson).

31 JAN

Blackburn R (1) 1 *(Jansen 25)*
Newcastle U (1) 2 *(Shearer 20, 79)* 29,946
Blackburn R: Kelly; Grayson, Davidson, Peacock, Dailly, Carsley (Johnson), McAteer, Frandsen, Blake, Jansen, Duff.
Newcastle U: Harper; Barton, Pistone, Dabizas, Helder (Hughes), Lee, Dyer (Maric), Gallacher (Domi), Shearer, Ferguson, Speed.

SIXTH ROUND

19 FEB

Bolton W (0) 1 *(Gudjohnsen 47)*
Charlton Ath (0) 0   20,131
Bolton W: Jaaskelainen; Holden, Whitlow, Elliott,
Bergsson, Fish, Johansen (Passi), Jensen, Gudjohnsen,
Taylor (Ritchie), Johnston (Gardner).
Charlton Ath: Kiely; Barness (Kinsella), Powell, Brown,
Rufus (Tiler), Todd (Salako), Newton, Stuart, Hunt,
Pringle, Robinson.

20 FEB

Chelsea (1) 5 *(Flo 16, Terry 49, Weah 50, Zola 85 (pen),
Morris 88)*
Gillingham (0) 0   34,205
Chelsea: De Goey; Lambourde, Harley, Deschamps,
Terry (Clement), Desailly, Poyet, Flo (Ambrosetti),
Weah (Sutton), Zola, Morris.
Gillingham: Bartram; Southall (Browning), Edge, Smith,
Ashby, Butters, Lewis, Hessenthaler, Thomson
(Nosworthy), Pennock (Asaba), Saunders.

Everton (1) 1 *(Moore 20)*
Aston Villa (2) 2 *(Stone 15, Carbone 45)*   35,331
Everton: Myhre; Weir, Unsworth, Pembridge
(Cadamarteri), Gough, Xavier (Jeffers), Collins, Barmby,
Campbell, Hutchison, Moore.
Aston Villa: Enckelman; Delaney, Wright, Southgate,
Ehiogu, Barry, Stone, Boateng, Joachim, Carbone,
Merson (Taylor).

Tranmere R (1) 2 *(Allison 45, Jones G 76)*
Newcastle U (2) 3 *(Speed 27, Domi 36, Ferguson 58)*
                                              15,776
Tranmere R: Murphy; Hazell, Roberts (Thompson),
Henry, Babb, Challinor, Mahon (Morgan), Parkinson
(Taylor S), Jones G, Allison, Kelly.
Newcastle U: Given; Barton, Domi, Dabizas, Helder,
Hughes, Dyer, Gallacher, Shearer, Ferguson, Speed.

SEMI-FINALS (at Wembley)

2 APR

Bolton W (0) 0
Aston Villa (0) 0   62,828
Bolton W: Jaaskelainen; Bergsson (O'Kane), Whitlow,
Elliott, Fish, Ritchie, Johansen, Jensen (Warhurst),
Gudjohnsen, Holdsworth, Johnston.
Aston Villa: James; Delaney, Wright, Southgate, Ehiogu,
Barry, Taylor (Stone), Boateng (Hendrie), Joachim,
Carbone (Dublin), Merson.
aet; Aston Villa won 4-1 on penalties.

9 APR

Newcastle United (0) 1 *(Lee 66)*
Chelsea (1) 2 *(Poyet 17, 72)*   73,876
Newcastle United: Given; Barton, Hughes (Ketsbaia),
Dabizas, Howey, Solano, Dyer, Lee, Shearer, Ferguson
(Domi), Speed.
Chelsea: De Goey; Ferrer (Petrescu), Harley,
Deschamps, Leboeuf, Desailly, Poyet, Di Matteo, Sutton
(Flo), Weah (Zola), Wise.

FINAL (at Wembley)

20 MAY

Aston Villa (0) 0
Chelsea (0) 1 *(Di Matteo 72)*   78,217
Aston Villa: James; Delaney, Wright (Hendrie),
Southgate, Ehiogu, Barry, Taylor (Stone), Boateng,
Dublin, Carbone (Joachim), Merson.
Chelsea: De Goey; Melchiot, Babayaro, Deschamps,
Leboeuf, Desailly, Poyet, Di Matteo, Weah (Flo), Zola
(Morris), Wise.
Referee: G. Poll (Tring).

Roberto Di Matteo takes advantage of David James' failure to grasp the ball and gives Chelsea victory over
Aston Villa. (Actionimages)

THE SCOTTISH SEASON 1999–2000

There were some 'very nearly' occasions this season; but not quite, alas!

Scotland very nearly reached the European finals.

Rangers very nearly reached the last stages of the Champions' League.

The Premier League was very nearly a one-horse race, and it must be hoped that Celtic, after all their various troubles, can, given sufficient time by their fans, again provide the kind of opposition which is needed, and can again aspire to a high rank in Europe. Is it too much to hope that some of the other teams might be able to make a sustained challenge for the top places?

With Rangers fast disappearing out of sight in the new year, interest was in who would finish in third place, with a European entry assured. Dundee United were the early runners, but after Billy Dodds moved to Rangers, United went rapidly down hill, and finished near the foot of the table. It was left to Hearts and Motherwell to chase the elusive place: Hearts, with several games left, looked to be sure of success, but they huffed and puffed, and Motherwell kept going. It all went to the last day when Hearts at last achieved the necessary point; but even then Motherwell beat Rangers, so there was not much to spare. This was only the second league defeat for Rangers – the other being by Dundee at Ibrox, a high point for the Tayside team in an otherwise undistinguished season where their main object was to maintain their place in the SPL. They did this with some ease, but their manager was out of a job at the end of it; it is good to see that the capable Jocky Scott has not stayed in the wilderness for long. Early on all relegation worries were removed from the large majority of teams by Aberdeen's appalling start. It was hard to understand and, although subsequently they reached two cup finals, their league performances showed only brief signs of improvement. For most of the season they were well anchored at the foot of the table; Kilmarnock were often within sight – they, too, could never recapture the form of the previous season – but they did enough to avoid the fate of relegation. So, as it happened, did the Dons. There was provision for a play-off between the bottom placed team in the SPL and the teams placed second and third in the First Division, with two of the three to move into next season's SPL. Unfortunately for Falkirk, who were third, their ground did not meet the SPL's requirements.

The new format in the Premier League is now as promised when the SPL began. It is hard to see how a twelve team group can function successfully, and further changes in due course look likely. However there is sure to be a good deal of exciting manoeuvring before the split, for the last part of the coming season, into a top group seeking honours and a lower group not wanting to be relegated.

If the SPL was predictable, the same was not true in the SFL.

There are many clubs which are suffering from extremely tight finance. Clydebank have managed to keep going somehow, but they could not cope with the First Division, and their points tally for the season only just reached double figures. In the normal season Airdrie would have been in serious trouble with relegation worries; on this occasion, only one team was to go down, so that Airdrie's problems did not include fighting against the drop. Of the teams new to the division, Inverness Caledonian Thistle made a very poor start, but once they found their feet they advanced into a mid-table position, not threatened from below nor pushing the clubs above. Livingston did better, but they could not quite maintain a challenge for the top places. Raith Rovers, too, failed to keep in the top trio. St Mirren really had a stunning run, and were well worth their position as First Division champions, Dunfermline were comfortable as runners-up, and the third place was taken by Falkirk.

The top end of the Second Division resolved itself during the last part of the season into a three-horse race. Clyde, Alloa Athletic and Ross County took the places with some ease, and in a group well ahead of the rest. The next six were not far apart: Arbroath went well for a time, but could not keep it up, whilst Partick Thistle had a poor start, followed

by a fine spell when they rushed up the table; there then came another indifferent period, and they finished in a disappointing fifth place. This is a team which must be looking to go up again soon. Queen of the South were stranded at the foot of the table, but they were reprieved when Hamilton were heavily penalised following their inability to fulfil a fixture.

In the Third Division, Queen's Park set off in great style, and went into a convincing lead. Their supporters kept their fingers crossed. When the almost inevitable fall from grace occurred, there was a bit of 'I-told-you-so'-ing, but the Spiders gritted their teeth, regained composure, and finished in high form at the top. Berwick worked their way up from a modest start, even took over briefly in first place, and finished soundly as runners-up. The fight for the vital third position was eventually to be settled only on the last day of the season when Forfar managed a rather indifferent win whilst East Fife were soundly beaten in front of a large crowd in Dumbarton's last game at Boghead. Perhaps the Fifers were unlucky to have to play a vital game on such an emotional occasion, but competent judges felt that the three best teams in this division gained promotion.

The changes in the SPL have meant that two new clubs join the SFL. Various teams hoped to join, and a small committee examined the credentials of the contenders, and finally selected Elgin City and Peterhead: here are two formidable Highland League members who may soon be pushing their claims for further advancement, as the last two from this league have done. Good luck to them.

The cups always provide shocks. From the start of this season the lesser were sometimes overcoming the greater.

The Bell's League Challenge came to its conclusion at Brockville with Alloa Athletic and Inverness Caledonian Thistle finishing, after extra time, with the score at 4-4. Penalties followed, and for Alloa, a Second Division team, victory. In the CIS Cup (the League Cup), East Fife had a good run against teams in divisions above them, and Alloa again proved a handful. In the end Celtic won a rather dull final against Aberdeen at Hampden. It was in the Scottish Cup that the biggest shock came when, at the first hurdle, Celtic lost comprehensively to Inverness. This, too, in front of their home crowd. In the subsequent uproar, the fact that Inverness were a good First Division team was somewhat forgotten, and heads rolled at Parkhead. Arbroath gave Motherwell some trouble, and Alloa were again in the picture, overcoming Kilmarnock, and only losing to Dundee United in a replay. Terry Christie had an outstanding season: in addition to all these cup successes, he led Alloa to promotion. In the later stages, battling Ayr United reached the semi-finals having disposed of Dundee and Motherwell on the way. The Scottish Cup Final was really over in a few minutes at the start: in a most unfortunate accident, Jim Leighton, who has made such a contribution both at international and club level, was seriously injured, and there was no substitute goalkeeper on the bench. Hard though the Dons tried, they could not stem the Rangers tide, and goals around half time settled the issue.

In the European matches, Rangers made headway, and had some good results; they reached the first 'league' pools, and narrowly missed reaching the second. They were clearly in a better position than last season, but still have a way to go if they are to reach the heights demanded by their astute manager. Celtic, Kilmarnock and St Johnstone made modest progress in the UEFA Cup.

At the international level there are the usual encouraging signs, with some good results, but without real progress where it matters. Both the senior team and the Under-21s had their days, and Craig Brown and his back room assistants did wonders with scant material. The training and encouraging of the young – of both sexes – is rightly a priority with the SFA, and much is being done. This has been a year of development in Scottish Women's football, and the A team is currently doing well in the UEFA Women's Championship.

Let us hope that our fans – always looking forward to the day when success is again ours – may continue to be welcome wherever and whenever they go abroad.

ALAN ELLIOTT

ABERDEEN   Premier League

Year Formed: 1903. *Ground & Address:* Pittodrie Stadium, Pittodrie St, Aberdeen AB24 5QH. *Telephone:* 01224 650400. *Fax:* 01224 644173.
Ground Capacity: all seated: 22,199. *Size of Pitch:* 110yd × 72yd.
Chairman: Stewart Milne. *Secretary:* Roy Johnston. *Operations Manager:* John Morgan.
Manager: Ebbe Skovdahl. *Assistant Manager:* Gardner Speirs. *Physios:* David Wylie, John Sharp.
Managers since 1975: Ally MacLeod; Billy McNeill; Alex Ferguson; Ian Porterfield; Alex Smith and Jocky Scott; Willie Miller; Roy Aitken; Alex Miller; Paul Hegarty. *Club Nicknames(s):* The Dons. *Previous Grounds:* None.
Record Attendance: 45,061 v Hearts, Scottish Cup 4th rd; 13 Mar, 1954.
Record Transfer Fee received: £1.75 million for Eoin Jess to Coventry City (February 1996).
Record Transfer Fee paid: £1m+ for Paul Bernard from Oldham Athletic (September 1995).
Record Victory: 13-0 v Peterhead, Scottish Cup; 9 Feb, 1923.
Record Defeat: 0-8 v Celtic, Division 1; 30 Jan, 1965.
Most Capped Players: Alex McLeish, 77, Scotland.
Most League Appearances: 556: Willie Miller, 1973-90.
Most League Goals in Season (Individual): 38: Benny Yorston, Division I; 1929-30.
Most Goals Overall (Individual): 199: Joe Harper.

ABERDEEN 1999–2000 LEAGUE RECORD

Match No.	Date	Venue	Opponents	Result	H/T Score	Lg. Pos.	Goalscorers	Attendance
1	Aug 1	H	Celtic	L 0-5	0-3	—		16,080
2	7	A	Kilmarnock	L 0-2	0-1	10		8378
3	14	H	Dundee	L 0-2	0-2	10		9041
4	22	A	Hearts	L 0-3	0-1	10		12,803
5	29	H	St Johnstone	L 0-3	0-1	10		9600
6	Sept 11	A	Rangers	L 0-3	0-1	10		49,226
7	18	H	Dundee U	L 1-2	0-1	10	Dow [50]	11,814
8	Oct 2	H	Hibernian	D 2-2	0-0	10	Jess [58], Gillies [85]	11,876
9	16	A	Celtic	L 0-7	0-3	10		59,931
10	20	A	Motherwell	W 6-5	4-2	—	Dow [3], Winters [8, 25, 59], Jess [39], Bernard [68]	5009
11	23	H	Kilmarnock	D 2-2	1-0	10	Bernard 2 [2, 57]	10,552
12	30	H	Rangers	L 1-5	1-1	10	Solberg (pen) [10]	16,846
13	Nov 6	A	Dundee U	L 1-3	0-0	10	Solberg (pen) [90]	8170
14	21	A	St Johnstone	D 1-1	0-0	10	Dow [71]	6279
15	27	A	Hibernian	L 0-2	0-2	10		11,627
16	Dec 8	H	Hearts	W 3-1	1-1	—	Jess [9], Stavrum [63], Guntweit [65]	10,274
17	11	H	Celtic	L 0-6	0-2	10		16,532
18	27	H	Dundee U	W 3-1	1-1	—	Zerouali [45], Belabed [73], Stavrum [88]	16,586
19	Jan 22	A	Rangers	L 0-5	0-3	10		50,023
20	26	H	Motherwell	D 1-1	0-1	—	Zerouali [89]	10,314
21	Feb 5	H	St Johnstone	W 2-1	1-1	9	Stavrum (pen) [23], Winters [50]	17,568
22	23	A	Dundee	W 3-1	0-0	—	Dow [47], Stavrum [55], Bernard [60]	5784
23	26	H	Hibernian	W 4-0	3-0	9	Stavrum 2 [18, 46], Guntweit [29], Anderson [43]	12,630
24	Mar 4	A	Motherwell	L 0-1	0-0	9		7528
25	22	A	Hearts	L 0-3	0-1	—		13,249
26	25	A	Dundee U	D 1-1	1-1	10	Stavrum [5]	6723
27	Apr 1	H	Rangers	D 1-1	1-1	10	Guntweit [16]	16,521
28	12	A	Kilmarnock	L 0-1	0-1	—		11,525
29	15	H	Hearts	L 1-2	1-0	10	Stavrum [13]	12,626
30	18	H	Dundee	L 0-1	0-0	—		12,403
31	22	H	Motherwell	W 2-1	1-1	10	Dow [32], Solberg [82]	9348
32	29	A	Hibernian	L 0-1	0-0	10		9659
33	May 2	A	St Johnstone	L 1-2	1-1	—	Winters [27]	3991
34	6	A	Celtic	L 1-5	0-3	10	Winters [64]	56,235
35	14	H	Kilmarnock	W 5-1	3-1	10	Zerouali [6], Rowson [29], Jess [44], Solberg [75], Winters [88]	9275
36	21	A	Dundee	W 2-0	1-0	10	Stavrum [26], Jess [63]	6449

Final League Position: 10   1998–99 8

Honours
League Champions: Division I 1954-55. Premier Division 1979-80, 1983-84, 1984-85; *Runners-up:* Division I 1910-11, 1936-37, 1955-56, 1970-71, 1971-72. Premier Division 1977-78, 1980-81, 1981-82, 1988-89, 1989-90, 1990-91, 1992-93, 1993-94.
Scottish Cup Winners: 1947, 1970, 1982, 1983, 1984, 1986, 1990; *Runners-up:* 1937, 1953, 1954, 1959, 1967, 1978, 1993, 2000.
League Cup Winners: 1955-56, 1976-77, 1985-86, 1989-90, (Coca Cola cup) 1995-96; *Runners-up:* 1946-47, 1978-79, 1979-80, 1987-88, 1988-89, 1992-93, 1999–2000.
Drybrough Cup Winners: 1971, 1980.

European: *European Cup:* 12 matches (1980-81, 1984-85, 1985-86); *Cup Winners' Cup:* 39 matches (1967-68, 1970-71, 1978-79, 1982-83 winners, 1983-84 semi-finals, 1986-87, 1990-91, 1993-94); *UEFA Cup:* 42 matches (*Fairs Cup:* 1968-69. *UEFA Cup:* 1971-72, 1972-73, 1973-74, 1977-78, 1979-80, 1981-82, 1987-88, 1988-89, 1989-90, 1991-92, 1994-95, 1996-97).

Club colours: Shirt, Shorts, Stockings: Red with white trim.

Goalscorers: *League (44):* Stavrum 9 (1 pen), Winters 7, Dow 5, Jess 5, Bernard 4, Solberg 4 (2 pens), Guntweit 3, Zerouali 3, Anderson 1, Belabed 1, Gillies 1, Rowson 1. *Scottish Cup (8):* Stavrum 2, Zerouali 2, Bernard 1, Dow 1, Guntweit 1, Jess 1. *CIS Cup (1):* Gillies 1.

Preece D 9+1	Smith B 6	Anderson R 34	Whyte D 19+1	Pepper C 4	Dow A 35	Bernard P 24+1	Jess E 25+1	Young Derek 9+5	Wyness D 1+2	Winters R 23+10	Hamilton J 3+4	Kiriakov 16+2	McAllister J 29+5	Gillies R 3+7	Hart M 2+1	Mackie D 2+2	Mayer A 20+1	Solberg T 26	Buchan J 5+3	Perry M 10+8	Lilley D 14+3	Bett B —+1	Leighton J 26	Guntweit C 20	Cobian J 2+1	Stavrum A 22	Rutkiewcz K 1+9	Belabed R 6+15	Zerouali H 6+8	McGuire P —+3	Clark C —+2	Young Darren 1+2	Rowson D 2+3	Esson R 1	Match No
1	2	3	4	5	6	7^3	8	9^1	10^2	11	12	13	14																						1
1	2	3	4	5	6	8^2	9	13	11^1	10	7^3	14	12																						2
1	2	3	4	5	6	8	11^3	14	13	7^1	12	9^2	10																						3
1	2	3	4	5	6	8	9^1	11^3	13	14	10	12	7^2																						4
1	2^2	5			6	14	8	12	3	10^1	11	9	4	7^3	13																				5
1	2	5			6	7^1	8	11^3	12	13	10^2	14	9	4	3																				6
1		5			6	8	13	3^1	12	9	4	7	2																						7
1		5			6	8	11^3	13	10	3^2	14	9	4	7	2	12																			8
1		5			6	8^1	9	11^3	14	12	10^2	7	4	3	2	13																			9
		5	4		6	7^3	8	9^1	10	11^2	12	13	3	14							2		1												10
		5	4		6	7^1	8	9^2	10	11	12	13	3								2		1												11
		5	4		6	7	8	9	10	11^1	3^3	12	14								2		1												12
		5	4		6	7	8^3	9^1		11	14	3					4^{2}	12			2^2		1	10	13										13
		5	12		6					11		3					8	4^1	13		2^2		1	9		7	10								14
		5	4		6	7	8^1			11^2		3					12				1		9	2^3	10	13	14								15
		5	4		6^2	7	8			11^1		3					2				1		9	10		14	13	12							16
		5	4		6^2	7	8^1			11		3					2^3				1		9	10		13	12	14							17
		5	4		6	7	8			13		3					2				1		9^1	10^3	14	12	11^2								18
		5	4		6	7^2	8^1			12		3					9				2		1	9^2		10	14	13	11^3						19
		5	4		6	7^3	8			11^1		3					2				1^2		8	10	13	11									20
		5^1			6^3	7				9^2		3					4				2		1	8	10	13	14	11	12						21
		5	4		6	7				11^2		3^3			14		2				1		9	10	8^1	13		12							22
15		5	4		6	7				11^1		3					2				1^6		9	10	12	8		13							23
		5			6	7^3				9^2		3^1					4				2		1	8	10	12	11	14	13						24
		5			6^3	8	12			11		7^1					4				2		1	10	14	13		9^2							25
		5			6^1	9	8^2			12		3					7	4			2		1	10		11		13							26
		5			6^1	9	8			12		3					7^2	4			2		1	10		11^3	13		14						27
		5	4		6^3	9^2	8	14		13		3					7^1				2		1	10		11	12								28
		5	4		6^2	9^1	8			3		7^3					2	14			1		10	11		12	13								29
		5	4		6	8^1	13			3		7^2	14				2				1		10	11^3		9	12								30
		5^1			6	13		10^2		3		7	4				12	2			1		9^3	11	14	8									31
		5	4		6^2	8				3^3		7^1	2		14			1			10		11	9		12		13							32
		5^2	4		7	8		10		3		13	2		1		9^2		11	9		12							6						33
			4		6	7	12	11		3		5	2				9^1	10^2	14	13			1				8^3								34
			4		6^2	7^1	8	10		13		5	2				9			11		12	1												35
		5			6^3	7	8			12		3					4	2			1		9^2	10	14	11^1		13							36

AIRDRIEONIANS First Division

Year Formed: 1878. *Ground & Address:* Shyberry Excelsior Stadium, Broomfield Park, Craigneuk Avenue, Airdrie ML6 8QZ. *Telephone:* 01236 622000.
Ground Capacity: all seated: 10,000. *Size of Pitch:* 112yd × 76yd.
Acting Secretary: Ethel Pattenden.
Manager: Gary Mackay.
Managers since 1975: I. McMillan; J. Stewart; R. Watson; W. Munro; A. MacLeod; D. Whiteford; G. McQueen; J. Bone; A. MacDonald. *Club Nickname(s):* The Diamonds or The Waysiders. *Previous Grounds:* Mavisbank, Broomfield Park.
Record Attendance: 26,000 v Hearts, Scottish Cup; 8 Mar, 1952 (at Broomfield Park). 8762 v Celtic, League Cup 3rd rd, 19 Aug 1998 (at Shyberry Excelsior Stadium).
Record Transfer Fee received: £200,000 for Sandy Clark to West Ham U (May 1982).
Record Transfer Fee paid: £175,000 for Owen Coyle from Clydebank (February 1990).
Record Victory: 15-1 v Dundee Wanderers, Division II; 1 Dec, 1894.
Record Defeat: 1-11 v Hibernian, Division I; 24 Oct, 1959.
Most Capped Player: Jimmy Crapnell, 9, Scotland.
Most League Appearances: 523: Paul Jonquin, 1962-79.
Most League Goals in Season (Individual): 53, Hugh Baird, Division II, 1954-55. *Most Goals Overall (Individual):* —

AIRDRIEONIANS 1999–2000 LEAGUE RECORD

Match No.	Date	Venue	Opponents	Result	H/T Score	Lg. Pos.	Goalscorers	Attendance
1	Aug 7	A	Clydebank	W 2-0	1-0	—	McCormick [4], Evans [77]	425
2	Aug 14	H	Dunfermline Ath	D 2-2	1-2	3	Moore [16], McCormick [47]	2930
3	Aug 21	A	Livingston	L 0-3	0-0	6		2837
4	Aug 28	H	Raith R	L 1-4	0-2	8	Jack (pen) [51]	1493
5	Sept 4	A	St Mirren	L 0-5	0-3	8		3117
6	Sept 11	A	Ayr U	L 0-2	0-0	9		1888
7	Sept 18	H	Falkirk	D 0-0	0-0	9		2868
8	Sept 25	A	Morton	W 2-0	1-0	8	Evans [21], McCann [55]	1126
9	Oct 2	H	Inverness CT	D 1-1	1-0	8	Evans [34]	2097
10	Oct 16	A	Dunfermline Ath	D 0-0	0-0	8		3964
11	Oct 23	H	Clydebank	W 1-0	0-0	7	Thompson N [55]	1390
12	Oct 30	H	Ayr U	W 2-1	1-1	6	McCormick [33], Evans [65]	1568
13	Nov 6	A	Falkirk	L 0-2	0-2	7		2644
14	Nov 12	H	St Mirren	L 0-2	0-0	7		3209
15	Nov 20	A	Raith R	D 1-1	0-0	6	Moore [57]	2353
16	Nov 27	A	Inverness CT	L 0-2	0-1	7		2022
17	Dec 7	H	Morton	W 1-0	0-0	—	Taylor [67]	1135
18	Dec 14	H	Livingston	L 2-3	1-1	—	McGuire [15], McCormick [84]	1492
19	Dec 18	A	Clydebank	D 1-1	0-0	7	McKeown [55]	307
20	Dec 27	A	Ayr U	L 0-5	0-4	—		2004
21	Jan 3	H	Falkirk	L 0-2	0-1	—		2418
22	Jan 8	A	St Mirren	L 1-3	1-1	8	Neil [8]	3636
23	Jan 15	H	Raith R	L 0-2	0-0	8		2098
24	Jan 22	A	Morton	L 0-4	0-1	9		1201
25	Feb 5	H	Inverness CT	L 1-4	0-2	9	McKeown [59]	1597
26	Feb 26	H	Dunfermline Ath	L 1-2	0-1	9	McKeown [90]	2304
27	Mar 4	H	Ayr U	D 0-0	0-0	9		1038
28	Mar 18	A	Falkirk	L 0-8	0-3	9		2927
29	Mar 25	A	Raith R	L 0-2	0-2	9		2056
30	Apr 1	H	St Mirren	L 0-1	0-1	9		2909
31	Apr 4	A	Livingston	L 2-3	0-3	—	Easton [46], Neil [79]	1473
32	Apr 8	H	Morton	W 3-0	0-0	9	Neil 2 [66, 89], Thompson N [90]	866
33	Apr 15	A	Inverness CT	W 5-1	4-0	9	Thompson N 3 [7, 22, 44], McCann (pen) [20], Neil [57]	1404
34	Apr 22	H	Clydebank	D 0-0	0-0	9		797
35	Apr 29	A	Dunfermline Ath	L 0-1	0-0	9		4378
36	May 6	H	Livingston	L 0-2	0-0	9		1493

Final League Position: 9   1998–99 4

Honours
League Champions: Division II 1902-03, 1954-55, 1973-74; *Runners-up:* Division I 1922-23, 1923-24, 1924-25, 1925-26.
First Division 1979-80, 1989-90, 1990-91, 1996–97. Division II 1900-01, 1946-47, 1949-50, 1965-66.
Scottish Cup Winners: 1924; *Runners-up:* 1975, 1992, 1995. *Scottish Spring Cup Winners:* 1976.
League Cup semi-finalists: 1991-92, 1994-95, 1998-99.
B&Q Cup Winners: 1994-95.

European: *Cup Winners' Cup:* 2 matches (1992-93).

Club colours: Shirt: White with red diamond. Shorts: White. Stockings: Red.

Goalscorers: *League (29):* Neil 5, Thompson 5, Evans 4, McCormick 4, McKeown 3, McCann 2 (1 pen), Moore 2, Easton 1, Jack 1 (pen), McGuire 1, Taylor 1. *Scottish Cup (1):* McCann 1 (pen). *CIS Cup (2):* McCormick 2. *Bell's League Cup (3):* Moore 2, Johnston 1.

Thomson S 22	Farrell G 20 + 1	Jack P 29 + 1	Conway F 5 + 5	Forrest E 28 + 3	Sandison J 25 + 2	Johnston F 16 + 3	Dick J 19 + 3	Evans G 25	McCormick S 17 + 4	Moore A 23 + 4	Taylor S 16 + 6	Stewart A 28 + 1	McGuire D 4 + 14	Farrell D 14 + 2	McCann A 25 + 4	Ingram S 7 + 5	McClelland J — + 1	Easton S 14 + 3	McKeown S 3 + 15	Wallace R — + 1	Thompson N 19 + 6	McGinty B 4	Gallacher P 9	Holsgrove P 4	Boyce S 6 + 1	Neil A 15 + 1	Wilson S 5	Brady D — + 4	Struthers W — + 3	Greacen S 2	Match No.
1	2²	3	4	5	6	7	8¹	9	10	11³	12	13	14																		1
1	2	3	12	5	6²	11	8	9	10¹	7			4	13																	2
1	2	5	12	13	6²	8		10	7			11	14	4¹	3	9²															3
1	2¹	3	4	5		11	8	9	10³	7²	12	6	13		14																4
1	13	3	4	5	6¹	7	8²			10	2	14		11	9³	12															5
1	2	6	4	5		8²	11	9	7¹	3		12			10	13															6
1	2	5		6	4¹	7	12	9		10²	3				11		8	13													7
1	2	5¹	12	6	4		7	10²	13	14	3				11		8		9³												8
1	2		13	4	6²	14	7	10⁹	12		3				5	11¹	8		9												9
1	2²	4¹	13	6		8	7	10			3	14	5	12				9³	11												10
1	2	4		6		7	10		3	5	11	12						9¹	8												11
1	2	4		6	13		7²	10	12	3		5	11				14	9³	8¹												12
1	2	4		6	14		7	10¹		3	13	5	11³				12	9	8²												13
1	2	4		6	8		7	12	11²	3¹		5	10				13	9													14
	2	4		6	8	10	7²	12	11¹		5	3					13	9	1												15
	2	4	5²	6	10³	14	7		11¹			13	3				12	9	1	8											16
	2	4		6	3²	8	9	7		12			5	14			13		11¹	1	10³										17
		4		6	2	10	9¹	7		13		12	5	3					11²	1	8										18
	3		4	6		10		9	11²		7¹	5			13 12				1	8	2										19
	2	3		4	6	12		7²			11	5	13	8¹	9³	14		1	10												20
		3		4		8		7¹	10	6	13		5	9²			11	1	2 12												21
	1	4		5		8²		12	7	10	6		3	9³	13 14				2¹ 11												22
8	4	5						7¹	10	6	12		3	9²				13	1	2 11											23
7²	4	5		8				12	11	6		13	3 14		10	1	2¹ 9³														24
1		5		2	8²	9		7		6	11¹	3		4	12	13			10												25
1	2²	5		13	6		8	7		10¹	9	4		3			12		11												26
1		4		5	6			8		7	10	2	13	3 12			9¹		11²												27
1		4		5	2		7		14	11	10²	6		3			12 13		9¹		8³										28
1		6		5			8	11¹	4	10²	3	14		2	12		9³			13	7										29
1			6	14			10	8		11	9¹	4	5³	3			2	12	13		7²										30
1	12		5				4	8		11	10¹	6	14	3			2	9²	13		7³										31
			6		4	8³		11	10¹	5	13	3		2	9²		12				7	1	14								32
	5		6			10	8³		7	12	4	13	3	2	14		9¹				11²	1									33
	5	14	6			8¹		7³	10	4			3	2¹			9				11	1	13	12							34
		3	6					7	10	4			8¹	2							9²		11	1	12	13	5				35
		14	6			9³		3	10¹	4	7²			8			2						11	1	12	13	5				36

ALBION ROVERS   Third Division

Year Formed: 1882. *Ground & Address:* Cliftonhill Stadium, Main St, Coatbridge ML5 3RB. *Telephone/Fax:* 01236 606334.
Ground capacity: total: 2496, seated: 538. *Size of Pitch:* 110yd × 72yd.
Chairman: Andrew Dick, *Company Secretary:* David Shanks BSc. *General Manager:* John Reynolds.
Commercial Manager: Dennis Newall.
Manager: John McVeigh. *Assistant Manager:* Pat McAuley. *Youth Development:* Jimmy Lindsay. *Physio:* Derek Kelly.
Managers since 1975: G. Caldwell; S. Goodwin; H. Hood; J. Baker; D. Whiteford; M. Ferguson; W. Wilson; B. Rooney;
A. Ritchie; T. Gemmell; D. Provan; M. Oliver; B. McLaren; T. Gemmell; T Spence; J. Crease; V. Moore; B. McLaren.
Club Nickname(s): The Wee Rovers. *Previous Grounds:* Cowheath Park, Meadow Park, Whifflet.
Record Attendance: 27,381 v Rangers, Scottish Cup 2nd rd; 8 Feb, 1936.
Record Transfer Fee received: £40,000 from Motherwell for Bruce Cleland.
Record Transfer Fee paid: £7000 for Gerry McTeague to Stirling Albion, September 1989.
Record Victory: 12-0 v Airdriehill, Scottish Cup; 3 Sept, 1887.
Record Defeat: 1-11 v Partick T, League Cup, 11 August 1993.
Most Capped Player: Jock White, 1 (2), Scotland.
Most League Appearances: 399, Murdy Walls, 1921-36.
Most League Goals in Season (Individual): 41: Jim Renwick, Division II; 1932-33.
Most Goals Overall (Individual): 105: Bunty Weir, 1928-31.

ALBION ROVERS 1999–2000 LEAGUE RECORD

Match No.	Date	Venue	Opponents	Result	H/T Score	Lg. Pos.	Goalscorers	Atten- dance
1	Aug 7	H	Dumbarton	L	1-3	1-2	—	Duncan [28]	308
2	14	A	Berwick R	D	1-1	0-1	9	Nesovic [87]	366
3	21	H	Brechin C	D	0-0	0-0	9		273
4	28	A	Forfar Ath	L	0-2	0-1	9		421
5	Sept 4	H	East Fife	L	1-3	0-1	9	McStay [55]	366
6	11	H	Montrose	L	1-3	0-2	9	Flannigan [53]	243
7	18	A	Queen's Park	L	0-2	0-0	10		642
8	25	H	East Stirling	D	1-1	1-0	10	Flannigan [4]	122
9	Oct 2	A	Cowdenbeath	D	0-0	0-0	10		382
10	16	H	Berwick R	L	0-3	0-1	10		360
11	23	A	Dumbarton	D	1-1	0-1	9	Tait [76]	590
12	30	A	Montrose	L	1-2	0-0	10	Harty [62]	261
13	Nov 6	H	Queen's Park	L	2-4	0-3	10	Diack [57], Smith [89]	513
14	14	A	East Fife	W	4-1	3-1	10	Tait [18], McStay [22], Duncan [29], Diack [76]	464
15	20	H	Forfar Ath	L	0-1	0-1	10		311
16	27	H	Cowdenbeath	L	1-4	0-0	10	McStay [86]	276
17	Dec 11	A	Brechin C	L	1-8	0-3	10	Lumsden [78]	256
18	18	H	Dumbarton	W	3-0	0-0	10	McLees [53], Duncan [63], McStay [68]	257
19	Jan 3	A	Queen's Park	W	1-0	1-0	—	McStay [18]	742
20	22	H	East Stirling	L	0-1	0-0	10		260
21	Feb 5	A	Cowdenbeath	L	0-5	0-2	10		303
22	12	A	Forfar Ath	L	1-3	1-1	10	Coulter [9]	395
23	19	H	East Fife	W	3-1	0-0	10	Prentice [51], Diack 2 [59, 63]	368
24	26	A	Berwick R	L	1-2	1-0	10	Flannigan [29]	756
25	29	A	East Stirling	L	3-4	2-0	10	Flannigan [29], McLees [45], McStay [89]	191
26	Mar 4	H	Brechin C	L	0-2	0-1	10		241
27	7	A	Montrose	L	0-2	0-2	—		159
28	11	A	Montrose	W	2-1	0-1	10	Diack [77], Hughes [81]	329
29	18	A	Queen's Park	L	0-3	0-0	10		531
30	25	H	Forfar Ath	L	0-1	0-1	10		307
31	Apr 1	A	East Fife	L	1-2	0-1	10	Deegan [46]	512
32	8	A	East Stirling	L	1-3	1-2	10	Tait [10]	206
33	15	H	Cowdenbeath	L	0-3	0-2	10		257
34	22	A	Dumbarton	D	0-0	0-0	10		415
35	29	H	Berwick R	D	0-0	0-0	10		443
36	May 6	A	Brechin C	L	2-3	1-1	10	Diack (pen) [45], McCarroll [71]	257

Final League Position: 10   1998–99 7

Honours
League Champions: Division II 1933-34, Second Division 1988-89; *Runners-up:* Division II 1913-14, 1937-38, 1947-48. *Scottish Cup Runners-up:* 1920. *League Cup:* —.

Club colours: Shirt: Yellow with red/black trim. Shorts: Red. Stockings: Yellow.

Goalscorers: *League (33):* Diack 7 (1 pen), McStay 6, Flannigan 4, Duncan 3, Tait 3, McLees 2, Coulter 1, Deegan 1, Hughes 1, Lumsden 1, McCarroll 1, Nesovic 1, Prentice 1, Smith 1. *Scottish Cup (6):* Flannigan 3, Duncan 1, McLees 1, McStay 1. *CIS Cup (0). Bell's League Cup (3):* Tait 2, Rae 1.

McLean M 30	Greenock R 5	McGowan N 2	McStay J 26 + 1	Duncan G 13	McLees J 27 + 4	Russell G 4 + 2	Tait T 30 + 1	Flannigan C 20 + 3	Nesovic A 9	Rae D 5	Silvestro C 23 + 6	McBride K 14 + 6	Coulter J 14 + 7	Robertson G 6	Lumsden T 26 + 1	Diack J 20 + 12	Harry M 5 + 9	McMillan R 5 + 5	Smith J 23 + 2	Hamilton J 11 + 2	McCondichie A 2	Fotheringham G 2 + 1	McMullen S 1 + 5	Bonar S 14 + 1	McCarroll J 13 + 3	Prentice A 9	Sutherland D — + 5	Deegan C 7	Lyon M 2	Vennard D 1	McIntyre J 1 + 1	Clyde R 4	Best R 1	Young F 2	Hughes M 4 + 1	Friels G 1	McKenzie J 3	McArthur S 4 + 1	Dobbins I — + 1	Martin C 7	Match No.
1	2	3	4	5	6¹	7	8	9²	10³	11	12	13	14																												1
1		3	4	5	12		7	8			9	11²	6¹		2	10	13																								2
1			4	5	6		7²	8			9	11	13	3	2	10	12																								3
1			4	2	7²		13	8			9	11	5	3¹	6	10	12																								4
1	2³		4	5	6		7²	8			10	11¹	9		3	12			13	14																					5
1	2		6		7		8	12	10		11				3	5	9¹		4																						6
	4¹		2	5			8	9	10		11				3	6	12		7	1																					7
			2		6		8	9	10		11				3	5	12		4	1	7¹																				8
1	2²		6		12		8	9	10		11	13			3	5			4		7¹																				9
1			6		7¹	12	8²	9			11				3	2	5		10³	4					14	13															10
1			4		14		8	9³			7	3	13		5	10³	12				6	11²		2																	11
1			4				8	9			7	3	12		5	13	10¹				6	11²		2																	12
1			4²	12			8	9			7¹		11		6	10	13		5					2	3																13
1			4	10	7		8	9					11		6²	12			5	13				2	3¹																14
1			4	10	7		8	9¹					11		12	13			5					2	3	6															15
1			4	10	7		8	9¹					12			13			5	11¹				2³	3	6															16
1					7³		8				6²	13			4	9	10		5	3				2	12	11¹	14														17
1	2²	9	8								3	13			6	12	14	5	4					7³		11					10¹										18
1	2	9	8								3	13	14		6	12		5	4²					7³		11					10¹										19
1	2	9	8								4	10¹	13	11²	3³	6	12		5	14				7																	20
1			4	9	8						7	10	11²		3	5	13		12					6	2¹																21
1	13				8						12	10	5		6	9	7¹		4					2	3²	11															22
1			4		8						7	10¹			5	9²	12							6	2³	3	11	14					1				13				23
1			4		6						7	10			12	9			5					8	2	3	11														24
1			4		8³						7	10	6²		12	2	9	14	5					3	11¹	13															25
1					8						7	10	11¹	13	2	6	9		4					12	3²							5									26
1					8							11¹		3	2	6	9		4					12								5	1		7	10					27
1					8							10		11	2²	6	9		4³					12	3¹	14						5			7	13					28
1												10	7²	11	2	3¹	9		4					12	13										6	8		5³	14		29
1		3									5	13		8		14	12	9	7¹					6²							10³			11			2			4	30
1			4		8						13				6	3	9		7							11¹					10²			12			2			5	31
1			6²								5	7³	8	3		9	13		12	14				11	10												2¹			4	32
1		3										5¹		6	12		9		2	13				11²	10	8							1			7				4	33
1													11		6	4			3	10	12	7	2			9¹													8	5	34
1													11	12	6	5			3	10²	13	7	2			9¹													8	4	35
													8	11	6	4			3	10	12	7²	2		13	9¹													5³	1	36

ALLOA ATHLETIC
First Division

Year Formed: 1883. *Ground & Address:* Recreation Park, Clackmannan Rd, Alloa FK10 1RR. *Telephone:* 01259 722695.
Ground Capacity: total: 3142, seated: 414. *Size of Pitch:* 110yd × 75yd.
Chairman: William McKie. *Secretary:* E. G. Cameron. *Commercial Manager:* Pat McAuley.
Manager: Terry Christie. *Assistant Manager:* Graeme Armstrong. *Physio:* Jim Law.
Managers since 1975: H. Wilson; A. Totten; W. Garner; J. Thomson; D. Sullivan; G. Abel; B. Little; H. McCann; W. Lamont; P. McAuley; T. Hendrie. *Club Nickname(s):* The Wasps. *Previous Grounds:* None.
Record Attendance: 13,000 v Dunfermline Athletic, Scottish Cup 3rd rd replay; 26 Feb, 1939.
Record Transfer Fee received: £60,000 for Paul Sheerin to Southampton (1992).
Record Transfer Fee paid: £10,000 for Douglas Lawrie from Stirling Albion.
Record Victory: 9-2 v Forfar Ath, Division II; 18 Mar, 1933.
Record Defeat: 0-10 v Dundee, Division II; 8 Mar, 1947: v Third Lanark, League Cup, 8 Aug, 1953.
Most Capped Player: Jock Hepburn, 1, Scotland.
Most League Appearances: —.
Most League Goals in Season (Individual): 49: William 'Wee' Crilley, Division II; 1921-22.
Most Goals Overall (Individual): —.

ALLOA ATHLETIC 1999–2000 LEAGUE RECORD

Match No.	Date	Venue	Opponents	Result	H/T Score	Lg. Pos.	Goalscorers	Attendance
1	Aug 7	A	Clyde	W 1-0	0-0	—	Irvine [69]	782
2	14	H	Partick Th	W 1-0	0-0	3	Cameron [76]	1178
3	21	A	Queen of the S	D 1-1	0-1	2	Menelaus [47]	1204
4	28	H	Hamilton A	D 1-1	0-1	3	McKechnie [51]	689
5	Sept 4	A	Arbroath	D 2-2	2-1	2	Cameron [20], Boyle [38]	851
6	11	H	Ross Co	W 2-0	0-0	3	Irvine [48], Little [52]	694
7	18	A	Stirling A	W 1-0	1-0	2	Clark G [6]	1196
8	25	H	Stenhousemuir	L 1-4	1-3	3	Cameron [34]	675
9	Oct 2	A	Stranraer	D 0-0	0-0	2		463
10	16	A	Partick Th	D 2-2	0-2	2	Irvine [50], Cameron [65]	1801
11	23	H	Clyde	W 1-0	0-0	2	Little [89]	814
12	30	A	Ross Co	L 0-1	0-1	2		2415
13	Nov 6	H	Stirling A	D 4-4	2-2	3	Clark G [26], Cameron [45], Irvine [67], Menelaus [75]	909
14	9	H	Arbroath	D 0-0	0-0	—		637
15	16	A	Hamilton A	W 2-1	1-0	—	Little [39], Irvine [75]	401
16	27	H	Stranraer	D 1-1	0-0	3	Cameron [53]	569
17	Dec 4	A	Stenhousemuir	W 3-1	1-0	2	Irvine [21], Cameron 2 [59, 86]	574
18	18	A	Clyde	D 0-0	0-0	2		1071
19	Jan 3	A	Stirling A	D 1-1	0-0	—	Clark G [48]	1398
20	Feb 26	H	Partick Th	D 1-1	1-0	5	Irvine [37]	1847
21	Mar 4	A	Queen of the S	L 1-2	1-0	6	Conway [34]	1018
22	7	H	Stenhousemuir	W 3-1	1-1	—	Irvine [44], Cameron [65], Walker [87]	492
23	11	A	Ross Co	W 4-3	0-1	2	Irvine 2 [57, 65], Clark G [70], Cameron [85]	2331
24	14	A	Ross Co	L 1-2	0-0	—	Little [75]	613
25	18	H	Stirling A	W 1-0	0-0	2	Cameron [65]	939
26	21	A	Stranraer	D 2-2	1-0	—	Clark D [10], Irvine [75]	388
27	25	A	Hamilton A	D 0-0	0-0	3		508
28	28	A	Arbroath	L 0-2	0-0	—		567
29	Apr 1	H	Arbroath	W 2-1	1-0	3	Irvine [5], Nish [80]	631
30	4	H	Hamilton A	W 2-0	1-0	—	Cameron [17], Nish [70]	482
31	8	A	Stenhousemuir	L 1-2	1-0	3	Little [35]	495
32	11	H	Queen of the S	W 3-1	0-0	—	Nish 2 [58, 64], Cameron [78]	620
33	15	H	Stranraer	W 4-0	3-0	2	Beaton [24], Clark D [42], Nish [44], Little [72]	605
34	22	H	Clyde	W 2-1	1-1	3	Cameron [1], Irvine [82]	1739
35	29	A	Partick Th	W 1-0	1-0	3	Cameron [33]	1803
36	May 6	H	Queen of the S	W 6-1	3-0	2	Christie [31], Little [38], Beaton [41], Walker 2 [48, 66], Robison (og) [55]	714

Final League Position: 2   1998–99 DIV 2 5

Honours
League Champions: Division II 1921-22; Third Division 1997–98. *Runners-up:* Division II 1938-39. Second Division 1976-77, 1981-82, 1984-85, 1988-89, 1999-2000.
Bell's League Challenge Cup: Winners 1999-2000.
Scottish Cup: —.
League Cup: —.

Club colours: Shirt: Gold with black trim. Shorts: Black. Stockings: Gold.

Goalscorers: *League (58):* Cameron 15, Irvine 13, Little 7, Nish 5, Clark G 4, Walker 3, Beaton 2, Clark D 2, Menelaws 2, Boyle 1, Christie 1, Conway 1, McKechnie 1, own goal 1. *Scottish Cup (5):* Cameron 2, Beaton 1, Irvine 1, McKechnie 1. *CIS Cup (6):* Cameron 2, Irvine 2, McKechnie 2. *Bell's League Cup (14):* Cameron 3, Irvine 2 (1 pen), Bannerman 1, Beaton 1, Clark G 1, Donaghy 1, Little 1, McKechnie 1, Nelson 1, Wilson 1, own goal 1.

Cairns M 20	Boyle J 14 + 2	Clark D 31 + 1	McAneny P 17 + 1	Beaton D 34	Valentine C 36	Wilson M 19 + 2	McKechnie G 4 + 5	Cameron M 35	Irvine W 36	Donaghy M 15 + 11	Nelson M 9 + 2	Menelaus D 6 + 12	Clark G 18 + 14	Sharp R 5 + 3	Little I 29	Christie M 20 + 4	Bannerman S 1 + 1	Cowan M 1 + 1	Conway F 13	Walker A 4 + 4	Stewart C 16	Farrell G 4 + 1	Nish C 9 + 4	Match No.
1	2	3	4	5	6	7	8¹	9	10	11	12													1
1	2	3	4	5	6		8¹	9	10	11	7²	12	13											2
1	2	3²	4	5	6	12		9	10	11		8¹	13		7									3
1	2	12		5	6		8	9¹	10	11	4		13	3²	7									4
1	2	3		5	6	12		9	10	11	4		8		7¹									5
1	2	3		5	6	13		9²	10	11	4		8	12	7¹									6
1	2	3		5	6			9	10	11²	4	12	8¹		7	13								7
1	2	3		5	6		8	9	10	4¹	11²	12			7	13								8
1	2			5	6		8	9	10	4	3		11		7									9
1	13	3	4	5	6	2²		9	10	8¹	12				7	11³	14							10
1	2	3	4	5	6	12		9	10	8					7	11¹								11
1	2	3²	4	5	6	11		9	10	12		13	8¹		7³	14								12
1		3	4²	5	6	2		9	10	11¹	12		8³		7	14	13							13
1		3		5	6	2¹		9	10	12	11		8		7			4						14
1	2	3	4	5	6			9	10	12			8		7¹	11								15
1	2¹	11		5	6		8²	9	10	13	12	4	3		7									16
1	11			5	6	2		9	10			4	3		7	8								17
1		3		5	6	2	7¹	9	10	13			8	12		11²			4					18
1	2³	3		5	6	13	12	9¹	10	14				7		11²			4	8				19
		3		5	6		13	9	10	11	2¹		8²	12		7			4		1			20
		3		5	6			9	10³	12	2²	14	13	11	7¹				4	8	1			21
		3		5	6			9	10	11¹	2		8		7				4	12	1			22
		3¹		5	6	11²		9	10	14		12	13	8	7				4		1		2³	23
	14			5³	6			9	10	13		12	3			11			7²	4	1		8¹	24
		3		5	6	2		9	10	7²			8¹	12		11			4		1		13	25
		3		5³	6		8	9²	10	14			13		7¹	11			4		1	2	12	26
		3		5	6			9²	10	7	2¹	13		12		11			4		1		8	27
	2			5	6			9	10	7			8			11			4		1	3¹	12	28
		3		5	6	2		9	10	11					7				4	8¹	1		12	29
		3	13	5	6			9	10³		2	12			7	11¹			4²	14	1		8	30
			4	5	6	2		9¹	10	3			11		7	12					1		8	31
		3	4	5²	6	2¹		9	10	13		12	11		7						1		8	32
		3	4	5	6	2		9²	10	12			11		7¹	13					1		8	33
		3	4	5	6			9	10		2¹		11		7						1	12	8	34
		3	4	5	6			9¹	10	12		13	11		7²						1	2	8	35
1		3	4²	5	6	2			10	13		14	12	11	7³	9							8¹	36

ARBROATH

Second Division

Year Formed: 1878. *Ground & Address:* Gayfield Park, Arbroath DD11 1QB. *Telephone and Fax:* 01241 872157.
Ground Capacity: 6488, seated: 715. *Size of Pitch:* 115yd × 71yd.
President: John D. Christison. *Secretary:* Charles Kinnear. *Commercial Manager:* Bill Thompson.
Manager: David Baikie. *Assistant Manager:* Graeme Irons. *Physio:* Ian Cardle. *Coach:* Ray McWalter.
Managers since 1975: A. Henderson; I. J. Stewart; G. Fleming; J. Bone; J. Young; W. Borthwick; M. Lawson,
D. McGrain MBE, J. Scott, J. Brogan, T. Campbell, G. Mackie.
Club Nickname(s): The Red Lichties. *Previous Grounds:* None.
Record Attendance: 13,510 v Rangers, Scottish Cup 3rd rd; 23 Feb, 1952.
Record Transfer Fee received: £120,000 for Paul Tosh to Dundee (Aug 1993).
Record Transfer Fee paid: £20,000 for Douglas Robb from Montrose (1981).
Record Victory: 36-0 v Bon Accord, Scottish Cup 1st rd; 12 Sept, 1885.
Record Defeat: 1-9 v Celtic, League Cup 3rd rd; 25 Aug 1993.
Most Capped Player: Ned Doig, 2 (5), Scotland.
Most League Appearances: 445: Tom Cargill, 1966-81.
Most League Goals in Season (Individual): 45: Dave Easson, Division II; 1958-59.
Most Goals Overall (Individual): 120: Jimmy Jack; 1966-71.

ARBROATH 1999–2000 LEAGUE RECORD

Match No.	Date		Venue	Opponents	Result		H/T Score	Lg. Pos.	Goalscorers	Atten- dance
1	Aug	7	A	Queen of the S	W	3-2	2-1	—	McGlashan [21], Crawford [28], Devine [53]	1118
2		14	H	Clyde	W	2-1	0-1	1	Sellars [50], McGlashan [82]	812
3		21	A	Partick Th	W	3-1	1-1	1	Brownlie [28], Bryce [46], Peters [78]	1915
4		28	A	Ross Co	L	0-2	0-0	1		2303
5	Sept	4	H	Alloa Ath	D	2-2	1-2	1	McGlashan [32], Gallagher [77]	851
6		11	H	Stirling A	W	2-1	1-0	1	Brownlie [27], Gallagher (pen) [90]	805
7		18	A	Stenhousemuir	W	3-1	1-0	1	Sellars [20], McGlashan [61], Bryce [72]	596
8		25	H	Stranraer	L	1-2	1-0	1	Mercer [18]	811
9	Oct	2	A	Hamilton A	D	2-2	1-0	1	Bryce [32], Mercer [79]	489
10		16	A	Clyde	D	0-0	0-0	1		887
11		23	H	Queen of the S	W	5-2	2-0	1	McGlashan 3 [5, 60, 87], Arbuckle 2 [25, 70]	851
12		30	A	Stirling A	W	4-3	1-0	1	Bryce 2 (2 pens) [25, 88], McGlashan [50], Mercer [86]	856
13	Nov	6	H	Stenhousemuir	L	0-3	0-3	1		866
14		9	A	Alloa Ath	D	0-0	0-0	—		637
15		20	H	Ross Co	L	0-1	0-0	2		972
16		27	H	Hamilton A	D	1-1	0-1	2	Tindal [76]	764
17	Dec	4	A	Stranraer	D	2-2	0-0	4	McGlashan [78], Mercer [84]	384
18		18	A	Queen of the S	L	0-1	0-1	5		837
19		27	H	Partick Th	D	0-0	0-0	—		1509
20	Jan	3	A	Stenhousemuir	L	0-3	0-3	—		381
21		22	H	Stranraer	D	1-1	1-1	4	Tosh [25]	720
22	Feb	5	A	Hamilton A	D	2-2	0-2	4	McGlashan [81], Thomson J [90]	407
23		12	A	Ross Co	D	1-1	0-1	5	Tosh [60]	2059
24		26	H	Clyde	D	1-1	1-1	6	McGlashan [35]	880
25		29	H	Stirling A	W	3-2	0-0	—	McGlashan 2 [62, 82], Sellars [70]	580
26	Mar	4	A	Partick Th	L	0-2	0-1	4		2210
27		11	A	Stirling A	D	1-1	1-0	5	Mercer [5]	681
28		18	H	Stenhousemuir	D	2-2	1-1	5	Arbuckle [25], Thomson J [65]	730
29		25	H	Ross Co	L	1-2	0-2	6	McGlashan [89]	804
30		28	H	Alloa Ath	W	2-0	0-0	—	Mercer [55], Brownlie [78]	567
31	Apr	1	A	Alloa Ath	L	1-2	0-1	5	McGlashan (pen) [65]	631
32		8	A	Stranraer	W	1-0	1-0	5	Brownlie [6]	412
33		15	H	Hamilton A	D	1-1	0-0	5	Bryce [47]	604
34		22	H	Queen of the S	L	1-2	1-2	5	Raeside [4]	589
35		29	A	Clyde	L	1-4	0-1	5	McGlashan [78]	1798
36	May	6	H	Partick Th	W	3-2	0-1	4	Peters [50], Sellars [70], Brownlie [80]	889

Final League Position: 4   1998–99 7

Honours
League Champions Runners-up: Division II 1934-35, 1958-59, 1967-68, 1971-72; Third Division 1997–98.
Scottish Cup: Quarter-finals: 1993.
League Cup: —.

Club colours: Shirt: Maroon with white trim. Shorts: Maroon with white trim. Stockings: Maroon with white hooped tops.

Goalscorers: *League (52):* McGlashan 16 (1 pen), Bryce 6 (2 pens), Mercer 6, Brownlie 5, Sellars 4, Arbuckle 3, Gallagher 2, Peters 2, Thomson J 2, Tosh 2, Crawford 1, Devine 1, Raeside 1, Tindal 1. *Scottish Cup (4):* Bryce 1, Devine 1, McGlashan 1, Mercer 1. *CIS Cup (0).* *Bell's League Cup (4):* McGlashan 2, Brownlie 1, Mercer 1.

Hinchcliffe C 26	Florence S 31+3	Gallagher J 14+5	McAulay J 35	Arbuckle D 31	Crawford J 29+2	Sellars B 33+2	Bryce T 32+3	McGlashan C 34	Devine C 7+14	Mercer J 31	Brownlie P 19+5	Thomson N 1+3	Peters S 11+5	Cooper C 6+10	Thomson J 15	Webster A 4	Desuarte F —+2	Raeside J 14	Mols T 3	Tindal K 4+11	Steel K 1+4	Wight C 10	Tosh P 3	King T 2	Match No.
1	2	3	4	5^1	6	7	8^1	9	10	11^2	12	13	14												1
1	2	3^1	4		6	7	8	9		11^1	10	13	12	5											2
1	2	3	4	11^1	6	7	8^2	9	14	10^2	12	13		5											3
1		3^1	4		6	11	8	9	13	12	2		7^2	5	10^3	14									4
1	2	3	4		6	7	8	9		11	10				5										5
1		3	4	2	6	7	8^1	9		11	10		12		5										6
1	12	3^1	4	2	6	7	8^1	9		11	10^2		14		5					13					7
1		3	4	2	6	7	8^2	9		11^1	10	13	12		5										8
1	13	3	4	2	6	7	8^1	9		11	10^2		12		5										9
1	2	3	4	10	12	7	8^1	9^2		11	13			6	5										10
1	2		4	7	6^3		8^2	9	10^1	11	12		14		5		3		11^1	13					11
1	12	3	4	2	6^1	7	8	9	13	11	10^2				5										12
1		3	4	2^2	12	7	8^3	9	14	11	10^1			6	5					13					13
1	2	3	4	11	6	7	8^1	9	10		12				5										14
1	2	3	4	10	6	7^2	8^1	9	12	11	13				5										15
1		3	4	2	6	7	8^1	9		11			12		5					13					16
	2	3	4	5	6	7	13	9^2	10^1	11			8							12		1			17
13		3^1	4	2	6	7	8^2	9	10^1	11			12		5			14				1			18
	11	3	4	2	6	7	8	9	10						5							1			19
	11	3	4	2	6	7	8	9		10^1			12		5							1			20
		3	4	2	6	7^2	8	9	13	10			12		5				11^1			1			21
	2	3	4		6	7	8^1	9	13	10	11^2		12		5							1			22
	2	3	4		6	7^1	8	9	10	11			12		5							1			23
	12	3	4	2	6	7^2	8	9	10^1	11					5					13		1			24
		3	4	2	6	7^2	8^1	9	10	11			12		5					13		1			25
	12	3	4	2	6	7	8^2	9	10^1	11					5					13		1			26
1		3	4	2	6	7	8^1	9	10	11			12		5										27
1		3	4	2	6	7	8^2	9	13	10	11^1		12		5										28
1	12	3^3	4	2^1		7	8^2	9	13	10	11			6	5			14							29
1		3	4	2	6	7	8	9		11	10				5										30
1		3^1	4	2	6	7	8^2	9	13	11	10^3		12					14							31
1		3	4	2	6	7	8	9	13	11	10^2		12		5										32
1		3	4	2	6	7^2	8	9	13	11^1	10		12		5										33
1		3	4	2	6	7^1	8^2		13	10	11		12		5										34
1		3	4	2		7	8	9	10^1	11			12	6	5									2	35
1		3	4			7	8	9	10^1		11^2		12	6							5			2	36

AYR UNITED　　　　　　　　　First Division

Year Formed: 1910. *Ground & Address:* Somerset Park, Tryfield Place, Ayr KA8 9NB. *Telephone:* 01292 263435.
Ground Capacity: 10,243, seated: 1549. *Size of Pitch:* 110yd × 72yd.
Chairman: W. J. Barr. *Administrator:* Brian Caldwell. *Secretary:* J. E. Eyley. *Lottery Manager:* Andrew Downie.
Manager: Gordon Dalziel. *Coach:* Iain Munro. *Youth Coach:* Campbell Money.
Managers since 1975: Alex Stuart; Ally MacLeod; Willie McLean; George Caldwell; Ally MacLeod; George Burley;
Simon Stainrod. *Club Nickname(s):* The Honest Men. *Previous Grounds:* None.
Record Attendance: 25,225 v Rangers, Division I; 13 Sept, 1969.
Record Transfer Fee received: £300,000 for Steven Nicol to Liverpool (Oct 1981).
Record Transfer Fee paid: £80,000 for Mark Campbell from Stranraer (March 1999).
Record Victory: 11-1 v Dumbarton, League Cup; 13 Aug, 1952.
Record Defeat: 0-9 in Division I v Rangers (1929); v Hearts (1931); B Division v Third Lanark (1954).
Most Capped Player: Jim Nisbet, 3, Scotland.
Most League Appearances: 459, John Murphy, 1963–78.
Most League League and Cup Goals in Season (Individual): 66, Jimmy Smith, 1927-28.
Most League and Cup Goals Overall (Individual): 213, Peter Price, 1955–61.

AYR UNITED 1999–2000 LEAGUE RECORD

Match No.	Date	Venue	Opponents	Result	H/T Score	Lg. Pos.	Goalscorers	Atten- dance
1	Aug 7	A	St Mirren	D 1-1	0-0	—	Bone [49]	3671
2	Aug 14	H	Livingston	L 1-2	0-1	7	Lennon [70]	2533
3	Aug 21	A	Falkirk	L 1-2	1-1	9	Hurst [40]	2938
4	Aug 28	H	Inverness CT	W 1-0	0-0	7	Hurst [89]	2157
5	Sept 4	A	Raith R	L 1-5	0-1	7	Bone [81]	2368
6	Sept 11	H	Airdrieonians	W 2-0	0-0	7	Jemson 2 (1 pen) [63 (p), 86]	1888
7	Sept 18	A	Clydebank	W 2-0	2-0	5	Campbell [20], Jemson (pen) [22]	476
8	Sept 25	A	Dunfermline Ath	L 1-2	0-2	6	Hurst [55]	4044
9	Oct 2	H	Morton	W 3-0	1-0	6	Jemson 2 (1 pen) [13, 85 (p)], Hurst [53]	2186
10	Oct 16	A	Livingston	L 1-4	1-1	6	Craig [33]	2332
11	Oct 23	H	St Mirren	L 0-3	0-2	6		3467
12	Oct 30	A	Airdrieonians	L 1-2	1-1	8	Campbell [44]	1568
13	Nov 6	H	Clydebank	D 0-0	0-0	8		1727
14	Nov 14	H	Raith R	L 0-1	0-0	9		1769
15	Nov 27	A	Morton	D 0-0	0-0	9		1168
16	Nov 30	A	Inverness CT	D 1-1	0-0	—	Grant [53]	1073
17	Dec 4	H	Dunfermline Ath	L 0-3	0-2	9		2113
18	Dec 11	H	Falkirk	D 1-1	1-0	8	Hansen [19]	1729
19	Dec 18	A	St Mirren	W 2-1	1-0	8	Grant [4], Tarrant [88]	3607
20	Dec 27	H	Airdrieonians	W 5-0	4-0	—	Wilson [5], Tarrant [12], Hurst 2 [43, 44], Hansen [83]	2004
21	Jan 3	A	Clydebank	W 2-0	1-0	—	Hurst [7], Rogers [48]	901
22	Jan 8	A	Raith R	L 0-2	0-1	7		2583
23	Jan 22	A	Dunfermline Ath	L 0-2	0-2	7		3684
24	Feb 5	H	Morton	W 3-2	2-1	7	Tarrant [1], Hurst 2 (1 pen) [45, 90 (p)]	1985
25	Feb 12	A	Falkirk	L 0-1	0-1	7		2729
26	Feb 29	H	Livingston	L 0-1	0-0	—		1765
27	Mar 4	A	Airdrieonians	D 0-0	0-0	7		1038
28	Mar 7	H	Inverness CT	L 1-3	1-1	—	Shepherd [23]	1274
29	Mar 18	H	Clydebank	W 4-0	1-0	7	Hurst 3 [22, 85, 86], Craig [79]	1661
30	Mar 25	A	Inverness CT	D 1-1	1-1	7	Wilson [43]	1790
31	Apr 1	A	Raith R	L 0-1	0-1	7		1841
32	Apr 11	H	Dunfermline Ath	L 0-2	0-0	—		1798
33	Apr 15	A	Morton	W 2-1	1-0	7	Hurst 2 [36, 72]	656
34	Apr 22	H	St Mirren	L 1-2	0-0	7	Craig [52]	4678
35	Apr 29	A	Livingston	L 1-3	0-0	7	Keane [88]	5729
36	May 6	H	Falkirk	D 3-3	2-1	7	Tarrant [2], Crilly [14], Bradford (pen) [88]	2667

Final League Position: 7　　　　1998–99 3

Honours
League Champions: Division II 1911-12, 1912-13, 1927-28, 1936-37, 1958-59, 1965-66. Second Division 1987-88, 1996–97; *Runners-up:* Division II 1910-11, 1955-56, 1968-69.
Scottish Cup: —. *League Cup:* —.
B&Q Cup Runners-up: 1990-91, 1991-92.

Club colours: Shirt: White with black trim. Shorts: Black. Stockings: Black and white.

Goalscorers: *League (42):* Hurst 14 (1 pen), Jemson 5 (3 pens), Tarrant 4, Craig 3, Bone 2, Campbell 2, Grant 2, Hansen 2, Wilson 2, Bradford 1 (pen), Crilly 1, Keane 1, Lennon 1, Rogers 1, Shepherd 1. *Scottish Cup (7):* Tarrant 3, Teale 2 (1 pen), Campbell 1, Duffy 1. *CIS Cup (2):* Bone 1, Reynolds 1. *Bell's League Cup (0).*

Appearances / goals grid (squad numbers shown, goals as superscripts):

Gill T 8	Prenderville B 3+2	Rogers D 13+3	Duffy C 28	Traynor J 1	Lennon D 3+4	Reynolds M 14+13	Davies J 7	Bradford J 5+1	Bone A 6+3	Lindau P 5+11	Kelly R 2+1	Scally N 15+3	Bowman G 5+1	Hurst G 25	Teale G 26+6	Robertson J 26+5	Craig D 23	Lyons A 16+9	Wilson M 23+1	Campbell M 19	Jemson N 9+3	Nelson C 18	Keane S —+2	Shepherd P 20+2	McMillan A 16+3	Adams D 4	McKeown J —+1	Nolan J 1	Knudsen J 4	Grant R 9+4	Hogg K 2+2	Crilly M 5+8	Tarrant N 15	Duncan L —+1	Hansen J 8	McNally M 5+3	Armstrong G —+2	Burns G 1+2	Rövde M 4	Dodds J 2	Match No
1	2	3	4	5	6	7³	8	9¹	10²	11	12	13	14																												1
1	2	5	4		6	12	8	9²	14	11¹				3	7	10³	13																								2
1	2	3	4			12	10	8¹		9²	14				7	13	5	6³	11																						3
1	12		4			13	8³	9		14				3	7	10²	2	6¹	11	5																					4
1	12		4			8	13	9		14				3	7	10³	2	11²	6	5¹																					5
1		3	4			12	13	9³		14			8		7²	2		11	6¹	5	10																				6
1		3	4¹			12	7	13		9²			8		14	2		11	6	5	10³																				7
1		3	4			12	8			11				7	9¹	2		13	6²	5	10																				8
		3⁶				12	8			13			11	7¹	9	4			6	5	10²	1	2																		9
		4¹				8				13			3	7²	12	2	6	14	11	5	10³	1	9																		10
		4				8		9²		14			7	13	12	6	3	11³	5	10		1	2																		11
		12								14			13	7	11³	3	6		4	5	10²	1¹	9	2	8																12
		13	6³			7							4	11	14	12		5	10¹	1	3	2	8	9²																	13
		3	4			12							6	7	9		11	5	10¹	1		2	8																		14
		3	5					14	9¹	4			8	7³	13	6²	11			12	2	10	1																		15
		5						8	3				10	7	6	11			1	4	2		9																		16
						8³			14	3²			10	7¹	6	11			12	1	4	2		9	5	13															17
		6				13							7²	3	12	8	5	14	1	4	2		9			10³	11¹														18
		6				13		14					7	3	5	12	8		1	4	2		9¹			10³	11²														19
		12	6			13							9	7	3	5	11²	8	14	1	2¹					10³	4														20
		3	6			12							9	7²	5	13	8		1	4	2		14			10³	11¹														21
		3¹	6										9	7	12	5	14	8	1	4	2		13			10³	11²														22
		3	6			12							9	7	11¹	5	8		1	4	2⁸		13	14	10²																23
		3²	6			11¹							9¹	7	2	5	8		1	4	13		12	14	10																24
			6			7²							9	13	3	5	8		1	12	2		10³	14	11¹	4															25
														7	3	5	8	6		1	9	12	11	10	4	2¹															26
		6				7					4¹			2³	3	8	5		14	1	9	12	10²	11		13															27
		11								8³				6	13	5¹		10	2	1	9	3²	7		4	12	14														28
		6				11			10³	4¹			9	7	3	5	13	8²		1	2		12	14																	29
		6¹				14							9⁹	7	3	11²	8	5	4	2	13	10	12		1																30
		11				14			4¹				9	7³	3	6	12	8²	5	1	2	13	10																		31
		11							7²				9	12	6	3¹	8	5		2	13	10	4	1																	32
		12²				13			4				9	7³	2	6	11	5¹		14	8	10	3	1																	33
		5				12							8	9	7	3	6	11¹		4	2	10	1																		34
		6						10¹					4²	7	3³	5	11	12		2		9	8	14	13	1															35
		6				7²	9						8	2	3	5	5¹	13		12			4	10	14	11³	1														36

BERWICK RANGERS   Second Division

Year Formed: 1881. *Ground & Address:* Shielfield Park, Tweedmouth, Berwick-upon-Tweed TD15 2EF. *Telephone:* 01289 307424. *Fax (to Secretary):* 01289 307424. Club 24 hour hotline 01891 800697. *Ground Capacity:* 4131, seated: 1366. *Size of Pitch:* 110yd × 70yd.
Chairman: Jamie Curle. *Vice-chairman:* Moray McLaren. *Chief Executive:* Tom Davidson. *Club Secretary:* Dennis McCleary.
Manager: Paul Smith. *Assistant Manager:* John Clark. *Physios:* Rev. Glyn Jones, Ian Smith. *Coaches:* Ian Oliver, Ian Smith
Managers since 1975: H. Melrose; G. Haig; W. Galbraith; D. Smith; F. Connor; J. McSherry; E. Tait; J. Thomson; J. Jefferies; J. Anderson, J. Crease, T. Hendrie, I. Ross, J. Thomson.
Club Nickname(s): The Borderers. *Previous Grounds:* Bull Stob Close, Pier Field, Meadow Field, Union Park, Old Shielfield.
Record Attendance: 13,365 v Rangers, Scottish Cup 1st rd; 28 Jan, 1967.
Record Victory: 8-1 v Forfar Ath. Division II; 25 Dec, 1965: v Vale of Leithen, Scottish Cup; Dec, 1966.
Record Defeat: 1-9 v Hamilton A, First Division; 9 Aug, 1980.
Most Capped Player: —.
Most League Appearances: 435: Eric Tait, 1970-87.
Most League Goals in Season (Individual): 38: Ken Bowron, Division II; 1963-64.
Most Goals Overall (Individual): 115: Eric Tait, 1970-87.

BERWICK RANGERS 1999–2000 LEAGUE RECORD

Match No.	Date	Venue	Opponents	Result	H/T Score	Lg. Pos.	Goalscorers	Atten- dance
1	Aug 7	A	East Fife	W 2-1	1-0	—	Watt [31], Leask [73]	549
2	14	H	Albion R	D 1-1	1-0	3	Patterson [13]	366
3	21	A	Montrose	W 2-1	2-0	2	Anthony [38], Rafferty [40]	313
4	28	H	Queen's Park	L 1-2	0-1	4	Smith [75]	710
5	Sept 4	A	Dumbarton	L 1-2	0-1	6	Ritchie [57]	324
6	11	H	Cowdenbeath	L 0-2	0-1	7		457
7	18	A	Forfar Ath	D 1-1	0-0	6	Haddow (pen) [47]	375
8	25	H	Brechin C	W 2-0	1-0	5	Ritchie [12], Anthony [75]	407
9	Oct 2	A	East Stirling	W 3-0	2-0	4	Ritchie 2 [34, 78], Findlay [39]	266
10	16	A	Albion R	W 3-0	1-0	4	Findlay 2 [40, 48], Anthony [69]	360
11	23	H	East Fife	L 0-1	0-1	5		506
12	30	A	Cowdenbeath	D 1-1	0-0	5	Haddow (pen) [68]	313
13	Nov 6	H	Forfar Ath	D 2-2	1-1	6	Findlay [15], Haddow (pen) [73]	328
14	14	H	Dumbarton	L 0-1	0-0	6		415
15	20	A	Queen's Park	W 4-1	3-1	5	Watt [19], Smith [26], Anthony 2 [35, 54]	678
16	27	H	East Stirling	W 1-0	0-0	5	McNicoll [72]	318
17	Dec 7	A	Brechin C	W 3-0	1-0	—	Smith 2 [39, 51], Anthony [58]	356
18	27	H	Montrose	D 0-0	0-0	—		472
19	Jan 15	H	Cowdenbeath	D 0-0	0-0	4		413
20	22	H	Brechin C	W 3-1	1-1	3	Patterson [25], Watt [48], Smith [90]	344
21	Feb 5	A	East Stirling	W 1-0	0-0	3	Wood [80]	255
22	12	H	Queen's Park	D 1-1	0-1	4	Laidlaw [78]	525
23	26	H	Albion R	W 2-1	0-0	4	Laidlaw [84], Anthony [89]	756
24	Mar 4	A	Montrose	W 3-2	2-1	3	Wood 2 (1 pen) [3, 73 (p)], Laidlaw [24]	302
25	7	A	Forfar Ath	L 0-2	0-1	—		482
26	11	A	Cowdenbeath	W 3-1	2-0	3	Wood 2 (1 pen) [14 (p), 34], Ramsay [83]	402
27	14	A	Dumbarton	W 2-0	2-0	—	Anthony [30], Smith [36]	330
28	18	H	Forfar Ath	W 2-0	0-0	—	Wood [48], Anthony [58]	614
29	21	A	East Fife	L 1-3	1-1	—	Ramsay [43]	551
30	25	A	Queen's Park	W 1-0	0-0	1	Neill A (pen) [76]	964
31	Apr 1	H	Dumbarton	D 0-0	0-0	2		560
32	8	A	Brechin C	W 2-1	2-0	1	Haddow [16], Wood [44]	267
33	15	H	East Stirling	W 3-0	1-0	1	Ritchie [44], Wood [67], Smith [88]	486
34	22	H	East Fife	L 0-1	0-0	2		942
35	29	A	Albion R	D 0-0	0-0	2		443
36	May 6	H	Montrose	W 2-1	1-1	2	Haddow [1], Findlay [60]	1224

Final League Position: 2   1998–99 DIV 3 5

Honours
League Champions: Second Division 1978-79; *Runners-up:* Second Division 1993-94. Third Division 1999–2000.
Scottish Cup: Quarter-finals: 1953-54, 1979-80.
League Cup: Semi-finals: 1963-64.

Club colours: Shirt: Black with 4 inch gold stripes. Shorts: Black with white trim. Stockings: Gold with black trim.

Goalscorers: *League (53):* Anthony 9, Wood 8 (2 pens), Smith 7, Findlay 5, Haddow 5 (3 pens), Ritchie 5, Laodlaw 3, Watt 3, Patterson 2, Ramsay 2, Leask 1, McNicoll 1, Neill A 1 (pen), Rafferty 1. *Scottish Cup (4):* Findlay 2, Haddow 2 (2 pens). *CIS Cup (1):* Patterson 1. *Bell's League Cup (5):* Patterson 2, Leask 1, Neil M 1, Neill A 1.

O'Connor G 29	Watt D 26+2	Haddow L 31	McNicoll G 26+1	Neill A 30+3	Ritchie J 29+2	Neil M 25+1	Patterson P 20+7	Leask M 4+7	Anthony M 32+2	Magee K 20+9	Forrester P 2+4	Smith D 28+7	Campbell C 19+3	Rafferty K 14+9	Humphreys M —+2	Hunter M 1+4	Porteous A —+1	Findlay C 12+14	Carr-Lawton C 4+3	McPherson D —+1	Wood G 15	Laidlaw S 9+3	Ramsay S 4+2	Oliver N 9	Scrimgour D 7	Harvey J —+1	Moonie D —+1	Match No.
1	2	3	4	5	6	7	8¹	9³	10	11²	12	13	14															1
1		3	2¹	5	6	9	8	11³	7	4²	14	10	12	13														2
1	13	3		5	6	4	8³	9¹	7	11²	12	10		2	14													3
1		3		5²	6	7	9		8	11		10	13	2				4¹	12									4
1	13	3²	2	5	6	7	9	12	8	11		10		4¹														5
1	4	3	2	5	6	7	11¹	9	8²			10		13				12										6
1	6	3		5	2	7	9³	12	8	11²	10¹	13	4		14													7
1	6³	3		5	2	7	8	12	10	11²	9¹	13	4		14													8
1	6	3		5	2	7	9		8	11¹	13	12	4								10²							9
1	6³	3	2	4		10	7²	14	8	11¹		12	5	13							9							10
1	6	3		5	2	7	8¹	12	10	11		13	4²								9							11
1	6	3	12	5¹	2	10	7²	13	8	14		11	4								9³							12
1		3³	5		2	7	12		8	11		10²	4	13							9	6¹	14					13
1		3²	5		2	6	13		7	11¹		10	4	12							9	8						14
1	7	3	2		5	6	13		10	11		8	4								9¹	12²						15
1	7	3	2	14	5	6	12		10³	11		8¹	4					13			9²							16
1	6²	3¹	2	14	5	8	7		10			11	4	13				12			9¹							17
1	6	3	2	14	5	8	7¹	13	10	12³		11	4								9²							18
1	8	3	2	5		7	10	12				11	4								9	6¹						19
1	6	3	2	5	12	7		8	11¹			10	4								9							20
1		3	2	5	12	7						11	6	4	8			13			9²	10¹						21
1			2	5	3	7¹		12				11	6	4²	8³			13			9	10	14					22
1	6		2	5								8	11	12	4³	7		13	14			10¹	9		3²			23
1	6		2	5							12	8	13	11²	4			14	7¹			10	9³		3			24
1	6		2	5							12	7²	8	11	4¹			13				10	9		3			25
1	6		2	5	4	8						10²	11¹	3		7		13	14				9³	12				26
1	6	11		5	4	8						10³	13	3		7			14				9¹	12	2²			27
1	6	11		5	4	8						10¹	14	3		7		13					9²	12	2³			28
1	6	11³		5	4	8						10²	13	3		7			14				9¹	12	2			29
	8	3¹	2	5	4	7						14	12	11²				13				10³	9	6	1			30
	8	3¹	2	5	4	7²						10	11					13				12	9	6	1			31
	8	3	2	5	4						12	10²	11	7¹				13					9	6	1			32
	8	3¹	2	5	4						12	10²	14	11	7¹			13					9	6	1			33
	8	3	2	5	4							10	11	7				12					9¹	6	1			34
		3	2	5	4	7¹						8	11	12				13				10	9²	6	1			35
		3¹	2	5	4							8	11	7				10					9¹	6	1	12	13	36

BRECHIN CITY
Third Division

Year Formed: 1906. *Ground & Address:* Glebe Park, Trinity Rd, Brechin, Angus DD9 6BJ. *Telephone:* 01356 622856.
Fax (to Secretary): 01356 625524.
Ground Capacity: total: 3980, seated: 1518. *Size of Pitch:* 110yd × 67yd.
Chairman: David Birse. *Vice-Chairman:* Hugh Campbell Adamson. *Secretary:* Ken Ferguson.
Manager: Dick Campbell. *Youth Coach:* Eddie Wolecki. *Physio:* Tom Gilmartin.
Managers since 1975: Charlie Dunn; Ian Stewart; Doug Houston; Ian Fleming; John Ritchie, Ian Redford. *Club Nickname(s):* The City. *Previous Grounds:* Nursery Park.
Record Attendance: 8122 v Aberdeen, Scottish Cup 3rd rd; 3 Feb, 1973.
Record Transfer Fee received: £100,000 for Scott Thomson to Aberdeen (1991).
Record Transfer Fee paid: £16,000 for Sandy Ross from Berwick Rangers (1991).
Record Victory: 12-1 v Thornhill, Scottish Cup 1st rd; 28 Jan, 1926.
Record Defeat: 0-10 v Airdrieonians, Albion R and Cowdenbeath, all in Division II; 1937-38.
Most Capped Player: —.
Most League Appearances: 459: David Watt, 1975-89.
Most League Goals in Season (Individual): 26: W. McIntosh, Division II; 1959-60.
Most Goals Overall (Individual): 131: Ian Campbell.

BRECHIN CITY 1999–2000 LEAGUE RECORD

Match No.	Date		Venue	Opponents	Result	H/T Score	Lg. Pos.	Goalscorers	Attendance
1	Aug	7	A	Forfar Ath	D 0-0	0-0	—		620
2		14	H	Queen's Park	L 1-2	1-1	8	Hutcheon [28]	311
3		21	A	Albion R	D 0-0	0-0	8		273
4		28	H	Dumbarton	L 0-2	0-1	8		357
5	Sept	4	A	Cowdenbeath	L 1-6	1-2	10	Dickson (pen) [5]	254
6		11	H	East Stirling	L 1-2	1-2	10	Kerrigan [35]	284
7		18	A	Montrose	W 1-0	1-0	9	Black [33]	512
8		25	A	Berwick R	L 0-2	0-1	9		407
9	Oct	2	H	East Fife	L 1-3	1-2	9	Kerrigan [42]	365
10		16	A	Queen's Park	L 3-5	0-3	9	Black 3 [60, 62, 75]	483
11		23	H	Forfar Ath	L 0-2	0-0	10		502
12		30	A	East Stirling	D 0-0	0-0	9		210
13	Nov	6	H	Montrose	W 1-0	0-0	9	Bailey [54]	366
14		14	H	Cowdenbeath	W 2-0	1-0	9	Bain [2], Hutcheon [57]	275
15		20	A	Dumbarton	W 3-1	1-1	8	Black [33], Hutcheon [47], Honeyman [48]	447
16		27	A	East Fife	L 0-1	0-1	9		463
17	Dec	7	H	Berwick R	L 0-3	0-1	—		356
18		11	H	Albion R	W 8-1	3-0	8	Bailey [8], Honeyman 2 [26, 41], Coulston [56], Black [64], Hutcheon 2 [68, 83], Kerrigan [85]	256
19	Jan	3	A	Montrose	L 0-1	0-1	—		798
20		22	A	Berwick R	L 1-3	1-1	9	Honeyman [12]	344
21	Feb	5	H	East Fife	W 3-1	1-0	9	Sorbie [19], Agostini (og) [49], Honeyman [73]	337
22		12	A	Dumbarton	L 1-2	0-1	9	Black [74]	278
23		19	A	Cowdenbeath	D 1-1	1-0	9	Sorbie [13]	222
24		26	H	Queen's Park	D 0-0	0-0	9		287
25		29	A	Forfar Ath	L 0-2	0-1	—		516
26	Mar	4	A	Albion R	W 2-0	1-0	8	Kerrigan [45], Black [65]	241
27		7	H	East Stirling	D 1-1	1-0	—	Honeyman [18]	207
28		11	A	East Stirling	W 3-0	3-0	8	Honeyman 2 [14, 25], Coulston [37]	259
29		18	H	Montrose	D 0-0	0-0	8		360
30		25	A	Dumbarton	L 1-2	0-0	8	Black [83]	365
31	Apr	1	H	Cowdenbeath	L 1-2	0-1	8	Kerrigan [60]	244
32		8	H	Berwick R	L 1-2	0-2	9	Kerrigan [57]	267
33		15	A	East Fife	D 1-1	0-1	9	Cusick (og) [75]	452
34		22	H	Forfar Ath	W 1-0	1-0	8	Honeyman [10]	548
35		29	A	Queen's Park	L 0-1	0-0	9		943
36	May	6	H	Albion R	W 3-2	1-1	8	Honeyman 2 [39, 47], Hutcheon [60]	257

Final League Position: 8 1998–99 3

Honours

League Champions: Second Division 1982-83. C Division 1953-54. Second Division 1989-90. *Runners-up:* 1992-93. Third Division Runners-up 1995-96.
Scottish Cup: —.
League Cup: —.

Club colours: Shirt, Shorts, Stockings: Red with white trimmings.

Goalscorers: *League (42):* Honeyman 11, Black 9, Hutcheon 6, Kerrigan 6, Bailey 2, Coulston 2, Sorbie 2, Bain 1, Dickson 1 (pen), own goals 2. *Scottish Cup (6):* Black 2, Bailey 1, Christie 1, Nairn 1, Smith 1. *CIS Cup (0). Bell's League Cup (0).*

Geddes R 36	Smith G 25	Christie G 15+1	Cairney H 31	Bain K 29	Riley P 28	Dickson J 3+3	Dailly M 1+2	Sorbie S 24+1	Price G 4+2	Campbell S 13+4	Kerrigan S 16+14	Coulston D 12+9	Hutcheon A 9+9	Durie J 4	Buck G 3+3	McKellar J 5+3	Black R 32+1	Armstrong G 1+2	Brown R 4	Boyle S 4	Williamson K 2+3	Bailey L 20+1	Donachie B 23	Nairn J 9	Honeyman B 19+3	Raynes S 24	Harris P —+2	Match No.
1	2	3	4	5	6^1	7	8^3	9	10	11^2	12	13	14															1
1	2		4	5	6	11^1	13	9	8						7	3	10^2	12										2
1	2^3	14	4	5	6	13		9	8^1	10	12				7	3	11^2											3
1	2		4	5	6	14		9	13	10	11^2				3^1	8	7^3	12										4
1	6^3		4	5	10	7		9	12	3^2	14				2	13	11	8^1										5
1	2			5	6	8		9	13	10^1	11^2				7	3	12	4										6
1	2			5	8			9		3	10				7	6			4	11								7
1	2			5	8			9		3	10^2	12			7^1	6	13		4	11								8
1	2			5	8			9		3^1	10^2	12			13	6			4	11	7							9
1		3	4	5	8	12			11	9	7^2	13			6				10	2^1								10
1	2	6	4	5	7			9			3	11^1	12				10					8						11
1		6	4	5				9		3^1	13						10				12	8	2	7	11^2			12
1		6	4	5				9									10					8	2	7	11	3		13
1		6	4	5						12	7^2						10				9	2	8	11	3		13	14
1		6	4	5				9^1		12							10				8	2	7	11	3			15
1		6	4	5				9^2		12	13						10				8	2	7	11^1	3			16
1	5	6	4					9		13							10				12	8	2	7	11^2	3		17
1		6	4	5				9^1		13	11	12					10				14	8^2	2^3	7		3		18
1	2	6	4	5						12	11						10					8^1	7		9	3		19
1		6	4	5	11					12	13	7^2					10					8^1	2		9	3^2		20
1		6	4	5	7	13	8^3			12	14						10				11		2		9^1	3^2		21
1	6		4	5	7^2		8			12	13						10				11^1		2		9	3		22
1	6		4	5	7		8			12							10				11		2		9^1	3		23
1	6		4	5	7		8	12	9	11^1							10						2		3			24
1	6		4	5	7^1		8	12	9	13							10				11^2		2		3			25
1	6		4	5	7		8	11^1	9								10						2		12	3		26
1	6		4	5	7		8^1	14	13	9^2							10				12		2		11^2	3		27
1	5		4		7		6	12	11								10				8		2		9^1	3		28
1	2		4	5	7			6		11^1			12				10				8^2				9	3	13	29
1	5		4	2			8	11		7		12	6				10								9^1	3		30
1	5		4		7		8	11^1	9								6				10	2			12	3		31
1	5		4		7		6	9	8^1	13							11				10^2	2			12	3		32
1	6		4	5	7		10	9		12							11				8^1	2				3		33
1	4			5	7		8			12	9						11					2	6		10^1	3		34
1	4	5			7		8		12	13	9^1						11					2	6^2		10	3		35
1		5	4		7		8			10		9		12			6					2			11^1	3		36

CELTIC   Premier League

Year Formed: 1888. *Ground & Address:* Celtic Park, Glasgow G40 3RE. *Telephone:* 0141 556 2611. *Fax:* 0141 551 8106.
Ground Capacity: all seated: 60,506. *Size of Pitch:* 110m × 68m.
Chairman: Brian Quinn. *Chief Executive:* Allan MacDonald. *Secretary:* Kevin Sweeney.
Manager: Martin O'Neill. *Coach:* Tommy Burns. *Head Youth Coach:* Willie McStay. *Kit Manager:* John Clark. *Physio:*
Brian Scott. *Assistant Physio:* Neil McLeod.
Managers since 1975: Jock Stein, Billy McNeill, David Hay, Billy McNeill, Liam Brady, Lou Macari, Tommy Burns,
Wim Jansen, Dr Jozef Venglos, John Barnes (Head Coach). *Club Nickname(s):* The Bhoys. *Previous Grounds:* None.
Record Attendance: 92,000 v Rangers, Division I; 1 Jan, 1938.
Record Transfer Fee received: £4,700,000 for Paolo Di Canio to Sheffield W (August 1997).
Record Transfer Fee paid: £6,000,000 for Chris Sutton from Chelsea (July 2000).
Record Victory: 11-0 Dundee, Division I; 26 Oct, 1895.
Record Defeat: 0-8 v Motherwell, Division I; 30 Apr, 1937.
Most Capped Player: Paddy Bonner, 80, Republic of Ireland.
Most League Appearances: 486: Billy McNeill 1957-75.
Most League Goals in Season (Individual): 50: James McGrory, Division I; 1935-36.
Most Goals Overall (Individual): 397: James McGrory; 1922-39.

CELTIC 1999–2000 LEAGUE RECORD

Match No.	Date		Venue	Opponents	Result		H/T Score	Lg. Pos.	Goalscorers	Attendance
-1	Aug	1	A	Aberdeen	W	5-0	3-0	—	Larsson 2 [4, 52], Viduka 2 [35, 42], Burchill [88]	16,080
2		7	H	St Johnstone	W	3-0	2-0	1	Mjallby [6], Viduka [28], Wieghorst [50]	60,282
3		15	A	Dundee U	L	1-2	0-2	3	Berkovic [81]	12,375
4		21	A	Dundee	W	2-1	0-0	2	Mahe [68], Larsson [89]	10,531
5		29	H	Hearts	W	4-0	2-0	2	Viduka [17], Larsson [36], Berkovic 2 [70, 72]	60,107
6	Sept	12	A	Kilmarnock	W	1-0	0-0	2	Burchill [72]	14,318
7		25	A	Hibernian	W	2-0	0-0	2	Viduka 2 [56, 66]	14,747
8	Oct	16	H	Aberdeen	W	7-0	3-0	2	Berkovic [16], Larsson 3 [40, 43, 75], Viduka 3 [61, 64, 89]	59,931
9		24	A	St Johnstone	W	2-1	0-1	2	Burchill [47], Wieghorst [89]	9066
10		27	H	Motherwell	L	0-1	0-1	—		57,898
11		30	H	Kilmarnock	W	5-1	0-1	2	Viduka 3 [52, 55, 57], Wright [78], Burley [85]	59,791
12	Nov	7	A	Rangers	L	2-4	2-2	2	Berkovic 2 [22, 42]	50,026
13		20	A	Hearts	W	2-1	0-1	2	Wright [71], Moravcik [89]	17,184
14		28	A	Motherwell	L	2-3	2-2	2	Berkovic [21], Viduka (pen) [27]	10,730
15	Dec	4	H	Hibernian	W	4-0	2-0	2	Viduka (pen) [18], Moravcik 2 [29, 58], Wieghorst [86]	60,092
16		11	A	Aberdeen	W	6-0	2-0	2	Lambert [21], Mahe [28], Moravcik [67], Viduka [75], Blinker [80], Wright [87]	16,532
17		18	H	Dundee U	W	4-1	0-1	2	Blinker [47], Viduka [51], Moravcik [61], Burchill [89]	58,181
18		27	H	Rangers	D	1-1	1-1	—	Viduka [18]	59,619
19	Jan	23	A	Kilmarnock	D	1-1	1-1	2	Viduka [31]	14,126
20	Feb	5	H	Hearts	L	2-3	2-1	2	Moravcik [18], Viduka [29]	59,735
21		12	A	Dundee	W	3-0	0-0	2	Mjallby [66], Viduka [69], Healy [83]	10,044
22	Mar	1	H	Dundee	W	6-2	5-0	2	Johnson 3 [17, 31, 64], Viduka 2 [36, 44], Petrov [42]	55,628
23		5	A	Hibernian	L	1-2	0-1	2	Viduka [73]	12,239
24		8	H	Rangers	L	0-1	0-0	—		59,220
25		11	A	St Johnstone	W	4-1	1-1	2	Burchill 2 [18, 71], Viduka 2 [65, 69]	59,331
26		26	A	Rangers	L	0-4	0-2	2		50,039
27	Apr	2	H	Kilmarnock	W	4-2	2-0	2	Johnson [11], Blinker [21], Berkovic [73], Burchill [83]	55,194
28		5	H	Motherwell	W	4-0	2-0	—	Johnson 2 [8, 75], Berkovic [32], Blinker [77]	55,689
29		8	A	Hearts	L	0-1	0-1	2		16,046
30		15	H	Dundee	D	2-2	2-1	2	Mahe [30], Burchill [44]	56,403
31		22	H	Hibernian	D	1-1	0-1	2	Mahe [80]	56,843
32		29	A	Motherwell	D	1-1	1-1	2	Burchill [15]	7405
33	May	2	A	Dundee U	W	1-0	1-0	—	Burchill [9]	7449
34		6	H	Aberdeen	W	5-1	3-0	2	Johnson 3 [25, 51, 54], Moravcik 2 [34, 44]	56,235
35		13	A	St Johnstone	D	0-0	0-0	2		6739
36		21	H	Dundee U	W	2-0	0-0	2	Lynch [52], Burchill [65]	56,749

Final League Position: 2   1998–99 2

Honours
League Champions: (36 times) Division I 1892-93, 1893-94, 1895-96, 1897-98, 1904-05, 1905-06, 1906-07, 1907-08, 1908-09, 1909-10, 1913-14, 1914-15, 1915-16, 1916-17, 1918-19, 1921-22, 1925-26, 1935-36, 1937-38, 1953-54, 1965-66, 1966-67, 1967-68, 1968-69, 1969-70, 1970-71, 1971-72, 1972-73, 1973-74. Premier Division 1976-77, 1978-79, 1980-81, 1981-82, 1985-86, 1987-88, 1997-98. *Runners-up:* 26 times.
Scottish Cup Winners: (30 times) 1892, 1899, 1900, 1904, 1907, 1908, 1911, 1912, 1914, 1923, 1925, 1927, 1931, 1933, 1937, 1951, 1954, 1965, 1967, 1969, 1971, 1972, 1974, 1975, 1977, 1980, 1985, 1988, 1989, 1995; *Runners-up:* 17 times.
League Cup Winners: (11 times) 1956-57, 1957-58, 1965-66, 1966-67, 1967-68, 1968-69, 1969-70, 1974-75, 1982-83, 1997-98, 1999–2000; *Runners-up:* 10 times.

European: *European Cup:* 82 matches (1966-67 winners, 1967-68, 1968-69, 1969-70 runners-up, 1970-71, 1971-72 semi-finals, 1972-73, 1973-74 semi-finals, 1974-75, 1977-78, 1979-80, 1981-82, 1982-83, 1986-87, 1988-89, 1998-99). *Cup Winners' Cup:* 39 matches (1963-64 semi-finals, 1965-66 semi-finals, 1975-76, 1980-81, 1984-85, 1985-86, 1989-90, 1995-96). *UEFA Cup:* 48 matches (*Fairs Cup:* 1962-63, 1964-65). *UEFA Cup:* 1976-77, 1983-84, 1987-88, 1991-92, 1992-93, 1993-94, 1996-97, 1997-98, 1998-99, 1999–2000).

Club colours: Shirt: Green and white hoops. Shorts: White. Stockings: White.

Goalscorers: *League (90):* Viduka 25 (2 pens), Burchill 11, Berkovic 9, Johnson 9, Moravcik 8, Larsson 7 (1 pen), Blinker 4, Mahe 4, Wieghorst 3, Wright 3, Mjallby 2, Burley 1, Healy 1, Lambert 1, Lynch 1, Petrov 1. *Scottish Cup (1):* Burchill 1. *CIS Cup (8):* Blinker 1, Johnson 1, Mjallby 1, Moravcik 1, Petta 1, Riseth 1, Viduka 1, Wieghorst 1.

Gould J 28+1	Boyd T 10	Riseth V 28	Mjallby J 26+4	Tebily O 19+3	Berkovic E 27+1	Wieghorst M 14+3	Lambert P 25	Moravcik L 29+1	Larsson H 8+1	Viduka M 28	Burchill M 12+16	Burley C 6+2	Petta B 2+10	Mahe S 19	Petrov S 21+6	Stubbs A 23	McNamara J 22	Blinker R 10+7	Kharine D 4	Brattbakk H —+4	Wright I 4+4	Healy C 8+2	Johnson T 7+3	Rafael I +2	Crainey S 5+4	Kennedy J 1+4	De Ornelas F —+2	Kerr S 4	Lynch S 1+1	Shields P —+1	Fotheringham M 1+1	Goodwin J 1	McColligan B 1	McCann R 1	Convery J —+1	Miller L —+1	Match No
1	2	3	4	5	6	7	8	9	10	11¹	12																										1
1	2	3	4	5	6	7¹	8	9²	10	11	12	13																									2
1		2	4	3	6	7¹	8	9	10	11				5	12																						3
1		3	14	4	6		8¹	9²	10	11³		12	13	5	7	2																					4
1		3	2				8¹	9	10	11²	12		7	13	5		6	14																			5
1		3	5	2			8	9¹	10	11			7	12	13	4²	6																				6
		3	2				8	9	10	11					6	4	5	7	1																		7
1		3	12	2	6²		8	9	10³	11	14			7¹	4	5	13																				8
1		3	12	2¹		7	8		11	10				5	6	4	9																				9
1		3	2¹	12		13	8	9	11	10³				5	6²	4		14																			10
1		3	2		14	8	9³		11²	13	7			12	4	5	6¹	10																			11
1		3	12	2	9		8¹		11	14	7			6²	4	5	13	10³																			12
1		3	2		8		9		11				5	7	4	6	12	10¹																			13
1		3	7¹	2	9	12		10²	11				5	8	4	6	13																				14
1		3¹	5	2	9²	7	8	10³	11	13	14		12	4	6			13																			15
1		3	2		9¹	7	8³	10²	11				5	12	4	6	14	13																			16
1		3	2		9	7¹	8	10³	11	13	14		12	4	5	6²																					17
1		3	5	2	9²		8	10	11				7¹	4	6	12	13																				18
1	2	3	4		9²			10	11				6		5	7¹	12	8	13																		19
1	2	3	7¹		9²			10	11	12			5²	6	4	14		8	13																		20
	2	3	4	13		7		9	11	12			5	8	6²	1		10¹	14																		21
	2	3	12	7		9¹		11	14				5²	8	4	6	1			10³	13																22
15	2	3	9¹	7		10		11	12				5	8	4	6	1⁶			13																	23
1	2	3	7¹		8			10	11	12			5	9	4	6				13																	24
1	2	3		12	9	7		11	10				5²	8	6³	13					4¹	14															25
1	2	3	4			8¹	9	11	12				5	7	6			10																			26
1		2¹	3	4	9³		8	10		13	14		6		7		5	11²	12																		27
1		3		9¹	7	8	12		11²	13			5		4	6			10³		2	14															28
1		2	3		9²	7	8	10		12			5		4	6¹		13	11³	14																	29
1		2	3	4	9			11	10				5¹	7	6²	8				12	13																30
1		2	3¹		9		8	10		11			5	6		7²			4		12	13															31
	2		4	9²		8			11	10	12	5	6¹				7			3				1	13												32
	2		7¹		8	9		11²	10³	13	5	4						6	12		3	14	1														33
	2		7	8	9			10²	14	5³	4						6	11			3¹	12		1			13										34
		2	7	8	9			10	5	4							6²	11			3¹	13	1			12											35
1		4	9¹	8		12		10					5	4				3				11			7	2²	5	6³	13	14							36

CLYDE

First Division

Year Formed: 1878. *Ground & Address:* Broadwood Stadium, Cumbernauld, G68 9NE. *Telephone:* 01236 451511.
Ground Capacity: all seated: 8200. *Size of Pitch:* 112yd × 76yd.
Chairman: W. B. Carmichael. *Secretary:* John D. Taylor. *Chief Executive:* Ronnie MacDonald.
Manager: Allan Maitland. *First Team Coach:* Denis McDaid. *Physio:* John Watson.
Managers since 1975: S. Anderson; C. Brown; J. Clark; A. Smith; G. Speirs. *Club Nickname(s):* The Bully Wee. *Previous Grounds:* Barrowfield & Shawfield Stadium.
Record Attendance: 52,000 v Rangers, Division I; 21 Nov, 1908.
Record Transfer Fee received: £175,000 for Scott Howie to Norwich City (Aug 1993).
Record Transfer Fee paid: £14,000 for Harry Hood from Sunderland (1966).
Record Victory: 11-1 v Cowdenbeath, Division II; 6 Oct, 1951.
Record Defeat: 0-11 v Dumbarton, Scottish Cup 4th rd, 22 Nov, 1879; v Rangers, Scottish Cup 4th rd, 13 Nov, 1880.
Most Capped Player: Tommy Ring, 12, Scotland.
Most League Appearances: 428: Brian Ahern.
Most League Goals in Season (Individual): 32: Bill Boyd, 1932-33.
Most Goals Overall (Individual): —.

CLYDE 1999–2000 LEAGUE RECORD

Match No.	Date	Venue	Opponents	Result	H/T Score	Lg. Pos.	Goalscorers	Atten- dance
1	Aug 7	H	Alloa Ath	L 0-1	0-0	—		782
2	14	A	Arbroath	L 1-2	1-0	8	Carrigan [35]	812
3	21	H	Stranraer	D 0-0	0-0	8		722
4	28	H	Stirling A	W 3-0	1-0	5	Carrigan [2], Keogh [78], McLauchlan Mart [85]	1003
5	Sept 4	A	Queen of the S	D 1-1	0-0	6	Keogh [80]	1186
6	11	H	Partick Th	W 2-0	1-0	4	McLauchlan Mart [21], McClay [75]	2356
7	18	A	Ross Co	L 0-2	0-1	5		2840
8	25	H	Hamilton A	W 2-1	1-1	5	Woods [43], Spittal [85]	865
9	Oct 2	A	Stenhousemuir	W 3-1	1-0	5	Cranmer [32], Grant [75], Carrigan [79]	715
10	16	H	Arbroath	D 0-0	0-0	4		887
11	23	A	Alloa Ath	L 0-1	0-0	5		814
12	30	A	Partick Th	D 0-0	0-0	5		2617
13	Nov 6	H	Ross Co	W 3-1	1-1	4	Carrigan 2 (2 pens) [45, 53], McLaughlin Mark [80]	894
14	9	H	Queen of the S	W 3-0	0-0	—	Woods [60], McClay [78], Carrigan [83]	640
15	20	A	Stirling A	W 2-1	1-1	1	McLaughlin Mark [39], Carrigan [50]	949
16	27	H	Stenhousemuir	W 1-0	1-0	1	McLaughlin Mark [3]	882
17	Dec 4	A	Hamilton A	W 3-2	1-2	1	Grant [42], Barrett [55], Keogh [70]	731
18	18	H	Alloa Ath	D 0-0	0-0	1		1071
19	27	A	Stranraer	D 2-2	2-1	—	Woods [36], Grant [38]	649
20	Jan 22	H	Hamilton A	W 1-0	0-0	1	Keogh [79]	975
21	Feb 5	A	Stenhousemuir	W 4-3	0-3	1	Carrigan [49], Mitchell [53], Grant [60], Keogh [63]	690
22	12	H	Stirling A	W 4-1	2-0	1	Keogh 2 [33, 43], Carrigan [65], McLauchlan Mart [90]	1027
23	26	A	Arbroath	D 1-1	1-1	1	McCusker [20]	880
24	29	H	Partick Th	W 1-0	1-0	—	McLaughlin Mark [43]	2781
25	Mar 7	A	Ross Co	D 2-2	0-0	—	Keogh [64], McGraw [82]	2002
26	14	A	Queen of the S	L 0-3	0-2	—		830
27	18	H	Ross Co	D 0-0	0-0	1		1107
28	21	A	Partick Th	W 2-1	1-1	—	Carrigan [43], McLaughlin Mark [71]	3012
29	25	A	Stirling A	W 6-3	2-1	1	Mitchell 3 [30, 35, 68], Ross [78], Grant [85], Carrigan [86]	1102
30	28	H	Stranraer	D 1-1	0-0	—	Carrigan [57]	785
31	Apr 1	H	Queen of the S	W 3-1	1-0	1	Carrigan 2 [15, 77], Barrett [47]	1101
32	8	A	Hamilton A	D 1-1	0-0	1	Carrigan [83]	851
33	15	H	Stenhousemuir	W 7-0	2-0	1	Grant 2 [11, 86], Keogh [44], Carrigan 2 [51, 55], Cranmer [71], McLaughlin Mark [76]	1033
34	22	A	Alloa Ath	L 1-2	1-1	1	Keogh [6]	1739
35	29	H	Arbroath	W 4-1	1-0	1	Cranmer 2 [18, 63], Keogh [78], McCusker [84]	1798
36	May 6	A	Stranraer	L 1-2	1-2	1	Carrigan [38]	471

Final League Position: 1   1998–99 DIV 2 3

Honours
League Champions: Division II 1904-05, 1951-52, 1956-57, 1961-62, 1972-73. Second Division 1977-78, 1981-82, 1992-93, 1999–2000.
Runners-up: Division II 1903-04, 1905-06, 1925-26, 1963-64.
Scottish Cup Winners: 1939, 1955, 1958; Runners-up: 1910, 1912, 1949.
League Cup: —

Club colours: Shirt: White with red and black trim. Shorts: Black. Stockings: Black with red and white tops.

Goalscorers: League (65): Carrigan 18 (2 pens), Keogh 11, Grant 7, McLaughlin 6, Cranmer 4, Mitchell 4, McLauchlan 3, Woods 3, Barrett 2, McClay 2, McCusker 2, McGraw 1, Ross 1, Spittal 1. Scottish Cup (8): Carrigan 5 (3 pens), Grant 1, McLaughlin 1, Woods 1. CIS Cup (5): Carrigan 2, Farrell 1, Murray 1, Woods 1. Bell's League Cup (0).

Wylie D 31	Farrell T 1+3	Cranmer C 24+1	Murray D 32	Smith B 35	Ross J 29+1	Convery S 5+5	McClay A 25	McLauchlan Mart 9+11	McCusker R 27+3	McLaughlin Mark 30+1	Carrigan B 31+2	Craib S —+2	Keogh P 26+4	Woods T 13+8	Mitchell J 15+9	Spittal 7	Grant A 24+5	Barrett J 9+17	McDonald I 2+3	McIntyre G 5	McGraw M 4+2	Hay P 2+11	Mols T 1	Quinn C 1+2	McGhee G 2+2	Dunn D —+3	Henderson N 6+1	Vickers S —+4	Match No.
1	2¹	3	4	5	6	7	8	9²	10³	11	12	13	14																1
1		3	2	5	6	7¹		14	10	8²	11	13	4		9²	12													2
1		3¹	2	5			8			7	12	10	6		9²	13	4	11³	14										3
1			2	5	6¹		8	13		7³			10		9²	12	4	11	14	3									4
1	13	3	2	5	6		8	11¹		7²			10		9²	12	4		14										5
	13	2²		5			8	11	12	3¹	7		10	9³	6		4		14	1									6
	12	3	2	5			8	11³		10	7			9²	6		4¹	13	14	1									7
		2		5		12	8		13	10	7²			9	6¹		4	11	14	1	3³								8
	14	3	2	5			8	11²	10		6		7³	9¹			4	13	12	1									9
	5¹	2	4				8	11	12	3	7		10	9²	6		13			1									10
1			5	2	4		8³	13	10	3	12		7				11²				9	14							11
1			5	2	4		8	13	10	3	7¹						12	11			9²		6						12
1			5	2	4	6	8		7¹	10	3	9³		13			11²	12	14										13
1			5	2	4	6³	8		7¹	10²	3	9		13			11	12	14										14
1			5	2	4	6¹	13	8		10²	3	7		12	14		11	9³											15
1			5	2	4	6	7¹	8		10³	3		14	12	13		11²	9											16
1			5	2	4	6	8		10¹	3	7		12	13			11³	9²	14										17
1			5	2		6	8			3¹	7		10	13	12		11	9²											18
1			5	2		8	14	13	10	3	7		4	9²			11³	12			6¹								19
1			5	2	4	6¹	7²	8	13	14	3	9		10			12	11³											20
1			5	4	2	13		12	8	3	7³		10	9¹	6		11²					14							21
1			2	4	6		12	8	5	7¹	10			9²	3		11³	13				14							22
1			2	4	6		8	3		10	9²		7	11¹	12		13					5							23
1			2	4	6³		8	3²	5	10	12		7	11	13		9¹	14											24
1			2	4	6		8	3¹	5	7	10			9	11²		12	13											25
1			4	6	9²		13	3	7	10	14		8	11				2¹				5²		12					26
1			5	2	4	6	8	13		3¹	7		10	11²			9¹	12									14		27
1			5		4	6	8		10	3	7		2	11			12										9¹		28
1			5²		4	6	8¹		10	3	7		2	11			12	13									9		29
1			5²		4	6	8		10	3	7		2	11¹			12				13						9³	14	30
1			2¹	4	6²		8		10	3	7		5	11			9³	13									12	14	31
1			2	4	6¹		8		10³	3	7		5	11			9²	13									12	14	32
1			5	2	4	6¹			10	3	7³		8	11			9²	13									12	14	33
1			5³	2	4	6			10²	3	7		8	11			9¹	13									12	14	34
1			5	2	4	6	13		10	3⁴	7		8	11²			9¹	14									12		35
1			2	4	6	13			10	3³	7		8	9²			5¹	14									12		36

CLYDEBANK Second Division

Year Formed: 1965. *Club Address:* c/o West of Scotland RFC, Burnbrae, Milngavie, G62 6HX. *Telephone:* 0141 955 9048.
Fax: 0141 955 9049. *Telephone (Match days only):* 01475 723571. *Ground:* (sharing with Morton) Cappielow Park, Sinclair
St, Greenock PA15 2TY. *Ground Capacity:* total: 14,891, seated: 5741. *Size of Pitch:* 110yd × 71yd.
Chairman: Dr John Hall. *Secretary:* Billy Hall.
Manager: Stephen Morrison.
Club Nickname(s): The Bankies. *Previous Ground:* Kilbowie Park.
Record Attendance: 14,900 v Hibernian, Scottish Cup 1st rd; 10 Feb, 1965.
Record Transfer Fee received: £175,000 for Owen Coyle from Airdrieonians (Feb 1990).
Record Transfer Fee paid: £50,000 for Gerry McCabe from Clyde.
Record Victory: 8-1 Arbroath, First Division; 3 Jan 1977.
Record Defeat: 1-9 v Gala Fairydean, Scottish Cup qual rd; 15 Sept, 1965.
Most Capped Player: —.
Most League Appearances: 620; Jim Fallon; 1968-86.
Most League Goals in Season (Individual): 29; Ken Eadie, First Division, 1990-91.
Most League Goals Overall (Individual): 138, Ken Eadie 1988-95.

CLYDEBANK 1999–2000 LEAGUE RECORD

Match No.	Date	Venue	Opponents	Result	H/T Score	Lg. Pos.	Goalscorers	Attendance
1	Aug 7	H	Airdrieonians	L	0-2	0-1	—	425
2	Aug 14	A	Morton	D	0-0	0-0	8	1433
3	Aug 21	H	Raith R	D	1-1	1-1	7	Gardner [37]	232
4	Aug 29	H	St Mirren	L	2-3	1-1	9	Cormack [32], Miller [86]	1513
5	Sept 4	A	Falkirk	L	2-3	0-2	9	Miller [63], McIntyre [84]	2496
6	Sept 11	A	Inverness CT	L	0-1	0-0	10		1697
7	Sept 18	H	Ayr U	L	0-2	0-2	10		476
8	Sept 25	A	Livingston	L	1-2	0-2	10	Gardner [72]	3290
9	Oct 9	H	Dunfermline Ath	L	1-4	0-2	10	Cormack [47]	475
10	Oct 16	H	Morton	L	1-3	1-1	10	O'Neil K [45]	758
11	Oct 23	A	Airdrieonians	L	0-1	0-0	10		1390
12	Oct 30	H	Inverness CT	L	0-3	0-2	10		184
13	Nov 6	A	Ayr U	D	0-0	0-0	10		1727
14	Nov 14	H	Falkirk	L	0-3	0-0	10		500
15	Nov 20	A	St Mirren	L	1-2	0-0	10	Scott [46]	4434
16	Nov 27	A	Dunfermline Ath	L	1-2	0-2	10	Scott [47]	4224
17	Dec 4	H	Livingston	L	1-5	0-2	10	Gardner [84]	346
18	Dec 18	A	Airdrieonians	D	1-1	0-0	10	Gardner [47]	307
19	Dec 27	A	Inverness CT	L	1-4	0-0	—	Cameron [66]	1640
20	Jan 3	H	Ayr U	L	0-2	0-1	—		901
21	Jan 8	A	Falkirk	L	0-4	0-3	10		2119
22	Jan 18	A	Raith R	L	0-1	0-0	—		2754
23	Jan 22	A	Livingston	L	0-3	0-0	10		3064
24	Feb 5	H	Dunfermline Ath	L	1-3	1-0	10	Tod (og) [20]	601
25	Feb 26	A	Morton	L	0-1	0-1	10		1052
26	Mar 4	H	Inverness CT	L	0-1	0-0	10		168
27	Mar 7	H	Raith R	W	2-1	2-1	—	Cameron 2 [12, 20]	256
28	Mar 11	A	St Mirren	L	0-8	0-3	10		3388
29	Mar 18	A	Ayr U	L	0-4	0-1	10		1661
30	Mar 25	H	St Mirren	D	0-0	0-0	10		2244
31	Apr 2	H	Falkirk	L	0-1	0-1	10		727
32	Apr 8	H	Livingston	L	1-2	0-1	10	Cameron [90]	316
33	Apr 15	A	Dunfermline Ath	L	0-6	0-4	10		4969
34	Apr 22	A	Airdrieonians	D	0-0	0-0	10		797
35	Apr 29	H	Morton	L	0-3	0-2	10		339
36	May 6	A	Raith R	D	0-0	0-0	10		1510

Final League Position: 10   1998–99 DIV 1 7

Honours
League Champions: Second Division 1975-76; *Runners-up:* 1997-98; *Runners-up:* First Division 1976-77, 1984-85.
Scottish Cup: Semi-finalists 1990. *League Cup:* —.

Club colours: Shirt: Vertical red and white stripes. Shorts: Black. Stockings: Black.

Goalscorers: *League (17):* Cameron 5, Gardner 4, Cormack 2, Miller 2, McIntyre 1, McKelvie 1, O'Neil 1, own goal 1. *Scottish Cup (2):* Gardner 1 (pen), Wishart 1. *CIS Cup (1):* Stewart 1. *Bell's League Cup (6):* Ewing 3, Cormack 1, McLaughlin 1, McWilliams 1.

Scott C 21	Wishart F 35	Stewart D 8+3	Murdoch S 18+4	McLaughlin J 12	Oliver N 18	McKinstrey J 25+6	McIntyre P 4+5	Miller G 24+11	Gardner L 33+1	McWilliams D 14+6	McKelvie D 13+16	Cormack P 19+1	Ewing C 3+7	Cameron I 28+4	McDonald P —+1	McDonald W 3+1	Roddie A 4	O'Neil M 9+8	Beach K 1	McCondichie A 1	O'Neil K 9+3	Geraghty M 5	Brannigan K 19	Jackson C 5	Morrison S 1+3	Stewart C 4	McCutcheon G 4	Murray S 12+1	Hunter M 8+5	Sutherland C 8	Aibache A 1	McKay J 10+2	O'Sullivan L 5	Pheury B 1	Beggs J 2	Stewart A 3+5	Hutchison S 6	Match No.
1	2^1	3^2	4^3	5	6	7	8	9	10	11	12	13	14																									1
1	2	6	4	5		7^3	8	9	10^1	13		3	11^2	12	14																							2
1	2	6	4	5		7	8^1	9^2	10		12	3	13	11																								3
1	2	13	4	5	6	7		12	10	11	14	3^2	9^3	8^1																								4
1	2	13	4	5	6		12	9	10	11		3^2	14					7^1			8^3																	5
1	6		4	5	2		7^2	13	9	10	11^1		3	14				12			8^3																	6
1	2	3^3	12	5		6^1	7	14	9	10			13	11			4	8^2																				7
1	2^3	6	4	5		7	13	12	10			3	9^2	11				8^1	14																			8
1	2		4	5		7		9	10	11^2		3	12	8				13	6^1																			9
	2	14	4^1	5^3		7		9^2	10	11		3	12	13	6						1	8																10
1	2	5		4	7		12	10	11	13		3^2		9				6^1			8																	11
1	2	5	4		6	7	13	9^1	10		14	3^4		12							8	11^3																12
1	2			5	7			12	10	11^1	13	3		4				14			8^2	9^3	6															13
1	2		4^2	5		7		13	10		12	3		11							8^1	9	6															14
1	2			5	7		12	10^2			4^1	3		11				13			8	9	6															15
1	2	12		5	7^1		14	10			13	3		11				8^2	9^3	6	4																	16
1	2^3	14		5	7		13	10	12		9	3		11				8^2			6	4^1																17
1	2		5^2	7			13	10	9^1	12	3		11				8			6	4																	18
	2	4		5	14	7^1	10^2	12	9	3		11					13	6	8^2	1																		19
	2	4^1		5	12	7		13	9	3		11					14	6	8^2	1	10^3																	20
	2	4		5	14	9		7	10^2	3		12					13	6	1	8^1	11^3																	21
	6	4	3	2		7^2	10	11	12			8					13		5	1	9^1																	22
	6	4	3	2^2		7	10	11^1	12			8					14		5	1	9^2	13																23
1	6	4		14		7	8	12	9^2			11					13		5					2^3	3	10^1												24
1^1	6	4			7	7^2	12	11	13			10^3					8		5					2	9	3	14											25
1	6	4^3		12	8	7	9					11^2					13		5					2	10^1	3	14	5										26
1^1	6			14	7	8	12	13				10^2					11^3							2	9	4		3	5									27
	6	12		13	7^3	8		14				10					11^1							2	9	4^2		3	5	1								28
	6			3		8		9				11^3					7^2					14			13	10^1	4	2	5		1	12						29
	4			11	7	8	12					10					6								2	9^1		3	5		10	1						30
	4			7	11^2	8	12					10					6				5				2	13		3			9^1	1						31
	4			7^3	12	8	9^2					11					6^1				5				2	13	10	3			14	1						32
	4			7	11	8	9^3					10									5^2	14			2	12	6^1	3			13	1						33
	4			6	7	8		11				10									5				2	9		3^1			12	1						34
	4^1			2	7	8		11				10									5	13			6	9^2		3			1	12						35
	4			2	7	8		9				10					6				5					12		3			11^1	1						36

COWDENBEATH   Third Division

Year Formed: 1881. *Ground & Address:* Central Park, Cowdenbeath KY4 9EY. *Telephone:* 01383 610166. *Fax:* 01383 512132.
Ground Capacity: total: 5268, seated: 1622. *Size of Pitch:* 107yd × 66yd.
Chairman: Gordon McDougall. *Secretary:* Tom Ogilvie. *General Manager:* Joe McNamara.
Manager: Craig Levein. *Assistant Manager:* Gary Kirk. *Physio:* Wendy McDonald.
Managers since 1975: D. McLindon; F. Connor; P. Wilson; A. Rolland; H. Wilson; W. McCulloch; J. Clark; J. Craig; R.
Campbell; J. Blackley; J. Brownlie, A. Harrow, J. Reilly, P Dolan, T. Steven, S. Conn. *Previous Grounds:* North End
Park, Cowdenbeath.
Record Attendance: 25,586 v Rangers, League Cup quarter-final; 21 Sept, 1949.
Record Transfer Fee received: £30,000 for Nicky Henderson to Falkirk (March 1994).
Record Transfer Fee paid: —
Record Victory: 12-0 v Johnstone, Scottish Cup 1st rd; 21 Jan, 1928.
Record Defeat: 1-11 v Clyde, Division II; 6 Oct, 1951.
Most Capped Player: Jim Paterson, 3, Scotland.
Most League and Cup Appearances: 491 Ray Allan 1972-75, 1979-89.
Most League Goals in Season (Individual): 54, Rab Walls, Division II, 1938-39.
Most Goals Overall (Individual): 127, Willie Devlin, 1922-26, 1929-30.

COWDENBEATH 1999–2000 LEAGUE RECORD

Match No.	Date	Venue	Opponents	Result	H/T Score	Lg. Pos.	Goalscorers	Atten- dance
1	Aug 7	A	Montrose	W 1-0	1-0	—	Bradley [36]	275
2	14	H	Forfar Ath	L 0-3	0-1	7		256
3	21	A	Queen's Park	L 0-1	0-0	7		578
4	28	A	East Stirling	W 1-0	1-0	6	Burns [5]	205
5	Sept 4	H	Brechin C	W 6-1	2-1	5	Burns 2 [7, 85], McDowell [15], Simpson 2 [51, 59], Wilson [84]	254
6	11	H	Berwick R	W 2-0	1-0	3	Simpson [7], Burns [84]	457
7	18	H	East Fife	W 4-0	1-0	2	Burns [43], Simpson [68], McDowell 2 [72, 75]	670
8	25	A	Dumbarton	D 1-1	1-0	2	Meechan (og) [44]	424
9	Oct 2	H	Albion R	D 0-0	0-0	2		382
10	16	H	Forfar Ath	L 1-3	1-3	3	McDowell [4]	399
11	23	H	Montrose	D 1-1	1-0	4	Bradley [1]	254
12	30	H	Berwick R	D 1-1	0-0	4	Sharp [70]	313
13	Nov 6	A	East Fife	W 3-2	2-1	4	Brown 3 [36, 44, 83]	569
14	14	A	Brechin C	L 0-2	0-1	5		275
15	20	H	East Stirling	L 1-2	1-2	6	Winter [15]	248
16	27	A	Albion R	W 4-1	0-0	4	McDowell [48], Winter [62], Burns [65], Bradley [85]	276
17	Dec 8	H	Dumbarton	L 0-2	0-0	—		262
18	18	A	Montrose	W 3-1	2-0	5	Carnie [37], Bradley [40], McDowell [77]	318
19	22	H	Queen's Park	L 0-2	0-2	—		221
20	Jan 3	H	East Fife	W 1-0	0-0	—	Brown [52]	639
21	15	A	Berwick R	D 0-0	0-0	3		413
22	22	A	Dumbarton	L 0-2	0-1	5		469
23	Feb 5	H	Albion R	W 5-0	2-0	4	Brown 2 [7, 40], McDowell [56], White [57], Winter [82]	303
24	12	A	East Stirling	W 4-0	3-0	3	McDowell 2 [19, 42], Brown [44], Gray [73]	224
25	19	H	Brechin C	D 1-1	0-1	3	McDowell [74]	222
26	26	H	Forfar Ath	W 4-1	1-0	2	Winter [37], Gray [50], Brown [53], McDowell [75]	354
27	Mar 4	A	Queen's Park	L 1-3	1-1	4	McDowell [15]	625
28	11	H	Berwick R	L 1-3	0-2	5	Brown [60]	402
29	18	A	East Fife	D 1-1	0-1	5	Porteous [86]	702
30	25	H	East Stirling	D 0-0	0-0	5		243
31	Apr 1	A	Brechin C	W 2-1	1-0	5	Brown [34], Gray [86]	244
32	8	H	Dumbarton	L 1-2	1-0	6	Gray [41]	284
33	15	A	Albion R	W 3-0	2-0	5	McDowell [8], White [24], Bradley [67]	257
34	22	H	Montrose	W 2-1	0-1	5	McDonald [64], Winter [70]	252
35	29	A	Forfar Ath	D 2-2	2-1	5	Bradley [6], Snedden [24]	556
36	May 6	H	Queen's Park	L 2-3	1-0	5	Brown 2 [27, 77]	813

Final League Position: 5   1998–99 9

Honours
League Champions: Division II 1913-14, 1914-15, 1938-39; *Runners-up:* Division II 1921-22, 1923-24, 1969-70. Second Division 1991-92.
Scottish Cup: Quarter-finals: 1931.
League Cup: Semi-finals: 1959-60, 1970-71.

Club colours: Shirt: Royal blue with white stripe down shoulder and sleeve; white round neck with one Royal blue stripe. Shorts: White with Royal blue stripe on side. Stockings: Royal blue with one white leg hoop.

Goalscorers: *League (59):* McDowell 13, Brown 12, Bradley 6, Burns 6, Winter 5, Gray 4, Simpson 4, White 2, Carnie 1, McDonald 1, Porteous 1, Sharp 1, Sneddon 1, Wilson 1, own goal 1. *Scottish Cup (2):* Brown 2. *CIS Cup (0).* Bell's *League Cup (0).*

Godfrey R 24	White D 34	Berry N 3	Snedden S 29	Thomson R 12	Wilson W 34 + 2	Winter C 32	Bradley M 31 + 4	Stewart W 10 + 13	Simpson P 11	Burns J 23 + 3	McDowell M 27 + 2	Brown G 23 + 9	McMillan C 9 + 7	Clark R — + 1	McCulloch K 23 + 1	Johnston D — + 1	King S 3 + 2	Hutchison S 12	Sharp R 5	Jackson C 5	Carnie G 4 + 8	Young C — + 5	Mitchell W 1	Neilson R 8	McDonald I 12	Simpson P 2 + 6	Gray D 8 + 2	Cunning J 4 + 5	Vaugh B — + 2	Nicol G 1 + 1	Porteous A 2 + 2	Lakie J 4	Match No.
1	2	3	4	5	6	7	8	9	10^2	11^1	12	13																					1
1	2		4	5	6^1	7	8	11	10		9		3	12																			2
1	6		4	2		7	8	11	9		10		3		5																		3
1	2			5	6	7	8	12	11^3	10^2	9^1	14	3		4			13															4
1	2		4		6	7	8	10^1	11	9	12		3		5																		5
1	2		4		6	7	8	12	10^2	11	9^1	13	3		5																		6
1	2		4		6	7	8	10	11	9	12				5^1		3																7
1	2		4		6	7	8	10^2	11^1	9	13	12			5		3																8
	2		4		6	7	8	10	11	9^1	12				5		3	1															9
1	2			5	6^1	7	8	12	10^2	11	9	13	3		4																		10
1	2		4	13		7	8	10^3	11^1	9					5		12				3	6^2		14									11
1	4		6	2		7	10	9^2	11	12					5						3	8^1		13									12
	4			2		7	8	9^1	11^2	10	12				5		1	3			6			13									13
	4			2		7	8^3	10^2	11	12	9	13			5		1	3			6			14									14
1	4			2		7	6	13		10^2	9	8^1			5						3	11		12									15
1	2		5	3	6	7	8	13		11	10^2	9	12		4^1																		16
1				3	8	7	6^2	12		11	10^1	9	2		5						13		4										17
1			4	3	2	7	6	9		11	10				5						8												18
1	2		5	3^2	14	7	8	9^3		11^1	10	12			4		13				6												19
	4	3		11		7	8	12		6^1	9	10			5		1				2												20
	4	3		6		7	8	13		9^1	10^2				5		1				2	11	12										21
	4	3		6^3		7		14		12	9^2	10			5^1		1				8	2	11	13									22
	4	5	3	8		7	12	13		9^2	10						1				14	2	11^3		6^1								23
	4	5	3	11		7	12			9	10^2						1				2	8^1	13	6									24
	4	5	3	11		7	8			9	10^2						1				2	13	6^1	12									25
	4	5	3	11		7	13			12	9	10					1				2		8^1	6^2									26
	2	5	3	11		7	13	14		9	10^3				4		1					8^2	6^3	12									27
	4			2		7	8^3	13		10					5		1				3	9	14	11^3	12	6^2							28
1	4	5		7		6		11^3	9^2	10					8						3	13	2^1			12	14						29
1	2	5			7	8		11	9	10^2					6^1						3	13	12			14							30
1	4	5		2	6			11^2	9	10					13						3		8	12		7^2							31
1	4	5		2	6			11^2	9		14				12	13					3	10	8^3			7^1							32
1	2	4			6	7	8			11^2	9	10^1			12						3		13				5						33
1	4			2	6^1	7	8	12		11^3	10	9^2			14						3		13				5						34
1	2		5	3	6^2	7	8	9		11^1	10	13			12								4										35
1	2		5		6^3	7	8	9^2		13	10	12			14						3^1		11				4						36

DUMBARTON   Third Division

Year Formed: 1872. Ground sharing with Albion Rovers at Cliftonhill. *Club Address:* c/o 62 Round Riding Road,
Dumbarton G82 2JB. *Telephone:* 01389 762569/767864. *Fax:* 01389 762629
Ground Capacity: total: 2496. *Size of Pitch:* 110yd × 72yd.
Chairman: D. Dalglish. *Club Secretary:* Colin J. Hosie. *Company Secretary:* John Benn.
Manager: Jimmy Brown. *Assistant Manager:* Tom Carson. *Coach:* John McCormack. *Physio:* David Steele.
Managers since 1975: A. Wright; D. Wilson; S. Fallon; W. Lamont; D. Wilson; D. Whiteford; A. Totten; M. Clougherty;
R. Auld; J. George; W. Lamont; M. MacLeod; J. Fallon; I. Wallace. *Club Nickname(s):* The Sons. *Previous Grounds:*
Broadmeadow, Ropework Lane, Townend Ground, Boghead Park.
Record Attendance: 18,000 v Raith Rovers, Scottish Cup; 2 Mar, 1957.
Record Transfer Fee received: £125,000 for Graeme Sharp to Everton (March 1982).
Record Transfer Fee paid: £50,000 for Charlie Gibson from Stirling Albion (1989).
Record Victory: 13-1 v Kirkintilloch Central. 1st Rd; 1 Sept, 1888.
Record Defeat: 1-11 v Albion Rovers, Division II; 30 Jan, 1926: v Ayr United, League Cup; 13 Aug, 1952.
Most Capped Player: James McAulay, 9, Scotland.
Most League Appearances: 297: Andy Jardine, 1957-67.
Most Goals in Season (Individual): 38: Kenny Wilson, Division II; 1971-72. *(League and Cup):* 46 Hughie Gallacher, 1955-56.

DUMBARTON 1999–2000 LEAGUE RECORD

Match No.	Date		Venue	Opponents	Result	H/T Score	Lg. Pos.	Goalscorers	Atten-dance
1	Aug	7	A	Albion R	W 3-1	2-1	—	Melvin 2 [1, 38], King [85]	308
2		14	H	Montrose	L 3-4	2-2	4	Flannery 2 [30, 37], Brown [53]	436
3		21	A	East Fife	L 0-1	0-0	5		591
4		28	A	Brechin C	W 2-0	1-0	5	Flannery [6], King [76]	357
5	Sept	4	H	Berwick R	W 2-1	1-0	4	Robertson [15], Flannery [62]	324
6		11	H	Queen's Park	L 0-1	0-0	5		539
7		18	A	East Stirling	W 3-1	3-1	4	Templeman 3 [12, 22, 39]	284
8		25	H	Cowdenbeath	D 1-1	0-1	4	Robertson [46]	424
9	Oct	2	A	Forfar Ath	L 0-5	0-3	6		397
10		16	A	Montrose	W 4-1	3-0	6	Smith 2 [7, 63], Grace [10], Flannery [40]	274
11		23	H	Albion R	D 1-1	1-0	6	Smith [17]	590
12		30	A	Queen's Park	L 2-3	0-3	6	Ward [47], Bradford [52]	713
13	Nov	6	H	East Stirling	W 1-0	1-0	5	Bradford [14]	415
14		14	H	Berwick R	W 1-0	0-0	3	Bradford [69]	415
15		20	H	Brechin C	L 1-3	1-1	4	Flannery [42]	447
16		27	H	Forfar Ath	D 3-3	2-0	6	Robertson [2], Stewart [10], Flannery [53]	469
17	Dec	8	A	Cowdenbeath	W 2-0	0-0	—	Brown A [57], Robertson [69]	262
18		18	A	Albion R	L 0-3	0-0	6		257
19	Jan	3	A	East Stirling	L 1-2	0-0	—	Flannery [66]	308
20		22	H	Cowdenbeath	W 2-0	1-0	6	Brown A [3], Flannery [62]	469
21		29	H	Queen's Park	D 1-1	0-1	6	Flannery [62]	492
22	Feb	5	A	Forfar Ath	L 3-4	1-3	6	Robertson [26], Flannery [79], Smith [89]	439
23		12	A	Brechin C	W 2-1	1-0	5	Flannery [3], Brown And [53]	278
24		26	H	Montrose	W 3-2	1-0	5	King [38], Robertson [81], Hringsson [89]	482
25	Mar	4	A	East Fife	L 1-2	1-0	6	Watters [25]	436
26		11	A	Queen's Park	L 0-2	0-2	6		788
27		14	H	Berwick R	L 0-2	0-2	—		330
28		18	H	East Stirling	W 3-0	1-0	6	Watters [5], Dillon [61], Hringsson [86]	367
29		25	H	Brechin C	W 2-1	0-0	6	Grace [57], Brittain [75]	365
30		28	H	East Fife	D 1-1	0-0	—	Hringsson [88]	394
31	Apr	1	A	Berwick R	D 0-0	0-0	6		560
32		8	A	Cowdenbeath	W 2-1	0-1	5	Flannery 2 [76, 86]	284
33		15	H	Forfar Ath	D 0-0	0-0	6		474
34		22	H	Albion R	D 0-0	0-0	6		415
35		29	A	Montrose	L 1-2	1-1	6	King [43]	267
36	May	1	H	East Fife	W 2-1	0-1	6	King [46], Robertson [65]	3031

Final League Position: 6   1998–99 4

Most Goals Overall (Individual): 169: Hughie Gallacher, 1954-62 (including C Division 1954-55). *(League and Cup):* 202 Hughie Gallacher, 1954-62

Honours
League Champions: Division I 1890-91 (shared with Rangers), 1891-92. Division II 1910-11, 1971-72. Second Division 1991-92; *Runners-up:* First Division 1983-84. Division II 1907-08.
Scottish Cup Winners: 1883; *Runners-up:* 1881, 1882, 1887, 1891, 1897. *League Cup:* —.

Club colours: Shirt: White with yellow horizontal band between two black bands. Shorts: White. Stockings: White with black and gold hooped tops.

Goalscorers: *League (53):* Flannery 14, Robertson 7, King 5, Andrew Brown 4, Smith 4, Bradford 3, Hringsson 3, Templeman 3, Grace 2, Melvin W 2, Watters 2, Brittain 1, Dillon 1, Stewart 1, Ward 1. *Scottish Cup (0).* CIS *Cup (2):* Flannery 2. *Bell's League Cup (1):* Dillon 1 (pen).

Meechan K 12	Dickie M 31	Brittain C 35	Bruce J 21	Jack S 34	King T 32	Melvin W 8 + 2	Grace A 26 + 1	Flannery P 27 + 2	Brown And 27 + 7	Robertson J 33 + 3	Ward H 3 + 10	McHarg S 1 + 6	Dillon J 17 + 8	Smith C 9 + 11	McCormack J 8 + 10	Templeman C 3	Barnes D 24	Melvin M 1 + 5	Bradford J 6	Stewart D 21	Finnigan P 2	McCann K 3	Hringsson H 3 + 10	Brown Alan — + 3	Watters W 6 + 1	Bonar S 3	Gentile C — + 2	Match No.
1	2	3	4	5	6	7³	8	9²	10	11¹	12	13	14															1
1	2	3	4	5	6	7	8	9	10	11																		2
1	2	3	4	5		7²	8	9	10	6	12	13	11¹															3
1	2	3	4	5	6	7¹	8	9	10²	11³			14	12	13													4
1	2	3		5	6	7³	8¹	9	10²	11	12	13	4	14														5
1	2	3		5	6	7³	8	9¹	10²	11	13	12	4	14														6
1	2	3³		5	6		8		14	11¹	7	10	12	13	4	9²												7
1	2	3		5	6		8	9		11		7¹	12		4	10												8
1	2¹	3		5	8	7²		9³	13	11		14	6	12	4	10												9
	3			5	6		8	9	10¹	11	13		4	7²	2		1	12										10
	3			5	6		8	9	13	11	12		4	7¹	2		1		10²									11
	3			5	6	14	8	9¹	12	11	13		4³	7²	2		1		10									12
	2	3		5	6²		8	9³	13	11	7¹			14	12		1		10	4								13
	2	3		5	6¹		8	9	14	11	13			12			1		10³	4	7²							14
	2			5	6	7²	8	9	13	11			3		12		1		10	4¹								15
1	2	3		8	6		7	9¹		11							12	10	4		5							16
1	2	3		8	6			9²	10³	11	12		14	13						4		5	7¹					17
1	2	3		8		12		9	10	11			6¹	14	4		8²							7³	13			18
	3	5	6			8	9	7	11²	12			10¹	2		1				4		13						19
	2	3	5	6			8	9	10²	11³			13	14			1	12		4	7¹							20
	2	3	5	8	6		7	9	10	11¹							1	12		4								21
	2	3	4	8	6		7¹	9	10	11			12				1			5								22
	2	3	5	8	6			9	10²	11³			14	7¹	12		1	13		4								23
	2	3	5	8²	6			10		11			13	7¹	14		1			4				12	9³			24
	2	3	5	8	6			10		11				7¹			1			4				12	9			25
	2	3		8	6		5	9	10¹	11			12				1			4					7			26
	2	3	5	8	6			9	10	7¹			11				1			4				12				27
	2	3	5	8³	6		7²		10	12			11¹	14			1			4				13	9			28
	2	3	5	8	6		7³	14	10	12			11¹				1			4				13	9²			29
	2	3	5	8	6		7³	13	10	12			11¹	9²			1			4				14				30
	2	3	4¹	8	6			9	10³	11			6				1							13	12		7	31
	2	3	4	8	6			9²	10	11			7¹				1			5				12	13			32
		3	4	8	6		2	9	10	11			7¹				1			5				12				33
	2	3	4	8	6		12		10	11			7¹				1			5				13	9²			34
	2	3	4		6		8		10³	11²			13	12			1			5				9¹		7	14	35
	2	3³	4		6		8		10¹	11			12	9²	14		1			5						7	13	36

DUNDEE

Premier League

Year Formed: 1893. *Ground & Address:* Dens Park Stadium, Sandeman St, Dundee DD3 7JY. *Telephone:* 01382 889966.
Fax: 01382 832284.
Ground Capacity: all seated: 12,371. *Size of Pitch:* 101m × 66m.
Chairman: Jim Marr. *Chief Executive:* Peter Marr.
Manager: Ivano Bonetti. *Assistant Manager:* Jimmy Bone. *Coach:* Billy Thomson. *Physio:* John McCreadie. *Youth Coach:* Ray Farningham. *Youth Development:* Kenny Cameron.
Managers since 1975: David White; Tommy Gemmell; Donald Mackay; Archie Knox; Jocky Scott; Dave Smith; Gordon Wallace; Iain Munro; Simon Stainrod; Jim Duffy, John McCormack, John Scott. *Club Nickname(s):* The Dark Blues or The Dee. *Previous Grounds:* Carolina Port 1893-98.
Record Attendance: 43,024 v Rangers, Scottish Cup; 1953.
Record Transfer Fee received: £500,000 for Tommy Coyne to Celtic (March 1989).
Record Transfer Fee paid: £200,000 for Jim Leighton (Feb 1992).
Record Victory: 10-0 Division II v Alloa; 9 Mar, 1947 and v Dunfermline Ath; 22 Mar, 1947.
Record Defeat: 0-11 v Celtic, Division I; 26 Oct, 1895.
Most Capped Player: Alex Hamilton, 24, Scotland.
Most League Appearances: 341: Doug Cowie 1945-61.
Most League Goals in Season (Individual): 52: Alan Gilzean, 1963-64.
Most Goals Overall (Individual): 113: Alan Gilzean.

DUNDEE 1999–2000 LEAGUE RECORD

Match No.	Date	Venue	Opponents	Result	H/T Score	Lg. Pos.	Goalscorers	Attendance
1	Jul 31	A	Dundee U	L 1-2	0-1	—	Falconer 53	11,693
2	Aug 8	H	Hibernian	L 3-4	0-1	8	Lovering (og) 57, McSkimming 58, Annand 73	6050
3	14	A	Aberdeen	W 2-0	2-0	6	Falconer 2 29, 39	9041
4	21	H	Celtic	L 1-2	0-0	8	Sharp 86	10,531
5	28	A	Motherwell	W 2-0	1-0	6	Annand 15, Falconer 83	6278
6	Sept 11	A	Hearts	L 0-4	0-1	7		13,378
7	19	H	St Johnstone	L 1-2	1-0	7	Yates 10	5283
8	25	A	Kilmarnock	W 2-0	1-0	6	Boyack 40, Rae 83	7433
9	Oct 2	H	Rangers	L 2-3	0-1	6	McSkimming 56, Falconer 69	10,494
10	17	H	Dundee U	L 0-2	0-1	6		9484
11	23	A	Hibernian	L 2-5	1-2	9	Falconer 2 5, 74	10,162
12	30	H	Hearts	W 1-0	1-0	8	Tweed 2	6018
13	Nov 6	A	St Johnstone	W 1-0	1-0	7	Annand 43	4917
14	20	H	Motherwell	L 0-1	0-1	7		4340
15	28	A	Rangers	W 2-1	1-0	6	Ireland 13, Rae 89	47,154
16	Dec 12	A	Dundee U	L 0-1	0-0	7		9185
17	27	H	St Johnstone	D 1-1	0-1	—	Falconer 77	6232
18	Jan 22	A	Hearts	L 0-2	0-1	8		13,112
19	26	H	Kilmarnock	D 0-0	0-0	—		4039
20	Feb 5	A	Motherwell	W 3-0	0-0	7	Robertson 49, Rae 65, Grady (pen) 89	5856
21	12	H	Celtic	L 0-3	0-0	7		10,044
22	23	H	Aberdeen	L 1-3	0-0	—	Bayne 87	5784
23	27	H	Rangers	L 1-7	1-6	8	Tweed 28	9297
24	Mar 1	A	Celtic	L 2-6	0-5	—	Robertson 57, Grady 76	55,628
25	4	A	Kilmarnock	D 2-2	0-1	8	Annand 74, Grady 82	8460
26	21	A	Hibernian	W 2-1	0-1	—	Falconer 2 62, 90	10,208
27	26	A	St Johnstone	L 1-2	0-1	8	Falconer 48	4655
28	Apr 1	H	Hearts	D 0-0	0-0	8		6291
29	8	H	Motherwell	W 4-1	0-1	8	Grady 2 52, 54, Billio 85, Luna 87	4701
30	15	A	Celtic	D 2-2	1-2	8	Luna 2, Gould (og) 54	56,403
31	18	A	Aberdeen	W 1-0	0-0	—	Artero 89	12,403
32	22	H	Kilmarnock	L 1-2	0-1	7	Luna 76	6208
33	30	A	Rangers	L 0-3	0-0	8		50,032
34	May 6	H	Dundee U	W 3-0	0-0	8	Falconer 2 50, 74, Grady 65	8580
35	14	H	Hibernian	W 1-0	0-0	7	Rae 54	5060
36	21	A	Aberdeen	L 0-2	0-1	7		6449

Final League Position: 7   1998–99 5

Honours
League Champions: Division I 1961-62. First Division 1978-79, 1991-92, 1997-98. Division II 1946-47; *Runners-up:* Division I 1902-03, 1906-07, 1908-09, 1948-49, 1980-81.
Scottish Cup Winners: 1910; *Runners-up:* 1925, 1952, 1964.
League Cup Winners: 1951-52, 1952-53, 1973-74; *Runners-up:* 1967-68, 1980-81. *(Coca-Cola Cup):* 1995–96.
B&Q (Centenary) Cup Winners: 1990-91; *Runners-up:* 1994-95.

European: *European Cup:* 8 matches (1962-63 semi-finals). *Cup Winners' Cup:* 2 matches: (1964-65).
UEFA Cup: 18 matches: *(Fairs Cup:* 1967-68 semi-finals. *UEFA Cup:* 1971-72, 1973-74, 1974-75).

Club colours: Shirt: Dark blue with red and white trim. Shorts: White. Stockings: Blue and white.

Goalscorers: *League (45):* Falconer 13, Grady 6, Annand 4 (1 pen), Rae 4, Luna 3, McSkimming 2, Robertson 2, Tweed 2, Artero 1, Bayne 1, Billio 1, Boyack 1, Ireland 1, Sharp 1, Yates 1, own goals 2. *Scottish Cup (1):* Rae 1. *CIS Cup (7):* Falconer 4, Boyack 2, Grady 1

Douglas R 35	Smith B 32	Miller W 10+2	Tweed S 34	Maddison L 19+1	Sharp L 11+3	Boyack S 32+4	Rae G 35	McSkimming S 20+2	Grady J 18+13	Falconer W 31	Coyne T —+2	Robertson H 15+9	Yates M 2+3	Van Eijs F 14+2	Annand E 18+9	Bayne G 3+10	Wilkie L 21+3	Matute R 1+4	Slater M —+1	Elliott J —+1	Ireland C 14	Billio P 16+1	Banger N 2+4	Langfield J 1	Raeside R 1	Artero J 6+3	Luna F 5+4	Match No.
1	2	3	4²	5	6²	7	8	9	10¹	11	12	13	14															1
1	2	3	4	5		7	8	12		11		6¹		9²	10	13												2
1	2	3	4	5		7	8	12		11		6¹		9²	10	13												3
1	2	3²	4		6	7	8	11	12			13		9¹	10		5											4
1	2	3	4	5		7²	8	6	9¹	11			14	12	10³		13											5
1	2	3	4	5		7	8	6²	9	11		13			10¹		12											6
1	2	3¹	4	5		7	8	6	10²	11				9³	13		12	14										7
1	2		4	5		7	8	9	12	11²		6			10¹		3	13										8
1	2		4	5	14	7³	8	9	12	11²		6			10¹		3	13										9
1		2²	4	5		7	8	6	9³	11		14		13	10¹		3	12										10
1		3¹	4		6	7	8	11	9	5¹		13	2		10²		12	14										11
1		3¹	4			7	8	6	12	11		5			10						2	9						12
1	2		4			7	8	6	12	11		5			10¹		3					9						13
1	2		4			7	8	6	13	11¹		5²			10		3					9	12					14
1	2		4			7	8	6	11²	12		5			10	13	3					9						15
1	2		4			7	8	6²	14	11		13			5²	10	3¹					9	12					16
1	2		4	5		7	8	12	11	13		6¹					3²					9	10					17
1	2		4	5	14	8	7	10¹	11			6²			12							9³	13					18
1	2		4	5		7²	8	6	11¹	10		12			3		5	13				9						19
1	2²		4			7	8	9	12	11		6			13	10¹	3	5										20
1	2		4	14		7	8	9¹	12	11		6²			13	10³	3	5										21
	2	3	4			7	8	9	10¹	11		6²	14		12	5							13³	1				22
1	2	3	4			6	12	8	10	11		9		7¹			5											23
1		4	13	5		7	8		11	9		6²	10¹	12	3		2											24
1	2		4			5	7	8		10	11	6		12	9¹	3												25
1	2		4	5¹		7	8	13	10	11		6²			12		3					9						26
1	2		4	5		7	8	9¹	11			6			10		3										12	27
1	2		4	5		7	8	10²	11			6³		13	14		3					9¹					12	28
1	2			5		7¹	8	10		6		13	4		3							9					11¹²	29
1	2	14		5	13	8³	6¹	10	12			4			3		7									9²	11	30
1	2		4	5		7²	9	11	6	13		3			8		12										10¹	31
1	2		4	5	14	8		11²	6³			10¹	12		3		9					7	13					32
1	2		4	5		7	8	12	11			3			6							9					10¹	33
1	2	13	4²	5		7	8³	12	11			14			3		6					9					10¹	34
1	2		4	5		7¹	8	10²	11			12			3		6					9	13					35
1	2		4	5	13	7	8	10	11³			6²		14	3							9¹					12	36

DUNDEE UNITED   Premier League

Year Formed: 1909 (1923). *Ground & Address:* Tannadice Park, Tannadice St, Dundee DD3 7JW. *Telephone:* 01382 833166. *Fax:* 01382 889398. *Ground Capacity:* total: 14,209 all seated: stands: east 2868, west 2096, south 2201, Fair Play 1601, George Fox 5151, executive boxes 292.
Size of Pitch: 110yd × 72yd.
Chairman: James Y. McLean. *Company Secretary:* Spence Anderson. *Commercial Manager:* Bill Campbell.
Manager: Paul Sturrock. *Assistant Manager:* John Blackley. *Coach:* Maurice Malpas. *Physio:* David Rankine.
Managers since 1975: J. McLean; I. Golac; W. Kirkwood; T. McLean. *Club Nickname(s):* The Terrors. *Previous Grounds:* None.
Record Attendance: 28,000 v Barcelona, Fairs Cup; 16 Nov, 1966.
Record Transfer Fee received: £4,000,000 for Duncan Ferguson from Rangers (July 1993).
Record Transfer Fee paid: £750,000 for Steven Pressley from Coventry C (July 1995).
Record Victory: 14-0 v Nithsdale Wanderers, Scottish Cup 1st rd; 17 Jan, 1931.
Record Defeat: 1-12 v Motherwell, Division II; 23 Jan, 1954.
Most Capped Player: Maurice Malpas, 55, Scotland.
Most League Appearances: 612, Dave Narey; 1973-94.
Most Appearances in European Matches: 76, Dave Narey (record for Scottish player).
Most League Goals in Season (Individual): 41: John Coyle, Division II; 1955-56.
Most Goals Overall (Individual): 158: Peter McKay.

DUNDEE UNITED 1999–2000 LEAGUE RECORD

Match No.	Date	Venue	Opponents	Result	H/T Score	Lg. Pos.	Goalscorers	Attendance
1	Jul 31	H	Dundee	W 2-1	1-0	—	Skoldmark [13], Ferraz [85]	11,693
2	Aug 7	A	Motherwell	D 2-2	0-2	4	Dodds [69], Ferraz [81]	6791
3	15	H	Celtic	W 2-1	2-0	2	Easton [13], Dodds [41]	12,375
4	21	H	Rangers	L 1-4	0-1	4	De Vos [87]	48,849
5	29	H	Kilmarnock	D 0-0	0-0	3		6621
6	Sept 11	H	Hibernian	W 3-1	1-0	3	Telesnikov [3], Hannah [72], Dodds (pen) [89]	8167
7	18	A	Aberdeen	W 2-1	1-0	3	Hannah [31], Dodds [65]	11,814
8	25	H	Hearts	L 0-2	0-1	3		8510
9	Oct 17	A	Dundee	W 2-0	1-0	3	Dodds [14], Thompson [51]	9484
10	23	H	Motherwell	L 0-2	0-1	3		6213
11	27	A	St Johnstone	W 1-0	0-0	—	Dodds [70]	4236
12	31	A	Hibernian	L 2-3	2-1	3	Dodds [5], Telesnikov [33]	11,073
13	Nov 6	H	Aberdeen	W 3-1	0-0	3	Dodds 2 [47, 81], Paterson J [55]	8170
14	20	A	Kilmarnock	D 1-1	0-0	3	Hannah [65]	7012
15	27	H	St Johnstone	W 1-0	1-0	3	Telesnikov [17]	6367
16	Dec 5	A	Hearts	L 0-3	0-1	3		10,598
17	12	H	Dundee	W 1-0	0-0	3	Ferraz [87]	9185
18	18	A	Celtic	L 1-4	1-0	3	Ferraz [27]	58,181
19	27	A	Aberdeen	L 1-3	1-1	—	Hannah [25]	16,586
20	Jan 22	H	Hibernian	D 0-0	0-0	3		7457
21	Feb 2	H	Rangers	L 0-4	0-2	—		11,241
22	26	A	St Johnstone	L 0-2	0-0	4		4732
23	Mar 4	H	Hearts	L 0-1	0-0	5		6928
24	15	H	Kilmarnock	D 2-2	0-1	—	Hannah [62], Ferraz [90]	6966
25	25	A	Aberdeen	D 1-1	1-1	7	Ferraz [27]	6723
26	Apr 1	A	Hibernian	L 0-1	0-1	7		10,264
27	4	A	Rangers	L 0-3	0-0	—		45,829
28	8	A	Kilmarnock	L 0-1	0-0	7		6037
29	15	H	Rangers	L 0-2	0-2	7		11,419
30	19	A	Motherwell	W 3-1	0-1	—	Mathie [46], Hannah [81], De Vos [83]	4271
31	22	H	Hearts	W 2-1	0-0	5	Mathie 2 [72, 87]	12,604
32	29	A	St Johnstone	L 0-1	0-0	6		5843
33	May 2	H	Celtic	L 0-1	0-1	—		7449
34	6	A	Dundee	L 0-3	0-0	7		8580
35	13	H	Motherwell	L 1-2	1-1	8	Hamilton [37]	5908
36	21	A	Celtic	L 0-2	0-0	8		56,749

Final League Position: 8   1998–99 9

Honours
League Champions: Premier Division 1982-83. Division II 1924-25, 1928-29; *Runners-up:* Division II 1930-31, 1959-60.
First Division Runners-up 1995-96.
Scottish Cup Winners: 1994; *Runners-up:* 1974, 1981, 1985, 1987, 1988, 1991.
League Cup Winners: 1979-80, 1980-81; *Runners-up:* 1981-82, 1984-85, 1997-98.
Summer Cup Runners-up: 1964-65. *Scottish War Cup Runners-up:* 1939-40.

European: *European Cup:* 8 matches (1983-84, semi-finals). *Cup Winners' Cup:* 10 matches (1974-75, 1988-89, 1994-95).
UEFA Cup: 84 matches (*Fairs Cup:* 1966-67, 1969-70, 1970-71. *UEFA Cup:* 1975-76, 1977-78, 1978-79, 1979-80, 1980-81, 1981-82, 1982-83, 1984-85, 1985-86, 1986-87 runners-up, 1987-88, 1989-90, 1990-91, 1993-94, 1997-98).

Club colours: Tangerine and black shirt, black shorts, tangerine and black hoops.

Goalscorers: *League (34):* Dodds 9 (1 pen), Ferraz 6, Hannah 6, Mathie 3, Telesnikov 3, De Vos 2, Easton 1, Hamilton 1, Paterson J 1, Skoldmark 1, Thompson 1. *Scottish Cup (10):* Hamilton 3, Hannah 2, Thompson 2, Ferraz 1, Mathie 1, Preget 1. *CIS Cup (8):* Thompson 3, Davidson 1, Dodds 1, Easton 1, Ferraz 1, Telesnikov 1.

Combe A 35	Pascual B 30+2	Skoldmark M 7+3	De Vos J 35	Worrell D 10+3	Jonsson S 14	Davidson H 17+7	Hannah D 33	Paterson J 8	Dodds W 15	Thompson S 16+10	Ferraz J 15+13	Easton C 22+10	Partridge D 29	Mathie A 10+2	Smith A 4+3	Telesnikov J 22+3	Delaunay J 1	Venetis A 12+5	McCulloch S 10+5	Bove R —+1	McConalogue S 9+7	Malpas M 8+4	Preget A 3+1	Byrne D —+1	Hamilton J 8+5	Gallacher P 1	Jenkins I 1	Patterson D 6	McQuillan J 11	O'Connor S 1	Jenkinson L 1+3	McCracken D 2	Match No.
1	2	3³	4	5	6	7	8	9	10	11¹	12	13																					1
1	2	3	4	5¹	6	7	8	9	10	11¹	12	13																					2
1	2	5	4		6	12	8		7¹	10	11	9	3																				3
1	2	5²	4				8	7³	10	11¹	12	9	3	13	14																		4
1	12	5¹	4			2	8	7	10	13	11¹²	9	3			6																	5
1	2	14	4				8	7¹²	10	12	11¹¹	9	3			6		5³	13														6
1	2		4	5	6		8		10	12	11¹	9	3			7																	7
1	2		4	5	13		8		7¹²		11¹	9	3			6		12															8
1	2	12	4		6¹		8			10	11	9	3			7		5															9
1	2³		4		6²		8		10	11	12	9¹	3			7		13	5		14												10
1	2		4	5	6¹		8		10	11	12		3			7		9															11
1	2		4	5	6²		8		10	11		9¹	3			7		12	13														12
1	2		4	5	6		8	9¹	10	12			3			7		13	11²														13
1	2		4	5¹	6²		8		10	11	13	9	3			7²		12	14														14
1	2		4	12	6		8		10	11		9	3			7		5¹															15
1	2		4	5²				13		11³	14	9	3			7		12		8	6¹	10											16
1	2		4	13	6		8			11	12	9	3			7²		5			10¹												17
1	2	6¹	4	5						11¹	10	9	3			8²		13			7	14											18
1	2	12	4	5	6¹	7²	8			11	10	9	3			13																	19
1	2		4	14	5		8			11²	13	9	3			10¹		6			7	12											20
1	2	5	4		6	7¹	8		10	11³	14	9²	3			13		12															21
	2				6¹		8			11²	14	9	3			12		13	3		7³	10				1	4	5					22
1	2		4		6		8			11	13	9¹	3			7³		14			12	10²						5					23
1	2¹		4	7	12		8			13		9¹	3	11²		14		6			10							5					24
1	2		4		6			12	11			9	3			7		8²			5	10¹							13				25
1	2		4		6		8		11¹	14		7²	3			9³		13	5		10							3	12				26
1	2		4		6		8		13	11³	10	5¹	3			7		9²			12							3	14				27
1	2		4	6¹			8		10	11²	7	5	3			14		12			13							3	9³				28
1			4			13	8		2	14	12	9¹	3			7		11³	6		10²							5	3				29
1	2		4			14	8			12		3¹	10²	9³	7		11	6			13							5					30
1	2		4			12	8			13		3	10	9²	7¹	11³	6				14							5					31
1	2		4			13	8			14	12	3	10	9²	7¹	11³	6											5					32
1			4				8	6¹		13	11³	12	5	10²		7		9			14							3				2	33
1	12		4				8			13	11	9³	3	10²		6		7¹			14							5	2				34
1			4				8			13		10²	5	6		7		11¹	12		9							2	3				35
1			4			6³	8			12	14	10	3	7		13		11²	5		9¹							2					36

DUNFERMLINE ATHLETIC   Premier League

Year Formed: 1885. *Ground & Address:* East End Park, Halbeath Rd, Dunfermline KY12 7RB. *Telephone:* 01383 724295. *Fax:* 01383 723468.
Ground Capacity: all seated: 12,500. *Size of Pitch:* 115yd × 71yd.
Chairman: John Yorkston. *Secretary:* P. A. M. D'Mello. *Commercial Manager:* Miss Audrey Bastianelli.
Manager: Jim Calderwood.
Physio: Philip Yeates, MCSP. *Coach and Youth Development Officer:* John Ritchie.
Managers since 1975: G. Miller; H. Melrose; P. Stanton; T. Forsyth; J. Leishman; I. Munro; J. Scott; B. Paton; Dick Campbell. *Club Nickname(s):* The Pars. *Previous Grounds:* None.
Record Attendance: 27,816 v Celtic, Division I, 30 April, 1968.
Record Transfer Fee received: £650,000 for Jackie McNamara to Celtic (Oct 1995).
Record Transfer Fee paid: £540,000 for Istvan Kozma from Bordeaux (Sept 1989).
Record Victory: 11-1 v Stenhousemuir, Division II, 27 Sept, 1930.
Record Defeat: 1-11 v Hibernian, Scottish Cup, 3rd rd replay, 26 Oct, 1889.
Most Capped Player: Colin Miller 15(59), Canada.
Most League Appearances: 497: Norrie McCathie; 1981-96.
Most League Goals in Season (Individual): 53: Bobby Skinner, Division II, 1925-26.
Most Goals Overall (Individual): 154: Charles Dickson.

DUNFERMLINE ATHLETIC 1999–2000 LEAGUE RECORD

Match No.	Date	Venue	Opponents	Result	H/T Score	Lg. Pos.	Goalscorers	Attendance
1	Aug 7	H	Inverness CT	W 4-0	1-0	—	May (pen) [20], Reid [61], Thomson [81], Petrie [90]	4677
2	Aug 14	A	Airdrieonians	D 2-2	2-1	2	Coyle 2 [9, 21]	2930
3	Aug 21	H	Morton	W 2-1	0-0	2	Smith 2 [63, 78]	4030
4	Aug 28	H	Falkirk	D 1-1	0-1	2	Graham [73]	6520
5	Sept 4	A	Livingston	W 1-0	0-0	2	Coyle [83]	5302
6	Sept 11	H	St Mirren	D 1-1	1-1	2	Huxford [44]	6128
7	Sept 18	A	Raith R	D 2-2	1-0	2	Reid [6], Smith [46]	6087
8	Sept 25	H	Ayr U	W 2-1	2-0	2	Coyle 2 [8, 9]	4044
9	Oct 9	A	Clydebank	W 4-1	2-0	1	Reid [28], Dair [32], Coyle [83], French [86]	475
10	Oct·16	H	Airdrieonians	D 0-0	0-0	2		3964
11	Oct 23	A	Inverness CT	D 1-1	1-0	2	Hampshire [28]	3006
12	Oct 30	A	St Mirren	L 1-3	0-1	2	Moss [51]	6130
13	Nov 6	H	Raith R	D 1-1	1-0	2	Moss [9]	6953
14	Nov 14	H	Livingston	W 3-0	2-0	2	Moss [43], Crawford 2 (1 pen) [35 lpl, 84]	4163
15	Nov 20	A	Falkirk	W 3-1	1-0	2	Coyle [2], Crawford 2 [56, 68]	4263
16	Nov 27	H	Clydebank	W 2-1	2-0	2	Crawford [32], Petrie [41]	4224
17	Dec 4	A	Ayr U	W 3-0	2-0	2	Crawford [40], French 2 [43, 75]	2113
18	Dec 11	A	Morton	W 3-0	0-0	2	Coyle [25], Skinner [32], Crawford [85]	1289
19	Dec 18	H	Inverness CT	W 1-0	0-0	2	Tod [90]	3775
20	Jan 3	A	Raith R	L 0-3	0-2	—		7464
21	Jan 8	A	Livingston	L 0-1	0-0	2		3800
22	Jan 15	H	Falkirk	D 2-2	1-0	2	Hampshire [1], Crawford [73]	7233
23	Jan 22	H	Ayr U	W 2-0	2-0	2	Hampshire [9], Ferguson [11]	3684
24	Feb 5	A	Clydebank	W 3-1	0-1	2	Bullen [67], Crawford 2 [70, 90]	601
25	Feb 12	H	Morton	D 1-1	1-1	2	Bullen [35]	4289
26	Feb 19	H	St Mirren	D 1-1	1-0	2	Petrie [44]	7132
27	Feb 26	A	Airdrieonians	W 2-1	1-0	2	Bullen [1], Potter [50]	2304
28	Mar 4	A	St Mirren	W 2-0	2-0	1	Crawford 2 [3, 27]	6938
29	Mar 18	H	Raith R	L 0-2	0-0	2		6694
30	Mar 25	A	Falkirk	D 1-1	0-0	3	Moss [66]	5242
31	Apr 1	H	Livingston	W 4-1	2-0	3	Coyle [16], May [44], Crawford [58], Bullen [73]	4337
32	Apr 11	A	Ayr U	W 2-0	0-0	—	Crawford [56], Bullen [58]	1798
33	Apr 15	H	Clydebank	W 6-0	4-0	2	Thomson [7], Crawford 2 [10, 24], Bullen [38], Ferguson [51], May [65]	4969
34	Apr 22	A	Inverness CT	W 2-1	2-0	2	Moss [20], Bullen [35]	2677
35	Apr 29	H	Airdrieonians	W 1-0	0-0	2	Graham [83]	4378
36	May 6	A	Morton	L 0-2	0-1	2		1039

Final League Position: 2   1998–99 PREM 10

Honours

League Champions: First Division 1988-89, 1995-96. Division II 1925-26. Second Division 1985-86; *Runners-up:* First Division 1986-87, 1993-94, 1994-95, 1999–2000. Division II 1912-13, 1933-34, 1954-55, 1957-58, 1972-73. Second Division 1978-79.
Scottish Cup Winners: 1961, 1968; *Runners-up:* 1965.
League Cup Runners-up: 1949-50, 1991-92.

European: *Cup Winners' Cup:* 14 matches (1961-62, 1968-69 semi-finals). *UEFA Cup:* 28 matches (*Fairs Cup:* 1962-63, 1964-65, 1965-66, 1966-67, 1969-70).

Club colours: Shirt: Black and white vertical stripes, stippled with red dots. Shorts: Black with white side panel. Stockings: White with red chevrons.

Goalscorers: *League (66):* Crawford 16 (1 pen), Coyle 9, Bullen 7, Moss 6, French 3, Hampshire 3, May 3 (1 pen), Petrie 3, Reid 3, Smith 3, Ferguson 2, Graham 2, Thomson 2, Dair 1, Huxford 1, Potter 1, Tod 1. *Scottish Cup (1):* Graham 1. *CIS Cup (4):* Coyle 2, Petrie 1, Smith 1. *Bell's League Cup (2):* Coyle 2.

Westwater I 22	Shields G 3	McGroarty C 13 + 7	Tod A 27 + 3	Reid B 21 + 2	Dolan J 19	Thomson S 28 + 1	May E 19 + 4	Smith A 11 + 1	Coyle O 23 + 7	Petrie S 32	Graham D — + 15	Ireland C 1 + 2	French H 13 + 8	Nish C — + 2	Dair J 22 + 2	Huxford R 2	Skinner J 26 + 2	Moss D 18 + 6	Potter J 17 + 4	Hampshire S 11 + 8	Crawford S 25	Mampaey K 14	Ferguson I 12	Bullen L 11 + 2	Doesburg M 5 + 1	Templeman C — + 1	McGarty M 1	Match No.
1	2	3	4	5²	6	7	8	9¹	10	11	12	13																1
1	2	3	4	5	6	7	8¹	9¹	10	11			12	13														2
1	2	13	4	5	6		8¹	9	10	11²		12	7		3													3
1		13	4	5	6	2	8	9²	10	11	12		7¹		3													4
1			4	5	6²		13	9¹	10	11	12		8		3	2	7											5
1		12	4	5	6			9	10			11²	13		3	2	7¹	8										6
1		3	4	5	6	7¹		9	10	11			12		2			8										7
1			5	6	13	2		9¹	10	11²	12			3		7	8	4										8
1			5	6¹	7	2		9²	10	11	13		12		3		8		4									9
1		12	5	6³	11	2¹		9	10		13				3		8	14	4	7²								10
1			4	5²	6	7	2			11			10²	13	3¹		8	12	14	9								11
1			4	5	6³	2		13		11			14		3¹		7	8	12	10³	9							12
1		3	4	5		2			10				6				11	8		7	9							13
1		3¹	4	5	6	2	12	9²	10								7	8		13	11							14
1		3	4	5	6	2			10	11							7	8¹		12	9							15
1			4	5	6	3	2		10	11¹			8				7			12	9							16
1		12	4	5	6	3	2¹		10²	11			8³				7	14		13	9							17
1		12	4²	5		3	2¹		10³	11			6				7	8	13	14	9							18
1		3	4	5¹					10	11	12		2				7	8	6		9							19
1		3	4	5¹	6²		13		10	11			2				7	8		12	9							20
1		3	4		6		7			11	12		2²		13		5	8¹		10	9							21
		6	4				2²		10¹	11³	14			3			5	13	12	7	9	1	8					22
		3	4	5		7			11	14		12		2²			6¹	13		10	9³	1	8					23
		12	4				2	7²		11³	13			3¹			6	5	14	9	1	8	10					24
		3	4				2	7¹	13	11²	12		14				6	5		9	1	8	10³					25
			4				3		12	11			2				6	5	7¹	9	1	8	10					26
		14	4				3		13	11			2			12	6¹	5	7	9²	1	8	10³					27
			4				2		14	11³		13		3²		12	6	5	7	9	1	8¹	10					28
			4			2	13		14	11		12		3²		8¹	6	5	7³	9	1		10					29
			4				3			10¹	11						7	6	5		9	1	8	12	2			30
		13				6	7²		10¹	11³	14			3			4		5		9	1	8	12	2			31
						6	7			11				3			4		5		9	1	8	10	2			32
		14				6	7		12	11	13			3¹			4		5		9	1	8³	10²	2			33
	3²					6	7		13	11							4	12	5		9	1	8¹	10	2			34
		12	6³	2					10²	11	13		8				4¹		5		9	1		7	14			35
1		12		6³					10²	11			8³				4		5	14	9			7		13	2	36

EAST FIFE
Third Division

Year Formed: 1903. *Ground & Address:* Bayview Stadium, Harbour View, Methil, Fife KY8 3RW. *Telephone:* 01333 426323. *Fax:* 01333 426376.
Ground Capacity: all seated: 2000. *Size of Pitch:* 115yd × 75yd.
Chairman: Julian Danskin. *Secretary:* Kenneth R. MacKay.
Manager: Rab Shannon. *Coaches:* Dave Gorman, Danny Hendry. *Stadium Controller:* Rob Scott. *Physio:* Neil Bryson.
Managers since 1975: Frank Christie; Roy Barry; David Clarke; Gavin Murray, Alex Totten, Steve Archibald, James Bone. *Club Nickname(s):* The Fifers. *Previous Ground:* Bayview Park.
Record Attendance: 22,515 v Raith Rovers, Division I; 2 Jan, 1950.
Record Transfer Fee received: £150,000 for Paul Hunter from Hull C (March 1990).
Record Transfer Fee paid: £70,000 for John Sludden from Kilmarnock (July 1991).
Record Victory: 13-2 v Edinburgh City, Division II; 11 Dec, 1937.
Record Defeat: 0-9 v Hearts, Division I; 5 Oct, 1957.
Most Capped Player: George Aitken, 5 (8), Scotland.
Most League Appearances: 517: David Clarke, 1968-86.
Most League Goals in Season (Individual): 41: Jock Wood, Division II; 1926-27 and Henry Morris, Division II; 1947-48.
Most Goals Overall (Individual): 225: Phil Weir (215 in League).

EAST FIFE 1999–2000 LEAGUE RECORD

Match No.	Date		Venue	Opponents	Result		H/T Score	Lg. Pos.	Goalscorers	Attendance
1	Aug	7	H	Berwick R	L	1-2	0-1	—	Ritchie (og) [49]	549
2		14	A	East Stirling	W	2-0	0-0	5	Moffat [72], Mackay [85]	300
3		21	H	Dumbarton	W	1-0	0-0	3	McGrillen [61]	591
4		28	H	Montrose	D	0-0	0-0	3		512
5	Sept	4	A	Albion R	W	3-1	1-0	2	Mackay [19], Robertson [49], Honeyman [88]	366
6		11	H	Forfar Ath	W	2-0	0-0	2	Kirk [48], Herd [86]	586
7		18	A	Cowdenbeath	L	0-4	0-1	3		670
8		25	H	Queen's Park	D	0-0	0-0	3		568
9	Oct	2	A	Brechin C	W	3-1	2-1	3	Mackay [14], Moffat 2 [25, 75]	365
10		16	H	East Stirling	W	1-0	1-0	2	Kirk [25]	446
11		23	A	Berwick R	W	1-0	1-0	2	Cusick [19]	506
12		30	A	Forfar Ath	L	2-3	2-2	2	Mackay [12], Moffat [39]	504
13	Nov	6	H	Cowdenbeath	L	2-3	1-2	3	Moffat 2 [42, 60]	569
14		14	H	Albion R	L	1-4	1-3	4	Lumsden (og) [33]	464
15		20	A	Montrose	W	2-1	1-0	3	Robertson [7], Wright [75]	440
16		27	H	Brechin C	W	1-0	1-0	2	Agostini [8]	463
17	Dec	4	A	Queen's Park	W	1-0	0-0	2	Munro [82]	742
18	Jan	3	A	Cowdenbeath	L	0-1	0-0	—		639
19		15	H	Forfar Ath	D	1-1	1-0	2	Robertson [5]	577
20		22	H	Queen's Park	D	0-0	0-0	2		631
21	Feb	5	A	Brechin C	L	1-3	0-1	5	Robertson [80]	337
22		15	H	Montrose	W	2-0	1-0	—	Sharpe [8], Forrest [64]	390
23		19	A	Albion R	L	1-3	0-0	5	Logan [74]	368
24		26	A	East Stirling	L	0-1	0-0	6		328
25	Mar	4	H	Dumbarton	W	2-1	0-1	5	McManus [64], Moffat [85]	436
26		11	A	Forfar Ath	W	1-0	1-0	4	Logan [3]	582
27		18	H	Cowdenbeath	D	1-1	1-0	4	Cusick [3]	702
28		21	H	Berwick R	W	3-1	1-1	—	Cusick [14], Robertson [71], Moffat [89]	551
29		25	A	Montrose	D	1-1	1-1	4	McManus [25]	442
30		28	A	Dumbarton	D	1-1	0-0	—	McCormick [80]	394
31	Apr	1	H	Albion R	W	2-1	1-0	4	McManus [44], Moffat [58]	512
32		11	A	Queen's Park	L	0-1	0-1	—		788
33		15	H	Brechin C	D	1-1	1-0	4	McCormick [5]	452
34		22	A	Berwick R	W	1-0	0-0	4	Moffat [89]	942
35		29	H	East Stirling	W	3-1	2-0	3	Cusick [11], McCormick [13], Moffat [75]	590
36	May	6	A	Dumbarton	L	1-2	1-0	4	Logan [11]	3031

Final League Position: 4   1998–99 DIV 2 9

Honours
League Champions: Division II 1947-48; *Runners-up:* Division II 1929-30, 1970-71. Second Division 1983-84, 1995-96.
Scottish Cup Winners: 1938; *Runners-up:* 1927, 1950.
League Cup Winners: 1947-48, 1949-50, 1953-54.

Club colours: Shirt: Gold with black shoulders. Shorts: Black. Stockings: Black.

Goalscorers: *League (45):* Moffat 11, Robertson 5, Cusick 4, Mackay 4, Logan 3, McCormick 3, McManus 3, Kirk 2, Agostini 1, Forrest 1, Herd 1, Honeyman 1, McGrillen 1, Munro 1, Sharp 1, Wright 1, own goals 2. *Scottish Cup (1):* O'Hara 1 *CIS Cup (4):* Agostini 1, Kirk 1, Logan 1, Robertson 1 (pen). *Bell's League Cup (2):* Robertson 1, Wright 1.

McCulloch W 36	Munro K 24+3	Gibb R 6+4	Ramsay S 6+3	Agostini D 31+1	Herd W 16	Robertson G 26+7	Mackay S 26+5	Wright D 4+14	Kirk S 5+6	Logan R 21+10	Porteous A —+1	Cusick J 23+3	Martin J —+1	Shannon R 24+1	Love G 13+3	Honeyman B 2+3	McGrillen P 3	Moffat B 28+2	Mooney R —+1	Forrest G 23+3	Clark P 1+3	Tinley G 1+2	O'Hara G 14	McAnally D 2	Sharpe R 14	McCloy B 14	Jackson C 11	McCormick S 11	McManus T 11	Match No
1	2	3	4	5	6	7	8	9	10^1	11	12	13	14																	1
1	13			4		6	11^2	8	14	7		5		2	3	9^1		10^3	12											2
1	4			14		6	7	8^1	12			11		5	2	3	13	9^2	10^3											3
1			4^3	5	6	7^1	8	14	13	11		12		2	3			9^2	10											4
1	3	12	4	5	6^1	7	8	14	9^3	11				2		13		10^2												5
1	3		4^3	5	6	9	8	13	12	7^2	11			2	14			10^1												6
1	3		11^3	5	6	9	8		12	7^2		4		2	14			10^1	13											7
1	2			13	5		11^1	8		9	7^2	4			3	12		10		6										8
1	3				5	6	8^2	11	13	12		4^1		2	9			10		7										9
1	12			5	6^1	9^3	11	13		7	14	4		2	3			10^2		8										10
1	12			5	6	9	11	13		7		4		2	3			10^2		8^1										11
1	14			5	6	9^3	11^2	13		7^1		4		2	3			10		8	12									12
1	3			5	6		7^2	12		9	13	4		2				10		8	11^1									13
1	14	3		5	6^3	9	8	11^1		12		4		2				10^2	13	7										14
1	2			5			11	7	9^1			8			6	3		10		12					4					15
1	2			5			9	11	13			7			8^1	6	3	10^2		12					4					16
1	2			5			11	9				7			6	3		10		8					4					17
1	2			5			11^2	9^1	13			7		12	6	3		10		8					4					18
1	2			5	6		9	11				7						10		8					4	3				19
1	2^1			5	6		9	13				12			8	3		10		7					4		11^2			20
1	2	3		13		6^2	11	10^1	9			7		8^3	4			12		14			5							21
1	2			5			11	10^2	13			6						7^1							3	4	8	9		22
1	2^2			5			11^1	10	13			6						7		12					3	4	8	9		23
1	2			5			12	6^1										10		7	13		4^2		3	8	11	9		24
1	2			5			12											10		11			5		3	4	8	9^1	7	25
1	2			5			12	13				8			6^2			10^1							3	4	11	9		26
1	2			5			7	8							6^1		12	10							3	4	11	9		27
1	3			5			11	13	12		14				6^2	2		10^3		7					4		8	9^1		28
1				5			11^1	12								2		10		7			6		3	4	8	9		29
1				5										4	2			10		6			3			8	7	9	11	30
1				5			12	13						4				10^2		7			6		3	2	8	9^1	11	31
1				5				13				7		2^2				10		12			6		3	4	8^1	9	11	32
1	2			5			12					8			6			10		7					3	4		9^1	11	33
1	2^1	14		5^3			13	7	12			8^1			6			10		11					3	4		9		34
1	2	12		5^1			8	14	13			6^2						10		7					3	4		9^3	11	35
1	2^3	5					12	11^2	13	8		6			14			10^1		7					3	4		9		36

EAST STIRLINGSHIRE   Third Division

Year Formed: 1880. *Ground & Address:* Firs Park, Firs St, Falkirk FK2 7AY. *Telephone:* 01324 623583. *Fax:* 01324 637 862
Ground Capacity: total: 1880, seated: 200. *Size of Pitch:* 112yd × 72yd.
Chairman: A. Mackin. *Vice Chairman:* Tom Kirk. *Secretary:* Leslie G. Thomson.
Manager: George Fairley. *Physio:* Paul Green.
Managers since 1975: I. Ure; D. McLinden; W. P. Lamont; A. Ferguson; W. Little; D. Whiteford; D. Lawson; J. D.
Connell; A. Mackin; Dom Sullivan; Bobby McCulley; Billy Little; John Brownlie; Hugh McCann. *Club Nickname(s):*
The Shire. *Previous Grounds:* Burnhouse, Randyford Park, Merchiston Park, New Kilbowie Park.
Record Attendance: 12,000 v Partick T, Scottish Cup 3rd rd; 21 Feb 1921.
Record Transfer Fee received: £35,000 for Jim Docherty to Chelsea (1978).
Record Transfer Fee paid: £6,000 for Colin McKinnon from Falkirk (March 1991).
Record Victory: 11-2 v Vale of Bannock, Scottish Cup 2nd rd; 22 Sept, 1888.
Record Defeat: 1-12 v Dundee United, Division II; 13 Apr, 1936.
Most Capped Player: Humphrey Jones, 5 (14), Wales.
Most League Appearances: 380: Gordon Russell, 1983-2000.
Most League Goals in Season (Individual): 36: Malcolm Morrison, Division II; 1938-39.
Most Goals Overall (Individual): —.

EAST STIRLINGSHIRE 1999–2000 LEAGUE RECORD

Match No.	Date	Venue	Opponents	Result	H/T Score	Lg. Pos.	Goalscorers	Attendance
1	Aug 7	A	Queen's Park	L	1-2	1-2	—	Barr [27]	450
2	14	H	East Fife	L	0-2	0-0	10		300
3	21	A	Forfar Ath	D	1-1	1-1	10	Muirhead [27]	416
4	28	H	Cowdenbeath	L	0-1	0-1	10		205
5	Sept 4	A	Montrose	W	2-1	2-1	8	Laidlaw [30], Higgins [43]	278
6	11	A	Brechin C	W	2-1	2-1	8	Laidlaw [16], Hardie [25]	284
7	18	H	Dumbarton	L	1-3	1-3	8	Laidlaw [44]	284
8	25	A	Albion R	D	1-1	0-1	7	Laidlaw [73]	122
9	Oct 2	H	Berwick R	L	0-3	0-2	8		266
10	16	A	East Fife	L	0-1	0-1	8		446
11	23	H	Queen's Park	D	1-1	1-0	8	Laidlaw [17]	354
12	30	H	Brechin C	D	0-0	0-0	8		210
13	Nov 6	A	Dumbarton	L	0-1	0-1	8		415
14	14	H	Montrose	W	2-0	1-0	8	Higgins [23], Storrar [89]	241
15	20	A	Cowdenbeath	W	2-1	2-1	7	Laidlaw 2 [10, 27]	248
16	27	A	Berwick R	L	0-1	0-0	8		318
17	Dec 18	A	Queen's Park	W	1-0	1-0	8	Higgins [19]	413
18	Jan 3	H	Dumbarton	W	2-1	0-0	—	Laidlaw 2 [54, 82]	308
19	22	A	Albion R	W	1-0	0-0	7	Hay [65]	260
20	29	H	Forfar Ath	L	0-2	0-1	7		201
21	Feb 5	H	Berwick R	L	0-1	0-0	7		255
22	12	H	Cowdenbeath	L	0-4	0-3	8		224
23	19	A	Montrose	D	0-0	0-0	8		327
24	26	H	East Fife	W	1-0	0-0	7	Higgins [76]	328
25	29	H	Albion R	W	4-3	0-2	—	Higgins 2 [58, 66], McPherson [75], Scott [78]	191
26	Mar 4	A	Forfar Ath	L	0-3	0-1	7		399
27	7	A	Brechin C	D	1-1	0-1	—	Higgins [69]	207
28	11	H	Brechin C	L	0-3	0-3	7		259
29	18	A	Dumbarton	L	0-3	0-1	7		367
30	25	A	Cowdenbeath	D	0-0	0-0	7		243
31	Apr 1	H	Montrose	W	1-0	1-0	7	Crawford [8]	205
32	8	H	Albion R	W	3-1	2-1	7	Higgins [13], Crawford [20], Storrar [88]	206
33	15	A	Berwick R	L	0-3	0-1	7		486
34	22	H	Queen's Park	L	0-1	0-1	7		497
35	29	A	East Fife	L	1-3	0-2	7	Higgins [69]	590
36	May 6	H	Forfar Ath	L	0-1	0-1	7		409

Final League Position: 7   1998–99 8

Honours
League Champions: Division II 1931-32; C Division 1947-48. *Runners-up:* Division II 1962-63. Second Division 1979-80. Division Three 1923-24.
Scottish Cup: —.
League Cup: —.

Club colours: Shirt: Black and white stripes. Shorts: Black and white. Stockings: Black with 3 tangerine bands on top.

Goalscorers: *League (28):* Higgins 9, Laidlaw 9, Crawford 2, Storrar 2, Barr 1, Hardie 1, Hay 1, McPherson 1, Muirhead 1, Scott 1. *Scottish Cup (2):* Hay 1, Higgins 1. *CIS Cup (2):* Higgins 1 (pen), Muirhead 1. *Bell's League Cup (1):* Hardie 1.

Butter J 36	Storrar A 36	Brown M 35+1	Ross B 7+1	Bowsher C 3	Muirhead D 36	Ferguson B 16+7	Barr A 10+7	Laidlaw S 19	Higgins G 22+4	Elliott A 19+3	Russell G 31+1	Gordon K 22+13	Lynes C 21+5	Hardie M 21	McNeill W 3+6	Donnelly S 2+3	McDonald G —+2	O'Hara G 2	MacMillan G 2	Menmuir S 1	Hay D 12+3	Campbell M 1+1	Allan G 3	Morrison S 3+3	Crawford G 7+6	Scott A 15+1	McPherson D 1+11	McCann K 7	Sutherland M 2+2	Abdulrahman K 1	Match No.
1	2	3¹	4	5	6	7³	8	9	10	11²	12	13	14																		1
1	2	12	4	5	6	8	7²	9	10	11¹	3	13																			2
1	2	4	5¹	6		7	9		11	3	14		8	10³	12²	13															3
1	2	4	6³	12	7¹	9		11²	3	14	8	10		5																	4
1	2	4	6	8	7¹	9	10³	12	3	14	11	13	5²																		5
1	2	4	6	7¹	9	10²	11³	3	12		8	13	14	5																	6
1	2	4	6	7	12	9	11¹	3	10		8		13	5²																	7
1	2	4	12	6	7³	11²	9	14	3	10		8	13	5¹																	8
1	2	4	5	6	13	7¹	9	11²	3	10		8	12	5																	9
1	3	4	5	6	2	13	9¹		10	11	8²	12		7																	10
1	3	4	5	6	2		9		10¹	11	8	12		7																	11
1	3	4	5	6¹	2	12	9	13		11	8	10²		7																	12
1	3	6	4¹	8	2	13	9		10	7²	11	12		5																	13
1	2	4	8	13	7²	9	10³	11	3	14	12	5	6¹																		14
1	2	4	8	12	7¹	9	10³	11	3	14	13	5	6²																		15
1	2	4	6	7	9	10	11¹	3	12		8	5																			16
1	2	4	8	7¹	13	9	10	11²	3	12	6	5																			17
1	2	4	8	12	7¹	9		3	13	6	5	10²	11																		18
1	2	4	6	7	12	9²	13	11	3	10	5		8¹																		19
1	2	5	6²	7¹	12	9	11	3	10	4	13		8³	14																	20
1	2	4	8	12	3	7¹	10	5				6	9	11																	21
1	2	4	8	12	14	6	10	13	5	3³	9¹	7	11²																		22
1	2	4	5		9	11²	3	10	6	8			12	7	13																23
1	2	5	4		9	10²	3	11	8	6			12	7	13																24
1	2	5	4		9²	10¹	3	11	8	6³		14		13	7	12															25
1	2	5	4³		9	10¹	3	11²	8	6		14		13	7	12															26
1	2	5	4		9	10¹	3	11²	8	6				13	7	12															27
1	2	5³	4		9¹	10²	3	11	8	6		14		12	7	13															28
1	2	6	4		3	7	8	10		5			9	11¹	12	8															29
1	2	6	4		9	3	12	11		8	7			5	10¹																30
1	2	6	4		9	3	12	11		8	7			5	10¹																31
1	2	6	4	12	9	3	10	11¹		8²	7	13		5																	32
1	2	6	4²	12	9	3	10	11		13	8¹	7¹	14	5																	33
1	2¹	6	4		9	3	10	11		12	7	13	5		8²																34
1	7	3		8	2	10	6	9²	11			5¹	12	4	13																35
1	2	6		8	4²	10	3	9¹	11			7	13	5	12																36

FALKIRK

First Division

Year Formed: 1876. *Ground & Address:* Brockville Park, Hope St, Falkirk FK1 5AX. *Telephone:* 01324 624121. *Fax:* 01324 612418.
Ground Capacity: total: 9706, seated: 2661. *Size of Pitch:* 110yd × 72yd.
Chairman: Martin Ritchie. *Secretary:* Alex Blackwood. *General Manager:* Crawford Baptie.
Manager: Alex Totten. *Assistant Manager:* Kevin McAllister. *Physio:* Alec McQueen.
Managers since 1975: J. Prentice; G. Miller; W. Little; J. Hagart; A. Totten; G. Abel; W. Lamont; D. Clarke; J. Duffy; W. Lamont; J. Jefferies; J. Lambie E. Bannon; A. Totten. *Club Nickname(s):* The Bairns. *Previous Grounds:* Randyford 1876–81; Blinkbonny Grounds 1881–83; Brockville Park 1883 to present.
Record Attendance: 23,100 v Celtic, Scottish Cup 3rd rd; 21 Feb, 1953.
Record Transfer Fee received: £380,000 for John Hughes to Celtic (Aug 1995).
Record Transfer Fee paid: £225,000 to Chelsea for Kevin McAllister (Aug 1991).
Record Victory: 12-1 v Laurieston, Scottish Cup 2nd rd; 23 Sept, 1893.
Record Defeat: 1-11 v Airdrieonians, Division I; 28 Apr, 1951.
Most Capped Player: Alex Parker, 14 (15), Scotland.
Most League Appearances: (post-war): 353, George Watson, 1975–87.
Most League Goals in Season (Individual): 43: Evelyn Morrison, Division I; 1928-29.
Most Goals Overall (Individual): Dougie Moran, 86, 1957–61 and 1964–67.

FALKIRK 1999–2000 LEAGUE RECORD

Match No.	Date	Venue	Opponents	Result	H/T Score	Lg. Pos.	Goalscorers	Attendance
1	Aug 7	H	Morton	L 2-4	0-1	—	McStay [67], Sinclair [82]	2945
2	Aug 14	A	Inverness CT	W 3-2	1-2	6	McDonald [21], Crabbe [70], Hutchison [86]	3022
3	Aug 21	H	Ayr U	W 2-1	1-1	4	Crabbe (pen) [39], Moss [80]	2938
4	Aug 28	A	Dunfermline Ath	D 1-1	1-0	4	Moss [31]	6520
5	Sept 4	H	Clydebank	W 3-2	2-0	3	McDonald 2 [1, 31], Moss [88]	2496
6	Sept 11	H	Livingston	L 0-2	0-1	4		3326
7	Sept 18	A	Airdrieonians	D 0-0	0-0	4		2868
8	Sept 25	H	St Mirren	W 3-1	3-0	4	Coyne [1], Henry 2 [15, 26]	4505
9	Oct 2	A	Raith R	L 1-2	0-1	5	Crabbe [86]	3182
10	Oct 16	H	Inverness CT	L 0-2	0-1	5		2403
11	Oct 23	A	Morton	W 3-2	1-0	5	McDonald 2 [12, 69], Crabbe [79]	1409
12	Oct 30	A	Livingston	D 1-1	0-0	5	Morris [70]	3482
13	Nov 6	H	Airdrieonians	W 2-0	2-0	4	Crabbe [1], Hagen [33]	2644
14	Nov 14	A	Clydebank	W 3-0	0-0	4	Nicholls [72], Hagen [79], Crabbe [82]	500
15	Nov 20	A	Dunfermline Ath	L 1-3	0-1	4	Nicholls [50]	4263
16	Nov 27	H	Raith R	W 2-1	1-0	3	Hagen [14], Crabbe [64]	2611
17	Dec 4	A	St Mirren	L 1-2	0-1	4	Nicholls [61]	4980
18	Dec 11	A	Ayr U	D 1-1	0-1	4	Nicholls [75]	1729
19	Dec 18	H	Morton	W 2-1	0-0	3	Hagen [73], McStay [90]	2015
20	Dec 27	H	Livingston	L 2-3	1-0	—	Nicholls 2 [34, 72]	3109
21	Jan 3	A	Airdrieonians	W 2-0	1-0	—	Nicholls [30], Lawrie [70]	2418
22	Jan 8	H	Clydebank	W 4-0	3-0	3	McDonald [20], Nicholls [25], Hagen [43], Crabbe [69]	2119
23	Jan 15	A	Dunfermline Ath	D 2-2	0-1	4	McKenzie [85], Den Bieman [90]	7233
24	Jan 22	H	St Mirren	W 2-0	1-0	4	Henry [6], Christie [66]	4746
25	Feb 5	A	Raith R	W 1-0	1-0	3	Hutchison [11]	4140
26	Feb 12	H	Ayr U	W 1-0	1-0	3	Lawrie [15]	2729
27	Feb 26	A	Inverness CT	W 3-0	2-0	3	Crabbe 2 [12, 45], Hutchison [88]	2727
28	Mar 4	A	Livingston	W 1-0	1-0	3	Nicholls [44]	4055
29	Mar 18	H	Airdrieonians	W 8-0	3-0	2	Crabbe 2 (2 pens) [4, 67], Nicholls 2 [20, 73], McAllister [45], Lawrie [58], Hutchison [68], Morris	2927
30	Mar 25	H	Dunfermline Ath	D 1-1	0-0	2	Christie [87]	5242
31	Apr 2	A	Clydebank	W 1-0	1-0	2	Hagen [34]	727
32	Apr 8	A	St Mirren	L 0-1	0-0	2		6742
33	Apr 15	H	Raith R	W 1-0	0-0	3	Lawrie [58]	4686
34	Apr 22	A	Morton	W 2-0	0-0	3	Hutchison [73], McAllister [86]	1037
35	Apr 29	H	Inverness CT	D 2-2	0-1	3	McQuilken [50], Crabbe [78]	4449
36	May 6	A	Ayr U	D 3-3	1-2	3	Crabbe [39], Nicholls [78], Kerr [90]	2667

Final League Position: 3 1998–99 2

Honours
League Champions: Division II 1935-36, 1969-70, 1974-75. First Division 1990-91, 1993-94. Second Division 1979-80; *Runners-up:* Division I 1907-08, 1909-10. First Division 1985-86, 1988-89. Division II 1904-05, 1951-52, 1960-61. *Scottish Cup Winners:* 1913, 1957; *Runners-up:* 1997. *League Cup Runners-up:* 1947-48. *B&Q Cup Winners:* 1993-94. *League Challenge Cup Winners:* 1997-98.

Club colours: Shirt: Navy blue. Shorts: White. Stockings: Navy blue.

Goalscorers: *League (67):* Crabbe 14 (3 pens), Nicholls 12, Hagen 6, McDonald 6, Hutchison 5, Lawrie 4, Henry 3, Moss 3, Christie 2, McAllister 2, McStay 2, Morris 2, Coyne 1, Den Bieman 1, Kerr 1, McKenzie 1, McQuilken 1, Sinclair 1. *Scottish Cup (7):* Crabbe 2, Hagen 2, Lawrie 1, McQuilken 1, Nicholls 1. *CIS Cup (3):* Crabbe 2, own goal 1. *Bell's League Cup (2):* Lawrie 1, McDonald 1.

Hogarth M 36	Rennie S 10 + 3	McQuilken J 28 + 3	Lawrie A 33 + 2	Sinclair D 19 + 3	McKenzie S 34	Hagen D 33 + 2	McStay G 2 + 4	Crabbe S 35	McDonald C 26 + 4	Hutchison G 22 + 10	Kerr M 2 + 5	Coyne T 6 + 2	Moss D 3 + 1	Nicholls D 32 + 1	Seaton A 9 + 10	Henry J 21	McAllister K 6 + 3	Morris 18 + 7	Pearson C — + 1	Innes C 2	Den Bieman I 15	Christie K 14	Waddell R — + 1	Match No
1	2	3	4	5	6	7	8	9^1	10	11	12													1
1	2	3	4	5	6	11^1		9	8	7				10	12									2
1	2	3	4	5	8	11^2		9	13	7				10^1	6	12								3
1	13	3	4	5	2	11^2		9	12	7				8^1	10	6								4
1	2	3	4	5		12		9	8	7				11^1	10	6								5
1	2^2	3	4^3	5	6	11^1	13	9		7				12	10	14	8							6
1		3	4	5	2	11^1		9	10	7				12	6	8								7
1		3	4	5	2	11^2		9	12	7				10^1	6	13	8							8
1	12		4	5	2			9	8^1	11		14	10	3	6^2	7^3	13							9
1	14	3	4	5	2	11		9	8^1	10^3				6	13		7^2	12						10
1			4	5	2	11^1	12	9	8	7				6	3	10								11
1			4	5	2	12		9	10	11^1				6	3	8	7							12
1		4	12	5^1	2	11		9	10	13				6	3	8	7^2							13
1		4	12	5^1	2	11		9	10	13				6	3	8	7^2							14
1		4	12	5	2	11^1		9	10	7				6	3	8								15
1		4	3		2	11^1		9	10	12				6	13	8^2	7		5					16
1		3	4		2	11		9	10	7^2				13	6	12	8		5^1					17
1		3	4	5	2	11		9	10					6	12	8	7^1							18
1	10^1	4	5		2	11	13	9		7^2				6	3	8	12							19
1		3	4	5	2	11	14	9^3	10^1	13				6	12	8	7^2							20
1		3			2	7		9^2	8^1	12				11		6		10			4	5	13	21
1		3^3			2	7^3	13	9	8^1					11	14	6	12	10			4	5		22
1		3			2	7		9	8^1	12				11		6		10			4	5		23
1		3			2	7		9	8					11		6		10			4	5		24
1		3			2	7		9	8^1	12				11		6		10			4	5		25
1		3			2	7		9	8^1	12				11		6		10			4	5		26
1		3			2	7		9	8^1	12				11		6		10			4	5		27
1		3			2	7	13	9	8^1	12				11		6		10^2			4	5		28
1		3			2^3	14		9	8^1	12				11	13	6	7^2	10			4	5		29
1		3			2	7^1		9	8	11					12	6		10			4	5		30
1		3			2	7^1		9	8	11					12	6		10			4	5		31
1		3			2	7^1		9	8	11					12	6		10			4	5		32
1		3			2	7		9	8	11					12	6		10^1			4	5		33
1		3		5	2	7		9	8^2	11					13	6	12	10^1			4			34
1	12	3		5^1	2	7^3		9	8	11					13	6^2	14	10			4			35
1		12	3	5^3	2	7		9	8	11					13	6	14	10^2			4^1			36

FORFAR ATHLETIC   Second Division

Year Formed: 1885. *Ground & Address:* Station Park, Carseview Road, Forfar. *Telephone:* 01307 463576/462259.
Fax: 01307 466956.
Ground Capacity: total: 8732, seated: 739. *Size of Pitch:* 115yd × 69yd.
Chairman and Secretary: David McGregor.
Manager: Ian McPhee. *Assistant Manager:* Billy Bennett. *Physio:* Jim Peacock. *Coaches:* Jim Moffat, Gordon Wallace.
Managers since 1975: Jerry Kerr; Archie Knox; Alex Rae; Doug Houston; Henry Hall; Bobby Glennie;
Paul Hegarty; Tommy Campbell. *Club Nickname(s):* Loons. *Previous Grounds:* None.
Record Attendance: 10,780 v Rangers, Scottish Cup 2nd rd; 2 Feb, 1970.
Record Transfer Fee received: £65,000 for David Bingham to Dunfermline Ath (September 1995).
Record Transfer Fee paid: £50,000 for Ian McPhee from Airdrieonians (1991).
Record Victory: 14-1 v Lindertis, Scottish Cup 1st rd; 1 Sept 1988.
Record Defeat: 2-12 v King's Park, Division II; 2 Jan, 1930.
Most Capped Player: —.
Most League Appearances: 484: Ian McPhee, 1978–88 and 1991–98.

FORFAR ATHLETIC 1999–2000 LEAGUE RECORD

Match No.	Date	Venue	Opponents	Result	H/T Score	Lg. Pos.	Goalscorers	Atten- dance
1	Aug 7	H	Brechin C	D 0-0	0-0	—		620
2	14	A	Cowdenbeath	W 3-0	1-0	2	Brand [30], Milne [49], McLean [86]	256
3	21	H	East Stirling	D 1-1	1-1	4	Brand [44]	416
4	28	H	Albion R	W 2-0	1-0	2	Brand [37], Milne [72]	421
5	Sept 4	A	Queen's Park	D 1-1	1-1	3	Taylor [29]	764
6	11	A	East Fife	L 0-2	0-0	4		586
7	18	H	Berwick R	D 1-1	0-0	5	McCheyne [90]	375
8	28	A	Montrose	L 0-2	0-0	—		281
9	Oct 2	H	Dumbarton	W 5-0	3-0	5	Milne 3 [6, 35, 84], MacDonald [12], Cargill [70]	397
10	16	H	Cowdenbeath	W 3-1	3-1	5	Milne 2 [9, 13], Cargill [24]	399
11	23	A	Brechin C	W 2-0	0-0	3	Taylor [60], Milne [65]	502
12	30	H	East Fife	W 3-2	2-2	3	Taylor [16], McIllravey 2 [18, 56]	504
13	Nov 6	A	Berwick R	D 2-2	1-1	2	Rattray [28], Milne [72]	328
14	14	H	Queen's Park	D 2-2	1-1	2	Brand [24], Taylor [50]	626
15	20	A	Albion R	W 1-0	1-0	2	Robson [22]	311
16	27	A	Dumbarton	D 3-3	0-2	3	Robson [60], Donaldson [75], Milne [81]	469
17	Dec 7	H	Montrose	L 1-2	0-0	—	Brand [63]	379
18	Jan 15	A	East Fife	D 1-1	0-0	5	Craig [90]	577
19	22	A	Montrose	W 5-1	2-1	4	Robson 2 [14, 33], Brand [67], Milne [72], McKellar [78]	588
20	29	A	East Stirling	W 2-0	1-0	2	Robson [26], Milne [71]	201
21	Feb 5	H	Dumbarton	W 4-3	3-1	2	McCheyne [18], Craig 2 [20, 35], Milne [80]	439
22	12	H	Albion R	W 3-1	1-1	1	McKellar [36], Craig [63], McLean [81]	395
23	19	A	Queen's Park	L 2-3	2-1	2	McCheyne [19], Craig [39]	818
24	26	A	Cowdenbeath	L 1-4	0-1	3	Milne [47]	354
25	29	H	Brechin C	W 2-0	1-0	—	Milne [20], Robson [47]	516
26	Mar 4	H	East Stirling	W 3-0	1-0	2	Craig 2 [21, 66], McKellar [86]	399
27	7	H	Berwick R	W 2-0	1-0	—	McCheyne [16], Rattray [54]	482
28	11	H	East Fife	L 0-1	0-1	2		582
29	18	A	Berwick R	L 0-2	0-0	3		614
30	25	A	Albion R	W 1-0	1-0	3	Craig [34]	307
31	Apr 1	H	Queen's Park	W 4-0	1-0	1	McIlravey 2 [21, 44], Robson [53], McPhee [85]	570
32	8	H	Montrose	L 1-2	0-0	2	Robson [54]	516
33	15	A	Dumbarton	D 0-0	0-0	3		474
34	22	A	Brechin C	L 0-1	0-1	3		548
35	29	H	Cowdenbeath	D 2-2	1-2	4	Farnan [39], Robson [53]	556
36	May 6	A	East Stirling	W 1-0	1-0	3	Milne [2]	409

Final League Position: 3   1998–99 DIV 2 10

Most League Goals in Season (Individual): 45: Dave Kilgour, Division II; 1929–30.
Most Goals Overall (Individual): 124, John Clark.

Honours
League Champions: Second Division 1983–84. Third Division 1994–95; *Runners-up:* 1996–97. C Division 1948–49.
Scottish Cup: Semi-finals 1982.
League Cup: Semi-finals 1977–78.

Club colours: Shirt: Sky blue with navy chest panel. Shorts: Navy. Stockings: Sky blue.

Goalscorers: *League (64):* Milne 16, Robson 9, Craig 8, Brand 6, McCheyne 4, McIlravey 4, Taylor 4, McKellar 3, Cargill 2, McLean 2, Rattray 2, Donaldson 1, Farnan 1, MacDonald 1, McPhee 1. *Scottish Cup (3):* Donaldson 1 (pen), Milne 1, Robson 1. *CIS Cup (1):* MacDonald 1. *Bell's League Cup (3):* Milne 2, Christie 1.

Garden S 36	Rattray A 31 + 1	Donaldson E 26 + 3	McCheyne G 31	Johnston G 13 + 2	McPhee G 22 + 7	McLean B 11 + 8	Taylor A 30 + 1	Brand R 17 + 6	Milne S 35	Cargill A 31	MacDonald I 6 + 7	McIlravey P 9 + 11	Ferguson G 3	Craig D 31	Nairn J 1 + 4	Christie S 3 + 4	Robson B 25	Morris R 3 + 5	McKellar J 7 + 15	Farnan C 19 + 2	Horn R 6	Match No.
1	2	3	4	5	6	7¹	8	9²	10	11	12	13										1
1	2	3	4	5	6	12	8	9²	10¹	11	13	7										2
1	2	3	4	5	6	11¹	8	9	10	12		7										3
1	2	3	4			7	8	9²	10	11¹	12		5	6	13							4
1	2	3	4	5	7	12	8	9	10	11¹				6								5
1	5	3	2	14	7	4²	8³	9	10	11¹	6	12	13									6
1	5	3¹	2	4	7	8	12		10	11	6		13	9²								7
1	2	13	4	5	8	7	9		10		12	14		3³			11¹	6²				8
1	5³	6	2	12	4	9²	10	8	7¹	13		14		3			11					9
1	5	6	2	12	4	9²	10³	8	7¹	14		13		3			11					10
1	5	6	2	13	11	4	9¹	10³	8	7²		14		3			12					11
1	5	6	2	7	11	4	10	8	9¹					3			12					12
1	5	6	2	7	4		8	9	10		12	13		3²			11¹					13
1	5	6	2	7	4²	9¹	10	8			12			3	13		11					14
1	2	6	5	7	4	9	10		8		12			3			11¹					15
1	2	6	12	5²	7¹	4	9	10	8		13	14		3²			11					16
1	5	6	2	7	4¹	9	10		8		12			3			11					17
1	2	6		8¹	4	9	10				12			3	13		11		7²	5		18
1	7	14	2		6	4²	8¹	9	10²		12			3			11		13	5		19
1	7	13	2		6	4		9	10		12			3			11²		8¹	5		20
1	7		2		6	4		9	10		12			3			11¹		8	5		21
1	7	13	2		6¹	4		9¹	10		12	14		3			11		8²	5		22
1	7		2		6²	4		9	10		12			3	13		11		8¹	5		23
1	7		2		6	4		9	10		12	14		3	13		11³		8²	5¹		24
1	7¹		2		6	4	8	9¹	10		12	14		3			11²		13	5		25
1	7¹		2		6	4³	8	9²	10		12	14		3			11		13	5		26
1	7		2		6	4	8²	9¹	10		12	14		3			11³		13	5		27
1	7¹		2		6	4	8	9²	10		12	13	14	3			11			5³		28
1	7	3	2		6	4	8¹	9	10		12						11			5		29
1	7		2		6	4	8¹	9	10		12			3		13	11²		12	4	5	30
1	7		2		6		8	9	10¹		12			3			11¹			4	5	31
1	7	13	2		6		8	9	10²		12			3			11¹			4	5	32
1	7¹		2		6	4²	8	9	10		12			3			11		13	5		33
1	7	3²	2		6	4	8	9¹	10		12						11		13	5		34
1	7		2			4²	8	9	10¹		12			3			11		13	5	6	35
1	7		2		6	4	8	9	10		12			3			11¹			5		36

HAMILTON ACADEMICAL Third Division

Year Formed: 1874. *Ground:* Firhill Stadium, 80 Firhill Road, Glasgow G20 7AL. *Telephone (match days only):* 0141 579
1971. *(Weekdays):* 01698 286103. *Club Address:* Enable Building, Prospect House, New Park St, Hamilton ML3 0BN.
Telephone: 01698 286103.
Ground Capacity: total: 14,538, seated: 8397. *Size of Pitch:* 110yd × 75yd.
Secretary: Scott A. Struthers BA. *Commercial Manager:* Gary Clark
Manager: Ally Dawson. *Assistant Manager:* Robert Prytz. *Physio:* Jim Fallon.
Managers since 1975: J. Eric Smith; Dave McParland; John Blackley; Bertie Auld; John Lambie; Jim Dempsey; John
Lambie; Billy McLaren; Iain Munro; Sandy Clark; Colin Miller. *Club Nickname(s):* The Accies. *Previous Grounds:*
Bent Farm, South Avenue, South Haugh, Douglas Park, Cliftonhill Stadium.
Record Attendance: 28,690 v Hearts, Scottish Cup 3rd rd; 3 Mar, 1937.
Record Transfer Fee received: £380,000 for Paul Hartley to Millwall (July 1996).
Record Transfer Fee paid: £60,000 for Paul Martin from Kilmarnock (Oct 1988) and for John McQuade from
Dumbarton (Aug 1993).
Record Victory: 11-1 v Chryston, Lanarkshire Cup; 28 Nov, 1885.
Record Defeat: 1-11 v Hibernian, Division I; 6 Nov, 1965.
Most Capped Player: Colin Miller, 29, Canada, 1988-94.
Most League Appearances: 452: Rikki Ferguson, 1974-88.

HAMILTON ACADEMICAL 1999–2000 LEAGUE RECORD

Match No.	Date	Venue	Opponents	Result	H/T Score	Lg. Pos.	Goalscorers	Atten-dance
1	Aug 7	A	Ross Co	L	1-2	0-1	—	McCormick [67]	2312
2	14	H	Queen of the S	L	0-3	0-1	10		630
3	21	A	Stirling A	L	0-2	0-2	10		656
4	28	A	Alloa Ath	D	1-1	1-0	10	Henderson N (pen) [13]	689
5	Sept 5	H	Stenhousemuir	D	1-1	0-0	10	Henderson D [64]	445
6	11	H	Stranraer	W	2-1	1-1	9	McCormick [9], Henderson D (pen) [90]	503
7	18	A	Partick Th	W	1-0	1-0	7	Hunter [2]	2312
8	25	A	Clyde	L	1-2	1-1	8	Henderson N [5]	865
9	Oct 2	H	Arbroath	D	2-2	0-1	8	Cunnington [50], Henderson N [64]	489
10	9	H	Ross Co	W	1-0	1-0	7	McFarlane D [26]	392
11	16	A	Queen of the S	L	2-3	2-0	8	Ferguson [18], Henderson N [20]	1027
12	30	A	Stranraer	W	2-0	1-0	7	McCormick [19], Crossley [88]	454
13	Nov 6	H	Partick Th	D	0-0	0-0	7		1828
14	10	A	Stenhousemuir	D	0-0	0-0	—		510
15	16	H	Alloa Ath	L	1-2	0-1	—	McFarlane D [74]	401
16	27	A	Arbroath	D	1-1	1-0	9	McFarlane D [74]	764
17	Dec 4	H	Clyde	L	2-3	2-1	9	MacLaren [15], McFarlane D [18]	731
18	27	H	Stirling A	L	0-2	0-1	—		431
19	Jan 3	A	Partick Th	D	2-2	2-0	—	Henderson D [21], Bonnar [26]	2755
20	15	H	Stranraer	W	2-0	0-0	9	Gaughan [66], Bonnar [86]	576
21	22	A	Clyde	L	0-1	0-0	9		975
22	29	A	Ross Co	W	1-0	1-0	9	Bonnar [33]	1860
23	Feb 5	H	Arbroath	D	2-2	2-0	8	Thomson [13], Bonnar [21]	407
24	26	H	Queen of the S	D	1-1	0-1	8	Henderson D [90]	553
25	Mar 4	A	Stirling A	W	4-1	2-0	8	Henderson D [29], Ferguson 2 [39, 49], Henderson N (pen) [90]	692
26	11	A	Stranraer	D	2-2	1-1	8	Ferguson [17], Henderson D [81]	405
27	14	H	Stenhousemuir	W	2-1	1-1	—	Cunnington [31], Henderson N [78]	347
28	18	H	Partick Th	L	0-1	0-1	8		2223
29	25	H	Alloa Ath	D	0-0	0-0	7		508
30	Apr 4	A	Alloa Ath	L	0-2	0-1	—		482
31	8	H	Clyde	D	1-1	0-0	7	Cunnington [61]	851
32	15	A	Arbroath	D	1-1	0-0	7	Coubrough [49]	604
33	18	A	Stenhousemuir	W	1-0	0-0	—	Cunnington [28]	309
34	22	H	Ross Co	L	0-3	0-2	7		693
35	29	A	Queen of the S	D	1-1	1-0	7	Quitongo [39]	2084
36	May 6	H	Stirling A	W	1-0	0-0	10	McFarlane D [79]	498

Final League Position: 10   1998–99 DIV 1 9

Most League Goals in Season (Individual): 35: David Wilson, Division I; 1936-37.
Most Goals Overall (Individual): 246: David Wilson, 1928-39.

Honours
League Champions: First Division 1985-86, 1987-88; *Runners-up:* Second Division 1996–97. Division II 1903-04; *Runners-up:* Division II 1952-53, 1964-65.
Scottish Cup Runners-up: 1911, 1935. *League Cup:* Semi-finalists three times.
B&Q Cup Winners: 1991-92, 1992-93.

Club colours: Shirt: Red and white hoops. Shorts: White. Stockings: White.

Goalscorers: *League (39):* Henderson D 6 (1 pen), Henderson N 6 (2 pens), McFarlane D 5, Bonnar 4, Cunnington 4, Ferguson 4, McCormick 3, Coubrough 1, Crossley 1, Gaughan 1, Hunter 1, MacLaren 1, Quitongo 1, Thomson 1.
Scottish Cup (1): Henderson D 1. *CIS Cup (3):* Henderson D 3. *Bell's League Cup (3):* Henderson N 1 (pen), McCormick 1, Moore 1.

Reid C 24	Martin M 15+3	Cunnington E 31+1	Miller C 1	MacLaren R 30+1	Thomson S 36	Muir D 2	Davidson W 22+1	McFarlane D 8+5	Moore M 6+8	Henderson N 19+2	McCormick S 20+8	Russell A —+6	Gaughan P 22+3	Lynn G 4+1	Renicks S 6+5	McAulay I 12+3	Kelly R 4+7	Bonnar M 30+1	Henderson D 27	Hunter G 21+1	Crossley O 8+9	Ferguson I 8+2	MacFarlane I 12	Hillcoat C 5+2	Quitongo J 15	Coubrough J 8	Match No.
1	2	3	4¹	5	6	7²	8	9	10³	11	12	13	14														1
1	12	3		2	6	7²	8		9	4	10	13	5	11¹													2
1	2	3		5²	6		4		11¹	10	9		12					7	8	13							3
1		3		5	6		4		9	8	10		12			2		11¹	7								4
1	12			5	6		4		9¹	7	10					2		8	11								5
1	12			5	8		4		10	9						2¹		7	11	6							6
1	2	3		5	8		4	13	10	9³			14			12		7	11²	6¹							7
1	2	3		5	6		4	12	10	9	13					8¹		7	11²								8
1	2²	3¹		5	8		4		10	9	12							7	11	6	13						9
1	2	3		5	6		4	12²	8	10¹			13					7	11		9						10
1	2²	3		5	6		4		8	10¹			13					7	11	12	9						11
1	2	3		5	6			12	10	9¹			13					7	11		4²	8					12
	2²	3		5	6			12	10	9¹			13					7	11	4	8		1				13
	2¹	3		5	6			13	10	9²			12					7	11	4	8		1				14
	2¹	3		5	6		9	13	10³				4	12	14			7²	11		8		1				15
		3		5	6		9		10				4		2	12		7¹	11		8		1				16
	1	3		5	6		4	9	10³	13			14		2	12		7²	11	8¹							17
1	2	3			6¹		8²		9	10			5		12	13		7	11	4							18
	2¹	3		12	6²			14		9³			5		10	7		8	11	4		1	13				19
1		3			6						5³				8¹	14		7	11	4	9²	13		12	10		20
1		2			6						5				8¹			7	11	4	12	9		3	10		21
1		2			6						5				8			7	11	4	12	9		3	10¹		22
1	13	2			6			9¹			5				8			7	11	4	12			3	10²		23
1		3			6		2¹			12	13				5	8		7²	11	4		9			10		24
1	10	2¹			6			12	14						5	8²	13		11	4	9³			3	7		25
1	10	2			6			12		7²	13				5	8			11	4		9		3¹			26
1	10	2			6		3			7	12				5	8¹			11	4	13					9²	27
1	10	2			6		3			9¹					5	8			11	4	12				7		28
1	3	2			6		8		10²		13				5	2¹			11	4	12				7	9	29
	10	2			6		3	12							5	8¹			11	4			1		7	9	30
	10	2			6		3	12							5	8			11¹	4	13		1		7	9²	31
	11	2			6		3	10	12						5	8				4¹			1		7	9	32
	11	2			6		3	10		4¹					5	8	13				12		1		7	9²	33
	11	2¹			6		4	12							5	8		3			10		1		7	9	34
	11				6		2²	10	12		13				5	8		3		4			1		7	9¹	35
		2			6			10	12	11					5	8²		3		4	13		1		7	9¹	36

HEART OF MIDLOTHIAN   Premier League

Year Formed: 1874. *Ground & Address:* Tynecastle Stadium, Gorgie Rd, Edinburgh EH11 2NL. *Telephone:* 0131 200
7200. *Fax:* 0131 200 7222. *Website:* www.heartsfc.co.uk.
Ground Capacity: 18,000. *Size of Pitch:* 108yd × 73yd.
Chairman: Douglas Smith. *Chief Executive:* Christopher Robinson. *Sales and Marketing Manager:* Kenny Wittmann.
Manager: Jim Jefferies. *Assistant Manager:* Billy Brown.
Physio: Alan Rae. *Coach:* Peter Houston.
Managers since 1975: J. Hagart; W. Ormond; R. Moncur; T. Ford; A. MacDonald; A. MacDonald & W. Jardine; A.
MacDonald; J. Jordan, S. Clark, T. McLean.
Club Nickname(s): Hearts, Jambo's. *Previous Grounds:* The Meadows 1874, Powderhall 1878, Old Tynecastle 1881,
(Tynecastle Park, 1886).
Record Attendance: 53,396 v Rangers, Scottish Cup 3rd rd; 13 Feb, 1932.
Record Transfer Fee received: £2,100,000 for Alan McLaren from Rangers (October 1994).
Record of Transfer paid: £750,000 for Derek Ferguson to Rangers (July 1990).
Record Victory: 21-0 v Anchor, EFA Cup 30th October 1880.
Record Defeat: 1-8 v Vale of Leven, Scottish Cup, 1888.
Most Capped Player: Bobby Walker, 29, Scotland.
Most League Appearances: 515: Gary Mackay, 1980-97.
Most League Goals in Season (Individual): 44: Barney Battles.
Most Goals Overall (Individual): 214: John Robertson, 1983-98.

HEART OF MIDLOTHIAN 1999–2000 LEAGUE RECORD

Match No.	Date	Venue	Opponents	Result	H/T Score	Lg. Pos.	Goalscorers	Attendance
1	Jul 31	A	St Johnstone	W 4-1	1-0	—	McSwegan [29], Flögel [67], Dods (og) [78], Cameron [79]	6707
2	Aug 7	H	Rangers	L 0-4	0-2	6		17,893
3	14	A	Hibernian	D 1-1	0-1	5	McSwegan [79]	15,858
4	22	H	Aberdeen	W 3-0	1-0	3	McSwegan 3 [44, 50, 76]	12,803
5	29	A	Celtic	L 0-4	0-2	5		60,107
6	Sept 11	H	Dundee	W 4-0	1-0	4	Adam [7], Jackson [75], Cameron [76], Severin [82]	13,378
7	25	A	Dundee U	W 2-0	1-0	4	Adam 2 [14, 90]	8510
8	Oct 16	H	St Johnstone	D 1-1	1-0	4	McSwegan [5]	12,872
9	27	A	Kilmarnock	D 2-2	0-0	—	Cameron [83], Juanjo [88]	12,541
10	30	A	Dundee	L 0-1	0-1	5		6018
11	Nov 6	H	Motherwell	D 1-1	1-0	6	McSwegan [6]	12,514
12	20	H	Celtic	L 1-2	1-0	6	Cameron [2]	17,184
13	23	A	Motherwell	L 1-2	0-1	—	McSwegan [46]	7793
14	27	A	Kilmarnock	D 2-2	2-0	7	McSwegan [7], Ritchie [21]	8326
15	Dec 5	H	Dundee U	W 3-0	1-0	5	Juanjo [5], Jackson [68], Adam [88]	10,598
16	8	A	Aberdeen	L 1-3	1-1	—	Severin [27]	10,274
17	19	H	Hibernian	L 0-3	0-2	6		17,954
18	22	A	Rangers	L 0-1	0-0	—		49,907
19	Jan 22	H	Dundee	W 2-0	1-0	6	Wales [23], Jackson [49]	13,112
20	Feb 5	A	Celtic	W 3-2	1-2	5	Cameron 2 (1 pen) [32, 82 (p)], Naysmith [55]	59,735
21	26	H	Kilmarnock	D 0-0	0-0	6		14,243
22	Mar 1	A	Motherwell	W 2-0	1-0	—	Jackson [45], Wales [59]	5588
23	4	A	Dundee U	W 1-0	0-0	4	Cameron (pen) [54]	6928
24	15	A	St Johnstone	W 1-0	0-0	—	McSwegan [65]	4468
25	18	A	Hibernian	L 1-3	1-1	3	Jackson [26]	15,908
26	22	H	Aberdeen	W 3-0	1-0	—	Cameron [9], Wales [47], Fulton [88]	13,249
27	25	H	Motherwell	D 0-0	0-0	3		13,702
28	Apr 1	A	Dundee	D 0-0	0-0	3		6291
29	8	H	Celtic	W 1-0	1-0	3	McSwegan [36]	16,046
30	12	H	Rangers	L 1-2	1-1	—	McSwegan [12]	16,314
31	15	A	Aberdeen	W 2-1	0-1	3	Wales [80], Jackson [84]	12,626
32	22	H	Dundee U	L 1-2	0-0	3	Wales [63]	12,604
33	29	A	Kilmarnock	W 1-0	0-0	3	Wales [53]	8057
34	May 6	H	St Johnstone	D 0-0	0-0	3		12,368
35	13	A	Rangers	L 0-1	0-1	3		49,140
36	21	H	Hibernian	W 2-1	1-0	3	Juanjo [30], McSwegan [62]	17,391

Final League Position: 3   1998–99 6

Honours
League Champions: Division I 1894-95, 1896-97, 1957-58, 1959-60. First Division 1979-80; *Runners-up:* Division I 1893-94, 1898-99, 1903-04, 1905-06, 1914-15, 1937-38, 1953-54, 1956-57, 1958-59, 1964-65. Premier Division 1985-86, 1987-88, 1991-92. First Division 1977-78, 1982-83.
Scottish Cup Winners: 1891, 1896, 1901, 1906, 1956, 1998; *Runners-up:* 1903, 1907, 1968, 1976, 1986, 1996.
League Cup Winners: 1954-55, 1958-59, 1959-60, 1962-63; *Runners-up:* 1961-62, 1996-97.

European: *European Cup:* 4 matches (1958-59, 1960-61). *Cup Winners' Cup:* 10 matches (1976-77, 1996-97, 1998-99). *UEFA Cup:* 33 matches (*Fairs Cup:* 1961-62, 1963-64, 1965-66. *UEFA Cup:* 1984-85, 1986-87, 1988-89, 1990-91, 1992-93, 1993-94).

Club colours: Shirt: Maroon. Shorts: White. Stockings: Maroon with white tops.

Goalscorers: *League (47):* McSwegan 13, Cameron 8 (2 pens), Jackson 6, Wales 6, Adam 4, Juanjo 3, Severin 2, Flögel 1, Fulton 1, Naysmith 1, Ritchie 1, own goal 1. *Scottish Cup (6):* Cameron 2 (2 pens), McSwegan 2, Jackson 1, Wales 1. *CIS Cup (5):* Jackson 2, Cameron 1, Holmes 1, Severin 1.

Rousset G 16	Pressley S 36	James K 8 + 2	Murray G 15 + 6	Severin S 18 + 6	Fulton S 16 + 10	Flögel T 28 + 1	Cameron C 31 + 1	Adam S 18 + 7	McSwegan G 23 + 7	Jackson D 31 + 4	Makel L 11 + 6	Juanjo 2 + 13	Wales G 17 + 7	Naysmith S 34 + 1	Locke G 9 + 4	Ritchie P 14	Quitongo J — + 1	McKinnon R 3	Leclercq F 8 + 2	McKenzie R 3 + 2	Graham A — + 1	Petric G 17 + 1	Niemi A 17	Simpson F 7 + 4	Milne K — + 1	Tomaschek R 13 + 1	Kirk A 1 + 3	Match No.
1	2	3	4	5	6	7	8	9²	10¹	11³	12	13	14															1
1	2	5	4	6³	7¹	9	8	10	11²	14	12		13	3														2
1	2	3		5	6²	7	8	9¹	10	11	12		13	4														3
1	2		4	6	12	7	8¹	9	10	11				3	5													4
1	2		4²	6	14	9³	8	12	10	11				3	7¹	5	13											5
1	2	4		6		7³	8	9¹	10²	11	12	13	14	3	5													6
1	2	4	12	6	13	7³	8	9	10	11¹				3	14	5²												7
1	2	4		6				10¹	11		12	9²	3		5													8
1	2	4²		6³	13	7	8	9¹	10	11			14	12	3		5											9
1	2	4¹		7		8	13	10	11³	14	12	9²	3	6	5													10
1	2		4	13	7	12	8	9	10³	11		14		3²	6¹	5												11
1	2		6¹	9	11	8		10²	13					3	7	5		4	12									12
1	2	14		8	9		10	11¹	13					3²	7	5		4³	6	12								13
	2	13	6	9	11¹	8³	12	10²	14					3	7	5		4		1								14
	2	13	4	6	7		9	10¹	11³		8²	12	3		5					1	14							15
	2		6	9		8	10²		11		13	12	3	7¹	4				1		5							16
	2¹	12		6	9		8	10		11		14	13	3		4³				5	1	7²						17
	2		4	12		8	11²	10¹						3	7		6			5	1	9	13					18
	2		4	6	9		8		11		13	10²	3	7¹		12				5	1							19
	2		4		9	8	12		11¹				10²	3						5	1	7		6	13			20
1	2		4		9	8		12	11		10	3						5				7¹	6					21
	2		4	12		9	8	14	13	11²			10³	3					5		1	7¹	6					22
	2		4		9	8		12	11				10¹	3					5		13	1	7²	6				23
	2		4	7		9	8	14	10²	13	12		11³	3					5		1		6¹					24
	2		4			8	12	9	11	13			10	3					6²		5	1		7¹				25
	2		6	7	8	9	13¹	11	5²				10¹	3						15³	4	1						26
1	2		6	7	8	9	12	11	5				10¹	3							4							27
	2		13	6³	7	8	9²	12	11	5			10¹	3							4	1	14					28
	2		13	7	8	9	10¹	11	5³		12		3							4	1	14		6				29
	2		8²	12	7		9	10¹	11	5			3							4	1	13		6				30
	2		12	14		8		9³	13	11	5		10	3						4¹	1	7²		6				31
	2		12	7	8¹		9	11³	5				10	3						4	1		6²	13				32
	2	13		12	7	8¹		9²	11³	5			10	3						4	1	14		6				33
	2		8²	7	12		9	11³	5¹	14	10	3	13							4	1		6					34
	2	5		14	9²	8		12	6	13	10¹	3								4	1		7	11³				35
	2	13	6		7	8		10²	11¹	5³	9		3							4	1		14	12				36

HIBERNIAN   Premier League

Year Formed: 1875. *Ground & Address:* Easter Road Stadium, Albion Rd, Edinburgh EH7 5QG. *Telephone:* 0131 661 2159. *Fax:* 0131 659 6488.
Ground Capacity: total: 16,032. *Size of Pitch:* 112yd × 74yd.
Managing Director: Rod Petrie. *Commercial Director:* Colin Deas. *Secretary:* Mary Anne McAdam.
Manager: Alex McLeish. *Assistant Manager:* Andrew Watson.
Physio: Malcolm Colquhoun. *Coach:* D. Park.
Managers since 1975: Eddie Turnbull; Willie Ormond; Bertie Auld; Pat Stanton; John Blackley, Alex Miller, Jim Duffy.
Club Nickname(s): Hibees. *Previous Grounds:* Meadows 1875-78, Powderhall 1878-79, Mayfield 1879-80, First Easter Road 1880-92, Second Easter Road 1892-.
Record Attendance: 65,860 v Hearts, Division I; 2 Jan, 1950.
Record Victory: 22-1 v 42nd Highlanders; 3 Sept, 1881.
Record Defeat: 0-10 v Rangers; 24 Dec, 1898.
Most Capped Player: Lawrie Reilly, 38, Scotland.
Most League Appearances: 446: Arthur Duncan.
Most League Goals in Season (Individual): 42: Joe Baker.
Most Goals Overall (Individual): 364: Gordon Smith.

HIBERNIAN 1999–2000 LEAGUE RECORD

Match No.	Date	Venue	Opponents	Result	H/T Score	Lg. Pos.	Goalscorers	Attendance
1	Jul 31	H	Motherwell	D 2-2	1-0	—	Lehmann 2 [44, 81]	13,015
2	Aug 8	A	Dundee	W 4-3	1-0	3	Lehmann [32], Sauzee 2 [61, 84], Miller [90]	6050
3	14	H	Hearts	D 1-1	1-0	4	Latapy [42]	15,858
4	21	A	St Johnstone	D 1-1	0-1	5	McAnespie (og) [69]	6165
5	28	H	Rangers	L 0-1	0-0	7		15,587
6	Sept 11	A	Dundee U	L 1-3	0-1	6	Latapy [49]	8167
7	19	H	Kilmarnock	L 0-3	0-1	9		11,219
8	25	H	Celtic	L 0-2	0-0	9		14,747
9	Oct 2	A	Aberdeen	D 2-2	0-0	8	Paatelainen [82], Jack [88]	11,876
10	16	A	Motherwell	D 2-2	1-1	8	Latapy (pen) [9], Paatelainen [57]	7559
11	23	H	Dundee	W 5-2	2-1	6	Miller [30], Latapy 2 [40, 80], Sauzee [63], Lehmann [89]	10,162
12	31	H	Dundee U	W 3-1	1-2	6	De Vos (og) [6], Latapy 2 (1 pen) [61 (p), 79]	11,073
13	Nov 6	A	Kilmarnock	W 2-0	0-0	4	Miller 2 [70, 87]	8735
14	20	A	Rangers	L 0-2	0-1	5		49,544
15	24	H	St Johnstone	L 0-1	0-1	—		9454
16	27	H	Aberdeen	W 2-0	2-0	5	McGinlay [24], Paatelainen [34]	11,627
17	Dec 4	A	Celtic	L 0-4	0-2	6		60,092
18	11	H	Motherwell	D 2-2	0-0	5	Paatelainen [63], McGinlay [88]	9955
19	19	A	Hearts	W 3-0	2-0	5	Lehmann [17], Sauzee [27], Miller [89]	17,954
20	27	H	Kilmarnock	D 2-2	0-2	—	Paatelainen [75], Miller [89]	11,900
21	Jan 22	A	Dundee U	D 0-0	0-0	5		7457
22	Feb 6	H	Rangers	D 2-2	0-0	5	Miller 2 [49, 67]	13,420
23	22	A	St Johnstone	L 0-1	0-1	—		8236
24	26	A	Aberdeen	L 0-4	0-3	7		12,630
25	Mar 5	H	Celtic	W 2-1	1-0	6	McGinlay [23], Miller [63]	12,239
26	18	H	Hearts	W 3-1	1-1	5	Latapy [37], Sauzee [60], Paatelainen [85]	15,908
27	21	H	Dundee	L 1-2	1-0	—	Paatelainen [22]	10,208
28	25	A	Kilmarnock	L 0-1	0-0	6		8068
29	Apr 1	H	Dundee U	W 1-0	1-0	5	Hartley [22]	10,264
30	15	H	St Johnstone	D 3-3	1-0	5	Latapy [12], Paatelainen [48], Lehmann [89]	9211
31	22	A	Celtic	D 1-1	1-0	6	Lovell [31]	56,843
32	29	A	Aberdeen	W 1-0	0-0	5	Miller [53]	9659
33	May 3	A	Rangers	L 2-5	0-2	—	Miller [48], Lehmann [71]	44,359
34	6	A	Motherwell	L 0-2	0-0	6		5426
35	14	A	Dundee	L 0-1	0-0	6		5060
36	21	A	Hearts	L 1-2	0-1	6	Paatelainen [57]	17,391

Final League Position: 6   1998–99 DIV 1 1

Honours

League Champions: Division I 1902-03, 1947-48, 1950-51, 1951-52. First Division 1980-81, 1998-99. Division II 1893-94, 1894-95, 1932-33; *Runners-up:* Division I 1896-97, 1946-47, 1949-50, 1952-53, 1973-74, 1974-75.

Scottish Cup Winners: 1887, 1902; *Runners-up:* 1896, 1914, 1923, 1924, 1947, 1958, 1972, 1979.

League Cup Winners: 1972-73, 1991-92; *Runners-up:* 1950-51, 1968-69, 1974-75, 1993-94.

European: *European Cup:* 6 matches (1955-56 semi-finals). *Cup Winners' Cup:* 6 matches (1972-73). *UEFA Cup:* 59 matches (*Fairs Cup:* 1960-61 semi-finals, 1961-62, 1962-63, 1965-66, 1967-68, 1968-69, 1970-71. *UEFA Cup:* 1973-74, 1974-75, 1975-76, 1976-77, 1978-79, 1989-90, 1992-93).

Club colours: Shirt: Green with white sleeves. Shorts: White. Stockings: Green with white trim.

Goalscorers: *League (49):* Miller 11, Latapy 9 (2 pens), Paatelainen 9, Lehmann 7, Sauzee 5, McGinlay 3, Hartley 1, Jack 1, Lovell 1, own goals 2. *Scottish Cup (12):* Latapy 3 (1 pen), Brebner 1, Collins 1, Hartley 1, Lehmann 1, Lovell 1, McGinlay 1, Miller 1, Murray 1, Sauzee 1. *CIS Cup (4):* McGinlay 2, Hartley 1, Miller 1.

Gottskalksson O 12	Lovering P 9+1	Renwick M 11+2	Dennis S 23+1	Jack M 20+2	Sauzee F 24+1	Henry F 6+3	Latapy R 28	Lovell S 19+7	Crawford S 1+2	Lehmann D 18+12	Hartley P 14+10	Skinner J 1+1	McGinlay P 22+9	Paatelainen M 25+6	Miller K 23+8	Collins D 23+1	Brebner G 27+1	Hughes J 20	Dempsie M 7+1	Smith T 21	Colgan N 24	Bannerman S —+1	Murray 18+1	Jean E —+5	McIntosh M 9	McManus T 1+1	Reid A —+1	Match No
1	2	3	4	5	6	7¹	8	9		10²	11	12	13															1
1	2	3	4	5	6	7²	8			11	13		9	10¹	12													2
1	2	3	4	5	9¹	7³	8			11²	12		6	10	13	14												3
1		3	4	5	9	6¹	8	12		11					10		2	7										4
1		3	4		6	12	8			11²	10³		9	13	14	2¹		7		5								5
1		2	4		6	5²	8	13		11¹			10	9	12			7	3									6
1		2³	4	3	6	5¹	8	12		11²			10	9	13	14		7										7
1	2	3	4	5	6		8	9²	12	13	11¹		10		14			7³										8
1		3	4	5		8³	9¹	13		11²	14		10	12		2		7	6									9
1		4	3		6	8²	13			12			9	10	11¹			7		5	2							10
1		4	3		6²	13	8			12			9	10	11¹			7		5	2							11
1		4	3		6²	13	8						9	10	11	12		7		5¹	2							12
			4		6¹		8			13	12		9	10²	11	2		7		5	1						3	13
			4		6³	14	8			13	10¹		9	12	11²	2		7		5	1						3	14
		13	4	12			8			14	9¹		6	10¹	11	2²		7		5	1						3	15
		4¹	12	6			8	14		11			9	10²	13	2		7		5	1						3¹	16
		4	6				8³	12		13	14		9¹	10²	11	2		7		5	1						3	17
		4		6¹			8	9		13				12	10	11²	2	7		5	1						3	18
		4		6			8³	9²		11¹			13	10	12	2	7		5	1	14						3	19
	3¹	4		6			8	9		11²			12	10	13	2	7		5	1								20
	3	4					8¹	9²		14	12		13	10	11	2	7		5	1		6³						21
		4	9			8			12			13	10¹	11	2	7		5	1		6²						22
	3	4					8			12				12	9	10	11	2	7		5	1	6²	13				23
		4	6				12				9²			10	11	2	7		5	1		8¹	13				24
			6				7	9						8	10	11¹	2		5	1			12	4			25
			6				8	7						9	10	11	2		5	1			4				26
							8	6			9			7	10	11	2		5	1			4				27
		4	6				8¹	7		12	9²		13	10	11	2			3	1			5				28
		4	12	6²			7			11	9		8	10		2³	13		3	1		14	5¹				29
2			4				8	6		12			9	10	11¹		7		5	3	1		4				30
2		4	6²				8	9		10¹	12		13	11³			7		5	3	1		14				31
		4	3				8	9		10	11			2	7		5			1		6					32
		3	4				8¹	10		9	12			11	2	7		5		1		6					33
14	12				6¹		9	8		7	10			11²	3	2¹	1		5			13	4				34
	12	4	3¹		6		10²	9		8	13		11		7³	2		1		5		14					35
		3					13			8	10		11		2	7		5		1		6²	4	9¹	12		36

INVERNESS CALEDONIAN THISTLE
First Division

Year Formed: 1994. *Ground & Address:* Caledonian Stadium, East Longman, Inverness IV1 1FF. *Telephone:* 01463 222880.
Ground Capacity: 5600, seated: 2200. *Size of Pitch:* 115yd × 75yd.
Chairman: David Sutherland. *Hon. Presidents:* John S. McDonald and Norman Miller. *Secretary:* Jim Falconer.
Manager: Steven W. Paterson. *Assistant Manager:* Duncan Shearer. *Coach:* Alex Young. *Physios:* Emily Goodlad and Ian Manning.
Record Attendance: 6290 v Aberdeen, Scottish Cup, 20 February 2000.
Record Victory: 8-1, v Annan Ath, Scottish Cup 3rd rd, 24 January 1998.
Record Defeat: 1-5, v Morton, First Division, 12 November 1999 and v Airdrieonians, First Division, 15 April 2000.
Most League Appearances: 196, Charlie Christie, 1995-2000.
Most League Goals in Season: 27, Ian Stewart, 1996-97.
Most Goals Overall (Individual): 68, Ian Stewart, 1995-99.

INVERNESS CALEDONIAN THISTLE 1999–2000 LEAGUE RECORD

Match No.	Date	Venue	Opponents	Result	H/T Score	Lg. Pos.	Goalscorers	Atten-dance
1	Aug 7	A	Dunfermline Ath	L	0-4	0-1	—	4677
2	Aug 14	H	Falkirk	L	2-3	2-1	10	Sheerin [7], Tokely [38]	3022
3	Aug 21	A	St Mirren	L	2-3	1-3	10	Sheerin (pen) [28], Teasdale [86]	3040
4	Aug 28	A	Ayr U	L	0-1	0-0	10		2157
5	Sept 4	H	Morton	D	0-0	0-0	10	Glancy [54]	2414
6	Sept 11	H	Clydebank	W	1-0	0-0	8	Sheerin (pen) [54]	1697
7	Sept 18	A	Livingston	D	2-2	2-1	8	Bavidge [35], Sheerin (pen) [39]	2584
8	Sept 25	H	Raith R	L	0-2	0-2	9		2961
9	Oct 2	A	Airdrieonians	D	1-1	0-1	8	Glancy [72]	2097
10	Oct 16	A	Falkirk	W	2-0	1-0	9	Wyness [9], McLean [84]	2403
11	Oct 23	H	Dunfermline Ath	D	1-1	0-1	9	Bavidge [89]	3006
12	Oct 30	A	Clydebank	W	3-0	2-0	7	Sheerin [24], Teasdale [41], Wilson [72]	184
13	Nov 6	H	Livingston	W	2-0	0-0	6	Golabek [76], McLean [90]	2474
14	Nov 12	A	Morton	L	1-5	1-2	6	Fridge [1]	812
15	Nov 27	H	Airdrieonians	W	2-0	1-0	6	Wilson [23], Xausa [48]	2022
16	Nov 30	H	Ayr U	D	1-1	0-0	—	Christie [80]	1073
17	Dec 4	A	Raith R	L	2-4	2-3	6	Sheerin [14], Bavidge [42]	1971
18	Dec 11	A	St Mirren	D	1-1	0-1	6	Wilson [51]	2893
19	Dec 18	A	Dunfermline Ath	L	0-1	0-0	6		3775
20	Dec 27	H	Clydebank	W	4-1	0-0	—	Sheerin 2 [53, 73], Wilson 2 [56, 87]	1640
21	Jan 3	A	Livingston	D	1-1	0-0	—	Wilson [73]	2656
22	Jan 8	H	Morton	W	6-2	0-0	6	Byers [49], Bavidge [60], Wilson 2 [67, 84], Sheerin [75], Tokely [90]	1524
23	Jan 22	H	Raith R	D	1-1	0-1	6	Glancy [84]	2302
24	Feb 5	A	Airdrieonians	W	4-1	2-0	6	Wyness [14], Sheerin [37], Xausa [71], Wilson [79]	1597
25	Feb 12	A	St Mirren	L	0-2	0-1	6		3742
26	Feb 26	H	Falkirk	L	0-3	0-2	6		2727
27	Mar 4	A	Clydebank	W	1-0	0-0	6	Wyness [64]	168
28	Mar 7	A	Ayr U	W	3-1	1-1	—	Wilson [42], Sheerin [51], Xausa [89]	1274
29	Mar 18	H	Livingston	W	4-1	2-0	6	Xausa 3 [11, 68, 86], Wyness [32]	2206
30	Mar 25	A	Ayr U	D	1-1	1-1	6	Wilson [17]	1790
31	Apr 1	A	Morton	W	2-0	0-0	6	Wyness [52], Xausa [83]	567
32	Apr 8	A	Raith R	L	0-2	0-0	6		2538
33	Apr 15	H	Airdrieonians	L	1-5	0-4	6	Wyness [51]	1404
34	Apr 22	H	Dunfermline Ath	L	1-2	0-2	6	Xausa [63]	2677
35	Apr 29	A	Falkirk	D	2-2	1-0	6	Xausa [4], Wilson [63]	4449
36	May 6	H	St Mirren	W	5-0	3-0	6	Xausa [25], McCulloch 2 [35, 89], Wilson [36], Bavidge [84]	3218

Final League Position: 6   1998–99 DIV 2 2

Honours
Scottish Cup: Quarter-finals 1996.
League Champions: Third Division 1996–97; *Runners-up:* Second Division 1998-99.
Bell's League Challenge Cup runners-up: 1999–2000.

Club colours: Shirts: Royal blue with red stripes. Shorts: Blue. Stockings: Blue.

Goalscorers: *League (60):* Wilson 13, Sheerin 11 (3 pens), Xausa 10, Wyness 6, Bavidge 5, Glancy 3, Tokely 3, McCulloch 2, McLean 2, Teasdale 2, Byers 1, Christie 1, Golabek 1. *Scottish Cup (4):* Mann 1, Sheerin 1 (pen), Wilson 1, own goal 1. *CIS Cup (5):* McLean 2, Byers 1, Sheerin 1 (pen), Wilson 1. *Bell's League Cup (11):* Sheerin 4, Stewart 2, Glancy 1, McLean 1, Robson 1, Teasdale 1, Wilson 1.

Fridge L 27	Tokely R 30	Golabek S 29 + 2	Teasdale M 23 + 4	Mann R 27	McCulloch M 35	Wilson B 30 + 2	Stewart I 3	McLean S 4 + 7	Christie C 22 + 6	Sheerin P 32	Allan A 4 + 1	Robson B 3 + 1	Glancy M 6 + 12	Hastings R 28	Shearer D — + 1	Bavidge M 12 + 15	Byers K 21 + 10	Xausa D 19	Wyness D 21 + 5	Calder J 9	Hind D 2 + 3	Munro G 3 + 1	Craig D 6 + 3	Macdonald N — + 1	Stewart G — + 1	Match No.
1	2	3	4	5	6	7¹	8³	9	10	11²	12	13	14													1
1	2	3	7	5	6		8¹	9²	10	11		12	4	13												2
1	2	3	7	5	6			12	10	11		9²		4		8¹	13									3
1		11	4	5	2	12	9	8²	10	6			3¹			13	7									4
1	2		4	5	6				10	11		8	3			9	7									5
1	2		4	5	6	12			10	11		13	3			9	7¹	8²								6
1	2	13	4	5	6	7¹			10	11		8²	3			9	12									7
1	2		4	5¹	6	7		13	10	8		11²	14	3		9³	12									8
1	2	13	4		5	7³		8¹	10	11		12	3			14	6²		9							9
1	2	11	4		5	7¹		13		6		8²	3			12	10		9							10
1	2	11²	4		5	7		12	13	6		8¹	3			14	10³		9							11
1	2	11	4		5	7		13	12	6		8³	3			14	10¹		9²							12
1	2	11	4		5	7		12	10	6		8¹	3			13	9²									13
1	2	11	4		5	7¹		14	10	6		8²	3²			13	12		9							14
1	2	11	12	4	5	7¹			10	6			3			9²	14	8³	13							15
1	2	11	14	4	5	7			10	6²			3			9¹	13	8³	12							16
1	2	11²	12	4	5	7			14	6			3			9²	10³	8	13							17
	11		2	4	5	7¹			10	6		12	3				8	9	1							18
	11	3	2	4	7				10	6		13	5			12		8²	9¹	1						19
	11¹	3	2	4	7³	9			10	6		14	5			13	12		8²	1						20
	11	3	2	4	7	9¹			10	6			5			12		8	1							21
	11	3	2	4	5¹	9			10	6						8	7			1	12					22
	2	3	4			9			10	6		13	5			11¹	7²	8	12	1						23
	7	3	2		4	9			10³	6		13	5			14	12	8²	11¹	1						24
	7	3	2		4	9				6			12			8¹	10²		11	1	13	5				25
	7	3¹	2	4	8	9			12	6			14			13	10²		11³	1		5				26
1	2	3		4	8	7				6			5			11¹	10²	9	12				13			27
1	2	3¹		4	8	7				6			5				13	9	10				12	11²		28
1	2	3		5	4	7				6						12	10	9	8				11¹			29
1	2	3		5	4	7					6					12	10¹	9	8				11			30
1	2	3¹		4	5	7				11			6			10	9	8					12			31
1		12	4	2	7					6			5			10	9	8				3	11¹			32
1	3		4	2	7			12		6²			5			10³	9¹	8	13			11	14			33
1	3		4	5	7			12	6							13	10	9	8²			2	11¹			34
1	3		4	5	7			10	6							11	9	8	2							35
1		3	4	2	7			10³	6							12	11¹	9²	8					14	13	36

KILMARNOCK   Premier League

Year Formed: 1869. *Ground & Address:* Rugby Park, Kilmarnock KA1 2DP. *Telephone:* 01563 545300. *Fax:* 01563 522181. *Website:* www.kilmarnockfc.co.uk.
Ground Capacity: all seated: 18,128. *Size of Pitch:* 114yd × 72yd.
Chairman: W. Costley. *Chief Executive:* I. Welsh. *Secretary:* Kevin Collins. *Commercial Manager:* J. McSherry. *Stadium Manager:* Bobby Williamson. *Assistant Managers:* Jim Clark, Gerry McCabe. *Physio:* A. MacFie.
Managers since 1975: W. Fernie; D. Sneddon; J. Clunie; E. Morrison; J. Fleeting; T. Burns; A. Totten. *Club Nickname(s):* Killie. *Previous Grounds:* Rugby Park (Dundonald Road); The Grange; Holm Quarry; Present ground since 1899.
Record Attendance: 35,995 v Rangers, Scottish Cup; 10 March, 1962.
Record Transfer Fee received: £300,000 for Shaun McSkimming to Motherwell (1995).
Record Transfer Fee paid: £300,000 for Paul Wright from St Johnstone (1995).
Record Victory: 11-1 v Paisley Academical, Scottish Cup; 18 Jan, 1930 (15-0 v Lanemark, Ayrshire Cup; 15 Nov, 1890).
Record Defeat: 1-9 v Celtic, Division I; 13 Aug, 1938.
Most Capped Player: Joe Nibloe, 11, Scotland.
Most League Appearances: 481: Alan Robertson, 1972-88.
Most League Goals in Season (Individual): 34: Harry 'Peerie' Cunningham 1927-28 and Andy Kerr 1960-61.
Most Goals Overall (Individual): 148: W. Culley; 1912-23.

KILMARNOCK 1999–2000 LEAGUE RECORD

Match No.	Date	Venue	Opponents	Result	H/T Score	Lg. Pos.	Goalscorers	Atten- dance
1	Jul 31	A	Rangers	L	1-2	0-1	—	Mitchell [65]	48,074
2	Aug 7	H	Aberdeen	W	2-0	1-0	5	Hay 2 [38, 62]	8378
3	15	A	St Johnstone	L	0-2	0-0	7		4681
4	21	H	Motherwell	L	0-1	0-1	9		7732
5	29	A	Dundee U	D	0-0	0-0	9		6621
6	Sept 12	H	Celtic	L	0-1	0-0	9		14,318
7	19	A	Hibernian	W	3-0	1-0	6	Reilly [11], Jeffrey [80], McCoist (pen) [88]	11,219
8	25	H	Dundee	L	0-2	0-1	7		7433
9	Oct 16	H	Rangers	D	1-1	0-1	7	Jeffrey [72]	15,795
10	23	A	Aberdeen	D	2-2	0-1	8	Cocard [50], Mitchell [86]	10,552
11	27	A	Hearts	D	2-2	0-0	—	MacPherson [67], Cocard [89]	12,541
12	30	A	Celtic	L	1-5	1-0	9	Cocard [36]	59,791
13	Nov 6	H	Hibernian	L	0-2	0-0	9		8735
14	20	H	Dundee U	D	1-1	0-0	9	Cocard (pen) [50]	7012
15	27	H	Hearts	D	2-2	0-2	9	Mahood [72], Reilly [89]	8326
16	Dec 11	A	Rangers	L	0-1	0-0	9		47,169
17	18	H	St Johnstone	L	1-2	0-2	9	Wright [49]	6002
18	27	A	Hibernian	D	2-2	2-0	—	Smith [15], Cocard [20]	11,900
19	Jan 23	H	Celtic	D	1-1	1-1	9	Reilly [40]	14,126
20	26	A	Dundee	D	0-0	0-0	—		4039
21	Feb 12	H	Motherwell	L	0-2	0-0	10		7057
22	22	A	Motherwell	W	4-0	2-0	—	Cocard 2 [29, 42], Vareille 2 [85, 89]	5813
23	26	A	Hearts	D	0-0	0-0	10		14,243
24	Mar 4	H	Dundee	D	2-2	1-0	10	Durrant [10], Dindeleux [56]	8460
25	15	A	Dundee U	D	2-2	1-0	—	Durrant 2 [44, 49]	6966
26	18	A	St Johnstone	D	0-0	0-0	9		4688
27	25	H	Hibernian	W	1-0	0-0	9	Vareille [52]	8068
28	Apr 2	A	Celtic	L	2-4	0-2	9	Wright [50], Lauchlan [58]	55,194
29	8	H	Dundee U	W	1-0	0-0	9	McQuillan (og) [79]	6037
30	12	H	Aberdeen	W	1-0	1-0	—	Wright [24]	11,525
31	16	A	Motherwell	L	0-2	0-1	9		5429
32	22	A	Dundee	W	2-1	1-0	8	Wright 2 [33, 75]	6208
33	29	H	Hearts	L	0-1	0-0	9		8057
34	May 7	H	Rangers	L	0-2	0-1	9		13,284
35	14	A	Aberdeen	L	1-5	1-3	9	Lauchlan [25]	9275
36	21	H	St Johnstone	W	3-2	1-0	9	Durrant [11], Bollan (og) [50], Cocard [67]	9192

Final League Position: 9   1998–99 4

Honours
League Champions: Division I 1964-65. Division II 1897-98, 1898-99; *Runners-up:* Division I 1959-60, 1960-61, 1962-63, 1963-64. First Division 1975-76, 1978-79, 1981-82, 1992-93. Division II 1953-54, 1973-74. Second Division 1989-90.
Scottish Cup Winners: 1920, 1929, 1997; *Runners-up:* 1898, 1932, 1938, 1957, 1960.
League Cup Runners-up: 1952-53, 1960-61, 1962-63.

European: *European Cup:* 4 matches (1965-66). *Cup Winners' Cup:* 4 matches (1997-98). *UEFA Cup:* 20 matches (*Fairs Cup:* 1964-65, 1966-67, 1969-70, 1970-71, *UEFA Cup:* 1998-99, 1999–2000).

Club colours: Shirt: Blue and white vertical stripes. Shorts: Blue. Stockings: Blue.

Goalscorers: *League (38):* Cocard 8, Wright 5, Durrant 4, Reilly 3, Vareille 3, Hay 2, Jeffrey 2, Lauchlan 2, Mitchell 2, Dindeleux 1, McCoist 1 (pen), MacPherson 1, Mahood 1, Smith 1, own goals 2. *Scottish Cup (0). CIS Cup (4):* McCoist 2, Jeffrey 1, Vareille 1.

Meldrum C 18	MacPherson A 30	Hay G 8+2	McGowne K 9	Dindeleux F 28	Reilly M 28+1	Holt G 35	Innes C 5	Mitchell A 22+4	Roberts M 2	Jeffrey M 10+8	Vareille J 13+10	Mahood A 6+12	Canero P 6+5	Lauchlan J 29	Henry J 1	Wright P 12+4	Bagan D 2+1	Baker M 11	Durrant I 32	McCoist A 5+4	Fowler J 1+4	Davidson S —+2	Burke A 3+6	Hessey S 7+4	Watt M 4	Cocard C 24+1	Smith A 11+4	McKinlay T 14+1	McCutcheon G —+2	Marshall G 14	Abou S 5+5	Beesley D 1+1	Match No.
1	2	3²	4	5	6	7	8	9		10¹	11	12	13																				1
1	2	3³	4	5	6²	7	8	9		10	11¹	12	13	14																			2
1	2³	3	4		6	7				11¹	10²	8	14	5	9	12	13																3
1	2²			5	6	7		12			9	13		4		10¹		3	8³	11	14												4
1	2			5	13	7		9			11			4		10¹		3	8	6²	12												5
1	2		5		7			9			11²			4		10	6¹	3	8³	13		12	14										6
1	2		5		6	7					13	9³		4¹		10²		3	8	11		12	14										7
1	2		4	5²	6	7		12			10¹	13				3	8	11		9³	14												8
	2		5		6²			9			12	10		4		3	8	11¹								1	13						9
	2		5		7		6	11			9			4		3	8									1	10						10
	2		5		6	7		9			11²	13	12	4		3	8¹									1	10						11
	2	12	5		6			9			11¹	13	7	4		3	8									1	10²						12
1	2	3	5		6¹	7		9			12	11		4		8										10							13
1	2¹	3	5		6	7		9			11			4		8				12						10							14
1	3¹		5		6	7		9			11¹	13	2	4		8²				14						10							15
1	3		5		6	7		9					2	4		8¹				12						10	11						16
1	3	5			6	7		13			14	12	2	4		9¹		8²								10	11³						17
1			5		6	7	3	9			12			2	4	13		8								10¹	11²						18
1	2		5		6	7³		9²			12		13	14	4	3	8									10	11¹						19
1	2		5		6	7					13	9²		4		3	8				4					10¹	11	12					20
1	2		5		6	7		9²			11¹			4		8				13						10	3	12					21
	2		5		6	7		9			13	14		4		8³				12						10	3¹		1	11²			22
	2		5		6	7		9			13			4¹		8				12						10²	3		1	11			23
	2		5		6	7		9			12	13		4		8										10¹	3		1	11²			24
	2¹		5		6	7							12	4		8										10	13	3		1	11²		25
	2		5		6	7		11²			9			4		8										10¹	13	3		1	12		26
	2		5		6	7		9²						4		8	11¹									10	3		1	12		27
	2		5		6	7		9²						4	13	8									12	10	3¹		1	11		28
	2		5		6	7					13			4	11¹	8²					3					10	9		1	12		29
	2		5		6	7					13			4	11²	8					3					10	9¹		1	12		30
	2		5		6	7					13			4	11³	8				10²						10	9¹	3	12	1	14		31
	2		5¹		7			10			9³	12		11		8			13	6²	4					14	3	1					32
	2				7	5	6	9¹						11		8					4					10	12	3	1				33
	2				7	5¹		9²			12			11		8	14	13	6	4						10³	3	1					34
					8¹	7		12				9	2	4		11	14	13	5							10³	3	1			6²		35
1	12	5¹			7			13			9	2	4		8³			6								10	11²	3			14		36

LIVINGSTON
First Division

Year Formed: 1974. *Ground:* West Lothian Courier Stadium, Alderton Road, Livingston EH54 7DN. *Telephone:* 01506 417000. *Fax:* 01506 418888. *Email:* livingstonfc@btinternet.com.
Ground Capacity: 10,004 (all seated). *Size of Pitch:* 105yd × 72yd.
Chairman: Dominic Keane. *Secretary:* J. R. S. Renton.
Team Manager: Jim Leishman. *Head Coach:* David Hay. *First Team Coach:* John Robertson. *Physios:* Michael McBride and Arthur Duncan.
Managers since 1975: John Bain; Alec Ness; Willie MacFarlane; Terry Christie; Michael Lawson. *Club Nickname:* Livvy Lions. *Previous Grounds:* None.
Record Attendance: 4000 v Albion Rovers, League Cup 1st rd; 9 Sept, 1974.
Record Transfer Fee received: £115,000 for John Inglis to St Johnstone (1990).
Record Transfer Fee paid: £28,000 for Victor Kasule from Albion Rovers (1987).
Record Victory: 6-0 v Raith R, Second Division; 9 Nov, 1985.
Record Defeat: 0-8 v Hamilton A. Division II; 14 Dec, 1974.
Most Capped Player (under 18): I. Little.
Most League Appearances: 446: Walter Boyd, 1979-89.
Most League Goals in Season (Individual): 21: John McGachie, 1986-87. *(Team):* 69; Second Division, 1986-87.
Most Goals Overall (Individual): 64: David Roseburgh, 1986-93.

LIVINGSTON 1999–2000 LEAGUE RECORD

Match No.	Date	Venue	Opponents	Result	H/T Score	Lg. Pos.	Goalscorers	Atten-dance
1	Aug 7	H	Raith R	D 1-1	1-0	—	Keith [14]	3116
2	Aug 14	A	Ayr U	W 2-1	1-0	5	Britton [44], Bingham [73]	2533
3	Aug 21	H	Airdrieonians	W 3-0	0-0	3	McPhee 2 [62, 65], Sweeney [75]	2837
4	Aug 28	A	Morton	D 2-2	2-1	3	Keith [12], Millar J [30]	1257
5	Sept 4	H	Dunfermline Ath	L 0-1	0-0	4		5302
6	Sept 11	A	Falkirk	W 2-0	1-0	3	Robertson [43], Bingham [65]	3326
7	Sept 18	H	Inverness CT	D 2-2	1-2	3	McPhee 2 [28, 66]	2584
8	Sept 25	H	Clydebank	W 2-1	2-0	3	Bingham 2 [7, 8]	3290
9	Oct 2	A	St Mirren	D 1-1	1-0	3	Britton [17]	4520
10	Oct 16	H	Ayr U	W 4-1	1-1	3	Britton [11], McCormick 2 [55, 61], McKinnon [75]	2332
11	Oct 23	A	Raith R	L 1-3	1-2	3	Millar M [25]	2942
12	Oct 30	H	Falkirk	D 1-1	0-0	4	Millar M [62]	3482
13	Nov 6	A	Inverness CT	L 0-2	0-0	5		2474
14	Nov 14	A	Dunfermline Ath	L 0-3	0-2	5		4163
15	Nov 20	H	Morton	W 2-1	0-0	5	Britton [49], Bingham [55]	2490
16	Nov 27	H	St Mirren	L 1-2	0-1	5	Deas [80]	4239
17	Dec 4	A	Clydebank	W 5-1	2-0	5	Bingham 2 [10, 89], McCormick [40], King [49], Fleming [69]	346
18	Dec 14	A	Airdrieonians	W 3-2	1-1	—	McCormick [35], Bingham 2 [61, 88]	1492
19	Dec 27	A	Falkirk	W 3-2	0-0	—	King [47], McPhee 2 [61, 84]	3109
20	Jan 3	H	Inverness CT	D 1-1	0-0	—	McPhee [80]	2656
21	Jan 8	H	Dunfermline Ath	W 1-0	0-0	4	Bingham [61]	3800
22	Jan 22	H	Clydebank	W 3-0	0-0	5	Keith 2 [66, 69], McPhee [89]	3064
23	Feb 5	A	St Mirren	W 2-0	1-0	4	Bingham [30], McPhee [54]	5015
24	Feb 29	A	Ayr U	W 1-0	0-0	—	Deas [65]	1765
25	Mar 4	H	Falkirk	L 0-1	0-1	5		4055
26	Mar 11	H	Raith R	D 0-0	0-0	5		2683
27	Mar 14	A	Morton	L 0-1	0-0	—		684
28	Mar 18	A	Inverness CT	L 1-4	0-2	5	McPhee [59]	2206
29	Mar 25	H	Morton	W 1-0	0-0	5	McCormick [83]	3252
30	Apr 1	A	Dunfermline Ath	L 1-4	0-2	5	May (og) [51]	4337
31	Apr 4	H	Airdrieonians	W 3-2	3-0	—	Smith [13], McKinnon [25], Rowson [26]	1473
32	Apr 8	A	Clydebank	W 2-1	1-0	5	Bingham [34], Millar J [60]	316
33	Apr 15	H	St Mirren	L 1-2	0-1	5	Bingham [60]	4531
34	Apr 22	A	Raith R	W 3-1	0-1	5	McPhee 2 [60, 88], Britton [87]	2129
35	Apr 29	H	Ayr U	W 3-1	0-0	4	Bingham [52], McCormick [75], McPhee [80]	5729
36	May 6	A	Airdrieonians	W 2-0	0-0	4	Bingham [55], McPhee [90]	1493

Final League Position: 4   1998–99 DIV 2 1

Honours

League Champions: Second Division 1986-87, 1998–99. Third Division 1995-96; *Runners-up:* Second Division 1982-83. First Division 1987-88.
Scottish Cup: —. *League Cup:* Semi-finals 1984-85. *B&Q Cup:* Semi-finals 1992-93, 1993-94.

Club colours: Shirt: Black with yellow trim. Shorts: Black. Stockings: Black.

Goalscorers: *League (60):* Bingham 15, McPhee 14, McCormick 6, Britton 5, Keith 4, Deas 2, King 2, McKinnon 2, Millar J 2, Millar M 2, Fleming 1, Robertson 1, Rowson 1, Smith 1, Sweeney 1, own goal 1. *Scottish Cup (8):* Keith 3, McKinnon 2, Bingham 1, McPhee 1, own goal 1. *CIS Cup (2):* Britton 2. *Bell's League Cup (5):* Bingham 2, Britton 1, McPhee 1, Millar M 1.

McCaldon I 23	Kelly P 30+2	Deas P 33	Watson G 1	Coughlan G 26+3	Millar J 27+3	King C 20+11	Millar M 24	Britton G 13+5	Bingham D 32	Keith M 8+1	McCormick M 16+12	McDonald W —+1	Little I 1+3	McManus A 28	McPhee B 20+13	Fleming D 17+8	Robertson J 1+4	Sweeney S 15+3	McCann G —+4	Feroz C 2+7	McKinnon R 17+2	McLaren A 5+4	Bennett N —+1	Courts T 2+2	Alexander N 13	Richardson L 6	Hart M 3	Smith J 5+1	Rowson D 6	Clark S 2	Moffat A —+1	Match No
1	2^3	3	4	5	6	7^1	8	9^2	10	11	12	13	14																			1
1	2	3		5	6	7^2	8	9^1	10^3	11				4	12	13	14															2
1	2	3			6	7^1	8	9^2	10					4	12	11	13	5														3
1	2	3		13	6^3	7^1	8	9^2	10	11				4	12			5	14													4
1		3		5	6	7	8	9^1	10^2	11^3				2	12			4	13	14												5
1	2	3			6	7	8	12	10	11^1				4					9^2		5	13										6
1	2	3		12	6	7^3	8	9^1	10				13	4	11	14					5^2											7
1	2			5	6^3	7	8	9^2	10^1					4	11	3				14	13											8
1	2	3		5	6	7^1	8	9^2					13	4	11^3	12					14	10										9
1	2	3		5	6	13	8^3	9^1			11			4	12						10	7^2	14									10
1	2	3		5	6	13	8	9^3			11			4^1	12						10	7^2	14									11
	2	3^2		5	6	12	8	14			11^1		13	4	9^3						10	7^2		1								12
1		3		5	6^1	13	8	14			11			2	9^1	12		4			10	7^3										13
1	2	3		5	6	7^2	8	9^1	10					12	11			4			13											14
	2	3		5	6	7^1		9^2	10				13	4	8	11		12							1							15
	2	3		5	6^3	7		9^1	10		12		13	4	8^2	11			14						1							16
	2^1	3		5	6	7	8^2	9	10					4	11	12					13				1							17
	2	3		5	6	7^3	8	9^2	10		12		13	4	11^1				14						1							18
	2	3		5^1	6	7	8	9	10		12		13	4	11^2										1							19
	2	3		5	6	7	8	9^1	10		12		13	4	11^2										1							20
	2	3		5	6	7	8	9^1	10		12		13	4	11^2										1							21
	2	3		5	6	7	8	9	10^2		12		13	4	11^1										1							22
1	2	3		5			8	9^2	10^1		12		13	4				7			6				11							23
1	2	3		5			8	9	10		12			4				7			6^1				11							24
1	2	3		5			8	9	10		12		13	4				7^1			6^2				11							25
1	2	3^3		5			8	9	10		13			4	12			7^1	14		6				11^2							26
1	2	3		5			8^2	9^1	10		13			4		12		7^3	14		6				11							27
1	2	3		5	6^1			9	10^2				13	4	12	11			14									7^3	8			28
1	2	3		5				9	10				13	4	12	11^1					6^2							7	8			29
	2	3		5^1				9	10				13	4	12	11			14						1	6^3		7^2	8			30
1	2	3		5				9	10				13	4	12	11^1					6^2							7	8			31
1	2	3		5				9	10					4	12	11					6							7^1	8			32
1	2	3		5				9^2	10^1				13	4	12	11^3		7	14		6								8			33
	2	3		5				9	10				13^3	4	12	11			14		6^2				1			7^1	8			34
		3		5	6			9	10				13	4^1	8^2	11		7^3	14		12				1					2		35
		3		5				9	10^2				13	4	12	11		8^1			6^3				1			7		2	14	36

MONTROSE
Third Division

Year Formed: 1879. *Ground & Address:* Links Park, Wellington St, Montrose DD10 8QD. *Telephone:* 01674 673200.
Ground Capacity: total: 4338, seated: 1338. *Size of Pitch:* 113yd × 70yd.
Chairman: John F. Paton. *Secretary:* Malcolm J. Watters.
Manager: Kevin Drinkell. *Assistant Manager:* John Sheran. *Physio:* Allan Borthwick.
Managers since 1975: A. Stuart; K. Cameron; R. Livingstone; S. Murray; D. D'Arcy; I. Stewart; C. McLelland; D. Rougvie;
J. Leishman, J Holt, A. Dornan, D. Smith; T. Campbell.
Club Nickname(s): The Gable Endies. *Previous Grounds:* None.
Record Attendance: 8983 v Dundee, Scottish Cup 3rd rd; 17 Mar, 1973.
Record Transfer Fee received: £50,000 for Gary Murray to Hibernian (Dec 1980).
Record Transfer Fee paid: £17,500 for Jim Smith from Airdrieonians (Feb 1992).
Record Victory: 12-0 v Vale of Leithen, Scottish Cup 2nd rd; 4 Jan, 1975.
Record Defeat: 0-13 v Aberdeen; 17 Mar, 1951.
Most Capped Player: Alexander Keillor, 2 (6), Scotland.
Most League Appearances: 426: David Larter, 1987-98.
Most League Goals in Season (Individual): 28: Brian Third, Division II; 1972-73.

MONTROSE 1999–2000 LEAGUE RECORD

Match No.	Date		Venue	Opponents	Result	H/T Score	Lg. Pos.	Goalscorers	Atten- dance
1	Aug	7	H	Cowdenbeath	L 0-1	0-1	—		275
2		14	A	Dumbarton	W 4-3	2-2	6	O'Driscoll 3 [7, 45, 80], Farnan [80]	436
3		21	H	Berwick R	L 1-2	0-2	6	Duffy [49]	313
4		28	A	East Fife	D 0-0	0-0	7		512
5	Sept	4	H	East Stirling	L 1-2	1-2	7	Paterson [27]	278
6		11	A	Albion R	W 3-1	2-0	6	Taylor [26], Craib [28], Meldrum [82]	243
7		18	H	Brechin C	L 0-1	0-1	7		512
8		28	H	Forfar Ath	W 2-0	0-0	—	Taylor [55], Mailer [84]	281
9	Oct	2	A	Queen's Park	L 1-2	1-1	7	Taylor [28]	688
10		16	H	Dumbarton	L 1-4	0-3	7	Mailer [61]	274
11		23	A	Cowdenbeath	D 1-1	0-1	7	Taylor [76]	254
12		30	H	Albion R	W 2-1	0-0	7	Shand [50], O'Driscoll [53]	261
13	Nov	6	A	Brechin C	L 0-1	0-0	7		366
14		14	A	East Stirling	L 0-2	0-1	7		241
15		20	H	East Fife	L 1-2	0-1	9	Love (og) [90]	440
16		27	H	Queen's Park	W 2-1	1-1	7	Scott [1], Taylor [57]	424
17	Dec	7	A	Forfar Ath	W 2-1	0-0	—	Craib M [66], Craib S [90]	379
18		18	A	Cowdenbeath	L 1-3	0-2	7	Craig M [48]	318
19		27	A	Berwick R	D 0-0	0-0	—		472
20	Jan	3	H	Brechin C	W 1-0	1-0	—	Craig D [42]	798
21		22	A	Forfar Ath	L 1-5	1-2	8	Taylor [44]	588
22	Feb	5	A	Queen's Park	D 1-1	0-0	8	McWilliam [66]	505
23		15	A	East Fife	L 0-2	0-1	—		390
24		19	H	East Stirling	D 0-0	0-0	7		327
25		26	A	Dumbarton	L 2-3	0-1	8	Taylor [69], Shand [73]	482
26	Mar	4	H	Berwick R	L 2-3	1-2	9	Mailer [19], O'Driscoll [57]	302
27		7	A	Albion R	W 2-0	2-0	—	Scott [28], Paterson [38]	159
28		11	H	Albion R	L 1-2	1-0	9	Taylor [20]	329
29		18	A	Brechin C	D 0-0	0-0	9		360
30		25	H	East Fife	D 1-1	1-1	9	Taylor [3]	442
31	Apr	1	A	East Stirling	L 0-1	0-1	9		205
32		8	A	Forfar Ath	W 2-1	0-0	8	Craib M [62], Bennett [64]	516
33		15	H	Queen's Park	L 0-2	0-0	8		393
34		22	A	Cowdenbeath	L 1-2	1-0	9	Taylor [37]	252
35		29	H	Dumbarton	W 2-1	1-1	8	Taylor [15], Ogboke [52]	267
36	May	6	A	Berwick R	L 1-2	1-1	9	Taylor [44]	1224

Final League Position: 9   1998–99 10

Honours
League Champions: Second Division 1984-85; *Runners-up:* 1990-91. Third Division, *Runners-up:* 1994-95.
Scottish Cup: Quarter-finals 1973, 1976.
League Cup: Semi-finals 1975-76.
B&Q Cup: Semi-finals 1992-93.
League Challenge Cup: Semi-finals: 1996-97.

Club colours: Shirt: Royal blue and white vertical stripes. Shorts: Royal blue. Stockings: Royal blue.

Goalscorers: *League (39):* Taylor 12, O'Driscoll 5, Mailer 3, Craib M 2, Craib S 2, Paterson 2, Scott 2, Shand 2, Bennett 1, Craig D 1, Craig M 1, Duffy 1, Farnan 1, McWilliam 1, Meldrum 1, Ogboke 1, own goal 1. *Scottish Cup (1):* O'Driscoll 1. *CIS Cup (1):* O'Driscoll 1. *Bell's League Cup (1):* Taylor 1 (pen).

McGlynn G 35	Mailer C 29	Scott W 25	Farnan C 12	Paterson G 24	Craib M 33	Shand M 7+11	Duffy K 11+11	Taylor S 35	McWilliam R 27+8	Meldrum G 11+9	Stevenson C —+2	Niddrie K 13+3	Dorward R —+1	Clark S 8	Bennett N 16	O'Driscoll J 20+4	Robertson S 13+9	Harrison T 1	Craig M 15+4	Craib S 6+3	Craig D 12	Black M 23	Ogboke C 3+11	Mitchell B 6	Jackson C 1	Young J 7	Fitzpatrick F 1	Dailly G 2	Match No.
1	2²	3	4	5	6	7¹	8	9	10	11³	12	13	14																1
1		3	4	5	6		7¹	9	12	11					2	8	10												2
1		3	4	5	6	13	7	9	12	11					2	10²	8¹												3
1		3	4	5	6	7²	8	9	13	11¹	12	14			2¹	10													4
1		3	8	5	6	14	7	10	2¹	13	12							4²	9³	11									5
1	8¹	3	4		6		7²	10	12	14	5				2	13			9³	11									6
1	8	3	11¹	4	6	7		9	13	14	5³				2	12	10²												7
1	8	3	4	5	6	13	12	9	10²	11					2	7¹													8
1	8	3	4	5	6	13	12	9¹	10²	11					2						7								9
1	7	3	8		6		12	9²	10	11³	5				2¹	13			14	4									10
1	8³	3	4		6		12	10¹	9	14	5					13	7²		11	2									11
1	8	3	4		6	7³	14	9	12	13	5					10¹			11²	2									12
1	4	3			6	7¹	8	9	12		5					10			11	2									13
1	4	3			6	7		9	12	11¹						10	8					2	5						14
1	8		4	5	6		12	9		11²						10	7¹					2	3	13					15
1	8	11		5	6			9¹	7							10			4		12	2	3						16
1	7			5	6		11	8								10			4	9¹	12	2	3						17
1	8			5	6	13		11¹	7							10²			4	9	12	2	3						18
1	8			5	6¹	13		11	7	12						10²			4	9		2	3						19
1	7	8		5		11	4	6								10			12	9¹		2	3						20
1	4	8	5¹		6	14		11	2	12						10²	7³			9			3	13					21
1				5	6	7		11								10¹			4	9²	12	2	3	13	8				22
1				5	6	8	7	11³		14						10¹			4	9²	12	2	3	13					23
1	4			5	6	7		10	11							8				9¹	12	2	3						24
1	4			5	6	7¹	12	10	11²	13						8				9		2	3						25
1	4			5	6	7¹		9	11							8	10					2	3						26
1	4	7		5	6			9	11²							8	10¹				12	2	3	13					27
1	4²	7			6	13		9¹	11	3						8	10²				12	2	5	14					28
1	7				6	13		11²			5					8	10¹		4	9	12	2	3						29
1	4	11			6	14		10	7³		5					8				9²	12	2¹	3	13					30
1	4	7			6			10	11²		5					8				9¹	12	2	3	13					31
1	4	10			6	7			11		5					8				9		2	3						32
1	4	10¹			6	14	12	11	7²		5					8				9³		2	3	13					33
1	7	4			6²	13		11	10		5					8				9¹	12	2	3			1			34
1	7				6	13		10	11		5					8				9¹	12	2	3					4²	35
1	7³	4				13		10	11²		5					8				9¹	12	2	3	14				6	36

MORTON

First Division

Year Formed: 1874. *Ground & Address:* Cappielow Park, Sinclair St, Greenock. *Telephone:* 01475 723571. *Fax:* 01475 781084
Ground Capacity: total: 14,891, seated: 5741. *Size of Pitch:* 110yd × 71yd.
Chairman: Hugh Scott. *Club Secretary:* George Carson.
Manager: Allan Evans. *Youth Coach:* Peter Weir.
Managers since 1975: Joe Gilroy; Benny Rooney; Alex Miller; Tommy McLean; Willie McLean; Allan McGraw; Billy Stark; Ian McCall. *Club Nickname(s):* The Ton. *Previous Grounds:* Grant Street 1874, Garvel Park 1875, Cappielow Park 1879, Ladyburn Park 1882, (Cappielow Park 1883).
Record Attendance: 23,500 v Celtic; 29 April, 1922.
Record Transfer Fee received: £350,000 for Neil Orr to West Ham U.
Record Transfer Fee paid: £150,000 for Allan Mahood from Nottingham Forest.
Record Victory: 11-0 v Carfin Shamrock, Scottish Cup 1st rd; 13 Nov, 1886.
Record Defeat: 1-10 v Port Glasgow Ath, Division II; 5 May, 1894 and v St Bernards, Division II; 14 Oct, 1933.
Most Capped Player: Jimmy Cowan, 25, Scotland.
Most League Appearances: 358: David Hayes, 1969-84.
Most League Goals in Season (Individual): 58: Allan McGraw, Division II; 1963-64.

MORTON 1999–2000 LEAGUE RECORD

Match No.	Date	Venue	Opponents	Result	H/T Score	Lg. Pos.	Goalscorers	Atten-dance
1	Aug 7	A	Falkirk	W 4-2	1-0	—	Anderson J [31], Thomas 2 [55, 60], Archdeacon [90]	2945
2	Aug 14	H	Clydebank	D 0-0	0-0	4		1433
3	Aug 21	A	Dunfermline Ath	L 1-2	0-0	5	Wright [83]	4030
4	Aug 28	H	Livingston	D 2-2	1-2	5	Murie [39], Connolly [67]	1257
5	Sept 4	A	Inverness CT	D 1-1	0-0	6	Connolly [76]	2414
6	Sept 11	H	Raith R	W 2-0	2-0	5	Connolly [17], Wright [33]	970
7	Sept 18	A	St Mirren	L 2-3	1-2	6	Connolly 2 (2 pens) [6, 63]	6773
8	Sept 25	H	Airdrieonians	L 0-2	0-1	7		1126
9	Oct 2	A	Ayr U	L 0-3	0-1	7		2186
10	Oct 16	A	Clydebank	W 3-1	1-1	7	McDonald [39], Tweedie [61], Wright [76]	758
11	Oct 23	H	Falkirk	L 2-3	0-1	8	Curran [64], Hawke [80]	1409
12	Oct 30	A	Raith R	L 1-3	0-0	9	Curran [88]	2664
13	Nov 6	H	St Mirren	L 1-4	0-3	9	Curran [48]	3733
14	Nov 12	H	Inverness CT	W 5-1	2-1	8	Wright [18], Curran [44], Morrison [59], Matheson [76], Aitken [84]	812
15	Nov 20	A	Livingston	L 1-2	0-0	8	Murie [76]	2490
16	Nov 27	H	Ayr U	D 0-0	0-0	8		1168
17	Dec 7	A	Airdrieonians	L 0-1	0-0	—		1135
18	Dec 11	H	Dunfermline Ath	L 0-3	0-0	9		1289
19	Dec 18	A	Falkirk	L 1-2	0-0	9	McPherson [66]	2015
20	Dec 27	H	Raith R	W 1-0	1-0	—	Curran [24]	1056
21	Jan 3	A	St Mirren	D 1-1	0-0	—	Hartley [68]	7266
22	Jan 8	A	Inverness CT	L 2-6	0-0	9	McPherson [83], Curran [89]	1524
23	Jan 22	H	Airdrieonians	W 4-0	1-0	8	McDonald 2 [45, 56], Anderson J [53], Earnshaw [67]	1201
24	Feb 5	A	Ayr U	L 2-3	1-2	8	Anderson D [38], Curran [64]	1985
25	Feb 12	A	Dunfermline Ath	D 1-1	1-1	8	Earnshaw [18]	4289
26	Feb 26	H	Clydebank	W 1-0	1-0	8	Anderson J [28]	1052
27	Mar 4	A	Raith R	L 0-3	0-1	8		2026
28	Mar 14	H	Livingston	W 1-0	0-0	—	Curran [73]	684
29	Mar 18	H	St Mirren	L 0-2	0-0	8		3768
30	Mar 25	A	Livingston	L 0-1	0-0	8		3252
31	Apr 1	H	Inverness CT	L 0-2	0-0	8		567
32	Apr 8	A	Airdrieonians	L 0-3	0-0	8		866
33	Apr 15	H	Ayr U	L 1-2	0-1	8	Whalen [78]	656
34	Apr 22	H	Falkirk	L 0-2	0-0	8		1037
35	Apr 29	A	Clydebank	W 3-0	2-0	8	Anderson J [14], Curran [27], Matheson [65]	339
36	May 6	H	Dunfermline Ath	W 2-0	1-0	8	McPherson [15], Anderson J [72]	1039

Final League Position: 8   1998–99 6

Honours
League Champions: First Division 1977-78, 1983-84, 1986-87. Division II 1949-50, 1963-64, 1966-67. Second Division 1994-95. *Runners-up:* Division 1 1916-17, Division II 1899-1900, 1928-29, 1936-37.
Scottish Cup Winners: 1922; *Runners-up:* 1948. *League Cup Runners-up:* 1963-64.
B&Q Cup Runners-up: 1992-93.

European: *UEFA Cup:* 2 matches (*Fairs Cup:* 1968-69).

Club colours: Shirt: Royal blue and white 4" Hoops. Shorts: White with royal blue panel down side. Stockings: Royal blue and white hoops.

Goalscorers: *League (45):* Curran 9, Anderson J 5, Connolly 5 (2 pens), Wright 4, McDonald 3, McPherson 3, Earnshaw 2, Matheson 2, Murie 2, Thomas 2, Aitken 1, Anderson D 1, Archdeacon 1, Hartley 1, Hawke 1, Morrison 1, Tweedie 1, Whalen 1. *Scottish Cup (1):* Anderson J 1. *CIS Cup (1):* Curran 1 *Bell's League Cup (2):* Hawke 1, Thomas 1.

Maxwell A 33	Murie D 33+1	Archdeacon O 4	Millen A 28	Anderson D 28	Fenwick P 14	Curran H 28	Anderson J 26+3	Wright K 17+6	Thomas K 2	Matheson R 33+1	Hawke N 9+6	Aitken S 19+10	McDonald P 16+8	Ferguson I 3+4	McPherson C 14+9	Connolly P 5	Slavin B 14+6	Tweedie G 10+8	Carlin A 3	Morrison G 20+1	Whalen S 15+6	Hartley P 3	Kerr B —+4	Hart M 1+9	Earnshaw R 3	Pluck C 3+1	Ross M —+2	Walker J 2+5	McDonald S 7	Rice B 1	Stevenson C 1+1	Aitken C 1+1	Robb R —+2	Match No.
1	2	3	4	5	6	7	8	9¹	10²	11³	12	13	14																					1
1	2	3²	4	5		7	6	9¹	10	8	11	12	13																					2
1	2	3²	4	5		7	6	12		11	10	8	9¹	13																				3
1	2	3	4	5	6	9		7³		8²	14	12	11¹	10	13																			4
1	2		4	5		7	6	8²		12		14	13	9³	10	3	11¹																	5
1	2		4	5	6	8	9	7²				13	11¹	12	10³	3	14																	6
1	2³		4	5	6	8	9²	7		11¹	3	13	12	10			14																	7
1	2		4	5	6	8		7		12	3		11¹	9²		10	13																	8
1	2		4	5		8	12	9²		7	10	3	11¹	13			6																	9
	2		4	5		8	12	9³		7	10	13	11¹				6²		1	3	14													10
1	2			5		8	4	9¹		7	10	11²	13				6		3	12														11
1	2		4	5	6	8		9²		7	10			12	11¹				3	13														12
1	2²		4	3	6	8	13	12		7	10				11¹					5	9													13
1	2		3	6	8	4	9	7³		13	12			14	11¹					5	10²													14
1	2		3		8	4²	9¹	7		14	6			12	13	11¹				5	10													15
1	2		3		8			12		7²	9¹	6	14	11³	4	13				5	10													16
1	2		4	3	6	8²	10	7³		12	14			11	13					5	9¹													17
1	2		3	6	8¹	10²		7		12	13			11	14	4³				5	9													18
1	2		4	3	6		9	7		8				11	10¹					5	12													19
1			4	6	8	5	9¹	7³							13		10		3	14	2	12	11²											20
1	2		4	6	8	5	9¹	7			3		11²								12	10	13											21
1²	2¹		4		8	5		7			6			11					3	12	9	10	13											22
1	2		4	3	6	10	8¹			14	11				12					5	9²							13	7³					23
1	2		4	3	6	10	8	9³					11²		12					5								13	7¹	14				24
1	2		4	3		10	9							12	11²	6	14			5								13	7³	8¹				25
1			4	3		10	8	7		9				12	11²		14		2²	5¹								6	13					26
1	2		4	3		10²	8	7³		9				11	12	13				5¹								6	14					27
1	2		4			10	8	13		9				11	6¹				3	5					7²				12					28
1	2		4			10	8	12		9				11	6¹				3	5					7²				13					29
	2		4			10	8	12		9				11	6²	5³			1						7¹	13		14	3					30
	2					9	11	10		6	1			7³			14							8¹	4	3²	5	12	13					31
1	2					7	11			3				6		5¹	9	13	14					8²	4			10³	12					32
1	2³					6		7		8¹			11²	3	10					5	9		13				14	4	12					33
1	12		4	6		10	5	7		3	8			13	9					11¹								2²						34
1	2		4	6		10	8²	7						9¹	3³					5								12	13	14	11			35
1	2¹		4	6		10	8³	7						9²	13	3	12			5								14	11					36

MOTHERWELL   Premier League

Year Formed: 1886. *Ground & Address:* Fir Park Stadium, Motherwell ML1 2QN. *Telephone:* 01698 333333. *Fax:* 01698 338001.
Ground Capacity: all seated: 13,742. *Size of Pitch:* 110yd × 75yd.
Chairman: John Boyle. *General Manager/Secretary:* Alisdair Barron. *Commercial Manager:* Karen Paterson.
Manager: Billy Davies. *First Team Coach:* Miodrag Krivokapic. *Physio:* John Porteous.
Managers since 1975: Ian St. John; Willie McLean; Rodger Hynd; Ally MacLeod; David Hay; Jock Wallace; Bobby
Watson; Tommy McLean; Alex McLeish; Harri Kampman.
Club Nickname(s): The Well. *Previous Grounds:* Roman Road, Dalziel Park.
Record Attendance: 35,632 v Rangers, Scottish Cup 4th rd replay; 12 Mar, 1952.
Record Transfer Fee received: £1,750,000 for Phil O'Donnell to Celtic (September 1994).
Record Transfer Fee paid: £500,000 for John Spencer from Everton (Jan 1999).
Record Victory: 12-1 v Dundee U, Division II; 23 Jan, 1954.
Record Defeat: 0-8 v Aberdeen, Premier Division; 26 Mar, 1979.
Most Capped Player: Tommy Coyne, 13, Republic of Ireland.
Most League Appearances: 626: Bobby Ferrier, 1918-37.
Most League Goals in Season (Individual): 52: Willie McFadyen, Division I; 1931-32.
Most Goals Overall (Individual): 283: Hugh Ferguson, 1916-25.

MOTHERWELL 1999–2000 LEAGUE RECORD

Match No.	Date	Venue	Opponents	Result	H/T Score	Lg. Pos.	Goalscorers	Attendance
1	Jul 31	A	Hibernian	D 2-2	0-1	—	Nevin [64], Nicholas [89]	13,015
2	Aug 7	H	Dundee U	D 2-2	2-0	7	McCulloch 2 [17, 36]	6791
3	15	A	Rangers	L 1-4	0-2	9	McCulloch [90]	45,264
4	21	A	Kilmarnock	W 1-0	1-0	6	Adams [32]	7732
5	28	H	Dundee	L 0-2	0-1	8		6278
6	Sept 11	A	St Johnstone	D 1-1	0-1	8	Spencer [61]	5468
7	Oct 16	H	Hibernian	D 2-2	1-1	9	McCulloch [31], McMillan [67]	7559
8	20	H	Aberdeen	L 5-6	2-4	—	Spencer 3 [28, 65, 71], Goodman [44], Teale [79]	5009
9	23	A	Dundee U	W 2-0	1-0	7	Spencer [44], Teale (pen) [69]	6213
10	27	A	Celtic	W 1-0	1-0	—	Twaddle [15]	57,898
11	30	H	St Johnstone	W 1-0	1-0	4	Twaddle [9]	6173
12	Nov 6	A	Hearts	D 1-1	0-1	5	Spencer [82]	12,514
13	20	A	Dundee	W 1-0	1-0	4	McCulloch [44]	4340
14	23	H	Hearts	W 2-1	1-0	—	McCulloch [24], Nevin [90]	7793
15	28	H	Celtic	W 3-2	2-2	4	Brannan [9], Townsley [44], Goodman [50]	10,730
16	Dec 11	A	Hibernian	D 2-2	0-0	4	Spencer 2 [70, 89]	9955
17	18	H	Rangers	L 1-5	0-3	4	Goodman [88]	12,640
18	Jan 22	A	St Johnstone	D 1-1	0-1	4	McMillan [85]	4158
19	26	A	Aberdeen	D 1-1	1-0	—	Spencer [23]	10,314
20	Feb 5	H	Dundee	L 0-3	0-0	4		5856
21	12	A	Kilmarnock	W 2-0	0-0	3	Spencer [66], McMillan [73]	7057
22	22	H	Kilmarnock	L 0-4	0-2	—		5813
23	Mar 1	H	Hearts	L 0-2	0-1	—		5588
24	4	H	Aberdeen	W 1-0	0-0	3	Goodman [52]	7528
25	18	A	Rangers	L 2-6	2-4	4	Kemble [18], McCulloch [41]	49,622
26	25	A	Hearts	D 0-0	0-0	4		13,702
27	Apr 1	H	St Johnstone	W 2-1	0-0	4	Brannan [77], Corrigan [89]	5934
28	5	A	Celtic	L 0-4	0-2	—		55,689
29	8	A	Dundee	L 1-4	1-0	4	Goodman [15]	4701
30	16	H	Kilmarnock	W 2-0	1-0	4	Brannan [22], McCulloch [55]	5429
31	19	H	Dundee U	L 1-3	1-0	—	McCulloch [23]	4271
32	22	A	Aberdeen	L 1-2	1-1	4	Brannan [40]	9348
33	29	H	Celtic	D 1-1	1-1	4	Brannan [43]	7405
34	May 6	H	Hibernian	W 2-0	0-0	4	Twaddle 2 [71, 74]	5426
35	13	A	Dundee U	W 2-1	1-1	4	Goodman 2 [33, 79]	5908
36	21	H	Rangers	W 2-0	0-0	4	Twaddle [64], Spencer [72]	12,310

Final League Position: 4   1998–99 7

Honours

League Champions: Division I 1931-32. First Division 1981-82, 1984-85. Division II 1953-54, 1968-69; *Runners-up:* Premier Division 1994-95. Division I 1926-27, 1929-30, 1932-33, 1933-34. Division II 1894-95, 1902-03. *Scottish Cup:* 1952, 1991; *Runners-up:* 1931, 1933, 1939, 1951.
League Cup: 1950-51. *Runners-up:* 1954-55. *Scottish Summer Cup:* 1944, 1965.

Club colours: Shirt: Amber with claret hoop and trimmings. Shorts: White. Stockings: Claret.

European: *Cup Winners' Cup:* 2 matches (1991-92). *UEFA Cup:* 6 matches (1994-95, 1995-96).

Goalscorers: *League (49):* Spencer 11, McCulloch 9, Goodman 7, Brannan 5, Twaddle 5, McMillan 3, Nevin 2, Teale 2 (1 pen), Adams 1, Corrigan 1, Kemble 1, Nicholas 1, Townsley 1. *Scottish Cup (6):* Goodman 3, McCulloch 2, Brannan 1 (pen). *CIS Cup (5):* Halliday 1, McCulloch 1, Teale 1, Townsley 1, own goal 1.

Goram A 22	Craigan S 3+2	McGowan J 10+3	Teale S 16	Thomas A 6	Townsley D 16+9	Brannan G 33	Valakari S 28+2	Adams D 15+2	Goodman D 25+4	McCulloch L 28+1	Nevin P 6+22	Doesburg M 17+2	Nicholas S 2+19	McMillan S 31	Matthaei R 2+1	Spencer J 25+3	Halliday S 1+4	Woods S 14+1	Twaddle K 18+7	Kemble B 25	Harvey P 6+7	Denham G 6	Davies J 7+1	Corrigan M 18+1	Curcic S 3+3	Strong G 10	Ramsay D —+2	Hammell S 3+1	Match No
1	2²	3	4	5	6³	7	8	9¹	10	11	12	13	14																1
1			4	5	12	7	8	14	9	11³		2	13	3	6¹	10²													2
1			4	5	13	7	8		11	12	2	9²	3	6¹	10														3
1	6	5	4		7		8¹	9	11³	14	2	3	12	10²	13														4
1	6	5¹	4		7	12	8²	9³	11	13	2	3	10	14															5
		4	5	6³	7	8	9¹	11²	12	2	14	3	10	13	1														6
1		4	5	6²	7	8	12	11¹	9³	2	14	3	10		13														7
1	12	4	5	6³	7	8	11	9²	2¹	3	10	13	14																8
1		4	13	7	8	12	11	9³	2	3	10¹		6²	5	14														9
1	12	4			9	11²	13	2	14	3	10¹		6³	5															10
1⁶	3	13	7	8	9²	11	12	2		10	15	6¹	5	4															11
1		4	12	7	8		11	9¹	2	3	10	1	6²	5	13														12
1		4	12	7	8		11	9¹	2	14	3	10³	1	6²	5	13													13
1		4	6	7	8	13	11	12	2²	3	10	1	9¹	5															14
1		4	6²	7	8	10	11³	12	2	13	3	1	9¹	5	14														15
1		4	6	7	8		9²	2	12	3	10	11¹	1	5	13														16
1		4	6¹	7	8	11	12	2	13	3	10	9²	5																17
1			6²		8	11	13	2¹	14	3	10	9³	5	4	7	12													18
1			7	8	9	11	12	13	3	10²	6¹	5	4	2															19
1			6¹	7	8	13	11²	12	3	10	9	5	4	2															20
1	5		7	8	9	11³	14	13	3	10²	12		4	6¹	2														21
1	5	13	7	12		11		3	10¹	14	6²	9²	4	8	2														22
1	4	6²	8	9¹	10	11³	12	13	3		5	14	7	2															23
1	4	6¹	8	9	11	13	12	3	10²		5	7	2																24
1	4		7	8	9³	11	12	13	3		6¹	5	14	2	10²														25
			7	8	9¹	10	11	12	3		1	6²	5	13	2	4													26
	12		7	8	6¹	9	11		13	3	1	14		5²	10³	4													27
	12		7		9²	11	13		14	3	1	8	5	6	2	10³	4¹												28
12	4		7		9	10²	11		14	3	1	8	5	6³	2¹	13													29
		6²	7	8	14	10¹	11		3	12	1	9³	5		2	13	4												30
1		6²	7	8	10	11		3	12	1	9¹	5		2	13	4													31
		5³	7	8	6²	10	11¹	14	9		12	1		5	6²	2		3	13	4									32
	12	7		8	10¹	11	13		14	9³	1		5	6²	2		4	3											33
	6¹	7		8²	10		13	3	11²	1	12	5	9	2		4	14												34
1		13	7	8	10	14		3¹	11		9	5	6²	2³	4	12													35
1			7	8	9	10	13		11²	12		5	6¹	2	4	3													36

PARTICK THISTLE

Second Division

Year Formed: 1876. *Ground & Address:* Firhill Stadium, 80 Firhill Rd, Glasgow G20 7AL. *Telephone:* 0141 579 1971. *Fax:* 0141 945 1525
Ground Capacity: total: 14,538, seated: 8397. *Size of Pitch:* 110yd × 75yd.
Chairman: T. Brown McMaster. *Secretary:* Alan C. Dick. *Commercial Manager:* Amanda Stark.
Manager: John Lambie. *Assistant Manager:* Gerry Collins. *Physio:* Walter Cannon. *Player/Coach:* Kenny Brannigan.
Managers since 1975: R. Auld; P. Cormack; B. Rooney; R. Auld; D. Johnstone; W. Lamont; S. Clark; J. Lambie; M. MacLeod; J. McVeigh; T. Bryce. *Club Nickname(s):* The Jags. *Previous Grounds:* Jordanvale Park; Muirpark; Inchview; Meadowside Park.
Record Attendance: 49,838 v Rangers, Division I; 18 Feb, 1922. *Ground Record:* 54,728, Scotland v Ireland, 25 Feb 1928.
Record Transfer Fee received: £200,000 for Mo Johnston to Watford.
Record Transfer Fee paid: £85,000 for Andy Murdoch from Celtic (Feb 1991).
Record Victory: 16-0 v Royal Albert, Scottish Cup 1st rd; 17 Jan, 1931.
Record Defeat: 0-10 v Queen's Park, Scottish Cup; 3 Dec, 1881.
Most Capped Player: Alan Rough, 51 (53), Scotland.
Most League Appearances: 410: Alan Rough, 1969-82.
Most League Goals in Season (Individual): 41: Alec Hair, Division I; 1926-27.

PARTICK THISTLE 1999–2000 LEAGUE RECORD

Match No.	Date		Venue	Opponents	Result		H/T Score	Lg. Pos.	Goalscorers	Attendance
1	Aug	7	H	Stenhousemuir	L	0-1	0-0	—		2072
2		14	A	Alloa Ath	L	0-1	0-0	9		1178
3		21	H	Arbroath	L	1-3	1-1	9	Dunn [27]	1915
4		28	H	Queen of the S	W	2-0	1-0	9	Elliot [5], McKeown [76]	1959
5	Sept	4	A	Stranraer	D	1-1	0-1	9	Elliot [81]	1138
6		11	A	Clyde	L	0-2	0-1	10		2356
7		18	H	Hamilton A	L	0-1	0-1	10		2312
8		25	H	Ross Co	L	0-2	0-1	10		2171
9	Oct	2	A	Stirling A	L	1-3	0-3	10	Miller [68]	1333
10		16	H	Alloa Ath	D	2-2	2-0	10	Docherty [21], Dunn [40]	1801
11		23	A	Stenhousemuir	W	1-0	1-0	10	Dunn [31]	1188
12		30	H	Clyde	D	0-0	0-0	10		2617
13	Nov	6	A	Hamilton A	D	0-0	0-0	9		1828
14		14	H	Stranraer	W	2-0	2-0	9	Dunn 2 [16, 43]	1825
15		20	A	Queen of the S	W	2-1	1-1	9	English [12], Lyle [71]	1462
16		27	H	Stirling A	W	1-0	0-0	7	Craig [89]	2812
17	Dec	4	A	Ross Co	L	1-2	0-1	7	Jacobs [77]	2392
18		18	H	Stenhousemuir	W	1-0	1-0	7	Landau [25]	1922
19		27	A	Arbroath	D	0-0	0-0	—		1509
20	Jan	3	H	Hamilton A	D	2-2	0-2	—	Paton [72], Lyle [81]	2755
21		22	H	Ross Co	W	4-2	2-1	7	Landau 2 [13, 89], Craig [43], Jacobs [53]	2698
22	Feb	5	A	Stirling A	W	2-0	1-0	5	Lyle [44], McLean [51]	1704
23		12	H	Queen of the S	W	5-4	2-1	2	Lennon [37], Lyle [41], Landau [69], Craig [72], Jacobs [79]	2605
24		26	A	Alloa Ath	D	1-1	0-1	4	Miller [82]	1847
25		29	A	Clyde	L	0-1	0-1	—		2781
26	Mar	4	H	Arbroath	W	2-0	1-0	2	Blom [13], Craig [67]	2210
27		7	A	Stranraer	L	1-3	0-2	—	McKeown [75]	628
28		18	A	Hamilton A	W	1-0	1-0	4	Lennon [41]	2223
29		21	H	Clyde	L	1-2	1-1	—	McWilliams [12]	3012
30		25	A	Queen of the S	D	1-1	0-1	4	McWilliams (pen) [47]	1813
31	Apr	1	H	Stranraer	D	1-1	1-0	4	Huggon [27]	2351
32		8	A	Ross Co	W	3-1	1-0	4	Hardie 2 [27, 73], McWilliams [47]	3511
33		15	H	Stirling A	D	1-1	0-1	4	Miller [87]	2160
34		22	A	Stenhousemuir	L	0-2	0-0	4		895
35		29	A	Alloa Ath	L	0-1	0-1	4		1803
36	May	6	A	Arbroath	L	2-3	1-0	5	Hardie [23], Kelly [88]	889

Final League Position: 5   1998–99 8

Honours

League Champions: First Division 1975-76. Division II 1896-97, 1899-1900, 1970-71; *Runners-up:* First Division 1991-92. Division II 1901-02.

Scottish Cup Winners: 1921; *Runners-up:* 1930.

League Cup Winners: 1971-72; *Runners-up:* 1953-54, 1956-57, 1958-59.

European: *Fairs Cup:* 4 matches (1963-64). *UEFA Cup:* 2 matches (1972-73).

Club colours: Shirt: Red and yellow hoops. Shorts: Black. Stockings: Red with two yellow leg bands, tops red with one broad yellow band.

Goalscorers: *League (42):* Dunn 5, Craig 4, Lindau 4, Lyle 4, Hardie 3, Jacobs 3, McWilliams 3 (1 pen), Miller 3, Elliot 2, Lennon 2, McKeown 2, Blom 1, Docherty 1, English 1, Huggon 1, Kelly 1, McLean 1, Paton 1. *Scottish Cup (6):* Lennon 2, Craig 1, Dunn 1, McLean 1, own goal 1. *CIS Cup (0). Bell's League Cup (0).*

Budinauckas K 33	Duncan G 12 + 8	McKeown D 31 + 1	Montgomerie R 31 + 1	Brannigan K 10	Archibald A 35	Paton E 20 + 6	Craig A 28 + 1	Miller S 13 + 5	Docherty S 17 + 1	English I 7 + 7	McGuiness E 1 + 4	Dunn R 18 + 9	Dallas S 1 + 1	Newall R —+ 3	Elliot D 10 + 1	McAllister T 1	Jacobs Q 22 + 5	Howie W —+ 1	Walker A 4	Ferguson D 7	Lyle D 9 + 13	Callaghan T 3 + 6	McCann K —+ 1	Nesovic A 1 + 1	McIntyre P 7 + 6	McVey W —+ 2	Martin B 12 + 4	Arthur K 3	Lennon D 19	McLean S 7	Lindau P 9	Rodden P —+ 1	Blom J 2	McWilliams D 7	Swan I —+ 2	Hardie M 6	Rogers D 6	Huggon R 3 + 1	Kelly R 1 + 1	Match No.
1	2	3	4	5	6	7	8	9	10¹	11²	12	13																												1
1	2	3	4	5	6	10	9	7²	11³	12	8¹	13	14																											2
1	2¹	3	4	5	6²	12	8	7	10	11		9			13																									3
1	2	3	4	5	6	14	8	9²	7³	12	13	10¹			11																									4
1	2		4	5	6	7		9		11¹	10		13	3	8²	12																								5
1	2	11	4	5	6	14	8		7³	13		10²		3¹		12	9																							6
1	2	10	4	5	6	13		7	8²	11¹		12	14	3³		9																								7
1	2	10	4	5	6	8²	13			14	12	7¹		3	11	9²																								8
1		10	4¹	5	6		12	7	2		9			3	11²	8³	13	14																						9
1		11¹		5²	6		8		2	14		9		3		7	4	10³	12	13																				10
1	13	11	5		6		8		2		9²			3		7	4	12	10																					11
1	12	11	5		6		8¹		2		9²			3		7	4³	14	10	13																				12
1		11	5		6		8		2²		12			3¹		10	4	14	13	9³	7																			13
1	3	5	6	8	2		11	9²						10		4¹	7	12		13																				14
1	13	3	5	6	8	2		11¹	9			10²		4		7	12																							15
1	13	3²	5	6	8¹	2		12	9			11		10¹	14		7	4																						16
1	2		4	3	6	8	13	12	14			9²			11	10³			7	5¹																				17
	12		4	3	8		2								11	10³			7	5¹	1	6	9²	10																18
1		3	5		6		8	2				12			11				7		4	9¹	10																	19
1		3	5		6	12	8		2³	10²					11		13	14	7¹		4	9																		20
1		3	5		6	7	8		2						11¹				12		4	9	10																	21
1	13		5		3	8	12	2				14			11¹		7²				6	4	9³	10																22
1		12	5		3	2	8					13			11		7³		14		6¹	4	10²	9																23
1		3	5		6	7	8	13	2¹			9			11²				12		4	10																		24
1	2	3		5	6	7	8			13		9³			11²		12				14	4	10¹																	25
1	2²	3		5	6	7	8					9			11¹		12		13	14	4			10³																26
1		3	5		6	7	8					12			13				2		4	11²	10¹	9																27
1	13		5		6	2	8	7²				11			12						4	9¹		10																28
1		3	5		6	2	8	9²				13			7				11¹		4		10	12																29
1		3	5		6	2¹	8	9¹				12			11				13	14	4		7	10³																30
1		3	2			12		9²				13			11				6		4		8	10	5	7¹	11													31
1		3		6	8			9¹				13			12			14	2	4		11¹	10²	5	7															32
1	11			6	8	13		9				12			10³				2²	5	4		14		3	7¹														33
1¹	11	14	3		2	8			12			7³								5	4		9²	10	6	13														34
	2²	11	6¹		8	9³			13			7				12		5	1	4		14		10	3															35
14	11¹	2	3		8	7²			13								5	1	4³		9			10	6			12												36

QUEEN OF THE SOUTH   Second Division

Year Formed: 1919. *Ground & Address:* Palmerston Park, Dumfries DG2 9BA. *Telephone and Fax:* 01387 254853.
Ground Capacity: total: 8352, seated: 3549. *Size of Pitch:* 112yd × 73yd.
Chairman: Norman Blount. *Secretary:* Richard Shaw MBE. *Commercial Manager:* Margaret Heuchan.
Manager: John Connolly. *Coach:* Ian Scott.
Managers since 1975: M. Jackson; W. Hunter; B. Little; G. Herd; H. Hood; A. Busby; R. Clark; M. Jackson; D. Wilson;
W. McLaren; F. McGarvey; A. MacLeod; D. Frye; W. McLaren; M. Shanks; R. Alexander. *Club Nickname(s):* The
Doonhamers. *Previous Grounds:* None.
Record Attendance: 24,500 v Hearts, Scottish Cup 3rd rd; 23 Feb, 1952.
Record Transfer Fee received: £250,000 for Andy Thomson to Southend U (1994).
Record Transfer Fee paid: £30,000 for Jim Butter from Alloa Athletic (1995).
Record Victory: 11-1 v Stranraer, Scottish Cup 1st rd; 16 Jan, 1932.
Record Defeat: 2-10 v Dundee, Division I; 1 Dec, 1962.
Most Capped Player: Billy Houliston, 3, Scotland.
Most League Appearances: 731: Allan Ball, 1963–82.
Most League Goals in Season (Individual): 37: Jimmy Gray, Division II; 1927-28.
Most Goals in Season: 41: Jimmy Rutherford, 1931–32.
Most Goals Overall (Individual): 250: Jim Patterson, 1949–63.

QUEEN OF THE SOUTH 1999–2000 LEAGUE RECORD

Match No.	Date	Venue	Opponents	Result	H/T Score	Lg. Pos.	Goalscorers	Attendance
1	Aug 7	H	Arbroath	L 2-3	1-2	—	Weir 18, Mallan 52	1118
2	14	A	Hamilton A	W 3-0	1-0	5	Caldwell 16, Findlay 80, Mallan 89	630
3	21	H	Alloa Ath	D 1-1	1-0	5	Caldwell 43	1204
4	28	A	Partick Th	L 0-2	0-1	6		1959
5	Sept 4	H	Clyde	D 1-1	0-0	7	Bailey 78	1186
6	11	H	Stenhousemuir	L 0-3	0-1	8		928
7	18	A	Stranraer	L 0-1	0-0	9		621
8	25	H	Stirling A	D 3-3	1-3	9	Rowe 12, Mallan 57, Harvey 68	1038
9	Oct 2	A	Ross Co	D 1-1	1-1	9	Boyle 17	2293
10	16	H	Hamilton A	W 3-2	0-2	9	Adams 55, Mallan 70, Harvey 81	1027
11	23	A	Arbroath	L 2-5	0-2	9	Caldwell 70, Rowe 86	851
12	30	A	Stenhousemuir	L 1-2	0-0	9	Dickson 80	447
13	Nov 6	H	Stranraer	L 0-5	0-0	10		1052
14	9	A	Clyde	L 0-3	0-0	—		640
15	20	H	Partick Th	L 1-2	1-1	1	Aitken 28	1462
16	27	H	Ross Co	L 0-2	0-0	10		862
17	Dec 11	A	Stirling A	L 0-3	0-0	10		534
18	18	H	Arbroath	W 1-0	1-0	10	Mallan 14	837
19	Jan 3	A	Stranraer	W 2-1	2-0	—	Hawke 4, Eadie 21	928
20	15	H	Stenhousemuir	W 3-1	3-0	10	Mallan 23, Watson (og) 24, Hawke 27	1017
21	22	H	Stirling A	L 2-3	1-2	10	Mallan 2, Eadie 90	1104
22	Feb 5	A	Ross Co	L 0-2	0-0	10		2018
23	12	A	Partick Th	L 4-5	1-2	10	Boyle 19, Mallan 56, Duncan 63, Preston 84	2605
24	26	A	Hamilton A	D 1-1	1-0	10	Adams 8	553
25	Mar 4	H	Alloa Ath	W 2-1	0-1	10	Mallan 2 75, 83	1018
26	11	A	Stenhousemuir	L 0-2	0-0	10		541
27	14	H	Clyde	W 3-0	2-0	—	Hodge 3, Hawke 7, Mallan 50	830
28	18	H	Stranraer	D 0-0	0-0	10		1165
29	25	H	Partick Th	D 1-1	1-0	10	Mallan 7	1813
30	Apr 1	A	Clyde	L 1-3	0-1	10	Kerr 83	1101
31	8	A	Stirling A	D 2-2	1-2	10	Adams 2 8, 75	520
32	11	A	Alloa Ath	L 1-3	0-0	—	Mallan 89	620
33	15	H	Ross Co	L 0-3	0-1	10		1010
34	22	A	Arbroath	W 2-1	2-1	10	Hawke 2, Eadie 13	589
35	29	H	Hamilton A	D 1-1	0-1	10	Rowe 48	2084
36	May 6	A	Alloa Ath	L 1-6	0-3	9	Eadie 88	714

Final League Position: 9   1998–99 4

Honours
League Champions: Division II 1950-51; *Runners-up:* Division II 1932-33, 1961-62, 1974-75. Second Division 1980-81, 1985-86.
Scottish Cup: semi-finalists 1949–50.
League Cup: semi-finalists 1950–51, 1960–61.
B&Q Cup: semi-finalists 1991–92. *League Challenge Cup:* runners-up 1997–98.

Club colours: Shirt: Royal blue. Shorts: White. Stockings: Royal blue with white tops.

Goalscorers: *League (45):* Mallan 13, Adams 4, Eadie 4, Hawke 4, Caldwell 3, Rowe 3, Boyle 2, Harvey 2, Aitken 1, Bailey 1, Dickson 1, Duncan 1, Findlay 1, Hodge 1, Kerr 1, Preston 1, Weir 1, own goal 1. *Scottish Cup (3):* Adams 1, Eadie 1, Hawke 1. *CIS Cup (2):* Bailey 1, Leslie 1. *Bell's League Cup (1):* Adams 1.

Hillcoat J 22	Lilley D 2	Kerr A 13 + 8	Stewart P 19 + 1	Aitken A 33	Cleeland M 21 + 1	Harvey P 9	Leslie S 13 + 1	Bailey L 4 + 3	Mallan S 29 + 3	Weir M 10 + 4	Adams C 18 + 12	Findlay W 3 + 4	Robison K 14 + 6	Caldwell B 12 + 5	Rowe G 27	Hodge A 26 + 1	Boyle D 17 + 1	Strain C 1 + 7	Dickson J 23 + 2	Gallacher I 1	McMillan A 15 + 1	McLean S 3	Paterson G 2	Hawke W 17	Preston A 6 + 2	Eadie K 5 + 4	Davidson S 1 + 1	Mathieson D 14	Duncan G 13	Gallagher J 3 + 3	Match No.
1		2	3	4	5	6	7²	8	9	10	11¹	12	13																		1
1		3	2	5	6	7²	8	13	10	12	9¹	14	4	11³																	2
1	2	3²		5	6³	7	8	12	10				13	14	11	4¹	3	9³													3
1		2			5	6	7	8²	14	10			13	12	11	4¹	3	9³													4
1		2			5	6	7		9	10¹	12				8	11	4	3													5
1		3²	2		5	6	7	13	9	12	10¹				8	11	4														6
1		3	2		5	6		8	9¹	10	12				7	11	4														7
1		3	2		5	6	7	8		10	9¹				11²	4		13	12												8
1			2		5	6	7	8		10	9¹					4	3	11	12												9
1	12		2		5	6	7			10	11		9²		13	4¹	3	8													10
1	14		2		5	6		8		10	11¹		9²		12	4	3¹		13		7										11
1		3	2		5	6		8		10	11		9¹			4			12		7										12
1			2		5	6		8		10	13		12		11	9	4	3²			7¹										13
1			3¹		5	6		8		10	12				11	9	4		13		7²		2								14
1		13			5	6²				10	11¹				4	3	8		12		7		2	9							15
1					5	6¹				12	10				4	3	8		7		2			9	11						16
1		8²	14		5	13				12	11				4	3	10¹		7		2			9	6³						17
1		8			5	6²				10			13		4	3			7		2			9	11¹	12					18
1					5	6				10	12				4	3		13	7		2			9²	11¹	8					19
1					5	6				10²	12				4	3			7³		2			9	13	11¹	14				20
1						6		8		10	13			5¹	4	3			7²		2			9	12	11					21
1					5	6				10	12		11		4		8		7²		2			9¹	3	13					22
					5					10					7	4	3		8		2			9	11			1	6		23
					5¹					10					9		12		4		3		8	7	2			1	6		24
		2			5					10	11¹				13	12	4		8		7²			9	3			1	6		25
		2²			5					10					13	11¹	4	12	8		7			9	3			1	6		26
		13	2		5					10	11¹				12	4	3	8²			7			9				1	6		27
		13	2		5					10³	11¹				4²	12	3	8			7			9		14		1	6		28
			2		5					10	12				4	3	8		7²					9				1	6	11¹	29
		12	2		5					10	13				4	3	8		7²					9				1	6	11¹	30
		5²	2¹							10	14	11			4	3	8		7³		12			9¹				1	6	13	31
		5								10	11	7			4	3			12					9¹				1	6	8	32
		12			5						11	13			4	10	3	8¹	7		2²			9				1	6		33
		13			5						11³	12	2		4	3		7¹	8					9		10²		1	6	14	34
					5						11¹	7	2		4	3			12		8			9		10		1	6		35
		2			5					10	11	9	4			3²	6¹		7		8					12		1		13	36

QUEEN'S PARK   Second Division

Year Formed: 1867. *Ground & Address:* Hampden Park, Mount Florida, Glasgow G42 9BA. *Telephone:* 0141 632 1275.
Fax: 0141 636 1612.
Ground Capacity: all seated: 52,000. *Size of Pitch:* 115yd × 75yd.
President: James Nicholson. *Secretary:* Alistair Mackay. *Commercial Director:* Garry Templeman.
Coach: John McCormack. *Physio:* R.C.Findlay.
Coaches since 1975: D. McParland, J. Gilroy, E. Hunter, H. McCann. *Club Nickname(s):* The Spiders. *Previous
Grounds:* 1st Hampden (Recreation Ground); (Titwood Park was used as an interim measure between 1st & 2nd
Hampdens); 2nd Hampden (Cathkin); 3rd Hampden.
Record Attendance: 95,772 v Rangers, Scottish Cup, 18 Jan, 1930.
Record for Ground: 149,547 Scotland v England, 1937.
Record Transfer Fee received: Not applicable due to amateur status.
Record Transfer Fee paid: Not applicable due to amateur status.
Record Victory: 16-0 v St. Peters, Scottish Cup 1st rd; 29 Aug, 1885.
Record Defeat: 0-9 v Motherwell, Division I; 26 Apr, 1930.
Most Capped Player: Walter Arnott, 14, Scotland.
Most League Appearances: 473: J. B. McAlpine.

QUEEN'S PARK 1999–2000 LEAGUE RECORD

Match No.	Date	Venue	Opponents	Result	H/T Score	Lg. Pos.	Goalscorers	Attendance
1	Aug 7	H	East Stirling	W 2-1	2-1	—	Orr 21, Gallagher 36	450
2	14	A	Brechin C	W 2-1	1-1	1	Connaghan 34, Whelan 78	311
3	21	H	Cowdenbeath	W 1-0	0-0	1	Whelan 72	578
4	28	A	Berwick R	W 2-1	1-0	1	Martin 19, Gallagher 84	710
5	Sept 4	H	Forfar Ath	D 1-1	1-1	1	Whelan 45	764
6	11	A	Dumbarton	W 1-0	0-0	1	Carroll 53	539
7	18	H	Albion R	W 2-0	0-0	1	Carroll 71, Brown 76	642
8	25	A	East Fife	D 0-0	0-0	1		568
9	Oct 2	H	Montrose	W 2-1	1-1	1	Gallagher 2 4, 89	688
10	16	H	Brechin C	W 5-3	3-0	1	Brown 2 3, 48, Whelan 16, Carroll 2 41, 56	483
11	23	A	East Stirling	D 1-1	0-1	1	Caven (pen) 86	354
12	30	H	Dumbarton	W 3-2	3-0	1	Carroll 3, Gallagher 13, Connaghan 14	713
13	Nov 6	A	Albion R	W 4-2	3-0	1	Caven 2 (2 pens) 34, 78, McGoldrick 38, Whelan 42	513
14	14	A	Forfar Ath	D 2-2	1-1	1	McGoldrick 11, Caven 60	626
15	20	H	Berwick R	L 1-4	1-3	1	Caven (pen) 5	678
16	27	A	Montrose	L 1-2	1-1	1	Gallagher 25	424
17	Dec 4	H	East Fife	L 0-1	0-0	1		742
18	18	H	East Stirling	L 0-1	0-1	1		413
19	22	A	Cowdenbeath	W 2-0	2-0	—	Gallagher 2 10, 28	221
20	Jan 3	A	Albion R	L 0-1	0-1	—		742
21	22	A	East Fife	D 0-0	0-0	1		631
22	29	A	Dumbarton	D 1-1	1-0	1	Carroll 34	492
23	Feb 5	A	Montrose	D 1-1	0-0	1	Gallagher 73	505
24	12	A	Berwick R	D 1-1	1-0	2	Whelan 16	525
25	19	H	Forfar Ath	W 3-2	1-2	1	Gallagher 30, Whelan 59, Connell 70	818
26	26	A	Brechin C	D 0-0	0-0	1		287
27	Mar 4	H	Cowdenbeath	W 3-1	1-1	1	Gallagher 42, Brown 2 72, 76	625
28	11	H	Dumbarton	W 2-0	2-0	1	Whelan 6, McGoldrick 35	788
29	18	A	Albion R	W 3-0	0-0	1	Gallagher 58, Brown 2 65, 74	531
30	25	H	Berwick R	L 0-1	0-0	2		964
31	Apr 1	A	Forfar Ath	L 0-4	0-2	3		570
32	11	H	East Fife	W 1-0	1-0	—	Walker 1	788
33	15	A	Montrose	W 2-0	0-0	2	Finlayson 71, Caven 89	393
34	22	A	East Stirling	W 1-0	1-0	1	Gallagher 8	497
35	29	H	Brechin C	W 1-0	0-0	1	Walker 89	943
36	May 6	A	Cowdenbeath	W 3-2	0-1	1	Ferry 63, Carroll 2 71, 77	813

Final League Position: 1   1998–99 DIV 3 6

Most League Goals in Season (Individual): 30: William Martin, Division I; 1937-38.
Most Goals Overall (Individual): 163: J. B. McAlpine.

Honours
League Champions: Division II 1922-23. B Division 1955-56. Second Division 1980-81. Third Division 1999–2000.
Scottish Cup Winners: 1874, 1875, 1876, 1880, 1881, 1882, 1884, 1886, 1890, 1893; *Runners-up:* 1892, 1900.
League Cup: —.
FA Cup runners-up: 1884, 1885.

Club colours: Shirt: White and black hoops. Shorts: White. Stockings: White with black hoops.

Goalscorers: *League (54):* Gallagher 13, Carroll 8, Whelan 8, Brown 7, Caven 6 (4 pens), McGoldrick 3, Connaghan 2, Walker 2, Connell 1, Ferry 1, Finlayson 1, Martin 1, Orr 1. *Scottish Cup (1):* Carroll 1. *CIS Cup (2):* Brown 1, McGoldrick 1. *Bell's League Cup (4):* Gallagher 2, Brown 1, Whelan 1.

Inglis N 36	Sinclair R 12 + 3	Connaghan D 30 + 3	Caven R 29 + 1	MacFarlane N 36	Connell G 30	Orr S 5 + 5	Gallagher M 35	Brown J 28 + 3	McGoldrick K 13 + 7	Edgar S 1 + 16	Whelan J 27 + 7	Little T 1 + 5	Ferry D 26 + 4	Carroll F 21 + 6	Borland P 19 + 5	Tyrrell P — + 1	Scobie R 2 + 12	Geoghegan J — + 1	Travers M 1 + 2	Elder G — + 1	Carmichael D 1	McKee C 2 + 5	Reid A — + 1	Finlayson K 8 + 2	Walker P 6 + 2	Match No
1	2	3	4	5	6	7	8^1	9^2	10^3	11	12	13	14													1
1		3	4	5	6	7	8^1	9	10	11^2	12	13		2												2
1		3	4	5	6	7	8^1	9	10^3	11^2	12	13		2	14											3
1	2	3^1	4	5	6	7		9		11^2	12	8	13	10^1	14											4
1	2	3	4	5	6		10	7^3			13	8	11^1	14	9^2		12									5
1	2^1	3	4		6	7		9	10		8	13	12	11^2	5											6
1		3	4		6	7^1	12	9^2	10		13	8	14	2	11^3		5									7
1		3	4		6		7^2	9	10		12	8		2	11^3	5^1	13	14								8
1		3	4	5	6	7		9	10	13		8		2^2	12		11^1									9
1		3^1	4	5	6	7		9	10^3	14		8		2	11^2		13	12								10
1	14	3	4	5	6	7			10	13	12	8^2		2	11^2		9^1									11
1	14	3	4	5	6	7		9^2	10^1	12	13	8^2		2	11											12
1	7^1	3	4	5^2	6		12	9	10	11^2	14	8		2			13									13
1	13	3	4	5	6			9^2	10	11^2	14	8		2	7^1		12									14
1		3	4	5	6		14	9	10	11^1		8^2		2	7^3		13	12								15
1	3^1		4	5	6			9	10	11^2	14	8^3		2	7		12	13								16
1	2	3	4	5^3	6	7	8^2	9^1	10		12			11	14				13							17
1	2	3	4	5^3	6	7^2		9			10^1	13	14	11	8		12									18
1	2	3	4	5	6^1	7		9	10		12			11^2	8		13									19
1	2	3	4	5	6	7	13	9	10^3	12	8^2								11^1	14						20
1		14	4	5	6	7		9	10^2		12	13		2	11		3^3							8^1		21
1			4	5	6	7		9	8	12			13	2	11^1		3					10^2				22
1	2	3	4	5	6	7		9^2	8				13	11^3			12					10^1	14			23
1		3	4	5	6	7		9^1	10		12	8		2	11^2		13									24
1		3	4	5^3	6	7		9	10^3	14		8		2	11^2		12	13								25
1		4	3		6	7		9	10^2	13		8		2	11^1		5	12								26
1		3			6	7	13	9	10	8			4^2	2	5									12	11^1	27
1		3			6	7		9	10^1	8			4	2	12		5^2							13	11	28
1		3	14		6	7		9^3	10^2	8			4	2	5								13	11^1	12	29
1		3^1		13	6	7		9	10^3	8			4	2	5								14	11^1	12	30
1		3			6	7		9^2		8^1			4	2	10		5						13	12	11	31
1	2^1		4	5	6	7		9			8		12	10^2	3									13	11	32
1			4	5	6	7		9			8			2	3									10	11	33
1	12		4	5	6	7		9^3	14		8			2	13		3^1							10^3	11	34
1	12		4	5	6	7		9^3	13		8^2			2	14		3^1							10	11	35
1			4	5	6	7		9	13		8			2	12		3							10^1	11^2	36

RAITH ROVERS   First Division

Year Formed: 1883. *Ground & Address:* Stark's Park, Pratt St, Kirkcaldy KY1 1SA. *Telephone:* 01592 263514. *Fax:* 01592 642833.
Ground Capacity: all seated: 10,104. *Size of Pitch:* 113yd × 70yd.
Chairman: William Gray. *Office Manager:* Keri Gooding.
Manager: Peter Hetherston. *Assistant Manager:* Kenny Black. *Youth Coach:* Davie Kirkwood. *Physio:* John Cooper.
Managers since 1975: R. Paton; A. Matthew; W. McLean; G. Wallace; R. Wilson; F. Connor; J. Nicholl; J. Thomson; T. McLean; I. Munro; J. Nicholl; J. McVeigh. *Club Nickname:* Rovers. *Previous Grounds:* Robbie's Park.
Record Attendance: 31,306 v Hearts, Scottish Cup 2nd rd; 7 Feb, 1953.
Record Transfer Fee received: £900,000 for S. McAnespie to Bolton Wanderers (Sept 1995).
Record Transfer Fee paid: £225,000 for Paul Harvey from Airdrieonians (1996).
Record Victory: 10-1 v Coldstream, Scottish Cup 2nd rd; 13 Feb, 1954.
Record Defeat: 2-11 v Morton, Division II; 18 Mar, 1936.
Most Capped Player: David Morris, 6, Scotland.
Most League Appearances: 430: Willie McNaught.
Most League Goals in Season (Individual): 38: Norman Haywood, Division II; 1937-38.
Most Goals Overall (Individual): 154: Gordon Dalziel (League), 1987-94.

RAITH ROVERS 1999–2000 LEAGUE RECORD

Match No.	Date	Venue	Opponents	Result	H/T Score	Lg. Pos.	Goalscorers	Attendance
1	Aug 7	A	Livingston	D 1-1	0-1	—	Tosh P [55]	3116
2	Aug 14	H	St Mirren	L 0-6	0-3	9		2787
3	Aug 21	A	Clydebank	D 1-1	1-1	8	Dargo [7]	232
4	Aug 28	A	Airdrieonians	W 4-1	2-0	6	Black [3], Agathe 3 [37, 64, 72]	1493
5	Sept 4	H	Ayr U	W 5-1	1-0	5	Dargo 2 [7, 63], Burns [61], Agathe [64], Clark [89]	2368
6	Sept 11	A	Morton	L 0-2	0-2	6		970
7	Sept 18	H	Dunfermline Ath	D 2-2	0-1	7	Dargo 2 [67, 80]	6087
8	Sept 25	A	Inverness CT	W 2-0	2-0	5	Andrews [8], Agathe [24]	2961
9	Oct 2	H	Falkirk	W 2-1	1-0	4	Dargo 2 [12, 59]	3182
10	Oct 16	A	St Mirren	L 2-3	1-1	4	Black [45], Stein [80]	3815
11	Oct 23	H	Livingston	W 3-1	2-1	4	Browne [22], Black (pen) [34], Shields [75]	2942
12	Oct 30	H	Morton	W 3-1	0-0	3	Agathe [72], Burns [77], Stein [83]	2664
13	Nov 6	A	Dunfermline Ath	D 1-1	0-1	3	Stein [81]	6953
14	Nov 14	A	Ayr U	W 1-0	0-0	3	Hetherston [86]	1769
15	Nov 20	H	Airdrieonians	D 1-1	0-0	3	Stein [64]	2353
16	Nov 27	A	Falkirk	L 1-2	0-1	4	Agathe [82]	2611
17	Dec 4	H	Inverness CT	W 4-2	3-2	3	Roberts [3], Burns 2 [38, 39], Browne [73]	1971
18	Dec 27	A	Morton	L 0-1	0-1	—		1056
19	Jan 3	H	Dunfermline Ath	W 3-0	2-0	—	Burns [3], Browne [21], Tosh S [86]	7464
20	Jan 8	H	Ayr U	W 2-0	1-0	5	Dargo (pen) [18], Tosh S [47]	2583
21	Jan 15	A	Airdrieonians	W 2-0	0-0	3	Burns [50], Stein [66]	2098
22	Jan 18	H	Clydebank	W 1-0	0-0	—	Tosh S [90]	2754
23	Jan 22	A	Inverness CT	D 1-1	1-0	3	Dargo [44]	2302
24	Feb 5	H	Falkirk	L 0-1	0-1	5		4140
25	Feb 26	H	St Mirren	L 1-2	0-0	5	Tosh P [85]	4662
26	Mar 4	H	Morton	W 3-0	1-0	4	Stein [44], Tosh P [62], Tosh S [90]	2026
27	Mar 7	A	Clydebank	L 1-2	1-2	—	Tosh P [25]	256
28	Mar 11	A	Livingston	D 0-0	0-0	4		2683
29	Mar 18	A	Dunfermline Ath	L 2-0	0-0	4	Browne [77], Dargo [78]	6694
30	Mar 25	H	Airdrieonians	W 2-0	2-0	4	Dargo [10], Owusu [26]	2056
31	Apr 1	A	Ayr U	W 1-0	1-0	4	Owusu [26]	1841
32	Apr 8	H	Inverness CT	W 2-0	0-0	4	Dargo [60], Tosh S [78]	2538
33	Apr 15	A	Falkirk	L 0-1	0-0	4		4686
34	Apr 22	H	Livingston	L 1-3	1-0	4	Owusu [23]	2129
35	Apr 29	A	St Mirren	L 0-3	0-0	5		8386
36	May 6	H	Clydebank	D 0-0	0-0	5		1510

Final League Position: 5   1998–99 8

Honours
League Champions: First Division: 1992-93, 1994-95. Division II 1907-08, 1909-10 (shared), 1937-38, 1948-49; *Runners-up:* Division II 1908-09, 1926-27, 1966-67. Second Division 1975-76, 1977-78, 1986-87. *Scottish Cup Runners-up:* 1913. *League Cup Winners: (Coca-Cola Cup):* 1994-95. *Runners-up:* 1948-49.

European: *UEFA Cup:* 6 matches (1995-96).

Club colours: Shirt: Navy blue, white trim. Shorts: White with navy blue edges. Stockings: Navy blue with white turnover.

Goalscorers: *League (55):* Dargo 12 (1 pen), Agathe 7, Burns 6, Stein 5, Tosh S 5, Browne 4, Tosh P 4, Black 3 (1 pen), Owugu 3, Hetherston 2, Andrews 1, Clark 1, Roberts 1, Shields 1. *Scottish Cup (1):* Dargo 1. *CIS Cup (3):* Black 1, Burns 1, Dargo 1. *Bell's League Cup (4):* Andrews 1, Clark 1, Dargo 1, own goal 1.

Van De Kamp G 32	Hamilton S 11 + 4	McCulloch G 13 + 9	Andrews M 29	Gaughan K 6 + 1	Black K 23 + 2	McEwan C 30 + 4	Tosh S 25 + 6	Tosh P 10 + 8	Burns A 34	Stein J 32 + 3	Shields P 1 + 8	Agnew P 2 + 2	Hetherston B 3 + 11	Kirkwood D 3 + 1	Clark A 3 + 15	McCondichie A 1	Ellis L 4	Browne P 34	Dargo C 25	Coyle C 3	Agathe D 30	Berthe M 1	Stewart A — + 1	Preget A 2	Craig S — + 2	Roberts M 3	Begue Y — + 2	Opinel S 15	Javary J 10 + 1	Owusu A 8 + 2	Fenwick P 2	Nicol K 1	Match No.
1	2	3	4	5	6[2]	7[1]	8	9[1]	10	11	12	13	14																				1
1	2	3	4	5	6[1]	12	7	9[1]	10	11[2]			8	13	14																		2
	7	12	4		14	2[1]	6		10	11[2]			9[3]		13	1	3	5	9														3
		13	4		6[2]	2	8		10[1]	11	12				14		3	5	9		7[3]	1											4
			4		6	2	8[1]	12	10	11					13		3	5	9		7[2]	1											5
		13	4		6[3]	2	8		10	11[1]	12				14		3	5	9[2]		7	1											6
1			4		6	2		12	10	11							3	5	9		7		8[1]										7
1	13		4		6	2	8		10	11							3	5	9[1]		7		12[2]										8
1			4		6[1]	2	8	12	10	11							3	5	9		7												9
1	9		4		6	2[1]	8		10	11	12[3]				13			5			7[2]							3	14				10
1			4		6	2	8		10	11	12							5	9[1]		7							3					11
1		3	4[2]		6	2	8		10	11	12				13			5	9[1]		7												12
1		3	4		6	2	8	12	10	11								5	9[1]		7												13
1		3	4		6	2	8		10	11[1]	12			13				5	9[2]		7												14
1		3	4		6	2	8[1]		10	11	12				13			5	9[2]		7												15
1		3[1]	4		6	2	8		10	11	12				14			5[3]	9[2]		7								13				16
1		3	4		6[3]	2	8		10	11[1]	12				14			5	9[2]		7								13				17
1	7		4		6	2	8[1]		10	11	12							5	9									3					18
1	12		4		6	2	8		10	11[2]					13			5	9		7							3[1]					19
1	12		4		6	2	8		10[3]	11			14		13			5	9[2]		7[1]							3					20
1	12		4		6	2	8		10	11[1]					13			5	9		7[2]							3					21
1			4		6	2	8		10	11	12				13			5	9[1]		7							3[2]					22
1			4		6	2	8		10	11[1]								5	9		7							3	12				23
1		3	4			2	8		10	11	12				13			5[1]	9		7									6[2]			24
1	13		4				8		10[3]	11[1]	12		14					5	9		7			2				3[2]		6			25
1			4		6		8[1]		10	11				13	14			5	9		7[1]			2				3[2]	12				26
1	7		4[2]				8		10	11[1]				13				5	9					2				3	12	6			27
1			4		6		8[3]	12	10	11[2]				13	14			5	9		7			2				3[1]					28
1			4			2		12	10	11				13				5	9		7							3		6[2]	8[1]		29
1		3	4			2		12	10	11				13				5	9		7[2]									6[1]	8		30
1			4			2		12	10	11[1]				13	14			5	9		7							3[3]		6[2]	8		31
1			4			2[2]		12	10	11				13	14			5	9		7[1]							3		6	8[3]		32
1			4			2		12	10	11[1]				13				5[2]	9		7							3		6	8		33
1			4			2[2]		12	10	11[1]				13	14			5	9		7[3]							3		6	8		34
1		3	4			2		12	10	11				13				5	9[2]		7									6[1]	8		35
1		3	4			2	8	12	10	11[3]				13				5	9[1]		7[2]								14			6	36

RANGERS   Premier League

Year Formed: 1873. *Ground & Address:* Ibrox Stadium, 150 Edmiston Drive, Glasgow G51 2XD.
Telephone: 0870 600 1972. *Fax:* 0870 600 1978.
Ground Capacity: all seated: 50,467. *Size of Pitch:* 115yd × 76yd.
Chairman: David Murray. *Secretary:* R. C. Ogilvie. *Commercial & Marketing Manager:* Martin Bain.
Manager: Dick Advocaat. *Assistant Manager:* Bert Van Lingen. *Physio:* Grant Downie. *Reserve team coaches:* John McGregor, John Brown.
Managers since 1975: Jock Wallace; John Greig; Jock Wallace; Graeme Souness. *Club Nickname(s):* The Gers.
Previous Grounds: Flesher's Haugh, Burnbank, Kinning Park, Old Ibrox.
Record Attendance: 118,567 v Celtic, Division I; 2 Jan, 1939.
Record Transfer Fee received: £5,580,000 for Trevor Steven to Marseille (Aug 1991).
Record Transfer Fee paid: £5.5 million for Andrei Kanchelskis from Fiorentina (July 1998).
Record Victory: 14-2 v Blairgowrie, Scottish Cup 1st rd; 20 Jan, 1934.
Record Defeat: 2-10 v Airdrieonians; 1886.
Most Capped Player: Ally McCoist, 60, Scotland.
Most League Appearances: 496: John Greig, 1962-78.
Most League Goals in Season (Individual): 44: Sam English, Division I; 1931–32.
Most Goals Overall (Individual): 355: Ally McCoist; 1985–98.

RANGERS 1999–2000 LEAGUE RECORD

Match No.	Date	Venue	Opponents	Result	H/T Score	Lg. Pos.	Goalscorers	Atten- dance
1	Jul 31	H	Kilmarnock	W 2-1	1-0	—	Wallace [39], Reyna [68]	48,074
2	Aug 7	A	Hearts	W 4-0	2-0	2	Reyna 2 [13, 73], Mols [44], Albertz [67]	17,893
3	15	H	Motherwell	W 4-1	2-0	1	Mols 4 [41, 44, 69, 81]	45,264
4	21	H	Dundee U	W 4-1	1-0	1	Reyna [22], Van Bronckhorst [51], Wallace [60], Vidmar [75]	48,849
5	28	A	Hibernian	W 1-0	0-0	1	Johansson [68]	15,587
6	Sept 11	H	Aberdeen	W 3-0	1-0	1	Mols 2 [17, 48], Albertz (pen) [85]	49,226
7	25	H	St Johnstone	W 3-1	1-0	1	Albertz 2 (1 pen) [32, 59 (p)], Mols [87]	47,475
8	Oct 2	A	Dundee	W 3-2	1-0	1	Kanchelskis [29], Wallace [80], Amato [84]	10,494
9	16	A	Kilmarnock	D 1-1	1-0	1	Van Bronckhorst [24]	15,795
10	30	A	Aberdeen	W 5-1	1-1	1	Johansson 3 [24, 78, 80], Mols [68], Amato [69]	16,846
11	Nov 7	H	Celtic	W 4-2	2-2	1	Johansson [20], Albertz (pen) [45], Amoruso [50], Amato [67]	50,026
12	20	H	Hibernian	W 2-0	1-0	1	Johansson [32], Albertz [46]	49,544
13	28	H	Dundee	L 1-2	0-1	1	Wallace [71]	47,154
14	Dec 11	H	Kilmarnock	W 1-0	0-0	1	Albertz [56]	47,169
15	18	A	Motherwell	W 5-1	3-0	1	Kanchelskis 2 [26, 58], Amoruso [35], Dodds 2 [45, 50]	12,640
16	22	H	Hearts	W 1-0	0-0	—	Albertz [90]	49,907
17	27	A	Celtic	D 1-1	1-1	1	Dodds [27]	59,619
18	Jan 22	H	Aberdeen	W 5-0	3-0	1	Moore [36], Van Bronckhorst [38], Numan [43], Wallace [60], Ferguson B [82]	50,023
19	Feb 2	A	Dundee U	W 4-0	2-0	—	Vidmar 2 [9, 23], Wallace [68], McCann [86]	11,241
20	6	A	Hibernian	D 2-2	0-0	1	Wallace [56], McCann [81]	13,420
21	15	A	St Johnstone	D 1-1	0-0	—	Vidmar [57]	9608
22	27	A	Dundee	W 7-1	6-1	1	Wallace 3 [2, 30, 34], Vidmar 2 [22, 96], Albertz [30], Rozental [45]	9297
23	Mar 4	H	St Johnstone	D 0-0	0-0	1		49,907
24	8	A	Celtic	W 1-0	0-0	1	Wallace [86]	59,220
25	18	H	Motherwell	W 6-2	4-2	1	Wallace 3 [20, 42, 69], Rozental (pen) [30], Albertz [36], Kerimoglu (pen) [89]	49,622
26	26	H	Celtic	W 4-0	2-0	1	Albertz 2 [3, 84], Kanchelskis [41], Van Bronckhorst [87]	50,039
27	Apr 1	A	Aberdeen	D 1-1	1-1	1	Ferguson B [39]	16,521
28	4	A	Dundee U	W 3-0	0-0	—	Albertz [62], Dodds [66], Wallace [72]	45,829
29	12	A	Hearts	W 2-1	1-1	—	Wallace [45], Dodds [64]	16,314
30	15	A	Dundee U	W 2-0	2-0	1	Ferguson B [21], Albertz [41]	11,419
31	23	A	St Johnstone	W 2-0	1-0	1	Dodds 2 [42, 60]	10,016
32	30	H	Dundee	W 3-0	0-0	1	Dodds [54], McCann [57], Rozental [73]	50,032
33	May 3	H	Hibernian	W 5-2	2-0	—	Ferguson B [10], Dennis (og) [45], Dodds [47], Albertz 2 [80, 85]	44,359
34	7	A	Kilmarnock	W 2-0	1-0	1	Reyna [42], Albertz [78]	13,284
35	13	H	Hearts	W 1-0	1-0	1	Dodds [21]	49,140
36	21	A	Motherwell	L 0-2	0-0	1		12,310

Final League Position: 1   1998–99 1

Honours

League Champions: (49 times) Division I 1890-91 (shared), 1898-99, 1899-1900, 1900-01, 1901-02, 1910-11, 1911-12, 1912-13, 1917-18, 1919-20, 1920-21, 1922-23, 1923-24, 1924-25, 1926-27, 1927-28, 1928-29, 1929-30, 1930-31, 1932-33, 1933-34, 1934-35, 1936-37, 1938-39, 1946-47, 1948-49, 1949-50, 1952-53, 1955-56, 1956-57, 1958-59, 1960-61, 1962-63, 1963-64, 1974-75. Premier Division: 1975-76, 1977-78, 1986-87, 1988-89, 1989-90, 1990-91, 1991-92, 1992-93, 1993-94, 1994-95, 1995-96, 1996-97, 1998-99;, 1999–2000 *Runners-up:* 24 times.

Scottish Cup Winners: (29 times) 1894, 1897, 1898, 1903, 1928, 1930, 1932, 1934, 1935, 1936, 1948, 1949, 1950, 1953, 1960, 1962, 1963, 1964, 1966, 1973, 1976, 1978, 1979, 1981, 1992, 1993, 1996, 1999, 2000; *Runners-up:* 17 times.

League Cup Winners: (21 times) 1946-47, 1948-49, 1960-61, 1961-62, 1963-64, 1964-65, 1970-71, 1975-76, 1977-78, 1978-79, 1981-82, 1983-84, 1984-85, 1986-87, 1987-88, 1988-89, 1990-91, 1992-93, 1993-94, 1996-97, 1998-99; *Runners-up:* 7 times.

European: *European Cup:* 101 matches (1956-57, 1957-58, 1959-60 semi-finals, 1961-62, 1963-64, 1964-65, 1975-76, 1976-77, 1978-79, 1987-88, 1989-90, 1990-91, 1991-92, 1992-93 final pool, 1993-94, 1994-95, 1995-96; 1996-97, 1997-98, 1999-2000). *Cup Winners' Cup:* 54 matches (1960-61 runners-up, 1962-63, 1966-67 runners-up, 1969-70, 1971-72 winners, 1973-74, 1977-78, 1979-80, 1981-82, 1983-84). *UEFA Cup:* 52 matches (*Fairs Cup:* 1967-68, 1968-69 semi-finals, 1970-71. *UEFA Cup:* 1982-83, 1984-85, 1985-86, 1986-87, 1988-89, 1997-98, 1998-99, 1999-2000).

Club colours: Shirt: Royal blue with white trim. Shorts: White with blue trim. Stockings: Black with red tops.

Goalscorers: *League (96):* Albertz 17 (3 pens), Wallace 16, Dodds 10, Mols 9, Johansson 6, Vidmar 6, Reyna 5, Ferguson B 4, Kanchelskis 4, Van Bronckhorst 4, Amato 3, McCann 3, Rozental 3 (1 pen), Amoruso 2, Kerimoglu 1, Moore 1, Numan 1, own goal 1. *Scottish Cup (18):* Dodds 5, Numan 2, Rozental 2, Van Bronckhorst 2, Albertz 1, Amoruso 1, Ferguson B 1, Kanchelskis 1, Moore 1, Vidmar 1, Wallace 1. *CIS Cup (0).*

Klos S 24	Adamczuk D 5 + 5	Moore C 22	Amoruso L 30	Numan A 23 + 1	Ferguson B 31	Reyna C 25 + 4	Van Bronckhorst G 27	Albertz J 30 + 5	Wallace R 25 + 3	Amato G 4 + 4	Porrini S 11 + 1	Johansson J 8 + 8	Vidmar A 21 + 6	Mols M 9	Ferguson I — + 2	Niemi A 1	McCann N 12 + 18	Charbonnier L 7	Kanchelskis A 25 + 3	Hendry C 1 + 1	McInnes D — + 1	Durie G 1 + 6	Brown M 1	Myhre T 3	Wilson S 9	Dodds W 16 + 2	Kerimoglu T 9 + 7	Nicholson B — + 1	Rozental S 6 + 5	Ross M — + 1	Penttila T 3	Malcolm R 1 + 2	Gibson J — + 1	Hughes S — + 1	Match No.
1	2	3¹	4³	5	6	7	8	9	10	11²	12	13	14																						1
1	12	3¹	4		7	6²		8	9	13	2	11²	5	10	14																				2
	13	3	4		7	6¹	8	12	10		2²	14	5	11		1	9³																		3
	12	3	4		7	6	8²	13	10		2¹		5	11			9	1																	4
	2	3	4		7	9	8	13				12	5²	11			10³	1	6¹	14															5
	3	4	13		7³	6	8¹	12		11	2		5	10			9²	1	14																6
	2	3		5	7¹		8	9	13			11²		10			12	1	6	4															7
	14	3	4	5¹	7		8	6	11	13	2²		12	10			1	9³																	8
1		3	4	5²	7		8	6	11			2³	14	13	10			12		9¹															9
1	13	3	4	9	7		8			12		2²	11	5¹	10³			6		14															10
1		3	4	5	7	6	8³	9		10¹	2	11²	14				12			13															11
	2	3	4	5		6	8	9	12	10		11¹					7				1														12
	2¹	3³	4	5	7	6²		9	11			10	12				8	13		14	1														13
		4	5	7	6³		8	11¹			2		14				9	12		13	1	3	10²												14
	3	4	5	7¹	12	8	9²	11			2						13	6		14	1	10³													15
	3	4	5²	7		8	6	11			2¹						12	1	9		13	10													16
	3	4	5	7	6	8	9	11¹	12		2							1				10													17
1		3	4	5	7	13	8³	9²	11		2						12	6				10¹	14												18
1		3	4	5	7	13	8³	9	11		2						12	6²				10¹	14												19
1		3	4	5	7	13	8	9	11		2²						12	6				10¹													20
1		3	4¹	5	7		8	9	11		2						13	6²		10				12											21
1			5		4²	7	9	11			2						12	6¹				3		8	10	13									22
1		4	5		3	7	9	11			2						13	6¹				12	8²	10											23
1		3	4	5	7	6	8	9	11		2						10																		24
1	2³	4			7		5	9	11								12	6¹				3	13	8	14	10²									25
1		4	5	7	2	8	9²	11									12	6				3	10¹	13											26
1		4	5	7	2		8	10¹		12							11	6				3	9												27
1		4	5	7	2		8	10									12	6³				3	11²	9¹		13		14						28
1		4	5	7	2¹	8	12	10									6					3	11	9										29
1		4	5	7	2	8	9³	10									13	6²				3	11¹	14		12								30
1		4	5	7	2	8²	9	10¹									13	6³				3	11	14		12								31
1		4	5³	7	2³		8			12	13			9	6							11¹	14		10		3							32
1		5	7¹	2	8			14	4			13	6									11³	9		10²		3	12						33
1		7		8	2	12	5				11²		6¹									10³	9	13		3	4	14						34
1		5	2		8	3	11¹	4			9²		6³				12					10	7	13					14					35
1		5	7³	2	9	8	13	3	11¹	4			12	6²								14	10											36

ROSS COUNTY   First Division

Year Formed: 1929. *Ground & Address:* Victoria Park, Dingwall IV15 9QW. *Telephone:* 01349 860860. *Fax:* 01349 866277.
Ground Capacity: total 5500, seated 2700. *Size of Ground:* 110×75yd.
Chairman: Roy McGregor. *Secretary:* Donnie MacBean. *Facilities Manager:* Brian Campbell.
Manager: Neale Cooper. *Assistant Manager:* Gordon Chisholm. *Physio:* Douglas Sim. *Record Attendance:* 6600, benefit match v Celtic, 31 August 1970.
Record Transfer Fee Received: £200,000 for Neil Tarrant to Aston Villa (April 1999).
Record Transfer Fee Paid: £25,000 for Barry Wilson from Southampton (Oct.1992).
Record Victory: 11-0 v St Cuthbert Wanderers, Scottish Cup, Dec.1993.
Record Defeat: 1-10 v Inverness Thistle, Highland League.
Most League Appearances: 124: W. Herd, 1995–98.
Most League Goals in Season: 22: D. Adams, 1996–97.
Most League Goals (Overall): 38: D. Adams, 1996–98.

ROSS COUNTY 1999–2000 LEAGUE RECORD

Match No.	Date	Venue	Opponents	Result	H/T Score	Lg. Pos.	Goalscorers	Atten-dance
1	Aug 7	H	Hamilton A	W 2-1	1-0	—	McGlashan [3], Irvine [79]	2312
2	14	A	Stranraer	D 0-0	0-0	4		475
3	21	H	Stenhousemuir	D 0-0	0-0	4		2612
4	28	H	Arbroath	W 2-0	0-0	2	Ferguson S [57], Shaw [62]	2303
5	Sept 4	A	Stirling A	L 1-2	0-2	4	McGlashan [66]	1015
6	11	A	Alloa Ath	L 0-2	0-0	5		694
7	18	H	Clyde	W 2-0	1-0	4	Kinnaird [18], Fraser [66]	2840
8	25	A	Partick Th	W 2-0	1-0	4	Maxwell [10], Wood [90]	2171
9	Oct 2	H	Queen of the S	D 1-1	1-1	4	Wood [39]	2293
10	9	A	Hamilton A	L 0-1	0-1	4		392
11	16	H	Stranraer	D 1-1	1-0	3	Shaw [11]	2168
12	30	H	Alloa Ath	W 1-0	1-0	3	Holmes [4]	2415
13	Nov 6	A	Clyde	L 1-3	1-1	6	Wood [25]	894
14	12	H	Stirling A	L 1-3	1-0	6	Holmes [19]	2693
15	20	A	Arbroath	W 1-0	0-0	6	Holmes [50]	972
16	27	A	Queen of the S	W 2-0	0-0	4	Kinnaird 2 [49, 65]	862
17	Dec 4	H	Partick Th	W 2-1	1-0	3	Shaw (pen) [22], McBain [48]	2392
18	Jan 22	H	Partick Th	L 2-4	1-2	6	Shaw [11], Holmes [46]	2698
19	29	H	Hamilton A	L 0-1	0-1	5		1860
20	Feb 5	H	Queen of the S	W 2-0	0-0	3	Kinnaird [60], Irvine [67]	2018
21	12	H	Arbroath	D 1-1	1-0	3	Ferguson S [25]	2059
22	19	A	Stirling A	L 1-3	0-1	3	Irvine [89]	661
23	26	A	Stranraer	W 2-0	0-0	2	Escalon [64], Ferguson [85]	472
24	Mar 7	H	Clyde	D 2-2	0-0	—	Ferguson S [55], Shaw [87]	2002
25	11	A	Alloa Ath	L 3-4	1-0	4	Holmes 2 [42, 54], Ferguson S [64]	2331
26	14	A	Alloa Ath	W 2-1	0-0	—	Ferguson S [48], Gilbert [58]	613
27	18	A	Clyde	D 0-0	0-0	3		1107
28	21	A	Stenhousemuir	W 2-0	0-0	—	Kinnaird [6], McGlashan [87]	358
29	25	A	Arbroath	W 2-1	2-0	2	Holmes [25], Shaw [36]	804
30	28	H	Stenhousemuir	W 2-0	2-0	—	Shaw [27], Kinnaird [36]	1771
31	Apr 1	H	Stirling A	W 5-1	2-0	2	Shaw 2 [38, 80], Holmes [42], Irvine [59], McGlashan [65]	2148
32	8	H	Partick Th	L 1-3	0-1	2	Irvine [82]	3511
33	15	A	Queen of the S	W 3-0	1-0	3	Irvine [39], Bone [61], Kinnaird [71]	1010
34	22	A	Hamilton A	W 3-0	2-0	2	Shaw 2 (1 pen) [10, 81 (p)], Bone [16]	693
35	29	H	Stranraer	W 3-1	2-1	2	Taggart [1], Bone [18], Shaw [75]	2812
36	May 6	A	Stenhousemuir	D 2-2	0-1	3	Bone [52], Shaw [57]	600

Final League Position: 3   1998–99 DIV 3 1

Honours
League Champions: Third Division: 1998-99.

Club colours: Navy blue, white and red.

Goalscorers: *League (57):* Shaw 13 (2 pens), Holmes 8, Kinnaird 7, Ferguson 6, Irvine 6, Bone 4, McGlashan 4, Wood 3, Escalon 1, Fraser 1, Gilbert 1, McBain 1, Maxwell 1, Taggart 1. *Scottish Cup (2):* Irvine 1, Shaw 1. *CIS Cup (3):* Escalon 1, Irvine 1, Shaw 1 (pen). *Bell's League Cup (8):* Shaw 3, Irvine 2, Fraser 1, Geraghty 1, Wood 1.

Walker N 25	Escalon F 12+1	McBain R 18+10	Maxwell I 35	Irvine B 32	Gilbert K 26+1	Shaw G 32+1	McGlashan J 13+3	Geraghty M 3+6	Finlayson K 3+8	Kinnaird P 22+6	Fraser J 16+10	Wood G 8+4	Tully C 12+1	Ferguson S 18+1	Mackay S —+1	Ross D 4+7	Campbell C —+2	Hateley M 2	Canning M 5+1	Mackay D 13+5	Lennon D 7	Holmes D 20+5	Duthie M 24	Mols T 1	Hamilton G 1	Cormack P 6	Ferguson D 10	Thomson P 3	Roddie A 1	Feroz C 4	Hamilton G 7	Taggart C 9	Boyle S —+3	Bone A 4+2	Match No
1	2	3	4	5	6	7	8	9^2	10^1	11	12	13																							1
1	10	3	4	5	12	7	8	9^3	14	11^1	6^2	13	2																						2
1		3	4	5	6^2	7	8	12		11^1	13	9^3	2	10	14																				3
1	8^2	3	4	5	6	7		12		13	9^1	2	10	11^3	14																				4
1	8	3	4	5^1	6	7	13	12		2	9	11^1		10																					5
1	8^3	3^1	4	5	6	7	14	12	11	2	9	13		10^2																					6
1	8	3	4	5		7	10^1	11^2	6	9	12	2		13						2	13														7
1	8^1	12	4	5	6	7	3	11^2		9	13	2		10																					8
1		8	4	5	6	7	3^3	13	11^2	14	9					2^1	12	10																	9
1		3	4	5	6	7	8^1	12		11	9^2	2		13					10																10
1	8^3	3	4	5	6	7		13	14	11^1		2		12						10^2	9														11
1	8^1	3	4	5		7^2				13	2	12		8^1						6	10	9	11												12
1		12	4	5	6	7				13	11	7^2	10^1	2						6	10^2	9	3												13
1		3	4	5						13	11	7^2	10^1		12					6	9	2	8												14
1		3	4		6	7				11^1	8			10		12				5		9	2												15
1		3	4		6	7				11	8			10						5		9	2												16
1		3	4		6	7	8			11	12			10						5		9^1	2												17
	11^1	4	5		7		13	12		6	8			9						2^2		1	3	10											18
8		4	5	6	7		12			10	13			9		2				3^2		1	11^1												19
12		4	5	6			11			8				7^1		9				2		3	10	1											20
1		7	4	5	6		11	12		8				9^1		2				3^2		1	0^1												21
1	14	7	5	6	13		12	11		4^3	2	8		9^1		3^2				10															22
1	2^1	12	4	5	6	7		11^1	8			9		13						3		10													23
1	2^1	12	4	5	6	7			8			9								13		3	10^2				11								24
		12	4	5	6	7				2^1		9								10		3		8		1	11								25
		12	4	5	6	7		13				9		2						8^1		10^2	3								11^1	1			26
		12	4	5	6	7		13				9	14						2^1	8^3		10	3								11^2	1			27
			4	5	6	7	13	11^3	2^2			9^1								12		10	3							1	8	14			28
			4	5		7	13	11^1	8^2		2									6		9	3							1	10	12			29
		12	4	5		7		11^2			2	13								8		6	3					8^1		1	10				30
		14	4	5		7		11^2	2^3			12								6		9^1	3				8^1			1	10	13			31
			4	5		7		11^1	2	14		13								6		9^3	3^2				8			1	10	12			32
1			4	5^1	6	7		11	2			12								8		13	3								10	9^2			33
1			4		7			11	2			8								5		12	3								10	9^1			34
1			4	5	6	7	2^2	11^3		13		14								12		3	8								10^1	9			35
1			4	5	6	7	2^1	11		13		14								12		3	8^3								10^2	9			36

ST JOHNSTONE — Premier League

Year Formed: 1884. *Ground & Address:* McDiarmid Park, Crieff Road, Perth PH1 2SJ. *Telephone:* 01738 459090. *Fax:* 01738 625 771. *Clubcall:* 0898 121559.
Ground Capacity: all seated: 10,673. *Size of Pitch:* 115yd × 75yd.
Chairman: G.S.Brown. *Secretary and Managing Director:* Stewart Duff.
Manager: Sandy Clark. *Sales Executive:* Helen Harcus. *Physio:* Nick Summersgill. *Coach:* Billy Kirkwood. *Youth Development Officer:* Alistair Stevenson.
Managers since 1975: J. Stewart; J. Storrie; A. Stuart; A. Rennie; I. Gibson; A. Totten, J. McClelland, P. Sturrock. *Club Nickname(s):* Saints. *Previous Grounds:* Recreation Grounds, Muirton Park.
Record Attendance: (McDiarmid Park): 10,545 v Dundee, Premier Division; 23 May, 1999.
Record Transfer Fee received: £1,750,000 for Calum Davidson to Blackburn R (March 1998).
Record Transfer Fee paid: £300,000 for Billy Dodds from Dundee (1994).
Record Victory: 9-0 v Albion R, League Cup; 9 March, 1946.
Record Defeat: 1-10 v Third Lanark, Scottish Cup; 24 January, 1903.
Most Capped Player: George O'Boyle, 10, Northern Ireland.
Most League Appearances: 298: Drew Rutherford.
Most League Goals in Season (Individual): 36: Jimmy Benson, Division II; 1931-32.
Most Goals Overall (Individual): 140: John Brogan, 1977-83.

ST JOHNSTONE 1999–2000 LEAGUE RECORD

Match No.	Date	Venue	Opponents	Result	H/T Score	Lg. Pos.	Goalscorers	Atten-dance
1	Jul 31	H	Hearts	L	1-4	0-1	—	McQuillan [83]	6707
2	Aug 7	A	Celtic	L	0-3	0-2	9		60,282
3	15	A	Kilmarnock	W	2-0	0-0	8	Bollan [53], Lowndes [58]	4681
4	21	H	Hibernian	D	1-1	1-0	7	Lowndes [36]	6165
5	29	A	Aberdeen	W	3-0	1-0	4	Thomas [26], Weir [67], Lowndes [74]	9600
6	Sept 11	H	Motherwell	D	1-1	1-0	5	Thomas [25]	5468
7	19	A	Dundee	W	2-1	0-1	4	Lowndes 2 [80, 83]	5283
8	25	A	Rangers	L	1-3	0-1	5	Simao [61]	47,475
9	Oct 16	A	Hearts	D	1-1	0-1	5	Lowndes [57]	12,872
10	24	H	Celtic	L	1-2	1-0	5	Lowndes [28]	9066
11	27	H	Dundee U	L	0-1	0-0	—		4236
12	30	A	Motherwell	L	0-1	0-1	7		6173
13	Nov 6	H	Dundee	L	0-1	0-1	8		4917
14	21	H	Aberdeen	D	1-1	0-0	8	Jones [75]	6279
15	24	A	Hibernian	W	1-0	1-0	—	Jones [17]	9454
16	27	A	Dundee U	L	0-1	0-1	8		6367
17	Dec 18	A	Kilmarnock	W	2-1	2-0	7	McBride [16], O'Neil [26]	6002
18	27	A	Dundee	D	1-1	1-0	—	Lowndes [44]	6232
19	Jan 22	H	Motherwell	D	1-1	1-0	7	Jones [44]	4158
20	Feb 5	A	Aberdeen	L	1-2	1-1	8	O'Neil [15]	17,568
21	15	H	Rangers	D	1-1	0-0	—	Lowndes [86]	9608
22	22	H	Hibernian	W	1-0	1-0	—	O'Halloran (pen) [27]	8236
23	26	H	Dundee U	W	2-0	0-0	5	Griffin [51], Lowndes [89]	4732
24	Mar 4	A	Rangers	D	0-0	0-0			49,907
25	11	A	Celtic	L	1-4	1-1	7	Connolly [34]	59,331
26	15	H	Hearts	L	0-1	0-0	—		4468
27	18	H	Kilmarnock	D	0-0	0-0	7		4688
28	25	H	Dundee	W	2-1	1-0	53	Bollan [45], Millar [90]	4655
29	Apr 1	A	Motherwell	L	1-2	0-0	6	Russell [60]	5934
30	15	A	Hibernian	D	3-3	0-1	6	O'Neil [68], McAnespie [72], Parker [88]	9211
31	23	H	Rangers	L	0-2	0-1	9		10,016
32	29	A	Dundee U	W	1-0	0-0	7	Dods [67]	5843
33	May 2	H	Aberdeen	W	2-1	1-1	—	Dods [30], Kane [89]	3991
34	6	A	Hearts	D	0-0	0-0	5		12,368
35	13	H	Celtic	D	0-0	0-0	5		6739
36	21	A	Kilmarnock	L	2-3	0-1	5	Millar [76], Parker [87]	9192

Final League Position: 5   1998–99 3

Honours
League Champions: First Division 1982–83, 1989–90, 1996–97. Division II 1923–24, 1959–60, 1962–63; *Runners-up:* Division II 1931–32. Second Division 1987–88.
Scottish Cup: Semi-finals 1934, 1968, 1989, 1991.
League Cup Runners-up: 1969, 1998.
League Challenge Cup Runners-up: 1996–97.

European: *UEFA Cup:* 10 matches (1971–72, 1999–2000).

Club colours: Shirt: Royal blue with white trim. Shorts: White. Stockings: Royal blue with white hoops.

Goalscorers: *League (36):* Lowndes 10, Jones 3, O'Neil 3, Bollan 2, Dods 2, Millar 2, Parker 2, Thomas 2, Connolly 1, Griffin 1, Kane 1, McAnespie 1, McBride 1, McQuillan 1, O'Halloran 1, Russell 1, Simao 1, Weir 1. *Scottish Cup (0).* *CIS Cup (1):* Griffin 1.

Main A 21	McQuillan J 18	Bollan G 34	Dods D 22	Weir J 31	O'Halloran K 31 + 1	McBride J 18 + 1	Kane P 33 + 1	Dasovic N 13	Simao M 6 + 11	Grant R 1 + 2	O'Neil J 31 + 2	Griffin D 26 + 3	McMahon G 9 + 10	Lowndes N 16 + 9	Lauchlan M —+5	McAnespie K 14 + 6	Thomas K 5 + 7	Parker K 6 + 4	O'Boyle G 4 + 4	McCluskey S 5 + 1	Jones G 15 + 4	Frail S 9	Connolly P 8 + 3	Ferguson A 3	Robertson S 12 + 1	Millar M 3 + 5	Russell C 1	Conway C —+1	Match No.
1	2	3	4	5	6¹	7	8³	9	10	11²	12	13	14																	1
1	2	3	4	5	6	7¹	8³	9	10		11²	12		13	14															2
1	2	3	4	5		8	6	12		9		7¹	10		11															3
1	2	3	4	5		8	6	14		9¹	12	7²	10³		11	13													4
1	2	3	4	5		8	7³	9¹	13	10	6		12	14		11²													5
1	2	3	4¹	5	12	8	7	9³		10	6			11²	13	14													6
1	2	3		5	6	8		12		7	4		10		9²	11¹		13											7
1	2	3		5	6	8²	7	12		9	4		10³		13	11¹	14												8
1	2	3		6		8¹	7	14		12	4		10³		9	13		11²	5										9
1	2	3		6		8	7	12			4		10¹		9		11	5											10
1	2	3		6²		8	7		12		4		10		9		13	11¹	5										11
1	2	3		6		14	8	13			4	7²	10		9¹	11³		12	5										12
1	2	3		5	6	8		13		9²	4	7	10	12			11¹												13
1	2	3		5	6	8		12		9	4	7	10¹			13			11²										14
1	2	3		5	6		9	8¹		10	4	7	12			13			11²										15
1	2	3		5	6		8	13		9	4	7²	10			12			11¹										16
1	2	3		5	6	7²	8			9	4	12	10³	13					11										17
1	2	3		5	6	7¹	8			9	4		10	12		13			11²										18
1		3		5	6	7	8	12		9	4		10¹					2	11										19
1		3		5	6³	7	8	9²		10	4	13	12	14				11¹	2										20
1		3	4	5	7¹	9³	8			10²	2		13				14	12	6	11									21
		3	4	5	6	7²	8			9		13	12				10¹	2	11	1									22
		3	4	5	7¹	9	8			10	2		12				13	6	11²	1									23
		3	4	5	7	9	8			10	2		13	14					6³	11²	1³	15							24
		3	4	5¹	7	9	8			10	2		13	12					6	11²	1								25
		3	4	5		7	8²			9	2	12	10						13	6¹	11	1							26
		3	4	5	6	7²	8			9	2	13	10¹						12		11	1							27
		3	4	5	7		8			10	2	9¹							11	6²	12		1	13					28
			4	5	6	7²	8			10	2	12		9					11				1	13	3¹				29
			4	5	6	7²	8			10	2	13		9		12				3¹	11		1						30
		3	4	5	6		8			7	2	12		10¹		9²					11		1	13					31
		3	2	4	6	5²	8			7				10	12	9¹			11				1	13					32
		3	2	4	6	5¹	8			7				10		9			11				1	12					33
		3	2	4	6		8			7		12		10¹	13	9²			11				1	5					34
		3	2	4	6	9²	8			7				13		10			11¹		12		1	5					35
		3	2		6	13	8			7²		4³		14	9¹	10			11				1	5			12		36

ST MIRREN   Premier League

Year Formed: 1877. *Ground & Address:* St Mirren Park, Love St, Paisley PA3 2EJ. *Telephone:* 0141 889 2558/0141 840 1337. *Fax:* 0141 848 6444.
Ground Capacity: 10,866 (all seated). *Size of Pitch:* 112yd × 73yd.
Chairman: Stewart Gilmour. *Vice-Chairman:* George Campbell. *Secretary:* Allan Marshall.
Manager: Tom Hendrie. *Physio:* Colin Brow. *Youth Development Officer:* Joe Hughes.
Managers since 1975: Alex Ferguson; Jim Clunie; Rikki MacFarlane; Alex Miller; Alex Smith; Tony Fitzpatrick; David Hay; Jimmy Bone; Tony Fitzpatrick. *Club Nickname(s):* The Buddies. *Previous Grounds:* Short Roods 1877-79, Thistle Park Greenhill 1879-83, Westmarch 1883-94.
Record Attendance: 47,438 v Celtic, League Cup, 20 Aug, 1949.
Record Transfer Fee received: £850,000 for Ian Ferguson to Rangers (1988).
Record Transfer Fee paid: £400,000 for Thomas Stickroth from Bayer Uerdingen (1990).
Record Victory: 15-0 v Glasgow University, Scottish Cup 1st rd; 30 Jan, 1960.
Record Defeat: 0-9 v Rangers, Division I; 4 Dec, 1897.
Most Capped Player: Godmundor Torfason, 29, Iceland.
Most League Appearances: 351: Tony Fitzpatrick, 1973-88.
Most League Goals in Season (Individual): 45: Dunky Walker, Division I; 1921-22.
Most Goals Overall (Individual): 221: David McCrae, 1923-34.

ST MIRREN 1999–2000 LEAGUE RECORD

Match No.	Date	Venue	Opponents	Result	H/T Score	Lg. Pos.	Goalscorers	Attendance
1	Aug 7	H	Ayr U	D 1-1	0-0	—	Brown [69]	3671
2	Aug 14	A	Raith R	W 6-0	3-0	1	Lavety [18], Walker [30], Ross [41], Yardley 2 [60, 64], McGarry [83]	2787
3	Aug 21	H	Inverness CT	W 3-2	3-1	1	Yardley [33], Walker [36], McGarry [39]	3040
4	Aug 29	A	Clydebank	W 3-2	1-1	1	Lavety 2 [4, 55], Brown [75]	1513
5	Sept 4	H	Airdrieonians	W 5-0	3-0	1	Mendes [6], Murray 2 [18, 54], Lavety [28], Ross [47]	3117
6	Sept 11	A	Dunfermline Ath	D 1-1	1-1	1	Brown [34]	6128
7	Sept 18	H	Morton	W 3-2	2-1	1	Yardley [28], Lavety [38], McLaughlin [57]	6773
8	Sept 25	A	Falkirk	L 1-3	0-3	1	Murray [75]	4505
9	Oct 2	H	Livingston	D 1-1	0-1	1	Lavety [51]	4520
10	Oct 16	H	Raith R	W 3-2	1-1	1	Lavety [37], Yardley [57], Turner [90]	3815
11	Oct 23	A	Ayr U	W 3-0	2-0	1	Lavety [13], Yardley 2 [28, 47]	3467
12	Oct 30	H	Dunfermline Ath	W 3-1	1-0	1	Lavety [33], Yardley [55], Tod (og) [84]	6130
13	Nov 6	A	Morton	W 4-1	3-0	1	Baltacha [10], Lavety [34], Yardley [43], Walker [60]	3733
14	Nov 12	A	Airdrieonians	W 2-0	0-0	1	Yardley [59], Lavety [62]	3209
15	Nov 20	H	Clydebank	W 2-1	0-0	1	McGarry (pen) [53], Yardley [82]	4434
16	Nov 27	A	Livingston	W 2-1	1-0	1	McGarry [14], McLaughlin [75]	4239
17	Dec 4	H	Falkirk	W 2-1	1-0	1	Yardley [5], Lavety [66]	4980
18	Dec 11	A	Inverness CT	D 1-1	1-0	1	Yardley [43]	2893
19	Dec 18	H	Ayr U	L 1-2	0-1	1	Lavety [65]	3607
20	Jan 3	H	Morton	D 1-1	0-0	—	Yardley [48]	7266
21	Jan 8	H	Airdrieonians	W 3-1	1-1	1	Mendes 2 [2, 52], McGarry [75]	3636
22	Jan 22	A	Falkirk	L 0-2	0-1	1		4746
23	Feb 5	H	Livingston	L 0-2	0-1	1		5015
24	Feb 12	H	Inverness CT	W 2-0	1-0	1	Yardley [22], Bowman [67]	3742
25	Feb 19	A	Dunfermline Ath	D 1-1	0-1	1	Nicolson [80]	7132
26	Feb 26	A	Raith R	W 2-1	0-0	1	Yardley [86], Mendes [88]	4662
27	Mar 4	H	Dunfermline Ath	L 0-2	0-2	2		6938
28	Mar 11	H	Clydebank	W 8-0	3-0	1	McGarry [9], Lavety 3 [20, 56, 71], Ross [26], Murray 2 [51, 65], Walker [69]	3388
29	Mar 18	A	Morton	W 2-0	0-0	1	Yardley [77], McGarry [85]	3768
30	Mar 25	A	Clydebank	D 0-0	0-0	1		2244
31	Apr 1	A	Airdrieonians	W 1-0	1-0	1	McLaughlin J [39]	2909
32	Apr 8	H	Falkirk	W 1-0	0-0	1	McKnight [84]	6742
33	Apr 15	A	Livingston	W 2-1	1-0	1	McGarry [23], Yardley [76]	4531
34	Apr 22	A	Ayr U	W 2-1	0-0	1	Mendes [49], McKnight [90]	4678
35	Apr 29	H	Raith R	W 3-0	0-0	1	Yardley [51], McGarry [55], McLaughlin B [58]	8386
36	May 6	A	Inverness CT	L 0-5	0-3	1		3218

Final League Position: 1   1998–99 DIV 1 5

Honours

League Champions: First Division 1976-77, 1999–2000. Division II 1967-68; *Runners-up:* 1935-36.
Scottish Cup Winners: 1926, 1959, 1987. *Runners-up:* 1908, 1934, 1962.
League Cup Runners-up: 1955-56.
B&Q Cup Runners-up: 1993-94. *Victory Cup:* 1919-20. *Summer Cup:* 1943-44. *Anglo-Scottish Cup:* 1979-80.

European: *Cup Winners' Cup:* 4 matches (1987-88). *UEFA Cup:* 10 matches (1980-81, 1983-84, 1985-86).

Club colours: Shirt: Black and white vertical stripes. Shorts: Black. Stockings: Black with white trim. Change colours: Predominantly red.

Goalscorers: *League (75):* Yardley 19, Lavety 16, McGarry 9 (1 pen), Mendes 5, Murray 5, Walker 4, Brown 3, McLaughlin B 3, Ross 3, McKnight 2, Baltacha 1, Bowman 1, McLaughlin J 1, Nicolson 1, Turner 1, own goal 1. *Scottish Cup (1):* McGarry 1. *CIS Cup (0).* *Bell's League Cup (0).*

Roy L 31	Nicolson I 33 + 1	Kerr C 3	Turner T 31	McLaughlin B 34	Walker S 33	Murray H 29	Ross I 30 + 1	McGarry S 22 + 10	Brown T 19 + 7	Baltacha S 18 + 9	Yardley M 33 + 2	Drew C — + 6	Lavety B 21 + 8	Mendes J 28 + 5	Rudden P 9 + 7	Bowman G 10 + 9	Robinson R — + 9	Scrimgour D 5	McLaughlin J 3	Paaslack I 1 + 1	McKnight P 1 + 3	Gillies R 2 + 2	Donnachie S — + 1	Match No.
1	2	3	4	5	6²	7	8	9	10	11¹	12	13												1
1	2	3	4	5	6²	7	8³	14	12	13	11		9¹	10										2
1	2	3²	4	5	6	7	8	12	13		11		9¹	10										3
1	2¹		4	5	6	7	3		8²	13	11	12	9	10										4
1	2		4	5²	6	7³	3	12	8	13	11		9	10¹	14									5
1	2		4	5	6	7	3		8	12	11¹		9	10										6
1	2		4	5	6	7¹	3	13		8	11	12	9	10²										7
1	2		4	5	6	7	3	13	9²	8¹	11	12		10										8
1	2		4	5	6	7	3	9¹	13	8²	12	14	11³	10										9
1	2		4	5	6	7	3	13	12	8¹	11		9²	10										10
1	2		4	5	6	7	3		13	8²	11	12	9¹	10										11
1	2		4	5	6	7	3	12		8	11		9¹	10										12
1	2³		4	5	6	7	3	13	12	8	11		9¹	10²	14									13
1	2		4		6	7	3		8	5	11		9	10¹		12²	13							14
1	2		4	5	6		3	10	8¹	7²	11		9		14	13	12³							15
1	2		4	5	6		3¹	10	8	7	11		9²		13	12								16
1	2		4	5	6			10	8	7	11¹		9	12		3								17
	2		4	5	6			10²	8¹	7	11		9	13		3	12	1						18
	2		4	5	6	7		10	12	8¹	11		9²	13		3		1						19
	2		4	5	6	7	3¹	9	8²	13	11		10		12									20
	2		4	5	6	7	3	9²	8	12	11		10¹		13		1							21
	2		4	5	6		3	9¹	8	7²	11		12	10		13		1						22
1	2		4	5	6		3	9⁴	8	7¹	11		13	10²	14	12								23
1	2¹		4	5	6			8	9	7	11		13	10²	12	3								24
1	2		4	5	6	7	8	13		11¹	9²		10	12		3								25
1			5	6	7	8	12		2²	11¹		9	10	4	3	13								26
1	2²		5	6	7	8	9¹		13	11		12	10	4	3									27
1	2		5	6	7	3	9	8²	14	11		12	10¹	4³	13									28
1	2²		5	6	7	8	9		11			10¹	3	4	12	13								29
1	2		4	5		7	3	9	8		11		12	10¹		13		6²						30
1	13		4	2		7	6²	9¹	8		11		10³		3			5	12	14				31
1			4	5		7		9	8	2²	11¹		12	3	6	13³			10	14				32
1	2		4	5	6		3¹	9			11		13	8					10²	12				33
1	2		4²	5	6	7		9³			11		14	10	3	8¹			13	12				34
1	2²		4	5	6	7	12	9			11		14	10³	3¹		13				8			35
1	2²			6	7	3	9		12			11³	10	4		13		5¹			8	14		36

STENHOUSEMUIR

Second Division

Year Formed: 1884. *Ground & Address:* Ochilview Park, Gladstone Rd, Stenhousemuir FK5 5QL. *Telephone:* 01324 562992. *Fax:* 01324 562980.
Ground Capacity: total: 2374, seated: 626. *Size of Pitch:* 110yd × 72yd.
Chairman: A Terry Bulloch. *Secretary:* David O.Reid. *Commercial Manager:* John Sharp.
Manager: Brian Fairley. *Assistant Manager:* Gordon Buchanan. *Physio:* Lee Campbell.
Managers since 1975: H. Glasgow; J. Black; A. Rose; W. Henderson; A. Rennie; J. Meakin; D. Lawson; T. Christie;
G. Armstrong. *Club Nickname(s):* The Warriors. *Previous Grounds:* Tryst Ground 1884-86, Goschen Park 1886-90.
Record Attendance: 12,500 v East Fife, Scottish Cup 4th rd; 11 Mar, 1950.
Record Transfer Fee received: £70,000 for Euan Donaldson to St Johnstone (May 1995).
Record Transfer Fee paid: £20,000 to Livingston for Ian Little (June 1995).
Record Victory: 9-2 v Dundee U, Division II; 19 Apr, 1937.
Record Defeat: 2-11 v Dunfermline Ath. Division II; 27 Sept, 1930.
Most Capped Player: —.
Most League Appearances: 360: Archie Rose.
Most League Goals in Season (Individual): 32: Robert Taylor, Division II; 1925-26.
Most Goals Overall (Individual): —.

STENHOUSEMUIR 1999–2000 LEAGUE RECORD

Match No.	Date		Venue	Opponents	Result	H/T Score	Lg. Pos.	Goalscorers	Atten- dance
1	Aug	7	A	Partick Th	W 1-0	0-0	—	Lorimer [87]	2072
2		14	H	Stirling A	W 2-1	1-1	2	Hamilton R [38], Watters [62]	703
3		21	A	Ross Co	D 0-0	0-0	3		2612
4		28	H	Stranraer	D 1-1	1-0	4	McKinnon [16]	427
5	Sept	5	A	Hamilton A	D 1-1	0-0	3	McKinnon [51]	445
6		11	A	Queen of the S	W 3-0	1-0	2	Hamilton R [12], Graham 2 [60, 66]	928
7		18	H	Arbroath	L 1-3	0-1	3	Mooney [87]	596
8		25	A	Alloa Ath	W 4-1	3-1	2	Mooney [34], Fisher [40], Valentine (og) [42], Hamilton R [70]	675
9	Oct	2	H	Clyde	L 1-3	0-1	3	Graham [87]	715
10		16	A	Stirling A	L 1-5	0-4	5	Fisher [85]	649
11		23	H	Partick Th	L 0-1	0-1	6		1188
12		30	H	Queen of the S	W 2-1	0-0	4	Hamilton R [85], McKinnon [88]	447
13	Nov	6	A	Arbroath	W 3-0	3-0	2	Mooney 3 [7, 23, 30]	866
14		10	H	Hamilton A	D 0-0	0-0	—		510
15		20	A	Stranraer	L 0-2	0-0	5		398
16		27	A	Clyde	L 0-1	0-1	6		882
17	Dec	4	H	Alloa Ath	L 1-3	0-1	6	Graham [70]	574
18		18	A	Partick Th	L 0-1	0-1	6		1922
19	Jan	3	H	Arbroath	W 3-0	3-0	—	Watson [20], Mooney [28], Hamilton R [41]	381
20		15	A	Queen of the S	L 1-3	0-3	7.	McKinnon [82]	1017
21	Feb	5	H	Clyde	L 3-4	3-0	9	Banks [13], Ross (og) [16], Fisher [20]	690
22		12	H	Stranraer	D 1-1	1-1	8	Fisher [18]	306
23		26	H	Stirling A	L 1-2	0-1	9	Fraser [65]	629
24	Mar	7	A	Alloa Ath	L 1-3	1-1	—	Fisher [42]	492
25		11	H	Queen of the S	W 2-0	0-0	9	Hamilton R [49], Fisher [86]	541
26		14	A	Hamilton A	L 1-2	1-1	—	Mooney [8]	347
27		18	A	Arbroath	D 2-2	1-1	9	Hamilton R [32], McKinnon [87]	730
28		21	A	Ross Co	L 0-2	0-0	—		358
29		25	A	Stranraer	D 2-2	0-2	9	McKinnon 2 [51, 62]	409
30		28	A	Ross Co	L 0-2	0-2			1771
31	Apr	8	H	Alloa Ath	W 2-1	0-1	0	McLauchlan [84], Welsh [89]	495
32		15	A	Clyde	L 0-7	0-2	9		1033
33		18	H	Hamilton A	L 0-1	0-1	—		309
34		22	H	Partick Th	W 2-0	0-0	9	Wood [59], Wright [82]	895
35		29	A	Stirling A	L 0-1	0-0	9		564
36	May	6	H	Ross Co	D 2-2	1-0	8	Wood [36], Mooney [72]	600

Final League Position: 8　　1998–99 DIV 3 2

Honours
League Champions: Third Division runners-up: 1998-99. *Scottish Cup:* Semi-finals 1902-03. Quarter-finals 1948–49, 1949–50, 1994-95. *League Cup:* Quarter-finals 1947-48, 1960-61, 1975-76. *League Challenge Cup:* Winners 1995-96.

Club colours: Shirt: Maroon. Shorts: White. Stockings: Maroon.

Goalscorers: *League (44):* Mooney 8, Hamilton R 7, McKinnon 7, Fisher 6, Graham 4, Wood 2, Banks 1, Fraser 1, Lorimer 1, McLauchlan 1, Watson 1, Watters 1, Welsh 1, Wright 1, own goals 2. *Scottish Cup (11):* Fisher 3, Graham 2, Hamilton R 2, Mooney 2, Forrester 1, own goal 1. *CIS Cup (1):* Mooney 1. *Bell's League Cup (2):* Hamilton R 1, Watters 1.

Hamilton L 33	Lawrence A 31+3	Gibson J 14	Armstrong G 22+7	Graham T 32	Davidson G 15+1	Lorimer D 9+7	Fisher J 30	Hamilton R 34+1	McKinnon C 35	Wood D 9+13	Watters W 4+15	Banks A 18+4	Cummings A 1+5	McGurk R 2	Mooney M 17+14	Roseburgh D —+2	Watson G 27	Forrester P 9+3	Hall M 9	Fraser G 15+4	Bradford J 8+5	Welsh B 8	McLauchlan M 8+1	Connolly J 1	Murphy S —+1	Wright K 4+1	Match No.
1	2	3	4	5	6	7	8	9	10	11¹	12																1
1	2¹	10	4	5	6	11²	7	8	12	9	3	13															2
1	2	11	4	5⁴	6	10	7	8	12	9	3¹	13															3
	2	11	4	5	6	10	7²	8	9¹	12	3				1		13										4
1	2	7	4	5	6	10	9¹	8	11²	13	3³	14			12												5
1	2		4	5	6	11	7³	8	14	9²	3	10¹			13		12										6
1	2	11³	4	5	6	10	7	8	14	9²	3¹				13		12										7
1	2	8³	4		6	10	9	5	11	12	13	14			7¹	3²											8
1	2	3¹	4	5	6	10	9	8³	11²	14	12	13			7												9
1	2	3⁴	4	5⁴	6	11	9	8	14	13	7¹				10		12										10
1	2	10	12	5	6¹	11	7	8	13						14		4	9¹	3²								11
1	2	10	6	5		11	7	8	12	13							4	9¹	3²								12
1	2	6		5		11	10	8³	13	12	7²				14		4	9¹	3								13
1	2	6		5		11	10	8	14	13	7³						4	9²	3¹	12							14
1	2	6		5		12	10³	8	14	13	7¹						4	9²	3	11							15
1	2	6				10	9	5	13	12	7²						4	8	3¹	11							16
1	2	6		5	10	11	7	8	13	12							4	9¹	3²								17
1	2	6		5		11	7	8	12		3¹				9		4		10								18
1	12	6		5		11¹	7	8	13	14	3				10³		4	9²									19
1	2¹	14		5		10³	11	7	8		3				9²		4	13	6	12							20
1	2	12		5	6	11	7	8			3¹				13		4	10	9²								21
1	2	6		5		12	10	7	8¹		3				11		4	9									22
1	2	6³		5	14	12	11	7	8		3				13		4	10¹	9²								23
	13	14		5	2³	12	11	7	8		3			1			10²	4¹	6	9							24
1	2	12	4¹	5		10²	11	7	8	13	3							9	6								25
1	2			5		10	11	7	8		3				9¹		4	12	6								26
1	2	6		5	14		7	8	13		3³				10¹		4	12	11	9²							27
1	2			5		11	7	8			3				12		4	10¹	6	9							28
1	2		4¹	5²			7	8			3				11		10	13	12	6	9						29
	2	13		5		10	7	8	12		3¹				11²		4		6	9³				1	14		30
1	2	13				10	11				3				12		4	8¹	6²	7	5	9					31
1	2	13		5		10²	7	8			3¹				12		4	14	6	9	11³						32
1	2			5		12	3	10	8¹	7²							4	13	6	9	11						33
1	2	3		5	6¹	11	7	8³	12	13					14		4	9²	10								34
1	14	3	2	5		10	7	8	11³	13							4	6¹	12	9²							35
1			2	5			8		11¹	13	3				7		4	10²	6	9³	14						36

STIRLING ALBION — Second Division

Year Formed: 1945. *Ground & Address:* Forthbank Stadium, Springkerse Industrial Estate, Stirling FK7 7UJ.
Telephone: 01786 450399. *Fax:* 01786 448592.
Ground Capacity: 3808, seated: 2508. *Size of Pitch:* 110yd × 74yd.
Chairman: Peter McKenzie. *Secretary:* Mrs Marlyn Hallam.
Manager: Ray Stewart. *Physio:* George Cameron.
Managers since 1975: A. Smith; G. Peebles; J. Fleeting; J. Brogan; K. Drinkell; J. Philliben. *Club Nickname(s):* The Binos.
Previous Grounds: Annfield 1945–92.
Record Attendance: 26,400 (at Annfield) v Celtic, Scottish Cup 4th rd; 14 Mar, 1959. 3808 v Aberdeen, Scottish Cup 4th rd, 15 February 1996 (Forthbank).
Record Transfer Fee received: £70,000 for John Philliben to Doncaster R (Mar 1984).
Record Transfer Fee paid: £25,000 for Craig Taggart from Falkirk (Aug 1994).
Record Victory: 20-0 v Selkirk, Scottish Cup 1st rd; 8 Dec, 1984.
Record Defeat: 0-9 v Dundee U, Division I; 30 Dec, 1967.
Most Capped Player: —.
Most League Appearances: 504: Matt McPhee, 1967-81.

STIRLING ALBION 1999–2000 LEAGUE RECORD

Match No.	Date	Venue	Opponents	Result	H/T Score	Lg. Pos.	Goalscorers	Attendance
1	Aug 7	H	Stranraer	D	1-1	1-1	—	Graham [13]	525
2	14	A	Stenhousemuir	L	1-2	1-1	7	Aitken [12]	703
3	21	H	Hamilton A	W	2-0	2-0	6	McQuade [12], Wood [21]	656
4	28	A	Clyde	L	0-3	0-1	8		1003
5	Sept 4	H	Ross Co	W	2-1	2-0	5	Graham [4], McQuade [43]	1015
6	11	A	Arbroath	L	1-2	0-1	6	McGrillen [88]	805
7	18	H	Alloa Ath	L	0-1	0-1	8		1196
8	25	A	Queen of the S	D	3-3	3-1	7	Graham 2 [7, 18], McGrillen [13]	1038
9	Oct 2	H	Partick Th	W	3-1	3-0	7	Graham [31], McGrillen [38], McCallion [42]	1333
10	16	H	Stenhousemuir	W	5-1	4-0	6	Gardner J [14], Taggart [28], McQuade 2 [36, 38], Graham [53]	649
11	23	A	Stranraer	L	1-2	0-1	7	Taggart [70]	446
12	30	H	Arbroath	L	3-4	0-1	8	Mortimer [49], Graham [51], McGrillen [82]	856
13	Nov 6	A	Alloa Ath	D	4-4	2-2	8	Taggart [13], McQuade [17], Wood [53], Graham [87]	909
14	12	A	Ross Co	W	3-1	0-1	7	McGrillen [60], McQuade 2 [79, 87]	2693
15	20	H	Clyde	L	1-2	1-1	7	Graham [19]	949
16	27	A	Partick Th	L	0-1	0-0	8		2812
17	Dec 11	A	Queen of the S	W	3-0	0-0	7	McQuade [53], Whiteford [78], Donald [89]	534
18	18	H	Stranraer	L	2-5	1-2	8	McQuade [35], McGrillen [58]	571
19	27	A	Hamilton A	W	2-0	1-0	—	McQuade [12], McGrillen [81]	431
20	Jan 3	H	Alloa Ath	D	1-1	0-0	—	McGrillen [63]	1398
21	22	A	Queen of the S	W	3-2	2-1	5	McQuade [15], Graham [31], McGrillen [80]	1104
22	Feb 5	H	Partick Th	L	0-2	0-1	7		1704
23	12	A	Clyde	L	1-4	0-2	7	McQuade [80]	1027
24	19	H	Ross Co	W	3-1	1-0	5	McQuade 2 [1, 74], Bone [53]	661
25	26	A	Stenhousemuir	W	2-1	1-0	3	Graham [17], Bone [76]	629
26	29	A	Arbroath	L	2-3	0-0	—	McQuade [48], Bone [77]	580
27	Mar 4	H	Hamilton A	L	1-4	0-2	5	McGrillen [72]	692
28	11	A	Arbroath	D	1-1	0-1	6	Bone [64]	681
29	18	A	Alloa Ath	L	0-1	0-0	7		939
30	25	H	Clyde	L	3-6	1-2	8	Paterson [45], McGrillen [47], Graham [49]	1102
31	Apr 1	A	Ross Co	L	1-5	0-2	8	Aitken [90]	2148
32	8	H	Queen of the S	D	2-2	2-1	8	Graham 2 [19, 44]	520
33	15	A	Partick Th	D	1-1	1-0	8	Graham [3]	2160
34	22	A	Stranraer	L	1-3	1-0	8	Graham [32]	447
35	29	H	Stenhousemuir	W	1-0	0-0	8	Graham [89]	564
36	May 6	A	Hamilton A	L	0-1	0-0	7		· 498

Final League Position: 7   1998–99 6

Most League Goals in Season (Individual): 27: Joe Hughes, Division II; 1969-70.
Most Goals Overall (Individual): 129: Billy Steele, 1971-83.

Honours
League Champions: Division II 1952-53, 1957-58, 1960-61, 1964-65. Second Division 1976-77, 1990-91, 1995-96; *Runners-up:* Division II 1948-49, 1950-51.
Scottish Cup: —. *League Cup:* —.

Club colours: Shirt: Red and white halves. Shorts: Red and white halves. Stockings: Red.

Goalscorers: *League (60):* Graham 17, McQuade 15, McGrillen 11, Bone 4, Taggart 3, Aitken 2, Wood 2, Donald 1, Gardner 1, McCallion 1, Mortimer 1, Paterson 1, Whiteford 1. *Scottish Cup (2):* Graham 1, Whiteford 1. *CIS Cup (2):* Graham 1 (pen), Wood 1. *Bell's League Cup (8):* Gardner 2, Graham 2, Aitken 1, McQuade 1, Paterson 1 (pen), Wood 1.

Gow G 8	Paterson A 32+1	Tortolano J 26+1	Donald G 36	Martin B 11	Wood C 18+5	McQuade J 34	Aitken N 4+10	Graham A 35	Taggart C 27+1	Gardner J 29	Mortimer P 20+8	Gardiner J 25	Philliben J 10+7	Bell D —+6	McGrillen P 23+6	McCallion K 4+9	McCallum D 12+8	Whiteford A 20	Clark P 11+3	Bone A 7+2	Williams A —+5	McAlpine J 3	Gardner G 1	Match No.
1¹	2	3	4	5	6	7	8	9	10	11	12													1
	2	3¹	4	5	6	7³	8²	9	10	11	14			1	12	13								2
	2	3	4	5¹	6	7	8²	9	10	11				1	12	13								3
	2	3	4	5	6	7	8¹	9²	10	11	13	1			12									4
	2¹	3	4	5	6	7	13	9²	10	11			1	12			8							5
	2	3	4	5	6	7		9	10	11	12	11			8									6
		3	4		6	7		9	10	11³	2	1		5	13	8²	12							7
	2	3	4	5	12	7		9	10	11¹	6	1			8									8
	2	3	4	5		7	13	9	10¹	11	8	1			12	6²								9
	2	3	4	5		7	13	9	10²	11	8	1			12	6¹								10
	2	3	4³	5		7	13	9	10	11²	8	1	14		12	6¹								11
	2	3	4	5	6	7¹		9	10	11²	8	1			12	13								12
	2¹	3	4		12	7		9	10	11²	6	1		5	8			13						13
	2	3	4		6	7	13	9	10	11	5	1	12		8²									14
	2	4¹	3		7	13	9	10	11	5	1	12		8		6²								15
	2	4	3		7		9¹		6	1	5	12	8		10									16
	2	4	3		7		9	10	11¹	6	1		8		12	5								17
	2	13	4	3³	7		9	10	11¹	6²	1		8	14	12	5								18
1	2	3²	4	6³	7¹		9	10	11	12			8	13		5	14							19
1	2	3	4	12	7		9	10	11¹	13			8		6²	5								20
1	2	3	4		7		9	10	11				8		6	5								21
1	2²	3¹	4	12	7³		9	10	11				8		6	5	13	14						22
1	13	4	10	7		9	14	11	6³	3²	8¹			5	2	12								23
	2¹	4	7		9	10²	11³	6	1	12	13		12	5	6	8	14							24
	2	3	4	7	9	10			1		12	5	6	8	11¹									25
	2	3	4	7	9	10			1		12	5	6	8	11¹									26
	2	3²	4	7	9	10	13	1		12	14	5	6²	8	11¹									27
	2	3	4	7³	9	10²	13	1		12	11¹	5	14	8		6								28
1	2	3	4	7	9	10			11	12	5	6¹	8											29
1	2	3	4	7	9		6¹	11	12	5	10	8												30
		3	4	7	13	9		8¹	1	6	11²	12	10³	5	2	14								31
	2	3	4	6	7¹	12	9	11²	1³	8	13	10	5	14										32
	2	4	7¹	9	11	3	1¹	6	8	12	10	5	13											33
	2	1	12	9	11	6	4	7	3¹	10	5	8												34
		1	6	7¹	13	9²	11	4	3	8	12	10	5	2										35
	2	1	8	13	9	11²	4	3¹	7³	12	10	5	6	14										36

STRANRAER

Second Division

Year Formed: 1870. *Ground & Address:* Stair Park, London Rd, Stranraer DG9 8BS. *Telephone:* 01776 703271.
Ground Capacity: total: 6100, seated: 1800. *Size of Pitch:* 110yd × 70yd.
Chairman/Secretary: Graham Rodgers. *Commercial Manager:* T. L. Sutherland.
Manager: Billy McLaren.
Managers since 1975: J. Hughes; N. Hood; G. Hamilton; D. Sneddon; J. Clark; R. Clark; A. McAnespie; C. Money.
Club Nickname(s): The Blues. *Previous Grounds:* None.
Record Attendance: 6500 v Rangers, Scottish Cup 1st rd; 24 Jan, 1948.
Record Transfer Fee received: £30,000 for Mark Campbell to Ayr Utd, 1999.
Record Transfer Fee paid: £15,000 for Colin Harkness from Kilmarnock (Aug 1989).
Record Victory: 7-0 v Brechin C, Division II; 6 Feb, 1965.
Record Defeat: 1-11 v Queen of the South, Scottish Cup 1st rd; 16 Jan, 1932.
Most Capped Player: —.
Most League Appearances: 256: Danny McDonald.
Most League Goals in Season (Individual): 27: Derek Frye, Second Division; 1977-78.
Most Goals Overall (Individual): —.

STRANRAER 1999–2000 LEAGUE RECORD

Match No.	Date		Venue	Opponents	Result	H/T Score	Lg. Pos.	Goalscorers	Attendance
1	Aug	7	A	Stirling A	D 1-1	1-1	—	Cahoon [6]	525
2		14	H	Ross Co	D 0-0	0-0	6		475
3		21	A	Clyde	D 0-0	0-0	7		722
4		28	A	Stenhousemuir	D 1-1	0-1	7	Smith [89]	427
5	Sept	4	H	Partick Th	D 1-1	1-0	8	McMartin (pen) [25]	1138
6		11	A	Hamilton A	L 1-2	1-1	7	McMartin (pen) [6]	503
7		18	H	Queen of the S	W 1-0	0-0	6	Smith [76]	621
8		25	A	Arbroath	W 2-1	0-1	6	Blaikie [62], Wright [90]	811
9	Oct	2	H	Alloa Ath	D 0-0	0-0	6		463
10		16	A	Ross Co	D 1-1	0-1	7	Young [81]	2168
11		23	H	Stirling A	W 2-1	1-0	4	Duthie [29], Roddie [74]	446
12		30	H	Hamilton A	L 0-2	0-1	6		454
13	Nov	6	A	Queen of the S	W 5-0	0-0	5	Roddie 2 [52, 56], Ronald 3 [70, 81, 82]	1052
14		14	A	Partick Th	L 0-2	0-2	5		1825
15		20	H	Stenhousemuir	W 2-0	0-0	4	George [57], Johnstone [65]	398
16		27	A	Alloa Ath	D 1-1	0-0	5	Johnstone [48]	569
17	Dec	4	H	Arbroath	D 2-2	0-0	5	Ronald [68], Jenkins [90]	384
18		18	A	Stirling A	W 5-2	2-1	4	Harty 3 [8, 48, 72], Smith J [20], Ronald [52]	571
19		27	H	Clyde	D 2-2	1-2	—	Smith J [29], Macdonald [81]	649
20	Jan	3	H	Queen of the S	L 1-2	0-2	—	Harty (pen) [53]	928
21		15	A	Hamilton A	L 0-2	0-0	3		576
22		22	A	Arbroath	D 1-1	1-1	3	Ronald [16]	720
23	Feb	12	A	Stenhousemuir	D 1-1	1-1	6	Ronald [9]	306
24		26	H	Ross Co	L 0-2	0-0	7		472
25	Mar	7	H	Partick Th	W 3-1	2-0	—	Ronald [9], Harty [11], Smith J [83]	628
26		11	A	Hamilton A	D 2-2	1-1	7	Blair [17], Harty [24]	405
27		18	A	Queen of the S	D 0-0	0-0	6		1165
28		21	H	Alloa Ath	D 2-2	0-1	—	Harty [60], Blaikie [69]	388
29		25	H	Stenhousemuir	D 2-2	2-0	5	Harty [17], Smith J [45]	409
30		28	A	Clyde	D 1-1	0-0	—	Knox [84]	785
31	Apr	1	A	Partick Th	D 1-1	0-1	6	Knox [84]	2351
32		8	H	Arbroath	L 0-1	0-1	6		412
33		15	A	Alloa Ath	L 0-4	0-3	6		605
34		22	H	Stirling A	W 3-1	0-1	6	Ronald 3 [71, 72, 90]	447
35		29	A	Ross Co	L 1-3	1-2	6	Smith J [16]	2812
36	May	6	H	Clyde	W 2-1	2-1	6	Edgar [24], Ronald [31]	471

Final League Position: 6   1998–99 DIV 1 10

Honours
League Champions: Second Division 1993-94, 1997-98.
Scottish Cup: —.
League Cup: —.
Qualifying Cup Winners: 1937.
League Challenge Cup Winners: 1996-97.

Club colours: Shirt: Blue with white side panels. Shorts: Blue with white side panels. Stockings: Blue with two white hoops.

Goalscorers: *League (47):* Ronald 12, Harty 8 (1 pen), Smith J 7, Roddie 3, Blaikie 2, Johnstone 2, Knox 2, McMartin 2 (2 pens), Blair 1, Cahoon 1, Duthie 1, Edgar 1, George 1, Jenkins 1, MacDonald 1, Wright 1, Young 1. *Scottish Cup (2):* Blaikie 1, Ronald 1. *CIS Cup (0). Bell's League Cup (3):* Blaikie 2, Knox 1.

McGeown M 36	Knox K 33	Black T 16 + 1	Furphy W 16	Smith J 30 + 2	Cahoon D 9 + 4	Bell R 9 + 5	George D 22	Harty I 30 + 2	Blaikie A 28 + 4	McMartin G 14 + 3	Walker P 8 + 12	Jenkins A 17 + 8	Johnstone D 17 + 6	Wright F 19 + 5	Young J 9 + 13	Watson P 19 + 5	Duthie M 4	Roddie A 9	Ronald P 17 + 2	Macdonald W 14	Ramsay D 4	Abbott S — + 2	Feroz C 2	Blair P 8 + 3	Mitchell A — + 1	Edgar S 3 + 6	Smith D 3 + 1	Match No.
1	2	3	4	5	6[2]	7[1]	8	9	10[3]	11	12	13	14															1
1	5	3	4[2]	2	6[3]		8	9	10	7	12	14	13	11[1]														2
1	6	3	4	2	12		8	9[2]	10[1]	11	13	14	5			7[3]												3
1	4	3		2	8[2]		6	11[3]	9[1]	7	12	13	5	10	14													4
1	7	3	4[1]	2	6[2]		8	9[3]	11	10		13	12	14		5												5
1	2			5			6	8		7		10	11	9[1]		3	12	4										6
1	7		4	2			8	9[2]		10		11	12	6		5[1]	13	3										7
1	6		4	2			10[2]	7	14	11[3]	5	12	8	13		9[1]		3										8
1	5		4	2			7	6	10[2]	9[1]	11	12	8	13				3										9
1	5		4	2			6	10[2]	12	7	11[1]		8	14	13	3[3]		9										10
1	2		4[2]	5			6	11	3[1]	8	13	9	7			10		12										11
1	3		4[1]	2			5[3]	7	14	11	9[2]	6	12	8		10		13										12
1	4	3		2			13	8[2]	9[1]	14	5	6	12	11					10[3]	7								13
1	4	3[2]		2			14	8[3]	9		5	6[1]	12	13	11				10	7								14
1	4			2	12		5	8[3]	11	14	3	9	13	6					10[2]	7[1]								15
1	4			2			5	9[2]	11	13	3	6	12	8[1]					10	7								16
1	4			2			7[1]	9	11	12	8	6[2]	13	5					10	3								17
1	4			2				9	11[1]	7	6	3	10	8					5	12								18
1	4			2				9	6[1]	10	8	3	12	11					7	5								19
1	3			5				9	12	11[1]	7[2]	2	13	6					10	8	4							20
1	8			2				9[1]	12	7	14	5	4	11					10[2]	6				3[3]	13			21
1	5			2	3			9	11		6	12	4	10					8					7[1]				22
1	2			14	12			6[1]	10	13	5	3	4	11					8					9[2]	7[3]			23
1	6	5						11	9[3]	12	8[2]	2	3[1]	13		4			10	7			14					24
1	2			4	5			8	9[1]	11	12	3		10					6					7				25
1	2			4	5			8	9	11	13	12	14	3					10[2]	6[1]				7[3]				26
1	3			4	2			6	9	7	12	8[1]		13		5			10							11[2]		27
1	2			4[2]	13	12		5[1]	9	11	8	3		6					14					7		10[3]		28
1	3	13		2			12	9	10[2]	5[1]		6	11	8					4					7[3]		14		29
1	2			4			7[2]	9	11	8[1]	6	5		10					3					12		13		30
1	2			4[3]			8	9	11	6[2]	5	13		10[1]					3	12			14	7				31
1	2			4[2]	14		7	6[3]	9	11	8	5		13					10[1]	3				12				32
1	5			4[1]	2		14	9	7[2]	8[3]	3	6		12					10							13	11	33
1	6			4	2		8	9	5	11	3		10					12							7[1]		34
1	8			4[1]	2		11	9	5	6	3		10					7[2]							12	13	35
1	8	3		2			6[1]	9	12	5	4		7					11							10		36

ELGIN CITY Third Division

Year Formed: 1893. *Ground and Address:* Borough Briggs, Borough Briggs Road, Elgin IV30 1AP.
Telephone: 01343 551114. *Fax:* 01343 547921.
Ground Capacity: 6500, seated 470. *Size of pitch:* 110yd × 75yd.
Chairman: Dennis J. Miller. *General Manager:* Harry McFadden. *Secretary:* John A. Milton.
Manager: Alex Caldwell. *Coach:* Neil MacLennan. *Physio:* Maurice O'Donnell. *Club Nickname(s):* City or Black &
Whites. *Previous Grounds:* Association Park, Milnfield Park, Station Park, Cooper Park.
Record Attendance: 12,608 v Arbroath, Scottish Cup, 17 Feb 1968.
Record Victory: 18-1 v Brora Rangers, North of Scotland Cup, 6 Feb 1960.
Record Defeat: 1-14 v Hearts, Scottish Cup, 4 Feb 1939.
Record Transfer Fee received: £32,000 for Michael Teasdale to Dundee, Jan 1994.

Honours
Scottish Cup, Quarter Finals 1968.
Highland League Champions: winners 14 times.
Scottish Qualifying Cup (North): winners 7 times.
North of Scotland Cup: winners 17 times.
Club colours: Shirt: Black and White vertical stripes; Shorts: Black; Stockings: Black.

PETERHEAD Third Division

Year Formed: 1891. *Ground and Address:* Balmoor Stadium, Lord Catto Park, Peterhead AB42 1EU.
Telephone: 01779 478256. *Fax:* 01779 490682. *Ground Capacity:* 3250, seated 1000.
Chairman: Roger Taylor. *General Manager:* Dave Watson. *Secretary:* George Moore.
Team Manager: Ian Wilson. *Assistant Manager:* Alan Lyons. *Physio:* Sandy Rennie.
Managers since 1975: C. Grant, D. Darcy, I. Taylor, J. Harper, D. Smith, J. Hamilton, G. Adams, J. Guyan, I. Wilson,
D. Watson, R. Brown, D. Watson, I. Wilson. *Club Nickname(s):* Blue Toon. *Previous Grounds:* Recreation Park.
Record Attendance: 6310 friendly v Celtic, 1948.
Record Victory: 17-0 v Fort William, 1998-99.
Record Defeat: 0-13 v Aberdeen, Scottish Cup 1923-24.

Honours
Highland League Champions: winners 5 times.
Scottish Qualifying Cup (North): winners 6 times.
North of Scotland Cup: winners 5 times.
Aberdeenshire Cup: winners 20 times.
Club colours: Shirt: Blue and White; Shorts: White; Stockings: Blue.

SCOTTISH LEAGUE TABLES 1999–2000

Premier Division

	P	Home W	D	L	Goals F	A	Away W	D	L	Goals F	A	Pts	GD
Rangers	36	16	1	1	52	12	12	5	1	44	14	90	70
Celtic	36	12	3	3	58	17	9	3	6	32	21	69	52
Hearts	36	7	6	5	25	18	8	3	7	22	22	54	7
Motherwell	36	8	3	7	27	34	6	7	5	22	29	52	−14
St Johnstone	36	5	7	6	16	18	5	5	7	20	26	42	−8
Hibernian	36	7	6	5	30	27	3	5	10	19	34	41	−12
Dundee	36	4	3	11	20	33	8	2	8	25	31	41	−19
Dundee U	36	6	4	8	16	22	5	2	10	18	35	39	−23
Kilmarnock	36	5	5	8	16	22	3	8	7	22	30	37	−14
Aberdeen	36	6	4	8	28	37	3	2	13	16	46	33	−39

First Division

	P	Home W	D	L	Goals F	A	Away W	D	L	Goals F	A	Pts	GD
St Mirren	36	12	3	3	42	19	11	4	3	33	20	76	36
Dunfermline Ath	36	10	7	1	34	13	10	4	4	32	20	71	33
Falkirk	36	11	2	5	38	23	9	6	3	29	17	68	27
Livingston	36	9	5	4	29	17	10	2	6	31	28	64	15
Raith R	36	11	3	4	35	21	6	5	7	20	19	59	15
Inverness CT	36	7	6	5	34	25	6	4	8	26	30	49	5
Ayr U	36	6	3	9	25	24	4	5	9	17	28	38	−10
Greenock Morton	36	7	3	8	22	23	3	3	12	23	38	36	−16
Airdrieonians	36	4	5	9	15	26	3	3	12	14	43	29	−40
Clydebank	36	1	3	14	11	40	0	4	14	6	42	10	−65

Second Division

	P	Home W	D	L	Goals F	A	Away W	D	L	Goals F	A	Pts	GD
Clyde	36	12	5	1	35	7	6	6	6	30	30	65	28
Alloa Ath	36	11	5	2	36	18	6	8	4	22	20	64	20
Ross Co	36	9	5	4	31	20	9	3	6	26	19	62	18
Arbroath	36	6	7	5	28	26	5	7	6	24	29	47	−3
Partick T	36	7	5	6	25	22	5	5	8	17	22	46	−2
Stranraer	36	6	8	4	25	22	3	10	5	22	24	45	1
Stirling Albion	36	7	4	7	34	33	4	3	11	26	39	40	−12
Stenhousemuir	36	6	4	8	24	26	4	4	10	20	33	38	−15
Queen of the S	36	5	6	7	24	32	3	3	12	21	43	33	−30
Hamilton A*	36	5	7	6	18	23	5	7	6	21	21	29	−5

*deducted 15 points for failing to field a team

Third Division

	P	Home W	D	L	Goals F	A	Away W	D	L	Goals F	A	Pts	GD
Queen's Park	36	11	2	5	28	20	9	7	2	26	17	69	17
Berwick R	36	7	6	5	20	14	12	3	3	33	16	66	23
Forfar Ath	36	10	5	3	39	18	7	5	6	25	22	61	24
East Fife	36	9	6	3	24	16	8	2	8	21	23	59	6
Cowdenbeath	36	6	5	7	30	23	9	4	5	29	20	54	16
Dumbarton	36	7	7	4	26	22	8	1	9	27	29	53	2
East Stirlingshire	36	6	2	10	15	27	5	5	8	13	23	40	−22
Brechin C	36	6	3	9	25	25	4	5	9	17	26	38	−9
Montrose	36	5	2	11	19	31	5	5	8	20	23	37	−15
Albion R	36	2	3	13	13	35	3	4	11	20	40	22	−42

SCOTTISH LEAGUE HONOURS 1890 to 2000

*On goal average (ratio)/difference.   †Held jointly after indecisive play-off.   ‡Won on deciding match.
††Held jointly.   ¶Two points deducted for fielding ineligible player.
Competition suspended 1940–45 during war; Regional Leagues operating.   ‡‡Two points deducted for registration
irregularities.

PREMIER LEAGUE

Maximum points: 108

	First	Pts	Second	Pts	Third	Pts
1998–99	Rangers	77	Celtic	71	St Johnstone	57
1999–2000	Rangers	90	Celtic	69	Hearts	54

PREMIER DIVISION

Maximum points: 72

	First	Pts	Second	Pts	Third	Pts
1975–76	Rangers	54	Celtic	48	Hibernian	43
1976–77	Celtic	55	Rangers	46	Aberdeen	43
1977–78	Rangers	55	Aberdeen	53	Dundee U	40
1978–79	Celtic	48	Rangers	45	Dundee U	44
1979–80	Aberdeen	48	Celtic	47	St Mirren	42
1980–81	Celtic	56	Aberdeen	49	Rangers*	44
1981–82	Celtic	55	Aberdeen	53	Rangers	43
1982–83	Dundee U	56	Celtic*	55	Aberdeen	55
1983–84	Aberdeen	57	Celtic	50	Dundee U	47
1984–85	Aberdeen	59	Celtic	52	Dundee U	47
1985–86	Celtic*	50	Hearts	50	Dundee U	47

Maximum points: 88

1986–87	Rangers	69	Celtic	63	Dundee U	60
1987–88	Celtic	72	Hearts	62	Rangers	60

Maximum points: 72

1988–89	Rangers	56	Aberdeen	50	Celtic	46
1989–90	Rangers	51	Aberdeen*	44	Hearts	44
1990–91	Rangers	55	Aberdeen	53	Celtic*	41

Maximum points: 88

1991–92	Rangers	72	Hearts	63	Celtic	62
1992–93	Rangers	73	Aberdeen	64	Celtic	60
1993–94	Rangers	58	Aberdeen	55	Motherwell	54

Maximum points: 108

1994–95	Rangers	69	Motherwell	54	Hibernian	53
1995–96	Rangers	87	Celtic	83	Aberdeen*	55
1996–97	Rangers	80	Celtic	75	Dundee U	60
1997–98	Celtic	74	Rangers	72	Hearts	67

FIRST DIVISION

Maximum points: 52

1975–76	Partick T	41	Kilmarnock	35	Montrose	30

Maximum points: 78

1976–77	St Mirren	62	Clydebank	58	Dundee	51
1977–78	Morton*	58	Hearts	58	Dundee	57
1978–79	Dundee	55	Kilmarnock*	54	Clydebank	54
1979–80	Hearts	53	Airdrieonians	51	Ayr U*	44
1980–81	Hibernian	57	Dundee	52	St Johnstone	51
1981–82	Motherwell	61	Kilmarnock	51	Hearts	50
1982–83	St Johnstone	55	Hearts	54	Clydebank	50
1983–84	Morton	54	Dumbarton	51	Partick T	46
1984–85	Motherwell	50	Clydebank	48	Falkirk	45
1985–86	Hamilton A	56	Falkirk	45	Kilmarnock	44

Maximum points: 88

1986–87	Morton	57	Dunfermline Ath	56	Dumbarton	53
1987–88	Hamilton A	56	Meadowbank T	52	Clydebank	49

Maximum points: 78

1988–89	Dunfermline Ath	54	Falkirk	52	Clydebank	48
1989–90	St Johnstone	58	Airdrieonians	54	Clydebank	44
1990–91	Falkirk	54	Airdrieonians	53	Dundee	52

Maximum points: 88

1991–92	Dundee	58	Partick T*	57	Hamilton A	57
1992–93	Raith R	65	Kilmarnock	54	Dunfermline Ath	52
1993–94	Falkirk	66	Dunfermline Ath	65	Airdrieonians	54

Maximum points: 108

1994–95	Raith R	69	Dunfermline Ath*	68	Dundee	68
1995–96	Dunfermline Ath	71	Dundee U*	67	Morton	67
1996–97	St Johnstone	80	Airdrieonians	60	Dundee*	58
1997–98	Dundee	70	Falkirk	65	Raith R*	60
1998–99	Hibernian	89	Falkirk	66	Ayr U	62
1999–2000	St Mirren	76	Dunfermline Ath	71	Falkirk	68

SECOND DIVISION

Maximum points: 52

	First	Pts	Second	Pts	Third	Pts
1975–76	Clydebank*	40	Raith R	40	Alloa	35

Maximum points: 78

	First	Pts	Second	Pts	Third	Pts
1976–77	Stirling A	55	Alloa	51	Dunfermline Ath	50
1977–78	Clyde*	53	Raith R	53	Dunfermline Ath	48
1978–79	Berwick R	54	Dunfermline Ath	52	Falkirk	50
1979–80	Falkirk	50	East Stirling	49	Forfar Ath	46
1980–81	Queen's Park	50	Queen of the S	46	Cowdenbeath	45
1981–82	Clyde	59	Alloa*	50	Arbroath	50
1982–83	Brechin C	55	Meadowbank T	54	Arbroath	49
1983–84	Forfar Ath	63	East Fife	47	Berwick R	43
1984–85	Montrose	53	Alloa	50	Dunfermline Ath	49
1985–86	Dunfermline Ath	57	Queen of the S	55	Meadowbank T	49
1986–87	Meadowbank T	55	Raith R*	52	Stirling A*	52
1987–88	Ayr U	61	St Johnstone	59	Queen's Park	51
1988–89	Albion R	50	Alloa	45	Brechin C	43
1989–90	Brechin C	49	Kilmarnock	48	Stirling A	47
1990–91	Stirling A	54	Montrose	46	Cowdenbeath	45
1991–92	Dumbarton	52	Cowdenbeath	51	Alloa	50
1992–93	Clyde	54	Brechin C*	53	Stranraer	53
1993–94	Stranraer	56	Berwick R	48	Stenhousemuir*	47

Maximum points: 108

	First	Pts	Second	Pts	Third	Pts
1994–95	Morton	64	Dumbarton	60	Stirling A	58
1995–96	Stirling A	81	East Fife	67	Berwick R	60
1996–97	Ayr U	77	Hamilton A	74	Livingston	64
1997–98	Stranraer	61	Clydebank	60	Livingston	59
1998–99	Livingston	77	Inverness CT	72	Clyde	53
1999–2000	Clyde	65	Alloa Ath	64	Ross Co	62

THIRD DIVISION

Maximum points: 108

	First	Pts	Second	Pts	Third	Pts
1994–95	Forfar Ath	80	Montrose	67	Ross Co	60
1995–96	Livingston	72	Brechin C	63	Caledonian T	57
1996–97	Inverness CT	76	Forfar Ath*	67	Ross Co	67
1997–98	Alloa Ath	76	Arbroath	68	Ross Co	67
1998–99	Ross Co	77	Stenhousemuir	64	Brechin C	59
1999–2000	Queen's Park	69	Berwick R	66	Forfar Ath	61

FIRST DIVISION to 1974–75

Maximum points: a 36; b 44; c 40; d 52; e 60; f 68; g 76; h 84.

	First	Pts	Second	Pts	Third	Pts
1890–91*a*	Dumbarton††	29	Rangers††	29	Celtic	21
1891–92*b*	Dumbarton	37	Celtic	35	Hearts	34
1892–93*a*	Celtic	29	Rangers	28	St Mirren	20
1893–94*a*	Celtic	29	Hearts	26	St Bernard's	23
1894–95*a*	Hearts	31	Celtic	26	Rangers	22
1895–96*a*	Celtic	30	Rangers	26	Hibernian	24
1896–97*a*	Hearts	28	Hibernian	26	Rangers	25
1897–98*a*	Celtic	33	Rangers	29	Hibernian	22
1898–99*a*	Rangers	36	Hearts	26	Celtic	24
1899–1900*a*	Rangers	32	Celtic	25	Hibernian	24
1900–01*c*	Rangers	35	Celtic	29	Hibernian	25
1901–02*a*	Rangers	28	Celtic	26	Hearts	22
1902–03*b*	Hibernian	37	Dundee	31	Rangers	29
1903–04*d*	Third Lanark	43	Hearts	39	Celtic*	38
1904–05*d*	Celtic‡	41	Rangers	41	Third Lanark	35
1905–06*e*	Celtic	49	Hearts	43	Airdrieonians	38
1906–07*f*	Celtic	55	Dundee	48	Rangers	45
1907–08*f*	Celtic	55	Falkirk	51	Rangers	50
1908–09*f*	Celtic	51	Dundee	50	Clyde	48
1909–10*f*	Celtic	54	Falkirk	52	Rangers	46
1910–11*f*	Rangers	52	Aberdeen	48	Falkirk	44
1911–12*f*	Rangers	51	Celtic	45	Clyde	42
1912–13*f*	Rangers	53	Celtic	49	Hearts*	41
1913–14*g*	Celtic	65	Rangers	59	Hearts*	54
1914–15*g*	Celtic	65	Hearts	61	Rangers	50
1915–16*g*	Celtic	67	Rangers	56	Morton	51
1916–17*g*	Celtic	64	Morton	54	Rangers	53
1917–18*f*	Rangers	56	Celtic	55	Kilmarnock*	43
1918–19*f*	Celtic	58	Rangers	57	Morton	47
1919–20*h*	Rangers	71	Celtic	68	Motherwell	57
1920–21*h*	Rangers	76	Celtic	66	Hearts	50
1921–22*h*	Celtic	67	Rangers	66	Raith R	51
1922–23*g*	Rangers	55	Airdrieonians	50	Celtic	46
1923–24*g*	Rangers	59	Airdrieonians	50	Celtic	46
1924–25*g*	Rangers	60	Airdrieonians	57	Hibernian	52
1925–26*g*	Celtic	58	Airdrieonians*	50	Hearts	50
1926–27*g*	Rangers	56	Motherwell	51	Celtic	49

	First	Pts	Second	Pts	Third	Pts
1927–28g	Rangers	60	Celtic*	55	Motherwell	55
1928–29g	Rangers	67	Celtic	51	Motherwell	50
1929–30g	Rangers	60	Motherwell	55	Aberdeen	53
1930–31g	Rangers	60	Celtic	58	Motherwell	56
1931–32g	Motherwell	66	Rangers	61	Celtic	48
1932–33g	Rangers	62	Motherwell	59	Hearts	50
1933–34g	Rangers	66	Motherwell	62	Celtic	47
1934–35g	Rangers	55	Celtic	52	Hearts	50
1935–36g	Celtic	66	Rangers*	61	Aberdeen	61
1936–37g	Rangers	61	Aberdeen	54	Celtic	52
1937–38g	Celtic	61	Hearts	58	Rangers	49
1938–39g	Rangers	59	Celtic	48	Aberdeen	46
1946–47e	Rangers	46	Hibernian	44	Aberdeen	39
1947–48e	Hibernian	48	Rangers	46	Partick T	36
1948–49e	Rangers	46	Dundee	45	Hibernian	39
1949–50e	Rangers	50	Hibernian	49	Hearts	43
1950–51e	Hibernian	48	Rangers*	38	Dundee	38
1951–52e	Hibernian	45	Rangers	41	East Fife	37
1952–53e	Rangers*	43	Hibernian	43	East Fife	39
1953–54e	Celtic	43	Hearts	38	Partick T	35
1954–55e	Aberdeen	49	Celtic	46	Rangers	41
1955–56f	Rangers	52	Aberdeen	46	Hearts*	45
1956–57f	Rangers	55	Hearts	53	Kilmarnock	42
1957–58f	Hearts	62	Rangers	49	Celtic	46
1958–59f	Rangers	50	Hearts	48	Motherwell	44
1959–60f	Hearts	54	Kilmarnock	50	Rangers*	42
1960–61f	Rangers	51	Kilmarnock	50	Third Lanark	42
1961–62f	Dundee	54	Rangers	51	Celtic	46
1962–63f	Rangers	57	Kilmarnock	48	Partick T	46
1963–64f	Rangers	55	Kilmarnock	49	Celtic*	47
1964–65f	Kilmarnock*	50	Hearts	50	Dunfermline Ath	49
1965–66f	Celtic	57	Rangers	55	Kilmarnock	45
1966–67f	Celtic	58	Rangers	55	Clyde	46
1967–68f	Celtic	63	Rangers	61	Hibernian	45
1968–69f	Celtic	54	Rangers	49	Dunfermline Ath	45
1969–70f	Celtic	57	Rangers	45	Hibernian	44
1970–71f	Celtic	56	Aberdeen	54	St Johnstone	44
1971–72f	Celtic	60	Aberdeen	50	Rangers	44
1972–73f	Celtic	57	Rangers	56	Hibernian	45
1973–74f	Celtic	53	Hibernian	49	Rangers	48
1974–75f	Rangers	56	Hibernian	49	Celtic	45

SECOND DIVISION to 1974–75

Maximum points: a 76; b 72; c 68; d 52; e 60; f 36; g 44.

	First	Pts	Second	Pts	Third	Pts
1893–94f	Hibernian	29	Cowlairs	27	Clyde	24
1894–95f	Hibernian	30	Motherwell	22	Port Glasgow	20
1895–96f	Abercorn	27	Leith Ath	23	Renton	21
1896–97f	Partick T	31	Leith Ath	27	Kilmarnock*	21
1897–98f	Kilmarnock	29	Port Glasgow	25	Morton	22
1898–99f	Kilmarnock	32	Leith Ath	27	Port Glasgow	25
1899–1900f	Partick T	29	Morton	28	Port Glasgow	20
1900–01f	St Bernard's	25	Airdrieonians	23	Abercorn	21
1901–02g	Port Glasgow	32	Partick T	31	Motherwell	26
1902–03g	Airdrieonians	35	Motherwell	28	Ayr U*	27
1903–04g	Hamilton A	37	Clyde	29	Ayr U	28
1904–05g	Clyde	32	Falkirk	28	Hamilton A	27
1905–06g	Leith Ath	34	Clyde	31	Albion R	27
1906–07g	St Bernard's	32	Vale of Leven*	27	Arthurlie	27
1907–08g	Raith R	30	Dumbarton*‡‡	27	Ayr U	27
1908–09g	Abercorn	31	Raith R*	28	Vale of Leven	28
1909–10g	Leith Ath‡	33	Raith R	33	St Bernard's	27
1910–11g	Dumbarton	31	Ayr U	27	Albion R	25
1911–12g	Ayr U	35	Abercorn	30	Dumbarton	27
1912–13d	Ayr U	34	Dunfermline Ath	33	East Stirling	32
1913–14g	Cowdenbeath	31	Albion R	27	Dunfermline Ath*	26
1914–15d	Cowdenbeath*	37	St Bernard's*	37	Leith Ath	37
1921–22a	Alloa	60	Cowdenbeath	47	Armadale	45
1922–23a	Queen's Park	57	Clydebank¶	50	St Johnstone¶	45
1923–24a	St Johnstone	56	Cowdenbeath	55	Bathgate	44
1924–25a	Dundee U	50	Clydebank	48	Clyde	47
1925–26a	Dunfermline Ath	59	Clyde	53	Ayr U	52
1926–27a	Bo'ness	56	Raith R	49	Clydebank	45
1927–28a	Ayr U	54	Third Lanark	45	King's Park	44
1928–29b	Dundee U	51	Morton	50	Arbroath	47
1929–30a	Leith Ath*	57	East Fife	57	Albion R	54
1930–31a	Third Lanark	61	Dundee U	50	Dunfermline Ath	47
1931–32a	East Stirling*	55	St Johnstone	55	Raith R*	46
1932–33c	Hibernian	54	Queen of the S	49	Dunfermline Ath	47

	First	Pts	Second	Pts	Third	Pts
1933–34c	Albion R	45	Dunfermline Ath*	44	Arbroath	44
1934–35c	Third Lanark	52	Arbroath	50	St Bernard's	47
1935–36c	Falkirk	59	St Mirren	52	Morton	48
1936–37c	Ayr U	54	Morton	51	St Bernard's	48
1937–38c	Raith R	59	Albion R	48	Airdrieonians	47
1938–39c	Cowdenbeath	60	Alloa*	48	East Fife	48
1946–47d	Dundee	45	Airdrieonians	42	East Fife	31
1947–48e	East Fife	53	Albion R	42	Hamilton A	40
1948–49e	Raith R*	42	Stirling A	42	Airdrieonians*	41
1949–50e	Morton	47	Airdrieonians	44	Dunfermline Ath*	36
1950–51e	Queen of the S*	45	Stirling A	45	Ayr U*	36
1951–52e	Clyde	44	Falkirk	43	Ayr U	39
1952–53e	Stirling A	44	Hamilton A	43	Queen's Park	37
1953–54e	Motherwell	45	Kilmarnock	42	Third Lanark*	36
1954–55e	Airdrieonians	46	Dunfermline Ath	42	Hamilton A	39
1955–56b	Queen's Park	54	Ayr U	51	St Johnstone	49
1956–57b	Clyde	64	Third Lanark	51	Cowdenbeath	45
1957–58b	Stirling A	55	Dunfermline Ath	53	Arbroath	47
1958–59b	Ayr U	60	Arbroath	51	Stenhousemuir	46
1959–60b	St Johnstone	53	Dundee U	50	Queen of the S	49
1960–61b	Stirling A	55	Falkirk	54	Stenhousemuir	50
1961–62b	Clyde	54	Queen of the S	53	Morton	44
1962–63b	St Johnstone	55	East Stirling	49	Morton	48
1963–64b	Morton	67	Clyde	53	Arbroath	46
1964–65b	Stirling A	59	Hamilton A	50	Queen of the S	45
1965–66b	Ayr U	53	Airdrieonians	50	Queen of the S	47
1966–67a	Morton	69	Raith R	58	Arbroath	57
1967–68b	St Mirren	62	Arbroath	53	East Fife	49
1968–69b	Motherwell	64	Ayr U	53	East Fife*	48
1969–70b	Falkirk	56	Cowdenbeath	55	Queen of the S	50
1970–71b	Partick T	56	East Fife	51	Arbroath	46
1971–72b	Dumbarton*	52	Arbroath	52	Stirling A	50
1972–73b	Clyde	56	Dumfermline Ath	52	Raith R*	47
1973–74b	Airdrieonians	60	Kilmarnock	58	Hamilton A	55
1974–75a	Falkirk	54	Queen of the S*	53	Montrose	53

Elected to First Division: 1894 Clyde; 1895 Hibernian; 1896 Abercorn; 1897 Partick T; 1899 Kilmarnock; 1900 Morton and Partick T; 1902 Port Glasgow and Partick T; 1903 Airdrieonians and Motherwell; 1905 Falkirk and Aberdeen; 1906 Clyde and Hamilton A; 1910 Raith R; 1913 Ayr U and Dumbarton.

RELEGATED FROM PREMIER LEAGUE

1998–99 Dunfermline Ath
1999–2000 *No relegation due to League reorganization*

RELEGATED FROM PREMIER DIVISION

1974–75 *No relegation due to League reorganization*
1975–76 Dundee, St Johnstone
1976–77 Hearts, Kilmarnock
1977–78 Ayr U, Clydebank
1978–79 Hearts, Motherwell
1979–80 Dundee, Hibernian
1980–81 Kilmarnock, Hearts
1981–82 Partick T, Airdrieonians
1982–83 Morton, Kilmarnock
1983–84 St Johnstone, Motherwell
1984–85 Dumbarton, Morton
1985–86 *No relegation due to League reorganization*
1986–87 Clydebank, Hamilton A
1987–88 Falkirk, Dunfermline Ath, Morton
1988–89 Hamilton A
1989–90 Dundee
1990–91 *None*
1991–92 St Mirren, Dunfermline Ath
1992–93 Falkirk, Airdrieonians
1993–94 *See footnote*
1994–95 Dundee U
1995–96 Partick T, Falkirk
1996–97 Raith R
1997–98 Hibernian

RELEGATED FROM DIVISION 1

1974–75 *No relegation due to League reorganization*
1975–76 Dunfermline Ath, Clyde
1976–77 Raith R, Falkirk
1977–78 Alloa Ath, East Fife
1978–79 Montrose, Queen of the S
1979–80 Arbroath, Clyde
1980–81 Stirling A, Berwick R
1981–82 East Stirling, Queen of the S
1982–83 Dunfermline Ath, Queen's Park
1983–84 Raith R, Alloa
1984–85 Meadowbank T, St Johnstone
1985–86 Ayr U, Alloa
1986–87 Brechin C, Montrose
1987–88 East Fife, Dumbarton
1988–89 Kilmarnock, Queen of the S
1989–90 Albion R, Alloa
1990–91 Clyde, Brechin C
1991–92 Montrose, Forfar Ath
1992–93 Meadowbank T, Cowdenbeath
1993–94 *See footnote*
1994–95 Ayr U, Stranraer
1995–96 Hamilton A, Dumbarton
1996–97 Clydebank, East Fife
1997–98 Partick T, Stirling A
1998–99 Hamilton A, Stranraer
1999–2000 Clydebank

RELEGATED FROM DIVISION 2

1994–95 Meadowbank T, Brechin C
1995–96 Forfar Ath, Montrose
1996–97 Dumbarton, Berwick R

1997–98 Stenhousemuir, Brechin C
1998–99 East Fife, Forfar Ath
1999–2000 Hamilton A**

RELEGATED FROM DIVISION 1 (TO 1973–74)

1921–22 *Queen's Park, Dumbarton, Clydebank	1951–52 Morton, Stirling A
1922–23 Albion R, Alloa Ath	1952–53 Motherwell, Third Lanark
1923–24 Clyde, Clydebank	1953–54 Airdrieonians, Hamilton A
1924–25 Third Lanark, Ayr U	1954–55 *No clubs relegated*
1925–26 Raith R, Clydebank	1955–56 Stirling A, Clyde
1926–27 Morton, Dundee U	1956–57 Dunfermline Ath, Ayr U
1927–28 Dunfermline Ath, Bo'ness	1957–58 East Fife, Queen's Park
1928–29 Third Lanark, Raith R	1958–59 Queen of the S, Falkirk
1929–30 St Johnstone, Dundee U	1959–60 Arbroath, Stirling A
1930–31 Hibernian, East Fife	1960–61 Ayr U, Clyde
1931–32 Dundee U, Leith Ath	1961–62 St Johnstone, Stirling A
1932–33 Morton, East Stirling	1962–63 Clyde, Raith R
1933–34 Third Lanark, Cowdenbeath	1963–64 Queen of the S, East Stirling
1934–35 St Mirren, Falkirk	1964–65 Airdrieonians, Third Lanark
1935–36 Airdrieonians, Ayr U	1965–66 Morton, Hamilton A
1936–37 Dunfermline Ath, Albion R	1966–67 St Mirren, Ayr U
1937–38 Dundee, Morton	1967–68 Motherwell, Stirling A
1938–39 Queen's Park, Raith R	1968–69 Falkirk, Arbroath
1946–47 Kilmarnock, Hamilton A	1969–70 Raith R, Partick T
1947–48 Airdrieonians, Queen's Park	1970–71 St Mirren, Cowdenbeath
1948–49 Morton, Albion R	1971–72 Clyde, Dunfermline Ath
1949–50 Queen of the S, Stirling A	1972–73 Kilmarnock, Airdrieonians
1950–51 Clyde, Falkirk	1973–74 East Fife, Falkirk

*Season 1921–22 – only 1 club promoted, 3 clubs relegated. ***15pts deducted for failing to field a team.*

Scottish League championship wins: Rangers 49, Celtic 36, Aberdeen 4, Hearts 4, Hibernian 4, Dumbarton 2, Dundee 1, Dundee U 1, Kilmarnock 1, Motherwell 1, Third Lanark 1.

At the end of the 1993–94 season four divisions were created assisted by the admission of two new clubs Ross County and Caledonian Thistle. Only one club was promoted from Division 1 and Division 2. The three relegated from the Premier joined with teams finishing second to seventh in Division 1 to form the new Division 1. Five relegated from Division 1 combined with those who finished second to sixth to form a new Division 2 and the bottom eight in Division 2 linked with the two newcomers to form a new Division 3. At the end of the 1997–98 season the nine clubs remaining in the Premier Division plus the promoted team from Division 1 formed a breakaway Premier League. At the end of the 1999–2000 season two teams were added to the Scottish League. There was no relegation from the Premier League but two promoted from the First Division and three from each of the Second and Third Divisions. One team was relegated from the First Division and one from the Second Division, leaving 12 teams in each division.

Scotland's national team pose before the Euro 2000 match with England. A 2-0 home defeat was followed by a 1-0 Scots win at Wembley. (ASP)

SCOTTISH LEAGUE CUP FINALS 1946–2000

Season	Winners	Runners-up	Score
1946–47	Rangers	Aberdeen	4-0
1947–48	East Fife	Falkirk	4-1 after 0-0 draw
1948–49	Rangers	Raith R	2-0
1949–50	East Fife	Dunfermline Ath	3-0
1950–51	Motherwell	Hibernian	3-0
1951–52	Dundee	Rangers	3-2
1952–53	Dundee	Kilmarnock	2-0
1953–54	East Fife	Partick T	3-2
1954–55	Hearts	Motherwell	4-2
1955–56	Aberdeen	St Mirren	2-1
1956–57	Celtic	Partick T	3-0 after 0-0 draw
1957–58	Celtic	Rangers	7-1
1958–59	Hearts	Partick T	5-1
1959–60	Hearts	Third Lanark	2-1
1960–61	Rangers	Kilmarnock	2-0
1961–62	Rangers	Hearts	3-1 after 1-1 draw
1962–63	Hearts	Kilmarnock	1-0
1963–64	Rangers	Morton	5-0
1964–65	Rangers	Celtic	2-1
1965–66	Celtic	Rangers	2-1
1966–67	Celtic	Rangers	1-0
1967–68	Celtic	Dundee	5-3
1968–69	Celtic	Hibernian	6-2
1969–70	Celtic	St Johnstone	1-0
1970–71	Rangers	Celtic	1-0
1971–72	Partick T	Celtic	4-1
1972–73	Hibernian	Celtic	2-1
1973–74	Dundee	Celtic	1-0
1974–75	Celtic	Hibernian	6-3
1975–76	Rangers	Celtic	1-0
1976–77	Aberdeen	Celtic	2-1
1977–78	Rangers	Celtic	2-1
1978–79	Rangers	Aberdeen	2-1
1979–80	Dundee U	Aberdeen	3-0 after 0-0 draw
1980–81	Dundee U	Dundee	3-0
1981–82	Rangers	Dundee U	2-1
1982–83	Celtic	Rangers	2-1
1983–84	Rangers	Celtic	3-2
1984–85	Rangers	Dundee U	1-0
1985–86	Aberdeen	Hibernian	3-0
1986–87	Rangers	Celtic	2-1
1987–88	Rangers	Aberdeen	3-3
		(Rangers won 5-3 on penalties)	
1988–89	Rangers	Aberdeen	3-2
1989–90	Aberdeen	Rangers	2-1
1990–91	Rangers	Celtic	2-1
1991–92	Hibernian	Dunfermline Ath	2-0
1992–93	Rangers	Aberdeen	2-1
1993–94	Rangers	Hibernian	2-1
1994–95	Raith R	Celtic	2-2
		(Raith R won 6-5 on penalties)	
1995–96	Aberdeen	Dundee	2-0
1996–97	Rangers	Hearts	4-3
1997–98	Celtic	Dundee U	3-0
1998–99	Rangers	St Johnstone	2-1
1999–2000	Celtic	Aberdeen	2-0

SCOTTISH LEAGUE CUP WINS

Rangers 21, Celtic 11, Aberdeen 5, Hearts 4, Dundee 3, East Fife 3, Dundee U 2, Hibernian 2, Motherwell 1, Partick T 1, Raith R 1.

APPEARANCES IN FINALS

Rangers 27, Celtic 23, Aberdeen 12, Hibernian 7, Dundee 6, Hearts 6, Dundee U 5, Partick T 4, East Fife 3, Kilmarnock 3, Dunfermline Ath 2, Motherwell 2, Raith R 2, St Johnstone 2, Falkirk 1, Morton 1, St Mirren 1, Third Lanark 1.

CIS SCOTTISH LEAGUE CUP 1999–2000

FIRST ROUND

31 JUL

Albion R (0) 0
Clyde (0) 3 *(Carrigan 99, Farrell 118, Murray 120)* 576
Albion R: McLean; Greenock (McBride), McGowan N, McStay, Duncan, McLees (Diack), Russell, Tait, Nesovic, Flannigan, Rae.
Clyde: Wylie; Mitchell, Cranmer, Spittal, Smith, Keogh (Farrell), Convery (Murray), McLay, Martin McLaughlan (Carrigan), McCusker, Barrett.
aet

Brechin C (0) 0
Dumbarton (0) 2 *(Flannery 49, 77)* 346
Brechin C: Geddes; Boylan (Durie), Smith, Cairney, Bain, Brown, Coulston (Dickson), Riley, Sorbie, Kerrigan (Dailly), Campbell.
Dumbarton: Meechan; Dickie, Brittain, Bruce, Jack, King, Melvin W (McHarg), Grace, Flannery, Brown, Robertson (Ward).

Clydebank (0) 1 *(Stewart 57)*
East Stirling (1) 2 *(Muirhead 34, Higgins 74 (pen))* 69
Clydebank: Scott; Wishart, Stewart, Murdoch (O'Neill), McLaughlin, Oliver, McKinstrey, McIntyre (Ewing), McKelvie (McCall), Gardner, McWilliams.
East Stirling: Butter; Storrar (Gordon), Brown, Ross, Bowsher, Muirhead, Barr, Hardie (Ferguson), Laidlaw, Higgins, Elliot (Russell).

Cowdenbeath (0) 0
Livingston (0) 2 *(Britton 17, 24)* 655
Cowdenbeath: Godfrey; Wilson, McMillan (Thomson), Berry (White), McCulloch, Snedden, Winter, Bradley, Stewart, Simpson, Burns (Brown).
Livingston: McCaldon; Kelly, Deas (Macdonald), Watson, Coughlan, Millar J, McCormick, Millar M, Britton (Keith), Bingham, Little.

East Fife (0) 2 *(Agostini 88, Kirk 115)*
Stirling Albion (0) 2 *(Graham 54 (pen), Wood 118)* 631
East Fife: McCulloch; Munro, Ramsay (Kirk), Mackay, Agostini, Herd, Robertson, Martin (Tinley), Wright, Logan, Grattan.
Stirling Albion: Gow; Paterson, Tortolano, Donald, Martin, Wood, McQuade (Mortimer), Aitken (Bell), Graham, Taggart, Gardner.
aet (East Fife won 8-7 on penalties)

Montrose (0) 1 *(O'Driscoll 55)*
Hamilton A (1) 2 *(Henderson D 16, 80)* 327
Montrose: McGlynn; Mailer, Scott, Farnan, Paterson, Craib, Duffy (Shand), Robertson (Stevenson), Taylor, O'Driscoll, Meldrum.
Hamilton A: Reid; Martin, Cunnington, Miller, MacLaren, Thomson, Muir (Henderson N), Davidson, Moore (McCormick), McFarlane, Henderson D.

Partick T (0) 0
Alloa Ath (0) 2 *(McKechnie 77, 80)* 2143
Partick T: Arthur; Duncan, McKeown, Montgomerie, Brannigan, Archibald, Paton (Newall), Craig, Miller, Docherty, English (Dallas).
Alloa Ath: Cairns; Boyle, Clark, McAneny, Beaton, Valentine, Wilson, Menelaws (McKechnie), Cameron, Irvine, Donaghy (Nelson).

Queen of the S (0) 1 *(Bailey 106)*
Arbroath (0) 0 986
Queen of the S: Hillcoat J; Lilley, Kerr, Rowe, Aitken, Cleeland (Adam S), Harvey, Leslie, Bailey (Robison), Mallan, Boyle (Findlay).
Arbroath: Hinchcliffe; McAulay, Florence, Arbuckle, Thomson J (Peters), Crawford, Mercer, Bryce (Devine), McGlashan, Brownlie (Cooper), Gallagher.
aet

Queen's Park (0) 2 *(McGoldrick 53, Brown 78)*
Berwick R (1) 1 *(Patterson 29)* 390
Queen's Park: Inglis; Ferry, Geoghegan, Caven, Martin, McFarlane, Connell, Orr (Whelan), Edgar, Brown, McGoldrick.
Berwick R: O'Connor; McNicoll (Leask), Haddow, Ritchie, Neill A, Neil M, Hunter, Anthony, Forrester (Campbell), Patterson (Watt), Magee.

Ross Co (1) 2 *(Irvine 39, Shaw 117 (pen))*
Forfar Ath (1) 1 *(MacDonald 23)* 1115
Ross Co: Walker; Tully, McBain, Maxwell, Irvine, Gilbert, Escalon (Geraghty), McGlashan, Shaw, Ferguson (Finlayson), Kinnaird (Fraser).
Forfar Ath: Moffat; McCheyne, Donaldson, Morris (Nairn), Rattray, McPhee, McLean, Taylor, Brand, Cargill, MacDonald (McIlravey).
aet

Stenhousemuir (0) 1 *(Mooney 79)*
Inverness CT (2) 3 *(McLean 1, 12, Wilson 68)* 528
Stenhousemuir: Hamilton L; Lawrence, Gibson, Armstrong (Banks), Graham, Davidson, Lorimer, Fisher, Watters (Mooney), Cummings (McKinnon), Wood.
Inverness CT: Fridge; Tokely, Golabek, Teasdale, Mann, McCulloch, Wilson, Stewart (Christie), McLean, Sheerin (Robson), Hastings (Glancy).

Stranraer (0) 0
Raith R (0) 1 *(Black 114)* 622
Stranraer: McGeown; Knox, Black, Furphy, Smith, George, McMartin, Bell, Harty, Blaikie (Walker), Wright (Jenkins).
Raith R: Van De Kamp; Hamilton, McCulloch, Andrews (Browne), Gaughan, Black, McEwan, Agnew, Tosh P (Shields) (Kirkwood), Burns, Stein.
aet

SECOND ROUND

17 AUG

Aberdeen (0) 1 *(Gillies 59)*
Livingston (0) 0 6756
Aberdeen: Preece; Smith, Anderson, Whyte, Dow, Gillies (Kiriakov), Pepper, Mayer (Hart), Mackie, Winters, Derek Young (Jess).
Livingston: McCaldon; Kelly, Deas, McManus, Coughlan, Millar J (Fleming), King (Robertson), Millar M, Britton, Bingham, Keith (McPhee).

Ayr U (0) 2 *(Reynolds 85, Bone 89)*
Hamilton A (0) 1 *(Henderson D 68)* 1789
Ayr U: Gill; Prenderville, Rogers, Duffy, Wilson (Robertson), Craig, Reynolds, Davies, Bone, Teale, Lyons (Lindau).
Hamilton A: Reid; Martin, Cunnington, Henderson N, MacLaren, Thomson, Renicks (Moore), Davidson, McCormick, McAulay (Kelly), Henderson D.

Clyde (2) 2 *(Woods 14, Carrigan 31)*
Hibernian (2) 2 *(McGinlay 8, Hartley 15)* 2008
Clyde: Wylie; Murray, Cranmer, Spittal, Smith, Keogh, Convery, Mark McLaughlin (Martin McLauchlan), Woods (Ross), McCusker (Craib), Carrigan.
Hibernian: Colgan; Smith, Lovering, Hughes, Marenkov (Jack), Skinner, Lovell, McGinlay, Crawford, Hartley (Miller), Lehmann (Latapy).
aet (Hibernian won 5-4 on penalties)

Dundee (3) 4 *(Boyack 17, 90, Falconer 31, 35)*
Dumbarton (0) 0 2675

Dundee: Douglas; Smith, Miller (Van Eijs), Tweed, Sharp, Robertson (McSkimming), Boyack, Rae, Yeats (Raeside), Annand, Falconer.
Dumbarton: Meechan K; Dickie, Brittain, Bruce, Jack, King, Melvin W (McHarg), Grace (Dillon), Flannery, Brown, Robertson (Melvin M).

East Fife (1) 2 *(Logan 45, Robertson 53 (pen))*
Airdrieonians (1) 2 *(McCormick 21, 49)* 741

East Fife: McCulloch; Munro, Love, Ramsay (Gibb), Cusick, Herd, Robertson, Mackay, McGrillen, Moffat (Wright), Logan (Honeyman).
Airdrieonians: Thomson; Farrell G, Jack, Forrest, Farrell D, Stewart (Conway), Moore (Ingram), Dick, Evans (McGuire), McCormick, Johnston.
aet (East Fife won 5-4 on penalties)

Inverness CT (0) 2 *(Sheerin 104 (pen), Byers 119)*
St Mirren (0) 0 1238

Inverness CT: Fridge; Tokely (Byers), Golabek, Hastings, Mann, McCulloch, Teasdale (Robson), Bavidge, McLean (Stewart), Christie, Sheerin.
St Mirren: Roy; Nicolson, Kerr, Turner (Baltacha), McLaughlin, Walker, Murray (Brown), Ross, Lavety, Mendes (McGarry), Yardley.
aet

Morton (1) 1 *(Curran 45)*
Alloa Ath (2) 3 *(Irvine 23, 68, Cameron 43)* 747

Morton: Maxwell; Murie (McDonald), Archdeacon, Millen, Anderson D, Anderson J, Curran, Matheson, Ferguson (Hawke), Thomas, McPherson.
Alloa Ath: Cairns; Boyle, Clark D, Nelson, Beaton, Valentine, Sharpe, Menelaws (Clark G), Cameron, Irvine, Donaghy.

18 AUG

Dundee U (1) 3 *(Ferraz 28, Thompson 113, 119)*
Ross Co (1) 1 *(Escalon 41)* 4673

Dundee U: Combe; Pascual, Partridge, De Vos, Worrell (Easton), Skoldmark, Davidson (Mathie), Hannah, Paterson J, Dodds, Ferraz (Thompson).
Ross Co: Walker; Tully, McBain, Maxwell, Irvine, Gilbert, Shaw, McGlashan, Finlayson (Geraghty), Escalon (Fraser), Ferguson (Wood).
aet

Dunfermline Ath (3) 4 *(Coyle 20, 39, Petrie 43, Smith 81)*
Queen's Park (0) 0 2546

Dunfermline Ath: Westwater; Shields, Dair, Tod, Reid (Ireland), Dolan, French (McGroarty) (Nish), May, Smith, Coyle, Petrie.
Queen's Park: Inglis; Ferry, Connaghan, Caven, Martin, McFarlane, Whelan (Geoghegan), Orr (Edgar), Gallagher (Carmichael), Brown, McGoldrick.

East Stirling (0) 0
Falkirk (0) 2 *(Crabbe 100, Bowsher (og) 102)* 1201

East Stirling: Butter; Storrar, Russell, Brown, Bowsher, Muirhead, Ferguson (Gordon), Hardie, Laidlaw, Higgins, Donnelly (Barr).
Falkirk: Hogarth; Rennie, McQuilken, Lawrie, Sinclair, McKenzie, McDonald (Seaton), Coyne (Nicholls), Crabbe, Moss, Hutchison (Hagen).
aet

Queen of the S (1) 1 *(Leslie 17)*
Hearts (0) 3 *(Jackson 46, 82, Severin 75)* 4633

Queen of the S: Hillcoat; Lilley, Kerr, Rowe, Aitken, Cleeland, Harvey (Findlay), Leslie, Adams (Bailey), Mallan, Caldwell.
Hearts: Rousset; Pressley, Naysmith, James, Ritchie, Locke, Severin, Cameron, Makel (Fulton), Juanjo (Jackson), McSwegan (Quitongo).

Raith R (0) 2 *(Burns 75, Dargo 85)*
Motherwell (1) 2 *(Browne (og) 5, Halliday 71)* 2393

Raith R: Van De Kamp; McEwan, Ellis, Andrews, Browne, Black (Hamilton), Tosh P, Tosh S (Agnew), Clark (Dargo), Burns, Stein.
Motherwell: Goram; Doesburg, McMillan, McGowan, Thomas, Townsley (Halliday), Brannan, Nevin (Nicholas), Adams, Spencer, Goodman.
aet (Motherwell won 5-4 on penalties)

THIRD ROUND

12 OCT

Aberdeen (0) 1 *(Lawrie (og) 49)*
Falkirk (0) 1 *(Crabbe 57)* 8166

Aberdeen: Preece; Perry, Anderson, Solberg, Buchan, Dow, Mayer (Derek Young), Jess, Gillies (McAllister), Hamilton (Hart), Winters.
Falkirk: Hogarth; McKenzie, McQuilken, Lawrie, Sinclair, Nicholls, McAllister (McDonald), Coyne, Crabbe, Hutchison, Hagen (Seaton).
aet (Aberdeen won 5-3 on penalties)

Alloa Ath (1) 1 *(Cameron 1)*
Dundee (2) 3 *(Falconer 20, 52, Grady 40)* 1344

Alloa Ath: Cairns; Boyle, Clark D, Clark G (Sharp), Beaton, Valentine, Bannerman (Menelaws), Wilson (Donaghy), Cameron, Irvine, Christie.
Dundee: Douglas; Smith, Miller, Tweed, Maddison, McSkimming, Boyack, Rae (Robertson), Grady, Annand, Falconer.

East Fife (0) 0
Hearts (1) 2 *(Cameron 41, Holmes 89)* 3337

East Fife: McCulloch; Shannon, Love, Cusick (Ramsay), Agostini, Herd, Logan (Honeyman), Forrest, Robertson, Moffat (Kirk), Mackay.
Hearts: Rousset; Pressley, McKinnon, Leclercq, Ritchie, Severin, Fulton (Holmes), Cameron, Floegel, McSwegan (Wales), Jackson.

Inverness CT (0) 0
Motherwell (0) 1 *(McCulloch 47)* 2195

Inverness CT: Fridge; Tokely, Hastings, Teasdale, McCulloch, Sheerin, Wilson, Glancy, Wyness, Christie, Golabek (Byers).
Motherwell: Goram; Doesburg, McMillan, Teale, Thomas, Townsley (Goodman), Brannan, Valakari, Nevin, Spencer (Halliday), McCulloch.

Kilmarnock (2) 3 *(McCoist 18, 26, Vareille 75)*
Hibernian (1) 2 *(McGinlay 40, Miller 80)* 6837

Kilmarnock: Meldrum (Mahood); MacPherson, Baker, McGowne, Dindeleux, Reilly, Holt, Durrant, Vareille (Cocard), Mitchell, McCoist (Jeffrey).
Hibernian: Colgan; Renwick, Lovering, Dennis, Jack (Dempsie M), Sauzee, Brebner, Latapy, McGinlay, Paatelainen, Miller (Lehmann).

Rangers (1) 1 *(Wallace 24)*
Dunfermline Ath (0) 0 30,024

Rangers: Brown; Adamczuk, Moore, Amoruso, Vidmar, Kanchelskis, McInnes, Albertz, Johansson (Mols), Wallace, Amato (Porrini).
Dunfermline Ath: Westwater; Thomson, Dair, Potter, Reid, Dolan (McGroarty), Graham, French, Smith (May), Coyle, Petrie.

St Johnstone (0) 1 *(Griffin 65)*
Dundee U (0) 2 *(Davidson 56, Telesnikov 87)* 4806

St Johnstone: Main; McQuillan, Bollan, Griffin, Kernaghan, O'Halloran, Simao (McMahon), Kane, Dasovic, O'Neil, Lowndes.
Dundee U: Combe; Pascual, Partridge, De Vos, Venetis, Bove (Davidson), Telesnikov, Hannah, Paterson J (Malpas), Dodds, Thompson (Ferraz).

13 OCT

Ayr U (0) 0

Celtic (0) 4 *(Viduka 58, Blinker 65, Mjallby 71, Petta 88)*
8421

Ayr U: Nelson; Robertson, Rogers, Duffy, Campbell, Craig (Teale), Hurst, Davies, Shepherd, Jemson (Reynolds), Wilson.
Celtic: Gould; Riseth, Mjallby, Stubbs, McNamara, Tebily, Burley (Wieghorst), Blinker, Moravcik (Petta), Viduka, Burchill.

QUARTER-FINALS

1 DEC

Aberdeen (0) 1 *(Dow 117)*

Rangers (0) 0   11,380

Aberdeen: Leighton; Cobian (Perry), McAllister, Whyte, Anderson, Dow, Bernard, Jess (Rutkiewicz), Guntweit (Belabed), Winters, Stavrum.
Rangers: Myhre; Wilson, Amoruso, Numan, Nicholson (Penttila), Kanchelskis, Ferguson B, Van Bronckhorst, McCann, Johansson (Carson), Durie (Ferguson I).
aet

Celtic (0) 1 *(Wieghorst 90)*

Dundee (0) 0   38,922

Celtic: Gould; Riseth (Burchill), Stubbs, Tebily, Mahe, McNamara, Mjallby, Wieghorst, Moravcik, Wright (Petrov), Viduka.
Dundee: Douglas; Smith, Van Eijs, Tweed, Wilkie, Sharp (Robertson), Boyack, Rae, Billio (Grady), Annand (Banger), Falconer.

Dundee U (2) 3 *(Dodds 26, Easton 43, Thompson 84)*

Motherwell (0) 2 *(Townsley 54, Teale 87)*   5086

Dundee U: Combe; Pascual, Partridge, De Vos, Worrall, Davidson (Ferraz), Telesnikov, Hannah, Easton, Dodds, Thompson (Malpas).
Motherwell: Woods; Doesburg, McMillan, Teale, Kemble, Townsley, Brannan, Valakari, Twaddle (Nevin), Halliday (Spencer), Goodman.

2 FEB

Kilmarnock (0) 1 *(Jeffrey 79)*

Hearts (0) 0   6648

Kilmarnock: Meldrum; MacPherson, Baker, Lauchlan, Dindeleux, Reilly, Holt, Durrant, Mahood (Bagan), Vareille (Burke), Jeffrey.
Hearts: Niemi; Pressley, Naysmith, Petric, Leclercq (Simpson), Murray, Fulton, Cameron, McSwegan, Wales, Jackson (Juanjo).

SEMI-FINALS

13 FEB

Aberdeen (0) 1 *(Stavrum 78)*

Dundee U (0) 0   9500

Aberdeen: Leighton; Solberg, McAllister, Whyte, Anderson, Dow, Bernard, Guntweit, Winters (Rutkiewicz), Zerouali (Belabed), Stavrum.
Dundee U: Combe; Pascual, Partridge, Malpas, Patterson, Telesnikov (Venetis), Preget (McConalogue), Hannah, Easton, Ferraz (Mathie), Thompson.

16 FEB

Celtic (0) 1 *(Moravcik 68)*

Kilmarnock (0) 0   22,926

Celtic: Kharine; Boyd, Riseth, Stubbs, Mahe, McNamara, Mjallby, Tebily, Moravcik, Burchill (Healy), Viduka.
Kilmarnock: Meldrum; MacPherson, McKinlay, Lauchlan, Dindeleux, Reilly, Holt, Durrant (Jeffrey), Mitchell (Bagan), McCutcheon (Burke), Cocard.

FINAL AT HAMPDEN PARK

19 MAR

Celtic (1) 2 *(Riseth 11, Johnson 58)*

Aberdeen (0) 0   50,073

Celtic: Gould; Boyd, Riseth, Mjallby, Mahe, McNamara, Wieghorst, Petrov, Moravcik (Stubbs), Johnson (Berkovic), Viduka.
Aberdeen: Leighton; Perry, McAllister, Solberg, Anderson, Dow, Bernard, Jess (Mayer), Guntweit (Belabed), Zerouali (Winters), Stavrum.
Referee: K. W. Clark (Paisley)

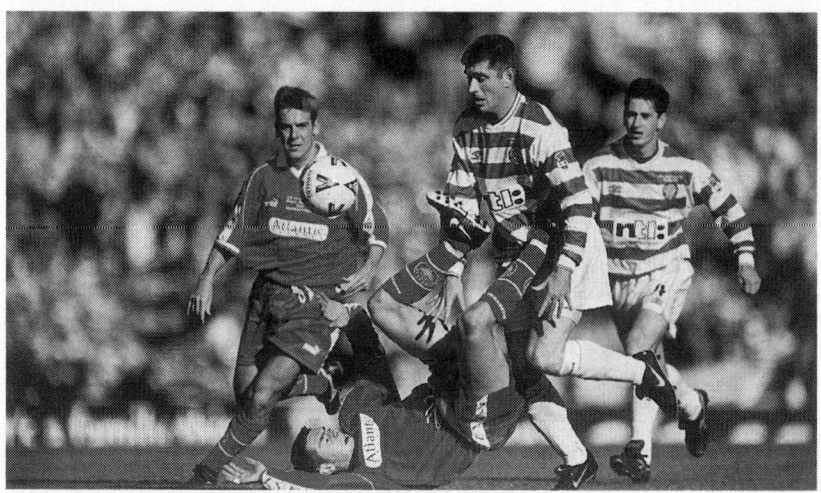

The hooped shirted Tommy Johnson in action for Celtic in the League Cup Final against Aberdeen. (Actionimages)

BELL'S CHALLENGE CUP 1999–2000

FIRST ROUND

10 AUG

Airdrieonians (1) 2 *(Moore 11, 56)*
Dumbarton (0) 1 *(Dillon 75 (pen))* 826
Airdrieonians: Thomson; Farrell G, Stewart, Farrell D, Conway, Johnston, Moore (McGuire), Dick, Evans, McCormick, McCann.
Dumbarton: Barnes; Dickie, Brittain, Bruce, Jack (Dillon), King, McHarg, Grace, Flannery, Brown (Smith), Ward (Melvin M).

Arbroath (0) 3 *(McGlashan 74, Mercer 88, Brownlie 89)*
East Fife (1) 2 *(Robertson 30, Wright 90)* 553
Arbroath: Hinchcliffe; Florence, Gallagher, McAulay, Arbuckle (Thomson), Crawford, Sellars, Bryce (Peters), McGlashan, Devine (Brownlie), Mercer.
East Fife: McCulloch; Shannon, Gibb, Ramsay, Cusick, Herd, Robertson, Logan, Honeyman (Wright), McGrillen, Mackay.

Ayr U (0) 0
Raith R (0) 1 *(Clark 88)* 1881
Ayr U: Nelson; Robertson, Rogers, Duffy, Traynor (Scally), Wilson, Hurst, Davies, Lindau (Bradford), Teale (Bone), Lennon.
Raith R: Van De Kamp; McEwan, Ellis, Andrews, Browne, Tosh S, Kirkwood, Agnew, Shields P (Shields D), Clark (McCulloch), Hetherston.

Berwick R (1) 4 *(Neil M 25, Leask 50, Neill A 56, Patterson 64)*
Queen of the S (0) 1 *(Adams 82)* 336
Berwick R: O'Connor; McNicoll (Humphries), Haddow, Rafferty, Neill A, Ritchie, Anthony, Patterson (Quinn), Neil M (Hunter), Smith, Leask.
Queen of the S: Hillcoat; Lilley, Kerr, Rowe, Aitken, Findlay (Cleeland), Harvey, Leslie, Bailey (Adams), Mallan, Boyle (Strain).

Brechin C (0) 0
Queen's Park (0) 1 *(Brown 48)* 224
Brechin C: Geddes; Christie, Smith, Cairney, Bain, Dailly, Dickson (Kerrigan), Price, Sorbie, Hutcheon, Coulston (Durie).
Queen's Park: Inglis; Sinclair, Connaghan, Caven, Martin, McFarlane, Connell, Orr (Whelan) (Edgar), Gallagher, Brown, McGoldrick.

Clyde (0) 0
Ross Co (2) 4 *(Fraser 17, Geraghty 33, Irvine 64, Shaw 81)* 586
Clyde: Wylie; Keogh, Mark McLaughlin, Spittal, Smith, Mitchell (Barrett), Convery, McLay, Carrigan, Ross, Martin McLauchlan (Craib).
Ross Co: Walker; Tully, McBain, Maxwell, Irvine, Fraser, Shaw, McGlashan, Geraghty (Finlayson), Escalon, Kinnaird (Gilbert).

Cowdenbeath (0) 0
Alloa Ath (3) 4 *(Cameron 4, Beaton 21, McKechnie 26, Snedden 49 (og))* 206
Cowdenbeath: Godfrey; Wilson, Thomson, Snedden, McCulloch, White, Perry (McDowall), Bradley, Stewart, Brown (McMillan), Burns.
Alloa Ath: Cairns; Boyle, Clark D, McAneny, Beaton, Valentine, Nelson (Bovill), McKechnie, Cameron (Sharp), Irvine, Donnachy (Clark G).

Dunfermline Ath (0) 2 *(Coyle 75, 84)*
Morton (2) 2 *(Hawke 28, Thomas 43)* 2892
Dunfermline Ath: Westwater; Shields, McGroarty, Tod, Reid, Dolan, Thomson, May (French), Smith, Coyle, Petrie (Graham).

Morton: Maxwell; Murie, McDonald (McPherson), Millen, Anderson D, Fenwick (Matheson), Curran, Anderson J, Ferguson, Thomas, Hawke (Aitken).
aet. Morton won 5-4 on penalties

East Stirling (0) 1 *(Hardie 76)*
Clydebank (0) 2 *(McLaughlin 79, Cormack 113)* 227
East Stirling: Butter; Storrar, Russell, Ross, Bowsher, Muirhead, Barr (Brown) (McDonald), Hardie, Laidlaw, Higgins, Elliot (Ferguson).
Clydebank: Scott; Wishart, Stewart (Cormack), Murdoch, McLaughlin, Oliver, McKinstrey, McIntyre (Morrison), Miller, Gardner, McKelvie (Ewing).
aet

Inverness CT (0) 1 *(Teasdale 88)*
St Mirren (0) 0 1343
Inverness CT: Fridge; Tokely, Golabek, Hastings, Mann, McCulloch, Teasdale, Stewart (Glancy), McLean, Christie, Sheerin (Robson).
St Mirren: Roy; Nicolson, Kerr, Turner, Baltacha, McLaughlin, Murray, Drew (Mendes), McGarry (Lavety), Brown, Yardley.

Montrose (0) 1 *(Taylor 80 (pen))*
Hamilton A (1) 3 *(Moore 35, Henderson N 55 (pen), McCormick 74)* 224
Montrose: McGlynn; Clark, Scott, Farnan (Stevenson), Paterson, Craib, Duffy, Bennett, Taylor, O'Driscoll, Meldrum (McWilliam).
Hamilton A: Reid; MacLaren, Cunnington, Henderson N, Gaughan, Thomson, Muir (Russell), Davidson (Bonar), Moore, McCormick, Henderson D (Lynn).

Partick T (0) 0
Albion R (1) 2 *(Rae 28, Tait 85)* 1231
Partick T: Budinaukas; Duncan, McKeown (English), Montgomerie, Brannigan, Archibald, Paton (Dallas), Craig, Miller (McGuiness), McAllister, Dunn.
Albion R: McLean; Greenock (McLees), McGowan, McStay, Duncan, Silvestro, Russell, Tait, Nesovic (Diack), Lumsden, Rae.

Stirling Albion (0) 2 *(Paterson 54 (pen), Gardner 91)*
Stenhousemuir (0) 2 *(Hamilton R 80, Watters 119)* 412
Stirling Albion: Gardiner; Paterson, Tortolano, Donald, Martin, Wood, McQuade, Mortimer (Bell), Aitken (McCallion), Taggart, Gardner (Philliben).
Stenhousemuir: Hamilton L; Lawrence, Banks, Davidson (Gibson), Graham, Fisher (Lorimer) (Cummings), Mooney, Hamilton R, Watters, McKinnon, Wood.
aet. Stirling Albion won 6-5 on penalties.

Stranraer (2) 2 *(Blaikie 7, 15)*
Falkirk (0) 2 *(McDonald 53, Lawrie 90)* 362
Stranraer: McGeown; Smith, Knox, Furphy, Johnstone, Black (Walker), McMartin, Cahoon (Jenkins), Harty, Blaikie, George.
Falkirk: Hogarth; Rennie, McQuilken, Lawrie, Sinclair, McKenzie, McStay (Deuchar), McDonald, Crabbe, Hutchison, Hagen.
aet. Stranraer won 5-4 on penalties.

SECOND ROUND

24 AUG

Airdrieonians (0) 1 *(Johnston 90)*
Alloa Ath (1) 2 *(Nelson 45, Little 49)* 765
Airdrieonians: Thomson; McClelland (Johnston), Farrell G, Jack, Forrest, Stewart, Moore (McKeown), Dick (Taylor), Ingram, McCormick, McCann.
Alloa Ath: Cairns; Boyle, Sharp, Nelson, Beaton, Valentine, Little, McKechnie (Clark), Cameron, Irvine, Donaghy.

Clydebank (3) 4 *(Ewing 20, 26, 58, McWilliams 32)*
Forfar Ath (2) 3 *(Christie 12, Milne 15, 84)* 179
Clydebank: Scott; Wishart, Cormack (Stewart), McWilliams (Murdoch), McLaughlin, Oliver, McKinstrey, Ewing (McKelvie), Miller, Gardner, Cameron.
Forfar Ath: Garden; Rattray, Donaldson, Ferguson (McCheyne), Johnston (Brand), Craig, MacDonald (McPhee), Taylor, Milne, Nairn, Christie.

Hamilton A (0) 0
Inverness CT (1) 3 *(Stewart 41, 59, McLean 84)* 298
Hamilton A: Reid; Martin (Muir), Cunnington, Kelly, Gaughan, Thomson, Renicks, Davidson (Moore), McCormick, Henderson N, Henderson D.
Inverness CT: Fridge; McCulloch, Hastings, Teasdale, Mann, Sheerin, Byers (Wilson), McLean, Stewart, Christie, Golabek.

Livingston (0) 2 *(Bingham 65, 104)*
Berwick R (1) 1 *(Patterson 27)* 1384
Livingston: McCaldon; Kelly, Deas, McManus, Sweeney, Millar J (King), McPhee, Macdonald, Britton (McCormick), Bingham, Fleming (Robertson).
Berwick R: O'Connor; Rafferty, Haddow, Hunter (Leask), Neill A, Ritchie, Patterson, Anthony (Humphreys), Smith (Watt), Neil M, Magee.
aet

Queen's Park (2) 3 *(Gallagher 22, 35, Whelan 73)*
Albion R (0) 1 *(Tait 68)* 480
Queen's Park: Inglis; Ferry, Connaghan, Caven (Sinclair), Martin, MacFarlane, Connell, Whelan, Gallagher (Orr), Carroll (Little), McGoldrick.
Albion R: McLean; Robertson (Rae), McBride (Harty), McStay, Duncan, Coulter (Silvestro), McLees, Tait, Nesovic, Lumsden, Diack.

Ross Co (1) 3 *(Irvine 22, Shaw 69, Wood 88)*
Morton (0) 0 1030
Ross Co: Walker; Canning, McBain, Maxwell, Irvine, Gilbert, Shaw, Fraser (Geraghty), Wood, Ferguson, Ross.
Morton: Carlin; Murie, Archdeacon (McPherson), Millen, Anderson D, Anderson J, Curran, Aitken, Ferguson (Wright), Hawke, Matheson.

Stirling Albion (1) 1 *(Graham 18)*
Arbroath (1) 1 *(McGlashan 42)* 427
Stirling Albion: Gardiner; Paterson, Tortolano, Donald, Martin, Wood, McQuade (Philliben), Aitken (Bell (McCallion)), Graham, Taggart, Mortimer.
Arbroath: Hinchcliffe; Florence, Gallagher, McAulay, Webster, Crawford, Cooper, Bryce (Thomson), McGlashan, Devine (Evans), Sellars.
aet (Stirling Albion won 4-3 on penalties.)

Stranraer (0) 1 *(Knox 47)*
Raith R (1) 2 *(Andrews 32, Dargo 89)* 351
Stranraer: McGeown; Smith, Black, Furphy (Jenkins), Johnstone, Knox, McMartin, George, Young, Cahoon, Harty (Walker).
Raith R: Coyle; McCulloch (Hamilton), Kirkwood, Andrews, Browne, Black (Tosh S), Tosh P, Agnew, Dargo, Clark, Hetherston (Stein).

QUARTER-FINALS

14 SEPT

Inverness CT (1) 2 *(Glancy 19, Robson 65)*
Clydebank (0) 0 635
Inverness CT: Fridge; Tokely, Hastings, Teasdale, Mann, McCulloch, Wilson (Byers), Glancy (Christie), Bavidge (Shearer), Robson, Sheerin.

Clydebank: Scott; Wishart, Stewart (Cormack), Murdoch (Cameron), McLaughlin, Oliver, McKinstrey, McIntyre, Miller, Gardner, Roddie (Ewing).

Livingston (2) 3 *(McPhee 1, Britton 29, Millar M 89)*
Raith R (1) 1 *(McManus (og) 30)* 2233
Livingston: McCaldon; Kelly, Deas, McManus, Sweeney, Millar J, King (Bingham), Millar M, Britton (McCormick), McPhee, McCann (Fleming).
Raith R: Van De Kamp; McEwan, Kirkwood (Shields), Andrews, Browne, Hamilton, Tosh P (Agathe), Tosh S, Dargo, Burns, Stein.

Ross Co (1) 1 *(Shaw 41)*
Alloa Ath (0) 2 *(Donaghy 82, Irvine 113)* 948
Ross Co: Walker; Canning, Fraser, Maxwell, Irvine, Gilbert, Shaw, Escalon, Wood (Ross), Ferguson (Finlayson), Kinnaird (McBain).
Alloa Ath: Cairns; Sharp (Boyle), Clark D, Nelson, Beaton, Valentine, Menelaws, Christie (Clark G), Cameron, McKechnie (Irvine), Donaghy.
aet

Stirling Albion (1) 4 *(Gardner 27, Aitken 53, Graham 68, Wood 75)*
Queen's Park (0) 0 535
Stirling Albion: Gardiner; Paterson, McCallion, Donald (Philliben), Martin, Wood, McQuade (Mortimer), Aitken (Bell), Graham, Taggart, Gardner.
Queen's Park: Inglis; Sinclair (Ferry), Connaghan, Caven, Borland, McFarlane, Connell, Whelan (Orr), Gallacher, Brown, Carroll (Little).

SEMI-FINALS

28 SEPT

Inverness CT (0) 1 *(Sheerin 89)*
Livingston (0) 0 1025
Inverness CT: Fridge; Tokely, Hastings, Teasdale, McCulloch, Byers, Wilson (Bavidge), McLean, Wyness, Christie (Golabek), Sheerin.
Livingston: McCaldon; Kelly, Deas, McManus, Coughlan, Sweeney, King (Britton), Millar M, Feroz (McCormick), McPhee, Fleming (McKinnon).

Stirling Albion (1) 1 *(McQuade 38)*
Alloa Ath (0) 2 *(Bannerman 75, Irvine 80 (pen))* 877
Stirling Albion: Gardiner; Paterson, Tortolano, Donald, Martin, Wood, McQuade, Mortimer (Aitken), Graham, Taggart, Gardner (McCallion).
Alloa Ath: Cairns; Boyle, Sharp, Nelson, Beaton, Valentine, Bannerman, Wilson, Cameron, Irvine, Christie (Clark G).

FINAL at Shyberry Excelsior Stadium, Airdrie

21 NOV

Alloa Ath (0) 4 *(Clark G 19, Wilson 34, Cameron 48, 103)*
Inverness CT (1) 4 *(Wilson 28, Sheerin 46, 53, 110)* 4047
Alloa Ath: Cairns; Boyle, Clark D, McAneny, Beaton, Valentine, Little, Clark G (Christie), Cameron, Irvine, Wilson (McKechnie).
Inverness CT: Fridge; Tokely, Hastings, Teasdale, McCulloch, Sheerin, Wilson, Xausa (Glancy), Wyness (Bavidge), Christie, Golabek (Byres).
aet (Alloa Ath won 5-4 on penalties)
Referee: Jim McCluskey

SCOTTISH CUP FINALS 1874–2000

Year	Winners	Runners-up	Score
1874	Queen's Park	Clydesdale	2-0
1875	Queen's Park	Renton	3-0
1876	Queen's Park	Third Lanark	2-0 after 1-1 draw
1877	Vale of Leven	Rangers	3-2 after 0-0 and 1-1 draws
1878	Vale of Leven	Third Lanark	1-0
1879	Vale of Leven*	Rangers	
1880	Queen's Park	Thornlibank	3-0
1881	Queen's Park†	Dumbarton	3-1
1882	Queen's Park	Dumbarton	4-1 after 2-2 draw
1883	Dumbarton	Vale of Leven	2-1 after 2-2 draw
1884	Queen's Park‡	Vale of Leven	
1885	Renton	Vale of Leven	3-1 after 0-0 draw
1886	Queen's Park	Renton	3-1
1887	Hibernian	Dumbarton	2-1
1888	Renton	Cambuslang	6-1
1889	Third Lanark§	Celtic	2-1
1890	Queen's Park	Vale of Leven	2-1 after 1-1 draw
1891	Hearts	Dumbarton	1-0
1892	Celtic¶	Queen's Park	5-1
1893	Queen's Park	Celtic	2-1
1894	Rangers	Celtic	3-1
1895	St Bernard's	Renton	2-1
1896	Hearts	Hibernian	3-1
1897	Rangers	Dumbarton	5-1
1898	Rangers	Kilmarnock	2-0
1899	Celtic	Rangers	2-0
1900	Celtic	Queen's Park	4-3
1901	Hearts	Celtic	4-3
1902	Hibernian	Celtic	1-0
1903	Rangers	Hearts	2-0 after 1-1 and 0-0 draws
1904	Celtic	Rangers	3-2
1905	Third Lanark	Rangers	3-1 after 0-0 draw
1906	Hearts	Third Lanark	1-0
1907	Celtic	Hearts	3-0
1908	Celtic	St Mirren	5-1
1909	••		
1910	Dundee	Clyde	2-1 after 2-2 and 0-0 draws
1911	Celtic	Hamilton A	2-0 after 0-0 draw
1912	Celtic	Clyde	2-0
1913	Falkirk	Raith R	2-0
1914	Celtic	Hibernian	4-1 after 0-0 draw
1920	Kilmarnock	Albion R	3-2
1921	Partick T	Rangers	1-0
1922	Morton	Rangers	1-0
1923	Celtic	Hibernian	1-0
1924	Airdrieonians	Hibernian	2-0
1925	Celtic	Dundee	2-1
1926	St Mirren	Celtic	2-0
1927	Celtic	East Fife	3-1
1928	Rangers	Celtic	4-0
1929	Kilmarnock	Rangers	2-0
1930	Rangers	Partick T	2-1 after 0-0 draw
1931	Celtic	Motherwell	4-2 after 2-2 draw
1932	Rangers	Kilmarnock	3-0 after 1-1 draw
1933	Celtic	Motherwell	1-0
1934	Rangers	St Mirren	5-0
1935	Rangers	Hamilton A	2-1
1936	Rangers	Third Lanark	1-0
1937	Celtic	Aberdeen	2-1
1938	East Fife	Kilmarnock	4-2 after 1-1 draw
1939	Clyde	Motherwell	4-0
1947	Aberdeen	Hibernian	2-1
1948	Rangers	Morton	1-0 after 1-1 draw
1949	Rangers	Clyde	4-1
1950	Rangers	East Fife	3-0
1951	Celtic	Motherwell	1-0
1952	Motherwell	Dundee	4-0
1953	Rangers	Aberdeen	1-0 after 1-1 draw
1954	Celtic	Aberdeen	2-1
1955	Clyde	Celtic	1-0 after 1-1 draw
1956	Hearts	Celtic	3-1
1957	Falkirk	Kilmarnock	2-1 after 1-1 draw
1958	Clyde	Hibernian	1-0
1959	St Mirren	Aberdeen	3-1
1960	Rangers	Kilmarnock	2-0
1961	Dunfermline Ath	Celtic	2-0 after 0-0 draw
1962	Rangers	St Mirren	2-0
1963	Rangers	Celtic	3-0 after 1-1 draw
1964	Rangers	Dundee	3-1
1965	Celtic	Dunfermline Ath	3-2
1966	Rangers	Celtic	1-0 after 0-0 draw

Year	Winners	Runners-up	Score
1967	Celtic	Aberdeen	2-0
1968	Dunfermline Ath	Hearts	3-1
1969	Celtic	Rangers	4-0
1970	Aberdeen	Celtic	3-1
1971	Celtic	Rangers	2-1 after 1-1 draw
1972	Celtic	Hibernian	6-1
1973	Rangers	Celtic	3-2
1974	Celtic	Dundee U	3-0
1975	Celtic	Airdrieonians	3-1
1976	Rangers	Hearts	3-1
1977	Celtic	Rangers	1-0
1978	Rangers	Aberdeen	2-1
1979	Rangers	Hibernian	3-2 after 0-0 and 0-0 draws
1980	Celtic	Rangers	1-0
1981	Rangers	Dundee U	4-1 after 0-0 draw
1982	Aberdeen	Rangers	4-1 (aet)
1983	Aberdeen	Rangers	1-0 (aet)
1984	Aberdeen	Celtic	2-1 (aet)
1985	Celtic	Dundee U	2-1
1986	Aberdeen	Hearts	3-0
1987	St Mirren	Dundee U	1-0 (aet)
1988	Celtic	Dundee U	2-1
1989	Celtic	Rangers	1-0
1990	Aberdeen	Celtic	0-0 (aet)
		(Aberdeen won 9-8 on penalties)	
1991	Motherwell	Dundee U	4-3 (aet)
1992	Rangers	Airdrieonians	2-1
1993	Rangers	Aberdeen	2-1
1994	Dundee U	Rangers	1-0
1995	Celtic	Airdrieonians	1-0
1996	Rangers	Hearts	5-1
1997	Kilmarnock	Falkirk	1-0
1998	Hearts	Rangers	2-1
1999	Rangers	Celtic	1-0
2000	Rangers	Aberdeen	4-0

*Vale of Leven awarded cup, Rangers failing to appear for replay after 1-1 draw.
†After Dumbarton protested the first game, which Queen's Park won 2-1.
‡Queen's Park awarded cup, Vale of Leven failing to appear.
§Replay by order of Scottish FA because of playing conditions in first match, won 3-0 by Third Lanark.
¶After mutually protested game which Celtic won 1-0.
••Owing to riot, the cup was withheld after two drawn games – between Celtic and Rangers 2-2 and 1-1.

SCOTTISH CUP WINS

Celtic 30, Rangers 29, Queen's Park 10, Aberdeen 7, Hearts 6, Clyde 3, Kilmarnock 3, St Mirren 3, Vale of Leven 3, Dunfermline Ath 2, Falkirk 2, Hibernian 2, Motherwell 2, Renton 2, Third Lanark 2, Airdrieonians 1, Dumbarton 1, Dundee 1, Dundee U 1, East Fife 1, Morton 1, Partick T 1, St Bernard's 1.

APPEARANCES IN FINAL

Celtic 48, Rangers 46, Aberdeen 15, Queen's Park 12, Hearts 12, Hibernian 10, Kilmarnock 8, Vale of Leven 7, Clyde 6, Dumbarton 6, Dundee U 7, Motherwell 6, St Mirren 6, Third Lanark 6, Renton 5, Airdrieonians 4, Dundee 4, Dunfermline Ath 3, East Fife 3, Falkirk 3, Hamilton A 2, Morton 2, Partick T 2, Albion R 1, Cambuslang 1, Clydesdale 1, Raith R 1, St Bernard's 1, Thornliebank 1.

TENNENT'S SCOTTISH CUP 1999–2000

FIRST ROUND

11 DEC

Hamilton A (0) 1 *(Henderson D 79)*
Clyde (1) 2 *(Carrigan 3 (pen), Grant 72)*   777
Hamilton A: Reid; McLaren, Cunnington, Davidson, Gaughan, Thomson, Renicks, Henderson N (Crossley (McAulay)), McFarlane, Bonnar (McCormick), Henderson
Clyde: Wylie; Murray, Martin McLaughlin, Keogh, Cranmer, Ross, Carrigan, McClay, Barrett (Woods), Mitchell, Grant.

Huntly (0) 0
East Stirling (0) 1 *(Higgins 88)*   467
Huntly: Morgan; Smith, Allan, Guild, Paterson, Black, Addicoat (Farmer), MacRonald, Stewart, Whyte, De Barros.
East Stirling: Butter; Storrar, Russell, Brown, Hay, Lynes (Elliott), Ferguson (Gordon), Muirhead, Laidlaw, Higgins (McMillan), Hardie.

Ross Co (1) 2 *(Shaw 5, Irvine 89)*
Forfar Ath (1) 2 *(Donaldson 37 (pen), Robson 79)*   749
Ross Co: Walker; Duthie, McBain, Maxwell, Mackay, Gilbert, Shaw, Geraghty (Irvine), Wood, Fraser (Finlayson), Kinnaird.
Forfar Ath: Garden; McCheyne, Craig, Rattray, Johnston, Donaldson, Morris, Farnan, Milne, Cargill, Robson.

Threave R (0) 0 *(Smith 85)*
Stenhousemuir (4) 7 *(Fisher 15, 37, Graham 25, 53, Mooney 41, Fraser 53 (og), Forrester 71)*   526
Threave R: McWilliam; Smith, Tuchewicz (Livingstone), Wilson (Adams), Fraser, McGinley, Kirkpatrick, McCulloch, Possee (Little), Hudson, Cook.
Stenhousemuir: Hamilton L; Lawrence, Banks, Davidson (Armstrong), Graham, Watson, Hamilton R, McKinnon, Mooney (Forrester), Fisher, Lorimer (Watters).

FIRST ROUND REPLAY

3 JAN

Forfar Ath (0) 0
Ross Co (0) 0   1057
Forfar Ath: Garden; McCheyne, Craig, Rattray, Johnston, Donaldson, Morris (McPhee), McLean (Brand), Milne, Cargill, Robson.
Ross Co: Walker; Duthie, Mackay, Maxwell, Irvine, Gilbert, Shaw, Geraghty, Holmes (Wood), Ferguson, Kinnaird (McBain).
aet (Forfar Ath won 4-2 on penalties)

SECOND ROUND

8 JAN

Albion R (0) 0
Dalbeattie Star (0) 0   422
Albion R: McLean; McStay, McBride, Hamilton, Smith, Lumsden, Bonar (Tait), McLees, Duncan, Lyon (Diack), Prentice (Coulter).
Dalbeattie Star: Fitzpatrick; MacMinn, Campbell, Skahill, Dingwall, McGinley, Pearson, Parker, Johnston, Black (Telfer), Rodgerson (Glendinning).

Arbroath (0) 0
Fraserburgh (0) 0   1235
Arbroath: Wight; Florence, Gallagher, McAulay, Thomson, Crawford, Cooper, Bryce (Brownlie), McGlashan, Arbuckle, Mercer (Sellars).
Fraserburgh: Gordon; Milne, McBride, Murray, Fleming, Geddes, Norris, Thomson, Wemyss (Young), Hunter, Stephen.

Brechin C (2) 2 *(Bailey 26, Smith 42)*
Annan Ath (0) 2 *(McGuffie 52, Sloan 89)*   396
Brechin C: Geddes; Smith, Raynes, Cairney, Bain, Christie, Nairn, Bailey, Honeyman, Black, Coulston (Kerrigan).
Annan Ath: Potter; Hannay, Leslie (Sloan), Proudfoot, Laurie, Irons, Nicoll, Jardine, Docherty (Thomson), McMenimin, McGuffie.

Cowdenbeath (0) 2 *(Brown 67, 72)*
Clyde (1) 3 *(Carrigan 20 (pen), 84, McLaughlin 76)*   622
Cowdenbeath: Hutchison; White, King, Snedden, McCulloch, Carnie (Stewart), Winter, Bradley, McDowell (Simpson), Brown, Wilson.
Clyde: McIntyre; Murray, McLaughlin, Smith, Cranmer, Ross (Mitchell), Carrigan, Mackay, Woods (Convery), Keogh, Grant (McLauchlan).

Dumbarton (0) 0
Stenhousemuir (1) 2 *(Fisher 17, Hamilton R 62)*   302
Dumbarton: Barnes; Dickie, Brittain, Stewart, Bruce, King, Grace (Hringsson), Jack, Flannery, Andrew Brown, Robertson.
Stenhousemuir: Hamilton L; Lawrence, Banks, Watson, Graham, Lorimer, Hamilton R, McKinnon, Mooney (Wood), Fisher, Fraser.

Montrose (0) 1 *(O'Driscoll 55)*
Queen of the S (1) 3 *(Eadie 40, Hawke 74, Adams 76)* 380
Montrose: McGlynn; Craig D, Black, McWilliam (Ogboke), Paterson, Craib M, Mailer, Scott, Craig M, O'Driscoll, Taylor.
Queen of the S: Hillcoat; McMillan, Hodge, Rowe. Robison, Cleeland, Dickson, Kerr (Leslie), Hawke, Mallan (Weir), Eadie (Adams).

Partick T (1) 2 *(Lennon 36, Brown 71 (og))*
East Stirling (0) 1 *(Hay 67)*   2262
Partick T: Budinauckas; Duncan, McKeown, Lennon, McCann (Martin), Archibald, Paton, Docherty, McLean, Lyle, Jacobs (Miller).
East Stirling: Butter; Storrar, Russell, Brown, Hay, Muirhead, Ferguson, Hardie, Laidlaw, Higgins (Gordon), Elliott.

Peterhead (1) 2 *(Clark G 6, Cheyne 63)*
Forfar Ath (1) 1 *(Milne 33)*   1130
Peterhead: Pirie; Clark S, Morrison, King, Simpson, Gibson, Yeats (Copeland), Clark G, Milne (Yule), Brown, Cheyne.
Forfar Ath: Garden; McCheyne, Craig, McPhee (Brand), Farnan, Donaldson, Morris (Taylor), McLean, Milne, Cargill, Robson (McKellar).

Queen's Park (1) 1 *(Carroll 3)*
Berwick R (1) 2 *(Haddow 34 (pen), Findlay 83)*   630
Queen's Park: Inglis; Ferry, Connaghan, Caven, Martin, McFarlane, Connell, Borland (Whelan), Gallagher, Carmichael (Brown), Carroll.
Berwick R: O'Connor; McNicoll, Haddow, Campbell, Neill A, Neill M, Patterson, Watt, Findlay, Anthony (Leask), Smith (Magee).

Stirling Albion (1) 2 *(Whiteford 12, Graham 56)*
East Fife (1) 1 *(O'Hara 7)*   728
Stirling Albion: Gow; Paterson, Tortolano, Donald (Clark), Whiteford, McCallum (Mortimer), McQuade, McGrillen (Wood), Graham, Taggart, Gardner.
East Fife: McCulloch; Munro, Gibb (Forrest), O'Hara (Herd), Agostini, Shannon, Logan, Cusick (Wright), Robertson, Moffat, Mackay.

Stranraer (0) 1 *(Blaikie 83)*
Clachnacuddin (0) 0   351
Stranraer: McGeown; Smith, Wright, Watson, Jenkins, McDonald, Walker, Ramsay, Harty, Ronald (Young), Roddie.
Clachnacuddin: Rae; MacCuish, MacLeod, Bennett, Sinclair, Douglas (McCraw), Williamson, Munro, Stewart (Holmes), Brennan, Richardson.

Whitehill Welfare (0) 2 *(Bird51, Samuel 88)*
Alloa Ath (1) 2 *(Irvine 29, McKechnie 85)*   813
Whitehill Welfare: Cantley; McLaren, Gowne, Malcolm, Steel, Bennett, Jardine, Samuel, Tulloch (McGovern), Bird (Hope), Manson (Smith).
Alloa Ath: Cairns; Wilson, Clark D, Conway, Beaton, Valentine, Clark G (Christie), Walker (McKechnie), Cameron, Irvine, Donaghy (Boyle).

SECOND ROUND REPLAYS

15 JAN

Annan Ath (1) 2 *(Docherty 24, Thomson 88)*
Brechin C (1) 3 *(Christie 44, Nairn 51, Black 105)*   1039
Annan Ath: Potter; Hannay, Leslie (Sloan), Proudfoot, Laurie, Irons, Nicol (Elliott), Jardine, Docherty (Thomson), McMenimin, McGuffie.
Brechin C: Geddes; Smith (Coulston), Raynes, Cairney, Bain, Christie, Nairn, Bailey (Kerrigan), Honeyman (Sorbie), Black, Donachie.
aet

Fraserburgh (0) 1 *(Florence (og) 72)*
Arbroath (1) 3 *(McGlashan 9, Mercer 48, Devine 90)* 1967
Fraserburgh: Gordon; Milne, McBride, Fleming, Stephen A (McLaren), Murray, Norris, Thomson, Wemyss (Young (Martin)), Mackie, Stephen M.
Arbroath: Wight; Arbuckle, Florence, McAulay, Thomson, Crawford, Cooper (Gallagher), Bryce (Devine), McGlashan, Sellars, Mercer.

19 JAN

Dalbeattie Star (1) 1 *(Parker 25)*
Albion R (1) 5 *(Flannigan 32, 82, 85, McLees 59, McStay 66)*   483
Dalbeattie Star: Fitzpatrick; MacMinn, Campbell, Skachill, Dingwall, McGinley, Pearson (Telfer), Parker, Johnston, Black (True), Rodgerson (Harkness).
Albion R: McLean; McStay, Coulter, Tait (McMillan), Smith, Lumsden, Hamilton (Diack), McLees, Duncan (Silvestro), Flannigan, Prentice.

29 JAN

Alloa Ath (2) 2 *(Donaghy 38, Cameron 43)*
Whitehill Welfare (0) 0   640
Alloa Ath: Cairns; Wilson, Clark D, Conway, Beaton (Boyle), Valentine, Clark G, Walker, Cameron, Irvine, Donaghy (Christie).
Whitehill Welfare: Cantley; McLaren, Gowrie, Malcolm, Steel (McGovern), Bennett, Jardine, Samuel, Hope, Bird (Tulloch), Manson (Smith).

THIRD ROUND

29 JAN

Albion R (0) 1 *(Duncan 86)*
Partick T (1) 2 *(Dunn 6, Lennon 89)*   1682
Albion R: McLean; Bonar, Smith, Tait, Lumsden, McStay, Silvestro, McLees, Duncan, Flannigan, Prentice (Diack).
Partick T: Budinauckas; Docherty, McKeown, Lennon, Montgomerie, Archibald, Paton (Miller), Craig, McLean, Dunn (Lyle), Jacobs (Martin).

Clyde (0) 3 *(Carrigan 76, 89 (pen), Woods 79)*
Raith R (1) 1 *(Dargo 35)*   1831
Clyde: Wylie; Keogh, Mark McLaughlin, Smith, Cranmer (Martin McLauchlan), Ross, Convery (Woods), McClay, Carrigan, Mitchell, Grant.

Raith R: Van De Kamp; McEwan, Andrews, Browne, Opinel, Black, Agathe, Tosh S, Dargo, Burns, Stein (Hetherston).

Clydebank (1) 1 *(Wishart 6)*
Stirling Albion (0) 0   355
Clydebank: Scott; Murray (Jackson), McLaughlin, McKinstrey, Murdoch, Miller (O'Neil), Brannigan, Gardner, Wishart, Cameron, McKelvie (Oliver).
Stirling Albion: Gow; Paterson, Tortolano, Donald, Whiteford, McCallum, McQuade, McGrillen (Wood), Graham, Taggart, Gardner.

Dundee (0) 0
Ayr U (0) 0   3925
Dundee: Douglas; Smith, Wilkie, Tweed, Ireland, McSkimming, Boyack (Bayne), Rae, Banger, Annand, Falconer.
Ayr U: Nelson; Robertson, Rogers, Scally, Craig, Duffy, Teale, Wilson, Hurst, Tarrant, Reynolds (Shepherd).

Falkirk (2) 3 *(Nicholls 6, Crabbe 35, Hagen 72)*
Peterhead (1) 1 *(Gibson 11)*   3165
Falkirk: Hogarth; Lawrie, McQuilken (Seaton), Den Bieman, Christie, Nicholls, Mackenzie, Donald (Hutchison), Crabbe, Henry, Hagen.
Peterhead: Pirie; Clark S (Watson), Morrison, King, Simpson, Cheyne, Yeats (Clark G), Yule, Milne (Copeland), Brown, Gibson.

Hearts (1) 3 *(Cameron 38 (pen), McSwegan 61, 88)*
Stenhousemuir (2) 2 *(Hamilton R 8, Mooney 29)*   11,752
Hearts: Niemi; Pressley, Naysmith, Petric, Murray (McSwegan), Locke, Tomaschek (Juanjo), Cameron, Fulton, Wales, Jackson.
Stenhousemuir: Hamilton L; Lawrence, Banks (Lorimer), Watson, Graham (Wood), Armstrong, Hamilton R, McKinnon, Mooney (Forrester); Fraser, Fisher.

Hibernian (2) 4 *(Miller 1, Brebner 38, Murray 66, Collins 85)*
Dunfermline Ath (1) 1 *(Graham 32)*   10,863
Hibernian: Colgan; Collins, Smith, Hughes, Jack, Sauzee, Brebner (Hartley), Latapy, Lovell (Murray), Paatelainen (Lehmann), Miller.
Dunfermline Ath: Mampaey; McGroarty, Dair, Tod, Reid (Coyle), Dolan (Moss), Thomson, Ferguson, Graham, Hampshire, Petrie.

Queen of the S (0) 0   1530
Livingston (1) 7 *(McKinnon 14, 89, Keith 50, 57, 63, Bingham 59, McPhee 68)*
Queen of the S: Hillcoat; McMillan (Kerr), Hodge (Adams), Rowe, Aitken, Cleeland, Dickson, Leslie, Hawke, Mallan, Eadie (Caldwell).
Livingston: McCaldon; Kelly, Deas (Bennett), McManus, Coughlan, McKinnon, King (McCormick), Millar M (Sweeney), Keith, Bingham, McPhee.

St Mirren (0) 1 *(McGarry 56)*
Aberdeen (0) 1 *(Zerouali 71)*   7319
St Mirren: Roy; Nicolson, Ross, Baltacha (Bowman), McLaughlin, Walker, Murray (Rodden), Brown, McGarry (Lavety), Mendes, Yardley.
Aberdeen: Leighton; Solberg, McAllister, Whyte, Anderson, Dow (Belabed), Bernard, Jess (Winters), Guntveit, Stavrum, Zerouali.

Stranraer (0) 1 *(Ronald 69)*
Berwick R (1) 2 *(Haddow 41 (pen), Findlay 65)*   423
Stranraer: McGeown; Smith, Wright, Watson, Kerr, MacDonald, Young, Jenkins (Cahoon), Harty (Johnstone), Ronald, Blaikie (Walker).
Berwick R: O'Connor; McNicoll, Haddow, Campbell, Neill A, Watt, Patterson, Anthony (Ritchie), Findlay (Carr-Lawton), Smith, Magee.

30 JAN

Dundee U (1) 4 *(Hannah 18, 80, Mathie 59, Ferraz 86)*
Airdrieonians (0) 1 *(McCann 58 (pen))* 5172
Dundee U: Combe; Pascual, Partridge, De Vos, Jonsson, Davidson, Telesnikov (Skoldmark), Hannah, Preget, Mathie (Ferraz), Thompson.
Airdrieonians: Thomson S; Johnston, McCann, Jack, Forrest, Stewart, Moore, Dick, Thompson N (McCormick), Evans (Neil), Easton (Taylor).

Morton (1) 1 *(Anderson J 25)*
Brechin C (0) 1 *(Black 84)* 900
Morton: Maxwell; Murie (Reid), Anderson D, Millen, Morrison, Fenwick, Matheson, Anderson J, Whalen, Curran (Tweedie), McDonald (McPherson).
Brechin C: Geddes; Donachie, Raynes, Cairney, Bain, Christie, Riley, Sorbie, Honeyman (Coulston), Black, Bailey (Kerrigan).

St Johnstone (0) 0
Rangers (1) 2 *(Numan 41, Van Bronckhorst 54)* 9099
St Johnstone: Main; Griffin, Bollan, Weir, Dods, O'Halloran, McBride (McAnespie), Kane, O'Neil, Lowndes (Simao), Jones.
Rangers: Klos; Vidmar, Moore, Amoruso, Numan, Kanchelskis (Reyna), Ferguson B, Van Bronckhorst, Albertz (Kerimoglu), Durie, Wallace (McCann).

1 FEB

Arbroath (1) 1 *(Bryce 34)*
Motherwell (1) 1 *(Goodman 25)* 2509
Arbroath: Wight; Florence, Peters, McAulay, Thomson, Arbuckle, Cooper, Bryce (Devine), McGlashan, Tindal, Mercer.
Motherwell: Goram; Doesburg, McMillan, Denham, Craigan, Townsley (Nevin), Brannan, Valakari, Twaddle, McCulloch, Goodman.

5 FEB

Kilmarnock (0) 0
Alloa Ath (0) 0 5584
Kilmarnock: Meldrum; MacPherson, Baker, Lauchlan, Dindeleux, Reilly, Holt, Durrant (Bagan), Burke, Vareille, Jeffrey (Smith).
Alloa Ath: Cairns; Wilson M, Clark D, Conway, Valentine (Clark G), Beaton, Christie, Walker (McKechnie), Cameron, Irvine, Donaghy.

8 FEB

Celtic (1) 1 *(Burchill 17)*
Inverness CT (2) 3 *(Wilson 12, Moravcik (og) 24, Sheerin 56 (pen))* 34,389
Celtic: Gould; Boyd, Riseth, Tebily, Mahe, Blinker, Healy, Berkovic, Moravcik, Viduka (Wright), Burchill.
Inverness CT: Calder; Teasdale, Golabek, Mann, Hastings, Sheerin, Tokely (Byers), McCulloch, Wilson (Glancy), Christie, Wyness (Bavidge).

THIRD ROUND REPLAYS

8 FEB

Aberdeen (0) 2 *(Zerouali53, Bernard 89)*
St Mirren (0) 0 12,947
Aberdeen: Leighton; Solberg, McAllister, Whyte, Anderson, Dow (Belabed), Bernard, Guntweit, Winters, Stavrum (Rutkiewicz), Zerouali.
St Mirren: Roy; Nicolson, Ross, Rodden, McLaughlin, Walker, Murray (McGarry), Bowman, Lavety (Turner), Mendes, Yardley (Baltacha).

Brechin C (0) 0
Morton (0) 0 623
Brechin C: Geddes; Donachie, Raynes, Cairney, Bain, Smith, Riley, Sorbie, Honeyman (Kerrigan), Black, Bailey.
Morton: Maxwell; Murie (Tweedie), Anderson D, Millen, Morrison, Slaven (Aitken), Whalen (Hart), Anderson J, Matheson, Curran, McDonald.
aet (Morton won 4-2 on penalties)

9 FEB

Alloa Ath (1) 1 *(Cameron 5)*
Kilmarnock (0) 0 1894
Alloa Ath: Cairns; Wilson, Clark D, Conway, Beaton, Valentine, Christie, Walker (McKechnie), Cameron, Irvine, Donaghy (Clark G).
Kilmarnock: Meldrum; MacPherson, Baker, Lauchlan, Dindeleux, Reilly (Durrant), Holt, Burke, Mitchell (Bagan), Smith, Cocard.

15 FEB

Ayr U (0) 1 *(Duffy 104)*
Dundee (0) 1 *(Rae 91)* 3029
Ayr U: Nelson; McMillan (Grant), Robertson, Scally (Cully), Craig, Duffy, Teale, Wilson, Hurst, Tarrant (Reynolds), Shepherd.
Dundee: Langfield; Smith, Raeside, Tweed, Wilkie, Robertson, Boyack (Banger), Rae, McSkimming (Sharp), Bayne (Grady), Falconer.
aet (Ayr U won 7-6 on penalties)

19 FEB

Motherwell (1) 2 *(Goodman 13, McCulloch 63)*
Arbroath (0) 0 5311
Motherwell: Goram; Doesburg, McMillan, McGowan, Denham, Davies J, Brannan, Valakari, Goodman (Twaddle), Spencer, McCulloch.
Arbroath: Wight; Peters, Gallagher, McAulay, Thomson, Webster, Cooper (Brownlie), Bryce (Devine), McGlashan, Sellars, Mercer.

FOURTH ROUND

19 FEB

Alloa Ath (2) 2 *(Beaton 5, Cameron 33)*
Dundee U (0) 2 *(Hamilton 55, 80)* 2570
Alloa Ath: Cairns (McKechnie); Wilson, Clark D, Conway, Beaton, Valentine, Christie, Little, Cameron, Irvine, Donaghy (Clark G).
Dundee U: Combe; Skoldmark (Mathie), Partridge, Malpas, Patterson D, Jenkins, Telesnikov (Smith), Hannah, Easton, Hamilton, Thompson (Ferraz).

Berwick R (0) 0
Falkirk (0) 0 1932
Berwick R: O'Connor; McNicoll, Haddow, Ritchie, Neill A, Watt, Rafferty, Anthony, Findlay (Carr-Lawton), Smith, Magee.
Falkirk: Hogarth; Lawrie, McQuilken, Den Bieman, Christie, Nicholls, Mackenzie, McDonald, Crabbe, Henry (Hutchison), Hagen.

Clyde (0) 0
Hearts (2) 2 *(Jackson 1, Wales 7)* 6416
Clyde: Wylie; Ross, Mark McLaughlin, Smith, Murray, Mitchell (Martin McLauchlan), Carrigan, McClay (McCusker), Woods (Barrett), Keogh, Grant.
Hearts: Niemi; Pressley, Naysmith, Petric, Murray, Tomaschek, Simpson, Cameron, Adam (Severin), Jackson (McSwegan), Wales.

Hibernian (0) 1 *(Hartley 66)*
Clydebank (0) 1 *(Gardner 63 (pen))* 9827
Hibernian: Colgan; Collins, Smith, Hughes, Jack, Murray, Brebner, Sauzee, Hartley (Lovell), Paatelainen (Lehmann), Miller.
Clydebank: Scott; Murray, Sutherland, Murdoch (McKinstrey (O'Neil)), Brannigan, Wishart, Miller, Gardner, McKelvie (Hunter), McWilliams, Cameron.

Morton (0) 0
Rangers (0) 1 *(Moore 50)* 8600
Morton: Maxwell; Murie, Anderson D, Millen, Morrison, Pluck, Earnshaw (Slavin), Anderson J (Aitken), Matheson, Curran, McDonald (Wright).
Rangers: Klos; Vidmar, Moore, Van Bronckhorst, Numan, Kanchelskis, Ferguson B, Kerimoglu, McCann (Albertz), Durie (Negri), Wallace.

Partick T (1) 2 *(Craig 40, McLean 83)*
Livingston (1) 1 *(Bingham 9)*   4850
Partick T: Budinauckas; Docherty, McKeown, Lennon, Montgomerie, Archibald, Lyle, Craig, Dunn, Miller (McLean), Jacobs.
Livingston: McCaldon; Kelly, Deas, McManus, Coughlan, McKinnon (Fleming), McCormick (King), Millar M, Keith (McPhee), Bingham, Richardson.

20 FEB
Inverness CT (0) 1 *(Mann 50)*
Aberdeen (0) 1 *(Guntweit 80)*   6290
Inverness CT: Calder; Tokely, Golabek, Teasdale, Mann, Sheerin, Bavidge (Byers), McCulloch, Wilson, Christie, Wyness (Glancy).
Aberdeen: Leighton; Solberg, McAllister, Whyte, Anderson, Dow, Bernard, Rutkiewicz (Belabed), Guntweit, Stavrum, Winters (Perry).

26 FEB
Motherwell (3) 3 *(McCulloch 23, Goodman 29, Brannan 35 (pen))*
Ayr U (3) 4 *(Teale 8, 32 (pen), Tarrant 39, 59)*   5222
Motherwell: Goram; Doesburg, McMillan, McGowan, Denham (Davies J), Townsley (Nevin), Brannan, Valakari, Twaddle (Nicholas), McCulloch, Goodman.
Ayr U: Nelson; McMillan, Robertson, Shepherd, Craig, Duffy, Teale, Wilson, Hurst, Tarrant (Crilly), Reynolds.

FOURTH ROUND REPLAYS
22 FEB
Dundee U (2) 4 *(Preget 38, Hamilton 39, Thompson 80, 83)*
Alloa Ath (0) 0   4913
Dundee U: Combe; Pascual, Partridge, Jenkins, Malpas, Davidson, Preget (Smith), Hannah, Easton, Hamilton (Ferraz), McConalogue (Thompson).
Alloa Ath: Parkyn; Boyle (McKechnie), Clark D, Conway, Beaton (McAneny), Valentine, Little, Walker (Donaghy), Cameron, Irvine, Clark G.

29 FEB
Aberdeen (0) 1 *(Stavrum 75)*
Inverness CT (0) 0   18,451
Aberdeen: Leighton; Perry, McAllister, Solberg, Anderson, Dow, Bernard, Mayer (Darren Young), Belabed (Rutkiewicz), Stavrum, Zerouali.
Inverness CT: Calder; Teasdale, Golabek, Mann, Hastings, Sheerin, Tokely, McCulloch (Byers), Wilson (Bavidge), Christie, Xausa (Wyness).

Clydebank (0) 0   2225
Hibernian (1) 3 *(Lovell 40, Lehmann 74, Sauzee 82)*
Clydebank: Morrison; Murray, Oliver, Murdoch, Brannigan, Wishart, Miller (Hunter), Gardner (O'Neil), McKelvie, Cameron, McWilliams.
Hibernian: Colgan; Collins, Smith, Hughes, Sauzee, Lovell, Brebner, Latapy, McGinlay, Lehmann, Miller.

Falkirk (1) 3 *(Crabbe 40, Hagen 49, McQuilken 51)*
Berwick R (0) 0   3708
Falkirk: Hogarth; Lawrie, McQuilken, Den Bieman, Christie, Nicholls (Sinclair), McKenzie, Henry, Crabbe (McDonald), Hutchison, Hagen (Seaton).
Berwick R: O'Connor; McNicoll, Haddow, Ritchie, Neill A, Watt (Carr-Lawton), Patterson, Smith (Campbell), Findlay (Rafferty), Anthony, Magee.

QUARTER-FINALS
11 MAR
Ayr U (1) 2 *(Campbell 25, Tarrant 50)*
Partick T (0) 0   8365
Ayr U: Nelson; McMillan, Craig, Scally, Campbell, Duffy, Teale (Grant), Shepherd, Hurst, Tarrant, Hansen (Robertson).

Partick T: Budinauckas; Martin, McKeown, Lennon, Montgomerie, Archibald, Paton, Craig, McLean, Dunn (English), Jacobs.

Hibernian (2) 3 *(Latapy 25, 42 (pen), McGinlay 89)*
Falkirk (1) 1 *(Lawrie 32)*   14,041
Hibernian: Colgan; Collins, Smith, Hughes, McIntosh, Sauzee, Lovell (Brebner), Latapy, McGinlay, Paatelainen (Lehmann), Miller.
Falkirk: Hogarth; Lawrie, McQuilken, Den Bieman, Christie, Nicholls, McKenzie, Henry (McDonald), Crabbe, Hutchison (McAllister), Hagen.

12 MAR
Dundee U (0) 0
Aberdeen (0) 1 *(Jess 83)*   6738
Dundee U: Combe; Pascual, Partridge, De Vos, McQuillan, Jonsson, McCulloch (Davidson), Hannah, Easton, Hamilton (Ferraz), Mathie.
Aberdeen: Leighton; Lilley (Perry), McAllister, Solberg, Anderson, Dow, Bernard, Jess, Mayer (Belabed), Guntweit, Stavrum.

Rangers (2) 4 *(Ferguson B 11, Numan 16, Amoruso 68, Dodds 79 (pen))*
Hearts (1) 1 *(Cameron 34 (pen))*   31,471
Rangers: Klos; Reyna (Wilson), Moore, Amoruso, Numan (Kanchelskis), Ferguson B, Albertz, Van Bronckhorst, McCann, Wallace, Rozental (Dodds).
Hearts: Niemi; Pressley, Naysmith, Murray (McSwegan), Leclercq, Tomaschek (Severin), Simpson (Adam), Cameron, Flogel, Wales, Jackson.

SEMI-FINALS
8 APR
Ayr U (0) 0   38,357
Rangers (3) 7 *(Rozental 19, 90, Kanchelskis 28, Wallace 42, Dodds 67, 72, 87)*
Ayr U: Roude; McMillan, Robertson, Shepherd (Scally), Campbell (Craig), Duffy, Teale, Wilson, Hurst, Tarrant, Reynolds (Lyons).
Rangers: Klos; Reyna, Wilson, Amoruso, Numan, Kanchelskis, Ferguson B, Van Bronckhorst (Kerimoglu), Albertz (McCann), Wallace (Dodds), Rozental.

9 APR
Hibernian (0) 1 *(Latapy 56)*
Aberdeen (0) 2 *(Stavrum 64, Dow 68)*   22,193
Hibernian: Colgan; Collins (Hartley), Smith, Hughes, McIntosh, Sauzee, Lovell, Latapy, McGinlay, Paatelainen (Lehmann), Miller.
Aberdeen: Leighton; Solberg, McAllister, Whyte, Anderson, Dow (Lilley), Bernard, Jess, Mayer, Guntweit, Stavrum (Belabed).

FINAL AT HAMPDEN PARK

27 MAY
Aberdeen (0) 0   50,685
Rangers (1) 4 *(Van Bronckhorst 36, Vidmar 47, Dodds 49, Albertz 51)*
Aberdeen: Leighton (Winters); Solberg, McAllister, Whyte, Anderson (Belabed), Dow, Bernard, Jess, Rowson, Guntweit, Stavrum (Zerouali).
Rangers: Klos; Reyna, Moore (Porrini), Vidmar, Numan, Kanchelskis, Ferguson B, Albertz, Van Bronckhorst (Kerimoglu), Wallace (McCann), Dodds.
Referee: Jim McCluskey

WELSH FOOTBALL 1999–2000

"I've never felt so good after a 3-0 beating."

So wrote a reader to the sports editor of the *Western Mail* newspaper a few days after Wales had taken on Brazil at the new Millennium Stadium in Cardiff last May. They may have been separated by a hundred ranking positions but for an hour, the new-look Welsh side – minus Ryan Giggs – had managed to contain the best team in the world before a ten-minute burst of brilliance from Rivaldo and co swept them away.

Despite closing the roof and narrowing the pitch in an attempt to disrupt the boys from Brazil, Wales were still powerless to prevent them from coasting to victory in front of a record 72,250 crowd. It was an historical night to remember. Roger Freestone, the Swansea City goalkeeper making his debut at the age of 31, could not be faulted with any of the goals, including a breathtaking header from the world's number one player himself, and although Brazil simply stepped up a gear when they needed to, Wales emerged from the game – and indeed the season – with hope that the corner had at last been turned.

The opening sentence of that reader's letter neatly summed up the general reaction to a typically spirited Welsh display. His final paragraph was equally apposite. "Da iawn (very good), lads. Keep it up. I can feel the pride returning each game."

Since replacing Bobby Gould as national manager, Mark Hughes has set about the task of re-building Welsh confidence with a quiet determination. Results may have been less than impressive – four defeats in his first six games in charge – but the Everton midfielder has put in place a more solid structure. After an inspirational 2-1 win in Belarus – with Giggs scoring the winner – Wales slipped up badly at home to Switzerland in their final Euro 2000 qualifying match before beating Qatar and then losing to Finland, Brazil and Portugal – three disappointing but not embarrassing defeats. With respect for both the manager and the red shirt restored, the team had more shape. A new generation is anxious to make its mark on the international stage with Norwich City's Craig Bellamy and Matthew Jones of Leeds United leading the way. At just 19, Jones might just be the man to take on the central, and hopefully more creative, midfield mantle while Bellamy has recovered well from a serious knee injury to stake a claim for a regular striker's spot.

That said, the honeymoon is now over and Hughes, having negotiated a four-and-a-half-year contract which allows him to continue playing in the Premiership for half of it, will now be judged on results rather than performances once the 2002 World Cup qualifying campaign begins. Armenia, Ukraine, Poland, Belarus and Norway stand in the way of Wales reaching the finals of a major international tournament for the first time in 44 years.

Domestically, it proved a mixed season for the three Nationwide League clubs. For the second year running, Wrexham struggled to make an impression in Division Two before concluding their campaign with five successive victories during which they conceded no goals. Cardiff City's promotion was sadly short-lived as they lost their manager, a lot of credibility and goodwill and, ultimately, their fight against relegation. An abortive takeover bid by a consortium led by the brother of soft-porn publisher David Sullivan de-stabilised the club, Frank Burrows was sacked and Cardiff slid slowly back towards Division Three. Adding insult to injury, they found themselves changing places with arch rivals Swansea City along the way.

The Swans were determined to avoid a repeat of the heartache of 1999 when they reached the play-off semi-finals. Automatic promotion was the name of the game and – bolstered by a tight defence marshalled superbly by Freestone, Division Three's best goalkeeper – they deservedly made it. Goals at the other end were also at a premium but, aided by a crucial mid-season contribution from their Jamaican joker-in-the-pack, the red-booted Walter Boyd, Swansea emerged as Third Division champions – despite a late stutter. A draw at challengers Rotherham United on the final day of the season secured the vital point but the celebrations were inevitably muted when it was discovered that a Swansea supporter, Terry Coles, a 41-year-old father-of-two, had been trampled to death by a police horse before the match.

After being sacked by Chelsea more than a decade ago, John Hollins restored his reputation by achieving promotion with little or no money but a bucketload of team spirit and enthusiasm. As they prepare to move to the Morfa Stadium at the end of the season, it is to be hoped that the Swans will learn from Cardiff's mistakes and buy a top-class striker on their return to Division Two.

Two of the three Welsh clubs playing in the English non-league pyramid experienced seasons they will want to forget. Both Merthyr and Colwyn Bay narrowly avoided relegation but Newport County finished seventh in the Premier Division of the Dr Martens League – their highest-ever position since being formed 11 years ago.

The four Welsh representatives in Europe all failed to negotiate the first hurdle. Aberystwyth Town lost 4-3 to Malta's Floriana in the Intertoto Cup while Barry Town went down 3-2 to the same island's top team Valletta in the Champions Cup. Cwmbran Town were unsurprisingly brushed aside by Celtic 10-0 while Inter Cardiff put up a brave fight before losing 2-1 on aggregate to Slovenia's NK Gorica and then ran into financial trouble. After a spell as Inter Cable-Tel, a merger with the students of the University of Wales Institute in the capital city means yet another name for the club – Uwic Inter Cardiff.

It was all change, too, in the League of Wales where, after four years of success, Barry were relieved of the championship title. In 1996, they lost a memorable Welsh Cup Final on penalties to the small Mid Wales village side of Llansantffraid. Last season, the same club but with a new name, Total Network Solutions, finished two points clear of Barry thanks to an impressive run during which they dropped only four points out of their last 42. A combination of the enthusiastic sponsorship of local computer company TNS, their effervescent managing director Mike Harris, team manager Andy Cale and general manager Grahame Breeze, means that Llansantffraid are back in the big time – in the Champions League. Barry, who also won the Gilbert League Cup by beating Bangor City 6-0, qualified for the UEFA Cup as league runners-up, along with Bangor who beat Cwmbran Town 1-0 in the Welsh Cup Final. Cwmbran had to be content with a place in the Intertoto Cup after finishing third in the League of Wales while Wrexham regained the FAW Premier Cup by easily overcoming a demoralised Cardiff City side 2-0 at the Racecourse.

Finally, a rare word of praise for the much-maligned members of the Welsh FA – for once, they got it right. Under pressure from Mark Hughes, the friendly against Finland was switched from Ninian Park to the Millennium Stadium and, after reducing prices to a standard £5, the FAW councillors hit the jackpot. A capacity 66,500 crowd turned up for the first football game at the home of Welsh rugby and then 5,750 extra seats were made available for the Brazil match where tickets were priced at £10 and £5 for adults and children respectively.

These two attendances demonstrate that, despite the long-standing but often overstated status of rugby, a huge appetite exists for football in Wales and the councillors deserve a pat on the back for setting the ball rolling by tapping into this reservoir of support. Having negotiated an improved deal with BBC Wales for television coverage, they now want to turn the Millennium Stadium into their permanent home. The only question now is whether Mark Hughes and his players can meet the expectations of a ravenous public and deliver on the pitch? Watch this space.

GRAHAME LLOYD

LEAGUE OF WALES

	Aberystwyth Town	Afan Lido	Bangor City	Barry Town	Caernarfon Town	Caersws	Carmarthen Town	Connah's Quay Nomads	Conwy United	Cwmbran Town	Flexys Cefn Druids	Haverfordwest County	Inter Cardiff	Llanelli	Newtown	Rhayader Town	Rhyl	Total Network Solutions
Aberystwyth Town	—	2-0	2-1	3-1	6-0	1-1	2-1	2-1	1-1	1-2	3-0	4-0	1-2	3-1	3-2	3-1	2-1	4-1
Afan Lido	2-1	—	4-0	0-2	4-0	3-0	0-0	1-1	3-0	0-0	2-2	4-3	3-0	0-0	2-1	3-0	0-1	0-0
Bangor City	1-3	4-1	—	3-3	1-0	1-3	0-1	0-2	8-0	1-1	3-3	1-0	3-1	1-3	3-2	1-0	3-2	0-2
Barry Town	3-3	5-0	5-2	—	3-0	1-0	3-1	3-3	4-1	3-1	7-0	3-1	5-1	4-2	4-0	2-0	1-1	5-1
Caernarfon Town	0-0	0-3	1-2	0-3	—	1-3	0-0	0-2	0-2	0-2	2-3	0-4	0-0	0-2	1-1	3-0	2-3	2-3
Caersws	0-3	3-0	2-5	1-2	3-1	—	2-1	0-2	3-3	0-1	3-0	1-0	0-3	0-2	0-1	1-1	0-1	0-1
Carmarthen Town	4-3	3-0	0-1	3-2	3-1	3-2	—	2-0	4-1	3-1	3-0	0-3	0-1	2-1	5-3	1-1	1-0	2-1
Connah's Quay Nomads	0-1	1-1	0-1	2-0	2-1	1-1	0-2	—	10-0	1-2	1-0	2-2	2-1	1-0	2-0	0-0	2-0	2-4
Conwy United	4-2	0-0	6-0	0-4	4-0	0-4	—	3-2	—	0-5	1-2	1-0	0-2	0-2	0-1	0-3	0-2	4-5
Cwmbran Town	2-1	3-2	0-2	0-4	4-0	1-1	3-1	0-2	3-1	—	2-1	1-0	3-1	3-1	3-2	1-2	5-0	0-2
Flexys Cefn Druids	2-0	1-0	1-2	0-1	3-0	1-3	3-1	0-2	3-1	2-1	—	2-3	2-1	2-1	2-1	0-2	4-0	0-1
Haverfordwest County	0-5	0-2	2-1	0-6	1-1	0-0	1-6	1-4	1-1	1-1	3-0	—	2-1	1-1	1-1	0-1	2-2	1-1
Inter Cardiff	0-1	1-1	1-0	1-5	1-1	2-7	0-4	2-0	2-0	1-4	0-1	0-0	—	0-3	0-0	1-1	2-1	1-2
Llanelli	5-0	4-2	4-1	2-1	5-0	3-2	7-2	2-0	3-2	1-3	2-1	3-2	3-1	—	0-4	2-0	7-0	0-2
Newtown	2-0	0-0	2-0	1-0	2-1	2-3	0-2	0-1	1-2	2-0	4-1	0-0	2-0	1-2	—	2-1	1-0	0-1
Rhayader Town	0-3	0-1	1-3	0-0	2-1	0-1	1-2	1-2	5-0	1-1	3-1	2-0	1-0	1-3	0-2	—	0-1	0-1
Rhyl	1-0	1-0	1-0	0-5	2-1	2-0	0-1	1-4	1-1	1-2	2-0	3-1	2-0	1-3	2-3	1-0	—	2-4
Total Network Solutions	4-1	3-0	2-1	0-2	4-0	0-0	2-1	1-0	7-0	1-3	0-3	4-1	2-0	2-0	0-0	3-1	2-1	—

LEAGUE OF WALES

	P	W	Home D	L	Goals F	A	W	Away D	L	Goals F	A	GD	Pts
Total Network Solutions	34	12	2	3	37	14	12	2	3	32	23	+32	76
Barry Town	34	14	3	0	61	17	9	2	6	37	17	+64	74
Cwmbran Town	34	13	1	3	41	17	8	5	4	30	20	+34	69
Carmarthen Town	34	13	1	3	39	21	9	2	6	29	21	+26	69
Llanelli	34	13	1	3	49	24	8	2	7	27	22	+30	66
Aberystwyth Town	34	13	2	2	43	16	6	2	9	27	30	+24	61
Connah's Quay Nomads	34	8	4	5	29	16	9	2	6	28	19	+22	57
Newtown	34	9	2	6	25	13	5	4	8	24	28	+8	48
Bangor City	34	8	3	6	34	27	7	0	10	22	34	−5	48
Afan Lido	34	9	6	2	31	11	3	4	10	13	31	+2	46
Rhyl	34	9	2	6	23	24	4	3	10	17	36	−20	44
Caersws	34	4	3	10	18	28	7	5	5	31	22	−1	41
Flexsys Cefn Druids	34	9	0	8	26	22	4	2	11	18	41	−19	41
Rhayader Town	34	5	3	9	20	23	4	4	9	14	24	−13	34
Haverfordwest County	34	4	5	8	15	31	4	1	12	15	31	−32	30
Inter Cardiff	34	3	8	6	17	34	3	3	11	20	31	−28	28*
Conwy United	34	4	1	12	17	38	2	4	11	16	59	−64	21**
Caernarfon Town	34	1	4	12	12	33	0	4	13	9	48	−60	11

*One point deducted for playing ineligible player.
**Two points deducted for failing to fulfil fixture.

WELSH CUP 1999–2000

First Round

Aberaman Athletic v Ammanford	0-4
Blaenrhondda v Skewen Athletic	1-0
British Aerospace v CPD Porthmadog	2-1
Briton Ferry Athletic v AFC Llwydcoed	1-0
Brymbo Broughton v Lex XI	2-3
Caerleon v Fields Park Pontllanfraith	2-1
Cemaes Bay v Amlwch Town	1-4
Chirk AAA v Llandyrnog United	1-2
Corwen Amateurs v Holyhead Hotspur	2-2
(Corwen won on penalties)	
Garden Village v Pontyclun	3-0
Garw Athletic v Porthcawl Town	4-4
(Garw won on penalties)	
Glan Conwy v Halkyn United	3-4
Guilsfield v Knighton Town	5-0
Hoover Sports v Chepstow Town	7-2
Kerry v Oswestry Town	1-4
Llandudno v Mold Alexandra	8-0
Llandudno Junction v Castell Alun Colts	2-1
Llanfairpwll v Ruthin Town	0-1
Llangefni Town w.o. Rhyl Delta withdrew	
Llanidloes Town v Llandrindod Wells	4-0
Llanwern v Caerau	4-2
Maesteg Park Athletic v Gwynfi United	2-0
Penrhiwceiber Rangers v Goytre United	1-2
CPD Penrhyncoch v Welshpool Town	3-0
Penycae v Denbigh Town	1-2
Porth Tywyn Suburbs v Pontlottyn Blast Furnace	2-2
(Porth Tywyn won on penalties)	
Port Talbot Athletic v Cardiff Civil Service	2-1
Prestatyn Town v Bala Town	2-0
Rhos Aelwyd v Buckley Town	0-2
Risca United v Bridgend Town	0-4
Taffs Well v Treowen Stars	0-3
Treharris Athletic v Ely Rangers	0-6
UWI Cardiff v Caldicot Town	6-0
Tredegar Town v Pontardawe Town	3-0

Second Round

Ely Rangers v Garden Village	1-2
Blaenrhondda v BP Llandarcy	2-1
AFC Rhondda v Afan Lido	1-2
Ton Pentre v Haverfordwest County	1-2
Garw Athletic v Goytre United	6-1
Maesteg Park Athletic v Caerleon	1-3
Llanelli v Briton Ferry Athletic	6-0
Rhayader Town v Tredegar Town	3-1
Hoover Sports v Port Talbot Athletic	2-2 aet
(Port Talbot Athletic won 5-4 on penalties)	
Llanwern v Ammanford	2-1
Bridgend Town v UWI Cardiff	0-1
Treowen Stars v Porth Tywyn Suburbs	1-2
Corwen Amateurs v Bangor City	1-2
Buckley Town v Rhydymwyn	1-3
Oswestry Town v Rhyl	0-1 aet
Llandyrnog United v Total Network Solutions	0-7

Newtown v Holywell Town	11-0
British Aerospace v Llandudno	3-5 aet
Flexsys Cefn Druids v Flint Town United	2-0
Ruthin Town v Amlwch Town	0-0 aet
(Amlwch Town won 4-2 on penalties)	
Halkyn United v Prestatyn Town	6-2 aet
Guilsfield v Connah's Quay Nomads	3-3 aet
(Guilsfield won 5-4 on penalties)	
Llanidloes Town v CPD Penrhyncoch	0-1 aet
Lex XI v Caernarfon Town	0-5
Denbigh Town v Llangefni Town	1-2
Caersws v Llandudno Junction	5-0

Third Round

UWI Cardiff v Afan Lido	0-2
CPD Penrhyncoch v Blaenrhondda	2-1 aet
Llanelli v Porth Tywyn Suburbs	7-1
Llanwern v Amlwch Town	0-1
Aberystwyth Town v Garw Athletic	3-1
Cwmbran Town v Caernarfon Town	0-0
(Cwmbran Town won 5-3 on penalties)	
Inter Cardiff v Garden Village	5-0
Rhyl v Guilsfield	1-0
Port Talbot Athletic v Carmarthen Town	0-1
Total Network Solutions v Newtown	2-0
Caersws v Flexsys Cefn Druids	1-0
Llangefni Town v Caerleon	1-3
Barry Town v Rhydymwyn	2-0
Conwy United v Rhayader Town	2-4 aet
Bangor City v Llandudno	5-0
Haverfordwest County v Halkyn United	0-1

Fourth Round

Afan Lido v Total Network Solutions	1-0
Bangor City v Inter Cardiff	4-0
Barry Town v Rhayader Town	3-0
Caersws v Cwmbran Town	1-2
Carmarthen Town v Aberystwyth Town	4-1
Halkyn United v Caerleon	2-3
Llanelli v Rhyl	3-0
CPD Penrhyncoch v Amlwch Town	6-1

Quarter-finals

Afan Lido v Llanelli	3-1 aet
Barry Town v CPD Penrhyncoch	5-0
Caerleon v Bangor City	1-4
Carmarthen Town v Cwmbran Town	2-3

Semi-finals

Afan Lido v Bangor City	2-4 aet
(At Newtown)	
Barry Town v Cwmbran Town	2-2 aet
(Cwmbran Town won 4-2 on penalties)	
(At Llanelli)	

Final
Bangor City (1) 1 Cwmbran Town (0) 0
(At the Racecourse, Wrexham 7 May 2000)

Bangor City: Mulliner; Johnson, Rowlands, Brett, Bird, Williams S, Williams R (Comley-Excell 83), Coady, Roberts, Allen, Williams E.
Scorer: Roberts 29.
Cwmbran Town: Wager; Carter (Davies 45), Wigley (Powell 87), Aizlewood, Blackie, O'Brien, Summers, Moore, Graham, Futcher (Pattimore 67), James.
Referee: B. Lawlor (Holyhead).
Attendance: 1125.

FAW PREMIER CUP

Group A	P	W	D	L	F	A	GD	Pts
Swansea City	6	5	0	1	18	3	+15	15
Caernarfon Tn	6	2	1	3	6	8	−2	7
Cwmbran Tn	6	2	1	3	7	12	−5	7
Inter Cardiff	6	1	2	3	4	12	−8	5

Group B	P	W	D	L	F	A	GD	Pts
Cardiff City	6	3	2	1	9	6	+3	11
Barry Town	6	2	4	0	8	6	+2	10
Merthyr Tydfil	6	1	2	3	5	7	−2	5
Newtown	6	1	2	3	4	7	−3	5

Group C	P	W	D	L	F	A	GD	Pts
Wrexham	6	6	0	0	18	2	+16	18
Aberystwyth	6	3	1	2	12	12	0	10
Total Network S	6	1	2	3	6	12	−6	5
Conwy United	6	0	1	5	2	12	−10	1

Quarter-finals

Cardiff City v Aberystwyth Town	4-0
Wrexham v Merthyr Tydfil	8-0
Barry Town v Cwmbran Town	2-0
Swansea City v Caernarfon Town	0-1

Semi-finals (two legs)

Wrexham v Barry Town	4-0
Barry Town v Wrexham	0-0
Caernarfon Town v Cardiff City	0-4
Cardiff City v Caernarfon Town	4-1

Final

Wrexham v Cardiff City	2-0

CC SPORTS WELSH LEAGUE

Division One

	P	W	D	L	F	A	Pts
Ton Pentre Athletic	34	25	5	4	111	34	80
Port Talbot Athletic*	34	22	9	3	85	33	75
Maesteg Park Athletic	34	18	11	5	67	41	65
BP Llandarcy	34	17	5	12	96	57	56
Cardiff Civil Service	34	15	9	10	70	49	54
AFC Rhondda	34	17	3	14	67	61	54
Bridgend Town	34	15	5	14	67	72	50
Briton Ferry Athletic	34	14	6	14	47	55	48
Gwynfi United	34	14	5	15	73	79	47
Penrhiwceiber Rangers	34	13	6	15	61	65	45
Goytre United	34	13	6	15	64	70	45
Porth Tywyn Suburbs	34	12	7	15	60	70	43
Treowen Stars	34	12	6	16	61	74	42
Pontardawe Town	34	11	8	15	56	63	41
UWI Cardiff	34	10	8	16	50	82	38
Ammanford	34	10	6	18	41	54	36
Cardiff Corries	34	9	7	18	45	71	34
Aberaman Town	34	2	2	30	47	138	8

Promoted instead of champions who declined place in League of Wales for third successive season.

HUWS GRAY – FITLOCK CYMRU ALLIANCE LEAGUE

	P	W	D	L	F	A	Pts
Oswestry Town*	32	21	4	7	64	43	64
Glantraeth	32	18	7	7	81	40	61
Cemaes Bay	32	17	8	7	74	44	59
Welshpool Town	32	17	6	9	60	41	57
CPD Porthmadog	32	17	5	10	64	40	56
Flint Town United	32	16	8	8	65	43	56
Llandudno	32	16	5	11	71	58	53
Rhydymwyn	32	15	5	12	55	54	50
Llangefni Town	32	13	10	9	60	43	49
Buckley Town	32	13	8	11	53	44	47
Ruthin Town	32	13	7	12	55	46	46
Holyhead Hotspur	32	9	6	17	52	67	33
Lex XI	32	9	3	20	55	92	30
Brymbo Broughton	32	7	8	17	32	49	29
Denbigh Town*	32	8	5	19	36	79	26
Holywell Town	32	7	4	21	41	69	25
Corwen Amateurs	32	5	3	24	25	91	18

*3 Points deducted

NORTHERN IRISH FOOTBALL 1999–2000

Northern Ireland football, both domestic and international, is now passing through a crisis phase – never has the situation been more serious or precarious with bankruptcy threatening several clubs. It is a sorry saga.

The non-existence of a political Assembly over the past decades has been a major contributory factor with Government grant aid for ground improvements unable to be released and, consequently, the deterioration at some stadia is alarming. Now, however, with an Administration operating again priority may be given to football. Smirnoff Premiership champions Linfield and Irish Cup holders Glentoran have each been forced to reduce the wage bill of £100,000, a major and vital cost-cutting exercise while clubs are placing an unofficial ceiling on their signing-on and wage structure with players given a take-it-or-leave-it message. "If the money isn't coming in we cannot pay it out – it is as simple as that," said one club official.

Ards, in receivership and with a new board appointed, are searching for a stadium after selling Castlereagh Park to a Scottish property developer to meet pressing creditors. The ground has been put on the market again, and, until it is sold, Ards must wait on their additional pay out. Nothing can be done until then.

Approaches to several other Irish League clubs for ground-sharing have failed while a number who did offer the facilities were unsuitable because of location. Unless a solution is found, Ards could be forced to play all their fixtures away.

They have been allocated a site, only a few hundred yards from Castlereagh Park by highly supportive Newtownards Borough Council, but this will take two years to complete and, of course, everything depends on the release of finance from the developers and various grants from various sources.

And it has been a disastrous year, too, for the Irish FA playing-wise and financially. Elimination from the European championship qualifiers, one win in eight matches, heralded the departure of Lawrie McMenemy and his managerial team, Joe Jordan, Chris Nicholl, and Pat Jennings who declined to take up an extension option on their contract. Sammy McIlroy, former Northern Ireland and Manchester United midfielder who had been with Macclesfield, took over, assisted by Jim Harvey, ex-Arsenal midfielder, now manager of Morecambe.

Meanwhile, after a near £1m profit last season due primarily to £900,000 from live televising and track advertising of the European championship game with Germany, David Bowen, Irish FA general secretary, reported they had made a gross trading loss of £842,000, the first since 1990 which, given the uncertainties of world football, is in itself a remarkable achievement. Cost of playing international football was £500,000 while income from home games had not kept pace with spiralling costs.

"The stark truth is that, when faced with such a financially unpromising World Cup draw against Czech Republic, Denmark, Bulgaria, Iceland and Malta it is imperative that sound fiscal planning and prudence shown previously is maintained," said Bowen.

"Those in decision-making positions must take a mature and measured view of their responsibilities. Participation in expensive and unnecessary matches and tournaments will have a negative effect on other parts of the Associations programmes. Such decisions must be weighed up carefully – balancing our commitments with the resources available for them will be an initial challenge in the new millennium."

McIlroy had initial success against Luxembourg and Malta, a cold douche of reality hit him with the 1-0 defeat by Hungary at Windsor Park and prospects of making an impact in the World Cup don't appear bright.

"I believe I have a reasonably good squad," says McIlroy. "I would, however, like more of them to be regularly competing in Premiership clubs but that could be difficult in view of the import of so many foreigners. I want them to play with passion and pride – just like the teams of the Eighties when we reached the 1982 and 1986 World Cup finals. Those qualities have been missing."

Linfield dominated the Irish Premiership with a soaraway 18-point success, won the Coca-Cola Floodlit Cup; Glentoran collected the Irish Cup, whose Bass sponsorship ended after 22 years, and also the Nationwide Gold Cup and Calor County Antrim Senior Shield while Coleraine, hovering in the relegation zone at Christmas, finished Premiership runners-up under newly-appointed manager Marty Quinn – an astonishing transformation.

Northern Ireland lost one of its football stalwarts with the death of Harry Cavan, CBE, distinguished Irish FA President for more than three decades and senior FIFA vice-president who served on various bodies including the Executive and World Cup Organising Committees.

His influence in the corridors of power was immense and, as a stand-in for ex-President Dr Joao Havelange, he earned global respect, especially in Africa and Asia where he had solved so many problems as an intermediary. The Irish FA owe a lot to his administrative expertise, business acumen and diplomatic handling of controversial and delicate issues. He was a true giant of football.

MALCOLM BRODIE

COCA-COLA FLOODLIT CUP

Semi-finals

Limavady United v Linfield (at Limavady)	0-1
Portadown v Coleraine (at Portadown)	0-2

Final

Linfield 4 Coleraine 0 (at The Oval)
Linfield: Mathers; Collier (McDonald), McShane, Marks, Murphy, Kelly (McCoosh), Larmour, Callaghan, Gorman, Morgan (Ferguson), Bailie.
Coleraine: McKeown; Clanaghan (McCann), Smyth, Gasgon, Devine, Stewart (Gray), Loughery, Picking, Keegan, McAllister, McHugh (Chillingsworth).
Scorers: Linfield: Gorman, Morgan, Larmour, McShane.
Referee: F. McDonald (Newry).
Attendance: 2963.

SMIRNOFF IFL

Premiership

	P	W	D	L	F	A	GD	Pts
Linfield	36	24	7	5	67	30	+37	79
Coleraine	36	18	7	11	64	42	+22	61
Glenavon	36	17	10	9	55	34	+21	61
Glentoran	36	18	7	11	59	51	+8	61
Portadown	36	15	7	14	64	62	+2	52
Newry Town	36	11	7	18	44	58	−14	40
Crusaders	36	9	13	14	41	55	−14	40
Ballymena United	36	6	16	14	45	62	−17	34
Cliftonville	36	7	13	16	38	59	−21	34
Lisburn Distillery	36	9	5	22	39	63	−24	32

Promotion and Relegation Play-Offs
First Leg
Ards 0 Cliftonville 2 *(Mulvenna 15, C Scannell 95)*
(At Castlereagh Park, Newtownards, May 2, 2000)
(Ards last game at Castlereagh Park which has been sold to a developer)

Second Leg
Cliftonville 1 *(C Scannell)*, Ards 0
(At Solitude, May 4, 2000)
Cliftonville retained senior status

First Division

	P	W	D	L	F	A	GD	Pts
Omagh Town	36	20	10	6	65	35	+30	70
Ards	36	16	16	4	65	36	+29	64
Limavady United	36	17	9	10	54	42	+12	60
Bangor	36	16	9	11	60	49	+11	57
Larne	36	15	9	12	56	53	+3	54
Institute	36	14	9	13	59	53	+6	51
Armagh City	36	10	10	16	50	61	−11	40
Dungannon Swifts	36	9	8	19	43	62	−19	35
Carrick Rangers	36	8	10	18	45	64	−19	34
Ballyclare Comrades	36	8	4	24	39	81	−42	28

Second Division

	P	W	D	L	F	A	GD	Pts
Dundela	22	16	5	1	65	17	+48	53
Loughgall	22	14	5	3	52	18	+34	47
Brantwood	22	13	6	3	51	29	+22	45
RUC	22	12	3	7	42	38	+4	39
H&W Welders	22	9	5	8	31	24	+7	32
Banbridge Town	22	8	7	7	43	37	+6	31
Ballinamallard Utd	22	8	5	9	32	38	−6	29
Ballymoney Utd	22	7	4	11	42	45	−3	25
Moyola Park	22	7	1	14	45	47	−2	22
Cookstown Utd	22	6	4	12	26	48	−22	22
Tobermore Utd	22	5	5	12	29	45	−16	20
Chimney Corner	22	1	2	19	23	94	−71	5

IFL Youth League

	P	W	D	L	F	A	GD	Pts
Linfield Rangers	18	12	3	3	54	17	+37	39
Cliftonville Str	18	11	4	3	53	27	+26	37
Ballymena Utd III	18	11	0	7	44	29	+15	33
Ards Colts	18	9	4	5	33	29	+4	31
Portadown III	18	7	5	6	30	40	−10	26
Glentoran Colts	18	7	3	8	41	32	+9	24
Crusaders Colts	18	5	3	10	29	38	−9	18
Glenavon III	18	5	2	11	23	43	−20	17
Ballyclare Com Clts	18	5	1	12	27	51	−24	16
Coleraine Colts	18	3	5	10	24	52	−28	14

IFL Reserve League

	P	W	D	L	F	A	GD	Pts
Linfield Swifts	34	28	3	3	95	31	+64	87
Crusaders Res	34	25	4	6	68	27	+41	79
Glenavon Res	34	19	4	10	64	43	+21	61
Cliftonville Olympic	34	17	7	10	90	51	+39	58
Ballymena Utd Res	34	18	4	12	53	40	+13	58
Glentoran II	34	16	6	12	61	48	+13	54
Dungannon Sw Res	34	15	7	12	54	47	+7	52
Coleraine Res	34	13	7	14	57	55	+2	46
Lisburn Distillery II	34	13	6	15	46	58	−12	45
Bangor Res	34	13	6	15	35	49	−14	45
Larne Olympic	34	10	12	12	59	76	−17	42
Ards II	34	12	5	17	48	53	−5	41
Portadown Res	34	10	10	14	47	62	−15	39
Carrick Rngrs Res	34	10	7	17	54	62	−8	37
Armagh City Res	34	10	7	17	49	75	−26	37
Ballyclare Com Res	34	8	4	22	41	74	−33	28
Institute Res	34	8	3	23	55	89	−34	27
Newry Town Res	34	6	9	19	42	76	−34	27

IRISH LEAGUE CHAMPIONSHIP WINNERS

1891	Linfield	1910	Cliftonville	1934	Linfield	1961	Linfield	1981	Glentoran
1892	Linfield	1911	Linfield	1935	Linfield	1962	Linfield	1982	Linfield
1893	Linfield	1912	Glentoran	1936	Belfast Celtic	1963	Distillery	1983	Linfield
1894	Glentoran	1913	Glentoran	1937	Belfast Celtic	1964	Glentoran	1984	Linfield
1895	Linfield	1914	Linfield	1938	Belfast Celtic	1965	Derry City	1985	Linfield
1896	Distillery	1915	Belfast Celtic	1939	Belfast Celtic	1966	Linfield	1986	Linfield
1897	Glentoran	1920	Belfast Celtic	1940	Belfast Celtic	1967	Glentoran	1987	Linfield
1898	Linfield	1921	Glentoran	1948	Belfast Celtic	1968	Glentoran	1988	Glentoran
1899	Distillery	1922	Linfield	1949	Linfield	1969	Linfield	1989	Linfield
1900	Belfast Celtic	1923	Linfield	1950	Linfield	1970	Glentoran	1990	Portadown
1901	Distillery	1924	Queen's Island	1951	Glentoran	1971	Linfield	1991	Portadown
1902	Linfield	1925	Glentoran	1952	Glenavon	1972	Glentoran	1992	Glentoran
1903	Distillery	1926	Belfast Celtic	1953	Glentoran	1973	Crusaders	1993	Linfield
1904	Linfield	1927	Belfast Celtic	1954	Linfield	1974	Coleraine	1994	Linfield
1905	Glentoran	1928	Belfast Celtic	1955	Linfield	1975	Linfield	1995	Crusaders
1906	Cliftonville	1929	Belfast Celtic	1956	Linfield	1976	Crusaders	1996	Portadown
	Distillery	1930	Linfield	1957	Glentoran	1977	Glentoran	1997	Crusaders
1907	Linfield	1931	Glentoran	1958	Ards	1978	Linfield	1998	Cliftonville
1908	Linfield	1932	Linfield	1959	Linfield	1979	Linfield	1999	Glentoran
1909	Linfield	1933	Belfast Celtic	1960	Glenavon	1980	Linfield	2000	Linfield

FIRST DIVISION

1996	Coleraine
1997	Ballymena United
1998	Newry Town
1999	Distillery
2000	Omagh Town

ULSTER CUP WINNERS

1949	Linfield	1960	Linfield	1971	Linfield	1981	Glentoran	1991	Bangor
1950	Larne	1961	Ballymena U	1972	Coleraine	1982	Glentoran	1992	Linfield
1951	Glentoran	1962	Linfield	1973	Ards	1983	Glentoran	1993	Crusaders
1952		1963	Crusaders	1974	Linfield	1984	Linfield	1994	Bangor
1953	Glentoran	1964	Linfield	1975	Coleraine	1985	Coleraine	1995	Portadown
1954	Crusaders	1965	Coleraine	1976	Glentoran	1986	Coleraine	1996	Portadown
1955	Glenavon	1966	Glentoran	1977	Linfield	1987	Larne	1997	Coleraine
1956	Linfield	1967	Linfield	1978	Linfield	1988	Glentoran	1998	Ballyclare Comrades
1957	Linfield	1968	Coleraine	1979	Linfield	1989	Glentoran	1999	Distillery
1958	Distillery	1969	Coleraine	1980	Ballymena U	1990	Portadown	2000	*No competition*
1959	Glenavon	1970	Linfield						

BASS IRISH CUP 1999–2000

Fifth Round

Ballinamallard v Killyleagh	1-2
Cliftonville v Portstewart	3-0
Limavady United v Armagh City	0-2
Coleraine v Comber Rec	7-0
Bangor v Carrick Rangers	3-0
Dungannon Swifts v Ards	0-0, 1-0
Loughgall v Ballymena United	0-1
Larne v Portadown	1-5
Glenavon v Newry Town	0-1
Tobermore United v Ballyclare Comrades	4-2
Bambridge Town v East Belfast	3-2
Lisburn Distillery v Omagh Town	2-1
Glentoran v Crusaders	3-0
Brantwood v Bessbrook United	2-3
Linfield v Enkalon	3-1
Institute v RUC	1-2

Sixth Round

Linfield v Killyleagh	1-0
Newry Town v RUC	3-0
Lisburn Distillery v Bambridge Town	3-0
Ballymena United v Bessbrook United	2-1
Bangor v Coleraine	3-3, 3-8
Dungannon Swifts v Tobermore United	4-0
Armagh City v Glentoran	2-2, 0-4
Portadown v Cliftonville	1-0

Quarter-finals

Linfield v Dungannon Swifts	2-2, 2-1 *(aet)*
Coleraine v Ballymena United	1-0
Newry Town v Glentoran	1-3
Lisburn Distillery v Portadown	0-2

Semi-finals

Coleraine v Portadown	0-0, 0-1

(first match at Ballymena; replay at Mourneview Park, Lurgan)

Glentoran v Linfield	3-2

(at Windsor Park)

Final

Glentoran 1 Portadown 0 *(at Windsor Park)*

Glentoran: Gough; Nixon, Kennedy, Dickson, McCombe, Young, McCann, Hamill, Russell (Gilzean), Batey, Elliott.

Portadown: Dalton; Brown, O'Hara, Byrne, Strain, Major, Larkin, Clarke, Sheridan, Arkins, Hill (Davidson).

Referee: J. Ferry (Londonderry).

Attendance: 8355.

Scorer: Gilzean

IRISH CUP FINALS (from 1946–47)

1946–47	Belfast Celtic 1, Glentoran 0
1947–48	Linfield 3, Coleraine 0
1948–49	Derry City 3, Glentoran 1
1949–50	Linfield 2, Distillery 1
1950–51	Glentoran 3, Ballymena U 1
1951–52	Ards 1, Glentoran 0
1952–53	Linfield 5, Coleraine 0
1953–54	Derry City 1, Glentoran 0
1954–55	Dundela 3, Glenavon 0
1955–56	Distillery 1, Glentoran 0
1956–57	Glenavon 2, Derry City 0
1957–58	Ballymena U 2, Linfield 0
1958–59	Glenavon 2, Ballymena U 0
1959–60	Linfield 5, Ards 1
1960–61	Glenavon 5, Linfield 1
1961–62	Linfield 4, Portadown 0
1962–63	Linfield 2, Distillery 1
1963–64	Derry City 2, Glentoran 0
1964–65	Coleraine 2, Glenavon 1
1965–66	Glentoran 2, Linfield 0
1966–67	Crusaders 3, Glentoran 1
1967–68	Crusaders 2, Linfield 0
1968–69	Ards 4, Distillery 2
1969–70	Linfield 2, Ballymena U 1
1970–71	Distillery 3, Derry City 0
1971–72	Coleraine 2, Portadown 1
1972–73	Glentoran 3, Linfield 2
1973–74	Ards 2, Ballymena U 1
1974–75	Coleraine 1:0:1, Linfield 1:0:0
1975–76	Carrick Rangers 2, Linfield 1
1976–77	Coleraine 4, Linfield 1
1977–78	Linfield 3, Ballymena U 1
1978–79	Cliftonville 3, Portadown 2
1979–80	Linfield 2, Crusaders 0
1980–81	Ballymena U 1, Glenavon 0
1981–82	Linfield 2, Coleraine 1
1982–83	Glentoran 1:2, Linfield 1:1
1983–84	Ballymena U 4, Carrick Rangers 1
1984–85	Glentoran 1:1, Linfield 1:0
1985–86	Glentoran 2, Coleraine 1
1986–87	Glentoran 1, Larne 0
1987–88	Glentoran 1, Glenavon 0
1988–89	Ballymena U 1, Larne 0
1989–90	Glentoran 3, Portadown 0
1990–91	Portadown 2, Glenavon 1
1991–92	Glenavon 2, Linfield 1
1992–93	Bangor 1:1:1, Ards 1:1:0
1993–94	Linfield 2, Bangor 0
1994–95	Linfield 3, Carrick Rangers 1
1995–96	Glentoran 1, Glenavon 0
1996–97	Glenavon 1, Cliftonville 0
1997–98	*Portadown awarded trophy after Cliftonville were eliminated for using an ineligible player in semi-final.*
1999–2000	Glentoran1, Portadown 0

NATIONWIDE GOLD CUP

Preliminary Round

Limavady United v Omagh Town	1-1

(aet; Limavady United won 3-2 on penalties)

Larne v Dungannon Swifts	1-2
Armagh City v Carrick Rangers	2-2

(aet; Carrick Rangers won 5-4 on penalties)

Bangor v Ards	1-2

First Round

Cliftonville v Portadown	3-1
Ards v Glentoran	1-2
Institute v Ballyclare Comrades	3-1
Ballymena United v Crusaders	3-2
Linfield v Dungannon Swifts	3-1
Carrick Rangers v Glenavon	1-3
Coleraine v Limavady United	2-3
Newry Town v Lisburn Distillery	1-0

Quarter-finals

Linfield v Ballymena United	3-1
Glenavon v Glentoran	1-2
Institute v Newry Town	2-0
Limavady United v Cliftonville	2-2

(Cliftonville won on penalties)

Semi-finals (two legs)

Linfield v Institute	4-0, 1-0
Glentoran v Cliftonville	0-0, 2-2

(aet; Glentoran won 4-3 on penalties)

Final

Glentoran 4 Linfield 2 *(at Windsor Park)*

Glentoran: Gough; Nixon, Ferguson, Walker, McCombe, Young, McCann, Hamill, Russell, Batey, Rainey (Leeman).

Linfield: Mathers; Collier, McShane, Marks, McLoughlin, Beatty, Larmour, McCoosh (Ferguson), Callaghan (Chisholm), Morgan, Bailie.

Scorers: Glentoran: Russell 2, Young, McCombe. *Linfield:* Larmour, Bailie.

Referee: A. Snoddy (Carryduff).

WHERE THE TROPHIES WENT

	Winners	*Runners-up*
Smirnoff Irish League		
Premier Division	Linfield	Glentoran
First Division	Omagh Town	Ards
Bass Irish Cup	Glentoran	Portadown
Nationwide Gold Cup	Glentoran	Portadown
Coca-Cola Irish League Floodlit Cup	Linfield	Coleraine
Calor County Antrim Senior Shield	Glentoran	Bangor
Calor County Antrim Junior Shield	Portaferry Rangers	FC Penarol
Smirnoff Knock-Out Cup	Moyola Park	H&W Welders
Belfast Telegraph Intermediate Cup	Dundela	Loughgall
Silverwood Golf Hotel Mid Ulster Cup	Newry Town	Banbridge Town
Calor Steel & Sons Cup	Dundela	Comber Rec
Harry Cavan Youth Cup	Linfield Rangers	Cliftonville Strollers
George Wilson Memorial Cup	Cliftonville Olympic	Ballymena
Irish League Second Division	Dundela	Loughgall
Irish Reserve League	Linfield Swifts	Crusaders Reserves
Sunday Mirror Irish Junior Cup Final	Lisnaskea	Enniskillen Rangers
Wilkinson Sword Charity Shield	Portadown	Glentoran
North West Senior Cup	Omagh Town	Limavady United

EUROPEAN CUP

EUROPEAN CUP FINALS 1956–2000

Year	Winners		Runners-up		Venue	Attendance	Referee
1956	Real Madrid	4	Reims	3	Paris	38,000	Ellis (E)
1957	Real Madrid	2	Fiorentina	0	Madrid	124,000	Horn (Ho)
1958	Real Madrid	3	AC Milan	2 *(aet)*	Brussels	67,000	Alsteen (Bel)
1959	Real Madrid	2	Reims	0	Stuttgart	80,000	Dutsch (WG)
1960	Real Madrid	7	Eintracht Frankfurt	3	Glasgow	135,000	Mowat (S)
1961	Benfica	3	Barcelona	2	Berne	28,000	Dienst (Sw)
1962	Benfica	5	Real Madrid	3	Amsterdam	65,000	Horn (Ho)
1963	AC Milan	2	Benfica	1	Wembley	45,000	Holland (E)
1964	Internazionale	3	Real Madrid	1	Vienna	74,000	Stoll (A)
1965	Internazionale	1	Benfica	0	Milan	80,000	Dienst (Sw)
1966	Real Madrid	2	Partizan Belgrade	1	Brussels	55,000	Kreitlein (WG)
1967	Celtic	2	Internazionale	1	Lisbon	56,000	Tschenscher (WG)
1968	Manchester U	4	Benfica	1 *(aet)*	Wembley	100,000	Lo Bello (I)
1969	AC Milan	4	Ajax	1	Madrid	50,000	Ortiz (Sp)
1970	Feyenoord	2	Celtic	1 *(aet)*	Milan	50,000	Lo Bello (I)
1971	Ajax	2	Panathinaikos	0	Wembley	90,000	Taylor (E)
1972	Ajax	2	Internazionale	0	Rotterdam	67,000	Helies (F)
1973	Ajax	1	Juventus	0	Belgrade	93,500	Guglovic (Y)
1974	Bayern Munich	1	Atletico Madrid	1	Brussels	49,000	Loraux (Bel)
Replay	Bayern Munich	4	Atletico Madrid	0	Brussels	23,000	Delcourt (Bel)
1975	Bayern Munich	2	Leeds U	0	Paris	50,000	Kitabdjian (F)
1976	Bayern Munich	1	St Etienne	0	Glasgow	54,864	Palotai (H)
1977	Liverpool	3	Moenchengladbach	1	Rome	57,000	Wurtz (F)
1978	Liverpool	1	FC Brugge	0	Wembley	92,000	Corver (Ho)
1979	Nottingham F	1	Malmo	0	Munich	57,500	Linemayr (A)
1980	Nottingham F	1	Hamburg	0	Madrid	50,000	Garrido (P)
1981	Liverpool	1	Real Madrid	0	Paris	48,360	Palotai (H)
1982	Aston Villa	1	Bayern Munich	0	Rotterdam	46,000	Konrath (F)
1983	Hamburg	1	Juventus	0	Athens	80,000	Rainea (R)
1984	Liverpool	1	Roma	1	Rome	69,693	Fredriksson (Se)
	(aet; Liverpool won 4–2 on penalties)						
1985	Juventus	1	Liverpool	0	Brussels	58,000	Daina (Sw)
1986	Steaua Bucharest	0	Barcelona	0	Seville	70,000	Vautrot (F)
	(aet; Steaua won 2–0 on penalties)						
1987	Porto	2	Bayern Munich	1	Vienna	59,000	Ponnet (Bel)
1988	PSV Eindhoven	0	Benfica	0	Stuttgart	70,000	Agnolin (I)
	(aet; PSV won 6–5 on penalties)						
1989	AC Milan	4	Steaua Bucharest	0	Barcelona	97,000	Tritschler (WG)
1990	AC Milan	1	Benfica	0	Vienna	57,500	Kohl (A)
1991	Red Star Belgrade	0	Marseille	0	Bari	56,000	Lanese (I)
	(aet; Red Star won 5–3 on penalties)						
1992	Barcelona	1	Sampdoria	0 *(aet)*	Wembley	70,827	Schmidhuber (G)
1993	Marseille*	1	AC Milan	0	Munich	64,400	Rothlisberger (Sw)
1994	AC Milan	4	Barcelona	0	Athens	70,000	Don (E)
1995	Ajax	1	AC Milan	0	Vienna	49,730	Craciunescu (Ro)
1996	Juventus	1	Ajax	1	Rome	67,000	Vega (Sp)
	(aet; Juventus won 4–2 on penalties)						
1997	Borussia Dortmund	3	Juventus	1	Munich	59,000	Puhl (H)
1998	Real Madrid	1	Juventus	0	Amsterdam	47,500	Krug (G)
1999	Manchester U	2	Bayern Munich	1	Barcelona	90,000	Collina (I)
2000	Real Madrid	3	Valencia	0	Paris	78,759	Braschi (I)

Subsequently stripped of title.

EUROPEAN CUP 1999–2000

FIRST QUALIFYING ROUND, FIRST LEG
Barry Town (0) 0, Valletta (0) 0   2005
HB Torshavn (0) 1 *(Lakjuni 47)*, Haka (0) 1 *(Popovic 60)*
                                                             1200
IBV (1) 1 *(Johannesson 45)*, SK Tirana (0) 0   790
Jeunesse Esch (0) 0, Skonto Riga (0) 2 *(Astafyev 66,*
  Miholap 73)   1000
Litets (2) 3 *(Hadji 11, Bushi 35 (pen), Petrov 82)*,
  Glentoran (0) 0   4000
Partizan Belgrade (3) 6 *(Ilic 12, Pekovic 25, 71, Ivic 36,*
  75, Kezman 54), Flora Tallinn (0) 0   10,000
Sloga (0) 1 *(Memedi 66)*, Kapaz (0) 0   5000
St Patrick's Athletic (0) 0, Zimbru Chisinau (3) 5
  (Berco 29, 41, Epureanu 35, 84, Boret 72)   3727
Zalgiris (1) 2 *(Stesjko I 45, Stesjko A 88)*, Tsement (0) 0
                                                             570

FIRST QUALIFYING ROUND, SECOND LEG
Flora Tallinn (0) 1 *(Viikmae 52)*, Partizan Belgrade (2) 4
  (Kezman 10, 69, Ilic 20, Tomic 82)   225
Glentoran (0) 0, Litets (0) 2 *(Haxhi 63, Bushi 89)*   5000
Haka (2) 6 *(Salli 26, Reynders 44, Nyyssonen 46, Wilson*
  63, Popovic 80, Torkkeli 90), HB Torshavn (0) 0   2200
Kapaz (1) 2 *(Mamedov 19, Rzayev 90 (pen))*, Sloga (1) 1
  (Arif 34)   8000
Skonto Riga (2) 8 *(Bleidelis 37, 50, Miholap 39, 55, 63, 85*
  (pen), 90 (pen), Koleschenko 77), Jeunesse Esch (0) 0
                                                             500
SK Tirana (0) 1 *(Bulku 82)*, IBV (2) 2 *(Johannesson 33,*
  Sigurdsson 48)   5000
Tsement (0) 0, Zalgiris (2) 3 *(Novikov 7, Jokshas 32,*
  Vasilauskas 65)   1500
Valletta (1) 3 *(Agius 42, 46, Chetcuti 55)*, Barry Town (0)
  2 *(Sloan 47, 56)*   2996
Zimbru Chisinau (3) 5 *(Tropanet 25, 40, Borets 31, 75,*
  Oprea 83 (pen)), St Patrick's Athletic (0) 0   4000

SECOND QUALIFYING ROUND, FIRST LEG
Anorthosis (1) 2 *(Obicu 28, 88 (pen))*, Slovan Bratislava
  (0) 1 *(Hrncar 53)*   7000
Besiktas (0) 1 *(Akhman 90)*, Hapoel Haifa (0) 1
  (Rosso 76)   12,000
CSKA Moscow (1) 2 *(Siskin 7, Khomukha 86)*,
  Molde (0) 0   8000
Dnepr Mogilev (0) 0, AIK Stockholm (0) 1
  (Tjernstrom 90)   5000
Dynamo Kiev (1) 2 *(Shatskikh 37, 78)*, Zalgiris (0) 0
                                                           14,500
Dynamo Tbilisi (0) 2 *(Tsitaishvili 82, Khomeriki 88)*,
  Zimbru Chisinau (0) 1 *(Berko 68)*   8000
Haka (0) 1 *(Niemi 51)*, Rangers (3) 4 *(Amoruso 18, Mols*
  28, 42, Johansson 85)   3341
IBV (0) 0, MTK Budapest (1) 2 *(Halmai 26, Preisinger*
  54)   1500
Litets (1) 4 *(Todorov 39, 80, Zivkovic 82 (pen), Dodrov*
  90), Widzew Lodz (1) 1 *(Wichniarek 89 (pen)*   3500
Maribor (2) 5 *(Balajic 25, Galic 62, Karic 69 (pen),*
  Simundza 77, Djuranovic 90), Genk (1) 1 *(Strupar 34)*
                                                            8000
Partizan Belgrade (2) 3 *(Ilic 10, Krstajic 22, 85)*, Rijeka
  (0) 1 *(Stipanovic 56)*   32,000
Rapid Bucharest (1) 3 *(Barbu 14, Schumacher 52, Mutica*
  73), Skonto Riga (2) 3 *(Chaladze 5, 32, Astafyev 65)*
                                                            6000
Rapid Vienna (0) 3 *(Dawe 54, Savicevic 74, Penksa 86)*,
  Valletta (0) 0   17,000
Sloga (0) 0, Brondby (1) 1 *(Daugaard 15)*   6000

SECOND QUALIFYING ROUND, SECOND LEG
AIK Stockholm (0) 2 *(Corneliusson 55, Gustafsson 85)*,
  Dnepr Mogilev (0) 0   8513
Brondby (1) 1 *(Daugaard 4 (pen))*, Sloga (0) 0   8000
Genk (1) 3 *(Gudjonsson T 45, 58, Horvath 62)*,
  Maribor (0) 0   8000
(in Liege).
Hapoel Haifa (0) 0, Besiktas (0) 0   11,500
Molde (0) 4 *(Tessem 47, Berg Hestad 65, Hoseth 67, 81)*,
  CSKA Moscow (0) 0   5203
MTK Budapest (3) 3 *(Illes 4, 41, Kuttor 25)*, IBV (0) 1
  (Moller 90)   2500
Rangers (2) 3 *(Wallace 15, Johansson 28, Amato 66)*,
  Haka (0) 0   46,443

Rijeka (0) 0, Partizan Belgrade (2) 3 *(Kezman 7, 83,*
  Ivic 19)   20,000
Skonto Riga (0) 2 *(Laizans 77, Rubins 87)*, Rapid
  Bucharest (1) 1 *(Raducanu 33)*   4900
Slovan Bratislava (0) 1 *(Timko 60)*, Anorthosis (0) 1
  (Obicu 58)   10,770
Valletta (0) 0, Rapid Vienna (0) 2 *(Dawe 71,*
  Lagonikakis 88)   3500
Widzew Lodz (1) 4 *(Gesior 14, Wichniarek 52, 60,*
  Michalski 75), Litets (1) 1 *(Todorov 30)*   4800
(Widzew Lodz won 3-2 on penalties).
Zalgiris (0) 0, Dynamo Kiev (1) 1 *(Rebrov 35)*   4000
Zimbru Chisinau (1) 2 *(Dodul 23, Epureanu 90)*,
  Dynamo Tbilisi (0) 0   10,000

THIRD QUALIFYING ROUND, FIRST LEG
Aalborg (0) 1 *(Strandli 55)*, Dynamo Kiev (2) 2 *(Rebrov*
  13, Shatskikh 39)   8462
AEK Athens (0) 0, AIK Stockholm (0) 0   25,000
Brondby (0) 1 *(Smith 65)*, Boavista (1) 2 *(Mario Silva 25,*
  Moreira 73)   9060
Chelsea (0) 3 *(Babayaro 76, Poyet 77, Sutton 84)*, Skonto
  Riga (0) 0   22,043
Croatia Zagreb (0) 0, MTK Budapest (0) 0   34,000
Fiorentina (1) 3 *(Adani 17, Cois 57, Rui Costa 90)*,
  Widzew Lodz (0) 1 *(Adani 73 (og))*   35,000
Hapoel Haifa (0) 0, Valencia (0) 2 *(Lopez 68,*
  Farinos 74)   14,500
Hertha Berlin (1) 2 *(Daei 2, Preetz 58)*,
  Anorthosis (0) 0   35,000
Lyon (0) 0, Maribor (0) 1 *(Filipovic 89)*   25,000
Molde (0) 0, Mallorca (0) 0   8573
Rangers (1) 2 *(Vidmar 32, Reyna 76)*, Parma (0) 0   49,263
Rapid Vienna (0) 0, Galatasaray (2) 3 *(Hakan Unsal 34,*
  Fatih 38, Hagi 90)   30,200
Spartak Moscow (1) 2 *(Shirko 39, Tikhonov 73)*,
  Partizan Belgrade (0) 0   45,000
Sturm Graz (2) 2 *(Vastic 35, Martens 44)*, Servette (1) 1
  (Lonfat 45)   12,000
Teplice (0) 0, Borussia Dortmund (0) 1 *(Nerlinger 66)*
                                                           15,000
Zimbru Chisinau (0) 0, PSV Eindhoven (0) 0   10,000

THIRD QUALIFYING ROUND, SECOND LEG
AIK Stockholm (0) 1 *(Novakovic 58)*,
  AEK Athens (0) 0   31,115
Anorthosis (0) 0, Hertha Berlin (0) 0   8000
Boavista (1) 4 *(Litos 13, Ahinful 99, 110, Rui Bento 117)*,
  Brondby (0) 2 *(Christensen 47, Bjur 90)*   9000
Borussia Dortmund (0) 1 *(Herrlich 90)*, Teplice (0) 0
                                                          48,000
Dynamo Kiev (0) 2 *(Gusin 74, Shatskikh 90)*,
  Aalborg (1) 2 *(Oper 9, Gaarde 47)*   15,000
Galatasaray (0) 1 *(Okan 52)*, Rapid Vienna (0) 0   15,000
Mallorca (1) 1 *(Stankovic 22 (pen))*, Molde (0) 1
  (Lund 85 (pen))   23,000
Maribor (0) 2 *(Simundza 24, Balajic 45)*, Lyon (0) 0   7600
MTK Budapest (0) 0, Croatia Zagreb (0) 2 *(Simic 60, 85)*
                                                           6000
Parma (0) 1 *(Walem 68)*, Rangers (0) 0   28,500
Partizan Belgrade (0) 1 *(Kezman 72)*, Spartak
  Moscow (1) 3 *(Shirko 19, 46, Titov 83 (pen))*   27,000
PSV Eindhoven (0) 2 *(Nilis 81, Ooijer 86)*, Zimbru
  Chisinau (0) 0   20,000
Servette (1) 2 *(Kocijan 54, Thurre 89)*, Sturm Graz (0) 2
  (De Souza 50, Vastic 78)   8829
Skonto Riga (0) 0, Chelsea (0) 0   5023
Valencia (0) 2 *(Sanchez 59, 66)*, Hapoel Haifa (0) 0
Widzew Lodz (0) 1, Fiorentina (1) 2 *(Chiesa 40, Cois 68)*
                                                           6500

CHAMPIONS LEAGUE

GROUP A
Dynamo Kiev (0) 0, Maribor (0) 1 *(Simundza 73)* 30,000
Leverkusen (1) 1 *(Neuville 14)*, Lazio (1) 1 *(Mihajlovic*
  18)   22,500
Lazio (0) 2 *(Negro 70, Salas 72)*, Dynamo Kiev (0) 1
  (Rebrov 68 (pen)   45,000
Maribor (0) 0, Leverkusen (0) 2 *(Zivkovic 82, Kirsten 90)*
                                                          10,000

Leverkusen (0) 1 *(Kirsten 52)*, Dynamo Kiev (0) 1
   (Gusin 71) 22,500
Lazio (0) 4 *(Inzaghi 61, Conceicao 62, Salas 71, 76)*,
   Maribor (0) 0 30,000
Dynamo Kiev (2) 4 *(Kossovski 4, Shatskikh 36, Golovko
   61, Vashchuk 89)*, Leverkusen (1) 2 *(Kirsten 12,
   Neuville 49)* 40,000
Maribor (0) 0, Lazio (1) 4 *(Mihajlovic 36, Inzaghi 50, 74,
   Stankovic 63)* 10,000
Lazio (1) 1 *(Nedved 2)*, Leverkusen (1) 1 *(Kirsten 44)*
   45,000
Maribor (0) 1 *(Balajic 50)*, Dynamo Kiev (1) 2
   (Rebrov 37, 84 (pen)) 9500
Leverkusen (0) 0, Maribor (0) 0 22,500
Dynamo Kiev (0) 0, Lazio (1) 1 *(Mamedov 18 (og))*
   70,000

FINAL TABLE	P	W	D	L	F	A	Pts
Lazio	6	4	2	0	13	3	14
Dynamo Kiev	6	2	1	3	8	8	7
Leverkusen	6	1	4	1	7	7	7
Maribor	6	1	1	4	2	12	4

GROUP B
AIK Stockholm (0) 1 *(Novakovic 72)*, Barcelona (0) 2
   (Abelardo 86, Dani 90) 30,543
Fiorentina (0) 0, Arsenal (0) 0 33,903
Arsenal (1) 3 *(Ljungberg 27, Henry 89, Suker 90)*,
   AIK Stockholm (0) 1 *(Nordin 52)* 71,227 *(at Wembley)*.
Barcelona (2) 4 *(Figo 7, Luis Enrique 10, Rivaldo 68
   (pen), 70)*, Fiorentina (0) 2 *(Batistuta 51, Chiesa 79)*
   75,000
AIK Stockholm (0) 0, Fiorentina (0) 0 30,195
Barcelona (1) 1 *(Luis Enrique 16)*, Arsenal (0) 1
   (Kanu 81) 85,000
Arsenal (1) 2 *(Bergkamp 44, Overmars 84)*, Barcelona
   (2) 4 *(Rivaldo 15 (pen), Luis Enrique 16, Figo 56,
   Cocu 69)* 73,091 *(at Wembley)*.
Fiorentina (2) 3 *(Batistuta 5, Chiesa 36, Balbo 86)*, AIK
   Stockholm (0) 0 30,000
Arsenal (0) 0, Fiorentina (0) 1 *(Batistuta 75)*
   73,336 *(at Wembley)*.
Barcelona (3) 5 *(Kluivert 15, 33, Zenden 43, Gabri 53,
   Dehu 56)*, AIK Stockholm (0) 0 45,000
AIK Stockholm (0) 2 *(Andersson A 41, 68)*, Arsenal (1) 3
   (Overmars 17, 52, Suker 56) 33,005
Fiorentina (1) 3 *(Bressan 14, Balbo 56, 69)*,
   Barcelona (2) 3 *(Figo 20, Rivaldo 43, 74)* 28,000

FINAL TABLE	P	W	D	L	F	A	Pts
Barcelona	6	4	2	0	19	9	14
Fiorentina	6	2	3	1	9	7	9
Arsenal	6	2	2	2	9	9	8
AIK Stockholm	6	0	1	5	4	16	1

GROUP C
Boavista (0) 0, Rosenborg (2) 3 *(Sorensen 10, Berg 43,
   Strand 73)* 8000
Feyenoord (0) 1 *(Van Wonderen 67)*, Borussia Dortmund
   (0) 1 *(Bobic 71)* 35,000
Borussia Dortmund (1) 3 *(Moller 40, Bobic 53, 65)*,
   Boavista (1) 1 *(Rui Bento 44)* 44,000
Rosenborg (2) 2 *(Carew 21, 24)*, Feyenoord (2) 2
   (Tomasson 12, Kalou 22) 20,000
Boavista (0) 1 *(Mario Silva 87)*, Feyenoord (0) 1
   (Bosvelt 62) 7000
Rosenborg (1) 2 *(Sorensen 35, Carew 68)*, Borussia
   Dortmund (2) 2 *(Barbarez 12, Kohler 22)* 14,068
Borussia Dortmund (0) 0, Rosenborg (1) 3 *(Sorensen 17,
   58, Winsnes 70)* 35,000
Feyenoord (0) 1 *(Tomasson 76)*, Boavista (0) 1
   (Timofte 83 (pen)) 35,000
Borussia Dortmund (1) 1 *(Addo 45)*, Feyenoord (0) 1
   (Van Vossen 72) 40,000
Rosenborg (0) 2 *(Berg 62, Dahlum 66)*, Boavista (0) 0
   14,167
Boavista (1) 1 *(Emanuel 16)*, Borussia Dortmund (0) 0
   9000
Feyenoord (0) 1 *(Somalia 86)*, Rosenborg (0) 0 39,000

FINAL TABLE	P	W	D	L	F	A	Pts
Rosenborg	6	3	2	1	12	5	11
Feyenoord	6	1	5	0	7	6	8
Borussia Dortmund	6	1	3	2	7	9	6
Boavista	6	1	2	3	4	10	5

GROUP D
Manchester United (0) 0, Croatia Zagreb (0) 0 53,250

Marseille (2) 2 *(Pires 9, Ravanelli 33)*, Sturm Graz (0) 0
   35,000
Croatia Zagreb (0) 1 *(Sokota 64)*, Marseille (1) 2
   (Bakayoko 5, Perez 77) 25,000
Sturm Graz (0) 0, Manchester United (3) 3 *(Keane 17,
   Yorke 31, Cole 33)* 16,480
Croatia Zagreb (2) 3 *(Rukavina 28, Sokota 34, 57 (pen))*,
   Sturm Graz (0) 0 20,000
Manchester United (0) 2 *(Cole 79, Scholes 83)*, Marseille
   (1) 1 *(Bakayoko 41)* 53,993
Marseille (0) 1 *(Gallas 69)*, Manchester United (0) 0
   57,745
Sturm Graz (1) 1 *(Kocijan 40)*, Croatia Zagreb (0) 0
   12,000
Croatia Zagreb (0) 1 *(Prosinecki 90)*, Manchester United
   (1) 2 *(Beckham 32, Keane 49)* 38,000
Sturm Graz (1) 3 *(Mahlich 19, Kocijan 61, 84)*,
   Marseille (0) 2 *(Dugarry 53, 78)* 14,850
Manchester United (0) 2 *(Solskjaer 56, Keane 69)*,
   Sturm Graz (0) 1 *(Vastic 87 (pen))* 53,745
Marseille (0) 2 *(Bakayoko 53, Diawara 89)*, Croatia
   Zagreb (1) 2 *(Mujcin 42, Mikic 84)* 37,887

FINAL TABLE	P	W	D	L	F	A	Pts
Manchester United	6	4	1	1	9	4	13
Marseille	6	3	1	2	10	8	10
Sturm Graz	6	2	0	4	5	12	6
Croatia Zagreb	6	1	2	3	7	7	5

GROUP E
Molde (0) 0, Porto (0) 1 *(Deco 88)* 9000
Olympiakos (1) 3 *(Giovanni 11, 64, Zahovic 67)*, Real
   Madrid (2) 3 *(Savio 24, Roberto Carlos 32, Raul 80)*
   80,000
Porto (1) 2 *(Esquerdinha 6, Jardel 47)*, Olympiakos (0) 0
   25,000
Real Madrid (1) 4 *(Morientes 27, Savio 60, 70 (pen), Guti
   81)*, Molde (0) 1 *(Lindbaek 80)* 15,000
Olympiakos (1) 3 *(Giovanni 16, 70, Luciano 77)*,
   Molde (0) 1 *(Lund 58)* 50,000
Real Madrid (2) 3 *(Morientes 23, Helguera 37, Hierro 68
   (pen))*, Porto (1) 1 *(Jardel 24)* 27,000
Molde (0) 3 *(Lund 55, 59, Hestad 74)*, Olympiakos (2) 2
   (Mavrogenidis 36, Zahovic 40) 10,230
Porto (2) 2 *(Jardel 13, 35)*, Real Madrid (0) 1
   (Peixe 68 (og)) 32,000
Porto (2) 3 *(Deco 1, 28, Jardel 57)*, Molde (0) 1
   (Hestad 82) 35,000
Real Madrid (1) 3 *(Raul 21, Morientes 64, Roberto Carlos
   83)*, Olympiakos (0) 0 9000
Molde (0) 0, Real Madrid (1) 1 *(Karembeu 43)* 10,785
Olympiakos (0) 1 *(Giannakopoulos 56)*, Porto (0) 0
   30,000

FINAL TABLE	P	W	D	L	F	A	Pts
Real Madrid	6	4	1	1	15	7	13
Porto	6	4	0	2	9	6	12
Olympiakos	6	2	1	3	9	12	7
Molde	6	1	0	5	6	14	3

GROUP F
Bayern Munich (1) 2 *(Paulo Sergio 11, 69)*, PSV
   Eindhoven (0) 1 *(Khokhlov 59)* 32,000
Valencia (0) 2 *(Moore 57 (og), Gonzalez 74)*,
   Rangers (0) 0 54,971
PSV Eindhoven (0) 1 *(Van Nistelrooij 72 (pen))*,
   Valencia (1) 1 *(Lopez 4)* 30,000
Rangers (1) 1 *(Albertz 22)*, Bayern Munich (0) 1
   (Tarnat 88) 49,960
Bayern Munich (1) 1 *(Elber 6)*, Valencia (0) 1
   (Gerard 80) 30,000
PSV Eindhoven (0) 0, Rangers (0) 1 *(Albertz 84)* 27,000
Rangers (2) 4 *(Amoruso 18, Mols 38, 79, McCann 55)*,
   PSV Eindhoven (1) 1 *(Van Nistelrooij 45 (pen))* 50,083
Valencia (1) 1 *(Ilie A 11)*, Bayern Munich (1) 1
   (Effenberg 18 (pen)) 42,000
PSV Eindhoven (1) 2 *(Van Nistelrooij 40, Nilis 57)*,
   Bayern Munich (0) 1 *(Santa Cruz 51)* 29,500
Rangers (0) 0 *(Moore 59)*, Valencia (2) 2 *(Mendieta 34,
   Lopez 45)* 50,063
Bayern Munich (1) 1 *(Strunz 32 (pen))*, Rangers (0) 0
   54,000
Valencia (0) 1 *(Lopez 70)*, PSV Eindhoven (0) 0 30,000

FINAL TABLE	P	W	D	L	F	A	Pts
Valencia	6	3	3	0	8	4	12
Bayern Munich	6	2	3	1	7	6	9
Rangers	6	2	1	3	7	7	7
PSV Eindhoven	6	1	1	4	5	10	4

GROUP G

Sparta Prague (0) 0, Bordeaux (0) 0   14,928
Willem II (0) 1 *(Arts 56)*, Spartak Moscow (2) 3
  (Tikhonov 27 (pen), 37, 53 (pen))   14,500
Bordeaux (2) 3 *(Victoria 17 (og), Laslandes 22,*
  Feindouno 82), Willem II (1) 2 *(Abdellaoui 40,*
  Sanou 70)   14,000
Spartak Moscow (0) 1 *(Bezrodny 73)*, Sparta Prague (1) 1
  (Lokvenc 17)   45,000
Bordeaux (1) 2 *(Wiltord 9, Micoud 56)*, Spartak
  Moscow (0) 1 *(Bezrodny 64)*   17,550
Sparta Prague (3) 4 *(Novotny 26, Prohaszka 29 (pen),*
  Rosicky 40, Jarosik 58), Willem II (0) 0   10,581
Spartak Moscow (0) 1 *(Tikhonov 55 (pen))*, Bordeaux (1)
  2 *(Micoud 23, Wiltord 76)*   48,000
Willem II (2) 3 *(Bombarda 1, Shoukov 6, Schenning 50)*,
  Sparta Prague (1) 4 *(Novotny 17, Labant 54 (pen), 90*
  (pen), Baranek 62)   14,000
Bordeaux (0) 0, Sparta Prague (0) 0   22,000
Spartak Moscow (1) 1 *(Bezrodny 25)*, Willem II (0) 1
  (Sanou 69)   20,000
Sparta Prague (2) 5 *(Lokvenc 1, 66, Rosicky 10, Fukal 49,*
  Labant 63 (pen)), Spartak Moscow (2) 2 *(Bulatov 34,*
  Bezrodny 45)   12,106
Willem II (0) 0, Bordeaux (0) 0   13,000

FINAL TABLE	P	W	D	L	F	A	Pts
Sparta Prague	6	3	3	0	14	6	12
Bordeaux	6	3	3	0	7	4	12
Spartak Moscow	6	1	2	3	9	12	5
Willem II	6	0	2	4	7	15	2

GROUP H

Chelsea (0) 0, AC Milan (0) 0   33,873
Galatasaray (1) 2 *(Hakan Sukur 24, Hagi 89 (pen))*,
  Hertha Berlin (2) 2 *(Preetz 12, Wosz 13)*   22,000
Hertha Berlin (1) 2 *(Daei 3, 70)*, Chelsea (0) 1 *(Leboeuf*
  86 (pen))   55,541
AC Milan (2) 2 *(Leonardo 44, Shevchenko 45)*,
  Galatasaray (0) 1 *(Umit 55)*   37,822
Chelsea (0) 1 *(Petrescu 55)*, Galatasaray (0) 0   33,426
AC Milan (0) 1 *(Bierhoff 74)*, Hertha Berlin (0) 1
  (Daei 69)   40,941
Galatasaray (0) 0, Chelsea (1) 5 *(Flo 32, 49, Zola 54,*
  Wise 79, Ambrosetti 87)   25,500
Hertha Berlin (1) 1 *(Wosz 41)*, AC Milan (0) 0   76,000
AC Milan (0) 1 *(Bierhoff 74)*, Chelsea (0) 1 *(Wise 77)*
   74,855
Hertha Berlin (1) 1 *(Rekdal 35 (pen))*, Galatasaray (0) 4
  (Hakan Sukur 48, 66, Tugay 81, Okan 90)   71,520
Chelsea (2) 2 *(Deschamps 11, Ferrer 44)*, Hertha Berlin
  (0) 0   33,623
Galatasaray (1) 3 *(Capone 27, Hakan Sukur 87, Umit 90*
  (pen)), AC Milan (1) 2 *(Weah 20, Giunti 51)*   30,000

FINAL TABLE	P	W	D	L	F	A	Pts
Chelsea	6	3	2	1	10	3	11
Hertha Berlin	6	2	2	2	7	10	8
Galatasaray	6	2	1	3	10	13	7
AC Milan	6	1	3	2	6	7	6

SECOND STAGE

GROUP A

Hertha Berlin (1) 1 *(Michalke 33)*, Barcelona (1) 1 *(Luis*
  Enrique 14)   65,000
Sparta Prague (0) 0, Porto (0) 2 *(Drulovic 77, Jardel 84)*
   14,625
Barcelona (2) 5 *(Kluivert 44, 63, Luis Enrique 45, 76,*
  Guardiola 60), Sparta Prague (0) 0   65,000
Porto (0) 1 *(Drulovic 79)*, Hertha Berlin (0) 0   24,000
Barcelona (3) 4 *(Rivaldo 16, 88, Frank de Boer 22,*
  Kluivert 45), Porto (1) 2 *(Jardel 5, 29)*   68,000
Hertha Berlin (1) 1 *(Veit 45)*, Sparta Prague (0) 1 *(Siegl*
  84)   30,337
Porto (0) 0, Barcelona (1) 2 *(Abelardo 38, Rivaldo 59)*
   45,500
Sparta Prague (0) 1 *(Fukal 90)*, Hertha Berlin (0) 0   9100
Barcelona (1) 3 *(Xavi 11, Gabri 49, Kluivert 83)*,
  Hertha Berlin (1) 1 *(Alves 7)*   48,000

Porto (1) 2 *(George Costa 16, Capucho 64)*, Sparta
  Prague (0) 2 *(Lokvenc 74, Fukal 90)*   27,400
Hertha Berlin (0) 0, Porto (0) 1 *(Clayton 70)*   30,506
Sparta Prague (1) 1 *(Svoboda 18)*, Barcelona (0) 2
  (Gabri 52, 89)   20,224

FINAL TABLE	P	W	D	L	F	A	Pts
Barcelona	6	5	1	0	17	5	16
Porto	6	3	1	2	8	8	10
Sparta Prague	6	1	2	3	5	12	5
Hertha Berlin	6	0	2	4	3	8	2

GROUP B

Fiorentina (1) 2 *(Batistuta 24, Balbo 52)*, Manchester
  United (0) 0   40,000
Valencia (0) 3 *(Farinos 60, Ilie A 68, Gonzalez 90)*,
  Bordeaux (0) 0   25,000
Bordeaux (0) 0, Fiorentina (0) 0   28,000
Manchester United (1) 3 *(Keane 38, Solskjaer 47, Scholes*
  69), Valencia (0) 0   54,606
Manchester United (1) 2 *(Giggs 42, Sheringham 84)*,
  Bordeaux (0) 0   59,786
Fiorentina (1) 1 *(Mijatovic 20 (pen))*, Valencia (0) 0
   27,000
Bordeaux (0) 1 *(Pavon 9)*, Manchester United (1) 2
  (Keane 33, Solskjaer 84)   33,100
Valencia (1) 2 *(Ilie A 35, Mendieta 90 (pen))*,
  Fiorentina (0) 0   50,000
Bordeaux (0) 1 *(Wiltord 54)*, Valencia (1) 4 *(Djukic 41,*
  Mendieta 48 (pen), Kili Gonzalez 72, Sanchez 90)
   27,000
Manchester United (2) 3 *(Cole 20, Keane 32, Yorke 70)*,
  Fiorentina (1) 1 *(Batistuta 16)*   59,926
Fiorentina (0) 3 *(Chiesa 47 (pen), Batistuta 61, Rua Costa*
  64), Bordeaux (1) 3 *(Wiltord 5, Zanotti 87, Battles 90)*
   27,000
Valencia (0) 0, Manchester United (0) 0   48,432

FINAL TABLE	P	W	D	L	F	A	Pts
Manchester United	6	4	1	1	10	4	13
Valencia	6	3	1	2	9	5	10
Fiorentina	6	2	2	2	7	8	8
Bordeaux	6	0	2	4	5	14	2

GROUP C

Dynamo Kiev (0) 1 *(Rebrov 86 (pen))*, Real Madrid (1) 2
  (Morientes 17, Raul 48)   15,000
Rosenborg (0) 1 *(Skammelsrud 47)*, Bayern Munich (1) 1
  (Jancker 10)   14,167
Bayern Munich (1) 2 *(Jancker 6, Sergio 80)*, Dynamo
  Kiev (0) 1 *(Rebrov 50)*   16,000
Real Madrid (1) 3 *(Raul 16, Savio 85, Roberto Carlos 90)*,
  Rosenborg (0) 1 *(Carew 48)*   20,000
Real Madrid (1) 2 *(Morientes 25, Raul 48)*, Bayern
  Munich (3) 4 *(Scholl 21, Effenberg 24, Fink 39, Paulo*
  Sergio 66)   72,000
Dynamo Kiev (2) 2 *(Khatskevich 10, Rebrov 29)*,
  Rosenborg (0) 1 *(Jakobsen 48)*   38,000
Bayern Munich (2) 4 *(Scholl 4, Elber 30, Zickler 79, 90)*,
  Real Madrid (0) 1 *(Helguera 69)*   59,000
Rosenborg (1) 1 *(Berg 38)*, Dynamo Kiev (1) 2
  (Rebrov 32, 67)   13,067
Bayern Munich (2) 2 *(Scholl 11, Paulo Sergio 39 (pen))*,
  Rosenborg (0) 1 *(Carew 64)*   19,000
Real Madrid (1) 2 *(Raul 14 (pen), Roberto Carlos 71)*,
  Dynamo Kiev (1) 2 *(Khatskevich 42, Hierro 56 (og))*
   72,000
Dynamo Kiev (1) 2 *(Kaladze 34, Demetradze 72)*,
  Bayern Munich (0) 0   65,000
Rosenborg (0) 0, Real Madrid (1) 1 *(Raul 3)*   13,000

FINAL TABLE	P	W	D	L	F	A	Pts
Bayern Munich	6	4	1	1	13	8	13
Real Madrid	6	3	1	2	11	12	10
Dynamo Kiev	6	3	1	2	10	8	10
Rosenborg	6	0	1	5	5	11	1

GROUP D

Chelsea (1) 3 *(Babayaro 45, Flo 67, 85)*, Feyenoord (0) 1
  (Cruz 90)   29,704
Marseille (0) 0, Lazio (0) 2 *(Stankovic 64, Conceicao 77)*
   55,000
Feyenoord (0) 3 *(Cruz 72, 90, Bosvelt 83)*, Marseille (0) 0
   45,000
Lazio (0) 0, Chelsea (0) 0   38,662
Lazio (1) 1 *(Veron 37)*, Feyenoord (0) 2 *(Tomasson 78,*
  84)   30,000

Marseille (1) 1 *(Pires 16)*, Chelsea (0) 0   40,000
Chelsea (1) 1 *(Wise 27)*, Marseille (0) 0   33,206
Feyenoord (0) 0, Lazio (0) 0   45,000
Feyenoord (0) 1 *(Kalou 59)*, Chelsea (1) 3 *(Zola 39,*
  Wise 64, Flo 69)   44,000
Lazio (3) 5 *(Inzaghi 17, 37, 38, 71, Boksic 81)*,
  Marseille (0) 1 *(Leroy 50)*   38,000
Chelsea (1) 1 *(Poyet 44)*, Lazio (0) 2 *(Inzaghi 54,*
  Mihajlovic 66)   34,260
Marseille (0) 0, Feyenoord (0) 0   9000

FINAL TABLE	P	W	D	L	F	A	Pts
Lazio	6	3	2	1	10	4	11
Chelsea	6	3	1	2	8	5	10
Feyenoord	6	2	2	2	7	7	8
Marseille	6	1	1	4	2	11	4

QUARTER-FINALS, FIRST LEG
Chelsea (3) 3 *(Zola 30, Flo 34, 38)*, Barcelona (0) 1
  (Figo 64)   33,662
Porto (0) 1 *(Jardel 46)*, Bayern Munich (0) 1 *(Sergio 80)*
    20,125
Real Madrid (0) 0, Manchester United (0) 0   64,119

Valencia (3) 5 *(Angulo 1, Gerard 4, 39, 79, Lopez 90)*,
  Lazio (1) 2 *(Inzaghi 28, Salas 86)*   46,000

QUARTER-FINALS, SECOND LEG
Barcelona (2) 5 *(Rivaldo 24, 98 (pen), Figo 45, Dani 83,*
  Kluivert 104), Chelsea (0) 1 *(Flo 60)*   100,000
Bayern Munich (1) 2 *(Sergio 15, Linke 90)*, Porto (0) 1
  (Jardel 89)   47,000
Lazio (0) 1 *(Veron 51)*, Valencia (0) 0   53,135
Manchester United (0) 2 *(Beckham 64, Scholes 88 (pen))*,
  Real Madrid (1) 3 *(Keane 20 (og), Raul 50, 52)*   59,178

SEMI-FINALS, FIRST LEG
Valencia (3) 4 *(Angulo 10, 43, Mendieta 45 (pen), Lopez*
  90), Barcelona (1) 1 *(Pellegrino 27 (og))*   55,124
Real Madrid (2) 2 *(Anelka 4, Jeremies 33 (og))*, Bayern
  Munich (0) 0   83,500

SEMI-FINALS, SECOND LEG
Barcelona (0) 2 *(Frank de Boer 78, Cocu 90)*, Valencia
  (0) 1 *(Mendieta 70)*   95,000
Bayern Munich (1) 2 *(Jancker 12, Elber 54)*, Real Madrid
  (1) 1 *(Anelka 31)*   60,234

FINAL

Real Madrid (1) 3, Valencia (0) 0

(in Paris, 24 May 2000, 78,759)

Real Madrid: Casillas; Michel Salgado (Hierro 84), Roberto Carlos, Campo, Helguera, Karanka, McManaman, Anelka (Sanchis 80), Raul, Morientes (Savio 72), Redondo.
Scorers: Morientes 39, McManaman 67, Raul 75.
Valencia: Canizares; Angloma, Gerardo, Mendieta, Djukic, Pellegrino, Kili Gonzalez, Farinos, Angulo, Lopez, Gerard (Ilie A 67).
Referee: Braschi (Italy).

Steve McManaman enjoyed his first season at Real Madrid and collected a European Cup medal at the end of it.
(ASP)

EUROPEAN CUP 1999–2000 – BRITISH AND IRISH CLUBS

FIRST QUALIFYING ROUND, FIRST LEG

14 JULY

Barry Town (0) 0

Valletta (0) 0 2005

Barry Town: Wells; Evans, Davies, Jones, York, Barrow, Barnett, Carter, Mitchell, Sloan, Ince (Perry 63).

Valletta: Cini; Giglio, Chetcuti, Radak, Debono, Buttigieg, Agius (Azzopardi 90), Saliba, Veselji (Camilleri 70), Ivanov, Theuma.

Litets (2) 3 *(Haxhi 12, Bushai 36, Petrov 81)*

Glentoran (0) 0 4000

Litets: Voutov; Ibraimov, Johnson, Emilov, Rusev, Dimitrov, Bushai, Motta, Zagorichi, Petrov, Todorov (Dimitr 65).

Glentoran: Gough; Young, Kennedy, Walker, Ferguson, Leeman, McCann (Young 46), Hamill, Elliott (Finlay 46), Batey, McBride (Rainey 60).

St Patricks Athletic (0) 0 3727

Zimbru Chisinau (3) 5 *(Berco 29, 41, Epureanu 35, 84, Boret 72)*

St Patricks Athletic: Wood; McGuinness, Campbell, Hawkins, Croly, Gormley, Osam (Harte 62), Russell (Hallows 46), Burke, Gilzean (Devereaux 85), Molloy.

Zimbru Chisinau: Romanenco; Kulik, Telesnenco, Catinsus, Dodul (Buzelizchi 90), Tropanet, Ghilazov, Oprea, Epureanu, Boret, Berco (Ryeakov 78).

FIRST QUALIFYING ROUND, SECOND LEG

21 JULY

Glentoran (0) 2 *(Haxhi 63, Bushai 90)* 3000

Litets (0) 2 *(Haxhi 63, Bushai 90)*

Glentoran: Gough; Nixon (Livingstone 30), Kennedy, Walker, Ferguson, Leeman, McCann (Young 60), Hamill (Rainey 74), Elliott, Batey, Young.

Litets: Voutov; Ibraimov (Rusev 80), Jelev, Kolev, Johnson, Dimitrov, Motta, Bushai, Zagorichi, Petrov (Emilov 67), Todorov (Dimitrov 69).

Valletta (1) 3 *(Agius 42, 46, Chetcuti 55)*

Barry Town (0) 2 *(Sloan 47, 56)* 2996

Valletta: Cini; Giglio, Chetcuti, Radak, Debono, Buttigieg, Agius, Saliba (Azzopardi 85), Veselji (Laferla 69), Ivanov (Camilleri 59), Theuma.

Barry Town: Wells; Evans, Davies, Jones, York, Barrow, Barnett (Pridham 85), Carter, Mitchell, Perry, Ince (Sloan 46).

27 JULY

Zimbru Chisinau (3) 5 *(Tropanet 25, 40, Boret 31, 75, Oprea 83 (pen))*

St Patricks Athletic (0) 0 4000

Zimbru Chisinau: Romanenco; Kulik, Telesnenco, Catinsus, Dodul, Ghilazov, Oprea, Tropanet (Butelschi 72), Boret, Epureanu (Gavriliuc 82), Berco (Mitirev 57).

St Patricks Athletic: Wood; Croly, McGuinness, Hawkins, Byrne (Campbell 46), Devereaux, Gormley, Morgan, Harte, Russell (Osam 46), Molloy.

SECOND QUALIFYING ROUND, FIRST LEG

28 JULY

Haka (0) 1 *(Niemi 51)*

Rangers (3) 4 *(Amoruso 18, Mols 28, 42, Johansson 85)* 3341

Haka: Vilnrotter; Hyokyvaara (Okkonen 83), Karjalainen, Pentilla, Rasanen, Reynders, Ivanov (Torkkeli 57), Wilson, Niemi (Nyyssonen 73), Savolainen, Popovic.

Rangers: Klos; Adamczuk, Amoruso, Moore, Numan, Ferguson, Van Bronckhorst (Albertz 69), Reyna, McCann, Wallace (Johansson 69), Mols.

SECOND QUALIFYING ROUND, SECOND LEG

4 AUG

Rangers (2) 3 *(Wallace 15, Johansson 28, Amato 66)*

Haka (0) 0 46,443

Rangers: Klos; Adamczuk, Moore, Amoruso, Numan (Vidmar 40), Ferguson (Nicholson 72), Johansson, Van Bronckhorst, Mols (Amato 46), Wallace, Albertz.

Haka: Vilnrotter; Pentilla, Karjalainen, Rasanen (Savolainen 62), Ivanov (Nyyssonen 55), Reynders, Popovic, Rantala, Wilson, Okkonen, Niemi (Torkkeli 72).

THIRD QUALIFYING ROUND, FIRST LEG

11 AUG

Chelsea (0) 3 *(Babayaro 76, Poyet 77, Sutton 84)*

Skonto Riga (0) 0 22,043

Chelsea: De Goey; Ferrer, Le Saux, Deschamps (Babayaro 65), Leboeuf, Desailly, Petrescu (Goldbaek 79), Poyet, Sutton, Zola (Flo 65), Wise.

Skonto Riga: Kolinko; Laizans, Silagadze, Zemlinsky, Tereskinas, Rekhviashvili, Bleidelis, Rubins, Astafyev, Mihalop (Menteshashvili 79), Chaladze (Blagonadezdin 39).

Rangers (1) 2 *(Vidmar 32, Reyna 76)*

Parma (0) 0 49,263

Rangers: Klos; Porrini, Moore, Amoruso, Vidmar (Albertz 55), Reyna, Ferguson, Van Bronckhorst, McCann, Wallace, Mols.

Parma: Buffon; Sartor, Thuram, Cannavaro, Serena, Boghossian, Walem, Dino Baggio (Fuser 60), Vanoli, Ortega (Torrisi 37), Di Vaio (Stanic 85).

THIRD QUALIFYING ROUND, SECOND LEG

25 AUG

Parma (0) 1 *(Walem 68)*

Rangers (0) 0 28,500

Parma: Buffon; Lassissi, Fuser, Dino Baggio, Crespo, Ortega, Boghossian (Walem 64), Torrisi, Di Vaio (Stanic 64), Thuram, Vanoli (Serena 78).

Rangers: Charbonnier; Porrini, Moore, Amoruso, Ferguson (Albertz 73), Van Bronckhorst, Mols, Wallace (McCann 60), Reyna, Vidmar, Adamczuk (Hendry 83).

Skonto Riga (0) 0

Chelsea (0) 0 5023

Skonto Riga: Kolinko; Laizans (Kolesnicenko 88), Silagadze, Zemlinsky, Blagonadezdin, Bleidelis (Menteshashvili 75), Astafyev (Babicev 62), Rekhviashvili, Rubins, Chaladze. Miholap.

Chelsea: De Goey (Cudicini 78); Petrescu, Babayaro, Goldbaek (Harley 82), Hogh, Desailly, Morris, Poyet (Nicholls 64), Flo, Forssell, Wise.

CHAMPIONS LEAGUE

GROUP B

14 SEPT

Fiorentina (0) 0

Arsenal (0) 0 33,903

Fiorentina: Toldo; Repka, Padalino, Pierini (Adani 84), Di Livio, Cois, Rui Costa, Heinrich, Batistuta, Chiesa, Mijatovic.

Arsenal: Manninger; Luzhny, Winterburn, Vieira, Keown, Adams, Ljungberg, Grimandi, Suker (Kanu 60), Bergkamp (Henry 81), Overmars.

22 SEPT

Arsenal (1) 3 *(Ljungberg 27, Henry 89, Suker 90)*

AIK Stockholm (0) 1 *(Nordin 52)* 71,227 *at Wembley*

Arsenal: Manninger; Dixon, Winterburn, Vieira, Keown, Adams, Ljungberg (Henry 68), Grimandi (Silvinho 55), Suker, Bergkamp, Overmars (Kanu 68).

AIK Stockholm: Asper; Kamark (Kjolo 46), Gustafsson, Lagerlof, Ljung, Brundin, Tjernstrom, Nordin, Andersson O (Corneliusson 89), Andersson A, Novakovic (Aslund 81).

29 SEPT

Barcelona (1) 1 *(Luis Enrique 16)*
Arsenal (0) 1 *(Kanu 81)* 85,000
Barcelona: Hesp; Frank de Boer, Bogarde, Reiziger (Ronald de Boer 69), Guardiola, Sergi, Luis Enrique (Litmanen 77), Cocu, Figo, Dani, Rivaldo.
Arsenal: Manninger; Dixon, Winterburn, Vieira, Keown, Adams, Parlour (Henry 73), Grimandi, Kanu, Bergkamp (Suker 73), Overmars (Ljungberg 79).

19 OCT

Arsenal (1) 2 *(Bergkamp 44, Overmars 84)*
Barcelona (2) 4 *(Rivaldo 15 (pen), Luis Enrique 16, Figo 56, Cocu 69)* 73,091 *at Wembley.*
Arsenal: Seaman; Dixon, Winterburn, Vieira, Keown (Upson 73), Adams, Parlour, Ljungberg (Henry 76), Kanu (Suker 76), Bergkamp, Overmars.
Barcelona: Arnau; Abelardo, Bogarde, Reiziger, Guardiola, Sergi, Luis Enrique (Gabri 70), Cocu, Figo, Kluivert, Rivaldo.

27 OCT

Arsenal (0) 0
Fiorentina (0) 1 *(Batistuta 75)* 73,336 *at Wembley.*
Arsenal: Seaman; Dixon (Suker 73), Winterburn, Vieira, Keown, Adams, Parlour (Ljungberg 57), Petit (Vivas 59), Kanu, Bergkamp, Overmars.
Fiorentina: Toldo; Repka, Firicano, Pierini, Di Livio, Cois (Adani 46), Rossitto, Heinrich, Rui Costa, Batistuta, Chiesa.

2 NOV

AIK Stockholm (1) 2 *(Andersson A 41, 68)*
Arsenal (1) 3 *(Overmars 17, 52, Suker 56)* 33,005
AIK Stockholm: Asper (Baxter 71); Lagerlof, Kjolo, Kamark, Gustafsson, Corneliusson (Aslund 71), Nordin, Andersson O, Tjernstrom, Novakovic, Andersson A.
Arsenal: Manninger; Dixon, Winterburn, Vieira, Luzhny (Vivas 77), Upson, Ljungberg, Petit (Malz 77), Suker (Hughes 77), Kanu, Overmars.

GROUP D
14 SEPT

Manchester United (0) 0
Croatia Zagreb (0) 0 53,250
Manchester United: Van der Gouw; Clegg (Fortune 75), Neville P, Berg, Wilson (Sheringham 60), Stam, Beckham, Scholes, Cole, Yorke, Giggs.
Croatia Zagreb: Ladic; Tokic, Juric, Tomas, Saric, Jurcic, Cvitanovic, Biscan, Rukavina (Sokota 89), Simic J (Mikic 66), Mujcin (Mumlek 69).

22 SEPT

Sturm Graz (0) 0 16,480
Manchester United (3) 3 *(Keane 17, Yorke 31, Cole 33)*
Sturm Graz: Sidorczuk; Prilasnig (Kutsupias 72), Foda, Fieldhofer (Korsos 74), Neukirchner, Mahlich (Reinmayr 76), Schupp, Martens, Kocijan, Strafner, Vastic.
Manchester United: Van der Gouw; Neville P, Irwin, Berg, Keane (Wilson 62), Stam, Beckham, Scholes, Cole (Solskjaer 77), Yorke, Cruyff (Sheringham 67).

29 SEPT

Manchester United (0) 2 *(Cole 79, Scholes 83)*
Marseille (1) 1 *(Bakayoko 41)* 53,993
Manchester United: Van der Gouw; Irwin, Neville P, Berg (Sheringham 77), Scholes, Stam, Beckham, Butt, Cole (Clegg 86), Yorke, Solskjaer (Fortune 72).
Marseille: Porato; Perez, Fischer, Gallas, Blondeau, Issa (Belmadi 82), Brando, Luccin (De La Pena 76), Dalmat, Ravanelli (Pires 61), Bakayoko.

19 OCT

Marseille (0) 1 *(Gallas 69)*
Manchester United (0) 0 57,745
Marseille: Porato; Perez, Gallas, Berizzo, Blondeau, Issa, Brando (De La Pena 64), Pires, Luccin, Dalmat (Reina 88), Ravanelli (Maurice 74).

Manchester United: Bosnich; Neville P, Irwin, Berg (Solskjaer 83), Keane, Stam, Beckham, Scholes, Cole, Yorke, Giggs.

27 OCT

Croatia Zagreb (0) 1 *(Prosinecki 90)*
Manchester United (1) 2 *(Beckham 32, Keane 49)* 38,000
Croatia Zagreb: Butina; Sedloski, Juric (Prosinecki 35), Tomas, Saric, Rukavina, Tokic, Mujcin, Cvitanovic (Mumiek 68), Sokota, Mikic (Simic J 55).
Manchester United: Bosnich; Neville P, Irwin, Berg, Keane, Stam, Beckham, Scholes (Greening 67), Cole (Cruyff 78), Yorke (Solskjaer 59), Giggs.

2 NOV

Manchester United (0) 2 *(Solskjaer 56, Keane 69)*
Sturm Graz (0) 1 *(Vastic 87 (pen))* 53,745
Manchester United: Bosnich; Neville G, Irwin (Higginbotham 76), Berg, Keane, May, Greening (Cruyff 65), Wilson (Neville P 52), Cole, Solskjaer, Giggs.
Sturm Graz: Schicklgruber; Prilasnig, Neukirchner, Strafner, Schopp, Mahlich, Angiebeaud (Bardel 71), Minavand, Martens (Reinmayr 71), Vastic, Kocijan (Bochtler 74).

GROUP F
15 SEPT

Valencia (0) 2 *(Moore 57 (og), Gonzalez 74)*
Rangers (0) 0 54,971
Valencia: Canizares; Angloma, Bjorklund, Pellegrino, Carboni, Mendieta, Gerard, Albeida, Gonzalez, Sanchez (Angulo 81), Lopez (Ilie A 72).
Rangers: Charbonnier; Porrini, Moore, Amoruso, Vidmar, Reyna, Ferguson B, Van Bronckhorst, McCann (Albertz 46), Amato, Mols (Johansson 86).

21 SEPT

Rangers (1) 1 *(Albertz 22)*
Bayern Munich (0) 1 *(Tarnat 88)* 49,960
Rangers: Charbonnier; Porrini, Moore, Amoruso, Numan, Reyna, Ferguson B, Van Bronckhorst, Mols (Hendry 83), Albertz, Johansson (McCann 90).
Bayern Munich: Wessels; Kuffour, Linke, Jeremies, Matthaus (Zickler 79), Tarnat, Effenberg, Lizarazu (Jancker 46), Salihamidzic, Elber (Santa Cruz 72), Scholl.

28 SEPT

PSV Eindhoven (0) 0
Rangers (0) 1 *(Albertz 84)* 27,000
PSV Eindhoven: Waterreus; Wielaert, Dirkx, Nikiforov, Heintze, Rommedahl (Kolkka 62), Van der Doelen (Bruggink 71), Stinga (Bouma 67), Khokhlov, Nilis, Van Nistelrooij.
Rangers: Charbonnier; Porrini, Numan, Ferguson B, Moore, Amoruso, Reyna (Albertz 23), Van Bronckhorst, Mols, Wallace, McCann.

20 OCT

Rangers (2) 4 *(Amoruso 18, Mols 38, 79, McCann 55)*
PSV Eindhoven (1) 1 *(Van Nistelrooij 45 (pen))* 50,083
Rangers: Klos; Porrini, Moore, Amoruso, Vidmar, McInnes, Ferguson B, Van Bronckhorst, McCann (Albertz 70), Mols (Johansson 80), Wallace (Kanchelskis 87).
PSV Eindhoven: Kralj; Wielaert (Kolkka 31), Nikiforov, Faber, Heintze, Stinga (Rommedahl 73), Vogel, Van Bommel, Khokhlov, Nilis (Bruggink 85), Van Nistelrooij.

26 OCT

Rangers (0) 1 *(Moore 59)*
Valencia (2) 2 *(Mendieta 34, Lopez 45)* 50,063
Rangers: Klos; Porrini, Moore, Amoruso, Vidmar (Albertz 60), McInnes (Kanchelskis 36), Ferguson B, Van Bronckhorst, Mols, McCann, Wallace (Johansson 74).
Valencia: Palop; Angulo, Djukic, Pellegrino, Carboni, Mendieta (Soria 80), Albelda, Gerard, Gonzalez (Farinos 66), Illie A (Sanchez 60), Lopez.

3 NOV

Bayern Munich (1) 1 *(Strunz 32 (pen))*
Rangers (0) 0 54,000
Bayern Munich: Kahn; Babbel, Matthaus, Linke, Strunz, Fink, Effenberg (Tarnat 74), Lizarazu, Scholl (Salihamidzic 62), Santa Cruz (Paulo Sergio 62), Elber.
Rangers: Klos; Porrini, Numan (McCann 72), Ferguson B, Moore, Amoruso, Reyna, Mols (Johansson 30), Wallace (Amato 79), Van Bronckhorst, Albertz.

GROUP H

15 SEPT

Chelsea (0) 0
AC Milan (0) 0 33,873
Chelsea: De Goey; Ferrer, Babayaro, Deschamps, Leboeuf (Hogh 81), Desailly, Petrescu, Poyet (Le Saux 80), Flo (Sutton 84), Zola, Wise.
AC Milan: Abbiati; Helveg, Guly, Costacurta, Ayala, Maldini, Shevchenko, Albertini, Bierhoff, Leonardo (Giunti 83), Gattuso.

21 SEPT

Hertha Berlin (1) 2 *(Daei 3, 70)*
Chelsea (0) 1 *(Leboeuf 86 (pen))* 55,541
Hertha Berlin: Kiraly; Herzog, Van Burik, Schmidt, Sanneh (Veit 67), Deisler, Wosz, Dardai (Helmer 80), Tretschok (Michalke 12), Preetz, Daei.
Chelsea: De Goey; Ferrer (Ambrosetti 64), Le Saux (Morris 73), Deschamps, Leboeuf, Desailly, Petrescu, Babayaro, Flo (Sutton 64), Zola, Wise.

28 SEPT

Chelsea (0) 1 *(Petrescu 55)*
Galatasaray (0) 0 33,426
Chelsea: De Goey; Ferrer, Babayaro, Morris, Leboeuf, Desailly (Hogh 62), Petrescu, Ambrosetti (Poyet 53), Sutton (Flo 85), Zola, Wise.
Galatasaray: Taffarel; Fatih, Gheorge Popescu, Capone, Unsal, Okan (Emre 72), Umit, Urgun, Hagi (Hasan 73), Hakan Sukur, Arif (Mehmet 34).

20 OCT

Galatasaray (0) 0 25,500
Chelsea (1) 5 *(Flo 32, 49, Zola 54, Wise 79, Ambrosetti 87)*
Galatasaray: Mehmet; Fatih (Umit 46), Capone, Popescu, Unsal, Okan, Tugay, Emre, Hagi (Sas 46), Hakan Sukur (Saffet 65), Erdem.
Chelsea: De Goey; Ferrer, Babayaro, Deschamps (Petrescu 67), Leboeuf, Desailly, Poyet (Wise 67), Morris, Flo, Zola (Ambrosetti 76), Le Saux.

26 OCT

AC Milan (0) 0 *(Bierhoff 74)*
Chelsea (0) 1 *(Wise 77)* 74,855
AC Milan: Abbiati; Guly, Serginho, Costacurta, Ayala, Maldini, Gattuso, Ambrosini, Shevchenko, Bierhoff, Leonardo.
Chelsea: De Goey; Ferrer, Babayaro, Deschamps, Leboeuf, Desailly, Poyet (Morris 46), Poyet (Di Matteo 75), Flo, Zola (Ambrosetti 81), Wise.

3 NOV

Chelsea (2) 2 *(Deschamps 11, Ferrer 44)*
Hertha Berlin (0) 0 33,623
Chelsea: De Goey; Ferrer, Babayaro, Deschamps, Hogh (Leboeuf 66), Desailly (Lambourde 85), Petrescu, Flo, Sutton, Zola (Poyet 62), Wise.
Hertha Berlin: Kiraly; Van Burik, Helmer (Schmidt 75), Rekdal, Sverrisson, Sanneh, Deisler, Wosz (Konstantinidis 46), Michalke, Daei, Preetz (Aracic 46).

SECOND STAGE

23 NOV

GROUP B

Fiorentina (1) 2 *(Batistuta 24, Balbo 52)*
Manchester United (0) 0 40,000
Fiorentina: Toldo; Pierini (Adani 80), Firicano, Repka, Torricelli, Cois, Di Livio (Rossitto 63), Heinrich, Rui Costa, Balbo (Bressan 80), Batistuta.
Manchester United: Bosnich; Neville G, Irwin, Berg (Neville P 63), Keane, Stam, Beckham, Scholes, Cole (Sheringham 63), Yorke (Solskjaer 63), Giggs.

8 DEC

Manchester United (1) 3 *(Keane 38, Solskjaer 47, Scholes 69)*
Valencia (0) 0 54,606
Manchester United: Van der Gouw; Neville P, Irwin, Neville G, Keane, Stam, Beckham, Scholes (Butt 70), Cole (Yorke 70), Solskjaer, Giggs.
Valencia: Palop; Angloma, Carboni, Djukic, Bjorklund, Pellegrino, Farinos, Milla, Lopez (Vlaovic 85), Oscar (Sanchez 68), Mendieta.

1 MAR

Manchester United (1) 2 *(Giggs 42, Sheringham 84)*
Bordeaux (0) 0 59,786
Manchester United: Van der Gouw; Neville G, Irwin, Silvestre, Keane (Fortune 88), Stam, Beckham, Butt, Cole (Neville P 81), Sheringham, Giggs (Solskjaer 88).
Bordeaux: Rame; Grenet, Afanou, Alicarte, Bonnissel, Martins (Ziani 65), Diabate, Pavon, Micoud, Laslandes, Wiltord.

7 MAR

Bordeaux (1) 1 *(Pavon 9)* 33,100
Manchester United (1) 2 *(Keane 33, Solskjaer 84)*
Bordeaux: Rame; Grenet, Saveljic, Afanou, Bonnissel, Ziani (Rouviere 60), Battles (Diabate 8), Pavon, Micoud, Laslandes, Wiltord (Feindouno 81).
Manchester United: Van der Gouw; Neville G, Irwin (Solskjaer 82), Silvestre, Keane, Stam, Beckham, Butt, Cole (Berg 85), Sheringham (Yorke 76), Giggs.

15 MAR

Manchester United (2) 3 *(Cole 20, Keane 32, Yorke 70)*
Fiorentina (1) 1 *(Batistuta 16)* 59,926
Manchester United: Bosnich; Neville G, Irwin, Berg, Keane, Stam, Beckham, Scholes, Cole, Yorke, Giggs.
Fiorentina: Toldo; Repka, Adani, Pierini, Torricelli (Tarozzi 75), Rossitto, Di Livio (Amoroso 75), Heinrich, Rui Costa, Mijatovic, Batistuta.

21 MAR

Valencia (0) 0
Manchester United (0) 0 48,432
Valencia: Canizares; Angloma, Pellegrino, Djukic, Carboni, Angulo, Farinos, Gerard, Gonzalez, Sanchez (Ilie A 71), Lopez.
Manchester United: Bosnich; Neville G, Irwin, Berg, Keane, Stam, Scholes, Butt, Solskjaer (Cruyff 66), Sheringham, Fortune.

24 NOV

GROUP D

Chelsea (1) 3 *(Babayaro 45, Flo 67, 85)*
Feyenoord (0) 1 *(Cruz 90)* 29,704
Chelsea: De Goey; Ferrer, Babayaro, Deschamps (Dalla Bona 86), Leboeuf, Desailly, Petrescu, Poyet (Di Matteo 86), Flo, Zola, Wise.
Feyenoord: Dudek; Van Gobbel, Konteiman, Van Wonderen, De Visser, Van Gastel, Kalou, Bosvelt, Van Vossen (Samardzic 60), Tomasson (Cruz 58), Somalia.

7 DEC

Lazio (0) 0
Chelsea (0) 0 38,662
Lazio: Marchegiani; Gottardi, Favalli, Simeone, Nesta, Fernando Couto, Lombardo (Boksic 68), Veron, Inzaghi (Salas 46), Mancini (Conceicao 79), Nedved.
Chelsea: De Goey; Ferrer, Babayaro, Deschamps (Di Matteo 75), Leboeuf, Desailly, Petrescu, Flo, Zola, Wise.

29 FEB

Marseille (1) 1 *(Pires 16)*
Chelsea (0) 0 40,000
Marseille: Trevisan; Blondeau, Cyprien, Luccin, Abardonado, Pires, Brando, Leroy J, Dalmat, Pouget (De La Pena 72), Bakayoko (Moses 90).
Chelsea: De Goey; Ferrer (Morris 81), Harley, Deschamps (Di Matteo 61), Leboeuf, Desailly, Petrescu, Poyet, Flo (Sutton 81), Zola, Wise.

8 MAR

Chelsea (1) 1 *(Wise 27)*

Marseille (0) 0 33,206

Chelsea: De Goey; Ferrer, Babayaro, Deschamps (Di Matteo 79), Leboeuf, Desailly, Poyet, Morris, Flo, Zola (Harley 79), Wise.
Marseille: Trevisan; Cyprien (De La Pena 66), Luccin, Abardonado, Perez (Fischer 37), Brando, Leroy J, Dalmat, Pires, Bakayoko, Pouget.

14 MAR

Feyenoord (0) 1 *(Kalou 59)* 44,000

Chelsea (1) 3 *(Zola 39, Wise 64, Flo 69)*

Feyenoord: Dudek; Van Gobbel, Konterman, Van Wonderen, Rzasa, Bosvelt, Van Gastel, Paauwe (Kalou 46), De Visser (Samardzic 69), Tomasson, Cruz.
Chelsea: De Goey; Petrescu, Babayaro, Deschamps, Leboeuf, Desailly, Poyet (Morris 76), Di Matteo, Flo, Zola (Ambrosetti 89), Wise.

22 MAR

Chelsea (1) 1 *(Poyet 44)*

Lazio (0) 2 *(Inzaghi 54, Mihajlovic 66)* 34,260

Chelsea: De Goey; Ferrer, Babayaro (Harley 73), Deschamps, Leboeuf (Hogh 61), Desailly, Petrescu, Di Matteo (Morris 73), Flo, Zola, Poyet.
Lazio: Marchegiani; Negro, Fernando Couto, Mihajlovic, Pancaro, Stankovic (Boksic 46), Simeone, Almeyda, Nedved, Veron, Inzaghi (Salas 63) (Gottardi 88).

QUARTER-FINALS, FIRST LEG

4 APR

Real Madrid (0) 0

Manchester United (0) 0 64,119

Real Madrid: Casillas; Michel Salgado, Karanka, Ivan Campo, Roberto Carlos, McManaman, Helguera, Redondo, Savio (Baljic 75), Raul, Morientes (Ognjenovic 86).
Manchester United: Bosnich; Neville G, Irwin (Silvestre 87), Berg, Keane, Stam, Beckham, Scholes (Butt 81), Cole, Yorke (Sheringham 76), Giggs.

5 APR

Chelsea (3) 3 *(Zola 30, Flo 34, 38)*

Barcelona (0) 1 *(Figo 64)* 33,662

Chelsea: De Goey; Ferrer, Babayaro, Deschamps, Emerson, Desailly, Petrescu (Di Matteo 71), Morris, Flo (Sutton 87), Zola, Wise.
Barcelona: Hesp; Puyol (Litmanen 46), Abelardo, Frank de Boer, Bogarde, Gabri, Xavi, Cocu, Figo, Kluivert (Dani 71), Rivaldo.

QUARTER-FINALS, SECOND LEG

18 APR

Barcelona (2) 5 *(Rivaldo 24, 98 (pen), Figo 45, Dani 83, Kluivert 104)*

Chelsea (0) 1 *(Flo 60)* *aet* 100,000

Barcelona: Hesp; Puyol (Abelardo 85), Frank de Boer, Reiziger (Sergi 105), Gabri, Guardiola, Cocu, Rivaldo, Figo, Kluivert, Zenden (Dani 72).
Chelsea: De Goey; Ferrer (Lambourde 46), Babayaro, Deschamps (Petrescu 101), Leboeuf, Desailly, Morris, Di Matteo, Flo, Zola (Poyet 105), Wise.

19 APR

Manchester United (0) 2 *(Beckham 64, Scholes 88 (pen))*

Real Madrid (1) 3 *(Keane 20 (og), Raul 50, 52)* 59,178

Manchester United: Van der Gouw; Neville G, Irwin (Silvestre 46), Berg (Sheringham 62), Keane, Stam, Beckham, Scholes, Cole (Solskjaer 62), Yorke, Giggs.
Real Madrid: Casillas; Michel Salgado, Campo, Helguera, Karanka, Roberto Carlos, McManaman (Julio Cesar 89), Redondo, Savio (Geremi 65), Raul, Morientes (Anelka 71).

Croatia Zagreb 1, Manchester United 2 and Ryan Giggs prepares to take on Goce Sedloski (left). (Actionimages)

EUROPEAN CUP-WINNERS' CUP

EUROPEAN CUP-WINNERS' CUP FINALS 1961–99

Year	Winners		Runners-up		Venue	Attendance	Referee
1961	Fiorentina	2	Rangers	0 *(1st Leg)*	Glasgow	80,000	Steiner (A)
	Fiorentina	2	Rangers	1 *(2nd Leg)*	Florence	50,000	Hernadi (H)
1962	Atletico Madrid	1	Fiorentina	1	Glasgow	27,389	Wharton (S)
Replay	Atletico Madrid	3	Fiorentina	0	Stuttgart	38,000	Tschenscher (WG)
1963	Tottenham Hotspur	5	Atletico Madrid	1	Rotterdam	49,000	Van Leuwen (Ho)
1964	Sporting Lisbon	3	MTK Budapest	3 *(aet)*	Brussels	3000	Van Nuffel (Bel)
Replay	Sporting Lisbon	1	MTK Budapest	0	Antwerp	19,000	Versyp (Bel)
1965	West Ham U	2	Munich 1860	0	Wembley	100,000	Szolt (H)
1966	Borussia Dortmund	2	Liverpool	1 *(aet)*	Glasgow	41,657	Schwinte (F)
1967	Bayern Munich	1	Rangers	0 *(aet)*	Nuremberg	69,480	Lo Bello (I)
1968	AC Milan	2	Hamburg	0	Rotterdam	53,000	Ortiz (Sp)
1969	Slovan Bratislava	3	Barcelona	2	Basle	19,000	Van Ravens (Ho)
1970	Manchester C	2	Gornik Zabrze	1	Vienna	8,000	Schiller (A)
1971	Chelsea	1	Real Madrid	1 *(aet)*	Athens	42,000	Scheurer (Sw)
Replay	Chelsea	2	Real Madrid	1 *(aet)*	Athens	35,000	Bucheli (Sw)
1972	Rangers	3	Moscow Dynamo	2	Barcelona	24,000	Ortiz (Sp)
1973	AC Milan	1	Leeds U	0	Salonika	45,000	Mihas (Gr)
1974	Magdeburg	2	AC Milan	0	Rotterdam	4000	Van Gemert (Ho)
1975	Dynamo Kiev	3	Ferencvaros	0	Basle	13,000	Davidson (S)
1976	Anderlecht	4	West Ham U	2	Brussels	58,000	Wurtz (F)
1977	Hamburg	2	Anderlecht	0	Amsterdam	65,000	Partridge (E)
1978	Anderlecht	4	Austria/WAC	0	Paris	48,679	Adlinger (WG)
1979	Barcelona	4	Fortuna Dusseldorf	3 *(aet)*	Basle	58,000	Palotai (H)
1980	Valencia	0	Arsenal	0	Brussels	36,000	Christov (Cz)
	(aet; Valencia won 5-4 on penalties)						
1981	Dynamo Tbilisi	2	Carl Zeiss Jena	1	Dusseldorf	9000	Lattanzi (I)
1982	Barcelona	2	Standard Liege	1	Barcelona	100,000	Eschweiler (WG)
1983	Aberdeen	2	Real Madrid	1 *(aet)*	Gothenburg	17,804	Menegali (I)
1984	Juventus	2	Porto	1	Basle	60,000	Prokop (EG)
1985	Everton	3	Rapid Vienna	1	Rotterdam	50,000	Casarin (I)
1986	Dynamo Kiev	3	Atletico Madrid	0	Lyon	39,300	Wohrer (A)
1987	Ajax	1	Lokomotiv Leipzig	0	Athens	35,000	Agnolin (I)
1988	Mechelen	1	Ajax	0	Strasbourg	39,446	Pauly (WG)
1989	Barcelona	2	Sampdoria	0	Berne	45,000	Courtney (E)
1990	Sampdoria	2	Anderlecht	0	Gothenburg	20,103	Galler (Sw)
1991	Manchester U	2	Barcelona	1	Rotterdam	42,000	Karlsson (Se)
1992	Werder Bremen	2	Monaco	0	Lisbon	16,000	D'Elia (I)
1993	Parma	3	Antwerp	1	Wembley	37,393	Assenmacher (G)
1994	Arsenal	1	Parma	0	Copenhagen	33,765	Krondl (Czr)
1995	Zaragoza	2	Arsenal	1	Paris	42,424	Ceccarini (I)
1996	Paris St Germain	1	Rapid Vienna	0	Brussels	37,500	Pairetto (I)
1997	Barcelona	1	Paris St Germain	0	Rotterdam	45,000	Merk (G)
1998	Chelsea	1	Stuttgart	0	Stockholm	30,216	Braschi (I)
1999	Lazio	2	Mallorca	1	Villa Park	33,021	Benko (A)

INTER-CITIES FAIRS & UEFA CUP

FAIRS CUP FINALS 1958–71
(Winners in italics)

Year	First Leg	Attendance	Second Leg	Attendance
1958	London 2 Barcelona 2	45,466	*Barcelona* 6 London 0	62,000
1960	Birmingham C 0 Barcelona 0	40,500	*Barcelona* 4 Birmingham C 1	70,000
1961	Birmingham C 2 Roma 2	21,005	*Roma* 2 Birmingham C 0	60,000
1962	Valencia 6 Barcelona 2	65,000	Barcelona 1 *Valencia* 1	60,000
1963	Dynamo Zagreb 1 Valencia 2	40,000	*Valencia* 2 Dynamo Zagreb 0	55,000
1964	*Zaragoza* 2 Valencia 1	50,000	(in Barcelona)	
1965	*Ferencvaros* 1 Juventus 0	25,000	(in Turin)	
1966	Barcelona 0 Zaragoza 1	70,000	Zaragoza 2 *Barcelona* 4	70,000
1967	Dynamo Zagreb 2 Leeds U 0	40,000	Leeds U 0 *Dynamo Zagreb* 0	35,604
1968	Leeds U 1 Ferencvaros 0	25,368	Ferencvaros 0 *Leeds U* 0	70,000
1969	Newcastle U 3 Ujpest Dozsa 0	60,000	Ujpest Dozsa 2 *Newcastle U* 3	37,000
1970	Anderlecht 3 Arsenal 1	37,000	*Arsenal* 3 Anderlecht 0	51,612
1971	Juventus 0 Leeds U 0 *(abandoned 51 minutes)*	42,000		
	Juventus 2 Leeds U 2	42,000	*Leeds U* 1* Juventus 1	42,483

UEFA CUP FINALS 1972–97
(Winners in italics)

1972	Wolverhampton W 1 Tottenham H 2	45,000	*Tottenham H* 1 Wolverhampton W 1	48,000
1973	Liverpool 0 Moenchengladbach 0			
	(abandoned 27 minutes)	44,967		
	Liverpool 3 Moenchengladbach 0	41,169	Moenchengladbach 2 *Liverpool* 0	35,000
1974	Tottenham H 2 Feyenoord 2	46,281	*Feyenoord* 2 Tottenham H 0	68,000
1975	Moenchengladbach 0 Twente 0	45,000	Twente 1 *Moenchengladbach* 5	24,500
1976	Liverpool 3 FC Brugge 2	56,000	FC Brugge 1 *Liverpool* 1	32,000
1977	Juventus 1 Athletic Bilbao 0	75,000	Athletic Bilbao 2 *Juventus* 1*	43,000
1978	Bastia 0 PSV Eindhoven 0	15,000	*PSV Eindhoven* 3 Bastia 0	27,000
1979	Red Star Belgrade 1 Moenchengladbach 1	87,500	*Moenchengladbach* 1 Red Star Belgrade 0	45,000
1980	Moenchengladbach 3 Eintracht Frankfurt 2	25,000	*Eintracht Frankfurt* 1* Moenchengladbach 0	60,000
1981	Ipswich T 3 AZ 67 Alkmaar 0	27,532	AZ 67 Alkmaar 4 *Ipswich T* 2	28,500
1982	Gothenburg 1 Hamburg 0	42,548	Hamburg 0 *Gothenburg* 3	60,000
1983	Anderlecht 1 Benfica 0	45,000	Benfica 1 *Anderlecht* 1	80,000
1984	Anderlecht 1 Tottenham H 1	40,000	*Tottenham H* 1[1] Anderlecht 1	46,258
1985	Videoton 0 Real Madrid 3	30,000	*Real Madrid* 0 Videoton 1	98,300
1986	Real Madrid 5 Cologne 1	80,000	Cologne 2 *Real Madrid* 0	15,000
1987	Gothenburg 1 Dundee U 0	50,023	Dundee U 1 *Gothenburg* 1	20,911
1988	Espanol 3 Bayer Leverkusen 0	42,000	*Bayer Leverkusen* 3[2] Espanol 0	22,000
1989	Napoli 2 Stuttgart 1	83,000	Stuttgart 3 *Napoli* 3	67,000
1990	Juventus 3 Fiorentina 1	45,000	Fiorentina 0 *Juventus* 0	32,000
1991	Internazionale 2 Roma 0	68,887	Roma 1 *Internazionale* 0	70,901
1992	Torino 2 Ajax 2	65,377	*Ajax* 0* Torino 0	40,000
1993	Borussia Dortmund 1 Juventus 3	37,000	*Juventus* 3 Borussia Dortmund 0	62,781
1994	Salzburg 0 Internazionale 1	47,500	*Internazionale* 1 Salzburg 0	80,326
1995	Parma 1 Juventus 0	23,000	Juventus 1 *Parma* 1	80,750
1996	Bayern Munich 2 Bordeaux 0	62,000	Bordeaux 1 *Bayern Munich* 3	36,000
1997	Schalke 1 Internazionale 0	56,824	Internazionale 1 *Schalke* 0[3]	81,670

*won on away goals   [1]*Tottenham H won 4-3 on penalties aet*   [2]*Bayer Leverkusen won 3-2 on penalties aet*
[3]*Schalke won 4-1 on penalties aet*

UEFA CUP FINALS 1998–2000

Year	Winners	Runners-up	Venue	Attendance	Referee
1998	Internazionale 3	Lazio 0	Paris	42,938	Nieto (Sp)
1999	Parma 3	Marseille 0	Moscow	61,000	Dallas (S)
2000	Galatasaray 0	Arsenal 0	Copenhagen	38,919	Nieto (Sp)

(aet; Galatasaray won 4-1 on penalties)

UEFA CUP 1999-2000

ROUND, FIRST LEG

Anderlect (3) 6 *(Goor 19, 41, Gunnarsson 40 (og),*
Zetterberg 53, Baseggio 56, Radzinski 68), Leiftur (1) 1
(De Boeck 26 (og))   20,514
Ankaragucu (1) 1 *(Unal 15)*, B36 (0) 0   5700
Apoel (0) 0, Levski Sofia (0) 0   4200
BATE Borisov (0) 1 *(Lisovski 72)*, Lokomotiv Moscow
(3) 7 *(Janashia 6, 34, 60, Loskov 24, Sarkissian 55,*
Bulykin 73, 86)   5500
Belshina (1) 1 *(Khrypack 21)*, Omonia (3) 5 *(Kalotheou*
8, Michalovic 26, Rauffmann 34, Kaiafas 56,
Konstantinidis 89)   3300
Bodo Glimt (1) 1 *(Staurvik 27)*, Vaduz (0) 0   1612
Cwmbran Town (0) 0, Celtic (3) 6 *(Berkovic 2, Tebily 20,*
Larsson 32, 61, Viduka 52, Brattbakk 83)
                                                                                 8920 *(at Cardiff)*.
Erevan (0) 0, Hapoel Tel Aviv (0) 2 *(Harazi R 55, 58)*   800
Ferencvaros (2) 3 *(Horvath 35, Fuzi 41, Kovacs 72)*,
Constructorul (0) 1 *(Comlionoc 81)*   5000
FK Riga (0) 0, Helsingborg (0) 0   340
Gorica (0) 2 *(Mitrakovic 75 (pen), Zlogar 83)*, Inter
Cardiff (0) 0   1100
IFK Gothenburg (1) 3 *(Andersson P 36, Karlsson 74, 87)*,
Cork City (0) 0   3278
Grasshoppers (1) 4 *(Chapuisat 30, 63, Isabella 78, 83)*,
Bray Wanderers (0) 0   5600
Hajduk Split (2) 5 *(Bulat 4, Baturina 24, Grdic 57, Leko*
68, Dranja 90), Dudelange (0) 0   4000
HJK Helsinki (1) 2 *(Rafael 21, Ylola 70)*, Shirak (0) 0   2500
Inter Bratislava (2) 3 *(Gwerich 16, Kratochvil 28, Pernis*
75), Bylis (0) 1 *(Jakupi 62)*   2552
KI (0) 0, Graz (3) 5 *(Radovic 7, 37, Standfest 9, 86, 90)*   763
Krivbas (2) 3 *(Ponomanenko 10, Paljaritsis 20, Moroz*
81), Shamkir (0) 0   1470
KR Reykjavik (0) 1 *(Hinriksson 87)*, Kilmarnock (0) 0
                                                                                                    3000
Lantana (0) 0, Torpedo Kutaisi (3) 5 *(Gwadachiani 2,*
Janashia D 34, Ioanidze 39, Chkhetiani 53,
Megreladze 66)   300
Lokomotiv Tbilisi (1) 1 *(Kebadze 24)*, Linfield (0) 0 5000
Lyngby (2) 7 *(Hermansen 29, 90, Jensen M 33, Jensen C*
47, Magleby 68, Luthje 82, Havlykke 87),
Birkirkara (0) 0   1350
Maccabi Tel Aviv (2) 3 *(Kubicka 13 (pen), 33, Basis 69)*,
Kaunas (1) 1 *(Papecko 19)*   5100
Metalurgs (1) 3 *(Boulders 36, Verpakovsky 53, Dragun*
62), Lech Poznan (1) 2 *(Zjuravski 24, Kajewski 59)* 4300
Mondercange (1) 2 *(Christophe 38, Neves 90)*, Dinamo
Bucharest (2) 6 *(Lupescu 21 (pen), Petre 26, Mihalcea*
50, Mutu 53, 79, Niculae 81)   850
Neftchi (1) 2 *(Vasiliev 27, 65)*, Red Star Belgrade (0) 3
(Boskovic 68, Pjanovic 69, Pantelic 70)   3500
Olimpija (1) 1 *(Moro 27)*, Kareda (0) 1 *(Fomenka 68)*   911
Portadown (0) 0, CSKA Sofia (1) 3 *(Mantchev 2,*
Kovacevic 77, Boukarev 85)   786
Serif (1) 1 *(Mujiri 10)*, Sigma Olomouc (1) 1
(Kovac 20)   5000
Shakhtjor Donetsk (0) 3 *(Seleznjov 61, Shtolcers 81, 88)*,
Sileks (0) 1 *(Gogic 90)*   8000
Sliema Wanderers (0) 0, Zurich (1) 3 *(Kavelashvili 36,*
Bartlett 80, Kebe 90)   365
Steaua (1) 1 *(Ilie S 40, 90, Ciocoiu 79)*, Levadia (0) 0 5000
Tulevik (0) 0, FC Brugge (0) 3 *(Deflandre 50 (pen),*
Jankauskas 59, 68)   364
Vardar (0) 0, Legia Warsaw (2) 5 *(Mieciel 9,*
Czereszewski 19, Srutna 57, 72, Wroblenski 65)   4900
Viking (3) 7 *(Aarsheim 5, Svensson 17, 48, Dadason 40,*
72, 82, Nygaard 64), Principat (0) 0   2090
Vllaznia (1) 1 *(Sinani 43)*, Spartak Trnava (1) 1
(Leitner 28)   2500
Vojvodina (2) 4 *(Suskavcevic 3, Jankovic 19 (pen), 47,*
Jovic 61), Ujpest (0) 0   3500
VPS Vaasa (1) 1 *(Pohja 40)*, St Johnstone (0) 1
(Lowndes 76)   2256

QUALIFYING ROUND, SECOND LEG

Birkirkara (0) 0, Lyngby (0) 0   1000
Bray Wanderers (0) 0, Grasshoppers (2) 4 *(Tikva 6, 39,*
De Napoli 53, Muff 64)   1600
Bylis (0) 0, Inter Bratislava (1) 2 *(Nemeth 34, 62)*   1500
B36 (0) 0, Ankaragucu (0) 1 *(Mkhalele 86)*   450

FC Brugge (0) 2 *(Jankauskas 47, De Brul 59)*,
Tulevik (0) 0   5000
Celtic (1) 4 *(Brattbakk 8, Smith 49, Mjallby 65,*
Johnson 90), Cwmbran Town (0) 0   46,757
Constructorul (1) 1 *(Zabolotny 38)*, Ferencvaros (1) 1
(Horvath 37)   1500
Cork City (1) 1 *(Morley 30)*, IFK Gothenburg (0) 0 5235
CSKA Sofia (2) 5 *(Petkov 15 (pen), Litera 27, 49,*
Hristov 61 (pen), Simeonov 78), Portadown (0) 0   8000
Dinamo Bucharest (4) 7 *(Mutu 8 (pen), 20,*
Niculae 22, 29, 73, Fogel 70 (og), Petre 90),
Mondercange (0) 0   4000
Dudelange (0) 1 *(Kabongo 48)*, Hajduk Split (0) 1
(Jazic 51)   1000
Graz (0) 4 *(Ramusch 47, Akwuegbo 73, Dimitrovic 81,*
Adu Tutu 88), KI (0) 0   9800
Hapoel Tel Aviv (0) 2 *(Pisont 81, Antebe 90)*,
Erevan (0) 1 *(Gogoladze 50)*   5000
Helsingborg (3) 5 *(Andersson C 4, Jonsson M 16,*
Powell 43, Prica 66, Bakkerud 84), FK Riga (0) 0   2624
Inter Cardiff (0) 1 *(Mainwaring 57)*, Gorica (0) 0   651
Kareda (0) 2 *(Fomenka 70, 72)*, Olimpija (1) 2 *(Moro 22,*
Kmetech 90)   3500
Kaunas (1) 2 *(Pacevicius 29, 48)*, Maccabi Tel Aviv (0) 1
(Basis 85)   3000
Kilmarnock (0) 2 *(Wright 90 (pen), Bagan 92)*, KR
Reyjkavik (0) 0   11,760
Lech Poznan (0) 3 *(Golinski 54, Kubicki 71,*
Mackiewicz 80), Metalurgs (0) 1 *(Boulders 87)*   7500
Legia Warsaw (2) 4 *(Czereszewski 5, Karwan 17,*
Sokolowski 54, Mieciel 77), Vardar (0) 0   4000
Leiftur (0) 3, Anderlecht (2) 3 *(Van Diemen 2,*
Zetterberg 41 (pen), 61 (pen))   200
Levadia (1) 1 *(Olumets 28)*, Steaua (0) 4
(Reghecampf 51, Rosu 67, 78, Ilie A 83)   500
Levski Sofia (0) 2 *(Sirakov 67, Pazin 75)*, Apoel (0) 0
                                                                                                 20,000
Linfield (0) 1 *(Larmour 68)*, Lokomotiv Tbilisi (0) 1
(Kebadze 79)   4000
Lokomotiv Moscow (3) 5 *(Chugainov 16, Loskov 23,*
Smertin 36, Kharlachyov 67, 75), BATE Borisov (0) 0
                                                                                                    9000
Omonia (0) 3 *(Rauffmann 65, 67, 73)*, Belshina (0) 0 7000
Principat (0) 0, Viking (5) 11 *(Dadason 37, 42, Berre 43,*
60, 75, Berland 44, 45, Sanne 64, 65, 67, Mathiassen 83)
                                                                                                     500
Red Star Belgrade (0) 1 *(Pantelic 77)*, Neftchi (0) 0 8000
Shamkir (0) 0, Krivbas (1) 2 *(Simakov 24, 67)*   3500
Shirak (1) 1 *(Bernetsian 28)*, HJK Helsinki (0) 0   5000
Sigma Olomouc (0) 0, Serif (0) 0   6371
Sileks (1) 2 *(Ignatov 16 (pen), Simovski 74)*,
Shakhtjor Donetsk (1) 1 *(Matvejev 40)*   2000
Spartak Trnava (0) 2 *(Uljaky 58, 89)*, Vllaznia (0) 0 6500
St Johnstone (0) 2 *(Simao 87, 90)*, VPS Vaasa (0) 0 8392
Torpedo Kutaisi (3) 4 *(Ioanidze 11, Megreladze 27, 31,*
72), Lantana (2) 2 *(Leitan 37, Dolinin 56)*   2500
Ujpest (0) 1 *(Kovacs 56)*, Vojvodina (0) 1 *(Bratis 87)* 1000
Vaduz (1) 1 *(Wegmann 39)*, Bodo Glimt (1) 2
(Saeternes 29, 83)   500
Zurich (0) 1 *(Kebe 70)*, Sliema Wanderers (0) 0   4000

FIRST ROUND, FIRST LEG

AB Copenhagen (0) 0, Grasshoppers (0) 2 *(Yakin 50,*
Ekoku 81)   2000
Ajax (2) 6 *(Verlaat 25 (pen), Reuser 26, Knopper 47,*
Mahlas 49, 64, Wamberto 72), Bystrica (1) 1
(Verlaat 14 (og))   26,145
Amica (1) 2 *(Dawidovski 23, Bosacki 69)*, Brondby (0) 0
                                                                                                   4000
Anderlecht (2) 3 *(Bajrektarevic 20 (og),*
Radzinski 35, 67), Olimpija (0) 1 *(Ekmecic 53)*   17,500
Anorthosis (0) 1 *(Engomitis 84)*, Legia Warsaw (0) 0 4000
Aris Salonika (1) 1 *(Matzios 13 (pen))*, Servette (0) 0
                                                                                                 25,000
Atletico Madrid (2) 3 *(Gamarra 41, Hasselbaink 45,*
Paunovic 57), Ankaragucu (0) 0   19,000
Beira Mar (1) 1 *(Fary 41)*, Vitesse (0) 2 *(Van Hooijdonk*
50, Grozdic 82)   10,000
Benfica (0) 0, Dinamo Bucharest (1) 1 *(Nastase 5)* 31,000
Bodo Glimt (0) 0, Werder Bremen (2) 5 *(Pizarro 12, 76,*
Bogdanovic 43, 53, Maximov 59)   1000
Celtic (1) 2 *(Larsson 25, 50 (pen))*, Hapoel Tel Aviv (0) 0
                                                                                                 45,171

CSKA Sofia (0) 0, Newcastle United (0) 2
(Solano 51, Ketsbaia 77) 20,260
Gorica (0) 0, Panathinaikos (1) 1 *(Limberopoulos 13)*
1700
Graz (2) 3 *(Akwuegbo 14, 56, Tuto 34),*
Spartak Trnava (0) 0 5000
Hajduk Split (0) 0, Levski Sofia (0) 0 20,000
Hapoel Haifa (3) 3 *(Tourgeman 19, 26, Sivilia 45),*
FC Brugge (0) 1 *(Jankauskas 65)* 7000
Helsingborg (0) 1 *(Jonsson 85),* Karpaty (1) 1
(Getsko 17) 3642
HJK Helsinki (0) 0, Lyon (1) 1 *(Vairelles 16)* 8103
Inter Bratislava (1) 1 *(Lalik 45),* Rapid Vienna (0) 0 6596
Ionikos (0) 1 *(Dimitriadis 90),* Nantes (0) 3 *(Lievres 54,*
Monterrubio 63, 80) 3000
Kaiserslautern (3) 3 *(Koch 30, Djorkaeff 37,*
Marschall 39), Kilmarnock (0) 0 21,000
Lausanne (2) 3 *(Kuzba 20, Mazzone 22, 58),*
Celta Vigo (0) 2 *(Rapo 62 (og), Karpin 67)* 7700
Lech Poznan (1) 1 *(Zurawski 45 (pen)),*
IFK Gothenburg (1) 2 *(Andersson P 33, Mild 83)* 8000
Lokomotiv Tbilisi (0) 0, PAOK Salonika (3) 7
(Georgiadis 15, 23, Sabri 42, Froussos 56, 62,
Marangos 66, Frantzeskos 67) 6000
Lyngby (0) 1 *(Bidstrup 69),* Lokomotiv Moscow (2) 2
(Chugainov 13, Bulykin 38) 1474
Maccabi Tel Aviv (1) 2 *(Kubicka 43, Ben Dayan 84),*
Lens (1) 2 *(Sakho 32, Job 54)* 4000
Monaco (0) 3 *(Simone 69, 89, Trezeguet 72),*
St Johnstone (0) 0 7000
MTK Budapest (0) 0, Fenerbahce (0) 0 5000
Omonia (0) 2 *(Kondolefteros 75, 86),* Juventus (4) 5
(Inzaghi 3, 16, Kovacevic 23, Esnaider 25, Del Piero 82)
12,585
Parma (2) 3 *(Di Vaio 15, 20, Dino Baggio 67),*
Krivbas (1) 2 *(Palynianitsa 5, Monarov 72)* 3887
Partizan Belgrade (1) 1 *(Tomic 20),* Leeds United (2) 3
(Bowyer 26, 82, Radebe 39) 4950 *(in Heerenveen).*
Red Star Belgrade (0) 0, Montpellier (1) 1 *(Loko 6)*
8500 *(in Sofia).*
Roda (2) 2 *(Doomernik 20, Zafarin 36),*
Shakhtjor Donetsk (0) 0 6500
Roma (4) 7 *(Aldair 12, Montella 13, Alenichev 15, 54, 75,*
Assuncao 39, Delvecchio 73), Setubal (0) 0 23,013
Sigma Olomouc (0) 1 *(Kobylik 63),* Mallorca (1) 3
(Engonga 12, Diego Tristan 53, Stankovic 76) 7000
Skonto Riga (1) 1 *(Astafyev 32),* Widzew Lodz (0) 0 650
Stabaek (0) 1 *(Finstad 57),* La Coruna (0) 0 3807
Steaua (0) 2 *(Ciocoiu 64, Danciulescu 82),*
LASK Linz (0) 0 3600
Teplice (1) 1 *(Frydek 32, Kolomazni 53, Rizek 71),*
Ferencvaros (1) 1 *(Kovacs 16)* 10,258
Torpedo Kutaisi (0) 0, AEK Athens (0) 1 *(Zikos 90)*
10,000
Tottenham Hotspur (2) 3 *(Leonhardsen 3, Perry 32,*
Sherwood 56), Zimbru Chisinau (0) 0 32,660
Udinese (1) 1 *(Sottil 9),* Aalborg (0) 0 17,661
Viking (0) 3 *(Svensson 57, Berre 70, Espevoll 78),*
Sporting Lisbon (0) 0 4080
Vojvodina (0) 0, Slavia Prague (0) 0 2000 *(in Skopje).*
West Ham United (1) 3 *(Wanchope 39, Di Canio 48,*
Lampard 58), Osijek (0) 0 25,331
Wolfsburg (0) 1 *(Akonnor 61, Juskowiak 87),*
Debrecen (0) 0 10,000
Zenit (0) 0, Bologna (1) 3 *(Ventola 39,*
Signori 65, 90 (pen)) 22,000
Zurich (1) 1 *(Jamarauli 29),* Lierse (0) 0 4200

FIRST ROUND, SECOND LEG
Aalborg (0) 1 *(Matovac 71),* Udinese (0) 2 *(Muzzi 63,*
Locatelli 90) 8473
AEK Athens (4) 6 *(Ciric 8 (pen), Bjekovic 22, Maladenis*
25, Kopitsis 43, 88, Nikolaidis 74), Torpedo Kutaisi (0)
1 *(Megreladze 73)* 5000
Ankaragucu (0) 1 *(Birol 84),* Atletico Madrid (0) 0 5000
Bologna (1) 2 *(Fontalan 39, Cipriani 74),* Zenit (1) 2
(Panov 35, Kondrasjov 89) 12,126
Brondby (1) 4 *(Madsen 37, 76, Da Silva 54, Christensen*
78), Amica (0) 3 *(Kryszalowicz 52, 68,*
Kukielka 63 (pen)) 5907
FC Brugge (2) 4 *(Verheyen 20, Borkelmans 26,*
Janssen 52, 90), Hapoel Haifa (1) 2 *(Rosso 18, 79)* 9000
Bystrica (1) 1 *(Malatinsky 45),* Ajax (0) 3 *(Arveladze 47,*
Bobsun 64, Laudrup 90) 9000
Celta Vigo (1) 4 *(McCarthy 10, 85, 90, Mostovoi 76),*
Lausanne (0) 0 16,000

Debrecen (0) 2 *(Sabo 54, 89),* Wolfsburg (0) 1
(Akpoborie 25) 4500
Dinamo Bucharest (0) 0, Benfica (1) 2 *(Maniche 26,*
Chano 72) 13,000
Fenerbahce (0) 0, MTK Budapest (0) 2 *(Kenesei 56, 63)*
20,000
Ferencvaros (0) 1 *(Matyus 57),* Teplice (0) 1 *(Rada 53)*
7000
Grasshoppers (0) 1 *(Magro 79),* AB Copenhagen (1) 1
(Hansen 30) 3800
Hapoel Tel Aviv (0) 0, Celtic (0) 1 *(Larsson 63)* 6400
IFK Gothenburg (0) 0, Lech Poznan (0) 0 4910
Juventus (2) 5 *(Kovacevic 21, 47, 88, Tacchinardi 55,*
Conte 90), Omonia (0) 0 32,000
Karpaty (0) 1 *(Getsko 90),* Helsingborg (0) 1
(Jonsson 89) 27,000
(Helsingborg won 4-2 on penalties).
Kilmarnock (0) 0, Kaiserslautern (2) 2 *(Djorkaeff 22,*
Ramzy 29) 8074
Krivbas (0) 0, Parma (2) 3 *(Boghossian 36, Crespo 40,*
Di Vaio 67) 30,000
La Coruna (1) 2 *(Jokanovic 37, Conceicao 62),*
Stabaek (0) 0 15,000
LASK Linz (1) 2 *(Stumpf 7, Sane 89),* Steaua (2) 3
(Ciociou 8, Sabrin 32, Duro 59) 5500
Leeds United (0) 1 *(Huckerby 55),*
Partizan Belgrade (0) 0 39,806
Legia Warsaw (0) 2 *(Mieciel 48, Czereszewski 68),*
Anorthosis (0) 0 6500
Lens (0) 2 *(Nouma 78, Delporte 80),*
Maccabi Tel Aviv (1) 1 *(Basis 23)* 37,000
Levski Sofia (2) 3 *(Ivankov 16 (pen), Bachev 32, Dimitrov*
84), Hajduk Split (0) 0 29,000
Lierse (1) 3 *(Van Meir 16, Huysegems 71, Zdebel 82),*
Zurich (1) 4 *(Jamarauli 2, Frick 57, Eydelie 87,*
Daems 89 (og)) 5400
Lokomotiv Moscow (2) 3 *(Kharlachyov 20, Drozdov 43,*
Janashia 44), Lyngby (0) 0 13,000
Lyon (3) 5 *(Anderson 11, Blanc 15, Linares 18, Vairelles*
71, 85), HJK Helsinki (1) 1 *(Lehkosuo 40)* 19,000
Mallorca (0) 0, Sigma Olomouc (0) 0 10,000
Montpellier (1) 2 *(Ouedec 35, Loko 52),* Red Star
Belgrade (0) 2 *(Jelic 49, Boskovic 54 (pen))* 9240
Nantes (0) 1 *(Da Rocha 48),* Ionikos (0) 0 28,000
Newcastle United (1) 2 *(Shearer 36, Robinson 88),* CSKA
Sofia (1) 2 *(Litera 29, Simeonov 90)* 36,228
Olimpja (0) 0, Anderlecht (0) 3 *(Koller 63,*
Radzinski 69, 72) 800
Osijek (0) 1 *(Bubalo 70),* West Ham United (1) 3
(Kitson 27, Ruddock 83, Foe 90) 15,000
Panathinaikos (1) 2 *(Sigurdsson 38, Nassiopoulos 69),*
Gorica (0) 0 8000
PAOK Salonika (0) 2 *(Valencia 52 (pen), Salpigidis 88),*
Lokomotiv Tbilisi (0) 0 6000
Rapid Vienna (0) 1 *(Zingler 65),* Inter Bratislava (1) 2
(Suchanok 45, Babnic 64) 7000
St Johnstone (2) 3 *(Leonard 5 (og), Dasovic 33, O'Neil*
76), Monaco (2) 3 *(Prso 9, Riise 24, Legwinski 69)* 7706
Servette (1) 1 *(Lonfat 35),* Aris Salonika (1) 2
(Andriolo 37, Kyzeridis 90) 6200
Setubal (0) 1 *(Maki 79),* Roma (0) 0 5000
Shakhtjor Donetsk (1) 1 *(Benjo 33),* Roda (1) 3
(Tchoutang 28, Van der Luer 81, Van Dessel 88) 20,000
Slavia Prague (1) 3 *(Petrous 39, Dosek 73, Zelenka 82),*
Vojvodina (1) 2 *(Belic 18, Bogdanovic 47)* 4000
Spartak Trnava (1) 2 *(Muzlay 45, 70),* Graz (1) 1
(Standfest 14) 2097
Sporting Lisbon (0) 1 *(Ayew 76 (pen)),* Viking (0) 0
32,000
Vitesse (0) 0, Beira Mar (0) 0 15,000
Werder Bremen (0) 1 *(Ailton 76),* Bodo Glimt (1) 1
(Staurvik 36) 15,291
Widzew Lodz (2) 2 *(Wichniarek 1, Gesior 43),*
Skonto Riga (0) 0 4000
Zimbru Chisinau (0) 0, Tottenham Hotspur (0) 0 7000

SECOND ROUND, FIRST LEG
Anderlecht (2) 2 *(Koller 19, 37),* Bologna (0) 1
(Signori 90) 21,000
Aris Salonika (1) 2 *(Andrioli 44, Kyzeridis 68),*
Celta Vigo (2) 2 *(Karpin 40, 42)* 18,000
Atletico Madrid (0) 1 *(Baraja 84),* Amica (0) 0 4000
Graz (2) 2 *(Lipa 57, Pamic 81),* Panathinaikos (0) 1
(Sypniewski 64) 6000
Hapoel Haifa (0) 0, Ajax (2) 3 *(Mahlas 3, Knopper 12,*
Laudrup 56) 14,500

IFK Gothenburg (0) 0, Roma (1) 2 _(Montella 37, 51)_
    18,319
Inter Bratislava (0) 0, Nantes (2) 3 _(Sibierski 25 (pen),_
    Da Rocha 35, Carriere 86)   7000
La Coruna (1) 3 _(Pauleta 17, Djalminha 47 (pen),_
    Makaay 53), Montpellier (1) 1 _(Romero 6 (og))_ 15,000
Leeds United (2) 4 _(Bowyer 27, 45, Smith 56, Kewell 83)_,
    Lokomotiv Moscow (0) 1 _(Loskov 81)_ 37,814
Lens (2) 4 _(Brunel 3, Nouma 17, Nyarko 74, Blanchard_
    _87)_, Vitesse (0) 1 _(Van Hooijdonk 72 (pen))_ 38,000
Levski Sofia (0) 1 _(Youffou 55)_, Juventus (1) 3
    (Oliseh 23, Kovacevic 53, 89) 30,000
Lyon (0) 1 _(Blanc 61)_, Celtic (0) 0 37,500
MTK Budapest (2) 2 _(Egressy 28, Eros 35)_,
    AEK Athens (0) 1 _(Ciric 62)_ 4000
PAOK Salonika (0) 1 _(Frantzeskos 81)_, Benfica (0) 2
    (Nuno Gomes 68, Ronaldo 90) 33,000
Parma (1) 1 _(Cannavaro 44)_, Helsingborg (0) 0 3530
Roda (0) 0, Wolfsburg (0) 0 7500
Slavia Prague (2) 3 _(Ulich 20, 50, Kuchar 39)_,
    Grasshoppers (1) 1 _(Yakin 23)_ 4555
Steaua (1) 2 _(Rosu 40, Ilie S 57)_, West Ham United (0) 0
    12,500
Teplice (0) 1 _(Verbir 66)_, Mallorca (2) 2 _(Tristan 27, 31)_
    5850
Tottenham Hotspur (1) 1 _(Iversen 34 (pen))_,
    Kaiserslautern (0) 0 35,177
Udinese (1) 1 _(Sosa 28)_, Legia Warsaw (0) 0 13,722
Werder Bremen (0) 0, Viking (0) 0 6000
Widzew Lodz (1) 1 _(Wichniarek 5 (pen))_, Monaco (1) 1
    (Giuly 39) 5000
Zurich (0) 1 _(Castillo 68)_, Newcastle United (0) 2
    (Maric 51, Shearer 60) 9600

SECOND ROUND, SECOND LEG
AEK Athens (0) 1 _(Ciric 74 (pen))_, MTK Budapest (0) 0
    7288
Ajax (0) 0, Hapoel Haifa (0) 1 _(Rosso 60 (pen))_ 38,765
Amica (1) 1 _(Jackiewicz 34)_, Atletico Madrid (3) 4
    (Hasselbaink 30, Capdevila 44, Baraja 45, Correa 85)
    6000
Benfica (1) 1 _(Kandourov 25)_, PAOK Salonika (2) 2
    (Marangos 28, Sabry 44) 30,000
Bologna (1) 3 _(Eriberto 45, Ze Elias 56, Nervo 90)_,
    Anderlecht (0) 0 21,548
Celta Vigo (0) 2 _(Djorovic 65, Turdo 90)_,
    Aris Salonika (0) 0 15,000
Celtic (0) 0, Lyon (1) 1 _(Vairelles 17)_ 54,291
Grasshoppers (0) 1 _(Yakin 76)_, Slavia Prague (0) 0 3300
Helsingborg (0) 1 _(Stavrum 86)_, Parma (3) 3
    (Di Vaio 11, 42, 43) 12,250
Juventus (0) 1 _(Kovacevic 79)_, Levski Sofia (1) 1
    (Atanassov 15) 2681
Kaiserslautern (0) 2 _(Buck 89, Carr 90 (og))_, Tottenham
    Hotspur (0) 0 29,044
Legia Warsaw (1) 1 _(Czereszewski 11)_, Udinese (1) 1
    (Sosa 41) 12,000
Lokomotiv Moscow (0) 0, Leeds United (3) 3
    (Harte 16 (pen), Bridges 28, 45) 8000
Mallorca (1) 3 _(Nadal 30, Stankovic 57, Nino 68)_,
    Teplice (0) 0 12,000
Monaco (0) 2 _(Lamouchi 50, Trezeguet 84)_,
    Widzew Lodz (0) 0 5133
Montpellier (0) 0, La Coruna (1) 2 _(Makaay 45,_
    Pauleta 83) 16,845
Nantes (0) 4 _(Sibierski 48, Monterrubio 61, Devineau 73,_
    Da Rocha 82), Inter Bratislava (0) 0 3700
Newcastle United (1) 3 _(Maric 33, Ferguson 58,_
    Speed 61), Zurich (1) 1 _(Jamarauli 17)_ 34,502
Panathinaikos (0) 1 _(Pflipsen 90 (pen))_, Graz (0) 0 15,000
Roma (0) 1 _(Fabio Junior 88)_, IFK Gothenburg (0) 0 9777
Viking (1) 2 _(Berland 3, Dadason 78)_,
    Werder Bremen (1) 2 _(Wiedener 43, Herzog 63)_ 6120
Vitesse (0) 1 _(Kreek 64)_, Lens (0) 1 _(Blanchard 90)_ 15,000
West Ham United (0) 0, Steaua (0) 0 24,514
Wolfsburg (0) 1 _(Akonnor 87)_, Roda (0) 0 7677

THIRD ROUND, FIRST LEG
AEK Athens (1) 2 _(Nikolaidis 45, 90)_, Monaco (1) 2
    (Giuly 25, Simone 77) 10,000
Ajax (0) 0, Mallorca (1) 1 _(Tristan 35)_ 42,000
Arsenal (1) 3 _(Overmars 13 (pen), Winterburn 81,_
    Bergkamp 90), Nantes (0) 0 36,118
Bologna (0) 1 _(Signori 68)_, Galatasaray (0) 1
    (Hakan Sukur 82) 20,000

Celta Vigo (4) 7 _(Karpin 16 (pen), 53, Makelele 30, Turdo_
    39, 50, Juanfran 43, Mostovoi 62), Benfica (0) 0 30,000
La Coruna (4) 4 _(Olivares 8 (og), Pauleta 13, Djalminha_
    15, Donato 30), Panathinaikos (1) 2 _(Warzycha 20,_
    Galetto 66) 25,000
Lens (0) 1 _(Schjonberg 84 (og))_, Kaiserslautern (2) 2
    (Sikora 31 (og), Wagner 38) 32,000
Lyon (2) 3 _(Anderson 12, 31, Vairelles 78)_, Werder
    Bremen (0) 0 25,000
Olympiakos (1) 1 _(Yannakopoulos 15)_, Juventus (1) 3
    (Tudor 27, Kovacevic 67, Inzaghi 88) 30,000
Parma (1) 2 _(Di Vaio 16, Stanic 62)_, Sturm Graz (1) 1
    (Schopp 21) 8000
Rangers (2) 2 _(Kohler 18 (og), Wallace 45)_, Borussia
    Dortmund (0) 0 49,268
Roma (0) 1 _(Totti 51 (pen))_, Newcastle United (0) 0
    45,655
Slavia Prague (2) 4 _(Dostalek 2, Horvath 38, 47,_
    Dosek 55), Steaua (0) 1 _(Lutu 81)_ 15,000
Spartak Moscow (1) 2 _(Shirko 38, Robson 65)_,
    Leeds United (1) 1 _(Kewell 14)_ 5485 _(in Sofia)_.
Udinese (0) 0, Leverkusen (0) 1 _(Ballack 77)_ 10,000
Wolfsburg (1) 2 _(Juskowiak 21, Akonnor 83 (pen))_,
    Atletico Madrid (2) 3 _(Aguilera 6, 58, Hasselbaink 35)_
    10,700

THIRD ROUND, SECOND LEG
Atletico Madrid (1) 2 _(Hasselbaink 4, Correa 86)_,
    Wolfsburg (0) 1 _(Akonnor 56 (pen))_ 5000
Benfica (0) 1 _(Caceres 79 (og))_, Celta Vigo (1) 1
    (McCarthy 18) 3000
Borussia Dortmund (1) 2 _(Ikpeba 28, Bobic 90)_,
    Rangers (0) 0 38,000
(Borussia Dortmund won 3-1 on penalties).
Galatasaray (2) 2 _(Sas 5, Umit 29)_, Bologna (1) 1
    (Ventola 8) 23,000
Juventus (1) 1 _(Kovacevic 2)_, Olympiakos (1) 2
    (Djordjevic 37, 82 (pen)) 16,331
Kaiserslautern (1) 1 _(Hristov 21)_, Lens (2) 4 _(Job 20, 40,_
    Strasser 56 (og), Nyarko 90) 25,000
Leeds United (0) 1 _(Radebe 84)_, Spartak Moscow (0) 0
    39,732
Leverkusen (1) 1 _(Ballack 24)_, Udinese (2) 2
    (Margiotta 9, 18) 22,500
Mallorca (1) 2 _(Soler 3 (pen), Biagini 73)_, Ajax (0) 0
    19,000
Monaco (1) 1 _(Simone 32)_, AEK Athens (0) 0 5000
Nantes (1) 3 _(Sibierski 12, 57, Vahirua 77)_, Arsenal (3) 3
    (Grimandi 24, Henry 31, Overmars 42) 28,000
Newcastle United (0) 0, Roma (0) 0 35,739
Panathinaikos (0) 1 _(Asanovic 77 (pen))_, La Coruna (0) 1
    (Makaay 90) 35,000
Steaua (0) 1 _(Ciocoiu 46)_, Slavia Prague (0) 1
    (Dostalek 49) 12,000
Sturm Graz (0) 3 _(Reinmayr 67, 94, Vastic 86)_,
    Parma (1) 3 _(Stanic 4, 108, Crespo 120)_ 13,400
Werder Bremen (2) 4 _(Bode 16, Herzog 39 (pen),_
    Baumann 54, Pizarro 78), Lyon (0) 0 9559

FOURTH ROUND, FIRST LEG
Atletico Madrid (1) 2 _(Hasselbaink 24, 77)_, Lens (1) 2
    (Dacourt 15, 76) 15,000
Arsenal (2) 5 _(Dixon 5, Henry 30, 67, Kanu 78, Bergkamp_
    _83)_, La Coruna (0) 1 _(Djalminha 55 (pen))_ 37,837
Borussia Dortmund (0) 0, Galatasaray (2) 2
    (Hakan Sukur 33, Hagi 45) 55,000
Juventus (0) 1 _(Kovacevic 49)_, Celta Vigo (0) 0 10,000
Mallorca (2) 4 _(Stankovic 42, 52 (pen), 60 (pen), Diego_
    Tristan 90), Monaco (1) 1 _(Simone 1)_ 24,000
Parma (1) 1 _(Crespo 5)_, Werder Bremen (0) 0 8398
Roma (0) 0, Leeds United (0) 0 37,726
Slavia Prague (0) 1 _(Zanchi 76 (og))_, Udinese (0) 0 13,149

FOURTH ROUND, SECOND LEG
Celta Vigo (2) 4 _(Makelele 1, Birindelli 33 (og),_
    McCarthy 46, 70), Juventus (0) 0 30,000
Galatasaray (0) 0, Borussia Dortmund (0) 0 35,000
La Coruna (2) 2 _(Victor 69, Ivan 90)_, Arsenal (0) 1
    (Henry 63) 20,000
Leeds United (0) 1 _(Kewell 67)_, Roma (0) 0 39,149
Lens (2) 4 _(Nouma 28, 53, Sakho 38, Brunel 71)_,
    Atletico Madrid (1) 2 _(Hasselbaink 45, Kiko 64)_ 40,000
Monaco (1) 1 _(Simone 33)_, Mallorca (0) 0 10,000
Udinese (1) 2 _(Fiore 22, Sosa 51)_, Slavia Prague (1) 1
    (Koller 41) 19,289

Werder Bremen (2) 3 *(Dabrovski 29, Bode 45,*
Cannavaro 66 (og)), Parma (1) 1 *(Stanic 32)*   30,050

QUARTER-FINALS, FIRST LEG
Arsenal (1) 2 *(Henry 21, Ljungberg 77),*
  Werder Bremen (0) 0   38,009
Celta Vigo (0) 0, Lens (0) 0   27,000
Leeds United (1) 3 *(Wilcox 39, Kewell 54, Bowyer 59),*
  Slavia Prague (0) 0   39,519
Mallorca (0) 1 *(Lauren 80),* Galatasaray (1) 4 *(Arif 45,*
Emre 48, Hakan Sukur 58, Okan 64)   20,000

QUARTER-FINALS, SECOND LEG
Galatasaray (1) 2 *(Capone 31, Hakan Sukur 46),*
  Mallorca (0) 1 *(Carlos 63)*   30,000
Lens (0) 2 *(Ismael 63 (pen), Nouma 75),* Celta Vigo (0) 1
(Revivo 59)   41,649

Slavia Prague (0) 2 *(Ulich 52, 79 (pen),*
  Leeds United (0) 1 *(Kewell 47)*   13,460
Werder Bremen (1) 2 *(Bode 41, Bogdanovic 60),*
  Arsenal (2) 4 *(Parlour 8, 25, 70, Henry 59)*   33,875

SEMI-FINALS, FIRST LEG
Arsenal (1) 1 *(Bergkamp 2),* Lens (0) 0   38,102
Galatasaray (2) 2 *(Hakan Sukur 12, Capone 43),*
  Leeds United (0) 0   18,000

SEMI-FINALS, SECOND LEG
Leeds United (1) 2 *(Bakke 16, 68),* Galatasaray (2) 2
(Hagi 5 (pen), Hakan Sukur 42)   38,406
Lens (0) 1 *(Nouma 73),* Arsenal (1) 2 *(Henry 43,*
Kanu 86)   41,043

FINAL

Galatasaray (0) 0, Arsenal (0) 0

(in Copenhagen, 17 May 2000, 38,919)

Galatasaray: Taffarel; Capone, Ergun, Suat (Ahmet 94), Popescu, Bulent, Okan (Hakan Unsal 83), Umit, Arif (Hasan 94), Hagi, Hakan Sukur.
Arsenal: Seaman; Dixon, Silvinho, Vieira, Keown, Adams, Parlour, Henry, Petit, Bergkamp (Kanu 74), Overmars (Suker 114).
(aet; Galatasaray won 4-1 on penalties; Ergun (scored) 1-0; Suker (hit post) 1-0; Hakan Sukur (scored) 2-0; Parlour (scored) 2-1; Umit (scored) 3-1; Vieira (hit bar) 3-1; Popescu (scored) 4-1).
Referee: Nieto (Spain).

Thierry Henry holds his head in anguish. A goal would have spared Arsenal's eventual penalty shoot embarrassment against Galatasaray. (Actionimages)

UEFA CUP 1999–2000 – BRITISH AND IRISH CLUBS

FIRST QUALIFYING ROUND, FIRST LEG

12 AUG

Cwmbran Town (0) 0   8920 *(at Cardiff)*.
Celtic (3) 6 *(Berkovic 2, Tebily 20, Larsson 32, 61, Viduka 52, Brattbakk 83)*
Cwmbran Town: O'Hagan; O'Brien, Wills, Dyson, John, Blackie, Evans (Thomas 58), Moore, Wigley (Aizlewood 72), Graham D, Summers (Hughes 84).
Celtic: Gould; Riseth, Petta (Blinker 46), Stubbs, Tebily, Mahre, Burley, Lambert, Larsson (Johnson 80), Berkovic, Viduka (Brattbakk 80).

Gorica (0) 2 *(Mitrakovic 75 (pen), Zlogar 83)*
Inter Cardiff (0) 0   1100
Gorica: Mavric; Srebrnic, Molefe (Drobne 26), Alomerovic, Ipavec, Vulic (Znidercic 55), Mitrakovic, Zlogar, Ribaric, Becaj, Halili.
Inter Cardiff: Wager; Poretta, Brazil, David, Philpott, Mardenborough (Evans 60), Wile, Murray, Davies, Williams, Misbah.

Grasshoppers (1) 4 *(Chapuisat 30, 63, Isabella 78, 83)*
Bray Wanderers (0) 0   5600
Grasshoppers: Huber; Haas, Gren, Hodel, Yakin (Isabella 74), Tikva (Lovvik 63), Sermeter (Cabanas 80), Smilijanic, Magro, Zanni, Chapuisat.
Bray Wanderers: Walsh; Tresson, Farrell, Kenny, Doohan, Keogh (Tierney 86), Byrne, Lynch (O'Brien 46), O'Brien, Fox, Connolly (O'Connor 59).

IFK Gothenburg (1) 3 *(Andersson P 36, Karlsson 74, 87)*
Cork City (0) 0   3278
IFK Gothenburg: Andersson B; Pedersen, Nilsson, Anegrund, Landberg, Persson, Mild, Erinkmark, Karlsson P, Hermansson (Tetteh 62), Andersson P.
Cork City: Mooney; Napier, Daly, Hill, Cronin, O'Brien, Flanagan, Freyne (Dobbs 82), Herrick, Cahill, Morley (Caulfield 82).

KR Reykjavik (0) 1 *(Hinriksson 87)*
Kilmarnock (0) 0   5000
KR Reykjavik: Finnbogason; Porsteinsson, Gislason, Egilsson, Winnie, Jonsson S, Juliusson (Birgisson 70), Danielsson, Hinriksson, Gunnlaugsson, Benediktsson.
Kilmarnock: Meldrum; MacPherson, Jeffrey (Wright 85), McGowne, Reilly, Holt, Mitchell, Dindeleux, Roberts (Vareille 61), Innes, Hay.

Lokomotiv Tbilisi (1) 1 *(Kebadze 24)*
Linfield (0) 0   5000
Lokomotiv Tbilisi: Janelidze; Balashuili, Barnovi, Chikhkadze, Baramidze (Katishuili 20), Gogichaishvili, Kebadze, Mikadze, Kobuladze, Shavbuildze (Melkadze 68), Chomakhidze (Aslanadze 68).
Linfield: Robinson; McDonald, Easton, Kelly, Murphy, Beatty, Larmour, Gorman, Callaghan, Marks, Bailie.

Portadown (0) 0   786
CSKA Sofia (1) 3 *(Mantchev 2, Kovacevic 77, Boukarev 85)*
Portadown: Dalton; McKeown, Davidson, Byrne (Quigley 75), Strain, major, Clarke, Dunne, Millar, Arkins, Campbell.
CSKA Sofia: Luckic; Kremenliev, Murkic, Chomakov, Trentchev, Litera, Paskov (Valentiov 64), Hristov (Boukarev 82), Simeonov, Sarac, Mantchev (Kovacevic 62).

VPS Vaasa (1) 1 *(Pohja 40)*
St Johnstone (0) 1 *(Lowndes 76)*   2256
VPS Vaasa: Toiuonem; Kaultonem, Suoste, Koko, Jallonen, Priha, Kangaskorpi, Enquist, Jaakkola, Pohja, Sykora (Kaijasilta 32).
St Johnstone: Main; McQuillan, Bollan, Dasovic, Weir, Dods, Simao (Grant 55), O'Neil, McAnespie, McMahon (Lowndes 70), Kane.

FIRST QUALIFYING ROUND, SECOND LEG

24 AUG

CSKA Sofia (2) 5 *(Petkov 15 (pen), Litera 27, 49, Hristov 61 (pen), Simeonov 78)*
Portadown (0) 0   8000
CSKA Sofia: Luckic; Kremenliev, Murkic, Trentchev, Sarac, Litera (Paskov 80), Chomakov, Petkov, Hristov, Berbatov (Simeonov 74), Kovacevic (Mantchev 62).
Portadown: Dalton; McKeown, Strain, Major, Davidson, Quigley, Clarke, Dunne, Irwin, Hill (O'Hara 87), Arkins.

26 AUG

Bray Wanderers (0) 0   1600
Grasshoppers (2) 4 *(Tikva 6, 39, De Napoli 53, Muff 64)*
Bray Wanderers: Walsh; Tresson, McKeever (O'Connor 77), Doohan, Farrell, Kenny (Larkin 70), Tierney, Smyth (Power 70), Byrne, Fox, O'Brien.
Grasshoppers: Huber; Zanni, De Nicola, Gren, Smilijanic, Isabella (Sermeter 67), Hodel, Cabanas, Magro, De Napoli, Tikva (Muff 63).

Celtic (1) 4 *(Brattbakk 8, Smith 49, Mjallby 65, Johnson 90)*
Cwmbran Town (0) 0   46,757
Celtic: Kharine; Riseth, Petta (Johnson 70), Stubbs, McKinlay, Wieghorst (Smith 46), Mjallby, Blinker, Burchill, Brattbakk, Healy.
Cwmbran Town: Morris; O'Brien (Graham B 79), Wills, Futcher, John, Blackie, Aizlewood, Moore, Wigley (Pattimore 88), Graham D, Summers (Goodridge 88).

Cork City (1) 1 *(Morley 30)*
IFK Gothenburg (0) 0   5235
Cork City: Mooney; Napier, Daly, Cronin, O'Brien C, Freyne, O'Brien L, Flanagan, Cahill (O'Halloran 71), Morley (Dobbs 69), Hill.
IFK Gothenburg: Andersson B; Nilsson, Anegrund, Erlingmark, Landberg, Hoiland, Mild, Henriksson, Karlsson P, Andersson P (Hermansson 86), Tetteh (Svensson 90).

Inter Cardiff (0) 1 *(Mainwaring 57)*
Gorica (0) 0   651
Inter Cardiff: Wager; Brazil, David, Philpott, Hewitt, Giles (Murray 80), Davies, King (Wile 89), Misbah, Tyler (Dyer 80), Mainwaring.
Gorica: Mavric; Srebrnic, Zlogar, Becaj, Halili, Mitrakovic, Ribaric, Molefe, Alomerovic, Ipavec (Znidercic 30), Vulic (Debenjak 89).

Kilmarnock (0) 2 *(Wright 90 (pen), Bagan 92)*
KR Reykjavik (0) 0   aet 11,760
Kilmarnock: Meldrum; MacPherson, Henry (Bagan 70), Holt, Wright, Baker, Dindeleux, Lauchlan, McCoist (Jeffrey 70), Mahood (Vareille 46), Durrant.
KR Reykjavik: Finnbogason; Porsteinsson, Gislason, Egilsson, Winnie, Jonsson S, Juliusson (Jonsson P 46), Danielsson, Hinriksson, Gunnlaugsson (Sigurdsson 82), Benediktsson (Birgisson 62).

Linfield (0) 1 *(Larmour 68)*
Lokomotiv Tbilisi (0) 1 *(Kebadze 79)*   4000
Linfield: Mathers; McDonald (Rogan 86), Easton (McMullan 66), Kelly, Murphy, Morgan (Semple 86), Larmour, Beatty, Callaghan, Marks, Bailie.
Lokomotiv Tbilisi: Aslanadze; Balashvili, Chikhkadze, Baramidze, Gogichaishvili, Kebadze, Malladze, Mikadze, Kobuladze, Gvelesiani, Chomakhidze (Katsiashvili 60).

St Johnstone (0) 2 *(Simao 87, 90)*
VPS Vaasa (0) 0   8392
St Johnstone: Main; McQuillan, Bollan, Dasovic, Weir, Dods, McAnespie (Grant 56), O'Neil, Lowndes (Simao 80), McMahon, Cane.
VPS Vaasa: Stringham (Sillampaa 70); Kaultonem, Koko, Jallonen, Kangaskorpi, Sihvonen, Enquist, Essandoh, Jaakkola (Nygard 84), Pohja, Kajasitta.

FIRST ROUND, FIRST LEG

14 SEPT

Partizan Belgrade (1) 1 *(Tomic 20)*   4950 *(in Heerenveen)*.

Leeds United (2) 3 *(Bowyer 26, 82, Radebe 39)*

Partizan Belgrade: Damjanac; Savic, Tomic, Stanojevic, Rasovic, Krstajic, Ivic (Stojakovic 88), Trobok, Iliev (Pekovic 70), Kezman, Ilic (Gerasimovski 81).
Leeds United: Martyn; Mills, Harte, Woodgate, Radebe, Batty, Hopkin, Kelly, Bridges (Smith 70), Kewell, Bowyer.

16 SEPT

Celtic (1) 2 *(Larsson 25, 50 (pen))*
Hapoel Tel Aviv (0) 0   45,171

Celtic: Gould; McNamara, Mahe, Stubbs, Tebily, Petta (Blinker 83), Burley, Lambert, Larsson, Burchill, Moravcik.
Hapoel Tel Aviv: Elimelech; Antebi, Gereson, Bakhar, Oharon, Pishont, Rutnik, Udi, Toema (Gohen 71), Cimirotic, Harazi R (Pikva 63).

CSKA Sofia (0) 0
Newcastle United (0) 2 *(Solano 51, Ketsbaia 77)*   20,260

CSKA Sofia: Lukic; Kremenliev (Ivanov G 60), Sarac, Velikov, Mrkic, Trentchev (Litera 55), Tchomakov, Petkov, Hristov (Ivanov I 55), Mantchev, Berbatov.
Newcastle United: Harper; Barton, Domi, Dabizas, Goma, Solano (Hamilton 83), Dyer, Lee, Shearer, Ferguson (Ketsbaia 18), Speed.

Kaiserslautern (3) 3 *(Koch 30, Djorkaeff 37, Marschall 39)*
Kilmarnock (0) 0   21,000

Kaiserslautern: Reinke; Ramzy, Hristov (Strasser 78), Wagner (Reich 71), Petterson, Sforza, Marschall, Djorkaeff, Ratinho (Sobotzik 82), Buck, Koch.
Kilmarnock: Meldrum; MacPherson, McGowne, Holt, Baker, Lauchlan, Bagan, Durrant (Reilly 76), Mitchell (Burke 79), Vareille (Jeffrey 70), Mahood.

Monaco (0) 3 *(Simone 69, 89, Trezeguet 72)*
St Johnstone (0) 0   7000

Monaco: Barthez; Marquez, Christanval, Lamouchi (Riise 55), Giuly (N'Diaye 82), Trezeguet, Gallardo, Simone, Leonard (Legwinski 84), Da Costa, Sagnol.
St Johnstone: Main; McQuillan, Bollan, McAnespie, Weir, Griffin, Simao, O'Neil, Thomas (Lowndes 64), O'Halloran, Kane.

Tottenham Hotspur (2) 3 *(Leonhardsen 3, Perry 32, Sherwood 56)*
Zimbru Chisinau (0) 0   32,660

Tottenham Hotspur: Walker; Carr, Taricco (Edinburgh 82), Freund, Young, Perry, Leonhardsen, Sherwood, Armstrong (Dominguez 76), Iversen, Ginola.
Zimbru Chisinau: Romanenco; Kulik, Catinsus, Oprea, Telesnenco, Tropanet (Fistican 46), Ghilazev, Dodul (Robu 46), Epureanu, Miterev (Gusila 82), Boret.

West Ham United (1) 3 *(Wanchope 39, Di Canio 48, Lampard 58)*
Osijek (0) 0   25,331

West Ham United: Hislop; Sinclair, Keller, Potts, Stimac, Margas, Moncur (Foe 88), Lampard, Wanchope, Di Canio (Kitson 85), Lomas.
Osijek: Galinovic; Gaspar, Besirevic (Balatinac 78), Beljan, Zebic, Vulca, Ergovic, Vranjes, Prisc (Mitu 57), Bubalo (Turkovic 80), Babic.

FIRST ROUND, SECOND LEG

30 SEPT

Hapoel Tel Aviv (0) 0
Celtic (0) 1 *(Larsson 63)*   6400

Hapoel Tel Aviv: Elimelech; Oharon, Bakhar (Ekayan 73), Gereson, Cohen (Balan 78), Toema (Harazi R 46), Pishont, Rutnik, Cimirotic, Antebi, Racunica.
Celtic: Gould; McNamara, Riseth, Tebiley, Stubbs, Petrov (Wieghorst 62), Burley, Lambert, Viduka (Berkovic 75), Larsson, Moravcik (Blinker 63).

Kilmarnock (0) 0   8074
Kaiserslautern (2) 2 *(Djorkaeff 22, Ramzy 29)*

Kilmarnock: Meldrum; MacPherson, Baker, McGowne, Dindeleux, Innes, Durrant, Reilly, Holt, McCoist (Mitchell 77), Vareille (Jeffrey 77).
Kaiserslautern: Reinke; Schjonberg, Ramzy, Wagner, Sforza (Sobotzik 58), Marschall (Buck 46), Komljenovic, Djorkaeff, Strasser, Koch, Rodrigues (Petterson 46).

Leeds United (0) 1 *(Huckerby 55)*
Partizan Belgrade (0) 0   39,806

Leeds United: Martyn; Kelly, Harte, Woodgate, Radebe, Batty, Hopkin (Bakke 80), Huckerby, Bridges (Smith 67), Kewell (Jones 85), Bowyer.
Partizan Belgrade: Damjanac; Stanojevic, Savic, Gerasimovski, Sabo, Trobok (Duljaj 66), Ivic (Stojakovic 87), Tomic, Pekovic, Stojisavlevic, Obradovic (Baljak 63).

Newcastle United (1) 2 *(Shearer 36, Robinson 88)*
CSKA Sofia (1) 2 *(Litera 29, Simeonov 90)*   36,228

Newcastle United: Harper; Barton, Domi, Dabizas, Goma, Marcelino, Lee (McClen 90), Maric (Robinson 72), Shearer (Glass 85), Solano, Speed.
CSKA Sofia: Lukic; Velikov, Mrkic, Antonov, Tomovski, Kremenliev, Litera (Deyanov 83), Kiosev, Ivanov D (Simeonov 54), Bukarev (Hristov 77), Berbatov.

Osijek (0) 1 *(Bubalo 70)*   15,000
West Ham United (1) 3 *(Kitson 27, Ruddock 83, Foe 90)*

Osijek: Malovan; Zebic, Beljan, Vuica, Prisc (Jukic 63), Ergovic, Vranjes (Zrilic 79), Besirevic, Dumitru, Bubalo (Turkovic 86), Babic.
West Ham United: Hislop; Sinclair (Newton 46), Keller, Potts, Ferdinand (Ruddock 63), Stimac, Foe, Lampard, Kitson, Di Canio (Wanchope 69), Lomas.

St Johnstone (2) 3 *(Leonard 5 (og), Dasovic 33, O'Neil 76)*   7706
Monaco (2) 3 *(Prso 9, Riise 24, Legwinski 69)*

St Johnstone: Main; McQuillan, Bollan, Dasovic, Kernaghan, Griffin, Simao, O'Neil, Lowndes (O'Boyle 78), O'Halloran (Grant 88), Kane (McAnespie 88).
Monaco: Barthez; Marquez, Lamouchi (Giuly 46), Simone (Trezeguet 46) Legwinski, Leonard, Sagnol, Prso, N'Diaye (Gallardo 60), Irles, Riise.

Zimbru Chisinau (0) 0
Tottenham Hotspur (0) 0   7000

Zimbru Chisinau: Romanenco; Dodul (Kulik 75), Oprea, Telesnenko, Catinsus, Ghilazev, Tropanet, Boret, Epureanu (Robu 87), Miterev, Berco (Gusila 84).
Tottenham Hotspur: Walker; Carr, Taricco (Edinburgh 86), Freund, Young, Perry, Leonhardsen, Nielsen, Armstrong (Dominguez 76), Iversen, Clemence.

SECOND ROUND, FIRST LEG

21 OCT

Leeds United (2) 4 *(Bowyer 27, 45, Smith 56, Kewell 83)*
Lokomotiv Moscow (0) 1 *(Loskov 81)*   37,814

Leeds United: Martyn; Kelly, Harte, Woodgate, Radebe, Batty, McPhail, Smith, Bridges (Huckerby 62), Kewell, Bowyer.
Lokomotiv Moscow: Nigmatulin; Arifullin, Chugainov, Pashinin (Hovhannisyan 61), Sarkisian (Maminov 75), Lavrik, Smertin, Drozdov, Khariatchev, Loskov, Janashia (Bulykin 38).

Lyon (0) 1 *(Blanc 61)*
Celtic (0) 0   37,500

Lyon: Coupet; Carteron, Laville, Bak (Malbranque 53), Violeau, Anderson, Dhorasoo, Vairelles (Caveglia 75), Blanc, Delmotte, Brechet.
Celtic: Gould; McNamara, Stubbs, Larsson (Burchill 13), Burley, Lambert, Tebily, Moravcik (Petta 66), Riseth, Mjallby, Viduka.

Steaua (1) 2 *(Rosu 40, Ilie S 57)*
West Ham United (0) 0 12,500
Steaua: Ritli; Reghecampf, Baciu, Miu, Bordeanu, Lincar, Duro, Danciulescu, Rosu, Ciocoiu (Ogararu 90), Ilie S (Luca 75).
West Ham United: Hislop; Sinclair, Lomas, Potts (Margas 61), Ferdinand, Ruddock, Moncur, Lampard, Wanchope, Di Canio (Cole 55), Foe.

Zurich (0) 1 *(Castillo 68)* 9600
Newcastle United (0) 2 *(Maric 51, Shearer 60)*
Zurich: Pascolo; Castillo, Stocklasa, Djordjevic, Kebe (Del Signore 65), Chassot (Douglas 65), Eydelie, Sant'Anna, Kavelashvili, Bartlett, Frick (Akale Kanga 77).
Newcastle United: Harper; Barton, Domi, Dabizas, Hughes, Solano (McClen 88), Dyer (Serrant 64), Lee, Shearer, Maric (Robinson 79), Speed.

28 OCT
Tottenham Hotspur (1) 1 *(Iversen 34 (pen))*
Kaiserslautern (0) 0 35,177
Tottenham Hotspur: Walker; Carr, Tarico, Freund, Campbell, Perry, Fox (Clemence 90), Sherwood, Iversen, Leonhardsen, Ginola.
Kaiserslautern: Reinke; Roos (Komdjenovic 73), Schjonberg, Strasser, Koch, Ramzy, Ratinho (Buck 46), Sforza, Marschall, Hristov, Wagner (Reich 46).

SECOND ROUND, SECOND LEG

4 NOV
Celtic (0) 0
Lyon (1) 1 *(Vairelles 17)* 54,291
Celtic: Gould; McNamara, Stubbs, Burley, Berkovic, Lambert, Tebily, Moravcik (Blinker 81), Burchill, Riseth, Viduka.
Lyon: Coupet; Carteron, Laville, Bak, Violeau, Anderson (Uras 87), Dhorasoo (Malbranque 65), Vairelles, Blanc (Devaux 78), Delmotte, Linares.

Kaiserslautern (0) 2 *(Buck 89, Carr 90 (og))*
Tottenham Hotspur (0) 0 29,044
Kaiserslautern: Reinke; Koch, Ramzy (Reich 85), Schjonberg (Tare 82), Sforza, Buck, Djorkaeff, Ratinho, Strasser, Marschall (Pettersson 74), Hristov.
Tottenham Hotspur: Walker; Carr, Edinburgh (Young 76), Freund, Campbell, Perry, Leonhardsen, Sherwood, Armstrong (Ginola 81), Iversen, Clemence.

Lokomotiv Moscow (0) 0 8000
Leeds United (3) 3 *(Harte 16 (pen), Bridges 28, 45)*
Lokomotiv Moscow: Nigmatulin; Arifullin, Chugainov (Semenenko 77), Ovannesian, Sarkisian, Lavrik, Smertin, Pashinin (Kharlachyov 46), Loskov, Bulykin (Piminov 73), Solomatin.
Leeds United: Martyn; Kelly, Harte, Woodgate, Radebe, Batty, McPhail (Hopkin 80), Bakke, Bridges, Kewell (Huckerby 66), Bowyer (Haaland 46).

Newcastle United (1) 3 *(Maric 33, Ferguson 58, Speed 61)*
Zurich (1) 1 *(Jamarauli 17)* 34,502
Newcastle United: Harper; Barton, Domi, Dabizas, Marcelino, Solano, Lee (McClen 82), Maric (Glass 86), Shearer, Ferguson (Robinson 82), Speed.
Zurich: Pascolo; Giannini (Castillo 72), Stocklasa, Djordjevic, Quentin, Kebe (Frick 46), Eydelie, Sant'Anna, Kavelashvili, Bartlett (Chassot 46), Jamarauli.

West Ham United (0) 0
Steaua (0) 0 24,514
West Ham United: Hislop; Sinclair, Keller (Kitson 64), Margas, Ferdinand, Ruddock, Lampard, Cole, Wanchope, Di Canio, Lomas.
Steaua: Ritli; Baciu, Duro, Miu, Reghecampf, Lincar (Lacatus 85), Danciulescu (Trica 67), Rosu, Bordeanu, Ciocoiu (Lutu 89), Ilie S.

THIRD ROUND, FIRST LEG

25 NOV
Arsenal (1) 3 *(Overmars 13 (pen), Winterburn 81, Bergkamp 90)*
Nantes (0) 0 36,118
Arsenal: Seaman; Vivas, Winterburn, Vieira, Grimandi, Adams, Ljungberg (Henry 69), Kanu (Suker 69), Petit (Parlour 38), Bergkamp, Overmars.
Nantes: Landreau; Deroff (Olembe 41), Chanelet, Savinaud, Gillet, Carriere, Piocelle, Leroy, Ahamada (Toure 52), Sibierski, Monterrubio (Gope-Fenepej 69).

Rangers (2) 2 *(Kohler 18 (og), Wallace 45)*
Borussia Dortmund (0) 0 49,268
Rangers: Myhre; Adamczuk, Numan, Ferguson B, Moore, Vidmar, Reyna (Kanchelskis 86), Wallace (McCann 68), Amato (Johansson 44), Van Bronckhorst, Albertz.
Borussia Dortmund: Lehmann; Worns, Stevic, Kohler, Feiersinger, Moller, Barbarez, Ricken (But 72), Addo (Reinhardt 46), Bobic (Herrlich 82), Evanilson.

Roma (0) 1 *(Totti 51 (pen))*
Newcastle United (0) 0 45,655
Roma: Antonioli; Zago, Cafu, Aldair, Rinaldi, Assuncao, Di Francesco, Candela, Totti, Montella, Delvecchio.
Newcastle United: Harper; Barton, Hughes, Dabizas, Charvet, Solano, Lee, Pistone, Shearer, Ketsbaia (Robinson 80), Speed.

2 DEC
Spartak Moscow (1) 2 *(Shirko 38, Robson 65)*
Leeds United (1) 1 *(Kewell 14)* 5485 *(in Sofia)*.
Spartak Moscow: Filimonov; Kovtun, Khlestov, Bouschmanov, Baranov, Bulatov, Titov, Parfionov, Bezrodny, Robson, Shirko.
Leeds United: Martyn; Kelly, Harte, Woodgate, Duberry, Haaland, McPhail, Bakke, Bridges (Huckerby 55), Kewell, Bowyer.

7 DEC
THIRD ROUND, SECOND LEG
Borussia Dortmund (1) 2 *(Ikpeba 28, Bobic 90)*
Rangers (0) 0 38,000
Borussia Dortmund: Lehmann; Nijhuis, Worns, Reuter, Nerlinger, Stevic (Tanko 72), But, Addo, Ikpeba, Ricken (Barbarez 82), Herrlich (Bobic 7).
Rangers: Myhre; Adamczuk (Kanchelskis 90), Numan, Ferguson B, Moore, Amoruso, Reyna, Wallace (Vidmar 90), McCann, Van Bronckhorst, Albertz (Durie 46).

9 DEC
Leeds United (0) 1 *(Radebe 84)*
Spartak Moscow (0) 0 39,732
Leeds United: Martyn; Kelly, Harte, Woodgate, Radebe, Bakke, McPhail, Smith (Huckerby), Bridges, Kewell, Bowyer.
Spartak Moscow: Filimonov (Smetanin 37); Parfionov, Evseev, Baranov, Khlestov, Bouschmanov, Bulatov, Tikhonov, Shirko, Robson, Titov.

Nantes (1) 3 *(Sibierski 12, 57, Vahirua 77)*
Arsenal (3) 3 *(Grimandi 24, Henry 31, Overmars 42)* 28,000
Nantes: Landreau; Olembe (Lievre 46), Leroy, Savinaud, Gillet, Toure, Carriere, Berson (Femillat 68), Bustos, Sibierski (Vahirua 77), De Rocha.
Arsenal: Manninger; Dixon, Winterburn, Vieira, Grimandi, Adams, Ljungberg (Vivas 80), Kanu, Petit, Henry (Suker 71), Overmars (Silvinho 64).

Newcastle United (0) 0
Roma (0) 0 35,739
Newcastle United: Harper; Solano, Pistone, Dabizas, Charvet, Dumas (Hughes 28), Dyer (Ferguson 73), Lee, Shearer, Ketsbaia (Glass 73), Speed.
Roma: Antonioli; Zago, Aldair, Mangone, Cafu, Tommasi, Assuncau, Candela, Totti, Montella (Di Francesco 64), Delvecchio.

FOURTH ROUND, FIRST LEG

2 MAR

Arsenal (2) 5 *(Dixon 5, Henry 30, 67, Kanu 78, Bergkamp 83)*

La Coruna (0) 1 *(Djalminha 55 (pen))*   37,837

Arsenal: Seaman; Dixon, Silvinho, Luzhny, Keown, Grimandi, Ljungberg, Henry (Suker 76), Petit, Bergkamp (Parlour 82), Overmars (Kanu 65).
La Coruna: Songo'o; Manuel Pablo, Donato, Naybet, Romero, Mauro Silva, Flavio, Djalminha, Jokanovic (Victor 53), Turu Flores (Fernando 68), Makaay (Pauleta 74).

Roma (0) 0

Leeds United (0) 0   37,726

Roma: Antonioli; Zago, Aldair, Mangone, Cafu, Nakata, Tommasi, Candela, Totti, Montella, Delvecchio.
Leeds United: Martyn; Kelly, Harte, Woodgate, Radebe, Haaland, Bakke, Jones, Bridges (Smith 70), Kewell, Bowyer.

FOURTH ROUND, SECOND LEG

9 MAR

La Coruna (0) 2 *(Victor 69, Ivan 90)*

Arsenal (0) 1 *(Henry 63)*   20,000

La Coruna: Kouba; Naybet, Ramis, Manel, Scaloni, Jaime (Fran 63), Mauro Silva, Turu Flores, Fernando (Ivan 79), Makaay (Victor 55), Pauleta.
Arsenal: Seaman; Dixon, Winterburn (Vernazza 83), Vieira, Luzhny, Silvinho, Parlour, Kanu (Malz 82), Petit, Henry (Suker 78), Ljungberg.

Leeds United (0) 1 *(Kewell 67)*

Roma (0) 0   39,149

Leeds United: Martyn; Kelly, Harte, Haaland, Radebe, Bakke (Jones 84), Bowyer, McPhail (Huckerby 89), Bridges (Smith 82), Kewell, Wilcox.
Roma: Antonioli; Zago, Aldair, Mangone, Rinaldi, Nakata (Di Francesco 77), Tommasi, Candela, Totti, Delvecchio, Montella.

QUARTER-FINALS, FIRST LEG

16 MAR

Arsenal (1) 2 *(Henry 21, Ljungberg 77)*

Werder Bremen (0) 0   38,009

Arsenal: Seaman; Dixon, Silvinho, Vieira, Luzhny, Adams, Parlour (Overmars 66), Grimandi, Henry (Suker 76), Bergkamp (Kanu 66), Ljungberg.
Werder Bremen: Rost; Tjikuzu, Barten, Baumann, Wiedener, Eilts, Frings, Herzog, Dabrowski, Ailton (Schierenbeck 82), Bode.

Leeds United (1) 3 *(Wilcox 39, Kewell 54, Bowyer 59)*

Slavia Prague (0) 0   39,519

Leeds United: Martyn; Kelly, Harte, Haaland, Radebe, Bakke, Bowyer, McPhail (Huckerby 76), Bridges (Smith 86), Kewell, Wilcox.
Slavia Prague: Radek; Vicek (Vagner 55), Rada, Koller, Dosek L, Kuchar, Dostalek (Hysky 64), Horvath, Petrous, Ulich, Dosek T.

QUARTER-FINALS, SECOND LEG

23 MAR

Slavia Prague (0) 2 *(Ulich 52, 79 (pen))*

Leeds United (0) 1 *(Kewell 47)*   13,460

Slavia Prague: Radek; Kozel, Koller, Hysky, Dosek L, Dostalek (Lerch 53), Kuchar (Vozabal 84), Skala, Ulich, Dosek T (Vagner 53), Zelenka.
Leeds United: Martyn; Kelly, Harte, Woodgate, Radebe, Haaland, Bakke, McPhail, Bridges (Smith 48), Kewell, Jones.

Werder Bremen (1) 2 *(Bode 41, Bogdanovic 60)*

Arsenal (2) 4 *(Parlour 8, 25, 70, Henry 59)*   33,875

Werder Bremen: Rost; Frings, Barten, Baumann, Eilts (Maximov 46), Trares (Bogdanovic 46), Herzog, Wiedener, Ailton, Pizarro, Bode.
Arsenal: Manninger; Dixon, Silvinho, Vieira (Winterburn 76), Luzhny, Adams (Petit 61), Parlour, Grimandi, Kanu (Overmars 68), Henry, Ljungberg.

SEMI-FINALS, FIRST LEG

6 APR

Arsenal (1) 1 *(Bergkamp 2)*

Lens (0) 0   38,102

Arsenal: Seaman; Dixon, Silvinho, Vieira, Keown, Grimandi, Parlour, Kanu, Petit, Bergkamp (Suker 82), Overmars (Ljungberg 74).
Lens: Warmuz; Sikora, Coly, Mawene, Queudrue, Blanchard, Nyarko, Moreira (Sakho 78), Coridon, Brunel, Nouma.

Galatasaray (2) 2 *(Hakan Sukur 12, Capone 43)*

Leeds United (0) 0   18,000

Galatasaray: Taffarel; Popescu, Korkmaz, Penbe, De Oliveira, Suat, Buruk (Unsal 62), Belozoglu, Hagi (Yildirim 89), Erdem (Sas 78), Hakan Sukur.
Leeds United: Martyn; Kelly, Harte, Woodgate, Radebe, Bakke, McPhail, Jones (Wilcox 65), Bridges (Huckerby 75), Kewell, Bowyer.

SEMI-FINALS, SECOND LEG

20 APR

Leeds United (1) 2 *(Bakke 16, 68)*

Galatasaray (2) 2 *(Hagi 5 (pen), Hakan Sukur 42)* 38,406

Leeds United: Martyn; Mills, Harte (Huckerby 46), Woodgate, Radebe, Bakke, Bowyer, McPhail, Bridges, Kewell, Wilcox.
Galatasaray: Taffarel; Capone, Popescu, Korkmaz, Penbe, Buruk (Sas 87), Kaya (Yildirim 81), Belozoglu, Hagi, Erdem (Unsal 46), Hakan Sukur.

Lens (0) 1 *(Nouma 73)*

Arsenal (1) 2 *(Henry 43, Kanu 86)*   41,043

Lens: Warmuz; Sikora, Pierre-Fanfan, Ismael, Queudrue, Nyarko, Coridon (Rodriguez 75), Dacourt, Brunel (Moreira 58), Sakho, Nouma (Job 89).
Arsenal: Seaman; Dixon, Silvinho, Vieira, Keown, Adams, Parlour, Henry (Grimandi 81), Petit, Bergkhamp (Kanu 70), Ljungberg (Overmars 70).

FINAL

(in Copenhagen, 17 May 2000, 38,919)

Galatasaray (0) 0

Arsenal (0) 0

Galatasaray: Taffarel; Capone, Ergun, Suat (Ahmet 94), Popescu, Bulent, Okan (Hakan Unsal 83), Umit, Arif (Hasan 94), Hagi, Hakan Sukur.
Arsenal: Seaman; Dixon, Silvinho, Vieira, Keown, Adams, Parlour, Henry, Petit, Bergkamp (Kanu 74), Overmars (Suker 114).
Referee: Nieto (Spain).
(aet; Galatasaray won 4-1 on penalties)

Summary of Appearances

EUROPEAN CUP (1955–2000)

English clubs
12 Liverpool
11 Manchester U
4 Arsenal
3 Nottingham F, Leeds U
2 Derby Co, Wolverhampton W, Everton, Aston Villa
1 Burnley, Tottenham H, Ipswich T, Manchester C, Blackburn R, Newcastle U, Chelsea

Scottish clubs
20 Rangers
16 Celtic
3 Aberdeen
2 Hearts
1 Dundee, Dundee U, Kilmarnock, Hibernian

Welsh clubs
3 Barry T
1 Cwmbran T

Northern Ireland clubs
18 Linfield
9 Glentoran
3 Crusaders
2 Portadown
1 Glenavon, Ards, Distillery, Derry C, Coleraine, Cliftonville

Eire clubs
7 Shamrock R, Dundalk
6 Waterford
3 Drumcondra, St Patrick's Ath
2 Bohemians, Limerick, Athlone T, Shelbourne, Derry C*
1 Cork Hibs, Cork Celtic, Cork City, Sligo R

Winners: Celtic 1966–67; Manchester U 1967–68, 1998–99; Liverpool 1976–77, 1977–78, 1980–81, 1983–84; Nottingham F 1978–79, 1979–80; Aston Villa 1981–82

Finalists: Celtic 1969–70; Leeds U 1974–75; Liverpool 1984–85

EUROPEAN CUP-WINNERS' CUP (1960–2000)

English clubs
6 Tottenham H
5 Manchester U, Liverpool, Chelsea
4 West Ham U
3 Arsenal, Everton
2 Manchester C
1 Wolverhampton W, Leicester C, WBA, Leeds U, Sunderland, Southampton, Ipswich T, Newcastle U

Scottish clubs
10 Rangers
8 Aberdeen, Celtic
3 Hearts
2 Dunfermline Ath, Dundee U
1 Dundee, Hibernian, St Mirren, Motherwell, Airdrieonians, Kilmarnock

Welsh clubs
14 Cardiff C
8 Wrexham
7 Swansea C
3 Bangor C
1 Borough U, Newport Co, Merthyr Tydfil, Barry T, Llansantfraid, Cwmbran T

Northern Ireland clubs
9 Glentoran
5 Glenavon
4 Ballymena U, Coleraine
3 Crusaders, Linfield
2 Ards, Bangor
1 Derry C, Distillery, Portadown, Carrick Rangers, Cliftonville

Eire clubs
6 Shamrock R
4 Shelbourne
3 Limerick, Waterford, Dundalk, Bohemians
2 Cork Hibs, Galway U, Sligo R, Derry C*, Cork City
1 Cork Celtic, St Patrick's Ath, Finn Harps, Home Farm, University College Dublin, Bray W

Winners: Tottenham H 1962–63; West Ham U 1964–65; Manchester C 1969–70; Chelsea 1970–71, 1997–98; Rangers 1971–72; Aberdeen 1982–83; Everton 1984–85; Manchester U 1990-91; Arsenal 1993–94

Finalists: Rangers 1960–61, 1966–67; Liverpool 1965–66; Leeds U 1972–73; West Ham U 1975–76; Arsenal 1979–80, 1994–95

EUROPEAN FAIRS CUP & UEFA CUP (1955–2000)

English clubs
11 Leeds U
9 Liverpool, Aston Villa, Arsenal
8 Ipswich T
7 Manchester U, Newcastle U
6 Everton, Tottenham H
5 Southampton, Nottingham F
4 Manchester C, Birmingham C, Wolverhampton W, WBA
3 Chelsea, Sheffield W
2 Stoke C, Derby Co, QPR, Blackburn R
1 Burnley, Coventry C, Norwich C, London Rep-XI, Watford, Leicester C, West Ham U

Scottish clubs
18 Dundee U
14 Hibernian
13 Aberdeen, Celtic
11 Rangers
9 Hearts
6 Kilmarnock
5 Dunfermline Ath
4 Dundee
3 St Mirren
2 Partick T, Motherwell, St Johnstone
1 Morton, Raith R

Welsh Clubs
3 Inter Cardiff (formerly Inter Cable-Tel)
2 Bangor C, Newtown
1 Afan Lido, Barry T, Cwmbran

Northern Ireland clubs
11 Glentoran
7 Coleraine, Linfield
5 Portadown
4 Glenavon
3 Crusaders
1 Ards, Ballymena U, Bangor

Eire clubs
11 Bohemians
5 Dundalk
4 Shamrock R, Shelbourne
3 Finn Harps, St Patrick's Ath, Cork City
2 Drumcondra, Derry C*
1 Cork Hibs, Athlone T, Limerick, Drogheda U, Galway U, Bray Wanderers

Winners: Leeds U 1967–68, 1970–71; Newcastle U 1968–69; Arsenal 1969–70; Tottenham H 1971–72, 1983–84; Liverpool 1972–73, 1975–76; Ipswich T 1980–81

Finalists: London 1955–58, Birmingham C 1958–60, 1960–61; Leeds U 1966–67; Wolverhampton W 1971–72; Tottenham H 1973–74; Dundee U 1986–87

* Now play in League of Ireland

INTERTOTO CUP 1999

FIRST ROUND
Aberystwyth v Floriana 2-2, 1-2
Ceahlaul v Ekranas 1-0, 1-0
Jokerit v Trans Narva 3-0, 4-1
Spartak Varna v St Truiden 1-2, 0-6
Bacau v Ararat Erevan 0-1, 0-1
Tsement v Kolkheti 4-2, 4-0
Pobeda v Trencin 3-1, 1-3
Pobeda won 4-3 on penalties.
Herfolge v Zilina 0-2, 0-2
IA Akranes v Teuta 5-1, 1-2
Polonia v Tiligul 4-0, 0-0
Lokomotiv 96 v Varteks 1-2, 2-2
Maccabi Haifa v Karabach 1-2, 1-0
Hrvatski v Newry Town 1-0, 0-2
Jedinstvo v GI Gotu 3-0, 0-1
Korotan v Basle 0-0, 0-6
Rudar v Halmstad 0-0, 2-2
Shelbourne v Neuchatel Xamax 0-0, 0-2
Hradec Kralove v Gomel 1-0, 0-0
Gomel won 3-1 on penalties.
Union Luxembourg v Vasas 1-3, 0-4
Valerengen v Ventspils 1-0, 0-2

SECOND ROUND
Perugia v Pobeda 1-0, 0-0
Ararat Erevan v St Truiden 0-2, 1-3
Basle v Boby Brno 0-0, 4-2
Ceahlaul v Jedinstvo 2-1, 3-1
Jokerit v Floriana 2-1, 1-1
Karabach v Montpellier 0-3, 0-6
FC Copenhagen v Polonia 0-3, 1-1
Tsement v Rostelmash 1-1, 1-2
Ventspils v Kocaeli 1-1, 0-2
Hammarby v Gomel 4-0, 2-2
Lokeren v IA Akranes 3-1, 3-1
Zilina v Metz 2-1, 0-3
Duisburg v Newry Town 2-0, 0-1
Neuchatel Xamax v Vasas 0-2, 0-1
Rudar v Lustenau 1-2, 1-2
Brann v Varteks 3-0, 0-3
Varteks won 5-4 on penalties.

THIRD ROUND
Ceahlaul v Juventus 1-1, 0-0
Hamburg v Basle 0-1, 3-2
St Truiden v FK Austria 0-2, 2-1
Kocaeli v Duisburg 0-3, 0-0
Polonia v Vasas 2-0, 2-1
Lokeren v Metz 1-2, 1-0
Varteks v Rostelmash 1-2, 1-0
Espanyol v Montpellier 0-2, 1-2
Lustenau v Rennes 2-1, 0-1
Heerenveen v Hammarby 2-0, 2-0
Trabzon v Perugia 1-2, 3-0
West Ham U v Jokerit 1-0, 1-1

SEMI-FINALS
Metz v Polonia 5-1, 1-1
Trabzon v Hamburg 2-2, 1-4
Duisburg v Montpellier, 1-1, 0-3
West Ham U v Heerenveen 1-0, 1-0
Rennes v FK Austria 2-0, 2-2
Rostelmash v Juventus 0-4, 1-5

FINALS
West Ham U v Metz 0-1, 3-1
Montpellier v Hamburg 1-1, 1-1
Montpellier won 3-0 on penalties.
Juventus v Rennes 2-0, 2-2
West Ham U, Montpellier and Juventus qualify for the UEFA Cup.

West Ham U (0) 1 *(Kitson 18)*
Jokerit (0) 0
West Ham U: Forrest; Lomas, Minto, Potts (Wright 46), Ferdinand, Ruddock, Lampard, Cole, Kitson, Di Canio, Sinclair (Keller 60).

Jokerit (0) 1 *(Koskela 33)*
West Ham U (0) 1 *(Lampard 71)*
West Ham U: Jones (Potts 46), Minto, Lomas, Ferdinand, Ruddock, Lampard, Keller (Carrick 80), Kitson, Di Canio (Lazaridis 76), Sinclair.

West Ham U (1) 1 *(Lampard 7)*
Heerenveen (0) 0   7485
West Ham U: Hislop; Potts, Minto, Lomas, Ferdinand, Ruddock (Pearce I 52), Lampard, Keller (Moncur 46), Wanchope, Di Canio (Kitson 78), Sinclair.

Heerenveen (0) 0
West Ham U (1) 1 *(Wanchope 26)*   13,500
West Ham U: Hislop; Lomas, Minto, Lampard, Ferdinand, Pearce I, Moncur (Cole 82), Foe, Wanchope, Di Canio (Kitson 69), Sinclair.

West Ham U (0) 0
Metz (1) 1 *(Saha 12)*   25,372
West Ham U: Hislop; Lomas, Minto, Lampard, Ferdinand, Potts, Moncur, Foe (Kitson 77), Wanchope, Di Canio, Sinclair.

Metz (0) 1 *(Jestrovic 68)*
West Ham U (2) 3 *(Sinclair 23, Lampard 43,*
Wanchope 78)   19,599
West Ham U: Hislop; Lomas, Keller, Foe, Ferdinand, Potts, Moncur, Lampard, Wanchope, Di Canio (Cole 81), Sinclair.

EUROPEAN CUP 2000–2001

FIRST QUALIFYING ROUND, FIRST LEG
12 JULY 2000
Birkirara 1 (1) *(Nwoko 28)*, KR Reykjavik 2 (0)
  (Sigthorsson 47, Juliusson 67)   2000
F91 Dudelange 0 (0), Levski Sofia 4 (2) *(Ivanov G 12, 16*
  (pen), 87, Isykhmeistruk 67)   1200
FC Haka 1 (0) *(Wilson 55)*, Linfield 0 (0)   1500
KI 0 (0), Red Star Belgrade 3 (1) *(Ilic 43, Stevanovic 78,*
  Mirkovic 90)   1000
SK Tirana 2 (2) *(Dede 13, Fortuzi 16)*, FC Zimbru 3 (2)
  (Berco 30, 60, Borets 45)   4000
Shirak Gumri 1 (1) *(Tahmazyan 31)*,
  BATE Borisov 1 (1) *(Kutuzov 24)*   2500
Skonto Riga 2 (0) *(Kolesnicenko 51, 90 (pen))*,
  Shamkir 1 (0) *(Kulikov 24)*   3200
Sloga 0 (0), Shelbourne 1 (0) *(Baker 84)*   8000
T.N.S. 2 (0) *(Wright 58, Toner 89)*, Levadia 2 (0) *(Bragin*
  51, Krasnopjorov 88)   1432
Zalgiris Kaunas 4 (3) *(Ksanavicius 13, 37, Kuta 19,*
  Tuotkalis 87), NK Brotnjo 0 (0)   2000

FIRST QUALIFYING ROUND, SECOND LEG
19 JULY 2000
BATE Borisov 2 (1) *(Rahozhkin 17, Lashankau 59)*,
  Shirak Gumri 1 (0) *(Tahmazyan 73)*
FC Zimbru 3 (2) *(Oprea 7, 30, Borets 85)*, SK Tirana 2 (2)
  (Dabulla 11, Kanesei 23)
KR Reykjavik 4 (2) *(Winnie 11, Benediktsson 45, Sigurdsson*
  60, Marteinsson 66), Birkirkara 1 (0) *(Spiteri 56)*
Levadia 4 (1) *(Krom 45, Fenin 58, Tselnokov 60,*
  Edwards 64 (og)), T.N.S. 0 (0)
Levski Sofia 2 (1) *(Ivanov G 35, Ivankov 53 (pen))*,
  F91 Dudelange 0 (0)
Linfield 2 (1) *(Ferguson 21 (pen), 73)*, FC Haka 1 (0)
  (Kovacs 87)
NK Brotnjo 3 (3) *(Katic 32, 41 (pen), Jurcic 39)*, Zalgiris
  Kaunas 0 (0)
Red Star Belgrade 2 (2) *(Boskovic 11 (pen), Drulic 17)*,
  KI 0 (0)
Shamkir 4 (1) *(Kvaratsckheliya 2, 90, 101, Kulikov 110)*,
  Skonto Riga 1 (1) *(Samusevas 29) aet*
Shelbourne 1 (0) *(Haylock 67)*, Sloga 1 (0) *(Nuhiji 81 (pen))*

WORLD CLUB CHAMPIONSHIP

Played annually up to 1974 and intermittently since then between the winners of the European Cup and the winners of the South American Champions Cup — known as the Copa Libertadores. In 1980 the winners were decided by one match arranged in Tokyo in February 1981 and the venue has been the same since. AC Milan replaced Marseille who had been stripped of their European Cup title in 1993.

1960	Real Madrid beat Penarol 0-0, 5-1	1981	Flamengo beat Liverpool 3-0
1961	Penarol beat Benfica 0-1, 5-0, 2-1	1982	Penarol beat Aston Villa 2-0
1962	Santos beat Benfica 3-2, 5-2	1983	Gremio Porto Alegre beat SV Hamburg 2-1
1963	Santos beat AC Milan 2-4, 4-2, 1-0	1984	Independiente beat Liverpool 1-0
1964	Inter-Milan beat Independiente 0-1, 2-0, 1-0	1985	Juventus beat Argentinos Juniors 4-2 on penalties
1965	Inter-Milan beat Independiente 3-0, 0-0		after a 2-2 draw
1966	Penarol beat Real Madrid 2-0, 2-0	1986	River Plate beat Steaua Bucharest 1-0
1967	Racing Club beat Celtic 0-1, 2-1, 1-0	1987	FC Porto beat Penarol 2-1 after extra time
1968	Estudiantes beat Manchester United 1-0, 1-1	1988	Nacional (Uru) beat PSV Eindhoven 7-6 on
1969	AC Milan beat Estudiantes 3-0		penalties after 1-1 draw
1970	Feyenoord beat Estudiantes 2-2, 1-0	1989	AC Milan beat Atletico Nacional (Col) 1-0 after
1971	Nacional beat Panathinaikos* 1-1, 2-1		extra time
1972	Ajax beat Independiente 1-1, 3-0	1990	AC Milan beat Olimpia 3-0
1973	Independiente beat Juventus* 1-0	1991	Red Star Belgrade beat Colo Colo 3-0
1974	Atlético Madrid* beat Independiente 0-1, 2-0	1992	Sao Paulo beat Barcelona 2-1
1975	Independiente and Bayern Munich could not	1993	Sao Paulo beat AC Milan 3-2
	agree dates; no matches.	1994	Velez Sarsfield beat AC Milan 2-0
1976	Bayern Munich beat Cruzeiro 2-0, 0-0	1995	Ajax beat Gremio Porto Alegre 4-3 on penalties
1977	Boca Juniors beat Borussia Moenchengladbach*		after 0-0 draw
	2-2, 3-0	1996	Juventus beat River Plate 1-0
1978	Not contested	1997	Borussia Dortmund beat Cruzeiro 2-0
1979	Olimpia beat Malmö* 1-0, 2-1	1998	Real Madrid beat Vasco da Gama 2-1
1980	Nacional beat Nottingham Forest 1-0		*European Cup runners-up; winners declined to take part.

1999

30 November in Tokyo

Manchester U (1) 1

Palmeiras (0) 0   53,372

Manchester U: Bosnich; Neville G, Irwin, Silvestre, Keane, Stam, Beckham, Butt, Solskjaer (York 46), Scholes (Sheringham 74), Giggs.
Scorer: Keane 35.
Palmeiras: Marcos; Arce, Roque Junior, Cesar Sampaio, Junior Baiano, Junior, Galeano (Evair 54), Alex, Asprilla (Oseas 56), Nunes (Euller 77), Zinho.
Referee: Krug (Germany).

EUROPEAN SUPER CUP

Played annually between the winners of the European Champions' Cup and the European Cup-Winners' Cup. AC Milan replaced Marseille in 1993–94.

1972	Ajax beat Rangers 3-1, 3-2	1993	Parma beat AC Milan 0-1, 2-0
1973	Ajax beat AC Milan 0-1, 6-0	1994	AC Milan beat Arsenal 0-0, 2-0
1974	Not contested	1995	Ajax beat Zaragoza 1-1, 4-0
1975	Dynamo Kiev beat Bayern Munich 1-0, 2-0	1996	Juventus beat Paris St. Germain 6-1, 3-1
1976	Anderlecht beat Bayern Munich 4-1, 1-2	1997	Barcelona beat Borussia Dortmund 2-0, 1-1
1977	Liverpool beat Hamburg 1-1, 6-0	1998	Chelsea beat Real Madrid 1-0
1978	Anderlecht beat Liverpool 3-1, 1-2		
1979	Nottingham F beat Barcelona 1-0, 1-1		
1980	Valencia beat Nottingham F 1-0, 1-2	**1999**	
1981	Not contested		
1982	Aston Villa beat Barcelona 0-1, 3-0	**27 August 1999, Monaco**	
1983	Aberdeen beat Hamburg 0-0, 2-0		
1984	Juventus beat Liverpool 2-0	**Lazio (1) 1** *(Salas 35)*	
1985	Juventus v Everton not contested due to UEFA	**Manchester U (0) 0**	14,461
	ban on English clubs		
1986	Steaua Bucharest beat Dynamo Kiev 1-0	*Lazio:* Marchegiani; Negro, Pancaro, Nedved (Simeone	
1987	FC Porto beat Ajax 1-0, 1-0	65), Nesta, Mihajlovic, Stankovic, Veron, Inzaghi (Salas	
1988	KV Mechelen beat PSV Eindhoven 3-0, 0-1	23), Mancini (Lombardo 83), Almeyda.	
1989	AC Milan beat Barcelona 1-1, 1-0	*Manchester U:* Van der Gouw; Neville G, Neville P, Berg,	
1990	AC Milan beat Sampdoria 1-1, 2-0	Keane, Stam (Curtis 56), Beckham (Cruyff 57), Scholes,	
1991	Manchester U beat Red Star Belgrade 1-0	Cole (Greening 77), Sheringham, Solskjaer.	
1992	Barcelona beat Werder Bremen 1-1, 2-1	*Referee:* Wojcik (Poland).	

FIFA CLUB WORLD CHAMPIONSHIP 2000

FIFA's Club World Championship as recorded in the official programme – contains contrasting entries respectively for the Champions, Corinthians and England's representatives Manchester United.

'O Corinthian Football Club, da Inglaterra, foi a fonte de inspiracao para a fundacao do clube paulista, em 1910'.

Translated: England's Corinthian Football Club inspired the foundation of the paulista club in 1910.

It went on to say that 'in 1999 alone, Manchester United made about 180m US dollars for merchandising, TV transmission, ticket selling and stock shares.

The two worlds of 1910 for the amateur English Corinthians and the professional Manchester United of today could not be more greatly contrasted, although oddly enough at the beginning of the 1910–11 Football League season, Manchester United were en route to that domestic championship!

In Aidan Hamilton's An Entirely Different Game: The British Influence on Brazilian Football, he has recorded: 'Stories abound about the precise nature of the events which led to the founding of Sport Club Corinthians Paulista. The bare facts are that a group of Brazilians, in the main Sao Paulo Railway employees, were inspired to form a club after watching the English Corinthians – either at the Velodromo or on film of the games screened at the Radium cinema in Sao Paulo. The first meeting is said to have taken place on the evening of 1st September under a street-lamp in the Bom Retiro district. Miguel Bataglia was elected president. Four days later, at a subsequent gathering, the name Corinthians was adopted. Most Corinthianos may not know it, but according to Charles Miller's cousin, Charles Rule, it was Miller who suggested the name to Bataglia.'

Charles Miller was an expatriate Englishman who is credited with bringing the game to Brazil, but the significance of the Corinthians influence was that the tour took place during the August summer holidays from the schools and the then vacation from the Law Courts. For the tour party comprised essentially schoolmasters and practising lawyers on leave from their daily routines. As Hamilton explained, the then Corinthians had been forced to intensify their own touring missionary activity simply because following a breakaway split from the FA with the creation of the Amateur Football Alliance, they were barred from competing against professional and other FA members.

Today, the Corinthian-Casuals, still flying the flag at Tolworth in Surrey, continue their missionary work, mainly in the schools; but during this Millennium year a reciprocal visit from the Sao Paulo Athletic Club of Brazil to Tolworth was a return gesture for the hospitality extended to Corinthian-Casuals a decade ago in 1988 when the great Socrates from the Brazil Corinthians donned a Casuals shirt for part of a match.

Two further contrasts between then and now can be seen from a biography of Charles Miller who died in 1994, by John R. Mills, and the Olympic Games of today. At a banquet ending the Corinthians tour, the visiting captain Morgan-Owen 'did not mention in his speech the small incident – because it was irrelevant and trivial – that had happened in the game against Paulistano. The ball hit the post and on its return, a Corinthian player made the goal, obviously validated by the referee. A barefoot boy, became so upset that he invaded the field, kicked Timmis in the buttocks, and quickly ran off the field. The English were unperturbed and laughed at the incident and the game continued in an atmosphere of perfect chivalry.'

– the last description hardly recognisable as a term for modern sport.

Closer at home, Great Britain represented by England had won the Olympic Games football tournament two years earlier in 1908 with a practising solicitor among its members, Harold Hardman. In due course he became Manchester United's chairman during the 1950s to lead his club into Europe in opposition to the Football League, but with the support of Sir Stanley Rous at the FA; and in turn his place as a solicitor on the United board is now seen through Maurice Watkins who has followed me as President of the British Association for Sport and Law, and is a Governor of Manchester Grammar School.

Thus the blend of the law and teaching professions which took the English Corinthians to inspire foundation of the first FIFA Club World Champions still exists at England's Premier professional League club. With Sir Alex Ferguson's brilliant analysis as told to Hugh McIlvanney in the Sunday Times for the schools to lead the way back to correct techniques, within the Laws of the Game, Old Trafford may yet have a different mission to that which the English Corinthian predecessors of the present Corinthian-Casuals demonstrated in the year of Manchester United's Football League championship season ninety years ago in 1910.

EDWARD GRAYSON
Life member Corinthian-Casuals

GROUP A

Sao Paulo, 5 January 2000, 17,000

Corinthians (0) 2 *(Luizao 50, Fabio Luciano 65)*

Raja (0) 0

Corinthians: Dida; Indio, Joao Carlos, Kieber, Fabio Luciano, Rincon, Vampeta (Edu 85), Ricardinho, Marcelinho Carioca (Senna 77), Edilson, Luizao (Dinei 80).

Raja: Chadli; Misbah, Talal El-Karkouri, El-Haimeur, Aboub Zakaria, Nejery, Jrindou, Reda Ereyahi, Safri, Moustaoudia, Khoubbache (Achami 60).

Referee: Braschi (Italy).

Real Madrid (1) 3 *(Anelka 21, Raul 62, Savio 71 (pen))*

Al Nassr (1) 1 *(Al-Husseini 45 (pen))*

Real Madrid: Casillas; Michel Salgado, Karembeu, Hierro, Roberto Carlos (Karanka 78), Geremi, Redondo, Guti (McManaman 62), Raul, Anelka, Savio.

Al Nassr: Khojali; Al-Shokia, Hadi Sharify, Mohsin Al-Harthi, Abdallah Al-Karni, Mansour Al-Moussa, Moussa Saib (Ismael Triki 67), Fuad Amin, Fahd Al-Husseini (Hamad Al-Khathran 79), Mohaysen Al-Jaman (Fahd Al-Mehalel 83), Ahmed Bahja.

Referee: Ruiz (Colombia).

GROUP B

Rio, 6 January 2000, 26,000

Manchester United (0) 1 *(Yorke 82)*

Necaxa (1) 1 *(Montecinos 15)*

Manchester United: Bosnich; Neville G, Irwin (Solskjaer 73), Silvestre, Keane, Stam, Beckham, Butt (Neville P 73), Cole (Sheringham 73), Yorke, Giggs.

Necaxa: Pineda; Vigna (Ambriz 80), Milian, Perez, Lopez, Almaguer, Higareda (Acosta 83), Aguinaga, Delgado, Montecinos (Vasquez 77), Cabrera.

Referee: Elizondo (Argentina).

Vasco da Gama (0) 2 *(Felipe 53, Edmundo 86)*

South Melbourne (0) 0

Vasco da Gama: Helton; Jorginho, Junior Baiano, Mauro Galvao, Felipe, Gilberto, Amaral, Juninho, Ramon (Alex de Oliveira 80), Romario, Edmundo (Viola 90).

South Melbourne: Jones; Iosifidis, Blatsis, Orlic, Lozanovski, Panopoulos, Trimboli (Anastasiadis 80), Clarkson, De Amicis, Liparoti, Curcija (Covney 74).

Referee: Jol (Holland).

GROUP A

Sao Paulo, 7 January 2000, 300

Al Nassr (1) 4 *(Fuad Amin 3, Ahmed Bahja 48, Al-Husseini 50, Moussa Saib 85)*

Raja (1) 3 *(Al-Husseini 24 (og), El-Moubarki 67, El-Karkouri 73)*

Al Nassr: Mohammed Babka (Mahda Al-Dossari 28); Al-Shokia, Mohsin Al-Harthi, Hadi Sharify, Abdallah Al-Karni (Nassip Al-Ghamdi 71), Mansour Al-Moussa, Moussa Saib, Fuad Amin, Mouhaisen Al-Dossari, Fahd Al-Husseini (Fahd A-Mehalel 76), Ahmed Bahja.

Raja: Chadli; Misbah, El-Haimeur, Talal El-Karkouri, Aboub Zakaria, Nejery (Nater 31), Jrindou (Achami 54), Reda Ereyahi (El-Moubarki 54), Safri, Moustaoudia, Khoubbache.

Referee: Rugg (New Zealand).

Corinthians (1) 2 *(Edilson 28, 63)*

Real Madrid (1) 2 *(Anelka 19, 70)*

Corinthians: Dida; Indio, Joao Carlos, Kieber, Fabio Luciano, Marcelinho Carioca, Rincon, Vampeta (Eta 74), Ricardinho (Senna 86), Edilson, Luizao (Dinei 89).

Real Madrid: Casillas; Michel Salgado, Karembeu, Hierro, Roberto Carlos, Geremi (McManaman 70), Redondo, Guti (Morientes 70), Raul, Anelka, Savio.

Referee: Vega (Czech Republic).

GROUP B

Rio, 8 January 2000, 5000

Necaxa (2) 3 *(Montecinos 18, Delgado 28, Cabrera 78)*

South Melbourne (0) 1 *(Anastasiadis 48)*

Necaxa: Pineda; Higareda, Almaguer, Lopez (Ambriz 65), Milian, Cabrera, Vigna, Perez, Aguinaga, Montecinos (Oliva 75), Delgado (Vasquez 85).

South Melbourne: Jones; Iosifidis, De Amicis, Orlic, Blatsis, Clarkson, Panopoulos (Curcija 70), Trimboli (Tsekinis 46), Coveny, Anastasiadis, Alagich.

Referee: Ndoye (Senegal).

Vasco da Gama (3) 3 *(Romario 24, 26, Edmundo 43)*

Manchester United (0) 1 *(Butt 81)*

Vasco da Gama: Helton; Jorginho (Paulo Miranda 65), Junior Baiano, Mauro Galvao, Gilberto, Amaral, Juninho (Alex de Oliveira 80), Felipe, Ramon (Nasa 75), Romario, Edmundo.

Manchester United: Bosnich; Neville G, Irwin, Silvestre, Keane, Stam (Cruyff 71), Neville P, Butt, Solskjaer (Sheringham 46), Yorke, Giggs (Fortune 77).

Referee: Mane (Kuwait).

GROUP A

Sao Paulo, 9 January 2000, 20,000

Al Nassr (0) 0

Corinthians (1) 2 *(Ricardinho 24, Rincon 81)*

Al Nassr: Mohammed Babka; Al-Shokia, Hadi Sharify, Mohsin Al-Harthi, Abdallah Al-Karni, Mansour Al-Moussa, Moussa Saib (Fahd Al-Mehalel 74), Fahd Al-Husseini (Al-Janoubi 41), Ahmed Bahja, Fuad Amin, Mouhaisen Al-Dossari (Ismael Triki 88).

Corinthians: Dida; Daniel, Joao Carlos (Adilson 10), Kieber, Fabio Luciano, Rincon, Vampeta (Dinei 74), Ricardinho (Edu 27), Marcelinho Carioca, Edilson, Luizao.

Referee: Jol (Holland).

Real Madrid (0) 3 *(Hierro 38, Morientes 52, Geremi 88)*

Raja (1) 2 *(Achami 28, Moustaoudia 59)*

Real Madrid: Casillas; Michel Salgado (Karanka 80), Hierro, Karembeu, Roberto Carlos, Guti, McManaman (Geremi 46), Redondo, Raul, Anelka (Morientes 37), Savio.

Raja: Chadli; Talal El-Karkouri, El-Haimeur, Aboub Zakaria, Kharbouch, Nater (Kherazi 90), Reda Ereyahi, El-Moubarki, Achami, Moustaoudia, Khoubbache.

Referee: Elizondo (Argentina).

GROUP B

Rio, 11 January 2000, 25,000

Manchester United (2) 2 *(Fortune 8, 20)*

South Melbourne (0) 0

Manchester United: Van der Gouw (Rachubka 82); Neville P, Higginbotham, Berg, Wallwork, Wilson (Beckham 75), Greening, Cruyff, Cole, Solskjaer, Fortune.

South Melbourne: Jones; Blatsis, Liparoti (Goutzioulis 31), Iosifidis, De Amicis, Clarkson (Tsekinis 71), Panopoulos, Lozanovski, Trimboli, Curcija, Anastasiadis (Coveny 66).

Referee: Braschi (Italy).

Vasco da Gama (1) 2 *(Odvan 14, Romario 69)*

Necaxa (1) 1 *(Aguinaga 5)*

Vasco da Gama: Helton; Paulo Miranda, Mauro Galvao, Junior Baiano (Odvan 10), Gilberto, Amaral, Felipe, Juninho, Ramon, Donizete (Edmundo 70), Romario.

Necaxa: Pineda; Cabrera, Almaguer, Lopez, Higareda, Vigna, Milian (Vasquez 84), Aguinaga, Perez, Delgado, Montecinos (Ambriz 72).

Referee: Costa (Colombia).

THIRD PLACE PLAY-OFF

Rio, 14 January 2000, 35,000

Real Madrid (1) 1 *(Raul 15)*

Necaxa (0) 1 *(Delgado 58)*

Real Madrid: Bizzarri; Sanchis, Hierro (Campo 52), Dorado, McManaman, Helguera, Geremi, Karanka, Raul (Etoo 67), Savio (Ognjenovic 52), Morientes.

Necaxa: Pineda; Almaguer, Lopez (Ambriz 46), Higareda, Vigna (Oliva 84), Cabrera, Milian, Perez, Delgado, Montecinos (Vasquez 46).

Necaxa won 4-3 on penalties.

Referee: Costa (Colombia).

FINAL

Rio, 14 January 2000, 73,000

Corinthians (0) 0

Vasco da Gama (0) 0

Corinthians: Dida; Indio, Adilson, Vampeta (Gilmar 91), Kieber, Marcelinho, Rincon, Fabio Luciano, Edilson (Fernando Baiano 113), Ricardinho (Edu 46), Luizao.

Vasco da Gama: Helton; Odvan, Amaral, Paulo Miranda, Mauro Galvao, Felipe (Alex de Oliveira 102), Juninho (Viola 96), Gilberto, Ramon (Donizete 111), Romario, Edmundo.

aet; Corinthians won 4-3 on penalties.

Referee: Jol (Holland).

INTERNATIONAL DIRECTORY

The latest available information has been given regarding numbers of clubs and players registered with FIFA, the world governing body. Where known, official colours are listed. With European countries, League tables show a number of signs. * indicates relegated teams, + play-offs, *+ relegated after play-offs, ++ promoted.

There are 197 member associations and one provisional member, Palestine. The four home countries, England, Scotland, Northern Ireland and Wales, are dealt with elsewhere in the Yearbook; but basic details appear in this directory.

EUROPE

ALBANIA

The Football Association of Albania, Rruga Dervish Hima Nr. 31, Tirana.
Founded: 1930; *Number of Clubs:* 49; *Number of Players:* 5,192; *National Colours:* All red.
Telephone: 00–355–42 27 877; *Cable:* ALBSPORT TIRANA; *Telex:* 2228 bfssh ab. *Fax:* 00 355–42 50 275.

International matches 1999
Macedonia (h) 2-0, Latvia (a) 0-0, Norway (h) 1-2, Slovenia (h) 0-1, Slovenia (a) 0-2, Latvia (h) 3-3, Greece (a) 0-2, Georgia (h) 2-1.

League Championship wins (1930-37; 1945–2000)
Dinamo Tirana 15; Partizani Tirana 15; SK Tirana 11; 17 Nentori 8; Vllaznia 8; Flamurtari 1; Labinoti 1; Skenderbeu 1, Teuta 1.

Cup wins (1948–2000)
Partizani Tirana 14; Dinamo Tirana 12; 17 Nentori 6; Vllaznia 5; SK Tirana 3; Flamurtari 2; Teuta 2; Labinoti 1; Elbasan 1; Apolonia 1.

Final League Table 1999–2000

	P	W	D	L	F	A	Pts
SK Tirana	26	16	4	6	40	14	52
Tomori	26	15	7	4	35	22	52
Teuta	26	15	4	7	36	16	49
Vllaznia	26	11	4	9	36	39	37
Bylis	26	10	7	9	28	28	37
Lushnja	26	10	5	11	34	31	35
Shkumbini	26	10	5	11	31	31	35
Skenderbeu	26	10	4	12	33	33	34
Shqiponja	26	8	9	9	21	21	33
Dinamo	26	8	7	10	27	31	31
Apolonia	26	9	4	13	24	39	31
Flamurtari	26	9	3	14	25	35	30
Elbasan*	26	8	5	13	19	22	39
Partizani*	26	6	6	14	21	35	24

Top scorer: Arberi (Tomori) 18.
Cup Final: Teuta 0, Lushnja 0.
Teuta won 5-4 on penalties.

ANDORRA

Federacio Andorrana de Futbol, C/Sant Salvador, 10-2-5, Edifici Galerias Plaza, Andorra la Vella, Principat d'Andorra.
Founded: 1994; *Number of Clubs:* 12; *Number of Players:* 300; *National Colours:* Yellow shirts, red shorts, yellow stockings.
Telephone: 00376 862003; *Fax:* 00376 862006.

International matches 1999
Faeroes (h) 0-0, Iceland (h) 0-2, Russia (a) 1-6, Ukraine (a) 0-4, France (h) 0-1, Portugal (a) 0-4, Iceland (a) 0-3, Russia (h) 1-2, Armenia (h) 0-3.

League Championship wins (1996-2000)
Principat 3; Dicoansa 1; Constelacio 1.

Cup wins (1996-2000)
Principat 4; Constelacio 1.

Final League Table 1999-2000

	P	W	D	L	F	A	Pts
Constelacio	12	12	0	0	71	6	36
Don Pernil	12	9	1	2	34	10	28
Construccions	12	6	2	4	24	25	20
Encamp	12	5	2	5	33	29	17
Matecosa	12	3	1	8	28	36	10
Principal	12	2	0	10	16	41	6
Sporting	12	1	2	9	12	66	5

Cup Final: Constelacio 6, Encamp 0.

ARMENIA

Football Federation of Armenia, 9, Abovian Str. 375001 Erevan, Armenia.
Founded: 1992; *Number of Clubs:* 32; *Number of Players:* 15,000; *National Colours:* Red shirts, blue shorts, orange stockings.
Telephone: 00374 2/589480; *Telex:* 243337 minor su; *Fax:* 00374 2/151573.

International matches 1999
Poland (a) 0-1, Russia (h) 0-3, France (a) 0-2, Iceland (a) 0-2, Ukraine (h) 0-0, Estonia (a) 0-2, Russia (a) 0-2, France (h) 2-3, Andorra (a) 3-0.

League Championship wins (1992–99)
Shirak Gyumri 4*; Pyunik 2; Ararat Erevan 2*; Homenmen 1; FC Erevan 1; Tsement 1.
*Includes one unofficial title.

Cup wins (1992–2000)
Ararat Erevan 4; Tsement 2; Banants 1; Pyunik 1; Mika 1.

Final League Table 1999

	P	W	D	L	F	A	Pts
Shirak	32	23	4	5	93	29	73
Ararat	32	22	6	4	63	21	72
Tsement	32	22	5	5	78	19	71
Zvartnots	32	16	6	10	50	38	54
FC Erevan	32	15	6	11	60	43	51
Erebouni	32	12	5	15	41	44	41
Kilikia	32	10	4	18	57	55	34
Dvinn*	32	2	2	28	20	116	8
Gyumri*	32	2	2	28	23	120	8

Top scorer: Sarikian (Tsement) 21.
Cup Final: Mika 2, Zvartnots 1.

AUSTRIA

Oesterreichischer Fussball-Bund, Ernst-Happel Stadion, Postfach 340, Meierestrasse, A-1021 Wien.
Founded: 1904; *Number of Clubs:* 2,081; *Number of Players:* 253,576; *National Colours:* White shirts, black shorts, white stockings.
Telephone: 0043 1 727 180; *Cable:* FOOTBALL WIEN; *Telex:* 111919 oefb a; *Fax:* 0043 1 728 1632.

International matches 1999
Switzerland (a) 4-2, Spain (a) 0-9, San Marino (h) 7-0, Israel (a) 0-5, Sweden (a) 0-0, Spain (h) 1-3, Cyprus (h) 3-1.

League Championship wins (1912–2000)
Rapid Vienna 30; FK Austria 22; Admira-Energie-Wacker 9; Tirol-Svarowski-Innsbruck 8; First Vienna 6; Wiener Sportklub 3; Austria Salzburg 3; Sturm Graz 2; FAC 1; Hakoah 1; Linz ASK 1; WAF 1; Voest Linz 1.

Cup wins (1919–2000)
FK Austria 25; Rapid Vienna 14; TS Innsbruck (prev. Wacker Innsbruck) 7; Admira-Energie-Wacker (prev. Sportklub Admira & Admira-Energie) 5; First Vienna 3; Sturm Graz 3; Graz 2; Linz ASK 1; Wacker Vienna 1; WAF 1; Wiener Sportklub 1; Stockerau 1; Ried 1.

Final League Table 1999–2000

	P	W	D	L	F	A	Pts
Innsbruck	36	24	5	7	54	30	77
Sturm Graz	36	22	8	6	77	32	74
Rapid	36	20	6	10	59	29	66
FK Austria	36	16	6	14	48	44	54
Ried	36	15	8	13	56	39	53
Austria Salzburg	36	12	10	14	39	45	46
Graz	36	12	6	18	41	62	42
Linz ASK	36	10	9	17	41	49	39
Bregenz	36	10	5	21	39	73	35
Lustenau*	36	4	7	25	22	74	19

Top scorer: Vastic (Sturm Graz) 32.
Cup Final: Graz 2, Salzburg 2.
Graz won 4-3 on penalties.

AZERBAIJAN

Association of Football Federations of Azerbaijan, Husu Haciyev kuc., 42, 370009 Baku, Azerbaijan.
Founded: 1992; *Number of Clubs:* 1,500;. *Number of Players:* 95,000; *National Colours:* White shirts with blue stripes, blue shorts, white stockings.
Telephone: 00994 12 94 49 16; *Cable:* FOOTBALL ASSOCIATION, AZ; *Fax:* 00994 12 98 93 93.

International matches 1999
Estonia (a) 2-2, Portugal (a) 0-7, Romania (h) 0-1, Liechtenstein (h) 4-0, Romania (a) 0-4, Portugal (h) 1-1, Hungary (a) 0-3, Slovakia (h) 0-1.

League Championship wins (1992–2000)
Kopaz 3; Karabach 2; Neftchi 2; Turan 1; Shamkir 1.

Cup wins (1992–2000)
Kopaz 4; Neftchi 3; Karabach 1; Inshatchi 1.

Final League Table 1999–2000

	P	W	D	L	F	A	Pts
Shamkir	22	17	4	1	46	11	55
Kopaz	22	14	2	6	46	24	44
Neftchi	22	13	4	5	35	17	43
Vilash	22	11	3	8	28	25	36
Pivani	22	10	2	10	24	28	32
Dinamo Baku	22	9	4	9	21	17	31
Shafa	22	8	3	11	22	32	27
Karabach	22	5	10	7	21	25	25
Kimyachi	22	7	1	14	23	34	22
Turan	22	5	5	12	17	36	20
Khazar Universitesi*	22	5	3	14	19	41	18
OLK*	22	3	3	16	11	41	12

Top scorer: Kvaratskhelia (Shamkir) 16.
Cup Final: Kopaz 2, Karabach 1.

BELARUS

Belarus Football Association, 8–2 Kyrov Str. 220600 Minsk, Belarus.
Founded: 1989; *Number of Clubs:* 455; *Number of Players:* 120,000; *National Colours:* All green.
Telephone: 007 0172 375 272325; *Telex:*252175 athlet su; *Fax:* 007 0172 27 29 20.

International matches 1999
Israel (a) 1-2, Switzerland (h) 0-1, Italy (a) 1-1, Russia (a) 1-1, Denmark (a) 0-1, Russia (h) 0-2, Wales (h) 1-2, Switzerland (a) 0-2, Italy (h) 0-0.

League Championship wins (1992–99)
Dynamo Minsk 6; MPKC Mozyr 1; Dnepr Mogilev 1; BATE Borisov 1.

Cup wins (1992–2000)
Dynamo Minsk 2; Belshina 2; Slavia Mozyr (formerly MPKC Mozyr) 2; Neman 1; Dynamo 93 Minsk 1; Lokomotiv 96 1.

Final League Table 1999

	P	W	D	L	F	A	Pts
BATE Borisov	30	24	5	1	80	22	77
Slavia	30	20	5	5	74	25	65
Gomel	30	19	6	5	57	28	63
Dnepr Mogilev	30	17	9	4	53	27	60
Shakhter	30	16	5	7	58	29	59
Dynamo Minsk	30	14	9	7	51	30	51
Dynamo Brest	30	14	4	12	59	52	46
Belshina	30	13	6	11	52	42	45
Neman	30	10	6	13	36	43	37
Torpedo Minsk	30	10	5	15	31	47	35
Lokomotiv 96	30	9	7	14	40	45	34
Naftan	30	8	4	18	39	63	28
Lida	30	7	4	19	27	64	25
Torpedo Kadino	30	6	5	19	30	69	24
Svisloch*	30	4	4	22	24	74	16
Molodechno*	30	2	5	23	21	71	11

Top scorer: Stripeikis (Slavia) 22.
Cup Final: Slavia Mozyr 2, Torpedo Minsk 1.

BELGIUM

Union Royale Belge Des Societes De Football Association, 145 Avenue Houba de Strooper, B-1020 Bruxelles.
Founded: 1895; *Number of Clubs:* 2,120; *Number of Players:* 390,468; *National Colours:* All red.
Telephone: 0032 2 477 12 11; *Cable:* URBSFA BRUXELLES; *Telex:* 23257 bvbfbf b; *Fax:* 0032 2 478 23 91.

International matches 1999
Cyprus (a) 1-0, Greece (a) 0-1, Czech Republic (a) 0-1, Bulgaria (h) 0-1, Egypt (h) 0-1, Romania (a) 0-1, Peru (h) 1-1, Japan (a) 0-0, South Korea (a) 2-1, Finland (a) 3-4, Holland (a) 5-5, Morocco (h) 4-0, England (a) 1-2, Italy (a) 3-1.

League Championship wins (1896–2000)
Anderlecht 25; Union St Gilloise 11; FC Brugge 11; Standard Liege 8; Beerschot 7; RC Brussels 6; FC Liege 5; Daring Brussels 5; Antwerp 4; Mechelen 4; Lierse SK 4; SV Brugge 3; Beveren 2; RWD Molenbeek 1; Genk 1.

Cup wins (1954–2000)
Anderlecht 9; FC Brugge 7; Standard Liege 5; Beerschot 2; Waterschei 2; Beveren 2; Gent 2; Antwerp 2; Lierse SK 2; Racing Doornik 1; Waregem 1; SV Brugge 1; Mechelen 1; FC Liege 1; Ekeren 1; Genk 1.

Final League Table 1998–2000

	P	W	D	L	F	A	Pts
Anderlecht	34	22	9	3	86	36	75
FC Brugge	34	21	4	9	70	32	67
Gent	34	20	3	11	78	54	63
Mouscron	34	16	9	9	67	45	57
Standard Liege	34	18	2	14	67	51	56
Westerlo	34	16	8	10	73	66	56
Antwerp	34	16	7	11	56	45	55
Genk	34	16	6	12	63	59	54
Lierse	34	15	7	12	65	47	52
Lokeren	34	12	11	11	56	58	47
Mechelen	34	12	5	17	47	77	41
Aalst	34	11	4	19	52	73	37
St Truiden	34	10	7	17	41	65	37
Harelbeke	34	10	5	19	56	72	35
Beveren	34	9	8	17	51	69	35
Charleroi	34	7	10	17	42	62	31
Geel*	34	5	13	16	32	60	28
Lommel*	34	5	12	17	35	66	27

Top scorer: Aarst (Gent) 30, Brogno T (Westerlo) 30.
Cup Final: Anderlecht 2, Mouscron 2.
Anderlecht won 4-3 on penalties.

BOSNIA HERZEGOVINA

Bosnia & Herzegovina Football Federation, Sime Milutinovico, 12/1 71000 Sarajevo.
Founded: 1992; *National Colours:* White shirts, blue shorts, white stockings.
Telephone: 00387 71/213881; *Fax:* 00387 71/444332.

International matches 1999
Malta (a) 1-2, Hungary (a) 1-1, Lithuania (h) 2-0, Faeroes (a) 2-2, Scotland (h) 1-2, Czech Republic (a) 0-3, Scotland (a) 0-1, Estonia (a) 4-1.

League Championship wins (1996-99)
Celik 2; Zeljeznicar 1; Sarajevo 1.

Cup wins (1996-99)
Sarajevo 2; Bosna 1; Celik 1.
There are three separate leagues in Bosnia, Muslim, Serbian and Croatian. No agreement has been reached on play-offs for an overall winner.

BULGARIA

Bulgarian Football Union, Karnigradska 19, BG-1000 Sofia.
Founded: 1923; *Number of Clubs:* 376; *Number of Players:* 48,240; *National Colours:* White shirts, green shorts, white stockings.
Telephone: 00359 2 987 74 90; *Cable:* BULFUTBOL SOFIA; *Telex:* 23145 bfs bg; *Fax:* 00359 2 986 2538.

International matches 1999
Egypt (a) 1-3, Hong Kong (h) 3-0, Slovakia (h) 2-0, Belgium (a) 1-0, Luxembourg (a) 2-0, Slovakia (a) 0-2, Poland (a) 0-2, England (h) 1-1, Ukraine (a) 1-1, Sweden (a) 0-1, Luxembourg (h) 3-0, Greece (a) 0-1.

League Championship wins (1925-2000)
CSKA Sofia 28; Levski Sofia 20; Slavia Sofia 7; Vladislav Varna 3; Lokomotiv Sofia 3; Litets 2; Trakia Plovdiv 2; AC 23 Sofia 1; Botev Plovdiv 1; SC Sofia 1; Sokol Varna 1; Spartak Plovdiv 1; Tichka Varna 1; JSZ Sofia 1; Beroe Stara Zagora 1; Etur 1.

Cup wins (1946-2000)
Levski Sofia 20; CSKA Sofia 16; Slavia Sofia 7; Lokomotiv Sofia 4; Botev Plovdiv 1; Spartak Plovdiv 1; Spartak Sofia 1; Marek Stanke 1; Trakia Plovdiv 1; Spartak Varna 1; Sliven 1.

Final League Table 1998–2000

	P	W	D	L	F	A	Pts
Levski Sofia	30	23	5	2	66	17	74
CSKA Sofia	30	20	4	6	60	26	64
Levski Kustendil	30	17	4	9	52	32	55
Neftochimik	30	14	11	5	42	21	53
Litets	30	15	4	11	61	34	49
Slavia Sofia	30	13	6	11	38	40	45
Spartak Varna	30	12	5	13	42	51	41
Botev Plovdiv	30	12	4	14	43	42	40
Lokomotiv Sofia	30	10	9	11	54	37	39
Chernomorets	30	10	7	13	31	40	37
Mineur	30	11	3	16	44	58	36
Dobrudja	30	10	5	15	29	43	35
Olimpik	30	10	4	16	28	47	34
Pirin*	30	10	3	17	31	50	33
Belasitsa*	30	9	6	15	28	57	33
Chumen*	30	3	2	25	13	67	11

*Top scorer:*Mihailov (Kustendil) 20.
Cup Final: Levski Sofia 2, Neftochimik 0.

CROATIA

Croatian Football Federation, Illica 31, CRO-10000 Zagreb, Croatia.
Founded: 1912; *Number of Clubs:* 1,221; *Number of Players:* 78,127; *National Colours:* Red/white shirts, white shorts, blue stockings.
Telephone: 00385 1/4554100. *Fax:* 00385 1 42 46 39.

International matches 1999
Denmark (h) 0-1, Greece (a) 2-3, Italy (h) 0-0, Spain (a) 1-3, Macedonia (a) 1-1, Spain (a) 2-2, Mexico (h) 2-1, South Korea (a) 1-1, Yugoslavia (a) 0-0, Malta (h) 2-1, Republic of Ireland (h) 1-0, Yugoslavia (h) 2-2, France (a) 0-3.

League Championship wins (1941-44; 1992-2000)
Dynamo Zagreb (Formerly Croatia Zagreb) 6; Hajduk Split 3; Gradanski 3; Concordia 1.

Cup wins (1993–2000)
Dynamo Zagreb (Formerly Croatia Zagreb) 4, Hajduk Split 3, Osijek 1.

Final League Table 1999–2000

	P	W	D	L	F	A	Pts
Dynamo Zagreb	33	23	6	4	83	25	75
Hajduk Split	33	17	10	6	58	30	61
Osijek	33	15	8	10	55	49	53
Rijeka	33	14	7	12	54	39	49
Slaven	33	12	13	8	34	34	49
Cibalia	33	11	12	10	42	39	45
Varteks	33	10	10	13	32	44	40
Zagreb	33	9	12	12	42	49	39
Sibenik	33	8	10	15	33	50	34
Hrvatski	33	8	9	16	36	58	33
Vukovar 91*	33	7	9	17	32	56	30
Istra*	33	8	6	19	33	61	30

Top scorer: Sokota (Dynamo Zagreb) 21.
Cup Final: Hajduk Split 2, 0, Dynamo Zagreb 0, 1.

CYPRUS

Cyprus Football Association, 1 Stasinos Str., Engomi, P.O. Box 5071, CY-2404 Nicosia.
Founded: 1934; *Number of Clubs:* 85; *Number of Players:* 6,000; *National Colours:* Blue shirts, white shorts, blue stockings.
Telephone: 00357 2 /352341; *Cable:* FOOTBALL CYPRUS; *Telex:* 3880 football cy; *Fax:* 00357 2/590544.

International matches 1999
Belgium (h) 0-1, San Marino (h) 4-0, Estonia (h) 1-2, Israel (a) 0-3, Romania (h) 2-2, Israel (h) 3-2, Spain (h) 0-8, Austria (a) 1-3.

League Championship wins (1935–2000)
Omonia 17; Apoel 16; Anorthosis 11; AEL 5; EPA 3; Olympiakos 3; Apollon 2; Pezoporikos 2; Chetin Kayal 1; Trast 1.

Cup wins (1935–2000)
Apoel 17; Omonia 11; AEL 6; EPA 5; Anorthosis 5; Apollon 4; Trast 3; Chetin Kayal 2; Olympiakos 1; Pezoporikos 1; Salamina 1.

Final League Table 1999–2000

	P	W	D	L	F	A	Pts
Anorthosis	26	21	2	3	82	28	65
Omonia	26	18	5	3	71	27	59
Apoel	26	14	4	8	58	31	46
Salamina	26	13	4	9	58	34	43
Apollon	26	13	3	10	49	44	42
AEL	26	13	3	10	45	42	42
AEK	26	13	2	11	42	39	41
ENP	26	11	3	12	51	50	36
Olympiakos	26	10	6	10	57	58	36
Ethnikos	26	10	5	11	42	36	35
APOP	26	9	5	12	38	47	32
Ethnikos Ashia*	26	9	4	13	35	38	31
Dherynia*	26	4	0	22	22	87	12
Alki*	26	1	0	25	20	109	3

Top scorer: Rauffmann (Omonia) 34.
Cup Final: Omonia 4, Apoel 2.

CZECH REPUBLIC

Football Association of Czech Republic, Diskarska 100, 169 00 Prague 6 - Strahov, Czech Republic.
Founded: 1901; *Number of Clubs:* 3,836; *Number of Players:* 319,500; *National Colours:* Red shirts, white shorts, blue stockings.
Telephone: 00422 20513575; *Cable:* SPORTSVAZ PRAHA; *Telex:* 122650 cstv c; *Fax:* 004202 3335 3107.

International matches 1999
Belgium (h) 0-1, Lithuania (h) 2-0, Scotland (a) 2-1, Poland (a) 1-2, Estonia (a) 2-0, Scotland (h) 3-2, Switzerland (h) 3-0, Lithuania (a) 4-0, Bosnia (h) 3-0, Faeroes (h) 2-0, Holland (a) 1-1.

League Championship wins (1926–93)
Sparta Prague 20; Slavia Prague 12; Dukla Prague (prev. UDA) 11; Slovan Bratislava 7; Spartak Trnava 5; Banik Ostrava 3; Inter-Bratislava 1; Spartak Hradec Kralove 1; Viktoria Zizkov 1; Zbrojovka Brno 1; Bohemians 1; Vitkovice 1.

Cup wins (1961–93)
Dukla Prague 8; Sparta Prague 8; Slovan Bratislava 5; Spartak Trnava 4; Banik Ostrava 3; Lokomotiv Kosice 3; TJ Gottwaldov 1; Dunajska Streda 1.
From 1993–94, there were two separate countries; the Czech Republic and Slovakia.

League Championship wins (1993–2000)
Sparta Prague 7; Slavia Prague 1.

Cup wins (1994–2000)
Slavia Prague 2; Viktoria Zizkov 1; Spartak Hradec Kralove 1; Sparta Prague 1; Jablonec 1, Slovan Liberec 1.

Final League Table 1998–2000

	P	W	D	L	F	A	Pts
Sparta Prague	30	24	4	2	81	23	76
Slavia Prague	30	21	5	4	53	25	68
Petra Drnovice	30	14	6	10	36	32	48
Boby Brno	30	12	6	12	35	33	42
Teplice	30	10	11	9	38	38	41
Dukla Prague	30	11	7	12	33	36	40
Bohemians	30	10	10	10	24	28	40
Slovan Liberec	30	9	11	10	21	24	38
Viktoria Zizkov	30	9	10	11	37	41	37
Chmel Blsany	30	10	7	13	28	45	37
Banik Ostrava	30	8	11	11	43	45	35
Sigma Olomouc	30	7	13	10	31	38	34
Jablonec	30	7	11	12	24	36	32
Ceske Budejovice	30	9	5	16	34	49	32
Kaucuk Opava*	30	6	10	14	31	39	28
Hradec Kralove*	30	4	11	15	21	38	23

Top scorer: Lokvenc (Sparta Prague) 22.
Cup Final: Slovan Liberec 2, Ratiskovice 1.

DENMARK

Danish Football Association, Idraettens Hus, Brondby Stadion 20, DK-2605, Brondby.
Founded: 1889; *Number of Clubs:* 1,555; *Number of Players:* 268,517; *National Colours:* Red shirts, white shorts, red stockings.
Telephone: 0045 43/262222; *Cable:* DANSKBOLDSPIL COPENHAGEN; *Telex:* 15545 dbu dk; *Fax:* 0045 43/262245.

International matches 1999
Croatia (a) 1-0, Italy (h) 1-2, South Africa (h) 1-1, Belarus (h) 1-0, Wales (a) 2-0, Holland (h) 0-0, Switzerland (h) 2-1, Italy (a) 3-2, Iran (h) 0-0, Israel (a) 5-0, Israel (h) 3-0.

League Championship wins (1913–2000)
KB Copenhagen 15; B 93 Copenhagen 10; AB (Akademisk) 9; Brondby 8; B 1903 Copenhagen 7; Frem 6; Esbjerg BK 5; Vejle BK 5; AGF Aarhus 5; Hvidovre 3; Odense BK 3; AaB Aalborg 2; B 1909 Odense 2; Koge BK 2; Lyngby 2; FC Copenhagen 1; Silkeborg 1; Herfolge 1.

Cup wins (1955–2000)
Aarhus GF 9; Vejle BK 6; Randers Freja 3; Lyngby 3; OB Odense 3; Brondby 3; B1909 Odense 2; Aalborg BK 2; Esbjerg BK 2; Frem 2; B 1903 Copenhagen 2; FC Copenhagen 2; B 93 Copenhagen 1; KB Copenhagen 1; Vanlose 1; Hvidovre 1; B1913 Odense 1, AB Copenhagen 1, Viborg 1.

Final League Table 1999–2000

	P	W	D	L	F	A	Pts
Herfolge	33	16	8	9	52	49	56
Brondby	33	15	9	9	56	37	54
AB Copenhagen	33	14	10	9	52	35	52
Viborg	33	15	7	11	56	50	52
Aalborg	33	12	13	8	57	40	49
Silkeborg	33	13	10	10	49	33	49
Lyngby	33	14	5	14	51	55	47
FC Copenhagen	33	12	8	13	44	37	44
Odense	33	11	10	12	42	44	43
Aarhus	33	9	9	15	37	56	36
Vejle*	33	7	11	15	38	68	32
Esbjerg*	33	8	4	21	41	71	28

Top scorer: Lassen (Silkeborg) 16.
Cup Final: Viborg 1, Aalborg 0.

ENGLAND

The Football Association, 16 Lancaster Gate, London W2 3LW.
Founded: 1863; *Number of Clubs:* 42,000; *Number of Players:* 2,250,000; *National Colours:* White shirts with navy blue collar, navy blue shorts, white stockings with light blue top.
Telephone: 0171 262 4542, 0171 402 7151; *Cable:* FOOTBALL ASSOCIATION LONDON W2; *Telex:* 261110 faldn g; *Fax:* 0171 402 0486.

ESTONIA

Estonian Football Association, Voidu 16, Tallinn EE 0012.
Founded: 1921; *Number of Clubs:* 40; *Number of Players:* 12,000; *National Colours:* Blue shirts, black shorts, white stockings.
Telephone: 00372 6/542715, 542716, 542717; *Fax:* 00372 6/542719.

International matches 1999
Israel (a) 0-7, Norway (h) 3-3, Romania (a) 0-2, Azerbaijan (h) 2-2, Cyprus (a) 2-1, Lithuania (a) 2-1, Czech Republic (h) 0-2, Lithuania (h) 1-2, Armenia (h) 2-0, Faeroes (a) 2-0, Scotland (h) 0-0, Bosnia (h) 1-4, Iraq (a) 1-1, UAE (a) 2-2, Turkmenistan (h) 1-1, Greece (a) 2-2.

League Championship wins (1922-40; 1992–2000)
Sport 8; Estonia 5; Flora Tallinn 4; Norma Tallinn 2; Tallinn JK 2; Kalev 2; LFLS 1; Olimpia 1; Lantana 1; Lavadia 1.

Cup wins (1992–2000)
Levadia 4 (merged with Sadam); VMV Tallinn 1; Nikol Tallinn 1; Norma Tallinn 1, Lantana 1; Flora Tallinn 1.

Final League Table 1999-2000

	P	W	D	L	F	A	Pts
Levadia	28	23	4	1	77	12	73
Tulevik	28	16	5	7	57	34	53
Flora	28	13	8	7	60	33	47
Trans	28	11	7	10	40	28	40
VMK	28	7	9	12	16	33	30
Lantana	28	6	9	13	31	52	27
Lelle*	28	5	9	14	25	45	24
Johvi*	28	2	7	19	12	81	28

Top scorer: Krom (Lavadia) 19.
Cup Final: Levadi 2, Tulevik 0.

FAEROE ISLANDS

Fotboltssamband Foroya, The Faeroes' Football Assn., Gundalur, P.O. Box 3028, FR-110, Torshavn.
Founded: 1979; *Number of Clubs:* 16; *Number of Players:* 1,014; *National Colours:* White shirts, blue shorts, white stockings.
Telephone: 00298 31 6707/457607; *Telex:* 81328 nspkkl fa; *Fax:* 00298 31 9079.

International matches 1999
Andorra (a) 0-0, Scotland (h) 1-1, Bosnia (h) 2-2, Iceland (h) 0-1, Estonia (h) 0-2, Lithuania (h) 0-1, Czech Republic (a) 0-2.

League Championship wins (1942–99)
KI Klaksvik 16; HB Torshavn 15; TB Tvoroyri 7; GI Gotu 7; B36 Torshavn 6; B68 Toftir 3; SI Sorvag 1; IF Fuglafjordur 1; B71 Sandur 1.

Cup wins (1955–99)
HB Torshavn 25; KI Klaksvik 5; TB Tvoroyri 4; GI Gotu 4; B36 Torshavn 1; VB Vagur 1; NSI Runavik 1; B71 Sandur 1.

Final League Table 1999

	P	W	D	L	F	A	Pts
KI	18	13	2	3	38	19	41
GI	18	12	3	3	46	24	39
B36	18	12	2	4	52	22	38
HB	18	11	4	3	41	16	37
NSI	18	6	5	7	25	26	23
VB	18	6	3	9	19	27	21
B68	18	5	3	9	22	41	18
B71	18	3	5	10	26	45	14
Sumba	18	2	5	11	22	43	11
IF*	18	2	4	12	20	48	10

Top scorer: Borg (B36) 17.
Cup Final: KI 3, B36 1.

FINLAND

Suomen Palloliitto Finlands Bollfoerbund, Lantinen Brahenkatu 2, P.O. Box 179, SF-00511 Helsinki.
Founded: 1907; *Number of Clubs:* 1,135; *Number of Players:* 66,100; *National Colours:* White shirts, blue shorts, white stockings.
Telephone: 00358 0 9701 01 01; *Cable:* SUOMIFOT-BOLL HELSINKI; *Telex:* 126033 spl sf; *Fax:* 00358 0 9701 01 099.

International matches 1999
Greece (a) 1-2, Cyprus (h) 1-2, Poland (a) 1-1, Germany (a) 0-2, Slovenia (a) 1-1, Turkey (h) 2-4, Moldova (a) 0-0, Belgium (h) 4-3, Germany (h) 1-2, Northern Ireland (h) 4-1.

League Championship wins (1949–99)
HJK Helsinki 10; Valkeakosken Haka 7; Turun Palloseura 5; Kuopion Palloseura 5; Kuusysi 4; Lahden Reipas 3; IF Kamraterna 3; Ilves-Kissat 2; Jazz Pori 2; Kotkan TP 2; OPS Oulu 2; Torun Pyrkiva 1; IF Kronohagens 1; Helsinki PS 1; Kokkolan PV 1; Vasa 1; TPV Tampere 1.

Cup wins (1955–99)
Valkeakosken Haka 10; Lahden Reipas 7; HJK Helsinki 6; Kotkan TP 4; Mikkeli 2; Kuusysi 2; Kuopion Palloseura 2; Ilves Tampere 2; TPS Turku 2; ; MyPa 2; IFK Abo 1; Drott 1; Helsinki PS 1; Pallo-Peikot 1; Rovaniemi PS 1, Jokerit 1 (formerly PK-35).

Qualifying Table 1999

	P	W	D	L	F	A	Pts
Haka	22	15	5	2	43	17	50
HJK Helsinki	22	14	5	3	43	14	47
Inter	22	10	4	8	28	25	34
Jokerit	22	9	6	7	26	22	33
MyPa	22	9	6	7	27	27	33
Jazz Pori	22	7	10	5	28	24	31
KTP Kotka	22	7	7	8	22	25	28
RoPS Rovaniemi	22	6	9	7	27	30	27
TPS Turku	22	7	6	9	27	31	27
Lahti	22	6	4	12	25	41	22
VPS	22	6	3	13	22	33	21
TPV Tampere*	22	1	5	16	13	42	8

Final Pool: Haka 67; HKJ Helsinki 65; MyPa 47; Jokerit 40; Inter 39; Jazz Pori 37; KTP Kotka 34; RoPS Rovaniemi 31.

Promotion/Relegation Pool:- TPS Turku 39; Lahti 30; VPS 29; TPV Tampere* 12.
Top scorer: Hiukka (RoPS Rovaniemi) 11.
Cup Final: Jokerit 2, Jaro 1.

FRANCE

Federation Francaise De Football, 60 Bis Avenue D'Iena, F-75783 Paris, Cedex 16.
Founded: 1919; *Number of Clubs:* 21,629; *Number of Players:* 1,692,205; *National Colours:* Blue shirts, white shorts, red stockings.
Telephone: 0033 1 44 31 73 00; *Cable:* CEFI PARIS 034; *Telex:* 640000 fedfoot f; *Fax:* 0033 1 47 20 82 96.

International matches 1999
Morocco (h) 1-0, England (a) 2-0, Ukraine (h) 0-0, Armenia (h) 2-0, Russia (h) 2-3, Andorra (a) 1-0, Northern Ireland (a) 1-0, Urkaine (a) 0-0, Armenia (a) 3-2, Iceland (h) 3-2, Croatia (h) 3-0.

League Championship wins (1933–2000)
Saint Etienne 10; Olympique Marseille 8; Nantes 7; AS Monaco 7; Stade de Reims 6; Girondins Bordeaux 5; OGC Nice 4; Lille OSC 3; Paris St Germain 2; FC Sete 2; Sochaux 2; Racing Club Paris 1; Roubaix-Tourcoing 1; Strasbourg 1; Auxerre 1; Lens 1.

Cup wins (1918–2000)
Olympique Marseille 10; Saint Etienne 6; Lille OSC 5; Racing Club Paris 5; Red Star 5; AS Monaco 5; Olympique Lyon 4; Paris St Germain 4; Girondins Bordeaux 3; OGC Nice 3; Nantes 3; CAS Genereaux 2; Nancy 2; Racing Club Strasbourg 2; Sedan 2; FC Sete 2; Stade de Reims 2; SO Montpellier 2; Stade Rennes 2; Auxerre 2; AS Cannes 1; Club Français 1; Excelsior Roubaix 1; Le Havre 1; Olympique de Pantin 1; CA Paris 1; Sochaux 1; Toulouse 1; Bastia 1; Metz 1.

Final League Table 1998–2000

	P	W	D	L	F	A	Pts
Monaco	34	20	5	9	69	38	65
Paris St Germain	34	16	10	8	54	40	58
Lyon	34	16	8	10	45	42	56
Bordeaux	34	15	9	10	52	40	54
Lens	34	14	7	13	42	41	49
St Etienne	34	13	9	12	46	47	48
Sedan	34	13	9	12	43	44	48
Auxerre	34	13	8	13	37	39	47
Strasbourg	34	13	7	14	42	52	46
Bastia	34	11	12	11	43	39	45
Metz	34	9	17	8	38	33	44
Nantes	34	12	7	15	39	40	43
Rennes	34	12	7	15	44	48	43
Troyes	34	13	4	17	36	52	43
Marseille	34	9	15	10	45	45	42
Nancy*	34	11	9	14	43	45	42
Le Havre*	34	9	7	18	30	52	34
Montpellier*	34	7	10	17	39	50	31

Top scorer: Anderson (Lyon) 23.
Cup Final: Nantes 2, Calais 1.

GEORGIA

Georgian Football Federation, 5 Shota Iamanidze Str, Tbilisi 380012, Georgia.
Founded: 1990; *Number of Clubs:* 4050. *Number of Players:* 115,000; *National Colours:* White shirts, black shorts, cherry stockings.
Telephone: 00995 32/960750; *Fax:* 00995 32/001128.

International matches 1999
Ukraine (h) 0-1, Slovenia (h) 1-1, Norway (h) 1-4, Norway (a) 0-1, Greece (h) 1-2, Slovenia (a) 1-2, Latvia (h) 2-2, Albania (a) 1-2.

League Championship wins (1990–2000)
Dynamo Tbilisi 10; Torpedo Kutaisi 1.

Cup wins (1992–2000)
Dynamo Tbilisi 7; Dynamo Batumi 1, Torpedo Kutaisi 1, Lokomotivi 1.

Championship Table 1999–2000

	P	W	D	L	F	A	Pts
Torpedo Kutaisi	14	8	4	2	37	11	46
WIT	14	8	5	1	15	7	41
Dynamo Tbilisi	14	5	9	0	19	4	41
Dynamo Batumi	14	8	2	4	22	10	39
Kolkheti	14	7	3	4	18	10	37
Sioni	14	3	1	10	13	32	21
Samtredia	14	2	2	10	6	29	17
Dila Gori	14	2	0	12	10	37	16

Relegation Table

	P	W	D	L	F	A	Pts
Merani 91	14	9	4	1	18	5	39
Lokomotivi	14	8	3	3	22	8	36
TSU	14	9	0	5	26	15	35
Gorda	14	8	2	4	25	10	34
Samgurali*	14	8	3	3	17	8	33
FC Tbilisi*	14	3	2	9	12	26	18
Arsenali*	14	3	0	11	11	27	14
Khobi*	14	1	0	13	13	45	8

Top scorer: Ionanidze (Torpedo Kutaisi) 25.
Cup Final: Lokomotivi 0, Torpedo Kutaisi 0.
Lokomotivi won 4-2 on penalties.

GERMANY

Deutsche Fussball-Bund, Postfach 710265, D-60492, Frankfurt Am Main.
Founded: 1900; *Number of Clubs:* 26,760; *Number of Players:* 5,260,320; *National Colours:* White shirts, black shorts, white stockings.
Telephone: 0049 69 678 80; *Telex:* 416815 dfb d; *Fax:* 0049 69 678 82 66.

International matches 1999

USA (a) 0-3, Colombia (a) 3-3, Northern Ireland (a) 3-0, Finland (h) 2-0, Scotland (h) 0-1, Moldova (h) 6-1, Brazil (a) 0-4, New Zealand (h) 2-0, USA (a) 0-2, Finland (a) 2-1, Northern Ireland (h) 4-0, Turkey (h) 0-0, Norway (a) 1-0.

League Championship wins (1903–2000)

Bayern Munich 16; IFC Nuremberg 9; Schalke 04 7; SV Hamburg 6; Borussia Moenchengladbach 5; Borussia Dortmund 5; VfB Stuttgart 4; IFC Kaiserslautern 4; VfB Leipzig 3; Sp Vgg Furth 3; IFC Cologne 3; Werder Bremen 3; Viktoria Berlin 2; Hertha Berlin 2; Hanover 96 2; Dresden SC 2; Munich 1860 1; Union Berlin 1; FC Freiburg 1; Phoenix Karlsruhe 1; Karlsruher FV 1; Holsten Kiel 1; Fortuna Dusseldorf 1; Rapid Vienna 1; VfB Mannheim 1; Rot-Weiss Essen 1; Eintracht Frankfurt 1; Eintracht Brunswick 1.

Cup wins (1935–2000)

Bayern Munich 10; IFC Cologne 4; Eintracht Frankfurt 4; Werder Bremen 4; IFC Nuremberg 3; SV Hamburg 3; Moenchengladbach 3; VfB Stuttgart 3; Dresden SC 2; Fortuna Dusseldorf 2; Karlsruhe SC 2; Munich 1860 2; Schalke 04 2; Borussia Dortmund 2; Kaiserslautern 2; First Vienna 1; VfB Leipzig 1; Kickers Offenbach 1; Rapid Vienna 1; Rot-Weiss Essen 1; SW Essen 1; Bayer Uerdingen 1; Hannover 96 1; Leverkusen 1.

Final League Table 1999–2000

	P	W	D	L	F	A	Pts
Bayern Munich	34	22	7	5	73	28	73
Leverkusen	34	21	10	4	74	36	73
Hamburg	34	16	11	7	63	39	59
Munich 1860	34	14	11	9	55	48	53
Kaiserslautern	34	15	5	14	54	59	50
Hertha	34	13	11	10	39	46	50
Wolfsburg	34	12	13	9	51	58	49
Stuttgart	34	14	6	14	44	47	48
Werder Bremen	34	13	8	13	65	52	47
Unterhaching	34	12	8	14	40	42	44
Borussia Dortmund	34	9	13	12	41	38	40
Freiburg	34	10	10	14	45	50	40
Eintracht Frankfurt	34	12	5	17	42	44	39
Schalke	34	8	15	11	42	44	39
Hansa Rostock	34	8	14	12	44	60	38
Ulm*	34	9	8	17	36	62	35
Bielefeld*	34	7	9	18	40	61	30
Duisburg*	34	4	10	20	37	71	22

Top scorer: Max (Munich 1860) 19.
Cup Final: Bayern Munich 3, Werder Bremen 0.

GREECE

Federation Hellenique De Football, Singrou Avenue 137, 17121 Athens.
Founded: 1926; *Number of Clubs:* 4,050; *Number of Players:* 180,000; *National Colours:* White shirts, blue shorts, white stockings.
Telephone: 0030 1 933 88 50; *Cable:* FOOTBALL ATHENS; *Telex:* 215328 epo gr; *Fax:* 0030 1 935 96 66.

International matches 1999

Finland (h) 2-1, Belgium (h) 1-0, Croatia (h) 3-2, Norway (h) 0-2, Latvia (a) 0-0, Switzerland (h) 1-1, Georgia (a) 2-1, Latvia (h) 1-2, Mexico (h) 3-2, El Salvador (h) 3-1, El Salvador (h) 3-0, Norway (a) 0-1, Albania (h) 2-0, Slovenia (a) 3-0, Nigeria (h) 2-0, Bulgaria (h) 1-0, Ghana (h) 1-1, Moldova (h) 2-0, Estonia (h) 2-2.

League Championship wins (1928–2000)

Olympiakos 29; Panathinaikos 18; AEK Athens 11; Aris Salonika 3; PAOK Salonika 2; Larissa 1.

Cup wins (1932–2000)

Olympiakos 21; Panathinaikos 16; AEK Athens 12; PAOK Salonika 2; Panionios 2; Aris Salonika 1; Ethnikos 1; Iraklis 1; Kastoria 1; Larissa 1; Ofi Crete 1.

Final League Table 1998–2000

	P	W	D	L	F	A	Pts
Olympiakos	34	30	2	2	86	18	92
Panathinaikos	34	28	4	2	92	24	88
AEK Athens	34	20	6	8	69	39	66
Ofi Crete	34	18	9	7	60	44	63
PAOK Salonika	34	15	10	9	63	43	55
Aris	34	14	8	12	50	46	50
Iraklis	34	15	5	14	58	58	50
Panionios	34	14	3	17	50	63	45
Kalamata	34	12	8	14	41	57	44
Xanthi	34	11	8	15	36	43	41
Ionikos	34	10	11	13	40	50	41
Astir	34	12	5	17	32	49	41
Paniliakos	34	12	4	18	44	48	40
Panachaiki	34	9	12	13	37	47	39
Kavala*	34	8	6	20	33	66	30
Proodeftiki*	34	7	7	20	27	55	28
Apollon*	34	6	6	22	30	59	24
Trikala*	34	5	6	23	35	74	21

Top scorer: Nalitzis (PAOK Salonika) 24.
Cup Final: AEK Athens 3, Ionikos 0.

HOLLAND

Koninklijke Nederlandsche Voetbalbond, Woudenbergseweg 56-58, Postbus 515, NL-3700 AM, Zeist.
Founded: 1889; *Number of Clubs:* 3,097; *Number of Players:* 962,397; *National Colours:* Orange shirts, white shorts, orange stockings.
Telephone: 0031343 499211; *Cable:* VOETBAL ZEIST; *Telex:* 40497 knvb nl; *Fax:* 0031343 499189.

International matches 1999

Portugal (h) 0-0, Argentina (h) 1-1, Morocco (h) 1-2, Brazil (a) 2-2, Brazil (a) 1-3, Denmark (a) 0-0, Belgium (h) 5-5, Brazil (h) 2-2, Czech Republic (h) 1-1.

League Championship wins (1898–2000)

Ajax Amsterdam 27; Feyenoord 15; PSV Eindhoven 15; HVV The Hague 8; Sparta Rotterdam 6; Go Ahead Deventer 4; HBS The Hague 3; Willem II Tilburg 3; RCH Haarlem 2; RAP 2; Heracles 2; ADO The Hague 2; Quick The Hague 1; BVV Schiedam 1; NAC Breda 1; Eindhoven 1; Enschede 1; Volewijckers Amsterdam 1; Limburgia 1; Rapid JC Haarlem 1; DOS Utrecht 1; DWS Amsterdam 1; Haarlem 1; Be Quick Groningen 1; SVV Schiedam 1; AZ 67 Alkmaar 1.

Cup wins (1899–2000)

Ajax Amsterdam 14; Feyenoord 10; PSV Eindhoven 8; Quick The Hague 4; AZ 67 Alkmaar 3; Rotterdam 3; DFC 2; Fortuna Geleen 2; Haarlem 2; HBS The Hague 2; RCH 2; Roda 2; VOC 2; Wageningen 2; Willem II Tilburg 2; FC Den Haag 2; Concordia Rotterdam 1; CVV 1; Eindhoven 1; HVV The Hague 1; Longa 1; Quick Nijmegen 1; RAP 1; Roermond 1; Schoten 1; Velocitas Breda 1; Velocitas Groningen 1; VSV 1; VUC 1; VVV Groningen 1; ZFC 1; NAC Breda 1; Twente Enschede 1; Utrecht 1.

Final League Table 1999–2000

	P	W	D	L	F	A	Pts
PSV Eindhoven	34	27	3	4	105	24	84
Heerenveen	34	21	5	8	65	36	68
Feyenoord	34	18	10	6	66	42	64
Vitesse	34	18	9	7	66	42	63
Ajax	34	18	7	9	72	51	61
Twente	34	16	12	6	57	37	60
AZ	34	17	4	13	69	59	55
Roda JC	34	16	7	11	62	53	55
Willem II	34	13	9	12	55	65	48
Utrecht	34	14	4	16	55	61	46
RKC Waalwijk	34	12	6	16	44	67	42
Fortuna Sittard	34	10	8	16	47	54	38
Sparta	34	11	4	19	48	75	37
De Graafschap	34	8	9	17	41	60	33
NEC Nijmegen	34	7	6	21	35	62	27
Maastricht+	34	6	7	21	38	68	25
Cambuur+	34	6	7	21	35	66	25
Den Bosch+	34	4	11	19	36	74	23

Top scorer: Van Nistelrooy (PSV Eindhoven) 29.
Cup Final: Roda JC 2, NEC Nijmegen 0.

HUNGARY

Hungarian Football Federation, Magyar Labdarugo Szovetseg, Istvanmezei ut. 3-5, Nepstadion (Toronyepulet), H-1146 Budapest. For correspondence: Pf. 106H-1581 Budapest.
Founded: 1901; *Number of Clubs:* 1944; *Number of Players* 95,986; *National Colours:* Red shirts, white shorts, green stockings.
Telephone: 0036 1 222 0343; *Telex:* 225782 misz h; *Fax:* 0036 1 222 0324/222 0344.

International matches 1999

Bosnia (h) 1-1, Liechtenstein (h) 5-0, Slovakia (a) 0-0, England (h) 1-1, Romania (a) 0-2, Slovakia (h) 0-1, Moldova (h) 1-1, Liechtenstein (a) 0-0, Azerbaijan (h) 3-0, Portugal (a) 0-3.

League Championship wins (1901–2000)

Ferencvaros 26; MTK-VM Budapest 21; Ujpest Dozsa 20; Honved 13; Vasas Budapest 6; Csepel 4; Raba Gyor 3; BTC 2; Nagyvarad 1; Vac 1; Dunaferr 1.

Cup wins (1910–2000)

Ferencvaros 17; MTK-VM Budapest 12; Ujpest Dozsa 8; Raba Gyor 4; Kispest Honved 4; Vasas Budapest 3; Diösgyör 2; Bocskai 1; III Ker 1; Kispesti AC 1; Soroksar 1; Szolnoki MAV 1; Siofok Banyasz 1; Bekescsaba 1; Pecs 1; Debrecen 1.
Cup not regularly held until 1964.

Final League Table 1999–2000

	P	W	D	L	F	A	Pts
Dunaferr	32	24	7	10	79	23	79
MTK	32	18	9	5	64	28	63
Vasas	32	19	4	9	58	32	61
Tatabanya	32	14	13	5	37	34	55
Ferencvaros	32	14	8	10	61	39	50
Debrecen	32	14	8	10	52	41	50
Gazszer	32	11	12	9	41	47	45
Gyori	32	12	8	12	52	36	44
Nyiregyhaza	32	12	8	12	32	42	44
Ujpest	32	10	11	11	47	42	41
Zalaegerszeg	32	8	15	9	34	31	39
Kispest Honved	32	10	9	13	27	39	39
Haladas	32	8	8	16	37	54	32
Nagykanizsa	32	7	10	15	27	44	31
Siofok*	32	7	7	18	26	51	25
Diosgyor*	32	5	9	18	26	56	24
Vac*	32	3	6	23	24	35	15

Szeged (excluded).
Top scorer: Tokoli (Dunaferr) 21.
Cup Final: MTK 3, Vasas 1.

ICELAND

Knattspyrnusamband Island, Laugardal, 104 Reykjavik.
Founded: 1929; *Number of Clubs:* 73; *Number of Players:* 23,673; *National Colours:* All blue.
Telephone: 00354 5102900; *Cable* KSI REYKJAVIK; *Telex:* 2314 isi is; *Fax:* 00354 75689793.

International matches 1999

Luxembourg (a) 2-1, Andorra (a) 2-0, Ukraine (a) 1-1, Malta (a) 2-1, Armenia (h) 2-0, Russia (a) 0-1, Faeroes (a) 1-0, Andorra (h) 3-0, Ukraine (h) 0-1, France (a) 2-3.

League Championship wins (1912–99)

KR 21; Valur 19; Fram 18; IA Akranes 17; Vikingur 5; IBV Vestmann 4; IBK Keflavik 3; KA Akureyri 1.

Cup wins (1960–99)

KR 10; Valur 8; Fram 7; IA Akranes 6; IBV Vestmann 4; IBK Keflavik 2; IBA Akureyri 1; Vikingur 1.

Final League Table 1999

	P	W	D	L	F	A	Pts
KR	18	14	3	1	43	13	45
IBV	18	11	5	2	31	14	38
Leiftur	18	6	8	4	22	26	26
IA	18	6	6	6	21	21	24
Breidablik	18	5	6	7	22	24	21
Grindavik	18	5	4	9	25	29	19
Fram	18	4	7	7	23	27	19
IBK	18	5	4	9	28	34	19
Valur*	18	4	6	8	28	38	18
Vikingur*	18	3	5	10	21	38	14

Top scorer: Johannesson (IBV) 12.
Cup Final: KR 3, IA 1.

REPUBLIC OF IRELAND

The Football Association of Ireland, (Cumann Peile Na H-Eireann), 80 Merrion Square, South Dublin 2.
Founded: 1921; *Number of Clubs:* 3,190; *Number of Players:* 124,615; *National Colours:* Green shirts, white shorts, green and white stockings.
Telephone: 00353 1 676 68 64; *Telex:* 91397 fai ei; *Fax:* 00353 1 661 09 31.

International matches 1999

Paraguay (h) 2-0, Sweden (h) 2-0, Northern Ireland (h) 1-0, Macedonia (h) 1-0, Yugoslavia (h) 2-1, Croatia (a) 0-1, Malta (a) 3-2, Macedonia (a) 1-1, Turkey (h) 1-1, Turkey (a) 0-0.

League Championship wins (1922–2000)

Shamrock Rovers 15; Dundalk 9; Shelbourne 9; St Patrick's Athletic 8; Bohemians 7; Waterford 6; Cork United 5; Drumcondra 5; St James's Gate 2; Cork Athletic 2; Sligo Rovers 2; Limerick 2; Athlone Town 2; Derry City 2; Dolphin 1; Cork Hibernians 1; Cork Celtic 1; Cork City 1.

Cup wins (1922–2000)

Shamrock Rovers 24; Dundalk 8; Shelbourne 6; Drumcondra 5; Bohemians 5; Cork Athletic 2; Cork United 2; St James's Gate 2; St Patrick's Athletic 2; Cork Hibernians 2; Limerick 2; Waterford 2; Derry City 2; Athlone Town 2; Sligo 2; Bray Wanderers 2; Alton United 1; Cork 1; Fordsons 1; Transport 1; Finn Harps 1; Home Farm 1; UCD 1; Galway United 1; Cork City 1.

Final League Table 1999–2000

	P	W	D	L	F	A	Pts
Shelbourne	33	19	12	2	49	20	69
Cork City	33	16	10	7	53	32	58
Bohemians	33	16	9	8	40	22	57
UCD	33	13	12	8	40	29	51
Shamrock Rovers	33	13	11	9	49	36	50
St Patrick's Ath	33	13	11	9	40	31	50
Derry City	33	12	10	11	32	38	46
Finn Harps	33	8	10	15	39	41	34
Galway United	33	8	10	15	32	49	34
Waterford United	33	7	12	14	24	38	33
Sligo Rovers*	33	5	10	18	31	60	25
Drogheda United*	33	4	11	18	20	53	23

Top scorer: Morley (Cork City) 20.
Cup Final: Shelbourne 0, 1, Bohemians 0, 0.

ISRAEL

Israel Football Association, Ramat-Gan Stadium, 299 Aba Hilell Street, Ramat-Gan 52594.
Founded: 1948; *Number of Clubs:* 544; *Number of Players:* 30,449; *National Colours:* Blue shirts, white shorts, blue stockings.

Telephone: 00972 3 570 59 99; *Cable:* CADUREGEL RAMAT-GAN; *Telex:* 361353 fa; *Fax:* 00972 3 570 20 44.

International matches 1999
Estonia (h) 7-0, Norway (h) 0-1, Belarus (h) 2-1, Latvia (h) 2-0, Romania (a) 2-0, Cyprus (h) 3-0, Austria (h) 5-0, Slovakia (a) 0-1, Cyprus (a) 2-3, San Marino (h) 8-0, Spain (a) 0-3, Denmark (h) 0-5, Denmark (a) 0-3.

League Championship wins (1932–2000)
Maccabi Tel Aviv 18; Hapoel Tel Aviv 13; Hapoel Petah Tikva 6; Maccabi Haifa 5; Maccabi Netanya 5; Beitar Jerusalem 4; Hakoah Ramat Gan 2; Hapoel Beersheba 2; Bnei Yehouda 1; British Police 1; Hapoel Kfar Sava 1; Hapoel Ramat Gan 1; Hapoel Haifa 1.

Cup wins (1928–2000)
Maccabi Tel Aviv 19; Hapoel Tel Aviv 11; Beitar Jerusalem 5; Maccabi Haifa 5; Hapoel Haifa 3; Hapoel Kfar Sava 3; Beitar Tel Aviv 2; Bnei Yehouda 2; Hakoah Ramat Gan 2; Hapoel Petah Tikva 2; Maccabi Petah Tikva 2; British Police 1; Hapoel Jerusalem 1; Hapoel Lod 1; Maccabi Netanya 1; Hapoel Beersheba 1.

Final League Table 1998–2000

	P	W	D	L	F	A	Pts
Hapoel Tel Aviv	39	26	7	6	76	28	85
Maccabi Haifa	39	22	10	7	86	35	76
Hapoel Petah Tikva	39	23	5	11	77	53	74
Maccabi Petah Tikva	39	18	6	15	50	47	60
Beitar Jerusalem	39	15	14	10	61	54	59
Maccabi Tel Aviv	39	18	7	14	66	42	58
Hapoel Haifa	39	13	18	8	53	39	57
Ironi Ashdod	39	13	13	13	48	49	52
Ironi Rishon	39	10	13	16	42	65	43
Maccabi Netanya	39	11	10	18	53	71	41
Bnei Yehuda	39	9	13	17	37	64	40
Hapoel Kfar Sabah*	39	8	14	17	40	56	38
Maccabi Herzliya*	39	9	8	22	33	73	35
Hapoel Jerusalem*	39	6	6	27	33	82	24

Top scorer: Toubi (Maccabi Petah Tikva) 27.
Cup Final: Hapoel Tel Aviv 2, Beitar Jerusalem 2.
Hapoel Tel Aviv won 4-2 on penalties.

ITALY

Federazione Italiana Giuoco Calcio, Via Gregorio Allegri 14, C.P. 2450, 1-00198, Roma.
Founded: 1898; *Number of Clubs:* 20,961; *Number of Players:* 1,420,160; *National Colours:* Blue shirts, white shorts, blue stockings with white trim.
Telephone: 0039 6 849 11; *Cable:* FEDERCALCIO ROMA; *Telex:* 624132 calcio i; *Fax:* 0039 6 849 12 526.

International matches 1999
Norway (h) 0-0, Denmark (a) 2-1, Belarus (h) 1-1, Croatia (a) 0-0, Wales (h) 4-0, Switzerland (a) 0-0, Denmark (h) 2-3, Belarus (a) 0-0, Belgium (h) 1-3.

League Championship wins (1898–2000)
Juventus 25; AC Milan 16; Inter-Milan 13; Genoa 9; Torino 8; Pro Vercelli 7; Bologna 7; Fiorentina 2; Lazio 2; Napoli 2; AS Roma 2; Casale 1; Novese 1; Cagliari 1; Verona 1; Sampdoria 1.

Cup wins (1922–2000)
Juventus 9; AS Roma 8; Fiorentina 5; Torino 4; AC Milan 4; Sampdoria 4; Lazio 3; Inter-Milan 3; Napoli 3; Bologna 2; Parma 2; Atalanta 1; Genoa 1; Vado 1; Venezia 1; Vicenza 1.

Final League Table 1999–2000

	P	W	D	L	F	A	Pts
Lazio	34	21	9	4	64	33	72
Juventus	34	21	8	5	46	20	71
AC Milan	34	16	13	5	65	40	61
Internazionale	34	17	7	10	58	36	58
Parma	34	16	10	8	52	37	58
Roma	34	14	12	8	57	34	54
Fiorentina	34	13	12	9	48	38	51
Udinese	34	13	11	10	55	45	50
Verona	34	10	13	11	40	45	43
Perugia	34	12	6	16	36	52	42
Bologna	34	9	13	12	32	39	40
Reggina	34	9	13	12	31	42	40
Lecce	34	10	10	14	33	49	40
Bari	34	10	9	15	34	48	39
Torino*	34	8	12	14	35	47	36
Venezia*	34	6	8	20	30	60	26
Cagliari*	34	3	13	18	29	54	22
Piacenza*	34	4	9	21	19	45	21

Top scorer: Shevchenko (AC Milan) 24.
Cup Final: Lazio 2, 0, Internazionale 1, 0.

LATVIA

Latvian Football Federation, Augsiela, 1, LV-1009, Riga.
Founded: 1921; *Number of Clubs:* 50; *Number of Players:* 12,000; *National Colours:* Carmine red shirts, white shorts, carmine red stockings.
Telephone: 00371 2 29 29 88; *Fax:* 00371 7828331.

International matches 1999
Israel (a) 0-2, Greece (h) 0-0, Albania (h) 0-0, Slovenia (h) 1-2, Greece (a) 2-1, Brazil (a) 0-3, Albania (a) 3-3, Georgia (a) 2-2, Norway (h) 1-2.

League Championship wins (1922–99)
ASK Riga 9; Skonto Riga 9; RFK Riga 8; Olympia Liepaya 7; Sarkanais Metalurgs Liepaya 7; VEF Riga 6; Energija Riga 4; Elektrons Riga 3; Torpedo Riga 3; Daugava Liepaya 2; ODO Riga 2; Khimikis Daugavpils 2; RAF Yelgava 2; Keisermezhs Riga 2; Dinamo Riga 1; Zhmilyeva Team 1; Darba Rezervi 1; REZ Riga 1; Start Brotseni 1; Venta Ventspils 1; Yurnieks Riga 1; Alfa Riga 1; Gauya Valmiera 1.

Cup wins (1937–2000)
Elektrons Riga 7; Sarkanais Metalurgs Liepaya 5; Skonto Riga 5; ODO Riga 3; VEF Riga 3; ASK Riga 3; Tseltnieks Riga 3; RAF Yelgava 3; RFK Riga 2; Daugava Liepaya 2; Start Brotseni 2; Selmash Liepaya 2; Yurnieks Riga 2; Khimikis Daugavpils 2; Rigas Vilki 1; Dinamo Liepaya 1; Dinamo Riga 1; REZ Riga 1; Voulkan Kouldiga 1; Baltija Liepaya 1; Venta Ventspils 1; Pilot Riga 1; Lielupe Yurmala 1; Energija Riga 1; Torpedo Riga 1; Daugava SKIF Riga 1; Tseltnieks Daugavpils 1; Olympia Riga 1; FK Riga 1.

Final League Table 1999

	P	W	D	L	F	A	Pts
Skonto Riga	28	23	0	5	88	15	69
Metalurgs Liepaya	28	19	3	6	73	25	60
FK Ventspils	28	18	2	8	62	26	56
Dinaburg Daugavpils	28	13	5	10	37	32	44
FK Valmiera	28	10	5	13	33	42	35
FK Riga	28	10	4	14	35	42	34
Police FK	28	5	5	18	25	93	20
FK Rezekne	28	1	2	25	12	90	5

Top scorer: Dobretsov (Metalurgs Liepaya) 22.
Cup Final 2000: Skonto Riga 4, Metalurgs Liepaya 1.

LIECHTENSTEIN

Liechtensteiner Fussball-Verband, Malbuner Huus Altenbach 11, Postfach 165, 9490 Vaduz.
Founded: 1934; *Number of Clubs:* 7; *Number of Players:* 1,247; *National Colours:* Blue shirts, red shorts, blue stockings.
Telephone: 004175 237 4747; *Cable:* FUSSBALLVER-BAND VADUZ; *Fax:* 004175 237 4748.

International matches 1999
Hungary (a) 0-5, Portugal (h) 0-5, Azerbaijan (a) 0-4, Portugal (a) 0-9, Hungary (h) 0-0, Slovakia (a) 0-2, Romania (h) 0-3.

Liechtenstein has no national league. Teams compete in Swiss regional leagues.

Cup wins (1946–2000)
Vaduz 29; Balzers 11; Triesen 8; Eschen/Mauren 4; Schaan 3.

LITHUANIA

Lithuanian Football Federation, Seimyniskiu str. 15, 2005 Vilnius.
Founded: 1922; *Number of Clubs:* 152; *Number of Players:* 16,600; *National Colours:* Yellow shirts, green shorts, yellow stockings.
Telephone: 00370 2/723654; *Fax:* 00370 2/723651.

International matches 1999
Czech Republic (a) 0-2, Estonia (h) 1-2, Bosnia (a) 0-2, Estonia (a) 2-1, Norway (a) 0-1, Czech Republic (h) 0-4, Faeroes (a) 1-0, Scotland (a) 0-3.

League Championship wins (1922–99)
Kovas Kaunas 6; KSS Klaipeda 6; LFLS Kaunas 4; Zalgiris Vilnius 4; LGSF Kaunas 2; Kareda 2; MSK Kaunas 1; Ekranas Panevezys 1; Romar Mazeikiai 1; Inkaras Grifas 1.

Cup wins (1992–2000)
Zalgiris Vilnius 3; Kareda 2; Ekranas 2; Inkaras 1.

Final League Table 1999–2000

	P	W	D	L	F	A	Pts
Kaunas	18	12	5	1	36	10	41
Zalgiris	18	10	6	2	33	9	36
Atlantas	18	9	6	3	34	24	33
Kareda	18	9	3	6	31	18	30
Ekranas	18	7	8	3	22	11	29
Inkaras	18	8	5	5	25	18	29
Nevezis	18	3	7	8	10	22	16
Banga	18	2	6	10	12	40	12
Ardena	18	2	5	11	10	26	11
Dainava*	18	1	3	14	9	44	6

Promotion/Relegation Play-Offs
Banga 5, 3, Tauras 1, 0.
Ardena 0, 1, Gelezinis 0, 1.
Top scorer: Vasiliauskas (Zalgiris 10).
Cup Final: Ekranas 1, Zalgiris 0.

LUXEMBOURG

Federation Luxembourgeoise De Football, (F.L.F.), 50, Rue De Strasbourg, L-2560, Luxembourg.
Founded: 1908; *Number of Clubs:* 126; *Number of Players:* 21,684; *National Colours:* All red.
Telephone: 00352 48 86 65; *Cable:* FOOTBALL LUXEMBOURG; *Telex:* 2426 flf l; *Fax:* 00352 40 02 01.

International matches 1999
Iceland (h) 1-2, Sweden (a) 0-2, Bulgaria (h) 0-2, Poland (h) 2-3, England (a) 0-6, Sweden (h) 0-1, Bulgaria (a) 0-3.

League Championship wins (1910–2000)
Jeunesse Esch 26; Spora Luxembourg 11; Stade Dudelange 10; Avenir Beggen 7; Red Boys Differdange 6; US Hollerich-Bonnevoie 5; Fola Esch 5; US Luxembourg 5; Aris Bonnevoie 3; Progres Niedercorn 3; F91 Dudelange 1.

Cup wins (1922–2000)
Red Boys Differdange 16; Jeunesse Esch 12; US Luxembourg 10; Spora Luxembourg 8; Avenir Beggen 6; Stade Dudelange 4; Progres Niedercorn 4; Fola Esch 3; Alliance Dudelange 2; US Rumelange 2; Grevenmacher 2; Aris Bonnevoie 1; US Dudelange 1; Jeunesse Hautcharage 1; National Schiffige 1; Racing Luxembourg 1; SC Tetange 1; Hesperange 1.

Qualifying Table 1999-2000

	P	W	D	L	F	A	Pts
Grevenmacher	22	11	8	3	42	18	41
F91 Dudelange	22	11	8	3	36	20	41
Avenir Beggen	22	12	4	6	32	19	40
Jeunesse Esch	22	10	8	4	36	26	38
Sporting Mertzig	22	11	4	7	35	25	37
Union	22	8	9	5	29	23	33
Hobscheid	22	9	5	8	35	26	32
Rumelange	22	8	5	9	28	38	29
FC Wiltz 71	22	6	7	9	34	37	25
Mondercange	22	7	4	11	35	45	25
Schifflange*	22	4	4	14	24	39	16
Bonnevoie*	22	1	2	19	14	64	5

Championship Play-offs:- F91 Dudelange 57; Juenesse Esch 46; Grevenmacher 46; Avenir Beggen 44.
Top scorer: Christophe (Mondercange) 26.
Cup Final: Jeunesse Esch 4, Mondercange 1.

MACEDONIA

Football Association of the Former Yugoslav Republic of Macedonia, VIII-ma Udarna Brigada 31A, PO Box 84, MAC-91000 Skopje.
Founded: 1948; *Number of Clubs:* 598; *Number of Players:* 15,165; *National Colours:* All red.
Telephone: 00389 1 22 90 42; *Fax:* 00389 1 23 54 48.

International matches 1999
Albania (a) 0-2, Croatia (h) 1-1, Republic of Ireland (a) 0-1, Yugoslavia (a) 1-3, Yugoslavia (h) 2-4, Republic of Ireland (h) 1-1.

League Championship wins (1993-2000)
Vardar 3; Sileks 3; Sloga 2.

Cup wins (1993-2000)
Vardar 4; Sileks 1; Sloga 1.

Final Table 1999–2000

	P	W	D	L	F	A	Pts
Sloga	26	18	7	1	55	13	61
Pobeda	26	15	7	4	57	23	52
Rabotnicki	26	16	2	8	41	26	50
Pelister	26	14	5	7	48	30	47
Cement	26	14	5	7	43	29	47
Sileks	26	11	7	8	43	29	40
Makedonia	26	10	6	10	29	28	36
Tikves	26	9	4	13	37	54	31
Borec	26	8	6	12	30	42	30
Veles	26	7	8	11	39	38	29
Sasa	26	7	7	12	23	35	28
Osogovo	26	7	5	14	34	53	26
Napredok*	26	4	8	14	30	48	20
Kumanovo*	26	2	3	21	16	77	9

Top scorer: Bekiri (Sloga) 19.
Cup Final: Sloga 6, Pobeda 0.

MALTA

Malta Football Association, 280 St. Paul Street, Valletta VLT07.
Founded: 1900; *Number of Clubs:* 252; *Number of Players:* 5,544; *National Colours:* Red shirts, white shorts, red stockings.
Telephone: 00356 22 26 97; *Cable:* FOOTBALL MALTA VALLETTA; *Fax:* 00356 24 51 36.

International matches 1999
Bosnia (h) 2-1, Poland (h) 0-1, Yugoslavia (h) 0-3, Moldova (h) 0-2, Iceland (h) 1-2, Yugoslavia (a) 1-4, Croatia (a) 1-2, Republic of Ireland (h) 2-3, Libya (h) 1-0.

League Championship wins (1910–2000)
Floriana 25; Sliema Wanderers 23; Valletta 17; Hibernians 8; Hamrun Spartans 7; Rabat Ajax 2; St George's 1; KOMR 1; Birkirkara 1.

Cup wins (1935–2000)
Floriana 18; Sliema Wanderers 18; Valletta 9; Hamrun Spartans 6; Hibernians 6; Gzira United 1; Melita 1; Zurrieq 1; Rabat Ajax 1.

Qualifying Table 1999–2000

	P	W	D	L	F	A	Pts
Birkirkara	18	15	2	1	39	9	47
Valletta	18	13	1	4	58	22	40
Floriana	18	11	1	6	35	24	34
Sliema Wanderers	18	10	3	5	41	23	33
Pieta Hotspurs	18	7	5	6	33	36	26
Hibernians	18	5	7	6	28	25	22
Naxxar Lions	18	4	4	10	27	40	16
Gozo	18	3	5	10	44	29	14
Zurrieq	18	3	3	12	20	55	12
Rabat Ajax	18	2	3	13	19	51	9

Final Table 1999-2000

	P	W	D	L	F	A	Pts
Birkirkara	28	22	3	3	61	14	46
Sliema Wanderers	28	17	4	7	62	36	39
Valletta	28	18	2	8	75	36	36
Floriana	28	14	2	12	50	44	27
Pieta Hotspurs	28	10	5	13	45	57	22
Hibernians	28	8	7	13	37	48	20

Promotion/Relegation Table 1999-2000

	P	W	D	L	F	A	Pts
Naxxar Lions	24	8	5	11	44	49	21
Rabat Ajax	24	5	6	13	34	62	17
Gozo*	24	4	7	13	22	39	12
Zurrieq*	24	4	3	17	32	77	9

Top scorer: Mifsud (Sliema Wanderers) 21.
Cup Final: Sliema Wanderers 4, Birkirkara 1.

MOLDOVA

Moldavian Football Federation, 39 Tricolorului Str, 2012, Chisinau.
Founded: 1990; *Number of Clubs:* 143; *Number of Players:* 75,000; *National Colours:* Blue shirts, red shorts, yellow stockings.
Telephone: 00373 2 247878. *Fax:* 00373 2 247890.

International matches 1999
Malta (a) 2-0, Turkey (a) 0-2, Northern Ireland (h) 0-0, Germany (a) 1-6, Finland (h) 0-0, Hungary (a) 1-1, Turkey (h) 1-1, Greece (a) 0-2.

League Championship wins (1992–2000)
Zimbru Chisinau 8; Constructorul 1.

Cup wins (1992–2000)
Tiligul 4; Zimbru Chisinau 2; Combat 1, Serif 1, Constructorul 1.

Final League Table 1999-2000

	P	W	D	L	F	A	Pts
Zimbru Chisinau	36	25	7	4	78	21	82
Serif	36	25	6	5	77	25	81
Constructorul	36	18	11	7	52	23	65
Otaci	36	16	11	9	53	28	59
Tiligul	36	12	13	11	35	33	49
Olimpia	36	13	7	16	42	51	46
Agro	36	10	10	16	36	56	40
Moldova-Gaz*	36	10	9	17	37	48	39
Roma*	36	8	6	22	28	66	30
Energia*	36	2	2	32	13	100	8

Top scorer: Rogaciov (Serif) 20.
Cup Final: Constructorul 1, Zimbru Chisinau 0.

NORTHERN IRELAND

Irish Football Association Ltd, 20 Windsor Avenue, Belfast BT9 6EG.
Founded: 1880; *Number of Clubs:* 1,555; *Number of Players:* 24,558; *National Colours:* Green shirts, white shorts, green stockings.
Telephone: 01232 66 94 58; *Cable:* FOOTBALL BELFAST; *Telex:* 747317 ifa ni g; *Fax:* 01232 66 76 20.

NORWAY

Norges Fotballforbund Ullevaal Stadion, Postboks 3823, Ulleval Hageby, 0805 Oslo 8.
Founded: 1902; *Number of Clubs:* 1,810; *Number of Players:* 300,000; *National Colours:* Red shirts, white shorts, blue stockings.
Telephone: 0047 22/024500 ; *Cable* FOTBALLFOR-BUND OSLO; *Telex:* 71722 nff n; *Fax:* 0047 22 95 10 10.

International matches 1999
Israel (a) 1-0, Estonia (a) 3-3, Italy (a) 0-0, Greece (a) 2-0, Georgia (a) 4-1, Jamaica (h) 6-0, Georgia (h) 1-0, Albania (a) 2-1, Lithuania (h) 1-0, Greece (h) 1-0, Slovenia (h) 4-0, Latvia (a) 2-1, Germany (h) 0-1.

League Championship wins (1938–99)
Rosenborg Trondheim 13; Fredrikstad 9; Viking Stavanger 8; Lillestroem 6; Valerengen 4; Larvik Turn 3;

Brann Bergen 2; Lyn Oslo 2; IK Start 2; Friedig 1; Fram 1; Skeid Oslo 1; Strömsgodset Drammen 1; Moss 1.

Cup wins (1902–99)
Odds Bk Skien 11; Fredrikstad 10; Lyn Oslo 8; Skeid Oslo 8; Rosenborg Trondheim 7; Sarpsborg FK 6; Brann Bergen 5; Orn F Horten 4; Lillestroem 4; Viking Stavanger 4; Strömsgodset Drammen 4; Frigg 3; Mjondalens F 3; Bodo-Glimt 2; Mercantile 2; Tromso 2; Valerengen 2; Grane Nordstrand 1; Kvik Halden 1; Sparta 1; Gjovik 1; Moss 1; Byrne 1; Molde 1; Stabaek 1.
(Known as the Norwegian Championship for HM The King's Trophy).

Final League Table 1999

	P	W	D	L	F	A	Pts
Rosenborg	26	18	2	6	75	33	56
Molde	26	16	2	8	49	37	50
Brann	26	16	1	9	45	40	49
Lillestrom	26	15	3	8	60	41	48
Stabaek	26	14	4	8	58	49	46
Tromso	26	13	5	8	70	46	44
Odd	26	12	3	11	42	48	39
Viking	26	11	3	12	51	48	36
Bodo-Glimt	26	10	4	12	52	54	34
Moss	26	9	2	15	39	46	29
Valerengen	26	8	4	14	40	53	28
Stromsgodset*	26	7	3	16	46	68	24
Skeid*	26	7	2	17	36	75	23
Kongsvinger*	26	6	2	18	34	59	20

Top scorer: Lange (Tromso) 23.
Cup Final: Rosenborg 2, Brann 0.

POLAND

Federation Polonaise De Foot-Ball, Al. Ujazdowskie 22, 00-478 Warszawa.
Founded: 1919; *Number of Clubs:* 5,881; *Number of Players:* 317,442; *National Colours:* White shirts, red shorts, white & red stockings.
Telephone: 0048 22 6223398; *Cable:* PEZETPEEN WARSZAWA; *Telex:* 825320 pzpn pl; *Fax:* 0048 22 629 24 89.

International matches 1999
Malta (a) 1-0, Finland (h) 1-1, Armenia (h) 1-0, England (a) 1-3, Sweden (h) 0-1, Czech Republic (h) 2-1, Bulgaria (h) 2-0, Luxembourg (a) 3-2, Spain (h) 1-2, England (h) 0-0, Sweden (a) 0-2.

League Championship wins (1921–2000)
Gornik Zabrze 14; Ruch Chorzow 13; Wisla Krakow 7; Legia Warsaw 6; Widzew Lodz 6; Lech Poznan 5; Pogon Lwow 4; Cracovia 3; Warta Poznan 2; Polonia Bytom 2; Stal Mielec 2; LKS Lodz 2; Polonia Warsaw 2; Garbarnia Krakow 1; Slask Wroclaw 1; Szombierki Bytom 1; Zaglebie Lubin 1.

Cup wins (1951–2000)
Legia Warsaw 12; Gornik Zabrze 6; Zaglebie Sosnowiec 4; Lech Poznan 3; GKS Katowice 3; Ruch Chorzow 3; Amica Wronki 3; Slask Wroclaw 2; Gwardia Warsaw 1; LKS Lodz 1; Polonia Warsaw 1; Wisla Krakow 1; Stal Rzeszow 1; Arka Gdynia 1; Lechia Gdansk 1; Widzew Lodz 1; Miedz Legnica 1.

Final League Table 1999–2000

	P	W	D	L	F	A	Pts
Polonia	30	20	5	5	56	25	65
Wisla	30	16	8	6	64	38	56
Ruch	30	15	10	5	53	32	55
Legia	30	14	10	6	53	34	52
Zaglebie Lubin	30	12	9	9	42	37	45
Amica	30	11	11	8	43	37	44
Widzew	30	11	7	12	48	54	40
Odra	30	10	7	13	34	38	37
Stomil	30	8	13	9	43	43	37
Radzionkow	30	11	4	15	38	49	37
Groclin	30	11	3	16	29	46	36
Pogon	30	8	10	12	42	53	34
Petrochemia	30	9	7	14	35	48	34
Gornik Zabrze	30	8	8	14	42	41	32
LKS Lodz*	30	7	7	16	28	42	28
Lech*	30	6	7	17	34	57	25

Top scorer: Kompala (Gornik Zabrze) 19.
Cup Final: Wisla 2, 0, Amica 2, 3.

PORTUGAL

Federacao Portuguesa De Futebol, Praca De Alegria N.25, Apartado 21.100, P-1127, Lisboa Codex.
Founded: 1914; *Number of Clubs:* 204; *Number of Players:* 79,235; *National Colours:* Red shirts, green shorts, red stockings.
Telephone: 00351 1 342 8207/8/9/0; *Cable:* FUTEBOL LISBOA; *Telex:* 13489 fpf p; *Fax:* 00351 1 346 72 31.

International matches 1999
Holland (a) 0-0, Azerbaijan (h) 7-0, Liechtenstein (a) 5-0, Slovakia (h) 1-0, Liechtenstein (h) 9-0, Andorra (h) 4-0, Azerbaijan (a) 1-1, Romania (a) 1-1, Hungary (h) 3-0.

League Championship wins (1935–2000)
Benfica 30; FC Porto 18; Sporting Lisbon 17; Belenenses 1.

Cup wins (1939–2000)
Benfica 23; Sporting Lisbon 12; FC Porto 10; Boavista 5; Belenenses 3; Vitoria Setubal 2; Academica Coimbra 1; Leixoes Porto 1; Sporting Braga 1; Amadora 1; Beira Mar 1.

Final League Table 1999–2000

	P	W	D	L	F	A	Pts
Sporting Lisbon	34	23	8	3	57	22	77
Porto	34	22	7	5	66	26	73
Benfica	34	21	6	7	58	33	69
Boavista	34	16	7	11	40	31	55
Gil Vicente	34	14	11	9	48	34	53
Maritimo	34	13	11	10	42	36	50
Guimaraes	34	14	6	14	48	43	48
Amadora	34	10	15	9	40	35	45
Braga	34	12	7	15	44	45	43
Uniao Leiria	34	10	12	12	31	35	42
Alverca	34	11	8	15	39	48	41
Belenenses	34	9	13	12	36	38	40
Campomaiorense	34	10	6	18	31	51	36
Farense	34	8	11	15	35	60	35
Salgueiros	34	9	7	18	30	49	34
Rio Ave*	34	8	9	17	34	54	33
Setubal*	34	9	6	19	25	49	33
Santa Clara*	34	7	10	17	35	50	31

Top scorer: Jardel (Porto) 38.
Cup Final: Sporting Lisbon 1, 0, Porto 1, 2.

ROMANIA

Federatia Romana De Fotbal, Str. Poligrafiei 3, Sector 1, 71556 Bucharest.
Founded: 1909; *Number of Clubs:* 414; *Number of Players:* 22,920; *National Colours:* All yellow.
Telephone: 0040 1 224 1993/224 2983; *Cable:* SPORTROM BUCURESTI-FOTBAL; *Telex:* 10097 frf r; *Fax:* 0040 1 224 0661.

International matches 1999
Estonia (h) 2-0, Israel (h) 0-2, Slovakia (h) 0-0, Azerbaijan (a) 1-0, Belgium (h) 1-0, Hungary (h) 2-0, Azerbaijan (h) 4-0, Cyprus (a) 2-2, Slovakia (a) 5-1, Portugal (h) 1-1, Liechtenstein (a) 3-0.

League Championship wins (1910–2000)
Steaua Bucharest 20; Dinamo Bucharest 15; Venus Bucharest 8; Chinezul Timisoara 6; UT Arad 6; Ripensia Temesvar 4; Uni Craiova 4; Petrolul Ploesti 3; Olimpia Bucharest 2; Colentina Bucharest 2; Arges Pitesti 2; ICO Oradea 2; ; Rapid Bucharest 2; Soc RA Bucharest 1; Prahova Ploesti 1; Coltea Brasov 1; Juventus Bucharest 1; Metalochimia Resita 1; Ploesti United 1; Unirea Tricolor 1.

Cup wins (1934–2000)
Steaua Bucharest 20; Rapid Bucharest 10; Dinamo Bucharest 8; Uni Craiova 6; UT Arad 2; Ripensia Temesvar 2; Politehnica Timisoara 2; Petrolul Ploesti 2; ICO Oradeo 1; Metalochimia Resita 1; Stinta Cluj 1; CFR Turnu Severin 1; Chimia Ramnicu Vilcea 1; Jiul Petroseni 1; Progresul Bucharest 1; Progresul Oradea 1; Gloria Bistrita 1.

Final League Table 1999–2000

	P	W	D	L	F	A	Pts
Dinamo	34	27	3	4	93	39	84
Rapid	34	22	6	6	65	38	72
Ceahlaul	34	17	6	11	56	48	57
Steaua	34	18	3	13	62	56	57
Arges	34	16	6	12	45	34	54
Gloria	34	17	2	15	54	49	53
Bacau	34	15	6	13	40	39	51
National	34	15	4	15	61	44	49
Otelul	34	15	4	15	58	55	49
Astra	34	13	8	13	43	41	47
Rocar	34	15	2	17	51	52	47
Petrolul	34	14	5	15	48	55	47
Brasov	34	14	4	16	53	43	46
Uni Craiova	34	13	7	14	45	41	46
Farul*	34	12	8	14	38	45	44
Onesti*	34	9	3	22	37	92	30
Resita*	34	5	8	21	35	73	23
Extensiv*	34	4	5	25	26	66	17

Top scorer: Savu (National) 20.
Cup Final: Dinamo 2, Uni Craiova 0.

RUSSIA

Football Union of Russia; Luzhnetskaya Naberezyhnaja, 8. SU-119871 Moscow.
Founded: 1912; *Number of Clubs:* 43,700; *Number of Players:*785,000; *National Colours:* White shirts, blue shorts, red stockings.
Telephone: 0070 95 2011637; *Telex:* 411287 priz su; *Fax:* 0070 95 2011303.

International matches 1999
Armenia (a) 3-0, Andorra (h) 6-1, Belarus (h) 1-1, France (a) 3-2, Iceland (h) 1-0, Belarus (a) 2-0, Armenia (h) 2-0, Andorra (a) 2-1, Ukraine (h) 1-1.

League Championship wins (1945–99)
Spartak Moscow 18; Dynamo Kiev 13; Dynamo Moscow 11; CSKA Moscow 7; Torpedo Moscow 3; Dynamo Tbilisi 2; Dnepr Dnepropetrovsk 2; Saria Voroshilovgrad 1; Ararat Erevan 1; Dynamo Minsk 1; Zenit Leningrad 1; Spartak Vladikavkaz 1.

Cup wins (1936–2000)
Spartak Moscow 12; Dynamo Kiev 10; Torpedo Moscow 7; Dynamo Moscow 7; CSKA Moscow 5; Lokomotiv Moscow 5; Donetsk Shaktyor 4; Dynamo Tbilisi 2; Ararat Erevan 2; Zenit Leningrad 2; Karpaty Lvov 1; SKA Rostov 1; Metallist Kharkov 1; Dnepr 1.

Final League Table 1999

	P	W	D	L	F	A	Pts
Spartak Moscow	30	22	6	2	75	24	72
Lokomotiv Moscow	30	20	5	5	62	30	65
CSKA Moscow	30	15	10	5	56	29	55
Torpedo Moscow	30	13	11	6	38	33	50
Dynamo Moscow	30	12	8	10	44	41	44
Vladikavkaz	30	12	7	11	54	45	43
Rostov	30	11	8	11	32	37	41
Zenit	30	9	12	9	36	34	39
Uralan	30	10	6	14	27	34	36
Saturn	30	8	10	12	30	38	34
Lokomotiv Nizhniy	30	9	6	15	33	48	33
Krylia Sovekov	30	8	7	15	39	49	31
Volgograd	30	7	10	13	36	51	31
Chernomorets	30	7	8	15	30	49	29
Sotchi*	30	5	11	14	29	55	26
Shinnik*	30	5	9	16	21	45	24

Top scorer: Demetradze (Vladikavkaz) 21.
Cup Final: Lokomotiv Moscow 3, CSKA Moscow 2 aet.

SAN MARINO

Federazione Sammarinese Giuoco Calcio, Viale Campo dei Giudei, 14; 47031-Rep. San Marino.
Founded: 1931; *Number of Clubs:* 17; *Number of Players:* 1,033; *National Colours:* All light blue.
Telephone: 00378 9990515; *Telex:* 0505284 cosmar so; *Fax:* 00378 9992348.

International matches 1999
Cyprus (a) 0-4, Spain (h) 0-6, Austria (a) 0-7, Spain (a) 0-9, Israel (a) 0-8.

League Championship wins (1986–2000)
Tre Fiori 4; Faetano 3; Folgore 3; Fiorita 2; Domagnano 1; Montevito 1, Libertas 1.

Cup wins (1986–99)
Domagnano 4; Libertas 3; Cosmos 2; Faetano 2, Fiorita 1, Tre Fiori 1; Murata 1.

SCOTLAND

The Scottish Football Association Ltd, 6 Park Gardens, Glasgow G3 7YF.
Founded: 1873; *Number of Clubs:* 6,148; *Number of Players:* 135,474; *National Colours:* Dark blue shirts, white shorts, red stockings with dark blue tops.
Telephone: 0141 332 6372; *Cable:* EXECUTIVE GLASGOW; *Telex:* 778904 sfa g; *Fax:* 0141 332 7559.

SLOVAKIA

Slovak Football Association, Junacka 6, 83280 Bratislava, Slovakia.
Founded: 1993; *Number of Clubs:* 2,140; *Number of Players:* 141,000; *National Colours:* All blue.
Telephone: 00421 75049151/5; *Fax:* 00421 75 049554.

International matches 1999
Bulgaria (a) 0-2, Romania (a) 0-0, Hungary (h) 0-0, Bulgaria (h) 2-0, Portugal (a) 0-1, Hungary (a) 1-0, Israel (h) 1-0, Romania (h) 1-5, Liechtenstein (h) 2-0, Azerbaijan (a) 1-0, Peru (a) 1-2, Colombia (a) 0-1, Guatemala (a) 1-0, Costa Rica (a) 0-4.

League Championship wins (1939-44; 1994–2000)
Slovan Bratislava 8; Kosice 2; Bystrica 1; OAP Bratislava 1; Inter 1.

Cup wins (1994–2000)
Inter 2; Slovan Bratislava 2; Tatran Presov 1; Humenne 1; Spartak Trnava 1.

Final League Table 1998–2000

	P	W	D	L	F	A	Pts
Inter	30	21	7	2	65	16	70
Kosice	30	19	4	7	57	31	61
Slovan Bratislava	30	16	9	5	52	18	57
Spartak Trnava	30	15	8	7	38	21	53
Odu Trencin	30	13	8	9	38	29	47
Tatran Presov	30	14	5	11	38	42	47
Ruzomberok	30	13	7	10	29	26	46
Zilina	30	12	5	13	39	37	41
Petrzalka	30	11	6	13	43	48	39
Koba*	30	9	10	11	33	36	37
Humenne*	30	10	7	13	31	43	37
Dubnica*	30	9	7	14	25	35	34
Nitra*	30	8	4	18	24	44	28
Streda*	30	6	9	15	24	42	27
Dukla Bystrica*	30	7	2	21	27	53	23
Prievidza*	30	6	4	20	29	71	22

Top scorer: Nemeth (Inter) 16.
Cup Final: Inter 1, Kosice 1.
Inter won 4-2 on penalties.

SLOVENIA

Football Association of Slovenia, P.P. 3986, 1001 Ljubljana, Slovenia.
Founded: 1920; *Number of Clubs:* 375; *Number of Players:* 20,117; *National Colours:* White shirts, green shorts, white stockings.
Telephone: 00386 61 1611500; *Fax:* 00386 61 612220.

International matches 1999
Switzerland (a) 0-2, Oman (h) 7-0, Georgia (a) 1-1, Finland (h) 1-1, Latvia (a) 1-1, Albania (a) 1-0, Albania (h) 2-0, Georgia (h) 2-1, Norway (a) 0-4, Greece (h) 0-3, Ukraine (h) 1-1.

League Championship wins (1992–2000)
SCT Olimpija 4; Maribor 4; Gorica 1.

Cup wins (1992–2000)
Maribor 4; SCT Olimpija 3; Mura 1; Rudar 1.

Final League Table 1999–2000

	P	W	D	L	F	A	Pts
Maribor Teatanic	33	25	6	2	90	29	81
Gorica	33	19	5	9	55	34	62
Rudar	33	17	7	9	48	35	58
Korotan	33	15	7	11	58	43	52
Primorje	33	13	11	9	56	49	50
Publikum	33	11	14	8	53	45	47
Olimpija	33	14	4	15	64	58	46
Dravograd	33	11	10	12	44	54	43
Domzale	33	11	8	14	50	51	41
Mura	33	10	6	17	47	53	36
Ruse*	33	4	6	23	26	73	18
Beltinci*	33	3	6	24	21	88	15

Top scorer: Bozgo (Maribor) 24.
Cup Final: Korotan 2, 0, Olimpija 1, 2.

SPAIN

Real Federacion Espanola De Futbol, Calle Alberto Bosch 13, Apartado Postal 347, E-28014 Madrid.
Founded: 1913; *Number of Clubs:* 10,240; *Number of Players:* 408,135; *National Colours:* Red shirts, blue shorts, blue stockings with red, blue & yellow border.
Telephone: 0034 91 420 1362; *Cable:* FUTBOL MADRID; *Fax:* 0034 91 420 2094.

International matches 1999
Austria (h) 9-0, San Marino (a) 6-0, Croatia (h) 3-1, San Marino (h) 9-0, Croatia (h) 2-2, Poland (a) 2-1, Austria (a) 3-1, Cyprus (h) 8-0, Israel (h) 3-0, Brazil (h) 0-0, Argentina (h) 0-2.

League Championship wins (1929-36; 1940–2000)
Real Madrid 27; Barcelona 16; Atletico Madrid 9; Athletic Bilbao 8; Valencia 4; Real Sociedad 2; Real Betis 1; Seville 1; La Coruna 1.

Cup wins (1902–2000)
Barcelona 24; Athletic Bilbao 23; Real Madrid 17; Atletico Madrid 9; Valencia 6; Real Zaragoza 4; Real Union de Irun 3; Seville 3; Espanyol 3; Arenas 1; Ciclista Sebastian 1; Racing de Irun 1; Vizcaya Bilbao 1; Real Betis 1; Real Sociedad 1, La Coruna 1.

Final League Table 1999–2000

	P	W	D	L	F	A	Pts
La Coruna	38	21	6	11	66	44	69
Barcelona	38	19	7	12	70	46	64
Valencia	38	18	10	10	59	39	64
Zaragoza	38	16	15	7	60	40	63
Real Madrid	38	16	14	8	58	48	62
Alaves	38	17	10	11	41	37	61
Celta	38	15	8	15	45	43	53
Valladolid	38	14	11	13	36	44	53
Rayo Vallecano	38	15	7	16	51	53	52
Mallorca	38	14	9	15	52	45	51
Athletic Bilbao	38	12	14	12	47	57	50
Malaga	38	11	15	12	55	50	48
Espanyol	38	12	11	15	51	48	47
Real Sociedad	38	11	14	13	42	49	47
Santander	38	10	16	12	52	50	46
Numancia	38	11	12	15	47	59	45
Oviedo	38	11	12	15	44	60	45
Betis*	38	11	9	18	33	56	42
Atletico Madrid*	38	9	11	18	48	64	38
Seville*	38	5	13	20	42	67	28

Top scorer: Salva (Santander) 27.
Cup Final: Espanyol 2, Atletico Madrid 1

SWEDEN

Svenska Fotbollfoerbundet, Box 1216, S-17123 Solna.
Founded: 1904; *Number of Clubs:* 3,250; *Number of Players:* 485,000; *National Colours:* Yellow shirts, blue shorts, yellow stockings.
Telephone: 0046 8 735 09 00; *Cable:* FOOTBALL-S; *Fax:* 0046 8 27 51 47.

International matches 1999

Tunisia (a) 1-0, Luxembourg (h) 2-0, Poland (a) 1-0, Republic of Ireland (a) 0-2, Jamaica (h) 2-1, England (a) 0-0, Austria (h) 0-0, Bulgaria (h) 1-0, Luxembourg (a) 1-0, Poland (h) 2-0, South Africa (a) 0-1.

League Championship wins (1896–1999)

IFK Gothenburg 18; Oergryte IS Gothenburg 14; Malmo FF 14; IFK Norrköping 11; AIK Stockholm 10; Djurgaarden 8; GAIS Gothenburg 6; IF Helsingborg 6; Boras IF Elfsborg 4; Oster Vaxjo 4; Halmstad 3; Atvidaberg 2; IFK Ekilstune 1; IF Gavic Brynas 1; IF Gothenburg 1; Fassbergs 1; Norrköping IK Sleipner 1.

Cup wins (1941–2000)

Malmo FF 13; AIK Stockholm 7; IFK Norrköping 6; IFK Gothenburg 4; Atvidaberg 2; Kalmar 2; Helsingborg 2; GAIS Gothenburg 1; IF Raa 1; Landskrona 1; Oster Vaxjo 1; Djurgaarden 1; Degerfors 1, Halmstad 1, Orgryte 1.

Final League Table 1999

	P	W	D	L	F	A	Pts
Helsingborg	26	17	3	6	44	24	54
AIK	26	16	5	5	42	14	53
Halmstad	26	14	6	6	43	22	48
Orgryte	26	11	10	5	41	23	43
Norrköping	26	11	6	9	41	36	39
IFK Gothenburg	26	11	5	10	27	33	38
Vastra	26	9	7	10	30	33	34
Trelleborg	26	9	6	11	39	47	33
Elfsborg	26	9	5	12	41	48	32
Hammarby	26	8	5	13	32	42	29
Kalmar	26	8	4	14	27	41	28
Orebro	26	8	3	15	24	36	27
Malmo*	26	7	4	15	30	48	25
Djurgaarden*	26	5	9	12	27	41	24

Top scorer: Allback (Orgryte) 15.
Cup Final: Orgryte 0, 2, AIK Stockholm 1, 0 .

SWITZERLAND

Schweizerisher Fussballverband, Postfach 3000 Berne 15. *Founded:* 1895; *Number of Clubs:* 1,473; *Number of Players:* 185,286; *National Colours:* Red shirts, white shorts, red stockings.
Telephone: 0041 31 950 81 11; *Cable:* SWISSFOOT BERNE; *Fax:* 0041 31 950 81 81.

International matches 1999

Slovenia (h) 2-0, Oman (a) 2-1, Austria (h) 2-4, Belarus (a) 1-0, Wales (h) 2-0, Greece (a) 1-1, Italy (h) 0-0, Czech Republic (a) 0-3, Denmark (a) 1-2, Belarus (h) 2-0, Wales (a) 2-0.

League Championship wins (1898–2000)

Grasshoppers 24; Servette 17; Young Boys Berne 11; FC Zurich 9; FC Basle 8; Lausanne 7; La Chaux-de-Fonds 3; FC Lugano 3; Winterthur 3; FX Aarau 3; Neuchatel Xamax 3; Sion 2; St Gallen 2; FC Anglo-American 1; FC Brühl 1; Cantonal-Neuchatel 1; Biel 1; Bellinzona 1; FC Etoile Le Chaux-de-Fonds 1; Lucerne 1.

Cup wins (1926–2000)

Grasshoppers 18; FC Sion 9; Lausanne 9; La Chaux-de-Fonds 6; Young Boys Berne 6; Servette 6; FC Zurich 6; FC Basle 5; Lucerne 2; FC Lugano 2; FC Granges 1; St Gallen 1; Urania Geneva 1; Young Fellows Zurich 1; Aarau 1.

Qualifying Table 1999–2000

	P	W	D	L	F	A	Pts
St Gallen	22	13	6	3	42	15	45
Basle	22	9	10	3	31	21	37
Lausanne	22	9	9	4	35	25	36
Grasshoppers	22	9	7	6	40	25	34
Yverdon	22	7	9	6	28	25	30
Lucerne	22	8	4	10	28	29	28
Servette	22	8	4	10	32	36	28
Zurich	22	6	9	7	22	27	27
Neuchatel Xamax	22	6	8	8	32	34	26
Aarau	22	7	5	10	30	42	26
Lugano	22	5	6	11	27	34	21
Delemont	22	4	5	13	24	48	17

Final Table 1999–2000

	P	W	D	L	F	A	Pts
St Gallen	14	9	4	1	33	14	54
Lausanne	14	8	2	4	22	13	44
Basle	14	5	6	3	16	16	40
Grasshoppers	14	5	5	4	30	26	37
Servette	14	4	5	5	25	21	31
Lucerne	14	5	2	7	17	30	31
Neuchatel Xamax	14	4	3	7	25	29	29
Yverdon	14	2	1	11	16	35	22

Teams take half points from qualifying table.

Promotion/Relegation Table 1999–2000

	P	W	D	L	F	A	Pts
Lugano	14	8	4	2	26	18	28
Sion	14	7	3	4	28	19	24
Zurich	14	7	3	4	17	12	24
Aarau	14	6	4	4	23	16	22
Bellinzona	14	4	8	2	21	14	20
Thun	14	4	4	6	17	18	16
Delemont	14	4	2	8	18	29	14
Baden	14	1	2	11	7	31	5

Top scorer: Amoah (St Gallen) 25.
Cup Final: Zurich 2, Lausanne 2 aet.
Zurich won 3-0 on penalties.

TURKEY

Turkiye Futbol Federasyonu, Konaklar Mah. Ihlamurlu Sok. 9, 80620 4 Levent, Istanbul.
Founded: 1923; *Number of Clubs:* 230; *Number of Players:* 64,521; *National Colours:* White shirts, white shorts, red and white stockings.
Telephone: 0090 212 282 70 10; *Cable:* ISTANBUL FUTBOL SPOR; *Telex:* 46308 btff tr; *Fax:* 0090 212 282 70 15.

International matches 1999

Moldova (h) 2-0, Finland (a) 4-2, Northern Ireland (a) 3-0, Moldova (a) 1-1, Germany (a) 0-0, Republic of Ireland (a) 1-1, Republic of Ireland (h) 0-0.

League Championship wins (1960–2000)

Galatasaray 14; Fenerbahce 13; Besiktas 10; Trabzonspor 6.

Cup wins (1963–2000)

Galatasaray 13; Besiktas 6; Trabzonspor 5; Fenerbahce 4; Goztepe Izmir 2; Altay Izmir 2; Ankaragucu 2; Eskisehirspor 1; Bursapor 1; Genclerbirligi 1; Sakaryaspor 1; Kocaeli 1.

Final League Table 1999–2000

	P	W	D	L	F	A	Pts
Galatasaray	34	24	7	3	77	23	79
Besiktas	34	23	6	5	74	27	75
Gaziantep	34	17	11	6	49	27	62
Fenerbahce	34	17	10	7	59	44	61
Genclerbirligi	34	16	8	10	57	47	56
Trabzonspor	34	15	8	11	47	41	53
Samsun	34	16	4	14	51	43	52
Denizli	34	13	8	13	55	57	47
Adana	34	13	6	15	51	55	45
Bursa	34	12	6	16	51	63	42
Antalya	34	11	8	15	42	58	41
Kocaeli	34	11	7	16	44	58	40
Ankaragucu	34	9	12	13	45	56	39
Erzurum	34	10	8	16	40	61	38
Istanbul	34	8	13	13	38	43	37
Altay*	34	10	7	17	34	43	37
Goztepe*	34	7	5	22	26	54	26
Van*	34	4	6	24	38	78	18

Top scorer: Aykut (Samsun) 30.
Cup Final: Galatasaray 5, Antalya 3 aet.

UKRAINE

Football Federation of Ukraine, Ulianovyh Street 1, P.O. Box 503, 252150 Kiev, Ukraine.
Founded: 1991; *Number of Clubs:* 1500; *Number of Players:* 759,500; *National Colours:* Yellow and blue shirts, blue shorts, yellow stockings.

Telephone: 00380 44 2528498; *Fax:* 00380 44 2528513 (or) 2692550; *Telex:* 631461 uff ux.

International matches 1999
Georgia (a) 1-0, France (a) 0-0, Iceland (h) 1-1, Andorra (h) 4-0, Armenia (a) 0-0, Bulgaria (h) 1-1, France (h) 0-0, Iceland (a) 1-0, Russia (a) 1-1, Slovenia (a) 1-2, Slovenia (h) 1-1.

League Championship wins (1992–2000)
Dynamo Kiev 7; Tavria Simferopol 1.

Cup wins (1992–2000)
Dynamo Kiev 5; Chernomorets 2; Shakhtjor Donetsk 2.

Final League Table 1999–2000

	P	W	D	L	F	A	Pts
Dynamo Kiev	30	27	3	0	85	18	84
Shakhtjor Donetsk	30	21	3	6	60	16	66
Krivbas	30	18	6	6	54	30	60
Vorskla	30	14	7	9	50	34	49
Metalurg Zapor	30	12	8	10	43	35	44
Metallist Charkov	30	12	8	10	41	39	44
Metalurg Donetsk	30	11	10	9	39	35	43
Metalurg Mariupol	30	13	3	14	49	48	42
Karpaty	30	12	4	14	39	38	40
CSKA	30	9	8	13	31	36	35
Dnepr	30	8	9	13	29	52	33
Ternopol	30	7	10	13	40	57	31
Simferopol	30	7	8	15	32	51	29
Prekarpate*	30	7	8	15	27	47	29
Chernomorets*	30	6	8	16	20	53	26
Kirovograd*	30	0	9	21	16	66	9

Top scorer: Chatskikh (Dynamo Kiev) 20.
Cup Final: Dynamo Kiev 1, Krivbas 0.

WALES

The Football Association of Wales Limited, Plymouth Chambers, 3 Westgate Street, Cardiff, South Glamorgan CF1 1DD.
Founded: 1876; *Number of Clubs:* 2,326; *Number of Players:* 53,926; *National Colours:* All red.
Telephone: 01222 372325; *Telex:* 497 363 faw g; *Cable:* WELSOCCER CARDIFF; *Fax:* 01222 343961.

YUGOSLAVIA

Yugoslav Football Association, P.O. Box 263, Terazije 35, 11000 Beograd.

Founded: 1919; *Number of Clubs:* 6,532; *Number of Players:* 229,024; *National Colours:* Blue shirts, white shorts, red stockings.
Telephone: 00381 11 323 3447; *Cable:* JUGOFUDBAL BEOGRAD; *Telex:* 11666 fsj yu; *Fax:* 00381 11 323 3433.

International matches 1999
Malta (a) 3-0, Malta (h) 4-1, Croatia (h) 0-0, Republic of Ireland (a) 1-2, Macedonia (h) 3-1, Macedonia (a) 4-2, Croatia (a) 2-2.

League Championship wins (1923–2000)
Red Star Belgrade 21; Partizan Belgrade 16; Hajduk Split 9; Gradjanski Zagreb 5; BSK Belgrade 5; Dynamo Zagreb 4; Jugoslavija Belgrade 2; Concordia Zagreb 2; FC Sarajevo 2; Vojvodina Novi Sad 2; HASK Zagreb 1; Zeljeznicar 1; Obilic 1.

Cup wins (1947–2000)
Red Star Belgrade 18; Hajduk Split 9; Dynamo Zagreb 8; Partizan Belgrade 8; BSK Belgrade 2; OFK Belgrade 2; Rijeka 2; Velez Mostar 2; Vardar Skopje 1; Borac Banjaluka 1.

Final League Table 1999–2000

	P	W	D	L	F	A	Pts
Red Star Belgrade	40	33	6	1	85	19	105
Partizan Belgrade	40	32	5	3	111	30	101
Obilic	40	28	5	7	71	32	89
Rad	40	17	9	14	56	46	60
Sutjeska	40	17	9	14	50	50	60
Cukaricki	40	15	11	14	42	43	56
OFK Belgrade	40	15	10	15	61	63	55
Zeleznik	40	15	9	16	55	47	54
Zemun	40	15	9	16	47	57	54
Vojvodina	40	15	8	17	55	50	53
Radnicki Nis	40	14	4	20	50	49	52
Buducnost	40	15	7	18	45	45	52
Radnicki Kragujevac	40	13	13	14	35	41	52
Hajduk Kula	40	15	7	18	39	46	52
Milicionar	40	14	9	17	52	52	51
Sartid 1913*	40	14	8	18	42	47	50
Proleter*	40	12	10	18	36	49	46
Hajduk B*	40	14	3	23	56	75	45
Mogren*	40	13	5	22	39	70	44
Spartak*	40	8	5	27	34	86	29
Borac*	40	6	4	30	36	100	22

Top scorer: Kezman (Partizan Belgrade) 28.
Cup Final: Red Star Belgrade 4, Napredak 0.

SOUTH AMERICA

ARGENTINA

Asociacion Del Futbol Argentina, Viamonte 1366/76, 1053 Buenos Aires.
Founded: 1893; *Number of Clubs:* 3,035; *Number of Players:* 306,365; *National Colours:* Light blue & white striped shirts, black shorts, white stockings.
Telephone: 00541 371 4276; *Cable:* FUTBOL BUENOS AIRES; *Telex:* 17848 AFA AR; *Fax:* 00541 375 4410.

International matches 1999
Venezuela (a) 2-0, Mexico (a) 1-0, Holland (a) 1 1, Mexico (h) 2-2, USA (a) 0-1, Lithuania (h) 0-0, Ecuador (n) 3-1, Colombia (n) 0-3, Uruguay (n) 2-0, Brazil (n) 1-2, Brazil (h) 2-0, Brazil (a) 2-4, Colombia (h) 2-1, Spain (a) 2-0.

BOLIVIA

Federacion Boliviana De Futbol, Av. Libertador Bolivar No. 1168, Casilla de Correo 484, Cochabamba, Bolivia.
Founded: 1925; *Number of Clubs:* 305; *Number of Players:* 15,290; *National Colours:* Green shirts with white borders, white shorts with green borders, green stockings.
Telephone: 0059142 44982; *Cable:* FEDFUTBOL COCHABAMBA; *Telex:* 6239 FEDBOL; *Fax:* 0059142 82132.

International matches 1999
USA (h) 0-0, Jamaica (h) 0-0, Guatemala (a) 3-0, Paraguay (h) 0-3, Mexico (a) 1-2, Guatemala (h) 1-2,

Chile (h) 1-1, Chile (a) 0-1, Paraguay (n) 0-0, Peru (n) 0-1, Japan (n) 1-1, Egypt (n) 2-2, Saudi Arabia (n) 0-0, Mexico (n) 0-1, Venezuela (h) 0-0, Paraguay (a) 0-0.

BRAZIL

Confederacao Brasileira De Futebol, Rua Da Alfandega, 70, P.O. Box 1078, 20.070 Rio De Janeiro.
Founded: 1914; *Number of Clubs:* 12,987; *Number of Players:* 551,358; *National Colours:* Yellow shirts with green collar/cuffs, blue shorts, white stockings with green-yellow border.
Telephone: 005521 509 5937; *Cable:* DESPORTOS RIO DE JANEIRO; *Telex:* 21509 CBDS BR; *Fax:* 005521 252 9294.

International matches 1999
South Korea (a) 0-1, Japan (a) 2-0, Holland (h) 2-2, Holland (h) 3-1, Latvia (h) 3-0, Venezuela (n) 7-0, Mexico (n) 2-1, Chile (n) 2-1, Argentina (n) 2-1, Mexico (n) 2-0, Uruguay (n) 3-0, Germany (n) 4-0, USA (n) 1-0, New Zealand (n) 2-0, Saudi Arabia (n) 8-2, Mexico (n) 3-4, Argentina (n) 0-2, Argentina (h) 4-2, Holland (a) 2-2, Spain (n) 0-0.

CHILE

Federacion De Futbol De Chile, Avda. Quillin No. 5635, Casilla postal 3733, Correo Central, Santiago de Chile.
Founded: 1895; *Number of Clubs:* 4,598; *Number of*

Players: 609,724; *National Colours:* Red shirts with white collar & cuffs, blue shorts, white stockings.
Telephone: 00562 2849000; *Cable:* FEDFUTBOL SANTIAGO DE CHILE; *Fax:* 00562 2843510.

International matches 1999
Guatemala (a) 1-1, USA (a) 1-2, Bolivia (a) 1-1, Costa Rica (h) 3-0, Bolivia (h) 1-0, Ecuador (h) 0-0, Mexico (n) 0-1, Venezuela (n) 3-0, Brazil (n) 1-2, Colombia (n) 3-2, Uruguay (n) 1-1, Mexico (n) 1-2.

COLOMBIA

Federacion Colombiana De Futbol, Avenida 32, No. 16-22 piso 40. Apartado Aereo 17602, Santafe de Bogota.
Founded: 1924; *Number of Clubs:* 3,685; *Number of Players:* 188,050; *National Colours:* Yellow shirts with tricolour borders, blue shorts, Red stockings with tricolour borders.
Telephone: 00571 2853320; *Cable:* COLFUTBOL BOGOTA; *Fax:* 00571 2889740.

International matches 1999
Denmark (h) 1-1, Germany (a) 3-3, Venezuela (a) 0-0, Venezuela (a) 1-1, Paraguay (a) 2-0, El Salvador (a) 1-2, Peru (h) 3-3, Paraguay (a) 1-2, Uruguay (n) 1-0, Argentina (n) 3-0, Ecuador (n) 2-1, Chile (n) 2-3, Trinidad & Tobago (a) 3-4, Argentina (a) 1-2, Mexico (a) 0-0, Slovakia (h) 1-0.

ECUADOR

Federacion Ecuatoriana del Futbol, km 4 via a la Costa (Avda. del Bombero), Guayaquil.
Founded: 1925; *Number of Clubs:* 170; *Number of Players:* 15,700; *National Colours:* Yellow shirts with blue and red fringes, blue shorts, red stockings.
Telephone: 005934 352 372/3; *Cable:* ECUAFUTBOL GUAYAQUIL; *Fax:* 005934 352 116.

International matches 1999
Costa Rica (a) 0-0, Denmark (h) 1-1, Guatemala (a) 0-0, Peru (a) 2-1, Peru (h) 1-2, Mexico (a) 0-0, Venezuela (h) 0-2, Iran (h) 1-1, Guatemala (a) 3-1, Canada (a) 2-1, Venezuela (a) 2-3, Chile (a) 0-0, Argentina (n) 1-3, Uruguay (n) 1-2, Colombia (n) 1-2, Uruguay (a) 0-0, Mexico (a) 0-0.

PARAGUAY

Asociacion Paraguaya de Futbol, Estadio De Sajonia, Calles Mayor Martinez Y Alejo Garcia, Asuncion.
Founded: 1906; *Number of Clubs:* 1,500; *Number of Players:* 140,000; *National Colours:* Red & white shirts, blue shorts, blue stockings.
Telephone: 0059521 480120; *Telex:* 38009 PY FUTBOL; *Fax:* 0059521 480124.

International matches 1999
Republic of Ireland (a) 0-2, Guatemala (a) 3-2, Jamaica (h) 3-1, Bolivia (a) 3-0, Jamaica (a) 0-3, Colombia (h) 0-2,

Mexico (h) 2-1, Uruguay (h) 2-3, Colombia (h) 2-1, Bolivia (h) 0-0, Japan (h) 4-0, Peru (h) 1-0, Uruguay (h) 1-1, Mexico (a) 1-0, Guatemala (a) 0-0, Bolivia (h) 0-0, Uruguay (a) 1-0.

PERU

Federacion Peruana De Futbol, Av. Aviacion Cdra. 20 s/n, San Luis, Lima.
Founded: 1922; *Number of Clubs:* 10,000; *Number of Players:* 325,650; *National Colours:* White shirts with red stripe, white shorts with red lines, white stockings with red line.
Telephone: 00511 2258236-9; *Cable* FEPEFUTBOL LIMA; *Fax:* 00511 2258240; *Telex:* 20066 FEPEFUT PE.

International matches 1999
Ecuador (h) 1-2, Ecuador (a) 2-1, Belgium (n) 1-1, Japan (n) 0-0, Colombia (a) 3-3, Venezuela (a) 0-3, Venezuela (h) 3-0, Japan (n) 3-2, Bolivia (n) 1-0, Paraguay (n) 0-1, Mexico (n) 3-3, Slovakia (h) 2-1, Honduras (h) 0-0.

URUGUAY

Asociacion Uruguaya De Futbol, Guayabo 1531, 11200 Montevideo.
Founded: 1900; *Number of Clubs:* 1,091; *Number of Players:* 134,310; *National Colours:* Sky blue shirts with white collar/cuffs, black shorts, black stockings with sky blue borders.
Telephone: 005982 4007101/06; *Cable:* FOOTBALL MONTEVIDEO; *Fax:* 005982 4007873; *Telex:* AUF UY 22607.

International matches 1999
Paraguay (a) 3-2, Colombia (n) 0-1, Ecuador (n) 2-1, Argentina (n) 0-2, Paraguay (n) 1-1, Chile (n) 1-1, Brazil (n) 0-3, Costa Rica (h) 5-4, Venezuela (h) 2-0, Ecuador (h) 0-0, Paraguay (h) 0-1.

VENEZUELA

Federacion Venezolana De Futbol, Avda S. Erminy, Torre Mega II Pent House B, e/Sabana Gr. y la Solano, Parroquia el Recreo, Caracas.
Founded: 1926; *Number of Clubs:* 1,753; *Number of Players:* 63,175; *National Colours:* Dark red shirts, white shorts, white stockings with black border.
Telephone: 00582 7620362; *Cable:* FEVEFUTBOL CARACAS; *Telex:* 26140 FVFCS VC; *Fax:* 00582 7620596.

International matches 1999
Denmark (h) 1-1, Argentina (h) 0-2, Colombia (h) 0-0, Colombia (h) 1-1, Ecuador (a) 2-0, Ecuador (h) 3-2, Peru (h) 3-0, Peru (a) 0-3, Brazil (n) 0-7, Chile (n) 0-3, Mexico (n) 1-3, Bolivia (a) 0-0, Uruguay (a) 0-2, Haiti (a) 2-3.

ASIA

AFGHANISTAN

Afghanistan Football Federation, c/o Afghanistan Olympic Committee, P.O. Box 1824, Kabul.
Founded: 1933; Number of Clubs: 30; Number of Players: 3,300; National Colours: All white with red lines.
Telephone: 0093 11420579; *Cable:* OLYMPIC KABUL.

BAHRAIN

Bahrain Football Association, P.O. Box 5464, Manama.
Founded: 1957; *Number of Clubs:* 25; *Number of Players:* 2,030; *National Colours:* All red.
Telephone: 00973 252929; *Cable:* BAHKORA BAHRAIN; *Telex:* 9040 FAB BN; *Fax:* 00973 255560.

BANGLADESH

Bangladesh Football Federation, National Stadium-1, Dhaka 1000.
Founded: 1972; *Number of Clubs:* 1,265; *Number of Players:* 30,385; *National Colours:* Orange shirts, white shorts, green stockings.
Telephone: 008802 9556072; *Cable:* FOOTBALFED DHAKA; *Fax:* 008802 9563419.

BRUNEI

The Football Association of Brunei Darussalam, P.O. Box 2010, 1920 Bandar Seri Begawan.
Founded: 1959; *Number of Clubs:* 22; *Number of Players:* 830; *National Colours:* Yellow shirts, black shorts, yellow stockings.
Telephone: 006732 383883; *Cable:* BAFA BRUNEI; *Telex:* BU 2575 Attn: BAFA; *Fax:* 006732 382900.

CAMBODIA

Cambodian Football Federation, PO Box 2327 PTT, Phnom-Penh 3.
Founded: 1933; *Number of Clubs:* 30; *Number of Players:* 650; *National Colours:* Blue, red and white shirts, white and blue shorts, red, white and blue stockings.
Telephone: 0085523 364889; *Cable:* CFF PHNOM PENH; *Fax:* 0088523 367191.

CHINA PR

Football Association of The People's Republic of China, 9 Tiyuguan Road, Beijing 100763.
Founded: 1924; *Number of Clubs:* 1,045; *Number of Players:* 2,250,000; *National Colours:* All white.

Telephone: 008610 67117019; *Cable:* SPORTSCHINE BEIJING; *Telex:* 22034 ACSF CN; *Fax:* 008610 67142533.

CHINA TAIPEI

Chinese Taipei Football Association, 100, Kuang-Fu South Road, Taipei, Taiwan.
Founded: 1936; *Number of Players:* 17,000; *National Colours:* Blue shirts, white shorts, red stockings.
Telephone: 008862 27117710; *Cable:* CTFA Taipei; *Fax:* 008862 27117713.

GUAM

Guam Soccer Association, P.O.Box 5093, Agana, Guam 96932.
Founded: 1975; *National Colours:* Blue shirts, white shorts, blue stockings.
Telephone: 00671 472 1824, 646 9609; *Fax:* 00671 4775424.

HONG KONG

The Hong Kong Football Association Ltd, 55 Fat Kwong Street, Homantin, Kowloon, Hong Kong.
Founded: 1914; *Number of Clubs:* 69; *Number of Players:* 3,274; *National Colours:* All Red.
Telephone: 00852 27129122; *Cable:* FOOTBALL HONG KONG; *Telex:* 40518 FAHKG HX; *Fax:* 00852 27604303.

INDIA

All India Football Federation , Mr KN Mour, Gen. Secretary, Youth Hostel Complex, Paltan Bazar, Guwahati - 781 008, Assam.
Founded: 1937; *Number of Clubs:* 2,000; *Number of Players:* 56,000; *National Colours:* Orange shirts, white shorts, green stockings.
Telephone: 0091361 525109; *Fax:* 0091 361525110.

INDONESIA

All Indonesia Football Federation, Wisma Karsa Pemuda, Jl.Gerbang Pemuda No. 3, PO Box 2305, Jakarta 10023.
Founded: 1930; *Number of Clubs:* 2,880; *Number of Players:* 97,000; *National Colours:* Red shirts, white shorts, red and white stockings.
Telephone: 006221 5722948; *Cable:* PSSI JAKARTA; *Telex:* 65739 PSSI IA; *Fax:* 006221 5734386.

IRAN

IR Iran Football Federation, Shahid Keshvari Sports Complex, Mirdamad Ave., Razan Jonoobi Str., PO Box 15875-6967 Tehran 15875.
Founded: 1920; *Number of Clubs:* 6,326; *Number of Players:* 306,000; *National Colours:* All white.
Telephone: 009821 2258116; *Cable:* FOOTBALL IRAN - TEHRAN; *Telex:* 212691 NOC IR; *Fax:* 009821 2258123.

IRAQ

Iraqi Football Association, Olympic Committee Building, Palestine Street, PO Box 484, Baghdad.
Founded: 1948; *Number of Clubs:* 155; *Number of Players:* 4,400; *National Colours:* All black.
Telephone: 009641 7729990; *Cable:* BALL BAGHDAD; *Telex:* 213409 IRFA IK; *Fax:* 009641 7744475.

JAPAN

Japan Football Association, 2nd Floor, Gotoh Ikueikai Bldg, 1-10-7 Dogenzaka, Shibuya-Ku, Tokyo 150, Japan.
Founded: 1921; *Number of Clubs:* 13,047; *Number of Players:* 358,989; *National Colours:* Blue shirts, white shorts, blue stockings.
Telephone: 00813 34762011; *Cable:* SOCCERJAPAN TOKYO; *Telex:* 2422975 FOTJPN J; *Fax:* 00813 34762291.

JORDAN

Jordan Football Association, P.O. Box 1054, Amman.
Founded: 1949; *Number of Clubs:* 98; *Number of Players:* 4,305; *National Colours:* All white and red.
Telephone: 009626 825450; *Cable:* JORDAN FOOT-BALL ASSN AMMAN; *Fax:* 009626 861530.

KAZAKHSTAN

The Football Association of the Republic of Kazakhstan, 44 Abai Street, 480072 Almaty, Kazakhstan.
Founded: 1914; *Number of Clubs:* 5,793; *Number of Players:* 260,000.
Telephone: 0073272 671885; *Telex:* 251347 TREK SU; *Fax:* 0073272 671885.

KOREA, NORTH

Football Association of The Democratic People's Rep. of Korea, Kumsong-dong 2, Mangyongdae Distr, Pyongyang.
Founded: 1945; *Number of Clubs:* 90; *Number of Players:* 3,420; *National Colours:* All white.
Telephone: 008502 3814164; *Cable:* DPR KOREA FOOTBALL PYONGYANG; *Telex:* 5472 KP; *Fax:* 008502 3814403.

KOREA, SOUTH

Korea Football Association, 110-39, Kyeonji-Dong, Chongro-Ku, Seoul.
Founded: 1928; *Number of Clubs:* 476; *Number of Players:* 2,047; *National Colours:* Red shirts, black shorts, red stockings.
Telephone: 00822 7336764; *Cable:* FOOTBALLKOREA SEOUL; *Telex:* KFASEL K 25373; *Fax:* 00822 7352755.

KUWAIT

Kuwait Football Association, P.O. Box 2029 Safat, 13021 Safat.
Founded: 1952; *Number of Clubs:* 14 (senior); *Number of Players:* 1,526; *National Colours:* Blue shirts, white shorts, blue stockings.
Telephone: 00965 2555851; *Cable:* FOOT KUWAIT; *Fax:* 00965 2549955.

KYRGYZSTAN

Football Association of Kyrgyz Republic, Frunze Street, 503 Bishkek 720040, Kyrgyzstan.
Founded: 1992; *Number of Players:* 20,000; *National Colours:* Red shirts, white shorts, red stockings.
Telephone: 00331 2223507; *Fax:* 00331 2225492.

LAOS

Federation Lao de Football, National Stadium, Vientiane, Laos.
Founded: 1951; *Number of Clubs:* 76; *Number of Players:* 2,060; *National Colours:* Red shirts, white shorts, blue stockings.
Telephone: 0085621 216008/9; *Cable:* FOOTBALL VIENTIANE; *Fax:* 0085621 216008.

LEBANON

Federation Libanaise De Football-Association, P.O. Box 4732, Verdun Street, Bristol, Radwan Centre Building, Beirut.
Founded: 1933; *Number of Clubs:* 105; *Number of Players:* 8,125; *National Colours:* Red shirts, white shorts, red stockings.
Telephone: 009611 347157; *Cable:* FOOTBALL BEIRUT; *Telex:* 21404 LIBALL; *Fax:* 009611 349529; *Internet:* http://www.lebanon-online.com/lfa; *E-mail:* lfa@lebanon-online.com.lb.

MACAO

Associacao De Futebol De Macau (AFM), P.O. Box 920, Macau.
Founded: 1939; *Number of Clubs:* 52; *Number of Players:* 800; *National Colours:* Green shirts, black shorts, green stockings.
Telephone: 00853 71996; *Cable:* FOOTBALL MACAU; *Fax:* 00853 260148.

MALAYSIA

Football Association of Malaysia, Wisma Fam, Tingkat 3, Jalan SS5A/9, Kelana Jaya, 47301 Petaling Jaya, Selangor.
Founded: 1933; *Number of Clubs:* 450; *Number of Players:* 11,250; *National Colours:* All yellow and black.
Telephone: 00603 7763766; *Cable:* FOOTB. PETALING JAYA SELANGO; *Telex:* FAM PJ MA 36701; *Fax:* 00603 7757984.

MALDIVES REPUBLIC

Football Association of Maldives, National Stadium Ghalolhu, Male 20-04.
Founded: 1982; *Number of Clubs: Number of Players:* *National Colours:* Green shirts, white shorts, red stockings.
Telephone: 0096031 7006; *Fax:* 0096031 7005.

MONGOLIA

Mongolia Football Federation, R413, Mongolia Youth Association Building, Baga Toiruu 10, Ulaanbaatar 10.
Telephone & fax: 009761 313145.

MYANMAR

Myanmar Football Federation, Attn Maj. Naw Tawng, Gen. Secr. Youth Training Centre, Thuwunna, Yangon.
Founded: 1947; *Number of Clubs:* 600; *Number of Players:* 21,000; *National Colours:* Red shirts, white shorts, red stockings.
Telephone: 00951 577366; *Cable:* FOOTBALL YANGON; *Telex:* 21253 SPED BM; *Fax:* 00951 571253.

NEPAL

All-Nepal Football Association, Dasharath Rangashala, Tripureshwor, PO Box 2090, Kathmandu.
Founded: 1951; *Number of Clubs:* 85; *Number of Players:* 2,550; *National Colours:* All red.
Telephone: 009771 241367; *Cable:* ANFA KATHMANDU; *Telex:* 2390 NSC NP; *Fax:* 009771 241365.

OMAN

Oman Football Association, P.O. Box 3462, Ruwi Postal Code 112.
Founded: 1978; *Number of Clubs:* 47; *Number of Players:* 2,340; *National Colours:* Red shirts with white sleeves, red/white shorts and stockings.
Telephone: 00968 787638/9; *Cable:* FOOTBALL MUSCAT; *Telex:* FOOTBALL 3223 ON; *Fax:* 00968 787632/33.

PAKISTAN

Pakistan Football Federation, 183, Abu Bakar Block, New Garden Town, Lahore, Pakistan.
Founded: 1948; *Number of Clubs:* 882; *Number of Players:* 21,000; *National Colours:* Green shirts, white shorts, green stockings.
Telephone: 009242 5832786; *Cable:* FOOTBALL LAHORE; *Telex:* 47643 PFF PK; *Fax:* 009242 7281541.

PALESTINE

Palestinian Football Federation, Al-Yarmouk, Gaza.
Telephone: 009727 829433; *Fax:* 009727 857020.

PHILIPPINES

Philippine Football Federation, Room 207 PSC, Administration Building, Rizal Memorial Sports Complex, P. Ocampo Street, Manila.
Founded: 1907; *Number of Clubs:* 650; *Number of Players:* 45,000; *National Colours:* Blue and red shirts, blue shorts, white stockings.
Telephone: 00632 5256502; *Cable:* FOOTBALL MANILA; *Telex:* 65014 POC PACA PN; *Fax:* 00632 5233741.

QATAR

Qatar Football Association, P.O. Box 5333, Doha.
Founded: 1960; *Number of Clubs:* 8 (senior); *Number of Players:* 1,380; *National Colours:* All white.
Telephone: 00974 434455; *Cable:* FOOTQATAR DOHA; *Telex:* 4749 QATFOT DH; *Fax:* 00974 411660.

SAUDI ARABIA

Saudi Arabian Football Federation, Al Mather Quarter (Olympic Complex), P.O. Box 5844, Riyadh 11432.
Founded: 1959; *Number of Clubs:* 120; *Number of Players:* 9,600; *National Colours:* White shirts, green shorts, white stockings.
Telephone: 009661 4822240; *Cable:* KURA RIYADH; *Telex:* 404300 SAFOTB SJ; *Fax:* 009661 4821215.

SINGAPORE

Football Association of Singapore, Jalan Besar Stadium, Tyrwhitt Road, Singapore 207542.
Founded: 1892; *Number of Clubs:* 250; *Number of Players:* 8,000; *National Colours:* All red.
Telephone: 0065 2931477; *Fax:* 0065 2933728.

SRI LANKA

Football Federation of Sri Lanka, No. 2, Old Grand Stand, Race Course, Reid Avenue, Colombo 7.
Founded: 1939; *Number of Clubs:* 600; *Number of Players:* 18,825; *National Colours:* Maroon and gold shirts, white shorts and stockings.
Telephone: 00941 696179; *Cable:* SOCCER COLOMBO; *Telex:* 21537 METALIX CE; *Fax:* 00941 682471.

SYRIA

Syrian Football Federation, Maysaloon St., PO Box 421, Damascus.
Founded: 1936; *Number of Clubs:* 102; *Number of Players:* 30,600; *National Colours:* All white.
Telephone: 0096311 3335866; *Cable:* FOOTBALL DAMASCUS; *Telex:* 411578 SPOFED SY; *Fax:* 0096311 3331511.

TAJIKISTAN

Tajikistan National Football Federation, 44, Rudaki Ave., PO Box 26, 734025 Dushanbe, Tajikistan.
Founded: 1991; *Number of Clubs:* 1,804; *Number of Players:* 71,400; *National Colours:* Green shirts, white shorts, green stockings.
Telephone: 0073772 212363; *Telex:* 116286 SHAKH; *Fax:* 0073772 212447.

THAILAND

The Football Association of Thailand, National Stadium, Rama I Road, Bangkok.
Founded: 1916; *Number of Clubs:* 168; *Number of Players:* 15,000; *National Colours:* All red.
Telephone: 00662 2141058; *Cable:* FOOTBALL BANGKOK; *Telex:* 20211 FAT TH; *Fax:* 00662 2154494.

TURKMENISTAN

Turkmenistan Football Federation, 10 Turkmenbashi Avenue, 744005 Ashgabat, Turkmenistan.
Founded: 1992; *Number of Players:* 75,000; *National Colours:* Green shirts, white shorts, green stockings.
Telephone: 00363 2353739; *Fax:* 00363 2355327; *Telex:* 116175 TINTO SU.

UNITED ARAB EMIRATES

United Arab Emirates Football Association, P.O. Box 916, Abu Dhabi.
Founded: 1971; *Number of Clubs:* 23 (senior); *Number of Players:* 1,787; *National Colours:* All white.
Telephone: 00971 2445600; *Cable:* FOOTBALL EMIRATES ABU DHABI; *Telex:* 22121 UAEFA EM; *Fax:* 00971 2448558.

UZBEKISTAN

Uzbekistan Football Federation, Massiv Almazar Furkat Street 15/1, 700003 Tashkent, Uzbekistan.
Founded: 1946; *Number of Clubs:* 15,000; *Number of Players:* 217,000; *National Colours:* Blue shirts, white shorts, green stockings.
Telephone: 0073712 457106; *Telex:* 116108 PTB SU; *Fax:* 0073712 454948.

VIETNAM

Vietnam Football Federation, 141 Nguyen Thai Hoc Str., Dis Dongda, Hanoi.
Founded: 1962; *Number of Clubs:* 55 (senior); *Number of Players:* 16,000; *National Colours:* All red.
Telephone: 008448 452480; *Cable:* AFBVN, 141 NGUYEN THAI HOC STR.; *Fax:* 008448 233119.

YEMEN

Yemen Football Association, P.O. Box 908, Sana'a.
Founded: 1962; *Number of Clubs:* 26; *Number of Players:* 1750; *National Colours:* All green.
Telephone: 009671 264159. *Cable:* SANA'A FOOTBALL; *Telex:* 2710 YOUTH YE; *Fax:* 009671 263182.

CONCACAF

ANGUILLA

Anguilla Football Association, P.O. Box 608, The Valley, Anguilla, BWI.
National Colours: All blue.
Telephone: 001264 4975214/4972416; *Fax:* 001264 4972326.

ANTIGUA & BARBUDA

The Antigua Football Association, P.O. Box 773, St. John's.
Founded: 1928; *Number of Clubs:* 60; *Number of Players:* 1,008; *National Colours:* Gold shirts, black shorts and stockings.
Telephone: 001268 4624863; *Cable:* AFA ANTIGUA; *Fax:* 001268 4624864.

ARUBA

Arubaanse Voetbal Bond, PO Box 376, Oranjestad, Aruba.
Founded: 1932; *Number of Clubs:* 50; *Number of Players:* 1,000; *National Colours:* Yellow shirts, blue shorts, yellow and blue stockings.
Telephone: 00297 829550; *Cable:* AVB ARUBA; *Fax:* 00297 820624.

BAHAMAS

Bahamas Football Association, P.O. Box N 8434, Nassau, N.P.
Founded: 1967; *Number of Clubs:* 14; *Number of Players:* 700; *National Colours:* Yellow shirts, black shorts, yellow stockings.
Telephone: 001809 3233426; *Cable:* BAHSOCA NASSAU; *Fax:* 001809 3288006.

BARBADOS

Barbados Football Association, P.OI. Box 1362, Bridgetown, Barbados.
Physical address: Hadley Court, Upper Collymore Rock, St. Michael.
Founded: 1910; *Number of Clubs:* 92; *Number of Players:* 1,100; *National Colours;* Royal blue and gold shirts, gold shorts, white, gold and blue stockings.
Tel: 001246 2281707; *Cable:* FOOTBALL BRIDGETOWN; *Fax:* 001246 2286484.

BELIZE

Belize National Football Association, P.O. Box 1742, Belize City.
Founded: 1980; *National Colours:* Red, white and blue shirts and shorts, red stockings.
Telephone: 005012 36563; *Fax:* 005012 36564.

BERMUDA

The Bermuda Football Association, P.O. Box HM 745, Hamilton HM CX.
Founded: 1928; *Number of Clubs:* 30; *Number of Players:* 1,947; *National Colours:* Royal blue shirts, white shorts and stockings.
Telephone: 001809 2952199; *Cable:* FOOTBALL BERMUDA; *Telex:* 3441 BFA BA; *Fax:* 001809 2950773.

BRITISH VIRGIN ISLANDS

British Virgin Islands Football Association, P.O. Box 29, Road Town, Tortola, BVI.
Telephone: 001284 4945655; *Fax:* 001284 4948968.

US VIRGIN ISLANDS

V.I. Soccer Federation, P.O. Box 2618, Kingshill, St. Croix, US.V.I. 00851-2618.
Telephone: 001 340 7737216; *Fax:* 001 340 7739686.

CANADA

The Canadian Soccer Association, Place Soccer Canada, 237 Metcalfe Street, Ottawa, ONT K2P 1R2.
Founded: 1912; *Number of Clubs:* 1,600; *Number of Players:* 224,290; *National Colours:* All red.
Telephone: 001613 2377678; *Cable:* SOCCANADA OTTAWA; *Fax:* 001613 2371516.

CAYMAN ISLANDS

Cayman Islands Football Association, PO Box 178 GT, George Town, Grand Cayman, Cayman Islands W1.
Founded: 1966; *Number of Clubs:* 25; *Number of Players:* 875; *National Colours:* Red shirts, blue shorts, white stockings.
Telephone: 001345 9497822328. *Fax:* 001345 945 7673.

COSTA RICA

Federacion Costarricense De Futbol, Apartado 670-1000, Calle 40, Avda CTL & I, San Jose.
Founded: 1921; *Number of Clubs:* 431; *Number of Players:* 12,429; *National Colours:* Red and white shirts, blue shorts, white stockings.
Telephone: 00506 2221544; *Cable:* FEDEFUTBOL SAN JOSE; *Telex:* 3394 DIDER CR; *Fax:* 00506 2552674.

CUBA

Federacion Cubana De Futbol, c/o Comite Olimpico Cubano, Calle 13 No. 601, Esq. C. Vedado, La Habana, ZP 4.
Founded: 1924; *Number of Clubs:* 70; *Number of Players:* 12,900; *National Colours:* White shirts with red collar & cuffs, dark blue shorts, white and red stockings.
Telephone: 00537 403581; *Cable:* FOOTBALL HABANA; *Telex:* 511332 INDER CU; *Fax:* 00537 409037.

DOMINICA

Dominica Football Association, P.O. Box 372, Roseau, Commonwealth of Dominica.
Founded: 1970; *Number of Clubs:* 30; *Number of Players:* 500; *National Colours:* Emerald green shirts, green shorts, yellow stockings.
Telephone & fax: 001767 4492173.

DOMINICAN REPUBLIC

Federacion Dominicana De Futbol, Apartado De Correos No. 1953, Santo Domingo.
Founded: 1953; *Number of Clubs:* 128; *Number of Players:* 10,706; *National Colours:* Navy blue shirts, white shorts, red stockings.
Telephone: 001809542 6923. *Cable:* FEDOFUTBOL SANTO DOMINGO; *Telex:* 817240; *Fax:* 001809547 5363.

EL SALVADOR

Federacion Salvadorena De Futbol, Av. J.M. Delgado, Col. Escalon, Frente Ctro Espanol, Apartado 1029, San Salvador.
Founded: 1935; *Number of Clubs:* 944; *Number of Players:* 21,294; *National Colours:* Blue shirts, white shorts, blue stockings.
Telephone: 00503 2637525/6; *Cable:* FESFUT SAN SALVADOR; *Fax:* 00503 2637583.

GRENADA

Grenada Football Association, P.O. Box 326, St. Juilles Street, St George's, Grenada, West Indies.
Founded: 1924; *Number of Clubs:* 15; *Number of Players:* 200; *National Colours:* Green & yellow striped shirts, red shorts, yellow stockings.
Telephone & fax: 001473 4401986; *Cable:* GRENBALL GRENADA; *Telex:* 3431 CW BUR.

GUATEMALA

Federacion Nacional De Futbol De Guatemala, Avenida Reforma 1-90 Zona 9, 11 Nivel, Edificio Masval, 01009 Ciudad Guatemala, C.A.
Founded: 1946; *Number of Clubs:* 1,611; *Number of Players:* 43,516; *National Colours:* Blue shirts, white shorts, blue stockings.
Telephone: 005023 314797; *Cable:* FEDFUTBOL GUATEMALA C.A.; *Fax:* 005023 600188.

GUYANA

Guyana Football Association, Lot 65 King Street, P.O. Box 10727 Georgetown.
Founded: 1902; *Number of Clubs:* 103; *Number of*

Players: 1,665; *National Colours:* Green shirts and shorts, yellow stockings.
Telephone & fax: 005922 62641;*Telex:* 2266 RICEBRD GY.

HAITI

Federation Haitienne De Football, P.O. Box 2258, Port-Au-Prince.
Founded: 1904; *Number of Clubs:* 40; *Number of Players:* 4,000; *National Colours:* Blue and red shirts, blue shorts, blue and red stockings.
Telephone: 00509 464509; *Cable:* FEDHAFOOB PORT-AU-PRINCE; *Fax:* 00509 573001.

HONDURAS

Federacion Nacional Autonoma De Futbol De Honduras, Apartado Postal 827, Costa Oeste Del Est. Nac, Tegucigalpa, D. C.
Founded: 1951; *Number of Clubs:* 1,050; *Number of Players:* 15,300; *National Colours:* Blue shirts, white shorts, blue stockings.
Telephone: 00504 231 1432/231 1463/ 232 1897/239 8826; *Cable* FENAFUTH TEGUCIGALPA; *Fax:* 00504 231 1428.

JAMAICA

Jamaica Football Federation, General Secretariat, Room 8, Nat. Arena, Institue of Sports, Independence Park, Kingston 6.
Founded: 1910; *Number of Clubs:* 266; *Number of Players:* 45,200; *National Colours:* Gold shirts, black shorts, gold stockings.
Telephone: 001809 9290484; *Cable:* FOOTBALL JAMAICA KINGSTON; *Telex:* 2224 FEDLASCO JA; *Fax:* 001809 9290483.

MEXICO

Federacion Mexicana De Futbol Asociacion, A.C., Abraham Gonzales 74, Col. Juarez, C.P. 06600, Mexico 6, D.F.
Founded: 1927; *Number of Clubs:* 77 (senior); *Number of Players:* 1,402,270; *National Colours:* Green shirts with white collar, white shorts, red stockings.
Telephone: 00525 5662155; *Cable:* MEXFUTBOL MEX-ICO; *Fax:* 00525 5667580.

MONSERRAT

Monserrat Football Association, P.O. Box 46, Church Road, Plymouth, Monserrat.
Telephone: 001664 4912346; *Fax:* 001664 4912719.

NETHERLANDS ANTILLES

Nederlands Antiliaanse Voetbal Unie, P.O. Box 341, Curacao, N.A.
Founded: 1921; *Number of Clubs:* 85; *Number of Players:* 4,500; *National Colours:* white shirts with red and blue strips, white shorts, red, white and blue stockings.
Telephone: 005999 4627222/4343862; *Cable:* NAVU CURACAO; *Telex:* 1046 ENNIA NA; *Fax:* 005999 4627087/4343837.

NICARAGUA

Federacion Nicaraguense De Futbol, Estadio Futbol Camilo Ortega (Cranshaw), Apdo Postal 976, Managua.
Founded: 1931; *Number of Clubs:* 31; *Number of Players:* 160 (senior); *National Colours:* Blue and white striped shirts, blue shorts, blue and white striped stockings.
Telephone: 005052 680006/7/8; *Cable:* FENIFUT MAN-AGUA; *Fax:* 005052 664134.

PANAMA

Federacion Panamena De Futbol, Apartado Postal 8-391, Zona 8, Panama.

Founded: 1937; *Number of Clubs:* 65; *Number of Players:* 4,225; *National Colours:* Red shirts, blue shorts, white stockings.
Telephone & fax: 00507 2282238.

PUERTO RICO

Federacion Puertorriquena De Futbol, Coliseo Roberto Clemente, P.O. Box 1944355, Hato Rey, P.R. 00919-4355.
Founded: 1940; *Number of Clubs:* 175; *Number of Players:* 4,200; *National Colours:* Blue shirts, blue and white shorts and stockings.
Telephone & fax: 001787 7642025.

SAINT LUCIA

St Lucia National Football Association, PO Box 255, Castries, St Lucia.
Founded: 1979; *Number of Clubs:* 100; *Number of Players:* 4,000; *National Colours:* Blue and white shirts, black shorts, blue stockings.
Telephone: 001758 0689; *Cable:* NFU ST. LUCIA; *Telex:* 6394 FOR AFF LC; *Fax:* 001758 2506.

SAINT KITTS & NEVIS

St Kitts-Nevis Football Association, P.O. Box 465, Basseterre, St Kitts, W.I.
Founded: 1932; *Number of Clubs:* 36; *Number of Players:* 600; *National Colours:* Green and yellow shirts, red shorts, yellow stockings.
Telephone: 001869 465 6809; *Cable:* HORSFORD ST. KITTS; *Telex:* 6822 HORSFDSKB KC; *Fax:* 001869 465 1190; *Internet:* www.skbee.com/sknfa; E-mail: sknfa@skbee.com.

SAINT VINCENT & THE GRENADINES

St Vincent & The Grenadines Football Federation, PO Box 1278, Kingstown, St Vincent, W.I.
Founded: 1979; *Number of Clubs:* 500; *Number of Players:* 5,000; *National Colours:* Green shirts with yellow border, blue shorts, yellow stockings.
Telephone: 001784 4561659; *Fax:* 001784 4571659.

SURINAM

Surinaamse Voetbal Bond, Letitia Vriesde Laan 7, P.O. Box 1223, Paramaribo.
Founded: 1920; *Number of Clubs:* 168; *Number of Players:* 4,430; *National Colours:* Red green and white shirts, white or green shorts and stockings.
Telephone: 00597 473112; *Cable:* SVB Paramaribo; *Fax:* 00597 479718.

TRINIDAD AND TOBAGO

Trinidad & Tobago Football Federation, Petrotrin Savannah Building, 9 Queen's Park West, P.O. Box 400, Port of Spain.
Founded: 1908; *Number of Clubs:* 124; *Number of Players:* 5,050; *National Colours:* Red shirts, black shorts, white stockings.
Telephone: 001809 6271011; *Fax:* 001809 6271007.

TURKS & CAICOS

Turks & Caicos Football Association, P.O. Box 180, Providenciales, Turks & Caicos Islands, BWI.
Telephone: 001649 9464650; *Fax:* 001649 9464663.

USA

US Soccer, Soccer House, 1801-1811 S. Prairie Avenue, Chicago, Illinois 60616.
Founded: 1913; *Number of Clubs:* 7,000; *Number of Players:* 1,411,500; *National Colours:* All white.
Telephone: 001312 8081300; *Telex:* 450024 US SOCCER FED; *Fax:* 001312 8081301.

OCEANIA

AMERICAN SAMOA

American Samoa Football Association, P.O. Box 282, Pago Pago.
Telephone: 00684 6882290; *Fax:* 00684 6882291.

AUSTRALIA

Soccer Australia, Sydney Football Stadium, Driver Avenue, P.O. Box 175, Paddington NSW 2021.
Founded: 1961; *Number of Clubs:* 6,816; *Number of Players:* 433,957; *National Colours:* Gold shirts with green trim, gold shorts, gold and green stockings.

Telephone: 0061 293806099; *Cable:* FOOTBALL SYD-NEY; *Fax:* 0061 293806155.

COOK ISLANDS

Cook Islands Football Federation, P.O. Box 29, Avarua, Rarotonga, Cook Islands.
Founded: 1971; *Number of Clubs:* 9; *National Colours:* Green shirts and shorts with golden stripes, gold and green stockings.
Telephone: 00682 21231; *Fax:* 00682 25912.

FIJI

Fiji Football Association, Bob S. Kumar, Hon. Secretary, Government Bldgs, P.O.Box 2514, Suva.
Founded: 1938; *Number of Clubs;* 140: *Number of Players:* 21,300; *National Colours:* White shirts, blue shorts and stockings.
Telephone: 00679 300453; *Fax:* 00679 304642.

NEW ZEALAND

Soccer New Zealand, 51 O'Rorke Road, Penrose, Auckland, New Zealand.
Founded: 1891; *Number of Clubs:* 312; *Number of Players:* 52,969; *National Colours:* White shirts with black trim, white shorts and stockings.
Telephone: 00649 5256120; *Fax:* 00649 5256123.

PAPUA NEW GUINEA

Papua New Guinea Football (Soccer) Association, c/o National Sports Institute, P.O. Box 337, Goroka, EHP 441.
Founded: 1962; *Number of Clubs:* 350; *Number of Players:* 8,250; *National Colours:* Red shirts, black shorts, red stockings.
Telephone: 00675 7321699; *Telex:* TOTOTRA NE 23436; *Fax:* 00675 7321941.

SOLOMAN ISLANDS

Soloman Islands Football Federation, PO Box 854, Honiara, Soloman Islands.
Founded: 1978; *Number of Players:* 4,000; *National Colours:* Green, yellow and blue shirts and shorts, white stockings.
Telephone: 00677 26496; *Telex:* HQ 66349; *Fax:* 00677 26497.

TAHITI

Federation Tahitienne de Football (F.T.F.), B.P.50 358, Pirae, Tahiti, French Polynesia.
Founded: 1989; *National Colours:* White shirts, red shorts, white stockings.
Telephone: 00689 540954; *Cable:* FOOTBALL TAHITI; *Fax:* 00689 419629.

TONGA

Tonga Football Association, P.O. Box 852, Nuku'Alofa, Tonga.
Founded: 1965; *Number of Clubs:* 23; *Number of Players:* 350; *National Colours:* Red shirts, white shorts, red and white stockings.
Telephone: 00676 24442; *Cable:* SOCCER NUKU'ALOFA; *Fax:* 00676 23340; *E-mail:* tfa@kalianet.to.

VANUATU

Vanuatu Football Federation, P.O. Box 226, Port Vila, Vanuatu.
Founded: 1934; *National Colours:* Gold and black shirts, black shorts, gold and black stockings.
Telephone: 00678 25236; *Cable:* FUTBOL BLONG VANUATU; *Fax:* 00678 25236.

WESTERN SAMOA

Samoa Football (Soccer) Association, P.O. Box 960, Apia.
Founded: 1968; *National Colours:* Royal blue shirts, white shorts, royal blue and white stockings.
Telephone: 00685 22822; *Telex:* 233 TREASURY SX; *Fax:* 00685 21312.

AFRICA

ALGERIA

Federation Algerienne De Foot-ball, Chemin Ahmed Ouaked, Boite Postale No. 39, Dely-Ibrahim-Alger.
Founded: 1962; *Number of Clubs:* 780; *Number of Players:* 58,567; *National Colours:* Green shirts, white shorts, green stockings.
Telephone: 002132 365938; *Cable:* FAFOOT ALGER; *Telex:* 61378. *Fax:* 002132 365949.

ANGOLA

Federation Angolaise De Football, Compl. da Cidadela Desportiva, B.P. 3449, Luanda.
Founded: 1979; *Number of Clubs:* 276; *Number of Players:* 4,269; *National Colours:* Red shirts, black shorts, red stockings.
Telephone: 002442 364948; *Cable:* FUTANGOLA; *Telex:* 2580 PALANCA AN; *Fax:* 002442 333147.

BENIN

Federation Beninoise De Football, B.P. 965, Cotonou.
Founded: 1962; *Number of Clubs:* 117; *Number of Players:* 6,700; *National Colours:* Yellow shirts, green shorts, red stockings.
Telephone: 00229 330537; *Cable:* FEBEFOOT COTO-NOU; *Telex:* 5245 SONACOP COTONOU; *Fax:* 00229 312485.

BOTSWANA

Botswana Football Association, P.O. Box 1396, Gabarone.
Founded: 1970; *National Colours:* Blue and white shirts, blue, white and black shorts, blue, white and black striped stockings.
Telephone: 00267 300279; *Cable:* BOTSBALL GABARONE; *Telex:* 2977 BD; *Fax:* 00267 300280.

BURKINA FASO

Federation Burkinabe De Foot-Ball, 01 B.P. 57, Ouagadougou 01.
Founded: 1960; *Number of Clubs:* 57; *Number of Players:* 4,672; *National Colours:* Red shirts, green shorts with yellow star, red stockings.
Telephone: 00226 318815; *Cable:* FEDEFOOT OUA-GADOUGOU; *Fax:* 00226 318843.

BURUNDI

Federation De Football Du Burundi, B.P. 3426, Bujumbura.
Founded: 1948; *Number of Clubs:* 132; *Number of Players:* 3,930; *National Colours:* Red shirts, white shorts, green stockings.
Telephone & fax: 00257 212891; *Cable:* FFB BUJA.

CAMEROON

Federation Camerounaise De Football, B.P. 1116, Yaounde.
Founded: 1959; *Number of Clubs:* 200; *Number of Players:* 9,328; *National Colours:* Green shirts, red shorts, yellow stockings.
Telephone: 00237 216662; *Cable:* FECAFOOT YAOUNDE; *Telex:* 8568 JEUNESPO KN; *Fax:* 00237 217403/202784.

CAPE VERDE ISLANDS

Federacao Cabo-Verdiana De Futebol, P.O. Box 234, Praia.
Founded: 1982; *National Colours:* All green.
Telephone & fax: 00238 611362; *Cable:* FUTEBOL PRAIA CV; *Telex:* 6005 ACAS CV.

CENTRAL AFRICAN REPUBLIC

Federation Centrafricaine De Football Amateur, B.P. 344, Bangui.
Founded: 1937; *Number of Clubs:* 256; *Number of Players:* 7,200; *National Colours:* Grey & blue shirts with Nat. emblem and star, white shorts, red stockings with yellow trim.
Telephone: 00236 612433; *Cable:* FOOTBANGUI BANGUI; *Fax:* 00236 615660.

CHAD

Federation Tchadienne de Footbal, B.P. 886, N'Djamena.
Founded: 1962; *National Colours:* Blue shirts, yellow shorts, red stockings.
Telephone: 00235/519204; *Telex:* 5248 kd; *Fax:* 00235/518648.

CONGO

Federation Congolaise De Football, B.P. 4041, Brazzaville.
Founded: 1962; *Number of Clubs:* 250; *Number of Players:* 5,940; *National Colours:* All red.
Telephone: 00242 834885; *Cable:* FECOFOOT BRAZ-ZAVILLE; *Telex:* 5210 KG; *Fax:* 00242 836199.

CONGO DR

Federation Congolaise De Football-Association (FECOFA), P.O. Box 1284, Av. De L'Enseignem. 210, Z/Kasa-Vubu, Kinshasa 1.
Founded: 1919; *Number of Clubs:* 3,800; *Number of Players:* 64,627; *National Colours:* Green shirts, yellow shorts, red stockings.
Telephone & fax: 001212 3769411; *Cable:* FECOFA KIN-SHASA.

DJIBOUTI

Federation Djiboutienne de Football, B.P. 2694, Djibouti.
Founded: 1977; *Number of Players:* 2,000; *National Colours:* Green shirts, white shorts, blue stockings.
Telephone: 00253 342049; *Fax:* 00253 356793.

EGYPT

Egyptian Football Association, 5, Shareh Gabalaya, Guezira, Al Borg Post Office, Cairo.
Founded: 1921; *Number of Clubs:* 247; *Number of Players:* 19,735; *National Colours:* Red shirts, white shorts, black stockings.
Telephone: 00202 3401793; *Cable:* KORA CAIRO; *Telex:* 93506 KORA UN; *Fax:* 00202 3417817.

ERITREA

The Eritrean National Football Federation, P.O. Box 3665, Asmara.
Telephone & fax: 002911 126821.

ETHIOPIA

Ethiopia Football Federation, Addis Ababa Stadium, P.O. Box 1080, Addis Ababa.
Founded: 1943; *Number of Clubs:* 767; *Number of Players:* 20,594; *National Colours:* Green shirts, yellow shorts, red stockings.
Telephone: 002511 514453; *Cable:* FOOTBALL ADDIS ABABA; *Telex:* 21377 NESCO ET; *Fax:* 002511 513345.

GABON

Federation Gabonaise De Football, B.P. 181, Libreville.
Founded: 1962; *Number of Clubs:* 320; *Number of Players:* 10,000; *National Colours:* Green, yellow and blue shirts, blue and yellow shorts, white stockings with tricolour trims.
Telephone: 00241 730460; *Cable:* FEGAFOOT LIBRE-VILLE; *Telex:* 5526 GO; *Fax:* 00241 746047.

GAMBIA

Gambia Football Association, Independence Stadium, Bakau, P.O. Box 523, Banjul.
Founded: 1952; *Number of Clubs:* 30; *Number of Players:* 860; *National Colours:* White shirts with striped band, white shorts, white stockings with red tops.
Telephone: 00220 496980; *Cable:* SPORTS GAMBIA BANJUL; *Telex:* 2262 FISCO GV.

GHANA

Ghana Football Association, P.O. Box 1272, Accra.
Founded: 1957; *Number of Clubs:* 347; *Number of Players:* 11,275; *National Colours:* All yellow.
Telephone: 0023321 666697; *Cable:* GFA ACCRA; *Telex:* 2519 SPORTS GH; *Fax:* 0023321 668590.

GUINEA

Federation Guineenne De Football, P.O. Box 3645, Conakry.
Founded: 1959; *Number of Clubs:* 351; *Number of Players:* 10,000; *National Colours:* Red shirts, yellow shorts, green stockings.
Telephone: 00224 461159; *Cable:* GUINEFOOT CONAKRY; *Telex:* 22302 MJ GE; *Fax:* 00224 411926.

GUINEA-BISSAU

Federacao De Football Da Guinea-Bissau, Rua 4 No. 10-C, Apartado 375, 1035 Bissau- Codex.
Founded: 1974; *National Colours:* All red..
Telephone & fax: 00245 201918; *Cable:* FUTEBOL BIS-SAU.

GUINEA, EQUATORIAL

Federacion Ecuatoguineana De Futbol, Malabo.
Founded: 1986; *National Colours:* All red.
Telephone: 002409 2392; *Cable:* FEGUIFUT MALABO; *Telex:* 9991111 EG; *Fax:* 002409 3353.

IVORY COAST

Federation Ivoirienne De Football, Av. 1 Treichville, 01 B.P. 1202, Abidjan 01.
Founded: 1960; *Number of Clubs:* 84 (senior); *Number of Players:* 3,655; *National Colours:* Orange shirts, white shorts, green stockings.
Telephone: 00225 242301; *Cable:* FIF ABIDJAN; *Telex:* 42344 FIF CI; *Fax:* 00225 257111.

KENYA

Kenya Football Federation, Nyayo National Stadium, P.O. Box 40234, Nairobi.
Founded: 1960; *Number of Clubs:* 351; *Number of Players:* 8,880; *National Colours:* Red, green and white shirts, red, green and black shorts and stockings.
Telephone: 002542 501825/35; *Cable:* KEFF NAIROBI; *Telex:* 24069 SPICERS KE; *Fax:* 002542 501120.

LESOTHO

Lesotho Football Association, P.O. Box 756, Maseru-100, Lesotho.
Founded: 1932; *Number of Clubs:* 88; *Number of Players:* 2,076; *National Colours:* Blue shirts, green shorts, white stockings.
Telephone: 00266 311879; *Cable:* LEFA MASERU; *Telex:* 4493, 4228; *Fax:* 00266 310586.

LIBERIA

Liberia Football Association, 110 Camp Johnson Road, P.O. Box 10-1066, 1000 Monrovia 10.
Founded: 1936; *National Colours:* Red shirts, white shorts, blue stockings.
Telephone: 00231 226284; *Cable:* LIBFOTASS MON-ROVIA; *Telex:* 44220 EXM IBR. *Fax:* 00231 225217.

LIBYA

Libyan Arab Football Federation, 7th October Stadium, P.O. Box 5137, Tripoli.
Founded: 1963; *Number of Clubs:* 89; *Number of Players:* 2,941; *National Colours:* Green shirts, white shorts, green stockings.
Telephone & fax: 0021821 4446610/3339150; *Telex:* 20896 LY.

MADAGASCAR

Federation Malagasy De Football, P. O. Box 4409, Antananarivo 101.
Founded: 1961; *Number of Clubs:* 775; *Number of Players:* 23,536; *National Colours:* Red shirts, white shorts, green stockings.
Telephone: 0026120 2228433; *Telex:* 22265 AROSUR MG; *Fax:* 0026120 2234464.

MALAWI

Football Association of Malawi, P.O. Box 865, Blantyre.
Founded: 1966; *Number of Clubs:* 465; *Number of Players:* 12,500; *National Colours:* Red shirts, red and green shorts, green stockings.
Telephone & fax: 00265 674290; *Cable:* FOOTBALL BLANTYRE; *Telex:* 4526 SPORTS MI.

MALI

Federation Malienne De Football, Stade Mamdou Konate, B.P. 1020, Bamako.
Founded: 1960; *Number of Clubs:* 128; *Number of Players:* 5,480; *National Colours:* Green shirts, yellow shorts, red stockings.
Telephone: 00223 224254; *Cable:* MALIFOOT BAMAKO; *Telex:* 0985 1200 MJ; *Fax:* 00356 245136.

MAURITANIA

Federation De Foot-Ball De La Rep. Islamique. De Mauritanie, B.P. 566, Nouakchott.
Founded: 1961; *Number of Clubs:* 59; *Number of Players:* 1,930; *National Colours:* Green and yellow shirts, yellow shorts, green stockings.
Telephone: 00222 291032 (or) 50424; *Cable:* FOOTRIM NOUAKCHOTT; *Telex:* 577 MTN NKTT RIM; *Fax:* 00222 291031 (or) 50424.

MAURITIUS

Mauritius Football Association, Chancery House, 2nd Floor Nos. 303-305, 14 Lislet Geoffroy Street, Port Louis.
Founded: 1952; *Number of Clubs:* 397; *Number of Players:* 29,375; *National Colours:* Red shirts, white shorts, red

stockings with white tops.
Telephone: 00230 2121418; *Cable:* MFA PORT LOUIS;
Fax: 00230 2084100.

MOROCCO

Federation Royale Marocaine De Football, Av. Ibn Sina,
C.N.S. Bellevue, B.P. 51, Rabat.
Founded: 1955; *Number of Clubs:* 350; *Number of Players:*
19,768; *National Colours:* All red.
Telephone: 002127 672706/08; *Cable:* FERMAFOOT
RABAT; *Telex:* 32940 FERMFOOT M. *Fax:* 002127
671070.

MOZAMBIQUE

Federacao Mocambicana De Futebol, Av. Samora Machel,
11-2, Caixa Postal 1467, Maputo.
Founded: 1978; *Number of Clubs:* 144; *National Colours:*
Red shirts, black shorts, black and red stockings.
Telephone: 002581 300366; *Cable:* MÔCAMBOLA
MAPUTO; *Telex:* 6-747 MCID MO; *Fax:* 002581 300367.

NAMIBIA

Namibia Football Federation, Abraham Mashego Street
8521, Katurua Council of Churches in Namibia, PO Box
1345, Windhoek, Namibia.
Founded: 1990*Number of Clubs:* 244; *Number of Players:*
7320; *National Colours:* All blue, red, green, yellow and
white.
Telephone & fax: 0026461 217621.

NIGER

Federation Nigerienne De Football (Fenifoot), Stade du 29
Juillet, B.P. 10299, Niamey.
Founded: 1967; *Number of Clubs:* 64; *Number of Players:*
1,525; *National Colours:* Orange shirts, white shorts, green
stockings.
Telephone: 00227 725127/722147; *Cable:* FEDERFOOT
NIGER NIAMEY; *Telex:* 5527; *Fax:* 00227 722147/ 734694.

NIGERIA

Nigeria Football Association, Plot 2033, Olusegun
Obasanjo Way, Wuse Zone 7, Abuja, Nigeria.
Founded: 1945; *Number of Clubs:* 326; *Number of Players:*
80,190; *National Colours:* Green shirts, white shorts, green
stockings.
Telephone: 002349 5237326; *Cable:* FOOTBALL ABUJA;
Telex: 26570 NFA NG; *Fax:* 002349 5237327.

RWANDA

Federation Rwandaise De Football Amateur, B.P. 2000,
Kigali.
Founded: 1972; *Number of Clubs:* 167; *National Colours:*
Red, green and yellow shirts, green shorts, red stockings.
Telephone: 00250 84999; *Cable:* FERWAFA KIGALI;
Telex: 22504 PUBLIC RW; *Fax:* 00250 76574.

SENEGAL

Federation Senegalaise De Football, Stade L.S. Senghor,
Route De L'Aeroport De Yoff, B.P. 130 21, Dakar.
Founded: 1960; *Number of Clubs:* 75 (senior); *Number of
Players:* 3,977; *National Colours:* Green shirts, yellow
shorts, red stockings.
Telephone & fax: 00221 8273524; *Cable:* SENEFOOT
DAKAR ; *Telex:* 13048 PUBLIDK SG.

SEYCHELLES

Seychelles Football Federation, P.O. Box 843, People's
Stadium, Victoria-Mahe, Seychelles.
Founded: 1979; *National Colours:* Red and blue shirts, blue
and red shorts, white stockings.
Telephone: 00248 323908 ext. 244; *Fax:* 00248 225468.

ST. THOMAS AND PRINCIPE

Federation Santomense De Futebol, P.O. Box 42, Sao
Tome.
Founded: 1975; *National Colours:* All green and yellow.
Telephone: 0023912 23431; *Telex:* 213 PUBLICÓ STP; *Fax:*
0023912 21365.

SIERRA LEONE

Sierra Leone Football Association, P.O. Box 672, National
Stadium, Brookfields, Freetown.
Founded: 1967; *Number of Clubs:* 104; *Number of Players:*
8,120; *National Colours:* Green, white and blue shirts, white
shorts, blue stockings with white tops.
Telephone & fax: 00232 2224 1872.

SOMALIA

Somali Football Federation, c/o Conf. Afric. de Football, 5
Gabalaya Street, 11567, El Borg, Cairo, Egypt.
Founded: 1951; *Number of Clubs:* 46 (senior); *Number of
Players:* 1,150; *National Colours:* All sky blue and white.
Telephone: 0020 2/3412497; *Cable:* SOMALIA FOOT-
BALL CAIRO; *Telex:* 93162 CAF UN; *Fax:* 0020
2/3420114 (CAF).

SOUTH AFRICA

South African Football Association, First National Bank
Stadium, Nasrec/ PO Box 910, Johannesburg 2000; South
Africa.
Founded: 1991; *Number of Teams:* 51,944; *Number of
Players:* 1,039,880; *National Colours:* Gold and black shirts,
green shorts, white stockings.
Telephone: 002711 4943522; *Fax:* 002711 4943013.

SUDAN

Sudan Football Association, P.O. Box 437, Khartoum.
Founded: 1936; *Number of Clubs:* 750; *Number of Players:*
42,200; *National Colours:* Green shirts, white shorts, green
stockings.
Telephone & fax: 0024911 776633; *Cable:* ALKOURA
KHARTOUM; *Telex:* 23007 KORA SD.

SWAZILAND

National Football Association of Swaziland, P.O. Box 641,
Mbabane.
Founded: 1968; *Number of Clubs:* 136; *National Colours:*
Blue shirts, gold shorts, white stockings.
Telephone: 00268 46852; *Telex:* 2245 EXP WD; *Fax:* 00268
46206.

TANZANIA

Football Association of Tanzania, Uhuru/Shaurimoyo
Road, Karume Memorial Stadium, W.A.O. Box 1574,
Ilala/Dar Es Salaam.
Founded: 1930; *Number of Clubs:* 51; *National Colours:*
Yellow shirts with black stripes, yellow shorts, yellow and
black stockings with horiz. stripe.
Telephone: 0025551 117931; *Cable:* FAT DAR- ES-
SALAAM; *Telex:* 41873 TZ; *Fax:* 0025551 117930.

TOGO

Federation Togolaise De Football, C.P. 5, Lome.
Founded: 1960; *Number of Clubs:* 144; *Number of Players:*
4,346; *National Colours:* White shirts, green shorts, red and
yellow stockings with green stripes.
Telephone: 00228 221412; *Cable:* TOGOFOOT LOME;
Telex: 5015 CNOT TG. *Fax:* 00228 221413.

TUNISIA

Federation Tunisienne De Football, 16 Rue de la Ligue
Arabe, El-Menzah VI, Tunis 1004.
Founded: 1956; *Number of Clubs:* 215; *Number of Players:*
18,300; *National Colours:* Red shirts, white shorts, red
stockings.
Telephone: 002161 233303; *Cable:* FOOTBALL TUNIS;
Telex: 14783 FTFOOT TN; *Fax:* 002161 767929.

UGANDA

Federation of Uganda Football Associations, P.O. Box
22518, Kampala, Uganda.
Founded: 1924; *Number of Clubs:* 400; *Number of Players:*
1,518; *National Colours:* Yellow shirts with black stripes,
black shorts with yellow stripes, yellow and red stockings.
Telephone: 0025641 342731; *Cable:* FUFA LUGOGO STA-
DIUM, KAMPALA; *Telex:* 61605; *Fax:* 0025641 342731.

ZAMBIA

Football Association of Zambia, P.O. Box 34751, Lusaka.
Founded: 1929; *Number of Clubs:* 20 (senior); *Number of
Players:* 4,100; *National Colours:* Copper shirts, black
shorts, copper stockings.
Telephone: 002601 750254; *Cable:* FOOTBALL LUSAKA;
Fax: 002601 225046.

ZIMBABWE

Zimbabwe Football Association, P.O. Box CY 114,
Causeway, Harare.
Founded: 1965; *National Colours:* Green shirts, gold shorts,
green and gold stockings.
Telephone: 002634 731262; *Cable:* SOCCER HARARE;
Telex: 22299 SOCCER ZW; *Fax:* 002634 731265.

THE WORLD CUP 1930-98

Year	Winners		Runners-up		Venue	Attendance	Referee
1930	Uruguay	4	Argentina	2	Montevideo	90,000	Langenus (B)
1934	Italy	2	Czechoslovakia	1	Rome	50,000	Eklind (Se)
	(after extra time)						
1938	Italy	4	Hungary	2	Paris	45,000	Capdeville (F)
1950	Uruguay	2	Brazil	1	Rio de Janeiro	199,854	Reader (E)
1954	West Germany	3	Hungary	2	Berne	60,000	Ling (E)
1958	Brazil	5	Sweden	2	Stockholm	49,737	Guigue (F)
1962	Brazil	3	Czechoslovakia	1	Santiago	68,679	Latychev (USSR)
1966	England	4	West Germany	2	Wembley	93,802	Dienst (Sw)
	(after extra time)						
1970	Brazil	4	Italy	1	Mexico City	107,412	Glockner (EG)
1974	West Germany	2	Holland	1	Munich	77,833	Taylor (E)
1978	Argentina	3	Holland	1	Buenos Aires	77,000	Gonella (I)
	(after extra time)						
1982	Italy	3	West Germany	1	Madrid	90,080	Coelho (Br)
1986	Argentina	3	West Germany	2	Mexico City	114,580	Filho (Br)
1990	West Germany	1	Argentina	0	Rome	73,603	Codesal (Mex)
1994	Brazil	0	Italy	0	Los Angeles	94,194	Puhl (H)
	(Brazil won 3-2 on penalties aet)						
1998	France	3	Brazil	0	St-Denis	75,000	Belqola (Mor)

GOALSCORING AND ATTENDANCES IN WORLD CUP FINAL ROUNDS

Venue	Matches	Goals (av)	Attendance (av)
1930, Uruguay	18	70 (3.9)	434,500 (24,138)
1934, Italy	17	70 (4.1)	395,000 (23,235)
1938, France	18	84 (4.6)	483,000 (26,833)
1950, Brazil	22	88 (4.0)	1,337,000 (60,772)
1954, Switzerland	26	140 (5.4)	943,000 (36,270)
1958, Sweden	35	126 (3.6)	868,000 (24,800)
1962, Chile	32	89 (2.8)	776,000 (24,250)
1966, England	32	89 (2.8)	1,614,677 (50,458)
1970, Mexico	32	95 (2.9)	1,673,975 (52,311)
1974, West Germany	38	97 (2.5)	1,774,022 (46,684)
1978, Argentina	38	102 (2.7)	1,610,215 (42,374)
1982, Spain	52	146 (2.8)	2,064,364 (38,816)
1986, Mexico	52	132 (2.5)	2,441,731 (46,956)
1990, Italy	52	115 (2.2)	2,515,168 (48,368)
1994, USA	52	141 (2.7)	3,567,415 (68,604)
1998, France	64	171 (2.6)	2,775,400 (43,366)

LEADING GOALSCORERS

Year	Player	Goals
1930	Guillermo Stabile (Argentina)	8
1934	Angelo Schiavio (Italy)	
	Oldrich Nejedly (Czechoslovakia)	
	Edmund Conen (Germany)	4
1938	Leonidas da Silva (Brazil)	8
1950	Ademir (Brazil)	9
1954	Sandor Kocsis (Hungary)	11
1958	Just Fontaine (France)	13
1962	Valentin Ivanov (USSR), Leonel Sanchez (Chile),	
	Garrincha, Vava (both Brazil), Florian Albert	
	(Hungary), Drazen Jerkovic (Yugoslavia)	4
1966	Eusebio (Portugal)	9
1970	Gerd Muller (West Germany)	10
1974	Grzegorz Lato (Poland)	7
1978	Mario Kempes (Argentina)	6
1982	Paolo Rossi (Italy)	6
1986	Gary Lineker (England)	6
1990	Salvatore Schillaci (Italy)	6
1994	Oleg Salenko (Russia)	
	Hristo Stoichkov (Bulgaria)	6
1998	Davor Suker (Croatia)	6

FIFA WORLD CUP 2002 FIXTURES

EUROPE
(Members 51, Entries 51)

Fourteen or fifteen teams qualify including France as world champions and play-offs between UEFA and Asia.

Group 1
Yugoslavia, Russia, Switzerland, Slovenia, Luxembourg, Faeroes
02.09.00 Luxembourg v Yugoslavia
02.09.00 Faeroes v Slovenia
02.09.00 Switzerland v Russia
07.10.00 Switzerland v Faeroes
07.10.00 Yugoslavia v Russia
07.10.00 Luxembourg v Slovenia
11.10.00 Russia v Luxembourg
11.10.00 Slovenia v Switzerland
11.10.00 Yugoslavia v Faeroes
24.03.01 Russia v Slovenia
24.03.01 Luxembourg v Faeroes
24.03.01 Yugoslavia v Switzerland
28.03.01 Slovenia v Yugoslavia
28.03.01 Russia v Faeroes
28.03.01 Switzerland v Luxembourg
02.06.01 Slovenia v Luxembourg
02.06.01 Faeroes v Switzerland
02.06.01 Russia v Yugoslavia
06.06.01 Switzerland v Slovenia
06.06.01 Faeroes v Yugoslavia
06.06.01 Luxembourg v Russia
01.09.01 Faeroes v Luxembourg
01.09.01 Switzerland v Yugoslavia
01.09.01 Slovenia v Russia
05.09.01 Yugoslavia v Slovenia
05.09.01 Faeroes v Russia
05.09.01 Luxembourg v Switzerland
06.10.01 Russia v Switzerland
06.10.01 Slovenia v Faeroes
06.10.01 Yugoslavia v Luxembourg

Group 2
Holland, Portugal, Republic of Ireland, Cyprus, Andorra, Estonia
16.08.00 Estonia v Andorra
02.09.00 Andorra v Cyprus
02.09.00 Holland v Republic of Ireland
03.09.00 Estonia v Portugal
07.10.00 Cyprus v Holland
07.10.00 Portugal v Republic of Ireland
07.10.00 Andorra v Estonia
11.10.00 Holland v Portugal
11.10.00 Republic of Ireland v Estonia
15.11.00 Cyprus v Andorra
14.02.01 Portugal v Andorra
24.03.01 Andorra v Holland
24.03.01 Cyprus v Republic of Ireland
28.03.01 Cyprus v Estonia
28.03.01 Andorra v Republic of Ireland
28.03.01 Portugal v Holland
24.04.01 Holland v Cyprus
25.04.01 Republic of Ireland v Andorra
02.06.01 Estonia v Holland
02.06.01 Republic of Ireland v Portugal
06.06.01 Portugal v Cyprus
06.06.01 Estonia v Republic of Ireland
15.08.01 Estonia v Cyprus
01.09.01 Republic of Ireland v Holland
01.09.01 Andorra v Portugal
05.09.01 Holland v Estonia
05.09.01 Cyprus v Portugal
06.10.01 Republic of Ireland v Cyprus
06.10.01 Holland v Andorra
06.10.01 Portugal v Estonia

Group 3
Czech Republic, Denmark, Bulgaria, Iceland, Northern Ireland, Malta
02.09.00 Iceland v Denmark
02.09.00 Northern Ireland v Malta
02.09.00 Bulgaria v Czech Republic
07.10.00 Czech Republic v Iceland
07.10.00 Northern Ireland v Denmark
07.10.00 Bulgaria v Malta
11.10.00 Iceland v Northern Ireland
11.10.00 Malta v Czech Republic
11.10.00 Denmark v Bulgaria
25.03.01 Malta v Denmark
25.03.01 Bulgaria v Iceland
25.03.01 Northern Ireland v Czech Republic
28.03.01 Czech Republic v Denmark
28.03.01 Bulgaria v Northern Ireland
25.04.01 Malta v Iceland
02.06.01 Iceland v Malta
02.06.01 Denmark v Czech Republic
02.06.01 Northern Ireland v Bulgaria
06.06.01 Denmark v Malta
06.06.01 Iceland v Bulgaria
06.06.01 Czech Republic v Northern Ireland
01.09.01 Denmark v Northern Ireland
01.09.01 Malta v Bulgaria
01.09.01 Iceland v Czech Republic
05.09.01 Northern Ireland v Iceland
05.09.01 Czech Republic v Malta
05.09.01 Bulgaria v Denmark
06.10.01 Czech Republic v Bulgaria
06.10.01 Malta v Northern Ireland
06.10.01 Denmark v Iceland

Group 4
Sweden, Turkey, Slovakia, Macedonia, Azerbaijan, Moldova
02.09.00 Slovakia v Macedonia
02.09.00 Azerbaijan v Sweden
02.09.00 Turkey v Moldova
07.10.00 Moldova v Slovakia
07.10.00 Macedonia v Azerbaijan
07.10.00 Sweden v Turkey
11.10.00 Azerbaijan v Turkey
11.10.00 Moldova v Macedonia
11.10.00 Slovakia v Sweden
24.03.01 Turkey v Slovakia
24.03.01 Azerbaijan v Moldova
24.03.01 Sweden v Macedonia
28.03.01 Moldova v Sweden
28.03.01 Slovakia v Azerbaijan
28.03.01 Macedonia v Turkey
02.06.01 Macedonia v Moldova
02.06.01 Sweden v Slovakia
02.06.01 Turkey v Azerbaijan
06.06.01 Azerbaijan v Slovakia
06.06.01 Turkey v Macedonia
06.06.01 Sweden v Moldova
01.09.01 Moldova v Azerbaijan
01.09.01 Slovakia v Turkey
01.09.01 Macedonia v Sweden
05.09.01 Turkey v Sweden
05.09.01 Azerbaijan v Macedonia
05.09.01 Slovakia v Moldova
07.10.01 Sweden v Azerbaijan
07.10.01 Moldova v Turkey
07.10.01 Macedonia v Slovakia

Group 5
Norway, Ukraine, Poland, Wales, Armenia, Belarus
02.09.00 Ukraine v Poland
02.09.00 Norway v Armenia
02.09.00 Belarus v Wales
07.10.00 Poland v Belarus
07.10.00 Armenia v Ukraine
07.10.00 Wales v Norway
10.10.00 Poland v Wales
10.10.00 Norway v Ukraine
10.10.00 Belarus v Armenia
24.03.01 Ukraine v Belarus
24.03.01 Norway v Poland
24.03.01 Armenia v Wales
27.03.01 Poland v Armenia
27.03.01 Wales v Ukraine
27.03.01 Belarus v Norway
02.06.01 Ukraine v Norway
02.06.01 Armenia v Belarus
02.06.01 Wales v Poland
05.06.01 Armenia v Poland
05.06.01 Ukraine v Wales
05.06.01 Norway v Belarus
01.09.01 Wales v Armenia
01.09.01 Belarus v Ukraine
01.09.01 Poland v Norway
04.09.01 Norway v Wales
04.09.01 Belarus v Poland
04.09.01 Ukraine v Armenia
06.10.01 Armenia v Norway
06.10.01 Poland v Ukraine
06.10.01 Wales v Belarus

Group 6
Belgium, Scotland, Croatia, Latvia, San Marino
02.09.00 Latvia v Scotland
02.09.00 Belgium v Croatia
07.10.00 Latvia v Belgium
07.10.00 San Marino v Scotland
11.10.00 Croatia v Scotland
15.11.00 San Marino v Latvia
14.02.01 Belgium v San Marino
24.03.01 Scotland v Belgium
24.03.01 Croatia v Latvia
28.03.01 Scotland v San Marino
25.04.01 Latvia v San Marino
02.06.01 Croatia v San Marino
02.06.01 Belgium v Latvia
06.06.01 San Marino v Belgium
06.06.01 Latvia v Croatia
01.09.01 Scotland v Croatia
05.09.01 Belgium v Scotland
05.09.01 San Marino v Croatia
06.10.01 Scotland v Latvia
06.10.01 Croatia v Belgium

Group 7
Spain, Austria, Israel, Bosnia, Liechtenstein
02.09.00 Bosnia v Spain
03.09.00 Israel v Liechtenstein
07.10.00 Liechtenstein v Austria
07.10.00 Spain v Israel
11.10.00 Israel v Bosnia
11.10.00 Austria v Spain
24.03.01 Bosnia v Austria
24.03.01 Spain v Liechtenstein
28.03.01 Austria v Israel
28.03.01 Liechtenstein v Bosnia
02.06.01 Spain v Bosnia
02.06.01 Liechtenstein v Israel
06.06.01 Austria v Liechtenstein
06.06.01 Israel v Spain
01.09.01 Spain v Austria
01.09.01 Bosnia v Israel
05.09.01 Liechtenstein v Spain
05.09.01 Austria v Bosnia
07.10.01 Bosnia v Liechtenstein
07.10.01 Israel v Austria

Group 8
Romania, Italy, Lithuania, Hungary, Georgia
02.09.00 Romania v Lithuania
02.09.00 Hungary v Italy
07.10.00 Italy v Romania

07.10.00 Lithuania v Georgia	05.09.01 Hungary v Romania	24.03.01 England v Finland
11.10.00 Lithuania v Hungary	06.10.01 Romania v Georgia	28.03.01 Albania v England
11.10.00 Italy v Georgia	06.10.01 Italy v Hungary	28.03.01 Greece v Germany
24.03.01 Hungary v Lithuania		02.06.01 Finland v Germany
24.03.01 Romania v Italy	**Group 9**	02.06.01 Greece v Albania
28.03.01 Georgia v Romania	Germany, England, Greece, Finland,	06.06.01 Greece v England
28.03.01 Italy v Lithuania	Albania	06.06.01 Albania v Germany
02.06.01 Romania v Hungary	02.09.00 Finland v Albania	01.09.01 Albania v Finland
02.06.01 Georgia v Italy	02.09.00 Germany v Greece	01.09.01 Germany v England
06.06.01 Lithuania v Romania	07.10.00 Greece v Finland	05.09.01 Finland v Greece
06.06.01 Hungary v Georgia	07.10.00 England v Germany	05.09.01 England v Albania
01.09.01 Lithuania v Italy	11.10.00 Finland v England	06.10.01 Germany v Finland
01.09.01 Georgia v Hungary	11.10.00 Albania v Greece	06.10.01 England v Greece
05.09.01 Georgia v Lithuania	24.03.01 Germany v Albania	

SOUTH AMERICA
(Members 10, Entries 10)

Four or five teams qualify including play-offs with Oceania

Rio, 28 June 2000, 47,715

Brazil (0) 1 *(Rivaldo 85 (pen))*
Uruguay (1) 1 *(Dario Silva 6)*

Brazil: Dida; Cafu, Antonio Carlos, Aldair, Roberto Carlos, Emerson, Vampeta (Ze Roberto 70), Rivaldo, Ronaldinho (Guilherme 46), Franca, Savio (Alex 46).
Uruguay: Carini; Tais, Lembo, Montero, Rodriguez, Garcia, O'Neill (Giacomazzi 82), Olivera, Dario Silva, Guigou.
Referee: Acosta (Colombia).

Santiago, 28 June 2000, 60,000

Chile (2) 3 *(Caniza 18 (og), Salas 35, Zamorano 78 (pen))*
Paraguay (0) 1 *(Cardoso 71)*

Chile: Tapia; Fuentes, Rojas, Reyes, Villarroel, Maldonado, Tello, Estay, Nunez (Piuzarro 68), Zamorano, Salas.
Paraguay: Chilavert; Caniza, Zelaya, Ayala, Toledo, Quintana, Struway (Gonzalez 46), Paredes, Acuna (Gabilan 37), Santa Cruz (Cardoso 76), Brizuela.
Referee: Martin (Argentina).

Bogota, 28 June 2000, 50,000

Colombia (1) 1 *(Oviedo 27)*
Argentina (2) 3 *(Batistuta 24, 45, Crespo 75)*

Colombia: Oscar Cordoba; Ivan Cordoba, Bermudez, Yepes, Bolano, Oviedo, Rincon, Dinas (Grisales 51)

(Candelo 85), Viveros, Angel, Castillo (Valenciano 58).
Argentina: Bonano; Sensini, Ayala, Samuel, Zanetti, Veron (Lopez G 70), Gonzalez, Ortega (Sorin 86), Simeone, Lopez C, Batistuta (Crespo 70).
Referee: Larrionda (Uruguay).

San Cristobal, 28 June 2000, 7000

Venezuela (2) 4 *(Vitali 23, Moran 38, Savaresse 61, Tortolero 67 (pen))*
Bolivia (0) 2 *(Moreno 49, Baldivieso 59)*

Venezuela: Angelucci; Gimenez, Gonzalez, Alvarado, Martinez, Urdaneta (Echenausi 90), Farias, Tortolero, Vitali, Moran, Savaresse (Galan 72).
Bolivia: Fernandez; Ribera, Etcheverry (Galindo 80), Pena, Sandy, Castillo, Cristaldo, Sanchez, Baldivieso, Suarez (Garcia 73), Botero (Moreno 46).
Referee: Zambrano (Ecuador).

Quito, 29 June 2000, 45,000

Ecuador (0) 2 *(Chala 16, Hurtado E 51)*
Peru (0) 1 *(Pajuelo 76)*

Ecuador: Cevallos; De La Cruz, Hurtado I, Poroso, Ayovi, Abregon, Blandon, Chala, Aguinaga (Burbano 70), Delgado (Graziani 70), Hurtado E (Kaviedes 74).
Peru: Ibanez; Soto, Rebosio, Pajuelo, Olivares (Zuniga 75), Solano, Del Solar, Jayo (Ciurlizza 75), Serrano (Soria 20), Palacios, Pizarro.
Referee: Simon (Brazil).

18.07.00 Uruguay v Venezuela	08.10.00 Argentina v Uruguay	15.08.01 Brazil v Paraguay
18.07.00 Paraguay v Brazil	14.11.00 Paraguay v Peru	15.08.01 Ecuador v Argentina
19.07.00 Bolivia v Chile	14.11.00 Brazil v Colombia	04.09.01 Peru v Uruguay
19.07.00 Argentina v Ecuador	15.11.00 Bolivia v Uruguay	04.09.01 Chile v Venezuela
19.07.00 Peru v Colombia	15.11.00 Venezuela v Ecuador	05.09.01 Argentina v Brazil
25.07.00 Uruguay v Peru	15.11.00 Chile v Argentina	05.09.01 Colombia v Ecuador
25.07.00 Ecuador v Colombia	27.03.01 Peru v Chile	05.09.01 Paraguay v Bolivia
25.07.00 Venezuela v Chile	27.03.01 Ecuador v Brazil	06.10.01 Venezuela v Peru
26.07.00 Brazil v Argentina	27.03.01 Argentina v Venezuela	06.10.01 Brazil v Chile
27.07.00 Bolivia v Paraguay	28.03.01 Uruguay v Paraguay	06.10.01 Paraguay v Argentina
15.08.00 Chile v Brazil	28.03.01 Colombia v Bolivia	06.10.01 Bolivia v Ecuador
15.08.00 Colombia v Uruguay	24.04.01 Venezuela v Colombia	06.10.01 Uruguay v Colombia
16.08.00 Ecuador v Bolivia	24.04.01 Ecuador v Paraguay	07.11.01 Venezuela v Paraguay
16.08.00 Argentina v Paraguay	24.04.01 Chile v Uruguay	07.11.01 Colombia v Chile
16.08.00 Peru v Venezuela	25.04.01 Bolivia v Argentina	07.11.01 Ecuador v Uruguay
02.09.00 Chile v Colombia	25.04.01 Brazil v Peru	07.11.01 Argentina v Peru
02.09.00 Paraguay v Venezuela	02.06.01 Paraguay v Chile	07.11.01 Bolivia v Brazil
03.09.00 Brazil v Bolivia	02.06.01 Peru v Ecuador	14.11.01 Chile v Ecuador
03.09.00 Peru v Argentina	03.06.01 Argentina v Colombia	14.11.01 Peru v Bolivia
03.09.00 Uruguay v Ecuador	03.06.01 Uruguay v Brazil	14.11.01 Uruguay v Argentina
07.10.00 Colombia v Paraguay	03.06.01 Bolivia v Venezuela	14.11.01 Paraguay v Colombia
08.10.00 Bolivia v Peru	14.08.01 Venezuela v Uruguay	14.11.01 Brazil v Venezuela
08.10.00 Venezuela v Brazil	14.08.01 Chile v Bolivia	
08.10.00 Ecuador v Chile	15.08.01 Colombia v Peru	

OCEANIA
(Members 11, Entries 10)

Either one or no team qualifies, play-offs with South America.

Group 1: Australia, Tonga, Fiji, American Samoa, Samoa.

Group 2: New Zealand, Tahiti, Solomon Islands, Vanuatu, Cook Islands.

ASIA
(Members 44, Entries 42)

Four or five teams qualify, including hosts South Korea and Japan plus play-offs with UEFA.

Group 1: Oman, Syria, Laos, Philippines.
Group 2: Iran, Tajikistan, Myanmar, Guam.
Group 3: Qatar, Malaysia, Hong Kong, Palestine.
Group 4: Kuwait, Singapore, Bahrain, Kyrgyzstan.
Group 5: Thailand, Lebanon, Sri Lanka, Pakistan.

Group 6: Iraq, Kazakhstan, Nepal, Macao.
Group 7: Uzbekistan, Jordan, Turkmenistan, Taiwan.
Group 8: UAE, India, Yemen, Brunei.
Group 9: China, Indonesia, Maldives, Cambodia.
Group 10: Saudi Arabia, Vietnam, Bangladesh, Mongolia.

CONCACAF
(Members 35, Entries 35)

Three teams qualify

Preliminary Round
Caribbean Zone 1: Barbados 2, Grenada 2; Grenada 2, Barbados 3; Cuba 4, Cayman Islands 0; Cayman Islands 0, Cuba 0; St Lucia 1, Surinam 0; Surinam 1, St Lucia 0 (Surinam won 3-1 on penalties); Aruba 4, Puerto Rico 2; Puerto Rico 2, Aruba 2.

Caribbean Zone 2: St Vincent & Grenadines 9, US Virgin Islands 0; US Virgin Islands 1, St Vincent & Grenadines 5; British Virgin Islands 1, Bermuda 5; Bermuda 9, British Virgin Islands 0; St Kitts & Nevis 8, Turks & Caicos Islands 0; Turks & Caicos Islands 0, St Kitts & Nevis; Guyana suspended, Antigua and Barbuda w.o.

Caribbean Zone 3: Trinidad & Tobago 5, Netherlands Antilles 0; Netherlands Antilles 1, Trinidad & Tobago 1; Anguilla 1, Bahamas 3; Bahamas 2, Anguilla 1; Dominican Republic 3, Montserrat 0; Montserrat 1, Dominican Republic 3; Haiti 4, Dominica 0; Dominica 1, Haiti 3.

Caribbean Zone 1
Second Round: Cuba 1, Surinam 0; Surinam 0, Cuba 0; Aruba 1, Barbados 3; Barbados 4, Aruba 0.

Third Round: Cuba 1, Barbados 1, Barbados 1, Cuba 1 *(Barbados won 5-4 on penalties).*

Caribbean Zone 2
Second Round: St Vincent & the Grenadines 1, St Kitts & Nevis 0; St Kitts & Nevis 1, St Vincent & the Grenadines 2; Antigua & Barbuda 0, Bermuda 0; Bermuda 1, Antigua & Barbuda 1.
Third Round: Antigua & Barbuda 2, St Vincent & the Grenadines 1; St Vincent & the Grenadines 4, Antigua & Barbuda 0.

Caribbean Zone 3
Second Round: Trinidad & Tobago 3, Dominican Republic 0; Dominican Republic 0, Trinidad & Tobago 1; Haiti 9, Bahamas 0; Bahamas 0, Haiti 4.

Third Round: Trinidad & Tobago 3, Haiti 1; Haiti 1, Trinidad & Tobago 1.

CENTRAL AMERICAN ZONE

Group A: El Salvador 5, Belize 0; Belize 1, Guatemala 2; Guatemala 0, El Salvador 1; Belize 1, El Salvador 3; El Salvador 1, Guatemala 0; Guatemala 0, Belize 0.

Group B: Honduras 3, Nicaragua 0; Nicaragua 0, Panama 2; Panama 1, Honduras 0; Nicaragua 0, Honduras 1; Honduras 3, Panama 1; Panama 4, Nicaragua 0

Inter zone round
Group 1: Cuba 0, Canada 1; Canada 0, Cuba 0.

Group 2: Antigua & Barbuda 0, Guatemala 1.

Group 3: Honduras 4, Haiti 0.

AFRICA
(Members 52, Entries 50)

Five teams qualify

First Round
Group A: Mauritania 1, Tunisia 2; Tunisia 3, Mauritania 0; Guinea Bissau 0, Togo 0; Togo 3, Guinea Bissau 0; Benin 1, Senegal 1; Senegal 1, Benin 0; Cape Verde Islands 0, Algeria 0; Algeria 2, Cape Verde Islands 0; Gambia 0, Morocco 1; Morocco 2, Gambia 0.

Group B: Botswana 0, Zambia 1; Zambia 1, Botswana 0; Madagascar 2, Gabon 0; Gabon 1, Madagascar 0; Lesotho 0, South Africa 2; South Africa 1, Lesotho 0; Sudan 1, Mozambique 0; Mozambique 2, Sudan 1; Swaziland 0, Angola 1; Angola 7, Swaziland 1.

Group C: Sao Tome e Principe 2, Sierra Leone 0; Sierra Leone 4, Sao Tome e Principe 0; Central African Republic 0, Zimbabwe 1; Zimbabwe 3, Central African Republic 1; Equatorial Guinea 1, Congo 3; Congo 2, Equatorial Guinea 1; Libya 3, Mali 0; Mali 3, Libya 1; Rwanda 2, Ivory Coast 2; Ivory Coast 2, Rwanda 0.

Group D: Djibouti 1, Congo DR 1; Congo DR 9, Djibouti 1; Seychelles 1, Namibia 1; Namibia 3, Seychelles 0; Eritrea 0, Nigeria 0; Nigeria 4, Eritrea 0; Mauritius 0, Egypt 2; Egypt 4, Mauritius 2; Somalia 0, Cameroon 3; Cameroon 3, Somalia 0.

Group E: Malawi 2, Kenya 0; Kenya v Malawi abandoned; Tanzania 0, Ghana 1; Ghana 3, Tanzania 0; Uganda 4, Guinea 4; Guinea 3, Uganda 0; Chad 0, Liberia 1; Liberia 0, Chad 0; Ethiopia 2, Burkina Faso 1; Burkina Faso 3, Ethiopia 0.

EUROPEAN FOOTBALL CHAMPIONSHIP
(formerly EUROPEAN NATIONS' CUP)

Year	Winners		Runners-up		Venue	Attendance
1960	USSR	2	Yugoslavia	1	Paris	17,966
1964	Spain	2	USSR	1	Madrid	120,000
1968	Italy	2	Yugoslavia	0	Rome	60,000
	After 1-1 draw					75,000
1972	West Germany	3	USSR	0	Brussels	43,437
1976	Czechoslovakia	2	West Germany	2	Belgrade	45,000
	(Czechoslovakia won on penalties)					
1980	West Germany	2	Belgium	1	Rome	47,864
1984	France	2	Spain	0	Paris	48,000
1988	Holland	2	USSR	0	Munich	72,308
1992	Denmark	2	Germany	0	Gothenburg	37,800
1996	Germany	2	Czech Republic	1	Wembley	73,611
	(Germany won on sudden death)					

EURO 2000 Qualifying Competition

GROUP 1

Minsk, 5 September 1998, 35,000

Belarus (0) 0
Denmark (0) 0

Belarus: Satsunkevich; Yakhimovic, Ostrovski, Shtanyuk, Romashchenko M (Geraschenko 40), Gurenko, Khatskevich, Baranov, Lavrik, Belkevich, Makovski V (Romashchenko MA 89).
Denmark: Schmeichel; Tobiasen, Rieper, Hogh, Heintze, Helveg, Nielsen A, Thomsen, Tomasson (Frederiksen 81), Jorgensen (Andersen 67), Moller (Gravesen 67).
Referee: Dardenne (Germany).

Anfield, 5 September 1998, 23,160

Wales (0) 0
Italy (1) 2 *(Fuser 19, Vieri 76)*

Wales: Jones P; Robinson, Barnard, Symons, Williams, Coleman, Speed, Johnson, Blake (Saunders 66), Hughes M (Savage 80), Giggs.
Italy: Peruzzi; Panucci, Pessotto, Albertini (Di Biagio 68), Cannavaro, Iuliano, Fuser, Dino Baggio, Vieri, Del Piero (Roberto Baggio 74), Di Francesco (Serena 82).
Referee: Hauge (Norway).

Udine, 10 October 1998, 35,247

Italy (1) 2 *(Del Piero 19, 61)*
Switzerland (0) 0

Italy: Buffon; Panucci, Cannavaro, Maldini, Torricelli, Fuser, Dino Baggio, Albertini, Di Francesco (Bachini 63), Inzaghi, Del Piero (Totti 70).
Switzerland: Hilfiker; Wolf (Chassot 68), Vega, Henchoz, Vogel, Wicky (Celestini 86), Sforza, Rothenbuhler, Sesa, Chapuisat, Muller P.
Referee: Sars (France).

Copenhagen, 10 October 1998, 36,009

Denmark (0) 1 *(Frederiksen 57)*
Wales (0) 2 *(Williams 58, Bellamy 86)*

Denmark: Krogh; Tobiasen, Rieper, Hogh, Heintze, Helveg, Frandsen (Gravesen 76), Steen-Nielsen, Jorgensen, Frederiksen, Beck (Sand 65).
Wales: Jones; Savage, Barnard, Williams, Symons, Coleman, Saunders (Robinson 81), Blake (Bellamy 69), Hughes M, Johnson (Pembridge 62), Speed.
Referee: Piller (Hungary).

Cardiff, 14 October 1998, 11,975

Wales (1) 3 *(Robinson 15, Coleman 54, Symons 85)*
Belarus (1) 2 *(Gurenko 21, Belkevich 48)*

Wales: Jones P; Robinson, Barnard, Savage, Symons, Coleman, Saunders, Johnson, Blake, Hughes M, Pembridge.
Belarus: Satsunkevich; Yakhimovic, Ostrovski, Lavrik, Shtanyuk, Baranov (Gerasimets 70), Khatskevich, Geraschenko (Romashchenko MA 88), Gurenko, Belkevich, Makovski V (Katchuro 73).
Referee: Sammut (Malta).

Zurich, 14 October 1998, 12,500

Switzerland (0) 1 *(Chapuisat 58)*
Denmark (0) 1 *(Tobiasen 90)*

Switzerland: Hilfiker; Jeanneret (Rothenbuhler 76), Sforza, Henchoz, Vogel, Wicky, Sesa (Haas 89), Fournier, Celestini, Chapuisat, Muller P (Di Jorio 78).
Denmark: Krogh; Tobiasen, Rieper, Hogh, Heintze, Helveg, Frandsen (Colding 59), Steen-Nielsen, Tomasson (Beck 78), Fredriksen (Sand 61), Jorgensen.
Referee: Radoman (Yugoslavia).

Minsk, 27 March 1999, 44,000

Belarus (0) 0
Switzerland (0) 1 *(Fournier 72)*

Belarus: Tumilovich; Lavrik, Lukhvich, Yakhimovic, Gurenko, Khatskevich, Belkevich, Geraschenko (Skripchenko 86), Baranov (Chaika 56), Romashchenko MA, Makovski V (Ostrovski 87).
Switzerland: Brunner; Hodel, Henchoz, Vogel, Fournier, Jeanneret, Wicky (Muller P 66), Sforza, Sesa (De Napoli 74), Chapuisat, Comisetti.
Referee: Sarvan (Turkey).

Copenhagen, 27 March 1999, 41,429

Denmark (0) 1 *(Sand 56)*
Italy (1) 2 *(Inzaghi 1, Conte 68)*

Denmark: Schmeichel; Helveg, Henriksen, Hogh, Heintze, Goldbaek (Colding 82), Thomsen, Nielsen A (Tofting 77), Gronkjaer (Molnar 53), Jorgensen, Sand.
Italy: Buffon; Panucci, Nesta, Cannavaro, Maldini, Fuser (Conte 46), Dino Baggio, Di Biagio, Di Francesco, Inzaghi, Chiesa (Totti 63).
Referee: Lopez (Spain).

Ancona, 31 March 1999, 20,735

Italy (1) 1 *(Inzaghi 31 (pen))*

Belarus (1) 1 *(Belkevich 24)*

Italy: Buffon; Panucci, Nesta, Cannavaro, Maldini, Conte, Dino Baggio, Di Biagio (Giannichedda 46), Totti (Di Francesco 46), Inzaghi, Chiesa (Roberto Baggio 64).
Belarus: Tumilovich; Lavrik, Lukhvich, Yakhimovic, Gurenko, Orlovski, Belkevich, Ostrovski, Baranov, Romashchenko MA, Makovski V.
Referee: Piraux (Belgium).

Zurich, 31 March 1999, 13,500

Switzerland (1) 2 *(Chapuisat 4, 70)*

Wales (0) 0

Switzerland: Brunner; Jeanneret, Henchoz, Wolf, Muller P, Vogel, Sforza, Fournier, Wicky, Chapuisat, Comisetti (Buhlmann 67).
Wales: Jones P (Crossley 26); Robinson, Pembridge, Symons, Coleman, Johnson, Saunders, Savage, Blake (Hartson 63), Hughes M (Bellamy 73), Speed.
Referee: Liba (Czech Republic).

Copenhagen, 5 June 1999, 24,876

Denmark (1) 1 *(Heintze 22)*

Belarus (0) 0

Denmark: Schmeichel; Colding, Henriksen, Hogh, Heintze, Goldbaek, Nielsen A, Tofting (Steen-Nielsen 87), Gronkjaer, Jorgensen, Sand (Molnar 78).
Belarus: Tumilovich; Lavrik, Lukhvich, Yakhimovic, Gurenko, Orlovski, Belkevic, Khatskevich (Kulchi 70), Ostrovski (Romashchenko MA 46), Baranov, Makovski V (Ryndyuk 85).
Referee: Baptista (Portugal).

Bologna, 5 June 1999, 12,392

Italy (3) 4 *(Vieri 6, Inzaghi 36, Maldini 39, Chiesa 89)*

Wales (0) 0

Italy: Buffon; Panucci, Maldini, Fuser (Di Livio 68), Negro, Cannavaro, Conte, Albertini, Vieri (Montella 46), Inzaghi (Chiesa 80), Di Francesco.
Wales: Jones P; Robinson (Jenkins 77), Barnard, Page, Melville, Williams, Giggs, Bellamy (Pembridge 79), Saunders (Hartson 46), Hughes M, Speed.
Referee: Steinborn (Germany).

Lausanne, 9 June 1999, 15,800

Switzerland (0) 0

Italy (0) 0

Switzerland: Huber; Wicky (Haas 70), Muller P, Hodel, Jeanneret (Di Jorio 78), Vogel, Sforza, Rothenbuhler, Sesa, Chapuisat, Comisetti (Celestini 57).
Italy: Buffon; Panucci (Pancaro 72), Negro, Cannavaro, Maldini, Fuser (Di Livio 61), Albertini, Conte, Vieri (Chiesa 61), Inzaghi, Di Francesco.
Referee: Poll (England).

Liverpool, 9 June 1999, 10,000

Wales (0) 0

Denmark (0) 2 *(Tomasson 84, Tofting 90 (pen))*

Wales: Jones P; Jenkins, Barnard (Legg 90), Robinson (Pembridge 87), Melville, Coleman, Speed, Saunders, Hartson (Bellamy 89), Hughes M, Giggs.
Denmark: Schmeichel; Colding, Heintze, Gronkjaer, Hogh, Henriksen, Goldbaek, Nielsen A (Tofting 85), Jorgensen (Frandsen 90), Sand, Molnar (Tomasson 72).
Referee: Ancion (Belgium).

Copenhagen, 4 September 1999, 41,667

Denmark (0) 2 *(Nielsen A 53, Tomasson 81)*

Switzerland (0) 1 *(Turkyilmaz 79)*

Denmark: Schmeichel; Helveg, Henriksen, Hogh, Heintze, Goldbaek (Colding 50), Nielsen A (Steen-Nielsen 80), Tofting, Jorgensen, Tomasson (Wieghorst 87), Sand.
Switzerland: Huber; Di Jorio (Turkyilmaz 59), Hodel, Jeanneret, Muller P, Buhlmann, Sforza, Vogel, Wicky (Wyss 88), Chapuisat, Sesa (Muller S 77).
Referee: Wojcik (Poland).

Minsk, 4 September 1999, 25,000

Belarus (1) 1 *(Baranov 30)*

Wales (1) 2 *(Saunders 42, Giggs 86)*

Belarus: Tumilovich; Lavrik, Lukhvich, Ostrovski, Tarlovski, Gurenko, Chaika, Baranov, Kulchi, Orlovski (Romashchenko MA 59), Makovski V.
Wales: Jones P; Robinson J, Barnard, Melville, Page, Coleman, Pembridge (Robinson C 81), Speed, Saunders, Blake, Giggs.
Referee: Ovrebo (Norway).

Naples, 8 September 1999, 46,919

Italy (2) 2 *(Fuser 10, Vieri 34)*

Denmark (1) 3 *(Jorgensen 39 (pen), Wieghorst 57, Tomasson 64)*

Italy: Buffon; Panucci, Nesta, Cannavaro, Pancaro, Fuser, Dino Baggio (Giannichedda 46), Albertini, Di Francesco (Conte 70), Inzaghi, Vieri (Totti 77).
Denmark: Schmeichel; Colding, Hogh, Henriksen, Heintze, Helveg (Goldbaek 52), Nielsen A, Tofting (Wieghorst 52), Jorgensen, Tomasson (Schjonberg 85), Sand.
Referee: Jol (Holland).

Lausanne, 8 September 1999, 12,000

Switzerland (0) 2 *(Turkyilmaz 68, 87 (pen))*

Belarus (0) 0

Switzerland: Huber; Hodel, Muller P (Wolf 78), Henchoz, Wicky, Vogel, Sforza, Di Jorio, Buhlmann (Sesa 71), Turkyilmaz, Chapuisat (Comisetti 62).
Belarus: Afanasenko; Lukhvich, Lavrik, Yakhimovic, Ostrovski, Gurenko, Kulchi (Katchuro 55), Chaika, Baranov, Tarlovski, Makovski V (Romashchenko MA 69).
Referee: Irvine (Northern Ireland).

Minsk, 9 October 1999, 32,000

Belarus (0) 0

Italy (0) 0

Belarus: Shantalosov; Lukhvich, Yakhimovic, Tarlovski, Orlovski, Gurenko, Romashchenko MA (Makovski V 46), Ostrovski, Chaika, Gerasimets (Kulchi 79), Baranov.
Italy: Buffon; Panucci, Nesta, Cannavaro, Maldini, Moriero, Conte, Di Biagio, Zambrotta, Inzaghi, Vieri (Del Piero 82).
Referee: Colombo (France).

Wrexham, 9 October 1999, 5064

Wales (0) 0

Switzerland (1) 2 *(Rey 17, Buhlmann 59)*

Wales: Jones P; Delaney, Barnard, Savage, Page, Coleman, Robinson J, Blake (Roberts N 78), Saunders (Hartson 67), Oster (Jones M 78), Speed.
Switzerland: Zuberbuhler; Hodel, Henchoz, Jacquet (Wyss 72), Haas, Vogel, Sesa, Di Jorio, Jeanneret, Buhlmann, Rey (Comisetti 67).
Referee: Papadakos (Greece).

Group 1 – Final Table	P	W	D	L	F	A	Pts
Italy	8	4	3	1	13	5	15
Denmark	8	4	2	2	11	8	14
Switzerland	8	4	2	2	9	5	14
Wales	8	3	0	5	7	16	9
Belarus	8	0	3	5	4	10	3

GROUP 2

Tbilisi, 5 September 1998, 35,000

Georgia (0) 1 *(Arveladze A 65)*
Albania (0) 0

Georgia: Gvaramadze; Kaladze, Tskitishvili, Silagadze (Kiknadze 42), Tsereteli, Kobiashvili, Nemsadze, Jamarauli, Ketsbaia (Janashia 56), Kinkladze, Iashvili (Arveladze A 60).
Albania: Strakosha; Lala, Shulku, Xhumba, Vata, Pinari, Haxhi, Bushi (Galo 74), Kola, Rrakli, Tare (Peco 67) (Maxhuni 87).
Referee: Tetrucci (Switzerland).

Athens, 6 September 1998, 29,000

Greece (0) 2 *(Mahlas 56 (pen), Frantzeskos 58)*
Slovenia (1) 2 *(Zahovic 19, 73)*

Greece: Atmatsidis; Kalitzakis, Ouzounidis, Dabizas, Borbokis (Liberopoulos 83), Markos, Zagorakis, Tsartas (Frantzeskos 46), Kassapis (Georgatos 78), Mahlas, Nikolaidis.
Slovenia: Simeunovic; Milanic, Galic, Knavs, Novak (Englaro 46), Ceh, Zahovic, Pavlin, Rudonja, Udovic, Osterc (Siljak 68) (Acimovic 72).
Referee: Trentalange (Italy).

Oslo, 6 September 1998, 11,030

Norway (1) 1 *(Solbakken 17)*
Latvia (1) 3 *(Pakhar 11, Shtolcers 53, Zemlinsky 65 (pen))*

Norway: Baardsen; Heggem (Berg 61), Bjornebye, Johnsen, Hoftun, Rekdal, Rudi (Flo H 79), Solbakken, Strandli, Flo T, Solskjaer (Flo J 62).
Latvia: Karavayev; Laizans (Lukashevich 51), Lobanyov, Zemlinsky, Ivanov, Bleidelis, Zakreshevsky, Babichev, Sharando (Boulders 73), Pakhar (Isakov 81), Shtolcers.
Referee: Shmolik (Belarus).

Riga, 10 October 1998, 1900

Latvia (1) 1 *(Shtolcers 2)*
Georgia (0) 0

Latvia: Karavayev; Lukashevich, Zemlinsky, Lobanyov, Sharando, Ivanov, Astafyev (Isakov 75), Bleidelis (Laizans 51), Babichev, Pakhar (Boulders 89), Shtolcers.
Georgia: Gvaramadze; Kaladze, Shekiladze, Kavelashvili, Gakhokidze (Demetradze 60), Kobiashvili, Nemsadze, Jamarauli, Ketsbaia, Kinkladze, Arveladze S.
Referee: Zotta (Romania).

Ljubljana, 10 October 1998, 7000

Slovenia (1) 1 *(Zahovic 24)*
Norway (1) 2 *(Flo T 43, Rekdal 80)*

Slovenia: Simeunovic; Galic, Milanic, Knavs, Rudonja, Novak, Ceh, Zahovic, Pavlin, Osterc (Englaro 46), Udovic (Acimovic 65).
Norway: Grodas; Haaland, Berg, Hoftun, Bjornebye, Heggem (Riseth 86), Strand (Hestad 77), Rekdal, Solbakken, Flo J, Flo T (Rushfeldt 89).
Referee: Schluchter (Switzerland).

Maroussi, 14 October 1998, 15,000

Greece (3) 3 *(Mahlas 13, Liberopoulos 15, Ouzounidis 36)*
Georgia (0) 0

Greece: Atmatsidis; Kalitzakis, Ouzounidis, Dabizas, Zagorakis, Markos, Poursanidis, Frantzeskos (Tsartas 74), Georgatos, Liberopoulos (Yannakopoulos 67), Mahlas (Mavroyenidis 85).
Georgia: Togonidze; Kobiashvili, Kaladze, Shelia, Nemsadze, Shekiladze, Ketsbaia, Jamarauli, Kinkladze, Kavelashvili (Gakhokidze 59), Arveladze S.
Referee: Ouzounov (Bulgaria).

Oslo, 14 October 1998, 17,770

Norway (0) 2 *(Rekdal 80 (pen), Berg 87)*
Albania (1) 2 *(Bushi 38, Tare 53)*

Norway: Grodas; Haaland (Iversen 12), Berg, Hoftun, Bjornebye, Heggem, Strand, Rekdal, Solbakken (Rushfeldt 90), Flo J (Solskjaer 57), Flo T.
Albania: Strakosha; Shulku, Lala, Xhumba, Haxhi, Bushi (Halili 84), Vata, Kola (Dalipi 90), Fakaj, Tare, Rrakli.
Referee: Grabher (Austria).

Maribor, 14 October 1998, 4700

Slovenia (0) 1 *(Udovic 86)*
Latvia (0) 0

Slovenia: Simeunovic; Galic, Milanic, Knavs (Gliha 46), Novak, Istenic (Acimovic 65), Pavlin, Englaro, Zahovic, Udovic (Milinovic 88), Rudonja.
Latvia: Karavayev; Lukashevich, Zemlinsky, Ivanov (Rimkus 87), Lobanyov, Sharando, Bleidelis (Mikholap 51), Astafyev (Boulders 79), Isakov, Pakhar, Shtolcers.
Referee: Nalbandyan (Armenia).

Tirana, 18 November 1998, 14,000

Albania (0) 0
Greece (0) 0

Albania: Strakosha; Dalipi (Halili 52), Haxhi, Vata, Xhumba, Shulku, Fakaj, Kola, Bushi, Rrakli, Tare.
Greece: Atmatsidis; Dabizas (Vokolos 90), Ouzounidis, Kalitzakis, Zagorakis, Poursanidis, Frantzeskos (Liberopoulos 46), Georgatos, Mahlas, Nikolaidis (Konstantinidis K 68), Markos.
Referee: Torres (Spain).

Tbilisi, 27 March 1999, 20,000

Georgia (1) 1 *(Janashia 42)*
Slovenia (0) 1 *(Zahovic 52)*

Georgia: Grishikashvili; Kaladze, Baslashvili, Chkhaidze, Tsereteli, Aleksidze (Kinkladze 46), Nemsadze, Jamarauli (Daraselia 82), Kobiashvili, Janashia, Demetradze (Kavelashvili 74).
Slovenia: Simeunovic; Karic, Milanic, Knavs, Rudonja (Mitrakovic 90) Bulajic, Milinovic, Ceh, Pavlin (Istenic 78), Udovic (Acimovic 60), Zahovic.
Referee: Hamer (Luxembourg).

Athens, 27 March 1999, 42,571

Greece (0) 0
Norway (1) 2 *(Solskjaer 38, 87)*

Greece: Atmatsidis; Dabizas, Ouzounidis, Anatolakis, Zagorakis (Mavroyenidis 46), Yannakopoulos, Poursanidis, Markos (Mahlas 55), Georgatos, Liberopoulos (Frantzeskos 75), Nikolaidis.
Norway: Myhre; Heggem, Berg, Johnsen, Bergdolmo (Halle 65), Iversen, Strand (Bohinen 60), Solbakken, Mykland, Rudi, Solskjaer (Carew 88).
Referee: Irvine (Republic of Ireland).

Riga, 31 March 1999, 3200

Latvia (0) 0
Greece (0) 0

Latvia: Karavayev; Lukashevich, Astafyev, Zemlinsky, Lobanyov, Ivanov (Isakov 27), Sharando (Stepanov 62), Mikholap (Boulders 46), Blagonadezhdin, Pakhar, Shtolcers.
Greece: Atmatsidis; Kassapis, Ouzounidis, Dabizas, Poursanidis, Mavroyenidis, Zagorakis (Yannakopoulos 75), Liberopoulos, Georgatos (Frantzeskos 75), Mahlas (Anastasiou 81), Nikolaidis.
Referee: Fisker (Denmark).

Riga, 28 April 1999, 2700

Latvia (0) 0

Albania (0) 0

Latvia: Karavayev; Stepanov (Sharando 84), Isakov, Lukashevich, Lobanyov, Blagonadezhdin, Ivanov, Boulders, Rubins, Mikholap (Dobretsov 70), Shtolcers (Laizans 60).

Albania: Strakosha; Lala, Shulku, Xhumba, Vata (Jupi 77), Fakaj, Haxhi, Bushi (Halili 87), Kola, Rrakli (Dalipi 82), Tare.

Referee: Romain (Belgium).

Tbilisi, 28 April 1999, 20,000

Georgia (0) 1 *(Janashia 58)*

Norway (4) 4 *(Shekiladze 16 (og), Flo T 26, 38, Solskjaer 35)*

Georgia: Togonidze; Shekiladze (Popkhadze 46), Didava, Tsereteli, Kaladze, Nemsadze, Rekhviashvili (Kiknadze 81), Jamarauli, Kobiashvili, Janashia, Ketsbaia (Demetradze 46).

Norway: Myhre; Haaland, Pedersen, Hoftun, Bergdolmo, Solskjaer (Strand 46), Iversen, Solbakken, Mykland, Rudi (Riseth 82), Flo T (Carew 88).

Referee: Puhl (Hungary).

Oslo, 30 May 1999, 18,236

Norway (1) 1 *(Iversen 4)*

Georgia (0) 0

Norway: Olsen; Heggem, Pedersen, Hoftun, Bergdolmo, Iversen (Dahlum 85), Leonhardsen (Rudi 46), Solbakken, Mykland, Riseth (Rekdal 70), Flo T.

Georgia: Gvaramadze; Guchua (Chichveishvili 62), Kaladze, Didava (Popkhadze 46), Tsereteli, Tskitishvili, Nemsadze, Ketsbaia, Jamarauli, Kavelashvili, Demetradze (Ashvetia 77).

Referee: Huyghe (Belgium).

Tbilisi, 5 June 1999, 15,000

Georgia (0) 1 *(Ketsbaia 55)*

Greece (0) 2 *(Mavroyenidis 88, Mahlas 90)*

Georgia: Gvaramadze; Chichveishvili (Didava 10), Khizaneishvili O, Akhvlediani (Khizaneishvili Z 67), Tsereteli, Tskitishvili (Aleksidze 56), Nemsadze, Ketsbaia, Jamarauli, Ashvetia, Kobiashvili.

Greece: Atmatsidis; Mavroyenidis, Ouzounidis, Anatolakis, Kassapis, Konstantinidis K (Froussas 46), Poursanidis, Zagorakis (Frantzeskos 81), Niniadis, Georgatos (Anastasiou 61), Mahlas.

Referee: Young (Scotland).

Tirana, 5 June 1999, 5000

Albania (1) 1 *(Tare 16)*

Norway (1) 2 *(Iversen 4, Flo T 83)*

Albania: Strakosha; Lala, Shulku, Xhumba, Vata, Haxhi, Bushi, Kola (Duro 69), Fakaj (Bellaj 62), Tare, Rrakli (Bogdani 80).

Norway: Olsen; Haaland, Pedersen (Bragstad 62), Hoftun, Bergdolmo, Iversen, Solbakken (Riseth 89), Rekdal, Mykland, Rudi (Dahlum 78), Flo T.

Referee: Stoica (Romania).

Riga, 5 June 1999, 2500

Latvia (1) 1 *(Pakhar 18)*

Slovenia (2) 2 *(Zahovic 25, 38 (pen))*

Latvia: Kolinko; Lukashevich, Astafyev (Rubins 41), Zemlinsky, Lobanyov (Korablyov 43), Sharando (Bleidelis 69), Laizans, Shtolcers, Pakhar, Babichev, Mikholap.

Slovenia: Simeunovic; Rudonja (Osterc 88), Milinovic, Karic, Galic, Knavs, Novak, Ceh, Udovic (Acimovic 66), Zahovic, Pavlin (Istenic 79).

Referee: Arceo (Spain).

Tirana, 9 June 1999, 8000

Albania (0) 0

Slovenia (1) 1 *(Zahovic 26 (pen))*

Albania: Strakosha; Lala, Shulku, Xhumba, Vata, Duro, Bushi, Bellaj, Bogdani (Dalipi 75), Rrakli (Halili 46), Tare.

Slovenia: Simeunovic; Galic, Knavs, Osterc (Istenic 80), Milinovic, Karic, Novak, Ceh, Udovic (Acimovic 66), Pavlin, Zahovic.

Referee: Stoica (Romania).

Athens, 9 June 1999, 15,000

Greece (1) 1 *(Niniadis 38 (pen))*

Latvia (1) 2 *(Verpakovskis 24, Zemlinsky 90 (pen))*

Greece: Atmatsidis; Mavroyenidis, Ouzounidis, Anatolakis, Kassapis, Zikos, Zagorakis, Frantzeskos (Anastasiou 60), Niniadis (Froussos 79), Georgatos (Markos 73), Mahlas.

Latvia: Kolinko; Lukashevich, Astafyev (Bleidelis 54), Zemlinsky, Rubins (Sismannovs 64), Pakhar, Babichev, Laizans, Verpakovskis (Mikholap 46), Korablyov, Lobanyov.

Referee: Pucek (Czech Republic).

Ljubljana, 18 August 1999, 8000

Slovenia (0) 2 *(Zahovic 49, Osterc 80)*

Albania (0) 0

Slovenia: Dabanovic; Osterc, Rudonja, Milanic (Milinovic 60), Galic, Knavs, Novak (Istenic 90), Zahovic, Ceh, Udovic (Acimovic 46), Pavlin.

Albania: Strakosha; Pinari, Xhumba, Vata, Shulku, Bellai, Haxhi, Murati (Halili 59), Kola, Rrakli (Bogdani 60), Tare.

Referee: Da Silva (Portugal).

Tirana, 4 September 1999, 3000

Albania (1) 3 *(Bushi 29, 79, Muka 90)*

Latvia (1) 3 *(Astafyev 20, 63, Shtolcers 69)*

Albania: Strakosha; Lala, Shulku, Xhumba, Vata, Fakaj (Bogdani 67), Haxhi, Bellai, Murati (Dalipi 46), Bushi, Tare (Muka 77).

Latvia: Kolinko; Stepanov, Zemlinsky, Lobanov, Lukashevich, Astafyev (Babichev 81), Ivanov (Blagonadezhdin 60), Bleidelis, Rubins, Shtolcers (Boulders 84), Mikholap.

Referee: Hamer (Luxembourg).

Oslo, 4 September 1999, 24,133

Norway (1) 1 *(Leonhardsen 34)*

Greece (0) 0

Norway: Olsen; Heggem, Berg, Hoftun, Bergdolmo, Iversen, Mykland, Skammelsrud, Leonhardsen (Riseth 73), Solskjaer (Rudi 67), Flo T.

Greece: Atmatsidis; Mavrogenidis, Kassapis, Dabizas, Ouzounidis, Poursanidis, Zagorakis (Mahlas 49), Georgatos, Niniadis (Yannakopoulos 46), Nikolaidis, Liberopoulos.

Referee: Merk (Germany).

Ljubljana, 4 September 1999, 8500

Slovenia (0) 2 *(Acimovic 48, Zahovic 80)*

Georgia (0) 1 *(Arveladze S 55)*

Slovenia: Simeunovic; Galic, Milanovic, Knavs, Ceh, Zahovic (Istenic 90), Pavlin, Novak, Osterc (Acimovic 46), Rudonja, Udovic (Karic 75).

Georgia: Gvaramadze; Kaladze, Kobiashvili, Tskitishvili, Didava, Sichinava, Akhvlediani (Shekiladze 46), Potskhveria, Kavelashvili, Arveladze A, Arveladze S.

Referee: Wegereef (Holland).

Tbilisi, 8 September 1999, 15,000

Georgia (1) 2 *(Arveladze S 30, Kavelashvili 52)*
Latvia (0) 2 *(Bleidelis 62, Stepanov 90)*
Georgia: Gvaramadze; Kaladze, Tskitishvili (Sichinava 70), Didava, Tsereteli, Shekiladze, Nemsadze, Jamarauli, Kobiashvili, Kavelashvili (Arveladze A 75), Arveladze S (Demetradze 72).
Latvia: Kolinko; Stepanov, Zemlinsky, Lobanov, Ivanov, Laizans (Boulders 83), Rubins, Bleidelis, Isakov (Babichev 60), Pakhar, Shtolcers (Sharando 74).
Referee: Radoman (Yugoslavia).

Oslo, 8 September 1999, 24,288

Norway (3) 4 *(Istenic 16 (og), Iversen 18, Solskjaer 30, Leonhardsen 68)*
Slovenia (0) 0
Norway: Olsen; Heggem, Berg, Hoftun, Bergdolmo, Iversen, Mykland, Skammelsrud (Sorensen 78), Leonhardsen, Solskjaer (Riseth 78), Flo T (Lund 88).
Slovenia: Simeunovic (Dabanovic 46); Milinovic, Istenic, Knavs, Novak, Ceh, Zahovic, Pavlin, Rudonja, Udovic (Karic 42), Osterc (Acimovic 84).
Referee: Veissiere (France).

Athens, 6 October 1999, 8000

Greece (1) 2 *(Tsartas 1, Georgiadis 87)*
Albania (0) 0
Greece: Atmatsidis; Amanatidis, Ouzounidis, Dabizas, Georgatos (Konstantinidis 66), Poursanidis, Zagorakis (Georgiadis 46), Tsartas (Niniadis 75), Zikos, Mahlas, Nikolaidis.
Albania: Strakosha; Lala, Bellaj (Bogdani 84), Xhumba, Vata, Haxhi, Murazi (Duro 55), Rakli, Bushi, Kola, Tare (Muka 67).
Referee: Ivanov (Bulgaria).

Tirana, 9 October 1999, 3000

Albania (0) 2 *(Rakli 30, Kola 36)*
Georgia (0) 1 *(Arveladze S 52)*
Albania: Beqaj; Lala, Shulku, Xhumba, Vata, Duro, Fakaj, Rakli (Muka 75), Bushi (Murati 54), Kola, Tare (Bogdani 90).
Georgia: Chanturia; Kobiashvili, Didava, Shekiladze, Gakhokidze, Nemsadze, Tskitishvili, Jamarauli, Kaladze, Arveladze S, Arveladze A (Janashia 83).
Referee: Michallef (Malta).

Riga, 9 October 1999, 3000

Latvia (0) 1 *(Pakhar 53)*
Norway (0) 2 *(Solskjaer 52, Flo T 86)*
Latvia: Kolinko; Lukashevich (Laizans 82), Zemlinsky, Lobanyov, Blagonadezhdin, Bleidelis, Ivanov, Astafyev, Rubins, Shtolcers, Pakhar.
Norway: Olsen; Heggem, Bergdolmo, Berg, Hoftun, Leonhardsen, Skammelsrud, Mykland (Solbakken 82), Iversen (Lund 46), Solskjaer (Riseth 87), Flo T.
Referee: Drabek (Austria).

Maribor, 9 October 1999, 2500

Slovenia (0) 0
Greece (2) 3 *(Tsartas 39, Georgiadis 43, Nikolaidis 73)*
Slovenia: Simeunovic; Bajrektarevic, Vugdalic (Englaro 84), Galic, Seslar, Rudonja, Novak, Acimovic, Ceh, Udovic (Karic 46), Simundza (Osterc 60).
Greece: Atmatsidis; Amanatidis, Zikos, Dabizas, Antzas (Zagorakis 71), Georgiadis, Poursanidis, Tsartas (Niniadis 69), Konstantinidis, Limberopoulos, Nikolaidis (Mahlas 75).
Referee: Ghandour (Egypt).

Group 2 – Final Table	P	W	D	L	F	A	Pts
Norway	10	8	1	1	21	9	25
Slovenia	10	5	2	3	12	14	17
Greece	10	4	3	3	13	8	15
Latvia	10	3	4	3	13	12	13
Albania	10	1	4	5	8	14	7
Georgia	10	1	2	7	8	18	5

GROUP 3

Helsinki, 5 September 1998, 18,716

Finland (2) 3 *(Kolkka 8, Johansson 44, Paatelainen 62)*
Moldova (2) 2 *(Oprea 10, 11)*
Finland: Niemi; Ylonen, Tuomela, Hyypia, Turpeinen (Reini 46), Wiss, Kautonen, Litmanen, Johansson (Sumiala 80), Paatelainen, Kolkka (Mahlio 73).
Moldova: Coselev; Fistican (Tabanov 76), Rebeja (Pusca 46), Testimitanu, Guzun, Stroenco, Oprea, Gaidamasciuc, Epureanu (Suharev 76), Curtianu, Clescenco.
Referee: Barber (England).

Istanbul, 5 September 1998, 26,500

Turkey (1) 3 *(Oktay 18, 58, Tayfur 49 (pen))*
Northern Ireland (0) 0
Turkey: Rustu; Saffet, Mert, Alpay, Okan (Arif 87), Sergen, Tayfur, Tugay (Oguz 75), Abdullah, Oktay (Hami 79), Hakan Sukur.
Northern Ireland: Fettis; Hughes A, Horlock, Mulryne, Hill, Morrow, Gillespie (Jim Whitley 78), Lennon, Dowie, Rowland (Quinn 46), Hughes M.
Referee: Wojcik (Poland).

Belfast, 10 October 1998, 10,002

Northern Ireland (1) 1 *(Rowland 31)*
Finland (0) 0
Northern Ireland: Fettis; Hughes A, Horlock, Mulryne, Morrow, Patterson, Gillespie (McCarthy 71), Lennon, Dowie (O'Boyle 80), Rowland (Quinn 89), Hughes M.
Finland: Niemi; Ylonen, Ilola, Hyypia, Kautonen, Reini, Riihilahti (Litmanen 75) Valakari, Kolkka, Paatelainen, Johansson.
Referee: Arsic (Yugoslavia).

Bursa, 10 October 1998, 20,000

Turkey (0) 1 *(Hakan Sukur 70)*
Germany (0) 0
Turkey: Rustu; Fatih, Ogun (Unsal 89), Alpay, Tayfur, Tayfur, Tugay (Oktay 61), Abdullah, Mert, Sergen (Saffet 81), Hakan Sukur.
Germany: Kahn; Babbel, Nowotny, Rehmer, Ricken (Bode 81), Ramelow, Beinlich, Jeremies, Heinrich (Neuville 76), Bierhoff, Kirsten.
Referee: Dallas (Scotland).

Chisinau, 14 October 1998, 5000

Moldova (1) 1 *(Guzun 6)*
Germany (3) 3 *(Kirsten 20, 36, Bierhoff 38)*
Moldova: Coselev; Fistican, Stroenco, Testimitanu, Gaidamasciuc, Rebeja, Guzun, Oprea, Curtianu (Suharev 53), Clescenco, Epureanu.
Germany: Kahn; Babbel, Nowotny, Rehmer, Ricken (Neuville 53), Ramelow, Beinlich (Wosz 83), Nerlinger, Tarnat, Kirsten (Jancker 74), Bierhoff.
Referee: Marin (Spain).

Istanbul, 14 October 1998, 25,000

Turkey (0) 1 *(Ogun 73)*
Finland (1) 3 *(Paatelainen 5, Johansson 51, Litmanen 90)*
Turkey: Rustu; Alpay, Ogun, Fatih, Okan (Hami 46), Tugay (Mert 46), Sergen (Hasan Sas 83), Tayfur, Abdullah, Hakan Sukur, Oktay.
Finland: Niemi; Reini, Ylonen (Kolkka 61), Hyypia, Kautonen, Tuomela, Riihilahti (Valakari 76), Litmanen, Ilola, Johansson (Saastamoinen 90), Paatelainen.
Referee: Krondl (Czech Republic).

Belfast, 18 November 1998, 11,137

Northern Ireland (0) 2 _(Dowie 49, Lennon 63)_
Moldova (1) 2 _(Gaidamasciuc 22, Testimitanu 57)_
Northern Ireland: Fettis; Griffin, Kennedy, Lomas, Patterson, Morrow, Gillespie (McCarthy 88), Lennon, Dowie, Rowland (Gray 77), Hughes M.
Moldova: Dinov; Fistican, Guzun (Pusca 71), Stroenco, Rebeja, Curtianu, Stratulat (Suharev 62), Testimitanu (Maievici 86), Epureanu, Gaidamasciuc, Clescenco.
Referee: Hrinak (Slovakia).

Belfast, 27 March 1999, 14,270

Northern Ireland (0) 0
Germany (2) 3 _(Bode 11, 42, Hamann 62)_
Northern Ireland: Taylor; Patterson, Horlock, Lomas, Williams, Morrow, Gillespie (McCarthy 84), Lennon (Sonner 68), Dowie, Rowland (Kennedy 69), Hughes M.
Germany: Kahn; Babbel, Worns, Jeremies, Matthaus (Nowotny 46), Strunz, Heinrich, Hamann, Bierhoff, Neuville (Jancker 69), Bode (Preetz 79).
Referee: Cesari (Italy).

Istanbul, 27 March 1999, 30,000

Turkey (1) 2 _(Hakan Sukur 34, Sergen 90)_
Moldova (0) 0
Turkey: Rustu; Fatih, Ogun, Alpay, Okan, Tugay (Ayhan 85), Sergen, Tayfur, Abdullah, Hakan Sukur, Oktay (Hami 9) (Arif 74).
Moldova: Dinov; Fistican, Rebeja, Tabanov, Guzun, Stroenco, Sischin, Stratulat, Gaidamasciuc, Epureanu, Clescenco (Suharev 81).
Referee: Plautz (Austria).

Nuremberg, 31 March 1999, 40,758

Germany (2) 2 _(Jeremies 31, Neuville 37)_
Finland (0) 0
Germany: Kahn; Babbel, Matthaus, Worns, Strunz, Hamann (Nowotny 72), Jeremies, Heinrich, Neuville (Kirsten 65), Bierhoff, Bode (Jancker 76).
Finland: Niemi; Reini (Lehkosuo 89), Hyypia, Ylonen, Kautonen (Kolkka 72), Kinnunen, Riihilahti, Litmanen, Ilola, Johansson, Paatelainen (Saastamoinen 46).
Referee: Koussainov (Russia).

Chisinau, 31 March 1999, 9237

Moldova (0) 0
Northern Ireland (0) 0
Moldova: Dinov; Fistican, Stroenco, Sosnovschi, Oprea (Stratulat 90), Gaidamasciuc, Epureanu, Rebeja, Guzun, Clescenco, Suharev.
Northern Ireland: Taylor; Patterson (Hughes A 62), Horlock, Lomas, Williams M, Morrow, Gillespie, Lennon, Dowie, Robinson, Hughes M.
Referee: Trivkovic (Croatia).

Leverkusen, 4 June 1999, 21,000

Germany (3) 6 _(Bierhoff 2, 56, 82, Kirsten 27, Bode 38, Scholl 71)_
Moldova (0) 1 _(Stratulat 76)_
Germany: Kahn; Nowotny, Matthaus (Babbel 75), Strunz, Hamann, Jeremies (Scholl 46), Heinrich, Neuville, Bierhoff, Kirsten (Ramelow 54), Bode.
Moldova: Dinov; Fistican, Maievici (Stratulat 55), Stroenco, Rebeja, Gaidamasciuc (Belous 74), Epureanu, Guzun, Curtianu, Oprea, Clescenco (Sischin 81).
Referee: Coroado (Portugal).

Helsinki, 5 June 1999, 36,042

Finland (2) 2 _(Tihinen 10, Paatelainen 14)_
Turkey (2) 4 _(Tayfur 25, 84, Hakan Sukur 34, 87)_
Finland: Niemi; Ylonen, Hyypia, Kuivasto, Tihinen, Riihilahti, Valakari, Litmanen, Kolkka, Paatelainen, Johansson.
Turkey: Rustu; Fatih, Ali Eren, Alpay, Saffet, Sergen (Umit 89), Tayfur, Abdullah (Unsal 90), Tayfun, Hakan Sukur, Ayhan (Tugay 74).

Referee: Jol (Holland).

Chisinau, 9 June 1999, 8000

Moldova (0) 0
Finland (0) 0
Moldova: Dinov; Fistican, Stratulat, Stroenco, Rebeja, Sischin (Belous 75), Guzun, Epureanu, Curtianu, Oprea (Gaidamasciuc 79), Suharev (Chirilov 89).
Finland: Niemi; Ylonen, Reini (Lehkosuo 85), Hyypia, Tininen (Kautonen 46), Riihilahti, Valakari, Paatelainen, Kolkka, Ilola, Johansson (Forssell 60).
Referee: Treossi (Italy).

Helsinki, 4 September 1999, 20,184

Finland (0) 1 _(Salli 63)_
Germany (2) 2 _(Bierhoff 2, 17)_
Finland: Niemi (Laaksonen 46); Saastamoinen, Hyypia, Kuivasto, Ylonen (Kuqi 46), Salli, Wiss, Riihilahti, Tainio, Johansson, Kottila.
Germany: Lehmann; Babbel, Nowotny, Linke, Jeremies, Matthaus, Scholl (Nerlinger 79), Ziege, Neuville (Strunz 85), Bierhoff, Kirsten (Schneider 32).
Referee: Nieto (Spain).

Belfast, 4 September 1999, 7500

Northern Ireland (0) 0
Turkey (0) 3 _(Arif 45, 46, 48)_
Northern Ireland: Taylor; Hughes A, Horlock, Lomas, Williams M, Hunter, McCarthy (Gillespie 62), Lennon, Dowie (Quinn 75), Hughes M, Kennedy.
Turkey: Rustu; Ali Eren, Ogun, Alpay, Tayfun, Tayfur, Tugay, Abdullah (Hakan Unsal 75), Sergen (Umit Karan 90), Arif (Okan 78), Hakan Sukur.
Referee: Sars (France).

Dortmund, 8 September 1999, 41,000

Germany (4) 4 _(Bierhoff 3, Ziege 16, 33, 45)_
Northern Ireland (0) 0
Germany: Lehmann; Linke, Matthaus, Babbel (Strunz 30), Jeremies, Nowotny (Worns 46), Scholl, Ziege, Neuville (Schneider 67), Bierhoff, Bode.
Northern Ireland: Taylor; Nolan, Horlock, Lomas, Williams, Morrow, McCarthy, Lennon (Gillespie 46), Dowie (Quinn 46), Hughes M, Kennedy.
Referee: Bikas (Greece).

Chisinau, 8 September 1999, 6000

Moldova (1) 1 _(Epureanu 3)_
Turkey (0) 1 _(Tayfur 76)_
Moldova: Dinov; Fistican, Stroenco, Boret, Gusin (Siskin 81), Oprea, Epureanu, Osipenco, Rebeja, Clescenco (Chirilov 84), Gaidamasciuc (Stratulat 46).
Turkey: Rustu; Ali Eren, Ogun, Alpay, Okan (Tugay 46), Tayfur, Fatih (Ayhan 46), Hakan Unsal, Sergen (Umit 88), Arif, Hakan Sukur.
Referee: Schluchter (Switzerland).

Helsinki, 9 October 1999, 8217

Finland (1) 4 _(Johansson 9, Hyypia 63, Kolkka 73, 83)_
Northern Ireland (0) 1 _(Jeff Whitley 59)_
Finland: Viander; Lehkosuo, Kuivasto, Hyypia, Tihinen, Wiss (Valakari 87), Litmanen, Riihilahti (Yla-Jussila 87), Kolkka, Paatelainen, Johansson.
Northern Ireland: Taylor; Jenkins (Jim Whitley 79), Nolan, Lennon, Williams, Morrow, McCarthy, Jeff Whitley, Quinn (Coote 68), Kennedy, Hughes M (Johnson 75).
Referee: Ancion (Belgium).

Munich, 9 October 1999, 63,572

Germany (0) 0

Turkey (0) 0

Germany: Kahn; Babbel, Matthaus, Linke, Schneider (Dogan 89), Hamann (Nerlinger 46), Jeremies, Ziege (Bode 76), Neuville, Bierhoff, Scholl.
Turkey: Rustu; Fatih, Ogun, Alpay, Ali Eren, Okan (Arif 72), Tayfun, Sergen, Tayfur (Oktay 85), Abdullah (Ergun 69), Hakan Sukur.
Referee: Collina (Italy).

Group 3 – Final Table	P	W	D	L	F	A	Pts
Germany	8	6	1	1	20	4	19
Turkey	8	5	2	1	15	6	17
Finland	8	3	1	4	13	13	10
N. Ireland	8	1	2	5	4	19	5
Moldova	8	0	4	4	7	17	4

GROUP 4

Erevan, 5 September 1998, 2300

Armenia (1) 3 *(Avalyan 40, Yessayan 71, 90)*

Andorra (0) 1 *(Lucendo 86 (pen))*

Armenia: Berezovski; Soukiassian, Krbachian, Hovsepian, Oganessian T (Khodgoyan 83), Vardanian, Sarkissian, Ara Adamian, Art Adamian (Gsepyan 86), Shahgeldian, Avalyan (Yessayan 68).
Andorra: Koldo; Ramirez, Chema, Martin, Lima, Escurza, Garcia, Oscar, Sanchez, Lucendo, Justo.
Referee: O'Hanlon (Republic of Ireland).

Reykjavik, 5 September 1998, 10,500

Iceland (1) 1 *(Dadason 33)*

France (1) 1 *(Dugarry 36)*

Iceland: Kristinsson B; Helgason A, Sigurdsson L, Sverrisson E, Marteinsson, Hreidarsson, Kolvidsson, Gudjonsson T, Kristinsson R, Dadason, Gunnlaugsson A (Thordarson 69).
France: Barthez; Karembeu, Thuram, Leboeuf, Lizarazu, Dugarry (Henry 66), Deschamps, Djorkaeff, Zidane, Pires, Laslandes.
Referee: Blareau (Belgium).

Kiev, 5 September 1998, 18,000

Ukraine (2) 3 *(Popov 14, Skachenko 24, Rebrov 74 (pen))*

Russia (0) 2 *(Varlamov 67, Onopko 87)*

Ukraine: Shovkovskyi; Gusin, Mikitin, Golovko, Vashchuk, Dmitrulin, Skachenko (Kalitvintsev 46), Popov, Kovalov (Kriventsov 87), Shevchenko, Rebrov.
Russia: Kharine; Minko, Chugainov, Kovtun, Yanovski, Semak (Cherchesov 72), Onopko, Alenichev (Mostovoi 64), Kanchelskis (Karpin 71), Kolyvanov, Varlamov.
Referee: Merk (Germany).

Andorra, 10 October 1998, 850

Andorra (0) 0

Ukraine (2) 2 *(Kossovski V 30, Rebrov 43)*

Andorra: Koldo; Ramirez, Chema, Martin, Lima A, Lima I, Pol, Oscar, Emiliano, Sanchez (Jimenez 87), Ruiz.
Ukraine: Shovkovskyi; Luzhny, Golovko, Vashchuk, Mikitin (Kovalov 46), Popov, Maximov (Kriventsov 51), Gusin, Kossovski V, Shevchenko (Mikhailenko 69), Rebrov.
Referee: Guetzov (Bulgaria).

Erevan, 10 October 1998, 6,000

Armenia (0) 0

Iceland (0) 0

Armenia: Berezovski; Soukiassian, Vardanian, Khachatrian V, Hovsepian, Sarkissian, Art Petrossian (Oganessian T 40), Art Adamian, Shahgeldian, Mikaelian, Assadourian (Yessayan 25).
Iceland: Kristinsson B; Jonsson S, Hreidarsson, Adolfsson, Helgason A, Kristinsson R, Kolvidsson, Gunnlaugsson A, Dadason, Gudjonsson T, Sigurdsson L.
Referee: Norman (Sweden).

Moscow, 10 October 1998, 32,500

Russia (1) 2 *(Yanovski 45, Mostovoi 55)*

France (2) 3 *(Anelka 12, Pires 28, Boghossian 81)*

Russia: Ovchinnikov; Kovtun, Onopko, Varlamov, Khlestov, Karpin, Yanovski, Alenichev (Semak 69), Mostovoi, Tikhonov, Bestchastnykh (Gerasimenko 62).
France: Lama; Thuram, Blanc, Desailly, Lizarazu, Deschamps, Petit (Boghossian 46), Pires, Zidane, Djorkaeff (Vieira 54), Anelka (Vairelles 88).
Referee: Ceccarini (Italy).

Paris, 14 October 1998, 75,000

France (0) 2 *(Candela 53, Djorkaeff 61)*

Andorra (0) 0

France: Lama; Candela, Leboeuf, Blanc, Lizarazu, Deschamps, Zidane, Djorkaeff (Boghossian 82), Dugarry (Pires 71), Trezeguet (Anelka 71), Vairelles.
Andorra: Koldo; Ramirez (Sanchez 80), Chema, Martin, Lima A, Lima I, Pol, Oscar, Lucendo (Jimenez 88), Ruiz, Emiliano.
Referee: Koren (Israel).

Reykjavik, 14 October 1998, 3500

Iceland (0) 1 *(Kovtun 88 (og))*

Russia (0) 0

Iceland: Kristinsson B; Jonsson S, Hreidarsson, Adolfsson, Helgason A, Kristinsson R, Kolvidsson (Thordarson 85), Gunnlaugsson A, Dadason, Sigurdsson L, Gudjonsson T (Sigurdsson H 6).
Russia: Cherchesov; Kovtun, Onopko, Smertin, Yanovski, Shalimov, Varlamov (Solomatin 59), Mostovoi, Tikhonov (Igonin 12), Karpin (Khokhlov 59), Titov.
Referee: Temmink (Holland).

Kiev, 14 October 1998, 25,000

Ukraine (1) 2 *(Skachenko 31, Gusin 83)*

Armenia (0) 0

Ukraine: Shovkovskyi; Luzhny, Dmitrulin, Golovko, Vashchuk, Popov (Maximov 75), Skachenko (Kovalov 61), Gusin, Kossovski V, Shevchenko (Kriventsov 80), Rebrov.
Armenia: Berezovski; Soukiassian, Vardanian, Khachatrian V, Hovsepian, Krbachian (Oganessian T 85), Art Petrossian, Ara Adamian, Shahgeldian, Mikaelian (Avalyan 65), Assadourian (Yessayan 73).
Referee: Lica (Romania).

La Vella, 27 March 1999, 1400

Andorra (0) 0

Iceland (0) 2 *(Sverrisson E 58, Adolfsson 67.)*

Andorra: Alvarez; Ramirez (Gonzalez 77), Garcia, Martin, Lima T, Lima I, Pol, Oscar, Jimenez (Sanchez 73), Lucendo, Ruiz (Imbernon 83).
Iceland: Kristinsson B; Jonsson S, Gunnarsson B (Hreidarsson 70), Adolfsson, Helgason A, Kristinsson R, Thordarson, Gunnlaugsson A (Gudmundsson T 81), Sverrisson E (Gretarsson 70), Sigurdsson H, Gudjonsson T.
Referee: Agius (Malta).

Erevan, 27 March 1999, 20,000

Armenia (0) 0

Russia (1) 3 *(Karpin 7, 63 (pen), Bestchastnykh 89)*

Armenia: Berezovski; Mkrchian, Hovsepian, Oganessian S, Karbanian (Harutyunian 65), Vardanian, Art Petrossian, Voskanian (Kakosian 78), Sarkissian, Shahgeldian, Mikalian (Yessayan 81).
Russia: Filimonov; Khlestov, Onopko, Drozdov, Tsymbalar, Karpin, Alenichev (Tikhonov 65), Yanovski, Titov, Yuran (Khokhlov 85), Panov (Bestchastnykh 46).
Referee: Hauge (Norway).

Saint Denis, 27 March 1999, 78,500

France (0) 0

Ukraine (0) 0

France: Barthez; Thuram, Lizarazu, Deschamps, Blanc, Desailly, Pires (Dhorasoo 85), Djorkaeff, Petit (Boghossian 78), Anelka, Dugarry (Wiltord 69).
Ukraine: Shovkovskyi; Luzhny, Vashchuk, Golovko, Mikitin, Gusin (Skrypnyk 85), Popov, Kovalov (Kossovski V 55), Rebrov, Skachenko (Maximov 69), Shevchenko.
Referee: Benko (Austria).

Saint Denis, 31 March 1999, 78,852

France (2) 2 *(Wiltord 3, Dugarry 45)*

Armenia (0) 0

France: Barthez; Thuram (Karembeu 79), Blanc, Desailly, Deschamps, Vieira, Djorkaeff (Pires 69), Boghossian, Anelka, Wiltord, Dugarry (Trezeguet 46).
Armenia: Berezovski; Soukiassian (Khachatrian V 40), Mkrchian, Vardanian, Hovsepian, Oganessian S, Art Petrossian, Voskanian (Hayrapetian 77), Sarkissian, Shahgeldian (Yessayan 53), Mikaelian.
Referee: Bikas (Greece).

Moscow, 31 March 1999, 20,000

Russia (3) 6 *(Titov 8, Bestchastnykh 11, 62, Onopko 42, Tsymbalar 50, Alenichev 90)*

Andorra (0) 1 *(Sanchez 73)*

Russia: Filimonov; Khlestov, Smertin, Tsymbalar, Yevseyev (Tikhonov 46), Alenichev, Onopko, Karpin, Titov, Shirko, Bestchastnykh.
Andorra: Alvarez; Alonso (Gonzalez 57), Garcia, Martin, Lima T, Lima I, Pol, Oscar, Jimenez, Lucendo (Sanchez 65), Ruiz.
Referee: Vuorela (Finland).

Kiev, 31 March 1999, 50,000

Ukraine (0) 1 *(Vashchuk 59)*

Iceland (0) 1 *(Sigurdsson L 66)*

Ukraine: Shovkovskyi; Luzhny, Vashchuk, Golovko, Mikitin, Gusin, Popov (Kalitvintsev 75), Kossovski V, Rebrov, Skachenko (Maximov 46), Shevchenko.
Iceland: Kristinsson B; Jonsson S, Gunnarsson B, Adolfsson, Helgason A, Kristinsson R (Kolvidsson 80), Sigurdsson L, Hreidarsson, Sverrisson E, Sigurdsson H (Sverrisson S 86), Gudjonsson T.
Referee: Dani (Israel).

Saint-Denis, 5 June 1999, 78,000

France (0) 2 *(Petit 48, Wiltord 54)*

Russia (1) 3 *(Panov 40, 75, Karpin 85)*

France: Barthez; Thuram, Blanc, Desailly, Candela (Pires 88), Deschamps, Petit, Djorkaeff (Boghossian 90), Dugarry (Vieira 59), Anelka, Wiltord.
Russia: Filimonov; Khlestov, Onopko, Smertin, Varlamov, Karpin, Semak (Bestchastnykh 60), Mostovoi (Khokhlov 26), Titov, Tikhonov (Tsymbalar 71), Panov.
Referee: Durkin (England).

Reykjavik, 5 June 1999, 5565

Iceland (1) 2 *(Dadason 30, Gunnarsson B 46)*

Armenia (0) 0

Iceland: Kristinsson B; Helgason A (Kolvidsson 72), Hreidarsson, Jonsson S, Marteinsson, Gunnarsson B, Kristinsson R, Sverrisson E, Sigurdsson H (Danielsson 81), Gudjonsson T, Dadason (Helguson 69).
Armenia: Berezovski; Soukiassian (Mkrchian 65), Khachatrian V, Hovsepian, Voskanian (Gregorian 84), Vardanian, Art Petrossian (Hayrapetian 75), Harutyunian, Sarkissian, Shahgeldian, Mikaelian.
Referee: Peltola (Finland).

Kiev, 5 June 1999, 45,000

Ukraine (2) 4 *(Popov 38, Rebrov 41, Dmitrulin 56, Gusin 89)*

Andorra (0) 0

Ukraine: Vorobiov; Luzhny, Mikitin (Mizin 72), Golovko, Vashchuk, Dmitrulin (Maximiuk 78), Tsykhmeistruk, Popov, Gusin, Shevchenko (Skachenko 67), Rebrov.
Andorra: Alvarez; Pol, Martin (Lucendo 53), Garcia, Lima T, Lima I, Gonzalez, Oscar, Ramirez, Sanchez, Ruiz.
Referee: Georgiou (Cyprus).

Barcelona, 9 June 1999, 4000

Andorra (0) 0

France (0) 1 *(Leboeuf 85 (pen))*

Andorra: Alvarez; Pol, Ramirez, Lima T, Lima I, Chema (Jonas 70), Gonzalez, Oscar, Ruiz, Jimenez (Genis 89), Lucendo (Martin 77).
France: Rame; Karembeu, Candela, Boghossian, Leboeuf, Desailly, Wiltord, Dugarry, Anelka, Petit (Vieira 56), Dhorasoo (Pires 60).
Referee: Ross (Northern Ireland).

Erevan, 9 June 1999, 10,000

Armenia (0) 0

Ukraine (0) 0

Armenia: Berezovski; Petrossian T (Gregorian 63), Khachatrian V, Hovsepian, Oganessian S (Harutyunian 46), Vardanian, Art Petrossian, Voskanian, Sarkissian, Shahgeldian, Mikaelian (Mkrchian 46).
Ukraine: Vorobiov; Luzhny, Mikitin, Golovko, Vashchuk, Dmitrulin, Tsykhmeistruk, Popov (Konovalov 34), Gusin, Shevchenko (Cardash 80), Rebrov (Skachenko 70).
Referee: Boggi (Italy).

Moscow, 9 June 1999, 36,000

Russia (1) 1 *(Karpin 44)*

Iceland (0) 0

Russia: Filimonov; Khlestov, Varlamov (Yanovski 56), Onopko, Semak (Bulatov 46), Smertin, Karpin, Khokhlov, Tikhonov, Bestchastnykh (Tsymbalar 71), Panov.
Iceland: Kristinsson B; Helgason A, Hreidarsson (Adolfsson 60), Jonsson S (Kolvidsson 46), Marteinsson, Kristinsson R, Gunnarsson B (Helguson 82), Sverrisson E, Sigurdsson L, Gudjonsson T, Dadason.
Referee: Tokat (Turkey).

Reykjavik, 4 September 1999, 5100

Iceland (2) 3 *(Gudjonsson T 29, Hreidarsson 32, Gudjohnsen E 90)*

Andorra (0) 0

Iceland: Kristinsson B; Helgason A, Hreidarsson, Jonsson S, Sigurdsson L (Vidarsson 26), Gudjonsson B, Gunnarsson, Gudmundsson, Sigurdsson H (Helguson 57), Gudjonsson T, Dadason (Gudjohnsen E 77).
Andorra: Koldo; Martin (Armand Godoy 61), Escura, Ramirez, Garcia J, Sonejee, Pol (Buxo 90), Gonzalez, Jimenez, Sanchez, Alex Godoy (Garcia G 67).
Referee: Liba (Czech Republic).

Moscow, 4 September 1999, 40,000

Russia (1) 2 *(Bestchastnykh 8 (pen), Karpin 70)*

Armenia (0) 0

Russia: Filimonov; Khlestov, Onopko, Smertin, Karpin, Khokhlov, Alenichev, Titov (Semak 80), Panov (Chirko 78), Bestchastnykh, Tikhonov (Yanovski 73).
Armenia: Berezovski; Mkrchian, Khachatrian V, Hovsepian, Oganessian S, Vardanian, Khachatrian R (Art Petrossian 85), Harutyunian (Kakossian 55), Voskanian, Shahgeldian (Devani 78), Mikaelian.
Referee: Agius (Malta).

Kiev, 4 September 1999, 70,000

Ukraine (0) 0
France (0) 0
Ukraine: Shovkovskyi; Luzhny, Golovko, Vashchuk, Dmitrulin (Mitikin 46), Popov, Maximov (Konovalov 70), Gusin (Tsykhmeistruk 84), Kossovski V, Shevchenko, Rebrov.
France: Barthez; Thuram, Blanc, Desailly, Lizarazu, Karembeu, Deschamps, Vieira, Djorkaeff (Pires 69), Zidane, Anelka (Laslandes 52).
Referee: Dallas (Scotland).

La Vella, 8 September 1999, 1000

Andorra (1) 1 *(Ruiz 39 (pen))*
Russia (1) 2 *(Onopko 22, 57)*
Andorra: Koldo; Ramirez, Lima I, Sonejee, Garcia T, Escura, Alex Godoy (Pol 59), Gonzalez, Jimenez, Ruiz, Sanchez (Armand Godoy 89).
Russia: Filimonov; Khlestov, Onopko, Smertin, Karpin, Khokhlov (Bezrodny 55), Alenichev (Yanovski 61), Titov, Bestchastnykh (Panov 46), Chirko, Tikhonov.
Referee: Larsen (Denmark).

Reykjavik, 8 September 1999, 7700

Iceland (0) 0
Ukraine (1) 1 *(Rebrov 43 (pen))*
Iceland: Kristinsson B; Helgason A, Hreidarsson, Jonsson S (Vidarsson 85), Sigurdsson L, Kristinsson R, Gunnarsson, Kolvidsson (Helguson 59), Marteinsson, Gudjonsson T, Dadason (Gudjohnsen E 73).
Ukraine: Shovkovskyi; Luzhny (Mitikin 80), Golovko, Vashchuk, Dmitrulin, Popov, Maximov, Konovalov (Tsykhmeistruk 66), Kossovski V, Shevchenko, Rebrov.
Referee: Pereira (Portugal).

Erevan, 8 September 1999, 20,000

Armenia (1) 2 *(Mikaelian 6, Shakhgeldian 90 (pen))*
France (1) 3 *(Djorkaeff 45 (pen), Zidane 67, Laslandes 74)*
Armenia: Berezovski; Mkrchian, Khachatrian V, Hovsepian, Khachatrian R (Kotcharian 75), Yessayan, Petrossian T, Harutyunian (Gregorian 63), Shakhgeldian, Mikaelian (Devani 67), Sarkissian.
France: Barthez; Thuram, Blanc, Desailly, Lizarazu, Karembeu, Deschamps, Djorkaeff, Zidane (Dehu 72), Wiltord (Robert 63), Laslandes.
Referee: Ouzunov (Bulgaria).

La Vella, 9 October 1999, 700

Andorra (0) 0
Armenia (1) 3 *(Art Petrossian 26, Yessayan 59, Shakhgeldian 65)*
Andorra: Koldo; Ramirez, Escura, Sonejee, Garcia T (Alonso 58), Lima I, Alex Godoy (Pol 46), Gonzalez (Soria 62), Jimenez, Sanchez, Ruiz.
Armenia: Abramian; Soukiassian, Voskanian, Vardanian, Mortigian, Khachatrian, Art Petrossian (Harobian 79), Petrossian T (Krpcharian 82), Sarkissian, Shakhgeldian (Minasian 78), Yessayan.
Referee: Jones (England).

Saint-Denis, 9 October 1999, 80,000

France (2) 3 *(Dadason 17 (og), Djorkaeff 39, Trezeguet 71)*
Iceland (0) 2 *(Sverrisson E 48, Gunnarsson 56)*
France: Lama; Thuram, Blanc, Desailly, Lizarazu, Deschamps, Boghossian (Vieira 90), Zidane, Djorkaeff, Laslandes (Trezeguet 67), Wiltord (Vairelles 84).
Iceland: Kristinsson B; Helgason A, Sigurdsson L, Marteinsson, Hreidarsson, Sverrisson E, Kristinsson R, Gunnarsson, Gudjonsson T (Gudjohnsen E 74), Sigurdsson H (Helguson 72), Dadason.
Referee: Heynemann (Germany).

Moscow, 9 October 1999, 80,000

Russia (0) 1 *(Karpin 72)*
Ukraine (0) 1 *(Shevchenko 87)*
Russia: Filimonov; Khlestov, Onopko, Smertin, Aleinichev, Khokhlov, Drozdov, Titov, Karpin, Panov (Semak 80), Tikhonov (Bestchastnykh 60).
Ukraine: Shovkovskyi; Luzhny, Golovko, Vashchuk, Mizin, Maximov (Moroz 76), Gusin, Dmitrulin (Kovalev 76), Shevchenko, Skachenko (Mikitin 42), Rebrov.
Referee: Elleray (England).

Group 4 – Final Table	P	W	D	L	F	A	Pts
France	10	6	3	1	17	10	21
Ukraine	10	5	5	0	14	4	20
Russia	10	6	1	3	22	12	19
Iceland	10	4	3	3	12	7	15
Armenia	10	2	2	6	8	15	8
Andorra	10	0	0	10	3	28	0

GROUP 5

Stockholm, 5 September 1998, 35,394

Sweden (2) 2 *(Andersson A 30, Mjallby 32)*
England (1) 1 *(Shearer 2)*
Sweden: Hedman; Nilsson, Andersson P, Bjorklund, Kamark (Lucic 82), Schwarz, Andersson A (Andersson D 90), Mjallby, Ljungberg, Larsson, Pettersson.
England: Seaman; Anderton (Lee 42), Le Saux, Southgate, Adams, Campbell (Merson 74), Redknapp, Ince, Shearer, Owen, Scholes (Sheringham 85).
Referee: Collina (Italy).

Bourgas, 6 September 1998, 20,000

Bulgaria (0) 0
Poland (2) 3 *(Czereszewski 19, 45, Iwan 47)*
Bulgaria: Zdravkov; Ginchev, Zagorcic (Petkov I 50), Yordanov, Petkov M (Trendafilov 46), Sirakov, Kishishev, Bachev, Borimirov (Gruev 46), Stoichkov, Donev.
Poland: Sidorczuk; Bak, Zielinski, Lapinski, Siadaczka, Hajto (Klos 68), Brzeczek, Czereszewski, Swierczewski (Michalski 76), Iwan, Trzeciak (Juskowiak 83).
Referee: Batta (France).

Wembley, 10 October 1998, 72,974

England (0) 0
Bulgaria (0) 0
England: Seaman; Anderton (Batty 67), Hinchcliffe (Le Saux 34), Neville G, Southgate, Campbell, Lee, Scholes (Sheringham 77), Shearer, Owen, Redknapp.
Bulgaria: Zdravkov; Yordanov, Zagorcic, Kirilov, Kishishev, Iliev (Gruiev 63), Yankov, Petkov M, Naidenov, Stoichkov (Bachev 60), Hristov (Ivanov G 90).
Referee: Vagner (Hungary).

Warsaw, 10 October 1998, 8000

Poland (2) 3 *(Brzeczek 18, Juskowiak 35, Trzeciak 65)*
Luxembourg (0) 0
Poland: Matysek; Zielinski, Lapinski, Ratajczyk (Siadaczka 69), Hajto (Majak 62), Czereszewski (Bak 75), Iwan, Brzeczek, Swierczewski, Juskowiak, Trzeciak.
Luxembourg: Koch; Ferron, Birsens, Funck, Strasser, Holtz (Afrika 69), Theis (Deville F 46), Saibene, Cardoni, Deville L, Christophe (Thill 63).
Referee: Pregia (Albania).

Bourgas, 14 October 1998, 12,000

Bulgaria (0) 0
Sweden (0) 1 *(Larsson 62)*
Bulgaria: Zdravkov; Zagorcic, Yordanov, Kirilov (Parushev 17), Naidenov (Ivanov G 69), Iliev (Bachev 61), Yankov, Petkov M, Petkov I, Stoichkov, Hristov.
Sweden: Hedman; Nilsson, Andersson P, Bjorklund, Lucic (Sundgren 76), Ljungberg, Mild, Mjallby, Schwarz, Larsson (Erlingmark 88), Aslund (Blomqvist 71).
Referee: Heynemann (Germany).

Luxembourg, 14 October 1998, 8000

Luxembourg (0) 0

England (2) 3 *(Owen 19, Shearer 40 (pen), Southgate 90)*

Luxembourg: Koch; Ferron, Deville L, Funck, Deville F, Theis (Holtz 62), Saibene, Strasser, Posing, Cardoni, Christophe.
England: Seaman; Anderton (Lee 64), Neville P, Southgate, Ferdinand, Campbell, Beckham, Batty, Shearer, Owen, Scholes (Wright 76).
Referee: Vorgias (Greece).

Wembley, 27 March 1999, 73,836

England (2) 3 *(Scholes 11, 21, 70)*

Poland (1) 1 *(Brzeczek 29)*

England: Seaman; Neville G, Le Saux, Sherwood, Keown, Campbell, Beckham (Neville P 77), Scholes (Redknapp 83), Shearer, Cole, McManaman (Parlour 69).
Poland: Matysek; Hajto, Zielinski, Lapinski, Ratajczyk, Swierczewski (Klos 46), Bak, Brzeczek, Siadaczka (Kowalczyk 87), Iwan, Trzeciak (Juskowiak 83).
Referee: Pereira (Portugal).

Gothenburg, 27 March 1999, 37,728

Sweden (1) 2 *(Mjallby 34, Larsson 87)*

Luxembourg (0) 0

Sweden: Hedman; Kamark (Lucic 68), Andersson P, Bjorklund, Sundgren, Schwarz, Alexandersson, Mjallby, Ljungberg (Andersson D 79), Larsson, Andersson K.
Luxembourg: Felgen; Ferron, Funck, Birsens, Strasser, Theis (Holtz 70), Vanek, Saibene (Deville F 89), Cardoni, Deville L, Christophe (Zaritski 81).
Referee: Melnitjuk (Ukraine).

Luxembourg, 31 March 1999, 3004

Luxembourg (0) 0

Bulgaria (2) 2 *(Stoichkov 18, Yordanov 38)*

Luxembourg: Felgen; Ferron (Holtz 75), Vanek, Strasser, Deville L, Saibene, Birsens, Theis (Deville F 88), Posing (Zaritski 46), Cardoni, Christophe.
Bulgaria: Zdravkov; Kishishev, Yankov, Stoianov (Petkov I 48), Petkov M, Markov, Yordanov, Petrov, Iliev, Yovov (Ivanov G 79), Stoichkov (Todorov 71).
Referee: Mitrovic (Slovakia).

Chorzow, 31 March 1999, 32,000

Poland (0) 0

Sweden (1) 1 *(Ljungberg 36)*

Poland: Sidorczuk; Waldoch, Lapinski, Zielinski, Siadaczka (Adamczuk 82), Iwan, Michalski (Bak 87), Brzeczek, Majak (Kowalczyk 70), Juskowiak, Trzeciak.
Sweden: Hedman; Kamark, Andersson P, Bjorklund, Lucic, Mild (Alexandersson 72), Schwarz, Mjallby, Ljungberg, Larsson (Pettersson 89), Andersson K.
Referee: Merk (Germany).

Warsaw, 4 June 1999, 8000

Poland (1) 2 *(Hajto 16, Iwan 62)*

Bulgaria (0) 0

Poland: Matysek; Waldoch, Lapinski, Zielinski, Hajto (Majak 80), Nowak (Brzeczek 73), Michalski, Iwan, Siadaczka, Wichniarek (Frankowski 64), Trzeciak.
Bulgaria: Ivankov; Kirilov, Zagorcic, Markov, Kishishev, Petrov, Stoilov, Petkov M, Petkov I (Iliev 80), Stoichkov (Ivanov G 63), Yovov (Bachev 46).
Referee: Braschi (Italy).

Wembley, 5 June 1999, 75,824

England (0) 0

Sweden (0) 0

England: Seaman; Neville P, Le Saux (Gray 46), Batty, Keown (Ferdinand R 35), Campbell, Beckham (Parlour 76), Sherwood, Shearer, Cole, Scholes.
Sweden: Hedman; Nilsson, Kamark, Schwarz, Andersson P, Bjorklund, Mild (Alexandersson 7), Mjallby (Andersson D 82), Andersson K, Larsson (Svensson 70), Ljungberg.
Referee: Aranda (Spain).

Sofia, 9 June 1999, 22,000

Bulgaria (1) 1 *(Markov 18)*

England (1) 1 *(Shearer 15)*

Bulgaria: Ivankov; Kirilov, Stoilov, Kishishev, Zagorcic, Markov, Petrov S, Iliev (Borimirov 61), Petkov M, Stoichkov (Bachev 75), Yovov (Petrov M 46).
England: Seaman; Neville P, Gray, Southgate, Woodgate (Parlour 65), Campbell, Redknapp, Batty, Shearer, Fowler (Heskey 81), Sheringham.
Referee: Van der Ende (Holland).

Luxembourg, 9 June 1999, 2806

Luxembourg (0) 2 *(Birsens 76, Vanek 82)*

Poland (2) 3 *(Siadaczka 22, Wichniarek 45, Iwan 68)*

Luxembourg: Felgen; Vanek, Funck, Birsens, Strasser, Saibene (Alverdi 80), Theis (Schneider 46), Deville F, Cardoni, Christophe, Zaritski (Posing 65).
Poland: Matysek; Waldoch, Lapinski, Klos, Hajto (Brzeczek 65), Nowak, Michalski, Iwan, Siadaczka, Wichniarek (Majak 87), Trzeciak.
Referee: Ivanov (Russia).

Wembley, 4 September 1999, 68,772

England (5) 6 *(Shearer 12 (pen), 28, 34, McManaman 30, 44, Owen 90)*

Luxembourg (0) 0

England: Martyn; Dyer (Neville G 46), Pearce, Batty, Keown, Adams (Neville P 64), Parlour, Beckham (Owen 64), Shearer, Fowler, McManaman.
Luxembourg: Felgen; Ferron, Schauls, Birsens, Funck, Posing (Deville F 83), Vanek, Schneider (Alverdi 46), Saibene, Theis, Christophe (Zaritski 62).
Referee: Shmolik (Belarus).

Stockholm, 4 September 1999, 35,640

Sweden (0) 1 *(Alexandersson 65)*

Bulgaria (0) 0

Sweden: Hedman; Nilsson R, Andersson P, Bjorklund, Kamark, Andersson D, Mild (Svensson 83), Mjallby, Ljungberg (Alexandersson 63), Larsson, Andersson K.
Bulgaria: Ivankov; Stoilov (Gruev 89), Zagorcic (Yankov 26), Petkov I, Markov, Kirilov, Petrov, Petkov M, Todorov, Borimirov, Hristov.
Referee: Koren (Israel).

Luxembourg, 8 September 1999, 4228

Luxembourg (0) 0

Sweden (1) 1 *(Alexandersson 39)*

Luxembourg: Felgen; Funck, Birsens, Schauls, Vanek, Strasser, Saibene (Holtz 87), Schneider (Zaritski 46), Alverdi (Theis 72), Posing, Christophe.
Sweden: Hedman; Nilsson R, Andersson P, Bjorklund, Lucic, Schwarz (Andersson D 81), Mjallby, Alexandersson, Svensson (Zetterberg 46), Larsson, Andersson K.
Referee: Hanacsek (Czech Republic).

Warsaw, 8 September 1999, 17,000

Poland (0) 0

England (0) 0

Poland: Matysek; Klos (Bak 90), Waldoch, Zelinski, Hajto, Iwan, Nowak, Michalski, Siadaczka, Trzeciak (Swierzcewski P 59), Gilewicz (Juskowiak 65).
England: Martyn; Neville G (Neville P 12), Pearce, Batty, Keown, Adams, Beckham, Scholes, Shearer, Fowler (Owen 66), McManaman (Dyer 80).
Referee: Benko (Austria).

Stockholm, 9 October 1999, 35,037

Sweden (0) 2 *(Andersson K 64, Larsson 90)*

Poland (0) 0

Sweden: Hedman; Nilsson R (Sundgren 46), Andersson P, Bjorklund, Kamark, Alexandersson, Mjallby, Schwarz, Ljungberg (Mild 83), Andersson K, Larsson.
Poland: Matysek; Siadaczka, Klos, Zielinski, Waldoch, Hajto, Swierczewski (Wichniarek 89), Michalski, Czereszewski (Nowak 73), Juskowiak (Kryszalowicz 81), Trzeciak.
Referee: Meier (Switzerland).

Sofia, 10 October 1999, 4000

Bulgaria (1) 3 *(Borimirov 40, Petkov I 68, Hristov R 78)*

Luxembourg (0) 0

Bulgaria: Zdravkov; Zagorcic (Ivanov B 84), Stoilov, Petkov I, Yordanov, Borimirov, Markov, Petrov, Bachev (Hristov R 51), Hristov M (Todorov 64), Alexandrov.
Luxembourg: Felgen; Vanek, Schauls, Birsens, Strasser, Alverdi (Theis 71), Saibene, Posing (Deville 59), Cardoni (Holtz 85), Zaritski, Christophe.
Referee: Gadosi (Slovenia).

Group 5 – Final Table	P	W	D	L	F	A	Pts
Sweden	8	7	1	0	10	1	22
England	8	4	1	3	14	4	13
Poland	8	4	1	3	12	8	13
Bulgaria	8	2	2	4	6	8	8
Luxembourg	8	0	0	8	2	23	0

GROUP 6

Vienna, 5 September 1998, 20,000

Austria (1) 1 *(Reinmayr 7)*

Israel (0) 1 *(Nimni 68 (pen))*

Austria: Wohlfahrt; Schottel (Hiden 73), Feiersinger, Pfeffer, Cerny (Stoger 74), Kuhbauer, Mahlich, Reinmayr, Amerhauser, Vastic, Haas (Mayrleb 73).
Israel: Cohen; Harazi A, Shelach (Nimni 46), Ben Shimon, Amsalem, Abuksis (Mizrahi A 46), Berkovic, Revivo, Benado, Harazi R (Ghrayib 61), Badir.
Referee: Frisk (Sweden).

Larnaca, 5 September 1998, 3500

Cyprus (1) 3 *(Engomitis 44, Gogic 48, Spoljaric 77)*

Spain (0) 2 *(Raul 72, Morientes 85)*

Cyprus: Panayiotou N; Costa, Ioannou D (Ioakim 84), Charalambous M, Pittas, Melanarkitis, Spoljaric, Christodolou M, Engomitis, Gogic (Agathocleous 61), Malekos (Pounas 55).
Spain: Canizares; Michel Salgado, Nadal (Amor 65), Alkorta, Sergi, Etxeberria J (Ezquerro 59), Hierro, Raul, Luis Enrique, Alfonso (Kiko 39), Morientes.
Referee: Guseinov (Russia).

Larnaca, 10 October 1998, 10,000

Cyprus (0) 0

Austria (0) 3 *(Cerny 53, 61, Reinmayr 74)*

Cyprus: Panayiotou N; Engomitis, Ioannou D, Costa, Charalambous M, Pittas (Georgiou 67), Spoljaric, Melanarkitis (Constandinou M 68), Christodolou M, Agathocleous (Okkas 46), Gogic.
Austria: Wohlfahrt; Hiden, Schottel, Pfeffer, Cerny, Kuhbauer, Mahlich, Reinmayr (Stoger 79), Wetl, Vastic (Glieder 82), Haas (Mayrleb 78).
Referee: Meese (Belgium).

Serravalle, 10 October 1998, 872

San Marino (0) 0

Israel (3) 5 *(Revivo 16, Nimni 19, Mizrahi A 31, 64, Ghrayib 83)*

San Marino: Gasperoni F; Gennari, Guerra, Valentini M, Bacciocchi S (Valentini V 55), Marani, Montagna (Gualtieri 78), Muccioli, Della Valle (Francini 67), Matteoni, Selva A.
Israel: Cohen; Harazi A, Ben Shimon, Telasnikov, Badir, Benado (Shelach 68), Nimni (Banin 59), Ghrayib, Revivo, Berkovic (Shitrit 74), Mizrahi A.
Referee: Khudiev (Azerbaijan).

Tel Aviv, 14 October 1998, 42,000

Israel (0) 1 *(Hazan 63)*

Spain (0) 2 *(Hierro 65, Etxeberria J 77)*

Israel: Cohen; Harazi A, Ben Shimon, Benado, Hazan (Banin 75), Badir, Telasnikov (Mizrahi A 59), Ghrayib, Nimni, Revivo, Berkovic.
Spain: Canizares; Michel Salgado, Hierro, Alkorta, Aranzabal, Luis Enrique, Engonga, Alkiza, De Pedro (Etxeberria J 72), Kiko (Urzaiz 88), Raul (Vales 90).
Referee: Elleray (England).

Serravalle, 14 October 1998, 1000

San Marino (0) 1 *(Selva A 80 (pen))*

Austria (0) 4 *(Vastic 58, Mayrleb 63, Hiden 68, Glieder 76)*

San Marino: Gasperoni F; Gennari, Guerra, Valentini M (Della Valle 80), Bacciocchi S, Marani, Muccioli, Francini (Valentini V 69), Ugolini (Montagna 62), Matteoni, Selva A.
Austria: Wohlfahrt; Hiden, Schottel, Pfeffer, Cerny, Kuhbauer, Heraf, Reinmayr (Mayrleb 46), Wetl, Vastic (Stoger 70), Haas (Glieder 66).
Referee: Onufer (Ukraine).

Serravalle, 18 November 1998, 600

San Marino (0) 0

Cyprus (1) 1 *(Spoljaric 41)*

San Marino: Gasperoni F; Gennari, Valentini M, Guerra, Valentini V, Marani, Gasperoni B, Muccioli (Mularoni 83), Matteoni (Francini 75), Montagna (Bacchiocchi N 67), Ugolini.
Cyprus: Panayiotou N; Pittas, Panayiotou P, Charalambous M, Sophocleous, Engomitis, Melanarkitis, Spoljaric, Agathocleous (Constandinou M 73), Malekos (Ioannou Y 73), Gogic (Okkas 86).
Referee: McDermott (Republic of Ireland).

Nicosia, 10 February 1999, 3000

Cyprus (3) 4 *(Melanarkitis 18, Constantinou M 32, 45, Christodoulou M 88)*

San Marino (0) 0

Cyprus: Panayiotou N; Theodotou, Christodoulou M, Ioakim, Charalambous M, Pittas, Melanarkitis, Spoljaric, Gogic (Ioannou Y 80), Constantinou M (Okkas 80), Malekos (Aristocleous 89).
San Marino: Gasperoni F; Gennari, Marani (Vannucci 84), Gobbi, Valentini V, Guerra, Zonzini, Della Valle (Manzaroli 70), Ugolini (Bacciocchi 46), Mularoni, Selva A.

Valencia, 27 March 1999, 40,000

Spain (5) 9 *(Raul 5, 17, 47, 74, Urzaiz 30, 44, Hierro 35 (pen), Wetl 76 (og), Fran 84)*

Austria (0) 0

Spain: Canizares; Michel Salgado, Hierro, Marcelino, Sergi, Etxeberria J (Dani 84), Guardiola, Valeron (Mendieta 71), Fran, Raul, Urzaiz (Munitis 61).
Austria: Wohlfahrt; Schottel, Feiersinger (Kogler 54), Pfeffer, Cerny, Mahlich, Neukirchner, Prosenik (Reinmayr 58), Wetl, Herzog, Haas (Mayrleb 69).
Referee: Veissiere (France).

Tel Aviv, 28 March 1999, 30,000

Israel (1) 3 *(Banin 11, Mizrahi A 47, 53)*

Cyprus (0) 0

Israel: Davidovich; Harazi A, Ghrayib, Shelach, Badir (Talker 46), Banin, Benado, Berkovic, Revivo (Tikva 85), Harazi R (Mizrahi A 46), Nimni.
Cyprus: Panayiotou N; Theodotou, Pittas, Ioannou D, Charalambous M, Constandinou M (Okkas 65), Melanarkitis, Spoljaric (Agathocleous 79), Malekos (Nicolaou 46), Sophocleous, Christodolou M.
Referee: Lica (Romania).

Serravalle, 31 March 1999, 1000

San Marino (0) 0
Spain (2) 6 *(Fran 20, Raul 45, 59, 66, Urzaiz 49, Etxeberria J 72)*
San Marino: Gasperoni F; Gennari, Marani, Valentini V, Zonzini, Valentini M, Manzaroli, Gasperoni B (Muccioli 75), Gobbi (Della Balda 51), Selva A, Montagna (Gualtieri 60).
Spain: Canizares; Michel Salgado, Marcelino, Paco, Sergi, Etxeberria J, Guardiola (Engonga 68), Valeron (Helguera 78), Fran, Raul, Urzaiz (Dani 61).
Referee: Maric (Croatia).

Graz, 28 April 1999, 15,000

Austria (3) 7 *(Mayrleb 24, 53, Vastic 42, 44, 84, Amerhauser 71, Herzog 82 (pen))*
San Marino (0) 0
Austria: Wohlfahrt; Winklhofer (Rohseano 80), Feiersinger, Neukirchner, Cerny (Kitzbichler 71), Schopp (Glieder 71), Herzog, Prosenik, Amerhauser, Mayrleb, Vastic.
San Marino: Gasperoni F; Gennari (Bacciocchi S 46), Della Balda, Guerra, Gobbi, Vannucci, Gasperoni B (Manzaroli 15), Zonzini, Muccioli, Selva A, Montagna (Selva R 78).
Referee: Vassaros (Greece).

Villarreal, 5 June 1999, 16,000

Spain (4) 9 *(Hierro 8 (pen), Luis Enrique 22, 67, 71, Etxeberria J 25, 45, Raul 56, Gennari 85 (og), Mendieta 90)*
San Marino (0) 0
Spain: Canizares; Michel Salgado (Munitis 60), Marcelino, Hierro, Aranzabal, Etxeberria J, Guardiola, Guerrero (Mendieta 74), Luis Enrique, Raul (Urzaiz 60), Morientes.
San Marino: Gasperoni F; Gennari (Vannucci 90), Marani, Della Balda, Gobbi, Guerra, Bacciocchi N, Della Valle, Zonzini, Manzaroli (Valentini V 75), Montagna (Ugolini 58).
Referee: Perry (Republic of Ireland).

Tel Aviv, 6 June 1999, 43,000

Israel (2) 5 *(Berkovic 26, 47, Revivo 45, Mizrahi A 54, Ghrayib 75)*
Austria (0) 0
Israel: Davidovich; Shelach, Benado, Harazi A, Ghrayib, Banin, Abuksis (Tal 82), Hazan, Mizrahi A (Tikva 78), Berkovic (Sivilia 77), Revivo.
Austria: Wohlfahrt; Winklhofer, Barisic, Kogler, Cerny, Mahlich, Herzog, Neukirchner, Amerhauser (Prosenik 46), Mayrleb (Haas 67), Vastic (Glieder 57).
Referee: Michel (Slovakia).

Vienna, 4 September 1999, 27,000

Austria (0) 1 *(Hierro 50 (og))*
Spain (1) 3 *(Raul 23, Hierro 54, Luis Enrique 89)*
Austria: Manninger; Streiter, Winklhofer, Hatz, Ibertsberger, Kuhbauer, Vastic, Mahlich (Schopp 60), Kirchler (Weissenberger 67), Cerny, Mayrleb.
Spain: Canizares; Michel Salgado, Hierro, Paco, Sergi, Etxeberria J (Mendieta 81), Valeron (Engonga 72), Guardiola, Luis Enrique, Morientes (Guerrero 88), Raul.
Referee: Piraux (Belgium).

Limassol, 5 September 1999, 16,000

Cyprus (1) 3 *(Engomitis 27, Spoljaric 53, 86 (pen))*
Israel (1) 2 *(Badir 31, Benayoun 82)*
Cyprus: Panayiotou; Engomitis, Pittas, Kostakis, Charalambous, Melanarkitis, Papavassiliou (Christodolou M 64), Kaiafas (Aristocleous 80), Spoljaric, Gogic (Constantinou 72), Okkas.
Israel: Davidovich; Hazan, Harazi A, Benado, Shelach (Civilia 65), Ghrayib, Abuksis (Benayoun 55), Banin, Berkovic (Badir 18), Revivo, Mizrahi A.
Referee: Barber (England).

Tel Aviv, 8 September 1999, 20,000

Israel (3) 8 *(Benayoun 25, 46, 71, Revivo 40, 69, Mizrahi A 38, Sivilia 84, Abuksis 90)*
San Marino (0) 0
Israel: Davidovich; Talkar, Harazi A, Benado (Halfon 66), Amsalem, Telesnikov, Hazan, Tikva (Abuksis 62), Benayoun, Revivo, Mizrahi A (Sivilia 46).
San Marino: Gasperoni F; Gennari, Tomassoni, Bacciocchi S, Della Balda, Pelliccioni, Bacciocchi N (Salva R 59), Gasperoni B, Salva A, Zonzini (Della Valle 75), Montagna (De Luigi 80).
Referee: Kaplan (Turkey).

Badajoz, 8 September 1999, 15,000

Spain (5) 8 *(Urzaiz 19, 25, 37, Guerrero 33, 42, 57, Cesar 82, Hierro 88)*
Cyprus (0) 0
Spain: Canizares (Toni 77); Michel Salgado, Cesar, Hierro, Aranzabal, Etxeberria J (Munitis 46), Guardiola, Guerrero, Luis Enrique (Mendieta 61), Raul, Urzaiz.
Cyprus: Panayiotou; Costa, Nicolaou (Aristocleous 46), Louka, Pittas (Theodotou 46), Melanarkitis, Engomitis, Christodoulou M, Papavassiliou, Gogic (Constandinou 88), Okkas.
Referee: Trentalange (Italy).

Vienna, 10 October 1999, 10,000

Austria (2) 3 *(Glieder 5, Vastic 23, Herzog 81)*
Cyprus (0) 1 *(Costa 64)*
Austria: Manninger; Winklhofer, Neukirchner (Herzog 46), Vastic, Ibertsberger, Cerny (Kauz 75), Kirchler, Kuhbauer, Mayrleb, Glieder, Weissenberger (Wimmer 83).
Cyprus: Panayiotou N; Costa, Christodolou M, Kaiafas, Charalambous M, Engomitis, Spoljaric, Melanarkitis (Demetriou 82), Alexandrou, Gogic (Agathocleous 26), Okkas (Theodotou 46).
Referee: Bazzoli (Italy).

Albacete, 10 October 1999, 12,000

Spain (2) 3 *(Morientes 30, Cesar 37, Raul 51)*
Israel (0) 0
Spain: Toni; Michel Salgado, Hierro (Cesar 22), Paco, Sergi, Etxeberria J, Guardiola, Guerrero (Mendieta 70), Luis Enrique, Morientes (Urzaiz 75), Raul.
Israel: Awat; Gershon, Amsalem, Shelah, Benado (Halfon 49), Hazan (Telesnikov 80), Banin, Tal, Berkovic (Benayoun 67), Revivo, Turgeman.
Referee: Krug (Germany).

Group 6 – Final Table	P	W	D	L	F	A	Pts
Spain	8	7	0	1	42	5	21
Israel	8	4	1	3	25	9	13
Austria	8	4	1	3	19	20	13
Cyprus	8	4	0	4	12	21	12
San Marino	8	0	0	8	1	44	0

GROUP 7

Bucharest, 2 September 1998, 6000

Romania (4) 7 *(Gheorge Popescu 18, Munteanu C 30, Ilie A 32, 45, 51, Moldovan 56, Haas 60 (og))*
Liechtenstein (0) 0
Romania: Stelea (Lobont 80); Petrescu, Batranu, Gheorge Popescu, Contra, Petre, Galca, Munteanu C (Sabau 72), Munteanu D, Moldovan, Ilie A (Mihalcea 69).
Liechtenstein: Oehry M; Hefti, Hanselmann, Michael Stocklasa, Telser M (Ender 89), Ritter, Zech, Lingg (Buchel 62), Beck T, Oehri R, Haas (Martin Stocklasa 63).
Referee: Prolic (Bosnia).

Kosice, 5 September 1998, 3243

Slovakia (3) 3 *(Fabus 17, Dubovsky 26 (pen), Moravcik 40)*
Azerbaijan (0) 0
Slovakia: Vencel; Varga, Tomaschek, Tittel, Spilar, Kinder, Sovic, Moravcik, Fabus (Jancula 62), Majoros (Ujlaky 46), Dubovsky (Zvara 62).
Azerbaijan: Kramarenko; Gaisumov, Abusev, Jabarov, Agayev, Lichkin (Rzayev 46), Nasurov (Guseynov 79), Asadov, Sirkhaev, Suleimanov (Kuliyev 46), Kurbanov K.
Referee: Snoddy (Northern Ireland).

Budapest, 6 September 1998, 50,000

Hungary (1) 1 *(Horvath 32)*

Portugal (0) 3 *(Sa Pinto 56, 76, Rui Costa 84)*

Hungary: Kiraly; Feher C (Korsos 78), Lakos, Hrutka, Matyus, Lisztes (Dardai 46), Halmai, Illes, Dombi (Kovacs Z 78), Horvath, Hamar.

Portugal: Vitor Baia; Secretario, Jorge Costa, Paulo Madeira, Dimas, Figo, Paulo Bento, Rui Costa, Paulinho Santos, Joao Pinto, Sa Pinto.

Referee: Meier (Switzerland).

Baku, 10 October 1998, 10,000

Azerbaijan (0) 0

Hungary (0) 4 *(Dardai 58, Illes 85 (pen), Pisont 87, Feher M 90)*

Azerbaijan: Kramarenko (Jidkov 59); Gaisumov, Agayev, Abusev, Kerimov, Asadov (Mamedov I 51), Lichkin, Sirkhaev, Rzayev, Kambarov (Kasumov 46), Kurbanov K.

Hungary: Kiraly; Sebok V (Korsos 65), Feher C, Hrutka, Matyus, Dardai, Pisont, Illes, Lisztes (Dombi 75), Horvath (Feher M 6), Hamar.

Referee: Bre (France).

Vaduz, 10 October 1998, 1900

Liechtenstein (0) 0

Slovakia (3) 4 *(Sovic 3, Dubovsky 13, Tomaschek 36, 61)*

Liechtenstein: Oehry M; Ritter, Hanselmann, Zech, Hefti (Lingg 76), Haas (Martin Stocklasa 33), Oehri R (Ospelt J 46), Hasler, Michael Stocklasa, Frick M, Telser M.

Slovakia: Vencel; Varga (Timko 65), Tittel, Spilar, Sovic, Tomaschek, Moravcik, Dubovsky, Kinder (Kozak 30), Majoros, Fabus (Jancula 61).

Referee: Antonov (Moldova).

Porto, 10 October 1998, 40,000

Portugal (0) 0

Romania (0) 1 *(Munteanu D 90)*

Portugal: Vitor Baia; Abel Xavier (Dani 85), Jorge Costa, Fernando Couto, Dimas, Figo, Paulo Bento (Conceicao 70), Rui Costa, Paulinho Santos, Joao Pinto (Nuno Gomes 79), Sa Pinto.

Romania: Stelea; Petrescu (Contra 83), Filipescu, Gheorge Popescu, Ciobotariu, Petre, Munteanu C (Lupescu 61), Galca, Munteanu D, Rosu, Moldovan (Mihalcea 89).

Referee: Krug (Germany).

Budapest, 14 October 1998, 40,000

Hungary (0) 1 *(Hrutka 82)*

Romania (0) 1 *(Moldovan 51)*

Hungary: Kiraly; Feher C, Sebok V, Hrutka, Matyus, Pisont, Dardai, Illes, Egressy (Lisztes 78), Feher M (Hamori 75), Hamar (Toth 70).

Romania: Stelea; Petrescu, Filipescu, Georghe Popescu, Ciobotariu, Petre (Serban 70), Galca, Lupescu, Munteanu D, Moldovan (Mihalcea 85), Craioveanu (Munteanu C 75).

Referee: Nielsen (Denmark).

Vaduz, 14 October 1998, 1900

Liechtenstein (0) 2 *(Frick M 47 (pen), Telser M 49)*

Azerbaijan (0) 1 *(Kurbanov K 59)*

Liechtenstein: Jehle; Ritter, Zech, Hasler, Martin Stocklasa, Bicker (Ospelt J 67), Lingg, Michael Stocklasa, Beck T (Buchel 74), Frick M, Telser M.

Azerbaijan: Jidkov; Yadullayev, Gaisumov, Agayev, Kerimov, Abusev (Kuliyev 76), KurbanovM (Suleimanov 25), Rzayev, Kambarov (Mamedov I 61), Kurbanov K, Sirkhaev.

Referee: Barr (N Ireland).

Bratislava, 14 October 1998, 22,059

Slovakia (0) 0

Portugal (2) 3 *(Joao Pinto 16, 31, Abel Xavier 72)*

Slovakia: Vencel; Spilar, Kinder (Kozak 46), Tittel, Varga, Sovic (Pinte 82), Tomaschek, Fabus (Nemeth S 57), Moravcik, Majoros, Dubovsky.

Portugal: Vitor Baia; Abel Xavier, Jorge Costa, Fernando Couto, Dimas, Figo (Capucho 89), Paulo Bento, Rui Costa (Da Costa 67), Paulinho Santos, Joao Pinto (Conceicao 46), Sa Pinto.

Referee: Sarvan (Turkey).

Guimaraes, 26 March 1999, 20,000

Portugal (2) 7 *(Sa Pinto 28, Joao Pinto 36, 77, Paulo Madeira 67, Conceicao 75, Pauleta 82, 83)*

Azerbaijan (0) 0

Portugal: Vitor Baia (Espinha 83); Secretario, Paulo Madeira, Fernando Couto, Dimas, Paulo Sousa, Rui Costa (Pedro Barbosa 83), Conceicao, Figo (Pauleta 74), Sa Pinto, Joao Pinto.

Azerbaijan: Kramarenko; Agayev, Asadov, Akhmedov, Stukas, Abusev, Kambarov (Vasiliev 72), Musayev (Rzayev 69), Sirkhaev, Lichkin, Kurbanov K.

Referee: Granat (Poland).

Budapest, 27 March 1999, 9534

Hungary (3) 5 *(Sebok J 17, Sebok V 33, 41, 86, Illes 74)*

Liechtenstein (0) 0

Hungary: Kiraly; Hrutka (Somogyi 79), Sebok V, Korsos, Matyus, Halmai, Sebok J (Dombi 71), Pisont, Illes, Feher M, Toth (Hamar 76).

Liechtenstein: Jehle; Hanselmann (Hefti 46), Martin Stocklasa, Lingg, Ritter, Michael Stocklasa, Wohlwend, Frick M, Hasler, Telser M, Beck M (Ospelt J 78).

Referee: Kapitanis (Cyprus).

Bucharest, 27 March 1999, 15,000

Romania (0) 0

Slovakia (0) 0

Romania: Stelea; Petrescu, Batranu, Gheorge Popescu, Rosu, Petre, Galca, Munteanu C (Lupescu 66), Munteanu D, Moldovan (Craioveanu 64), Ilie A.

Slovakia: Konig; Varga, Zeman, Karhan, Kratochvil, Zatek (Dzurik 75), Tomaschek, Balis, Labant, Dubovsky (Suchancok 78), Majoros (Slicho 62).

Referee: Barber (England).

Baku, 31 March 1999, 25,000

Azerbaijan (0) 0

Romania (0) 1 *(Petre 49)*

Azerbaijan: Magomedov; Kerimov, Poshekhontsev, Asadov, Agayev (Kuliyev 75), Tagizade (Kambarov 69), Kurbanov M (Rzayev 67), Akhmedov, Lichkin, Sirkhaev, Kurbanov K.

Romania: Lobont; Contra, Filipescu, Ciobotariu, Munteanu D, Petre, Galca, Lupescu, Rosu (Florea 75), Moldovan, Craioveanu (Mihalcea 89).

Referee: Luinge (Holland).

Vaduz, 31 March 1999, 3000

Liechtenstein (0) 0

Portugal (1) 5 *(Rui Costa 16 (pen), 79, Figo 49, Paulo Madeira 54, 60)*

Liechtenstein: Jehle; Lingg, Hasler, Hanselmann (Ospelt J 84), Martin Stocklasa, Ritter, Telser M, Frick C, Michael Stocklasa (Beck M 66), Wohlwend (Burgmaier 83), Frick M.

Portugal: Vitor Baia; Secretario, Paulo Madeira, Fernando Couto, Dimas, Conceicao (Capucho 88), Paulo Sousa, Rui Costa, Figo, Sa Pinto (Pauleta 61), Joao Pinto (Nuno Gomes 75).

Referee: Orrason (Iceland).

Bratislava, 31 March 1999, 19,400

Slovakia (0) 0
Hungary (0) 0
Slovakia: Konig; Kratochvil, Zeman (Dzurik 13), Varga, Karhan, Balis, Tomaschek, Dubovsky, Zatek (Hrncar 79), Majoros, Pinte (Slicho 83).
Hungary: Kiraly; Korsos, Sebok V, Hrutka, Matyus, Pisont, Halmai, Illes, Sebok J (Dombi 56), Feher M (Hamar 64), Toth.
Referee: Colombo (France).

Bucharest, 5 June 1999, 23,000

Romania (2) 2 *(Ilie A 2, Munteanu D 15)*
Hungary (0) 0
Romania: Lobont; Petrescu, Filipescu, Gheorge Popescu, Nanu, Petre, Hagi (Lupescu 46), Galca, Munteanu D, Moldovan (Ganea 64), Ilie A (Craioveanu 86).
Hungary: Kiraly; Sebok V, Hrutka, Matyus, Korsos, Dardai, Halmai, Illes (Preisinger 81), Egressy, Sebok J (Herczeg 76), Feher M (Pisont 46).
Referee: Pedersen (Norway).

Baku, 5 June 1999, 8500

Azerbaijan (2) 4 *(Kurbanov K 16, Lichkin 42, Tagizade 60, Isaiev 73)*
Liechtenstein (0) 0
Azerbaijan: Kramarenko; Agayev, Yadullayev, Akhmedov, Kerimov, Kurbanov M, Tagizade (Isaiev 68), Vasiliev (Khankishiev 61), Sirkhaev, Lichkin (Stukas 74), Kurbanov K.
Liechtenstein: Jehle; Lingg, Hasler, Zech, Martin Stocklasa, Ritter, Telser M, Michael Stocklasa (Wohlwend 74), Frick C, Bicker (Beck M 59), Benz (Beck T 46).
Referee: Stadskaar (Denmark).

Lisbon, 5 June 1999, 25,000

Portugal (0) 1 *(Capucho 62)*
Slovakia (0) 0
Portugal: Vitor Baia; Abel Xavier (Conceicao 31), Fernando Couto, Paulo Madeira, Dimas, Paulo Sousa, Paulo Bento, Rui Costa, Figo (Barbosa 89), Joao Pinto (Capucho 61), Sa Pinto.
Slovakia: Konig; Varga, Timko, Karhan, Kratochvil, Zvara (Valachovic 30), Tomaschek, Pinte (Slicho 64), Labant, Dubovsky, Majoros (Kozuch 83).
Referee: Larsen (Denmark).

Gyor, 9 June 1999, 16,500

Hungary (0) 0
Slovakia (0) 1 *(Fabus 53)*
Hungary: Kiraly; Sebok V, Hrutka, Matyus, Korsos, Dardai, Halmai (Pisont 73), Illes, Egressy (Dombi 60), Sebok J, Somogyi (Preisinger 78).
Slovakia: Konig; Varga, Timko, Karhan, Kratochvil, Zvara (Dzurik 81), Valachovic, Pinte, Labant, Nemeth P, Fabus.
Referee: Vega (Spain).

Coimbra, 9 June 1999, 25,000

Portugal (3) 8 *(Sa Pinto 28, 44, Joao Pinto 40, 59, 67, Ritter 52 (og), Rui Costa 80, 90 (pen))*
Liechtenstein (0) 0
Portugal: Vitor Baia; Secretario (Capucho 14), Fernando Couto, Paulo Madeira, Dimas, Paulo Sousa (Barbosa 63), Conceicao, Rui Costa, Figo, Joao Pinto, Sa Pinto.
Liechtenstein: Jehle; Zech, Hasler, Ospelt J, Ritter, Telser D (Lingg 53), Michael Stocklasa (Burgmaier 67), Wohlwend, Telser M (Buchel 73), Bicker, Beck T.
Referee: Drabek (Austria).

Bucharest, 9 June 1999, 8000

Romania (2) 4 *(Ganea 35, Munteanu D 44 (pen), Vladoiu 50, Rosu 90)*
Azerbaijan (0) 0
Romania: Lobont; Petrescu, Filipescu, Gheorge Popescu, Nanu, Petre (Moldovan 68), Galca, Lupescu, Munteanu D, Ganea (Craioveanu 59), Vladoiu (Rosu 79).
Azerbaijan: Kramarenko; Agayev (Getman 71), Jadullayev, Akhmedov, Lichkin (Vasiliev 82), Kerimov, Kurbanov M (Musayev 59), Tagizade, Kurbanov K, Poshekhontsev, Sirkhaev.
Referee: Siric (Croatia).

Baku, 4 September 1999, 8000

Azerbaijan (0) 1 *(Tagizade 51)*
Portugal (0) 1 *(Figo 90)*
Azerbaijan: Kramarenko; Poshekhontsev, Kuliev, Akhmedov, Agayev, Niftaliev, Getman, Tagizade, Musayev (Kurbanov M 58), Vasiliev (Gambarov 54), Lichkin (Stukas 90).
Portugal: Vitor Baia; Secretario, Fernando Couto, Paulo Madeira, Dimas, Paulo Bento (Pauleta 29), Paulo Sousa (Capucho 68), Rui Costa, Figo, Joao Pinto, Sa Pinto (Conceicao 46).
Referee: Gallagher (England).

Vaduz, 4 September 1999, 1700

Liechtenstein (0) 0
Hungary (0) 0
Liechtenstein: Jehle; Zech, Ospelt J, Hasler, Hefti, Gigon, Martin Stocklasa, Telser (Ritter 66), Michael Stocklasa, Frick M (Beck M 90), Beck T (Bicker 83).
Hungary: Kiraly; Korsos, Sebok V, Halmai, Matyus, Dardai, Illes, Feher M (Lendvai 46), Dombi (Sowoumni 60), Horvath (Herczeg 76), Egressy.
Referee: Kaldma (Estonia).

Bratislava, 4 September 1999, 8143

Slovakia (1) 1 *(Labant 22)*
Romania (2) 5 *(Ilie A 6, Hagi 30, Ciobotariu 65, Moldovan 88, 90)*
Slovakia: Konig; Kratochvil (Hrabal 74), Valachovic, Varga, Karhan, Balis (Jancula 68), Nemeth P, Janocko, Labant, Nemeth S, Fabus (Uljaky 81).
Romania: Stelea; Petrescu, Gheorge Popescu, Ciobotariu, Filipescu, Sabau (Stinga 83), Galca, Hagi (Lupescu 75), Munteanu D, Ganea (Moldovan 58), Ilie A.
Referee: Cesari (Italy).

Bucharest, 8 September 1999, 23,000

Romania (1) 1 *(Ilie A 37)*
Portugal (1) 1 *(Figo 45)*
Romania: Stelea; Petrescu (Nanu 46), Gheorge Popescu, Filipescu, Ciobotariu, Sabau, Galca, Hagi, Munteanu D, Moldovan (Lupescu 69), Ilie A (Ganea 85).
Portugal: Vitor Baia; Rui Bento, Fernando Couto, Paulo Madeira, Dimas, Paulo Bento, Paulo Sousa (Conceicao 69), Rui Costa, Figo, Joao Pinto (Pauleta 80), Sa Pinto.
Referee: Strampe (Germany).

Dudnica, 8 September 1999, 3052

Slovakia (1) 2 *(Nemeth S 4, Karhan 56)*
Liechtenstein (0) 0
Slovakia: Susko; Valachovic, Varga, Karhan, Balis, Dzurik, Janocko (Hrabal 41), Uljaky, Labant, Nemeth S (Kozuch 76), Fabus (Nemeth P 61).
Liechtenstein: Jehle; Ospelt J, Ritter, Martin Stocklasa, Zech, Gigon (Wohlwend 57), Hasler, Telser, Michael Stocklasa (Buchel 12) (Beck M 57), Frick M, Beck T.
Referee: Georgiou (Cyprus).

Budapest, 8 September 1999, 3500

Hungary (1) 3 *(Sebok V 28, Egressy 51, Sowunmi 55)*

Azerbaijan (0) 0

Hungary: Kiraly; Korsos, Sebok V, Hrutka, Matyus, Lendvai, Halmai, Illes, Herczeg (Horvath 74), Sowunmi (Fuzi 89), Egressy.
Azerbaijan: Gassan; Poshekhontsev, Kerimov (Gambarov 61), Getman, Niftialiev, Kuliyev, Asadov, Musayev, Yadullayev, Lichkin (Stukas 68), Vasiliev (Ismailov 90).
Referee: Lazarevski (Macedonia).

Baku, 9 October 1999, 8000

Azerbaijan (0) 0

Slovakia (0) 1 *(Labant 70)*

Azerbaijan: Kramarenko; Agayev (Kerimov 80), Poshekhontsev, Akhmedov, Isayev (Ismailov 56), Getman, Yadullayev, Gambarov (Lichkin 46), Vasiliev, Musayev, Niftalijev.
Slovakia: Susko; Kozak, Sucanchak, Kratochvil, Varga, Labant (Kozuch 84), Timko, Karhan (Zeman 86), Janocko (Pinter 90), Nemeth S, Fabus.
Referee: Vassaras (Greece).

Vaduz, 9 October 1999, 2900

Liechtenstein (0) 0

Romania (1) 3 *(Rosu 26, Ganea 65, 73)*

Liechtenstein: Jehle; Ospelt J, Martin Stocklasa, Hefti, Zech, Ritter, Frick C (Wohlwend 89), Frick M, Telser M (Bicker 69), Beck M, Beck T.
Romania: Stelea; Petrescu, Gheorge Popescu, Ciobotariu, Nanu, Petre, Galca (Lupescu 68), Hagi (Stinga 70), Rosu, Moldovan (Ganea 62), Ilie A.
Referee: Butenko (Russia).

Lisbon, 9 October 1999, 65,000

Portugal (2) 3 *(Rui Costa 15, Joao Pinto 16, Abel Xavier 58)*

Hungary (0) 0

Portugal: Vitor Baia; Secretario (Abel Xavier 46), Paulo Madeira, Jorge Costa, Dimas, Figo, Paulo Sousa, Rui Costa (Paulo Bento 84), Conceicao, Pauleta, Joao Pinto (Sa Pinto 89).
Hungary: Kiraly; Korsos, Dragoner, Lakos, Matyus, Lendvai, Halmai, Pisont (Dardai 24), Sowunmi (Kovacs 83), Egressy, Horvath (Kuttor 75).
Referee: Nielsen (Denmark).

Group 7 – Final Table	P	W	D	L	F	A	Pts
Romania	10	7	3	0	25	3	24
Portugal	10	7	2	1	32	4	23
Slovakia	10	5	2	3	12	9	17
Hungary	10	3	3	4	14	10	12
Azerbaijan	10	1	1	8	6	26	4
Liechtenstein	10	1	1	8	2	39	4

GROUP 8

Dublin, 5 September 1998, 34,000

Republic of Ireland (2) 2 *(Irwin 4 (pen), Roy Keane 15)*

Croatia (0) 0

Republic of Ireland: Given; Irwin, Staunton, McAteer, Cunningham, Babb, Kinsella, Roy Keane, O'Neill (Cascarino 9), Robbie Keane (Carsley 62), Duff (Kenna 46).
Croatia: Ladic; Soldo (Tokic 77), Stimac, Simic D, Tudor (Krpan 62), Jurcic, Boban, Asanovic, Jarni, Stanic, Maric (Pamic 46).
Referee: Pereira (Portugal).

Skopje, 6 September 1998, 5000

Macedonia (1) 4 *(Bozinov 20, 48, Sakiri 75, 80)*

Malta (0) 0

Macedonia: Milosevski; Lazarevski, Stojkovski (Gosev 80), Nikolovski (Sainovski 78), Sedloski, Micevski, Stojanoski (Sakiri 70), Trenevski, Zaharievski, Stavrevski, Bozinov.
Malta: Muscat; Said, Overand, Debono, Chetcuti, Turner, Agius (Suda 70), Brincat, Zahra (Carabott 78), Busuttil, Camilleri.
Referee: Wegereef (Holland).

Ta'Qali, 10 October 1998, 8000

Malta (1) 1 *(Suda 28 (pen))*

Croatia (0) 4 *(Simic D 54, Vugrinec 68, 74, Suker 85)*

Malta: Muscat; Buttigieg, Spiteri, Debono, Chetcuti, Suda (Turner 57), Agius (Zammit 11), Brincat, Zahra (Sixsmith 77), Busuttil, Camilleri.
Croatia: Ladic; Simic D (Tokic 81), Soldo, Tudor, Saric, Maric, Boban, Asanovic, Jarni (Cvitanovic 87), Suker, Vucko (Vugrinec 60).
Referee: Benedik (Slovakia).

Zagreb, 14 October 1998, 20,000

Croatia (2) 3 *(Suker 16, Boban 45, 70)*

Macedonia (1) 2 *(Ciric 2, Sainovski 55)*

Croatia: Ladic; Tudor, Stimac, Simic D, Stanic (Jurcic 81), Soldo, Boban, Asanovic (Saric 61), Jarni, Maric, Suker.
Macedonia: Milosevski; Sedloski, Stavrevski, Nikolovski (Stojanoski 77), Sainovski, Zaharievski, Micevski (Gosev 46), Lazarevski (Bozinov 60), Trenevski, Sakiri, Ciric.
Referee: Levnikov (Russia).

Dublin, 14 October 1998, 34,500

Republic of Ireland (2) 5 *(Robbie Keane 16, 18, Roy Keane 54, Quinn 63, Breen 82)*

Malta (0) 0

Republic of Ireland: Given; Kenna, Staunton, McAteer (Carsley 85), Cunningham, Breen, Kinsella, Roy Keane, Quinn (Cascarino 66), Robbie Keane (Kennedy 81), Duff.
Malta: Cini; Debono, Buttigieg, Spiteri, Carabott, Brincat, Zahra (Zammit 70), Sixsmith (Camilleri 66), Chetcuti, Turner, Suda (Agius 65).
Referee: Olsen (Norway).

Valletta, 18 November 1998, 4000

Malta (0) 0 *(Sixsmith 69)*

Macedonia (0) 2 *(Nikolovski 49, Zaharievski 62)*

Malta: Muscat; Sixsmith, Camilleri, Buttigieg, Spiteri, Debono, Busuttil, Saliba (Turner 67), Brincat, Nwoko (Carabott 54), Cutajar (Agius 59).
Macedonia: Milosevski; Veselinovski, Nikolovski, Sedloski, Babunski, Stavrevski, Zaharievski, Micevski, Sainovski, Bozinov (Trenevski 65), Sakiri.
Referee: Smolik (Belarus).

Belgrade, 18 November 1998, 44,000

Yugoslavia (0) 1 *(Mijatovic 65)*

Republic of Ireland (0) 0

Yugoslavia: Kralj; Djukic, Djorovic, Mihajlovic, Jokanovic, Jugovic (Grodzic 77), Stojkovic (Kovacevic 46), Stankovic J, Stankovic D, Mijatovic, Milosevic (Drulovic 77).
Republic of Ireland: Given; Cunningham, Irwin, McLoughlin (Connolly 72), Breen, Staunton, Kinsella, Roy Keane, Quinn (Cascarino 72), McAteer (O'Neill 83), Duff.
Referee: Nilsson (Sweden).

Valletta, 10 February 1999, 7000

Malta (0) 0

Yugoslavia (1) 3 *(Nadj 22, 55, Milosevic 90)*

Malta: Barry; Said, Turner, Spiteri, Camilleri (Sixsmith 73), Buttigieg, Busuttil, Saliba, Carabott, Nwoko (Cutajar 82), Agius (Bencini 59).

Yugoslavia: Kralj; Mirkovic, Djorovic, Jokanovic, Djukic, Mihajlovic, Stankovic D (Grodzic 88), Nadj, Stankovic J (Tomic 75), Mijatovic, Kovacevic (Milosevic 70).

Referee: Garibian (France).

Skopje, 5 June 1999, 14,000

Macedonia (0) 1 *(Hristov 80)*

Croatia (1) 1 *(Suker 19)*

Macedonia: Milosevski; Nikolovski, Stojanovski, Stavrevski, Babunski (Zaharievski 60), Sainovski, Micevski, Trenevski (Bozinov 46), Trajcov (Hristov 80), Sakiri, Ciric.

Croatia: Ladic; Juric, Simic D, Soldo, Saric, Boban, Asanovic, Vugrinec (Vlaovic 19), Jarni, Suker, Boksic (Rapaic 19).

Referee: Dallas (Scotland).

Salonika, 8 June 1999, 2000

Yugoslavia (1) 4 *(Mijatovic 36, Milosevic 49, 90, Kovacevic 75)*

Malta (1) 1 *(Saliba 7)*

Yugoslavia: Kralj; Mirkovic, Djukic, Djorovic, Saveljic, Stojkovic (Drulovic 77), Nadj (Milosevic 46), Jokanovic, Stankovic D (Grozdic 63), Mijatovic, Kovacevic.

Malta: Barry; Buhagiar (Cutajar 80), Said, Debono, Chetcuti, Buttigieg, Saliba, Camilleri (Brincat 64), Carabott, Busuttil, Nwoko (Sultana 83).

Referee: Stahl (Sweden).

Dublin, 9 June 1999, 28,108

Republic of Ireland (0) 1 *(Quinn 67)*

Macedonia (0) 0

Republic of Ireland: Kelly; Carr, Irwin, Duff (Kilbane 63), Cunningham, Breen, Kennedy, Kinsella, Quinn (Connolly 83), Robbie Keane (Cascarino 67), Carsley.

Macedonia: Milosevski; Stavrevski, Babunski, Stojanoski, Trajcev (Memedi 46), Micevski, Trenevski (Hristov 75), Sainovski (Sedloski 70), Nikolovski, Ciric, Sakiri.

Referee: Meier (Switzerland).

Belgrade, 18 August 1999, 52,600

Yugoslavia (0) 0

Croatia (0) 0

Yugoslavia: Kocic; Mirkovic, Djukic, Mihajlovic, Djorovic G (Drulovic 46), Nadj, Jokanovic, Stankovic D, Stankovic J, Mijatovic, Kovacevic (Milosevic 62).

Croatia: Ladic; Kovac, Stimac, Simic D, Jarni, Asanovic, Soldo, Boban (Biscan 75), Jurcic, Stanic, Suker.

Referee: Nielsen (Denmark).

Zagreb, 21 August 1999, 20,000

Croatia (1) 2 *(Stanic 34, Soldo 55)*

Malta (0) 1 *(Carabott 61)*

Croatia: Mrmic; Biscan, Stimac, Simic D, Rapaic, Asanovic, Soldo, Boban (Saric 16), Simic J (Boksic 46), Stanic (Vlaovic 46), Suker.

Malta: Barry; Said, Vella S, Debono, Camilleri, Carabott, Busuttil (Okonkwo 72), Saliba, Nwoko (Mifsud 89), Brincat, Agius (Sultana 83).

Referee: Ouzouniv (Bulgaria).

Dublin, 1 September 1999, 31,400

Republic of Ireland (0) 2 *(Robbie Keane 54, Kennedy 70)*

Yugoslavia (0) 1 *(Stankovic D 61)*

Republic of Ireland: Kelly A; Irwin (Carr 66), Staunton, Breen, Cunningham, Roy Keane (Carsley 69), Kinsella, Robbie Keane, Quinn (Cascarino 80), Kilbane, Kennedy.

Yugoslavia: Kocic; Komljenovic, Djukic, Mihajlovic (Saveljic 68), Bolic, Savicevic (Drulovic 53), Stankovic D, Govedarica, Nadj (Kovacevic 74), Mijatovic, Milosevic.

Referee: Collina (Italy).

Zagreb, 4 September 1999, 25,000

Croatia (0) 1 *(Suker 90)*

Republic of Ireland (0) 0

Croatia: Ladic; Bilic (Rukavina 46), Stimac, Simic D, Stanic (Simic J 84), Kovac, Soldo, Asanovic, Jarni, Suker, Rapaic.

Republic of Ireland: Kelly A; Carr, Kelly G (Harte 72), Breen, Cunningham, Staunton, Carsley, Kinsella, Cascarino (Quinn 82), McLoughlin, Duff (Kilbane 56).

Referee: Vega (Spain).

Belgrade, 5 September 1999, 22,000

Yugoslavia (1) 3 *(Stojkovic 37, 54, Savicevic 77)*

Macedonia (0) 1 *(Ciric 64 (pen))*

Yugoslavia: Kralj; Mirkovic, Krstajic, Jokanovic, Djukic, Saveljic, Stankovic D (Govedarica 75), Mijatovic, Milosevic (Kovacevic 82), Stojkovic (Savicevic 66), Drulovic.

Macedonia: Milosevski; Stavrevski, Jovanovski (Serafimovski 59), Lazarevski, Babunski, Savevski, Veselinovski, Micevski (Gerasimovski 53), Hristov, Ciric (Memedi 77), Sakiri.

Referee: Frisk (Sweden).

Skopje, 8 September 1999, 14,000

Macedonia (0) 2 *(Sakiri 60, Ciric 90)*

Yugoslavia (2) 4 *(Milosevic 1, Babunski 4 (og), Stankovic D 14, Drulovic 38)*

Macedonia: Milosevski; Stavrevski, Jovanovski, Lazarevski, Babunski, Savevski (Gerasimovski 46), Veselinovski (Serafimovski 40), Micevski (Sainovski 40), Hristov, Ciric, Sakiri.

Yugoslavia: Kralj; Mirkovic (Komljenovic 46), Djukic, Mihajlovic, Krstajic, Stankovic D, Stojkovic (Savicevic 46), Jokanovic, Drulovic, Mijatovic, Milosevic (Kovacevic 82).

Referee: Michel (Slovakia).

Valletta, 8 September 1999, 6200

Malta (0) 2 *(Said 62, Carabott 69 (pen))*

Republic of Ireland (2) 3 *(Robbie Keane 13, Breen 21, Staunton 74)*

Malta: Barry; Debono, Buttigieg (Vella S 30), Said, Carabott, Saliba, Camilleri, Agius (Theuma 67), Chetcuti (Buhagiar 24), Busuttil, Nwoko.

Republic of Ireland: Kelly A; Carr, Staunton, Carsley, Cunningham, Breen (Harte 75), Kennedy (McLoughlin 55), Robbie Keane, Quinn, Kilbane (Duff 65), Kinsella.

Referee: Corpodean (Romania).

Zagreb, 9 October 1999, 40,000

Croatia (1) 2 *(Boksic 20, Stanic 47)*

Yugoslavia (2) 2 *(Mijatovic 26, Stankovic D 31)*

Croatia: Ladic; Juric, Kovak (Biscan 61), Tudor (Rapajic 82), Rukavina, Stanic, Soldo, Asanovic, Jarni, Suker, Boksic (Simic J 77).

Yugoslavia: Kralj; Mirkovic, Djukic, Mihajlovic, Djorovic, Jokanovic, Stojkovic (Bolic 54), Nadj (Drulovic 58), Stankovic D, Mijatovic (Savicevic 73), Milosevic.

Referee: Aranda (Spain).

Skopje, 9 October 1999, 4500

Macedonia (0) 1 *(Stavrevski 90)*

Republic of Ireland (1) 1 *(Quinn 19)*

Macedonia: Filevski; Stavrevski, Sedloski, Babunski, Jovanovski (Memedi 78), Gerasimovski, Sainovski, Stanic (Zaharievski 71), Stojanoski (Bekiri 55), Savevski, Hristov.

Republic of Ireland: Kelly A; Irwin, Staunton, McLoughlin, Cunningham, Breen, Kelly G, Kinsella, Robbie Keane (O'Neill 65), Quinn (Cascarino 78), Kennedy (Holland 85).

Referee: Marin (Spain).

Group 8 – Final Table	P	W	D	L	F	A	Pts
Yugoslavia	8	5	2	1	18	8	17
Republic of Ireland	8	5	1	2	14	6	16
Croatia	8	4	3	1	13	9	15
Macedonia	8	2	2	4	13	14	8
Malta	8	0	0	8	6	27	0

GROUP 9

Tallinn, 4 June 1998, 3500

Estonia (2) 5 *(Viikmae 13, Reim 43 (pen), Terehhov 76, Oper 87, Kirs 90)*

Faeroes (0) 0

Estonia: Poom; Lemsalu, Kirs, Hohlov-Simson, Meet, Viikmae (O'Konnell-Bronin 80), Terehhov, Oper, Kristal, Reim, Zilinski.
Faeroes: Knudsen; Dam, Hansen J, Thorsteinsson, Hansen O (Jarnskor H 83), Morkore A, Johannesen, Johnsson, Petersen, Muller (Mikkelsen 41), Jonsson (Arge 83).

Sarajevo, 19 August 1998, 20,000

Bosnia (0) 1 *(Baljic 65)*

Faeroes (0) 0

Bosnia: Dedic; Kapetanovic, Barbarez (Mujdza 75), Konjic, Varesanovic, Hibic, Bolic (Mujcin 65), Halilovic, Kodro, Salihamidzic (Sabic 81), Baljic.
Faeroes: Mikkelsen; Hansen H, Hansen JK, Thorsteinsson, Johannesen O, Jarnskor H, Joensen S, Johnsson, Morkore A, Arge (Borg 77), Petersen.
Referee: Mikulski (Poland).

Vilnius, 5 September 1998, 5112

Lithuania (0) 0

Scotland (0) 0

Lithuania: Stauce; Sugzda (Buitkus 61), Semberas, Zutautas R, Zvirgzdauskas, Mikulenas (Slekys 90), Skerla, Baltusnikas, Preiksaitis, Jankauskas, Skarbalius.
Scotland: Leighton; Dailly, Boyd, Elliott, Hendry, Calderwood (Davidson 70), Lambert, Gallacher, McCoist (McCann 82), Jackson (Ferguson B 56), Collins.
Referee: Zotta (Romania).

Sarajevo, 5 September 1998, 21,000

Bosnia (0) 1 *(Barbarez 75 (pen))*

Estonia (1) 1 *(Hibic 28 (og))*

Bosnia: Dedic; Varesanovic, Konjic, Hibic, Kapetanovic, Salihamidzic, Katana (Mujcin 65), Halilovic (Bolic 77), Mujdza (Sabic 65), Barbarez, Baljic.
Estonia: Poom; Rooba U (Meet 81), Kirs, Hohlov-Simson, Reim, Smirnov, Terehov, Kristal, Alonen, Zelinski (Viikmae 81), Oper.
Referee: Agius (Malta).

Toftir, 6 September 1998, 2000

Faeroes (0) 0

Czech Republic (0) 1 *(Smicer 84)*

Faeroes: Mikkelsen; Johannesen O, Hansen JK, Thorsteinsson, Hansen H, Jarnskor H, Arge (Jarnskor M 78), Johnsson, Morkore A, Jonsson T, Petersen.
Czech Republic: Postulka; Rada, Bejbl (Latal 81), Suchoparek, Votava, Cizek (Berger 55), Nemec, Nedved, Lokvenc, Poborsky (Sloncik 81), Smicer.
Referee: Hirviniemi (Finland).

Sarajevo, 10 October 1998, 30,000

Bosnia (0) 1 *(Topic 88)*

Czech Republic (1) 3 *(Baranek 13, Smicer 59, Kuka 90)*

Bosnia: Dedic; Varesanovic, Konjic, Hibic, Kapetanovic, Salihamidzic (Demirovic 66), Katana, Halilovic, Mujcin (Topic 63), Barbarez, Baljic (Besirevic 71).
Czech Republic: Postulka; Baranek (Rada 71), Repka, Suchoparek, Latal, Votava, Nemec, Bejbl, Lokvenc (Kuka 80), Smicer (Sloncik 85), Berger.
Referee: Messina (Italy).

Vilnius, 10 October 1998, 1500

Lithuania (0) 0

Faeroes (0) 0

Lithuania: Stauce; Skerla, Mikalajunas (Zvingilas 74), Zutautas R, Baltusnikas, Zvirgzdauskas, Mikulenas (Buitkus 46), Ivanauskas, Skarbalius, Preiksaitis, Jankauskas.
Faeroes: Mikkelsen; Johannesen O, Hansen JK, Thorsteinsson, Hansen H, Joensen S, Jarnskor H, Johnsson, Arge (Borg 88), Jonsson T, Petersen.
Referee: Schaack (Luxembourg).

Edinburgh, 10 October 1998, 16,930

Scotland (0) 3 *(Dodds 70, 85, Hohlov-Simson 78 (og))*

Estonia (1) 2 *(Hohlov-Simson 35, Smirnov 76)*

Scotland: Leighton; Weir, Davidson, Calderwood (Donnelly 56), Hendry, Boyd, McKinlay W, Durrant, McCoist (Dodds 68), Gallacher (Jackson 17), Johnston.
Estonia: Poom; Kirs, Hohlov-Simson, Reim, Rooba U, Kristal, Smirnov, Alonen, Terehov, Zelinski (Viikmae 86), Oper.
Referee: Marques (Portugal).

Teplice, 14 October 1998, 13,123

Czech Republic (4) 4 *(Nedved 8, Berger 21, 41, Meet 44 (og))*

Estonia (0) 1 *(Arbeiter 90)*

Czech Republic: Postulka; Latal, Suchoparek, Repka, Votava (Rada 53), Nedved, Nemec, Bejbl (Cizek 80), Berger, Lokvenc (Kuka 61), Smicer.
Estonia: Poom; Smirnov (Nommik 46), Meet, Hohlov-Simson, Rooba U, Alonen, Terehov (O'Konnel-Bronin 63), Oper, Viikmae (Arbeiter 46), Reim, Zelinski.
Referee: Olafsson (Iceland).

Vilnius, 14 October 1998, 2000

Lithuania (0) 4 *(Ivanauskas 10, 67, 75, Baltusnikas 90)*

Bosnia (0) 2 *(Konjic 4, Baljic 68)*

Lithuania: Stauce; Skerla, Mikalajunas (Baltusnikas 87), Zutautas R, Gleveckas, Zvirgzdauskas, Semberas, Ivanauskas, Skarbalius (Zvingilas 62), Preiksaitis, Jankauskas (Danilevicius 79).
Bosnia: Dedic; Varesanovic, Konjic, Ramcic, Kapetanovic (Mujdza 80), Salihamidzic, Katana (Topic 75), Halilovic, Mujcin (Besirevic 80), Barbarez, Baljic.
Referee: Schuttengruber (Austria).

Aberdeen, 14 October 1998, 18,517

Scotland (2) 2 *(Burley 22, Dodds 45)*

Faeroes (0) 1 *(Petersen 86 (pen))*

Scotland: Sullivan; Weir, Davidson, Elliott, Hendry, Boyd, McKinlay W (Durrant 46), Donnelly, Dodds, Burley, Johnston (Glass 79).
Faeroes: Mikkelsen; Hansen H, Johannesen O, Hansen JK, Thorsteinsson, Petersen, Joensen S, Johnsson, Jarnskor H (Hansen J 80), Arge (Borg 69), Jonsson T.
Referee: Kapitanis (Cyprus).

Teplice, 27 March 1999, 14,658

Czech Republic (1) 2 *(Hornak 10, Berger 74 (pen))*

Lithuania (0) 0

Czech Republic: Srnicek; Repka, Suchoparek, Hornak, Poborsky (Kuka 63), Hasek, Nemec, Berger, Nedved, Lokvenc (Koller 71), Smicer (Baranek 80).
Lithuania: Stauce; Skerla, Zvirgzdauskas, Zutautas D, Semberas, Vainoras, Preiksaitis, Skarbalius, Mikalajunas (Mikulenas 78), Ivanauskas (Buitkus 83), Jankauskas (Zvingilas 67).
Referee: Juhos (Hungary).

Vilnius, 31 March 1999, 3000

Lithuania (0) 1 *(Fomenka 83)*

Estonia (0) 2 *(Terehov 49, 77)*

Lithuania: Stauce; Skerla, Zutautas R, Zvirgzdauskas, Semberas, Vainoras, Preiksaitis, Maciulevicius, Mikalajunas, Skarbalius (Gleveckas 35) (Buitkus 52), Mikulenas (Fomenka 46).
Estonia: Poom; Lemsalu, Kirs, Hohlov-Simson, Saviauk, Shvets (Kristal 69), Terehov, Oper (Zelinski 67), Viikmae, Smirnov (Alonen 90), Reim.
Referee: Trentalange (Italy).

Glasgow, 31 March 1999, 44,513

Scotland (0) 1 *(Jess 68)*

Czech Republic (2) 2 *(Elliott 27 (og), Smicer 35)*

Scotland: Sullivan; Hopkin, Davidson (Johnston 51), Elliott, Boyd, Weir, Burley, Lambert, McCann, McAllister (Hutchison 62), Jess.
Czech Republic: Srnicek; Hornak, Votava, Suchoparek, Poborsky (Rada 74), Hasek, Nedved, Berger, Nemec, Smicer (Baranek 82), Lokvenc (Kuka 69).
Referee: Nielsen (Denmark).

Sarajevo, 5 June 1999, 5000

Bosnia (1) 2 *(Kodro 26 (pen), Bolic 90)*
Lithuania (0) 0
Bosnia: Dedic; Smajic, Kapetanovic, Varesanovic, Hibic, Repuh (Bolic 87), Besirevic, Sabic, Topic (Turkovic 90), Kodro (Mujcin 79), Salihamidzic.
Lithuania: Leusas; Skerla, Skinderis, Gvildys, Kancelskis, Mikalajunas, Zvirgzdauskas, Semberas (Mikulenas 64), Maciulevicius (Fomenka 46), Ivanauskas, Preiksaitis.
Referee: Ibanez (Spain).

Tallin, 5 June 1999, 3000

Estonia (0) 0
Czech Republic (1) 2 *(Berger 45, Koller 83)*
Estonia: Poom; Lemsalu, Kirs, Hohlov-Simson, Saviauk, Alonen (Smirnov 65) (O'Konnel-Bronin 74), Terehov (Shvets 80), Kristal, Oper, Reim, Viikmae.
Czech Republic: Srnicek; Suchoparek, Repka, Hornak, Poborsky, Hasek, Nedved (Galasek 85), Berger, Nemec, Smicer (Kuka 65), Lokvenc (Koller 70).
Referee: Roca (Spain).

Toftir, 5 June 1999, 4500

Faeroes (0) 1 *(Hansen H)*
Scotland (1) 1 *(Johnston 38)*
Faeroes: Mikkelsen; Johannesen O, Hansen H, Thorsteinsson, Hansen O (Hansen J 87), Johnsson, Joensen J (Borg 73), Joensen S, Jonsson T, Morkore A, Petersen (Arge 82).
Scotland: Sullivan; Weir, Davidson, Elliott, Calderwood, Boyd, Durrant (Cameron 46), Gallacher (Jess 88), Dodds, Lambert, Johnston (Gemmill 85).
Referee: Kalt (France).

Prague, 9 June 1999, 22,000

Czech Republic (0) 3 *(Repka 65, Kuka 75, Koller 87)*
Scotland (1) 2 *(Ritchie 30, Johnston 62)*
Czech Republic: Srnicek; Poborsky (Kuka 68), Berger, Hornak, Suchoparek, Repka, Nedved, Hasek (Baranek 60), Nemec, Lokvenc (Koller 68), Smicer.
Scotland: Sullivan; Johnston, Davidson, Weir, Boyd, Ritchie, Lambert, Calderwood, Gallacher, Dodds, Durrant (Jess 70).
Referee: Krug (Germany).

Tallinn, 9 June 1999, 2500

Estonia (1) 1 *(Oper 10)*
Lithuania (0) 2 *(Ramelis 52, Maciulevicius 56)*
Estonia: Poom; Lemsalu, Kirs, Kaal, Viikmae, Alonen, Terehov (O'Konnel-Bronin 73), Kristal (Shvets 80), Oper, Reim, Zelinski.
Lithuania: Leusas; Skerla, Skinderis, Zutautas D (Maciulevicius 46), Zutautas R, Mikalajunas, Zvirgzdauskas, Ramelis, Razanauskas, Skarbalius, Ivanauskas (Preiksaitis 87).
Referee: Albrecht (Germany).

Toftir, 9 June 1999, 4600

Faeroes (1) 2 *(Arge 38, 48)*
Bosnia (1) 2 *(Bolic 13, 50)*
Faeroes: Mikkelsen; Johannesen O, Joensen S, Thorsteinsson, Hansen O (Jarnskor H 65), Johnsson, Hansen H, Arge (Joensen J 85), Morkore A, Jonsson T, Petersen.
Bosnia: Dedic; Smajic, Besirevic, Varesanovic, Hibic, Repuh (Osmanhodzic 78), Sabic, Topic, Turkovic (Joldic 63), Bolic, Mujcin (Muratovic 85).
Referee: Jones (England).

Sarajevo, 4 September 1999, 26,000

Bosnia (1) 1 *(Bolic 23)*
Scotland (2) 2 *(Hutchison 13, Dodds 45)*
Bosnia: Dedic; Joldic (Repuh 77), Konjic, Hibic, Mujdza (Demirovic 77), Besirevic, Topic, Halilovic (Mujcin 62), Kodro, Barbarez, Bolic.
Scotland: Sullivan; Weir, Burley, Calderwood (Dailly 46), Hendry, Ferguson B (Durrant 69), Hopkin, Collins, Dodds, Hutchison, McCann (Gallacher 75).
Referee: Levnikov (Russia).

Torshavn, 4 September 1999, 2300

Faeroes (0) 0
Estonia (0) 2 *(Reim 88, Piroja 90)*
Faeroes: Mikkelsen; Johannesen O, Hansen JK, Hansen F, Thorsteinsson (Hansen O 75), Johannesen (Jarnskor H 90), Johnsson J, Petersen, Morkore A, Jonsson T, Arge (Borg 90).
Estonia: Poom; Saviauk (Lemsalu 90), Piroja, Hohlov-Simson, Alonen, Terehov, Anniste (O'Konnel Bronin 67), Reim, Kirs, Kristal, Zelinski (Ustritski 75).
Referee: Trivkovic (Croatia).

Vilnius, 4 September 1999, 3000

Lithuania (0) 0
Czech Republic (0) 4 *(Nedved 60, 63, Koller 68, 90)*
Lithuania: Stauce; Semberas (Skerla 55), Zvirgzdauskas, Lencevicius, Zutautas D, Razanauskas, Preiksaitis (Danilevicius 77), Mikalajunas, Tereskinas, Ivanauskas (Ramelis 38), Jankauskas.
Czech Republic: Srnicek; Repka, Rada, Nikl, Poborsky (Sloncik 79), Bejbl, Nedved (Horvath 70), Berger, Nemec (Baranek 78), Kuka, Koller.
Referee: Granat (Poland).

Teplice, 8 September 1999, 10,125

Czech Republic (1) 3 *(Koller 26, Berger 59 (pen), Poborsky 67)*
Bosnia (0) 0
Czech Republic: Srnicek; Niki, Suchoparek, Repka, Nemec, Poborsky, Bejbl, Nedved, Berger (Hasek 83), Kuka (Baranek 79), Koller (Lokvenc 59).
Bosnia: Dedic; Konjic, Barbarez, Hibic, Joldic (Repuh 70), Varesanovic, Ihtijarevic (Bolic 70), Sabic, Besirevic, Kodro, Topic (Demirovic 70).
Referee: Nilsson (Sweden).

Tallinn, 8 September 1999, 4500

Estonia (0) 0
Scotland (0) 0
Estonia: Poom; Kirs, Hohlov-Simson, Piiroja, Saviauk, Kristal, Anniste, Reim, Terehov, O'Konnel-Bronin (Zelinski 46), Oper.
Scotland: Sullivan; Weir, Burley, Davidson, Hendry, Dailly, Durrant (Ferguson B 67), Collins, Dodds, Hutchison, Johnston (McCann 55).
Referee: Stuchlik (Austria).

Torshavn, 8 September 1999, 450

Faeroes (0) 0
Lithuania (0) 1 *(Ramelis 55)*
Faeroes: Mikkelsen; Johannesen O, Hansen JK, Hansen F, Thorsteinsson, Hansen O, Jarnskor H (Lakjuni 84), Johnsson J (Benjaminsen 65), Morkore A, Jonsson T, Arge (Borg 46).
Lithuania: Stauce (Rodimanskas 79); Semberas, Zvrigzdauskas, Vencevicius, Zutautas D, Razanauskas (Skerla 74), Preiksaitis (Danilevicius 88), Mikalajunas, Tereskinas, Ramelis, Skinderis.
Referee: Romain (Belgium).

Ibrox Park, 5 October 1999, 30,574

Scotland (1) 1 *(Collins 26 (pen))*

Bosnia (0) 0

Scotland: Sullivan; Weir, Davidson, Burley, Dailly, Hendry (Calderwood 36), Hopkin, Lambert, Dodds (McSwegan 89), Gallacher (Burchill 79), Collins.
Bosnia: Guso; Hujdorovic, Varesanovic, Barbarez, Kapetanovic, Ihtijarevic (Topic 79), Sabic, Besirevic, Mujcin (Avdic 90), Baljic, Bolic.
Referee: Sundell (Sweden).

Prague, 9 October 1999, 21,326

Czech Republic (1) 2 *(Koller 11, Verbir 84)*

Faeroes (0) 0

Czech Republic: Srnicek; Repka, Suchoparek (Verbir 74), Rada, Poborsky, Baranek (Hornak 58), Nemec, Berger, Bejbl (Horvath 66), Koller, Smicer.
Faeroes: Knudsen; Johannesen O, Hansen JK, Thorsteinsson, Hansen HF, Hansen HJ (Hansen O 88), Johannesen, Johnsson J, Petersen (Jakosen 72), Morkore A, Jonsson T.
Referee: Lica (Romania).

Tallinn, 9 October 1999, 1200

Estonia (1) 1 *(Oper 4)*

Bosnia (1) 4 *(Baljic 42, 57, 67, 87)*

Estonia: Kaalma; Piiroja, Kirs, Hohlov-Simson, Anniste (Saviauk 61), Terehov (O'Konnel-Bronin 74), Alonen, Kristal, Reim, Oper, Zelinski (Viikmae 40).
Bosnia: Guso; Joldic, Kapetanovic, Hujdorovic, Varesanovic, Ihtijarevic, Besirevic, Sabic (Duro 60), Topic, Bolic (Mujcin 80), Baljic (Avdic 89).
Referee: Luinge (Holland).

Hampden Park, 9 October 1999, 22,059

Scotland (0) 3 *(Hutchison 48, McSwegan 50, Cameron 88)*

Lithuania (0) 0

Scotland: Gould; Weir, Davidson, O'Neil, Dailly, Ritchie, Burley (Cameron 46), Lambert, Burchill (Dodds 79), McSwegan (Gallacher 82), Hutchison.
Lithuania: Leus; Zvirgzdauskas, Skinderis, Zutautas D, Skerla, Stumbrys (Vencevicius 54), Razanauskas, Mikalajunas, Tereskinas (Fomenko 65), Dancenko (Maciulevicius 54), Mikulenas.
Referee: Bre (France).

Group 9 – Final Table	P	W	D	L	F	A	Pts
Czech Republic	10	10	0	0	26	5	30
Scotland	10	5	3	2	15	10	18
Estonia	10	3	2	5	15	17	11
Bosnia	10	3	2	5	14	17	11
Lithuania	10	3	2	5	8	16	11
Faeroes	10	0	3	7	4	17	3

PLAY-OFFS FIRST LEG

Tel Aviv, 13 November 1999, 45,000

Israel (0) 0

Denmark (2) 5 *(Tomasson 2, 34, Tofting 67, Jorgensen 68, Steen-Nielsen 72)*

Israel: Awat; Harazi A, Amsalem, Benado, Ben Shimon (Tal 38), Hazan, Banin (Telesnikov 79), Berkovic, Revivo, Turjeman, Abuksis (Benayoun 38).
Denmark: Schmeichel; Tofting (Goldbaek 79), Henriksen, Hogh, Heintze, Helveg, Steen-Nielsen, Jorgensen (Schjonberg 86), Gronkjaer, Tomasson (Andersen S 79), Sand.
Referee: Elleray (England).

Dublin, 13 November 1999, 33,610

Republic of Ireland (0) 1 *(Robbie Keane 79)*

Turkey (0) 1 *(Tayfur 83 (pen))*

Republic of Ireland: Kelly A (Kiely 62); Carr, Irwin, Breen, Cunningham, Carsley, Delap (Duff 54), Roy Keane, Robbie Keane, Cascarino (Connolly 76), Kilbane.

Turkey: Rustu; Tayfun, Abdullah, Ali Eren, Alpay, Ogun, Sergen (Korkmaz 86), Umit (Arif 46), Tayfur, Hakan Unsal (Tugay 68), Hakan Sukur.
Referee: Frisk (Sweden).

Hampden Park, 13 November 1999, 50,132

Scotland (0) 0

England (2) 2 *(Scholes 21, 42)*

Scotland: Sullivan; Burley, Ritchie, Weir, Hendry, Dailly, Gallacher (Burchill 83), Ferguson B, Dodds, Hutchison, Collins.
England: Seaman; Campbell, Neville P, Redknapp, Keown, Adams, Beckham, Scholes, Shearer, Owen (Cole 68), Ince.
Referee: Vega (Spain).

Ljubljana, 13 November 1999, 16,000

Slovenia (0) 2 *(Zahovic 53, Asimovic 82)*

Ukraine (1) 1 *(Shevchenko 33)*

Slovenia: Dabanovic; Knavs, Milanic (Osterc 73), Milinovic, Novak, Karic, Ceh, Pavlin, Zahovic, Udovic (Asimovic 46), Rudonja.
Ukraine: Shovkovskyi; Parfionov, Golovko, Vashchuk, Dmitrulin, Popov, Gusin, Kandarov (Kardach 56), Kossovski V, Shevchenko, Rebrov.
Referee: Meier (Switzerland).

PLAY-OFFS SECOND LEG

Copenhagen, 17 November 1999, 41,186

Denmark (2) 3 *(Sand 4, Steen-Nielsen 14, Tomasson 65)*

Israel (0) 0

Denmark: Schmeichel (Sorensen 17); Helveg (Laursen 70), Hogh, Henriksen, Heintze, Tofting, Steen-Nielsen, Gronkjaer (Schjonberg 83), Jorgensen, Sand, Tomasson.
Israel: Elimelech; Talkar, Shelah, Amsalem (Badir 43), Harazi A, Hazan, Banin, Tal (Telesnikov 28), Berkovic (Gershon 72), Benayoun, Turgeman.
Referee: Pereira (Portugal).

Wembley, 17 November 1999, 75,848

England (0) 0

Scotland (1) 1 *(Hutchison 39)*

England: Seaman; Campbell, Neville P, Ince, Southgate, Adams, Beckham, Redknapp, Shearer, Owen (Heskey 64), Scholes (Parlour 90).
Scotland: Sullivan; Burley, Davidson, Weir, Hendry, Dailly, Collins, Ferguson B, Dodds, Hutchison, McCann (Burchill 75).
Referee: Collina (Italy).

Bursa, 17 November 1999, 21,000

Turkey (0) 0

Republic of Ireland (0) 0

Turkey: Rustu (Engin 37); Ali Eren, Ogun, Alpay, Okan, Tayfur, Tayfun (Fatih 46), Abdullah, Arif (Umit 83), Sergen, Hakan Sukur.
Republic of Ireland: Kiely; Carr (Kenna 5) (Cascarino 80), Irwin, Delap, Cunningham, Breen, Kinsella, Roy Keane, Quinn, Connolly (Duff 70), Kilbane.
Referee: Veissiere (France).

Kiev, 17 November 1999, 45,000

Ukraine (0) 1 *(Rebrov 65 (pen))*

Slovenia (1) 1 *(Pavlin 74)*

Ukraine: Shovkovskyi; Luzhny, Golovko, Vashchuk, Dmitrulin, Kandarov (Kovalev 46), Fedorov, Kossovski V (Popov 74), Skachenko (Moroz G 57), Rebrov, Shevchenko.
Slovenia: Dabanovic; Galic, Milanic, Milinovic, Karic (Osterc 74), Novak, Ceh, Pavlin, Zahovic, Udovic (Acimovic 57), Rudonja.
Referee: Heynemann (Germany).

EURO 2000 Finals

So who cares that England returned from Euro 2000 with the three Lions' tails between their legs? The FA Carling Premiership provided players for all but four of the 16 competing nations. Even one of that quartet consisting of Spain, Italy, Slovenia and Yugoslavia managed to have a former Premier League player on duty, none other than Savo Milosevic, once of Aston Villa. Moreover he finished joint leading scorer with Holland's Patrick Kluivert on five goals.

There was the contrast in the final one team fielding a succession of mercenaries, the other with entirely home grown talent. That Italy came close to pulling off a surprise victory over France, might provide further ammunition for those who consider the English game is suffering from a surfeit of foreigners. But 'twas ever so.

For well over a century we have had Scots, Welsh and Irish gracing our game. With one or two exceptions when their actual birthplace was either misplaced or misinterpreted, they have been unable to play international football for England. Nobody made much of a complaint about that situation.

Tiredness clearly cost Italy dearly in the final with France. They were badly treated by having to play their semi-final with Holland a day after France had beaten Portugal. Moreover they had had to battle against the Dutch with ten men for much of the game.

That said, France deserved their overall success because of their commitment to attack, but Italy must have rued the several chances they had of increasing their lead before the French managed a dramatic last gasp equaliser. In fact drama played a leading role in both semi-finals.

Holland having qualified for the last four thanks to a sparkling 6-1 drubbing of Yugoslavia during which there were thoughts of the 'total' football produced by the Dutch a quarter of a century earlier, were right off their game with the Italians.

In addition to playing against ten men, Holland missed two penalties – Frank de Boer having his effort saved and Kluivert hitting a post. They had no excuses. Once again the Dutch temperament let them down at the wrong time. And you knew they would not survive the penalty shoot-out.

France and Portugal seemed to have cancelled each other out in the other semi-final before the match was decided by sudden death in a controversial incident. Abel Xavier handled the ball by the post and after the furore which followed, Zinedine Zidane converted the penalty in the 117th minute.

The tournament as a whole was well received. It got off to a splendidly entertaining start when Belgium beat Sweden 2-1 in Brussels. Alas neither reproduced this form in subsequent matches and failed to qualify.

England threw away a two-goal lead against Portugal and lost 3-2, albeit to a vastly superior outfit and Germany appeared as poor as their pre-match billing had forecast. England did manage to beat Germany for the first time in a competitive match since the 1966 World Cup final, but it was wretched fare. Worse after further examples English exported hooliganism, UEFA threatened to ban us from the tournament.

Portugal went from strength to strength and Romania deservedly beat England 3-2, even though it was a careless tackle by Phil Neville which presented the Romanians with late victory.

Spain appeared to be flattering to deceive again, but participated in what has been described as the finest European Championship game of all time, in which they came back from 3-2 down to snatch injury-time victory over Yugoslavia.

Few tournaments of this nature take place without one meaningless match and Euro 2000 was no exception. Both Holland and France had qualified for the quarter-finals when they met in Amsterdam, the largely French reserves losing 3-2 to Holland.

The quarter-finals saw Portugal beat Turkey 2-0, Italy overcome Romania by the same margin and France edge Spain out 2-1. Holland as previously mentioned clinically disposed of Yugoslavia.

In the final, Italy took the lead after the best move of the game through Marco Delvecchio after 55 minutes and failed to capitalize on other chances. The French stuck gamely to their task against tiring opponents and triumphed with goals from two substitutes, Sylvain Wiltord and David Trezeguet. Wiltord latched onto a tired, attempted headed clearance and fired into the far corner in injury time to force the extra period.

Italy who had been apparently playing out time were stunned and there seemed only one likely winner from then on. As it was a superb volley from David Trezeguet settled it in the 103rd minute.

Outstanding individuals were Zinedine Zidane, Thierry Henry and Laurent Blanc of France; Francesco Toldo and Alessandro Nesta (Italy), Luis Figo (Portugal), Cristian Chivu (Romania) and Edgar Davids (Holland).

The statistics of Euro 2000, the first major competition to be played in two countries Holland and Belgium, produced 85 goals in 31 matches, 126 yellow and 10 red cards. The attendance aggregate was 1,101,650 and the average crowd 35,537.

FINAL COMPETITION (played in Holland and Belgium)

GROUP A

Liege, 12 June 2000, 30,000

Germany (1) 1 *(Scholl 29)*
Romania (1) 1 *(Moldovan 5)*

Germany: Kahn; Babbel, Ziege, Linke (Rehmer 46), Matthaus (Deisler 77), Nowotny, Jeremies, Hassler (Hamann 73), Scholl, Bierhoff, Rink.
Romania: Stelea; Petrescu (Contra 69), Chivu, Ciobotariu, Popescu, Filipescu, Munteanu D, Galca, Moldovan (Lupescu 85), Ilie A, Hagi (Mutu 73).
Referee: Nielsen (Denmark).

Eindhoven, 12 June 2000, 33,000

Portugal (2) 3 *(Figo 22, Joao Pinto 38, Nuno Gomes 60)*
England (2) 2 *(Scholes 3, McManaman 18)*

Portugal: Vitor Baia; Xavier, Dimas, Paulo Bento, Fernando Couto, Jorge Costa, Figo, Rui Costa (Beto 84), Nuno Gomes (Capucho 90), Joao Pinto (Conceicao 75), Vidigal.
England: Seaman; Neville G, Neville P, Ince, Campbell, Adams (Keown 81), Beckham, Scholes, Shearer, Owen (Heskey 46), McManaman (Wise 57).
Referee: Frisk (Sweden).

Charleroi, 17 June 2000, 30,000

England (0) 1 *(Shearer 53)*
Germany (0) 0

England: Seaman; Neville G, Neville P, Ince, Keown, Campbell, Beckham, Scholes (Barmby 72), Shearer, Owen (Gerrard 61), Wise.
Germany: Kahn; Babbel, Ziege, Hamann, Matthaus, Nowotny, Deisler (Ballack 72), Scholl, Jancker, Kirsten (Rink 70), Jeremies (Bode 78).
Referee: Collina (Italy).

Arnhem, 17 June 2000, 18,000

Romania (0) 0
Portugal (0) 1 *(Constinha 90)*

Romania: Stelea; Contra, Chivu, Munteanu D, Popescu, Filipescu, Petrescu (Petr 64), Galca, Moldovan (Ganea 69), Ilie A (Rosu 78), Hagi.
Portugal: Vitor Baia; Secretario, Dimas, Vidigal, Fernando Couto, Jorge Costa, Figo, Paulo Bento, Joao Pinto (Conceicao 56), Rui Costa (Constinha 87), Nuno Gomes (Sa Pinto 56).
Referee: Veissiere (France).

Charleroi, 20 June 2000, 30,000

England (2) 2 *(Shearer 40 (pen), Owen 45)*
Romania (2) 3 *(Chivu 22, Munteanu D 48, Ganea 89 (pen))*

England: Martyn; Neville G, Neville P, Ince, Keown, Campbell, Beckham, Scholes (Southgate 81), Shearer, Owen (Heskey 67), Wise (Barmby 75).
Romania: Stelea; Petrescu, Chivu, Contra, Popescu (Belodedici 31), Filipescu, Mutu, Galca (Rosu 68), Moldovan, Ilie A (Ganea 74), Munteanu D.
Referee: Meier (Switzerland).

Rotterdam, 20 June 2000, 44,000

Portugal (1) 3 *(Conceicao 35, 54, 71)*
Germany (0) 0

Portugal: Espinha; Conceicao, Capucho, Beto, Fernando Couto, Jorge Costa, Costinha, Paulo Sousa, Sa Pinto, Pauleta (Nuno Gomez 66), Rui Jorge.
Germany: Kahn; Deisler, Linke, Rehmer, Matthaus, Nowotny, Ballack (Rink 46), Hamann, Jancker, Scholl (Hassler 59), Bode.
Referee: Jol (Holland).

GROUP B

Brussels, 10 June 2000, 50,000

Belgium (1) 2 *(Goor 43, Mpenza E 46)*
Sweden (0) 1 *(Mjallby 53)*

Belgium: De Wilde; Deflandre, Leonard (Van Kerckhoven 72), Verheyen (Peeters 88), Valgaeren, Staelens, Vanderhaeghe, Wilmots, Mpenza E, Strupar (Nilis 69), Goor.
Sweden: Hedman; Nilsson (Lucic 46), Mellberg, Andersson D (Osmanovski 70), Andersson P, Bjorklund, Alexandersson, Mjallby, Andersson K, Pettersson (Larsson 49), Ljungberg.
Referee: Merk (Germany).

Arnhem, 11 June 2000, 25,000

Turkey (0) 1 *(Okan 62)*
Italy (0) 2 *(Conte 52, Inzaghi 70 (pen))*

Turkey: Rustu; Alpay, Fatih, Okan (Ergun 89), Abdullah, Temizkanoglu, Tayfur, Korkut, Hakan Sukur, Sergen (Arif 81), Umit (Tugay 76).
Italy: Toldo; Zambrotta, Pessotto (Iuliano 62), Cannavaro, Nesta, Maldini, Conte, Albertini, Totti (Di Livio 83), Inzaghi, Fiore (Del Piero 74).
Referee: Dallas (Scotland).

Brussels, 14 June 2000, 46,000

Italy (1) 2 *(Totti 6, Fiore 66)*
Belgium (0) 0

Italy: Toldo; Cannavaro, Maldini, Albertini, Nesta, Iuliano, Conte, Zambrotta, Totti (Del Piero 64), Inzaghi (Delvecchio 77), Fiore (Ambrosini 83).
Belgium: De Wilde; Deflandre, Van Kerckhoven (Hendrikx 44), Verheyen (Mpenza M 67), Valgaeren, Staelens, Vanderhaeghe, Wilmots, Mpenza E, Strupar (Nilis 58), Goor.
Referee: Aranda (Spain).

Eindhoven, 15 June 2000, 24,500

Sweden (0) 0
Turkey (0) 0

Sweden: Hedman; Lucic, Sundgren, Mild, Mellberg, Bjorklund, Alexandersson (Andersson A 62), Mjallby, Andersson K (Pettersson 46), Larsson (Svensson 78), Ljungberg.
Turkey: Rustu; Alpay, Unsal, Okan, Fatih, Ogun (Tugay 59), Umit (Tayfun 46), Suat, Hakan Sukur, Izzet (Sergen 58), Arif.
Referee: Jol (Holland).

Eindhoven, 19 June 2000, 25,000

Italy (1) 2 *(Di Biagio 39, Del Piero 88)*
Sweden (0) 1 *(Larsson 77)*

Italy: Toldo; Negro, Pessotto, Ferrara, Iuliano, Maldini (Nesta 42), Di Livio (Fiore 64), Di Biagio, Montella, Del Piero, Ambrosini.
Sweden: Hedman; Svensson (Alexandersson 52), Gustafsson (Andersson K 75), Mellberg, Andersson P, Bjorklund, Mjallby (Andersson D 56), Osmanovski, Mild, Larsson, Ljungberg.
Referee: Pereira (Portugal).

Brussels, 19 June 2000, 48,000

Turkey (1) 2 *(Hakan Sukur 45, 70)*
Belgium (0) 0

Turkey: Rustu; Tayfun, Abdullah, Fatih, Ogun, Alpay, Okan (Ergun 77), Suat, Hakan Sukur, Tugay (Tayfur 37), Arif (Osman 84).
Belgium: De Wilde; Deflandre, Van Kerckhoven, Verheyen (Strupar 64), Staelens, Valgaeren, Vanderhaeghe, Wilmots, Mpenza E, Nilis (De Bilde 77), Goor (Hendrikx 59).
Referee: Nielsen (Denmark) (Benko (Austria) 40).

GROUP C

Rotterdam, 13 June 2000, 45,000

Spain (0) 0
Norway (0) 1 *(Iversen 66)*

Spain: Molina; Michel Salgado, Aranzabal, Guardiola, Paco, Hierro, Etxeberria (Alfonso 71), Valeron (Helguera 80), Raul, Urzaiz, Fran (Mendieta 71).
Norway: Myhre; Heggem, Bergdolmo, Skammelsrud, Berg (Eggen 59), Bragstad, Bakke, Mykland, Flo (Carew 69), Iversen (Riseth 90), Solskjaer.
Referee: Gandour (Egypt).

Charleroi, 13 June 2000, 15,000

Yugoslavia (0) 3 *(Milosevic 67, 73, Drulovic 70)*
Slovenia (2) 3 *(Zahovic 23, 57, Pavlin 52)*

Yugoslavia: Kralj; Jugovic, Nadj, Dudic, Mihajlovic, Djukic, Stankovic D (Stojkovic 36), Jokanovic, Mijatovic (Kezman 82), Kovacevic (Milosevic 52), Drulovic.
Slovenia: Dabanovic; Novak, Karic (Osterc 78), Milinovic, Milanic, Galic, Pavlin (Pavlovic 74), Ceh, Zahovic, Udovic (Acimovic 65), Rudonja.
Referee: Pereira (Portugal).

Liege, 18 June 2000, 24,000

Norway (0) 0
Yugoslavia (1) 1 *(Milosevic 8)*

Norway: Myhre; Heggem (Bjornebye 35), Bergdolmo, Skammelsrud, Eggen, Bragstad, Bakke (Strand 75), Mykland, Flo, Iversen, Solskjaer.
Yugoslavia: Kralj; Saveljic, Djorovic, Jokanovic (Govedarcia 89), Djukic, Komljenovic, Stojkovic (Nadj 83), Jugovic, Milosevic, Mijatovic (Kezman 86), Drulovic.
Referee: Dallas (Scotland).

Amsterdam, 18 June 2000, 45,000

Slovenia (0) 1 *(Zahovic 59)*
Spain (1) 2 *(Raul 5, Etxeberria 60)*

Slovenia: Dabanovic; Novak, Karic, Galic, Milanic (Knavs 67), Milinovic, Pavlin (Acimovic 81), Ceh, Udovic (Osterc 46), Zahovic, Rudonja.
Spain: Canizares; Michel Salgado, Aranzabal, Guardiola (Helguera 81), Hierro, Abelardo, Etxeberria, Valeron (Engonga 89), Raul, Alfonso (Urzaiz 71), Mendieta.
Referee: Merk (Germany).

Arnhem, 21 June 2000, 21,000

Slovenia (0) 0
Norway (0) 0

Slovenia: Dabanovic; Novak, Karic, Milinovic, Galic (Acimovic 83), Knavs, Ceh, Pavlin, Siljak (Osterc 86), Zahovic, Rudonja.
Norway: Myhre; Bergdolmo, Bjornebye, Solbakken, Eggen, Bragstad, Carew (Bakke 61) (Strand 82), Mykland, Flo, Iversen, Solskjaer.
Referee: Poll (England).

Bruges, 21 June 2000, 22,000

Yugoslavia (1) 3 *(Milosevic 31, Govedarica 51, Komljenovic 75)*
Spain (1) 4 *(Alfonso 39, 90, Munitis 53, Mendieta 89 (pen))*

Yugoslavia: Kralj; Komljenovic, Djorovic (Stankovic J 13), Jokanovic, Djukic, Mihaljovic, Stojkovic (Saveljic 69), Jugovic (Govedarica 46), Milosevic, Mijatovic, Drulovic.
Spain: Canizares; Michel Salgado (Munitis 46), Barjuan, Guardiola, Abelardo, Jemez (Urzaiz 64), Helguera, Mendieta, Raul, Alfonso, Gonzalez (Etxeberria 23).
Referee: Veissiere (France).

GROUP D

Bruges, 11 June 2000, 29,000

France (1) 3 *(Blanc 16, Henry 65, Wiltord 90)*
Denmark (0) 0

France: Barthez; Thuram, Lizarazu, Deschamps, Blanc, Desailly, Djorkaeff (Vieira 58), Petit, Henry, Zidane, Anelka (Wiltord 82).
Denmark: Schmeichel; Colding, Heintze, Nielsen A, Schjonberg, Henriksen, Bisgaard (Gravesen 72), Tomasson (Beck 80), Sand, Tofting (Jorgensen 72), Gronkjaer.
Referee: Benko (Austria).

Amsterdam, 11 June 2000, 50,000

Holland (0) 1 *(Frank de Boer 89 (pen))*
Czech Republic (0) 0

Holland: Van der Sar; Reiziger, Van Bronckhorst, Cocu, Frank de Boer, Stam (Konterman 75), Seedorf (Ronald de Boer 57), Davids, Kluivert, Bergkamp, Zenden (Overmars 79).
Czech Republic: Srnicek; Latal (Bejbl 70), Gabriel, Nedved, Rada, Repka, Poborsky, Nemec, Koller, Smicer (Kuka 83), Rosicky.
Referee: Collina (Italy).

Bruges, 16 June 2000, 25,000

Czech Republic (1) 1 *(Poborsky 35 (pen))*
France (1) 2 *(Henry 7, Djorkaeff 60)*

Czech Republic: Srnicek; Poborsky, Nedved, Repka, Rada, Gabriel (Fukal 46), Rosicky (Jankulovski 61), Bejbl, Smicer, Koller, Nemec.
France: Barthez; Thuram, Candela, Vieira, Blanc, Desailly, Deschamps, Petit (Djorkaeff 46), Anelka (Dugarry 64), Zidane, Henry (Wiltord 90).
Referee: Poll (England).

Rotterdam, 16 June 2000, 50,000

Holland (0) 3 *(Kluivert 58, Ronald de Boer 66, Zenden 77)*
Denmark (0) 0

Holland: Van der Sar (Westerveld 88); Reiziger, Van Bronckhorst, Cocu, Konterman, Frank de Boer, Zenden, Davids, Kluivert, Bergkamp (Winter 75), Overmars (Ronald de Boer 61).
Denmark: Schmeichel; Colding, Heintze, Nielsen A, Henriksen, Schjonberg (Helveg 83), Bisgaard, Gravesen, Tomasson, Sand, Gronkjaer.
Referee: Meier (Switzerland).

Liege, 21 June 2000, 25,000

Denmark (0) 0
Czech Republic (0) 2 *(Smicer 64, 67)*

Denmark: Schmeichel; Schjonberg, Helveg, Tofting, Henriksen, Heintze (Colding 68), Goldbaek, Steen-Nielsen, Beck (Molnar 74), Tomasson, Gronkjaer.
Czech Republic: Srnicek; Repka, Nedved, Nemec, Rada, Fukal, Poborsky, Bejbl (Jankulovski 62), Koller (Kuka 74), Smicer (Lokvenc 79), Berger.
Referee: Ghandour (Egypt).

Amsterdam, 21 June 2000, 50,000

France (2) 2 *(Dugarry 8, Trezeguet 32)*
Holland (1) 3 *(Kluivert 14, Frank de Boer 51, Zenden 59)*

France: Lama; Karembeu, Candela, Vieira (Deschamps 90), Leboeuf, Desailly, Pires, Dugarry (Djorkaeff 68), Trezeguet, Wiltord (Anelka 80), Micoud.
Holland: Westerveld; Bosvelt, Numan, Cocu, Frank de Boer, Stam, Zenden, Davids, Kluivert (Makaay 59), Bergkamp (Winter 78), Overmars (Van Vossen 90).
Referee: Frisk (Sweden).

QUARTER-FINALS

Brussels, 24 June 2000, 42,500

Italy (2) 2 *(Totte 34, Inzaghi 43)*
Romania (0) 0

Italy: Toldo; Zambrotta, Maldini (Pessotto 46), Cannavaro, Nesta, Iuliano, Conte (Di Biagio 59), Albertini, Inzaghi, Totti (Del Piero 78), Fiore.
Romania: Stelea; Petre, Chivu, Ciobotariu, Belodedici, Filipescu, Mutu, Galca (Lupescu 69), Moldovan (Ganea 54), Munteanu D, Hagi.
Referee: Pereira (Portugal).

Amsterdam, 24 June 2000, 42,000

Portugal (1) 2 *(Nuno Gomes 44, 56)*
Turkey (0) 0

Portugal: Vitor Baia; Conceicao, Dimas, Paulo Bento, Fernando Couto, Jorge Costa, Figo, Costinha (Paulo Sousa 46), Joao Pinto, Nuno Gomes (Sa Pinto 74), Rui Costa (Capucho 87).
Turkey: Rustu; Tayfun, Unsal, Fatih, Ogun (Yalcin 85), Alpay, Tayfur, Okan (Derelioglu 62), Ergun, Hakan Sukur, Arif (Kaya 62).
Referee: Jol (Holland).

Bruges, 25 June 2000, 30,000

France (2) 2 *(Zidane 32, Djorkaeff 44)*
Spain (1) 1 *(Mendieta 38 (pen))*

France: Barthez; Thuram, Lizarazu, Vieira, Blanc, Desailly, Deschamps, Dugarry, Henry (Anelka 81), Zidane, Djorkaeff.
Spain: Canizares; Michel Salgado, Aranzabal, Guardiola, Paco, Abelardo, Helguera (Gerard 77), Munitis (Exteberria 73), Alfonso, Raul, Mendieta (Urzaiz 57).
Referee: Collina (Italy).

Rotterdam, 25 June 2000, 50,000

Holland (2) 6 *(Kluivert 23, 38, 54, Govedarica 51 (og), Overmars 78, 90)*
Yugoslavia (0) 1 *(Milosevic 90)*

Holland: Van der Sar (Westerveld 64); Bosvelt, Numan, Cocu, Frank de Boer, Stam, Zenden (Ronald de Boer 79), Davids, Kluivert (Makaay 59), Bergkamp, Overmars.
Yugoslavia: Kralj; Komljenovic, Djukic, Govedarica, Saveljic (Stankovic J 56), Mihajlovic, Stojkovic (Stankovic D 51), Jugovic, Milosevic, Mijatovic, Drulovic (Kovanevic 69).
Referee: Aranda (Spain).

SEMI-FINALS

Brussels, 28 June 2000, 50,000

France (0) 2 *(Henry 51, Zidane 117 (pen))*
Portugal (1) 1 *(Nuno Gomes 19)*

France: Barthez; Thuram, Lizarazu, Vieira, Blanc, Desailly, Deschamps, Anelka (Wiltord 71), Henry (Trezeguet 105), Zidane, Petit (Pires 87).
Portugal: Vitor Baia; Xavier, Dimas (Rui Jorge 91), Conceicao, Fernando Couto, Jorge Costa, Costinha, Vidigal (Paulo Bento 60), Figo, Rui Costa (Joao Pinto 76), Nuno Gomes.
France won on sudden death.
Referee: Benko (Austria).

Amsterdam, 29 June 2000, 50,000

Italy (0) 0
Holland (0) 0

Italy: Toldo; Cannavaro, Zambrotta, Nesta, Maldini, Iuliano, Di Biagio, Albertini (Pessotto 78), Inzaghi (Delvecchio 67), Del Piero, Fiore (Totti 82).
Holland: Van der Sar; Bosvelt, Van Bronckhorst, Cocu (Winter 95), Frank de Boer, Stam, Zenden (Van Vossen 77), Davids, Kluivert, Bergkamp (Seedorf 86), Overmars.
aet; Italy won 3-1 on penalties. Di Biagio scored 1-0; Frank de Boer saved 1-0; Pessotto scored 2-0; Stam shot over 2-0; Totti scored 3-0; Kluivert saved 3-1; Maldini saved 3-1; Bosvelt saved 3-1.
Referee: Merk (Germany).

FINAL

Rotterdam, 2 July 2000, 50,000

France (0) 2 *(Wiltord 90, Trezeguet 103)*
Italy (0) 1 *(Delvecchio 55)*

France: Barthez; Thuram, Lizarazu (Pires 85), Vieira, Blanc, Desailly, Deschamps, Dugarry (Wiltord 56), Henry, Zidane, Djorkaeff (Trezeguet 75).
Italy: Toldo; Cannavaro, Maldini, Pessotto, Nesta, Iuliano, Di Biagio (Ambrosini 65), Albertini, Totti, Delvecchio (Montella 85), Fiore (Del Piero 52).
France won on sudden death.
Referee: Frisk (Sweden).

David Trezeguet hits a spectacular volley to end Italy's dream of lifting the European Championship and give France a 2-1 win. (Colorsport)

BRITISH AND IRISH INTERNATIONAL RESULTS 1872–2000

Note: In the results that follow, wc=World Cup, ec=European Championship, ui=Umbro International Trophy. tf = Tournoi de France. For Ireland, read Northern Ireland from 1921.

ENGLAND v SCOTLAND
Played: 110; England won 45, Scotland won 41, Drawn 24. *Goals:* England 192, Scotland 169.

Year	Date	Venue	E	S	Year	Date	Venue	E	S
1872	30 Nov	Glasgow	0	0	1932	9 Apr	Wembley	3	0
1873	8 Mar	Kennington Oval	4	2	1933	1 Apr	Glasgow	1	2
1874	7 Mar	Glasgow	1	2	1934	14 Apr	Wembley	3	0
1875	6 Mar	Kennington Oval	2	2	1935	6 Apr	Glasgow	0	2
1876	4 Mar	Glasgow	0	3	1936	4 Apr	Wembley	1	1
1877	3 Mar	Kennington Oval	1	3	1937	17 Apr	Glasgow	1	3
1878	2 Mar	Glasgow	2	7	1938	9 Apr	Wembley	0	1
1879	5 Apr	Kennington Oval	5	4	1939	15 Apr	Glasgow	2	1
1880	13 Mar	Glasgow	4	5	1947	12 Apr	Wembley	1	1
1881	12 Mar	Kennington Oval	1	6	1948	10 Apr	Glasgow	2	0
1882	11 Mar	Glasgow	1	5	1949	9 Apr	Wembley	1	3
1883	10 Mar	Sheffield	2	3	wc1950	15 Apr	Glasgow	1	0
1884	15 Mar	Glasgow	0	1	1951	14 Apr	Wembley	2	3
1885	21 Mar	Kennington Oval	1	1	1952	5 Apr	Glasgow	2	1
1886	31 Mar	Glasgow	1	1	1953	18 Apr	Wembley	2	2
1887	19 Mar	Blackburn	2	3	wc1954	3 Apr	Glasgow	4	2
1888	17 Mar	Glasgow	5	0	1955	2 Apr	Wembley	7	2
1889	13 Apr	Kennington Oval	2	3	1956	14 Apr	Glasgow	1	1
1890	5 Apr	Glasgow	1	1	1957	6 Apr	Wembley	2	1
1891	6 Apr	Blackburn	2	1	1958	19 Apr	Glasgow	4	0
1892	2 Apr	Glasgow	4	1	1959	11 Apr	Wembley	1	0
1893	1 Apr	Richmond	5	2	1960	9 Apr	Glasgow	1	1
1894	7 Apr	Glasgow	2	2	1961	15 Apr	Wembley	9	3
1895	6 Apr	Everton	3	0	1962	14 Apr	Glasgow	0	2
1896	4 Apr	Glasgow	1	2	1963	6 Apr	Wembley	1	2
1897	3 Apr	Crystal Palace	1	2	1964	11 Apr	Glasgow	0	1
1898	2 Apr	Glasgow	3	1	1965	10 Apr	Wembley	2	2
1899	8 Apr	Birmingham	2	1	1966	2 Apr	Glasgow	4	3
1900	7 Apr	Glasgow	1	4	ec1967	15 Apr	Wembley	2	3
1901	30 Mar	Crystal Palace	2	2	ec1968	24 Jan	Glasgow	1	1
1902	3 Mar	Birmingham	2	2	1969	10 May	Wembley	4	1
1903	4 Apr	Sheffield	1	2	1970	25 Apr	Glasgow	0	0
1904	9 Apr	Glasgow	1	0	1971	22 May	Wembley	3	1
1905	1 Apr	Crystal Palace	1	0	1972	27 May	Glasgow	1	0
1906	7 Apr	Glasgow	1	2	1973	14 Feb	Glasgow	5	0
1907	6 Apr	Newcastle	1	1	1973	19 May	Wembley	1	0
1908	4 Apr	Glasgow	1	1	1974	18 May	Glasgow	0	2
1909	3 Apr	Crystal Palace	2	0	1975	24 May	Wembley	5	1
1910	2 Apr	Glasgow	0	2	1976	15 May	Glasgow	1	2
1911	1 Apr	Everton	1	1	1977	4 June	Wembley	1	2
1912	23 Mar	Glasgow	1	1	1978	20 May	Glasgow	1	0
1913	5 Apr	Chelsea	1	0	1979	26 May	Wembley	3	1
1914	14 Apr	Glasgow	1	3	1980	24 May	Glasgow	2	0
1920	10 Apr	Sheffield	5	4	1981	23 May	Wembley	0	1
1921	9 Apr	Glasgow	0	3	1982	29 May	Glasgow	1	0
1922	8 Apr	Aston Villa	0	1	1983	1 June	Wembley	2	0
1923	14 Apr	Glasgow	2	2	1984	26 May	Glasgow	1	1
1924	12 Apr	Wembley	1	1	1985	25 May	Glasgow	0	1
1925	4 Apr	Glasgow	0	2	1986	23 Apr	Wembley	2	1
1926	17 Apr	Manchester	0	1	1987	23 May	Glasgow	0	0
1927	2 Apr	Glasgow	2	1	1988	21 May	Wembley	1	0
1928	31 Mar	Wembley	1	5	1989	27 May	Glasgow	2	0
1929	13 Apr	Glasgow	0	1	ec1996	15 June	Wembley	2	0
1930	5 Apr	Wembley	5	2	ec1999	13 Nov	Glasgow	2	0
1931	28 Mar	Glasgow	0	2	ec1999	17 Nov	Wembley	0	1

ENGLAND v WALES
Played: 97; England won 62, Wales won 14, Drawn 21. *Goals:* England 239, Wales 90.

Year	Date	Venue	E	W	Year	Date	Venue	E	W
1879	18 Jan	Kennington Oval	2	1	1882	13 Mar	Wrexham	3	5
1880	15 Mar	Wrexham	3	2	1883	3 Feb	Kennington Oval	5	0
1881	26 Feb	Blackburn	0	1	1884	17 Mar	Wrexham	4	0

			E	W					E	W
1885	14 Mar	Blackburn	1	1		1934	29 Sept	Cardiff	4	0
1886	29 Mar	Wrexham	3	1		1936	5 Feb	Wolverhampton	1	2
1887	26 Feb	Kennington Oval	4	0		1936	17 Oct	Cardiff	1	2
1888	4 Feb	Crewe	5	1		1937	17 Nov	Middlesbrough	2	1
1889	23 Feb	Stoke	4	1		1938	22 Oct	Cardiff	2	4
1890	15 Mar	Wrexham	3	1		1946	13 Nov	Manchester	3	0
1891	7 May	Sunderland	4	1		1947	18 Oct	Cardiff	3	0
1892	5 Mar	Wrexham	2	0		1948	10 Nov	Aston Villa	1	0
1893	13 Mar	Stoke	6	0		wc1949	15 Oct	Cardiff	4	1
1894	12 Mar	Wrexham	5	1		1950	15 Nov	Sunderland	4	2
1895	18 Mar	Queen's Club,				1951	20 Oct	Cardiff	1	1
		Kensington	1	1		1952	12 Nov	Wembley	5	2
1896	16 Mar	Cardiff	9	1		wc1953	10 Oct	Cardiff	4	1
1897	29 Mar	Sheffield	4	0		1954	10 Nov	Wembley	3	2
1898	28 Mar	Wrexham	3	0		1955	27 Oct	Cardiff	1	2
1899	20 Mar	Bristol	4	0		1956	14 Nov	Wembley	3	1
1900	26 Mar	Cardiff	1	1		1957	19 Oct	Cardiff	4	0
1901	18 Mar	Newcastle	6	0		1958	26 Nov	Aston Villa	2	2
1902	3 Mar	Wrexham	0	0		1959	17 Oct	Cardiff	1	1
1903	2 Mar	Portsmouth	2	1		1960	23 Nov	Wembley	5	1
1904	29 Feb	Wrexham	2	2		1961	14 Oct	Cardiff	1	1
1905	27 Mar	Liverpool	3	1		1962	21 Oct	Wembley	4	0
1906	19 Mar	Cardiff	1	0		1963	12 Oct	Cardiff	4	0
1907	18 Mar	Fulham	1	1		1964	18 Nov	Wembley	2	1
1908	16 Mar	Wrexham	7	1		1965	2 Oct	Cardiff	0	0
1909	15 Mar	Nottingham	2	0		EC1966	16 Nov	Wembley	5	1
1910	14 Mar	Cardiff	1	0		EC1967	21 Oct	Cardiff	3	0
1911	13 Mar	Millwall	3	0		1969	7 May	Wembley	2	1
1912	11 Mar	Wrexham	2	0		1970	18 Apr	Cardiff	1	1
1913	17 Mar	Bristol	4	3		1971	19 May	Wembley	0	0
1914	16 Mar	Cardiff	2	0		1972	20 May	Cardiff	3	0
1920	15 Mar	Highbury	1	2		wc1972	15 Nov	Cardiff	1	0
1921	14 Mar	Cardiff	0	0		wc1973	24 Jan	Wembley	1	1
1922	13 Mar	Liverpool	1	0		1973	15 May	Wembley	3	0
1923	5 Mar	Cardiff	2	2		1974	11 May	Cardiff	2	0
1924	3 Mar	Blackburn	1	2		1975	21 May	Wembley	2	2
1925	28 Feb	Swansea	2	1		1976	24 Mar	Wrexham	2	1
1926	1 Mar	Crystal Palace	1	3		1976	8 May	Cardiff	1	0
1927	12 Feb	Wrexham	3	3		1977	31 May	Wembley	0	1
1927	28 Nov	Burnley	1	2		1978	3 May	Cardiff	3	1
1928	17 Nov	Swansea	3	2		1979	23 May	Wembley	0	0
1929	20 Nov	Chelsea	6	0		1980	17 May	Wrexham	1	4
1930	22 Nov	Wrexham	4	0		1981	20 May	Wembley	0	0
1931	18 Nov	Liverpool	3	1		1982	27 Apr	Cardiff	1	0
1932	16 Nov	Wrexham	0	0		1983	23 Feb	Wembley	2	1
1933	15 Nov	Newcastle	1	2		1984	2 May	Wrexham	0	1

ENGLAND v IRELAND

Played: 96; England won 74, Ireland won 6, Drawn 16. *Goals:* England 319, Ireland 80.

			E	I					E	I
1882	18 Feb	Belfast	13	0		1903	14 Feb	Wolverhampton	4	0
1883	24 Feb	Liverpool	7	0		1904	12 Mar	Belfast	3	1
1884	23 Feb	Belfast	8	1		1905	25 Feb	Middlesbrough	1	1
1885	28 Feb	Manchester	4	0		1906	17 Feb	Belfast	5	0
1886	13 Mar	Belfast	6	1		1907	16 Feb	Everton	1	0
1887	5 Feb	Sheffield	7	0		1908	15 Feb	Belfast	3	1
1888	31 Mar	Belfast	5	1		1909	13 Feb	Bradford	4	0
1889	2 Mar	Everton	6	1		1910	12 Feb	Belfast	1	1
1890	15 Mar	Belfast	9	1		1911	11 Feb	Derby	2	1
1891	7 Mar	Wolverhampton	6	1		1912	10 Feb	Dublin	6	1
1892	5 Mar	Belfast	2	0		1913	15 Feb	Belfast	1	2
1893	25 Feb	Birmingham	6	1		1914	14 Feb	Middlesbrough	0	3
1894	3 Mar	Belfast	2	2		1919	25 Oct	Belfast	1	1
1895	9 Mar	Derby	9	0		1920	23 Oct	Sunderland	2	0
1896	7 Mar	Belfast	2	0		1921	22 Oct	Belfast	1	1
1897	20 Feb	Nottingham	6	0		1922	21 Oct	West Bromwich	2	0
1898	5 Mar	Belfast	3	2		1923	20 Oct	Belfast	1	2
1899	18 Feb	Sunderland	13	2		1924	22 Oct	Everton	3	1
1900	17 Mar	Dublin	2	0		1925	24 Oct	Belfast	0	0
1901	9 Mar	Southampton	3	0		1926	20 Oct	Liverpool	3	3
1902	22 Mar	Belfast	1	0		1927	22 Oct	Belfast	0	2

			E	I				E	I
1928	22 Oct	Everton	2	1	1962	20 Oct	Belfast	3	1
1929	19 Oct	Belfast	3	0	1963	20 Nov	Wembley	8	3
1930	20 Oct	Sheffield	5	1	1964	3 Oct	Belfast	4	3
1931	17 Oct	Belfast	6	2	1965	10 Nov	Wembley	2	1
1932	17 Oct	Blackpool	1	0	EC1966	20 Oct	Belfast	2	0
1933	14 Oct	Belfast	3	0	EC1967	22 Nov	Wembley	2	0
1935	6 Feb	Everton	2	1	1969	3 May	Belfast	3	1
1935	19 Oct	Belfast	3	1	1970	21 Apr	Wembley	3	1
1936	18 Nov	Stoke	3	1	1971	15 May	Belfast	1	0
1937	23 Oct	Belfast	5	1	1972	23 May	Wembley	0	1
1938	16 Nov	Manchester	7	0	1973	12 May	Everton	2	1
1946	28 Sept	Belfast	7	2	1974	15 May	Wembley	1	0
1947	5 Nov	Everton	2	2	1975	17 May	Belfast	0	0
1948	9 Oct	Belfast	6	2	1976	11 May	Wembley	4	0
wc1949	16 Nov	Manchester	9	2	1977	28 May	Belfast	2	1
1950	7 Oct	Belfast	4	1	1978	16 May	Wembley	1	0
1951	14 Nov	Aston Villa	2	0	EC1979	7 Feb	Wembley	4	0
1952	4 Oct	Belfast	2	2	1979	19 May	Belfast	2	0
wc1953	11 Nov	Everton	3	1	EC1979	17 Oct	Belfast	5	1
1954	2 Oct	Belfast	2	0	1980	20 May	Wembley	1	1
1955	2 Nov	Wembley	3	0	1982	23 Feb	Wembley	4	0
1956	10 Oct	Belfast	1	1	1983	28 May	Belfast	0	0
1957	6 Nov	Wembley	2	3	1984	24 Apr	Wembley	1	0
1958	4 Oct	Belfast	3	3	wc1985	27 Feb	Belfast	1	0
1959	18 Nov	Wembley	2	1	wc1985	13 Nov	Wembley	0	0
1960	8 Oct	Belfast	5	2	EC1986	15 Oct	Wembley	3	0
1961	22 Nov	Wembley	1	1	EC1987	1 Apr	Belfast	2	0

SCOTLAND v WALES

Played: 102; Scotland won 60, Wales won 19, Drawn 23. *Goals:* Scotland 238, Wales 112.

			S	W				S	W
1876	25 Mar	Glasgow	4	0	1921	12 Feb	Aberdeen	2	1
1877	5 Mar	Wrexham	2	0	1922	4 Feb	Wrexham	1	2
1878	23 Mar	Glasgow	9	0	1923	17 Mar	Paisley	2	0
1879	7 Apr	Wrexham	3	0	1924	16 Feb	Cardiff	0	2
1880	3 Apr	Glasgow	5	1	1925	14 Feb	Tynecastle	3	1
1881	14 Mar	Wrexham	5	1	1925	31 Oct	Cardiff	3	0
1882	25 Mar	Glasgow	5	0	1926	30 Oct	Glasgow	3	0
1883	12 Mar	Wrexham	3	0	1927	29 Oct	Wrexham	2	2
1884	29 Mar	Glasgow	4	1	1928	27 Oct	Glasgow	4	2
1885	23 Mar	Wrexham	8	1	1929	26 Oct	Cardiff	4	2
1886	10 Apr	Glasgow	4	1	1930	25 Oct	Glasgow	1	1
1887	21 Mar	Wrexham	2	0	1931	31 Oct	Wrexham	3	2
1888	10 Mar	Edinburgh	5	1	1932	26 Oct	Edinburgh	2	5
1889	15 Apr	Wrexham	0	0	1933	4 Oct	Cardiff	2	3
1890	22 Mar	Paisley	5	0	1934	21 Nov	Aberdeen	3	2
1891	21 Mar	Wrexham	4	3	1935	5 Oct	Cardiff	1	1
1892	26 Mar	Edinburgh	6	1	1936	2 Dec	Dundee	1	2
1893	18 Mar	Wrexham	8	0	1937	30 Oct	Cardiff	1	2
1894	24 Mar	Kilmarnock	5	2	1938	9 Nov	Edinburgh	3	2
1895	23 Mar	Wrexham	2	2	1946	19 Oct	Wrexham	1	3
1896	21 Mar	Dundee	4	0	1947	12 Nov	Glasgow	1	2
1897	20 Mar	Wrexham	2	2	wc1948	23 Oct	Cardiff	3	1
1898	19 Mar	Motherwell	5	2	1949	9 Nov	Glasgow	2	0
1899	18 Mar	Wrexham	6	0	1950	21 Oct	Cardiff	3	1
1900	3 Feb	Aberdeen	5	2	1951	14 Nov	Glasgow	0	1
1901	2 Mar	Wrexham	1	1	wc1952	18 Oct	Cardiff	2	1
1902	15 Mar	Greenock	5	1	1953	4 Nov	Glasgow	3	3
1903	9 Mar	Cardiff	1	0	1954	16 Oct	Cardiff	1	0
1904	12 Mar	Dundee	1	1	1955	9 Nov	Glasgow	2	0
1905	6 Mar	Wrexham	1	3	1956	20 Oct	Cardiff	2	2
1906	3 Mar	Edinburgh	0	2	1957	13 Nov	Glasgow	1	1
1907	4 Mar	Wrexham	0	1	1958	18 Oct	Cardiff	3	0
1908	7 Mar	Dundee	2	1	1959	4 Nov	Glasgow	1	1
1909	1 Mar	Wrexham	2	3	1960	20 Oct	Cardiff	0	2
1910	5 Mar	Kilmarnock	1	0	1961	8 Nov	Glasgow	2	0
1911	6 Mar	Cardiff	2	2	1962	20 Oct	Cardiff	3	2
1912	2 Mar	Tynecastle	1	0	1963	20 Nov	Glasgow	2	1
1913	3 Mar	Wrexham	0	0	1964	3 Oct	Cardiff	2	3
1914	28 Feb	Glasgow	0	0	EC1965	24 Nov	Glasgow	4	1
1920	26 Feb	Cardiff	1	1	EC1966	22 Oct	Cardiff	1	1

			S	W				S	W
1967	22 Nov	Glasgow	3	2	wc1977	12 Oct	Liverpool	2	0
1969	3 May	Wrexham	5	3	1978	17 May	Glasgow	1	1
1970	22 Apr	Glasgow	0	0	1979	19 May	Cardiff	0	3
1971	15 May	Cardiff	0	0	1980	21 May	Glasgow	1	0
1972	24 May	Glasgow	1	0	1981	16 May	Swansea	0	2
1973	12 May	Wrexham	2	0	1982	24 May	Glasgow	1	0
1974	14 May	Glasgow	2	0	1983	28 May	Cardiff	2	0
1975	17 May	Cardiff	2	2	1984	28 Feb	Glasgow	2	1
1976	6 May	Glasgow	3	1	wc1985	27 Mar	Glasgow	0	1
wc1976	17 Nov	Glasgow	1	0	wc1985	10 Sept	Cardiff	1	1
1977	28 May	Wrexham	0	0	1997	27 May	Kilmarnock	0	1

SCOTLAND v IRELAND

Played: 92; Scotland won 61, Ireland won 15, Drawn 16. *Goals:* Scotland 254, Ireland 81.

			S	I				S	I
1884	26 Jan	Belfast	5	0	1934	20 Oct	Belfast	1	2
1885	14 Mar	Glasgow	8	2	1935	13 Nov	Edinburgh	2	1
1886	20 Mar	Belfast	7	2	1936	31 Oct	Belfast	3	1
1887	19 Feb	Glasgow	4	1	1937	10 Nov	Aberdeen	1	1
1888	24 Mar	Belfast	10	2	1938	8 Oct	Belfast	2	0
1889	9 Mar	Glasgow	7	0	1946	27 Nov	Glasgow	0	0
1890	29 Mar	Belfast	4	1	1947	4 Oct	Belfast	0	2
1891	28 Mar	Glasgow	2	1	1948	17 Nov	Glasgow	3	2
1892	19 Mar	Belfast	3	2	1949	1 Oct	Belfast	8	2
1893	25 Mar	Glasgow	6	1	1950	1 Nov	Glasgow	6	1
1894	31 Mar	Belfast	2	1	1951	6 Oct	Belfast	3	0
1895	30 Mar	Glasgow	3	1	1952	5 Nov	Glasgow	1	1
1896	28 Mar	Belfast	3	3	1953	3 Oct	Belfast	3	1
1897	27 Mar	Glasgow	5	1	1954	3 Nov	Glasgow	2	2
1898	26 Mar	Belfast	3	0	1955	8 Oct	Belfast	1	2
1899	25 Mar	Glasgow	9	1	1956	7 Nov	Glasgow	1	0
1900	3 Mar	Belfast	3	0	1957	5 Oct	Belfast	1	1
1901	23 Feb	Glasgow	11	0	1958	5 Nov	Glasgow	2	2
1902	1 Mar	Belfast	5	1	1959	3 Oct	Belfast	4	0
1903	21 Mar	Glasgow	0	2	1960	9 Nov	Glasgow	5	2
1904	26 Mar	Dublin	1	1	1961	7 Oct	Belfast	6	1
1905	18 Mar	Glasgow	4	0	1962	7 Nov	Glasgow	5	1
1906	17 Mar	Dublin	1	0	1963	12 Oct	Belfast	1	2
1907	16 Mar	Glasgow	3	0	1964	25 Nov	Glasgow	3	2
1908	14 Mar	Dublin	5	0	1965	2 Oct	Belfast	2	3
1909	15 Mar	Glasgow	5	0	1966	16 Nov	Glasgow	2	1
1910	19 Mar	Belfast	0	1	1967	21 Oct	Belfast	0	1
1911	18 Mar	Glasgow	2	0	1969	6 May	Glasgow	1	1
1912	16 Mar	Belfast	4	1	1970	18 Apr	Belfast	1	0
1913	15 Mar	Dublin	2	1	1971	18 May	Glasgow	0	1
1914	14 Mar	Belfast	1	1	1972	20 May	Glasgow	2	0
1920	13 Mar	Glasgow	3	0	1973	16 May	Glasgow	1	2
1921	26 Feb	Belfast	2	0	1974	11 May	Glasgow	0	1
1922	4 Mar	Glasgow	2	1	1975	20 May	Glasgow	3	0
1923	3 Mar	Belfast	1	0	1976	8 May	Glasgow	3	0
1924	1 Mar	Glasgow	2	0	1977	1 June	Glasgow	3	0
1925	28 Feb	Belfast	3	0	1978	13 May	Glasgow	1	1
1926	27 Feb	Glasgow	4	0	1979	22 May	Glasgow	1	0
1927	26 Feb	Belfast	2	0	1980	17 May	Belfast	0	1
1928	25 Feb	Glasgow	0	1	wc1981	25 Mar	Glasgow	1	1
1929	23 Feb	Belfast	7	3	1981	19 May	Glasgow	2	0
1930	22 Feb	Glasgow	3	1	wc1981	14 Oct	Belfast	0	0
1931	21 Feb	Belfast	0	0	1982	28 Apr	Belfast	1	1
1931	19 Sept	Glasgow	3	1	1983	24 May	Glasgow	0	0
1932	12 Sept	Belfast	4	0	1983	13 Dec	Belfast	0	2
1933	16 Sept	Glasgow	1	2	1992	19 Feb	Glasgow	1	0

WALES v IRELAND

Played: 90; Wales won 42, Ireland won 27, Drawn 21. *Goals:* Wales 181, Ireland 127.

			W	I				W	I
1882	25 Feb	Wrexham	7	1	1886	27 Feb	Wrexham	5	0
1883	17 Mar	Belfast	1	1	1887	12 Mar	Belfast	1	4
1884	9 Feb	Wrexham	6	0	1888	3 Mar	Wrexham	11	0
1885	11 Apr	Belfast	8	2	1889	27 Apr	Belfast	3	1

			W	I
1890	8 Feb	Shrewsbury	5	2
1891	7 Feb	Belfast	2	7
1892	27 Feb	Bangor	1	1
1893	8 Apr	Belfast	3	4
1894	24 Feb	Swansea	4	1
1895	16 Mar	Belfast	2	2
1896	29 Feb	Wrexham	6	1
1897	6 Mar	Belfast	3	4
1898	19 Feb	Llandudno	0	1
1899	4 Mar	Belfast	0	1
1900	24 Feb	Llandudno	2	0
1901	23 Mar	Belfast	1	0
1902	22 Mar	Cardiff	0	3
1903	28 Mar	Belfast	0	2
1904	21 Mar	Bangor	0	1
1905	18 Apr	Belfast	2	2
1906	2 Apr	Wrexham	4	4
1907	23 Feb	Belfast	3	2
1908	11 Apr	Aberdare	0	1
1909	20 Mar	Belfast	3	2
1910	11 Apr	Wrexham	4	1
1911	28 Jan	Belfast	2	1
1912	13 Apr	Cardiff	2	3
1913	18 Jan	Belfast	1	0
1914	19 Jan	Wrexham	1	2
1920	14 Feb	Belfast	2	2
1921	9 Apr	Swansea	2	1
1922	4 Apr	Belfast	1	1
1923	14 Apr	Wrexham	0	3
1924	15 Mar	Belfast	1	0
1925	18 Apr	Wrexham	0	0
1926	13 Feb	Belfast	0	3
1927	9 Apr	Cardiff	2	2
1928	4 Feb	Belfast	2	1
1929	2 Feb	Wrexham	2	2
1930	1 Feb	Belfast	0	7
1931	22 Apr	Wrexham	3	2
1931	5 Dec	Belfast	0	4
1932	7 Dec	Wrexham	4	1
1933	4 Nov	Belfast	1	1
1935	27 Mar	Wrexham	3	1

			W	I
1936	11 Mar	Belfast	2	3
1937	17 Mar	Wrexham	4	1
1938	16 Mar	Belfast	0	1
1939	15 Mar	Wrexham	3	1
1947	16 Apr	Belfast	1	2
1948	10 Mar	Wrexham	2	0
1949	9 Mar	Belfast	2	0
wc1950	8 Mar	Wrexham	0	0
1951	7 Mar	Belfast	2	1
1952	19 Mar	Swansea	3	0
1953	15 Apr	Belfast	3	2
wc1954	31 Mar	Wrexham	1	2
1955	20 Apr	Belfast	3	2
1956	11 Apr	Cardiff	1	1
1957	10 Apr	Belfast	0	0
1958	16 Apr	Cardiff	1	1
1959	22 Apr	Belfast	1	4
1960	6 Apr	Wrexham	3	2
1961	12 Apr	Belfast	5	1
1962	11 Apr	Cardiff	4	0
1963	3 Apr	Belfast	4	1
1964	15 Apr	Cardiff	2	3
1965	31 Mar	Belfast	5	0
1966	30 Mar	Cardiff	1	4
ec1967	12 Apr	Belfast	0	0
ec1968	28 Feb	Wrexham	2	0
1969	10 May	Belfast	0	0
1970	25 Apr	Swansea	1	0
1971	22 May	Belfast	0	1
1972	27 May	Wrexham	0	0
1973	19 May	Everton	0	1
1974	18 May	Wrexham	1	0
1975	23 May	Belfast	0	1
1976	14 May	Swansea	1	0
1977	3 June	Belfast	1	1
1978	19 May	Wrexham	1	0
1979	25 May	Belfast	1	1
1980	23 May	Cardiff	0	1
1982	27 May	Wrexham	3	0
1983	31 May	Belfast	1	0
1984	22 May	Swansea	1	1

OTHER BRITISH INTERNATIONAL RESULTS 1908–2000

ENGLAND

		v ALBANIA	E	A
wc1989	8 Mar	Tirana	2	0
wc1989	26 Apr	Wembley	5	0

		v ARGENTINA	E	A
1951	9 May	Wembley	2	1
1953	17 May	Buenos Aires	0	0
(abandoned after 21 mins)				
wc1962	2 June	Rancagua	3	1
1964	6 June	Rio de Janeiro	0	1
wc1966	23 July	Wembley	1	0
1974	22 May	Wembley	2	2
1977	12 June	Buenos Aires	1	1
1980	13 May	Wembley	3	1
wc1986	22 June	Mexico City	1	2
1991	25 May	Wembley	2	2
wc1998	30 June	St Etienne	2	2
2000	23 Feb	Wembley	0	0

		v AUSTRALIA	E	A
1980	31 May	Sydney	2	1
1983	11 June	Sydney	0	0
1983	15 June	Brisbane	1	0
1983	18 June	Melbourne	1	1
1991	1 June	Sydney	1	0

		v AUSTRIA	E	A
1908	6 June	Vienna	6	1
1908	8 June	Vienna	11	1

			E	A
1909	1 June	Vienna	8	1
1930	14 May	Vienna	0	0
1932	7 Dec	Chelsea	4	3
1936	6 May	Vienna	1	2
1951	28 Nov	Wembley	2	2
1952	25 May	Vienna	3	2
wc1958	15 June	Boras	2	2
1961	27 May	Vienna	1	3
1962	4 Apr	Wembley	3	1
1965	20 Oct	Wembley	2	3
1967	27 May	Vienna	1	0
1973	26 Sept	Wembley	7	0
1979	13 June	Vienna	3	4

		v BELGIUM	E	B
1921	21 May	Brussels	2	0
1923	19 Mar	Highbury	6	1
1923	1 Nov	Antwerp	2	2
1924	8 Dec	West Bromwich	4	0
1926	24 May	Antwerp	5	3
1927	11 May	Brussels	9	1
1928	19 May	Antwerp	3	1
1929	11 May	Brussels	5	1
1931	16 May	Brussels	4	1
1936	9 May	Brussels	2	3
1947	21 Sept	Brussels	5	2

			E	B
1950	18 May	Brussels	4	1
1952	26 Nov	Wembley	5	0
wc1954	17 June	Basle	4	4*
1964	21 Oct	Wembley	2	2
1970	25 Feb	Brussels	3	1
EC1980	12 June	Turin	1	1
wc1990	27 June	Bologna	1	0*
1998	29 May	Casablanca	0	0
1999	10 Oct	Sunderland	2	1

*After extra time

v BOHEMIA			E	B
1908	13 June	Prague	4	0

v BRAZIL			E	B
1956	9 May	Wembley	4	2
wc1958	11 June	Gothenburg	0	0
1959	13 May	Rio de Janeiro	0	2
wc1962	10 June	Vina del Mar	1	3
1963	8 May	Wembley	1	1
1964	30 May	Rio de Janeiro	1	5
1969	12 June	Rio de Janeiro	1	2
wc1970	7 June	Guadalajara	0	1
1976	23 May	Los Angeles	0	1
1977	8 June	Rio de Janeiro	0	0
1978	19 Apr	Wembley	1	1
1981	12 May	Wembley	0	1
1984	10 June	Rio de Janeiro	2	0
1987	19 May	Wembley	1	1
1990	28 Mar	Wembley	1	0
1992	17 May	Wembley	1	1
1993	13 June	Washington	1	1
UI1995	11 June	Wembley	1	3
TF1997	10 June	Paris	0	1
2000	27 May	Wembley	1	1

v BULGARIA			E	B
wc1962	7 June	Rancagua	0	0
1968	11 Dec	Wembley	1	1
1974	1 June	Sofia	1	0
EC1979	6 June	Sofia	3	0
EC1979	22 Nov	Wembley	2	0
1996	27 Mar	Wembley	1	0
EC1998	10 Oct	Wembley	0	0
EC1999	9 June	Sofia	1	1

v CAMEROON			E	C
wc1990	1 July	Naples	3	2*
1991	6 Feb	Wembley	2	0
1997	15 Nov	Wembley	2	0

*After extra time

v CANADA			E	C
1986	24 May	Burnaby	1	0

v CHILE			E	C
wc1950	25 June	Rio de Janeiro	2	0
1953	24 May	Santiago	2	1
1984	17 June	Santiago	0	0
1989	23 May	Wembley	0	0
1998	11 Feb	Wembley	0	2

v CHINA			E	C
1996	23 May	Beijing	3	0

v CIS			E	C
1992	29 Apr	Moscow	2	2

v COLOMBIA			E	C
1970	20 May	Bogota	4	0
1988	24 May	Wembley	1	1
1995	6 Sept	Wembley	0	0
wc1998	26 June	Lens	2	0

v CROATIA			E	C
1996	24 Apr	Wembley	0	0

v CYPRUS			E	C
EC1975	16 Apr	Wembley	5	0
EC1975	11 May	Limassol	1	0

v CZECHOSLOVAKIA			E	C
1934	16 May	Prague	1	2
1937	1 Dec	Tottenham	5	4
1963	29 May	Bratislava	4	2
1966	2 Nov	Wembley	0	0
wc1970	11 June	Guadalajara	1	0
1973	27 May	Prague	1	1
EC1974	30 Oct	Wembley	3	0
EC1975	30 Oct	Bratislava	1	2
1978	29 Nov	Wembley	1	0
wc1982	20 June	Bilbao	2	0
1990	25 Apr	Wembley	4	2
1992	25 Mar	Prague	2	2

v CZECH REPUBLIC			E	C
1998	18 Nov	Wembley	2	0

v DENMARK			E	D
1948	26 Sept	Copenhagen	0	0
1955	2 Oct	Copenhagen	5	1
wc1956	5 Dec	Wolverhampton	5	2
wc1957	15 May	Copenhagen	4	1
1966	3 July	Copenhagen	2	0
EC1978	20 Sept	Copenhagen	4	3
EC1979	12 Sept	Wembley	1	0
EC1982	22 Sept	Copenhagen	2	2
EC1983	21 Sept	Wembley	0	1
1988	14 Sept	Wembley	1	0
1989	7 June	Copenhagen	1	1
1990	15 May	Wembley	1	0
EC1992	11 June	Malmo	0	0
1994	9 Mar	Wembley	1	0

v ECUADOR			E	Ec
1970	24 May	Quito	2	0

v EGYPT			E	Eg
1986	29 Jan	Cairo	4	0
wc1990	21 June	Cagliari	1	0

v FIFA			E	FIFA
1938	26 Oct	Highbury	3	0
1953	21 Oct	Wembley	4	4
1963	23 Oct	Wembley	2	1

v FINLAND			E	F
1937	20 May	Helsinki	8	0
1956	20 May	Helsinki	5	1
1966	26 June	Helsinki	3	0
wc1976	13 June	Helsinki	4	1
wc1976	13 Oct	Wembley	2	1
1982	3 June	Helsinki	4	1
wc1984	17 Oct	Wembley	5	0
wc1985	22 May	Helsinki	1	1
1992	3 June	Helsinki	2	1

v FRANCE			E	F
1923	10 May	Paris	4	1
1924	17 May	Paris	3	1
1925	21 May	Paris	3	2
1927	26 May	Paris	6	0
1928	17 May	Paris	5	1
1929	9 May	Paris	4	1
1931	14 May	Paris	2	5
1933	6 Dec	Tottenham	4	1
1938	26 May	Paris	4	2
1947	3 May	Highbury	3	0
1949	22 May	Paris	3	1
1951	3 Oct	Highbury	2	2

			E	F
1955	15 May	Paris	0	1
1957	27 Nov	Wembley	4	0
EC1962	3 Oct	Sheffield	1	1
EC1963	27 Feb	Paris	2	5
WC1966	20 July	Wembley	2	0
1969	12 Mar	Wembley	5	0
WC1982	16 June	Bilbao	3	1
1984	29 Feb	Paris	0	2
1992	19 Feb	Wembley	2	0
EC1992	14 June	Malmo	0	0
TF1997	7 June	Montpellier	1	0
1999	10 Feb	Wembley	0	2

		v GEORGIA	E	G
WC1996	9 Nov	Tbilisi	2	0
WC1997	30 Apr	Wembley	2	0

		v GERMANY	E	G
1930	10 May	Berlin	3	3
1935	4 Dec	Tottenham	3	0
1938	14 May	Berlin	6	3
1991	11 Sept	Wembley	0	1
1993	19 June	Detroit	1	2
EC1996	26 June	Wembley	1	1*
EC2000	17 June	Charleroi	1	0

		v EAST GERMANY	E	EG
1963	2 June	Leipzig	2	1
1970	25 Nov	Wembley	3	1
1974	29 May	Leipzig	1	1
1984	12 Sept	Wembley	1	0

		v WEST GERMANY	E	WG
1954	1 Dec	Wembley	3	1
1956	26 May	Berlin	3	1
1965	12 May	Nuremberg	1	0
1966	23 Feb	Wembley	1	0
WC1966	30 July	Wembley	4	2*
1968	1 June	Hanover	0	1
WC1970	14 June	Leon	2	3*
EC1972	29 Apr	Wembley	1	3
EC1972	13 May	Berlin	0	0
1975	12 Mar	Wembley	2	0
1978	22 Feb	Munich	1	2
WC1982	29 June	Madrid	0	0
1982	13 Oct	Wembley	1	2
1985	12 June	Mexico City	3	0
1987	9 Sept	Dusseldorf	1	3
WC1990	4 July	Turin	1	1*
After extra time				

		v GREECE	E	G
EC1971	21 Apr	Wembley	3	0
EC1971	1 Dec	Athens	2	0
EC1982	17 Nov	Athens	3	0
EC1983	30 Mar	Wembley	0	0
1989	8 Feb	Athens	2	1
1994	17 May	Wembley	5	0

		v HOLLAND	E	H
1935	18 May	Amsterdam	1	0
1946	27 Nov	Huddersfield	8	2
1964	9 Dec	Amsterdam	1	1
1969	5 Nov	Amsterdam	1	0
1970	14 Jun	Wembley	0	0
1977	9 Feb	Wembley	0	2
1982	25 May	Wembley	2	0
1988	23 Mar	Wembley	2	2
EC1988	15 June	Dusseldorf	1	3
WC1990	16 June	Cagliari	0	0
WC1993	28 Apr	Wembley	2	2
WC1993	13 Oct	Rotterdam	0	2
EC1996	18 June	Wembley	4	1

		v HUNGARY	E	H
1908	10 June	Budapest	7	0
1909	29 May	Budapest	4	2
1909	31 May	Budapest	8	2
1934	10 May	Budapest	1	2
1936	2 Dec	Highbury	6	2
1953	25 Nov	Wembley	3	6
1954	23 May	Budapest	1	7
1960	22 May	Budapest	0	2
WC1962	31 May	Rancagua	1	2
1965	5 May	Wembley	1	0
1978	24 May	Wembley	4	1
WC1981	6 June	Budapest	3	1
WC1982	18 Nov	Wembley	1	0
EC1983	27 Apr	Wembley	2	0
EC1983	12 Oct	Budapest	3	0
1988	27 Apr	Budapest	0	0
1990	12 Sept	Wembley	1	0
1992	12 May	Budapest	1	0
1996	18 May	Wembley	3	0
1999	28 Apr	Budapest	1	1

		v ICELAND	E	I
1982	2 June	Reykjavik	1	1

		v REPUBLIC OF IRELAND	E	RI
1946	30 Sept	Dublin	1	0
1949	21 Sept	Everton	0	2
WC1957	8 May	Wembley	5	1
WC1957	19 May	Dublin	1	1
1964	24 May	Dublin	3	1
1976	8 Sept	Wembley	1	1
EC1978	25 Oct	Dublin	1	1
EC1980	6 Feb	Wembley	2	0
1985	26 Mar	Wembley	2	1
EC1988	12 June	Stuttgart	0	1
WC1990	11 June	Cagliari	1	1
EC1990	14 Nov	Dublin	1	1
EC1991	27 Mar	Wembley	1	1
1995	15 Feb	Dublin	0	1
(abandoned after 27 mins)				

		v ISRAEL	E	I
1986	26 Feb	Ramat Gan	2	1
1988	17 Feb	Tel Aviv	0	0

		v ITALY	E	I
1933	13 May	Rome	1	1
1934	14 Nov	Highbury	3	2
1939	13 May	Milan	2	2
1948	16 May	Turin	4	0
1949	30 Nov	Tottenham	2	0
1952	18 May	Florence	1	1
1959	6 May	Wembley	2	2
1961	24 May	Rome	3	2
1973	14 June	Turin	0	2
1973	14 Nov	Wembley	0	1
1976	28 May	New York	3	2
WC1976	17 Nov	Rome	0	2
WC1977	16 Nov	Wembley	2	0
EC1980	15 June	Turin	0	1
1985	6 June	Mexico City	1	2
1989	15 Nov	Wembley	0	0
WC1990	7 July	Bari	1	2
WC1997	12 Feb	Wembley	0	1
TF1997	4 June	Nantes	2	0
WC1997	11 Oct	Rome	0	0

		v JAPAN	E	J
UI1995	3 June	Wembley	2	1

		v KUWAIT	E	K
WC1982	25 June	Bilbao	1	0

v LUXEMBOURG			E	L
1927	21 May	Esch-sur-Alzette	5	2
wc1960	19 Oct	Luxembourg	9	0
wc1961	28 Sept	Highbury	4	1
wc1977	30 Mar	Wembley	5	0
wc1977	12 Oct	Luxembourg	2	0
EC1982	15 Dec	Wembley	9	0
EC1983	16 Nov	Luxembourg	4	0
EC1998	14 Oct	Luxembourg	3	0
EC1999	4 Sept	Wembley	6	0

v MALAYSIA			E	M
1991	12 June	Kuala Lumpur	4	2

v MALTA			E	M
EC1971	3 Feb	Valletta	1	0
EC1971	12 May	Wembley	5	0
2000	3 June	Valletta	2	1

v MEXICO			E	M
1959	24 May	Mexico City	1	2
1961	10 May	Wembley	8	0
wc1966	16 July	Wembley	2	0
1969	1 June	Mexico City	0	0
1985	9 June	Mexico City	0	1
1986	17 May	Los Angeles	3	0
1997	29 Mar	Wembley	2	0

v MOLDOVA			E	M
wc1996	1 Sept	Chisinau	3	0
wc1997	10 Sept	Wembley	4	0

v MOROCCO			E	M
wc1986	6 June	Monterrey	0	0
1998	27 May	Casablanca	1	0

v NEW ZEALAND			E	NZ
1991	3 June	Auckland	1	0
1991	8 June	Wellington	2	0

v NIGERIA			E	N
1994	16 Nov	Wembley	1	0

v NORWAY			E	N
1937	14 May	Oslo	6	0
1938	9 Nov	Newcastle	4	0
1949	18 May	Oslo	4	1
1966	29 June	Oslo	6	1
wc1980	10 Sept	Wembley	4	0
wc1981	9 Sept	Oslo	1	2
wc1992	14 Oct	Wembley	1	1
wc1993	2 June	Oslo	0	2
1994	22 May	Wembley	0	0
1995	11 Oct	Oslo	0	0

v PARAGUAY			E	P
wc1986	18 June	Mexico City	3	0

v PERU			E	P
1959	17 May	Lima	1	4
1962	20 May	Lima	4	0

v POLAND			E	P
1966	5 Jan	Everton	1	1
1966	5 July	Chorzow	1	0
wc1973	6 June	Chorzow	0	2
wc1973	17 Oct	Wembley	1	1
wc1986	11 June	Monterrey	3	0
wc1989	3 June	Wembley	3	0
wc1989	11 Oct	Katowice	0	0
EC1990	17 Oct	Wembley	2	0
EC1991	13 Nov	Poznan	1	1
wc1993	29 May	Katowice	1	1
wc1993	8 Sept	Wembley	3	0
wc1996	9 Oct	Wembley	2	1
wc1997	31 May	Katowice	2	0
EC1999	27 Mar	Wembley	3	1
EC1999	8 Sept	Warsaw	0	0

v PORTUGAL			E	P
1947	25 May	Lisbon	10	0
1950	14 May	Lisbon	5	3
1951	19 May	Everton	5	2
1955	22 May	Oporto	1	3
1958	7 May	Wembley	2	1
wc1961	21 May	Lisbon	1	1
wc1961	25 Oct	Wembley	2	0
1964	17 May	Lisbon	4	3
1964	4 June	São Paulo	1	1
wc1966	26 July	Wembley	2	1
1969	10 Dec	Wembley	1	0
1974	3 Apr	Lisbon	0	0
EC1974	20 Nov	Wembley	0	0
EC1975	19 Nov	Lisbon	1	1
wc1986	3 June	Monterrey	0	1
1995	12 Dec	Wembley	1	1
1998	22 Apr	Wembley	3	0
EC2000	12 June	Eindhoven	2	3

v ROMANIA			E	R
1939	24 May	Bucharest	2	0
1968	6 Nov	Bucharest	0	0
1969	15 Jan	Wembley	1	1
wc1970	2 June	Guadalajara	1	0
wc1980	15 Oct	Bucharest	1	2
wc1981	29 April	Wembley	0	0
wc1985	1 May	Bucharest	0	0
wc1985	11 Sept	Wembley	1	1
1994	12 Oct	Wembley	1	1
wc1998	22 June	Toulouse	1	2
EC2000	20 June	Charleroi	2	3

v SAN MARINO			E	SM
wc1992	17 Feb	Wembley	6	0
wc1993	17 Nov	Bologna	7	1

v SAUDI ARABIA			E	SA
1988	16 Nov	Riyadh	1	1
1998	23 May	Wembley	0	0

v SOUTH AFRICA			E	SA
1997	24 May	Old Trafford	2	1

v SPAIN			E	S
1929	15 May	Madrid	3	4
1931	9 Dec	Highbury	7	1
wc1950	2 July	Rio de Janeiro	0	1
1955	18 May	Madrid	1	1
1955	30 Nov	Wembley	4	1
1960	15 May	Madrid	0	3
1960	26 Oct	Wembley	4	2
1965	8 Dec	Madrid	2	0
1967	24 May	Wembley	2	0
EC1968	3 Apr	Wembley	1	0
EC1968	8 May	Madrid	2	1
1980	26 Mar	Barcelona	2	0
EC1980	18 June	Naples	2	1
1981	25 Mar	Wembley	1	2
wc1982	5 July	Madrid	0	0
1987	18 Feb	Madrid	4	2
1992	9 Sept	Santander	0	1
EC 1996	22 June	Wembley	0	0

v SWEDEN			E	S
1923	21 May	Stockholm	4	2
1923	24 May	Stockholm	3	1
1937	17 May	Stockholm	4	0
1947	19 Nov	Highbury	4	2
1949	13 May	Stockholm	1	3
1956	16 May	Stockholm	0	0
1959	28 Oct	Wembley	2	3
1965	16 May	Gothenburg	2	1
1968	22 May	Wembley	3	1
1979	10 June	Stockholm	0	0
1986	10 Sept	Stockholm	0	1
wc1988	19 Oct	Wembley	0	0
wc1989	6 Sept	Stockholm	0	0
EC1992	17 June	Stockholm	1	2
UI1995	8 June	Leeds	3	3
EC1998	5 Sept	Stockholm	1	2
EC1999	5 June	Wembley	0	0

v SWITZERLAND

			E	S
1933	20 May	Berne	4	0
1938	21 May	Zurich	1	2
1947	18 May	Zurich	0	1
1948	2 Dec	Highbury	6	0
1952	28 May	Zurich	3	0
wc1954	20 June	Berne	2	0
1962	9 May	Wembley	3	1
1963	5 June	Basle	8	1
EC1971	13 Oct	Basle	3	2
EC1971	10 Nov	Wembley	1	1
1975	3 Sept	Basle	2	1
1977	7 Sept	Wembley	0	0
wc1980	19 Nov	Wembley	2	1
wc1981	30 May	Basle	1	2
1988	28 May	Lausanne	1	0
1995	15 Nov	Wembley	3	1
EC1996	8 June	Wembley	1	1
1998	25 Mar	Berne	1	1

v TUNISIA

			E	T
1990	2 June	Tunis	1	1
wc1998	15 June	Marseilles	2	0

v TURKEY

			E	T
wc1984	14 Nov	Istanbul	8	0
wc1985	16 Oct	Wembley	5	0
EC1987	29 Apr	Izmir	0	0
EC1987	14 Oct	Wembley	8	0
EC1991	1 May	Izmir	1	0
EC1991	16 Oct	Wembley	1	0
wc1992	18 Nov	Wembley	4	0
wc1993	31 Mar	Izmir	2	0

v UKRAINE

			E	U
2000	31 May	Wembley	2	0

v URUGUAY

			E	U
1953	31 May	Montevideo	1	2
wc1954	26 June	Basle	2	4
1964	6 May	Wembley	2	1
wc1966	11 July	Wembley	0	0
1969	8 June	Montevideo	2	1
1977	15 June	Montevideo	0	0
1984	13 June	Montevideo	0	2
1990	22 May	Wembley	1	2
1995	29 Mar	Wembley	0	0

v USA

			E	USA
wc1950	29 June	Belo Horizonte	0	1
1953	8 June	New York	6	3
1959	28 May	Los Angeles	8	1
1964	27 May	New York	10	0
1985	16 June	Los Angeles	5	0
1993	9 June	Foxboro	0	2
1994	7 Sept	Wembley	2	0

v USSR

			E	USSR
1958	18 May	Moscow	1	1
wc1958	8 June	Gothenburg	2	2
wc1958	17 June	Gothenburg	0	1
1958	22 Oct	Wembley	5	0
1967	6 Dec	Wembley	2	2
EC1968	8 June	Rome	2	0
1973	10 June	Moscow	2	1
1984	2 June	Wembley	0	2
1986	26 Mar	Tbilisi	1	0
EC1988	18 June	Frankfurt	1	3
1991	21 May	Wembley	3	1

v YUGOSLAVIA

			E	Y
1939	18 May	Belgrade	1	2
1950	22 Nov	Highbury	2	2
1954	16 May	Belgrade	0	1
1956	28 Nov	Wembley	3	0
1958	11 May	Belgrade	0	5
1960	11 May	Wembley	3	3
1965	9 May	Belgrade	1	1
1966	4 May	Wembley	2	0
EC1968	5 June	Florence	0	1
1972	11 Oct	Wembley	1	1
1974	5 June	Belgrade	2	2
EC1986	12 Nov	Wembley	2	0
EC1987	11 Nov	Belgrade	4	1
1989	13 Dec	Wembley	2	1

SCOTLAND

v ARGENTINA

			S	A
1977	18 June	Buenos Aires	1	1
1979	2 June	Glasgow	1	3
1990	28 Mar	Glasgow	1	0

v AUSTRALIA

			S	A
wc1985	20 Nov	Glasgow	2	0
wc1985	4 Dec	Melbourne	0	0
1996	27 Mar	Glasgow	1	0

v AUSTRIA

			S	A
1931	16 May	Vienna	0	5
1933	29 Nov	Glasgow	2	2
1937	9 May	Vienna	1	1
1950	13 Dec	Glasgow	0	1
1951	27 May	Vienna	0	4
wc1954	16 June	Zurich	0	1
1955	19 May	Vienna	4	1
1956	2 May	Glasgow	1	1
1960	29 May	Vienna	1	4
1963	8 May	Glasgow	4	1
(abandoned after 79 mins)				
wc1968	6 Nov	Glasgow	2	1
wc1969	5 Nov	Vienna	0	2
EC1978	20 Sept	Vienna	2	3
EC1979	17 Oct	Glasgow	1	1
1994	20 Apr	Vienna	2	1
wc1996	31 Aug	Vienna	0	0
wc1997	2 Apr	Celtic Park	2	0

v BELARUS

			S	B
wc1997	8 June	Minsk	1	0
wc1997	7 Sept	Aberdeen	4	1

v BELGIUM

			S	B
1947	18 May	Brussels	1	2
1948	28 Apr	Glasgow	2	0
1951	20 May	Brussels	5	0
EC1971	3 Feb	Liège	0	3
EC1971	10 Nov	Aberdeen	1	0
1974	2 June	Brussels	1	2
EC1979	21 Nov	Brussels	0	2
EC1979	19 Dec	Glasgow	1	3
EC1982	15 Dec	Brussels	2	3
EC1983	12 Oct	Glasgow	1	1
EC1987	1 Apr	Brussels	1	4
EC1987	14 Oct	Glasgow	2	0

v BOSNIA

			S	B
EC1999	4 Sept	Sarajevo	2	1
EC1999	5 Oct	Glasgow	1	0

v BRAZIL

			S	B
1966	25 June	Glasgow	1	1
1972	5 July	Rio de Janeiro	0	1
1973	30 June	Glasgow	0	1
wc1974	18 June	Frankfurt	0	0
1977	23 June	Rio de Janeiro	0	2
wc1982	18 June	Seville	1	4
1987	26 May	Glasgow	0	2
wc1990	20 June	Turin	0	1
wc1998	10 June	Sant-Denis	1	2

v BULGARIA

			S	B
1978	22 Feb	Glasgow	2	1
EC1986	10 Sept	Glasgow	0	0
EC1987	11 Nov	Sofia	1	0
EC1990	14 Nov	Sofia	1	1
EC1991	27 Mar	Glasgow	1	1

v CANADA		S	C
1983	12 June Vancouver	2	0
1983	16 June Edmonton	3	0
1983	20 June Toronto	2	0
1992	21 May Toronto	3	1

v CHILE		S	C
1977	15 June Santiago	4	2
1989	30 May Glasgow	2	0

v CIS		S	C
EC1992	18 June Norrkoping	3	0

v COLOMBIA		S	C
1988	17 May Glasgow	0	0
1996	30 May Miami	0	1
1998	23 May New York	2	2

v COSTA RICA		S	CR
wc1990	11 June Genoa	0	1

v CYPRUS		S	C
wc1968	17 Dec Nicosia	5	0
wc1969	11 May Glasgow	8	0
wc1989	8 Feb Limassol	3	2
wc1989	26 Apr Glasgow	2	1

v CZECHOSLOVAKIA		S	C
1937	22 May Prague	3	1
1937	8 Dec Glasgow	5	0
wc1961	14 May Bratislava	0	4
wc1961	26 Sept Glasgow	3	2
wc1961	29 Nov Brussels	2	4*
1972	2 July Porto Alegre	0	0
wc1973	26 Sept Glasgow	2	1
wc1973	17 Oct Prague	0	1
wc1976	13 Oct Prague	0	2
wc1977	21 Sept Glasgow	3	1

*After extra time

v CZECH REPUBLIC		S	C
EC1999	31 Mar Glasgow	1	2
EC1999	9 June Prague	2	3

v DENMARK		S	D
1951	12 May Glasgow	3	1
1952	25 May Copenhagen	2	1
1968	16 Oct Copenhagen	1	0
EC1970	11 Nov Glasgow	1	0
EC1971	9 June Copenhagen	0	1
wc1972	18 Oct Copenhagen	4	1
wc1972	15 Nov Glasgow	2	0
EC1975	3 Sept Copenhagen	1	0
EC1975	29 Oct Glasgow	3	1
wc1986	4 June Nezahualcayotl	0	1
1996	24 Apr Copenhagen	0	2
1998	25 Mar Glasgow	0	1

v ECUADOR		S	E
1995	24 May Toyama	2	1

v EGYPT		S	E
1990	16 May Aberdeen	1	3

v ESTONIA		S	E
wc1993	19 May Tallinn	3	0
wc1993	2 June Aberdeen	3	1
wc1997	11 Feb Monaco	0	0
wc1997	29 Mar Kilmarnock	2	0
EC1998	10 Oct Edinburgh	3	2
EC1999	8 Sept Tallinn	0	0

v FAEROES		S	F
EC1994	12 Oct Glasgow	5	1
EC1995	7 June Toftir	2	0
EC1998	14 Oct Aberdeen	2	1
EC1999	5 June Toftir	1	1

v FINLAND		S	F
1954	25 May Helsinki	2	1
wc1964	21 Oct Glasgow	3	1
wc1965	27 May Helsinki	2	1
1976	8 Sept Glasgow	6	0

		S	F
1992	25 Mar Glasgow	1	1
EC1994	7 Sept Helsinki	2	0
EC1995	6 Sept Glasgow	1	0
1998	22 Apr Edinburgh	1	1

v FRANCE		S	F
1930	18 May Paris	2	0
1932	8 May Paris	3	1
1948	23 May Paris	0	3
1949	27 Apr Glasgow	2	0
1950	27 May Paris	1	0
1951	16 May Glasgow	1	0
wc1958	15 June Orebro	1	2
1984	1 June Marseilles	0	2
wc1989	8 Mar Glasgow	2	0
wc1989	11 Oct Paris	0	3
1997	12 Nov St Etienne	1	2
2000	29 Mar Glasgow	0	2

v GERMANY		S	G
1929	1 June Berlin	1	1
1936	14 Oct Glasgow	2	0
EC1992	15 June Norrkoping	0	2
1993	24 Mar Glasgow	0	1
1998	28 Apr Bremen	1	0

v EAST GERMANY		S	EG
1974	30 Oct Glasgow	3	0
1977	7 Sept East Berlin	0	1
EC1982	13 Oct Glasgow	2	0
EC1983	16 Nov Halle	1	2
1985	16 Oct Glasgow	0	0
1990	25 Apr Glasgow	0	1

v WEST GERMANY		S	WG
1957	22 May Stuttgart	3	1
1959	6 May Glasgow	3	2
1964	12 May Hanover	2	2
wc1969	16 Apr Glasgow	1	1
wc1969	22 Oct Hamburg	2	3
1973	14 Nov Glasgow	1	1
1974	27 Mar Frankfurt	1	2
wc1986	8 June Queretaro	1	2

v GREECE		S	G
EC1994	18 Dec Athens	0	1
EC1995	16 Aug Glasgow	1	0

v HOLLAND		S	H
1929	4 June Amsterdam	2	0
1938	21 May Amsterdam	3	1
1959	27 May Amsterdam	2	1
1966	11 May Glasgow	0	3
1968	30 May Amsterdam	0	0
1971	1 Dec Rotterdam	1	2
wc1978	11 June Mendoza	3	2
1982	23 Mar Glasgow	2	1
1986	29 Apr Eindhoven	0	0
EC1992	12 June Gothenburg	0	1
1994	23 Mar Glasgow	0	1
1994	27 May Utrecht	1	3
EC1996	10 June Birmingham	0	0
2000	26 Apr Arnhem	0	0

v HUNGARY		S	H
1938	7 Dec Glasgow	3	1
1954	8 Dec Glasgow	2	4
1955	29 May Budapest	1	3
1958	7 May Glasgow	1	1
1960	5 June Budapest	3	3
1980	31 May Budapest	1	3
1987	9 Sept Glasgow	2	0

v ICELAND		S	I
wc1984	17 Oct Glasgow	3	0
wc1985	28 May Reykjavik	1	0

v IRAN

			S	I
wc1978	7 June	Cordoba	1	1

v REPUBLIC OF IRELAND

			S	RI
wc1961	3 May	Glasgow	4	1
wc1961	7 May	Dublin	3	0
1963	9 June	Dublin	0	1
1969	21 Sept	Dublin	1	1
EC1986	15 Oct	Dublin	0	0
EC1987	18 Feb	Glasgow	0	1
2000	30 May	Dublin	2	1

v ISRAEL

			S	I
wc1981	25 Feb	Tel Aviv	1	0
wc1981	28 Apr	Glasgow	3	1
1986	28 Jan	Tel Aviv	1	0

v ITALY

			S	I
1931	20 May	Rome	0	3
wc1965	9 Nov	Glasgow	1	0
wc1965	7 Dec	Naples	0	3
1988	22 Dec	Perugia	0	2
wc1992	18 Nov	Glasgow	0	0
wc1993	13 Oct	Rome	1	3

v JAPAN

			S	J
1995	21 May	Hiroshima	0	0

v LATVIA

			S	L
wc1996	5 Oct	Riga	2	0
wc1997	11 Oct	Glasgow	2	0

v LITHUANIA

			S	L
EC1998	5 Sept	Vilnius	0	0
EC1999	9 Oct	Glasgow	3	0

v LUXEMBOURG

			S	L
1947	24 May	Luxembourg	6	0
EC1986	12 Nov	Glasgow	3	0
EC1987	2 Dec	Esch	0	0

v MALTA

			S	M
1988	22 Mar	Valletta	1	1
1990	28 May	Valletta	2	1
wc1993	17 Feb	Glasgow	3	0
wc1993	17 Nov	Valletta	2	0
1997	1 June	Valletta	3	2

v MOROCCO

			S	M
wc1998	23 June	St Etienne	0	3

v NEW ZEALAND

			S	NZ
wc1982	15 June	Malaga	5	2

v NORWAY

			S	N
1929	28 May	Oslo	7	3
1954	5 May	Glasgow	1	0
1954	19 May	Oslo	1	1
1963	4 June	Bergen	3	4
1963	7 Nov	Glasgow	6	1
1974	6 June	Oslo	2	1
EC1978	25 Oct	Glasgow	3	2
EC1979	7 June	Oslo	4	0
wc1988	14 Sept	Oslo	2	1
wc1989	15 Nov	Glasgow	1	1
1992	3 June	Oslo	0	0
wc1998	16 June	Bordeaux	1	1

v PARAGUAY

			S	P
wc1958	11 June	Norrkoping	2	3

v PERU

			S	P
1972	26 Apr	Glasgow	2	0
wc1978	3 June	Cordoba	1	3
1979	12 Sept	Glasgow	1	1

v POLAND

			S	P
1958	1 June	Warsaw	2	1
1960	4 June	Glasgow	2	3
wc1965	23 May	Chorzow	1	1
wc1965	13 Oct	Glasgow	1	2
1980	28 May	Poznan	0	1
1990	19 May	Glasgow	1	1

v PORTUGAL

			S	P
1950	21 May	Lisbon	2	2
1955	4 May	Glasgow	3	0
1959	3 June	Lisbon	0	1
1966	18 June	Glasgow	0	1
EC1971	21 Apr	Lisbon	0	2
EC1971	13 Oct	Glasgow	2	1
1975	13 May	Glasgow	1	0
EC1978	29 Nov	Lisbon	0	1
EC1980	26 Mar	Glasgow	4	1
wc1980	15 Oct	Glasgow	0	0
wc1981	18 Nov	Lisbon	1	2
wc1992	14 Oct	Glasgow	0	0
wc1993	28 Apr	Lisbon	0	5

v ROMANIA

			S	R
EC1975	1 June	Bucharest	1	1
EC1975	17 Dec	Glasgow	1	1
1986	26 Mar	Glasgow	3	0
EC1990	12 Sept	Glasgow	2	1
EC1991	16 Oct	Bucharest	0	1

v RUSSIA

			S	R
EC1994	16 Nov	Glasgow	1	1
EC1995	29 Mar	Moscow	0	0

v SAN MARINO

			S	SM
EC1991	1 May	Serravalle	2	0
EC1991	13 Nov	Glasgow	4	0
EC1995	26 Apr	Serravalle	2	0
EC1995	15 Nov	Glasgow	5	0

v SAUDI ARABIA

			S	SA
1988	17 Feb	Riyadh	2	2

v SPAIN

			S	Sp
wc1957	8 May	Glasgow	4	2
wc1957	26 May	Madrid	1	4
1963	13 June	Madrid	6	2
1965	8 May	Glasgow	0	0
EC1974	20 Nov	Glasgow	1	2
EC1975	5 Feb	Valencia	1	1
1982	24 Feb	Valencia	0	3
wc1984	14 Nov	Glasgow	3	1
wc1985	27 Feb	Seville	0	1
1988	27 Apr	Madrid	0	0

v SWEDEN

			S	Sw
1952	30 May	Stockholm	1	3
1953	6 May	Glasgow	1	2
1975	16 Apr	Gothenburg	1	1
1977	27 Apr	Glasgow	3	1
wc1980	10 Sept	Stockholm	1	0
wc1981	9 Sept	Glasgow	2	0
wc1990	16 June	Genoa	2	1
1995	11 Oct	Stockholm	0	2
wc1996	10 Nov	Glasgow	1	0
wc1997	30 Apr	Gothenburg	1	2

v SWITZERLAND

			S	Sw
1931	24 May	Geneva	3	2
1948	17 May	Berne	1	2
1950	26 Apr	Glasgow	3	1
wc1957	19 May	Basle	2	1
wc1957	6 Nov	Glasgow	3	2
1973	22 June	Berne	0	1
1976	7 Apr	Glasgow	1	0

			S	Sw
EC1982	17 Nov	Berne	0	2
EC1983	30 May	Glasgow	2	2
EC1990	17 Oct	Glasgow	2	1
EC1991	11 Sept	Berne	2	2
wc1992	9 Sept	Berne	1	3
wc1993	8 Sept	Aberdeen	1	1
EC1996	18 June	Birmingham	1	0

v TURKEY			S	T
1960	8 June	Ankara	2	4

v URUGUAY			S	U
wc1954	19 June	Basle	0	7
1962	2 May	Glasgow	2	3
1983	21 Sept	Glasgow	2	0
wc1986	13 June	Nezahualcoyotl	0	0

v USA			S	USA
1952	30 Apr	Glasgow	6	0
1992	17 May	Denver	1	0
1996	26 May	New Britain	1	2
1998	30 May	Washington	0	0

v USSR			S	USSR
1967	10 May	Glasgow	0	2
1971	14 June	Moscow	0	1
wc1982	22 June	Malaga	2	2
1991	6 Feb	Glasgow	0	1

v YUGOSLAVIA			S	Y
1955	15 May	Belgrade	2	2
1956	21 Nov	Glasgow	2	0
wc1958	8 June	Vasteras	1	1
1972	29 June	Belo Horizonte	2	2
wc1974	22 June	Frankfurt	1	1
1984	12 Sept	Glasgow	6	1
wc1988	19 Oct	Glasgow	1	1
wc1989	6 Sept	Zagreb	1	3

v ZAIRE			S	Z
wc1974	14 June	Dortmund	2	0

WALES

v ALBANIA			W	A
EC1994	7 Sept	Cardiff	2	0
EC1995	15 Nov	Tirana	1	1

v ARGENTINA			W	A
1992	3 June	Tokyo	0	1

v AUSTRIA			W	A
1954	9 May	Vienna	0	2
EC1955	23 Nov	Wrexham	1	2
EC1974	4 Sept	Vienna	1	2
1975	19 Nov	Wrexham	1	0
1992	29 Apr	Vienna	1	1

v BELARUS			W	B
EC1998	14 Oct	Cardiff	3	2
EC1999	4 Sept	Minsk	2	2

v BELGIUM			W	B
1949	22 May	Liège	1	3
1949	23 Nov	Cardiff	5	1
EC1990	17 Oct	Cardiff	3	1
EC1991	27 Mar	Brussels	1	1
wc1992	18 Nov	Brussels	0	2
wc1993	31 Mar	Cardiff	2	0
wc1997	29 Mar	Cardiff	1	2
wc1997	11 Oct	Brussels	2	3

v BRAZIL			W	B
wc1958	19 June	Gothenburg	0	1
1962	12 May	Rio de Janeiro	1	3
1962	16 May	São Paulo	1	3
1966	14 May	Rio de Janeiro	1	3
1966	18 May	Belo Horizonte	0	1
1983	12 June	Cardiff	1	1
1991	11 Sept	Cardiff	1	0
1997	12 Nov	Brasilia	0	3
2000	23 May	Cardiff	0	3

v BULGARIA			W	B
EC1983	27 Apr	Wrexham	1	0
EC1983	16 Nov	Sofia	0	1
EC1994	14 Dec	Cardiff	0	3
EC1995	29 Mar	Sofia	1	3

v CANADA			W	C
1986	10 May	Toronto	0	2
1986	20 May	Vancouver	3	0

v CHILE			W	C
1966	22 May	Santiago	0	2

v COSTA RICA			W	CR
1990	20 May	Cardiff	1	0

v CYPRUS			W	C
wc1992	14 Oct	Limassol	1	0
wc1993	13 Oct	Cardiff	2	0

v CZECHOSLOVAKIA			W	C
wc1957	1 May	Cardiff	1	0
wc1957	26 May	Prague	0	2
EC1971	21 Apr	Swansea	1	3
EC1971	27 Oct	Prague	0	1
wc1977	30 Mar	Wrexham	3	0
wc1977	16 Nov	Prague	0	1
wc1980	19 Nov	Cardiff	1	0
wc1981	9 Sept	Prague	0	2
EC1987	29 Apr	Wrexham	1	1
EC1987	11 Nov	Prague	0	2
wc1993	28 Apr	Ostrava†	1	1
wc1993	8 Sept	Cardiff†	2	2

†Czechoslovakia played as RCS (Republic of Czechs and Slovaks).

v DENMARK			W	D
wc1964	21 Oct	Copenhagen	0	1
wc1965	1 Dec	Wrexham	4	2
EC1987	9 Sept	Cardiff	1	0
EC1987	14 Oct	Copenhagen	0	1
1990	11 Sept	Copenhagen	0	1
EC1998	10 Oct	Copenhagen	2	1
EC1999	9 June	Liverpool	0	2

v ESTONIA			W	E
1994	23 May	Tallinn	2	1

v FINLAND			W	F
EC1971	26 May	Helsinki	1	0
EC1971	13 Oct	Swansea	3	0
EC1987	10 Sept	Helsinki	1	1
EC1987	1 Apr	Wrexham	4	0
wc1988	19 Oct	Swansea	2	2
wc1989	6 Sept	Helsinki	0	1
2000	29 Mar	Cardiff	1	2

v FAEROES			W	F
wc1992	9 Sept	Cardiff	6	0
wc1993	6 June	Toftir	3	0

v FRANCE			W	F
1933	25 May	Paris	1	1
1939	20 May	Paris	1	2
1953	14 May	Paris	1	6
1982	2 June	Toulouse	1	0

v GEORGIA

			W	G
EC1994	16 Nov	Tbilisi	0	5
EC1995	7 June	Cardiff	0	1

v GERMANY

			W	G
EC1995	26 Apr	Dusseldorf	1	1
EC1995	11 Oct	Cardiff	1	2

v EAST GERMANY

			W	EG
wc1957	19 May	Leipzig	1	2
wc1957	25 Sept	Cardiff	4	1
wc1969	16 Apr	Dresden	1	2
wc1969	22 Oct	Cardiff	1	3

v WEST GERMANY

			W	WG
1968	8 May	Cardiff	1	1
1969	26 Mar	Frankfurt	1	1
1976	6 Oct	Cardiff	0	2
1977	14 Dec	Dortmund	1	1
EC1979	2 May	Wrexham	0	2
EC1979	17 Oct	Cologne	1	5
wc1989	31 May	Cardiff	0	0
wc1989	15 Nov	Cologne	1	2
EC1991	5 June	Cardiff	1	0
EC1991	16 Oct	Nuremberg	1	4

v GREECE

			W	G
wc1964	9 Dec	Athens	0	2
wc1965	17 Mar	Cardiff	4	1

v HOLLAND

			W	H
wc1988	14 Sept	Amsterdam	0	1
wc1989	11 Oct	Wrexham	1	2
1992	30 May	Utrecht	0	4
wc1996	5 Oct	Cardiff	1	3
wc1996	9 Nov	Eindhoven	1	7

v HUNGARY

			W	H
wc1958	8 June	Sanviken	1	1
wc1958	17 June	Stockholm	2	1
1961	28 May	Budapest	2	3
EC1962	7 Nov	Budapest	1	3
EC1963	20 Mar	Cardiff	1	1
EC1974	30 Oct	Cardiff	2	0
EC1975	16 Apr	Budapest	2	1
1985	16 Oct	Cardiff	0	3

v ICELAND

			W	I
wc1980	2 June	Reykjavik	4	0
wc1981	14 Oct	Swansea	2	2
wc1984	12 Sept	Reykjavik	0	1
wc1984	14 Nov	Cardiff	2	1
1991	1 May	Cardiff	1	0

v IRAN

			W	I
1978	18 Apr	Teheran	1	0

v REPUBLIC OF IRELAND

			W	RI
1960	28 Sept	Dublin	3	2
1979	11 Sept	Swansea	2	1
1981	24 Feb	Dublin	3	1
1986	26 Mar	Dublin	1	0
1990	28 Mar	Dublin	0	1
1991	6 Feb	Wrexham	0	3
1992	19 Feb	Dublin	1	0
1993	17 Feb	Dublin	1	2
1997	11 Feb	Cardiff	0	0

v ISRAEL

			W	I
wc1958	15 Jan	Tel Aviv	2	0
wc1958	5 Feb	Cardiff	2	0
1984	10 June	Tel Aviv	0	0
1989	8 Feb	Tel Aviv	3	3

v ITALY

			W	I
1965	1 May	Florence	1	4
wc1968	23 Oct	Cardiff	0	1
wc1969	4 Nov	Rome	1	4
1988	4 June	Brescia	1	0
1996	24 Jan	Terni	0	3
EC1998	5 Sept	Liverpool	0	2
EC1999	5 June	Bologna	0	4

v JAMAICA

			W	J
1998	25 Mar	Cardiff	0	0

v JAPAN

			W	J
1992	7 June	Matsuyama	1	0

v KUWAIT

			W	K
1977	6 Sept	Wrexham	0	0
1977	20 Sept	Kuwait	0	0

v LUXEMBOURG

			W	L
EC1974	20 Nov	Swansea	5	0
EC1975	1 May	Luxembourg	3	1
EC1990	14 Nov	Luxembourg	1	0
EC1991	13 Nov	Cardiff	1	0

v MALTA

			W	M
EC1978	25 Oct	Wrexham	7	0
EC1979	2 June	Valletta	2	0
1988	1 June	Valletta	3	2
1998	3 June	Valletta	3	0

v MEXICO

			W	M
wc1958	11 June	Stockholm	1	1
1962	22 May	Mexico City	1	2

v MOLDOVA

			W	M
EC1994	12 Oct	Kishinev	2	3
EC1995	6 Sept	Cardiff	1	0

v NORWAY

			W	N
EC1982	22 Sept	Swansea	1	0
EC1983	21 Sept	Oslo	0	0
1984	6 June	Trondheim	0	1
1985	26 Feb	Wrexham	1	1
1985	5 June	Bergen	2	4
1994	9 Mar	Cardiff	1	3

v POLAND

			W	P
wc1973	28 Mar	Cardiff	2	0
wc1973	26 Sept	Katowice	0	3
1991	29 May	Radom	0	0

v PORTUGAL

			W	P
1949	15 May	Lisbon	2	3
1951	12 May	Cardiff	2	1
2000	2 June	Chaves	0	3

v QATAR

			W	Q
2000	23 Feb	Doha	1	0

v ROMANIA

			W	R
EC1970	11 Nov	Cardiff	0	0
EC1971	24 Nov	Bucharest	0	2
1983	12 Oct	Wrexham	5	0
wc1992	20 May	Bucharest	1	5
wc1993	17 Nov	Cardiff	1	2

v SAN MARINO

			W	SM
wc1996	2 June	Serravalle	5	0
wc1996	31 Aug	Cardiff	6	0

v SAUDI ARABIA

			W	SA
1986	25 Feb	Dahran	2	1

v SPAIN

			W	S
wc1961	19 Apr	Cardiff	1	2
wc1961	18 May	Madrid	1	1
1982	24 Mar	Valencia	1	1
wc1984	17 Oct	Seville	0	3
wc1985	30 Apr	Wrexham	3	0

v SWEDEN		W	S
wc1958	15 June	Stockholm	0	0
1988	27 Apr	Stockholm	1	4
1989	26 Apr	Wrexham	0	2
1990	25 Apr	Stockholm	2	4
1994	20 Apr	Wrexham	0	2

v SWITZERLAND		W	S
1949	26 May	Berne	0	4
1951	16 May	Wrexham	3	2
1996	24 Apr	Lugano	0	2
EC1999	31 Mar	Zurich	0	2
EC1999	9 Oct	Wrexham	0	2

v TUNISIA		W	T
1998	6 June	Tunis	0	4

v TURKEY		W	T
EC1978	29 Nov	Wrexham	1	0
EC1979	21 Nov	Izmir	0	1
wc1980	15 Oct	Cardiff	4	0
wc1981	25 Mar	Ankara	1	0
wc1996	14 Dec	Cardiff	0	0
wc1997	20 Aug	Istanbul	4	6

v REST OF UNITED KINGDOM		W	UK
1951	5 Dec	Cardiff	3	2
1969	28 July	Cardiff	0	1

v URUGUAY		W	U
1986	21 Apr	Wrexham	0	0

v USSR		W	USSR
wc1965	30 May	Moscow	1	2
wc1965	27 Oct	Cardiff	2	1
wc1981	30 May	Wrexham	0	0
wc1981	18 Nov	Tbilisi	0	3
1987	18 Feb	Swansea	0	0

v YUGOSLAVIA		W	Y
1953	21 May	Belgrade	2	5
1954	22 Nov	Cardiff	1	3
EC1976	24 Apr	Zagreb	0	2
EC1976	22 May	Cardiff	1	1
EC1982	15 Dec	Titograd	4	4
EC1983	14 Dec	Cardiff	1	1
1988	23 Mar	Swansea	1	2

NORTHERN IRELAND

v ALBANIA		NI	A
wc1965	7 May	Belfast	4	1
wc1965	24 Nov	Tirana	1	1
EC1982	15 Dec	Tirana	0	0
EC1983	27 Apr	Belfast	1	0
wc1992	9 Sept	Belfast	3	0
wc1993	17 Feb	Tirana	2	1
wc1996	14 Dec	Belfast	2	0
wc1997	10 Sept	Zurich	0	1

v ALGERIA		NI	A
wc1986	3 June	Guadalajara	1	1

v ARGENTINA		NI	A
wc1958	11 June	Halmstad	1	3

v ARMENIA		NI	A
wc1996	5 Oct	Belfast	1	1
wc1997	30 Apr	Erevan	0	0

v AUSTRALIA		NI	A
1980	11 June	Sydney	2	1
1980	15 June	Melbourne	1	1
1980	18 June	Adelaide	2	1

v AUSTRIA		NI	A
wc1982	1 July	Madrid	2	2
EC1982	13 Oct	Vienna	0	2
EC1983	21 Sept	Belfast	3	1
EC1990	14 Nov	Vienna	0	0
EC1991	16 Oct	Belfast	2	1
EC1994	12 Oct	Vienna	2	1
EC1995	15 Nov	Belfast	5	3

v BELGIUM		NI	B
wc1976	10 Nov	Liège	0	2
wc1977	16 Nov	Belfast	3	0
1997	11 Feb	Belfast	3	0

v BRAZIL		NI	B
wc1986	12 June	Guadalajara	0	3

v BULGARIA		NI	B
wc1972	18 Oct	Sofia	0	3
wc1973	26 Sept	Sheffield	0	0
EC1978	29 Nov	Sofia	2	0
EC1979	2 May	Belfast	2	0

v CANADA		NI	C
1995	22 May	Edmonton	0	2
1999	27 Apr	Belfast	1	1

v CHILE		NI	C
1989	26 May	Belfast	0	1
1995	25 May	Edmonton	1	2

v COLOMBIA		NI	C
1994	4 June	Boston	0	2

v CYPRUS		NI	C
EC1971	3 Feb	Nicosia	3	0
EC1971	21 Apr	Belfast	5	0
wc1973	14 Feb	Nicosia	0	1
wc1973	8 May	London	3	0

v CZECHOSLOVAKIA		NI	C
wc1958	8 June	Halmstad	1	0
wc1958	17 June	Malmo	2	1*

*After extra time

v DENMARK		NI	D
EC1978	25 Oct	Belfast	2	1
EC1979	6 June	Copenhagen	0	4
1986	26 Mar	Belfast	1	1
EC1990	17 Oct	Belfast	1	1
EC1991	13 Nov	Odense	1	2
wc1992	18 Nov	Belfast	0	1
wc1993	13 Oct	Copenhagen	0	1

v FAEROES		NI	F
EC1991	1 May	Belfast	1	1
EC1991	11 Sept	Landskrona	5	0

v FINLAND		NI	F
wc1984	27 May	Pori	0	1
wc1984	14 Nov	Belfast	2	1
EC1998	10 Oct	Belfast	1	0
EC1998	9 Oct	Helsinki	1	4

v FRANCE		NI	F
1951	12 May	Belfast	2	2
1952	11 Nov	Paris	1	3
wc1958	19 June	Norrkoping	0	4
1982	24 Mar	Paris	0	4
wc1982	4 July	Madrid	1	4
1986	26 Feb	Paris	0	0
1988	27 Apr	Belfast	0	0
1999	18 Aug	Belfast	0	1

v GERMANY		NI	G
1992	2 June	Bremen	1	1
1996	29 May	Belfast	1	1
wc1996	9 Nov	Nuremberg	1	1

			NI	G
wc1997	20 Aug	Belfast	1	3
EC1999	27 Mar	Belfast	0	3
EC1999	8 Sept	Dortmund	0	4

v WEST GERMANY			NI	WG
wc1958	15 June	Malmo	2	2
wc1960	26 Oct	Belfast	3	4
wc1961	10 May	Hamburg	1	2
1966	7 May	Belfast	0	2
1977	27 Apr	Cologne	0	5
EC1982	17 Nov	Belfast	1	0
EC1983	16 Nov	Hamburg	1	0

v GREECE			NI	G
wc1961	3 May	Athens	1	2
wc1961	17 Oct	Belfast	2	0
1988	17 Feb	Athens	2	3

v HOLLAND			NI	H
1962	9 May	Rotterdam	0	4
wc1965	17 Mar	Belfast	2	1
wc1965	7 Apr	Rotterdam	0	0
wc1976	13 Oct	Rotterdam	2	2
wc1977	12 Oct	Belfast	0	1

v HONDURAS			NI	H
wc1982	21 June	Zaragoza	1	1

v HUNGARY			NI	H
wc1988	19 Oct	Budapest	0	1
wc1989	6 Sept	Belfast	1	2
2000	26 Apr	Belfast	0	1

v ICELAND			NI	I
wc1977	11 June	Reykjavik	0	1
wc1977	21 Sept	Belfast	2	0

v REPUBLIC OF IRELAND			NI	RI
EC1978	20 Sept	Dublin	0	0
EC1979	21 Nov	Belfast	1	0
wc1988	14 Sept	Belfast	0	0
wc1989	11 Oct	Dublin	0	3
wc1993	31 Mar	Dublin	0	3
wc1993	17 Nov	Belfast	1	1
EC1994	16 Nov	Belfast	0	4
EC1995	29 Mar	Dublin	1	1
1999	29 May	Dublin	1	0

v ISRAEL			NI	I
1968	10 Sept	Jaffa	3	2
1976	3 Mar	Tel Aviv	1	1
wc1980	26 Mar	Tel Aviv	0	0
wc1981	18 Nov	Belfast	1	0
1984	16 Oct	Belfast	3	0
1987	18 Feb	Tel Aviv	1	1

v ITALY			NI	I
wc1957	25 Apr	Rome	0	1
1957	4 Dec	Belfast	2	2
wc1958	15 Jan	Belfast	2	1
1961	25 Apr	Bologna	2	3
1997	22 Jan	Palermo	0	2

v LATVIA			NI	L
wc1993	2 June	Riga	2	1
wc1993	8 Sept	Belfast	2	0
EC1995	26 Apr	Riga	1	0
EC1995	7 June	Belfast	1	2

v LIECHTENSTEIN			NI	L
EC1994	20 Apr	Belfast	4	1
EC1995	11 Oct	Eschen	4	0

v LITHUANIA			NI	L
wc1992	28 Apr	Belfast	2	2
wc1993	25 May	Vilnius	1	0

v LUXEMBOURG			NI	L
2000	23 Feb	Luxembourg	3	1

v MALTA			NI	M
wc1988	21 May	Belfast	3	0
wc1989	26 Apr	Valletta	2	0
2000	28 Mar	Valletta	3	0

v MEXICO			NI	M
1966	22 June	Belfast	4	1
1994	11 June	Miami	0	3

v MOLDOVA			NI	M
EC1998	18 Nov	Belfast	2	2
EC1999	31 Mar	Chisinau	0	0

v MOROCCO			NI	M
1986	23 Apr	Belfast	2	1

v NORWAY			NI	N
EC1974	4 Sept	Oslo	1	2
EC1975	29 Oct	Belfast	3	0
1990	27 Mar	Belfast	2	3
1996	27 Mar	Belfast	0	2

v POLAND			NI	P
EC1962	10 Oct	Katowice	2	0
EC1962	28 Nov	Belfast	2	0
1988	23 Mar	Belfast	1	1
1991	5 Feb	Belfast	3	1

v PORTUGAL			NI	P
wc1957	16 Jan	Lisbon	1	1
wc1957	1 May	Belfast	3	0
wc1973	28 Mar	Coventry	1	1
wc1973	14 Nov	Lisbon	1	1
wc1980	19 Nov	Lisbon	0	1
wc1981	29 Apr	Belfast	1	0
EC1994	7 Sept	Belfast	1	2
EC1995	3 Sept	Lisbon	1	1
wc1997	29 Mar	Belfast	0	0
wc1997	11 Oct	Lisbon	0	1

v ROMANIA			NI	R
wc1984	12 Sept	Belfast	3	2
wc1985	16 Oct	Bucharest	1	0
1994	23 Mar	Belfast	2	0

v SLOVAKIA			NI	S
1998	25 Mar	Belfast	1	0

v SPAIN			NI	S
1958	15 Oct	Madrid	2	6
1963	30 May	Bilbao	1	1
1963	30 Oct	Belfast	0	1
EC1970	11 Nov	Seville	0	3
EC1972	16 Feb	Hull	1	1
wc1982	25 June	Valencia	1	0
1985	27 Mar	Palma	0	0
wc1986	7 June	Guadalajara	1	2
wc1988	21 Dec	Seville	0	4
wc1989	8 Feb	Belfast	0	2
wc1992	14 Oct	Belfast	0	0
wc1993	28 Apr	Seville	1	3
1998	2 June	Santander	1	4

v SWEDEN			NI	S
EC1974	30 Oct	Solna	2	0
EC1975	3 Sept	Belfast	1	2
wc1980	15 Oct	Belfast	3	0
wc1981	3 June	Solna	0	1
1996	24 Apr	Belfast	1	2

v SWITZERLAND			NI	S
wc1964	14 Oct	Belfast	1	0
wc1964	14 Nov	Lausanne	1	2
1998	22 Apr	Belfast	1	0

v THAILAND			NI	T
1997	21 May	Bangkok	0	0

v TURKEY			NI	T
wc1968	23 Oct	Belfast	4	1
wc1968	11 Dec	Istanbul	3	0
EC1983	30 Mar	Belfast	2	1
EC1983	12 Oct	Ankara	0	1

			NI	T
wc1985	1 May	Belfast	2	0
wc1985	11 Sept	Izmir	0	0
EC1986	12 Nov	Izmir	0	0
EC1987	11 Nov	Belfast	1	0
EC1998	5 Sept	Istanbul	0	3
EC1999	4 Sept	Belfast	0	3

		v UKRAINE	NI	U
wc1996	31 Aug	Belfast	0	1
wc1997	2 Apr	Kiev	1	2

		v URUGUAY	NI	U
1964	29 Apr	Belfast	3	0
1990	18 May	Belfast	1	0

		v USSR	NI	USSR
wc1969	19 Sept	Belfast	0	0
wc1969	22 Oct	Moscow	0	2
EC1971	22 Sept	Moscow	0	1
EC1971	13 Oct	Belfast	1	1

		v YUGOSLAVIA	NI	Y
EC1975	16 Mar	Belfast	1	0
EC1975	19 Nov	Belgrade	0	1
wc1982	17 June	Zaragoza	0	0
EC1987	29 Apr	Belfast	1	2
EC1987	14 Oct	Sarajevo	0	3
EC1990	12 Sept	Belfast	0	2
EC1991	27 Mar	Belgrade	1	4

REPUBLIC OF IRELAND

		v ALBANIA	RI	A
wc1992	26 May	Dublin	2	0
wc1993	26 May	Tirana	2	1

		v ALGERIA	RI	A
1982	28 Apr	Algiers	0	2

		v ARGENTINA	RI	A
1951	13 May	Dublin	0	1
1979	29 May	Dublin	0	0*
1980	16 May	Dublin	0	1
1998	22 Apr	Dublin	0	2

* Not considered a full international

		v AUSTRIA	RI	A
1952	7 May	Vienna	0	6
1953	25 Mar	Dublin	4	0
1958	14 Mar	Vienna	1	3
1962	8 Apr	Dublin	2	3
EC1963	25 Sept	Vienna	0	0
EC1963	13 Oct	Dublin	3	2
1966	22 May	Vienna	0	1
1968	10 Nov	Dublin	2	2
EC1971	30 May	Dublin	1	4
EC1971	10 Oct	Linz	0	6
EC1995	11 June	Dublin	1	3
EC1995	6 Sept	Vienna	1	3

		v BELGIUM	RI	B
1928	12 Feb	Liège	4	2
1929	30 Apr	Dublin	4	0
1930	11 May	Brussels	3	1
wc1934	25 Feb	Dublin	4	4
1949	24 Apr	Dublin	0	2
1950	10 May	Brussels	1	5
1965	24 Mar	Dublin	0	2
1966	25 May	Liège	3	2
wc1980	15 Oct	Dublin	1	1
wc1981	25 Mar	Brussels	0	1
EC1986	10 Sept	Brussels	2	2
EC1987	29 Apr	Dublin	0	0
wc1997	29 Oct	Dublin	1	1
wc1997	16 Nov	Brussels	1	2

		v BOLIVIA	RI	B
1994	24 May	Dublin	1	0
1996	15 June	New Jersey	3	0

		v BRAZIL	RI	B
1974	5 May	Rio de Janeiro	1	2
1982	27 May	Uberlandia	0	7
1987	23 May	Dublin	1	0

		v BULGARIA	RI	B
wc1977	1 June	Sofia	1	2
wc1977	12 Oct	Dublin	0	0
EC1979	19 May	Sofia	0	1
EC1979	17 Oct	Dublin	3	0

			RI	B
wc1987	1 Apr	Sofia	1	2
wc1987	14 Oct	Dublin	2	0

		v CHILE	RI	C
1960	30 Mar	Dublin	2	0
1972	21 June	Recife	1	2
1974	12 May	Santiago	2	1
1982	22 May	Santiago	0	1
1991	22 May	Dublin	1	1

		v CHINA	RI	C
1984	3 June	Sapporo	1	0

		v CROATIA	RI	C
1996	2 June	Dublin	2	2
EC1998	5 Sept	Dublin	2	0
EC1999	4 Sept	Zagreb	0	1

		v CYPRUS	RI	C
wc1980	26 Mar	Nicosia	3	2
wc1980	19 Nov	Dublin	6	0

		v CZECHOSLOVAKIA	RI	C
1938	18 May	Prague	2	2
EC1959	5 Apr	Dublin	2	0
EC1959	10 May	Bratislava	0	4
wc1961	8 Oct	Dublin	1	3
wc1961	29 Oct	Prague	1	7
EC1967	21 May	Dublin	0	2
EC1967	22 Nov	Prague	2	1
wc1969	4 May	Dublin	1	2
wc1969	7 Oct	Prague	0	3
1979	26 Sept	Prague	1	4
1981	29 Apr	Dublin	3	1
1986	27 May	Reykjavik	1	0

		v CZECH REPUBLIC	RI	C
1994	5 June	Dublin	1	3
1996	24 Apr	Prague	0	2
1998	25 Mar	Olomouc	1	2
2000	23 Feb	Dublin	3	2

		v DENMARK	RI	D
wc1956	3 Oct	Dublin	2	1
wc1957	2 Oct	Copenhagen	2	0
wc1968	4 Dec	Dublin	1	1
(abandoned after 51 mins)				
wc1969	27 May	Copenhagen	0	2
wc1969	15 Oct	Dublin	1	1
EC1978	24 May	Copenhagen	3	3
EC1979	2 May	Dublin	2	0
wc1984	14 Nov	Copenhagen	0	3
wc1985	13 Nov	Dublin	1	4
wc1992	14 Oct	Copenhagen	0	0
wc1993	28 Apr	Dublin	1	1

		v ECUADOR	RI	E
1972	19 June	Natal	3	2

v EGYPT			RI	E
wc1990	17 June	Palermo	0	0

v ENGLAND			RI	E
1946	30 Sept	Dublin	0	1
1949	21 Sept	Everton	2	0
wc1957	8 May	Wembley	1	5
wc1957	19 May	Dublin	1	1
1964	24 May	Dublin	1	3
1976	8 Sept	Wembley	1	1
EC1978	25 Oct	Dublin	1	1
EC1980	6 Feb	Wembley	0	2
1985	26 Mar	Wembley	1	2
EC1988	12 June	Stuttgart	1	0
wc1990	11 June	Cagliari	1	1
EC1990	14 Nov	Dublin	1	1
EC1991	27 Mar	Wembley	1	1
1995	15 Feb	Dublin	1	0
(abandoned after 27 mins)				

v FINLAND			RI	F
wc1949	8 Sept	Dublin	3	0
wc1949	9 Oct	Helsinki	1	1
1990	16 May	Dublin	1	1

v FRANCE			RI	F
1937	23 May	Paris	2	0
1952	16 Nov	Dublin	1	1
wc1953	4 Oct	Dublin	3	5
wc1953	25 Nov	Paris	0	1
wc1972	15 Nov	Dublin	2	1
wc1973	19 May	Paris	1	1
wc1976	17 Nov	Paris	0	2
wc1977	30 Mar	Dublin	1	0
wc1980	28 Oct	Paris	0	2
wc1981	14 Oct	Dublin	3	2
1989	7 Feb	Dublin	0	0

v GERMANY			RI	G
1935	8 May	Dortmund	1	3
1936	17 Oct	Dublin	5	2
1939	23 May	Bremen	1	1
1994	29 May	Hanover	2	0

v WEST GERMANY			RI	WG
1951	17 Oct	Dublin	3	2
1952	4 May	Cologne	0	3
1955	28 May	Hamburg	1	2
1956	25 Nov	Dublin	3	0
1960	11 May	Dusseldorf	1	0
1966	4 May	Dublin	0	4
1970	9 May	Berlin	1	2
1975	1 Mar	Dublin	1	0†
1979	22 May	Dublin	1	3
1981	21 May	Bremen	0	3†
1989	6 Sept	Dublin	1	1
†v West Germany 'B'				

v GREECE			RI	G
2000	26 Apr	Dublin	0	1

v HOLLAND			RI	N
1932	8 May	Amsterdam	2	0
1934	8 Apr	Amsterdam	2	5
1935	8 Dec	Dublin	3	5
1955	1 May	Dublin	1	0
1956	10 May	Rotterdam	4	1
wc1980	10 Sept	Dublin	2	1
wc1981	9 Sept	Rotterdam	2	2
EC1982	22 Sept	Rotterdam	1	2
EC1983	12 Oct	Dublin	2	3
EC1988	18 June	Gelsenkirchen	0	1
wc1990	21 June	Palermo	1	1
1994	20 Apr	Tilburg	1	0
wc1994	4 July	Orlando	0	2
EC1995	13 Dec	Liverpool	0	2
1996	4 June	Rotterdam	1	3

v HUNGARY			RI	H
1934	15 Dec	Dublin	2	4
1936	3 May	Budapest	3	3
1936	6 Dec	Dublin	2	3
1939	19 Mar	Cork	2	2
1939	18 May	Budapest	2	2
wc1969	8 June	Dublin	1	2
wc1969	5 Nov	Budapest	0	4
wc1989	8 Mar	Budapest	0	0
wc1989	4 June	Dublin	2	0
1991	11 Sept	Gyor	2	1

v ICELAND			RI	I
EC1962	12 Aug	Dublin	4	2
EC1962	2 Sept	Reykjavik	1	1
EC1982	13 Oct	Dublin	2	0
EC1983	21 Sept	Reykjavik	3	0
1986	25 May	Reykjavik	2	1
wc1996	10 Nov	Dublin	0	0
wc1997	6 Sept	Reykjavik	4	2

v IRAN			RI	I
1972	18 June	Recife	2	1

v N. IRELAND			RI	NI
EC1978	20 Sept	Dublin	0	0
EC1979	21 Nov	Belfast	0	1
wc1988	14 Sept	Belfast	0	0
wc1989	11 Oct	Dublin	3	0
wc1993	31 Mar	Dublin	3	0
wc1993	17 Nov	Belfast	1	1
EC1994	16 Nov	Belfast	4	0
EC1995	29 Mar	Dublin	1	1
1999	29 May	Dublin	0	1

v ISRAEL			RI	I
1984	4 Apr	Tel Aviv	0	3
1985	27 May	Tel Aviv	0	0
1987	10 Nov	Dublin	5	0

v ITALY			RI	I
1926	21 Mar	Turin	0	3
1927	23 Apr	Dublin	1	2
EC1970	8 Dec	Rome	0	3
EC1971	10 May	Dublin	1	2
1985	5 Feb	Dublin	1	2
wc1990	30 June	Rome	0	1
1992	4 June	Foxboro	0	2
wc1994	18 June	New York	1	0

v LATVIA			RI	L
wc1992	9 Sept	Dublin	4	0
wc1993	2 June	Riga	2	1
EC1994	7 Sept	Riga	3	0
EC1995	11 Oct	Dublin	2	1

v LIECHTENSTEIN			RI	L
FC1994	12 Oct	Dublin	4	0
EC1995	3 June	Eschen	0	0
wc1996	31 Aug	Eschen	5	0
wc1997	21 May	Dublin	5	0

v LITHUANIA			RI	L
wc1993	16 June	Vilnius	1	0
wc1993	8 Sept	Dublin	2	0
wc1997	20 Aug	Dublin	0	0
wc1997	10 Sept	Vilnius	2	1

v LUXEMBOURG			RI	I
1936	9 May	Luxembourg	5	1
wc1953	28 Oct	Dublin	4	0
wc1954	7 Mar	Luxembourg	1	0
EC1987	28 May	Luxembourg	2	0
EC1987	9 Sept	Dublin	2	1

v MACEDONIA

			RI	M
wc1996	9 Oct	Dublin	3	0
wc1997	2 Apr	Skopje	2	3
EC1999	9 June	Dublin	1	0
EC1999	9 Oct	Skopje	1	1

v MALTA

			RI	M
EC1983	30 Mar	Valletta	1	0
EC1983	16 Nov	Dublin	8	0
wc1989	28 May	Dublin	2	0
wc1989	15 Nov	Valletta	2	0
1990	2 June	Valletta	3	0
EC1998	14 Oct	Dublin	5	0
EC1999	8 Sept	Valletta	3	2

v MEXICO

			RI	M
1984	8 Aug	Dublin	0	0
wc1994	24 June	Orlando	1	2
1996	13 June	New Jersey	2	2
1998	23 May	Dublin	0	0
2000	4 June	Chicago	2	2

v MOROCCO

			RI	M
1990	12 Sept	Dublin	1	0

v NORWAY

			RI	N
wc1937	10 Oct	Oslo	2	3
wc1937	7 Nov	Dublin	3	3
1950	26 Nov	Dublin	2	2
1951	30 May	Oslo	3	2
1954	8 Nov	Dublin	2	1
1955	25 May	Oslo	3	1
1960	6 Nov	Dublin	3	1
1964	13 May	Oslo	4	1
1973	6 June	Oslo	1	1
1976	24 Mar	Dublin	3	0
1978	21 May	Oslo	0	0
wc1984	17 Oct	Oslo	0	1
wc1985	1 May	Dublin	0	0
1988	1 June	Oslo	0	0
wc1994	28 June	New York	0	0

v PARAGUAY

			RI	P
1999	10 Feb	Dublin	2	0

v POLAND

			RI	P
1938	22 May	Warsaw	0	6
1938	13 Nov	Dublin	3	2
1958	11 May	Katowice	2	2
1958	5 Oct	Dublin	2	2
1964	10 May	Kracow	1	3
1964	25 Oct	Dublin	3	2
1968	15 May	Dublin	2	2
1968	30 Oct	Katowice	0	1
1970	6 May	Dublin	1	2
1970	23 Sept	Dublin	0	2
1973	16 May	Wroclaw	0	2
1973	21 Oct	Dublin	1	0
1976	26 May	Poznan	2	0
1977	24 Apr	Dublin	0	0
1978	12 Apr	Lodz	0	3
1981	23 May	Bydgoszcz	0	3
1984	23 May	Dublin	0	0
1986	12 Nov	Warsaw	0	1
1988	22 May	Dublin	3	1
EC1991	1 May	Dublin	0	0
EC1991	16 Oct	Poznan	3	3

v PORTUGAL

			RI	P
1946	16 June	Lisbon	1	3
1947	4 May	Dublin	0	2
1948	23 May	Lisbon	0	2
1949	22 May	Dublin	1	0
1972	25 June	Recife	1	2

			RI	P
1992	7 June	Boston	2	0
EC1995	26 Apr	Dublin	1	0
EC1995	15 Nov	Lisbon	0	3
1996	29 May	Dublin	0	1

v ROMANIA

			RI	R
1988	23 Mar	Dublin	2	0
wc1990	25 June	Genoa	0	0*
wc1997	30 Apr	Bucharest	0	1
wc1997	11 Oct	Dublin	1	1

*After extra time

v RUSSIA

			RI	R
1994	23 Mar	Dublin	0	0
1996	27 Mar	Dublin	0	2

v SCOTLAND

			RI	S
wc1961	3 May	Glasgow	1	4
wc1961	7 May	Dublin	0	3
1963	9 June	Dublin	1	0
1969	21 Sept	Dublin	1	1
EC1986	15 Oct	Dublin	0	0
EC1987	18 Feb	Glasgow	1	0

v SOUTH AFRICA

			RI	SA
2000	11 June	New Jersey	2	1
2000	30 May	Dublin	1	2

v SPAIN

			RI	S
1931	26 Apr	Barcelona	1	1
1931	13 Dec	Dublin	0	5
1946	23 June	Madrid	1	0
1947	2 Mar	Dublin	3	2
1948	30 May	Barcelona	1	2
1949	12 June	Dublin	1	4
1952	1 June	Madrid	0	6
1955	27 Nov	Dublin	2	2
EC1964	11 Mar	Seville	1	5
EC1964	8 Apr	Dublin	0	2
wc1965	5 May	Dublin	1	0
wc1965	27 Oct	Seville	1	4
wc1965	10 Nov	Paris	0	1
EC1966	23 Oct	Dublin	0	0
EC1966	7 Dec	Valencia	0	2
1977	9 Feb	Dublin	0	1
EC1982	17 Nov	Dublin	3	3
EC1983	27 Apr	Zaragoza	0	2
1985	26 May	Cork	0	0
wc1988	16 Nov	Seville	0	2
wc1989	26 Apr	Dublin	1	0
wc1992	18 Nov	Seville	0	0
wc1993	13 Oct	Dublin	1	3

v SWEDEN

			RI	S
wc1949	2 June	Stockholm	1	3
wc1949	13 Nov	Dublin	1	3
1959	1 Nov	Dublin	3	2
1960	18 May	Malmo	1	4
EC1970	14 Oct	Dublin	1	1
EC1970	28 Oct	Malmo	0	1
1999	28 Apr	Dublin	2	0

v SWITZERLAND

			RI	S
1935	5 May	Basle	0	1
1936	17 Mar	Dublin	1	0

			RI	S
1937	17 May	Berne	1	0
1938	18 Sept	Dublin	4	0
1948	5 Dec	Dublin	0	1
EC1975	11 May	Dublin	2	1
EC1975	21 May	Berne	0	1
1980	30 Apr	Dublin	2	0
WC1985	2 June	Dublin	3	0
WC1985	11 Sept	Berne	0	0
1992	25 Mar	Dublin	2	1

v TRINIDAD & TOBAGO			RI	TT
1982	30 May	Port of Spain	1	2

v TUNISIA			RI	T
1988	19 Oct	Dublin	4	0

v TURKEY			RI	T
EC1966	16 Nov	Dublin	2	1
EC1967	22 Feb	Ankara	1	2
EC1974	20 Nov	Izmir	1	1
EC1975	29 Oct	Dublin	4	0
1976	13 Oct	Ankara	3	3
1978	5 Apr	Dublin	4	2
1990	26 May	Izmir	0	0
EC1990	17 Oct	Dublin	5	0
EC1991	13 Nov	Istanbul	3	1
EC2000	13 Nov	Dublin	1	1
EC2000	17 Nov	Bursa	0	0

v URUGUAY			RI	U
1974	8 May	Montevideo	0	2
1986	23 Apr	Dublin	1	1

v USA			RI	USA
1979	29 Oct	Dublin	3	2
1991	1 June	Boston	1	1

			RI	USA
1992	29 Apr	Dublin	4	1
1992	30 May	Washington	1	3
1996	9 June	Boston	1	2
2000	6 June	Boston	1	1

v USSR			RI	USSR
WC1972	18 Oct	Dublin	1	2
WC1973	13 May	Moscow	0	1
EC1974	30 Oct	Dublin	3	0
EC1975	18 May	Kiev	1	2
WC1984	12 Sept	Dublin	1	0
WC1985	16 Oct	Moscow	0	2
EC1988	15 June	Hanover	1	1
1990	25 Apr	Dublin	1	0

v WALES			RI	W
1960	28 Sept	Dublin	2	3
1979	11 Sept	Swansea	1	2
1981	24 Feb	Dublin	1	3
1986	26 Mar	Dublin	0	1
1990	28 Mar	Dublin	1	0
1991	6 Feb	Wrexham	3	0
1992	19 Feb	Dublin	0	1
1993	17 Feb	Dublin	2	1
1997	11 Feb	Cardiff	0	0

v YUGOSLAVIA			RI	Y
1955	19 Sept	Dublin	1	4
1988	27 Apr	Dublin	2	0
EC1998	18 Nov	Belgrade	0	1
EC1999	1 Sept	Dublin	2	1

Christian Dailly (Scotland) tackles Michael Owen during the first leg of the Euro 2000 play-off with England. (ASP)

OTHER BRITISH AND IRISH INTERNATIONAL MATCHES 1999-2000

FRIENDLIES

Sunderland, 10 October 1999, 40,897

England (1) 2 *(Shearer 6, Redknapp 66)*

Belgium (1) 1 *(Strupar 14)*

England: Seaman (Martyn 46); Dyer (Neville P 57), Guppy, Keown, Adams, Southgate, Lampard (Wise 75), Redknapp, Shearer (Heskey 85), Phillips (Owen 57), Ince.
Belgium: De Vlieger (Gaspercic 46); Deflandre, Peeters, Van Meir, Oyen, Tanghe (Walem 46), Vanderhaeghe, Wilmots, Van Kerckhoven, De Bilde, Strupar (Brogno 72).
Referee: Frisk (Sweden).

Wembley, 23 February 2000, 74,008

England (0) 0

Argentina (0) 0

England: Seaman; Dyer (Neville P 59), Wilcox, Southgate, Keown (Ferdinand R 46), Campbell, Beckham (Parlour 73), Scholes, Shearer (Phillips 78), Heskey (Cole 79), Wise.
Argentina: Cavallero; Zanetti, Arruabarrena (Vivas 67), Ayala, Sensini (Pochettino 34), Chamot, Simeone, Veron, Batistuta (Crespo 57), Ortega (Lopez 90), Gonzalez.
Referee: Merk (Germany).

Wembley, 27 May 2000, 73,956

England (1) 1 *(Owen 38)*

Brazil (1) 1 *(Franca 45)*

England: Seaman; Neville G, Neville P, Ince (Parlour 60 (Barmby 90)), Keown, Campbell, Beckham, Scholes, Shearer (Fowler 84), Owen (Phillips 84), Wise.
Brazil: Dida; Carlos (Carvalho 81), Aldair, Cafu, Cesar Sampaio, Emerson, Silvinho (Roberto Carlos 60), Ze Roberto, Franca, Rivaldo, Amoroso (Denilson 68).
Referee: Wojcik (Poland).

Wembley, 31 May 2000, 55,975

England (1) 2 *(Fowler 44, Adams 68)*

Ukraine (0) 0

England: Martyn; Gerrard (Dyer 81), Neville P (Barry 73), Southgate, Adams, Campbell, Beckham, Scholes (Barmby 73), Shearer, Fowler (Heskey 46), McManaman.
Ukraine: Kernozenko (Virt 84); Luzhny, Dmitrulin, Golovko, Popov, Vashchuk, Kandaurov (Moroz 46), Tymoschuk, Shevchenko, Rebrov, Gusin.
Referee: Michel (Slovakia).

Valletta, 3 June 2000, 10,023

Malta (1) 1 *(Wright 29 (og))*

England (1) 2 *(Keown 23, Heskey 75)*

Malta: Barry (Muscat 90); Debono (Camilleri 33), Buttigieg (Chetcuti 54), Said (Okonkwo 77), Carabott (Ciantar 90), Brincat (Holland 82), Vella (Theuma 41), Turner (Veselji 86), Spiteri (Dimech 77), Busuttil (Nwoko 46), Agius (Mallia 59).
England: Wright; Neville G, Neville P, Wise (Ince 68), Keown (Southgate 58), Campbell, Beckham (Barry 79), Barmby, Shearer (Heskey 50), Phillips (Fowler 58), Scholes (McManaman 68).
Referee: Braschi (Italy).

Hampden Park, 29 March 2000, 48,157

Scotland (0) 0

France (0) 2 *(Wiltord 54, Henry 89)*

Scotland: Sullivan; Telfer (Johnston 68), Davidson, Dailly, Hendry, Ritchie (Pressley 46), Cameron (McCann 46), Ferguson B, Dodds, Gallacher (Burchill 79), Hutchison.
France: Rame; Thuram, Lizarazu, Deschamps (Vieira 59), Blanc, Desailly, Giuly (Wiltord 46), Dugarry (Pires 72), Henry, Djorkaeff (Micoud 46), Petit.
Referee: Pedersen (Norway).

Arnhem, 26 April 2000, 24,500

Holland (0) 0

Scotland (0) 0

Holland: Van der Sar; Ooijer, Numan, Bosvelt, Konterman, Frank de Boer, Makaay (Talan 60), Hasselbaink (Van Hooijdonk 66), Bergkamp (Kluivert 46), Davids, Overmars (Zenden 46).
Scotland: Sullivan; McNamara (Burchill 66), Ritchie, Dailly (O'Neil 84), Elliott, Weir, Burley (Durrant 46), Lambert, Dodds, Hutchison, McCann.
Referee: Strampe (Germany).

Dublin, 30 May 2000, 30,213

Republic of Ireland (1) 1 *(Kennedy 2)*

Scotland (2) 2 *(Hutchison 15, Ferguson B 27)*

Republic of Ireland: Kelly A; Carr, Kilbane, McAteer, Breen (Dunne 75), Babb, Finnan, Kennedy (Duff 64), McPhail (Phelan 63), Quinn (Foley 75), Robbie Keane.
Scotland: Sullivan; Burley, Naysmith (Holt 89), O'Neil, Elliott, Dailly, Ferguson B (Cameron 84), Lambert (Johnston 75), Dodds (Gallacher 46), Hutchison, McCann (Pressley 90).
Referee: Pereira (Portugal).

Doha, 23 February 2000, 2000

Qatar (0) 0

Wales (1) 1 *(Robinson J 10)*

Qatar: Khalil (Hussain 81); Z Al Kuwari (Saad 65), Al Tamimi, Fatah, Al Nobbi, Kuwari, Jassim (Obaildy 71), Nadmi (Hasan 90), Hasan (Mohd 78), F Al Kuwari, Salim Al Enizi (Mubarek 63).
Wales: Jones P; Delaney, Barnard (Simons 90), Page, Coleman, Melville, Robinson J, Jones M, Blake, Pembridge, Speed.
Referee: Aziz (Bahrain).

Millennium Stadium, Cardiff, 29 March 2000, 66,500

Wales (0) 1 *(Giggs 60)*

Finland (2) 2 *(Litmanen 21, Blake 42 (og))*

Wales: Crossley; Savage (Johnson 79), Barnard (Roberts G 70), Page, Coleman, Melville, Robinson J, Pembridge (Roberts I 85), Blake (Saunders 79), Speed, Giggs.
Finland: Enckelman (Moilanen 46); Reini, Tihinen, Hyypia, Saastamoinen (Tuomela 46), Kolkka, Valakari (Wiss 65), Litmanen (Lehkuoso 70), Forssell (Paatelainen 46), Riihilahti, Nurmela.
Referee: Ross (Northern Ireland).

Millennium Stadium, Cardiff, 23 May 2000, 72,500

Wales (0) 0

Brazil (0) 3 *(Elber 62, Cafu 70, Rivaldo 72)*

Wales: Freestone; Delaney, Roberts G, Page, Melville, Savage (Bellamy 75), Robinson J, Jones M (Johnson 75), Saunders (Barnard 84), Roberts I, Speed.
Brazil: Dida; Carlos (Assuncao 83), Silvinho, Cafu, Aldair (Denilson 71), Cesar Sampaio (Carvalho 83), Ze Roberto, Emerson, Rivaldo (Evanilson 83), Elber, Franca.
Referee: Pereira (Portugal).

Chaves, 2 June 2000, 11,000

Portugal (2) 3 *(Figo 21, Sa Pinto 44, Capucho 66)*

Wales (0) 0

Portugal: Vitor Baia; Secretario (Costinha 59), Dimas (Rui Jorge 69), Fernando Couto, Jorge Costa, Vidigal (Conceicao 46), Paulo Bento, Figo (Capucho 79), Rui Costa, Joao Pinto (Pauleta 78), Sa Pinto (Nuno Gomes 62).
Wales: Ward; Delaney, Roberts G (Weston 83), Page, Melville, Barnard (Robinson C 66), Robinson J, Jones M, Roberts I, Bellamy, Speed (Johnson 31).
Referee: Bleeckere (Belgium).

Windsor Park, Belfast, 18 August 2000, 11,804
Northern Ireland (0) 0

France (0) 1 *(Laslandes 67)*
Northern Ireland: Taylor (Wright 46); Hughes A, Horlock, Lomas, Williams M, Hunter, McCarthy, Lennon, Dowie (Quinn 55), Hughes M, Kennedy (Gillespie 74).
France: Barthez; Thuram, Lizarazu (Candela 55), Vieira (Dehu 83), Blanc, Desailly (Leboeuf 65), Pires, Boghossian, Laslandes (Vairelles 75), Micoud, Wiltord (Robert 55).
Referee: Young (Scotland).

Luxembourg, 23 February 2000, 1818

Luxembourg (1) 1 *(Cardoni 41)*

Northern Ireland (1) 3 *(Healy 21, 48, Quinn 87)*
Luxembourg: Besic; Vanek, Schaack, Birsens (Alverdi 5), Strasser, Saibene, Deville F, Holtz (Huss 75), Braun (Zaritski 61), Cardoni, Schneider (Christophe 46).
Northern Ireland: Carroll (Taylor 75); Nolan, Hughes A, Griffin (McGibbon 87), Williams M (Murdock 65), Lomas, Magilton (Sonner 75), Johnson (Hughes M 77), Quinn (Coote 87), Healy, Gillespie (Robinson 87).
Referee: Schutiengruber (Austria).

Valletta, 28 March 2000, 956

Malta (0) 0

Northern Ireland (3) 3 *(Hughes M 13 (pen), Quinn 15, Healy 41)*
Malta: Barry (Muscat 46); Said, Debono, Buttigieg (Turner 46), Chetcuti, Carabott (Ifeanyi 46), Busuttil (Veselji 63), Vella (Azzopardi 56), Ciantar, Nwoko (Mallia 78), Agius (Miscud 46).
Northern Ireland: Carroll (Taylor 86); Nolan, Griffin, Lomas, Williams M, Murdock (Sonner 46), Gillespie (Johnson 63), Quinn (Coote 70), Healy, Hughes M (Horlock 77).
Referee: De Santis (Italy).

Windsor Park, Belfast, 26 April 2000, 9140
Northern Ireland (0) 0

Hungary (0) 1 *(Horvath 61)*
Northern Ireland: Taylor; Griffin (Johnson 72), Nolan, Lennon, Hughes A, Taggart (Williams M 58), Gillespie (Murdock 73), Sonner, Kirk (Coote 58), Healy, Hughes M.
Hungary: Kiraly; Hrutka, Sebok V, Matyus, Feher C, Lendvai, Dardai (Halmai 46), Illes, Peto (Korsos 56), Preisinger (Herczeg 77), Horvath (Hamar 88).
Referee: Richards (Wales).

Dublin, 23 February 2000, 30,543
Republic of Ireland (2) 3 *(Rada 16 (og), Harte 43, Robbie Keane 87)*

Czech Republic (2) 2 *(Koller 4, 35)*
Republic of Ireland: Kelly A; Kelly G, Harte, Kilbane (Staunton 83), Cunningham, Butler (Babb 46), Kennedy (McAteer 46), Kinsella, Quinn, Robbie Keane (Connolly 90), Roy Keane.
Czech Republic: Maier; Repka (Suchoparek 46), Rada, Gabriel, Poborsky, Bejbl, Nedved (Rosicky 83), Nemec (Latal 63), Smicer (Wagner 66), Koller (Kuka 69), Berger (Horvath 73).
Referee: Coue (France).

NIKE CUP
Chicago, 4 June 2000
Republic of Ireland (0) 2 *(Dunne 59, Foley 71)*

Mexico (1) 2 *(Osorno 37, Sanchez 53)*
Republic of Ireland: Kiely; Carr, Phelan, Breen, Dunne (Babb 81), Holland, McAteer, Quinn B (Kilbane 41), Quinn N, Robbie Keane (Foley 46), Kennedy.
Mexico: Bernal; Beltran, Ramirez (Giminez 69), Alpizar, Lopez, Torrado, Perez, Sancho, Sanchez (Galinda 81), Gonzalez, Osorno.
Referee: Stott (USA).

Boston, 6 June 2000
Republic of Ireland (1) 1 *(Foley 31)*

USA (0) 1 *(Razov 68)*
Republic of Ireland: Kelly; Carr, Phelan, Breen, Babb, Holland, Farrelly (Kennedy 72), McPhail (McAteer 37), Doherty (Quinn N 72), Foley (Quinn B 88), Kilbane.
USA: Friedel; Hejduk, Berhalter, Brown, Vanney, O'Brien (Reyna 58), Kirovski, Olsen (Zanneh 75), Ralston (Stewart 46), Kreis (Jones 65), Razov (McBride 88).
Referee: Archondia (Mexico).

New Jersey, 11 June, 2000
Republic of Ireland (1) 2 *(McPhail 43, Quinn N 69)*

South Africa (1) 1 *(Bartlett 17)*
Republic of Ireland: Given; Carr, Phelan, Breen, Babb, Holland, McAteer (Kennedy 44), McPhail (Quinn B 85), Quinn N (Doherty 76), Foley (Robbie Keane 46), Mahon (Kilbane 42).
South Africa: Arendse; Lekgetho, Rabuta, Mokoena, Nzama, Buckley, Fortune (Swane 76), Ngobe (Mayo 46), Mhkalele (Mngomeni 76), McCartay (Sheppard 46), Bartlett.
Referee: Badilla (Mexico).

INTERNATIONAL APPEARANCES 1872–2000

This is a list of full international appearances by Englishmen, Irishmen, Scotsmen and Welshmen in matches against the Home Countries and against foreign nations. It does not include unofficial matches against Commonwealth and Empire countries. The year indicated refers to the season; ie 2000 is the 1999-2000 season.

Explanatory code for matches played by all five countries: A represents Austria; Alb, Albania; Alg, Algeria; An, Angola; Arg, Argentina; Arm, Armenia; Aus, Australia; B, Bohemia; Bel, Belgium; Bl, Belarus; Bol, Bolivia; Bos, Bosnia; Br, Brazil; Bul, Bulgaria; C,CIS; Ca, Canada; Cam, Cameroon; Ch, Chile; Chn, China; Co, Colombia; Cr, Costa Rica; Cro, Croatia; Cy, Cyprus; Cz, Czechoslovakia; CzR, Czech Republic; D, Denmark; E, England; Ec, Ecuador; Ei, Republic of Ireland; EG, East Germany; Eg, Egypt; Es, Estonia; F, France; Fa, Faeroes; Fi, Finland; G, Germany; Ge, Georgia; Gr, Greece; H, Hungary; Ho, Holland; Hon, Honduras; I, Italy; Ic, Iceland; Ir, Iran; Is, Israel; J, Japan; Jam, Jamaica; K, Kuwait; L, Luxembourg; La, Latvia; Li, Lithuania; Lie, Liechtenstein; M, Mexico; Ma, Malta; Mac, Macedonia; Mal, Malaysia; Mol, Moldova; Mor, Morocco; N, Norway; Ni, Ng, Nigeria; Ni, Northern Ireland; Nz, New Zealand; P, Portugal; Para, Paraguay; Pe, Peru; Pol, Poland; Q, Qatar; R, Romania; RCS, Republic of Czechs and Slovaks; R of E, Rest of Europe; R of UK, Rest of United Kingdom; R of W, Rest of World; Ru, Russia; S.Af, South Africa; S.Ar, Saudi Arabia; S, Scotland; Se, Sweden; Slo, Slovakia; Sm, San Marino; Sp, Spain; Sw, Switzerland; T, Turkey; Th, Thailand; Tr, Trinidad & Tobago; Tun, Tunisia; U, Uruguay; Uk, Ukraine; US, United States of America; USSR, Soviet Union; W, Wales; WG, West Germany; Y, Yugoslavia; Z, Zaire.
As at July 2000.

ENGLAND

Abbott, W. (Everton), 1902 v W (1)

A'Court, A. (Liverpool), 1958 v Ni, Br, A, USSR; 1959 v W (5)

Adams, T. A. (Arsenal), 1987 v Sp, T, Br; 1988 v WG, T, Y, Ho, H, S, Co, Sw, Ei, Ho, USSR; 1989 v D, Se, S.Ar.; 1991 v Ei (2); 1993 v N, T, Sm, T, Ho, Pol, N; 1994 v Pol, Ho, D, Gr, N; 1995 v US, R, Ei, U; 1996 v Co, N, Sw, P, Chn, Sw, S, Ho, Sp, G; 1997 v Ge (2); 1998 v I, Ch, P, S.Ar, Tun, R, Co, Arg; 1999 v Se, F; 2000 v L, Pol, Bel, S (2), Uk, P (64)

Adcock, H. (Leicester C), 1929 v F, Bel, Sp; 1930 v Ni, W (5)

Alcock, C. W. (Wanderers), 1875 v S (1)

Alderson, J. T. (C Palace), 1923 v F (1)

Aldridge, A. (WBA), 1888 v Ni; (with Walsall Town Swifts), 1889 v S (2)

Allen, A. (Stoke C) 1960 v Se, W, Ni (3)

Allen, A. (Aston Villa), 1888 v Ni (1)

Allen, C. (QPR), 1984 v Br (sub), U, Ch; (with Tottenham H), 1987 v T; 1988 v Is (5)

Allen, H. (Wolverhampton W), 1888 v S, W, Ni; 1889 v S; 1890 v S (5)

Allen, J. P. (Portsmouth), 1934 v Ni, W (2)

Allen, R. (WBA), 1952 v Sw; 1954 v Y, S; 1955 v WG, W (5)

Alsford, W. J. (Tottenham H), 1935 v S (1)

Amos, A. (Old Carthusians), 1885 v S; 1886 v W (2)

Anderson, R. D. (Old Etonians), 1879 v W (1)

Anderson, S. (Sunderland), 1962 v A, S (2)

Anderson, V. (Nottingham F), 1979 v Cz, Se; 1980 v Bul, Sp; 1981 v N, R, W, S; 1982 v Ni, Ic; 1984 v Ni; (with Arsenal), 1985 v T, Ni, Ei, R, Fi, S, M, US; 1986 v USSR, M; 1987 v Se, Ni (2), Y, Sp, T; (with Manchester U), 1988 v WG, H, Co (30)

Anderton, D. R. (Tottenham H), 1994 v D, Gr, N; 1995 v US, Ei, U, J, Se, Br; 1996 v H, Chn, Sw, S, Ho, Sp, G; 1998 v S.Ar, Mor, Tun, R, Co, Arg; 1999 v Se, Bul, L, CzR, F (27)

Angus, J. (Burnley), 1961 v A (1)

Armfield, J. C. (Blackpool), 1959 v Br, Pe, M, US; 1960 v Y, Sp, H, S; 1961 v L, P, Sp, M, I, A, W, Ni, S; 1962 v A, Sw, Pe, W, Ni, S, L, P, H, Arg, Bul, Br; 1963 v F (2), Br, EG, Sw, Ni, W, S; 1964 v R of W, W, Ni, S; 1966 v Y, Fi (43)

Armitage, G. H. (Charlton Ath), 1926 v Ni (1)

Armstrong, D. (Middlesbrough), 1980 v Aus; (with Southampton), 1983 v WG; 1984 v W (3)

Armstrong, K. (Chelsea), 1955 v S (1)

Arnold, J. (Fulham), 1933 v S (1)

Arthur, J. W. H. (Blackburn R), 1885 v S, W, Ni; 1886 v S, W; 1887 v W, Ni (7)

Ashcroft, J. (Woolwich Arsenal), 1906 v Ni, W, S (3)

Ashmore, G. S. (WBA), 1926 v Bel (1)

Ashton, C. T. (Corinthians), 1926 v Ni (1)

Ashurst, W. (Notts Co), 1923 v Se (2); 1925 v S, W, Bel (5)

Astall, G. (Birmingham C), 1956 v Fi, WG (2)

Astle, J. (WBA), 1969 v W; 1970 v S, P, Br (sub), Cz (5)

Aston, J. (Manchester U), 1949 v W, D, Sw, Se, N, F; 1950 v S, W, Ni, Ei, I, P, Bel, Ch, US; 1951 v Ni (17)

Athersmith, W. C. (Aston Villa), 1892 v Ni, 1897 v S, W, Ni; 1898 v S, W, Ni; 1899 v S, W, Ni; 1900 v S, W (12)

Atyeo, P. J. W. (Bristol C), 1956 v Br, Se, Sp; 1957 v D, Ei (2) (6)

Austin, S. W. (Manchester C), 1926 v Ni (1)

Bach, P. (Sunderland), 1899 v Ni (1)

Bache, J. W. (Aston Villa), 1903 v W; 1904 v W, Ni; 1905 v S; 1907 v Ni; 1910 v Ni; 1911 v S (7)

Baddeley, T. (Wolverhampton W), 1903 v S, Ni; 1904 v S, W, Ni (5)

Bagshaw, J. J. (Derby Co), 1920 v Ni (1)

Bailey, G. R. (Manchester U), 1985 v Ei, M (2)

Bailey, H. P. (Leicester Fosse), 1908 v W, A (2), H, B (5)

Bailey, M. A. (Charlton Ath), 1964 v US; 1965 v W (2)

Bailey, N. C. (Clapham Rovers), 1878 v S; 1879 v S, W; 1880 v S; 1881 v S; 1882 v S, W; 1883 v S, W; 1884 v S, W, Ni; 1885 v S, W, Ni; 1886 v S, W; 1887 v S, W (19)

Baily, E. F. (Tottenham H), 1950 v Sp; 1951 v Y, Ni, W; 1952 v A (2), Sw, W; 1953 v Ni (9)

Bain, J. (Oxford University), 1887 v S (1)

Baker, A. (Arsenal), 1928 v W (1)

Baker, B. H. (Everton), 1921 v Bel; (with Chelsea), 1926 v Ni (2)

Baker, J. H. (Hibernian), 1960 v Y, Sp, H, Ni, S; (with Arsenal) 1966 v Sp, Pol, Ni (8)

Ball, A. J. (Blackpool), 1965 v Y, WG, Se; 1966 v S, Sp, Fi, D, U, Arg, P, WG (2), Pol (2); (with Everton), 1967 v W, S, Ni, A, Cz, Sp; 1968 v W, S, USSR, Sp (2), Y, WG; 1969 v Ni, W, S, R (2), M, Br, U; 1970 v P, Co, Ec, R, Br, Cz (sub), WG, S, Bel; 1971 v Ma, EG, Gr, Ma (sub), Ni, S; 1972 v Sw, Gr (with Arsenal), WG (2), S; 1973 v W (3), Y, S (2), Cz, Ni, Pol; 1974 v P (sub); 1975 v WG, Cy (2), Ni, W, S (72)

Ball, J. (Bury), 1928 v Ni (1)

Balmer, W. (Everton), 1905 v Ni (1)

Bamber, J. (Liverpool), 1921 v W (1)

Bambridge, A. L. (Swifts), 1881 v S; 1883 v W; 1884 v Ni (3)

Bambridge, E. C. (Swifts), 1879 v S; 1880 v S; 1881 v S; 1882 v S, W, Ni; 1883 v W; 1884 v S, W, Ni; 1885 v S, W, Ni; 1886 v S, W; 1887 v S, W, Ni (18)

Bambridge, E. H. (Swifts), 1876 v S (1)

Banks, G. (Leicester C), 1963 v S, Br, Cz, EG; 1964 v W, Ni, S, R of W, U, P (2), US, Arg; 1965 v Ni, S, H, Y, WG, Se; 1966 v Ni, S, Sp, Pol (2), WG (2), Y, Fi, U, M, F, Arg, P; 1967 v Ni, W, S, Cz; (with Stoke C), 1968 v W, Ni, S, USSR (2), Sp, WG, Y; 1969 v Ni, S, R (2), F, U, Br; 1970 v W, Ni, S, Ho, Bel, Co, Ec, R, Br, Cz; 1971 v Gr, Ma (2), Ni, S; 1972 v Sw, Gr, WG (2), S (73)

Banks, H. E. (Millwall), 1901 v Ni (1)

Banks, T. (Bolton W), 1958 v USSR (3), Br, A; 1959 v Ni (6)

Bannister, W. (Burnley), 1901 v W; (with Bolton W), 1902 v Ni (2)

Barclay, R. (Sheffield U), 1932 v S; 1933 v Ni; 1936 v S (3)

Bardsley, D. J. (QPR), 1993 v Sp (sub), Pol (2)

Barham, M. (Norwich C), 1983 v Aus (2) (2)

Barkas, S. (Manchester C), 1936 v Bel; 1937 v S; 1938 v W, Ni, Cz (5)

Barker, J. (Derby Co), 1935 v I, Ho, S, W, Ni; 1936 v G, A, S, W, Ni; 1937 v W (11)

Barker, R. (Herts Rangers), 1872 v S (1)

Barker, R. R. (Casuals), 1895 v W (1)

Barlow, R. J. (WBA), 1955 v Ni (1)

Barmby, N.J. (Tottenham H), 1995 v U (sub), Se (sub); (with Middlesbrough), 1996 v Co, N, P, Chn, Sw (sub), Ho (sub), Sp (sub); 1997 v Mol; (with Everton), 2000 v Br (sub), Uk (sub), Ma, G (sub), R (sub) (15)

Barnes, J. (Watford), 1983 v Ni (sub), Aus (sub), Aus (2); 1984 v D, L (sub), F (sub), S, USSR, Br, U, Ch; 1985 v EG, Fi, T, Ni, R, Fi, S, I (sub), M, WG (sub), US (sub); 1986 v R (sub), Is (sub), M (sub), Ca (sub), Arg (sub); 1987 v Se, T (sub), Br; (with Liverpool), 1988 v WG, T, Y, Is, Ho, S, Co, Sw, Ei, Ho, USSR; 1989 v Se, Gr, Alb, Pol, D; 1990 v Se, I, Br, D, U, Tun, Ei, Ho, Eg, Bel, Cam; 1991 v H, Pol, Cam, Ei, T, USSR, Arg; 1992 v Cz, Fi; 1993 v Sm, T, Ho, Pol, US, G; 1995 v US, R, Ng, U, Se; 1996 v Co (sub) (79)

Barnes, P. S. (Manchester C), 1978 v I, WG, Br, W, S, H; 1979 v D, Ei, Cz, Ni (2), S, Bul, A; (with WBA), 1980 v D, W; 1981 v Sp (sub), Br, W, Sw (sub); (with Leeds U), 1982 v N (sub), Ho (sub) (22)

Barnet, H. H. (Royal Engineers), 1882 v Ni (1)

Barrass, M. W. (Bolton W), 1952 v W, Ni; 1953 v S (3)

Barrett, A. F. (Fulham), 1930 v Ni (1)

Barrett, E. D. (Oldham Ath), 1991 v Nz; 1993 v Br, G (3)

Barrett, J. W. (West Ham U), 1929 v Ni (1)

Barry, G. (Aston Villa), 2000 v Uk (sub), Ma (sub) (2)

Barry, L. (Leicester C), 1928 v F, Bel; 1929 v F, Bel, Sp (5)

Barson, F. (Aston Villa), 1920 v W (1)

Barton, J. (Blackburn R), 1890 v Ni (1)

Barton, P. H. (Birmingham), 1921 v Bel; 1922 v Ni; 1923 v F; 1924 v Bel, S, W; 1925 v Ni (7)

Barton, W. D. (Wimbledon), 1995 v Ei; (with Newcastle U), Se, Br (sub) (3)

Bassett, W. I. (WBA), 1888 v Ni, 1889 v S, W; 1890 v S, W; 1891 v S, Ni; 1892 v S; 1893 v S, W; 1894 v S; 1895 v S, Ni; 1896 v S, W, Ni (16)

Bastard, S. R. (Upton Park), 1880 v S (1)

Bastin, C. S. (Arsenal), 1932 v W; 1933 v I, Sw; 1934 v S, Ni, W, H, Cz; 1935 v S, Ni, I; 1936 v S, W, G, A; 1937 v W, Ni; 1938 v S, G, Sw, F (21)

Batty, D. (Leeds U), 1991 v USSR (sub), Arg, Aus, Nz, Mal; 1992 v G, T, H (sub), F, Se; 1993 v N, Sm, US, Br; (with Blackburn R), 1994 v D (sub); 1995 v J, Br; (with Newcastle U), 1997 v Mol (sub), Ge, I, M, Ge, S.Af (sub), Pol (sub), F; 1998 v Mol, I, Ch, Se (sub), P, S.Ar, Tun, R, Co (sub), Arg (sub); 1999 v Bul (sub), L; (with Leeds U), H, Se, Bul; 2000 v L, Pol (42)

Baugh, R. (Stafford Road), 1886 v Ni; (with Wolverhampton W), 1890 v Ni (2)

Bayliss, A. E. J. M. (WBA), 1891 v Ni (1)

Baynham, R. L. (Luton T), 1956 v Ni, D, Sp (3)

Beardsley, P. A. (Newcastle U), 1986 v Eg (sub), Is, USSR, M, Ca (sub), P (sub), Pol, Para, Arg; 1987 v Ni (2), Y, Sp, Br, S; (with Liverpool), 1988 v WG, T, Y, Is, Ho, H, S, Co, Sw, Ei, Ho; 1989 v D, Se, S.Ar, Gr (sub), Alb (sub+1), Pol, D; 1990 v Se, Pol, I, Br, U (sub), Tun (sub), Ei, Eg (sub), Cam (sub), WG, I; 1991 v Pol (sub), Ei (2), USSR (sub); (with Newcastle U), 1994 v D, Gr, N; 1995 v Ng, Ei, U, J, Se; 1996 v P (sub), Chn (sub) (59)

Beasant, D. J. (Chelsea), 1990 v I (sub), Y (sub) (2)

Beasley, A. (Huddersfield T), 1939 v S (1)

Beats, W. E. (Wolverhampton W), 1901 v W; 1902 v S (2)

Beattie, T. K. (Ipswich T), 1975 v Cy (2), S; 1976 v Sw, P; 1977 v Fi, I (sub), Ho; 1978 v L (sub) (9)

Beckham, D. R. J. (Manchester U), 1997 v Mol, Pol, Ge, I, Ge, S.Af (sub), Pol, I, F; 1998 v Mol, I, Cam, P, S.Ar, Bel (sub), R (sub), Co, Arg; 1999 v L, CzR, F, Pol, Se; 2000 v L, Pol, S (2), Arg, Br, Uk, Ma, P, G, R (34)

Becton, F. (Preston NE), 1895 v Ni; (with Liverpool), 1897 v W (2)

Bedford, H. (Blackpool), 1923 v Se; 1925 v Ni (2)

Bell, C. (Manchester C), 1968 v Se, WG; 1969 v W, Bul, F, U, Br; 1970 v Ni (sub), Ho (2), P, Br (sub), Cz, WG (sub); 1972 v Gr, WG (2), W, Ni, S; 1973 v W (3), Y, S (2), Ni, Cz, Pol; 1974 v A, Pol, I, W, Ni, S, Arg, EG, Bul, Y; 1975 v Cz, P, WG, Cy (2), Ni, S; 1976 v Sw, Cz (48)

Bennett, W. (Sheffield U), 1901 v S, W (2)

Benson, R. W. (Sheffield U), 1913 v Ni (1)

Bentley, R. T. F. (Chelsea), 1949 v Se; 1950 v S, P, Bel, Ch, USA; 1953 v W, Bel; 1955 v W, WG, Sp, P (12)

Beresford, J. (Aston Villa), 1934 v Cz (1)

Berry, A. (Oxford University), 1909 v Ni (1)

Berry, J. J. (Manchester U), 1953 v Arg, Ch, U; 1956 v Se (4)

Bestall, J. G. (Grimsby T), 1935 v Ni (1)

Betmead, H. A. (Grimsby T), 1937 v Fi (1)

Betts, M. P. (Old Harrovians), 1877 v S (1)

Betts, W. (Sheffield W), 1889 v W (1)

Beverley, J. (Blackburn R), 1884 v S, W, Ni (3)

Birkett, R. H. (Clapham Rovers), 1879 v S (1)

Birkett, R. J. E. (Middlesbrough), 1936 v Ni (1)

Birley, F. H. (Oxford University), 1874 v S; (with Wanderers), 1875 v S (2)

Birtles, G. (Nottingham F), 1980 v Arg (sub), I; 1981 v R (3)

Bishop, S. M. (Leicester C), 1927 v S, Bel, L, F (4)

Blackburn, F. (Blackburn R), 1901 v S; 1902 v Ni; 1904 v S (3)

Blackburn, G. F. (Aston Villa), 1924 v F (1)

Blenkinsop, E. (Sheffield W), 1928 v F, Bel; 1929 v S, W, Ni, F, Bel, Sp; 1930 v S, W, Ni, G, A; 1931 v S, W, Ni, F, Bel; 1932 v S, W, Ni, Sp; 1933 v S, W, Ni, A (26)

Bliss, H. (Tottenham H), 1921 v S (1)

Blissett, L. (Watford), 1983 v WG (sub), L, W, Gr (sub), H, Ni, S (sub), Aus (1+1 sub); (with AC Milan), 1984 v D (sub), H, W (sub), S, USSR (14)

Blockley, J. P. (Arsenal), 1973 v Y (1)

Bloomer, S. (Derby Co), 1895 v S, Ni; 1896 v W, Ni; 1897 v S, W, Ni; 1898 v S; 1899 v S, W, Ni; 1900 v S; 1901 v S, W; 1902 v S, W, Ni; 1904 v S; 1905 v S, W, Ni; (with Middlesbrough), 1907 v S, W (23)

Blunstone, F. (Chelsea), 1955 v W, S, F, P; 1957 v Y (5)

Bond, R. (Preston NE), 1905 v Ni, W; 1906 v S, W, Ni; (with Bradford C), 1910 v S, W, Ni (8)

Bonetti, P. P. (Chelsea), 1966 v D; 1967 v Sp, A; 1968 v Sp; 1970 v Ho, P, WG (7)

Bonsor, A. G. (Wanderers), 1873 v S; 1875 v S (2)

Booth, F. (Manchester C), 1905 v Ni (1)

Booth, T. (Blackburn R), 1898 v W; (with Everton), 1903 v S (2)

Bould, S. A. (Arsenal), 1994 v Gr, N (2)

Bowden, E. R. (Arsenal), 1935 v W, I; 1936 v W, Ni, A; 1937 v H (6)

Bower, A. G. (Corinthians), 1924 v Ni, Bel; 1925 v W, Bel; 1927 v W (5)

Bowers, J. W. (Derby Co), 1934 v S, Ni, W (3)

Bowles, A. (QPR), 1974 v P, W, Ni; 1977 v I, Ho (5)

Bowser, S. (WBA), 1920 v Ni (1)

Boyer, P. J. (Norwich C), 1976 v W (1)

Boyes, W. (WBA), 1935 v Ho; (with Everton), 1939 v W, R of É (3)

Boyle, T. W. (Burnley), 1913 v Ni (1)

Brabrook, P. (Chelsea), 1958 v USSR; 1959 v Ni; 1960 v Sp (3)

Bracewell, P. W. (Everton), 1985 v WG (sub), US; 1986 v Ni (3)

Bradford, G. R. W. (Bristol R), 1956 v D (1)

Bradford, J. (Birmingham), 1924 v Ni; 1925 v Bel; 1928 v S; 1929 v Ni, W, F, Sp; 1930 v S, Ni, G, A; 1931 v W (12)

Bradley, W. (Manchester U), 1959 v I, US, M (sub) (3)

Bradshaw, F. (Sheffield W), 1908 v A (1)

Bradshaw, T. H. (Liverpool), 1897 v Ni (1)

Bradshaw, W. (Blackburn R), 1910 v W, Ni; 1912 v Ni; 1913 v W (4)

Brann, G. (Swifts), 1886 v S, W; 1891 v W (3)

Brawn, W. F. (Aston Villa), 1904 v W, Ni (2)

Bray, J. (Manchester C), 1935 v W; 1936 v S, W, Ni, G; 1937 v S (6)

Brayshaw, E. (Sheffield W), 1887 v Ni (1)

Bridges, B. J. (Chelsea), 1965 v S, H, Y; 1966 v A (4)

Bridgett, A. (Sunderland), 1905 v S; 1908 v S, A (2), H, B; 1909 v Ni, W, A (11)

Brindle, T. (Darwen), 1880 v S, W (2)

Brittleton, J. T. (Sheffield W), 1912 v S, W, Ni; 1913 v S; 1914 v W (5)

Britton, C. S. (Everton), 1935 v S, W, Ni, I; 1937 v S, Ni, H, N, Se (9)

Broadbent, P. F. (Wolverhampton W), 1958 v USSR; 1959 v S, W, Ni, I, Br; 1960 v S (7)

Broadis, I. A. (Manchester C), 1952 v S, A, I; 1953 v S, Arg, Ch, U, US; (with Newcastle U), 1954 v S, H, Y, Bel, Sw, U (14)

Brockbank, J. (Cambridge University), 1872 v S (1)

Brodie, J. B. (Wolverhampton W), 1889 v S, Ni; 1891 v Ni (3)

Bromilow, T. G. (Liverpool), 1921 v W; 1922 v S, W; 1923 v Bel; 1926 v Ni (5)

Bromley-Davenport, W. E. (Oxford University), 1884 v S, W (2)

Brook, E. F. (Manchester C), 1930 v Ni; 1933 v Sw; 1934 v S, W, Ni, F, H, Cz; 1935 v S, W, Ni, I; 1936 v S, W, Ni; 1937 v H; 1938 v W, Ni (18)

Brooking, T. D. (West Ham U), 1974 v P, Arg, EG, Bul, Y; 1975 v Cz (sub), P; 1976 v P, W, Br, I, Fi; 1977 v Ei, Fi, I, Ho, Ni, W; 1978 v I, WG, W, S (sub), H; 1979 v D, Ei, Ni, W (sub), S, Bul, Se (sub), A; 1980 v D, Ni, Arg (sub), W, Ni, S, Bel, Sp; 1981 v Sw, Sp, R, H; 1982 v H, S, Fi, Sp (sub) (47)

Brooks, J. (Tottenham H), 1957 v W, Y, D (3)

Broome, F. H. (Aston Villa), 1938 v G, Sw, F; 1939 v N, I, R, Y (7)

Brown, A. (Aston Villa), 1882 v S, W, Ni (3)

Brown, A. S. (Sheffield U), 1904 v W; 1906 v Ni (2)

Brown, A. (WBA), 1971 v W (1)

Brown, G. (Huddersfield T), 1927 v S, W, Ni, Bel, L, F; 1928 v W; 1929 v S; (with Aston Villa), 1933 v W (9)

Fleming, H. J. (Swindon T), 1909 v S, H (2); 1910 v W, Ni; 1911 v W, Ni; 1912 v Ni; 1913 v S, W; 1914 v S (11)

Fletcher, A. (Wolverhampton W), 1889 v W; 1890 v W (2)

Flowers, R. (Wolverhampton W), 1955 v F; 1959 v S, W, I, Br, Pe, US, M (sub); 1960 v W, Ni, S, Se, Y, Sp, H; 1961 v Ni, W, S, L, P, Sp, M, I, A; 1962 v W, Ni, S, A, Sw, Pe, L, P, H, Arg, Bul, Br; 1963 v Ni, W, S, F (2), Sw; 1964 v Ei, US, P; 1965 v W, Ho, WG; 1966 v N (49)

Flowers, T. D. (Southampton), 1993 v Br; (with Blackburn R), 1994 v Gr; 1995 v Ng, U, J, Se, Br; 1996 v Chn; 1997 v I; 1998 v Sw, Mor (11)

Forman, Frank (Nottingham F), 1898 v S, Ni; 1899 v S, W, Ni; 1901 v S; 1902 v S, Ni; 1903 v W (9)

Forman, F. R. (Nottingham F), 1899 v S, W, Ni (3)

Forrest, J. H. (Blackburn R), 1884 v W; 1885 v S, W, Ni; 1886 v S, W; 1887 v S, W, Ni; 1889 v S; 1890 v Ni (11)

Fort, J. (Millwall), 1921 v Bel (1)

Foster, R. E. (Oxford University), 1900 v W; (with Corinthians), 1901 v W, Ni, S; 1902 v W (5)

Foster, S. (Brighton & HA), 1982 v Ni, Ho, K (3)

Foulke, W. J. (Sheffield U), 1897 v W (1)

Foulkes, W. A. (Manchester U), 1955 v Ni (1)

Fowler, R. B. (Liverpool), 1996 v Bul (sub), Cro, Chn (sub), Ho (sub), Sp (sub); 1997 v M; 1998 v Cam; 1999 v CzR (sub), Bul; 2000 v L, Pol, Br (sub), Uk, Ma (sub) (14)

Fox, F. S. (Millwall), 1925 v F (1)

Francis, G. C. J. (QPR), 1975 v Cz, P, W, S; 1976 v Sw, Cz, P, W, Ni, S, Br, Fi (12)

Francis, T. (Birmingham C), 1977 v Ho, L, S, Br; 1978 v Sw, L, I (sub), WG (sub), Br, W, S, H; (with Nottingham F), 1979 v Bul (sub), Se, A (sub); 1980 v Ni, Bul, Sp; 1981 v Sp, R, S (sub), Sw; (with Manchester C), 1982 v N, Ni, W, S (sub), Fi (sub), F, Cz, K, WG, Sp; (with Sampdoria), 1983 v D, Gr, H, Ni, S, Aus (3); 1984 v D, Ni, USSR; 1985 v EG (sub), T (sub), Ni (sub), R, Fi, S, I, M; 1986 v S (52)

Franklin, C. F. (Stoke C), 1947 v S, W, Ni, Ei, Ho, F, Sw, P; 1948 v S, W, Ni, Bel, Se, I; 1949 v S, W, Ni, D, Sw, N, F, Se; 1950 v W, S, Ni, Ei, I (27)

Freeman, B. C. (Everton), 1909 v S, W; (with Burnley), 1912 v S, W, Ni (5)

Froggatt, J. (Portsmouth), 1950 v Ni, I; 1951 v S; 1952 v S, A (2), I, Sw; 1953 v Ni, W, S, Bel, US (13)

Froggatt, R. (Sheffield W), 1953 v W, S, Bel, US (4)

Fry, C. B. (Corinthians), 1901 v Ni (1)

Furness, W. I. (Leeds U), 1933 v I (1)

Galley, T. (Wolverhampton W), 1937 v N, Se (2)

Gardner, T. (Aston Villa), 1934 v Cz; 1935 v Ho (2)

Garfield, B. (WBA), 1898 v Ni (1)

Garratty, W. (Aston Villa), 1903 v W (1)

Garrett, T. (Blackpool), 1952 v S, I; 1954 v W (3)

Gascoigne, P. J. (Tottenham H), 1989 v D (sub), S.Ar (sub), Alb (sub), Ch, S (sub); 1990 v Se (sub), Br (sub), Cz, D, U, Tun, Ei, Ho, Eg, Bel, Cam, WG; 1991 v H, Pol, Cam; (with Lazio), 1993 v N, T, Sm, T, Ho, Pol, N; 1994 v Pol, D; 1995 v J (sub), Se (sub), Br (sub); (with Rangers), 1996 v Co, Sw, P, Bul, Cro, Chn, Sw, S, Ho, Sp, G; 1997 v Mol, Pol, Ge, S.Af, Pol, I (sub), F, Br; 1998 v Mol, I, Cam; (with Middlesbrough), S.Ar (sub), Mor, Bel (57)

Gates, E. (Ipswich T), 1981 v N, R (2)

Gay, L. H. (Cambridge University), 1893 v S; (with Old Brightonians), 1894 v S, W (3)

Geary, F. (Everton), 1890 v Ni; 1891 v S (2)

Geaves, R. L. (Clapham Rovers), 1875 v S (1)

Gee, C. W. (Everton), 1932 v W, Sp; 1937 v Ni (3)

Geldard, A. (Everton), 1933 v I, Sw; 1935 v S; 1938 v Ni (4)

George, C. (Derby Co), 1977 v Ei (1)

George, W. (Aston Villa), 1902 v S, W, Ni (3)

Gerrard, S. G. (Liverpool), 2000 v Uk, G (sub) (2)

Gibbins, W. V. T. (Clapton), 1924 v F; 1925 v F (2)

Gidman, J. (Aston Villa), 1977 v L (1)

Gillard, I. T. (QPR), 1975 v WG, W; 1976 v Cz (3)

Gilliat, W. E. (Old Carthusians), 1893 v Ni (1)

Goddard, P. (West Ham U), 1982 v Ic (sub) (1)

Goodall, F. R. (Huddersfield T), 1926 v S; 1927 v S, F, Bel, L; 1928 v S, W, F, Bel; 1930 v S, G, A; 1931 v S, W, Ni, Bel; 1932 v Ni; 1933 v W, Ni, A, I, Sw; 1934 v W, Ni, F (25)

Goodall, J. (Preston NE), 1888 v S, W; 1889 v S, W; (with Derby Co), 1891 v S, W; 1892 v S; 1893 v W; 1894 v S; 1895 v S, Ni; 1896 v S, W; 1898 v W (14)

Goodhart, H. C. (Old Etonians), 1883 v S, W, Ni (3)

Goodwyn, A. G. (Royal Engineers), 1873 v S (1)

Goodyer, A. C. (Nottingham F), 1879 v S (1)

Gosling, R. C. (Old Etonians), 1892 v W; 1893 v S; 1894 v W; 1895 v W, S (5)

Gosnell, A. A. (Newcastle U), 1906 v Ni (1)

Gough, H. C. (Sheffield U), 1921 v S (1)

Goulden, L. A. (West Ham U), 1937 v Se, N; 1938 v W, Ni, Cz, G, Sw, F; 1939 v S, W, R of E, I, R, Y (14)

Graham, L. (Millwall), 1925 v S, W (2)

Graham, T. (Nottingham F), 1931 v F; 1932 v Ni (2)

Grainger, C. (Sheffield U), 1956 v Br, Se, Fi, WG; 1957 v W, Ni; (with Sunderland), 1957 v S (7)

Gray, A. A. (C Palace), 1992 v Pol (1)

Gray, M. (Sunderland), 1999 v H (sub), Se (sub), Bul (3)

Greaves, J. (Chelsea), 1959 v Pe, M, US; 1960 v W, Se, Y, Sp; 1961 v Ni, W, S, L, P, Sp, I, A; (with Tottenham H), 1962 v S, Sw, Pe, H, Arg, Bul, Br; 1963 v Ni, W, S, F (2), Br, Cz, Sw; 1964 v W, Ni, R of W, P (2), Ei, Br, U, Arg; 1965 v Ni, S, Bel, Ho, H, Y; 1966 v W, A, Y, N, D, Pol, U, M, F; 1967 v S, Sp, A (57)

Green, F. T. (Wanderers), 1876 v S (1)

Green, G. H. (Sheffield U), 1925 v F; 1926 v S, Bel, W; 1927 v W, Ni; 1928 v F, Bel (8)

Greenhalgh, E. H. (Notts Co), 1872 v S; 1873 v S (2)

Greenhoff, B. (Manchester U), 1976 v W, Ni; 1977 v Ei, Fi, I, Ho, Ni, W, S, Br, Arg, U; 1978 v Br, W, Ni, S (sub), H (sub); (with Leeds U), 1980 v Aus (sub) (18)

Greenwood, D. H. (Blackburn R), 1882 v S, Ni (2)

Gregory, J. (QPR), 1983 v Aus (3); 1984 v D, H, W (6)

Grimsdell, A. (Tottenham H), 1920 v S, W; 1921 v S, Ni; 1923 v W, Ni (6)

Grosvenor, A. T. (Birmingham), 1934 v Ni, W, F (3)

Gunn, W. (Notts Co), 1884 v S, W (2)

Guppy, S. (Leicester C), 2000 v Bel (1)

Gurney, R. (Sunderland), 1935 v S (1)

Hacking, J. (Oldham Ath), 1929 v S, W, Ni (3)

Hadley, N. (WBA), 1903 v Ni (1)

Hagan, J. (Sheffield U), 1949 v D (1)

Haines, J. T. W. (WBA), 1949 v Sw (1)

Hall, A. E. (Aston Villa), 1910 v Ni (1)

Hall, G. W. (Tottenham H), 1934 v F; 1938 v S, W, Ni, Cz; 1939 v S, Ni, R of E, I, Y (10)

Hall, J. (Birmingham C), 1956 v S, W, Ni, Br, Se, Fi, WG, D, Sp; 1957 v S, W, Ni, Y, D (2), Ei (2) (17)

Halse, H. J. (Manchester U), 1909 v A (1)

Hammond, H. E. D. (Oxford University), 1889 v S (1)

Hampson, J. (Blackpool), 1931 v Ni, W; 1933 v A (3)

Hampton, H. (Aston Villa), 1913 v S, W; 1914 v S, W (4)

Hancocks, J. (Wolverhampton W), 1949 v Sw; 1950 v W; 1951 v Y (3)

Hapgood, E. (Arsenal), 1933 v I, Sw; 1934 v S, Ni, W, H, Cz; 1935 v S, Ni, W, I, Ho; 1936 v S, Ni, W, G, A, Bel; 1937 v Fi; 1938 v S, G, Sw, F; 1939 v S, W, Ni, R of E, N, I, Y (30)

Hardinge, H. T. W. (Sheffield U), 1910 v S (1)

Hardman, H. P. (Everton), 1905 v W; 1907 v S, Ni; 1908 v W (4)

Hardwick, G. F. M. (Middlesbrough), 1947 v S, W, Ni, Ei, Ho, F, Sw, P; 1948 v S, W, Ni, Bel, Se (13)

Hardy, H. (Stockport Co), 1925 v Bel (1)

Hardy, S. (Liverpool), 1907 v S, W, Ni; 1908 v S; 1909 v S, W, Ni, H (2), A; 1910 v S, W, Ni; 1912 v Ni; (with Aston Villa), 1913 v S; 1914 v Ni, W, S; 1920 v Ni, W (21)

Harford, M. G. (Luton T), 1988 v Is (sub); 1989 v D (2)

Hargreaves, F. W. (Blackburn R), 1880 v W; 1881 v W; 1882 v Ni (3)

Hargreaves, J. (Blackburn R), 1881 v S, W (2)

Harper, E. C. (Blackburn R), 1926 v S (1)

Harris, G. (Burnley), 1966 v Pol (1)

Harris, P. P. (Portsmouth), 1950 v Ei; 1954 v H (2)

Harris, S. S. (Cambridge University), 1904 v S; (with Old Westminsters), 1905 v Ni, W; 1906 v S, W, Ni (6)

Harrison, A. H. (Old Westminsters), 1893 v S, Ni (2)

Harrison, G. (Everton), 1921 v Bel; 1922 v Ni (2)

Harrow, J. H. (Chelsea), 1923 v Ni, Se (2)

Hart, E. (Leeds U), 1929 v W; 1930 v W, Ni; 1933 v S, A; 1934 v S, H, Cz (8)

Hartley, F. (Oxford C), 1923 v F (1)

Harvey, A. (Wednesbury Strollers), 1881 v W (1)

Harvey, J. C. (Everton), 1971 v Ma (1)

Hassall, H. W. (Huddersfield T), 1951 v S, Arg, P; 1952 v F; (with Bolton W), 1954 v Ni (5)

Hateley, M. (Portsmouth), 1984 v USSR (sub), Br, U, Ch; (with AC Milan), 1985 v EG (sub), Fi, Ei, Fi, S, I, M; 1986 v R, T, Eg, S, M, Ca, P, Mor, Para (sub); 1987 v T (sub), Br (sub); (with Monaco), 1988 v WG (sub), Ho (sub), H (sub), Co (sub), Ho (sub), USSR (sub); (with Rangers), 1992 v Cz (32)

Hawkes, R. M. (Luton T), 1907 v Ni; 1908 v A (2), H, B (5)

Haworth, G. (Accrington), 1887 v Ni, W, S; 1888 v S; 1890 v S (5)

Hawtrey, J. P. (Old Etonians), 1881 v S, W (2)
Haygarth, E. B. (Swifts), 1875 v S (1)
Haynes, J. N. (Fulham), 1955 v Ni; 1956 v S, Ni, Br, Se, Fi, WG, Sp; 1957 v W, Y, D, Ei (2); 1958 v W, Ni, S, F, P, Y, USSR (3), Br, A; 1959 v S, Ni, USSR, I, Br, Pe, M, US; 1960 v Ni, Y, Sp, H; 1961 v Ni, W, S, L, P, Sp, M, I, A; 1962 v W, Ni, S, A, Sw, Pe, P, H, Arg, Bul, Br (56)
Healless, H. (Blackburn R), 1925 v Ni; 1928 v S (2)
Hector, K. J. (Derby Co), 1974 v Pol (sub), I (sub) (2)
Hedley, G. A. (Sheffield U), 1901 v Ni (1)
Hegan, K. E. (Corinthians), 1923 v Bel, F; 1924 v Ni, Bel (4)
Hellawell, M. S. (Birmingham C), 1963 v Ni, F (2)
Hendrie, L. A. (Aston Villa), 1999 v CzR (sub) (1)
Henfrey, A. G. (Cambridge University), 1891 v Ni; (with Corinthians), 1892 v W; 1895 v W; 1896 v S, W (5)
Henry, R. P. (Tottenham H), 1963 v F (1)
Heron, F. (Wanderers), 1876 v S (1)
Heron, G. H. H. (Uxbridge), 1873 v S; 1874 v S; (with Wanderers), 1875 v S; 1876 v S; 1878 v S (5)
Heskey, E. W. (Leicester C), 1999 v H (sub), Bul (sub); 2000 v Bel (sub), S (sub), Arg; (with Liverpool), Uk (sub), Ma (sub), P (sub), R (sub) (9)
Hibbert, W. (Bury), 1910 v S (1)
Hibbs, H. E. (Birmingham), 1930 v S, W, A, G; 1931 v S, W, Ni; 1932 v W, Ni, Sp; 1933 v S, W, Ni, A, I, Sw; 1934 v Ni, W, F; 1935 v S, W, Ni, Ho; 1936 v G, W (25)
Hill, F. (Bolton W), 1963 v Ni, W (2)
Hill, G. A. (Manchester U), 1976 v I; 1977 v Ei (sub), Fi (sub), L; 1978 v Sw (sub), L (6)
Hill, J. H. (Burnley), 1925 v W; 1926 v S; 1927 v S, Ni, Bel, F; 1928 v Ni, W; (with Newcastle U), 1929 v F, Bel, Sp (11)
Hill, R. (Luton T), 1983 v D (sub), WG; 1986 v Eg (sub) (3)
Hill, R. H. (Millwall), 1926 v Bel (1)
Hillman, J. (Burnley), 1899 v Ni (1)
Hills, A. F. (Old Harrovians), 1879 v S (1)
Hilsdon, G. R. (Chelsea), 1907 v Ni; 1908 v S, W, Ni, A, H, B; 1909 v Ni (8)
Hinchcliffe, A. G. (Everton), 1997 v Mol, Pol, Ge; 1998 v Cam; (with Sheffield W), Sw, S.Ar; 1999 v Bul (7)
Hine, E. W. (Leicester C), 1929 v W, Ni; 1930 v W, Ni; 1932 v W, Ni (6)
Hinton, A. T. (Wolverhampton W), 1963 v F; (with Nottingham F), 1965 v W, Bel (3)
Hirst, D. E. (Sheffield W), 1991 v Aus, Nz (sub); 1992 v F (3)
Hitchens, G. A. (Aston Villa), 1961 v M, I, A; (with Inter-Milan), 1962 v Sw, Pe, H, Br (7)
Hobbis, H. H. F. (Charlton Ath), 1936 v A, Bel (2)
Hoddle, G. (Tottenham H), 1980 v Bul, W, Aus, Sp; 1981 v Sp, W, S; 1982 v N, Ni, W, Ic, Cz (sub), K; 1983 v L (sub), Ni, S; 1984 v H, L, F; 1985 v Ei (sub), S, I (sub), M, WG, US; 1986 v R, T, Ni, Is, USSR, S, M, Ca, P, Mor, Pol, Para, Arg; 1987 v Se, Ni, Y, Sp, T, S; (with Monaco), 1988 v WG, T (sub), Y (sub), Ho (sub), H (sub), Co (sub), Ei (sub), Ho, USSR (53)
Hodge, S. B. (Aston Villa), 1986 v USSR (sub), S, Ca, P (sub), Mor (sub), Pol, Para, Arg; 1987 v Se, Ni, Y; (with Tottenham H), Sp, Ni, T, S; (with Nottingham F), 1989 v D; 1990 v I (sub), Y (sub), Cz, D, U, Tun; 1991 v Cam (sub), T (sub) (24)
Hodgetts, D. (Aston Villa), 1888 v S, W, Ni; 1892 v S, Ni; 1894 v Ni (6)
Hodgkinson, A. (Sheffield U), 1957 v S, Ei (2), D; 1961 v W (5)
Hodgson, G. (Liverpool), 1931 v S, Ni, W (3)
Hodkinson, J. (Blackburn R), 1913 v W, S; 1920 v Ni (3)
Hogg, W. (Sunderland), 1902 v S, W, Ni (3)
Holdcroft, G. H. (Preston NE), 1937 v W, Ni (2)
Holden, A. D. (Bolton W), 1959 v S, I, Br, Pe, M (5)
Holden, G. H. (Wednesbury OA), 1881 v S; 1884 v S, W, Ni (4)
Holden-White, C. (Corinthians), 1888 v W, S (2)
Holford, T. (Stoke), 1903 v Ni (1)
Holley, G. H. (Sunderland), 1909 v S, W, H (2), A; 1910 v W; 1912 v S, W, Ni; 1913 v S (10)
Holliday, E. (Middlesbrough), 1960 v W, Ni, Se (3)
Hollins, J. W. (Chelsea), 1967 v Sp (1)
Holmes, R. (Preston NE), 1888 v Ni; 1891 v S; 1892 v S; 1893 v S, W; 1894 v Ni; 1895 v Ni (7)
Holt, J. (Everton), 1890 v W; 1891 v S, W; 1892 v S, Ni; 1893 v S; 1894 v S, Ni; 1895 v S; (with Reading), 1900 v Ni (10)
Hopkinson, E. (Bolton W), 1958 v W, Ni, S, F, P, Y; 1959 v S, I, Br, Pe, M, US; 1960 v W, Se (14)
Hossack, A. H. (Corinthians), 1892 v W; 1894 v W (2)
Houghton, W. E. (Aston Villa), 1931 v Ni, W, F, Bel; 1932 v S, Ni; 1933 v A (7)

Houlker, A. E. (Blackburn R), 1902 v S; (with Portsmouth), 1903 v S, W; (with Southampton), 1906 v W, Ni (5)
Howarth, R. H. (Preston NE), 1887 v Ni; 1888 v S, W; 1891 v S; (with Everton), 1894 v Ni (5)
Howe, D. (WBA), 1958 v S, W, Ni, F, P, Y, USSR (3), Br, A; 1959 v S, W, Ni, USSR, I, Br, Pe, M, US; 1960 v W, Ni, Se (23)
Howe, J. R. (Derby Co), 1948 v I; 1949 v S, Ni (3)
Howell, L. S. (Wanderers), 1873 v S (1)
Howell, R. (Sheffield U), 1895 v Ni; (with Liverpool) 1899 v S (2)
Howey, S. N. (Newcastle U), 1995 v Ng; 1996 v Co, P, Bul (4)
Hudson, A. A. (Stoke C), 1975 v WG, Cy (2)
Hudson, J. (Sheffield), 1883 v Ni (1)
Hudspeth, F. C. (Newcastle U), 1926 v Ni (1)
Hufton, A. E. (West Ham U), 1924 v Bel; 1928 v S, Ni; 1929 v F, Bel, Sp (6)
Hughes, E. W. (Liverpool), 1970 v W, Ni, S, Ho, P, Bel; 1971 v EG, Ma (2), Gr, W; 1972 v Sw, Gr, WG (2), W, Ni, S; 1973 v W (3), S (2), Pol, USSR, I; 1974 v A, Pol, I, W, Ni, S, Arg, EG, Bul, Y; 1975 v Cz, P, Cy (sub), Ni; 1977 v I, L, W, S, Br, Arg, U; 1978 v Sw, L, I, WG, Ni, S, H; 1979 v D, Ei, Ni, W, Se; (with Wolverhampton W), 1980 v Sp (sub), Ni, S (sub) (62)
Hughes, L. (Liverpool), 1950 v Ch, US, Sp (3)
Hulme, J. H. A. (Arsenal), 1927 v S, Bel, F; 1928 v S, Ni, W; 1929 v Ni, W; 1933 v S (9)
Humphreys, P. (Notts Co), 1903 v S (1)
Hunt, G. S. (Tottenham H), 1933 v I, Sw, S (3)
Hunt, Rev K. R. G. (Leyton), 1911 v S, W (2)
Hunt, R. (Liverpool), 1962 v A; 1963 v EG; 1964 v S, US, P; 1965 v W; 1966 v S, Sp, Pol (2), WG (2), Fi, N, U, M, F, Arg, P; 1967 v Ni, W, Cz, Sp, A; 1968 v W, Ni, USSR (2), Sp (2), Se, Y; 1969 v R (2) (34)
Hunt, S. (WBA), 1984 v S (sub), USSR (sub) (2)
Hunter, J. (Sheffield Heeley), 1878 v S; 1880 v S, W; 1881 v S, W; 1882 v S, W (7)
Hunter, N. (Leeds U), 1966 v WG, Y, Fi, Sp (sub); 1967 v A; 1968 v Sp, Se, Y, WG, USSR; 1969 v R, W; 1970 v Ho, WG (sub); 1971 v Ma; 1972 v WG (2), W, Ni, S; 1973 v W (2) USSR (sub); 1974 v A, Pol, Ni (sub), S; 1975 v Cz (28)
Hurst, G. C. (West Ham U), 1966 v S, WG (2), Y, Fi, D, Arg, P; 1967 v Ni, W, S, Cz, Sp, A; 1968 v W, Ni, S, Se (sub), WG, USSR (2); 1969 v Ni, S, R (2), Bul, F, M, U, Br; 1970 v W, Ni, S, Ho (1+1 sub), Bel, Co, Ec, R, Br, WG; 1971 v EG, Gr, W, S; 1972 v Sw (2), Gr, WG (49)

Ince, P. E. C. (Manchester U), 1993 v Sp, N, T (2), Ho, Pol, US, Br, G; 1994 v Pol, Ho, Sm, D, N; 1995 v R, Ei; (with Internazionale), 1996 v Bul, Cro, H, Sw, S, Ho, G; 1997 v Mol, Pol, Ge, I, M, Ge, Pol, I, F (sub), Br; (with Liverpool), 1998 v I, Cam, Ch (sub), Sw, P, Mor, Tun, R, Co, Arg; 1999 v Se, F; (with Middlesbrough), 2000 v Bel, S (2), Br, Ma (sub), P, G, R (53)
Iremonger, J. (Nottingham F), 1901 v S; 1902 v Ni (2)

Jack, D. N. B. (Bolton W), 1924 v S, W; 1928 v F, Bel; (with Arsenal), 1930 v S, G, A; 1933 v W, A (9)
Jackson, E. (Oxford University), 1891 v W (1)
James, D. B. (Liverpool), 1997 v M (1)
Jarrett, B. G. (Cambridge University), 1876 v S; 1877 v S; 1878 v S (3)
Jefferis, F. (Everton), 1912 v S, W (2)
Jezzard, B. A. G. (Fulham), 1954 v H; 1956 v Ni (2)
Johnson, D. E. (Ipswich T), 1975 v W, S; 1976 v Sw; (with Liverpool), 1980 v Ei, Arg, Ni, S, Bel (8)
Johnson, E. (Saltley College), 1880 v W; (with Stoke C), 1884 v Ni (2)
Johnson, J. A. (Stoke C), 1937 v N, Se, Fi, S, Ni (5)
Johnson, T. C. F. (Manchester C), 1926 v Bel; 1930 v W; (with Everton), 1932 v S, Sp; 1933 v Ni (5)
Johnson, W. H. (Sheffield U), 1900 v S, W, Ni; 1903 v S, W, Ni (6)
Johnston, H. (Blackpool), 1947 v S, Ho; 1951 v S; 1953 v Arg, Ch, U, US; 1954 v W, Ni, H (10)
Jones, A. (Walsall Swifts), 1882 v S, W; (with Great Lever), 1883 v S (3)
Jones, H. (Blackburn R), 1927 v S, Bel, L, F; 1928 v S, Ni (6)
Jones, H. (Nottingham F), 1923 v F (1)
Jones, M. D. (Sheffield U), 1965 v WG, Se; (with Leeds U), 1970 v Ho (3)
Jones, R. (Liverpool), 1992 v F; 1994 v Pol, Gr, N; 1995 v US, R, Ng, U (8)
Jones, W. (Bristol C), 1901 v Ni (1)
Jones, W. H. (Liverpool), 1950 v P, Bel (2)
Joy, B. (Casuals), 1936 v Bel (1)

Kail, E. I. L. (Dulwich Hamlet), 1929 v F, Bel, Sp (3)

Kay, A. H. (Everton), 1963 v Sw (1)

Kean, F. W. (Sheffield W), 1923 v S, Bel; 1924 v W; 1925 v Ni; 1926 v Ni, Bel; 1927 v L; (with Bolton W), 1929 v F, Sp (9)

Keegan, J. K. (Liverpool), 1973 v W (2); 1974 v W, Ni, Arg, EG, Bul, Y; 1975 v Cz, WG, Cy (2), Ni, S; 1976 v Sw, Cz, P, W (2), Ni, S, Br, Fi; 1977 v Ei, Fi, I, Ho, L; (with SV Hamburg), W, Br, Arg, U; 1978 v Sw, I, WG, Br, H; 1979 v D, Ei, Cz, Ni, W, S, Bul, Se, A; 1980 v D, Ni, Ei, Sp (2), Arg, Bel, I; (with Southampton), 1981 v Sp, Sw, H; 1982 v N, H, Ni, S, Fi, Sp (sub) (63)

Keen, E. R. L. (Derby Co), 1933 v A; 1937 v W, Ni, H (4)

Kelly, R. (Burnley), 1920 v S; 1921 v S, W, Ni; 1922 v S, W; 1923 v S; 1924 v Ni; 1925 v Ni, S; (with Sunderland), 1926 v W; (with Huddersfield T), 1927 v L; 1928 v S (14)

Kennedy, A. (Liverpool), 1984 v Ni, W (2)

Kennedy, R. (Liverpool), 1976 v W (2), Ni, S; 1977 v L, W, S, Br (sub), Arg (sub); 1978 v Sw, L; 1980 v Bul, Sp, Arg, W, Bel (sub), I (17)

Kenyon-Slaney, W. S. (Wanderers), 1873 v S (1)

Keown, M. R. (Everton), 1992 v F, Cz, C, H, Br, Fi, D, Fe, Se; (with Arsenal), 1993 v Ho, G (sub); 1997 v M, S.Af, I, Br; 1998 v Sw, Mor, Bel; 1999 v CzR, F, Pol, H, Se; 2000 v L, Pol, Bel, S, Arg, Br, Ma, P (sub), G, R (33)

Kevan, D. T. (WBA), 1957 v S; 1958 v W, Ni, S, P. Y, USSR (3), Br, A; 1959 v M, US; 1961 v M (14)

Kidd, B. (Manchester U), 1970 v Ni, Ec (sub) (2)

King, R. S. (Oxford University), 1882 v Ni (1)

Kingsford, R. K. (Wanderers), 1874 v S (1)

Kingsley, M. (Newcastle U), 1901 v W (1)

Kinsey, G. (Wolverhampton W), 1892 v W; 1893 v S; (with Derby Co), 1896 v W, Ni (4)

Kirchen, A. J. (Arsenal), 1937 v N, Se, Fi (3)

Kirton, W. J. (Aston Villa), 1922 v Ni (1)

Knight, A. E. (Portsmouth), 1920 v Ni (1)

Knowles, C. (Tottenham H), 1968 v USSR, Sp, Se, WG (4)

Labone, B. L. (Everton), 1963 v Ni, W, F; 1967 v Sp, A; 1968 v S, Sp, Se, Y, USSR, WG; 1969 v Ni, S, R, Bul, M, U, Br; 1970 v S, W, Bel, Co, Ec, R, Br, WG (26)

Lampard, F. J. (West Ham U), 2000 v Bel (1)

Lampard, F. R. G. (West Ham U), 1973 v Y; 1980 v Aus (2)

Langley, E. J. (Fulham), 1958 v S, P, Y (3)

Langton, B. (Blackburn R), 1947 v W, Ni, Ei, Ho, F, Sw; 1948 v Se; (with Preston NE), 1949 v D, Se; (with Bolton W), 1950 v S; 1951 v Ni (11)

Latchford, R. D. (Everton), 1978 v I, Br, W; 1979 v D, Ei, Cz (sub), Ni (2), W, S, Bul, A (12)

Latheron, E. G. (Blackburn R), 1913 v W; 1914 v Ni (2)

Lawler, C. (Liverpool), 1971 v Ma, W, S; 1972 v Sw (4)

Lawton, T. (Everton), 1939 v S, W, Ni, R of E, N, I, R, Y; (with Chelsea), 1947 v S, W, Ni, Ei, Ho, F, Sw, P; 1948 v W, Ni, Bel; (with Notts Co), 1948 v S, Se, I; 1949 v D (23)

Leach, T. (Sheffield W), 1931 v W, Ni (2)

Leake, A. (Aston Villa), 1904 v S, Ni; 1905 v S, W, Ni (5)

Lee, E. A. (Southampton), 1904 v W (1)

Lee, F. H. (Manchester C), 1969 v Ni, W, S, Bul, F, M, U; 1970 v W, Ho (2), P, Bel, Co, Ec, R, Br, WG; 1971 v EG, Gr, Ma, Ni, W, S; 1972 v Sw (2), Gr, WG (27)

Lee, J. (Derby Co), 1951 v Ni (1)

Lee, R. M. (Newcastle U), 1995 v R, Ng; 1996 v Co (sub), N, Sw, Bul (sub), H; 1997 v M, Ge, S.Af, Pol, F (sub), Br (sub); 1998 v Cam (sub), Ch, Sw, Bel, Co (sub); 1999 v Se (sub), Bul, L (sub) (21)

Lee, S. (Liverpool), 1983 v Gr, L, W, Gr, H, S, Aus; 1984 v D, H, L, F, Ni, W, Ch (sub) (14)

Leighton, J. E. (Nottingham F), 1886 v Ni (1)

Le Saux, G. P. (Blackburn R), 1994 v D, Gr, N; 1995 v US, R, Ng, Ei, U, Se, Br; 1996 v Co, P (sub); 1997 v I, M, Ge, S.Af, Pol, I, F, Br; (with Chelsea), 1998 v I, Ch (sub), P, Mor, Bel, Tun, R, Co, Arg; 1999 v Se, Bul (sub), CzR, F, Pol, Se (35)

Le Tissier, M. P. (Southampton), 1994 v D (sub), Gr (sub), N (sub); 1995 v R, Ng (sub), Ei; 1997 v Mol (sub), I (8)

Lilley, H. E. (Sheffield U), 1892 v W (1)

Linacre, H. J. (Nottingham F), 1905 v W, S (2)

Lindley, T. (Cambridge University), 1886 v S, W, Ni; 1887 v S, W, Ni; 1888 v S, W, Ni; (with Nottingham F), 1889 v S; 1890 v S, W; 1891 v Ni (13)

Lindsay, A. (Liverpool), 1974 v Arg, EG, Bul, Y (4)

Lindsay, W. (Wanderers), 1877 v S (1)

Lineker, G. (Leicester C), 1984 v S (sub); 1985 v Ei, R (sub), S (sub), I (sub), WG, US; (with Everton), 1986 v R, T, Ni, Eg, USSR, Ca, P, Mor, Pol, Para, Arg; (with Barcelona), 1987 v Ni (2), Y, Sp, T, Br; 1988 v WG, T, Y, Ho, H, S, Co, Sw, Ei, Ho, USSR; 1989 v Se, S.Arr, Gr, Alb (2), Pol, D; (with Tottenham H) 1990 v Se, Pol, I, Y, Br, Cz, D, U, Tun, Ei,

Ho, Eg, Bel, Cam, WG, I; 1991 v H, Pol, Ei (2), Cam, T, Arg, Aus, Nz, Mal; 1992 v G, T, Pol, F (sub), Cz (sub), C, H, Br, Fi, D, F, Se (80)

Lintott, E. H. (QPR), 1908 v S, W, Ni; (with Bradford C), 1909 v S, Ni, H (2) (7)

Lipsham, H. B. (Sheffield U), 1902 v W (1)

Little, B. (Aston Villa), 1975 v W (sub) (1)

Lloyd, L. V. (Liverpool), 1971 v W; 1972 v Sw, Ni; (with Nottingham F), 1980 v W (4)

Lockett, A. (Stoke C), 1903 v Ni (1)

Lodge, L. V. (Cambridge University), 1894 v W; 1895 v S, W; (with Corinthians), 1896 v S, Ni (5)

Lofthouse, J. M. (Blackburn R), 1885 v S, W, Ni; 1887 v S, W; (with Accrington), 1889 v Ni; (with Blackburn R), 1890 v Ni (7)

Lofthouse, N. (Bolton W), 1951 v Y; 1952 v W, Ni, S, A (2), I, Sw; 1953 v W, Ni, S, Bel, Arg, Ch, U, US; 1954 v W, Ni, R of E, Bel, U; 1955 v Ni, S, F, Sp, P; 1956 v W, S, Sp, D, Fi (sub); 1959 v W, USSR (33)

Longworth, E. (Liverpool), 1920 v S; 1921 v Bel; 1923 v S, W, Bel (5)

Lowder, A. (Wolverhampton W), 1889 v W (1)

Lowe, E. (Aston Villa), 1947 v F, Sw, P (3)

Lucas, T. (Liverpool), 1922 v Ni; 1924 v F; 1926 v Bel (3)

Luntley, E. (Nottingham F), 1880 v S, W (2)

Lyttelton, Hon. A. (Cambridge University), 1877 v S (1)

Lyttelton, Hon. E. (Cambridge University), 1878 v S (1)

McCall, J. (Preston NE), 1913 v S, W; 1914 v S; 1920 v S; 1921 v Ni (5)

McDermott, T. (Liverpool), 1978 v Sw, L; 1979 v Ni, W, Se; 1980 v D, Ni (sub), Ei, Ni, S, Bel (sub), Sp; 1981 v N, R, Sw, R (sub), Br, Sw (sub), H; 1982 v N, H, W (sub), Ho, S (sub), Ic (25)

McDonald, C. A. (Burnley), 1958 v USSR (3), Br, A; 1959 v W, Ni, USSR (8)

McFarland, R. L. (Derby Co), 1971 v Gr, Ma (2), Ni, S; 1972 v Sw, Gr, WG, W, S; 1973 v W (3), Ni, S, Cz, Pol, USSR, I; 1974 v A, Pol, I, W, Ni; 1976 v Cz, S; 1977 v Ei, I (28)

McGarry, W. H. (Huddersfield T), 1954 v Sw, U; 1956 v W, D (4)

McGuinness, W. (Manchester U), 1959 v Ni, M (2)

McInroy, A. (Sunderland), 1927 v Ni (1)

McMahon, S. (Liverpool), 1988 v Is, H, Co, USSR; 1989 v D (sub); 1990 v Se, Pol, I, Y (sub), Br, Cz (sub), D, Ei (sub), Eg, Bel, I; 1991 v Ei (17)

McManaman, S. (Liverpool), 1995 v Ng (sub), U (sub), J (sub); 1996 v Co, N, Sw, P (sub), Bul, Cro, Chn, Sw, S, Ho, Sp, G; 1997 v Pol, I, M; 1998 v Cam, Sw, Mor, Co (sub); 1999 v Pol, H; (with Real Madrid), 2000 v L, Pol, Uk, Ma (sub), P (29)

McNab, R. (Arsenal), 1969 v Ni, Bul, R (1+1 sub) (4)

McNeal, R. (WBA), 1914 v S, W (2)

McNeil, M. (Middlesbrough), 1961 v W, Ni, S, L, P, Sp, M, I; 1962 v L (9)

Mabbutt, G. (Tottenham H), 1983 v WG, Gr, L, W, Gr, H, Ni, S; 1984 v H; 1987 v Y, Ni, T; 1988 v WG; 1992 v T, Pol, Cz (16)

Macaulay, R. H. (Cambridge University), 1881 v S (1)

Macdonald, M. (Newcastle U), 1972 v W, Ni, S (sub); 1973 v USSR (sub); 1974 v P, S (sub), Y (sub); 1975 v WG, Cy (2), Ni; 1976 v Sw (sub), Cz, P (14)

Macrae, S. (Notts Co), 1883 v S, W, Ni; 1884 v S, Ni (5)

Maddison, F. B. (Oxford University), 1872 v S (1)

Madeley, P. E. (Leeds U), 1971 v Ni; 1972 v Sw (2), Gr, WG (2), W, S; 1973 v S, Cz, Pol, USSR, I; 1974 v A, Pol, I; 1975 v Cz, P, Cy; 1976 v Cz, P, Fi; 1977 v Ei, Ho (24)

Magee, T. P. (WBA), 1923 v W, Se; 1925 v S, Bel, F (5)

Makepeace, H. (Everton), 1906 v S; 1910 v S; 1912 v S, W (4)

Male, C. G. (Arsenal), 1935 v S, Ni, Ho; 1936 v S, W, Ni, G, A, Bel; 1937 v S, Ni, H, N, Se, Fi; 1939 v I, R, Y (19)

Mannion, W. J. (Middlesbrough), 1947 v S, W, Ni, Ei, Ho, F, Sw, P; 1948 v W, Ni, Bel, Se, I; 1949 v N, F; 1950 v S, Ei, P, Bel, Ch, US; 1951 v Ni, W, S, Y; 1952 v F (26)

Mariner, P. (Ipswich T), 1977 v L (sub), Ni; 1978 v L, W (sub), S; 1980 v W, Ni (sub), S, Aus, I (sub), Sp (sub); 1981 v N, Sw, Sp, Sw, H; 1982 v N, H, Ho, S, Fi, F, Cz, K, WG, Sp; 1983 v D, WG, Gr, W; 1984 v D, H, L; (with Arsenal), 1985 v EG, R (35)

Marsden, J. T. (Darwen), 1891 v Ni (1)

Marsden, W. (Sheffield W), 1930 v W, S, G (3)

Marsh, R. W. (QPR), 1972 v Sw (sub); (with Manchester C), WG (sub+1), W, Ni, S; 1973 v W (2), Y (9)

Marshall, T. (Darwen), 1880 v W; 1881 v W (2)

Martin, A. (West Ham U), 1981 v Br, S (sub); 1982 v H, Fi; 1983 v Gr, L, W, Gr, H; 1984 v H, L, W; 1985 v Ni; 1986 v Is, Ca, Para; 1987 v Se (17)

Martin, H. (Sunderland), 1914 v Ni (1)

Martyn, A. N. (C Palace), 1992 v C (sub), H; 1993 v G; (with Leeds U), 1997 v S.Af; 1998 v Cam, Ch, Bel; 1999 v CzR, F (sub); 2000 v L, Pol, Bel (sub), Uk, R (14)

Marwood, B. (Arsenal), 1989 v S.Ar (sub) (1)

Maskrey, H. M. (Derby Co), 1908 v Ni (1)

Mason, C. (Wolverhampton W), 1887 v Ni; 1888 v W; 1890 v Ni (3)

Matthews, R. D. (Coventry C), 1956 v S, Br, Se, WG; 1957 v Ni (5)

Matthews, S. (Stoke C), 1935 v W, I; 1936 v G; 1937 v S; 1938 v S, W, Cz, G, Sw, F; 1939 v S, W, Ni, R of E, N, I, Y; 1947 v S; (with Blackpool), 1947 v Sw, P; 1948 v S, W, Ni, Bel, I; 1949 v S, W, Ni, D, Sw; 1950 v Sp; 1951 v Ni, S; 1954 v Ni, R of E, H, Bel, U; 1955 v Ni, W, S, F, WG, Sp, P; 1956 v W, Br; 1957 v S, W, Ni, Y, D (2), Ei (54)

Maynard, W. J. (1st Surrey Rifles), 1872 v S; 1876 v S (2)

Meadows, J. (Manchester C), 1955 v S (1)

Medley, L. D. (Tottenham H), 1951 v Y, W; 1952 v F, A, W, Ni (6)

Meehan, T. (Chelsea), 1924 v Ni (1)

Melia, J. (Liverpool), 1963 v S, Sw (2)

Mercer, D. W. (Sheffield U), 1923 v Ni, Bel (2)

Mercer, J. (Everton), 1939 v S, Ni, I, R, Y (5)

Merrick, G. H. (Birmingham C), 1952 v Ni, S, A (2), I, Sw; 1953 v Ni, W, S, Bel, Arg, Ch, U; 1954 v W, Ni, S, R of E, H (2), Y, Bel, Sw, U (23)

Merson, P. C. (Arsenal), 1992 v G (sub), Cz, H, Br (sub), Fi (sub), D, Se (sub); 1993 v Sp (sub), N (sub), Ho (sub), Br (sub), G; 1994 v Ho, Gr; 1997 v I (sub); (with Middlesbrough), 1998 v Sw, P (sub), Bel, Arg (sub); 1999 v Se (sub); (with Aston Villa), CzR (21)

Metcalfe, V. (Huddersfield T), 1951 v Arg, P (2)

Mew, J. W. (Manchester U), 1921 v Ni (1)

Middleditch, B. (Corinthians), 1897 v Ni (1)

Milburn, J. E. T. (Newcastle U), 1949 v S, W, Ni, Sw; 1950 v W, P, Bel, Sp; 1951 v W, Arg, P; 1952 v F; 1956 v D (13)

Miller, B. G. (Burnley), 1961 v A (1)

Miller, H. S. (Charlton Ath), 1923 v Se (1)

Mills, G. R. (Chelsea), 1938 v W, Ni, Cz (3)

Mills, M. D. (Ipswich T), 1973 v Y; 1976 v W (2), Ni, S, Br, I (sub), Fi; 1977 v Fi (sub), I, Ni, W, S; 1978 v WG, Br, W, Ni, S, H; 1979 v D, Ei, Ni (2), S, Bul, A; 1980 v D, Ni, Sp (2); 1981 v Sw (2), H; 1982 v N, H, S, Fi, F, Cz, K, WG, Sp (42)

Milne, G. (Liverpool), 1963 v Br, Cz, EG; 1964 v W, Ni, S, R of W, U, P, Ei, Br, Arg; 1965 v Ni, Bel (14)

Milton, C. A. (Arsenal), 1952 v A (1)

Milward, A. (Everton), 1891 v S, W; 1897 v S, W (4)

Mitchell, C. (Upton Park), 1880 v W; 1881 v S; 1883 v S, W; 1885 v W (5)

Mitchell, J. F. (Manchester C), 1925 v Ni (1)

Moffat, H. (Oldham Ath), 1913 v W (1)

Molyneux, G. (Southampton), 1902 v S; 1903 v S, W, Ni (4)

Moon, W. R. (Old Westminsters), 1888 v S, W; 1889 v S, W; 1890 v S, W; 1891 v S (7)

Moore, H. T. (Notts Co), 1883 v Ni; 1885 v W (2)

Moore, J. (Derby Co), 1923 v Se (1)

Moore, R. F. (West Ham U), 1962 v Pe, H, Arg, Bul, Br; 1963 v W, Ni, S, F (2), Br, Cz, EG, Sw; 1964 v W, Ni, S, R of W, U, P (2), Ei, Br, Arg; 1965 v Ni, S, Bel, H, Y, WG, Se; 1966 v W, Ni, S, A, Sp, Pol (2), WG (2), N, D, U, M, F, Arg, P; 1967 v W, Ni, S, Cz, Sp, A; 1968 v W, Ni, S, USSR (2), Sp (2), Se, Y, WG; 1969 v Ni, W, S, R, Bul, F, M, U; 1970 v W, Ni, S, Ho, P, Bel, Co, Ec, R, Br, Cz, WG; 1971 v EG, Gr, Ma, Ni, S; 1972 v Sw (2), Gr, WG (2), W, S; 1973 v W (3), Y, S (2), Ni, Cz, Pol, USSR, I; 1974 v I (108)

Moore, W. G. B. (West Ham U), 1923 v Se (1)

Mordue, J. (Sunderland), 1912 v Ni; 1913 v Ni (2)

Morice, C. J. (Barnes), 1872 v S (1)

Morley, A. (Aston Villa), 1982 v H (sub), Ni, W, Ic; 1983 v D, Gr (6)

Morley, H. (Notts Co), 1910 v Ni (1)

Morren, T. (Sheffield U), 1898 v Ni (1)

Morris, F. (WBA), 1920 v S; 1921 v Ni (2)

Morris, J. (Derby Co), 1949 v N, F; 1950 v Ei (3)

Morris, W. W. (Wolverhampton W), 1939 v S, Ni, R (3)

Morse, H. (Notts Co), 1879 v S (1)

Mort, T. (Aston Villa), 1924 v W, F; 1926 v S (3)

Morten, A. (C Palace), 1873 v S (1)

Mortensen, S. H. (Blackpool), 1947 v P; 1948 v W, S, Ni, Bel, Se, I; 1949 v S, W, Ni, Se, N; 1950 v S, W, Ni, I, P, Bel, Ch, US, Sp; 1951 v S, Arg; 1954 v R of E, H (25)

Morton, J. R. (West Ham U), 1938 v Cz (1)

Mosforth, W. (Sheffield W), 1877 v S; (with Sheffield Albion), 1878 v S; 1879 v S, W; 1880 v S, W; (with Sheffield W), 1881 v W; 1882 v S, W (9)

Moss, F. (Arsenal), 1934 v S, H, Cz; 1935 v I (4)

Moss, F. (Aston Villa), 1922 v S, Ni; 1923 v Ni; 1924 v S, Bel (5)

Mosscrop, E. (Burnley), 1914 v S, W (2)

Mozley, B. (Derby Co), 1950 v W, Ni, Ei (3)

Mullen, J. (Wolverhampton W), 1947 v S; 1949 v N, F; 1950 v Bel (sub), Ch, US; 1954 v W, Ni, S, R of E, Y, Sw (12)

Mullery, A. P. (Tottenham H), 1965 v Ho; 1967 v Sp, A; 1968 v W, Ni, S, USSR, Sp (2), Se, Y; 1969 v Ni, S, R, Bul, F, M, U, Br; 1970 v W, Ni, S (sub), Ho (sub), Bel, P, Co, Ec, R, Cz, WG, Br; 1971 v Ma, EG, Gr; 1972 v Sw (35)

Neal, P. G. (Liverpool), 1976 v W, I; 1977 v W, S, Br, Arg, U; 1978 v Sw, I, WG, Ni, S, H; 1979 v D, Ei, Ni (2), S, Bul, A; 1980 v D, Ni, Sp, Arg, W, Bel, I; 1981 v R, Sw, Sp, Br, H; 1982 v N, H, W, Ho, Ic, F (sub), K; 1983 v D, Gr, L, W, Gr, H, Ni, S, Aus (2); 1984 v D (50)

Needham, E. (Sheffield U), 1894 v S; 1895 v S; 1897 v S, W, Ni; 1898 v S, W; 1899 v S, W, Ni; 1900 v S, Ni; 1901 v S, W, Ni; 1902 v W (16)

Neville, G. A. (Manchester U), 1995 v J, Br; 1996 v Co, N, Sw, P, Bul, Cro, H, Chn, Sw, S, Ho, Sp; 1997 v Mol, Pol, I, Ge, Pol, I (sub), F, Br (sub); 1998 v Mol, Ch, P, S.Ar, Bel, R, Co, Arg; 1999 v Bul, Pol; 2000 v L (sub), Pol, Br, Ma, P, G, R (39)

Neville, P. J. (Manchester U), 1996 v Chn; 1997 v S.Af, Pol (sub), I, F, Br; 1998 v Mol, Cam, Ch, P (sub), S.Ar (sub), Bel; 1999 v L, Pol (sub), H, Se, Bul; 2000 v L (sub), Pol (sub), Bel, S (2), Arg (sub), Br, Uk, Ma, P, G, R (29)

Newton, K. R. (Blackburn R), 1966 v S, WG; 1967 v Sp, A; 1968 v W, S, Sp, Se, Y, WG; 1969 v Ni, W, S, R, Bul, M, U, Br, F; (with Everton), 1970 v Ni, S, Ho, Co, Ec, R, Cz, WG (27)

Nicholls, J. (WBA), 1954 v S, Y (2)

Nicholson, W. E. (Tottenham H), 1951 v P (1)

Nish, D. J. (Derby Co), 1973 v Ni; 1974 v P, W, Ni, S (5)

Norman, M. (Tottenham H), 1962 v Pe, H, Arg, Bul, Br; 1963 v S, F, Br, Cz, EG; 1964 v W, Ni, S, R of W, U, P (2), US, Br, Arg; 1965 v Ni, Bel, Ho (23)

Nuttall, H. (Bolton W), 1928 v W, Ni; 1929 v S (3)

Oakley, W. J. (Oxford University), 1895 v W; 1896 v S, W, Ni; (with Corinthians), 1897 v S, W, Ni; 1898 v S, W, Ni; 1900 v S, W, Ni; 1901 v S, W, Ni (16)

O'Dowd, J. P. (Chelsea), 1932 v S; 1933 v Ni, Sw (3)

O'Grady, M. (Huddersfield T), 1963 v Ni; (with Leeds U), 1969 v F (2)

Ogilvie, R. A. M. M. (Clapham R), 1874 v S (1)

Oliver, L. F. (Fulham), 1929 v Bel (1)

Olney, B. A. (Aston Villa), 1928 v F, Bel (2)

Osborne, F. R. (Fulham), 1923 v Ni, F; (with Tottenham H), 1925 v Bel; 1926 v Bel (4)

Osborne, R. (Leicester C), 1928 v W (1)

Osgood, P. L. (Chelsea), 1970 v Bel, R (sub), Cz (sub); 1974 v I (4)

Osman, R. (Ipswich T), 1980 v Aus; 1981 v Sp, R, Sw; 1982 v N, Ic; 1983 v D, Aus (3); 1984 v D (11)

Ottaway, C. J. (Oxford University), 1872 v S; 1874 v S (2)

Owen, J. R. B. (Sheffield), 1874 v S (1)

Owen, M. J. (Liverpool), 1998 v Ch, Sw, P (sub), Mor (sub), Bel (sub), Tun (sub), R (sub), Co, Arg; 1999 v Se, Bul, L, F; 2000 v L (sub), Pol (sub), Bel (sub), S (2), Br, P, G, R (22)

Owen, S. W. (Luton T), 1954 v H, Y, Bel (3)

Page, L. A. (Burnley), 1927 v S, W, Bel, L, F; 1928 v W, Ni (7)

Paine, T. L. (Southampton), 1963 v Cz, EG; 1964 v W, Ni, S, R of W, U, US, P; 1965 v Ni, H, Y, WG, Se; 1966 v W, A, Y, N, M (19)

Pallister, G. A. (Middlesbrough), 1988 v H; 1989 v S.Ar; (with Manchester U), 1991 v Cam (sub), T; 1992 v G; 1993 v N, US, Br, G; 1994 v Pol, Ho, Sm, D; 1995 v US, R, Ei, U, Se; 1996 v N, Sw; 1997 v Mol, Pol (sub) (22)

Palmer, C. L. (Sheffield W), 1992 v C, H, Br, Fi (sub), D, F, Se; 1993 v Sp (sub), N (sub), T, Sm, T, Ho, Pol, N, US, Br (sub); 1994 v Ho (18)

Pantling, H. H. (Sheffield U), 1924 v Ni (1)

Paravacini, P. J. de (Cambridge University), 1883 v S, W, Ni (3)

Parker, P. A. (QPR), 1989 v Alb (sub), Ch, D; 1990 v Y, U, Ho, Eg, Bel, Cam, WG, I; 1991 v H, Pol, USSR, Aus, Nz; (with Manchester U), 1992 v G; 1994 v Ho, D (19)

Parker, T. R. (Southampton), 1925 v F (1)

Parkes, P. B. (QPR), 1974 v P (1)
Parkinson, J. (Liverpool), 1910 v S, W (2)
Parlour, R. (Arsenal), 1999 v Pol (sub), Se (sub), Bul (sub); 2000 v L, S (sub), Arg (sub), Br (sub) (7)
Parr, P. C. (Oxford University), 1882 v W (1)
Parry, E. H. (Old Carthusians), 1879 v W; 1882 v W, S (3)
Parry, R. A. (Bolton W), 1960 v Ni, S (2)
Patchitt, B. C. A. (Corinthians), 1923 v Se (2) (2)
Pawson, F. W. (Cambridge University), 1883 v Ni; (with Swifts), 1885 v Ni (2)
Payne, J. (Luton T), 1937 v Fi (1)
Peacock, A. (Middlesbrough), 1962 v Arg, Bul; 1963 v Ni, W; (with Leeds U), 1966 v W, Ni (6)
Peacock, J. (Middlesbrough), 1929 v F, Bel, Sp (3)
Pearce, S. (Nottingham F), 1987 v Br, S; 1988 v WG (sub), Is, H; 1989 v D, Se, S.Ar, Gr, Alb (2), Ch, S, Pol, D; 1990 v Se, Pol, I, Y, Br, Cz, D, U, Tun, Ei, Ho, Eg, Bel, Cam, WG; 1991 v H, Pol, Ei (2), Cam, T, Arg, Aus, Nz (2), Mal; 1992 v T, Pol, F, Cz, Br (sub), Fi, D, F, Se; 1993 v Sp, N, T; 1994 v Pol, Sm, Gr (sub); 1995 v R (sub), J, Br; 1996 v N, Sw, P, Bul, Cro, H, Sw, S, Ho, Sp, G; 1997 v Mol, Pol, I, M, S.Af, I; (with West Ham U), 2000 v L, Pol (78)
Pearson, H. F. (WBA), 1932 v S (1)
Pearson, J. H. (Crewe Alex), 1892 v Ni (1)
Pearson, J. S. (Manchester U), 1976 v W, Ni, S, Br, Fi; 1977 v Ei, Ho (sub), W, S, Br, Arg, U; 1978 v I (sub), WG, Ni (15)
Pearson, S. C. (Manchester U), 1948 v S; 1949 v S, Ni; 1950 v Ni, I; 1951 v P; 1952 v S, I (8)
Pease, W. H. (Middlesbrough), 1927 v W (1)
Pegg, D. (Manchester U), 1957 v Ei (1)
Pejic, M. (Stoke C), 1974 v P, W, Ni, S (4)
Pelly, F. R. (Old Foresters), 1893 v Ni; 1894 v S, W (3)
Pennington, J. (WBA), 1907 v S, W; 1908 v S, W, Ni, A; 1909 v S, W, H (2), A; 1910 v S, W; 1911 v S, W, Ni; 1912 v S, W, Ni; 1913 v S, W; 1914 v S, Ni; 1920 v S, W (25)
Pentland, F. B. (Middlesbrough), 1909 v S, W, H (2), A (5)
Perry, C. (WBA), 1890 v Ni; 1891 v Ni; 1893 v W (3)
Perry, T. (WBA), 1898 v W (1)
Perry, W. (Blackpool), 1956 v Ni, S, Sp (3)
Perryman, S. (Tottenham H), 1982 v Ic (sub) (1)
Peters, M. (West Ham U), 1966 v Y, Fi, Pol, M, F, Arg, P, WG; 1967 v Ni, W, S, Cz; 1968 v W, Ni, S, USSR (2), Sp (2), Se, Y; 1969 v Ni, S, R, Bul, F, M, U, Br; 1970 v Ho (2), P (sub), Bel; (with Tottenham H), W, Ni, S, Co, Ec, R, Br, Cz, WG; 1971 v EG, Gr, Ma (2), Ni, W, S; 1972 v Sw, Gr, WG (1+1 sub), Ni (sub); 1973 v S (2), Ni, W, Cz, Pol, USSR, I; 1974 v A, Pol, I, P, S (67)
Phelan, M. C. (Manchester U), 1990 v I (sub) (1)
Phillips, K. (Sunderland), 1999 v H; 2000 v Bel, Arg (sub), Br (sub), Ma (5)
Phillips, L. H. (Portsmouth), 1952 v Ni; 1955 v W, WG (3)
Pickering, F. (Everton), 1964 v US; 1965 v Ni, Bel (3)
Pickering, J. (Sheffield U), 1933 v S (1)
Pickering, N. (Sunderland), 1983 v Aus (1)
Pike, T. M. (Cambridge University), 1886 v Ni (1)
Pilkington, B. (Burnley), 1955 v Ni (1)
Plant, J. (Bury), 1900 v S (1)
Platt, D. (Aston Villa), 1990 v I (sub), Y (sub), Br, D (sub), Tun (sub), Ho (sub), Eg (sub), Bel (sub), Cam, WG, I; 1991 v H, Pol, Ei (2), T, USSR, Arg, Aus, Nz (2), Mal; (with Bari), 1992 v G, T, Pol, Cz, Č, Br, Fi, D, F, Se; (with Juventus), 1993 v Sp, N, T, Sm, T, Ho, Pol, N, Br (sub), G; (with Sampdoria), 1994 v Pol, Ho, Sm, D, Gr, N; 1995 v US, Ng, Ei, U, J, Se, Br; (with Arsenal), 1996 v Bul (sub), Cro, H, Sw (sub), Ho (sub), Sp, G (62)
Plum, S. L. (Charlton Ath), 1923 v F (1)
Pointer, R. (Burnley), 1962 v W, L, P (3)
Porteous, T. S. (Sunderland), 1891 v W (1)
Priest, A. E. (Sheffield U), 1900 v Ni (1)
Prinsep, J. F. M. (Clapham Rovers), 1879 v S (1)
Puddefoot, S. C. (Blackburn R), 1926 v S, Ni (2)
Pye, J. (Wolverhampton W), 1950 v Ei (1)
Pym, R. H. (Bolton W), 1925 v S, W; 1926 v W (3)

Quantrill, A. (Derby Co), 1920 v S, W; 1921 v W, Ni (4)
Quixall, A. (Sheffield W), 1954 v W, Ni, R of E; 1955 v Sp, P (sub) (5)

Radford, J. (Arsenal), 1969 v R; 1972 v Sw (sub) (2)
Raikes, G. B. (Oxford University), 1895 v W; 1896 v W, Ni, S (4)
Ramsey, A. E. (Southampton), 1949 v Sw; (with Tottenham H), 1950 v S, I, P, Bel, Ch, US, Sp; 1951 v S, Ni, W, Y, Arg, P; 1952 v S, W, Ni, F, A (2), I, Se; 1953 v Ni, W, S, Bel, Arg, Ch, U, US; 1954 v R of E, H (32)
Rawlings, A. (Preston NE), 1921 v Bel (1)

Rawlings, W. E. (Southampton), 1922 v S, W (2)
Rawlinson, J. F. P. (Cambridge University), 1882 v Ni (1)
Rawson, H. E. (Royal Engineers), 1875 v S (1)
Rawson, W. S. (Oxford University), 1875 v S; 1877 v S (2)
Read, A. (Tufnell Park), 1921 v Bel (1)
Reader, J. (WBA), 1894 v Ni (1)
Reaney, P. (Leeds U), 1969 v Bul (sub); 1970 v P; 1971 v Ma (3)
Redknapp, J. F. (Liverpool), 1996 v Co, N, Sw, Chn, S (sub); 1997 v M (sub), Ge (sub), S.Af; 1999 v Se, Bul, F, Pol (sub), H (sub), Bul; 2000 v Bel, S (2) (17)
Reeves, K. (Norwich C), 1980 v Bul; (with Manchester C), Ni (2)
Regis, C. (WBA), 1982 v Ni (sub), W (sub), Ic; 1983 v WG; (with Coventry C), 1988 v T (sub) (5)
Reid, P. (Everton), 1985 v M (sub), WG, US (sub); 1986 v R, S (sub), Ca (sub), Pol, Para, Arg; 1987 v Br; 1988 v WG, Y (sub), Sw (sub) (13)
Revie, D. G. (Manchester C), 1955 v Ni, S, F; 1956 v W, D; 1957 v Ni (6)
Reynolds, J. (WBA), 1892 v S; 1893 v S, W; (with Aston Villa), 1894 v S, Ni; 1895 v S; 1897 v S, W (8)
Richards, C. H. (Nottingham F), 1898 v Ni (1)
Richards, G. H. (Derby Co), 1909 v A (1)
Richards, J. P. (Wolverhampton W), 1973 v Ni (1)
Richardson, J. R. (Newcastle U), 1933 v I, Sw (2)
Richardson, K. (Aston Villa), 1994 v Gr (1)
Richardson, W. G. (WBA), 1935 v Ho (1)
Rickaby, S. (WBA), 1954 v Ni (1)
Rigby, A. (Blackburn R), 1927 v S, Bel, L, F; 1928 v W (5)
Rimmer, E. J. (Sheffield W), 1930 v S, G, A; 1932 v Sp (4)
Rimmer, J. J. (Arsenal), 1976 v I (1)
Ripley, S. E. (Blackburn R), 1994 v Sm; 1998 v Mol (sub) (2)
Rix, G. (Arsenal), 1981 v N, R, Sw (sub), Br, W, S; 1982 v Ho (sub), Fi (sub), F, Cz, K, WG, Sp; 1983 v D, WG (sub), Gr (sub); 1984 v Ni (17)
Robb, G. (Tottenham H), 1954 v H (1)
Roberts, C. (Manchester U), 1905 v Ni, W, S (3)
Roberts, F. (Manchester C), 1925 v S, W, Bel, F (4)
Roberts, G. (Tottenham H), 1983 v Ni, S; 1984 v F, Ni, S, USSR (6)
Roberts, H. (Arsenal), 1931 v S (1)
Roberts, H. (Millwall), 1931 v Bel (1)
Roberts, R. (WBA), 1887 v S; 1888 v Ni; 1890 v Ni (3)
Roberts, W. T. (Preston NE), 1924 v W, Bel (2)
Robinson, J. (Sheffield W), 1937 v Fi; 1938 v G, Sw; 1939 v W (4)
Robinson, J. W. (Derby Co), 1897 v S, Ni; (with New Brighton Tower), 1898 v S, W, Ni; (with Southampton), 1899 v W, S; 1900 v S, W, Ni; 1901 v Ni (11)
Robson, B. (WBA), 1980 v Ei, Aus; 1981 v N, R, Sw, Sp, R, Br, W, S, Sw, H; 1982 v V; (with Manchester U), H, Ni, W, Ho, S, Fi, F, Cz, WG, Sp; 1983 v D, Gr, L, S; 1984 v H, L, F, Ni, S, USSR, Br, U, Ch; 1985 v EG, Fi, T, Ei, R, Fi, S, M, I, WG, US; 1986 v R, T, Is, M, P, Mor; 1987 v Ni (2), Sp, T, Br, S; 1988 v T, Y, Ho, H, S, Co, Ho, USSR; 1989 v S, Se, S.Ar, Gr, Alb (2), Ch, S, Pol, D; 1990 v Pol, I, Y, Cz, U, Tun, Ei, Ho; 1991 v Cam, Ei; 1992 v T (90)
Robson, R. (WBA), 1958 v F, USSR (2), Br, A; 1960 v Sp, H; 1961 v Ni, W, S, L, P, Sp, M, I; 1962 v W, Ni, Sw, L, P (20)
Rocastle, D. (Arsenal), 1989 v D, S.Ar, Gr, Alb (2), Pol (sub), D; 1990 v Se (sub), Pol, Y, D (sub); 1992 v Pol, Cz, Br (sub) (14)
Rose, W. C. (Wolverhampton W), 1884 v S, W, Ni; (with Preston NE), 1886 v Ni; (with Wolverhampton W), 1891 v Ni (5)
Rostron, T. (Darwen), 1881 v S, W (2)
Rowe, A. (Tottenham H), 1934 v F (1)
Rowley, J. F. (Manchester U), 1949 v Sw, Se, F; 1950 v Ni, I; 1952 v S (6)
Rowley, W. (Stoke C), 1889 v Ni; 1892 v Ni (2)
Royle, J. (Everton), 1971 v Ma; 1973 v Y; (with Manchester C), 1976 v Ni (sub), I; 1977 v Fi, L (6)
Ruddlesdin, H. (Sheffield W), 1904 v W, Ni; 1905 v S (3)
Ruddock, N. (Liverpool), 1995 v Ng (1)
Ruffell, J. W. (West Ham U), 1926 v S; 1927 v Ni; 1929 v S, W, Ni; 1930 v W (6)
Russell, B. B. (Royal Engineers), 1883 v W (1)
Rutherford, J. (Newcastle U), 1904 v S; 1907 v S, Ni, W; 1908 v S, Ni, W, A (2), H, B (11)

Sadler, D. (Manchester U), 1968 v Ni, USSR; 1970 v Ec (sub); 1970 v EG (4)
Sagar, C. (Bury), 1900 v Ni; 1902 v W (2)
Sagar, E. (Everton), 1936 v S, Ni, A, Bel (4)

Salako, J. A. (C Palace), 1991 v Aus (sub), Nz (sub + 1), Mal; 1992 v G (5)
Sandford, E. A. (WBA), 1933 v W (1)
Sandilands, R. R. (Old Westminsters), 1892 v W; 1893 v Ni; 1894 v W; 1895 v W; 1896 v W (5)
Sands, J. (Nottingham F), 1880 v W (1)
Sansom, K. (C Palace), 1979 v W; 1980 v Bul, Ei, Arg, W (sub), Ni, S, Bel, I; (with Arsenal), 1981 v N, R, Sw, Sp, R, Br, W, S, Sw; 1982 v Ni, W, Ho, S, Fi, F, Cz, WG, Sp; 1983 v D, WG, Gr, L, Gr, H, Ni, S; 1984 v D, H, L, F, S, USSR, Br, U, Ch; 1985 v EG, Fi, T, Ni, Ei, R, Fi, S, I, M, WG, US; 1986 v R, T, Ni, Eg, Is, USSR, S, M, Ca, P, Mor, Pol, Para, Arg; 1987 v Se, Ni (2), Y, Sp, T; 1988 v WG, T, Y, Ho, S, Co, Sw, Ei, Ho, USSR (86)
Saunders, F. E. (Swifts), 1888 v W (1)
Savage, A. H. (C Palace), 1876 v S (1)
Sayer, J. (Stoke C), 1887 v Ni (1)
Scales, J. R. (Liverpool), 1995 v J, Se (sub), Br (3)
Scattergood, E. (Derby Co), 1913 v W (1)
Schofield, J. (Stoke C), 1892 v W; 1893 v W; 1895 v Ni (3)
Scholes, P. (Manchester U), 1997 v S.Af (sub), I, Br; 1998 v Mol, Cam, P, S.Ar, Tun, R, Co, Arg; 1999 v Se, Bul, L, F (sub), Pol, Se; 2000 v Pol, S (2), Arg, Br, Uk, Ma, P, G, R (27)
Scott, L. (Arsenal), 1947 v S, W, Ni, Ei, Ho, F, Sw, P; 1948 v S, W, Ni, Bel, Se, I; 1949 v W, Ni, D (17)
Scott, W. R. (Brentford), 1937 v W (1)
Seaman, D. A. (QPR), 1989 v S.Ar, D (sub); 1990 v Cz (sub); (with Arsenal), 1991 v Cam, Ei, T, Arg; 1992 v Cz, H (sub); 1994 v Pol, Ho, Sm, D, N; 1995 v US, R, Ei; 1996 v Co, N, Sw, P, Bul, Cro, H, Sw, S, Ho, Sp, G; 1997 v Mol, Pol, Ge (2), Pol, F, Br; 1998 v Mol, I, P, S.Ar, Tun, R, Co, Arg; 1999 v Se, Bul, L, F, Pol, H, Se, Bul; 2000 v Bel, S (2), Arg, Br, P, G (59)
Seddon, J. (Bolton W), 1923 v F, Se (2); 1924 v Bel; 1927 v W; 1929 v S (6)
Seed, J. M. (Tottenham H), 1921 v Bel; 1923 v W, Ni, Bel; 1925 v S (5)
Settle, J. (Bury), 1899 v S, W, Ni; (with Everton), 1902 v S, Ni; 1903 v Ni (6)
Sewell, J. (Sheffield W), 1952 v Ni, A, Sw; 1953 v Ni; 1954 v H (2) (6)
Sewell, W. R. (Blackburn R), 1924 v W (1)
Shackleton, L. F. (Sunderland), 1949 v W, D; 1950 v W; 1955 v W, WG (5)
Sharp, J. (Everton), 1903 v Ni; 1905 v S (2)
Sharpe, L. S. (Manchester U), 1991 v Ei (sub); 1993 v T (sub), N, US, Br, G; 1994 v Pol, Ho (8)
Shaw, G. E. (WBA), 1932 v S (1)
Shaw, G. L. (Sheffield U), 1959 v S, W, USSR, I; 1963 v W (5)
Shea, D. (Blackburn R), 1914 v W, Ni (2)
Shearer, A. (Southampton), 1992 v F, C, F; (with Blackburn R), 1993 v Sp, N, T; 1994 v Ho, D, Gr, N; 1995 v US, R, Ng, Ei, J, Se, Br; 1996 v Co, N, Sw, P, H (sub), Chn, Sw, S, Ho, Sp, G; (with Newcastle U), 1997 v Mol, Pol, I, Ge, Pol, F, Br; 1998 v Ch (sub), Sw, P, S.Ar, Tun, R, Co, Arg; 1999 v Se, Bul, L, F, Pol, H, Se, Bul; 2000 v L, Pol, Bel, S (2), Arg, Br, Uk, Ma, P, G, R (63)
Shellito, K. J. (Chelsea), 1963 v Cz (1)
Shelton, A. (Notts Co), 1889 v Ni; 1890 v S, W; 1891 v S, W; 1892 v S (6)
Shelton, C. (Notts Rangers), 1888 v Ni (1)
Shepherd, A. (Bolton W), 1906 v S; (with Newcastle U), 1911 v Ni (2)
Sherwood, T. A. (Tottenham H), 1999 v Pol, H, Se (3)
Sheringham, E. P. (Tottenham H), 1993 v Pol, N; 1995 v US, R (sub), Ng (sub), U, J (sub), Se, Br; 1996 v Co (sub), N (sub), Sw, Bul, Cro, H, Sw, S, Ho, Sp, G; 1997 v Ge, M, Ge, S.Af, Pol, I, F (sub), Br; (with Manchester U), 1998 v I, Ch, Sw (sub), P, S.Ar, Tun, R; 1999 v Se (sub), Bul (sub), Bul (38)
Shilton, P. L. (Leicester C), 1971 v EG, W; 1972 v Sw, Ni; 1973 v Y, S (2), Ni, W, Cz, Pol, USSR, I; 1974 v A, Pol, I, W, Ni, S, Arg; (with Stoke C), 1975 v Cy; 1977 v Ni, W; (with Nottingham F), 1978 v W; 1979 v Cz, Se, A; 1980 v Ni, Sp, I; 1981 v N, Sw, R; 1982 v H, Ho, S, F, Cz, K, WG, Sp; (with Southampton), 1983 v D, WG, Gr, W, Gr, H, Ni, S, Aus (3); 1984 v D, H, F, Ni, W, S, USSR, Br, U, Ch; 1985 v EG, Fi, T, Ni, R, Fi, S, I, WG; 1986 v R, T, Ni, Eg, Is, USSR, S, M, Ca, P, Mor, Para, Arg; 1987 v Se, Ni (2), Sp, Br; (with Derby Co), 1988 v WG, T, Y, Ho, S, Co, Sw, Ei, Ho; 1989 v D, Se, Gr, Alb (2), Ch, S, Pol, D; 1990 v Se, Pol, I, Y, Br, Cz, D, U, Tun, Ei, Ho, Eg, Bel, Cam, WG, I (125)
Shimwell, E. (Blackpool), 1949 v Se (1)
Shutt, G. (Stoke C), 1886 v Ni (1)
Silcock, J. (Manchester U), 1921 v S, W; 1923 v Se (3)
Sillett, R. P. (Chelsea), 1955 v F, Sp, P (3)

Simms, E. (Luton T), 1922 v Ni (1)
Simpson, J. (Blackburn R), 1911 v S, W, Ni; 1912 v S, W, Ni; 1913 v S; 1914 v W (8)
Sinton, A. (QPR), 1992 v Pol, C, H (sub), Br, F, Se; 1993 v Sp, T, Br, G; (with Sheffield W), 1994 v Ho (sub), Sm (12)
Slater, W. J. (Wolverhampton W), 1955 v W, WG; 1958 v S, P, Y, USSR (3), Br, A; 1959 v USSR; 1960 v S (12)
Smalley, T. (Wolverhampton W), 1937 v W (1)
Smart, T. (Aston Villa), 1921 v S; 1924 v S, W; 1926 v Ni; 1930 v W (5)
Smith, A. (Nottingham F), 1891 v S, W; 1893 v Ni (3)
Smith, A. K. (Oxford University), 1872 v S (1)
Smith, A. M. (Arsenal), 1989 v S.Ar (sub), Gr, Alb (sub), Pol (sub); 1991 v T, USSR, Arg; 1992 v G, T, Pol (sub), H (sub), D, Se (sub) (13)
Smith, B. (Tottenham H), 1921 v S; 1922 v W (2)
Smith, C. E. (C Palace), 1876 v S (1)
Smith, G. O. (Oxford University), 1893 v Ni; 1894 v W, S; 1895 v W; 1896 v Ni, W, S; (with Old Carthusians), 1897 v Ni, W, S; 1898 v Ni, W, S; (with Corinthians), 1899 v Ni, W, S; 1899 v Ni, W, S; 1901 v S (20)
Smith, H. (Reading), 1905 v W, S; 1906 v W, Ni (4)
Smith, J. (WBA), 1920 v Ni; 1923 v Ni (2)
Smith, Joe (Bolton W), 1913 v Ni; 1914 v S, W; 1920 v W, Ni (5)
Smith, J. C. R. (Millwall), 1939 v Ni, N (2)
Smith, J. W. (Portsmouth), 1932 v Ni, W, Sp (3)
Smith, Leslie (Brentford), 1939 v R (1)
Smith, Lionel (Arsenal), 1951 v W; 1952 v W, Ni; 1953 v W, S, Bel (6)
Smith, R. A. (Tottenham H), 1961 v Ni, W, S, L, P, Sp; 1962 v S; 1963 v S, F, Br, Cz, EG; 1964 v W, Ni, R of W (15)
Smith, S. (Aston Villa), 1895 v S (1)
Smith, S. C. (Leicester C), 1936 v Ni (1)
Smith, T. (Birmingham C), 1960 v W, Se (2)
Smith, T. (Liverpool), 1971 v W (1)
Smith, W. H. (Huddersfield T), 1922 v W, S; 1928 v S (3)
Sorby, T. H. (Thursday Wanderers, Sheffield), 1879 v W (1)
Southgate, G. (Aston Villa), 1996 v P (sub), Bul, H (sub), Chn, Sw, S, Ho, Sp, G; 1997 v Mol, Pol, Ge, M, Ge (sub), S.Af, Pol, I, F, Br; 1998 v Mol, I, Cam, Sw, S.Ar, Mor, Tun, Arg (sub); 1999 v Se, Bul, L, Bul; 2000 v Bel, S, Arg, Uk, Ma (sub), R (sub) (37)
Southworth, J. (Blackburn R), 1889 v W; 1891 v W; 1892 v S (3)
Sparks, F. J. (Herts Rangers), 1879 v S; (with Clapham Rovers), 1880 v S, W (3)
Spence, J. W. (Manchester U), 1926 v Bel; 1927 v Ni (2)
Spence, R. (Chelsea), 1936 v A, Bel (2)
Spencer, C. W. (Newcastle U), 1924 v S; 1925 v W (2)
Spencer, H. (Aston Villa), 1897 v S, W; 1900 v W; 1903 v Ni; 1905 v W, S (6)
Spiksley, F. (Sheffield W), 1893 v S, W; 1894 v S, Ni; 1896 v Ni; 1898 v S, W (7)
Spilsbury, B. W. (Cambridge University), 1885 v Ni; 1886 v Ni, S (3)
Spink, N. (Aston Villa), 1983 v Aus (sub) (1)
Spouncer, W. A. (Nottingham F), 1900 v W (1)
Springett, R. D. G. (Sheffield W), 1960 v Ni, S, Y, Sp, H; 1961 v Ni, S, L, P, Sp, M, I, A; 1962 v W, Ni, S, A, Sw, Pe, L, P, H, Arg, Bul, Br; 1963 v Ni, W, F (2), Sw; 1966 v W, A, N (33)
Sproston, B. (Leeds U), 1937 v W; 1938 v S, W, Ni, Cz, G, Sw, F; (with Tottenham H), 1939 v W, R of E; (with Manchester C), N (11)
Squire, R. T. (Cambridge University), 1886 v S, W, Ni (3)
Stanbrough, M. H. (Old Carthusians), 1895 v W (1)
Staniforth, R. (Huddersfield T), 1954 v S, H, Y, Bel, Sw, U; 1955 v W, WG (8)
Starling, R. W. (Sheffield W), 1933 v S; (with Aston Villa), 1937 v S (2)
Statham, D. (WBA), 1983 v W, Aus (2) (3)
Steele, F. C. (Stoke C), 1937 v S, W, Ni, N, Se, Fi (6)
Stein, B. (Luton T), 1984 v F (1)
Stephenson, C. (Huddersfield T), 1924 v W (1)
Stephenson, G. T. (Derby Co), 1928 v F, Bel; (with Sheffield W), 1931 v F (3)
Stephenson, J. E. (Leeds U), 1938 v S; 1939 v Ni (2)
Stepney, A. C. (Manchester U), 1968 v Se (1)
Sterland, M. (Sheffield W), 1989 v S.Ar (1)
Steven, T. M. (Everton), 1985 v Ni, Ei, R, Fi, I, US (sub); 1986 v T (sub), Eg, USSR, M (sub), Pol, Para, Arg; 1987 v Se, Y (sub), Sp (sub); 1988 v T, Y, Ho, H, S, Sw, Ho, USSR; 1989 v S; (with Rangers), 1990 v Cz, Cam (sub), WG (sub), I; 1991 v Cam; (with Marseille), 1992 v G, C, Br, Fi, D, F (36)

Stevens, G. A. (Tottenham H), 1985 v Fi (sub), T (sub), Ni; 1986 v S (sub), M (sub), Mor (sub), Para (sub) (7)
Stevens, M. G. (Everton), 1985 v I, WG; 1986 v R, T, Ni, Eg, Is, S, Ca, P, Mor, Pol, Para, Arg; 1987 v Br, S; 1988 v T, Y, Is, Ho, H (sub), S, Sw, Ei, Ho, USSR; (with Rangers), 1989 v D, Se, Gr, Alb (2), S, Pol; 1990 v Se, Pol, I, Br, D, Tun, Ei, I; 1991 v USSR; 1992 v C, H, Br, Fi (46)
Stewart, J. (Sheffield W), 1907 v S, W; (with Newcastle U), 1911 v S (3)
Stewart, P. A. (Tottenham H), 1992 v G (sub), Cz (sub), C (sub) (3)
Stiles, N. P. (Manchester U), 1965 v S, H, Y, Se; 1966 v W, Ni, S, A, Sp, Pol (2), WG (2), N, D, U, M, F, Arg, P; 1967 v Ni, W, S, Cz; 1968 v USSR; 1969 v R; 1970 v Ni, S (28)
Stoker, J. (Birmingham), 1933 v W; 1934 v S, H (3)
Stone, S. B. (Nottingham F), 1996 v N (sub), Sw (sub), P, Bul, Cro, Chn (sub), Sw (sub), S (sub), Sp (sub) (9)
Storer, H. (Derby Co), 1924 v F; 1928 v Ni (2)
Storey, P. E. (Arsenal), 1971 v Gr, Ni, S; 1972 v Sw, WG, W, Ni, S; 1973 v W (3), Y, S (2), Ni, Cz, Pol, USSR, I (19)
Storey-Moore, I. (Nottingham F), 1970 v Ho (1)
Strange, A. H. (Sheffield W), 1930 v S, A, G; 1931 v S, W, Ni, F, Bel; 1932 v S, W, Ni, Sp; 1933 v S, Ni, A, I, Sw; 1934 v Ni, W, F (20)
Stratford, A. H. (Wanderers), 1874 v S (1)
Streten, B. (Luton T), 1950 v Ni (1)
Sturgess, A. (Sheffield U), 1911 v Ni; 1914 v S (2)
Summerbee, M. G. (Manchester C), 1968 v S, Sp, WG; 1972 v Sw, WG (sub), W, Ni; 1973 v USSR (sub) (8)
Sunderland, A. (Arsenal), 1980 v Aus (1)
Sutcliffe, J. W. (Bolton W), 1893 v W; 1895 v S, Ni; 1901 v S; (with Millwall), 1903 v W (5)
Sutton, C. R. (Blackburn R), 1998 v Cam (sub) (1)
Swan, P. (Sheffield W), 1960 v Y, Sp, H; 1961 v Ni, W, S, L, P, Sp, M, I, A; 1962 v W, Ni, S, A, Sw, L, P (19)
Swepstone, H. A. (Pilgrims), 1880 v S; 1882 v S, W; 1883 v S, W, Ni (6)
Swift, F. V. (Manchester C), 1947 v S, W, Ni, Ei, Ho, F, Sw, P; 1948 v S, W, Ni, Bel, Se, I; 1949 v S, W, Ni, D, N (19)

Tait, G. (Birmingham Excelsior), 1881 v W (1)
Talbot, B. (Ipswich T), 1977 v Ni (sub), S, Br, Arg, U; (with Arsenal), 1980 v Aus (6)
Tambling, R. V. (Chelsea), 1963 v W, F; 1966 v Y (3)
Tate, J. T. (Aston Villa), 1931 v F, Bel; 1933 v W (3)
Taylor, E. (Blackpool), 1954 v H (1)
Taylor, E. H. (Huddersfield T), 1923 v S, W, Ni, Bel; 1924 v S, Ni, F; 1926 v S (8)
Taylor, J. G. (Fulham), 1951 v Arg, P (2)
Taylor, P. H. (Liverpool), 1948 v W, Ni, Se (3)
Taylor, P. J. (C Palace), 1976 v W (sub+1), Ni, S (4)
Taylor, T. (Manchester U), 1953 v Arg, Ch, U; 1954 v Bel, Sw; 1956 v S, Br, Se, Fi, WG; 1957 v Ni, Y (sub), D (2), Ei (2); 1958 v W, Ni, F (19)
Temple, D. W. (Everton), 1965 v WG (1)
Thickett, H. (Sheffield U), 1899 v S, W (2)
Thomas, D. (Coventry C), 1983 v Aus (1+1 sub) (2)
Thomas, D. (QPR), 1975 v Cz (sub), P, Cy (sub+1), W, S (sub); 1976 v Cz (sub), P (sub) (8)
Thomas, G. R. (C Palace), 1991 v T, USSR, Arg, Aus, Nz (2), Mal; 1992 v Pol, F (9)
Thomas, M. L. (Arsenal), 1989 v S.Ar; 1990 v Y (2)
Thompson, P. (Liverpool), 1964 v P (2), Ei, US, Br, Arg; 1965 v Ni, W, S, Bel, Ho; 1966 v Ni; 1968 v Ni, WG; 1970 v S, Ho (sub) (16)
Thompson, P. B. (Liverpool), 1976 v W (2), Ni, S, Br, I, Fi; 1977 v Fi; 1979 v Ei (sub), Cz, Ni, S, Bul, Se (sub), A; 1980 v D, Ni, Bul, Ei, Sp (2), Arg, W, S, Bel, I; 1981 v N, R, H; 1982 v N, H, W, Ho, S, Fi, F, Cz, K, WG, Sp; 1983 v WG, Gr (42)
Thompson, T. (Aston Villa), 1952 v W; (with Preston NE), 1957 v S (2)
Thomson, R. A. (Wolverhampton W), 1964 v Ni, US, P, Arg; 1965 v Bel, Ho, Ni, W (8)
Thornewell, G. (Derby Co), 1923 v Se (2); 1924 v F; 1925 v F (4)
Thornley, I. (Manchester C), 1907 v W (1)
Tilson, S. F. (Manchester C), 1934 v H, Cz; 1935 v W; 1936 v Ni (4)
Titmuss, F. (Southampton), 1922 v W; 1923 v W (2)
Todd, C. (Derby Co), 1972 v Ni; 1974 v P, W, Ni, S, Arg, EG, Bul, Y; 1975 v P (sub), WG, Cy (2), Ni, W, S; 1976 v Sw, Cz, P, Ni, S, Br, Fi; 1977 v Ei, Fi, Ho (sub), Ni (27)
Toone, G. (Notts Co), 1892 v S, W (2)
Topham, A. G. (Casuals), 1894 v W (1)

Topham, R. (Wolverhampton W), 1893 v Ni; (with Casuals) 1894 v W (2)
Towers, M. A. (Sunderland), 1976 v W, Ni (sub), I (3)
Townley, W. J. (Blackburn R), 1889 v W; 1890 v Ni (2)
Townrow, J. E. (Clapton Orient), 1925 v S; 1926 v W (2)
Tremelling, D. R. (Birmingham), 1928 v W (1)
Tresadern, J. (West Ham U), 1923 v S, Se (2)
Tueart, D. (Manchester C), 1975 v Cy (sub), Ni; 1977 v Fi, Ni, W (sub), S (sub) (6)
Tunstall, F. E. (Sheffield U), 1923 v S; 1924 v S, W, Ni, F; 1925 v Ni, S (7)
Turnbull, R. J. (Bradford), 1920 v Ni (1)
Turner, A. (Southampton), 1900 v Ni; 1901 v Ni (2)
Turner, H. (Huddersfield T), 1931 v F, Bel (2)
Turner, J. A. (Bolton W), 1893 v W; (with Stoke C) 1895 v Ni; (with Derby Co) 1898 v Ni (3)
Tweedy, G. J. (Grimsby T), 1937 v H (1)

Ufton, D. G. (Charlton Ath), 1954 v R of E (1)
Underwood A. (Stoke C), 1891 v Ni; 1892 v Ni (2)
Unsworth, D. G. (Everton), 1995 v J (1)
Urwin, T. (Middlesbrough), 1923 v Se (2); 1924 v Bel; (with Newcastle U), 1926 v W (4)
Utley, G. (Barnsley), 1913 v Ni (1)

Vaughton, O. H. (Aston Villa), 1882 v S, W, Ni; 1884 v S, W (5)
Veitch, C. C. M. (Newcastle U), 1906 v S, W, Ni; 1907 v W; 1909 v W (6)
Veitch, J. G. (Old Westminsters), 1894 v W (1)
Venables, T. F. (Chelsea), 1965 v Ho, Bel (2)
Venison, B. (Newcastle U), 1995 v US, U (2)
Vidal, R. W. S. (Oxford University), 1873 v S (1)
Viljoen, C. (Ipswich T), 1975 v Ni, W (2)
Viollet, D. S. (Manchester U), 1960 v H; 1962 v L (2)
Von Donop (Royal Engineers), 1873 v S; 1875 v S (2)

Wace, H. (Wanderers), 1878 v S; 1879 v S, W (3)
Waddle, C. R. (Newcastle U), 1985 v Ei, R (sub), Fi (sub), S (sub), I, M (sub), WG, US; (with Tottenham H), 1986 v R, T, Ni, Is, USSR, S, M, Ca, P, Mor, Pol (sub), Arg (sub); 1987 v Se (sub), Ni (2), Y, Sp, T, Br, S; 1988 v WG, Is, H, S (sub), Co, Sw (sub), Ei, Ho (sub); 1989 v Se, S.Ar, Alb (2), Ch, S, Pol, D (sub); (with Marseille), 1990 v Se, Pol, I, Y, Br, D, U, Tun, Ei, Ho, Eg, Bel, Cam, WG, I (sub); 1991 v H (sub), Pol (sub); 1992 v T (62)
Wadsworth, S. J. (Huddersfield T), 1922 v S; 1923 v S, Bel; 1924 v S, Ni; 1925 v S, Ni; 1926 v W; 1927 v Ni (9)
Wainscoat, W. R. (Leeds U), 1929 v S (1)
Waiters, A. K. (Blackpool), 1964 v Ei, Br; 1965 v W, Bel, Ho (5)
Walden, F. I. (Tottenham H), 1914 v S; 1922 v W (2)
Walker, D. S. (Nottingham F), 1989 v D (sub), Se (sub), Gr, Alb (2), Ch, S, Pol, D; 1990 v Se, Pol, I, Y, Br, Cz, D, U, Tun, Ei, Ho, Eg, Bel, Cam, WG, I; 1991 v H, Pol, Ei (2), Cam, T, Arg, Aus, Nz (2), Mal; 1992 v T, Pol, F, Cz, C, H, Br, Fi, D, F, Se; (with Sampdoria), 1993 v Sp, N, T, Sm, T, Ho, Pol, N, US (sub), Br, G; (with Sheffield W), 1994 v Sm (59)
Walker, I. M. (Tottenham H), 1996 v H (sub), Chn (sub); 1997 v I (3)
Walker, W. H. (Aston Villa), 1921 v Ni; 1922 v Ni, W, S; 1923 v Se (2); 1924 v S; 1925 v Ni, W, S, Bel, F; 1926 v Ni, W, S; 1927 v Ni, W; 1933 v A (18)
Wall, G. (Manchester U), 1907 v W; 1908 v Ni; 1909 v S; 1910 v W, S; 1912 v S; 1913 v Ni (7)
Wallace, C. W. (Aston Villa), 1913 v W; 1914 v Ni; 1920 v S (3)
Wallace, D. L. (Southampton), 1986 v Eg (1)
Walsh, P. (Luton T), 1983 v Aus (2 + 1 sub); 1984 v F, W (5)
Walters, A. M. (Cambridge University), 1885 v S, N; 1886 v S; 1887 v S, W; (with Old Carthusians), 1889 v S, W; 1890 v S, W (9)
Walters, K. M. (Rangers), 1991 v Nz (1)
Walters, P. M. (Oxford University), 1885 v S, Ni; (with Old Carthusians), 1886 v S, W; 1887 v S, W; 1888 v S, Ni; 1889 v S, W; 1890 v S, W (13)
Walton, N. (Blackburn R), 1890 v Ni (1)
Ward, J. T. (Blackburn Olympic), 1885 v W (1)
Ward, P. (Brighton & HA), 1980 v Aus (sub) (1)
Ward, T. V. (Derby Co), 1948 v Bel; 1949 v N (2)
Waring, T. (Aston Villa), 1931 v F, Bel; 1932 v S, W, Ni (5)
Warner, C. (Upton Park), 1878 v S (1)
Warren, B. (Derby Co), 1906 v S, W, Ni; 1907 v S, W, Ni; 1908 v S, W, Ni; (with Chelsea), 1909 v S, Ni, W, H (2), A; 1911 v S, Ni, W (22)
Waterfield, G. S. (Burnley), 1927 v W (1)

Watson, D. (Norwich C), 1984 v Br, U, Ch; 1985 v M, US (sub); 1986 v S; (with Everton), 1987 v Ni; 1988 v Is, Ho, S, Sw (sub), USSR (12)

Watson, D. V. (Sunderland), 1974 v P, S (sub), Arg, EG, Bul, Y; 1975 v Cz, P, WG, Cy (2), Ni, W, S; (with Manchester C), 1976 v Sw, Cz (sub), P; 1977 v Ho, L, Ni, W, S, Br, Arg, U; 1978 v Sw, L, I, WG, Br, W, Ni, S, H; 1979 v D, Ei, Cz, Ni (2), W, S, Bul, Se, A; (with Werder Bremen), 1980 v D; (with Southampton), Ni, Bul, Ei, Sp (2), Arg, Ni, S, Bel, I; 1981 v N, R, Sw, R, W, S, Sw, H; (with Stoke C), 1982 v Ni. Ic (65)

Watson, V. M. (West Ham U), 1923 v W, S; 1930 v S, G, A (5)

Watson, W. (Burnley), 1913 v S; 1914 v Ni; 1920 v Ni (3)

Watson, W. (Sunderland), 1950 v Ni, I; 1951 v W, Y (4)

Weaver, S. (Newcastle U), 1932 v S, 1933 v S, Ni (3)

Webb, G. W. (West Ham U), 1911 v S, W (2)

Webb, N. J. (Nottingham F), 1988 v WG (sub), T, Y, Is, Ho, S, Sw, Ei, USSR (sub); 1989 v D, Se, Gr, Alb (2), Ch, S, Pol, D; (with Manchester U), 1990 v Se, I (sub); 1992 v F, H, Br (sub), Fi, D (sub), Se (26)

Webster, M. (Middlesbrough), 1930 v S, A, G (3)

Wedlock, W. J. (Bristol C), 1907 v S, Ni, W; 1908 v S, Ni, W, A (2), H, B; 1909 v S, W, Ni, H (2), A; 1910 v S, W, Ni; 1911 v S, W, Ni; 1912 v S, W, Ni; 1914 v W (26)

Weir, D. (Bolton W), 1889 v S, Ni (2)

Welch, R. de C. (Wanderers), 1872 v S; (with Harrow Chequers), 1874 v S (2)

Weller, K. (Leicester C), 1974 v W, Ni, S, Arg (4)

Welsh, D. (Charlton Ath), 1938 v G, Sw; 1939 v R (3)

West, G. (Everton), 1969 v W, Bul, M (3)

Westwood, R. W. (Bolton W), 1935 v S, W, Ho; 1936 v Ni, G; 1937 v W (6)

Whateley, O. (Aston Villa), 1883 v S, Ni (2)

Wheeler, J. E. (Bolton W), 1955 v Ni (1)

Wheldon, G. F. (Aston Villa), 1897 v Ni; 1898 v S, Ni (4)

White, D. (Manchester C), 1993 v Sp (1)

White, T. A. (Everton), 1933 v I (1)

Whitehead, J. (Accrington), 1893 v W; (with Blackburn R), 1894 v Ni (2)

Whitfeld, H. (Old Etonians), 1879 v W (1)

Whitham, M. (Sheffield U), 1892 v Ni (1)

Whitworth, S. (Leicester C), 1975 v WG, Cy, Ni, W, S; 1976 v Sw, P (7)

Whymark, T. J. (Ipswich T), 1978 v L (sub) (1)

Widdowson, S. W. (Nottingham F), 1880 v S (1)

Wignall, F. (Nottingham F), 1965 v W, Ho (2)

Wilcox, J. M. (Blackburn R), 1996 v Ni; 1999 v F (sub); (with Leeds U), 2000 v Arg (3)

Wilkes, A. (Aston Villa), 1901 v S, W; 1902 v S, W, Ni (5)

Wilkins, R. G. (Chelsea), 1976 v I; 1977 v Ei, Fi, Ni, Br, Arg, U; 1978 v Sw (sub), L, I, WG, W, Ni, S, H; 1979 v D, Ei, Cz, Ni, W, S, Bul, Se (sub), A; (with Manchester U), 1980 v D, Ni, Bul, Sp (2), Arg, W (sub), Ni, S, Bel, I; 1981 v Sp (sub), R, Br, W, S, Sw, H (sub); 1982 v Ni, W, Ho, S, Fi, F, Cz, K, WG, Sp; 1983 v D, WG; 1984 v D, Ni, W, S, USSR, Br, U, Ch; (with AC Milan), 1985 v EG, Fi, T, Ni, Ei, R, Fi, S, I, M; 1986 v T, Ni, Is, Eg, USSR, S, M, Ca, P, Mor; 1987 v Se, Y (sub) (84)

Wilkinson, B. (Sheffield U), 1904 v S (1)

Wilkinson, L. R. (Oxford University), 1891 v W (1)

Williams, B. F. (Wolverhampton W), 1949 v F; 1950 v S, W, Ei, I, P, Bel, Ch, US, Sp; 1951 v Ni, W, S, Y, Arg, P; 1952 v W, F; 1955 v S, WG, F, Sp, P; 1956 v W (24)

Williams, O. (Clapton Orient), 1923 v W, Ni (2)

Williams, S. (Southampton), 1983 v Aus (1+1 sub); 1984 v F; 1985 v EG, Fi, T (6)

Williams, W. (WBA), 1897 v Ni; 1898 v W, Ni, S; 1899 v W, Ni (6)

Williamson, E. C. (Arsenal), 1923 v Se (2) (2)

Williamson, R. G. (Middlesbrough), 1905 v Ni; 1911 v Ni, S, W; 1912 v S, W; 1913 v Ni (7)

Willingham, C. K. (Huddersfield T), 1937 v Fi; 1938 v S, G, Sw, F; 1939 v S, W, Ni, R of E, N, I, Y (12)

Willis, A. (Tottenham H), 1952 v F (1)

Wilshaw, D. J. (Wolverhampton W), 1954 v W, Sw, U; 1955 v S, F, Sp, P; 1956 v W, Ni, Fi, WG; 1957 v Ni (12)

Wilson, C. P. (Hendon), 1884 v S, W (2)

Wilson, C. W. (Oxford University), 1879 v W; 1881 v S (2)

Wilson, G. (Sheffield W), 1921 v S, W, Bel; 1922 v S, Ni; 1923 v S, W, Ni, Bel; 1924 v W, Ni, F (12)

Wilson, G. P. (Corinthians), 1900 v S, W (2)

Wilson, R. (Huddersfield T), 1960 v S, Y, Sp, H; 1962 v W, Ni, S, A, Sw, Pe, P, H, Arg, Bul, Br; 1963 v Ni, F, Br, Cz, EG, Sw; 1964 v W, S, R of W, U, P (2), Ei, Br, Arg; (with

Everton), 1965 v S, H, Y, WG, Se; 1966 v WG (sub), W, Ni, A, Sp, Pol (2), Y, Fi, D, U, M, F, Arg, P, WG; 1967 v Ni, W, S, Cz, A; 1968 v Ni, S, USSR (2), Sp (2), Y (63)

Wilson, T. (Huddersfield T), 1928 v S (1)

Winckworth, W. N. (Old Westminsters), 1892 v W; 1893 v Ni (2)

Windridge, J. E. (Chelsea), 1908 v S, W, Ni, A (2), H, B; 1909 v Ni (8)

Wingfield-Stratford, C. V. (Royal Engineers), 1877 v S (1)

Winterburn, N. (Arsenal), 1990 v I (sub); 1993 v G (sub) (2)

Wise, D. F. (Chelsea), 1991 v T, USSR, Aus (sub), Nz (2); 1994 v N; 1995 v R (sub), Ng; 1996 v Co, N, P, H (sub); 2000 v Bel (sub), Arg, Br, Ma, P (sub), G, R (19)

Withe, P. (Aston Villa), 1981 v Br, W, S; 1982 v N (sub), W, Ic; 1983 v H, Ni, S; 1984 v H (sub); 1985 v T (11)

Wollaston, C. H. R. (Wanderers), 1874 v S; 1875 v S; 1877 v S; 1880 v S (4)

Wolstenholme, S. (Everton), 1904 v S; (with Blackburn R), 1905 v W, Ni (3)

Wood, H. (Wolverhampton W), 1890 v S, W; 1896 v S (3)

Wood, R. E. (Manchester U), 1955 v Ni, W; 1956 v Fi (3)

Woodcock, A. S. (Nottingham F), 1978 v Ni; 1979 v Ei (sub), Cz, Bul (sub), Se; 1980 v Ni; (with Cologne), Bul, Ei, Sp (2), Arg, Bel, I; 1981 v N, R, Sw, R, W (sub), S; 1982 v Ni (sub), Ho, Fi (sub), WG (sub), Sp; (with Arsenal), 1983 v WG (sub), Gr, L, Gr; 1984 v L, F (sub), Ni, W, S, Br, U (sub); 1985 v EG, Fi, T, Ni; 1986 v R (sub), T (sub), Is (sub) (42)

Woodgate, J. S. (Leeds U), 1999 v Bul (1)

Woodger, G. (Oldham Ath), 1911 v Ni (1)

Woodhall, G. (WBA), 1888 v S, W (2)

Woolley, V. R. (Chelsea), 1937 v S, N, Se, Fi; 1938 v S, W, Ni, Cz, G, Se, F; 1939 v S, W, Ni, R of E, N, I, R, Y (19)

Woods, C. C. E. (Norwich C), 1985 v US; 1986 v Eg (sub), Is (sub), Ca (sub); (with Rangers), 1987 v Y, Sp (sub), Ni (sub), T, S; 1988 v Is, H, Sw (sub), USSR; 1989 v D (sub); 1990 v Br (sub), D (sub); 1991 v H, Pol, Ei, USSR, Aus, Nz (2), Mal; (with Sheffield W), 1992 v G, T, Pol, F, C, Br, Fi, D, F, Se; 1993 v Sp, N, T, Sm, T, Ho, Pol, N, US (43)

Woodward, V. J. (Tottenham H), 1903 v S, W, Ni; 1904 v S, Ni; 1905 v S, W, Ni; 1907 v S; 1908 v S, W, Ni, A (2), H, B; 1909 v W, Ni, H (2), A; (with Chelsea), 1910 v Ni; 1911 v W (23)

Woosnam, M. (Manchester C), 1922 v W (1)

Worrall, F. (Portsmouth), 1935 v Ho; 1937 v Ni (2)

Worthington, F. S. (Leicester C), 1974 v Ni (sub), S, Arg, EG, Bul, Y; 1975 v Cz, P (sub) (8)

Wreford-Brown, C. (Oxford University), 1889 v Ni; (with Old Carthusians), 1894 v W; 1895 v W; 1898 v S (4)

Wright, E. G. D. (Cambridge University), 1906 v W (1)

Wright, I. E. (C Palace), 1991 v Cam, Ei (sub), USSR, Nz; (with Arsenal), 1992 v H (sub); 1993 v N, T (2), Pol (sub), N (sub), US (sub), Br, G (sub); 1994 v Pol, Ho (sub), Sm, Gr (sub), N (sub); 1995 v US (sub), R; 1997 v Ge (sub), I (sub), M (sub), S.Af, I, F, Br (sub); 1998 v Mol, I, S.Ar (sub), Mor; (with West Ham U), 1999 v L (sub), CzR (33)

Wright, J. D. (Newcastle U), 1939 v N (1)

Wright, M. (Southampton), 1984 v W; 1985 v EG, Fi, T, Ei, R, I, WG; 1986 v R, T, Ni, Eg, USSR; 1987 v Y, S; (with Derby Co), 1988 v Is, Ho (sub), Co, Sw, Ei, Ho; 1990 v Cz (sub), Tun (sub), Ho, Eg, Bel, Cam, WG, I; 1991 v H, Pol, Ei (2), Cam, USSR, Arg, Aus, Nz, Mal; (with Liverpool), 1992 v F, Fi; 1993 v Sp; 1996 v Cro, H (45)

Wright, R. I. (Ipswich T), 2000 v Ma (1)

Wright, T. J. (Everton), 1968 v USSR; 1969 v R (2), M (sub), U, Br; 1970 v W, Ho, Bel, R (sub), Br (11)

Wright, W. A. (Wolverhampton W), 1947 v S, W, Ni, Ei, Ho, F, Sw, P; 1948 v S, W, Ni, Bel, Se, I; 1949 v S, W, Ni, D, Sw, Se, N, F; 1950 v S, W, Ni, Ei, I, P, Bel, Ch, US, Sp; 1951 v Ni, S, Arg; 1952 v W, Ni, S, F, A (2), I, Sw; 1953 v Ni, W, S, Bel, Arg, Ch, U, US; 1954 v W, Ni, S, R of E, H (2), Y, Bel, Sw, U; 1955 v W, Ni, S, WG, F, Sp, P; 1956 v Ni, W, S, Br, Se, Fi, WG, D, Sp; 1957 v S, W, Ni, Y, D (2), Ei (2); 1958 v W, Ni, S, P, Y, USSR (3), Br, A, F; 1959 v W, Ni, S, USSR, I, Br, Pe, M, US (105)

Wylie, J. S. (Wanderers), 1878 v S (1)

Yates, J. (Burnley), 1889 v Ni (1)

York, R. E. (Aston Villa), 1922 v S; 1926 v S (2)

Young, A. (Huddersfield T), 1933 v W; 1937 v S, H, N, Se; 1938 v G, Se, F; 1939 v W (9)

Young, G. M. (Sheffield W), 1965 v W (1)

R. E. Evans also played for Wales against E, Ni, S; J. Reynolds also played for Ireland against E, W, S.

NORTHERN IRELAND

Aherne, T. (Belfast C), 1947 v E; 1948 v S; 1949 v W; (with Luton T), 1950 v W (4)

Alexander, T. E. (Cliftonville), 1895 v S (1)

Allan, C. (Cliftonville), 1936 v E (1)

Allen, J. (Limavady), 1887 v E (1)

Anderson, T. (Manchester U), 1973 v Cy, E, S, W; 1974 v Bul, P; (with Swindon T), 1975 v S (sub); 1976 v Is; 1977 v Ho, Bel, WG, E, S, W, Ic; 1978 v Ic, Ho, Bel; (with Peterborough U), S, E, W; 1979 v D (sub) (22)

Anderson, W. (Linfield), 1898 v W, E, S; (with Cliftonville), 1899 v S (4)

Andrews, W. (Glentoran), 1908 v S; (with Grimsby T), 1913 v E, S (3)

Armstrong, G. J. (Tottenham H), 1977 v WG, E, W (sub), Ic (sub); 1978 v Bel, S, E, W; 1979 v Ei, D, Bul, E, Bul, E, S, W, D; 1980 v E, Ei, Is, S, E, W, Aus (3); 1981 v Se; (with Watford), P, S, P, S, Se; 1982 v S, Is, E, F, W, Y, Hon, Sp, A, F; 1983 v A, T, Alb, S, E, W; (with Real Mallorca), 1984 v A, WG, E, W, Fi; 1985 v R, Fi, E, Sp; (with WBA), 1986 v T, R (sub), E (sub), F (sub); (with Chesterfield), D (sub), Br (sub) (63)

Baird, G. (Distillery), 1896 v S, E, W (3)

Baird, H. C. (Huddersfield T), 1939 v E (1)

Balfe, J. (Shelbourne), 1909 v E; 1910 v W (2)

Bambrick, J. (Linfield), 1929 v W, S, E; 1930 v W, S, E; 1932 v W; (with Chelsea), 1935 v W; 1936 v E, S; 1938 v W (11)

Banks, S. J. (Cliftonville), 1937 v W (1)

Barr, H. H. (Linfield), 1962 v E; (with Coventry C), 1963 v E, Pol (3)

Barron, J. H. (Cliftonville), 1894 v E, W, S; 1895 v S; 1896 v S; 1897 v E, W (7)

Barry, J. (Cliftonville), 1888 v W, S; 1889 v E (3)

Barry, J. (Bohemians), 1900 v S (1)

Baxter, R. A. (Distillery), 1887 v S (1)

Baxter, S. N. (Cliftonville), 1887 v W (1)

Bennett, L. V. (Dublin University), 1889 v W (1)

Best, G. (Manchester U), 1964 v W, U; 1965 v E, Ho (2), S, Sw (2), Alb; 1966 v S, E, Alb; 1967 v E; 1968 v S; 1969 v E, S, W, T; 1970 v S, E, W, USSR; 1971 v Cy (2), Sp, E, S, W; 1972 v USSR, Sp; 1973 v Bul; 1974 v P; (with Fulham), 1977 v Ho, Bel, WG; 1978 v Ic, Ho (37)

Bingham, W. L. (Sunderland), 1951 v F; 1952 v E, S, W; 1953 v E, S, F, W; 1954 v E, S, W; 1955 v E, S, W; 1956 v E, S, W; 1957 v E, S, W, P (2), I; 1958 v S, E, W, I (2), Arg, Cz (2), WG, F; (with Luton T), 1959 v E, S, W, Sp; 1960 v S, E, W; (with Everton), 1961 v E, S, WG (2), Gr, I; 1962 v E, Gr; 1963 v E, S, Pol (2), Sp; (with Port Vale), 1964 v S, E, Sp (56)

Black, K. T. (Luton T), 1988 v Fr (sub), Ma (sub); 1989 v Ei, H, Sp (2), Ch (sub); 1990 v H, N, U; 1991 v Y (2), D, A, Pol, Fa; (with Nottingham F), 1992 v Fa, A, D, S, Li, G; 1993 v Sp, D (sub), Alb, Ei (sub), Sp; 1994 v D (sub), Ei (sub), R (sub) (30)

Black, T. (Glentoran), 1901 v E (1)

Blair, H. (Portadown), 1931 v S; 1932 v S; (with Swansea), 1934 v S (3)

Blair, J. (Cliftonville), 1907 v W, E, S; 1908 v E, S (5)

Blair, R. V. (Oldham Ath), 1975 v Se (sub), S (sub), W; 1976 v Se, Is (5)

Blanchflower, J. (Manchester U), 1954 v W; 1955 v E, S; 1956 v S, W; 1957 v S, E, P; 1958 v S, E, I (2) (12)

Blanchflower, R. D. (Barnsley), 1950 v S, W; 1951 v E, S; (with Aston Villa), F; 1952 v W; 1953 v E, S, W, F; 1954 v E, S, W; 1955 v E, S; (with Tottenham H), W; 1956 v E, S, W; 1957 v E, S, W, I, P (2); 1958 v E, S, W, I (2), Cz (2), Arg, F, WG; 1959 v E, S, W, Sp; 1960 v E, S, W; 1961 v E, S, W, WG (2); 1962 v E, S, W, Gr, Ho; 1963 v E, S, Pol (2) (56)

Bookman, L. J. O. (Bradford C), 1914 v W; (with Luton T), 1921 v S, W; 1922 v E (4)

Bothwell, A. W. (Ards), 1926 v S, E, W; 1927 v E, W (5)

Bowler, G. C. (Hull C), 1950 v E, S, W (3)

Boyle, P. (Sheffield U), 1901 v E; 1902 v E; 1903 v S, W; 1904 v É (5)

Braithwaite, R. M. (Linfield), 1962 v W; 1963 v P, Sp; (with Middlesbrough), 1964 v W, U; 1965 v E, S, Sw (2), Ho (10)

Breen, T. (Belfast C), 1935 v E, W; 1937 v E, S; (with Manchester U), 1937 v W; 1938 v E, S; 1939 v W, S (9)

Brennan, B. (Bohemians), 1912 v W (1)

Brennan, R. A. (Luton T), 1949 v W; (with Birmingham C), 1950 v E, S, W; (with Fulham), 1951 v E (5)

Briggs, W. R. (Manchester U), 1962 v W; (with Swansea T), 1965 v Ho (2)

Brisby, D. (Distillery), 1891 v S (1)

Brolly, T. H. (Millwall), 1937 v W; 1938 v W; 1939 v E, W (4)

Brookes, E. A. (Shelbourne), 1920 v S (1)

Brotherston, N. (Blackburn R), 1980 v S, E, W, Aus (3); 1981 v Se, P; 1982 v S, Is, E, F, S, W, Hon (sub), A (sub); 1983 v A (sub), WG, Alb, T, Alb, S (sub), E (sub), W; 1984 v T; 1985 v Is (sub), T (27)

Brown, J. (Glenavon), 1921 v W; (with Tranmere R), 1924 v E, W (3)

Brown, J. (Wolverhampton W), 1935 v E, W; 1936 v E; (with Coventry C), 1937 v E, W; 1938 v S, W; (with Birmingham C), 1939 v E, S, W (10)

Brown, N. M. (Limavady), 1887 v E (1)

Brown, W. G. (Glenavon), 1926 v W (1)

Browne, F. (Cliftonville), 1887 v E, S, W; 1888 v E, S (5)

Browne, R. J. (Leeds U), 1936 v E, W; 1938 v E, W; 1939 v E, S (6)

Bruce, W. (Glentoran), 1961 v S; 1967 v W (2)

Buckle, H. R. (Sunderland), 1904 v E; (with Bristol R), 1908 v W (2)

Buckle, J. (Cliftonville), 1882 v E (1)

Burnett, J. (Distillery), 1894 v E, W, S; (with Glentoran), 1895 v E, W (5)

Burnison, J. (Distillery), 1901 v E, W (2)

Burnison, S. (Distillery), 1908 v E; 1910 v E, S; (with Bradford), 1911 v E, S, W; (with Distillery), 1912 v E; 1913 v W (8)

Burns, J. (Glenavon), 1923 v E (1)

Butler, M. P. (Blackpool), 1939 v W (1)

Campbell, A. C. (Crusaders), 1963 v W; 1965 v Sw (2)

Campbell, D. A. (Nottingham F), 1986 v Mor (sub), Br; 1987 v E (2), T, Y; (with Charlton Ath), 1988 v Y, T (sub), Gr (sub), Pol (sub) (10)

Campbell, James (Cliftonville), 1897 v E, S, W; 1898 v E, S, W; 1899 v E; 1900 v E, S; 1901 v S, W; 1902 v S; 1903 v E; 1904 v S (14)

Campbell, John (Cliftonville), 1896 v W (1)

Campbell, J. P. (Fulham), 1951 v E, S (2)

Campbell, R. M. (Bradford C), 1982 v S, W (sub) (2)

Campbell, W. G. (Dundee), 1968 v S, E; 1969 v T; 1970 v S, W, USSR (6)

Carey, J. J. (Manchester U), 1947 v E, S, W; 1948 v E; 1949 v E, S, W (7)

Carroll, E. (Glenavon), 1925 v S (1)

Carroll, R. E. (Wigan Ath), 1997 v Th (sub); 1999 v Ei (sub); 2000 v L, Ma (4)

Casey, T. (Newcastle U), 1955 v W; 1956 v W; 1957 v E, S, W, I, P (2); 1958 v WG, F; (with Portsmouth), 1959 v E, Sp (12)

Caskey, W. (Derby Co), 1979 v Bul, E, Bul, E, S (sub), D (sub); 1980 v E (sub); (with Tulsa R), 1982 v F (sub) (8)

Cassidy, T. (Newcastle U), 1971 v E (sub); 1972 v USSR (sub); 1974 v Bul (sub), S, E, W; 1975 v N; 1976 v S, E, W; 1977 v WG (sub); 1980 v E, Ei (sub), Is, S, E, W, Aus (3); (with Burnley), 1981 v Se, P; 1982 v Is, Sp (sub) (24)

Caughey, M. (Linfield), 1986 v F (sub), D (sub) (2)

Chambers, R. J. (Distillery), 1921 v W; (with Bury), 1928 v E, S, W; 1929 v E, S, W; 1930 v S, W; (with Nottingham F), 1932 v E, S, W (12)

Chatton, H. A. (Partick T), 1925 v E, S; 1926 v E (3)

Christian, J. (Linfield), 1889 v S (1)

Clarke, C. J. (Bournemouth), 1986 v F, D, Mor, Alg (sub), Sp, Br; (with Southampton), 1987 v E, T, Y; 1988 v Y, T, Gr, Pol, F, Ma; 1989 v Ei, H, Sp (1+1 sub); (with QPR), Ma, Ch; 1990 v H, Ei, N; (with Portsmouth), 1991 v Y (sub), D, A, Pol, Y (sub), Fa; 1992 v Fa, D, S, G; 1993 v Alb, Sp, D (38)

Clarke, R. (Bradford C), 1901 v E, S (2)

Cleary, J. (Glentoran), 1982 v S, W; 1983 v W (sub); 1984 v T (sub); 1985 v Is (5)

Clements, D. (Coventry C), 1965 v W, Ho; 1966 v M; 1967 v S, W; 1968 v S, E; 1969 v T (2), S, W; 1970 v S, E, W, USSR (2); 1971 v Sp, E, S, W, Cy; (with Sheffield W), 1972 v USSR (2), Sp, E, S, W; 1973 v Bul, Cy (2), P, E, S, W; (with Everton), 1974 v Bul, P, S, E, W; 1975 v N, Y, E, S, W; 1976 v Se, Y; (with New York Cosmos), E, W (48)

Clugston, D. (Cliftonville), 1888 v W; 1889 v W, S, E; 1890 v E, S; 1891 v E, W; 1892 v E, S, W; 1893 v E, S, W (14)

Cochrane, D. (Leeds U), 1939 v E, W; 1947 v E, S, W; 1948 v E, S, W; 1949 v S, W; 1950 v E, S (12)

Cochrane, G. T. (Coleraine), 1976 v N (sub); (with Burnley), 1978 v S (sub), E (sub), W (sub); 1979 v Ei (sub); (with Middlesbrough), D, Bul, E, Bul, E; 1980 v Is, E (sub), Aus (1+2 sub); 1981 v Se (sub), P (sub), S, P, S, Se; 1982 v E (sub), F; (with Gillingham), 1984 v S, Fi (sub) (26)

Cochrane, M. (Distillery), 1898 v S, W, E; 1899 v E; 1900 v E, S, W; (with Leicester Fosse), 1901 v S (8)

Collins, F. (Celtic), 1922 v S (1)

Condy, J. (Distillery), 1882 v W; 1886 v E, S (3)

Connell, T. E. (Coleraine), 1978 v W (sub) (1)

Connor, J. (Glentoran), 1901 v S, E; (with Belfast C), 1905 v E, S, W; 1907 v E, S; 1908 v E, S; 1909 v W; 1911 v S, E, W (13)

Connor, M. J. (Brentford), 1903 v S, W; (with Fulham), 1904 v E (3)

Cook, W. (Celtic), 1933 v E, W, S; (with Everton), 1935 v E; 1936 v S, W; 1937 v E, S, W; 1938 v E, S, W; 1939 v E, S, W (15)

Cooke, S. (Belfast YMCA), 1889 v E; (with Cliftonville), 1890 v E, S (3)

Coote, A. (Norwich C), 1999 v Ca, Ei (sub); 2000 v Fi (sub), L (sub), Ma (sub), H (sub) (6)

Coulter, J. (Belfast C), 1934 v E, S, W; (with Everton), 1935 v E, S, W; 1937 v S, W; (with Grimsby T), 1938 v S, W; (with Chelmsford C), 1939 v S (11)

Cowan, J. (Newcastle U), 1970 v E (sub) (1)

Cowan, T. S. (Queen's Island), 1925 v W (1)

Coyle, F. (Coleraine), 1956 v E, S; 1957 v P; (with Nottingham F), 1958 v Arg (4)

Coyle, L. (Derry C), 1989 v Ch (sub) (1)

Coyle, R. I. (Sheffield W), 1973 v P, Cy (sub), W (sub); 1974 v Bul (sub), P (sub) (5)

Craig, A. B. (Rangers), 1908 v E, S, W; 1909 v S; (with Morton), 1912 v S, W; 1914 v E, S, W (9)

Craig, D. J. (Newcastle U), 1967 v W; 1968 v W; 1969 v T (2), E, S, W; 1970 v E, S, W, USSR; 1971 v Cy (2), Sp, S (sub); 1972 v USSR, S (sub); 1973 v Cy (2), E, S, W; 1974 v Bul, P; 1975 v N (25)

Crawford, A. (Distillery), 1889 v E, W; (with Cliftonville), 1891 v E, S, W; 1893 v E, W (7)

Croft, T. (Queen's Island), 1924 v E (1)

Crone, R. (Distillery), 1889 v S; 1890 v E, S, W (4)

Crone, W. (Distillery), 1882 v W; 1884 v E, S, W; 1886 v E, S, W; 1887 v E; 1888 v E, W; 1889 v S; 1890 v W (12)

Crooks, W. J. (Manchester U), 1922 v W (1)

Crossan, E. (Blackburn R), 1950 v S; 1951 v E; 1955 v W (3)

Crossan, J. A. (Sparta-Rotterdam), 1960 v E; (with Sunderland), 1963 v W, P, Sp; 1964 v E, S, W, U, Sp; 1965 v E, S, Sw (2); (with Manchester C), W, Ho (2), Alb; 1966 v S, E, Alb, WG; 1967 v E, S; (with Middlesbrough), 1968 v S (24)

Crothers, C. (Distillery), 1907 v W (1)

Cumming, L. (Huddersfield T), 1929 v W, S; (with Oldham Ath), 1930 v S (3)

Cunningham, W. (Ulster), 1892 v S, E, W; 1893 v E (4)

Cunningham, W. E. (St Mirren), 1951 v W; 1953 v E; 1954 v S; 1955 v S; (with Leicester C), 1956 v E, S, W; 1957 v E, S, W, I, P (2); 1958 v S, W, I, Cz (2), Arg, WG, F; 1959 v E, S, W; 1960 v E, S, W; (with Dunfermline Ath), 1961 v W; 1962 v W, Ho (30)

Curran, S. (Belfast C), 1926 v S, W; 1928 v S (3)

Curran, J. J. (Glenavon), 1922 v W; (with Pontypridd), 1923 v E, S; (with Glenavon), 1924 v E (4)

Cush, W. W. (Glenavon), 1951 v E, S; 1954 v S, E; 1957 v W, I, P (2); (with Leeds U), 1958 v I (2), W, Cz (2), Arg, WG, F; 1959 v E, S, W, Sp; 1960 v E, S, W; (with Portadown), 1961 v WG, Gr; 1962 v Gr (26)

Dalton, W. (YMCA), 1888 v S; (with Linfield), 1890 v S, W; 1891 v S, W; 1892 v E, S, W; 1894 v E, S, W (11)

D'Arcy, S. D. (Chelsea), 1952 v W; 1953 v E; (with Brentford), 1953 v S, W, F (5)

Darling, J. (Linfield), 1897 v E, S, 1900 v S; 1902 v E, S, W; 1903 v E, S, W; 1905 v E, S, W; 1906 v E, S, W; 1908 v W; 1909 v E; 1910 v E, S, W; 1912 v S (21)

Davey, H. H. (Reading), 1926 v E; 1927 v E, S; 1928 v E; (with Portsmouth), 1928 v W (5)

Davis, T. L. (Oldham Ath), 1937 v E (1)

Davison, A. J. (Bolton W), 1996 v Se; (with Bradford C), 1997 v Th; (with Grimsby T), 1998 v G (3)

Davison, J. R. (Cliftonville), 1882 v E, W; 1883 v E, W; 1884 v E, W, S; 1885 v E (8)

Dennison, R. (Wolverhampton W), 1988 v F, Ma; 1989 v H, Sp Ch (sub); 1990 v Ei, U; 1991 v Y (2), A. Pol, Fa (sub); 1992 v Fa, A, D (sub); 1993 v Sp (sub); 1994 v Co (sub); 1997 v I (sub) (18)

Devine, A. O. (Limavady), 1886 v E, W; 1887 v W; 1888 v W (4)

Devine, J. (Glentoran), 1990 v U (sub) (1)

Dickson, D. (Coleraine), 1970 v S (sub), W; 1973 v Cy, P (4)

Dickson, T. A. (Linfield), 1957 v S (1)

Dickson, W. (Chelsea), 1951 v W, F; 1952 v E, S, W; 1953 v E, S, W, F; (with Arsenal), 1954 v E, W; 1955 v E (12)

Diffin, W. J. (Belfast C), 1931 v W (1)

Dill, A. H. (Knock), 1882 v E, W; (with Down Ath), 1883 v W; (with Cliftonville), 1884 v E, S, W; 1885 v E, S, W (9)

Doherty, I. (Belfast C), 1901 v E (1)

Doherty, J. (Cliftonville), 1933 v E, W (2)

Doherty, L. (Linfield), 1985 v Is; 1988 v T (sub) (2)

Doherty, M. (Derry C), 1938 v S (1)

Doherty, P. D. (Blackpool), 1935 v E, W; 1936 v E, S; (with Manchester C), 1937 v E, W; 1938 v E, S; 1939 v E, W; (with Derby Co), 1947 v E; (with Huddersfield T), 1947 v W; 1948 v E, W; 1949 v S; (with Doncaster R), 1951 v S (16)

Donaghy, M. M. (Luton T), 1980 v S, E, W; 1981 v Se, P, S (sub); 1982 v S, Is, E, F, S, W, Y, Hon, Sp, F; 1983 v A, WG, Alb, T, Alb, S, E, W; 1984 v A, T, WG, S, E, W, Fi; 1985 v R, Fi, E, Sp, T; 1986 v T, R, E, F, D, Mor, Alg, Sp, Br; 1987 v E (2), T, Is, Y; 1988 v Y, T, Gr, Pol, F, Ma; 1989 v H; (with Manchester U), Sp (2), Ma, Ch; 1990 v Ei, N; 1991 v Y (2), D, A, Pol, Fa; 1992 v Fa, A, D, S, Li, G; (with Chelsea), 1993 v Alb, Sp, D, Alb, Ei, Sp, Li, La; 1994 v La, D, Ei, R, Lie, Co, M (91)

Donnelly, L. (Distillery), 1913 v W (1)

Doran, J. F. (Brighton), 1921 v E; 1922 v E, W (3)

Dougan, A. D. (Portsmouth), 1958 v Cz; (with Blackburn R), 1960 v S; 1961 v E, W, I, Gr; (with Aston Villa), 1963 v S, Pol (2); (with Leicester C), 1966 v S, E, W, M, Alb, WG; 1967 v E, S; (with Wolverhampton W), 1967 v W; 1968 v S, W,; 1969 v Is, T (2), E, S, W; 1970 v S, E, USSR (2); 1971 v Cy (2), Sp, E, S, W; 1972 v USSR (2), E, S, W; 1973 v Bul, Cy (43)

Douglas, J. P. (Belfast C), 1947 v E (1)

Dowd, H. O. (Glenavon), 1974 v W; (with Sheffield W), 1975 v N (sub), Se (3)

Dowie, I. (Luton T), 1990 v N (sub), U; 1991 v Y, D, A (sub), (with West Ham U), Y, Fa; (with Southampton), 1992 v Fa, A, D (sub), S (sub), Li; 1993 v Alb (2), Ei, Sp (sub), Li, La; 1994 v La, D, Ei (sub), R (sub), Lie, Co, M (sub); 1995 v A, Ei; (with C Palace), Ei, La, Ca, Ch, La; 1996 v P; (with West Ham U), A, N, G; 1997 v Uk, Arm, G, Alb, P, Uk, Arm, Th; 1998 v Alb, P; (with QPR), Slo, Sw, Sp; 1999 v T, Fi, Mol, G, Mol, Ca, Ei; 2000 v F, T, G (59)

Duggan, H. A. (Leeds U), 1930 v E; 1931 v E, W; 1933 v E; 1934 v E; 1935 v S, W; 1936 v S (8)

Dunlop, G. (Linfield), 1985 v Is; 1987 v E, Y; 1990 v Ei (4)

Dunne, J. (Sheffield U), 1928 v W; 1931 v W, E; 1932 v E, S; 1933 v E, W (7)

Eames, W. L. E. (Dublin U), 1885 v E, S, W (3)

Eglington, T. J. (Everton), 1947 v S, W; 1948 v E, S, W; 1949 v E (6)

Elder, A. R. (Burnley), 1960 v W; 1961 v S, E, W, WG (2), Gr; 1962 v E, S, Gr; 1963 v E, S, W, Pol (2); 1964 v W, U; 1965 v E, S, W, Sw (2), Ho (2), Alb; 1966 v E, S, W, M, Alb; 1967 v E, S, W; (with Stoke C), 1968 v E, W; 1969 v E (sub), S, W; 1970 v USSR (40)

Elleman, A. R. (Cliftonville), 1889 v W; 1890 v E (2)

Elwood, J. H. (Bradford), 1929 v W; 1930 v E (2)

Emerson, M. (Glentoran), 1920 v E, S, W; 1921 v E; 1922 v E, S; (with Burnley), 1922 v W; 1923 v E, S, W; 1924 v E (11)

English, S. (Rangers), 1933 v W, S (2)

Enright, J. (Leeds C), 1912 v S (1)

Falloon, E. (Aberdeen), 1931 v S; 1933 v S (2)

Farquharson, T. G. (Cardiff C), 1923 v S, W; 1924 v E, S, W; 1925 v S (7)

Farrell, P. (Distillery), 1901 v S, W (2)

Farrell, P. (Hibernian), 1938 v W (1)

Farrell, P. D. (Everton), 1947 v S, W; 1948 v E, S, W; 1949 v E, W (7)

Feeney, J. M. (Linfield), 1947 v S; (with Swansea T), 1950 v E (2)

Feeney, W. (Glentoran), 1976 v Is (1)

Ferguson, G. (Glentoran), 1999 v Ca (sub) (1)

Ferguson, W. (Linfield), 1966 v M; 1967 v E (2)

Ferris, J. (Belfast C), 1920 v E, W; (with Chelsea), 1921 v S, E; (with Belfast C), 1928 v S (5)

Ferris, R. O. (Birmingham C), 1950 v S; 1951 v F; 1952 v S (3)

Fettis, A. W. (Hull C), 1992 v D, Li; 1993 v D; 1994 v M; 1995 v P, Ei, La, Ca, Ch, La; 1996 v P, Lie, A; (with Nottingham F), v N; 1997 v Uk, Arm (2); (with Blackburn R), 1998 v P, Slo, Sw, Sp; 1999 v T, Fi, Mol (25)

Finney, T. (Sunderland), 1975 v N, E (sub), S, W; 1976 v N, Y, S; (with Cambridge U), 1980 v E, Is, S, E, W, Aus (2) (14)

Fitzpatrick, J. C. (Bohemians), 1896 v E, S (2)

Flack, H. (Burnley), 1929 v S (1)

Fleming, J. G. (Nottingham F), 1987 v E (2), Is, Y; 1988 v T, Gr, Pol; 1989 v Ma, Ch; (with Manchester C), 1990 v H, Ei; (with Barnsley), 1991 v Y; 1992 v Li (sub), G; 1993 v Alb, Sp, D, Alb, Sp, Li, La; 1994 v La, D, Ei, R, Lie, Co, M; 1995 v P, A, Ei (31)

Forbes, G. (Limavady), 1888 v W; (with Distillery), 1891 v E, S (3)

Forde, J. T. (Ards), 1959 v Sp; 1961 v E, S, WG (4)

Foreman, T. A. (Cliftonville), 1899 v S (1)

Forsyth, J. (YMCA), 1888 v E, S (2)

Fox, W. T. (Ulster), 1887 v E, S (2)

Fulton, R. P. (Belfast C), 1930 v W; 1931 v E, S, W; 1932 v W, E; 1933 v E, S; 1934 v E, W, S; 1935 v E, W, S; 1936 v S, W; 1937 v E, S, W; 1938 v W (20)

Gaffikin, G. (Linfield Ath), 1890 v S, W; 1891 v S, W; 1892 v E, S, W; 1893 v E, S, W; 1894 v E, S, W; 1895 v E, W (15)

Galbraith, W. (Distillery), 1890 v W (1)

Gallagher, P. (Celtic), 1920 v E, S; 1922 v S; 1923 v S, W; 1924 v S, W; 1925 v S, W, E; (with Falkirk), 1927 v S (11)

Gallogly, C. (Huddersfield T), 1951 v E, S (2)

Gara, A. (Preston NE), 1902 v E, S, W (3)

Gardiner, A. (Cliftonville), 1930 v S, W; 1931 v S; 1932 v E, S (5)

Garrett, J. (Distillery), 1925 v W (1)

Gaston, R. (Oxford U), 1969 v Is (sub) (1)

Gaukrodger, G. (Linfield), 1895 v W (1)

Gaussen, A. D. (Moyola Park), 1884 v E, S; (with Magherafelt), 1888 v E, W; 1889 v E, W (6)

Geary, J. (Glentoran), 1931 v S; 1932 v S (2)

Gibb, J. T. (Wellington Park) 1884 v S, W; 1885 v S, E, W; 1886 v S; 1887 v S, E, W; (with Cliftonville), 1889 v S (10)

Gibb, T. J. (Cliftonville), 1936 v W (1)

Gibson W. K. (Cliftonville), 1894 v S, W, E; 1895 v S; 1897 v W; 1898 v S, W, E; 1901 v S, W, E; 1902 v S, W (13)

Gillespie, K. R. (Manchester U), 1995 v P, A, Ei; (with Newcastle U), Ei, La, Ca, Ch (sub), La (sub); 1996 v P, A, N, G; 1997 v Uk, Arm, Bel, P, Uk; 1998 v G, Alb, Slo, Sw; 1999 v T, Fi, Mol; (with Blackburn R), G, Mol; 2000 v F (sub), T (sub), G (sub), L, Ma, H (32)

Gillespie, S. (Hertford), 1886 v E, S, W; 1887 v E, S, W (6)

Gillespie, W. (Sheffield U), 1913 v E, S; 1914 v E, W; 1920 v S, W; 1921 v E; 1922 v E, S, W; 1923 v E, S, W; 1924 v E, S, W; 1925 v E, S; 1926 v S, W; 1927 v E, W; 1928 v E; 1929 v E; 1931 v E (25)

Gillespie, W. (West Down), 1889 v W (1)

Goodall, A. L. (Derby Co), 1899 v S, W; 1900 v E, W; 1901 v E; 1902 v S; 1903 v E, W; (with Glossop), 1904 v E, W (10)

Goodbody, M. F. (Dublin University), 1889 v E; 1891 v W (2)

Gordon, H. (Linfield), 1895 v E; 1896 v E, S (3)

Gordon R. W. (Linfield), 1891 v S; 1892 v W, E, S; 1893 v E, S, W (7)

Gordon, T. (Linfield), 1894 v W; 1895 v E (2)

Gorman, W. C. (Brentford), 1947 v E, S, W; 1948 v W (4)

Gowdy, J. (Glentoran), 1920 v E; (with Queen's Island), 1924 v W; (with Falkirk), 1926 v E, S; 1927 v E, S (6)

Gowdy, W. A. (Hull C), 1932 v S; (with Sheffield W), 1933 v S; (with Linfield), 1935 v E, S, W; (with Hibernian), 1936 v W (6)

Graham, W. G. L. (Doncaster R), 1951 v W, F; 1952 v E, S, W; 1953 v S, F; 1954 v E, W; 1955 v S, W; 1956 v E, S; 1959 v E (14)

Gray, P. (Luton T), 1993 v D (sub), Alb, Ei, Sp; (with Sunderland), 1994 v La, D, Ei, R, Lie (sub); 1995 v P, A, Ei, Ca, Ch (sub); 1996 v P (sub), Lie, A; (with Nancy), 1997 v Uk, Arm, G (sub); (with Luton T), 1999 v Mol (sub) (21)

Greer, W. (QPR), 1909 v E, S, W (3)

Gregg, H. (Doncaster R), 1954 v W; 1957 v E, S, W, I, P (2); 1958 v E, I; (with Manchester U), 1958 v Cz, Arg, WG, F, W; 1959 v E, W; 1960 v S, E, W; 1961 v E, S; 1962 v S, Gr; 1964 v S, E (25)

Griffin, D. J. (St Johnstone), 1996 v G; 1997 v Uk, I, Bel (sub), Th; 1998 v G (sub), Alb; 1999 v Mol, Ei (sub); 2000 v L, Ma, H (12)

Hall, G. (Distillery), 1897 v E (1)

Halligan, W. (Derby Co), 1911 v W; (with Wolverhampton W), 1912 v E (2)

Hamill, M. (Manchester U), 1912 v E; 1914 v E, S; (with Belfast C), 1924 v E, S, W; (with Manchester C), 1921 v S (7)

Hamill, R. (Glentoran), 1999 v Ca (sub) (1)

Hamilton, B. (Linfield), 1969 v T; 1971 v Cy (2), E, S, W; (with Ipswich T), 1972 v USSR (1+1 sub), Sp; 1973 v Bul, Cy (2), P, E, S, W; 1974 v Bul, S, E, W; 1975 v N, Se, Y, E; 1976 v Se, N, Y; (with Everton), Is, S, E, W; 1977 v Ho, Bel, WG, E, S, W, Ic; (with Millwall), 1978 v S, E, W; 1979 v Ei (sub); (with Swindon T), Bul (2), E, S, W, D; 1980 v Aus (2 sub) (50)

Hamilton, J. (Knock), 1882 v E, W (2)

Hamilton, R. (Rangers), 1928 v S; 1929 v E; 1930 v S, E; 1932 v S (5)

Hamilton, W. D. (Dublin Association), 1885 v W (1)

Hamilton, W. J. (Distillery), 1908 v W (1)

Hamilton, W. J. (Dublin Association), 1885 v W (1)

Hamilton, W. R. (QPR), 1978 v S (sub); (with Burnley), 1980 v S, E, W, Aus (2); 1981 v Se, P, S, P, S, Se; 1982 v S, Is, E, W, Y, Hon, Sp, A, F; 1983 v A, WG, Alb (2), S, E, W; 1984 v A, T, WG, S, E, W, Fi; (with Oxford U), 1985 v R, Sp; 1986 v Mor (sub), Alg, Sp (sub), Br (sub) (41)

Hampton, H. (Bradford C), 1911 v E, S, W; 1912 v E, W; 1913 v E, S, W; 1914 v E (9)

Hanna, J. (Nottingham F), 1912 v S, W (2)

Hanna, J. D. (Royal Artillery, Portsmouth), 1899 v W (1)

Hannon, D. J. (Bohemians), 1908 v E, S; 1911 v E, S; 1912 v W; 1913 v E (6)

Harkin, J. T. (Southport), 1968 v W; 1969 v T; (with Shrewsbury T), W (sub); 1970 v USSR; 1971 v Sp (5)

Harland, A. I. (Linfield), 1923 v E (1)

Harris, J. (Cliftonville), 1921 v W (1)

Harris, V. (Shelbourne), 1906 v E; 1907 v E, W; 1908 v E, W, S; (with Everton), 1909 v E, W, S; 1910 v E, S, W; 1911 v E, S, W; 1912 v E; 1913 v E, S; 1914 v S, W (20)

Harvey, M. (Sunderland), 1961 v I; 1962 v Ho; 1963 v W, Sp; 1964 v S, E, W, U, Sp; 1965 v E, S, W, Sw (2), Ho (2), Alb; 1966 v S, E, W, M, Alb, WG; 1967 v E, S; 1968 v E, W; 1969 v Is, T (2), E; 1970 v USSR; 1971 v Cy, W (sub) (34)

Hastings, J. (Knock), 1882 v E, W; (with Ulster), 1883 v W; 1884 v E, S; 1886 v E, S (7)

Hatton, S. (Linfield), 1963 v S, Pol (2)

Hayes, W. E. (Huddersfield T), 1938 v E, S; 1939 v E, S (4)

Healy, D. J. (Manchester U), 2000 v L, Ma, H (3)

Healy, P. J. (Coleraine), 1982 v S, W, Hon (sub); (with Glentoran), 1983 v A (sub) (4)

Hegan, D. (WBA), 1970 v USSR; (with Wolverhampton W), 1972 v USSR, E, S, W; 1973 v Bul, Cy (7)

Henderson, J. (Ulster), 1885 v E, S, W (3)

Hewison, G. (Moyola Park), 1885 v E, S (2)

Hill, C. F. (Sheffield U), 1990 v N, U; 1991 v Pol, Y; 1992 v A, D; (with Leicester C) 1995 v Ei, La; 1996 v P, Lie, A, N, Se, G; 1997 v Uk, Arm, G, Alb, P, Uk, Arm, Th; (with Trelleborg), 1998 v G, Alb, P; (with Northampton T), Slo; 1999 v T (27)

Hill, M. J. (Norwich C), 1959 v W; 1960 v W; 1961 v WG; 1962 v S; (with Everton), 1964 v S, E, Sp (7)

Hinton, E. (Fulham), 1947 v S, W; 1948 v S, E, W; (with Millwall), 1951 v W, F (7)

Hopkins, J. (Brighton), 1926 v E (1)

Horlock, K. (Swindon T), 1995 v La, Ca; 1997 v G, Alb, I; (with Manchester C), v Bel, Uk, Arm, Th; 1998 v G, Alb, P; 1999 v T, Fi, G, Mol, Ca; 2000 v F, T, G, Ma (sub) (21)

Houston, J. (Linfield), 1912 v S, W; 1913 v W; (with Everton), 1913 v S; 1914 v S (5)

Houston, W. (Linfield), 1933 v W (1)

Houston, W. J. (Moyola Park), 1885 v E, S (2)

Hughes, A. W. (Newcastle U), 1998 v Slo, Sw, Sp (sub); 1999 v T, Fi, Mol (sub), Ca, Ei; 2000 v F, T, L, H (12)

Hughes, M. E. (Manchester C), 1992 v D, S, Li, G; (with Strasbourg), 1993 v Alb, Sp, D, Ei, Sp, Li, La; 1994 v La, D, Ei, R, Lie, Co, M; 1995 v P, A, Ei (2) La, Ca, Ch, La; 1996 v P, Lie, A, N, G; (with West Ham U), 1997 v Uk, Arm, G, Alb, I, Uk; 1998 v G; (with Wimbledon), P, Slo, Sw, Sp; 1999 v T, Fi, Mol, G, Mol; 2000 v F, T, G, Fi, L (sub), Ma, H (54)

Hughes, P. A. (Bury), 1987 v E, T, Is (3)

Hughes, W. (Bolton W), 1951 v W (1)

Humphries, W. M. (Ards), 1962 v W; (with Coventry C), 1962 v Ho; 1963 v E, S, W, Pol, Sp; 1964 v S, E, Sp; 1965 v S, Ho; (with Swansea T), 1965 v W, Alb (14)

Hunter, A. (Distillery), 1905 v W; 1906 v W, E, S; (with Belfast C), 1908 v W; 1909 v W, E, S (8)

Hunter, A. (Blackburn R), 1970 v USSR; 1971 v Cy (2), E, S, W; (with Ipswich T), 1972 v USSR (2), Sp, E, S, W; 1973 v Bul, Cy (2), P, E, S, W; 1974 v Bul, S, E, W; 1975 v N, Se, Y, E, S, W; 1976 v Se, N, Y, Is, S, E, W; 1977 v Ho, Bel, WG, E, S, W, Ic; 1978 v Ic, Ho, Bel; 1979 v Ei, D, S, W; 1980 v E, Ei (53)

Hunter, B. V. (Wrexham), 1995 v La; 1996 v P, Lie, A, Se, G; (with Reading), 1997 v Arm, G, Alb, I, Bel; 1999 v Ca, Ei; 2000 v F, T (15)

Hunter, R. J. (Cliftonville), 1884 v E, S, W (3)

Hunter, V. (Coleraine), 1962 v E; 1964 v Sp (2)

Irvine, R. J. (Linfield), 1962 v Ho; 1963 v E, S, W, Pol (2), Sp; (with Stoke C), 1965 v W (8)

Irvine, R. W. (Everton), 1922 v S; 1923 v E, W; 1924 v E, S; 1925 v E; 1926 v E; 1927 v E, W; 1928 v E, S; (with Portsmouth), 1929 v E; 1930 v S; (with Connah's Quay), 1931 v E; (with Derry C), 1932 v W (15)

Irvine, W. J. (Burnley), 1963 v W, Sp; 1965 v S, W, Sw, Ho (2), Alb; 1966 v S, E, W, M, Alb; 1967 v E, S; 1968 v E, W; (with Preston NE), 1969 v Is, T, E; (with Brighton), 1972 v E, S, W (23)

Irving, S, J. (Dundee), 1923 v S, W; 1924 v S, E, W; 1925 v S, E, W; 1926 v S, W; (with Cardiff C), 1927 v S, E, W; 1928 v S, E, W; (with Chelsea), 1929 v E; 1931 v W (18)

Jackson, T. A. (Everton), 1969 v Is, E, S, W; 1970 v USSR (1+1 sub); (with Nottingham F), 1971 v Sp; 1972 v E, S, W; 1973 v Cy, E, S, W; 1974 v Bul, P, S (sub), E (sub), W (sub); 1975 v N (sub), Se, Y, E, S, W; (with Manchester U); 1976 v Se, N, Y; 1977 v Ho, Bel, WG, E, S, W, Ic (35)

Jamison, J. (Glentoran), 1976 v N (1)

Jenkins, I. (Chester C), 1997 v Arm, Th; 1998 v Slo; (with Dundee U), Sw, Sp; 2000 v Fi (6)

Jennings, P. A. (Watford), 1964 v W, U; (with Tottenham H), 1965 v E, S, Sw (2), Ho, Alb; 1966 v S, E, W, Alb, WG; 1967 v E, S; 1968 v S, E, W; 1969 v Is, T (2), E, S, W; 1970 v S, E, USSR (2); 1971 v Cy (2), E, S, W; 1972 v USSR, Sp, S, E, W; 1973 v Bul, Cy, P, E, S, W; 1974 v P, S, E, W; 1975 v N, Se, Y, E, S, W; 1976 v Se, N, Y, Is, S, E, W; 1977 v Ho, Bel, WG, E, S, W, Ic; (with Arsenal), 1978 v Ic, Ho, Bel; 1979 v Ei, D, Bul, E, Bul, E, S, W, D; 1980 v E, Ei, Is; 1981 v S, P, S, Se; 1982 v S, Is, E, W, Y, Hon, Sp, F; 1983 v Alb, S, E, W; 1984 v A, T, WG, S, W, Fi; 1985 v R, Fi, E, Sp, T; (with Tottenham H), 1986 v T, R, E, F, D; (with Everton), Mor; (with Tottenham H), Alg, Sp, Br (119)

Johnson, D. M. (Blackburn R), 1999 v Ei (sub); 2000 v Fi (sub), L, Ma (sub), H (sub) (5)

Johnston, H. (Portadown), 1927 v W (1)

Johnston, R. S. (Distillery), 1882 v W; 1884 v E; 1886 v E, S (4)

Johnston, R. S. (Distillery), 1905 v W (1)

Johnston, S. (Linfield), 1890 v W; 1893 v S, W; 1894 v E (4)

Johnston, W. (Oldpark), 1885 v S, W (2)

Johnston, W. C. (Glenavon), 1962 v W; (with Oldham Ath), 1966 v M (sub) (2)

Jones, J. (Linfield), 1930 v S, W; 1931 v S, W, E; 1932 v S, E; 1933 v S, E, W; 1934 v S, E, W; 1935 v S, E, W; 1936 v E, S; (with Hibernian), 1936 v W; 1937 v E, W, S; (with Glenavon), 1938 v E (23)

Jones, J. (Glenavon), 1956 v W; 1957 v E, W (3)

Jones, S. (Distillery), 1934 v E; (with Blackpool), 1934 v W (2)

Jordan, T. (Linfield), 1895 v E, W (2)

Kavanagh, P. J. (Celtic), 1930 v E (1)

Keane, T. R. (Swansea T), 1949 v S (1)

Kearns, A. (Distillery), 1900 v E, S, W; 1902 v E, S, W (6)

Kee, P. V. (Oxford U), 1990 v N; 1991 v Y (2), D, A, Pol, Fa; (with Ards), 1995 v A, Ei (9)

Keith, R. M. (Newcastle U), 1958 v E, W, Cz (2), Arg, I, WG, F; 1959 v E, S, W, Sp; 1960 v S, E; 1961 v S, E, W, I, WG (2), Gr; 1962 v W, Ho (23)

Kelly, H. R. (Fulham), 1950 v E, W; (with Southampton), 1951 v E, S (4)

Kelly, J. (Glentoran), 1896 v E (1)

Kelly, J. (Derry C), 1932 v E, W; 1933 v E, W, S; 1934 v W; 1936 v E, S, W; 1937 v S, E (11)

Kelly, P. J. (Manchester C), 1921 v E (1)

Kelly, P. M. (Barnsley), 1950 v S (1)

Kennedy, A. L. (Arsenal), 1923 v W; 1925 v E (2)

Kennedy, P. H. (Watford), 1999 v Mol, G (sub); 2000 v F, T, G, Fi (6)

Kernaghan, N. (Belfast C), 1936 v W; 1937 v S; 1938 v E (3)

Kirk, A. (Hearts), 2000 v H (1)

Kirkwood, H. (Cliftonville), 1904 v W (1)

Kirwan, J. (Tottenham H), 1900 v W; 1902 v E, W; 1903 v E, S, W; 1904 v E, S, W; 1905 v E, S, W; (with Chelsea), 1906 v E, S, W; 1907 v W; (with Clyde), 1909 v S (17)

Lacey, W. (Everton), 1909 v E, S, W; 1910 v E, S, W; 1911 v E, S, W; 1912 v E; (with Liverpool), 1913 v W; 1914 v E, S, W; 1920 v E, S, W; 1921 v E, S, W; 1922 v E, S; (with New Brighton), 1925 v E (23)

Lawther, R. (Glentoran), 1888 v E, S (2)

Lawther, W. I. (Sunderland), 1960 v W; 1961 v I; (with Blackburn R), 1962 v S, Ho (4)

Leatham, J. (Belfast C), 1939 v W (1)

Ledwidge, J. J. (Shelbourne), 1906 v S, W (2)

Lemon, J. (Glentoran), 1886 v W; (with Belfast YMCA), 1888 v S; 1889 v W (3)

Lennon, N. F. (Crewe Alex), 1994 v M (sub); 1995 v Ch; 1996 v P, Lie, A; (with Leicester C), v N; 1997 v Uk, Arm, G, Alb, Bel, P, Uk, Arm, Th; 1998 v G, Alb, P, Slo, Sw, Sp; 1999 v T, Fi, Mol, G, Mol, Ei; 2000 v F, T, G, Fi, Ma, H (33)

Leslie, W. (YMCA), 1887 v E (1)

Lewis, J. (Glentoran), 1899 v S, E, W; (with Distillery), 1900 v S (4)

Lockhart, H. (Russell School), 1884 v W (1)

Lockhart, N. H. (Linfield), 1947 v E; (with Coventry C), 1950 v W; 1951 v W; 1952 v W; (with Aston Villa), 1954 v S, E; 1955 v W; 1956 v W (8)

Lomas, S. M. (Manchester C), 1994 v R, Lie, Co (sub), M; 1995 v P, A; 1996 v P, Lie, A, N, Se, G; 1997 v Uk, Arm, G, Alb, I, Bel; (with West Ham U), P, Uk, Arm, Th; 1998 v Alb, P, Slo, Sw; 1999 v Mol, G, Mol, Ca; 2000 v F, T, G, L, Ma (35)

Loyal, J. (Clarence), 1891 v S (1)

Lutton, R. J. (Wolverhampton W), 1970 v S, E; (with West Ham U), 1973 v Cy (sub), S (sub), W (sub); 1974 v P (6)

Lyner, D. R. (Glentoran), 1920 v E, W; 1922 v S, W; (with Manchester U), 1923 v E; (with Kilmarnock), 1923 v W (6)

Lytle, J. (Glentoran), 1898 W (1)

McAdams, W. J. (Manchester C), 1954 v W; 1955 v S; 1957 v E; 1958 v S, I; (with Bolton W), 1961 v E, S, W, I, WG (2), Gr; 1962 v E, Gr; (with Leeds U), Ho (15)

McAlery, J. M. (Cliftonville), 1882 v E, W (2)

McAlinden, J. (Belfast C), 1938 v S; 1939 v S; (with Portsmouth), 1947 v E; (with Southend U), 1949 v E (4)

McAllen, J. (Linfield), 1898 v E; 1899 v E, S, W; 1900 v E, S, W; 1901 v W; 1902 v S (9)

McAlpine, S. (Cliftonville), 1901 v S (1)

McArthur, A. (Distillery), 1886 v W (1)

McAuley, J. L. (Huddersfield T), 1911 v E, W; 1912 v E, S; 1913 v E, S (6)

McAuley, P. (Belfast C), 1900 v S (1)

McBride, S. D.(Glenavon), 1991 v D (sub), Pol (sub); 1992 v Fa (sub), D (4)

McCabe, J. J. (Leeds U), 1949 v S, W; 1950 v E; 1951 v W; 1953 v W; 1954 v S (6)

McCabe, W. (Ulster), 1891 v E (1)

McCambridge, J. (Ballymena), 1930 v S, W; (with Cardiff C), 1931 v W; 1932 v E (4)

McCandless, J. (Bradford), 1912 v W; 1913 v W; 1920 v W, S; 1921 v E (5)

McCandless, W. (Linfield), 1920 v E, W; 1921 v E; (with Rangers), 1921 v W; 1922 v S; 1924 v W, S; 1925 v S; 1929 v W (9)

McCann, P. (Belfast C), 1910 v E, S, W; 1911 v E; (with Glentoran), 1911 v S; 1912 v E; 1913 v W (7)

McCarthy, J. D. (Port Vale), 1996 v Se; 1997 v I, Arm, Th; (with Birmingham C), 1998 v P (sub), Slo (sub), Sp; 1999 v Fi (sub), Mol (sub), G (sub), Ca, Ei; 2000 v F, T, G, Fi (16)

McCartney, A. (Ulster), 1903 v S, W; (with Linfield), 1904 v S, W; (with Everton), 1905 v E, S; (with Belfast C), 1907 v E, S, W; 1908 v E, S, W; (with Glentoran), 1909 v E, S, W (15)

McCashin, J. (Cliftonville), 1896 v W; 1898 v S, W; 1899 v S (4)

McCavana, W. T. (Coleraine), 1955 v S; 1956 v E, S (3)

McCaw, D. (Malone), 1882 v E (1)

McCaw, J. (Linfield), 1927 v W; 1930 v S; 1931 v E, S, W (5)

McClatchey, J. (Distillery), 1886 v E, S, W (3)

McClatchey, T. (Distillery), 1895 v S (1)

McCleary, J. W. (Cliftonville), 1955 v W (1)

McCleery, W. (Linfield), 1930 v E; 1931 v E, S, W; 1932 v S, W; 1933 v E, W (9)

McClelland, J. T. (Arsenal), 1961 v W, I, WG (2), Gr; (with Fulham), 1966 v M (6)

McClelland, J. (Mansfield T), 1980 v S (sub), Aus (3); 1981 v Se, S; (with Rangers), S, Se (sub); 1982 v S, W, Y, Hon, Sp, A, F; 1983 v A, WG, Alb, T, Alb, S, E, W; 1984 v A, T, WG, S, E, W, Fi; 1985 v R, Is; (with Watford), Fi, E, Sp, T; 1986 v T, F (sub); 1987 v E (2), T, Is, Y; 1988 v T, Gr, F, Ma; 1989 v Ei, H, Sp (2), Ma; (with Leeds U), 1990 v N (53)

McCluggage, A. (Bradford), 1924 v E; (with Burnley), 1927 v S, W; 1928 v S, E, W; 1929 v S, E, W; 1930 v W; 1931 v E, W (12)

McClure, G. (Cliftonville), 1907 v S, W; 1908 v E; (with Distillery), 1909 v E (4)

McConnell, E. (Cliftonville), 1904 v S, W; (with Glentoran), 1905 v S; (with Sunderland), 1906 v E; 1907 v E; 1908 v S, W; (with Sheffield W), 1909 v S, W; 1910 v S, W, E (12)

McConnell, P. (Doncaster R), 1928 v W; (with Southport), 1932 v E (2)

McConnell, W. G. (Bohemians), 1912 v W; 1913 v E, S; 1914 v E, S, W (6)

McConnell, W. H. (Reading), 1925 v W; 1926 v E, W; 1927 v E, S, W; 1928 v E, W (8)

McCourt, F. J. (Manchester C), 1952 v E, W; 1953 v E, S, W, F (6)

McCoy, R. K. (Coleraine), 1987 v Y (sub) (1)

McCoy, S. (Distillery), 1896 v W (1)

McCracken, R. (C Palace), 1921 v E; 1922 v E, S, W (4)

McCracken, W. R. (Distillery), 1902 v E, W; 1903 v E; 1904 v E, S, W; (with Newcastle U), 1905 v E, S, W; 1907 v E; 1920 v E; 1922 v E, S, W; (with Hull C), 1923 v S (15)

McCreery, D. (Manchester U), 1976 v S (sub), E, W; 1977 v Ho, Bel, WG, E, S, W, Ic; 1978 v Ic, Ho, Bel, S, E, W; 1979 v Ei, D, Bul, E, Bul, W, D; (with QPR), 1980 v E, Ei, S (sub), E (sub), W (sub), Aus (1+1 sub); 1981 v Se (sub), P (sub); (with Tulsa R), S, P, Se; 1982 v S, Is, E (sub), F, Y, Hon, Sp, A, F; (with Newcastle U), 1983 v A; 1984 v T (sub); 1985 v R, Sp (sub); 1986 v T (sub), R, E, F, D, Alg, Sp, Br; 1987 v T, E, Y; 1988 v Y; 1989 v Sp, Ma, Ch; (with Hearts), 1990 v H, Ei, N, U (sub) (67)

McCrory, S. (Southend U), 1958 v E (1)

McCullough, K. (Belfast C), 1935 v W; 1936 v E; (with Manchester C), 1936 v S; 1937 v E, S (5)

McCullough, W. J. (Arsenal), 1961 v I; 1963 v Sp; 1964 v S, E, W, U, Sp; 1965 v E, Sw; (with Millwall), 1967 v E (10)

McCurdy, C. (Linfield), 1980 v Aus (sub) (1)

McDonald, A. (QPR), 1986 v R, E, F, D, Mor, Alg, Sp, Br; 1987 v E (2), T, Is, Y; 1988 v Y, T, Pol, F, Ma; 1989 v Ei, H, Sp, Ch; 1990 v H, Ei, U; 1991 v Y, D, A, Fa; 1992 v Fa, S, Li. G; 1993 v Alb, Sp, D, Alb, Ei, Li, La; 1994 v D, Ei; 1995 v P, A, Ei, La, Ca, Ch, La; 1996 v A (sub), N (52)

McDonald, R. (Rangers), 1930 v S; 1932 v E (2)

McDonnell, R. (Bohemians), 1911 v E, S; 1912 v W; 1913 v W (4)

McElhinney, G. M. A. (Bolton W), 1984 v WG, S, E, W, Fi; 1985 v R (6)

McFaul, W. S. (Linfield), 1967 v E (sub); (with Newcastle U), 1970 v W; 1971 v Sp; 1972 v USSR; 1973 v Cy; 1974 v Bul (6)

McGarry, J. K. (Cliftonville), 1951 v W, F, S (3)

McGaughey, M. (Linfield), 1985 v Is (sub) (1)

McGibbon, P. C. G. (Manchester U), 1995 v Ca (sub), Ch, La; 1996 v Lie (sub); 1997 v Th; (with Wigan Ath), 1998 v Alb; 2000 v L (sub) (7)

McGrath, R. C. (Tottenham H), 1974 v S, E, W; 1975 v N; 1976 v Is (sub); 1977; (with Manchester U), Ho, Bel, WG, E, S, W, Ic; 1978 v Ic, Ho, Bel, S, E, W; 1979 v Bul (sub), E (2 sub) (21)

McGregor, S. (Glentoran), 1921 v S (1)

McGrillen, J. (Clyde), 1924 v S; (with Belfast C), 1927 v S (2)

McGuire, E. (Distillery), 1907 v S (1)

McIlroy, H. (Cliftonville), 1906 v E (1)

McIlroy, J. (Burnley), 1952 v E, S, W; 1953 v E, S, W; 1954 v E, S, W; 1955 v E, S, W; 1956 v E, S, W; 1957 v E, S, W, I, P (2); 1958 v E, S, W, I (2), Cz (2), Arg, WG, F; 1959 v E, S, W, Sp; 1960 v E, S, W; 1961 v E, W, WG (2), Gr; 1962 v E, S, Gr, Ho; 1963 v E, S, Pol (2); (with Stoke C), 1963 v W; 1966 v S, E, Alb (55)

McIlroy, S. B. (Manchester U), 1972 v Sp, S (sub); 1974 v S, E, W; 1975 v N, Se, Y, E, S, W; 1976 v Se, N, Y, S, E, W; 1977 v Ho, Bel, E, S, W, Ic; 1978 v Ic, Ho, Bel, S, E, W; 1979 v Ei, D, Bul, E, Bul, S, W, D; 1980 v E, Ei, S, S, E, W; 1981 v Se, P, S, P, Se; 1982 v S, Is; (with Stoke C), E, F, S, W, Y, Hon, Sp, A, F; 1983 v A, WG, Alb, T, Alb, S, E, W; 1984 v A, T, S, E, W, Fi; 1985 v Fi, E, T; (with Manchester C), 1986 v T, R, E, F, D, Mor, Alg, Sp, Br; 1987 v E (sub) (88)

McIlvenny, P. (Distillery), 1924 v W (1)

McIlvenny, R. (Distillery), 1890 v E; (with Ulster), 1891 v E (2)

McKeag, W. (Glentoran), 1968 v S, W (2)

McKee, F. W. (Cliftonville), 1906 v S, W; (with Belfast C), 1914 v E, S, W (5)

McKelvey, H. (Glentoran), 1901 v W (1)

McKenna, J. (Huddersfield), 1950 v E, S, W; 1951 v E, S, F; 1952 v E (7)

McKenzie, H. (Distillery), 1923 v S (1)

McKenzie, R. (Airdrie), 1967 v W (1)

McKeown, N. (Linfield), 1892 v E, S, W; 1893 v S, W; 1894 v S, W (7)

McKie, H. (Cliftonville), 1895 v E, S, W (3)

McKinney, D. (Hull C), 1921 v S; (with Bradford C), 1924 v S (2)

McKinney, V. J. (Falkirk), 1966 v WG (1)

McKnight, A. D. (Celtic), 1988 v Y, T, Gr, Pol, F, Ma; (with West Ham U) 1989 v Ei, H, Sp (2) (10)

McKnight, J. (Preston NE), 1912 v S; (with Glentoran), 1913 v S (2)

McLaughlin, J. C. (Shrewsbury T), 1962 v E, S, W, Gr; 1963 v W; (with Swansea T), 1964 v W, U; 1965 v E, W, Sw (2); 1966 v W (12)

McLean, T. (Limavady), 1885 v S (1)

McMahon, G. J. (Tottenham H), 1995 v Ca (sub), Ch, La; 1996 v Lie, N (sub), Se, G; (with Stoke C), 1997 v Arm (sub), Alb (sub), Bel, P (sub), Uk (sub), Arm (sub), Th (sub); 1998 v G (sub), Alb (sub), P (sub) (17)

McMahon, J. (Bohemians), 1934 v S (1)

McMaster, G. (Glentoran), 1897 v E, S, W (3)

McMichael, A. (Newcastle U), 1950 v E, S; 1951 v E, S, F; 1952 v E, S, W; 1953 v E, S, W, F; 1954 v E, S, W; 1955 v E, W; 1956 v W; 1957 v E, S, W, I, P (2); 1958 v E, S, W, I (2), Cz (2), Arg, WG, F; 1959 v S, W, Sp; 1960 v E, S, W (40)

McMillan, G. (Distillery), 1903 v E; 1905 v W (2)

McMillan, S. T. (Manchester U), 1963 v E, S (2)

McMillen, W. S. (Manchester U), 1934 v E; 1935 v S; 1937 v S; (with Chesterfield), 1938 v S, W; 1939 v E, S (7)

McMordie, A. S. (Middlesbrough), 1969 v Is, T (2), E, S, W; 1970 v E, S, W, USSR; 1971 v Cy (2), E, S, W; 1972 v USSR, Sp, E, S, W; 1973 v Bul (21)

McMorran, E. J. (Belfast C), 1947 v E; (with Barnsley), 1951 v E, S, W; 1952 v E, S, W; 1953 v E, S, F; (with Doncaster R), 1953 v W; 1954 v E; 1956 v W; 1957 v I, P (15)

McMullan, D. (Liverpool), 1926 v E, W; 1927 v S (3)

McNally, B. A. (Shrewsbury T), 1986 v Mor; 1987 v T (sub); 1988 v Y, Gr, Ma (sub) (5)

McNinch, J. (Ballymena), 1931 v S; 1932 v S, W (3)

McParland, P. J. (Aston Villa), 1954 v W; 1955 v E, S; 1956 v E, S; 1957 v E, S, W, P; 1958 v E, S, W, I (2), Cz (2), Arg, WG, F; 1959 v E, S, Sp; 1960 v E, S, W; 1961 v E, S, W, I, WG (2), Gr; (with Wolverhampton W), 1962 v Ho (34)

McShane, J. (Cliftonville), 1899 v S; 1900 v E, S, W (4)

McVeigh, P. (Tottenham H), 1999 v Ca (sub) (1)

McVicker, J. (Linfield), 1888 v E; (with Glentoran), 1889 v S (2)

McWha, W. B. R. (Knock), 1882 v E, W; (with Cliftonville), 1883 v E, W; 1884 v E; 1885 v E, W (7)

Mackie, J. (Arsenal), 1923 v W; (with Portsmouth), 1935 v S, W (3)

Madden, O. (Norwich C), 1938 v E (1)

Magee, G. (Wellington Park), 1885 v E, S, W (3)

Magill, E. J. (Arsenal), 1962 v E, S, Gr; 1963 v E, S, W, Pol (2); Sp; 1964 v E, S, W, U, Sp; 1965 v E, S, Sw (2), Ho, Alb; 1966 v S, (with Brighton), E, Alb, W, WG, M (26)

Magilton, J. (Oxford U), 1991 v Pol, Y, Fa; 1992 v Fa, A, D, S, Li, G; 1993 v Alb, D, Alb, Ei, Li, La; 1994 v La, D, Ei;(with Southampton), R, Lie, Co, M; 1995 v P, A, Ei (2), Ca, Ch, La; 1996 v P, N, G; 1997 v Uk (sub), Arm (sub), Bel, P; 1998 v G; (with Sheffield W), P, Sp; (with Ipswich T), 2000 v L (40)

Maginnis, H. (Linfield), 1900 v E, S, W; 1903 v S, W; 1904 v E, S, W (8)

Mahood, J. (Belfast C), 1926 v S; 1928 v E, S, W; 1929 v E, S, W; 1930 v W; (with Ballymena), 1934 v S (9)

Manderson, R. (Rangers), 1920 v W, S; 1925 v S, E; 1926 v S (5)

Mansfield, J. (Dublin Freebooters), 1901 v E (1)

Martin, C. (Bo'ness), 1925 v S (1)

Martin, C. (Cliftonville), 1882 v E, W; 1883 v E (3)

Martin, C. J. (Glentoran), 1947 v S; (with Leeds U), 1948 v E, S, W; (with Aston Villa), 1949 v E; 1950 v W (6)

Martin, D. K. (Belfast C), 1934 v E, S, W; 1935 v S; (with Wolverhampton W), 1935 v E; 1936 v W; (with Nottingham F), 1937 v S; 1938 v E, S; 1939 v S (10)

Mathieson, A. (Luton T), 1921 v W; 1922 v E (2)

Maxwell, J. (Linfield), 1902 v W; 1903 v W, E; (with Glentoran), 1905 v W, S; (with Belfast C), 1906 v W; 1907 v S (7)

Meek, H. L. (Glentoran), 1925 v W (1)

Mehaffy, J. A. (Queen's Island), 1922 v W (1)

Meldon, P. A. (Dublin Freebooters), 1899 v S, W (2)

Mercer, H. V. A. (Linfield), 1908 v E (1)

Mercer, J. T. (Distillery), 1898 v E, S, W; 1899 v E; (with Linfield), 1902 v E, W; (with Distillery), 1903 v S, W; (with Derby Co), 1904 v E, W; 1905 v S (11)

Millar, W. (Barrow), 1932 v W; 1933 v S (2)

Miller, J. (Middlesbrough), 1929 v W, S; 1930 v E (3)

Milligan, D. (Chesterfield), 1939 v W (1)

Milne, R. G. (Linfield), 1894 v E, S, W; 1895 v E, W; 1896 v E, S, W; 1897 v E, S; 1898 v E, S, W; 1899 v E, W; 1901 v W; 1902 v S, W; 1903 v E, S; 1904 v E, S, W; 1906 v E, S, W (27)

Mitchell, E. J. (Cliftonville), 1933 v S; (with Glentoran), 1934 v W (2)
Mitchell, W. (Distillery), 1932 v E, W; 1933 v E, W; (with Chelsea), 1934 v W, S; 1935 v S, E; 1936 v S, E; 1937 v E, S, W; 1938 v E, S (15)
Molyneux, T. B. (Ligoniel), 1883 v E, W; (with Cliftonville), 1884 v S; 1885 v E, W; 1886 v E, W, S; 1888 v S (11)
Montgomery, F. J. (Coleraine), 1955 v E (1)
Moore, C. (Glentoran), 1949 v W (1)
Moore, P. (Aberdeen), 1933 v E (1)
Moore, R. (Linfield Ath), 1891 v E, S, W (3)
Moore, R. L. (Ulster), 1887 v S, W (2)
Moore, W. (Falkirk), 1923 v S (1)
Moorhead, F. W. (Dublin University), 1885 v E (1)
Moorhead, G. (Linfield), 1923 v S; 1928 v S; 1929 v S (3)
Moran, J. (Leeds C), 1912 v W (1)
Moreland, V. (Derby Co), 1979 v Bul (2 sub), E, S; 1980 v E, Ei (6)
Morgan, F. G. (Linfield), 1923 v E; (with Nottingham F), 1924 v S; 1927 v E; 1928 v E, S, W; 1929 v E (7)
Morgan, S. (Port Vale), 1972 v Sp; 1973 v Bul (sub), P, Cy, E, S, W; (with Aston Villa), 1974 v Bul, P, S, E; 1975 v Se; 1976 v Se (sub), N, Y; (with Brighton & HA), S, W (sub); (with Sparta Rotterdam), 1979 v D (18)
Morrison, R. (Linfield Ath), 1891 v E, W (2)
Morrison, T. (Glentoran), 1895 v E, S, W; (with Burnley), 1899 v W; 1900 v W; 1902 v E, S (7)
Morrogh, D. (Bohemians), 1896 v S (1)
Morrow, S. J. (Arsenal), 1990 v U (sub); 1991 v A (sub), Pol, Y; 1992 v Fa, S (sub), G (sub); 1993 v Sp (sub), Alb, Ei; 1994 v R, Co, M (sub); 1995 v P, Ei (2), La; 1996 v P, Se; 1997 v Uk, G, Alb, I, Bel; (with QPR), P, Uk, Arm; 1998 v G, Slo, Sw, Sp; 1999 v T, Fi, Mol, G, Mol; 2000 v G, Fi (39)
Morrow, W. J. (Moyola Park), 1883 v E, W; 1884 v S (3)
Muir, R. (Oldpark), 1885 v S, W (2)
Mulholland, S. (Celtic), 1906 v S, E (2)
Mullan, G. (Glentoran), 1983 v S, E, W, Alb (sub) (4)
Mulligan, J. (Manchester C), 1921 v S (1)
Mulryne, P. P. (Manchester U), 1997 v Bel (sub), Arm (sub), Th; 1998 v Alb (sub), Sp (sub); 1999 v T, Fi; (with Norwich C), Ca (8)
Murdock, C. J. (Preston NE), 2000 v L (sub), Ma, H (sub) (3)
Murphy, J. (Bradford C), 1910 v E, S, W (3)
Murphy, N. (QPR), 1905 v E, S, W (3)
Murray, J. M. (Motherwell), 1910 v E, S; (with Sheffield W), 1910 v W (3)

Napier, R. J. (Bolton W), 1966 v WG (1)
Neill, W. J. T. (Arsenal), 1961 v I, Gr, WG; 1962 v E, S, W, Gr; 1963 v E, W, Pol, Sp; 1964 v S, E, W, U, Sp; 1965 v E, S, W, Sw, Ho (2), Alb; 1966 v S, E, W, Alb, WG, M; 1967 v S, W; 1968 v S, E; 1969 v E, S, W, Is, T (2); 1970 v S, E, W, USSR (2); (with Hull C), 1971 v Cy, Sp; 1972 v USSR (2), Sp, S, E, W; 1973 v Bul, Cy (2), P, E, S, W (59)
Nelis, P. (Nottingham F), 1923 v E (1)
Nelson, S. (Arsenal), 1970 v W, E (sub); 1971 v Cy, Sp, E, S, W; 1972 v USSR (2), Sp, E, S, W; 1973 v Bul, Cy, P; 1974 v S, E; 1975 v Se, Y; 1976 v Se, N, Is, E; 1977 v Bel (sub), WG, W, Ic; 1978 v Ic, Ho, Bel; 1979 v Ei, D, Bul, E, Bul, E, S, W, D; 1980 v E, Ei, Is; 1981 v S, P, S, Se; (with Brighton & HA), 1982 v E, S, Sp (sub), A (51)
Nicholl, C. J. (Aston Villa), 1975 v Se, Y, E, S, W; 1976 v Se, N, Y, S, E, W; 1977 v W; (with Southampton), 1978 v Bel (sub), S, E, W; 1979 v Ei, Bul, E, Bul, E, W; 1980 v Ei, Is, S, E, W, Aus (3); 1981 v Se, P, S, P, S, Se; 1982 v S, Is, E, F, W, Y, Hon, Sp, A, F; 1983 v S (sub), E, W; (with Grimsby T), 1984 v A, T (51)
Nicholl, H. (Belfast C), 1902 v E, W; 1905 v E (3)
Nicholl, J. M. (Manchester U), 1976 v Is, W (sub); 1977 v Ho, Bel, E, S, W, Ic; 1978 v Ic, Ho, Bel, S, E, W; 1979 v Ei, D, Bul, E, Bul, E, S, W, D; 1980 v E, Ei, Is, S, E, W, Aus (3); 1981 v Se, P, S, P, S, Se; 1982 v S, Is, E; (with Toronto B), F, W, Y, Hon, Sp, A, F; (with Sunderland), 1983 v A, WG, Alb, T, Alb; (with Toronto B), S, E, W; 1984 v T; (with Rangers), WG, S, E; (with Toronto B), Fi; 1985 v R; (with WBA), Fi, E, Sp, T; 1986 v T, R, E, F, Alg, Sp, Br (73)
Nicholson, J. J. (Manchester U), 1961 v S, W; 1962 v E, W, Gr, Ho; 1963 v E, S, Pol (2); (with Huddersfield T), 1965 v W, Ho (2), Alb; 1966 v S, E, W, Alb, M; 1967 v S, W; 1968 v S, E, W; 1969 v S, E, W, T (2); 1970 v S, E, W, USSR (2); 1971 v Cy (2), S, W; 1972 v USSR (2) (41)
Nixon, R. (Linfield), 1914 v S (1)
Nolan, I. R. (Sheffield W), 1997 v Arm, G, Alb, P, Uk; 1998 v G, P; 2000 v G, Fi, L, Ma, H (12)
Nolan-Whelan, J. V. (Dublin Freebooters), 1901 v E, W; 1902 v S, W (4)

O'Boyle, G. (Dunfermline Ath), 1994 v Co (sub), M; (with St Johnstone), 1995 v P (sub), La (sub), Ca (sub), Ch (sub); 1996 v Se (sub), G (sub); 1997 v I (sub), Bel (sub); 1998 v Slo (sub), Sw (sub); 1999 v Fi (sub) (13)
O'Brien, M. T. (QPR), 1921 v S; (with Leicester C), 1922 v S, W; 1924 v S, W; (with Hull C), 1925 v S, E, W; 1926 v W; (with Derby Co), 1927 v W (10)
O'Connell, P. (Sheffield W), 1912 v E, S; (with Hull C), 1914 v E, S, W (5)
O'Doherty, A. (Coleraine), 1970 v E, W (sub) (2)
O'Driscoll, J. F. (Swansea T), 1949 v E, S, W (3)
O'Hagan, C. (Tottenham H), 1905 v S, W; 1906 v S, W, E; (with Aberdeen), 1907 v E, S, W; 1908 v S, W; 1909 v E (11)
O'Hagan, W. (St Mirren), 1920 v E, W (2)
O'Hehir, J. C. (Bohemians), 1910 v W (1)
O'Kane, W. J. (Nottingham F), 1970 v E, W, S (sub); 1971 v Sp, E, S, W; 1972 v USSR (2); 1973 v P, Cy; 1974 v Bul, P, S, E, W; 1975 v N, Se, E, S (20)
O'Mahoney, M. T. (Bristol R), 1939 v S (1)
O'Neill, C. (Motherwell), 1989 v Ch (sub); 1990 v Ei (sub); 1991 v D (3)
O'Neill, J. (Sunderland), 1962 v W (1)
O'Neill, J. P. (Leicester C), 1980 v Is, S, E, W, Aus (3); 1981 v P, S, P, S, Se; 1982 v S, Is, E, F, S, F (sub); 1983 v A, WG, Alb, T, Alb, S; 1984 v S (sub); 1985 v Is, Fi, E, Sp, T; 1986 v T, R, E, F, D, Mor, Alg, Sp, Br (39)
O'Neill, M. A. M. (Newcastle U), 1988 v Gr, Pol, F, Ma; 1989 v Ei, H, Sp (sub), Sp (sub), Ma (sub), Ch; (with Dundee U), 1990 v H (sub), Ei; 1991 v Pol; 1992 v Fa (sub), S (sub), G (sub); 1993 v Alb (sub + 1), Ei, Sp, Li, La; (with Hibernian), 1994 v Lie (sub); 1995 v A (sub), Ei; 1996 v Lie, A, N, Se; (with Coventry C), 1997 v Uk (sub), Arm (sub) (31)
O'Neill, M. H. M. (Distillery), 1972 v USSR (sub), (with Nottingham F), Sp (sub), W (sub); 1973 v P, Cy, E, S, W; 1974 v Bul, P, E (sub), W; 1975 v Se, Y, E, S; 1976 v Y (sub); 1977 v E (sub), S; 1978 v Ic, Ho, S, E, W; 1979 v Ei, D, Bul, E, Bul, D; 1980 v Ei, Is, Aus (3); 1981 v Se, P; (with Norwich C), P, S, Se; (with Manchester C), 1982 v S; (with Norwich C), E, F, S, Y, Hon, Sp, A, F; 1983 v A, WG, Alb, T, Alb, S, E; (with Notts Co), 1984 v A, T, WG, E, W, Fi; 1985 v R, Fi (64)
O'Reilly, H. (Dublin Freebooters), 1901 v S, W; 1904 v S (3)

Parke, J. (Linfield), 1964 v S; (with Hibernian), 1964 v E, Sp; (with Sunderland), 1965 v Sw, S, W, Ho (2), Alb; 1966 v WG; 1967 v E, S; 1968 v S, E (14)
Patterson, D. J. (C Palace), 1994 v Co (sub), M (sub); 1995 v Ei (sub+1), La, Ca, Ch (sub), La (sub); (with Luton T), 1996 v N (sub), Se; 1998 v Sw, Sp; (with Dundee U), 1999 v Fi, Mol, G, Mol, Ei (17)
Peacock, R. (Celtic), 1952 v S; 1953 v F; 1954 v W; 1955 v E, S; 1956 v E, S; 1957 v W, I, P; 1958 v S, E, W, I (2), Arg, Cz (2), WG; 1959 v E, S, W; 1960 v S, E; 1961 v E, S, I, WG (2), Gr; (with Coleraine), 1962 v S (31)
Peden, J. (Distillery), 1887 v S, W; 1888 v W, E; 1889 v S, E; 1890 v W, S; 1891 v W, E; 1892 v W, E; 1893 v E, S, W; 1896 v W, E, S; 1897 v W, S; 1898 v W, E, S; 1899 v W (24)
Penney, S. (Brighton & HA), 1985 v Is; 1986 v T, R, E, F, D, Mor, Alg, Sp; 1987 v E, T, Is; 1988 v Pol, F, Ma; 1989 v Ei, Sp (17)
Percy, J. C. (Belfast YMCA), 1889 v W (1)
Platt, J. A. (Middlesbrough), 1976 v Is (sub); 1978 v S, E, W; 1980 v S, E, W, Aus (3); 1981 v Se, P; 1982 v F, S, W (sub), A; 1983 v A, WG, Alb, T; (with Ballymena U), 1984 v E, W (sub); (with Coleraine), 1986 v Mor (sub) (23)
Ponsonby, J. (Distillery), 1895 v S, W; 1896 v E, S, W; 1897 v E, S, W; 1899 v E (9)
Potts, R. M. C. (Cliftonville), 1883 v E, W (2)
Priestley, T. J. M. (Coleraine), 1933 v S; (with Chelsea), 1934 v E (2)
Pyper, Jas. (Cliftonville), 1897 v S, W; 1898 v S, E, W; 1899 v S; 1900 v E (7)
Pyper, John (Cliftonville), 1897 v E, S, W; 1899 v E, W; 1900 v E, W, S; 1902 v S (9)
Pyper, M. (Linfield), 1932 v W (1)

Quinn, J. M. (Blackburn R), 1985 v Is, Fi, E, Sp, T; 1986 v T, R, E, F, D (sub), Mor (sub); 1987 v E (sub), T; (with Swindon T), 1988 v Y (sub), T, Gr, Pol, F (sub), Ma; (with Leicester C), 1989 v Ei, H (sub), Sp (sub+1); (with Bradford C), Ma, Ch; 1990 v H, (with West Ham U), N; 1991 v Y (sub); (with Bournemouth), 1992 v Li; (with Reading), 1993 v Sp, D, Alb (sub), Ei (sub), La (sub); 1994 v La, D (sub), Ei, R, Lie, Co, M; 1995 v P, A (sub), La (sub); 1996 v Lie, A (sub) (46)

Quinn, S. J. (Blackpool), 1996 v Se (sub); 1997 v Alb (sub), I, Bel, P, Uk (sub), Arm, Th (sub); 1998 v G, Alb; (with WBA), Slo, Sw; 1999 v T (sub), Fi (sub), Ei; 2000 v F (sub), T (sub), G (sub), Fi, L, Ma (21)

Rafferty, P. (Linfield), 1980 v E (sub) (1)
Ramsey, P. C. (Leicester C), 1984 v A, WG, S; 1985 v Is, E, Sp, T; 1986 v T, Mor; 1987 v Is, E, Y (sub); 1988 v Y; 1989 v Sp (14)
Rankine, J. (Alexander), 1883 v E, W (2)
Rattray, D. (Avoniel), 1882 v E; 1883 v E, W (3)
Rea, R. (Glentoran), 1901 v E (1)
Redmond, R. (Cliftonville), 1884 v W (1)
Reid, G. H. (Cardiff C), 1923 v S (1)
Reid, J. (Ulster), 1883 v E; 1884 v W; 1887 v S; 1889 v W; 1890 v S, W (6)
Reid, S. E. (Derby Co), 1934 v E, W; 1936 v E (3)
Reid, W. (Hearts), 1931 v E (1)
Reilly, M. M. (Portsmouth), 1900 v E; 1902 v E (2)
Renneville, W. T. J. (Leyton), 1910 v S, E, W; (with Aston Villa), 1911 v W (4)
Reynolds, J. (Distillery), 1890 v E, W; (with Ulster), 1891 v E, S, W (5)
Reynolds, R. (Bohemians), 1905 v W (1)
Rice, P. J. (Arsenal), 1969 v Is; 1970 v USSR; 1971 v E, S, W; 1972 v USSR, Sp, E, S, W; 1973 v Bul, Cy, E, S, W; 1974 v Bul, P, S, E, W; 1975 v N, Y, E, S, W; 1976 v Se, N, Y, Is, S, E, W; 1977 v Ho, Bel, WG, E, S, Ic; 1978 v Ic, Ho, Bel; 1979 v Ei, D, E (2), S, W, D; 1980 v E (49)
Roberts, F. C. (Glentoran), 1931 v S (1)
Robinson, P. (Distillery), 1920 v S; (with Blackburn R), 1921 v W (2)
Robinson, S. (Bournemouth), 1997 v Th (sub); 1999 v Mol, Ei; 2000 v L (sub), H (sub) (5)
Rogan, A. (Celtic), 1988 v Y (sub), Gr, Pol (sub); 1989 v Ei (sub), H, Sp (2), Ma (sub), Ch; 1990 v H, N (sub), U; 1991 v Y (2), D, A; (with Sunderland), 1992 v Li (sub); (with Millwall), 1997 v G (sub) (18)
Rollo, D. (Linfield), 1912 v W; 1913 v W; 1914 v W, E; (with Blackburn R), 1920 v S, W; 1921 v E, S, W; 1922 v E; 1923 v E; 1924 v W; 1925 v W; 1926 v E; 1927 v E (16)
Roper, E. O. (Dublin University), 1886 v W (1)
Rosbotham, A. (Cliftonville), 1887 v E, S, W; 1888 v E, S, W; 1889 v E (7)
Ross, W. E. (Newcastle U), 1969 v Is (1)
Rowland, K. (West Ham U), 1994 v La (sub); 1995 v Ca, Ch, La; 1996 v P (sub), Lie (sub), N (sub), Se, G (sub); 1997 v Uk, Arm, I (sub); 1998 v Alb; (with QPR), 1999 v T, Fi, Mol, G, Ca, Ei (19)
Rowley, R. W. M. (Southampton), 1929 v S, W; 1930 v W, E; (with Tottenham H), 1931 v W; 1932 v S (6)
Russell, A. (Linfield), 1947 v E (1)
Russell, S. R. (Bradford C), 1930 v E, S; (with Derry C), 1932 v E (3)
Ryan, R. A. (WBA), 1950 v W (1)

Sanchez, L. P. (Wimbledon), 1987 v T (sub); 1989 v Sp, Ma (3)
Scott, L. (Liverpool), 1920 v S; 1921 v E, S, W; 1922 v E; 1925 v W; 1926 v E, S, W; 1927 v E, S, W; 1928 v E, S, W; 1929 v E, S, W; 1930 v E; 1931 v E; 1932 v W; 1933 v E, S, W; 1934 v E, S, W; (with Belfast C), 1935 v S; 1936 v E, S, W (31)
Scott, J. (Grimsby), 1958 v Cz, F (2)
Scott, J. E. (Cliftonville), 1901 v S (1)
Scott, L. J. (Dublin University), 1895 v S, W (2)
Scott, P. W. (Everton), 1975 v W; 1976 v Y; (with York C), Is, S, E (sub), W; 1978 v S, E, W; (with Aldershot), 1979 v S (sub) (10)
Scott, T. (Cliftonville), 1894 v E, S; 1895 v S, W; 1896 v S, E, W; 1897 v E, W; 1898 v E, S, W; 1900 v W (13)
Scott, W. (Linfield), 1903 v E, S, W; 1904 v E, S, W; (with Everton), 1905 v E, S, W; 1906 v E, S; 1908 v E, S, W; 1909 v E, S, W; 1910 v E, S; 1911 v E, S, W; 1912 v E; (with Leeds City), 1913 v E, S, W (25)
Scraggs, M. J. (Glentoran), 1921 v W; 1922 v E (2)
Seymour, H. C. (Bohemians), 1914 v W (1)
Seymour, J. (Cliftonville), 1907 v W; 1909 v W (2)
Shanks, T. (Woolwich Arsenal), 1903 v S; 1904 v W; (with Brentford), 1905 v E (3)
Sharkey, P. G. (Ipswich T), 1976 v S (1)
Sheehan, Dr G. (Bohemians), 1899 v S; 1900 v E, W (3)
Sheridan, J. (Everton), 1903 v W, E, S; 1904 v E, S; (with Stoke C), 1905 v E (6)
Sherrard, J. (Limavady), 1885 v S; 1887 v W; 1888 v W (3)
Sherrard, W. C. (Cliftonville), 1895 v E, W, S (3)
Sherry, J. J. (Bohemians), 1906 v E; 1907 v W (2)

Shields, R. J. (Southampton), 1957 v S (1)
Silo, M. (Belfast YMCA), 1888 v E (1)
Simpson, W. J. (Rangers), 1951 v W, F; 1954 v E, S; 1955 v E; 1957 v I, P; 1958 v S, E, W, I; 1959 v S (12)
Sinclair, J. (Knock), 1882 v E, W (2)
Slemin, J. C. (Bohemians), 1909 v W (1)
Sloan, A. S. (London Caledonians), 1925 v W (1)
Sloan, D. (Oxford U), 1969 v Is; 1971 v Sp (2)
Sloan, H. A. de B. (Bohemians), 1903 v E; 1904 v S; 1905 v E; 1906 v W; 1907 v E, W; 1908 v W; 1909 v S (8)
Sloan, J. W. (Arsenal), 1947 v W (1)
Sloan, T. (Cardiff C), 1926 v S, W, E; 1927 v W, S; 1928 v E, W; 1929 v E; (with Linfield), 1930 v W, S; 1931 v S (11)
Sloan, T. (Manchester U), 1979 v S, W (sub); 1980 v S (sub) (3)
Small, J. M. (Clarence), 1887 v E; (with Cliftonville), 1893 v E, S, W (4)
Smith, E. E. (Cardiff C), 1921 v S; 1923 v W, E; 1924 v E (4)
Smith, J. E. (Distillery), 1901 v S, W (2)
Smyth, R. H. (Dublin University), 1886 v W (1)
Smyth, S. (Wolverhampton W), 1948 v E, S, W; 1949 v S, W; 1950 v E, S, W; (with Stoke C), 1952 v E (9)
Smyth, W. (Distillery), 1949 v E, S; 1954 v S, E (4)
Snape, A. (Airdrie), 1920 v E (1)
Sonner, D. J. (Ipswich T), 1998 v Alb (sub); (with Sheffield W), 1999 v G (sub), Ca (sub); 2000 v L (sub), Ma (sub), H (6)
Spence, D. W. (Bury), 1975 v Y, E, S, W; 1976 v Se, Is, E, W, S (sub); (with Blackpool), 1977 v Ho (sub), WG (sub), E (sub), S (sub), W (sub), Ic (sub); 1979 v Ei, D (sub), E (sub), Bul (sub), E (sub), S, W, D; 1980 v Ei; (with Southend U), Is (sub), Aus (sub); 1981 v S (sub), Se (sub); 1982 v F (sub) (29)
Spencer, S. (Distillery), 1890 v E, S; 1892 v E, S, W; 1893 v E (6)
Spiller, E. A. (Cliftonville), 1883 v E, W; 1884 v E, W, S (5)
Stanfield, O. M. (Distillery), 1887 v E, S, W; 1888 v E, S, W; 1889 v E, S, W; 1890 v E, S; 1891 v E, S, W; 1892 v E, S, W; 1893 v E, W; 1894 v E, S, W; 1895 v E, S; 1896 v E, S, W; 1897 v E, S, W (30)
Steele, A. (Charlton Ath), 1926 v W, S; (with Fulham), 1929 v W, S (4)
Stevenson, A. E. (Rangers), 1934 v E, S, W; (with Everton), 1935 v E, S; 1936 v S, W; 1937 v E, W; 1938 v E, W; 1939 v E, S, W; 1947 v S, W; 1948 v S (17)
Stewart, A. (Glentoran), 1967 v W; 1968 v S, E; (with Derby Co), 1968 v W; 1969 v Is, T (1+1 sub) (7)
Stewart, D. C. (Hull C), 1978 v Bel (1)
Stewart, I. (QPR), 1982 v F (sub); 1983 v A, WG, Alb, T, Alb, S, E, W; 1984 v A, T, WG, S, E, W, Fi; 1985 v R, Fi, Is, E, Sp, T; (with Newcastle U), 1986 v R, E, D, Mor, Alg (sub), Sp (sub), Br; 1987 v E, Is (sub) (31)
Stewart, R. K. (St Columb's Court), 1890 v E, S, W; (with Cliftonville), 1892 v E, S, W; 1893 v E, W; 1894 v E, S, W (11)
Stewart, T. C. (Linfield), 1961 v W (1)
Swan, S. (Linfield), 1899 v S (1)

Taggart, G. P. (Barnsley), 1990 v N, U; 1991 v Y, D, A, Pol, Fa; 1992 v Fa, A, D, S, Li, G; 1993 v Alb, Sp, D, Alb, Ei, Sp, Li, La; 1994 v La, D, Ei, R, Lie, Co, M; 1995 v P (sub), A, Ei (2), Ca, Ch, La; (with Bolton W), 1997 v G, Alb, I, Bel, P, Uk, Arm; 1998 v G, P, Sp; (with Leicester C), 2000 v H (46)
Taggart, J. (Walsall), 1899 v W (1)
Taylor, M. S. (Fulham), 1999 v G, Mol, Ca, Ei; 2000 v F, T, G, Fi, L (sub), Ma (sub), H (11)
Thompson, F. W. (Cliftonville), 1910 v E, S, W; (with Linfield), 1911 v W; (with Bradford C), 1911 v E; 1912 v E, W; 1913 v E, S, W; (with Clyde), 1914 v E, S (12)
Thompson, J. (Belfast Ath), 1889 v S (1)
Thompson, J. (Distillery), 1897 v S (1)
Thunder, P. J. (Bohemians), 1911 v W (1)
Todd, S. J. (Burnley), 1966 v M (sub); 1967 v E; 1968 v W; 1969 v E, S, W; 1970 v S, USSR; (with Sheffield W), 1971 v Cy (2), Sp (sub) (11)
Toner, J. (Arsenal), 1922 v W; 1923 v W; 1924 v W, E; 1925 v E, S; (with St Johnstone), 1927 v E, S (8)
Torrans, R. (Linfield), 1893 v S (1)
Torrans, S. (Linfield), 1889 v S; 1890 v S, W; 1891 v S, W; 1892 v E, S, W; 1893 v E, S; 1894 v E, S, W; 1895 v E; 1896 v E, S, W; 1897 v E, S, W; 1898 v E, S; 1899 v E, W; 1901 v S, W (26)
Trainor, D. (Crusaders), 1967 v W (1)
Tully, C. P. (Celtic), 1949 v E; 1950 v E; 1952 v S; 1953 v E, S, W, F; 1954 v S; 1956 v E; 1959 v Sp (10)
Turner, E. (Cliftonville), 1896 v E, W (2)

Turner, W. (Cliftonville), 1886 v E, S; 1888 v S (3)
Twoomey, J. F. (Leeds U), 1938 v W; 1939 v E (2)

Uprichard, W. N. M. C. (Swindon T), 1952 v E, S, W; 1953 v E, S; (with Portsmouth), 1953 v W, F; 1955 v E, S, W; 1956 v E, S, W; 1958 v S, I, Cz; 1959 v S, Sp (18)

Vernon, J. (Belfast C), 1947 v E, S; (with WBA), 1947 v W; 1948 v E, S, W; 1949 v E, S, W; 1950 v E, S; 1951 v E, S, W, F; 1952 v S, E (17)

Waddell, T. M. R. (Cliftonville), 1906 v S (1)
Walker, J. (Doncaster R), 1955 v W (1)
Walker, T. (Bury), 1911 v S (1)
Walsh, D. J. (WBA), 1947 v S, W; 1948 v E, S, W; 1949 v E, S, W; 1950 v W (9)
Walsh, W. (Manchester C), 1948 v E, S, W; 1949 v E, S (5)
Waring, J. (Cliftonville), 1899 v E (1)
Warren, P. (Shelbourne), 1913 v E, S (2)
Watson, J. (Ulster), 1883 v E, W; 1886 v E, S, W; 1887 v S, W; 1889 v E, W (9)
Watson, P. (Distillery), 1971 v Cy (sub) (1)
Watson, T. (Cardiff C), 1926 v S (1)
Wattie, J. (Distillery), 1899 v E (1)
Webb, C. G. (Brighton), 1909 v S, W; 1911 v S (3)
Weir, E. (Clyde), 1939 v W (1)
Welsh, E. (Carlisle U), 1966 v W, WG, M; 1967 v W (4)
Whiteside, N. (Manchester U), 1982 v Y, Hon, Sp, A, F; 1983 v WG, Alb, T; 1984 v A, T, WG, S, E, W, Fi; 1985 v R, Fi, Is, E, Sp, T; 1986 v R, E, F, D, Mor, Alg, Sp, Br; 1987 v E (2), Is, Y; 1988 v T, Pol, F; (with Everton), 1990 v H, Ei (38)
Whiteside, T. (Distillery), 1891 v E (1)
Whitfield, E. R. (Dublin University), 1886 v W (1)
Whitley, Jeff (Manchester C), 1997 v Bel (sub), Th (sub); 1998 v Sp (sub); 2000 v Fi (4)
Whitley, Jim (Manchester C), 1998 v Sp; 1999 v T (sub); 2000 v Fi (sub) (3)
Williams, J. R. (Ulster), 1886 v E, S (2)
Williams, M. S. (Chesterfield), 1999 v G, Mol, Ca, Ei; (with Watford), 2000 v F, T, G, Fi, L, Ma, H (sub) (11)
Williams, P. A. (WBA), 1991 v Fa (sub) (1)

Williamson, J. (Cliftonville), 1890 v E; 1892 v S; 1893 v S (3)
Willighan, T. (Burnley), 1933 v W; 1934 v S (2)
Willis, G. (Linfield), 1906 v S, W; 1907 v S; 1912 v S (4)
Wilson, D. J. (Brighton & HA), 1987 v T, Is, E (sub); (with Luton T), 1988 v Y, T, Gr, Pol, F, Ma; 1989 v Ei, H, Sp, Ma, Ch; 1990 v H, Ei, N, U; (with Sheffield W), 1991 v Y, D, A, Fa; 1992 v A (sub), S (24)
Wilson, H. (Linfield), 1925 v W (1)
Wilson, K. J. (Ipswich T), 1987 v Is, E, Y; (with Chelsea), 1988 v Y, T, Gr (sub), Pol (sub), F (sub); 1989 v H (sub), Sp (2), Ma, Ch; 1990 v Ei (sub), N, U; 1991 v Y (2), A, Pol, Fa; 1992 v Fa, A, D, S; (with Notts Co), Li, G; 1993 v Alb, Sp, D, Sp, Li, La; 1994 v La, D, Ei, R, Lie, Co, M; (with Walsall), 1995 v Ei (sub), La (42)
Wilson, M. (Distillery), 1884 v E, S, W (3)
Wilson, R. (Cliftonville), 1888 v S (1)
Wilson, S. J. (Glenavon), 1962 v S; 1964 v S; (with Falkirk), 1964 v E, W, U, Sp; 1965 v E, Sw; (with Dundee), 1966 v W, WG; 1967 v S; 1968 v E (12)
Wilton, J. M. (St Columb's Court), 1888 v E, W; 1889 v S, E; (with Cliftonville), 1890 v E; (with St Columb's Court); 1893 v W, S (7)
Wood, T. J. (Walsall), 1996 v Lie (sub) (1)
Worthington, N. (Sheffield W), 1984 v W, Fi (sub); 1985 v Is, Sp (sub); 1986 v T, R (sub), E (sub), D, Alg, Sp; 1987 v E (2), T, Is, Y; 1988 v Y, T, Gr, Pol, F, Ma; 1989 v Ei, H, Sp, Ma; 1990 v H, Ei, U; 1991 v Y, D, A, Fa; 1992 v A, D, S, Li, G; 1993 v Alb, Sp, D, Ei, Sp, Li, La; 1994 v La, D, Ei, Lie, Co, M; (with Leeds U), 1995 v P, A, Ei (2), La, Ca (sub), Ch, La; 1996 v P, Lie, A, N, Se, G; (with Stoke C), 1997 v I, Bel (sub) (66)
Wright, J. (Cliftonville), 1906 v E, S, W; 1907 v E, S, W (6)
Wright, T. J. (Newcastle U), 1989 v Ma, Ch; 1990 v H, U; 1992 v Fa, A, S, G; 1993 v Alb, Sp, Alb, Ei, Sp, Li, La; 1994 v La; (with Nottingham F), D, Ei, R, Lie, Co, M (sub); 1997 v G, Alb, I, Bel; (with Manchester C), P, Uk; 1998 v Alb; 1999 v Ca (sub); 2000 v F (sub) (31)

Young, S. (Linfield), 1907 v E, S; 1908 v E, S; (with Airdrie), 1909 v E; 1912 v S, W; (with Linfield), 1914 v E, S, W (9)

SCOTLAND

Adams, J. (Hearts), 1889 v Ni; 1892 v W; 1893 v Ni (3)
Agnew, W. B. (Kilmarnock), 1907 v Ni; 1908 v W, Ni (3)
Aird, J. (Burnley), 1954 v N (2), A, U (4)
Aitken, A. (Newcastle U), 1901 v E; 1902 v E; 1903 v E, W; 1904 v E; 1905 v E, W; 1906 v E; (with Middlesbrough), 1907 v E, W; 1908 v E; (with Leicester Fosse), 1910 v E; 1911 v E, Ni (14)
Aitken, G. G. (East Fife), 1949 v E, F; 1950 v W, Ni, Sw; (with Sunderland), 1953 v W, Ni; 1954 v E (8)
Aitken, R. (Dumbarton), 1886 v E; 1888 v Ni (2)
Aitken, R. (Celtic), 1980 v Pe (sub), Bel, W (sub), E, Pol; 1983 v Bel, Ca (1+1 sub); 1984 v Bel (sub), W (sub); 1985 v E, Ic; 1986 v W, EG, Aus (2), Is, R, E, D, WG, U; 1987 v Bul, Ei (2), L, Bel, E, Br; 1988 v H, Bel, Bul, L, S.Ar, Ma, Sp, Co, E; 1989 v N, Y, I, Cy, F, Cy, E, Ch; 1990 v Y, F, N; (with Newcastle U), Arg (sub), Pol, Ma, Cr, Se, Br; (with St Mirren), 1992 v R (sub) (57)
Aitkenhead, W. A. C. (Blackburn R), 1912 v Ni (1)
Albiston, A. (Manchester U), 1982 v Ni; 1984 v U, Bel, EG, W, E; 1985 v Y, Ic, Sp (2), W; 1986 v EG, Ho, U (14)
Alexander, D. (East Stirlingshire), 1894 v W, Ni (2)
Allan, D. S. (Queen's Park), 1885 v E, W; 1886 v W (3)
Allan, G. (Liverpool), 1897 v E (1)
Allan, H. (Hearts), 1902 v W (1)
Allan, J. (Queen's Park), 1887 v E, W (2)
Allan, T. (Dundee), 1974 v WG, N (2)
Ancell, R. F. D. (Newcastle U), 1937 v W, Ni (2)
Anderson, A. (Hearts), 1933 v E; 1934 v A, E, W, Ni; 1935 v E, W, Ni; 1936 v E, W, Ni; 1937 v G, E, W, Ni, A; 1938 v W, Ni, Cz, Ho; 1939 v W, H (23)
Anderson, F. (Clydesdale), 1874 v E (1)
Anderson, G. (Kilmarnock), 1901 v Ni (1)
Anderson, H. A. (Raith R), 1914 v W (1)
Anderson, J. (Leicester C), 1954 v Fi (1)
Anderson, K. (Queen's Park), 1896 v Ni; 1898 v E, Ni (3)
Anderson, W. (Queen's Park), 1882 v W; 1883 v E, W; 1884 v E; 1885 v E, W (6)
Andrews, P. (Eastern), 1875 v E (1)

Archibald, A. (Rangers), 1921 v W; 1922 v W, E; 1923 v Ni; 1924 v E, W; 1931 v E; 1932 v E (8)
Archibald, S. (Aberdeen), 1980 v P (sub); (with Tottenham H), Ni, Pol, H; 1981 v Se (sub), Is, Ni, Is, Ni, E; 1982 v Ni, P, Sp (sub), Ho, Nz (sub), Br, USSR; 1983 v EG, Sw (sub), Bel; 1984 v EG, E, F; (with Barcelona), 1985 v Sp, E, Ic (sub); 1986 v WG (27)
Armstrong, M. W. (Aberdeen), 1936 v W, Ni; 1937 v G (3)
Arnott, W. (Queen's Park), 1883 v W; 1884 v E, Ni; 1885 v E, W; 1886 v E; 1887 v E, W; 1888 v E; 1889 v E; 1890 v E; 1891 v E; 1892 v E; 1893 v E (14)
Auld, J. R. (Third Lanark), 1887 v E, W; 1889 v W (3)
Auld, R. (Celtic), 1959 v H, P; 1960 v W (3)

Baird, A. (Queen's Park), 1892 v Ni; 1894 v W (2)
Baird, D. (Hearts), 1890 v Ni; 1891 v E; 1892 v W (3)
Baird, H. (Airdrieonians), 1956 v A (1)
Baird, J. C. (Vale of Leven), 1876 v E; 1878 v W; 1880 v E (3)
Baird, S. (Rangers), 1957 v Y, Sp (2), Sw, WG; 1958 v F, Ni (7)
Baird, W. U. (St Bernard), 1897 v Ni (1)
Bannon, E. (Dundee U), 1980 v Bel; 1983 v Ni, W, E, Ca; 1984 v EG; 1986 v Is, R, E, D (sub), WG (11)
Barbour, A. (Renton), 1885 v Ni (1)
Barker, J. B. (Rangers), 1893 v W; 1894 v W (2)
Barrett, F. (Dundee), 1894 v Ni; 1895 v W (2)
Battles, B. (Celtic), 1901 v E, W, Ni (3)
Battles, B. jun. (Hearts), 1931 v W (1)
Bauld, W. (Hearts), 1950 v E, Sw, P (3)
Baxter, J. C. (Rangers), 1961 v N, Ei (2), Cz; 1962 v Ni, W, E, Cz, U; 1963 v W, Ni, E, A, N, Ei, Sp; 1964 v W, E, N, WG; 1965 v W, Ni, Fi; (with Sunderland), 1966 v P, Br, Ni, W, E, I; 1967 v W, E, USSR; 1968 v W (34)
Baxter, R. D. (Middlesbrough), 1939 v E, W, H (3)
Beattie, A. (Preston NE), 1937 v E, A, Cz; 1938 v E; 1939 v W, Ni, H (7)
Beattie, R. (Preston NE), 1939 v W (1)
Begbie, I. (Hearts), 1890 v Ni; 1891 v E; 1892 v W; 1894 v E (4)
Bell, A. (Manchester U), 1912 v Ni (1)

Bell, J. (Dumbarton), 1890 v Ni; 1892 v E; (with Everton), 1896 v E; 1897 v E; 1898 v E; (with Celtic), 1899 v E, W, Ni; 1900 v E, W (10)

Bell, M. (Hearts), 1901 v W (1)

Bell, W. J. (Leeds U), 1966 v P, Br (2)

Bennett, A. (Celtic), 1904 v W; 1907 v Ni; 1908 v W; (with Rangers), 1909 v W, Ni, E; 1910 v E, W; 1911 v E, W; 1913 v Ni (11)

Bennie, R. (Airdrieonians), 1925 v W, Ni; 1926 v Ni (3)

Bernard, P. R. J. (Oldham Ath), 1995 v J (sub), Ec (2)

Berry, D. (Queen's Park), 1894 v W; 1899 v W, Ni (3)

Berry, W. H. (Queen's Park), 1888 v E; 1889 v E; 1890 v E; 1891 v E (4)

Bett, J. (Rangers), 1982 v Ho; 1983 v Bel; (with Lokeren), 1984 v Bel, W, E, F; 1985 v Y, Ic, Sp (2), W, E, Ic; (with Aberdeen), 1986 v W, Is, Ho; 1987 v Bel; 1988 v H (sub); 1989 v Y; 1990 v F (sub), N, Arg, Eg, Ma, Cr (25)

Beveridge, W. W. (Glasgow University), 1879 v E, W; 1880 v W (3)

Black, A. (Hearts), 1938 v Cz, Ho; 1939 v H (3)

Black, D. (Hurlford), 1889 v Ni (1)

Black, E. (Metz), 1988 v H (sub), L (sub) (2)

Black, I. H. (Southampton), 1948 v E (1)

Blackburn, J. E. (Royal Engineers), 1873 v E (1)

Blacklaw, A. S. (Burnley), 1963 v N, Sp; 1966 v I (3)

Blackley, J. (Hibernian), 1974 v Cz, E, Bel, Z; 1976 v Sw; 1977 v W, Se (7)

Blair, D. (Clyde), 1929 v W, Ni; 1931 v E, A, I; 1932 v W, Ni; (with Aston Villa), 1933 v W (8)

Blair, J. (Sheffield W), 1920 v E, Ni; (with Cardiff C), 1921 v E; 1922 v E; 1923 v E, W, Ni; 1924 v W (8)

Blair, J. (Motherwell), 1934 v W (1)

Blair, J. A. (Blackpool), 1947 v W (1)

Blair, W. (Third Lanark), 1896 v W (1)

Blessington, J. (Celtic), 1894 v E, Ni; 1896 v E, Ni (4)

Blyth, J. A. (Coventry C), 1978 v Bul, W (2)

Bone, J. (Norwich C), 1972 v Y (sub); 1973 v D (2)

Booth, S. (Aberdeen), 1993 v G (sub), Es (2 subs); 1994 v Sw, Ma (sub); 1995 v Fa, Ru; 1996 v Fi, Sm, Aus (sub), US, Ho, Sw (sub); (with Borussia Dortmund), 1998 v D, Fi, Co (sub), Mor (sub) (17)

Bowie, J. (Rangers), 1920 v E, Ni (2)

Bowie, W. (Linthouse), 1891 v Ni (1)

Bowman, D. (Dundee U), 1992 v Fi, US (sub); 1993 v G, Es; 1994 v Sw, I (6)

Bowman, G. A. (Montrose), 1892 v W (1)

Boyd, J. M. (Newcastle U), 1934 v Ni (1)

Boyd, R. (Mossend Swifts), 1889 v Ni; 1891 v W (2)

Boyd, T. (Motherwell), 1991 v R (sub), Sw, Bul, USSR; (with Chelsea), 1992 v Sw, R; (with Celtic), Fi, Ca, N, C; 1993 v Sw, P, I, Ma, G, Es (2); 1994 v I, Ma (sub), Ho (sub), A; 1995 v Fi, Fa, Ru, Gr, Ru, Sm; 1996 v Gr, Fi, Se, Sm, Aus, D, US, Co, Ho, E, Sw; 1997 v A, La, Se, Es (2), A, Se, W, Ma, Bl; 1998 v Bl, La, F, D, Fi (sub), Co, US, Br, N, Mor; 1999 v Li, Es, Fa, CzR, G, Fa, CzR (65)

Boyd, W. G. (Clyde), 1931 v I, Sw (2)

Brackenbridge, T. (Hearts), 1888 v Ni (1)

Bradshaw, T. (Bury), 1928 v E (1)

Brand, R. (Rangers), 1961 v Ni, Cz, Ei (2); 1962 v Ni, W, Cz, U (8)

Branden, T. (Blackburn R), 1896 v E (1)

Brazil, A. (Ipswich T), 1980 v Pol (sub), H; 1982 v Sp, Ho (sub), Ni, W, E, Nz, USSR (sub); 1983 v EG, Sw, (with Tottenham H), W, E (sub) (13)

Bremner, D. (Hibernian), 1976 v Sw (sub) (1)

Bremner, W. J. (Leeds U), 1965 v Sp; 1966 v E, Pol, P, Br, I (2); 1967 v W, Ni, E; 1968 v W, E; 1969 v W, E, Ni, D, A, WG, Cy (2); 1970 v Ei, WG, A; 1971 v W, E; 1972 v P, Bel, Ho, Ni, W, E, Y, Cz, Br; 1973 v D (2), E (2), Ni (sub), Sw, Br; 1974 v Cz, WG, Ni, W, E, Bel, N, Z, Br, Y; 1975 v Sp (2); 1976 v D (54)

Brennan, F. (Newcastle U), 1947 v W, Ni; 1953 v W, Ni, E; 1954 v Ni, E (7)

Breslin, B. (Hibernian), 1897 v W (1)

Brewster, G. (Everton), 1921 v E (1)

Brogan, J. (Celtic), 1971 v W, Ni, P, E (4)

Brown, A. (Middlesbrough), 1904 v E (1)

Brown, A. (St Mirren), 1890 v W; 1891 v W (2)

Brown, A. D. (East Fife), 1950 v Sw, P, F; (with Blackpool), 1952 v USA, D; 1953 v W; 1954 v W, E, N (2), Fi, A, U (14)

Brown, G. C. P. (Rangers), 1931 v W; 1932 v E, W, Ni; 1933 v E; 1934 v A; 1935 v E, W; 1936 v E, W; 1937 v G, E, W, Ni, Cz; 1938 v E, W, Cz, Ho (19)

Brown, H. (Partick T), 1947 v W, Bel, L (3)

Brown, J. (Cambuslang), 1890 v W (1)

Brown, J. B. (Clyde), 1939 v W (1)

Brown, J. G. (Sheffield U), 1975 v R (1)

Brown, R. (Dumbarton), 1884 v W, Ni (2)

Brown, R. (Rangers), 1947 v Ni; 1949 v Ni; 1952 v E (3)

Brown, R. jun. (Dumbarton), 1885 v W (1)

Brown, W. D. F. (Dundee), 1958 v F; 1959 v E, W, Ni; (with Tottenham H), 1960 v W, Ni, Pol, A, H, T; 1962 v Ni, W, E, Cz; 1963 v W, Ni, E, A; 1964 v Ni, W, N; 1965 v E, Fi, Pol, Sp; 1966 v Ni, Pol, I (28)

Browning, J. (Celtic), 1914 v W (1)

Brownlie, J. (Hibernian), 1971 v USSR; 1972 v Pe, Ni, E; 1973 v D (2); 1976 v R (7)

Brownlie, J. (Third Lanark), 1909 v E, Ni; 1910 v E, W, Ni; 1911 v W, Ni; 1912 v W, Ni, E; 1913 v W, Ni, E; 1914 v W, Ni, E (16)

Bruce, D. (Vale of Leven), 1890 v W (1)

Bruce, R. F. (Middlesbrough), 1934 v A (1)

Buchan, M. M. (Aberdeen), 1972 v P (sub), Bel; (with Manchester U), W, Y, Cz, Br; 1973 v D (2), E; 1974 v WG, Ni, W, N, Br, Y; 1975 v EG, Sp, P; 1976 v D, R; 1977 v Fi, Cz, Ch, Arg, Br; 1978 v EG, W (sub), Ni, Pe, Ir, Ho; 1979 v A, N, P (34)

Buchanan, J. (Cambuslang), 1889 v Ni (1)

Buchanan, J. (Rangers), 1929 v E; 1930 v E (2)

Buchanan, P. S. (Chelsea), 1938 v Cz (1)

Buchanan, R. (Abercorn), 1891 v W (1)

Buckley, P. (Aberdeen), 1954 v N; 1955 v W, Ni (3)

Buick, A. (Hearts), 1902 v W, Ni (2)

Burchill, M. J. (Celtic), 2000 v Bos (sub), Li, E (sub + sub), F (sub), Ho (sub) (6)

Burley, C. W. (Chelsea), 1995 v J, Ec, Fa; 1996 v Gr, Se, Aus, D, US, Co (sub), Ho (sub), E (sub), Sw; 1997 v A, La, Se, Es, A, Se, Ma, Bl; (with Celtic), 1998 v Bl, La, F, Co, US (sub), Br, N, Mor; 1999 v Fa, CzR; 2000 v Bos, Es, Bos, Li, E (2); (with Derby Co), Ho, Ei (38)

Burley, G. (Ipswich T), 1979 v W, Ni, E, Arg, N; 1980 v P, Ni, E (sub), Pol; 1982 v W (sub), E (11)

Burness, F. (Manchester U), 1970 v A (1)

Burns, K. (Birmingham C), 1974 v WG; 1975 v EG (sub), Sp (2); 1977 v Cz (sub), W, Se, W (sub); (with Nottingham F), 1978 v Ni (sub), W, E, Pe, Ir; 1979 v N; 1980 v Pe, A, Bel; 1981 v Is, Ni, W (20)

Burns, T. (Celtic), 1981 v Ni; 1982 v Ho (sub), W; 1983 v Bel (sub), Ni, Ca (1 + 1 sub); 1988 v E (sub) (8)

Busby, M. W. (Manchester C), 1934 v W (1)

Cairns, T. (Rangers), 1920 v W; 1922 v E; 1923 v E, W; 1924 v Ni; 1925 v W, E, Ni (8)

Calderhead, D. (Queen of the South), 1889 v Ni (1)

Calderwood, C. (Tottenham H), 1995 v Ru, Sm, J, Ec, Fa; 1996 v Gr, Fi, Se, Sm, US, Co, Ho, E, Sw; 1997 v A, La, Se, Es (2), A, Se; 1998 v Bl, La, F, D, Fi, Co, US, Br, N; 1999 v Li, Es; (with Aston Villa) Fa, CzR; 2000 v Bos (1 + sub) (36)

Calderwood, R. (Cartvale), 1885 v Ni, E, W (3)

Caldow, E. (Rangers), 1957 v Sp (2), Sw, WG, E; 1958 v Ni, W, Sw, Par, H, Pol, Y, F; 1959 v E, W, Ni, WG, Ho, P; 1960 v E, W, Ni, A, H, T; 1961 v E, W, Ni, Ei (2); 1962 v Ni, W, E, Cz (2), U; 1963 v W, Ni, E (40)

Callaghan, P. (Hibernian), 1900 v Ni (1)

Callaghan, W. (Dunfermline Ath), 1970 v Ei (sub), W (2)

Cameron, C. (Hearts), 1999 v G (sub), Fa (sub); 2000 v Li (sub), F, Ei (sub) (5)

Cameron, J. (Rangers), 1886 v Ni (1)

Cameron, J. (Queen's Park), 1896 v Ni (1)

Cameron, J. (St Mirren), 1904 v Ni; (with Chelsea), 1909 v E (2)

Campbell, C. (Queen's Park), 1874 v E; 1876 v W; 1877 v E, W; 1878 v E; 1879 v E; 1880 v E; 1881 v E; 1882 v E, W; 1884 v E; 1885 v E; 1886 v E (13)

Campbell, H. (Renton), 1889 v W (1)

Campbell, Jas (Sheffield W), 1913 v W (1)

Campbell, J. (South Western), 1880 v W (1)

Campbell, J. (Kilmarnock), 1891 v Ni; 1892 v W (2)

Campbell, John (Celtic), 1893 v E, Ni; 1898 v E, Ni; 1900 v E, Ni; 1901 v E, Ni; 1902 v W, Ni; 1903 v W (12)

Campbell, John (Rangers), 1899 v E, W, Ni; 1901 v Ni (4)

Campbell, K. (Liverpool), 1920 v E, W, Ni; (with Partick T), 1921 v W, Ni; 1922 v W, Ni, E (8)

Campbell, P. (Rangers), 1878 v W; 1879 v W (2)

Campbell, P. (Morton), 1898 v W (1)

Campbell, R. (Falkirk), 1947 v Bel, L; (with Chelsea), 1950 v Sw, F, F (5)

Campbell, W. (Morton), 1947 v Ni; 1948 v E, Bel, Sw, F (5)

Carabine, J. (Third Lanark), 1938 v Ho; 1939 v E, Ni (3)

Dougall, J. (Preston NE), 1939 v E (1)
Dougan, R. (Hearts), 1950 v Sw (1)
Douglas, A. (Chelsea), 1911 v Ni (1)
Douglas, J. (Renfrew), 1880 v W (1)
Dowds, P. (Celtic), 1892 v Ni (1)
Downie, R. (Third Lanark), 1892 v W (1)
Doyle, D. (Celtic), 1892 v E; 1893 v W; 1894 v E; 1895 v E, Ni; 1897 v E; 1898 v E, Ni (8)
Doyle, J. (Ayr U), 1976 v R (1)
Drummond, J. (Falkirk), 1892 v Ni; (with Rangers), 1894 v Ni; 1895 v Ni, E; 1896 v E, Ni; 1897 v Ni; 1898 v E; 1900 v E; 1901 v E; 1902 v E, W, Ni; 1903 v Ni (14)
Dunbar, M. (Cartvale), 1886 v Ni (1)
Duncan, A. (Hibernian), 1975 v P (sub), W, Ni, E, R; 1976 v D (sub) (6)
Duncan, D. (Derby Co), 1933 v E, W; 1934 v A, W; 1935 v E, W; 1936 v E, W, Ni; 1937 v G, E, W, Ni; 1938 v W (14)
Duncan, D. M. (East Fife), 1948 v Bel, Sw, F (3)
Duncan, J. (Alexandra Ath), 1878 v W; 1882 v W (2)
Duncan, J. (Leicester C), 1926 v W (1)
Duncanson, J. (Rangers), 1947 v Ni (1)
Dunlop, J. (St Mirren), 1890 v W (1)
Dunlop, W. (Liverpool), 1906 v E (1)
Dunn, J. (Hibernian), 1925 v W, Ni; 1927 v Ni; 1928 v Ni, E; (with Everton), 1929 v W (6)
Durie, G. S. (Chelsea), 1988 v Bul (sub); 1989 v I (sub), Cy; 1990 v Y, EG, Eg, Se; 1991 v Sw (sub), Bul (2), USSR (sub), Sm; (with Tottenham H), 1992 v Sw, R, Sm, Ni (sub), Fi, Ca, N (sub), Ho, G; 1993 v Sw, I; 1994 v Sw, I; (with Rangers), Ho (2); 1996 v US, Ho, E, Sw; 1997 v A (sub), Se (sub), Ma (sub), Bl; 1998 v Bl, La, F, Fi (sub), Co, Br, N, Mor (43)
Durrant, I. (Rangers), 1988 v H, Bel, Ma, Sp; 1989 v N (sub); 1993 v Sw (sub), P (sub), I, P (sub); 1994 v I (sub), Ma; (with Kilmarnock), 1999 v Es, Fa (sub), G, Fa, CzR; 2000 v Bos (sub), Eo, Ho (sub) (19)
Dykes, J. (Hearts), 1938 v Ho; 1939 v Ni (2)

Easson, J. F. (Portsmouth), 1931 v A, Sw; 1934 v W (3)
Elliott, M. S. (Leicester C), 1998 v F (sub), D, Fi; 1999 v Li, Fa, CzR, Fa; 2000 v Ho, Ei (9)
Ellis, J. (Mossend Swifts), 1892 v Ni (1)
Evans, A. (Aston Villa), 1982 v Ho, Ni, E, Nz (4)
Evans, R. (Celtic), 1949 v E, W, Ni, F; 1950 v W, Ni, Sw, P; 1951 v A; 1952 v Ni; 1953 v Se; 1954 v Ni, W, E, N, Fi; 1955 v Ni, P, Y, A, H; 1956 v E, Ni, W, A; 1957 v WG, Sp; 1958 v Ni, W, E, Sw, H, Pol, Y, Par, F; 1959 v E, WG, Ho, P; 1960 v E, Ni, W, Pol; (with Chelsea), 1960 v A, H, T (48)
Ewart, J. (Bradford C), 1921 v E (1)
Ewing, T. (Partick T), 1958 v W, E (2)

Farm, G. N. (Blackpool), 1953 v W, Ni, E, Se; 1954 v Ni, W, E; 1959 v WG, Ho, P (10)
Ferguson, B. (Rangers), 1999 v Li; 2000 v Bos, Es (sub), E (2), F, Ei (7)
Ferguson, Derek (Rangers), 1988 v Ma, Co (sub) (2)
Ferguson, Duncan (Dundee U), 1992 v US (sub), Ca, Ho (sub); 1993 v G; (with Everton), 1995 v Gr; 1997 v A, Es (7)
Ferguson, I. (Rangers), 1989 v I, Cy (sub); F; 1993 v Ma (sub), Es; 1994 v Ma, A (sub), Ho (sub); 1997 v Es (sub) (9)
Ferguson, J. (Vale of Leven), 1874 v E; 1876 v E, W; 1877 v E, W; 1878 v W (6)
Ferguson, R. (Kilmarnock), 1966 v W, E, Ho, P, Br; 1967 v W, Ni (7)
Fernie, W. (Celtic), 1954 v Fi, A, U; 1955 v W, Ni; 1957 v E, Ni, W, Y; 1958 v W, Sw, Par (12)
Findlay, R. (Kilmarnock), 1898 v W (1)
Fitchie, T. T. (Woolwich Arsenal), 1905 v W; 1906 v W, Ni; (with Queen's Park), 1907 v W (4)
Flavell, R. (Airdrieonians), 1947 v Bel, L (2)
Fleck, R. (Norwich C), 1990 v Arg, Se, Br (sub); 1991 v USSR (4)
Fleming, C. (East Fife), 1954 v Ni (1)
Fleming, J. W. (Rangers), 1929 v G, Ho; 1930 v E (3)
Fleming, R. (Morton), 1886 v Ni (1)
Forbes, A. R. (Sheffield U), 1947 v Bel, L, E; 1948 v W, Ni; (with Arsenal), 1950 v E, P, F; 1951 v W, Ni, A; 1952 v W, D, Se (14)
Forbes, J. (Vale of Leven), 1884 v E, W, Ni; 1887 v W, E (5)
Ford, D. (Hearts), 1974 v Cz (sub), WG (sub), W (3)
Forrest, J. (Rangers), 1966 v W, I; (with Aberdeen), 1971 v Bel (sub), D, USSR (5)
Forrest, J. (Motherwell), 1958 v E (1)
Forsyth, A. (Partick T), 1972 v Y, Cz, Br; 1973 v D; (with Manchester U), E; 1975 v Sp, Ni (sub), R, EG; 1976 v D (10)

Forsyth, C. (Kilmarnock), 1964 v E; 1965 v W, Ni, Fi (4)
Forsyth, T. (Motherwell), 1971 v D; (with Rangers), 1974 v Cz; 1976 v Sw, Ni, W, E; 1977 v Fi, Se, W, Ni, E, Ch, Arg, Br; 1978 v Cz, W, Ni, W (sub), E, Pe, Ir (sub), Ho (22)
Foyers, R. (St Bernards), 1893 v W; 1894 v W (2)
Fraser, D. M. (WBA), 1968 v Ho; 1969 v Cy (2)
Fraser, J. (Moffat), 1891 v Ni (1)
Fraser, M. J. E. (Queen's Park), 1880 v W; 1882 v W, E; 1883 v W, E (5)
Fraser, J. (Dundee), 1907 v Ni (1)
Fraser, W. (Sunderland), 1955 v W, Ni (2)
Fulton, W. (Abercorn), 1884 v Ni (1)
Fyfe, J. H. (Third Lanark), 1895 v W (1)

Gabriel, J. (Everton), 1961 v W; 1964 v N (sub) (2)
Gallacher, H. K. (Airdrieonians), 1924 v Ni; 1925 v E, W, Ni; 1926 v W; (with Newcastle U), 1926 v E, Ni; 1927 v E, W, Ni; 1928 v E, W; 1929 v E, W, Ni; 1930 v W, Ni, F; (with Chelsea), 1934 v E; (with Derby Co), 1935 v E (20)
Gallacher, K. W. (Dundee U), 1988 v Co, E (sub); 1989 v N, I; (with Coventry C), 1991 v Sm; 1992 v R (sub), Sm (sub), Ni (sub), N (sub), Ho (sub), G (sub), C; 1993 v Sw (sub), P; (with Blackburn R), P, Es (2); 1994 v I, Ma; 1996 v Aus (sub), D, Co (sub), Ho; 1997 v Se (sub), Es (2), A, Se, W, Ma, Bl; 1998 v Bl, La, F, Fi (sub), US, Br, N, Mor; 1999 v Li, Es, Fa, CzR; 2000 v Bos (sub); (with Newcastle U), Bos, Li (sub), E, F, Ei (sub) (49)
Gallacher, P. (Sunderland), 1935 v Ni (1)
Galloway, M. (Celtic), 1992 v R (1)
Galt, J. H. (Rangers), 1908 v W, Ni (2)
Gardiner, I. (Motherwell), 1958 v W (1)
Gardner, D. R. (Third Lanark), 1897 v W (1)
Gardner, R. (Queen's Park), 1872 v E; 1873 v E; (with Clydesdale), 1874 v E; 1875 v E; 1878 v E (5)
Gemmell, T. (St Mirren), 1955 v P, Y (2)
Gemmell, T. (Celtic), 1966 v E; 1967 v W, Ni, E, USSR; 1968 v Ni, E; 1969 v W, Ni, E, D, A, WG, Cy; 1970 v E, Ei, WG; 1971 v Bel (18)
Gemmill, A. (Derby Co), 1971 v Bel; 1972 v P, Ho, Pe, Ni, W, E; 1976 v D, R, Ni, W, E; 1977 v Fi, Cz, W (2), Ni (sub), E (sub), Ch (sub), Arg, Br; 1978 v EG (sub); (with Nottingham F), Bul, Ni, W, E (sub), Pe (sub), Ir, Ho; 1979 v A, N, P, N; (with Birmingham C), 1980 v A, P, Ni, W, E, H; 1981 v Se, P, Is, Ni (43)
Gemmill, S. (Nottingham F), 1995 v J, Ec, Fa (sub); 1996 v Sm, D (sub), US; 1997 v Es, Se (sub), W, Ma (sub), Bl (sub); 1998 v D, Fi; (with Everton), 1999 v G, Fa (sub) (15)
Gibb, W. (Clydesdale), 1873 v E (1)
Gibson, D. W. (Leicester C), 1963 v A, N, Ei, Sp; 1964 v Ni; 1965 v W, Fi (7)
Gibson, J. D. (Partick T), 1926 v E, W, Ni; (with Aston Villa), 1928 v E, W; 1930 v W, Ni (8)
Gibson, N. (Rangers), 1895 v E, Ni; 1896 v E, Ni; 1897 v E, Ni; 1898 v E; 1899 v E, Ni; 1900 v E, Ni; 1901 v W; (with Partick T), 1905 v Ni (14)
Gilchrist, J. E. (Celtic), 1922 v E (1)
Gilhooley, M. (Hull C), 1922 v W (1)
Gillespie, G. (Rangers), 1880 v W; 1881 v E, W; 1882 v E; (with Queen's Park), 1886 v W; 1890 v W; 1891 v Ni (7)
Gillespie, G. T. (Liverpool), 1988 v Bel, Sw, Sp; 1989 v N, F, Ch; 1990 v Y, EG, Eg, Pol, Ma, Br (sub); 1991 v Bul (13)
Gillespie, Jas (Third Lanark), 1898 v W (1)
Gillespie, John (Queen's Park), 1896 v W (1)
Gillespie, R. (Queen's Park), 1927 v W; 1931 v W; 1932 v F; 1933 v E (4)
Gillick, T. (Everton), 1937 v A, Cz; 1939 v W, Ni, H (5)
Gilmour, J. (Dundee), 1931 v W (1)
Gilzean, A. J. (Dundee), 1964 v W, E, N, WG; 1965 v Ni, (with Tottenham H), Sp; 1966 v Ni, W, Pol, I; 1968 v W; 1969 v W, E, WG, Cy (2), A (sub); 1970 v Ni, E (sub), WG, A; 1971 v P (22)
Glass, S. (Newcastle U), 1999 v Fa (sub) (1)
Glavin, R. (Celtic), 1977 v Se (1)
Glen, A. (Aberdeen), 1956 v E, Ni (2)
Glen, R. (Renton), 1895 v W; 1896 v W; (with Hibernian), 1900 v Ni (3)
Goram, A. L. (Oldham Ath), 1986 v EG (sub), R, Ho; 1987 v Br; (with Hibernian) 1989 v Y, I; 1990 v EG, Pol, Ma; 1991 v R, Sw, Bul (2), USSR, Sm; (with Rangers), 1992 v Sw, R, Sm, Fi, N, Ho, G, C; 1993 v Sw, P, I, Ma, P; 1994 v Ma, La, Es; 1998 v D (sub) (43)
Gordon, J. E. (Rangers), 1912 v E, Ni; 1913 v E, Ni, W; 1914 v E, Ni; 1920 v W, E, Ni (10)
Gossland, J. (Rangers), 1884 v Ni (1)
Goudie, J. (Abercorn), 1884 v Ni (1)

Gough, C. R. (Dundee U), 1983 v Sw, Ni, W, E, Ca (3); 1984 v U, Bel, EG, Ni, W, E, F; 1985 v Sp, E, Ic; 1986 v W, EG, Aus, Is, R, E, D, WG, U; (with Tottenham H), 1987 v Bul, L, Ei (2), Bel, E, Br; 1988 v H; (with Rangers), S.Ar, Sp, Co, E; 1989 v Y, I, Cy, F, Cy; 1990 v F, Arg, EG, Eg, Pol, Ma, Cr; 1991 v USSR, Bul; 1992 v Sm, Ni, Ca, N, Ho, G, C; 1993 v Sw, P (61)

Gould, J. (Celtic), 2000 v Li (1)

Gourlay, J. (Cambuslang), 1886 v Ni; 1888 v W (2)

Govan, J. (Hibernian), 1948 v E, W, Bel, Sw, F; 1949 v Ni (6)

Gow, D. R. (Rangers), 1888 v E (1)

Gow, J. J. (Queen's Park), 1885 v E (1)

Gow, J. R. (Rangers), 1888 v Ni (1)

Graham, A. (Leeds U), 1978 v EG (sub); 1979 v A (sub), N, W, Ni, E, Arg, N; 1980 v A; 1981 v W (10)

Graham, G. (Arsenal), 1972 v P, Ho, Ni, Y, Cz, Br; 1973 v D (2); (with Manchester U), E, W, Ni, Br (sub) (12)

Graham, J. (Annbank), 1884 v Ni (1)

Graham, J. A. (Arsenal), 1921 v Ni (1)

Grant, J. (Hibernian), 1959 v W, Ni (2)

Grant, P. (Celtic), 1989 v E (sub), Ch (2)

Gray, A. (Hibernian), 1903 v Ni (1)

Gray, A. M. (Aston Villa), 1976 v R, Sw; 1977 v Fi, Cz; 1979 v A, N; (with Wolverhampton W), 1980 v P, E (sub); 1981 v Se, P, Is (sub), Ni; 1982 v Se (sub), Ni (sub); 1983 v Ni, W, E, Ca (1+1 sub); (with Everton), 1985 v Ic (20)

Gray, D. (Rangers), 1929 v W, Ni, G, Ho; 1930 v W, E, Ni; 1931 v W; 1933 v W, Ni (10)

Gray, E. (Leeds U), 1969 v E, Cy; 1970 v WG, A; 1971 v W, Ni; 1972 v Bel, Ho; 1976 v W, E; 1977 v Fi, W (12)

Gray, F. T. (Leeds U), 1976 v Sw; 1979 v N, P, W, Ni, E, Arg (sub); (with Nottingham F), 1980 v Bel (sub); 1981 v Se, P, Is, Ni, Is, W; (with Leeds U), Ni, E; 1982 v Se, Ni, P, Sp, Ho, W, Nz, Br, USSR; 1983 v EG, Sw, Bel, Sw, W, E, Ca (32)

Gray, W. (Pollokshields Ath), 1886 v E (1)

Green, A. (Blackpool), 1971 v Bel (sub), P (sub), Ni, E; (with Newcastle U), 1972 v W, E (sub) (6)

Greig, J. (Rangers), 1964 v E, WG; 1965 v W, Ni, E, Fi (2), Sp, Pol; 1966 v Ni, W, E, Pol, I (2), P, Ho, Br; 1967 v W, Ni, E; 1968 v Ni, W, E, Ho; 1969 v W, Ni, E, D, A, WG, Cy (2); 1970 v W, E, Ei, WG, A; 1971 v D, Bel, W (sub), Ni, E; 1976 v D (44)

Groves, W. (Hibernian), 1888 v W; (with Celtic), 1889 v Ni; 1890 v E (3)

Guilliland, W. (Queen's Park), 1891 v W; 1892 v Ni; 1894 v E; 1895 v E (4)

Gunn, B. (Norwich C), 1990 v Eg; 1993 v Es (2); 1994 v Sw, I, Ho (sub) (6)

Haddock, H. (Clyde), 1955 v E, H (2), P, Y; 1958 v E (6)

Haddow, D. (Rangers), 1894 v E (1)

Haffey, F. (Celtic), 1960 v E; 1961 v E (2)

Hamilton, A. (Queen's Park), 1885 v E, W; 1886 v E; 1888 v E (4)

Hamilton, A. W. (Dundee), 1962 v Cz, U, W, E; 1963 v W, Ni, E, A, N, Ei; 1964 v Ni, W, E, N, WG; 1965 v Ni, W, E, Fi (2), Pol, Sp; 1966 v Pol, Ni (24)

Hamilton, G. (Aberdeen), 1947 v Ni; 1951 v Bel, A; 1954 v N (2) (5)

Hamilton, G. (Port Glasgow Ath), 1906 v Ni (1)

Hamilton, J. (Queen's Park), 1892 v W; 1893 v E, Ni (3)

Hamilton, J. (St Mirren), 1924 v Ni (1)

Hamilton, R. C. (Rangers), 1899 v E, W, Ni; 1900 v W; 1901 v E, Ni; 1902 v W, Ni; 1903 v E; 1904 v Ni; (with Dundee), 1911 v W (11)

Hamilton, T. (Hurlford), 1891 v Ni (1)

Hamilton, T. (Rangers), 1932 v E (1)

Hamilton, W. M. (Hibernian), 1965 v Fi (1)

Hannah, A. B. (Renton), 1888 v W (1)

Hannah, J. (Third Lanark), 1889 v W (1)

Hansen, A. D. (Liverpool), 1979 v W, Arg; 1980 v Bel, P; 1981 v Se, P, Is; 1982 v Se, Ni, P, Sp, Ni (sub), W, E, Nz, Br, USSR; 1983 v EG, Sw, Bel, Sw; 1985 v W (sub); 1986 v R (sub); 1987 v E (2), L (26)

Hansen, J. (Partick T), 1972 v Bel (sub), Y (sub) (2)

Harkness, J. D. (Queen's Park), 1927 v E, Ni; 1928 v E; (with Hearts), 1929 v W, E, Ni; 1930 v E, W; 1932 v W, F; 1934 v Ni (11)

Harper, J. M. (Aberdeen), 1973 v D (1+1 sub); (with Hibernian), 1976 v D; (with Aberdeen), 1978 v Ir (sub) (4)

Harper, W. (Hibernian), 1923 v E, Ni, W; 1924 v E, Ni, W; 1925 v E, Ni, W; (with Arsenal), 1926 v E, Ni (11)

Harris, J. (Partick T), 1921 v W, Ni (2)

Harris, N. (Newcastle U), 1924 v E (1)

Harrower, W. (Queen's Park), 1882 v E; 1884 v Ni; 1886 v W (3)

Hartford, R. A. (WBA), 1972 v Pe, W (sub), E, Y, Cz, Br; (with Manchester C), 1976 v D, R, Ni (sub); 1977 v Cz (sub), W (sub), Se, W, Ni, E, Ch, Arg, Br; 1978 v EG, Cz, W, Bul, W, E, Pe, Ir, Ho; 1979 v A, N, P, W, Ni, E, Arg, N; (with Everton), 1980 v Pe, Bel; 1981 v Ni (sub), Is, W, Ni, E; 1982 v Se; (with Manchester C), Ni, P, Sp, Ni, W, E, Br (50)

Harvey, D. (Leeds U), 1973 v D; 1974 v Cz, WG, Ni, W, E, Bel, Z, Br, Y; 1975 v EG, Sp (2); 1976 v D (2); 1977 v Fi (sub) (16)

Hastings, A. C. (Sunderland), 1936 v Ni; 1938 v Ni (2)

Haughney, M. (Celtic), 1954 v E (1)

Hay, D. (Celtic), 1970 v Ni, W, E; 1971 v D, Bel, W, P, Ni; 1972 v P, Bel, Ho; 1973 v W, Ni, E, Sw, Br; 1974 v Cz (2), WG, Ni, W, E, Bel, N, Z, Br, Y (27)

Hay, J. (Celtic), 1905 v Ni; 1909 v Ni; 1910 v W, Ni, E; 1911 v Ni, E; (with Newcastle U), 1912 v E, W; 1914 v E, Ni (11)

Hegarty, P. (Dundee U), 1979 v W, Ni, E, Arg, N (sub); 1980 v W, E; 1983 v Ni (8)

Heggie, C. (Rangers), 1886 v Ni (1)

Henderson, G. H. (Rangers), 1904 v Ni (1)

Henderson, J. G. (Portsmouth), 1953 v Se; 1954 v Ni, E, N; 1956 v W; (with Arsenal), 1959 v W, Ni (7)

Henderson, W. (Rangers), 1963 v W, Ni, E, A, N, Ei, Sp; 1964 v W, Ni, E, N, WG; 1965 v Fi, Pol, E, Sp; 1966 v Ni, W, Pol, I, Ho; 1967 v W, Ni; 1968 v Ho; 1969 v Ni, E, Cy; 1970 v Ei; 1971 v P (29)

Hendry, E. C. J. (Blackburn R), 1993 v Es (2); 1994 v Ma, Ho, A, Ho; 1995 v Fi, Fa, Gr, Ru, Sm; 1996 v Fi, Se, Sm, Aus, D, US, Co, Ho, E, Sw; 1997 v A, Se, Es (2), A, Se; 1998 v La, D, Fi, Co, US, Br, N, Mor; (with Rangers), 1999 v Li, Es, Fa, G; 2000 v Bos, Es, Bos, E (2); (with Coventry C), F (45)

Hepburn, J. (Alloa Ath), 1891 v W (1)

Hepburn, R. (Ayr U), 1932 v Ni (1)

Herd, A. C. (Hearts), 1935 v Ni (1)

Herd, D. G. (Arsenal), 1959 v E, W, Ni; 1961 v Ei, Cz (5)

Herd, G. (Clyde), 1958 v E; 1960 v H, T; 1961 v W, Ni (5)

Herriot, J. (Birmingham C), 1969 v Ni, E, D, Cy (2), W (sub); 1970 v Ei (sub), WG (8)

Hewie, J. D. (Charlton Ath), 1956 v E, A; 1957 v E, Ni, W, Y, Sp (2), Sw, WG; 1958 v H, Pol, Y, F; 1959 v Ho, P; 1960 v Ni, W, Pol (19)

Higgins, A. (Kilmarnock), 1885 v Ni (1)

Higgins, A. (Newcastle U), 1910 v E, Ni; 1911 v E, Ni (4)

Highet, T. C. (Queen's Park), 1875 v E; 1876 v E, W; 1878 v E (4)

Hill, D. (Rangers), 1881 v E, W; 1882 v W (3)

Hill, D. A. (Third Lanark), 1906 v Ni (1)

Hill, F. R. (Aberdeen), 1930 v F; 1931 v W, Ni (3)

Hill, J. (Hearts), 1891 v E; 1892 v W (2)

Hogg, G (Hearts), 1896 v E, Ni (2)

Hogg, J. (Ayr U), 1922 v Ni (1)

Hogg, R. M. (Celtic), 1937 v Cz (1)

Holt, G. J. (Kilmarnock), 2000 v Ei (sub) (1)

Holm, A. H. (Queen's Park), 1882 v W; 1883 v E, W (3)

Holt, D. D. (Hearts), 1963 v A, N, Ei, Sp; 1964 v WG (sub) (5)

Holton, J. A. (Manchester U), 1973 v W, Ni, E, Sw, Br; 1974 v Cz, WG, Ni, W, E, N, Z, Br, Y; 1975 v EG (15)

Hope, R. (WBA), 1968 v Ho; 1969 v D (2)

Hopkin, D. (Crystal Palace), 1997 v Ma, Bl; (with Leeds U), 1998 v Bl (sub), F (sub); 1999 v CzR; 2000 v Bos (2) (7)

Houliston, W. (Queen of the South), 1949 v E, Ni, F (3)

Houston, S. M. (Manchester U), 1976 v D (1)

Howden, W. (Partick T), 1905 v Ni (1)

Howe, R. (Hamilton A), 1929 v N, Ho (2)

Howie, H. (Hibernian), 1949 v W (1)

Howie, J. (Newcastle U), 1905 v E; 1906 v E; 1908 v E (3)

Howieson, J. (St Mirren), 1927 v Ni (1)

Hughes, J. (Celtic), 1965 v Pol, Sp; 1966 v Ni, I (2); 1968 v E; 1969 v A; 1970 v Ei (8)

Hughes, W. (Sunderland), 1975 v Se (sub) (1)

Humphries, W. (Motherwell), 1952 v Se (1)

Hunter, A. (Kilmarnock), 1972 v Pe, Y; (with Celtic), 1973 v E; 1974 v Cz (4)

Hunter, J. (Dundee), 1909 v W (1)

Hunter, J. (Third Lanark), 1874 v E; (with Eastern), 1875 v E; (with Third Lanark), 1876 v E; 1877 v W (4)

Hunter, R. (St Mirren), 1890 v Ni (1)

Hunter, W. (Motherwell), 1960 v H, T; 1961 v W (3)

Husband, J. (Partick T), 1947 v W (1)

Hutchison, D. (Everton), 1999 v CzR (sub), G; 2000 v Bos, Es, Li, E (2), F, Ho, Ei (10)

Hutchison, T. (Coventry C), 1974 v Cz (2), WG (2), Ni, W, Bel (sub), N, Z (sub), Y (sub); 1975 v EG, Sp (2), P, E (sub), R (sub); 1976 v D (17)

Hutton, J. (Aberdeen), 1923 v E, W, Ni; 1924 v Ni; 1926 v W, E, Ni; (with Blackburn R), 1927 v Ni; 1928 v W, Ni (10)

Hutton, J. (St Bernards), 1887 v Ni (1)
Hyslop, T. (Stoke C), 1896 v E; (with Rangers), 1897 v E (2)

Imlach, J. J. S. (Nottingham F), 1958 v H, Pol, Y, F (4)
Imrie, W. N. (St Johnstone), 1929 v N, G (2)
Inglis, J. (Kilmarnock Ath), 1884 v Ni (1)
Inglis, J. (Rangers), 1883 v E, W (2)
Irons, J. H. (Queen's Park), 1900 v W (1)
Irvine, B. (Aberdeen), 1991 v R; 1993 v G, Es (2); 1994 v Sw, I, Ma, A, Ho (9)

Jackson, A. (Cambuslang), 1886 v W; 1888 v Ni (2)
Jackson, A. (Aberdeen), 1925 v E, W, Ni; (with Huddersfield T), 1926 v E, W, Ni; 1927 v W, Ni; 1928 v E, W; 1929 v E, W, Ni; 1930 v E, W, Ni, F (17)
Jackson, C. (Rangers), 1975 v Se, P (sub), W; 1976 v D, R, Ni, W, E (8)
Jackson, D. (Hibernian), 1995 v Ru, Sm, J, Ec, Fa; 1996 v Gr, Fi (sub), Se (sub), Sm (sub), Aus (sub), D (sub), US; 1997 v La, Se, Es, A, Se, W, Ma, Bl; (with Celtic), 1998 v D, Fi, Co, US, Br, N; 1999 v Li, Es (sub) (28)
Jackson, J. (Partick T), 1931 v A, I, Sw; 1933 v E; (with Chelsea), 1934 v E; 1935 v E; 1936 v W, Ni (8)
Jackson, T. A. (St Mirren), 1904 v W, E, Ni; 1905 v W; 1907 v W, Ni (6)
James, A. W. (Preston NE), 1926 v W; 1928 v E; 1929 v E, Ni; (with Arsenal), 1930 v E, W, Ni; 1933 v W (8)
Jardine, A. (Rangers), 1971 v D (sub); 1972 v P, Bel, Ho; 1973 v E, Sw, Br; 1974 v Cz (2), WG (2), Ni, W, E, Bel, N, Z, Br, Y; 1975 v EG, Sp (2), Se, P, W, Ni, E; 1977 v Se (sub), Ch (sub), Br (sub); 1978 v Cz, W, Ni, Ir; 1980 v Pe, A, Bel (2) (38)
Jarvie, A. (Airdrieonians), 1971 v P (sub), Ni (sub), E (sub) (3)
Jenkinson, T. (Hearts), 1887 v Ni (1)
Jess, E. (Aberdeen), 1993 v I (sub), Ma; 1994 v Sw (sub), I, Ho (sub), A, Ho (sub); 1995 v Fi (sub); 1996 v Se (sub), Sm; (with Coventry C), US, Co (sub), E (sub); (with Aberdeen), 1998 v D (sub); 1999 v CzR, G (sub), Fa (sub), CzR (sub) (18)
Johnston, A. (Sunderland), 1999 v Es, Fa, CzR (sub), G, Fa, CzR; 2000 v Es, F (sub), Ei (sub) (9)
Johnston, L. H. (Clyde), 1948 v Bel, Sw (2)
Johnston, M. (Watford), 1984 v W (sub), E (sub), F; 1985 v Y; (with Celtic), Ic, Sp (2), W; 1986 v EG; 1987 v Bul, Ei (2), L; (with Nantes), 1988 v H, Bel, L, S.Ar, Sp, Co, E; 1989 v N, Y, I, Cy, F, Cy, E, Ch (sub); (with Rangers), 1990 v F, N, EG, Pol, Ma, Cr, Se, Br; 1992 v Sw, Sm (sub) (38)
Johnston, R. (Sunderland), 1938 v Cz (1)
Johnston, W. (Rangers), 1966 v W, E, Pol, Ho; 1968 v W, E; 1969 v Ni (sub); 1970 v Ni; 1971 v D; (with WBA), 1977 v Se, W (sub), Ni, E, Ch, Arg, Br; 1978 v EG, Cz, W (2), E, Pe (22)
Johnstone, D. (Rangers), 1973 v W, Ni, E, Sw, Br; 1975 v EG (sub), Se (sub); 1976 v Sw, Ni (sub), E (sub); 1978 v Bul (sub), Ni, W; 1980 v Bel (14)
Johnstone, J. (Abercorn), 1888 v W (1)
Johnstone, J. (Celtic), 1965 v W, Fi; 1966 v E; 1967 v W, USSR; 1968 v W; 1969 v A, WG; 1970 v E, WG; 1971 v D, E; 1972 v P, Bel, Ho, Ni, E (sub); 1974 v W, E, Bel, N; 1975 v EG, Sp (23)
Johnstone, Jas (Kilmarnock), 1894 v W (1)
Johnstone, J. A. (Hearts), 1930 v W; 1933 v W, Ni (3)
Johnstone, R. (Hibernian), 1951 v E, D, F; 1952 v Ni, E; 1953 v E, Se; 1954 v W, E, N, Fi; 1955 v Ni, H; (with Manchester C), 1955 v E; 1956 v E, Ni, W (17)
Johnstone, W. (Third Lanark), 1887 v Ni; 1889 v W; 1890 v E (3)
Jordan, J. (Leeds U), 1973 v E (sub), Sw (sub), Br; 1974 v Cz (sub+1), WG (sub), Ni (sub), W, E, Bel, N, Z, Br, Y; 1975 v EG, Sp (2); 1976 v Ni, W, E; 1977 v Cz, W, Ni, E; 1978 v EG, Cz, W; (with Manchester U), Bul, Ni, E, Pe, Ir, Ho; 1979 v A, P, W (sub), Ni, E, N; 1980 v Bel, Ni (sub), W, E, Pol; 1981 v Is, W, E; (with AC Milan), 1982 v Se, Ho, W, E, USSR (52)

Kay, J. L. (Queen's Park), 1880 v E; 1882 v E, W; 1883 v E, W; 1884 v W (6)
Keillor, A. (Montrose), 1891 v W; 1892 v Ni; (with Dundee), 1894 v Ni; 1895 v W; 1896 v W; 1897 v W (6)
Keir, L. (Dumbarton), 1885 v W; 1886 v Ni; 1887 v E, W; 1888 v E (5)
Kelly, H. T. (Blackpool), 1952 v USA (1)
Kelly, J. (Renton), 1888 v E; (with Celtic), 1889 v E; 1890 v E; 1892 v E; 1893 v E, Ni; 1894 v W; 1896 v Ni (8)
Kelly, J. C. (Barnsley), 1949 v W, Ni (2)

Kelso, R. (Renton), 1885 v W, Ni; 1886 v W; 1887 v E, W; 1888 v E, Ni; (with Dundee), 1898 v Ni (8)
Kelso, T. (Dundee), 1914 v W (1)
Kennaway, J. (Celtic), 1934 v W, A (2)
Kennedy, A. (Eastern), 1875 v E; 1876 v E, W; (with Third Lanark), 1878 v E; 1882 v W; 1884 v W (6)
Kennedy, J. (Celtic), 1964 v W, E, WG; 1965 v W, Ni, Fi (6)
Kennedy, J. (Hibernian), 1897 v W (1)
Kennedy, S. (Aberdeen), 1978 v Bul, W, E, Pe, Ho; 1979 v A, P; 1982 v P (sub) (8)
Kennedy, S. (Partick T), 1905 v W (1)
Kennedy, S. (Rangers), 1975 v Se, P, W, Ni, E (5)
Ker, G. (Queen's Park), 1880 v E; 1881 v E, W; 1882 v W, E (5)
Ker, W. (Granville), 1872 v E; (with Queen's Park), 1873 v E (2)
Kerr, A. (Partick T), 1955 v A, H (2)
Kerr, P. (Hibernian), 1924 v Ni (1)
Key, G. (Hearts), 1902 v Ni (1)
Key, W. (Queen's Park), 1907 v Ni (1)
King, A. (Hearts), 1896 v E, W; (with Celtic), 1897 v Ni; 1898 v Ni; 1899 v Ni, W (6)
King, J. (Hamilton A), 1933 v Ni; 1934 v Ni (2)
King, W. S. (Queen's Park), 1929 v W (1)
Kinloch, J. D. (Partick T), 1922 v Ni (1)
Kinnaird, A. F. (Wanderers), 1873 v E (1)
Kinnear, D. (Rangers), 1938 v Cz (1)

Lambert, P. (Motherwell), 1995 v J, Ec (sub); (with Borussia Dortmund), 1997 v La (sub), Se (sub), A, Se, Bl; 1998 v Bl, La; (with Celtic), Fi (sub), Co, US, Br, N, Mor; 1999 v Li, CzR, G, Fa, CzR; 2000 v Bos, Li, Ho, Ei (24)
Lambie, J. A. (Queen's Park), 1886 v Ni; 1887 v Ni; 1888 v E (3)
Lambie, W. A. (Queen's Park), 1892 v Ni; 1893 v W; 1894 v E; 1895 v E, Ni; 1896 v E, Ni; 1897 v E, Ni (9)
Lamont, D. (Pilgrims), 1885 v Ni (1)
Lang, A. (Dumbarton), 1880 v W (1)
Lang, J. J. (Clydesdale), 1876 v W; (with Third Lanark), 1878 v W (2)
Latta, A. (Dumbarton), 1888 v W; 1889 v E (2)
Law, D. (Huddersfield T), 1959 v W, Ni, Ho, P; 1960 v Ni, W; (with Manchester C), 1960 v E, Pol, A; 1961 v E, Ni; (with Torino), 1962 v Cz (2), E; (with Manchester U), 1963 v W, Ni, E, A, Ni, E, Sp; 1964 v W, E, N, WG; 1965 v W, Ni, E, Fi (2), Pol, Sp; 1966 v Ni, E, Pol; 1967 v W, E, USSR; 1968 v Ni; 1969 v Ni, A, WG; 1972 v Pe, Ni, W, E, Y, Cz, Br; (with Manchester C), 1974 v Cz (2), WG (2), Ni, Z (55)
Law, G. (Rangers), 1910 v E, Ni, W (3)
Law, T. (Chelsea), 1928 v E; 1930 v E (2)
Lawrence, J. (Newcastle U), 1911 v E (1)
Lawrence, T. (Liverpool), 1963 v Ei; 1969 v W, WG (3)
Lawson, D. (St Mirren), 1923 v E (1)
Leckie, R. (Queen's Park), 1872 v E (1)
Leggat, G. (Aberdeen), 1956 v E; 1957 v W; 1958 v Ni, H, Pol, Y, Par; (with Fulham), 1959 v E, W, Ni, WG, Ho; 1960 v E, Ni, W, Pol, A, H (18)
Leighton, J. (Aberdeen), 1983 v EG, Sw, Bel, Sw, W, E, Ca (2); 1984 v U, Bel, Ni, W, E, F; 1985 v Y, Ic, Sp (2), W, E, Ic; 1986 v W, EG, Aus (2), Is, D, WG, U; 1987 v Bul, Ei (2), L, Bel, E; 1988 v H, Bel, Bul, L, S.Ar, Ma, Sp; (with Manchester U), Co, E; 1989 v N, Cy, F, Cy, E, Ch; 1990 v Y, F, N, Arg, Ma (sub, Cr, Se, Br; (with Hibernian), 1994 v Ma, A, Ho; 1995 v Gr (sub), Ru, Sm, J, Ec, Fa; 1996 v Gr, Fi, Se, Sm, Aus, D, US; 1997 v Se, Es, A, Se, W (sub), Ma, Bl; (with Aberdeen), 1998 v Bl, La, D, Fi, US, Br, N, Mor; 1999 v Li, Es (91)
Lennie, W. (Aberdeen), 1908 v W, Ni (2)
Lennox, R. (Celtic), 1967 v Ni, E, USSR; 1968 v W, L; 1969 v D, A, WG, Cy (sub); 1970 v W (sub) (10)
Leslie, L. G. (Airdrieonians), 1961 v W, Ni, Ei (2), Cz (5)
Levein, C. (Hearts), 1990 v Arg, EG, Eg (sub), Pol, Ma (sub), Se; 1992 v R, Sm; 1993 v P, G, P; 1994 v Sw, Ho; 1995 v Fi, Fa, Ru (16)
Liddell, W. (Liverpool), 1947 v W, Ni; 1948 v E, W, Ni; 1950 v E, W, P, F; 1951 v W, Ni, E, A; 1952 v W, Ni, E, USA, D, Se; 1953 v W, Ni, E; 1954 v W; 1955 v P, Y, A, H; 1956 v Ni (28)
Liddle, D. (East Fife), 1931 v A, I, Sw (3)
Lindsay, D. (St Mirren), 1903 v Ni (1)
Lindsay, J. (Dumbarton), 1880 v W; 1881 v W, E; 1884 v W, E; 1885 v W, E; 1886 v E (8)
Lindsay, J. (Renton), 1888 v E; 1893 v E, Ni (3)
Linwood, A. B. (Clyde), 1950 v W (1)
Little, R. J. (Rangers), 1953 v Se (1)

Livingstone, G. T. (Manchester C), 1906 v E; (with Rangers), 1907 v W (2)
Lochhead, A. (Third Lanark), 1889 v W (1)
Logan, J. (Ayr U), 1891 v W (1)
Logan, T. (Falkirk), 1913 v Ni (1)
Logie, J. T. (Arsenal), 1953 v Ni (1)
Loney, W. (Celtic), 1910 v W, Ni (2)
Long, H. (Clyde), 1947 v Ni (1)
Longair, W. (Dundee), 1894 v Ni (1)
Lorimer, P. (Leeds U), 1970 v A (sub); 1971 v W, Ni; 1972 v Ni (sub), W, E; 1973 v D (2), E (2); 1974 v WG (sub), E, Bel, N, Z, Br, Y; 1975 v Sp (sub); 1976 v D (2), R (sub) (21)
Love, A. (Aberdeen), 1931 v A, I, Sw (3)
Low, A. (Falkirk), 1934 v Ni (1)
Low, T. P. (Rangers), 1897 v Ni (1)
Low, W. L. (Newcastle U), 1911 v E, W; 1912 v Ni; 1920 v E, Ni (5)
Lowe, J. (Cambuslang), 1891 v Ni (1)
Lowe, J. (St Bernards), 1887 v Ni (1)
Lundie, J. (Hibernian), 1886 v W (1)
Lyall, J. (Sheffield W), 1905 v E (1)

McAdam, J. (Third Lanark), 1880 v W (1)
McAllister, B. (Wimbledon), 1997 v W, Ma, Bl (sub) (3)
McAllister, G. (Leicester C), 1990 v EG, Pol, Ma (sub); (with Leeds U), 1991 v R, Sw, Bul, USSR (sub), Sm; 1992 v Sw (sub), Sm, Ni, Fi (sub), US, Ca, N, Ho, G, C; 1993 v Sw, P, I, Ma; 1994 v Sw, I, Ma, Ho, A, Ho; 1995 v Fi, Ru, Gr, Ru, Sm; 1996 v Gr, Fi, Se, Sm, Aus, D, US (sub), Co, Ho, E, Sw; (with Coventry C), 1997 v A, La, Es (2), A, Se, W, Ma, Bl; 1998 v Bl, La, F; 1999 v CzR (57)
McArthur, D. (Celtic), 1895 v E, Ni; 1899 v W (3)
McAtee, A. (Celtic), 1913 v W (1)
McAulay, J. (Arthurlie), 1884 v Ni (1)
McAulay, J. D. (Dumbarton), 1882 v W; 1883 v E, W; 1884 v E; 1885 v E, W; 1886 v E; 1887 v E, W (9)
McAuley, R. (Rangers), 1932 v Ni, W (2)
McAvennie, F. (West Ham U), 1986 v Aus (2), D (sub), WG (sub); (with Celtic), 1988 v S.Ar (5)
McBain, E. (St Mirren), 1894 v W (1)
McBain, N. (Manchester U), 1922 v E; (with Everton), 1923 v Ni; 1924 v W (3)
McBride, J. (Celtic), 1967 v W, Ni (2)
McBride, P. (Preston NE), 1904 v E; 1906 v E; 1907 v E, W; 1908 v E; 1909 v W (6)
McCall, J. (Renton), 1886 v W; 1887 v E, W; 1888 v E; 1890 v E (5)
McCall, S. M. (Everton), 1990 v Arg, EG, Eg (sub), Pol, Ma, Cr, Br; 1991 v Sw, USSR, Sm; (with Rangers), 1992 v Sw, R, Sm, US, Ca, N, Ho, G, C; 1993 v Sw, P (2); 1994 v I, Ho, A (sub), Ho; 1995 v Fi (sub), Ru, Gr; 1996 v Gr, D, US (sub), Co, Ho, E, Sw; 1997 v A, La; 1998 v D (sub) (40)
McCalliog, J. (Sheffield W), 1967 v E, USSR; 1968 v Ni; 1969 v D; (with Wolverhampton W), 1971 v P (5)
McCallum, N. (Renton), 1888 v Ni (1)
McCann, N. (Hearts), 1999 v Li (sub); (with Rangers), CzR; 2000 v Bos, Es (sub), E, F (sub), Ho, Ei (8)
McCann, R. J. (Motherwell), 1959 v WG; 1960 v E, Ni, W; 1961 v E (5)
McCartney, W. (Hibernian), 1902 v Ni (1)
McClair, B. (Celtic), 1987 v L, Ei, E, Br (sub); (with Manchester U), 1988 v Bul, Ma (sub), Sp (sub); 1989 v N, Y, I (sub), Cy, F (sub); 1990 v N (sub), Arg (sub); 1991 v Bul (2), Sm; 1992 v Sw (sub), R, Ni, US, Ca (sub), N, Ho, G, C; 1993 v Sw, P (sub), Es (2) (30)
McCloy, P. (Ayr U), 1924 v E; 1925 v E (2)
McCloy, P. (Rangers), 1973 v W, Ni, Sw, Br (4)
McCoist, A. (Rangers), 1986 v Ho; 1987 v L (sub), Ei (sub), Bel, E, Br; 1988 v H, Bel, Ma, Sp, Co, E; 1989 v Y (sub), F, Cy, E; 1990 v Y, F, N, EG (sub), Eg, Pol, Ma (sub), Cr (sub), Se (sub), Br; 1991 v R, Sw, Bul (2), USSR; 1992 v Sw, Sm, Ni, Fi (sub), US, Ca, N, Ho, G, C; 1993 v Sw, P, I, Ma, P; 1996 v Gr (sub), Fi (sub), Sm (sub), Aus, D (sub), Co, E (sub), Sw; 1997 v A, Se (sub), Es (sub), A (sub); 1998 v Bl (sub); (with Kilmarnock), 1999 v Li, Es (61)
McColl, A. (Renton), 1888 v Ni (1)
McColl, I. M. (Rangers), 1950 v E, F; 1951 v W, Ni, Bel; 1957 v E, Ni, W, Y, Sp, Sw, WG; 1958 v Ni, E (14)
McColl, R. S. (Queen's Park), 1896 v W, Ni; 1897 v Ni; 1898 v Ni; 1899 v Ni, E, W; 1900 v E, W; 1901 v E, W; (with Newcastle U), 1902 v E; (with Queen's Park), 1908 v Ni (13)
McColl, W. (Renton), 1895 v W (1)
McCombie, A. (Sunderland), 1903 v E, W; (with Newcastle U), 1905 v E, W (4)
McCorkindale, J. (Partick T), 1891 v W (1)

McCormick, R. (Abercorn), 1886 v W (1)
McCrae, D. (St Mirren), 1929 v N, G (2)
McCredie, A. (Rangers), 1893 v W; 1894 v E (2)
McCreadie, E. G. (Chelsea), 1965 v E, Sp, Fi, Pol; 1966 v P, Ni, W, Pol, I; 1967 v E, USSR; 1968 v Ni, W, E, Ho; 1969 v W, Ni, E, D, A, WG, Cy (2) (23)
McCulloch, D. (Hearts), 1935 v W; (with Brentford), 1936 v E; 1937 v W, Ni; 1938 v Cz; (with Derby Co), 1939 v H, W (7)
MacDonald, A. (Rangers), 1976 v Sw (1)
McDonald, A. (Edinburgh University), 1886 v E (1)
McDonald, J. (Sunderland), 1956 v W, Ni (2)
MacDougall, E. J. (Norwich C) 1975 v Se, P, W, Ni, E; 1976 v D, R (sub) (7)
McDougall, J. (Liverpool), 1931 v I, A (2)
McDougall, J. (Airdrieonians), 1926 v Ni (1)
McDougall, J. (Vale of Leven), 1877 v E, W; 1878 v E; 1879 v E, W (5)
McFadyen, W. (Motherwell), 1934 v A, W (2)
Macfarlane, A. (Dundee), 1904 v W; 1906 v W; 1908 v W; 1909 v Ni; 1911 v W (5)
Macfarlane, W. (Hearts), 1947 v L (1)
McFarlane, R. (Greenock Morton), 1896 v W (1)
McGarr, E. (Aberdeen), 1970 v Ei, A (2)
McGarvey, F. P. (Liverpool), 1979 v Ni (sub), Arg; (with Celtic), 1984 v U, Bel (sub), EG (sub), Ni, W (7)
McGeoch, A. (Dumbreck), 1876 v E, W; 1877 v E, W (4)
McGhee, J. (Hibernian), 1886 v W (1)
McGhee, M. (Aberdeen), 1983 v Ca (1+1 sub); 1984 v Ni (sub), E (4)
McGinlay, J. (Bolton W), 1994 v A, Ho; 1995 v Fa, Ru, Gr, Ru, Sm, Fa; 1996 v Se; 1997 v Se, Es (1 + sub), A (sub) (13)
McGonagle, W. (Celtic), 1933 v E; 1934 v A, E, Ni; 1935 v Ni, W (6)
McGrain, D. (Celtic), 1973 v W, Ni, E, Sw, Br; 1974 v Cz (2), WG, W (sub), E, Bel, N, Z, Br, Y; 1975 v Sp, Se, P, W, Ni, E, R; 1976 v D (2), Sw, Ni, W, E; 1977 v Fi, Cz, W (2), Se, Ni, E, Ch, Arg, Br; 1978 v EG, Cz; 1980 v Bel, P, Ni, W, E, Pol, H; 1981 v Se, P, Is, Ni, Is, W (sub), Ni, E; 1982 v Se, Sp, Ho, Ni, E, Nz, USSR (sub) (62)
McGregor, C. (Vale of Leven), 1877 v E, W; 1878 v E; 1880 v E (4)
McGrory, J. E. (Kilmarnock), 1965 v Ni, Fi; 1966 v P (3)
McGrory, J. (Celtic), 1928 v Ni; 1931 v E; 1932 v Ni, W; 1933 v E, Ni; 1934 v Ni (7)
McGuire, W. (Beith), 1881 v E, W (2)
McGurk, F. (Birmingham), 1934 v W (1)
McHardy, H. (Rangers), 1885 v Ni (1)
McInally, A. (Aston Villa), 1989 v Cy (sub), Ch; (with Bayern Munich), 1990 v Y (sub), F (sub), Arg, Pol (sub), Ma, Cr (8)
McInally, J. (Dundee U), 1987 v Bel, Br; 1988 v Ma (sub); 1991 v Bul (2); 1992 v US (sub), N (sub), C (sub); 1993 v G, P (10)
McInally, T. B. (Celtic), 1926 v Ni; 1927 v W (2)
McInnes, T. (Cowlairs), 1889 v Ni (1)
McIntosh, W. (Third Lanark), 1905 v Ni (1)
McIntyre, A. (Vale of Leven), 1878 v E; 1882 v E (2)
McIntyre, H. (Rangers), 1880 v W (1)
McIntyre, J. (Rangers), 1884 v W (1)
MacKay, D. (Celtic), 1959 v E, WG, Ho, P; 1960 v E, Pol, A, H, T; 1961 v W, Ni; 1962 v Ni, Cz, U (sub) (14)
Mackay, D. C. (Hearts), 1957 v Sp; 1958 v F; 1959 v W, Ni; (with Tottenham H), 1959 v WG, E; 1960 v W, Ni, A, Pol, H, T; 1961 v W, Ni, E; 1963 v E, A, N; 1964 v Ni, W, N; 1966 v Ni (22)
Mackay, G. (Hearts), 1988 v Bul (sub), L (sub), S.Ar (sub), Ma (4)
McKay, J. (Blackburn R), 1924 v W (1)
McKay, R. (Newcastle U), 1928 v W (1)
McKean, R. (Rangers), 1976 v Sw (sub) (1)
McKenzie, D. (Brentford), 1938 v Ni (1)
Mackenzie, J. A. (Partick T), 1954 v W, E, N, Fi, A, U; 1955 v E, H; 1956 v A (9)
McKeown, M. (Celtic), 1889 v Ni; 1890 v E (2)
McKie, J. (East Stirling), 1898 v W (1)
McKillop, T. R. (Rangers), 1938 v Ho (1)
McKimmie, S. (Aberdeen), 1989 v E, Ch; 1990 v Arg, Eg, Cr (sub), Br; 1991 v R, Sw, Bul, Sm; 1992 v Sw, R, Ni, Fi, US, Ca (sub), N (sub), Ho, G, C; 1993 v P, Es (sub); 1994 v Sw, I, Ho, A, Ho; 1995 v Fi, Fa, Ru, Gr, Ru, Fa; 1996 v Gr, Fi, Se, D, Co, Ho, E (40)
McKinlay, D. (Liverpool), 1922 v W, Ni (2)
McKinlay, T. (Celtic), 1996 v Gr, Fi, D, Co, E, Sw; 1997 v A, La, Se, Es (sub + 1), A, Se, W, Ma, Bl; 1998 v Bl, La (sub), F (sub), US, Br (sub), Mor (sub) (22)

McKinlay, W. (Dundee U), 1994 v Ma, Ho (sub), A, Ho; 1995 v Fa (sub), Ru, Gr, Ru (sub), Sm (sub), J, Ec, Fa; 1996 v Fi (sub), Se (sub); (with Blackburn R), Sm (sub), Aus, D (sub), Ho (sub); 1997 v Se, Es (sub); 1998 v La (sub), F, D, Fi, Co (sub), US, Br (sub); 1999 v Es, Fa (29)

McKinnon, A. (Queen's Park), 1874 v E (1)

McKinnon, R. (Rangers), 1966 v W, E, I (2), Ho, Br; 1967 v W, Ni, E; 1968 v Ni, W, E, Ho; 1969 v D, A, WG, Cy; 1970 v Ni, W, E, Ei, WG, A; 1971 v D, Bel, P, USSR, D (28)

McKinnon, R. (Motherwell), 1994 v Ma; 1995 v J, Fa (3)

MacKinnon, W. (Dumbarton), 1883 v E, W; 1884 v E, W (4)

MacKinnon, W. W. (Queen's Park), 1872 v E; 1873 v E; 1874 v E; 1875 v E; 1876 v E, W; 1877 v E; 1878 v E; 1879 v E (9)

McLaren, A. (St Johnstone), 1929 v N, G, Ho; 1933 v W, Ni (5)

McLaren, A. (Preston NE), 1947 v E, Bel, L; 1948 v W (4)

McLaren, A. (Hearts), 1992 v US, Ca, N; 1993 v I, Ma, G, Es (sub + 1); 1994 v I, Ma, Ho, A; 1995 v Fi, Fa; (with Rangers), Ru, Gr, Ru, Sm, J, Ec, Fa; 1996 v Fi, Se, Sm (24)

McLaren, J. (Hibernian), 1888 v W; (with Celtic), 1889 v E; 1890 v E (3)

McLean, A. (Celtic), 1926 v W, Ni; 1927 v W, E (4)

McLean, D. (St Bernards), 1896 v W; 1897 v Ni (2)

McLean, D. (Sheffield W), 1912 v E (1)

McLean, G. (Dundee), 1968 v Ho (1)

McLean, T. (Kilmarnock), 1969 v D, Cy, W; 1970 v Ni, W; 1971 v D (6)

McLeish, A. (Aberdeen), 1980 v P, Ni, W, E, Pol, H; 1981 v Se, Is, Ni, Is, Ni, E; 1982 v Se, Sp, Ni, Br (sub); 1983 v Bel, Sw (sub), W, E, Ca (3); 1984 v U, Bel, EG, Ni, W, E; 1985 v Y, Ic, Sp (2), W, E, Ic; 1986 v W, EG, Aus (2), E, Ho, D; 1987 v Bel, E, Br; 1988 v Bel, Bul, L, S.Ar (sub), Ma, Sp, Co, E; 1989 v N, Y, I, Cy, F, Cy, E, Ch; 1990 v Y, F, N, Arg, EG, Eg, Cr, Se, Br; 1991 v R, Sw, USSR, Bul; 1993 v Ma (77)

McLeod, D. (Celtic), 1905 v Ni; 1906 v E, W, Ni (4)

McLeod, J. (Dumbarton), 1888 v Ni; 1889 v W; 1890 v Ni; 1892 v E; 1893 v W (5)

MacLeod, J. M. (Hibernian), 1961 v E, Ei (2), Cz (4)

MacLeod, M. (Celtic), 1985 v E (sub); 1987 v Ei, L, E, Br; (with Borussia Dortmund), 1988 v Co, E; 1989 v I, Ch; 1990 v Y, F, N (sub), Arg, EG, Pol, Se Br; (with Hibernian) 1991 v R, Sw, USSR (sub) (20)

McLeod, W. (Cowlairs), 1886 v Ni (1)

McLintock, A. (Vale of Leven), 1875 v E; 1876 v E; 1880 v E (3)

McLintock, F. (Leicester C), 1963 v N (sub), Ei, Sp; (with Arsenal), 1965 v Ni; 1967 v USSR; 1970 v Ni; 1971 v W, Ni, E (9)

McLuckie, J. S. (Manchester C), 1934 v W (1)

McMahon, A. (Celtic), 1892 v E; 1893 v E, Ni; 1894 v E; 1901 v Ni; 1902 v W (6)

McMenemy, J. (Celtic), 1905 v Ni; 1909 v Ni; 1910 v E, W; 1911 v Ni, W, E; 1912 v W; 1914 v W, Ni, E; 1920 v Ni (12)

McMenemy, J. (Motherwell), 1934 v W (1)

McMillan, I. L. (Airdrieonians), 1952 v E, USA, D; 1955 v E; 1956 v E; (with Rangers), 1961 v Cz (6)

McMillan, J. (St Bernards), 1897 v W (1)

McMillan, T. (Dumbarton), 1887 v Ni (1)

McMullan, J. (Partick T), 1920 v W; 1921 v W, Ni, E; 1924 v E, Ni; 1925 v E; 1926 v W; (with Manchester C), 1926 v E; 1927 v E, W; 1928 v E, W; 1929 v W, E, Ni (16)

McNab, A. (Morton), 1921 v E, Ni (2)

McNab, A. (Sunderland), 1937 v A; (with WBA), 1939 v E (2)

McNab, C. D. (Dundee), 1931 v E, W, A, I, Sw; 1932 v E (6)

McNab, J. S. (Liverpool), 1923 v W (1)

McNair, A. (Celtic), 1906 v W; 1907 v Ni; 1908 v E, W; 1909 v E; 1910 v W; 1912 v E, W, Ni; 1913 v E; 1914 v E, Ni; 1920 v E, W, Ni (15)

McNamara, J. (Celtic), 1997 v La (sub), Se, Es, W (sub); 1998 v D, Co, US (sub), N (sub), Mor; 2000 v Ho (10)

McNaught, W. (Raith R), 1951 v A, W, Ni; 1952 v E; 1955 v Ni (5)

McNiel, H. (Queen's Park), 1874 v E; 1875 v E; 1876 v E, W; 1877 v W; 1878 v E; 1879 v E, W; 1881 v E, W (10)

McNiel, M. (Rangers), 1876 v W; 1880 v E (2)

McNeill, W. (Celtic), 1961 v E, Ei (2), Cz; 1962 v Ni, E, Cz, U; 1963 v Ei, Sp; 1964 v W, E, WG; 1965 v E, Fi, Pol, Sp; 1966 v Ni, Pol; 1967 v USSR; 1968 v E; 1969 v Cy, W, E, Cy (sub); 1970 v WG; 1972 v Ni, W, E (29)

McPhail, J. (Celtic), 1950 v W; 1951 v W, Ni, A; 1954 v Ni (5)

McPhail, R. (Airdrieonians), 1927 v E; (with Rangers), 1929 v W; 1931 v E, Ni; 1932 v W, Ni, F; 1933 v E, Ni; 1934 v A, Ni; 1935 v E; 1937 v G, E, Cz; 1938 v W, Ni (17)

McPherson, D. (Kilmarnock), 1892 v Ni (1)

McPherson, D. (Hearts), 1989 v Cy, E; 1990 v N, Ma, Cr, Se, Br; 1991 v Sw, Bul (2), USSR (sub), Sm; 1992 v Sw, R, Sm, Ni, Fi, US, Ca, N, Ho, G, C; (with Rangers), 1993 v Sw, I, Ma, P (27)

McPherson, J. (Clydesdale), 1875 v E (1)

McPherson, J. (Vale of Leven), 1879 v E, W; 1880 v E; 1881 v W; 1883 v E, W; 1884 v E; 1885 v Ni (8)

McPherson, J. (Kilmarnock), 1888 v W; (with Cowlairs), 1889 v E; 1890 v Ni, E; (with Rangers), 1892 v W; 1894 v E; 1895 v E, Ni; 1897 v Ni (9)

McPherson, J. (Hearts), 1891 v E (1)

McPherson, R. (Arthurlie), 1882 v E (1)

McQueen, G. (Leeds U), 1974 v Bel; 1975 v Sp (2), P, W, Ni, E, R; 1976 v D; 1977 v Cz, W (2), Ni, E; 1978 v EG, Cz, W; (with Manchester U), Bul, Ni, W; 1979 v A, N, P, Ni, E, N; 1980 v Pe, A, Bel; 1981 v W (30)

McQueen, M. (Leith Ath), 1890 v W; 1891 v W (2)

McRorie, D. M. (Morton), 1931 v W (1)

McStay, P. (Celtic), 1984 v U, Bel, EG, Ni, W, E (sub); 1985 v Y, Ic, Sp (2), W; 1986 v EG (sub), Aus, Is, U; 1987 v Bul, Ei (1+1 sub), L (sub), Bel, E, Br; 1988 v H, Bel, Bul, L, S.Ar, Sp, Co, E; 1989 v N, Y, I, Cy, F, Cy, E, Ch; 1990 v Y, F, N, Arg, EG (sub), Eg, Pol (sub), Ma, Cr, Se (sub), Br; 1991 v R, USSR, Bul; 1992 v Sm, Fi, US, Ca, N, Ho, G, C; 1993 v Sw, P, I, Ma, P, Es (2); 1994 v I (sub), Ho; 1995 v Fi, Fa, Ru; 1996 v Aus; 1997 v Es (2), A (sub) (76)

McStay, W. (Celtic), 1921 v W, Ni; 1925 v E, Ni, W; 1926 v E, Ni, W; 1927 v E, Ni, W; 1928 v W, Ni (13)

McSwegan, G. (Hearts), 2000 v Bos (sub), Li (2)

McTavish, J. (Falkirk), 1910 v Ni (1)

McWattie, G. C. (Queen's Park), 1901 v W, Ni (2)

McWilliam, P. (Newcastle U), 1905 v E; 1906 v E; 1907 v E, W; 1909 v E, W; 1910 v E; 1911 v W (8)

Macari, L. (Celtic), 1972 v W (sub), E, Y, Cz, Br; 1973 v D; (with Manchester U), E (2), W (sub), Ni (sub); 1975 v Se, P (sub), W, E (sub), R; 1977 v Ni (sub), E (sub), Ch, Arg; 1978 v EG, W, Bul, Pe (sub), Ir (24)

Macauley, A. R. (Brentford), 1947 v E; (with Arsenal), 1948 v E, W, Ni, Bel, Sw, F (7)

Madden, J. (Celtic), 1893 v W; 1895 v W (2)

Main, F. R. (Rangers), 1938 v W (1)

Main, J. (Hibernian), 1909 v Ni (1)

Maley, W. (Celtic), 1893 v E, Ni (2)

Malpas, M. (Dundee U), 1984 v F; 1985 v E, Ic; 1986 v W, Aus (2), Is, E, Ho, D, WG; 1987 v Bul, Ei, Bel; 1988 v Bel, Bul, L, S.Ar, Ma; 1989 v N, Y, I, Cy, F, Cy, E, Ch; 1990 v Y, F, N, Arg, EG, Pol, Ma, Cr, Se, Br; 1991 v R, Bul (2), USSR, Sm; 1992 v Sw, R, Sm, Ni, Fi, US, Ca (sub), N, Ho, G; 1993 v Sw, P, I (55) (55)

Marshall, G. (Celtic), 1992 v US (1)

Marshall, H. (Celtic), 1899 v W; 1900 v Ni (2)

Marshall, J. (Middlesbrough), 1921 v E, W, Ni; 1922 v E, W, Ni; (with Llanelly), 1924 v W (7)

Marshall, J. (Third Lanark), 1885 v Ni; 1886 v W; 1887 v E, W (4)

Marshall, J. (Rangers), 1932 v E; 1933 v E; 1934 v E (3)

Marshall, R. W. (Rangers), 1892 v Ni; 1894 v Ni (2)

Martin, B. (Motherwell), 1995 v J, Ec (2)

Martin, F. (Aberdeen), 1954 v N (2), A, U; 1955 v E, H (6)

Martin, N. (Hibernian), 1965 v Fi, Pol; (with Sunderland), 1966 v I (3)

Martis, J. (Motherwell), 1961 v W (1)

Mason, J. (Third Lanark), 1949 v E, Ni; 1950 v Ni; 1951 v Ni, Bel, A (7)

Massie, A. (Hearts), 1932 v Ni, W, F; 1933 v Ni; 1934 v E, Ni; 1935 v E, Ni, W; 1936 v W, Ni; (with Aston Villa), 1936 v E; 1937 v G, E, W, Ni, A; 1938 v W (18)

Masson, D. S. (QPR), 1976 v Ni, W, E; 1977 v Fi, Cz, W, Ni, E, Ch, Arg, Br; 1978 v EG, Cz, W; (with Derby Co), Ni, E, Pe (17)

Mathers, D. (Partick T), 1954 v Fi (1)

Maxwell, W. S. (Stoke C), 1898 v E (1)

May, J. (Rangers), 1906 v W, Ni; 1908 v E, Ni; 1909 v W (5)

Meechan, P. (Celtic), 1896 v Ni (1)

Meiklejohn, D. D. (Rangers), 1922 v W; 1924 v W; 1925 v W, Ni, E; 1928 v W, Ni; 1929 v E, Ni; 1930 v E, Ni; 1931 v E; 1932 v W, Ni; 1934 v A (15)

Menzies, A. (Hearts), 1906 v E (1)

Mercer, R. (Hearts), 1912 v W; 1913 v Ni (2)

Middleton, R. (Cowdenbeath), 1930 v Ni (1)

Millar, A. (Hearts), 1939 v W (1)

Millar, J. (Rangers), 1897 v E; 1898 v E, W (3)

Millar, J. (Rangers), 1963 v A, Ei (2)

Miller, J. (St Mirren), 1931 v E, I, Sw; 1932 v F; 1934 v E (5)

Miller, P. (Dumbarton), 1882 v E; 1883 v E, W (3)

Miller, T. (Liverpool), 1920 v E; (with Manchester U), 1921 v E, Ni (3)

Miller, W. (Third Lanark), 1876 v E (1)
Miller, W. (Celtic), 1947 v E, W, Bel, L; 1948 v W, Ni (6)
Miller, W. (Aberdeen), 1975 v R; 1978 v Bul; 1980 v Bel, W, E, Pol, H; 1981 v Se, P, Is (sub), Ni, W, Ni, E; 1982 v Ni, P, Ho, Br, USSR; 1983 v EG, Sw (2), W, E, Ca (3); 1984 v U, Bel, EG, W, E, F; 1985 v Y, Ic, Sp (2), W, E, Ic; 1986 v W, EG, Aus (2), Is, R, E, Ho, D, WG, U; 1987 v Bul, E, Br; 1988 v H, L, S.Ar, Ma, Sp, Co, E; 1989 v N, Y; 1990 v Y, N (65)
Mills, W. (Aberdeen), 1936 v W, Ni; 1937 v W (3)
Milne, J. V. (Middlesbrough), 1938 v E; 1939 v E (2)
Mitchell, D. (Rangers), 1890 v Ni; 1892 v E; 1893 v E, Ni; 1894 v E (5)
Mitchell, J. (Kilmarnock), 1908 v Ni; 1910 v Ni, W (3)
Mitchell, R. C. (Newcastle U), 1951 v D, F (2)
Mochan, N. (Celtic), 1954 v N, A, U (3)
Moir, W. (Bolton W), 1950 v E (1)
Moncur, R. (Newcastle U), 1968 v Ho; 1970 v Ni, W, E, Ei; 1971 v D, Bel, W, P, Ni, E, D; 1972 v Pe, Ni, W, E (16)
Morgan, H. (St Mirren), 1898 v W; (with Liverpool), 1899 v E (2)
Morgan, W. (Burnley), 1968 v Ni; (with Manchester U), 1972 v Pe, Y, Cz, Br; 1973 v D (2), E (2), W, Ni, Sw, Br; 1974 v Cz (2), WG (2), Ni, Bel (sub), Br, Y (21)
Morris, D. (Raith R), 1923 v Ni; 1924 v E, Ni; 1925 v E, W, Ni (6)
Morris, H. (East Fife), 1950 v Ni (1)
Morrison, T. (St Mirren), 1927 v E (1)
Morton, A. L. (Queen's Park), 1920 v W, Ni; (with Rangers), 1921 v E; 1922 v E, W; 1923 v E, W, Ni; 1924 v E, W, Ni; 1925 v E, W, Ni; 1927 v E, Ni; 1928 v E, W, Ni; 1929 v E, W, Ni; 1930 v E, W, Ni; 1931 v E, W, Ni; 1932 v E, W, F (31)
Morton, H. A. (Kilmarnock), 1929 v G, Ho (2)
Mudie, J. K. (Blackpool), 1957 v W, Ni, E, Y, Sw, Sp (2), WG; 1958 v Ni, E, W, Sw, H, Pol, Y, Par, F (17)
Muir, W. (Dundee), 1907 v Ni (1)
Muirhead, T. A. (Rangers), 1922 v Ni; 1923 v E; 1924 v W; 1927 v Ni; 1928 v Ni; 1929 v W, Ni; 1930 v W (8)
Mulhall, G. (Aberdeen), 1960 v Ni; (with Sunderland), 1963 v Ni; 1964 v Ni (3)
Munro, A. D. (Hearts), 1937 v W, Ni; (with Blackpool), 1938 v Ho (3)
Munro, F. M. (Wolverhampton W), 1971 v Ni (sub), E (sub), D, USSR; 1975 v Se, W (sub), Ni, E, R (9)
Munro, I. (St Mirren), 1979 v Arg, N; 1980 v Pe, A, Bel, W, E (7)
Munro, N. (Abercorn), 1888 v W; 1889 v E (2)
Murdoch, J. (Motherwell), 1931 v Ni (1)
Murdoch, R. (Celtic), 1966 v W, E, I (2); 1967 v Ni; 1968 v Ni; 1969 v W, Ni, E, WG, Cy; 1970 v A (12)
Murphy, F. (Celtic), 1938 v Ho (1)
Murray, J. (Renton), 1895 v W (1)
Murray, J. (Hearts), 1958 v E, H, Pol, Y, F (5)
Murray, J. W. (Vale of Leven), 1890 v W (1)
Murray, P. (Hibernian), 1896 v Ni; 1897 v W (2)
Murray, S. (Aberdeen), 1972 v Bel (1)
Mutch, G. (Preston NE), 1938 v E (1)

Napier, C. E. (Celtic), 1932 v E; 1935 v E, W; (with Derby Co), 1937 v Ni, A (5)
Narey, D. (Dundee U), 1977 v Se (sub); 1979 v P, Ni (sub), Arg; 1980 v P, Ni, Pol, H; 1981 v W, E (sub); 1982 v Ho, W, E, Nz (sub), Br, USSR; 1983 v EG, Sw, Bel, Ni, W, E, Ca (3); 1986 v Is, R, Ho, WG, U; 1987 v Bul, E, Bel; 1989 v I, Cy (35)
Naysmith, G. A. (Hearts), 2000 v Ei (1)
Neil, R. G. (Hibernian), 1896 v W; (with Rangers), 1900 v W (2)
Neill, R. W. (Queen's Park), 1876 v W; 1877 v E, W; 1878 v W; 1880 v E (5)
Nellies, P. (Hearts), 1913 v Ni; 1914 v W (2)
Nelson, J. (Cardiff C), 1925 v W, Ni; 1928 v E; 1930 v F (4)
Nevin, P. K. F. (Chelsea), 1986 v R (sub), E (sub); 1987 v L, Ei, Bel (sub); 1988 v L; (with Everton), 1989 v Cy, E; 1991 v R (sub), Bul (sub), Sm (sub); 1992 v US, G (sub), C (sub); (with Tranmere R), 1993 v Ma, P (sub), Es; 1994 v Sw, Ma, Ho, A (sub), Ho; 1995 v Fa, Ru (sub), Sm; 1996 v Se (sub), Sm, Aus (sub) (28)
Niblo, T. D. (Aston Villa), 1904 v E (1)
Nibloe, J. (Kilmarnock), 1929 v E, N, Ho; 1930 v W; 1931 v E, Ni, A, I, Sw; 1932 v E, F (11)
Nicholas, C. (Celtic), 1983 v Sw, Ni, E, Ca (3); (with Arsenal), 1984 v Bel, F (sub); 1985 v Y (sub), Ic (sub), Sp (sub), W (sub); 1986 v Is, R (sub), E, D, U (sub); 1987 v Bul, E (sub); (with Aberdeen), 1989 v Cy (sub) (20)

Nicol, S. (Liverpool), 1985 v Y, Ic, Sp, W; 1986 v W, EG, Aus, E, D, WG, U; 1988 v H, Bul, S.Ar, Sp, Co, E; 1989 v N, Y, Cy, F; 1990 v Y, F; 1991 v Sw, USSR, Sm; 1992 v Sw (27)
Nisbet, J. (Ayr U), 1929 v N, G, Ho (3)
Niven, J. B. (Moffatt), 1885 v Ni (1)

O'Donnell, F. (Preston NE), 1937 v E, A, Cz; 1938 v W; (with Blackpool), E, Ho (6)
O'Donnell, P. (Motherwell), 1994 v Sw (sub) (1)
Ogilvie, D. H. (Motherwell), 1934 v A (1)
O'Hare, J. (Derby Co), 1970 v W, Ni, E; 1971 v D, Bel, W, Ni; 1972 v P, Bel, Ho (sub), Pe, Ni, W (13)
O'Neil, B. (Celtic), 1996 v Aus; (with Wolfsburg), 1999 v G (sub); 2000 v Li, Ho (sub), Ei (5)
Ormond, W. E. (Hibernian), 1954 v E, N, Fi, A, U; 1959 v E (6)
O'Rourke, F. (Airdrieonians), 1907 v Ni (1)
Orr, J. (Kilmarnock), 1892 v W (1)
Orr, R. (Newcastle U), 1902 v E; 1904 v E (2)
Orr, T. (Morton), 1952 v Ni, W (2)
Orr, W. (Celtic), 1900 v Ni; 1903 v Ni; 1904 v W (3)
Orrock, R. (Falkirk), 1913 v W (1)
Oswald, J. (Third Lanark), 1889 v E; (with St Bernards), 1895 v E; (with Rangers), 1897 v W (3)

Parker, A. H. (Falkirk), 1955 v P, Y, A; 1956 v E, Ni, W, A; 1957 v Ni, W, Y; 1958 v Ni, W, E, Sw; (with Everton), Par (15)
Parlane, D. (Rangers), 1973 v W, Sw, Br; 1975 v Sp (sub), Se, P, W, Ni, E, R; 1976 v D (sub); 1977 v W (12)
Parlane, R. (Vale of Leven), 1878 v W; 1879 v E, W (3)
Paterson, G. D. (Celtic), 1939 v Ni (1)
Paterson, J. (Leicester C), 1920 v E (1)
Paterson, J. (Cowdenbeath), 1931 v A, I, Sw (3)
Paton, A. (Motherwell), 1952 v D, Se (2)
Paton, D. (St Bernards), 1896 v W (1)
Paton, M. (Dumbarton), 1883 v E; 1884 v W; 1885 v W, E; 1886 v E (5)
Paton, R. (Vale of Leven), 1879 v E, W (2)
Patrick, J. (St Mirren), 1897 v E, W (2)
Paul, H. McD. (Queen's Park), 1909 v E, W, Ni (3)
Paul, W. (Partick T), 1888 v W; 1889 v W; 1890 v W (3)
Paul, W. (Dykebar), 1891 v Ni (1)
Pearson, T. (Newcastle U), 1947 v E, Bel (2)
Penman, A. (Dundee), 1966 v Ho (1)
Pettigrew, W. (Motherwell), 1976 v Sw, Ni, W; 1977 v W (sub), Se (5)
Phillips, J. (Queen's Park), 1877 v E, W; 1878 v W (3)
Plenderleith, J. B. (Manchester C), 1961 v Ni (1)
Porteous, W. (Hearts), 1903 v Ni (1)
Pressley, S. J. (Hearts), 2000 v F (sub), Ei (sub) (2)
Pringle, C. (St Mirren), 1921 v W (1)
Provan, D. (Rangers), 1964 v Ni, N; 1966 v I (2), Ho (5)
Provan, D. (Celtic), 1980 v Bel (2 sub), P (sub), Ni (sub); 1981 v Is, W, E; 1982 v Se, P, Ni (10)
Pursell, P. (Queen's Park), 1914 v W (1)

Quinn, J. (Celtic), 1905 v Ni; 1906 v Ni, W; 1908 v Ni, E; 1909 v E; 1910 v E, Ni, W; 1912 v E, W (11)
Quinn, P. (Motherwell), 1961 v E, Ei (2); 1962 v U (4)

Rae, J. (Third Lanark), 1889 v W; 1890 v Ni (2)
Raeside, J. S. (Third Lanark), 1906 v W (1)
Raisbeck, A. G. (Liverpool), 1900 v E; 1901 v E; 1902 v E; 1903 v E, W; 1904 v E; 1906 v E; 1907 v E (8)
Rankin, G. (Vale of Leven), 1890 v Ni; 1891 v E (2)
Rankin, R. (St Mirren), 1929 v N, G, Ho (3)
Redpath, W. (Motherwell), 1949 v W, Ni; 1951 v E, D, F, Bel, A; 1952 v Ni, E (9)
Reid, J. G. (Airdrieonians), 1914 v W; 1920 v W; 1924 v Ni (3)
Reid, R. (Brentford), 1938 v E, Ni (2)
Reid, W. (Rangers), 1911 v E, W, Ni; 1912 v Ni; 1913 v E, W, Ni; 1914 v E, Ni (9)
Reilly, L. (Hibernian), 1949 v E, W, F; 1950 v W, Ni, Sw, F; 1951 v W, E, D, F, Bel, A; 1952 v Ni, W, E, USA, D, Se; 1953 v Ni, W, E, Se; 1954 v W; 1955 v H (2), P, Y, A, E; 1956 v E, W, Ni, A; 1957 v E, Ni, W, Y (38)
Rennie, H. G. (Hearts), 1900 v E, Ni; (with Hibernian), 1901 v E; 1902 v E, Ni, W; 1903 v Ni, W; 1904 v Ni; 1905 v W; 1906 v Ni; 1908 v Ni, W (13)
Renny-Tailyour, H. W. (Royal Engineers), 1873 v E (1)
Rhind, A. (Queen's Park), 1872 v E (1)
Richmond, A. (Queen's Park), 1906 v W (1)
Richmond, J. T. (Clydesdale), 1877 v E; (with Queen's Park), 1878 v E; 1882 v W (3)

Ring, T. (Clyde), 1953 v Se; 1955 v W, Ni, E, H; 1957 v E, Sp (2), Sw, WG; 1958 v Ni, Sw (12)
Rioch, B. D. (Derby Co), 1975 v P, W, Ni, E, R; 1976 v D (2), R, Ni, W, E; 1977 v Fi, Cz, W; (with Everton), W, Ni, E, Ch, Br; 1978 v Cz; (with Derby Co), Ni, E, Pe, Ho (24)
Ritchie, A. (East Stirlingshire), 1891 v W (1)
Ritchie, H. (Hibernian), 1923 v W; 1928 v Ni (2)
Ritchie, J. (Queen's Park), 1897 v W (1)
Ritchie, P. S. (Hearts), 1999 v G (sub), CzR; 2000 v Li, E; (with Bolton W), F, Ho (6)
Ritchie, W. (Rangers), 1962 v U (sub) (1)
Robb, D. T. (Aberdeen), 1971 v W, E, P, D (sub), USSR (5)
Robb, W. (Rangers), 1926 v W; (with Hibernian), 1928 v W (2)
Robertson, A. (Clyde), 1955 v P, A, H; 1958 v Sw, Par (5)
Robertson, D. (Rangers), 1992 v Ni; 1994 v Sw, Ho (3)
Robertson, G. (Motherwell), 1910 v W; (with Sheffield W), 1912 v W; 1913 v E, Ni (4)
Robertson, G. (Kilmarnock), 1938 v Cz (1)
Robertson, H. (Dundee), 1962 v Cz (1)
Robertson, J. (Dundee), 1931 v A, I (2)
Robertson, J. (Hearts), 1991 v R, Sw, Bul (sub), Sm (sub); 1992 v Sm, Ni (sub), Fi; 1993 v I (sub), Ma (sub), G, Es; 1995 v J (sub), Ec, Fa (sub); 1996 v Gr (sub), Se (16)
Robertson, J. G. (Tottenham H), 1965 v W (1)
Robertson, J. N. (Nottingham F), 1978 v Ni, W (sub), Ir; 1979 v P, N; 1980 v Pe, A, Bel (2), P; 1981 v Se, P, Is, Ni, Is, Ni, E; 1982 v Se, Ni (2), E (sub), Nz, Br, USSR; 1983 v EG, Sw; (with Derby Co), 1984 v U, Bel (28)
Robertson, J. T. (Everton), 1898 v E; (with Southampton), 1899 v E; (with Rangers), 1900 v E, W; 1901 v W, Ni, E; 1902 v W, Ni, E; 1903 v E, W; 1904 v E, W, Ni; 1905 v W (16)
Robertson, P. (Dundee), 1903 v Ni (1)
Robertson, T. (Queen's Park), 1889 v Ni; 1890 v E; 1891 v W; 1892 v Ni (4)
Robertson, T. (Hearts), 1898 v Ni (1)
Robertson, W. (Dumbarton), 1887 v E, W (2)
Robinson, R. (Dundee), 1974 v WG (sub); 1975 v Se, Ni, R (sub) (4)
Rough, A. (Partick T), 1976 v Sw, Ni, W, E; 1977 v Fi, Cz, W (2), Se, Ni, E, Ch, Arg, Br; 1978 v Cz, W, Ni, E, Pe, Ir, Ho; 1979 v A, P, W, Arg, N; 1980 v Pe, A, Bel (2), P, W, E, Pol, H; 1981 v Se, P, Is, Ni, Is, W, E; 1982 v Se, Ni, Sp, Ho, W, E, Nz, Br, USSR; (with Hibernian), 1986 v W (sub), E (53)
Rougvie, D. (Aberdeen), 1984 v Ni (1)
Rowan, A. (Caledonian), 1880 v E; (with Queen's Park), 1882 v W (2)
Russell, D. (Hearts), 1895 v E, Ni; (with Celtic), 1897 v W; 1898 v Ni; 1901 v W, Ni (6)
Russell, J. (Cambuslang), 1890 v Ni (1)
Russell, W. F. (Airdrieonians), 1924 v W; 1925 v E (2)
Rutherford, E. (Rangers), 1948 v F (1)

St John, I. (Motherwell), 1959 v WG; 1960 v E, Ni, W, Pol, A; 1961 v E; (with Liverpool), 1962 v Ni, W, E, Cz (2), U; 1963 v W, Ni, E, N, Ei (sub); Sp; 1964 v Ni; 1965 v E (21)
Sawers, W. (Dundee), 1895 v W (1)
Scarff, P. (Celtic), 1931 v Ni (1)
Schaedler, E. (Hibernian), 1974 v WG (1)
Scott, A. S. (Rangers), 1957 v Ni, Y, WG; 1958 v W, Sw; 1959 v P; 1962 v Ni, W, E, Cz, U; (with Everton), 1964 v W, N; 1965 v Fi; 1966 v P, Br (16)
Scott, J. (Hibernian), 1966 v Ho (1)
Scott, J. (Dundee), 1971 v D (sub), USSR (2)
Scott, M. (Airdrieonians), 1898 v W (1)
Scott, R. (Airdrieonians), 1894 v Ni (1)
Scoular, J. (Portsmouth), 1951 v D, F, A; 1952 v E, USA, D, Se; 1953 v W, Ni (9)
Sellar, W. (Battlefield), 1885 v E; 1886 v E; 1887 v E, W; 1888 v E; (with Queen's Park), 1891 v E; 1892 v E; 1893 v E, Ni (9)
Semple, W. (Cambuslang), 1886 v W (1)
Shankly, W. (Preston NE), 1938 v E; 1939 v E, W, Ni, H (5)
Sharp, G. M. (Everton), 1985 v Ic; 1986 v W, Aus (2 sub), Is, R, U; 1987 v Ei; 1988 v Bel (sub), Bul, L, Ma (12)
Sharp, J. (Dundee), 1904 v W; (with Woolwich Arsenal), 1907 v W, E; 1908 v E; (with Fulham), 1909 v W (5)
Shaw, D. (Hibernian), 1947 v W, Ni; 1948 v E, Bel, Sw, F; 1949 v W, Ni (8)
Shaw, F. W. (Pollokshields Ath), 1884 v E, W (2)
Shaw, J. (Rangers), 1947 v E, Bel, L; 1949 v Ni (4)
Shearer, D. (Aberdeen), 1994 v A (sub), Ho (sub); 1995 v Fi, Ru (sub), Sm, Fa; 1996 v Gr (7)
Shearer, R. (Rangers), 1961 v E, Ei (2), Cz (4)

Sillars, D. C. (Queen's Park), 1891 v Ni; 1892 v E; 1893 v W; 1894 v E; 1895 v W (5)
Simpson, J. (Third Lanark), 1895 v E, W, Ni (3)
Simpson, J. (Rangers), 1935 v E, W; 1936 v E, W, Ni; 1937 v G, E, W, Ni, A, Cz; 1938 v W, Ni (14)
Simpson, N. (Aberdeen), 1983 v Ni; 1984 v U (sub), F (sub); 1987 v E; 1988 v E (5)
Simpson, R. C. (Celtic), 1967 v E, USSR; 1968 v Ni, E; 1969 v A (5)
Sinclair, G. L. (Hearts), 1910 v Ni; 1912 v W, Ni (3)
Sinclair, J. W. E. (Leicester C), 1966 v P (1)
Skene, L. H. (Queen's Park), 1904 v W (1)
Sloan, T. (Third Lanark), 1904 v W (1)
Smellie, R. (Queen's Park), 1887 v Ni; 1888 v W; 1889 v E; 1891 v E; 1893 v E, Ni (6)
Smith, A. (Rangers), 1898 v E; 1900 v E, Ni, W; 1901 v E, Ni, W; 1902 v E, Ni, W; 1903 v E, Ni, W; 1904 v Ni; 1905 v W; 1906 v E, Ni; 1907 v W; 1911 v E, Ni (20)
Smith, D. (Aberdeen), 1966 v Ho; (with Rangers), 1968 v Ho (2)
Smith, G. (Hibernian), 1947 v E, Ni; 1948 v W, Bel, Sw, F; 1952 v E, USA; 1955 v P, Y, A, H; 1956 v E, Ni, W; 1957 v Sp (2), Sw (18)
Smith, H. G. (Hearts), 1988 v S.Ar (sub); 1992 v Ni, Ca (3)
Smith, J. (Rangers), 1935 v Ni; 1938 v Ni (2)
Smith, J. (Ayr U), 1924 v E (1)
Smith, J. (Aberdeen), 1968 v Ho (sub); (with Newcastle U), 1974 v WG, Ni (sub), W (sub) (4)
Smith, J. E. (Celtic), 1959 v H, P (2)
Smith, Jas (Queen's Park), 1872 v E (1)
Smith, John (Mauchline), 1877 v E, W; 1879 v E, W; (with Edinburgh University), 1880 v E; (with Queen's Park), 1881 v W, E; 1883 v E, W; 1884 v E (10)
Smith, N. (Rangers), 1897 v E; 1898 v W; 1899 v E, Ni; 1900 v E, W, Ni; 1901 v Ni, W; 1902 v E, Ni (12)
Smith, R. (Queen's Park), 1872 v E; 1873 v E (2)
Smith, T. M. (Kilmarnock), 1934 v E; (with Preston NE), 1938 v E (2)
Somers, P. (Celtic), 1905 v E, Ni; 1907 v Ni; 1909 v W (4)
Somers, W. S. (Third Lanark), 1879 v E, W; (with Queen's Park), 1880 v W (3)
Somerville, G. (Queen's Park), 1886 v E (1)
Souness, G. J. (Middlesbrough), 1975 v EG, Sp, Se; (with Liverpool), 1978 v Bul, W, E (sub), Ho; 1979 v A, N, W, Ni, E; 1980 v Pe, A, Bel, P, Ni; 1981 v P, Is (2); 1982 v Ni, P, Sp, W, E, Nz, Br, USSR; 1983 v EG, Sw, Bel, Sw, W, E, Ca (2 + 1 sub); 1984 v U, Ni, W; (with Sampdoria), 1985 v Y, Ic, Sp (2), W, E, Ic; 1986 v EG, Aus (2), R, E, D, WG (54)
Speedie, D. R. (Chelsea), 1985 v E; 1986 v W, EG (sub), Aus, E; (with Coventry C), 1989 v Y (sub), I (sub), Cy (1+1 sub), Ch (10)
Speedie, F. (Rangers), 1903 v E, W, Ni (3)
Speirs, J. H. (Rangers), 1908 v W (1)
Spencer, J. (Chelsea), 1995 v Ru (sub), Gr (sub), Sm (sub), J; 1996 v Fi, Aus, D, US (sub), Co, Ho (sub), E, Sw (sub); 1997 v La; (with QPR), W (sub) (14)
Stanton, P. (Hibernian), 1966 v Ho; 1969 v Ni; 1970 v Ei, A; 1971 v D, Bel, P, USSR, D; 1972 v P, Bel, Ho, W; 1973 v W, Ni; 1974 v WG (16)
Stark, J. (Rangers), 1909 v E, Ni (2)
Steel, W. (Morton), 1947 v E, Bel, L; (with Derby Co), 1948 v F, E, W, Ni; 1949 v E, W, Ni, F; 1950 v E, W, Sw, P, F; (with Dundee), 1951 v W, Ni, E, A (2), D, F, Bel; 1952 v W; 1953 v W, E, Ni, Se (30)
Steele, D. M. (Huddersfield), 1923 v E, W, Ni (3)
Stein, C. (Rangers), 1969 v W, Ni, D, E, Cy (2); 1970 v A (sub), Ni (sub), W, E, Ei, WG; 1971 v D, USSR, Bel, D; 1972 v Cz (sub); (with Coventry C), 1973 v E (2 sub), W (sub), Ni (21)
Stephen, J. F. (Bradford), 1947 v W; 1948 v W (2)
Stevenson, G. (Motherwell), 1928 v W, Ni; 1930 v Ni, E, F; 1931 v E, W; 1932 v W, Ni; 1933 v Ni; 1934 v E; 1935 v Ni (12)
Stewart, A. (Queen's Park), 1888 v Ni; 1889 v W (2)
Stewart, A. (Third Lanark), 1894 v W (1)
Stewart, D. (Dumbarton), 1888 v Ni (1)
Stewart, D. (Queen's Park), 1893 v W; 1894 v Ni; 1897 v Ni (3)
Stewart, D. S. (Leeds U), 1978 v EG (1)
Stewart, G. (Hibernian), 1906 v W, E; (with Manchester C), 1907 v E, W (4)
Stewart, J. (Kilmarnock), 1977 v Ch (sub); (with Middlesbrough), 1979 v N (2)
Stewart, R. (West Ham U), 1981 v W, Ni, E; 1982 v Ni, P, W; 1984 v F; 1987 v Ei (2), L (10)
Stewart, W. E. (Queen's Park), 1898 v Ni; 1900 v Ni (2)
Storrier, D. (Celtic), 1899 v E, W, Ni (3)

Strachan, G. (Aberdeen), 1980 v Ni, W, E, Pol, H (sub); 1981 v Se, P; 1982 v Ni, P, Sp, Ho (sub), Nz, Br, USSR; 1983 v EG, Sw, Bel, Sw, Ni (sub); W, E, Ca (2 + 1 sub); 1984 v EG, Ni, E, F; (with Manchester U), 1985 v Sp (sub), E, Ic; 1986 v W, Aus, R, D, WG, U; 1987 v Bul, Ei (2); 1988 v H; 1989 v F (sub); (with Leeds U), 1990 v F; 1991 v USSR, Bul, Sm; 1992 v Sw, R, Ni, Fi (50)

Sturrock, P. (Dundee U), 1981 v W (sub), Ni, E (sub); 1982 v P, Ni (sub), W (sub), E (sub); 1983 v EG (sub), Sw, Bel (sub), Ca (3); 1984 v W; 1985 v Y (sub); 1986 v Is (sub), Ho, D, U; 1987 v Bel (20)

Sullivan, N. (Wimbledon), 1997 v W; 1998 v F, Co; 1999 v Fa, CzR, G, Fa, CzR; 2000 v Bos, Es, Bos, E (2), F, Ho, Ei (16)

Summers, W. (St Mirren), 1926 v E (1)

Symon, J. S. (Rangers), 1939 v H (1)

Tait, T. S. (Sunderland), 1911 v W (1)

Taylor, J. (Queen's Park), 1872 v E; 1873 v E; 1874 v E; 1875 v E; 1876 v E, W, (6)

Taylor, J. D. (Dumbarton), 1892 v W; 1893 v W; 1894 v Ni; (with St Mirren), 1895 v Ni (4)

Taylor, W. (Hearts), 1892 v E (1)

Telfer, P. N. (Coventry C), 2000 v F (1)

Telfer, W. (Motherwell), 1933 v Ni; 1934 v Ni (2)

Telfer, W. D. (St Mirren), 1954 v W (1)

Templeton, R. (Aston Villa), 1902 v E; (with Newcastle U), 1903 v E, W; 1904 v E; (with Woolwich Arsenal), 1905 v W; (with Kilmarnock), 1908 v Ni; 1910 v E, Ni; 1912 v E, Ni; 1913 v W (11)

Thomson, A. (Arthurlie), 1886 v Ni (1)

Thomson, A. (Third Lanark), 1889 v W (1)

Thomson, A. (Airdrieonians), 1909 v Ni (1)

Thomson, A. (Celtic), 1926 v E; 1932 v F; 1933 v W (3)

Thomson, C. (Hearts), 1904 v Ni; 1905 v E, Ni, W; 1906 v W, Ni; 1907 v E, W, Ni; 1908 v E, W, Ni; (with Sunderland), 1909 v W; 1910 v E; 1911 v Ni; 1912 v E, W; 1913 v E, W; 1914 v E, Ni (21)

Thomson, C. (Sunderland), 1937 v Cz (1)

Thomson, D. (Dundee), 1920 v W (1)

Thomson, J. (Celtic), 1930 v F; 1931 v E, W, Ni (4)

Thomson, J. J. (Queen's Park), 1872 v E; 1873 v E; 1874 v E (3)

Thomson, J. R. (Everton), 1933 v W (1)

Thomson, R. (Celtic), 1932 v W (1)

Thomson, R. W. (Falkirk), 1927 v E (1)

Thomson, S. (Rangers), 1884 v W, Ni (2)

Thomson, W. (Dumbarton), 1892 v W; 1893 v W; 1898 v Ni, W (4)

Thomson, W. (Dundee), 1896 v W (1)

Thornton, W. (Rangers), 1947 v W, Ni; 1948 v E, Ni; 1949 v F; 1952 v D, Se (7)

Thomson, W. (St Mirren), 1980 v Ni; 1981 v Ni (sub+1) 1982 v P; 1983 v Ni, Ca; 1984 v EG (7)

Toner, W. (Kilmarnock), 1959 v W, Ni (2)

Townsley, T. (Falkirk), 1926 v W (1)

Troup, A. (Dundee), 1920 v E; 1921 v W, Ni; 1922 v Ni; (with Everton), 1926 v E (5)

Turnbull, E. (Hibernian), 1948 v Bel, Sw; 1951 v A; 1958 v H, Pol, Y, Par, F (8)

Turner, T. (Arthurlie), 1884 v W (1)

Turner, W. (Pollokshields Ath), 1885 v Ni; 1886 v Ni (2)

Ure, I. F. (Dundee), 1962 v W, Cz; 1963 v W, Ni, E, A, N, Sp; (with Arsenal), 1964 v Ni, N; 1968 v Ni (11)

Urquhart, D. (Hibernian), 1934 v W (1)

Vallance, T. (Rangers), 1877 v E, W; 1878 v E; 1879 v E, W; 1881 v E, W (7)

Venters, A. (Cowdenbeath), 1934 v Ni; (with Rangers), 1936 v E; 1939 v E (3)

Waddell, T. S. (Queen's Park), 1891 v Ni; 1892 v E; 1893 v E, Ni; 1895 v E, Ni (6)

Waddell, W. (Rangers), 1947 v W; 1949 v E, W, Ni, F; 1950 v E, Ni; 1951 v E, D, F, Bel, A; 1952 v Ni, W; 1954 v Ni; 1955 v W, Ni (17)

Wales, H. M. (Motherwell), 1933 v W (1)

Walker, A. (Celtic), 1988 v Co (sub); 1995 v Fi, Fa (sub) (3)

Walker, F. (Third Lanark), 1922 v W (1)

Walker, G. (St Mirren), 1930 v F; 1931 v Ni, A, Sw (4)

Walker, J. (Hearts), 1895 v Ni; 1897 v W; 1898 v Ni; (with Rangers), 1904 v W, Ni (5)

Walker, J. (Swindon T), 1911 v E, W, Ni; 1912 v E, W, Ni; 1913 v E, W, Ni (9)

Walker, J. N. (Hearts), 1993 v G; (with Partick T), 1996 v US (sub) (2)

Walker, R. (Hearts), 1900 v E, Ni; 1901 v E, W; 1902 v E, W, Ni; 1903 v E, W, Ni; 1904 v E, W, Ni; 1905 v E, W, Ni; 1906 v Ni; 1907 v E, Ni; 1908 v E, W, Ni; 1909 v E, W; 1912 v E, W, Ni; 1913 v E, W (29)

Walker, T. (Hearts), 1935 v E, W; 1936 v E, W, Ni; 1937 v G, E, W, Ni, A, Cz; 1938 v E, W, Ni, Cz, Ho; 1939 v E, W, Ni, H (20)

Walker, W. (Clyde), 1909 v Ni; 1910 v Ni (2)

Wallace, I. A. (Coventry C), 1978 v Bul (sub); 1979 v P (sub), W (3)

Wallace, W. S. B. (Hearts), 1965 v Ni; 1966 v E, Ho; (with Celtic), 1967 v E, USSR (sub); 1968 v Ni; 1969 v E (sub) (7)

Wardhaugh, J. (Hearts), 1955 v H; 1957 v Ni (2)

Wark, J. (Ipswich T), 1979 v W, Ni, E, Arg, N (sub); 1980 v Pe, A, Bel (2); 1981 v Is, Ni; 1982 v Se, Sp, Ho, Ni, Nz, Br, USSR; 1983 v EG, Sw (2), Ni, E (sub); 1984 v U, Bel, EG; (with Liverpool), E, F; 1985 v Y (29)

Watson, A. (Queen's Park), 1881 v E, W; 1882 v E (3)

Watson, J. (Sunderland), 1903 v E, W; 1904 v E, W; 1905 v E; (with Middlesbrough), 1909 v E, Ni (6)

Watson, J. (Motherwell), 1948 v Ni; (with Huddersfield T), 1954 v Ni (2)

Watson, J. A. K. (Rangers), 1878 v W (1)

Watson, P. R. (Blackpool), 1934 v A (1)

Watson, R. (Motherwell), 1971 v USSR (1)

Watson, W. (Falkirk), 1898 v W (1)

Watt, F. (Kilbirnie), 1889 v W, Ni; 1890 v W; 1891 v E (4)

Watt, W. W. (Queen's Park), 1887 v Ni (1)

Waugh, W. (Hearts), 1938 v Cz (1)

Weir, A. (Motherwell), 1959 v WG; 1960 v E, P, A, H, T (6)

Weir, D. G. (Hearts), 1997 v W, Ma (sub); 1998 v F, D (sub), Fi (sub), N (sub), Mor; 1999 v Es, Fa; (with Everton), CzR, G, Fa, CzR; 2000 v Bos, Es, Bos, Li, E (2), Ho (20)

Weir, J. (Third Lanark), 1887 v Ni (1)

Weir, J. B. (Queen's Park), 1872 v E; 1874 v E; 1875 v E; 1878 v W (4)

Weir, P. (St Mirren), 1980 v Ni, W, Pol (sub), H; (with Aberdeen), 1983 v Sw; 1984 v Ni (6)

White, John (Albion R), 1922 v W; (with Hearts), 1923 v Ni (2)

White, J. A. (Falkirk), 1959 v WG, Ho, P; 1960 v Ni; (with Tottenham H), 1960 v W, Pol, A, T; 1961 v W; 1962 v Ni, W, E, Cz (2); 1963 v W, Ni, E; 1964 v Ni, W, E, N, WG (22)

White, W. (Bolton W), 1907 v E; 1908 v E (2)

Whitelaw, A. (Vale of Leven), 1887 v Ni; 1890 v W (2)

Whyte, D. (Celtic), 1988 v Bel (sub), L; 1989 v Ch (sub); 1992 v US (sub); (with Middlesbrough), 1993 v P, I; 1995 v J (sub), Ec; 1996 v US; 1997 v La; (with Aberdeen), 1998 v Fi; 1999 v G (sub) (12)

Wilson, A. (Sheffield W), 1907 v E; 1908 v E; 1912 v E; 1913 v E, W; 1914 v Ni (6)

Wilson, A. (Portsmouth), 1954 v Fi (1)

Wilson, A. N. (Dunfermline), 1920 v E, W, Ni; 1921 v E, W, Ni; (with Middlesbrough), 1922 v E, W, Ni; 1923 v E, W, Ni (12)

Wilson, D. (Queen's Park), 1900 v W (1)

Wilson, D. (Oldham Ath), 1913 v E (1)

Wilson, D. (Rangers), 1961 v E, W, Ni, Ei (2), Cz; 1962 v Ni, W, E, Cz, U; 1963 v W, E, A, N, Ei, Sp; 1964 v E, WG; 1965 v Ni, E, Fi (22)

Wilson, G. W. (Hearts), 1904 v W; 1905 v E, Ni; 1906 v W; (with Everton), 1907 v E; (with Newcastle U), 1909 v E (6)

Wilson, Hugh, (Newmilns), 1890 v W; (with Sunderland), 1897 v E; (with Third Lanark), 1902 v W; 1904 v Ni (4)

Wilson, I. A. (Leicester C), 1987 v E, Br; (with Everton), 1988 v Bel, Bul, L (5)

Wilson, J. (Vale of Leven), 1888 v W; 1889 v E; 1890 v E; 1891 v E (4)

Wilson, P. (Celtic), 1926 v Ni; 1930 v F; 1931 v Ni; 1933 v E (4)

Wilson, P. (Celtic), 1975 v W (sub) (1)

Wilson, R. P. (Arsenal), 1972 v P, Ho (2)

Winters, R. (Aberdeen), 1999 v G (sub) (1)

Wiseman, W. (Queen's Park), 1927 v W; 1930 v Ni (2)

Wood, G. (Everton), 1979 v Ni, E, Arg (sub); (with Arsenal), 1982 v Ni (4)

Woodburn, W. A. (Rangers), 1947 v E, Bel, L; 1948 v W, Ni; 1949 v E, F; 1950 v E, W, Ni, P, F; 1951 v E, W, Ni, A (2), D, F, Bel; 1952 v E, W, Ni, USA (24)

Wotherspoon, D. N. (Queen's Park), 1872 v E; 1873 v E (2)

Wright, K. (Hibernian), 1992 v Ni (1)

Wright, S. (Aberdeen), 1993 v G, Es (2)

Wright, T. (Sunderland), 1953 v W, Ni, E (3)

Wylie, T. G. (Rangers), 1890 v Ni (1)

Yeats, R. (Liverpool), 1965 v W; 1966 v I (2)

Yorston, B. C. (Aberdeen), 1931 v Ni (1)

Yorston, H. (Aberdeen), 1955 v W (1)

Young, A. (Hearts), 1960 v E, A (sub), H, T; 1961 v W, Ni; (with Everton), Ei; 1966 v P (8)
Young, A. (Everton), 1905 v E; 1907 v W (2)
Young, G. L. (Rangers), 1947 v E, Ni, Bel, L; 1948 v E, Ni, Bel, Sw, F; 1949 v E, W, Ni, F; 1950 v E, W, Ni, Sw, P, F; 1951 v E, W, Ni, A (2), D, F, Bel; 1952 v E, W, Ni, USA, D,

Se; 1953 v W, E, Ni, Se; 1954 v Ni, W; 1955 v W, Ni, P, Y; 1956 v Ni, W, E, A; 1957 v E, Ni, W, Y, Sp, Sw (53)
Young, J. (Celtic), 1906 v Ni (1)
Younger, T. (Hibernian), 1955 v P, Y, A, H; 1956 v E, Ni, W, A; (with Liverpool), 1957 v E, Ni, W, Y, Sp (2), Sw, WG; 1958 v Ni, W, E, Sw, H, Pol, Y, Par (24)

WALES

Adams, H. (Berwyn R), 1882 v Ni, E; (with Druids), 1883 v Ni, E (4)
Aizlewood, M. (Charlton Ath), 1986 v S.Ar, Ca (2); 1987 v Fi; (with Leeds U), USSR, Fi (sub); 1988 v D (sub), Se, Ma, I; 1989 v Ho, Se (sub), WG; (with Bradford C), 1990 v Fi, WG, Ei, Cr; (with Bristol C), 1991 v D, Bel (2), L, Ei, Ic, Pol, WG; 1992 v Br, L, Ei, A, R, Ho, Arg, J; 1993 v Ei, Bel, Fa; 1994 v RCS, Cy; (with Cardiff C), 1995 v Bul (39)
Allchurch, I. J. (Swansea T), 1951 v E, Ni, P, Sw; 1952 v E, S, Ni, R of UK; 1953 v S, E, Ni, F, Y; 1954 v S, E, Ni, A; 1955 v S, E, Ni, Y; 1956 v E, S, Ni, A; 1957 v E, S; 1958 v Ni, Is (2), H (2), M, Sw, Br; (with Newcastle U), 1959 v E, S, Ni; 1960 v E, S; 1961 v Ni, H, Sp (2); 1962 v E, S, Br (2), M; (with Cardiff C), 1963 v S, E, Ni, H (2); 1964 v E; 1965 v S, E, Ni, Gr, I, USSR; (with Swansea T), 1966 v USSR, E, S, D, Br (2), Ch (68)
Allchurch, L. (Swansea T), 1955 v Ni; 1956 v A; 1958 v S, Ni, EG, Is; 1959 v S; (with Sheffield U), 1962 v S, Ni, Br; 1964 v E (11)
Allen, B. W. (Coventry C), 1951 v S, E (2)
Allen, M. (Watford), 1986 v S.Ar (sub), Ca (1 + 1 sub); (with Norwich C), 1989 v Is (sub); 1990 v Ho, WG; (with Millwall), Ei, Se, Cr (sub); 1991 v L (sub), Ei (sub); 1992 v A; 1993 v Ei (sub); (with Newcastle U), 1994 v R (sub) (14)
Arridge, S. (Bootle), 1892 v S, Ni; (with Everton), 1894 v Ni; 1895 v Ni; 1896 v E; (with New Brighton Tower), 1898 v E, Ni; 1899 v E (8)
Astley, D. J. (Charlton Ath), 1931 v Ni; (with Aston Villa), 1932 v E; 1933 v E, S, Ni; 1934 v E, S; 1935 v S; 1936 v E, Ni; (with Derby Co), 1939 v E, S; (with Blackpool), F (13)
Atherton, R. W. (Hibernian), 1899 v E, Ni; 1903 v E, S, Ni; (with Middlesbrough), 1904 v E, S, Ni; 1905 v Ni (9)

Bailiff, W. E. (Llanelly), 1913 v E, S, Ni; 1920 v Ni (4)
Baker, C. W. (Cardiff C), 1958 v M; 1960 v S, Ni; 1961 v S, E, Ei; 1962 v S (7)
Baker, W. G. (Cardiff C), 1948 v Ni (1)
Bamford, T. (Wrexham), 1931 v E, S, Ni; 1932 v Ni; 1933 v F (5)
Barnard, D. S. (Barnsley), 1998 v Jam; 1999 v I, D, Bl, I, D; 2000 v Bl, Sw, Q, Fi, Br (sub), P (12)
Barnes, W. (Arsenal), 1948 v E, S, Ni; 1949 v E, S, Ni; 1950 v E, S, Ni, Bel; 1951 v E, S, Ni, P; 1952 v E, S, Ni, R of UK; 1954 v E, S; 1955 v S, Y (22)
Bartley, T. (Glossop NE), 1898 v E (1)
Bastock, A. M. (Shrewsbury), 1892 v Ni (1)
Beadles, G. H. (Cardiff C), 1925 v E, S (2)
Bell, W. S. (Shrewsbury Engineers), 1881 v E, S; (with Crewe Alex), 1886 v E, S, Ni (5)
Bellamy, C. D. (Norwich C), 1998 v Jam (sub), Ma, Tun; 1999 v D (sub), Sw (sub), I, D (sub); 2000 v Br (sub), P (9)
Bennion, S. R. (Manchester U), 1926 v S; 1927 v S; 1928 v S, E, Ni; 1929 v S, E, Ni; 1930 v S; 1932 v Ni (10)
Berry, G. F. (Wolverhampton W), 1979 v WG; 1980 v Ei, WG (sub), T; (with Stoke C), 1983 v E (sub) (5)
Blackmore, C. G. (Manchester U), 1985 v N (sub); 1986 v S (sub), H (sub), S.Ar, Ei, U; 1987 v Fi (2), USSR, Cz; 1988 v D (2), Cz, Y, Se, Ma, I; 1989 v Ho, Fi, Is, WG; 1990 v Ho, WG, Cr; 1991 v Bel, L; 1992 v Ei (sub), A, R (sub), Ho, Arg, J; 1993 v Fa, Cy, Bel, RCS; 1994 v Se (sub); (with Middlesbrough), 1997 v Bel (39)
Blake, N. A. (Sheffield U), 1994 v N, Se (sub); 1995 v Alb, Mol; 1996 v G (with Bolton W), I (sub); 1998 v T; 1999 v I, D, Bl; (with Blackburn R), Sw; 2000 v Bl, Sw, Q, Fi (15)
Blew, H. (Wrexham), 1899 v E, S, Ni; 1902 v S, Ni; 1903 v E, S; 1904 v E, S, Ni; 1905 v S, Ni; 1906 v E, S, Ni; 1907 v S; 1908 v E, S, Ni; 1909 v E, S; 1910 v E (22)
Boden, T. (Wrexham), 1880 v E (1)
Bodin, P. J. (Swindon T), 1990 v Cr; 1991 v D, Bel, L, Ei; (with C Palace), Bel, Ic, Pol, WG; 1992 v Br, G, L (sub); (with Swindon T), Ei (sub), Ho, Arg; 1993 v Ei, Bel, RCS, Fa; 1994 v R, Se, Es (sub); 1995 v Alb (23)
Boulter, L. M. (Brentford), 1939 v Ni (1)

Bowdler, H. E. (Shrewsbury), 1893 v S (1)
Bowdler, J. C. H. (Shrewsbury), 1890 v Ni; (with Wolverhampton W), 1891 v S; 1892 v Ni; (with Shrewsbury), 1894 v E (4)
Bowen, D. L. (Arsenal), 1955 v S, Y; 1957 v Ni, Cz, EG; 1958 v E, S, Ni, EG, Is (2), H (2), M, Se, Br; 1959 v E, S, Ni (19)
Bowen, E. (Druids), 1880 v S; 1883 v S (2)
Bowen, J. P. (Swansea C), 1994 v Es; (with Birmingham C), 1997 v Ho (2)
Bowen, M. R. (Tottenham H), 1986 v Ca (2 sub); (with Norwich C), 1988 v Y (sub); 1989 v Fi (sub), Is, Se, WG (sub); 1990 v Fi (sub), Ho, WG, Se; 1992 v Br (sub), G, L, Ei, A, R, Ho (sub), J; 1993 v Fa, Cy, Bel (1 + sub), RCS (sub); 1994 v RCS, Se; 1995 v Mol, Ge, Bul (2), G, Ge; 1996 v Mol, G, Alb, Sw, Sm; (with West Ham U), 1997 v Sm, Ho (2), Ei (sub) (41)
Bowsher, S. J. (Burnley), 1929 v Ni (1)
Boyle, T. (C Palace), 1981 v Ei, S (sub) (2)
Britten, T. J. (Parkgrove), 1878 v S; (with Presteigne), 1880 v S (2)
Brookes, S. J. (Llandudno), 1900 v E, Ni (2)
Brown, A. I. (Aberdare Ath), 1926 v Ni (1)
Browning, M. T. (Bristol R), 1996 v I (sub), Sm; 1997 v Sm, Ho (with Huddersfield T), S (sub) (5)
Bryan, T. (Oswestry), 1886 v E, Ni (2)
Buckland, T. (Bangor), 1899 v E (1)
Burgess, W. A. R. (Tottenham H), 1947 v E, S, Ni; 1948 v E, S; 1949 v E, S, Ni, P, Bel, Sw; 1950 v E, S, Ni, Bel; 1951 v S, Ni, P, Sw; 1952 v E, S, Ni, R of UK; 1953 v S, E, Ni, F, Y; 1954 v S, E, Ni, A (32)
Burke, T. (Wrexham), 1883 v E; 1884 v S; 1885 v E, S, Ni; (with Newton Heath), 1887 v E, S; 1888 v S (8)
Burnett, T. B. (Ruabon), 1877 v S (1)
Burton, A. D. (Norwich C), 1963 v Ni, H; (with Newcastle U), 1964 v E; 1969 v S, E, Ni, I, EG; 1972 v Cz (9)
Butler, J. (Chirk), 1893 v E, S, Ni (3)
Butler, W. T. (Druids), 1900 v S, Ni (2)

Cartwright, L. (Coventry C), 1974 v E (sub), S, Ni; 1976 v S (sub); 1977 v WG (sub); (with Wrexham), 1978 v Ir (sub); 1979 v Ma (7)
Carty, T. See McCarthy (Wrexham).
Challen, J. B. (Corinthians), 1887 v E, S; 1888 v E; (with Wellingborough GS), 1890 v E (4)
Chapman, T. (Newtown), 1894 v E, S, Ni; 1895 v S, Ni; (with Manchester C), 1896 v E; 1897 v E (7)
Charles, J. M. (Swansea C), 1981 v Cz, T (sub), S (sub), USSR (sub); 1982 v Ic; 1983 v N (sub), Sp (sub), Bul (sub), S, Ni, Br; 1984 v Bul (sub); (with QPR), Y (sub), S; (with Oxford U), 1985 v Ic (sub), Sp, Ic; 1986 v Ei; 1987 v Fi (19)
Charles, M. (Swansea T), 1955 v Ni; 1956 v E, S, A; 1957 v E, Ni, Cz, EG; 1958 v E, S, EG, Is (2), H (2), M, Se, Br; 1959 v E, S; (with Arsenal), 1961 v Ni, H, Sp (2); 1962 v E, S; (with Cardiff C), 1962 v Br, Ni; 1963 v S, H (31)
Charles, W. J. (Leeds U), 1950 v Ni; 1951 v Sw; 1953 v Ni, F, Y; 1954 v E, S, Ni, A; 1955 v S, E, Ni, Y; 1956 v E, S, A, Ni; 1957 v E, S, Ni, Cz (2), EG; (with Juventus), 1958 v Is (2), H (2) M, Se; 1960 v S; 1962 v E, Br (2), M; (with Leeds U), 1963 v S; (with Cardiff C), 1964 v S; 1965 v S, USSR (38)
Clarke, R. J. (Manchester C), 1949 v E; 1950 v S, Ni, Bel; 1951 v E, S, Ni, P, Sw; 1952 v S, E, Ni, R of UK; 1953 v S, E; 1954 v E, S, Ni; 1955 v Y, S, E; 1956 v Ni (22)
Coleman, C. (C Palace), 1992 v A (sub); 1993 v Ei (sub); 1994 v N, Es; 1995 v Alb, Mol, Ge, Bul (2), G; 1996 v Mol; (with Blackburn R), I, Sw, Sm; 1997 v Sm; 1998 v Br; (with Fulham), Jam, Ma, Tun; 1999 v I, D, Bl, Sw, D; 2000 v Bl, Sw, Q, Fi (28)
Collier, D. J. (Grimsby T), 1921 v S (1)
Collins, W. S. (Llanelly), 1931 v S (1)
Conde, C. (Chirk), 1884 v E, S, Ni (3)
Cook, F. C. (Newport Co), 1925 v E, S; (with Portsmouth), 1928 v E, S; 1930 v E, S, Ni; 1932 v E (8)
Cornforth, J.M. (Swansea C), 1995 v Bul (sub), Ge (2)

Coyne, D. (Tranmere R), 1996 v Sw (1)
Crompton, W. (Wrexham), 1931 v E, S, Ni (3)
Cross, E. A. (Wrexham), 1876 v S; 1877 v S (2)
Crosse, K. (Druids), 1879 v S; 1881 v E, S (3)
Crossley, M. G. (Nottingham F), 1997 v Ei; 1999 v Sw (sub); 2000 v Fi (3)
Crowe, V. H. (Aston Villa), 1959 v E, Ni; 1960 v E, Ni; 1961 v S, E, Ni, Ei, H, Sp (2); 1962 v E, S, Br, M; 1963 v H (16)
Cumner, R. H. (Arsenal), 1939 v E, S, Ni (3)
Curtis, A. (Swansea C), 1976 v E, Y (sub), S, Ni, Y (sub), E; 1977 v WG, S (sub), Ni (sub); 1978 v WG, E, S; 1979 v WG, S; (with Leeds U), E, Ni, Ma; 1980 v Ei, WG, T; (with Swansea C), 1982 v Cz, Ic, USSR, Sp, E, S, Ni; 1983 v N; 1984 v R (sub); (with Southampton), S; 1985 v Sp, N (1 + 1 sub); 1986 v H; (with Cardiff C), 1987 v USSR (35)
Curtis, E. R. (Cardiff C), 1928 v S; (with Birmingham), 1932 v S; 1934 v Ni (3)

Daniel, R. W. (Arsenal), 1951 v E, Ni, P; 1952 v E, S, Ni, R of UK; 1953 v S, E, Ni, F, Y; (with Sunderland), 1954 v E, S, Ni; 1955 v E, Ni; 1957 v S, E, Ni, Cz (21)
Darvell, S. (Oxford University), 1897 v S, Ni (2)
Davies, A. (Manchester U), 1983 v Ni, Br; 1984 v E, Ni; 1985 v Ic (2), N; (with Newcastle U), 1986 v H; (with Swansea C), 1988 v Ma, I; 1989 v Ho; (with Bradford C), 1990 v Fi, Ei (13)
Davies, A. (Wrexham), 1876 v S; 1877 v S (2)
Davies, A. (Druids), 1904 v S; (with Middlesbrough), 1905 v S (2)
Davies, A. O. (Barmouth), 1885 v Ni; 1886 v E, S; (with Swifts), 1887 v E, S; 1888 v E, Ni; (with Wrexham), 1889 v S; (with Crewe Alex), 1890 v E (9)
Davies, A. T. (Shrewsbury), 1891 v Ni (1)
Davies, C. (Charlton Ath), 1972 v R (sub) (1)
Davies, D. (Bolton W), 1904 v S, Ni; 1908 v E (sub) (3)
Davies, D. C. (Brecon), 1899 v Ni; (with Hereford); 1900 v Ni (2)
Davies, D. W. (Treharris), 1912 v Ni; (with Oldham Ath), 1913 v Ni (2)
Davies, E. Lloyd (Stoke C), 1904 v E; 1907 v E, S, Ni; (with Northampton T), 1908 v S; 1909 v Ni; 1910 v Ni; 1911 v E, S; 1912 v E, S; 1913 v E, S; 1914 v Ni, E, S (16)
Davies, E. R. (Newcastle U), 1953 v S, E; 1954 v E, S; 1958 v E, EG (6)
Davies, G. (Fulham), 1980 v T, Ic; 1982 v Sp (sub), F (sub); 1983 v E, Bul, S, Ni, Br; 1984 v R (sub), S (sub), E, Ni; 1985 v Ic; (with Manchester C), 1986 v S.Ar, Ei (16)
Davies, Rev. H. (Wrexham), 1928 v Ni (1)
Davies, Idwal (Liverpool Marine), 1923 v S (1)
Davies, J. E. (Oswestry), 1885 v E (1)
Davies, Jas (Wrexham), 1878 v S (1)
Davies, John (Wrexham), 1879 v S (1)
Davies, Jos (Newton Heath), 1888 v E, S, Ni; 1889 v S; 1890 v E; (with Wolverhampton W), 1892 v E; 1893 v E (7)
Davies, Jos (Everton), 1889 v S, Ni; (with Chirk), 1891 v Ni; (with Ardwick), v E, S; (with Sheffield U), 1895 v E, S, Ni; (with Manchester C), 1896 v E; (with Millwall), 1897 v E; (with Reading), 1900 v E (11)
Davies, J. P. (Druids), 1883 v E, Ni (2)
Davies, Ll. (Wrexham), 1907 v Ni; 1910 v Ni, S, E; (with Everton), 1911 v S, Ni; (with Wrexham), 1912 v Ni, S, E; 1913 v Ni, S, E; 1914 v Ni (13)
Davies, L. S. (Cardiff C), 1922 v E, S, Ni; 1923 v E, S, Ni; 1924 v E, S, Ni; 1925 v S, Ni; 1926 v E, Ni; 1927 v E, Ni; 1928 v S, Ni, E; 1929 v S, Ni, E; 1930 v E, S (23)
Davies, O. (Wrexham), 1890 v S (1)
Davies, R. (Wrexham), 1883 v Ni; 1884 v Ni; 1885 v Ni (3)
Davies, R. (Druids), 1885 v E (1)
Davies, R. O. (Wrexham), 1892 v Ni, E (2)
Davies, R. T. (Norwich C), 1964 v Ni; 1965 v E; 1966 v Br (2), Ch; (with Southampton), 1967 v S, E, Ni; 1968 v S, Ni, WG; 1969 v S, E, Ni, I, WG, R of UK; 1970 v E, S, Ni; 1971 v Cz, S, E, Ni; 1972 v R, E, S, N; (with Portsmouth), 1974 v E (29)
Davies, R. W. (Bolton W), 1964 v E; 1965 v E, S, Ni, D, Gr, USSR; 1966 v E, S, Ni, USSR, D, Br (2), Ch (sub); 1967 v S; (with Newcastle U), E; 1968 v S, Ni, WG; 1969 v S, E, Ni, I; 1970 v EG; 1971 v R, Cz; (with Manchester C), 1972 v E, S, Ni; (with Manchester U), 1973 v E, S (sub), Ni; (with Blackpool), 1974 v Pol (34)
Davies, S. I. (Manchester U), 1996 v Sw (sub) (1)
Davies, Stanley (Preston NE), 1920 v E, S, Ni; (with Everton), 1921 v E, S, Ni; (with WBA), 1922 v E, S, Ni; 1923 v S; 1925 v S, Ni; 1926 v E, S, Ni; 1927 v S; 1928 v S; (with Rotherham U), 1930 v Ni (18)
Davies, T. (Oswestry), 1886 v E (1)
Davies, T. (Druids), 1903 v E, Ni, S; 1904 v S (4)

Davies, W. (Wrexham), 1884 v Ni (1)
Davies, W. (Swansea T), 1924 v E, S, Ni; (with Cardiff C), 1925 v E, S, Ni; 1926 v E, S, Ni; 1927 v S; 1928 v Ni; (with Notts Co), 1929 v E, S, Ni; 1930 v E, S, Ni (17)
Davies, William (Wrexham), 1903 v Ni; 1905 v Ni; (with Blackburn R), 1908 v E, S; 1909 v E, S, Ni; 1911 v E, S, Ni; 1912 v Ni (11)
Davies, W. C. (C Palace), 1908 v S; (with WBA), 1909 v E; 1910 v S; (with C Palace), 1914 v E (4)
Davies, W. D. (Everton), 1975 v H, L, S, E, Ni; 1976 v Y (2), E, Ni; 1977 v WG, S (2), Cz, E, Ni; 1978 v K; (with Wrexham), S, Cz, WG, Ir, E, S, Ni; 1979 v Ma, T, WG, S, E, Ni, Ma; 1980 v Ei, WG, T, E, S, Ni, Ic; 1981 v T, Cz, Ei, T, S, E, USSR; (with Swansea C), 1982 v Cz, Ic, USSR, Sp, E, S, F; 1983 v Y (52)
Davies, W. H. (Oswestry), 1876 v S; 1877 v S; 1879 v E; 1880 v E (4)
Davies, W. O. (Millwall Ath), 1913 v E, S, Ni; 1914 v S, Ni (5)
Davis, G. (Wrexham), 1978 v Ir, E (sub), Ni (3)
Day, A. (Tottenham H), 1934 v Ni (1)
Deacy, N. (PSV Eindhoven), 1977 v Cz, S, E, Ni; 1978 v K (sub), S (sub), Cz (sub), WG, Ir, S (sub), Ni; (with Beringen), 1979 v T (12)
Dearson, D. J. (Birmingham), 1939 v S, Ni, F (3)
Delaney, M. A. (Aston Villa), 2000 v Sw, Q, Br, P (4)
Derrett, S. C. (Cardiff C), 1969 v S, WG; 1970 v I; 1971 v Fi (4)
Dewey, F. T. (Cardiff Corinthians), 1931 v E, S (2)
Dibble, A. (Luton T), 1986 v Ca (1+1 sub); (with Manchester C), 1989 v Is (3)
Doughty, J. (Druids), 1886 v S; (with Newton Heath), 1887 v S, Ni; 1888 v E, S, Ni; 1889 v S; 1890 v E (8)
Doughty, R. (Newton Heath and Druids), 1888 v S, Ni (2)
Durban, A. (Derby Co), 1966 v Br (sub); 1967 v Ni; 1968 v E, S, Ni, WG; 1969 v EG, S, E, Ni, WG; 1970 v E, S, Ni, EG, I; 1971 v R, S, E, Ni, Cz, Fi; 1972 v Fi, Cz, E, S, Ni (27)
Dwyer, P. (Cardiff C), 1978 v Ir, E, S, Ni; 1979 v T, S, E, Ni, Ma (sub); 1980 v WG (10)

Edwards, C. (Wrexham), 1878 v S (1)
Edwards, C. N. H. (Swansea C), 1996 v Sw (sub) (1)
Edwards, G. (Birmingham), 1947 v E, S, Ni; 1948 v E, S, Ni; (with Cardiff C), 1949 v Ni, P, Bel, Sw; 1950 v E, S (12)
Edwards, H. (Wrexham Civil Service), 1878 v S; 1880 v E, S; 1882 v S; 1883 v S; 1884 v Ni; 1887 v Ni (8)
Edwards, J. H. (Wanderers), 1876 v S (1)
Edwards, J. H. (Shrewsbury), 1895 v Ni; 1897 v E, Ni (3)
Edwards, J. H. (Aberystwyth), 1898 v Ni (1)
Edwards, L. T. (Charlton Ath), 1957 v Ni, EG (2)
Edwards, R. I. (Chester), 1978 v K (sub); 1979 v Ma, WG; (with Wrexham), 1980 v T (sub) (4)
Edwards, R. W. (Bristol C), 1998 v T (sub), Bel, Ma (sub), Tun (sub) (4)
Edwards, T. (Linfield), 1932 v S (1)
Egan, W. (Chirk), 1892 v S (1)
Ellis, B. (Motherwell), 1932 v E; 1933 v E; 1934 v S; 1936 v E; 1937 v S (6)
Ellis, E. (Nunhead), 1931 v S; (with Oswestry), E; 1932 v Ni (3)
Emanuel, W. J. (Bristol C), 1973 v E (sub), Ni (sub) (2)
England, H. M. (Blackburn R), 1962 v Ni, Br, M; 1963 v Ni, H; 1964 v E, S, Ni; 1965 v E, D, Gr (2), USSR, Ni, I; 1966 v S, Ni, USSR, D; (with Tottenham H), 1967 v S, E; 1968 v E, Ni, WG; 1969 v EG; 1970 v R of UK, EG, E, S, Ni, I; 1971 v R; 1972 v Fi, E, S, Ni; 1973 v E (3), S; 1974 v Pol; 1975 v H, L (44)
Evans, B. C. (Swansea C), 1972 v Fi, Cz; 1973 v E (2), Pol, S; (with Hereford U), 1974 v Pol (7)
Evans, D. G. (Reading), 1926 v Ni; 1927 v Ni, E; (with Huddersfield T), 1929 v S (4)
Evans, H. P. (Cardiff C), 1922 v E, S, Ni; 1924 v E, S, Ni (6)
Evans, I. (C Palace), 1976 v A, E, Y (2), E, Ni; 1977 v WG, S (2), Cz, Ni; 1978 v K (13)
Evans, J. (Oswestry), 1893 v Ni; 1894 v E, Ni (3)
Evans, J. (Cardiff C), 1912 v Ni; 1913 v Ni; 1914 v S; 1920 v S, Ni; 1922 v Ni; 1923 v E, Ni (8)
Evans, J. H. (Southend U), 1922 v E, S, Ni; 1923 v S (4)
Evans, Len (Aberdare Ath), 1927 v Ni; (with Cardiff C), 1931 v E, S; (with Birmingham), 1934 v Ni (4)
Evans, M. (Oswestry), 1884 v E (1)
Evans, R. (Clapton), 1902 v Ni (1)
Evans, R. E. (Wrexham), 1906 v E, S; (with Aston Villa), Ni; 1907 v E; 1908 v E, S; (with Sheffield U), 1909 v S; 1910 v E, S, Ni (10)
Evans, R. O. (Wrexham), 1902 v Ni; 1903 v E, S, Ni; (with Blackburn R), 1908 v Ni; (with Coventry C), 1911 v E, Ni; 1912 v E, S, Ni (10)

Evans, R. S. (Swansea T), 1964 v Ni (1)
Evans, T. J. (Clapton Orient), 1927 v S; 1928 v E, S; (with Newcastle U), Ni (4)
Evans, W. (Tottenham H), 1933 v Ni; 1934 v E, S; 1935 v E; 1936 v E, Ni (6)
Evans, W. A. W. (Oxford University), 1876 v S; 1877 v S (2)
Evans, W. G. (Bootle), 1890 v E; 1891 v E; (with Aston Villa), 1892 v E (3)
Evelyn, E. C. (Crusaders), 1887 v E (1)
Eyton-Jones, J. A. (Wrexham), 1883 v Ni; 1884 v Ni, E, S (4)

Farmer, G. (Oswestry), 1885 v E, S (2)
Felgate, D. (Lincoln C), 1984 v R (sub) (1)
Finnigan, R. J. (Wrexham), 1930 v Ni (1)
Flynn, B. (Burnley), 1975 v L (2 sub), H (sub), S, E, Ni; 1976 v A, E, Y (2), E, Ni; 1977 v WG (sub), S (2), Cz, E, Ni; 1978 v K (2), S; (with Leeds U), Cz, WG, Ir (sub), E, S, Ni; 1979 v Ma, T, S, E, Ni, Ma; 1980 v Ei, WG, E, S, Ni, Ic; 1981 v T, Cz, Ei, T, S, E, USSR; 1982 v Cz, USSR, E, S, Ni, F; 1983 v N; (with Burnley), Y, E, Bul, S, Ni, Br; 1984 v N, R, Bul, Y, S, N, Is (66)
Ford, T. (Swansea T), 1947 v S; (with Aston Villa), 1947 v Ni; 1948 v S, Ni; 1949 v E, S, Ni, P, Bel, Sw; 1950 v E, S, Ni, Bel; 1951 v S; (with Sunderland), 1951 v E, Ni, P, Sw; 1952 v E, S, Ni, R of UK; 1953 v S, E, Ni, F, Y; (with Cardiff C), 1954 v A; 1955 v S, E, Ni, Y; 1956 v S, Ni, E, A; 1957 v S (38)
Foulkes, H. E. (WBA), 1932 v Ni (1)
Foulkes, W. I. (Newcastle U), 1952 v E, S, Ni, R of UK; 1953 v E, S, F, Y; 1954 v E, S, Ni (11)
Foulkes, W. T. (Oswestry), 1884 v Ni; 1885 v S (2)
Fowler, J. (Swansea T), 1925 v E; 1926 v E, Ni; 1927 v S; 1928 v S; 1929 v E (6)
Freestone, R. (Swansea C), 2000 v Br (1)

Garner, J. (Aberystwyth), 1896 v S (1)
Giggs, R. J. (Manchester U), 1992 v G (sub), L (sub), R (sub); 1993 v Fa (sub), Bel (sub + 1), RCS, Fa; 1994 v RCS, Cy, R; 1995 v Alb, Bul; 1996 v G, Alb, Sm; 1997 v Sm, T, Bel; 1998 v T, Bel; 1999 v I (2), D; 2000 v Bl, Fi (26)
Giles, D. (Swansea C), 1980 v E, S, Ni, Ic; 1981 v T, Cz, T (sub), E (sub), USSR (sub); (with C Palace), 1982 v Sp (sub); 1983 v Ni (sub), Br (12)
Gillam, S. G. (Wrexham), 1889 v S (sub), Ni; (with Shrewsbury), 1890 v E, Ni; (with Clapton), 1894 v S (5)
Glascodine, G. (Wrexham), 1879 v E (1)
Glover, E. M. (Grimsby T), 1932 v S; 1934 v Ni; 1936 v S; 1937 v E, S, Ni; 1939 v Ni (7)
Godding, G. (Wrexham), 1923 v S, Ni (2)
Godfrey, B. C. (Preston NE), 1964 v Ni; 1965 v D, I (3)
Goodwin, U. (Ruthin), 1881 v E (1)
Goss, J. (Norwich C), 1991 v Ic, Pol (sub); 1992 v A; 1994 v Cy (sub), R (sub), Se; 1995 v Alb; 1996 v Sw (sub), Sm (sub) (9)
Gough, R. T. (Oswestry White Star), 1883 v S (1)
Gray, A. (Oldham Ath), 1924 v E, S, Ni; 1925 v E, S, Ni; 1926 v E, S; 1927 v S; (with Manchester C), 1928 v E, S; 1929 v E, S, Ni; (with Manchester Central), 1930 v S; (with Tranmere R), 1932 v E, S, Ni; (with Chester), 1937 v E, S, Ni; 1938 v E, S, Ni (24)
Green, A. W. (Aston Villa), 1901 v Ni; (with Notts Co), 1903 v E; 1904 v S, Ni; 1906 v Ni, E; (with Nottingham F), 1907 v E; 1908 v S (8)
Green, C. R. (Birmingham C), 1965 v USSR, I; 1966 v E, S, USSR, Br (2); 1967 v E; 1968 v E, S, Ni, WG; 1969 v S, I, Ni (sub) (15)
Green, G. H. (Charlton Ath), 1938 v Ni; 1939 v E, Ni, F (4)
Green, R. M. (Wolverhampton W), 1998 v Ma, Tun (2)
Grey, Dr W. (Druids), 1876 v S; 1878 v S (2)
Griffiths, A. T. (Wrexham), 1971 v Cz (sub); 1975 v A, H (2), L (2), E, Ni; 1976 v A, E, S, E (sub), Ni, Y (2); 1977 v WG, S (17)
Griffiths, F. J. (Blackpool), 1900 v E, S (2)
Griffiths, G. (Chirk), 1887 v Ni (1)
Griffiths, J. H. (Swansea T), 1953 v Ni (1)
Griffiths, L. (Wrexham), 1902 v S (1)
Griffiths, M. W. (Leicester C), 1947 v Ni; 1949 v P, Bel; 1950 v E, S, Bel; 1951 v E, Ni, P, Sw; 1954 v A (11)
Griffiths, P. (Chirk), 1884 v E, Ni; 1888 v E; 1890 v S, Ni; 1891 v Ni (6)
Griffiths, P. H. (Everton), 1932 v S (1)
Griffiths, T. P. (Everton), 1927 v E, Ni; 1929 v E; 1930 v E; 1931 v Ni; 1932 v Ni, S, E; (with Bolton W), 1933 v E, S, Ni; (with Middlesbrough), F; 1934 v E, S; 1935 v E, Ni; 1936 v S; (with Aston Villa), Ni; 1937 v E, S, Ni (21)

Hall, G. D. (Chelsea), 1988 v Y (sub), Ma, I; 1989 v Ho, Fi, Is; 1990 v Ei; 1991 v Ei; 1992 v A (sub) (9)

Hallam, J. (Oswestry), 1889 v E (1)
Hanford, H. (Swansea T), 1934 v Ni; 1935 v S; 1936 v E; (with Sheffield W), 1936 v Ni; 1938 v E, S; 1939 v F (7)
Harrington, A. C. (Cardiff C), 1956 v Ni; 1957 v E, S; 1958 v S, Ni, Is (2); 1961 v S, E; 1962 v E, S (11)
Harris, C. S. (Leeds U), 1976 v E, S; 1978 v WG, Ir, E, S, Ni; 1979 v Ma, T, WG, E (sub), Ma; 1980 v Ni (sub), Ic (sub); 1981 v T, Cz (sub), Ei, T, S, E, USSR; 1982 v Cz, Ic, E (sub) (24)
Harris, W. C. (Middlesbrough), 1954 v A; 1957 v EG, Cz; 1958 v E, S, EG (6)
Harrison, W. C. (Wrexham), 1899 v E; 1900 v E, S, Ni; 1901 v Ni (5)
Hartson, J. (Arsenal), 1995 v Bul, G (sub), Ge (sub); 1996 v Mol (sub), Sw; 1997 v Ho, T (sub), Ei; (with West Ham U), Bel (sub), S; 1998 v Bel, Jam, Ma, Tun; (with Wimbledon), 1999 v Sw (sub), I (sub), D; 2000 v Sw (sub) (18)
Haworth, S. O. (Cardiff C), 1997 v S (sub); (with Coventry C), 1998 v Br, Jam (sub), Ma (sub), Tun (sub) (5)
Hayes, A. (Wrexham), 1890 v Ni; 1894 v Ni (2)
Hennessey, W. T. (Birmingham C), 1962 v Ni, Br (2); 1963 v S, E, H (2); 1964 v E, S; 1965 v S, E, D, Gr, USSR; 1966 v E, USSR; (with Nottingham F), 1966 v S, Ni, D, Br (2), Ch; 1967 v S, E; 1968 v E, S, Ni; 1969 v WG, EG, R of UK; 1970 v EG; (with Derby Co), E, S, Ni; 1972 v Fi, Cz, E, S; 1973 v E (39)
Hersee, A. M. (Bangor), 1886 v S, Ni (2)
Hersee, R. (Llandudno), 1886 v Ni (1)
Hewitt, R. (Cardiff C), 1958 v Ni, Is, Se, H, Br (5)
Hewitt, T. J. (Wrexham), 1911 v E, S, Ni; (with Chelsea), 1913 v E, S, Ni; (with South Liverpool), 1914 v E, S (8)
Heywood, D. (Druids), 1879 v E (1)
Hibbott, H. (Newtown Excelsior), 1880 v E, S; (with Newtown), 1885 v S (3)
Higham, G. G. (Oswestry), 1878 v S; 1879 v E (2)
Hill, M. R. (Ipswich T), 1972 v Cz, R (2)
Hockey, T. (Sheffield U), 1972 v Fi, R; 1973 v E (2); (with Norwich C), Pol, S, E, Ni; (with Aston Villa), 1974 v Pol (9)
Hoddinott, T. F. (Watford), 1921 v E, S (2)
Hodges, G. (Wimbledon), 1984 v N (sub), Is (sub); 1987 v USSR, Fi, Cz; (with Newcastle U), 1988 v D; (with Watford), D (sub), Cz (sub), Se, Ma (sub), I (sub); 1990 v Se, Cr; (with Sheffield U), 1992 v Br (sub), Ei (sub), A; 1996 v G (sub), I (18)
Hodgkinson, A. V. (Southampton), 1908 v Ni (1)
Holden, A. (Chester C), 1984 v Is (sub) (1)
Hole, B. G. (Cardiff C), 1963 v Ni; 1964 v Ni; 1965 v S, E, Ni, D, Gr (2), USSR, I; 1966 v E, S, Ni, USSR, D, Br (2), Ch; (with Blackburn R), 1967 v S, E, Ni; 1968 v E, S, Ni, WG; (with Aston Villa), 1969 v I, WG, EG; 1970 v I; (with Swansea C), 1971 v R (30)
Hole, W. J. (Swansea T), 1921 v Ni; 1922 v E; 1923 v E, Ni; 1928 v E, S, Ni; 1929 v E, S (9)
Hollins, D. M. (Newcastle U), 1962 v Br (sub), M; 1963 v Ni, H; 1964 v E; 1965 v Ni, Gr, I; 1966 v S, D, Br (11)
Hopkins, I. J. (Brentford), 1935 v S, Ni; 1936 v E, Ni; 1937 v E, S, Ni; 1938 v E, Ni; 1939 v E, S, Ni (12)
Hopkins, J. (Fulham), 1983 v Ni, Br; 1984 v N, R, Bul, Y, S, E, Ni, N, Is; 1985 v Ic (1 + 1 sub), N; (with C Palace), 1990 v Ho, Cr (16)
Hopkins, M. (Tottenham H), 1956 v Ni; 1957 v Ni, S, E, Cz (2), EG; 1958 v E, S, Ni, EG, Is (2), H (2), M, Se, Br; 1959 v E, S, Ni; 1960 v E, S; 1961 v Ni, H, Sp (2); 1962 v Ni, Br (2), M; 1963 v S, Ni, H (34)
Horne, B. (Portsmouth), 1988 v D (sub), Y, Se (sub), Ma, I; 1989 v Ho, Fi, Is; (with Southampton), Se, WG; 1990 v WG (sub), Ei, Se, Cr; 1991 v D, Bel (2), Ei, Ic, Pol, WG; 1992 v Br, G, L, Ei, A, R, Ho, Arg, D; (with Everton), 1993 v Fa, Cy, Bel, Ei, Bel, RCS, Fa; 1994 v RCS, Cy, R, N, Se, Es; 1995 v Mol, Ge, Bul, G, Ge; 1996 v Mol, G, I, Sw, Sm; (with Birmingham C), 1997 v Sm, Ho, T, Ei, Bel (59)
Howell, E. G. (Builth), 1888 v Ni; 1890 v E; 1891 v E (3)
Howells, R. G. (Cardiff C), 1954 v E, S (2)
Hugh, A. R. (Newport Co), 1924 v Ni (1)
Hughes, A. (Rhos), 1894 v E, S (2)
Hughes, A. (Chirk), 1907 v Ni (1)
Hughes, C. M. (Luton T), 1992 v Ho (sub); 1994 v N (sub), Se (sub), Es; 1996 v Alb; 1997 v Ei (sub); (with Wimbledon), 1998 v T, Bel (8)
Hughes, E. (Everton), 1899 v S, Ni; (with Tottenham H), 1901 v E, S; 1902 v Ni; 1904 v E, Ni, S; 1905 v E, Ni, S; 1906 v E, Ni; 1907 v E (14)
Hughes, E. (Wrexham), 1906 v S; (with Nottingham F), 1906 v Ni; 1908 v S, E; 1910 v Ni, E, S; 1911 v Ni, E, S; (with Wrexham), 1912 v Ni, E, S; (with Manchester C), 1913 v E, S; 1914 v N (16)

Hughes, F. W. (Northwich Victoria), 1882 v E, Ni; 1883 v E, Ni, S; 1884 v S (6)
Hughes, I. (Luton T), 1951 v E, Ni, P, Sw (4)
Hughes, J. (Cambridge University), 1877 v S; (with Aberystwyth), 1879 v S (2)
Hughes, J. (Liverpool), 1905 v E, S, Ni (3)
Hughes, J. I. (Blackburn R), 1935 v Ni (1)
Hughes, L. M. (Manchester U), 1984 v E, Ni; 1985 v Ic, Sp, Ic, N, S, Sp, N; 1986 v S, H, U; (with Barcelona), 1987 v USSR, Cz; 1988 v D (2), Cz, Se, Ma, I; (with Manchester U), 1989 v Ho, Fi, Is, Se, WG; 1990 v Fi, WG, Cr; 1991 v D, Bel (2), I, Ic, Pol, WG; 1992 v Br, G, L, Ei, R, Ho, Arg, J; 1993 v Fa, Cy, Bel, Ei, Bel, RCS, Fa; 1994 v RCS, Cy, N; 1995 v Ge, Bul, G, Ge; (with Chelsea), 1996 v Mol, I, Sm; 1997 v Sm, Ho, T, Ei, Bel; 1998 v T; (with Southampton), 1999 v I, D, Bl, Sw, I, D (72)
Hughes, P. W. (Bangor), 1887 v Ni; 1889 v Ni, E (3)
Hughes, W. (Bootle), 1891 v E; 1892 v S, Ni (3)
Hughes, W. A. (Blackburn R), 1949 v E, Ni, P, Bel, Sw (5)
Hughes, W. M. (Birmingham), 1938 v E, Ni, S; 1939 v E, Ni, S, F; 1947 v E, S, Ni (10)
Humphreys, J. V. (Everton), 1947 v Ni (1)
Humphreys, R. (Druids), 1888 v Ni (1)
Hunter, A. H. (FA of Wales Secretary), 1887 v Ni (1)

Jackett, K. (Watford), 1983 v N, Y, E, Bul, S; 1984 v N, R, Y, S, Ni, N, Is; 1985 v Ic, Sp, Ic, N, S, Sp, N; 1986 v S, H, S.Ar, Ei, Ca (2); 1987 v Fi (2); 1988 v D, Cz, Y, Se (31)
Jackson, W. (St Helens Rec), 1899 v Ni (1)
James, E. (Chirk), 1893 v E, Ni; 1894 v E, S, Ni; 1898 v S, E; 1899 v Ni (8)
James, E. G. (Blackpool), 1966 v Br (2), Ch; 1967 v Ni; 1968 v S; 1971 v Cz, S, E, Ni (9)
James, L. (Burnley), 1972 v Cz, R, S (sub); 1973 v E (3), Pol, S, Ni; 1974 v Pol, E, S, Ni; 1975 v A, H (2), L (2), S, E, Ni; 1976 v A; (with Derby Co), S, E, Y (2), Ni; 1977 v WG, S (2), Cz, E, Ni; 1978 v K (2); (with QPR), WG; (with Burnley), 1979 v T; (with Swansea C), 1980 v E, S, Ni, Ic; 1981 v T, Ei, T, S, E; 1982 v Cz, Ic, USSR, E (sub), S, Ni, F; (with Sunderland), 1983 v E (sub) (54)
James, R. M. (Swansea C), 1979 v Ma, WG (sub), S, E, Ni, Ma; 1980 v WG; 1982 v Cz (sub), Ic, Sp, E, S, Ni, F; 1983 v N, Y, E, Bul; (with Stoke C), 1984 v N, R, Bul, Y, S, E, Ni, N, Is; 1985 v Ic, Sp, Ic; (with QPR), N, S, Ni; 1986 v S, S.Ar, Ei, U, Ca (2); 1987 v Fi (2), USSR, Cz; (with Leicester C), 1988 v D (2); (with Swansea C), Y (47)
James, W. (West Ham U), 1931 v Ni; 1932 v Ni (2)
Jarrett, R. H. (Ruthin), 1889 v Ni; 1890 v S (2)
Jarvis, A. L. (Hull C), 1967 v S, E, Ni (3)
Jenkins, E. (Lovell's Ath), 1925 v E (1)
Jenkins, J. (Brighton), 1924 v Ni, E, S; 1925 v S, Ni; 1926 v E, S; 1927 v S (8)
Jenkins, R. W. (Rhyl), 1902 v Ni (1)
Jenkins, S. R. (Swansea C), 1996 v G; (with Huddersfield T), Alb, I; 1997 v Ho (sub), T, S; 1998 v T, Bel, Br, Jam; 1999 v I (sub), D (12)
Jenkyns, C. A. L. (Small Heath), 1892 v E, S, Ni; 1895 v E; (with Woolwich Arsenal), 1896 v S; (with Newton Heath), 1897 v Ni; (with Walsall), 1898 v S, E (8)
Jennings, W. (Bolton W), 1914 v E, S; 1920 v S; 1923 v Ni, E; 1924 v E, S, Ni; 1927 v S, Ni; 1929 v S (11)
John, R. F. (Arsenal), 1923 v S, Ni; 1925 v Ni; 1926 v E; 1927 v E; 1928 v E, Ni; 1930 v E, S; 1932 v E; 1933 v F, Ni; 1935 v Ni; 1936 v S; 1937 v E (15)
John, W. R. (Walsall), 1931 v Ni; (with Stoke C), 1933 v E, S, Ni, F; 1934 v E, S; (with Preston NE), 1935 v E, S; (with Sheffield U), 1936 v E, S, Ni; (with Swansea T), 1939 v E, S (14)
Johnson, A. J. (Nottingham F), 1999 v I, D, Bl, Sw; 2000 v Fi (sub), Br (sub), P (sub) (7)
Johnson, M. G. (Swansea T), 1964 v Ni (1)
Jones, A. (Port Vale), 1987 v Fi, Cz (sub); 1988 v D, (with Charlton Ath), D (sub), Cz (sub); 1990 v Hol (sub) (6)
Jones, A. F. (Oxford University), 1877 v S (1)
Jones, A. T. (Nottingham F), 1905 v E; (with Notts Co), 1906 v E (2)
Jones, Bryn (Wolverhampton W), 1935 v Ni; 1936 v E, S, Ni; 1937 v E, S, Ni; 1938 v E, S, Ni; (with Arsenal), 1939 v E, S, Ni; 1947 v S, Ni; 1948 v E; 1949 v S (17)
Jones, B. S. (Swansea T), 1963 v S, E, Ni, H (2); 1964 v S, Ni; (with Plymouth Arg), 1965 v D; (with Cardiff C), 1969 v S, E, Ni, I (sub), WG, EG, R of UK (15)
Jones, Charlie (Nottingham F), 1926 v E; 1927 v S, Ni; 1928 v E; (with Arsenal), 1930 v E, S; 1932 v E; 1933 v F (8)
Jones, Cliff (Swansea T), 1954 v A; 1956 v E, Ni, S, A; 1957 v E, S, Ni, Cz (2), EG; 1958 v EG, E, S, Is (2); (with

Tottenham H), 1958 v Ni, H (2), M, Se, Br; 1959 v Ni; 1960 v E, S, Ni; 1961 v S, E, Ni, Sp, H, Ei; 1962 v E, Ni, S, Br (2), M; 1963 v S, Ni, H; 1964 v E, S, Ni; 1965 v E, S, Ni, D, Gr (2), USSR, I; 1967 v S, E; 1968 v E, S, WG; (with Fulham), 1969 v I, R of UK (59)
Jones, C. W. (Birmingham), 1935 v Ni; 1939 v F (2)
Jones, D. (Chirk), 1888 v S, Ni; (with Bolton W), 1889 v E, S, Ni; 1890 v E; 1891 v S; 1892 v Ni; 1893 v E; 1894 v E; 1895 v E; 1898 v S; (with Manchester C), 1900 v E, Ni (14)
Jones, D. E. (Norwich C), 1976 v S, E (sub); 1978 v S, Cz, WG, Ir, E; 1980 v E (8)
Jones, D. O. (Leicester C), 1934 v E, Ni; 1935 v E, S; 1936 v E, Ni; 1937 v Ni (7)
Jones, Evan (Chelsea), 1910 v S, Ni; (with Oldham Ath), 1911 v E, S; 1912 v E, S; (with Bolton W), 1914 v Ni (7)
Jones, F. R. (Bangor), 1885 v E, Ni; 1886 v S (3)
Jones, F. W. (Small Heath), 1893 v S (1)
Jones, G. P. (Wrexham), 1907 v S, Ni (2)
Jones, H. (Aberaman), 1902 v Ni (1)
Jones, Humphrey (Bangor), 1885 v E, Ni, S; 1886 v E, Ni, S; (with Queen's Park), 1887 v E; (with East Stirlingshire), 1889 v E, Ni; 1890 v E, S, Ni; (with Queen's Park), 1891 v E, S (14)
Jones, Ivor (Swansea T), 1920 v S, Ni; 1921 v Ni, E; 1922 v S, Ni; (with WBA), 1923 v E, Ni; 1924 v S; 1926 v Ni (10)
Jones, Jeffrey (Llandrindod Wells), 1908 v Ni; 1909 v Ni; 1910 v S (3)
Jones, J. (Druids), 1876 v S (1)
Jones, J. (Berwyn Rangers), 1883 v S, Ni; 1884 v S (3)
Jones, J. (Wrexham), 1925 v Ni (1)
Jones, J. L. (Sheffield U), 1895 v E, S, Ni; 1896 v Ni, S, E; 1897 v Ni, S, E; (with Tottenham H), 1898 v Ni, E, S; 1899 v S, Ni; 1900 v S; 1902 v E, S, Ni; 1904 v E, S, Ni (21)
Jones, J. Love (Stoke C), 1906 v S; (with Middlesbrough), 1910 v Ni (2)
Jones, J. O. (Bangor), 1901 v S, Ni (2)
Jones, J. P. (Liverpool), 1976 v A, E, S; 1977 v WG, S (2), Cz, E, Ni; 1978 v K (2), S, Cz, WG, Ir, E, S, Ni; (with Wrexham), 1979 v Ma, T, WG, S, E, Ni, Ma; 1980 v Ei, WG, T, E, S, Ni, Ic; 1981 v T, Ei, T, S, E, USSR; 1982 v Cz, Ic, USSR, Sp, E, S, Ni, F; 1983 v N; (with Chelsea), Y, E, Bul, S, Ni, Br; 1984 v N, R, Bul, Y, S, E, Ni, N, Is; 1985 v Ic, N, S, N; (with Huddersfield T), 1986 v S, H, Ei, U, Ca (2) (72)
Jones, J. T. (Stoke C), 1912 v E, S, Ni; 1913 v E, Ni; 1914 v S, Ni; 1920 v E, S, Ni; (with C Palace), 1921 v E, S; 1922 v E, S, Ni (15)
Jones, K. (Aston Villa), 1950 v S (1)
Jones, Leslie J. (Cardiff C), 1933 v F; (with Coventry C), 1935 v Ni; 1936 v S; 1937 v E, S, Ni; (with Arsenal), 1938 v E, S, Ni; 1939 v E, S (11)
Jones, M. G. (Leeds U), 2000 v Sw (sub), Q, Br, P (4)
Jones, P. L. (Liverpool), 1997 v S (sub); (with Tranmere R), 1998 v T (sub) (2)
Jones, P. S. (Stockport Co), 1997 v S (sub); (with Southampton), 1998 v T (sub), Br, Jam, Ma; 1999 v I, D, Bl, Sw, I, D; 2000 v Bl, Sw, Q (14)
Jones, P. W. (Bristol R), 1971 v Fi (1)
Jones, R. (Bangor), 1887 v S; 1889 v E; (with Crewe Alex), 1890 v E (3)
Jones, R. (Leicester Fosse), 1898 v S (1)
Jones, R. (Druids), 1899 v S (1)
Jones, R. (Bangor), 1900 v S, Ni (2)
Jones, R. (Millwall), 1906 v S, Ni (2)
Jones, R. A. (Druids), 1884 v E, Ni, S; 1885 v S (4)
Jones, R. A. (Sheffield W), 1994 v Es (1)
Jones, R. S. (Everton), 1894 v Ni (1)
Jones, S. (Wrexham), 1887 v Ni; (with Chester), 1890 v S (2)
Jones, S. (Wrexham), 1893 v S, Ni; (with Burton Swifts), 1895 v S; 1896 v E, Ni; (with Druids), 1899 v E (6)
Jones, T. (Manchester U), 1926 v Ni; 1927 v E, Ni; 1930 v Ni (4)
Jones, T. D. (Aberdare), 1908 v Ni (1)
Jones, T. G. (Everton), 1938 v Ni; 1939 v E, S, Ni; 1947 v E, S; 1948 v E, S, Ni; 1949 v E, Ni, P, Bel, Sw; 1950 v E, S, Bel (17)
Jones, T. J. (Sheffield W), 1932 v Ni; 1933 v F (2)
Jones, V. P. (Wimbledon), 1995 v Bul (2), G, Ge; 1996 v Sw; 1997 v Ho, T, Ei, Bel (9)
Jones, W. E. A. (Swansea T), 1947 v E, S; (with Tottenham H), 1949 v E, S (4)
Jones, W. J. (Aberdare), 1901 v E, S; (with West Ham U), 1902 v E, S (4)
Jones, W. Lot (Manchester C), 1905 v E, Ni; 1906 v E, S, Ni; 1907 v E, S, Ni; 1908 v S; 1909 v E, S, Ni; 1910 v E; 1911 v E; 1913 v E, S; 1914 v S, Ni; (with Southend U), 1920 v E, Ni (20)

Jones, W. P. (Druids), 1889 v E, Ni; (with Wynstay), 1890 v S, Ni (4)
Jones, W. R. (Aberystwyth), 1897 v S (1)

Keenor, F. C. (Cardiff C), 1920 v E, Ni; 1921 v E, Ni, S; 1922 v Ni; 1923 v E, Ni, S; 1924 v E, Ni, S; 1925 v E, Ni, S; 1926 v S; 1927 v E, Ni, S; 1928 v E, Ni, S; 1929 v E, Ni, S; 1930 v E, Ni, S; 1931 v E, Ni, S; (with Crewe Alex), 1933 v S (32)
Kelly, F. C. (Wrexham), 1899 v S, Ni; (with Druids), 1902 v Ni (3)
Kelsey, A. J. (Arsenal), 1954 v Ni, A; 1955 v S, Ni, Y; 1956 v E, Ni, S, A; 1957 v E, Ni, S, Cz (2), EG; 1958 v E, S, Ni, Is (2), H (2), M, Se, Br; 1959 v E, S; 1960 v E, Ni, S; 1961 v E, Ni, S, H, Sp (2); 1962 v E, S, Ni, Br (2) (41)
Kenrick, S. L. (Druids), 1876 v S; 1877 v S; (with Oswestry), 1879 v E, S; (with Shropshire Wanderers), 1881 v E (5)
Ketley, C. F. (Druids), 1882 v Ni (1)
King, J. (Swansea T), 1955 v E (1)
Kinsey, N. (Norwich C), 1951 v Ni, P, Sw; 1952 v E; (with Birmingham C), 1954 v Ni; 1956 v E, S (7)
Knill, A. R. (Swansea C), 1989 v Ho (1)
Krzywicki, R. L. (WBA), 1970 v EG, I; (with Huddersfield T), Ni, E, S; 1971 v R, Fi; 1972 v Cz (sub) (8)

Lambert, R. (Liverpool), 1947 v S; 1948 v E; 1949 v P. Bel, Sw (5)
Latham, G. (Liverpool), 1905 v E, S; 1906 v S; 1907 v E, S, Ni; 1908 v E; 1909 v Ni; (with Southport Central), 1910 v E; (with Cardiff C), 1913 v Ni (10)
Law, B. J. (QPR), 1990 v Se (1)
Lawrence, E. (Clapton Orient), 1930 v Ni; (with Notts Co), 1932 v S (2)
Lawrence, S. (Swansea T), 1932 v Ni; 1933 v F; 1934 v S, E, Ni; 1935 v E, S; 1936 v S (8)
Lea, A. (Wrexham), 1889 v E; 1891 v S, Ni; 1893 v Ni (4)
Lea, C. (Ipswich T), 1965 v Ni, I (2)
Leary, P. (Bangor), 1889 v Ni (1)
Leek, K. (Leicester C), 1961 v S, E, Ni, H, Sp (2); (with Newcastle U), 1962 v S; (with Birmingham C), v Br (sub), M; 1963 v E; 1965 v S, Gr; (with Northampton T), 1965 v Gr (13)
Legg, A. (Birmingham C), 1996 v Sw, Sm (sub); 1997 v Ho (sub), Ei; (with Cardiff C), 1999 v D (sub) (5)
Lever, A. R. (Leicester C), 1953 v S (1)
Lewis, B. (Chester), 1891 v Ni; (with Wrexham), 1892 v S, E, Ni; (with Middlesbrough), 1893 v S, E; (with Wrexham), 1894 v S, E, Ni; 1895 v S (10)
Lewis, D. (Arsenal), 1927 v E; 1928 v Ni; 1930 v E (3)
Lewis, D. (Swansea C), 1983 v Br (sub) (1)
Lewis, D. J. (Swansea T), 1933 v E, S (2)
Lewis, D. M. (Bangor), 1890 v Ni, S (2)
Lewis, J. (Bristol R), 1906 v E (1)
Lewis, J. (Cardiff C), 1926 v S (1)
Lewis, T. (Wrexham), 1881 v E, S (2)
Lewis, W. (Bangor), 1885 v E; 1886 v E, S; 1887 v E, S; 1888 v E; 1889 v E, Ni, S; (with Crewe Alex), 1890 v E; 1891 v E, S; 1892 v E, S, Ni; 1894 v E, S, Ni; (with Chester), 1895 v S, Ni, E; 1896 v E, S, Ni; (with Manchester C), 1897 v E, S; (with Chester), 1898 v Ni (27)
Lewis, W. L. (Swansea T), 1927 v E, Ni; 1928 v E, Ni; 1929 v S; (with Huddersfield T), 1930 v E (6)
Llewellyn, C. M. (Norwich C), 1998 v Ma (sub), Tun (sub) (2)
Lloyd, B. W. (Wrexham), 1976 v A, E, S (3)
Lloyd, J. W. (Wrexham), 1879 v S; (with Newtown), 1885 v S (2)
Lloyd, R. A. (Ruthin), 1891 v Ni; 1895 v S (2)
Lockley, A. (Chirk), 1898 v Ni (1)
Lovell, S. (C Palace), 1982 v USSR (sub); (with Millwall), 1985 v N; 1986 v S (sub), H (sub), Ca (1+1 sub) (6)
Lowrie, G. (Coventry C), 1948 v E, S, Ni; (with Newcastle U), 1949 v P (4)
Lowndes, S. (Newport Co), 1983 v S (sub), Br (sub); (with Millwall), 1985 v N (sub); 1986 v S.Ar (sub), Ei, U, Ca (2); (with Barnsley), 1987 v Fi (sub); 1988 v Se (sub) (10)
Lucas, P. M. (Leyton Orient), 1962 v Ni, M; 1963 v S, E (4)
Lucas, W. H. (Swansea T), 1949 v S, Ni, P, Bel, Sw; 1950 v E; 1951 v E (7)
Lumberg, A. (Wrexham), 1929 v Ni; 1930 v E, S; (with Wolverhampton W), 1932 v S (4)

McCarthy, T. P. (Wrexham), 1899 v Ni (1)
McMillan, R. (Shrewsbury Engineers), 1881 v E, S (2)
Maguire, G. T. (Portsmouth), 1990 v Fi (sub), Ho, WG, Ei, Se; 1992 v Br (sub), G (7)
Mahoney, J. F. (Stoke C), 1968 v E; 1969 v EG; 1971 v Cz; 1973 v E (3), Pol, S, Ni; 1974 v Pol, E, S, Ni; 1975 v A, H (2),

L (2), S, E, Ni; 1976 v A, Y (2), E, Ni; 1977 v WG, Cz, S, E, Ni; (with Middlesbrough), 1978 v K (2), S, Cz, Ir, E (sub), S, Ni; 1979 v WG, S, E, Ni, Ma; (with Swansea C), 1980 v Ei, WG, T (sub); 1982 v Ic, USSR; 1983 v Y, E (51)
Mardon, P. J. (WBA), 1996 v G (sub) (1)
Marriott, A. (Wrexham), 1996 v Sw (sub); 1997 v S; 1998 v Bel, Br (sub), Tun (5)
Martin, T. J. (Newport Co), 1930 v Ni (1)
Marustik, C. (Swansea C), 1982 v Sp, E, S, Ni, F; 1983 v N (6)
Mates, J. (Chirk), 1891 v Ni; 1897 v E, S (3)
Mathews, R. W. (Liverpool), 1921 v Ni; (with Bristol C), 1923 v E; (with Bradford), 1926 v Ni (3)
Matthews, W. (Chester), 1905 v Ni; 1908 v E (2)
Matthias, J. S. (Brymbo), 1896 v S, Ni; (with Shrewsbury), 1897 v E, S; (with Wolverhampton W), 1899 v S (5)
Matthias, T. J. (Wrexham), 1914 v S, E; 1920 v Ni, S, E; 1921 v S, E, Ni; 1922 v S, E, Ni; 1923 v S (12)
Mays, A. W. (Wrexham), 1929 v Ni (1)
Medwin, T. C. (Swansea T), 1953 v Ni, F, Y; (with Tottenham H), 1957 v E, S, Ni, Cz (2), EG; 1958 v E, S, Ni, Is (2), H (2), M, Br; 1959 v E, S, Ni; 1960 v E, S, Ni; 1961 v S, Ei, E, Sp; 1963 v E, H (30)
Melville, A. K. (Swansea C), 1990 v WG, Ei, Se, Cr (sub); (with Oxford U), 1991 v Ic, Pol, WG; 1992 v Br, G, L, R, Ho, J (sub); 1993 v RCS, Fa (sub); (with Sunderland), 1994 v RCS (sub), R, N, Se, Es; 1995 v Alb, Mol (sub), Ge, Bul; 1996 v G, Alb, Sm; 1997 v Sm, Ho (2), T; 1998 v T; (with Fulham), 1999 v I, D; 2000 v Bl, Q, Fi, Br, P (39)
Meredith, S. (Chirk), 1900 v S; 1901 v S, E, Ni; (with Stoke C), 1902 v E; 1903 v Ni; 1904 v E; (with Leyton), 1907 v E (8)
Meredith, W. H. (Manchester C), 1895 v E, Ni; 1896 v E, Ni; 1897 v E, Ni, S; 1898 v E, Ni; 1899 v E; 1900 v E, Ni; 1901 v E, Ni; 1902 v E, S; 1903 v E, S, Ni; 1904 v E; 1905 v E, S; (with Manchester U), 1907 v E, S, Ni; 1908 v E, Ni; 1909 v E, S, Ni; 1910 v E, S, Ni; 1911 v E, S, Ni; 1912 v E, S, Ni; 1913 v E, S, Ni; 1914 v E, S, Ni; 1920 v E, S, Ni (48)
Mielczarek, R. (Rotherham U), 1971 v Fi (1)
Millership, H. (Rotherham Co), 1920 v E, S, Ni; 1921 v E, S, Ni (6)
Millington, A. H. (WBA), 1963 v S, E, H; (with C Palace), 1965 v E, USSR; (with Peterborough U), 1966 v Ch, Br; 1967 v E, Ni; 1968 v Ni, WG; 1969 v I, EG; (with Swansea T), 1970 v E, S, Ni; 1971 v Cz, Fi; 1972 v Fi (sub), Cz, R (21)
Mills, T. J. (Clapton Orient), 1934 v E, Ni; (with Leicester C), 1935 v E, S (4)
Mills-Roberts, R. H. (St Thomas' Hospital), 1885 v E, S, Ni; 1886 v E; 1887 v E; (with Preston NE), 1888 v E, Ni; (with Llanberis), 1892 v E (8)
Moore, G. (Cardiff C), 1960 v E, S, Ni; 1961 v Ei, Sp; (with Chelsea), 1962 v Br; 1963 v Ni, H; (with Manchester U), 1964 v S, Ni; (with Northampton T), 1966 v Ni, Ch; (with Charlton Ath), 1969 v S, E, Ni, R of UK; 1970 v E, S, Ni, I; 1971 v R (21)
Morgan, J. R. (Cambridge University), 1877 v S; (with Swansea T), 1879 v S; (with Derby School Staff), 1880 v E, S; 1881 v E, S; 1882 v E, S, Ni; (with Swansea T), 1883 v E (10)
Morgan, J. T. (Wrexham), 1905 v Ni (1)
Morgan-Owen, H. (Oxford University), 1902 v S; 1906 v E, Ni; (with Welshpool), 1907 v S (5)
Morgan-Owen, M. M. (Oxford University), 1897 v S, Ni; 1898 v E, S; 1899 v S; 1900 v E; (with Corinthians), 1901 v S, E; 1903 v S; 1906 v S, E, Ni; 1907 v E (13)
Morley, E. J. (Swansea T), 1925 v E; (with Clapton Orient), 1929 v E, S, Ni (4)
Morris, A. G. (Aberystwyth), 1896 v E, Ni, S; (with Swindon T), 1897 v E; 1898 v S; (with Nottingham F), 1899 v E, S; 1903 v E, S; 1905 v E, S; 1907 v E, S; 1908 v E; 1910 v E, S, Ni; 1911 v E, S, Ni; 1912 v E (21)
Morris, C. (Chirk), 1900 v E, S, Ni; (with Derby Co), 1901 v E, S, Ni; 1902 v E; 1903 v E, S, Ni; 1904 v Ni; 1905 v E, S, Ni; 1906 v S; 1907 v S; 1908 v E, S; 1909 v E, S, Ni; 1910 v E, S, Ni; (with Huddersfield T), 1911 v E, S, Ni (27)
Morris, E. (Chirk), 1893 v E, S, Ni (3)
Morris, H. (Sheffield U), 1894 v S; (with Manchester C), 1896 v E; (with Grimsby T), 1897 v E (3)
Morris, J. (Oswestry), 1887 v S (1)
Morris, J. (Chirk), 1898 v Ni (1)
Morris, R. (Chirk), 1900 v E, Ni; 1901 v Ni; 1902 v S; (with Shrewsbury T), 1903 v E, Ni (6)
Morris, R. (Druids), 1902 v E, S; (with Newtown), Ni; (with Liverpool), 1903 v S, Ni; 1904 v E, S, Ni; (with Leeds C), 1906 v S; (with Grimsby T), 1907 v Ni; (with Plymouth Arg), 1908 v Ni (11)
Morris, S. (Birmingham), 1937 v E, S; 1938 v E, S; 1939 v F (5)

Morris, W. (Burnley), 1947 v Ni; 1949 v E; 1952 v S, Ni, R of UK (5)
Moulsdale, J. R. B. (Corinthians), 1925 v Ni (1)
Murphy, J. P. (WBA), 1933 v F, E, Ni; 1934 v E, S; 1935 v E, S, Ni; 1936 v E, S, Ni; 1937 v S, Ni; 1938 v E, S (15)

Nardiello, D. (Coventry C), 1978 v Cz, WG (sub) (2)
Neal, J. E. (Colwyn Bay), 1931 v E, S (2)
Neilson, A. B. (Newcastle U), 1992 v Ei; 1994 v Se, Es; 1995 v Ge; (with Southampton), 1997 v Ho (5)
Newnes, J. (Nelson), 1926 v Ni (1)
Newton, L. F. (Cardiff Corinthians), 1912 v Ni (1)
Nicholas, D. S. (Stoke C), 1923 v S; (with Swansea T), 1927 v E, Ni (3)
Nicholas, P. (C Palace), 1979 v S (sub), Ni (sub), Ma; 1980 v Ei, WG, T, E, S, Ni, Ic; 1981 v T, Cz, E; (with Arsenal), T, S, E, USSR; 1982 v Cz, Ic, USSR, Sp, E, S, Ni, F; 1983 v Y, Bul, S, Ni; 1984 v N, Bul, N, Is; (with C Palace), 1985 v Sp; (with Luton T), N, S, Sp, N; 1986 v S, H, S.Ar, Ei, U, Ca (2); 1987 v Fi (2) USSR, Cz; (with Aberdeen), 1988 v D (2), Cz, Y, Se; (with Chelsea), 1989 v Ho, Fi, Is, Se, WG; 1990 v Fi, Ho, WG, Ei, Se, Cr; 1991 v D (sub), Bel, L, Ei; (with Watford), Bel, Pol, WG; 1992 v L (73)
Nicholls, J. (Newport Co), 1924 v E, Ni; (with Cardiff C), 1925 v E, S (4)
Niedzwiecki, E. A. (Chelsea), 1985 v N (sub); 1988 v D (2)
Nock, W. (Newtown), 1897 v Ni (1)
Nogan, L. M. (Watford), 1992 v A (sub); (with Reading), 1996 v Mol (2)
Norman, A. J. (Hull C), 1986 v Ei (sub), U, Ca; 1988 v Ma, I (5)
Nurse, M. T. G. (Swansea T), 1960 v E, Ni; 1961 v S, E, H, Ni, Ei, Sp (2); (with Middlesbrough), 1963 v E, H; 1964 v S (12)

O'Callaghan, E. (Tottenham H), 1929 v Ni; 1930 v S; 1932 v S, E; 1933 v Ni, S, E; 1934 v Ni, S, E; 1935 v E (11)
Oliver, A. (Blackburn R), 1905 v E; (with Bangor), S (2)
Oster, J. M. (Everton), 1998 v Br, Jam; (with Sunderland), 2000 v Sw (3)
O'Sullivan, P. A. (Brighton), 1973 v S (sub); 1976 v S; 1979 v Ma (sub) (3)
Owen, D. (Oswestry), 1879 v E (1)
Owen, E. (Ruthin Grammar School), 1884 v E, Ni, S (3)
Owen, G. (Chirk), 1888 v S; (with Newton Heath), 1889 v S, Ni; 1893 v Ni (4)
Owen, J. (Newton Heath), 1892 v E (1)
Owen, Trevor (Crewe Alex), 1899 v E, S (2)
Owen, T. (Oswestry), 1879 v E (1)
Owen, W. (Chirk), 1884 v E; 1885 v Ni; 1887 v E; 1888 v E; 1889 v E, Ni, S; 1890 v S, Ni; 1891 v E, S, Ni; 1892 v E, S; 1893 v Ni (16)
Owen, W. P. (Ruthin), 1880 v E, S; 1881 v E, S; 1882 v E, S, Ni; 1883 v E, S; 1884 v E, S, Ni (12)
Owens, J. (Wrexham), 1902 v S (1)

Page, M. E. (Birmingham C), 1971 v Fi; 1972 v S, Ni; 1973 v E (1+1 sub), Ni; 1974 v S, Ni; 1975 v H, L, S, E, Ni; 1976 v E, Y (2), Ei, Ni; 1977 v WG, S; 1978 v K (sub+1), WG, Ir, E, S; 1979 v Ma, WG (28)
Page, R. J. (Watford), 1997 v T, Bel, S; 1998 v T, Bel (sub), Br, I; 2000 v Bl, Sw, Q, Fi, Br, P (13)
Palmer, D. (Swansea T), 1957 v Cz; 1958 v E, EG (3)
Parris, J. E. (Bradford), 1932 v Ni (1)
Parry, B. J. (Swansea T), 1951 v S (1)
Parry, J. (Everton), 1891 v E, S; 1893 v E; 1894 v E; 1895 v E, S; (with Newtown), 1896 v E, S, Ni; 1897 v Ni; 1898 v E, S, Ni (13)
Parry, E. (Liverpool), 1922 v S; 1923 v E, Ni; 1925 v Ni; 1926 v Ni (5)
Parry, M. (Liverpool), 1901 v E, S, Ni; 1902 v E, S, Ni; 1903 v E, S; 1904 v E, Ni; 1906 v E; 1908 v E, S, Ni; 1909 v E, S (16)
Parry, T. D. (Oswestry), 1900 v E, S, Ni; 1901 v E, S, Ni; 1902 v E (7)
Parry, W. (Newtown), 1895 v Ni (1)
Pascoe, C. (Swansea C), 1984 v N, Is; (with Sunderland), 1989 v Fi, Is, WG (sub); 1990 v Ho (sub), WG (sub); 1991 v Ei, Ic (sub); 1992 v Br (10)
Paul, R. (Swansea T), 1949 v E, S, Ni, P, Sw; 1950 v E, S, Ni, Bel; (with Manchester C), 1951 v S, E, Ni, P, Sw; 1952 v E, S, Ni, R of UK; 1953 v S, E, Ni, F, Y; 1954 v E, S, Ni; 1955 v S, E, Y; 1956 v E, Ni, S, A (33)
Peake, E. (Aberystwyth), 1908 v Ni; (with Liverpool), 1909 v Ni, S, E; 1910 v S, Ni; 1911 v Ni; 1912 v E; 1913 v E, Ni; 1914 v Ni (11)
Peers, E. J. (Wolverhampton W), 1914 v Ni, S, E; 1920 v E, S; 1921 v S, Ni, E; (with Port Vale), 1922 v E, S, Ni; 1923 v E (12)

Pembridge, M. A. (Luton T), 1992 v Br, Ei, R (with Derby Co), Ho, J (sub); 1993 v Bel (sub), Ei; 1994 v N (sub); 1995 v Alb (sub), Mol, Ge (sub); (with Sheffield W), 1996 v Mol, G, Alb, Sw, Sm; 1997 v Sm, Ho (2), T, Ei, Bel, S; 1998 v Bel, Br, Jam, Ma, Tun; (with Benfica), 1999 v D (sub), Bl, Sw, I (sub), D (sub); (with Everton), 2000 v Bl, Q, Fi (36)
Perry, E. (Doncaster R), 1938 v E, S, Ni (3)
Perry, J. (Cardiff C), 1994 v N (1)
Phennah, E. (Civil Service), 1878 v S (1)
Phillips, C. (Wolverhampton W), 1931 v Ni; 1932 v E; 1933 v S; 1934 v E, S, Ni; 1935 v E, S, Ni; 1936 v S; (with Aston Villa), 1936 v E, Ni; 1938 v S (13)
Phillips, D. (Plymouth Arg), 1984 v E, Ni, N; (with Manchester C), 1985 v Sp, Ic, S, Sp, N; 1986 v S, H, S.Ar, Ei, U; (with Coventry C), 1987 v Fi, Cz; 1988 v D (2), Cz, Y, Se; 1989 v Se, WG; (with Norwich C), 1990 v Fi, Ho, WG, Ei, Se; 1991 v D, Bel, Ic, Pol, WG; 1992 v L, Ei, A, R, Ho (sub), Arg, J; 1993 v Fa, Cy, Bel, Ei, Bel, RCS, Fa; (with Nottingham F), 1994 v RCS, Cy, R, N, Se, Es; 1995 v Alb, Mol, Ge, Bul (2), G, Ge; 1996 v Mol (sub), Alb, I (62)
Phillips, L. (Cardiff C), 1971 v Cz, S, E, Ni; 1972 v Cz, R, S, Ni; 1973 v E; 1974 v Pol (sub), Ni; 1975 v A; (with Aston Villa), H (2), L (2), S, E, Ni; 1976 v A, E, Y (2), E, Ni; 1977 v WG, S (2), Cz, E; 1978 v K (2), S, Cz, WG, E, S; 1979 v Ma; (with Swansea C), T, WG, S, E, Ni, Ma; 1980 v Ei, WG, T, S (sub), Ni, Ic; 1981 v T, Cz, T, S, E, USSR; (with Charlton Ath), 1982 v Cz, USSR (58)
Phillips, T. J. S. (Chelsea), 1973 v E; 1974 v E; 1975 v H (sub); 1978 v K (4)
Phoenix, H. (Wrexham), 1882 v S (1)
Poland, G. (Wrexham), 1939 v Ni, F (2)
Pontin, K. (Cardiff C), 1980 v E (sub), S (2)
Powell, A. (Leeds U), 1947 v E, S; 1948 v E, S, Ni; (with Everton), 1949 v E; 1950 v Bel; (with Birmingham C), 1951 v S (8)
Powell, D. (Wrexham), 1968 v WG; (with Sheffield U), 1969 v S, E, Ni, I, WG; 1970 v E, S, Ni, EG; 1971 v R (11)
Powell, I. V. (QPR), 1947 v E; 1948 v E, S, Ni; (with Aston Villa), 1949 v Bel; 1950 v S, Bel; 1951 v S (8)
Powell, J. (Druids), 1878 v S; 1880 v E, S; 1882 v E, S, Ni; 1883 v E, S, Ni; (with Bolton W), 1884 v E; (with Newton Heath), 1887 v E, S; 1888 v E, S, Ni (15)
Powell, Seth (WBA), 1885 v S; 1886 v E, Ni; 1891 v E, S; 1892 v E, S (7)
Price, H. (Aston Villa), 1907 v S; (with Burton U), 1908 v Ni; (with Wrexham), 1909 v S, E, Ni (5)
Price, J. (Wrexham), 1877 v S; 1878 v S; 1879 v E; 1880 v E, S; 1881 v E, S; (with Druids), 1882 v S, E, Ni; 1883 v S, Ni (12)
Price, P. (Luton T), 1980 v E, S, Ni, Ic; 1981 v T, Cz, Ei, T, S, E, USSR; (with Tottenham H), 1982 v USSR, Sp, F; 1983 v N, Y, E, Bul, S, Ni; 1984 v N, R, Bul, Y, S (sub) (25)
Pring, K. D. (Rotherham U), 1966 v Ch, D; 1967 v Ni (3)
Pritchard, H. K. (Bristol C), 1985 v N (sub) (1)
Pryce-Jones, A. W. (Newtown), 1895 v E (1)
Pryce-Jones, W. E. (Cambridge University), 1887 v S; 1888 v S, E, Ni; 1890 v Ni (5)
Pugh, A. (Rhostyllen), 1889 v S (sub) (1)
Pugh, D. H. (Wrexham), 1896 v S, Ni; 1897 v S, Ni; (with Lincoln C), 1900 v S; 1901 v S, E (7)
Pugsley, J. (Charlton Ath), 1930 v Ni (1)
Pullen, W. J. (Plymouth Arg), 1926 v E (1)

Rankmore, F. E. J. (Peterborough), 1966 v Ch (sub) (1)
Ratcliffe, K. (Everton), 1981 v Cz, Ei, T, S, E, USSR; 1982 v Cz, Ic, USSR, Sp, E; 1983 v Y, E, Bul, S, Ni, Br; 1984 v N, R, Bul, Y, S, E, Ni, N, Is; 1985 v Ic, Sp, Ic, N, S, Sp; 1986 v S, H, S.Ar, U; 1987 v Fi (2), USSR, Cz; 1988 v D (2), Cz; 1989 v Fi, Is, Se, WG; 1990 v Fi; 1991 v D, Bel (2), L, Ei, Ic, Pol, WG; 1992 v Br, G; (with Cardiff C), 1993 v Bel (59)
Rea, J. C. (Aberystwyth), 1894 v Ni, S, E; 1895 v S; 1896 v S, Ni; 1897 v S, Ni; 1898 v Ni (9)
Ready, K. (QPR), 1997 v Ei; 1998 v Bel, Br, Ma, Tun (5)
Reece, G. I. (Sheffield U), 1966 v E, S, Ni, USSR; 1967 v S; 1969 v R of UK (sub); 1970 v I (sub); 1971 v S, E, Ni, Fi; 1972 v Fi, R, E (sub), S, Ni; (with Cardiff C), 1973 v E (sub), Ni; 1974 v Pol (sub), E, S, Ni; 1975 v A, H (2), L (2), S, Ni (29)
Reed, W. G. (Ipswich T), 1955 v S, Y (2)
Rees, A. (Birmingham C), 1984 v N (sub) (1)
Rees, J. M. (Luton T), 1992 v A (sub) (1)
Rees, R. R. (Coventry C), 1965 v S, E, Ni, D, Gr (2), I, R; 1966 v E, S, Ni, R, D, Br (2), Ch; 1967 v E, Ni; 1968 v E, S, Ni; (with WBA), WG; 1969 v I; (with Nottingham F), 1969 v WG, EG, S (sub), R of UK; 1970 v E, S, Ni, EG, I; 1971 v Cz, R, E (sub), Ni (sub), Fi; 1972 v Cz (sub), R (39)

Rees, W. (Cardiff C), 1949 v Ni, Bel, Sw; (with Tottenham H), 1950 v Ni (4)
Richards, A. (Barnsley), 1932 v S (1)
Richards, D. (Wolverhampton W), 1931 v Ni; 1933 v E, S, Ni; 1934 v E, S, Ni; 1935 v E, S, Ni; 1936 v S; (with Brentford), 1936 v E, Ni; 1937 v S, E; (with Birmingham), Ni; 1938 v E, S, Ni; 1939 v E, S (21)
Richards, G. (Druids), 1899 v E, S, Ni; (with Oswestry), 1903 v Ni; (with Shrewsbury), 1904 v S; 1905 v Ni (6)
Richards, R. W. (Wolverhampton W), 1920 v E, S; 1921 v Ni; 1922 v E, S; (with West Ham U), 1924 v E, S, Ni; (with Mold), 1926 v S (9)
Richards, S. V. (Cardiff C), 1947 v E (1)
Richards, W. E. (Fulham), 1933 v Ni (1)
Roach, J. (Oswestry), 1885 v Ni (1)
Robbins, W. W. (Cardiff C), 1931 v E, S; 1932 v Ni, E, S; (with WBA), 1933 v F, E, S, Ni; 1934 v S; 1936 v S (11)
Roberts, A. M. (QPR), 1993 v Ei (sub); 1997 v Sm (sub) (2)
Roberts, D. F. (Oxford U), 1973 v Pol, E (sub), Ni; 1974 v E, S; 1975 v A; (with Hull C), L, Ni; 1976 v S, Ni, Y; 1977 v E (sub), Ni; 1978 v K (1+1 sub), S, Ni (17)
Roberts, G. W. (Tranmere R), 2000 v Fi (sub), Br, P (3)
Roberts, I. W. (Watford), 1990 v Ho; (with Huddersfield T), 1992 v A, Arg, J; (with Leicester C), 1994 v Se; 1995 v Alb (sub), Mol; (with Norwich C), 2000 v Fi (sub), Br, P (10)
Roberts, Jas (Wrexham), 1913 v S, Ni (2)
Roberts, J. (Corwen), 1879 v S; 1880 v E, S; 1882 v E, S, Ni; (with Berwyn R), 1883 v E (7)
Roberts, J. (Ruthin), 1883 v S; 1882 v S (2)
Roberts, J. (Bradford C), 1906 v Ni; 1907 v Ni (2)
Roberts, J. G. (Arsenal), 1971 v S, E, Ni, Fi; 1972 v Fi, E, Ni; (with Birmingham C), 1973 v E (2), Pol, S, Ni; 1974 v Pol, E, S, Ni; 1975 v A, H, S, E; 1976 v E, S (22)
Roberts, J. H. (Bolton), 1949 v Bel (1)
Roberts, N. W. (Wrexham), 2000 v Sw (sub) (1)
Roberts, P. S. (Portsmouth), 1974 v E; 1975 v A, H, L (4)
Roberts, R. (Druids), 1884 v S; (with Bolton W), 1887 v S; 1888 v S, E; 1889 v S, E; 1890 v S; 1892 v Ni; (with Preston NE), S (9)
Roberts, R. (Wrexham), 1886 v Ni; 1887 v Ni; 1891 v Ni (3)
Roberts, R. (Rhos), 1891 v Ni; (with Crewe Alex), 1893 v E (2)
Roberts, R. L. (Chester), 1890 v Ni (1)
Roberts, W. (Llangollen), 1879 v E, S; 1880 v E, S; (with Berwyn R), 1881 v S; 1883 v S (6)
Roberts, W. (Wrexham), 1886 v E, S, Ni; 1887 v Ni (4)
Roberts, W. H. (Ruthin), 1882 v E, S; 1883 v E, S, Ni; (with Rhyl), 1884 v S (6)
Robinson, C. P. (Wolverhampton W), 2000 v Bl (sub), P (sub) (2)
Robinson, J. R. C. (Charlton Ath), 1996 v Alb (sub), Sw, Sm; 1997 v Sm, Ho (1 + sub), Ei, S; 1998 v Bel, Br; 1999 v I, D (sub), Bl, Sw, I, D; 2000 v Bl, Sw, Q, Fi, Br, P (22)
Rodrigues, P. J. (Cardiff C), 1965 v Ni, Gr (2); 1966 v USSR, E, S, D; (with Leicester C), Ni, Br (2), Ch; 1967 v S; 1968 v E, S, Ni; 1969 v E, Ni, EG, R of UK; 1970 v E, S, Ni, EG; (with Sheffield W), 1971 v R, E, S, Cz, Ni; 1972 v Fi, Cz, R, E, Ni (sub); 1973 v E (3), Pol, S, Ni; 1974 v Pol (40)
Rogers, J. P. (Wrexham), 1896 v E, S, Ni (3)
Rogers, W. (Wrexham), 1931 v E, S (2)
Roose, L. R. (Aberystwyth), 1900 v Ni; (with London Welsh), 1901 v E, S, Ni; (with Stoke C), 1902 v E, S; 1904 v E; (with Everton), 1905 v S, E; (with Stoke C), 1906 v E, S, Ni; 1907 v E, S, Ni; (with Sunderland), 1908 v E, S; 1909 v E, S, Ni; 1910 v E, S, Ni; 1911 v S (24)
Rouse, R. V. (C Palace), 1959 v Ni (1)
Rowlands, A. C. (Tranmere R), 1914 v E (1)
Rowley, T. (Tranmere R), 1959 v Ni (1)
Rush, I. (Liverpool), 1980 v S (sub), Ni; 1981 v E (sub); 1982 v Ic (sub), USSR, E, S, Ni, F; 1983 v N, Y, E, Bul; 1984 v N, R, Bul, Y, S, E, Ni; 1985 v Ic, N, S, Sp; 1986 v S, S.Ar, Ei, U; 1987 v Fi (2), USSR, Cz; (with Juventus), 1988 v D, Cz, Y, Se, Ma, I; (with Liverpool), 1989 v Ho, Fi, Se, WG; 1990 v Fi, Ei; 1991 v D, Bel (2), L, Ei, Pol, WG; 1992 v G, L, R; 1993 v Fa, Cy, Bel (2), RCS, Fa; 1994 v RCS, Cy, R, N, Se, Es; 1995 v Alb, Ge, Bul, G, Ge; 1996 v Mol, I (73)
Russell, M. R. (Merthyr T), 1912 v S, Ni; 1914 v E; (with Plymouth Arg), 1920 v E, S, Ni; 1921 v E, S, Ni; 1922 v E, Ni; 1923 v E, S, Ni; 1924 v E, S, Ni; 1925 v E, S; 1926 v E, S; 1928 v S; 1929 v E (23)

Sabine, H. W. (Oswestry), 1887 v Ni (1)
Saunders, D. (Brighton & HA), 1986 v Ei (sub), Ca (2); 1987 v Fi, USSR (sub); (with Oxford U), 1988 v Y, Se, Ma, I (sub); 1989 v Ho (sub), Fi; (with Derby Co), Is, Se, WG; 1990 v Fi, Ho, WG, Se, Cr; 1991 v D, Bel (2), L, Ei, Ic, Pol,

WG; (with Liverpool), 1992 v Br, G, Ei, R, Ho, Arg, J; 1993 v Fa; (with Aston Villa), Cy, Bel (2), RCS, Fa; 1994 v RCS, Cy, R, N (sub); 1995 v Ge, Bul (2), G, Ge; (with Galatasaray), 1996 v G, Alb, Sm; (with Nottingham F), 1997 v Sm, Ho (2), T, Bel, S; 1998 v T, Bel, Br; (with Sheffield U), Ma, Tun; 1999 v I (sub), D, Bl; (with Benfica) Sw, I, D; (with Bradford C), 2000 v Bl, Sw, Fi (sub), Br (73)
Savage, R. W. (Crewe Alex), 1996 v Alb (sub), Sw (sub), Sm (sub); 1997 v Ei (sub), S; (with Leicester C), 1998 v T, Bel, Jam, Tun; 1999 v I (sub), D, Bl, Sw; 2000 v Sw, Fi, Br (16)
Savin, G. (Oswestry), 1878 v S (1)
Sayer, P. (Cardiff C), 1977 v Cz, S, E, Ni; 1978 v K (2), S (7)
Scrine, F. H. (Swansea T), 1950 v E, Ni (2)
Sear, C. R. (Manchester C), 1963 v E (1)
Shaw, E. G. (Oswestry), 1882 v Ni; 1884 v S, Ni (3)
Sherwood, A. T. (Cardiff C), 1947 v E, Ni; 1948 v S, Ni; 1949 v E, S, Ni, P, Sw; 1950 v E, S, Ni, Bel; 1951 v E, S, Ni, P, Sw; 1952 v E, S, Ni, R of UK; 1953 v S, E, Ni, F, Y; 1954 v E, S, Ni, A; 1955 v S, E, Y, Ni; 1956 v E, S, Ni, A; (with Newport Co), 1957 v E, S (41)
Shone, W. W. (Oswestry), 1879 v E (1)
Shortt, W. W. (Plymouth Arg), 1947 v Ni; 1950 v Ni, Bel; 1952 v E, S, Ni, R of UK; 1953 v S, E, Ni, F, Y (12)
Showers, D. (Cardiff C), 1975 v E (sub), Ni (2)
Sidlow, C. (Liverpool), 1947 v E, S; 1948 v E, S, Ni; 1949 v S; 1950 v E (7)
Sisson, H. (Wrexham Olympic), 1885 v Ni; 1886 v S, Ni (3)
Slatter, N. (Bristol R), 1983 v S; 1984 v N (sub), Is; 1985 v Ic, Sp, Ic, N, S, Sp, N; (with Oxford U), 1986 v H (sub), S.Ar, Ca (2); 1987 v Fi (sub), Cz; 1988 v D (2), Cz, Ma, I; 1989 v Is (sub) (22)
Smallman, D. P. (Wrexham), 1974 v E (sub), S (sub), Ni; (with Everton), 1975 v H (sub), E, Ni (sub); 1976 v A (7)
Southall, N. (Everton), 1982 v Ni; 1983 v N, E, Bul, S, Ni, Br; 1984 v N, R, Bul, Y, S, E, Ni, N, Is; 1985 v Ic, Sp, Ic, N, S, Sp, N; 1986 v S, H, S.Ar, Ei; 1987 v USSR, Fi, Cz; 1988 v D, Cz, Y, Se; 1989 v Ho, Fi, Se, WG; 1990 v Fi, Ho, WG, Ei, Se, Cr; 1991 v D, Bel (2), L, Ei, Ic, Pol, WG; 1992 v Br, G, L, Ei, A, R, Ho, Arg, J; 1993 v Fa, Cy, Bel, Ei, Bel, RCS, Fa; 1994 v RCS, Cy, R, N, Se, Es; 1995 v Alb, Mol, Ge, Bul (2), G, Ge; 1996 v Mol, G, Alb, I, Sm; 1997 v Sm, Ho (2), T, Bel; 1998 v T (92)
Speed, G. A. (Leeds U), 1990 v Cr (sub); 1991 v D, L (sub), Ei (sub), Ic, WG (sub); 1992 v Br, G (sub), L, Ei, R, Ho,Arg,J; 1993 v Fa, Cy, Bel, Ei, Bel, Fa (sub); 1994 v RCS (sub), Cy, R, N, Se; 1995 v Alb, Mol, Ge, Bul (2), G; 1996 v Mol, G, I, Sw (sub); (with Everton), 1997 v Sm (sub), Ho (2), T, Ei, Bel, S; 1998 v T, Br; (with Newcastle U), Jam, Ma, Tun; 1999 v I, D, Sw, I, D; 2000 v Bl, Sw, Q, Fi, Br, P (58)
Sprake, G. (Leeds U), 1964 v S, Ni; 1965 v S, D, Gr; 1966 v E, Ni, USSR; 1967 v S; 1968 v E, S; 1969 v S, E, Ni, WG, R of UK; 1970 v EG, I; 1971 v R, S, E, Ni; 1972 v Fi, E, S, Ni; 1973 v E (2), Pol, S, Ni; 1974 v Pol; (with Birmingham C), S, Ni; 1975 v A, H, L (37)
Stansfield, F. (Cardiff C), 1949 v S (1)
Stevenson, B. (Leeds U), 1978 v Ni; 1979 v Ma, T, S, E, Ni, Ma; 1980 v WG, T, Ic (sub); 1982 v Cz; (with Birmingham C), Sp, S, Ni, F (15)
Stevenson, N. (Swansea C), 1982 v E, S, Ni; 1983 v N (4)
Stitfall, R. F. (Cardiff C), 1953 v E; 1957 v Cz (2)
Sullivan, D. (Cardiff C), 1953 v Ni, F, Y; 1954 v Ni; 1955 v E, Ni; 1957 v E, S; 1958 v Ni, H (2), Se, Br; 1959 v S, Ni; 1960 v E, S (17)
Symons, C. J. (Portsmouth), 1992 v Ei, Ho, Arg, J; 1993 v Fa, Cy, Bel, Ei, RCS, Fa; 1994 v RCS, Cy, R; 1995 v Mol, Ge (sub), Bul, G, Ge; (with Manchester C), 1996 v Mol, G, I, Sw; 1997 v Ho (2), Ei, Bel, S; (with Fulham), 1999 v I, D, Bl, Sw; 2000 v Q (sub) (32)

Tapscott, D. R. (Arsenal), 1954 v A; 1955 v S, E, Ni, Y; 1956 v E, Ni, S, A; 1957 v Ni, Cz, EG; (with Cardiff C), 1959 v E, Ni (14)
Taylor, G. K. (C Palace), 1996 v Alb, I (sub); (with Sheffield U), Sw; 1997 v Sm (sub), Ho (sub), Ei (sub); 1998 v Bel (sub), Jam (8)
Taylor, J. (Wrexham), 1898 v E (1)
Taylor, O. D. S. (Newtown), 1893 v S, Ni; 1894 v S, Ni (4)
Thomas, D. (Druids), 1899 v Ni; 1900 v S (2)
Thomas, D. A. (Swansea T), 1957 v Cz; 1958 v EG (2)
Thomas, D. S. (Fulham), 1948 v E, S, Ni; 1949 v S (4)
Thomas, E. (Cardiff Corinthians), 1925 v E (1)
Thomas, G. (Wrexham), 1885 v E, S (2)
Thomas, H. (Manchester U), 1927 v E (1)

Thomas, M. (Wrexham), 1977 v WG, S (1+1 sub); Ni (sub); 1978 v K (sub), S, Cz, Ir, E, Ni (sub); 1979 v Ma; (with Manchester U), T, WG, Ma (sub); 1980 v Ei, WG (sub), T, E, S, Ni; 1981 v Cz, S, E, USSR; (with Everton), 1982 v Cz; (with Brighton & HA), USSR (sub), Sp, E, S (sub), Ni (sub); 1983 (with Stoke C), v N, Y, E, Bul, S, Ni, Br; 1984 v R, Bul, Y; (with Chelsea), S, E; 1985 v Ic, Sp, Ic, S, Sp, N; 1986 v S; (with WBA), H, S.Ar (sub) (51)

Thomas, M. R. (Newcastle U), 1987 v Fi (1)

Thomas, R. J. (Swindon T), 1967 v Ni; 1968 v WG; 1969 v E, Ni, I, WG, R of UK; 1970 v E, S, Ni, EG, I; 1971 v S, E, Ni, R, Cz; 1972 v Fi, Cz, R, E, S, Ni; 1973 v E (3), Pol, S, Ni; 1974 v Pol; (with Derby Co), E, S, Ni; 1975 v H (2), L (2), S, E, Ni; 1976 v A, Y, E; 1977 v Cz, S, E, Ni; 1978 v K, S; (with Cardiff C), Cz (50)

Thomas, T. (Bangor), 1898 v S, Ni (2)

Thomas, W. R. (Newport Co), 1931 v E, S (2)

Thomson, D. (Druids), 1876 v S (1)

Thomson, G. F. (Druids), 1876 v S; 1877 v S (2)

Toshack, J. B. (Cardiff C), 1969 v S, E, Ni, WG, EG, R of UK; 1970 v EG, I; (with Liverpool), 1971 v S, E, Ni, Fi; 1972 v Fi, E; 1973 v E (3), Pol, S; 1975 v A, H (2), L (2), S, E; 1976 v Y (2), E; 1977 v S; 1978 v K (2), S, Cz; (with Swansea C), 1979 v WG (sub), S, E, Ni, Ma; 1980 v WG (40)

Townsend, W. (Newtown), 1887 v Ni; 1893 v Ni (2)

Trainer, H. (Wrexham), 1895 v E, S, Ni (3)

Trainer, J. (Bolton W), 1887 v S; (with Preston NE), 1888 v S; 1889 v E; 1890 v S; 1891 v S; 1892 v Ni, S; 1893 v E; 1894 v Ni, E; 1895 v Ni, E; 1896 v S; 1897 v Ni, S, E; 1898 v S, E; 1899 v Ni, S (20)

Trollope, P. J. (Derby Co), 1997 v S; 1998 v Br (sub); (with Fulham), Jam (sub), Ma, Tun (5)

Turner, H. G. (Charlton Ath), 1937 v E, S, Ni; 1938 v E, S, Ni; 1939 v Ni, F (8)

Turner, J. (Wrexham), 1892 v E (1)

Turner, R. E. (Wrexham), 1891 v E, Ni (2)

Turner, W. H. (Wrexham), 1887 v E, Ni; 1890 v S; 1891 v E, S (5)

Van Den Hauwe, P. W. R. (Everton), 1985 v Sp; 1986 v S, H; 1987 v USSR, Fi, Cz; 1988 v D (2), Cz, Y, I; 1989 v Fi, Se (13)

Vaughan, Jas (Druids), 1893 v E, S, Ni; 1899 v E (4)

Vaughan, John (Oswestry), 1879 v S; 1880 v S; 1881 v E, S; 1882 v E, S, Ni; 1883 v E, S, Ni; (with Bolton W), 1884 v E (11)

Vaughan, J. O. (Rhyl), 1885 v Ni; 1886 v Ni, E, S (4)

Vaughan, N. (Newport Co), 1983 v Y (sub), Br; 1984 v N; (with Cardiff C), R, Bul, Y, Ni (sub), N, Is; 1985 v Sp (sub) (10)

Vaughan, T. (Rhyl), 1885 v E (1)

Vearncombe, G. (Cardiff C), 1958 v EG; 1961 v Ei (2)

Vernon, T. R. (Blackburn R), 1957 v Ni, Cz (2), EG; 1958 v E, S, EG, Se; 1959 v S; (with Everton), 1960 v Ni; 1961 v S, E, Ei; 1962 v Ni, Br (2), M; 1963 v S, E, H; 1964 v E, S; (with Stoke C), 1965 v Ni, Gr, I; 1966 v E, S, Ni, USSR, D; 1967 v Ni; 1968 v E (32)

Villars, A. K. (Cardiff C), 1974 v E, S, Ni (sub) (3)

Vizard, E. T. (Bolton W), 1911 v E, S, Ni; 1912 v E, S; 1913 v S; 1914 v E, Ni; 1920 v E; 1921 v E, S, Ni; 1922 v E, S; 1923 v E, Ni; 1924 v E, S, Ni; 1926 v E, S; 1927 v S (22)

Walley, J. T. (Watford), 1971 v Cz (1)

Walsh, I. (C Palace), 1980 v Ei, T, E, S, Ic; 1981 v T, Cz, Ei, T, S, E, USSR; 1982 v Cz (sub), Ic; (with Swansea C), Sp, S (sub), Ni (sub), F (18)

Ward, D. (Bristol R), 1959 v E; (with Cardiff C), 1962 v E (2)

Ward, D. (Notts Co), 2000 v P (1)

Warner, J. (Swansea T), 1937 v E; (with Manchester U), 1939 v F (2)

Warren, F. W. (Cardiff C), 1929 v Ni; (with Middlesbrough), 1931 v Ni; 1933 v F, E; (with Hearts), 1937 v Ni; 1938 v Ni (6)

Watkins, A. E. (Leicester Fosse), 1898 v E, S; (with Aston Villa), 1900 v E, S; (with Millwall), 1904 v Ni (5)

Watkins, W. M. (Stoke C), 1902 v E; 1903 v E, S; (with Aston Villa); 1904 v E, S, Ni; (with Sunderland), 1905 v E, S, Ni; (with Stoke C), 1908 v Ni (10)

Webster, C. (Manchester U), 1957 v Cz; 1958 v H, M, Br (4)

Weston, R. D. (Arsenal), 2000 v P (sub) (1)

Whatley, W. J. (Tottenham H), 1939 v E, S (2)

White, P. F. (London Welsh), 1896 v Ni (1)

Wilcock, A. R. (Oswestry), 1890 v Ni (1)

Wilding, J. (Wrexham Olympians), 1885 v E, S, Ni; 1886 v E, Ni; (with Bootle), 1887 v E; 1888 v S, Ni; (with Wrexham), 1892 v S (9)

Williams, A. (Reading), 1994 v Es; 1995 v Alb, Mol, G (sub), Ge; 1996 v Mol, I; (with Wolverhampton W), 1998 v Br (sub), Jam; 1999 v I, D, I (12)

Williams, A. L. (Wrexham), 1931 v E (1)

Williams, A. P. (Southampton), 1998 v Br (sub), Ma (2)

Williams, B. (Bristol C), 1930 v Ni (1)

Williams, B. D. (Swansea T), 1928 v Ni, E; 1930 v E, S; (with Everton), 1931 v Ni; 1932 v E; 1933 v E, S, Ni; 1935 v Ni (10)

Williams, D. G. (Derby Co), 1988 v Cz, Y, Se, Ma, I; 1989 v Ho, Is, Se, WG; 1990 v Fi, Ho; (with Ipswich T), 1993 v Ei; 1996 v G (sub) (13)

Williams, D. M. (Norwich C), 1986 v S.Ar (sub), U, Ca (2); 1987 v Fi (5)

Williams, D. R. (Merthyr T), 1921 v E, S; (with Sheffield W), 1923 v S; 1926 v S; 1927 v E, Ni; (with Manchester U), 1929 v E, S (8)

Williams, E. (Crewe Alex), 1893 v E, S (2)

Williams, E. (Druids), 1901 v E, Ni, S; 1902 v E, Ni (5)

Williams, G. (Chirk), 1893 v S; 1894 v S; 1895 v E, S, Ni; 1898 v Ni (6)

Williams, G. E. (WBA), 1960 v Ni; 1961 v S, E, Ei; 1963 v Ni, H; 1964 v E, S, Ni; 1965 v S, E, Ni, D, Gr (2), USSR; 1966 v Ni, Br (2), Ch; 1967 v S, E, Ni; 1968 v Ni; 1969 v I (26)

Williams, G. G. (Swansea T), 1961 v Ni, H, Sp (2); 1962 v E (5)

Williams, G. J. J. (Cardiff C), 1951 v Sw (1)

Williams, G. O. (Wrexham), 1907 v Ni (1)

Williams, H. J. (Swansea T), 1965 v Gr (2); 1972 v R (3)

Williams, H. T. (Newport Co), 1949 v Ni, Sw; (with Leeds U), 1950 v Ni; 1951 v S (4)

Williams, J. H. (Oswestry), 1884 v E (1)

Williams, J. J. (Wrexham), 1939 v F (1)

Williams, J. T. (Middlesbrough), 1925 v Ni (1)

Williams, J. W. (C Palace), 1912 v S, Ni (2)

Williams, R. (Newcastle U), 1935 v S, E (2)

Williams, R. P. (Caernarvon), 1886 v S (1)

Williams, S. G. (WBA), 1954 v A; 1955 v E, Ni; 1956 v E, S, A; 1958 v E, S, Ni, Is (2), H (2), M, Se, Br; 1959 v E, S, Ni; 1960 v E, S, Ni; 1961 v Ni, Ei, H, Sp (2); 1962 v E, S, Ni, Br (2), M; (with Southampton), 1963 v S, E, H (2); 1964 v E, S; 1965 v S, E, D; 1966 v D (43)

Williams, W. (Druids), 1876 v S; 1878 v S; (with Oswestry), 1879 v E, S; (with Druids), 1880 v E; 1881 v E, S; 1882 v E, S, Ni; 1883 v Ni (11)

Williams, W. (Northampton T), 1925 v S (1)

Witcomb, D. F. (WBA), 1947 v E, S; (with Sheffield W), 1947 v Ni (3)

Woosnam, A. P. (Leyton Orient), 1959 v S; (with West Ham U), E; 1960 v E, S, Ni; 1961 v S, E, Ni, Ei, Sp, H; 1962 v E, S, Ni, Br; (with Aston Villa), 1963 v Ni, H (17)

Woosnam, G. (Newton White Star), 1879 v S (1)

Worthington, T. (Newtown), 1894 v S (1)

Wynn, G. A. (Wrexham), 1909 v E, S, Ni; (with Manchester C), 1910 v E; 1911 v Ni; 1912 v E, S; 1913 v E, S; 1914 v E, S (11)

Wynn, W. (Chirk), 1903 v Ni (1)

Yorath, T. C. (Leeds U), 1970 v I; 1971 v S, E, Ni; 1972 v Cz, E, S, Ni; 1973 v E, Pol, S; 1974 v Pol, E, S, Ni; 1975 v A, H (2), L (2), S; 1976 v A, E, S, Y (2), E, Ni; (with Coventry C), 1977 v WG, S (2), Cz, E, Ni; 1978 v K (2), S, Cz, WG, Ir, E, S, Ni; 1979 v T, WG, S, E, Ni; (with Tottenham H), 1980 v Ei, T, E, S, Ni, Ic; 1981 v T, Cz; (with Vancouver W), Ei, T, USSR (59)

Young, E. (Wimbledon), 1990 v Cr; (with C Palace), 1991 v D, Bel (2), L, Ei; 1992 v G, L, Ei, A; 1993 v Fa, Cy, Bel, Ei, Bel, Fa; 1994 v RCS, Cy, R, N; (with Wolverhampton W) 1996 v Alb (21)

REPUBLIC OF IRELAND

Aherne, T. (Belfast C), 1946 v P, Sp; (with Luton T), 1950 v Fi, E, Fi, Se, Bel; 1951 v N, Arg, N; 1952 v WG (2), A, Sp; 1953 v F; 1954 v F (16)

Aldridge, J. W. (Oxford U), 1986 v W, U, Ic, Cz; 1987 v Bel, S, Pol; (with Liverpool), S, Bul, Bel, Br, L; 1988 v Bul, Pol, N, E, USSR, Ho; 1989 v Ni, Tun, Sp, F (sub), H, Ma (sub), H; 1990 v WG; (with Real Sociedad), Ni, Ma, Fi (sub), T, E, Eg, Ho, R, I; 1991 v T, E (2), Pol; (with Tranmere R), 1992 v H (sub), T, W (sub), Sw (sub), US (sub), Alb, I, P (sub); 1993 v La, D, Sp, D, Alb, La, Li; 1994 v Li, Ni, CzR, I (sub), M (sub), N; 1995 v La, Ni, P, Lie; 1996 v La, P, Ho, Ru; 1997 v Mac (sub) (69)

Ambrose, P. (Shamrock R), 1955 v N, Ho; 1964 v Pol, N, E (5)

Anderson, J. (Preston NE), 1980 v Cz (sub), US (sub); 1982 v Ch, Br, Tr; (with Newcastle U), 1984 v Chn; 1986 v W, Ic, Cz; 1987 v Bul, Bel, Br, L; 1988 v R (sub), Y (sub); 1989 v Tun (16)

Andrews, P. (Bohemians), 1936 v Ho (1)

Arrigan, T. (Waterford), 1938 v N (1)

Babb, P. A. (Coventry C), 1994 v Ru, Ho, Bol, G, CzR (sub), I, M, N, Ho; (with Liverpool), 1995 v La, Lie, Ni (2), P, Lie, A; 1996 v La, P, Ho, CzR; 1997 v Ic; 1998 v Li (sub), R, Arg (sub), M; 1999 v Cro, Para (sub), Se (sub), Ni; 2000 v CzR (sub), S, M (sub), US, S.Af (34)

Bailham, E. (Shamrock R), 1964 v E (1)

Barber, E. (Shelbourne), 1966 v Sp; (with Birmingham C), 1966 v Bel (2)

Barry, P. (Fordsons), 1928 v Bel; 1929 v Bel (2)

Beglin, J. (Liverpool), 1984 v Chn; 1985 v M, D, I, Is, E, N, Sw; 1986 v Sw, USSR, D, W; 1987 v Bel (sub), S, Pol (15)

Bermingham, J. (Bohemians), 1929 v Bel (1)

Bermingham, P. (St James' Gate), 1935 v H (1)

Braddish, S. (Dundalk), 1978 v T (sub), Pol (2)

Bonner, P. (Celtic), 1981 v Pol; 1982 v Alg; 1984 v Ma, Is, Chn; 1985 v I, Is, E, N; 1986 v U, Ic; 1987 v Bel (2), S (2), Pol, Bul, Br, L; 1988 v Bul, R, Y, N, E, USSR, Ho; 1989 v Sp, F, H, Sp, Ma, H; 1990 v WG, Ni, Ma, W, Fi, T, E, Eg, Ho, R, I; 1991 v Mor, T, E (2), W, Pol, US; 1992 v H, Pol, T, W, Sw, Alb, I; 1993 v La, D, Sp, W, Ni, D, Alb, La, Li; 1994 v I, Sp, Ni, Ru, Ho, Bol, CzR, I, M, N, Ho; 1995 v Lie; 1996 v M, Bol (sub) (80)

Bradshaw, P. (St James' Gate), 1939 v Sw, Pol, H (2), G (5)

Brady, F. (Fordsons), 1926 v I; 1927 v I (2)

Brady, T. R. (QPR), 1964 v A (2), Sp (2), Pol, N (6)

Brady, W. L. (Arsenal), 1975 v USSR, T, Sw, USSR, Sw, WG; 1976 v T, N, Pol; 1977 v E, T, F (2), Sp, Bul; 1978 v Bul, N; 1979 v Ni, E, D, Bul, WG; 1980 v W, Bul, E, Cy; (with Juventus), 1981 v Ho, Bel, F, Cy, Bel; 1982 v Ho, F, Ch, Br, Tr; (with Sampdoria), 1983 v Ho, Sp, Ic, Ma; 1984 v Ic, Ho, Ma, Pol, Is; (with Internazionale), 1985 v USSR, N, D, I, E, N, Sp, Sw; 1986 v Sw, USSR, D, W; (with Ascoli), 1987 v Bel, S (2), Pol; (with West Ham U), Bul, Bel, Br, L; 1988 v L, Bul; 1989 v F, H (sub), H (sub); 1990 v WG, Fi (72)

Branagan, K. G. (Bolton W), 1997 v W (1)

Breen, G. (Birmingham C), 1996 v P (sub), Cro, Ho, US, M, Bol (sub); 1997 v Lie, Mac, Ic; (with Coventry C), v Mac; 1998 v Li (sub), R, CzR, Arg, M; 1999 v Ma, Y, Para, Se, Mac; 2000 v Y, Cro, Ma, Mac, T (2), Gr, S, M, US, S.Af (31)

Breen, T. (Manchester U), 1937 v Sw, F; (with Shamrock R), 1947 v E, Sp, P (5)

Brennan, F. (Drumcondra), 1965 v Bel (1)

Brennan, S. A. (Manchester U), 1965 v Sp; 1966 v Sp, A, Bel; 1967 v Sp, T, Sp; 1969 v Cz, D, H; 1970 v S, Cz, D, H, Pol (sub), WG; (with Waterford), 1971 v Pol, Se, I (19)

Brown, J. (Coventry U), 1937 v Sw, F (2)

Browne, W. (Bohemians), 1964 v A, Sp, E (3)

Buckley, L. (Shamrock R), 1984 v Pol (sub); (with Waregem), 1985 v M (2)

Burke, F. (Cork Ath), 1952 v WG (1)

Burke, J. (Cork), 1934 v Bel (1)

Burke, J. (Shamrock R), 1929 v Bel (1)

Butler, P. J. (Sunderland), 2000 v CzR (1)

Byrne, A. B. (Southampton), 1970 v D, Pol, WG; 1971 v Pol, Se (2), I (2), A; 1973 v F, USSR (sub), F, N; 1974 v Pol (14)

Byrne, D. (Shelbourne), 1929 v Bel; (with Shamrock R), 1932 v Sp; (with Coleraine), 1934 v Bel (3)

Byrne, J. (Bray Unknowns), 1928 v Bel (1)

Byrne, J. (QPR), 1985 v I, Is (sub), E (sub), Sp (sub); 1987 v S (sub), Bel (sub), Br, L (sub); 1988 v L, Bul (sub), Is, R, Y (sub), Pol (sub); (with Le Havre), 1990 v WG (sub), W, Fi, T (sub), Ma; (with Brighton & HA), 1991 v W; (with Sunderland), 1992 v T, W; (with Millwall), 1993 v W (23)

Byrne, P. (Shamrock R), 1984 v Pol, Chn; 1985 v M; 1986 v D (sub), W (sub), U (sub), Ic (sub), Cz (8)

Byrne, P. (Dolphin), 1931 v Sp; 1932 v Ho; (with Drumcondra), 1934 v Ho (3)

Byrne, S. (Bohemians), 1931 v Sp (1)

Campbell, A. (Santander), 1985 v I (sub), Is, Sp (3)

Campbell, N. (St Patrick's Ath), 1971 v A (sub); (with Fortuna, Cologne), 1972 v Ir, Ec, Ch, P; 1973 v USSR, F (sub); 1975 v WG; 1976 v N; 1977 v Sp, Bul (sub) (11)

Cannon, H. (Bohemians), 1926 v I; 1928 v Bel (2)

Cantwell, N. (West Ham U), 1954 v L; 1956 v Sp, Ho; 1957 v D, WG, E (2); 1958 v D, Pol, A; 1959 v Pol, Cz (2); 1960 v Se, Ch, Se; 1961 v N; (with Manchester U), S (2); 1962 v Cz (2), A; 1963 v Ic (2), S; 1964 v A, Sp, E; 1965 v Pol, Sp; 1966 v Sp (2), A, Bel; 1967 v Sp, T (36)

Carey, B. P. (Manchester U), 1992 v US (sub); 1993 v W; (with Leicester C), 1994 v Ru (3)

Carey, J. J. (Manchester U), 1938 v N, Cz, Pol; 1939 v Sw, Pol, H (2), G; 1946 v P, Sp; 1947 v E, Sp, P; 1948 v P, Sp; 1949 v Sw, Bel, P, Se, Sp; 1950 v Fi, E, Fi, Se; 1951 v N, Arg, N; 1953 v F, A, Sp (29)

Carolan, J. (Manchester U), 1960 v Se, Ch (2)

Carr, S. (Tottenham H), 1999 v Se, Ni, Mac; 2000 v Y (sub), Cro, Ma, T (2), S, M, US, S.Af (12)

Carroll, B. (Shelbourne), 1949 v Bel; 1950 v Fi (2)

Carroll, T. R. (Ipswich T), 1968 v Pol; 1969 v Pol, A, D; 1970 v Cz, Pol, WG; 1971 v Se; (with Birmingham C), 1972 v Ir, Ec, Ch, P; 1973 v USSR (2), Pol, F, N (17)

Carsley, L. K. (Derby Co), 1998 v R, Bel (1 + sub), CzR, Arg, M; 1999 v Cro (sub), Ma (sub), Para (sub); (with Blackburn R) Ni, Mac; 2000 v Y (sub), Cro, Ma, T (15)

Cascarino, A. G. (Gillingham), 1986 v Sw, USSR, D; (with Millwall), 1988 v Pol, N (sub), USSR (sub), Ho (sub); 1989 v Ni, Tun, Sp, F, H, Sp, Ma, H; 1990 v WG (sub), Ni, Ma; (with Aston Villa), W, Fi, T, E, Eg, Ho (sub), R (sub), I (sub); 1991 v Mor (sub),T (sub), E (2 sub), Pol (sub), Ch (sub), US; (with Celtic), 1992 v Pol, T; (with Chelsea), W, Sw, US (sub); 1993 v W, Ni (sub), D (sub), Alb (sub), La (sub); 1994 v Li (sub), Sp (sub), Ni (sub), Ru, Bol (sub), G, CzR, Ho (sub); (with Marseille), 1995 v La (sub), Ni (sub), P (sub), Lie (sub), A (sub); 1996 v A (sub), P (sub), Ho (sub), P, Cro (sub), Ho; 1997 v Lie (sub), Mac, Ic; (with Nancy), v W, Mac, R (sub), Lie (sub); 1998 v Li (sub), Ic (sub), Li, R, Bel (2); 1999 v Cro (sub), Ma (sub), Y (sub), Para (sub), Se (sub), Ni (sub), Mac (sub); 2000 v Y (sub), Cro, Mac (sub), T (1 + sub) (88)

Chandler, J. (Leeds U), 1980 v Cz (sub), US (2)

Chatton, H. A. (Shelbourne), 1931 v Sp; (with Dumbarton), 1932 v Sp; (with Cork), 1934 v Ho (3)

Clarke, J. (Drogheda U), 1978 v Pol (sub) (1)

Clarke, K. (Drumcondra), 1948 v P, Sp (2)

Clarke, M. (Shamrock R), 1950 v Bel (1)

Clinton, T. J. (Everton), 1951 v N; 1954 v F, L (3)

Coad, P. (Shamrock R), 1947 v E, Sp, P; 1948 v P, Sp; 1949 v Sw, Bel, P, Se; 1951 v N (sub); 1952 v Sp (11)

Coffey, T. (Drumcondra), 1950 v Fi (1)

Colfer, M. D. (Shelbourne), 1950 v Bel; 1951 v N (2)

Collins, F. (Jacobs), 1927 v I (1)

Conmy, O. M. (Peterborough U), 1965 v Bel; 1967 v Cz; 1968 v Cz, Pol; 1970 v Cz (5)

Connolly, D. J. (Watford), 1996 v P, Ho, US, M; 1997 v R, Lie; (with Feyenoord), 1998 v Li, Ic, Li, Bel (1 + sub), CzR, M; (with Wolverhampton W), 1999 v Y, Para (sub), Se, Ni (sub), Mac (sub); (with Excelsior), 2000 v T (1 + sub), CzR (sub), Gr (22)

Connolly, H. (Cork), 1937 v G (1)

Connolly, J. (Fordsons), 1926 v I (1)

Conroy, G. A. (Stoke C), 1970 v Cz, D, H, Pol, WG; 1971 v Pol, Se (2), I; 1973 v USSR, F, USSR, N; 1974 v Pol, Br, U, Ch; 1975 v T, Sw, USSR, SW (sub); 1976 v T (sub), Pol; 1977 v E, T, Pol (27)

Conway, J. P. (Fulham), 1967 v Sp, T, Sp; 1968 v Cz; 1969 v A (sub), H; 1970 v S, Cz, D, H, Pol, WG; 1971 v I, A; 1974 v Ch; 1975 v WG (sub); 1976 v N, Pol; (with Manchester C), 1977 v Pol (20)

Corr, P. J. (Everton), 1949 v P, Sp; 1950 v E, Se (4)

Courtney, E. (Cork U), 1946 v P (1)

Coyle, O. C. (Bolton W), 1994 v Ho (1)

Coyne, T. (Celtic), 1992 v Sw, US, Alb (sub), US (sub), I (sub), P (sub); 1993 v W, US (sub), La (sub); (with Tranmere R), Ni; (with Motherwell), 1994 v Ru (sub), Ho, Bol, G (sub), CzR (sub), I, M, Ho; 1995 v Lie, Ni (sub), A; 1996 v Ru (sub); 1998 v Bel (sub) (22)

Cummins, G. P. (Luton T), 1954 v L (2); 1955 v N (2), WG; 1956 v Y, Sp; 1958 v D, Pol, A; 1959 v Pol, Cz (2); 1960 v Se, Ch, WG, Se; 1961 v S (2) (19)

Cuneen, T. (Limerick), 1951 v N (1)

Cunningham, K. (Wimbledon), 1996 v CzR, P, Cro, Ho (sub), US, Bol; 1997 v Ic (sub), W, R, Lie; 1998 v Li, Ic, Li, Bel (2), CzR; 1999 v Cro, Ma, Y, Para, Se, Ni, Mac; 2000 v Y, Cro, Ma, Mac, T (2), CzR, Gr (31)

Curtis, D. P. (Shelbourne), 1957 v D, WG; (with Bristol C), 1957 v E (2); 1958 v D, Pol, A; (with Ipswich T), 1959 v Pol; 1960 v Se, Ch, WG, Se; 1961 v N, S; 1962 v A; 1963 v Ic; (with Exeter C), 1964 v A (17)

Cusack, S. (Limerick), 1953 v F (1)

Daish, L. S. (Cambridge U), 1992 v W, Sw (sub); (with Coventry C), 1996 v CzR (sub), Cro, M (5)

Daly, G. A. (Manchester U), 1973 v Pol (sub), N; 1974 v Br (sub), U (sub); 1975 v Sw (sub), WG; 1977 v E, T, F; (with Derby Co), F, Bul; 1978 v Bul, T, D; 1979 v Ni, E, D, Bul; 1980 v Ni, E, Cy, Sw, Arg; (with Coventry C), 1981 v WG'B', Ho, Bel, Cy, W, Bel, Cz, Pol (sub); 1982 v Alg, Ch, Br, Tr; 1983 v Ho, Sp (sub); 1984 v Is (sub), Ma; (with Birmingham C), 1985 v M (sub), N, Sp, Sw; 1986 v Sw; (with Shrewsbury T), U, Ic (sub), Cz (sub); 1987 v S (sub) (48)

Daly, J. (Shamrock R), 1932 v Ho; 1935 v Sw (2)

Daly, M. (Wolverhampton W), 1978 v T, Pol (2)

Daly, P. (Shamrock R), 1950 v Fi (sub) (1)

Davis, T. L. (Oldham Ath), 1937 v G, H; (with Tranmere R), 1938 v Cz, Pol (4)

Deacy, E. (Aston Villa), 1982 v Alg (sub), Ch, Br, Tr (4)

Delap, R. J. (Derby Co), 1998 v CzR (sub), Arg (sub), M (sub); 2000 v T (2), Gr (sub) (6)

De Mange, K. J. P. P. (Liverpool), 1987 v Br (sub); (with Hull C), 1989 v Tun (sub) (2)

Dempsey, J. T. (Fulham), 1967 v Sp, Cz; 1968 v Cz, Pol; 1969 v Pol, A, D; (with Chelsea), 1969 v Cz, D; 1970 v H, WG; 1971 v Pol, Se (2), I; 1972 v Ir, Ec, Ch, P (19)

Dennehy, J. (Cork Hibernians), 1972 v Ec (sub), Ch; (with Nottingham F), 1973 v USSR (sub), Pol, F, N; 1974 v Pol (sub); 1975 v T (sub), WG (sub); (with Walsall), 1976 v Pol (sub); 1977 v Pol (sub) (11)

Desmond, P. (Middlesbrough), 1950 v Fi, E, Fi, Se (4)

Devine, J. (Arsenal), 1980 v Cz, Ni; 1981 v WG'B', Cz; 1982 v Ho, Alg; 1983 v Sp, Ma; (with Norwich C), 1984 v Ic, Ho, Is; 1985 v USSR, N (13)

Doherty, G. M. T. (Luton T), 2000 v Gr (sub); (with Tottenham H), US, S.Af (sub) (3)

Donnelly, J. (Dundalk), 1935 v H, Sw, G; 1936 v Ho, Sw, H, L; 1937 v G, H; 1938 v N (10)

Donnelly, T. (Drumcondra), 1938 v N; (Shamrock R), 1939 v Sw (2)

Donovan, D. C. (Everton), 1955 v N, Ho, N, WG; 1957 v E (5)

Donovan, T. (Aston Villa), 1980 v Cz; 1981 v WG'B'(sub) (2)

Dowdall, C. (Fordsons), 1928 v Bel; (with Barnsley), 1929 v Bel; (with Cork), 1931 v Sp (3)

Doyle, C. (Shelbourne), 1959 v Cz (1)

Doyle, D. (Shamrock R), 1926 v I (1)

Doyle, L. (Dolphin), 1932 v Sp (1)

Duff, D. A. (Blackburn R), 1998 v CzR, M; 1999 v Cro, Ma, Y, Para, Se (sub), Ni, Mac; 2000 v Cro, Ma (sub), T (sub + sub), S (sub) (14)

Duffy, B. (Shamrock R), 1950 v Bel (1)

Duggan, H. A. (Leeds U), 1927 v I; 1930 v Bel; 1936 v H, L; (with Newport Co), 1938 v N (5)

Dunne, A. P. (Manchester U), 1962 v A; 1963 v Ic, S; 1964 v A, Sp, Pol, N, E; 1965 v Pol, Sp; 1966 v Sp (2), A, Bel; 1967 v Sp, T, Sp; 1969 v Pol, D, H; 1970 v H; 1971 v Se, I, A; (with Bolton W), 1974 v Br (sub), U, Ch; 1975 v T, Sw, USSR, Sw, WG; 1976 v T (33)

Dunne, J. (Sheffield U), 1930 v Bel; (with Arsenal), 1936 v Sw, H, L; (with Southampton), 1937 v Sw, F; (with Shamrock R), 1938 v N (2), Cz, Pol; 1939 v Sw, Pol, H (2), G (15)

Dunne, J. C. (Fulham), 1971 v A (1)

Dunne, L. (Manchester C), 1935 v Sw, G (2)

Dunne, P. A. J. (Manchester U), 1965 v Sp; 1966 v Sp (2), WG; 1967 v T (5)

Dunne, R. P. (Everton), 2000 v Gr, S (sub), M (3)

Dunne, S. (Luton T), 1953 v F, A; 1954 v F, L; 1956 v Sp, Ho; 1957 v D, WG, E; 1958 v D, Pol, A; 1959 v Pol; 1960 v WG, Se (15)

Dunne, T. (St Patrick's Ath), 1956 v Ho; 1957 v D, WG (3)

Dunning, P. (Shelbourne), 1971 v Se, I (2)

Dunphy, E. M. (York C), 1966 v Sp; (with Millwall), 1966 v WG; 1967 v T, Sp, T, Cz; 1968 v Cz, Pol; 1969 v Pol, A, D (2), H; 1970 v D, H, Pol, WG (sub); 1971 v Pol, Se (2), I (2), A (23)

Dwyer, N. M. (West Ham U), 1960 v Se, Ch, WG, Se; (with Swansea T), 1961 v W, N, S (2); 1962 v Cz (2); 1964 v Pol (sub), N, E; 1965 v Pol (14)

Eccles, P. (Shamrock R), 1986 v U (sub) (1)

Egan, R. (Dundalk), 1929 v Bel (1)

Eglington, T. J. (Shamrock R), 1946 v P, Sp; (with Everton), 1947 v E, Sp, P; 1948 v P; 1949 v Sw, P, Se; 1951 v N, Arg; 1952 v WG (2), A, Sp; 1953 v F, A; 1954 v F, L, F; 1955 v N, Ho, WG; 1956 v Sp (24)

Ellis, P. (Bohemians), 1935 v Sw, G; 1936 v Ho, Sw, L; 1937 v G, H (7)

Evans, M. J. (Southampton), 1998 v R (sub) (1)

Fagan, E. (Shamrock R), 1973 v N (sub) (1)

Fagan, F. (Manchester C), 1955 v N; 1960 v Se; (with Derby Co), 1960 v Ch, WG, Se; 1961 v W, N, S (8)

Fagan, J. (Shamrock R), 1926 v I (1)

Fairclough, M. (Dundalk), 1982 v Ch (sub), Tr (sub) (2)

Fallon, S. (Celtic), 1951 v N; 1952 v WG (2), A, Sp; 1953 v F; 1955 v N, WG (8)

Fallon, W. J. (Notts Co), 1935 v H; 1936 v H; 1937 v H, Sw, F; 1939 v Sw, Pol; (with Sheffield W), 1939 v H, G (9)

Farquharson, T. G. (Cardiff C), 1929 v Bel; 1930 v Bel; 1931 v Sp; 1932 v Sp (4)

Farrell, P. (Hibernian), 1937 v Sw, F (2)

Farrell, P. D. (Shamrock R), 1946 v P, Sp; (with Everton), 1947 v Sp, P; 1948 v P, Sp; 1949 v Sw, P (sub), Sp; 1950 v E, Fi, Se; 1951 v Arg, N; 1952 v WG (2), A, Sp; 1953 v F, A; 1954 v F (2); 1955 v N, Ho, WG; 1956 v Y, Sp; 1957 v E (28)

Farrelly, G. (Aston Villa), 1996 v P, US, Bol; (with Everton), 1998 v CzR, M; (with Bolton W), 2000 v US (6)

Feenan, J. J. (Sunderland), 1937 v Sw, F (2)

Finnan, S. (Fulham), 2000 v Gr, S (2)

Finucane, A. (Limerick), 1967 v T, Cz; 1969 v Cz, D, H; 1970 v S, Cz; 1971 v Se, I (1+1 sub); 1972 v A (11)

Fitzgerald, F. J. (Waterford), 1955 v Ho; 1956 v Ho (2)

Fitzgerald, P. J. (Leeds U), 1961 v W, N, S; (with Chester), 1962 v Cz (2) (5)

Fitzpatrick, K. (Limerick), 1970 v Cz (1)

Fitzsimons, A. G. (Middlesbrough), 1950 v Fi, Bel; 1952 v WG (2), A, Sp; 1953 v F, A; 1954 v F, L, F; 1955 v Ho, N, WG; 1956 v Y, Sp, Ho; 1957 v D, WG, E (2); 1958 v D, Pol, A; 1959 v Pol; (with Lincoln C), 1959 v Cz (26)

Fleming, C. (Middlesbrough), 1996 v CzR (sub), P, Cro (sub), Ho (sub), US (sub), M, Bol; 1997 v Lie (sub); 1998 v R (sub), M (10)

Flood, J. J. (Shamrock R), 1926 v I; 1929 v Bel; 1930 v Bel; 1931 v Sp; 1932 v Sp (5)

Fogarty, A. (Sunderland), 1960 v WG, Se; 1961 v S; 1962 v Cz (2); 1963 v Ic (2), S (sub); 1964 v A (2); (with Hartlepools U), Sp (11)

Foley, D. J. (Watford), 2000 v S (sub), M (sub), US, S.Af (4)

Foley, J. (Cork), 1934 v Bel, Ho; (with Celtic), 1935 v H, Sw, G; 1937 v G, H (7)

Foley, M. (Shelbourne), 1926 v I (1)

Foley, T. C. (Northampton T), 1964 v Sp, Pol, N; 1965 v Pol, Bel; 1966 v Sp (2), WG; 1967 v Cz (9)

Foy, T. (Shamrock R), 1938 v N; 1939 v H (2)

Fullam, J. (Preston NE), 1961 v N; (with Shamrock R), 1964 v Sp, Pol, N; 1966 v A, Bel; 1968 v Pol; 1969 v Pol, A, D; 1970 v Cz (sub) (11)

Fullam, R. (Shamrock R), 1926 v I; 1927 v I (2)

Gallagher, C. (Celtic), 1967 v T, Cz (2)

Gallagher, M. (Hibernian), 1954 v L (1)

Gallagher, P. (Falkirk), 1932 v Sp (1)

Galvin, A. (Tottenham H), 1983 v Ho, Ma; 1984 v Ho (sub), Is (sub); 1985 v M, USSR, N, D, I, N, Sp; 1986 v U, Ic, Cz; 1987 v Bel (2), S, Bul, L; (with Sheffield W), 1988 v L, Bul, R, Pol, N, E, USSR, Ho; 1989 v Sp; (with Swindon T), 1990 v WG (29)

Gannon, E. (Notts Co), 1949 v Sw; (with Sheffield W), 1949 v Bel, P, Se, Sp; 1950 v Fi; 1951 v N; 1952 v WG, A; 1954 v L, F; 1955 v N; (with Shelbourne), 1955 v N, WG (14)

Gannon, M. (Shelbourne), 1972 v A (1)

Gaskins, P. (Shamrock R), 1934 v Bel, Ho; 1935 v H, Sw, G; (with St James' Gate), 1938 v Cz, Pol (7)

Gavin, J. T. (Norwich C), 1950 v Fi (2); 1953 v F; 1954 v L; (with Tottenham H), 1955 v Ho, WG; (with Norwich C), 1957 v D (7)

Geoghegan, M. (St James' Gate), 1937 v G; 1938 v N (2)

Gibbons, A. (St Patrick's Ath), 1952 v WG; 1954 v L; 1956 v Y, Sp (4)

Gilbert, R. (Shamrock R), 1966 v WG (1)

Giles, C. (Doncaster R), 1951 v N (1)

Giles, M. J. (Manchester U), 1960 v Se, Ch; 1961 v W, N, S (2); 1962 v Cz (2), A; 1963 v Ic, S; (with Leeds U), 1964 v A (2), Sp (2), Pol, N, E; 1965 v Sp; 1966 v Sp (2), A, Bel; 1967 v Sp, T (2); 1969 v A, D, Cz; 1970 v S, Pol, WG; 1971 v I; 1973 v F, USSR; 1974 v Br, U, Ch; 1975 v USSR, T, Sw, USSR, Sw; (with WBA), 1976 v T; 1977 v E, T, F (2), Pol, Bul; (with Shamrock R), 1978 v Bul, T, Pol, N, D; 1979 v Ni, D, Bul, WG (59)

Given, S. J. J. (Blackburn R), 1996 v Ru, CzR, P, Cro, Ho, US, Bol; 1997 v Lie (2); (with Newcastle U), 1998 v Li, Ic, Li, Bel (2), CzR, Arg, M; 1999 v Cro, Ma, Y, Para, Se, Ni; 2000 v Gr, S.Af (25)

Givens, D. J. (Manchester U), 1969 v D, H; 1970 v S, Cz, D, H; (with Luton T), 1970 v Pol, WG; 1971 v Se, I (2), A; 1972 v Ir, Ec, P; (with QPR), 1973 v F, USSR, Pol, F, N; 1974 v Pol, Br, U, Ch; 1975 v USSR, T, Sw, USSR, Sw, WG; 1976 v T, N, Pol; 1977 v E, T, F (2), Sp, Bul; 1978 v Bul, N, D; (with Birmingham C), 1979 v Ni (sub), E, D, Bul, WG; 1980 v US (sub), Ni (sub), Sw, Arg; 1981 v Ho, Bel, Cy (sub), W; (with Neuchatel X), 1982 v F (sub) (56)

Glen, W. (Shamrock R), 1927 v I; 1929 v Bel; 1930 v Bel; 1932 v Sp; 1936 v Ho, Sw, H, L (8)

Glynn, D. (Drumcondra), 1952 v WG; 1955 v N (2)

Godwin, T. F. (Shamrock R), 1949 v P, Se, Sp; 1950 v Fi, E; (with Leicester C), 1950 v Fi, Se, Bel; 1951 v N; (with Bournemouth), 1956 v Ho; 1957 v E; 1958 v D, Pol (13)

Golding, J. (Shamrock R), 1928 v Bel; 1930 v Bel (2)

Goodman, J. (Wimbledon), 1997 v W, Mac, R (sub), Lie (sub) (4)

Gorman, W. C. (Bury), 1936 v Sw, H, L; 1937 v G, H; 1938 v N, Cz, Pol; 1939 v Sw, Pol (with Brentford) H; 1947 v E, P (13)

Grace, J. (Drumcondra), 1926 v I (1)

Grealish, A. (Orient), 1976 v N, Pol; 1978 v N, D; 1979 v Ni, E, WG; (with Luton T), 1980 v W, Cz, Bul, US, Ni, E, Cy, Sw, Arg; 1981 v WG'B', Ho, Bel, F, Cy, W, Bel, Pol; (with Brighton & HA), 1982 v Ho, Alg, Ch, Br, Tr; 1983 v Ho, Sp, Ic, Sp; 1984 v Ic, Ho; (with WBA), Pol, Chn; 1985 v M, USSR, N, D, Sp (sub), Sw; 1986 v USSR, D (45)

Gregg, E. (Bohemians), 1978 v Pol, D (sub); 1979 v E (sub), D, Bul, WG; 1980 v W, Cz (8)

Griffith, R. (Walsall), 1935 v H (1)

Grimes, A. A. (Manchester U), 1978 v T, Pol, N (sub); 1980 v Bul, US, Ni, E, Cy; 1981 v WG'B' (sub), Cz, Pol; 1982 v Alg; 1983 v Sp (2); (with Coventry C), 1984 v Pol, Is; (with Luton T), 1988 v L, R (18)

Hale, A. (Aston Villa), 1962 v A; (with Doncaster R), 1963 v Ic; 1964 v Sp (2); (with Waterford), 1967 v Sp; 1968 v Pol (sub); 1969 v Pol, A, D; 1970 v S, Cz; 1971 v Pol (sub); 1972 v A (sub); 1974 v Pol (sub) (14)

Hamilton, T. (Shamrock R), 1959 v Cz (2) (2)

Hand, E. K. (Portsmouth), 1969 v Cz (sub); 1970 v Pol, WG; 1971 v Pol, A; 1973 v USSR, F, USSR, Pol, F; 1974 v Pol, Br, U, Ch; 1975 v T, Sw, USSR, Sw, WG; 1976 v T (20)

Harrington, M. (Cork), 1936 v Ho, Sw, H, L; 1938 v Pol (sub) (5)

Harte, I. P. (Leeds U), 1996 v Cro (sub), Ho, M, Bol; 1997 v Lie, Mac, Ic (sub), W, Mac (sub), R, Lie; 1998 v Li, Ic, Li, Bel (2), Arg, M; 1999 v Para; 2000 v Cro (sub), Ma (sub), CzR (22)

Hartnett, J. B. (Middlesbrough), 1949 v Sp; 1954 v L (2)

Haverty, J. (Arsenal), 1956 v Ho; 1957 v D, WG, E (2); 1958 v D, Pol, A; 1959 v Pol; 1960 v Se, Ch; 1961 v W, N, S (2); (with Blackburn R), 1962 v Cz (2); (with Millwall), 1963 v S; 1964 v A, Sp, Pol, N, E; (with Celtic), 1965 v Pol; (with Bristol R), 1965 v Sp; (with Shelbourne), 1966 v Sp (2), WG, A, Bel; 1967 v T, Sp (32)

Hayes, A. W. P. (Southampton), 1979 v D (1)

Hayes, W. E. (Huddersfield T), 1947 v E, P (2)

Hayes, W. J. (Limerick), 1949 v Bel (1)

Healey, B. (Cardiff C), 1977 v Pol; 1980 v E (sub) (2)

Heighway, S. D. (Liverpool), 1971 v Pol, Se (2), I, A; 1973 v USSR; 1975 v USSR, T, USSR, WG; 1976 v T, N; 1977 v T, E, F (2), Bul; 1978 v Bul, N, D; 1979 v Ni, Bul; 1980 v Bul, US, Ni, E, Cy, Arg; 1981 v Bel, F, Cy, W, Bel; (with Minnesota K), 1982 v Ho (34)

Henderson, B. (Drumcondra), 1948 v P, Sp (2)

Hennessy, J. (Shelbourne), 1965 v Pol, Bel, Sp; 1966 v WG; (with St Patrick's Ath), 1969 v A (5)

Herrick, J. (Cork Hibernians), 1972 v A, Ch (sub); (with Shamrock R), 1973 v F (sub) (3)

Higgins, J. (Birmingham C), 1951 v Arg (1)

Holland, M. R. (Ipswich T), 2000 v Mac (sub), M, US, S.Af (4)

Holmes, J. (Coventry C), 1971 v A (sub); 1973 v F, USSR, Pol, F, N; 1974 v Pol, Br; 1975 v USSR, Sw; 1976 v T, N, Pol;

1977 v E, T, F, Sp; (with Tottenham H), F, Pol, Bul; 1978 v Bul, T, Pol, N, D; 1979 v Ni, E, D, Bul; (with Vancouver W), 1981 v W (30)

Horlacher, A. F. (Bohemians), 1930 v Bel; 1932 v Sp, Ho; 1934 v Ho (sub); 1935 v H; 1936 v Ho, Sw (7)

Houghton, R. J. (Oxford U), 1986 v W, U, Ic, Cz; 1987 v Bel (2), S (2), Pol, L; 1988 v L, Bul; (with Liverpool), Is, Y, N, E, USSR, Ho; 1989 v Ni, Tun, Sp, F, H, Sp, Ma, H; 1990 v Ni, Ma, Fi, E, Eg, Ho, R, I; 1991 v Mor, T, E (2), Pol, Ch, US; 1992 v H, Alb, US, I, P; (with Aston Villa), 1993 v D, Sp, Ni, D, Alb, La, Li; 1994 v Li, Sp, Ni, Bol, G (sub), I, M, N, Ho; (with C Palace), 1995 v P, A; 1996 v A, CzR; 1997 v Lie, R, Lie; (with Reading), 1998 v Li, R, Bel (1 + sub) (73)

Howlett, G. (Brighton & HA), 1984 v Chn (sub) (1)

Hoy, M. (Dundalk), 1938 v N; 1939 v Sw, Pol, H (2), G (6)

Hughton, C. (Tottenham H), 1980 v US, E, Sw, Arg; 1981 v Ho, Bel, F, Cy, W, Bel, Pol; 1982 v F; 1983 v Ho, Sp, Ma, Sp; 1984 v Ic, Ho, Ma; 1985 v M (sub), USSR, N, I, Is, E, Sp; 1986 v Sw, USSR, U, Ic; 1987 v Bel, Bul; 1988 v Is, Y, Pol, N, E, USSR, Ho; 1989 v Ni, F, H, Sp, Ma, H; 1990 v W (sub), USSR (sub), Fi, T (sub), Ma; 1991 v T; (with West Ham U), Ch; 1992 v T (53)

Hurley, C. J. (Millwall), 1957 v E; (with Sunderland), 1958 v D, Pol, A; 1959 v Cz (2); 1960 v Se, Ch, W, Se; 1961 v W, N, S (2); 1962 v Cz (2), A; 1963 v Ic (2), S; 1964 v A, Sp (2), Pol, N; 1965 v Sp; 1966 v WG, A, Bel; 1967 v T, Sp, T, Cz; 1968 v Cz, Pol; 1969 v Pol, D, Cz, (with Bolton W), H (40)

Hutchinson, F. (Drumcondra), 1935 v Sw, G (2)

Irwin, D. J. (Manchester U), 1991 v Mor, T, W, E, Pol, US; 1992 v H, Pol, W, US, Alb, US (sub), I; 1993 v La, D, Sp, Ni, D, Alb, La, Li; 1994 v Li, Sp, Ni, Bol, G, I, M; 1995 v La, Lie, Ni, E, N, P, Lie, A; 1996 v A, P, Ho, CzR; 1997 v Lie, Mac, Ic, Mac, R; 1998 v Li, Bel, Arg (sub); 1999 v Cro, Y, Para, Mac; 2000 v Y, Mac, T (2) (56)

Jordan, D. (Wolverhampton W), 1937 v Sw, F (2)

Jordan, M. (Bohemians), 1934 v Ho; 1938 v N (2)

Kavanagh, G. A. (Stoke C), 1998 v CzR (sub); 1999 v Se (sub), Ni (sub) (3)

Kavanagh, P. J. (Celtic), 1931 v Sp; 1932 v Sp (2)

Keane, R. D. (Wolverhampton W), 1998 v CzR (sub), Arg, M; 1999 v Cro, Ma, Para, Se (sub), Ni, Mac; (with Coventry C), 2000 v Y, Ma, Mac, T, CzR, Gr, S, M, S.Af (sub) (18)

Keane, R. M. (Nottingham F), 1991 v Ch; 1992 v H, Pol, W, Sw, Alb, US; 1993 v La, D, Sp, Ni, D, Alb, La, Li; (with Manchester U), 1994 v Li, Sp, Ni, Bol, G, CzR (sub), I, M, N, Ho; 1995 v Ni (2); 1996 v A, Ru; 1997 v Ic, W, Mac, R, Lie; 1998 v Li, Li; 1999 v Cro, Ma, Y, Para; 2000 v Y, T (2), CzR (46)

Keane, T. R. (Swansea T), 1949 v Sw, P, Se, Sp (4)

Kearin, M. (Shamrock R), 1972 v A (1)

Kearns, F. T. (West Ham U), 1954 v L (1)

Kearns, M. (Oxford U), 1971 v Pol (sub); (with Walsall), 1974 v Pol (sub), U, Ch; 1976 v N, Pol; 1977 v E, T, F (2), Sp, Bul; 1978 v N, D; 1979 v Ni, E; (with Wolverhampton W), 1980 v US, Ni (18)

Kelly, A. T. (Sheffield U), 1993 v W (sub); 1994 v Ru (sub), G; 1995 v La, Ni, E, Ni, P, Lie, A; 1996 v A, La, P, Ho; 1997 v Mac, Ic, Mac, R (sub); 1999 v Para (sub), Mac; (with Blackburn R), 2000 v Y, Cro, Ma, Mac, T, CzR, S, US (30)

Kelly, D. T. (Walsall), 1988 v Is, R, Y; (with West Ham U), 1989 v Tun (sub); (with Leicester C), 1990 v USSR, Ma; 1991 v Mor, W (sub), Ch, US; 1992 v H; (with Newcastle U), I (sub), P; 1993 v Sp (sub), Ni; (with Wolverhampton W), 1994 v Ru, N (sub); 1995 v E, Ni; (with Sunderland), 1996 v La (sub); 1997 v Ic, W (sub), Mac (sub); (with Tranmere R), 1998 v Li (sub), R, Bel (sub) (26)

Kelly, G. (Leeds U), 1994 v Ru, Ho, Bol (sub), G (sub), CzR, N, Ho; 1995 v La, Lie, Ni (2), P, Lie, A; 1996 v A, La, P, Ho; 1997 v W (sub), R, Lie; 1998 v Ic, Li, Bel (2), CzR, Arg, M; 2000 v Cro, Mac, CzR (31)

Kelly, J. (Derry C), 1932 v Ho; 1934 v Bel; 1936 v Sw, L (4)

Kelly, J. A. (Drumcondra), 1957 v WG, E; (with Preston NE), 1962 v A; 1963 v Ic (2), S; 1964 v A (2), Sp (2), Pol; 1965 v Bel; 1966 v A, Bel; 1967 v Sp (2), T, Cz; 1968 v Pol, Cz; 1969 v Pol, A, D, Cz, D, H; 1970 v S, D, H, Pol, WG; 1971 v Pol, Se (2), I (2), A; 1972 v Ir, Ec, Ch, P; 1973 v USSR, F, USSR, Pol, F, N (47)

Kelly, J. P. V. (Wolverhampton W), 1961 v W, N, S; 1962 v Cz (2) (5)

Kelly, M. J. (Portsmouth), 1988 v Y, Pol (sub); 1989 v Tun; 1991 v Mor (4)

Kelly, N. (Nottingham F), 1954 v L (1)

Kendrick, J. (Everton), 1927 v I; (with Dolphin) 1934 v Bel, Ho; 1936 v Ho (4)

Kenna, J. J. (Blackburn R), 1995 v P (sub), Lie (sub), A (sub); 1996 v La, P, Ho, Ru (sub), CzR, P, Cro, Ho, US; 1997 v Lie, Mac, Ic, R (sub), Lie; 1998 v Li, Ic, R, Bel (1 + sub), CzR, Arg; 1999 v Cro (sub), Ma; 2000 v T (sub) (27)

Kennedy, M. J. (Liverpool), 1996 v A, La (sub), P, Ru, CzR, Cro, Ho (sub), US (sub), M, Bol (sub); 1997 v R, Lie; 1998 v Li, Ic (sub), R, Bel (2); (with Wimbledon), M (sub); 1999 v Ma (sub), Se, Ni, Mac; (with Manchester C), 2000 v Y, Ma, Mac, CzR, S, M, US (sub), S.Af (sub) (30)

Kennedy, M. F. (Portsmouth), 1986 v Ic, Cz (sub) (2)

Kennedy, W. (St James' Gate), 1932 v Ho; 1934 v Bel, Ho (3)

Keogh, J. (Shamrock R), 1966 v WG (sub) (1)

Keogh, S. (Shamrock R), 1959 v Pol (1)

Kernaghan, A. N. (Middlesbrough), 1993 v La, D (2), Alb, La, Li; 1994 v Li; (with Manchester C), Sp, Ni, Bol (sub), CzR; 1995 v Lie, E; 1996 v A, P (sub), Ho (sub), Ru, P, Cro (sub), Ho, US, Bol (22)

Kiely, D. L. (Charlton Ath), 2000 v T (sub + 1), Gr (sub), M (4)

Kiernan, F. W. (Shamrock R), 1951 v Arg, N; (with Southampton), 1952 v WG (2), A (5)

Kilbane, K. D. (WBA), 1998 v Ic, CzR (sub), Arg; 1999 v Se (sub), Mac (sub); 2000 v Y, Cro (sub), Ma, T (2); (with Sunderland), CzR, Gr, S, M (sub), US, S.Af (sub) (16)

Kinnear, J. P. (Tottenham H), 1967 v T; 1968 v Cz, Pol; 1969 v A; 1970 v Cz, D, H, Pol; 1971 v Se (sub), I; 1972 v Ir, Ec, Ch, P; 1973 v USSR, F; 1974 v Pol, Br, U, Ch; 1975 v USSR, T, Sw, USSR, WG; (with Brighton & HA), 1976 v T (sub) (26)

Kinsella, J. (Shelbourne), 1928 v Bel (1)

Kinsella, M. A. (Charlton Ath), 1998 v CzR, Arg; 1999 v Cro, Ma, Y, Para, Se, Ni, Mac; 2000 v Y, Cro, Ma, Mac, T, CzR, Gr (16)

Kinsella, O. (Shamrock R), 1932 v Ho; 1938 v N (2)

Kirkland, A. (Shamrock R), 1927 v I (1)

Lacey, W. (Shelbourne), 1927 v I; 1928 v Bel; 1930 v Bel (3)

Langan, D. (Derby Co), 1978 v T, N; 1980 v Sw, Arg; (with Birmingham C), 1981 v WG'B', Ho, Bel, F, Cy, W, Bel, Cz, Pol; 1982 v Ho, F; (with Oxford U), 1985 v N, Sp, Sw; 1986 v W, U; 1987 v Bel, S, Pol, Br (sub), L (sub); 1988 v L (26)

Lawler, J. F. (Fulham), 1953 v A; 1954 v L, F; 1955 v N, H, N, WG; 1956 v Y (8)

Lawlor, J. C. (Drumcondra), 1949 v Bel; (with Doncaster R), 1951 v N, Arg (3)

Lawlor, M. (Shamrock R), 1971 v Pol, Se (2), I (sub); 1973 v Pol (5)

Lawrenson, M. (Preston NE), 1977 v Pol; (with Brighton), 1978 v Bul, Pol, N (sub), D; 1979 v Ni, E; 1980 v E, Cy, Sw; 1981 v Ho, Bel, F, Cy, Pol; (with Liverpool), 1982 v Ho, F; 1983 v Ho, Sp, Ic, Ma, Sp; 1984 v Ic, Ho, Ma, Is; 1985 v USSR, N, D, I, E, N; 1986 v Sw, USSR, D; 1987 v Bel, S; 1988 v Bul, Is (39)

Leech, M. (Shamrock R), 1969 v Cz, D, H; 1972 v A, Ir, Ec, P; 1973 v USSR (sub) (8)

Lennon, C. (St James' Gate), 1935 v H, Sw, G (3)

Lennox, G. (Dolphin), 1931 v Sp; 1932 v Sp (2)

Lowry, D. (St Patrick's Ath), 1962 v A (sub) (1)

Lunn, R. (Dundalk), 1939 v Sw, Pol (2)

Lynch, J. (Cork Bohemians), 1934 v Bel (1)

McAlinden, J. (Portsmouth), 1946 v P, Sp (2)

McAteer, J. W. (Bolton W), 1994 v Ru, Ho (sub), Bol (sub), G, CzR (sub), I (sub), M (sub), N, Ho (sub); 1995 v La, Lie, Ni (2 sub), Lie; (with Liverpool), 1996 v La, P, Ho (sub), Ru; 1997 v Mac, Ic, W, Mac; 1998 v Ic (sub), Li, R; 1999 v Cro, Ma, Y; (with Blackburn R), Para, Se; 2000 v CzR (sub), S, M, US (sub), S.Af (35)

McCann, J. (Shamrock R), 1957 v WG (1)

McCarthy, J. (Bohemians), 1926 v I; 1928 v Bel; 1930 v Bel (3)

McCarthy, M. (Manchester C), 1984 v Pol, Chn; 1985 v M, D, I, Is, E, Sp, Sw; 1986 v Sw, USSR, W (sub), U, Ic, Cz; 1987 v S (2), Pol, Bul, Bel; (with Celtic), Br, L; 1988 v Bul, Is, R, Y, N, E, USSR, Ho; 1989 v Ni, Tun, Sp, F, H, Sp; (with Lyon), 1990 v WG, Ni; (with Millwall), W, USSR, Fi, T, E, Eg, Ho, R, I; 1991 v Mor, T, E, US; 1992 v H, T, Alb, (sub), US, I, P (57)

McCarthy, M. (Shamrock R), 1932 v Ho (1)

McConville, T. (Dundalk), 1972 v A; (with Waterford), 1973 v USSR, F, USSR, Pol, F (6)

McDonagh, Jacko (Shamrock R), 1984 v Pol (sub), Ma (sub); 1985 v M (sub) (3)

McDonagh, J. (Everton), 1981 v WG'B', W, Bel, Cz; (with Bolton W), 1982 v Ho, F, Ch, Br; 1983 v Ho, Sp, Ic, Ma, Sp; (with Notts Co), 1984 v Ic, Ho, Pol; 1985 v M, USSR, N, D, Sp, Sw; 1986 v Sw, USSR; (with Wichita Wings) D (25)

McEvoy, M. A. (Blackburn R), 1961 v S (2); 1963 v S; 1964 v A, Sp (2), Pol, N, E; 1965 v Pol, Bel, Sp; 1966 v Sp (2); 1967 v Sp, T, Cz (17)

McGee, P. (QPR), 1978 v T, N (sub), D (sub); 1979 v Ni, E, D (sub), Bul (sub); 1980 v Cz, Bul; (with Preston NE), US, Ni, Cy, Sw, Arg; 1981 v Bel (sub) (15)

McGoldrick, E. J. (C Palace), 1992 v Sw, US, I, P (sub); 1993 v D, W, Ni (sub), D; (with Arsenal), 1994 v Ni, Ru, Ho, CzR; 1995 v La (sub), Lie, E (15)

McGowan, D. (West Ham U), 1949 v P, Se, Sp (3)

McGowan, J. (Cork U), 1947 v Sp (1)

McGrath, M. (Blackburn R), 1958 v A; 1959 v Pol, Cz (2); 1960 v Se, WG, Se; 1961 v W; 1962 v Cz (2); 1963 v S; 1964 v A (2), E; 1965 v Pol, Bel, Sp; 1966 v Sp; (with Bradford), 1966 v WG, A, Bel; 1967 v T (22)

McGrath, P. (Manchester U), 1985 v I (sub), Is, E, N (sub), Sw (sub); 1986 v Sw (sub), D, W, Ic, Cz; 1987 v Bel (2), S (2), Pol, Bul, Br; 1988 v L, Bul, Y, Pol, N, E, Ho; 1989 v Ni, F, H, Sp, Ma, H; (with Aston Villa), 1990 v WG, Ma, USSR, Fi, T, E, Eg, Ho, R, I; 1991 v E (2), W, Pol, Ch (sub), US; 1992 v Pol, T, Sw, US, Alb, US, I, P; 1993 v La, Sp, Ni, D, La, Li; 1994 v Sp, Ni, G, CzR, I, M, N, Ho; 1995 v La, Ni, E, Ni, P, Lie, A; 1996 v A, La, P, Ho, Ru, CzR; (with Derby Co), 1997 v W (83)

McGuire, W. (Bohemians), 1936 v Ho (1)

McKenzie, G. (Southend U), 1938 v N (2), Cz, Pol; 1939 v Sw, Pol, H (2), G (9)

Mackey, G. (Shamrock R), 1957 v D, WG, E (3)

McLoughlin, A. F. (Swindon T), 1990 v Ma, E (sub), Eg (sub); 1991 v Mor (sub), E (sub); (with Southampton), W, Ch (sub); 1992 v H (sub), W (sub); (with Portsmouth), US (1 + sub), I (sub), P; 1993 v W; 1994 v Ni (sub), Ru, Ho (sub); 1995 v Lie (sub); 1996 v P, Cro, Ho, US, M, Bol (sub); 1997 v Lie, Mac, Ic, W, Mac; 1998 v Li (sub), Ic, Li, R, Bel, CzR (sub); 1999 v Y, Para (sub), Se, Ni (sub); 2000 v Cro, Ma (sub), Mac (42)

McLoughlin, F. (Fordsons), 1930 v Bel; (with Cork), 1932 v Sp (2)

McMillan, W. (Belfast Celtic), 1946 v P, Sp (2)

McNally, J. B. (Luton T), 1959 v Cz; 1961 v S; 1963 v Ic (3)

McPhail, S. (Leeds U), 2000 v S, US, S.Af (3)

Macken, A. (Derby Co), 1977 v Sp (1)

Madden, O. (Cork), 1936 v H (1)

Maguire, J. (Shamrock R), 1929 v Bel (1)

Mahon, A. J. (Tranmere R), 2000 v Gr (sub), S.Af (2)

Malone, G. (Shelbourne), 1949 v Bel (1)

Mancini, T. J. (QPR), 1974 v Pol, Br, U, Ch; (with Arsenal), 1975 v USSR (5)

Martin, C. (Bo'ness), 1927 v I (1)

Martin, C. J. (Glentoran), 1946 v P (sub), Sp; 1947 v E; (with Leeds U), 1947 v Sp; 1948 v P, Sp; (with Aston Villa), 1949 v Sw, Bel, P, Se, Sp; 1950 v Fi, E, Fi, Se, Bel; 1951 v Arg; 1952 v WG, A, Sp; 1954 v F (2), L; 1955 v N, Ho, N, WG; 1956 v Y, Sp, Ho (30)

Martin, M. P. (Bohemians), 1972 v A, Ir, Ec, Ch, P; 1973 v USSR; (with Manchester U), 1973 v USSR, Pol, F, N; 1974 v Pol, Br, U, Ch; 1975 v USSR, T, Sw, USSR, Sw, WG; (with WBA), 1976 v T, N, Pol; 1977 v E, T, F (2), Sp, Pol, Bul; (with Newcastle U), 1979 v D, Bul, WG; 1980 v W, Cz, Bul, US, Ni; 1981 v WG'B', F, Bel, Cz; 1982 v Ho, F, Alg, Ch, Br, Tr; 1983 v Ho, Sp, Ma, Sp (52)

Maybury, A. (Leeds U), 1998 v CzR; 1999 v Ni (2)

Meagan, M. K. (Everton), 1961 v S; 1962 v A; 1963 v Ic; 1964 v Sp; (with Huddersfield T), 1965 v Bel; 1966 v Sp (2), A, Bel; 1967 v Sp, T, Sp, T, Cz; 1968 v Cz, Pol; (with Drogheda), 1970 v S (17)

Meehan, P. (Drumcondra), 1934 v Ho (1)

Milligan, M. J. (Oldham Ath), 1992 v US (sub) (1)

Monahan, P. (Sligo R), 1935 v Sw, G (2)

Mooney, J. (Shamrock R), 1965 v Pol, Bel (2)

Moore, A. (Middlesbrough), 1996 v CzR, Cro (sub), Ho, M, Bol; 1997 v Lie (sub), Mac (sub), Ic (sub) (8)

Moore, P. (Shamrock R), 1931 v Sp; 1932 v Ho; (with Aberdeen), 1934 v Bel, Ho; 1935 v H, G; (with Shamrock R), 1936 v Ho; 1937 v G, H (9)

Moran, K. (Manchester U), 1980 v Sw, Arg; 1981 v WG'B', Bel, F, Cy, W (sub); Bel, Cz, Pol; 1982 v F, Alg; 1983 v Ic; 1984 v Ic, Ho, Ma, Is; 1985 v M; 1986 v D, Ic, Cz; 1987 v Bel (2), S (2), Pol, Bul, Br, L; 1988 v L, Bul, Is, R, Y, Pol, N, E, USSR, Ho; (with Sporting Gijon), 1989 v Ni, Sp, H, Sp, Ma, H; 1990 v Ni, Ma; (with Blackburn R), W, USSR (sub), Ma, E, Eg, Ho, R, I; 1991 v T (sub), W, E, Pol, Ch, US; 1992 v Pol, US; 1993 v D, Sp, Ni, Alb; 1994 v Li, Sp, Ho, Bol (71)

Moroney, T. (West Ham U), 1948 v Sp; 1949 v P, Se, Sp; 1950 v Fi, E, Fi, Bel; 1951 v N (2); 1952 v WG; (with Evergreen U), 1954 v F (12)

Morris, C. B. (Celtic), 1988 v Is, R, Y, Pol, N, E, USSR, Ho; 1989 v Ni, Tun, Sp, F, H (1+1 sub); 1990 v WG, Ni, Ma (sub), W, USSR, Fi (sub), T, E, Eg, Ho, R, I; 1991 v E; 1992 v H (sub), Pol, W, Sw, US (2), P; (with Middlesbrough), 1993 v W (35)

Moulson, C. (Lincoln C), 1936 v H, L; (with Notts Co), 1937 v H, Sw, F (5)

Moulson, G. B. (Lincoln C), 1948 v P, Sp; 1949 v Sw (3)

Mucklan, C. (Drogheda U), 1978 v Pol (1)

Muldoon, T. (Aston Villa), 1927 v I (1)

Mulligan, P. M. (Shamrock R), 1969 v Cz, D, H; 1970 v S, Cz, D; (with Chelsea), 1970 v H, Pol, WG; 1971 v Pol, Se, I; 1972 v A, Ir, Ec, Ch, P; (with C Palace), 1973 v F, USSR, Pol, F, N; 1974 v Pol, Br, U, Ch; 1975 v USSR, T, Sw, USSR, Sw; (with WBA), 1976 v T, Pol; 1977 v E, T, F (2), Pol, Bul; 1978 v Bul, N, D; 1979 v E, D, Bul (sub), WG; (with Shamrock R), 1980 v W, Cz, Bul, US (sub) (50)

Munroe, L. (Shamrock R), 1954 v L (1)

Murphy, A. (Clyde), 1956 v Y (1)

Murphy, B. (Bohemians), 1986 v U (1)

Murphy, J. (C Palace), 1980 v W, US, Cy (3)

Murray, T. (Dundalk), 1950 v Bel (1)

Newman, W. (Shelbourne), 1969 v D (1)

Nolan, R. (Shamrock R), 1957 v D, WG, E; 1958 v Pol; 1960 v Ch, WG, Se; 1962 v Cz (2); 1963 v Ic (10)

O'Brien, F. (Philadelphia F), 1980 v Cz, E, Cy (sub) (3)

O'Brien, L. (Shamrock R), 1986 v U; (with Manchester U), 1987 v Br; 1988 v Is (sub), R (sub), Y (sub), Pol (sub); 1989 v Tun; (with Newcastle U), Sp (sub); 1992 v Sw (sub); 1993 v W; (with Tranmere R), 1994 v Ru; 1996 v Cro, Ho, US, Bol; 1997 v Mac (sub) (16)

O'Brien, M. T. (Derby Co), 1927 v I; (with Walsall), 1929 v Bel; (with Norwich C), 1930 v Bel; (with Watford), 1932 v Ho (4)

O'Brien, R. (Notts Co), 1976 v N, Pol; 1977 v Sp, Pol; 1980 v Arg (sub) (5)

O'Byrne, L. B. (Shamrock R), 1949 v Bel (1)

O'Callaghan, B. R. (Stoke C), 1979 v WG (sub); 1980 v W, US; 1981 v W; 1982 v Br, Tr (6)

O'Callaghan, K. (Ipswich T), 1981 v WG'B', Cz, Pol; 1982 v Alg, Ch, Br, Tr (sub); 1983 v Sp, Ic (sub), Ma (sub), Sp (sub); 1984 v Ic, Ho, Ma; 1985 v M (sub), N (sub), D (sub); (with Portsmouth), E (sub); 1986 v Sw (sub), USSR (sub); 1987 v Br (21)

O'Connell, A. (Dundalk), 1967 v Sp; (with Bohemians), 1971 v Pol (sub) (2)

O'Connor, T. (Shamrock R), 1950 v Fi, E, Fi, Se (4)

O'Connor, T. (Fulham), 1968 v Cz; (with Dundalk), 1972 v A, Ir (sub), Ec (sub), Ch; (with Bohemians), 1973 v F (sub), Pol (sub) (7)

O'Driscoll, J. F. (Swansea T), 1949 v Sw, Bel, Se (3)

O'Driscoll, S. (Fulham), 1982 v Ch, Br, Tr (sub) (3)

O'Farrell, F. (West Ham U), 1952 v A; 1953 v A; 1954 v F; 1955 v Ho, N; 1956 v Y, Ho; (with Preston NE), 1958 v D; 1959 v Cz (9)

O'Flanagan, K. P. (Bohemians), 1938 v N, Cz, Pol; 1939 v Pol, H (2), G; (with Arsenal), 1947 v E, Sp, P (10)

O'Flanagan, M. (Bohemians), 1947 v E (1)

O'Hanlon, K. G. (Rotherham U), 1988 v Is (1)

O'Kane, P. (Bohemians), 1935 v H, Sw, G (3)

O'Keefe, E. (Everton), 1981 v W; (with Port Vale), 1984 v Chn; 1985 v M, USSR (sub), E (5)

O'Keefe, J. (Cork), 1934 v Bel; (with Waterford), 1938 v Cz, Pol (3)

O'Leary, D. (Arsenal), 1977 v E, F (2), Sp, Bul; 1978 v Bul, N, D; 1979 v E, Bul, WG; 1980 v W, Bul, Ni, E, Cy; 1981 v WG'B', Ho, Cz, Pol; 1982 v Ho, F; 1983 v Ho, Ic, Sp; 1984 v Pol, Is, Chn; 1985 v USSR, N, D, Is, E (sub), N, Sp, Sw; 1986 v Sw, USSR, D, W; 1989 v Sp, Ma, H; 1990 v WG, Ni (sub), Ma, W (sub), USSR, Fi, T, Ma, R (sub); 1991 v Mor, T, E (2), Pol, Ch; 1992 v H, Pol, T, W, Sw, US, Alb, I, P; 1993 v W (68)

O'Leary, P. (Shamrock R), 1980 v Bul, US, Ni, E (sub) Cz, Arg; 1981 v Ho (7)

O'Mahoney, M. T. (Bristol R), 1938 v Cz, Pol; 1939 v Sw, Pol, H, G (6)

O'Neill, F. S. (Shamrock R), 1962 v Cz (2); 1965 v Pol, Bel, Sp; 1966 v Sp (2), WG, A; 1967 v Sp, T, Sp, T; 1969 v Pol, A, D, Cz, D (sub), H (sub); 1972 v A (20)

O'Neill, J. (Everton), 1952 v Sp; 1953 v F, A; 1954 v F, L, F; 1955 v N, Ho, N, WG; 1956 v Y, Sp; 1957 v D; 1958 v A; 1959 v Pol, Cz (2) (17)

O'Neill, J. (Preston NE), 1961 v W (1)

O'Neill, K. P. (Norwich C), 1996 v P (sub), Cro, Ho (sub), US (sub), M, Bol; 1997 v Lie, Mac (1 + sub); 1999 v Cro, Y (sub); (with Middlesbrough), Ni (sub); 2000 v Mac (sub) (13)

O'Neill, W. (Dundalk), 1936 v Ho, Sw, H, L; 1937 v G, H, Sw, F; 1938 v N; 1939 v H, G (11)

O'Regan, K. (Brighton & HA), 1984 v Ma, Pol; 1985 v M, Sp (sub) (4)

O'Reilly, J. (Brideville), 1932 v Ho; (with Aberdeen), 1934 v Bel, Ho; (with Brideville), 1936 v Ho; Sw, H, L; (with St James' Gate), 1937 v G, H, Sw, F; 1938 v N (2), Cz, Pol; 1939 v Sw, Pol, H (2), G (20)

O'Reilly, J. (Cork U), 1946 v P, Sp (2)

Peyton, G. (Fulham), 1977 v Sp (sub); 1978 v Bul, T, Pol; 1979 v D, Bul, WG; 1980 v W, Cz, Bul, E, Cy, Sw, Arg; 1981 v Ho, Bel, F, Cy; 1982 v Tr; 1985 v M (sub); 1986 v W, Cz; (with Bournemouth), 1988 v L, Pol; 1989 v Ni, Tun; 1990 v USSR, Ma; 1991 v Ch; (with Everton) 1992 v US (2), I (sub), P (33)

Peyton, N. (Shamrock R), 1957 v WG; (with Leeds U), 1960 v WG, Se (sub); 1961 v W; 1963 v Ic, S (6)

Phelan, T. (Wimbledon), 1992 v H, Pol (sub), T, W, Sw, US, I (sub), P; (with Manchester C), 1993 v La (sub), D, Sp, Ni, Alb, La, Li; 1994 v Li, Sp, Ni, Ho, Bol, G, CzR, I, M, Ho; 1995 v E; 1996 v La; (with Chelsea), Ho, Ru, P, Cro, Ho, US, M (sub), Bol; (with Everton), 1997 v W, Mac; 1998 v R; (with Fulham), 2000 v S (sub), M, US, S.Af (42)

Quinn, B. S. (Coventry C), 2000 v Gr, M, US (sub), S.Af (sub) (4)

Quinn, N. J. (Arsenal), 1986 v Ic (sub), Cz; 1987 v Bul (sub), Br (sub); 1988 v L (sub), Bul (sub), Is, R (sub), Pol (sub), E (sub); 1989 v Tun (sub), Sp, H (sub); (with Manchester C), 1990 v USSR, Ma, Eg (sub), Ho, R, I; 1991 v Mor, T, E(2) W, Pol; 1992 v H, W (sub), US, Alb, US, I (sub), P; 1993 v La, D, Sp, Ni, D, Alb, La, Li; 1994 v Li, Sp, Ni; 1995 v La, Lie, Ni, E, Ni, P, Lie, A; 1996 v A, La, P, Ru, CzR, P (sub), Cro, Ho (sub), US; (with Sunderland), 1997 v Lie; 1998 v Li, Arg; 1999 v Ma, Y, Para, Se, Ni, Mac; 2000 v Y, Cro (sub), Ma, Mac, T, CzR, S, M, US (sub), S.Af (79)

Reid, C. (Brideville), 1931 v Sp (1)

Richardson, D. J. (Shamrock R), 1972 v A (sub); (with Gillingham), 1973 v N (sub); 1980 v Cz (3)

Rigby, A. (St James' Gate), 1935 v H, Sw, G (3)

Ringstead, A. (Sheffield U), 1951 v Arg, N; 1952 v WG (2), A, Sp; 1953 v A; 1954 v F; 1955 v N; 1956 v Y, Sp, Ho; 1957 v E (2); 1958 v D, Pol, A; 1959 v Pol, Cz (2) (20)

Robinson, J. (Bohemians), 1928 v Bel; (with Dolphin), 1931 v Sp (2)

Robinson, M. (Brighton & HA), 1981 v WG'B', F, Cy, Bel, Pol; 1982 v Ho, F, Alg, Ch; 1983 v Ho, Sp, Ic, Ma; (with Liverpool), 1984 v Ic, Ho, Is; 1985 v USSR, N; (with QPR), N, Sp, Sw; 1986 v D (sub), W, Cz (24)

Roche, P. J. (Shelbourne), 1972 v A; (with Manchester U), 1975 v USSR, T, Sw, USSR, Sw, WG; 1976 v T (8)

Rogers, E. (Blackburn R), 1968 v Cz, Pol; 1969 v Pol, A, D, Cz, D, H; 1970 v S, D, H; 1971 v I (2), A; (with Charlton Ath), 1972 v Ir, Ec, Ch, P; 1973 v USSR (19)

Ryan, G. (Derby Co), 1978 v T; (with Brighton & HA), 1979 v E, WG; 1980 v W, Cy (sub), Sw, Arg (sub); 1981 v WG'B' (sub), F (sub), Pol (sub); 1982 v Br (sub), Ho (sub), Alg (sub), Ch (sub), Tr; 1984 v Pol, Chn; 1985 v M (18)

Ryan, R. A. (WBA), 1950 v Se, Bel; 1951 v N, Arg, N; 1952 v WG (2), A, Sp; 1953 v F, A; 1954 v F, L, F; 1955 v N; (with Derby Co), 1956 v Sp (16)

Savage, D. P. T. (Millwall), 1996 v P (sub), Cro (sub), US (sub), M, Bol (5)

Saward, P. (Millwall), 1954 v L; (with Aston Villa), 1957 v E (2); 1958 v D, Pol, A; 1959 v Pol, Cz; 1960 v Se, Ch, WG, Se; 1961 v W, N; (with Huddersfield T), 1961 v S; 1962 v A; 1963 v Ic (2) (18)

Scannell, T. (Southend U), 1954 v L (1)

Scully, P. J. (Arsenal), 1989 v Tun (sub) (1)

Sheedy, K. (Everton), 1984 v Ho (sub), Ma; 1985 v D, I, Is, Sw; 1986 v Sw, D; 1987 v S, Pol; 1988 v Is, R, Pol, E (sub); USSR; 1989 v Ni, Tun, H, Sp, Ma, H; 1990 v Ni, Ma, W (sub), USSR, Fi, T, E, Eg, Ho, R, I; 1991 v W, E, Pol, Ch, US; 1992 v H, Pol, T, W; (with Newcastle U), Sw (sub), Alb; 1993 v La, W (sub) (45)

Sheridan, J. J. (Leeds U), 1988 v R, Y, Pol, N (sub); 1989 v Sp; (with Sheffield W), 1990 v W, T (sub), Ma, I (sub); 1991 v Mor (sub), T, Ch, US (sub); 1992 v H; 1993 v La; 1994 v Sp (sub), Ho, Bol, G, CzR, I, M, N, Ho; 1995 v La, Lie, Ni, E, Ni, P, Lie, A; 1996 v A, Ho (34)

Slaven, B. (Middlesbrough), 1990 v W, Fi, T (sub), Ma; 1991 v W, Pol (sub); 1993 v W (7)

Sloan, J. W. (Arsenal), 1946 v P, Sp (2)

Smyth, M. (Shamrock R), 1969 v Pol (sub) (1)

Squires, J. (Shelbourne), 1934 v Ho (1)

Stapleton, F. (Arsenal), 1977 v T, F, Sp, Bul; 1978 v Bul, N, D; 1979 v Ni, E (sub), D, WG; 1980 v W, Bul, Ni, E, Cy; 1981 v WG'B', Ho, Bel, F, Cy, Bel, Cz, Pol; (with Manchester U), 1982 v Ho, F, Alg; 1983 v Ho, Sp, Ic, Ma, Sp; 1984 v Ic, Ho, Ma, Pol, Is, Chn; 1985 v N, D, I, Is, E, N, Sw; 1986 v Sw, USSR, D, U, Ic, Cz (sub); 1987 v Bel (2), S (2), Pol, Bul, L; (with Ajax), 1988 v L, Bul, R, Y, N, E, USSR, Ho; (with Le Havre), 1989 v F, Sp, Ma; (with Blackburn R), 1990 v WG, Ma (sub) (71)

Staunton, S. (Liverpool), 1989 v Tun, Sp (2), Ma, H; 1990 v WG, Ni, Ma, W, USSR, Fi, T, Ma, E, Eg, Ho, R, I; 1991 v Mor, T, E (2), W, Pol, Ch, US; (with Aston Villa), 1992 v Pol, T, Sw, US, Alb, US, I, P; 1993 v La, Sp, Ni, D, Alb, La, Li; 1994 v Li, Sp, Ho, Bol, G, CzR, I, M, N, Ho; 1995 v La, Lie, Ni, E, Ni, P, Lie, A; 1996 v La, P, Ru; 1997 v Lie, Mac (2), W, R, Lie; 1998 v Li, Ic, Li, Bel (2), Arg; (with Liverpool), 1999 v Cro, Ma, Y, Se; 2000 v Y, Cro, Ma, Mac, CzR (sub), Gr (84)

Stevenson, A. E. (Dolphin), 1932 v Ho; (with Everton), 1947 v E, Sp, P; 1948 v P, Sp; 1949 v Sw (7)

Strahan, F. (Shelbourne), 1964 v Pol, N, E; 1965 v Pol; 1966 v WG (5)

Sullivan, J. (Fordsons), 1928 v Bel (1)

Swan, M. M. G. (Drumcondra), 1960 v Se (sub) (1)

Synnott, N. (Shamrock R), 1978 v T, Pol; 1979 v Ni (3)

Taylor, T. (Waterford), 1959 v Pol (sub) (1)

Thomas, P. (Waterford), 1974 v Pol, Br (2)

Townsend, A. D. (Norwich C), 1989 v F, Sp (sub), Ma (sub), H; 1990 v WG (sub), Ni, Ma, W, USSR, Fi (sub), T, Ma (sub), E, Eg, Ho, R, I; (with Chelsea), 1991 v Mor, T, E (2), W, Pol, Ch, US; 1992 v Pol, W, US, Alb, US, I; 1993 v La, D, Sp, Ni, D, Alb, La, Li; (with Aston Villa), 1994 v Li, Ni, Ho, Bol, G, CzR, I, M, N, Ho; 1995 v La, Ni, E, Ni, P; 1996 v A, La, Ho, Ru, CzR, P; 1997 v Lie, Mac (2), Ic, R, Lie; 1998 v Li; (with Middlesbrough), Ic, Bel (2) (70)

Traynor, T. J. (Southampton), 1954 v L; 1962 v A; 1963 v Ic (2), S; 1964 v A (2), Sp (8)

Treacy, R. C. P. (WBA), 1966 v WG; 1967 v Sp, Cz; 1968 v Cz; (with Charlton Ath), 1968 v Pol; 1969 v Pol, Cz, D; 1970 v S, D, H (sub), Pol (sub), WG (sub); 1971 v Pol, Se (sub+1), I, A; (with Swindon T), 1972 v Ir, Ec, Ch, P; 1973 v USSR, F, USSR, Pol, F, N; 1974 v Pol; (with Preston NE), Br; 1975 v USSR, Sw (2), WG; 1976 v T, N (sub), Pol (sub); (with WBA), 1977 v F, Pol; (with Shamrock R), 1978 v T, Pol; 1980 v Cz (sub) (42)

Tuohy, L. (Shamrock R), 1956 v Y; 1959 v Cz (2); (with Newcastle U), 1962 v A; 1963 v Ic (2); (with Shamrock R), 1964 v A; 1965 v Bel (8)

Turner, C. J. (Southend U), 1936 v Sw; 1937 v G, H, Sw, F; 1938 v N (2); (with West Ham U) Cz, Pol; 1939 v H (10)

Turner, P. (Celtic), 1963 v S; 1964 v Sp (2)

Vernon, J. (Belfast C), 1946 v P, Sp (2)

Waddock, G. (QPR), 1980 v Sw, Arg; 1981 v W, Pol (sub); 1982 v Alg; 1983 v Ic, Ma, Sp, Ho (sub); 1984 v Ma (sub), Ic, Ho, Is; 1985 v I, Is, E, N, Sp; 1986 v USSR; (with Millwall), 1990 v USSR, T (21)

Walsh, D. J. (Linfield), 1946 v P, Sp; (with WBA), 1947 v Sp, P; 1948 v P, Sp; 1949 v Sw, P, Se, Sp; 1950 v E, Fi, Se; 1951 v N; (with Aston Villa), Arg, N; 1952 v Sp; 1953 v A; 1954 v F (2) (20)

Walsh, J. (Limerick), 1982 v Tr (1)

Walsh, M. (Blackpool), 1976 v N, Pol; 1977 v F (sub), Pol; (with Everton), 1979 v Ni (sub); (with QPR), D (sub), Bul, WG (sub); (with Porto), 1981 v Bel (sub), Cz; 1982 v Alg (sub); 1983 v Sp, Ho (sub), Sp (sub); 1984 v Ic (sub), Ma, Pol, Chn; 1985 v USSR, N (sub), D (21)

Walsh, M. (Everton), 1982 v Ch, Br, Tr; 1983 v Ic (4)

Walsh, W. (Manchester C), 1947 v E, Sp, P; 1948 v P, Sp; 1949 v Bel; 1950 v E, Se, Bel (9)

Waters, J. (Grimsby T), 1977 v T; 1980 v Ni (sub) (2)

Watters, F. (Shelbourne), 1926 v I (1)

Weir, E. (Clyde), 1939 v H (2), G (3)

Whelan, R. (St Patrick's Ath), 1964 v A, E (sub) (2)

Whelan, R. (Liverpool), 1981 v Cz (sub); 1982 v Ho (sub), F; 1983 v Ic, Ma, Sp; 1984 v Is; 1985 v USSR, N, I (sub), Is, E, N (sub), Sw); 1986 v USSR (sub), W; 1987 v Bel (sub), S, Bul, Bel, Br, L; 1988 v L, Bul, Pol, N, E, USSR, Ho; 1989 v Ni, F, H, Sp, Ma; 1990 v WG, Ni, Ma, W, Ho (sub); 1991 v Mor, E; 1992 v Sw; 1993 v La, W (sub), Li (sub); 1994 v Li (sub), Sp, Ru, Ho, G (sub), N (sub); (with Southend U), 1995 v Lie, A (53)

Whelan, W. (Manchester U), 1956 v Ho; 1957 v D, E (2) (4)

White, J. J. (Bohemians), 1928 v Bel (1)

Whittaker, R. (Chelsea), 1959 v Cz (1)

Williams, J. (Shamrock R), 1938 v N (1)

BRITISH & IRISH INTERNATIONAL MANAGERS

England
Walter Winterbottom 1946–1962 (after period as coach); Alf Ramsey 1963–1974; Joe Mercer (caretaker) 1974; Don Revie 1974–1977; Ron Greenwood 1977–1982; Bobby Robson 1982–1990; Graham Taylor 1990–1993; Terry Venables (coach) 1994–1996; Glenn Hoddle 1996–1999; Kevin Keegan from May 1999.

Northern Ireland
Peter Doherty 1951–1952; Bertie Peacock 1962–1967; Billy Bingham 1967–1971; Terry Neill 1971–1975; Dave Clements (player-manager) 1975–1976; Danny Blanchflower 1976–1979; Billy Bingham 1980–1994; Bryan Hamilton 1994–1998; Lawrie McMenemy 1998–1999; Sammy McIlroy from January 2000.

Scotland (since 1967)
Bobby Brown 1967–1971; Tommy Docherty 1971–1972; Willie Ormond 1973–1977; Ally MacLeod 1977–1978; Jock Stein 1978–1985; Alex Ferguson (caretaker) 1985–1986 Andy Roxburgh (coach) 1986–1993; Craig Brown from September 1993.

Wales (since 1974)
Mike Smith 1974–1979; Mike England 1980–1988; David Williams (caretaker) 1988; Terry Yorath 1988–1993; John Toshack 1994 for one match; Mike Smith 1994–1995; Bobby Gould 1995–1999; Mark Hughes from November 1999.

Republic of Ireland
Liam Tuohy 1971–1972; Johnny Giles 1973–1980 (after period as player-manager); Eoin Hand 1980–1985; Jack Charlton 1986–1996; Mick McCarthy from February 1996.

BRITISH AND IRISH INTERNATIONAL GOALSCORERS SINCE 1872

Where two players with the same surname and initials have appeared for the same country, and one or both have scored, they have been distinguished by reference to the club which appears *first* against their name in the international appearances section.

ENGLAND

A'Court, A.	1
Adams, T. A.	5
Adcock, H.	1
Alcock, C. W.	1
Allen, A.	3
Allen, R.	2
Amos, A.	1
Anderson, V.	2
Anderton, D. R.	7
Astall, G.	1
Athersmith, W. C.	3
Atyeo, P. J. W.	5
Bache, J. W.	4
Bailey, N. C.	2
Baily, E. F.	5
Baker, J. H.	3
Ball, A. J.	8
Bambridge, A. L.	1
Bambridge, E. C.	11
Barclay, R.	2
Barmby, N. J.	3
Barnes, J.	11
Barnes, P. S.	4
Barton, J.	1
Bassett, W. I.	8
Bastin, C. S.	12
Beardsley, P. A.	9
Beasley, A.	1
Beattie, T. K.	1
Beckham, D. R. J.	1
Becton, F.	2
Bedford, H.	1
Bell, C.	9
Bentley, R. T. F.	9
Bishop, S. M.	1
Blackburn, F.	1
Blissett, L.	3
Bloomer, S.	28
Bond, R.	2
Bonsor, A. G.	1
Bowden, E. R.	1
Bowers, J. W.	2
Bowles, S.	1
Bradford, G. R. W.	1
Bradford, J.	7
Bradley, W.	2
Bradshaw, F.	3
Brann, G.	1
Bridges, B. J.	1
Bridgett, A.	3
Brindle, T.	1
Britton, C. S.	1
Broadbent, P. F.	2
Broadis, I. A.	8
Brodie, J. B.	1
Bromley-Davenport, W.	2
Brook, E. F.	10
Brooking, T. D.	5
Brooks, J.	2
Broome, F. H.	3
Brown, A.	4
Brown, A. S.	1
Brown, G.	5
Brown, J.	3
Brown, W.	1
Buchan, C. M.	4
Bull, S. G.	4
Bullock, N.	2
Burgess, H.	4
Butcher, T.	3
Byrne, J. J.	8
Camsell, G. H.	18
Carter, H. S.	7
Carter, J. H.	4
Chadwick, E.	3
Chamberlain, M.	1
Chambers, H.	5
Channon, M. R.	21
Charlton, J.	6
Charlton, R.	49
Chenery, C. J.	1
Chivers, M.	13
Clarke, A. J.	10
Cobbold, W. N.	6
Cock, J. G.	2
Common, A.	2
Connelly, J. M.	7
Coppell, S. J.	7
Cotterill, G. H.	2
Cowans, G.	2
Crawford, R.	1
Crawshaw, T. H.	1
Crayston, W. J.	1
Creek, F. N. S.	1
Crooks, S. D.	7
Currey, E. S.	2
Currie, A. W.	3
Cursham, A. W.	2
Cursham, H. A.	5
Daft, H. B.	3
Davenport, J. K.	2
Davis, G.	1
Davis, H.	1
Day, S. H.	2
Dean, W. R.	18
Devey, J. H. G.	1
Dewhurst, F.	11
Dix, W. R.	1
Dixon, K. M.	4
Dixon, L. M.	1
Dorrell, A. R.	1
Douglas, B.	11
Drake, E. J.	6
Ducat, A.	1
Dunn, A. T. B.	2
Eastham, G.	2
Edwards, D.	5
Elliott, W. H.	3
Evans, R. E.	1
Ferdinand, L.	5
Finney, T.	30
Fleming, H. J.	9
Flowers, R.	10
Forman, Frank	1
Forman, Fred	3
Foster, R. E.	3
Fowler, R. B.	3
Francis, G. C. J.	3
Francis, T.	12
Freeman, B. C.	3
Froggatt, J.	2
Froggatt, R.	2
Galley, T.	1
Gascoigne, P. J.	10
Geary, F.	3
Gibbins, W. V. T.	3
Gilliatt, W. E.	3
Goddard, P.	1
Goodall, J.	12
Goodyer, A. C.	1
Gosling, R. C.	2
Goulden, L. A.	4
Grainger, C.	3
Greaves, J.	44
Grosvenor, A. T.	2
Gunn, W.	1
Haines, J. T. W.	2
Hall, G. W.	9
Halse, H. J.	2
Hampson, J.	5
Hampton, H.	2
Hancocks, J.	2
Hardman, H. P.	1
Harris, S. S.	2
Hassall, H. W.	4
Hateley, M.	9
Haynes, J. N.	18
Hegan, K. E.	4
Henfrey, A. G.	2
Heskey, E. W.	1
Hilsdon, G. R.	14
Hine, E. W.	4
Hinton, A. T.	1
Hirst, D. E.	1
Hitchens, G. A.	5
Hobbis, H. H. F.	1
Hoddle, G.	8
Hodgetts, D.	1
Hodgson, G.	1
Holley, G. H.	8
Houghton, W. E.	5
Howell, R.	1
Hughes, E. W.	1
Hulme, J. H. A.	4
Hunt, G. S.	1
Hunt, R.	18
Hunter, N.	2
Hurst, G. C.	24
Ince, P. E. C.	2
Jack, D. N. B.	3
Johnson, D. E.	6
Johnson, E.	2
Johnson, J. A.	2
Johnson, T. C. F.	5
Johnson, W. H.	1
Kail, E. I. L.	2
Kay, A. H.	1
Keegan, J. K.	21
Kelly, R.	8
Kennedy, R.	3
Kenyon-Slaney, W. S.	2
Keown, M. R.	2
Kevan, D. T.	8
Kidd, B.	1
Kingsford, R. K.	1
Kirchen, A. J.	2
Kirton, W. J.	1
Langton, R.	1
Latchford, R. D.	5
Latherton, E. G.	1
Lawler, C.	1
Lawton, T.	22
Lee, F.	10
Lee, J.	1
Lee, R. M.	2
Lee, S.	2
Le Saux, G. P.	1
Lindley, T.	14
Lineker, G.	48
Lofthouse, J. M.	3
Lofthouse, N.	30
Hon. A. Lyttelton	1
Mabbutt, G.	1
Macdonald, M.	6
Mannion, W. J.	11
Mariner, P.	13
Marsh, R. W.	1
Matthews, S.	11
Matthews, V.	1
McCall, J.	1
McDermott, T.	3
McManaman, S.	3
Medley, L. D.	1
Melia, J.	1
Mercer, D. W.	1
Merson, P. C.	3
Milburn, J. E. T.	10
Miller, H. S.	1
Mills, G. R.	3
Milward, A.	3
Mitchell, C.	5
Moore, J.	1
Moore, R. F.	2
Moore, W. G. B.	2
Morren, T.	1
Morris, F.	1
Morris, J.	3
Mortensen, S. H.	23
Morton, J. R.	1
Mosforth, W.	3
Mullen, J.	6
Mullery, A. P.	1
Neal, P. G.	5
Needham, E.	3
Nicholls, J.	1
Nicholson, W. E.	1
O'Grady, M.	3
Osborne, F. R.	3
Owen, M. J.	7
Own goals	23
Page, L. A.	1
Paine, T. L.	7
Palmer, C. L.	1
Parry, E. H.	1
Parry, R. A.	1
Pawson, F. W.	1
Payne, J.	2
Peacock, A.	3
Pearce, S.	5
Pearson, J. S.	5
Pearson, S. C.	5
Perry, W.	2
Peters, M.	20
Pickering, F.	5

Platt, D. 27
Pointer, R. 2

Quantrill, A. 1

Ramsay, A. E. 3
Revie, D. G. 4
Redknapp, J. F. 1
Reynolds, J. 3
Richardson, J. R. 2
Rigby, A. 3
Rimmer, E. J. 2
Roberts, F. 2
Roberts, H. 1
Roberts, W. T. 2
Robinson, J. 3
Robson, B. 26
Robson, R. 4
Rowley, J. F. 6
Royle, J. 2
Rutherford, J. 3

Sagar, C. 1
Sandilands, R. R. 3
Sansom, K. 1
Schofield, J. 1
Scholes, P. 10
Seed, J. M. 1
Settle, J. 6
Sewell, J. 3
Shackleton, L. F. 1
Sharp, J. 1
Shearer, A. 30
Shelton, A. 1
Shepherd, A. 2
Sheringham, E. P. 9
Simpson, J. 1
Smith, A. M. 2
Smith, G. O. 11
Smith, Joe 1
Smith, J. R. 2
Smith, J. W. 4
Smith, R. 13
Smith, S. 1
Sorby, T. H. 1
Southgate, G. 1
Southworth, J. 3
Sparks, F. J. 3
Spence, J. W. 1
Spiksley, F. 5
Spilsbury, B. W. 5
Steele, F. C. 8
Stephenson, G. T. 2
Steven, T. M. 4
Stewart, J. 2
Stiles, N. P. 1
Storer, H. 1
Stone, S. B. 2
Summerbee, M. G. 1

Tambling, R. V. 1
Taylor, P. J. 2
Taylor, T. 16
Thompson, P. B. 1
Thornewell, G. 1
Tilson, S. F. 6
Townley, W. J. 2
Tueart, D. 2

Vaughton, O. H. 6
Veitch, J. G. 3
Violett, D. S. 1

Waddle, C. R. 6
Walker, W. H. 9
Wall, G. 2
Wallace, D. 1
Walsh, P. 1
Waring, T. 4
Warren, B. 2
Watson, D. V. 4
Watson, V. M. 4
Webb, G. W. 1
Webb, N. 4
Wedlock, W. J. 2
Weller, K. 1
Welsh, D. 1
Whateley, O. 2
Wheldon, G. F. 6
Whitfield, H. 1
Wignall, F. 2
Wilkes, A. 1
Wilkins, R. G. 3
Willingham, C. K. 1
Wilshaw, D. J. 10
Wilson, G. P. 1
Winckworth, W. N. 1
Windridge, J. E. 7
Wise, D. F. 1
Withe, P. 1
Wollaston, C. H. R. 1
Wood, H. 1
Woodcock, T. 16
Woodhall, G. 1
Woodward, V. J. 29
Worrall, F. 2
Worthington, F. S. 2
Wright, I. E. 9
Wright, M. 1
Wright, W. A. 3
Wylie, J. G. 1

Yates, J. 3

NORTHERN IRELAND

Anderson, T. 4
Armstrong, G. 12

Bambrick, J. 12
Barr, H. H. 1
Barron, H. 3
Best, G. 9
Bingham, W. L. 10
Black, K. 1
Blanchflower, D. 2
Blanchflower, J. 1
Brennan, B. 1
Brennan, R. A. 1
Brotherston, N. 3
Brown, J. 1
Browne, F. 2

Campbell, J. 1
Campbell, W. G. 1
Casey, T. 2
Caskey, W. 1
Cassidy, T. 1
Chambers, J. 3
Clarke, C. J. 13
Clements, D. 2
Cochrane, T. 1
Condy, J. 1
Connor, M. J. 1
Coulter, J. 1
Croft, T. 1
Crone, W. 1
Crossan, E. 1
Crossan, J. A. 10
Curran, S. 2
Cush, W. W. 5

Dalton, W. 4
D'Arcy, S. D. 1
Darling, J. 1
Davey, H. H. 1
Davis, T. L. 1
Dill, A. H. 1
Doherty, L. 1
Doherty, P. D. 3
Dougan, A. D. 8
Dowie, I. 12
Dunne, J. 4

Elder, A. R. 1
Emerson, W. 1
English, S. 1

Feeney, W 1
Ferguson, W. 1
Ferris, J. 1
Ferris, R. O. 1
Finney, T. 2

Gaffkin, J. 4
Gara, A. 3
Gaukrodger, G. 1
Gibb, J. T. 2
Gibb, T. J. 1
Gillespie, K. R. 1
Gillespie, W. 12
Goodall, A. L. 2
Griffin, D. J. 1
Gray, P. 5

Halligan, W. 1
Hamill, M. 1
Hamilton, B. 4
Hamilton, W. R. 5
Hannon, D. J. 1
Harkin, J. T. 2
Harvey, M. 3
Healy, D. J. 3
Hill, C. F. 1
Hughes, M. 4
Humphries, W. 1
Hunter, A. (*Distillery*) 1
Hunter, A. (*Blackburn R*) 1
Hunter, B. V. 1

Irvine, R. W. 3
Irvine, W. J. 8

Johnston, H. 2
Johnston, S. 2
Johnston, W. C. 1
Jones, S. 1
Jones, J. 1

Kelly, J. 4
Kernaghan, N. 2
Kirwan, J. 2

Lacey, W. 3
Lemon, J. 2
Lennon, N. F. 2
Lockhart, N. 3
Lomas, S. M. 2

Magilton, J. 5
Mahood, J. 2
Martin, D. K. 3
Maxwell, J. 2
McAdams, W. J. 7
McAllen, J. 1
Mcauley, J. L. 1
McCandless, J. 3
McCaw, J. H. 1
McClelland, J. 1
McCluggage, A. 2
McCracken, W. 1
McCrory, S. 1
McCurdy, C. 1
McDonald, A. 3
McGarry, J. K. 1
McGrath, R. C. 4
McIlroy, J. 10
McIlroy, S. B. 5
McKnight, J. 2
McLaughlin, J. C. 6
McMahon, G. J. 2
McMordie, A. S. 3
McMorran, E. J. 4
McParland, P. J. 10
McWha, W. B. R. 1
Meldon, J. 1
Mercer, J. T. 1
Millar, W. 1
Milligan, D. 1
Milne, R. G. 2
Molyneux, T. B. 1
Moreland, V. 1
Morgan, S. 3
Morrow, S. J. 1
Morrow, W. J. 1
Mulryne, P. P. 1
Murphy, N. 1

Neill, W. J. T. 2
Nelson, S. 1
Nicholl, C. J. 3
Nicholl, J. M. 1
Nicholson, J. J. 6

O'Boyle, G. 1
O'Hagan, C. 2
O'Kane, W. J. 1
O'Neill, J. 2
O'Neill, M. A. 4
O'Neill, M. H. 8
Own goals 6

Patterson, D. J. 1
Peacock, R. 2
Peden, J. 7
Penney, S. 2
Pyper, James 2
Pyper, John 1

Quinn, J. M. 12
Quinn, S. J. 3

Reynolds, J. 1
Rowland, K. 1
Rowley, R. W. M. 2

Sheridan, J. 2
Sherrard, J. 1
Sherrard, W. C. 2
Simpson, W. J. 5
Sloan, H. A. de B. 4
Smyth, S. 5
Spence, D. W. 3
Stanfield, O. M. 11
Stevenson, A. E. 5
Stewart, I. 2

Taggart, G. P. 7
Thompson, F. W. 2
Torrans, S. 1
Tully, C. P. 3
Turner, E. 1

Walker, J. 1
Walsh, D. J. 5
Welsh, E. 1
Whiteside, N. 9
Whiteside, T. 1
Whitley, Jeff 1
Williams, J. R. 1
Williamson, J. 1
Wilson, D. J. 1
Wilson, K. J. 6
Wilson, S. J. 7
Wilton, J. M. 2

Young, S. 2

SCOTLAND

Aitken, R. (*Celtic*) 1
Aitken, R. (*Dumbarton*) 1
Aitkenhead, W. A. C. 2
Alexander, D. 1
Allan, D. S. 4
Allan, J. 2
Anderson, F. 1
Anderson, W. 4

Smith, John	13	Davies, L. S.	6	Mays, A. W.	1	Williams, W.	1
Somerville, G.	1	Davies, R. T.	9	Medwin, T. C.	6	Woosnam, A. P.	3
Souness, G. J.	4	Davies, R. W.	6	Melville, A. K	3	Wynn, G. A.	1
Speedie, F.	2	Davies, S.	5	Meredith, W. H.	11		
St John, I.	9	Davies, W.	6	Mills, T. J.	1	Yorath, T. C.	2
Steel, W.	12	Davies, W. H.	1	Moore, G.	1	Young, E.	1
Stein, C.	10	Davies, William	5	Morgan, J. R.	2		
Stevenson, G.	4	Davis, W. O.	1	Morgan-Owen, H.	1	**REPUBLIC OF**	
Stewart, A.	1	Deacy, N.	4	Morgan-Owen, M. M.	2	**IRELAND**	
Stewart, R.	1	Doughty, J.	6	Morris, A. G.	9	Aldridge, J.	19
Stewart, W. E.	1	Doughty, R.	2	Morris, H.	2	Ambrose, P.	1
Strachan, G.	5	Durban, A.	2	Morris, R.	1	Anderson, J.	1
Sturrock, P.	3	Dwyer, P.	2	Morris, S.	2	Bermingham, P.	1
						Bradshaw, P.	4
Taylor, J. D.	1	Edwards, G.	2	Nicholas, P.	2	Brady, L.	9
Templeton, R.	1	Edwards, R. I.	4			Breen, G.	4
Thomson, A.	1	England, H. M.	4	O'Callaghan, E.	3	Brown, D.	1
Thomson, C.	4	Evans, I.	1	O'Sullivan, P. A.	1	Byrne, J. (*Bray*)	1
Thomson, R.	1	Evans, J.	1	Owen, G.	2	Byrne, J. (*QPR*)	4
Thomson, W.	1	Evans, R. E.	2	Owen, W.	4		
Thornton, W.	1	Evans, W.	1	Owen, W. P.	6	Cantwell, J.	14
		Eyton-Jones, J. A.	1	Own goals	13	Carey, J.	3
Waddell, T. S.	1					Carroll, T.	1
Waddell, W.	6	Flynn, B.	7	Palmer, D.	3	Cascarino, A.	19
Walker, J.	2	Ford, T.	23	Parry, T. D.	3	Coad, P.	3
Walker, R.	7	Foulkes, W. I.	1	Paul, R.	1	Connolly, D. J.	7
Walker, T.	9	Fowler, J.	3	Peake, E.	1	Conroy, T.	2
Wallace, I. A.	1			Pembridge, M.	5	Conway, J.	3
Wark, J.	7	Giles, D.	2	Perry, E.	1	Coyne, T.	6
Watson, J. A. K.	1	Giggs, R. J.	7	Phillips, C.	5	Cummings, G.	5
Watt, F.	2	Glover, E. M.	7	Phillips, D.	2	Curtis, D.	8
Watt, W. W.	1	Godfrey, B. C.	2	Powell, A.	1		
Weir, A.	1	Green, A. W.	3	Powell, D.	1	Daly, G.	13
Weir, J. B.	2	Griffiths, A. T.	6	Price, J.	4	Davis, T.	4
White, J. A.	3	Griffiths, M. W.	2	Price, P.	1	Dempsey, J.	1
Wilson, A.	2	Griffiths, T. P.	3	Pryce-Jones, W. E.	3	Dennehy, M.	2
Wilson, A. N.	13			Pugh, D. H.	2	Donnelly, J.	4
Wilson, D. (*Queen's*		Harris, C. S.	1			Donnelly, T.	1
Park)	2	Hartson, J.	2	Reece, G. I.	2	Duffy, B.	1
Wilson, D. (*Rangers*)	9	Hersee, R.	1	Rees, R. R.	3	Duggan, H.	1
Wilson, H.	1	Hewitt, R.	1	Richards, R. W.	1	Dunne, J.	13
Wylie, T. G.	1	Hockey, T.	1	Roach, J.	2	Dunne, L.	1
		Hodges, G.	2	Robbins, W. W.	4	Dunne, R. P.	1
Young, A.	5	Hole, W. J.	1	Roberts, J. (*Corwen*)	1		
		Hopkins, I. J.	2	Roberts, Jas.	1	Eglington, T.	2
WALES		Horne, B.	2	Roberts, P. S.	1	Ellis, P.	2
Allchurch, I. J.	23	Howell, E. G.	3	Roberts, R. (*Druids*)	1		
Allen, M.	3	Hughes, L. M.	16	Roberts, W. (*Llangollen*)	2	Fagan, F.	5
Astley, D. J.	12			Roberts, W. (*Wrexham*)	1	Fallon, S.	2
Atherton, R. W.	2	James, E.	2	Roberts, W. H.	1	Fallon, W.	2
		James, L.	10	Robinson, J. R. C.	3	Farrell, P.	3
Bamford, T.	1	James, R.	7	Rush, I.	28	Fitzgerald, P.	2
Barnes, W.	1	Jarrett, R. H.	3	Russell, M. R.	1	Fitzgerald, J.	1
Bellamy, C. D.	2	Jenkyns, C. A.	1			Fitzsimmons, A.	7
Blackmore, C. G.	1	Jones, A.	1	Sabine, H. W.	1	Flood, J. J.	4
Blake, N. A.	2	Jones, Bryn	6	Saunders, D.	22	Fogarty, A.	3
Bodin, P. J.	3	Jones, B. S.	2	Savage, R. W.	1	Foley, D.	2
Boulter, L. M.	1	Jones, Cliff	16	Shaw, E. G.	2	Fullam, J.	1
Bowdler, J. C. H.	3	Jones, C. W.	1	Sisson, H.	4	Fullam, R.	1
Bowen, D. L.	1	Jones, D. E.	1	Slatter, N.	2		
Bowen, M.	3	Jones, Evan	1	Smallman, D. P.	1	Galvin, A.	1
Boyle, T.	1	Jones, H.	1	Speed, G. A.	3	Gavin, J.	2
Bryan, T.	1	Jones, I.	1	Symons, C. J.	2	Geoghegan, M.	2
Burgess, W. A. R.	1	Jones, J. L.	1			Giles, J.	5
Burke, T.	1	Jones, J. O.	1	Tapscott, D. R.	4	Givens, D.	19
Butler, W. T.	1	Jones, J. P.	1	Thomas, M.	4	Glynn, D.	1
		Jones, Leslie J.	1	Thomas, T.	1	Grealish, T.	8
Chapman, T.	2	Jones, R. A.	2	Toshack, J. B.	12	Grimes, A. A.	1
Charles, J.	1	Jones, W. L.	6	Trainer, H.	2		
Charles, M.	6					Hale, A.	2
Charles, W. J.	15	Keenor, F. C.	2	Vaughan, John	2	Hand, E.	2
Clarke, R. J.	5	Krzywicki, R. L.	1	Vernon, T. R.	8	Harte, I. P.	3
Coleman, C.	4			Vizard, E. T.	1	Haverty, J.	3
Collier, D. J.	1	Leek, K.	5			Holmes, J.	1
Crosse, K.	1	Lewis, B.	4	Walsh, I.	7	Horlacher, A.	2
Cumner, R. H.	1	Lewis, D. M.	2	Warren, F. W.	3	Houghton, R.	6
Curtis, A.	6	Lewis, W.	8	Watkins, W. M.	4	Hughton, C.	1
Curtis, E. R.	3	Lewis, W. L.	3	Wilding, J.	4	Hurley, C.	1
		Lovell, S.	1	Williams, A.	1		
Davies, D. W.	1	Lowrie, G.	2	Williams, D. R.	2	Irwin, D.	4
Davies, E. Lloyd	1			Williams, G. E.	1		
Davies, G.	2	Mahoney, J. F.	1	Williams, G. G.	1	Jordan, D.	1

Kavanagh, G. A.	1	McGrath, P.	8	O'Neill, F.	1	Squires, J.	1
Keane, R. D.	6	McLoughlin, A. F.	2	O'Neill, K. P.	4	Stapleton, F.	20
Keane, R. M.	5	McPhail, S. J. P.	1	O'Reilly, J. (*Brideville*)	2	Staunton, S.	6
Kelly, D.	9	Mancini, T.	1	O'Reilly, J. (*Cork*)	1	Strahan, J.	1
Kelly, G.	1	Martin, C.	6	Own goals	8	Sullivan, J.	1
Kelly, J.	2	Martin, M.	4				
Kennedy, M.	1	Mooney, J.	1	Quinn, N.	20	Townsend, A. D.	7
Kernaghan, A. N.	1	Moore, P.	7			Treacy, R.	5
		Moran, K.	6	Ringstead, A.	7	Touhy, L.	4
Lacey, W.	1	Moroney, T.	1	Robinson, M.	4		
Lawrenson, M.	5	Mulligan, P.	1	Rogers, E.	5	Waddock, G.	3
Leech, M.	2			Ryan, G.	1	Walsh, D.	5
		O'Callaghan, K.	1	Ryan, R.	3	Walsh, M.	3
McAteer, J. W.	1	O'Connor, T.	2			Waters, J.	1
McCann, J.	1	O'Farrell, F.	2	Sheedy, K.	9	White, J. J.	2
McCarthy, M.	2	O'Flanagan, K.	3	Sheridan, J.	5	Whelan, R.	3
McEvoy, A.	6	O'Keefe, E.	1	Slaven, B.	1		
McGee, P.	4	O'Leary, D. A.	1	Sloan, W.	1		

INTERNATIONAL RECORDS

MOST GOALS IN AN INTERNATIONAL

Record	Sophus Nielsen (Denmark) 10 goals v France, at White City (Olympics)	22.10.1908
	Gottfried Fuchs (Germany) 10 goals v Russia, in Stockholm (Olympics)	1.7.1912
World Cup	Gary Cole (Australia) 7 goals v Fiji, in Melbourne	14.8.1981
	Karim Bagheri (Iran) 7 goals v Maldives, in Damascus	2.6.1997
England	Malcolm Macdonald (Newcastle U) 5 goals v Cyprus, at Wembley	16.4.1975
	Willie Hall (Tottenham H) 5 goals v Ireland, at Old Trafford	16.11.1938
	Steve Bloomer (Derby Co) 5 goals v Wales, at Cardiff	16.3.1896
	Howard Vaughton (Aston Villa) 5 goals v Ireland, at Belfast	18.2.1882
Northern Ireland	Joe Bambrick (Linfield) 6 goals v Wales, at Belfast	1.2.1930
Wales	John Price (Wrexham) 4 goals v Ireland, at Wrexham	25.2.1882
	Mel Charles (Cardiff C) 4 goals v Ireland, at Cardiff	11.4.1962
	Ian Edwards (Chester) 4 goals v Malta, at Wrexham	25.10.1978

MOST GOALS IN AN INTERNATIONAL CAREER

		Goals	Games
England	Bobby Charlton (Manchester U)	49	106
Scotland	Denis Law (Huddersfield T, Manchester C, Torino, Manchester U)	30	55
	Kenny Dalglish (Celtic, Liverpool)	30	102
Northern Ireland	Colin Clarke (Bournemouth, Southampton, QPR, Portsmouth)	13	38
Wales	Ian Rush (Liverpool, Juventus)	28	73
Republic of Ireland	Frank Stapleton (Arsenal, Manchester U, Ajax, Derby Co, Le Havre, Blackburn R)	20	70
	Niall Quinn (Arsenal, Manchester C, Sunderland)	20	79

HIGHEST SCORES

World Cup Match	Iran	17	Maldives	0	1997
European Championship	Spain	12	Malta	1	1983
Olympic Games	Denmark	17	France	1	1908
	Germany	16	USSR	0	1912
Other International Match	Libya	21	Oman	0	1966
European Cup	Feyenoord	12	K R Reykjavik	2	1969
European Cup-Winners' Cup	Sporting Lisbon	16	Apoel Nicosia	1	1963
Fairs & UEFA Cups	Ajax	14	Red Boys	0	1984

GOALSCORING RECORDS

World Cup Final	Geoff Hurst (England) 3 goals v West Germany	1966
World Cup Final tournament	Just Fontaine (France) 13 goals	1958
Career	Artur Friedenreich (Brazil) 1329 goals	1910–30
	Pelé (Brazil) 1281 goals	*1956–78
	Franz 'Bimbo' Binder (Austria, Germany) 1006 goals	1930–50

Pelé subsequently scored two goals in Testimonial matches making his total 1283.

MOST CAPPED INTERNATIONALS IN BRITISH ISLES

England	Peter Shilton	125 appearances	1970–90
Northern Ireland	Pat Jennings	119 appearances	1964–86
Scotland	Kenny Dalglish	102 appearances	1971–86
Wales	Neville Southall	92 appearances	1982–97
Republic of Ireland	Paul McGrath	83 appearances	1984–97

SOUTH AMERICA

COPA LIBERTADORES 2000

PRELIMINARY ROUND
Dep Tachira 2, Atlas 2
Ital-Chacao 3, Atlas 3
Ital-Chacao 0, Dep Tachira 0
Atlas 6, America (Mexico) 3
America (Mexico) 6, Dep Tachira 0
Atlas 3, Dep Tachira 0
America (Mexico) 1, Ital-Chacao 1
Atlas 2, Ital-Chacao 2

GROUP 1	P	W	D	L	F	A	Pts
Paranaense	6	5	1	0	11	2	16
Nacional (Uru)	6	3	1	2	8	7	10
Alianza	6	1	2	3	7	12	5
Emelec	6	0	2	4	3	8	2

GROUP 2	P	W	D	L	F	A	Pts
Boca Juniors	6	4	1	1	14	5	13
Penarol	6	2	3	1	12	9	9
Blooming	6	2	1	3	9	17	7
Univ Catolica	6	1	1	4	10	14	4

GROUP 3	P	W	D	L	F	A	Pts
Corinthians	6	4	1	1	17	9	13
America (Mex)	6	3	1	2	15	9	10
Olimpia	6	2	2	2	13	17	8
LDU Quito	6	0	2	4	3	13	2

GROUP 4	P	W	D	L	F	A	Pts
River Plate	6	2	3	1	11	9	9
Atlas	6	2	2	2	13	10	8
Univ de Chile	6	2	2	2	10	10	8
At Nacional	6	2	1	3	11	16	7

GROUP 5	P	W	D	L	F	A	Pts
At Junior	6	4	0	2	7	4	12
Cerro Porteno	6	3	1	2	9	6	10

GROUP A	P	W	D	L	F	A	Pts
America (Col)	6	4	2	0	13	8	14
El Nacional	6	2	1	3	10	14	7
At Nacional	6	1	3	2	11	9	6
Universitario	6	1	2	3	7	10	5

GROUP B	P	W	D	L	F	A	Pts
Alianza	6	4	1	1	8	4	13
Barcelona	6	2	3	1	9	5	9
Millonarios	6	2	1	3	8	8	7
The Strongest	6	1	1	4	7	15	4

GROUP A	P	W	D	L	F	A	Pts
Cruzeiro	6	5	1	0	16	2	16
Palmeiras	6	3	2	1	19	10	11
River Plate	6	2	1	3	8	11	7
Racing Club	6	0	0	6	2	22	0

GROUP B	P	W	D	L	F	A	Pts
Independiente	6	3	2	1	7	5	11
Corinthians	6	3	1	2	10	5	10
Gremio	6	2	2	2	5	6	8
Velez Sarsfield	6	0	3	3	3	9	3

GROUP C	P	W	D	L	F	A	Pts
San Lorenzo	6	4	0	2	11	8	12
Boca Juniors	6	3	1	2	10	5	10
Sao Paulo	6	3	1	2	11	8	10
Univ Catolica	6	1	0	5	2	13	3

GROUP D	P	W	D	L	F	A	Pts
Penarol	6	3	3	0	10	7	12
Nacional	6	3	1	2	10	6	10
Vasco da Gama	6	2	2	2	9	8	8
Cerro Porteno	6	0	2	4	9	17	2

	P	W	D	L	F	A	Pts
San Lorenzo	6	2	2	2	10	9	8
Universitario	6	1	1	4	2	9	4

GROUP 6	P	W	D	L	F	A	Pts
America (Col)	6	5	1	0	20	10	16
Rosario Central	6	2	3	1	19	17	9
Sporting Cristal	6	1	1	4	9	13	4
Colegiales	6	1	1	4	10	18	4

GROUP 7	P	W	D	L	F	A	Pts
Palmeiras	6	3	1	2	16	10	10
El Nacional	6	3	1	2	10	7	10
Juventude	6	2	1	3	8	12	7
The Strongest	6	2	1	3	10	15	7

GROUP 8	P	W	D	L	F	A	Pts
Bolivar	6	3	1	2	12	9	10
At Mineiro	6	3	0	3	9	7	9
Bella Vista	6	2	2	2	8	5	8
Cobreloa	6	1	3	2	7	15	6

SECOND ROUND, FIRST LEG
America (Mex) 2, America (Col) 1
At Mineiro 1, Paranaense 0
Atlas 2, At Junior 0
El Nacional 0, Boca Juniors 0
Nacional (Uru) 3, Bolivar 0
Rosario Central 3, Corinthians 2
Cerro Porteno 0, River Plate 4
Penarol 2, Palmeiras 0

SECOND ROUND, SECOND LEG
America (Col) 2, America (Mex) 3
Boca Juniors 5, El Nacional 3
Corinthians 3, Rosario Central 2
(Corinthians won 4-3 on penalties)
At Junior 1, Atlas 3

MERCONORTE CUP

GROUP C	P	W	D	L	F	A	Pts
Indep Santa Fe	6	4	1	1	10	3	13
Caracas	6	4	0	2	9	8	12
Emelec	6	3	0	3	9	9	9
Sporting Cristal	6	0	1	5	7	15	1

SEMI-FINALS, FIRST LEG
America (Col) 3, Alianza 1
Caracas 1, Indep Santa Fe 1

SEMI-FINALS, SECOND LEG
Alianza 2, America (Col) 0

MERCOSUR CUP

GROUP E	P	W	D	L	F	A	Pts
Olimpia	6	4	0	2	10	7	12
Flamengo	6	3	1	2	16	8	10
Colo Colo	6	2	2	2	6	8	8
Univ de Chile	6	1	1	4	4	13	4

*Corinthians qualified after toss of coin
v Boca Juniors.*

**QUARTER-FINALS,
FIRST LEG**
Olimpia 1, Penarol 0
San Lorenzo 2, Corinthians 1
Palmeiras 7, Cruzeiro 3
Independiente 1, Flamengo 1

**QUARTER-FINALS,
SECOND LEG**
Corinthians 1, San Lorenzo 2
Penarol 3, Olimpia 0
Cruzeiro 2, Palmeiras 0
Flamengo 4, Independiente 0

Bolivar 3, Nacional 0
(Bolivar won 5-3 on penalties)
River Plate 1, Cerro Porteno 0
Paranaense 2, At Mineiro 1
(At Mineiro won 5-3 on penalties)
Palmeiras 3, Penarol 1
(Palmeiras won 3-2 on penalties)

QUARTER-FINALS, FIRST LEG
America (Mex) 2, Bolivar 0
River Plate 2, Boca Juniors 1
Atlas 0, Palmeiras 2
At Mineiro 1, Corinthians 1

**QUARTER-FINALS, SECOND
LEG**
Corinthians 2, At Mineiro 1
Boca Juniors 3, River Plate 0
Palmeiras 3, Atlas 2
Bolivar 1, America (Mex) 2

SEMI-FINALS, FIRST LEG
Corinthians 4, Palmeiras 3
Boca Juniors 4, America (Mex) 1

SEMI-FINALS, SECOND LEG
Palmeiras 3, Corinthians 2
(Palmeiras won 5-4 on penalties)
America (Mex) 3, Boca Juniors 1

FINAL, FIRST LEG
Boca Juniors 2, Palmeiras 2

FINAL, SECOND LEG
Palmeiras 0, Boca Juniors 0
(Boca Juniors won 4-2 on penalties)

America (Col) won 4-3 on penalties.
Indep Santa Fe 1, Caracas 1
Indep Santa Fe won 4-2 on penalties.

FINAL, FIRST LEG
America (Col) 1, Indep Santa Fe 2

FINAL, SECOND LEG
Indep Santa Fe 0, America (Col) 1
America (Col) won 5-3 on penalties.

SEMI-FINALS, FIRST LEG
San Lorenzo 1, Palmeiras 0
Flamengo 3, Penarol 0

SEMI-FINALS, SECOND LEG
Palmeiras 3, San Lorenzo 0
Penarol 3, Flamengo 2

FINAL, FIRST LEG
Flamengo 4, Palmeiras 3

FINAL, SECOND LEG
Palmeiras 3, Flamengo 3

CONMEBOL CUP

FIRST ROUND, FIRST LEG
Rosario Central 2, Dep Concepcion 2
Estudiantes (Ven) 2, Quindio 0
Dep Cuenca 2, Sport Boys 2
Parana 1, San Lorenzo 0
Indep Petrolero 4, Talleres 1
Huila 1, Sao Raimundo 2
Alagoano 2, Vila Nova 0

FIRST ROUND, SECOND LEG
Quindio 2, Estudiantes (Ven) 0
(Estudiantes won 5-3 on penalties)
Sport Boys 0, Dep Cuenca 0
(Sport Boys won 4-3 on penalties)
San Lorenzo 2, Parana 1
(Parana won 3-1 on penalties)

Talleres 3, Indep Petrolero 0
(Talleres won 4-3 on penalties)
Dep Concepcion 2, Rosario Central 1
Sao Raimundo 2, Huila 1
Vila Nova 2, Alagoano 0
(Alagoano won 4-3 on penalties)

SECOND ROUND, FIRST LEG
Talleres 1, Parana 0
Estudiantes (Ven) 0, Alagoano 0
Sport Boys 1, Sao Raimundo 1
Dep Concepcion bye

SECOND ROUND, SECOND LEG
Sao Raimundo 4, Sport Boys 0
Parana 1, Talleres 0
(Talleres won 3-1 on penalties)

Alagoano 3, Estudiantes (Ven) 1

SEMI-FINALS, FIRST LEG
Sao Raimundo 1, Alagoano 0
Talleres 2, Dep Concepcion 1

SEMI-FINALS, SECOND LEG
Alagoano 2, Sao Raimundo 1
(Alagoano won 5-4 on penalties)
Dep Concepcion 1, Talleres 1

FINAL, FIRST LEG
Alagoano 4, Talleres 2

FINAL, SECOND LEG
Talleres 3, Alagoano 0

FIFA CONFEDERATIONS CUP (in Mexico)

GROUP A
Bolivia 2, Egypt 2
Mexico 5, Saudi Arabia 1
Saudi Arabia 0, Bolivia 0
Mexico 2, Egypt 2
Egypt 1, Saudi Arabia 5
Bolivia 0, Mexico 1

GROUP B
Brazil 4, Germany 0
New Zealand 1, USA 2
Germany 2, New Zealand 0
Brazil 1, USA 0
USA 3, Germany 0
New Zealand 0, Brazil 2

SEMI-FINALS
Mexico 1, USA 0 *aet*
Brazil 8, Saudi Arabia 2

THIRD/FOURTH PLACE
USA 2, Saudi Arabia 0

FINAL
Mexico 4, Brazil 3

	P	W	D	L	F	A	Pts
Mexico	3	2	1	0	8	3	7
Saudi Arabia	3	1	1	1	6	6	4
Bolivia	3	0	2	1	2	3	2
Egypt	3	0	2	1	5	9	2

	P	W	D	L	F	A	Pts
Brazil	3	3	0	0	7	0	9
USA	3	2	0	1	4	2	6
Germany	3	1	0	2	2	6	3
New Zealand	3	0	0	3	1	6	0

GOLD CUP

FIRST ROUND

GROUP A
Colombia 1, Jamaica 0
Jamaica 0, Honduras 2
Honduras 2, Colombia 0

GROUP B
USA 3, Haiti 0
Haiti 1, Peru 1
USA 1, Peru 0

GROUP C
Mexico 4, Trinidad & Tobago 0
Trinidad & Tobago 4, Guatemala 2
Mexico 1, Guatemala 1

GROUP D
Costa Rica 2, Canada 2
South Korea 0, Canada 0
South Korea 2, Costa Rica 2
Canada qualified on the toss of a coin.

QUARTER-FINALS
USA 2, Colombia 2
Colombia won 2-1 on penalties.
Peru 5, Honduras 3
Mexico 1, Canada 2
Costa Rica 1, Trinidad & Tobago 2

SEMI-FINALS
Colombia 2, Peru 1
Trinidad & Tobago 0, Canada 1

FINAL
Canada 2, Colombia 0

AFRICAN NATIONS' CUP 2000

(Finals in Ghana and Nigeria)

FIRST ROUND

GROUP A
Ghana 1, Cameroon 1
Ivory Coast 1, Togo 1
Ghana 2, Togo 0
Cameroon 3, Ivory Coast 0
Ghana 0, Ivory Coast 2
Cameroon 0, Togo 1

GROUP B
Gabon 1, South Africa 3
Algeria 0, DR Congo 0
DR Congo 0, South Africa 1
Gabon 1, Algeria 3
Gabon 0, DR Congo 0
Algeria 1, South Africa 1

GROUP C
Egypt 2, Zambia 0
Burkina Faso 1, Senegal 3
Egypt 1, Senegal 0
Zambia 1, Burkina Faso 1
Egypt 4, Burkina Faso 2
Senegal 2, Zambia 2

GROUP D
Nigeria 4, Tunisia 2
Morocco 1, Congo 0
Nigeria 0, Congo 0
Morocco 0, Tunisia 0
Nigeria 2, Morocco 0
Congo 0, Tunisia 1

QUARTER-FINALS
Cameroon 2, Algeria 1
Ghana 0, South Africa 1
Egypt 0, Tunisia 1
Nigeria 2, Senegal 1

SEMI-FINALS
Nigeria 2, South Africa 0
Cameroon 3, Tunisia 0

THIRD PLACE
South Africa 2, Tunisia 2
South Africa won 4-3 on penalties.

FINAL
Nigeria 2, Cameroon 2
Cameroon won 4-3 on penalties.

UEFA UNDER-21 CHAMPIONSHIP 1998–2000

GROUP 1
Belarus 0, Denmark 2
Wales 1, Italy 2
Denmark 2, Wales 2
Italy 1, Switzerland 0
Switzerland 2, Denmark 0
Wales 0, Belarus 0
Denmark 1, Italy 2
Switzerland 1, Wales 0
Italy 4, Belarus 1
Denmark 2, Belarus 0
Italy 6, Wales 2
Wales 1, Denmark 2
Switzerland 0, Italy 0
Belarus 1, Switzerland 0
Belarus 1, Wales 0
Denmark 1, Switzerland 3
Switzerland 2, Belarus 1
Italy 3, Denmark 1
Wales 0, Switzerland 0
Belarus 1, Italy 2

GROUP 2
Latvia 1, Georgia 2
Georgia 0, Albania 1
Slovenia 1, Norway 3
Norway 4, Albania 1
Greece 3, Georgia 2
Slovenia 0, Latvia 1
Norway 2, Latvia 0
Greece 2, Slovenia 2
Albania 0, Greece 5
Greece 2, Norway 1
Georgia 0, Slovenia 0
Latvia 0, Greece 2
Georgia 0, Norway 3
Latvia 0, Albania 0
Norway 0, Georgia 0
Albania 1, Norway 2
Georgia 1, Greece 1
Latvia 1, Slovenia 1
Albania 1, Slovenia 4
Greece 6, Latvia 0
Norway 2, Greece 1
Georgia 4, Latvia 2
Norway 3, Slovenia 0
Greece 5, Albania 2
Slovenia 0, Greece 5
Latvia 2, Norway 1
Albania 0, Georgia 0
Albania 1, Latvia 1
Slovenia 2, Georgia 2
Slovenia 0, Albania 1

GROUP 3
Turkey 2, N Ireland 0
N Ireland 1, Finland 1
Turkey 2, Germany 0
Moldova 0, Germany 2
Turkey 1, Finland 1
Finland 1, Moldova 0
N Ireland 1, Moldova 1
N Ireland 1, Germany 0
Turkey 2, Moldova 0
Moldova 0, N Ireland 0
Germany 2, Finland 0
Germany 2, Moldova 0
Finland 0, Turkey 0
Moldova 1, Finland 1
Finland 3, Germany 1
N Ireland 1, Turkey 2
Germany 1, N Ireland 0
Moldova 1, Turkey 1
Finland 2, N Ireland 1
Germany 1, Turkey 1

GROUP 4
Ukraine 1, Russia 0
Armenia 3, Iceland 1
Russia 2, France 1
Ukraine 8, Armenia 0
Iceland 1, Russia 2
Iceland 0, France 2
France 4, Ukraine 0
Armenia 0, Russia 2
Ukraine 5, Iceland 1
France 3, Armenia 1
Iceland 2, Armenia 0

France 2, Russia 0
Armenia 1, Ukraine 1
Russia 3, Iceland 0
Ukraine 0, France 0
Armenia 1, France 4
Russia 6, Armenia 0
Iceland 4, Ukraine 1
France 2, Iceland 0
Russia 2, Ukraine 0

GROUP 5
Sweden 0, England 2
England 1, Bulgaria 0
Poland 5, Luxembourg 0
Bulgaria 2, Sweden 1
Luxembourg 0, England 5
Bulgaria 2, Poland 2
Sweden 3, Luxembourg 0
England 5, Poland 0
Poland 2, Sweden 0
Luxembourg 0, Bulgaria 3
England 3, Sweden 0
Poland 3, Bulgaria 3
Bulgaria 0, England 1
Luxembourg 0, Poland 4
England 5, Luxembourg 0
Poland 3, England 1
Luxembourg 0, Sweden 1
Sweden 1, Poland 2
Bulgaria 3, Luxembourg 0
Sweden 1, Bulgaria 4

GROUP 6
Austria 0, Israel 1
Cyprus 1, Spain 3
Cyprus 2, Austria 1
Holland 3, Israel 0
Israel 0, Spain 4
Holland 3, Austria 2
Cyprus 0, Holland 3
Spain 4, Austria 0
Israel 1, Cyprus 1
Holland 0, Spain 1
Austria 0, Holland 1
Spain 4, Holland 1
Israel 2, Austria 1
Holland 5, Cyprus 1
Austria 1, Spain 2
Israel 0, Holland 1
Spain 1, Cyprus 1
Spain 2, Israel 1
Austria 3, Cyprus 0
Cyprus 1, Israel 1

GROUP 7
Portugal 1, Romania 1
Azerbaijan 2, Hungary 1
Slovakia 1, Portugal 0
Hungary 1, Romania 2
Hungary 0, Portugal 3
Slovakia 2, Azerbaijan 1
Portugal 5, Azerbaijan 1
Romania 0, Slovakia 1
Azerbaijan 0, Romania 2
Slovakia 4, Hungary 1
Romania 2, Hungary 1
Portugal 1, Slovakia 1
Romania 1, Azerbaijan 1
Hungary 3, Slovakia 0
Romania 2, Portugal 3
Azerbaijan 0, Slovakia 3
Portugal 0, Hungary 1
Azerbaijan 0, Portugal 2
Slovakia 0, Romania 1
Hungary 4, Azerbaijan 1

GROUP 8
Republic of Ireland 2, Croatia 2
Malta 0, Croatia 3
Republic of Ireland 2, Malta 1
Croatia 4, Macedonia 0
Macedonia 1, Malta 0
Yugoslavia 1, Republic of Ireland 1
Malta 5, Macedonia 1
Malta 1, Yugoslavia 5
Macedonia 0, Croatia 2

Republic of Ireland 0, Macedonia 0
UEFA awarded Republic of Ireland a 3-0 win; Macedonia fielded a suspended player.
Yugoslavia 7, Malta 0
Republic of Ireland 0, Yugoslavia 2
Croatia 5, Republic of Ireland 1
Malta 1, Republic of Ireland 3
Macedonia 0, Yugoslavia 8
Macedonia 0, Republic of Ireland 1
Croatia 2, Yugoslavia 2
Yugoslavia 2, Macedonia 0
Croatia 1, Malta 0
Yugoslavia 2, Croatia 6

GROUP 9
Lithuania 0, Scotland 0
Scotland 2, Estonia 0
Bosnia 0, Czech Republic 0
Lithuania 0, Belgium 1
Lithuania 4, Bosnia 0
Czech Republic 3, Estonia 0
Belgium 2, Scotland 0
Belgium 0, Czech Republic 2
Bosnia 3, Estonia 2
Scotland 2, Belgium 2
Czech Republic 1, Lithuania 0
Lithuania 4, Estonia 1
Scotland 0, Czech Republic 1
Belgium 4, Bosnia 0
Bosnia 1, Lithuania 2
Estonia 0, Czech Republic 3
Czech Republic 3, Scotland 2
Estonia 0, Lithuania 3
Belgium 5, Estonia 0
Lithuania 0, Czech Republic 2
Estonia 0, Scotland 4
Czech Republic 1, Bosnia 0
Belgium 3, Lithuania 0
Scotland 2, Bosnia 0
Scotland 1, Lithuania 2
Czech Republic 1, Belgium 3
Estonia 0, Bosnia 2
Bosnia 2, Scotland 5
Estonia 1, Belgium 7
Bosnia 3, Belgium 4

PLAY-OFFS
FIRST LEG
Czech Republic 3, Greece 0
Holland 2, Belgium 2
Norway 1, Spain 3
Portugal 2, Croatia 0
Russia 0, Slovakia 1
France 1, Italy 1

PLAY-OFFS
SECOND LEG
Belgium 0, Holland 2
Croatia 3, Portugal 0
Greece 1, Czech Republic 0
Slovakia 3, Russia 1
Italy 2, France 1

1 game: England 3, Yugoslavia 0

FINALS (in Slovakia)
GROUP A
Croatia 1, Holland 2
Spain 1, Czech Republic 1
Czech Republic 3, Holland 1
Spain 0, Croatia 0
Holland 0, Spain 1
Czech Republic 4, Croatia 3

GROUP B
Italy 2, England 0
Slovakia 2, Turkey 1
England 6, Turkey 0
Italy 1, Slovakia 1
England 0, Slovakia 2
Turkey 1, Italy 3

THIRD PLACE PLAY-OFF
Spain 1, Slovakia 0

FINAL
Czech Republic 1, Italy 2

18TH UEFA UNDER-16 CHAMPIONSHIP

(Finals in Israel)

GROUP A
England 2, Russia 3
Portugal 1, Republic of Ireland 0
England 1, Portugal 2
Russia 3, Republic of Ireland 0
Republic of Ireland 2, England 1
Russia 2, Portugal 1

GROUP B
Czech Republic 3, Denmark 1
Slovakia 2, Finland 2
Czech Republic 2, Slovakia 2
Denmark 5, Finland 2
Finland 3, Czech Republic 7
Denmark 1, Slovakia 2

GROUP C
Israel 0, Holland 2
Hungary 1, Germany 4
Israel 1, Hungary 3
Holland 0, Germany 1
Germany 2, Israel 2
Holland 2, Hungary 0

GROUP D
Spain 7, Poland 2
Romania 0, Greece 1
Spain 1, Romania 0
Poland 3, Greece 3
Greece 2, Spain 1
Poland 3, Romania 0

QUARTER-FINALS
Russia 0, Holland 3
Germany 1, Portugal 1
(Portugal won on penalties)
Czech Republic 2, Spain 0
Greece 2, Slovakia 2
(Greece won on penalties)

SEMI-FINALS
Holland 1, Czech Republic 2
Portugal 2, Greece 1

MATCH FOR THIRD PLACE
Holland 5, Greece 0

FINAL
Czech Republic 1, Portugal 2 *aet*

8TH FIFA UNDER-17 WORLD CHAMPIONSHIP

(Finals in New Zealand)

GROUP A
New Zealand 1, USA 2
Uruguay 1, Poland 1
New Zealand 0, Uruguay 5
USA 1, Poland 1
Poland 1, New Zealand 2
USA 1, Uruguay 0

GROUP B
Ghana 1, Spain 1
Mexico 4, Thailand 0
Spain 6, Thailand 0
Ghana 4, Mexico 0
Thailand 1, Ghana 7
Spain 0, Mexico 1

GROUP C
Brazil 2, Australia 1
Mali 0, Germany 0
Australia 2, Germany 1
Brazil 0, Mali 0
Germany 0, Brazil 0
Australia 1, Mali 0

GROUP D
Jamaica 0, Burkina Faso 1

Paraguay 2, Qatar 0
Burkina Faso 1, Qatar 2
Jamaica 0, Paraguay 5
Qatar 4, Jamaica 0
Burkina Faso 2, Paraguay 2

QUARTER-FINALS
USA 3, Mexico 2
Ghana 3, Uruguay 2
(Ghana won on sudden death)
Australia 1, Qatar 0
Paraguay 1, Brazil 4

SEMI-FINALS
USA 2, Australia 2
(Australia won 7-6 on penalties)
Ghana 2, Brazil 2
(Brazil won 4-2 on penalties)

MATCH FOR THIRD PLACE
USA 0, Ghana 2

FINAL
Brazil 0, Australia 0
(aet; Brazil won 8-7 on penalties)

16TH UEFA UNDER-18 CHAMPIONSHIP

(Finals in Sweden)

GROUP A
Portugal 0, Greece 0
Sweden 0, France 0
France 1, Greece 1
Sweden 1, Portugal 3
France 0, Portugal 1
Greece 1, Sweden 1

GROUP B
Italy 2, Georgia 0
Spain 0, Republic of Ireland 1

Republic of Ireland 3, Georgia 3
Spain 3, Italy 3
Georgia 1, Spain 4
Republic of Ireland 0, Italy 2

MATCH FOR THIRD PLACE
Republic of Ireland 1, Greece 0

FINAL
Portugal 1, Italy 0

OLYMPIC FOOTBALL

Previous medallists

1896	Athens*	1 Denmark	1932	Los Angeles		1968	Mexico City	1 Hungary
		2 Greece		no tournament				2 Bulgaria
1900	Paris*	1 Great Britain	1936	Berlin	1 Italy			3 Japan
		2 France			2 Austria	1972	Munich	1 Poland
1904	St Louis**	1 Canada			3 Norway			2 Hungary
		2 USA	1948	London	1 Sweden			3 E Germany/USSR
1908	London	1 Great Britain			2 Yugoslavia	1976	Montreal	1 East Germany
		2 Denmark			3 Denmark			2 Poland
		3 Holland	1952	Helsinki	1 Hungary			3 USSR
1912	Stockholm	1 England			2 Yugoslavia	1980	Moscow	1 Czechoslovakia
		2 Denmark			3 Sweden			2 East Germany
		3 Holland	1956	Melbourne	1 USSR			3 USSR
1920	Antwerp	1 Belgium			2 Yugoslavia	1984	Los Angeles	1 France
		2 Spain			3 Bulgaria			2 Brazil
		3 Holland	1960	Rome	1 Yugoslavia			3 Yugoslavia
1924	Paris	1 Uruguay			2 Denmark	1988	Seoul	1 USSR
		2 Switzerland			3 Hungary			2 Brazil
		3 Sweden	1964	Tokyo	1 Hungary			3 West Germany
1928	Amsterdam	1 Uruguay			2 Czechoslovakia	1992	Barcelona	1 Spain
		2 Argentina			3 East Germany			2 Poland
		3 Italy						3 Ghana
						1996	Atlanta	1 Nigeria
								2 Argentina
								3 Brazil

* No official tournament
** No official tournament but gold medal later awarded by IOC

Olympic Football Tournament Sydney 2000

QUALIFYING TOURNAMENT

European Zone

(See results in European Under-21 Tournament)

Italy, Czech Republic, Spain and Slovakia qualified for finals.

Asian Zone

GROUP 1
Yemen 0, Qatar 3
UAE 6, Yemen 1
UAE 0, Qatar 1
Qatar 3, Yemen 1
Yemen 0, UAE 5
Qatar 2, UAE 2

GROUP 2
Oman 2, Kuwait 2
Syria 1, Kuwait 2
Oman 1, Syria 5
Kuwait 3, Syria 2
Syria 0, Oman 1
Kuwait 3, Oman 1

GROUP 3
Jordan 1, Saudi Arabia 3
Iraq 4, Jordan 2
Saudi Arabia 1, Iraq 1
Saudi Arabia 3, Jordan 1
Jordan 5, Iraq 0
Iraq 2, Saudi Arabia 2

GROUP 4
Iran 2, Bahrain 1
Bahrain 2, Lebanon 1
Lebanon 2, Iran 0
Bahrain 2, Iran 0
Lebanon 0, Bahrain 2
Iran 1, Lebanon 1

GROUP 5
Uzbekistan 3, Kyrgyzstan 0
Tajikistan 1, Turkmenistan 2
Uzbekistan 3, Tajikistan 0
Tajikistan 0, Kazakhstan 0

Turkmenistan 1, Uzbekistan 1
Kyrgyzstan 1, Tajikistan 0
Kazakhstan 4, Turkmenistan 1
Uzbekistan 0, Kazakhstan 2
Turkmenistan 3, Kyrgyzstan 0
Kyrgyzstan 2, Turkmenistan 1
Kazakhstan 3, Uzbekistan 1
Tajikistan 1, Kyrgyzstan 2
Turkmenistan 3, Kazakhstan 2
Uzbekistan 3, Turkmenistan 0
Kazakhstan 5, Tajikistan 1
Kazakhstan 1, Kyrgyzstan 1
Kyrgyzstan 2, Kazakhstan 3
Tajikistan 0, Uzbekistan 2
Kyrgyzstan 0, Uzbekistan 2
Turkmenistan 6, Tajikistan 1

GROUP 6
Hong Kong 1, Nepal 2
Philippines 0, Japan 13
Hong Kong 2, Malaysia 2
Nepal 0, Japan 5
Malaysia 0, Japan 4
Philippines 0, Nepal 1
Hong Kong 1, Japan 4
Malaysia 6, Philippines 1
Hong Kong 4, Philippines 1
Nepal 1, Malaysia 1
Japan 9, Nepal 0
Philippines 0, Hong Kong 1
Japan 4, Malaysia 0
Nepal 1, Hong Kong 2
Malaysia 0, Hong Kong 3
Nepal 2, Philippines 2
Japan 2, Hong Kong 0
Philippines 0, Malaysia 5
Japan 11, Philippines 0
Malaysia 3, Nepal 2

GROUP 7
Myanmar 0, North Korea 1
Vietnam 0, China 4
Myanmar 0, China 4
Vietnam 1, North Korea 2
North Korea 0, China 1
Vietnam 1, Myanmar 2

China 3, Vietnam 0
North Korea 6, Myanmar 0
China 6, Myanmar 0
North Korea 1, Vietnam 1
Myanmar 0, Vietnam 0
China 2, North Korea 0

GROUP 8
Taiwan 1, Indonesia 2
South Korea 5, Sri Lanka 0
Indonesia 2, Sri Lanka 1
South Korea 7, Taiwan 0
Taiwan 4, Sri Lanka 1
South Korea 7, Indonesia 0

GROUP 9
Thailand 2, India 0
India 0, Thailand 0

SECOND STAGE

GROUP A
Qatar 4, Saudi Arabia 1
Saudi Arabia 2, Kuwait 1
Kuwait 4, Qatar 0
Saudi Arabia 2, Qatar 0
Kuwait 3, Saudi Arabia 0
Qatar 1, Kuwait 2

GROUP B
South Korea 1, China 0
China 2, Bahrain 1
Bahrain 0, South Korea 1
China 1, South Korea 1
Bahrain 1, China 0
South Korea 2, Bahrain 1

GROUP C
Kazakhstan 0, Thailand 0
Kazakhstan 0, Japan 2
Japan 3, Thailand 1
Thailand 1, Kazakhstan 4
Japan 3, Kazakhstan 1
Thailand 0, Japan 6

Kuwait, South Korea and Japan qualified for the finals.

Concacaf Zone

CARIBBEAN GROUP 1
Aruba 0, Antigua 6
Guyana 4, Surinam 1
Antigua 7, Aruba 1
Surinam 3, Guyana 4
Guyana 1, Antigua 1
Antigua 0, Guyana 0

CARIBBEAN GROUP 2
Dominican Republic 1, St Kitts & Nevis 1
St Kitts & Nevis 2, Dominican Republic 0
St Kitts & Nevis 1, Jamaica 3
Jamaica 2, St Kitts & Nevis 1

CARIBBEAN GROUP 3
Haiti 3, Dominica 2
Dominica 1, Haiti 0
Dominica 0, Cuba 4

CARIBBEAN GROUP 4
St Vincent 1, Trinidad & Tobago 5
Trinidad & Tobago 4, St Vincent 0
St Lucia 2, Barbados 1
Barbados 4, St Lucia 1
Tinidad & Tobago 4, Barbados 1

Central America

GROUP 1
Belize 1, Guatamala 3
Guatamala 6, Belize 1

GROUP 3
El Salvador 1, Panama 2
Panama 1, El Salvador 1

GROUP 4
Nicaragua 0, Honduras 6
Honduras 4, Nicaragua 2

QUALIFYING ROUND

GROUP A
Canada 0, Guatemala 0
Trinidad & Tobago 6, Netherlands Antilles 0
Canada 1, Netherlands Antilles 0
Trinidad & Tobago 0, Guatemala 0
Guatemala 9, Netherlands Antilles 1
Trinidad & Tobago 0, Canada 2

GROUP B
Jamaica 1, Costa Rica 2
Mexico 2, Honduras 2
Costa Rica 1, Honduras 1
Mexico 5, Jamaica 0
Jamaica 0, Honduras 2
Mexico 5, Costa Rica 1

GROUP C
Panama 1, Bermuda 0
Cuba 0, Bermuda 0
Panama 1, Cuba 1

FINAL ROUND

GROUP D
USA 3, Honduras 0
Canada 0, Honduras 2
USA 0, Canada 0

GROUP E
Panama 1, Guatemala 2
Mexico 1, Guatemala 1
Mexico 3, Panama 0

SEMI-FINALS
Mexico 0, Honduras 0
Honduras won 5-4 on penalties.
USA 4, Guatemala 0

THIRD/FOURTH PLACE
Mexico 5, Guatemala 0

FINAL
Honduras 2, USA 1

Honduras and USA qualified for finals.

African Zone

PRELIMINARY COMPETITION
Kenya 1, Tanzania 0
Uganda 2, Sudan 1
Namibia 0, Mozambique 0
Botswana 3, Swaziland 0
Congo Brazzaville 1, Guinea 0
Seychelles 0, Mauritius 2
Guinea 1, Congo Brazzaville 1
Mauritius 4, Seychelles 0
Mozambique 3, Namibia 3
Sudan 0, Uganda 0
Swaziland 2, Botswana 2
Tanzania 2, Kenya 0

FINAL ROUND

GROUP A
Nigeria 2, Angola 0
Uganda 0, Zimbabwe 3
Angola 3, Uganda 1
Zimbabwe 2, Nigeria 1
Zimbabwe 3, Angola 2
Uganda 2, Nigeria 3
Nigeria 1, Uganda 0
Angola 4, Zimbabwe 2
Angola 3, Nigeria 1
Zimbabwe 1, Uganda 0
Uganda 0, Angola 1
Nigeria 4, Zimbabwe 0

GROUP B
Ghana 2, South Africa 2
Guinea 0, Cameroon 3
South Africa 3, Guinea 1
Cameroon 2, Ghana 2
Ghana 2, Guinea 0
South Africa 2, Cameroon 0
Cameroon 2, South Africa 0
Guinea 1, Ghana 2
South Africa 1, Ghana 0
Cameroon 2, Guinea 1
Guinea 1, South Africa 4
Ghana 0, Cameroon 3

GROUP C
Morocco 1, Egypt 0
Tunisia 1, Ivory Coast 1
Egypt 2, Tunisia 1
Ivory Coast 4, Morocco 1
Ivory Coast 3, Egypt 3
Tunisia 2, Morocco 4
Morocco 2, Tunisia 0
Egypt 2, Ivory Coast 1
Ivory Coast 3, Tunisia 1
Egypt 1, Morocco 1

Morocco 2, Ivory Coast 1
Tunisia 0, Egypt 3

Nigeria, Cameroon and Morocco qualified for finals; South Africa met New Zealand for further place.

South America

GROUP A
Colombia 4, Ecuador 2
Brazil 1, Chile 1
Chile 2, Ecuador 1
Colombia 1, Venezuela 1
Chile 3, Venezuela 0
Brazil 2, Ecuador 0
Colombia 5, Chile 1
Brazil 3, Venezuela 0
Ecuador 2, Venezuela 4
Brazil 9, Colombia 0

GROUP B
Uruguay 2, Peru 0
Argentina 3, Paraguay 1
Paraguay 3, Bolivia 1
Argentina 1, Peru 1
Paraguay 3, Peru 4
Uruguay 2, Bolivia 1
Uruguay 1, Paraguay 0
Argentina 2, Bolivia 0
Peru 5, Bolivia 2
Argentina 1, Uruguay 2

FINAL ROUND
Uruguay 1, Chile 4
Brazil 4, Argentina 2
Uruguay 0, Argentina 3
Brazil 3, Chile 1
Chile 1, Argentina 0
Brazil 2, Uruguay 2

Brazil and Chile qualified for finals.

Oceania

GROUP A
Solomon Islands 7, Tonga 0
Fiji 4, Samoa 0
Solomon Islands 2, Samoa 1
Fiji 9, Tonga 0
Solomon Islands 2, Fiji 0
Samoa 4, Tonga 1

GROUP B
New Zealand 4, Vanuatu 0
Papua New Guinea 2, Vanuatu 0
Papua New Guinea 0, New Zealand 5

SEMI-FINALS
Solomon Islands 3, Papua New Guinea 1
New Zealand 5, Fiji 2

THIRD/FOURTH PLACE
Papua New Guinea 0, Fiji 3

FINAL
New Zealand 4, Solomon Islands 1

PLAY-OFF
New Zealand 2, South Africa 3
South Africa 1, New Zealand 0

Australia qualified as hosts and South Africa as fourth African qualifier.

ENGLAND UNDER-21 RESULTS 1976–2000

EC UEFA Competition for Under-21 Teams

Year	Date		Venue	Eng	Opp
		v ALBANIA		Eng	Alb
EC1989	Mar	7	Shkroda	2	1
EC1989	April	25	Ipswich	2	0
		v ANGOLA		Eng	Ang
1995	June	10	Toulon	1	0
1996	May	28	Toulon	0	2
		v ARGENTINA		Eng	Arg
1998	May	18	Toulon	0	2
2000	Feb	22	Fulham	1	0
		v AUSTRIA		Eng	Aus
1994	Oct	11	Kapfenberg	3	1
1995	Nov	14	Middlesbrough	2	1
		v BELGIUM		Eng	Bel
1994	June	5	Marseille	2	1
1996	May	24	Toulon	1	0
		v BRAZIL		Eng	B
1993	June	11	Toulon	0	0
1995	June	6	Toulon	0	2
1996	June	1	Toulon	1	2
		v BULGARIA		Eng	Bul
EC1979	June	5	Pernik	3	1
EC1979	Nov	20	Leicester	5	0
1989	June	5	Toulon	2	3
EC1998	Oct	9	West Ham	1	0
EC1999	June	8	Vratsa	1	0
		v CROATIA		Eng	Cro
1996	Apr	23	Sunderland	0	1
		v CZECHOSLOVAKIA		Eng	Cz
1990	May	28	Toulon	2	1
1992	May	26	Toulon	1	2
1993	June	9	Toulon	1	1
		v CZECH REPUBLIC		Eng	CzR
1998	Nov	17	Ipswich	0	1
		v DENMARK		Eng	Den
EC1978	Sept	19	Hvidovre	2	1
EC1979	Sept	11	Watford	1	0
EC1982	Sept	21	Hvidovre	4	1
EC1983	Sept	20	Norwich	4	1
EC1986	Mar	12	Copenhagen	1	0
EC1986	Mar	26	Manchester	1	1
1988	Sept	13	Watford	0	0
1994	Mar	8	Brentford	1	0
1999	Oct	8	Bradford	4	1
		v EAST GERMANY		Eng	EG
EC1980	April	16	Sheffield	1	2
EC1980	April	23	Jena	0	1
		v FINLAND		Eng	Fin
EC1977	May	26	Helsinki	1	0
EC1977	Oct	12	Hull	8	1
EC1984	Oct	16	Southampton	2	0
EC1985	May	21	Mikkeli	1	3
		v FRANCE		Eng	Fra
EC1984	Feb	28	Sheffield	6	1
EC1984	Mar	28	Rouen	1	0
1987	June	11	Toulon	0	2
EC1988	April	13	Besancon	2	4
EC1988	April	27	Highbury	2	2
1988	June	12	Toulon	2	4
1990	May	23	Toulon	7	3
1991	June	3	Toulon	1	0
1992	May	28	Toulon	0	0
1993	June	15	Toulon	1	0
1994	May	31	Aubagne	0	3
1995	June	10	Toulon	0	2
1998	May	14	Toulon	1	1
1999	Feb	9	Derby	2	1
		v GEORGIA		Eng	Geo
EC1996	Nov	8	Batumi	1	0
EC1997	April	29	Charlton	0	0
		v GERMANY		Eng	Ger
1991	Sept	10	Scunthorpe	2	1
		v GREECE		Eng	Gre
EC1982	Nov	16	Piraeus	0	1
EC1983	Mar	29	Portsmouth	2	1
1989	Feb	7	Patras	0	1
EC1997	Nov	13	Heraklion	0	2
EC1997	Dec	17	Norwich	4	2
		v HOLLAND		Eng	H
EC1993	April	27	Portsmouth	3	0
EC1993	Oct	12	Utrecht	1	1
		v HUNGARY		Eng	Hun
EC1981	June	5	Keszthely	2	1
EC1981	Nov	17	Nottingham	2	0
EC1983	April	26	Newcastle	1	0
EC1983	Oct	11	Nyiregyhaza	2	0
1990	Sept	11	Southampton	3	1
1992	May	12	Budapest	2	2
1999	April	27	Budapest	2	2
		v ITALY		Eng	Italy
EC1978	Mar	8	Manchester	2	1
EC1978	April	5	Rome	0	0
EC1984	April	18	Manchester	3	1
EC1984	May	2	Florence	0	1
EC1986	April	9	Pisa	0	2
EC1986	April	23	Swindon	1	1
EC1997	Feb	12	Bristol	1	0
EC1997	Oct	10	Rieti	1	0
EC2000	May	27	Bratislava	0	2
		v ISRAEL		Eng	Isr
1985	Feb	27	Tel Aviv	2	1
		v LATVIA		Eng	Lat
1995	April	25	Riga	1	0
1995	June	7	Burnley	4	0
		v LUXEMBOURG		Eng	Lux
EC1998	Oct	13	Greven Macher	5	0
EC1999	Sept	3	Reading	5	0
		v MALAYSIA		Eng	Mal
1995	June	8	Toulon	2	0
		v MEXICO		Eng	Mex
1988	June	5	Toulon	2	1
1991	May	29	Toulon	6	0
1992	May	25	Toulon	1	1
		v MOLDOVA		Eng	Mol
EC1996	Aug	31	Chisinau	2	0
EC1997	Sept	9	Wycombe	1	0
		v MOROCCO		Eng	Mor
1987	June	7	Toulon	2	0
1988	June	9	Toulon	1	0
		v NORWAY		Eng	Nor
EC1977	June	1	Bergen	2	1
EC1977	Sept	6	Brighton	6	0
1980	Sept	9	Southampton	3	0
1981	Sept	8	Drammen	0	0
EC1992	Oct	13	Peterborough	0	2
EC1993	June	1	Stavanger	1	1
1995	Oct	10	Stavanger	2	2
		v POLAND		Eng	Pol
EC1982	Mar	17	Warsaw	2	1
EC1982	April	7	West Ham	2	2
EC1989	June	2	Plymouth	2	1
EC1989	Oct	10	Jastrzebie	3	1
EC1990	Oct	16	Tottenham	0	1
EC1991	Nov	12	Pila	1	2
EC1993	May	28	Zdroj	4	1
EC1993	Sept	7	Millwall	1	2
EC1996	Oct	8	Wolverhampton	0	0
EC1997	May	30	Katowice	1	1
EC1999	Mar	26	Southampton	5	0
EC1999	Sept	7	Plock	1	3
		v PORTUGAL		Eng	Por
1987	June	13	Toulon	0	0
1990	May	21	Toulon	0	1
1993	June	7	Toulon	2	0
1994	June	7	Toulon	2	0
EC1994	Sept	6	Leicester	0	0
1995	Sept	2	Lisbon	0	2
1996	May	30	Toulon	1	3

			v REPUBLIC OF IRELAND	Eng	RoI
1981	Feb	25	Liverpool	1	0
1985	Mar	25	Portsmouth	3	2
1989	June	9	Toulon	0	0
EC1990	Nov	13	Cork	3	0
EC1991	Mar	26	Brentford	3	0
1994	Nov	15	Newcastle	1	0
1995	Mar	27	Dublin	2	0
			v ROMANIA	Eng	Rom
EC1980	Oct	14	Ploesti	0	4
EC1981	April	28	Swindon	3	0
EC1985	April	30	Brasov	0	0
EC1985	Sept	10	Ipswich	3	0
			v RUSSIA	Eng	Rus
1994	May	30	Bandol	2	0
			v SAN MARINO	Eng	SM
EC1993	Feb	16	Luton	6	0
EC1993	Nov	17	San Marino	4	0
			v SENEGAL	Eng	Sen
1989	June	7	Toulon	6	1
1991	May	27	Toulon	2	1
			v SCOTLAND	Eng	Sco
1977	April	27	Sheffield	1	0
EC1980	Feb	12	Coventry	2	1
EC1980	Mar	4	Aberdeen	0	0
EC1982	April	19	Glasgow	1	0
EC1982	April	28	Manchester	1	1
EC1988	Feb	16	Aberdeen	1	0
EC1988	Mar	22	Nottingham	1	0
1993	June	13	Toulon	1	0
			v SLOVAKIA	Eng	Slo
EC2000	June	1	Bratislava	0	2
			v SOUTH AFRICA	Eng	SA
1998	May	16	Toulon	3	1
			v SPAIN	Eng	Spa
EC1984	May	17	Seville	1	0
EC1984	May	24	Sheffield	2	0
1987	Feb	18	Burgos	2	1
1992	Sept	8	Burgos	1	0
			v SWEDEN	Eng	Swe
1979	June	9	Vasteras	2	1
1986	Sept	9	Ostersund	1	1
EC1988	Oct	18	Coventry	1	1

				Eng	Swe
EC1989	Sept	5	Uppsala	0	1
EC1998	Sept	4	Sundvall	2	0
EC1999	June	4	Huddersfield	3	0
			v SWITZERLAND	Eng	Swit
EC1980	Nov	18	Ipswich	5	0
EC1981	May	31	Neuenburg	0	0
1988	May	28	Lausanne	1	1
1996	April	1	Swindon	0	0
1998	Mar	24	Brugglifeld	0	2
			v USA	Eng	USA
1989	June	11	Toulon	0	2
1994	June	2	Toulon	3	0
			v TURKEY	Eng	Tur
EC1984	Nov	13	Bursa	0	0
EC1985	Oct	15	Bristol	3	0
EC1987	April	28	Izmir	0	0
EC1987	Oct	13	Sheffield	1	1
EC1991	April	30	Izmir	2	2
1991	Oct	15	Reading	2	0
EC1992	Nov	17	Orient	0	1
EC1993	Mar	30	Izmir	0	0
EC2000	May	29	Bratislava	6	0
			v USSR	Eng	USSR
1987	June	9	Toulon	0	0
1988	June	7	Toulon	1	0
1990	May	25	Toulon	2	1
1991	May	31	Toulon	2	1
			v WALES	Eng	Wales
1976	Dec	15	Wolverhampton	0	0
1979	Feb	6	Swansea	1	0
1990	Dec	5	Tranmere	0	0
			v WEST GERMANY	Eng	WG
EC1982	Sept	21	Sheffield	3	1
EC1982	Oct	12	Bremen	2	3
1987	Sept	8	Ludenscheid	0	2
			v YUGOSLAVIA	Eng	Yugo
EC1978	April	19	Novi Sad	1	2
EC1978	May	2	Manchester	1	0
EC1986	Nov	11	Peterborough	1	1
EC1987	Nov	10	Zemun	5	1
EC2000	Mar	29	Barcelona	3	0

ENGLAND B RESULTS 1949–2000

Year	Date		Venue		
			v ALGERIA	Eng	Alg
1990	Dec	11	Algiers	0	0
			v AUSTRALIA	Eng	Aust
1980	Nov	17	Birmingham	1	0
			v AUSTRIA	Eng	Aus
1979†	June	12	Klagenfurt	1	0

†Abandoned 60 mins; waterlogged pitch.

			v CHILE	Eng	Ch
1998	Feb	10	West Bromwich	1	2
			v CIS	Eng	CIS
1992	April	28	Moscow	1	1
			v CZECHOSLOVAKIA	Eng	Cz
1978	Nov	28	Prague	1	0
1990	April	24	Sunderland	2	0
1992	Mar	24	Budejovice	1	0
			v FINLAND	Eng	Fin
1949	May	15	Helsinki	4	0
			v FRANCE	Eng	Fra
1952	May	22	Le Havre	1	7
1992	Feb	18	Loftus Road	3	0
			v WEST GERMANY	Eng	WG
1954	Mar	24	Gelsenkirchen	4	0
1955	Mar	23	Sheffield	1	1
1978	Feb	21	Augsburg	2	1
			v HOLLAND	Eng	Hol
1949	May	18	Amsterdam	4	0
1950	Feb	15	Newcastle	1	0
1952	Mar	26	Amsterdam	1	0

			v ICELAND	Eng	Ice
1989	May	19	Reykjavik	2	0
1991	April	27	Watford	1	0
			v ITALY	Eng	Italy
1950	May	11	Milan	0	5
1989	Nov	14	Brighton	1	1
			v LUXEMBOURG	Eng	Lux
1950	May	21	Luxembourg	2	1
			v MALAYSIA	Eng	Mal
1978	May	30	Kuala Lumpur	1	1
			v MALTA	Eng	Mal
1987	Oct	14	Ta'Qali	2	0
			v NEW ZEALAND	Eng	NZ
1978	June	7	Christchurch	4	0
1978	June	11	Wellington	3	1
1978	June	14	Auckland	4	0
1979	Oct	15	Leyton	4	1
1984	Nov	13	Nottingham	2	0
			v NORTHERN IRELAND	Eng	NI
1994	May	10	Sheffield	4	2
			v NORWAY	Eng	Nor
1989	May	22	Stavanger	1	0
			v REPUBLIC OF IRELAND	Eng	RoI
1990	Mar	27	Cork	1	4
1994	Dec	13	Liverpool	2	0
			v RUSSIA	Eng	Rus
1998	Apr	21	Loftus Road	4	1

			v SCOTLAND	Eng	Sco
1953	Mar	11	Edinburgh	2	2
1954	Mar	3	Sunderland	1	1
1956	Feb	29	Dundee	2	2
1957	Feb	6	Birmingham	4	1

			v SINGAPORE	Eng	Sin
1978	June	18	Singapore	8	0

			v SPAIN	Eng	Sp
1980	Mar	26	Sunderland	1	0
1981	Mar	25	Granada	2	3
1991*	Dec	18	Castellon	1	0

*Spanish Olympic XI

			v SWITZERLAND	Eng	Swit
1950	Jan	18	Sheffield	5	0
1954	May	22	Basle	0	2
1956	Mar	21	Southampton	4	1
1989	May	16	Winterthur	2	0
1991	May	20	Walsall	2	1

			v USA	Eng	USA
1980	Oct	14	Manchester	1	0

			v WALES	Eng	Wales
1991	Feb	5	Swansea	1	0

			v YUGOSLAVIA	Eng	Yugo
1954	May	16	Ljubljana	1	2
1955	Oct	19	Manchester	5	1
1989	Dec	12	Millwall	2	1

BRITISH AND IRISH UNDER-21 TEAMS 1999–2000

ENGLAND UNDER-21 INTERNATIONALS

3 Sept

England (2) 5 *(Gerrard 12, Jeffers 31, Hendrie 60, Cort 69, Lampard 79)*
Luxembourg (0) 0   18,094
England: Weaver; Mills, Ball, Gerrard, Carragher, Upson (King 69), Lampard (Thompson 82), Chadwick, Heskey (Cort 49), Jeffers, Hendrie.

7 Sept

Poland (0) 3 *(Kubik 46, Dawidowski 57, Sobczak 61)*
England (0) 1 *(Mills 48)*   1500
England: Weaver; Curtis (Woodhouse 65), Robinson, Carragher, Mills, Upson, Greening (Thompson 80), Gerrard, Beattie, Cort (Vassell 46), Morris.

8 Oct

England (2) 4 *(Smith 19, Bowyer 30, Cort 83, Thompson 90)*
Denmark (0) 1 *(Magleby 72)*   15,220
England: Robinson; Mills, Johnson (Ball 83), Carragher (Young 75), Gerrard, Upson, Chadwick, Bowyer (Thompson 65), Smith, Hendrie, Bridges (Cort 75).

22 Feb

England (0) 1 *(Hendrie 68)*
Argentina (0) 0   15,748
England: Weaver; Mills (Young 46), Naylor (Johnson 69), Carragher, Lampard, Woodgate, Chadwick, Bowyer (Cole 46), Cort, Hendrie, Jeffers (Smith 8 (Harley 80)).

29 Mar

England (1) 3 *(Campbell 24, Lampard 49 (pen), Hendrie 64)*
Yugoslavia (0) 0   1000
England: Wright; Dyer, Johnson, Carragher, Ferdinand, Barry, Lampard, Gerrard, Heskey (Davies 77), Hendrie (Mills 87), Campbell (Cadamarteri 86).

27 May

Italy (2) 2 *(Comandini 24, Pirlo 45 (pen))*
England (0) 0
England: Weaver; Mills, Carragher, King, Thompson (Chadwick 74), Lampard, Murphy, Johnson, Hendrie (Dunn 46), Cort (Jansen 66), Jeffers.

29 May

England (2) 6 *(Lampard 28, Jeffers 45, Cort 66, King 73, Mills 77, Campbell 90)*
Turkey (0) 0   250
England: Weaver; Young, Carragher, King, Mills, Murphy (Thompson 79), Lampard, Dunn, Johnson (Harley 79), Cort, Jeffers (Campbell 75).

1 June

England (0) 0
Slovakia (0) 2 *(Babnic 67, Nemeth 74)*   9113
England: Weaver; Young, Carragher, King, Mills, Murphy, Lampard, Dunn (Campell 46), Harley (Hendrie 46), Cort, Jeffers (Chadwick 78).

SCOTLAND UNDER-21 INTERNATIONALS

4 Sept

Bosnia 3
Scotland 2 *(Hughes, Thompson)*
Scotland: Gallacher; Anderson R (Nicholson), Wilson, Lauchlan, Naysmith (O'Brien), Anderson I (Campbell), Brebner, Rae, Hughes, Burchill, Thompson.

7 Sept

Estonia (0) 0   350
Scotland (3) 4 *(Rae 20, Burchill 22, Thompson 38, Dalglish 89 (pen))*
Scotland: Gallacher; Anderson R, Hughes (Davidson), Lauchlan, Naysmith, Nicholson, Rae, Severin, Burchill (Dalglish), Thompson (Tarrant), Paterson.

5 Oct

Scotland 2 *(Lauchlan, Dalglish)*
Bosnia 0
Scotland: Gallacher; Rae (Murray), Wilkie (Jordan), Lauchlan, Baltacha, Naysmith, Nicholson, Severin, Paterson, Thompson (Tarrant), Dalglish.

8 Oct

Scotland (1) 1 *(Easton 40)*
Lithuania (2) 2 *(Ksanavicius 1, Laurisas 43)*   1805
Scotland: Esson; Nicholson, Jordan, Lauchlan, Naysmith, Davidson (Severin), Strachan (Baltacha), Easton, Paterson, Notman, Tarrant (Dalglish).

28 Mar

Scotland (0) 0
France (0) 2 *(Sorltn 72, Reveillere 89)*   4357
Scotland: Gallacher; Canero (Baltacha), Wilkie (Milne), Jordan, Cummings (Crainey), Davidson (Murray), Easton, Severin, Caldwell G, Miller, Wales (Notman).

29 May

Northern Ireland (0) 1 *(Kirk 56)*
Scotland (1) 1 *(Notman 25)*   300
Scotland: Esson; Neilson, Cummings (Fraser), Wilkie, Caldwell G, Doig, Notman, Severin, Miller, Stewart (Murray), McAnespie (Tarrant).

31 May

Wales (0) 0
Scotland (1) 1 *(Miller 8)*   100
Scotland: Langfield; Fraser, McAnespie, Wilkie, Caldwell G, Doig, Notman, Severin, Miller, Murray I, Young.

WALES UNDER-21 INTERNATIONALS

3 Sept

Belarus (0) 1 *(Lanko 90)*
Wales (0) 0   3000
Wales: Tony Williams; Price, Jenkins, Gabbidon, Jarman, Green, Andrew Williams, Williams D (Roberts S 68), Haworth, Jeanne, Llewellyn (Thomas 78).

8 Oct

Wales (0) 0
Switzerland (0) 0   1050
Wales: Tony Williams, Price, Roberts G, Gabbidon, Hughes, Jenkins, Andrew Williams, Jones M (Maxwell 68), Haworth (Roberts N 46), Jeanne (Slatter 46), Llewellyn.

31 May

Wales (0) 0
Scotland (1) 1 *(Miller 8)*   100
Wales: Walsh; Green, Gabbidon, Jenkins, Stephen Roberts (Day 46), Slatter (Gibson 46), Williams D, Davies, Llewellyn, Jeanne (Earnshaw 78), Maxwell.

2 June

Wales (1) 2 *(Jeanne 3, Maxwell 84)*   852
Northern Ireland (1) 2 *(Friars 38 (pen), Hamilton 67)*
Wales: Walsh; Green, Gabbidon, Jenkins, Day (Jones E 67), Stuart Roberts, Williams D, Gibson (Folland 69), Tipton (Earnshaw 74), Jeanne, Maxwell.

NORTHERN IRELAND UNDER-21 INTERNA-TIONALS

17 Aug

Northern Ireland (1) 3 *(Coote 33, Healy 57, 88)*
France (1) 1 *(Kanoute 36)*   2000
Northern Ireland: Miskelly; Griffin, McGlinchey, Jeff Whitley, Burns, Waterman, Johnson (Clarke 72), Graham G, Coote (Graham R 72), McVeigh (Healy 46), Friars.

3 Sept

Northern Ireland (1) 1 *(Griffin 20)*
Turkey (2) 2 *(Albayrak 6, Goktan 8)*   1571
Northern Ireland: Carroll; Griffin (Ferguson 90), McGlinchey, Jeff Whitley, Burns, Waterman, Johnson, Graham G, Coote, Healy (Graham R 84), Friars (McVeigh 71).

7 Sept

Germany (0) 1 *(Voigt 73 (pen))*
Northern Ireland (0) 0   3724
Northern Ireland: Carroll; Lyttle, McGlinchey, Jeff Whitley, Burns, Waterman, Johnson, Graham G, Coote (Graham R 85), Healy, Friars (McVeigh 78).

8 Oct

Finland (1) 2 *(Niemi 20, Tainio 70)*
Northern Ireland (1) 1 *(Feeney 25)*
Northern Ireland: Carroll; Lyttle, McGlinchey, Burns, Waterman, Dolan (Nixon 64), Graham G, Feeney, Graham R (Carlisle 88), Healy, McVeigh.

28 Mar

Malta (1) 1 *(Galea 23)*
Northern Ireland (1) 2 *(Kirk 5, Harkin 89)*   462
Northern Ireland: Miskelly; Dolan, McAreavey (McFlynn 50), Skates (Toner 56), Kelly D, Holmes, Carson, Jeff Whitley, Kirk (Hamilton 56), Graham R (Harkin 56), Friars (Ferguson 89).

29 May

Northern Ireland (0) 1 *(Kirk 56)*
Scotland (1) 1 *(Notman 25)*   300
Northern Ireland: Miskelly; McAreavey (McCann 61), Graham R, Convery, Dolan, Holmes, Clarke (Toner 81), Jeff Whitley, Kirk, Hamilton (Harkin 46), Friars.

2 June

Northern Ireland (1) 2 *(Friars 38 (pen), Hamilton 67)*
Wales (1) 2 *(Jeanne 3, Maxwell 84)*   852
Northern Ireland: Miskelly; Graham R (Clarke 75), McCann, Convery, Kelly D, Holmes, Jeff Whitley, Toner, Kirk (Hamilton 35), Harkin, Friars (McFlynn 78).

REPUBLIC OF IRELAND UNDER-21 INTERNATIONALS

31 Aug

Republic of Ireland (0) 0
Yugoslavia (0) 2 *(Djokaj 56, 82)*   2200
Republic of Ireland: O'Reilly; Maybury, O'Brien, Dunne, Ryan, Rowlands, Quinn, McPhail, Mahon (Barry-Murphy 63), Lee (Conlon 60), Clare (Folan 60).

3 Sept

Croatia (3) 5 *(Filipovic 12, Sokota 22, Mikic 24, Balaban 88, 90)*
Republic of Ireland (1) 1 *(Hawkins 41)*
Republic of Ireland: O'Reilly; Boxall, Worrell, Hawkins, Ryan, Dunne, O'Brien, McPhail (Rowlands 7), Fenn, Conlon (Clare 58), Quinn (Mahon 72).

7 Sept

Malta (0) 1 *(Mamo 88)*   1280
Republic of Ireland (1) 3 *(Lee 37, Mahon 71, Fenn 86)*
Republic of Ireland: O'Reilly; Boxall (Ryan 58), Maybury, O'Brien, Hawkins, Worrell, Quinn, Barry-Murphy (Cummins 70), Lee (Conlon 83), Fenn, Mahon.

8 Oct

Macedonia (0) 0
Republic of Ireland (1) 1 *(Rowlands 33)*   750
Republic of Ireland: O'Reilly; Heary, O'Brien A, Clarke, Ryan, Rowlands, Quinn, Healy (O'Brien R 75), Partridge, George (Baker 79), Doherty (Sadlier 79).

22 Feb

Republic of Ireland (1) 1 *(Doherty 12)*
Czech Republic (0) 2 *(Dosek 61, Baros 83)*   650
Republic of Ireland: O'Reilly (Delaney 46); Heary (Ferguson 46), Clarke (Murphy 46), Dunne, O'Brien, Quinn B, Partridge, George (Barrett 46), Doherty, Rowlands, Quinn A (Healy 71).

25 Apr

Republic of Ireland (0) 1 *(Baker 90)*
Greece (0) 2 *(Charisteas 57, Loboutis 87)*
Republic of Ireland: Delaney; Heary, Delaney, McGovern, Murphy (McGrath 46), Healy, Crossley, Billington (O'Grady 76), Partridge (Martyn 76), Freeman (Baker 46), Barrett (Reddy 65).

25 May

Republic of Ireland (0) 0
Colombia (0) 1 *(Moreno 74)*
Republic of Ireland: Murphy; Heary, Ferguson, McGovern, Clarke, Rowlands (Baker 73), Quinn B, O'Connor, Quinn A (Partride 63), Barrett, Doherty.

27 May

Republic of Ireland (2) 2 *(Reddy 8, Quinn B 10)*
Ghana (0) 0
Republic of Ireland: Delaney; O'Halloran, O'Shea, Ferguson, Clarke, Quinn B, O'Connor, Quinn A (McGrath 78), Partridge, Doherty (Barrett 70), Reddy (George 59).

29 May

Republic of Ireland (0) 0
Portugal (1) 3 *(Tonel 37, Miguel 49, Ednilson 74)*
Republic of Ireland: Murphy; O'Halloran, O'Shea, Ferguson, Clarke, Quinn B, Partridge (Baker 58), O'Connor (Rowlands 64), Quinn A, Reddy (McGrath 58), Barrett.

BRITISH UNDER-21 APPEARANCES 1976–2000

ENGLAND

Ablett, G. (Liverpool), 1988 v F (1)
Adams, A. (Arsenal). 1985 v Ei, Fi; 1986 v D; 1987 v Se, Y (5)
Adams, N. (Everton), 1987 v Se (1)
Allen, B. (QPR), 1992 v H, M, Cz, F; 1993 v N (sub), T, P, Cz (sub) (8)
Allen, C. A. (Oxford U), 1995 v Br (sub), F (sub) (2)
Allen, C. (QPR), 1980 v EG (sub); (with C Palace), 1981 v N, R (3)
Allen, M. (QPR), 1987 v Se (sub); 1988 v Y (sub) (2)
Allen, P. (West Ham U), 1985 v Ei, R; (with Tottenham H), 1986 v R (3)
Allen, R. W. (Tottenham H), 1998 v F (sub), S.Af, Arg (sub) (3)
Anderson, V. A. (Nottingham F), 1978 v I (1)
Anderton, D. R. (Tottenham H), 1993 v Sp, Sm, Ho, Pol, N, P, Cz, Br, S, F; 1994 v Pol, Sm (12)
Andrews, I. (Leicester C), 1987 v Se (1)
Ardley, N. C. (Wimbledon), 1993 v Pol, N, P, Cz, Br, S, F, 1994 v Pol (sub), Ho, Sm (10)
Ashcroft, L. (Preston NE), 1992 v H (sub) (1)
Atherton, P. (Coventry C), 1992 v T (1)
Atkinson, B. (Sunderland), 1991 v W (sub), Sen, M, USSR (sub), F; 1992 v Pol (sub) (6)
Awford, A. T. (Portsmouth), 1993 v Sp, N, T, P, Cz, Br, S, F; 1994 v Ho (9)

Bailey, G. R. (Manchester U), 1979 v W, Bul; 1980 v D, S (2), EG; 1982 v N; 1983 v D, Gr; 1984 v H, F (2), I, Sp (14)
Baker, G. E. (Southampton), 1981 v N, R (2)
Ball, M. J. (Everton), 1999 v Se, Bul, L, CzR, Pol; 2000 v L, D (sub) (7)
Barker, S. (Blackburn R), 1985 v Is (sub), Ei, R; 1986 v I (4)
Barmby, N. J. (Tottenham H), 1994 v D; 1995 v P, A (sub); (with Everton), 1998 v Sw (4)
Bannister, G. (Sheffield W), 1982 v Pol (1)
Barnes, J. (Watford), 1983 v D, Gr (2)
Barnes, P. S. (Manchester C), 1977 v W (sub), S, Fi, N; 1978 v N, Fi, I (2), Y (9)
Barrett, E. D. (Oldham Ath), 1990 v P, F, USSR, Cz (4)
Barry, G. (Aston Villa), 1999 v CzR, F, H; 2000 v Y (4)
Bart-Williams, C. G. (Sheffield W), 1993 v Sp, N, T; 1994 v D, Ru, F, Bel, P; 1995 v P, A, Ei (2), La (2); (with Nottingham F) 1996 v P (sub), A (16)
Batty, D. (Leeds U), 1988 v Sw (sub); 1989 v Gr (sub), Bul, Sen, Ei, US; 1990 v Pol (7)
Bazeley, D. S. (Watford), 1992 v H (sub) (1)
Beagrie, P. (Sheffield U), 1988 v WG, T (2)
Beardsmore, R. (Manchester U), 1989 v Gr, Alb (sub), Pol, Bul, USA (5)
Beattie, J. S. (Southampton), 1999 v CzR (sub), F (sub), Pol, H; 2000 v Pol (5)
Beckham, D. R. J. (Manchester U), 1995 v Br, Mal, An, F; 1996 v P, A (sub), Bel, An, P (9)
Bent, M. N. (Crystal Palace), 1998 v S.Af (sub), Arg (2)
Beeston, C. (Stoke C), 1988 v USSR (1)
Bertschin, K. E. (Birmingham C), 1977 v S; 1978 v Y (2) (3)
Birtles, G. (Nottingham F), 1980 v Bul, EG (sub) (2)
Blackwell, D. R. (Wimbledon), 1991 v W, T, Sen (sub), M, USSR, F (6)
Blake, M. A. (Aston Villa), 1990 v F (sub), Cz (sub); 1991 v H, Pol, Ei (2), W; 1992 v Pol (8)
Blissett, L. L. (Watford), 1979 v W, Bul (sub), Se; 1980 v D (4)
Booth, A. D. (Huddersfield T), 1995 v La (2 subs); 1996 v N (3)
Bowyer, L. D. (Charlton Ath), 1996 v N (sub), Bel, P, Br; (with Leeds U), 1997 v Mol, I, Sw, Ge; 1998 v Mol; 1999 v F, Pol; 2000 v D, Arg (13)
Bracewell, P. (Stoke C), 1983 v D, Gr (1 + 1 sub), H; 1984 v D, H, F (2), I (2), Sp (2); 1985 v T (13)
Bradbury, L. M. (Portsmouth), 1997 v Pol; (with Manchester C), 1998 v Mol (sub), I (sub) (3)
Branch, P. M. (Everton), 1997 v Pol (sub) (1)
Bradshaw, P. W. (Wolverhampton W), 1977 v W, S; 1978 v Fi, Y (4)
Breacker, T. (Luton T), 1986 v I (2) (2)
Brennan, M. (Ipswich T), 1987 v Y, Sp, T, Mor, F (5)
Bridge, W. M. (Southampton), 1999 v H (sub) (1)

Bridges, M. (Sunderland), 1997 v Sw (sub); 1999 v F; (with Leeds U), 2000 v D (3)
Brightwell, I. (Manchester C), 1989 v D, Alb; 1990 v Se (sub), Pol (4)
Briscoe, L. S. (Sheffield W), 1996 v Cro, Bel (sub), An, Br; 1997 v Sw (sub) (5)
Brock, K. (Oxford U), 1984 v I, Sp (2); 1986 v I (4)
Broomes, M. C. (Blackburn R), 1997 v Sw, Ge (2)
Brown, M. R. (Manchester C), 1996 v Cro, Bel, An, P (4)
Brown, W. M. (Manchester U), 1999 v Se, Bul, L, CzR, Pol, Se, Bul (7)
Bull, S. G. (Wolverhampton W), 1989 v Alb (2) Pol; 1990 v Se, Pol (5)
Bullock, M. J. (Barnsley), 1998 v Gr (sub) (1)
Burrows, D. (WBA), 1989 v Se (sub); (with Liverpool), Gr, Alb (2), Pol; 1990 v Se, Pol (7)
Butcher, T. I. (Ipswich T), 1979 v Se; 1980 v D, Bul, S (2), EG (2) (7)
Butt, N. (Manchester U), 1995 v Ei (2), La; 1996 v P, A; 1997 v Ge, Pol (7)
Butters, G. (Tottenham H), 1989 v Bul, Sen (sub), Ei (sub) (3)
Butterworth, I. (Coventry C), 1985 v T, R; (with Nottingham F), 1986 v R, T, D (2), I (2) (8)

Cadamarteri, D. L. (Everton), 1999 v CzR (sub); 2000 v Y (sub) (2)
Caesar, G. (Arsenal), 1987 v Mor, USSR (sub), F (3)
Callaghan, N. (Watford), 1983 v D, Gr (sub), H (sub); 1984 v D, H, F (2), I, Sp (9)
Campbell, A. P. (Middlesbrough), 2000 v Y, T (sub), Slo (sub) (3)
Campbell, K. J. (Arsenal), 1991 v H, T (sub); 1992 v G, T (4)
Campbell, S. (Tottenham), 1994 v D, Ru, F, US, Bel, P; 1995 v P, A, Ei; 1996 v N, A (11)
Carbon, M. P. (Derby Co), 1996 v Cro (sub); 1997 v Ge, I, Sw (4)
Carr, C. (Fulham), 1985 v Ei (sub) (1)
Carr, F. (Nottingham F), 1987 v Se, Y, Sp (sub), Mor, USSR; 1988 v WG (sub), T, Y, F (9)
Carragher, J. L. (Liverpool), 1997 v I (sub), Sw, Ge, Pol; 1998 v Mol (sub), I, Gr, Sw (sub), F, S.Af, Arg; 1999 v Se, Bul, L, CzR, F, Pol, Se, Bul; 2000 v L, Pol, D, Arg, Y, I, T, Slo (27)
Casper, C. M. (Manchester U), 1995 v Mal (1)
Caton, T. (Manchester C), 1982 v N, H (sub), Pol (2), S; 1983 v WG (2), Gr; 1984 v D, H, F (2), I (2) (14)
Chadwick, L. H. (Manchester U), 2000 v L, D, Arg, I (sub), Slo (sub) (5)
Challis, T. M. (QPR), 1996 v An, P (2)
Chamberlain, M. (Stoke C), 1983 v Gr; 1984 v F (sub), I, Sp (4)
Chapman, L. (Stoke C), 1981 v Ei (1)
Charles, G. A. (Nottingham F), 1991 v H, W (sub), Ei; 1992 v T (4)
Chettle, S. (Nottingham F), 1988 v M, USSR, Mor, F; 1989 v D, Se, Gr, Alb (2), Bul; 1990 v Se, Pol (12)
Clark, L. R. (Newcastle U), 1992 v Cz, F; 1993 v Sp, N, T, Ho (sub), Pol (sub), Cz, Br, S; 1994 v Ho (11)
Clegg, M. J. (Manchester U), 1998 v Fr (sub), S.Af (sub) (2)
Clemence, S. N. (Tottenham H), 1999 v Se (sub) (1)
Clough, N. (Nottingham F), 1986 v D (sub); 1987 v Se, Y, T, USSR, F (sub), P; 1988 v WG, T, Y, S (2), M, Mor, F (15)
Cole, A. A. (Arsenal), 1992 v H, Cz (sub), F (sub); (with Bristol C), 1993 v Sm; (with Newcastle U), Pol, N; 1994 v Pol, Ho (8)
Cole, J. J. (West Ham U), 2000 v Arg (sub) (1)
Coney, D. (Fulham), 1985 v T (sub); 1986 v R; 1988 v T, WG (4)
Connor, T. (Brighton & HA), 1987 v Y (1)
Cooke, R. (Tottenham H), 1986 v D (sub) (1)
Cooke, T. J. (Manchester U), 1996 v Cro, Bel, An (sub), P (4)
Cooper, C. (Middlesbrough), 1988 v F (2), M, USSR, Mor; 1989 v D, Se, Gr (8)
Corrigan, T. J. (Manchester C), 1978 v I (2), Y (3)
Cort, C. E. R. (Wimbledon), 1999 v L (sub), CzR, H (sub), Se, Bul; 2000 v L (sub), Pol, D (sub), Arg, I, T, Slo (12)
Cottee, A. (West Ham U), 1985 v Fi (sub), Is (sub), Ei, R, Fi; 1987 v Sp, P; 1988 v WG (8)

Couzens, A. J. (Leeds U), 1995 v Mal (sub), An, F (sub) (3)
Cowans, G. S. (Aston Villa), 1979 v W, Se; 1980 v Bul, EG; 1981 v R (5)
Cox, N. J. (Aston Villa), 1993 v T, Ho, Pol, N; 1994 v Pol, Sm (6)
Cranson, I. (Ipswich T), 1985 v Fi, Is, R; 1986 v R, I (5)
Cresswell, R. P. W. (York C), 1999 v F (sub); (with Sheffield W) H (sub), Se, Bul (4)
Croft, G. (Grimsby T), 1995 v Br, Mal, An, F (4)
Crooks, G. (Stoke C), 1980 v Bul, S (2), EG (sub) (4)
Crossley, M. G. (Nottingham F), 1990 v P, USSR, Cz (3)
Cundy, J. V. (Chelsea), 1991 v Ei (2); 1992 v Pol (3)
Cunningham, L. (WBA), 1977 v S, Fi, N (sub); 1978 v N, Fi, I (6)
Curbishley, L. C. (Birmingham C), 1981 v Sw (1)
Curtis, J. C. K. (Manchester U), 1998 v I (sub), Gr, Sw, F, S.Af, Arg; 1999 v Se (sub), Bul, L, CzR, F, Pol (sub), H, Se (sub), Bul; 2000 v Pol (16)

Daniel, P. W. (Hull C), 1977 v S, Fi, N; 1978 v Fi, I, Y (2) (7)
Davies, K. C. (Southampton), 1998 v Gr (sub); (with Blackburn R), 1999 v CzR; (with Southampton), 2000 v Y (sub) (3)
Davis, K. G. (Luton T), 1995 v An; 1996 v Cro (sub), P (3)
Davis, P. (Arsenal), 1982 v Pol, S; 1983 v D, Gr (1 + 1 sub), H (sub); 1987 v T; 1988 v WG, T, Y, Fr (11)
Day, C. N. (Tottenham H), 1996 v Cro, Bel, Br; (with Crystal Palace), 1997 v Mol, Ge, Sw (6)
D'Avray, M. (Ipswich T), 1984 v I, Sp (sub) (2)
Deehan, J. M. (Aston Villa), 1977 v N; 1978 v N, Fi, I; 1979 v Bul, Se (sub); 1980 v D (7)
Dennis, M. E. (Birmingham C), 1980 v Bul; 1981 v N, R (3)
Dichio, D. S. E. (QPR), 1996 v N (sub) (1)
Dickens, A. (West Ham U), 1985 v Fi (sub) (1)
Dicks, J. (West Ham U), 1988 v Sw (sub), M, Mor, F (4)
Digby, F. (Swindon T), 1987 v Sp (sub), USSR, P; 1988 v T; 1990 v Pol (5)
Dillon, K. P. (Birmingham C), 1981 v R (1)
Dixon, K. (Chelsea), 1985 v Fi (1)
Dobson, A. (Coventry C), 1989 v Bul, Sen, Ei, US (4)
Dodd, J. R. (Southampton), 1991 v Pol, Ei, T, Sen, M, F; 1992 v G, Pol (8)
Donowa, L. (Norwich C), 1985 v Is, R (sub), Fi (sub) (3)
Dorigo, A. (Aston Villa), 1987 v Se, Sp, T, Mor, USSR, F, P; (with Chelsea) 1988 v WG, Y, S (2) (11)
Dozzell, J. (Ipswich T), 1987 v Se, T (sub), Sp, USSR, F, P; 1989 v Se, Gr (sub); 1990 v Se (sub) (9)
Draper, M. A. (Notts Co), 1991 v Ei (sub); 1992 v G, Pol (3)
Duberry, M. W. (Chelsea), 1997 v Mol, Pol, Ge; 1998 v Mol, Gr (5)
Dunn, D. J. I. (Blackburn R), 1999 v CzR (sub); 2000 v I (sub), T, Slo (4)
Duxbury, M. (Manchester U), 1981 v Sw (sub), Ei (sub), R (sub), Sw; 1982 v N; 1983 v WG (2) (7)
Dyer, B. A. (Crystal Palace), 1994 v Ru, F, US, Bel, P; 1995 v P (sub); 1996 v Cro; 1997 v Mol, Ge; 1998 v Mol, Gr (10)
Dyer, K. C. (Ipswich T), 1998 v Mol, I, Gr, Sw, S.Af, Arg; 1999 v Se, Bul, CzR, Se; (with Newcastle U), 2000 v Y (11)
Dyson, P. I. (Coventry C), 1981 v N, R, Sw, Ei (4)

Eadie, D. M. (Norwich C), 1994 v F (sub), US; 1997 v Mol, Ge (2), I; 1998 v I (7)
Ebbrell, J. (Everton), 1989 v Sen, Ei, US (sub); 1990 v P, F, USSR, Cz; 1991 v H, Pol, Ei, W, T; 1992 v G, T (14)
Edghill, R. A. (Manchester C), 1994 v Ru; 1995 v A (3)
Ehiogu, U. (Aston Villa), 1992 v H, M, Cz, F; 1993 v Sp, N, T, Sm, T, Ho, Pol, N; 1994 v Pol, Ho, Sm (15)
Elliott, P. (Luton T), 1985 v Fi; 1986 v T, D (3)
Elliott, R. J. (Newcastle U), 1996 v P, A (2)
Elliott, S. W. (Derby Co), 1998 v F, Arg (sub) (2)
Euell, J. (Wimbledon), 1998 v F, Arg (sub); 1999 v Se (sub), Bul (se), Pol (sub), H (6)

Fairclough, C. (Nottingham F), 1985 v T, Is, Ei; 1987 v Sp, T; (with Tottenham H), 1988 v Y, F (7)
Fairclough, D. (Liverpool), 1977 v W (1)
Fashanu, J. (Norwich C), 1980 v EG; 1981 v N (sub), R, Sw, Ei (sub), H; (with Nottingham F), 1982 v N, H, Pol, S; 1983 v WG (sub) (11)
Fear, P. (Wimbledon), 1994 v Ru, F, US (sub) (3)
Fenton, G. A. (Aston Villa), 1995 v Ei (1)

Fenwick, T. W. (C Palace), 1981 v N, R, Sw, Ei; (with QPR), R; 1982 v N, H, S (2); 1983 v WG (2) (11)
Ferdinand, R. G. (West Ham U), 1997 v Sw, Ge; 1998 v I, Gr; 2000 v Y (5)
Fereday, W. (QPR), 1985 v T, Ei (sub). Fi; 1986 v T (sub), I (5)
Flitcroft, G. W. (Manchester C), 1993 v Sm, Hol, N, P, Cz, Br, S, F; 1994 v Pol, Ho (10)
Flowers, T. (Southampton), 1987 v Mor, F; 1988 v WG (sub) (3)
Ford, M. (Leeds U), 1996 v Cro; 1997 v Mol (2)
Forster, N. M. (Brentford), 1995 v Br, Mal, An, F (4)
Forsyth, M. (Derby Co), 1988 v Sw (1)
Foster, S. (Brighton & HA), 1980 v EG (sub) (1)
Fowler, R. B. (Liverpool), 1994 v Sm, Ru (sub), F, US; 1995 v P, A; 1996 v P, A (8)
Froggatt, S. J. (Aston Villa), 1993 v Sp, Sm (sub) (2)
Futcher, P. (Luton T), 1977 v W, S, Fi, N; (with Manchester C), 1978 v N, Fi, I (2), Y (2); 1979 v D (11)

Gabbiadini, M. (Sunderland), 1989 v Bul, USA (2)
Gale, A. (Fulham), 1982 v Pol (1)
Gallen, K. A. (QPR), 1995 v Ei, La (2); 1996 v Cro (4)
Gascoigne, P. (Newcastle U), 1987 v Mo, USSR, P; 1988 v WG, Y, S (2), F (2), Sw, M, USSR (sub), Mor (13)
Gayle, H. (Birmingham C), 1984 v I, Sp (2) (3)
Gernon, T. (Ipswich T), 1983 v Gr (1)
Gerrard, P. W. (Oldham Ath), 1993 v T, Ho, Pol, N, P, Cz, Br, S, F; 1994 v D, Ru; 1995 v P, A, Ei (2), La (2); 1996 v P (18)
Gerrard, S. G. (Liverpool), 2000 v L, Pol, D, Y (4)
Gibbs, N. (Watford), 1987 v Mor, USSR, F, P; 1988 v T (5)
Gibson, C. (Aston Villa), 1982 v N (1)
Gilbert, W. A. (C Palace), 1979 v W, Bul; 1980 v Bul; 1981 v N, R, Sw, R, Sw, H; 1982 v N (sub), H (11)
Goddard, P. (West Ham U), 1981 v N, Sw, Se (sub); 1982 v N (sub), Pol, S; 1983 v WG (2) (8)
Gordon, D. (Norwich C), 1987 v T (sub), Mor (sub), F, P (4)
Gordon, D. D. (Crystal Palace), 1994 v Ru, F, US, Bel, P; 1995 v P, A, Ei (2), La (2); 1996 v P, N (13)
Grant, A. J. (Everton), 1996 v An (sub) (1)
Granville, D. P. (Chelsea), 1997 v Ge (sub), Pol; 1998 v Mol (3)
Gray, A. (Aston Villa), 1988 v S, F (2)
Greening, J. (Manchester U), 1999 v H, Se (sub), Bul; 2000 v Pol (4)
Griffin, A. (Newcastle U), 1999 v H (1)
Guppy, S. A. (Leicester C), 1998 v Sw (1)

Haigh, P. (Hull C), 1977 v N (sub) (1)
Hall, M. T. J. (Coventry C), 1997 v Pol (2), I, Sw, Ge; 1998 v Mol, Gr (2) (8)
Hall, R. A. (Southampton), 1992 v H (sub), F; 1993 v Sm, T, Ho, Pol, P, Cz, Br, S, F (11)
Hamilton, D. V. (Newcastle U), 1997 v Pol (1)
Hardyman, P. (Portsmouth), 1987 v Ei; 1986 v D (2)
Harley, J. (Chelsea), 2000 v Arg (sub), T (sub), Slo (3)
Hateley, M. (Coventry C), 1982 v Pol, S; 1983 v Gr (2), H; (with Portsmouth), 1984 v F (2), I, Sp (2) (10)
Hayes, M. (Arsenal), 1987 v Sp, T; 1988 v F (sub) (3)
Hazell, R. J. (Wolverhampton W), 1979 v D (1)
Heaney, N. A. (Arsenal), 1992 v H, M, Cz, F; 1993 v N, T (6)
Heath, A. (Stoke C), 1981 v R, Sw, H; 1982 v N, H; (with Everton), Pol, S; 1983 v WG (8)
Hendon, I. M. (Tottenham H), 1992 v H, M, Cz, F; 1993 v Sp, N, T (7)
Hendrie, L. A. (Aston Villa), 1996 v Cro (sub); 1998 v Sw (sub); 1999 v Se, Bul, L, F, Pol; 2000 v L, D, Arg, Y, I, Slo (sub) (13)
Hesford, I. (Blackpool), 1981 v Ei (sub), Pol (2), S (2); 1983 v WG (2) (7)
Heskey, E. W. I. (Leicester C), 1997 v I, Ge, Pol (2); 1998 v I, Gr (2), Sw, F, S.Af, Arg; 1999 v Se, Bul, L; 2000 v L; (with Liverpool), Y (16)
Hilaire, V. (C Palace), 1980 v Bul, S (1+1 sub), EG (2); 1981 v N, R, Sw (sub); 1982 v Pol (sub) (9)
Hill, D. R. L. (Tottenham H), 1995 v Br, Mal, An, F (4)
Hillier, D. (Arsenal), 1991 v T (1)
Hinchcliffe, A. (Manchester C), 1989 v D (1)
Hinshelwood, P. A. (C Palace), 1978 v N; 1980 v EG (2)
Hirst, D. (Sheffield W), 1988 v USSR, F; 1989 v D, Bul (sub), Sen, Ei, US (7)
Hislop, N. S. (Newcastle U), 1998 v Sw (1)

Hoddle, G. (Tottenham H), 1977 v W (sub); 1978 v Fi (sub), I (2), Y; 1979 v D, W, Bul; 1980 v S (2), EG (2) (12)

Hodge, S. (Nottingham F), 1983 v Gr (sub); 1984 v D, F, I, Sp (2); (with Aston Villa), 1986 v R, T (8)

Hodgson, D. J. (Middlesbrough), 1981 v N, R (sub), Sw, Ei; 1982 v Pol; 1983 v WG (6)

Holdsworth, D. (Watford), 1989 v Gr (sub) (1)

Holland, C. J. (Newcastle U), 1995 v La; 1996 v N (sub), A (sub), Cro, Bel, An, Br; 1997 v Mol, Pol, Sw (10)

Holland, P. (Mansfield T), 1995 v Br, Mal, An, F (4)

Holloway, D. (Sunderland), 1998 v Sw (sub) (1)

Horne, B. (Millwall), 1989 v Gr (sub), Pol, Bul, Ei, US (5)

Howe, E. J. F. (Bournemouth), 1998 v S.Af (sub), Arg (2)

Hucker, P. (QPR), 1984 v I, Sp (2)

Huckerby, D. (Coventry C), 1997 v I (sub), Sw, Ge (sub), Pol (sub) (4)

Hughes, S. J. (Arsenal), 1997 v I, Sw, Ge, Pol; 1998 v Mol, I, Gr, Sw (sub) (8)

Humphreys, R. J. (Sheffield W), 1997 v Pol, Ge (sub), Sw (3)

Impey, A. R. (QPR), 1993 v T (1)

Ince, P. (West Ham U), 1989 v Alb; 1990 v Se (2)

Jackson, M. A. (Everton), 1992 v H, M, Cz, F; 1993 v Sm (sub), T, Ho, Pol, N; 1994 v Pol (10)

James, D. (Watford), 1991 v Ei (2), T, Sen, M, USSR, F; 1992 v G, T, Pol (10)

James, J. C. (Luton T), 1990 v F, USSR (2)

Jansen, M. B (Crystal Palace), 1999 v Se, Bul, L; (with Blackburn R) F (sub), Pol; 2000 v I (sub) (6)

Jeffers, F. (Everton), 2000 v L, Arg, I, T, Slo (5)

Jemson, N. B. (Nottingham F), 1991 v W (1)

Joachim, J. K. (Leicester C), 1994 v D (sub); 1995 v P, A, Ei, Br, Mal, An, F; 1996 v N (9)

Johnson, S. A. M. (Crewe Alex), 1999 v L (sub), CzR (sub), F (sub), Pol; (with Derby Co), Se, Bul; 2000 v D, Arg (sub), Y, I, T (11)

Johnson, T. (Notts Co), 1991 v H (sub), Ei (sub); 1992 v G, T, Pol; (with Derby Co), M, Cz (sub) (7)

Johnston, C. P. (Middlesbrough), 1981 v N, Ei (2)

Jones, D. R. (Everton), 1977 v W (1)

Jones, C. H. (Tottenham H), 1978 v Y (sub) (1)

Jones, R. (Liverpool), 1993 v Sm, Ho (2)

Keegan, G. A. (Manchester C), 1977 v W (1)

Kenny, W. (Everton), 1993 v T (1)

Keown, M. (Aston Villa), 1987 v Sp, Mor, USSR, P; 1988 v T, S, F (2) (8)

Kerslake, D. (QPR), 1986 v T (1)

Kilcline, B. (Notts C), 1983 v D, Gr (2)

King, A. E. (Everton), 1977 v W; 1978 v Y (2)

King, L. (Tottenham H), 2000 v L (sub), I, T, Slo (4)

Kitson, P. (Leicester C), 1991 v Sen (sub), M, F; 1992 v Pol; (with Derby Co), M, Cz, F (7)

Knight, A. (Portsmouth), 1983 v Gr, H (2)

Knight, I. (Sheffield W), 1987 v Se (sub), Y (2)

Kozluk, R. (Derby Co), 1998 v F, Arg (sub) (2)

Lake, P. (Manchester C), 1989 v D, Alb (2), Pol; 1990 v Pol (5)

Lampard, F. J. (West Ham U), 1998 v Gr (2), Sw, F, S.Af, Arg; 1999 v Se, Bul, L, CzR, F, Pol, Se; 2000 v L, Arg, Y, I, T, Slo (19)

Langley, T. W. (Chelsea), 1978 v I (sub) (1)

Lee, D. J. (Chelsea), 1990 v F; 1991 v H, Pol, Ei (2), T, Sen, USSR, F; 1992 v Pol (10)

Lee, R. (Charlton Ath), 1986 v I (sub); 1987 v Se (sub) (2)

Lee, S. (Liverpool), 1981 v R, Sw, H; 1982 v S; 1983 v WG (2) (6)

Le Saux, G. (Chelsea), 1990 v P, F, USSR, Cz (4)

Lowe, D. (Ipswich T), 1988 v F, Sw (sub) (2)

Lukic, J. (Leeds U), 1981 v N, R, Ei, R, Sw, H; 1982 v H (7)

Lund, G. (Grimsby T), 1985 v T; 1986 v R, T (3)

McCall, S. H. (Ipswich T), 1981 v Sw, H; 1982 v H, S; 1983 v WG (2) (6)

McDonald, N. (Newcastle U), 1987 v Se (sub), Sp, T; 1988 v WG, Y (sub) (5)

McGrath, L. (Coventry C), 1986 v D (1)

MacKenzie, S. (WBA), 1982 v N, S (2) (3)

McLeary, A. (Millwall), 1988 v Sw (1)

McMahon, S. (Everton), 1981 v Ei; 1982 v Pol; 1983 v D, Gr (2); (with Aston Villa), 1984 v H (6)

McManaman, S. (Liverpool), 1991 v N, M (sub); 1993 v N, T, Sm, T; 1994 v Pol (7)

Mabbutt, G. (Bristol R), 1982 v Pol (2), S; (with Tottenham H), 1983 v D; 1984 v F; 1986 v D, I (7)

Makin, C. (Oldham Ath), 1994 v Ru (sub), F, US, Bel, P (5)

Marriott, A. (Nottingham F), 1992 v M (1)

Marsh, S. T. (Oxford U), 1998 v F (1)

Marshall, A. J. (Norwich C), 1995 v Mal, An; 1997 v Pol, I (4)

Marshall, L. K. (Norwich C), 1999 v F (sub) (1)

Martin, L. (Manchester U), 1989 v Gr (sub), Alb (sub) (2)

Martyn, N. (Bristol R), 1988 v S (sub), M, USSR, Mor, F; 1989 v D, Se, Gr, Alb (2); 1990 v Se (11)

Matteo, D. (Liverpool), 1994 v F (sub), Bel, P; 1998 v Sw (4)

Matthew, D. (Chelsea), 1990 v P, USSR (sub), Cz; 1991 v Ei, M, USSR, F; 1992 v G (sub), T (9)

May, A. (Manchester C), 1986 v I (sub) (1)

Merson, P. (Arsenal), 1989 v D, Gr, Pol (sub); 1990 v Pol (4)

Middleton, J. (Nottingham F), 1977 v Fi, N; (with Derby Co), 1978 v N (3)

Miller, A. (Arsenal), 1988 v Mor (sub); 1989 v Sen; 1991 v H, Pol (4)

Mills, D. J. (Charlton Ath), 1999 v Se, Bul (sub), L, Pol, H, Se; (with Leeds U), 2000 v L, Pol, D, Arg, Y (sub), I, T, Slo (14)

Mills, G. R. (Nottingham F), 1981 v R; 1982 v N (2)

Mimms, R. (Rotherham U), 1985 v Is (sub), Ei (sub); (with Everton), 1986 v I (3)

Minto, S. C. (Charlton Ath), 1991 v W; 1992 v H, M, Cz; 1993 v T; 1994 v Ho (6)

Moore, I. (Tranmere R), 1996 v Cro (sub), Bel (sub), An, P, Br; 1997 v Mol (sub); (with Nottingham F), Sw (sub) (7)

Moran, S. (Southampton), 1982 v N (sub); 1984 v F (2)

Morgan, S. (Leicester C), 1987 v Se, Y (2)

Morris, J. (Chelsea), 1997 v Pol (sub), Sw (sub), Ge (sub); 1999 v Bul (sub), L (sub), CzR; 2000 v Pol (7)

Mortimer, P. (Charlton Ath), 1989 v Sen, Ei (2)

Moses, A. P. (Barnsley), 1997 v Pol; 1998 v Gr (sub) (2)

Moses, R. M. (WBA), 1981 v N (sub), Sw, Ei, R, Sw, H; 1982 v N (sub); (with Manchester U), H (8)

Mountfield, D. (Everton), 1984 v Sp (1)

Muggleton, C. D. (Leicester C), 1990 v F (1)

Mullins, H. I. (Crystal Palace), 1999 v Pol (sub), H, Bul (3)

Murphy, D. B. (Liverpool), 1998 v Mol, Gr (sub); 2000 v T, Slo (4)

Murray, P. (QPR), 1997 v I, Pol; 1998 v I, Gr (4)

Mutch, A. (Wolverhampton W), 1989 v Pol (1)

Myers. A. (Chelsea), 1995 v Br, Mal, An (sub), F (4)

Naylor, L. M. (Wolverhampton W), 2000 v Arg (1)

Nethercott, S. (Tottenham), 1994 v D, Ru, F, US, Bel, P; 1995 v La (2) (8)

Neville, P. J. (Manchester U), 1995 v Br, Mal, An, F; 1996 v P, N (sub); 1997 v Ge (7)

Newell, M. (Luton T), 1986 v D (1 + 1 sub), I (1 + 1 sub) (4)

Newton, E. J. I. (Chelsea), 1993 v T (sub); 1994 v Sm (2)

Newton, S. O. (Charlton Ath), 1997 v Mol, Pol, Ge (3)

Nicholls, A. (Plymouth Arg), 1994 v F (1)

Oakes, M. C. (Aston Villa), 1994 v D (sub), F (sub), US, Bel, P; 1996 v A (6)

Oakes, S. J. (Luton T), 1993 v Br (sub) (1)

Oakley, M. (Southampton), 1997 v Ge; 1998 v F, S.Af, Arg (4)

O'Brien, A. J. (Bradford C), 1999 v F (1)

O'Connor, J. (Everton), 1996 v Cro, An, Br (3)

Oldfield, D. (Luton T), 1989 v Se (1)

Olney, I. A. (Aston Villa), 1990 v P, F, USSR, Cz; 1991 v H, Pol, Ei (2), T; 1992 v Pol (sub) (10)

Ord, R. J. (Sunderland), 1991 v W, M, USSR (3)

Osman, R. C. (Ipswich T), 1979 v W (sub), Se; 1980 v D, S (2), EG (2) (7)

Owen, G. A. (Manchester C), 1977 v S, Fi, N; 1978 v N, Fi, I (2), Y; 1979 v D, W; (with WBA), Bul, Se (sub); 1980 v D, S (2), EG; 1981 v Sw, R; 1982 v N (sub), H; 1983 v WG (2) (22)

Owen, M. J. (Liverpool), 1998 v Gr (1)

Painter, I. (Stoke C), 1986 v I (1)

Palmer, C. (Sheffield W), 1989 v Bul, Sen, Ei, US (4)

Parker, G. (Hull C), 1986 v I (2); (with Nottingham F), F; 1987 v Se, Y (sub), Sp (6)

Parker, P. (Fulham), 1985 v Fi, T, Is (sub), Ei, R, Fi; 1986 v T, D (8)

Parkes, P. B. F. (QPR), 1979 v D (1)
Parkin, S. (Stoke C), 1987 v Sp (sub); 1988 v WG (sub), T, S (sub), F (5)
Parlour, R. (Arsenal), 1992 v H, M, Cz, F; 1993 v Sp, N, T; 1994 v D, Ru, Bel, P; 1995 v A (12)
Peach, D. S. (Southampton), 1977 v S, Fi, N; 1978 v N, I (2) (6)
Peake, A. (Leicester C), 1982 v Pol (1)
Pearce, I. A. (Blackburn R), 1995 v Ei, La; 1996 v N (3)
Pearce, S. (Nottingham F), 1987 v Y (1)
Pickering N. (Sunderland), 1983 v D (sub), Gr, H; 1984 v F (sub + 1), I (2), Sp; 1985 v Is, R, Fi; 1986 v R, T; (with Coventry C), D, I (15)
Platt, D. (Aston Villa), 1988 v M, Mor, F (3)
Plummer, C. S. (QPR), 1996 v Cro (sub), Bel, An, P (sub), Br (5)
Pollock, J. (Middlesbrough), 1995 v Ei (sub); 1996 v N, A (3)
Porter, G. (Watford), 1987 v Sp (sub), T, Mor, USSR, F, P (sub); 1988 v T (sub), Y, S (2), F, Sw (12)
Potter, G. S. (Southampton), 1997 v Mol (1)
Pressman, K. (Sheffield W), 1989 v D (sub) (1)
Proctor, M. (Middlesbrough), 1981 v Ei (sub), Sw; (with Nottingham F) 1982 v N, Pol (4)
Purse, D. J. (Birmingham C), 1998 v F. S.Af (2)

Quashie, N. F. (QPR), 1997 v Pol; 1998 v Mol, Gr, Sw (4)
Quinn, W. R. (Sheffield U), 1998 v Mol (sub), I (2)

Ramage, C. D. (Derby Co), 1991 v Pol (sub), W; 1992 v Fr (sub) (3)
Ranson, R. (Manchester C), 1980 v Bul, EG; 1981 v R (sub), R, Sw (1 + 1 sub), H, Pol (2), S (10)
Redknapp, J. F. (Liverpool), 1993 v Sm, Pol, N, P, Cz, Br, S, F; 1994 v Pol, Ho (sub), D, Ru, F, US, Bel, P; 1995 v P, A; 1998 v Sw (19)
Redmond, S. (Manchester C), 1988 v F (2), M, USSR, Mor, F; 1989 v D, Se, Gr, Alb (2), Pol; 1990 v Se, Pol (14)
Reeves, K. P. (Norwich C), 1978 v I, Y (2); 1979 v N, W, Bul, Sw; 1980 v D, S; (with Manchester C), EG (10)
Regis, C. (WBA), 1979 v D, Bul, Se; 1980 v S, EG; 1983 v D (6)
Reid, N. S. (Manchester C), 1981 v H (sub); 1982 v H, Pol (2), S (2) (6)
Reid, P. (Bolton W), 1977 v S, Fi, N; 1978 v Fi, I, Y (6)
Richards, D. I. (Wolverhampton W), 1995 v Br, Mal, An, F (4)
Richards, J. P. (Wolverhampton W), 1977 v Fi, N (2)
Rideout, P. (Aston Villa), 1985 v Fi, Is, Ei (sub), R; (with Bari), 1986 v D (5)
Ripley, S. (Middlesbrough), 1988 v USSR, F (sub); 1989 v D (sub), Se, Gr, Alb (2); 1990 v Se (8)
Ritchie, A. (Brighton & HA), 1982 v Pol (1)
Rix, G. (Arsenal), 1978 v Fi (sub), Y; 1979 v D, Se; 1980 v D (sub), Bul, S (7)
Roberts, A. J. (Millwall), 1995 v Ei, La (2); (with C Palace), 1996 v N, A (5)
Roberts, B. J. (Middlesbrough), 1997 v Sw (sub) (1)
Robins, M. G. (Manchester U), 1990 v P, F, USSR, Cz; 1991 v H (sub), Pol (6)
Robinson, P. P. (Watford), 1999 v Se, Bul; 2000 v Pol (3)
Robinson, P. W. (Leeds U), 2000 v D (1)
Robson, B. (WBA), 1979 v W, Bul (sub), Se; 1980 v D, Bul, S (2) (7)
Robson, S. (Arsenal), 1984 v I; 1985 v Fi, Is, Fi; 1986 v R, I (with West Ham U); 1988 v S, Sw (8)
Rocastle, D. (Arsenal), 1987 v Se, Y, Sp, T; 1988 v WG, T, Y, S (2), F (2 subs), M, USSR, Mor (14)
Rodger, G. (Coventry C), 1987 v USSR, F, P; 1988 v WG (4)
Rogers, A. (Nottingham F), 1998 v F, S.Af, Arg (3)
Rosario, R. (Norwich C), 1987 v T (sub), Mor, F, P (sub) (4)
Rose, M. (Arsenal), 1997 v Ge (sub), I (2)
Rowell, G. (Sunderland), 1977 v Fi (1)
Ruddock, N. (Southampton), 1989 v Bul (sub), Sen, Ei, US (4)
Rufus, R. R. (Charlton Ath), 1996 v Cro, Bel, An, P, Br; 1997 v I (6)
Ryan, J. (Oldham Ath), 1983 v H (1)
Ryder, S.H. (Walsall), 1995 v Br, An, F (3)

Samways, V. (Tottenham H), 1988 v Sw (sub), USSR, F; 1989 v D, Se (5)
Sansom, K. G. (C Palace), 1979 v D, W, Bul, Se; 1980 v S (2), EG (2) (8)
Scimeca, R. (Aston Villa), 1996 v P; 1997 v Mol, Pol, Ge, I; 1998 v Mol, I, Gr (2) (9)

Scowcroft, J. B. (Ipswich T), 1997 v Pol, Ge (2), I (sub); 1998 v Gr (sub) (5)
Seaman, D. (Birmingham C), 1985 v Fi, T, Is, Ei, R, Fi; 1986 v R, F, D, I (10)
Sedgley, S. (Coventry C), 1987 v USSR, F (sub), P; 1988 v F; 1989 v D (sub), Se, Gr, Alb (2), Pol; (with Tottenham H), 1990 v Se (11)
Sellars, S. (Blackburn R), 1988 v S (sub), F, Sw (3)
Selley, I. (Arsenal), 1994 v Ru (sub), F (sub), US (3)
Serrant, C. (Oldham Ath), 1998 v Gr (2) (2)
Sharpe, L. (Manchester U), 1989 v Gr; 1990 v P (sub), F, USSR, Cz; 1991 v H, Pol (sub), Ei (8)
Shaw, G. R. (Aston Villa), 1981 v Ei, Sw, H; 1982 v H, S; 1983 v WG (2) (7)
Shearer, A. (Southampton), 1991 v Fi (2), W, T, Sen, M, USSR, F; 1992 v G, T, Pol (11)
Shelton, G. (Sheffield W), 1985 v Fi (1)
Sheringham, T. (Millwall), 1988 v Sw (1)
Sheron, M. N. (Manchester C), 1992 v H, F; 1993 v N (sub), T (sub), Sm, Ho, Pol, N, P, Cz, Br, S, F; 1994 v Pol (sub), Ho, Sm (16)
Sherwood, T. A. (Norwich C), 1990 v P, F, USSR, Cz (4)
Shipperley, N. J. (Chelsea), 1994 v Sm (sub); (with Southampton) 1995 v Ei, La (2); 1996 v P, N, A (7)
Simonsen, S. P. A. (Tranmere R), 1998 v F; (with Everton), 1999 v CzR, F, Bul (4)
Simpson, P. (Manchester C), 1986 v D (sub); 1987 v Y, Mor, F, P (5)
Sims, S. (Leicester C), 1977 v W, S, Fi, N; 1978 v N, Fi, I (2), Y (2) (10)
Sinclair, T. (QPR), 1994 v Ho, Sm, D, Ru, F, US, Bel, P; 1995 v P, Ei (2), La; 1996 v P; (with West Ham U), 1998 v Sw (5)
Sinnott, L. (Watford), 1985 v Is (sub) (1)
Slade, S. A. (Tottenham H), 1996 v Bel, An, P, Br (4)
Slater, S. I. (West Ham U), 1990 v P, USSR (sub), Cz (sub) (3)
Small, B. (Aston Villa), 1993 v Sm, T, Ho, Pol, N, P, Cz, Br, S, F; 1994 v Pol, Sm (12)
Smith, A. (Leeds U), 2000 v D, Arg (sub) (2)
Smith, D. (Coventry C), 1988 v M, USSR (sub), Mor; 1989 v D, Se, Alb (2), Pol; 1990 v Se, Pol (10)
Smith, M. (Sheffield W), 1981 v Ei, R, Sw, H; 1982 v Pol (sub) (5)
Smith, M. (Sunderland), 1995 v Ei (sub) (1)
Snodin, I. (Doncaster R), 1985 v T, Is, R, Fi (4)
Statham, B. (Tottenham H), 1988 v Sw; 1989 v D (sub), Se (3)
Statham, D. J. (WBA), 1978 v Fi, 1979 v W, Bul, Se; 1980 v D; 1983 v D (6)
Stein, B. (Luton T), 1984 v D, H, I (3)
Sterland, M. (Sheffield W), 1984 v D, H, F (2), I, Sp (2) (7)
Steven, T. (Everton), 1985 v Fi, T (2)
Stevens, G. (Brighton & HA), 1983 v H; (with Tottenham H), 1984 v H, F (1+1 sub), I (sub), Sp (1+1 sub); 1986 v I (8)
Stewart, P. (Manchester C), 1988 v F (1)
Stuart, G. C. (Chelsea), 1990 v P (sub), F, USSR, Cz; 1991 v T (sub) (5)
Stuart, J. C. (Charlton Ath), 1996 v Bel, An, P, Br (4)
Suckling, P. (Coventry C), 1986 v D; (with Manchester C), 1987 v Se (sub), Y, Sp, T; (with C Palace), 1988 v S (2), F (2), Sw (10)
Summerbee, N.J. (Swindon T), 1993 v P (sub), S (sub), F (3)
Sunderland, A. (Wolverhampton W), 1977 v W (1)
Sutton, C. R. (Norwich), 1993 v Sp (sub), T (sub + 1),Ho, P (sub), Cz, Br, S, F; 1994 v Pol, Ho, Sm, D (13)
Swindlehurst, D. (C Palace), 1977 v W (1)
Sutch, D. (Norwich C), 1992 v H, M, Cz; 1993 v T (4)

Talbot, B. (Ipswich T), 1977 v W (1)
Thatcher, B. D. (Millwall), 1996 v Cro; (with Wimbledon), 1997 v Mol, Pol; 1998 v I (4)
Thomas, D. (Coventry C), 1981 v Ei; 1983 v WG (2), Gr, H; (with Tottenham H), I, Sp (7)
Thomas, M. (Luton T), 1986 v T, D, I (3)
Thomas, M. (Arsenal), 1988 v Y, S, F (2), M, USSR, Mor; 1989 v Gr, Alb (2), Pol; 1990 v Se (12)
Thomas, R. E. (Watford), 1990 v P (1)
Thompson, A. (Bolton W), 1995 v La; 1996 v P (2)
Thompson, D. A. (Liverpool), 1997 v Pol (sub), Ge; 2000 v L (sub), Pol (sub), D (sub), I, T (sub) (7)
Thompson, G. L. (Coventry C), 1981 v R, Sw, H; 1982 v N, H, S (6)
Thorn, A. (Wimbledon), 1988 v WG (sub). Y, S, F, Sw (5)
Thornley, B. L. (Manchester U), 1996 v Bel, P, Br (3)

Tiler, C. (Barnsley), 1990 v P, USSR, Cz; 1991 v H, Pol, Ei (2), T, Sen, USSR, F; (with Nottingham F), 1992 v G, T (13)

Unsworth, D. G. (Everton), 1995 v A, Ei (2), La; 1996 v N, A (6)

Upson, M. J. (Arsenal), 1999 v Se, Bul, L, F; 2000 v L, Pol, D (7)

Vassell, D. (Aston Villa), 1999 v H (sub); 2000 v Pol (sub) (2)

Venison, B. (Sunderland), 1983 v D, Gr; 1985 v Fi, T, Is, Fi; 1986 v R, T, D (2) (10)

Vinnicombe, C. (Rangers), 1991 v H (sub), Pol, Ei (2), T, Sen, M, USSR (sub), F; 1992 v G, T, Pol (12)

Waddle, C. (Newcastle U), 1985 v Fi (1)

Wallace, D. (Southampton), 1983 v Gr, H; 1984 v D, H, F (2), I, Sp (sub); 1985 v Fi, T, Is; 1986 v R, D, I (14)

Wallace, Ray (Southampton), 1989 v Bul, Sen (sub), Ei; 1990 v Se (4)

Wallace, Rod (Southampton), 1989 v Bul, Ei (sub), US; 1991 v H, Pol, Ei, T, Sen, M, USSR, F (11)

Walker, D. (Nottingham F), 1985 v Fi; 1987 v Se, T; 1988 v WG, T, S (2) (7)

Walker, I. M. (Tottenham H), 1991 v W; 1992 v H, Cz, F; 1993 v Sp, N, T, Sm; 1994 v Pol (9)

Walsh, G. (Manchester U), 1988 v WG, Y (2)

Walsh, P. M. (Luton T), 1983 v D (sub), Gr (2), H (4)

Walters, K. (Aston Villa), 1984 v D (sub), H (sub); 1985 v Is, Ei, R; 1986 v R, T, D, I (sub) (9)

Ward, P. D. (Brighton & HA), 1978 v N; 1980 v EG (2)

Warhurst, P. (Oldham Ath), 1991 v H, Pol, W, Sen, M (sub), USSR, F (sub); (with Sheffield W), 1992 v G (8)

Watson, D. (Norwich C), 1984 v D, F (2), I (2), Sp (2) (7)

Watson, D. N. (Barnsley), 1994 v Ho, Sm; 1995 v Br, F; 1996 v N (5)

Watson, D. (Sheffield W), 1991 v Sen, USSR (2)

Watson, S. C. (Newcastle U), 1993 v Sp (sub), N; 1994 v Sm (sub), D; 1995 v P, A, Ei (2), La (2); 1996 v N, A (12)

Weaver, N. J. (Manchester C), 2000 v L, Pol, Arg, I, T, Slo (6)

Webb, N. (Portsmouth), 1985 v Ei; (with Nottingham F), 1986 v D (2) (3)

Whelan, P. J. (Ipswich T), 1993 v Sp, T (sub), P (3)

Whelan, N. (Leeds U), 1995 v A (sub), Ei (2)

White, D. (Manchester U), 1988 v S (2), F, USSR; 1989 v Se; 1990 v Pol (6)

Whyte, C. (Arsenal), 1982 v S (1+1 sub); 1983 v D, Gr (4)

Wicks, S. (QPR), 1982 v S (1)

Wilkins, R. C. (Chelsea), 1977 v W (1)

Wilkinson, P. (Grimsby T), 1985 v Ei, R (sub); (with Everton), 1986 v R (sub), I (4)

Williams, D. (Sunderland), 1998 v Sw (sub); 1999 v F (2)

Williams, P. (Charlton Ath), 1989 v Bul, Sen, Ei, US (sub) (4)

Williams, P. D. (Derby Co), 1991 v Sen, M, USSR; 1992 v G, T, Pol (6)

Williams, S. C. (Southampton), 1977 v S, Fi, N; 1978 v N, I (1 + 1 sub), Y (2); 1979 v D, Bul, Se (sub); 1980 v D, EG (2) (14)

Winterburn, N. (Wimbledon), 1986 v I (1)

Wise, D. (Wimbledon), 1988 v Sw (1)

Woodcook, A. S. (Nottingham F), 1978 v Fi, I (2)

Woodgate, J. S. (Leeds U), 2000 v Arg (1)

Woodhouse, C. (Sheffield U), 1999 v H, Se, Bul; 2000 v Pol (sub) (4)

Woods, C. C. E. (Nottingham F), 1979 v W (sub), Se; (with QPR), 1980 v Bul, EG; 1981 v Sw; (with Norwich C), 1984 v D (6)

Wright, A. G. (Blackburn), 1993 v Sp, N (2)

Wright, M. (Southampton), 1983 v Gr, H; 1984 v D, H (4)

Wright, R. I. (Ipswich T), 1997 v Ge, Pol; 1998 v Mol, I, Gr (2), S.Af, Arg; 1999 v Se, Bul, L, Pol, H, Se; 2000 v Y (15)

Wright, W. (Everton), 1979 v D, W, Bul; 1980 v D, S (2) (6)

Yates, D. (Notts Co), 1989 v D (sub), Bul, Sen, Ei, US (5)

Young, L. P. (Tottenham H), 1999 v H; 2000 v D (sub), Arg (sub), T, Slo (5)

SCOTLAND

Aitken, R. (Celtic), 1977 v Cz, W, Sw; 1978 v Cz, W; 1979 v P, N (2); 1980 v Bel, E; 1984 v EG, Y (2); 1985 v WG, Ic, Sp (16)

Albiston, A. (Manchester U), 1977 v Cz, W, Sw; 1978 v Sw, Cz (5)

Alexander, N. (Stenhousemuir), 1997 v P (sub); 1998 v Bl, Ei, I; (with Livingston), 1999 v Li, Es, Bel (2), CzR, G (10)

Anderson, I. (Dundee), 1997 v Co (sub), US, CzR, P; 1998 v Bl, La, Fi, D (sub), Ei (sub), Ni; 1999 v G (sub), Ei, Ni, CzR; (with Toulouse), 2000 v Bos (15)

Anderson, R. (Aberdeen), 1997 v Es, A, Se; 1998 v La (sub), Fi, Ei, I; 1999 v Es, Bel, G, Ei, Ni, CzR; 2000 v Bos, Es (15)

Anthony, M. (Celtic), 1997 v La (sub), Es (sub), Col (3)

Archdeacon, O. (Celtic), 1987 v WG (sub) (1)

Archibald, A. (Partick T), 1998 v Fi, Ei, Ni, I; 1999 v Li (5)

Archibald, S. (Aberdeen), 1980 v B, E (2), WG; (with Tottenham H), 1981 v D (5)

Bagen, D. (Kilmarnock), 1997 v Es, A (sub), Se (sub), Bl (4)

Bain, K. (Dundee), 1993 v P, I, Ma, P (4)

Baker, M. (St. Mirren), 1993 v F, M, E; 1994 v Ma, A; 1995 v Gr, M, F (sub), Sk (sub); 1996 v H (sub) (10)

Baltacha, S. S. (St Mirren), 2000 v Bos, Li (sub), F (sub) (3)

Bannon, E. J. P. (Hearts), 1979 v US; (with Chelsea), P, N (2); (with Dundee U), 1980 v Bel, WG, E (7)

Beattie, J. (St Mirren), 1992 v D, US, P, Y (4)

Beaumont, D. (Dundee U), 1985 v Ic (1)

Bell, D. (Aberdeen), 1981 v D; 1984 v Y (2)

Bernard, P. R. J. (Oldham Ath), 1992 v R (sub), D, Se (sub), US; 1993 v Sw, P, I, Ma, P, F, Bul, M, E; 1994 v I, Ma (15)

Bett, J. (Rangers), 1981 v Se, D; 1982 v Se, D, I, E (2) (7)

Black, E. (Aberdeen), 1983 v EG, Sw (2), Bel; 1985 v Ic, Sp (2), Ic (8)

Blair, A. (Coventry C), 1980 v E; 1981 v Se; (with Aston Villa), 1982 v Se, D, I (5)

Bollan, G. (Dundee U), 1992 v D, G (sub), US, P, Y; 1993 v Sw, P, I, P, F, Bul, M, E; 1994 v Sw; 1995 v Gr; (with Rangers) v Ru, Sm (17)

Bonar, P. (Raith R), 1997 v A, La, Es (sub), Se (4)

Booth, S. (Aberdeen), 1991 v R (sub), Bul (sub + 1), Pol, F (sub); 1992 v Sw, R, D, Se, US, P, Y; 1993 v Ma, P (14)

Bowes, M. J. (Dunfermline Ath), 1992 v D (sub) (1)

Bowman, D. (Hearts), 1985 v WG (sub) (1)

Boyack, S. (Rangers), 1997 v Se (1)

Boyd, T. (Motherwell), 1987 v WG, Ei (2), Bel; 1988 v Bel (5)

Brazil, A. (Hibernian), 1978 v W (1)

Brazil, A. (Ipswich T), 1979 v N; 1980 v Bel (2), E (2), WG; 1981 v Se; 1982 v Se (8)

Brebner, G. I. (Manchester U), 1997 v Col, CzR (sub), US (sub), P; 1998 v Bl, La, Fi, D; (with Reading), 1999 v Li, Es, Bel (2), CzR, G, Ei, Ni, CzR; (with Hibernian), 2000 v Bos (18)

Brough, J. (Hearts), 1981 v D (1)

Browne, P. (Raith R), 1997 v A (1)

Buchan, J. (Aberdeen), 1997 v Se, Col, CzR, P; 1998 v Bl, La, Fi; 1999 v Li, Es, Bel, CzR, G, Ei (13)

Burchill, M. (Celtic), 1998 v Fi, D (sub); 1999 v Li, Es (sub), Bel (2), CzR, Ei, Ni, CzR; 2000 v Bos, Es (12)

Burke, A. (Kilmarnock), 1997 v Es, A, Bl (sub); 1998 v Ei (sub) (4)

Burley, G. E. (Ipswich T), 1977 v Cz, W, Sw; 1978 v Sw, Cz (5)

Burley, C. (Chelsea), 1992 v D; 1993 v Sw, P, I, P; 1994 v Sw, I (sub) (7)

Burns, H. (Rangers), 1985 v Sp, Ic (sub) (2)

Burns, T. (Celtic), 1977 v Cz, W, E; 1978 v Sw; 1982 v E (5)

Caldwell, G. (Newcastle U), 2000 v F, Ni, W (3)

Campbell, S. (Dundee), 1989 v N (sub), Y, F (3)

Campbell, S. P. (Leicester C), 1998 v Fi (sub), D, Ei, Ni (sub), I; 1999 v Li, Es, Bel (2), CzR, G, Ei, Ni, CzR (sub); 2000 v Bos (sub) (15)

Canero, P. (Kilmarnock), 2000 v F (1)

Carey, L. A. (Bristol C), 1998 v D (1)

Casey, J. (Celtic), 1978 v W (1)

Christie, M. (Dundee), 1992 v D, P (sub), Y (3)

Clark, R. (Aberdeen), 1977 v Cz, W, Sw (3)

Clarke, S. (St Mirren), 1984 v Bel, EG, Y; 1985 v WG, Ic, Sp (2), Ic (8)

Cleland, A. (Dundee U), 1990 v F, N (2); 1991 v R, Sw, Bul; 1992 v Sw, R, G, Se (2) (11)

Lavety, B. (St. Mirren), 1993 v Ic, Bul (sub), M (sub), E; 1994 v Ma, A (sub), Eg (sub), Bel (sub); 1995 v Fi (sub) (9)

Lavin, G. (Watford), 1993 v F, Bul, M; 1994 v Ma, Eg, P, Bel (7)

Leighton, J. (Aberdeen), 1982 v I (1)

Levein, C. (Hearts), 1985 v Sp, Ic (2)

Liddell, A. M. (Barnsley), 1994 v Ma (sub); 1995 v Sm (sub), M (sub), F, Sk; 1996 v Gr, Fi, Sm, H (2), Sp, F (sub) (12)

Lindsey, J. (Motherwell), 1979 v US (1)

Locke, G. (Hearts), 1994 v Ma, A, Eg, P; 1995 v Fi; 1996 v Fi, H; 1997 v Es, A, Bl (10)

Love, G. (Hibernian), 1995 v Ru (1)

McAllister, G. (Leicester C), 1990 v N (1)

McAlpine, H. (Dundee U), 1983 v EG, Sw (2), Bel; 1984 v Bel (5)

McAnespie, K. (St Johnstone), 1998 v Fi (sub); 1999 v G (sub); 2000 v Ni, W (4)

McAuley, S. (St. Johnstone), 1993 v P (sub) (1)

McAvennie, F. (St Mirren), 1982 v I, E; 1985 v Is, Ei, R (5)

McBride, J. (Everton), 1981 v D (1)

McBride, J. P. (Celtic), 1998 v Ni (sub), I (sub) (2)

McCall, S. (Bradford C), 1988 v E; (with Everton), 1990 v F (2)

McCann, N. (Dundee), 1994 v A, Eg, P, Bel; 1995 v Fi, Gr (sub), Sm; 1996 v Fi, Sm (9)

McClair, B. (Celtic), 1984 v Bel (sub), EG, Y (1 + 1 sub); 1985 v WG, Ic, Sp, Ic (8)

McCluskey, G. (Celtic), 1979 v US, P; 1980 v Bel (2); 1982 v D, I (6)

McCluskey, S. (St Johnstone), 1997 v Es (2), A, Se, Col, US, CzR; 1998 v Bl, La, D, Ei (sub), Ni, I; 1999 v Li (14)

McCoist, A. (Rangers), 1984 v Bel (1)

McConnell, I. (Clyde), 1997 v A (sub) (1)

McCulloch, A. (Kilmarnock); 1981 v Se (1)

McCulloch, I. (Notts Co), 1982 v E (2)

McCulloch, L. (Motherwell), 1997 v La (sub), Es (1 + sub), Se (sub + 1), A (sub), Col (sub); 1998 v Bl (sub), Fi (sub), D, Ei, Ni; 1999 v CzR, G (14)

MacDonald, C. (Rangers), 1980 v WG (sub); 1981 v Se; 1982 v Se (sub), L, I (2), E (2 sub) (8)

McDonald, C. (Falkirk), 1995 v Fi (sub), Ru, M (sub), F (sub), Br (sub) (5)

McEwan, C. (Clyde), 1997 v Col, US (sub), CzR (sub), P; (with Raith R), 1998 v Bl, La, Fi, D, Ei, Ni, I; 1999 v Li, Es (sub), Bel (2), CzR, G (sub) (17)

McFarlane, D. (Hamilton A), 1997 v Col, US (sub), P (sub) (3)

McGarry, S. (St Mirren), 1997 v US, CzR, P (sub) (3)

McGarvey, F. (St Mirren), 1977 v E; 1978 v Cz; (with Celtic), 1982 v D (3)

McGarvey, S. (Manchester U), 1982 v E (sub); 1983 v Bel, Sw; 1984 v Bel (4)

McGhee, M. (Aberdeen), 1981 v D (1)

McGinnis, G. (Dundee U), 1985 v Sp (1)

McGrillen, P. (Motherwell), 1994 v Sw (sub), I (2)

McInally, J. (Dundee U), 1989 v F (1)

McKenzie, R. (Hearts), 1997 v Es, Bl (2)

McKimmie, S. (Aberdeen), 1985 v WG, Ic (2) (3)

McKinlay, T. (Dundee), 1984 v EG (sub); 1985 v WG, Ic, Sp (2), Ic (6)

McKinlay, W. (Dundee U), 1989 v N, Y (sub), F; 1990 v Y, F, N (6)

McKinnon, R. (Dundee U), 1991 v R, Pol (sub); 1992 v G (2), Se (2) (6)

McLaren, A, (Hearts), 1989 v F; 1990 v Y, N; 1991 v Sw, Bul, Pol, F; 1992 v R, G, Se (2) (11)

McLaren, A. (Dundee U), 1993 v I, Ma (sub); 1994 v Sw, I (sub) (4)

McLaughlin, B. (Celtic), 1995 v Ru, Sm, M, Sk (sub), Br (sub); 1996 v Gr (sub), Sm (sub), H (8)

McLaughlin, J. (Morton), 1981 v D; 1982 v Se, D, I, E (2); 1983 v EG, Sw (2), Bel (10)

McLeish, A. (Aberdeen), 1978 v W; 1979 v US; 1980 v Bel, E (2); 1987 v Ei (6)

MacLeod, A. (Hibernian), 1979 v P, N (2) (3)

MacLeod, J. (Dundee U), 1989 v N; 1990 v F (2)

MacLeod, M. (Dumbarton), 1979 v US; (with Celtic), P (sub), N (2); 1980 v Bel (5)

McMillan, S. (Motherwell), 1997 v A (sub + sub), Se, Bl (4)

McNab, N. (Tottenham H), 1978 v W (1)

McNally, M. (Celtic), 1991 v Bul; 1993 v Ic (2)

McNamara, J. (Dunfermline Ath), 1994 v A, Bel; 1995 v Gr, Ru, Sm; 1996 v Gr, Fi; (with Celtic), Sm, H (2), Sp, F (12)

McNichol, J. (Brentford), 1979 v P, N (2); 1980 v Bel (2), WG, E (7)

McNiven, D. (Leeds U), 1977 v Cz, W (sub), Sw (sub) (3)

McNiven, S. A. (Oldham Ath), 1996 v Sm (sub) (1)

McPherson, D. (Rangers), 1984 v Bel; 1985 v Sp; (with Hearts), 1989 v N, Y (4)

McQuilken, J. (Celtic), 1993 v Bul, E (2)

McStay, P. (Celtic), 1983 v EG, Sw (2); 1984 v Y (2) (5)

McWhirter, N. (St Mirren), 1991 v Bul (sub) (1)

Main, A. (Dundee U), 1988 v E; 1989 v Y; 1990 v N (3)

Malpas, M. (Dundee U), 1983 v Bel, Sw (1+1 sub); 1984 v Bel, EG, Y (2); 1985 v Sp (8)

Marshall, S. R. (Arsenal), 1995 v Ru, Gr; 1996 v H, Sp, F (5)

Mason, G. R. (Manchester C), 1999 v Li (sub) (1)

Mathieson, D. (Queen of the South), 1997 v Col; 1998 v La; 1999 v G (sub) (3)

May, E. (Hibernian), 1989 v Y (sub), F (2)

Meldrum, C. (Kilmarnock), 1996 v F (sub); 1997 v A (2), La, Es, Se (6)

Melrose, J. (Partick Th), 1977 v Sw; 1979 v US, P, N (2); 1980 v Bel (sub), WG, E (8)

Miller, C. (Rangers), 1995 v Gr, Ru; 1996 v Gr, Sp, F; 1997 v A, La, Es (8)

Miller, J. (Aberdeen), 1987 v Ei (sub); 1988 v Bel; (with Celtic), E; 1989 v N, Y; 1990 v F, N (7)

Miller, K. (Hibernian), 2000 v F, Ni, W (3)

Miller, W. (Aberdeen), 1978 v Sw, Cz (2)

Miller, W. (Hibernian), 1991 v R, Sw, Bul, Pol, F; 1992 v R, G (sub) (7)

Milne, K. (Hearts), 2000 v F (1)

Milne, R. (Dundee U), 1982 v Se (sub); 1984 v Bel, EG (3)

Money, I. C. (St Mirren), 1987 v Ei; 1988 v Bel; 1989 v N (3)

Muir, L. (Hibernian), 1977 v Cz (sub) (1)

Murray, H. (St Mirren), 2000 v F (sub), Ni (sub), W (sub) (3)

Murray, N. (Rangers), 1993 v P (sub), Ma, Ic, P; 1994 v Sw, I; 1995 v Fi, Ru, Gr, Sm; 1996 v Gr (sub), Fi, Sm, H (2), F (16)

Murray, R. (Bournemouth) 1993 v Ic (sub) (1)

Narey, D. (Dundee U), 1977 v Cz, Sw; 1978 v Sw, Cz (4)

Naysmith, G. (Hearts), 1997 v La, Es (1 + sub), Se, A, Col, US, CzR, P; 1998 v La, D; 1999 v Es, Bel (2), CzR, G, Ei, CzR; 2000 v Bos, Es, Bos, Li (22)

Neilson, R. (Hearts), 2000 v Ni (1)

Nevin, P. (Chelsea), 1985 v WG, Ic, Sp (2), Ic (5)

Nicholas, C. (Celtic), 1981 v Se; 1982 v Se; 1983 v EG, Sw, Bel; (with Arsenal), 1984 v Y (6)

Nicholson, B. (Rangers), 1999 v G, Ni, CzR (sub); 2000 v Bos (sub), Es, Bos, Li (7)

Nicol, S. (Ayr U), 1981 v Se; 1982 v Se, D; (with Liverpool), I (2), E (2); 1983 v EG, Sw (2), Bel; 1984 v Bel, EG, Y (14)

Nisbet, S. (Rangers), 1989 v N, Y, F; 1990 v Y, F (5)

Notman, A. M. (Manchester U), 1999 v Li (sub), Es, Bel (sub+sub); 2000 v Li, F (sub), Ni, W (8)

O'Brien, B. (Blackburn R), 1999 v Ei (sub), Ni (sub), CzR (sub); 2000 v Bos (sub) (4)

O'Donnell, P. (Motherwell), 1992 v Sw (sub), R, D, G (2), Se (1 + 1 sub); 1993 v P (8)

O'Neil, B. (Celtic), 1992 v D, G, Se (2); 1993 v Sw, P, I (7)

O'Neil, J. (Dundee U), 1991 v Bul (sub) (1)

O'Neill, M. (Clyde), 1995 v Ru (sub), F, Sk, Br; 1997 v Se (sub), Bl (sub) (6)

Orr, N. (Morton), 1978 v W (sub); 1979 v US, P, N (2); 1980 v Bel, E (7)

Parlane, D. (Rangers), 1977 v W (1)

Paterson, C. (Hibernian), 1981 v Se; 1982 v I (2)

Paterson, J. (Dundee U), 1997 v Col, US, CzR; 1999 v Bel (sub+sub); 2000 v Es, Bos, Li (8)

Payne, G. (Dundee U), 1978 v Sw, Cz, W (3)

Peacock, L. A. (Carlisle U), 1997 v Bl (1)

Pressley, S. (Rangers), 1993 v Ic, F, Bul, M, E; 1994 v Sw, I, M, A, Eg, P, Bel; 1995 v Fi; (with Coventry C), Ru (2), Sm, M, F, Sk, Br; (with Dundee U), 1996 v Gr, Sm, H (2), Sp, F (26)

Provan, D. (Kilmarnock), 1977 v Cz (sub) (1)

Rae, A. (Millwall), 1991 v Bul (sub + 1), F (sub); 1992 v Sw, R, G (sub), Se (2) (8)

Rae, G. (Dundee), 1999 v Ei (sub), Ni, CzR; 2000 v Bos, Es, Bos (6)
Redford, I. (Rangers), 1981 v Se (sub); 1982 v Se, D, I (2), E (6)
Reid, B. (Rangers), 1991 v F; 1992 v D, US, P (4)
Reid, C. (Hibernian), 1993 v Sw, P, I (3)
Reid, M. (Celtic), 1982 v E; 1984 v Y (2)
Reid, R. (St Mirren), 1977 v W, Sw, E (3)
Renicks, S. (Hamilton A), 1997 v Bl (1)
Rice, B. (Hibernian), 1985 v WG (1)
Richardson, L. (St Mirren), 1980 v WG, E (sub) (2)
Ritchie, A. (Morton), 1980 v Bel (1)
Ritchie, P. R. (Hearts), 1996 v H; 1997 v A (2), La, Es (2), Se (7)
Robertson, A. (Rangers) 1991 v F (1)
Robertson, C. (Rangers), 1977 v E (sub) (1)
Robertson, D. (Aberdeen), 1987 v Ei (sub); 1988 v E (2); 1989 v N, Y; 1990 v Y, N (7)
Robertson, H. (Aberdeen), 1994 v Eg; 1995 v Fi (2)
Robertson, J. (Hearts), 1985 v WG, Ic (sub) (2)
Robertson, L. (Rangers), 1993 v F, M (sub), E (sub) (3)
Robertson, S. (St Johnstone), 1998 v Fi, Ni (2)
Roddie, A. (Aberdeen), 1992 v US, P; 1993 v Sw (sub), P, Ic (5)
Ross, T. W. (Arsenal), 1977 v W (1)
Rowson, D. (Aberdeen), 1997 v La, Es, Se (2), Bl (5)
Russell, R. (Rangers), 1978 v W; 1980 v Bel; 1984 v Y (3)

Salton, D. B. (Luton T), 1992 v D, US, P, Y; 1993 v Sw, I (6)
Scott, P. (St Johnstone), 1994 v A (sub), Eg (sub), P, Bel (4)
Scrimgour, D. (St Mirren), 1997 v US, CzR; 1998 v D (3)
Seaton, A. (Falkirk), 1998 v Bl (sub) (1)
Severin, S. D. (Hearts), 2000 v Es, Bos, Li (sub), F, Ni, W (6)
Shannon, R. (Dundee), 1987 v WG, Ei (2), Bel; 1988 v Bel, E (2) (7)
Sharp, G. (Everton), 1982 v E (1)
Sharp, R. (Dunfermline Ath), 1990 v N (sub); 1991 v R, Sw, Bul (4)
Sheerin, P. (Southampton), 1996 v Sm (1)
Shields, G. (Rangers), 1997 v A, La (2)
Simpson, N. (Aberdeen), 1982 v I (2), E; 1983 v EG, Sw (2), Bel; 1984 v Bel, EG, Y; 1985 v Sp (11)
Sinclair, G. (Dumbarton), 1977 v E (1)
Skilling, M. (Kilmarnock), 1993 v Ic (sub); 1994 v I (2)
Smith, B. M. (Celtic), 1992 v G (2), US, P, Y (5)
Smith, G. (Rangers), 1978 v W (1)
Smith, H. G. (Hearts), 1987 v WG, Bel (2)
Sneddon, A. (Celtic), 1979 v US (1)
Speedie, D. (Chelsea), 1985 v Sp (1)
Spencer, J. (Rangers), 1991 v Sw (sub), F; 1992 v Sw (3)
Stanton, P. (Hibernian), 1977 v Cz (1)
Stark, W. (Aberdeen), 1985 v Ic (1)
Stephen, R. (Dundee), 1983 v Bel (sub) (1)
Stevens, G. (Motherwell), 1977 v E (1)
Stewart, J. (Kilmarnock), 1978 v Sw, Cz; (with Middlesbrough), 1979 v P (3)
Stewart, M. J. (Manchester U), 2000 v Ni (1)
Stewart, R. (Dundee U), 1979 v P, N (2); (with West Ham U), 1980 v Bel (2), E (2), WG; 1981 v D; 1982 v I (2), E (12)
Stillie, D. (Aberdeen), 1995 v Ru (2), Sm, M, F, Sk, Br; 1996 v Gr, Fi, Sm, H (2), Sp, F (14)
Strachan, G. D. (Aberdeen), 1980 v Bel (1)
Strachan, G. D. (Coventry C), 1998 v D, Ei; 1999 v Li, Es, Bel (2); 2000 v Li (7)
Sturrock, P. (Dundee U), 1977 v Cz, W, Sw, E; 1978 v Sw, Cz; 1982 v Se, I, E (9)
Sweeney, S. (Clydebank), 1991 v R, Sw (sub), Bul (2), Pol; 1992 v Sw, R (7)

Tarrant, N. K. (Aston Villa), 1999 v Ni (sub); 2000 v Es (sub), Bos (sub), Li, Ni (sub) (5)
Teale, G. (Clydebank), 1997 v La (sub), Es, Bl; (with Ayr U), 1999 v CzR (sub), G (sub), Ei (sub) (6)
Telfer, P. (Luton T), 1993 v Ma, P; 1994 v Sw (3)
Thomas, K. (Hearts), 1993 v F (sub), Bul, M, E; 1994 v Sw, Ma; 1995 v Gr; 1997 v A (8)
Thompson, S. (Dundee U), 1997 v US, CzR, P; 1998 v Bl, La; 1999 v G (sub), Ei, Ni, CzR; 2000 v Bos, Es, Bos (12)
Thomson, W. (Partick Th), 1977 v E (sub); 1978 v W; (with St Mirren), 1979 v US, N (2); 1980 v Bel (2), E (2), WG (10)
Tolmie, J. (Morton), 1980 v Bel (sub) (1)

Tortolano, J. (Hibernian), 1987 v WG, Ei (2)
Tweed, S. (Hibernian), 1993 v Ic; 1994 v Sw, I (3)

Wales, G. (Hearts), 2000 v F (1)
Walker, A. (Celtic), 1988 v Bel (1)
Wallace, I. (Coventry C), 1978 v Sw (1)
Walsh, C. (Nottingham F), 1984 v EG, Sw (2), Bel; 1984 v EG (5)
Wark, J. (Ipswich T), 1977 v Cz, W, Sw; 1978 v W; 1979 v P; 1980 v E (2), WG (8)
Watson, A. (Aberdeen), 1981 v Se, D; 1982 v D, I (sub) (4)
Watson, K. (Rangers), 1977 v E; 1978 v Sw (sub) (2)
Watt, M. (Aberdeen), 1991 v R, Sw, Bul (2), Pol, F; 1992 v Sw, R, G (2), Se (2) (12)
Whiteford, A. (St Johnstone), 1997 v US (1)
Whyte, D. (Celtic), 1987 v Ei (2), Bel; 1988 v E (2); 1989 v N, Y; 1990 v Y, N (9)
Wilkie, L. (Dundee), 2000 v Bos, F, Ni, W (4)
Will, J. A. (Arsenal), 1992 v D (sub), Y; 1993 v Ic (sub) (3)
Wilson, S. (Rangers), 1999 v Es, Bel (2), G, Ei, CzR; 2000 v Bos (7)
Wilson, T. (St Mirren), 1983 v Sw (sub) (1)
Wilson, T. (Nottingham F), 1988 v E; 1989 v N, Y; 1990 v F (4)
Winnie, D. (St Mirren), 1988 v Bel (1)
Wright, P. (Aberdeen), 1989 v Y, F; (with QPR), 1990 v Y (sub) (3)
Wright, S. (Aberdeen), 1991 v Bul, Pol, F; 1992 v Sw, G (2), Se (2); 1993 v Sw, P, I, Ma; 1994 v I, Ma (14)
Wright, T. (Oldham Ath), 1987 v Bel (sub) (1)

Young, D. (Aberdeen), 1997 v Es (sub), Se, Col, CzR (sub), P; 1998 v La (sub); 1999 v CzR (sub), G (sub); 2000 v W (9)

WALES

Aizlewood, M. (Luton T), 1979 v E; 1981 v Ho (2)

Baddeley, L. M. (Cardiff C), 1996 v Mol (sub), G (sub) (2)
Balcombe, S. (Leeds U), 1982 v F (sub) (1)
Barnhouse, D. J. (Swansea), 1995 v Mol; 1996 v Mol, Sm (3)
Bater, P. T. (Bristol R), 1977 v E, S (2)
Bellamy, C. (Norwich C), 1996 v Sm (sub); 1997 v Sm, T, Bel; 1998 v T, Bel, I; 1999 v I (8)
Bird, A. (Cardiff C), 1993 v Cy (sub); 1994 v Cy (sub); 1995 v Mol, Ge (sub), Bul; 1996 v G (sub) (6)
Blackmore, C. (Manchester U), 1984 v N, Bul, Y (3)
Blake, N. (Cardiff C), 1991 v Pol (sub); 1993 v Cy, Bel, RCS; 1994 v RCS (5)
Blaney, S. D. (West Ham U), 1997 v Sm, Ho, T (3)
Bodin, P. (Cardiff C), 1983 v Y (1)
Bowen, J. P. (Swansea C), 1993 v Cy, Bel (2); 1994 v RCS, R (sub) (5)
Bowen, M. (Tottenham H), 1983 v N; 1984 v Bul, Y (3)
Boyle, T. (C Palace), 1982 v F (1)
Brace, D. P. (Wrexham), 1995 v Ge, Bul (2); 1997 v Sm Ho; 1998 v T (6)

Cegielski, W. (Wrexham), 1977 v E (sub), S (2)
Chapple, S. R. (Swansea C), 1992 v R; 1993 v Cy, Bel (2), RCS; 1994 v RCS; Bul (2) (8)
Charles, J. M. (Swansea C), 1979 v E; 1981 v Ho (2)
Clark, J. (Manchester U), 1978 v S; (with Derby Co), 1979 v E (2)
Coates, J. S. (Swansea C), 1996 v Mol, G; 1997 v Ho, T (sub); 1998 v T (sub) (5)
Coleman, C. (Swansea C), 1990 v Pol; 1991 v E, Pol (3)
Coyne, D. (Tranmere R), 1992 v R; 1994 v Cy (sub), R; 1995 v Mol, Ge, Bul (2) (7)
Curtis, A. T. (Swansea C), 1977 v E (1)

Davies, A. (Manchester U), 1982 v F (2), Ho; 1983 v N, Y, Bul (6)
Davies, D. (Barry T), 1999 v D (sub) (1)
Davies, G. M. (Hereford U), 1993 v Bel, RCS; 1995 v Mol (sub), Ge, Bul (2); (with C Palace) 1996 v Mol (7)
Davies, I. C. (Norwich C), 1978 v S (sub) (1)
Davies, S. (Peterborough U), 1999 v D, Bl, Sw, I, D; (with Tottenham H), 2000 v S (6)
Day, R. (Manchester C), 2000 v S (sub), Ni (2)
Deacy, N. (PSV Eindhoven), 1977 v S (1)
Dibble, A. (Cardiff C), 1983 v Bul; 1984 v N, Bul (3)
Doyle, S. C. (Preston NE), 1979 v E (sub); (with Huddersfield T), 1984 v N (2)
Dwyer, P. J. (Cardiff C), 1979 v E (1)

Earnshaw, R. (Cardiff C), 1999 v P (sub), I, D; 2000 v S, Ni (5)
Ebdon, M. (Everton), 1990 v Pol; 1991 v E (2)
Edwards, C. N. H. (Swansea C), 1996 v G; 1997 v Sm, Ho (2), T, Bel; 1998 v T (7)
Edwards, R. I. (Chester), 1977 v S; 1978 v W (2)
Edwards, R. W. (Bristol C), 1991 v Pol; 1992 v R; 1993 v Cy, Bel (2), RCS; 1994 v RCS, Cy, R; 1995 v Ge, Bul; 1996 v Mol, G (13)
Evans, A. (Bristol R), 1977 v E (1)
Evans, K. (Leeds U), 1999 v I (sub), D (2)
Evans, P. S. (Shrewsbury T), 1996 v G (1)
Evans, T. (Cardiff C), 1995 v Bul (sub); 1996 v Mol, G (3)

Folland, R. W. (Oxford U), 2000 v Ni (sub) (1)
Foster, M. G. (Tranmere R), 1993 v RCS (1)
Freestone, R. (Chelsea), 1990 v Pol (1)

Gabbidon, D. L. (WBA), 1999 v D, P, Sw, I (sub), D; 2000 v Bl, Sw, S, Ni (9)
Gale, D. (Swansea C), 1983 v Bul; 1984 v N (sub) (2)
Gibson, N. D. (Tranmere R), 1999 v D (sub), Bl (sub), P; 2000 v S (sub), Ni (5)
Giggs, R. (Manchester U), 1991 v Pol (1)
Giles, D. C. (Cardiff C), 1977 v S; 1978 v S; (with Swansea C), 1981 v Ho; (with C Palace), 1983 v Y (4)
Giles, P. (Cardiff C), 1982 v F (2), Ho (3)
Graham, D. (Manchester U), 1991 v E (1)
Green, R. M. (Wolverhampton W), 1998 v I; 1999 v I, D, Bl, Sw, I, D; 2000 v Bl, S, Ni (10)
Griffith, C. (Cardiff C), 1990 v Pol (1)
Griffiths, C. (Shrewsbury T), 1991 v Pol (sub) (1)

Hall, G. D. (Chelsea), 1990 v Pol (1)
Hartson, J. (Luton T), 1994 v Cy, R; 1995 v Mol, Ge, Bul; (with Arsenal), 1996 v G, Sm; 1997 v Sm, Ho (9)
Haworth, S. O. (Cardiff C), 1997 v Ho, T, Bel; (with Coventry C), 1998 v T, Bel; I; 1999 v I, D; (with Wigan Ath) Bl, Sw; 2000 v Bl, Sw (12)
Hodges, K. (Wimbledon), 1983 v Y (sub), Bul (sub); 1984 v N, Bul, Y (5)
Holden, A. (Chester), 1984 v Y (sub) (1)
Holloway, C. D. (Exeter C), 1999 v P, D (2)
Hopkins, J. (Fulham), 1982 v F (sub), Ho; 1983 v N, Y, Bul (5)
Hopkins, S. A. (Wrexham), 1999 v P (sub) (1)
Huggins, D. S. (Bristol C), 1996 v Sm (1)
Hughes, D. R. (Southampton), 1994 v R (1)
Hughes, R. D. (Aston Villa), 1996 v Sm; 1997 v Sm (sub), Ho (2), T, Bel; 1998 v T, Bel, I; 1999 v I, Sw, I; (with Shrewsbury T), 2000 v Sw (13)
Hughes, I. (Bury), 1992 v R; 1993 v Cy, Bel (sub), RCS; 1994 v Cy, R; 1995 v Mol, Ge, Bul; 1996 v Mol (sub), G (11)
Hughes, L. M. (Manchester U), 1983 v N, Y; 1984 v N, Bul, Y (5)
Hughes, W. (WBA), 1977 v E, S; 1978 v S (3)

Jackett, K. (Watford), 1981 v Ho; 1982 v F (2)
James, R. M. (Swansea C), 1977 v E, S; 1978 v S (3)
Jarman, L. (Cardiff C), 1996 v Sm; 1997 v Sm, Ho (2), Bel; 1998 v T, Bel; 1999 v I, P; 2000 v Bl (10)
Jeanne, L. C. (QPR), 1999 v P (sub), Sw, I; 2000 v Bl, Sw, S, Ni (7)
Jelleyman, G. A. (Peterborough U), 1999 v D (sub) (1)
Jenkins, L. D. (Swansea C), 1998 v T (sub); 2000 v Bl, Sw, S, Ni (4)
Jenkins, S. R. (Swansea C), 1993 v Cy (sub), Bel (2)
Jones, E. P. (Blackpool), 2000 v Ni (sub) (1)
Jones, F. (Wrexham), 1981 v Ho (1)
Jones, L. (Cardiff C), 1982 v F (2), Ho (3)
Jones, M. G. (Leeds U), 1998 v Bel; 1999 v I, D, Bl, Sw, I; 2000 v Sw (7)
Jones, P. L. (Liverpool), 1992 v R; 1993 v Cy, Bel (2), RCS; 1994 v RCS (sub), Cy, R; 1995 v Mol, Ge; 1996 v Mol, G (12)
Jones, R. (Sheffield W), 1994 v R; 1995 v Bul (2) (3)
Jones, V. (Bristol R), 1979 v E; 1981 v Ho (2)

Kendall, M. (Tottenham H), 1978 v S (1)
Kenworthy, J. R. (Tranmere R), 1994 v Cy; 1995 v Mol, Bul (3)
Knott, G. R. (Tottenham H), 1996 v Sm (1)

Law, B. J. (QPR), 1990 v Pol; 1991 v E (2)
Letheran, G. (Leeds U), 1977 v E, S (2)

Lewis, D. (Swansea C), 1982 v F (2), Ho; 1983 v N, Y, Bul; 1984 v N, Bul, Y (9)
Lewis, J. (Cardiff C), 1983 v N (1)
Llewellyn, C. M. (Norwich C), 1998 v T (sub), Bel (sub), I; 1999 v I, D, Bl, I; 2000 v Bl, Sw, S (10)
Loveridge, J. (Swansea C), 1982 v Ho; 1983 v N, Bul (3)
Low, J. D. (Bristol R), 1999 v P (1)
Lowndes, S. R. (Newport Co), 1979 v E; 1981 v Ho; (with Millwall), 1984 v Bul, Y (4)

McCarthy, A. J. (QPR), 1994 v RCS, Cy, R (3)
Maddy, P. (Cardiff C), 1982 v Ho; 1983 v N (sub) (2)
Margetson, M. W. (Manchester C), 1992 v R; 1993 v Cy, Bel (2), RCS; 1994 v RCS, Cy (7)
Martin, A. P. (Crystal Palace), 1999 v D (1)
Marustik, C. (Swansea C), 1982 v F (2); 1983 v Y, Bul; 1984 v N, Bul, Y (7)
Maxwell, L. J. (Liverpool), 1999 v Sw (sub), I; 2000 v Sw (sub), S, Ni (5)
Meaker, M. J. (QPR), 1994 v RCS (sub), R (sub) (2)
Melville, A. K. (Swansea C), 1990 v Pol; (with Oxford U), 1991 v E (2)
Micallef, C. (Cardiff C), 1982 v F, Ho; 1983 v N (3)
Morgan, A. M. (Tranmere R), 1995 v Mol, Bul; 1996 v Mol, G (4)
Mountain, P. D. (Cardiff C), 1997 v Ho, T (2)

Nardiello, D. (Coventry C), 1978 v S (1)
Neilson, A. B. (Newcastle U), 1993 v Cy, Bel (2), RCS; 1994 v RCS, Cy, R (7)
Nicholas, P. (C Palace), 1978 v S; 1979 v E; (with Arsenal), 1982 v F (3)
Nogan, K. (Luton T), 1990 v Pol; 1991 v E (2)
Nogan, L. (Oxford U) 1991 v E (1)

Oster, J. M. (Grimsby T), 1997 v Sm (sub), Ho (sub), T, Bel; (with Everton), 1998 v T, Bel, I; 1999 v I, Sw (9)
Owen, G. (Wrexham), 1991 v E (sub), Pol; 1992 v R; 1993 v Cy, Bel (2); 1994 v Cy, R (8)

Page, R. J. (Watford), 1995 v Mol, Ge, Bul; 1996 v Mol (4)
Partridge, D. W. (West Ham U), 1997 v T (1)
Pascoe, C. (Swansea C), 1983 v Bul (sub); 1984 v N (sub), Bul, Y (4)
Pembridge, M. (Luton T), 1991 v Pol (1)
Perry, J. (Cardiff C), 1990 v Pol; 1991 v E, Pol (3)
Peters, M. (Manchester C), 1992 v R; (with Norwich C), 1993 v Cy, RCS (3)
Phillips, D. (Plymouth Arg), 1984 v N, Bul, Y (3)
Phillips, L. (Swansea C), 1979 v E; (with Charlton Ath), 1983 v N (2)
Pontin, K. (Cardiff C), 1978 v S (1)
Powell, A. (Southampton), 1991 v Pol (sub); 1992 v R (sub); 1993 v Bel (sub); 1994 v RCS (4)
Price, J. J. (Swansea C), 1998 v I (sub); 1999 v I (sub), D, Bl, P; 2000 v Bl, Sw (7)
Price, P. (Luton T), 1981 v Ho (1)
Pugh, D. (Doncaster R), 1982 v F (2) (2)
Pugh, S. (Wrexham), 1993 v Bel (2 subs) (2)

Ramasut, M. W. T. (Bristol R), 1997 v Ho, Bel; 1998 v T, I (4)
Ratcliffe, K. (Everton), 1981 v Ho; 1982 v F (2)
Ready, K. (QPR), 1992 v R; 1993 v Bel (2); 1994 v RCS, Cy (5)
Rees, A. (Birmingham C), 1984 v N (1)
Rees, J. (Luton T), 1990 v Pol; 1991 v E, Pol (3)
Roberts, A. (QPR), 1991 v E, Pol (2)
Roberts, C. J. (Cardiff C), 1999 v D (sub) (1)
Roberts, G. (Hull C), 1983 v Bul (1)
Roberts, G. W. (Liverpool), 1997 v Ho, T, Bel; 1998 v T, I; 1999 v I, D, Bl, P; (with Panionios) D; (with Tranmere R), 2000 v Sw (11)
Roberts, J. G. (Wrexham), 1977 v E (1)
Roberts, N. W. (Wrexham), 1999 v I (sub), P; 2000 v Sw (sub) (3)
Roberts, P. (Porthmadog), 1997 v Ho (sub) (1)
Roberts, S. I. (Swansea C), 1999 v Sw, I (sub), D; 2000 v Bl (sub), Ni (5)
Roberts, S. W. (Wrexham), 2000 v S (1)
Robinson, C. P. (Wolverhampton W), 1996 v Sm; 1997 v Sm, Ho (2), T, Bel (6)
Robinson, J. (Brighton & HA), 1992 v R; (with Charlton Ath), 1993 v Bel; 1994 v RCS, Cy, R (5)
Rowlands, A. J. R. (Manchester C), 1996 v Sm; 1997 v Sm, Ho (1 + sub), T (sub) (5)
Rush, I. (Liverpool), 1981 v Ho; 1982 v F (2)

Savage, R. W. (Crewe Alex), 1995 v Bul; 1996 v Mol, G (3)
Sayer, P. A. (Cardiff C), 1977 v E, S (2)
Searle, D. (Cardiff C), 1991 v Pol (sub); 1992 v R; 1993 v Cy, Bel (2), RCS; 1994 v RCS (6)
Slatter, D. (Chelsea), 2000 v Sw (sub), S (2)
Slatter, N. (Bristol R), 1983 v N, Y, Bul; 1984 v N, Bul, Y (6)
Speed, G. A. (Leeds U), 1990 v Pol; 1991 v E, Pol (3)
Stevenson, N. (Swansea C), 1982 v F, Ho (2)
Stevenson, W. B. (Leeds U), 1977 v E, S; 1978 v S (3)
Symons, K. (Portsmouth), 1991 v E, Pol (2)

Taylor, G. K. (Bristol R), 1995 v Ge, Bul (2); 1996 v Mol (4)
Thomas, D. J. (Watford), 1998 v T, Bel (2)
Thomas, J. A. (Blackburn R), 1996 v Sm; 1997 v Sm, Ho (2), T, Bel; 1998 v Bel; 1999 v D, Bl, P; 2000 v Bl (sub) (11)
Thomas, Martin R. (Bristol R), 1979 v E; 1981 v Ho (2)
Thomas, Mickey R. (Wrexham), 1977 v E; 1978 v S (2)
Thomas, D. G. (Leeds U), 1977 v E; 1979 v E; 1984 v N (3)
Tibbott, L. (Ipswich T), 1977 v E, S (2)
Tipton, M. J. (Oldham Ath), 1998 v I (sub); 1999 v P, Sw (sub); 2000 v Ni (4)
Twiddy, C. (Plymouth Arg), 1995 v Mol, Ge; 1996 v G (sub) (3)

Vaughan, N. (Newport Co), 1982 v F, Ho (2)

Walsh, D. (Wrexham), 2000 v S, Ni (2)
Walsh, I. P. (C Palace), 1979 v E; (with Swansea C), 1983 v Bul (2)
Walton, M. (Norwich C.), 1991 v Pol (sub) (1)
Ward, D. (Notts Co), 1996 v Mol, G (2)
Williams, A. P. (Southampton), 1998 v Bel, I; 1999 v I, D (sub), Bl, Sw, I; 2000 v Bl, Sw (9)
Williams, A. S. (Blackburn R), 1996 v Sm; 1997 v Sm, Ho, Bel; 1998 v T, Bel, I; 1999 v I, D, Bl, P, Sw, I, D; 2000 v Bl, Sw (16)
Williams, D. (Bristol R), 1983 v Y (1)
Williams, D. I. L. (Liverpool), 1998 v I; 1999 v D, Bl; (with Wrexham) I, D; 2000 v Bl, S, Ni (8)
Williams, E. (Caernarfon T), 1997 v Ho (sub), T (sub) (2)
Williams, G. (Bristol R), 1983 v Y, Bul (2)
Williams, S. J. (Wrexham), 1995 v Mol, Ge, Bul (2) (4)
Wilmot, R. (Arsenal), 1982 v F (2), Ho; 1983 v N, Y; 1984 v Y (6)
Wright, A. A. (Oxford U), 1998 v Bel, I (sub); 1999 v D (sub) (3)

Young, S. (Cardiff C), 1996 v Sm; 1997 v Sm, Ho (2), Bel (sub) (5)

NORTHERN IRELAND

Bailie, N. (Linfield), l990 v Is; 1994 v R (sub) (2)
Beatty, S. (Chelsea), 1990 v Is; (with Linfield), 1994 v R (2)
Black, K. T. (Luton T), 1990 v Is (1)
Blackledge, G. (Portadown), 1978 v Ei (1)
Boyle, W. S. (Leeds U), 1998 v Sw (sub), S (sub) (2)
Brotherston, N. (Blackburn R), 1978 v Ei (sub) (1)
Burns, L. (Port Vale), 1998 v Sw, S, Ei; 1999 v T, Fi, Mol, G, Mol, Ei; 2000 v F, T, G, Fi (13)

Carlisle, W. T. (Crystal Palace), 2000 v Fi (sub) (1)
Carroll, R. E. (Wigan Ath), 1998 v S, Ei; 1999 v T, Fi, Mol, G, Mol, Ei; 2000 v T, G, Fi (11)
Carson, S. (Rangers), 2000 v Ma (1)
Clarke, R. D. J. (Portadown), 1999 v Ei (sub); S; 2000 v F (sub), S, W (sub) (5)
Connell, T. E. (Coleraine), 1978 v Ei (sub) (1)
Coote, A. (Norwich C), 1998 v Sw (sub), S, Ei; 1999 v T, Fi,Mol, G, Mol, Ei; 2000 v F, T, G (12)
Convery, J. (Celtic), 2000 v S, W (2)

Devine, D. (Omagh T), 1994 v R (1)
Devine, J. (Glentoran), 1990 v Is (1)
Dolan, J. (Millwall), 2000 v Fi, Ma, S (3)
Donaghy, M. M. (Larne), 1978 v Ei (1)
Dowie, I. (Luton T), 1990 v Is (1)
Elliott, S. (Glentoran), 1999 v Fi (sub), Ei, S (sub) (3)

Feeney, L. (Linfield), 1998 v Ei (sub); 1999 v T, Fi, Mol; (with Rangers), G (sub), Ei, S; 2000 v Fi (8)
Ferguson, M. (Glentoran), 2000 v T (sub), Ma (sub) (2)
Fitzgerald, D. (Rangers), 1998 v Sw, S; 1999 v T (sub), Fi (4)
Friars, S. M. (Liverpool), 1998 v Sw, S, Ei; (with Ipswich T), 1999 v T, Fi, Mol, G, Mol; 2000 v F, T, G, Ma, S, W (14)

Gillespie, K. R. (Manchester U), 1994 v R (1)
Glendinning, M. (Bangor), 1994 v R (1)
Graham, G. L. (Crystal Palace), 1999 v S; 2000 v F, T, G, Fi (5)
Graham, R. S. (QPR), 1999 v Fi (sub), Mol, Ei (sub); 2000 v F (sub), T (sub), G (sub), Fi (sub), Ma, S, W, (10)
Gray, P. (Luton T), 1990 v Is (sub) (1)
Griffin, D. J. (St Johnstone), 1998 v S (sub), Ei; 1999 v T, Fi, G, Mol, Ei, S; 2000 v F, T (10)

Hamilton, G. (Blackburn R), 2000 v Ma (sub), S, W (sub) (3)
Hamilton, W. R. (Linfield), 1978 v Ei (1)
Harkin, M. P. (Wycombe W), Ma (sub), S (sub), W (3)
Harvey, J. (Arsenal), 1978 v Ei (1)
Hayes, T. (Luton T), 1978 v Ei (1)
Healy, D. J. (Manchester U), 1999 v Mol (sub), G (sub), Ei (sub), S; 2000 v F (sub), T, G, Fi (8)
Holmes, S. (Manchester C), Ma, S, W (3)
Hughes, M. E. (Manchester C), 1990 v Is (sub)

Johnson, D. M. (Blackburn R), 1998 v Sw, S, Ei; 1999 v T, Fi, G, Mol, Ei; 2000 v F, T, G (11)
Johnston, B. (Cliftonville), 1978 v Ei (1)

Kee, P. V. (Oxford U), 1990 v Is (1)
Kelly, D. (Derry C), 2000 v Ma, W (2)
Kelly, N. (Oldham Ath), 1990 v Is (sub) (1)
Kirk, A. (Hearts), 1999 v S; 2000 v Ma, S, W (4)

Lennon, N. F. (Manchester C), 1990 v Is; (with Crewe Alex), 1994 v R (2)
Lyttle, G. (Celtic), 1998 v Sw, S; (with Peterborough U), 1999 v T (sub), Mol (2), S; 2000 v G, Fi (8)

Magee, J. (Bangor), 1994 v R (sub) (1)
Magilton, J. (Liverpool), 1990 v Is (1)
Matthews, N. P. (Blackpool), 1990 v Is (1)
McAreavey, P. (Swindon T), 2000 v Ma, S (2)
McBride, J. (Glentoran), 1994 v R (sub) (1)
McCallion, E. (Coleraine), 1998 v Sw (sub) (1)
McCann, G. S. (West Ham U), 2000 v S (sub), W (2)
McCoy, R. K. (Coleraine), 1990 v Is (1)
McCreery, D. (Manchester U), 1978 v Ei (1)
McGibbon, P. C. G. (Manchester U), 1994 v R (1)
McGlinchey, B. (Manchester C), 1998 v Sw, S, Ei; (with Port Vale), 1999 v T, Fi, Mol, G, Mol, Ei, S; (with Gillingham), 2000 v F, G, T, Fi (14)
McIlroy, T. (Linfield), 1994 v R (sub) (1)
McKnight, P. (Rangers), 1998 v Sw; 1999 v T (sub), Mol (sub) (3)
McFlynn, T. (QPR), 2000 v Ma (sub), W (sub) (2)
McMahon, G. J. (Tottenham H),1994 v R (sub) (1)
McVeigh, P. F. (Tottenham H), 1998 v S (sub), Ei; 1999 v T, Mol, G, Mol, Ei; 2000 v F, T (sub), G (sub), Fi (11)
Millar, W. P. (Port Vale), 1990 v Is (1)
Miskelly, D. T. (Oldham Ath), 2000 v F, Ma, S, W (4)
Moreland, V. (Glentoran), 1978 v Ei (sub) (1)
Morgan, M. P. T. (Preston NE), 1999 v S (1)
Mulryne, P. P. (Manchester U), Sw, S, Ei; (with Norwich C), 1999 v G, Mol (5)
Murray, M. (Linfield), 1978 v Ei (sub) (1)

Nicholl, J. M. (Manchester U), 1978 v Ei (1)
Nixon, C. (Glentoran), 2000 v Fi (sub) (1)

O'Hara, G. (Leeds U), 1994 v R (1)
O'Neill, M. A. M. (Hibernian), 1994 v R (1)
O'Neill, P. (Leicester C), 1978 v Ei (1)

Patterson, D. J. (Crystal Palace), 1994 v R (1)

Quinn, S. J. (Blackpool), 1994 v R (1)

Robinson, S. (Tottenham H), 1994 v R (1)

Skates, G. (Blackburn R), 2000 v Ma (1)
Sloan, T. (Ballymena U), 1978 v Ei (1)

Taylor, M. S. (Fulham), 1998 v Sw (1)
Toner, C. (Tottenham H), 2000 v Ma (sub), S (sub), W (3)

Waterman, D. G. (Portsmouth), 1998 v Sw, S, Ei; 1999 v T, Fi, Mol, G, Mol, Ei, S; 2000 v F, T, G, Fi (14)
Wells, D. P. (Barry T), 1999 v S (1)
Whitley, Jeff (Manchester C), 1998 v Sw, S, Ei; 1999 v T, Fi, Mol, G, Ei, S; 2000 v F, G, T, Ma, S, W (15)

FA SCHOOLS & YOUTH GAMES 1999–2000

ENGLAND UNDER-18

7 Sept

England 0   Switzerland 1

England: Bywater (West Ham U) [Kirkland (Coventry C) 46]; Iriekpen (West Ham U) [Tann (Cambridge U) 85], Konchesky (Charlton Ath), Prutton (Nottingham F), Samuel (Aston Villa), Barry (Aston Villa), Armstrong (Liverpool) [Johnson A (Birmingham C) 46], Murray (Derby Co) [Turner (Nottingham F) 60], Stonebridge (Plymouth Arg), Cole (West Ham U) [Pead (Coventry C) 18] [Carrick (West Ham U) 46], Etherington (Peterborough U) [McSheffrey (Coventry C) 75].

6 Oct

Spain 2   England 0

England: Bywater (West Ham U); Iriekpen (West Ham U) [Tann (Cambridge U) 83], Konchesky (Charlton Ath), Carrick (West Ham U), Samuel (Aston Villa), Barry (Aston Villa), Webber (Manchester U), Prutton (Nottingham F), Stonebridge (Plymouth Arg), Cole (West Ham U) [Etherington (Peterborough U) 64], McSheffrey (Coventry C) [Johnson A (Birmingham C) 75].

8 Oct

England 3 *(Barry 63, Stonebridge 73, Prutton 87)*
Cyprus 0

England: Bywater (West Ham U); Pead (Coventry C), Konchesky (Charlton Ath), Carrick (West Ham U), Samuel (Aston Villa), Barry (Aston Villa), Webber (Manchester U) [Armstrong (Liverpool) 66], Prutton (Nottingham F), Stonebridge (Plymouth Arg), Cole (West Ham U) [Tann (Cambridge U) 90], Etherington (Peterborough U) [McSheffrey (Coventry C) 58].

10 Oct

England 9 *(Barry 11, 66, 89, Iriekpen 35, 88, Armstrong 16, Carrick 14, Stonebridge 73, McSheffrey 90)*
San Marino 0

England: Rachubka (Manchester U); Tann (Cambridge U) [Webber (Manchester U) 73], Konchesky (Charlton Ath), Barry (Aston Villa), Iriekpen (West Ham U), Hanson (Middlesbrough), Armstrong (Liverpool), Prutton (Nottingham F) [Pead (Coventry C) 46], Mike (Manchester C) [Stonebridge (Plymouth Arg) 56)], Carrick (West Ham U), McSheffrey (Coventry C).

8 Mar

England 0   France 3

England: Kirkland (Coventry C) [Bywater (West Ham U) 46]; Parnaby (Middlesbrough), Konchesky (Charlton Ath), Halls (Arsenal), Clarke (Everton), Samuel (Aston Villa), Defoe (West Ham U) [Hamshaw (Sheffield W) 63], McMaster (Leeds U) [Brackstone (Middlesbrough) 71], Bothroyd (Arsenal) [Logan (Ipswich T) 51], Noble (Arsenal), McSheffrey (Coventry C) [Richardson (Leeds U) 88].

27 Apr

England 2 *(Knight 20, Hamshaw 25)*   **Luxembourg 0**

England: Evans (Chelsea) [Howarth (York C) 60]; Tann (Cambridge U) [Amankwaah (Bristol C) 70], Jenkins (Wimbledon), Jackson (Tottenham H) [Crane (Sheffield W) 80], Clarke (Everton), Lescott (Wolverhampton W), Knight (Chelsea), Jackson (Middlesbrough) [Jagielka (Sheffield U) 46], Logan (Ipswich T) [Richards (Blackburn R) 46], Bewers (Aston Villa) [Fallon (Barnsley) 65], Hamshaw (Sheffield W) [Keenan (Chelsea) 30].

ENGLAND UNDER-16/UNDER-17

1 July 1999

England 1 *(Chopra 55)*   **France 1**

England: Allaway; Sherman (Austin 64), Hylton, Clark (Moore 51), Bowditch, Otsemobor, Pennant (Muirhead 77), Spicer, Brown (Johnson 51), Chopra, Howard.

4 July 1999

England 2 *(Howard 21, Chopra 74)*   **Argentina 1**

England: Allaway; Sherman, Hylton, Clark, Bowditch, Johnson (Otsemobor 54), Pennant (Prince 69), Spicer, Moore (Brown 63), Chopra, Howard (Muirhead 57).

2 Aug 1999

England 3 *(Brown 16, Wood 36, Morgan 79)*   **Iceland 0**

England: Lonergan (Preston NE); Duncan (Newcastle U), Bailey (Arsenal), Willetts (Everton), Austin (Barnsley) [Emanuel (Bradford C) 65], Morgan (Wimbledon), Cooke (Aston Villa), Muirhead (Manchester U) [Jenas (Nottingham F) 52], Brown (Bristol C) [Sutton (Tottenham H) 77], Wood (Manchester U), Spicer (Arsenal) [Johnson (Leeds U) 59].

3 Aug 1999

England 4 *(Spicer 14, Johnson 25 (pen), Brown 50, Fox 59)*
Sweden 1

England: Lonergan (Preston NE); Duncan (Newcastle U), Emanuel (Bradford C), Willetts (Everton), Fox (Exeter C), Muirhead (Manchester U), Jenas (Nottingham F), Johnson (Leeds U), Brown (Bristol C), Spicer (Arsenal) [Cooke (Aston Villa) 79], Sutton (Tottenham H) [Almond (Manchester C) 75].

5 Aug 1999

England 1   Qatar 0

England: Lonergan (Preston NE) [Bell (Newcastle U) 79]; Duncan (Newcastle U), Bailey (Arsenal) [Spicer (Arsenal) 40], Emanuel (Bradford C), Willetts (Everton), Morgan (Wimbledon) [Muirhead (Manchester U) 53], Cooke (Aston Villa), Almond (Manchester C) [Jenas (Nottingham F) 40], Johnson (Leeds U), Wood (Manchester U), Sutton (Tottenham H) [Brown (Bristol C) 79].

6 Aug 1999

England 4 *(Johnson 27, Brown 37, Spicer 58, Jenas 60)*
Finland 5 *aet*

England: Lonergan (Preston NE); Duncan (Newcastle U), Bailey (Arsenal) [Muirhead (Manchester U) 26], Emanuel (Bradford C), Willetts (Everton), Cooke (Aston Villa), Jenas (Nottingham F), Johnson (Leeds U), Brown (Bristol C), Spicer (Arsenal) [Fox (Exeter C) 70], Sutton (Tottenham H) [Morgan (Wimbledon) 49].

9 Mar 2000

England 8 *(Clark 2, 55, Moore 28, 31, 33, Chopra 43, Duncan 57, Brown 74)*
Andorra 0

England: Grant (Derby Co); Duncan (QPR), Hylton (Aston Villa), Spicer (Arsenal) [Young (Swindon T) 64], Clark (Sunderland), Davenport (Coventry C), Pennant (Arsenal) [Brown (Bristol C) 56], Chopra (Newcastle U), Moore (Aston Villa), Prince (Liverpool), Morgan (Wimbledon) [Jenas (Nottingham F) 48].

11 Mar 2000

Luxembourg 0   England 1 *(Bowditch 63)*

England: Grant (Derby Co) [Lonergan (Preston NE) 74]; Austin (Barnsley), Willetts (Aston Villa), Bowditch (Tottenham H), Clark (Sunderland), Parker (Birmingham C) [Hylton (Aston Villa) 43], Pennant (Arsenal), Spicer (Arsenal), Brown (Bristol C), Chopra (Newcastle U) [Cooke (Aston Villa) 68], Morgan (Wimbledon).

27 Mar 2000

Mexico 1   England 4 *(Chopra 30, 40, Bowditch 75, Pennant 89)*

England: Grant (Derby Co); Austin (Barnsley), Willetts (Aston Villa), Bowditch (Tottenham H), Clark (Sunderland), Pennant (Arsenal), Brown (Bristol C) [Morgan (Wimbledon) 46], Chopra (Newcastle U), Cooke (Aston Villa) [Muirhead (Manchester U) 84], Otsemobor (Liverpool), Prince (Liverpool) [Johnson (Leeds U) 67].

28 Mar 2000

Trinidad & Tobago 0   England 5 *(Moore 39, 63, 75, Brown 70, 87)*

England: Lonergan (Preston NE); Austin (Barnsley) [Brown (Bristol C) 68], Willetts (Aston Villa) [Cooke (Aston Villa) 79], Clark (Sunderland) [Prince (Liverpool) 62], O'Hanlon (Everton), Spicer (Arsenal), Morgan (Wimbledon), Muirhead (Manchester U), Moore (Aston Villa), Johnson (Leeds U), Otsemobor (Liverpool).

30 Mar 2000

USA 1   England 1 *(Cooke 38)*

England: Grant (Derby Co); Austin (Barnsley), Willetts (Aston Villa), Bowditch (Tottenham H), Clark (Sunderland), Pennant (Arsenal), Chopra (Newcastle U) [Brown (Bristol C) 65], Cooke (Aston Villa) [Spicer (Arsenal) 79], Moore (Aston Villa), Otsemobor (Liverpool), Prince (Liverpool) [Morgan (Wimbledon) 46].

1 May 2000

England 2 *(Bowditch 22, Moore 25)*   **Russia 3**

England: Grant (Derby Co); Austin (Barnsley), Willetts (Aston Villa), Bowditch (Tottenham H), Clark (Sunderland), O'Hanlon (Everton), Pennant (Arsenal), Spicer (Arsenal) [Brown (Bristol C) 68], Moore (Aston Villa), Chopra (Newcastle U), Howard (Southampton) [Morgan (Wimbledon) 68].

3 May 2000

England 1 *(Clark 63)*   **Portugal 2**

England: Grant (Derby Co); Austin (Barnsley), Willetts (Aston Villa) [Spicer (Arsenal) 33], Bowditch (Tottenham H), Clark (Sunderland), Pennant (Arsenal), Chopra (Newcastle U), Brown (Bristol C), Cooke (Aston Villa) [Howard (Southampton) 48], Morgan (Wimbledon) [Moore (Aston Villa) 48], Otsemobor (Liverpool).

5 May 2000

Republic of Ireland 2   England 1 *(Chopra 49)*

England: Lonergan (Preston NE); Austin (Barnsley), Willetts (Aston Villa), Clark (Sunderland), O'Hanlon (Everton), Moore (Aston Villa), Chopra (Newcastle U), Prince (Liverpool) [Brown (Bristol C) 40], Howard (Southampton) [Morgan (Wimbledon) 74], Muirhead (Manchester U), Otsemobor (Liverpool) [Bowditch (Tottenham H) 14].

ADIDAS VICTORY SHIELD

15 Oct

England 2 *(Donnelly 6, Gordon 42)*   **Northern Ireland 1**

England: Pidgeley (Chelsea); Kamara (Nottingham F), Shippen (Sunderland), Schumacher (Everton), Johnson (West Ham U), Welsh (Liverpool), Westcarr (Nottingham F) [Gordon (Arsenal) 40], Donnelly (Blackburn R), Samba (Millwall) [Bent (Ipswich T) 85], Bentley (Arsenal) [Moogan (Everton) 69], Harding (Wimbledon) [Sweeney (Millwall) 65].

28 Oct

England 3 *(Bent 3, Samba 38, Donnelly 65)*   **Wales 1**

England: Parry (Barnsley); Kamara (Nottingham F), Moogan (Everton) [McKie (Tottenham H) 77], Schumacher (Everton), Johnson (West Ham U), Foster (Tottenham H), Bent (Ipswich T), Donnelly (Blackburn R) [Williamson (Leicester C) 79], Samba (Millwall), Sweeney (Millwall) [Frempong (Fulham) 75], Harding (Wimbledon) [Westcarr (Nottingham F) 40].

11 Nov

Scotland   England 2 *(Johnson 36, Schumacher 57)*

England: Pidgeley (Chelsea); Welsh (Liverpool), Foster (Tottenham H), Johnson (West Ham U), Shippen (Sunderland) [Moogan (Everton) 55], Bentley (Arsenal), Schumacher (Everton), Donnelly (Blackburn R), Gordon (Arsenal) [Westcarr (Nottingham F) 60], Samba (Millwall), Harding (Wimbledon) [Bent (Ipswich T) 40].

WALKERS CRISPS UNDER-15

24 Mar

England 1   Holland 0

England: Pidgeley (Chelsea); Arndale (Bristol R), Shippen (Sunderland) [Moogan (Everton) 70], Schumacher (Everton), Johnson (West Ham U), Killgallon (Leeds U) [Taylor (Manchester U) 62], Westcarr (Nottingham F), Bentley (Arsenal) [Watt (Blackburn R) 70], Bell (Blackburn R) [Poole (Manchester U) 72], Donnelly (Blackburn R), Buari (Fulham) [Samba (Millwall) 46].

7 Apr

England 2 *(Kitamike 30, Bentley 80)*   **Italy 2**

England: Holloway (Arsenal); Arndale (Bristol R), Moogan (Everton), Schumacher (Everton), Kitamike (Chelsea), Welsh (Liverpool), Westcarr (Nottingham F), Donnelly (Blackburn R) [Cade (Middlesbrough) 72], Samba (Millwall), Croft (Manchester U) [Bentley (Arsenal) 60], Gordon (Arsenal) [Bell (Blackburn R) 54].

MONTAIGU TOURNAMENT UNDER-15

21 Apr

England 1 *(Schumacher 45 (pen))*   **Argentina 0**

England: Pidgeley (Chelsea); Arndale (Bristol R), McKie (Tottenham H), Schumacher (Everton), Johnson (West Ham U), Beck (Everton), Donnelly (Blackburn R), Bentley (Arsenal), Samba (Millwall) [Camp (Derby Co) 50], Westcarr (Nottingham F) [Bell (Blackburn R) 46], Harding (Wimbledon) [Hopton (Watford) 52].

22 Apr

England 1 *(Johnson 18)*   **France 0**

England: Pidgeley (Chelsea); Arndale (Bristol R), McKie (Tottenham H), Schumacher (Everton), Johnson (West Ham U), Beck (Everton), Killgallon (Leeds U) [Frempong (Fulham) 50], Gordon (Arsenal) [Hopton (Watford) 30], Samba (Millwall), Donnelly (Blackburn R), Bell (Blackburn R).

23 Apr

England 4 *(Bell 10, 25, Bentley 20, Frempong 55)*   **Burkina Faso 0**

England: Camp (Derby Co); Frempong (Fulham), Shippen (Sunderland), Schumacher (Everton) [McKie (Tottenham H) 20], Killgallon (Leeds U), Hopton (Watford), Westcarr (Nottingham F), Bentley (Arsenal), Gordon (Arsenal), Bell (Blackburn R) [Arndale (Bristol R) 35], Harding (Wimbledon).

FINAL

24 Apr

England 0   Italy 0

England: Pidgeley (Chelsea); Arndale (Bristol R), McKie (Tottenham H), Schumacher (Everton), Johnson (West Ham U), Beck (Everton), Westcarr (Nottingham F), Killgallon (Leeds U), Samba (Millwall), Donnelly (Blackburn R), Bell (Blackburn R) [Frempong (Fulham) 60].

(Italy won 4-2 on penalties)

BALLYMENA TOURNAMENT

24 Apr

England 0   Switzerland 1

England: Stephenson (Blackburn R); Moogan (Everton), Kitamike (Chelsea), Taylor (Manchester U) [Murphy (Middlesbrough) 70], Hand (Watford), Bailey (Preston NE), Poole (Manchester U), Larvin (Leeds U) [Lambu (Millwall) 48], Haskins (Nottingham F), Croft (Manchester C) [Bent (Ipswich T) 60], Kamara (Arsenal) [Sims (Manchester U) 58].

25 Apr

England 4 *(Bent 20, 30, 36, 58)*   **Finland 0**

England: Wizik (Chelsea); Sims (Manchester U), Murphy (Middlesbrough), Kitamike (Chelsea), Hand (Watford), Cade (Middlesbrough) [Moogan (Everton) 42], Bent (Ipswich T), Bailey (Preston NE) [Poole (Manchester U) 47], Kanu S (Arsenal), Haskins (Nottingham F) [Taylor (Manchester U) 35], Lambu (Millwall) [Larvin (Leeds U) 47].

26 Apr

England 1 *(Bent 66)*   **Israel 2**

England: Stephenson (Blackburn R); Sims (Manchester U) [Lambu (Millwall) 66], Kitamike (Chelsea), Taylor (Manchester U), Murphy (Middlesbrough), Cade (Middlesbrough), Hand (Watford), Moogan (Everton) [Haskins (Nottingham F) 56], Poole (Manchester U), Bent (Ipswich T), Bailey (Preston NE) [Croft (Manchester C) 61].

28 Apr

England 2 *(Taylor 2, Moogan 23)*   **USA 2**

England: Wizik (Chelsea); Kamara (Arsenal) [Sims (Manchester U) 71], Kanu S (Arsenal), Kitamike (Chelsea), Taylor (Manchester U), Haskins (Nottingham F), Hand (Watford), Moogan (Everton) [Lambu (Millwall) 15], Bent (Ipswich T), Poole (Manchester U), Bailey (Preston NE) [Croft (Manchester C) 22].

(USA won 5-4 on penalties)

THIRD/FOURTH PLACE

29 Apr

England 3 *(Taylor 8, Bent 38, Cade 46)*   **Holland 2**

England: Stephenson (Blackburn R); Kamara (Arsenal), Kitamike (Chelsea), Hand (Watford), Taylor (Manchester U), Cade (Middlesbrough), Bailey (Preston NE), Croft (Manchester C) [Poole (Manchester U) 46], Lambu (Millwall), Bent (Ipswich T), Larvin (Leeds U) [Sims (Manchester U) 60].

WOMEN'S FOOTBALL 1999–2000

Effectively the three strongest clubs contested all the major honours last season. Croydon Ladies won the most prestigious title – that of the National Division for the second successive season with Doncaster Belles and Arsenal Ladies in second and third places respectively. Croydon also appeared in both of the Finals in the Cup competitions.

The AXA F.A. Women's Cup was won by Croydon, who defeated the Doncaster Belles 2-1, with goals from Carmaine Walker and Gemma Hunt, with a consolation goal for Doncaster scored by Vicky Exley. The game was played at Brammal Lane in front of 3,434 spectators.

Arsenal refused to be denied and they took the Premier League Cup with a 4-1 victory of Croydon at Barnet's Underhill ground with over 1,000 spectators present. This was their third successive triumph and their sixth in all, in this competition. They thus attained their twelfth Trophy in eight seasons. They were also successful in winning both the League and Cup in the Women's Premier League Reserve Section. These competitions were introduced for the first time last season. In the League Arsenal finished eleven points clear of Southampton Saints notching 107 goals in the process, whilst in the Cup Final they defeated Leeds 5-1.

In the other lower two divisions of the National League the Northern Section was won by Blyth Spartans Kestrels, with Bangor City thirteen points behind. Bradford City and Arnold Town were relegated. In the Southern Division, Barry Town were champions on goal difference from Brighton with Three Bridges and Whitehawk relegated.

Both the Northern and Southern Divisions were expanded to twelve apiece, confirming the still growing trend in the onward development of Women's football. This has seen the game promoted by Sky Sports with whom a contract has been signed and the commitment shown by the Football Association to try to move to a professional League in the next three years.

There are now 31 Centres of Excellence giving specialised coaching to girls between the ages of ten and sixteen and 8 Licensed Academies for the older age groups, with more on the way. The pilot scheme was at the East Durham Community College.

The F.A. Women's Football Awards were won by the following

AXA PLAYER'S PLAYER OF THE YEAR
National Division   Karen Walker   Doncaster Belles
Northern Division   Rachel Mander   Sheffield W
Southern Division   Trudy Williams   Barry Town

NATIONWIDE INTERNATIONAL PLAYER OF THE YEAR
Becky Easton – Everton

THE TIMES SPECIAL ACHIVEMENT AWARD
Gillian Coulthard – Doncaster Belles

WALKERS YOUNG PLAY OF THE YEAR
Carly Hunt – Croydon

AXA MANAGER OF THE YEAR
Julie Chipchase – Doncaster Belles

UMBRO MOST IMPROVED TEAM
Blyth Spartans Kestrels

The current structure of of Women's football consists of Mr Ray Kiddell, the Chairman of the F.A. Women's Committee; Kelly Simmons, the Women's Football Co-ordinator plus five Regional Directors. These are Julie Lewis (North-East); Ros Pots (South-East); Lucy Wellings (South-West); Donna McIvor (East Midlands) and Rachel Pavlou (West Midlands and North-West), whilst Tessa Hayward is an adminstrator who makes up the team. Hope Powell is the English National Coach and the Secretary of the F.A. Women's Premier League is Ms Sue Barwick. Although there is a Women's Football department at the F.A.'s Headquarters at Lancester Gate, most the administrative functions are carried out from the F.A.'s other address at 9 Wylotts Place, Potters Bar, Hertfordshire EN6 2JD – Telephone: 01707-671805, Fax: 01707-644190.

KEN GOLDMAN

RESULTS 1999–2000 Season: National Division	Arsenal	Aston Villa	Croydon	Doncaster Belles	Everton	Liverpool	Millwall Lionesses	Reading Royals	Southampton Saints	Tranmere Rovers
Arsenal	—	10-1	3-0	2-1	5-0	2-0	6-0	9-0	3-0	8-1
Aston Villa	1-8	—	0-4	0-6	2-4	0-0	0-1	0-1	1-3	0-7
Croydon	1-0	6-0	—	2-2	3-0	2-0	1-0	7-2	0-0	1-0
Doncaster Belles	2-0	9-0	0-2	—	3-1	2-1	2-1	6-1	3-0	4-1
Everton	1-1	6-0	4-5	1-4	—	1-1	5-1	13-0	3-0	3-0
Liverpool	1-1	1-0	0-4	1-3	2-4	—	0-3	3-1	2-1	1-0
Millwall Lionesses	0-7	2-0	0-4	1-5	1-1	3-0	—	3-0	1-1	1-1
Reading Royals	0-3	3-0	1-10	0-10	1-6	0-0	4-1	—	1-3	3-6
Southampton Saints	1-3	5-1	0-1	0-2	2-5	5-1	1-0	1-1	—	0-2
Tranmere Rovers	3-2	5-0	1-5	0-2	0-4	6-1	5-0	3-1	2-0	—

National Division	P	W	D	L	F	A	GD	Pts
Croydon	18	15	2	1	58	13	+45	47
Doncaster Belles	18	15	1	2	66	14	+52	46
Arsenal	18	13	2	3	73	13	+60	41
Everton	18	10	3	5	62	31	+31	33
Tranmere Rovers	18	9	1	8	43	36	+7	28
Southampton Saints	18	5	3	10	23	32	−9	18
Millwall Lionesses	18	5	3	10	19	43	−24	18
Liverpool	18	4	4	10	15	38	−23	16
Reading Royals	18	3	2	13	20	84	−64	11
Aston Villa	18	0	1	17	6	81	−75	1

RESULTS 1999–2000 Season: Northern Division	Arnold Town	Bangor City	Birmingham City	Blyth SK	Bradford City	Coventry City	Garswood Saints	Huddersfield Town	Ilkeston Town	Leeds United	Sheffield Weds	Wolverhampton
Arnold Town	—	0-0	0-1	0-2	0-2	2-1	1-2	0-0	2-0	1-2	1-2	0-3
Bangor City	2-0	—	1-1	0-2	3-1	6-1	2-3	4-1	3-1	4-0	2-0	2-1
Birmingham City	2-0	1-1	—	1-6	4-1	1-2	1-3	0-1	0-3	3-6	3-1	1-1
Blyth SK	10-1	1-1	11-1	—	7-2	2-0	3-1	5-0	4-0	2-1	1-2	4-3
Bradford City	6-1	1-3	0-5	3-5	—	4-0	1-4	1-3	1-4	1-3	0-2	3-9
Coventry City	3-0	1-2	2-1	0-3	3-2	—	1-1	1-1	1-2	2-2	1-2	1-3
Garswood Saints	4-1	1-1	1-1	0-2	3-1	4-0	—	5-4	2-4	0-2	2-2	1-1
Huddersfield Town	1-2	1-2	2-1	1-4	0-5	0-1	3-2	—	1-1	0-4	2-2	2-3
Ilkeston Town	4-1	0-1	1-0	1-2	0-0	1-1	1-1	6-0	—	0-3	0-2	0-4
Leeds United	4-1	0-1	0-1	2-5	1-1	5-0	1-1	1-2	2-0	—	0-2	3-0
Sheffield Weds	3-0	2-2	2-2	1-6	2-3	3-2	1-2	4-3	4-2	1-3	—	2-3
Wolverhampton	7-0	0-1	2-1	0-3	7-1	1-0	5-2	2-0	5-2	2-3	2-2	—

Northern Division	P	W	D	L	F	A	GD	Pts
Blyth Spartans Kestrels	22	20	1	1	90	21	+69	61
Bangor City	22	14	6	2	44	19	+25	48
Wolverhampton Wanderers	22	13	3	6	64	34	+30	42
Leeds United	22	12	3	7	48	39	+18	39
Sheffield Wednesday	22	10	5	7	44	42	+2	35
Garswood Saints	22	9	7	6	45	39	+6	34
Ilkeston Town	22	7	4	11	33	40	−7	25
Birmingham City	22	6	5	11	32	47	−15	23
Coventry City	22	5	4	13	24	48	−24	19
Huddersfield Town	22	5	4	13	28	56	−28	19
Bradford City	22	5	2	15	40	69	−29	17
Arnold Town	22	3	2	17	14	61	−47	11

RESULTS 1999–2000 Season: Southern Division	Barking	Barnet	Barry Town	Berkhamsted Town	Brighton & Hove A	Cardiff City	Ipswich Town	Langford	Three Bridges	Wembley Mill Hill	Whitehawk	Wimbledon
Barking	—	3-4	2-4	0-4	3-1	5-1	2-0	1-2	2-2	1-2	9-0	4-1
Barnet	7-4	—	2-1	2-2	1-2	3-1	0-3	1-1	1-1	0-6	6-2	4-3
Barry Town	4-0	7-0	—	3-0	1-2	4-0	2-0	5-0	5-1	3-2	5-0	5-1
Berkhamsted Town	2-6	3-2	2-4	—	1-1	2-2	4-2	3-1	1-1	0-2	3-1	1-1
Brighton & Hove A	2-2	2-0	1-1	5-0	—	1-1	5-0	2-1	5-1	3-2	5-0	2-0
Cardiff City	3-2	2-2	1-3	1-2	0-5	—	3-1	0-3	1-2	0-1	6-0	0-5
Ipswich Town	4-3	1-0	4-3	2-0	2-3	4-0	—	2-1	3-2	3-6	11-0	3-2
Langford	2-2	0-0	1-0	3-0	1-0	4-0	0-2	—	2-0	0-2	6-1	4-2
Three Bridges	1-3	1-1	1-3	1-3	1-2	1-2	0-1	2-2	—	0-2	6-2	2-1
Wembley Mill Hill	5-0	0-0	1-2	2-1	0-3	11-0	0-1	0-1	3-0	—	4-0	1-0
Whitehawk	1-9	1-4	1-7	3-5	0-5	0-4	0-5	0-9	2-3	0-2	—	0-4
Wimbledon	5-4	4-0	3-1	1-2	4-2	2-3	5-0	4-2	1-1	2-2	7-1	—

Southern Division	P	W	D	L	F	A	GD	Pts
Barry Town	22	16	1	5	73	25	+48	49
Brighton & Hove Albion	22	15	4	3	59	22	+37	49
Wembley Mill Hill	22	14	2	6	56	20	+36	44
Ipswich Town	22	14	0	8	54	41	+13	42
Langford	22	11	4	7	46	29	+17	37
Berkhamsted Town	22	9	5	8	41	46	−5	32
Wimbledon	22	9	3	10	58	44	+14	30
Barnet	22	7	7	8	40	50	−10	28
Barking	22	8	3	11	67	57	+10	27
Cardiff City	22	6	3	13	31	63	−32	21
Three Bridges	22	4	6	12	30	48	−18	18
Whitehawk	22	0	0	22	15	125	−110	0

AXA FA WOMEN'S CUP 1999–2000

EXTRA PRELIMINARY ROUND

Bolton Wanderers (Supporters) v Barnsley	1-0
Kirklees v Stockport County	0-8
Selby Town v Newsham PH	1-2
Hull City w.o. v Bridge Ladies (Rochdale) removed from competition	

Corwen v AFC Preston	0-5
Burnley Borough v Stockport Celtic	4-3
Manchester City v Norton	26-0
Thorpe United v Trafford	2-4
Scunthorpe United v Brazil Girls	7-2
Darlington v Morley Spurs	5-2

Killingworth v Lancaster City	4-2
Billesley United v Kettering Amazons	5-0
Steel City Wanderers v ES Barwell	5-0
Leicester City v Atherstone United	0-0
Leicester City won 3-1 on penalties.	
Stafford Rangers v Lichfield Diamonds	0-1
Leicester Vixens v Willenhall Town	6-2
Kidderminster Harriers v Tipton Town	4-0
West Bromwich Albion v Nottingham Forest	0-4
Leighton Linslade v Chesham United	0-4
Haverhill Rovers v Woking	2-6
London Womens v Kings Lynn	1-0
Redbridge Raiders withdrew v London Ladies w.o.	
Walkern withdrew v Haywards Heath w.o.	
Malling v Basingstoke Town	2-3
Tottenham Hotspur v Teynham Gunners	6-0
Hackney v Newport Pagnell Town	5-1
Bishop's Stortford v Witney Town	2-3
Newham withdrew v Gillingham Girls w.o.	
Stanway v Hastings Town	2-1
Bristol United v Penzance	1-2
Barnstaple Town v Dorchester	3-8
Elmore Eagles v Okeford United	1-7
Penryn w.o. v Mousehole withdrew	
Cogan Coronation v North Malton Sports	1-4
Swindon Spitfires v Red Star	0-2
North Prospect Oak Villa v Corfe Hills United	3-6

PRELIMINARY ROUND

Newton Aycliffe v Bury Girls & Ladies	0-10
Wakefield v Scunthorpe United	2-6
Carlisle Wanderers v Billingham	1-2
Killingworth v Kippax Welfare	8-5
Trafford v Manchester City	2-1
Warrington Grange v Newsham PH	2-1
AFC Preston v Wigan	5-0
Bolton Wanderers (Supporters) v Hull City	5-4
Sheffield Hallam United v Burnley Borough	1-14
Deans v Darlington	2-4
Stockport County v Chorley	1-1
Stockport County won 4-3 on penalties.	
Grantham Town v Kidderminster Harriers	0-1
Steel City Wanderers v Loughborough Dynamo	1-3
Leicester Vixens v Nottingham Forest	0-3
Billesley United v Loughborough Students	2-3
Calverton MW w.o. v Piccadilly Panthers removed	
Leicester City v Ilkeston	3-2
Lichfield Diamonds v Bromsgrove Rovers	2-3
Belper Town v Nettleham	2-1
Luton v Welwyn Garden City	5-1
Billericay Town v Tesco Country Club	2-3
Rangers v Woking	2-7
Slough v London Ladies	5-0
West Ham United v Hackney	10-1
Stanway v Haywards Heath	4-0
Chesham United v Redbridge Wanderers	7-1
Gillingham Girls v Croydon Postal	2-4
London Womens v Barnet Copthall	4-3
Tring v Tottenham Hotspur	1-8
Basingstoke Town v Maidstone United	2-2
Maidstone United won 4-2 on penalties.	
Cambridge City v Queens Park Rangers	2-4
Witney Town v Fulham	0-10
Penzance v Red Star	0-1
Exeter Rangers v Clevedon	1-5
Dorchester v Okeford United	2-8
Penryn v Corfe Hills United	0-5
Keynsham Town v North Malton Sports	1-2

FIRST ROUND

Middlesbrough v Preston North End	0-2
Darlington v Trafford	3-4
Manchester United v Oldham Curzon	4-3
Doncaster Rovers v Bolton Wanderers (Supporters)	4-1
Scunthorpe United v Killingworth	5-4
Stockport v Billingham	2-1
Worksop Town v Blackburn Rovers	0-3
Blackpool (Wren) Rovers v Newcastle	4-0
Burnley Borough v Leeds City Vixens	1-11
Bury Girls & Ladies v Warrington Grange	5-3
Stockport County v AFC Preston	4-3
Calverton MW v Telford United	0-9
Newcastle Town v Rea Valley Rovers	6-0
Shrewsbury Town v Leicester City	4-4
Shrewsbury Town won 3-2 on penalties.	
Stowmarket v Bromsgrove Rovers	5-0
Racers v Wyrley Rangers	0-1

Nottingham Forest v Derby County	2-1
Peterborough United v Chesterfield	2-1
Belper Town v Loughborough Dynamo	5-0
Mansfield Town v Loughborough Students	2-4
Highfield Rangers withdrew v Kidderminster Harriers w.o.	
West Ham United v Portsmouth	2-1
Croydon Postal v Slough	4-0
Woking v Crowborough Athletic	0-2
Tesco Country Club v Hampton	0-1
Fulham v Abbey Rangers	16-1
Charlton v Bedford Town Bells	2-1
London Womens v Maidstone United	4-2
Tottenham Hotspur v Chesham United	5-0
Enfield v Stanway	10-1
Luton v Clapton	2-3
Queens Park Rangers v Chelsea	0-5
Watford v Northampton Town & County	4-3
Swindon Town v Bristol Rovers	2-5
Corfe Hills United v Yeovil Town	2-1
Denham United v Clevedon	4-1
Southampton v Okeford United	0-6
Bristol City v Oxford United	3-2
North Malton Sports v Red Star	4-2
Newport Strikers v Saltash Pilgrims	4-1

SECOND ROUND

Scunthorpe United v Blackpool (Wren) Rovers	2-3
Trafford v Newcastle Town	2-1
Belper Town v Bury Girls & Ladies	0-3
Shrewsbury Town v Stockport County	1-3
Loughborough Students v Telford United	1-1
Loughborough Students won 3-1 on penalties.	
Blackburn Rovers v Doncaster Rovers	2-1
Nottingham Forest v Wyrley Rangers	1-1
Wyrley won 13-12 on penalties.	
Leeds City Vixens v Stockport	6-1
Preston North End v Manchester United	1-0
Hampton v Clapton	3-3
Hampton won 4-3 on penalties.	
Fulham v Okeford United	5-0
Bristol City v Corfe Hills United	5-4
Newport Strikers v Denham United	3-1
Enfield v North Malton Sports	9-1
Tottenham Hotspur v Stowmarket	1-1
Tottenham Hotspur won 8-7 on penalties.	
Chelsea v West Ham United	2-1
Croydon Postal v Bristol Rovers	1-5
Kidderminster Harriers v Charlton	6-8
Crowborough Athletic v Peterborough United	2-3
Watford v London Womens	6-4

THIRD ROUND

Garswood Saints v Ilkeston Town	4-1
Leeds United v Stockport County	9-0
Blyth Spartans Kestrels v Blackpool (Wren) Rovers	1-0
Wolverhampton Wanderers v Leeds City Vixens	6-0
Arnold Town v Birmingham City	1-2
Bradford City v Trafford	1-2
Preston North End v Sheffield Wednesday	0-4
Loughborough Students v Bangor City	1-0
Blackburn Rovers v Bury Girls & Ladies	2-2
Bury Girls & Ladies won 3-1 on penalties.	
Huddersfield Town v Wyrley Rangers	2-0
Whitehawk v Brighton & Hove Albion	0-6
Barking v Peterborough United	8-2
Wimbledon v Three Bridges	3-1
Charlton v Bristol Rovers	5-0
Enfield v Ipswich Town	1-6
Wembley Mill Hill v Barry Town	1-1
Wembley Mill Hill won 4-3 on penalties.	
Newport Strikers v Hampton	2-1
Cardiff City v Chelsea	1-1
Cardiff City won 4-2 on penalties.	
Bristol City v Tottenham Hotspur	0-2
Fulham v Berkhamsted Town	8-0
Watford v Coventry City	1-3
Langford v Barnet	4-3

FOURTH ROUND

Loughborough Students v Ipswich Town	2-1
Leeds United v Wimbledon	2-1
Bury Girls & Ladies v Tottenham Hotspur	1-1
Bury Girls & Ladies won 5-4 on penalties.	
Croydon v Tranmere Rovers	4-0
Doncaster Belles v Brighton & Hove Albion	1-0
Wembley Mill Hill v Birmingham City	5-1
Reading Royals v Millwall Lionesses	3-2

Southampton Saints v Huddersfield Town	5-0
Charlton v Wolverhampton Wanderers	0-3
Garswood Saints v Langford	5-2
Blyth Spartans Kestrels v Sheffield Wednesday	3-2
Everton v Coventry City	6-0
Aston Villa v Liverpool	0-5
Cardiff City v Arsenal	1-8
Newport Strikers v Fulham	0-3
Trafford v Barking	2-3

FIFTH ROUND

Wolverhampton Wanderers v Bury Girls & Ladies	7-0
Fulham v Barking	3-0
Garswood Saints v Doncaster Belles	0-4
Leeds United v Southampton Saints	3-2
Liverpool v Croydon	0-4
Wembley Mill Hill v Loughborough Students	3-0
Arsenal v Reading Royals	5-0
Everton v Blyth Spartans Kestrels	6-2

SIXTH ROUND

Everton v Croydon	1-2

Doncaster Belles v Wembley Mill Hill	3-0
Fulham v Arsenal	0-7
Wolverhampton Wanderers v Leeds United	0-1

SEMI-FINALS

Doncaster Belles v Arsenal	3-2
Leeds United v Croydon	1-2

FINAL (at Bramall Lane)

1 MAY

Croydon (1) 2 *(Walker 24, Hunt 67)*
Doncaster Belles (1) 1 *(Exley 40)*   3434

Croydon: Cope; Arnold, Fletcher, Barber, Wylie, Loizou, Hunt (Mapes 79), Broadhurst, Walker, Proctor, Bampton.
Doncaster Belles: Hall; Thomas (Borman 75), Embleton, Jackson, Utley, Gomersall, Exley, Coultard, Walker, Garside (Abrahams 79), Lowe.
Referee: J. Frampton.

AXA FA WOMEN'S PREMIER LEAGUE CUP 1999–2000

PRELIMINARY ROUND

Ilkeston Town v Cardiff City	4-0
Leeds United v Birmingham City	2-0

FIRST ROUND

Tranmere Rovers v Ipswich Town	4-2
Barry Town v Aston Villa	0-0
Aston Villa won 6-5 on penalties.	
Coventry City v Leeds United	0-5
Barnet v Garswood Saints	5-3
Wolverhampton Wanderers v Sheffield Wednesday	3-1
Three Bridges v Everton	0-4
Ilkeston Town v Wembley Mill Hill	0-1
Berkhamsted Town v Liverpool	0-5
Reading Royals v Arnold Town	1-0
Brighton & Hove Albion v Millwall Lionesses	2-2
Brighton & Hove Albion won 4-2 on penalties.	
Bradford City v Doncaster Belles	0-5
Bangor City v Blyth Spartans Kestrels	3-2
Croydon v Wimbledon	4-0
Arsenal v Langford	6-0
Barking v Southampton Saints	3-5
Whitehawk v Huddersfield Town	1-2

SECOND ROUND

Southampton Saints v Wolverhampton Wanderers	5-0
Bangor City v Leeds United	4-3
Everton v Brighton & Hove Albion	3-0
Reading Royals v Doncaster Belles	0-4
Croydon v Liverpool	4-1
Aston Villa v Arsenal	1-7
Tranmere Rovers v Barnet	2-1
Wembley Mill Hill v Huddersfield Town	5-1

THIRD ROUND

Everton v Doncaster Belles	2-1
Southampton Saints v Tranmere Rovers	1-8
Arsenal v Bangor City	6-1
Croydon v Wembley Mill Hill	4-0

SEMI-FINALS

Everton v Arsenal	1-2
Croydon v Tranmere Rovers	5-0

FINAL

Arsenal v Croydon	4-1

Croydon's Tara Proctor battles it out with Claire Utley of Doncaster Belles. (Actionimages)

NATIONWIDE CONFERENCE 1999–2000

		Home			Goals		Away			Goals		
	P	W	D	L	F	A	W	D	L	F	A	Pts
Kidderminster Harriers	42	16	3	2	47	16	10	4	7	28	24	85
Rushden & Diamonds	42	11	8	2	37	18	10	5	6	34	24	76
Morecambe	42	10	7	4	46	29	8	9	4	24	19	70
Scarborough	42	10	6	5	36	14	9	6	6	24	21	69
Kingstonian	42	9	4	8	30	24	11	3	7	28	20	67
Dover Athletic	42	10	7	4	43	26	8	5	8	22	30	66
Yeovil Town	42	11	4	6	37	28	7	6	8	23	35	64
Hereford United	42	9	6	6	43	31	6	8	7	18	21	59
Southport	42	10	5	6	31	21	5	8	8	24	35	58
Stevenage Borough	42	8	5	8	26	20	8	4	9	34	34	57
Hayes	42	7	3	11	24	28	9	5	7	33	30	56
Doncaster Rovers	42	7	5	9	19	21	8	4	9	27	27	54
Kettering Town	42	8	10	3	25	19	4	6	11	19	31	52
Woking	42	5	6	10	17	27	8	7	6	28	26	52
Nuneaton Borough	42	7	6	8	28	25	5	9	7	21	28	51
Telford United	42	12	4	5	34	21	2	5	14	22	45	51
Hednesford Town	42	10	3	8	27	23	5	3	13	18	45	51
Northwich Victoria	42	10	8	3	33	25	3	4	14	20	53	51
Forest Green Rovers	42	11	2	8	35	23	2	6	13	19	40	47
Welling United	42	6	5	10	27	32	7	3	11	27	34	47
Altrincham	42	6	8	7	31	26	3	11	7	20	34	46
Sutton United	42	4	8	9	23	32	4	2	15	16	43	34

ATTENDANCES BY CLUB 1999–2000

	Aggregate 1999–2000	Average 1999–2000	Average 1998–99	% Change
Altrincham	20,687	985	798	+20.0
Doncaster Rovers	62,611	2,981	3,380	–11.8
Dover Athletic	23,151	1,102	1,083	+1.8
Forest Green Rovers	20,233	963	854	+12.8
Hayes	15,711	748	760	–1.5
Hednesford Town	24,078	1,147	1,088	+5.4
Hereford United	42,309	2,015	1,976	+2.0
Kettering Town	31,491	1,500	2,033	–26.2
Kidderminster Harriers	59,990	2,857	1,944	+47.0
Kingstonian	25,028	1,192	1,300	–8.3
Morecambe	31,365	1,494	1,163	+28.5
Northwich Victoria	22,753	1,083	1,140	–5.0
Nuneaton Borough	45,053	2,145	1,679	+27.8
Rushden & Diamonds	69,273	3,299	3,044	+8.4
Scarborough	33,861	1,612	2,210	–27.0
Southport	27,455	1,307	1,158	+12.9
Stevenage Borough	45,649	2,174	2,551	–14.8
Sutton United	18,255	869	879	–1.1
Telford United	22,847	1,088	858	+26.8
Welling United	15,483	737	682	+8.0
Woking	42,379	2,018	2,235	–9.7
Yeovil Town	48,346	2,302	2,406	–4.3
Conference Total:	748,008	1,619	1,627	–0.47

HIGHEST ATTENDANCES 1999–2000

6,250	Kidderminster Harriers	2-0	Rushden & Diamonds	8.4.00
5,721	Rushden & Diamonds	2-1	Stevenage Borough	21.12.99
5,301	Kidderminster Harriers	3-3	Forest Green Rovers	1.5.00
4,752	Rushden & Diamonds	2-0	Kettering Town	28.3.00
4,706	Doncaster Rovers	0-1	Scarborough	27.12.99
4,606	Kidderminster Harriers	1-1	Hereford United	27.12.99
4,490	Nuneaton Borough	1-1	Rushden & Diamonds	2.11.99
4,473	Stevenage Borough	2-2	Rushden & Diamonds	3.1.00
4,437	Hereford United	1-1	Kidderminster Harriers	27.12.99
4,302	Doncaster Rovers	3-2	Forest Green Rovers	14.8.99
4,285	Doncaster Rovers	1-1	Southport	24.8.99
4,187	Doncaster Rovers	0-1	Rushden & Diamonds	19.2.00
4,144	Rushden & Diamonds	1-1	Nuneaton Borough	1.4.00
4,022	Rushden & Diamonds	0-0	Hereford United	25.3.00
4,017	Stevenage Borough	3-0	Kettering Town	30.8.99
3,764	Rushden & Diamonds	1-0	Kingstonian	9.10.99

NATIONWIDE CONFERENCE LEADING GOALSCORERS 1999–2000

Conf.			FAC	NM	UT
29	Justin Jackson (Morecambe)	+	1	—	1
24	Carl Alford (Stevenage Borough)	+	—	1	1
18	Neil Davis (Hereford United)	+	1	—	2
17	Ian Foster (Kidderminster Harriers)	+	—	—	—
15	Joff Vansittart (Dover Athletic)	+	—	—	4
14	Ian Arnold (Southport)	+	1	—	3
	Kevin Ellison (Altrincham)	+	1	—	—
13	Steve Brodie (Scarborough)	+	—	1	2
	Lee Charles (Hayes)	+	5	—	—
	Robin Elmes (Hereford United)	+	1	—	1
	Paul Fewings (Hereford United)	+	2	—	—
	Warren Patmore (Yeovil Town)	+	—	2	2
12	Nassim Akrour (Woking)	+	—	2	3
	Stewart Hadley (Kidderminster Harriers)	+	—	—	—
	Ritchie Hanlon (Welling United)	+	—	1	1
	Richard Landon (Altrincham)	+	1	—	1
	David Leworthy (Kingstonian)	+	2	1	2
	Marc McGregor (Forest Green Rovers)	+	1	—	1
	Val Owen (Northwich Victoria)	+	1	—	—
11	Darren Collins (Rushden & Diamonds)	+	2	—	2
	Phil Eastwood (Morecambe)	+	—	—	2
	Lee Elam (Southport)	+	—	—	1
	Mike McElhatton (Rushden & Diamonds)	+	2	—	—
	Zeke Rowe (Welling United)	+	—	—	—
	Dave Stevens (Hayes)	+	—	—	—
	Mark Watson (Sutton United)	+	—	—	1

FAC: FA Cup; NM: Nationwide Macmillan Trophy; UT Umbro Trophy.

CLUB REVIEW

	NC	UT	NM	FAC
Altrincham	21	3	QF	4q
1998-99	*1UL*	*5*	*-*	*2q*
Doncaster Rovers	12	4	W	1
	16	*2*	*W*	*2*
Dover Athletic	6	5	1	4q
	11	*3*	*1*	*4q*
Forest Green Rovers	19	4	1	2
	12	*F*	*1*	*3q*
Hayes	11	2	SF	2
	3	*2*	*QF*	*1*
Hednesford Town	17	3	1	1
	10	*3*	*2*	*2*
Hereford United	8	3	2	3
	13	*2*	*QF*	*3q*
Kettering Town	13	F	2	1
	2	*3*	*1*	*3q*
Kidderminster H	1	2	1	4q
	15	*2*	*2*	*1*
Kingstonian	5	F	F	1
	8	*F*	*1*	*2*
Morecambe	3	3	1	1
	14	*2*	*SF*	*4q*
Northwich Victoria	18	2	2	4q
	7	*QF*	*QF*	*3q*
Nuneaton Borough	15	2	2	4q
	1DM	*2*	*-*	*3q*
Rushden & Diamonds	2	QF	2	3
	4	*4*	*2*	*3*
Scarborough	4	5	QF	4q
	24DS	*-*	*-*	*1*
Southport	9	QF	2	1
	18	*QF*	*2*	*3*
Stevenage Borough	10	3	2	4q
	6	*4*	*2*	*2*
Sutton United	22	SF	1	4q
	1RL	*3*	*-*	*4q*
Telford United	16	SF	SF	4q
	17	*4*	*1*	*1*
Welling United	20	3	2	1
	20	*2*	*1*	*1*
Woking	14	5	QF	4q
	9	*5*	*QF*	*1*
Yeovil Town	7	5	QF	1
	5	*5*	*2*	*3*

HIGHEST AGGREGATE SCORE

6-2	Telford United v Hednesford Town	3.1.00
6-2	Morecambe v Sutton United	4.12.99
5-3	Rushden & Diamonds v Kidderminster H	21.9.99
5-3	Hereford United v Doncaster Rovers	4.9.99
4-4	Hereford United v Scarborough	2.10.99
2-6	Northwich Victoria v Kettering Town	24.4.00

LARGEST HOME MARGIN

6-0	Rushden & Diamonds v Northwich Victoria	29.1.00
5-0	Hednesford Town v Altrincham	5.2.00
5-0	Kidderminster H v Southport	13.11.99
5-0	Morecambe v Northwich Victoria	11.4.00
5-0	Scarborough v Forest Green Rovers	15.4.00
5-0	Scarborough v Yeovil Town	14.8.99

LARGEST AWAY MARGIN

2-6	Northwich Victoria v Kettering Town	24.4.00
0-4	Sutton United v Rushden & Diamonds	28.8.99

CONSECUTIVE VICTORIES

6	Kidderminster Harriers, Southport, Stevenage Borough
5	Kidderminster Harriers, Morecambe, Woking
4	Kingstonian, Rushden & Diamonds, Scarborough, Yeovil Town

CONSECUTIVE DEFEATS

7	Sutton United
6	Hednesford Town
5	Southport, Stevenage Borough

MATCHES WITHOUT DEFEAT

17	Morecambe
14	Altrincham
12	Kidderminster Harriers
11	Hereford United, Rushden & Diamonds
10	Dover Athletic, Kidderminster Harriers

MATCHES WITHOUT SUCCESS

12	Morecambe
11	Altrincham
10	Sutton United
9	Nuneaton Borough, Southport

NATIONWIDE CONFERENCE 1999–2000

APPEARANCES AND GOALSCORERS

Altrincham
Appearances: Adams, D. 41; Burke, B. 18(4); Carmody, M. 0; Chambers, L. 20(6); Coburn, S. 9; Crowe, B. 0(1); Doherty, M. 1(3); Ellender, P. 11; Ellison, K. 36(1); Gallagher, J. 36(1); Gardiner, D. 1; Goodier, O. 0; Goodwin, S. 11(2); Greygoose, D. 18(1); Harris, R. 0; Hart, P. 0; Hawse, S. 25(3); Hemmings, T. 0(2); Hodson, S. 33(1); Hoyland, J. 0(1); Hulston, W. 0(1); Key, L. 15; Kielty, G. 8(3); Landon, R. 14(22); Lovelock, A. 4(27); Maddox, M. 17(2); McDonald, M. 0; Morrell, M. 8(4); Pickering, A. 5; Power, P. 17(7); Price, G. 6(2); Quinn, S. 1; Russell, K. 29; Senior, I. 0(1); Shepherd, G. 0; Skelton, C. 1(2); Talbot, G. 38; Timons, C. 34(1); Trees, R. 2; Turkington, E. 0; Walker, S. 0(1); Wallace, R. 1; Wilson, S. 3(2).
Goals (51): Burke, B. 2, Chambers, L. 1, Ellison, K. 14, Gallagher, J. 2, Kielty, G. 1, Landon, R. 12, Lovelock, A. 1, Morrell, M. 2, Power, P. 3, Price, G. 2, Russell, K. 4, Talbot, G. 4, Timons, C. 2, OG, 1.

Doncaster Rovers
Appearances: Atkins, M. 16; Barnard, M. 35(2); Bubalovic, M. 0(1); Campbell, N. 8(2); Caudwell, M. 17(6); Duerden, I. 18(3); Foster, M. 21(7); Futcher, A. 5; Goodwin, S. 8(2); Hume, M. 2(7); Illman, N. 0(1); Kirkwood, G. 10(10); Maamria, D. 20(15); Marples, S. 22, Maxfield, S. 18(3); McIntyre, K. 29(1); Minett, J. 33(6); Newell, M. 18(1); Penney, D. 29(6); Shaw, S. 8, Snodin, I. 1(1); Sutherland, C. 7(2); Walling, D. 39(1); Warren, L. 27(5); Warrington, A. 42; Watson, A. 13(11); Whitman, T. 0(2); Williams, G. 3(9); Wright, T. 4(4).
Goals (46): Atkins, M. 3; Barnard, M. 1, Campbell, N. 1, Caudwell, M. 1, Duerden, I. 4, Foster, M. 1, Hume, M. 2, Kirkwood, G. 3, Maamria, D. 10, McIntyre, K. 5, Minett, J. 3, Newell, M. 2, Penney, D. 6, Warren, L. 1, Williams, G. 1, OG, 2.

Dover Athletic
Appearances: Beard, S. 32(2); Bolt, D. 4(1); Brown, S. 30(3); Browne, T. 30(3); Carruthers, M. 13(12); Clarke, D. 31(0); Clarke, M. 0(3); Coates, M. 6(1); Daniels, S. 1(1); Dunne, J. 11(1); Godden, R. 3(3); Hogg, A. 2(1); Hudson, K. 1(0); Hyde, P. 40(0); Hynes, M. 12(19); Leberl, J. 37(1); Le Bihan, N. 21(2); Livett, S. 0(1); Manning, P. 0(3); Mitten, C. 1(0); Morrison, D. 9(2); Munday, S. 25(0); Norman, S. 35(3); Shearer, L. 40; Strouts, J. 8(7); Vansittart, J. 33(0); Virgo, J. 14(6); Wormull, S. 23(1).
Goals (65): Brown, S. 8, Carruthers, M. 2, Clarke, D. 2, Coates, M. 1, Dunne, J. 2, Hynes, M. 7, Leberl, J. 5, Le Bihan, N. 2, Morrison, D. 3, Norman, S. 4, Shearer, L. 9, Vansittart, J. 15, Wormull, S. 3, OG, 2.

Forest Green Rovers
Appearances: Bailey, D. 34(5); Barnett, D. 3; Bennett, F. 9; Burns, C. 33; Catley, A. 0(2); Chapple, S. 2(1); Clark, B. 36(1); Cook, R. 13(4); Daley, T. 26; Drysdale, J. 32(1); Forbes, D. 18(9); Hatswell, W. 30(4); Hedges, I. 41; Honor, C. 12(1); Hunt, P. 10(18); Kilgour, M. 12(3); Lightfoot, N. 0; Little, G. 0;McGregor, M. 25(3); McMullen, L. 0; Meyhew, D. 8(14); Mings, A. 8(11); Norton, D. 18; Perrin, S. 26(1); Randall, A. 9(2); Shuttlewood, J. 16; Smith, C. 0(2); Sykes, A. 30(9); Thomas, B. 8(7); Winter, S. 3(3).
Goals (54): Bailey, D. 9, Bennett, F. 1, Burns, C. 5, Clark, B. 3, Cook, R. 1, Daley, T. 4, Drysdale, J. 2, Hatswell, W. 2, Hedges, I. 1, Hunt, P. 4, McGregor, M. 12, Norton, D. 1, Randall, A. 1, Sykes, A. 7, Thomas, B. 1.

Hayes
Appearances: Ansell, G. 4(1); Boyce, M. 24(9); Broad, S. 3; Bunce, N. 32; Carter, W. 1(2); Charles, L. 38(2); Coppard, D. 11(9); Flynn, L. 37; Gallen, B. 6(4); Goodliffe, J. 38; Gothard, P. 32(1); Hodson, B. 6(5); Hodson, M. 6; McKimm, S. 36(2); Metcalfe, C. 12; Molesley, M. 1; Moore, B. 24(3); O'Brien, A. 3; Onwere, U. 3; Patton, A. 8(4); Preson, M. 2(5); Roddis, N. 29(4); Smith, C. 4(1); Sparks, C. 0(2); Spencer, R. 15(12); Stevens, D. 21; Sullivan, A. 0(1); Telemaque, E. 6(3); Tilbury, D. 1; Trebble, N. 20(13); Tucker, J. 2; Watts, A. 31(3); Whitby, I. 2; Wilkerson, P. 4; Witter, T. 2.
Goals (57): Ansell, G. 2, Bunce, N. 2, Charles, L. 13, Flynn, L. 7, Goodliffe, J. 1, Hodson, B. 2, Mckimm, S. 3, Moore, B. 6, Preston, M. 1, Roddis, N. 2, Spencer, R. 2, Stevens, D. 10, Telemaque, E. 2, Trebble, N. 1, OG, 3.

Hednesford Town
Appearances: Airdrie, S. 16(10); Amos, N. 0(1); Bagshaw, P. 9; Bettney, S. 5; Bradley, R. 16; Brindley, C. 36(1); Colkin, L. 33;

Comyn, A. 15...
Comyn, A. 15; Davis, N. 32; Evans, S. 38(1); Ford, S. 13; Goodwin, S. 24(1); Hayward, P. 1; Hibbins, J. 3; Hickey, B. 2(1); Hunter, C. 4(4); Kelly, J. 30; Kimmins, G. 22(4); Lake, S. 32(2); Lampkin, K. 1; Mike, A. 16(3); Morgan, P. 20; Norbury, M. 12(2); Norman, J. 8(7); O'Connor, S. 7(5); Reece, D. 3(3); Rhodes, R. 1(2); Robinson, I. 34; Sedgemore, J. 2(1); Shakespeare, A. 0(1); Stewart, B. 5; Szewcyzk, P. 5(2); Twynham, G. 14(9); Wilson, P. 3.
Goals (45): Brindley, C. 1, Colkin, L. 1, Davis, N. 18, Kimmins, G. 8, Lake, S. 2, Mike, A. 1, Norman, J. 2, Robinson, I. 6, Szewcyzk, P. 1, Twynham, G. 1, OG, 1.

Hereford United
Appearances: Beale, M. 0(1); Clarke, M. 28(2); Cooksey, S. 17; Cotterill, J. 0(3); Elmes, R. 29(8); Fewings, P. 16(9); Hanson, C. 6(5); James, T. 34(3); Jones, M. 16(1); Lane, C. 27(2); May, L. 20(10); Parry, P. 24(7); Piearce, S. 9(2); Quy, A. 9; Rodgerson, I. 33(3); Shirley, J. 0(3); Snape, J. 38(2); Sturgess, P. 32(2); Taylor, M. 35(1); Wall, J. 11(2); White, T. 16; Williams, G. 29(11); Wright, I. 33.
Goals (61): Elmes, R. 13, Fewings, P. 12, Hanson, C. 1, James, P. 2, May, L. 4, Parry, P. 4, Piearce, S. 4, Rodgerson, I. 2, Snape, J. 2, Taylor, M. 2, Wall, J. 1, Williams, G. 6, Wright, I. 6, OG, 2.

Kettering Town
Appearances: Abrahams, P. 6(3); Adams, C. 38(1), Banya, S. 10(10); Broomes, D. 0(1); Brown, P. 29(5); Browne, B. 0; Chambers, L. 3; Cox, P. 29(1); Diuk, W. 30(6); Doane, B. 3; Dyer, W. 2; Fisher, M. 31(3); Foster, L. 0; Hailstone, R. 1(1); Haydon, N. 4(4); Hopkins, C. 6(7); Hudson, L. 9(21); Lock, T. 2; McNamara, B. 29(5); Norman, C. 38; Paul, M. 0(2); Perkins, C. 9(1); Ridgway, I. 20(6); Setchell, G. 22(7); Shutt, C. 17(8); Smith, P. 0; Sollitt, A. 42; Storer, S. 5(2); Tomlinson, P. 1; Tucker, M. 0; Vowden, C. 41; Watkins, D. 23; Weale, R. 0; Williams, S. 0(2); Wilson, S. 0(3).
Goals (44): Abrahams, P. 1, Adams, C. 4, Banya, S. 1, Brown, P. 4, Chambers, L. 1, Diuk, W. 2, Fisher, M. 4, Hudson, L. 1, McNamara, B. 3, Norman, C. 9, Perkins, C. 1, Setchell, G. 2, Shutt, C. 4, Vowden, C. 1, Watkins, 4, OG, 2.

Kidderminster Harriers
Appearances: Barnett, G. 4(5); Bennett, D. 42; Brock, S. 11; Brownrigg, A. 18(2); Bugler, A. 0; Burgess, R. 12; Clarke, T. 29(1); Clarkson, T. 28; Collins, J. 6; Corbett, A. 0; Creighton, M. 0; Cunnington, S. 9(3); Davies, B. 1(1); Druce, B. 19(5); Foster, I. 35(3); Hadley, S. 30(8); Hall, A. 0; Harman, J. 2; Hines, L. 23(3); Hinton, C. 42; Kelsall, K. 0; King, P. 18(1); Marsh, M. 23(1); Midgley, N. 5; Petersen, R. 19(1); Pope, S. 17(6); Skovbjerg, T. 32; Smith, A. 42; Stamps, S. 34(1); Taylor, S. 6(6); Tiptton, D. 0; Tucker, M. 0; Webb, P. 36; Weir, M. 6; Williams, L. 2.
Goals (75): Barnett, G. 2, Bennett, D. 10, Brownrigg, A. 3, Clarkson, I. 1, Druce, M. 7, Foster, I. 17, Hadley, S. 12, Hinton, C. 2, King, P. 2, Marsh, M. 4, Midgley, N. 2, Petersen, R. 3, Pope, S. 1, Skovbjerg, T. 4, Smith, A. 1, Stamps, S. 2, Taylor, S. 1, Webb, P. 1, OG, 1.

Kingstonian
Appearances: Akuamoah, E. 26(5); Allan, D. 28(1); Basford, L. 8(8); Boylan, L. 5(6); Brown, K. 2(0); Bryson, T. 0; Crossley, M. 37; Drewett, G. 4(4); Farrelly, S. 40(0); Green, R. 4(2); Harris, M. 30(3); Hendry, I. 2(4); Hurst, R. 2(0); Kadi, J. 8(8); Langley, S. 0(0); Lester, M. 2(1); Leworthy, D. 25(6); Luckett, C. 33(0); Lyttle, G. 1; Marshall, D. 8(4); Mustafa, T. 38(1); Newman, D. 0(2); O'Connor, J. 8(10); Patterson, G. 38; Pitcher, G. 38(1); Robson, D. 0; Saunders, E. 9(2); Simba, A. 8; Smith, D. 0(1); Stewart, S. 22(1); Taylor, R. 5(2); Thomas, D. 0; Thompson, R. 1(1); Walker, J. 0(1); Wingfield, P. 30(4).
Goals (58): Akuamoah, E. 8, Allan, D. 1, Crossley, M. 1; Drewett, G. 1, Harris, M. 4, Leworthy, D. 12, Luckett, C. 2, Marshall, D. 1, O'Connor, J. 2, Pitcher, G. 9. Simba, A. 6, Stewart, S. 2, Wingfield, P. 6, OG, 3.

Morecambe
Appearances: Banks, A. 33(2); Black, R. 0(6); Brown, G. 13(4); Burns, P. 22(3); Curtis, W. 0(1); Drummond, S. 39; Eastwood, P. 25(7); Farrell, A. 30(1); Fensome 40; Gardner, D. 4(3); Hall, D. 0; Hardiker, J. 18(4); Hardy, J. 17(14); Heald, A. 7(5); Holcroft, P. 0; Hughes, A. 0; Jackson, J. 38; Keeling, B. 3(19); Knowles, M. 18(3); Lyons, D. 23(2); McGuire, P. 7(12); McIlhargey, S. 9; McKearney, D. 41; Milner, A. 0(4); Morton, N. 2(1); Norman, J. 11(1); Rushton, P. 1(1); Smith, L. 5(11); Somerfield, P. 0; Swannick, D. 1(1); Takano, K. 20(2); Thompson, G. 14(8); Ward, P. 1; Wright, M. 20.

Goals (70): Brown, G. 1, Burns, P. 3, Drummond, S. 4, Eastwood, P. 11, Gardiner, D. 1, Hardy, J. 9, Jackson, J. 29, Knowles, M. 1, Lyons , D. 3, McGuire, P. 1, Norman, J. 4, Thompson, G. 1, OG, 2.

Northwich Victoria

Appearances: Bailey, M. 12(3); Bates, J. 30(3); Birch, M. 31(3); Burke, J. 1(1); Castro-Pearson, D. 0(2); Cooke; I. 26(3); Crookes, D. 16(5); Devlin, M. 34(1); Doherty, M. 0(1); Eatock, D. 0(2); Ellis, N. 14(9); Fletcher, G. 10(8); Gann, J. 1(1); Gardiner, M. 4(2); Gray, D. 9(9); Grobbelaar, B. 0; Heverin, M. 0; Holt, M. 5; Illman, N. 1(5); Key, L. 18; Logan, D. 0; Milner, A. 2(2); Owen, V. 25(4); Peel, N. 3(4); Pell, R. 4; Poland, L. 5(3); Prendergast, R. 6(1); Rigby, M. 23; Robertson, J. 33(1); Robinson, L. 14(1); Royle, C. 0(2); Simpson, W. 28(1) Terry, S. 18(11); Thomas, S. 1(2); Vicary, D. 37(1); Walker, R. 10; Walsh, S. 2; Walters, S. 27(1); West, C. 2; Williams, P. 0(1).

Goals (53): Bailey, M. 1 Bates, J. 1, Cooke, I. 7, Devlin, M. 4, Ellis, N. 3, Fletcher, G. 2, Gray, D. 2, Owen, V. 12, Pell, R. 1, Poland, L. 3, Robertson, J. 1, Robinson, L. 3, Simpson, W. 3, Vicary, D. 2, Walters, S. 6, OG. 2.

Nuneaton Borough

Appearances: Angus,T. 34; Blake, M. 1(7); Bradshaw, M. 5; Brennan, K. 1(2); Broughton, D. 10; Brown, J. 28(3); Carty, P. 1(1); Crowley, D. 22; Ducros, A. 30(5); Everitt, L. 0(1); Francis, D. 19(13); Hanson, D. 21(4); Kotyeo, K. 1(4); McKenzie, C. 41(1); McDermott, W. 11(2); Muir, I. 12(7); Murphy, G. 12(5); O'Brien, A. 1(1); O'Connor, J. 11(3); Prendergast, R. 3(4); Prindiville, S. 31; Reed, I. 8(5); Ryder, S. 20; Simpson, W. 30(3); Straw, R. 2(3); Thackeray, A. 37; Ware, P. 2; Weaver, S. 4(1); Williams, B. 31(1); Wray, S. 25(4); Young, R. 1.

Goals (49): Angus,T. 1, Broughton, D. 2, Ducros, A. 9, Francis, D. 6, Hanson , D. 3, McDermott, W. 2, Muir, I. 3, Murphy, G. 1, O'Connor, J. 3, Prindiville, S. 2, Ryder, S. 1, Straw, R. 1, Thackeray, A. 3, Ware, P. 3, Williams, B. 3, Wray, S. 4, OG, 2.

Rushden & Diamonds

Appearances: Aldridge, M. 1; Bertocchi, M. 0; Bradshaw, D. 11(3); Brady, J. 23(4); Bullock, D. 4; Burgess, A. 12(8); Butterworth, G. 41; Collins, D. 22(8); Cooper, M. 11(1); Cramman, K. 5(4); Desouza, M. 19(9); Hamsher, J. 17(2); Heggs, C. 1(8); Lowe, D. 13; McElhatton, M. 30; Mills, G. 8(8); Mison, M. 7(5); Naylor, S. 2; Peters, M. 27(5); Rodwell, J. 31(1); Sale, M. 6(2); Sigere, J-M. 6(1); Stowell, M. 4(1); Town, D. 13(4); Turley, B. 40; Underwood, P. 41; Warburton, R. 39; West, C. 0(3); Wooding, T. 16(5); Wormull, S. 9(2).

Goals (71): Brady, J. 3, Burgess, A. 5, Butterworth, G. 1, Collins, D. 11, Cooper, M. 1, Desouza, M. 7, Hamsher, J. 2, Lowe, D. 4, McElhatton, M. 11, Mison, M. 1, Peters, M. 6, Rodwell, J. 1, Sigere, J-M. 4, Town, D. 5, Underwood, 4, Warburton, R. 2, West, C. 1, OG, 2.

Scarborough

Appearances: Alkhatib, M. 0(4); Atkinson, P. 0; Bass, D. 17(2); Betts, S. 38; Bogan, D. 1; Brodie, S. 36; Brunton, D. 0(1); Carr, G. 1; Ellender, P. 23; Faure, R. 0; Gildea, A. 1(7); Harriot, M. 20(6); Ingram, D. 11; Jones, M. 35(1); Martin, K. 8; McAlindon, G. 11(3); McGinty, B. 8; McNaughton, M. 1(7); McNiven, D. 5; Middlesmass, S. 9; Milbourne, I. 2(4); Morris, A. 6(3); Morris, S. 5(15); Newton, P. 0; Rennison, S. 25(6); Roberts, D. 29(6); Russell, M. 19; Quinn, A. 1; Sinnot, L. 22; Stoker, G. 35; Tate, C. 22; Thompson, N. 9; Tremble, D. 0; Tyrrell, M. 9(3); Williams, G. 19; Woods, A. 34.

Goals (60): Bass, D. 1, Betts, S. 5, Brodie, S. 13, Harriot, M. 1, Jones, M. 1, McAlindon, G. 3, McNaughton, M. 1; McNiven, M. 2; Morris, A. 2; Morris, S. 2; Rennison, S. 2, Roberts, D. 7, Russell, M. 1, Quinn, A. 1, Stoker, G. 4, Tate, C. 9, Thompson, N. 1, OG, 4.

Southport

Appearances: Arnold, I. 40(1); Bolland, P. 35; Clark, M. 35(2); Connolly, J. 0(1); Courtney, G. 0(2); Devereux, R. 3 (4); Dickinson, S. 42; Elam, L. 31(10); Ellison, L. 8(8); Formby, K. 16(5); Furlong, L. 9(20); Gouck, A. 30(1); Grayston, N. 34(7); Gummer, S. 0(1); Guyett, S. 38; Lyons, D. 0(1); McNiven, D. 8(4); Mike, A. 9(6); Morley, D. 32(3); Pell, R. 6(3); Ryan, T. 39; Stuart, M. 35(1); Takano, K. 2(2); Taylor, P. 0(1); Trundle, L. 0(5); Woods, N. 9(4).

Goals (55): Arnold, I. 14, Bolland,P. 3, Clark, M. 1, Elam, L. 11, Furlong, L. 3, Gouck, A. 2, Grayston, N. 1, Guyett, S. 4, McNiven, D. 1, Mike,A. 1, Morley, D. 1, Pell, R. 2, Stuart, M 8, Woods, N. 2, OG, 1.

Stevenage Borough

Appearances: Alford, C. 38(1); Armstrong, P. 0(3); Ayres, J. 6; Barr, G. 0(1); Bass, D. 9; Behzadi, B. 0; Collins, C. 4(1); Field, L. 0(1); Forbes, S. 4(2); Futcher, A. 2; Gallagher, D. 1; Harrison, R.

10(10); Harvey, L. 30(1); Hassell, J. 2; Highton, B. 0; Hockton, D. 18(2); Houghton, R. 3; Howarth, L. 35(2); Kersey, L. 3(1); King, I. 17(2); Kirby, R. 34(5); Leadbeater, R. 15(20); Love, M. 32(3); Martin, D. 20(3); McGhee, D. 0(2); McMahon, S. 9; Miller, R. 8(1); Morrison, D. 3(1); Naylor, D. 1(1); Ougham, J. 0(1); Pearson, C. 1(6); Pluck, C. 3; Plummer, D. 2(4); Samuels, J. 13(9); Smith, M. 38(1); Strouts, J. 18(1); Taylor, C. 39; Trott, R. 21; Wraight, G. 22(5).

Goals (60): Alford, C. 24, Forbes, S. 1, Hockton, D. 6, Howarth, L. 1, Kirby, R. 3, Leadbeater, R. 5, Love, M. 2, Martin, D. 3, McMahon, S. 1, Miller, R. 1, Morrison, D. 1, Pearson, C. 1, Samuels, J. 5, Strouts, J. 3, Trott, R. 1, Wraight, G. 2.

Sutton United

Appearances: Baker, J. 0(2); Barclay, D. 0(5); Berry, G. 33; Brodrick, D. 7(4); Brooker, D. 30(2); Dack, J. 28(2); Ekoku, N. 22(4); Forrester, S. 1(7); Harford, P. 33(1); Harlow, D. 40; Howells, G. 41; Hutchinson, E. 10(6); Laker, B. 30(1); Lee, M. 5; Little, A. 1; Mackie, J. 10; McCormack, F. 1(1); Newhouse, A. 17(1); Riley, A. 21(1); Rogers, J. 0; Rowlands, K. 8(13); Salako, A. 4(2); Sears, P. 14(5); Simpson, C. 4(1); Skelly, R. 41; Vines, F. 0(5); Watson, M. 25(12); Westcott, J. 1; Winston, S. 35(4).

Goals (39): Dack, J. 4, Forrester, S. 1, Harford, P. 2, Harlow, D. 1, Hutchinson, E. 4, Laker, B. 2, Newhouse, A. 3, Riley, A. 1, Rowlands, K. 1, Skelly, R. 1, Watson, M. 11, Winston, S. 8.

Telford United

Appearances: Albrighton, M. 16; Bentley, J. 24; Bray, J. 7(2); Bridgwater, D. 0(1); Cooper, M. 4; Corns, S. 0(5); Doyle, M. 17(7); Edwards, J. 21(4); Fitzpatrick, G. 32(2); Ford, J. 29(2); Fowler, L. 26(1); Gayle, B. 9; Hartfield, C. 18(2); Henshaw, B. 0; Huckerby, S. 1(19); Macauley, C. 29(3); Malkin, C. 18(12); Martindale, G. 5(1); McGorry, B. 30; Moore, N. 4; Murphy, G. 28(8); Mutch, A. 0(1); Naylor, M. 7(12); Palmer, S. 28(4); Preece, R. 9; Price, R. 16; Sandwith, K. 17(5); Travis, S. 27(7); Williams, D. 17.

Goals (56): Albrighton, M. 1, Bentley, J. 4, Cooper, M. 1, Edwards, J. 9, Fitzpatrick, G. 4, Ford, J. 3, Hartfield, C. 3, Huckerby, S. 2, Macauley, C. 1, Malkin, C. 5, Martindale, G. 4, McGorry, B. 1, Murphy, G. 10, Naylor, M. 1, Palmer, S. 4, Sandwith, K. 1, OG, 2.

Welling United

Appearances: Adams, D. 3(1); Bailey, D. 19(3); Baker, J. 2(6); Barnes, S. 8; Belleness, G. 0(1); Braithwaite, L. 30(4); Budden, J. 25; Chapman, D. 30(3); Clarke, C. 2(3); Dennis, K. 16(3); Edwards, R. 35(1); Farley, J. 1(2); Gwillim, G. 0; Hanlon, R. 20; Harle, M. 23(1); Harney, M. 10(4); Harris, A. 8; Hogarth, D. 0; Holland, J. 0, Hollidge, K. 0; Hone, M. 41; Jackman, W. 0; Kasap, S. 0; Martin, J. 14; O'Sullivan, D. 0(1); Rivere, A. 29(5); Rowe, Z. 35, Rutherford, M. 37(3); Samuels, D. 0; Saunders, S. 0; Side, C. 4(16); Standen, D. 1(1); Taylor, S. 0; Twin, D. 0; Watts, L. 32; Watts, S. 3(1); Wilkerson, P. 34.

Goals (54): Bailey, D. 2, Barnes, S. 2, Braithwaite, L. 6, Budden, J. 1, Dennis, K. 3, Edwards, R. 1, Hanlon, R. 12, Hone, M. 2, Martin, J. 4, Riviere, A. 3, Rowe, Z. 11, Rutherford, M. 3, Watts, S. 2, OG, 2.

Woking

Appearances: Akrour, N. 36(3); Alighieri, D. 6(2); Batty, L. 17; Bolt, D. 6(13); Brown, K. 10(1); Bullen, M. 0(1); Charles, J. 4(6); Danzey, M. 21; Flahavan, D. 23(1); French, S. 1; Girdler, S. 11(5); Goddard, R. 7(5); Gridelet, P. 14; Hayfield, M. 11(1); Hay, D. 7(9); Hendry, I. 0; Hollingdale, R. 33; Miller, B. 15; Panter, D. 3(3); Payne, G. 8(4); Perkins, S. 29(2); Saunders, E. 5; Simpson, R. 1; Smith, P. 16(1); Smith, R. 7, Smith, S. 37; Steele, S. 30(4); Stott, S. 6(1); West, S. 34(1); White, R. 0(1); Wilkinson, D. 22(9).

Goals (45): Akrour, N. 11, Bolt, D. 2, Goddard, R. 2, Hay, D. 8, Hayfield, M. 2, Payne, G. 3, Perkins, S. 3, Steele, S. 6, West, S. 7, OG, 1.

Yeovil Town

Appearances: Archer, L. 4(1); Belgrave, B. 7; Bent, J. 3(4); Brown, K. 38(3); Browne, S. 0(4); Chandler, D. 16(2); Cousins, R. 32(3); Eaton, J. 11(14); Fishlock, M. 9(1); Foster, A. 20(6); Giles, C. 0(1); Griffin, C. 3; Hale, M. 11(1); Hayfield, M. 19(4); Lapgood, L 0; Lindegaard, A. 9; Malessa, T. 0; Metheringham, P. 0; Norton, D. 7(4); Patmore, W. 37(1); Pennock, T. 42; Piper, D. 30(4); Pitman, J. 34(1); Poole, G. 8(3); Pounder, T. 7(10); Simpson, P. 0(2); Skiverton, T. 32(2); Smith, B. 30(6); Sparks, C. 15; Steele, P. 10(1); Stott, S. 16; Stowell, M. 7; Thompson, S. 1(3); Tisdale, P. 11(4); Tonkin, A. 12; Wilmot, K. 1(3).

Goals (60): Belgrave, B. 1, Bent, J. 2, Cousins, R. 1, Eaton, J. 2, Foster, A. 9, Griffin, C. 1, Hale, M. 2, Hayfield, M. 8, Lindegaard, A. 1, Norton, D. 1, Patmore, W. 13, Piper, D. 1, Pitman, J. 2, Skiverton, T. 6, Smith, B. 4, Steele, P. 3, Thompson, S. 1, Tisdale, P. 1, OG, 1.

NATIONWIDE CONFERENCE: MEMBERS CLUBS SEASON 2000–2001

Club: BOSTON UNITED
Colours: Amber and black striped shirts, black
shorts amber trim
Ground: York Street Ground, York Street,
Boston, Lancashire, PE21 6HN
Tel: 01205 364406
Year Formed: 1934
Record Gate: 10,086 (1955 v Corby Town)
Nickname: The Pilgrims
Manager: Steve Evans
Secretary: John Blackwell

Club: CHESTER CITY
Colours: Blue and white striped shirts, blue and
white shorts
Ground: Deva Stadium, Bumpers Lane, Chester,
CH1 4LT
Tel: 01244 541281
Year Formed: 1885
Record Gate: 20,500 (1952 v Chelsea FA Cup
Third Round Proper)
Nickname: The Blues
Manager: Graham Barrow
Secretary: Michael Fair

Club: DAGENHAM & REDBRIDGE
Colours: Red shirt with white flash, white shorts
Ground: Victoria Road, Dagenham, Essex,
RM10 7XL
Tel: 0208 5927194
Year Formed: 1992
Record Gate: 5,300 (1992 v Leyton Orient FA
Cup First Round Proper)
Nickname: Daggers
Manager: Garry Hill
Secretary: Derek Almond

Club: DONCASTER ROVERS
Colours: Red shirt with navy insert, navy shorts
Ground: Belle Vue, Doncaster, DN4 5HT
Tel: 01302 539441
Year Formed: 1879
Record Gate: 37,149 (1948 v Hull City)
Nickname: Rovers
Manager: Steve Wignall
Secretary: Joan Oldale

Club: DOVER ATHLETIC
Colours: White shirts, black shorts
Ground: Crabble Athletic Ground, Lewisham
Road, River, Dover, Kent, CT17 0PB
Tel: 01304 240041
Year Formed: 1983
Record Gate: 4,035 (1992 v Bromsgrove Rovers)
Nickname: Whites
Manager: Bill Williams
Secretary: John F. Durrant

Club: FOREST GREEN ROVERS
Colours: Black and white striped shirts, black shorts
Ground: The Lawn, Nympsfield Road, Forest
Green, Nailsworth, Glos. GL6 0ET
Tel: 01453 834860
Year Formed: 1890
Record Gate: 3,002 (1999 v St. Albans City)
Nickname: Rovers
Manager: Frank Gregan
Secretary: David Honeybill

Club: HAYES
Colours: Red and white striped shirts, black
shorts
Ground: Townfield House, Church Road, Hayes,
Middlesex, UB3 3LE
Tel: 0208 5732075
Year Formed: 1909
Record Gate: 15,370 (1951 v Bromley)
Nickname: Missioners
Manager: Terry Brown
Secretary: John Bond (Jnr)

Club: HEDNESFORD TOWN
Colours: White shirt with red and black stripe at
front, black shorts
Ground: Keys Park, Hill Street, Hednesford,
WS12 5DW
Tel: 01543 422870
Year Formed: 1880
Record Gate: 10,000 (1927 v Walsall)
Nickname: The Pitmen
Manager: John Baldwin
Secretary: Richard Murning

Club: HEREFORD UNITED
Colours: White and black shirts, black shorts
Ground: Edgar Streets, Hereford, HR4 9JU
Tel: 01432 276666
Year Formed: 1924
Record Gate: 18,114 (1958 v Sheffield
Wednesday)
Nickname: United
Manager: Graham Turner
Secretary: Joan Fennessy

Club: KETTERING TOWN
Colours: Red and black shirts, red shorts
Ground: Rockingham Road, Kettering,
Northants, NN16 9AW
Tel: 01536 483028/410815
Year Formed: 1875
Record Gate: 11,536 (1947 v Peterborough)
Nickname: The Poppies
Manager: Peter Morris
Secretary: Graham Starmer

Club: KINGSTONIAN
Colours: Red and white hooped shirts, white
shorts
Ground: Kingsmeadow Stadium
Tel: 0208 547 3335
Year Formed: 1885
Record Gate: 4,582 (v Chelsea 1995)
Nickname: The K's
Manager: Geoff Chapple
Secretary: Derek Powell

Club: LEIGH RMI
Colours: Red and white shirts, black shorts
Ground: Hilton Park, Kirkhall Lane, Leigh
Tel: 01942 743743
Year Formed: 1896
Record Gate: 31,800 (1953 v St. Helens)
Nickname: Railwaymen
Manager: Steve Waywell
Secretary: Alan Robinson

Club: MORECAMBE
Colours: Red shirts, white socks
Ground: Christie Park, Lancaster Road,
    Morecambe, LA4 5TJ
Tel: 01524 411797
Year Formed: 1920
Record Gate: 9,326 (1962 FA Cup Third Round
    Proper v Weymouth)
Nickname: The Shrimps
Manager: Jim Harvey
Secretary: Neil W. Marsdin

Club: NORTHWICH VICTORIA
Colours: Green shirts with white trim, white
    shorts
Ground: The Drill Field, Northwich, Cheshire,
    CW9 5HN
Tel: 01606 41450
Year Formed: 1874
Record Gate: 12,000 (1977 FA Cup Fourth
    Round Proper v Watford)
Nickname: The Vics
Manager: Mark Gardiner
Secretary: Derek Nuttall

Club: NUNEATON BOROUGH
Colours: Blue and white striped shirts, blue
    shorts with white trim
Ground: Manor Park, Beaumont Road,
    Nuneaton, Warwickshire, CV11 5HD
Tel: 024 76385738
Year Formed: 1937
Record Gate: 22,114 (1967 FA Cup Third
    Round Proper v Rotherham)
Nickname: The Boro
Manager: Brendan Phillips
Secretary: Peter Humphreys

Club: RUSHDEN & DIAMONDS
Colours:
Ground: Nene Park, Diamond Way,
    Irthlingborough, Northants, NN9 5QF
Tel: 01933 652000
Year Formed: 1992
Record Gate: 6,431 (1999 v Leeds United)
Nickname: Diamonds
Manager: Brian Talbot
Secretary: David M. Joyce

Club: SCARBOROUGH
Colours: Red shirt with white banner
Ground: McCain Stadium, Seamer Road,
    Scarborough, YO12 4HF
Tel: 01723 375094
Year Formed: 1879
Record Gate: 11,130 (1987 FA Cup Third
    Round Proper v Luton)
Nickname: The Boro
Manager: Colin Addison
Secretary (Acting): Jade Sprintall

Club: SOUTHPORT
Colours: Old gold and black shirts, black shorts
Ground: Haig Avenue, Southport, PR8 6JZ
Tel: 01704 533422
Year Formed: 1881
Record Gate: 20,010 (1932 v Newcastle United)
Nickname: The Sandgrounders
Manager: Mark Wright
Secretary: Ken Hilton

Club: STEVENAGE BOROUGH
Colours: Red and white striped shirt, black
    shorts
Ground: Broadhall Way, Stevenage, Herts, SG2
    8RH
Tel: 01438 223223
Year Formed: 1976
Record Gate: 15,365 (1997 v Birmingham City at
    St. Andrews)
Nickname: The Boro
Manager: Paul Fairclough
Secretary: Roger Austin

Club: TELFORD UNITED
Colours: White shirts, black shorts
Ground: Bucks Head, Watling Street,
    Wellington, Telford, Shropshire, TF1 2NT
Tel: 01543 273507
Year Formed: 1877
Record Gate: 13,000 (1935 v Shrewsbury)
Nickname: The Bucks
Manager: Jake King
Secretary: Mike Ferriday

Club: WOKING
Colours: Red and white shirts, black shorts
Ground: Kingfield Sports Ground, Kingfield,
    Woking, Surrey, GU22 9AA
Tel: 01483 772470
Year Formed: 1889
Record Gate: 6,084 (1997 v Coventry City)
Nickname: The Cardinals
Manager: Colin Lippiatt
Secretary: Phil Ledger

Club: YEOVIL TOWN
Colours: Green and white shirts, white shorts
Ground: Huish Park, Lufton Way, Yeovil,
    Somerset, BA22 8YF
Tel: 01935 423662
Year Formed: 1896
Record Gate: 8,612 (1993 v Arsenal)
Nickname: The Glovers
Manager: David Webb
Secretary: Jean Cotton

NATIONWIDE CONFERENCE RESULTS 1999–2000

	Altrincham	Doncaster Rovers	Dover Athletic	Forest Green Rovers	Hayes	Hednesford Town	Hereford United	Kettering Town	Kidderminster Harriers	Kingstonian	Morecambe	Northwich Victoria	Nuneaton Borough	Rushden & Diamonds	Scarborough	Southport	Stevenage Borough	Sutton United	Telford United	Welling United	Woking	Yeovil Town
Altrincham	—	1-2	3-0	1-1	1-2	0-1	2-1	1-1	0-0	1-3	2-2	2-0	2-2	1-2	2-1	3-0	0-1	3-0	3-3	0-1	1-1	2-2
Doncaster Rovers	0-1	—	0-1	3-2	0-0	2-1	2-2	2-1	1-0	1-0	0-1	2-0	0-1	0-1	0-1	1-1	1-2	1-0	2-0	1-1	0-0	0-3
Dover Athletic	2-2	1-3	—	4-0	2-2	4-1	2-0	1-1	1-2	0-1	3-1	4-1	3-1	0-4	1-1	1-1	4-2	0-1	3-0	2-1	2-2	3-0
Forest Green Rovers	1-1	1-0	4-0	—	0-1	3-0	0-1	2-0	3-1	0-3	1-2	5-1	1-2	1-0	0-1	1-0	3-2	3-2	5-2	1-2	0-0	3-0
Hayes	1-1	3-4	1-2	3-0	—	2-1	0-1	0-1	2-1	1-2	0-1	2-1	3-0	0-5	0-1	0-2	3-0	6-2	1-2	0-1	3-0	2-3
Hednesford Town	5-0	2-1	1-0	1-0	2-1	—	3-0	4-2	3-0	2-3	1-3	1-0	0-0	1-2	0-3	1-2	0-1	0-0	2-1	1-2	3-2	1-0
Hereford United	2-2	5-3	2-0	1-0	0-2	3-0	—	0-1	2-0	1-1	1-1	3-0	1-1	4-0	4-4	2-1	1-2	4-1	2-2	1-2	2-4	0-1
Kettering Town	0-0	2-2	2-0	1-0	1-1	4-2	4-2	—	1-0	2-1	2-1	1-1	1-1	1-1	0-0	0-3	1-0	1-0	0-0	4-1	0-0	1-2
Kidderminster Harriers	1-1	1-0	1-2	3-3	2-1	3-0	2-0	1-0	—	2-0	1-1	1-1	1-2	4-0	2-0	5-0	3-1	4-0	2-0	1-0	3-0	4-0
Kingstonian	2-2	0-1	4-1	0-1	1-3	0-2	1-1	2-0	2-0	—	0-0	3-1	2-0	1-1	2-0	4-2	3-3	4-1	4-2	2-1	2-4	0-1
Morecambe	3-3	3-3	2-0	1-1	1-4	4-0	3-2	2-1	1-1	1-2	—	5-0	1-1	2-0	0-1	3-3	3-3	1-0	5-2	3-2	0-0	2-2
Northwich Victoria	1-1	2-1	1-1	0-0	0-0	3-2	0-0	2-6	1-1	0-3	0-0	—	3-1	0-1	2-0	0-1	0-1	4-0	2-1	4-3	3-1	2-0
Nuneaton Borough	3-1	0-0	0-2	2-3	2-1	3-0	0-1	0-1	2-3	2-0	1-1	3-1	—	0-0	1-1	0-2	2-1	3-0	1-1	2-0	0-1	2-0
Rushden & Diamonds	1-0	0-0	1-1	3-2	1-0	1-1	0-1	5-3	5-3	1-0	0-2	6-0	1-1	—	0-0	4-2	1-3	1-1	1-1	0-0	1-3	0-1
Scarborough	1-0	1-0	2-0	5-0	4-1	1-1	3-0	0-0	0-0	0-1	0-2	3-0	1-1	2-1	—	3-0	2-1	0-2	2-0	3-2	3-2	1-1
Southport	2-0	0-0	1-2	2-1	4-1	2-0	0-3	0-1	0-1	0-0	1-1	0-1	2-0	2-1	2-2	—	1-1	3-0	1-3	0-1	4-1	3-0
Stevenage Borough	1-1	1-0	3-1	1-1	3-0	0-1	1-1	3-0	0-2	0-1	1-2	3-1	2-1	2-2	0-1	1-1	—	1-0	2-0	2-3	0-1	2-3
Sutton United	3-0	3-0	0-1	3-2	2-2	0-0	1-1	1-1	0-3	2-2	0-1	2-2	1-2	0-4	1-2	0-0	0-2	—	2-1	2-1	1-1	1-0
Telford United	0-1	1-0	1-1	2-0	1-2	6-2	0-3	3-1	3-2	1-0	3-2	0-1	0-0	1-1	1-0	4-1	2-1	1-0	—	2-1	1-2	2-1
Welling United	2-2	0-1	1-1	1-1	1-2	0-1	1-1	1-0	1-2	0-1	0-0	1-3	1-1	1-3	2-1	0-0	2-1	2-3	2-1	—	1-2	0-1
Woking	0-1	0-2	1-1	1-1	0-3	3-0	2-4	1-1	1-0	1-1	1-0	1-1	1-1	1-3	0-2	1-2	0-2	1-1	1-0	1-1	—	1-1
Yeovil Town	3-0	1-3	1-1	1-0	2-4	3-0	1-0	2-0	1-0	3-2	2-0	3-2	1-3	5-1	1-2	1-1	2-2	1-2	2-1	1-1	0-3	—

THE NATIONWIDE MACMILLAN TROPHY 1999–2000

First Round

Forest Green Rovers 1 *(Mehew)* Telford United 2 *(McGorry, Fitzpatrick)*	424

Hednesford Town 1 *(Szewcyzk)* Nuneaton Borough 2 *(O'Connor 2)*	456

Altrincham 1 *(Burke)* Kidderminster 0	370

Hereford United 2 *(May 2)* Sutton United 0	625

Morecambe 1 *(Milner)* Southport 2 *(Ellison, Courtney)*	468

Welling United 3 *(Hanlon, Dennis, Rutherford)* Dover Athletic 0	361

Second Round

Doncaster Rovers 4 *(Foster, Walling, Duerden,* *Maamria)* Nuneaton Borough 0	1,245

Northwich Victoria 1 *(Cooke)* Altrincham 6 *(Power, Gallagher 2, Kielty, Talbot,* *Timons)*	402

Rushden & Diamonds 0 Telford United 1 *(McGorry)*	1,451

Southport 1 *(Stuart)* Scarborough 2 *(Betts, Brodie)*	339

Kettering Town 0 Hayes 1 *(Moore)*	302

Welling United 0 Kingstonian 1 *(Mustafa)*	206

Woking 3 *(Akrour 2, West)* Stevenage Borough 1 *(Alford)*	791

Yeovil Town 3 *(Poole, Patmore 2)* Hereford United 0	823

Quarter Final

Scarborough 1 *(Roberts)* Doncaster Rovers 2 *(Wright, Williams)*	1,188

Altrincham 1 *(Price)* Telford United 3 *(Hartfield, Naylor, Edwards)*	319

Hayes 2 *(Roddis, Trebble)* Yeovil Town 1 *(Eaton)*	364

Semi-Final (two legs)

Telford United 1 *(Edwards)* Doncaster Rovers 2 *(Williams, Warren)*	735

Doncaster Rovers 1 *(Penney)* Telford United 0	1,867

Hayes 0 Kingstonian 0	531

Kingstonian 1 *(Green)* Hayes 0	306

Final

Doncaster Rovers 2 *(Minnett, Penney)* Kingstonian 0	3,837

THE MAIL ON SUNDAY
Monthly Awards

Goalscorer Of The Month	Team Performance Of The Month	Manager Of The Month
AUGUST		
David Leworthy *Kingstonian*	*Scarborough* (5-0 v Yeovil Town (H) 14/8)	Richard Hill *Stevenage Borough*
SEPTEMBER		
Paul Fewings *Hereford United* Ritchie Hanlon *Welling United*	*Sutton United* (2-1 v Yeovil Town (A) 18/9)	Geoff Chapple *Kingstonian*
OCTOBER		
Carl Alford *Stevenage Borough*	*Forest Green Rovers* (3-2 v Stevenage Borough (H) 2/10)	Brian Talbot *Rushden & Diamonds*
NOVEMBER		
Nassim Akrour *Woking*	*Yeovil Town* (5-1 v Rushden & Diamonds (H) 13/11)	Bill Williams *Dover Athletic*
DECEMBER		
Neil Davis *Hednesford Town*	*Forest Green Rovers* (3-2 v Nuneaton Borough (A) 4/12)	Brian Talbot *Rushden & Diamonds*
JANUARY		
Ian Foster *Kidderminster Harriers*	*Hayes* (4-1 v Morecambe (A) 22/1)	Jan Molby *Kidderminster Harriers*
FEBRUARY		
Dennis Bailey *Forest Green Rovers*	*Kettering Town* (3-1 v Kidderminster Harriers (H) 19/2)	Geoff Chapple *Kingstonian*
MARCH		
Nassim Akrour *Woking*	*Woking* (4-2 v Hereford United (A) 14/3)	Jan Molby *Kidderminster Harriers*
APRIL/MAY		
Justin Jackson *Morecambe*	*Woking* (1-0 v Kidderminster Harriers (A) 29/4)	Jim Harvey *Morecambe*

UNIBOND LEAGUE 1999–2000

Premier Division		Home			Goals		Away			Goals		
	P	W	D	L	F	A	W	D	L	F	A	Pts
Leigh RMI	44	15	3	4	42	17	13	5	4	49	28	92
Hyde United	44	14	5	3	47	20	10	8	4	30	24	85
Gateshead	44	12	6	4	41	17	11	7	4	38	24	82
Marine	44	10	9	3	40	25	11	7	4	38	21	79
Emley	44	9	7	6	25	18	11	5	6	29	23	72
Lancaster City	44	14	4	4	40	18	6	7	9	25	37	71
Stalybridge Celtic	44	13	5	4	42	27	5	7	10	22	27	66
Bishop Auckland	44	9	8	5	33	23	9	3	10	30	38	65
Runcorn	44	11	4	7	36	25	7	6	9	28	30	64
Worksop Town	44	10	3	9	44	29	9	3	10	34	36	63
Gainsborough Trinity	44	12	6	4	40	22	4	9	9	19	27	63
Whitby Town	44	11	7	4	38	24	4	6	12	28	42	58
Barrow	44	6	7	9	35	40	8	8	6	30	19	57
Blyth Spartans	44	10	2	10	39	34	5	7	10	23	33	54
Droylsden	44	9	4	9	26	26	5	8	9	27	34	54
Frickley Athletic	44	8	8	6	39	40	7	1	14	25	45	54
Bamber Bridge	44	7	7	8	38	32	7	4	11	32	35	53
Hucknall Town	44	11	5	6	33	22	3	6	13	22	39	53
Leek Town	44	8	5	9	30	34	6	5	11	28	45	52
Colwyn Bay	44	5	7	10	20	35	7	5	10	26	50	48
Spennymoor United**	44	6	10	6	23	24	4	3	15	18	47	42
Guiseley	44	3	8	11	23	36	5	9	8	29	36	41
Winsford United	44	2	3	17	24	58	1	4	17	16	58	16

** –1 point deducted for breach of rule

First Division		Home			Goals		Away			Goals		
	P	W	D	L	F	A	W	D	L	F	A	Pts
Accrington Stanley	42	14	5	2	55	19	11	4	6	41	24	84
Burscough	42	13	6	2	46	18	9	12	0	35	17	84
Witton Albion	42	13	6	2	49	24	10	9	2	39	22	84
Bradford Park Avenue	42	15	5	1	48	19	8	4	9	29	29	78
Radcliffe Borough	42	11	7	3	36	21	11	5	5	35	27	78
Farsley Celtic	42	12	5	4	34	20	7	6	8	32	32	68
Matlock Town	42	10	7	4	44	30	7	9	5	28	25	67
Ossett Town	42	10	5	6	39	24	7	3	11	38	31	59
Stocksbridge Park Steels	42	11	2	8	30	30	5	6	10	25	40	56
Eastwood Town*	42	8	5	8	35	29	7	6	8	29	36	55
Harrogate Town	42	7	8	6	31	26	7	4	10	34	41	54
Congleton Town	42	8	5	8	31	30	6	7	8	32	43	54
Chorley	42	4	10	7	26	31	9	5	7	27	33	54
Ashton United	42	6	9	6	33	31	6	7	8	32	36	52
Workington	42	8	4	9	26	27	5	9	7	23	28	52
Lincoln United	42	8	5	8	31	37	5	7	9	21	43	51
Belper Town	42	8	5	8	31	31	5	6	10	28	41	50
Trafford	42	3	8	10	27	29	8	4	9	28	34	45
Gretna	42	7	5	9	32	34	4	2	15	16	44	40
Netherfield Kendal	42	5	6	10	26	36	3	3	15	20	46	33
Flixton	42	6	3	12	28	37	1	6	14	19	48	30
Whitley Bay	42	3	6	12	24	45	4	3	14	17	42	30

* –1 point deducted for breach of rule

LEADING GOALSCORERS
(In order of League Goals)

Premier Division

Lge	Cup	Tot	
23	14	37	Simon Yeo (Hyde United)
21	9	30	Simon Parke (Guiseley)
21	6	27	Andy Whittaker (Bamber Bridge)
20	13	33	Paul Kiely (Leek Town, now Stafford Rangers)
19	15	34	Andy Hayward (Frickley Athletic)
19	8	27	Nicky Peverill (Barrow)

First Division

Lge	Cup	Tot	
33	0	33	Ryan Lowe (Burscough)
26	2	28	Scott Jackson (Ossett Town)
25	5	30	Ian Blackstone (Farsley Celtic)
19	12	31	Carl Cunningham (Belper Town)
19	0	19	Paul Hennin (Witton Albion)
18	4	22	Paul Mullin (Radcliffe Borough)

UNIBOND CLUB OF THE MONTH AWARD

August	Marine
September	Lancaster City
October	Gateshead
November	Marine
December	Gateshead
January	Barrow
February	Bishop Auckland
March	Whitby Town
April/May	Hyde United

UNIBOND CLUB OF THE MONTH AWARD

August	Burscough
September	Belper Town
October	Eastwood Town
November	Accrington Stanley
December	Radcliffe Borough
January	Accrington Stanley
February	Ossett Town
March	Burscough
April/May	Witton Albion

ATTENDANCES
Premier Division
Highest Attendance: 2400 Barrow v Winsford United

ATTENDANCES
Division One
Highest Attendance: 2468 Accrington Stanley v Farsley Celtic

UNIBOND LEAGUE — PREMIER DIVISION RESULTS 1999-2000

	Bamber Bridge	Barrow	Bishop Auckland	Blyth Spartans	Colwyn Bay	Droylsden	Emley	Frickley Athletic	Gainsborough Trinity	Gateshead	Guiseley	Hucknall Town	Hyde United	Lancaster City	Leek Town	Leigh RMI	Marine	Runcorn	Spennymoor United	Stalybridge Celtic	Whitby Town	Winsford United	Worksop Town
Bamber Bridge	—	2-3	4-0	1-2	1-3	2-0	3-0	2-0	1-0	2-1	2-4	2-1	0-0	6-1	5-0	2-2	0-2	2-0	2-0	1-4	2-2	2-1	2-3
Barrow	4-0	—	1-3	1-1	0-3	0-3	0-0	2-5	1-3	0-0	0-0	0-3	1-2	2-2	1-4	2-2	2-2	0-2	1-0	1-1	0-3	0-0	2-3
Bishop Auckland	0-1	1-3	—	4-0	1-0	2-0	4-2	4-1	0-0	0-3	1-0	1-1	2-2	1-1	1-1	1-1	0-2	2-0	0-3	1-0	4-0	4-1	1-2
Blyth Spartans	1-2	1-1	0-2	—	3-0	1-2	1-2	4-1	2-0	6-0	2-2	2-2	3-4	0-2	2-3	0-1	3-1	4-2	2-3	1-4	2-0	1-0	2-1
Colwyn Bay	0-7	0-0	1-0	4-1	—	1-2	1-2	1-1	0-4	1-1	2-0	3-3	2-3	1-1	1-1	3-5	0-5	1-1	0-2	0-0	2-0	2-0	3-1
Droylsden	2-0	0-3	2-0	1-2	1-2	—	3-0	2-0	3-0	3-0	3-0	0-0	1-3	3-4	1-2	0-2	0-1	1-0	0-1	1-0	3-2	3-0	0-2
Emley	3-0	0-0	4-2	1-2	1-2	3-0	—	2-0	1-0	2-3	1-1	2-0	0-1	0-0	0-0	3-1	0-2	1-0	2-0	0-1	2-1	3-2	1-2
Frickley Athletic	2-0	2-5	4-1	4-1	1-1	2-0	2-0	—	0-0	3-1	2-2	3-2	3-1	3-2	1-1	2-4	2-2	1-2	1-1	1-1	2-1	3-1	1-3
Gainsborough Trinity	1-0	1-3	0-0	2-0	0-4	3-0	1-0	0-0	—	5-2	0-0	4-3	1-1	1-0	3-2	4-3	0-0	1-1	4-0	1-1	1-1	3-0	2-0
Gateshead	2-1	0-0	0-3	6-0	1-1	3-0	2-3	3-1	5-2	—	3-1	0-0	2-3	4-0	2-1	1-1	2-0	0-3	6-2	2-0	0-0	2-0	3-2
Guiseley	2-4	0-0	1-0	2-2	2-0	3-0	1-1	2-2	0-0	3-1	—	1-1	0-1	0-1	1-1	0-3	1-3	2-2	3-1	2-2	0-1	2-2	0-1
Hucknall Town	2-1	0-3	1-1	2-2	3-3	0-0	2-0	3-2	4-3	0-0	1-2	—	0-1	1-3	2-0	1-2	2-0	1-1	0-0	4-0	3-2	4-0	0-1
Hyde United	3-1	1-0	1-0	3-0	2-0	1-3	4-3	3-1	1-1	2-3	0-1	4-3	—	4-1	1-2	1-2	1-1	0-0	2-1	1-0	4-1	2-0	0-0
Lancaster City	1-1	1-0	1-4	3-0	4-0	3-4	0-0	3-2	1-0	4-0	0-1	1-0	1-0	—	1-3	1-3	1-1	3-2	3-0	3-2	1-2	4-1	0-0
Leek Town	0-0	2-1	4-1	0-2	0-0	1-2	0-0	1-1	3-2	2-1	1-1	2-2	1-0	1-3	—	2-0	2-4	0-1	1-0	0-0	2-1	2-0	3-1
Leigh RMI	3-0	1-0	3-1	1-2	1-2	0-2	3-1	2-4	4-3	1-1	0-3	1-0	2-0	2-0	2-0	—	2-1	2-0	4-0	2-0	2-1	3-2	2-2
Marine	0-3	1-0	2-0	1-1	3-2	0-1	0-2	2-2	0-0	2-0	1-3	3-0	0-0	3-1	2-1	1-1	—	0-1	3-0	1-3	3-3	3-1	3-2
Runcorn	2-0	2-2	0-1	1-2	1-1	1-0	1-0	1-2	1-1	0-3	2-2	0-1	0-0	2-1	6-1	0-2	2-1	—	3-2	0-0	3-1	1-0	2-0
Spennymoor United	3-1	0-0	5-0	1-1	1-1	0-1	2-0	1-1	4-0	6-2	3-1	1-1	0-3	0-0	5-0	1-3	1-2	3-0	—	1-0	1-1	0-0	2-1
Stalybridge Celtic	2-2	3-1	2-2	3-1	0-0	1-0	0-1	1-1	1-1	2-0	2-2	2-1	0-0	0-1	3-1	1-3	0-0	1-1	1-0	—	0-3	4-1	4-3
Whitby Town	1-1	1-1	2-5	1-1	5-2	3-2	2-1	2-1	1-1	0-0	0-1	2-1	3-1	1-0	3-2	2-0	0-3	4-0	1-1	1-1	—	2-2	2-1
Winsford United	1-5	0-2	1-2	1-2	1-1	3-0	3-2	3-1	3-0	2-0	2-2	1-2	1-1	0-2	3-1	0-5	0-3	1-6	3-0	1-2	1-1	—	1-3
Worksop Town	0-2	0-2	1-2	4-2	1-1	0-2	1-2	1-3	2-0	3-2	0-1	1-0	1-1	4-1	2-0	0-3	0-1	0-3	5-1	2-1	4-1	9-0	—

UNIBOND LEAGUE — FIRST DIVISION RESULTS 1999–2000

	Accrington Stanley	Ashton United	Belper Town	Bradford Park Avenue	Burscough	Chorley	Congleton Town	Eastwood Town	Farsley Celtic	Flixton	Gretna	Harrogate Town	Lincoln United	Matlock Town	Netherfield Kendal	Ossett Town	Radcliffe Borough	Stocksbridge Park Steels	Trafford	Whitley Bay	Witton Albion	Workington
Accrington Stanley	—	2-1	4-1	2-1	2-2	0-0	1-0	2-2	3-0	2-0	3-2	5-0	10-1	0-0	4-1	2-1	1-3	4-1	1-2	3-0	0-0	4-1
Ashton United	1-2	—	3-0	2-2	0-0	1-2	1-1	3-1	1-1	2-0	3-1	2-1	2-3	1-1	1-0	2-4	1-4	2-2	0-1	2-2	2-2	1-1
Belper Town	1-2	4-1	—	0-0	0-3	1-1	1-2	1-1	0-3	5-1	2-1	1-0	0-2	1-0	2-2	2-1	3-2	0-1	3-2	1-2	2-2	1-2
Bradford Park Avenue	1-0	2-3	2-1	—	1-1	4-1	3-2	1-0	1-1	3-1	6-0	2-2	4-1	4-3	3-0	1-0	1-1	2-0	3-0	1-0	2-2	1-0
Burscough	1-1	1-0	3-1	1-2	—	1-0	5-0	5-0	2-0	3-0	4-0	2-2	1-1	2-2	4-3	3-2	1-2	4-1	1-0	1-0	1-1	0-0
Chorley	2-3	1-1	1-1	2-1	2-2	—	0-1	0-0	3-0	1-1	0-1	3-1	1-1	1-2	3-0	3-3	1-1	0-3	0-4	0-0	1-1	0-0
Congleton Town	2-3	1-1	2-0	0-1	2-2	2-1	—	2-2	2-1	1-0	2-1	0-3	1-2	1-2	5-1	1-0	2-0	0-0	1-2	1-3	0-1	1-2
Eastwood Town	1-7	0-0	2-0	0-1	0-2	0-1	1-2	—	2-5	1-0	0-1	3-1	3-0	1-2	2-1	2-1	4-0	2-1	4-0	6-0	1-3	1-1
Farsley Celtic	2-1	2-1	3-1	4-1	0-0	0-1	2-5	1-3	—	3-1	0-1	4-3	1-2	1-1	2-1	2-1	1-2	2-1	4-0	2-0	1-0	1-1
Flixton	0-5	1-3	2-1	0-1	0-1	1-2	3-3	2-3	2-1	—	4-0	2-2	1-1	0-1	1-3	1-3	1-2	2-4	3-5	1-0	0-3	1-3
Gretna	0-1	1-1	3-4	1-2	0-2	3-2	5-0	0-0	0-5	1-1	—	2-0	4-1	2-5	4-1	2-0	0-1	1-0	1-1	1-0	0-3	1-3
Harrogate Town	0-2	1-1	2-2	0-3	1-2	1-3	0-2	2-0	0-5	0-0	3-2	—	0-0	1-1	3-0	0-1	1-1	6-1	1-1	1-0	1-1	2-0
Lincoln United	1-0	2-2	1-1	2-1	0-1	1-2	2-2	2-2	2-2	3-3	1-0	2-1	—	3-2	2-1	1-5	1-2	1-2	0-3	2-1	1-2	3-2
Matlock Town	2-1	1-1	3-4	2-2	1-1	1-2	1-2	2-1	3-0	3-2	2-1	3-3	0-0	—	1-2	2-1	0-1	3-1	3-1	5-0	2-2	3-2
Netherfield Kendal	1-0	3-4	1-1	1-1	4-7	1-1	0-0	1-3	0-1	3-0	0-2	0-1	2-1	1-0	—	1-1	0-0	0-1	3-3	3-2	0-4	0-1
Ossett Town	2-2	4-0	2-1	3-1	1-1	3-0	3-3	1-2	2-0	3-2	2-1	1-2	1-2	3-1	1-0	—	2-2	4-1	0-1	1-2	1-2	3-1
Radcliffe Borough	2-3	2-0	1-1	2-1	0-0	1-1	3-1	3-1	1-1	2-0	0-0	3-1	1-2	3-1	1-0	2-2	—	3-1	0-1	4-1	1-0	1-0
Stocksbridge Park Steels	1-3	2-1	1-0	2-1	0-2	1-2	3-1	0-2	0-1	3-1	1-0	2-1	2-0	0-1	3-2	0-2	2-4	—	1-0	3-2	1-2	1-1
Trafford	2-4	0-2	1-2	2-0	1-1	6-0	2-2	1-2	1-3	2-0	0-1	2-3	2-0	0-1	0-0	0-0	3-3	3-3	—	1-2	1-1	1-1
Whitley Bay	1-1	1-3	2-1	1-3	1-1	1-3	3-3	0-1	2-3	3-1	6-1	1-2	0-1	0-0	1-3	1-7	1-6	1-0	1-1	—	2-4	1-2
Witton Albion	0-0	3-2	0-2	0-2	1-1	2-0	5-3	4-1	2-2	2-0	3-1	1-2	3-1	1-1	2-1	3-2	3-0	1-1	2-0	2-0	—	2-2
Workington	1-0	2-4	2-3	0-2	0-3	1-1	1-2	2-0	3-1	1-0	3-1	4-0	0-1	0-1	2-0	0-3	0-1	0-0	2-0	2-0	1-1	—

UNIBOND LEAGUE – CUP COMPETITIONS

FIRST GROUP STAGE

Group 1
Gretna 1, Netherfield Kendal 1
Netherfield Kendal 0, Workington 2
Workington 1, Gretna 0

Group 2
Barrow 3, Bamber Bridge 4
Bamber Bridge 1, Lancaster City 2
Lancaster City 0, Barrow 0

Group 3
Marine 3, Chorley 0
Chorley 1, Burscough 0
Burscough 2, Marine 2

Group 4
Leigh RMI 2, Ashton United 1
Ashton United 1, Radcliffe Borough 2
Radcliffe Borough 0, Leigh RMI 2

Group 5
Hyde United 2, Trafford 2
Trafford 6, Flixton 0
Flixton 1, Hyde United 2

Group 6
Runcorn 3, Colwyn Bay 1
Colwyn Bay 5, Witton Albion 2
Witton Albion 2, Runcorn 2

Group 7
Leek Town 3, Winsford United 3
Congleton Town 1, Leek Town 3
Winsford United 1, Congleton Town 2

Group 8
Stocksbridge Park Steels 0, Belper Town 1
Belper Town 1, Matlock Town 1
Matlock Town 1, Stocksbridge Park Steels 1

Group 9
Worksop Town 1, Hucknall Town 0
Hucknall Town 1, Eastwood Town 2
Eastwood Town 2, Worksop Town 2

Group 10
Gainsborough Trinity 1, Frickley Athletic 0
Frickley Athletic 4, Lincoln United 1
Lincoln United 3, Gainsborough Trinity 1

Group 11
Emley 0, Bradford Park Avenue 0
Bradford Park Avenue 2, Ossett Town 1
Ossett Town 1, Emley 3

Group 12
Guiseley 1, Harrogate Town 0
Harrogate Town 1, Farsley Celtic 0
Farsley Celtic 1, Guiseley 1

Group 13
Whitby Town 3, Spennymoor United 1
Spennymoor United 2, Bishop Auckland 2
Bishop Auckland 0, Whitby Town 1

Group 14
Gateshead 4, Blyth Spartans 1
Blyth Spartans 7, Whitley Bay 0
Whitley Bay 0, Gateshead 1

Group 15
Stalybridge Celtic 0, Accrington Stanley 3
Accrington Stanley 3, Droylsden 1
Droylsden 0, Stalybridge Celtic 2

SECOND GROUP STAGE

Group A
Leigh RMI 2, Lancaster City 2
Lancaster City 1, Workington 0
Workington 0, Leigh RMI 0

Group B
Bamber Bridge 2, Hyde United 0
Hyde United 1, Accrington Stanley 3
Accrington Stanley 3, Bamber Bridge 1

Group C
Trafford 4, Colwyn Bay 3
Marine 1, Trafford 1
Colwyn Bay 2, Marine 5

Group D
Congleton Town 2, Runcorn 2
Runcorn 4, Radcliffe Borough 1
Radcliffe Borough 2, Congleton Town 1

Group E
Guiseley 2, Blyth Spartans 0
Blyth Spartans 4, Bradford Park Avenue 0
Bradford Park Avenue 6, Guiseley 2

Group F
Gateshead 2, Whitby Town 3
Whitby Town 0, Frickley Athletic 2
Frickley Athletic 3, Gateshead 1

Group G
Worksop Town 1, Emley 1
Emley 0, Lincoln United 2
Lincoln United 2, Worksop Town 3

Group H
Belper Town 3, Eastwood Town 2
Leek Town 1, Belper Town 2
Eastwood Town 5, Leek Town 3

LEAGUE CUP QUARTER-FINALISTS
Accrington Stanley, Belper Town, Bradford Park Avenue, Frickley Athletic, Lancaster City, Marine, Runcorn, Worksop Town.

PRESIDENT'S CUP QUARTER-FINALISTS
Bamber Bridge, Blyth Spartans, Eastwood Town, Leigh RMI, Lincoln United, Radcliffe Borough, Trafford, Whitby Town.

UNIFILLA CUP QUARTER-FINALISTS
Colwyn Bay, Congleton Town, Emley, Gateshead, Guiseley, Hyde United, Leek Town, Workington.

CHALLENGE CUP QUARTER-FINALS
Accrington Stanley 2, Belper Town 1
Frickley Athletic 2, Marine 1
Lancaster City 1, Bradford Park Avenue 0
Worksop Town 1, Runcorn 0

SEMI-FINALS
Frickley Athletic 2, Lancaster City 3
Accrington Stanley 1, Worksop Town 1
Replay Worksop Town 1, Accrington Stanley 1
(Worksop Town won 4-3 on penalties aet).

FINAL
Lancaster City 1, Worksop Town 0

PRESIDENT'S CUP QUARTER-FINALS
Blyth Spartans 2, Bamber Bridge 2
Leigh RMI 1, Eastwood Town 0
Lincoln United 1, Trafford 1
Replay Trafford 3, Lincoln United 2
Radcliffe Borough 0, Whitby Town 2

SEMI-FINALS
Blyth Spartans 0, Trafford 1
Leigh RMI 1, Whitby Town 3

FINAL (two legs)
Trafford 2, Whitby Town 1
Whitby Town 4, Trafford 3
(Trafford won 4-2 on penalties aet).

UNIFILLA CUP QUARTER-FINALS
Guiseley 1, Emley 1
Emley 2, Guiseley 2
(Emley won on penalties aet).
Hyde United 2, Gateshead 0
Leek Town 2, Congleton Town 0
Workington 0, Colwyn Bay 1

SEMI-FINALS
Hyde United 3, Leek Town 2
Emley 6, Colwyn Bay 2

FINAL
Hyde United 2, Emley 0

DR MARTENS LEAGUE 1999–2000

Premier Division

	P	W	D	L	F	A	Pts	GD
Boston United	42	27	11	4	102	39	92	63
Burton Albion	42	23	9	10	73	43	78	30
Margate	42	23	8	11	64	43	77	21
Bath City	42	19	15	8	70	49	72	21
King's Lynn	42	19	14	9	59	43	71	16
Tamworth	42	20	10	12	80	51	70	29
Newport County	42	16	18	8	67	50	66	17
Clevedon Town	42	18	9	15	52	52	63	0
Ilkeston Town	42	16	12	14	77	69	60	8
Weymouth	42	14	16	12	60	51	58	9
Halesowen Town	42	14	14	14	52	54	56	−2
Crawley Town	42	15	8	19	68	82	53	−14
Havant & Waterlooville	42	13	13	16	63	68	52	−5
Cambridge City	42	14	10	18	52	66	52	−14
Worcester City	42	13	11	18	60	66	50	−6
Salisbury City	42	14	8	20	70	84	50	−14
Merthyr Tydfil	42	13	9	20	51	63	48	−12
Dorchester Town	42	10	17	15	56	65	47	−9
Grantham Town	42	14	5	23	63	76	47	−13
Gloucester City	42	8	14	20	40	82	38	−42
Rothwell Town	42	5	14	23	48	85	29	−37
Atherstone United	42	5	13	24	30	76	28	−46

Western Division

	P	W	D	L	F	A	Pts	GD
Stafford Rangers	42	29	6	7	107	47	93	60
Moor Green	42	26	12	4	85	33	90	52
Hinckley United	42	25	12	5	89	47	87	42
Tiverton Town	42	26	7	9	91	44	85	47
Solihull Borough	42	20	11	11	85	66	71	19
Blakenall	42	19	12	11	70	46	69	24
Cirencester Town	42	20	8	14	72	64	68	8
Bilston Town	42	16	18	8	66	52	66	14
Cinderford Town	42	17	11	14	62	64	62	−2
Redditch United	42	17	10	15	73	65	61	8
Gresley Rovers	42	14	15	13	54	49	57	5
Weston-Super-Mare	42	15	9	17	55	55	57	0
Sutton Coldfield Town	42	13	17	12	49	52	56	−3
Evesham United	42	13	12	17	69	61	51	8
Bedworth United	42	13	10	19	52	71	49	−19
Rocester	42	12	12	18	63	78	48	−15
Bromsgrove Rovers	42	13	7	22	59	72	46	−13
Shepshed Dynamo	42	12	7	23	46	66	43	−20
Paget Rangers	42	11	4	27	44	82	37	−38
Racing Club Warwick	42	7	14	21	41	82	35	−41
Stourbridge	42	10	3	29	45	101	33	−56
Yate Town	42	3	3	36	28	108	12	−80

Eastern Division

	P	W	D	L	F	A	Pts	GD
Fisher Athletic London	42	31	5	6	107	42	98	65
Folkestone Invicta	42	30	7	5	101	39	97	62
Newport (IW)	42	25	7	10	74	40	82	34
Chelmsford City	42	24	8	10	74	38	80	36
Hastings Town	42	22	9	11	76	56	75	20
Ashford Town	42	21	9	12	70	49	72	21
Tonbridge Angels	42	20	10	12	82	60	70	22
Dartford	42	17	6	19	52	58	57	−6
Burnham	42	15	9	18	55	64	54	−9
Baldock Town	42	14	10	18	57	69	52	−12
Erith & Belvedere	42	14	9	19	62	68	51	−6
Witney Town	42	13	11	18	48	60	50	−12
VS Rugby	42	13	11	18	58	79	50	−21
Wisbech Town	42	14	7	21	58	66	49	−8
Spalding United	42	14	6	22	52	71	48	−19
Sittingbourne	42	13	7	22	48	75	46	−27
Stamford	42	9	18	15	50	62	45	−12
St Leonards	42	11	12	19	67	81	45	−14
†Raunds Town	42	11	12	19	44	63	45	−19
Bashley	42	12	7	23	56	95	43	−39
*Corby Town	42	11	12	19	56	62	42	−6
Fleet Town	42	8	8	26	54	104	32	−50

(*Corby Town 3 pts deducted – ineligible player)
(†Raunds Town gave notice to withdraw and take place of 2nd relegated club – but have since sought to be re-selected)

LEADING GOALSCORERS
(League and Cup)
(up to and including Saturday 6 May 2000)

Premier Division

Mark Hallam (Tamworth)	35
James Taylor (Havant & Waterlooville)	32
Christian Moore (Burton Albion)	29
Paul Sales (Salisbury City)	27
Philip Collins (Margate)	25
Mark Owen (Worcester City)	24
Martin Paul (Bath City)	20
Mark Rawle (Boston United)	20
James Smith (Salisbury City)	20
Carl Dale (Newport County)	19
Daniel O'Hagan (Dorchester Town)	19
Warren Haughton (Tamworth)	18
David Laws (Weymouth)	18
Ian Cambridge (Cambridge City)	14

Western Division

Richard Mitchell (Stafford Rangers)	36
Derek Hall (Moor Green)	32
Scott Voice (Bilston Town)	27
Kevin Nancekivell (Tiverton Town)	25
David Sadler (Hinckley United)	22
Simon Windsor (Racing Warwick)	21
Jody Bevan (Cinderford Town)	20
Joseph Dowling (Solihull Borough)	20
Mark Shepherd (Moor Green)	19
Scott Griffin (Cirencester Town)	17
Christie McKenzie (Stourbridge)	17
David Toomey (Cinderford Town)	17
Ian Drewitt (Bedworth United)	16
Anthony Eccleston (Stafford Rangers)	16
Jamie Lenton (Hinckley United)	16
John Muir (Blakenall)	16
Paul Corcoran (Cirencester Town)	15
Philip Everett (Tiverton Town)	15
Peter Varley (Tiverton Town)	15

Eastern Division

Stephen Portway (Fisher Athletic London)	28
David Arter (Tonbridge Angels)	25
Terry White (Hastings Town)	25
Oliver Berquez (Chelmsford City)	23
Nicholas Dent (Folkestone Invicta)	23
Gary Walker (Baldock Town)	22
Bryn Charles (Fisher Athletic London)	19
Hamid Barr (Fisher Athletic London)	18
Andrew Furnell (Wisbech Town)	18
Carl Henry (Witney Town)	18
Lee McRobert (Ashford Town)	18
Mark Frampton (Fleet Town)	16
Lee Guiver (Dartford)	15
Stephen Lawrence (Folkestone Invicta)	15
Philip Andrews (Bashley)	14
Stephen Leigh (Newport (IW))	14
Stuart Myall (Hastings Town)	14
Gavin Smith (Fleet Town)	14
Stephen White (Erith & Belvedere)	14

DR MARTENS LEAGUE CUP

PRELIMINARY ROUND
Tiverton Town 4, Cirencester Town 2
Dartford 2, Burnham 0

FIRST ROUND
Boston United 2, Wisbech Town 3
Chelmsford City 0, Erith & Belvedere 2
Dartford 1, Fleet Town 1
Fleet Town won 7-6 on penalties.
Worcester City 6, Redditch United 1
Baldock Town 3, Crawley Town 0
Bath City 2, Merthyr Tydfil 1
Blakenall 4, Rocester 1
Bromsgrove Rovers 0, Stafford Rangers 1
Burton Albion 4, Bedworth United 3
Cleveland Town 1, Weston-Super-Mare 1
Weston-Super-Mare won 6-5 on penalties.
Evesham United 1, Halesowen Town 2
Folkestone Invicta 0, Fisher Athletic London 2
Gloucester City 4, Yate Town 1
Gresley Rovers 3, Hinckley United 2
Hastings Town 4, Ashford Town 1
Havant & Waterlooville 5, Bashley 1
Paget Rangers 1, Moor Green 2
Racing Club Warwick 0, Sutton Coldfield 4
Raunds Town 0, Cambridge City 1
Rothwell Town 1, Grantham Town 2
Salisbury City 1, Newport (IW) 4
Shepshed Dynamo 3, Solihull Borough 5
Sittingbourne 0, Margate 2
Spalding United 0, King's Lynn 1
King's Lynn won 4-3 on penalties.
Stamford 1, Ilkeston Town 2
Stourbridge 0, Bilston Town 1
Tamworth 4, Atherstone United 0
Tiverton Town 2, Newport County 1
Tonbridge Angels 3, St Leonards 1
VS Rugby 2, Corby Town 2
VS Rugby won 4-3 on penalties.
Weymouth 1, Dorchester Town 2
Witney Town 2, Cinderford Town 1

SECOND ROUND
Worcester City 3, Moor Green 1
Burton Albion 3, Halesowen Town 2
Gloucester City 3, Solihull Borough 1
Grantham Town 2, Cambridge City 1
Hastings Town 2, Erith & Belvedere 0
Havant & Waterlooville 4, Dorchester Town 3
Sutton Coldfield 2, Stafford Rangers 4
Tonbridge Angels 1, Fleet Town 4
Weston-Super-Mare 1, Witney Town 3
Tiverton Town 1, Bath City 2
VS Rugby 4, Wisbech Town 1
Margate 4, Baldock Town 2
Fisher Athletic London 1, Newport (IW) 5
Tamworth 3, Gresley Rovers 1
Blakenall 3, Bilston Town 1
Ilkeston Town 1, King's Lynn 1
King's Lynn won 4-3 on penalties.

THIRD ROUND
Worcester City 4, Blakenall 2
Bath City 3, Gloucester City 0
Havant & Waterlooville 3, Witney Town 1
King's Lynn 1, Grantham Town 0
Tamworth 4, Stafford Rangers 0
VS Rugby 0, Burton Albion 4
Fleet Town 2, Margate 5
Hastings Town 5, Newport (IW) 2

FOURTH ROUND
Bath City 0, Havant & Waterlooville 1
King's Lynn 1, Tamworth 1
King's Lynn won 4-3 on penalties.
Hastings Town 3, Margate 1
Burton Albion 1, Worcester City 0

SEMI-FINAL
Hastings Town 4, Havant & Waterlooville 2
Burton Albion 2, King's Lynn 0

FINAL
Hastings Town 1, Burton Albion 2
Burton Albion 4, Hastings Town 1

ATTENDANCES

Premier Divison
Aggregate: 291,545
Highest Individual crowd: 4137 Boston United v Grantham Town

Eastern Division
Aggregate: 108,457
Highest Individual crowd: 1235 Ashford Town v Folkestone Invicta

Western Division
Aggregate: 118,526
Highest Individual crowd: 1971 Stafford Rangers v Bilston Town

DR MARTENS LEAGUE — PREMIER DIVISION RESULTS 1999–2000

	Atherstone United	Bath City	Boston United	Burton Albion	Cambridge City	Clevedon Town	Crawley Town	Dorchester Town	Gloucester City	Grantham Town	Halesowen Town	Havant & Waterlooville	Ilkeston Town	King's Lynn	Margate	Merthyr Tydfil	Newport County	Rothwell Town	Salisbury City	Tamworth	Weymouth	Worcester City
Atherstone United	—	0-0	1-1	0-2	0-1	1-3	0-1	1-1	1-0	0-2	4-5	0-1	3-2	0-2	0-1	0-3	0-1	3-1	0-3	0-5	1-1	2-1
Bath City	2-0	—	2-0	2-1	2-2	2-1	7-0	1-1	5-1	1-3	0-3	1-2	2-2	4-1	1-1	0-2	0-1	1-0	1-3	3-2	3-0	1-1
Boston United	3-0	1-1	—	3-1	5-0	5-1	1-0	3-0	6-1	0-3	1-1	4-2	3-2	1-1	3-0	0-2	1-1	2-0	6-0	1-0	2-2	2-1
Burton Albion	5-1	3-0	1-1	—	3-0	1-0	3-0	5-0	3-0	2-1	0-1	3-0	3-1	1-0	0-1	2-0	1-1	2-1	4-1	1-1	1-2	2-3
Cambridge City	3-2	0-2	0-2	0-1	—	1-1	3-2	0-1	2-1	2-0	1-2	4-1	3-2	0-0	0-0	1-0	1-0	1-0	1-3	4-0	0-0	4-2
Clevedon Town	1-0	3-0	0-0	0-0	1-0	—	1-1	2-1	3-0	2-0	3-0	0-0	1-2	1-0	1-0	1-2	1-0	1-0	1-2	4-1	0-1	1-0
Crawley Town	0-0	4-1	1-6	1-4	1-2	1-3	—	3-1	2-1	4-2	1-0	1-0	2-0	1-0	1-0	2-3	0-1	3-3	4-1	3-0	4-0	2-5
Dorchester Town	2-2	0-0	3-4	0-1	1-2	2-1	0-2	—	1-2	0-2	0-1	1-2	3-1	4-1	1-1	2-0	0-0	1-1	4-4	1-1	2-2	4-4
Gloucester City	1-1	1-1	2-2	2-1	1-0	1-5	1-1	1-2	—	1-1	1-0	1-1	1-0	2-0	3-0	5-0	2-1	2-0	5-1	1-1	4-1	4-0
Grantham Town	6-0	1-3	0-3	2-1	2-0	2-0	4-2	0-2	1-1	—	1-0	2-0	1-0	3-4	0-4	1-0	0-1	3-1	3-3	0-3	3-3	0-2
Halesowen Town	0-1	0-3	1-1	0-1	1-2	3-0	1-0	0-1	4-2	1-0	—	1-0	3-0	0-0	0-3	0-1	2-0	5-2	3-1	0-3	0-0	1-0
Havant & Waterlooville	1-1	1-2	3-3	6-0	3-1	1-2	1-0	1-2	1-1	2-0	1-0	—	2-3	2-1	3-3	1-2	3-3	5-0	0-1	0-2	1-2	0-3
Ilkeston Town	1-0	2-2	1-0	4-1	2-2	4-1	2-0	3-1	1-0	1-0	3-0	2-3	—	2-1	1-2	2-1	2-2	3-3	6-0	4-1	2-2	2-1
King's Lynn	1-1	4-1	0-0	0-1	0-0	1-0	1-0	4-1	2-0	3-4	0-0	2-1	2-1	—	1-0	0-0	1-2	2-1	2-0	3-0	1-0	1-1
Margate	2-0	1-1	2-1	1-0	1-2	2-1	1-0	1-1	3-0	0-4	0-3	3-3	1-2	1-0	—	0-0	3-4	3-1	2-0	2-0	4-2	1-3
Merthyr Tydfil	2-0	0-2	0-2	1-1	1-0	2-0	2-3	1-1	5-0	1-0	0-1	1-2	2-1	0-0	0-0	—	2-5	2-0	1-1	1-1	1-2	2-1
Newport County	1-1	0-1	2-2	1-1	1-0	5-0	0-1	0-0	2-1	0-1	2-0	3-3	2-2	1-2	3-4	2-5	—	2-0	0-0	2-0	2-1	0-1
Rothwell Town	3-3	2-3	0-2	1-1	2-2	0-1	3-3	1-1	2-0	3-1	5-2	5-0	3-3	2-1	3-1	2-0	1-1	—	1-1	4-2	3-0	0-0
Salisbury City	1-0	1-3	1-2	0-3	1-4	1-2	4-1	1-4	2-1	3-3	3-1	0-1	2-1	2-3	0-2	2-0	1-2	1-1	—	1-2	1-0	2-3
Tamworth	4-0	3-2	1-2	1-1	1-2	4-1	3-0	1-1	1-1	0-3	0-3	0-2	4-1	3-0	2-0	3-1	4-2	4-2	1-2	—	3-1	0-1
Weymouth	0-0	3-0	2-2	1-2	0-0	0-1	4-0	2-2	4-1	3-3	0-0	1-2	2-2	1-0	4-2	2-1	2-1	3-0	1-0	3-1	—	1-1
Worcester City	0-0	0-1	1-2	2-2	3-2	1-0	2-5	4-4	4-0	0-2	1-0	0-3	2-1	1-1	1-3	3-4	3-4	0-0	2-3	0-1	1-1	—

DR MARTENS LEAGUE — WESTERN DIVISION RESULTS 1999–2000

	Bedworth United	Bilston Town	Blakenall	Bromsgrove Rovers	Cinderford Town	Cirencester Town	Evesham United	Gresley Rovers	Hinckley United	Moor Green	Paget Rangers	Racing Club Warwick	Redditch United	Rocester	Shepshed Dynamo	Solihull Borough	Stafford Rangers	Stourbridge	Sutton Coldfield Town	Tiverton Town	Weston-Super-Mare	Yate Town
Bedworth United	—	1-1	0-1	3-0	0-0	0-2	0-5	1-1	0-1	1-4	3-1	2-0	2-0	3-2	1-2	2-2	2-1	3-0	0-0	0-0	0-0	2-0
Bilston Town	3-0	—	1-1	1-0	1-2	0-4	3-3	3-1	1-1	2-2	1-1	4-0	1-0	2-2	3-1	3-1	1-5	1-0	1-1	1-0	2-0	3-1
Blakenall	6-0	1-1	—	1-0	0-1	2-3	3-3	1-0	1-0	4-0	3-0	3-0	0-0	5-3	4-0	1-1	1-1	2-3	0-1	1-0	2-0	1-0
Bromsgrove Rovers	0-1	1-2	1-1	—	0-1	1-2	3-3	3-4	1-2	1-2	4-1	1-1	1-3	5-1	0-2	3-0	4-3	4-1	0-2	1-2	2-2	3-0
Cinderford Town	2-1	1-0	1-1	0-4	—	1-2	2-3	1-1	0-2	0-0	4-1	1-0	1-0	3-2	1-0	2-3	2-0	1-0	0-3	1-0	2-1	6-0
Cirencester Town	2-2	2-2	0-1	1-0	1-2	—	2-3	1-1	2-1	1-5	6-2	1-0	2-3	3-2	0-0	4-3	1-2	4-2	1-3	0-3	2-1	3-0
Evesham United	2-1	1-3	0-1	0-2	0-0	1-2	—	1-1	2-3	1-1	3-1	3-1	0-3	1-2	2-0	4-3	1-4	4-0	0-0	0-0	0-1	1-1
Gresley Rovers	2-1	3-1	0-1	0-0	1-1	0-0	1-1	—	2-2	0-1	4-1	1-1	2-1	0-0	0-0	4-2	0-1	3-0	3-1	1-3	0-0	5-2
Hinckley United	1-0	3-1	1-0	1-0	1-1	5-2	1-3	2-0	—	1-1	4-1	4-0	1-1	1-1	3-1	2-1	3-1	3-0	1-1	1-1	4-1	3-2
Moor Green	3-1	1-0	0-5	5-0	3-0	0-0	2-0	4-1	2-0	—	2-0	1-2	0-1	1-1	3-0	0-0	0-0	7-1	0-0	1-1	2-0	6-0
Paget Rangers	2-4	0-2	2-1	0-1	2-1	1-0	1-6	4-1	4-1	2-0	—	1-2	0-1	2-4	0-2	2-1	2-0	0-0	3-2	3-2	0-2	3-0
Racing Club Warwick	1-2	0-0	1-1	3-3	5-2	0-1	3-1	1-1	4-0	1-2	1-2	—	1-1	3-1	1-0	4-2	4-1	3-1	0-0	1-0	1-0	3-1
Redditch United	3-0	1-0	2-4	3-1	5-2	3-0	0-7	2-1	1-1	0-1	0-1	1-1	—	2-3	4-0	2-2	1-0	5-3	1-1	3-5	2-1	1-2
Rocester	1-1	1-1	1-1	4-0	3-3	3-4	3-4	0-0	1-1	1-5	2-3	3-0	2-3	—	1-5	1-4	0-1	4-2	4-1	1-1	3-0	1-0
Shepshed Dynamo	3-3	0-1	0-1	0-0	2-5	1-0	4-3	0-0	3-1	3-0	0-2	1-3	4-0	2-1	—	1-3	1-5	4-2	3-0	0-2	1-0	5-0
Solihull Borough	3-0	1-1	2-1	3-0	2-0	1-3	5-0	4-2	2-1	0-0	2-1	1-3	2-2	4-2	1-3	—	3-2	2-1	1-1	2-1	1-0	0-1
Stafford Rangers	2-1	1-1	2-2	3-1	3-1	1-3	1-0	0-1	3-1	0-0	2-0	5-0	1-0	3-0	4-2	2-1	—	7-2	4-1	2-1	5-2	4-0
Stourbridge	3-1	1-4	1-2	0-3	1-3	1-3	1-0	3-0	3-0	3-1	0-2	0-4	5-3	0-1	0-2	0-3	0-2	—	1-1	1-5	0-2	3-1
Sutton Coldfield Town	4-1	1-1	0-2	0-3	0-3	2-1	0-0	3-1	1-1	0-0	2-2	0-0	1-1	4-1	3-0	6-1	1-1	0-1	—	0-2	0-1	0-0
Tiverton Town	3-1	5-2	2-1	2-0	6-1	2-0	2-2	1-3	1-1	1-0	2-1	1-0	3-5	1-0	2-2	6-1	2-1	2-0	0-1	—	5-1	4-2
Weston-Super-Mare	1-3	2-0	3-0	5-2	3-2	2-2	2-2	0-0	4-1	2-0	0-2	1-0	2-1	1-0	2-2	1-0	2-2	3-0	2-2	5-1	—	4-1
Yate Town	1-2	0-4	0-2	3-0	1-2	1-1	1-2	5-2	3-2	6-0	3-0	3-1	1-2	1-0	5-0	0-1	4-0	3-1	0-0	4-2	4-1	—

DR MARTENS LEAGUE — EASTERN DIVISION RESULTS 1999–2000

	Ashford Town	Baldock Town	Bashley	Burnham	Chelmsford City	Corby Town	Dartford	Erith & Belvedere	Fisher Athletic London	Fleet Town	Folkestone Invicta	Hastings Town	Newport (IW)	Raunds Town	Sittingbourne	Spalding United	St Leonards	Stamford	Tonbridge Angels	VS Rugby	Wisbech Town	Witney Town
Ashford Town	—	0-2	2-4	0-2	2-1	0-2	1-2	1-2	3-0	0-1	1-1	2-0	2-1	0-0	1-3	3-1	2-0	0-1	2-2	2-3	4-2	0-0
Baldock Town	0-2	—	1-1	1-1	0-1	1-3	0-3	2-2	4-1	3-2	1-1	0-1	2-0	3-0	2-2	3-1	2-0	0-1	2-3	1-0	4-1	0-1
Bashley	2-4	1-1	—	1-1	1-1	0-1	1-2	2-1	2-4	4-0	3-1	6-1	0-1	1-0	5-0	4-1	2-0	1-0	5-0	0-2	1-1	1-1
Burnham	3-0	4-1	1-1	—	1-0	0-0	3-2	0-1	3-0	1-1	4-1	1-0	3-0	0-6	0-1	2-3	2-4	0-0	1-2	2-1	1-3	2-2
Chelmsford City	1-0	0-0	0-1	3-1	—	1-1	0-2	3-0	2-1	1-1	0-3	1-1	3-1	1-0	0-6	0-1	0-1	1-2	2-1	5-1	1-0	1-1
Corby Town	1-2	0-1	1-2	3-0	1-1	—	1-2	2-2	2-0	2-1	0-0	2-1	2-0	1-1	0-2	1-0	1-0	0-0	2-3	3-2	2-0	1-2
Dartford	3-1	1-0	3-1	0-1	2-0	0-1	—	3-0	4-0	1-0	4-1	1-1	0-0	2-2	3-2	2-2	1-0	2-4	1-2	0-2	0-1	3-1
Erith & Belvedere	2-2	0-1	0-0	1-0	1-0	5-1	0-0	—	0-2	4-2	0-1	1-2	2-2	3-2	0-3	1-4	1-2	1-1	1-0	2-1	1-2	2-1
Fisher Athletic London	1-3	3-4	2-5	1-0	1-2	1-2	0-3	0-2	—	2-0	1-0	3-2	0-2	0-1	0-1	1-2	1-1	1-4	0-1	0-1	1-1	2-5
Fleet Town	4-0	2-0	4-2	4-1	1-2	5-0	2-1	4-3	3-2	—	2-0	1-1	3-1	1-2	2-0	1-1	6-3	3-1	2-0	4-0	2-1	2-0
Folkestone Invicta	1-3	1-6	0-3	1-2	5-1	0-1	1-3	1-2	2-2	0-5	—	3-0	0-1	3-0	0-0	1-2	1-4	2-1	3-0	6-1	3-1	2-0
Hastings Town	2-1	0-1	1-3	0-5	0-0	1-2	4-2	2-3	4-2	2-3	3-0	—	2-1	3-0	4-3	0-0	0-3	4-1	1-1	3-0	0-1	0-0
Newport (IW)	1-1	1-2	1-2	3-4	1-0	1-1	1-2	0-2	0-1	3-2	2-1	2-2	—	1-0	1-4	1-0	1-1	0-1	3-3	1-0	2-1	2-1
Raunds Town	2-1	1-1	2-1	1-0	2-1	2-2	2-0	1-1	3-0	1-4	3-0	2-1	3-0	—	2-0	2-3	1-3	1-0	1-0	1-1	0-0	0-1
Sittingbourne	7-0	1-1	2-1	2-0	1-0	1-3	1-2	2-3	3-0	0-1	3-2	3-3	2-0	0-0	—	0-2	2-2	4-0	0-0	2-0	2-0	2-0
Spalding United	2-0	3-0	1-3	2-0	1-3	0-2	2-1	2-0	0-0	1-1	5-0	2-3	1-0	2-1	1-0	—	3-2	2-1	3-1	2-1	0-0	1-2
St Leonards	1-0	3-2	0-2	2-2	2-0	6-2	0-0	1-0	3-1	2-2	4-1	5-2	1-0	0-4	2-2	4-1	—	0-0	3-3	1-1	3-0	1-1
Stamford	1-2	2-2	1-0	4-3	2-1	3-3	2-0	1-1	6-0	1-1	2-4	3-0	1-1	1-1	3-1	1-1	0-0	—	4-0	0-0	2-1	1-1
Tonbridge Angels	0-0	0-2	0-3	3-3	3-0	2-2	3-0	0-2	0-2	2-3	3-0	1-0	0-3	2-2	1-4	4-2	2-1	2-2	—	1-1	2-3	1-0
VS Rugby	0-1	5-1	2-2	2-0	5-1	4-2	2-0	5-3	3-2	3-3	6-1	2-0	1-0	0-1	3-5	1-1	1-2	0-2	2-0	—	3-1	0-1
Wisbech Town	3-1	4-3	5-0	0-0	1-0	2-1	0-0	1-2	3-1	2-3	3-1	2-0	2-1	3-1	2-1	4-3	4-0	1-0	2-2	2-2	—	1-1
Witney Town	0-0	1-0	2-5	2-0	1-1	1-1	0-1	3-1	5-0	3-2	2-0	2-1	3-0	2-3	2-0	0-3	1-0	1-1	1-1	0-1	1-1	—

RYMAN FOOTBALL LEAGUE 1999–2000

Premier Division

	P	W	D	L	F	A	W	D	L	F	A	Pts
			Home						*Away*			
Dagenham & Redbridge	42	20	1	0	58	13	12	4	5	39	22	101
Aldershot Town	42	13	2	6	39	23	11	3	7	32	28	77
Chesham United	42	11	6	4	33	21	9	4	8	31	29	70
Purfleet	42	10	8	3	39	22	8	7	6	31	26	69
Canvey Island	42	13	2	6	37	18	8	4	9	33	35	69
St Albans City	42	8	6	7	37	26	11	4	6	38	29	67
Billericay Town	42	10	6	5	36	28	8	6	7	26	34	66
Hendon	42	11	4	6	38	31	7	4	10	23	33	62
Slough Town	42	10	3	8	37	30	7	6	8	24	29	60
Dulwich Hamlet	42	10	2	9	32	31	7	3	11	30	37	56
Gravesend & Northfleet	42	9	6	6	36	25	6	4	11	30	42	55
Farnborough Town	42	8	5	8	25	19	6	6	9	27	36	53
Hampton & Richmond	42	8	4	9	26	28	5	9	7	23	29	52
Enfield	42	9	6	6	42	34	4	5	12	22	34	50
Heybridge Swifts	42	7	5	9	34	33	6	6	9	23	32	50
Hitchin Town	42	10	4	7	36	29	3	7	11	23	43	50
Carshalton Athletic	42	6	9	6	30	30	6	3	12	25	35	48
Basingstoke Town	42	10	6	5	31	24	3	3	15	25	47	48
Harrow Borough	42	7	4	10	31	26	7	2	12	23	44	48
Aylesbury United	42	9	4	8	38	33	4	5	12	26	48	48
Boreham Wood	42	3	6	12	21	40	8	4	9	23	31	43
Walton & Hersham	42	4	4	13	19	38	7	4	10	25	32	41

Division One

	P	W	D	L	F	A	W	D	L	F	A	Pts
			Home						*Away*			
Croydon	42	10	8	3	39	23	15	1	5	46	24	84
Grays Athletic	42	11	5	5	44	23	10	7	4	36	21	75
Maidenhead United	42	11	5	5	36	24	9	10	2	36	21	75
Thame United	42	10	8	3	31	16	10	5	6	30	22	73
Worthing	42	9	6	6	45	34	10	6	5	35	26	69
Staines Town	42	10	7	4	36	30	9	5	7	27	22	69
Whyteleafe	42	10	5	6	31	23	10	4	7	29	26	69
Bedford Town	42	9	6	6	27	22	8	6	7	32	30	63
Bromley	42	10	4	7	36	31	7	5	9	26	34	60
Uxbridge	42	10	4	7	41	23	5	9	7	19	21	58
Bishop's Stortford	42	6	6	9	26	29	10	4	7	31	33	58
Barton Rovers	42	9	4	8	29	30	7	4	10	35	53	56
Oxford City	42	10	2	9	30	24	7	2	12	27	31	55
Braintree Town	42	11	6	4	40	26	4	4	13	25	48	55
Yeading	42	7	8	6	30	28	5	10	6	23	26	54
Wealdstone	42	8	5	8	27	26	5	7	9	24	32	51
Bognor Regis Town	42	3	7	11	19	30	9	6	6	28	23	49
Harlow Town	42	3	9	9	26	39	8	4	9	36	37	46
Romford	42	5	3	13	21	36	8	7	6	30	34	45
Leatherhead	42	4	4	13	22	36	5	9	7	25	34	40
Chertsey Town	42	5	3	13	28	43	4	2	15	22	41	32
Leyton Pennant	42	4	5	12	17	43	3	4	14	17	42	30

Division Two

	P	W	D	L	F	A	W	D	L	F	A	Pts
			Home						*Away*			
Hemel Hempstead Town	42	18	3	0	66	15	13	5	3	32	12	101
Northwood	42	18	1	2	64	17	11	8	2	45	23	96
Ford United	42	17	3	1	59	13	11	5	5	49	28	92
Berkhamsted Town	42	15	3	3	47	25	7	5	9	28	27	74
Windsor & Eton	42	10	6	5	43	32	10	7	4	30	21	73
Wivenhoe Town	42	11	6	4	32	20	9	3	9	29	27	69
Barking	42	8	7	6	35	24	10	6	5	35	27	67
Marlow	42	12	2	7	42	22	8	2	11	44	44	64
Metropolitan Police	42	14	3	4	45	27	4	4	13	30	44	61
Banstead Athletic	42	11	5	5	32	17	5	6	10	23	39	59
Tooting & Mitcham Utd	42	10	5	6	38	28	6	2	13	34	46	55
Wokingham Town	42	8	3	10	30	42	7	6	8	28	38	54
Wembley	42	8	4	9	23	26	6	7	8	24	27	53
Edgware Town	42	7	8	6	37	35	6	3	12	35	36	50
Hungerford Town	42	9	4	8	38	34	4	6	11	23	44	49
Cheshunt	42	5	8	8	25	32	7	4	10	28	33	48
Horsham	42	8	6	7	45	37	5	2	14	21	44	47
Leighton Town	42	6	3	12	33	39	7	5	9	32	45	47
Molesey	42	5	7	9	24	28	5	5	11	30	41	42
Wingate & Finchley	42	8	5	8	33	39	3	2	16	21	58	40
Witham Town	42	6	5	10	23	49	1	4	16	16	61	30
Chalfont St Peter	42	2	4	15	22	53	0	4	17	17	71	14

Division Three

		Home					Away					
	P	W	D	L	F	A	W	D	L	F	A	Pts
East Thurrock United	40	16	2	2	54	18	10	5	5	35	24	85
Great Wakering Rovers	40	13	5	2	48	21	12	2	6	33	20	82
Tilbury	40	13	5	2	41	15	8	7	5	26	24	75
Hornchurch	40	14	4	2	47	22	5	8	7	25	35	69
Croydon Athletic	40	11	5	4	52	26	8	6	6	33	26	68
Epsom & Ewell	40	9	10	1	40	22	9	2	9	27	24	66
Lewes	40	10	6	4	34	20	8	4	8	39	31	64
Bracknell Town	40	9	7	4	40	29	6	9	5	41	35	61
Aveley	40	9	6	5	42	25	8	4	8	31	39	61
Corinthian Casuals	40	9	3	8	32	27	7	7	6	27	24	58
Flackwell Heath	40	12	2	6	47	35	5	4	11	27	41	57
Ware	40	9	5	6	42	28	7	3	10	32	34	56
Egham Town	40	9	5	6	27	19	7	5	8	21	24	55
Hertford Town	40	6	6	8	28	31	9	4	7	35	29	55
Abingdon Town	40	5	5	10	18	31	5	7	8	30	33	42
Kingsbury Town	40	6	5	9	29	32	5	3	12	26	54	41
Camberley Town	40	7	5	8	25	29	4	2	14	19	50	40
Tring Town	40	6	4	10	29	29	4	5	11	17	35	39
Dorking	40	7	5	8	33	27	2	5	13	20	42	37
Clapton	40	6	3	11	25	37	3	4	13	25	56	34
Southall	40	1	3	16	21	58	2	2	16	12	65	14

LEADING GOALSCORERS

Premier Division

		Lge	RLC	PC
29	Gary Abbott (Aldershot Town)	29		
27	George Georgiou (Purfleet)	20		7
25	Steve Darlington (Farnborough Town)	19	5	1
23	Paul Coombs (Purfleet)	15	1	7
22	Terry Bowes (Chesham United)	18	3	1
21	Wayne Andrews (Aldershot Town)	17	2	2
	(includes while at St Albans City)	11	2	2
21	Simon Parker (Heybridge Swifts)	16	5	

Division One

30	Gordon Guile (Barton Rovers)	24	6	
22	Robbie Reinelt (Braintree Town)	19	3	
22	Matt Edwards (Yeading)	19		3
22	Mark Butler (Staines Town)	18	3	1
22	Eben Allen (Croydon)	18	2	2

Division Two

				VT
43	Jeff Wood (Ford United)	42		1
43	Lawrence Yaku (Northwood)	36	2	5
33	Leon Constantine (Edgware Town)	32		1
32	Dennis Greene (Windsor & Eton)	27	3	2

Division Three

36	Mark Cox (East Thurrock United)	36		
	(includes while at Grays Athletic)	4		
33	John Fowler (Croydon Athletic)	33		
30	Stuart White (Dorking)	28	1	1
27	Lee Watson (Flackwell Heath)	27		

Lge: Ryman League; RLC: Ryman League Cup; FMC: Full Members Cup; VT: Vandanel Trophy

ATTENDANCES

Premier Divison
Highest Individual crowd: 5518 Aldershot Town v Farnborough Town 27.12.99
Aggregate: 248,366

Division One
Highest Individual crowd: 919 Bedford Town v Barton Rovers 27.12.99
Aggregate: 103,729

Division Two
Highest Individual crowd: 464 Northwood v Hemel Hempstead Town 29.04.00
Aggregate: 49,116

Division Three
Highest Individual crowd: 521 Hertford Town v Ware 27.12.99
Aggregate: 34,489

PREVIOUS SEASONS

SEASON	CLUBS	GAMES	AGG	AVE
1988–1989	86	1764	323,197	183
1989–1990	87	1806	387,441	215
1990–1991	88	1848	404,703	219
1991–1992	86	1764	397,553	225
1992–1993	85	1724	430,518	247
1993–1994	87	1806	423,306	234
1994–1995	87	1806	433,703	240
1995–1996	86	1764	440,285	250
1996–1997	83	1658	461,944	278
1997–1998	86	1766	456,454	258
1998–1999	86	1766	446,637	253

RYMAN FOOTBALL LEAGUE—PREMIER DIVISION RESULTS 1999-2000

	Aldershot Town	Aylesbury United	Basingstoke Town	Billericay Town	Boreham Wood	Canvey Island	Carshalton Athletic	Chesham United	Dagenham & Redbridge	Dulwich Hamlet	Enfield	Farnborough Town	Gravesend & Northfleet	Hampton & Richmond	Harrow Borough	Hendon	Heybridge Swifts	Hitchin Town	Purfleet	Slough Town	St Albans City	Walton & Hersham
Aldershot Town	—	1-1	5-2	0-1	1-0	3-1	4-0	4-1	1-0	3-2	0-4	1-0	2-1	1-1	1-2	2-1	0-1	5-1	0-2	2-0	0-2	3-0
Aylesbury United	3-0	—	3-0	0-1	0-1	3-3	3-2	3-2	0-2	2-3	1-0	1-2	4-1	2-2	3-1	2-3	2-2	3-1	0-3	2-2	0-2	1-0
Basingstoke Town	2-1	4-2	—	2-0	1-1	3-1	2-0	0-1	0-4	2-3	2-2	2-2	2-0	2-0	2-0	1-1	1-2	1-1	2-2	1-0	0-2	1-3
Billericay Town	3-2	5-0	1-0	—	1-0	0-0	2-0	3-5	0-4	3-5	0-0	0-3	3-3	1-0	5-0	0-1	1-2	1-1	1-1	3-1	3-1	0-3
Boreham Wood	2-5	2-2	3-4	0-2	—	3-2	0-1	0-0	0-4	0-0	1-1	1-1	3-4	0-4	1-3	0-1	6-1	0-3	1-1	1-3	2-3	1-0
Canvey Island	2-1	2-3	2-1	3-0	3-1	—	1-1	0-3	3-1	0-0	1-0	2-0	4-1	1-1	2-0	0-0	1-1	0-3	2-0	2-0	0-1	1-1
Carshalton Athletic	3-0	2-1	3-3	3-3	3-0	2-1	—	1-2	1-1	0-1	2-0	2-1	1-2	1-1	3-1	0-0	1-1	2-1	0-0	1-1	0-1	1-1
Chesham United	2-0	1-1	1-0	5-0	3-0	2-0	2-0	—	3-0	1-2	1-0	1-1	1-1	1-0	1-2	0-1	2-0	2-1	1-0	1-1	3-4	2-1
Dagenham & Redbridge	3-1	4-1	3-2	2-0	2-0	3-1	3-1	3-0	—	3-0	4-0	3-2	2-1	5-0	4-1	4-0	2-1	4-1	3-1	2-1	2-1	2-0
Dulwich Hamlet	1-2	3-0	2-0	1-2	1-1	2-0	1-3	1-2	0-0	—	1-3	1-3	1-5	2-0	2-0	1-0	2-1	1-2	3-2	2-3	3-2	1-0
Enfield	1-4	3-1	3-0	1-1	0-2	1-1	3-2	3-2	1-1	3-2	—	3-0	0-1	2-3	0-3	5-3	3-2	1-1	1-2	1-3	4-0	4-1
Farnborough Town	0-0	3-1	2-0	3-0	0-2	1-2	4-1	0-5	0-1	0-0	1-1	—	3-2	0-1	0-0	0-1	0-1	1-1	1-1	0-1	1-0	1-2
Gravesend & Northfleet	1-1	5-0	2-1	0-1	3-0	0-1	0-5	1-0	1-2	3-0	2-0	5-1	—	0-0	4-1	1-0	1-1	1-1	1-2	1-0	1-2	1-1
Hampton & Richmond	0-1	2-1	2-1	1-2	1-1	0-2	0-1	2-1	0-0	0-1	2-1	1-0	1-0	—	3-1	1-2	1-4	2-1	1-1	1-1	2-2	0-2
Harrow Borough	0-1	4-1	1-1	1-1	1-3	1-3	0-0	1-0	0-2	0-2	1-2	1-3	6-0	3-0	—	2-1	2-0	4-0	2-3	0-1	0-2	0-1
Hendon	1-2	1-0	4-3	3-2	2-1	0-1	0-2	1-2	0-1	1-3	2-2	5-3	2-0	1-0	0-1	—	2-0	1-1	1-3	1-1	0-3	2-2
Heybridge Swifts	1-3	0-0	2-0	1-2	0-1	0-2	0-2	1-1	5-4	0-1	2-1	1-2	2-4	2-2	1-2	2-1	—	2-3	0-0	1-1	2-1	5-1
Hitchin Town	1-2	4-3	1-0	4-0	3-3	2-0	3-2	2-0	0-2	1-0	1-1	1-1	1-1	4-0	1-1	1-0	1-2	—	1-0	1-2	2-2	0-2
Purfleet	2-4	0-2	1-2	0-2	3-2	1-1	2-0	2-0	1-1	0-0	4-2	4-0	2-1	0-0	1-1	4-1	1-0	3-0	—	2-0	3-3	3-1
Slough Town	0-0	1-2	1-4	4-0	2-3	2-0	4-0	1-1	2-1	3-0	2-1	1-2	2-1	1-1	3-2	1-1	2-1	3-0	3-0	—	0-3	3-1
St Albans City	0-1	1-1	4-1	1-2	0-0	4-0	1-1	3-0	4-1	2-4	5-0	0-0	0-1	1-1	3-2	3-0	2-0	2-1	2-4	0-1	—	3-1
Walton & Hersham	0-1	0-3	1-0	0-1	3-1	0-3	1-1	2-1	0-3	0-3	4-1	1-3	2-2	1-3	3-1	1-2	0-1	4-3	0-3	2-2	1-1	—

RYMAN FOOTBALL LEAGUE—DIVISION ONE RESULTS 1999–2000

	Barton Rovers	Bedford Town	Bishop's Stortford	Bognor Regis Town	Braintree Town	Bromley	Chertsey Town	Croydon	Grays Athletic	Harlow Town	Leatherhead	Leyton Pennant	Maidenhead United	Oxford City	Romford	Staines Town	Thame United	Uxbridge	Wealdstone	Whyteleafe	Worthing	Yeading
Barton Rovers	—	0-1	2-3	3-1	1-1	1-2	0-3	2-1	0-2	0-3	2-1	0-2	1-1	3-1	3-2	0-1	1-0	1-1	2-1	1-0	2-2	4-1
Bedford Town	1-0	—	1-0	2-1	1-1	1-2	3-3	1-0	1-1	3-3	1-1	1-0	2-2	2-0	0-1	0-2	0-2	1-0	4-0	0-1	2-3	1-0
Bishop's Stortford	1-2	2-3	—	0-0	0-0	0-2	2-1	1-0	0-1	2-1	0-1	2-0	1-1	0-3	0-0	2-3	0-3	1-2	3-0	4-2	4-4	0-0
Bognor Regis Town	2-2	1-1	0-1	—	0-1	0-0	0-1	1-2	1-3	0-1	1-3	2-2	1-2	2-1	1-2	0-1	1-2	2-1	1-1	0-0	1-3	1-1
Braintree Town	2-2	3-1	3-0	4-0	—	2-2	2-0	0-2	0-1	2-1	2-1	3-2	0-0	1-3	3-3	1-1	0-0	1-0	2-1	2-1	1-2	4-0
Bromley	4-1	0-2	0-2	3-2	1-3	—	2-0	3-2	1-2	1-0	1-1	1-0	1-2	2-0	2-5	0-4	0-1	4-1	4-1	3-2	1-4	2-2
Chertsey Town	2-1	2-1	3-5	1-1	4-1	0-0	—	2-4	2-1	1-3	0-1	1-2	1-2	2-0	2-5	0-4	2-2	0-1	1-3	0-2	2-3	0-1
Croydon	1-2	1-1	1-1	0-2	6-1	3-1	2-4	—	0-0	1-0	2-2	3-0	2-2	2-0	1-1	1-0	2-4	1-1	1-3	3-0	1-0	2-0
Grays Athletic	4-1	3-0	1-3	0-0	4-0	5-0	3-4	0-0	—	2-2	2-2	4-0	2-2	1-0	2-1	1-1	0-2	1-0	0-1	4-1	3-1	1-1
Harlow Town	2-3	0-5	2-2	0-3	1-1	2-2	1-2	3-4	4-4	—	0-1	1-0	1-1	0-1	0-1	1-1	3-2	1-3	0-0	0-1	1-1	1-1
Leatherhead	1-2	2-0	0-2	0-2	4-1	0-2	1-1	1-2	1-3	2-5	—	2-1	1-3	1-2	1-1	1-2	2-2	1-0	0-2	0-0	1-2	0-1
Leyton Pennant	0-3	1-0	0-2	0-1	1-5	2-0	3-1	1-4	0-3	2-2	1-1	—	0-3	1-5	2-1	0-0	1-2	0-1	0-2	0-4	0-2	2-2
Maidenhead United	2-2	2-1	0-1	1-1	4-3	3-2	2-0	1-0	3-1	2-2	1-1	1-3	—	0-1	4-0	3-2	0-1	2-2	2-0	0-1	1-1	2-1
Oxford City	2-0	1-2	5-0	0-1	2-0	3-1	0-2	0-2	2-1	0-2	5-0	1-1	1-3	—	0-3	1-0	2-4	1-1	2-1	0-1	0-1	1-0
Romford	1-2	2-2	0-1	1-2	2-1	2-1	0-1	0-2	0-1	0-2	2-1	1-1	1-3	1-2	—	1-1	1-1	0-0	1-3	1-2	0-3	0-1
Staines Town	2-2	1-1	0-0	1-4	3-2	4-1	1-1	2-6	1-1	2-1	0-2	1-0	1-0	2-2	3-1	—	3-1	0-0	2-1	1-3	1-0	2-2
Thame United	2-0	0-1	3-2	1-2	3-0	1-0	3-0	0-0	2-1	3-0	2-2	5-1	1-0	3-1	1-1	1-1	—	1-0	1-1	1-1	0-0	0-0
Uxbridge	5-1	0-1	5-1	3-2	3-1	2-0	6-0	1-2	1-1	6-0	5-0	3-0	0-4	1-0	1-3	0-1	0-0	—	1-1	2-3	0-1	1-1
Wealdstone	4-1	1-1	0-2	0-0	2-0	1-3	3-1	1-2	0-2	3-1	1-1	2-2	0-1	2-1	2-0	0-2	1-0	1-1	—	3-1	2-1	1-3
Whyteleafe	4-2	2-1	0-1	1-0	1-2	1-1	3-1	0-5	0-4	3-1	2-1	4-0	1-1	2-1	0-1	2-0	0-1	0-0	2-1	—	1-1	0-0
Worthing	8-2	3-4	3-2	1-2	2-0	0-2	1-5	1-1	0-1	3-0	3-1	3-0	1-1	1-1	4-0	3-1	2-0	1-1	1-1	1-1	—	1-5
Yeading	3-4	3-3	2-0	1-1	3-1	1-2	1-2	0-2	1-1	1-1	1-1	2-2	2-1	2-1	2-2	2-1	1-0	1-1	1-1	0-2	2-0	—

RYMAN FOOTBALL LEAGUE—DIVISION TWO RESULTS 1999–2000

	Banstead Athletic	Barking	Berkhamsted Town	Chalfont St Peter	Cheshunt	Edgware Town	Ford United	Hemel Hempstead Town	Horsham	Hungerford Town	Leighton Town	Marlow	Metropolitan Police	Molesey	Northwood	Tooting & Mitcham United	Wembley	Windsor & Eton	Wingate & Finchley	Witham Town	Wivenhoe Town	Wokingham Town
Banstead Athletic	—	0-1	3-1	4-1	3-0	2-0	0-0	1-2	1-0	1-1	0-0	3-2	1-0	2-1	1-3	0-0	0-2	1-0	1-0	7-1	0-1	1-1
Barking	1-1	—	2-2	0-0	0-0	1-1	1-3	0-1	3-1	2-0	2-4	6-0	1-0	3-0	3-1	2-2	0-1	1-2	3-1	2-0	1-1	1-3
Berkhamsted Town	3-1	1-3	—	0-0	2-1	3-1	2-0	0-2	4-1	3-2	4-0	3-1	1-0	1-0	1-1	4-3	4-1	4-4	2-1	1-0	3-0	1-3
Chalfont St Peter	1-1	2-2	1-3	—	1-2	0-3	0-6	0-1	2-3	2-3	2-3	3-0	3-3	2-4	0-3	0-6	1-0	1-2	0-2	0-0	0-2	1-4
Cheshunt	1-1	1-4	0-2	2-1	—	3-1	2-2	0-0	1-2	1-1	3-2	0-1	0-2	1-4	2-3	2-0	0-0	1-1	0-1	0-0	3-3	2-1
Edgware Town	1-2	0-0	2-2	4-0	1-1	—	1-1	0-8	3-0	2-1	5-1	2-4	3-0	2-2	1-1	4-3	1-1	0-0	2-3	2-1	1-3	3-1
Ford United	2-0	1-1	3-1	8-1	2-0	2-1	—	0-0	4-0	6-0	3-1	2-0	2-0	4-2	1-1	1-0	2-1	3-1	6-1	4-0	3-1	0-1
Hemel Hempstead Town	8-0	3-0	3-1	2-1	3-0	3-0	1-0	—	3-1	1-1	4-1	1-0	7-1	3-0	2-2	5-2	2-0	0-0	2-1	4-1	4-2	5-1
Horsham	4-0	1-2	1-2	5-2	2-2	0-2	2-5	3-1	—	2-1	1-1	1-1	5-2	0-0	2-5	3-0	4-1	1-2	2-2	5-3	2-1	0-0
Hungerford Town	3-0	0-2	0-4	3-2	0-2	1-1	1-4	2-3	2-1	—	5-0	3-2	2-0	1-4	1-3	2-1	1-1	1-2	4-0	6-2	2-2	0-1
Leighton Town	2-2	2-0	0-1	5-0	1-1	2-3	1-3	0-0	1-2	2-1	—	2-5	1-3	3-3	0-5	0-1	1-2	0-2	4-1	4-1	0-2	2-0
Marlow	2-1	3-0	2-0	10-0	1-0	2-1	0-2	0-1	3-0	1-2	2-0	—	2-2	4-1	0-0	3-0	0-3	0-2	3-1	3-1	0-3	5-1
Metropolitan Police	1-2	2-0	2-0	2-0	2-0	3-0	3-1	1-5	1-3	4-2	3-2	3-2	—	4-2	1-2	5-2	0-0	2-1	2-2	2-0	1-0	3-2
Molesey	0-0	0-3	2-0	1-1	0-1	2-3	2-2	1-2	1-2	1-1	1-1	1-3	1-1	—	0-3	3-0	0-2	3-0	4-0	0-0	2-1	1-1
Northwood	2-0	6-2	1-0	7-2	4-0	1-0	0-3	0-0	2-0	7-1	2-3	1-0	2-0	2-0	—	4-2	2-1	0-2	7-2	5-0	1-0	4-0
Tooting & Mitcham United	1-2	1-1	0-0	2-0	3-2	2-1	2-2	0-1	3-1	1-2	2-2	3-0	6-5	3-2	0-1	—	1-2	0-1	3-1	3-0	2-1	1-1
Wembley	0-1	2-2	0-1	2-1	1-4	2-0	1-6	0-1	3-1	2-0	0-1	2-1	2-1	1-1	0-0	0-1	—	1-1	1-0	4-0	2-1	1-1
Windsor & Eton	2-1	1-1	1-1	3-3	2-1	3-2	4-0	1-1	2-1	3-1	3-5	3-4	0-0	2-0	3-2	1-4	1-1	—	2-0	5-2	1-2	1-2
Wingate & Finchley	2-1	1-2	1-1	4-1	0-1	0-9	4-2	3-1	0-0	2-1	1-1	2-5	0-3	1-2	1-1	2-1	1-1	2-0	—	5-2	0-1	3-1
Witham Town	2-1	0-4	0-5	2-1	2-7	0-4	1-3	1-0	2-2	0-0	2-1	0-6	1-0	0-2	1-3	1-3	2-2	2-2	4-2	—	0-1	1-1
Wivenhoe Town	1-1	0-3	1-0	3-0	1-0	1-1	0-1	1-0	2-0	0-0	0-2	1-1	4-2	2-0	2-2	0-1	2-1	2-1	2-0	2-1	—	5-2
Wokingham Town	0-5	0-2	3-1	2-0	2-3	3-1	0-3	1-2	1-0	1-1	0-1	2-6	0-5	0-0	1-3	4-2	2-1	0-3	4-0	2-2	2-1	—

RYMAN FOOTBALL LEAGUE—DIVISION THREE RESULTS 1999–2000

	Abingdon Town	Aveley	Bracknell Town	Camberley Town	Clapton	Corinthian Casuals	Croydon Athletic	Dorking	East Thurrock United	Egham Town	Epsom & Ewell	Flackwell Heath	Great Wakering Rovers	Hertford Town	Hornchurch	Kingsbury Town	Lewes	Southall	Tilbury	Tring Town	Ware
Abingdon Town	—	1-2	0-1	0-1	1-1	0-0	1-3	0-4	2-2	1-0	1-2	0-1	1-0	1-2	1-1	2-2	1-5	0-2	2-1	2-1	1-0
Aveley	1-2	—	1-1	6-1	4-0	0-3	1-1	2-0	0-1	2-2	0-1	2-1	2-1	2-2	4-1	5-1	0-1	3-0	4-3	0-0	3-3
Bracknell Town	1-1	3-3	—	3-1	5-1	1-1	2-0	1-1	0-2	5-2	1-3	3-1	2-3	1-2	2-1	3-3	2-1	1-1	1-0	2-2	1-0
Camberley Town	0-0	0-2	3-1	—	2-0	3-1	0-3	0-2	0-1	1-2	1-0	2-2	1-2	1-4	2-1	3-4	1-1	2-0	2-2	1-0	1-0
Clapton	1-2	1-2	0-6	3-2	—	3-1	2-4	1-0	0-1	1-1	1-2	3-3	0-4	0-1	0-0	3-1	0-2	4-0	1-2	1-0	0-3
Corinthian Casuals	1-1	5-1	2-2	0-1	3-0	—	3-1	0-0	0-2	2-1	0-3	1-4	0-0	4-2	3-1	1-3	4-1	3-1	0-3	1-2	2-1
Croydon Athletic	1-1	5-1	5-3	3-0	6-0	0-1	—	1-1	3-4	1-0	4-1	1-2	4-3	1-5	2-2	2-1	1-2	4-0	1-2	3-0	4-3
Dorking	1-0	1-2	4-4	5-1	1-2	0-0	1-1	—	2-2	2-0	2-1	1-1	0-1	2-1	0-0	0-1	4-0	4-0	0-1	5-0	1-2
East Thurrock United	2-1	4-1	1-1	3-1	3-2	2-0	3-2	5-0	—	2-0	0-4	3-0	2-1	0-1	3-0	6-2	1-0	6-0	3-0	2-2	3-1
Egham Town	0-5	2-4	1-1	3-1	3-0	3-1	1-0	3-1	0-0	—	1-0	3-0	1-2	2-2	0-1	2-0	1-0	1-1	0-1	0-0	0-0
Epsom & Ewell	1-1	0-0	1-1	2-1	2-2	1-1	0-3	3-2	2-1	1-0	—	2-1	3-1	1-1	0-1	2-1	3-3	4-0	6-1	3-3	3-0
Flackwell Heath	3-1	6-2	4-2	3-0	3-5	1-4	2-1	2-1	1-0	1-1	2-1	—	1-0	3-1	6-2	5-0	1-6	2-1	0-1	3-0	2-4
Great Wakering Rovers	3-3	2-0	2-2	1-0	5-0	2-2	1-1	3-1	0-3	0-1	3-1	1-0	—	3-1	4-1	4-0	2-1	5-0	1-1	3-1	2-1
Hertford Town	2-1	1-3	1-1	4-1	1-1	0-1	3-3	2-1	2-1	2-2	0-0	3-1	0-3	—	1-3	2-0	1-2	4-1	0-0	0-2	2-4
Hornchurch	2-1	2-0	2-3	2-2	3-3	3-1	1-1	3-2	2-1	0-1	3-0	3-2	1-0	1-3	—	4-0	3-2	3-0	0-0	4-1	3-1
Kingsbury Town	2-0	0-3	1-3	3-0	2-0	0-2	0-3	2-2	3-3	0-1	2-1	3-1	1-3	0-1	1-3	—	1-1	7-2	0-2	0-2	1-1
Lewes	4-1	1-0	4-1	1-1	2-1	1-1	0-2	1-1	5-2	1-1	0-2	2-1	1-3	3-1	1-1	4-0	—	2-0	0-0	1-0	0-1
Southall	2-3	2-3	1-5	1-2	4-5	0-3	1-1	3-1	0-3	1-1	0-3	1-3	1-1	1-4	1-1	0-3	1-6	—	1-4	0-1	0-3
Tilbury	4-2	0-0	1-0	3-0	2-1	0-1	2-1	5-0	1-1	2-0	1-1	2-1	0-1	2-2	1-3	2-0	2-0	5-0	—	2-0	2-3
Tring Town	1-1	2-1	1-0	1-3	1-0	2-2	0-1	2-0	0-3	0-4	0-1	2-2	1-0	1-0	1-1	0-2	2-3	2-3	1-1	—	3-1
Ware	1-3	1-1	1-2	3-1	3-1	3-1	1-1	3-0	1-2	1-1	2-0	5-1	1-3	0-2	0-0	5-2	3-1	3-0	1-1	2-0	—

RYMAN LEAGUE CUP 1999–2000

Preliminary Round

Aveley	0-1	Wingate & Finchley
Banstead Athletic	3-4	Ford United
Bracknell Town	2-1	Berkhamsted Town
Camberley Town	1-0	East Thurrock United
Cheshunt	3-2	Harlow Town
Clapton	0-4	Epsom & Ewell
Dorking	4-7	Windsor & Eton *(aet)*
Edgware Town	0-2	Tring Town
Flackwell Heath	1-0	Egham Town
Hemel Hempstead T	3-0	Barking
Hertford Town	1-0	Corinthian Casuals
Hungerford Town	5-3	Ware
Kingsbury Town	1-3	Leighton Town
Marlow	5-4	Hornchurch *(aet)*
Metropolitan Police	1-2	Abingdon Town *(aet)*
Molesey	1-2	Bedford Town
Northwood	0-0	Tilbury
Tilbury	*0-5*	*Northwood*
Southall	1-1	Chalfont St P *(aet)*
Chalfont St Peter	*3-3*	*Southall AET*
Southall won 4-2 on pens		
Thame United	3-1	Croydon Ath *(aet)*
Tooting & Mitcham Utd	1-3	Wembley
Witham Town	2-4	Lewes *(aet)*
Wivenhoe Town	5-2	Horsham
Wokingham Town	2-4	Great Wak R *(aet)*

First Round

Abingdon Town	2-1	Cheshunt
Basingstoke Town	3-1	Walton & Hersham
Bedford Town	0-2	Oxford City
Billericay Town	3-2	Wembley
Boreham Wood	0-2	Bishop's Stortford
Bracknell T	0-1	Gt Wakering Rovers
Braintree Town	3-1	Aylesbury United
Bromley	1-2	Maidenhead United
Camberley T	0-1	Lewes
Canvey Island	1-3	Romford
Carshalton Athletic	0-0	Bognor Regis Town
Bognor Regis Town	*0-2*	*Carshalton Athletic*
Chertsey Town	5-3	Southall *(aet)*
Croydon	5-0	Dagenham & Red
Dulwich Hamlet	6-2	Wivenhoe Town
Enfield	1-2	Barton Rovers *(aet)*
Epsom & Ewell	1-1	Staines Town *(aet)*
Staines Town	*3-0*	*Epsom & Ewell*
Farnborough Town	2-0	Yeading
Ford United	2-1	Flackwell Heath
Gravesend & Northfleet	1-2	Hendon
Hampton & Rich Boro	0-2	St Albans City
Hemel Hempstead T	1-3	Aldershot Town *(aet)*
Hertford Town	3-4	Wealdstone
Heybridge Swifts	5-1	Harrow Borough
Hungerford Town	1-2	Tring Town
Leyton Pennant	2-0	Thame United
Marlow	1-0	Leatherhead
Northwood	3-3	Chesham Utd *(aet)*
Chesham United	*2-1*	*Northwood AET*
Purfleet	2-0	Leighton Town

Slough Town	1-0	Grays Athletic
Uxbridge	1-2	Hitchin Town
Windsor & Eton	2-1	Worthing
Wingate & Finchley	0-5	Whyteleafe

Second Round

Abingdon Town	0-3	Aldershot Town
Barton Rovers	3-1	Hendon
Bishop's Stortford	2-2	Tring Town
Tring	1-2	Bishop's Stort(*(aet)*)
Dulwich Hamlet	1-2	Croydon
Ford United	0-5	Chesham Utd
Heybridge Swifts	2-1	Windsor & Eton
Hitchin Town	3-3	Farnborough Town*
Lewes	1-3	Billericay Town
Maidenhead United	2-1	Basingstoke Town
Oxford City	5-1	Marlow
Purfleet	2-1	Chertsey Town
Romford	0-0	Braintree Town
Braintree Town	1-1	Romford
Braintree won 5-4 on pens		
St Albans City	4-2	Great Wakering R
Slough Town	0-1	Carshalton Ath
Wealdstone	1-0	Leyton Pennant
Whyteleafe	3-2	Staines Town(*(aet)*)
* Hitchin Town removed from the competition		

Third round

Aldershot Town	1-2	Farnborough Town *(aet)*
Barton Rovers	5-0	Carshalton Athletic
Billericay Town	1-2	St Albans City *(aet)*
Chesham United	1-0	Purfleet
Croydon	0-2	Bishops Stortford
Heybridge Swifts	3-1	Braintree Town
Wealdstone	0-1	Oxford City
Whyteleafe	1-2	Maidenhead United

Fourth round

Chesham United	0-2	Billericay Town*
Farnborough Town	2-7	Heybridge Swifts
Maidenhead Utd	2-1	Bishop's Stortford
Oxford City	0-0	Barton Rovers *(aet)*
Barton Rovers	1-1	Oxford City *(aet)*
Barton won 2-1 on pens		
*St Albans City removed from the competition		

Semi Finals First Leg

Barton Rovers	1-1	Farnborough Town*
Billericay Town	1-1	Maidenhead United
*Heybridge Swifts removed from the competition		

Semi Finals Second Leg

Farnborough Town	2-0	Barton Rovers
Maidenhead United	0-0	Billericay Town
Maidenhead won 4-3 on pens		

FINAL

Farnborough Town	1-0	Maidenhead Utd
(aet)		

FULL MEMBERS CUP

Barton Rovers	0-3	Grays Athletic
Billericay Town	0-2	Bedford Town
Bromley	3-1	Aldershot Town
Croydon	1-1	Bognor Regis Town
(aet – Croydon won 3-2 on pens)		
Dulwich Hamlet	0-3	Farnborough Town
Hampton & Richmond	2-4	Worthing
Harrow Borough	3-3	Chertsey Town
(aet – Chertsey won 3-2 on pens)		
Hendon	2-2	Wealdstone
(aet – Wealdstone won 7-6 on pens)		
Maidenhead United	2-0	Walton & Hersham
Purfleet	5-0	Bishop's Stortford
St Albans City	2-1	Chesham United
Slough Town	4-1	Staines Town

Second Round

Aylesbury United	1-2	Oxford City AET
Basingstoke Town	2-0	Maidenhead United
Braintree Town	2-5	Gravesend & Northfleet
Bromley	1-0	Worthing
Croydon	3-0	Farnborough Town
Dagenham & Red	2-0	Romford
Harlow Town	1-5	Grays Athletic
Heybridge Swifts	2-4	Purfleet
Hitchin Town	2-1	Enfield
Leatherhead	4-1	Whyteleafe
Leyton Pennant	2-1	Canvey Island
Slough Town	2-1	Carshalton Athletic
St Albans City	2-2	Bedford Town
Bedford won 4-3 on pens		

Thame United	1-0	Uxbridge
Wealdstone	3-0	Boreham Wood
Yeading	3-2	Chertsey Town

Third Round

Bromley	1-0	Basingstoke Town
Croydon	1-0	Oxford City
Gravesend & Northfleet	3-1	Wealdstone
Grays Athletic	3-4	Purfleet AET
Hitchin Town	3-2	Bedford Town
Leatherhead	0-3	Slough Town
Leyton Pennant	1-5	Dagenham & Redbridge
Yeading	2-1	Thame United

Fourth Round

Croydon	2-1	Bromley
Gravesend & N	3-2	Slough Town
Hitchin Town	1-3	Yeading
Purfleet	5-2	Dagenham & Redbridge

Semi-Finals

| Gravesend & Nth | 1-2 | Croydon |
| Yeading | 2-3 | Purfleet |

FINAL

| Croydon | 2-0 | Purfleet |

VANDANEL TROPHY

First Round

Cheshunt	1-2	Ware
Clapton	0-1	Hertford Town (aet)
Flackwell Heath	1-1	Chalfont St Peter
(aet – Chalfont won 4-3 on pens)		
Great Wakering Rovers	1-1	Aveley
(aet – Aveley won 3-1 on pens)		
Horsham	2-6	Epsom & Ewell
Hungerford Town	2-2	Abingdon Town
(aet – Hungerford won 4-2 on pens)		
Leighton Town	0-1	Northwood
Marlow	2-0	Metropolitan Police
Molesey	1-2	Camberley Town
Wembley	1-2	Wivenhoe Town(aet)
Windsor & Eton	3-1	Dorking

Second Round

Aveley	1-2	Wivenhoe
Banstead Athletic	4-0	Wokingham Town
Berkhamsted Town	2-0	Witham Town
Bracknell Town	5-1	Egham Town
Chalfont St Peter	2-1	Hungerford Town
Corinthian Casuals	1-2	Windsor
Croydon Athletic	0-2	Marlow
East Thurrock United	1-1	Hornchurch
East Thurrock won 4-2 on pens		
Hertford	2-1	Edgware Town
Lewes	2-4	Camberley Town
Northwood	4-1	Hemel Hempstead
Tilbury	0-2	Barking

Tooting & Mitcham	4-1	Epsom & Ewell
Tring Town	0-1	Southall
Ware	5-1	Kingsbury Town
Wingate & Finchley	4-2	Ford United

Third Round

Berkhamsted Town	3-0	Wingate & Finchley
Camberley Town	1-3	Windsor & Eton AET
Chalfont St Peter	1-2	Banstead Athletic
East Thurrock United	1-5	Barking
Marlow	1-0	Bracknell Town
Tooting & Mitcham Utd	4-1	Southall
Ware	2-3	Northwood
Wivenhoe Town	3-0	Hertford Town

Fourth Round

Banstead Athletic	1-1	Marlow AET
Marlow won 6-5 on pens		
Berkhamsted Town	1-1	Barking AET
Barking won 3-1 on pens		
Northwood	2-1	Wivenhoe Town AET
Tooting & Mitcham Utd	3-4	Windsor & Eton AET

Semi-Finals

| Barking | 3-1 | Windsor & Eton |
| Northwood | 3-0 | Marlow |

FINAL

| Barking | 1-2 | Northwood |

CUP ATTENDANCES

Ryman League Cup	14,381
Full Members Cup	6,381
Vandanel Trophy	3,314

AWARDS

Spall Sports Manager of the Season Awards

Premier Division	Garry Hill	Dagenham & Redbridge
Division One	Ken Jarvie	Croydon
Division Two	Neil Price	Hemel Hempstead Town
Division Three	Lee Patterson	East Thurrock United

FA UMBRO TROPHY 1999–2000

FIRST ROUND

Bromsgrove Rovers v Halesowen Town	2-5
Guiseley v Flixton	2-0
Leigh RMI v Boston United	1-0
Gresley Rovers v Redditch United	0-1
Solihull Borough v Runcorn	1-2
Atherstone United v Ossett Town	0-3
Lincoln United v Hucknall Town	2-3
Blyth Spartans v Stourbridge	3-0
Burscough v Ilkeston Town	2-6
Hinckley United v Congleton Town	5-1
Grantham Town v Matlock Town	1-3
Corby Town v Belper Town	2-1
Barrow v Netherfield Kendal	4-0
Frickley Athletic v Ashton United	1-1, 4-2
Emley v Colwyn Bay	2-0
Rocester v Farsley Celtic	1-1, 2-0
Chorley v Moor Green	0-1
Spalding United v Shepshed Dynamo	2-1
Paget Rangers v Spennymoor United	0-1
Burton Albion v Trafford	1-1, 3-1
Leek Town v Accrington Stanley	2-2, 4-5
Gateshead v Bradford (Park Avenue)	4-1
Romford v Bashley	1-1, 1-2
Bishop's Stortford v Gravesend & Northfleet	1-3
Salisbury City v Tonbridge Angels	2-0
Racing Club Warwick v Harlow Town	1-3
Hitchin Town v Harrow Borough	1-1, 1-2
Purfleet v Dagenham & Redbridge	2-0
Basingstoke Town v Bognor Regis Town	1-1, 0-2
Sittingbourne v Chelmsford City	1-3
Gloucester City v Chesham United	4-2
Bath City v Baldock Town	1-3
Raunds Town v Maidenhead United	0-0, 1-0
Heybridge Swifts v Weston-Super-Mare	2-0
Cinderford Town v Merthyr Tydfil	1-2
Cirencester Town v Cambridge City	3-2
Braintree Town v Clevedon Town	3-2
Newport County v Yeading	2-1
Rothwell Town v Boreham Wood	0-0, 5-3
Fisher Athletic v Burnham	1-3
Worthing v Fleet Town	5-1
Leatherhead v Kings Lynn	2-0
Chertsey Town v Hampton & Richmond Borough	1-2
Slough Town v Hendon	0-2
St Albans City v Thame United	1-2
Havant & Waterlooville v Aylesbury United	0-0, 4-2
Croydon v Margate	0-0, 0-5
Oxford City v Hastings Town	2-0
Tiverton Town v Dorchester Town	1-1, 1-1

Tiverton Town won 5-3 on penalties.

SECOND ROUND

Barrow v Southport	2-3
Stocksbridge Park Steels v Redditch United	1-1, 4-3
Rocester v Tamworth	1-2
Leigh RMI v Worksop Town	1-1, 1-3
Accrington Stanley v Spalding United	2-2, 0-1
Morecambe v Hucknall Town	6-1
Wisbech Town v Bishop Auckland	1-2
Kidderminster Harriers v Telford United	2-4
Hyde United v Whitley Bay	6-0
Stafford Rangers v Emley	1-4
Ilkeston Town v Scarborough	2-4
Blakenall v Eastwood Town	3-1
Runcorn v Northwich Victoria	2-0
Spennymoor United v Gretna	2-1
Bedworth United v Hednesford Town	0-2
Matlock Town v Harrogate Town	1-1, 0-1
Hinckley United v Marine	1-1, 0-1
Halesowen Town v Sutton Coldfield Town	3-1
Frickley Athletic v Droylsden	4-3
Ossett Town v Doncaster Rovers	0-1
Stalybridge Celtic v Gainsborough Trinity	1-1, 3-1
Bilston Town v Workington	2-2, 2-3
Winsford United v VS Rugby	1-1, 0-2
Lancaster City v Corby Town	3-0
Radcliffe Borough v Moor Green	1-6
Guiseley v Nuneaton Borough	2-0
Bamber Bridge v Burton Albion	0-2
Whitby Town v Stamford	4-1

Blyth Spartans v Witton Albion	2-0
Altrincham v Gateshead	1-0
Rothwell Town v Evesham United	4-1
Hereford United v Barton Rovers	1-0
Heybridge Swifts v Witney Town	3-2
Enfield v Newport (IW)	2-2, 0-1
Hayes v Worcester City	0-2
Rushden & Diamonds v Havant & Waterlooville	1-0
Purfleet v Raunds Town	5-0
Harlow Town v Dover Athletic	2-3
Bromley v Chelmsford City	2-0
Cirencester Town v Forest Green Rovers	0-3
Folkestone Invicta v Kingstonian	0-1
Leatherhead v Bedford Town	0-0, 0-2
Bath City v Erith & Belvedere	5-0
Hendon v Grays Athletic	1-0
Weymouth v Yeovil Town	0-0, 1-2
Merthyr Tydfil v Stevenage Borough	0-0, 0-4
Yate Town v Billericay Town	0-2
Dulwich Hamlet v Burnham	1-1, 0-1
Bashley v Newport County	1-2
Ashford Town v Woking	0-5
Harrow Borough v Oxford City	0-0, 2-3
Tiverton Town v Farnborough Town	0-4
Hampton & Richmond Borough v Carshalton Athletic	1-2
Bognor Regis Town v Walton & Hersham	1-2
Crawley Town v Wealdstone	0-2
Uxbridge v Canvey Island	0-2
Welling United v Gloucester City	2-1
Gravesend & Northfleet v Worthing	2-0
Whyteleafe v St Leonards	4-2
Leyton Pennant v Staines Town	0-3
Margate v Dartford	0-0, 2-2

Dartford won 4-2 on penalties.

Kettering Town v Thame United	2-2, 1-0
Aldershot Town v Braintree Town	3-1
Salisbury City v Sutton United	2-5

THIRD ROUND

VS Rugby v Moor Green	1-4
Emley v Frickley Athletic	2-1
Blakenall v Morecambe	2-1
Tamworth v Runcorn	0-1
Stalybridge Celtic v Blyth Spartans	1-0
Doncaster Rovers v Halesowen Town	1-1, 3-2
Stocksbridge Park Steels v Scarborough	0-0, 0-5
Worksop Town v Lancaster City	1-1, 3-0
Workington v Burton Albion	1-1, 0-0

Workington won 4-2 on penalties.

Spennymoor United v Harrogate Town	1-1, 2-3

Match ordered to be replayed; Harrogate Town produced incorrect team sheet.

	2-0
Whitby Town v Telford United	1-3
Marine v Guiseley	2-1
Southport v Altrincham	0-0, 1-1

Southport won 4-3 on penalties.

Spalding United v Bishop Auckland	2-2, 0-2
Hednesford Town v Hyde United	1-1, 0-2
Sutton United v Canvey Island	1-0
Rothwell Town v Walton & Hersham	1-1, 0-1
Purfleet v Newport (IW)	1-1, 1-2
Forest Green Rovers v Hendon	4-1
Gravesend & Northfleet v Dover Athletic	1-1, 1-2
Oxford City v Burnham	1-5
Billericay Town v Hereford United	3-1
Aldershot Town v Staines Town	4-1
Wealdstone v Kingstonian	0-5
Carshalton Athletic v Farnborough Town	0-1
Kettering Town v Welling United	2-0
Bath City v Rushden & Diamonds	1-2
Worcester City v Bromley	2-1
Woking v Whyteleafe	4-2
Yeovil Town v Stevenage Borough	2-1
Dartford v Heybridge Swifts	1-2
Bedford Town v Newport County	0-0, 1-0

FOURTH ROUND

Heybridge Swifts v Newport (IW)	1-0
Bedford Town v Yeovil Town	0-4

Hyde United v Runcorn	0-0, 2-3
Spennymoor United v Bishop Auckland	0-3
Kingstonian v Moor Green	2-1
Kettering Town v Walton & Hersham	2-2, 2-0
Billericay Town v Rushden & Diamonds	0-0, 1-2
Burnham v Scarborough	1-1, 0-6
Woking v Aldershot Town	0-0, 1-0
Telford United v Farnborough Town	2-1
Blakenall v Marine	0-1
Sutton United v Forest Green Rovers	3-0
Southport v Emley	2-0
Worksop Town v Workington	1-1, 0-1
Dover Athletic v Doncaster Rovers	1-0
Stalybridge Celtic v Worcester City	0-1

FIFTH ROUND

Workington v Kettering Town	0-1
Southport v Woking	3-0
Yeovil Town v Kingstonian	0-1
Bishop Auckland v Scarborough	2-1
Rushden & Diamonds v Marine	1-0
Sutton United v Dover Athletic	2-1
Runcorn v Heybridge Swifts	2-1
Telford United v Worcester City	4-1

SIXTH ROUND

Kingstonian v Southport	0-0, 1-0
Sutton United v Rushden & Diamonds	1-1, 3-1
Kettering Town v Bishop Auckland	2-2, 2-0
Telford United v Runcorn	2-0

SEMI-FINALS (two legs)

Sutton United v Kingstonian	1-1, 0-6
Kettering Town v Telford United	1-0, 0-0

FINAL (at Wembley)

13 MAY

Kettering Town (0) 2 *(Vowden 55, Norman 64 (pen))*
Kingstonian (1) 3 *(Akuamoah 40, 69, Simba 75)*　20,034

Kettering Town: Solitt; Shutt, Setchell (Hopkins 80), Perkins, Vowden, Norman (Diuk 73), Brown, Fisher, McNamara, Watkins (Hudson 46), Adams.
Kingstonian: Farrelly; Mustafa, Luckett, Stewart (Saunders 75), Crossley, Harris, Pitcher, Kadi (Leworthy 82), Akuamoah, Simba, Green (Basford 85).
Referee: S. Dunn (Gloucester).

Ronnie Green of Kingstonian (left) in action against Colin Vowden (Kettering Town) in the Umbro Trophy Final at Wembley. (Actionimages)

FA CARLSBERG VASE 1999–2000

FIRST QUALIFYING ROUND

Chadderton v Fleetwood Freeport	0-4
Squires Gate v Sheffield	2-1
Bridlington Town v Newcastle Blue Star	2-1
Atherton Collieries v Shildon	3-1
Nelson v Skelmersdale United	0-6
Woodleigh Sports v Billingham Synthonia	0-3
Evenwood Town v Poulton Victoria	2-1
Eccleshill United v Blackpool Mechanics	10-1
Hallam v Thackley	1-3
Easington Colliery v Brandon United	0-3
Louth United v Salford City	3-2
Worsbro Bridge MW v Shotton Comrades	1-2
Denaby United v Bacup Borough	1-0
Rossington Main v Liversedge	1-3
Knypersley Victoria v Boston Town	3-0
Bridgnorth Town v Alvechurch	2-1
Stafford Town v Birstall United	0-0, 0-1
Wednesfield v Stratford Town	1-2
Halesowen Harriers v Quorn	0-7
Holbeach United v Bourne Town	1-0
Barwell v Holwell Sports	1-3
Blackstone v Stewarts & Lloyds	5-4
Shifnal Town v Kings Heath	3-1
Highfield Rangers v Cradley Town	2-3
Long Eaton United v Southam United	6-2
Kingsbury Town v Letchworth	0-1
Chalfont St Peter v Brache Sparta	3-1
Harpenden Town v Cornard United	0-2
Saffron Walden Town v Downham Town	1-3
Cockfosters v Dareham Town	1-0
March Town United v Norwich United	2-0
Lowestoft Town v Haverhill Rovers	5-0
Marlow v Brightlingsea United	6-0
Cheshunt v Brimsdown Rovers	3-0
Mildenhall Town v Brentwood	3-1
Harwich & Parkeston v Wallingford	2-4
Hullbridge Sports v Witham Town	3-0
St Margaretsbury v Royston Town	4-2
Buckingham Town v Gorleston	0-2
Leverstock Green v Hadleigh United	2-1
Portsmouth Royal Navy v Faversham Town	2-4
Moneyfields v Godalming & Guildford	7-2
Beckenham Town v Chatham Town	0-1
Gosport Borough v AFC Totton	0-4
Arundel v Eastbourne Town	1-2
Langney Sports v Redhill	1-2
Hillingdon Borough v Raynes Park Vale	4-1
Fareham Town v Peacehaven & Telscombe	7-0
VCD Athletic v Lewes	3-2
Whitehawk v Cove	1-0
Sandhurst Town v Abingdon United	0-1
BAT Sports v Eastbourne United	2-0
Wick v Ashford Town (Middlesex)	2-0
Wimborne Town v Warminster Town	7-0
Minehead Town v Tuffley Rovers	1-2
Almondsbury Town w.o. v Newquay withdrew	
Bodmin Town v Keynsham Town	2-1
Chard Town v Street	2-1
Bideford v Downton	3-2
Cirencester Academy v Devizes Town	0-1
Elmore v Shortwood United	1-0
Ilfracombe Town v Melksham Town	2-1

SECOND QUALIFYING ROUND

Crook Town v Bootle	5-0
Selby Town v St Helens Town	4-1
Shotton Comrades v Skelmersdale United	0-2
Peterlee Newtown v Darwen	1-1, 4-2
Thackley v Hebburn	3-0
Abbey Hey v Pontefract Collieries	1-0
Harrogate Railway v Marske United	1-6
Liversedge v Armthorpe Welfare	0-1
Thornaby-on-Tees v Holker Old Boys	3-0
Evenwood Town v Parkgate	1-4
Rossendale United v Curzon Ashton	2-3
Eccleshill United v Prudhoe Town	4-2
Washington Ikeda Hoover v Ramsbottom United	0-7
Prescot Cables v West Auckland Town	2-3
Penrith v Consett	3-4
Pickering Town v Fleetwood Freeport	3-1

Louth United v Hall Road Rangers	1-1, 3-6
Kennek Ryhope CA v East Manchester	3-1
Glasshoughton Welfare v Ashington	2-1
Brandon United v Denaby United	5-1
Horden CW v Billingham Synthonia	1-6
Morpeth Town v Jarrow Roofing Boldon CA	3-2
Oldham Town v Castleton Gabriels	0-3
Guisborough Town v Tadcaster Albion	2-0
Yorkshire Amateur v Squires Gate	1-1, 1-2
Durham City v Hatfield Main	7-1
Cheadle Town v Esh Winning	6-0
Northallerton Town v West Allotment Celtic	0-4
Bridlington Town v Brodsworth	3-1
Whickham v South Shields	2-1
Atherton LR v Atherton Collieries	1-3
Willington v Maine Road	3-0
Goole v Garforth Town	4-0
Holwell Sports v Nettleham	0-1
Rainworth MW v Barrow Town	2-3
Sandiacre Town v Nantwich Town	0-1
Sandwell Borough v Wolverhampton Casuals	2-1
Bridgnorth Town v West Midlands Police	0-2
Arnold Town v Kington Town	3-1
Ludlow Town v Cogenhoe United	0-5
Heanor Town v Dunkirk	1-0
Bugbrooke St Michaels v Cradley Town	1-0
St Andrews v Quorn	3-4
South Normanton Athletic v Gornal Athletic	1-2
Pelsall Villa v Cheslyn Hay	2-0
Star v Holbeach United	1-2
Shirebrook Town v Knypersley Victoria	0-2
Tividale v Anstey Nomads	4-5
Gedling Town v Downes Sports	6-4
Long Eaton United v Kimberley Town	3-0
Long Buckby v Chasetown	1-5
Stourport Swifts v Glapwell	1-0
Shifnal Town v Rushall Olympic	2-0
Northampton Spencer v Malvern Town	2-3
Blackstone v Glossop North End	0-2
Willenhall Town v Stapenhill	2-0
Ford Sports Daventry v Bolehall Swifts	1-3
Ibstock Welfare v Handrahan Timbers	1-1, 2-0
Stratford Town v Birstall United	5-1
Friar Lane OB v Walsall Wood	5-1
Mickleover Sports v Leek CSOB	4-3
Westfields v Kirby Muxloe	0-3
Wellingborough Town v Meir KA	0-4
Borrowash Victoria v Lye Town	3-1
Blidworth Welfare w.d. v Studley BKL w.o.	
Bury Town v Wivenhoe Town	1-0
Wootton Blue Cross v Gorleston	2-0
Leighton Town v Swaffham Town	5-1
Tring Town v March Town United	2-1
Stowmarket Town v Tiptree United	3-0
Ely City v Hullbridge Sports	3-0
Somersett Ambury V&E v Letchworth	3-4
Arlesey Town v Banbury United	2-4
Barking v Chalfont St Peter	3-3, 5-2
Beaconsfield SYCOB v Southall	3-0
Hoddesdon Town v Wingate & Finchley	1-4
Tilbury v St Neots Town	3-1
Kempston Rovers v Southend Manor	5-2
Felixstowe Port & Town v Warboys Town	0-3
Milton Keynes City v Downham Town	6-2
Newmarket Town v Harefield United	1-2
Leverstock Green v Flackwell Heath	1-4
Lowestoft Town v Ware	0-1
Welwyn Garden City v Somersham Town	2-3
Langford v Wallingford	1-1, 0-3
Sawbridgeworth Town v Marlow	1-2
Cockfosters v Watton United	2-3
Needham Market v Whitton United	1-3
Stanway Rovers v Haringey Borough	4-3
Halstead Town v Edgware Town	3-1
St Margaretsbury v Holmer Green	2-4
Ipswich Wanderers v London Colney	0-2
Chatteris Town v Hertford Town	0-4
Hornchurch v Burnham Ramblers	1-2
Soham Town Rangers v East Thurrock United	4-1
Concord Rangers v Ilford	1-5
Bedford United v Mildenhall Town	2-3
Brook House w.o. v Barkingside removed	

Clapton v Cheshunt	1-5
Yaxley v Eynesbury Rovers	3-1
Aveley v Potton United	7-0
Maldon Town v Bicester Town	5-1
Stotfold v Cornard United	3-1
Waltham Abbey v Ruislip Manor	4-1
Biggleswade Town v Stansted	4-2
Corinthian Casuals v Littlehampton Town	3-0
Kintbury Rangers removed v Oakwood w.o.	
Whitehawk v Didcot Town	1-1, 0-3
Thamesmead Town v Farnham Town	2-0
Erith Town v Three Bridges	3-1
BAT Sports v Hassocks	3-2
Sidley United v Eastleigh	0-2
Abingdon United v Chessington & Hook United	4-1
Hailsham Town v Viking Greenford	1-0
Ringmer v Hythe United	1-3
Walton Casuals v Selsey	1-0
Ash United v Shoreham	5-1
Fareham Town v East Cowes Victoria	1-0
Southwick v Lancing	2-1
Croydon Athletic v Romsey Town	4-0
Reading Town v Lordswood	5-0
Whitstable Town v Chatham Town	0-2
Faversham Town v Blackfield & Langley	3-2
Merstham v Egham Town	1-4
AFC North Leigh v Cobham	3-4
Totton v Horsham	3-1
Metropolitan Police v Sheppey United	3-3, 2-0
Dorking v Canterbury City	3-1
Tunbridge Wells v Epsom & Ewell	1-2
Wick v VCD Athletic	1-1, 1-2
Eastbourne Town v Slade Green	2-0
Cray Wanderers v Hillingdon Borough	1-2
Windsor & Eton v Redhill	3-0
Cowes Sports v Portfield	8-1
Brockenhurst v East Preston	2-4
Moneyfields v Bracknell Town	0-1
Bedfont v Wantage Town	4-0
Chichester City v Whitchurch United	2-0
Willand Rovers v Tuffley Rovers	1-0
Almondsbury Town v Dawlish Town	1-3
Bideford v Wellington Town	6-2
Ilfracombe Town v Fairford Town	3-2
Christchurch v Backwell United	3-1
Mangotsfield United v Barnstaple Town	2-1
Bishop Sutton v Torrington	2-0
Falmouth Town v Bodmin Town	2-0
Bridgwater Town v Welton Rovers	4-1
Bournemouth v Hallen	2-0
Odd Down v Ross Town	4-0
Chard Town v Devizes Town	0-3
Westbury United v St Blazey	1-1
St Blazey w.o., Westbury United unable to fulfil fixture.	
Glastonbury v Elmore	2-4
Harrow Hill v Wimborne Town	1-3
Brislington v Pershore Town	2-1
Paulton Rovers v Calne Town	2-0
Frome Town v Bridport	1-0
Newcastle Town v Dudley Town	4-0
Clacton Town v Basildon Town	2-1
Thetford Town v Hanwell Town	1-2

West Midlands Police v Cogenhoe United	3-2
Long Eaton United v Newcastle Town	0-5
Brigg Town v Barrow Town	5-2
Friar Lane OB v Anstey Nomads	0-0, 0-2
Borrowash Victoria v Boldmere St Michaels	4-1
Mickleover Sports v Bugbrooke St Michaels	8-1
Shifnal Town v Studley BKL	4-2
Quorn v Kirby Muxloe	1-1, 5-2
Arnold Town v Pelsall Villa	6-1
Knypersley Victoria v Gornal Athletic	2-1
Glossop North End v Bolehall Swifts	4-2
Stourport Swifts v Staveley MW	2-0
Willenhall Town v Gedling Town	1-2
Stratford Town v Holbeach United	4-1
Buxton v Desborough Town	1-2
Malvern Town v Ibstock Welfare	4-2
Nettleham v Heanor Town	0-1
Oldbury United v Kings Norton Town	3-2
Harefield United v Great Wakering Rovers	0-4
Hertford Town v Warboys Town	2-0
Beaconsfield SYCOB v Potters Bar Town	0-2
Witton United v Hemel Hempstead Town	0-3
Ware v Stotfold	2-3
Bury Town v Flackwell Heath	4-1
Banbury United v Ely City	2-1
Maldon Town v Burnham Ramblers	1-2
Marlow v Waltham Abbey	4-0
Fakenham Town v Kempston Rovers	6-1
Cheshunt v Leighton Town	2-1
Somersham Town v Great Yarmouth Town	1-2
Hanwell Town v Soham Town Rangers	1-2
Letchworth v Yaxley	2-1
Tring Town v Clacton Town	0-0, 1-1
Clacton Town won 4-1 on penalties.	
Mildenhall Town v Diss Town	0-2
Histon v Stowmarket Town	3-2
Milton Keynes City v Biggleswade Town	
(abandoned 78 minutes; waterlogged pitch)	2-0
Aveley v Ilford	0-2
Halstead Town v Tilbury	1-3
Wootton Blue Cross v London Colney	0-1
Wallingford v Barking	0-1
Holmer Green v Watton United	1-1, 1-3
Brook House v Wingate & Finchley	3-1
Stanway Rovers v Abingdon Town	3-1
Hythe United v Walton Casuals	1-0
Hillingdon Borough v East Preston	0-4
Bedfont v Southwick	2-0
Eastbourne Town v Reading Town	5-2
Chipstead v Greenwich Borough	5-2
Erith Town v Oakwood	5-0
Didcot Town v Hailsham Town	1-0
Wokingham Town v Metropolitan Police	2-5
Ash United v Epsom & Ewell	2-5
Corinthian Casuals v Dorking	3-0
Saltdean United v Chichester City	2-1
Horsham YMCA v Thatcham Town	5-3
Bracknell Town v Cowes Sports	1-4
AFC Totton v Egham Town	2-1
Chatham Town v Faversham Town	5-2
Windsor & Eton v Croydon Athletic	5-2
Fareham Town v Abingdon United	0-0
(abandoned 20 minutes; waterlogged pitch)	2-3
Thamesmead Town v VCD Athletic	3-0
Eastleigh v Deal Town	3-4
Cobham v BAT Sports	2-4
Christchurch v Bridgwater Town	1-0
Ilfracombe Town v Elmore	0-2
St Blazey v Swindon Super Marine	2-2, 2-3
Brislington v Bishop Sutton	3-1
Highworth Town v Carterton Town	2-3
Odd Down v Bideford	1-0
Devizes Town v Mangotsfield United	0-2
Frome Town v Paulton Rovers	1-2
Newbury v Hungerford Town	2-1
Dawlish Town v Bournemouth	1-0
Wimborne Town v Chippenham Town	1-3
Willand Rovers v Falmouth Town	0-3

FIRST ROUND

Hall Road Rangers v Armthorpe Welfare	3-2
Curzon Ashton v Warrington Town	3-3, 1-3
Bridlington Town v Eccleshill United	0-1
Abbey Hey v Parkgate	3-0
Morpeth Town v Durham City	4-1
Thornaby-on-Tees v North Ferriby United	2-3
West Allotment Celtic v Peterlee Newtown	1-2
Whickham v Pickering Town	0-1
Consett v Kennek Ryhope CA	1-0
Billingham Synthonia v Guisborough Town	0-3
Crook Town v Cheadle Town	3-1
Goole v Castleton Gabriels	1-0
Brandon United v Prescot Cables	0-1
Skelmersdale United v Glasshoughton Welfare	2-0
Atherton Collieries v Thackley	4-1
Marske United v Seaham Red Star	2-0
Chester-Le-Street Town v Billingham Town	1-3
Squires Gate v Ramsbottom United	3-3, 3-5
Willington v Selby Town	1-3
Nantwich Town v Meir KA	2-2, 4-2
Chasetown v Sandwell Borough	2-1

SECOND ROUND

Morpeth Town v Clitheroe	1-2
Great Harwood Town v Crook Town	0-4
Prescot Cables v Consett	2-3
Tow Law Town v Ramsbottom United	1-1, 2-1
Ossett Albion v Marske United	0-0, 2-1

Dunston FB v Warrington Town	1-2	Histon v Wembley	4-1
North Ferriby United v Pickering Town	3-0	AFC Totton v Barking	2-0
Mossley v Billingham Town	2-1	Berkhamsted Town v Stourport Swifts	2-0
Hall Road Rangers v Peterlee Newtown	1-0	Hemel Hempstead Town v Great Wakering Rovers	0-1
Vauxhall v Atherton Collieries	2-0	Fakenham Town v Saltdean United	2-3
Guisborough Town v Eccleshill United	3-4	Bideford v Woodbridge Town	1-2
Selby Town v Bedlington Terriers	1-1, 3-3	Letchworth v Stotfold	3-1
Bedlington Terriers won 3-0 on penalties.		Chippenham Town v Northwood	2-0
Abbey Hey v Skelmersdale United	1-2	Taunton Town v Tooting & Mitcham United	4-1
Shifnal Town v Stourport Swifts	2-3	Horsham YMCA v Diss Town	4-2
Gedling Town v Anstey Nomads	0-3	Marlow v Metropolitan Police	1-1, 0-1
West Midlands Police v Oldbury United	3-1	Lymington & New Milton v Ramsgate	1-2
Alfreton Town v Knypersley Victoria	4-0	Burgess Hill Town v Newbury	3-0
Arnold Town v Brigg Town	1-3	Paulton Rovers v Corinthian Casuals	2-0
Oadby Town v Chasetown	0-2	Tilbury v Falmouth Town	1-1, 0-0
Nantwich Town v Kidsgrove Athletic	4-0	*Tilbury won 2-0 on penalties.*	
Newcastle Town v Desborough Town	2-1	London Colney v Elmore	7-0
Malvern Town v Glossop North End	2-2, 0-3	Wroxham v BAT Sports	0-0, 1-1
Borrowash Victoria v Stratford Town	2-1	*Wroxham won 4-2 on penalties.*	
Heanor Town v Goole	2-0		
Mickleover Sports v Quorn	1-0	**FOURTH ROUND**	
London Colney v Potters Bar Town	4-0	Metropolitan Police v Burgess Hill Town	3-2
Watton United v Ilford	2-1	Crook Town v Deal Town	0-3
Sudbury v Northwood	3-4	Letchworth v Newcastle Town	0-2
Burnham Ramblers v Letchworth	0-0, 0-2	Cowes Sports v Tilbury	1-0
Great Wakering Rovers v Clacton Town	2-0	Bedlington Terriers v Histon	1-0
Banbury United v Histon	0-1	Great Wakering Rovers v Vauxhall	1-2
Brook House v Berkhamsted Town	4-4, 0-1	Woodbridge Town v Ossett Albion	3-0
Marlow v Hertford Town	4-1	Glossop North End v Chippenham Town	0-1
Stanway Rovers v Barking	3-3, 1-2	Consett v Alfreton Town	0-1
Wembley v Brackley Town	3-1	Wroxham v Paulton Rovers	3-2
Ford United v Hemel Hempstead Town	1-4	AFC Totton v Horsham YMCA	1-0
Bury Town v Tilbury	2-2, 2-4	Ramsgate v Berkhamsted Town	0-0, 0-0
Fakenham Town v Soham Town Rangers	2-1	*Ramsgate won 4-3 on penalties.*	
Bowers United v Wroxham	1-3	Mossley v Saltdean United	5-1
Great Yarmouth Town v Woodbridge Town	2-2, 0-2	Skelmersdale United v Taunton Town	2-3
Cheshunt v Stotfold	0-2	Chasetown v Porthleven	0-0, 2-1
Milton Keynes City v Diss Town	0-3	London Colney v Eccleshill United	3-4
Saltdean United v Windsor & Eton	3-1		
Deal Town v East Preston	3-0		
Chipstead v Metropolitan Police	1-2	**FIFTH ROUND**	
Banstead Athletic v Molesey	3-2	Bedlington Terriers v AFC Totton	5-0
Chatham Town v BAT Sports	2-3	Chasetown v Newcastle Town	0-0, 0-0
Burgess Hill Town v Camberley Town	3-1	*Newcastle Town won 3-1 on penalties.*	
Tooting & Mitcham United v Thamesmead Town	2-0	Ramsgate v Woodbridge Town	2-1
AFC Totton v Didcot Town	4-0	Mossley v Alfreton Town	1-0
Bedfont v Hythe United	2-1	Chippenham Town v Wroxham	3-1
Epsom & Ewell v Cowes Sports	1-1, 0-1	Cowes Sports v Taunton Town	0-7
Corinthian Casuals v Erith Town	3-1	Vauxhall v Eccleshill United	2-0
Ramsgate v Herne Bay	4-2	Metropolitan Police v Deal Town	2-5
Horsham YMCA v Eastbourne Town	4-3		
Newbury v Mangotsfield United	2-1		
Chippenham Town v Swindon Super Marine	3-0	**SIXTH ROUND**	
Abingdon United v Paulton Rovers	0-1	Chippenham Town v Bedlington Terriers	2-2, 0-1
Bideford v Dawlish Town	1-0	Ramsgate v Newcastle Town	0-1
Bemerton Heath Harlequins v Taunton Town	0-2	Deal Town v Mossley	3-1
Christchurch v Elmore	0-3	Taunton Town v Vauxhall	1-5
Falmouth Town v Brislington	7-2		
Carterton Town v Porthleven	0-4	**SEMI-FINALS (two legs)**	
Andover v Lymington & New Milton	1-2	Vauxhall v Chippenham Town	0-0, 0-1
		Newcastle Town v Deal Town	0-2, 1-1

THIRD ROUND

Glossop North End v Brigg Town	3-2
Skelmersdale United v Hall Road Rangers	3-2
Tow Law Town v Consett	0-0, 0-1
Mossley v Nantwich Town	5-1
Chasetown v Mickleover Sports	1-0
Vauxhall v Warrington Town	2-1
Bedlington Terriers v North Ferriby United	3-1
Ossett Albion v Anstey Nomads	5-1
Crook Town v West Midlands Police	3-1
Eccleshill United v Heanor Town	2-1
Newcastle Town v Clitheroe	2-1
Alfreton Town v Borrowash Victoria	2-1
Porthleven v Bedfont	1-0
Deal Town v Watton United	2-1
Cowes Sports v Banstead Athletic	3-1

FINAL (at Wembley)

6 MAY

Chippenham Town (0) 0
Deal Town (0) 1 *(Graham 87)*   20,083

Chippenham Town: Jones; James (Tiley 89), Andrews, Woods, Murphy, Burns, Collier, Charity, Godley (Cutler 69), Tweddle, Brown (Godwin 90).
Deal Town: Tucker; Ribbens, Monteith (Roberts 10), Ash (Warden 73), Martin, Best, Kempster, Seager, Lovell (Turner 58), Marshall, Graham.
Referee: D. Laws (Whitley Bay).

THE TIMES FA YOUTH CUP 1999–2000

FIRST QUALIFYING ROUND

Northwich Victoria v Morecambe	0-6
Rossington Main v Leigh RMI	0-2
Chadderton v Runcorn	0-4
Garforth Town v Crook Town	1-2
Harrogate Town v Congleton Town	5-0
Stalybridge Celtic v Gretna	0-5
Guiseley v Yorkshire Amateur	2-2, 3-1
Burscough v Farsley Celtic	3-2
Stocksbridge Park Steels w.o. v Nantwich Town withdrew	
Louth United v Brigg Town	0-2
Worksop Town v Lancaster City	3-1
Selby Town v Clitheroe	3-2
Altrincham v Scarborough	2-4
Blackpool Mechanics v Doncaster Rovers	0-2
Kettering Town v Ilkeston Town	3-5
Hednesford Town v Sutton Coldfield Town	3-1
Willenhall Town v Rushden & Diamonds	0-1
Bedworth United v Hinckley United	0-2
Corby Town v Malvern Town	0-3
Atherstone United v Bugbrooke St Michaels	1-2
Northampton Spencer v Kidderminster Harriers	0-1
Gornal Athletic v Leek Town	4-3
Stourbridge v Long Buckby	1-3
Holwell Sports v VS Rugby	2-1
Bridgnorth Town v Racing Club Warwick	1-2
Belper Town v Chasetown	2-2, 4-2
Matlock Town v Bilston Town	0-5
Nuneaton Borough v Lincoln United	0-2
Bromsgrove Rovers v Tamworth	4-1
Boldmere St Michaels v Newcastle Town	2-3
Walsall Wood v Cradleigh Town	5-3
Glossop North End v Coggenhoe United	3-2
Gresley Rovers v Birstall United	1-4
Wingate & Finchley v Aylesbury United	2-0
Chesham United v Burnham Ramblers	1-1, 3-2
Thetford Town v Harefield United	2-0
Brentwood v St Albans City	1-0
Soham Town Rangers v Ware	3-0
Wembley v Hemel Hempstead Town	3-1
Wisbech Town v Newmarket Town	6-2
Hullbridge Sports v Tring Town	2-1
Kempston Rovers v Marlow	3-1
Royston Town v Hornchurch	2-2, 0-3
Ipswich Wanderers v Bowers United	4-0
Brook House v Staines Town	2-0
(abandoned 57 minutes; fog)	
Bedford Town v Leyton	1-1, 4-4
Bedford Town won 5-4 on penalties.	
Uxbridge v Cheshunt	1-2
Concord Rangers v Ilford	2-2
Ilford won 5-4 on penalties.	
Hitchin Town v Welwyn Garden City	6-0
Clapton v Bishop's Stortford	3-0
Harlow Town v Cambridge City	1-2
Barkingside v Fakenham Town	2-0
Witham Town v Leighton Town	3-0
Waltham Abbey v East Thurrock United	1-3
Chelmsford City v Canvey Island	0-4
Histon w.o. v Barking withdrew	
Northwood v Great Wakering Rovers	2-3
Hendon v Hayes	3-3, 2-2
Hayes won 5-4 on penalties.	
Banbury United v Beaconsfield SYCOB	3-2
Sandhurst Town w.o. v Viking Greenford withdrew	
Aldershot Town v Erith Town	4-1
North Leigh v Dartford	3-1
Bracknell Town v Woking	2-4
Moneyfields v Lewisham	2-2, 1-2
Bedfont v Farnborough Town	4-1
Chatham Town v Oakwood	2-4
Lordswood v Molesey	3-2
Croydon v Maidenhead United	0-1
Newbury v Bromley	2-2, 1-5
Merstham v Thatcham Town	4-4, 1-3
Tooting & Mitcham United v Welling United	1-2
Margate v Abingdon Town	1-0
Thamesmead Town v Thame United	2-1
Oxford City v Leatherhead	2-0
Folkestone Invicta v Basingstoke Town	2-0
Eastbourne Town v Cobham	4-5
Herne Bay v Dover Athletic	0-3

Hillingdon Borough v Littlehampton Town	0-2
(abandoned 50 minutes; fog)	3-1
Whitstable Town v Three Bridges	3-2
Wokingham Town v Greenwich Borough	1-4
Saltdean United v Tonbridge Angels	2-4
Sittingbourne v Kingstonian	0-2
Camberley Town v Walton & Hersham	0-6
Gloucester City v Newport County	2-2
Gloucester City won 3-1 on penalties.	
Evesham United v Worcester City	0-7
Weston-Super-Mare v Hereford United	6-3
Weymouth v Forest Green Rovers	0-7
Street v Eastleigh	2-4
Warminster Town w.o.v Yate Town withdrew	
Pershore Town v Cinderford Town	9-4
Bashley v Chippenham Town	3-2
Paulton Rovers v Cirencester Town	0-6

SECOND QUALIFYING ROUND

Brigg Town v Runcorn	1-5
Gretna v Stocksbridge Park Steels	0-1
Emley v Worksop Town	7-3
Morecambe v Scarborough	1-2
Harrogate Town v Guiseley	1-3
Doncaster Rovers v Selby Town	6-1
Leigh RMI v Burscough	0-2
Ashton United w.o. v Flixton withdrew	
Frickley Athletic v Crook Town	1-6
Gornal Athletic v Malvern Town	4-2
Ilkeston Town v Racing Club Warwick	10-0
Stratford Town v Glossop North End	0-11
Holwell Sports v Kidderminster Harriers	0-3
Bilston Town v Lincoln United	0-3
Hinckley United v Redditch United	2-0
Belper Town v Bromsgrove Rovers	7-1
Bugbrooke St Michaels v Newcastle Town	1-3
Walsall Wood v Long Buckby	1-1, 1-2
Birstall United v Hednesford Town	1-0
Rushden & Diamonds v Burton Albion	2-3
Canvey Island v Somersett Ambury V&E	6-0
Ilford v Kempston Rovers	0-0, 6-3
Hornchurch v Hullbridge Sports	1-4
Cheshunt v Ruislip Manor	2-2, 5-2
Thetford Town v Wingate & Finchley	0-3
Stevenage Borough v Lowestoft Town	4-0
Hampton & Richmond Borough v Bedford Town	1-1, 0-5
Soham Town Rangers v Histon	0-4
Banbury United v Clapton	0-2
Hayes v Wisbech Town	5-0
Basildon United v Wembley	4-1
Great Wakering Rovers v Kingsbury Town	2-2, 3-1
Chesham United v Staines Town	0-6
Barkingside v Cambridge City	2-5
Braintree Town v Southend Manor	2-2, 1-5
Stowmarket Town v Ipswich Wanderers	0-2
East Thurrock United v Potters Bar Town	2-3
Witham Town v Hitchin Town	2-3
Brentwood v Maldon Town	2-0
Bromley v Peacehaven & Telscombe	6-1
Margate v Maidenhead United	1-3
Chipstead v Whyteleafe	4-2
Tonbridge Angels v Hillingdon Borough	6-0
North Leigh v Dover Athletic	2-3
Sandhurst Town v Whitstable Town	4-3
Oakwood v Woking	0-3
Greenwich Borough v Bedfont	5-3
Burgess Hill Town v Reading Town	2-3
Didcot Town v Folkestone Invicta	1-4
Thamesmead Town v Cobham	4-2
Kingstonian v Welling United	5-2
Banstead Athletic v Oxford City	5-2
Carshalton Athletic v Lordswood	4-4, 1-1
Lordswood won 5-4 on penalties.	
Thatcham Town v Sutton United	2-3
Abingdon United v Aldershot Town	0-5
Dorking v Hailsham Town	0-5
Lewisham v Walton & Hersham	2-2, 0-1
Salisbury City v Yeovil Town	1-2
Weston-Super-Mare v Brislington	1-2
Worcester City v Gloucester City	11-2
Pershore Town v Eastleigh	1-5

Cirencester Town v Bashley	4-1
Warminster Town v Forest Green Rovers	3-3, 0-4
Mangotsfield United v Bath City	0-4

THIRD QUALIFYING ROUND

Doncaster Rovers v Emley	3-2
Scarborough v Burscough	2-2, 2-3
Stocksbridge Park Steels v Ashton United	4-0
Crook Town v Guiseley	0-0, 1-0
Newcastle Town v Long Buckby	4-0
Runcorn v Lincoln United	0-0, 1-3
Kidderminster Harriers v Burton Albion	2-0
Birstall United v Ilkeston Town	0-3
Belper Town v Gornal Athletic	1-0
Hinckley United v Glossop North End	4-1
Cheshunt v Canvey Island	2-0
Staines Town v Ilford	4-2
Bedford Town v Ipswich Wanderers	1-3
Hayes v Histon	0-1
Hullbridge Sports v Brentwood	2-1
Hitchin Town v Basildon United	3-1
Stevenage Borough v Great Wakering Rovers	3-0
Southend Manor v Wingate & Finchley	1-0
Cambridge City v Clapton	1-0
Tonbridge Angels v Bromley	9-2
Banstead Athletic v Maidenhead United	0-3
Woking v Hailsham Town	2-2, 3-3
Hailsham Town won 6-5 on penalties.	
Folkestone Invicta v Greenwich Borough	3-1
Chipstead v Potters Bar Town	5-0
Walton & Hersham v Thamesmead Town	4-1
Sandhurst Town v Welling United	0-4
Sutton United v Dover Athletic	9-0
Lordswood v Burgess Hill Town	4-0
Eastleigh v Yeovil Town	0-1
Brislington v Cirencester Town	0-3
Aldershot Town v Forest Green Rovers	2-4
Bath City v Worcester City	5-2

FIRST ROUND

Carlisle United v York City	0-2
Mansfield Town v Burnley	1-1, 3-1
Chesterfield v Rochdale	2-2, 3-0
Hartlepool United v Preston North End	1-1, 1-3
Blackpool v Stocksbridge Park Steels	2-0
Shrewsbury Town v Hull City	1-1, 1-6
Scunthorpe United v Bury	3-1
Stoke City v Notts County	0-0, 3-4
Burscough v Rotherham United	1-3
Darlington v Crook Town	1-1, 3-0
Halifax Town v Chester City	1-3
Oldham Athletic v Wrexham	2-5
Lincoln United v Lincoln City	1-1, 4-1
Wigan Athletic v Doncaster Rovers	0-2
Hitchin Town v Ipswich Wanderers	4-3
Barnet v Staines Town	3-0
Southend Manor v Newcastle Town	0-1
Belper Town v Cambridge United	1-7
Reading v Histon	2-1
Hinckley United v Colchester United	0-2
Hullbridge Sports v Cheshunt	2-2, 3-2
Northampton Town v Stevenage Borough	0-2
Kidderminster Harriers v Cambridge City	2-4
Ilkeston Town v Peterborough United	1-1, 1-3
Chipstead v Welling United	1-3
Maidenhead United v Romford	2-1
Wycombe Wanderers v Tonbridge Angels	2-2, 3-0
Bath City v Brentford	0-6
Luton Town v Sutton United	2-0
Bristol Rovers v Gillingham	3-3, 1-1
Gillingham won 6-5 on penalties.	
Southend United v Exeter City	1-1, 1-0
Plymouth Argyle v Bournemouth	2-2, 2-1
Brighton & Hove Albion v Yeovil Town	5-0
Lordswood v Folkestone Invicta	0-2
Hailsham Town v Cirencester Town	1-3
Cheltenham Town v Swansea City	3-1
Leyton Orient v Walton & Hersham	7-1
Torquay United v Cardiff City	0-3
Bristol City v Forest Green Rovers	4-0
Oxford United v Millwall	1-3

SECOND ROUND

Chesterfield v Lincoln United	2-1
Hull City v Darlington	1-0
Preston North End v Rotherham United	1-1, 4-1
Blackpool v Notts County	0-2
Chester City v Doncaster Rovers	2-1
Mansfield Town v Wrexham	5-1
Scunthorpe United v York City	0-0, 3-1
Cambridge City v Brentford	1-1, 0-2
Stevenage Borough v Hullbridge Sports	1-1, 0-2
Newcastle Town v Hitchin Town	2-3
Wycombe Wanderers v Southend United	2-2, 2-2
Wycombe Wanderers won 6-4 on penalties.	
Luton Town v Maidenhead United	5-0
Cambridge United v Colchester United	1-2
Barnet v Cardiff City	1-1, 1-0
Peterborough United v Welling United	2-2, 1-3
Leyton Orient v Gillingham	5-0
Cirencester Town v Reading	1-1, 0-4
Millwall v Folkestone Invicta	6-0
Plymouth Argyle v Bristol City	1-2
Cheltenham Town v Brighton & Hove Albion	1-1, 0-2

THIRD ROUND

Tottenham Hotspur v Swindon Town	3-0
Hitchin Town v Leicester City	1-6
West Bromwich Albion v Liverpool	0-1
Notts County v Bradford City	1-3
Welling United v Luton Town	1-3
Brentford v Brighton & Hove Albion	0-2
Reading v Southampton	1-2
Colchester United v Walsall	3-2
Stockport County v Sunderland	2-3
Norwich City v Everton	0-1
Chesterfield v Coventry City	0-3
Manchester United v Nottingham Forest	1-2
Scunthorpe United v Preston North End	0-0, 1-1
Preston NE won 4-3 on penalties.	
Crystal Palace v Barnet	3-2
Manchester City v Bristol City	2-1
Derby County v Wolverhampton Wanderers	0-0, 2-1
West Ham United v Charlton Athletic	4-1
Barnsley v Mansfield Town	2-2, 1-2
Chelsea v Crewe Alexandra	1-2
Wimbledon v Sheffield Wednesday	0-0, 1-0
Huddersfield Town v Hull City	0-0, 2-1
Tranmere Rovers v Portsmouth	0-0, 1-2
Fulham v Aston Villa	1-4
Newcastle United v Millwall	2-0
Bolton Wanderers v Port Vale	1-0
Leyton Orient v Chester City	2-0
Grimsby Town v Middlesbrough	1-1, 1-3
Sheffield United v Arsenal	0-2
Ipswich Town v Leeds United	0-1
Queens Park Rangers v Watford	1-1, 1-2
Hullbridge Sports v Blackburn Rovers	0-6
Birmingham City v Wycombe Wanderers	0-1

FOURTH ROUND

Bolton Wanderers v Leicester City	2-1
Arsenal v Watford	3-1
Middlesbrough v Crystal Palace	6-0
Portsmouth v Wimbledon	0-2
Leyton Orient v Huddersfield Town	1-1, 0-1
Coventry City v Tottenham Hotspur	1-0
Southampton v Luton Town	4-0
Newcastle United v Wycombe Wanderers	1-0
Nottingham Forest v Liverpool	2-1
West Ham United v Blackburn Rovers	1-1, 4-1
Bradford City v Manchester City	0-6
Mansfield Town v Sunderland	1-1, 0-4
Leeds United v Colchester United	0-0, 0-0
Leeds United won 4-3 on penalties.	
Crewe Alexandra v Preston North End	1-0
Everton v Brighton & Hove Albion	1-0
Derby County v Aston Villa	2-0

FIFTH ROUND

Bolton Wanderers v Southampton	0-1
Everton v Crewe Alexandra	0-1
Huddersfield Town v Coventry City	1-4
West Ham United v Middlesbrough	0-2
Sunderland v Newcastle United	1-1, 1-2

Arsenal v Nottingham Forest	0-0, 1-0
Derby County v Manchester City	1-0
Leeds United v Wimbledon	1-0

SIXTH ROUND

Coventry City v Derby County	0-0, 2-1
Arsenal v Leeds United	1-1, 5-2
Crewe Alexandra v Southampton	1-2
Middlesbrough v Newcastle United	2-1

SEMI-FINALS (two legs)

Arsenal v Middlesbrough	1-0, 1-1
Coventry City v Southampton	1-1, 1-0

FINAL First Leg

4 MAY

Coventry City (0) 1 *(McSheffrey 85)*   10,280
Arsenal (0) 3 *(Thomas 48, Barratt 65, Sidwell 68)*

Coventry City: Montgomery; Spong, Hall D, Davenport, Cudworth, Betts, Pead (Grant 75), Strachan C, Parkinson (Ashby 67), McSheffrey, Fowler.

Arsenal: Stack; Da Silva, Chilvers, Noble, Halls, Galli, Sidwell, Ricketts, Barratt, Bothroyd, Thomas (Osei-Kuffour 79).
Referee: S. Bennett (Orpington).

FINAL Second Leg

12 MAY

Arsenal (1) 2 *(Bothroyd 38, Sidwell 72)*
Coventry City (0) 0   14,706

Arsenal: Stack; Volz, Chilvers, Noble, Halls, Galli, Pennant, Ricketts, Barratt, Bothroyd, Sidwell.
Coventry City: Montgomery; Spong, Hall D, Betts, Cudworth, Davenport, Strachan C (Shanahan 85), Fowler, Pead, McSheffrey (Parkinson 57), Ashby (Magennis 73).
Referee: S. Bennett (Orpington).

SEMI-PROFESSIONAL INTERNATIONALS

1 Mar
Italy 1
England 1 *(Watkins)*   1035
England: Farrelly (Kingstonian) [Sollitt (Kettering Town)]; Marples (Doncaster Rovers) [Cousins (Yeovil Town)], Underwood (Rushden & Diamonds), Goodliffe (Hayes) [Adie Smith (Kidderminster Harriers)], Mark Smith (Stevenage Borough), Ryan (Southport), Pitcher (Kingstonian) [Drummond (Morecambe)], Butterworth (Rushden & Diamonds), Patmore (Yeovil Town) [McGregor (Forest Green Rovers)], Watkins (Kettering Town), Patterson (Kingstonian).

21 Mar
England 1 *(Watkins)*
Holland 0   1150
England: Farrelly (Kingstonian) [Sollitt (Kettering Town)]; Marples (Doncaster Rovers) [McIntyre (Doncaster Rovers)], Wormull (Rushden & Diamonds), Goodliffe (Hayes) [Cousins (Yeovil Town)], Mark Smith (Stevenage Borough) [Adie Smith (Kidderminster Harriers)], Ryan (Southport), Pitcher (Kingstonian), Drummond (Morecambe), Patmore (Yeovil Town) [McGregor (Forest Green Rovers)], Watkins (Kettering Town), Patterson (Kingstonian).

16 May
Wales 1
England 1 *(Watkins (pen))*   517
England: Sollitt (Kettering Town) [Farrelly (Kingstonian)]; Wormull (Rushden & Diamonds), McIntyre (Doncaster Rovers), Goodliffe (Hayes), Adie Smith (Kidderminster Harriers), Ryan (Southport), Pitcher (Kingstonian) [Cousins (Yeovil Town)], Drummond (Morecambe), Jackson (Morecambe) [Foster (Kidderminster Harriers)], Watkins (Kettering Town) [Bennett (Kidderminster Harriers)], Patterson (Kingstonian) [Mark Smith (Stevenage Borough)].

FA UMBRO SUNDAY CUP 1999–2000

FIRST ROUND

Eden Vale v Sandon	0-3
Manfast v Pineapple	2-1
A3 (Canada) v Britannia	1-3
Bulford v Tithe Barn	4-0
Hartlepool Lion Hotel v Lobster	3-1
Shankhouse United v Nicosia	1-2
Fairfield v Caldway	1-5
Greyhound Dog v Cheadle United	1-2
Clifton Albion v Stockland Star	3-2
Broseley Town w.o. v Olympic Star withdrew	
Melton Youth Old Boys v Grosvenor Park	1-2
Sawston Keys withdrew v Leicester City Bus w.o.	
Slade Celtic v Rangers	2-4
FC Houghton Centre v Park Inn	3-0
Coach & Horses withdrew v Bournemouth Electric w.o.	
Theale (Sunday) v Continental	3-2
Belstone v Fryerns	4-1
Shenley Hotel v Beaufort	6-2
Hammer v Ouzavich	3-0
Oakwood Sports v Courage	2-1
The Cutters Friday v Old Oak	1-0

Old Oak successfully protested against the ground facilities; The Cutters Friday withdrew from the competition.

Santos v Stathams Solicitors	4-1
Oxford Supporters v Lea Bridge Rangers	4-6

Byes: Aidan Rangers, Albion Sports, Aspect Sports, Azaad Sports, Bolton Woods, Capel Plough, Cavaliers, Caversham Park Village, Celtic SC, Dudley & Weetslade, Duke of York, Edwards Birmingham Celtic, Gossoms End, Idsall Rangers, Hanham Sunday, Leominster British Legion, Longfleet St Marys, Luton Old Boys, Mackadown Lane S&S, Mainstay, Marston Sports, Northwood, Oakenshaw, Oakview, Orchard Park, Packaging DKS (withdrew), Prestige Brighams, Queens Park, Queensbury, Reading Borough, Salerno, Seymour, St Josephs (South Oxhey), The Charlton, Watford Labour.

Exemptions: Little Paxton, Littlewoods Athletic, Lodge Cottrell, St Josephs (Luton).

SECOND ROUND

Caldway v Littlewoods Athletic	0-3
Prestige Brighams v Nicosia	3-0
Britannia v Salerno	2-1
Mainstay v Queens Park	0-4
Manfast v Queensbury	3-0
Seymour v Broseley Town	3-2
Northwood v Oakenshaw	3-1
Orchard Park v Dudley & Weetslade	4-1
Hartlepool Lion Hotel v Sandon	3-2
Albion Sports v Clifton Albion	4-0
Marston Sports v Idsall Rangers	5-0
Leicester City Bus v Keith J Alarms	1-4
Cheadle United v Bolton Woods	1-1, 1-3
Bulford v Azaad Sports	0-0, 0-0

Azaad Sports won 4-2 on penalties.

Oakview v Lodge Cottrell	1-4
Lebeq Tavern v Grosvenor Park	1-3
Celtic SC v Hanham Sunday	5-1

Luton Old Boys v Little Paxton	4-2
Leominster British Legion v Oakwood Sports	4-7
Lea Bridge Rangers v Old Oak	4-2
The Charlton v St Josephs (Luton)	0-3
St Josephs (South Oxhey) v Aspect Sports	1-3
Belstone v Capel Plough	1-0
FC Houghton Centre v Gossoms End	4-1
Duke of York v Shenley Hotel	3-3, 2-0
Cavaliers v Santos	1-0
Bournemouth Electric v Aidan Rangers	1-2
Watford Labour v Rangers	1-4
Reading Borough withdrew v Edwards Birmingham Celtic w.o.	
Caversham Park Village v Mackadown Lane S&S	1-2
Longfleet St Marys v Hammer	1-2

Bye: Theale (Sunday).

THIRD ROUND

Northwood v Keith J Alarms	1-1, 1-0
Bolton Woods v Orchard Park	4-1
Britannia v Azaad Sports	1-2
Seymour v Albion Sports	0-3
Prestige Brighams v Littlewoods Athletic	5-1
Hartlepool Lion Hotel v Queens Park	0-2
Manfast v Marston Sports	1-3
Grosvenor Park v Aspect Sports	7-1
Lea Bridge Rangers v Celtic SC	2-5
Mackadown Lane S&S v FC Houghton Centre	1-3
Lodge Cottrell v St Josephs (Luton)	1-2
Duke of York v Rangers	3-2
Belstone v Oakwood Sports	0-3
Cavaliers v Edwards Birmingham Celtic	0-4
Aidan Rangers v Theale (Sunday)	3-0
Hammer v Luton Old Boys	1-3

FOURTH ROUND

Albion Sports v FC Houghton Centre	2-2, 2-2

Albion Sports won 4-2 on penalties.

Duke of York v Luton Old Boys	0-1
Edwards Birmingham Celtic v Azaad Sports	2-0
Queens Park v Grosvenor Park	2-2, 0-1
Aidan Rangers v Marston Sports	1-0
Celtic SC v Prestige Brighams	1-1, 1-2
Northwood v Oakwood Sports	4-4, 2-4
St Josephs (Luton) v Bolton Woods	1-0

FIFTH ROUND

Oakwood Sports v Grosvenor Park	0-6
Edwards Birmingham Celtic v Albion Sports	0-1
Luton Old Boys v Prestige Brighams	2-2, 0-2
Aidan Rangers v St Josephs (Luton)	0-3

SEMI-FINALS

Albion Sports v Grosvenor Park	1-0
Prestige Brighams v St Josephs (Luton)	1-0

FINAL

Prestige Brighams v Albion Sports	1-0

FA COUNTY YOUTH CHALLENGE CUP 1999–2000

FIRST ROUND

Sheffield & Hallamshire v Liverpool	3-1
Isle of Man v Lincolshire	2-1
North Riding v Nottinghamshire	5-0
Manchester v Northumberland	4-3
East Riding v Birmingham	1-2
Suffolk v Huntingdonshire	4-0
Dorset v Middlesex	1-0
Kent v Hampshire	1-2
Herefordshire v Hertfordshire	2-0
Army v Cornwall	2-3
Bedfordshire v Cambridgeshire	1-1, 4-7
Oxfordshire v London	3-2

Surrey v Suffolk	6-0
Herefordshire v Oxfordshire	2-1

THIRD ROUND

Surrey v Lancashire	5-1
Dorset v Norfolk	0-2
Berks & Bucks v Devon	2-3
Manchester v North Riding	0-3
Durham v West Riding	1-2
Gloucestershire v Northamptonshire	0-2
Leicestershire & Rutland v Herefordshire	3-1
Hampshire v Birmingham	2-6

SECOND ROUND

Isle of Man v Durham	3-4
Lancashire v Staffordshire	5-0
West Riding v Shropshire	1-0
Leicestershire & Rutland v Cumberland	4-1
North Riding v Cheshire	1-0
Manchester v Sheffield & Hallamshire	3-2
Birmingham v Westmoreland	3-2
Somerset v Dorset	1-4
Sussex v Berks & Bucks	3-3, 2-5
Worcestershire v Hampshire	3-4
Cambridgeshire v Gloucestershire	2-4
Essex v Norfolk	0-1
Devon v Wiltshire	2-1
Northamptonshire v Cornwall	4-3

FOURTH ROUND

Norfolk v West Riding	1-0
Birmingham v Devon	2-0
Northamptonshire v Surrey	1-2
Leicestershire & Rutland v North Riding	1-3

SEMI-FINALS

Norfolk v Surrey	1-3
Birmingham v North Riding	2-1

FINAL

Birmingham v Surrey	2-1

FA XI REPRESENTATIVE MATCHES

7 Dec

FA XI 0

Southern League 0

FA XI: Sollitt (Kettering Town) [Clarke (Kidderminster Harriers)]; Clarkson (Kidderminster Harriers) [Elam (Southport)], Hollis (Accrington Stanley), Guyett (Southport), Vowden (Kettering Town) [Adie Smith (Kidderminster Harriers)], Ryan (Southport), Williams (Nuneaton Borough), Brunskill (Runcorn), Druce (Kidderminster Harriers), Foster (Kidderminster Harriers), Kelly (Hednesford Town) [Bennett (Kidderminster Harriers)].

8 Dec

FA XI 3 *(Akuamoah, Patmore, West)*

Isthmian League 1

FA XI: Farrelly (Kingstonian) [Wilkerson (Welling United)]; Watts (Welling United) [Pitman (Yeovil Town)], Hollingdale (Woking) [Wingfield (Kingstonian)], Crossley (Kingstonian) [West (Woking)], Goodliffe (Hayes), Danzey (Woking), Hanlon (Welling United), Perkins (Woking), Patmore (Yeovil Town), Charles (Hayes) [Akuamoah (Kingstonian)], Patterson (Kingstonian).

10 Jan

FA XI 4 *(Elmes, McGregor, Thackeray, Moore)*

Combined Services 0

FA XI: McKenzie (Nuneaton Borough) [Shuttlewood (Forest Green Rovers)]; Thackeray (Nuneaton Borough) [Angus (Nuneaton Borough)], Travis (Telford United), Wright (Hereford United), Cousins (Yeovil Town), Comyn (Hednesford Town), Taylor (Hereford United) [Twynham (Hednesford Town)], Drummond (Morecambe), Elmes (Hereford United) [Moore (Ilkeston Town)], McGregor (Forest Green Rovers), Ducros (Nuneaton Borough).

31 Jan

FA XI 0

British Universities 1

FA XI: Edwards (Tiverton Town) [Dungey (Dorchester Town)]; O'Brien (Dorchester Town) [Loram (Taunton Town)], Hale (Weymouth), Browne (Weymouth), Thorne (Gloucester City), Rose (Gloucester City), Davis (Bath City) [Nancekivell (Tiverton Town)], Holloway (Bath City), Laight (Taunton Town), Lynch (Taunton Town) [Robinson (Weymouth)], Sullivan (Dorchester Town) [Hare (Weymouth)].

UNIVERSITY FOOTBALL 1999–2000

116th UNIVERSITY MATCH

(at Craven Cottage, Fulham, att: 2000)

Oxford 1, Cambridge 0 (h-t 0-0)

Oxford: Fletcher; Souster, Redmaine, Cairnes, Spencer, Hendra, Rishworth, Studin, Davis, Costello, Durnford. *Subs*: Rutter, Addley, Stevenson, Ratcliffe.

Scorer: Hendra 89.

Cambridge: Madden; Challis, Kerr, Paxton, Hepburn, Mowat, Walsh, Fearnley A, Kelly, Glamocak, Fearnley T. *Subs*: Garrood, Brooksbank, Elliott, Squires.

Referee: M. Gillin (AFA).

Cambridge have not won the fixture for 12 years and Oxford levelled the series at 45 wins each with 26 drawn.

UNIVERSITY OF LONDON MEN'S LEAGUE

PREMIER DIVISION:	P	W	D	L	F	A	Pts
King's College	14	9	3	2	26	15	30
R Holloway College	14	9	2	3	33	16	29
Goldsmiths' College	14	9	1	4	28	22	28
Q. Mary Westfield College	14	7	2	5	32	26	23
Imperial College	14	5	1	8	30	31	16
GKT (formerly UMDS)	14	4	2	8	19	27	14
University College	14	3	3	8	12	24	12
Lon. School Economics	14	2	2	10	25	44	8

DIVISION ONE	P	W	D	L	F	A	Pts
Imperial College Med Sch	18	15	3	0	62	17	48
R Sch Mines (IC)	18	9	5	4	46	35	32
Goldsmiths' College Res	18	8	2	8	35	47	26
St Bart's & R Lon'n Med Sch	18	7	4	7	39	40	25
R Free UC & Mx Hosp Med Sch	18	8	0	10	34	26	24
Royal Holloway College Res	18	6	4	8	49	49	22
Imperial College Res	18	7	1	10	33	42	22
Q Mary Westfield College Res	18	6	3	9	36	47	21
London School Economics Res	18	5	5	8	26	37	20
University College Res	18	4	3	11	23	43	15

DIVISION TWO	P	W	D	L	F	A	Pts
St George's Hospital MS	18	13	3	2	50	20	42
King's College Res	18	9	2	7	47	42	29
Imperial College Med Sch Res	18	9	1	8	33	32	28
King's College 3rd	18	9	1	8	33	34	28
London Sch Economics 3rd	18	7	5	6	36	31	26
University College 3rd	18	8	2	8	31	35	26
Royal Veterinary College	18	7	4	7	45	40	25
Royal Holloway College 3rd	18	8	4	6	38	37	25*
Sch.Orien'l African Studies	18	6	1	11	36	42	19
R.Free UC & Mx Hosp Res	18	2	1	15	17	53	7

(*3 pts deducted – breaches of Rule)

DIVISION THREE	P	W	D	L	F	A	Pts
King's College 4th	17	12	2	3	58	21	38
London Sch Economics 4th	18	12	2	4	45	28	38
Imperial College 3rd	18	10	2	6	41	34	32
University College 4th	17	9	0	8	40	44	27
Q. Mary Westf'd College 3rd	18	8	3	7	40	44	27
Q. Mary Westf'd College 4th	18	8	2	8	32	36	26
Imperial College 4th	18	7	2	9	39	48	23
Wye College	18	5	4	9	29	27	19
GKT Res	18	4	6	8	31	39	18
R Free UC & Mx Hosp 3rd	18	2	1	15	13	47	7

DIVISION FOUR–9 Teams – Won by University College 5th

DIVISION FIVE–10 Teams – Won by Won by Imperial College 5th

DIVISION SIX–6 Teams – Won by Won by King's College 6th

DIVISION SEVEN–7 Teams – Won by Heythrop College

Challenge Cup–Imperial College 4 London School of Economics 0

Upper Reserves Cup–IC Medical School Res 4 Goldsmiths' College Res 0

Lower Reserves Cup–Q Mary Westfield 6th 2 University College 5th 1

United Hospitals Cups

Senior Cup–No results advised

Junior Cup–No results advised

BRITISH UNIVERSITIES SPORTS ASSOCIATION CHAMPIONSHIP

Finals (Men)

First XI

Newcastle 4, Crewe & Alsager 1

Second XI

UWIC 2, Salford 0

Third XI

Staffordshire/Stoke 4, De Montfort Bedford 3

Fourth XI

Loughborough 4, Crewe & Alsager 3

Women's

Brunel, West London 3, Loughborough 2

BUSA Games

England Men: v Northern Ireland 2-0
v Scotland 2-1
v Wales 2-1

Position 1st

England Women: v Northern Ireland 6-0
v Scotland 4-0
v Wales 18-0

Position 1st

UNIVERSITY OF LONDON WOMEN'S LEAGUE

PREMIER DIVISION	P	W	D	L	F	A	Pts
Royal Holloway College	16	16	0	0	77	18	48
Q. Mary Westf'd College	16	12	0	4	54	17	36
University College	16	11	0	5	88	29	33
GKT	16	11	0	5	59	30	33
Imperial College	16	5	2	9	27	61	17
London School of Economics	15	4	2	9	20	44	14
SOAS	14	2	4	8	35	62	10
King's College	16	2	2	12	31	80	8
Goldsmiths' College	15	2	0	13	12	62	6

DIVISION ONE	P	W	D	L	F	A	Pts
Royal Free Hospital	12	7	5	0	49	9	26
St George's Hospital	12	7	2	3	42	10	23
R. Holloway College Res	12	6	4	2	23	13	22
Royal Veterinary	11	4	2	5	17	2	14
GKT Res	12	4	2	6	12	32	14
Royal Free Hospital Res	11	2	2	7	8	32	8
Wye College	12	2	1	9	5	58	7

Royal Free Hospital 3rd Withdrawn 11th March 2000
University College Res Withdrawn 2nd February 2000

Womens' Challenge Cup–Q Mary Westfield 1*:2p Royal Holloway 1*:3p

SCHOOLS FOOTBALL 1999–2000

BOODLE & DUNTHORNE INDEPENDENT SCHOOLS FA CUP 1999-2000

FIRST ROUND
Repton 4, Wolverhampton GS 0; Aldenham 3, Victoria College, Jersey 1; Batley GS 0, Eton 6; Hulme GS 1, John Lyon 1 *(aet; Hulme won 4-3 on penalties)*; QEGS, Blackburn 3, St Bede's 0; Malvern 3, Wellingborough 1

SECOND ROUND
Kimbolton 1, Forest 0; Bury GS 2, Repton 0; Ardingly 4, Alleyn's 1; Manchester GS 2, City of London 0; Hampton 6, Grange 2; KES, Witley 0, Haileybury 0 *(aet; KES, Witley won 4-2 on penalties)*; Hulme GS 4, Highgate 2; Malvern 0, Millfield 4; Charterhouse 2, Winchester 0; King's, Chester 3, Bolton 2 *aet*; Latymer Upper 6, Westminster 2; QEGS, Blackburn 9, Oswestry 1; Brentwood 4, Eton 1; St Edmund's, Canterbury 2, Lancing 0; Bradfield 4, Aldenham 0; Chigwell 0, Shrewsbury 2

THIRD ROUND
Ardingly 6, Kimbolton 1; Brentwood 4, Manchester GS 0; Hampton 0, King's, Chester 1; Bury GS 8, KES, Witley 0; Latymer Upper 3, Millfield 2 *aet*; Hulme GS 0, Bradfield 1; QEGS, Blackburn 2, Charterhouse 2 *(aet; Charterhouse won 5-4 on penalties)*; Shrewsbury 2, St Edmunds, Canterbury 0

FOURTH ROUND
Bury GS 1, Charterhouse 2; Brentwood 1, Latymer Upper 1 *(Brentwood won 5-4 on penalties)*; Shrewsbury 3, Ardingly 2; King's, Chester 3, Bradfield 1

SEMI-FINALS
Brentwood 0, Charterhouse 2; Shrewsbury 2, King's, Chester 1

FINAL (at Leicester City)
Charterhouse 0
Shrewsbury 1 *(Chapman)* 1702
Charterhouse: D Heaton-Watson; A Mezzetti, M Bailey, J Byrne, S Spinks (T Goodrich), C Shelton, I MacAuslan (T Blake), W Clark, M Smith, J Jackson, J Toller.
Shrewsbury: L Briggs; S Kemp, R Champion, C Marlow, R Bainbridge, R Gardner, J Elcock, A McLaren (T Wainwright-Lee), B Chapman, T Evans, M Jones (C Stockbridge).
Referee: S. Lodge (Barnsley).

CENTENARY SHIELD 1999-2000

UNDER-18	P	W	D	L	F	A	Pts
Scotland	3	2	1	0	4	2	7
Northern Ireland	3	1	2	0	3	1	5
England	3	1	0	2	2	4	3
Wales	3	0	1	2	4	6	1

ESFA UNDER-18 1999-2000
Republic of Ireland 1, England 1 - Galway, 11 February
Northern Ireland 2, England 0 - Armagh, 3 March
Wales 1, England 2 - Newtown, 17 March
England 0, Hungary 1 - Wembley, 25 March
England 0, Scotland 1 - Bradford City FC, 31 March
England 4, Austria 1 - Torquay United FC, 2 May

Overall Record...Played 6, Won 2, Drew 1, Lost 3, Goals For 7, Goals Against 7
Scorers: Onions (2), Thompson (2), Borley, Ward, Willock.

ESFA WAGONWHEELS 5-A-SIDE COMPETITION
U.12 FINALS
Staged at Aston Villa Sports Centre

BOYS FINAL:
St Thomas Apostle College (South London) 3, Crawshaw School (Leeds) 1

GIRLS FINAL:
Cottingham School (East Riding) 4, Durham Johnston School (Bishop Auckland) 0

ESFA U.11 ADIDAS PREDATOR PREMIER FINAL 7-A-SIDE TROPHY
FINAL:
Chester-Le-Street 0, Oxford 0
Trophy Shared. Played at Wembley.

ESFA U.11 ADIDAS PREDATOR FINAL 6-A-SIDE TROPHY
FINAL:
Headington Middle School (Oxford) 0, Clifton Without Primary School (York) 0
Trophy Shared.
Played at Old Trafford.

ESFA U.19 INTER-COUNTY PREMIER LEAGUE COMPETITION
FINAL:
Northumberland 0, Suffolk 2
Played at Derby County FC, 9 May.

ESFA U.19 INDIVIDUAL SCHOOLS TROPHY
FINAL:
Maidstone GS (Kent) 0, Kingsway School (Cheshire) 1
Played at West Bromwich Albion FC, 12 May.

ESFA U.19 SCHOOLS & COLLEGES TROPHY
FINAL:
Lancaster & Morecambe (Lancashire) 1, Cirencester College (Gloucestershire) 2
Played at West Bromwich Albion FC, 12 May.

ESFA U.16 INDIVIDUAL SCHOOLSNET CUP
FINAL:
Arnold Hill School (Nottinghamshire) 1, St Aloysius College (Inner London) 2 aet
Played at Wolverhampton Wanderers FC, 5 May.

ESFA U.16 UNITED NORWEST CO-OP TROPHY
FINAL:
Cheshire 0, Hampshire 1
Played at Blackburn Rovers FC, 17 May.

ESFA U.16 UNITED NORWEST CO-OP CUP
FINAL:
Helsby School (Cheshire) 4, Guildford County School (Surrey) 1
Played at Chester City FC, 8 May.

ESFA U.16 INTER COUNTY PREMIER LEAGUE TROPHY
FINAL:
West Midlands 0, Sussex 1
Played at Derby County FC, 9 May.

ESFA U.15 HEINZ KETCHUP INTER ASSOCIATION TROPHY
FINAL (two legs):
Cardiff 0, Salford 1
Played at Cardiff City FC
Salford 3, Cardiff 1
Played at Manchester United FC

ESFA U.14 HEINZ KETCHUP CUP
FINAL:
Ernest Bevin College (Inner London) 1, Barking Abbey School (Essex) 3
Played at Arsenal FC, 18 May.

ESFA/MANCHESTER UNITED 7-A-SIDE FOR YEAR 6 & YEAR 7 PUPILS
YEAR 6:
Golcar School (Huddersfield) 2, Lytchett Matravers School (Poole) 0

YEAR 7:
Drayton Manor School (London) 1, Langdon School (London) 0

PREDATOR COMMUNITY CUP (ESFA/PFA U.11 6-A-SIDE)
FINAL:
Headington Middle School (Oxford) 1, St Cuthbert's Primary School (Hartlepool) 0
Played at Wembley.

ESFA SMALL SCHOOLS PRIMARY COMPETITION (PILOT SCHEME - AREA 4)
FINAL:
Underwood School (Notts) 0, Newton School (Derbyshire) 2
Played at Leicester City FC

AVON INSURANCE COMBINATION 1999–2000

Millwall deservedly won the Avon Insurance Combination, narrowly seeing off the challenge of Queens Park Rangers and Ipswich Town. A 1-0 win in their last match over a strong Wycombe Wanderers team aided and abetted by a last minute penalty save by Nigel Spink gave the Lions their first Combination title since 1993.

Queens Park Rangers, Ipswich, Fulham and Bristol City were always in the running but Millwall finally triumphed by a three point margin in what was a close and exciting title race.

Steve Gritt did an excellent job in welding together a potent mix of youngsters and experienced professionals who lost only one game all season, with former Arsenal striker Paul Shaw leading the way with ten goals in as many games. Spink, Bobby Bowry and Jamie Stuart provided the necessary experience with youngsters Leke Odunsi, Leon Cort, Byron Bubb, Joe Dolan and Ronnie Bull all showing great promise for the future.

For the second season running Ipswich provided the League's leading scorer in the Swede Jonas Axeldal and Fulham's Kevin Betsy also emphasised his prowess in front of goal.

The main purpose of the Combination is to encourage the development of young talent and even without the presence of the Premiership teams last season, many players emerged who are likely to make their names in the near future.

Sean Davis of Fulham who scored a wonder goal against Brighton, Nathan Lamey and Tom Youngs of Cambridge United, KK Opara of Colchester United, Richard Logan of Ipswich, Ben Strevens of Barnet, Gary O'Neil of Portsmouth, Chris McPhee of Brighton, Damien Spencer and Simon of Bristol City and Bobby Zamora of Bristol Rovers amongst many others, are all names to take note of.

Congratulations are also due to Plymouth Argyle (Division Two Champions), AFC Bournemouth (League Cup Winners) and Cardiff City (Division Two League Cup Winners).

Norwich City won the Avon Insurance Enterprise Award for their excellent Family Night Football and Junior Roadshow schemes.

Avon Insurance are about to enter the seventh season of their sponsorship which has been extended to the end of the 2002-03 season by which time it will be one of the longest lasting sponsorships in English football.

From the start of the 2000-01 season, Avon Insurance will, in addition, be sponsoring the Avon Insurance League (formerly the Pontin's League) ensuring sponsorship of Nationwide League reserve team football on a national basis and providing additional opportunities for Avon Insurance to enhance their Broker relationships.

1999-2000 SEASON SUMMARY
Champions – Millwall
League Cup Winners – AFC Bournemouth
Division Two Champions – Plymouth Argyle
Division Two League Cup Winners – Cardiff City
Top Scorer – Jonas Axeldal (Ipswich Town)
Fair Play Award – Southend United
Avon Insurance Enterprise Award – Norwich City
Avon Insurance Programme Award – Barnet

Millwall League appearances: Alimi 2; Astafjevs 1; Biander 2; Blackwood 1; Bowry 9+5; Braniff 4; Bubb 14+1; Bull 14; Cook 0+2; Cort 14+1; Deegan 1; Dolan 12+2; Dunne 6+3; Dyche 3+2; Fitzgerald 1; Gilkes 5; Hamzo 1; Harris 3; Hicks 6+2; Hockton 3; Honey 1; Ifill 3; Johansson 1; Karaiskos 2+3; Kinet 4; Kuipers 1; Law 6+2; Livermore 5; Mead 2; Moody 5; Neill 1; Newman 7; Odunsi 17; Pereira 2; Phillips 2+1; Reid 12, Ryan 2; Sadlier 4; Shaw 10; Smith 6; Spink 12; Stuart 14; Trialist 1; Tyne 6+4; Williams 2; Wirmola 1.
Goals: Shaw 10, Harris 5, Bubb 3, Bull 3, Cort 3, Sadlier 3, Tyne 3, Hockton 2, Moody 2, Braniff 1, Hicks 1, Reid 1, Stuart 1.

Division One

	P	W	D	L	F	A	GD	Pts
Millwall	21	14	8	1	40	14	+26	48
QPR	21	14	3	4	53	21	+32	45
Ipswich T	21	13	4	4	49	27	+22	43
Fulham	21	12	5	4	42	21	+21	41
Bristol C	21	12	5	4	37	25	+12	41
Swindon T	21	12	4	5	38	26	+12	40
Bournemouth	21	10	4	7	35	33	+2	34
Peterborough U	21	9	5	7	39	27	+12	32
Cambridge U	21	9	4	8	39	33	+6	31
Bristol R	21	8	6	7	28	27	+1	30
Brighton & HA	21	8	5	8	34	30	+4	29
Norwich C	21	7	6	8	30	24	+6	27
Leyton Orient	21	7	5	9	30	40	–10	26
Colchester U	21	6	7	8	29	39	–10	25
Portsmouth	21	7	4	10	29	40	–11	25
Gillingham	21	6	5	10	23	39	–16	23
Northampton T	21	6	4	11	27	36	–9	22
Barnet	21	5	6	10	26	33	–7	21
Southend U	21	5	2	14	25	48	–23	17
Luton T	21	3	7	11	19	33	–14	16
Oxford U	21	4	4	13	27	45	–18	16
Wycombe W	21	2	3	16	19	57	–38	9

Division Two

	P	W	D	L	F	A	GD	Pts
Plymouth Arg	8	6	1	1	11	8	+3	19
Cardiff C	8	3	3	2	16	10	+6	12
Exeter C	8	4	0	4	11	9	+2	12
Swansea C	8	3	1	4	11	10	+1	10
Torquay U	8	1	1	6	8	20	–12	4

Avon Insurance Combination – League Cup Winners
Division One – Bournemouth
Division Two – Cardiff C

PONTIN'S LEAGUE 1999–2000

Premier Division	P	W	D	L	F	A	Pts
Manchester C	22	13	5	4	42	24	44
Huddersfield T	22	12	4	6	35	22	40
Birmingham C	22	9	8	5	31	22	35
Port Vale	22	8	8	6	32	26	32
Tranmere R	22	9	3	10	28	31	30
Wolverhampton W	22	9	3	10	27	30	30
Oldham Ath	22	7	8	7	35	34	29
Preston NE	22	7	8	7	35	36	29
WBA	22	8	5	9	23	24	29
Burnley	22	6	9	7	29	34	27
Stoke C	22	3	8	11	21	37	17
Grimsby T	22	2	9	11	23	41	15

Division One	P	W	D	L	F	A	Pts
Rotherham U	22	11	6	5	30	18	39
Stockport Co	22	11	5	6	39	26	38
Wrexham	22	10	6	6	36	27	36
Blackpool	22	9	6	7	27	22	33
Scunthorpe U	22	9	5	8	29	27	32

	P	W	D	L	F	A	Pts
Lincoln C	22	8	7	7	25	27	31
Sheffield U	22	8	6	8	30	26	30
York C	22	9	3	10	23	33	30
Shrewsbury T	22	6	9	7	19	23	27
Walsall	22	6	6	10	34	33	24
Notts Co	22	6	6	10	32	37	24
Scarborough	22	3	7	12	17	42	16

Division Two	P	W	D	L	F	A	Pts
Wigan Ath	20	12	5	3	39	21	41
Darlington	20	13	1	6	48	25	40
Bury	20	13	1	6	44	26	40
Hull C	20	9	4	7	32	26	31
Chesterfield	20	7	7	6	30	28	28
Macclesfield T	20	7	4	9	27	29	25
Hartlepool U	20	7	4	9	27	32	25
Mansfield T	20	7	3	10	27	36	24
Halifax T	20	5	4	11	20	34	19
Rochdale	20	4	6	10	23	38	18
Chester C	20	5	3	12	29	51	18

FA PREMIER RESERVE LEAGUE

NORTH	P	W	D	L	F	A	W	D	L	F	A	GD	Pts
			Home		Goals		Away			Goals			
Liverpool	24	7	5	0	28	9	9	2	1	27	9	+37	55
Sunderland	24	8	4	0	21	4	4	1	7	14	23	+8	41
Blackburn R	24	7	1	4	22	13	4	5	3	15	13	+11	39
Bradford C	24	7	2	3	24	16	5	1	6	20	29	−1	39
Newcastle U	24	8	0	4	21	12	3	4	5	16	23	+2	37
Manchester U	24	7	2	3	29	14	4	1	7	17	18	+14	36
Leeds U	24	6	3	3	30	19	4	3	5	18	19	+10	36
Middlesbrough	24	6	2	4	18	18	4	4	4	16	15	+1	36
Everton	24	4	5	3	21	17	3	5	4	23	23	+4	31
Aston Villa	24	3	3	6	18	24	5	2	5	19	18	−5	29
Bolton W	24	4	2	6	13	25	2	2	8	9	34	−37	22
Sheffield W	24	5	1	6	23	21	0	3	9	12	31	−17	19
Barnsley	24	2	4	6	14	22	1	1	10	8	26	−27	14

SOUTH	P	W	D	L	F	A	W	D	L	F	A	GD	Pts
			Home		Goals		Away			Goals			
Derby Co	24	9	3	0	22	9	5	3	4	23	19	+17	48
Charlton Ath	24	8	1	3	34	19	7	1	4	23	17	+21	47
Tottenham H	24	6	4	2	19	16	6	2	4	23	19	+7	42
Southampton	24	7	3	2	28	13	5	2	5	15	14	+16	41
Coventry C	24	5	3	4	18	17	6	3	3	20	13	+8	39
Arsenal	24	6	3	3	28	15	4	4	4	21	17	+17	37
Chelsea	24	4	6	2	14	13	4	3	5	17	17	+1	33
Wimbledon	24	5	3	4	21	17	3	4	5	17	18	+3	31
Nottingham F	24	6	3	3	19	13	1	4	7	15	25	−4	28
Leicester C	24	3	4	5	17	20	4	3	5	19	24	−8	28
West Ham U	24	4	0	8	17	25	3	3	6	10	18	−16	24
Watford	24	3	2	7	15	20	2	2	8	12	30	−23	19
Crystal Palace	24	2	2	8	8	24	1	3	8	6	29	−39	14

FA ACADEMY UNDER-19 LEAGUE 1999–2000

GROUP A	P	W	D	L	F	A	GD	Pts
Sunderland	22	15	5	2	62	24	+38	50
Barnsley	22	12	4	6	52	38	+14	40
Sheffield W	22	10	1	11	39	49	−10	31
Middlesbrough	22	9	2	11	32	40	−8	29
Leeds U	22	7	4	11	32	48	−16	25
Newcastle U	22	7	3	12	37	53	−16	24
Huddersfield T	22	4	1	17	34	68	−34	13

GROUP B	P	W	D	L	F	A	GD	Pts
Blackburn R	22	15	5	2	55	18	+37	50
Everton	22	14	3	5	38	22	+16	45
Manchester U	22	11	5	6	47	22	+25	38
Manchester C	22	12	2	8	45	32	+13	38
Liverpool	22	11	3	8	45	37	+8	36
Crewe Alex	22	7	8	7	29	34	−5	29
Bolton W	22	3	3	16	18	55	−37	12

GROUP C	P	W	D	L	F	A	GD	Pts
Nottingham F	22	15	2	5	63	29	+34	47
Leicester C	22	11	5	6	32	29	+3	38
Coventry C	22	11	4	7	38	33	+5	37
Aston Villa	22	8	6	8	34	31	+3	30
Derby Co	22	6	5	11	26	33	−7	23

	P	W	D	L	F	A	GD	Pts
Peterborough U	22	5	6	11	29	41	−12	21
Birmingham C	22	6	3	13	23	36	−13	21
Stoke C	22	3	5	14	17	47	−30	14

GROUP D	P	W	D	L	F	A	GD	Pts
Arsenal	22	14	4	4	50	25	+25	46
Fulham	22	11	7	4	43	25	+18	40
Bristol C	22	9	5	8	35	24	+11	32
Crystal Palace	22	9	5	8	37	31	+6	32
Millwall	22	9	1	12	35	34	−9	28
Chelsea	22	7	6	9	26	28	−2	27
Southampton	22	6	4	12	28	46	−18	22
Reading	22	6	3	13	27	40	−13	21

GROUP E	P	W	D	L	F	A	GD	Pts
West Ham U	22	13	5	4	46	20	+26	44
Wimbledon	22	12	5	5	30	22	+8	41
QPR	22	9	9	4	39	29	+10	36
Charlton Ath	22	8	6	8	35	39	−4	30
Tottenham H	22	7	7	8	36	31	+5	28
Watford	22	6	4	12	34	49	−15	22
Ipswich T	22	6	3	13	26	41	−15	21
Norwich C	22	4	1	17	19	60	−41	13

UNDER-19 PLAY-OFFS

First Round
Southampton 1 Ipswich T 3
Peterborough U 2 Norwich C 0
Watford 1 Reading 1*
Chelsea 3 Stoke C 0
Newcastle U 4 Bolton W 1
Birmingham C 0 Huddersfield T 2

Second Round
Blackburn R 3 Ipswich T 1
Middlesbrough 2 Aston Villa 2*
Manchester U 6 Leeds U 1
West Ham U 3 Peterborough U 0
Barnsley 0 Crewe Alex 2
Wimbledon 3 Liverpool 4 *(aet)*
Coventry C 2 Charlton Ath 1
Sunderland 4 Reading 0
Nottingham F 3* Chelsea 3

Bristol C 1 Manchester C 1*
Fulham 2 Derby Co 0
Leicester C 1 Newcastle U 4
Everton 1 Tottenham H 0
Sheffield W 2 Crystal Palace 1
QPR 0 Millwall 1
Arsenal 2 Huddersfield T 1

Third Round
Blackburn R 4 Aston Villa 1
West Ham U 5 Manchester U 0
Crewe Alex 2 Liverpool 1
Sunderland 0 Coventry C 1
Nottingham F 3 Manchester C 2
Newcastle U 1 Fulham 2
Everton 2 Sheffield W 0
Arsenal 2 Millwall 0

Fourth Round
Blackburn R 1 West Ham U 2
Coventry C 0 Crewe Alex 1
Nottingham F 1 Fulham 2
Arsenal 2 Everton 0

Semi-finals
Crewe Alex 0 West Ham U 1
Arsenal 4 Fulham 1

Final (2 legs)
West Ham U 5 Arsenal 5
Arsenal 1 West Ham U 1*
*(6-6 on aggregate. West Ham U won
4-2 on penalties)*

* = won on penalties

FA ACADEMY UNDER-17 LEAGUE 1999–2000

GROUP A	P	W	D	L	F	A	GD	Pts
Newcastle U	22	11	5	6	37	30	+7	38
Sunderland	22	11	4	7	29	23	+6	37
Middlesbrough	22	9	9	4	44	25	+19	36
Sheffield W	22	9	6	7	41	33	+8	33
Leeds U	22	9	0	13	46	52	−6	27
Barnsley	22	4	2	16	22	76	−54	14

GROUP B	P	W	D	L	F	A	GD	Pts
Crewe Alex	22	13	3	6	74	35	+39	42
Manchester U	22	13	2	7	59	29	+30	41
Blackburn R	22	11	5	6	43	34	+9	38
Liverpool	22	12	2	8	41	32	+9	38
Manchester C	22	11	2	9	42	25	+17	35
Bolton W	22	3	1	18	19	61	−42	10

GROUP C	P	W	D	L	F	A	GD	Pts
Aston Villa	22	14	6	2	57	29	+28	48
Leicester C	22	9	6	7	29	25	+4	33
Coventry C	22	8	7	7	40	33	+7	31
Nottingham F	22	9	3	10	31	45	−14	30
Birmingham C	22	3	6	13	27	60	−33	15

GROUP D	P	W	D	L	F	A	GD	Pts
Arsenal	22	17	4	1	65	13	+52	55
Bristol C	22	9	6	7	28	28	+0	33
Millwall	22	9	4	9	41	36	+5	31
Reading	22	8	7	7	33	31	+2	31
Southampton	22	3	7	12	34	52	−18	16
Crystal Palace	22	4	4	14	24	52	−28	16
Fulham	22	3	5	14	22	59	−37	14

GROUP E	P	W	D	L	F	A	GD	Pts
West Ham U	22	14	3	5	48	21	+27	45
Watford	22	11	4	7	37	35	+2	37
QPR	22	10	6	6	40	32	+8	36
Wimbledon	22	8	5	9	31	30	+1	29
Charlton Ath	22	5	4	13	25	49	−24	19
Tottenham H	22	2	8	12	17	41	−24	14

UNDER-17 PLAY-OFFS

First Round
Blackburn R 1 Sheffield W 3
Sunderland 2 Birmingham C 1
Aston Villa 6 Bolton W 2
Manchester U 3 Leeds U 1
Coventry C 5 Liverpool 1
Middlesbrough 2 Manchester C 3
Crewe Alex 7 Barnsley 2
QPR 2 Reading 1
Leicester C 4 Southampton 2
Bristol C 2 Tottenham H 1
Watford 3 Crystal Palace 2
Millwall 3 Charlton Ath 2
Wimbledon 1 Nottingham F 0
West Ham U 2* Fulham 2

Second Round
Newcastle U 3 Sheffield W 0
Aston Villa 2 Sunderland 0
Manchester U 2 Coventry C 3
Crewe Alex 1 Manchester C 0
Arsenal 3 QPR 0
Bristol C 2 Leicester C 3
Watford 1 Millwall 1*
West Ham U 3 Wimbledon 1

Third Round
Newcastle U 1 Aston Villa 3
Crewe Alex 4 Coventry C 1
Arsenal 2 Leicester C 0
West Ham U 1 Millwall 0

Semi-finals
Crewe Alex 1 Aston Villa 0
West Ham U 2 Arsenal 3

Final (2 legs)
Crewe Alex 1 Arsenal 0
Arsenal 4 Crewe 2
(Arsenal won 4-3 on aggregate)

* = won on penalties

NON-LEAGUE TABLES 1999–2000

ARNOTT NORTHERN LEAGUE

Division One	P	W	D	L	F	A	Pts
Bedlington Terriers	38	25	8	5	89	26	83
Seaham Red Star	38	23	5	10	64	49	74
Dunston Federation	38	20	7	11	73	41	67
Marske United	38	19	8	11	67	45	65
West Auckland Town	38	17	14	7	65	43	65
Billingham Synthonia	38	17	6	15	72	64	57
Jarrow Roofing	38	15	12	11	64	61	57
Morpeth Town	38	14	15	9	55	56	57
Consett	38	12	18	8	57	43	54
Tow Law Town	38	15	8	15	65	55	53
Billingham Town	38	13	13	12	58	47	52
Guisborough Town	38	15	7	16	57	62	52
Chester-le-Street Town	38	14	9	15	57	67	51
Crook Town	38	13	11	14	55	57	50
Durham City	38	11	13	14	50	61	46
Peterlee Newtown	38	13	7	18	56	76	46
Easington Colliery	38	10	11	17	57	74	41
Thornaby-on-Tees	38	7	12	19	47	68	33
Shotton Comrades	38	4	9	25	37	88	21
South Shields	38	3	7	28	33	95	16

Division Two	P	W	D	L	F	A	Pts
Brandon United	36	25	9	2	83	24	84
Newcastle Blue Star	36	24	5	7	94	43	77
Hebburn	36	22	4	10	71	34	70
Northallerton Town	36	21	5	10	76	48	68
Shildon	36	20	7	9	62	44	67
Willington	36	21	3	12	81	41	66
Washington	36	19	7	10	95	57	64
Norton & Stockton Ancients	36	18	8	10	70	51	62
Ashington	36	17	10	9	92	37	61
Penrith	36	15	11	10	69	40	56
Alnwick Town	36	16	7	13	78	58	55
Horden CW	36	13	10	13	53	57	49
Prudhoe Town	36	11	9	16	59	74	39
Evenwood Town	36	11	6	19	57	100	39
Esh Winning	36	11	2	23	59	81	35
Kennek Ryhope CA	36	9	7	20	49	70	34
Whickham	36	6	7	23	27	69	25
Murton	36	1	4	31	20	132	7
Eppleton CW	36	0	3	33	22	156	3

NORTHERN COUNTIES EAST LEAGUE

Premier Division	P	W	D	L	F	A	Pts
North Ferriby United	38	25	10	3	87	31	85
Brigg Town	38	25	6	7	73	38	81
Glasshoughton Welfare	38	20	6	12	68	57	66
Liversedge	38	20	5	13	76	45	65
Alfreton Town	38	17	11	10	73	49	62
Brodsworth MW	38	15	10	13	66	69	55
Ossett Albion	38	15	9	14	70	60	54
Arnold Town	38	14	11	13	60	47	53
Selby Town	38	13	14	11	53	49	53
Eccleshill United	38	15	8	15	59	65	53
Armthorpe Welfare	38	14	10	14	45	50	52
Hallam	38	14	9	15	72	67	51
Denaby United	38	13	11	14	46	41	50
Sheffield	38	12	13	13	62	55	49
Garforth Town	38	10	11	17	53	65	41
Harrogate Railway Ath	38	11	6	21	54	95	39
Maltby Main	38	8	12	18	36	58	36
Buxton (–3)	38	11	6	21	35	67	36
Staveley MW	38	9	8	21	53	83	35
Thackley	38	6	10	22	39	89	28

Division One	P	W	D	L	F	A	Pts
Goole	30	22	5	3	66	19	71
Glapwell	30	18	6	6	74	36	60
Borrowash Victoria	30	14	8	8	48	35	50
Mickleover Sports	30	14	7	9	52	44	49
Bridlington Town	30	15	4	11	43	36	49
Winterton Rangers	30	13	9	8	52	31	48
Yorkshire Amateurs	30	14	5	11	55	37	47
Hall Road Rangers	30	14	5	11	58	49	47
Louth United	30	12	4	14	51	62	40
Worsborough Bridge	30	11	6	13	44	46	39
Pickering Town	30	11	5	14	46	36	38
Parkgate	30	11	5	14	58	59	38
Pontefract Collieries	30	8	9	13	34	50	33
Tadcaster Albion	30	7	3	20	33	84	24
Rossington Main	30	5	7	18	27	62	22
Hatfield Main	30	5	4	21	36	91	19

FIRST NORTH-WESTERN TRAINS LEAGUE

Division One	P	W	D	L	F	A	Pts
Vauxhall	42	29	7	6	101	32	94
Newcastle Town	42	26	7	9	82	35	85
Ramsbottom United	42	23	10	9	87	53	79
Mossley	42	23	10	9	80	50	79
Rossendale United	42	23	9	10	77	46	78
Skelmersdale United	42	22	9	11	91	53	75
Fleetwood Freeport	42	21	10	11	75	45	73
Prescot Cables	42	21	10	11	83	55	73
St Helens Town	42	20	13	9	81	59	73
Clitheroe	42	21	7	14	75	49	70
Salford City	42	17	7	18	70	69	58
Atherton Collieries	42	16	6	20	58	68	54
Kidsgrove Athletic	42	14	9	19	47	66	51
Abbey Hey	42	14	8	20	50	75	50
Nantwich Town	42	13	9	20	60	73	48
Great Harwood Town	42	12	9	21	55	81	45
Glossop North End	42	10	11	21	52	73	41
Cheadle Town	42	8	13	21	49	85	37
Maine Road	42	9	10	23	59	100	37
Leek CSOB	42	8	10	24	49	101	34
Bootle	42	6	8	28	29	90	26
Atherton LR	42	4	12	26	51	103	24

Division Two	P	W	D	L	F	A	Pts
Woodley Sports	34	24	6	4	85	29	78
Curzon Ashton	34	24	6	4	78	26	78
Nelson	34	21	8	5	77	31	71
Darwen	34	20	6	8	69	35	66
Bacup Borough	34	15	11	8	68	42	56
Squires Gate	34	16	7	11	70	49	55
Tetley Walker	34	16	4	14	56	70	52
Castleton Gabriels	34	15	6	13	67	67	51
Warrington Town	34	14	8	12	66	44	50
Chadderton	34	12	12	10	52	57	48
Formby	34	12	8	14	52	68	44
Alsager	34	11	8	15	48	64	41
Colne	34	12	2	20	44	70	38
Holker Old Boys	34	8	11	15	59	73	35
Blackpool Mechanics	34	9	6	19	49	74	33
Daisy Hill	34	7	5	22	41	75	26
Oldham Town	34	4	6	24	43	86	18
Ashton Town	34	5	2	27	30	94	17

INTERLINK EXPRESS MIDLAND ALLIANCE

	P	W	D	L	F	A	Pts
Oadby Town	42	27	7	8	107	48	88
Stratford Town	42	22	12	8	73	47	78
Willenhall Town	42	20	13	9	77	42	73
Wednesfield	42	21	9	12	71	56	72
Boldmere St Michaels	42	20	12	10	61	48	72
Stourport Swifts	42	19	13	10	73	57	70
Rushall Olympic	42	20	9	13	75	65	69
Shifnal Town	42	17	16	9	66	50	67
Barwell	42	18	12	12	85	57	66
Oldbury United	42	17	13	12	62	45	64
Chasetown	42	18	7	17	61	62	61
Knypersley Victoria (–1)	42	17	10	15	75	71	60
West Midlands Police	42	15	8	19	62	71	53
Bridgnorth Town	42	15	7	20	70	72	52
Halesowen Harriers	42	14	8	20	63	71	50
Sandwell Borough	42	12	13	17	53	69	49
Bloxwich Town	42	11	13	18	57	84	46
Kings Norton Town	42	9	16	17	60	68	43
Cradley Town	42	10	12	20	56	87	42
Pelsall Villa	42	9	10	23	57	88	37
Stapenhill	42	8	6	28	42	91	30
Pershore Town	42	7	6	29	46	103	27

UNITED COUNTIES LEAGUE

Premier Division	P	W	D	L	F	A	Pts
Ford Sports Daventry	38	28	7	3	80	25	91
Cogenhoe United	38	27	6	5	135	39	87
Boston Town	38	27	6	5	88	30	87
Stotfold	38	24	7	7	70	24	79
Northampton Spencer	38	23	6	9	96	48	75
Blackstone	38	23	5	10	79	53	74
Kempston Rovers	38	20	10	8	70	38	70
Desborough Town	38	21	6	11	95	55	69
S & L Corby	38	20	3	15	86	70	63
Bugbrooke St Michaels	38	18	3	17	53	50	57
Wootton Blue Cross	38	15	7	16	81	63	52
Bourne Town	38	15	4	19	60	52	49
St Neots Town	38	13	5	20	61	60	44
Yaxley	38	10	7	21	43	60	37
Wellingborough Town	38	11	4	23	49	81	37
Holbeach United	38	10	5	23	48	71	35
Eynesbury Rovers	38	9	2	27	45	120	29
Potton United	38	6	6	26	47	97	24
Buckingham Town	38	5	1	32	27	172	16
Long Buckby	38	3	4	31	29	134	13

Division One	P	W	D	L	F	A	Pts
Cottingham	34	21	8	5	90	33	71
Thrapston Town	34	21	5	8	83	38	68
Deeping Rangers	34	18	13	3	73	28	67
Harrowby United	34	18	11	5	84	31	65
Daventry Town	34	19	7	8	65	36	64
St Ives Town	34	16	7	11	74	46	55
Newport Pagnell Town	34	15	7	12	69	57	52
Blisworth	34	14	9	11	57	51	51
Olney Town	34	15	5	14	61	57	50
Woodford United	34	15	5	14	71	73	50
Northampton Vanaid	34	13	9	12	57	48	48
Burton Park Wanderers	34	13	9	12	57	50	48
Rothwell Corinthians	34	9	11	14	46	69	38
Wellingborough Whitworths	34	10	6	18	46	74	36
Northampton ON Chenecks	34	8	5	21	47	88	29
Sharnbrook	34	6	6	22	34	96	24
Higham Town	34	4	8	22	35	104	20
Irchester United	34	4	3	27	26	96	15

JEWSON EASTERN COUNTIES

Premier Division	P	W	D	L	F	A	Pts
Histon	40	29	6	5	95	42	93
Wroxham	40	28	8	4	86	39	92
AFC Sudbury	40	28	6	6	106	48	90
Clacton Town	40	22	9	9	92	59	75
Lowestoft Town	40	20	10	10	58	36	70
Mildenhall Town	40	18	9	13	62	52	63
Woodbridge Town	40	17	9	14	63	51	60
Diss Town	40	17	9	14	69	62	60
Maldon Town	40	18	6	16	61	63	60
Ipswich Wanderers	40	16	8	16	59	60	56
Fakenham Town	40	14	12	14	55	55	54
Great Yarmouth Town	40	14	10	16	50	52	52
Gorleston	40	14	9	17	76	69	51
Newmarket Town	40	14	8	18	60	69	50
Warboys Town	40	13	9	18	55	65	48
Soham Town Rangers	40	12	5	23	52	76	41
Bury Town	40	8	12	20	38	65	36
Halstead Town	40	8	8	24	52	89	32
Stowmarket Town	40	8	8	24	40	83	32
Harwich & Parkeston	40	7	8	25	42	84	29
Felixstowe Port & Town	40	7	7	26	32	84	28

Division One	P	W	D	L	F	A	Pts
Tiptree United	34	23	9	2	89	19	78
Ely City	34	23	4	7	89	33	73
Stanway Rovers	34	21	8	5	68	31	71
Downham Town	34	22	4	8	77	36	70
Needham Market (−1)	34	20	5	9	76	46	64
Cambridge City Reserves	34	18	6	10	70	44	60
Dereham Town	34	16	5	13	53	36	53
Hadleigh United	34	15	7	12	52	44	52
Swaffham Town	34	16	4	14	47	42	52
Cornard United	34	14	10	10	42	44	52
Whitton United	34	14	6	14	65	58	48
Somersham Town	34	14	6	14	55	58	48
March Town United	34	10	7	17	48	78	37
Haverhill Rovers	34	9	7	18	48	70	34
Norwich United	34	6	3	25	44	99	21
Chatteris Town	34	4	7	23	30	75	19
Brightlingsea United	34	5	4	25	31	84	19
Thetford Town	34	3	4	27	27	105	13

COMPLETE MUSIC HELLENIC LEAGUE

Premier Division	P	W	D	L	F	A	Pts
Banbury United	36	29	5	2	87	22	92
Highworth Town	36	25	4	7	90	54	79
Swindon Supermarine	36	23	4	9	74	27	73
Tuffley Rovers	36	22	4	10	76	44	70
Brackley Town	36	21	6	9	66	32	69
North Leigh	36	19	7	10	81	53	64
Didcot Town	36	17	10	9	61	50	61
Abingdon United	36	17	6	13	58	55	57
Carterton Town	36	15	6	15	47	50	51
Pegasus Juniors	36	15	5	16	62	61	50
Shortwood United	36	13	10	13	54	55	49
Wantage Town	36	15	4	17	50	64	49
Hallen (−6)	36	13	7	16	55	60	40
Cirencester Academy	36	10	6	20	34	53	36
Bicester Town	36	9	5	22	42	73	32
Fairford Town	36	7	8	21	32	69	29
Almondsbury Town	36	7	5	24	42	83	26
Harrow Hill	36	7	1	28	44	96	22
Milton United	36	3	7	26	36	90	16

Division One	P	W	D	L	F	A	Pts
Cheltenham Saracens	28	23	2	3	61	20	71
Ardley United	28	16	6	6	63	38	54
Wootton Bassett Town	28	15	7	6	54	32	52
Worcester College OB	28	13	6	9	53	46	45
Bishops Cleeve	28	12	8	8	44	43	44
Middle Barton	28	12	5	11	49	45	41
Letcombe	28	11	5	12	57	45	38
Easington Sports	28	10	6	12	50	58	36
Purton	28	10	4	14	42	56	34
Ross Town	28	8	8	12	32	32	32
Old Woodstock Town	28	8	8	12	43	51	32
Kidlington	28	9	5	14	36	50	32
Cirencester United	28	10	1	17	38	50	31
Clanfield	28	6	6	16	33	58	24
Headington Amateurs	28	6	5	17	29	60	23

KENT BREWERS BASS LEAGUE

	P	W	D	L	F	A	Pts
Deal Town	34	26	5	3	87	28	83
Thamesmead Town (−3)	34	23	6	5	75	29	72
Chatham Town	34	23	3	8	76	40	72
VCD Athletic	34	18	10	6	53	32	64
Ramsgate	34	18	9	7	75	41	63
Greenwich Borough	34	17	5	12	70	44	56
Erith Town	34	16	8	10	56	54	56
Hythe United	34	14	6	14	38	50	48
Sheppey United (+3)	34	12	6	16	45	60	45
Beckenham Town	34	12	8	14	45	51	44
Lordswood	34	12	6	16	55	63	42
Herne Bay (−3)	34	12	8	14	56	48	41
Cray Wanderers (+3)	34	10	3	21	42	80	36
Tunbridge Wells	34	9	6	19	49	72	33
Slade Green	34	8	6	20	41	65	30
Whitstable Town	34	6	9	19	38	56	27
Faversham Town	34	6	6	22	39	70	24
Canterbury City	34	6	4	22	35	92	24

SCREWFIX DIRECT WESTERN LEAGUE

Premier Division	P	W	D	L	F	A	Pts
Taunton Town	36	30	4	2	116	37	94
Mangotsfield United	36	23	9	4	95	31	78
Brislington	36	20	5	11	63	43	65
Chippenham Town	36	18	9	9	69	41	63
Paulton Rovers	36	16	11	9	53	34	59
Melksham Town	36	15	11	10	50	46	56
Backwell United	36	15	9	12	50	44	54
Bridport	36	12	13	11	56	56	49
Dawlish Town	36	12	11	13	51	45	47
Yeovil Town Reserves	36	11	14	11	64	63	47
Elmore	36	13	8	15	51	63	47
Bishop Sutton	36	13	4	19	73	73	43
Bideford	36	10	10	16	46	68	40
Bridgwater Town	36	10	8	18	42	53	38
Barnstaple Town	36	9	7	20	35	51	34
Westbury United	36	9	7	20	39	67	34
Bristol Manor Farm	36	8	9	19	48	78	33
Odd Down	36	6	6	21	36	82	33
Minehead Town	36	9	5	22	60	101	32

Division One	P	W	D	L	F	A	Pts
Devizes Town	32	23	9	0	88	30	78
Welton Rovers	32	22	4	6	74	19	70
Clyst Rovers	32	19	5	8	83	39	62
Exmouth Town	32	16	9	7	67	43	57
Keynsham Town	32	16	9	7	48	34	57
Bitton	32	16	6	10	60	47	54
Torrington	32	16	6	10	62	50	54
Street	32	13	10	9	56	40	49
Larkhall Athletic	32	11	8	13	45	55	41
Wellington	32	11	7	14	46	44	40
Ilfracombe Town	32	12	2	18	59	65	38
Warminster Town	32	10	6	16	40	77	36
Calne Town	32	10	5	17	48	71	35
Pewsey Vale	32	10	2	20	51	88	32
Chard Town	32	8	7	17	31	52	31
Corsham Town	32	5	5	22	36	86	20
Frome Town	32	3	2	27	30	84	11

Division Three	P	W	D	L	F	A	Pts
Bosham	30	24	3	3	109	36	75
Wealden	30	22	2	6	78	38	68
Ansty Rangers	30	21	3	6	80	33	66
Crowborough Athletic	30	17	7	6	65	44	58
Haywards Heath	30	17	6	7	74	38	57
Uckfield Town	30	16	3	11	55	48	51
Bexhill Town	30	15	4	11	62	60	49
Seaford Town	30	14	3	13	65	60	45
Forest	30	13	6	11	42	48	45
St Francis	30	10	6	14	42	50	36
Franklands Village	30	9	5	16	39	52	32
Steyning Town	30	9	3	18	55	76	30
Ifield	30	5	6	19	43	69	21
Hurstpierpoint	30	5	5	20	44	81	20
Newhaven	30	5	2	23	34	104	17
Royal & Sun Alliance	30	4	4	22	33	83	16

JEWSON WESSEX LEAGUE

	P	W	D	L	F	A	Pts
Wimborne Town	40	31	4	4	126	33	100
Lymington & New Milton	40	31	7	2	115	27	100
Andover	40	25	7	8	147	60	82
AFC Totton	40	24	8	8	93	30	80
BAT Sports	40	24	8	8	88	48	80
Moneyfields	40	22	9	9	76	64	75
Eastleigh	40	20	8	12	67	46	68
AFC Newbury	40	17	12	11	67	51	63
Cowes Sports	40	17	11	12	73	55	62
Bemerton Heath H	40	17	9	14	75	66	60
Fareham Town	40	14	14	12	72	71	56
Christchurch	40	16	7	17	68	67	55
Thatcham Town	40	15	7	18	62	69	52
Gosport Borough	40	8	12	20	40	70	36
Downton	40	10	6	24	74	113	36
Hamble ASSC	40	7	11	22	44	89	32
Whitchurch United	40	7	10	23	53	89	31
Brockenhurst	40	7	7	26	43	114	28
Bournemouth (−2)	40	7	8	25	54	110	27
Portsmouth Royal Navy	40	5	10	25	47	114	25
East Cowes Victoria	40	5	5	30	43	141	20

MINERVA SPARTAN SOUTH MIDLANDS LEAGUE

Premier Division	P	W	D	L	F	A	Pts
Arlesey Town	40	30	3	7	98	45	93
Brook House (+2)	40	27	6	7	102	33	89
Beaconsfield SYCOB (−1)	40	26	4	10	87	42	81
Potters Bar Town	40	26	2	12	105	66	80
London Colney	40	22	11	6	87	38	77
Waltham Abbey	40	23	4	13	78	64	73
Brache Sparta	40	19	13	8	85	48	70
Hoddesdon Town	40	21	7	12	85	55	70
Milton Keynes City	40	21	5	14	80	53	68
Hanwell Town	40	20	6	14	73	52	66
Royston Town	40	15	8	17	53	54	53
Ruislip Manor	40	14	4	20	61	81	52
New Bradwell St Peter	40	12	13	15	65	75	49
Hillingdon Borough	40	14	6	20	56	63	48
Holmer Green	40	12	10	18	56	92	46
St Margaretsbury	40	10	9	21	67	93	39
Biggleswade Town	40	9	7	24	49	73	34
Haringey Borough	40	10	1	28	56	99	31
Welwyn Garden City	40	6	11	23	49	98	29
Somersett Ambury V&E	40	7	5	28	48	102	26
Harpenden Town	40	4	3	33	41	155	15

The Haringey v London Colney match on May 4 was abandoned after 69 mins. The result is subject to a yet to be convened County FA disciplinary hearing.

Senior Division	P	W	D	L	F	A	Pts
Tring Athletic	36	27	5	4	103	29	86
Ampthill Town	36	23	6	7	86	46	75
Bedford United	36	22	5	9	106	48	71
Biggleswade United	36	18	10	8	71	55	64
Letchworth	36	17	10	9	74	57	61
Cockfosters	36	17	9	10	79	55	60
Bridger Packing	36	19	3	14	74	63	60
Brimsdown Rovers (+2)	36	17	5	14	74	52	58
Amersham Town	36	15	11	10	63	48	56
Totternhoe	36	15	11	10	56	46	56
Langford	36	14	9	13	59	60	51
Leverstock Green	36	12	10	14	61	59	46
Greenacres	36	11	9	16	56	66	42
Stony Stratford	36	11	6	19	60	86	39
Harefield United (−1)	36	8	13	15	40	49	36
Risborough Rangers	36	6	7	23	44	73	25
Caddington	36	6	6	24	40	127	24
Luton Old Boys	36	5	7	24	35	89	22
Shillington	36	6	4	26	46	119	22

Division One	P	W	D	L	F	A	Pts
Dunstable Town	32	26	6	0	115	17	84
De Havilland	32	24	4	4	113	31	76
Pistone & Ivinghoe	32	22	7	3	97	28	73
Winslow United	32	21	5	6	84	34	68
Scot (−3)	32	19	1	12	92	64	55
Mursley United	32	16	6	10	62	42	54
Old Dunstablians	32	15	3	14	51	53	48
Crawley Green	32	14	5	13	67	47	47
Kent Athletic	32	14	1	17	55	60	43
Buckingham Athletic	32	12	5	15	50	55	41
Flamstead	32	12	5	15	53	59	41
Abbey National	32	10	6	16	46	75	36
The 61 FC	32	9	7	16	52	72	34
Newport Athletic	32	8	5	19	49	91	29
Leighton Athletic	32	6	7	19	45	98	25
Old Bradwell United (+3)	32	3	4	25	26	101	16
Markyate	32	1	3	32	18	148	16

UNIJET SUSSEX COUNTY LEAGUE

Division One	P	W	D	L	F	A	Pts
Langney Sports	38	31	6	1	101	25	99
Burgess Hill Town	38	26	7	5	78	37	85
Saltdean United	38	24	7	7	97	45	79
East Preston	38	21	5	12	83	52	68
Horsham YMCA	38	18	10	10	78	53	64
Sidley United	38	17	10	11	63	54	61
Hassocks	38	18	5	15	56	45	59
Littlehampton Town	38	17	6	15	53	55	57
Eastbourne Town	38	14	14	10	73	49	56
Selsey	38	16	7	15	80	67	55
Whitehawk	38	16	7	15	58	59	55
Redhill	38	12	12	14	63	58	48
Portfield	38	14	3	21	64	105	45
Three Bridges	38	11	9	18	53	76	42
Eastbourne United	38	11	8	19	62	80	41
Pagham	38	10	9	19	46	68	39
Chichester City	38	9	7	22	64	77	34
Wick	38	9	4	25	49	102	31
Ringmer	38	7	5	26	47	95	26
Shoreham	38	7	3	28	43	109	24

Division Two	P	W	D	L	F	A	Pts
Sidlesham	34	25	6	3	85	29	81
Arundel	34	23	5	6	89	37	74
Lancing (+2)	34	17	10	7	64	43	63
Crawley Down	34	18	8	8	54	33	62
Oving	34	15	6	13	59	43	51
East Grinstead	34	13	8	13	71	57	47
Hailsham Town	34	12	11	11	59	48	47
Southwick	34	13	8	13	75	76	47
Westfield	34	13	8	13	45	47	47
Storrington	34	12	8	14	52	57	44
Mile Oak (−1)	34	12	8	14	63	61	43
Broadbridge Heath	34	11	9	14	62	67	42
Oakwood	34	11	7	16	52	77	40
Peacehaven & Telscombe	34	9	10	15	52	70	37
Worthing United	34	10	7	17	46	80	37
Withdean	34	8	6	20	40	64	30
Shinewater Association	34	8	6	20	40	77	30
Lingfield	34	8	5	21	42	84	29

SCHWEPPES ESSEX SENIOR LEAGUE

	P	W	D	L	F	A	Pts
Saffron Walden Town	28	19	5	4	85	33	62
Southend Manor	28	19	5	4	81	33	62
Burnham Ramblers	28	19	5	4	68	32	62
Ilford	28	18	4	6	70	34	58
Brentwood	28	17	2	9	49	40	53
Bowers United	28	14	6	8	51	42	48
Sawbridgeworth Town	28	11	10	7	65	48	43
Concord Rangers	28	11	9	8	46	41	42
Leyton	28	9	5	14	45	55	32
Hullbridge Sports	28	8	3	17	44	63	27
East Ham United	28	5	8	15	30	65	23
Eton Manor (–4)	28	6	8	14	41	61	22
Basildon United (–2)	28	6	6	16	37	61	22
Woodford Town	28	5	3	20	46	99	18
Stansted	28	2	3	23	35	86	9

COURAGE COMBINED COUNTIES LEAGUE

	P	W	D	L	F	A	Pts
Ashford Town (+3)	40	31	6	3	123	37	102
Ash United	40	31	6	3	132	50	99
Bedfont	40	23	8	9	100	55	77
Chipstead	40	21	10	9	88	49	73
Walton Casuals (+3)	40	20	10	10	80	64	73
Wallingford	40	20	11	9	77	50	71
Godalming & Guildford	40	18	7	15	89	69	61
Cove	40	17	9	14	68	61	60
Westfield	40	15	13	12	60	47	58
Farnham Town	40	15	10	15	51	60	55
Cobham	39	15	8	16	74	65	53
Reading Town	40	14	10	16	64	74	52
Merstham	40	14	10	16	76	95	52
Chessington & Hook	40	11	13	16	57	66	46
Feltham	40	13	4	23	54	83	43
Raynes Park Vale	40	13	4	23	59	90	43
Viking Greenford (–3)	40	11	6	23	55	104	36
Sandhurst Town	39	8	9	22	70	96	33
Chessington United (–3)	40	9	9	22	45	92	33
Hartley Wintney	40	7	10	23	59	95	31
Cranleigh	40	4	5	31	35	114	17

Sandhurst Town v Cobham – Management Committee decision awaited.

REDFERNS CENTRAL MIDLANDS LEAGUE

Supreme Division

	P	W	D	L	F	A	Pts
Lincoln Moorlands	36	22	8	6	90	37	74
Shirebrook Town	36	22	7	7	67	33	73
Sandiacre Town	36	21	7	8	90	51	70
Gedling Town	36	22	4	10	77	51	70
Heanor Town	36	19	9	8	61	37	66
Dunkirk	36	21	2	13	81	48	65
South Normanton Athletic	36	19	6	11	80	55	63
Hucknall Rolls Royce	36	18	8	10	77	57	62
Selston	36	14	11	11	60	54	53
Sneinton	36	11	13	12	61	69	46
Collingham	36	13	6	17	64	82	45
Grimethorpe MW	36	12	7	17	54	70	43
Kimberley Town	36	11	9	16	60	60	42
Nettleham	36	10	9	17	49	62	39
Clipstone Welfare	36	10	7	19	60	80	37
Welbeck CW	36	10	6	20	56	78	36
Long Eaton United	36	10	3	23	38	77	33
Harworth CI	36	7	3	26	45	119	24
Blackwell MW	36	6	3	27	48	98	21

Premier

	P	W	D	L	F	A	Pts
Holbrook	30	19	6	5	84	34	63
Graham St Prims	30	18	5	7	67	32	59
Mickleover RBL	30	16	10	4	69	28	58
Shardlow St James	30	17	5	8	71	44	56
Stanton Ilkeston	30	17	4	9	53	46	55
Radford	30	15	7	8	58	45	52
Askern Welfare	30	15	7	8	49	38	52
Thorne Colliery	30	14	9	7	55	41	51
Greenwood Meadows	30	13	6	11	56	48	45
Yorkshire Main	30	11	5	14	47	58	38
Grantham Rangers	30	9	6	15	44	59	33
Ripley Town	30	9	3	18	47	71	30
Kiveton Park	30	7	4	19	49	71	25
Mexborough T Athletic	30	6	5	19	46	66	23
Teversal Grange	30	4	5	21	32	72	17
Blidworth Welfare	30	4	5	21	41	96	17

BANKS WEST MIDLANDS LEAGUE

Premier Division

	P	W	D	L	F	A	Pts
Stafford Town	42	35	4	3	113	32	109
Causeway United	42	34	2	6	88	35	104
Darlaston Town	42	30	5	7	115	63	95
Bandon	42	26	7	9	83	46	85
Wolverhampton Casuals	42	25	6	11	99	54	81
Kington Town (–6)	42	25	3	14	88	68	72
Tividale	42	19	9	14	66	58	66
Heath Hayes	42	19	4	19	64	66	61
Malvern Town	42	17	7	18	73	55	58
Little Drayton Rangers	42	16	10	16	64	66	58
Lye Town	42	15	9	18	65	66	54
Dudley Town	42	13	13	16	53	59	52
Gornal Athletic	42	14	4	24	58	75	46
Tipton Town	42	12	9	21	61	87	45
Smethwick Rangers	42	12	8	22	66	95	44
Ettingshall Holy Trinity	42	11	10	21	53	91	43
Brierley Hill Town	42	11	8	23	51	73	41
Ludlow Town	42	10	11	21	52	75	41
Bustleholme	42	10	9	23	68	95	39
Westfields	42	9	9	24	56	89	36
Walsall Wood	42	8	10	24	55	99	34
Star	42	8	9	25	37	81	33

JEWSON WESTERN LEAGUE

	P	W	D	L	F	A	Pts
Falmouth Town	34	24	8	2	88	25	80
St Blazey	34	25	5	4	97	36	80
Porthleven	34	23	9	2	91	41	78
Liskeard Athletic	34	18	7	9	80	40	61
Millbrook	34	17	9	8	68	47	60
Saltash United	34	18	3	13	61	50	57
Wadebridge Town	34	17	4	13	66	59	55
Tavistock	34	14	9	11	51	46	51
Plymouth Parkway	34	15	6	13	57	73	51
Newquay	34	14	5	15	67	76	47
Bodmin Town	34	14	4	16	60	64	46
Truro City	34	10	5	19	55	71	35
Penzance	34	10	4	20	51	76	34
Torpoint Athletic	34	9	6	19	53	74	33
Holsworthy	34	7	10	17	51	63	31
Callington Town	34	7	6	21	41	85	27
Launceston	34	5	5	24	35	95	20
St Austell	34	4	5	25	31	82	17

RAPIDE MIDLAND COMBINATION

Premier Division

	P	W	D	L	F	A	Pts
Nuneaton Griff	38	25	10	3	118	41	85
Kings Heath	38	22	10	6	79	42	76
Studley BKL	38	21	7	10	85	50	70
Marconi (Coventry)	38	20	9	9	81	51	69
Meir KA	38	18	10	10	81	48	64
Coventry Sphinx	38	18	7	13	69	47	61
Massey Ferguson	38	17	10	11	75	59	61
Cheslyn Hay	38	17	9	12	82	60	60
Feckenham	38	16	11	11	60	47	59
Alvechurch	38	17	8	13	74	77	59
Continental Star	38	14	11	13	62	75	53
Handrahan Timbers	38	15	7	16	51	61	52
Northfield Town	38	15	6	17	57	57	51
Bolehall Swifts	38	14	8	16	90	63	50
Blackheath Electrodrives	38	13	9	16	54	73	48
Southam United	38	11	8	19	64	78	41
Alveston	38	11	5	22	52	93	38
Highgate United	38	8	7	23	53	88	31
Coleshill Town (–3)	38	5	5	28	52	124	17
Kenilworth Town	38	3	3	32	34	139	12

CARLSBERG WEST CHESHIRE LEAGUE

Division One	P	W	D	L	F	A	Pts
Poulton Victoria	30	23	6	1	84	36	75
Cammell Laird	30	18	9	3	80	36	63
Vauxhall Motors	30	17	9	4	71	38	60
Ashville	30	15	9	6	62	25	54
Heswall	30	14	12	4	64	29	54
Stork	30	14	6	10	62	60	48
Capenhurst	30	13	9	8	47	45	48
Mersey Royal	30	13	8	9	71	55	47
Christleton	30	9	12	9	52	45	39
General Chemicals	30	10	7	13	52	57	37
Maghull	30	10	4	16	40	48	34
Mond Rangers	30	9	4	17	52	75	31
Shell Tessuti	30	5	5	20	37	84	20
Blacon Youth Club (–3)	30	6	4	20	55	105	19
Newton	30	3	7	20	29	70	16
Merseyside Police	30	4	3	23	35	85	15

EVERARDS LEICESTER SENIOR LEAGUE

Premier Division	P	W	D	L	F	A	Pts
Highfield Rangers	34	23	7	4	79	28	76
St Andrews SC	34	21	9	4	97	30	72
Quorn	34	19	7	8	69	44	64
Downes Sports	34	18	9	7	73	41	63
Kirby Muxloe SC	34	19	6	9	72	44	63
Ibstock Welfare	34	16	6	12	58	53	54
Thringstone United	34	14	7	13	64	61	49
Friar Lane OB	34	13	8	13	71	71	47
Thurmaston Town	34	12	9	13	60	53	45
Holwell Sports	34	11	11	12	58	66	44
Coalville Town	34	11	10	13	45	48	43
Barrow Town	34	10	9	15	58	64	39
Birstall United	34	9	11	14	46	60	38
Anstey Nomads	34	10	6	18	51	69	36
Cottesmore Amateurs	34	8	10	16	79	96	34
Aylestone Park OB	34	8	9	17	48	72	33
Ellistown	34	6	6	22	32	109	24
Lutterworth Town	34	6	4	24	39	90	22

DORSET COMBINATION

	P	W	D	L	F	A	Pts
Portland United	36	27	5	4	100	30	86
Dorchester Res	36	27	2	7	102	38	83
Swanage T & H	36	23	7	6	82	32	76
Hamworthy Eng	36	23	3	10	115	67	72
Parley Sports (–6)	36	23	5	8	100	59	68
Gillingham Town	36	17	8	11	87	70	59
Blandford United	36	17	7	12	65	43	58
Hamworthy United	36	16	8	12	63	53	56
Westland Sports	36	16	7	13	71	73	55
Flight Refuelling	36	15	9	12	84	65	54
Bridport Res	36	16	6	14	62	50	54
Allendale	36	14	9	13	66	55	51
Wareham Rangers	36	11	8	17	51	69	41
Sturm. Newton U	36	12	4	20	61	65	40
Weymouth Sports	36	9	7	20	53	89	34
Sherborne Town	36	8	9	19	40	91	33
Shaftesbury	36	6	4	26	39	91	22
Witchampton United	36	2	5	29	26	122	11
Bournemouth Sports	36	2	3	31	35	140	9

SLG SEAT CARS WEST LANCS PREMIER

	P	W	D	L	F	A	Pts
Kirkham & Wesham	30	24	3	3	98	22	75
Dalton United	30	19	4	7	80	47	61
Freckleton	30	17	5	8	60	40	56
Charnock Richard	30	17	4	9	66	45	55
Blackrod Town (–3)	30	17	3	10	58	51	51
Barnoldswick United	30	15	4	11	63	56	49
Vickers SC	30	14	6	10	49	41	48
Springfields	30	13	3	14	57	65	42
Leyland Motors Athletic	30	12	2	16	53	64	38
Norcross & Warb.	30	9	7	14	53	66	34
Wyre Villa	30	10	3	17	40	65	33
Eagley	30	9	5	16	43	57	32
Burnley United	30	10	1	19	52	76	31
Fulwood Ams (–3)	30	8	6	16	55	55	27
Lansil	30	6	7	17	49	86	25
Feniscowles	30	7	3	20	23	63	24

STRUCTURAL REVISIONS

The entire peak of the pyramid system in non-league football will be changed in two years time. Following meetings with the Northern Premier, Southern and Isthmian Leagues, the Nationwide Conference intends that as from the commencement of the 2002–03 season, the Northern Premier League and Southern Football League will be the only recognised feeder leagues to the Nationwide Conference.

The constitution of both competitions will be derived from the clubs in the Northern Premier, Southern and Isthmian Leagues. It is anticipated that this will create the opportunity for increased promotion into the Nationwide Conference.

AMATEUR FOOTBALL ALLIANCE 1999–2000

AFA SENIOR CUP

1st Round Proper
Old Salopians 3 National Westminster Bank 2
Cardinal Manning O B 3 Kew Association 4
Carshalton 3:5* Mill Hill Village 3:3*
Old Wilsonians 1 HSBC 2
Nottsborough 1 Old Owens 3
Old Reptonians 1 Old Danes 5
Broomfield 0 Old Esthameians 1
Old Hamptonians 0 Merton 2
Fulham Compton O B 1 West Wickham 3
Old Actonians Association 5* Old Aloysians 1*
Alexandra Park 1 Polytechnic 2
East Barnet Old Grammarians 2 Old Minchendenians 1
Civil Service 7 Old Southallians 1
Crouch End Vampires 1 Old Cholmeleians 0
Old Parmiterians 4*:4p Old Manorians 4*:3p
Old Challoners 3* Old Finchleians 5*
Old Ignatians 2 Honourable Artillery Company 1
Old Woodhouseians 5 Wandsworth Borough 4
Silhill 1 Old Salesians 2
Old Bromleians 2 Old Meadonians 5
Lloyds TSB Bank 1*:4p Old Tenisonians 1*:3p
Old Chigwellians 2 Southgate County 3
Old Vaughanians 3 Old Sedcopians 0
St. Mary's College 2 Old Salvatorians 0
Alleyn Old Boys 2 Old Tiffinians 1
Old Buckwellians 4 Shene Old Grammarians 2
UCL Academicals 6 Southgate Olympic 0
Old Grammarians 2 Old Isleworthians 1
Old Parkonians 2 Barclays Bank 1
Old Foresters 2*:1p Norsemen 2*:3p
Bank of England 4 CGU Cuaco Club 0

2nd Round Proper
Old Salopians 1 Kew Association 4
Carshalton 1 South Bank 0

HSBC 3*:3p Old Owens 3*:4p
Old Danes 2 Old Esthameians 5
Merton 2*:3p West Wickham 2*:4p
Old Actonians Ass'n 0*:2p Polytechnic 0*:4p
East Barnet Old Gramm'ns 1 Civil Service 2
Crouch End Vampires 5 Old Parmiterians 1
Old Finchleians 3 Old Ignatians 0
Old Woodhouseians 2 Old Salesians 1
Old Meadonians 3 Lloyds TSB Bank 2
Southgate County 3 Old Vaughanians 0
St Mary's College 3 Alleyn Old Boys 1
Old Buckwellians 1 UCL Academicals 2
Old Grammarians 1 Barclays Bank 3
Norsemen 0 Bank of England 3

3rd Round Proper
Kew Association 3* Carshalton 1*
Old Owens 1 Old Esthameians 2
West Wickham 2 Polytechnic 3
Civil Service 1*:3p Crouch End Vampires 1*:5p
Old Finchleians 4* Old Woodhouseians 1*
Old Meadonians 2 Southgate County 3
UCL Academicals 2 St Mary's College 1
Barclays Bank 2 Bank of England 1

4th Round Proper
Kew Association 3*:1p Old Esthameians 3*:4p
Polytechnic 3*:0p Crouch End Vampires 3*:3p
Old Finchleians 1 Southgate County 2
UCL Academicals 3 Barclays Bank 3

Semi-finals
Old Esthameians 0 Crouch End Vampires 2
Southgate County 1 UCL Academicals 2

Final
Crouch End Vampires 1*:2p UCL Academicals 1*:4p
(* after extra time; p – kicks from penalty mark)

OTHER AFA CUP RESULTS

Intermediate
Bank of England Res 4 Old Woodhouseians Res 1
Junior
East Barnet O G Res 0* Globe Rangers 1st 2*
Minor
HSBC 4th 2 Old Actonians 4th 1
Senior Novets
Old Aloysians 5th 6 Old Suttonians 5th 0
Intermediate Novets
Nat'l Westmin'r Bank 6th 2 Old Actonians 6th 0
Junior Novets
Old Actonians 7th 1 Polytechnic 7th 2
Veterans
Winchmore Hill 1 Old Buckwellians Vets 2
Open Veterans
Old Parmiterians 2* Port of London Auth'y 0*
Youth
Norsemen Youth 8 Old Parmiterians Youth 0
Essex Divisional Senior
Hale End Athletic 1 Old Brentwoods 0
Middlesex Divisional Senior
Old Actonians Assoc'n 2* Old Isleworthians 1*
Surrey Divisional Senior
Lloyds TSB Bank 2 Merton 1
Essex Divisional Intermediate
Old Egbertians 1st 2 Hale End Athletic Res 3
Kent Divisional Intermediate
West Wickham Res 3 Morgan Guaranty 1st 1
Middlesex Divisional Intermediate
Old Hamptonians Res 3 Old Vaughanians 4
Surrey Divisional Intermediate
Royal Sun Alliance 1st 4 Carshalton Res 1
W E Greenland Memorial
Old Ignatians 2 Old Actonians 1
(*after extra time)

AFA REPRESENTATIVE XI

v Civil Service National XI (Trial)	Lost	1-2	
v Oxford University	Lost	3-5	
v Army F A	Won	2-0	
v Royal Navy F A	Won	2-1	
v Royal Air Force F A	Lost	2-4	
v Cambridge University	Lost	1-4	
v London F A	Won	3-2	
v London University	Canc	Rain	

ARTHUR DUNN CUP FINAL
Lancing Old Boys 3 Old Foresters 0

ARTHURIAN LEAGUE

PREMIER DIVISION	P	W	D	L	F	A	Pts
Old Brentwoods	16	10	2	4	42	26	22
Old Carthusians	16	7	4	5	35	27	18
Old Chigwellians	16	6	6	4	33	31	18
Old Cholmeleians	16	8	2	6	28	27	18
Old Reptonians	16	5	7	4	25	22	17
Old Salopians	16	8	1	7	32	33	17
Lancing Old Boys	16	5	6	5	30	32	16
Old Foresters	16	7	2	7	32	26	13*
Old Malvernians	16	0	2	14	17	50	2

DIVISION 1	P	W	D	L	F	A	Pts
Old Harrovians	14	13	0	1	56	19	26
Old Etonians	14	10	0	4	40	21	20
Old Haberdashers	14	7	2	5	36	30	16
Old Bradfieldians	14	6	1	7	33	27	13
Old Wellingburians	14	6	0	8	25	42	12
Old Witleians	14	4	2	8	22	35	10
Old Wykehamists	14	4	1	9	31	43	9
Old Aldenhamians	14	3	0	11	21	47	6

DIVISION 2	P	W	D	L	F	A	Pts
Old Etonians Res	16	14	2	0	50	12	30
Old Brentwoods Res	16	8	5	3	39	21	21
Old Chigwellians Res	16	7	3	6	29	32	17
Old Salopians Res	16	7	2	7	30	32	16
Lancing Old Boys Res	16	4	6	6	32	32	14
Old Cholmeleians Res	16	5	4	7	21	33	14
Old Etonians 3rd	16	5	4	7	27	40	14
Old Carthusians Res	16	3	5	8	26	32	11
Old Millhillians	16	2	3	11	24	44	3*

DIVISION 3	P	W	D	L	F	A	Pts
Old Westminsters	14	12	1	1	66	13	25
Old Haberdashers Res	14	11	0	3	45	23	22
Old Foresters Res	14	6	2	6	34	33	14
Old Aldenhamians Res	14	6	1	7	34	25	13
Old Foresters 3rd	14	5	2	7	33	34	12
Old Harrovians Res	14	5	1	8	28	34	11
Old Reptonians Res	14	5	0	9	27	48	10
Old Cholmeleians 3rd	14	2	1	11	17	49	5

DIVISION 4	P	W	D	L	F	A	Pts
Old Carthusians 3rd	14	9	2	3	40	33	20
Old Bradfieldians Res	14	8	3	3	24	9	19
Old Eastbournians	14	7	2	5	42	29	16
Old Haileyburians	14	6	4	4	44	38	16
Old Cholmeleians 4th	14	6	1	7	25	30	13
Old Malvernians Res	14	6	2	6	35	32	12*
Old Brentwoods 3rd	14	4	1	9	28	38	9
Old Cholmeleians 5th	13	1	2	10	27	56	4

(*Points deducted - breach of Rule*)

DIVISION 5–8 Teams – Won by Old Brentwoods 4th

LONDON FINANCIAL FA

DIVISION ONE	P	W	D	L	F	A	Pts
Morgan Guaranty	16	13	2	1	56	23	41
Coutts	16	10	1	5	41	29	31
Royal Sun Alliance	16	8	1	7	46	33	25
Granby	16	7	4	5	32	29	25
Citibank	16	7	4	5	29	27	25
Bank of America	16	6	3	7	32	40	21
Dresdner Kleinwort Benson	16	3	1	12	28	40	10
Royal Bank of Scotland	16	3	1	12	26	43	10
Eagle Star	16	2	3	11	37	63	6***

DIVISION TWO	P	W	D	L	F	A	Pts
Mount Pleasant Post Office	14	13	1	0	68	17	40
Foreign & Commonwealth	14	8	4	2	44	22	28
Chase Manhattan Bank	14	7	2	5	45	26	23
Marsh	14	6	2	6	42	38	20
Standard Chartered Bank	14	4	4	6	23	30	16
Temple Bar	14	4	2	8	33	44	14
Abbey National	14	4	1	9	26	50	13
Customs and Excise	14	0	4	10	14	68	3***

DIVISION THREE	P	W	D	L	F	A	Pts
Royal Sun Alliance Res	16	14	2	0	46	18	44
Chelsea Exiles	16	10	4	2	88	37	34
Bank America Res	16	9	3	4	39	28	30
Eagle Star Res	16	8	3	5	40	35	27
Cabinet Office & Treasury	16	6	3	7	39	41	21
C. Hoare & Co.	16	5	1	10	43	60	16
Salomon Smith Barney	16	4	2	10	33	44	14
ANZ Banking Group	16	3	2	11	28	51	11
Royal Bank of Scotland Res	16	1	4	11	13	55	7

DIVISION FOUR	P	W	D	L	F	A	Pts
British Gas (Bromley)	16	12	3	1	73	30	39
Marsh Res	16	9	3	4	58	32	30
Coutts Res	16	5	7	4	28	25	22
Royal Sun Alliance Res	16	6	4	6	36	39	22
Granby Res	16	5	6	5	34	27	21
Citibank Res	16	5	5	6	38	44	20
Bank of Ireland	16	3	9	4	27	34	18
Credit Suisse First Boston	16	4	2	10	23	46	14
Noble Lowndes	16	1	5	10	21	61	18

DIVISION FIVE	P	W	D	L	F	A	Pts
UCB Home Loans	21	15	4	2	73	24	49
Marsh 3rd	21	13	3	5	54	38	42
Standard Chartered Res	21	11	3	7	57	59	36
Eagle Star 3rd	21	7	5	9	49	52	26
Granby 3rd	21	6	7	8	35	42	25
CGU Cuaco 5th	21	7	3	11	62	71	24
Temple Bar Res	21	4	7	10	33	49	19
Royal Bank of Scotland 3rd	21	2	6	13	42	70	12
Noble Lowndes Res. Withdrawn							

(***** *Points deducted – breach of rule*)

Challenge Cup–HSBC 4 Dresdner Kleinwort Benson 1
Senior Cup–Morgan Guaranty 3 Dresdner Kleinwort Benson 0
Junior Cup–Chelsea Exiles 7 Granby Res 1
Minor Cup–UCB Home Loans 3 Temple Bar Res 1
Veterans' Cup–Lensbury 1 Bank of England 0

W A Jewell Mem'l V-a-S–Won by Mount Pleasant P O
Saunders Shield V-a-S–Won by Temple Bar
Sportsmanship Shield–Won by Gaflac

Representative Matches

LFFA	v	Stock Exchange F A	Lost	2-3
(1999 Daily Telegraph Cup)				
LFFA	v	Southern Olympian League	Lost	1-8
LFFA	v	Royal Marines	Lost	0-9
LFFA	v	Southern Amateur League	Lost	1-5
LFFA	v	Old Boys' League	Won	4-3
LFFA	v	Bristol Insurance Institute	Lost	0-3
LFFA	v	Stock Exchange F A	Won	2-0
(2000 Daily Telegraph Cup)				

LONDON LEGAL LEAGUE

DIVISION ONE	P	W	D	L	F	A	Pts
Denton Wilde Sapte "A"	18	14	1	3	64	22	43
K.P.M.G.	18	12	3	3	42	22	39
Slaughter & May	18	12	1	5	59	24	36*
Lovell White Durrant	18	10	4	4	43	34	34
Gray's Inn	18	10	1	7	47	31	30*
Clifford Chance	18	8	3	7	37	41	26*
Linklaters & Paines	18	7	3	8	45	46	23*
Cameron Markby Hewitt	18	3	2	13	20	32	11
Rosling King	18	2	1	15	18	55	7
Taylor Joynson Garrett	18	1	3	14	18	66	5*

DIVISION TWO	P	W	D	L	F	A	Pts
Norton Rose	18	10	6	2	44	21	36
Nabarro Nathanson	18	11	3	4	36	18	36
Pegasus (Inner Temple)	18	10	3	5	51	34	33
Simmons & Simmons	18	8	7	3	39	21	31
Nicholson Graham & Jones	18	8	2	8	30	33	26
Freshfields	18	5	5	8	27	33	20
Watson Farley & Williams	18	5	3	10	28	33	18
Herbert Smith	18	6	0	12	28	50	18
Stephenson Harwood	18	5	3	10	28	39	16**
Denton Wilde Sapte "B"	18	4	4	10	18	47	16

DIVISION THREE	P	W	D	L	F	A	Pts
Eversheds	18	13	3	2	63	23	42
Baker & McKenzie	18	13	1	4	71	40	40
S.J. Berwin	18	11	1	6	38	24	34
Edge Ellison	18	8	3	7	27	43	27
Titmus Sainer Dechert	18	8	2	8	35	32	25*
Barlow Lyde & Gilbert	18	6	6	6	42	38	24
Allen & Overy	18	6	3	9	41	59	21
Richards Butler	18	6	1	11	24	40	19
Stock Exchange	18	5	3	10	38	44	18
Macfarlanes	18	1	3	14	30	57	4**

(*Points deducted – breach of Rule*)

League Challenge Cup–Gray's Inn 5 Slaughter & May 1
Weavers Arms Cup–Norton Rose 5 Linklaters & Paines 2

LONDON OLD BOYS' CUPS

Senior–Old Wilsonians 1 Old Ignatians 0
Intermediate–Queen Mary College O B 2 Latymer Old Boys Res 1
Junior–Old Actonians 3rd 2 Old Tollingtonians Res 1
Minor–Clapham Old Xaverians 4th 3 Old Aloysians 4th 1
Novets–Old Suttonians 5th 2 Old Edmontonians 4th 1
Drummond–Old Actonians Assn. 6th 2 Old Wilsonians 6th 0
Nemean–Old Aloysians 7th 5 Old Actonians 7th 3
Veterans'–Old Tenisonians Vets 3 Old Salvatorians Vets 0

OLD BOYS' INVITATION CUPS

Senior–Old Bromleians 2 Old Owens 1
Junior–Old Tenisonians Res 0 Old Finchleians Res 3
Minor–Old Salesians 3rd 1 Old Tenisonians 3rd 2
4th XIs–Old Wilsonians 4th 2 Old Finchleians 4th 7
5th XIs–Old Westminster Citizens 5th 3 Old Suttonians 5th 4
6th XIs–Old Finchleians 6th 9 Old Stationers 6th 2
7th Xis–Old Finchleians 7th 3 Old Finchleians 8th 1
Veterans'–Old Tenisonians Vets 1 Old Westminster Citizens Vets 0

MIDLAND AMATEUR ALLIANCE

PREMIER DIVISION	P	W	D	L	F	A	Pts
A S C Dayncourt	20	14	5	1	70	25	47
Old Elizabethans	20	14	0	6	64	34	42
Bassingfield	20	11	4	5	53	27	37
Caribbean Cavaliers	20	12	1	7	53	51	37
Nottingham Irish Centre	20	10	4	6	71	48	34
Kirton Brick Works	20	9	0	11	48	47	27
Lady Bay	20	7	5	8	51	49	26
Horse & Jockey	20	6	4	10	54	74	22
Pannell Kerr Foster Steelers	20	6	2	12	29	54	20
Parkhead Academicals	20	4	1	15	29	75	13
Beeston Old Boys Assn	20	3	2	15	20	58	11

DIVISION ONE	P	W	D	L	F	A	Pts
Woodborough United	28	20	1	7	96	47	61
A S C Dayncourt Res	28	19	3	6	83	48	60
Hucknall Sports YC	28	16	5	7	74	35	53
Wollaton 3rd	28	17	2	9	77	41	53
Old Elizabethans Res	28	15	4	9	67	51	49
City & Sherwood Res	28	13	6	9	63	49	45
Clifton Res	28	12	6	10	54	53	42
Magdala Amateurs Res	28	12	3	13	51	54	39
Radcliffe Olympic Res	28	11	5	12	56	55	38
Nottinghamshire	28	11	3	14	57	54	36
Derbyshire Amateurs Res	28	10	4	14	53	66	34
Tibshelf Old Boys	28	8	6	14	57	76	30
Bassingfield Res	28	7	3	18	63	101	24
Dynamo Baptist	28	5	6	17	36	77	21
Edwinstowe	28	4	3	21	33	113	15

DIVISION TWO	P	W	D	L	F	A	Pts
Chaffoteaux Res	26	23	2	1	99	18	71
Old Bemrosians	26	20	2	4	95	34	62
Linby Colliery Res	26	19	4	3	102	28	61
Fleet Cars	26	16	4	6	80	33	52
Southwell Amateurs	26	11	3	12	65	52	36
Wollaton 4th	26	9	6	11	54	52	33
Ilkeston Rangers	26	9	5	12	66	76	32
Brunts Old Boys	26	10	2	14	33	79	32
Magdala Amateurs 3rd	26	8	3	15	56	79	27
Nottinghamshire Res	26	7	5	14	40	64	26
Cadland Chilwell	26	6	6	14	42	86	24
Horse & Jockey Res	26	7	3	16	38	86	24
Lady Bay Res	26	6	4	16	62	107	22
Old Elizabethans 3rd	26	5	3	18	45	83	18

DIVISION THREE	P	W	D	L	F	A	Pts
Ashland Rovers	26	23	2	1	115	33	71
County Nalgo	26	16	4	6	88	48	52
A S C Dayncourt 3rd	26	16	4	6	80	40	52
Sherwood Forest	26	14	3	9	68	59	45
Derbyshire Amateurs 3rd	26	14	1	11	99	91	43
Beeston Old Boys Res	26	11	6	9	69	59	39
E M T E C	26	12	2	12	83	84	38
West Bridgford United	26	11	3	12	60	64	36
Wollaton 5th	26	10	6	10	65	78	36
Horse & Jockey 3rd	26	11	2	13	74	63	35
Nottinghamshire 3rd	26	6	7	13	69	76	25
Ilkeston Rangers Res	26	7	3	16	47	72	24
Old Bemrosians Res	26	4	4	18	36	100	16
Tibshelf Old Boys Res	26	2	3	21	30	116	9

League Cups:
Senior–Caribbean Cavaliers 3 Woodborough United 1
Intermediate–A S C Dayncourt Res 0*:5p Old Bemrosians Res 0*:4p
Minor–Ashland Rovers 3 Sherwood Forest 1
H.B. Poole Trophy– *Now ceased*

OLD BOYS' AMATEUR FOOTBALL LEAGUE

Premier Division	P	W	D	L	F	A	Pts
Old Ignatians	20	10	7	3	44	25	27
Old Aloysians	20	9	6	5	43	35	24
Old Vaughanians	20	10	4	6	36	28	24
Phoenix Old Boys	20	10	3	7	41	31	23
Old Wilsonians	20	9	4	7	36	30	22
Old Meadonians	20	9	3	8	30	24	21
Cardinal Manning OB	20	9	3	8	19	29	21
Old Tenisonians	20	6	4	10	22	27	16
Old Hamptonians	20	4	7	9	25	31	15
Old Salvatorians	20	6	3	11	29	51	15
Old Buckwellians	20	5	2	13	32	46	12

Senior Division One	P	W	D	L	F	A	Pts
Glyn Old Boys	20	14	1	5	52	21	29
Shene Old Grammarians	20	13	2	5	55	27	28
Latymer Old Boys	20	12	3	5	53	25	27
Old Dorkinians	20	9	5	6	41	32	23
Old Minchendenians	20	10	1	9	44	39	21
Old Isleworthians	20	9	3	8	39	38	21
Old Suttonians	20	6	7	7	33	41	19
Old Manorians	20	7	4	9	45	39	18
Enfield Old Grammarians	20	7	4	9	28	30	18
Old Vaughanians Res	20	4	2	14	28	69	10
Old Kingsburians	20	2	2	16	28	85	6

Senior Division Two	P	W	D	L	F	A	Pts
Old Danes	20	13	4	3	45	17	30
Old Sinjuns	20	14	2	4	57	34	30
Old Tiffinians	20	10	4	6	37	21	24
John Fisher Old Boys	20	6	8	6	39	35	20
Old Reigatians	20	7	6	7	33	40	20
Clapham Old Xaverians	20	7	5	8	49	40	19
Phoenix Old Boys Res	20	7	5	8	31	35	19
Chertsey Old Salesians	20	7	3	10	44	45	17
Latymer Old Boys Res	20	5	7	8	34	41	17
Old Meadonians Res	20	4	5	11	30	56	13
Old Tenisonians Res	20	4	3	13	19	54	11

Senior Division Three	P	W	D	L	F	A	Pts
Q. Mary College OB	20	16	2	2	60	16	34*
Old Sedcopians	20	11	5	4	55	29	27
Old Wokingians	20	9	6	5	49	29	24
Old Hamptonians Res	20	11	1	8	42	35	23
Old Wilsonians Res	20	8	6	6	48	43	22
Old Aloysians Res	20	8	5	7	44	43	21
Old Manorians Res	20	9	1	10	38	43	19
Old Tenisonians 3rd	20	8	3	9	34	42	19
Old Salvatorians Res	20	7	3	10	35	37	17*
Old Uffintonians	20	5	0	15	36	70	10
Old Southallians	20	1	2	17	20	74	4

final unplayed game entered as a 0-0 draw

Intermediate Division N–12 Teams
Won by Wood Green Old Boys
Intermediate Division S–11 Teams
Won by Old Wokingians Res
Division One North–10 Teams
Won by Old Tollingtonians Res
Division One South–10 Teams
Won by Fitzwilliam Old Boys
Division One West–10 Teams
Won by Old Salvatorians 3rd
Division Two North–12 Teams
Won by Old Tollingtonians 3rd
Division Two South–10 Teams
Won by John Fisher Old Boys Res
Division Two West–12 Teams
Won by Old Challoners Res
Division Three North–11 Teams
Won by Old Aloysians 5th
Division Three South–11 Teams
Won by Old Suttonians 5th
Division Three West– 9 Teams
Won by Old Salvatorians 5th
Division Four North–12 Teams
Won by Old Egbertians 4th
Division Four South–12 Teams
Won by Fitzwilliam Old Boys Res
Division Four West–11 Teams
Won by Old Manorians 5th
Division Five North– 9 Teams
Won by Old Minchendenians 5th
Division Five South–11 Teams
Won by Old Thorntonians Res
Division Five West–10 Teams
Won by Old Hendonians 3rd
Division Six North–10 Teams
Won by Ravenscroft Old Boys 3rd
Division Six South–11 Teams
Won by Chertsey Old Salesians 4th
Division Six West– 9 Teams
Won by Phoenix Old Boys 6th
Division Seven South–11 Teams
Won by Old Paulines 3rd
Division Eight South 10 Teams
Won by Glyn Old Boys 8th
Division Nine South–10 Teams
Won by Glyn Old Boys 8th

SOUTHERN AMATEUR LEAGUE

SENIOR SECTION

FIRST DIVISION	P	W	D	L	F	A	Pts
Old Actonians Association	22	15	2	5	51	23	47
Polytechnic	22	11	7	4	54	32	40
Crouch End Vampires	22	12	2	8	49	34	38
Norsemen	22	10	6	6	41	34	36
Old Owens	22	9	5	8	44	37	32
Carshalton	22	9	4	9	29	32	31
Barclays Bank	22	9	3	10	43	41	30
East Barnet Old Grammarians	22	9	2	11	39	43	29
Old Bromleians	22	8	5	9	40	49	27**
National Westminster Bank	22	6	5	11	39	53	23
Lloyds TSB Bank	22	6	5	11	36	52	23
Old Parmiterians	22	3	4	15	26	61	13

SECOND DIVISION	P	W	D	L	F	A	Pts
Alleyn Old Boys	22	14	3	5	54	33	45
Old Esthameians	22	12	6	4	49	23	42
West Wickham	22	11	8	3	45	21	41
Old Salesians	22	11	4	7	56	38	37
HSBC	22	8	7	7	51	32	31
Old Stationers	22	7	7	8	38	38	28
Alexandra Park	22	9	1	12	38	55	28
Lensbury	22	8	4	10	37	64	28
Civil Service	22	7	6	9	43	40	27
Old Finchleians	22	8	2	12	55	60	26
Old Parkonians	22	5	6	11	27	32	21
South Bank	22	3	4	15	29	86	13

THIRD DIVISION	P	W	D	L	F	A	Pts
Broomfield	22	17	1	4	54	29	52
Winchmore Hill	22	16	3	3	40	16	51
Kew Association	22	14	2	6	51	31	44
Bank of England	22	14	1	7	42	21	43
Old Lyonians	22	11	4	7	50	39	37
Southgate Olympic	22	10	5	7	47	42	35
Merton	22	8	5	9	45	45	29
Old Westminster Citizens	22	9	2	11	34	40	29
Ibis	22	5	4	13	32	43	16***
CGU Cuaco	22	3	5	14	25	49	14
Old Latymerians	22	4	2	16	24	56	14
Brentham	22	3	2	17	22	55	11

(*Points deducted – breach of Rule*)

RESERVE TEAMS SECTION
First Division–12 Teams Won by East Barnet Old Grammarians Res
Second Division–12 Teams Won by Old Finchleians Res
Third Division–12 Teams Won by Bank of England Res

3RD TEAMS SECTION
First Division–12 Teams Won by East Barnet Old Grammarians 3rd
Second Division–12 Teams Won by Alleyn Old Boys 3rd
Third Division–12 Teams Won by Old Parmiterians 3rd

4TH TEAMS SECTION
First Division–12 Teams Won by Norsemen 4th
Second Division–11 Teams Won by Old Finchleians 4th
Third Division–10 Teams Won by Kew Association 4th

5TH TEAMS SECTION
First Division–11 Teams Won by Polytechnic 5th
Second Division–10 Teams Won by Old Stationers 5th
Third Division–9 Teams Won by Old Bromleians 5th

6TH TEAMS SECTION
First Division–8 Teams Won by Old Actonians Association 6th
Second Division–8 Teams Won by Old Finchleians 6th
Third Division–8 Teams Won by Old Salesians 6th

MINOR SECTION:
First Division–9 Teams Won by National Westminster Bank 7th
Second Division–9 Teams Won by Old Finchleians 7th
Third Division–9 Teams Won by Civil Service 8th
Fourth Division–10 Teams Won by Kew Association 8th

CHALLENGE CUPS
Junior–Bank of England 3rd 3 Old Parmiterians 3rd 1
Minor–HSBC 4th 4 Polytechnic 4th 1
Senior Novets–Norsemen 5th 1*:7p Polytechnic 5th 1*:6p
Intermediate Novets–Old Actonians Ass'n 6th 3 Old Finchleians 6th 1
Junior Novets–Old Parmiterians 7th 1 Barclays Bank 8th 0
Hamilton Trophy for Hospitality & Sportsmanship – Old Owens
Wilkinson Sword for Disciplinary Conduct – Not Awarded

SOUTHERN OLYMPIAN LEAGUE

SENIOR SECTION:

DIVISION ONE	P	W	D	L	F	A	Pts.
Hon Artillery Company	18	14	1	3	62	17	29
Hale End Athletic	18	12	4	2	56	27	28
UCL Academicals	18	11	4	3	52	22	26
Nottsborough	18	9	4	5	43	25	22
Old Grammarians	18	9	3	6	44	38	21
Mill Hill Village	18	7	3	8	30	43	17
Old Woodhouseians	18	5	3	10	31	46	13
Ulysses	18	3	5	10	24	42	11
Parkfield	18	2	3	13	23	52	7
City of London	18	2	2	14	27	80	6

DIVISION TWO	P	W	D	L	F	A	Pts.
Albanian	18	14	3	1	51	16	31
Wandsworth Borough	18	12	4	2	52	25	28
Southgate County	18	11	3	4	56	22	25
St Mary's College	18	7	5	6	28	29	19
Old Colfeians	18	6	5	7	39	39	17
Old Bealonians	18	4	7	7	27	33	15
Pegasus	18	3	7	8	26	46	13
University of Hertford	18	5	2	11	33	34	12
Fulham Compton OB	18	3	6	9	34	56	10**
Ealing Association	18	3	2	13	20	66	8

DIVISION THREE	P	W	D	L	F	A	Pts.
Duncombe Sports	16	13	1	2	59	21	27
Kings Old Boys	16	11	1	4	53	33	23
BBC	16	9	4	3	54	32	22
Mayfield Athletic	16	7	4	5	40	34	18
Brent	16	7	3	6	30	24	17
Hampstead Heathens	16	8	1	7	43	41	17
London Welsh	16	3	2	11	20	41	8
The Comets	16	2	3	11	24	63	7
Inland Revenue	16	1	3	12	27	61	5

Tesco Country Club Withdrawn

DIVISION FOUR	P	W	D	L	F	A	Pts.
The Cheshunt Club	21	17	0	3	72	31	32**
Centymca	21	13	4	4	72	43	30
The Rugby Clubs	21	14	3	3	78	36	30*
Economicals	21	11	4	6	84	43	26
Witan	21	9	4	8	43	43	22
Westerns	21	4	4	13	35	68	10
London Airways	21	3	3	15	38	63	9
Birkbeck College	21	0	2	19	17	112	2

(**Points deducted – breach of Rule*)

Intermediate Section:
Division One–10 Teams Won by Old Woodhouseians Res.
Division Two–10 Teams Won by Albanian 3rd
Division Three–10 Teams Won by Centymca Res
Division Four–*Section Deleted*

Junior Section:
Division One N–11 Teams Won by Albanian 5th
Division Two N–11 Teams Won by Mill Hill Village 4th
Division Three N–10 Teams Won by Southgate County 5th
Division Four N–*Section Deleted*
Division One S&W–10 Teams Won by Old Grammarians 3rd
Division Two S&W– 9 Teams Won by Witan 3rd
Division Three S&W–10 Teams Won by Brent 3rd
Senior Challenge Bowl–Won by Nottsborough
Senior Challenge Shield–Won by Old Woodhouseians
Intermediate Challenge Cup–Won by Albanian Res
Intermediate Challenge Shield–Won by Nottsborough Res
Junior Challenge Cup–Won by Old Bealonians 3rd
Junior Challenge Shield–Won by Old Woodhouseians 3rd
Mander Cup–Won by Old Woodhouseians 4th
Mander Shield–Won by Albanian 4th
Burntwood Trophy–Won by Albanian 5th
Burntwood Shield–Won by Old Grammarians 5th
Veterans' Challenge Cup–Won by The Cheshunt Club Vets
Veterans' Challenge Shield–Won by Albanian Vets

RECORDS

Major British Records

HIGHEST WINS

First-Class Match		Arbroath	36	Bon Accord	0	12 Sept 1885
		(Scottish Cup 1st Round)				
International Match		England	13	Ireland	0	18 Feb 1882
FA Cup		Preston NE	26	Hyde U	0	15 Oct 1887
		(1st Round)				
League Cup		West Ham U	10	Bury	0	25 Oct 1983
		(2nd Round, 2nd Leg)				
		Liverpool	10	Fulham	0	23 Sept 1986
		(2nd Round, 1st Leg)				
FA PREMIER LEAGUE						
	(Home)	Manchester U	9	Ipswich T	0	4 March 1995
	(Away)	Nottingham F	1	Manchester U	8	6 Feb 1999
FOOTBALL LEAGUE						
Division 1	*(Home)*	WBA	12	Darwen	0	4 April 1892
		Nottingham F	12	Leicester Fosse	0	21 April 1909
	(Away)	Newcastle U	1	Sunderland	9	5 Dec 1908
		Cardiff C	1	Wolverhampton W	9	3 Sept 1955
Division 2	*(Home)*	Newcastle U	13	Newport Co	0	5 Oct 1946
	(Away)	Burslem PV	0	Sheffield U	10	10 Dec 1892
Division 3	*(Home)*	Gillingham	10	Chesterfield	0	5 Sept 1987
	(Away)	Halifax T	0	Fulham	8	16 Sept 1969
Division 3(S)	*(Home)*	Luton T	12	Bristol R	0	13 April 1936
	(Away)	Northampton T	0	Walsall	8	2 Feb 1947
Division 3(N)	*(Home)*	Stockport Co	13	Halifax T	0	6 Jan 1934
	(Away)	Accrington S	0	Barnsley	9	3 Feb 1934
Division 4	*(Home)*	Oldham Ath	11	Southport	0	26 Dec 1962
	(Away)	Crewe Alex	1	Rotherham U	8	8 Sept 1973
Aggregate Division 3(N)		Tranmere R	13	Oldham Ath	4	26 Dec 1935
SCOTTISH LEAGUE						
Premier	*(Home)*	Aberdeen	8	Motherwell	0	26 March 1979
Division	*(Away)*	Hamilton A	0	Celtic	8	5 Nov 1988
Division 1	*(Home)*	Celtic	11	Dundee	0	26 Oct 1895
	(Away)	Airdrieonians	1	Hibernian	11	24 Oct 1950
Division 2	*(Home)*	Airdrieonians	15	Dundee Wanderers	1	1 Dec 1894
	(Away)	Alloa Ath	0	Dundee	10	8 March 1947

LEAGUE CHAMPIONSHIP HAT-TRICKS

Huddersfield T	1923–24 to 1925–26
Arsenal	1932–33 to 1934–35
Liverpool	1981–82 to 1983–84

MOST GOALS FOR IN A SEASON

		Goals	*Games*	*Season*
FA PREMIER LEAGUE				
	Manchester U	97	38	1999–2000
FOOTBALL LEAGUE				
Division 1	Aston V	128	42	1930–31
Division 2	Middlesbrough	122	42	1926–27
Division 3(S)	Millwall	127	42	1927–28
Division 3(N)	Bradford C	128	42	1928–29
Division 3	QPR	111	46	1961–62
Division 4	Peterborough U	134	46	1960–61
SCOTTISH LEAGUE				
Premier Division	Rangers	101	44	1991–92
	Dundee U	90	36	1982–83
	Celtic	90	36	1982–83
	Celtic	90	44	1986–87
Division 1	Hearts	132	34	1957–58
Division 2	Raith R	142	34	1937–38
New Division 1	Dunfermline Ath	93	44	1993–94
	Motherwell	92	39	1981–82
New Division 2	Ayr U	95	39	1987–88
New Division 3	Alloa	78	36	1997–98

FEWEST GOALS FOR IN A SEASON

		Goals	Games	Season
FA PREMIER LEAGUE	Leeds U	28	38	1996–97
FOOTBALL LEAGUE	(minimum 42 games)			
Division 1	Stoke C	24	42	1984–85
Division 2	Watford	24	42	1971–72
	Leyton Orient	30	46	1994–95
Division 3(S)	Crystal Palace	33	46	1950–51
Division 3(N)	Crewe Alex	32	42	1923–24
Division 3	Stockport Co	27	46	1969–70
Division 4	Crewe Alex	29	46	1981–82
SCOTTISH LEAGUE	(minimum 30 games)			
Premier Division	Hamilton A	19	36	1988–89
	Dunfermline Ath	22	44	1991–92
Division 1	Brechin C	30	44	1993–94
	Ayr U	20	34	1966–67
Division 2	Lochgelly U	20	38	1923–24
New Division 1	Stirling Alb	18	39	1980–81
	Dumbarton	23	36	1995–96
New Division 2	Brechin C	22	36	1994–95
New Division 3	Alloa	26	36	1995–96

MOST GOALS AGAINST IN A SEASON

		Goals	Games	Season
FA PREMIER LEAGUE	Swindon T	100	42	1993–94
FOOTBALL LEAGUE				
Division 1	Blackpool	125	42	1930–31
Division 2	Darwen	141	34	1898–99
Division 3(S)	Merthyr T	135	42	1929–30
Division 3(N)	Nelson	136	42	1927–28
Division 3	Accrington S	123	46	1959–60
Division 4	Hartlepools U	109	46	1959–60
SCOTTISH LEAGUE				
Premier Division	Morton	100	36	1984–85
	Morton	100	44	1987–88
Division 1	Leith Ath	137	38	1931–32
Division 2	Edinburgh C	146	38	1931–32
New Division 1	Queen of the S	99	39	1988–89
	Cowdenbeath	109	44	1992–93
New Division 2	Meadowbank T	89	39	1977–78
New Division 3	Albion R	82	36	1994–95

FEWEST GOALS AGAINST IN A SEASON

		Goals	Games	Season
FA PREMIER LEAGUE	Arsenal	17	38	1998–99
FOOTBALL LEAGUE	(minimum 42 games)			
Division 1	Liverpool	16	42	1978–79
Division 2	Manchester U	23	42	1924–25
	West Ham U	34	46	1990–91
Division 3(S)	Southampton	21	42	1921–22
Division 3(N)	Port Vale	21	46	1953–54
Division 3	Gillingham	20	46	1995–96
Division 4	Lincoln C	25	46	1980–81
SCOTTISH LEAGUE	(minimum 30 games)			
Premier Division	Rangers	19	36	1989–90
	Rangers	23	44	1986–87
	Celtic	23	44	1987–88
Division 1	Celtic	14	38	1913–14
Division 2	Morton	20	38	1966–67
New Division 1	St Johnstone	23	36	1996–97
	Hibernian	24	39	1980–81
	Falkirk	32	44	1993–94
New Division 2	St Johnstone	24	39	1987–88
	Stirling Alb	24	39	1990–91
New Division 3	Brechin C	21	36	1995–96

MOST POINTS IN A SEASON

(under old system of two points for a win)

FOOTBALL LEAGUE		Points	Games	Season
Division 1	Liverpool	68	42	1978–79
Division 2	Tottenham H	70	42	1919–20
Division 3	Aston V	70	46	1971–72
Division 3(S)	Nottingham F	70	46	1950–51
	Bristol C	70	46	1954–55
Division 3(N)	Doncaster R	72	42	1946–47
Division 4	Lincoln C	74	46	1975–76
SCOTTISH LEAGUE				
Premier Division	Aberdeen	59	36	1984–85
	Rangers	73	44	1992–93
Division 1	Rangers	76	42	1920–21
Division 2	Morton	69	38	1966–67
New Division 1	St Mirren	62	39	1976–77
	Falkirk	66	44	1993–94
New Division 2	Forfar Ath	63	39	1983–84

(three points for a win)

		Points	Games	Season
FA PREMIER LEAGUE	Manchester U	92	42	1993–94
FOOTBALL LEAGUE				
Division 1	Sunderland	105	46	1998–99
	Everton	90	42	1984–85
	Liverpool	90	40	1987–88
Division 2	Fulham	101	46	1998–99
Division 3	Notts Co	99	46	1997–98
Division 4	Swindon T	102	46	1985–86
SCOTTISH LEAGUE				
Premier Division	Rangers	87	36	1995–96
New Division 1	Hibernian	89	36	1998–99
New Division 2	Stirling Alb	81	36	1995–96
New Division 3	Forfar Ath	80	36	1994–95

FEWEST POINTS IN A SEASON

		Points	Games	Season
FA PREMIER LEAGUE	Watford	24	38	1999–2000
FOOTBALL LEAGUE	(minimum 34 games)			
Division 1	Stoke C	17	42	1984–85
Division 2	Doncaster R	8	34	1904–05
	Loughborough T	8	34	1899–1900
Division 3	Doncaster R	20	46	1997–98
Division 3(S)	Merthyr T	21	42	1924–25 & 1929–30
	QPR	21	42	1925–26
Division 3(N)	Rochdale	11	40	1931–32
Division 4	Workington	19	46	1976–77
SCOTTISH LEAGUE	(minimum 30 games)			
Premier Division	St Johnstone	11	36	1975–76
	Morton	16	44	1987–88
Division 1	Stirling Alb	6	30	1954–55
Division 2	Edinburgh C	7	34	1936–37
New Division 1	Queen of the S	10	39	1988–89
	Cowdenbeath	13	44	1992–93
New Division 2	Berwick R	16	39	1987–88
	Stranraer	16	39	1987–88
New Division 3	Albion R	18	36	1994–95

MOST WINS IN A SEASON

		Wins	Games	Season
FA PREMIER LEAGUE	Manchester U	28	38	1999–2000
FOOTBALL LEAGUE				
Division 1	Tottenham H	31	42	1960–61
Division 2	Tottenham H	32	42	1919–20
Division 3(S)	Millwall	30	42	1927–28
	Plymouth Arg	30	42	1929–30
	Cardiff C	30	42	1946–47
	Nottingham F	30	46	1950–51
	Bristol C	30	46	1954–55

Division 3(N)	Doncaster R	33	42	1946–47
Division 3	Aston V	32	46	1971–72
Division 4	Lincoln C	32	46	1975–76
	Swindon T	32	46	1985–86

SCOTTISH LEAGUE

Premier Division	Rangers	27	36	1995–96
	Aberdeen	27	36	1984–85
	Rangers	33	44	1991–92
	Rangers	33	44	1992–93
Division 1	Rangers	35	42	1920–21
Division 2	Morton	33	38	1966–67
New Division 1	Hibernian	28	36	1998–99
New Division 2	Forfar Ath	27	39	1983–84
	Ayr U	27	39	1987–88
New Division 3	Forfar Ath	25	36	1994–95

RECORD HOME WINS IN A SEASON

Brentford won all 21 games in Division 3(S), 1929–30

UNDEFEATED AT HOME

Liverpool 85 games (63 League, 9 League Cup, 7 European, 6 FA Cup), Jan 1978–Jan 1981

RECORD AWAY WINS IN A SEASON

Doncaster R won 18 of 21 games in Division 3(N), 1946–47

FEWEST WINS IN A SEASON

		Wins	Games	Season
FA PREMIER LEAGUE	Swindon T	5	42	1993–94
FOOTBALL LEAGUE				
Division 1	Stoke C	3	22	1889–90
	Woolwich Arsenal	3	38	1912–13
	Stoke C	3	42	1984–85
Division 2	Loughborough T	1	34	1899–1900
	Cambridge U	4	42	1983–84
Division 3(S)	Merthyr T	6	42	1929–30
	QPR	6	42	1925–26
Division 3(N)	Rochdale	4	40	1931–32
Division 3	Rochdale	2	46	1973–74
Division 4	Southport	3	46	1976–77
SCOTTISH LEAGUE				
Premier Division	St Johnstone	3	36	1975–76
	Kilmarnock	3	36	1982–83
	Morton	3	44	1987–88
Division 1	Vale of Leven	0	22	1891–92
Division 2	East Stirlingshire	1	22	1905–06
	Forfar Ath	1	38	1974–75
New Division 1	Queen of the S	2	39	1988–89
	Cowdenbeath	3	44	1992–93
New Division 2	Forfar Ath	4	26	1975–76
	Stranraer	4	39	1987–88
New Division 3	Albion R	5	36	1994–95

MOST DEFEATS IN A SEASON

		Defeats	Games	Season
FA PREMIER LEAGUE	Ipswich T	29	42	1994–95
FOOTBALL LEAGUE				
Division 1	Stoke C	31	42	1984–85
Division 2	Tranmere R	31	42	1938–39
	Chester C	33	46	1992–93
Division 3	Doncaster R	34	46	1997–98
Division 3(S)	Merthyr T	29	42	1924–25
	Walsall	29	46	1952–53
	Walsall	29	46	1953–54
Division 3(N)	Rochdale	33	40	1931–32
Division 4	Newport Co	33	46	1987–88
SCOTTISH LEAGUE				
Premier Division	Morton	29	36	1984–85
Division 1	St Mirren	31	42	1920–21
Division 2	Brechin C	30	36	1962–63
	Lochgelly	30	38	1923–24
New Division 1	Queen of the S	29	39	1988–89
	Dumbarton	31	36	1995–96
	Cowdenbeath	34	44	1992–93
New Division 2	Berwick R	29	39	1987–88
New Division 3	Albion R	28	36	1994–95

HAT-TRICKS

Career 34 Dixie Dean (Tranmere R, Everton, Notts Co, England)
Division 1 (one season post-war) 6 Jimmy Greaves (Chelsea), 1960–61
Three for one team one match
West, Spouncer, Hooper, Nottingham F v Leicester Fosse, Division 1, 21 April 1909
Barnes, Ambler, Davies, Wrexham v Hartlepools U, Division 4, 3 March 1962
Adcock, Stewart, White, Manchester C v Huddersfield T, Division 2, 7 Nov 1987
Loasby, Smith, Wells, Northampton T v Walsall, Division 3S, 5 Nov 1927
Bowater, Hoyland, Readman, Mansfield T v Rotherham U, Division 3N, 27 Dec 1932

FEWEST DEFEATS IN A SEASON
(Minimum 20 games)

		Defeats	Games	Season
FA PREMIER LEAGUE	Manchester U	3	38	1999–2000
	Manchester U	3	38	1998–99
	Chelsea	3	38	1998–99
FOOTBALL LEAGUE				
Division 1	Preston NE	0	22	1888–89
	Arsenal	1	38	1990–91
	Liverpool	2	40	1987–88
	Leeds U	2	42	1968–69
Division 2	Liverpool	0	28	1893–94
	Burnley	2	30	1897–98
	Bristol C	2	38	1905–06
	Leeds U	3	42	1963–64
	Chelsea	5	46	1988–89
Division 3	QPR	5	46	1966–67
	Bristol R	5	46	1989–90
	Notts Co	5	46	1997–98
Division 3(S)	Southampton	4	42	1921–22
	Plymouth Arg	4	42	1929–30
Division 3(N)	Port Vale	3	46	1953–54
	Doncaster R	3	42	1946–47
	Wolverhampton W	3	42	1923–24
Division 4	Lincoln C	4	46	1975–76
	Sheffield U	4	46	1981–82
	Bournemouth	4	46	1981–82
SCOTTISH LEAGUE				
Premier Division	Rangers	3	36	1995–96
	Celtic	3	44	1987–88
Division 1	Rangers	0	18	1898–99
	Rangers	1	42	1920–21
Division 2	Clyde	1	36	1956–57
	Morton	1	36	1962–63
	St Mirren	1	36	1967–68
New Division 1	Partick T	2	26	1975–76
	St Mirren	2	39	1976–77
	Raith R	4	44	1992–93
	Falkirk	4	44	1993–94
New Division 2	Raith R	1	26	1975–76
	Clydebank	3	26	1975–76
	Forfar Ath	3	39	1983–84
	Raith R	3	39	1986–87
	Livingston	3	36	1998–99
New Division 3	Forfar Ath	6	36	1994–95
	Inverness T	6	36	1996–97

MOST DRAWN GAMES IN A SEASON

		Draws	Games	Season
FA PREMIER LEAGUE	Manchester C	18	42	1993–94
	Sheffield U	18	42	1993–94
	Southampton	18	42	1994–95
FOOTBALL LEAGUE				
Division 1	Norwich C	23	42	1978–79
Division 3	Cardiff C	23	46	1997–98
	Hartlepool U	23	46	1997–98
Division 4	Exeter C	23	46	1986–87
SCOTTISH LEAGUE				
Premier Division	Aberdeen	21	44	1993–94
New Division 1	East Fife	21	44	1986–87

MOST GOALS IN A GAME

FA PREMIER LEAGUE	Alan Shearer (Newcastle U) 5 goals v Sheffield W	19 Sept 1999
	Andy Cole (Manchester U) 5 goals v Ipswich T	4 Mar 1995

FOOTBALL LEAGUE

Division 1	Ted Drake (Arsenal) 7 goals v Aston V	14 Dec 1935
	James Ross (Preston NE) 7 goals v Stoke	6 Oct 1888
Division 2	Tommy Briggs (Blackburn R) 7 goals v Bristol R	5 Feb 1955
	Neville Coleman (Stoke C) 7 goals v Lincoln C	23 Feb 1957
Division 3(S)	Joe Payne (Luton T) 10 goals v Bristol R	13 April 1936
Division 3(N)	Bunny Bell (Tranmere R) 9 goals v Oldham Ath	26 Dec 1935
Division 3	Steve Earle (Fulham) 5 goals v Halifax T	16 Sept 1969
	Barrie Thomas (Scunthorpe U) 5 goals v Luton T	24 April 1965
	Keith East (Swindon T) 5 goals v Mansfield T	20 Nov 1965
	Alf Wood (Shrewsbury T) 5 goals v Blackburn R	2 Oct 1971
	Tony Caldwell (Bolton W) 5 goals v Walsall	10 Sept 1983
	Andy Jones (Port Vale) 5 goals v Newport Co	4 May 1987
	Steve Wilkinson (Mansfield T) 5 goals v Birmingham C	3 April 1990
Division 4	Bert Lister (Oldham Ath) 6 goals v Southport	26 Dec 1962
FA CUP	Ted MacDougall (Bournemouth) 9 goals v Margate (*1st Round*)	20 Nov 1971
LEAGUE CUP	Frankie Bunn (Oldham Ath) 6 goals v Scarborough	25 Oct 1989

SCOTTISH LEAGUE

Premier Division	Paul Sturrock (Dundee U) 5 goals v Morton	17 Nov 1984
Division 1	Jimmy McGrory (Celtic) 8 goals v Dunfermline Ath	14 Sept 1928
Division 2	Owen McNally (Arthurlie) 8 goals v Armadale	1 Oct 1927
	Jim Dyet (King's Park) 8 goals v Forfar Ath	2 Jan 1930
	John Calder (Morton) 8 goals v Raith R	18 April 1936
	Norman Hayward (Raith R) 8 goals v Brechin C	20 Aug 1937
SCOTTISH CUP	John Petrie (Arbroath) 13 goals v Bon Accord (*1st Round*)	12 Sept 1885

MOST LEAGUE GOALS IN A SEASON

		Goals	*Games*	*Season*
FA PREMIER LEAGUE	Andy Cole (Newcastle U)	34	40	1993–94
	Alan Shearer (Blackburn R)	34	42	1994–95
Division 1	Dixie Dean (Everton)	60	39	1927–28
Division 2	George Camsell (Middlesbrough)	59	37	1926–27
Division 3(S)	Joe Payne (Luton T)	55	39	1936–37
Division 3(N)	Ted Harston (Mansfield T)	55	41	1936–37
Division 3	Derek Reeves (Southampton)	39	46	1959–60
Division 4	Terry Bly (Peterborough U)	52	46	1960–61
FA CUP	Jimmy Ross (Preston NE)	20	8	1887–88
LEAGUE CUP	Clive Allen (Tottenham H)	12	9	1986–87

SCOTTISH LEAGUE

		Goals	*Games*	*Season*
Division 1	William McFadyen (Motherwell)	52	34	1931–32
Division 2	Jim Smith (Ayr U)	66	38	1927–28

MOST LEAGUE GOALS IN A CAREER

		Goals	*Games*	*Season*
FOOTBALL LEAGUE				
Arthur Rowley	WBA	4	24	1946–48
	Fulham	27	56	1948–50
	Leicester C	251	303	1950–58
	Shrewsbury T	152	236	1958–65
		434	619	
SCOTTISH LEAGUE				
Jimmy McGrory	Celtic	1	3	1922–23
	Clydebank	13	30	1923–24
	Celtic	396	375	1924–38
		410	408	

MOST CUP GOALS IN A CAREER

FA CUP (post-war)

Ian Rush   43   (Chester, Liverpool)
Pre-war: Henry Cursham   48   (Notts Co)

LEAGUE CUP

Geoff Hurst   49   (West Ham U, Stoke C)
Ian Rush   49   (Chester, Liverpool, Newcastle U)

A CENTURY OF LEAGUE AND CUP GOALS IN CONSECUTIVE SEASONS

George Camsell	Middlesbrough	59 Lge	5 Cup	1926–27
(101 goals)		33	4	1927–28
Steve Bull	Wolverhampton W	34 Lge	18 Cup	1987–88
(102 goals)		37	13	1988–89

(Camsell's cup goals were all scored in the FA Cup; Bull had 12 in the Sherpa Van Trophy, 3 Littlewoods Cup, 3 FA Cup in 1987–88; 11 Sherpa Van Trophy, 2 Littlewoods Cup in 1988–89.)

LONGEST SEQUENCE OF CONSECUTIVE SCORING (Individual)

FA PREMIER LEAGUE
Mark Stein (Chelsea)	9 in 7 games	1993–94

FOOTBALL LEAGUE RECORD
Dixie Dean (Everton)	23 in 12 games	1930–31

LONGEST WINNING SEQUENCE

FOOTBALL LEAGUE		*Games*	*Season*
Division 1	Tottenham H	13	1959–60 (2)
			and 1960–61 (11)
	Preston NE	13	1891–92
	Sunderland	13	1891–92
Division 2	Manchester U	14	1904–05
	Bristol C	14	1905–06
	Preston NE	14	1950–51
Division 3	Reading	13	1985–86
From Season's start			
Division 1	Tottenham H	11	1960–61
Division 3	Reading	13	1985–86

LONGEST WINNING SEQUENCE IN A SEASON

FOOTBALL LEAGUE		*Games*	*Season*
Division 1	Tottenham H	11	1960–61
Division 2	Manchester U	14	1904–05
Division 2	Bristol C	14	1905–06
Division 2	Preston NE	14	1950–51
SCOTTISH LEAGUE			
Division 2	Morton	23	1963–64

LONGEST UNBEATEN SEQUENCE

FOOTBALL LEAGUE		*Games*	*Seasons*
Division 1	Nottingham F	42	Nov 1977–Dec 1978

LONGEST UNBEATEN CUP SEQUENCE

Liverpool   25 rounds   League/Milk Cup   1980–84

LONGEST UNBEATEN SEQUENCE IN A SEASON

FOOTBALL LEAGUE		*Games*	*Season*
Division 1	Burnley	30	1920–21

LONGEST UNBEATEN START TO A SEASON

FOOTBALL LEAGUE		*Games*	*Season*
Division 1	Leeds U	29	1973–74
Division 1	Liverpool	29	1987–88

LONGEST SEQUENCE WITHOUT A WIN IN A SEASON

FOOTBALL LEAGUE		*Games*	*Season*
Division 2	Cambridge U	31	1983–84

LONGEST SEQUENCE WITHOUT A WIN FROM SEASON'S START

Division 1	Sheffield U	16	1990–91

LONGEST SEQUENCE OF CONSECUTIVE DEFEATS

FOOTBALL LEAGUE		*Games*	*Season*
Division 2	Darwen	18	1898–99

GOALKEEPING RECORDS (WITHOUT CONCEDING A GOAL)

British record (all competitive games)
Chris Woods, Rangers, in 1196 minutes from 26 November 1986 to 31 January 1987.
Football League
Steve Death, Reading, 1103 minutes from 24 March to 18 August 1979.

PENALTIES

Most in a Season (individual)		*Goals*	*Season*
Division 1	Francis Lee (Manchester C)	13	1971–72
Most awarded in one game			
Five	Crystal Palace (4 – 1 scored, 3 missed) v Brighton & HA (1 scored), Div 2		1988–89
Most saved in a Season			
Division 1	Paul Cooper (Ipswich T)	8 (of 10)	1979–80

MOST LEAGUE APPEARANCES (750+ matches)

1005 Peter Shilton (286 Leicester City, 110 Stoke City, 202 Nottingham Forest, 188 Southampton, 175 Derby County, 34 Plymouth Argyle, 1 Bolton Wanderers, 9 Leyton Orient)1966–97
879 Graeme Armstrong (204 Stirling A, 83 Berwick R, 353 Meadowbank T, 239 Stenhousemuir) 1975–99
876 Tony Ford (355 Grimsby T, 9 Sunderland (loan), 112 Stoke C, 114 WBA, 68 Grimsby T, 5 Bradford C (loan), 76 Scunthorpe U, 103 Mansfield T, 34 Rochdale) 1975–2000
863 Tommy Hutchison (165 Blackpool, 314 Coventry City, 46 Manchester City, 92 Burnley 178 Swansea City, 68 Alloa) 1965–91
824 Terry Paine (713 Southampton, 111 Hereford United) 1957–77
782 Robbie James (484 Swansea C, 48 Stoke C, 87 QPR, 23 Leicester C, 89 Bradford C, 51 Cardiff C) 1973–94
777 Alan Oakes (565 Manchester C, 211 Chester C, 1 Port Vale) 1959–84
771 John Burridge (27 Workington, 134 Blackpool, 65 Aston Villa, 6 Southend U (loan), 88 Crystal Palace, 39 QPR, 74 Wolverhampton W, 6 Derby Co (loan), 109 Sheffield U, 62 Southampton, 67 Newcastle U, 65 Hibernian, 3 Scarborough, 4 Lincoln C, 3 Aberdeen, 3 Dumbarton, 3 Falkirk, 4 Manchester C, 3 Darlington, 6 Queen of the South) 1968–96
770 John Trollope (all for Swindon Town) 1960–80†
764 Jimmy Dickinson (all for Portsmouth) 1946–65
761 Roy Sproson (all for Port Vale) 1950–72
760 Mick Tait (64 Oxford U, 106 Carlisle U, 33 Hull C, 240 Portsmouth, 99 Reading, 79 Darlington, 139 Hartlepool U) 1974–94
758 Ray Clemence (48 Scunthorpe United, 470 Liverpool, 240 Tottenham Hotspur) 1966–87
758 Billy Bonds (95 Charlton Ath, 663 West Ham U) 1964–88
757 Pat Jennings (48 Watford, 472 Tottenham Hotspur, 237 Arsenal) 1963–86
757 Frank Worthington (171 Huddersfield T, 210 Leicester C, 84 Bolton W, 75 Birmingham C, 32 Leeds U, 195 Sunderland, 34 Southampton, 31 Brighton & HA, 59 Tranmere R, 23 Preston NE, 19 Stockport Co) 1966–88
† record for one club

Consecutive
401 Harold Bell (401 Tranmere R; 459 in all games) 1946–55

FA CUP
88 Ian Callaghan (79 Liverpool, 7 Swansea C, 2 Crewe Alex)

Most Senior Matches
1390 Peter Shilton (1005 League, 86 FA Cup, 102 League Cup, 125 Internationals, 13 Under-23, 4 Football League XI, 20 European Cup, 7 Texaco Cup, 5 Simod Cup, 4 European Super Cup, 4 UEFA Cup, 3 Screen Sport Super Cup, 3 Zenith Data Systems Cup, 2 Autoglass Trophy, 2 Charity Shield, 2 Full Members Cup, 1 Anglo-Italian Cup, 1 Football League play-offs, 1 World Club Championship)

MOST FA CUP FINAL GOALS

Ian Rush (Liverpool) 5: 1986(2), 1989(2), 1992(1)

MOST LEAGUE MEDALS

Phil Neal (Liverpool) 8: 1976, 1977, 1979, 1980, 1982, 1983, 1984, 1986
Alan Hansen (Liverpool) 8: 1979, 1980, 1982, 1983, 1984, 1986, 1988, 1990

OTHER RECORDS

YOUNGEST PLAYERS
FA Premier League   Andy Campbell, 16 years, 352 days, Middlesbrough v Sheffield W, 5.4.96.
FA Premier League scorer   Andy Turner, 17 years 166 days, Tottenham H v Everton, 5.9.92.
Football League   Albert Geldard, 15 years 158 days, Bradford Park Avenue v Millwall, Division 2, 16.9.29; and Ken Roberts, 15 years 158 days, Wrexham v Bradford Park Avenue, Division 3N, 1.9.51
Football League scorer
   Ronnie Dix, 15 years 180 days, Bristol Rovers v Norwich City, Division 3S, 3.3.28.
Division 1
   Derek Forster, 15 years 185 days, Sunderland v Leicester City, 22.8.64.
Division 1 scorer
   Jason Dozzell, 16 years 57 days as substitute Ipswich Town v Coventry City, 4.2.84
Division 1 hat-tricks
   Alan Shearer, 17 years 240 days, Southampton v Arsenal, 9.4.88
   Jimmy Greaves, 17 years 10 months, Chelsea v Portsmouth, 25.12.57
FA Cup (any round)
   Andy Awford, 15 years 88 days as substitute Worcester City v Boreham Wood, 3rd Qual. rd, 10.10.87

FA Cup proper
Scott Endersby, 15 years 288 days, Kettering v Tilbury, 1st rd, 26.11.77
FA Cup Final
James Prinsep, 17 years 245 days, Clapham Rovers v Old Etonians, 1879
FA Cup Final scorer
Norman Whiteside, 18 years 18 days, Manchester United v Brighton & Hove Albion, 1983
FA Cup Final captain
David Nish, 21 years 212 days, Leicester City v Manchester City, 1969
League Cup Final scorer
Norman Whiteside, 17 years 324 days, Manchester United v Liverpool, 1983
League Cup Final captain
Barry Venison, 20 years 7 months 8 days, Sunderland v Norwich City, 1985

OLDEST PLAYERS
Football League
Neil McBain, 52 years 4 months, New Brighton v Hartlepools United, Div 3N, 15.3.47 (McBain was New Brighton's manager and had to play in an emergency)
Division 1
Stanley Matthews, 50 years 5 days, Stoke City v Fulham, 6.2.65

SENDINGS-OFF

Season	371 (League alone)	1998–99
Day	15 (all League)	31 Oct 1998
	15 (3 League, 12 FA Cup*)	20 Nov 1982
	worst overall FA Cup total	
	26 (14 English, 12 Scottish)	16 Oct 1999
	(On 17 Oct 1999 a further 1 English made it 27 for the weekend)	
Weekend	15 (League alone)	22/23 Dec 1990
FA Cup Final	Kevin Moran, Manchester U v Everton	1985
Quickest	Walter Boyd, Swansea C v Darlington Div 3 as substitute in zero seconds	23 Nov 1999
Most in one game	Five: Chesterfield (2) v Plymouth Arg (3)	22 Feb 1997
	Five: Wigan Ath (1) v Bristol R (4)	2 Dec 1997
Most in one team	Wigan Ath (1) v Bristol R (4)	2 Dec 1997
	Hereford U (4) v Northampton T (0)	11 Nov 1992

RECORD ATTENDANCES

FA Premier League	61,629	Manchester U v Tottenham H	6.5.2000
Football League	83,260	Manchester U v Arsenal, Maine Road	17.1.1948
Scottish League	118,567	Rangers v Celtic, Ibrox Stadium	2.1.1939
FA Cup Final	126,047*	Bolton W v West Ham U, Wembley	28.4.1923
European Cup	135,826	Celtic v Leeds U, semi-final at Hampden Park	15.4.1970
Scottish Cup	146,433	Celtic v Aberdeen, Hampden Park	24.4.37
World Cup	199,854†	Brazil v Uruguay, Maracana, Rio	16.7.50

* It has been estimated that as many as 70,000 more broke in without paying.
† 173,830 paid.

TOP TEN TRANSFERS

Player	From	To	Month	Fee
Hernan Crespo	Parma	Lazio	July 2000	£35.7m
Christian Vieri	Lazio	Internazionale	June 1999	£31m
Nicholas Anelka	Arsenal	Real Madrid	August 1999	£23.9m
Denilson	Sao Paulo	Real Betis	August 1998	£21.4m
Marcio Amoroso	Udinese	Parma	June 1999	£18m
Ronaldo	Barcelona	Internazionale	July 1997	£18m
Juan Sebastian Veron	Parma	Lazio	June 1999	£17.5m
Christian Vieri	Atletico Madrid	Lazio	June 1997	£17m
Rivaldo	La Coruna	Barcelona	August 1997	£16m
Andriy Shevchenko	Kiev Dynamo	AC Milan	June 1999	£15.7m

IMPORTANT ADDRESSES

The Football Association: The Secretary, 16 Lancaster Gate, London W2 3LW. *0171 262 4542*

Scotland: David Taylor, 6 Park Gardens, Glasgow G3 7YE. *0141 332 6372*

Northern Ireland (Irish FA): D. I. Bowen, 20 Windsor Avenue, Belfast BT9 6EG. *01232 669458*

Wales: A. Evans, 3 Westgate Street, Cardiff, South Glamorgan CF1 1JF. *01222 372325*

Republic of Ireland (FA of Ireland): B. O'Byrne, 80 Merrion Square South, Dublin 2. *00353 16766864*

International Federation (FIFA): M. Zen-Ruffinen, P. O. Box 85 8030 Zurich, Switzerland. *00 411 384 9595. Fax: 00 411 384 9696*

Union of European Football Associations: G. Aigner, Route de Geneve 46, Case Postale CH-1260 Nyon, Switzerland. *0041 22 994 44 44. Fax: 0041 22 994 44 88*

THE LEAGUES

The Premier League: The Secretary, 11 Connaught Place, London W2 2ET *0171-298-1600*

The Football League: J. D. Dent, F.C.I.S., The Football League, Unit 5, Edward VII Quay, Navigation Way, Preston, Lancashire PR2 2YF. *01772 325800. Fax 01772 325801*

Scottish Premier League: R. Mitchell, Hampden Park, Somerville Drive, Glasgow G42 9BA. *0141 646 6962*

The Scottish League: P. Donald, 188 West Regent Street, Glasgow G2 4RY. *0141 248 3844*

The Irish League: H. Wallace, 87 University Street, Belfast BT7 1HP. *01232 242888*

Football League of Ireland: E. Morris, 80 Merrion Square South, Dublin 2. *003531 765120*

Nationwide Conference: J. A. Moules, Chief Executive, Riverside House, 14b High Street, Crayford, DA1 4HG. *01322 411021*

Central League: A. Williamson, The Football League, Unit 5, Edward VII Quay, Navigation Way, Preston, Lancashire PR2 2YF. *01772 325800. Fax 01772 325801*

North West Counties League: M. Darby, 87 Hillary Road, Hyde, Cheshire SK14 4EB

Eastern Counties League: B. A. Badcock, 41 The Copse, Southwood, Farnborough, Hampshire GU14 0QD. *01252 387588*

Football Combination: N. Chamberlain, 2 Vicarage Close, Old Costessey, Norwich NR8 5DL. *01603 743998*

Hellenic League: B. King, 83 Queens Road, Carterton, Oxon OX18 3YF. *01793 493502*

Kent League: R. Vinter, Bakery House, The Street, Chilham, Canterbury, Kent CT4 8BX. *01227 730457*

Leicestershire Senior League: R. J. Holmes, 8 Huntsman Close, Markfield, Leics LE67 9XE. *01530 243093*

Manchester League: J. Hall, 31 Sunhill Close, Rochdale, OL16 4RU. *01706 719829*

Midland Combination: N. Harvey, 115 Millfield Road, Handsworth Wood, Birmingham B20 1ED. *0121 357 4172*

Northern Premier: R. D. Bayley, 22 Woburn Drive, Hale, Altrincham, Cheshire WA15 8LZ. *0161-980 7007*

Northern League: T. Golightly, 85 Park Road North, Chester-le-Street, Co Durham DH3 3SA. *0191 3882056*

Isthmian League: N. Robinson, 226 Rye Lane, Peckham SE15 4NL. *020 8409 1978. Fax: 020 7639 5726*

South-East Counties League: A. Leather, 66 Green Acres, Chichester Road, Croydon, Surrey CR0 5UX. *0181-681 7100*

Southern League: D. J. Strudwick, P. O. Box 90, Worcester, WR3 8RX. *01905 757509*

Spartan South Midlands League: M. Mitchell, 26 Leighton Court, Dunstable, Beds LU6 1EW. *01582 667291*

United Counties League: R. Gamble, 8 Bostock Avenue, Northampton NN1 4LW. *01604 637766*

Western League: K. A. Clarke, 32 Westmead Lane, Chippenham, Wilts SN15 3HZ. *01249 464467*

West Midlands Regional League: N. R. Juggins, 14 Badger Way, Blackwell, Bromsgrove, Worcs B60 1EX. *0121 447 8167*

Northern Counties (East): B. Wood, 6 Restmore Avenue, Guiseley, Leeds LS20 9DG. *01943 874558*

Central Midlands Football League: Frank Harwood, 103 Vestry Road, Oakwood, Derby, Derbyshire DE21 2BN. *01332 832372*

Combined Counties League: Clive R. Tidey, 22 Silo Road, Farncombe, Godalming, Surrey GU7 3PA. *01483 428453*

Essex Senior League: David Walls, 77 Thorpedene Gardens, Shoeburyness, Essex SS3 9JE. *01702 294047*

Lancashire Football League: Barbara Howarth, 86 Windsor Road, Great Harwood, Blackburn, Lancs BB6 7RR. *01254 886267*

Midland Football Alliance: Peter Dagger, 32 Drysdale Close, Wickhamford, Worcs WR11 6RZ. *01386 831763*

North West Counties Football League: Mike Darby, 87 Hillary Road, Hyde, Cheshire SK14 4EB. *0161 368 6243*

Wessex League: Tom Lindon, 63 Downs Road, South Wonston, Winchester, Hants SO21 3EW. *01264 884760*

South Western League: Wendy Donohue, 115 Longfield, Falmouth, Cornwall TR11 4SL. *01326 316642*

COUNTY FOOTBALL ASSOCIATIONS

Bedfordshire: P. D. Brown, Century House, Skimpot Road, Dunstable, Beds LU5 4JU. *01582 565111*

Berks and Bucks: B. G. Moore, 15a London Street, Faringdon, Oxon SN7 7HD. *01367 242099*

Birmingham County: M. Pennick, County FA Offices, Rayhall Lane, Great Barr, Birmingham B43 6JF. *0121 357 4278*

Cambridgeshire: R. K. Pawley, 3 Signet Court, Swanns Road, Cambridge CB5 8LA. *01223 576770*

Cheshire: Mrs M. Dunford, The Cottage, Hartford Moss Rec Centre, Winnington, Northwich CW8 4BG. *01606 871166*

Cornwall: B. Cudmore, 1 High Cross Street, St. Austell, Cornwall PL25 4AB. *01726 74080*

Cumberland: J. A. Murphy, 17 Oxford Street, Workington, Cumbria CA14 2AL. *01900 872310*

Derbyshire: K. Compton, The Grandstand, Moorways Stadium, Moor Lane, Derby DE24 8FB. *01332 361422*

Devon County: C. Davidson, County HQ, Coach Road, Newton Abbot, Devon TQ12 1EJ. *01626 332077*

Dorset County: P. Hough, County Ground, Blandford Close, Hamsworthy, Poole, Dorset BH15 4BF. *01202 682375*

Durham: J. Topping, 'Codeslaw', Ferens Park, Durham DH1 1JZ. *0191 3848653*

East Riding County: D. R. Johnson, 50 Boulevard, Hull HU3 2TB. *01482 221158*

Essex County: P. Sammons, 31 Mildmay Road, Chelmsford, Essex CM2 0DN. *01245 357727*

Gloucestershire: P. Britton, Oaklands Park, Almondsbury, Bristol BS34 4AG. *01454 615888*

Guernsey: D. Dorey, Haut Regard, St. Clair Hill, St. Sampson's, Guernsey, GY2 4DT, CI. *01481 246231*

Hampshire: R. G. Barnes, William Pickford House, 8 Ashwood Gardens, off Winchester Road, Southampton SO16 7NP. *01703 791110*

Herefordshire: J. S. Lambert, 1 Muirfield Close, Holmer, Hereford HR1 1QB. *01432 270308*

Hertfordshire: A. G. Kibble, County Ground, Baldock Road, Letchworth, Herts SG6 2EN. *01462 677622*

Huntingdonshire: M. M. Armstrong, Cromwell Chambers, 8 St Johns Street, Huntingdon, Cambs PE18 6DD. *01480 414422*

Isle of Man: Mrs A. Garrett, P.O. Box 53, The Bowl, Douglas IOM IM99 1GY. *01624 615576*
Jersey: S. Monks, Rocqueberg View Guest House, Rue De Samares, St. Clement, Jersey JE2 6LS. *01534 852642*
Kent County: K. T. Masters, 69 Maidstone Road, Chatham, Kent ME4 6DT. *01634 843824*
Lancashire: J. Kenyon, County Ground, Thurston Road, Leyland, Preston, Lancs PR5 1LF. *01772 624000*
Leicestershire and Rutland: P. Morrison, Holmes Park, Dog and Gun Lane, Whetstone, Leicester LE8 3LJ. *0116 2867828*
Lincolnshire: J. Griffin, PO Box 26, 12 Dean Road, Lincoln LN2 4DP. *01522 524917*
Liverpool County: F. L. J. Hunter, Liverpool Soccer Centre, Walton Hall Park, Walton Hall Avenue, Liverpool L4 9XP. *0151 523 4488*
London: D. Fowkes, 6 Aldworth Grove, London SE13 6HY. *0181 690 9626*
Manchester County: John Dutton, Brantingham Road, Chorlton, Manchester M21 0TT. *0161-881 0299*
Middlesex County: P. J. Clayton, 39 Roxborough Road, Harrow, Middx HA1 1NS. *0181 424 8524*
Norfolk County: R. J. Howlett, Plantation Park, Blofield, Norwich, Norfolk, NR13 4PL. *01603 717177*
Northamptonshire: B. Walden, 2 Duncan Close, Moulton Park, Northampton NN3 6WL. *01604 670741*
North Riding County: M. Jarvis, Southlands Centre, Ormesby Road, Middlesbrough TS3 0HB. *01642 318603*

Northumberland: R. E. Maughan, Seymour House, 10 Brenkley Way, Blezard Bus Park, Seaton Burn, Newcastle upon Tyne NE13 6DT. *0191 236 8020*
Nottinghamshire: M. Kilbee, 7 Clarendon Street, Nottingham NG1 5HS. *0115 9418954*
Oxfordshire: D. J. Hovard, Rhoslyn, Burford Road, Chipping Norton, Oxon OX7 5EB. *01608 644488*
Sheffield and Hallamshire: G. Thompson, Clegg House, 5 Onslow Road, Sheffield S11 7AF. *01142 670068*
Shropshire: D. Rowe, Gay Meadow, Abbey Foregate, Shrewsbury SY2 6AB. *01743 362769*
Somerset & Avon (South): Mrs H. Marchment, 30 North Road, Midsomer Norton, Bath BA3 2QD. *01761 410280*
Staffordshire: B. J. Adshead, County Showground, Weston Road, Stafford ST18 0DB. *01785 256994*
Suffolk County: W. M. Steward, 2 Millfields, Haughley, Stowmarket, Suffolk IP14 3PU. *01449 673481*
Surrey County: R. Ward, 321 Kingston Road, Leatherhead, Surrey KT22 7TU. *01372 373543*
Sussex County: Ken Benham, County Office, Culver Road, Lancing, Sussex BN15 9AX. *01903 753547*
Westmorland: P. G. Ducksbury, Unit 1, Angel Court, 21 Highgate, Kendal, Cumbria LA9 4DA. *01539 730946*
West Riding County: R. Carter, Fleet Lane, Woodlesford, Leeds LS26 8NX. *0113 2821222*
Wiltshire: M. G. Benson, 16 Robins Green, Covingham, Swindon SN3 5AY. *01793 525245*
Worcestershire: M. R. Leggett Fermain, 12 Worcester Road, Evesham, Worcs WR11 4JU. *01386 443215*

OTHER USEFUL ADDRESSES

Amateur Football Alliance: M. L. Brown, 55 Islington Park Street, London N1 1QB. *0171 359 3493*
English Schools FA: M. R. Berry, 1/2 Eastgate Street, Stafford ST16 2NN. *01785 51142*
Oxford University: M. H. Matthews, University College, Oxford OX1 4BH. *01865 276648*
Cambridge University: Dr J. A. Little, St Catherine's College, Cambridge CB2 1RL. *01223 338366*
Army: Major T. C. Knight ASCB (MOD), Clayton Barracks, Thornhill Road, Aldershot, Hants GU11 2BG. *01252 348571/4*
Royal Air Force: WG CDR R. N. Williams, RAF, FA OC OPS WG RAF 8 Birch Crescent, Uxbridge, Middlesex UB10 0RW. *01895 23667*
Royal Navy: Lt-Cdr J. Danks, R.N. Sports Office, H.M.S. Temeraire, Portsmouth, Hants PO1 2HB. *01705 722671*
British Universities Sports Association: G. Gregory-Jones, Chief Executive: BUSA, 8 Union Street, London SE1 1SZ. *0171 357 8555*
British Olympic Association: 6 John Prince's Street, London W1N 0DH. *0171 408 2029*
National Federation of Football Supporters' Clubs: Chairman: Ian D. Todd MBE, 8 Wyke Close, Wyke Gardens, Isleworth, Middlesex TW7 5PE. *0181 847 2905 (and fax). Mobile: 0961 558908.* National Secretary: Mark Agate, "The Stadium", 14 Coombe Close, Lordswood, Chatham, Kent ME5 8NU. *01634 319461 (and fax)*
National Playing Fields Association: Col R. Satterthwaite, O.B.E., 578b Catherine Place, London, SW1.
The Scottish Football Commercial Managers Association: J. E. Hillier (Chairman), c/o Keith FC Promotions Office, 60 Union Street, Keith, Banffshire, Scotland.
Professional Footballers' Association: G. Taylor, 2 Oxford Court, Bishopsgate, Off Lower Mosley Street, Manchester M2 3WQ. *0161 236 0575*
Referees' Association: A. Smith, 1 Westhill Road, Coundon, Coventry CV6 2AD *01203 601701*
Women's Football Alliance: Miss K. Simmons, 9 Wyllyotts Place, Potters Bar, Herts EN6 2JD. *01707 651840*
Institute of Football Management and Administration:

44 Holy Walk, Leamington Spa, Warwickshire, CV32 4YS. *01926 882313. Fax: 01926 886829*
Football Administrators Association: as above.
Commercial and Marketing Managers Association: as above.
Management Statts Association: as above.
League Managers Association: as above.
The Association of Football Statisticians: R. J. Spiller, PO Box 5828, Basildon, Essex SS15 5GQ. *01268 416020 (and fax 01268-543559)*
The Football Programme Directory: David Stacey, 'The Beeches', 66 Southend Road, Wickford, Essex SS11 8EN. *01268 732041 (and fax)*
England Football Supporters' Association: Publicity Officer, David Stacey, 'The Beeches', 66 Southend Road, Wickford, Essex SS11 8EN. *01268 732041 (and fax)*
World Cup (1966) Association: as above.
The Ninety-Two Club: 104 Gilda Crescent, Whitchurch, Bristol BS14 9LD.
Scottish 38 Club: Mark Byatt, 6 Greenfields Close, Loughton, Essex IG10 3HG. *0181 508 6088*
The Football Trust: Second Floor, Walkden House, 10 Melton Street, London NW1 2EJ. *0171 388 4504*
Association of Provincial Football Supporters Clubs in London: Stephen Moon, 32 Westminster Gardens, Barking, Essex IG11 0BJ. *0181 594 2367*
World Association of Friends of English Football: Carlisle Hill, Gluck, Habichthof 2, D24939 Flensburg, Germany. *01049 461 4700222*
Football Postcard Collectors Club: PRO: Bryan Horsnell, 275 Overdown Road, Tilehurst, Reading RG31 6NX. *Telephone and Fax: 0118 9424448*
UK Programme Collectors Club: Secretary, John Litster, 46 Milton Road, Kirkcaldy, Fife KY1 1TL. *01592 268718. Fax: 01592 595069*
Programme Monthly: as above.
Scottish Football Historians Association: as above.
Phil Gould (Licensed Football Agent), c/o Whoppit Management Ltd, P. O. Box 27204, London N11 2WS. *07071 732 468. Fax: 07070 732 469*
The Scandinavian Union of Supporters of British Football: Postboks, 15 Stovner, N-0913 Oslo, Norway.

FOOTBALL AWARDS 2000

FOOTBALLER OF THE YEAR

The Football Writers' Association for the Sir Stanley Matthews Trophy for the Footballer of the Year went to Roy Keane of Manchester United and the Republic of Ireland.

THE PFA AWARDS 2000

Player of the Year: Roy Keane.
Young Player of the Year: Harry Kewell, Leeds United.
Merit Award: Gary Mabbutt.

THE SCOTTISH FOOTBALL WRITERS' ASSOCIATION

Player of the Year: Barry Ferguson, Rangers.

THE SCOTTISH PFA AWARDS 2000

Player of the Year: Mark Viduka, Celtic.
Young Player of the Year: Kenny Miller, Hibernian (now Rangers).
Division One: Steve Crawford, Dunfermline Ath.
Division Two: Barry Carrigan, Clyde.
Division Three: Steve Milne, Forfar Ath.

EUROPEAN FOOTBALLER OF THE YEAR 1999

Rivaldo, Barcelona and Brazil.

WORLD PLAYER OF THE YEAR 1999

Rivaldo.

WORLD TEAM OF THE YEAR

Manchester United

CARLING PLAYER OF THE YEAR

Kevin Phillips, Sunderland and England.

CARLING MANAGER OF THE YEAR

Sir Alex Ferguson

Roy Keane PFA Player of the Year and Football Writers' Award winner as well. (Colorsport)

LEAGUE MANAGERS ASSOCIATION

The League Managers Association has developed into a major representative voice in the administration of football, which has brought increasing benefits for its members who are drawn from the professional ranks of the game.

With headquarters in Leamington Spa, the LMA was formed coincidentally in the year of the inauguration of the Premier League. Leading among the pioneers in its formation was Watford and former England manager Graham Taylor whose vision was collective representation for all Premiership and football League managers as the profile and demands on them became increasingly relevant.

The last decade has been one of overwhelming change for football and perhaps the most eventful period in the game's development. The formation of the Premier League itself heralded a change in structure and this was followed by the escalation in television rights through the associations with Sky and the Bosman judgement, which so dramatically affected the movement of players and heralded the arrival in this country of many overseas players from around the world. All these factors directly affected the role of the manager within the game.

Taylor's own motivation was a conviction that managers generally possessed a vast store of knowledge and experience, which was not being transmitted back for the benefit of the game as a whole. There was no recognised way for them to express their views to the legislators and decision makers.

By forming an association into which this information could be channelled the managers therefore won the recognition of both the Football Association and the Premier and Football Leagues. As the years have passed there has been an ever-increasing input from the managerial ranks and advice is sought from the LMA on a regular basis.

One of the most significant early breakthroughs was the introduction into the Premier League regulations of a Code of Conduct governing the appointment of managers and the termination of their contracts. This now means that LMA members in that league have a greater protection in the event of losing their jobs than they have ever had with similar safeguards for the clubs in relation to their managers being approached during the period of their contracts. Most club managers have realised that by using the LMA to fine-tune the wording of their contracts they now have a greater job protection than they have ever enjoyed.

There have been numerous other initiatives in regard to pensions, disciplinary procedures, the setting up of academies and the study of youth development both here and abroad.

In keeping with the developments in Information Technology, the LMA have, in partnership with Cisco Systems, introduced its members to the use of the Internet with the aim being that every club manager will eventually have a means of communication in keeping with the new century.

Part of that development has been the formation of the LMA website which not only features football news items but which contains a directory and CV of all members and on which can be found all the latest information connected to the organisation. This can be found on www.leaguemanagers.com.

The LMA has continued with its Performance of the Week award, which in the last season was once again sponsored by Scottish Mutual. A dedicated panel of managers, chaired by LMA chairman Howard Wilkinson, and including Graham Taylor, Sir Alex Ferguson, David Bassett and Barry Fry make the selections.

A new innovation last season was the introduction of a 'Cisco Kid' a panel of current and former international managers chaired by Bobby Robson selecting a young player of each month.

In addition the LMA has its own annual awards dinner at which members recognise the achievements of their colleagues in each division with the supreme award of Managers Manager of the Year, a title awarded in 1999–2000 to Charlton's Alan Curbishley.

The Carling Premiership award went to Sir Alex Ferguson with David Moyes winning the Division Two award and John Hollins Division Three. A further special award went to David Sexton for his services to football, the presentations being made by England coach Kevin Keegan.

The late John Camkin, whose own drive was a significant factor in the LMA's early development was the first Chief Executive of the LMA and at various stages since Frank Clark, Steve Coppell, Jim Smith and Gordon Milne have filled the position.

Since 1996, however, the LMA have had the benefit of a Chief Executive who took a conscious decision to make the job a career. John Barnwell, the former Peterborough, Wolves, Notts County, Walsall and Northampton manager has been a real driving force in progressing the status and influence of the LMA combining a lifetime's experience in football with a shrewd business brain which has helped improve the status of football managers. His deputy, Olaf Dixon, has been with the LMA since its inauguration and lends his invaluable experience into running the headquarters in Leamington.

REFEREES AND THE LAWS OF THE GAME

For the second successive year there were very few changes to the Laws of the Game. However, one fundamental alteration is likely to revolutionise universally the way football is played. It is yet another variation to the form in which the goalkeeper is allowed to fashion his/her art but this time it is positive and not restrictive. For the first time in more than half a century the 'keeper is free to control and carry the ball without having to drop it, bounce it or watch his steps. Provided he does not infringe the rules about receiving the ball from a colleague's foot or throw-in, he now has 6 seconds from clear control to part with it or drop it to his feet. This is an amalgam of the current 5/6 seconds provision and what was prevalent (although prohibited by the Laws) in the Italian Leagues some four to five years ago. Indeed one might go so far as to say, had this Law been introduced earlier, with a 4-second limit, there would have been no need to have created what is commonly referred to as the "back-pass" rule. Three areas that the Officials will now have to watch out for are (a) the strict timing of the 6 seconds (b) the re-use of the fair shoulder charge and (c) goalkeepers "cutting the line" of the penalty area with their feet or hands.

It will now be a sending-off offence to use offensive gestures. This area had previously been omitted and was inconsistent with the cautioning provisions on dissent. Heavy pressure from the North Middlesex Referees' Society encouraged this change which will be immensely helpful in junior football.

Another problem has been solved in respect of penalty shoot-outs. Although not part of the open play, they seem to have assumed enormous importance in cup competitions. Formerly it was unclear what happened if one team finished with more players than the other and all the kicks had been equally successful or unsuccessful. The new rule indicates that when a team finishes the match with a greater number of players than their opponents, they should reduce their numbers to equate with that of their opponents.

The International Board has reiterated their prohibition against advertising on the surrounds of the pitch i.e. Technical area, a metre on the ground outside the field and the goal-line and goal-nets. The Fourth Official receives some additional responsibility and Referees are reminded to demand a penalty re-take on encroachment.

Whilst all of these rules apply to football at all levels world wide, there is to be a further experiment, this time in the Premier and Nationwide Leagues, of penalising teams who are guilty of unsporting behaviour. Where players show dissent, encroach or delay a restart, the Referee apart from issuing a caution, is allowed to move the ball forward ten yards inwards towards the direction of the goal. This can only happen once unless the offence is repeated. Unfortunately if it is moved into the penalty area, it becomes a direct free kick and not a penalty thus leading to considerable confusion. If successful it is expected that this system will be implemented into the Laws next season.

On the domestic front although there has been a blending of Officials again, in the Four Divisions, thus altering the elite system, nonetheless the Premiership retains its own list of Referees and "Assistants". Two who disappear from the Premier list are Messrs Alcock and Rennie who are replaced by Messrs Dean, Styles and Taylor. Well-known Referees who have retired include Messrs Read, Wilkie, Burns, Lynch and Heilbron. One of those, Alan Wilkie refereed last season's Worthington Cup Final in which Wendy Toms as Assistant Referee became the first woman to officiate in a leading men's Cup Final at Wembley. The FA Cup Final went to Graham Poll who was also England's refereeing representative at Euro 2000 whilst Assistant Referee Phil Sharp officiated there in one Semi-final. The said Mrs Toms has been chosen as a Great Britain refereeing representative at the forthcoming Olympic Games.

KEN GOLDMAN

NATIONAL LIST OF REFEREES FOR SEASON 2000–2001

Alcock, P.E. (Halstead, Kent)
*Armstrong, P. (Thatcham, Berkshire)
Baines, S.J. (Chesterfield)
Barber, G.P. (Tring, Hertfordshire)
Barry, N.S. (Roxby, N. Lincolnshire)
Bates, A. (Stoke-on-Trent)
Beeby, R.J. (Northampton)
Bennett, S.G. (Orpington, Kent)
Brandwood, M.J. (Lichfield, Staffordshire)
Burns, W.C. (Scarborough)
Butler, A.N. (Sutton-in-Ashfield, Notts)
Cable, L.E. (Woking)
Cain, G. (Seaforth, Merseyside)
*Clattenburg, M. (Chester-le-Street)
*Cooper, M.A. (Walsall)
Cowburn, M.G. (Blackpool)
Crick, D.R. (Worcester Park, Surrey)
*Curson, B. (Hinckley, Leicestershire)
Danson, P.S. (Leicester)
¶Dean, M.L. (Heswall, Wirral)
Dowd, P. (Stoke-on-Trent)
Dunn, S.W. (Bristol)
Durkin, P.A. (Portland, Dorset)
D'Urso, A.P. (Billericay, Essex)
Elleray, D.R. (Harrow-on-the-Hill)

Fletcher, M. (Wolverley, Worcestershire)
Foy, C.J. (St Helens, Merseyside)
Frankland, G.B. (Middlesbrough)
Furnandiz, R.D. (Doncaster)
Gallagher, D.J. (Banbury, Oxfordshire)
Hall, A.R. (Birmingham)
Halsey, M.R. (Welwyn Garden City)
Harris, R.J. (Oxford)
Hill, K.D. (Royston, Hertfordshire)
Jones, M.J. (Chester)
Jones, P. (Loughborough)
Jones, T. (Dalton-in-Furness, Cumbria)
Jordan, W.M. (Tring, Hertfordshire)
Joslin, P.J. (Newark, Nottinghamshire)
Kaye, A. (Wakefield)
Knight, B. (Orpington, Kent)
Laws, D. (Whitley Bay)
Laws, G. (Whitley Bay)
Leake, A.R. (Darwen, Lancashire)
Lodge, S.J. (Barnsley)
Lomas, E. (Manchester)
Mathieson, S.W. (Stockport)
Messias, M.D. (York)
*North, M.J. (Poole, Dorset)
Olivier, R.J. (Sutton Coldfield)

Parkes, T.A. (Birmingham)
Pearson, R. (Peterlee, Durham)
Pike, M.S. (Barrow-in-Furness)
Poll, G. (Tring, Hertfordshire)
*Prosser, P.J. (Abbeymead, Glos)
Pugh, D. (Bebington, Merseyside)
Rejer, D. (Droitwich Spa, Worcestershire)
Rennie, U.D. (Sheffield)
Richards, P.R. (Darwen, Lancashire)
Riley, M.A. (Leeds)
Robinson, J.P. (Hull)
Ryan, M. (Preston)
Stretton, F.G. (Nottingham)
¶Styles, R. (Waterlooville, Hampshire)
¶Taylor, P. (Cheshunt, Hertfordshire)
Tomlin, S.G. (Lewes, East Sussex)
Walton, P. (Long Buckby, Northants)
Warren, M.R. (Walsall)
*Webb, H.M. (Rotherham)
*Webster, C.H. (Shotley Bridge, Durham)
Wiley, A.G. (Burntwood, Staffordshire)
Wilkes, C.R. (Gloucester)
Winter, J.T. (Stockton-on-Tees)
Wolstenholme, E.K. (Blackburn)

* New for season 2000–2001   ¶ New to Premier League 2000–2001

ASSISTANT REFEREES

Artis, S.G. (Norwich)
Aston, G.A. (Kingswinford)
Atkins, G. (Bradford)
Atkinson, M. (Leeds)
Babski, D.S. (Scunthorpe)
Baker, B.D. (Andover, Hampshire)
Baker, L. (Watchet, Somerset)
Bannister, N. (Goole, E. Yorkshire)
Barker, C. (Leeds)
Barnes, K.G. (Swindon)
Barnes, P.W. (Peterborough)
Barston, P.S. (Loughborough)
Bassindale, C. (Doncaster)
Beadle, J. (Gravesend)
Beale, G.A. (Taunton)
Bentley, I.F. (West Whickham, Kent)
Birkett, D.J. (Gainsborough)
Bishop, M.E. (Southfleet, Kent)
Bone, R. (Orpington, Kent)
Booth, R.J. (Sutton-in Ashfield, Notts)
Boyeson, C. (Hull)
Brand, S.R. (Wirral)
Bratt, S.J. (Walsall)
Brayne, R.E. (Harlow, Essex)
Brittain, G.M. (Doncaster)
Broadhurst, P. (West Kirby, Wirral)
Brown, A.R. (Preston)
Bryan, D.S. (Stamford)
Buller, K.R. (Bridgwater)
Burton, R. (Burton-on-Trent)
Butler, A.N. (Wigan)
Cairns, M.J. (Basingstoke)
Canadine, P. (Rotherham)
Carter, J.E. (Sunderland)
Castle, S. (Wolverhampton)
Chapman, G.J. (Stroud, Gloucestershire)
Chittenden, S. (St Albans)
Clingo, S.G. (Kings Lynn, Norfolk)
Clyde, A.L. (Doncaster)
Cockwill, N.R. (Barnstaple, North Devon)
Coffey, S. (Liverpool)
Conn, A. (Royston, Hertfordshire)
Crossley, P.T. (Bromley)
Cordy, J. (Bristol)
Deadman, D. (Cheshunt, Hertfordshire)
Denniff, A.P. (Sheffield)
Desmond, R.P. (Swindon)
Devine, J.P. (Middlesbrough)
Dexter, M.C. (Leicester)
Dorr, S.J. (Worcester)
Downs, D.G. (Norwich)
Drysdale, D. (Sleaford, Lincolnshire)
East, R. (Wilton, Wiltshire)
Eastwood, P. (Manchester)
Ebbage, M. (Burnham, Buckinghamshire)
Edwards, C.D. (Oldham)
Enright, D.J. (Bolton)
Evans, E.M. (Manchester)
Evans, R.J. (Beckenham, Kent)
Evetts, G.S. (Hoddesdon, Hertfordshire)
Faulkner, I.L. (Liverpool)
Foulkes, G.W. (Liverpool)
Francis, C.J. (Ely, Cambridgeshire)
Friend, K.A. (Leicester)
Gagen, S.L. (New Maiden, Surrey)
Garratt, A.M. (Walsall)
Garrett, L.P. (Rochford, Essex)
Gibbs, P.N. (Solihull Lodge, West Midlands)
Gosling, I.J. (Ashford, Kent)
Gould, R. (Swadlincote, Derbyshire)
Graham, E. (Stanford-le-Hope, Essex)
Greaves, A.J. (Doncaster)
Green, A.J. (Hinckley, Leicestershire)
Griffin, P.J. (Hornchurch, Essex)
Griggs, R.P. (Cambridge)
Habgood, S.D. (Chippenham, Wiltshire)
Hall, G.A. (Hixon, Nr Stafford)

Hancox, N. (Walsall Wood, W. Midlands)
Harris, I.R. (Torpoint, Cornwall)
Harvey, A.C. (Croxley Green, Hertfordshire)
Hawken, M.A. (St Austell, Cornwall)
Hawkes, K.J. (Quedgeley, Gloucestershire)
Haxby, M.D. (New Brighton, Wirral)
Head, S.C. (Stokenchurch, Buckinghamshire)
Hegley, G.K. (Bishops Stortford)
Higgins, L.G. (Manchester)
Hills, C.J. (Ely, Cambridgeshire)
Hilton, G. (Wigan)
Hine, D.J. (Worcester)
Hogg, A.S. (Sheffield)
Holbrook, J.H. (Telford)
Horton, A.J. (Wolverhampton)
Horwood, G.D. (Luton)
Howes, T.P. (Norwich)
Hubbard, J.R. (Leicester)
Hutchinson, S.M. (Bingham, Notts)
Ilderton, E.L. (Cullercoats, Tyne & Wear)
Ingram, K.R. (Kingswinford)
Ives, G.L. (Hornchurch)
Ives, M. (Biggleswade, Bedfordshire)
James, R.G. (Milton Keynes)
Jones, L.C. (Bournemouth)
Jones, N.L. (Plymouth)
Kellett, D.G. (Bradford)
Kettle, T.M. (Maidenhead)
King, E.A. (Northumberland)
Lawson, K.D. (Scunthorpe)
Lee, R. (Brentwood, Essex)
Lewis, G.J. (Shelford, Cambridgeshire)
Lewis, R.L. (Shrewsbury)
Lockhart, R. (Newcastle-upon-Tyne)
Lomas, W.D. (Wales, Nr Sheffield)
McCallum, D.A. (Whitley Bay)
McCoy, M.T. (Herne Bay, Kent)
McGee, A. (Knowsley Village, Merseyside)
McGuffog, P. (Manchester)
Marriner, A.M. (Coventry)
Martin, A.J. (Penkridge, Staffordshire)
Martin, E.A.C. (Williton, Somerset)
Martin, R.W. (Sheffield)
Mason, L.S. (Bolton)
Massey, T. (Stockport)
Maynard, M.A. (Hertford)
Mazonowicz, M.J. (Swindon)
Meads, C.J. (Wetherby)
Melin, P.W. (Frimley, Surrey)
Mellor, G.S. (Rotherham)
Merchant, K. (West Ewell, Surrey)
Miller, D.G. (Bristol)
Miller, K.J. (Northumberland)
Miller, N.S. (Witton Gilbert, Durham)
Morrison, D.P. (Littleover, Derbyshire)
Mullarkey, M. (Exeter)
Naylor, D. (Sutton-in-Ashfield, Notts)
Nicholson, A.R. (Halifax)
Nicholson, P.W. (Burnhope, Durham)
Nind, K.J. (Bromsgrove)
Norman, P.V. (Sherborne, Dorset)
Oliver, C.W. (Ashington, Northumberland)
Page, A. (Ilkeston, Derbyshire)
Palmer, R. (Bath)
Parry, B. (Peterlee)
Pashley, R.A. (Chesterfield)
Payne, R.G. (Ampthill, Bedfordshire)
Peacock, D. (Redcar, Cleveland)
Pearce, J.E. (Dagenham)
Pearson, G.D. (Kidderminster)
Penn, A.M. (Wall Heath, West Midlands)
Penton, C. (Woodingdean, E. Sussex)
Perkin, N.F. (Gravesend)
Perlejewski, A.J. (Ryme Intrinseca,

Dorset)
Pettitt, J.W. (Welling, Kent)
Pike, K. (Gillingham, Dorset)
Pollard, T.J. (Bury St Edmunds)
Pollock, R.M. (Maghull, Merseyside)
Postles, M.D. (Coneyhurst Common, W. Sussex)
Powell, K. (Hartlepool)
Probert, L.W. (Bridgwater)
Proctor-Green, S.R.M. (Rotherham)
Ramsay, M. (Coventry)
Ramsdale, P.A. (Mansfield)
Rawcliffe, A. (Manchester)
Reynolds, K.S. (East Barnet)
Richards, D.C. (Llanelli, Carmarthenshire)
Robinson, M.G. (Darlington)
Ross, J.J. (London)
Rubery, S.P. (Ilford)
Rushton, G.N. (Nelson, Lancashire)
Sainsbury, A. (Devizes, Wiltshire)
Salisbury, G. (Preston)
Sharp, P.R. (St Albans)
Shaw, G. (Bramhall, Cheshire)
Shaw, I.D. (Crewe)
Shaw, M.A. (Macclesfield)
Shaw, W. (Blackburn)
Sheffield, J.A. (Burntwood, Staffordshire)
Short, M. (Barnsley)
Short, M.L. (Grantham, Lincolnshire)
Simpson, G. (Leeds)
Singh, J. (Hounslow, Middlesex)
Smith, A.N. (Castleford, W. Yorkshire)
Smith, R.G. (Chelmsford)
Snartt, S. (Bristol)
Spicer, D.R. (Totton, Hampshire)
Steans, R.J. (Loughborough)
Stott, G.T. (Manchester)
Stroud, K.P. (Bournemouth)
Sygmuta, B.C. (Northallerton)
Tanner, S.J. (Bristol)
Tarry, E.J. (Manchester)
Tattan, J.F. (Liverpool)
Taylor, J.T. (Blackburn)
Thiarra, S.S. (Bedford)
Thorpe, M. (Ipswich)
Tiffin, R. (Houghton-le-Spring)
Tincknell, S.W. (Watford)
Tingey, M. (High Wycombe, Buckinghamshire)
Toms, W. (Mrs) (Poole)
Torrance, K.R. (Camberley, Surrey)
Townsend, K.N. (Brierley Hill, W. Midlands)
Turner, G.B. (Chesterfield)
Unsworth, D. (Bolton)
Vosper, P.A. (London)
Wade, B. (Isle of Wight)
Wallace, G. (New Herrington, Tyne & Wear)
Walsh, E.J. (Bromsgrove)
Webb, A.J. (Winnersh, Berkshire)
West, M. (Foxhole, Nr St Austell, Cornwall)
Whitby, D. (Liverpool)
Whitehouse, I. (Calne, Wiltshire)
Whitestone, D. (Northampton)
Wilkins, A.M. (Gravesend, Kent)
Wilkinson, K. (Blyth)
Williams, M.A. (Hereford)
Williamson, I.G. (Reading)
Wood, D. (Ilkley, W. Yorkshire)
Wood, P.M. (Fleetwood, Lancashire)
Woodroffe, J.D. (Wicken, Cambridgeshire)
Woodward, I.J. (Westerham, Kent)
Woolmer, K.A. (Northampton)
Wright, K.K. (Peterborough)
Yates, N.A. (Blackburn)
Yerby, M.S. (Ashford, Kent)
Young, G.R. (Dunstable, Bedfordshire)

FOOTBALL AND THE LAW

Football and the Law in the New Millennium is more a story of off-field activities than of what happens on it. The deaths of two Leeds United supporters in Turkey were an echo of the greater tragedy at Hillsborough in 1989. This still haunts wider memories beyond the bereaved while criminal manslaughter proceedings are taking place as these pages are being prepared; and in entirely unrelated criminal proceedings, professional players with Leeds United are awaiting trial, again for circumstances occurring beyond the fields of play.

Yet again, with echoes of the recent past, the anticipated crowd riots at Brussels during the Euro 2000 competition recalled the troubles at Marseilles during the World Cup competition of 1998.

The questions of what should be done raised queries of civil liberties. The German authorities, fired up by the fatality to a police officer and injuries caused in France apparently legislated for passport surrender on suspicion of anticipated offences, while the United Kingdom Parliament was unable to create any effective deterrent, with the ultimate threat by UEFA of expulsion from the tournament.

During the inevitable inquests, the most significant comment came from retired High Court judge, Sir Oliver Popplewell, who had reported on the Bradford City Valley Parade fire disaster of 1985. He wrote to *The Times* how, while his report was gathering dust in the Home Office, much evidence was produced about the cause of hooliganism which would inform the Home Secretary without his being much the wiser. That goes to the root of the problem which no one has yet been able to identify with clarity and thereby provide a remedy. What is often over-looked, however, is our editor Jack Rollin's assessment under the head of "Soccer Behaviour" in an Appendix to the 3rd Edition of *Sport and the Law*:

"During the inter-war years, two fifths of the 88 Football League clubs attracted their highest attendance figures. None of these events was accompanied by serious crowd disturbances." He then proceeded to identify contrasting patterns of playing behaviour before and after the Second World War of 1939-1945.

In the following Appendix, my solicitor son Harry, at my special request, produced under the title of *Hooligan-free Football Grounds: Record Attendances in England and Wales (1919-39)* the following lists in order of crowd size during national unemployment of an estimated three million; but no recorded violence or criminality appears at any of the crowd attendance records listed below:

Club	Crowd	Date	Occasion
Manchester City	84,569	3 Mar 1934	FA Cup 6
(British record for any game outside London or Glasgow)			
Chelsea	82,905	12 Oct 1935	FA Cup 5
Manchester United	76,926	25 Mar 1939	FA Cup
(Wolves v Grimsby Town)			Semi-final
Sunderland	75,118	8 Mar 1933	FA Cup 6
Tottenham Hotspur	75,038	5 Mar 1938	FA Cup 6
Charlton Athletic	75,031	12 Feb 1938	FA Cup 5
Arsenal	73,295	9 Mar 1935	Div 1
Sheffield Wednesday	72,841	17 Feb 1934	FA Cup 5
Bolton Wanderers	69,912	18 Feb 1933	FA Cup
Birmingham City	68,844	11 Feb 1939	FA Cup 5
Newcastle United	68,386	3 Sept 1930	Div 1
Sheffield United	68,287	15 Feb 1936	FA Cup 5
Huddersfield Town	67,037	27 Feb 1932	FA Cup 6
West Bromwich Albion	64,815	6 Mar 1937	FA Cup 6
Blackburn Rovers	61,783	2 Mar 1929	FA Cup 6
Wolverhampton Wanderers	61,315	11 Feb 1939	FA Cup 5
Burnley	54,775	25 Feb 1924	FA Cup 3
Stoke City	51,380	29 Mar 1937	Div 1
Fulham	49,335	8 Oct 1938	Div 2
Millwall	48,672	20 Feb 1937	FA Cup 5
Oldham Athletic	47,671	25 Jan 1930	FA Cup 4
Leicester City	47,298	18 Feb 1928	FA Cup 5
Plymouth Argyle	43,596	10 Oct 1936	Div 2
Bristol City	43,335	16 Feb 1935	FA Cup 5
Preston NE	42,684	23 Apr 1938	Div 1
Barnsley	40,255	15 Feb 1936	FA Cup 5
Brentford	39,626	5 Mar 1938	FA Cup 5
Reading	33,042	19 Feb 1927	FA Cup 5
Grimsby Town	31,657	20 Feb 1937	FA Cup
Chesterfield	30,968	7 Apr 1939	Div 2
York City	28,123	5 Mar 1938	FA Cup 5
Newport County	24,268	16 Oct 1937	Div 3 (S)
Exeter City	20,984	4 Mar 1931	FA Cup 6
Wimbledon	18,000	1932/33	FA Amateur Cup

On three occasions at Burnley (1924), Huddersfield Town (1932) and Fulham (1938), casualties were caused by crush crowd circumstances; but not by violence.

Thus, as Sir Oliver Popplewell explains, we may be better informed, but shall we ever be wiser in trying to understand why the beautiful game today attracts thuggery off the field which it never experienced during the periods listed above?

EDWARD GRAYSON
Founder President, British Association for Sport and Law.

The FOOTBALL TRUST
Helping the game

NATIONAL SHAME TO NATIONAL PRIDE
TRUST CLOSURE SIGNALS END OF A GLORIOUS ERA OF STADIUM REBUILDING FOLLOWING HILLSBOROUGH TRAGEDY

From the shame of Hillsborough to stadia fit to stage a World Cup Finals, the closure of the Football Trust signals the end of its role in the most groundbreaking era of stadia redevelopment ever seen anywhere in the world.

The Trust's work will be taken over by a brand new body with a new remit dedicated towards investing in the grassroots of the game. The new body will be called the Football Foundation and will be funded by the Premier League, the Football Association, Sport England and the Government.

The Football Trust has invested some £400 million in our national game at all levels, from junior sides right the way up to rebuilding our magnificent homes of football throughout the United Kingdom.

Our grounds have been transformed from crumbling edifices to some of the best and safest in Europe if not the world, supporters have flocked back to the game in record numbers and the industry, certainly at the top level, is continuing to boom.

Our legacy includes:

* 15 new grounds
* 160 new and refurbished stands
* 55 new community and family facilities
* 25 new facilities for spectators with disabilities
* 100 new PA systems
* 50 new sets of floodlights
* 30 new stadium control rooms

The introduction of CCTV surveillance equipment throughout football has proved the single most important measure in the campaign against football hooliganism and this has largely been paid for by the Trust.

The Football in the Community Programme owes its existence to the Trust and its investment of some £5.5m. Substantial investment has been made in training facilities and youth development.

The major projects at our professional clubs for the last financial year include:

Taylor Grants 1999/2000

Team	Grant (£)	Project (£)	
Barnet	39,000	77,000	Barrier work
Blackpool	25,000	31,500	Barrier work
Bradford City	990,000	2.77m	New North Stand
Bristol Rovers	34,000	51,385	Barrier work
Bury	1.5m	1.94m	New East Stand
Cambridge United	41,120	60,744	Barrier work
Cardiff City	50,000	75,972	Barrier work
Charlton Athletic	150,000	3.7m	West Stand, 2nd Phase
Crewe Alexandra	1.75m	4.8m	New South Stand
Darlington	36,500	56,273	Barrier work
Exeter City	1.8m	2.5m	Two new stands and barrier work
Gillingham	1.25m		Redfrean Avenue and Rainham End stands
Halifax Town	1.8m	2.66m	Redevelopment of the ground
Hull City	55,770	69,873	Barrier work
Ipswich Town	1.7m	2.5m	Redevelopment of the Churchman Road Stand
Leyton Orient	867,200	1.1m	New South Stand, seating and barrier improvements
Lincoln City	30,000	46,000	Seating the Stacey West Stand
Mansfield Town	1.55m	4.95m	Three new stands
Peterborough United	150,000	216,261	New barriers and roofing two stands
Plymouth Argyle	18,000	25,524	Barrier work
Port Vale	1.3m	4m	New Lorne Street Stand
Preston North End	250,000	2.4m	New North Stand
	35,750	71,500	Barrier work
Rochdale	1.1m	142,000	New Willbutts Land Stand and Sandy Lane Terrace
Rotherham United	287,822	338,951	Seating and toilets, Railway Terrace
Shrewsbury Town	22,000	27,456	Barrier work
Southampton	2.75m		New stadium
Walsall	3,000	3,765	Barrier work
Wigan Athletic	1m	24m	New stadium
Wrexham	1m,	2.7m	New Mold Road Stand and seating projects
	32,620	41,279	Barrier work
York City	7,000	8,781	Barrier work

Chairman Tom Pendry MP stated:

"The implementation of the Taylor Report's recommendations has transformed football and the Trust has played a huge part in this transformation. From Newcastle United to Northampton Town supporters in every division can now enjoy safe and comfortable facilities. We are proud of our achievements.

"Thanks to our investment this country can boast the finest football grounds in the world. Grounds to grace the 2006 World Cup.

"With the stadium rebuilding work all but complete, football must now turn its attention to tackling the problems at the grassroots of the game and we will be doing just that with the imminent launch of the Football Foundation."

FOOTBALL CLUB CHAPLAINCY

ENCOURAGING COMPARISONS

The autumn 1999 Football Chaplains' Conference occurred at around the fifteenth anniversary of the first such gathering and, naturally, therefore presented an interesting opportunity for some comparisons to be made – interesting, and particularly for those who understand or who have experienced first hand the huge advantages that a well appointed chaplain can bring to a football club, most encouraging.

Back in 1984 a dozen or so chaplains from Football League clubs met in conference for the first time. They were representative of some sixteen or eighteen such men and, whilst some clubs even then had had chaplains for perhaps twenty years, this was in most cases a relatively new, even experimental, area of Christian ministry. By 1999 there were nearly a hundred serving football chaplains in the country with perhaps a quarter of them to be found in non-league outfits and a growing representation in Scotland and Northern Ireland reflecting the advances among the Premiership and Football League clubs.

However, numbers alone do not tell the full story. Whilst the pioneer chaplains from the 1984 conference who were present at its 1999 successor were thrilled (and humbled) by the sheer size of it, the fact is that the standing and the involvement of the football chaplains have similarly increased.

RESPECT IN FOOTBALL AND CHURCH

This was to be discerned in several ways. Firstly, the respect with which both football and the churches regard the chaplains has grown significantly over the last decade and a half, and was witnessed at the 1999 conference by the presence as major speakers both of Mr John Barnwell, the Chief Executive since 1996 of the League Managers' Association, and the Rev David Coffey, the General Secretary of the Baptist Union of Great Britain (the Baptist equivalent of the Archbishop of Canterbury, as the Conference members were helpfully informed in their briefing packs!). Men of such authority as this simply do not and cannot give of their precious time to speak to fringe gatherings or ones that lack credibility. Equally, Mr Howard Wells, the Chief Executive of Premier League club Watford, was evidently pleased to address the 1999 chaplains' conference on its final morning.

Another example of the way in which our sport regards football chaplaincy in general and individual chaplains in particular lies in the fact that that their annual conferences are now sponsored by the Premier League and are hosted at the National Sport and Recreation Centre at Lilleshall – although readers who might therefore hope to see the Premiership logo appearing on chaplains' surplices or preaching gowns as a result of this backing will remain disappointed for some while to come!

Nevertheless, the attitude or style of the football chaplains is perhaps rather different from that of more typical churchmen. It can be seen in the fact that they *do* choose to gather at Lilleshall rather than at one of the acknowledged retreat and conference centres which the churches own that are sited around the country. These clergy are just as much at home and at ease worshipping in a lecture hall as in a chapel and in the company of men and women (the Great Britain Olympics ladies hockey team was also at Lilleshall at the same time!) of the world as they are with their regular congregations and especially is this so with other sports persons.

INSPIRATION

Interestingly too, our football chaplains have become the inspiration (no pun intended!) for the opening up of chaplaincies in several other sports, major and minor, team and individual, and as the validity and worth of their ministry is increasingly understood and recognised so the number of clergy who are engaged full time in sports ministry has grown steadily.

'PASTORS AND TEACHERS'

Finally, it has often been pointed out to regular readers of this page that the pastoral caring role of a football chaplain can be and has frequently proved to have been of enormous value to a football club and its employees – one of the football based speakers at the 1999 conference described it as being 'of vital importance' – but the Adidas Football Scholarship Scheme, about to enter its third season, has prompted a widening of his role at the clubs which have established an Academy. Not only has the Professional Footballers' Association, who were prime movers in the establishment of the details of the Academies' curriculum, asked clubs to engage their chaplains, *or to provide one*, to deliver certain of the modules, but some clubs are discovering that their chaplain is also a gifted teacher and communicator as well as an experienced pastor, who has been able to offer and present other areas of the curriculum as well – to the various pleasure, delight and relief of their hard-pressed Education and Welfare officers, even if, initially at least, it was also to the astonishment of the young student footballers whose dealings and understanding of clergymen had previously been somewhat limited!
THE REV

OFFICIAL CHAPLAINS TO FA PREMIERSHIP AND FOOTBALL LEAGUE CLUBS

Rev Steven Hawkins—Bristol Rovers; Rev Catherine Bell—Luton T; Rev Richard Chewter—Exeter C; Rev Peter Bye—Carlisle U; Rev Ken Howles—Blackburn Rovers; Rev David Langdon—QPR; Rev Andrew Taggart—Torquay U; Rev Gary Piper—Fulham; Rev David Jeans—Sheffield W; Rev Peter Amos—Barnsley; Rev Nigel Sands—Crystal Palace; Rev Barry Kirk—Reading; Rev Graham Spencer—Leicester C; Rev David Bunbury—Bradford C; Rev Philip Miller—Ipswich T; Rev John Boyers—Manchester U; Rev Allen Bagshawe—Hull C; Rev Martin Butt—Walsall; Rev David Tully—Newcastle U; Rev Steve Riley and Capt Andrew Vertigan—Leeds U; Rev Derek Cleave—Bristol City; Rev Fr Alan Poulter and Fr Gerald Courell—Tranmere R; Rev Brian Rice—Hartlepool U; Rev Mark Kichenside and Rev Jeffrey Heskins—Charlton Ath; Revs Andy Cowley and John Graham—Watford; Rev Owen Beament—Millwall; Rev Michael Chantry—Oxford U; Rev Elwin Cockett—West Ham U; Rev Michael Futens—Derby C; Rev Mick Woodhead—Sheffield U; Rev Ken Hawkins—Birmingham C; Rev Alan Comfort—Leyton Orient; Rev Simon Stevenette—Swindon Town; Rev John Hall-Matthews—Wolverhampton W; Rev Canon Michael Hunter—Grimsby T; Rev Steve Collis—Port Vale; Rev Chris Cullwick—York C; Rev Ken Baker—Northampton T; Rev Mark Hirst—Burnley; Rev Steve Halliwell—Barnet; Rev Tony Porter—Manchester C; Rev Richard Hayton—Gillingham; Rev Piers Lane—Darlington; Rev Clive Andrews—Notts Co; Fr Andrew McMahon—Southampton; Rev Chris Nelson—Preston North End; Rev Henry Corbett and Rev Harry Ross—Everton; Rev Paul Brown—Wrexham; Rev Jeff Howden—Plymouth Argyle; Major Graham Carey—Portsmouth; Rev Alan Hayday—Scunthorpe U; Rev Tim Welch—Shrewsbury T; Rev James Booth—Southend U; Rev Philip Hearn—Kidderminster H.

The chaplains hope that those who read this page will see the value and benefit of chaplaincy work in football and will take appropriate steps to spread the word where this is possible. They would also like to thank the editors of the Rothmans Yearbook *for their continued support for this specialist and growing area of work.*

The following addresses may be helpful: SCORE (Sports Chaplaincy Offering Resources and Encouragement), PO Box 123, Sale, Manchester M33 4ZA and Christians in Sport, PO Box 93, Oxford OX2 7YP.

OBITUARY
THE REV MICHAEL LOWE

Michael Lowe was the ebullient, larger than life chaplain at Bournemouth for seven years before his death in December 1999. His ministry was hugely respected and appreciated at Dean Court, indeed in the entire Bournemouth area, and even when suffering increasingly from the motor neurone disease which forced his retirement from Christchurch Priory in 1997, he continued to serve The Cherries as fully as his condition would allow. As Bournemouth's Chairman, Trevor Watkins, put it: 'Michael was a friend, a confidant to everyone at our club, and a tremendous supporter of it.' Bournemouth fans are joined in their loss by the other chaplains who mourn their former colleague.

OBITUARIES

Thomas 'Bud' Aherne (b Limerick 26.1.19; d 1.00). A full-back, 'Bud' started out with Belfast Celtic after the Second World War and went on to win 16 caps for the Republic of Ireland. He also gained four caps for Northern Ireland. He joined Luton Town in March, 1949 and went on to play 267 League games for the Hatters.

Emilio Aldecoa (b Bilbao, Spain 30.11.22; d Spain 9.99). An inside-left, Emilio was a Basque refugee from the Spanish Civil War, who came to England in 1937. He joined Wolves in 1943 and was their leading goalscorer in wartime League and Cup matches with 11 goals in 30 games. In 1945, he joined Coventry and made 29 appearances. He returned to Spain in 1947 and played for Barcelona.

Martin Aldridge (b Northampton 6.12.74; d 30.1.00). Martin died tragically in a car crash following a match for Rushden and Diamonds earlier this year. He was on loan to them from Blackpool, but also played for Northampton Town, Oxford United and had further loan spells with Dagenham and Redbridge and Southend United. A forward with good pace, Martin scored 44 goals in a total of 175 League games.

George Ashall (b Killamarsh 29.9.11; d 5.98). George played pre-war football for Wolves, scoring 14 times in 84 League games. before moving to Coventry City in 1938, where he hit a further ten goals in 62 League matches.

Chris Balderstone (b Huddersfield 16.11.40; d 6.3.00). A highly successful cricketer (with Yorkshire and Leicestershire) and footballer, who went on to become a first class umpire. On one occasion, he was playing cricket for Leicestershire until 6.30pm, but having scored 51 not out, he was required to play for Doncaster Rovers an hour later. He took part in a one-all draw against Brentford that evening, then resumed his innings the following day to complete a century and take three wickets! On the football field, he was a clever forward who played for Huddersfield Town (117 League appearances), Carlisle United (376 League games), Doncaster Rovers (39 League matches) and Queen of the South (24 League appearances).

Les Bennett (b Wood Green 10.1.18; d 29.4.99). A Tottenham forward who hit 102 goals in 272 League games for Spurs between 1946 and 1954. He completed his first class career with West Ham United (26 League appearances, 3 goals).

Dave Bickles (b West Ham 6.4.44; d 11.99). A half-back, who played alongside Bobby Moore and Martin Peters at West Ham between 1963 and 1967. After 25 League games, he moved on to Crystal Palace, but left for Colchester United (68 League games and 3 goals) before he had made a League appearance for Palace.

Ronald William Charles Bower (b Wrexham 17.11.11; d 12.98). An amateur with New Brighton in 1930, he made 20 League appearances as a defender, before moving to South Liverpool in 1935. He joined Bolton Wanderers in 1936, but only played three League games, then left for Millwall in 1937, but failed to make an appearance.

George Bradley (b Maltby 7.11.17; d 8.12.98). A tough defender, who played pre-war football for Rotherham and Newcastle. After hostilities, he joined Millwall and scored twice in 74 League games.

Ray Bunkell (b Edmonton 18.9.49; d 15.3.00). A talented midfielder who played for Swindon (56 League games) and Colchester (129 League appearances) between 1971 and 1980.

Johnny 'Budgie' Byrne (b West Horsley 13.5.38; d Cape Town 27.10.99). Immensely skilful inside forward who, at his first club, Crystal Palace, became the first Fourth Division player to win England Under-23 honours when he was capped in 1961. He also made 11 full international appearances and was the first Palace player to win major England honours since 1923. In 1962, he moved to West Ham and won an F.A. Cup winners' medal in 1964. After 156 League games and 79 goals, he returned to Palace in 1967, then joined Fulham in 1968. In all he made 238 League appearances (90 goals) for Palace. A year later he left England to pursue a new career in South Africa, where he managed Durban City with great success. Later he enjoyed managerial posts with Hellenic and Cape Town Spurs.

Edwin Carr (b Wheatley Hill 3.10.17; d 6.98). Joined Arsenal in 1935 and made his debut in 1938. His goals helped the Gunners win the title – 7 in 11 matches. The war then intervened and after hostilities he joined Newport County and hit 48 goals in 98 League games. In October, 1949, he moved to Bradford City and scored a further 49 times in 94 League outings. He completed his first class career at Darlington and eventually became manager at Feethams.

John 'Jack' Connor (b Todmorden 21.12.19; d 12.98). A centre-forward, who signed for Ipswich Town in 1944, but moved to Carlisle in 1946 where he had been stationed during the war. Following a loan spell to Ards in Northern Ireland, 'Jack' signed for Rochdale in 1948 and scored 42 goals in 88 League games. In April, his goalscoring feats persuaded Bradford City to sign him, but after seven goals in 14 League

outings Stockport County, who had long pursued him, snapped him up for £2,500. He became a legend at Edgeley Park, amassing 140 goals in 217 League and Cup games, including 17 hat-tricks; three of those were in consecutive games! In September, 1956, he left for Crewe Alexandra, where he saw out his first class career.

Reginald Horace Cumner (b Aberdare 31.3.18; d 1.99). Reg started out as an outside-left with Arsenal in 1935, then loaned to Margate and Hull City before being recalled to make his debut in 1938, when he scored the only goal of the game at Wolves. He played 12 matches before the outbreak of war and won three caps for Wales, scoring once. Following hostilities he played for Notts County, Watford and Scunthorpe United.

Richard 'Dickie' Davis (b Birmingham 22.1.22; d 8.99). Signed for Sunderland in 1939 but, because of hostilities, made his debut after the war. He scored 72 goals in 144 League games for the Rokerites, including 25 in 1949-50, and was a great foil for Len Shackleton. In 1954, he moved to Darlington, where he bagged a further 32 goals in 93 League games.

Alfred Dickinson (b Saltney 1915; d 8.98). Alf signed for Everton in 1934, but he only made one appearance, replacing Dixie Dean up front in a 5-1 defeat at Portsmouth in April, 1935.

Bill Dodgin (Senior) (b Gateshead 17.4.09; d 10.99). Following spells with Huddersfield Town and Lincoln City, Bill joined Charlton in 1934. A half-back, he won a Third Division South Championship medal a year later. In 1936, he joined Bristol Rovers, but after 12 months was on the move to Clapton Orient. Another summer move came in 1939, this time to Southampton, but the war intervened and, following hostilities he was appointed coach, then manager. After twice missing out on promotion for Second Division Saints, he joined Fulham, who were then in the top Division. In 1953, he was sacked and joined Brentford, but in 1957, he went to Sampdoria, where he remained for two years. He managed Yiewsley (Hillingdon Borough) between 1959 and 1961, then went to Bristol Rovers as chief scout, a post he occupied until 1969, when he became the club's manager.

Bill Dodgin (Junior) (b Durham 4.11.31; d 6.00). When Bill Dodgin became manager of Fulham in December, 1968, it was only the second ever father–son succession. Bill junior's teams, like his father's, were attractive to watch, always attempting to play entertaining football. Following the war, his playing career began with Southampton, whom his father managed at the time. Bill started out on an amateur basis, then followed his father to Fulham, for whom he signed professional forms in September, 1949. A centre-half, he made 35 appearances for the Cottagers, before moving to Arsenal in December, 1952. At Highbury he had 191 League outings and made an Under-23 appearance for England against Italy. In March, 1961, he returned to Craven Cottage, but a broken leg after 69 League appearances, effectively ended his playing career in the early sixties. In 1965, he joined Millwall as a coach, then took up a similar position with Queen's Park Rangers in January, 1968, before becoming manager that same season. He left Rangers in August of that year and took over the hot seat at Fulham in December, 1968. But, as at QPR, he was unable to prevent the club being relegated. In 1971, however, Fulham were promoted, after finishing Third Division runners-up, but Bill was dismissed a year later. Following a spell as coach at Leicester City, he took over at Northampton Town and guided to Cobblers to promotion from the Fourth Division in 1976. He did the same with Brentford two years later.

James Dougal (b Denny 3.10.13; d 17.10.99). Jimmy could play in any of the forward positions and it was his adaptability that persuaded Preston to sign him from Falkirk in January, 1934. He was in the North End side that lost to Sunderland in the 1937 F.A. Cup final, but missed the following year's Wembley success through injury. He played for the club during the war and was in the side when North End beat Arsenal in the Wartime League Cup final in 1941. Jimmy made one international appearance for Scotland against England in 1939 and scored Scotland's goal in their 2-1 defeat. In 1946, he joined Carlisle United, having played 171 League games (51 goals) for Preston. After two seasons with Carlisle, he saw out his first class career with Halifax Town.

James Dyson (b Middleton 4.3.07; d 1.00). Jimmy was a creative inside forward who joined Oldham Athletic in 1928. After 22 League appearances and 39 goals he was signed by Grimsby Town in 1932 and scored 38 goals in 139 League appearances, helping the Mariners to finish in their highest ever League position – fifth in the First Division in 1934-35. In February, 1938, he left for Nottingham Forest, where he remained until the war years. During hostilities, Jimmy played for Accrington Stanley.

George Eastham (Senior) (b Blackpool 13.8.14; d South Africa 1.00). George, a talented inside-forward, started out with Bolton Wanderers in 1932 and was a member of the side that finished Second Division runners-up in 1935. He also made his one and only international appearance for England against Holland that same year. In June, 1937, after 114 League games and 16 goals, he joined Brentford, but his stay was brief. In November, 1938, he joined Blackpool, playing pre and post war football for the Tangerines. He scored nine times in 44 League games before having short spells with Swansea Town, Rochdale and Lincoln City. He then held a player-manager position with Ards, before retiring from the playing side in 1955. He then had further managerial posts with Accrington Stanley, Distillery, Ards, Hellenic (South Africa) and Glentoran.

Henry 'Harry' Eastham (b Blackpool 30.6.17; d 9.98). The younger brother of George who signed professionally for Blackpool in July, 1934. In 1936, he signed for Liverpool and played 63 League games scoring

three times. In 1947, he won a First Division Championship medal. A year later, he joined Tranmere Rovers and scored 13 goals in 154 League matches. Harry completed his first class playing career with Accrington Stanley.

Arthur Ellis (b Halifax 8.7.14; d 23.5.99). Famous Football League referee who took charge of the F.A. Cup semi-final between Tottenham and Blackpool in 1948 then, in 1950, he refereed West Germany's first ever international against Switzerland, He also officiated at the 1950 World Cup finals and then took charge of the 1952 F.A. Cup final between Arsenal and Newcastle. In total he refereed 73 internationals and the 1956 European Champions' Cup final.

Dennis Evans (b Ellesmere Port 18.7.30; d 23.2.00). Arsenal full-back of the fifties, Dennis made his debut against Huddersfield Town in August, 1953. He represented London against Lausanne in the very first Inter Cities Fairs Cup (UEFA Cup) in 1957. A broken ankle suffered in 1959 curtailed his playing career and his final Arsenal appearance (189th) came in 1960 against Tottenham.

Dave Ewing (b Perth 10.5.29; d 7.99). Dave joined Manchester City in 1949 and made his debut four years later in a local derby against Manchester United. He played in the F.A. Cup finals of 1955 and 1956, emerging victorious in the latter. After 13 years and 279 League games, he joined Crewe Alexandra in July, 1962 and made 62 League appearances before returning to City as coach. He also served Sheffield Wednesday, Bradford City and Crystal Palace in a similar capacity and had a spell as manager at Hibernian.

John 'Jack' Fairbrother (b Burton 16.8.17; d 10.99). An outstanding goalkeeper, Jack signed for Preston before the war and played 107 times for North End during hostilities, as well as guesting for Blackburn, Burnley and Chester. After the war he made 41 League appearances for the Deepdale club, before leaving for Newcastle in 1947. He won a Second Division Championship medal with the Magpies and won an F.A. Cup winners' medal in 1951. Jack made 133 League appearances for United, then moved to Non-League Peterborough United as player manager in 1952. He went on to manage Coventry City a year later, coached the Israel national side in 1955, then returned to manage Peterborough in 1962.

Arthur Douglas Frost (b Liverpool 1.12.15; d 10.98). One of the many players whose career was wrecked by the Second World War. A prolific goalscorer, Frost signed for professional forms for New Brighton in August, 1938, and bagged 18 goals in 23 League games. Newcastle signed him in March, 1939, and he scored once in the remaining five matches of that season. He never played for the Magpies again and became player manager of South Liverpool in the 1946-47 season.

Alfred Garnham (b Birtley 22.6.14; d 4.98). Essentially a half-back, Alf signed for Newcastle United in April, 1934. In August, 1939, after making 48 League appearances, he was transferred to Queen of the South, but returned to the Magpies to guest for the club during the war.

Arthur Glover (b Barnsley 27.3.18; d 9.98). Arthur played for Barnsley and Yorkshire Schools and joined his local club in March, 1935 making his debut in 1938 against Stockport County. A centre-half, he played pre and post war football for the Tykes and made 186 League appearances, retiring at the end of the 1952-53 season.

Freddie Green (b Sheffield 9.9.16; d 9.98). A full-back who joined Torquay United in 1935. After 88 League games, he moved to Brighton and Hove Albion in 1938. He played just two League games before the war, then resumed his career in 1946-47 with a further 24 League outings.

Stan Gullan (b Southend 1926; d 1999). Stan played for Dumbarton after the war before being transferred to Clyde, for whom he kept goal in the 1949 Scottish Cup final against Rangers. In the summer of '49, he was sold to Queens Park Rangers, where he remained for five seasons. He had a spell in English Non-League football, then returned to Scotland to play for Berwick Rangers, Third Lanark, Montrose and Stenhousemuir.

Albert Edward Hankey (b Stoke 24.5.14; d 9.98). A goalkeeper, Albert signed for Southend in October, 1937 and made his debut against Watford the same month. His career resumed after the war years and he made a total of 125 League appearances for the Shrimpers.

Leo Harden (b West Hartlepool 7.5.23; d 5.12.99). Spent 10 seasons (1946-1956) with Hartlepools United. Leo, an outside-left, made his debut in the first League game following the war and scored on his debut against Barrow. A great character and a part-time professional, he was nicknamed 'the Flying Dustman' because he drove a dustcart for a living. He played 170 League games for Hartlepools and scored 47 goals, including four in one match against Rochdale in 1953.

Fred Harris (b Birmingham 2.7.12; d 10.98). Fred had a great career with Birmingham City either side of the war and, as first a goalscoring inside-forward, then a wing-half, hit 61 goals in 280 League games. In 1949, he won a place in The Football League side that opposed The Scottish League at Ibrox and played alongside Tom Finney, Jackie Milburn and Stan Mortensen.

Charles 'Midge' John Hill (b Cardiff 6.9.18; d 12.98). Signed for his hometown club, Cardiff City in 1938. An inside-forward or half-back, he made his debut in October of the year and had played 19 League

games (four goals) by the time war intervened. After hostilities, 'Midge' joined Torquay United (July, 1947) and he scored 15 goals in 63 League appearances before moving to Queens Park Rangers (20 League games, one goal). He completed his first class playing career with Swindon, with four appearances.

Joseph Kenneth Horton (b Preston 26.8.22; d 10.2.00). Signed for Preston North End in 1940, but had to wait until the end of the Second World War before he made his official League debut. He started out as a half-back, but converted to inside-forward in 1950-51. It was an inspired move, because he poached 22 goals that season as North End won the Second Division title. In October, 1952, he was sold to Hull City and remained there for three seasons before signing for Barrow in August, 1955. After 22 League games he went to Non-League Morecambe and scored 58 goals in 110 League and Cup games.

Jack Johnston (b Dundee 1922; d Queensland, Australia 12.98). Jack represented Raith Rovers, Queens Park, Dundee Violet and YM Anchorage. He also played for Scotland against England while on military duty.

Len Jones (b Barnsley 9.6.13; d 4.98). A right-half, Len started out as an amateur with Huddersfield Town before joining Barnsley on professional forms in August, 1933. After 51 League games, he surprisingly left for Non-League Chelmsford City in 1938. Just prior to the outbreak of the war, Len joined Plymouth Argyle and made 30 wartime appearances for the Pilgrims. After hostilities, he continued to play for Argyle and had a further 40 League outings. In August, 1949, he left Home Park for Southend United, where he made 29 League appearances; then moved to Colchester United for whom he played 71 times.

Walter Joyce (b Oldham 10.9.37; d 10.99). A wing-half who served Burnley (1960-63), Blackburn Rovers (1963-67) and Oldham Athletic (1967-69) before becoming coach at Oldham, then manager of Rochdale in July, 1973 to May, 1976. He was also a coach and assistant manager at Spotland and then occupied similar positions with Preston North End from the mid-eighties until 1992. He was later responsible for youth development at Bury, then became a youth scout at Manchester United.

John 'Jack' Kelly (b Hetton-le-Hole 2.3.13; d 2.00). A centre-forward, Jack began with Burnley in October, 1930. In April, he was transferred to Newcastle United, but after only five appearances he left for Leeds United, where he made 59 League appearances and scored 17 goals. In January, 1938, he joined Birmingham City, then in May, 1939, he signed for Bury, where he saw out his first class playing career.

Gordon Kennedy (b Dundee 15.4.24; d 24.10.99). A full-back with Blackpool during, and immediately following, the war years. However, after nine League games, Gordon moved to Bolton Wanderers, where he had 17 League outings. In 1953, he joined Stockport County and played 20 times, before returning to Dundee in the mid-fifties.

Fred Kenyon (b Carlisle 14.9.22; d 20.12.98). Fred signed for Carlisle United in 1943 and made four League appearances at centre-half in the 1947-48 season.

John 'Jerry' Kerr (b West Lothian 1912; d 8.11.99). Played pre-war football as a full-back for Rangers, Alloa and Dundee United. After the war he took up coaching before managing Berwick Rangers, Alloa, Dundee United and Forfar. He also had spells as a scout with West Brom and a youth coach with Dundee.

Ken Keyworth (b Rotherham 24.2.34; d 7.1.00). Ken started out in the early fifties with Rotherham United, where he played as a wing-half, but it was with Leicester City that he starred as a centre-forward, whom he joined in 1958. At Leicester he played in two F.A. Cup finals (1961 and 1963) and it was in the latter, against Manchester United, that he scored with a spectacular diving header. In 1964, he won a League Cup winners' medal as the Filberts defeated Stoke City in the two-legged final. After 63 goals in 177 League appearances, he completed his first class career with Coventry City and Swindon Town.

Len Kingswell (b Rossyth 31.5.18; d 12.98). A centre-half, who started out with Plymouth Argyle, but having made no League appearances he joined Torquay United in 1936. He had one League outing in 1937-38 and two in 1938-39 before the war intervened.

George Kirby (b 20.12.23; d 24.3.00). Former Manager of Halifax Town and Watford, who also held similar posts in Kuwait, Iceland, Indonesia and Saudi Arabia, and who had a nomadic career as a player between 1952 and 1969. George was a strong, battling centre-forward who scored his fair share of goals for Everton (26 League appearances; 9 goals), Sheffield Wednesday (3 League appearances; 0 goals), Plymouth Argyle (93 League appearances; 38 goals), Southampton (64 League appearances; 28 goals), Coventry City (18 League appearances; 10 goals), Swansea City (26 League appearances; 9 goals), Walsall (75 League appearances; 25 goals), Brentford (5 League appearances; 1 goal).

Willie Laird (b Carronshore 1918; d 9.99). Formerly with East Stirling, Willie made his name with East Fife and played a total of 219 League and Cup games for the club, winning a Scottish Cup winners' medal in 1938. He left the Fifers in the 1950-51 season and completed his first class playing career with Dunfermline.

Cliff Lloyd O.B.E. (b Frodsham 14.11.16; 8.1.00). Former secretary of the Professional Footballers' Association between 1953 and 1981, Cliff was on the books of Liverpool and joined Wrexham in 1938, operating on the wing or at inside forward. The arrival of hostilities, however, meant he never made his

League debut for the latter, but did play wartime football for Wrexham, Brentford and Fulham. He played two League matches for the Cottagers after the war, then went to Bristol Rovers in May, 1950, but made no League appearances for the Pirates.

Tommy Lowder (b Blyth 24.10.24; d 13.5.99). An outside-left who began with Rotherham United in 1947 and scored 5 goals in eight League games before joining Southampton in October, 1949. At The Dell he scored twice in 39 League outings, then completed his first class playing career with Southend United (21 League games, 3 goals).

Malcolm MacDonald (b Scotland 26.10.13; d 26.9.99). Malcolm started out with Celtic in April, 1932. An inside-forward, he won Championship medals in 1936 and 1938. After the war, he joined Kilmarnock, then became a Brentford player in 1946, eventually taking up a coaching position at Griffin Park. He returned to Kilmarnock in 1950 as Manager, had a spell in charge of Brentford from the late fifties to 1965, before returning once more to the hot seat at Rugby Park. Later he scouted for Tottenham and Celtic.

Donald MacLeod (b Edinburgh 1.11.17; d 20.6.99). Don joined the Royal Navy in the war years and guested for Portsmouth when available. Following hostilities, he joined Motherwell and was a member of the side that reached the Scottish Cup final in 1951. He was later assistant trainer and physiotherapist at Hearts.

Wilf Mannion (b 16.5.18: d 14.4.00). Wilf was known as 'the Golden Boy', because of his blond hair, supreme dribbling skills and wonderful pace. He signed professionally for Middlesbrough in January, 1937 and made his debut later that month against Portsmouth. He became a regular from 1938 until the war years. During hostilities, Wilf made four international appearances for England and also played for the Army side. He served with the Green Howard regiment and was evacuated from Dunkirk. He later served in the Middle East and Italy, but was invalided out of the army with shellshock. Following the war, Wilf became one of the greatest players in the British game. He scored a hat-trick in England's first post-war international – a 7-2 victory over Northern Ireland. In 1947, he was selected for Great Britain against the Rest of Europe and scored twice in a fine 6-1 win. His last international was in 1951 against Scotland, but he was unfortunately stretchered from the field after fracturing a cheekbone. Wilf won 26 caps and scored 11 goals. He left Middlesbrough (341 League appearances and 99 goals) for Hull City in 1954, where he made 16 appearances, scoring once. He later played Non-League football for Poole Town, Cambridge United, Kings Lynn, Haverhill Rovers and Earlestown, for whom he was player-manager.

John Mapson (b Birkenhead 2.5.17; d 8.99). A goalkeeper, John started out at Reading in 1935 and saved a penalty on his debut. He conceded four goals in his second game, but still finished on the winning side! Just days later, he was sold to Sunderland (March, 1936) and the following season won an F.A. Cup winners' medal. During the war he played in an international against Wales and, when football resumed after hostilities, he continued playing for the Rokerites, making a total of 345 League appearances before retiring in 1954.

Reuben 'Ben' John Marden (b Fulham 10.2.27; d 1.2.00). An outside-left who played for Arsenal between 1950 and 1955 (42 League appearances; 11 goals) and Watford between 1955 and 1957 (41 League appearances; 11 goals). He then served Non-League sides Bedford Town and Romford.

Arthur Masters (b Coppell 17.8.10; d 7.98). Arthur began with Nottingham Forest in 1932 and made 109 League appearances, scoring 24 goals, before he moved to Port Vale in 1937. Prior to the outbreak of the war, he scored 13 goals in 66 League outings from the right-wing berth.

Stanley James E. Mather (b Bolton 1905; d 7.98). Joined Crewe Alexandra in 1931 and made 17 League appearances in two seasons, scoring three times, before moving to Southport.

Sir Stanley Matthews (b Hanley 1.2.15; d 5.5.99). The supremely gifted winger, one of the greatest players to grace the world stage, possessed dazzling dribbling skills, wonderful ball control and had the ability to cross with uncanny accuracy. Stan's close control was simply mesmeric and, together with his acceleration off the mark, he was a tormentor-in-chief of the very best defences. Stan became a professional with Stoke City in March, 1932. In 1933, he won a Second Division Championship medal. He made his international debut in 1934 against Wales and scored in a 4-0 victory. In 1937, he scored a hat-trick against Czechoslovakia. However, the war years took a major chunk of his playing career. Stan joined the RAF and was stationed near Blackpool, for whom he guested during hostilities, along with Crewe Alexandra, Manchester United, Wrexham, Arsenal, Rangers and Greenock Morton. After the war, Stan returned to Stoke, but found himself out of favour following an injury. Despite vigorous protestations from the Stoke fans, he was sold to Blackpool for £11,500 and renewed his England partnership with Stan Mortensen. Blackpool drew massive attendances wherever they played and the club had wonderful Cup runs, culminating in final appearances in 1948 and 1951. Following defeats in both, they won the trophy in sensational fashion two years later, courtesy of some of the finest wing play ever seen. Three-one down against Bolton with 20 minutes remaining, the 38 year-old Matthews took centre stage. Blackpool won the most incredible match 4-3, with Stan Mortensen hitting a hat-trick, but Stan took the plaudits in a game that will forever be known as 'the Matthews Final'. Three years later, he was part of a great Blackpool side that finished runners-up to Manchester United in the First Division. He won his 54th cap in 1957, making him the oldest international ever to represent England. In October, 1961, aged 46, he returned to relegation-

threatened Stoke for £2,500. The crowd immediately increased from 8,400 to 36,000! The following season, Stan helped the Potters win the Second Division Championship, playing 31 games. He made his final appearance in the First Division, aged 50 years and five days, on the 6th February, 1965. That same year he received a knighthood, to add to a CBE, awarded in 1957. He was voted Footballer of the Year in 1948 and 1963 and European Footballer of the Year in 1956.

William McGlen (b Bedlinton 27.4.21; d 12.99). Joined Manchester United in 1946 and played 110 games, scoring twice for the club. He moved to Lincoln City in July, 1952, but after just 13 League outings he was off to Oldham Athletic, where he made 68 appearances, scoring three goals.

Andy McGowan (b Corby 17.5.56; 5.5.99). An England Youth international with three caps, Andy signed for Northampton Town in 1975 and scored on his debut against Bradford City. In 1976, the Cobblers finished runners-up to Lincoln City and Andy made 42 appearances in midfield. In 1979, after 105 League outings and 15 goals, he was forced to leave the club after a lengthy injury. He then played Non-League football for Rushden and scored one of the goals that helped Stamford win the F.A. Vase in 1980.

William McGregor (b Levenbank 1903; d 3.98). Bill made nine League appearances on the wing for Coventry in the mid-twenties, but a motor cycle accident brought a premature end to his first class career.

Alexander McIntosh (b Inverurie 19.10.23; d 19.10.98). Alex made 89 appearances for Barrow at full-back before moving to Carlisle United in October, 1949. He was signed by then Carlisle manager Bill Shankly and went on to play 228 League matches for the Cumbrians, scoring four goals.

William McKee (b Burtonwood 6.6.28; d 21.4.99). Bill was with Blackburn Rovers between November, 1949 and July, 1953, but after only one League appearance, he was sadly injured, which brought about a premature close to his playing career.

George McNestry (b Chopwell 7.1.08; d 3.98). A right-winger who played pre-war football between 1926 and 1937 for Bradford Park Avenue, Doncaster Rovers, Leeds United, Sunderland, Luton Town (69 League games, 26 goals), Bristol Rovers (112 League matches, 42 goals) and Coventry City (46 League outings, 21 goals).

Norman Millar (b Dunadry 30.11.08; d 8.98). A former player with Glentoran and Linfield, who made 21 League appearances between 1937 and 1939 for Bournemouth, scoring one goal.

Geoffrey Dalgleish Morton (b Acton 27.7.24; d 28.1.00). A goalkeeper who joined Watford in October, 1948 and went on to play 107 League games before moving to Southend in February, 1952, where he had 25 League outings. He saw out his first class playing career with Exeter City, for whom he made six appearances.

George Muir (b Stirling 1940; d 13.12.99). A former club captain of Partick Thistle in the sixties, who spent ten years with the club before moving to Dumbarton.

Robert Owen (b Sunderland 5.5.24; d 10.99). A wing-half and a great servant to Lincoln City, Bobby made 246 League appearances between 1947 and 1955. He won Third Division North Championship medals with the Red Imps in 1948 and 1952. He went on to captain South Shields between 1955 and 1963 and was highly regarded by everyone at the club.

John Paterson (b Colchester 1926; d 14.1.00). A fine central defender for Hibernian, John joined the Easter Road club in 1944, and helped the club win the Scottish title in 1952.

Hubert Perry (b Manchester 1911; d 1.98). An inside-forward, Hubert played one match for Bristol City on the 26th December, 1929, and also saw service with Bridgwater Town and Bath City

Derek Priestly (b Bradford 22.12.25; d 6.99). A left-winger, Derek made 145 League appearances for Halifax Town between 1950 and 1956, scoring 19 goals.

Robert Ireland Pryde (b Methil, Fife 25.4.13; d 6.98). A centre-half with Blackburn Rovers between 1933 and 1949, he made a total of 320 League appearances, scoring 11 times. In 1947, he played for The Football League against The League of Ireland and celebrated a 3-1 win alongside Matthews, Mortensen and Mercer. He later became player manager of Wigan Athletic.

Norrie Rattray (b Kelty 1939; d Barbados 1999). Norrie played for Dunfermline in the late fifties, then moved to St. Johnstone where he saw out his first class playing career.

Charles Revell (b Belvedere 5.6.19; d 11.12.99). Charlie was originally a winger, who converted to a half-back. He made 104 League appearances for Charlton Athletic between 1946 and 1951, scoring 15 times. In March, 1951, he moved to Derby County where he had 22 League outings and scored seven goals.

John Roberts (b Pentre Broughton 22.7.28; d 13.3.00). John, a right-winger, made one League appearance for Wrexham in April, 1951. He won a Welsh amateur international cap in 1959.

Sir Stanley Matthews

Wilf Mannion

Alan Ross (b Glasgow 26.5.42; d 2.11.99). A wonderful, loyal servant to Carlisle United, Alan was a fine goalkeeper, who made a total of 537 League and Cup appearances for the Cumbrians. He actually started out with Luton Town in April, 1962, then moved to Brunton Park the following summer. He made his League debut in September, 1963 and retired in 1978. During that time, Alan won a Third Division Championship medal in 1965 and promotion from the Second Division to the top flight in 1974. At the beginning of the following season, the Cumbrians held top spot in the First Division. Alan, of course, held the 'number one' spot at Carlisle at the time and went on to become part of Carlisle United folklore.

Sammy Salt (b Southport 30.12.38; d 18.5.99). Sammy was a half-back who made 18 League appearances for Blackpool in the early sixties.

Laurie Scott (b Sheffield 23.4.17; d 7.99). Laurie started out as a winger with Bradford City, but when he made his League debut for the Bantams in February, 1936, he had been converted to a full-back. A year later he was on his way to Arsenal, but because of the intervening war years he didn't make his Gunners debut until 1946! Exceptionally quick and consistent, he played in the Arsenal side of 1948 that won the League title and also in the victorious F.A. Cup team of 1950. He also represented England in the first 17 internationals after the war years. In October, 1951, he left Highbury to take the player-manager's job at Crystal Palace and made a further 28 League appearances.

William Spalding (b Glasgow 24.11.26; d 18.12.99). A right-winger who began with Aberdeen, then went to Ballymena in Northern Ireland. He joined Bristol City in January, 1950 and made 10 League appearances for the Robins, before signing for Bideford Town.

Bert Sproston (b Elworth 22.6.15; d 27.1.00). Bert made his League debut for Leeds in 1933 and went on to play 130 League games at full-back for the Yorkshire club. He also won 11 caps for England in the thirties. In June, 1938, he was sold to Tottenham Hotspur for a massive fee of £9,500, but he didn't settle, and nine games later joined Manchester City for £10,000. The war interrupted his career, but following hostilities he won a Second Division Championship medal with City in 1947.

John 'Jack' Swain M.B.E. (b Grimsby 13.4.14; d 1.00). A left-winger, 'Jack' made his debut for Grimsby Town in November, 1936 and played 22 League games for the Mariners prior to the outbreak of the war, scoring six times. He signed for Scunthorpe United in the summer of 1939, but never played a competitive match for his new club.

Hamish Thomson M.B.E., JP (b Dumbarton 14.9.10; d 22.9.99). Played for Scotland Schoolboys and later Cowdenbeath. He received an MBE award for bravery during the war.

Jack Connor

Bert Sproston

Theodore Michael Thresher (b Cullompton 9.3.31; d 28.12.99). Mike was a great servant to Bristol City, joining the Robins in January, 1954. A talented and dependable full-back, he made his debut in December of that year at Reading and remained a regular for ten years. He won a Third Division South Championship medal in 1955 and went on to amass a total of 378 League appearances, scoring once, before leaving for Bath City in 1965.

William Tovey (b Bristol 18.10.31; d 8.1.00). A wing-half with Bristol City, whom he joined in December, 1948. He played for City until 1953, making 57 League appearances and scoring once.

Bob Veck (b Titchfield 1.4.20; d 14.5.99). A centre-forward, Bob signed for Southampton in 1938 and made 28 League appearances, scoring six times before the war intervened. After hostilities, he continued in the Saints side, playing a further 23 League matches and scoring twice, before joining Gillingham In July, 1950. He scored 12 goals in 36 League outings for the Gills and then left for Southern League Chelmsford.

James Watters (b Buckhaven 1927; d 10.10.99). Made 75 League appearances for Hearts in the fifties and was with the Edinburgh side for a total of 12 years. He also played part-time football for East Fife and served the club as a director, before holding a similar position with Dunfermline, where he became Chairman in 1982.

S. Hastie Weir (b Glasgow 1930; d 21.12.99). A goalkeeper, who signed for Queens Park in 1949 and made his debut in the 1950-51 season. A regular thereafter, he joined Motherwell in 1954 and played in the Scottish League Cup final against Hearts that same year. He saw out his first class career at Fir Park.

Richard Witham (b Bowburn 4.5.15; d 29.10.99). A full-back, who signed for Huddersfield Town in 1930. He played 150 League games for the Terriers before the outbreak of war and, following hostilities, he joined Oldham Athletic where he had five League outings.

Alex Wright (b Glasgow 1930; 12.1.00). A forward with Partick Thistle, for whom he signed in 1948 and played for 14 years. Following his playing career, Alex held coaching positions with East Fife, Clyde and Partick, before becoming manager of St. Mirren in 1966. He led them to the Second Division title in 1968 and became an executive director of Dumbarton in 1970 until 1990.

THE FA CARLING PREMIERSHIP
and NATIONWIDE FOOTBALL LEAGUE
FIXTURES 2000–2001

Reproduced under Copyright Licence No. AP20.003.
Copyright © the FA Premier League Limited 2000. Copyright © the Football League Limited 2000.

Saturday, 12 August 2000
Nationwide Football League Division 1
Barnsley v Norwich C
Blackburn R v Crystal Palace
Bolton W v Burnley
Fulham v Crewe Alex
Gillingham v Stockport Co
Grimsby T v Preston NE
Huddersfield T v Watford
Nottingham F v WBA
QPR v Birmingham C
Sheffield U v Portsmouth
Wimbledon v Tranmere R

Nationwide League Division 2
Bristol R v AFC Bournemouth
Cambridge U v Bury
Luton T v Notts Co
Millwall v Reading
Northampton T v Brentford
Oldham Ath v Port Vale
Oxford U v Peterborough U
Rotherham U v Walsall
Stoke C v Wycombe W
Swansea C v Wigan Ath
Swindon T v Colchester U
Wrexham v Bristol C

Nationwide League Division 3
Barnet v Shrewsbury T
Blackpool v Hull C
Carlisle U v Halifax T
Cheltenham T v Mansfield T
Chesterfield v York C
Exeter C v Cardiff C
Kidderminster H v Torquay U
Lincoln C v Hartlepool U
Macclesfield T v Scunthorpe U
Plymouth Arg v Leyton Orient
Rochdale v Darlington
Southend U v Brighton & HA

Nationwide Football League Division 1
Wolverhampton W v Sheffield W
(12.30)

Friday, 18 August 2000
Birmingham C v Fulham (7.45)

Saturday, 19 August 2000
FA Carling Premiership
Charlton Ath v Manchester C
Chelsea v West Ham U
Coventry C v Middlesbrough
Derby Co v Southampton
Leeds U v Everton
Leicester C v Aston Villa
Liverpool v Bradford C
Sunderland v Arsenal
Tottenham H v Ipswich T

Nationwide Football League Division 1
Burnley v Wimbledon
Crewe Alex v Blackburn R
Norwich C v Nottingham F
Portsmouth v Grimsby T
Preston NE v Sheffield U
Sheffield W v Huddersfield T

Stockport Co v Wolverhampton W
Tranmere R v Gillingham
Watford v Barnsley
WBA v Bolton W

Nationwide League Division 2
AFC Bournemouth v Cambridge U
Brentford v Swansea C
Bristol C v Stoke C
Bury v Wrexham
Colchester U v Rotherham U
Notts Co v Millwall
Peterborough U v Bristol R
Port Vale v Oxford U
Reading v Swindon T
Walsall v Oldham Ath
Wigan Ath v Luton T
Wycombe W v Northampton T

Nationwide League Division 3
Brighton & HA v Rochdale
Cardiff C v Blackpool
Darlington v Exeter C
Halifax T v Lincoln C
Hartlepool U v Chesterfield
Hull C v Plymouth Arg
Leyton Orient v Carlisle U
Mansfield T v Barnet
Scunthorpe U v Kidderminster H
Shrewsbury T v Macclesfield T
Torquay U v Southend U
York C v Cheltenham T

Sunday, 20 August 2000
FA Carling Premiership
Manchester Uv Newcastle U (4.00)

Nationwide Football League Division 1
Crystal Palace v QPR (1.00)

Monday, 21 August 2000
FA Carling Premiership
Arsenal v Liverpool (8.00)

Tuesday, 22 August 2000
FA Carling Premiership
Bradford C v Chelsea
Ipswich T v Manchester U
Middlesbrough v Tottenham H

Wednesday, 23 August 2000
FA Carling Premiership
Aston Villa v Leeds U
Everton v Charlton Ath
Manchester C v Sunderland
Newcastle U v Derby Co
Southampton v Coventry C
West Ham U v Leicester C

Friday, 25 August 2000
Nationwide Football League Division 1
Gillingham v Portsmouth (7.45)

Saturday, 26 August 2000
FA Carling Premiership
Arsenal v Charlton Ath
Bradford C v Leicester C

Everton v Derby Co
Ipswich T v Sunderland
Manchester C v Coventry C
Middlesbrough v Leeds U
Newcastle U v Tottenham H
Southampton v Liverpool
West Ham U v Manchester U

Nationwide Football League Division 1
Barnsley v WBA
Blackburn R v Norwich C
Bolton W v Preston NE
Fulham v Stockport Co
Gillingham v Portsmouth
Grimsby T v Sheffield W
Huddersfield T v Crystal Palace
Nottingham F v Birmingham C
QPR v Crewe Alex
Sheffield U v Tranmere R
Wimbledon v Watford
Wolverhampton W v Burnley

Nationwide League Division 2
Bristol R v Port Vale
Cambridge U v Bristol C
Luton T v AFC Bournemouth
Millwall v Wycombe W
Northampton T v Reading
Oldham Ath v Peterborough U
Oxford U v Brentford
Rotherham U v Bury
Stoke C v Notts Co
Swansea C v Colchester U
Swindon T v Walsall
Wrexham v Wigan Ath

Nationwide League Division 3
Barnet v Cardiff C
Blackpool v Leyton Orient
Carlisle U v York C
Cheltenham T v Torquay U
Chesterfield v Shrewsbury T
Exeter C v Hartlepool U
Kidderminster H v Halifax T
Lincoln C v Brighton & HA
Macclesfield T v Hull C
Plymouth Arg v Mansfield T
Rochdale v Scunthorpe U
Southend U v Darlington

Sunday, 27 August 2000
FA Carling Premiership
Aston Villa v Chelsea (4.00)

Monday, 28 August 2000
Nationwide Football League Division 1
Birmingham C v Barnsley
Burnley v Gillingham
Crewe Alex v Grimsby T
Crystal Palace v Nottingham F
Norwich C v Fulham
Portsmouth v Wolverhampton W
Preston NE v Wimbledon
Sheffield W v Blackburn R (8.00)
Stockport Co v Huddersfield T
Tranmere R v Bolton W
Watford v Sheffield U
WBA v QPR

Nationwide League Division 2
AFC Bournemouth v Wrexham
Brentford v Bristol R
Bristol C v Rotherham U
Bury v Northampton T
Colchester U v Oldham Ath
Notts Co v Cambridge U
Peterborough U v Swansea C
Port Vale v Swindon T
Reading v Stoke C
Walsall v Oxford U
Wigan Ath v Millwall
Wycombe W v Luton T

Nationwide League Division 3
Brighton & HA v Kidderminster H
Cardiff C v Southend U
Darlington v Plymouth Arg
Halifax T v Rochdale
Hartlepool U v Cheltenham T
Hull C v Lincoln C
Leyton Orient v Exeter C
Mansfield T v Macclesfield T
Scunthorpe U v Chesterfield
Shrewsbury T v Carlisle U
Torquay U v Blackpool
York C v Barnet

Friday, 1 September 2000
Nationwide Football League Division 1
Tranmere R v Stockport Co (7.45)

Saturday, 2 September 2000
Nationwide Football League Division 1
Barnsley v Blackburn R
Bolton W v QPR
Burnley v Crewe Alex
Gillingham v Wolverhampton W
Norwich C v Birmingham C
Preston NE v Portsmouth
Sheffield U v Fulham
Watford v Sheffield W
WBA v Crystal Palace
Wimbledon v Grimsby T

Nationwide League Division 2
Brentford v Wycombe W
Bristol R v Millwall
Colchester U v AFC Bournemouth
Northampton T v Stoke C
Oldham Ath v Notts Co
Oxford U v Cambridge U
Peterborough U v Bury
Port Vale v Reading
Rotherham U v Luton T
Swansea C v Bristol C
Swindon T v Wrexham
Walsall v Wigan Ath

Nationwide League Division 3
Brighton & HA v Torquay U
Chesterfield v Barnet
Darlington v York C
Exeter C v Mansfield T
Halifax T v Leyton Orient
Hartlepool U v Shrewsbury T
Hull C v Cheltenham T
Kidderminster H v Carlisle U
Lincoln C v Southend U
Plymouth Arg v Macclesfield T
Rochdale v Cardiff C
Scunthorpe U v Blackpool

Sunday, 3 September 2000
Nationwide League Division 3
Nottingham F v Huddersfield T (1.00)

Tuesday, 5 September 2000
FA Carling Premiership
Charlton Ath v Southampton

Leeds U v Manchester C
Sunderland v West Ham U
Tottenham H v Everton

Wednesday, 6 September 2000
FA Carling Premiership
Chelsea v Arsenal (8.00)
Coventry C v Newcastle U
Derby Co v Middlesbrough
Leicester C v Ipswich T
Liverpool v Aston Villa
Manchester Uv Bradford C

Friday, 8 September 2000
Nationwide League Division 2
Wycombe W v Oxford U (7.45)

Saturday, 9 September 2000
FA Carling Premiership
Bradford C v Arsenal
Coventry C v Leeds U
Ipswich T v Aston Villa
Leicester C v Southampton
Liverpool v Manchester C
Manchester Uv Sunderland
Middlesbrough v Everton
Newcastle U v Chelsea

Nationwide Football League Division 1
Birmingham C v Sheffield U
Blackburn R v Nottingham F
Crewe Alex v Norwich C
Crystal Palace v Burnley
Fulham v Barnsley
Grimsby T v Gillingham
Huddersfield T v Bolton W
Portsmouth v Watford
QPR v Preston NE
Sheffield W v Wimbledon
Stockport Co v WBA
Wolverhampton W v Tranmere R

Nationwide League Division 2
AFC Bournemouth v Port Vale
Bristol C v Swindon T
Bury v Walsall
Cambridge U v Rotherham U
Luton T v Northampton T
Millwall v Swansea C
Notts Co v Bristol R
Reading v Brentford
Stoke C v Peterborough U
Wigan Ath v Colchester U
Wrexham v Oldham Ath

Nationwide League Division 3
Barnet v Kidderminster H
Blackpool v Hartlepool U
Cardiff C v Brighton & HA
Carlisle U v Rochdale
Cheltenham T v Chesterfield
Leyton Orient v Hull C
Macclesfield T v Exeter C
Mansfield T v Halifax T
Shrewsbury T v Darlington
Southend U v Plymouth Arg
Torquay U v Lincoln C
York C v Scunthorpe U

Sunday, 10 September 2000
FA Carling Premiership
Derby Co v Charlton Ath (4.00)

Nationwide Football League Division 1
Fulham v Burnley (1.00)

Monday, 11 September 2000
FA Carling Premiership
Tottenham H v West Ham U (8.00)

Tuesday, 12 September 2000
Nationwide Football League Division 1
Birmingham C v Preston NE
Crewe Alex v WBA
Crystal Palace v Barnsley
Grimsby T v Bolton W
Huddersfield T v Wimbledon (8.00)
Portsmouth v Tranmere R
Stockport Co v Norwich C
Wolverhampton W v Sheffield U

Nationwide League Division 2
AFC Bournemouth v Swindon T
Bristol C v Brentford
Bury v Colchester U
Cambridge U v Port Vale
Luton T v Walsall
Millwall v Northampton T
Notts Co v Swansea C
Reading v Oldham Ath
Wigan Ath v Peterborough U
Wrexham v Rotherham U
Wycombe W v Bristol R

Nationwide League Division 3
Barnet v Exeter C
Blackpool v Brighton & HA
Cardiff C v Halifax T
Carlisle U v Chesterfield
Cheltenham T v Darlington
Leyton Orient v Scunthorpe U
Macclesfield T v Lincoln C
Mansfield T v Hull C
Shrewsbury T v Plymouth Arg
Southend U v Kidderminster H
Torquay U v Hartlepool U
York C v Rochdale

Wednesday, 13 September 2000
Nationwide Football League Division 1
Blackburn R v Watford
QPR v Gillingham
Sheffield W v Nottingham F

Nationwide League Division 2
Stoke C v Oxford U

Friday, 15 September 2000
Nationwide Football League Division 1
Sheffield U v Blackburn R (7.45)

Saturday, 16 September 2000
FA Carling Premiership
Arsenal v Coventry C
Aston Villa v Bradford C
Charlton Ath v Tottenham H
Chelsea v Leicester C
Everton v Manchester U
Leeds U v Ipswich T
Southampton v Newcastle U
Sunderland v Derby Co
West Ham U v Liverpool

Nationwide Football League Division 1
Barnsley v QPR
Bolton W v Portsmouth
Burnley v Grimsby T
Gillingham v Huddersfield T
Norwich C v Crystal Palace
Nottingham F v Fulham
Preston NE v Stockport Co
Tranmere R v Sheffield W
Watford v Crewe Alex
WBA v Birmingham C
Wimbledon v Wolverhampton W

Nationwide League Division 2
Brentford v Millwall
Bristol R v Wigan Ath
Colchester U v Wrexham

Northampton T v Notts Co
Oldham Ath v Bristol C
Oxford U v Bury
Peterborough U v Reading
Rotherham U v Wycombe W
Swansea C v Luton T
Swindon T v Cambridge U
Walsall v AFC Bournemouth

Nationwide League Division 3
Brighton & HA v Cheltenham T
Chesterfield v Mansfield T
Darlington v Barnet
Exeter C v York C
Halifax T v Southend U
Hartlepool U v Macclesfield T
Hull C v Shrewsbury T
Kidderminster H v Leyton Orient
Lincoln C v Blackpool
Plymouth Arg v Carlisle U
Rochdale v Torquay U
Scunthorpe U v Cardiff C

Sunday, 17 September 2000
FA Carling Premiership
Manchester C v Middlesbrough (4.00)

Nationwide League Division 2
Port Vale v Stoke C (1.00)

Friday, 22 September 2000
Nationwide Football League Division 3
Macclesfield T v Darlington (7.45)

Saturday, 23 September 2000
FA Carling Premiership
Bradford C v Southampton
Coventry C v West Ham U
Derby Co v Leeds U
Ipswich T v Arsenal
Liverpool v Sunderland
Manchester Uv Chelsea (11.30)
Middlesbrough v Aston Villa
Newcastle U v Charlton Ath
Tottenham H v Manchester C

Nationwide Football League Division 1
Birmingham C v Tranmere R
Blackburn R v Bolton W
Crewe Alex v Barnsley
Crystal Palace v Sheffield U
Fulham v Gillingham
Grimsby T v Nottingham F
Huddersfield T v Burnley
Portsmouth v WBA
QPR v Wimbledon
Sheffield W v Preston NE
Stockport Co v Watford

Nationwide League Division 2
AFC Bournemouth v Oldham Ath
Bristol C v Colchester U
Bury v Port Vale
Cambridge U v Bristol R
Luton T v Swindon T
Millwall v Oxford U
Notts Co v Brentford
Reading v Swansea C
Stoke C v Rotherham U
Wigan Ath v Northampton T
Wrexham v Walsall
Wycombe W v Peterborough U

Nationwide League Division 3
Barnet v Hull C
Blackpool v Chesterfield
Cardiff C v Kidderminster H
Carlisle U v Exeter C
Cheltenham T v Plymouth Arg
Leyton Orient v Lincoln C

Mansfield T v Hartlepool U
Shrewsbury T v Rochdale
Southend U v Scunthorpe U
Torquay U v Halifax T
York C v Brighton & HA

Sunday, 24 September 2000
FA Carling Premiership
Leicester C v Everton (4.00)

Nationwide League Division 1
Wolverhampton W v Norwich C (1.00)

Friday, 29 September 2000
Nationwide League Division 3
Kidderminster H v Blackpool (7.45)

Saturday, 30 September 2000
FA Carling Premiership
Aston Villa v Derby Co
Charlton Ath v Coventry C
Chelsea v Liverpool
Everton v Ipswich T
Leeds U v Tottenham H
Manchester C v Newcastle U
Southampton v Middlesbrough
Sunderland v Leicester C
West Ham U v Bradford C

Nationwide Football League Division 1
Barnsley v Grimsby T
Bolton W v Fulham
Burnley v Portsmouth
Gillingham v Sheffield W
Norwich C v Huddersfield T
Nottingham F v Wolverhampton W
Preston NE v Crystal Palace
Sheffield U v QPR
Tranmere R v Crewe Alex
WBA v Blackburn R
Wimbledon v Stockport Co

Nationwide League Division 2
Brentford v AFC Bournemouth
Bristol R v Luton T
Colchester U v Stoke C
Northampton T v Wrexham
Oldham Ath v Cambridge U
Oxford U v Bristol C
Peterborough U v Millwall
Port Vale v Wycombe W
Rotherham U v Reading
Swansea C v Bury
Swindon T v Wigan Ath
Walsall v Notts Co

Nationwide League Division 3
Brighton & HA v Leyton Orient
Chesterfield v Macclesfield T
Darlington v Carlisle U
Exeter C v Cheltenham T
Halifax T v Shrewsbury T
Hartlepool U v York C
Hull C v Cardiff C
Lincoln C v Mansfield T
Plymouth Arg v Barnet
Rochdale v Southend U
Scunthorpe U v Torquay U

Sunday, 1 October 2000
FA Carling Premiership
Arsenal v Manchester U (4.00)

Nationwide Football League Division 1
Watford v Birmingham C (1.00)

Friday, 6 October 2000
Nationwide Football League Division 1
Blackburn R v Preston NE (7.45)

Saturday, 7 October 2000
Nationwide Football League Division 1
Crewe Alex v Birmingham C
Crystal Palace v Wimbledon
Gillingham v Bolton W
Huddersfield T v Barnsley
Norwich C v Watford
Nottingham F v Sheffield U
Sheffield W v WBA
Stockport Co v Portsmouth
Tranmere R v Burnley
Wolverhampton W v Grimsby T

Nationwide League Division 2
Bristol C v AFC Bournemouth
Bury v Bristol R
Colchester U v Walsall
Luton T v Millwall
Northampton T v Swansea C
Peterborough U v Port Vale
Rotherham U v Oldham Ath
Stoke C v Brentford
Swindon T v Oxford U
Wigan Ath v Reading
Wrexham v Cambridge U
Wycombe W v Notts Co

Nationwide League Division 3
Barnet v Macclesfield T
Blackpool v Southend U
Cardiff C v Lincoln C
Cheltenham T v Carlisle U
Chesterfield v Plymouth Arg
Hartlepool U v Darlington
Hull C v Brighton & HA
Kidderminster H v Rochdale
Scunthorpe U v Halifax T
Shrewsbury T v Exeter C
Torquay U v Leyton Orient
York C v Mansfield T

Sunday, 8 October 2000
Nationwide Football League Division 1
QPR v Fulham (1.00)

Saturday, 14 October 2000
FA Carling Premiership
Arsenal v Aston Villa
Coventry C v Tottenham H
Everton v Southampton
Ipswich T v West Ham U
Leeds U v Charlton Ath
Leicester C v Manchester U
Manchester C v Bradford C
Sunderland v Chelsea

Nationwide Football League Division 1
Barnsley v Nottingham F
Birmingham C v Crystal Palace
Bolton W v Wolverhampton W
Burnley v Stockport Co
Grimsby T v Huddersfield T
Portsmouth v Sheffield W
Preston NE v Tranmere R
Sheffield U v Crewe Alex
Watford v QPR
WBA v Norwich C
Wimbledon v Gillingham

Nationwide League Division 2
AFC Bournemouth v Rotherham U
Brentford v Peterborough U
Bristol R v Northampton T
Cambridge U v Luton T
Millwall v Bury
Notts Co v Wigan Ath
Oldham Ath v Swindon T
Oxford U v Wrexham
Port Vale v Colchester U
Reading v Wycombe W
Swansea C v Stoke C
Walsall v Bristol C

Nationwide League Division 3
Brighton & HA v Scunthorpe U
Carlisle U v Barnet
Darlington v Torquay U
Exeter C v Chesterfield
Halifax T v Hull C
Leyton Orient v Cardiff C
Lincoln C v Kidderminster H
Macclesfield T v Cheltenham T
Mansfield T v Shrewsbury T
Plymouth Arg v Blackpool
Rochdale v Hartlepool U
Southend U v York C

Sunday, 15 October 2000
FA Carling Premiership
Derby Co v Liverpool (4.00)

Nationwide Football League Division 1
Fulham v Blackburn R (1.00)

Monday, 16 October 2000
FA Carling Premiership
Middlesbrough v Newcastle U (8.00)

Tuesday, 17 October 2000
Nationwide Football League Division 1
Barnsley v Tranmere R
Birmingham C v Stockport Co
Bolton W v Nottingham F
Burnley v Sheffield W
Fulham v Crystal Palace
Grimsby T v QPR
Portsmouth v Crewe Alex
Preston NE v Norwich C
Sheffield U v Huddersfield T
Watford v Gillingham
WBA v Wolverhampton W (8.00)
Wimbledon v Blackburn R

Nationwide League Division 2
AFC Bournemouth v Wigan Ath
Brentford v Colchester U
Bristol R v Rotherham U
Cambridge U v Stoke C
Millwall v Bristol C
Notts Co v Bury
Oldham Ath v Wycombe W
Oxford U v Luton T
Port Vale v Northampton T
Reading v Wrexham
Swansea C v Swindon T
Walsall v Peterborough U

Nationwide League Division 3
Brighton & HA v Hartlepool U
Carlisle U v Cardiff C
Darlington v Kidderminster H
Exeter C v Hull C
Halifax T v Cheltenham T
Leyton Orient v Shrewsbury T
Lincoln C v York C
Macclesfield T v Torquay U
Mansfield T v Blackpool
Plymouth Arg v Scunthorpe U
Rochdale v Chesterfield
Southend U v Barnet

Saturday, 21 October 2000
FA Carling Premiership
Bradford C v Ipswich T
Charlton Ath v Middlesbrough
Chelsea v Coventry C
Liverpool v Leicester C
Manchester Uv Leeds U (11.30)
Newcastle U v Everton
Tottenham H v Derby Co
West Ham U v Arsenal

Nationwide Football League Division 1
Blackburn R v Grimsby T
Crewe Alex v Wimbledon
Crystal Palace v Portsmouth
Gillingham v Barnsley
Huddersfield T v Preston NE
Norwich C v Sheffield U
Nottingham F v Watford
QPR v Burnley
Stockport Co v Bolton W
Tranmere R v WBA
Wolverhampton W v Fulham

Nationwide League Division 2
Bristol C v Reading
Bury v AFC Bournemouth
Colchester U v Cambridge U
Luton T v Brentford
Northampton T v Oldham Ath
Peterborough U v Notts Co
Rotherham U v Oxford U
Stoke C v Millwall
Swindon T v Bristol R
Wigan Ath v Port Vale
Wrexham v Swansea C
Wycombe W v Walsall

Nationwide League Division 3
Barnet v Halifax T
Blackpool v Macclesfield T
Cardiff C v Mansfield T
Cheltenham T v Rochdale
Chesterfield v Brighton & HA
Hartlepool U v Plymouth Arg
Hull C v Southend U
Kidderminster H v Exeter C
Scunthorpe U v Darlington
Shrewsbury T v Lincoln C
Torquay U v Carlisle U
York C v Leyton Orient

Sunday, 22 October 2000
FA Carling Premiership
Aston Villa v Sunderland (4.00)

Nationwide Football League Division 1
Sheffield W v Birmingham C (1.00)

Monday, 23 October 2000
FA Carling Premiership
Southampton v Manchester C (8.00)

Tuesday, 24 October 2000
Nationwide Football League Division 1
Barnsley v Wolverhampton W
Birmingham C v Gillingham
Crewe Alex v Huddersfield T
Crystal Palace v Grimsby T
Fulham v Preston NE
Norwich C v Portsmouth
Sheffield U v Stockport Co
Watford v Bolton W (8.00)
WBA v Wimbledon

Nationwide League Division 2
AFC Bournemouth v Notts Co
Bristol C v Peterborough U
Bury v Reading
Cambridge U v Northampton T
Colchester U v Bristol R
Oldham Ath v Luton T
Oxford U v Wigan Ath
Port Vale v Brentford
Rotherham U v Swansea C
Swindon T v Millwall
Walsall v Stoke C
Wrexham v Wycombe W

Nationwide League Division 3
Blackpool v Carlisle U

Brighton & HA v Plymouth Arg
Cardiff C v Darlington
Halifax T v York C
Hull C v Hartlepool U
Kidderminster H v Chesterfield
Leyton Orient v Barnet
Lincoln C v Cheltenham T
Rochdale v Macclesfield T
Scunthorpe U v Shrewsbury T
Southend U v Exeter C
Torquay U v Mansfield T

Wednesday, 25 October 2000
Nationwide Football League Division 1
Blackburn R v Tranmere R
Nottingham F v Burnley
QPR v Sheffield W

Friday, 27 October 2000
Nationwide Football League Division 1
Preston NE v Barnsley (7.45)

Saturday, 28 October 2000
FA Carling Premiership
Arsenal v Manchester C
Aston Villa v Charlton Ath
Chelsea v Tottenham H
Ipswich T v Middlesbrough
Leicester C v Derby Co
Liverpool v Everton
Manchester Uv Southampton
Sunderland v Coventry C
West Ham U v Newcastle U

Nationwide Football League Division 1
Bolton W v Crystal Palace
Burnley v Norwich C
Gillingham v Crewe Alex
Huddersfield T v Blackburn R
Portsmouth v Birmingham C
Sheffield U v Fulham
Stockport Co v Nottingham F
Tranmere R v QPR
Wimbledon v Sheffield U
Wolverhampton W v Watford

Nationwide League Division 2
Brentford v Walsall
Bristol R v Oldham Ath
Luton T v Wrexham
Millwall v Cambridge U
Northampton T v Rotherham U
Notts Co v Swindon T
Peterborough U v Colchester U
Reading v Oxford U
Stoke C v AFC Bournemouth
Swansea C v Port Vale
Wigan Ath v Bury
Wycombe W v Bristol C

Nationwide League Division 3
Barnet v Lincoln C
Carlisle U v Scunthorpe U
Cheltenham T v Blackpool
Chesterfield v Cardiff C
Darlington v Brighton & HA
Exeter C v Rochdale
Hartlepool U v Leyton Orient
Macclesfield T v Halifax T
Mansfield T v Southend U
Plymouth Arg v Kidderminster H
Shrewsbury T v Torquay U
York C v Hull C

Sunday, 29 October 2000
FA Carling Premiership
Bradford C v Leeds U (4.00)

Nationwide Football League Division 1
Grimsby T v WBA (1.00)

Saturday, 4 November 2000
FA Carling Premiership
Charlton Ath v Bradford C
Coventry C v Manchester U
Leeds U v Liverpool (11.30)
Manchester C v Leicester C
Middlesbrough v Arsenal
Newcastle U v Ipswich T
Southampton v Chelsea
Tottenham H v Sunderland

Nationwide Football League Division 1
Birmingham C v Bolton W
Blackburn R v Stockport Co
Crewe Alex v Wolverhampton W
Crystal Palace v Sheffield W
Fulham v Huddersfield T
Norwich C v Tranmere R
Nottingham F v Preston NE
QPR v Portsmouth
Sheffield U v Gillingham
Watford v Grimsby T
WBA v Burnley

Nationwide League Division 2
AFC Bournemouth v Peterborough U
Bristol C v Notts Co
Bury v Luton T
Cambridge U v Brentford
Colchester U v Northampton T
Oldham Ath v Swansea C
Oxford U v Bristol R
Port Vale v Millwall
Rotherham U v Wigan Ath
Swindon T v Wycombe W
Walsall v Reading
Wrexham v Stoke C

Nationwide League Division 3
Blackpool v Shrewsbury T
Brighton & HA v Carlisle U
Cardiff C v York C
Halifax T v Exeter C
Hull C v Darlington
Kidderminster H v Cheltenham T
Leyton Orient v Mansfield T
Lincoln C v Chesterfield
Rochdale v Barnet
Scunthorpe U v Hartlepool U
Southend U v Macclesfield T
Torquay U v Plymouth Arg

Sunday, 5 November 2000
FA Carling Premiership
Everton v Aston Villa (4.00)

Nationwide Football League Division 1
Barnsley v Wimbledon (1.00)

Monday, 6 November 2000
FA Carling Premiership
Derby Co v West Ham U (8.00)

Friday, 10 November 2000
Nationwide Football League Division 1
Preston NE v Crewe Alex (7.45)

Saturday, 11 November 2000
FA Carling Premiership
Arsenal v Derby Co
Aston Villa v Tottenham H
Bradford C v Everton
Ipswich T v Charlton Ath
Leicester C v Newcastle U
Liverpool v Coventry C
Manchester Uv Middlesbrough
Sunderland v Southampton
West Ham U v Manchester C

Nationwide Football League Division 1
Bolton W v Barnsley
Burnley v Sheffield U
Grimsby T v Birmingham C
Huddersfield T v WBA
Portsmouth v Blackburn R
Sheffield W v Norwich C
Stockport Co v QPR
Tranmere R v Watford
Wimbledon v Fulham
Wolverhampton W v Crystal Palace

Nationwide League Division 2
Brentford v Rotherham U
Bristol R v Walsall
Luton T v Bristol C
Millwall v Wrexham
Northampton T v AFC Bournemouth
Notts Co v Port Vale
Peterborough U v Swindon T
Reading v Colchester U
Stoke C v Oldham Ath
Swansea C v Oxford U
Wigan Ath v Cambridge U
Wycombe W v Bury

Nationwide League Division 3
Barnet v Blackpool
Carlisle U v Southend U
Cheltenham T v Leyton Orient
Chesterfield v Hull C
Darlington v Halifax T
Exeter C v Scunthorpe U
Hartlepool U v Kidderminster H
Macclesfield T v Brighton & HA
Mansfield T v Rochdale
Plymouth Arg v Lincoln C
Shrewsbury T v Cardiff C
York C v Torquay U

Sunday, 12 November 2000
FA Carling Premiership
Chelsea v Leeds U (4.00)

Nationwide Football League Division 1
Gillingham v Nottingham F (1.00)

Saturday, 18 November 2000
FA Carling Premiership
Charlton Ath v Chelsea
Derby Co v Bradford C
Everton v Arsenal
Leeds U v West Ham U
Manchester C v Manchester U (11.30)
Middlesbrough v Leicester C
Newcastle U v Sunderland
Southampton v Aston Villa

Nationwide Football League Division 1
Barnsley v Sheffield W
Birmingham C v Burnley
Blackburn R v Wolverhampton W
Crewe Alex v Stockport Co
Crystal Palace v Tranmere R
Fulham v Portsmouth
Norwich C v Bolton W
Nottingham F v Wimbledon
QPR v Huddersfield T
Sheffield U v Grimsby T
Watford v Preston NE
WBA v Gillingham

Sunday, 19 November 2000
FA Carling Premiership
Tottenham H v Liverpool (4.00)

Monday, 20 November 2000
FA Carling Premiership
Coventry C v Ipswich T (8.00)

Saturday, 25 November 2000
FA Carling Premiership
Charlton Ath v Sunderland
Coventry C v Aston Villa
Derby Co v Manchester U
Everton v Chelsea
Leeds U v Arsenal
Manchester C v Ipswich T
Middlesbrough v Bradford C
Newcastle U v Liverpool
Southampton v West Ham U
Tottenham H v Leicester C

Nationwide Football League Division 1
Barnsley v Portsmouth
Birmingham C v Huddersfield T
Blackburn R v Gillingham
Crewe Alex v Sheffield W
Crystal Palace v Stockport Co
Fulham v Grimsby T
Norwich C v Wimbledon
Nottingham F v Tranmere R
QPR v Wolverhampton W
Sheffield U v Bolton W
Watford v Burnley
WBA v Preston NE

Nationwide League Division 2
AFC Bournemouth v Reading
Bristol C v Wigan Ath
Bury v Brentford
Cambridge U v Swansea C
Colchester U v Wycombe W
Oldham Ath v Millwall
Oxford U v Notts Co
Port Vale v Luton T
Rotherham U v Peterborough U
Swindon T v Stoke C
Walsall v Northampton T
Wrexham v Bristol R

Nationwide League Division 3
Blackpool v Darlington
Brighton & HA v Shrewsbury T
Cardiff C v Hartlepool U
Halifax T v Chesterfield
Hull C v Carlisle U
Kidderminster H v York C
Leyton Orient v Macclesfield T
Lincoln C v Exeter C
Rochdale v Plymouth Arg
Scunthorpe U v Mansfield T
Southend U v Cheltenham T
Torquay U v Barnet

Saturday, 2 December 2000
FA Carling Premiership
Arsenal v Southampton
Aston Villa v Newcastle U
Bradford C v Coventry C
Ipswich T v Derby Co
Leicester C v Leeds U
Liverpool v Charlton Ath
Manchester Uv Tottenham H
West Ham U v Middlesbrough

Nationwide Football League Division 1
Bolton W v Watford
Burnley v Nottingham F
Gillingham v Birmingham C
Grimsby T v Crystal Palace
Huddersfield T v Crewe Alex
Portsmouth v Norwich C
Preston NE v Fulham
Sheffield W v QPR
Stockport Co v Sheffield U
Tranmere R v Blackburn R
Wimbledon v WBA
Wolverhampton W v Barnsley

Nationwide League Division 2
Brentford v Wigan Ath
Bristol C v Bury
Colchester U v Notts Co
Northampton T v Swindon T
Oldham Ath v Oxford U
Peterborough U v Wrexham
Reading v Cambridge U
Rotherham U v Millwall
Stoke C v Luton T
Swansea C v Bristol R
Walsall v Port Vale
Wycombe W v AFC Bournemouth

Nationwide League Division 3
Brighton & HA v Halifax T
Carlisle U v Lincoln C
Cheltenham T v Barnet
Chesterfield v Leyton Orient
Darlington v Mansfield T
Exeter C v Plymouth Arg
Hartlepool U v Southend U
Kidderminster H v Macclesfield T
Rochdale v Blackpool
Scunthorpe U v Hull C
Torquay U v Cardiff C
York C v Shrewsbury T

Sunday, 3 December 2000
FA Carling Premiership
Chelsea v Manchester C

Monday, 4 December 2000
FA Carling Premiership
Sunderland v Everton

Saturday, 9 December 2000
FA Carling Premiership
Arsenal v Newcastle U
Bradford C v Tottenham H
Charlton Ath v Manchester U
Chelsea v Derby Co
Liverpool v Ipswich T
Manchester C v Everton
Southampton v Leeds U
Sunderland v Middlesbrough
West Ham U v Aston Villa

Nationwide Football League Division 1
Barnsley v Sheffield U
Birmingham C v Wimbledon
Blackburn R v QPR
Bolton W v Crewe Alex
Crystal Palace v Watford
Huddersfield T v Wolverhampton W
Norwich C v Gillingham
Nottingham F v Portsmouth
Preston NE v Burnley
Sheffield W v Stockport Co
Tranmere R v Grimsby T
WBA v Fulham

Sunday, 10 December 2000
FA Carling Premiership
Coventry C v Leicester C

Saturday, 16 December 2000
FA Carling Premiership
Aston Villa v Manchester C
Derby Co v Coventry C
Everton v West Ham U
Ipswich T v Southampton
Leeds U v Sunderland
Leicester C v Charlton Ath
Middlesbrough v Chelsea
Newcastle U v Bradford C

Nationwide Football League Division 1
Crewe Alex v Crystal Palace
Fulham v Tranmere R

Gillingham v Preston NE
Grimsby T v Norwich C
Portsmouth v Huddersfield T
QPR v Nottingham F
Sheffield U v Sheffield W (11.30)
Stockport Co v Barnsley
Watford v WBA
Wimbledon v Bolton W
Wolverhampton W v Birmingham C

Nationwide League Division 2
AFC Bournemouth v Swansea C
Bristol R v Stoke C
Bury v Oldham Ath
Cambridge U v Peterborough U
Luton T v Colchester U
Millwall v Walsall
Notts Co v Reading
Oxford U v Northampton T
Port Vale v Bristol C
Swindon T v Rotherham U
Wigan Ath v Wycombe W
Wrexham v Brentford

Nationwide League Division 3
Barnet v Scunthorpe U
Blackpool v Exeter C
Cardiff C v Cheltenham T
Halifax T v Hartlepool U
Hull C v Torquay U
Leyton Orient v Darlington
Lincoln C v Rochdale
Macclesfield T v Carlisle U
Mansfield T v Brighton & HA
Plymouth Arg v York C
Shrewsbury T v Kidderminster H
Southend U v Chesterfield

Sunday, 17 December 2000
FA Carling Premiership
Manchester Uv Liverpool

Nationwide Football League Division 1
Burnley v Blackburn R (4.00)

Monday, 18 December 2000
FA Carling Premiership
Tottenham H v Arsenal

Friday, 22 December 2000
Nationwide Football League Division 1
Bristol C v Bristol R (7.45)

Saturday, 23 December 2000
FA Carling Premiership
Charlton Ath v Everton
Chelsea v Bradford C
Coventry C v Southampton
Derby Co v Newcastle U
Leeds U v Aston Villa
Leicester C v West Ham U
Liverpool v Arsenal
Manchester Uv Ipswich T
Sunderland v Manchester C
Tottenham H v Middlesbrough

Nationwide Football League Division 1
Birmingham C v QPR
Burnley v Bolton W
Crewe Alex v Fulham
Crystal Palace v Blackburn R
Norwich C v Barnsley
Portsmouth v Sheffield U
Preston NE v Grimsby T
Sheffield W v Wolverhampton W
Stockport Co v Gillingham
Tranmere R v Wimbledon
Watford v Huddersfield T
WBA v Nottingham F

Nationwide League Division 2
AFC Bournemouth v Millwall
Brentford v Oldham Ath
Bury v Swindon T
Colchester U v Oxford U
Notts Co v Wrexham
Peterborough U v Northampton T
Port Vale v Rotherham U
Reading v Luton T
Walsall v Cambridge U
Wigan Ath v Stoke C
Wycombe W v Swansea C

Nationwide League Division 3
Brighton & HA v Exeter C
Cardiff C v Macclesfield T
Darlington v Lincoln C
Halifax T v Plymouth Arg
Hartlepool U v Barnet
Hull C v Kidderminster H
Leyton Orient v Rochdale
Mansfield T v Carlisle U
Scunthorpe U v Cheltenham T
Shrewsbury T v Southend U
Torquay U v Chesterfield
York C v Blackpool

Tuesday, 26 December 2000
FA Carling Premiership
Arsenal v Leicester C
Aston Villa v Manchester U
Bradford C v Sunderland
Everton v Coventry C
Ipswich T v Chelsea
Manchester C v Derby Co
Middlesbrough v Liverpool
Newcastle U v Leeds U
West Ham U v Charlton Ath

Nationwide Football League Division 1
Barnsley v Burnley
Blackburn R v Birmingham C
Bolton W v Sheffield W
Fulham v Watford
Gillingham v Crystal Palace
Grimsby T v Stockport Co
Huddersfield T v Tranmere R
Nottingham F v Crewe Alex
QPR v Norwich C
Sheffield U v WBA
Wimbledon v Portsmouth
Wolverhampton W v Preston NE

Nationwide League Division 2
Bristol R v Reading
Cambridge U v Wycombe W
Luton T v Peterborough U
Millwall v Colchester U
Northampton T v Bristol C
Oldham Ath v Wigan Ath
Oxford U v AFC Bournemouth
Rotherham U v Notts Co
Stoke C v Bury
Swansea C v Walsall
Swindon T v Brentford
Wrexham v Port Vale

Nationwide League Division 3
Barnet v Brighton & HA
Blackpool v Halifax T
Carlisle U v Hartlepool U
Cheltenham T v Shrewsbury T
Chesterfield v Darlington
Exeter C v Torquay U
Kidderminster H v Mansfield T
Lincoln C v Scunthorpe U
Macclesfield T v York C
Plymouth Arg v Cardiff C
Rochdale v Hull C
Southend U v Leyton Orient

Wednesday, 27 December 2000
FA Carling Premiership
Southampton v Tottenham H (8.00)

Saturday, 30 December 2000
FA Carling Premiership
Arsenal v Sunderland
Aston Villa v Leicester C
Bradford C v Liverpool
Everton v Leeds U
Ipswich T v Tottenham H
Manchester C v Charlton Ath
Middlesbrough v Coventry C
Newcastle U v Manchester U
Southampton v Derby Co
West Ham U v Chelsea

Nationwide Football League Division 1
Barnsley v Watford
Blackburn R v Crewe Alex
Bolton W v WBA
Fulham v Birmingham C
Gillingham v Tranmere R
Grimsby T v Portsmouth
Huddersfield T v Sheffield U
Nottingham F v Norwich C
QPR v Crystal Palace
Sheffield U v Preston NE
Wimbledon v Burnley
Wolverhampton W v Stockport Co

Nationwide League Division 2
Bristol R v Peterborough U
Cambridge U v AFC Bournemouth
Luton T v Wigan Ath
Millwall v Notts Co
Northampton T v Wycombe W
Oldham Ath v Walsall
Oxford U v Port Vale
Rotherham U v Colchester U
Stoke C v Bristol C
Swansea C v Brentford
Swindon T v Reading
Wrexham v Bury

Nationwide League Division 3
Barnet v Mansfield T
Blackpool v Cardiff C
Carlisle U v Leyton Orient
Cheltenham T v York C
Chesterfield v Hartlepool U
Exeter C v Darlington
Kidderminster H v Scunthorpe U
Lincoln C v Halifax T
Macclesfield T v Shrewsbury T
Plymouth Arg v Hull C
Rochdale v Brighton & HA
Southend U v Torquay U

Monday, 1 January 2001
FA Carling Premiership
Charlton Ath v Arsenal
Chelsea v Aston Villa
Coventry C v Manchester C
Derby Co v Everton
Leeds U v Middlesbrough
Leicester C v Bradford C
Liverpool v Southampton
Manchester U v West Ham U
Sunderland v Ipswich T
Tottenham H v Newcastle U

Nationwide Football League Division 1
Birmingham C v Nottingham F
Burnley v Wolverhampton W
Crewe Alex v QPR
Crystal Palace v Huddersfield T
Norwich C v Blackburn R
Portsmouth v Gillingham
Preston NE v Bolton W

Sheffield W v Grimsby T
Stockport Co v Fulham
Tranmere R v Sheffield U
Watford v Wimbledon
WBA v Barnsley

Nationwide League Division 2
AFC Bournemouth v Luton T
Brentford v Oxford U
Bristol C v Cambridge U
Bury v Rotherham U
Colchester U v Swansea C
Notts Co v Stoke C
Peterborough U v Oldham Ath
Port Vale v Bristol R
Reading v Northampton T
Walsall v Swindon T
Wigan Ath v Wrexham
Wycombe W v Millwall

Nationwide League Division 3
Brighton & HA v Southend U
Cardiff C v Exeter C
Darlington v Rochdale
Halifax T v Carlisle U
Hartlepool U v Lincoln C
Hull C v Blackpool
Leyton Orient v Plymouth Arg
Mansfield T v Cheltenham T
Scunthorpe U v Macclesfield T
Shrewsbury T v Barnet
Torquay U v Kidderminster H
York C v Chesterfield

Saturday, 6 January 2001
Nationwide Football League Division 2
AFC Bournemouth v Bristol R
Brentford v Northampton T
Bristol C v Wrexham
Bury v Cambridge U
Colchester U v Swindon T
Notts Co v Luton T
Peterborough U v Oxford U
Port Vale v Oldham Ath
Reading v Millwall
Walsall v Rotherham U
Wigan Ath v Swansea C
Wycombe W v Stoke C

Nationwide League Division 3
Brighton & HA v Lincoln C
Cardiff C v Barnet
Darlington v Southend U
Halifax T v Kidderminster H
Hartlepool U v Exeter C
Hull C v Macclesfield T
Leyton Orient v Blackpool
Mansfield T v Plymouth Arg
Scunthorpe U v Rochdale
Shrewsbury T v Chesterfield
Torquay U v Cheltenham T
York C v Carlisle U

Saturday, 13 January 2001
FA Carling Premiership
Arsenal v Chelsea
Aston Villa v Liverpool
Bradford C v Manchester U
Everton v Tottenham H
Ipswich T v Leicester C
Manchester C v Leeds U
Middlesbrough v Derby Co
Newcastle U v Coventry C
Southampton v Charlton Ath
West Ham U v Sunderland

Nationwide Football League Division 1
Barnsley v Birmingham C
Blackburn R v Sheffield W
Bolton W v Tranmere R
Fulham v Norwich C

Gillingham v Burnley
Grimsby T v Crewe Alex
Huddersfield T v Stockport Co
Nottingham F v Crystal Palace
QPR v WBA
Sheffield U v Watford
Wimbledon v Preston NE
Wolverhampton W v Portsmouth

Nationwide League Division 2
Bristol R v Brentford
Cambridge U v Notts Co
Luton T v Wycombe W
Millwall v Wigan Ath
Northampton T v Bury
Oldham Ath v Colchester U
Oxford U v Walsall
Rotherham U v Bristol C
Stoke C v Reading
Swansea C v Peterborough U
Swindon T v Port Vale
Wrexham v AFC Bournemouth

Nationwide League Division 3
Barnet v York C
Blackpool v Torquay U
Carlisle U v Shrewsbury T
Cheltenham T v Hartlepool U
Chesterfield v Scunthorpe U
Exeter C v Leyton Orient
Kidderminster H v Brighton & HA
Lincoln C v Hull C
Macclesfield T v Mansfield T
Plymouth Arg v Darlington
Rochdale v Halifax T
Southend U v Cardiff C

Saturday, 20 January 2001
FA Carling Premiership
Charlton Ath v West Ham U
Chelsea v Ipswich T
Coventry C v Everton
Derby Co v Manchester C
Leeds U v Newcastle U
Leicester C v Arsenal
Liverpool v Middlesbrough
Manchester U v Aston Villa
Sunderland v Bradford C
Tottenham H v Southampton

Nationwide Football League Division 1
Birmingham C v Blackburn R
Burnley v Barnsley
Crewe Alex v Nottingham F
Crystal Palace v Gillingham
Norwich C v QPR
Portsmouth v Wimbledon
Preston NE v Wolverhampton W
Sheffield W v Bolton W
Stockport Co v Grimsby T
Tranmere R v Huddersfield T
Watford v Fulham
WBA v Sheffield U

Nationwide League Division 2
AFC Bournemouth v Oxford U
Brentford v Swindon T
Bristol C v Northampton T
Bury v Stoke C
Colchester U v Millwall
Notts Co v Rotherham U
Peterborough U v Luton T
Port Vale v Wrexham
Reading v Bristol R
Walsall v Swansea C
Wigan Ath v Oldham Ath
Wycombe W v Cambridge U

Nationwide League Division 3
Brighton & HA v Barnet
Cardiff C v Plymouth Arg

Darlington v Chesterfield
Halifax T v Blackpool
Hartlepool U v Carlisle U
Hull C v Rochdale
Leyton Orient v Southend U
Mansfield T v Kidderminster H
Scunthorpe U v Lincoln C
Shrewsbury T v Cheltenham T
Torquay U v Exeter C
York C v Macclesfield T

Saturday, 27 January 2001
Nationwide Football League Division 2
Bristol R v Bristol C
Cambridge U v Walsall
Luton T v Reading
Millwall v AFC Bournemouth
Northampton T v Peterborough U
Oldham Ath v Brentford
Oxford U v Colchester U
Rotherham U v Port Vale
Stoke C v Wigan Ath
Swansea C v Wycombe W
Swindon T v Bury
Wrexham v Notts Co

Nationwide League Division 3
Barnet v Hartlepool U
Blackpool v York C
Carlisle U v Mansfield T
Cheltenham T v Scunthorpe U
Chesterfield v Torquay U
Exeter C v Brighton & HA
Kidderminster H v Hull C
Lincoln C v Darlington
Macclesfield T v Cardiff C
Plymouth Arg v Halifax T
Rochdale v Leyton Orient
Southend U v Shrewsbury T

Tuesday, 30 January 2001
FA Carling Premiership
Arsenal v Bradford C
Charlton Ath v Derby Co
Leeds U v Coventry C
Sunderland v Manchester U

Wednesday, 31 January 2001
FA Carling Premiership
Aston Villa v Ipswich T
Chelsea v Newcastle U
Everton v Middlesbrough
Manchester C v Liverpool
Southampton v Leicester C
West Ham U v Tottenham H

Saturday, 3 February 2001
FA Carling Premiership
Bradford C v Aston Villa
Coventry C v Arsenal
Derby Co v Sunderland
Ipswich T v Leeds U
Leicester C v Chelsea
Liverpool v West Ham U
Manchester U v Everton
Middlesbrough v Manchester C
Newcastle U v Southampton
Tottenham H v Charlton Ath

Nationwide Football League Division 1
Birmingham C v Norwich C
Blackburn R v Barnsley
Crewe Alex v Burnley
Crystal Palace v WBA
Fulham v Sheffield U
Grimsby T v Wimbledon
Huddersfield T v Nottingham F
Portsmouth v Preston NE
QPR v Bolton W
Sheffield W v Watford

Stockport Co v Tranmere R
Wolverhampton W v Gillingham

Nationwide League Division 2
AFC Bournemouth v Colchester U
Bristol C v Swansea C
Bury v Peterborough U
Cambridge U v Oxford U
Luton T v Rotherham U
Millwall v Bristol R
Notts Co v Oldham Ath
Reading v Port Vale
Stoke C v Northampton T
Wigan Ath v Walsall
Wrexham v Swindon T
Wycombe W v Brentford

Nationwide League Division 3
Barnet v Chesterfield
Blackpool v Scunthorpe U
Cardiff C v Rochdale
Carlisle U v Kidderminster H
Cheltenham T v Hull C
Leyton Orient v Halifax T
Macclesfield T v Plymouth Arg
Mansfield T v Exeter C
Shrewsbury T v Hartlepool U
Southend U v Lincoln C
Torquay U v Brighton & HA
York C v Darlington

Saturday, 10 February 2001
FA Carling Premiership
Arsenal v Ipswich T
Aston Villa v Middlesbrough
Charlton Ath v Newcastle U
Chelsea v Manchester U
Everton v Leicester C
Leeds U v Derby Co
Manchester C v Tottenham H
Southampton v Bradford C
Sunderland v Liverpool
West Ham U v Coventry C

Nationwide Football League Division 1
Barnsley v Fulham
Bolton W v Huddersfield T
Burnley v Crystal Palace
Gillingham v Grimsby T
Norwich C v Crewe Alex
Nottingham F v Blackburn R
Preston NE v QPR
Sheffield U v Birmingham C
Tranmere R v Wolverhampton W
Watford v Portsmouth
WBA v Stockport Co
Wimbledon v Sheffield W

Nationwide League Division 2
Brentford v Reading
Bristol R v Notts Co
Colchester U v Wigan Ath
Northampton T v Luton T
Oldham Ath v Wrexham
Oxford U v Wycombe W
Peterborough U v Stoke C
Port Vale v AFC Bournemouth
Rotherham U v Cambridge U
Swansea C v Millwall
Swindon T v Bristol C
Walsall v Bury

Nationwide League Division 3
Brighton & HA v Cardiff C
Chesterfield v Cheltenham T
Darlington v Shrewsbury T
Exeter C v Macclesfield T
Halifax T v Mansfield T
Hartlepool U v Blackpool
Hull C v Leyton Orient
Kidderminster H v Barnet

Lincoln C v Torquay U
Plymouth Arg v Southend U
Rochdale v Carlisle U
Scunthorpe U v York C

Saturday, 17 February 2001
Nationwide Football League Division 1
Birmingham C v WBA
Blackburn R v Sheffield U
Crewe Alex v Watford
Crystal Palace v Norwich C
Fulham v Nottingham F
Grimsby T v Burnley
Huddersfield T v Gillingham
Portsmouth v Bolton W
QPR v Barnsley
Sheffield W v Tranmere R
Stockport Co v Preston NE
Wolverhampton W v Wimbledon

Nationwide League Division 2
AFC Bournemouth v Walsall
Bristol C v Oldham Ath
Bury v Oxford U
Cambridge U v Swindon T
Luton T v Swansea C
Millwall v Brentford
Notts Co v Northampton T
Reading v Peterborough U
Stoke C v Port Vale
Wigan Ath v Bristol R
Wrexham v Colchester U
Wycombe W v Rotherham U

Nationwide League Division 3
Barnet v Darlington
Blackpool v Lincoln C
Cardiff C v Scunthorpe U
Carlisle U v Plymouth Arg
Cheltenham T v Brighton & HA
Leyton Orient v Kidderminster H
Macclesfield T v Hartlepool U
Mansfield T v Chesterfield
Shrewsbury T v Hull C
Southend U v Halifax T
Torquay U v Rochdale
York C v Exeter C

Tuesday, 20 February 2001
Nationwide Football League Division 1
Barnsley v Crystal Palace
Bolton W v Grimsby T
Burnley v Fulham
Gillingham v QPR
Norwich C v Stockport Co
Preston NE v Birmingham C
Sheffield U v Wolverhampton W
Tranmere R v Portsmouth
Watford v Blackburn R
WBA v Crewe Alex
Wimbledon v Huddersfield T

Nationwide League Division 2
Brentford v Bristol C
Bristol R v Wycombe W
Colchester U v Bury
Northampton T v Millwall
Oldham Ath v Reading
Oxford U v Stoke C
Peterborough U v Wigan Ath
Port Vale v Cambridge U
Rotherham U v Wrexham
Swansea C v Notts Co
Swindon T v AFC Bournemouth
Walsall v Luton T

Nationwide League Division 3
Brighton & HA v Blackpool
Chesterfield v Carlisle U
Darlington v Cheltenham T
Exeter C v Barnet

Halifax T v Cardiff C
Hartlepool U v Torquay U
Hull C v Mansfield T
Kidderminster H v Southend U
Lincoln C v Macclesfield T
Plymouth Arg v Shrewsbury T
Rochdale v York C
Scunthorpe U v Leyton Orient

Wednesday, 21 February 2001
Nationwide Football League Division 1
Nottingham F v Sheffield W

Saturday, 24 February 2001

FA Carling Premiership
Bradford C v West Ham U
Coventry C v Charlton Ath
Derby Co v Aston Villa
Ipswich T v Everton
Leicester C v Sunderland
Liverpool v Chelsea
Manchester Uv Arsenal
Middlesbrough v Southampton
Newcastle U v Manchester C
Tottenham H v Leeds U

Nationwide Football League Division 1
Barnsley v Crewe Alex
Bolton W v Blackburn R
Burnley v Huddersfield T
Gillingham v Fulham
Norwich C v Wolverhampton W
Nottingham F v Grimsby T
Preston NE v Sheffield W
Sheffield U v Crystal Palace
Tranmere R v Birmingham C
Watford v Stockport Co
WBA v Portsmouth
Wimbledon v QPR

Nationwide League Division 2
Brentford v Notts Co
Bristol R v Cambridge U
Colchester U v Bristol C
Northampton T v Wigan Ath
Oldham Ath v AFC Bournemouth
Oxford U v Millwall
Peterborough U v Wycombe W
Port Vale v Bury
Rotherham U v Stoke C
Swansea C v Reading
Swindon T v Luton T
Walsall v Wrexham

Nationwide League Division 3
Brighton & HA v York C
Chesterfield v Blackpool
Darlington v Macclesfield T
Exeter C v Carlisle U
Halifax T v Torquay U
Hartlepool U v Mansfield T
Hull C v Barnet
Kidderminster H v Cardiff C
Lincoln C v Leyton Orient
Plymouth Arg v Cheltenham T
Rochdale v Shrewsbury T
Scunthorpe U v Southend U

Saturday, 3 March 2001

FA Carling Premiership
Arsenal v West Ham U
Coventry C v Chelsea
Derby Co v Tottenham H
Everton v Newcastle U
Ipswich T v Bradford C
Leeds U v Manchester U
Leicester C v Liverpool
Manchester C v Southampton
Middlesbrough v Charlton Ath
Sunderland v Aston Villa

Nationwide Football League Division 1
Birmingham C v Watford
Blackburn R v WBA
Crewe Alex v Tranmere R
Crystal Palace v Preston NE
Fulham v Bolton W
Grimsby T v Barnsley
Huddersfield T v Norwich C
Portsmouth v Burnley
QPR v Sheffield U
Sheffield W v Gillingham
Stockport Co v Wimbledon
Wolverhampton W v Nottingham F

Nationwide League Division 2
AFC Bournemouth v Brentford
Bristol C v Oxford U
Bury v Swansea C
Cambridge U v Oldham Ath
Luton T v Bristol R
Millwall v Peterborough U
Notts Co v Walsall
Reading v Rotherham U
Stoke C v Colchester U
Wigan Ath v Swindon T
Wrexham v Northampton T
Wycombe W v Port Vale

Nationwide League Division 3
Barnet v Plymouth Arg
Blackpool v Kidderminster H
Cardiff v Hull C
Carlisle U v Darlington
Cheltenham T v Exeter C
Leyton Orient v Brighton & HA
Macclesfield T v Chesterfield
Mansfield T v Lincoln C
Shrewsbury T v Halifax T
Southend U v Rochdale
Torquay U v Scunthorpe U
York C v Hartlepool U

Tuesday, 6 March 2001
Nationwide Football League Division 1
Crewe Alex v Sheffield U
Crystal Palace v Birmingham C
Gillingham v Wimbledon
Huddersfield T v Grimsby T
Norwich C v WBA
Stockport Co v Burnley
Tranmere R v Preston NE
Wolverhampton W v Bolton W

Nationwide League Division 2
Bristol C v Walsall
Bury v Millwall
Colchester U v Port Vale
Luton T v Cambridge U
Northampton T v Bristol R
Peterborough U v Brentford
Rotherham U v AFC Bournemouth
Swindon T v Oldham Ath
Wigan Ath v Notts Co
Wrexham v Oxford U
Wycombe W v Reading

Nationwide League Division 3
Barnet v Carlisle U
Blackpool v Plymouth Arg
Cardiff C v Leyton Orient
Cheltenham T v Macclesfield T
Chesterfield v Exeter C
Hartlepool U v Rochdale
Hull C v Halifax T
Kidderminster H v Lincoln C
Scunthorpe U v Brighton & HA
Shrewsbury T v Mansfield T
Torquay U v Darlington
York C v Southend U

Wednesday, 7 March 2001
Nationwide Football League Division 1
Blackburn R v Fulham
Nottingham F v Barnsley
QPR v Watford
Sheffield W v Portsmouth

Nationwide League Division 2
Stoke C v Swansea C

Saturday, 10 March 2001
Nationwide Football League Division 1
Barnsley v Huddersfield T
Birmingham C v Crewe Alex
Bolton W v Gillingham
Burnley v Tranmere R
Fulham v QPR
Grimsby T v Wolverhampton W
Portsmouth v Stockport Co
Preston NE v Blackburn R
Sheffield U v Nottingham F
Watford v Norwich C
WBA v Sheffield W
Wimbledon v Crystal Palace

Nationwide League Division 2
AFC Bournemouth v Bristol C
Brentford v Stoke C
Bristol R v Bury
Cambridge U v Wrexham
Millwall v Luton T
Notts Co v Wycombe W
Oldham Ath v Rotherham U
Oxford U v Swindon T
Port Vale v Peterborough U
Reading v Wigan Ath
Swansea C v Northampton T
Walsall v Colchester U

Nationwide League Division 3
Brighton & HA v Hull C
Carlisle U v Cheltenham T
Darlington v Hartlepool U
Exeter C v Shrewsbury T
Halifax T v Scunthorpe U
Leyton Orient v Torquay U
Lincoln C v Cardiff C
Macclesfield T v Barnet
Mansfield T v York C
Plymouth Arg v Chesterfield
Rochdale v Kidderminster H
Southend U v Blackpool

Saturday, 17 March 2001
FA Carling Premiership
Aston Villa v Arsenal
Bradford C v Manchester C
Charlton Ath v Leeds U
Chelsea v Sunderland
Liverpool v Derby Co
Manchester Uv Leicester C
Newcastle U v Middlesbrough
Southampton v Everton
Tottenham H v Coventry C
West Ham U v Ipswich T

Nationwide Football League Division 1
Blackburn R v Wimbledon
Crewe Alex v Portsmouth
Crystal Palace v Fulham
Gillingham v Watford
Huddersfield T v Sheffield U
Norwich C v Preston NE
Nottingham F v Bolton W
QPR v Grimsby T
Sheffield W v Burnley
Stockport Co v Birmingham C
Tranmere R v Barnsley
Wolverhampton W v WBA

Nationwide League Division 2
Bristol C v Millwall
Bury v Notts Co
Colchester U v Brentford
Luton T v Oxford U
Northampton T v Port Vale
Peterborough U v Walsall
Rotherham U v Bristol R
Stoke C v Cambridge U
Swindon T v Swansea C
Wigan Ath v AFC Bournemouth
Wrexham v Reading
Wycombe W v Oldham Ath

Nationwide League Division 3
Barnet v Southend U
Blackpool v Mansfield T
Cardiff C v Carlisle U
Cheltenham T v Halifax T
Chesterfield v Rochdale
Hartlepool U v Brighton & HA
Hull C v Exeter C
Kidderminster H v Darlington
Scunthorpe U v Plymouth Arg
Shrewsbury T v Leyton Orient
Torquay U v Macclesfield T
York C v Lincoln C

Saturday, 24 March 2001
Nationwide Football League Division 1
Barnsley v Gillingham
Birmingham C v Sheffield W
Bolton W v Stockport Co
Burnley v QPR
Fulham v Wolverhampton W
Grimsby T v Blackburn R
Portsmouth v Crystal Palace
Preston NE v Huddersfield T
Sheffield U v Norwich C
Watford v Nottingham F
WBA v Tranmere R
Wimbledon v Crewe Alex

Nationwide League Division 2
AFC Bournemouth v Bury
Brentford v Luton T
Bristol R v Swindon T
Cambridge U v Colchester U
Millwall v Stoke C
Notts Co v Peterborough U
Oldham Ath v Northampton T
Oxford U v Rotherham U
Port Vale v Wigan Ath
Reading v Bristol C
Swansea C v Wrexham
Walsall v Wycombe W

Nationwide League Division 3
Brighton & HA v Chesterfield
Carlisle U v Torquay U
Darlington v Scunthorpe U
Exeter C v Kidderminster H
Halifax T v Barnet
Leyton Orient v York C
Lincoln C v Shrewsbury T
Macclesfield T v Blackpool
Mansfield T v Cardiff C
Plymouth Arg v Hartlepool U
Rochdale v Cheltenham T
Southend U v Hull C

Saturday, 31 March 2001
FA Carling Premiership
Arsenal v Tottenham H
Bradford C v Newcastle U
Charlton Ath v Leicester C
Chelsea v Middlesbrough
Coventry C v Derby Co
Liverpool v Manchester U
Manchester C v Aston Villa

Southampton v Ipswich T
Sunderland v Leeds U
West Ham U v Everton

Nationwide Football League Division 1
Barnsley v Stockport Co
Birmingham C v Wolverhampton W
Blackburn R v Burnley
Bolton W v Wimbledon
Crystal Palace v Crewe Alex
Huddersfield T v Portsmouth
Norwich C v Grimsby T
Nottingham F v QPR
Preston NE v Gillingham
Sheffield W v Sheffield U
Tranmere R v Fulham
WBA v Watford

Nationwide League Division 2
Brentford v Wrexham
Bristol C v Port Vale
Colchester U v Luton T
Northampton T v Oxford U
Oldham Ath v Bury
Peterborough U v Cambridge U
Reading v Notts Co
Rotherham U v Swindon T
Stoke C v Bristol R
Swansea C v AFC Bournemouth
Walsall v Millwall
Wycombe W v Wigan Ath

Nationwide League Division 3
Brighton & HA v Mansfield T
Carlisle U v Macclesfield T
Cheltenham T v Cardiff C
Chesterfield v Southend U
Darlington v Leyton Orient
Exeter C v Blackpool
Hartlepool U v Halifax T
Kidderminster H v Shrewsbury T
Rochdale v Lincoln C
Scunthorpe U v Barnet
Torquay U v Hull C
York C v Plymouth Arg

Saturday, 7 April 2001
FA Carling Premiership
Aston Villa v West Ham U
Derby Co v Chelsea
Everton v Manchester C
Ipswich T v Liverpool
Leeds U v Southampton
Leicester C v Coventry C
Manchester U v Charlton Ath
Middlesbrough v Sunderland
Newcastle U v Arsenal
Tottenham H v Bradford C

Nationwide Football League Division 1
Burnley v Preston NE
Crewe Alex v Bolton W
Fulham v WBA
Gillingham v Norwich C
Grimsby T v Tranmere R
Portsmouth v Nottingham F
QPR v Blackburn R
Sheffield U v Barnsley
Stockport Co v Sheffield W
Watford v Crystal Palace
Wimbledon v Birmingham C
Wolverhampton W v Huddersfield T

Nationwide League Division 2
AFC Bournemouth v Wycombe W
Bristol R v Swansea C
Bury v Bristol C
Cambridge U v Reading
Luton T v Stoke C
Millwall v Rotherham U
Notts Co v Colchester U

Oxford U v Oldham Ath
Port Vale v Walsall
Swindon T v Northampton T
Wigan Ath v Brentford
Wrexham v Peterborough U

Nationwide League Division 3
Barnet v Cheltenham T
Blackpool v Rochdale
Cardiff C v Torquay U
Halifax T v Brighton & HA
Hull C v Scunthorpe U
Leyton Orient v Chesterfield
Lincoln C v Carlisle U
Macclesfield T v Kidderminster H
Mansfield T v Darlington
Plymouth Arg v Exeter C
Shrewsbury T v York C
Southend U v Hartlepool U

Saturday, 14 April 2001
FA Carling Premiership
Arsenal v Middlesbrough
Aston Villa v Everton
Bradford C v Charlton Ath
Chelsea v Southampton
Ipswich T v Newcastle U
Leicester C v Manchester C
Liverpool v Leeds U
Manchester U v Coventry C
Sunderland v Tottenham H
West Ham U v Derby Co

Nationwide Football League Division 1
Bolton W v Birmingham C
Burnley v WBA
Gillingham v Sheffield U
Grimsby T v Watford
Huddersfield T v Fulham
Portsmouth v QPR
Preston NE v Nottingham F
Sheffield W v Crystal Palace
Stockport Co v Blackburn R
Tranmere R v Norwich C
Wimbledon v Barnsley
Wolverhampton W v Crewe Alex

Nationwide League Division 2
Brentford v Port Vale
Bristol R v Colchester U
Luton T v Oldham Ath
Millwall v Swindon T
Northampton T v Cambridge U
Notts Co v AFC Bournemouth
Peterborough U v Bristol C
Reading v Bury
Stoke C v Walsall
Swansea C v Rotherham U
Wigan Ath v Oxford U
Wycombe W v Wrexham

Nationwide League Division 3
Barnet v Leyton Orient
Carlisle U v Blackpool
Cheltenham T v Lincoln C
Chesterfield v Kidderminster H
Darlington v Cardiff C
Exeter C v Southend U
Hartlepool U v Hull C
Macclesfield T v Rochdale
Mansfield T v Torquay U
Plymouth Arg v Brighton & HA
Shrewsbury T v Scunthorpe U
York C v Halifax T

Monday, 16 April 2001
FA Carling Premiership
Charlton Ath v Aston Villa
Coventry C v Sunderland
Derby Co v Leicester C
Everton v Liverpool

Leeds U v Bradford C
Manchester C v Arsenal
Middlesbrough v Ipswich T
Newcastle U v West Ham U
Southampton v Manchester U
Tottenham H v Chelsea

Nationwide Football League Division 1
Barnsley v Preston NE
Birmingham C v Portsmouth
Blackburn R v Huddersfield T
Crewe Alex v Gillingham
Crystal Palace v Bolton W
Fulham v Sheffield W
Norwich C v Burnley
Nottingham F v Stockport Co
QPR v Tranmere R
Sheffield U v Wimbledon
Watford v Wolverhampton W
WBA v Grimsby T

Nationwide League Division 2
AFC Bournemouth v Stoke C
Bristol C v Wycombe W
Bury v Wigan Ath
Cambridge U v Millwall
Colchester U v Peterborough U
Oldham Ath v Bristol R
Oxford U v Reading
Port Vale v Swansea C
Rotherham U v Northampton T
Swindon T v Notts Co
Walsall v Brentford
Wrexham v Luton T

Nationwide League Division 3
Blackpool v Cheltenham T
Brighton & HA v Darlington
Cardiff C v Chesterfield
Halifax T v Macclesfield T
Hull C v York C
Kidderminster H v Plymouth Arg
Leyton Orient v Hartlepool U
Lincoln C v Barnet
Rochdale v Exeter C
Scunthorpe U v Carlisle U
Southend U v Mansfield T
Torquay U v Shrewsbury T

Saturday, 21 April 2001
FA Carling Premiership
Arsenal v Everton
Aston Villa v Southampton
Bradford C v Derby Co
Chelsea v Charlton Ath
Ipswich T v Coventry C
Leicester C v Middlesbrough
Liverpool v Tottenham H
Manchester Uv Manchester C
Sunderland v Newcastle U
West Ham U v Leeds U

Nationwide Football League Division 1
Bolton W v Norwich C
Burnley v Birmingham C
Gillingham v WBA
Grimsby T v Sheffield U
Huddersfield T v QPR
Portsmouth v Fulham
Preston NE v Watford
Sheffield W v Barnsley
Stockport Co v Crewe Alex
Tranmere R v Crystal Palace
Wimbledon v Nottingham F
Wolverhampton W v Blackburn R

Nationwide League Division 2
Brentford v Cambridge U
Bristol R v Oxford U
Luton T v Bury
Millwall v Port Vale
Northampton T v Colchester U
Notts Co v Bristol C
Peterborough U v AFC Bournemouth
Reading v Walsall
Stoke C v Wrexham
Swansea C v Oldham Ath
Wigan Ath v Rotherham U
Wycombe W v Swindon T

Nationwide League Division 3
Barnet v Rochdale
Carlisle U v Brighton & HA
Cheltenham T v Kidderminster H
Chesterfield v Lincoln C
Darlington v Hull C
Exeter C v Halifax T
Hartlepool U v Scunthorpe U
Macclesfield T v Southend U
Mansfield T v Leyton Orient
Plymouth Arg v Torquay U
Shrewsbury T v Blackpool
York C v Cardiff C

Saturday, 28 April 2001
FA Carling Premiership
Charlton Ath v Ipswich T
Coventry C v Liverpool
Derby Co v Arsenal
Everton v Bradford C
Leeds U v Chelsea
Manchester C v West Ham U
Middlesbrough v Manchester U
Newcastle U v Leicester C
Southampton v Sunderland
Tottenham H v Aston Villa

Nationwide Football League Division 1
Barnsley v Bolton W
Birmingham C v Grimsby T
Blackburn R v Portsmouth
Crewe Alex v Preston NE
Crystal Palace v Wolverhampton W
Fulham v Wimbledon
Norwich C v Sheffield W
Nottingham F v Gillingham
QPR v Stockport Co
Sheffield U v Burnley
Watford v Tranmere R
WBA v Huddersfield T

Nationwide League Division 2
AFC Bournemouth v Northampton T
Bristol C v Luton T
Bury v Wycombe W
Cambridge U v Wigan Ath
Colchester U v Reading
Oldham Ath v Stoke C
Oxford U v Swansea C
Port Vale v Notts Co
Rotherham U v Brentford
Swindon T v Peterborough U
Walsall v Bristol R
Wrexham v Millwall

Nationwide League Division 3
Blackpool v Barnet
Brighton & HA v Macclesfield T
Cardiff C v Shrewsbury T
Halifax T v Darlington
Hull C v Chesterfield
Kidderminster H v Hartlepool U

Leyton Orient v Cheltenham T
Lincoln C v Plymouth Arg
Rochdale v Mansfield T
Scunthorpe U v Exeter C
Southend U v Carlisle U
Torquay U v York C

Saturday, 5 May 2001
FA Carling Premiership
Arsenal v Leeds U
Aston Villa v Coventry C
Bradford C v Middlesbrough
Chelsea v Everton
Ipswich T v Manchester C
Leicester C v Tottenham H
Liverpool v Newcastle U
Manchester Uv Derby Co
Sunderland v Charlton Ath
West Ham U v Southampton

Nationwide Football League Division 2
Brentford v Bury
Bristol R v Wrexham
Luton T v Port Vale
Millwall v Oldham Ath
Northampton T v Walsall
Notts Co v Oxford U
Peterborough U v Rotherham U
Reading v AFC Bournemouth
Stoke C v Swindon T
Swansea C v Cambridge U
Wigan Ath v Bristol C
Wycombe W v Colchester U

Nationwide League Division 3
Barnet v Torquay U
Carlisle U v Hull C
Cheltenham T v Southend U
Chesterfield v Halifax T
Darlington v Blackpool
Exeter C v Lincoln C
Hartlepool U v Cardiff C
Macclesfield T v Leyton Orient
Mansfield T v Scunthorpe U
Plymouth Arg v Rochdale
Shrewsbury T v Brighton & HA
York C v Kidderminster H

Sunday, 6 May 2001
Nationwide Football League Division 1
Bolton W v Sheffield U
Burnley v Watford
Gillingham v Blackburn R
Grimsby T v Fulham
Huddersfield T v Birmingham C
Portsmouth v Barnsley
Preston NE v WBA
Sheffield W v Crewe Alex
Stockport Co v Crystal Palace
Tranmere R v Nottingham F
Wimbledon v Norwich C
Wolverhampton W v QPR

Saturday, 19 May 2001
FA Carling Premiership
Charlton Ath v Liverpool
Coventry C v Bradford C
Derby Co v Ipswich T
Everton v Sunderland
Leeds U v Leicester C
Manchester C v Chelsea
Middlesbrough v West Ham U
Newcastle U v Aston Villa
Southampton v Arsenal
Tottenham H v Manchester U

FA CARLING PREMIERSHIP FIXTURES 2000–2001

Reproduced under Copyright Licence No. AP20.003. Copyright © the FA Premier League Limited 2000.

Home \ Away	Arsenal	Aston Villa	Bradford C	Charlton Ath	Chelsea	Coventry C	Derby Co	Everton	Ipswich T	Leeds U	Leicester C	Liverpool	Manchester C	Manchester U	Middlesbrough	Newcastle U	Southampton	Sunderland	Tottenham H	West Ham U
Arsenal	—	14.10	30.1	26.8	13.1	16.9	11.11	21.4	10.2	5.5	26.12	21.8	28.10	1.10	14.4	9.12	2.12	30.12	31.3	3.3
Aston Villa	17.3	—	16.9	28.10	27.8	5.5	30.9	14.4	31.1	23.8	30.12	13.1	16.12	26.12	10.2	2.12	21.4	22.10	11.11	7.4
Bradford C	9.9	3.2	—	14.4	22.8	2.10	21.4	11.1	21.10	29.10	26.8	30.12	17.3	13.1	5.5	31.3	23.9	26.12	9.12	24.2
Charlton Ath	1.1	16.4	4.11	—	18.11	30.9	30.1	23.12	28.4	17.3	26.8	19.5	19.8	9.12	21.10	31.1	5.9	25.11	16.9	20.1
Chelsea	6.9	1.1	23.12	21.4	—	21.10	9.12	5.5	20.1	12.11	16.9	30.9	3.12	10.2	31.3	31.1	14.4	17.3	16.9	19.8
Coventry C	3.2	25.11	19.5	24.2	3.3	—	31.3	20.1	20.1	9.9	10.12	28.4	1.1	4.11	6.9	6.9	23.12	16.4	14.10	23.9
Derby Co	28.4	24.2	18.11	10.9	7.4	16.12	—	1.1	19.5	23.9	10.12	16.4	25.11	16.9	6.9	23.12	19.8	3.2	3.3	6.11
Everton	18.11	5.11	28.4	23.8	25.11	16.12	26.8	—	30.9	30.12	10.2	15.10	7.4	16.9	31.1	3.3	14.10	19.5	13.1	16.12
Ipswich T	23.9	9.9	3.3	11.11	26.12	21.4	2.12	24.2	—	3.2	13.1	7.4	5.5	22.8	1.1	14.4	16.12	26.8	30.12	14.10
Leeds U	26.11	23.12	16.4	14.10	28.4	30.1	10.2	19.8	16.9	—	19.5	7.4	5.9	3.3	21.4	20.1	7.4	16.12	30.9	18.11
Leicester C	20.1	19.8	1.1	16.12	3.2	7.4	28.10	24.9	6.9	2.12	—	3.3	14.4	14.10	1.1	11.11	9.9	24.2	5.5	23.12
Liverpool	23.12	6.9	19.8	2.12	24.2	11.11	17.3	28.10	9.12	14.4	21.10	—	9.9	31.3	17.9	5.5	1.1	23.9	21.4	3.2
Manchester C	16.4	31.3	14.10	30.12	19.5	26.8	26.12	9.12	25.11	13.1	4.11	31.1	—	18.11	11.11	30.9	3.3	23.8	10.2	28.4
Manchester U	24.2	20.1	5.9	7.4	23.9	14.4	5.5	3.2	23.12	21.10	17.3	17.12	21.4	—	18.11	20.8	28.10	9.9	2.12	1.1
Middlesbrough	4.11	23.9	25.11	3.3	16.12	30.12	23.8	9.9	16.4	26.8	18.11	26.12	3.2	28.4	—	16.10	24.2	7.4	22.8	19.5
Newcastle U	7.4	19.5	16.12	23.9	9.9	13.1	3.8	21.10	4.11	26.12	28.4	25.11	24.2	30.12	17.3	—	3.2	18.11	26.8	16.4
Southampton	19.5	18.11	10.2	13.1	4.11	23.8	30.12	17.3	31.3	9.12	31.1	26.8	23.10	16.4	30.9	16.9	—	28.4	27.12	25.11
Sunderland	19.8	3.3	20.1	5.5	14.10	28.10	16.9	4.12	1.1	31.3	30.9	10.2	23.12	30.1	9.12	21.4	11.11	—	14.4	5.9
Tottenham H	18.12	28.4	7.4	3.2	16.4	17.3	21.10	5.9	19.8	24.2	25.11	19.11	23.9	19.5	23.12	1.1	20.1	4.11	—	11.9
West Ham U	21.10	9.12	30.9	26.12	30.12	10.2	14.4	31.3	17.3	21.4	23.8	16.9	11.11	26.8	2.12	28.10	5.5	13.1	31.1	—

NATIONWIDE FOOTBALL LEAGUE FIXTURES 2000–2001

Reproduced under Copyright Licence No. AP20.003. Copyright © the Football League Limited 2000.

DIVISION ONE

	Barnsley	Birmingham C	Blackburn R	Bolton W	Burnley	Crewe Alex	Crystal Palace	Fulham	Gillingham	Grimsby T	Huddersfield T	Norwich C	Nottingham F	Portsmouth	Preston NE	QPR	Sheffield U	Sheffield W	Stockport Co	Tranmere R	Watford	WBA	Wimbledon	Wolverhampton W
Barnsley	—	13.1	2.9	28.4	26.12	24.2	20.2	10.2	24.3	30.9	10.3	12.8	14.10	25.11	16.4	16.9	9.12	18.11	31.3	17.10	30.12	26.8	5.11	24.10
Birmingham C	28.8	—	20.1	4.11	18.11	10.3	14.10	18.8	24.10	28.4	25.11	3.2	1.1	16.4	12.9	23.12	9.9	24.3	17.10	23.9	3.3	17.2	9.12	31.3
Blackburn R	3.2	26.12	—	23.9	31.3	30.12	12.8	7.3	25.11	21.10	16.4	26.8	9.9	28.4	6.10	9.12	4.11	13.1	4.11	25.10	13.9	3.3	17.3	18.11
Bolton W	11.11	14.4	24.2	—	12.8	9.12	28.10	30.9	25.11	16.4	10.2	21.4	17.10	16.9	26.8	2.9	6.5	26.12	24.3	13.1	2.12	30.12	31.3	14.10
Burnley	20.1	21.4	17.12	23.12	—	2.9	10.2	20.2	20.8	16.9	20.2	28.10	2.12	30.9	26.8	6.5	11.11	17.10	14.10	10.3	6.5	14.4	19.8	1.1
Crewe Alex	23.9	8.10	19.8	7.4	3.2	—	16.12	16.9	10.2	6.3	24.10	9.9	26.12	17.10	7.4	11.11	10.11	10.2	26.8	16.9	7.4	20.2	24.3	4.11
Crystal Palace	12.9	6.3	15.10	16.4	10.2	16.12	—	17.10	26.12	2.12	1.1	17.2	13.1	24.3	30.9	24.2	23.9	16.4	24.2	7.4	9.12	3.2	8.10	28.4
Fulham	10.9	30.12	17.3	7.3	20.2	16.9	17.10	—	23.9	24.2	28.10	2.12	28.4	21.4	11.11	6.5	1.1	30.9	1.1	16.9	11.11	21.10	21.10	24.3
Gillingham	21.10	2.12	25.11	25.11	20.8	10.2	26.12	23.9	—	9.9	14.10	2.12	30.9	23.12	31.3	4.11	29.8	12.8	9.12	7.4	17.3	21.4	6.3	2.9
Grimsby T	3.3	11.11	21.10	16.4	16.9	6.3	2.12	6.5	9.9	—	14.10	16.12	24.2	25.8	16.12	10.2	4.11	26.8	24.3	7.4	14.4	29.10	3.2	10.3
Huddersfield T	7.10	6.5	16.4	10.2	20.2	24.10	1.1	28.10	14.10	14.10	—	3.3	21.10	17.3	21.10	21.4	17.3	30.12	13.1	7.4	12.8	11.11	12.9	9.12
Norwich C	23.12	2.9	26.8	21.4	28.10	9.9	17.2	2.12	7.4	16.12	14.10	—	3.3	24.10	2.12	30.12	26.12	28.14	20.2	2.12	7.3	6.3	12.9	24.9
Nottingham F	14.10	1.1	9.9	17.10	20.1	28.2	17.2	7.4	12.11	23.9	3.2	19.8	—	7.4	30.12	11.11	8.10	21.2	16.12	14.4	21.10	21.4	18.11	3.3
Portsmouth	25.11	16.4	28.4	16.9	30.9	17.3	21.10	18.11	25.8	30.12	12.8	24.10	9.12	—	3.2	9.12	8.10	14.10	16.4	25.11	21.10	10.2	20.1	13.1
Preston NE	27.10	20.2	10.3	19.8	14.4	14.10	30.9	2.9	30.12	6.3	18.11	14.4	9.9	3.2	—	10.2	23.9	24.2	28.4	16.4	21.4	6.5	28.8	20.1
QPR	17.2	12.8	2.12	21.10	9.12	24.3	3.3	6.5	10.3	20.2	17.10	17.3	4.11	3.2	10.2	—	10.2	25.10	24.10	14.10	10.3	13.1	17.4	25.11
Sheffield U	7.4	9.9	4.11	6.5	11.11	10.11	23.9	1.1	29.8	4.11	17.3	26.12	8.10	8.10	23.9	10.2	—	16.12	3.3	25.11	16.4	12.8	23.9	20.2
Sheffield W	18.11	24.3	13.1	26.12	17.10	10.2	16.4	30.9	12.8	26.8	30.12	28.14	21.2	14.10	24.2	25.10	16.12	—	7.4	2.9	10.3	10.2	10.2	13.8
Stockport Co	31.3	17.10	4.11	24.3	14.10	18.11	25.11	26.8	12.8	26.12	13.1	20.2	16.4	16.9	28.4	24.10	9.12	16.12	—	24.2	1.9	23.9	20.1	23.12
Tranmere R	17.10	23.9	25.10	13.1	3.3	18.11	16.12	30.12	7.4	3.2	21.10	20.2	4.11	25.11	12.9	14.10	16.4	26.8	28.4	—	7.3	6.3	25.11	9.9
Watford	30.12	3.3	13.9	2.12	23.9	21.4	7.4	20.1	31.3	9.12	12.8	31.3	16.4	2.9	24.2	10.3	13.1	24.3	10.2	24.3	—	11.11	24.10	28.10
WBA	1.1	16.9	30.9	19.8	20.2	30.9	9.12	18.11	14.10	23.12	28.4	14.10	23.12	6.5	20.2	10.2	13.1	26.12	2.9	24.3	31.3	—	16.12	17.3
Wimbledon	14.4	7.4	18.10	16.12	30.12	20.2	24.3	10.3	20.2	2.9	18.11	24.2	25.11	26.12	13.1	28.8	28.8	2.9	10.3	10.2	26.8	2.12	—	16.9
Wolverhampton W	2.12	16.12	21.4	6.3	26.8	14.4	6.5	24.9	3.3	10.3	7.4	24.9	21.4	13.1	26.12	6.5	20.2	13.8	30.12	9.9	28.10	17.3	17.3	—

NATIONWIDE FOOTBALL LEAGUE FIXTURES 2000–2001

Reproduced under Copyright Licence No. AP20.003. Copyright © the Football League Limited 2000.

DIVISION TWO

	AFC Bournemouth	Brentford	Bristol C	Bristol R	Bury	Cambridge U	Colchester U	Luton T	Millwall	Northampton T	Notts Co	Oldham Ath	Oxford U	Peterborough U	Port Vale	Reading	Rotherham U	Stoke C	Swansea C	Swindon T	Walsall	Wigan Ath	Wrexham	Wycombe W
AFC Bournemouth	—	3.3	10.3	6.1	24.3	19.8	3.2	1.1	23.12	28.4	24.10	23.9	20.1	4.11	9.9	25.11	14.10	17.4	16.12	12.9	17.2	17.10	29.8	7.4
Brentford	30.9	—	20.2	28.8	5.5	21.4	17.10	24.3	16.9	6.1	24.2	23.12	1.1	14.10	14.4	10.2	11.11	10.3	19.8	20.1	28.10	2.12	31.3	2.9
Bristol C	6.10	12.9	—	22.12	2.12	1.1	23.9	28.4	17.3	20.1	4.11	17.2	3.3	24.10	31.3	21.10	28.8	19.8	3.2	9.9	6.3	25.11	6.1	16.4
Bristol R	12.8	13.1	27.1	—	10.3	24.2	14.4	30.9	2.9	14.10	10.2	28.10	21.4	30.12	26.8	21.10	17.10	16.12	7.4	24.3	11.11	16.9	5.5	20.2
Bury	21.10	25.11	7.4	6.10	—	6.1	12.9	4.11	6.3	28.8	17.3	16.12	17.2	3.2	23.9	26.12	17.10	20.1	3.3	23.12	11.11	16.9	19.8	28.4
Cambridge U	30.12	4.11	26.8	23.9	12.8	—	24.3	14.10	16.4	24.10	13.1	16.12	3.2	16.12	12.9	7.4	9.9	17.10	25.11	17.2	9.9	16.4	10.3	26.12
Colchester U	2.9	17.3	24.2	24.10	20.2	2.12	—	31.3	2.12	29.8	6.3	3.3	22.12	17.4	6.3	28.4	19.8	30.9	1.1	17.2	6.10	10.2	16.9	25.11
Luton T	26.8	21.10	11.11	3.3	21.4	21.10	7.10	—	7.10	12.8	14.4	2.12	29.8	22.12	26.12	6.3	27.1	3.2	7.4	17.2	6.10	30.12	16.9	26.8
Millwall	27.1	17.2	17.10	3.2	14.10	5.5	12.9	7.10	—	12.9	16.9	21.10	23.9	3.3	5.5	26.8	3.2	7.4	9.9	14.4	16.12	13.1	11.11	26.8
Northampton T	11.11	12.8	26.12	6.3	13.1	21.10	16.9	12.9	20.2	—	16.9	3.2	27.1	27.1	28.10	26.8	28.10	2.9	28.10	17.2	5.5	24.2	30.9	30.12
Notts Co	14.4	23.9	21.4	9.9	26.12	16.9	30.12	16.9	16.9	16.9	—	3.2	5.5	26.8	11.11	16.12	24.3	2.9	12.9	28.10	3.3	14.10	30.9	10.3
Oldham Ath	24.2	27.1	16.9	16.4	30.9	3.2	2.9	24.10	17.10	24.3	2.9	—	2.12	26.8	12.8	20.2	10.3	28.4	4.11	14.10	30.12	26.12	10.2	17.10
Oxford U	26.12	26.8	30.9	4.11	16.9	2.9	25.11	17.10	24.2	16.12	25.11	2.12	—	12.8	30.12	16.4	24.3	20.2	28.4	28.8	13.1	24.10	24.10	10.2
Peterborough U	21.4	6.3	14.4	19.8	2.9	31.3	2.9	1.1	23.12	21.10	12.8	8.10	6.1	—	30.12	16.9	5.5	22.12	28.8	11.11	17.3	20.2	2.12	24.2
Port Vale	10.2	26.8	16.12	1.1	14.4	6.3	14.10	25.11	30.9	23.12	21.10	28.4	19.8	10.3	—	2.9	22.12	17.9	16.4	28.8	7.4	24.3	2.12	30.9
Reading	5.5	9.9	24.3	1.1	28.10	16.12	4.11	13.1	31.3	1.1	31.3	12.9	28.10	17.2	3.2	—	3.3	23.9	19.8	31.3	21.4	10.3	17.10	14.10
Rotherham U	6.3	28.4	13.1	17.3	26.8	10.2	30.12	16.4	3.2	10.3	26.12	20.2	28.4	25.11	17.2	30.9	—	24.2	24.10	31.3	12.8	4.11	17.10	16.9
Stoke C	28.10	7.10	30.12	31.3	26.12	30.9	20.2	26.12	26.8	3.2	26.8	21.4	11.11	13.1	28.10	24.2	14.1	—	7.3	5.5	26.12	12.8	21.4	12.8
Swansea C	31.3	30.12	2.9	2.12	30.9	21.4	16.9	24.2	10.2	20.2	7.4	6.3	11.11	8.10	13.1	24.2	14.1	14.10	—	17.10	26.8	30.9	24.3	27.1
Swindon T	20.2	26.12	10.2	21.10	27.1	16.9	12.8	24.2	24.10	25.11	30.9	13.1	28.4	17.10	2.12	30.12	6.1	25.11	17.3	—	26.8	30.9	2.9	4.11
Walsall	16.9	17.4	14.10	28.4	10.2	23.12	9.9	19.8	31.3	6.3	2.12	4.11	17.10	6.1	21.10	6.10	21.4	23.12	20.1	1.1	—	2.9	24.2	24.3
Wigan Ath	17.3	7.4	5.5	17.2	28.10	11.11	9.9	19.8	7.11	23.9	6.3	20.1	14.4	12.9	21.10	6.10	21.4	23.12	6.1	3.3	3.2	—	1.1	16.12
Wrexham	13.1	16.12	12.8	25.11	30.12	6.10	17.2	16.4	28.4	3.3	27.1	9.9	6.3	7.4	26.12	17.3	12.9	4.11	21.10	3.2	23.9	26.8	—	24.10
Wycombe W	2.12	3.2	28.10	12.9	11.11	20.1	5.5	28.8	1.1	19.8	7.10	17.3	8.9	23.9	3.3	6.3	17.2	6.1	23.12	21.4	21.10	31.3	14.4	—

NATIONWIDE FOOTBALL LEAGUE FIXTURES 2000–2001

Reproduced under Copyright Licence No. AP20.003. Copyright © the Football League Limited 2000.

DIVISION THREE

	Bar	Bla	Bri	Car	Carl	Che T	Ches	Dar	Exe	Hal	Hart	Hull	Kid	Ley	Linc	Macc	Mans	Ply	Roch	Scun	Shrew	South	Torq	York
Barnet	—	11.11	26.12	26.8	6.3	7.4	3.2	17.2	12.9	21.10	27.1	23.9	9.9	14.4	28.10	8.10	19.8	3.3	21.4	16.12	12.8	17.3	5.5	13.1
Blackpool	28.4	—	12.9	30.12	24.10	16.4	23.9	25.11	16.12	26.12	9.9	12.8	3.3	26.8	17.2	21.10	17.3	6.3	7.4	3.2	4.11	7.10	13.1	27.1
Brighton & HA	20.1	20.2	—	10.2	4.11	16.9	24.3	16.4	22.12	2.12	18.10	10.3	28.8	30.9	6.1	28.4	31.3	24.10	19.8	14.10	1.1	2.9	24.2	24.2
Cardiff C	6.1	19.8	9.9	—	17.3	16.12	24.3	24.10	1.1	12.9	18.10	3.3	23.9	6.3	7.10	23.12	21.10	20.1	3.2	14.10	28.4	28.8	2.9	4.11
Carlisle U	14.10	14.4	21.4	17.10	—	10.3	14.10	3.3	23.9	17.3	26.8	5.5	30.12	11.11	14.4	31.3	27.1	23.9	9.9	28.10	13.1	11.11	24.3	26.8
Cheltenham T	2.12	28.10	17.2	31.3	6.10	—	9.9	12.9	3.3	12.8	13.1	3.2	28.4	24.10	14.10	1.1	24.2	25.11	16.12	23.12	6.1	11.1	30.12	19.8
Chesterfield	2.9	24.2	21.10	28.10	20.2	20.1	—	26.12	19.8	14.10	28.4	11.11	21.4	2.12	23.12	13.1	10.3	16.12	1.1	13.1	10.3	31.3	12.8	30.12
Darlington	16.9	5.5	28.10	14.4	30.9	26.12	26.12	—	30.12	17.3	9.9	21.4	17.3	16.12	27.1	3.3	22.9	7.4	13.1	13.1	12.8	21.10	6.3	3.2
Exeter C	20.2	31.3	27.1	12.8	24.2	30.9	20.1	30.12	—	21.4	24.10	17.10	6.1	2.9	25.11	16.4	2.9	23.12	6.3	21.4	30.9	20.1	20.2	24.10
Halifax T	24.3	20.1	2.12	7.4	1.1	12.8	30.12	17.3	21.4	—	16.12	14.10	6.3	24.10	28.10	30.12	9.9	3.2	14.4	13.1	10.2	31.3	23.9	14.4
Hartlepool U	23.12	10.2	18.10	20.2	20.1	2.9	19.8	7.10	16.12	16.12	—	26.8	7.4	16.4	14.10	17.2	23.9	24.3	13.1	4.11	27.1	3.2	12.9	3.3
Hull C	24.2	1.1	10.3	5.5	25.11	4.11	28.4	4.11	14.4	14.10	26.8	—	23.12	10.2	14.10	2.12	20.2	19.8	6.3	28.10	5.5	28.10	31.3	17.3
Kidderminster H	9.9	29.9	13.1	24.2	2.9	28.4	7.4	17.3	21.10	2.9	17.2	14.4	—	16.9	24.2	16.9	7.10	16.4	23.12	12.8	31.3	20.2	12.8	5.5
Leyton Orient	10.2	6.1	3.3	14.10	19.8	24.10	4.11	16.12	28.8	3.2	16.4	10.2	16.9	—	24.2	30.9	13.1	1.1	16.4	12.9	17.10	20.1	10.3	21.10
Lincoln C	16.4	16.9	26.8	10.3	7.4	14.10	3.3	27.1	25.11	11.11	14.10	13.1	14.10	24.2	—	20.2	30.9	28.4	16.12	26.12	2.12	2.9	10.2	17.10
Macclesfield T	10.3	24.3	11.11	27.1	16.12	14.10	17.2	10.3	16.9	16.9	6.3	2.12	25.11	20.2	31.3	—	13.1	28.4	24.10	28.4	19.8	3.3	4.11	20.1
Mansfield T	30.12	17.10	16.12	24.3	22.12	24.2	10.3	2.12	3.2	9.9	23.9	17.2	16.12	5.5	21.4	13.1	—	6.1	26.8	13.1	6.3	12.9	21.4	6.10
Plymouth Arg	30.9	14.10	14.4	26.12	16.9	25.11	16.12	7.4	7.4	3.2	24.3	10.3	28.10	12.8	27.1	2.9	26.8	—	6.1	25.11	9.9	10.2	21.4	14.10
Rochdale	4.11	2.9	2.12	2.9	16.4	16.12	23.12	13.1	16.4	14.4	13.1	31.3	23.12	16.12	23.12	14.4	11.11	5.5	—	17.10	23.9	3.3	17.2	12.9
Scunthorpe U	31.3	21.4	14.10	2.9	10.2	23.12	17.10	13.1	24.10	13.1	4.11	28.10	12.9	26.12	12.8	14.4	3.2	6.1	17.10	—	14.4	26.8	23.9	9.9
Shrewsbury T	1.1	5.5	12.8	16.9	28.4	6.1	6.1	3.3	28.4	10.2	27.1	17.2	16.12	17.3	2.12	6.3	25.11	6.3	21.4	24.10	—	22.12	27.1	16.4
Southend U	17.10	10.3	2.9	2.9	21.10	11.11	16.12	21.10	20.1	31.3	3.2	24.10	17.3	20.2	31.3	28.4	1.1	6.1	5.5	17.10	24.10	—	2.12	6.3
Torquay U	25.11	13.1	24.2	2.12	6.1	10.2	6.3	6.3	17.2	16.9	12.9	13.1	26.12	10.3	21.4	30.9	13.1	9.9	3.3	23.9	16.9	19.8	—	11.11
York C	28.8	22.12	23.9	21.4	28.4	19.8	1.1	3.2	17.2	14.4	3.3	28.10	5.5	21.10	17.10	20.1	6.10	31.3	12.9	9.9	2.12	6.3	11.11	—

THE SCOTTISH PREMIERSHIP and FOOTBALL LEAGUE FIXTURES 2000–2001

Reproduced under Copyright Licence No. 117.
Copyright © the Scottish Premier League Limited 2000. Copyright © the Scottish Football League 2000.

Saturday, 29 July 2000
Scottish Premier League
Dunfermline Ath v Aberdeen
Hearts v Hibernian
Motherwell v Dundee
Rangers v St Johnstone
St Mirren v Kilmarnock

Sunday, 30 July 2000
Scottish Premier League
Dundee U v Celtic

Saturday, 5 August 2000
Scottish Premier League
Aberdeen v St Mirren
Celtic v Motherwell
Dundee v Dunfermline Ath
Hibernian v Dundee U
Kilmarnock v Rangers

Scottish League Division 1
Ayr U v Ross Co
Clyde v Falkirk
Inverness CT v Airdrieonians
Greenock Morton v Livingston
Raith R v Alloa Ath

Scottish League Division 2
Arbroath v Partick T
Queen's Park v Berwick R
Stenhousemuir v Queen of the S
Stirling A v Clydebank
Stranraer v Forfar Ath

Scottish League Division 3
Albion R v East Fife
Brechin C v Elgin
East Stirlingshire v Cowdenbeath
Hamilton A v Dumbarton
Peterhead v Montrose

Sunday, 6 August 2000
Scottish Premier League
St Johnstone v Hearts

Saturday, 12 August 2000
Scottish Premier League
Dundee U v Motherwell
Dunfermline Ath v St Johnstone
Hibernian v Dundee

Scottish League Division 1
Airdrieonians v Raith R
Alloa Ath v Ayr U
Falkirk v Greenock Morton
Livingston v Inverness CT
Ross Co v Clyde

Scottish League Division 2
Berwick R v Arbroath
Clydebank v Stenhousemuir
Forfar Ath v Queen's Park
Partick T v Stranraer
Queen of the S v Stirling A

Scottish League Division 3
Cowdenbeath v Albion R
Dumbarton v Brechin C
East Fife v Peterhead
Elgin v Hamilton A
Montrose v East Stirlingshire

Sunday, 13 August 2000
Scottish Premier League
Aberdeen v Hearts
Celtic v Kilmarnock
St Mirren v Rangers

Tuesday, 15 August 2000
Scottish Premier League
Dundee v Dundee U

Wednesday, 16 August 2000
Scottish Premier League
Hearts v St Mirren
Kilmarnock v Hibernian
Motherwell v Dunfermline Ath
Rangers v Aberdeen
St Johnstone v Celtic

Saturday, 19 August 2000
Scottish Premier League
Aberdeen v Hibernian
Dundee U v St Johnstone
Hearts v Celtic
Kilmarnock v Motherwell
Rangers v Dunfermline Ath
St Mirren v Dundee

Scottish League Division 1
Ayr U v Airdrieonians
Clyde v Livingston
Inverness CT v Falkirk
Greenock Morton v Alloa Ath
Raith R v Ross Co

Scottish League Division 2
Arbroath v Clydebank
Queen's Park v Queen of the S
Stenhousemuir v Partick T
Stirling A v Forfar Ath
Stranraer v Berwick R

Scottish League Division 3
Albion R v Elgin
Brechin C v Cowdenbeath
East Stirlingshire v East Fife
Hamilton A v Montrose
Peterhead v Dumbarton

Saturday, 26 August 2000
Scottish Premier League
Dunfermline Ath v Dundee U
Hibernian v St Mirren
St Johnstone v Kilmarnock

Scottish League Division 1
Alloa Ath v Livingston
Ayr U v Falkirk
Clyde v Greenock Morton
Raith R v Inverness CT
Ross Co v Airdrieonians

Scottish League Division 3
Cowdenbeath v Albion R
Dumbarton v Brechin C
East Fife v Peterhead
Elgin v Hamilton A
Montrose v East Stirlingshire

Scottish League Division 2
Clydebank v Queen of the S
Forfar Ath v Stenhousemuir
Partick T v Berwick R
Stirling A v Queen's Park
Stranraer v Arbroath

Scottish League Division 3
Albion R v Dumbarton
Cowdenbeath v Elgin
East Stirlingshire v Hamilton A
Montrose v East Fife
Peterhead v Brechin C

Sunday, 27 August 2000
Scottish Premier League
Celtic v Rangers
Dundee v Hearts
Motherwell v Aberdeen

Saturday, 9 September 2000
Scottish Premier League
Aberdeen v St Johnstone
Celtic v Hibernian
Dundee v Rangers
Hearts v Dunfermline Ath
Kilmarnock v Dundee U
St Mirren v Motherwell

Scottish League Division 1
Airdrieonians v Alloa Ath
Falkirk v Raith R
Inverness CT v Clyde
Livingston v Ayr U
Greenock Morton v Ross Co

Scottish League Division 2
Arbroath v Forfar Ath
Berwick R v Clydebank
Queen of the S v Stranraer
Queen's Park v Partick T
Stenhousemuir v Stirling A

Scottish League Division 3
Brechin C v Montrose
Dumbarton v East Stirlingshire
East Fife v Cowdenbeath
Elgin v Peterhead
Hamilton A v Albion R

Saturday, 16 September 2000
Scottish Premier League
Dundee U v St Mirren
Hibernian v Motherwell
Kilmarnock v Aberdeen
Rangers v Hearts
St Johnstone v Dundee

Scottish League Division 1
Clyde v Airdrieonians
Falkirk v Alloa Ath
Inverness CT v Ross Co
Livingston v Raith R
Greenock Morton v Ayr U

Scottish League Division 2
Arbroath v Stenhousemuir
Berwick R v Queen of the S
Forfar Ath v Clydebank
Partick T v Stirling A
Stranraer v Queen's Park

Scottish League Division 3
Albion R v Brechin C
Cowdenbeath v Hamilton A
East Fife v Elgin
Montrose v Dumbarton
Peterhead v East Stirlingshire

Monday, 18 September 2000
Scottish Premier League
Dunfermline Ath v Celtic

Saturday, 23 September 2000
Scottish Premier League
Celtic v Dundee
Dundee U v Aberdeen
Dunfermline Ath v Hibernian
Motherwell v Rangers
St Mirren v St Johnstone

Scottish League Division 1
Airdrieonians v Livingston
Alloa Ath v Inverness CT
Ayr U v Clyde
Raith R v Greenock Morton
Ross Co v Falkirk

Scottish League Division 2
Clydebank v Partick T
Queen of the S v Forfar Ath
Queen's Park v Arbroath
Stenhousemuir v Berwick R
Stirling A v Stranraer

Scottish League Division 3
Brechin C v East Fife
Dumbarton v Cowdenbeath
East Stirlingshire v Albion R
Elgin v Montrose
Hamilton A v Peterhead

Sunday, 24 September 2000
Scottish Premier League
Hearts v Kilmarnock

Saturday, 30 September 2000
Scottish Premier League
Aberdeen v Celtic
Dundee v Kilmarnock
Hearts v Motherwell
St Johnstone v Hibernian
St Mirren v Dunfermline Ath

Scottish League Division 1
Ayr U v Inverness CT
Clyde v Raith R
Falkirk v Livingston
Greenock Morton v Airdrieonians
Ross Co v Alloa Ath

Scottish League Division 2
Arbroath v Queen of the S
Berwick R v Stirling A
Partick T v Forfar Ath
Queen's Park v Stenhousemuir
Stranraer v Clydebank

Scottish League Division 3
Albion R v Peterhead
Brechin C v East Stirlingshire
Cowdenbeath v Montrose
East Fife v Hamilton A
Elgin v Dumbarton

Sunday, 1 October 2000
Scottish Premier League
Rangers v Dundee U

Saturday, 7 October 2000
Scottish League Division 1
Airdrieonians v Falkirk
Alloa Ath v Clyde
Inverness CT v Greenock Morton
Livingston v Ross Co
Raith R v Ayr U

Scottish League Division 2
Clydebank v Queen's Park
Forfar Ath v Berwick R
Queen of the S v Partick T
Stenhousemuir v Stranraer
Stirling A v Arbroath

Scottish League Division 3
Dumbarton v East Fife
East Stirlingshire v Elgin
Hamilton A v Brechin C
Montrose v Albion R
Peterhead v Cowdenbeath

Saturday, 14 October 2000
Scottish Premier League
Aberdeen v Dundee
Celtic v St Mirren
Dundee U v Hearts
Hibernian v Rangers
Kilmarnock v Dunfermline Ath
Motherwell v St Johnstone

Scottish League Division 1
Airdrieonians v Inverness CT
Alloa Ath v Raith R
Falkirk v Clyde
Livingston v Greenock Morton
Ross Co v Ayr U

Scottish League Division 2
Berwick R v Queen's Park
Clydebank v Stirling A
Forfar Ath v Stranraer
Partick T v Arbroath
Queen of the S v Stenhousemuir

Scottish League Division 3
Cowdenbeath v East Stirlingshire
Dumbarton v Hamilton A
East Fife v Albion R
Elgin v Brechin C
Montrose v Peterhead

Saturday, 21 October 2000
Scottish Premier League
Aberdeen v Dunfermline Ath
Celtic v Dundee U
Dundee v Motherwell
Kilmarnock v St Mirren
St Johnstone v Rangers

Scottish League Division 1
Ayr U v Alloa Ath
Clyde v Ross Co
Inverness CT v Livingston
Greenock Morton v Falkirk
Raith R v Airdrieonians

Scottish League Division 2
Arbroath v Berwick R
Queen's Park v Forfar Ath
Stenhousemuir v Clydebank
Stirling A v Queen of the S
Stranraer v Partick T

Scottish League Division 3
Albion R v Cowdenbeath
Brechin C v Dumbarton
East Stirlingshire v Montrose
Hamilton A v Elgin
Peterhead v East Fife

Sunday, 22 October 2000
Scottish Premier League
Hibernian v Hearts

Saturday, 28 October 2000
Scottish Premier League
Dundee U v Hibernian
Dunfermline Ath v Dundee
Hearts v St Johnstone
Rangers v Kilmarnock
St Mirren v Aberdeen

Scottish League Division 1
Airdrieonians v Ross Co
Falkirk v Ayr U
Inverness CT v Raith R
Livingston v Alloa Ath
Greenock Morton v Clyde

Scottish League Division 2
Arbroath v Stranraer
Berwick R v Partick T
Queen of the S v Clydebank
Queen's Park v Stirling A
Stenhousemuir v Forfar Ath

Scottish League Division 3
Brechin C v Peterhead
Dumbarton v Albion R
East Fife v Montrose
Elgin v Cowdenbeath
Hamilton A v East Stirlingshire

Sunday, 29 October 2000
Scottish Premier League
Motherwell v Celtic

Saturday, 4 November 2000
Scottish Premier League
Hearts v Aberdeen
Kilmarnock v Celtic
Motherwell v Dundee U
Rangers v St Mirren
St Johnstone v Dunfermline Ath

Scottish League Division 1
Alloa Ath v Airdrieonians
Ayr U v Livingston
Clyde v Inverness CT
Raith R v Falkirk
Ross Co v Greenock Morton

Scottish League Division 2
Clydebank v Berwick R
Forfar Ath v Arbroath
Partick T v Queen's Park
Stirling A v Stenhousemuir
Stranraer v Queen of the S

Scottish League Division 3
Albion R v Hamilton A
Cowdenbeath v East Fife
East Stirlingshire v Dumbarton
Montrose v Brechin C
Peterhead v Elgin

Sunday, 5 November 2000
Scottish Premier League
Dundee v Hibernian

Saturday, 11 November 2000
Scottish Premier League
Celtic v St Johnstone
Dundee U v Dundee
Dunfermline Ath v Motherwell
Hibernian v Kilmarnock
St Mirren v Hearts

Scottish League Division 1
Clyde v Ayr U
Falkirk v Ross Co
Inverness CT v Alloa Ath
Livingston v Airdrieonians
Greenock Morton v Raith R

Scottish League Division 2
Arbroath v Queen's Park
Berwick R v Stenhousemuir
Forfar Ath v Queen of the S
Partick T v Clydebank
Stranraer v Stirling A

Scottish League Division 3
Albion R v East Stirlingshire
Cowdenbeath v Dumbarton
East Fife v Brechin C
Montrose v Elgin
Peterhead v Hamilton A

Sunday, 12 November 2000
Scottish Premier League
Aberdeen v Rangers

Saturday, 18 November 2000
Scottish Premier League
Celtic v Hearts
Dundee v St Mirren
Dunfermline Ath v Rangers
Hibernian v Aberdeen
Motherwell v Kilmarnock
St Johnstone v Dundee U

Scottish League Division 1
Airdrieonians v Clyde
Alloa Ath v Falkirk
Ayr U v Greenock Morton
Raith R v Livingston
Ross Co v Inverness CT

Scottish League Division 2
Clydebank v Forfar Ath
Queen of the S v Berwick R
Queen's Park v Stranraer
Stenhousemuir v Arbroath
Stirling A v Partick T

Scottish League Division 3
Brechin C v Albion R
Dumbarton v Montrose
East Stirlingshire v Peterhead
Elgin v East Fife
Hamilton A v Cowdenbeath

Saturday, 25 November 2000
Scottish Premier League
Aberdeen v Motherwell
Dundee U v Dunfermline Ath
Hearts v Dundee
Kilmarnock v St Johnstone
St Mirren v Hibernian

Scottish League Division 1
Ayr U v Raith R
Clyde v Alloa Ath
Falkirk v Airdrieonians
Greenock Morton v Inverness CT
Ross Co v Livingston

Scottish League Division 2
Arbroath v Stirling A
Berwick R v Forfar Ath
Partick T v Queen of the S
Queen's Park v Clydebank
Stranraer v Stenhousemuir

Scottish League Division 3
Albion R v Montrose
Brechin C v Hamilton A
Cowdenbeath v Peterhead
East Fife v Dumbarton
Elgin v East Stirlingshire

Sunday, 26 November 2000
Scottish Premier League
Rangers v Celtic

Wednesday, 29 November 2000
Scottish Premier League
Dundee U v Kilmarnock
Dunfermline Ath v Hearts
Hibernian v Celtic
Motherwell v St Mirren
Rangers v Dundee
St Johnstone v Aberdeen

Saturday, 2 December 2000
Scottish Premier League
Aberdeen v Kilmarnock
Celtic v Dunfermline Ath
Dundee v St Johnstone
Hearts v Rangers
Motherwell v Hibernian
St Mirren v Dundee U

Scottish League Division 1
Airdrieonians v Greenock Morton
Alloa Ath v Ross Co
Inverness CT v Ayr U
Livingston v Falkirk
Raith R v Clyde

Scottish League Division 2
Clydebank v Stranraer
Forfar Ath v Partick T
Queen of the S v Arbroath
Stenhousemuir v Queen's Park
Stirling A v Berwick R

Scottish League Division 3
Dumbarton v Elgin
East Stirlingshire v Brechin C
Hamilton A v East Fife
Montrose v Cowdenbeath
Peterhead v Albion R

Saturday, 9 December 2000
Scottish Premier League
Aberdeen v Dundee U
Dundee v Celtic
Hibernian v Dunfermline Ath
Kilmarnock v Hearts
Rangers v Motherwell
St Johnstone v St Mirren

Scottish League Division 1
Airdrieonians v Ayr U
Alloa Ath v Greenock Morton
Falkirk v Inverness CT
Livingston v Clyde
Ross Co v Raith R

Saturday, 16 December 2000
Scottish Premier League
Celtic v Aberdeen
Dundee U v Rangers
Dunfermline Ath v St Mirren

Hibernian v St Johnstone
Kilmarnock v Dundee
Motherwell v Hearts

Scottish League Division 1
Ayr U v Ross Co
Clyde v Falkirk
Inverness CT v Airdrieonians
Greenock Morton v Livingston
Raith R v Alloa Ath

Scottish League Division 2
Arbroath v Partick T
Queen's Park v Berwick R
Stenhousemuir v Queen of the S
Stirling A v Clydebank
Stranraer v Forfar Ath

Scottish League Division 3
Albion R v East Fife
Brechin C v Elgin
East Stirlingshire v Cowdenbeath
Hamilton A v Dumbarton
Peterhead v Montrose

Saturday, 23 December 2000
Scottish Premier League
Dundee v Aberdeen
Dunfermline Ath v Kilmarnock
Hearts v Dundee U
Rangers v Hibernian
St Johnstone v Motherwell
St Mirren v Celtic

Tuesday, 26 December 2000
Scottish Premier League
Dundee U v Celtic
Dunfermline Ath v Aberdeen
Hearts v Hibernian
Motherwell v Dundee
Rangers v St Johnstone
St Mirren v Kilmarnock

Scottish League Division 1
Airdrieonians v Alloa Ath
Falkirk v Raith R
Inverness CT v Clyde
Livingston v Ayr U
Greenock Morton v Ross Co

Scottish League Division 2
Berwick R v Stranraer
Clydebank v Arbroath
Forfar Ath v Stirling A
Partick T v Stenhousemuir
Queen of the S v Queen's Park

Scottish League Division 3
Cowdenbeath v Brechin C
Dumbarton v Peterhead
East Fife v East Stirlingshire
Elgin v Albion R
Montrose v Hamilton A

Saturday, 30 December 2000
Scottish Premier League
Aberdeen v St Mirren
Celtic v Motherwell
Dundee v Dunfermline Ath
Hibernian v Dundee U
Kilmarnock v Rangers
St Johnstone v Hearts

Scottish League Division 1
Alloa Ath v Livingston
Ayr U v Falkirk
Clyde v Greenock Morton
Raith R v Inverness CT
Ross Co v Airdrieonians

Scottish League Division 2
Clydebank v Queen of the S
Forfar Ath v Stenhousemuir
Partick T v Berwick R
Stirling A v Queen's Park
Stranraer v Arbroath

Scottish League Division 3
Albion R v Dumbarton
Cowdenbeath v Elgin
East Stirlingshire v Hamilton A
Montrose v East Fife
Peterhead v Brechin C

Tuesday, 2 January 2001
Scottish Premier League
Aberdeen v Hearts
Celtic v Kilmarnock
Dundee U v Motherwell
Dunfermline Ath v St Johnstone
Hibernian v Dundee
St Mirren v Rangers

Scottish League Division 1
Clyde v Airdrieonians
Falkirk v Alloa Ath
Inverness CT v Ross Co
Livingston v Raith R
Greenock Morton v Ayr U

Scottish League Division 2
Arbroath v Forfar Ath
Berwick R v Clydebank
Queen of the S v Stranraer
Queen's Park v Partick T
Stenhousemuir v Stirling A

Scottish League Division 3
Brechin C v Montrose
Dumbarton v East Stirlingshire
East Fife v Cowdenbeath
Elgin v Peterhead
Hamilton A v Albion R

Saturday, 6 January 2001
Scottish League Division 1
Airdrieonians v Livingston
Alloa Ath v Inverness CT
Ayr U v Clyde
Raith R v Greenock Morton
Ross Co v Falkirk

Saturday, 13 January 2001
Scottish League Division 1
Ayr U v Inverness CT
Clyde v Raith R
Falkirk v Livingston
Greenock Morton v Airdrieonians
Ross Co v Alloa Ath

Scottish League Division 2
Arbroath v Stenhousemuir
Berwick R v Queen of the S
Forfar Ath v Clydebank
Partick T v Stirling A
Stranraer v Queen's Park

Scottish League Division 3
Albion R v Brechin C
Cowdenbeath v Hamilton A
East Fife v Elgin
Montrose v Dumbarton
Peterhead v East Stirlingshire

Saturday, 20 January 2001
Scottish League Division 1
Airdrieonians v Falkirk
Alloa Ath v Clyde
Inverness CT v Greenock Morton

Livingston v Ross Co
Raith R v Ayr U

Scottish League Division 2
Clydebank v Partick T
Queen of the S v Forfar Ath
Queen's Park v Arbroath
Stenhousemuir v Berwick R
Stirling A v Stranraer

Scottish League Division 3
Brechin C v East Fife
Dumbarton v Cowdenbeath
East Stirlingshire v Albion R
Elgin v Montrose
Hamilton A v Peterhead

Wednesday, 31 January 2001
Scottish Premier League
Dundee v Dundee U
Hearts v St Mirren
Kilmarnock v Hibernian
Motherwell v Dunfermline Ath
Rangers v Aberdeen
St Johnstone v Celtic

Saturday, 3 February 2001
Scottish Premier League
Aberdeen v Hibernian
Dundee U v St Johnstone
Hearts v Celtic
Kilmarnock v Motherwell
Rangers v Dunfermline Ath
St Mirren v Dundee

Scottish League Division 1
Ayr U v Airdrieonians
Clyde v Livingston
Inverness CT v Falkirk
Greenock Morton v Alloa Ath
Raith R v Ross Co

Scottish League Division 2
Clydebank v Queen's Park
Forfar Ath v Berwick R
Queen of the S v Partick T
Stenhousemuir v Stranraer
Stirling A v Arbroath

Scottish League Division 3
Dumbarton v East Fife
East Stirlingshire v Elgin
Hamilton A v Brechin C
Montrose v Albion R
Peterhead v Cowdenbeath

Saturday, 10 February 2001
Scottish Premier League
Celtic v Rangers
Dundee v Hearts
Dunfermline Ath v Dundee U
Hibernian v St Mirren
Motherwell v Aberdeen
St Johnstone v Kilmarnock

Scottish League Division 1
Airdrieonians v Raith R
Alloa Ath v Ayr U
Falkirk v Greenock Morton
Livingston v Inverness CT
Ross Co v Clyde

Scottish League Division 2
Arbroath v Queen of the S
Berwick R v Stirling A
Partick T v Forfar Ath
Queen's Park v Stenhousemuir
Stranraer v Clydebank

Scottish League Division 3
Albion R v Peterhead
Brechin C v East Stirlingshire
Cowdenbeath v Montrose
East Fife v Hamilton A
Elgin v Dumbarton

Saturday, 17 February 2001
Scottish Football League Championship
Scottish League Division 2
Arbroath v Clydebank
Queen's Park v Queen of the S
Stenhousemuir v Partick T
Stirling A v Forfar Ath
Stranraer v Berwick R

Scottish League Division 3
Albion R v Elgin
Brechin C v Cowdenbeath
East Stirlingshire v East Fife
Hamilton A v Montrose
Peterhead v Dumbarton

Saturday, 24 February 2001
Scottish Premier League
Aberdeen v St Johnstone
Celtic v Hibernian
Dundee v Rangers
Hearts v Dunfermline Ath
Kilmarnock v Dundee U
St Mirren v Motherwell

Scottish League Division 1
Airdrieonians v Ross Co
Falkirk v Ayr U
Inverness CT v Raith R
Livingston v Alloa Ath
Greenock Morton v Clyde

Scottish League Division 2
Berwick R v Arbroath
Clydebank v Stenhousemuir
Forfar Ath v Queen's Park
Partick T v Stranraer
Queen of the S v Stirling A

Scottish League Division 3
Cowdenbeath v Albion R
Dumbarton v Brechin C
East Fife v Peterhead
Elgin v Hamilton A
Montrose v East Stirlingshire

Saturday, 3 March 2001
Scottish Premier League
Dundee U v St Mirren
Dunfermline Ath v Celtic
Hibernian v Motherwell
Kilmarnock v Aberdeen
Rangers v Hearts
St Johnstone v Dundee

Scottish League Division 1
Alloa Ath v Airdrieonians
Ayr U v Livingston
Clyde v Inverness CT
Raith R v Falkirk
Ross Co v Greenock Morton

Scottish League Division 2
Clydebank v Berwick R
Forfar Ath v Arbroath
Partick T v Queen's Park
Stirling A v Stenhousemuir
Stranraer v Queen of the S

Scottish League Division 3
Albion R v Hamilton A
Cowdenbeath v East Fife
East Stirlingshire v Dumbarton
Montrose v Brechin C
Peterhead v Elgin

Saturday, 10 March 2001
Scottish Football League Championship
Scottish League Division 2
Arbroath v Stranraer
Berwick R v Partick T
Queen of the S v Clydebank
Queen's Park v Stirling A
Stenhousemuir v Forfar Ath

Scottish League Division 3
Brechin C v Peterhead
Dumbarton v Albion R
East Fife v Montrose
Elgin v Cowdenbeath
Hamilton A v East Stirlingshire

Saturday, 17 March 2001
Scottish Premier League
Celtic v Dundee
Dundee U v Aberdeen
Dunfermline Ath v Hibernian
Hearts v Kilmarnock
Motherwell v Rangers
St Mirren v St Johnstone

Scottish League Division 1
Clyde v Ayr U
Falkirk v Ross Co
Inverness CT v Alloa Ath
Livingston v Airdrieonians
Greenock Morton v Raith R

Scottish League Division 2
Arbroath v Queen's Park
Berwick R v Stenhousemuir
Forfar Ath v Queen of the S
Partick T v Clydebank
Stranraer v Stirling A

Scottish League Division 3
Albion R v East Stirlingshire
Cowdenbeath v Dumbarton
East Fife v Brechin C
Montrose v Elgin
Peterhead v Hamilton A

Saturday, 31 March 2001
Scottish Premier League
Aberdeen v Celtic
Dundee v Kilmarnock
Hearts v Motherwell
Rangers v Dundee U
St Johnstone v Hibernian
St Mirren v Dunfermline Ath

Scottish League Division 1
Airdrieonians v Clyde
Alloa Ath v Falkirk

Ayr U v Greenock Morton
Raith R v Livingston
Ross Co v Inverness CT

Scottish League Division 2
Clydebank v Forfar Ath
Queen of the S v Berwick R
Queen's Park v Stranraer
Stenhousemuir v Arbroath
Stirling A v Partick T

Scottish League Division 3
Brechin C v Albion R
Dumbarton v Montrose
East Stirlingshire v Peterhead
Elgin v East Fife
Hamilton A v Cowdenbeath

Saturday, 7 April 2001
Scottish Premier League
Aberdeen v Dundee
Celtic v St Mirren
Dundee U v Hearts
Hibernian v Rangers
Kilmarnock v Dunfermline Ath
Motherwell v St Johnstone

Scottish League Division 1
Ayr U v Raith R
Clyde v Alloa Ath
Falkirk v Airdrieonians
Greenock Morton v Inverness CT
Ross Co v Livingston

Scottish League Division 2
Arbroath v Stirling A
Berwick R v Forfar Ath
Partick T v Queen of the S
Queen's Park v Clydebank
Stranraer v Stenhousemuir

Scottish League Division 3
Albion R v Montrose
Brechin C v Hamilton A
Cowdenbeath v Peterhead
East Fife v Dumbarton
Elgin v East Stirlingshire

Saturday, 14 April 2001
Scottish League Division 1
Airdrieonians v Greenock Morton
Alloa Ath v Ross Co
Inverness CT v Ayr U
Livingston v Falkirk
Raith R v Clyde

Scottish League Division 2
Clydebank v Stranraer
Forfar Ath v Partick T
Queen of the S v Arbroath
Stenhousemuir v Queen's Park
Stirling A v Berwick R

Scottish League Division 3
Dumbarton v Elgin
East Stirlingshire v Brechin C
Hamilton A v East Fife

Montrose v Cowdenbeath
Peterhead v Albion R

Saturday, 21 April 2001
Scottish League Division 1
Airdrieonians v Inverness CT
Alloa Ath v Raith R
Falkirk v Clyde
Livingston v Greenock Morton
Ross Co v Ayr U

Scottish League Division 2
Berwick R v Queen's Park
Clydebank v Stirling A
Forfar Ath v Stranraer
Partick T v Arbroath
Queen of the S v Stenhousemuir

Scottish League Division 3
Cowdenbeath v East Stirlingshire
Dumbarton v Hamilton A
East Fife v Albion R
Elgin v Brechin C
Montrose v Peterhead

Saturday, 28 April 2001
Scottish League Division 1
Ayr U v Alloa Ath
Clyde v Ross Co
Inverness CT v Livingston
Greenock Morton v Falkirk
Raith R v Airdrieonians

Scottish League Division 2
Arbroath v Berwick R
Queen's Park v Forfar Ath
Stenhousemuir v Clydebank
Stirling A v Queen of the S
Stranraer v Partick T

Scottish League Division 3
Albion R v Cowdenbeath
Brechin C v Dumbarton
East Stirlingshire v Montrose
Hamilton A v Elgin
Peterhead v East Fife

Saturday, 5 May 2001
Scottish League Division 1
Airdrieonians v Ayr U
Alloa Ath v Greenock Morton
Falkirk v Inverness CT
Livingston v Clyde
Ross Co v Raith R

Scottish League Division 2
Berwick R v Stranraer
Clydebank v Arbroath
Forfar Ath v Stirling A
Partick T v Stenhousemuir
Queen of the S v Queen's Park

Scottish League Division 3
Cowdenbeath v Brechin C
Dumbarton v Peterhead
East Fife v East Stirlingshire
Elgin v Albion R
Montrose v Hamilton A

OTHER FIXTURES 2000-2001

July 2000

1 Sat	UEFA Intertoto Cup 2 (1)
2 Sun	Euro 2000 Final
8 Sat	UEFA Intertoto Cup 2 (2)
11 Tue	U16 Nationwide Tournament – England v Thailand *at York City FC – 7.15pm*
12 Wed	UEFA Champions League 1Q (1)
15 Sat	UEFA Intertoto Cup 3 (1)
16 Sun	U16 Nationwide Tournament – England v Brazil *at Sunderland AFC – 2.30pm*
19 Wed	UEFA Champions League 1Q (2)
22 Sat	UEFA Intertoto Cup 3 (2)
26 Wed	UEFA Champions League 2Q (1) UEFA Intertoto Cup SF (1)

August 2000

2 Wed	UEFA Champions League 2Q (2) UEFA Intertoto Cup SF (2)
5 Sat	
8/9 Tue/Wed	UEFA Champions League 3Q (1)
9 Wed	UEFA Intertoto Cup Final (1)
10 Thu	UEFA Cup Qualifying Round (1)
12 Sat	Start of Football League
13 Sun	One2One Charity Shield
16 Wed	International – Friendly
19 Sat	Start of F.A. Premier League
22/23 Tue/Wed	UEFA Champions Leagues 3Q (2)
23 Wed	UEFA Intertoto Cup Final (2) Worthington Cup 1 (1)
24 Thu	UEFA Cup Qualifying Round (2)
25 Fri	UEFA Super Cup
26 Sat	F.A. Cup sponsored by AXA Extra Preliminary Round
28 Mon	Bank Holiday

September 2000

2 Sat	France v England – Friendly International F.A. Cup sponsored by AXA Preliminary Round AXA F.A. Youth Cup 1Q*
6 Wed	Worthington Cup 1 (2)
9 Sat	F.A. Carlsberg Vase 1Q
10 Sun	AXA F.A. Women's Cup Extra Preliminary Round AXA F.A. Premier League Cup Preliminary Round
12/13 Tue/Wed	UEFA Champions League – Group 1 – Match Day 1
14 Thu	UEFA Cup 1 (1)
16 Sat	F.A. Cup sponsored by AXA 1Q
19/20 Tue/Wed	UEFA Champions League – Group 1 – Match Day 2
20 Wed	Worthington Cup 2 (1)
23 Sat	F.A. Carlsberg Vase 2Q AXA F.A. Youth Cup 2Q*
24 Sun	AXA F.A. Women's Cup Preliminary Round AXA F.A. Women's Premier League Cup 1
26/27 Tue/Wed	UEFA Champions League – Group 1 – Match Day 3
27 Wed	Worthington Cup 2 (2)
28 Thu	UEFA Cup 1 (2)
30 Sat	F.A. Cup sponsored by AXA 2Q

October 2000

1 Sun	F.A. Umbro Sunday Cup 1
7 Sat	England v Germany – FIFA World Cup Qualifier AXA F.A. Youth Cup 3Q* F.A. County Youth Cup 1*
11 Wed	Finland v England – FIFA World Cup Qualifier
14 Sat	F.A. Cup sponsored by AXA 3Q
17/18 Tue/Wed	UEFA Champions League – Group 1 – Match Day 4
20 Fri	U15 Victory Shield – Northern Ireland v England – venue tbc
21 Sat	F.A. Carlsberg Vase 1P
24/25 Tue/Wed	UEFA Champions League – Group 1 – Match Day 5
26 Thu	UEFA Cup 2 (1)
28 Sat	F.A. Cup sponsored by AXA 4Q AXA F.A. Youth Cup 1P*
29 Sun	AXA F.A. Women's Cup 1 AXA F.A. Women's Premier League Cup 2

November 2000

1 Wed	Worthington Cup 3
3 Fri	U15 Victory Shield – Wales v England – venue tbc
4 Sat	F.A. Umbro Trophy 1
5 Sun	F.A. Umbro Sunday Cup 2
7/8 Tue/Wed	UEFA Champions League – Group 1 – Match Day 6
9 Thu	UEFA Cup 2 (2)
11 Sat	F.A. Carslberg Vase 2P AXA F.A. Youth Cup 2P* F.A. County Youth Cup 2*
12 Sun	AXA F.A. Women's Premier League 3
15 Wed	International – Friendly
18 Sat	F.A. Cup sponsored by AXA 1P
19 Sun	AXA F.A. Women's Cup 2
20 Mon	F.A. XI v Northern Premier League
21 Tue	F.A. XI v Southern League
21/22 Tue/Wed	UEFA Champions League – Group 2 – Match Day 1
22 Wed	F.A. XI v Isthmian League
23 Thu	UEFA Cup 3 (1)
25 Sat	
28 Tue	Inter-Continental Cup
29 Wed	F.A. Cup sponsored by AXA 1P replays Worthington Cup 4

December 2000

1 Fri	U15 Victory Shield – England v Scotland – venue tbc
2 Sat	F.A. Umbro Trophy 2
3 Sun	F.A. Umbro Sunday Cup 3
5/6 Tue/Wed	UEFA Champions League – Group 2 – Match Day 2
7 Thu	UEFA Cup 3 (2)
9 Sat	F.A. Cup sponsored by AXA 2P F.A. Carlsberg Vase 3P AXA F.A. Youth Cup 3P*
10 Sun	AXA F.A. Women's Cup 3
13 Wed	Worthington Cup 5
16 Sat	F.A. County Youth Cup 3
17 Sun	AXA F.A. Women's Premier League Cup SF
20 Wed	F.A. Cup sponsored by AXA 2P replays
25 Mon	Christmas Day
26 Tue	Boxing Day
30 Sat	

January 2001

1 Mon	New Year's Day
6 Sat	F.A. Cup sponsored by AXA 3P
7 Sun	AXA F.A. Women's Cup 4
8 Mon	F.A. XI v British Universities
10 Wed	Worthington Cup SF1
13 Sat	F.A. Umbro Trophy 3
14 Sun	F.A. Umbro Sunday Cup 4
17 Wed	F.A. Cup sponsored by AXA 3P replays
20 Sat	F.A. Carlsberg Vase 4P
	AXA F.A. Youth Cup 4P*
24 Wed	Worthington Cup SF2
27 Sat	F.A. Cup sponsored by AXA 4P
	F.A. County Youth Cup 4*
28 Sun	AXA F.A. Women's Cup 5
30 Mon	F.A. XI v Combined Services

February 2001

3 Sat	F.A. Umbro Trophy 4
4 Sun	F.A. Umbro Sunday Cup 5
7 Wed	F.A. Cup sponsored by AXA 4P replays
10 Sat	F.A. Carslberg Vase 5P
	AXA F.A. Youth Cup 5P*
13 Tue	England Semi-Professional International
13/14 Tue/Wed	UEFA Champions League – Group 2 – Match Day 3
14 Wed	International – Friendly
15 Thu	UEFA Cup 4 (1)
17 Sat	F.A. Cup sponsored by AXA 5P
18 Sun	AXA F.A. Women's Cup 6
20/21 Tue/Wed	UEFA Champions League – Group 2 – Match Day 4
22 Thu	UEFA Cup 4 (2)
24 Sat	F.A. Umbro Trophy 5
25 Sun	F.A. Umbro Sunday Cup SF
28 Wed	F.A. Cup sponsored by AXA 5P replays
	International Friendly

March 2001

3 Sat	F.A. Carlsberg Vase 6P
	AXA F.A. Youth Cup 6P*
4 Sun	Worthington Cup Final
6/7 Tue/Wed	UEFA Champions League – Group 2 – Match Day 5
8 Thu	UEFA Cup QF (1)
10 Sat	F.A. Cup sponsored by AXA 6P
	F.A. Umbro Trophy 6
	F.A. County Youth Cup SF*
11 Sun	AXA F.A. Women's Premier League Cup Final
13/14 Tue/Wed	UEFA Champions League – Group 2 – Match Day 6
15 Thu	UEFA Cup QF (2)
17 Sat	F.A. Carlsberg Vase SF1
	AXA F.A. Youth Cup SF1*
20 Tue	England Semi-Professional International
21 Wed	F.A. Cup sponsored by AXA 6P replays
24 Sat	England v Finland – FIFA World Cup Qualifier
	F.A. Carlsberg Vase SF2
25 Sun	AXA F.A. Women's Cup SF
28 Wed	Albania v England – FIFA World Cup Qualifier
31 Sat	F.A. Umbro Trophy SF1

April 2001

3/4 Tue/Wed	UEFA Champions League QF (1)
5 Thu	UEFA Cup SF (1)
7 Sat	F.A. Umbro Trophy SF2
	AXA F.A. Youth Cup SF2*
8 Sun	F.A. Cup sponsored by AXA SF
13 Fri	Good Friday
14 Sat	
15 Sun	Easter Sunday
16 Mon	Easter Monday
17/18 Tue/Wed	UEFA Champions League QF (2)
19 Thu	UEFA Cup SF (2)
25 Wed	International – Friendly
28 Sat	F.A. County Youth Cup Final (fixed date)

May 2001

1/2 Tue/Wed	UEFA Champions League SF (1)
5 Sat	Football League ends
7 Mon	AXA F.A. Women's Cup Final
	Bank Holiday
9 Wed	UEFA Champions League SF (2)
11 Fri	AXA F.A. Youth Cup Final (1)
12 Sat	F.A. Cup sponsored by AXA Final
13 Sun	Football League Play-Off SF (1)
16 Wed	UEFA Cup Final
	Football League Play-Off SF (2)
18 Fri	AXA F.A. Youth Cup Final (2)
19 Sat	Premier League ends
23 Wed	UEFA Champions League Final
26 Sat	Football League Division 3 Play-Off Final
27 Sun	Football League Division 2 Play-Off Final
28 Mon	Football League Division 1 Play-Off Final

June 2001

2 Sat	International (World Cup Qualifier) – no England fixture
6 Wed	Greece v England – FIFA World Cup Qualifier

September 2001

1 Sat	Germany v England – FIFA World Cup Qualifier

.* = closing date of Round
to be decided:
F.A. Carlsberg Vase Final
F.A. Umbro Trophy Final
F.A. Umbro Sunday Cup Final

STOP PRESS

£1.65 billion TV and communications cash to pour into football and ITV beats BBC who lose MOTD, but gain FA Cup! ... World Cup 2006 voting fiasco: Germany wins, South Africa loses, NZ stalls, England nowhere ... North Korea may host two WC 2002 matches ... Euro 2000 coaches depart: Ribbeck, Coelho, Johansson, Denizli, Rijkaard and Zoff ... Keith Harris (without Orville) is new FL Independent Chairman ... Intertoto: Bradford sink Atlantas and double Dutch RKC; Villa check Czechs ... Manchester U announce record English League receipts £1,701,000 v Spurs 6 May and appoint new Chief Executive Peter Kenyon ... 13 dead in World Cup stampede in Harare ... Brazil beaten 2-1 by Paraguay ... Bolton's £25,000 fine for play-off fracas is suspended ... Ken Bates says not enough good English players ... Luis Figo, Barcelona to Real Madrid for world record £37.4m ... Batistuta, Roma bargain and Anelka back to PSG, another snip, both at £22m ... Terry (father of) Brady buys Swindon ... One Darlington player earned nearly £140,000 last year ... Leeds to play 1860 Munich in Euro Cup ... Government to cough up for grass roots revival ...

Top Transfers: Jimmy Floyd Hasselbaink, Atletico Madrid to **Chelsea** £15m; Sergei Rebrov, Dynamo Kiev to **Tottenham H** £11m; Fabien Barthez, Monaco to **Manchester U** £7.8m; Olivier Dacourt, Lens to **Leeds U** £7.2m; Lauren Etame Mayer, Mallorca to **Arsenal** £7.2m; Carl Cort, Wimbledon to **Newcastle U** £7m.

Moves completed and pending: **Arsenal:** Robert Pires (Marseille); **Aston Villa:** Luc Nilis (PSV Eindhoven); Alpay Ozalan (Fenerbahce); **Bradford C:** David Hopkin (Leeds U); Peter Atherton (Sheffield W); Ian Nolan (Sheffield W); **Charlton Ath:** Ben Roberts (Middlesbrough); Claus Jensen (Bolton W) – £4m club record; **Chelsea:** Jimmy Floyd Hasselbaink (Atletico Madrid); Mario Stanic (Parma); Eidur Gudjohnsen (Bolton W); Carlo Cudicini (Castel di Sangro); **Coventry C:** Jay Bothroyd (Arsenal); Ivan Guerrero (Motagua); **Derby Co:** Danny Higginbotham (Manchester U); Simo Valakari (Motherwell); **Everton:** Alessandro Pistone (Newcastle U); Steve Watson (Aston Villa); Paul Gascoigne (Middlesbrough); Niclas Alexandersson (Sheffield W); Alex Nyarko (Lens); **Ipswich T:** Martijn Reuser (Vitesse); John Scales (Tottenham H); **Leeds U:** Olivier Dacourt (Lens); Mark Viduka (Celtic); **Leicester C:** Gary Rowett (Birmingham C); Callum Davidson (Blackburn R); Trevor Benjamin (Cambridge U); Simon Royce (Charlton Ath); **Liverpool:** Bernard Diomede (Auxerre); Pegguy Arphexad (Leicester C); Markus Babbel (Bayern Munich); Gary McAllister (Coventry C); Nick Barmby (Everton); **Manchester C:** Alf Inge Haaland (Leeds U); **Manchester U:** Fabien Barthez (Monaco); Daniel Nardiello (Wolverhampton W); **Middlesbrough:** Christian Karembeu (Real Madrid); Paul Okon (Fiorentina); Mark Crossley (Nottingham F); **Newcastle U:** Carl Cort (Wimbledon); Christian Bassedas (Velez Sarsfield); Daniel Cordone (Racing Club); **Southampton:** Mark Draper (Aston Villa); Uwe Rosler (Tennis Berlin); Patrice Tano (Monaco); **Sunderland:** Don Hutchison (Everton); Tom Peeters (Mechelen); Jurgen Macho (FC Vienna); **Tottenham H:** Sergei Rebrov (Dynamo Kiev); Ben Thatcher (Wimbledon); Neil Sullivan (Wimbledon); **West Ham U:** Frederic Kanoute (Lyon); Davor Suker (Arsenal); Nigel Winterburn (Arsenal).

Scottish moves: **Celtic:** Chris Sutton (Chelsea) £6m; **Dundee:** Georgi Nemsadze (Grasshoppers); Marcello Marrocco (Modena); Javier Artero (San Lorenzo); Marco de Marchi (Vitesse); Fabian Caballero (Sol de America); Juan Sara (Cerro Porteno); Ivano Bonetti (Setrese); **Dundee U:** Jamie Buchan (Aberdeen); Hasney Aljofree (Bolton W); Danny Griffin (St Johnstone); Neil Heaney (Darlington); **Dunfermline Ath:** Marco Ruitenbeet (Go Ahead); Michel Doesberg (Motherwell); Robert Matthaei (Motherwell); Andreas Skerla (PSV Eindhoven); Youssef Rossi (Rennes); Rob McKay (Motherwell); **Hibernian:** Paul Fenwick (Raith R); Ulrik Laursen (Odense); John O'Neil (St Johnstone); Hakim Temsoury (Nantes); Ian Westwater (Dunfermline Ath); Didier Agathe (Raith R); Gary Smith (Aberdeen); **Kilmarnock:** Andy McLaren (Reading); Neil MacFarlane (Queen's Park); Craig Dargo (Raith R); **Motherwell:** Greg Strong (Bolton W); **Rangers:** Allan Johnston (Sunderland); Bert Konterman (Feyenoord); Peter Lovenkrands (AB Copenhagen); Kenny Miller (Hibernian); Fernando Ricksen (AZ); Paul Ritchie (Bolton W); Paul Reid (Carlisle U); **St Johnstone:** Paul Hartley (Hibernian); Tommy Lovenkrands (AB Copenhagen); Craig Russell (Manchester C); **St Mirren:** Scott McKenzie (Falkirk); Jamie McGowan (Motherwell); Ricky Gillies (Aberdeen); Paul McKnight (Rangers).

Tommy Black, Arsenal to Crystal Palace; Julian Gray, Arsenal to Crystal Palace; Narada Bernard, Arsenal to Bournemouth; Darren Byfield, Aston Villa to Walsall; Anthony Barness, Charlton Ath to Bolton W; Keith Jones, Charlton Ath to Reading; John Turner, Charlton Ath to Stockport Co; Neil Clement, Chelsea to WBA; David Burrows, Coventry C to Birmingham C; Chuck Eribenne, Coventry C to Bournemouth; Richard Knight, Derby Co to Oxford U; Tony Dorigo, Derby Co to Stoke C; Marc Bridge-Wilkinson, Derby Co to Port Vale; Mitch Ward, Everton to Barnsley; Dean Delany, Everton to Port Vale; John Hodges, Leicester C to Plymouth Arg; Stig-Inge Bjornebye, Liverpool to Blackburn R (via Brondby); John Boardman, Liverpool to Burnley; Craig Russell, Manchester C to St Johnstone; John Curtis, Manchester U to Blackburn R; David Cunningham, Newcastle U to Livingston; Sam Aiston, Sunderland to Shrewsbury T; Ian Feuer, West Ham U to Wimbledon; Paul Robinson, Newcastle U to Wimbledon; Des Byrne, St Patrick's Ath to Wimbledon; Manny Omoyinmi, West Ham U to Oxford U; Steve Purches, West Ham U to Bournemouth; Alex Neil, Airdrie to Barnsley; Lee Jones, Tranmere R to Barnsley; Carl Regan, Everton to Barnsley; Geoff Horsfield, Fulham to Birmingham C (club record £2.25m); Nicky Eaden, Barnsley to Birmingham C; Paul Wheatcroft, Manchester U to Bolton W; Ian Woan, Nottingham F to Bolton W; Per Frandsen, Blackburn R to Bolton W; Maikel Renfrum, NEC to Bolton W; Michael Ricketts, Walsall to Bolton W; Simon Charlton, Birmingham C to Bolton W; Lee Briscoe, Sheffield W to Burnley; Phil Gray, Luton T to Burnley; Louis Saha, Metz to Fulham; John Collins, Everton to Fulham; Paul Shaw, Millwall to Gillingham; Chris Hope, Scunthorpe U to Gillingham; Marlon King, Barnet to Gillingham; Paul Raven, WBA to Grimsby T; Steen Nedergaard, Odense to Norwich C; George Jones, Tranmere R to Nottingham F; Iain Anderson, Toulouse to Preston NE; Steve Robinson, Bournemouth to Preston NE; Clarke Carlisle, Blackpool to QPR; Karl Connolly, Wrexham to QPR; Christer Warren, Bournemouth to QPR; Patrick Suffo, Nantes to Sheffield U; Keith Curle, Wolverhampton W to Sheffield U; Georges Santos, WBA to Sheffield U; David Kelly, Tranmere R to Sheffield U; Brian Carrigan, Clyde to Stockport Co; Peter Clark, Carlisle U to Stockport Co; Lee Jones, Bristol R to Stockport Co; Stuart Barlow, Wigan Ath to Tranmere R; Wayne Gill, Blackburn R to Tranmere R; Sean Flynn, WBA to Tranmere R; Paul Rideout, USA/China to Tranmere R; Mark Williams, Watford to Wimbledon; Michael Thomas, Benfica to Wimbledon; Peter Grant, Reading to Bournemouth; Olafur Gottskalksson, Hibs to Brentford; Paul Gibbs, Plymouth Arg to Brentford; Mark McCammon, Charlton Ath to Brentford; Mark Lever, Grimsby T to Bristol C; Che Wilson, Norwich C to Bristol R; John Dreyer, Bradford C to Cambridge U; Tom Cowan, Burnley to Cambridge U; Simon Clark, Leyton Orient to Colchester U; Mark Stein, Bournemouth to Luton T; Marco Gabbiadini, Darlington to Northampton T; Chris Hargreaves, Plymouth Arg to Northampton T; Ian McGuckin, Fulham to Oxford U; John Robertson, Ayr U to Oxford U; Mark Goodlad, Nottingham F to Port Vale; Sinclair Le Geyt, Derby Co to Port Vale; Adrian Viveash, Walsall to Reading; Adrian Williams, Wolverhampton W to Reading; Ian Gray, Stockport Co to Rotherham U; Stewart Talbot, Port Vale to Rotherham U; Marvin Bryan, Bury to Rotherham U; Mark Robins, Walsall to Rotherham U; Stefan Thordarson, Uerdingen to Stoke C; Bart Griemink, Peterborough U to Swindon T; Keith O'Halloran, St Johnstone to Swindon T; Brett Angell, Stockport Co to Walsall; Gino Padula, Walsall to Wigan Ath; Stewart Castledine, Wimbledon to Wycombe W; Steve Jones, Bristol C to Wycombe W (loan).

Leaving the country: Esteban Fuertes, Derby Co to Lens; Mikkel Beck, Derby Co to Lille; Marco Holster, Ipswich T to Go Ahead; Martin Hiden, Leeds U to FK Austria; Tommy Knarvik, Leeds U to Brann; Fernando Pasquinelli, Leicester C to Boca Juniors; Theo Zagorakis, Leicester C to AEK Athens; Phil Babb, Liverpool to Sporting Lisbon; Massimo Taibi, Manchester U to Reggina; Jordi Cruyff, Manchester U to Alaves; Silvio Maric, Newcastle U to Porto; Marc-Vivien Foe, West Ham U to Lyon; Georgi Ilristov, Barnsley to NEC; Carlos Merino, Nottingham F to Athletic Bilbao; Thierry Bonalair, Nottingham F to Zurich; Pavel Srnicek, Sheffield W to Brescia; Alan Mahon, Tranmere R to Sporting Lisbon.

Coaching and Admin: Brian Kidd, Leeds U Director of Youth development.

If you enjoyed this book here is a selection of other bestselling sports titles from Headline

PLAYFAIR FOOTBALL ANNUAL 2000–2001	Glenda Rollin and Jack Rollin	£5.99 ☐
ROTHMANS BOOK OF FOOTBALL RECORDS	Jack Rollin	£25.00 ☐
PSYCHO	Stuart Pearce	£17.99 ☐
KICKING WITH BOTH FEET	Frank Clark	£7.99 ☐
RED VOICES	Stephen F. Kelly	£7.99 ☐
JOHN BARNES: The Autobiography	John Barnes	£6.99 ☐
LEFT FOOT FORWARD	Garry Nelson	£6.99 ☐
DERBY DAYS	Dougie and Eddy Brimson	£6.99 ☐
BARMY ARMY	Dougie Brimson	£6.99 ☐
MANCHESTER UNITED RUINED MY LIFE	Colin Shindler	£5.99 ☐

Headline books are available at your local bookshop or newsagent. Alternatively, books can be ordered direct from the publisher. Just tick the titles you want and fill in the form below. Prices and availability subject to change without notice.

Buy four books from the selection above and get free postage and packaging and delivery within 48 hours. Just send a cheque or postal order made payable to *Bookpoint Ltd* to the value of the total cover price of the four books. Alternatively, if you wish to buy fewer than four books the following postage and packaging applies:

UK and BFPO £4.30 for one book; £6.30 for two books; £8.30 for three books.

Overseas and Eire: £4.80 for one book; £7.10 for two or three books (surface mail).

Please enclose a cheque or postal order made payable to *Bookpoint Limited*, and send to: Headline Book Publishing Ltd, 39 Milton Park, Abingdon, OXON OX14 4TD, UK.

E-mail address: orders@bookpoint.co.uk

If you prefer to pay by credit card, our call team would be delighted to take your order by telephone. Our direct line is 01235 400 414 (lines open 9.00 am–6.00 pm Monday to Saturday, 24 hour message answering service). Alternatively you can send a fax on 01235 400 454.

Name ....

Address ....

....

....

If you would prefer to pay by credit card, please complete:

Please debit my Visa/Access/Diner's Card/American Express (delete as applicable) card number:

Signature .... Expiry Date ....